THE LAROUSSE
DESK
REFERENCE

General Editor
JAMES HUGHES

LAROUSSE

LAROUSSE
Larousse Kingfisher Chambers Inc.
95 Madison Avenue
New York, New York 10016

First American edition 1995

2 4 6 8 10 9 7 5 3 1

Copyright © Larousse plc 1995

LIBRARY OF CONGRESS CATALOGING-IN-PUBLICATION DATA

The Larousse desk reference–1st American ed.

p. cm.

Includes index.

1. Encyclopedias and dictionaries

AG6.L.4 1995

031–dc20 94-37198 CIP

ISBN 0–7523–5006–4

Printed in Italy

CONTRIBUTORS

General Editor	James Hughes
Managing Editors	Judy Garlick, Nancy Bliss
Coordinating Editor	Sean Connolly
Editors	Michèle Byam
	Nigel Cawthorne
	Margaret Doyle
	Annabel Else
	Alex Gray
	Frances Halpin
	Sarah Hewetson
	Nina Hathway
	Emily Kent
	Rebecca Lister
	Elizabeth Longley
	Dorothy Mitchell-Smith
	Madeleine Phelan
	Matthew Rake
	Catherine Rubinstein
Cartographic Editors	Annabel Else
	Alan Whittaker
Project Coordinator	Rebecca Lister
Editorial Assistants	Lucy Firth
	Nicola Garrett
	Ingrid Karikari
General Consultant	Bill Shapiro
Contributors	
Earth and the Universe	Christopher Cooper
	Martin Redfern
Life on Earth	Michael Chinery
	Richard Walker
	Joyce Pope
People	Dr. Paul Bahn
	Chris Turner
	Mike Darton
	Yvonne McFarlane
	Greville Healey
	Neil McCarthy
	Norman Barrett
	David Hunn
	Richard O'Neill
History	Robert Stewart
	James Harpur
	Neil Grant
	Danielle Allen
Science and Technology	John Clark
	Maggie Ramsay
	Vivianne Croot
	Reg Harman
	Simon Leech
Art and Culture	Richard O'Neill
	Elizabeth Eger
	Victor Stevenson
	Ian Chilvers
	Bette Spektorov
	Andrew Bean
	Amanda O'Neill
	Angela Holroyd
	Tim Huggins
	Tracey Kelly
	Andy Butler
International World	Madeleine Phelan
	Neil Grant
Index	Angela Hipkin
Production Managers	Linda Edmonds
	Oonagh Phelan
Production Assistant	Stephen Lang
Project Designer	Malcolm Smythe
Designers	Paul Calver
	Ch'en Ling
	Shaun Deal
	Robert Perry
Illustrators	Stefan Chabluk
	Sandra Doyle
	Chris Forsey
	Bob Garwood
	Elsa Godfrey
	Sally Goodden
	Ron Hayward
	Karen Hiscock
	Ruth Lindsay
	Kevin Madison
	Mainline Design
	Carol Merryman
	Patrick Mulrey
	James Robins
	Rob Shone
	Les Smith
	E.T'Budge
	David Webb
	Simon Williams
	Philip Winton
Additional artwork preparation	Matthew Gore
	Janet Woronkowicz
	Smiljka Surla
DTP coordinators	Tracey McNerney
	Beverley Shields
DTP operators	Angie Allison
	Primrose Burton
	Matt Barbieri
	Deborah Thompson
	Michael Preston
	Jason Smith
	Geo Frangos
Media conversion	Rapid Reprographics
Researcher	Melanie Porte
Picture Research	Elaine Willis
	Su Alexander
Publishing Director	Jim Miles
Design Director	Paul Wilkinson

CONTENTS

4 HISTORY

5 SCIENCE AND TECHNOLOGY

6 ARTS AND CULTURE

7
INTERNATIONAL WORLD

SECTION ICONS
The seven main sections of the book are divided into subsections for easy cross-referencing by subject heading. Each subsection is indexed by its own clearly recognizable icon. The icons of each subsection are listed below.

 The Universe

 Earth Sciences

 The Natural World

 Human Beings

 Peoples and Languages

 Thought and Belief

 Politics and Society

 Business and Economics

 Sports and Leisure

 Warfare

 World History

 Physics

 Chemistry

 Math and Computing

 Food and Agriculture

 Resources and Energy

 Technology and Engineering

 **Transportation and
Communications**

 Literature and Drama

 **Theater, Film, and
Television**

 Music and Dance

 Art and Architecture

 Decorative Arts

 Photography

 Fashion and Design

 Countries of the World

LAROUSSE DESK REFERENCE ENCYCLOPEDIA:
STRUCTURE AND ORGANIZATION

Arranged in seven major topic areas and twenty-six subsections, the Desk Reference Encyclopedia presents its information in the form of timelines (chronological lists of events), brief essays, charts, tables, short biographies and glossaries. The timelines provide a chronological context for the text and tabular material. All the material has been planned and illustrated to provide a maximum of information in an easily accessible and visually attractive form. Each subsection is accompanied by biographical sketches specific to the subject, and a comprehensive list of terms.

Cross-references
Sections are prefaced by a complete table of contents. Icons at the top of each page refer to the seven main sections and twenty-six subsections of the book, and are highlighted to locate the relevant subject area. SMALL CAPITALS are used to cross-refer to entries within lists of terms and prominent people. References to additional information elsewhere in the book are shown in parentheses with page numbers in *italic*. A comprehensive index identifies principal text areas and captions as well as individual entries.

Units
Inch-pound units, followed by S.I. (Système International) metric units are used where applicable, with their standard abbreviations. A "billion" is one thousand million.

Abbreviations
Abbreviations used in the Desk Reference that may not be familiar to all readers are explained where relevant or on their first occurrence on each page (e.g. mya = million years ago). Others include:

CIS	Commonwealth of Independent States
DM	Deutsche Mark(s)
EC	European Community
EEC	European Economic Community
EFTA	European Free Trade Association
EU	European Union
GDP	Gross Domestic Product
GNP	Gross National Product
GMT	Greenwich Mean Time
IDP	International Driver's Permit
NAFTA	North American Free Trade Agreement
NATO	North Atlantic Treaty Organization
NASA	National Aeronautics and Space Administration
OPEC	Organization of Petroleum Exporting Countries
PLO	Palestine Liberation Organization

Accuracy
Every effort has been made to ensure that the information is as accurate and up-to-date as possible at the time of going to press. A team of fact-checkers with specialized knowledge in the relevant areas has verified the text.

1 EARTH AND THE UNIVERSE
The Universe: astronomical instruments, from optical telescopes to radio interferometers, followed by coverage of the Solar System and our Galaxy, extending into deep space. A history of space exploration, with comprehensive astronomical tables, 70 biographical sketches of prominent astronomers, and a glossary of terms.

Earth Sciences: structure and composition of the planet, including its geology and mineralogy. Geological timeline of the Earth, from Pre-Cambrian to Cenozoic. Natural landscaping, structure and composition of the atmosphere, climate and weather, mapping. The human impact on the physical Earth, with charts and statistics. The subsection concludes with numerous biographical sketches of prominent geographers and more than 120 terms.

2 LIFE ON EARTH
The Natural World: genetic and evolutionary factors underlying life, with illustrated tabular coverage of major animal and plant species, systematically organized according to accepted international convention, with descriptions of habitats, distinguishing features, endangered species, etc. The human impact, together with the latest conservation strategies. Biographies of prominent zoologists and technical terms.

Human Being: anatomical descriptions, from skeleton to skin. Lists of drugs and their properties. Information on nutrition, food values, dietary charts and eating disorders. Tabular material on diseases, diagnosis, and treatment: drugs, alternative medicine, surgery, and first aid. Key dates in medical history and healthcare around the world.

3 PEOPLE
Peoples and Languages: human origins and development, chronologically outlined, with boxed information encapsulating recent work in paleontology, anthropology, archaeology, ethnography, and linguistics. About 50 biographies of workers in these fields, together with a glossary of terms.

Thought and Belief: chronological account of the world's faiths and philosophies, from Paleolithic times to late 20th-century trends. Boxed information, illustrations, and brief essays refine and extend the chronological material, with full-length features on the major religions. A coverage of philosophical and religious terms, together with more than 100 biographical sketches of leading figures.

Politics and Society: key political definitions and institutions, including flowcharts. Timeline of Civil Rights and a list of Nobel Peace Prize winners. Comparison of various legislative systems, criminal statistics, and biographical sketches of famous criminals. Tables of educational institutions, comparative levels of world education, and literacy rates.

Business and Economics: the world's economic systems, trade organizations, multinational companies and the workings of a stock exchange. The flow of money from one nation to another in terms of aid and trade. About 40 biographies of important economists and a glossary of terms.

Sports and Leisure: types of sport, presented thematically, including ball and racket games, track and field events, gymnastics, water sports, winter sports, equestrian sports, and many more, outlining the history of the sport and itemizing rules, past winners, and records, together with artworks of the playing area and equipment. A breakdown of card and board games is followed by a full listing of popular leisure activities and pastimes and more than 100 biographical sketches of prominent sporting figures.

Warfare: organized into early and modern periods, a survey of the world's decisive battles and developments in weaponry and military strategy from 8000 B.C. Military ranks and formations, descriptions of the latest weapons, armies, and intelligence systems, and about 50 biographies of key figures in military history.

4 HISTORY

World History, 5000 B.C. – A.D. 1994: geographically organized timelines covering all important dates from the earliest historical period to the present day. Artworks, photographs, lists, charts, and brief essays expanding and refining the chronological material. Timelines of contemporaneous cultural developments. Double-page spreads dealing in greater detail with key historical periods. Biographies of distinguished historians.

People in History: more than 300 biographical sketches of major historical figures with their dates, achievements, and place in history.

Rulers and Leaders: family trees of ruling families, with lists of political leaders in the major countries of the world.

5 SCIENCE AND TECHNOLOGY

Physics: timeline of discoveries, inventions, applications, and developments in physics, with 28 text pieces, from the discovery of gravity to the world of subatomic particles.

Chemistry: chronological account, from alchemy to plastics, with boxed information, charts, and diagrams. The subsection closes with a coverage of famous physicists and chemists, and a glossary of terms.

Math and Computing: thematically organized information covering all areas of mathematical theory and method, including computer theory and practice. A timeline of the history and development of information technology and a glossary of computer-programming terminology.

Food and Agriculture: chronology of relevant developments from the earliest times to the present day. Coverage of food plants, plant and animal products, farming methods, and agribusiness, and detailed information of food production techniques with a comprehensive list of food additives. Features on the production of wine worldwide and international cuisine.

Resources and Energy: nature and distribution of energy resouces; their extraction and exploitation; the generation, distribution, and consumption of energy. Metallic, nonmetallic minerals and semiprecious stones, mineral producers, including minerals from the sea, uses of minerals. The conservation of resources and the recyling of manufactured materials.

Technology and Engineering: timelines of inventions and developments in the areas of construction and machinery are accompanied by brief essays on important topics and extensive tabular information. Analysis of the manufacturing industry electronics and computer applications.

Transportation and Communications: timelines of inventions developments covering transportation, from the wheel to rocket launchers. Writing, printing, photography, and all forms of media, including multimedia publishing, the Internet, and the information superhighway. About 100 biographies and a glossary of terms.

6 ARTS AND CULTURE

Literature and Drama: chronological coverage from pre-literate epic poetry to 20th-century spy fiction, with illustrated information boxes on important movements and genres. Great libraries, bestsellers, poets laureate, and Nobel, Pulitzer and Booker prize winners. The subsection ends with more than 200 biographical sketches of leading writers together with their works.

Theater, Film, and Television: chronological timeline, from Greek tragedy to TV soap operas, with 20 essays covering genres and movements. Academy Award (Oscar) winners listed, with more than 200 biographical sketches of leading performers.

Music and Dance: divided into classical and popular forms; with a timeline for classical music and dance, together with numerous essays. Coverage of popular music includes musicals, blues, soul, rock, pop, and world music.

About 250 biographies of classical composers, jazz, rock, and pop performers.

Art and Architecture: organized chronologically from ancient Egyptian to Post-Modernist art, with 32 illustrated essays describing movements and genres. Lists of great collections and major architectural styles. About 180 biographical sketches of leading artists and architects and their works.

Decorative Arts: timeline covering all decorative arts, with 20 illustrated essays describing major movements and artists. A glossary of terms and about 80 biographical sketches close the subsection.

Photography and Fashion: divided into two parts, beginning with a chronological survey of photography from the invention of the camera to holographic techniques. Fashion timelines run from the mid-19th to the late 20th century, with features on leading couturiers and movements. About 130 biographies of leading photographers and designers.

7 INTERNATIONAL WORLD:

Continents and Countries: organized by continent, detailed color maps of the world's countries, each accompanied by lists of physical features, population statistics, economic and social data, resources, and key dates. Travel boxes list practical advice such as visa requirements and tourist features. Sixteen "flashpoint" maps and explanatory text trace the historical development of conflicts and areas of special interest.

International Tables: geographical, demographic, and sociological statistics.

Map Index: more than 10,000 place names, together with their map references.

Tables: conversion tables for temperature, area, length, weight, capacity; international sizes and symbols; calendars of religious holidays.

Index

SECTION 1
EARTH AND THE UNIVERSE

OBJECTS IN THE SKY

Ancient astronomers regarded the universe of the stars as radically different in nature from the lower world of the air, land, and ocean. Below, all was change, with storms, earthquakes, growth, and decay. Above was the eternal universe of the unchanging stars. Between the two came the less constant but still orderly and reliable Sun, Moon, and planets.

The "fixed" stars are, with very few exceptions, mere points of light to even the most powerful telescopes. They seem to rise and set together, and over many centuries they show no movement in relation to each other. This apparent movement of the stars is the reflection of the Earth's daily rotation from west to east. But astronomers still find it convenient to imagine that the stars are shining points fixed to a vast sphere centered on the Earth (below), and that this sphere revolves from east to west.

The Sun (p. 16) also seems to move from east to west, but not quite as fast as the fixed stars. In relation to them, the Sun "slips" eastward, by an amount roughly equal to 1° or twice the Sun's apparent diameter, each day. At the same time it swings alternately north and south, giving summer and winter to the Earth's Northern and Southern hemispheres in turn. A year is the time it takes the Sun to move around the sky.

Five "stars" break the rule of orderly motion. These are the naked-eye planets, or "wanderers." Two of them, Mercury and Venus, swing from side to side of the Sun. We now know that this is because they move around the Sun with orbits that lie within the Earth's, and we view their motion from outside, as it were. The other naked-eye planets, Mars, Jupiter, and Saturn, move outside the Earth's orbit. They seem to us to move around the whole sky, from west to east in relation to the fixed stars, except for short periods when they stop and temporarily reverse. This is known as the retrograde motion of planets.

Another planet, Uranus, is just visible to the naked eye, but it is so dim and its movement so sluggish—it takes 84 years

Distance and brightness of the stars

Aurorae and meteors take place within 620 mi./1,000 km of the Earth's surface. The Moon is 250,000 mi./400,000 km from Earth, and the Sun 375 times farther. Saturn at its closest is nearly a billion miles from Earth, but the stars are thousands of times farther still. The nearest is Alpha Centauri, the brightest star in the constellation of Centaurus. It is 4.3 light-years away—i.e. light takes 4.3 years to reach Earth from the star. One light-year is almost 6 trillion miles.

The seeming brightness of a star depends on both its true brightness and its distance from us. Many of the faintest naked-eye stars are intrinsically enormously bright—as much as a mil-lion times as bright as the Sun—but very remote and therefore dim.

Astronomers use different methods to calculate the precise distance of a celestial body. The nearest objects, within 15,000 light-years, are measured by parallax (below, right); objects up to ten million light-years distant are measured using Cepheid variable stars; up to 600 million light-years, supernovae explosions are compared to calculate distance; from 50 million to 3 billion light-years distant, large, luminous galaxies are used as standards; and from 100 million to 15 billion light-years or more, an object's red shift (below, left) is used as a measure.

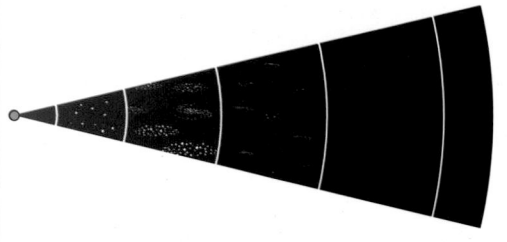

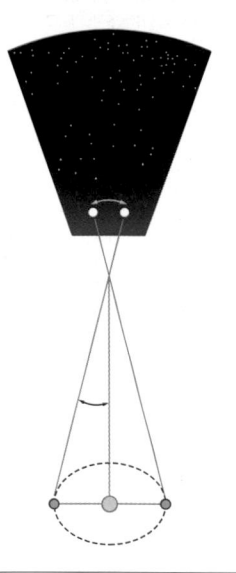

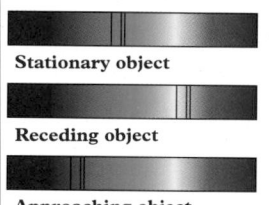

Stationary object

Receding object

Approaching object

Parallax (right) uses the apparent shift in a nearby star's position as the Earth completes half an orbit. Trigonometry is used to calculate the Earth–star distance. The absorption lines in a spectrum (left) shift to the red or blue end as a distant object moves.

to move around the sky—that it was not recognized as a planet until telescopes were turned on it in the 1700s.

Comets (p. 23) are objects at planetary distances, but which are only temporarily visible to us. They appear to develop slowly over weeks or months. A comet first appears as a faint, fuzzy patch and then, in favorable cases, develops a tail as it approaches the Sun. When it moves

away from the Sun again, the tail shrinks and then fades.

The Moon also moves from west to east in relation to the fixed stars, because it is revolving around the Earth. The Earth's gravitational pull keeps one face of the Moon always turned toward us, but differing amounts of it are illuminated by the Sun at different times, and this gives rise to the Moon's changing phases.

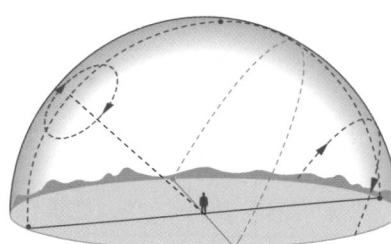

Stargazers visualize heavenly bodies as lying on the inside of a celestial sphere (above). Circumpolar stars never set, but most stars do, describing arcs across the celestial sphere.

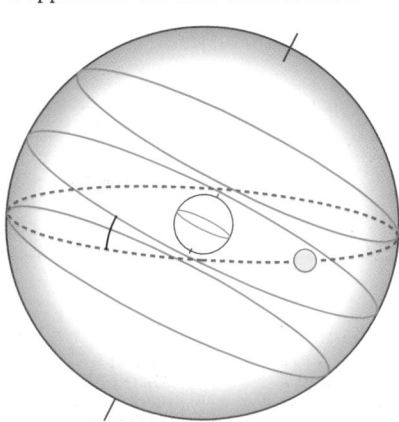

If we imagine the sky as a complete globe (left), the apparent path of the Sun in one year (ecliptic) crosses the celestial equator at the spring and fall equinoxes and, the tropics at the summer and winter solstices.

The axial tilt of the Earth by 23° produces the seasonal variations in each hemisphere as the planet follows its orbital path around the Sun (above). In June, the Sun is directly over the Tropic of Cancer, producing summer in the Northern Hemisphere; six months later it is directly over the Tropic of Capricorn.

Much closer to home are the aurorae—gently moving arcs, bands, and sheets of color that glow in the night sky, generally in polar regions. They occur where atoms in the upper atmosphere, 100— 62–620 mi./ 1,000 km above Earth, have been stimulated to glow by the bombardment of subatomic particles spilling over from the Van Allen Belts (Magnetism, p. 43). These are two reservoirs of solar particles, 6,200 mi./10,000 km and 14,300 mi./23,000 km above Earth.

"Shooting stars," or meteors, are closer still. They occasionally dart across the sky, disappearing after only a few seconds, sometimes leaving a briefly glowing trail. They have nothing to do with the fixed stars and are just the burning up of a grain of interplanetary dust, or occasionally a piece of rock, by friction as it falls through the atmosphere to Earth.

Brightness and magnitude

The apparent brightness of a star is represented by a number called its magnitude. The larger the number, the fainter the star. The bright star Arcturus, in the constellation Boötes, has a magnitude of almost exactly zero. It is 2.51 times as bright as a star of magnitude 1, which is 2.51 times as bright as a star of magnitude 2, and so on. This ratio is chosen so that a difference of five magnitudes represents a brightness ratio of precisely 100. The faintest stars visible to the naked eye are slightly fainter than magnitude 6. There are two stars—Sirius and Canopus—that are brighter than Arcturus and are therefore given negative magnitudes. Altogether there are billions of stars in the sky but only about 6,000 stars are visible to the naked eye.

Eclipses, transits, and occultations

In their constant movement, the planets, Sun, and Moon often block our view of each other. When the Moon passes in front of the Sun, there is a solar eclipse.

During a total solar eclipse the Moon blocks out light from the Sun so that only the solar corona is visible, streaming into space.

By chance, the apparent sizes of the Moon and Sun are almost identical, so the Moon just cuts off the disk of the Sun, as viewed from a point in the central region of the Moon's shadow on the Earth. At other points lying in the Moon's shadow there is a partial eclipse. In an annular eclipse a ring-shaped part of the Sun remains visible.

When the Moon passes on exactly the opposite side of the Earth from the Sun, it enters the Earth's shadow and there is a lunar eclipse (*below*). The Moon's disk is darkened, but rarely completely: red light refracted into the shadow by the Earth's atmosphere usually bathes the Moon in a coppery glow.

The inner planets, Mercury and Venus, sometimes pass directly between the

Solar eclipse

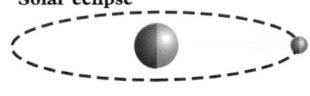

Lunar eclipse

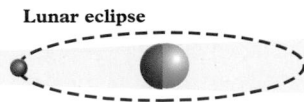

When atoms of nitrogen and oxygen are bombarded by subatomic particles they emit characteristic colors, as seen in the aurorae.

Earth and the Sun. Observations at such times first revealed that Venus has an atmosphere, while Mercury has none, and also yielded information about the relative distances of the other planets from the Sun.

The planets beyond the Earth all have satellites, which are visible only with telescopes. They can often be seen to pass behind and in front of the parent planet's disk and to disappear suddenly when they enter its shadow.

Planets and their satellites sometimes pass in front of some star or other celestial body. Accurate observations of the extinction of the light or radio waves from the distant body reveal a great deal about any atmosphere or ring systems that the nearer one may possess.

Solar eclipses

Date	Total/Annular	Visible from parts of
11/3/1994	Total	Indian Ocean, S. Atlantic, South America, mid-Pacific
10/24/1995	Total	Middle East, S. Asia, S. Pacific
3/9/1997	Total	C. and N. Asia, Arctic
2/26/1998	Total	Mid-Pacific, Central America, N. Atlantic
8/22/1998	Annular	Indonesia, S. Pacific, Indian Ocean
2/16/1999	Annular	Indian Ocean, Australia
8/11/1999	Total	N. Atlantic, N. Europe, Middle East, N. India
6/21/2001	Total	S. Atlantic, South Africa, Madagascar
12/14/2001	Annular	Pacific, Central America
6/10/2002	Annular	Indonesia, Pacific, Mexico
12/4/2002	Total	S. Africa, Indian Ocean, Australia
5/31/2003	Annular	Iceland, Greenland
11/23/2003	Total	Antarctic
4/8/2005	Annular/Total	Pacific, Panama, Venezuela
10/3/2005	Annular	Atlantic, Spain, Libya, Indian Ocean
3/29/2006	Total	Atlantic, Libya, Turkey, Russia
9/22/2006	Annular	Guyana, Atlantic, Indian Ocean

The twenty brightest stars

Star name	Distance (light-yrs.)	Apparent magnitude	Absolute magnitude
Sirius A	8.6	−1.46	+1.4
Canopus	98	−0.72	−8.5
Arcturus	36	−0.06	−0.3
Alpha Centauri A	4.3	−0.01	+4.4
Vega	26.5	+0.04	+0.5
Capella	45	+0.05	−0.7
Rigel	900	+0.14	−6.8
Procyon A	11.2	+0.37	+2.6
Betelgeuse	520	+0.41	−5.5
Achernar	118	+0.51	−1.0
Beta Centauri	490	+0.63	−5.1
Altair	16.5	+0.77	+2.2
Aldebaran	68	+0.86	−0.2
Spica	220	+0.91	−3.6
Antares	520	+0.92	−4.5
Pollux	35	+1.16	+0.8
Fomalhaut	22.6	+1.19	+2.0
Deneb	1,500	+1.26	−6.9
Beta Crucis	490	+1.28	−4.6
Alpha Crucis	120	+0.83	−4.0

TELESCOPES AND OBSERVATORIES

A telescope improves our view of the skies, partly by forming a large image that magnifies the detail in objects, but even more importantly by gathering more light than the human eye can, thus revealing very faint objects. The major challenge in telescope building is to construct a broad mirror or lens that will gather plenty of light yet is sufficiently accurately shaped to create a sharp image.

The main mirror in a reflecting telescope consists of a thin metal film on an accurately shaped base that can be supported over its whole area. The largest single-mirror telescope of relatively traditional design was the 20-foot (6-m) Bolshoi telescope on Mt. Patukhov in the Caucasus.

Astronomical telescopes are housed in rotating domes that can be completely enclosed to keep the weather out when the instrument is not observing. The dome is unheated to prevent disturbance of the air by rising currents. New large optical observatories are multinational collaborations, sited on mountaintops such as Mauna Kea in Hawaii or La Palma in the Canary Islands. Here they are above the bulk of the dust, water vapor, and smoke pollution of the lower atmosphere and far from the "light pollution" of cities. The same observatories now observe infrared radiation, which cannot penetrate to lower layers of the atmosphere. Since breathing is difficult at these altitudes, the observatories are increasingly designed for remote control from stations at lower altitudes and even

Centaurus A, optically, is an extensive elliptical galaxy: the dark band of dust and gas is a stellar birthplace. It is also the source of intense radio emissions, the result of a past explosion.

thousands of miles away.

Observations in visible light benefit even more from being made completely outside the atmosphere. The Hubble Space Telescope has a main mirror that is 95 in./2.4 m in diameter. The instrument was launched in 1990 into an orbit 375 mi./ 600 km high. It can form images of unprecedented sharpness, but it remains to be seen whether the Hubble telescope can compete with the new technological advances developing in ground telescopes in terms of both performance and cost efficiency.

The Hubble telescope is used for pinpointing areas near black holes and measuring the effect of gravity on starlight. It produces high-resolution images of objects billions of light years away.

The principle of a refracting telescope (A) is for light from the object that is being viewed to pass through a convex lens (the objective), producing an image. A strong eyepiece of short focal length magnifies the image so that it can be seen in detail. The images produced are always inverted. In a terrestrial telescope these are made upright by the introduction of another convex lens. In a reflecting telescope (B) light is collected by a concave mirror and brought to a focus, forming an image.

A

B

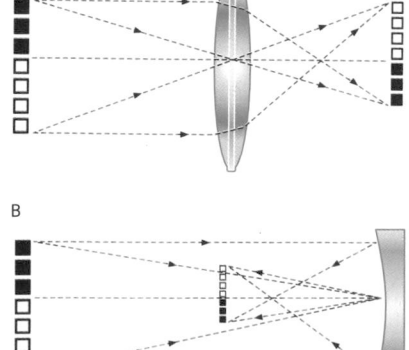

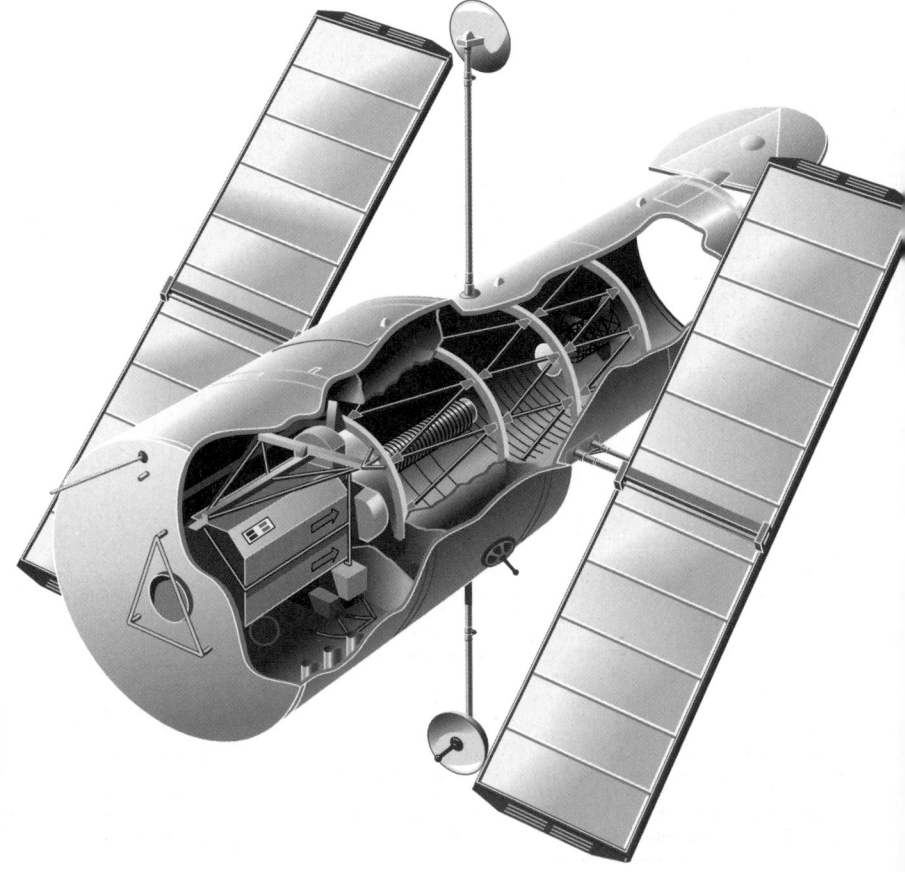

New telescope technologies

The photographic camera long ago replaced the human eye for all major astronomical work. Now photography is being largely replaced by electronic detectors. Instead of film they use microchips, which are more sensitive and yield an image in electronic form. Computers can process these directly, to enhance images by improving their contrast or adding false color to clarify them, and to analyze them mathematically.

The light-gathering power of mirrors is being enormously increased. Each of the twin Keck telescopes on Mauna Kea in Hawaii has a 33 ft./10 m main mirror constructed from 36 hexagonal segments (*right*). It is easier to shape these individually and keep them all aligned than to build a single equivalent mirror.

A telescope with adaptive optics can overcome the shimmering of the Earth's atmosphere that causes the image to break up and dance. The mirror is pulled and pushed hundreds of times a second in dozens of different places by mechanical "actuators" to compensate for the different effects of atmospheric turbulence on the light rays arriving at those parts of the mirror.

Fine details can be seen by combining the light from widely separated optical telescopes. This technique is already familiar to radio astronomers, who sometimes combine data from radio telescopes located in different continents. It is now becoming possible for the far shorter wavelengths of visible light to be combined. Thus an experimental array of four 20 in./50 cm optical telescopes spaced 330 ft./100 m apart will have the resolving power (though not the light-gathering power) of one 3,960 in./100 m telescope.

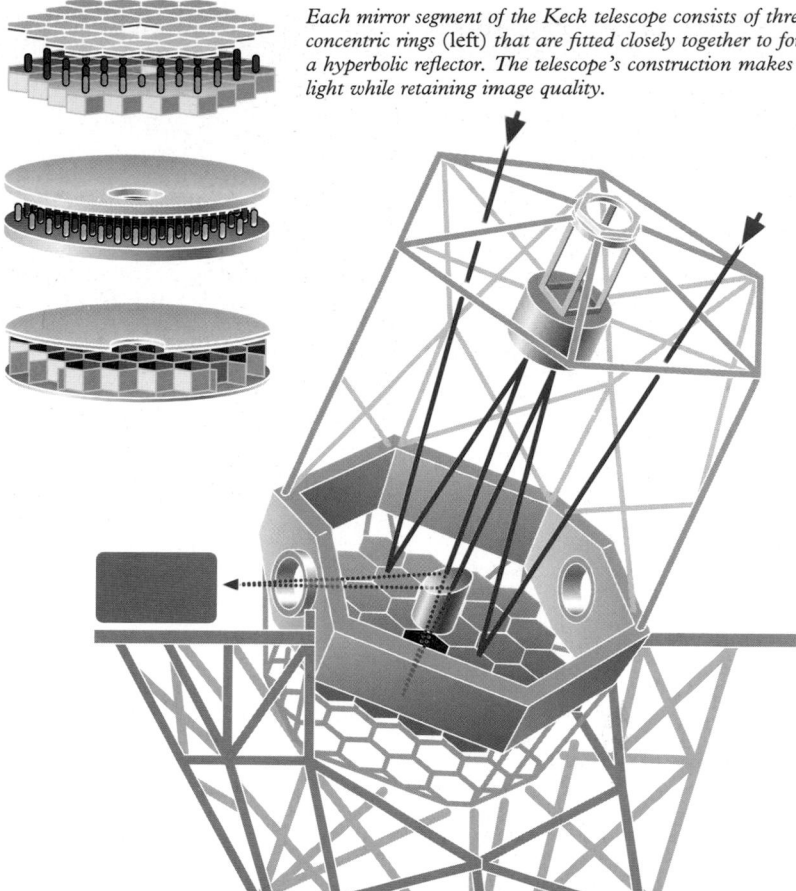

Each mirror segment of the Keck telescope consists of three concentric rings (left) *that are fitted closely together to form a hyperbolic reflector. The telescope's construction makes it light while retaining image quality.*

The Keck telescope aligns 36 hexagonal segments to form the primary mirror, creating an array equaling a single 33 ft./10 m hyperbolic mirror. Light received at the primary mirror is focused and passed on to a series of other mirrors and finally redirected to the Nasmyth focus or Cassegrain focus. Because of the advanced electronic techniques used, the collecting area is about four times as great as other contemporary telescopes.

Key astronomical advances

1600 B.C. Babylonian star catalogs compiled.
270 B.C. Aristarchus proposes the Earth revolves around the Sun.
230 B.C. Eratosthenes measures Earth's circumference: 252,000 stadia.
135 B.C. Hipparchus discovers precession of the equinoxes.
A.D. 127 Ptolemy develops Earth-centered theory of the universe.
1006 Supernovae observed by Chinese.
1543 Copernicus revives idea of Sun-centered universe.
1572 Tycho Brahe shows "new star" lies beyond the Moon.
1609 Kepler decribes planets' orbital shapes and periods.
1609–10 Galileo first to use telescope for astronomy.
1655 Christiaan Huygens discovers Saturn's rings and moon.
1668 Isaac Newton makes first reflecting telescope.
1675 Ole Rømer estimates speed of light.
1687 Isaac Newton publishes theories of mechanics and gravitation.
1705 Edmund Halley discovers periodic return of comets.
1781 William Herschel discovers Uranus.
1786 William Herschel describes shape of Milky Way galaxy.
1801 Giuseppe Piazzi discovers first asteroid (Ceres).
1802 William Herschel discovers double stars.
1838 Wilhelm Bessel measures distance of star (61 Cygni).
1846 Leverrier and Adams predict existence of Neptune
1864 William Huggins demonstrates that nebulae are gaseous.
1872 Henry Draper photographs spectrum of star (Vega).
1912 Henrietta Leavitt discovers Cepheid variables.
1920 Vesto Slipher discovers that most "nebulae" are receding.
1923 Edwin Hubble establishes that certain "nebulae" are galaxies.
1938 Bethe and Weizsäcker propose fusion as source of stellar energy.
1963 Maarten Schmidt discovers quasar 3C273.
1987 Supernova 1987A observed in Larger Magellanic Cloud.
1990 M. Hawkins discovers first brown dwarf.

Major optical and infrared telescopes

Name, site, and altitude	Mirror size
Hubble Space Telescope, 370-mile orbit	8 ft./2.4 m
VLT (Very Large Telescope) Paranal, Chile	53 ft./16 m equivalent
National New Technology Telescope, Mauna Kea, Hawaii	50 ft./15 m equivalent
Keck Telescope, Mauna Kea, Hawaii (36 segments) (13,600 ft.)	33 ft./10 m
Bolshoi Altazimuth Telescope, Mt. Pastukhov, Russia (6,900 ft.)	20 ft/6.0 m
Hale Telescope, Palomar Mountain, California (23,000 ft.)	16 ft./5 m
MMT (Multiple Mirror Telescope) Mt. Hopkins, Arizona (8,550 ft.)	15 ft./4.5 m (to be replaced with 21 ft./6.5 m mirror)
William Herschel Telescope, La Palma, Canary Islands (8,000 ft.)	14 ft./4.2 m
Cerro Tololo, Chile (7,000 ft.)	13 ft./4 m
Anglo-Australian Telescope, Siding Spring, New South Wales	12.5 ft./3.9 m
Mayall Telescope, Kitt Peak, Arizona	13 ft./4 m
UKIRT (U.K. Infrared Telescope), Mauna Kea, Hawaii (13,700 ft.)	12 ft./3.6 m
CFHT (Canada-France-Hawaii Telescope), Mauna Kea, Hawaii (13,700 ft.)	12 ft./3.6 m
ESO New Technology Telescope, Cerro Tololo, Chile (7,000 ft.)	12 ft./3.6 m
ESO 3.6m Cerro La Silla, Chile (8,000 ft.)	12 ft./3.6 m
Calar Alto, Spain (700ft.)	11.5 ft./3.5 m
Shane Telescope, Mt. Hamilton,	10 ft./3 m

RADIO ASTRONOMY

The first invisible region of the electromagnetic spectrum to be explored was the radio spectrum. Since World War II, steerable radio dishes up to 330ft./100 m in diameter have been built. Some radio telescopes have consisted of arrays of wire "clotheslines" spread over large areas. Such an instrument can be made to "look" in different directions by electronic means without physical movement being needed. By combining observations of the same object made at different times of day, from positions separated by thousands of miles because of the Earth's rotation, very fine detail can be observed. The largest radio dish is built into a smoothed-out volcanic crater at Areçibo, in Puerto Rico.

The signals from widely separated radio telescopes can be combined to give exceptionally detailed images. Networks of instruments in individual countries are regularly operated in this way, and they can be combined into worldwide groupings for special purposes. Signals are usually recorded and combined later.

The signals received from radio telescopes can be processed and enhanced by computer to yield images that superficially resemble those now obtained from optical telescopes.

Spectroscopy

All natural light originates from incandescent sources and is a mixture of wavelengths. Each wavelength of visible light corresponds to a certain color: red light has a wavelength of about three-fourths of a micrometer. (A micrometer is a millionth of a meter, or a thousandth of a millimeter.) Blue light has a wavelength of about half of this. Successively shorter wavelengths in the electromagnetic spectrum (*right*) represent ultraviolet radiation, X rays, and gamma rays. Wavelengths longer than those of red light are, successively, infrared radiation, microwave radiation, and radio waves. Spectroscopy is the analysis of electromagnetic radiation by wavelength.

Sunlight can be split into its component wavelengths by means of a prism or a device called a diffraction grating. The rainbow-colored band so formed is called a spectrum. Starlight similarly reveals a spectrum but one that is crossed by dark lines where certain wavelengths are "missing." These wavelengths are absorbed by cool gases surrounding the star—producing an absorption spectrum. Other spectra exhibit bright lines because extra light is being produced by hot gas surrounding the star: these are known as emission spectra. The light from planets, interstellar gas clouds, and whole galaxies can likewise be analyzed from spectra, which reveal an enormous amount about the sources' constituent chemical elements and compounds, as well as their temperature and pressure.

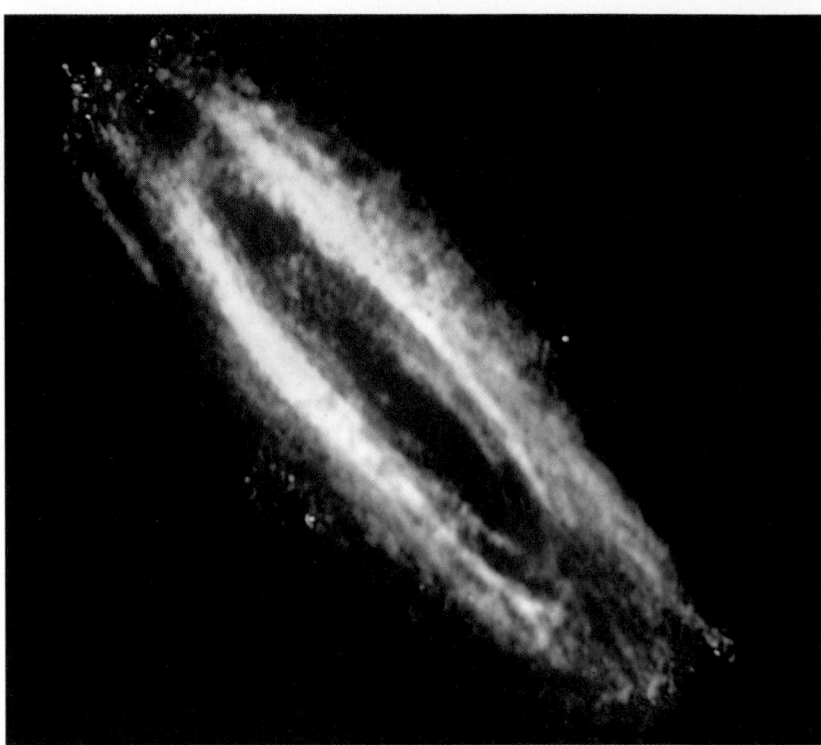

A radio image of hydrogen emissions from the Andromeda galaxy (above) *has been color coded to reveal the velocity of recession and approach in different parts of the galaxy as it rotates like a cartwheel relative to the position of the Earth. Green and blue regions are approaching, while yellow and red regions are receding.*

The electromagnetic spectrum (below), *from the shortest-wavelength gamma rays to the longest-wavelength radio waves, includes a very small "window" of visible light.*

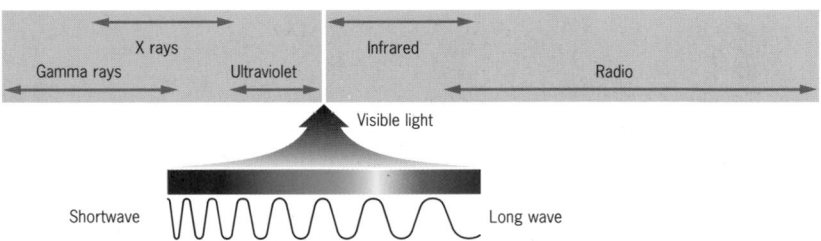

Key discoveries in radio astronomy
1931 Karl Jansky in New Jersey sets up makeshift antennae to study static but picks up radio waves from Milky Way galaxy.
1937 Grote Reber constructs first steerable radio telescope and makes first radio map of the sky.
1951 H. Ewen and E. Purcell detect cold hydrogen at 8 in.(21 cm) wavelength, predicted in 1944 by H. C. van de Hulst.
1961 Radio astronomers at Cambridge, U.K., discover quasars.
1965–66 Arno Penzias and Robert Wilson in New Jersey discover microwave background radiation—strong evidence for the Big Bang and predicted by Ralph Alpher and Robert Herman in1948.
1966 Jocelyn Bell in Cambridge, U.K., discovers pulsars.
1992 COBE (Cosmic Background Explorer satellite) discovers "wrinkles" in cosmic background radiation, believed to be earliest structures formed after the Big Bang.

Major radio telescopes
Australia Telescope, New South Wales, 200-mile array between Australia, Japan, and TDR satellite
VLA (Very Large Array), Socorro, New Mexico, 2.2-mile Y-shaped array
JCMT (James Clerk Maxwell Telescope) (13,600 ft.), Mauna Kea, Hawaii, 50 ft.
California Submillimeter Observatory (13,600 ft.), Mauna Kea, Hawaii, 34 ft.
Ryle, Cambridge, U.K., 3-mile array
CSIRO Radioheliograph, Culgoora, Australia, 2-mile array
Molonglo, Australia, 1 mile x 40 ft. array
Westerbork, Netherlands, 1-mile array
MERLIN (Multi-Element Radio-Linked Interferometer Network), U.K., 150-mile array
Areçibo, Puerto Rico, 980 ft.
Effelsberg Radio Telescope, Effelsberg, Germany, 330 ft.
Greenbank, West Virginia, 300 ft.
Jodrell Bank, Cheshire, U.K., 250 ft. and 216 ft. Parkes, New South Wales, 210 ft.

Infrared and millimetric astronomy

Infrared wavelengths range from just beyond the longest visible wavelengths, slightly less than one micrometer, to a maximum that is conventionally taken to be one millimeter. Here they shade into the shortest radio waves. Infrared radiation is described as heat radiation because it is given out by all bodies in the form of heat energy moving from an area of higher temperature to one of low temperature. An infrared telescope has to be placed on a mountaintop or in orbit since infrared radiation from space does not reach the ground. It also has to be protected from the flood of infrared radiation given out from objects around. It has to be immersed in a low-temperature liquid, such as liquid nitrogen or helium, to quench its own heat radiation.

Ultraviolet, X ray, and gamma-ray astronomy

Apart from visible light, the only wavelengths that can penetrate our atmosphere are some infrared and ultraviolet wavelengths, and part of the radio spectrum. To study other wavelengths, appropriate types of telescope have been launched on artificial satellites to make observations from above the atmosphere. Among many other things, IRAS (Infrared Astronomical Satellite) discovered infrared radiation from the birth of planetary systems around distant stars. COBE (Cosmic Background Explorer) observed the microwave radiation that fills the sky and discovered "ripples" in it that signal

An optical image of Andromeda shows the galaxy's familiar disk shape and central bulge.

the first building up of structures in the hot gas blasting outward from the Big Bang, less than a million years after the birth of the universe. Gamma-ray observatories have observed mysterious

gamma-ray "bursters," originating from violent events of an unknown nature, apparently beyond our galaxy. Gamma rays have the shortest wavelengths and are produced in nuclear reactions.

The data received from the dishes (above) of the Very Large Array radio interferometer are combined to produce a single radio image. Computers in the control center produce time delays between the signals from the different dishes. The delays make the signals from a radio wave come together at the same time and reinforce them in the same way as light waves are focused by a mirror. There are 27 receivers in all, running on railroad tracks forming a Y-shape (right). Each arm of the Y is about 12 mi./20 km long.

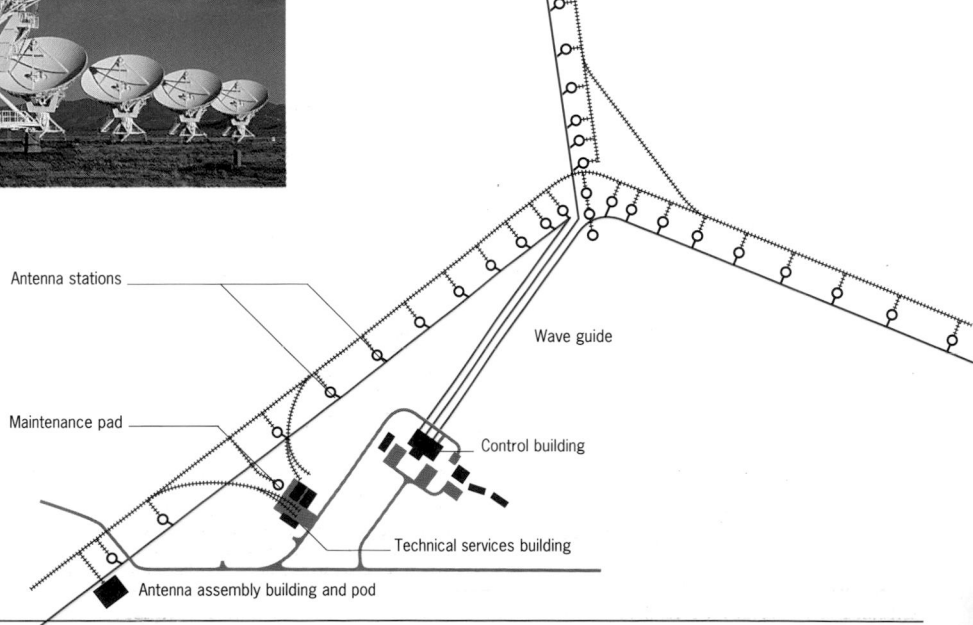

Antenna stations

Wave guide

Maintenance pad

Control building

Technical services building

Antenna assembly building and pod

STRUCTURE OF THE SUN

The Sun is an incandescent ball of gas 864,000 miles (1.4 million km) across, "burning" by nuclear processes like those unleashed in the hydrogen bomb. Its total mass is 2,000 trillion trillion tons, 300,000 times that of the Earth. It consists mainly of hydrogen, and to a lesser extent of helium. Throughout the Sun atoms are broken down by the high temperature into their positively charged nuclei and electrons; the hydrogen becomes a plasma. There are about 12 hydrogen nuclei for every helium nucleus.

At the Sun's center the pressure rises to 250 billion times that of the Earth's atmosphere at sea level, and the temperature is 27 million °F (15 million°C). Within a region extending about one-fourth of the way to the surface, hydrogen nuclei are fused together to form helium nuclei. In this process there is a conversion of some of the mass of the atoms into vast amounts of energy. This is transported to the surface of the Sun by radiation and by currents of hot rising gas in the outer layers (*inset, right*). The process takes so long that if the processes in the center of the Sun were turned off now, it would be a million years before the surface started to cool and darken. The Sun is made up of several layers of gas (*right*). The energy is produced via nuclear reactions at the core (1) and passes into the radiative zone (2), where some energy is absorbed. It then moves on to the turbulent convective layer (3), and on into the photosphere (4)—the visible surface of the Sun. The energy eventually escapes into space via the chromosphere and corona.

Astronomical telescopes reveal that the brilliant white surface of the Sun (the photosphere, or sphere of light) is mottled: the brighter areas, which are 600-1,200 miles (1,000–2,000 km) across, are

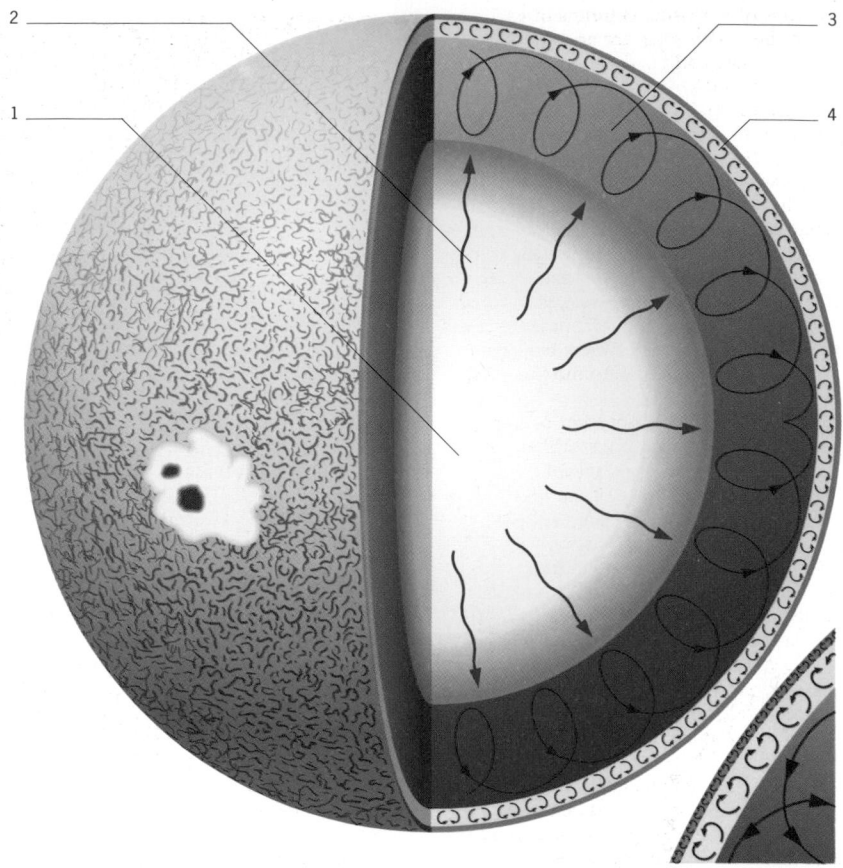

A giant prominence caused by changes in the Sun's magnetic field (far right).

Sunspots (below) are areas of cooler gas; they appear and disappear in regular cycles.

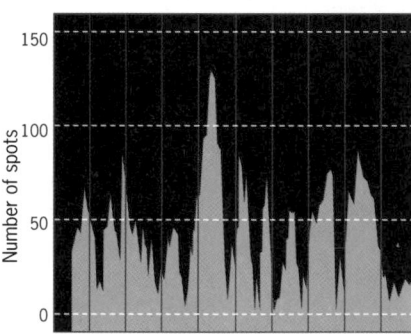

The fluctuation of sunspots as recorded over a ten-month period.

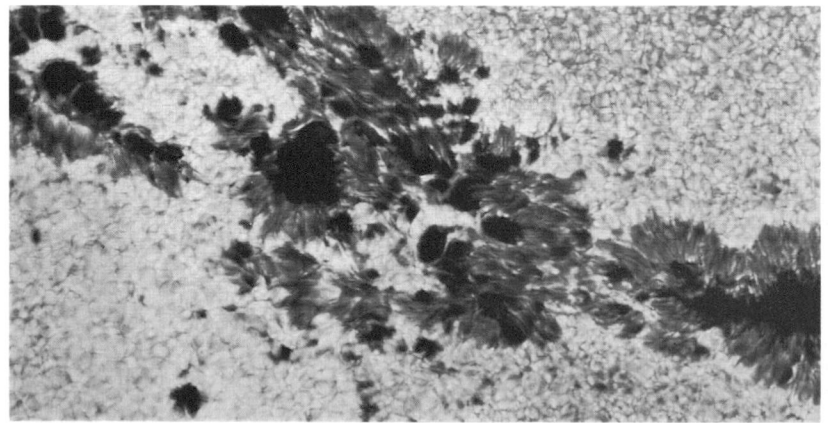

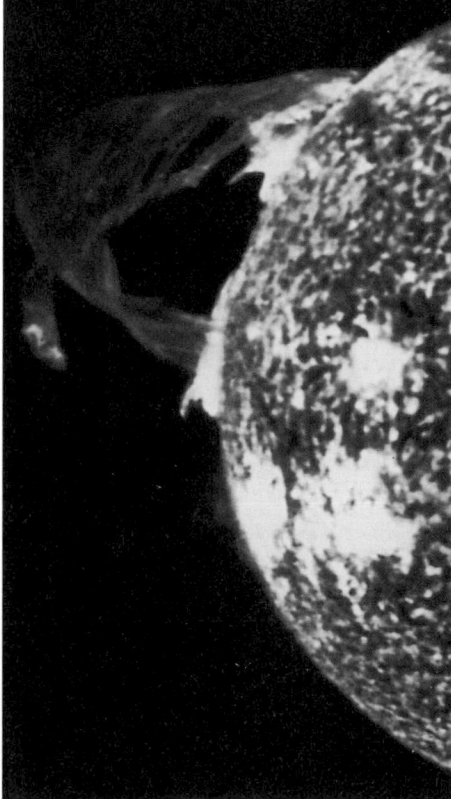

the tops of hot rising columns of gas, while the darker ones are areas where the gas has cooled and is descending. The surface is usually marked in areas near the equator by large sunspots (*far left, opposite*), which can be far larger than the Earth. They come in pairs, marking places where loops of the Sun's magnetic field have broken through the surface. Huge arches of glowing gas called prominences curve above the Sun's surface, but paradoxically they represent gas falling in toward the Sun and following the curved magnetic field. Occasionally flares explode on the Sun's surface, blasting a pulse of X rays and subatomic particles into space.

The chromosphere is a layer of tenuous gas, its hydrogen glowing a brilliant red. This is visible during a total eclipse as a red rim around the disk of the Moon.

Extending around the Sun to a distance of several times its radius is the pearly white corona (crown), which has a temperature of millions of degrees, yet is so rarefied that it would present no danger to a spacecraft.

The Sun's life cycle

The Sun has billions of years of life behind and ahead of it. About 4.6 billion years ago it began like other stars, as a cold mass of hydrogen and helium left over from the Big Bang, which began to shrink under its own gravity. As it collapsed, the temperature of its core rose from friction-al heating as gas molecules collided. When the temperature reached about 18 million °F, thermonuclear reactions began.

A star of mass similar to the Sun, having shone as a yellow star for millions of years, will enter its red-giant phase, ending its cycle as a white dwarf.

The Sun has about another five billion years of life ahead of it, as it turns hydrogen into helium in its core. When the hydrogen fuel runs low, it will burn some helium nuclei, fusing those into heavier nuclei. At the same time it will swell into a giant red star, and Earth will be destroyed. A few million years later, the Sun will release some outer layers and shrink into a white dwarf, with an intensely hot surface, too small to give out much light. It will then cool off for the rest of time.

The solar cycles

The Sun's activity follows an 11-year cycle, during which sunspot numbers build to a maximum and then decline again. After a time of sunspot minimum, when the surface may be completely unblemished, the first spots of the new cycle appear in mid-latitudes. These gradually migrate toward the equator, while further spots continue to appear in the higher latitudes. At the same time flares and prominences become more numerous, prompted by the same fluctuation in the magnetic field, and the corona grows bigger. This continues for five or six years, after which the rate at which new spots appear gradually drops and other forms of activity decline.

This characteristic movement of the sunspots across the Sun is positive proof that it spins. The cycle is caused by the progressive tangling and untangling of magnetic fields within the Sun, owing to the differential rates of rotation, with regions of gas near to the poles taking a few days longer to complete their rotation than the equatorial areas. Unlike the planets, the whole mass does not spin at the same rate.

Radiation

The Sun puts out its maximum radiation in the yellow part of the optical spectrum, but it radiates substantially in the ultraviolet and infrared and to a lesser extent at the X ray and radio wavelengths. These make up the electromagnetic spectrum of transverse waves, which all have the same velocity in space. The source of this energy is the conversion of mass into energy caused by nuclear fusion reactions that occur within the core. This reaction will only occur at extremely high temperatures and pressures, when gas turns to plasma. In this reaction hydrogen nuclei fuse together to form helium. Each helium nucleus produced has slightly less mass than the hydrogen nuclei that went into it, and this difference is converted into energy, in accordance with Einstein's famous principle of the equivalence of mass and energy $E = mc^2$, where c represents the speed of light and m represents mass. The heat produced by this reaction is sufficent to activate further reactions and so it is self-sustaining. Four million tons of matter are converted to energy each second in the Sun and will continue to do so for the next five billion years.

Sun data

Physical characteristics of the Sun

Diameter	864,000 mi.
Volume	3.387×10^{17} cu. mi.
Mass	2.19×10^{27} tons

Chemical composition of photosphere

Element	% weight	Element	% weight
Hydrogen	73.46	Nitrogen	0.09
Helium	24.85	Silicon	0.07
Oxygen	0.77	Magnesium	0.05
Carbon	0.29	Sulfur	0.04
Iron	0.16	Other	0.10
Neon	0.12		

Density (water = 1):

Mean density of entire Sun	1.410g cm^{-3}
Interior (center of Sun)	150g cm^{-3}
Surface (photosphere)	10^{-3}g cm^{-3}
Chromosphere	10^{-6}g cm^{-3}
Low corona	1.7×10^{-16}g cm^{-3}

Temperature:

Interior (center)	15,000,000K
Surface (photosphere)	6,050K
Sunspot umbra (typical)	4,240K
Penumbra (typical)	5,680K
Chromosphere	4,300 to 50,000K
Corona	800,000 to 5,000,000K

Rotation (as seen from Earth):

Of solar equator	26.8 days
At solar latitude 30°	28.2 days
At solar latitude 60°	30.8 days
At solar latitude 75°	31.8 days

SOLAR SYSTEM

The solar system is dominated by the gravitation of the Sun. About 99.85 percent of the mass of the system resides in the Sun, 0.14 percent in the planets, and the rest in the satellites, asteroids, comets, and meteoric matter that also circle the central star.

The planets all circle the Sun in the same direction, in almost exactly the same plane. Viewed from "above," that is the side on which the Earth's Northern Hemisphere lies, the direction of the planetary motion is counter clockwise. The asteroids, or minor planets, do the same. But the orbits of the comets are oriented randomly. They can approach the Sun, and recede from it, at any angle.

The farthest planet from the Sun, normally, is Pluto, which at its maximum reaches 4.5 billion miles from the Sun. But the farthest members of the Sun's group are believed to be an enormous group of unseen comets that form Oort's Cloud, named after the Dutch astronomer who deduced their presence. The comets spend most of their time in the outermost reaches of their orbits, at a distance of about two light-years from the Sun. They mark the true outer limit of the solar system, the region in which the Sun's gravity becomes feebler than that of its neighboring stars.

The birth of a solar system

When the Sun was born about 4.6 billion years ago, it was encircled by a disk of matter left over from the parent cloud. Such a cloud would consist of gas, mostly hydrogen and helium, mixed with solid grains (*right*, 1). In the cooler outer regions of the cloud, the grains would consist of rocky matter and of "ices"— frozen water, carbon dioxide, methane, and ammonia. The ices could relatively easily be turned into vapor, so in the inner regions of the cloud only the rocky material condensed (2) as it was warmed by the newly born star.

Grains of dust in the disk collided, accumulated, and built up into small bodies called planetoids (3). These rapidly swept the surrounding space clear of the remaining dust. The inner planetoids consisted of rock and were fairly small: in the outer system, the planetoids also included the icy materials. Because they were more massive, the outer planetoids gathered large atmospheres of hydrogen and helium around them. The smaller inner planetoids could not retain atmospheres: the warmth from the central star also helped to drive off these light gases. The process of planetoid formation was repeated in miniature around the larger outer planets, which formed systems of numerous satellites, or moons.

For hundreds of millions of years the young planets and moons were bombarded by leftover debris. Finally the plane-

The presence of a dust disk around Beta Pictoris means it may have a planetary system.

tary system became established (4): in our case, four small, rocky inner planets, and four giant outer planets mostly consisting of hydrogen and helium, and their systems of moons; an oddball rocky planet, Pluto, in the "wrong" place at the edge of the system; and assorted debris of rock and ice—the asteroids, comets, and meteoric bodies.

Planets of other stars

Most stars probably evolved with disks of gas and dust around them, so the process of planet formation may well have been repeated many times throughout our

galaxy. We cannot observe planets of other stars directly, since their feeble light would be swamped by the light of the parent star. But there is indirect evidence for such planets.

Some stars appear to "wobble" in the sky because of an invisible companion whose gravity pulls on them, and the mass of that companion can be calculated. In the majority of cases the companion must be a faint star, and sometimes it can be observed by a sufficiently powerful telescope. But other bodies seem to have a mass not much greater than that of Jupiter, the largest planet in our Solar System. In 1992, three strong candidates for planetary-system status were identified. They are companions to a pulsar, a fast-spinning dead star. Two are about three times the mass of the Earth, which means they are planets. The other is only a hundredth the size of the Earth, which makes it roughly the size of the Moon, and almost planet-sized.

Infrared (heat) radiation has been detected coming from dust disks encircling other stars, such as Beta Pictoris (*above left*), in the constellation of Pictor. It is believed that planets may be forming from this dust. There is some evidence of empty zones in these disks, swept clear by planetoids, but this is not established. The present consensus, however, is that planetary systems are probably common in our galaxy.

The theoretical evolution of a typical planetary system.

INNER PLANETS

Mercury

The innermost planet is tiny Mercury, less than half the diameter of the Earth. Its orbit is the most tilted and least circular of all the planets except Pluto, with the result that at its closest approach to the Sun, the planet is 79 percent as far as when it is at its farthest. It is too hot to retain an atmosphere or any water, and on the hottest parts of the surface, when the Sun is overhead and the planet is nearest to the Sun, the temperature is high enough to melt lead. Mercury is too small to have kept its primordial heat and there is no volcanic activity. The unchanging surface retains the craters created by the age of meteoric bombardment soon after the planets' birth and resembles the cratered areas of the Moon.

Mercury's rotation period is 58.65 days, exactly two-thirds of its "year" (88 days). This means that the time between sunrise and sunset at a given place on the planet is also 88 days, one Mercurian year.

Venus

The second planet from the Sun, Venus, is slightly smaller and less massive than the Earth, but its gravity is strong enough to retain a dense atmosphere. There may have been water on the early Venus, brought to the inner planets by the bombardment of icy comets from the outer solar system. But the planet was too hot because of its closeness to the Sun to have kept water vapor in its atmosphere. Without rain and oceans to dissolve the carbon dioxide it could not be removed from the atmosphere in the way it is on Earth. A thick heavy atmosphere of carbon dioxide built up, outgassed from volcanoes. This trapped heat from sunlight, leading to a runaway greenhouse effect. Today the atmosphere is almost wholly carbon dioxide and is so massive that the surface pressure is over 90 times that of the Earth.

The surface temperature is 837°F (447°C) and most of the space probes that have landed on Venus' surface have been roasted and crushed into silence within minutes. The longest-lasting survived for 127 minutes. But the probes have sent back pictures of a rocky landscape, glowing orange in the light filtered by the clouds of sulfuric acid that swathe the planet.

Earth

The Earth is the largest of the inner planets and is unique in its retention of the water that arrived in comets from the outer solar system when the planets were in their infancy. The carbon dioxide on Earth acts in a constructive manner, unlike on Venus, helping to moderate temperatures and allowing plant life to photosynthesize and so produce oxygen. Much of the Earth's carbon dioxide is dissolved in the oceans and rocks.

The solar system's innermost planet, Mercury, has a heavily cratered surface.

The Earth has the most active surface of any of the inner planets. The volcanic activity that drives the continents over the surface constantly swallows surface rocks and keeps carbon dioxide locked in the crust. The Earth's surface, like those of the other inner planets, was raised to red-heat by the bombardment of meteoric debris early in its life. Although the planet cooled off, heat from the radioactive elements within it softened its core, and metals, mostly iron and nickel, melted and sank to the center. The heat flowing out from the core keeps the surface in constant turbulence.

A radical consequence of the retention of water was the appearance of life within a billion years of the Earth's birth. Plants developed that gave out oxygen and built up the atmosphere of today— one-fifth oxygen and the rest mainly nitrogen. This oxygen-rich atmosphere, unique in the solar system, permits the profusion of life that exists today.

Mars

Mars is about half the diameter of the Earth. As a result of its small size, volcanic activity has ceased; dead volcanoes include Olympus Mons, the largest mountain in the solar system, 16 mi./25 km high and 375 mi./600 km broad at its

The planet Earth, as viewed from Apollo 17 on its journey to the Moon in 1972.

The rocky surface of Venus as investigated by the planetary probe Magellan.

base. The Martian atmosphere consists almost wholly of carbon dioxide, but it is so thin that the pressure at ground level is less than a hundredth of that of the Earth. Nevertheless, winds can blow that are strong enough to raise enormous dust storms which can obscure the entire planetary surface for weeks. To an observer on the surface of Mars, the sky would often appear pink because of the suspended dust, which is red because it largely consists of iron oxide rust.

The Martian poles are covered with a thin frosting of frozen water and carbon dioxide, and grow and shrink with the seasons. There is no free water on Mars today, but large quantities of water once flowed, carving gigantic valley systems, a single branch of which could easily swallow the Earth's Grand Canyon. The climate was apparently warmer in the past, and the atmosphere denser. Both these factors have led to speculation about the existence of life on Mars in the past. In more recent times the growth of huge volcanoes might have altered the tilt of the Martian poles, changing the climate and causing carbon dioxide in the atmosphere to freeze out at the poles. Or huge oceans might have caused the carbon dioxide to be used up in rock formation, thinning the atmosphere.

Volcanoes, including the giant Olympus Mons, feature on the Martian surface.

OUTER PLANETS

Jupiter

The largest planet in the solar system, Jupiter has a diameter more than ten times that of the Earth and could contain all the other planets in the solar system within its confines. The planet consists almost entirely of gas. The visible surface is banded by light and dark regions of brownish and yellowish clouds, which consist of methane and ammonia crystals. Enormous storms swirl within these clouds. One, called the Great Red Spot, has existed since the 1600s, when telescopes first focused on it.

Jupiter's atmosphere consists of hydrogen and helium in pretty much the same proportions as in the primordial cloud out of which the planets were formed. The gas extends almost to the center of the planet but is crushed by the colossal pressure into a liquid form, and then, still deeper, into a solid, metallike state. At the very center of Jupiter there may be a core of rock and ice.

Saturn

Saturn is a globe of hydrogen and helium, like Jupiter, although with a surface that seen through ordinary telescopes is relatively featureless. But the most powerful instruments, such as the Hubble Space Telescope, reveal bands of clouds and vast rotating storms, like those of the larger planet. The overall density of Saturn is less than that of water.

The planet is graced with a splendid system of rings. Saturn takes 30 years to orbit the Sun, and because of the tilt of the rings, it presents them to us at varying angles. Twice during that period they are edge-on to us and disappear in all but the most powerful telescopes. Twice they are fully opened out and make the planet a dazzling sight.

Uranus

The third of the gas giants has a bluish, featureless surface. The clouds are almost invisible because they form lower in the atmosphere than those of Jupiter and Saturn. Deep within the planet the

Jupiter's swirling bands of cloud are dominated by the Great Red Spot.

Saturn's rings make the planet the most distinctive and beautiful member of the outer solar system.

hydrogen and helium atmosphere gives way to an ocean of hot water under immense pressure, beneath which is a core of rock and ice. The heat is left over from the formation of Uranus, and the planet's interior continues to cool.

Uranus has an axis of rotation that is tilted at more than 90°: that is, its north pole lies just "below" the plane of the planet's orbit, making Uranus unique in the solar system. Each pole points toward the Sun for half of the planet's 84-year period of revolution and in fact these are the warmest regions of the planet. The planet's 15 known satellites revolve in the plane of its equator.

Neptune

The outermost of the gas giants became the outermost planet of the solar system in 1979 when Pluto, making its closest approach to the Sun, passed "inside" Neptune's orbit (though the two planets are always many millions of miles apart).

Temperatures on Neptune fall to –360°F (217°C), only 100°F (56°C) above absolute zero. Neptune shows more surface activity than Uranus, and occasionally white cloud-tops of methane crystals are just visible through the pale blue haze. Like Uranus, it probably has a central rocky core covered by a deep ocean of hot water, the temperature raised by left-over heat from the planet's formation.

Pluto

The outermost of the known planets is really a double planet. The diameter of Pluto's satellite Charon is half that of Pluto itself, making Charon larger in relation to Pluto than the Moon is to the Earth. Pluto has a highly elliptical orbit and its closest approach to the Sun brings it to three-fourths of its maximum distance. Pluto's orbital inclination is greater than that of any other planet. The planet has a core of rock covered with water-ice, and frozen methane covers the poles. Pluto and Charon resemble the satellites of the giant planets and would probably have become moons of Neptune if, by some gravitational chance, they had not been flung into their present positions.

Planet X

Could there be a tenth planet beyond Pluto? Neptune was "discovered" on paper in 1846, a year before it was seen; its orbit was calculated from its gravitational effect on the orbit of Uranus. But it did not seem to explain all the disturbance of Uranus that was observed, and the search for a further planet began. It was not until 1930 that Clyde Tombaugh discovered Pluto. Pluto does not seem to be massive enough to be responsible for all the gravitational disturbance of Uranus and Neptune that has been observed, and at least one more planet may lie beyond Pluto. Computer analysis of the orbits of Uranus and Neptune gives some "best bets" for the distance and mass of possible planets. Some predictions indicate a planet up to five times the mass of the Earth, several times as far from the Sun as Neptune, and possibly in a tilted orbit.

The blue-green color of Uranus is due to methane mixed in hydrogen and helium.

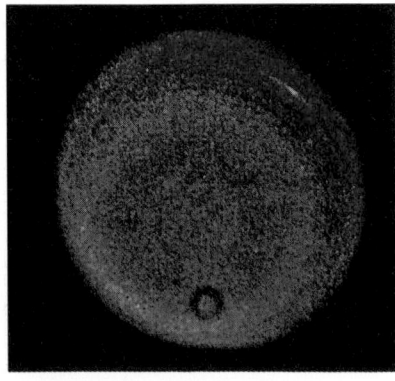

Neptune is similar in nature to Uranus but is more active and contains less methane.

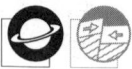

PLANETARY MOONS

Many small bodies formed from the dust left over after the planets had evolved. Some formed as satellites, or moons, of the four giant planets. But none formed around the small, rocky inner planets.

The Earth acquired the Moon when it collided with an asteroid-sized body during the intense bombardment that affected the young solar system until 3.8 billion years ago. The force of the collision melted the intruder and a large part of the Earth, and light rock from the outer parts of the Earth mingled with the new body. Fragments of the embryo Moon were flung into orbit around the Earth and coalesced to form the relatively large satellite we see today. The Moon continued to be scarred by meteoric bombardment, and the cratering survives on its highlands. The lowlands were flooded by rock melted by the bombardment, forming dark "maria," or "seas."

Mars managed to capture two small bodies from elsewhere. Phobos and Deimos are so small that their gravity is not strong enough to pull them into a spherical shape. Phobos is so close to Mars that it revolves faster than the planet turns, so it seems to rise in the west and set in the east as viewed from Mars. Phobos is scarred by a giant crater, Stickney, fully half of Phobos' diameter.

The satellites of the four gas giants are of two kinds: those that formed along with the parent planets from the same cloud of gas and dust, and those that were captured later from the general solar system debris. The former are relatively large, spherical bodies, several hundreds of miles in diameter, revolving in the plane of the parent planet's equator. The latter are smaller, irregularly shaped, and often moving in tilted retrograde orbits.

Jupiter's moons

Four giant satellites have been known since Galileo first observed the sky with a telescope, and the brightest can sometimes be glimpsed with the naked eye by the most sharp-sighted observer. The innermost Galilean moon, Io (*below, left*),

The near side of the Moon shows the familiar craters and "seas."

is unique among satellites in being geologically active. The moon is colored red, orange, and yellow by volcanic sulfur compounds. The next moons out, Europa and Ganymede (*below, center*), are responsible for the vulcanism of Io that is squeezed between their gravitational fields and that of Jupiter, and the continual flexing of Io heats it up.

Europa looks as smooth and white as a billiard ball because its surface is covered with ice. There are cracks in the surface, but all trace of meteoric craters has been removed by movements of ice.

The third of the Galilean satellites, Ganymede, is the largest known satellite in the solar system. With a diameter of over 3,200 mi./5,200 km, it is larger than Mercury. Its surface is covered with extensive cracks and with craters, many of them filled with ice.

Callisto is heavily cratered, and a huge set of concentric rings, formed by a giant impact in the past, marks one hemisphere like a bull's-eye. The craters have gentler contours than those of the Earth's Moon, because of the softness of the mixture of rock and ice that make up the surface.

Four small satellites revolve within the Galilean moons. Three of them move in the tenuous rings that circle Jupiter. Two other groups of captured moons orbit Jupiter. They are all less than about 50 mi./80 km in diameter. The inner four

Irregular-shaped Phobos is the innermost and largest of the two moons of Mars.

have strongly tilted orbits, while the outermost four have "retrograde" motion—they revolve the "wrong" way relative to the majority motion in the solar system.

Saturn's moons

The largest of Saturn's moons, Titan, has the densest atmosphere of any satellite. It consists of a reddish smog, made up of compounds formed by reactions triggered by sunlight in the high atmosphere. The atmosphere is composed mainly of nitrogen and is ten times as massive as the Earth's, with a pressure at the surface 50 percent greater. Titan's atmospheric circulation is driven by methane as the Earth's is driven by water, and there may be methane lakes on the surface.

The major satellite closest to Saturn is Mimas, whose surface is covered in bright, cratered ice. Seven satellites, including the major moon Enceladus, move within one of Saturn's rings. The material of the ring consists of ice grains thrown off from Enceladus.

Several of the moons share orbits. Only the outermost, dark-colored Phoebe, has retrograde motion. Phoebe also has a tilted orbit, as does Iapetus. Hyperion has no fixed period of rotation on its own axis, but tumbles chaotically as a result of the gravitational perturbation of the next satellite out, Titan.

Io's color is due to its volcanoes spewing out vast quantities of sulfur compounds.

Ganymede is the largest of all satellites within the solar system.

Miranda has a grooved surface with valleys and ridges.

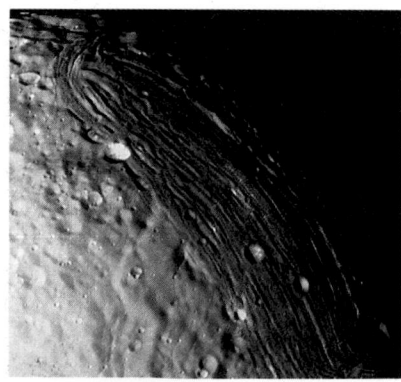

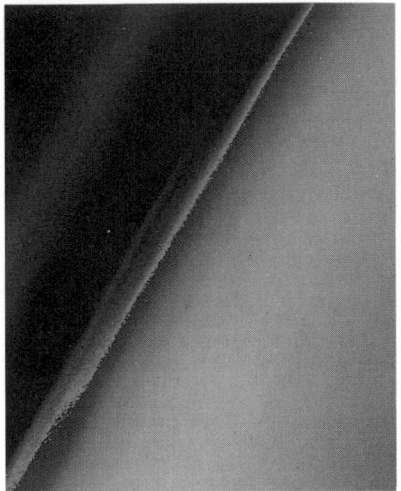

Titan, the largest of Saturn's moons, has dense orange clouds in its atmosphere.

Moons of Uranus

Five satellites of Uranus had been discovered from Earth before the Voyager spacecraft flew by the planet. Four of them are rock-ice mixtures, scarred by craters, and three of these are cracked by internal "volcanic" activity, with a mixture of water and methane or ammonia playing the role of lava. The fifth moon, Miranda (*p. 21*), is so fantastically scarred and grooved that it may once have been smashed into several fragments that came together again.

Ten smaller satellites move within the orbits of the larger moons. They are dark, and all are less than 125 mi./200 km across.

Neptune's moons

The coldest places in the solar system, with temperatures down to –390°F (-235°C), are to be found on the one large satellite of Neptune, Triton. "Snow" of frozen nitrogen, thrown out by volcanoes, coats the poles. Triton moves in a tilted and retrograde orbit, and is a captured body. The much smaller satellite Nereid is also captured, and its orbit is highly eccentric. The farthest satellite in the solar system is so dark that it has never been observed from Earth.

Pluto and Charon

The existence of Charon was not suspected until 1978, when a small bump was noticed on Pluto's image on a photographic plate. From 1985 to 1990, Charon's orbit was positioned so that the satellite passed repeatedly in front of and behind Pluto. This revealed a great deal about both bodies. They both revolve about their common center of gravity, a point in space between them. Their motion showed Pluto's mass to be only a five-hundredth of the Earth's, and Charon's a tenth of that.

During a Saturnian year (29.5 Earth years) the rings are viewed from different angles.

1995

2000

2005

2009

2013

2018

There are thousands of narrow rings circling Saturn, each made up of tiny fragments.

Rings

The four gas giants are all girdled by a system of rings. Those of Saturn are the best known. They are so broad, bright, and spectacular that they were observed with the very earliest telescopes. They are made up of billions of tiny bodies, consisting of rock and ice, and ranging in size from smaller than a grain of dust to yards across, each in effect a miniature satellite in its own orbit. This material forms broad sheets 41,000 mi./66,000 km across, but less than a mile thick. There are gaps in the rings where "moonlets" cannot linger because of the gravitational influence of Saturn's inner satellites. The Voyager space probes first revealed in detail the unsuspected fine structure of Saturn's ring system and sent back spectacular and revealing images. The rings are made up of more than 100,000 thin "ringlets," some of which appear to be kinked and braided.

The rings of the other giant planets are puny affairs by comparison, thin and faint. Those of Uranus and Neptune were first discovered by the brief twinkling of stars when the rings passed in front of them. The rings of Jupiter were discovered by Voyager. The rings of Jupiter, Uranus, and Neptune have very dark surfaces in contrast to those of Saturn. They may contain carbon, or frozen methane darkened by particle bombardment.

Neptune's rings were thought to be incomplete from Earth observations, but Voyager showed that they have bright patches, where moonlets clump together.

All rings are placed at a distance from the parent planet where a single moon could not survive because it would be pulled apart by the gravitational influence of the planet. The rings may have formed by the disintegration of an ordinary satellite that wandered too close to the planet. Or they could consist of matter left over from the formation of the planet that was prevented by gravitation from collecting into a single moon.

Jupiter's rings backlit by the Sun.

COSMIC DEBRIS

Meteors and meteorites

Untold numbers of grains of dust orbit the Sun, left over from the cloud of matter that formed the planets. As one of these meteoroids falls through the Earth's atmosphere, frictional heat causes it to burn up in a brief flash of light—known as a shooting star, or meteor. Very rarely a larger meteoroid survives its passage through the atmosphere and falls to the ground as a meteorite.

Meteors can come in regular showers, once a year. This happens when the Earth crosses the dust-strewn path of a comet, surviving or extinct.

Meteorites are of several types. Some are stony; others are mainly iron; others are of intermediate composition. Dating them by their weak natural radioactivity shows the minerals in them to have formed soon after the birth of the solar system. The different types of meteoroid are believed to have come from different parts of one or more planetoids, or embryo planets, that had grown large enough to begin separating into a dense metal core and a stony exterior.

The asteroids

Most of the thousands of known asteroids, or minor planets, move in a belt in the large gap between Mars and Jupiter. The largest, Ceres, the first to be discovered, is only 578 mi./930 km across, and only 200 are more than 60 mi./100 km across. They are too small for their own gravity to pull them into a spherical shape. They fall into types that match the meteorite types.

The asteroids are probably debris left over from the birth of the solar system, debris that failed to coalesce into a full-sized planet because of the disturbing gravitational pull of Jupiter. Some of them were deflected by collisions or close encounters into orbits outside the main asteroid belt. The so-called Earth-grazers come within Earth's orbit. Other asteroids have been observed moving beyond the orbit of Saturn, and there may be more. Two groups of asteroids share the orbit of Jupiter, one 60° ahead of the planet, and one 60° behind.

Comets

The comets that visit the Sun occasionally from the farthest limits of the solar system differ from the asteroids in having a greater quantity of water-ice and frozen gases mixed with their rock. They formed at the birth of the solar system in the cooler regions beyond Mars, where ices could survive. Encounters with the giant planets flung them into vast, stretched-out orbits that carried them to the limits of the Sun's gravitational field.

As the comet nucleus approaches the Sun these "ices" warm up, turn into gas, and blow rock and dust into space. A halo of gas and dust, called the coma,

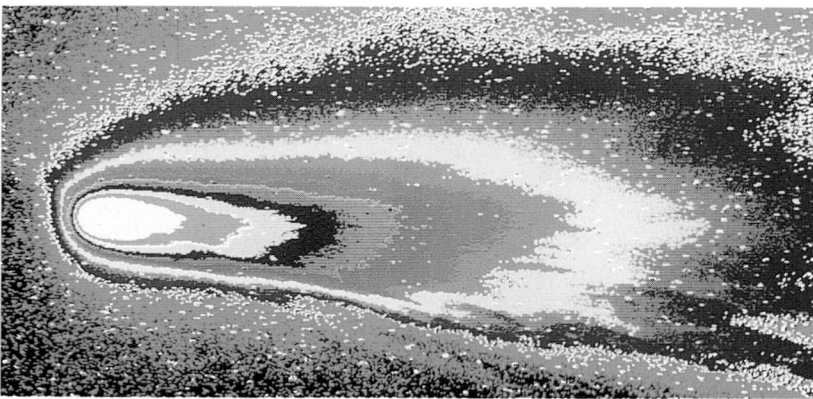

This false color image of Halley's comet reveals its structure by grades of brightness.

The Barringer Crater in Arizona, caused by a meteor impact 25,000 years ago.

forms around the nucleus. A long straight tail of gas, glowing blue, is driven off by radiation from the Sun, and a yellowish dust tail also streams from the nucleus. The tails point away from the Sun all the time that the comet sweeps past, though the more sluggish dust tail is curved because it lags slightly.

Most observed comets have been seen only once in human history, because they take millions of years to complete an orbit. And often in that time they are

Comets take an elliptical orbit around the Sun, their tails always pointing away.

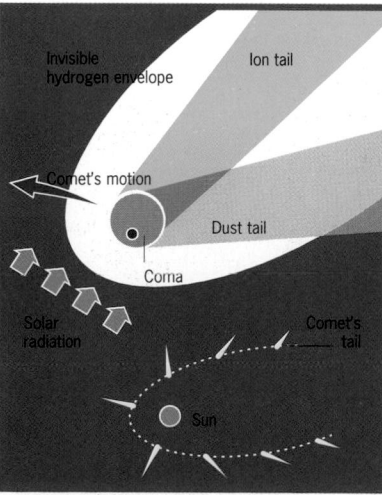

deflected by one of the giant planets into a new orbit that keeps them away. But a steady supply of new comets is sent in toward the inner solar system by gravitational disturbances in the comet cloud that envelops the Sun at a distance of several light-years. A few are closer in and reappear at intervals measured in years. They wear out a little at each pass and ultimately fade or break up.

Impacts

In 1994, the comet Shoemaker-Levy 9 demonstrated the power of a cometary impact with a planet. The "target" was Jupiter, but there have undoubtedly been many collisions between the Earth and comets or asteroids in the past. Traces of some craters survive: one off the Yucatán peninsula in Mexico seems to mark the impact of a body 6 mi./10 km wide 65 million years ago. Although the theory is contested, many scientists believe that the dust cloud generated by this impact resulted in significant climatic change. The closest known approach to the Earth by any asteroid in historical times was within 106,000 mi./170,000 km, less than half the distance of the Moon, in 1991.

The dark brown areas are the impact sites of the Shoemaker-Levy Comet on Jupiter.

STARS AND NEBULAE

Great clouds of gas and dust, called nebulae, extend across space. Bright clouds are limited regions stimulated to shine by the light of nearby hot stars. An example is the faint patch of light just discernible in the sword of the constellation Orion. In reality this is a nebula about 15 light-years across, the birthplace of thousands of new stars.

More extensive are the dark nebulae. The bulk of these is transparent gas, but the dust in them blocks the light from stars beyond. The dark "lanes" that we see in the Milky Way (p. 26) are actually dust clouds blocking our view of the piled-up banks of stars lying beyond and preventing us from seeing to the center of the galaxy, 30,000 light-years away.

Gas in the galaxy is pretty much the same as the primordial matter that emerged from the Big Bang (p. 30), and from which the galaxy formed perhaps 12 billion years ago. Three-fourths of its mass consists of hydrogen, nearly all the rest of helium, but some of the gas and all of the dust consists of new elements formed since then in stars. The hydrogen, though dark, can be mapped by its ultra high frequency radio emissions.

The birth of stars

A nebula can be considered as the birthplace of stars. If a gas cloud is dense enough—perhaps because it has been compressed by the shock waves from a nearby star that has exploded—it will begin to collapse. As it does so, its atoms and molecules speed up as gravitational energy is turned into kinetic energy—the energy of movement. Friction among the particles heats the cloud. Warm, dense clouds, apparently swathing such gravitationally heated "protostars," can be detected by heat radiation.

When the core has risen to about 18 million °F, nuclear reactions begin. Hydrogen nuclei are fused together to form helium nuclei. The surrounding matter is blown away in powerful streams, and the new star, though less bright than the protostar, is now visible.

Star types

The great majority of stars, including the Sun, are "dwarfs." Only a minority that are approaching death have swollen to become "giants" or "supergiants." Stars vary in color according to their temperature, from the cooler red stars to the hottest blue/white stars. By comparing magnitude and color it is possible to classify stars (right).

If the core of the star-forming gas cloud is less than one-twelfth as massive as the Sun, nuclear reactions can never begin, and the object glows dimly as a reddish ball of gas, a so-called "brown dwarf." The search is on for brown dwarfs.

Stars only slightly less massive than the Sun are reddish, with surface temperatures of a few thousand °F. They burn so slowly that they will live for hundreds of billions of years before fading away.

Stars of mass similar to the Sun are called "yellow dwarfs" because they give out most of their radiation as yellow light. (The mixture of all the wavelengths in their light is actually white.) The surface temperature of such a star is similar to that of the Sun, about 10,000°F, and its lifetime as a normal hydrogen-burning star is about ten billion years. After this it will briefly extend its life by "burning"' helium into heavier nuclei in the core, swelling to hundreds of times its original diameter as a red giant, with a cool surface, but still intensely bright because of its huge size. As the helium runs low, a red giant grows unstable and becomes a variable star, swelling and shrinking and becoming brighter and fainter as it does so. It puffs off shells of gas (*top, right*) and finally a collapsed core is left behind as an extremely dense white dwarf, with the mass of a star squeezed into the volume of the Earth. Though hot, it is small and faint, and it continues to cool and fade.

The most massive stars are about a hundred times as massive as the Sun. They burn fuel so quickly that they are blue-hot, with surfaces over 45,000°F, and diameters ten times greater than the 862,000 mi./1,390,000 km of the Sun. They use up their fuel in a few million years, rather than ten billion. Then they swell into giant or supergiant stars such

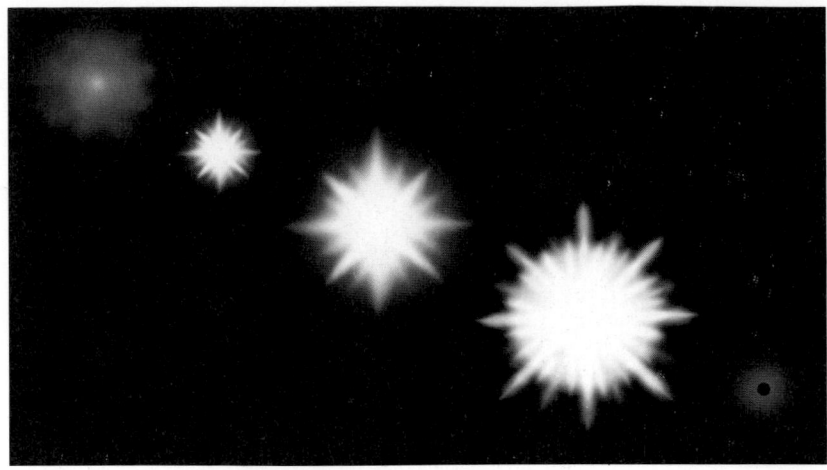

A brilliant hot star of 30 solar masses eventually suffers a massive explosion, or supernova, leaving extremely dense matter that collapses into a black hole.

The Hertzsprung Russell diagram plots a star's relative magnitude against temperature. The evolutionary path of the Sun is superimposed on it, plus the positions of well-known stars.

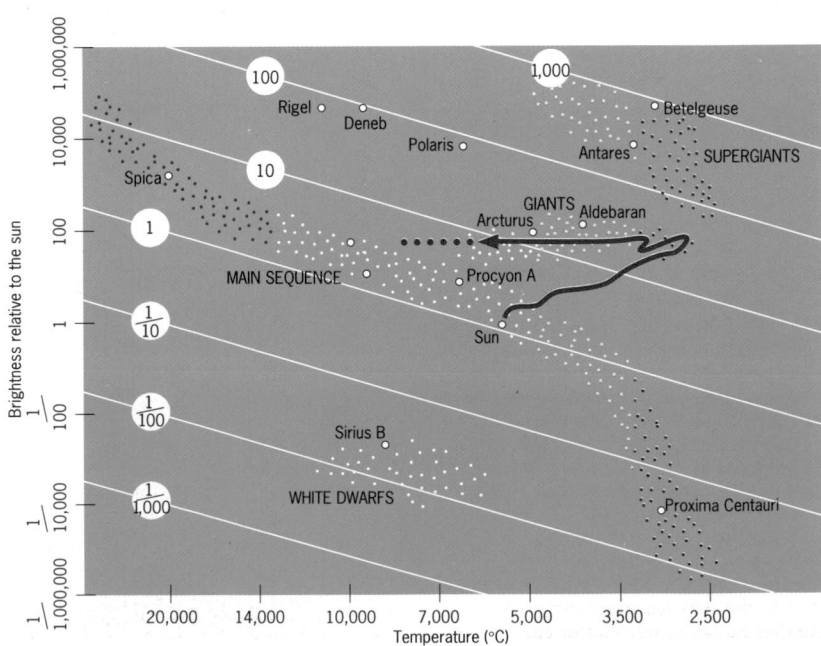

A planetary nebula is formed when a star in its giant phase of evolution produces a final burst of nuclear energy that blows an expanding shell of gas into space. This is the Helix nebula.

The 20 nearest stars			
Star name	**DLY**	**M¹**	**M²**
Proxima Centauri	4.3	+11.05	+15.5
Alpha Centauri A	4.3	0.01	+4.4
Alpha Centauri B	4.3	+1.33	+5.7
Barnard's Star	5.9	+9.54	+13.3
Wolf 359	7.6	+13.53	+16.7
Lalande 21185	8.1	+7.50	+10.5
Sirus A	8.6	-1.46	+1.4
Sirus B	8.6	+8.68	+11.6
Luyten 726-8 A	8.9	+12.45	+15.3
UV Ceti (726-8 B)	8.9	+12.95	+15.3
Ross 154	9.4	+10.6	+13.3
Ross 248	10.3	+12.29	+14.8
Epsilon Eridani	10.8	+3.73	+6.1
Ross 128	10.8	+11.10	+13.5
Luyten 789-6	10.8	+12.18	+14.6
61 Cygni A	11.1	+5.22	+7.6
61 Cygni B	11.1	+6.03	+8.4
Epsilon Indi	11.2	+4.68	+7.0
Procyon A	11.2	+0.37	+2.7
Procyon B	11.2	+10.70	+13.0

DLY = Distance (in light-years)
M^1 = Apparent magnitude
M^2 = Absolute magnitude

as Antares. In their intensely hot, dense cores, they burn first helium and then heavier nuclei. They build a range of nuclei. In the last seconds of the star's life it builds nuclei as heavy as those of iron. These cannot be burned, and the star, its internal power supply cut off, collapses and then explodes as a supernova.

Supernovae

A supernova flares up until it is briefly brighter than the hundred billion fellow stars of its galaxy. The heavy atomic nuclei that it has synthesized at the end of its life are flung across space, mixing with the interstellar nebulae and forming raw materials for new planetary systems around new stars, whose formation may be triggered by the shock waves emanating from the supernova.

Remnants of supernova explosions can be seen as enormous rings and globes of gas. At the center there may remain a fragment of the original star, with a mass similar to the Sun's, enormously compressed into a sphere perhaps 12 mi./20 km across. Here electrons and atomic nuclei are crushed together to form a ball of neutrons (the uncharged particles found in the heart of all atoms). One teaspoonful of this neutron star, or pulsar, has a mass of 100 million tons. Beams of radiation jet from its poles, generated by gas falling onto it and focused by the neutron star's intense magnetic field. The star spins a few tens or hundreds of times a second, and if one of the radiation beams sweeps across the direction of the Earth, we observe it as a pulsating radio source or pulsar.

When a star of around ten solar masses (a supergiant) dies, the remnant it leaves may be even more dense than a neutron star and becomes a black hole. The gravitation of such a body is so intense that it begins a collapse that continues forever toward a geometric point; the more it shrinks the stronger its gravity becomes. Neither radiation nor matter can escape

from within a sphere only a few miles across, the boundary of which is called the event horizon. Such matter has effectively left the universe.

But paradoxically black holes can be at the heart of intensely bright objects. Gas falling into a black hole—perhaps from a companion star—releases enormous amounts of energy, much of it at very short X ray wavelengths.

Multiple stars

Most stars have companions. Two, three, or more stars, born from the same gas cloud, may orbit each other. Some giant stars are in contact as they orbit each other. The members of other multiple systems are so far apart, they may not belong to one system.

The more massive star of a pair will go through its life cycle more rapidly, and its death may be affected by its companion. In some binary systems, one star has aged until it has become a white dwarf. When the second star at last ages and swells, gas from its outer layers can be sucked onto the surface of the white dwarf, which

Orion nebula; radiation emitted from hot newborn stars causes hydrogen to glow red.

flares up as a bright, seemingly "new" star, a nova, over 100,000 times brighter than the Sun. The white dwarf blows away the excess matter and subsides.

But if the mass of the white dwarf is above a certain limit, there can be a much more massive explosion—a supernova but caused in a different way from those discussed above.

Star clusters

The enormous sphere of gas that was to become our galaxy first gave birth to thousands of "globular clusters," tightly packed balls of stars that contain the oldest stars in our galaxy and fill a roughly spherical volume around the disk of the galaxy. Planets could probably not form or survive around the stars of such a cluster, which are less than a light-year apart.

Later, when the disk of the galaxy was formed, stars continued to be born. These were in looser showers—"open clusters"—of up to thousands at a time. These groupings were gradually dispersed, but many survive today (*below*).

The well-known Pleiades open cluster of stars in the constellation of Taurus.

MILKY WAY GALAXY

Evolution of the galaxy

The solar system is located in a spiral galaxy known as the Milky Way. The galaxy formed from an ill-defined globe of hydrogen and helium gas approximately 12–14 billion years ago. This "protogalaxy" gradually shrank under its own gravitational attraction. As it did so, smaller concentrations of gas condensed within it. These were the basis of globular clusters of stars, each orbiting the center of what was to become the galaxy. Each in turn broke into hundreds of thousands of smaller knots of gas, which evolved into stars.

The bulk of the protogalaxy collapsed into the center without forming part of a globular cluster. As the gas collapsed, it whirled faster around the center, as water whirls down a drain. Most of the matter formed a huge flattened globe—the galaxy's central bulge. Most of this gas broke up into stars, but some was spun out into a great rotating disk (*below*), 100,000 light-years across. The rotation of the disk slowed the condensing of gas into stars, which continues today.

Sister galaxy to the Milky Way, Andromeda shows a classic spiral structure and central bulge.

Structure of the galaxy

The globular clusters contain the galaxy's oldest stars and consequently look reddish, because many of their stars have expanded to become giants or supergiants. The clusters orbit the galaxy's center and often pass through the disk, but there are no collisions among the stars, which are enormous distances apart even within the relatively closely packed globular clusters. There is almost certainly a vast amount of undetected "dark matter" spread through the halo of every galaxy. It might consist of huge numbers of brown dwarfs—too dim to be seen—but many astronomers think this matter consists of undiscovered types of subatomic particles.

The stars near the center of the galaxy are also old and reddish, and relatively little gas was left over here from the process of star formation. But there are gas clouds in a central region of ten light-

Star clouds in Sagittarius lie in the direction of the center of the galaxy.

years or so in diameter that can be probed only with radio telescopes. The clouds are violently agitated by some

object—or objects—at the center with a mass of a few million Suns. That object may be a black hole, swallowing mass of the equivalent of ten Suns a year, or the remains of supermassive stars that may have exploded there within the last 100 million years or so.

The disk of the galaxy is 100,000 light-years across. The Sun lies about two-thirds of the way out from the center and takes about 230 million years to orbit the galactic center. Two, or perhaps four, tightly coiled spiral arms are marked out by bright bluish stars. The arms are regions where gravitational effects are believed to cause ripples of slightly increased density though this is poorly understood. Stars and gas clouds pass through the arms but their passage is slowed. Starbirth is triggered here. Though all kinds of stars are born, the minority of short-lived, fast-burning, blue-hot massive stars are conspicuous, marking out the arms.

A protogalaxy consists of a nucleus surrounded by star-forming gas. The movement of the gas produces an orbital motion around the nucleus which concentrates in the galaxy's equatorial plane. Finally, spiral arms develop within the disk structure.

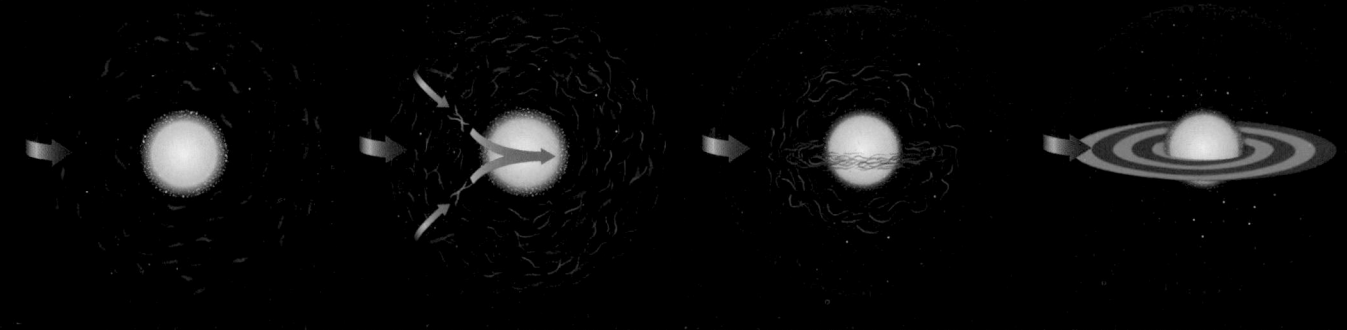

TYPES OF GALAXY

Only about one-fourth of all galaxies are spirals, and one-fourth are irregulars. The most numerous type are elliptical galaxies, with shapes ranging from that of a football to globular. Ellipticals vary greatly in size, from around ten million stars up to the largest galaxies known, with a hundred trillion (a hundred million million) members. They contain little gas and few young stars, so they are predominantly reddish in color. There are no large elliptical galaxies in the Local Group, but some small ones are satellite galaxies of Andromeda.

Spiral galaxies can have tightly coiled arms, emerging from large central disks, or less tightly coiled ones emerging from smaller disks. The same range of forms appears in a type of galaxy described as a barred spiral (*below*), in which a spiral arm emerges from each end of a central bulge that takes a bar-shaped rather than circular form.

Edwin Hubble's classification of galaxies divides regulars into ellipticals and spirals.

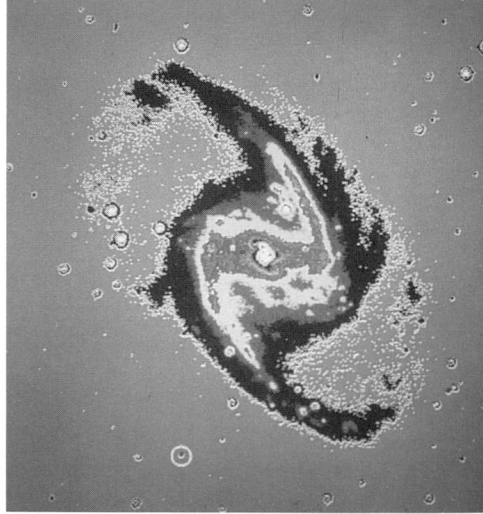

False-color image of a barred spiral galaxy.

The Local Group

Galaxies tend to cluster together. The Milky Way galaxy belongs to a small cluster, consisting of at least 25 galaxies. Four are visible to the naked eye. One is a small spiral that can just be seen under good conditions in Triangulum. The others are the Andromeda galaxy (*left*) and the Large (*below*) and Small Magellanic Clouds (LMC and SMC).

The Local Group of galaxies is dominated by two spirals, the Milky Way galaxy and the Andromeda galaxy, and the two are often compared. Both are larger than the average spiral, but Andromeda is twice as broad as ours and the largest member of the Local Group. It is approaching our galaxy at a speed of 170 mps/ 275 kps.—a negligible speed in comparison with its distance of over two million light-years.

The Magellanic Clouds

The Large and Small Magellanic Clouds are satellite galaxies of the Milky Way. They are visible as two patches of light close to the Milky Way in the southern sky. The LMC is 170,000 light-years distant and 30,000 light-years across; the SMC is 190,000 light-years away and 16,000 light-years in diameter. Both are classified as spiral, though they have been heavily distorted by the Milky Way.

The Large Magellanic Cloud (LMC) is the nearest galaxy to Earth. Its nebulae glow pink from energized hydrogen.

Local Group members		
Name	**Type***	**Distance (million light-years)**
M31 Andromeda	S	2.4
Milky Way Galaxy	S	–
M33 Triangulum	S	2.6
LMC	S	0.16
SMC	S	0.19
IC 10	I	2.0
NGC 205	E	2.4
M32	E	2.4
NGC 6822	I	1.6
WLM	I	3.1
NGC 185	E	2.1
NGC 147	E	2.1
IC 5152	I	3.0
IC 1613	I	2.3
DDO 210	Dwarf I	2.0
Pegasus	Dwarf I	3.0
SAGDIG	Dwarf I	2.0
Fornax	Dwarf I	0.8
Sculptor	Dwarf E	0.27
Andromeda I	Dwarf E	2.0
Andromeda II	Dwarf E	2.0
Andromeda III	Dwarf E	2.0
Leo I	Dwarf E	0.9
LGS 3	Dwarf I	2.0
Leo II	Dwarf E	0.75
Carina	Dwarf E	0.55
Draco	Dwarf E	0.33
Ursa Minor	Dwarf E	0.22

*S: Spiral, I: Irregular, E: Elliptical

UNIVERSE OF GALAXIES

Clusters and superclusters

Galaxies are grouped into clusters, typically tens of millions of light-years across,
with hundreds or thousands of members.
These are held together by their mutual
gravitation, and each galaxy moves
around the center of gravity of the cluster. Their speed of movement shows that
they experience a greater gravitational
pull than can be accounted for by the
observed galaxies. Some of this missing
mass consists of dim galaxies too faint to
be detectable, and some is dark intergalactic gas, which emits X rays that can
be detected. But there must be much
more "dark matter" than has so far been
accounted for. Furthermore, our theories

of the origin of the universe suggest that
there must be a hundred times as much
matter in the universe as we can detect.

Interacting galaxies

A typical galaxy will have had a collision
or a near miss with another galaxy half a
dozen times in its life so far. Pairs of
galaxies that are in the process of near-
collision can be observed now. One pair
is called the Mice because of the stream-
ers of stars, resembling mouse tails, that
they are pulling from each other; similar
features in another pair have led to the
galaxies being dubbed the Antennae.

One galaxy can score a direct hit on
another and pass right through. The individual stars are much more widely spaced

*A cluster of galaxies in the direction of the
constellation of Virgo may well be close to the
center of the Local Supercluster, of which the
Local Group of galaxies is a member.*

*One of the effects of interaction between two galaxies in the constella-
tion of Boötes is increased star formation in the smaller companion.*

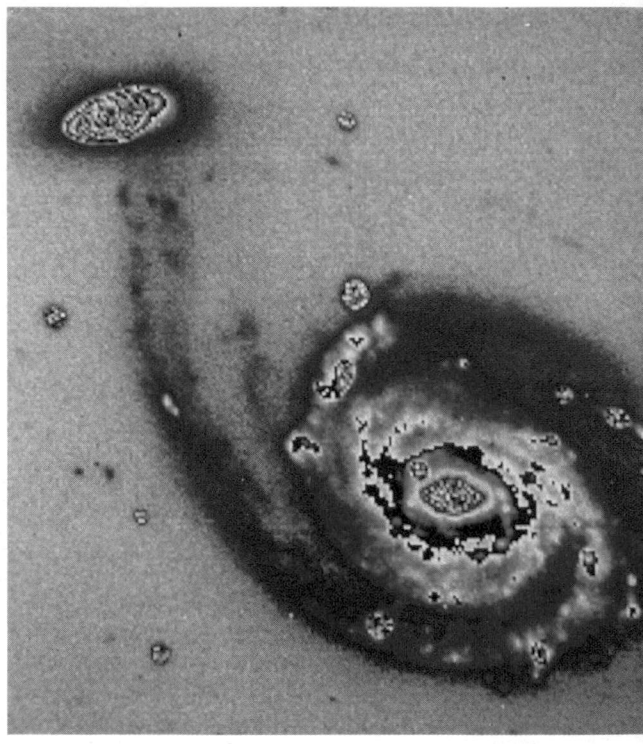

*The longer spiral galaxy extends one of its spiral arms toward its com-
panion, an elliptical galaxy, as the two orbit around each other.*

*In a computer model of galactic
interaction, two spiral galaxies,
spinning in opposite directions,
meet head on (1). They then
recede, their disks having been
distorted by gravitational forces
(2). They are drawn together
again as their orbits decay (3).
Most of their mass lies at the
common boundary; some stars
break free of their parent bodies.
After a second collision (4), stars
from both systems mix and begin
to move around a new galactic
center (5). Two billion years
after the initial collision, the two
have completely merged into an
elliptical galaxy (6).*

1   2   3

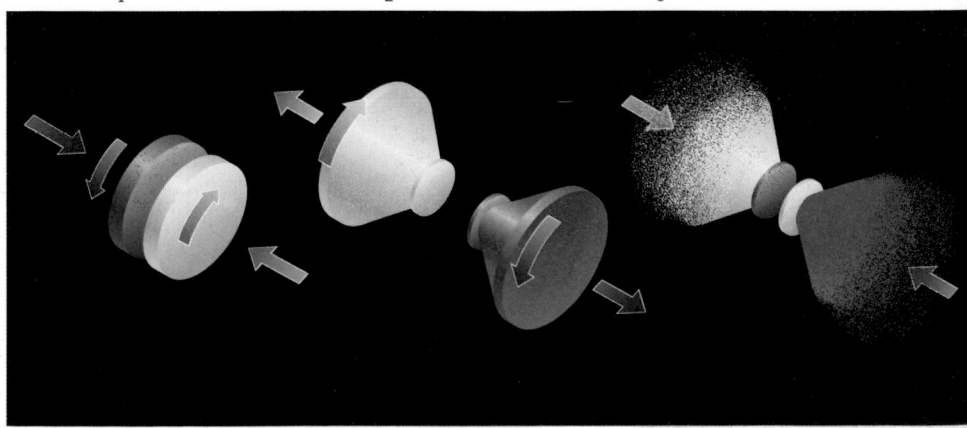

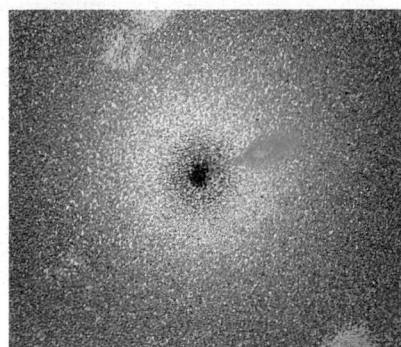

A jet of charged particles is powered by a black hole at the center of this galaxy.

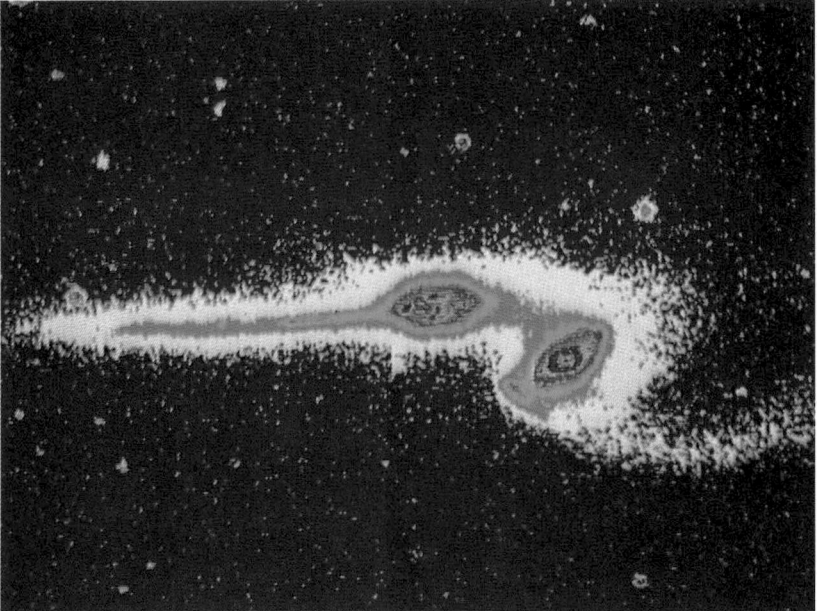

Two spirals have produced "tails" as a result of gravitational effects as they pass each other.

in relation to their diameters than galaxies are, and they do not collide. But gas clouds in the two galaxies can collide and generate intense radiation, thus spawning millions of new stars. Such objects are called "starburst" galaxies. When the intruding galaxy has departed, a ripple of matter may be left, spreading to the edge of the "target" galaxy, giving it a bright rim of young stars. Several such "cartwheel" galaxies are known.

When spirals collide (*below*), they often merge to form a large elliptical galaxy. Ellipticals can merge to form larger ellipticals, in which several nuclei—the remnants of individual galaxies—can often be seen. Galaxies can grow in this way until they become supergiant galaxies.

Superclusters

Counts of galaxies show that the clusters are themselves grouped into "superclusters"—chains and sheets separated by apparently empty voids and measuring hundreds and thousands of millions of light-years across. Whether this "frothy" texture of the universe was present in the gas from which the protogalaxies condensed, or whether the galaxies gathered into these structures after their formation, is still not understood.

Active galaxies

At the heart of many nearby galaxies, and of the Milky Way, there seems to be great

activity, hidden behind dense gas clouds. Stars are being whirled around by intense gravitational fields, and high-energy X ray radiation is being emitted. In some galaxies there is even greater activity, and these can be detected at greater distances—hundreds of millions of light-years away.

Many active galaxies are throwing out great jets of radiation, together with charged particles, which show up clearly at radio wavelengths (*above, left*). The jets collide with the intergalactic gas and are halted to form puffs of radio-emitting matter, called radio lobes, mainly consisting of fast-moving charged particles, but including a scattering of stars.

The most intense activity is shown by the quasars, the nearest of which is two billion light-years from us. A quasar is a quasistellar object, i.e. it looks like a star but radiates in other regions of the electromagnetic spectrum like a galaxy. Not only can we see more quasars at great distances, because they are so bright, but there really are more. Most are found so

far away that their light left them 9–11 billion years ago—only a few billion years after the Big Bang. The outpouring of radiation seems to come from a tiny region at the center of a galaxy.

Galactic black holes

The source of energy for all these different types of active galaxy is almost certainly a black hole. When a typical galaxy was formed, some of the stars near the center fell together and merged to form a massive black hole. For perhaps 50 million years this black hole swallowed stars, gas, and dust, emitting vast quantities of radiation as it did so. Then the matter at the core of the galaxy was used up and the quasar faded. Quasar activity flared up and died away in galaxies over a two-billion-year period.

Similar activity continued on a smaller scale thereafter. The various sorts of active galaxy that we see today may be similar objects but they are viewed from different angles.

4   5   6

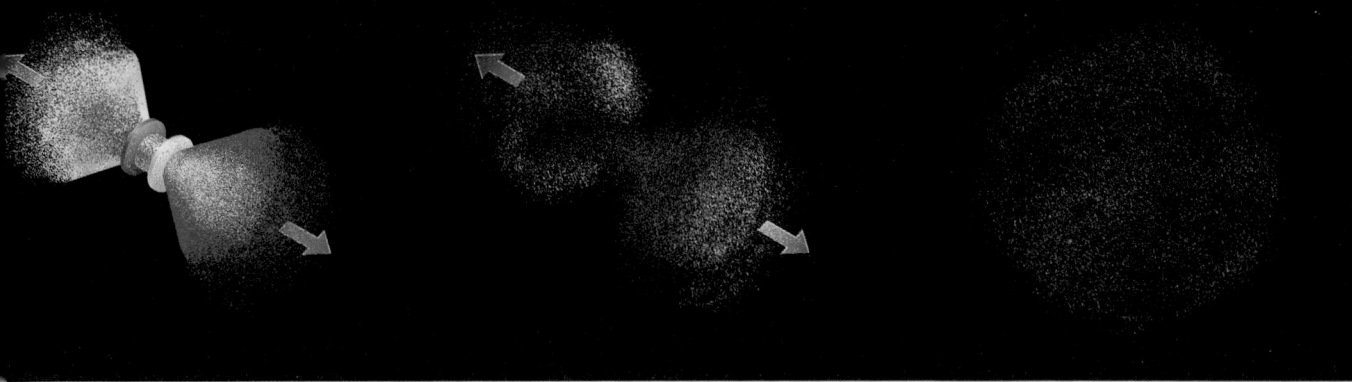

THE EVOLUTION OF THE UNIVERSE

Although galaxies move randomly within a cluster, the clusters are rushing apart from each other. This is revealed by their red shifts (*p. 10*). The galaxies' motion has no center: viewed from any galaxy, all other galaxies (outside one's own cluster) seem to be rushing away. The farther away the galaxy, the faster it recedes. The speed of recession is 11–19mps (17–30kps). for every million light-years of distance. Owing to uncertain estimates of the distances of galaxies complicates measurements.

The Big Bang

Galaxies seem to be flying apart as a result of an enormous explosion that occurred 10–20 billion years ago. Cosmologists believe this "Big Bang" began with all matter and energy in the universe packed into a tiny space, smaller than an atom, with density and temperature at unimaginable levels. The known laws of physics cannot describe or account for the very beginning. But cosmologists can describe what happens from an incredibly tiny fraction of a second afterward. At first, every possible particle existed, all of them colliding and changing into each other every moment. Many were particles unknown to us or only fleetingly glimpsed in experiments.

In today's universe there are four fundamental forces: gravitation, electromagnetism, and two forces that act within the nucleus, a strong and a weak. But at the colossal temperatures of the newly born universe, these were all merged into one "superforce" felt equally by all particles. However, 10^{-43} seconds after the beginning, gravity became a separate force. Then, at 10^{-35} seconds, there was an enormous "inflation" of the universe, in which it blew up from the size of an atom to that of a beach ball in a split second. Then the strong nuclear force separated out, and finally the weak force and elec-

tromagnetism split, all well within a billionth of a second.

As the universe expanded, it thinned and cooled. Short-lived, exotic particles "decayed" into the longer-lived, more familiar particles that we recognize today. Quarks were built up into the protons and neutrons that were to be the building blocks of atoms. But they were still too hot to stick to each other or to join up with electrons to form atoms.

All this took place within the first hundredth of a second. When the universe was 25 seconds old it consisted mostly of radiation at a temperature of several billion degrees, and a thousand times denser than water is today, outweighing matter a hundred thousand times. Matter was knocked around by energetic photons, "bullets" of radiation.

During the first three minutes, neutrons stuck to protons to form nuclei of helium, with traces of one or two other kinds of light atom. But helium nuclei were outnumbered 12 to one by single protons, or hydrogen nuclei. The temperature had fallen below one billion °F.

For 300,000 years the universe continued to expand. Then, as the temperature fell to about 5,000°F, electrons joined with atomic nuclei to form uncharged atoms. Radiation no longer interacted strongly with matter. After another few hundred million years, the thinning gas broke up into giant lumps—the protogalaxies. The first stars may have begun to shine at this time.

The cosmic background radiation

When complete atoms formed, radiation was liberated. Their radiation is still traveling, but it has been stretched and cooled a thousandfold by the expansion of the universe, and is now at a temperature of 5°F above absolute zero. It is detectable as microwave radiation filling the universe. Minute ripples in its intensity show that as matter and radiation broke free of each other, the matter was already beginning to break up into lumps.

Dark matter

Theories of the Big Bang, and the existence of the ripples in the background radiation, suggest that the "ordinary" matter we know about must have been greatly outweighed by "dark" matter. It did not interact with ordinary matter in any way except by gravity. The entire visible universe may be only a thin "froth" on this dark ocean of matter.

The far future

If the amount of matter in the universe consists only of what we can observe plus the dark matter, then its gravitational pull is not enough to reverse the expansion of the universe. The clusters of galaxies will recede ever farther apart and fade from each other's view. Black holes at the centers of the galaxies will grow, swallowing some of the matter in each galaxy, while the rest will disperse into intergalactic space. The last stars will be born a trillion (10^{12}) years from now. After 100 trillion years, even the longest-lived stars, the low-mass red dwarfs, will have faded. After 10^{19} years, most dead stars and other matter in galaxies will have dispersed, while the remainder will have been swallowed up by black holes. After 10^{32} years, even the protons in atoms may break down into lighter particles. After 10^{117} years, even black holes will have evaporated into radiation, and the universe will consist of a featureless, enormously diluted sea of lightweight particles and low-energy radiation.

A Big Crunch?

But if there is more matter, or if the universe is smaller than we think, then gravity will finally defeat expansion, and the galaxy clusters will fall together. The background radiation will be squeezed and will heat up, finally boiling the stars away. Matter will merge in a furnace that will replay the Big Bang in reverse. Finally there may be a "rebound" that will set the cosmos off on the next cycle of an infinitely repeating history.

Within a fraction of a second all matter in the universe came into being in a flash of creation. The fundamental forces—starting

with gravity—separated out, causing expansion and the split-second evolution of a "soup" made up of quarks and electrons.

These evolved into protons and neutrons which, by primordial nucleosynthesis, formed the atoms for the first galaxies and stars.

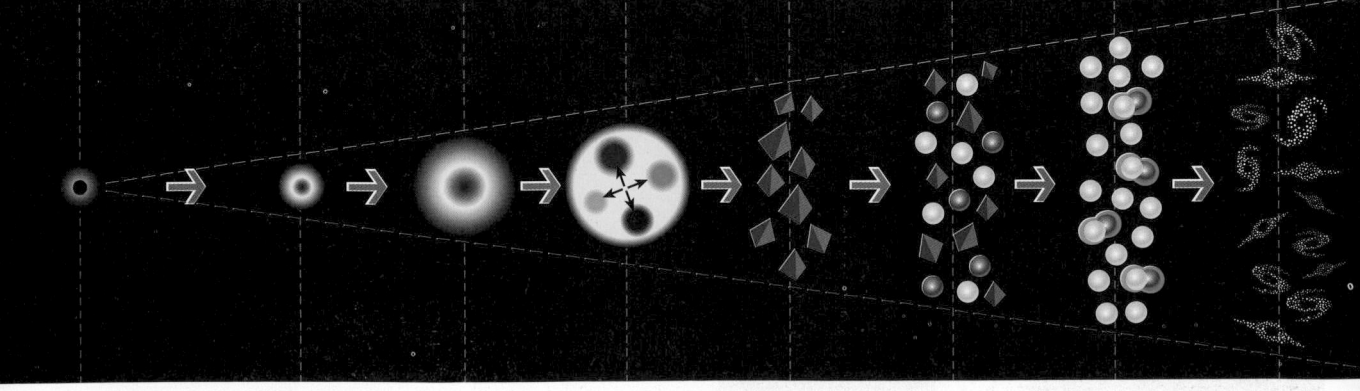

INTRODUCTION

It was in 1903 that the Russian theorist Konstantin Tsiolkovsky published *A Rocket into Cosmic Space*, in which he explained that the rocket is the only practical means of traveling beyond the Earth's atmosphere. A rocket is a device that does not need atmospheric oxygen to burn its fuel, since it carries its own, either separately or in chemical combination with the fuel. In 1919, the American visionary Robert Goddard published a paper called *A Method of Reaching Extreme Altitudes*, in which he described a project to fire a projectile to the Moon, setting off an explosive charge to signal its arrival when it crashed on the surface. Goddard went on to build liquid-fueled rockets, some reaching altitudes of about 1 mi./1.6 km, and some traveling faster than the speed of sound.

An enormous advance in rocketry was made in World War II when a German team led by Wernher Von Braun built the A-4 (or V2) rocket. Powered by ethyl alcohol and liquid oxygen, it had a range of about 220 mi./350 km, and reached a maximum height of about 162 mi./100 km.

The V2 was the basis for the U.S. space effort after the war. The Soviet Union developed its own more powerful launchers and in 1957 put the 182 lb./83 kg Sputnik I into a highly elliptical orbit. It broadcast scientific data for 21 days and survived for 57 days before atmospheric drag destroyed it.

Within four months the United States had launched the 30 lb./14 kg Explorer 1. But the scientific successes of its satellites, especially in discovering the Van Allen radiation belts around the Earth, counted for little in the propaganda war compared with the eye-catching Soviet feats. Within a year the Soviet Union had launched a 1.3-ton satellite, and the first man in space, Yuri Gagarin, made a single orbit of the Earth in 1961.

Artificial satellites

A projectile fired horizontally from a point just outside the atmosphere at about 5mps (8kps) would go into a circular orbit around the Earth. It would not need any further motive power, since without air resistance it could travel for ever. It would not have escaped gravity: on the contrary, gravity would be holding it in its orbit. An object moving in a circular orbit is constantly falling toward the center of the Earth under the influence of the planet's gravity, in the same way as an object near the Earth's surface is doing so.

If the object's speed is boosted, it will go into an elliptical orbit, traveling slower where it is farther from the Earth, and faster where it is closer in. If the projectile is given escape velocity, a speed of about 7mps (11kps), it will escape completely, traveling away from the Earth more and more slowly, but never quite coming to a complete halt.

Scientific satellites can observe wavelengths that never penetrate the Earth's atmosphere. IRAS (Infrared Astronomical Satellite) observed heat radiation from young planetary systems and from comet debris in our solar system. The Einstein X ray satellite observed X rays from remote quasars and from superdense objects in binary systems in the galaxy.

Surveillance satellites in low orbits only a few hundred miles high take 90 minutes to orbit the Earth. Communications satellites are stationed over the equator at heights of about 22,000 mi./36,000 km, in orbits that take precisely the same time as the Earth takes to rotate once (geostationary orbits).

Race to the Moon

Having lost the race to launch the first satellite and the first human being into space, the U.S.A. in 1961 declared its intention to send a man to the Moon and back. On July 20, 1969, Apollo 11 landed on the Sea of Tranquillity and stayed on the Moon for 21 hours 36 minutes. In all, six Apollo landings were made, the last three making use of an electrically powered Lunar Roving Vehicle. The U.S.S.R. had its own manned Moon program until repeated failures of the giant booster rocket led to its cancellation in 1972.

Astronauts aboard the Apollo 11 spacecraft observed this memorable earth-rise above the lunar landscape.

Thousands of satellites serve a variety of purposes including weather forecasting, communications, and scientific and military surveying.

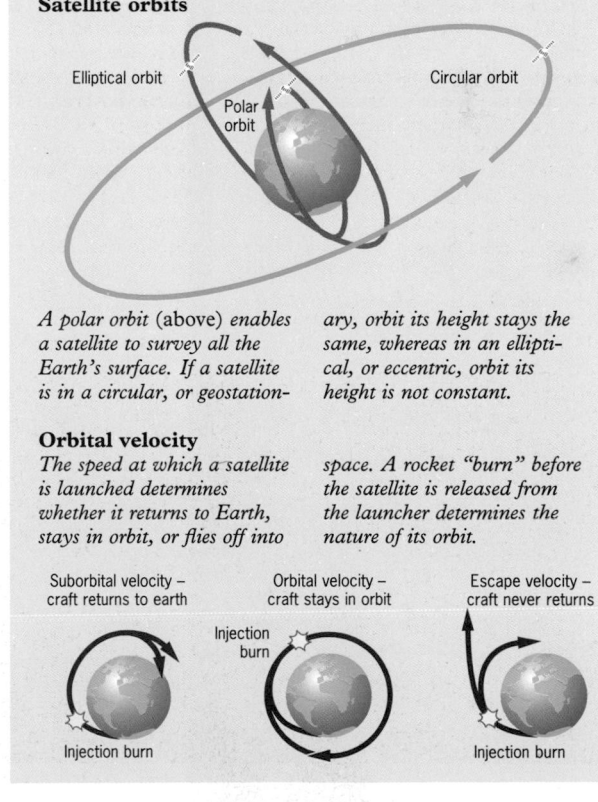

Satellite orbits

Elliptical orbit   Polar orbit   Circular orbit

A polar orbit (above) enables a satellite to survey all the Earth's surface. If a satellite is in a circular, or geostation- *ary, orbit its height stays the same, whereas in an elliptical, or eccentric, orbit its height is not constant.*

Orbital velocity
The speed at which a satellite is launched determines whether it returns to Earth, stays in orbit, or flies off into *space. A rocket "burn" before the satellite is released from the launcher determines the nature of its orbit.*

Suborbital velocity – craft returns to earth   Orbital velocity – craft stays in orbit   Escape velocity – craft never returns

Injection burn   Injection burn   Injection burn

Planetary probes

Unmanned space probes have flown by, or landed on, every planet except Pluto, and have made close studies of most of the solar system's scores of satellites. The Soviet Luna and Zond probes orbited the Moon, and in 1970, Luna 16 brought Moon rocks back to Earth; while the American Apollo craft explored the lunar surface (*below*). Soviet probes succeeded in landing on Venus and sent back pictures before they were destroyed by the tremendous heat and pressure on the planet's surface.

Soviet Missions to Mars were less successful, but in 1976, twin U.S. Viking craft landed on Mars and began observations that lasted for six years. They failed to find any clear signs of life.

The range of American missions to the planets has been enormously increased by the technique of "gravity assist." A probe swings by a planet and is flung onward by the planet's gravity field, with little expenditure of fuel. Voyager 1 and 2, launched in 1977, traveled from giant planet to giant planet in this way, taking advantage of a rare alignment. Finally they left the solar system altogether, still transmitting data.

Other probes have made multiple flybys of Mercury and Venus using gravity assist. Galileo, launched in 1989, followed a convoluted route, heading in toward the Sun to begin with, swinging by Venus and then Earth on the way to Jupiter in 1995. The U.S. Magellan probe was launched in 1989 and orbited Venus, scanning the surface with cloud-piercing radar and building up panoramas of the Venusian landscape.

This composite image shows the Galileo spacecraft arriving at Jupiter in 1995. The probe investigates the Jovian atmosphere before moving on to look at some of Jupiter's moons.

MAJOR SPACE FIRSTS

Mercury flyby

Probe	Nation	Launch date	Notes
Mariner 10	U.S.A	11/3/73	Three Mercury encounters, following Venus flyby.

Venus landings: "firsts"

Probe	Nation	Launch date	Notes
Venera 3	U.S.S.R.	11/16/65	Crushed by atmospheric pressure during parachute descent.
Venera 7	U.S.S.R.	8/18/70	Transmitted for 23 minutes after landing.
Pioneer-Venus 2	U.S.A	8/8/78	Multiple payload: four probes landed, one returned data for 67 minutes.
Venera 13	U.S.S.R.	10/30/81	Transmitted for over two hours after landing; analyzed soil.
Vega 1	U.S.S.R.	12/15/84	On way to Halley's Comet. Lander transmitted for 20 minutes after landing; balloon explored atmosphere.

Venus: major flybys

Probe	Nation	Launch date	Notes
Mariner 2	U.S.A	8/27/62	First successful flyby.
Pioneer-Venus 1	U.S.A	5/20/78	Orbiter
Venera 15	U.S.S.R.	6/2/83	Polar orbiter: radar mapping.
Magellan	U.S.A	5/5/89	Orbiter: radar mapping.

Mars

Probe	Nation	Launch date	Notes
Mariner 4	U.S.A	11/28/64	Flyby
Mariner 6	U.S.A	2/24/69	Flyby
Mariner 7	U.S.A	3/27/69	Flyby
Mars 2	U.S.S.R.	5/19/71	Orbiter; dropped Soviet flag to surface.
Mars 3	U.S.S.R.	5/28/71	Orbiter; lander transmitted for 20 seconds.
Mariner 9	U.S.A.	5/30/71	Orbiter
Viking 1	U.S.A.	8/20/75	Orbiter and lander; lander transmitted for over six years.
Viking 2	U.S.A.	9/9/75	Orbiter and lander; lander transmitted for four years.

Outer planets: flybys

Probe	Nation	Launch date	Notes
Pioneer 10	U.S.A.	3/2/72	Jupiter 12/73
Pioneer 11	U.S.A.	4/5/73	Jupiter 12/74 Saturn 9/79
Voyager 1	U.S.A.	9/5/77	Jupiter 3/79 Saturn 11/80
Voyager 2	U.S.A.	8/20/77	Jupiter 7/79 Saturn 8/81 Uranus 1/86 Neptune 8/89
Galileo	U.S.A.	10/18/89	Jupiter 1995; orbiter; atmosphere entry probe.
Ulysses	U.S.A.	10/6/90	Jupiter 2/92; went on to fly over poles of Sun.

SPACE SHUTTLE

The launch of the first space shuttle, *Columbia*, in 1981, marked a new development in space exploration—the deployment of reusable vehicles. The reuse element was an important factor in NASA's plans for space stations served by vehicles that could take off like a rocket—with a substantial payload—and land like a plane, shuttling to and from Earth many times.

The shuttle weighs as much as 2,000 tons on launch, and is designed to make up to 100 missions during a 20-year lifetime. It rapidly became important as a satellite-launcher, with the advantage that astronauts can make last-minute adjustments before a satellite is released from the cargo bay. Shuttles have since carried a variety of payloads (*below*), and made possible space repairs and retrieval. In future they will transport and assemble an international space station.

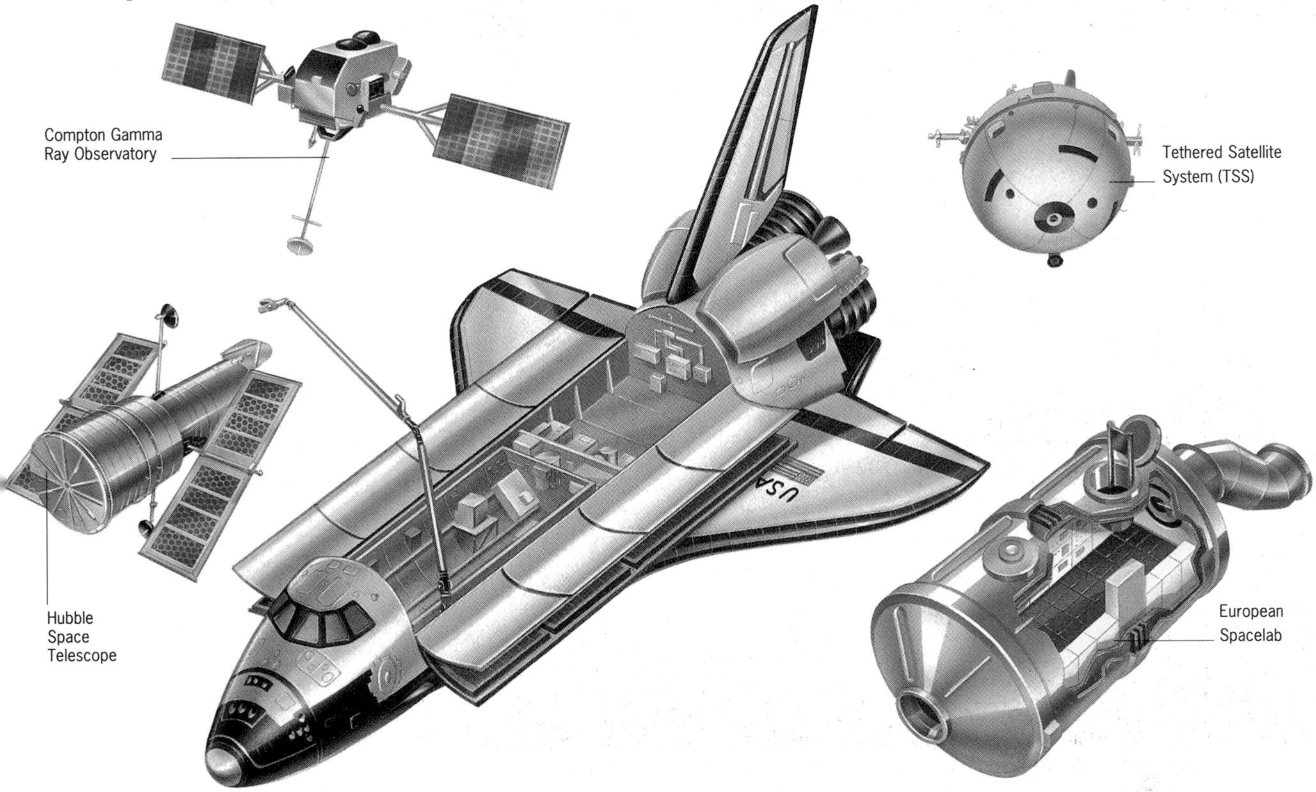

Compton Gamma
Ray Observatory

Tethered Satellite
System (TSS)

Hubble
Space
Telescope

European
Spacelab

PLANETARY PROBES

Mission/*Nation*	Launch	Event	Event description
Sputnik 1/U.S.S.R.	10/4/57	10/4/57	Satellite around Earth
Sputnik 2/U.S.S.R.	11/3/57	11/3/57	Dog in satellite
Explorer 1/U.S.A.	2/1/58	2/1/58	Van Allen belts discovered
Luna 1/U.S.S.R.	1/2/59	1/2/59	Escaped Earth's gravity
Vanguard 2/U.S.A.	2/17/59	2/17/59	Photographed Earth
Luna 2/U.S.S.R.	9/12/59	9/14/59	Lunar impact
Luna 3/U.S.S.R.	10/4/59	10/7/59	Pictures of lunar far side
TIROS 1/U.S.A.	4/1/60	4/1/60	Weather satellite
Transit lB/U.S.A.	4/13/60	4/13/60	Navigation satellite
ECHO 1/U.S.A.	8/12/60	8/12/60	Communications satellite
Sputnik 5/U.S.S.R.	8/19/60	8/20/60	Two dogs returned alive
Vostok 1/U.S.S.R.	4/12/61	4/12/61	Manned orbital flight
Mariner 2/U.S.A.	8/26/62	12/14/62	Venus flyby
Vostok 6/U.S.S.R.	6/16/63	6/16/63	Woman in orbit
Ranger VII/U.S.A.	7/28/64	7/31/64	TV pictures of Moon
Mariner 4/U.S.A.	11/28/64	7/15/65	Mars flyby pictures
Early Bird/U.S.A.	4/6/65	4/6/65	Commercial geostationary communications satellite
Venera 3/U.S.S.R.	11/16/65	3/1/66	Venus impact
A-1 Asterix/France	11/26/65	11/26/65	French launched satellite
Gemini 6/U.S.A.	12/15/65	12/15/65	Manned rendevous
Luna 9/U.S.S.R.	1/31/66	2/3/66	Lunar soft landing
Gemini 8/U.S.A.	3/16/66	3/16/66	Manned docking
Luna 10/U.S.S.R.	3/31/66	4/3/66	Lunar orbiter
Surveyor 1/U.S.A.	5/30/66	6/2/66	U.S. soft landing on Moon
Lunar orbiter 1/U.S.A.	8/10/66	10/29/66	U.S. lunar orbiter
Cosmos 186/188/U.S.A.	10/22/67 10/28/67	10/27/67 10/29/67	Automatic docking
Zond 5/U.S.S.R.	9/14/68	9/21/68	Animals around the Moon
Apollo 8/U.S.A.	12/21/68	12/24/68	Manned lunar orbit
Soyuz 4/U.S.S.R.	1/14/69		As Soyuz 5
Soyuz 5/U.S.S.R.	1/15/69	1/16/69	Transfer of crews
Apollo 11/U.S.A.	7/16/69	7/20/69	Manned lunar landing
Oshumi/Japan	2/11/70	2/11/70	Japanese-launched satellite
Long March/**China**	4/24/70	4/24/70	Chinese-launched satellite
Venera 7/U.S.S.R.	8/17/70	12/15/70	Venus soft landing
Luna 16/U.S.S.R.	9/12/70	9/21/70	Unmanned sample return
Luna 17/U.S.S.R.	11/10/70	11/17/70	Unmanned Moon rover
Mars 2/U.S.S.R.	5/19/71	11/27/71	Mars orbit
Mars 3/U.S.S.R.	5/28/71	12/2/71	Mars soft landing; no data
Mariner 9/U.S.A.	5/30/71	11/13/71	Mars orbit
Prospero/U.K.	10/28/71	10/28/71	U.K.-launched satellite
Pioneer 10/U.S.A.	3/3/72	12/3/73	Jupiter flyby; escaped solar system 6/14/83
Pioneer 11/U.S.A.	4/6/73	4/74	Jupiter flyby (Saturn 9/79).
Mariner 10/U.S.A.	11/3/73 3/74	2/5/74 4/75	Venus flyby Three Mercury flybys
Venera 9/U.S.S.R.	6/8/75	10/22/75	Venus orbit
Apollo/Soyuz/ U.S.A./U.S.S.R.	7/15/75	7/17/75	Manned international cooperative mission
Viking 1/U.S.A.	8/20/75	7/20/76	Mars surface operations
Viking 2/U.S.A.	9/9/75	9/3/76	As Viking 1
Voyager 2/U.S.A.	8/20/77	7/9/79	Jupiter flyby (Saturn, 8/26/81; Uranus, 1/24/86; Neptune, 8/24/89)
Voyager 1/U.S.A.	9/5/77	3/5/79	Jupiter (Saturn, 11/13/80)
ISEE-C/U.S.A.	8/12/78	9/85	Comet intercept
Ariane/CAT/ESA	12/24/79	12/24/79	European launcher
Rohini/India	7/18/80	7/18/80	Indian-launched satellite
STS1/U.S.A.	4/12/81	4/12/81	Space shuttle flight
STS2/U.S.A.	11/12/81	11/12/81	Launch vehicle reuse
Soyuz T9/U.S.S.R.	6/27/83	6/27/83	Construction in space

SPACE STATIONS

The Soviet Union built up unparalleled experience with long-endurance flights on permanent orbiting vessels, or space stations, leading up to the launch of *Mir* in 1986. Crew members' length of stay was further built up until, in 1991, Musa Manarov became the first cosmonaut to have stayed in orbit for 500 days.

Long exposure to weightlessness poses severe threats to health. The cosmonauts' bones lost calcium, and their heart muscles were weakened. They undertook a strict regime of exercise every day and experimented with elastic suits that required constant muscular exertion if the wearer were to stay erect.

The U.S.A.'s longest experiment in living in space was *Skylab*, which basically consisted of an empty fuel tank from a Saturn rocket booster. Three crews occupied it during 1973 and 1974, the longest period being 84 days.

Space shuttle

The space shuttle (*p. 33*) is a reusable vehicle. It is a spaceplane that glides back to Earth from orbit, covered with heat-resistant ceramic tiles. It is boosted on launch by two solid-fuel boosters that

The future in space

The Commonwealth of Independent States, successor to the U.S.S.R., will market its space-travel capabilities, but is a spent force as far as pushing back the frontiers of space is concerned. In the United States, enthusiasts are striving to obtain a government commitment to a manned mission to Mars.

Possible targets in space include the establishment of observatories on the far side of the Moon, shielded from the radio and light pollution of the Earth; permanent settlements on Mars; and perhaps even the "terraforming" of the planet, by the warming of its climate by orbiting mirrors or heat-absorbing powder scattered on its polar caps.

Whether or not manned spaceflight

has a future without the Cold War to fuel it financially remains to be seen. Robotic space probes have plenty to challenge them, whether it is searching for the early stages of life beneath the red smog of Saturn's largest moon, Titan, or under the Martian polar caps; parachuting into the depths of the gas giants; or investigating the clues to the origins of the solar system locked in asteroids and comets. And closer to home there will be the *Freedom* space station, an American initiative with international participation. It will be of modular construction, growing as units are ferried from Earth by the space shuttle. The plans are for four-astronaut crews to occupy the station for 90 days

later detach and are parachuted back to the ground. Only a large liquid-fuel tank, on the back of which the space shuttle sits on launch, is lost, burned up in the atmosphere when it is jettisoned. The shuttle's own rockets take it into its final orbit.

The shuttle fleet was intended to construct and maintain an American space

station. Plans for that space station have been deferred on a number of occasions-for lack of financial commitment, and the shuttle's program has been dogged by technical difficulties and tragedy—with the explosion in 1986 of the *Challenger* and the death of seven crew members. Since then the shuttle has attained only about four flights per year.

The year 1995 saw the space shuttle Atlantis *dock with the Russian* Mir *space station, seen below in an artist's impression. Such cooperation is an important preamble to future collaboration in the construction of an international space station.*

Northern Hemisphere

Southern Hemisphere

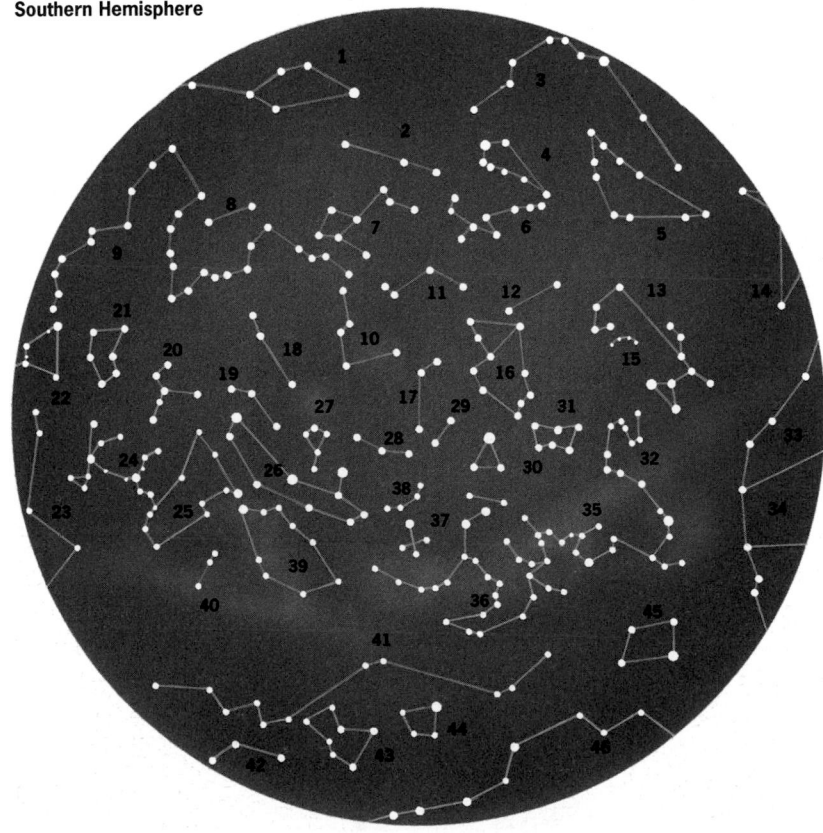

THE CONSTELLATIONS

The maps show the major constellations of the northern and southern skies. A constellation is a group of stars with a defined area of the celestial sphere (*p. 10*) that has internationally agreed boundaries. The largest is Hydra (the Water Snake) in the Northern Hemisphere; the smallest is Crux (the Cross) in the Southern Hemisphere.

Northern Hemisphere

1 *Equuleus* Little Horse; 2 *Delphinus* Dolphin; 3 *Pegasus* Pegasus; 4 *Pisces* Fish; 5 *Cetus* Whale; 6 *Aries* Ram; 7 *Triangulum* Triangle; 8 *Andromeda* Andromeda; 9 *Lacerta* Lizard; 10 *Cygnus* Swan; 11 *Sagitta* Arrow; 12 *Aquila* Eagle; 13 *Lyra* Lyre; 14 *Cepheus* Cepheus; 15 *Cassiopeia* Cassiopeia; 16 *Perseus* Perseus; 17 *Camelopardus* Giraffe; 18 *Auriga* Charioteer; 19 *Taurus* Bull; 20 *Orion* Orion; 21 *Lynx* Lynx; 22 *Polaris* Pole Star; 23 *Ursa Minor* Little Bear; 24 *Draco* Dragon; 25 *Hercules* Hercules; 26 *Ophiuchus* Serpent Bearer; 27 *Serpens* Serpent; 28 *Corona Borealis* Northern Crown; 29 *Boötes* Herdsman; 30 *Ursa Major* Great Bear; 31 *Gemini* Twins; 32 *Cancer* Crab; 33 *Canis Minor* Little Dog; 34 *Hydra* Water Snake; 35 *Leo* Lion; 36 *Leo Minor* Little Lion; 37 *Canes Venatici* Hunting Dogs; 38 *Coma Berenices* Bernice's Hair; 39 *Virgo* Virgin.

Southern Hemisphere

1 *Cetus* Whale; 2 *Sculptor* Sculptor; 3 *Aquarius* Water Bearer; 4 *Piscis Austranis* Southern Fish; 5 *Capricornus* SeaGoat; 6 *Grus* Crane; 7 *Phoenix* Phoenix; 8 *Fornax* Furnace; 9 *Eridanus* Eridanus River; 10 *Hydrus* Lesser Water Snake; 11 *Tucana* Toucan; 12 *Indus* Indian; 13 *Sagittarius* Archer; 14 *Aquila* Eagle; 15 *Corona Australis* Southern Crown; 16 *Pavo* Peacock; 17 *Octans* Octant; 18 *Dorado* Swordfish; 19 *Pictor* Painter; 20 *Columba* Dove; 21 *Lepus* Hare; 22 *Orion* Orion (hunter); 23 *Monoceros* Unicorn; 24 *Canis Major* Great Dog; 25 *Puppis* Poop (of Argo); 26 *Carina* Keel (of Argo); 27 *Volans* Flying Fish; 28 *Chamaeleon* Chameleon; 29 *Apus* Bird of Paradise; 30 *Triangulum Australe* Southern Triangle; 31 *Ara* Altar; 32 *Scorpius* Scorpion; 33 *Serpens* Serpent; 34 *Ophiuchus* Serpent Bearer; 35 *Lupus* Wolf; 36 *Centaurus* Cantaur; 37 *Crux* (Southern) Cross; 38 *Musca* Fly; 39 *Vela* Sails (of Argo); 40 *Pyxis* Mariner's Compass; 41 *Hydra* Water Snake; 42 *Sextans* Sextant; 43 *Crater* Cup; 44 *Corvus* Crow; 45 *Libra* Scales; 46 *Virgo* Virgin.

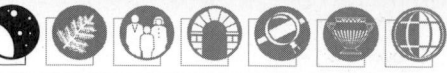

LUNAR ECLIPSES 1991–2008

Date	Eclipse type	Mid-eclipse	Where visible
December 21, 1991	Partial	10.34	Pacific, North America (W. coast), Japan, Australia
June 15, 1992	Partial	04.58	North, Central, and South America, W. Africa
December 9–10, 1992	Total	23.45	Africa, Europe, Middle East, part of South America
June 4, 1993	Total	13.02	Pacific, Australia, Southeast Asia
November 29, 1993	Total	06.26	North and South America
May 25, 1994	Partial	03.32	Central and South America, part of North America, W. Africa
April 15, 1995	Partial	12.19	Pacific, Australia, Southeast Asia
April 4, 1996	Total	00.11	Africa, S.E. Europe, South America
September 27, 1996	Total	02.55	Central and South America, part of North America, W. Africa
March 24, 1997	Partial	04.41	Central and South America, part of North America, W. Africa
September 16, 1997	Total	18.47	South Africa, E. Africa, Australia
July 28, 1999	Partial	11.34	Pacific, Australia, Southeast Asia
January 21, 2000	Total	04.45	North America, part of South America, S.W. Europe, W. Africa
July 16, 2000	Total	13.57	Pacific, Australia, Southeast Asia
January 9, 2001	Total	20.22	Europe, Asia, Africa
July 5, 2001	Partial	14.57	Asia, Australia, Pacific
May 16, 2003	Total	03.41	North, Central, and South America, Europe, Africa
November 8–9, 2003	Total	01.20	North, Central, and South America, Europe, Africa, W. Asia
May 4, 2004	Total	20.32	Europe, Africa, Asia
October 28, 2004	Total	03.05	North, Central, and South America, Europe, Africa
October 17, 2005	Partial	12.05	E. Asia, Pacific, North America
September 7, 2006	Partial	18.53	Australia, Asia, E. Africa
March 3, 2007	Total	23.22	Europe, Asia, Africa
August 28, 2007	Total	10.39	Australia, Pacific, part of North America
February 2,1 2008	Total	03.27	North, Central, and South America, Europe, Africa
August 16, 2008	Partial	21.12	Europe, Africa, W. Asia

THE INNER PLANETS: ORBITAL DATA AND PHYSICAL DATA

Orbital and rotational data

	Distance from Sun (million mi.)	Tilt of orbit (°) (Earth = 0)	Year	Day (equatorial) d h m			Polar tilt
Mercury	36	7.005	87.97	58	15	30	0.00
Venus	67	3.3948	224.70	243	0	26	177.33
Earth	93	0.000	365.256		23	56	23.49
Mars	142	1.850	686.98	1	0	37	25.19

Physical data

	Equatorial diameter (mi.)	Mass (Earth = 1)	Mass of Sun/ Mass of planet	Density (water = 1)
Mercury	3,032	0.0553	6,023,600	5.43
Venus	7,521	0.815	408,523.5	5.24
Earth	7,927	1	328,900.5	5.515
Mars	4,222	0.1074	3,098,710	3.94

METEORS

Shower	Begins	Max	Ends	Max. ZHR (Measure of rate)
Quadrantids	January 1	January 4	January 6	60
Virginids	February 1	March 12	April 18	5
Lyrids	April 19	April 21	April 25	10
η Aquarids	April 24	May 5	May 20	35
α Scorpiids	April 20	May 13	May 19	5
Ophiuchids	May 19	June 9	July	5
α Cygnids	July	July 21	August	5
Capricornids	July	Mid-July	August	5
δ Aquarids	July 15	July 29	August 20	20
Piscis Australids	July 15	July 31	August 20	5
α Capricornids	July 15	August 2	August 25	5
ι Aquarids	July 15	August 6	August 25	8
Perseids	July 23	August 12	August 20	75
Piscids	September	September 8	October	10
Orionids	October 16	October 22	October 27	25
Draconids	October 10	October 10	October 10	var.
Taurids	October 20	November 3	November 30	10
Leonids	November 15	November 17	November 20	var.
Andromedids	November 15	November 20	December 6	v. low
Puppids-Velids	November 27	December 9	January	15
Geminids	December 7	December 13	December 16	75
Ursids	December 17	December 23	December 25	5

Permanent daytime meteor showers include the Arietids (March 29 to June 17), the ξ Perseids (June 1 to 15) and the β Taurids (June 23 to July 7). The β Taurids are believed to be associated with Encke's Comet.

METEORITE CRATERS

Name/location	Diameter (mi.)
Acraman, Australia	100
Sudbury, Ontario, Canada	87
Vredefort, South Africa	87
Popigay, Russia	62
Manicouagan, Quebec, Canada	43
Kara, Russia	31
Manson, Iowa, U.S.A.	22
Clearwater Lake, Quebec, Canada	20
Steen River, Alberta, Canada	16
Meteor Crater, Arizona, U.S.A.	0.7

THE OUTER PLANETS: ORBITAL DATA AND PHYSICAL DATA

Orbital and rotational data

	Distance from Sun (million mi.)	Tilt of orbit (°) (Earth = 0)	Year	Day (equatorial) d h m			Polar tilt
Jupiter	483	1.3046	11.86	9	50		3.13
Saturn	887	2.486	29.46	10	13		25.33
Uranus	1,784	0.773	84.07	17	14		97.86
Neptune	2,794	1.77	164.82	16	6		28.31
Pluto	3,674	17.12	248.6	6	9	17	122.52

Physical data

	Equatorial diameter (mi.)	Mass (Earth = 1)	Mass of Sun/ Mass of planet	Density (water = 1)
Jupiter	88,849	317.83	1,047.355	1.33
Saturn	74,900	95.16	3,498.5	0.70
Uranus	31,764	14.50	22,869	1.30
Neptune	30,776	17.20	19,314	1.76
Pluto	1,430	0.0025	3,000,000	1.1

SATELLITES: ORBITAL DATA

Planet		Satellite	Orbital period	Distance from planet (thousand mi.)	Inclination of orbit to planet's equator (°)
Earth		Moon	27.321661	239	18.28–28.58
Mars	I	Phobos	0.31891023	5.8	1.0
	II	Deimos	1.2624407	15	0.9-2.7
Jupiter	I	Io	1.769137786	262	0.04
	II	Europa	3.551181041	417	0.47
	III	Ganymede	7.15455296	665	0.21
	IV	Callisto	26.6890184	1,170	0.51
	V	Amalthea	0.49817905	112	0.40
	VI	Himalia	250.5662	7,133	27.63
	VII	Elara	259.6528	7,293	24.77
	VIII	Pasiphae	735 R	14,603	145.0
	IX	Sinope	758 R	14,727	153.0
	X	Lysithea	259.22	7,283	29.02
	XI	Carme	692 R	14,043	164.0
	XII	Ananke	631 R	13,173	147.0
	XIII	Leda	238.72	6,894	26.07
	XIV	Thebe	0.6745	138	0.8
	XV	Adrastea	0.29826	80	
	XVI	Metis	0.294780	79	
Saturn	I	Mimas	0.942421813	115	1.53
	II	Enceladus	1.370217855	148	0.02
	III	Tethys	1.887802160	183	1.86
	IV	Dione	2.736914742	234	0.02
	V	Rhea	4.517500436	327	0.35
	VI	Titan	15.94542068	758	0.33
	VII	Hyperion	21.2766088	920	0.43
	VIII	Iapetus	79.3301825	2,213	14.72
	IX	Phoebe	550.48 R	8,048	175.0
	X	Janus	0.6945	94	0.14
	XI	Epimetheus	0.6942	94	0.34
	XI	Helene	2.7369	234	0.0
	XIII	Telesto	1.8878	183	
	XIV	Calypso	1.8878	183	
	XV	Atlas	0.6019	86	0.3
	XVI	Prometheus	0.6130	86	0.0
	XVII	Pandora	0.6285	88	0.0
	XVIII	Pan	0.5750	83	
Uranus	I	Ariel	2.52037935	119	0.3
	II	Umbriel	4.1441772	165	0.36
	III	Titania	8.7058717	271	0.14
	IV	Oberon	13.4632389	363	0.10
	V	Miranda	1.41347925	80	3.4
	VI	Cordelia	0.335033	31	0.1
	VII	Ophelia	0.376409	34	0.1
	VIII	Bianca	0.434577	37	0.2
	IX	Cressida	0.463570	38	0.0
	X	Desdemona	0.473651	39	0.2
	XI	Juliet	0.493066	40	0.1
	XII	Portia	0.513196	41	0.1
	XIII	Rosalind	0.558459	43	0.3
	XIV	Belinda	0.623525	47	0.0
	XV	Puck	0.761832	53	0.31
Neptune	I	Triton	5.8768541 R	220	157.345
	II	Nereid	360.13619	3,426	27.6
	III	Naiad	0.294396	30	4.74
	IV	Thalassa	0.311485	31	0.21
	V	Despina	0.334655	33	0.07
	VI	Galatea	0.428745	38	0.05
	VII	Larissa	0.554654	55	0.20
	VIII	Proteus	1.122315	73	0.55
Pluto	I	Charon	5.9 R	12	99.0

R = Retrograde

SATELLITES: PHYSICAL DATA

Planet		Satellite	Mass relative to planet	Diameter mi. †	Sidereal period of rotation ††
Earth		Moon	0.01230002	2,160	S
Mars	I	Phobos	1.5 x 10⁻⁸	17	S
	II	Deimos	3 x 10⁻⁹	9	S
Jupiter	I	Io	4.68 x 10⁻⁵	2,256	S
	II	Europa	2.52 x 10⁻⁵	2,113	S
	III	Ganymede	7.80 x 10⁻⁵	3,270	S
	IV	Callisto	5.66 x 10⁻⁵	2,983	S
	V	Amalthea	38 x 10⁻¹⁰	168	S
	VII	Elara	4 x 10⁻¹⁰	47	0.5
	VIII	Pasiphae	1 x 10⁻¹⁰	31	
	IX	Sinope	0.4 x 10⁻¹⁰	22	
	X	Lysithea	0.4 x 10⁻¹⁰	22	
	XI	Carme	0.5 x 10⁻¹⁰	25	
	XII	Ananke	0.2 x 10⁻¹⁰	19	
	XIII	Leda	0.03 x 10⁻¹⁰	10	
	XIV	Thebe	4 x 10⁻¹⁰	68	S
	XV	Adrastea	0.1 x 10⁻¹⁰	16	
	XVI	Metis	0.5 x 10⁻¹⁰	25	
Saturn	I	Mimas	8.0 x 10⁻⁸	244	S
	II	Enceladus	1.3 x 10⁻⁷	311	S
	III	Tethys	1.3 x 10⁻⁶	659	S
	IV	Dione	1.85 x 10⁻⁶	696	S
	V	Rhea	4.4 x 10⁻⁶	951	S
	VI	Titan	2.38 x 10⁻⁴	3,200	S
	VII	Hyperion	3 x 10⁻⁸	255	
	VIII	Iapetus	3.3 x 10⁻⁶	907	S
	IX	Phoebe	7 x 10⁻¹⁰	137	0.4
	X	Janus		137	S
	XI	Epimetheus		87	S
	XI	Helene		22	
	XIII	Telesto		21	
	XIV	Calypso		21	
	XV	Atlas		25	
	XVI	Prometheus		87	
	XVII	Pandora		68	
	XVIII	Pan		12	
Uranus	I	Ariel	1.56 x 10⁻⁵	720	S
	II	Umbriel	1.35 x 10⁻⁵	728	S
	III	Titania	4.06 x 10⁻⁵	982	S
	IV	Oberon	3.47 x 10⁻⁵	947	S
	V	Miranda	0.08 x 10⁻⁵	298	S
	VI	Cordelia		16	
	VII	Ophelia		19	
	VIII	Bianca		26	
	IX	Cressida		38	
	X	Desdemona		34	
	XI	Juliet		52	
	XII	Portia		67	
	XIII	Rosalind		34	
	XIV	Belinda		41	
	XV	Puck		96	
Neptune	I	Triton	2.09 x 10⁻⁴	1,681	S
	II	Nereid	2 x 10⁻⁷	211	
	III	Naiad		36	
	IV	Thalassa		50	
	V	Despina		92	
	VI	Galatea		98	
	VII	Larissa		129	
	VIII	Proteus		271	
Pluto	I	Charon	0.22	737	S

† = In the case of nonspherical satellites the greatest diameter is quoted.
†† = Synchronous: rotation period same as orbital period, so one side of satellite is permanently turned toward the planet.

PROMINENT PEOPLE

ADAMS, John Couch (1819–92) Co-discoverer of planet Neptune. From perturbations of the orbit of Uranus, he calculated the position of the unknown planet, but it was discovered with the aid of calculations made independently by Urbain LEVERRIER.

ANGSTRÖM, Anders (1814–74) Swedish physicist who studied the spectrum of the Sun in detail and was the first to study the spectra of aurorae.

ANTONIADI, Eugenios (1870–1944) Greek-born French astronomer who made detailed maps of the planets Mercury and Mars.

APOLLONIUS (c. 250–200 B.C.) Greek geometer who developed the analysis of planetary motions in terms of epicycles, or complex combinations of circular motions.

ARISTOTLE (384–322 B.C.) One of the foremost Greek philosophers, who developed the theory that the heavenly bodies are attached to crystal spheres that revolve around the Earth.

BAADE, Wilhelm Heinrich Walter (1893–1959) Dutch-born American observer. His observations of Cepheid variables caused the accepted scale of the universe to be doubled.

BAYER, Johann (1572–1625) German lawyer who drew up a star catalog and devised the system of naming stars by assigning them letters of the Greek alphabet.

BESSEL, Friedrich Wilhelm (1784–1846) German observer who made the first measurement of the distance of a star (61 Cygni) from its parallax.

BETHE, Hans Albrecht (b. 1906) German-born American physicist who in 1939 proposed hydrogen fusion as the energy source of the stars. In 1948, he lent his support to Ralph Alpher and George GAMOW's suggestion that all the atoms heavier than those of hydrogen were built up from hydrogen in a primordial explosion (known as the "Big Bang").

BODE, Johann Elert (1747–1826) German astronomer who drew attention to the Titius-Bode law of planetary distances, first enunciated by J. D. Titius.

BRAHE, Tycho (1546–1601) Danish observer. He made the most precise observations of pretelescopic times. He proposed a compromise between the Ptolemaic and Copernican systems, in which the Earth remained fixed at the center of the universe, while the planets revolved around the Sun, which in turn revolved around the Earth.

BRADLEY, James (1692–1762) English astronomer who discovered the aberration of light, which results from the movement of the Earth through space.

CANNON, Annie Jump (1863–1941) American observer whose system of classifying stellar spectra is the basis of the modern one.

CASSINI, Giovanni Domenico (1625–1712) Italian observer who discovered four satellites of Saturn and the division in its rings that is named after him.

COPERNICUS, Nicolaus (1473–1543) Polish church official who revived the ancient idea of a Sun-centered universe in his posthumously published book *On the Revolutions of the Heavenly Orbs* (1543). He saw the planets as being of the same nature as the Earth. As in the generally held Ptolemaic system, their complex movements were composed of simple circular movements.

DE LA RUE, Warren (1859–89) English pioneer of astronomical photography. In 1860 he took pictures of a solar eclipse that showed that prominences belong to the Sun.

DESCARTES, René (1596–1650) French philosopher, mathematician, and scientist who proposed that the planets were swept around the Sun by vortices in an ether that filled space.

DOLLOND, John (1706–61) English optician who invented an achromatic lens, which reduced the color aberrations that plagued refracting telescopes.

DREYER, John Louis Emil (1852–1926) Danish-born astronomer. He compiled the New General Catalog (NGC) of star clusters and "nebulae" (gas clouds and galaxies). Many celestial objects are still identified by their NGC numbers.

EDDINGTON, Sir Arthur Stanley (1882–1945) English astrophysicist and cosmologist. His greatest book was called *The Internal Constitution of the Stars* (1926), and he won fame by leading an expedition to observe the solar eclipse of 1919, in which he observed the bending of starlight by the Sun, exactly as predicted by EINSTEIN's general theory of relativity.

EINSTEIN, Albert (1879–1955), German-Swiss-American physicist who published the special theory of relativity in 1905 and followed it with the general theory of relativity in 1916. These are part of the foundations of all modern physics, and attempts to explain the large-scale structure and development of the universe are now made on the basis of the general relativity wedded to quantum theory.

ERATOSTHENES (c. 276–196 B.C.) Greek philosopher. He calculated the circumference of the Earth from differences in the apparent position of the Sun.

EUDOXUS (c. 408–355 B.C.) Greek astronomer and mathematician who developed the theory that the planets and stars are fixed to different concentric spheres. This model dominated astronomy to the time of COPERNICUS.

FABRICIUS, David (1564–1617) Dutch observer who pioneered telescopic observation of the sky and discovered the first variable star, Mira.

FABRICIUS, Johann (1587–1616) Pioneer telescopic observer, son of David Fabricius, who independently discovered the existence of sunspots.

FLAMMARION, Camille (1842–1925) French observer, especially of Mars, and author of many books on astronomy.

FLAMSTEED, John (1646–1720) English observer who was the first holder of the post Astronomer Royal.

FRAUNHOFER, Joseph von (1787–1826) German spectroscopist. He invented the diffraction grating, studied the spectrum of the Sun, and discovered the dark Fraunhofer lines, which reveal the chemical composition of the Sun.

GALILEI, Galileo (1564–1642) Italian physicist and astronomer. He revolutionized mechanics and championed the theory of the heliocentric universe of COPERNICUS. He was one of the first to turn the newly invented telescope to the skies and described the Moon as a rocky world like the Earth, breaking down the Aristotelian distinction between terrestrial and celestial matter. He observed phases of Venus, showing it moves around the Sun, and discovered the four major satellites of Jupiter, showing the Earth is not the only centre of revolution in the solar system.

GALLE, Johann Gottfried (1812–1910), German astronomer who with Heinrich D'Arrest first observed Neptune in approximately the position predicted by LEVERRIER. He also used asteroid observations to determine the distance of the Earth from the Sun.

GAMOW, George (1904–68) Russian-born American physicist who in 1948 developed with Ralph Alpher the theory that atoms of hydrogen were built up into heavier atoms in the first few minutes of the universe.

HALE, George Ellery (1868–1938) American observer. He invented the spectroheliograph and discovered that magnetic fields are associated with sunspots. He was responsible for the building of the large reflectors at Mt. Wilson and Mt. Palomar.

HALL, Asaph (1829–1907) American planetary observer who discovered the two moons of Mars.

HALLEY, Edmond (1656–1742) English astronomer who studied the motions of comets and predicted the return of the comet now named after him. He cataloged the southern stars, made important stellar observations, and discovered the proper motions of some stars.

HARRIOT, Thomas (1560–1621) English astronomer and mathematician who was one of the first to observe the skies with a telescope, and drew maps of the Moon even before GALILEI.

HAWKING, Stephen William (b. 1942) English physicist and cosmologist. Hawking has worked on the relationship between quantum theory and gravitation in the context of extremely dense matter, as in black holes and in the first moments of the Big Bang. He has proposed "closed" models of the universe in which there is no beginning and no end to time. He became the most famous scientist

since EINSTEIN with the publication of *A Brief History of Time* (1988).

HERACLIDES of Pontus (*c.* 388–315 B.C.) Greek philosopher who stated that the daily motion of the skies is due to the rotation of the Earth and that Mercury and Venus revolve around the Sun.

HERSCHEL, John (1792–1871) English observer, son of William HERSCHEL. Among his observations were six years of cataloging southern stars from the Cape of Good Hope.

HERSCHEL, William (Friedrich Wilhelm) (1738–1822) One of the greatest of observers. He was German-born, but worked in England, assisted by his sister Caroline. He discovered the planet Uranus, and drew up catalogs of double stars and southern-sky stars.

HERTZSPRUNG, Ejnar (1873–1967) Danish observer who devised his own version of what is now called the Hertzsprung-Russell, or HR, diagram of stellar brightness against temperature, which is fundamental to the classification of stars.

HIPPARCHUS (fl. 140 B.C.) Greek astronomer who worked in Rhodes. He cataloged the stars and discovered the precession of the equinoxes.

HOYLE, Sir Fred (b. 1915) , British astrophysicist and cosmologist. He proposed in 1948 the steady-state theory as an alternative to the Big Bang theory of the origin of the universe. He made important contributions to the theory of stellar nucleosynthesis, the building-up of heavier atomic nuclei from hydrogen nuclei in stars. While now accepting the reality of a Big Bang, he continues to develop theories in which it is only one of many such episodes in an eternal universe.

HUBBLE, Edwin Powell (1889–1953) American observer who established the nature of the galaxies and the expansion of the universe. Using the 100–in (2.5m) reflector on Mount Wilson, in California, Hubble detected Cepheid variables in what was then called the Great Nebula in Andromeda and showed that it lay beyond the Milky Way and like the latter was made of stars. His measurements of red-shifts in the light of the galaxies established Hubble's law.

HUYGENS, Christiaan (1629–95) Dutch scientist and astronomical observer. He explained that the strange shape of Saturn was due to its possession of a system of rings, and he discovered Saturn's largest satellite, Titan.

JANSKY, Karl Guthe (1905–49) Czech-born American engineer who discovered the first radio waves from space.

KANT, Immanuel (1724–1804) Prussian philosopher and astronomical theorist. He proposed the nebular hypothesis, that the Sun, planets, and other members of the solar system formed by condensing from a rotating cloud of gas.

KEPLER, Johannes (1571–1630) German theorist and observer, assistant to Tycho BRAHE, and discoverer of important laws of planetary motion. Kepler was an early adherent of the Copernican system but came to realize that the planets moved in ellipses, not combinations of circular orbits.

KIRCHOFF, Gustav Robert (1824–87) German physicist who mapped the spectrum of the Sun and explained how the dark Fraunhofer lines are caused.

LAGRANGE, Joseph Louis De (1736–1813) French mathematician who analyzed many astronomical topics, including the Moon's motion and whether the solar system is stable in the long term.

LAPLACE, Pierre Simon (1749–1827) French mathematician who contributed to the analysis of many astronomical problems, and wrote *Mécanique céleste* (1799–1825). He also further developed KANT's nebular hypothesis.

LEAVITT, Henrietta Swan (1868–1921) American observer who established the relationship between luminosity and the period of variation of the Cepheid variables. This makes Cepheids invaluable as standards of brightness.

LEMAITRE, Georges (1894–1966) Belgian priest and mathematician, who proposed that the universe was born in the explosion of a "primeval atom." This theory has developed into today's Big Bang theory.

LEVERRIER, Urbain Jean Joseph (1811–77) Codiscoverer of the planet Neptune. The position of the planet was calculated independently by John Couch ADAMS. Leverrier also calculated the orbit of the Leonid meteors.

LOMONOSOV, Mikhail (1711–65) Russian writer, scholar, and scientist. He discovered the atmosphere of Venus and championed the work of COPERNICUS and NEWTON.

LOVELL, Sir (Alfred Charles) Bernard (b. 1913) British radio astronomer, first director of the Jodrell Bank Experimental Station, now part of the Nuffield Radio Astronomy Laboratories, Cheshire, England. At Jodrell Bank he won funding for the 250–ft. (75–m) steerable radio dish, for some time the largest in the world, which is now called the Lovell Telescope after him.

LOWELL, Percival (1855–1916) American astronomer mainly remembered for his claim that there was intelligent life on Mars, and that he had observed straight-line markings on Mars which he believed to be canals. Lowell attempted to calculate the position of a hypothetical planet beyond Neptune, but it was probably merely a lucky chance that this led to the discovery of Pluto in 1930.

MESSIER, Charles (1730–1817) French observer. He prepared a famous catalogue of nebulous objects to enable astronomers to distinguish them from comets. They include nebulae, galaxies, and clusters of stars.

NEWTON, Sir Isaac (1643–1727) English physicist and mathematician, arguably the greatest scientist of all time. His *Principia Mathematica Philosophiae Naturalis* (1687) revolutionized mechanics, described his theory of gravitation, and explained numerous astronomical phenomena, including KEPLER's laws of planetary motion, much of the motion of the Moon, and the tides. Newton also built the first reflecting telescope.

OLBERS, Heinrich Wilhelm Matthias (1758–1840) German amateur observer who discovered two asteroids and studied comets.

PIAZZI, Giuseppe (1746–1826) Italian astronomer who was the first to discover an asteroid, Ceres, in 1801.

PTOLEMY (Claudius Ptolemaeus) (*c.* 120–180) Greek astronomer and geographer who worked in Alexandria, Egypt. In his *Almagest* he extended the star catalog of Hipparchus and elaborated a description of the universe in which the heavenly bodies circled the Earth.

RICCIOLI, Giovanni Battista (1598–1671) Italian observer and Jesuit priest. He mapped the Moon and devised the system of nomenclature that is still used.

ROMER, Ole (1644–1710) Danish observer. He invented many observing instruments and estimated the speed of light from the delay in the apparent times of the eclipses of Jupiter's satellites.

RUSSELL, Henry Norris (1877–1957) American observer who independently devised his own version of what is now called the Hertzsprung-Russell, or HR, diagram.

SAGAN, Carl (b. 1934) U.S. astronomer, cosmologist, author, and broadcaster whose ability as a natural communicator has enabled him to explain difficult concepts to readers and television viewers.

SCHIAPARELLI, Giovanni Virginio (1835–1910) Italian astronomer who showed that meteors shower are produced by comets.

SCHWABE, Heinrich (1789–1875) German amateur astronomer who discovered the 11–year sunspot cycle.

SEYFERT, Carl (1911–60) American observer. He studied galaxies and identified a class of galaxy with bright centers, now called Seyfert galaxies.

SHAPLEY, Harlow (1885–1972) American astronomer. He studied variable stars especially, and used Cepheid variables to map out the distribution of globular clusters and thus determine the shape and size of the galaxy.

ULUGH-BEG (or Ulugbek) (1394–1449) Mongol ruler of Turkestan, grandson of Timur. He founded an observatory at Samarkand and compiled a star catalog and tables of the movements of the Moon and planets.

WOLF, Max(imilian Franz Joseph Cornelius) (1863–1932) German astronomer who studied the behavior of comets and asteroids.

TERMS

Aberration 1. Failure of a lens to focus light rays accurately. 2. Apparent change in the direction of motion of a celestial object because the movement of the Earth alters the apparent motion of light rays from the source.

Absolute magnitude The true brightness of a star or other celestial object, expressed as the apparent magnitude that it would have when viewed from a standard distance of 10 PARSECs. The absolute magnitude of the Sun is 4.83.

Accretion disk A disk of gas and possibly solid matter circling a body such as a black hole.

Achromatic lens A lens consisting of a combination of component lenses, designed to reduce CHROMATIC ABERRATION.

Albedo The light-reflecting power of a nonluminous celestial body.

Angström (or ångström unit) A unit of length still used in spectroscopy, equal to a ten-billionth of a meter, or one-tenth of a nanometer.

Aphelion The point in the orbit of a planet, asteroid, etc. that is farthest from the Sun.

Apogee The point in the orbit of a satellite or spacecraft that is farthest from the Earth.

Apparent magnitude The apparent brightness of a celestial body expressed on a scale on which fainter objects are represented by larger numbers.

Asteroid A minor planet, or planetoid.

Astronomical unit (AU) A unit of distance originally defined as the average Earth-Sun distance. It's now equal to 92.96 million mi./149.6 million km.

Aurora Shifting patterns of light in the sky, normally in polar regions. It is an atmospheric phenomenon, caused by charged particles escaping from the VAN ALLEN BELTS.

Azimuth The angle between true north and the point on the horizon directly below a celestial object, measured clockwise.

Binary star A stellar system consisting of two individual stars revolving around one another.

Black hole A region surrounding an object that is so massive, or so dense, that no matter or radiation can escape from it. Black holes probably power QUASARS and SEYFERT GALAXIES.

Blue giant A MAIN SEQUENCE star of several times the radius and mass of the Sun, which "burns" rapidly.

Blue shift A shortening in the wavelength of light caused by its approach. Features in the spectrum are shifted toward, or beyond, the blue (short-wavelength) end.

Brown dwarf A hypothetical "failed star," born with insufficient mass to become a true star, but glowing faintly, deriving its energy from slow shrinkage.

Celestial equator The imaginary line around the celestial sphere that lies directly over the Earth's equator.

Cepheid variables A type of variable star whose average brightness is related to its period, or time of variation; the brighter the star, the longer its period.

Chromatic aberration The focusing of different colors at different points, resulting in colored fringes in an image.

Chromosphere A layer of the Sun's atmosphere lying above the photosphere.

Circumpolar stars Stars that do not appear to set as viewed from a given location.

Color index The difference between measurements of the magnitude of a star at different wavelengths, which is a measure of the star's color and hence temperature.

Conjunction The apparent coming together of two celestial bodies. *See* OPPOSITION.

Corona A pearly white atmosphere extending to several times the radius of the Sun. It is intensely hot, but extremely rarefied. It is visible to the naked eye during a total solar eclipse.

Coronagraph An instrument that cuts out the light of the Sun to permit the CORONA to be seen at times other than an eclipse.

Cosmic rays Primary cosmic rays consist of subatomic particles, mostly electrons, that travel through space at very high energies; some of them reach the Earth's surface. Secondary cosmic rays consist of particles produced by the collision of primary cosmic-ray particles with atoms in the Earth's atmosphere and bombard the Earth's surface.

Declination The angular distance of a celestial body north or south of the celestial equator.

Doppler effect A change in wavelength of light or sound caused by the relative motion of the source and the observer.

Eclipsing binary A BINARY STAR in which each component happens to pass between the other and the Earth, causing the apparent combined brightness to drop suddenly and making the system variable.

Ecliptic The apparent yearly path of the Sun eastward around the celestial sphere. All the planets follow apparent paths close to the ecliptic.

Elongation The angle between a planet and the Sun, or between a satellite and its planet, as viewed from the Earth.

Equinox Either of two positions on the celestial sphere at which the ECLIPTIC crosses the CELESTIAL EQUATOR; or the times (in spring and fall) at which the Sun reaches these points.

Escape velocity A speed sufficient to carry an object away from the Earth or any celestial body to infinity without any further boost being required.

Flare A violent explosion on the Sun's surface, which emits fast-moving particles and high-energy radiation.

Forbidden lines Lines in some astronomical spectra that do not match those of any known element under terrestrial conditions. They are produced by familiar elements, such as oxygen and nitrogen, but under conditions of very low pressure.

Fraunhofer lines Dark lines crossing the spectrum of a star. They represent elements in the outer, cooler layers of the body that are absorbing particular wavelengths of light from the continuous spectrum produced by the hotter surface below.

H I and H II regions Parts of interstellar space occupied by gas consisting of, respectively, neutral hydrogen atoms and hydrogen ions. An H I region is dark but reveals itself by the radio waves that it emits. An H II region glows red.

Halo A region around a galaxy occupied by many globular clusters and much invisible gas. An atmospheric phenomenon in which a ring of light appears around the Moon or Sun when seen through clouds consisting of ice crystals.

Hertzsprung-Russell (HR) diagram A chart on which stars are plotted according to their SPECTRAL TYPE (effectively, their temperature) and their brightness.

Hubble constant The ratio between the speed of recession of a galaxy cluster and its distance from us. It is currently believed to lie in the range 9–18mps (15–30kps) per million light-years.

Kepler's laws Three laws of planetary motion: 1. Every planet moves in an ellipse, with the Sun at one focus. 2. An imaginary line drawn from the planet to the Sun sweeps out equal areas in equal times (therefore the planet moves faster when closer to the Sun). 3. The squares of the planets' periods (their "years") are proportional to the cubes of their average distances from the Sun.

Libration An apparent "swaying" of the Moon from east to west and from north to south, allowing us to see a little of the far side.

Local Group The grouping of about 25 galaxies to which the Milky Way galaxy belongs.

Magnetosphere The region around a celestial body in which its magnetic field is stronger than the magnetic field in the surrounding space.

Main sequence A band in the HERTZSPRUNG-RUSSELL DIAGRAM on which most stars lie.

Meridian 1. A circle on the surface of a celestial body or the Earth running through both poles. 2. The circle on the celestial sphere running through both celestial poles and the zenith.

Meteor The visible phenomenon seen when a METEOROID hurtles into the atmosphere and is burned away by the frictional heat.

Meteorite A fragment sometimes found

on the Earth after the fall of a METEO-ROID.

Meteoroid A small solid body orbiting the Sun, typically a minute grain of dust but sometimes with a mass measured in pounds.

Multiple star A system of several individual stars, all of which revolve around a common center of gravity.

Nadir The unseen point on the celestial sphere directly beneath the observer, opposite to the ZENITH.

Nebula A mass of gas and dust in interstellar space.

Neutron star An extremely dense, fast-spinning body left behind after the explosion of a SUPERNOVA, having mass comparable with the Sun's squeezed into the volume of the Earth. Its atoms have been crushed to form the subatomic particles called neutrons. Some neutron stars are PULSARS.

Node Point at which the apparent path of a celestial body circling the Sun cuts the ECLIPTIC.

Nova A sudden flaring up of a star to hundreds or thousands of times its former brightness, so that it may appear as a "new star."

Nutation A nodding motion of the Earth, caused by the Moon's gravitational pull on the Earth's equatorial bulge.

Occultation The hiding of one celestial body by another. Jupiter occults its satellites when they pass behind it as viewed from Earth.

Opposition The position of an outer planet, or of the Moon, when it is exactly opposite the Sun as viewed from the Earth.

Parallax The apparent shift in position of an object due to a shift in the observer's position.

Parsec A unit of distance equal to 3.26 light-years.

Penumbra The lighter, outer part of a shadow or of a sunspot.

Perigee The point in the orbit of the Moon or an artificial satellite that is closest to the Earth.

Perihelion The point in the orbit of a planet, comet, etc. that is closest to the Sun.

Photosphere The bright white visible surface of the Sun.

Planetary nebula A bright compact gas cloud, so named because when seen in early telescopes such objects resembled planets. The nebula has been released by an aging, disturbed star, often visible at the center.

Planetoid *See* ASTEROID.

Populations I and **II** Two groups into which stars are classified. Population I stars are found where new stars are still being born; the brightest stars are hot, blue, short-lived ones. Among Population II stars the brightest are red giants.

Precession A "wobbling" motion of a rotating object. The Earth "wobbles" once in 26,300 years, causing the celes-

tial poles to move in circles and the EQUINOXES to precess westward along the ECLIPTIC.

Primary A body around which another one revolves. A satellite's primary is the planet that it circles; a planet's primary is the star to which it belongs.

Prominence Filaments of glowing hydrogen gas, often in the form of arches and loops, that rise tens and hundreds of thousands of miles above the Sun's surface.

Proper motion The motion of a celestial body at right angles to the line of sight in relation to the overall background of fixed stars.

Protostar A mass of gas that has condensed from a NEBULA and is on the verge of becoming a true star. It shines by gravitational energy released by its slow shrinking. Visible light cannot escape from the hot core through the surrounding gas, but the protostar is bright at infrared wavelengths.

Pulsar A NEUTRON STAR that happens to be oriented in such a way that beams of radiation emitted from its poles sweep repeatedly across the Earth like the beams of a lighthouse. It appears as a radio source pulsating at intervals ranging from about a thousandth of a second to several seconds.

Quasar An immensely bright object pouring out as much energy as tens or hundreds of billions of stars from a region only a few light-years across.

Radiant The point in the sky from which trails of meteors belonging to the same swarm seem to radiate.

Red dwarf A MAIN SEQUENCE star of mass significantly lower than the Sun's, which therefore "burns" its hydrogen fuel slowly. It is both cool and small, which means it is faint.

Red giant A star near the end of its life that has used up most of its hydrogen fuel and has begun to burn helium; this causes it to swell up. It becomes cool and reddish, but also large and therefore bright. It lies well above the MAIN SEQUENCE.

Red shift A lengthening of the wavelength of light from a source caused by its recession. Features in the spectrum are shifted toward, or beyond, the red (long-wavelength) end.

Reflector Telescope in which the main, or primary, image is formed by a concave mirror or mirrors. All major astronomical telescopes are reflectors.

Refractor Telescope in which the main, or primary, image is formed by a lens.

Retrograde motion Apparent motion of a celestial body in the opposite direction to normal.

Right ascension The angular position of a celestial body measured eastward from the vernal EQUINOX, the celestial equivalent of terrestrial longitude.

Roche limit The distance from a body such as a planet within which a satellite could not survive but would be torn

apart by gravitational forces.

Scintillation The twinkling of a star caused by turbulence in the Earth's atmosphere; the analogous variation in apparent "brightness" of a radio source caused by shifting interstellar gases.

Seyfert galaxy A type of galaxy that has a very bright, pointlike center.

Sidereal period The time in which a celestial body rotates or revolves in relation to the fixed stars.

Solar wind A stream of charged particles continually blowing outward from the Sun through the solar system.

Solstices The northernmost and southernmost points on the ECLIPTIC; times when the Sun reaches those points.

Spectral type One of the classes into which stars are grouped on the basis of their spectra. They range from O-type, the hottest, to S-type, the coolest.

Spectroheliograph An instrument that images the Sun at one particular wavelength.

Spectroscopic binary A BINARY STAR whose components are too close to be separated in the telescope, but which reveal themselves to the spectroscope.

Spectroscopy The analysis of light by splitting it up into its component wavelengths.

Spherical aberration The focusing of rays passing through the edge of a lens differently from those passing through the center of the lens, reducing the quality of the image.

Supernova The explosion, at the end of its life, of a star more than about 40 percent more massive than the Sun. Its peak brightness is tens of billions of times that of the Sun.

Synodic period The period of revolution of a celestial body in relation to the Earth, rather than, for example, the fixed stars. Thus the synodic period of a planet is the period from one CONJUNCTION to the next.

Terminator The boundary between the daylight and night-time hemispheres of a planet or satellite.

Transit The passage of a smaller celestial body in front of a larger one—for example, of Venus in front of the Sun, or of one of Jupiter's satellites in front of the parent body.

Umbra The darker, central part of a shadow or of a sunspot.

Van Allen belts Two zones surrounding the Earth in which electrons and atomic nuclei from the SOLAR WIND are trapped by the Earth's magnetic field.

Variable stars Stars that show repeated changes in brightness.

White dwarf A dense, hot star that has run out of hydrogen and helium fuel, and has passed through RED GIANT and highly disturbed phases. Though retaining a mass comparable to the Sun's, it has shrunk to about the size of the Earth.

Zenith The point on the celestial sphere directly above the observer.

INTRODUCTION

Earth Sciences examines our planet's structure and the geological processes at work within it and on its surface. It considers rock formation and composition, and the geological evolution of the Earth. Land-sculpting agents, weather, and mapping conclude the study.

DYNAMIC EARTH

Planet Earth is a small, dense, rocky planet that is unusual in several respects. It has free oxygen in its atmosphere; water is present in three phases—ice, liquid, and vapor; and surface temperatures are maintained in a relatively narrow range. Life forms play a key role in maintaining the balance of conditions on Earth.

The interior is layered (*right*). Radioactive decay in the interior releases heat which slowly rises to the surface. Convection currents within the semisolid mantle (*p. 43*) produce volcanic hotspots. The currents create new ocean crust and push the continents around like floating rafts (*p. 44*).

Formation of the Earth

About 4.7 billion years ago, the young Sun began to shine, blowing the remaining material of the solar nebula into a ring of dust, gas, and ice (*p. 18*). Rocky silicates condensed out nearest the Sun; gases and ices were driven farther.

Gravity and impacts helped the rocky material clump together. Radioactivity and the heat of impacts melted the larger protoplanets so that iron could sink and form a core. Depressions in the young Earth's surface which became the ocean basins may have been created by impacting comets. The first atmosphere was composed of gases expelled by volcanoes. A Mars-sized object hitting the planet may have produced the Moon (*p. 21*).

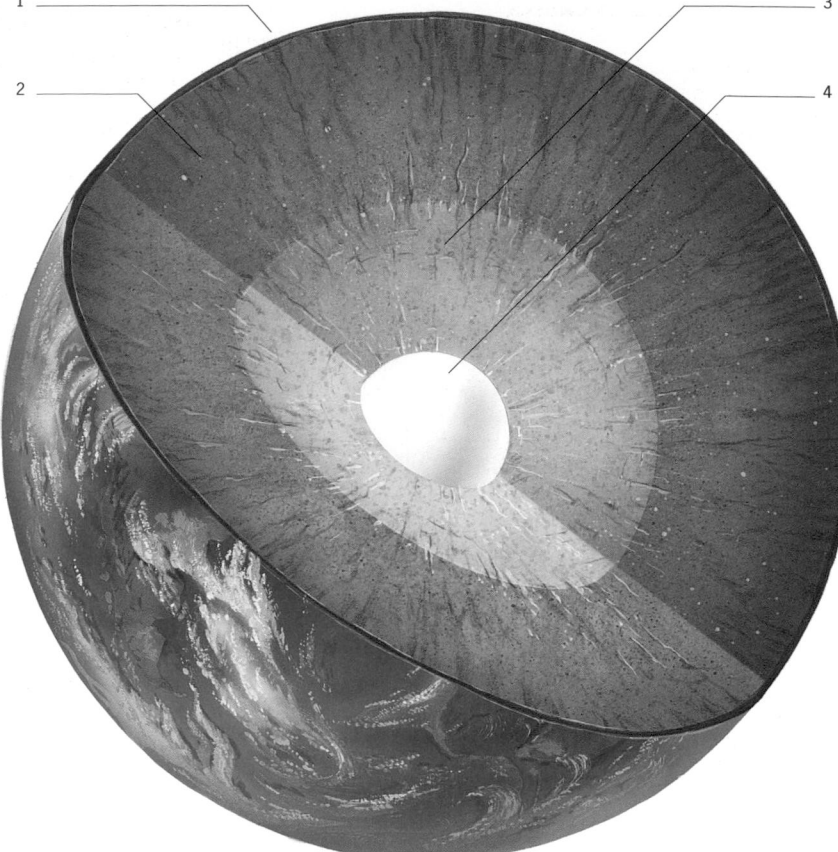

Lithosphere (1)
The crust and cold top of mantle are separated by the Mohorovicic discontinuity. The continents sit on huge tectonic plates, which have moved over geological time.

Mantle (2)
The mantle is composed of semi-solid silicates of magnesium and iron. It moves slowly by convection; there are separate circulations in the upper and lower mantle.

Outer core (3)
At 7,000°F and composed of molten iron and nickel, the outer core is fluid. Its rapid circulation and the electric currents within it create the Earth's magnetic field.

Inner core (4)
The inner core is solid, possibly made up of crystalline iron and nickel. Its temperature is around 11,000°F, but the enormous pressure of the rock above it stops it "melting."

Seismic clues

Earthquakes (*pp. 46-47*) produce shock waves that reverberate outward through rock from a central point of energy release. Different kinds of waves can be identified and their paths plotted (*right*). Rayleigh waves and Love waves only travel around the surface of the Earth. P waves (primary waves) and S waves (secondary waves) travel through the Earth, although S waves cannot cross the boundary of the molten outer core. They are reflected off that boundary, thus revealing the deep structure. Waves picked up by receivers across the globe are used to build up a structural cross-section.

Shock waves

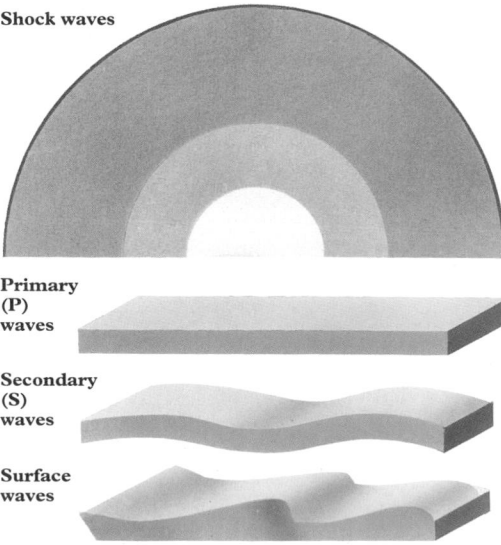

Primary (P) waves

Secondary (S) waves

Surface waves

Planetary data

Equatorial diameter	7,926 mi.
Polar diameter	7,900 mi.
Mass	6.6 sextillion tons
Density	5.52 of water
Surface gravity	$9.78ms^{-2}$
Escape velocity	6.95mps
Period of revolution	23.9345 hrs.
Year length	365.256 days
Axial inclination	23.44°
Distance from Sun	Min. 91 million mi.
	Max. 94 million mi.
Surface area	196 million mi.²
Land surface	57 million mi.²
Atmosphere	N_2 78%, O_2 21%
Ocean cover	70.8% of surface
Av. ht of land	2,756ft. above sea level
Av. depth of ocean	12,490 ft.
Continental crust	22 mi. thick (average)
Oceanic crust	4 mi. thick (average)
Lithosphere	To 46 mi. depth
Mantle	1,800 mi. thick
Outer core	1,367 mi. thick
Inner core	746 mi. thick

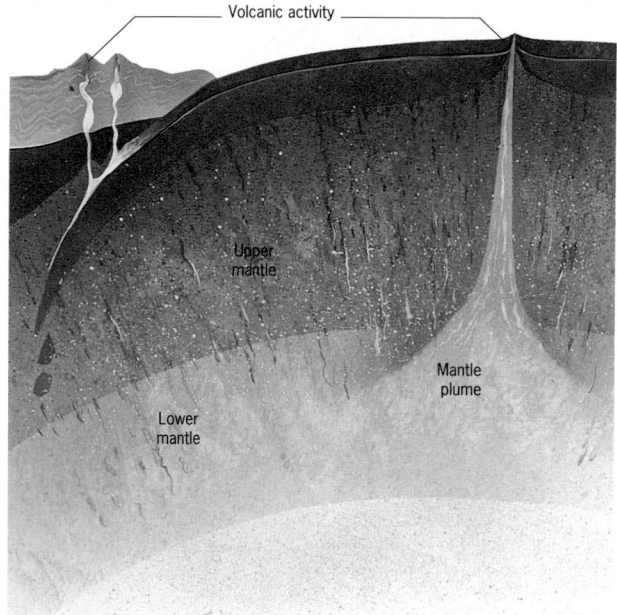

Volcanic activity

Upper mantle

Mantle plume

Lower mantle

Depth and density

As they travel through the Earth's crustal layer, the velocity of seismic waves is highest in hard, dense rocks. However, seismic waves travel faster through the semimolten mantle than the solid lithosphere above it. This apparent mystery is explained by the Earth's gravity, which compresses the planet into a ball, both making the interior extremely hot and subjecting it to great pressure. The immense pressure generated within the mantle means that the hot rock of which it is composed can remain molten but also be incredibly dense at the same time. The density changes encountered with increasing depth (*right*) can cause traveling seismic waves to be refracted.

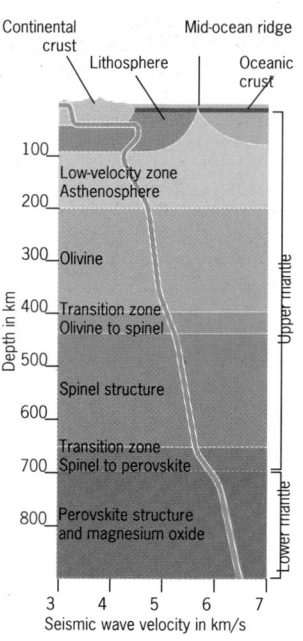

Continental crust
Mid-ocean ridge
Lithosphere
Oceanic crust

Low-velocity zone
Asthenosphere

Olivine
Transition zone
Olivine to spinel

Spinel structure

Transition zone
Spinel to perovskite

Perovskite structure
and magnesium oxide

Depth in km

Upper mantle
Lower mantle

Seismic wave velocity in km/s

Mantle convection

Heat rises through the mantle in convection currents (*above*), like those in a pan of water on a stove. But does semimolten rock circulate through the whole mantle or are there two separate circulations like a double boiler? Density estimates suggest the upper and lower mantles are chemically different, and are therefore not mixed by whole-mantle circulation. But seismic evidence shows slabs of cold material descending through the lower mantle: some volcanic rocks carry chemical signatures of the lower mantle. There is a barrier to flow about 400 mi./ 650 km down, but it may only be a temporary holding layer. To descend farther, rocks may have to change into denser mineral forms.

Structure of the Earth

	Depth to base (mi.)	Mineral phase	Temperature (°F)	P wave velocity (km/s)
Continental crust	22	Aluminum silicate	0–1,800	5.8–6.4
Ocean crust/	4	Magnesium silicate	0–1,100	6.5–6.9
Lithosphere	47		600–2,000	6.1–7.5
Asthenosphere	155	Olivine	1,000–3,000	*c.* 8
Upper mantle	403	Spinel	1,000–3,000	8–10
Lower mantle	1,647	Perovskite	3,000–5,000	10.5–13.5
D layer	1,796	Iron oxide, silicates	*c.* 5,000	*c.* 13.5
Outer core	3,203	Molten iron	6,000–7,000	7.5–10.2
Inner core	3,961	Solid iron	up to 9,000	10.5–11.6

Magnetism

The Earth has a strong dipolar magnetic field (*inset*), as if there was a large bar magnet in the core. In fact, electrical currents in the churning, liquid outer core produce a self-sustaining dynamo. The influence of the magnetic field extends beyond the planet (*top, right*). The field meets charged particles streaming from the Sun in a shock wave about 30,000 mi. above the Earth and slows them from 250 to 150mps. The solar wind, as these particles are known, sweeps the Earth's magnetic field into a 4 million-mile tail. Solar flares on the surface of the Sun result in magnetic storms on Earth two days later. There are belts of solar particles trapped in the magnetic field about 2,000 and 15,000 mi. above the equator, called the Van Allen belts. Aurorae occur where charged particles trapped by the Earth's magnetic field stream toward the poles.

The Earth's magnetic axis is 11° west of the North Pole and is slowly wandering. Eddy currents in the core and magnetism trapped in rocks produce local anomalies (*bottom, right*). In the geological past, the magnetic field has reversed

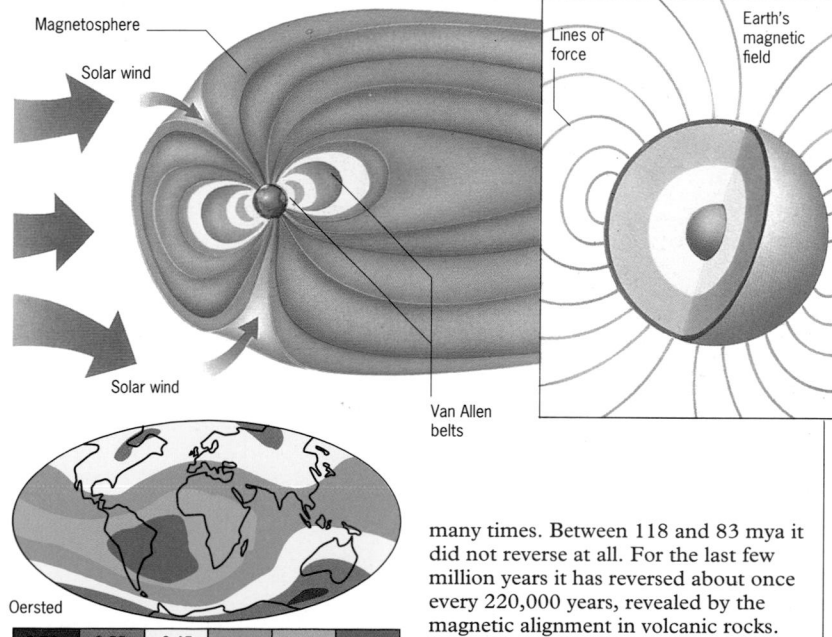

Magnetosphere

Solar wind

Solar wind

Van Allen belts

Lines of force

Earth's magnetic field

Oersted

| 0.70 | 0.55 | 0.45 | 0.35 | 0.30 | 0.25 |

many times. Between 118 and 83 mya it did not reverse at all. For the last few million years it has reversed about once every 220,000 years, revealed by the magnetic alignment in volcanic rocks. We are overdue for another reversal.

EARTH'S CRUST

The Earth's crust only accounts for 0.6 percent of the planet's volume, yet we have not penetrated through even that. Oceanic crust is 3–6 miles (5–10 km) thick and made mostly of dark, dense basalt, capped by sediments. The continents are much thicker—up to 53 miles (85 km) under the Himalayas—and generally made of less dense rocks, including granite and thick accumulations of sediment. The continental crust resembles the scum on the surface of a cauldron.

The oldest regions of continents, made of material that has been piling up for billions of years, have been "cooked" by heat and pressure and are made of crystalline metamorphic rocks. At the base of the crust is a boundary that reflects seismic waves, called the Mohorovicic discontinuity, or Moho. Beneath it are the rocky slabs of lithospheric mantle, composed mostly of iron and magnesium-rich peridotite, on which the crust floats. The more laden the crust, the lower it sinks. Mountainous areas have "roots" within the mantle which are significantly greater than the height of the mountains above. The balance maintained is called isostasy.

Tectonic crustal plates

The crust is divided into relatively rigid plates, some made of ocean crust, some of continents (*below*). Over geological time the plates jostle around as the convecting mantle moves beneath them, triggering earthquakes. Ocean crust is created where molten rock wells up along mid-ocean ridges, and is destroyed where it is subsumed under continental plates. Continental crust can be roasted, stretched, and split by mantle plumes, or uplifted, warped, and eroded at the surface, but ancient continental cores remain intact.

It is possible to trace the history of the movements of continents' waltzes around the globe over hundreds of millions of years. Their edges fit together like the pieces of a jigsaw: the similarities between their fossils and rock strata, the past climates they experienced, and the orientation of magnetic minerals, frozen in volcanic rocks like tiny compass needles, all record their travels. Precise laser measurements taken from satellites reveal the present rate of continental drift. It is roughly comparable to the rate at which fingernails grow—a mere 1.5–2 in.(4–5 cm) a year across the Atlantic, 4.5-5 in.(12–14 cm) a year across parts of the Pacific.

The continental waltz

Using the residual magnetism of particles locked in various rocks, geologists can work out their orientation when the rocks were formed. By comparing their magnetic alignment, scientists can trace how the continents have moved (*right*).

Two hundred million years ago almost all the continents were joined together in the supercontinent of Pangaea (1). By 100 million years ago, it had split into Laurasia and Gondwanaland, which also began to split (2). Fifty million years ago the Atlantic was just opening (3). In 50 million years' time, the face of the Earth will have changed once more (4).

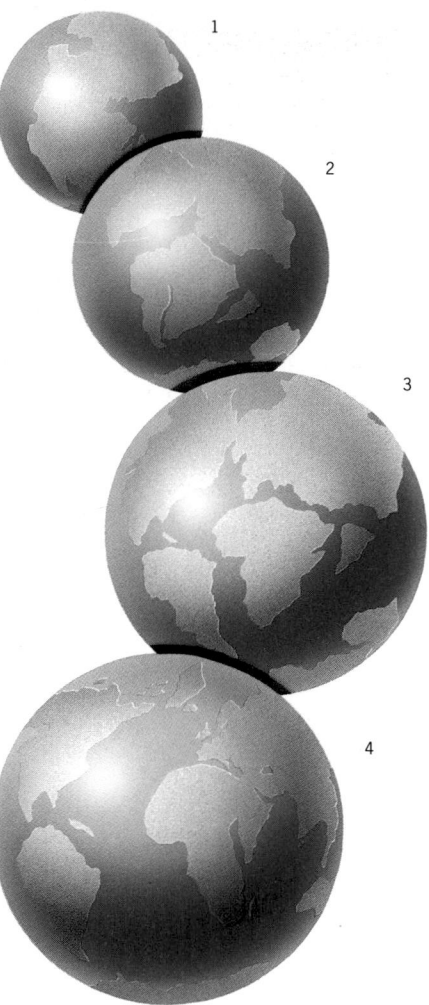

The Earth's solid surface is in effect a jigsaw consisting of variously sized crustal—or continental—plates, whose movement is determined by mantle convection currents.

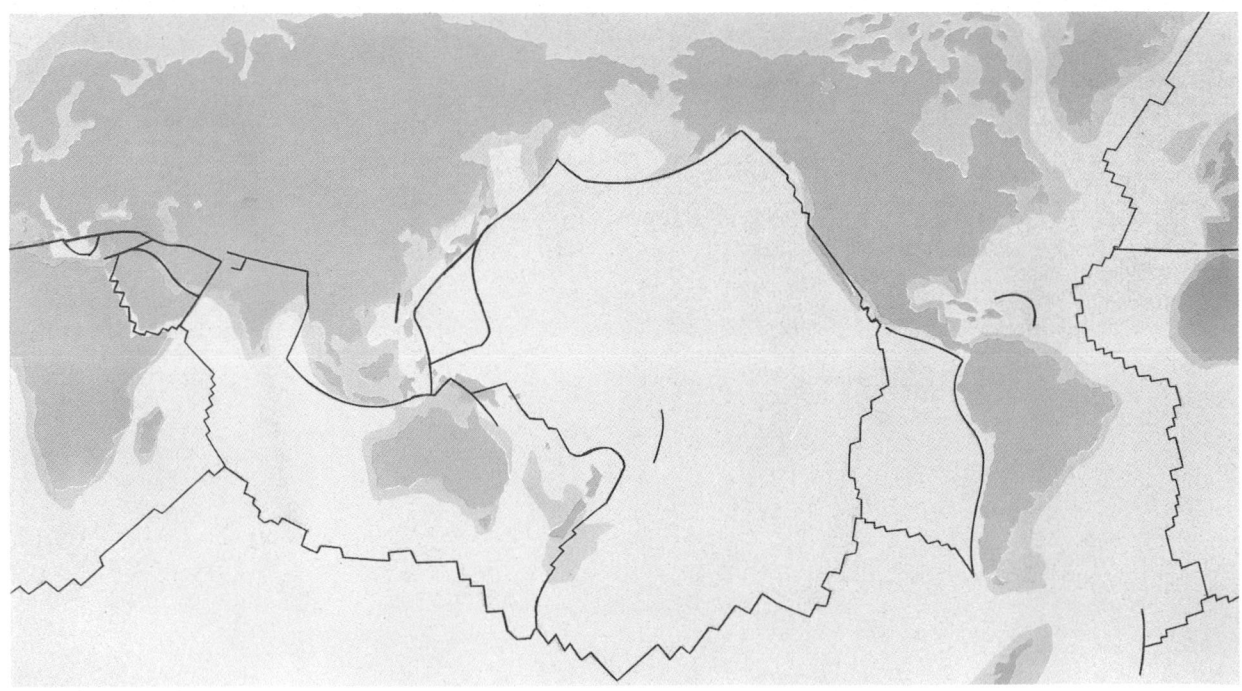

Plate boundaries

Tectonic plates are ringed with destructive boundaries (*right and below*) marked by earthquakes and volcanoes.

Most new plate forms under the sea at mid-ocean ridges (1). The ridge system is, in effect, the longest mountain chain on Earth at 45,000 mi.(70,000 km) long. Crust produced along a line will not fit over the spherical surface of the Earth so the ridges buckle and are punctuated by 90° transform faults.

Where an ocean plate meets another plate, it takes a dive at what is termed a subduction zone (2). This can result in an ocean trench fringed with volcanic atolls above the descend-

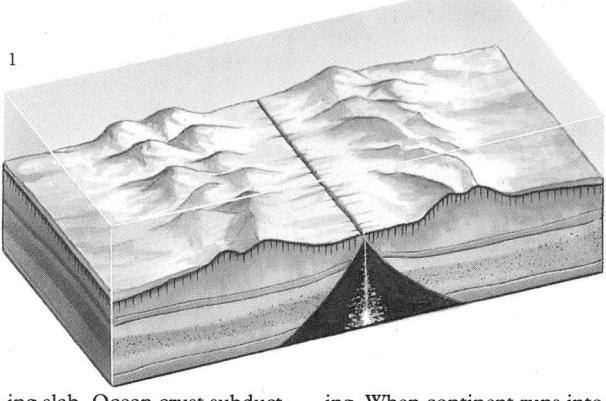

ing slab. Ocean crust subducting beneath a continent scrapes off accumulated sediment and carries seawater as it goes. This results in volcanic activity and mountain build-

ing. When continent runs into continent, massive buckling occurs (3). Neither continental plate can sink so the rocks are uplifted into high mountain ranges.

Magnetic memory

As lava from a mid-ocean ridge cools, it "freezes" the prevailing magnetism. Over time the Earth's reversing magnetic field results in a striped pattern of magnetism (*below*) either side of a ridge, a record of seafloor spreading.

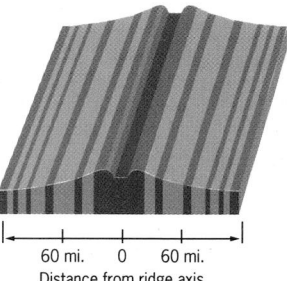

60 mi.   0   60 mi.
Distance from ridge axis

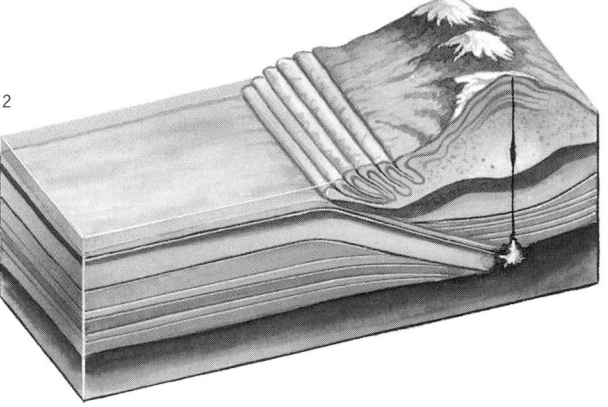

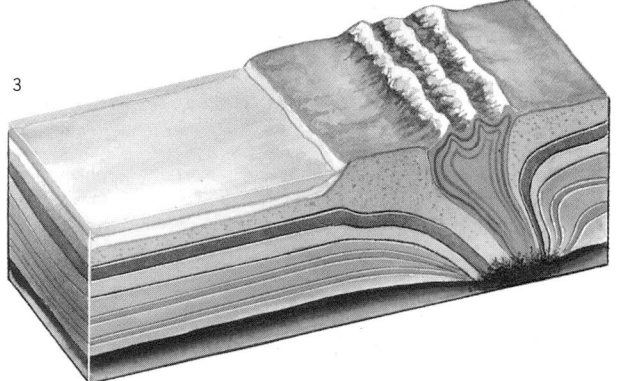

Profile of a continent

Geologists use explosives or hydraulic rams on giant-sized trucks to generate artificial seismic waves. As the waves reflect off the various layers within the Earth's interior, they reveal the continental structure, past and present.

Beneath the continent of North America (*below*), seismic studies show up great sheets of basalt that may have been injected under the conti-

nent as it was stretched by the circulatory motion of convection currents in the mantle. An ancient, Precambrian "shield" forms the nucleus of the continent. It is mostly overlain by ancient sedimentary rocks—known as a "stable platform"—deposited when an ocean covered the area. To either side are younger, orogenic areas, formed by continental impact or at crustal margins.

CRUSTAL COMPARISON

	Ocean crust	Continental crust
Thickness	3-6 miles	12-50 miles
Composition	Sima (magnesium silicates)	Sial (aluminium silicates)
Specific gravity	2.9–3.0	2.4–2.8
P wave velocity	4-4.3 mi./s	3.8-4 mi./s
Age range	0–100 million years	Up to 3.5 billion years
Rock formation	Old rock subducts into the Earth's interior; new rock is formed from rising magma	Very old rock that is not subducting into mantle
Typical rocks	Basalt, gabbro, dolerite	Sediments, granite, metamorphic massifs

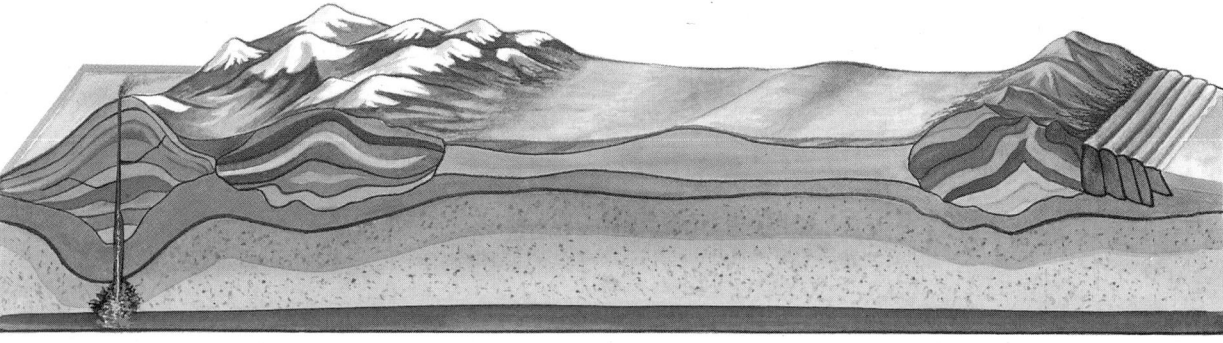

EARTHQUAKES

The continents slowly slip past one another, rising, falling, straining, and distorting as they go. Their passage is seldom smooth. With little lubrication, strain builds up until the rock can withstand it no longer and the ground cracks. The resulting earthquake can release tremendous amounts of energy in the form of seismic waves that run through the ground, shaking buildings with a destructive force. Movement along the fracture or fault line can extend for many yards, and can occur horizontally and vertically. Seismic seabed movement can generate seemingly harmless waves in deep water, but the waves travel at up to 500 mph (800 kph). They are slowed down in shallow water but their amplitude increases so that they reach heights of 160ft. (50m). These tidal waves, or tsunamis, wreak great havoc on coastal areas.

Severity scales

The Richter scale measures the amplitude of seismic waves on a logarithmic scale. Thus the waves from a magnitude 7 quake are ten times bigger than those of magnitude 6. The Mercalli scale (*below*) records damage in the absence of instruments.

I Seldom felt, but would be recorded by instruments.
II Felt by people at rest on upper floors.
III Obvious shaking felt indoors; hanging objects swing.
IV Standing cars rock; windows and dishes rattle; trees shake.
V Sleepers awake; doors swing open; liquids spill.
VI Felt by all; people walk unsteadily; windows and glassware break; pictures fall off walls.
VII Difficult to stand; furniture breaks; masonry damaged; large bells ring; waves on ponds.
VIII Car steering affected; chimneys fall; cracks in wet ground; branches broken from trees.
IX General panic; damage to foundations; underground pipes break; conspicuous cracks in ground appear.
X Most buildings destroyed; water thrown on banks of rivers; rails bent slightly; landslides.
XI Rails bent greatly; roads break up; underground pipelines completely out of service
XII Total destruction; large rock masses displaced; objects thrown into the air.

Volcano and earthquake zones

Most earthquakes, like volcanoes, take place in specific zones (*right*) that correspond to the boundaries of tectonic plates (*p. 45*). Shallow earthquakes happen where one plate moves against another on the surface, as in California, and where displacement is horizontal. Deeper earthquakes occur where one plate is sliding beneath another, described as a subduction zone. This is happening along the west coast of South America, where the ocean crust dives beneath the continent. Volcanoes occur in the same regions, as magma is produced at both constructive (where crust is being generated) and destructive (where it is disappearing) margins. The most violent eruptions occur at destructive margins and are known as Andesite volcanoes (after the Andes mountains).

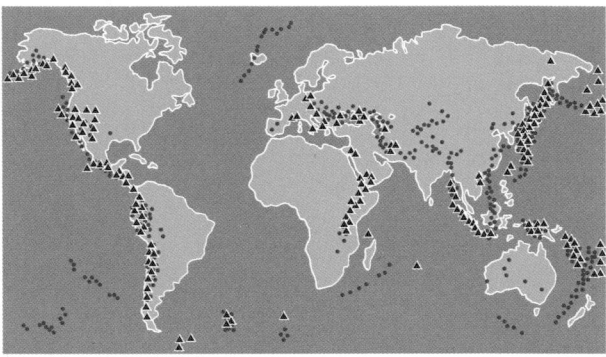

Mapping earthquakes from space

Better knowledge of why earthquakes happen is a major step toward improved prediction. In 1992, a 7.4 magnitude earthquake in California was mapped by combining satellite radar images taken before and after the shock (*below*). The closest contours around the fault show the zone of maximum ground displacement. Multiple faulting caused the confused zone near the epicenter. Radar mapping is more accurate than field surveys, which require monitoring equipment to be set up before a shock.

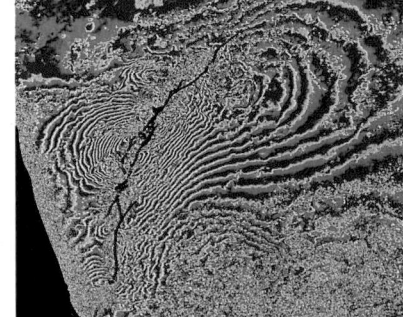

Epicentre

Although displacement in an earthquake is usually along the plane of a fault, seismic waves appear to radiate out in all directions from a single point (*above*). The epicenter of a quake is the point on the ground directly above that focus, which is called the hypocenter. The focus may be many miles deep within the Earth. Quakes on subducting crustal plates can occur at such a depth that the surrounding rock is more molten and therefore too soft to sustain a brittle fracture. These earthquakes happen when minerals suddenly change into a denser phase as a result of increases in temperature and pressure (*metamorphic rocks p. 50*).

San Andreas fault

The San Andreas fault (*below*) in California is the most famous crack in the world. Since the great earthquake of 1906 in San Francisco, no one has doubted the fault's destructive power, released as the Pacific crustal plate slides slowly north past the North American plate. In places the fault lines cross urban and industrial areas, where earthquake activity could be potentially devastating.

Stream beds crossing the fault are displaced by several yards.

Seismic gaps

The motion of one plate past another is inexorable, but close to the actual fault line, friction blocks the movement and the surrounding rock takes the strain. Eventually something gives: the longer the gap between quakes, the bigger the resulting quake. Displacement is measured along a fault: the "quiet" spots —or seismic gaps (*below*)— where quakes have not occurred recently, are most at risk.

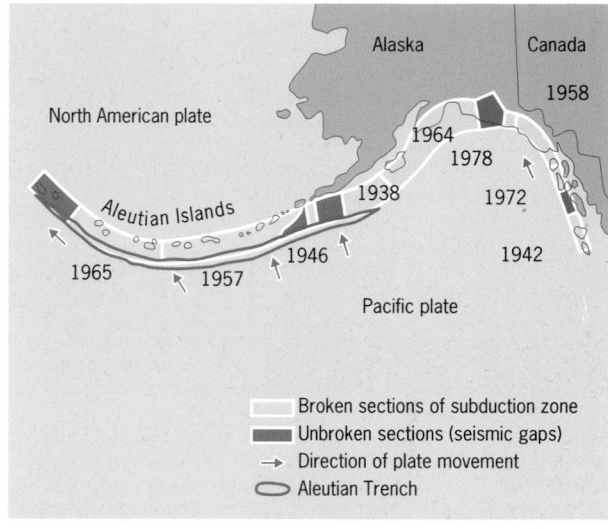

Prediction

An earthquake can happen anywhere and anytime. Clearly they are most likely near faults, but a prediction that a major quake is likely sometime in the next 50 years is not much use. A few faults seem more regular: quakes had occurred at Parkfield in California every 22 years, but the one expected in 1989 has still not come.

Short-term prediction is notoriously difficult. A small isolated quake looks like the foreshock to a major one. In 1975, observations of natural phenomena in China led to a successful prediction and many lives were saved, but a year later another Chinese quake killed 240,000. Accurate predictions only give a warning of seconds: sensors can raise the alarm at the speed of light, while shock waves take

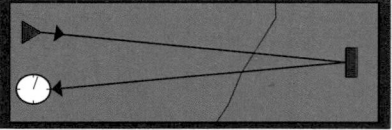

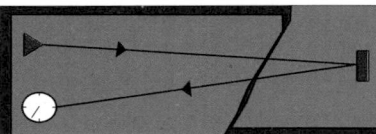

Laser beams between survey points detect land deformation prior to earth tremors.

longer to travel: that may be enough to stop trains and elevators, save computer data, and stop pumping dangerous chemicals.

Prevention

No one can prevent an earthquake from happening, but water pumped into boreholes can lubricate a fault, thus reducing friction and releasing stress. This could still result in damage, however, with expensive legal consequences, and is an option not without its own risk.

The way a building is constructed can reduce potential damage by earthquakes. Houses made of adobe and inadequately reinforced concrete can fall easily with great loss of life, especially if built on soft sediments. Modern earthquake-resistant buildings are stiffened or built on rubber bearings to dampen out vibrations. Some Japanese buildings have active systems that move weights to cancel out the effects of seismic shock waves.

MAJOR EARTHQUAKES

Location	Year	Mag.	Deaths	Location	Year	Mag.	Deaths	Location	Year	Mag.	Deaths
Kobe, Japan	1995	7.2	5,100	N.E. Iran	1978	7.7	25,000	Gansu, China	1920	8.6	180,000
Los Angeles	1994	6.6	63	Tangshan, China	1976	8.2	242,000	Avezzano, Italy	1915	7.5	30,000
S. India	1993	6.4	16,000	Guatemala City	1976	7.5	22,778	Messina, Italy	1908	7.5	120,000
N. Japan	1993	7.8	185	Kashmir	1974	6.3	5,200	Valparaiso, Chile	1906	8.6	20,000
S. California	1992	7.4	1	Nicaragua	1972	6.2	5,000	San Francisco	1906	8.3	500
N. India	1991	6.1	744	S. Iran	1972	6.9	5,000	Ecuador/Colombia	1868	–	70,000
Philippines	1990	7.7	1,653	Peru	1970	7.7	66,000	Calabria, Italy	1783	–	50,000
N.W. Iran	1990	7.5	36,000	N.E. Iran	1968	7.4	11,600	Portugal	1755	–	70,000
N. Peru	1990	5.8	200	Alaska	1964	8.5	131	Calcutta, India	1737	–	300,000
Romania	1990	6.6	70	N.W. Iran	1962	7.1	12,000	Hokkaido, Japan	1730	–	137,000
Philippines	1990	7.7	40	Morocco	1960	5.8	12,000	Catania, Italy	1693	–	60,000
San Francisco	1989	6.9	59	E. Turkey	1939	7.9	23,000	Caucasia	1667	–	80,000
Armenia	1988	7.0	25,000	Chillan, Chile	1939	7.8	30,000	Shensi, China	1556	–	830,000
Mexico City	1985	8.1	7,200	Quetta, India	1935	7.5	60,000	Chihli, China	1290	–	100,000
N. Yemen	1982	6.0	2,800	Gansu, China	1932	7.6	70,000	Silicia, Asia Minor	1268	–	60,000
S. Italy	1980	7.2	4,500	Nan-shan, China	1927	8.3	200,000	Corinth, Greece	856	–	45,000
Algeria	1980	7.3	5,000	Tokyo, Japan	1923	8.3	143,000	Antioch, Turkey	526		250,000

VOLCANOES

Although the Earth's mantle is solid, it can still flow slowly in the same way as a glacier does. Plumes of hot mantle rock rise and as they do so the pressure drops and some of the minerals begin to melt. Not everything melts, so the composition of the melt or magma is different from the bulk composition of the mantle. If the angles between the remaining grains (the dihedral angles) are big enough, the magma can flow out and upward, accumulating in large volumes called magma chambers. The nature of the subsequent volcanic eruption depends on the source and chemistry of the magma.

The ratio of different helium isotopes in bubbles of gas contained in the mantle plume suggests that some of them come from great depth, possibly the base of the lower mantle. These produce the vast basalt flows on which the Hawaiian islands are built. In the past they have produced even bigger eruptions. Sixty-five million years ago millions of cubic miles of basalt erupted over what is now western India. The effects on climate of large amounts of volcanic gases are considerable and may have caused the demise of the dinosaur. Such shield volcanoes produce copious quantities of runny, alkaline lava which spreads over a wide area. Acidic lavas are more viscous and produce more explosive eruptions and ash clouds, particularly if they contain a lot of water or dissolved gas.

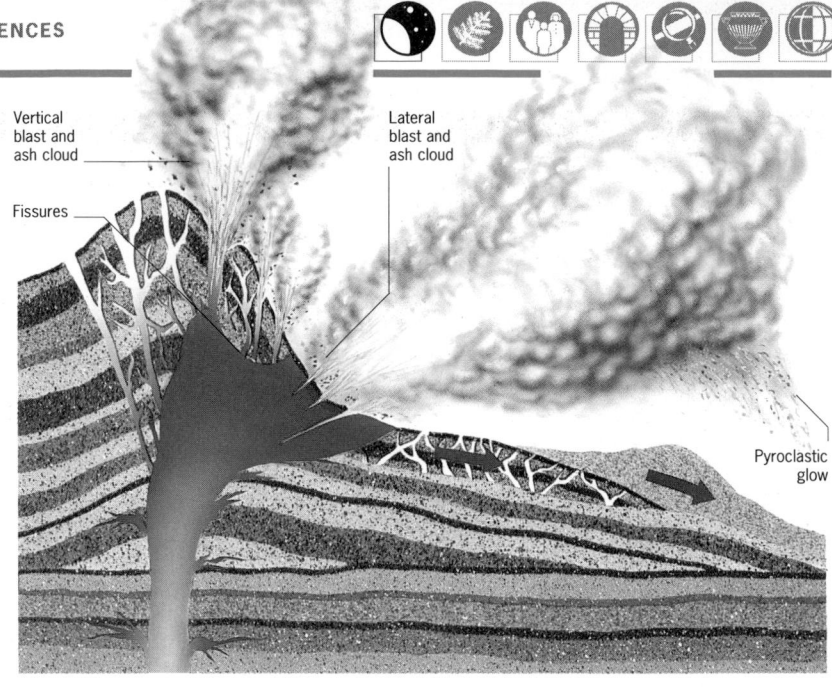

Vertical blast and ash cloud

Lateral blast and ash cloud

Fissures

Pyroclastic glow

Types of eruption

Apart from hot spots over mantle plumes, volcanoes frequent crustal plate boundaries, making a "ring of fire" around the Pacific. The ocean ridge system is a chain of submarine volcanoes. Where it breaks the surface, in Iceland for example, it coincides with a mantle plume. The volcanoes of the Rift Valley of East Africa represent a new ocean trying to open. Where ocean crust dives beneath a continent, it takes with it water locked in minerals. As the rocks heat and melt, the wet magma rises like uncorked champagne to produce some of the most violent eruptions.

Mt. St. Helens

Mt. St. Helens in the state of Washington is one of many volcanoes above the subducting Pacific plate. The wet magma ascends periodically like a pressure cooker letting off steam. Up to May 1980, geologists had monitored 10,000 small earthquakes in the region and had used lasers to measure the growing bulge on the mountain's north flank. By May 12 parts of the bulge were 450 ft./138 m higher than before and very unstable. Suddenly on May 18, the entire north flank collapsed in three great landslides only seconds apart. The second exposed pressurized molten magma which erupted in a tremendous lateral blast, flattening trees up to 18 mi./30 km away. The third block to slide exposed the top of the magma column itself, which erupted upward sending ash more than 11 mi./19 km high and coating 19,000 sq. mi. /50,000 km² with 540 million tons of ash.

Cinder (or composite) volcano

Fissure zone (Icelandic type)

Shield volcanoes (Hawaiian type)

MAJOR VOLCANOES

Name	Ht.(ft.)	Major eruptions	Last	Name	Ht.(ft.)	Major eruptions	Last
Bezymianny, U.S.S.R.	9,186	1955–56	1984	Mauna Loa, Hawaii	4,172	Frequent	1987
Cotopaxi, Ecuador	19,350	1877	1877	Nevado del Ruiz, Colombia	17,716	Frequent, esp. 1985	1992
El Chichón, Mexico	4,426	1982	1982	Nyamuragira, Zaire	3,056	1921–38, 1971, 1980	1988
Erebus, Antarctica	13,200	1947, 1972	1991	Paricutin, Mexico	3,188	1943–52	1952
Etna, Italy	10,616	Frequent	1992	Mt. Pelée, Martinique	1,397	1902, 1929-32	1932
Mt. Fuji, Japan	12,390	1707	1707	Pinatubo, Philippines	1,758	1391, 1991	1991
Galunggung, Indonesia	7,152	1822, 1918	1982	Popocatepetl, Mexico	5,483	1920	1943
Hekla, Iceland	4,890	1693, 1845, 1947–48, 1970	1981	Mt. Rainier, Washington	4,392	100s B.C., 1820	1882
Helgafell, Iceland	705	1973	1973	Ruapehu, New Zealand	2,796	1945, 1953, 1969, 1975	1986
Hibokhibok, Philippines	4,363	1951	1951	Mt. St. Helens, Washington	2,549	Frequent, esp. 1980	1987
Katmai, Alaska	7,540	1912, 1920, 1921	1931	Santorini, Greece	1,315	Frequent, esp. 1470 B.C.	1950
Kilauea, Hawaii	4,091	Frequent	1992	Stromboli, Italy	931	Frequent	1990
Klyuchevskoy, Russia	15,912	Frequent	1985	Surtsey, Iceland	174	1963-67	1967
Krakatau, Indonesia	2,684	Frequent, esp. 1883	1980	Tambora, Indonesia	2,868	1815	1880
La Soufrière, St. Vincent	4,042	1718, 1812, 1902, 1971–72	1979	Unzen, Japan	1,360	1360, 1791	1991
Lassen Peak, California	10,452	1914–15	1921	Vesuvius, Italy	1,289	Frequent, esp. 79 A.D.	1944

ROCK CYCLE

The Moon is dead. With no atmosphere and a cold, solidified interior, most features on the surface are several billion years old. The Earth is very different and little survives the aeons intact. Even great mountain ranges arise and are eroded over a few hundred million years. The rocks on the Earth's surface are perpetually being recycled. Magma rises from deep inside the Earth. Some is trapped underground and hardens into intrusive igneous rock. Some erupts onto the surface as extrusive igneous rock. Pressure and heat from below cook or metamorphose the rocks, and colliding continents push them up to the surface. Wind, rain, and ice erode the rock and, with the help of gravity, carry away the sediment. Rivers deposit it along their flood plains or at the bottom of lakes and seas, where it builds up in layers and hardens under pressure into sedimentary rocks. These sink into the ground and are metamorphosed by heat and pressure, or folded and uplifted again by more tectonic activity, continuing the cycle.

ROCK TYPES

Where formed	Igneous	Metamorphic	Sedimentary
Where formed	Where magma is extruded from volcanoes or intruded into the crust.	Where igneous or sedimentary rocks are subjected to heat and/or pressure through burial or nearby intrusions.	River valleys and deltas, shallow seas, reefs, and continental shelves, deserts, lakes, and glacial margins.
How rock is produced	By cooling and solidifying of molten magma.	By intense heat and/or pressure.	By compaction and/or cementation of particles.
Structure of rock formation	Large intrusions (batholiths), smaller intrusions (dikes and sills) and volcanic cones, flows and ash deposits.	Margins of major intrusions. Deep fault zones and cores of uplifted massifs.	Layered deposits, sedimentary basins, and geosynclines. Estuarine and deep-sea current bedding.
Texture of resulting rock	Crystalline, fine grained if cooled rapidly, coarse grained if cooled slowly.	Folded, foliated or banded, often crystalline, fine or medium texture.	Fine to coarse texture, grains rounded or angular rather than crystalline; often layered, sometimes containing fossils.
Mineral composition changes	By partial melting of source rock, by settling out of crystalline material from the melt.	Mixing and partial melting, diagenesis by percolating mineralizing fluids.	Removal by leaching, replacement by precipitation mineralization and cementation.

Energy flow

The rock cycle is powered from above and below. Heat from within the Earth (ultimately derived from radioactive decay and the slow solidification of the inner core) causes the upwelling of intrusive and extrusive rocks and produces the process of metamorphism of rocks. It also drives the drifting continents, uplifting mountain ranges. The energy of the Sun heats and expands rocks at the surface and ultimately drives the wind, waves, and precipitation that cause erosion. Gravity causes landslides which contribute to the circulation of rocks.

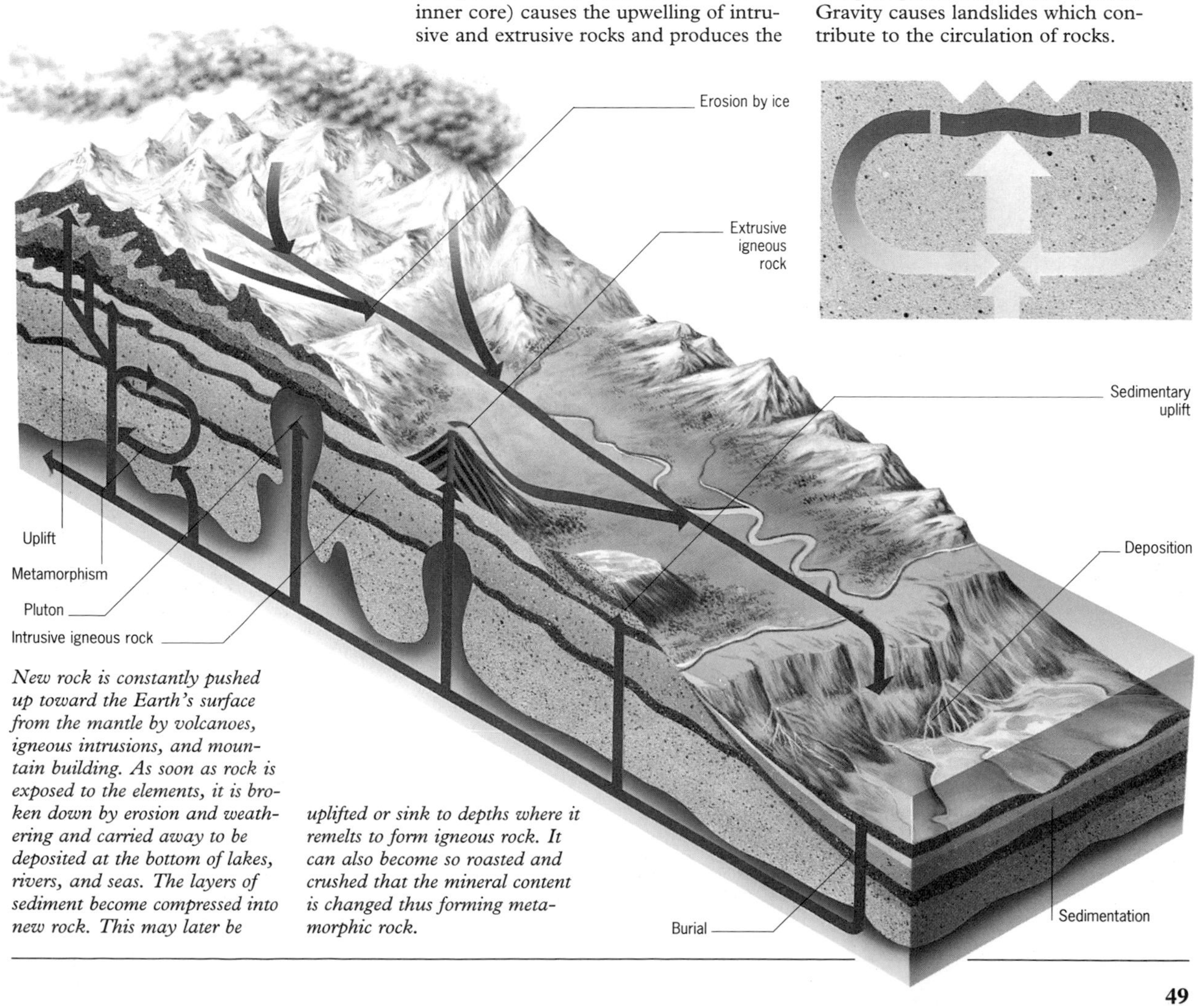

Erosion by ice

Extrusive igneous rock

Sedimentary uplift

Deposition

Uplift

Metamorphism

Pluton

Intrusive igneous rock

New rock is constantly pushed up toward the Earth's surface from the mantle by volcanoes, igneous intrusions, and mountain building. As soon as rock is exposed to the elements, it is broken down by erosion and weathering and carried away to be deposited at the bottom of lakes, rivers, and seas. The layers of sediment become compressed into new rock. This may later be uplifted or sink to depths where it remelts to form igneous rock. It can also become so roasted and crushed that the mineral content is changed thus forming metamorphic rock.

Burial

Sedimentation

ROCK TYPES

The rocks on Earth are constantly shaped by geological processes at work both within and on the surface. Igneous rocks result from volcanic activity in the Earth's crust and upper mantle; metamorphic rocks are produced when pressure and heat cause changes in existing rocks; and sedimentary rocks result from the deposition of materials transported by rivers.

Igneous rocks

Igneous rocks all form from molten magma. They are classified by their texture, composition, and origin. Acidic rocks tend to be light in color and low in density. They contain plenty of quartz, often with various minerals of the feldspar family. Basic igneous rocks are darker and denser with no free quartz and various combinations of amphibole, pyroxene, and olivine. The ultrabasic rocks are probably close in composition to the upper mantle. Igneous rocks are either intrusive—pushed up beneath overlying rocks in large plutons and along dikes and sills—or extrusive—erupted from volcanoes or into dikes and sills. The texture of igneous rocks depends on how fast they cool. If they cool slowly in large intrusions, big crystals can grow. Sometimes these settle out to form pegmatite or get caught up as large phe-

Sugar Loaf Mountain in Rio de Janeiro, extrusive igneous rock from an extinct volcano.

nocrysts in finer-grained material. If the magma cools rapidly, it will be finer-grained or even glassy, possibly trapping bubbles of gas or even large fragments of surrounding rock (xenoliths).

Metamorphic rocks

When igneous and sedimentary rocks are subjected to high temperatures and pressures, their structure and sometimes their mineral components can change. Hot percolating fluids can add or remove different minerals. These are metamorphic rocks—literally, rocks of changed form. Their grains can become aligned and any layering distorted, stretched, or destroyed. Metamorphic forces can exceed 100 atmospheres pressure and 750°F. The resulting rocks are classified according to texture, chemistry, and source rock.

PRINCIPAL IGNEOUS ROCKS

Rock	Texture	Type	Composition	Origin	Features	Varieties
Granite	Coarse	Acid	>20% quartz, K-feldspars, mica	Intrusive batholiths	Occasional phenocrysts	Pink, white, and microgranite
Pegmatite	Coarse	Acid	>20% quartz, mica, and feldspar	Deep batholiths and dikes	Very large crystals	Occasional rare minerals
Diorite	Coarse	Intermediate	Plagioclase feldspar and hornblende	Dikes associated with granite	Biotite and pyroxene	Granodiorite with quartz
Syenite	Coarse	Intermediate	Little or no quartz otherwise like granite	Dikes and sills near granite	Often pink	Nepheline syenite, quartz syenite
Gabbro	Coarse	Basic	Plagioclase, pyroxene, and olivine	Large layered intrusions	Layers of magnetite	Olivine gabbro
Larvikite	Coarse	Intermediate	Feldspar crystals with pyroxene, mica, and amphibolitebanks	Small sills	Popular for cladding banks	None
Anorthosite	Coarse	Basic	>90% plagioclase feldspar	Layered intrusions, on Moon	Aligned mineral grains	Can include olivine and pyroxene
Dolerite	Medium	Basic	<10% quartz with plagioclase and pyroxene	Dikes and sills near basalt	Dark color	None
Dunite	Medium	Ultrabasic	Almost entirely olivine	Deep sourced intrusions	Can contain chromite	None
Kimberlite	Coarse	Ultrabasic	Dense ferromagnesian minerals	Pipes of deep ancient volcanoes	Sometimes contains diamonds	None
Peridotite	Coarse	Ultrabasic	No quartz or feldspar, mostly olivine and garnet	Caught up in intrusions	Possibly derived from mantle	With pyroxene and hornblende
Rhyolite	Fine	Acid	As granite	Explosive volcanic eruptions	Phenocrysts and gas bubbles	Banded form
Obsidian	Glassy	Acid	Silica-rich glass	Rapid cooling of acid lava	Black, glassy	Snowflake obsidian
Lamprophyre	Medium	Acid to basic	Amphibole pyroxene and biotite	Dikes and sills around granite	Phenocrysts of biotite and hornblende	None
Andesite	Fine	Intermediate	Mainly plagioclase	Volcanoes above subduction zones	Dark with white phenocrysts	With vesicles of zeolite
Trachyte	Fine	Intermediate	<10% quartz, rich in alkali feldspar	Lava flows, dikes, and sills	Not many	Sometimes porphyritic
Basalt	Fine	Basic	Plagioclase and pyroxene	Volcanic eruptions	Dark—the commonest lava	Bubbles and vesicles
Tuff	Fine	Acid to basic	Consolidated volcanic fragments	Thrown out by volcanic vents	Variable	Tuff-breccia, lapilli-tuff
Pumice	Fine	Acid to basic	Glass and minute silicate crystals	Rapidly quenched frothy lava	Can sometimes float	Bubbles and vesicles

PRINCIPAL METAMORPHIC ROCKS

	Texture	Origin
Slate	Aligned minerals produce perfect cleavage; not necessarily aligned with bedding	Sedimentary shale and clay
Phyllite	As slate, but coarser, with small-scale folding	Medium grain sediments
Schist	Flaky minerals such as mica give glittery, foliated texture	Sediments buried deep in mountain belts, e.g. siltstones
Gneiss	Medium/coarse grain; quartz, feldspar and mica with darker layers or lines	High pressure and temperature, from sediment or granite; abundant deep under continents
Migmatite	Mixture of dark schist and light granitic rock; highly folded	Extensive deep metamorphism of sediments
Eclogite	Coarse grain; mostly green pyroxene and red garnet	Very high temperature and pressure close to mantle
Amphibolite	Coarse grain; often foliated; mostly hornblende	Highly metamorphosed igneous dolerite
Marble	Crystalline, soft and sugary; made of calcium carbonate	Limestone heated by igneous intrusion
Hornfels	Fine grain; dark colored with quartz, mica, and pyroxene	Sediments closest to hot igneous intrusions
Quartzite	Medium grain; of even texture with fused quartz crystals; very hard	Sandy sediment heated by intrusion or regional metamorphism
Serpentenite	Coarse grain; green serpentine minerals minerals	Intense metamorphism of olivine-rich rock

CLASSIFICATION OF SEDIMENTARY ROCKS

Clastic

Conglomerate	Large, rounded, cemented
Breccia	Coarse, angular, cemented
Gritstone	Coarse
Sandstone	Medium
Greensand	With glauconite
Graywacke	Deep ocean sediments
Siltstone	Fine, with more quartz than shale
Loess	Fine, angular particles
Marl	Fine silt or clay with limestone cement
Shale	Very fine laminated clay and detritus
Mudstone	Clay and very fine grains cemented with iron or calcite
Clay	Very fine; absorbs water

Chemical

Limestones:	Calcium carbonate
Chalk	Soft white limestone, mostly microfossils
Tufa	Calcium carbonate; precipitated from fresh water
Dolomite	Calcium and magnesium carbonate
Ironstone	Limestone or chert enriched in iron, often Pre-Cambrian
Chert & flint	Hard silicatious nodules or sheets in chalk or limestone

Organic

Peat	Plant material
Lignite	Soft, carbonaceous
Coal	Hard, brittle, carbonaceous
Jet	Hard, black, coallike

Sedimentary rocks

Three-fourths of all sedimentary rocks are made up of the eroded remnants of earlier rocks. They are known as clastic rocks. The particles can range from large rocks to the finest clays and be rounded and worn or angular and broken. They can be loose or unconsolidated, compressed together or cemented with another material such as calcium carbonate or iron oxide. The remaining sediments are either chemical (precipitated out of solution such as limestone) or organic (from living material). Sedimentary rocks all originate near the suface of the Earth at normal temperatures, usually under water, though they can be buried, compressed, and heated later.

Rock slices

Slices of rock polished so thin that they are almost transparent allow geologists to study the individual mineral grains in a rock one by one, even in fine-grained rock. Polarized light reveals different minerals in different colors. A fine beam of energetic electrons can analyze the composition of each grain. The illustrations (*below*) show the magnified micrographs of various types of rock. The variations in grain size and mineral content allow easy identification.

Granite; a coarse-grained igneous rock.

Andesite; extrusive igneous, large crystals.

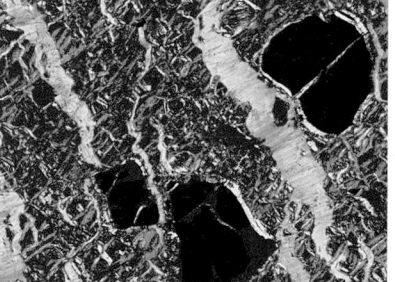

Serpentine; a low-grade metamorphic rock.

Gneiss; a medium/coarse metamorphic rock.

Sedimentary limestone; containing seashells.

Gypsum; a chemical sedimentary rock.

ROCK-FORMING MINERALS

The bulk of the rocks of the Earth's crust consists of silicates. They have a plethora of names, compositions, and complex structures, but the most important ones can be grouped into families.

Quartz

These are the most abundant of all minerals at the Earth's surface: spiral chains of silicate (SiO_4) tetrahedra linked at the corners; often transparent and crystalline. Acid rocks are at least ten percent quartz.

Feldspars

These make up 50–60 percent of the mass of all igneous rocks: 3-D framework of silicate tetrahedra with aluminum and varying amounts of potassium, sodium, calcium, and aluminum. There are two families of feldspars: orthoclase feldspars have varying amounts of aluminum and potassium; plagioclase feldspars have varying amounts of sodium and calcium.

Olivine

This dense, ultrabasic family of minerals is common in the Earth's mantle and igneous rocks originating from a deep source: dense, close-packed silicate tetrahedra containing magnesium and iron; glassy in appearance.

Pyroxene

This is a family of chain silicates in igneous rocks containing magnesium (in the case of enstatite), calcium and magnesium (in diopside), or iron and aluminum (in augite).

Amphibole

These have double chains of silicates containing iron and magnesium. Many amphiboles are described as fellomagnesium and one of the best-known examples is hornblende.

Mica

Mica consists of layered silicates that cleave easily into flakes or sheets, and include muscovite (white mica) and biotite (dark mica): a common constituent of gneiss and granite.

Naturally occurring rock crystal (a form of quartz) has the beauty of cut and polished stones.

Identifying minerals

Geologists have a whole battery of techniques at their disposal for identifying minerals by eye and by instrument, in the field and in the laboratory. These methods include the study of a rock's crystal system (*below*) and shape or other forms—which can be described variously as massive, dentritic, fibrous, tabular, or kidney-shaped (reniform).

Many minerals cleave or break apart more easily in one direction than another. Some break along an atomic, or cleavage plane, and this may be a basal, rhombic or cubic cleavage (p. 53). Those minerals that do not follow a cleavage plane but break at other angles are said to fracture (p. 53); the resulting pieces of rock may

CRYSTAL SYSTEMS

Crystal system	Crystal axes	Crystal forms	Examples
Cubic	3 equal axes at 90°	Cube, dodecahedron	Rock salt, pyrite, garnet
Tetragonal	3 axes at 90°, 1 of different length	Short prisms	Zircon, cassiterite
Hexagonal	3 equal axes at 120°, 1 at 90° to their plane	Hexagonal prisms and pyramids	Beryl, quartz, apatite
Trigonal	As hexagonal	Rhombohedra, triangular prisms	Calcite, dolomite, tourmaline
Orthorhombic	3 unequal axes at 90°	Prismatic or tabular	Olivine, barytes
Monoclinic	3 unequal axes, 2 not at 90°, 1 at 90° to their plane	Often long prisms	Pyroxene, orthoclase (50 percent of all crystalline substances)
Triclinic	3 unequal axes, none at 90°	Often tabular	Plagioclase, axinite

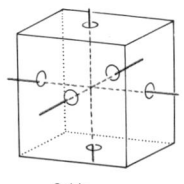

Cubic

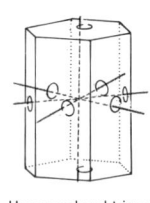

Tetragonal

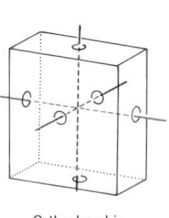

Hexagonal and trigonal

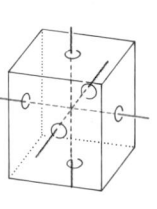

Orthorhombic

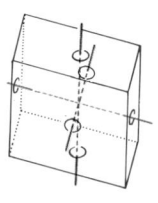

Monoclinic

Triclinic

Cleavage

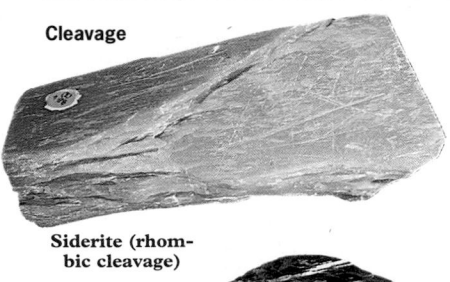

Siderite (rhombic cleavage)

Steatite (basal cleavage)

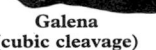
Galena (cubic cleavage)

Fracture

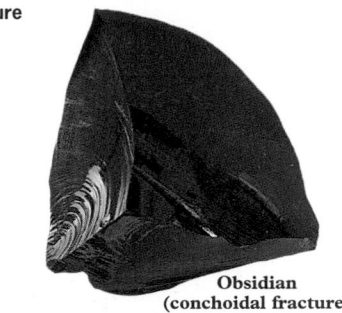

Obsidian (conchoidal fracture)

Platinum (hackly fracture)

Luster

Cinnabar (adamantine luster)

Antimony (metallic luster)

Barytes (vitreous luster)

Opal (waxy or resinous luster)

Talc (pearly luster)

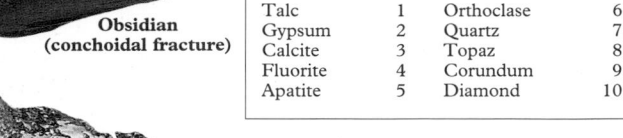

Mohs' hardness scale

Friedrich Mohs, a German mineralogist, created a scale of hardness based on ten minerals. Sets of hardness pencils are used to test specimens to see what will scratch them. Other useful instruments include:

Fingernail	2.5	Steel knife	5.5
Copper coin	3.5	Glass	6.0

The standard minerals are as follows:

Talc	1	Orthoclase	6
Gypsum	2	Quartz	7
Calcite	3	Topaz	8
Fluorite	4	Corundum	9
Apatite	5	Diamond	10

be decribed as conchoidal (shell-like), hackly (jagged), or splintery.

The optical properties of rock are investigated not only by their color but also by transparency, refractive index, luster (*right*)—the way in which light is reflected from the surface—and streak (the color left when the rock is scratched across an unglazed tile). The density, or more often the specific gravity, of a rock, i.e. its density compared to an equal volume of water, is also recorded, along with the hardness factor (*above right*).

PROPERTIES OF COMMON MINERALS

Name	Type	Hardness	Specific gravity	Crystal	Optical	Fracture
Talc	Silicate	1	2.6–2.8	Monoclinic	Pale green or gray, pearly luster	Uneven
Graphite	Element	1–2	2.1–2.3	Trigonal/hexagonal	Gray metallic luster	Perfect basal cleavage
Gypsum	Sulfate	2	2.32	Monoclinic	White to transparent	Splintery
Calcite	Carbonate	3	2.71	Trigonal/hexagonal	Double refraction	Perfect rhombic cleavage
Barytes	Sulfate	3–3.5	4.5	Orthorhombic	Pale, translucent	Perfect cleavage
Aragonite	Carbonate	3.5–4	2.95	Orthorhombic	Translucent white streak	Subconchoidal
Dolomite	Carbonate	3.5–4	2.85	Trigonal/hexagonal	Pale, translucent	Rhombohedral cleavage
Fluorite	Halide	4	3.18	Cubic	Many colors, fluorescent	Perfect octahedral cleavage
Apatite	Phosphate	5	3.1–3.2	Trigonal/hexagonal	Usually green	Uneven
Sodalite	Silicate	5.5–6	2.2–2.4	Cubic	Blue	Uneven
Pyrite	Sulfide	6–6.5	5.0	Cubic	"Fool's gold"	Uneven
Quartz	Oxide	7	2.65	Trigonal/hexagonal	Translucent, also microcrystalline	Uneven
Garnet	Silicate	7	3.5–4.3	Cubic	Various forms, often plum red	Uneven
Tourmaline	Silicate	7–7.5	3.0–3.2	Trigonal/hexagonal	Pink and green	Uneven
Zircon	Silicate	7.5	4.3	Tetragonal	Often brown	Uneven
Beryl	Silicate	7–8	2.6–2.9	Trigonal/hexagonal	Many colors, emerald green	Uneven
Spinel	Oxide	7.5–8	3.5–4.1	Cubic	Many colors, vitreous luster	Uneven
Corundum	Oxide	9	4.0–4.1	Trigonal/hexagonal	Various forms including ruby and sapphire	Uneven
Diamond	Element	10	3.52	Cubic	Transparent, sparkles if cut	Octahedral cleavage

FORMATION AND USES OF MINERALS

For a mineral to become economically important, it has to occur naturally in concentrated form. There are several ways in which concentration occurs.

Magmatic separation

As molten rock or magma cools, different minerals begin to crystallize out at different depths. Diamond forms very deep in the Earth's mantle and was already present as crystals when the kimberlite volcanoes of South Africa brought it to the surface (*right*). Dense crystals can settle out of otherwise molten magma, forming layers of, for example, magnetite, chromite, and platinum-rich pyroxenite. Late-crystallizing but dense minerals can form between crystals of other silicates, or be injected along faults and fissures as in the copper and nickel deposits of Norway and Canada and magnetite in Sweden.

Contact metamorphism

Rocks are altered by contact with the heat of an igneous intrusion. The result can be a change in their mineral content: some minerals are "donated" by the magma, as seen in magnetite deposits in Utah and copper deposits in Arizona.

Hydrothermal

Underground jets of mineral-rich hot water percolating through fissures in rock can coat or replace the fissure walls with minerals. This has produced copper, lead, and zinc deposits in many places, and gold seams in California.

Sedimentary

Many minerals dissolve easily in water and can be concentrated by evaporation, e.g. salt and potash deposits in Germany, Canada, the U.K. and U.S.A. Sedimentary rocks can be unusually rich

The splendid mask of Tutankhamen was made from gold, then inlaid with lapis lazuli.

in certain elements, e.g. iron in France and the U.S.A.. Hard or dense minerals can be concentrated in the detritus of erosion, e.g. the placer gold deposits of Australia, California, Alaska, and South Africa, titanium in India and Australia, and diamond placers in Namibia.

Residual deposits

Weathering can wash down or leach dissolved minerals through the soil, leaving valuable ones behind, e.g. iron ores in Cuba, Spain, and the U.S.A., and barytes in the U.S.A. Weathering and further leaching can also enrich the valuable mineral itself, e.g. aluminum (bauxite) in France, Hungary, Jamaica, and Guyana.

Mineral extraction and refining

The extraction of metals from their ores depends on how reactive the metal is. Few are sufficiently stable to occur in their elemental or native form, though this may be one reason why such great value has been placed on gold since ancient times.

The extraction of copper, lead, and zinc may have begun accidentally when ancient people noticed the metal appearing on lumps of ore placed against the charcoal of a hot hearth fire. That is the principle of smelting: heating ore in a reducing atmosphere. Nowadays coke is normally used to soak up the oxygen. In the case of iron, the furnace must be hotter (a blast furnace) and limestone is needed to soak up silicates that float above the molten iron to form slag.

The most reactive elements have to be extracted by electrolysis—of molten ore in the case of aluminum—or by chemical reaction with even more reactive metals (in the case of titanium). These processes consume much more energy and are therefore expensive, but justified by the value of the product. Various physical processes are often used to concentrate the ore from crushed rock: panning in the case of gold and froth flotation for tin.

Experimental biological processes are also under investigation, using, for example, plants or bacteria to concentrate the products. The rich ore deposits around the world are finite, so eventually techniques will have to be developed for using lower-grade ore or for using current sources more efficiently. This is especially true for another sort of mineral deposit—the fossil fuels coal, oil, and natural gas.

PRINCIPAL ORE MINERALS

Ore of	Mineral	Composition	Features
Aluminum	Bauxite	Hydroxide	Various shades of brown
	Cryolite	Na_3AlF_6	White, extracted by electrolysis
Antimony	Stibnite	Sulfide	Gray metallic
Arsenic	Realgar	Sulfide	Red
	Orpiment	Sulfide	Yellow
Chromium	Chromite	Iron chromate	Dark, opaque
Copper	Chalcopyrite	Sulfide	Brassy yellow
	Cuprite	Oxide	Black
	Malachite	Carbonate	Green
Gold	Native	Metal	Golden
Iron	Pyrite	Sulfide	Brassy yellow
	Magnetite	Oxide	Black
	Hematite	Hematite	Black/reddish
	Siderite	Carbonate	Orange
Lead	Galena	Sulfide	Metallic black
Mercury	Cinnabar	Sulfide	Red
Nickel	Nickeline	Arsenide	Silver metallic
Platinum	Native	Metal	Metal
Silver	Native	Metal	Silver
Tin	Cassiterite	Oxide	Black/brown
Titanium	Ilmenite	Oxide	Black opaque
Tungsten	Wolframite	$(FeMn)WO_4$	Dark, submetallic
Uranium	Uraninite	Oxide	Dull brown/black
Vanadium	Vanadanite	$Pb_5(VO_4)_3Cl$	Red/orange

PRECIOUS AND SEMIPRECIOUS STONES

Name	Type	Hardness	Color	Principal sources
Diamond	Element	10	Transparent	South Africa
Ruby	Corundum	9	Pink and red	Myanmar (Burma)
Sapphire	Corundum	9	Blue and yellow	Sri Lanka
Emerald	Beryl	8	Green	Colombia
Aquamarine	Beryl	7.5	Blue-green	Brazil
Tourmaline	Silicate	7–7.5	Green/pink	Madagascar
Topaz	Silicate	8	Yellow	Brazil
Zircon	Silicate	7.5	Various	Sri Lanka
Garnet	Silicate	7	Plum red	Czech Republic
Rock crystal	Quartz	7	Transparent and many varieties	Various
Amethyst	Quartz	7	Purple	Brazil
Carnelian	Chalcedony	7	Reddish brown and many varieties	Various
Opal	Hydrous silica	6	White iridescent or red	S.E. Australia
Lapis lazuli	Silicate	5.5	Dark blue	Afghanistan
Jade	Silicate	6–7	Soft green	China
Amber	Fossil resin	2–2.5	Amber	Poland

The Taj Mahal, India's most famous monument, is constructed from various marbles.

The Great Wall of China is built of brick, granite, and assorted local rock types.

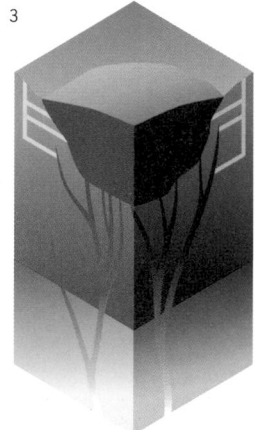

1   2   3

Diamonds, the world's most precious stones, are produced under intense heat and pressure deep within the Earth's crust. Under such conditions, gas rises up rock fissures and eventually explodes, creating depressions in the Earth's surface (1). Diamond-bearing kimberlite then wells up the fissures—known as kimberlite pipes—to fill the hollows (2). Mining shafts are sunk to reach all the diamond-bearing rock (3).

METAL USES AND PRODUCERS

Metals	Uses	Leading producers	Metals	Uses	Leading producers
Aluminum	Due to aluminum's high tensile strength and low density it is used in the production of lightweight machinery and sports equipment, power cables, and food packaging.	U.S.A., C.I.S., Canada, Australia, Brazil	Manganese	Compounds of manganese are present in dry batteries and paints; it is a vital alloy in steel-making.	C.I.S., South Africa, Brazil, India, China, Australia
			Nickel	Electroplating (stainless), dry batteries, electronics batteries; an alloy in steel-making.	C.I.S., Canada, Australia, New Caledonia (France)
Chromium	Chromium's shiny nonreactive finish is used in electroplating and the production of stainless steel.	South Africa, Zimbabwe	Platinum	Chemical containers, jewelry, surgical instruments, electronics.	C.I.S., South Africa, Canada, Japan, Australia
Copper	Copper is a good conductor of electricity and is used in electrical wiring; also used for pipes. Brass and bronze are alloys of copper.	U.S.A., Canada, C.I.S., Zambia, Zaire	Silver	Used for coinage, jewelry, dentistry, photographic film, and paper.	Mexico, Peru, C.I.S., U.S.A., Canada, Poland, Australia
Gold	Gold's malleability and low reactivity makes it suitable for gold leaf and jewelry. Also used in electronic circuits.	South Africa, C.I.S., Canada, U.S.A., China, Australia	Tin	Used as plate on steel cans to prevent corrosion; in solder (with lead), bronze, toothpaste, roofing.	Malaysia, Peru, C.I.S., U.S.A., Canada, Poland, Australia
			Titanium	Titanium dioxide in paint, paper, tools; as an alloy in aircraft.	C.I.S., Japan, U.S.A., Canada, U.K., China
Iron	Iron ore is abundant and iron relatively cheap to extract. It is easily molded. Most is used for production of stainless steel.	C.I.S., Brazil, Australia, China, Canada, South Africa, Sweden	Tungsten	Tungsten is extremely strong and is added to steel to increase the strength of steel. Also used for heating filaments in electronic equipment.	China, U.S.A., Canada, South Korea, Australia, Portugal
Lead	Can be used to store charge in lead acid batteries; used in paints, machine bearings, and as gasoline additive.	U.S.A., C.I.S., Mexico, Australia, Canada, Peru, China, North Korea	Zinc	In alloys (brass, with copper), batteries, paints, electroplating, cosmetics.	Canada, C.I.S., Peru, Australia, Mexico, China, Chile

ROCK RECORD

The rocks beneath our feet are mostly built up from layers. Each one resembles a page in a history book, recording conditions on Earth during its formation. In a sedimentary rock the grain size and shape can record the energy of the environment in which it was deposited. Coarse pebbles or rock fragments indicate rapid erosion of a nearby landmass by waves and weather. Fine clays and silts indicate slower accumulation in still waters. Angular grains may come from a desert, rounded ones from a river. Chemical deposits, such as limestone, imply accumulation away from a source of eroded sand and mud. Many rocks contain fossils, visible by eye or by microscope, and these can suggest the conditions in which the creatures lived. There are chemical clues too, to the salinity of seas and the temperature and even composition of the atmosphere at the time of rock formation.

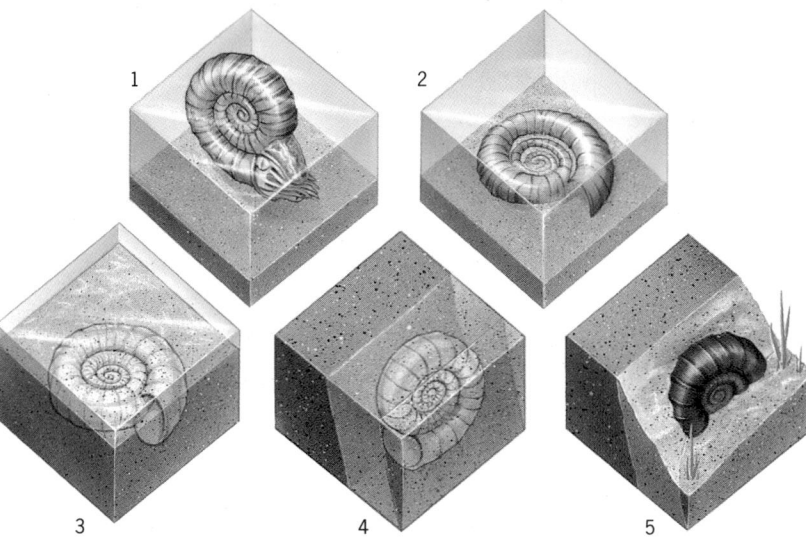

A dead animal sinks to the seabed (1). Its shell becomes part of the sediment (2) and is eventually buried (3). The sediment hardens into rock (4) which eventually is eroded, leaving the fossil exposed (5).

Molecular paleontology

If the theory of evolution is right, every living thing contains molecular clues to its past. Genes are living fossils. If there is a constant rate of random mutation, DNA is like a molecular clock: the genetic differences between species record the time since they shared an ancestor. The differences also reveal which species are related; humans are genetically only one percent different from chimpanzees. Genes and proteins have been recovered from extinct species—rom museum specimens of the marsupial wolf, and from a woolly mammoth in Siberian ice. DNA has even been found in a 100 million-year-old weevil preserved in amber. Dinosaur DNA may survive in bone but not in sufficient quantities to create a Jurassic Park.

Atomic messengers

Fossils and most sediments contain atoms from the atmosphere at the time they were laid down. These atoms carry messages. For example, oxygen comes in different forms or isotopes—seawater contains O_{16} and O_{18}. O_{16} is lighter and evaporates more easily to fall as snow: it thus becomes locked in polar ice caps, and the proportion of O_{18} or O_{16} remaining in the shells of tiny fossils indicates the amount of polar ice. Carbon, too, comes in different forms. Plankton take up C_{12} more readily than C_{13}. If that carbon continues down the chain to bottom-dwelling species, the atmosphere is depleted in C_{12}, as are subsequent plankton. Thus a comparison of C_{13} in surface- and bottom-dwelling microfossils reveals biological activity at the time.

Rock strata

Reading the stratigraphical notebook is not just a question of opening the pages. A geological map of the world today is in effect a patchwork of different environmental conditions, and the same was true at each stage in the past. That limestone was forming in one place a hundred million years ago does not imply that limestone was forming everywhere at that time. While rocks are deposited in one place, another place may be uplifted into mountains and eroded.

There are, however, gaps in the record, and things are not always what they seem. Although younger rocks are deposited on top of older ones, folding and faulting can be so intense that the younger rocks end up underneath the old. Layers can be folded up to steep angles, or the original layers may be sloping, such as current bedding at a river delta or a continental slope. Thick shale beds may have taken a few hundred thousand years to form and be tens of yards thick: in the same strata there may be another layer only a few inches thick that was five million years in the making. So thickness is no certain clue to age; neither is apparent depth of water. Sea level can change by tens of yards, land level by hundreds. Nor is present latitude much help, when continents have skated across the globe. Britain was once on the equator and there were glaciers in what is now the Sahara. But there are plenty of clues for geologists and, with their knowledge of processes at work, they can compare stratigraphical evidence from around the world to confirm their theories of geological processes and timescales.

Comparison of rock strata reveals the history of different sites.

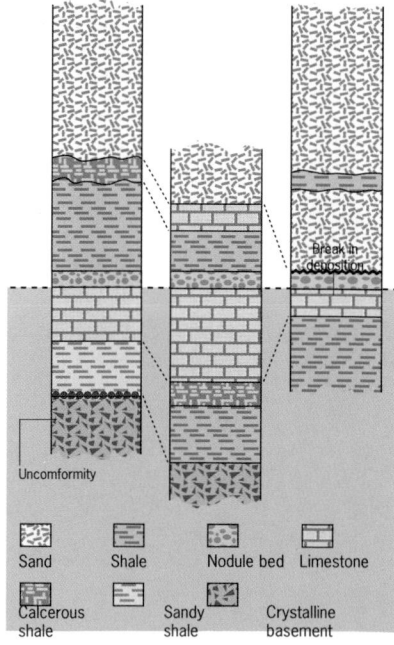

RADIO ISOTOPES USED FOR DATING			
Isotope	Product	Half-life (millions of years)	Use
Carbon 14	Carbon 12	0.005730	Dating organic remains up to 50,000 years old
Uranium 235	Lead 207	710	Dating rock intrusions
Uranium 238	Lead 206	4,500	Dating ancient crust
Potassium 40	Argon 40	11,850	Dating volcanic rocks
Rubidium 87	Strontium 87	50,000	Dating individual grains in ancient rock
Samarium 147	Neodymium 143	250,000	Dating ancient meteorites

FOSSILS

Sedimentary rocks contain a record of the changing forms of life on Earth. It is not a complete record: most creatures get eaten, rot, or are otherwise destroyed. Many do not have any resistant parts and, of those that do, the remains may later be eroded or never found. Although material from the original shell or bone may survive, it may alternatively be replaced by other minerals or leave just a faint imprint in the rock.

Even so, fossils provide a remarkably detailed picture of life on Earth. It is a picture of rapid diversification and great inventiveness to suit every ecological niche, punctuated by rapid extinctions when times get hard. Thus the changing fossil record provides a powerful means of dating rocks. So-called zone or index fossils (*right*) have been picked as key markers for each time. Ideally they are common, free-swimming species that can help correlate rocks of the same age wherever in the world they are found. Sometimes, finding assemblages of different fossils together at one location can narrow the time down further.

Dating techniques

Fossils and stratigraphy reveal relative ages of rocks, but not an absolute age. For that, geologists have other techniques. They can simply count the growth rings in trees—some bristlecone pines in the Rocky Mountains are over a thousand years old. Matching their record of drought, frost, and growth like a bar code with even older trees now dead extends the record back. Annual growth lines in shells, layers in ice cores and meltwater lakes reach still farther back.

Geologists also use carbon-14 dating. Cosmic rays convert C_{12} atoms in the air into radioactive C_{14}. Once out of the air in plants, the C_{14} decays at a fixed rate (*below*), so what is left reveals the age. Longer-lived isotopes date older rocks (*opposite*). The key to accuracy is purity of the sample. Potassium/argon dates are particularly accurate, since the decay product is a gas. If the sample comes from a lava, its melting will have released any previous gas and reset the clock. Modern mass spectrometers can measure even the slightest trace of an isotope, so tiny crystals can each be dated. Thus the oldest minerals on Earth were found: grains of zircon over four billion years old, eroded and redeposited later.

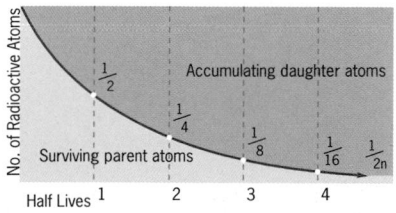

INDEX FOSSILS

Period	Fossil type
Cenozoic	Foraminifera (plankton)
Upper Cretaceous	Foraminifera, echinoderms, bivalves, and belemnites
Lower Cretaceous	Ammonites
Jurassic	Ammonites plus ostracods (tiny crustacea) and bivalves
Triassic	Ammonites
Permian	Foraminifera, ammonites, and goniatites (ammonite ancestors)
Carboniferous	Foraminifera, goniatites, freshwater bivalves, and plants
Lower Carboniferous	Corals and brachiopods
Devonian	Goniatites, fish, and plants
Silurian	Graptolites (thin, branching, free swimming, corallike)
Ordovician	Graptolites, trilobites (small crustacea)
Cambrian	Trilobites and brachiopods

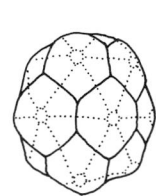
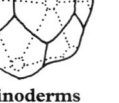
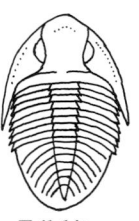
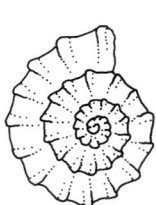
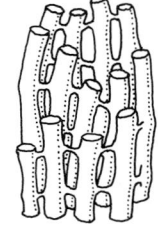

| Echinoderms Marsupites | Trilobites Ogygiocaris | Ammonites Echioceras | Corals Syringopora |

21	Quaternary	Cenozoic
	Pliocene	
	Miocene	
	Oligocene	
65	Paleocene and Eocene	
	Cretaceous	Mesozoic
135		
	Jurassic	
195		
225	Triassic	
280	Permian	
	Carboniferous	Paleozoic
345		
	Devonian	
395		
430	Silurian	
	Ordovician	
500		
	Cambrian	
570		
	Precambrian	
Mya		

GEOLOGICAL TIMELINE

If the evolution of life on Earth seems to go back a long way, it may be put into a geological context by comparing the age of the planet with the lifetime of a person now 47 years old. Fossils only tell us about life since the Pre-cambrian era began 600 million years ago (*left*), but by then our person would have already celebrated their 40th birthday. Soon after, multi-cellular life in the sea diversified into thousands of species. Two years later on the human timescale, plants and insects emerged onto land, followed by amphibious animals. Then things began to speed up. It is only a year since the age of the dinosaurs, a week since the last Ice Age and a mere four hours since our own species, *Homo sapiens*, first walked on the planet. During the Earth's lifetime, the solar system has moved around the galactic center (*p. 26*) about 25 times. The ocean crust has been recycled 50 times. The continents have accumulated, crashed into each other and broken apart (*p. 44*). Landscapes have been eroded and weathered (*p. 64-70*), and the atmosphere has been altered by life forms (*pp. 58-59*). Now the globe is being transformed by humans. Judging from the evolutionary path of the Sun, the Earth has five billion years to go.

Timeline

4,700 mya (million years ago) Solar nebula forms (*p. 17*); protoplanets start to form (*p. 18*).

4,600 Earth complete; still partially molten from radioactivity and heat of impacts; iron sinking to form core.

4,500 Impact of Mars-sized body throws off material to form the Moon.

4,450 Extensive volcanic activity adds steam and carbon dioxide to atmosphere. Bombarding comets add water.

4,400 Condensing water forms oceans.

4,000 First life on Earth; simple bacteria feed off organic molecules.

3,900 Rain of comets lessens.

3,800 Photosynthesis established.

3,500 Stromatolite reefs form.

3,000 Moon solidifies, ceases to be active and loses its magnetic field.

2,900 Volcanoes bring metal-rich minerals to the Earth's surface.

2,800 Formation of ancient cores of major continents.

2,500 First big iron oxide deposits, as life makes oxygen via photosynthesis.

2,300 Land grouped together in first supercontinent.

2,100 The first single-celled animals and fungi appear.

2,000 Uranium deoposits in West Africa are activated in what amounts to a natural nuclear reaction.

1,800 Free oxygen appears in the atmosphere.

1,750 Oxygen kills many bacteria; those that survive adapt to using oxygen or live in anaerobic conditions.

1,500 Second supercontinent forms. Some plant cells develop the ability to respire and photosynthesize.

1,300 First complex multicellular organism—a seaweed.

1,000 First sexual reproduction.

950 First evidence of ice ages.

800 Third supercontinent forms.

770 Ice ages.

670 Ice ages; first true animals.

650 Mountain building; formation of Gondwanaland.

620 First common worms with tube like body and primitive nervous system.

570 Start of Cambrian period; massive diversification of life.

550 Major marine extinctions.

510 Start of Ordovician period; first vertebrates.

460 Europe collides with North America.

440 Ice ages; mass extinction; start of Silurian period.

430 Start of long warm period; formation of coral reefs and limestone deposits.

425 First life on land; first jawed fish.

410 Start of Devonian period.

400 First lungfish.

395 First insects on land—millipedes, mites, spiders, scorpions, and springtails.

370 Mass extinction, especially in the sea. Tsunamis, possibly caused by asteroid impacts, devastate coral reefs. First amphibians, first forests.

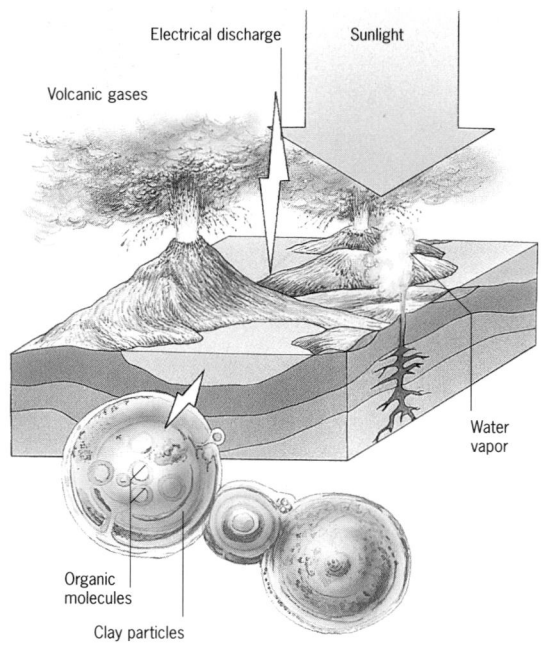

Electrical discharge   Sunlight

Volcanic gases

Water vapor

Organic molecules

Clay particles

The origin of life

The new planet Earth was hot, possibly molten, with no ocean and little atmosphere. Life probably began in muddy puddles or along the shores of shallow "lakes" (*left*). The complexities of RNA and DNA (*p. 90*) and the enzymes that make them replicate could never have occurred by chance, all at once. Lightning and radiation may have built up simple organic molecules which were absorbed onto the surfaces of clay particles (*inset, left*). Fatty layers around such particles formed the basis of the first cells. Once these particles could take in chemicals and were able to reproduce themselves, evolution could begin.

The first living things were microscopic bacteria and protozoa. The first visible sign of life was probably a film of algae. Some algae or filamentous bacteria grew in large mats in shallow water near the tidemark, binding sand among them to form layered mounds. Still found growing in warm seas today, fossil stromatolites form the oldest macroscopic fossils in 3.5 billion-year-old deposits in Australia and Zimbabwe.

Evidence of the oldest known multicellular animals is to be found in the late Precambrian Ediacara formation in southern Australia. These animals were without shells or skeletons but were preserved as impressions in sandstone. They include rounded jellyfish-like creatures, elongated and possibly segmented worms, branching "sea pens" possibly attached to the bottom, and odd shield-

shaped creatures (1). Plankton took up carbon dioxide and made it available to animals, via the food chain, to be incorporated in protective hard parts and shells that leave fossils. By the Cambrian period many groups of animals we know today were emerging (2): corals, sponges, and bivalve mollusks, and rarer groups such as brachiopods, and ones that are extinct such as graptolites and trilobites.

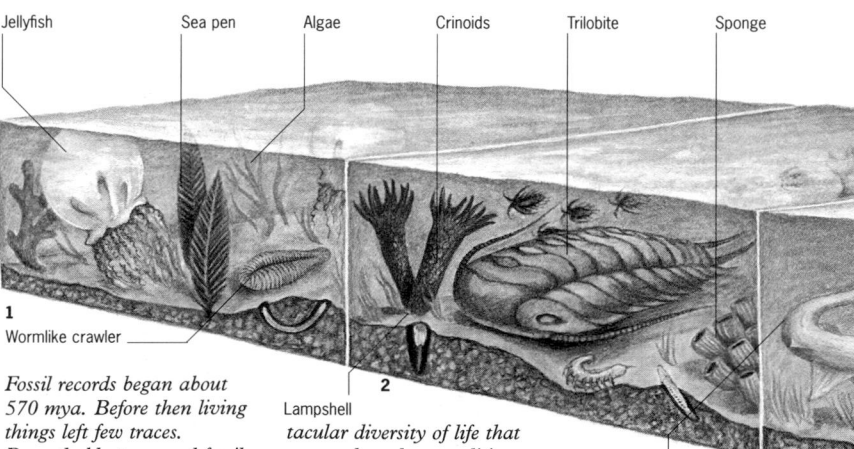

Jellyfish   Sea pen   Algae   Crinoids   Trilobite   Sponge

1
Wormlike crawler

2
Lampshell

Early shark (*Cladoselache*)   3

Fossil records began about 570 mya. Before then living things left few traces. Remarkably preserved fossils from the Cambrian Burgess shale of Canada reveal a vast fauna of soft-bodied creatures unlike anything alive today. Given names such as Anomalocaris and Hallucogenia that reflect their bizarre spines and tentacles, they show the spec-

tacular diversity of life that can evolve when conditions are right. The first worms and arthropods arrived 620 mya: the first creatures to have nerve cells connected together into a primitive brain. Life advanced rapidly, and about 510 mya the first vertebrates appeared. They were very

primitive fish without jaws but with bony protective scales around their heads and three eyes. In later evolution the third eye became the pineal gland in humans.

Evolution of the atmosphere

The first atmosphere on Earth was mostly carbon dioxide and water vapor. It was made up of gases exhaled by volcanoes and given off from comets colliding with Earth. The carbon dioxide had a warming effect and provided "food" for primitive bacteria and algae—the first "life" (*opposite*). They consumed carbon dioxide and released oxygen (*right*) as waste. Colonies of algae formed stromatolites (*inset, right*) which produced more oxygen. By 1.8 billion years ago free oxygen persisted in the atmosphere; 670 million years ago, when the first animals appeared, it was 60% of its present level. Solar radiation then turned some into ozone in the stratosphere (*p. 000*).

FIRST APPEARANCES

Age (mya)	Organism
4,000	First life
3,500	Stromatolites
2,100	Protozoa
1,600	Blue-green algae
1,300	Seaweed
670	Multicelled animals
620	Arthropods, worms
600	Brachiopods,
570	Corals, mollusks, crustacea
510	Jawless fish
425	Jawed fish
400	Lungfish
395	Insects
370	Amphibians, land plants
340	Reptiles
330	Winged insects
256	Mammallike reptiles
235	Dinosaurs, flowering plants
216	Mammals
195	Birds
125	Marsupial mammals
114	Modern mammals
75	Primates
55	Whales
10	Orangutans
7	Elephants
4	Mammoths
1.9	*Homo erectus*

Insignificant invertebrates, the protochordates, have a body plan very similar to that of laval fish and amphibians, which were probably their successors in the Cambrian. By the Devonian period (3), the age of the fish was at its height. Jawless fish, such as Pteraspis *and* Hemiclaspis, *had bony plates and shovel like mouths. Many fish were able to adapt to fresh water. The Devonian also saw the first sharks. Since their skeletons were made of cartilage, there are fewer fossils, but their sharp teeth often survive. During the Devonian, the first fishes came out of the water. Lobe-finned fish developed auxiliary lungs and could haul themselves out of the water if supplies of oxygen ran low. From them evolved the lungfish and an even closer relative that still lives in the Indian Ocean—the coelacanth. By the Carboniferous, amphibious creatures called labyrinthodonts, with fully formed feet, had established themselves on land (4).*

First continents

Rocks on Earth go back 3.8 billion years: the oldest are in Greenland, followed by ones in Australia, Canada, and South Africa. Most present-day continents formed 3,000–2,500 mya and have broken apart and regrouped (*below*).

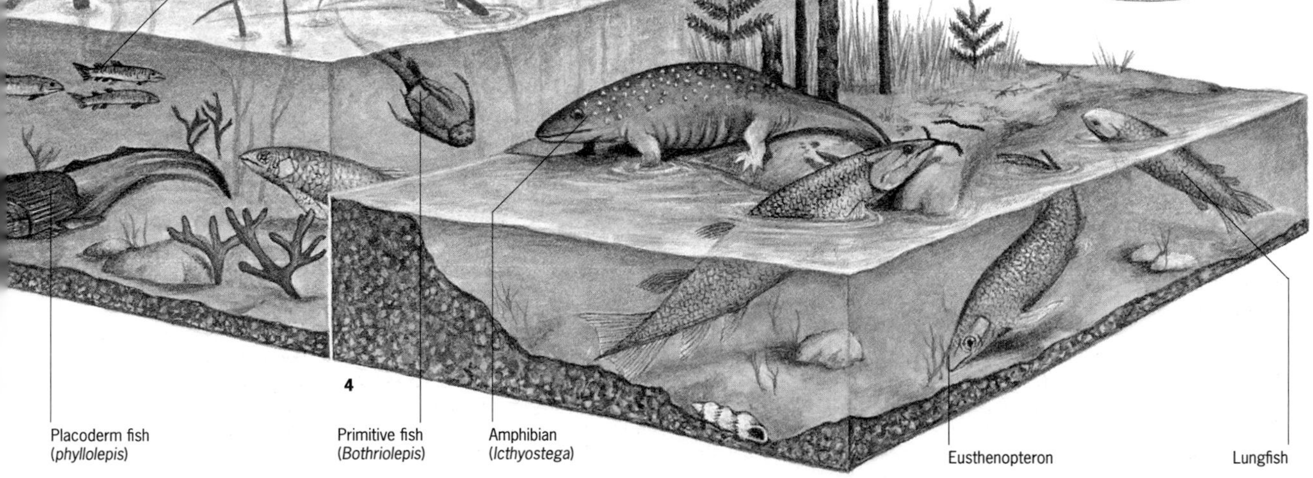

Giant weed

Lobe-finned fish

Early insect (Rhynia)

Vascular plant

Clubmosses

Ferns

4

Placoderm fish (*phyllolepis*)

Primitive fish (*Bothriolepis*)

Amphibian (*Icthyostega*)

Eusthenopteron

Lungfish

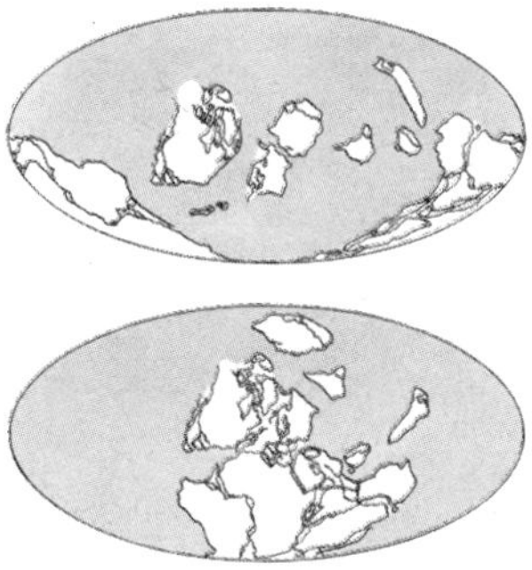

Timeline

355 mya (million years ago) Start of the Carboniferous period and the development of a cooler climate.

350 Euro-America collides with Gondwanaland; Hercynian and Appalachian mountains begin to form; huge amounts of carbon dioxide converted into limestone.

340 First reptiles; first eggs with (leathery) shells.

330 First winged insects.

320 Coal formation begins in swampy forests; continues for 80 million years.

310 Pelycosaurs—first large reptiles to walk on land.

300 Siberia collides with Europe; start of Permian period.

290 Ice ages: south polar ice sheet over Gondwanaland, present-day Australia and India.

275 First marine reptiles (nothosaurs).

255 Mammallike reptiles become the dominant reptiles on land.

245 Major extinctions: 52 percent of animal families lost; Triassic period begins.

235 First dinosaurs, flowers, and froglike amphibians on land; first ammonite mollusks and modern corals in the sea.

225 First giant herbivorous dinosaurs and winged reptiles.

220 Supercontinent of Pangaea complete.

216 Norian catastrophe (possibly linked to impact crater in Quebec): many extinctions; end of large nondinosaur reptiles; first mammals.

210 Pangaea begins to break up as proto-Atlantic opens up between W. Africa and North America.

205 Start of Jurassic period: warm seas, abundant life.

170 Peak formation of oil; volcanoes in Africa. Huge herbivorous dinosaurs (brachiosaurs).

150 Archaeopteryx flies.

145 Many extinctions on land and sea; Stegosaurs and Ichthyosaurs extinct.

140 Eurasia and North America breaking away from S. continent; equatorial ocean forming.

135 Start of Cretaceous period: many new dinosaurs including Iguanodon.

125 First modern flowering plants; first marsupial mammals which migrate to Australia and Antarctica before the split from Africa.

114 First placental mammals.

100 India breaks away from Antarctica.

95 Marine extinctions; extinction of Iguanodon. First primate ancestors.

90 Warm, productive seas; very high sea levels; peak production of chalk, for example in S.E. England, and oil, for example Middle East.

85 South America splits from Africa.

75 Tyrannosaurus is dominant carnivore. First primates.

65 Mass extinctions, notably dinosaurs. Volcanoes in India and Scotland. Start of the Tertiary period. Frequent magnetic reversals.

Tropical forests

During the early Carboniferous period, the Southern Hemisphere was in the grip of an ice age, but equatorial regions were experiencing a warmer climate and rising sea levels. This caused flooding of the low coastal plains, forming delta swamps which were rapidly colonized into tropical forests. The plants and trees that grew in this environment (*right*) were at first very specialized: they included various horsetails (1 and 2), including one that grew to a height of 30 feet (9 m) (*Calamites*), clubmoss relatives (3 and 4), and primitive conifers. The forest vegetation became varied, lush, and dense.

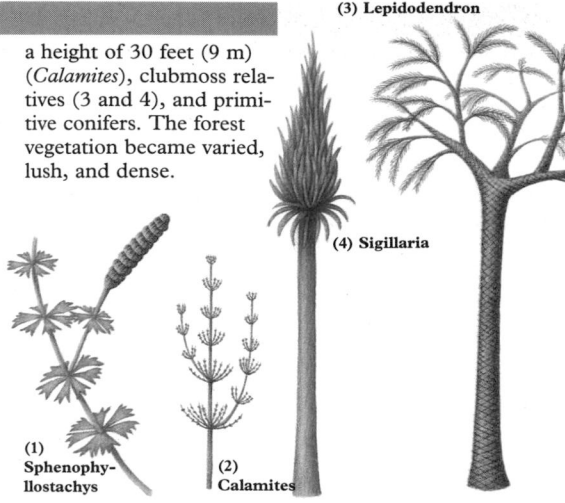

(3) Lepidodendron

(4) Sigillaria

(1) Sphenophyllostachys

(2) Calamites

The formation of coal

The branches and leaves of the lush tropical forest trees accumulated on the forest floor faster than organisms could rot them. The swampy ground was frequently flooded and the debris collected into thick carbonaceous layers, firstly of peat (1). Periodically, the sea flooded in, depositing thick layers of sediment on top of the organic remains, which became compressed into lignite (2). Further compression under the weight of more layers of sediment produced bituminous coal (3). Eventually the remains were buried under such a volume of sediment that they slowly sagged toward the heat of the Earth's interior, becoming lightly metamorphosed into anthracite (4)—hard, black, and rich in carbon.

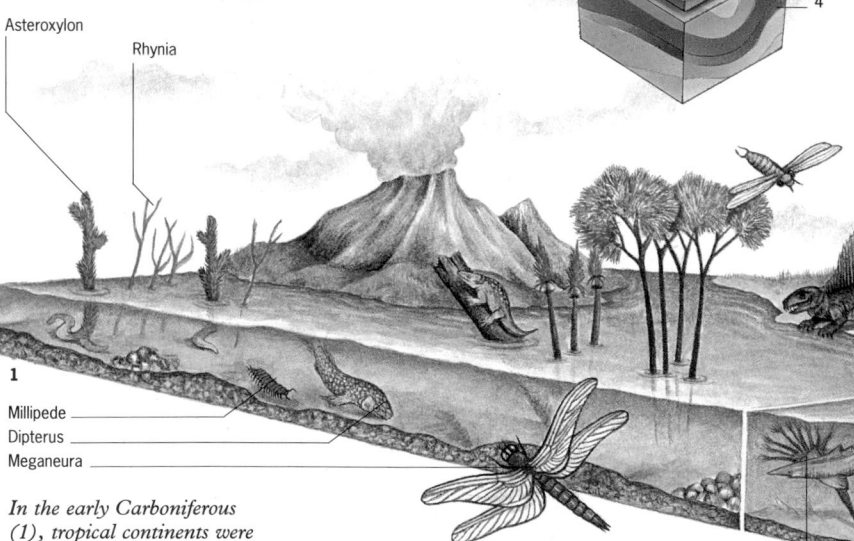

Asteroxylon

Rhynia

1

Millipede
Dipterus
Meganeura

Scapanorhynchus

In the early Carboniferous (1), tropical continents were fringed with vast lagoons. Coral reefs abounded, populated by fish, mollusks, brachiopods, and goniatites (the ancestors of ammonites). The deposits of limestone show how life stabilized the warming climate by turning carbon dioxide into carbonates in the form of stone.

In the Upper Carboniferous, coal swamps, great treeferns flourished along with club mosses and giant horsetails. Among them flew dragonflies with wingspans of up to a yard. Amphibians were also abundant. The first of the reptiles evolved from amphibians.

As the sea level fell, drier conditions began to take over. Only plants with resistant pollen and seeds could flourish. By the Triassic period there were extensive deserts that left thick sandstone deposits behind them.

Mountain building

Most great mountain ranges were formed by collisions of continents and occurred in phases. The first was the Caledonian (460 mya) as Europe collided with North America; next was the Appalachian uplift in the eastern U.S.A.; about 300 mya the collision between Europe, America, and Gondwanaland saw the Hercynian phase; and in the last ten million years the Alps (*below*) and Himalayas have developed. The Alps were formed by the collision of the Eurasian and African continental plates (1), and were then deformed and faulted by thrusting (2 and 3).

Dinosaur domination

From their rise 235 mya, dinosaurs dominated the land. More than 800 species of dinosaurs have been identified. The biggest, Brachiosaurus, grew to a height of 92 feet (28 m) and may have weighed as much as 100 tons. There were two main groups of dinosaur: the Saurischian, or lizard-hipped, and the Ornithischian, or bird-hipped. Though the dinosaurs are long gone, their descendants, the birds, are still abundant.

The great extinction

Geological history is peppered with catastrophes that may have been the reason why many animals suddenly became extinct. One such group was the dinosaurs that disappeared 65 mya. The most popular theory is that a large asteroid collided with the Earth, throwing dust and steam into the air, blotting out the Sun, and changing the climate. A large impact crater off the Yucatan Peninsula in Mexico is often cited as possible evidence of this.

Alps folded and deformed

Faulting

Eurasian plate

African plate

Deep crustal rocks brought to surface

Thrusting

THE DINOSAUR HUNTERS

When viewing the great hall of the Carnegie Museum in Pittsburgh, steel tycoon and benefactor Andrew Carnegie ordered, "Fill that room with something big." So paleontologist Earl Douglass and museum director Dr. W. J. Holland set out in 1908 to do just that. Eventually they found promising rocks in the hills of Colorado. About 145 mya a large river wound its way across a plain. This river must have been prone to serious flooding because, in a near vertical cliff that had once been a sandbar in the river, Douglass uncovered what must have once been a log-jam of dead dinosaurs piled up on the shore. Almost 350 tons of fossils have been collected from this site to fill the museums of North America, and more than 1,000 bones are still exposed in situ in what is now the Dinosaur National Monument.

Dimetrodon

Pterodactylus

Rhamphorhynchus

By the mid-Jurassic (2), dinosaurs were flourishing. Apatosaurs and slender Diplodocuses grazed off the plant life, were hunted by Allosaurus, and scavenged by small packs of Ornitholestes. Stegosaurus survived thanks to bony scales and spines. Volcanoes periodically flooded *whole continents with basalt. The Deccan Traps of western India represents millions of cubic miles of basalt that erupted at the end of the Cretaceous period.*

While dinosaurs ruled the land, the sea level was higher than it has ever been and life flourished in the extensive shelf seas and warm climate. Ammonites — relatives of the squid — were common, as were brachiopods, mollusks, and corals. The marine reptile Ichthyosaurus was the principal predator.

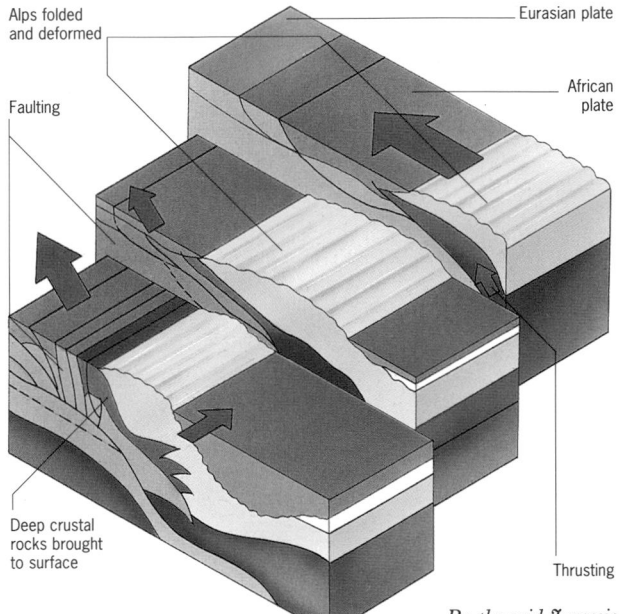

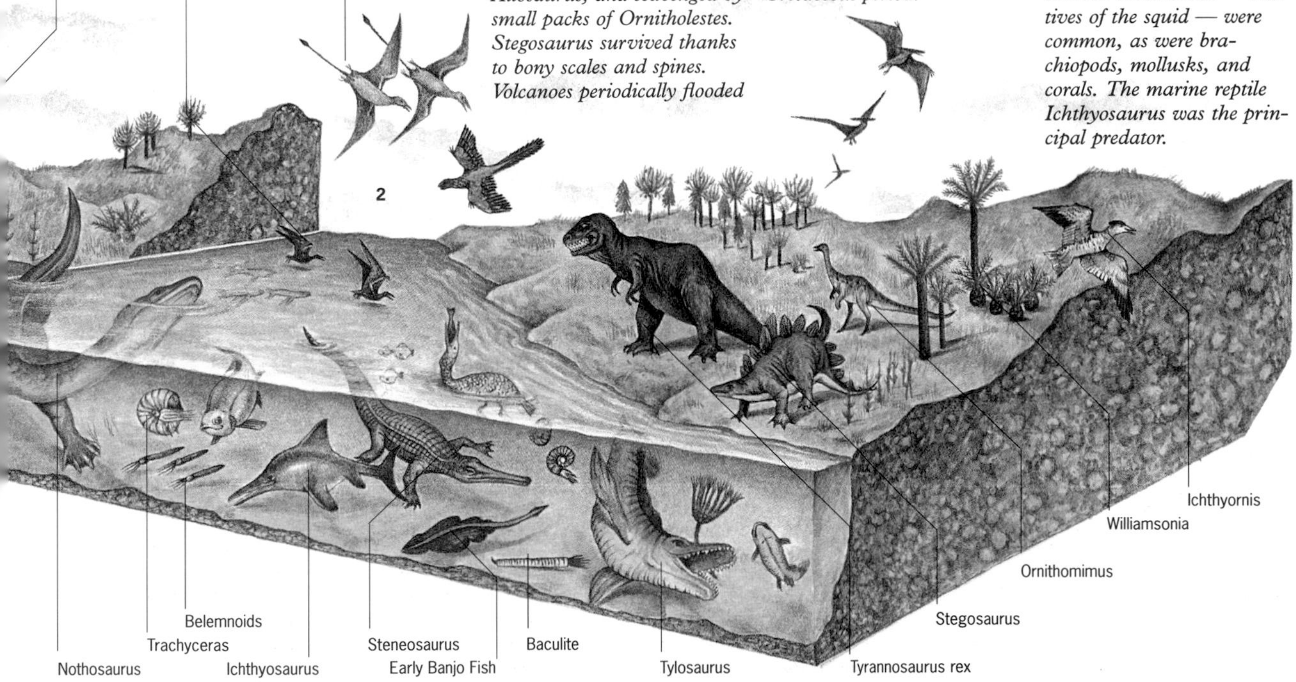

2

Ichthyornis

Williamsonia

Ornithomimus

Stegosaurus

Belemnoids

Trachyceras

Nothosaurus

Ichthyosaurus

Steneosaurus

Early Banjo Fish

Baculite

Tylosaurus

Tyrannosaurus rex

Timeline

64 mya (million years ago) Frequent magnetic reversals; falling sea levels; cooling climate.

62 Fall in sea level completes emergence of North America.

60 North America breaks from Europe. Volcanoes in N.W. Scotland. Rocky Mountains begin to form.

55 New mammals emerge: whales, elephants, and big cats. First grasses suitable for grazing.

50 Australia breaks from Antarctica, leaving Antarctica over South Pole. Oceans cool further.

45 India collides with Eurasia; Himalayas start to form.

40 Many new mammals and birds appear; primitive mammals die out.

37 End of the Eocene: temperatures begin to tumble; marine extinctions.

30 Antarctic circumpolar current begins. Japan breaks from Eurasia; Arabia breaks from Africa; major volcanoes in Indonesia and the Philippines.

24 Grass becomes widespread; grazing animals soon follow.

21 Apes split off from monkeys. Peak of collision of Africa with Eurasia.

16 Cooling of global temperatures resumes. Large herds of grazing mammals widespread. Massive eruptions in the Rockies.

15 Many extinctions; large impact crater in Germany. Sea level falls; climate oscillates.

14 Many volcanic eruptions. East Antarctic ice sheet forms.

10 Maximum activity in formation of the Alps, as Italy pushes into Europe.

9 Northern Hemisphere glaciers develop.

8 Uplift of North America.

6.6 West Antarctic ice sheet forms. Sea level drops 130 feet (40 m).

6.3 Mediterranean dries out.

5.3 Mediterranean re-formed via huge Gibraltar waterfall.

5 Uplift of Himalayas. Apes and ape men divide.

4.5 Andean uplift.

3.5 Oceanlike crust opens the Red Sea. North and South America join up.

3.25 Most recent Ice Age begins.

2.4 First stone tools. Ice Age intensifies.

1.9 *Homo erectus* emerges. Hunting begins.

1.6 Humans make fire.

1 Peak of large mammals. Great volcanic activity.

0.73 Asteroid impact near Australia: many extinctions; magnetic reversal.

0.6 *Homo sapiens* emerges.

0.15 Woolly mammoths evolve.

0.073 Huge volcano erupts in Indonesia; climate cools.

0.04 Modern man (*Homo sapiens sapiens*) emerges.

0.034 Neanderthals are extinct.

0.018 Peak of last Ice Age.

0.014 Thaw starts.

0.010 Brief refreeze (Younger Dryas).

Parallel evolution on different continents

The distribution of animal groups was influenced by land routes that were, in their turn, determined by continental drift (*p. 44*). A land bridge between the Americas (1) enabled more advanced mammals to "invade" the south, while the armadillo and opossum moved north. Before the desert barrier wasd established in north-ern Africa, animals now typical of the plains moved un from the north, while African animals such as the elephant migrated north (2). In the east, some oriental and Australian species reached a transitional area between Asia and Australia, while others such as the squirrel and the tree kangaroo, were unable to do so.

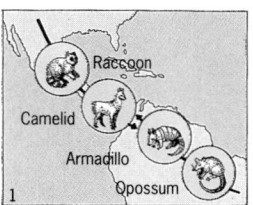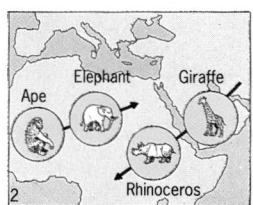

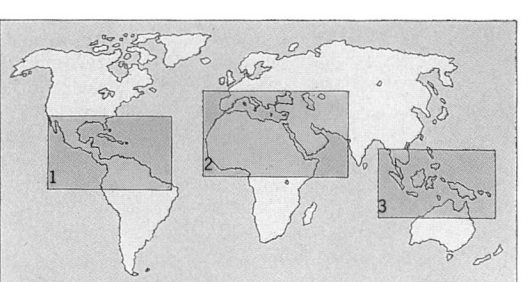

During the Tertiary period (1) the climate became steadily cooler. Forests gave way to grasslands, and mammals and birds replaced the dinosaurs. Continental landmasses continued to collide during the Tertiary and started to take their present shape. Alpine mountain building peaked only 10 mya *and the Himalayan just 5 mya and is still continuing. The Andes in South America are also still rising. In the Eocene period about 50 mya, the south of England stood on a shoreline, rather like a modern mangrove swamp, but domi-* *nated by the Nipa palm with woody vines, magnolias, bay, and laurel. The seeds of these plants were buried in the mud and can still be found in the clay on which London is built.*

The rise of mammals

The first mammals appeared 216 mya, although there was a setback in their evolution with a resurgence 114 mya. Early mammals were small and probably laid eggs. Hoofed mammals, carnivorous bats, and rodents had all diverged from the primate line before the Cretaceous catastrophe. After this period there was rapid development and diversification. Most modern mammals developed around 35 mya. The Ice Age saw the emergence of many giant mammals, most now extinct. More extinctions were to follow due to indiscriminate hunting by humans.

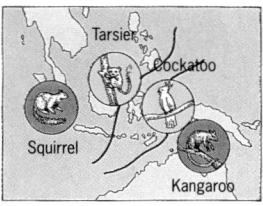

○ Endemic

● Transitional

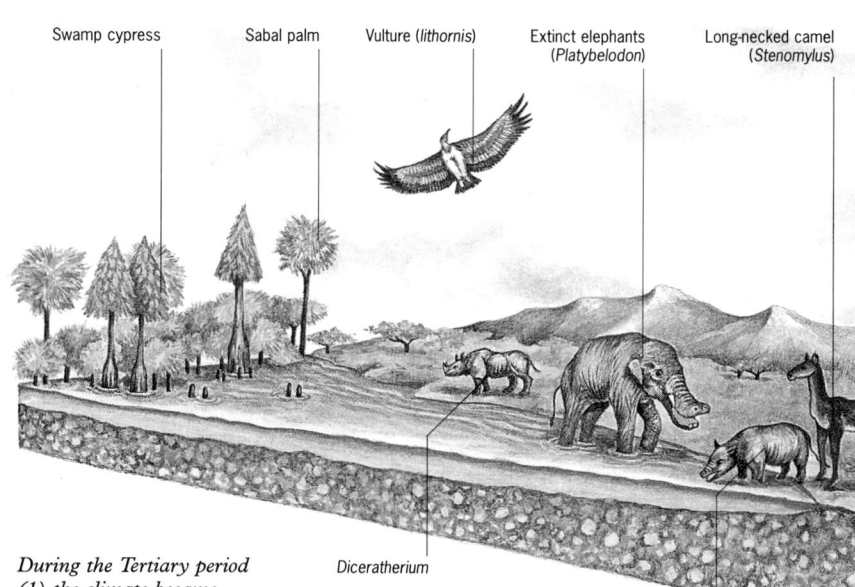

Swamp cypress · Sabal palm · Vulture (*lithornis*) · Extinct elephants (*Platybelodon*) · Long-necked camel (*Stenomylus*)

Diceratherium

Moeritherium

The family of primates

Dinosaurs still roamed the Earth when the first primatelike mammal appeared: a tree shrew called Pergatorius. By 55 mya there were tarsierlike primates with grasping hands and feet, binocular vision, and relatively large brains. By 30 mya the hang-nose Eastern Hemisphere monkeys and the broad-nose Western Hemisphere monkeys had split; ten million years later the ancestral apes split off. Eight million-year-old *Sivapithecus*, once thought to be ancestral to man, was probably closer to the orangutan. Molecular evidence suggests human ancestors split from those of chimpanzees 5 mya. Hominid fossils are rare, but the best candidate for our early ancestor is probably *Australopithecus afarensis* which lived in East Africa about 4 mya. It was small but had legs that could each be placed under its center of gravity, allowing it to walk upright. Footprints in Tanzania suggest it did so. *Homo habilis*, the first member of our

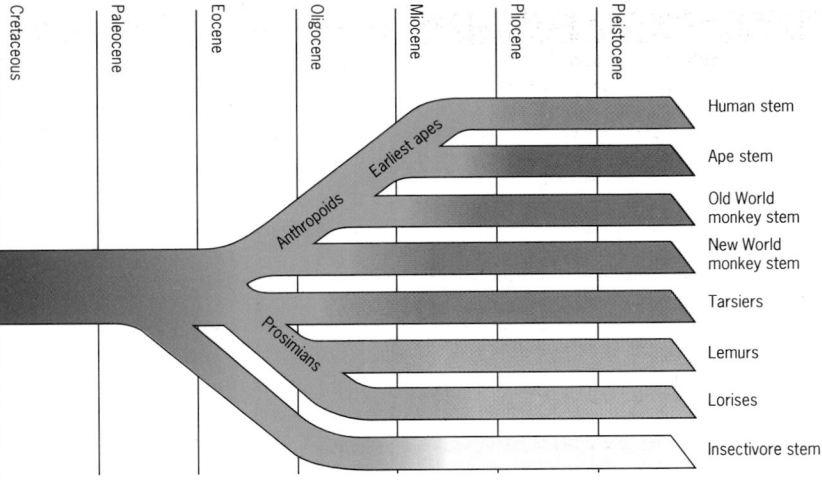

genus, made simple stone tools and had a bulge in its brain corresponding to the area we use for speech. Walking upright may have been the key to human success, allowing the brain cavity to expand without obscuring vision, freeing the hands and putting a bend in the windpipe that we now employ in speech (*p. 204*).

The last two million years witnessed evolution trying out some imaginative ideas on mammals (2). After the shrew-sized primates, rabbit-sized antelope and dog-sized horses of the Eocene, mammals grew large. Large bodies were perhaps better able to control their temperature as the Ice Age set in, or were better suited to migration. Many dinosaur traits were to be seen, such as huge horns and antlers, in creatures like giant elks, rhinoceros, beavers, and woolly mammoths.

By the peak of the last Ice Age, some 18,000–20,000 years ago, humans were systematically hunting wild animals, in some cases to extinction. In the Middle East hunters began shadowing wild herds of goat and gazelle: domestication was only a step away. At first animals were kept for meat, but around 10,000 years ago, it is believed, sheep were kept for their wool and milk in Iran and Afghanistan. The Chinese at this time domesticated water buffalo and pigs.

THE CHANGING CLIMATE

For the last 3.25 million years the world has been in and out of ice ages (*p. 000*). The present comparatively mild climate may only be another brief interglacial period.

14,000 yrs ago	Thaw begins		
10,900	Sudden, severe cold snap, perhaps as a result of cold, fresh meltwater disrupting North Atlantic salinity current		wet in Africa
		5,800	Sharp cooling
		4,920	Sharp warming; biblical flood
		3,280	Sharp cooling
		A.D. 390	Very warm
10,300	Slow warming	A.D.1530–1850	
9,800	Warm monsoon in India		Cooling; "little ice age"
9,000	Warm in Europe,	1900	Global warming due to human activity

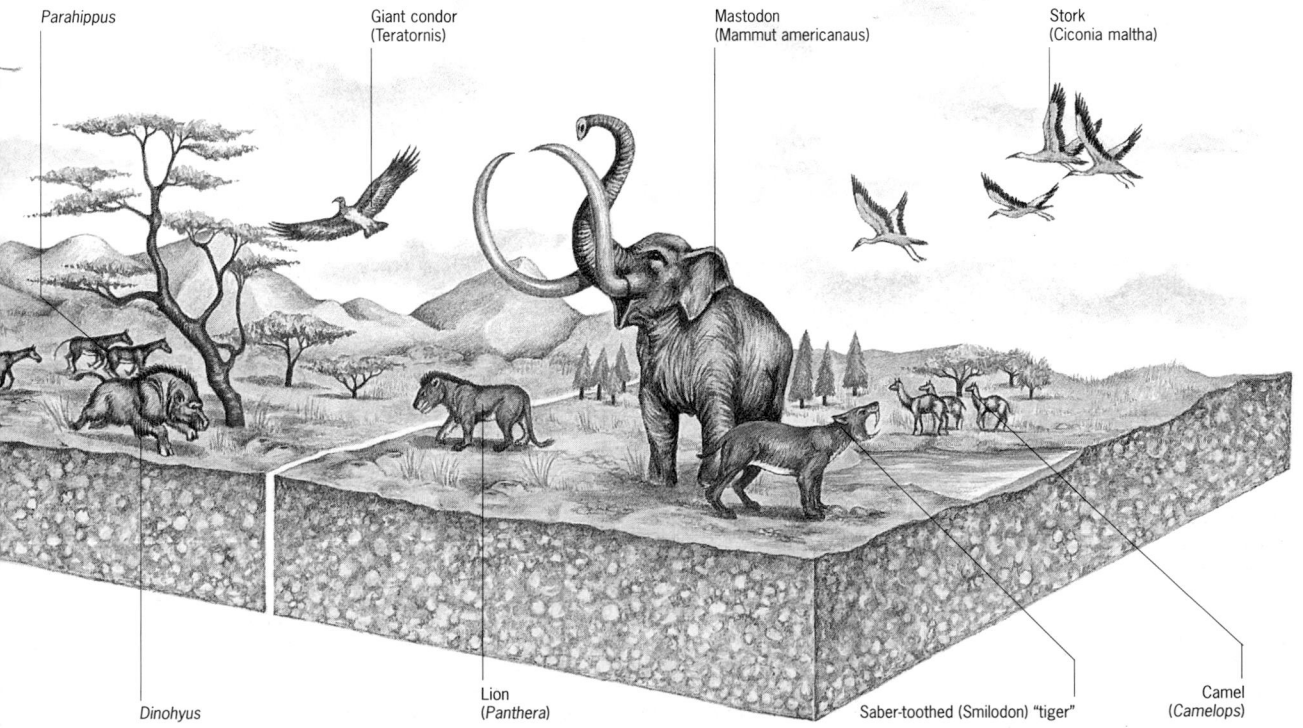

Parahippus

Giant condor (Teratornis)

Mastodon (Mammut americanaus)

Stork (Ciconia maltha)

Dinohyus

Lion (Panthera)

Saber-toothed (Smilodon) "tiger"

Camel (Camelops)

THE FACE OF THE EARTH

The Earth's surface is the scene of a constant battle between the upward forces of mountain building and the erosional forces of wind, water, and waves, aided and abetted by gravity. In the midst of all this, humans too have made their mark in their attempts to hold back the sea, concrete over the surface, and reclaim land. By removing vegetation, humans aid erosion rather than prevent it.

The features of landscape can be classified according to the predominant forces at work and the timescale during which they have been at work. In the Andes and Himalayas, mountain building still dominates over erosion: parts of Scotland and Canada, where once the mountains were higher, are now eroded by old age. The form the erosion takes depends very much on the climate. Where temperatures frequently drop below freezing, ice can act like a wedge, chiseling great boulders from the mountains. Glaciers grind out broad valleys and transport the debris far away. Rivers cut into the hillsides and wash millions of tons of rock and soil away, depositing them on wide flood plains, in deltas, and in deep sedimentary basins out at sea. Wind scours deserts with blown sand and spreads dunes far and wide. Eventually all this material gets pressed into rock and pushed back into mountains.

World relief

A relief map of the world (*above*) reveals the structure of global mountain systems: the great backbone of both North and South America from the Rockies to the Andes, where the Pacific has pushed underneath spouting volcanoes; the high peaks of the Alps and Himalayas where continental landmasses have collided; and the ridges and wrinkles that mark ancient oceans long since squeezed out of existence. With the oceans drained, other even larger features become visible. The ocean ridge system, where new crust is formed, consists of long mountain ranges. Isolated groups of volcanoes such as the Hawaiian chain stand out as great underwater mountains composed of millions of cubic miles of basalt. The ocean trenches, where crust is swallowed, plunge up to 46,000 feet (14,000 m) beneath the sea, and are flanked by volcanic atolls. Though the ancient wrinkles reveal a long history, continuing activity shows that the Earth is still a dynamic planet.

Rifts

Squeeze the crust together and blocks move upward either in folds or, through brittle fracture, faults. Stretch the crust and the result is rifting (*right*). In its simplest form a single block moves downward leaving a steep ridge on either side. More often the process happens many times, so in effect a flight of steps is produced on either side (1). This is often accompanied by uplift since it is not pulling from the sides but the pushing of upwelling mantle rock underneath that does the stretching. So the process is often accompanied by volcanoes. The same process operates at mid-ocean ridges: beneath continents it is as if a new ocean is trying to open. Recent examples of rifting processes at work include the valley of the Rhine River and Africa's Great Rift Valley.

The East African rift

Forty mya (million years ago) upwelling in the mantle was splitting Africa apart. It lifted the Atlas Mountains and split open the Red Sea (2). The crack continued down East Africa forming the Great Rift Valley. The stretching was at its greatest 3.5 mya when volcanoes erupted. In Kenya the volcanic material filled up the valley as fast as it was created. On the western branch of the rift, that did not happen and deep lakes fill the valley (3).

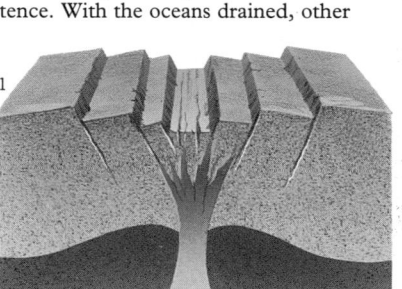

Faults

The Earth's crust can fracture in many different ways, depending on the nature of the rock and the direction of forces within them. Movement between plates of the Earth's crust tends to be accommodated by faulting (*right*) near the surface, where the rocks are cold and brittle. At depth, where temperature and pressure are higher, rocks are more likely to fold. An oblique fault has both horizontal and vertical movement. A normal fault is where one block slides down the fault face compared with the other block. A strike-slip fault (*below*) is where one plate grates alongside another. The movement in this case is not vertical but horizontal. Features called horsts (uplifted rocks) and grabens (downthrown blocks) result from blocks moving up or down between two faults.

The San Andreas Fault

The most famous strike-slip fault in the world runs from San Francisco in the north to the hills behind Los Angeles. It is the San Andreas Fault and, with its branches and tributaries, has been on the move almost continuously for thousands of years. Hardly a day goes by without a few tremors. Quakes in 1989 and 1994 brought San Francisco and Los Angeles respectively, to a halt, but the last big ones were in 1906 and 1857.

FOLDING

Rocks that are deeply buried have nowhere to go if they fault, so instead they form folds. They can be broad, gentle folds like those under southeast England, where the top of the fold or anticline has eroded away leaving the North and South Downs exposed and the London basin full of sediments. Such gentle folds are the comparatively minor knock-on effects of the formation of the Alps. There, the collision of Africa with Europe compressed the sediments so much that folds piled northward one on top of another in great overfolds, or nappes: a vertical cliff can expose a repeating sequence of layers.

Stair Hole, Lulworth Cove, England.

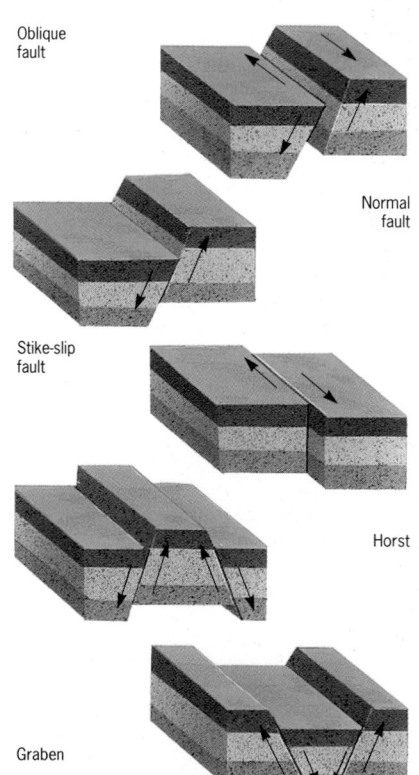

Oblique fault

Normal fault

Stike-slip fault

Horst

Graben

The life cycle of a mountain range

In a wide sedimentary basin, deposits accumulate layer by layer, sinking under their own weight and hardening as they are compressed. These sediment-laden troughs—which are known as geosynclines—are the potential birthplace of mountain ranges if they occur between two colliding continental plates. Colliding continents begin to uplift the sediment, deforming it by folding and compression. Simple folding produces symmetric anticlines (1) and synclines. Continuing pressure may cause uneven folding—and therefore asymmetric anticlines (2) and synclines—which eventually produces a recumbent fold (3). The anticline is now in effect above the syncline, and the rock layers on one side of the anticline are inverted. Further pressure may break the inverted layer, resulting in an overthrust fold (4). A nappe (5) is formed when this layer disappears due to stretching and fracturing as uplift and folding continues.

Tall mountain ranges are produced by large-scale faulting, the intrusion of magma domes, and extrusive volcanic activity, but most importantly by large-scale folding. As soon as mountains are formed (1) weathering processes break up the rock surface and water and ice erode incisions into the mountainsides (2). Landslides, glaciers, and rivers carry material away. The mature landscape (3) stabilizes as rocky peaks become gently rounded hills, rivers widen and slow, and vegetation stabilizes the soil.

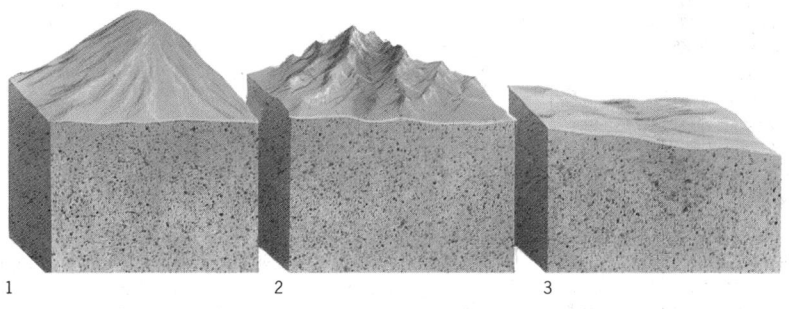

MOUNTAIN BUILDING PERIODS

Major mountain-building episodes

Period (mya)	Name	Region affected
2,800–2,300	Kenoran, Scourian, Saamide Dnieprovian, Singbhun, Dharwar, Limpopo, Yilgarn	North America and Europe, Ukraine, India, Africa, Australia
2,200–1,950	Hudsonian, Eburnean and others, Aravalli, Transamazonian, Laxfordian	North America, Africa, India, South America, Europe
1,400–800	Ankolean, Riphean, Grenville and Moinian	Africa, Europe, North America, Scotland
460–390	Caledonian	Europe, North America
380	Acadian	North America
370–280	Hercynian	Euramerica, Gondwanaland
370–260	Uralian	Urals, Siberia, Euramerica
350–280	Tien Shan	C. Asia, Siberia
230	Chin Ling	China
200–50	Yenshanian	China, Korea, Japan
150	Atlas	N. Africa
60	Caucasus	Georgia
40	Pyrenees	France, Spain
20	Zagross-Bitlis	Iran, Turkey
10	Alpine	Europe
8	Basin, Range, Rockies	W. North America
5	Himalayan	Himalayas
4.5	Andean	Andes

Lowest land levels (feet below sea level)

Asia	Dead Sea	1,310	South America	Valdés Peninsula, Argentina	130
Africa	Lake Assal	508			
North America	Death Valley, California	282	Europe	Caspian Sea	92
			Australia	Lake Eyre	52

LANDSCAPING BY WATER

The Earth is the only planet in the solar system on which water exists in three phases—ice, liquid, and vapor. The reason it is anything other than ice is because of sunshine. The Sun not only warms the land but evaporates water from the sea and powers weather systems so that it rains back down on the hills. The winds that whip up waves are also indirectly caused by solar power. The force of the water in a waterfall or a crashing wave represents a tremendous power. Worldwide, hydroelectric power accounts for as much energy production as nuclear power, and could provide a lot more. Every yard of the Atlantic coastline of North America receives an average of 50kW of power in the form of waves. Water can quite literally, in geologically short timescales, move cliffs and mountains, wearing them down, grinding them up, and washing their remains away.

Coastlines

The line where land meets sea stretches for hundreds of thousands of miles around the world. Water may appear to be a soft chisel, but it never fails to find the weakest points in rocks, splitting off boulders and cutting caves and arches through the headlands.

Waves break onto a shore in a circular motion, throwing sand or stones up the beach then dragging them back. If there is a current along the coast, the sand or stones zigzag their way with the current, gradually stripping the beach and building a long spit downstream. Over geological timescales sea level has varied by hundreds of yards, leaving raised beaches half way up present-day cliffs, drowning valleys once occupied by glaciers (fjords) and turning river valleys into natural harbors (rias). In some places cliffs are being washed away into the sea faster than humans can defend them.

The Dorset coast in southern England exhibits splendid features of coastal erosion.

A mountain stream scours a deep, V-shaped valley (1) with waterfalls (2) and rapids (3). The fast-flowing water rolls stones and boulders and picks up finer sediment into suspension. As the course levels out (4), the river slows and cannot hold as much sediment. Many rivers overflow their banks seasonally, depositing fertile material on the flood plain (5). The river starts to meander (6), scouring the bank away on the outside and depositing silt on the inside of each bend. Eventually the river breaks through the neck of land, leaving an ox-bow lake (7). Much material is deposited at the rivers mouth, forming a delta (8).

LONGEST RIVERS

Name	Outflow	Length (mi.)
Nile and tributaries	Mediterranean Sea (Egypt)	4,157
Amazon and tributaries	Atlantic Ocean (Brazil)	4,082
Mississippi and tributaries	Gulf of Mexico (U.S.A.)	3,741
Chang Jiang (Yangtze)	East China Sea (China)	3,716
Yenisey and tributaries	Kara Sea (Russia)	3,647
Amur and tributaries	Tartar Strait (Russia)	3,592
Ob and tributaries	Gulf of Ob (Russia)	3,362
Plata and tributaries	Atlantic Ocean (Argentina)	3,032
Huang He (Yellow River)	Yellow Sea (China)	3,007
Congo and tributaries	Atlantic Ocean (Angola/Zaire)	2,877
Lena and tributaries	Laptev Sea (Russia)	2,734
Mackenzie and tributaries	Beaufort Sea (Canada)	2,635
Mekong and tributaries	South China Sea (Vietnam)	2,597
Niger	Gulf of Guinea (Nigeria)	2,548

LARGEST LAKES

Name, location	Area (mi.²)	Name/location	Area (mi.²)
Caspian Sea, Iran/ Russia/Azerbaijan/ Turkmenistan/ Kazakhstan	143,200	Erie, U.S.A./Canada	9,930
		Winnipeg, Canada	9,420
		Malawi/Nyasa, E. Africa	8,680
Superior, U.S.A./Canada	31,760	Balkhash, Kazakhstan	6,560–8,490
Aral Sea, Kazakhstan/ Uzbekistan	24,900	Ontario, Canada	7,440
		Ladoga, Russia	7,000
Victoria, E. Africa	24,300	Chad, W. Africa	3,860–10,000
Huron, U.S.A./Canada	23,000	Maracaibo, Venezuela	5,020
Michigan, U.S.A.	22,400	Patos, Brazil	3,910
Tanganyika, E. Africa	12,350	Onega, Russia	3,780
Baikal, Russia	12,160	Rudolf, E. Africa	3,510
Great Bear, Canada	12,100	Eyre, Australia	3,400
Great Slave, Canada	11,030	Titicaca, Peru	3,200

Flood control

Since the time of King Canute, man has tried to control the sea and the flow of rivers. Rich agricultural land has been reclaimed from the sea behind dikes and sea walls, e.g. in the Netherlands around the southern North Sea. But the land is slowly sinking and global warming could soon make sea levels rise. Already, onshore gales, spring tides, and low atmospheric pressure can combine to put many of the world's major cities such as London at risk. Countries such as Bangladesh suffer from flooding rivers and cyclonic storms which threaten homes, crops, and lives. Artificially raised river banks do not necessarily give complete protection, as the Mississippi floods of 1993 unfortunately proved. Those floods killed 50 people and left 70,000 homeless in nine states. Some 20 million acres of farming land were inundated, leading to $20 billion in damage.

CAVES

Rainwater is a weak acid: it contains dissolved carbon dioxide and humic acids, and is capable of dissolving away rock such as limestone.

In limestone regions, streams (1) flowing over what is known as limestone pavement (9) often suddenly disappear underground down a swallow hole (2). They continue to flow underground, sometimes through great cave systems (4). Streams tend to follow a steplike path, seeking out the weakest passage along bedding plains and down vertical joints (6) in the limestone. In the early stage of development of an underground cave system (phreatic stage), water completely fills the passage and dissolves out a near circular tunnel. As the volume of water increases, the stream widens and cuts down into the bottom of the tun-

nels: the stream is now free-flowing (vadose stage) (7). Eventually, it may open up and follow a new and lower set of passageways, leaving empty, dry caves above it.

The solution of limestone to calcium bicarbonate is reversible. As the saturated water drips from the ceiling or splashes on the floor it evaporates and calcium carbonate precipitates out again, forming stalactites and stalagmites (3). These may eventually join up to form columns (8). Sometimes part of the roof of the passage or cave collapses, opening a pothole or chimney (5).

Caves are also formed when the sea erodes into the weaker parts of a cliff. Meltwater can carve out ice caves in glaciers, and molten lava draining from flow tubes can leave tunnels behind.

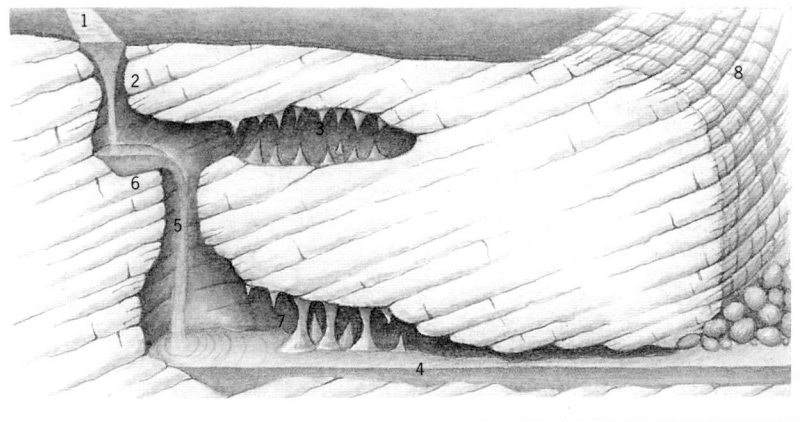

HIGHEST WATERFALLS

Name	Height (ft.)
Angel (upper falls), Venezuela	2,648
Itatinga, Brazil	2,060
Tugels, South Africa	2,014
Cuquenan, Guyana/Venezuela	2,000
Giessbach, Switzerland	1,981
Sutherland, New Zealand	1,903
Ormeli, Norway	1,847
Tysse, Norway	1,749
Pilao, Brazil	1,719
Ribbon, California	1,611
Vestre Mardola, Norway	1,535
Yosemite (upper falls), California	1,430

DEEPEST CAVES

Name and Location	Depth (ft.)
Jean Bernard, France	4,900
Snezhnaya, Russia	4,396
Puertas de Illamina, Spain	4,390
Pierre-Saint-Martin, France	4,334
Sistema Huautla, Mexico	4,068
Gouffre Berger, France	3,930
Vqerdi, Spain	3,921
Dachstein-Mammuthöhle, Austria	3,852
Zitu, Spain	3,737
Badalona, Spain	3,707
Batmanhöhle, Austria	3,625
Schneeloch, Austria	3,612
GES Malaga, Spain	3,510

LANDSCAPING BY ICE

Ice sheets once covered huge areas of both the Northern and Southern hemispheres. Today they have retreated and are restricted to polar regions and the highest mountain areas, but the landscapes carved during those earlier icy times still remain.

We tend to regard ice as a solid, yet under pressure, it can flow in the same sort of way that rocks flow within the Earth's mantle. The structure of ice is very similar to that of rock, too. As snow compacts, air is squeezed out and it slowly turns from a white crumbly texture into a blue crystalline substance, the crystals being of ice rather than minerals. They are lubricated by a microscopic film of water that is kept as a liquid by dissolved salts.

Ice can truly transform the Earth's landscape. It occupies a greater volume than water so, as it freezes in crevices and joints, it acts like a wedge, gradually breaking off pieces of rock or even boulders. Meanwhile, snow accumulates

Erosion by ice

A corrie lake fills the armchair-shaped depression at the head of a former glacier.

As ice flows, it carves out a deep U-shaped valley. Smaller glaciers join it, their surfaces roughly on a level, but their bases at different heights. When the ice melts, it leaves hanging valleys with waterfalls. Moraines from the side valleys join up to form stripes or medial moraines down the main glacier. As the glacier widens out, different flow rates can curve these moraines into complex patterns. The ice flows around resistant rock masses leaving eroded nunataks (a word originating in Greenland). When the ice begins to melt, the glacier's snout develops ice caves carrying meltwater. The melting of ice sheets unleashes torrents of water that can create giant rivers or channels known as coulees, or that feed existing lakes and streams. Large terminal moraines of clay and rock build up and include giant boulders or erratics. The rate of retreat (or advance) of glaciers is important for measuring long-term climate change. If a glacier flows into the sea, the floating snout is flexed up and down by the tides, absorbing a significant fraction of their energy and slowing the Earth's rotation. Eventually icebergs break off (or calve) and float away.

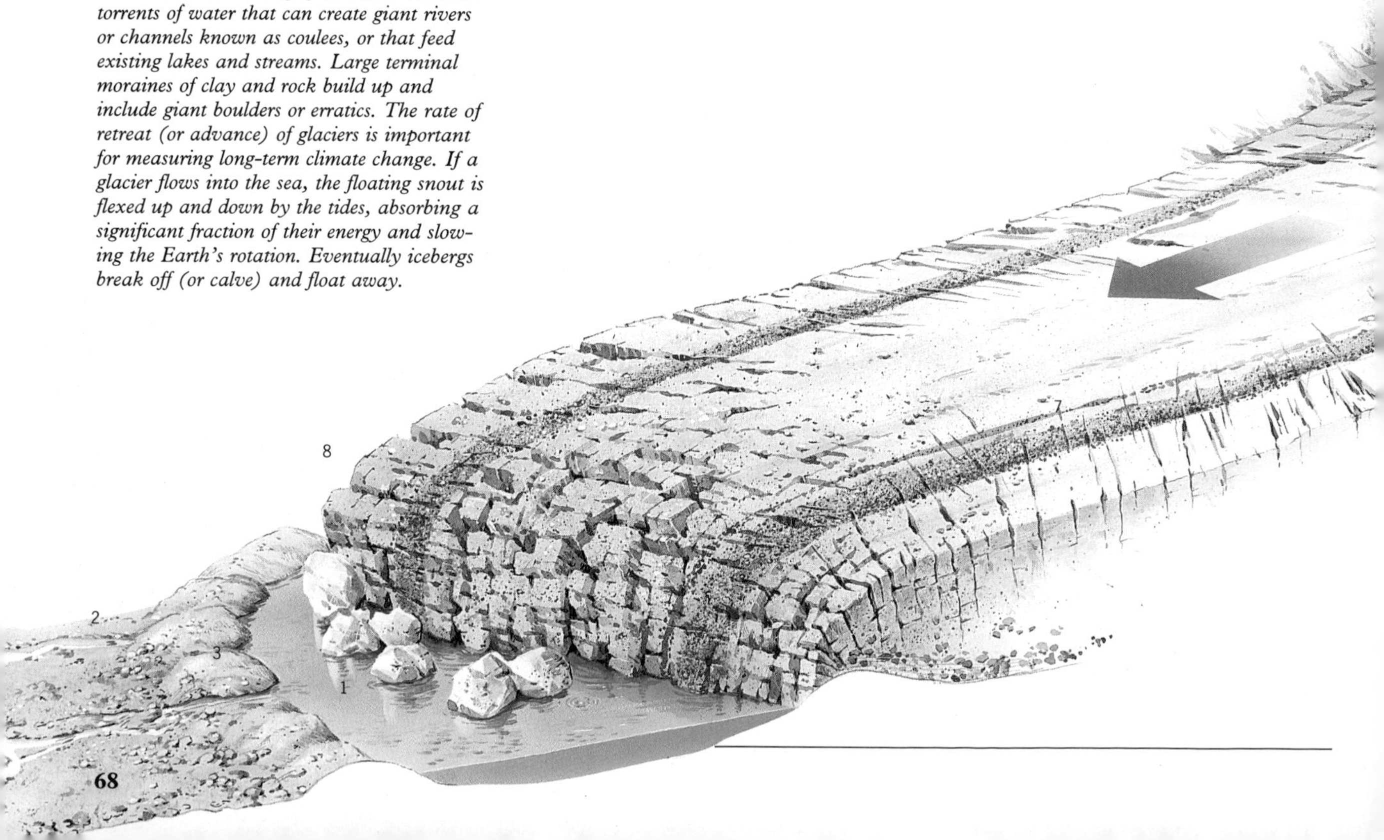

around mountain peaks, either triggering avalanches or compressing into ice.

Eventually, the ice begins to flow, making a scooping action as it starts to move down the mountainside. At very high latitudes ice covers everything in a sheet that may be hundreds of yards thick. Within it, there may be faster-flowing ice streams as the ground underneath falls away, is lubricated by mud, or is even warmed by volcanic activity (as is the case in part of Antarctica). As it thins, the sheet can part around rocky outcrops, or nunataks, to

form valley glaciers and then reunite on the other side into what are called Piedmont glaciers.

The flow rate of ice sheets and glaciers can be very slow—between a few and a few hundred yards a year. So to maintain the same flow as even a small mountain stream, a glacier has to fill the whole valley. As it goes, it grinds the rocks underneath it into a fine flour, and boulders embedded within it leave deep striations in the sides of the U-shaped valley that is being carved by its path.

Deposition by ice

Glaciers produce many kinds of debris and drift. As the ice progresses, a thick layer of fine clay builds up underneath. The pressure may be enough to keep the water liquid at the base even though the temperature is below 32°F (0°C). This lubricates the flow and leaves mounds of clay called drumlins. At the snout of the glacier, where ice is melting, it deposits the rest of its load of sediment and rock as a terminal moraine that can block in a subsequent lake. The moraine in front of New Zealand's Franz Josef glacier is 1,410 ft./430 m high. If an ice sheet retreats, as happened at the end of the last ice age, it leaves the countryside coat-ed with what is known as boulder clay or till—a completely unsorted rock mixture ranging from the finest clay to house-sized boulders. Sometimes a block of ice is left behind in the clay and when that melts it leaves a deep pond or kettle hole. Melting can result in stratigraphical puzzles with, for example, big blocks of ancient rock sitting randomly on top of much younger material (*right*). Known as erratics, their rock type often gives clues to the path taken by the ice.

Erratics are often deposited in areas of different rock type. They perch precariously if they were dropped by rapidly melting ice.

LAST ICE AGE

In four main periods during the last ice age, a vast sheet of ice advanced south from the North Pole, covering Canada, Greenland, Siberia, Scandinavia, and most of Britain including the North Sea. The courses of great rivers, such as the Thames in Great Britain, were altered when they were blocked by moraines. The Great Lakes are the remains of great meltwater lakes created at the end of the last ice age. As the ice retreated the lakes filled until they drained over higher ground to the south. When the ice retreated from the St. Lawrence, vast quantities of cold, fresh water flooded into the Atlantic, disrupting ocean currents and causing a brief refreeze since fresh water freezes at higher temperatures than salt water.

The first ice ages that left their mark in the rock record occurred during the Pre-Cambrian period. An ice age during the Ordovician affected what is now the Sahara. One in the Carboniferous period caught much of the Southern Hemisphere. The most recent ice age began about 3.5 million years ago and is probably still in progress, though we are

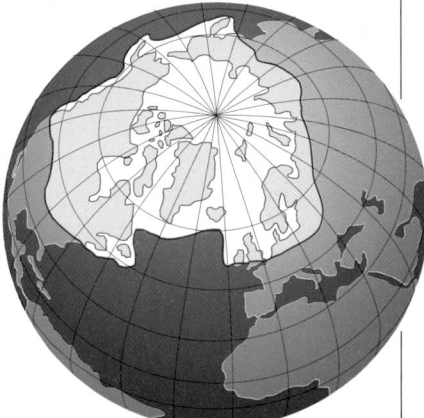

The extent of the ice sheet in the Northern Hemisphere during the last ice age.

at present in a relatively mild spell. The temperature appears to have fluctuated between two relatively stable states about 35 times during the Earth's history, triggered perhaps by the wobble of the Earth on its axis and variations in the Sun's activity.

Ice in snowfields high in mountains compacts and begins to flow, leaving a corrie, cwym or cirque (an armchair-shaped hollow) at the head of the valley. Back-to-back cirques leave jagged arêtes and pyramidal peaks. As the glacier pulls away or the surface bends, crevasses open. Screes fall from the hillsides and build up lateral moraines. As long as the surface goes downhill, the base of the ice can "over-deepen" a valley and then appear to travel uphill. Where it falls down a steep slope, it forms a jagged crevassed icefall.

FJORDS

Fjords (also, fiords) are deep, narrow coastal inlets that are "drowned" glaciated valleys. They are steep-sided and U-shaped and are found in recently glaciated coastal regions such as Norway, southern Chile, and the south island of New Zealand. The deepest fjord in the world is in Chile and has a depth of 4,225 ft./1,288 m.

Fjords were the sites of large valley glaciers during the last ice age. The glaciers by this stage had reached sea level and were therefore thick, carving out deep troughs. The sea level was lower then because large amounts of water were locked up in glaciers and ice caps. When they melted, the seas rose and the coastal valleys were flooded.

LANDSCAPING BY WIND

On its own, wind has little effect on rocks. But let it transport sand particles and it can blast a desert landscape. Deserts tend to form under consistently high-pressure weather systems, or close to cold ocean currents which prevent evaporation into rain clouds. Clear skies expose rocks to intense heat by day and allow them to cool by night. The constant heating and cooling expands and contracts the surfaces of rocks, powdering them to dust or making sheets flake off, producing smooth, rounded hills or inselbergs such as Ayers Rock in Australia.

Weathering processes produce a mixture of sand and rock and, although the popular image of a desert is of an endless expanse of sand, sandy deserts make up only 20 percent of the total. One reason is because wind whips up sand and dust and blows it away, leaving a layer of heavier pebbles as a protective crust. The pebbles receive an intense blasting of sand which wears away the windward side. If the prevailing wind changes or the pebble overbalances, another side is presented and the resulting pebble has several flat faces and is known as a dreikanter.

Where sand does dominate, it does not lie flat but builds into dunes such as barchans and seif dunes (*above, right*). If there is an obstacle such as a rocky outcrop or a bush, sand can build up in front and behind it, producing a long tail of sand in the lee of the obstacle.

Although it seldom rains in deserts, when it does occur the storms can be heavy. With little or no vegetation to retain it, the water produces flash floods which race down steep-sided water courses, called wadis, scouring sand and rock as they go. Eventually this leads to a highly eroded landscape, a good example being the badlands of Arizona.

Ridges of sand build up parallel to the wind direction in sandy deserts (1, bottom left). The sides of the ridges slow the wind by friction and produce eddies that scallop one side of the ridge (center).

The classic sand dune is crescent-shaped with a sharp ridge along the top: this is called a barchan (top right). The wind piles sand up on the back of the crescent until it spills over the

top. Turbulent eddies scour out the downwind side, keeping it steep. The dune forms a crescent shape because there is less sand to the sides so they advance faster. Where sand is blown across rock, seif (longitudinal) dunes develop parallel to the wind direction (bottom right). Star-shaped dunes are produced by irregular winds (top left). Wind blows sand along, but the surface area to weight ratio of sand grains is such that they cannot be lifted more than about a yard off the ground. The result is that they undercut rocks, forming long undercut tables called yardangs and smaller mushroom-shaped rocks called zeugens (2).

Rocky deserts, as in parts of the Sahara in Algeria, are far more common than sandy deserts.

THE WORLD'S LARGEST DESERTS

Name and location	Area (mi²)
Sahara, N. Africa	3,500,000
Arabian, Saudi Arabia	899,600
Gobi, Mongolia/N.E. China	500,000
Patagonian, Argentina	260,000
Great Victoria, S.W. Australia	250,000
Great Basin, S.W. U.S.A.	190,000
Chihuahuan, Mexico	140,000
Great Sandy, N.W. Australia	140,000
Sonoran, S.W. U.S.A.	120,000
Kyzyl Kum, Uzbekistan	116,000
Taklimakan, N. China	104,000
Kalahari, S.W. Africa	100,000
Kara Kum, Turkmenistan	100,000
Kavir, Iran	100,000
Syrian, Saudi Arabia/Jordan/ Syria/Iraq	100,000
Nubian, Sudan	100,000
Thar, India/Pakistan	77,000
Ust'-Urt, Kazakhstan	62,000
Bet-Pak-Dala, Kazakhstan	60,000
Simpson, C. Australia	56,000
Dzungaria, China	55,000
Atacama, Chile	54,000
Namib, S.W. Africa	52,000

SOILS

Plants, and hence all life, depend on the soil. Rock breaks up chemically and physically to form different soil types (*right*). The physical breakup produces sand and silt, but chemical decomposition is more complex. Chalk and limestone dissolve away leaving little residue and therefore are overlain by thin soils. Silicates on the other hand slowly react with water to form clay minerals. What happens then depends on the flow of water through the soil. If, as in temperate climates, rainfall continues through most of the year, chemicals such as iron hydroxide will tend to wash out of the top 12 inches (30 cm) or so, leaving pale gray earth, or podzol, and redepositing the iron underneath as a darker layer that can develop into an impervious hardpan, often eliminated by plowing. In the tropics, high rainfall during the wet season mobilizes the iron, but evaporation concentrates it near the surface. During the dry season plants draw water from farther down, bringing iron and aluminum hydroxide to the surface and producing red laterite. If this continues, the laterite becomes hard and impervious, making the soil infertile.

Another important soil type is the black chernosem of the steppes. During the dry summers grass draws up calcareous solutions which make the humus black and insoluble so that iron hydroxides are not leached out.

Intensive agriculture can eradicate such soil profiles, but the physical nature of the soil is still important. If it is sandy, it

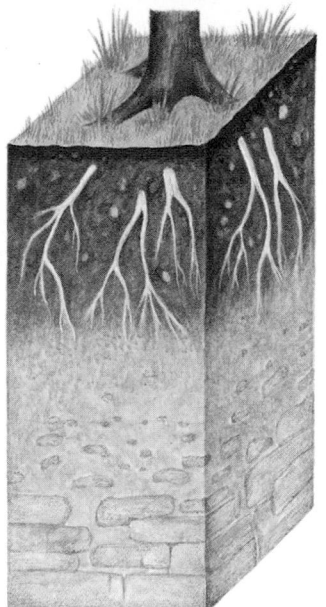

 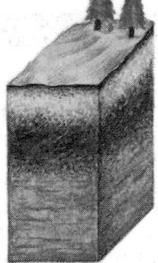 

Tundra Subpolar   **Coniferous Mountainous**   **Prairie Temperate**

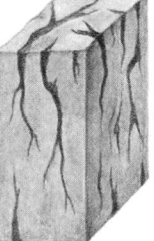  

Savanna   **Rain forest Tropical**   **Desert**

Soil profile

is light and easily drained but holds little organic matter, and nutrients soon wash away. Clay, by contrast, is heavy and waterlogged when wet and hard when dry, but it does retain nutrients. Vegetable matter can form soil too, such as peat, which retains water well. The most fertile soils are a mixture of sand and clay —loam—with plenty of organic matter.

Soils are valuable and vulnerable. If exposed to acidic pollution they can release aluminum salts that poison plants

and water. If vegetation is removed they get washed away altogether.

Soil profile

The uppermost layer, or topsoil, is rich in organic matter, but short of minerals. This layer is penetrated by roots and has its own established ecosystem. Beneath is the subsoil, rich in minerals but short of organic materials. Underneath is a layer of weathered rock and still deeper is the unweathered bedrock.

The distribution of soil types across the globe corresponds very closely to climate and vegetation zones.

Podzolized soils
- Podzolized soils (incl. brown)
- Gray-brown
- Red-yellow
- Terra rossa and brown forest soil

Lateritic soils
- Latosolic
- Black and dark gray

Grassland soils
- Prairie and chernozem soils (incl. denegrated chernozems)
- Chestnut and brown soils
- Reddish prairie, reddish-chestnut, and reddish-brown soils

Soils of arid regions
- Gray desert soils and red desert soil
- Tundra (incl. arctic brown forest soil)
- Undifferentiated highlands

OCEANS

Oceans cover 71 percent of the Earth's surface. Since the early Earth was probably too hot for liquid water to condense, all the water in today's oceans probably came out of volcanoes and from falling comets. Today, the oceans average more than 11,500 ft./3,500 m in depth and the deepest part, the Mariana Trench in the Pacific, goes down 36,200 ft./11,034 m. The shallow shelves around many continents are, geologically, extensions of those continents. They support a wide range of marine life as well as concealing extensive oil deposits. They are bounded by the continental slope, down which sediments fall, producing graded beds of coarse to fine sediment called turbidites.

The surface of the ocean provides an important source of moisture and warmth that controls the Earth's climate. The deep ocean floor is relatively unexplored. It has been mapped by sonar to reveal ridges, canyons, volcanoes, and seamounts. Deep-sea fishing and occasional visits by submersibles exploring the cold, dark, and crushing pressure of the ocean deeps provide glimpses of bizarre life forms—giant invertebrates, fish that carry their own lanterns, and entire communities that never see the Sun, depending for nutrients on hot submarine springs.

Where the water is

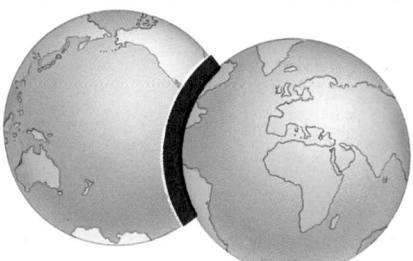

	Pacific Ocean	Atlantic Ocean	Indian Ocean
Area (millions mi.²)	69	41	111
Volume (millions mi.³)	170	80	70
Av. depth (ft.)	12,930	10,860	12,600

Waves and tides

The Earth's layer of water making up the oceans, often referred to as the hydrosphere, will according to the laws of gravity find its own level. The Earth's gravity, however, varies over its surface according to the density of the rocks beneath: hot, low-density rock, rising in a convection current through the mantle, will lead to a weaker gravitational pull and hence less water above it, whereas thick, cold, dense rock will have greater gravitational pull and so will have more water above it. This accounts for variations of several yards, revealed by satellite surveys.

The strongest influence on the height of the oceans is the gravitational pull of the

Currents and salinity

The sea is salty. If all the oceans evaporated and the salt spread out evenly, it would form a solid layer 245 ft./75 m thick. It is likely that the first oceans were of almost fresh water. Four billion years of rain, rivers, and erosion have progressively washed more and more soluble material out of continental rocks and down to the sea. The salinity varies widely from place to place. In the Baltic there is low evaporation and a regular input of fresh water from melting snow, and its salinity is about 5,000 parts per million. In the Red Sea and Persian Gulf, however, it can exceed 40,000 ppm. Salt plays an important role in the global transportation of ocean currents. As water evaporates, the sea becomes saltier and as a result more dense. Eventually, particularly if it cools, the salt water sinks downward. In this way, salt and sunshine drive great conveyor belts that carry heat from equatorial waters in surface currents and return salt in deep currents. The best example of this is in the North Atlantic, where the Gulf Stream brings rain and warm weather to western Europe and the salt returns south at depth. If this conveyor belt is disrupted, it can trigger an ice age. Ocean currents depend on the positions of the continents, and continental drift (p. 44) has caused major climatic change in the past. About 30 mya (million years ago) an eastward circumpolar current established itself around Antarctica, isolating the continent from other weather systems and leading to the development of the ice cap. A modern example of the effects of changing currents is El Niño (the Child, so called because it occurs at Christmas) a warm current that can develop in the Pacific and move toward the coast of Peru. It causes disruption to fisheries and triggers equatorial drought and tropical storms.

The hydrological cycle

The world's water is forever going around in circles—not just in ocean currents, but between atmosphere and ocean by evaporation from lakes, rivers, and seas (1), transportation in clouds (2), precipitation as rain or snow (3), seepage (4) from ground water and lakes, and the flow of rivers. This is the hydrological cycle. Ninety-seven percent of the world's water is contained in oceans and saline lakes; the remaining three percent is fresh water. Three-fourths of fresh water is stored as ice and nearly one-fourth is in underground aquifers. All rivers, lakes, and clouds contain less than one percent of the world's fresh water, or 0.03 percent of the total.

Moon, which causes a bulge of ocean that is pulled toward it. A similar bulge appears on the opposite side of the globe, as if in a falling-away response, which is caused by the Earth's spin. The result is two high tides during the course of a day, separated by about 12 hours as the Earth completes its orbit. (Since the Moon is also in orbit, the time of high tide varies by just under an hour each day.) The Sun also exerts a gravitational influence on the tides: when it pulls in the same direction as the Moon the tides are at their largest and are known as spring tides. When the Sun pulls at right angles to the Moon it has a diluting effect and the tidal range is less: this causes neap tides—the lowest high tides.

The surface of the ocean is constantly stirred by the wind, producing waves of a transverse nature. A wave may travel for many miles, and each particle of water within it moves in a small circular motion. As the wave comes into the shallow water of the shore, there is a change in speed, with the bottom part of the wave slowing down at a greater rate than the top water. The top part in effect overtakes the bottom, causing the wave to break. Depending on the angle at which the wave hits the shallow water, there can also be a change in direction of the wave since refraction will occur. The return flow of water down the beach becomes a current or undertow that can be a danger to swimmers or surfers.

OCEAN TEMPERATURE

The top few feet of the oceans store more heat than the entire atmosphere. So the oceans are a vital buffer in keeping the Earth's climate equitable. Still tropical waters tend to stratify as they warm, with the hottest water floating on the surface reaching temperatures of up to 75°F, while 33,000 ft./1,000 m down they are a meagre 40°F and below this they can plummet to 32-36°F. These layers are identified as the epilimnion (top), thermocline (middle) and hypolimnion (bottom). Only when they are stirred by wind and currents or become dense due to salt do different layers mix. One possible outcome of global warming might be an even greater stratification of the oceans, polarizing climate zones still further. As it is, warm ocean currents bring mild wet weather to some parts such as northwest Europe, while cold currents with low evaporation rates cause cold winters in eastern Canada and desertlike conditions in Chile, southwest Africa and Western Australia. Where cold and warm currents meet, they interact, forming eddies and fronts very similar to those of weather systems. As warm water mixes with nutrient-rich cold water, ideal conditions for rapid plankton growth are created, sometimes resulting in spring blooms of phytoplankton. Ocean temperatures and circulation are so important to climate that the complex computer simulations used for weather forecasting have to expend more computer power in monitoring the oceans than the atmosphere.

Minerals from the sea

Beneath the oceans are rich deposits of oil and natural gas, and valuable sources of aggregates (gravel and sand) used by the construction industry. In dry areas of the world the freshwater content of oceans is important, even though distilling it is an energy-intensive process. The salt, too, can be a valuable product. Most of it is sodium chloride that is often extracted by evaporation in salt pans for use in seasoning and food preserving. Sea water is also used to produce magnesium and most of the world's supply of bromine and iodine. If nuclear fusion reactors become commercial, their principal fuel is likely to be lithium, extracted from sea water. In the deep ocean, strange and poorly understood chemical processes are at work producing potato-shaped, mineral-rich manganese nodules on the ocean floor. So far, their extraction is not economic, but their presence raises important political and ethical issues over mineral rights in international waters.

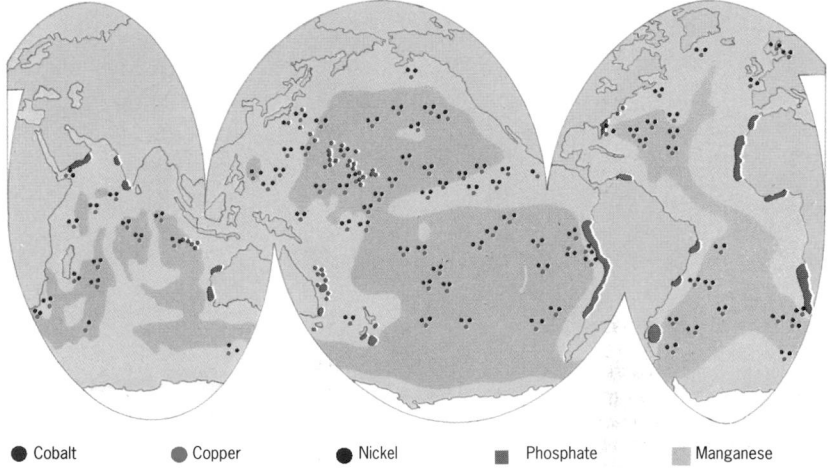

● Cobalt ● Copper ● Nickel ■ Phosphate ▨ Manganese

Exploitation of minerals in the sea is increasing as land reserves diminish. The most valuable are copper, cobalt, nickel, and manganese—often found in manganese nodules. These cover up to 20% of the ocean floor but are more common in deep-ocean basins. Other mineral deposits result from movements of the ocean floor and sediment deposition. Phosphorite accumulations occur on continental margins and upper continental slopes.

Sea-floor profile

The true margin of a continent is not its coastline but the edge of the continental shelf (1), seldom more than 660 ft./200 m deep. The continental slope (2) descends 10,000 ft./3,000 m or more to the abyssal plain (3). Landslides of sediment can fall down the slope to accumulate layers of turbidite. In places, steep seamounts, former submarine volcanoes, rise above the plain (4). Sometimes these break the surface to form islands. Measured from the ocean floor, they can be larger than the highest mountains on land. Mid-ocean ridge systems (5) run like a backbone for thousands of miles, occasionally offset by transform faults. Often there is a double ridge with a rift in between, from which submarine "pillow" lavas erupt. This is the youngest part of the ocean floor, and there is little accumulation of sediment. Sometimes there are hydrothermal vents associated with the volcanic activity, belching hot, black, mineral-laden water like a factory smokestack, and supporting strange life forms. Where two slabs of continental crust collide, one plunges down to form a deep ocean trench, 33,000 ft./10,000 m or more deep (6). On the other side, trapped magma creates volcanoes that can erupt to produce chains of islands (7) that are often surrounded by coral reefs or atolls.

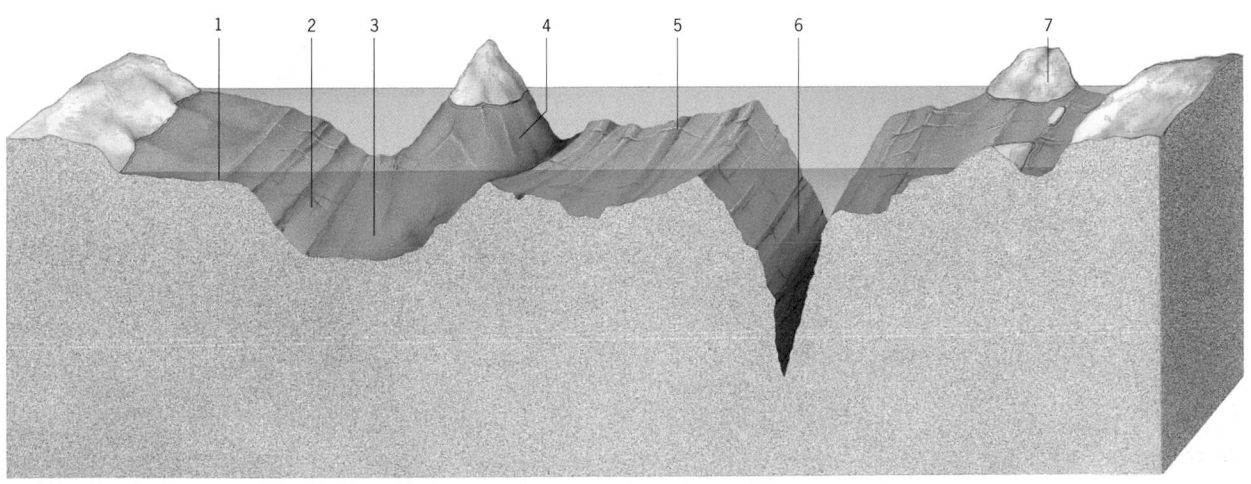

ATMOSPHERE

The Earth is shrouded in a thin veil of gas called the atmosphere. At sealevel it provides the air we breathe, the wind, and the weather, but with increasing height, it becomes more and more rarefied, slowly blending into the virtual vacuum of space. The atmosphere has no easily defined top: technically the height at which space shuttles orbit is within the atmosphere. Our atmosphere has evolved so that there is both carbon dioxide and oxygen held in balance by photosynthesis and respiration. This combination supports life on Earth, making it unique among the planets of the solar system.

Composition

Nitrogen accounts for approximately 80 percent of the volume of the Earth's atmosphere and oxygen most of the remainder. At lower levels water vapor is significant, forming large clouds that can reflect sunlight out and keep heat in. Water vapor, carbon dioxide, and methane are all what are called greenhouse gases, allowing the Sun's light to pass in and warm the ground but preventing heat radiation leaving. Thus they insulate the Earth and keep it warm. Although increasing the greenhouse effect by releasing more of these gases through human activities could have serious consequences, the basic greenhouse effect is essential to life. Without it, average surface temperatures on Earth would be about -31°F (-35°C).

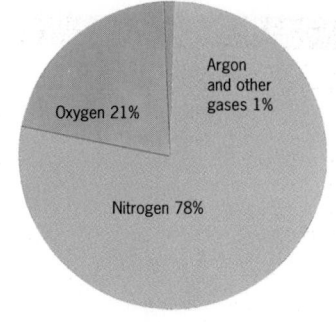

Oxygen 21%

Argon and other gases 1%

Nitrogen 78%

Thermosphere

Above about 280 mi.(450 km) any gas molecules are on their way out into space, so this is called the exosphere. Below that, down to about 50 mi. (80 km), is the thermosphere (1). This is the hottest layer of the atmosphere, where molecules of gas absorb ultraviolet radiation coming from the Sun, creating temperatures as high as 3,600°F (2,000°C.).

Mesosphere

The mesosphere (2), down to 30 mi.(50 km), is too low to be warmed by direct radiation and too thin to be warmed by convection. It includes most of the ionosphere, consisting of variable layers of atoms with one or more electrons stripped off to give them an electrical charge. Certain parts of the ionosphere can reflect shortwave radio signals and filter out X rays from space.

Stratosphere

From about 9–30 mi. (15–50 km) above us is the stratosphere (3), at temperatures below 32°F (0°C). Violent volcanic eruptions can propel gas and dust to this level, where they slowly spread around the globe. But generally, the stratosphere remains horizontally stratified. This layer screens out most solar ultraviolet radiation.

Ozone

Within the stratosphere ozone (4) forms a thin layer at a height of about 15 mi. (25 km). This screens out damaging solar ultraviolet rays. It is produced by the action of solar radiation on oxygen. Certain man-made substances reach the stratosphere, where chlorine contained in them is destroying the ozone layer.

Troposphere

The bottom 9 mi. (15 km) of the atmosphere, the layer in which weather conditions occur, is the troposphere (5). It contains 80 percent (by mass) of all the atmospheric gases. It is warmed by radiation from Earth and so is normally warmed from the bottom. The boundary with the stratosphere varies from 6 mi. (10 km) at the poles to 12 mi. (20 km) at the equator.

Aurorae

When charged particles from the Sun enter the upper atmosphere through gaps in the magnetosphere (magnetism *p. 43*) they can collide with atoms, making them emit their characteristic colors (oxygen-red and yellow; nitrogen-violet, blue, and red) (6). These are the Aurora Borealis and Aurora Australis.

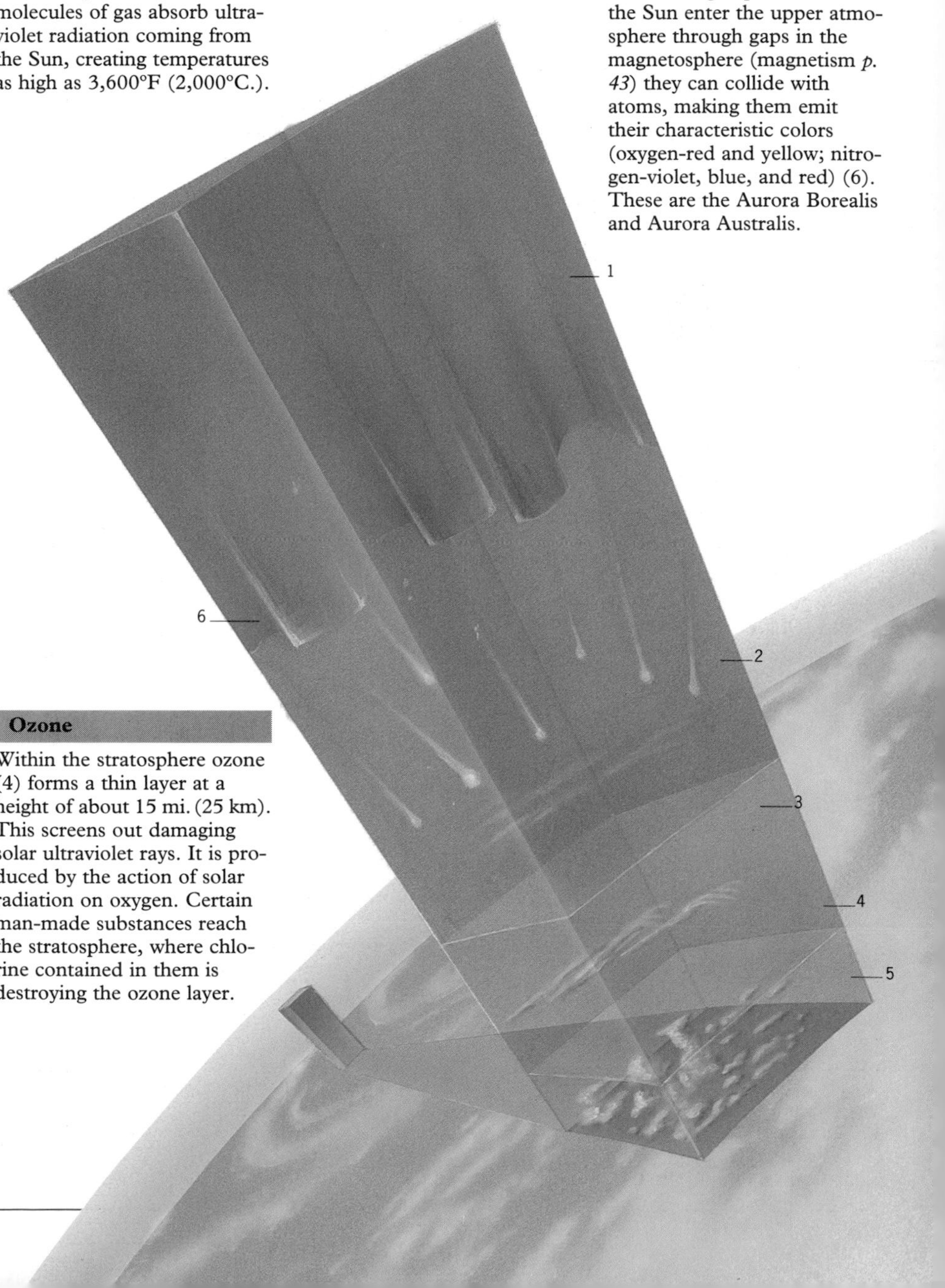

AN EVOLVING ATMOSPHERE

The first atmosphere of the Earth was very different from that of today. There was no free oxygen but high levels of carbon dioxide produced by continual volcanic eruptions. This provided the original greenhouse effect, allowing the Earth to be warmed by the trapped rays of the Sun. By 1,800 mya (million years ago) oxygen began to be produced by algae photosynthesizing and first appeared in the atmosphere. The amount of oxygen continued to increase but was still probably only two-thirds of the present level when the first animals appeared 670 mya. Only after the ozone layer formed did it become safe for animals to leave the sea, and respiration became mainly aerobic.

During the Mesozoic era there may have been more oxygen than today as a result of algal blooms. It cannot have been more than about 24 percent or forest fires would have raged out of control. One theory suggests that dinosaurs achieved their large size thanks to abundant oxygen and became extinct when levels fell. The other side of the story of increasing oxygen has been one of decreasing carbon dioxide. As the Sun warmed, life kept pace with it by consuming the greenhouse gases and converting carbon dioxide into thick deposits of limestone, chalk, and fossil fuels. Now humans are burning those fuels, releasing the carbon dioxide back into the air. And the forests that recycle it back into oxygen and organic matter are being felled, so the greenhouse effect is increasing. Various predictions suggest that average global temperatures could rise by several degrees as a result.

Temperature and pressure

The temperature of the atmosphere is the balance between convection and radiation. The amount of heat contained at any level depends on the pressure or density as well as the temperature. In the thermosphere the temperature may be as high as 3,600°F (2,000°C), but the pressure is only a millionth of a billionth of that at sea level. The temperature falls steadily as the influence of solar radiation lessens, reaching a minimum about 50 mi. (80 km) above the ground; then it rises again. Temperatures fall through the stratosphere, where typical pressures are still only a hundredth of those on the surface, but through the troposphere it warms again, as anyone coming down a mountain will notice.

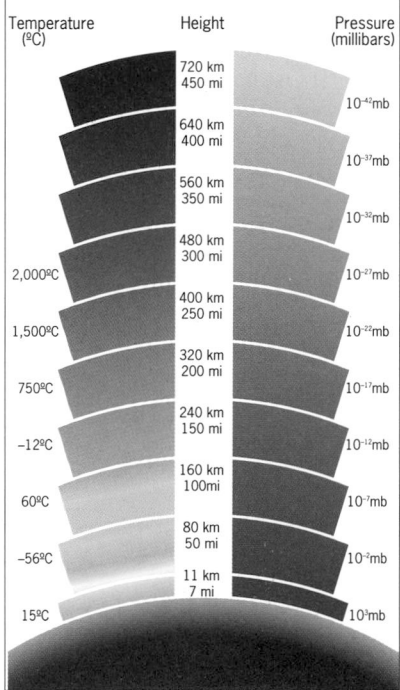

Temperature (°C)	Height	Pressure (millibars)
	720 km / 450 mi	10^{-42}mb
	640 km / 400 mi	10^{-37}mb
	560 km / 350 mi	10^{-32}mb
	480 km / 300 mi	10^{-27}mb
2,000°C	400 km / 250 mi	
1,500°C	320 km / 200 mi	10^{-22}mb
750°C	240 km / 150 mi	10^{-17}mb
−12°C	160 km / 100mi	10^{-12}mb
60°C	80 km / 50 mi	10^{-7}mb
−56°C	11 km / 7 mi	10^{-2}mb
15°C		10^{3}mb

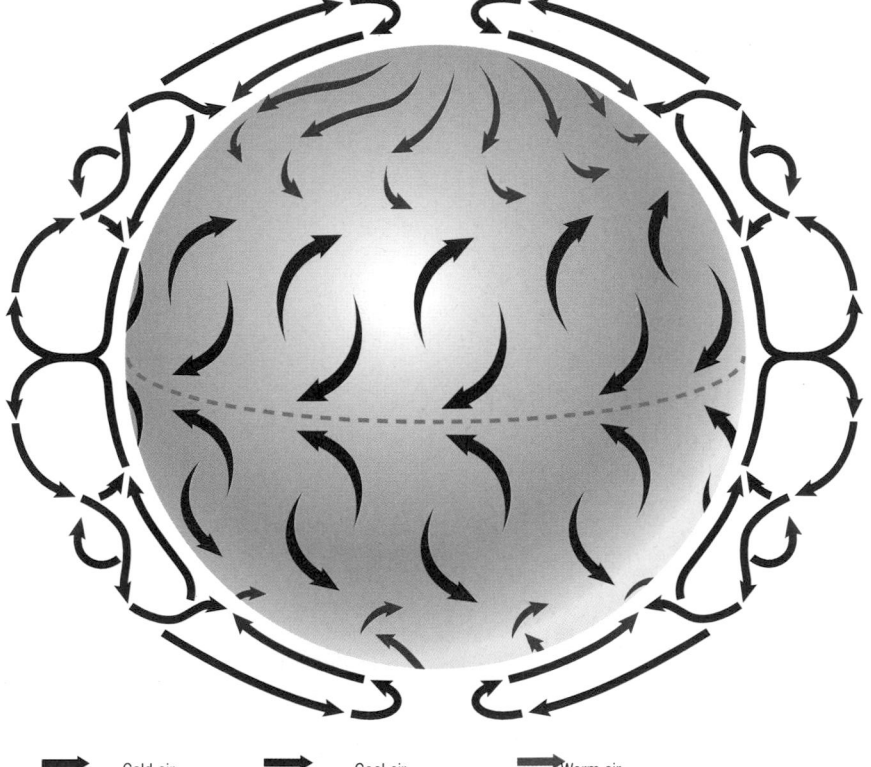

Cold air ➡   **Cool air** ➡   **Warm air** ➡

Heat circulation

The weather systems of the troposphere are constantly circulating like the cogs in a giant solar-powered engine. The Earth receives most solar energy around the equator and this causes evaporation and convection. Replacement air is drawn in from north and south, and convection cells transfer the heat in jet streams away from the equator. They descend in a band of high-pressure systems about 30°N and 30°S of the equator. That produces warm southwesterly winds near the ground. As the heat continues to move out from the equator, the next series of convection cells are completed by updrafts and accompanying low-pressure systems at latitudes of about 60°N and 60°S. These are often associated with heavy rains or snow. The poles are capped by relatively stable, high-pressure systems. At the same time, the rotation of the Earth produces the Coriolis force, which deflects weather systems to the east in the Northern Hemisphere and to the west in the Southern Hemisphere. It is against the backdrop of this global heat engine and consequent circulatory systems that weather patterns unfold.

COMPARISON OF PLANETARY ATMOSPHERES (% by weight)

Gas	Earth	Venus	Mars
Nitrogen	76.084	Trace	2.7
Oxygen	20.946		0.13
Carbon dioxide	0.031	97.0	95.32
Water	<1.0	0.1	0.03
Methane	0.00015		
Carbon monoxide	Trace	0.005	0.07
Inert gases	0.94	Trace	1.65
Halides		Trace	
Surface temp.	70°F	850°F	-180°F
Surface pressure	1 Bar	90 Bar	0.01 Bar

SEASONS

The most obvious seasonal variations on Earth are due to the 23.5° inclination of the Earth's axis to the plane of its rotation around the Sun. This produces hot summers and cold winters as a simple consequence of the different amounts of sunshine received at mid and high latitudes. Nearer the equator, seasonal temperature variations are less marked than variations in rainfall, so there the year is often divided into wet and dry seasons.

The most spectacular season is that of the monsoon in Southern Asia. Between April and October warm Southwesterly winds blow in off the Indian Ocean. This is released as extremely heavy rain when the winds rise over the heated land and begin to cool. Sri Lanka has rainy seasons in spring and fall, because the equatorial rain belt passes over it twice.

There are climatic cycles over much longer timescales—the Milankovitch cycles. The eccentricity of the Earth's orbit varies from nearly circular to more elliptical and back over a period of about 90,000 years. The time of year of the Earth's closest approach to the Sun varies over a period of 21,000 years. It currently occurs during the Southern Hemisphere summer, but that will be reversed in 10,000 years. These cycles all produce long-term climatic variations.

Climate change

There have clearly been many variations in the Earth's climate other than those produced by the cycles and wobbles of its orbit. Some changes are due to variations in the radiation reaching Earth from the Sun. Over its lifetime the Sun has been getting slowly brighter, but Earth has compensated for this by lowering carbon dioxide levels and reducing the greenhouse effect (*p. 74*). The Sun also has periods of low sunspot activity, known as Maunder minima, during which its radiation falls by a few percent. One such period caused the "little ice age" between 1530 and 1850, when fairs were held on the frozen Thames River in London.

Long-term trends in climate are very difficult to measure against the background of seasonal and annual variation. But there is evidence to suggest that average world temperatures have risen by about 1°F (0.5°C) during the last century. This follows closely the increasing levels of carbon dioxide caused by the large-scale clearing of the world's forests and the burning of fossil fuels. Climate models in computers mostly agree that, if the present trend continues, the overall climate could warm by about 4.5°F (2.5°C) by the year 2050. That may not seem much, but this is an average figure and local variations could be much more extreme. Some models suggest that the climate will become more polarized, with droughts in the tropics and more rainfall and storms in temperate zones.

New York and Oporto are on the same latitude but experience different winter climates.

December 21: the Sun is directly overhead at the Tropic of Capricorn and never sets, day or night, in Antarctica.

June 23: the Sun is overhead at the Tropic of Cancer and never sets in the Arctic. The Northern Hemisphere has its longest day.

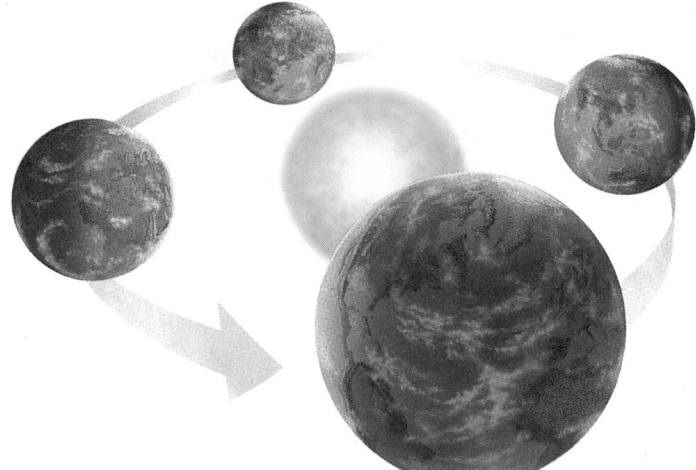

March 21: the Sun is directly overhead at the equator and everywhere on Earth has a 12-hour day (vernal equinox).

September 23: the Sun is overhead at the equator for autumnal equinox, which means equal day and night.

Climate extremes

The hottest place on Earth (annual average) is Dallol, Ethiopia, at 94°F (34.4°C).

The hottest recorded shade temperature was at al'Aziz yah, Libya, September 13, 1922, at 136°F (58°C).

The coldest place (on average) is Plateau Station, Antarctica, at -128°F (-89°C).

The driest place is the Atacama Desert near Calama, Chile, where no rainfall was recorded in over 400 years to 1972.

The most rainfall in 24 hours fell on Cilaos, Réunion, in the Indian Ocean, in March 1952: 74 in.(1,870 mm).

The greatest snowfall in 12 months fell at Paradise, Mt. Rainier, in Washington State, in 1971–72: 1,225 in. (31,102 mm).

The most rainy days in a year are the 350 experienced on Mt. Waialeali, Kaunai, Hawaii.

The least sunshine occurs at the North and South poles, where the Sun does not rise for 182 days of winter.

The maximum sunshine received is in the eastern Sahara: more than 4,300 hours a year (97% of daylight hours).

The highest surface wind speed was recorded on Mt. Washington, New Hampshire: 231 mph. (371 km/h).

CLIMATE

Whereas the weather anywhere on Earth can fluctuate day by day, even hour by hour, in ways that are very hard to predict in detail, climate describes the general weather conditions of a location, season by season, year by year, averaged out to something that is constant and predictable. That is not to say that the climate has remained constant over geological timescales. There have been huge variations with the changing composition of the atmosphere, the output of the Sun, and the changing positions of continents and ocean currents. For example, the onset of the Indian monsoon can be timed as coinciding with the initial uplift of the Himalayas which drive it. The climate is bound to change in the future too, with or without human help.

Atmospheric circulation

The different regional climates on Earth are governed by atmospheric circulation and to some extent by oceans. Both are driven by heat from the Sun. The cells of atmospheric circulation (*right*) reach several miles up into the troposphere (*p. 74*). The deepest, called the Hadley cell, rises at the equator and transports warm air north and south, returning cool air nearer the surface. The circulation continues across mid-latitudes in the lower Ferrel cell. Above that, between 3 and 6 mi. (5 and 10 km) up and not affected by friction from the land's surface, are jet streams that carry weather systems from west to east around the poles. They form a series of constantly shifting waves around regions of low and high pressure. The Ferrel cell underneath thus becomes complicated by eddies.

Tropical and polar air meet at the polar front. Where warm air rises above cooler air to form a front, moisture in it condenses to form clouds and heavy rain—the characteristic low-pressure system that often sweeps over Western Europe from the Atlantic. The position of the jet

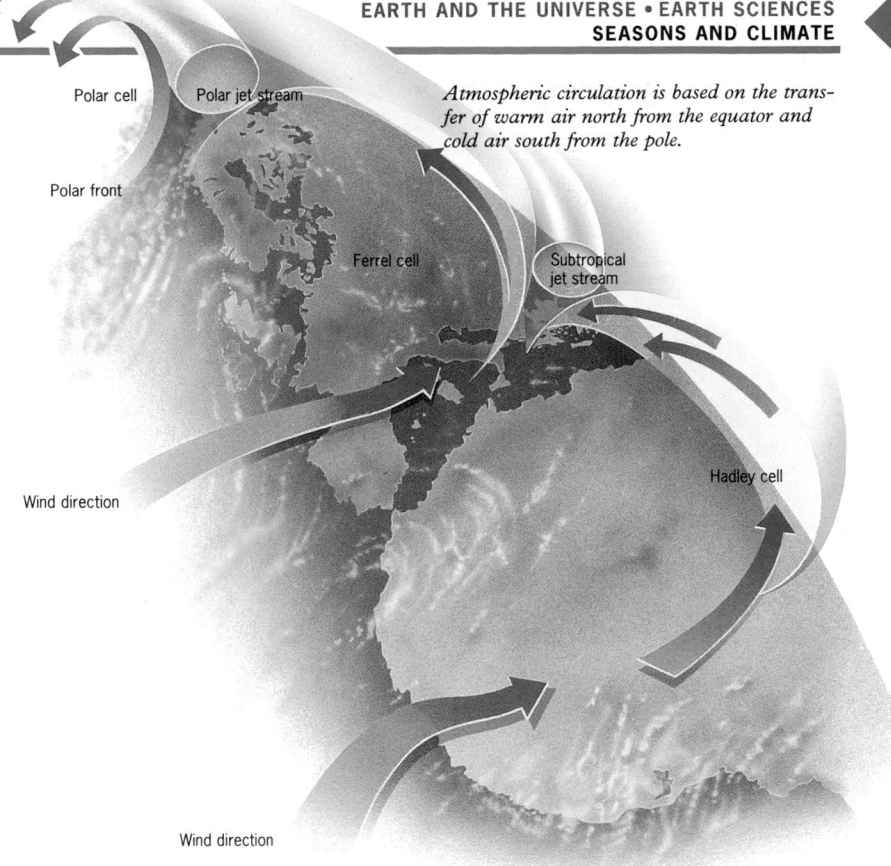

Polar cell
Polar jet stream
Polar front
Ferrel cell
Subtropical jet stream
Hadley cell
Wind direction
Wind direction

Atmospheric circulation is based on the transfer of warm air north from the equator and cold air south from the pole.

High-level jet streams are sometimes revealed by long strings of cirrus clouds.

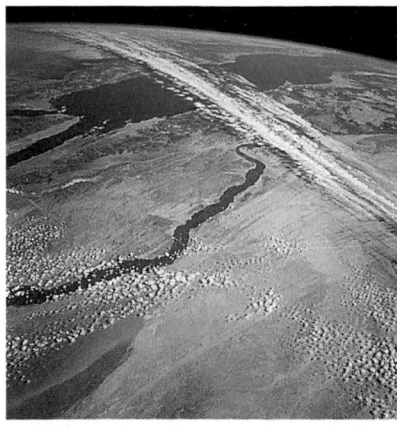

stream is important in determining whether the rain will fall on Iceland or London.

Climate zone factors

Averaged out over the year, temperatures are closely zoned to latitude. Temperatures in continental interiors tend to be more extreme—hotter in summer and colder in winter—than latitude would indicate, whereas oceans have a moderating influence—cooling the tropics but warming higher latitudes. Patterns of rainfall are more complex, although there is a tendency for continental interiors to be drier at subtropical latitudes but wetter closest to the equator.

Climate zones

There have been various systems of classifying climate, some with complex subsections, but essentially there are eight categories based on temperature and rainfall and thus vegetation. These are tropical/subtropical, steppe, arid, savanna, temperate/marine, continental, mountainous, and subpolar/polar. Within these there are local interactions of ocean and atmospheric circulation, continental position, and relief to be considered.

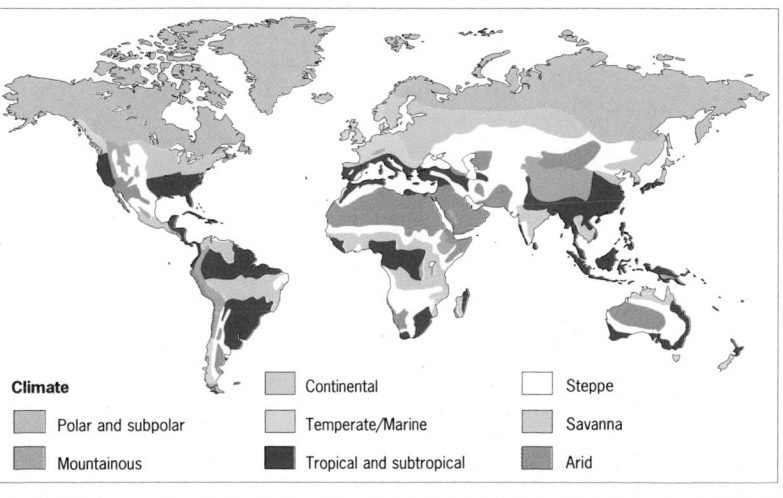

Climate
Polar and subpolar
Mountainous
Continental
Temperate/Marine
Tropical and subtropical
Steppe
Savanna
Arid

WEATHER

Climate affects whole regions and refers to weather patterns averaged out season by season over decades or even longer. Weather describes how the details of atmospheric conditions change day by day, or hour by hour, and refers to conditions at a much more local level.

Weather forecasting

Weather is determined by many factors — atmospheric pressure, humidity, temperature and winds. Small, unpredictable variations in any one of these factors can have cumulative and subsequently major effects on the others and the resulting weather systems. Meteorologists are, however, getting better at predicting the weather several days in advance. To do so requires thousands of measurements of existing weather conditions all over the world, from manned and automatic stations on the ground and at sea, from balloons, and from satellites in space. A variety of measuring instruments are used, the most common being the thermometer (temperature) and the barometer (atmospheric pressure).

Measurements are fed into a supercomputer which performs calculations based on mathematical models of typical weather systems. It calculates what is likely to happen at a series of points on the ground and in the air. The closer together those points are, the more accurate the forecast will be. A weather model can contain data for millions of points in the atmosphere. Even so, details of the forecast are sometimes wrong, but forecasts can generally predict accurately up to a week in advance.

Global winds

If the Earth were a smooth solid and not rotating, understanding wind systems would be easy. Heat would rise in the equatorial regions and warm, high-level winds would blow due north and south, returning toward the equator as cool winds at the surface (*p. 75*). But the Earth is spinning and has oceans and continents, hence the more complex patterns (*p. 77*). The Earth's rotation pulls the equator-bound winds to the west, creating the trade winds from the northeast in the region of the Tropic of Cancer and from the southeast at the Tropic of Capricorn. Other circulation cells provide the prevailing westerlies in the Northern Hemisphere and easterlies in the Southern Hemisphere. This is further complicated by the continents. During the Northern-Hemisphere winter, cold, dense air tends to flow out from the cold continental masses of Asia and North America. In July those continents are warmer and the air flow is reversed. The most spectacular example of this is the monsoon: warm, moist air blows into Asia from the Indian Ocean, depositing heavy rain as it crosses the Indian subcontinent and rises over the Himalayas.

Fronts

Much of the weather at temperate latitudes is dominated by the interaction between masses of cold and warm air.

WEATHER SYMBOLS

Accurate weather forecasting is based on synoptic charts compiled from data over a wide area, which is represented graphically by a variety of symbols.

Cloud types

⟋	Thick altostratus	⟍	Thin altostratus
⌐⟍	Scattered cirrus	⌐⟍⟍	Dense cirrus patches
⌐ᒑ	Partial cirrus cover	Ꝝᒑ	Complete cirrus cover
⟋ᵕ	Bands of thin altostratus	⟋	Patches of thin altostratus
⌒	Cumulus	⌄	Stratocumulus
- - -	Bad weather fractocumulus	—	Fair weather stratus

Cloud cover (octals – 1/8 parts)

○	Clear sky	◑	3/8	◗	6/8
◐	1/8	◑	4/8	◕	7/8
◔	2/8	◑	5/8	●	Completely overcast

Wind direction and speed (knots)

○	Calm	⟋	1–2	⟍	3–7
⟍	8–12	⟍	13–17	⟍⟍	18–22
⟍⟍	23–27	⟍⟍⟍	28–47	⟍	48–52

Precipitation

=	Mist	≡	Fog	∞	Haze	●	Rain
?	Drizzle	▽	Showers	✳	Snow	▲	Hail
△	Sleet	▽̇	Rain showers	▽̇	Rain and snow	✳̇	Snow showers
⌐	Thunderstorm	↯	Hurricane				
⌐	Sandstorm	)(	Tornado				

Fronts

▼▼▼	Cold front	▲▲▲	Warm front
▲▲▲	Occluded front	▲▲⌒	Stationary front

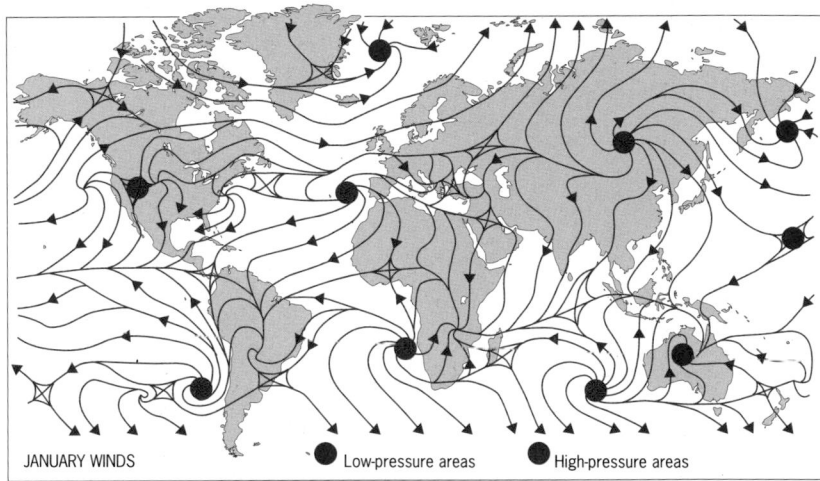

JANUARY WINDS   ● Low-pressure areas   ● High-pressure areas

The pattern of winds in January (above) and July (below) are basically produced by the presence of cells of low pressure, into which air flows, and high pressure, out of which air flows, but are complicated by the Earth's rotation and the distribution of land and sea.

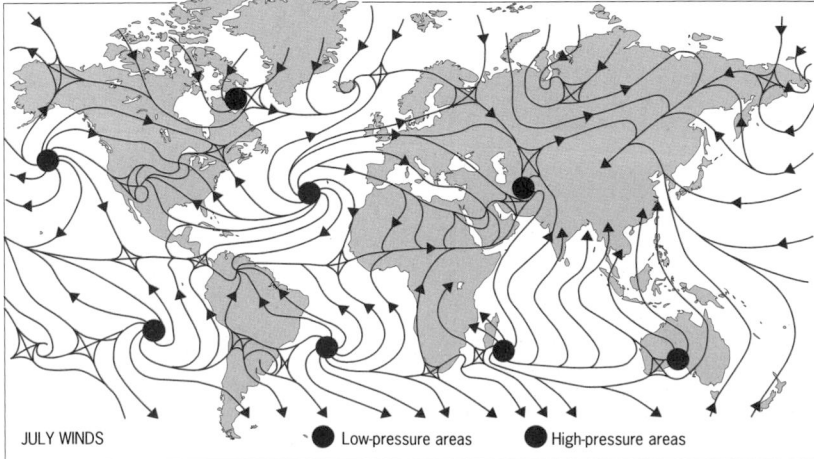

JULY WINDS   ● Low-pressure areas   ● High-pressure areas

They meet at what is known as a front (*right*), but do not mix. At a warm front, warm air rises above cold, creating a low-pressure system. Moisture in the warm air builds into clouds which may produce light precipitation. At a cold front cold air wedges in under warm air, clouds build again, this time resulting in heavier, more prolonged precipitation. As the warm air rises, the fronts eventually combine and lift off the ground to form what is known as an occluded front. The warm air then rises more slowly, the low-pressure system weakens and any precipitation eases off.

Clouds

Clouds are simply accumulations of condensed water vapor in the air. But their ever-changing patterns are quite revealing as to how and why they formed and what kind of weather they are heralding. There are three basic types of clouds — first described in 1804 by the English chemist Luke Howard: cirrus clouds, which are light and wispy, the word deriving from the Latin for "curl of hair;" cumulus, meaning a pile or heap; and stratus, describing clouds that spread out in a horizontal layer.

The height at which clouds form is also important. Cirrus clouds are usually very high — at an altitude of more than 16,500ft. (5,000m). Their drawn-out wisps are a sign of strong winds and changeable weather to come. Middle-altitude cumulus clouds include the white, piled-up fair-weather clouds, as well as altocumulus clouds, which bring light showers of rain. If they occur at lower altitudes, cumulus clouds can build into heavy rain clouds and dark, anvil-shaped cumulonimbus storm clouds. The latter can tower from 1,000–39,500ft. (300-12,000m) and result in thunderstorms.

Weather over northwestern Europe is dominated by low-pressure systems, or depressions, moving in from the North Atlantic. This false-color image of a frontal system shows clearly the results of the meeting of a mass of cold air with a mass of warm air. A swirling mass of clouds (low-level clouds are yellow, high-level clouds are white) is produced as warm air rises above cold at the warm front and cold air slides beneath warm at the cold front. This results in steady rainfall as the warm front passes and strong bursts of heavy, showery rain as the cold front passes.

Hurricanes, typhoons, cyclones, and tornadoes

Over very warm areas of ocean, warm, moist air starts rising so fast that it creates a region of intense low pressure beneath it, pulling more warm, moist air in from the sides. The phenomenon can develop into a vast spiraling weather system — a hurricane. Once formed, hurricanes can continue for many days. They tend to drift in the direction of the prevailing trade winds until they strike land. By then, the spiraling winds can reach speeds of 186mph(300km/h), and the whole weather system may be 500mi.(800km) across. In the middle — known as the eye — the air can be clear and deceptively still. But the other side of the storm is not far behind.

Huge cumulonimbus clouds release torrential rain and the winds whip up high waves on the surface of the ocean beneath the hurricane. The intense low pressure can temporarily raise sea-levels

Hurricane Juan photographed in 1985 from the space shuttle Challenger.

by as much as 25ft.(8m) in what is known as a storm surge, which can cause serious flooding. Once a hurricane is traveling over land, its supply of moist air is cut off and the storm eventually subsides.

Storms that arise in the North Atlantic and batter the Caribbean and southeastern U.S.A. are called hurricanes. Those in the Pacific that threaten Southeast Asia are typhoons, and those in the Indian Ocean that have caused such extensive flooding and damage in the Indian subcontinent are cyclones.

Tornadoes are also caused by rapidly rising spirals of air but they are on a much smaller scale than hurricanes, pulling air up into a thundercloud. Though affecting a smaller area, they can be just as devastating as hurricanes, tearing off roofs and sucking up almost anything in their path, resulting in some surprising objects raining down later.

HUMAN IMPACT

Humans have inhabited the Earth for only a fraction of its history, yet they have changed the face of the planet. Their impact is obvious to the eye, even from space: city lights and gas flares by night, sprawling urban areas and the unnaturally straight lines of intensive agriculture by day. With other sensors, vast tracts of pollution are obvious on land, in water, and in the atmosphere. Mapped over just a few decades, the destruction of forests, the spread of deserts, the reduction in stratospheric ozone, and the increase in greenhouse gases are dramatic. All are the result of human activity. In the past, the Earth has displayed a remarkable resilience, globally if not locally: today, an exploding population that demands ever-increasing affluence may be pushing the limits of the Earth's resources and its ability to process waste materials.

Interactive processes

At almost every stage the complex natural cycles between land, sea, and atmosphere can be influenced, augmented or upset by human activity (*below*). Most emissions follow the hydrological cycle. They can wash into ground water and rivers, dissolve in water vapor in clouds, and fall again to Earth in rain.

Mining and industry can release toxic metals and other wastes into ground water, and they release metals into the atmosphere as fine particles. They produce acidic gases, such as sulfur dioxide and nitrogen oxides, and greenhouse gases (*Composition, p. 74*), notably carbon dioxide. Human activities, using fossil fuels, notably power generation and transportation, are the biggest net emitters of greenhouse gases since they extract carbon

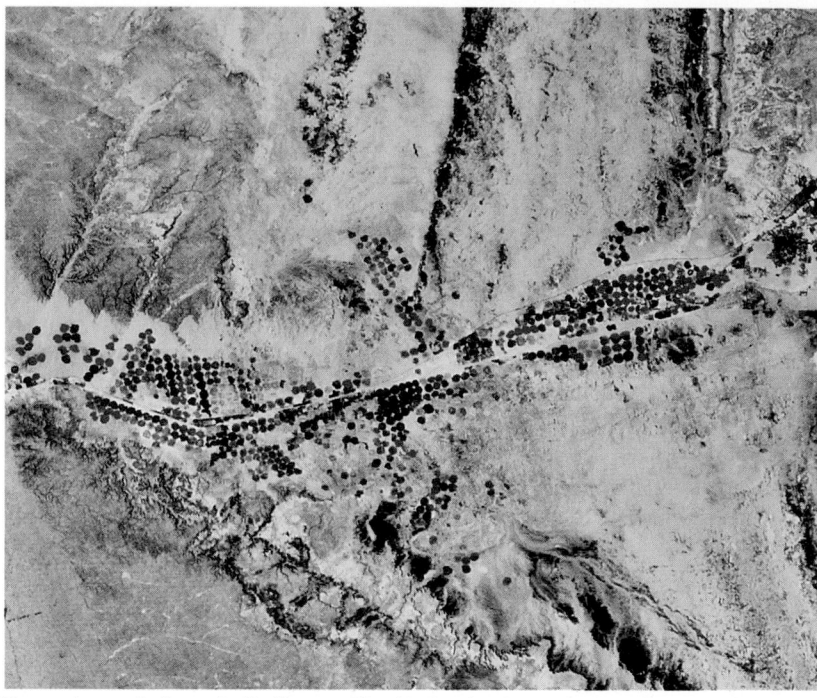

Human impact is dramatically illustrated by this Landsat image of pivotally irrigated wheat fields in a naturally barren region of Saudi Arabia. Young crops are red, mature ones black.

from nonrenewable energy sources.

Farming practices result in the release of nitrates and phosphates from fertilizers and animal waste into ground water and rivers, adding to sewage already released into rivers and seas and causing blooms of algae which subsequently deplete the oxygen in water. Although crops absorb carbon dioxide as they grow, they do not store it to the extent that a forest does, and rice cultivation and cattle raising produce another greenhouse gas, methane.

Clearance of natural vegetation releases carbon dioxide into the air and soil minerals into water and increases the likelihood of soil erosion.

Natural systems absorb some, but not all, of the excesses of human activity. Alkaline soils can neutralize acidic gases washed out of the air; forests, grasslands, and plankton can absorb carbon dioxide; some waste decomposes and some nutrients are recycled. But few human activities are sustainable in the long term.

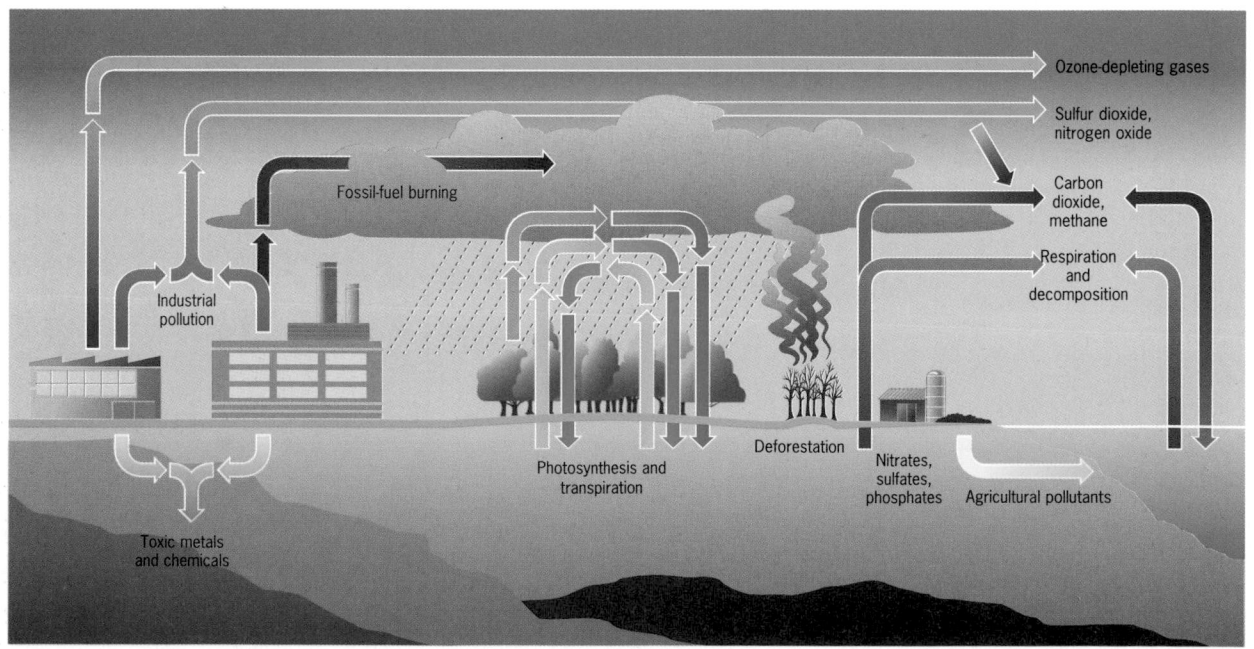

Riches from the Earth

The Earth is mined for building materials, metals, chemicals, and fuels. Powerful machinery, industrial processing, and international trade mean that individual deposits are exploited on a scale far beyond local needs. An estimated 23 billion tons of nonfuel minerals are extracted each year, about twice the amount of sediment carried each year by the world's river systems. As a result, an estimated 12 million acres of land are scarred each year. As the most concentrated ore deposits become exhausted, lower-grade ores are used, such that to produce an estimated nine million tons of copper in 1990, 990 million tons of ore had to be mined. The open pit Bingham Canyon copper mine in Utah, 2,500 ft.(775 m) deep, is the largest human excavation in the world.

The legacy of mining is not only the hole in the ground and the pile of spoil left behind: it can affect air and water over great distances. The Ilo smelter in Peru emits 600,000 tons of sulfur compounds each year, and cyanide in the waste affects marine life in a 500,000-acre area. Small-scale gold mining by hundreds of thousands of miners in the Amazon basin releases an estimated 100 tons of mercury into the river system each year.

Urbanization

As the world's population expands past the six billion mark, it becomes more and more unevenly distributed. The great concentrations do not always occur on the most productive land; and people tend to gravitate toward what are often already large cities. In 1950, the largest metropolitan areas were all in the developed world—New York, London, Tokyo, and Paris. Now those have been overtaken dramatically by Mexico City and São Paulo, with Shanghai, Calcutta, Bombay, and Jakarta rising rapidly on the list. The developing world's urban population is now larger than the total population of Europe, North America, and Japan combined. Many of the cities have grown beyond the control of planners and include illegal slums that pack millions of people together and concentrate pollution and disease. An estimated 600 million people in the cities of the developing world lack clean water, sanitation, and secure homes. Even if living standards improve, cities seem set to expand, putting more land under concrete and producing more fumes from industry and vehicles in congested streets.

Agriculture

Humans have farmed for thousands of years, but in just the last few decades burgeoning populations have called for more agricultural ingenuity than ever before. The breeding of new crop varieties, the use of fertilizers and pesticides and the bringing of more and more land under cultivation have kept production ahead of population growth throughout most of history. Since 1985, however, the limit seems to have been reached and per capita grain production has started to fall. In 1987, world grain reserves were sufficient for 100 days; by 1989 there were only enough for 54 days, yet there are 93 million more people to feed every year. There have been hidden costs to the increases in productivity. It is thought that about 40,000 people in the developing world die of pesticide poisoning every year. Twenty-four billion tons of topsoil are lost from crop lands each year, eroded by wind and water. Irrigation is lowering the water table beneath eight states in the Great Plains. by three feet (1 m) a year, and the diversion of rivers for irrigation in the former Soviet Union has reduced the Aral Sea to about a third of the size it was 25 years ago. One-tenth of the Earth's land surface is currently given over to agriculture but there will have to be yet further changes before food production is sustainable.

The changing atmosphere

The Earth's atmosphere is now changing more quickly than at any time in the past. In the last 150 years there has been a 25 percent increase in carbon dioxide and a 100 percent increase in methane in the atmosphere, largely as a result of the burning of fossil fuels, the expansion of agriculture, and rapid deforestation. Over the same period, the world has warmed by an average of 1°F (0.5°C), as greenhouse gases trap the Sun's heat within the atmosphere. Computer models predict a continued warming of 0.3°F (0.2°C) a decade unless steps are taken to limit emissions. The warming would be greater were it not for pollutants such as sulfur dioxide which scatter sunlight back into space. Other gases—notably CFCs (chlorofluorocarbons) from refrigerators, aerosols, and fire extinguishers—are damaging the tenuous layer of ozone (*below*) in the stratosphere which screens out ultraviolet radiation from the Sun. Steps have been taken to phase out CFCs. They are also powerful greenhouse gases, but legislation to reduce other greenhouse gases will be harder to implement since the practices that produce them are central to modern life. Many nations have pledged to reduce emissions to their 1990 levels by the year 2000, but stronger measures will be needed if global warming is to be averted.

Satellite images of the development of an ozone "hole" in the stratosphere over a ten-year period (1980, below left, to 1990) give cause for concern. First seen in 1979, the hole has grown steadily and is visible as the blue area covering most of Antarctica (outlined in black).

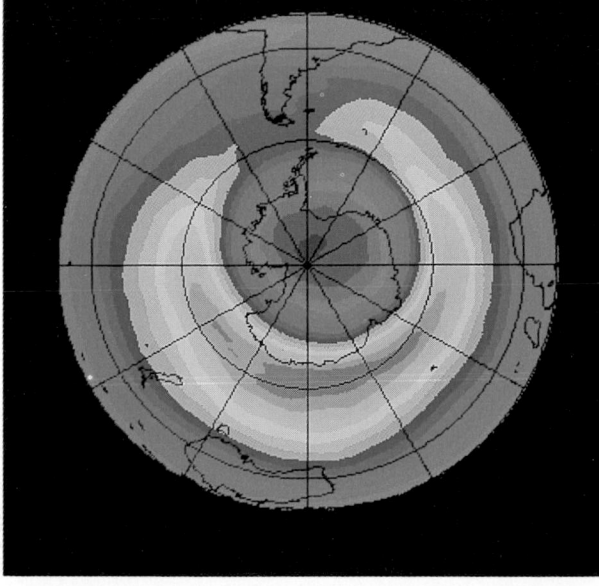
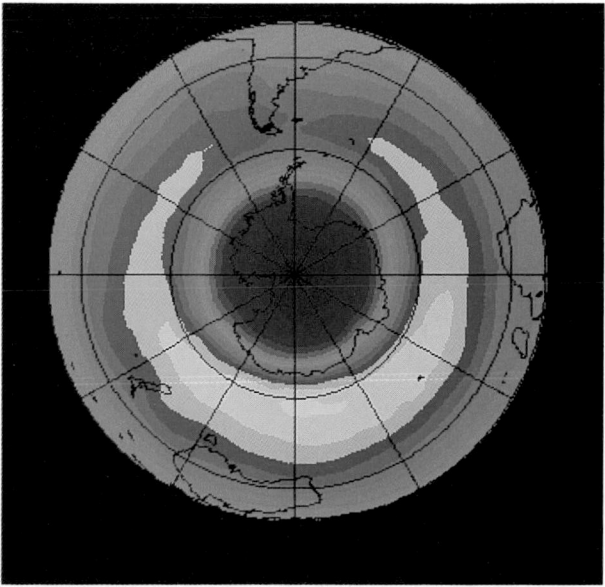

MAPMAKING

A map is a schematic representation of an area. Maps are primarily used to help locate places or plan a journey, and can range from a plan of a farm to a map of the world. Maps may also be used to illustrate information about a particular area; for example, distribution of population, resources, or climate. These specialized maps are known as thematic maps.

In any map the way reality is represented depends on the amount of information it contains, the use of diagrams and other graphic devices, and the scale—the size of the map in relation to the area it shows. The oldest surviving maps were made by the Babylonians more than 4,000 years ago. Many ancient map-makers assumed that the Earth was flat, but the circumnavigation of the globe in the 1400s led to great improvements in the accuracy of mapmaking.

Maps show a range of information by the use of symbols and approximations. The first stage of mapmaking is to construct a network of fixed points, from which everything else can be located. That way, subsequent errors will not accumulate and cause major distortions. Before mapmakers had aerial photographs and satellite images to help them, the fixed points were plotted by a process called triangulation. Triangulation points are set up on landmarks such as hilltops. From the angles between these points, distances can be calculated without the need to take measurements on the ground. Adding vertical angle measurements gives the heights. Height information on maps is normally shown as contours—lines linking points of the same elevation. It was by setting up a triangulation system across India from the coast to the Himalayas that cartographers first established that Mount Everest was the highest mountain in the world. Today, satellite images provide the framework and maps are stored on computer so that they can be updated quickly without the need for redrawing.

Latitude and longitude

Lines of latitude and longitude form a grid from which the position of any point on the Earth's surface can be measured. An obvious reference point is the equator and latitude is the angle of a place north or south of it as measured from the center of the Earth. Lines of latitude form horizontal rings around the Earth parallel with the equator. They become shorter as they get closer to the poles. Lines of longitude divide up the Earth through its poles, like the segments of an orange. Each line is a great circle going around the Earth. Lines of longitude have no obvious reference point such as the equator, so English navigators used the longitude of their home port, Greenwich, on the Thames River in London. Longitude is still measured east or west of the Greenwich meridian. Early navigators used the stars to find their position. Latitude was calculated from the heights of the stars in the sky or the position of the Sun as it rose, set, or reached its zenith. Longitude is also measured against the stars but it is necessary to know the exact time because the stars move east to west across the sky. It was only after the perfection of the marine chronometer by John Harrison in the mid-1700s that accurate longitude measurements, and hence accurate map-making, became possible.

Scales and symbols

A large-scale map can show a relatively high level of detail, whereas a small-scale map contains more information in relation to its size. The scale of a map is expressed as the ratio between the size of the map and the size of the corresponding area on the ground. This can be expressed as a simple ratio, for example 1:100, where one unit on a map is equal to 100 of the same units on the ground. Alternatively, the ratio may be expressed using different units, for example 1 inch:1 mile, in which one inch on the map represents one mile on the ground. Many maps also show scale in the form of a scale bar that can be used to calculate any distance on the map. The scale dictates the level of detail shown by the map. Because maps are smaller than the areas they represent, symbols are used to indicate the features on the ground. Many symbols do not resemble the things they represent and so they are often explained in a key.

Satellite photographs, such as this image of Moscow, have improved the accuracy of mapping.

Lines of longitude extend from pole to pole, north to south, and measure the angular distance east or west of the Greenwich meridian.

Lines of latitude run around the globe horizontally and measure the angular distance north and south of the equator.

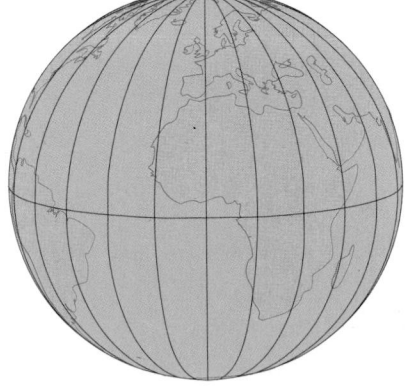

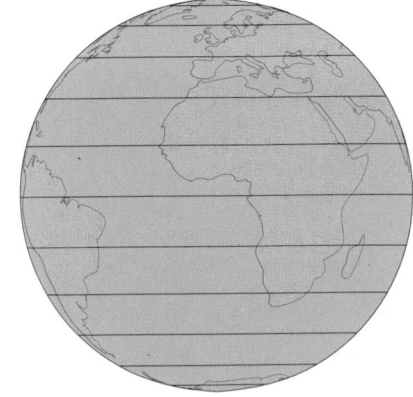

Map projections

Representing a globe on a flat plane requires the use of projections. Cylindrical projections are created by wrapping a piece of paper around the equator to form a cylinder. This was the principle used by the Flemish geographer Gerardus Mercator to draw one of the first reasonably accurate maps of the world in 1569. A Mercator projection shows equatorial regions very accurately and has the advantage that the shapes of the landmasses on the map are the same as on the ground, which is useful for navigators. However, away from the equator, the actual areas of the landmasses become more and more distorted so that Greenland seems bigger than Africa. A mercator projection is most distorted at the poles because the point of each pole is stretched out into a line as long as the equator.

Arno Peters, a German historian, devised an alternative in 1973. The Peters' projection is also cylindrical but it differs in that the north-south scale is adjusted so that the actual areas of the landmasses are accurately represented at all latitudes. Although Peters' projection shows the correct areas of all landmasses, it distorts their shapes. For example, Africa appears to have been stretched while Greenland seems squashed.

Another form of projection is the zenithal or azimuthal projection. The paper remains flat and touches the globe at one point. If this point is the North or South pole, lines of longitude show their correct angles. For this reason such projections are often used to represent polar regions.

A conical projection, in which the paper is rolled into a cone and placed over the globe to touch it along one line of latitude, shows countries with the minimum of distortion. Goode's projection is not strictly a projection but a series of manipulations of the curved surface of the sphere. Such maps look rather like the skin of an orange after it has been removed in one piece and rolled out flat. The continents are shown accurately but the oceans are opened up (interrupted) to stretch the segments onto the paper.

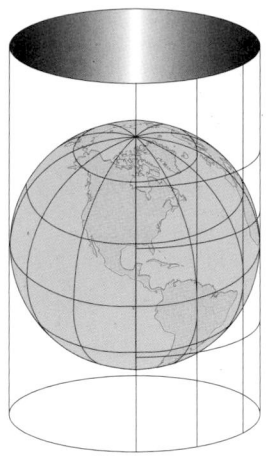

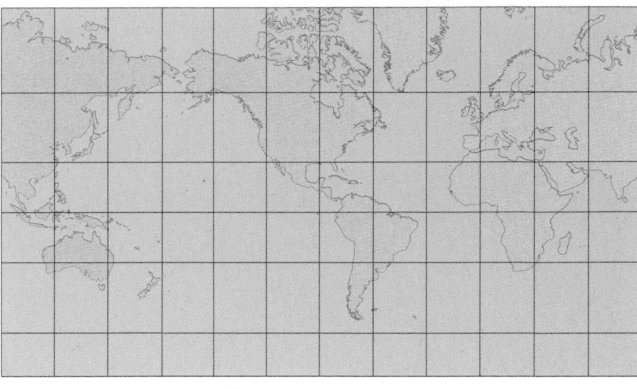

Mercator's projection (cylindrical)

Conical projection

Zenithal or azimuthal projection

Peters' projection (equal area) (*right*)

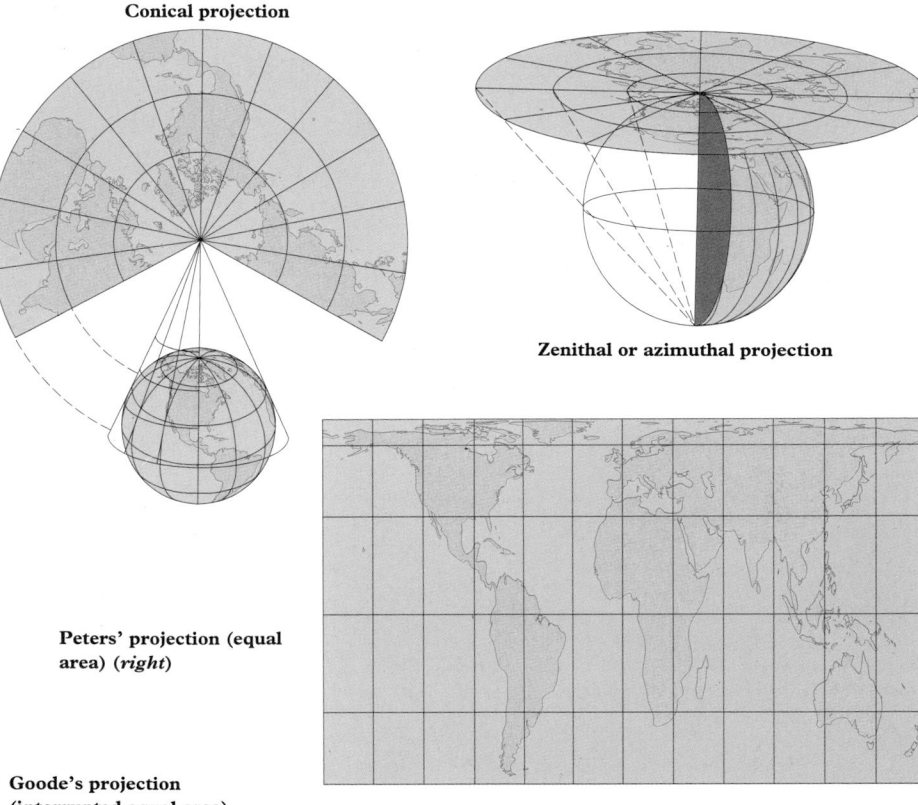

Goode's projection (interrupted equal area)

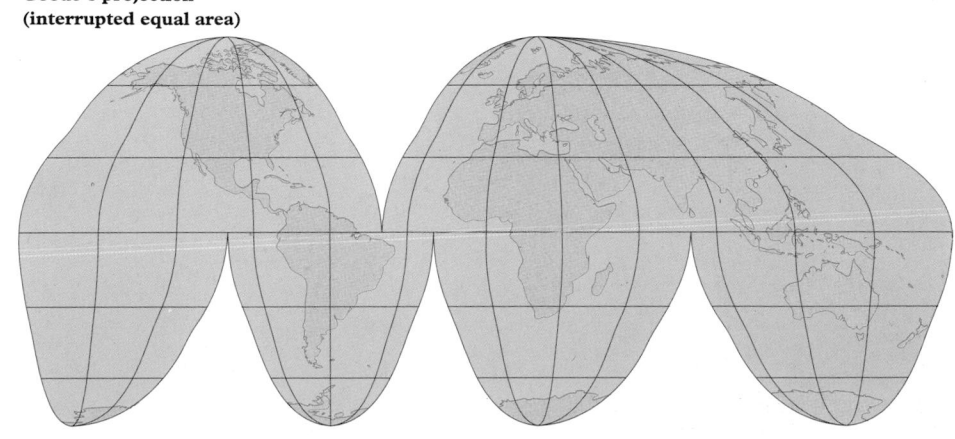

PROMINENT PEOPLE

AGASSIZ, Jean Louis (1807–73) Swiss-American glaciologist whose observations of the glacial transportation of rock material showed that glaciers move. He developed the concept of ice ages.

AGRICOLA, Georgius (1494–1555) German mineralogist and metallurgist. He recognized the erosive power of rivers and wrote a classification of minerals.

AKI, Keiiti (b. 1930) Japanese-American seismologist who introduced several concepts that formed the basis for measuring earthquake severity. He also developed seismic tomography.

BENIOFF, Victor Hugo (1899–1968) American geophysicist who developed seismic recording drums. He gave his name to the WADATI-Benioff zones where ocean crust subducts into the mantle.

BUFFON, Georges, Comte de (1707–88) French naturalist who anticipated aspects of evolutionary theory—that similar species are related—and recognized that landscape features were produced by processes still at work today.

BULLARD, Sir Edward (1907–80) English geophysicist who measured heat flow through the Earth's crust and developed the dynamo theory of the Earth's magnetism. He used computers to show how continents have moved.

BULLEN, Keith (1906–76) New Zealand geophysicist who determined the velocity of seismic waves through rocks of different densities, pinpointing earthquake epicenters and confirming the layered structure of the Earth.

CHAMBERLAIN, Thomas (1843–1928) U.S. geologist who confirmed the existence of Precambrian glaciations. He suggested that the Earth was formed from many smaller bodies and argued that it was at least 100 million years old.

COLBERT, Edwin (b. 1905) U.S. paleontologist who excavated dinosaur fossils and provided paleontological evidence for the theory of continental drift.

COX, Allan (1927–87) U.S. geophysicist who provided evidence of magnetic reversals over geological time and proved sea-floor spreading.

CUVIER, Baron Georges (1769–1832) French anatomist whose studies of comparative anatomy were vital in establishing the classification of fossils, extending the system of LINNAEUS.

DANA, James Dwight (1813–1895) U.S. geologist, mineralogist, and naturalist. Developed new theories on mountain building, volcanic activity, and the origins of continents and ocean basins. His *Manual of Geology* (1862) was an important textbook.

EWING, Maurice (1906–74) U.S. marine geologist who showed that ocean crust is thinner than continental crust. He determined the extent of mid–ocean ridges, their structure, and mapped ocean sediments around such ridges, supporting the theory of sea-floor spreading.

GILBERT, William (1544–1603) English amateur scientist who recognized that the Earth behaved like a giant magnet, and showed that magnetic declination could determine latitude at sea.

GUTENBERG, Beno (1889–1960) German–born American geophysicist who deduced from earthquake waves the existence of a zone in the mantle where seismic waves travel with low velocities. He correctly determined the depth of the Earth's core and its liquid nature.

HALL, Sir James (1761–1832) Scottish geologist who demonstrated the igneous origin of basalt and dolerite.

HALL, James (1811–1898) U.S. geologist and paleontologist. Made important studies of mountain formation, noting how the build up of sediment forces basins downward, while creating mountains around the edge of these depressions.

HESS, Harry (1906–69) U.S. marine geologist who discovered seamounts. Attracted by the idea of mantle convection proposed by HOLMES, he believed ocean crust was young and constantly renewed along mid-ocean ridges.

HOLMES, Arthur (1890–1965) English geologist who pioneered the dating of rocks from their radioactive constituents. He supported WEGENER's theory of continental drift and proposed that heat from radioactive decay could power it through mantle convection.

LINNAEUS, Carolus (1707–78) Swedish naturalist who founded the modern system of nomenclature for plants and animals, which is also used for fossil species.

LONSDALE, William (1794–1871) English geologist who proposed the Devonian geological period and postulated evolution ahead of Darwin.

LOVE, Augustus (1863–1940) English geophysicist who studied the propagation of waves in or on deformable solids, and introduced the concept of Love waves over the surface of a solid.

LYELL, Sir Charles (1797–1875) Scottish geologist whose uniformitarian principle suggested that, over long periods, forces at work today can bring about all observed geological features.

MARSH, Othniel Charles (1831–1899) U.S. paleontologist who conducted extensive expeditions of western North America. Credited with the discovery of more tha 1,000 fossil vertebrates and the description of 500 others.

MICHELL, John (1724–93) English geologist who, after the Lisbon earthquake of 1755, proposed that earthquakes set up wave motions in the Earth.

MILANKOVITCH, Milutin (1879–1958) Yugoslav geophysicist who linked the 21,000-year precession of the Earth's orbit and the 40,000-year period of variation in the tilt of the planets rotational axis to the amount of solar radiation reaching the Earth and hence with climatic cycles.

MOHOROVICIC, Andrija (1857–1936) Yugoslav seismologist who observed two distinct seismic-wave arrivals. He deduced that the slower followed a direct route from the earthquake focus while the faster was refracted from a discontinuity that marks the transition between the crust and the denser mantle.

MOHS, Friedrich (1773–1839) German mineralogist who developed a system for classifying minerals based on their physical as well as chemical properties. His concept of six crystal systems is still in use, as is his scale of hardness.

NAMIAS, Jerome (b. 1910) U.S. meteorologist who explored ocean-atmosphere interactions and developed weather forecasting.

OLDHAM, Richard (1858–1936) Irish seismologist who proved the existence of the Earth's core.

OSBORN, Henry (1857–1935) U.S. paleontologist and geographer. He helped usher in a modern era of museum displays but was also noted for his theory of adaptive radiation, whereby a single animal will evolve into different species in order to occupy ecological niches.

OWEN, Sir Richard (1804–92) English paleontologist who named and reconstructed many fossil skeletons. He first coined the term "dinosaur".

RICHTER, Charles (1900–85) U.S. seismologist who, with GUTENBERG, created a scale of earthquake magnitudes.

ROSSBY, Carl-Gustaf (1898–1957) Swedish-born American meteorologist who recognized the large-scale wavelike motions in the upper atmosphere.

SMITH, William (1769–1839) English civil engineer who was the first to use fossils to identifiy and date rock strata.

STENO, Nicolaus (1638–86) Danish anatomist who found what he recognized as shark's teeth far inland. He championed the organic nature of fossils and believed that sedimentary strata were laid down in ancient seas.

SUESS, Eduard (1831–1914) Austrian geologist who studied the evolution of mountains. He investigated deep ocean trenches and volcanic islands, and proposed the existence of an ancient supercontinent long before the theory of continental drift.

VINE, Frederick (1939–88) English geophysicist who used maps of marine magnetic anomalies to confirm the hypothesis of sea-floor spreading.

WADATI, Kiyoo (b. 1902) Japanese seismologist who first detected deep earthquakes. With BENIOFF he named the zones where ocean crust subducts into the Earth's mantle.

WEGENER, Alfred (1880–1930) German meteorologist and geophysicist. He suggested that the continents had once been joined as the supercontinent of Pangaea. No mechanism was known for continental drift and his hypothesis remained controversial until the 1960s.

WERNER, Abraham Gottlob (1749–1817) German geologist who was one of the first to classify rocks.

TERMS

For rock, mineral, and fossil names and names of geological periods, see tables or text in relevant sections.

Abyssal plain The deep and relatively level floor of the ocean, typically 6,500–20,000 ft.(2,000–6,000 m) deep with a slope of less than 1:1,000.

Accretion i) The process of enlargement of a continent by the addition of crustal fragments. ii) The formation of planetary bodies from coalescing fragments.

Acidic rock An IGNEOUS ROCK with more than 63% quartz.

Active margin A continental margin characterized by earthquakes, volcanoes, or mountain building as a result of a converging crustal plate.

Aeolian deposits Sediments deposited by wind and consisting of sand or dust.

Alluvium Sand, silt, and mud deposited by a river or flood.

Amber Fossilized tree sap commonly containing the bodies of extinct insects and plants that became stuck in the sap thousands of years ago when it was in a liquid state.

Ammonite An extinct group of cephalopods usually with a coiled shell and consisting of successive body chambers.

Anticline A type of rock fold shaped like an arch.

Aquifer Rock formation containing water in recoverable quantities.

Arenaceous rock SEDIMENTARY ROCK composed principally of particles the size of sand grains.

Argillaceous rock SEDIMENTARY ROCK composed of particles the size of silt or clay.

Asthenosphere The upper MANTLE: the layer of the Earth below the LITHOSPHERE. Low SEISMIC WAVE velocities suggest it is partly molten.

Auriole Area surrounding an igneous INTRUSION affected by metamorphic changes.

Basalt A fine-grained volcanic rock, dark in color and composed of plageoclase feldspar and pyroxene.

Basic rock IGNEOUS ROCK with low silica content.

Batholith A large body of intrusive igneous rock, frequently GRANITE.

Bedding The layering in SEDIMENTARY ROCKS due to chemical, physical, or biological changes between successive layers.

Benioff zone A plane beneath an OCEAN TRENCH or dipping under continents associated with earthquake activity where ocean CRUST subducts.

Biostratigraphy The identification and correlation of rock layers based on the fossils within them.

Bioturbation Structures or mixing in layered sediments due to organisms burrowing within them.

Breccia Coarse-grained rock made up of angular fragments of pre-existing rocks.

Calcareous rock Sediment containing a large amount of calcium carbonate, e.g. chalk or limestone.

Carbonaceous rocks Sedimentary deposits containing carbon derived from plants, e.g. coal, peat, and lignite.

Cleavage The splitting of a crystal along planes parallel to possible crystal faces, or the splitting of a rock into thin sheets.

Continental drift The process proposed by Alfred Wegener in 1912 to explain the shapes and distribution of the continents. He suggested that they once formed a single landmass and have drifted apart.

Continental shelf A gently sloping zone on the ocean floor, underlying a relatively shallow sea, between land and the deep ocean.

Core The central part of the Earth below 1,800 mi.(2,900 km), believed to be made of iron and nickel.

Coriolis force The deflection of bodies relative to the Earth's surface caused by the Earth's rotation.

Craton The ancient, stable part of a continent.

Crust The outermost layer of the Earth's LITHOSPHERE composed of relatively low-density rocks. Continental crust is largely granitic, oceanic crust is largely basaltic in composition.

D layer The discontinuous layer up to 125mi.(200km) thick at the base of the lower MANTLE.

Dendrochronology The use of tree rings for establishing the age or relative age of timber or the deposits in which it is found.

Deposition The laying down of eroded material after being transported by an erosive agent, e.g. wind or rivers.

Diagenesis Changes in a SEDIMENTARY ROCK after DEPOSITION that take place at low temperatures and pressures, e.g. compaction and cementation.

Dike Nearly vertical sheet of intrusive igneous rock.

Dip The angle that a rock bed makes with the horizontal.

Doldrums Meteorological term used to describe a humid area either side of the equator where the northeast and southeast trade winds converge, creating an area of low pressure, characterized by little or no wind, interrupted by sudden violent storms.

Drift A general name for superficial sediments often dating from the last ice ages.

El Niño A warm Pacific current moving east toward South America. It develops around Christmas every two to seven years and causes widespread climatic disturbance.

Epicenter The point on the surface of the Earth lying immediately above the focus of an earthquake.

Erosion Process by which material is broken down and transported by agents such as water, wind, gravity, ice, or living organisims, including human activity: e.g. the removal of sediment by a river that is carried downstream and eventually

deposited (*see also* WEATHERING).

Fault A fracture in rocks along which displacement has taken place, normally during an earthquake.

Folding The bending of strata usually as a result of compression.

Foraminifera Marine microorganisms with complex chambered, usually calcareous shells, often used as zone fossils.

Front The boundary between masses of cold and warm air or water.

Gaia hypothesis The concept of the Earth as a single, self-regulating entity proposed by James Lovelock.

Gastropod Class of mollusk usually with a single coiled, typically helical, calcareous shell, e.g. snails, whelks, and limpets.

Glaciation The processes and products arising from the presence of ice masses on the Earth.

Gondwanaland The Paleozoic continent of the Southern Hemisphere that is believed to have broken up to form South America, Africa, India, Australia, and Antarctica.

Goniatite Order of cephalopod pre-dating and possibly ancestral to AMMONITES.

Granite A coarse-grained IGNEOUS ROCK containing about 25% quartz, abundant feldspar, and mica or other minerals.

Graptolite Group of extinct colonial marine organisms of the Paleozoic era with individuals arrayed along one or more branches or stipes.

Greenhouse effect Phenomenon by which thermal radiation from the Sun is trapped in the Earth's atmosphere by water, carbon dioxide, and other gases that prevent its reemission from the planet's surface and cause an increase in the surface temperatures.

Ground water Water within the hydrological cycle that flows beneath the surface of the Earth but on the top of impermeable rock which may flow into a body of water or be stored in the form of AQUIFERS.

Gulf Stream Ocean current that flows from the Gulf of Mexico across the Atlantic Ocean and becomes known as the North Atlantic Drift. The current brings warm water and has a moderating affect on the climate of northern Europe.

Hardness The resistance of a mineral to abrasion, measured on Mohs' scale by comparison with ten standards ranging from talc to diamond.

Horizon The surface or thin layer between two beds of rock.

Hot spot Geothermal or volcanic activity on the Earth's surface resulting from heat and/or MAGMA rising in a MANTLE PLUME.

Humus Dark brown, nutrient-rich, organic material that is found in the top layer of soil, formed by the decomposition of plant and animal matter.

Hydrothermal vents Submarine outflows of geothermally heated water, often containing dissolved minerals and usually associated with a MID-OCEAN RIDGE.

Igneous rock Rock believed to have

formed by the solidification of MAGMA injected into the Earth's CRUST or extruded on to its surface.

Intrusion Mass of IGNEOUS ROCK formed by the injection of MAGMA into pre-existing rock.

Inversion layer Layer of cooler air overlying warm air.

Ionosphere Region of the upper atmosphere where high-energy solar radiation ionizes atoms, forming a layer which reflects shortwave radio signals.

Island arc A chain of volcanic islands formed above a convergent ocean plate boundary.

Joint An actual or potential crack in a rock, often perpendicular to the BEDDING, with no displacement.

Laurasia The supercontinent in the Northern Hemisphere that corresponded to GONDWANALAND in the Southern Hemisphere.

Lava The molten rock material that issues from a volcanic vent or fissure.

Leaching 1. The removal of soluble minerals from soil by percolating water. 2. The extraction of metallic compounds from ores using solvent.

Lithosphere The outer rigid shell of the Earth above the ASTHENOSPHERE. It includes the CRUST and hard top of the MANTLE that comprise tectonic plates.

Loess Homogenous blanket deposit of fine dust originally wind blown.

Luster A property describing the quality and quantity of light reflected from a mineral surface, e.g. metallic, vitreous, silky, resinous.

Mafic Mnemonic for ferromagnesian minerals in an IGNEOUS ROCK.

Magma Molten rock formed by melting at depth which rises to the surface as LAVA or solidifies underground as an INTRUSION.

Magnetic reversal A change of the polarity of the Earth's magnetic field. Often recorded by magnetic minerals trapped in volcanic rocks and used as the first proof of SEA-FLOOR SPREADING.

Magnetosphere The region surrounding the Earth in which charged particles are affected by the Earth's magnetic field.

Mantle The bulk of the Earth between CRUST and CORE, i.e. approximately 25–1,800mi.(40–2,900km) in depth.

Mantle plume Upwelling of hot and therefore less dense MANTLE rock, often partially melting as it rises and giving rise to MAGMA.

Mesophere Layer of the Earth's atmosphere above the STRATOSPHERE and below the THERMOSPHERE, between about 30mi.(50km) and 50mi.(80km) above the ground.

Metamorphic rock A rock changed in mineral or structural characteristics by heat and/or pressure.

Mid-ocean ridge A major, largely submarine mountain range where two crustal plates are pulled apart and new volcanic LITHOSPHERE is created.

Milankovitch cycle Theory that changes

in the amount of solar radiation received on Earth resulting from changes in its axial inclination account for climate changes such as the ice ages.

Mineralization The process by which minerals are introduced into a rock, e.g. in percolating solutions.

Mohorovicic discontinuity (Moho) The boundary between the Earth's CRUST and MANTLE, marked by a change in SEISMIC WAVE velocity.

Moraine Material deposited by a glacier or ice sheet.

Nappe Huge recumbent fold produced by a combination of compression and gravity during the building of mountain chains such as the Alps.

Ocean trench A long, narrow, deep depression in the ocean floor produced by movements in the Earth's CRUST.

Orogeny Formation of mountain ranges by upward displacement of the Earth's crust.

Ostracod Small arthropod with a bivalve shell. Range from Cambrian to present, used as zone fossils in the Jurassic.

Pangaea A supercontinent pre-dating GONDWANALAND and LAURASIA.

Permafrost Subsoil or rock which is permanently frozen, often found in polar and sub-polar regions such as the Antarctic and Arctic.

Phenocryst Large crystals found in a finer-grained IGNEOUS ROCK, resulting from earlier, slower partial crystallization.

Pillow lava LAVA with a pillowlike structure resulting from rapid quenching in an underwater eruption.

Pyroclastic flow Mixture of LAVA fragments and steam or gas which can flow from a volcano at high velocities.

Reservoir Geological term used to describe porous rock containing deposits of oil and/or gas.

Richter scale Logarithmic scale of earthquake magnitude devised by Charles Richter in 1935.

Rift valley An elongated downthrown block of the Earth's CRUST bounded by faults along either side.

Scarp and **dip** The two slopes formed by outcropping of a bed of SEDIMENTARY ROCK. A scarp is usually a steep slope and a dip is more gentle.

Sea-floor spreading Process by which new ocean CRUST is created as a result of the upwelling of MAGMA at MID-OEAN RIDGES.

Seam Horizontal, layered deposit of a mineral, especially used to describe deposits of coal.

Seamount Mountain rising from the ocean floor.

Sedimentary rock Rock that results from the DEPOSITION of the eroded remains of pre-existing rocks or formed from the remains of organisms or deposited from solution.

Seismic surveying Method of surveying using shock waves generated by explosives to map the rock layers below the Earth's surface.

Seismic tomography The imaging of structures within the Earth using data from numerous earthquakes.

Seismic waves Shock waves transmitted through the Earth from earthquake foci.

Sial The discontinuous shell of granitic composition that forms the foundations of the continents: composed of siliceous and aluminous minerals.

Sill A sheet-like intrusion of IGNEOUS ROCK more or less parallel to the BEDDING planes of rocks.

Silt material of an earthy character intermediate in grain size between sand and clay.

Sima The lower layer of the Earth's CRUST made of dense rocks containing silicon and magnesium.

Stalactite An iciclelike mass of limestone attached to the roof of a cave.

Stalagmite A mass of limestone sticking up from the floor of a cave formed by the water dripping off a STALACTITE.

Stratosphere Layer of the Earth's atmosphere above the TROPOSPHERE and below the MESOSPHERE.

Streak The color of the line of powder produced when a mineral is scratched or rubbed across unglazed porcelain.

Stromatolite A layered or domed calcareous sediment formed by algal mats.

Subduction The process in which a crustal plate moves under an over-riding plate.

Syncline A concave, U-shaped fold in rocks.

Tectonics The study of the structures that form the Earh's CRUST and the forces that change it, either large- or small-scale.

Thermosphere Layer of the Earth's atmosphere above the MESOSPHERE (50mi.[80km] and above). Includes the IONOSPHERE.

Trilobite Extinct marine arthropod with a segmented oval body found from the Cambrian to the Permian period.

Tropopause The boundary between the TROPOSPHERE and the STRATOSPHERE.

Troposphere The lower 8.5mi.(13.5km) of the Earth's atmosphere in which most clouds are found and where commercial aircraft fly.

Tsunami A destructive sea wave caused by an earthquake or submarine volcanic eruption.

Ultra-basic rock IGNEOUS ROCK containing less than 45 percent silica and large amounts of MAFIC minerals.

Van Allen belts Radiation belts consisting of charged particles from the Sun that become trapped in the Earth's magnetic field at a height of 1,200mi.(1,900km) above the Earth.

Weathering Process by which material is broken down in situ and not transported as in the case of EROSION, e.g. the action of water freezing to ice and chipping parts of a rock away.

Xenolith A fragment of extraneous rock incorporated in MAGMA and often metamorphosed by it.

SECTION 2
LIFE ON EARTH

THE ORIGIN OF LIFE

The earliest traces of life on earth have been found in rocks about 3.5 billion years old. They are layered structures similar to those formed by some of today's marine bacteria, and it is generally accepted that the first forms of life were some kind of bacteria. We do not know exactly how these first living things or organisms were produced, and probably never will, but laboratory experiments suggest that energy from lightning or from ultraviolet radiation could have caused gases, such as methane and ammonia, to combine with simple minerals to produce proteins and life's other building blocks. Such reactions probably took place in shallow water.

As more and more of life's building blocks were formed, they inevitably mingled and reacted with each other to form new compounds. Eventually, a chance combination gave rise to a molecule of DNA, a self-replicating material that is the basis of all living matter (*p. 90*). Here, perhaps, was the "spark of life," and the scene was then set for the appearance of the first cells and the subsequent evolution of all life on earth. Since the beginning of life, millions of different kinds of organisms have come and gone. It is estimated that there are about 300,000 different kinds of plants in the world at the present time, and there may be more than five million kinds of animals—or by some estimates, nearer ten million—although only a little over a million of these have so far been described.

The five kingdoms of life

Until fairly recently, all living things were classified as either plants or animals. This simple division is perfectly adequate for nonscientific purposes, but most biologists now recognize five separate kingdoms of life, based largely on microscopic structure and biochemical activity. These are the bacterial kingdom, or Prokaryotae (*right*); the Protoctista (*right*); the fungal kingdom (*pp. 92–93*); the plant kingdom (*pp. 94–113*); and the animal kingdom (*pp. 114–43*).

The characteristics of living things

Although we cannot give a simple definition of life, there are seven distinctive features that are shared by all living things and distinguish them from inanimate objects. These characteristics are:
Movement
Excretion (elimination of waste products)
Respiration or breathing
Reproduction
Irritability (also called sensitivity)
Nutrition or feeding
Growth
The initial letters of these features form the word MERRING, a convenient mnemonic for keeping them in mind.

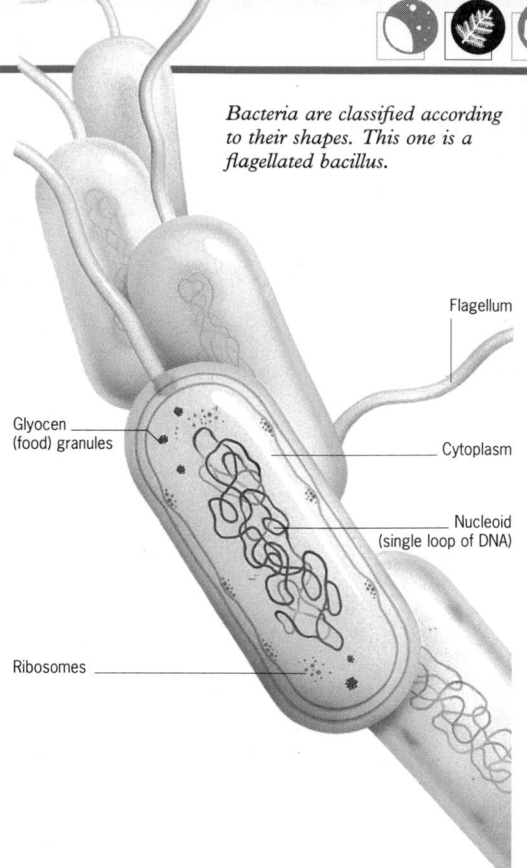

Bacteria are classified according to their shapes. This one is a flagellated bacillus.

Glyocen (food) granules

Ribosomes

Flagellum

Cytoplasm

Nucleoid (single loop of DNA)

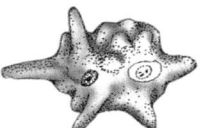

Amoeba

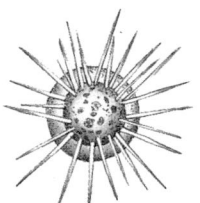

Ammodiscus

The kingdom Protoctista

This kingdom contains all the single-celled organisms in which there is a distinct nucleus enclosed in a membrane and in which there are also other discrete organelles, such as mitochondria and endoplasmic reticula (*p. 89*). It includes all those microscopic organisms, such as amoeba (*left*) and paramecium, that were once regarded as single-celled animals and placed in the phylum Protozoa. It also includes the slime molds.

The kingdom Prokaryotae

This kingdom contains the bacteria. These are all microscopic, single-celled organisms, but their structure is very different from that of other single-celled organisms, with no obvious nuclei or other well-defined structures—organelles—within the cells. There is no sexual reproduction, and increase in numbers is brought about solely by cell division, sometimes as often as once every 15 minutes. Some bacteria can carry out photosynthesis using the energy of sunlight, as plants do, but most rely on other chemical reactions to provide their energy.

Bacteria play a major role in the natural world, where they are heavily involved in the breakdown of dead plants and animals and the return of minerals to the soil. Many others, of course, cause diseases of plants and animals, including humans.

These strange organisms, whose lives involve several changes of form, have variously been regarded as fungi and animals. The Protoctista also contains almost all the algae. The latter were originally treated as plants because they contain chlorophyll and make food by photosynthesis (*p. 94*). The large seaweeds (*below*) are included in the Protoctista because, although they are multicellular organisms, their cells are all alike and not easily distinguished from single-celled algae.

Seaweeds

The seaweeds include species with fronds many meters long and made up of millions of cells, but they are included with the single-celled organisms in the Protoctista because their cells are all more or less alike. Some biologists regard the seaweeds as assemblages of cells rather than truly multicellular organisms. There are three major groups or phyla—the green seaweeds (Chlorophyta), the brown seaweeds (Phaeophyta), and the red seaweeds (Rhodophyta). All contain chlorophyll and make their food by photosynthesis, but the brown and red seaweeds contain other pigments that mask the chlorophyll. They have a variety of reproductive strategies.

ANIMAL AND PLANT CELLS

All living things are made of cells and, except for those of the bacteria (*p. 88*), the cells all have much the same internal structure, although their external appearance varies enormously according to the jobs they have to do. A variety of animal cells are shown on the right below. There are several hundred different kinds of cells in the human body, and the total number of cells may exceed ten trillion. Most of them are obviously extremely small, and it is only recently that powerful microscopes have revealed their detailed structure.

The nucleus, the most conspicuous of the internal structures or organelles, is the cell's control center. It is bounded by the nuclear membrane and it contains the chromosomes that carry all the hereditary material. The nucleolus produces the ribosomes, which themselves are responsible for the formation of the cell's proteins. This takes place on the surface of the endoplasmic reticulum, which is a network of flattened tubes connected to the nuclear membrane and spreading throughout the cell. The golgi complex is a sort of warehouse where proteins are sorted and assembled and then dispatched to other parts of the cell or secreted to the outside. The mitochondria are the cell's generators, combining food and oxygen to release the energy needed to power all the cell's other activities. The cell membrane keeps the cell's components together, but it has numerous pores through which food and other vital materials can diffuse in and out of the cell. The cytoplasm, often called protoplasm, is a watery material containing a range of organelles where most of the cell's chemical reactions take place.

All of the above cell components or organelles can be found in both animal and plant cells, but plant cells have an additional feature—a rigid cell wall made of cellulose. Most plant cells also contain a large fluid-filled space called the vacuole, and it is the pressure of this fluid that gives the green tissues their rigidity. If a plant cannot get sufficient water, its cells become limp and the whole plant is in danger of collapsing.

"Typical" animal cell

Lysosome

Cell membrane

Mitochondrion

Golgi complex

Nucleus

Chromosomes

Endoplasmic reticulum

"Typical" plant cell

Vacuole

Nucleolus

Nuclear membrane

Ribosomes

Cell wall

Chloroplast

Cell membrane

White blood cell

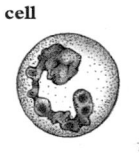

Epithelial cell

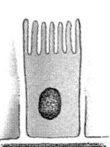

Osteocytes (bone cell)

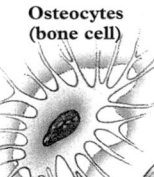

Smooth muscle cell

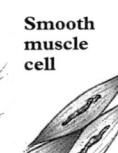

Conductive cell

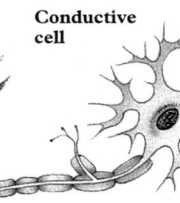

Viruses

Viruses are on the borderline of living and nonliving things and do not fit into the five kingdoms of the living world. They are much smaller than bacteria, and each consists simply of a lump of DNA inside a protein envelope.

There are many different kinds of viruses and they all produce disease in plants and animals by invading living cells and interfering with their normal functions. The viruses can be converted to a crystalline form, in which they can survive for a very long time, but they cannot grow or reproduce on their own. They need the help of the host cells for this. The virus DNA takes control of the cell nucleus and "instructs" it to make more virus matter. The new virus particles then escape from the host cell and rapidly infect other cells. Human diseases caused by viruses include the common cold, measles, polio, and AIDS.

Classification

Every different kind of organism is called a species, and closely related species are grouped together into genera (the singular of which is genus). Each species has a two-part scientific name, composed of its generic name and its species name. For example, the housefly, which belongs to the genus *Musca*, is scientifically known as *Musca domestica*. Where a number of members of the genus *Musca* are mentioned, later examples may be abbreviated to, for instance, *M. domestica*. (By convention the genus name begins with a capital letter.)

Related genera are grouped into families, related families are grouped into orders, orders are grouped into classes, and classes are grouped into phyla. The latter are the largest divisions of each kingdom. Family names in the animal kingdom always end in ...*idea*, while plant families always end in ...*aceae*.

DNA

Deoxyribonucleic acid, or DNA, is the molecule that carries the blueprint for construction of all the cells of an organism and all instructions that control their activities, and which enables these instructions to be passed on from one generation to the next. DNA is found in all living organisms except certain

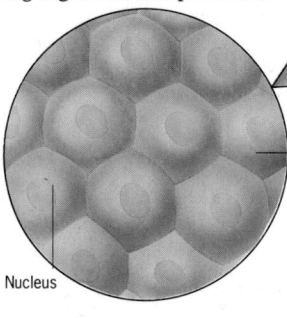

Nucleus

viruses which contain RNA (ribonucleic acid), a closely related molecule.

In eukaryotic cells—which make up the majority of organisms—DNA is found in the membrane-bound sphere

Sugar and phosphate backbone

called the nucleus. Here, it forms structures known as chromosomes, normally long threads (but in cells that are about to divide, chromosomes form separate X-shapes as

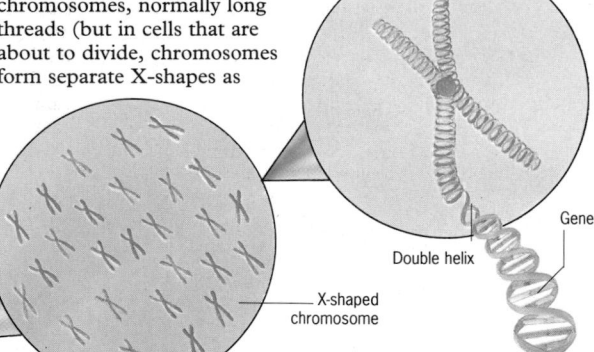

Cell containing DNA

X-shaped chromosome

Double helix

Genes

they duplicate themselves). Within the chromosome, DNA is tightly packed in coils and supercoils.

Once unraveled, DNA can be seen to consist of two long strands wound around each other in a spiral structure or double helix, like a twisted ladder. The "rungs" of this ladder are made from four different bases: adenine, cytosine, guanine, and thymine. A

"rung" is formed when adenine from one DNA strand binds with thymine on the other, or cytosine binds with guanine. The arrangement of bases along the double helix constitutes the genetic code, which controls production of the protein molecules that facilitate all cell activities, including metabolism and construction.

Each small unit of DNA, or gene, controls production of a particular protein. To do this, that part of the DNA "unzips" and the information within it is transferred to a messenger molecule which controls the synthesis of the protein outside the nucleus. The DNA in each human cell contains between about 50,000 and 100,000 genes.

DNA is unique among biological molecules in its ability to replicate itself. The two strands of the double helix separate along its length to form complementary copies of themselves, producing two new strands identical to each other and the "parent" strand.

Genetic engineering

Genes from one species may be introduced into another. The gene controlling insulin production is extracted from human DNA (1) and introduced into a bacterial cell (2),

where it fuses with the bacterial DNA (3). The bacterium divides repeatedly (4), creating clones that use the "foreign" gene to produce human insulin, which can be extracted and used in the treatment of diabetes.

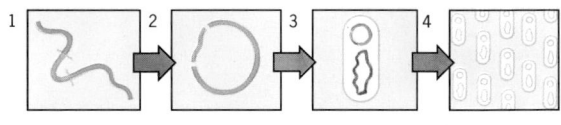

Human chromosome

Every human body cell, except for sperm and egg cells, contains 46 chromosomes. These contain around 100,000 genes that between them determine all of an individual's characteristics, from hair color to potential height. Sperm and egg cells each contain 23 chromosomes. When they fuse during fertilization, the chromosome number is restored to 46, or 23 pairs of chromosomes. Thus every body cell nucleus contains 23 paternal chromosomes paired with 23 maternal chromosomes.

DNA fingerprinting

Also known as genetic fingerprinting, this process is used to reveal the genetic identity of an individual. The arrangement of bases within his or her DNA is unique to that individual, just as his or her fingerprints are; the only exceptions are identical twins, who share the same DNA. A tissue sample, usually of blood, is taken from the person and DNA is extracted. The DNA molecules are then cut into small pieces and separated. By adding a radioactive probe and using an X-ray film, a banded strip is pro-

duced, unique to its owner. The more closely two people are related, the greater the similarity between the pattern of bands.

Genetic fingerprinting was used to confirm that human remains found in Russia were those of the Romanovs, the Russian royal family, by comparing DNA fingerprints from the remains with those of the Romanovs' living relatives. Genetic fingerprinting is similarly used to prove paternity. In criminal cases such as rape, DNA extracted from the perpetrator's semen or other body fluids can be used to confirm his identity.

DNA and taxonomy

The sequence of bases along the DNA molecule may be compared between species. If the base sequences are similar, then the species are closely related. For example, there is a 1.2 percent difference between the DNA of humans and that of chimpanzees, and a 1.4 percent difference between humans and gorillas, making the chimpanzee a closer relative to humans than is the gorilla. Humans and orangutans share 97.6 percent of their DNA, but this does not match the 98.8 percent shared by chimp and human.

EVOLUTION

Evolution is the process of gradual change by which the characteristics of living organisms are altered from generation to generation. The changes in a given organism eventually become so great that it can no longer be regarded as the same species. Fossil records show that such replacement of one species by a more advanced one has been taking place for many millions of years, and that most species have survived for only about ten million years.

The idea that living things have all evolved from simple ancestors was first put forward by the ancient Greeks, but until Charles Darwin and Alfred Russel Wallace published their work on natural selection no one could give a satisfactory explanation. Darwin and Wallace noticed that plants and animals produce large numbers of offspring and that there is a struggle for existence among the progeny —competition to find food and avoid predators as well as a struggle against adverse environmental factors. They also realized that the progeny vary, and they reasoned that only those most suited to their surroundings would survive. The progressive improvement shown throughout evolution is thus brought about by natural means—that is, by natural selection of the best in each generation.

The history of the horse

Few animals have such a clear fossil record as the horse. The oldest known fossils of this family, from rocks some 55 million years old, are of a fox-sized creature called *Hyracotherium*. Its teeth indicate that it ate leaves, and it probably lived in the forests. Fossils from successively younger rock layers show that the descendants of *Hyracotherium* gradually became larger and were represented by several distinct genera before producing the modern horse about two million years ago. Their toes were reduced to one on each foot and their teeth became larger and stronger to deal with tough grasses.

In less than 60 million years, the fox-sized Hyracotherium *evolved into the modern, fast-running horse adapted for life on the plains.*

Hyracotherium (55 million years ago) **Mesohippus** (38) **Merychippus** (20) **Pliohippus** (5) **Przewalski's horse** (2) **Modern horse**

Divergence

Divergent evolution is the evolution of one kind of animal or plant in several directions. One of the best examples concerns the finches of the Galápagos Islands, often called Darwin's finches because Charles Darwin was the first to study them. These birds differ in size and beak structure, indicating that they have different diets, but they share common ancestors who, having arrived originally from South America, found few other birds on the islands with whom to compete. The finches gradually adopted a range of different diets and evolved into the 13 different species that are found living on these islands today.

Galápagos finches

Vegetarian finch

Large cactus finch

Warbler finch

Small ground finch

Cactus finch

Large tree finch

Woodpecker finch

Large ground finch

Convergence

Convergent evolution is a common phenomenon in which unrelated plants or animals come to resemble each other because they have adapted to similar ways of life. The similarity of some species of American cacti and certain desert-living spurges in Africa is a good example. Seals and penguins (*right*) are apparently very different animals, but both are superbly adapted for swimming. Their limbs and general body shapes appear similar when observed in the water.

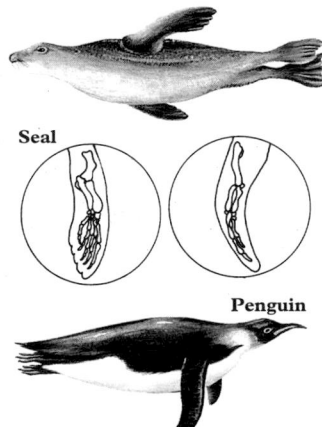

Seal

Penguin

Evolving peppered moths

Peppered moths (*Biston betularia*) exist in two main forms —speckled, and black or melanic. Most peppered moths in Britain used to be of the speckled variety until the mid-1800s, when the number of black moths increased significantly. This was because air pollution blackened the tree trunks and the resting black moths were better camouflaged than the speckled variety. Birds found and ate speckled moths, leaving the black ones to breed and dominate the population—a rapid evolutionary change that was brought about by a rapidly changing environment.

The melanic black moth (left) *is barely visible against a dark tree, whereas the normal (speckled) moth stands out clearly.*

FUNGI

The fungi were once regarded as simple plants, but their chemical makeup is very different from that of plants, and they are now placed in a separate kingdom. A fungus consists essentially of a mass of slender threads, called hyphae, which absorb food from other living or dead organisms. The familiar mushrooms and toadstools are the reproductive stages of the fungi and are often called fruiting bodies. They are composed of tightly compacted hyphae, and their role is to produce and scatter the dustlike spores. If a spore reaches a place with enough food and moisture for survival, it will grow by sending out a hypha.

The name *mushroom* was originally used for just one or two species of fungi with edible fruiting bodies; all the other fungi with umbrella-shaped fruiting bodies were called *toadstools*. The modern tendency, however, is for all umbrella-shaped fruiting bodies, whether edible or not, to be called mushrooms. Although many species are edible and very tasty, they contain little food value.

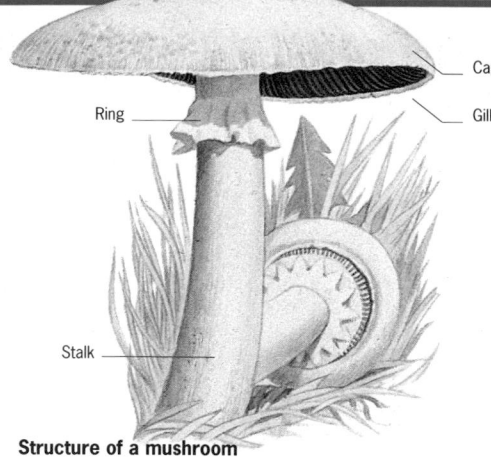

Structure of a mushroom

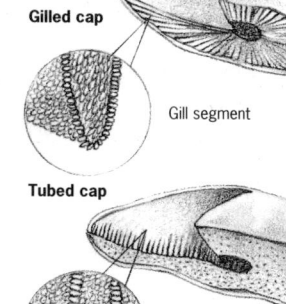

Gilled cap

Gill segment

Tubed cap

Tube

Gills and pores

The typical mushroom gets its food from decaying matter in the ground. Its fruiting body is spherical when it first bursts through the soil, but it quickly expands to form a cap and a stalk. The latter, often called the stipe, may have a ring showing where the rim of the cap was originally attached, and there may be a cup, or volva, at the base. Under the cap, most species bear numerous fragile gills, arranged like spokes in a wheel. The gill surfaces release millions of spores, the equivalent of seeds in flowering plants. Other mushrooms look more like sponges, scattering their spores from thousands of minute pores.

Poisonous fungi

Relatively few of the 100,000 or more known fungi are really poisonous, but a handful are truly deadly. The death cap (*Amanita phalloides*) probably kills more people than any other fungus. Growing in broad-leaved woodlands, this fungus has a greenish cap with white gills. One specimen is more than enough to kill a person, causing a slow and painful death. Several related fungi can produce severe illness if eaten, although they are not necessarily deadly. These include the fly agaric (*Amanita muscaria*), common under birch and pine trees, the blusher (*Amanita rubescens*), common in both deciduous and coniferous woodland, and the verdigris fungus (*Stropharia aeruginosa*), common in grass and woodland.

Death cap

Fly agaric

Blusher

Verdigris fungus

Molds

Molds are simple fungi that do not form fruiting bodies. The pin-mold (*Mucor*) is very common on stale bread. It bears its spores in tiny black capsules at the tips of some of its hyphae.

Penicillin

This important antibiotic, which has saved many thousands of lives, is obtained from bluish-green *Penicillium* molds like those that form velvetlike mats on rotting fruit and other materials. Penicillin was discovered by British scientist Sir Alexander Fleming in 1928; large-scale production of the drug began in the mid-1940s. To produce it, the molds are grown in huge vats that are full of nutrient-rich fluids.

Truffles

Truffles are subterranean fungi with solid, globular fruiting bodies. They grow mainly in broad-leaved woods. The Périgord truffle (*Tuber melanosporum*) of southern France is a much-prized and very expensive delicacy. The traditional way of finding truffles is to train pigs or dogs to sniff them out. Most attempts at cultivating truffles commercially have failed.

Truffle: Périgord truffle

Lichens

Lichens are among the hardiest of all organisms, growing in some of the hottest and coldest places. They clothe much of the Arctic tundra. Each of the many species is actually a combination of a fungus and an alga. The alga can exist alone, but the fungus cannot, so lichens are regarded as special kinds of fungi that rely on algae to provide much of their food.

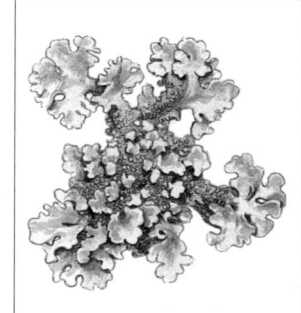

Lichen: *Parmelia caperata*

FUNGI

All these fungi occur in North America and Europe, and many are almost worldwide. Unless otherwise stated, they all have the familiar umbrella shape.

Family/Name	Form and color	Habitat	Edibility
FUNGI WITH GILLS			
Amanitaceae			
Death cap *Amanita phalloides*	Cup and ring; greenish cap and white gills.	Broad-leaved woodland floor	*Deadly*
Destroying angel *Amanita virosa*	Cup and ring; pure white cap, gills, and stalk.	Broad-leaved woodland floor	*Deadly*
Fly agaric *Amanita muscaria*	Scarlet cap with white flecks; ringed stalk, swollen at base.	Under birch and pine trees	*Poisonous*
Lepiotaceae			
Parasol *Lepiota procera*	Broad cap with brown patches; thin stem with double ring.	Fields and other grassy places	*Excellent*
Tricholomataceae			
Honey mushroom *Armillariella mellea*	Honey-colored with brown scales on the cap.	Living and dead wood	*Edible with care*
Russulaceae			
Emetic russula *Russula emetica*	Shiny red cap and white gills; white stalk with no ring.	Under pines	*Poisonous*
Pleurotaceae			
Oyster mushroom *Pleurotus ostreatus*	Bluish-gray cap with white gills; stalk on one side.	Clustered on dead tree trunks	*Good*
Agaricaceae			
Horse mushroom *Agaricus arvensis*	Broad whitish cap with pink to brown gills; toothed ring.	Grassland	*Very good*
Meadow mushroom *Agaricus campestris*	White cap; pink gills become brown with age; ringed stalk.	Pastureland	*Excellent*
Yellow-foot agaricus *Agaricus xanthodermus*	Very like field mushroom, but turns yellow when bruised.	Grassland and light woodland	*Poisonous*
Strophariaceae			
Liberty cap *Psilocybe semilanceata*	Brown, sharply pointed cap on thin stalk; also known as "magic mushroom" because of hallucinogenic properties.	Grassland	*Poisonous*
Coprinaceae			
Non-inky coprinus *Coprinus disseminatus*	Thimble-shaped grayish cap; dark gray to purple gills.	Dead wood and tree stumps	*Edible*
Shaggy mane *Coprinus comatus*	Cap white, clothed with soft, curly scales; egg-shaped at first, but soon opens and "melts" into a black liquid.	Grassy places and arable fields	*Edible when young*
Sulfur tuft *Hypholoma fasciculare*	Dirty yellow cap; gills yellow at first, then dark brown.	Tree stumps and dead wood	*Inedible*
Cantharellaceae			
Chanterelle *Cantharellus cibarius*	Funnel shaped; bright yellow; smells of apricots.	Woodland floor	*Excellent*
Horn of plenty *Craterellus cornucopioides*	Funnel shaped; brown or black with indistinct gills.	Broad-leaved woodland	*Very good*
FUNGI WITHOUT GILLS			
Boletaceae			
King bolete *Boletus edulis*	Shiny brown cap with pale pores below—the French *cèpe*.	Woodland floor	*Excellent*
Fistulinaceae			
Beefsteak polypore *Fistulina hepatica*	Tongue- or fan-shaped bracket with pores below; color and texture of raw meat.	Oak and sweet chestnut trunks	*Edible*
Polyporaceae			
Dryad's saddle *Polyporus squamosus*	Shelflike bracket up to 20 inches across; stalked at one side.	Trunks of deciduous trees	*Edible*
Auriculariaceae			
Auricularia auricula judae	Gelatinous, ear-shaped fruit body; spores cover surface.	Dead branches, elder bushes	*Inedible*
Geastraceae			
Earthstars (numerous species)	Globular fruit body, but outer coat splits like rays of a star.	Woodland floor	*Inedible*
Lycoperdaceae			
Puffballs (numerous species)	Globular fruit body, opening by pores or cracks to release clouds of spores when touched.	Grassland and woodland	*Most edible when young*
Phallaceae			
Stinkhorn *Phallus impudicus*	Penis-shaped fruit body, clothed with spore-carrying slime; stench attracts flies, which carry away the spores.	Woodland	*Inedible*
Morchellaceae			
Morel *Morchella* (several species)	Stalked, conical fruit body with a honeycomb texture.	Grassland and open woodland	*Good*
Tuberaceae			
European white truffle *Tuber magnatum*	Globular; subterranean; yellow-brown with whitish flesh.	Deciduous woods in N. Italy	*Excellent*
Périgord truffle *Tuber melanosporum*	Globular; subterranean; shiny black with red-brown flesh.	Under oaks in S. Europe	*Excellent*
Summer truffle *Tuber aestivum*	Globular; subterranean; brown warty with yellowish flesh.	Near beech trees; chalky soils	*Very good*

Family Pleurotaceae
Oyster mushroom

Family Agaricaceae
Meadow mushroom

Family Cantharellaceae
Chanterelle

Family Boletaceae
King bolete

Family Polyporaceae
Dryad's saddle

Family Lycoperdaceae
Puffball

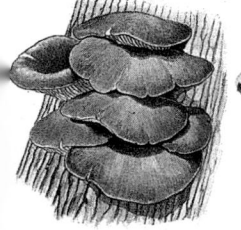   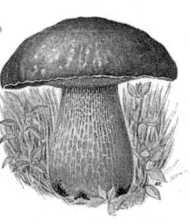  

INTRODUCTION

With something in the region of 300,000 different kinds or species, plants make up one of the two great kingdoms of the living world. The chlorophyll they contain is responsible for the essentially green nature of the planet. Unlike animals, plants can manufacture their own food from simple inorganic materials—mainly water and the carbon dioxide gas in the air. They are thus the primary producers of food, and all terrestrial animal life depends on them, either directly or indirectly, for food.

Most animals stop growing when they reach maturity, and each species has a fixed shape. But plants go on growing throughout their lives and, although the leaves and flowers of a particular species generally have a fixed shape, the overall shape and size of the plant can vary a good deal according to its situation.

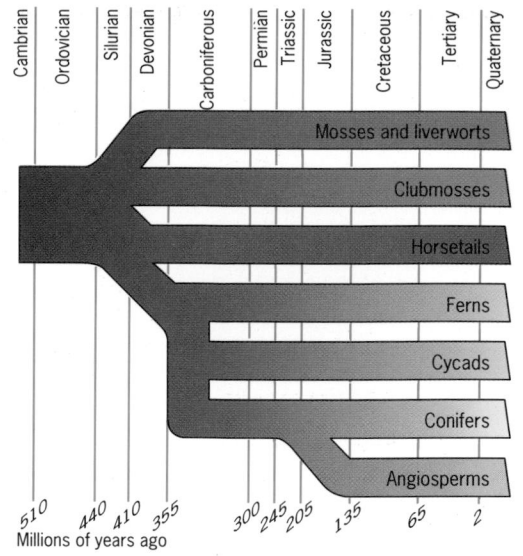

Cambrian | Ordovician | Silurian | Devonian | Carboniferous | Permian | Triassic | Jurassic | Cretaceous | Tertiary | Quaternary

Mosses and liverworts
Clubmosses
Horsetails
Ferns
Cycads
Conifers
Angiosperms

510 440 410 355 300 245 205 135 65 2
Millions of years ago

Plant evolution

The earliest plants all lived in water and did not invade the land until about 435 million years ago. The first invaders were simple plants, without leaves or flowers, but they did have water-absorbing roots and canals to carry the water through their bodies. They carried spores in small capsules and were the ancestors of our ferns and horsetails, but we can only guess at their origin from some kind of alga. Mosses appeared soon afterwards, possibly from another kind of alga. Cone-bearing plants, the cycads and conifers, and flowering plants evolved much later from fern-like ancestors.

The plant body

Leaving aside the flowers or other reproductive organs, a typical plant has three main regions—root, stem, and leaf.

The root anchors the plant and absorbs water and dissolved minerals from the soil by means of osmosis. Growth takes place by elongation of the cells just behind the tip, and this forces the root down. Delicate root hairs just behind the growing region absorb the water and pass it to tubes in the center of the root.

The stem, which may be soft (herbaceous) or woody (arboreal), carries water and dissolved minerals from the roots to the leaves through a ring of tubes. Another set of tubes carries manufactured food down from the leaves and distributes it around the plant. The stem also arranges the leaves in the most efficient way for catching sunlight (Photosynthesis, *right*) and, in flowering plants, displays the flowers in the best position for achieving pollination.

The leaves are the plant's food factories. They are usually flat and have a number of veins. Continuous with the tubes in the stems, the veins carry water to the leaf tissues for photosynthesis and also carry away the manufactured food. The undersides of the leaves carry thousands of microscopic breathing pores (stomata) that allow carbon dioxide in and oxygen out. They also release a lot of water vapor by evapotranspiration.

Parts of a typical plant

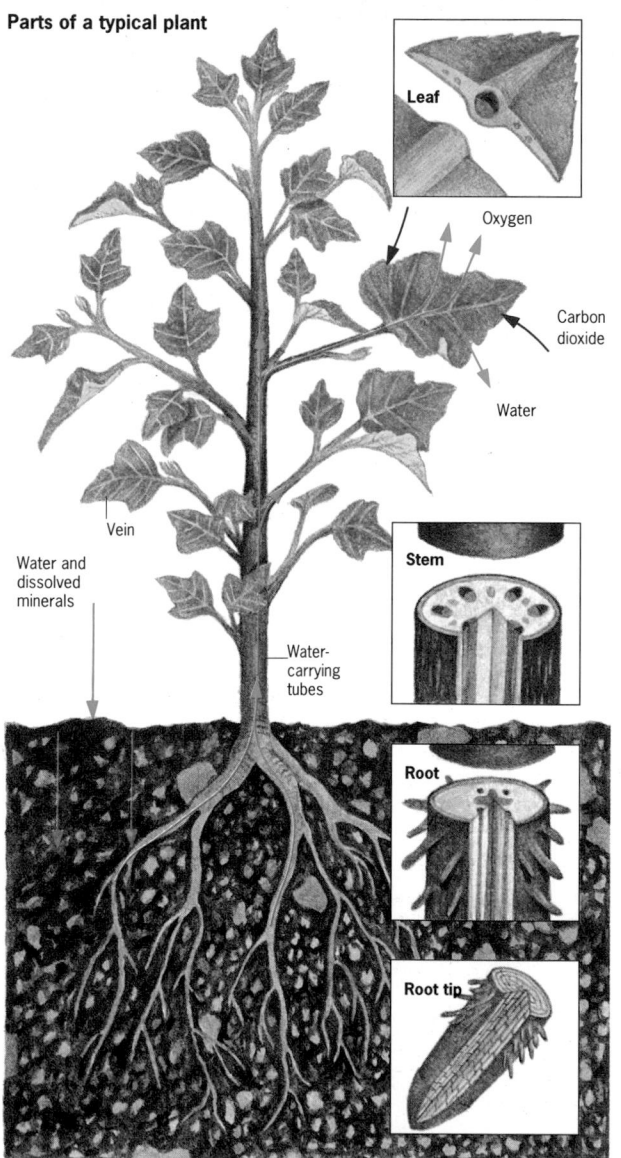

Leaf

Oxygen

Carbon dioxide

Water

Vein

Water and dissolved minerals

Water-carrying tubes

Stem

Root

Root tip

Photosynthesis

Photosynthesis is the process by which plants make glucose (sugar) from water and carbon dioxide. It takes place in the chloroplasts in the cells of the leaves and other green parts, and the energy needed comes from sunlight. Chlorophyll—the green pigment in the chloroplasts—absorbs the light and uses its energy in a series of reactions during which the water and carbon dioxide combine to form the glucose and give off oxygen. The glucose provides energy for other activities and is also converted into structural cellulose. Together with minerals from the soil, it is the starting point for making proteins.

Plant lifespans

Annual plants are those that complete their lives in one growing season or less.

Biennial plants need two growing seasons: they make and store food in the first one and flower and die during the second one.

Perennial plants live for several or many years, the record being held by the bristlecone pines of North America, some of which are nearly 5,000 years old.

At the other end of the scale are some desert-living annuals. Their seeds germinate as soon as the annual rains arrive, and the plants grow so rapidly that they can flower and scatter a new crop of seeds in just two weeks.

Flowerless plants

Mosses and ferns reproduce by scattering dustlike spores that grow indirectly into new plants. There are two distinct stages in the fern's life cycle. The fern itself produces the spores, and these grow into short-lived green disks called prothalli. Male and female sex cells produced on the disks must join before new ferns can grow. The sex cells need moisture, so ferns grow best in damp places. Conifers have seeds but no real flowers. They carry their seeds in woody cones instead of fruits. Conifers are the best known of the cone-bearing plants, known as gymnosperms.

Swan-necked moss

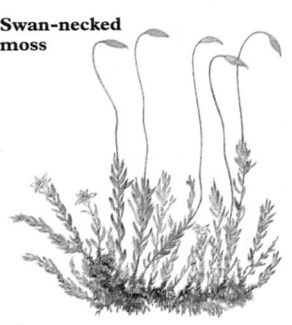

Mosses

Mosses and the closely related liverworts carry spores in stalked capsules. The capsules form only after the union of male and female sex cells. As in ferns, the cells need moist conditions, so mosses flourish mainly in damp environments.

Broad buckler fern

Ferns

Ferns generally carry their spores in little capsules under the leaves. The related horsetails carry theirs in fleshy cones at the tips of the stems. Although the reproductive process requires water, mature ferns can survive in dry places.

Atlas cedar

Conifers

Conifers bear seeds on the scales of their cones. The cones are small and soft at first but swell and become woody after pollination. When the seeds are ripe the cones either open slightly or fall to pieces to release them.

Flowering plants

Flowering plants, or angiosperms, make up the bulk of the world's vegetation. There are more than 250,000 species, which fall into two major groups. Dicotyledons have two seed leaves (cotyledons) in their seeds and their normal leaves have a network of veins. Monocotyledons have a single seed leaf and their normal leaves are strap-shaped with parallel veins. Flowers are the reproductive parts of the plant: their role is to produce fruits and seeds.

Flower structure

Despite a huge range of forms, flower parts can normally be recognized. The sepals protect the flower before it opens. The petals, which are brightly colored, attract pollinating insects. The stamens are the male, pollen-producing parts, and the carpels are the female organs. The carpel comprises ovary, style, and stigma.

The ovules or female cells that form the seeds after pollination are in the ovary. The ovary becomes the fruit enclosing the seeds.

Monocotyledon: daffodil

Dicotyledon: dog rose

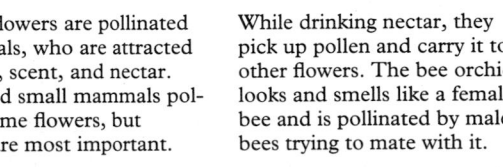

Stigma — Stamen
Carpel Style —
Ovary —
Petal
Sepal —
Receptacle — Stalk

Pollination

Seeds form after pollination. Pollen from the same kind of flower must reach the stigmas and thence the ovules. Many flowers rely on the wind to carry pollen: these include grasses and hazel catkins (*below left*), which have no nectar or scent and little color; many lack petals.

Most flowers are pollinated by animals, who are attracted by color, scent, and nectar. Birds and small mammals pollinate some flowers, but insects are most important.

While drinking nectar, they pick up pollen and carry it to other flowers. The bee orchid looks and smells like a female bee and is pollinated by male bees trying to mate with it.

Wind pollination: hazel catkin

Animal pollination: hummingbird

Animal pollination: mouse

Insect pollination: bee

Seed dispersal

A seed is a neatly packaged reproductive unit holding a miniature plant or embryo and enough food to see it through the early stages of growth or germination. It has a tough outer coat and can usually survive adverse conditions, such as drought, for a considerable time. The seeds of flowering plants are enclosed in fruits at first. The fruits are either dry or fleshy when ripe and may or may not split open to release the seeds.

Most flowering plants have some way of scattering their seeds so that the seeds reach new areas and do not compete with each other. Fleshy fruits are usually eaten by animals, but the hard seeds pass right through and may be dropped miles from the parent plants. Many fruits and seeds, such as the dandelion (*left*), have wings or feathery parachutes and are carried away by the wind. Poppy capsules (*below left*) have small holes through which seeds are scattered like pepper from a shaker when the stems sway in the wind. Many dry fruits, such as the noogoora (*Xanthium occidentale*) from Australia (*right*), have hooks that catch in the fur of animals. They can be carried a long way before they fall off. The pods of the pea family explode when ripe and throw their seeds far away.

Dandelion fruit

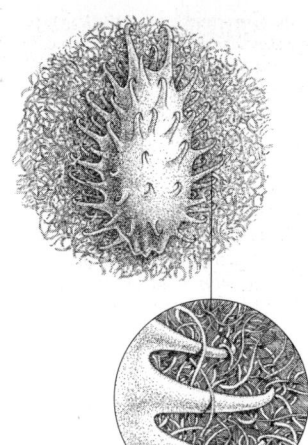

Poppy capsule

Noogoora hook

Unusual adaptations

Flowering plants have evolved in many directions, becoming adapted to a wide range of habitats and acquiring many life-styles.

Plants growing on high mountains or on the northern tundra usually form mats or cushions close to the ground to escape violent winds. The dwarf willow (*Salix herbacea*), for example, is a true willow but it has underground stems and its aerial branches are rarely more than 1.2 inches (3 cm) above ground.

The leaves and flowers of many montane plants are darker than those of their lowland relatives: dark colors absorb heat more efficiently in the cold climate.

Toothwort

Suckers on host root

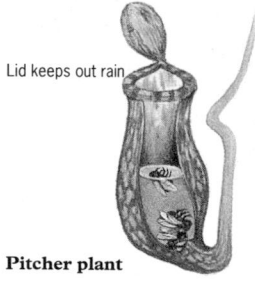

Lid keeps out rain

Pitcher plant

Orchid

Parasites

Parasitic plants lack chlorophyll and make no food for themselves. They steal what they need from other plants. The toothwort sends suckers into the roots of shrubs and trees and absorbs food from them. Saprophytes are similar plants, but they absorb food from decaying matter.

Flesh-eaters

A number of plants augment their food supplies by catching insects. The pitcher plant traps insects in fluid-filled pitchers at the tips of its leaves. The insects drown in the fluid and are digested. Insect-eating plants grow mainly in bogs and other areas of poor soil.

Epiphytes

Epiphytes grow on the bark of trees but are not parasites. They make their own food, absorbing moisture from the air and minerals from dust and animal droppings on the bark. Epiphytes are common in tropical forests with plenty of rain. They include many orchids and ferns.

Plants of the desert

Many plants manage to live in deserts despite the scarcity of water. Some of them are quick-growing annuals that complete their life cycles in a short time and are not affected by the drought, but the typical desert plants store water through the dry season. Waxy or hairy coatings and breathing pores sunk in deep grooves ensure that evaporation is cut to a minimum. Many of the plants have very small leaves or none at all, although some species sprout leaves when the rains come and then drop them for the dry season.

Cacti nearly all grow in the American deserts and can survive prolonged drought. They have no actual leaves and their ribbed green stems make all their food. Wide-spreading roots catch nearly all the rain that falls in the wet season, and the stems swell up (*below left*) as they take up water. The stems shrink as they use up water in the dry season, and the grooves become deeper (*insets below*). The breathing pores in the grooves thus become better protected from the dry air. Spines protect the cacti from grazing animals seeking moisture.

Cactus after the rains

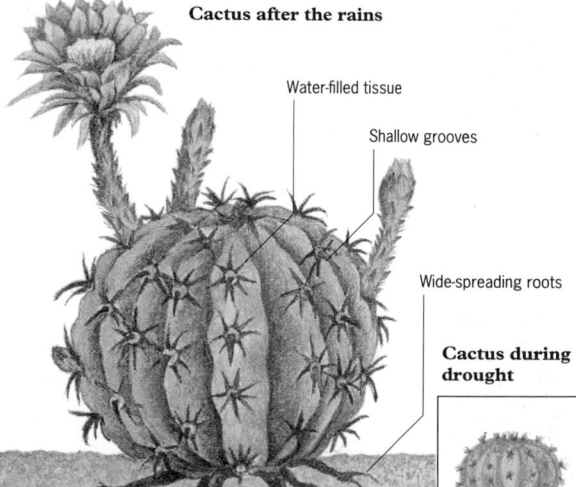

Water-filled tissue

Shallow grooves

Wide-spreading roots

Cactus during drought

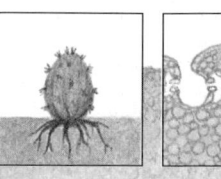

HERBACEOUS FLOWERS

Flowers—large and small

The world's biggest flower is that of rafflesia (*Rafflesia arnoldii*) from Indonesia. It is up to 35 inches (90 cm) across, brick-red, and in many ways it looks like a giant fungus. It smells like rotting meat and attracts swarms of small flies for pollination. Rafflesia is a parasite and has no leaves or stems. Its vegetative parts consist of a network of threads inside the stems and roots of woody climbers, and the plant is invisible until its flowers burst through the host tissues.

The smallest flowers belong to the duckweeds that cover many ponds in the summer. They are carried in little pouches at the edges of the disks. Each flower has just one or two stamens or a single carpel—no petals or sepals—and you need a very strong lens to see it.

Rafflesia　　　　　　　**Duckweed**

Indoor plants

The aspidistra (*Aspidistra elatior*), very popular during the early 1900s, was one of the earliest plants grown in houses as living ornaments. Today, we have a huge range of houseplants with attractive flowers or foliage. Many come from tropical forests, where little light reaches the ground, so they are well suited for life in poorly lit rooms. Cacti also make good houseplants because they can cope with the dry air and owners who forget to water them.

St. Bernard's lily or spider plant

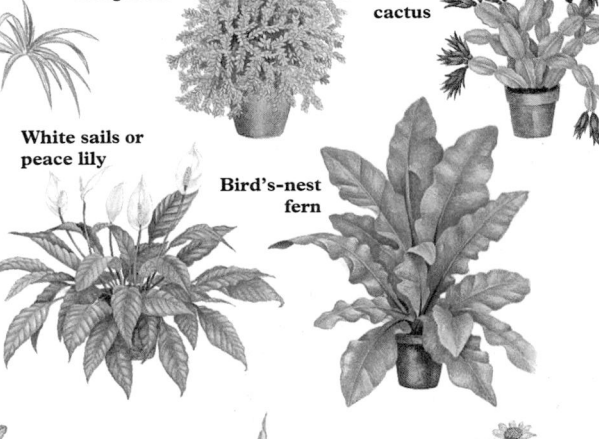

Selaginella

Easter cactus

White sails or peace lily

Bird's-nest fern

Weeds

Weeds are commonly defined as plants growing where we do not want them. Some are aliens that reach new countries and become troublesome—like the thistle in New Zealand. Most weeds, however, are simply wild plants that invade farms and gardens and compete with the cultivated plants for sunlight, water, and minerals in the soil. Some are annuals, producing lots of seeds, while others are vigorous, deep-rooted perennials. All weeds are very difficult to eradicate.

Locoweed

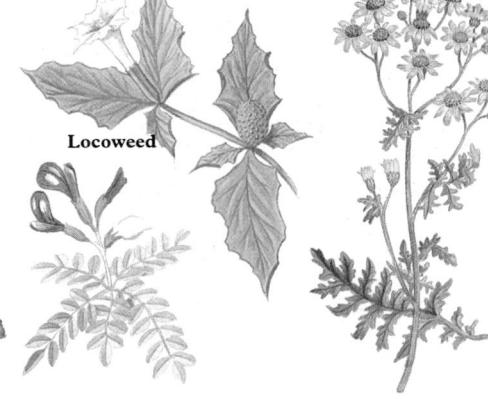

Welted thistle　　**Jimsonweed**　　**Ox-eye daisy**　　**Red deadnettle**　　**Ragwort**

Flowers for scent

Most garden flowers have a certain amount of scent, designed to attract pollinating insects, but many varieties have been bred for the sake of their unusually fragrant scents. These plants include pinks, freesias, and sweet peas, and are especially useful for making pleasantly scented gardens. Some plants, including nicotianas—commonly known as tobacco plants—and evening primrose, release their scent at night.

Sweet violet　　**Marsh marigold**　　　　**Cyclamen**　　　　**Verbena**

HERBACEOUS FLOWERS

[▲ = endangered species]

Family/Name	Color; season	Growth form	Habitat and features	Original home
DICOTYLEDONS				
Water lily/Nymphaeaceae	**(c. 75 species)**			
White water lily *Nymphaea alba*	White; summer	Aquatic perennial; floating leaves and flowers	Shallow water; the ancestor of many cultivated forms.	*Europe*
Lotus/Nelumbonaceae	**(2 species)**			
East Indian lotus *Nelumbo nucifera*	Pink; all year	Aquatic perennial; leaves and flowers above water	Sacred in India and S.E. Asia; edible seeds and rhizomes.	*Asia, Australia and Oceania*
Buttercup/Ranunculaceae	**(c. 2,000 species)**			
Christmas rose *Helleborus niger*	White or pink; early spring	Perennial	Rocky places; popular in gardens for its early flowers.	*S. Europe*
Columbine *Aquilegia* (*c.* 100 species)	Various; spring	Perennials with spurred, bonnet-shaped flowers	Woods and grassland; many cultivars are grown in gardens.	*N. Hemisphere*
Creeping buttercup *Ranunculus repens*	Yellow; summer	Creeping perennial	Damp habitats; a garden weed.	*Eurasia*
Delphinium *Delphinium* (many species)	Blue, purple, red, or white; summer	Tall annuals and perennials	Many cultivated hybrids.	*N. Hemisphere*
Pasque flower *Pulsatilla vulgaris*	Purple; spring	Short, hairy perennial	Limestone grassland; flowers at Easter (*Pâques* in French).	*Europe*
Poppy anemone *Anemone coronaria*	Various brilliant colors; spring	Tuberous perennial	Open habitats; much grown in gardens and used by florists.	*Mediterranean*
Peony/Paeoniaceae	**(c. 35 species)**			
Peony *Paeonia* (several species)	Pink, red, white, or yellow; summer	Perennial herbs and shrubs	Numerous cultivars grown for color and scent.	*Eurasia*
Poppy/Papaveraceae	**(c. 200 species)**			
Field poppy *Papaver rhoeas*	Red; summer	Hairy annual	Wasteground; long-lived seeds spring up whenever ground is disturbed.	*Europe*
Pitcher (American)/Sarraceniaceae	**(c. 17 species)**			
Pitcher plant *Sarracenia* (10 species)	Green, orange, red; summer	Low-growing perennials with tubular leaves (pitchers)	Bogs and marshes; colorful pitchers attract insects, which drown in them and are digested.	*North America*
Hop/Cannabaceae	**(4 species)**			
Hemp *Cannabis sativa*	Green with pink tinge; summer	Tall annual	Widely grown for its fibers as well as for its narcotic properties.	*C. Asia*
Hop *Humulus lupulus*	Green; late summer	Climbing perennial	Hedgerows and woodland; female flowers flavor beer.	*N. Hemisphere*
Stinging nettle/Urticaceae	**(c. 550 species)**			
Stinging nettle *Urtica dioica*	Green, in hanging catkins; spring/summer	Creeping perennial	Disturbed ground; glassy hairs inject acid when touched.	*Europe*
Dock/Polygonaceae	**(c. 800 species)**			
Dock *Rumex* (*c.* 200 species)	Green or reddish; summer	Upright, long-rooted perennials	Often troublesome farm and garden weeds.	*Worldwide*
Mesembryanthemum/Aizoaceae	**(c. 1,200 species)**			
Livingstone daisy *Dorotheanthus bellidiflorus*	Various; summer	Succulent, sprawling annual	Many varieties cultivated for the brilliant daisylike flowers.	*South Africa*
Stone plant *Lithops* (*c.* 50 species)	Various; summer	Perennials	Juicy leaves easily mistaken for stones; daisylike flowers.	*South African deserts*
Beet/Chenopodiaceae	**(c. 1,400 species)**			
Glasswort *Salicornia europaea*	Green, very small; late summer	Short succulent annual	Muddy seashores; the ash was once used in glassmaking.	*Europe*

Lotus
East Indian lotus

Buttercup
Columbine

Peony
Peony

Poppy
Field poppy

Dock
Dock

Family/Name	Color; season	Growth form	Habitat and features	*Original home*
Pink/Caryophyllaceae	**(*c.* 1,750 species)**			
Carnation *Dianthus caryophyllus*	White, pink, or yellow; summer	Low-growing perennial with many cultivars	Many cultivars are hybrids with other *Dianthus* species.	*S. Europe*
Sweet william *Dianthus barbatus*	White, pink, or red; summer	Biennial or short-lived perennial	Stony and grassy places.	*S. Europe*
Cabbage/Brassicaceae	**(*c.* 3,200 species)**			
Purple rock cress *Aubrieta deltoide*	Pink or purple; spring	Sprawling perennial	Stony, dry places; very popular rock garden plant.	*Mediterranean and W. Asia*
Rape *Brassica napus*	Yellow; spring	Annual or biennial	Widely grown for oil-rich seeds and as a forage crop.	*Europe*
Wallflower *Cheiranthus cheiri*	Yellow in the wild form; spring/summer	Short perennial; woody at base	Dry places; cultivated in many colors from cream to purple.	*Mediterranean*
Woad *Isatis tinctoria*	Yellow; spring	Biennial or perennial	Roadsides, riverbanks, waste-land; leaves yield blue dye.	*Europe*
Cactus/Cactaceae	**(*c.* 2,000 species)**			
Prickly pear *Opuntia vulgaris*	Yellow; spring/summer	Spiny perennial; stems in flat, oval sections	Grown in many warm areas; fruits are edible.	*Tropical Americas*
Violet/Violaceae	**(*c.* 900 species)**			
Garden pansy *Viola tricolor*	Various; all year in cultivation	Low-growing perennial	Grassy places; many varieties derived from the wild plant.	*Europe*
Begonia/Begoniaceae	**(*c.* 950 species)**			
Begonia *Begonia* (*c.* 900 species)	Various; all year	Perennials, often with tubers and watery stems	Many species and hybrids are cultivated.	*Tropics and subtropics*
Primrose/Primulaceae	**(*c.* 1,000 species)**			
Cyclamen *Cyclamen* (*c.* 15 species)	Pink or white; spring/fall	Perennials with a large round corm	Many cultivated forms grown as houseplants.	*Mediterranean and W. Asia*
Polyanthus *Primula* x *polyantha*	Various, clustered on leafless stems; spring	Low-growing hardy perennial	Complex hybrids of primrose and other *Primula* species.	*Europe*
Mallow/Malvaceae	**(*c.* 1,000 species)**			
Cotton *Gossypium* (several species)	White, yellow, or pink; all year	Bushy annuals or perennials	Cotton fiber comes from the hairs surrounding the seeds.	*Tropics*
Hollyhock *Alcea rosea*	Various; summer	Tall biennial/perennial	Many cultivars grown in gardens.	*Probably China*
Linden or Lime/Tiliaceae	**(*c.* 450 species)**			
Jute *Corchorus capsularis*	Yellow; all year	Bushy annual up to 15 feet (4.5 m)	Stem fibers used for sacking, burlap, and carpet backing.	*E. Asia*
Spurge/Euphorbiaceae	**(*c.* 5,000 species)**			
Caper spurge *Euphorbia lathyris*	Green; summer	Tall biennial; fruits resemble capers	A cultivated weed, often said to repel moles; poisonous.	*Europe*
Stonecrop/Crassulaceae	**(*c.* 1,500 species)**			
Gold moss or stone crop *Sedum acre*	Yellow; summer	Succulent mat-forming perennial	Dry, bare places, often on roofs.	*Europe*
Houseleek *Sempervivum* (several species)	Pink or yellow; spring/summer	Rosette perennials with succulent leaves	Mainly mountains; a popular rock garden plant.	*S. Europe*
Pea/Fabaceae	**(More than 10,000 species)**			
Clover *Trifolium* (*c.* 300 species)	White or pink; summer	Sprawling or upright annuals or perennials	Usually in grassland; grown everywhere as forage plants.	*N. Hemisphere*
Lucerne or alfalfa *Medicago sativa*	Mauve; summer	Deep-rooted, drought-resistant perennial	Now grown nearly all over the world as a major forage crop.	*S.W. Asia*
Lupin *Lupinus* (several species)	Various, usually in long spikes; summer	Annual or perennial herbs; sometimes shrubby	Many colorful hybrids are grown in gardens.	*North America, Mediterranean*
Sweet pea *Lathyrus odoratus*	Various; summer	Climbing annual with many cultivars	Cultivated worldwide for its colorful, scented flowers.	*Probably S. Europe*

Cabbage	**Cactus**	**Begonia**	**Mallow**	**Pea**
Wallflower	Prickly pear	Begonia	Cotton	Lupin

Family/Name	**Color; season**	Growth form	Habitat and features	*Original home*
Sundew/Droseraceae	**(c. 100 species)**			
Sundew *Drosera* (several species)	White; summer	Rosette perennials	Bogs; sticky hairs on leaves, trap insects for food.	*Worldwide*
▲ Venus's fly-trap *Dionaea muscipula*	White; summer	Rosette perennial	Bogs; the ends of the leaves form spiky "gin traps" for insects.	*North America*
Willowherb/Onagraceae	**(c. 650 species)**			
Evening primrose *Oenothera biennis*	Yellow; summer, giving out scent at night	Upright biennial	Widely grown in gardens and often escapes into the wild.	*North America*
Fireweed or rosebay willow-herb *Chamaenerion angustifolium*	Pink; summer	Tall, patch-forming perennial	Burned, cleared, and disturbed ground.	*N. Hemisphere*
Flax/Linaceae	**(c. 300 species)**			
Flax *Linum usitatissimum*	Blue; summer	Slender annual with slightly drooping heads	Grown for linen fibers in stems and linseed oil in seeds.	*Probably Europe*
Geranium/Geraniaceae	**(c. 750 species)**			
Crane's bill *Geranium* (several species)	Blue, pink, or mauve; spring to fall	Annuals or perennials; upright or sprawling	Named for beak-shaped fruit.	*Worldwide; mainly in temperate lands*
Geranium *Pelargonium* (several species)	Red, pink, or white; all year in cultivation	Upright or trailing perennials	Widely grown in gardens and greenhouses and as houseplants.	*South Africa*
Herb robert *Geranium robertianum*	Pink; spring/fall	Weak annual or biennial	Shady places; a common garden weed with foxlike smell.	*Eurasia*
Nasturtium/Tropaeolaceae	**(c. 100 species)**			
Nasturtium *Tropaeolum majus*	Red, orange, or yellow; summer	Tender climbing or sprawling annual	Leaves edible, with a slightly hot taste; many cultivars.	*Tropical Americas*
Balsam/Balsaminaceae	**(c. 600 species)**			
Busy-lizzy *Impatiens wallerana sultanii*	Various; all year in cultivation	Tender perennial with watery stems	Many cultivars grown as houseplants.	*Tropical Africa*
Carrot/Apiaceae	**(c. 3,000 species)**			
Hemlock *Conium maculatum*	White, in domed heads; summer	Tall, smelly biennial with purple spots on the stem	Riverbanks and damp ground; very poisonous.	*Europe*
Mistletoe/Loranthaceae	**(c. 900 species)**			
Mistletoe *Viscum album*	Green; spring	Woody perennial with forked branches	A parasite, forming evergreen "bushes" on poplars and other trees; white berries in winter.	*Eurasia*
Rafflesia/Rafflesiaceae	**(c. 50 species)**			
Rafflesia *Rafflesia arnoldii*	Brick-red, up to 35 inches (90 cm) across and up to 15 pounds (7 kg); all year	Leafless parasite growing on woody plants	World's largest flower; smells like carrion to attract flies for pollination; flowers sporadically.	*Southeast Asia*
Gentian/Gentianaceae	**(c. 900 species)**			
▲ Spring gentian *Gentiana verna*	Brilliant blue; spring/summer	Low-growing perennial	Flowers as soon as snow melts; a popular rock garden plant.	*Eurasian mountains*
Bedstraw/Rubiaceae	**(c. 6,000 species)**			
Madder *Rubia tinctorum*	Yellow, starlike; summer	Scrambling evergreen perennial	Formerly grown for the red dye obtained from its roots.	*Mediterranean and W. Asia*
Bindweed/Convolvulaceae	**(c. 1,700 species)**			
Hedge bindweed *Calystegia sepium*	White, bell-shaped; summer	Herbaceous climbing perennial	Scrambles over hedges and fences, smothering other plants.	*N. Hemisphere*
Morning glory *Ipomoea purpurea*	Blue, purple, pink, or white; summer	Climbing annual	Widely grown in gardens; flowering in morning.	*Tropical Americas*
Dodder/Cuscutaceae	**(c. 175 species)**			
Dodder *Cuscuta* (several species)	Pink; summer	Leafless parasites	Threadlike reddish stems cling to other plants and suck food.	*Worldwide*

Sundew	**Geranium**	**Nasturtium**	**Mistletoe**	**Bindweed**
Sundew	Crane's bill	Nasturtium	Mistletoe	Hedge bindweed

Family/Name	Color; season	Growth form	Habitat and features	Original home
Potato/Solanaceae	**(More than 2,000 species)**			
Cape gooseberry or Chinese lantern *Physalis alkekengi*	Cream; summer	Upright perennial	After flowering, calyx inflates, turns orange, forms a "lantern."	China
Jimsonweed *Datura stramonium*	White, trumpet shaped; summer/fall	Bushy, smelly annual	Disturbed, bare ground; often a cultivated weed.	North America
Tobacco *Nicotiana tabacum*	White or pink; summer	Tall, leafy annual	Now widely cultivated.	North America
Snapdragon/Scrophulariaceae	**(c. 3,000 species)**			
Ivy-leaved toadflax *Cymbalaria muralis*	Lilac with yellow center; spring/fall	Sprawling perennial	Mainly rocks and walls.	S. Europe
Snapdragon *Antirrhinum majus*	Pink, red, or yellow; spring/fall	Bushy perennial, woody at base	Rocks and dry places; many cultivars (antirrhinums).	Europe
Sesame/Pedaliaceae	**(c. 50 species)**			
Sesame *Sesamum indicum*	Yellow; summer	Tall, grasslike annual	Grown in tropics for the oil extracted from its seeds.	Tropical Asia
Gloxinia/Gesneriaceae	**(c. 2,000 species)**			
African violet *Saintpaulia ionantha*	Mauve, pink, or white; all year in cultivation	Low-growing perennial with hairy leaves	Popular as a houseplant because it tolerates shade.	African forests
Acanthus/Acanthaceae	**(c. 2,500 species)**			
Bear's breech *Acanthus mollis*	White with purple veins; summer	Bushy perennial with tall flower spikes	Often grown in parks for its large, shiny leaves.	Mediterranean
Plantain/Plantaginaceae	**(c. 300 species)**			
Plantain *Plantago* (c. 250 species)	Brown with white or lilac stamens; spring/fall	Low-growing plants; flowers in long spikes	Grassland and wasteland; a weed, but also fodder plant.	Worldwide
Mint/Lamiaceae	**(c. 3,500 species)**			
Bugle *Ajuga reptans*	Blue, in leafy spike; spring	Creeping perennial	Damp woods and grassland.	Eurasia
White deadnettle *Lamium album*	White, in whorls on stem; spring/fall	Creeping, patch-forming perennial; aromatic	Roadsides and wasteland; leaves without stinging hairs.	Eurasia
Bellflower/Campanulaceae	**(c. 2,000 species)**			
Harebell *Campanula rotundifolia*	Blue; bell shaped on slender stems	Low-growing perennial	Dry grassland.	N. Hemisphere
Daisy/Asteraceae	**(More than 13,000 species)**			
Chrysanthemum *Dendrathema*	Various; fall	Tall or bushy perennial	Many complex hybrids are grown in gardens.	E. Asia
Dahlia *Dahlia pinnata*	Various; summer/fall	Tuberous perennial	Many cultivars now grown, with florets of many shapes.	Central America
Dandelion *Taraxacum officinale*	Yellow; spring/summer	Low-growing rosette plant	Grassland and wasteland; a weed, but grown as salad crop.	N. Hemisphere
▲ Dwarf sunflower *Helianthus annuus*	Yellow and very large; summer	Tall annual	Grown in gardens and on a large scale for its oil-rich seeds.	North America
Edelweiss *Leontopodium alpinum*	White, in furry heads; summer	Low-growing perennial	Becoming rare through collecting for rock gardens.	European mountains
Fleabane *Pulicaria dysenterica*	Yellow; summer/fall	Upright, hairy perennial	Damp places; once strewn in houses to combat fleas.	Eurasia
Strawflower *Helichrysum bracteatum*	Various, with papery bracts; summer	Upright annual	Grown as "everlasting flowers" for dried flower displays.	Australia

MONOCOTYLEDONS

Family/Name	Color; season	Growth form	Habitat and features	Original home
Lily/Liliaceae	**(c. 4,000 species)**			
Asphodel *Asphodelus* (c. 12 species)	White or yellow in spikes; spring/summer	Slender annuals or tuberous perennial	Wasteland and burned ground; several species are cultivated.	S. Europe and Asia
Hyacinth *Hyacinthus orientalis*	Blue in the wild; spring	Bulbous perennial	Open habitats; cultivated varieties in many colors.	Mediterranean and W. Asia
Spanish bluebell *Endymion hispanicus*	Blue; spring	Bulbous perennial	Woodland.	Europe

Potato	**Snapdragon**	**Plantain**	**Bellflower**	**Daisy**
Chinese lantern	Snapdragon	Plantain	Harebell	Sunflower

Family/Name	Color; season	Growth form	Habitat and features	Original home
Lily of the valley *Convallaria majalis*	White, strongly scented; spring	Creeping rhizomatous perennial	Woodlands; tiny bell-shaped flowers.	Europe
Meadow saffron *Colchicum autumnale*	Pink or purple; fall	Bulbous perennial; leaves appear in spring	Damp meadows; often grown in gardens; poisonous.	Europe and C. Asia
Snake's head fritillary *Fritillaria meleagris*	Mottled purple; spring	Bulbous perennial	Old, damp grassland.	Europe
Solomon's seal *Polygonatum* (*c.* 50 species)	White, in drooping spikes; spring	Creeping rhizomatous perennials	Shady places; bear scars similar to mystic seal of Solomon.	Probably Eurasia
Tulip *Tulipa* (*c.* 100 species)	Various; spring	Bulbous perennials	Dry, grassy regions; many cultivars.	Eurasia, especially Turkey
Daffodil/Amaryllidaceae	**(*c.* 1,100 species)**			
Snowdrop *Galanthus* (*c.* 20 species)	White; early spring	Short bulbous perennials	Flower has three petals with no inner trumpet.	Eurasia and W. Asia
Snowflake *Leucojum* (12 species)	White, bell shaped; spring/fall	Bulbous perennials	Petals form a simple bell with no inner trumpet.	S. Europe and N. Africa
Iris/Iridaceae	**(*c.* 1,600 species)**			
Crocus *Crocus* (*c.* 75 species)	Purple, yellow, or white; spring	Low-growing perennials with corms	Very popular for rock gardens; some species becoming rare.	Europe and S. Asia
Freesia *Freesia* (*c.* 20 species)	Various; all year in cultivation	Perennials with corms	Widely grown for glorious scent; many hybrids now in existence.	South Africa
Gladiolus *Gladiolus* (*c.* 300 species)	Various; summer	Upright, slighlty stiff perennials with corms	Garden gladioli are hybrids, mostly of South African origin.	Africa and Eurasia
Iris *Iris* (*c.* 300 species)	Various; spring/summer	Upright perennials with bulbs, rhizomes, or corms	Many cultivated varieties include colorful "flag irises."	N. Hemisphere
Orchid/Orchidaceae	**(*c.* 17,000 species)**			
Bee orchid *Ophrys apifera*	Pink with a furry, brown, beelike lip; summer	Short, upright plant with tubers	Grassland and scrub mainly in tropics; in S. Europe bees pollinate it; normally self-pollinated.	Europe, N. Africa, W. Asia
Sedge/Cyperaceae	**(*c.* 4,000 species)**			
Cotton grass *Eriophorum* (*c.* 20 species)	Brownish; summer	Tufted or creeping perennials	Cool bogs; seedheads clothed with white, cottonlike hairs.	N. Hemisphere
Egyptian paper-plant or papyrus *Cyperus papyrus*	Brownish; summer	Up to 20 feet (6 m) high, leaves bunched at top	Marshlands; papyrus sheets made from compacted pith.	Upper Nile Valley, C. Africa
Grass/Poaceae	**(*c.* 10,000 species)**			
Blue grama grass *Bouteloua gracilis*	Brownish green; summer	Fine-leaved perennial with brushlike heads	One of the major grasses of the prairies.	North America
Common reed *Phragmites australis*	Silvery brown; summer	Tall perennial	Shallow water; stems much used for thatching.	Worldwide
Couch grass *Agropyron repens*	Green, in slender spikes; summer	Tough perennial with creeping rhizomes	Abundant on roadsides; a troublesome garden weed.	N. Hemisphere
Marram grass *Ammophila arenaria*	Brown; summer	Tall, tough perennial with creeping rhizomes	Widely planted to stabilize sand dunes.	Coasts of W. Europe
Pampas grass *Cortaderia selloana*	Silvery brown; summer	Tall perennial; with sharp-edged leaves	Planted for ornament; similar species occurs in New Zealand.	South America
Red oat grass *Themeda triandra*	Brownish; wet season	Tufted annual	Savannas; seeds, screwed into earth, avoid dry-season fires.	Africa
Spinifex grass *Triodia pungens*	Brownish; wet season	Tough, drought-resistant perennial	A major component of the grasslands.	Australia
Arum/Araceae	**(*c.* 2,000 species)**			
Lords and ladies *Arum maculatum*	Green and brown; spring/summer	Short perennial	Woods and hedgerows; flowers enclosed in spathe, followed by red berries; poisonous.	Europe
Reedmace/Typhaceae	**(155 species)**			
Bulrush or reedmace *Typha latifolia*	Brown, in cylindrical spike; summer	Tall perennial with straplike leaves	Swamps; fluffy seeds scattered in spring.	Worldwide

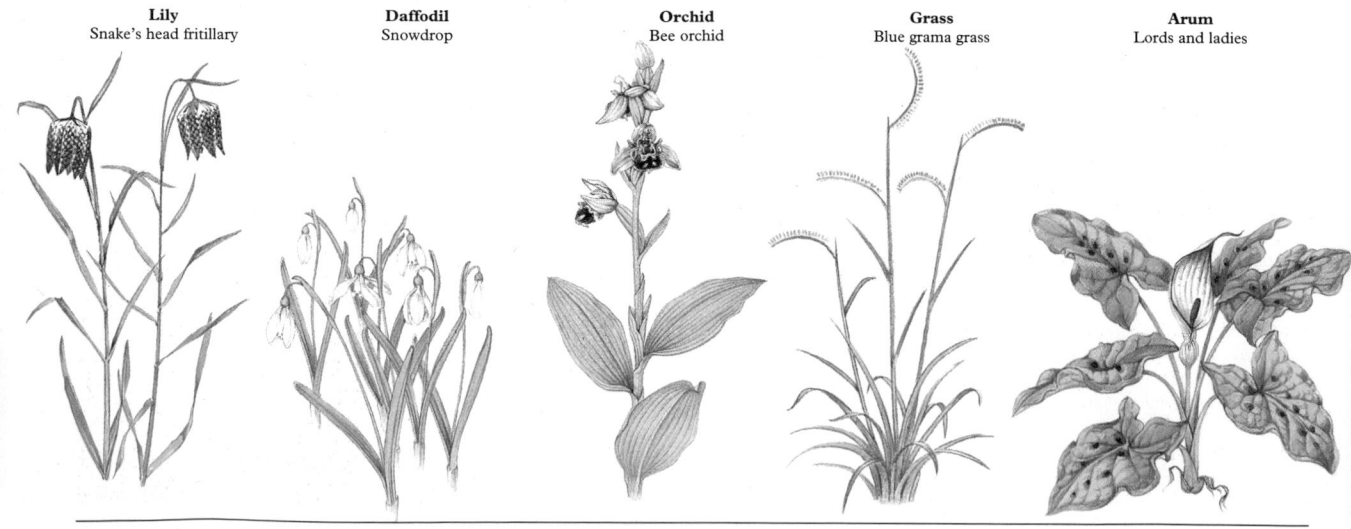

Lily
Snake's head fritillary

Daffodil
Snowdrop

Orchid
Bee orchid

Grass
Blue grama grass

Arum
Lords and ladies

TREES AND SHRUBS

Trees and shrubs are perennial plants with woody stems. Trees normally have a single main stem, called a trunk, with branches diverging from it some way above the ground, while shrubs normally have several main stems arising at or near ground level. Bush is a less precise term, used for any fairly short, much-branched woody plant: it may be a true shrub or else a tree that has been pruned to encourage branching.

Trees and shrubs include both flowering plants and conifers, and they belong to a great many different families. With the exception of the palms, however, very few of them are categorized as members of the group known as monocotyledons (*p. 95*).

Trees live longer than any other organism, with some of the bristlecone pines of North America known to be about 5,000 years old. Trees are also the biggest living things. Some eucalyptus trees in Australia and some of California's giant redwoods have grown taller than 330 feet (100 m). One of the largest sequoias, known as General Sherman, is more than 260 feet (80 m) high and weighs an estimated 2,000 tons, making it the largest of all living things.

As well as providing all our timber (*below*), trees provide much of the fruit we eat and many other materials that have proved very useful to humans, including rubber and medicinal drugs such as quinine. Forests also play a part in the conservation of soil and water resources.

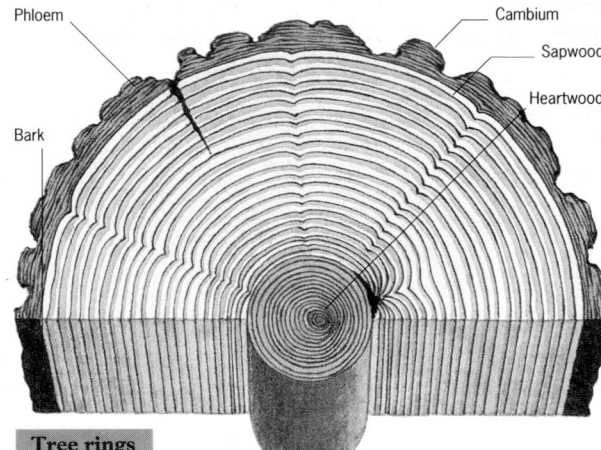

Phloem · Cambium · Sapwood · Heartwood · Bark

Tree rings

Trees grow by adding a new ring of wood under the cambium each year. These annual rings can be counted to find the age of a tree. Sapwood carries water to the leaves. Heartwood has been crushed and is very dense; it no longer carries water. The phloem carries food from the leaves. Constantly renewed from the cambium, it is gradually transformed into the protective bark.

Bonsai

Bonsai is the Japanese art of growing miniaturized trees and shrubs, which is becoming increasingly popular in many parts of the western world as well as in its country of origin. The plants are usually grown in shallow dishes and can make very decorative living ornaments. Their branches are pruned and trained into the desired shapes, and the roots are carefully pruned in order to reduce the plants' vigor.

The resulting bonsai trees become true miniatures, with dwarfed leaves as well as miniature trunks and branches. It is possible for almost any tree seedling to be grown as a bonsai, but conifers and other evergreens have generally proved to be the most popular.

Formal upright shape

Semicascade shape

Nuts

Botanically speaking, a nut is a dry fruit containing a single seed and having a hard, woody outer coat. Hazelnuts and sweet chestnuts are true nuts, and so are cashews and macadamia nuts, but in fact most of the other "nuts" that are available to buy and eat are not nuts at all. They are mostly the inner parts of other kinds of fruits.

Walnuts, pecans, and almonds, for example, are the equivalents of peach or plum stones, and until they fall from the trees they are enclosed in tough, leathery cases that correspond to the flesh of the peach or plum. Even the hard-shelled coconuts are the inner parts of the fruit, although in these the outer part is thick and fibrous—it is used for coconut matting.

Brazil nuts are actually hard-shelled seeds that are obtained from ball-shaped woody fruits. Peanuts are the seeds of a leguminous plant and are carried in pods. In all these examples, the parts that we actually eat are the seeds or kernels—the embryonic next generation of plants and their food reserves.

Softwoods and hardwoods

Timber has been used for building shelters ever since humans first evolved on the earth, and it still plays a major role in the construction and furnishing of our houses. Boats were once built entirely from wood, and even now many small boats have a mainly wooden construction. Other forms of transportation also relied largely on timber in the past. Paper generally comes from wood, and many tools and sporting goods have wooden handles.

Each kind of timber has its own special qualities and uses, but there are two major groups of timber—softwood and hardwood. Softwood comes from coniferous trees and is generally more easily worked than hardwood, which comes from broad-leaved or flowering trees. With some notable exceptions, softwoods are more susceptible to decay than hardwoods, but with modern timber treatments this is not a problem.

Softwood uses

Pine General construction work

Spruce General construction work

Douglas fir Building work

Redwood Roof shingles, cladding

Western red cedar Roof shingles, sheds

Hardwood uses

Birch Plywood, broomstick heads, brush handles

Beech Furniture

Ash Tool handles, sports equipment

Oak Furniture, building; formerly ships

Maple Furniture

Teak High-class furniture, paneling, boats

Tapping trees

Resin from various pine species yields turpentine, used in many artists' paints. The resin is collected in pots attached to slashed pine trunks.

A similar process is used each spring to collect sap from sugar maples, which is boiled down to produce maple syrup.

TREES AND SHRUBS

Trees that regularly reach heights of more than 100 feet (30 m) are described as tall; those less than about 20 feet (6 m) high are described as small.
[▲ = endangered species; (D) = deciduous; (E) = evergreen]

Family/Name	Notable features	Original home
CONE-BEARING TREES (GYMNOSPERMS)		
Ginkgo/Ginkgoaceae	**(1 species)**	
Maidenhair tree *Ginkgo biloba* (D)	Leathery, fan-shaped leaves. The sole survivor of an ancient group.	*China*
Monkey puzzle/Araucariaceae	**(38 species)**	
▲ Kauri pine *Agathis australis* (E)	Tall timber tree endangered through overexploitation.	*New Zealand*
Monkey puzzle tree *Araucaria araucana* (E)	Clothed with sharp-edged leaves that would "puzzle a monkey."	*Chile*
Cypress/Cupressaceae	**(c. 130 species)**	
Common juniper *Juniperus communis* (E)	Slender tree or sprawling bush; berrylike cones flavor gin.	*N. Hemisphere*
Leyland cypress *Cupressocyparis leylandii* (E)	Tall, quick-growing hybrid of the Alaska-cedar and Monterey cypress.	*North America*
Port-Orford cedar *Chamaecyparis lawsoniana* (E)	Tall and slender; many cultivars used for hedging.	*North America*
Western redcedar *Thuja plicata* (E)	Tall, often conical tree yielding soft, reddish, rot-proof timber.	*North America*
Pine/Pinaceae	**(250 species)**	
Balsam fir *Abies balsamea* (E)	Produces a useful yellow gum; also used for wood pulp.	*North America*
Bristlecone pine *Pinus aristata* (E)	Spiny cones; a montane tree that has lived for 5,000 years.	*W. North America*
Cedar-of-Lebanon *Cedrus libani* (E)	Tall cedar with oily, scented timber.	*Asia*
Common silver fir *Abies alba* (E)	Fast-growing timber tree; reaches heights of up to 180 feet (55 m).	*European mountains*
Deodar *Cedrus deodara* (E)	Massive tree with horizontal branches and strongly scented timber.	*Asia*
Douglas-fir *Pseudotsuga menziesii* (E)	One of world's tallest trees—up to 330 feet (100 m); a major timber tree.	*North America*
European larch *Larix decidua* (D)	Tall timber tree with whorled needles and thin-scaled cones.	*European mountains*
Lodgepole pine *Pinus contorta* (E)	Tall and very hardy; the strong timber was used for building huts.	*W. North America*
Maritime pine *Pinus pinaster* (E)	Tall and quick growing; trunks are tapped for turpentine.	*Mediterranean*
Monterey pine *Pinus radiata* (E)	Tall, fast-growing tree much planted for shelter and ornament.	*California*
Norway spruce *Picea abies* (E)	Tall, much-planted timber tree; young ones used as Christmas trees.	*Europe*
Scotch pine *Pinus sylvestris* (E)	Tall timber tree with orange-brown bark on upper trunk.	*Europe and Asia*
Stone pine *Pinus pinea* (E)	Umbrella-shaped crown and edible seeds; also called umbrella pine.	*Mediterranean*
Tamarack *Larix laricina* (D)	Very hardy larch yielding valuable timber.	*North America*
Podocarp/Podocarpaceae	**(c. 125 species)**	
Huon pine *Dacrydium franklinii* (E)	Slow-growing tree producing very durable and valuable timber.	*Tasmania*
▲ Kahikatea *Podocarpus dacrydioides* (E)	Valuable timber tree; drooping branchlets clothed with scale leaves.	*New Zealand*
Rimu *Dacrydium cupressinum* (E)	Valuable timber tree; drooping branchlets with triangular leaves.	*New Zealand*
Redwood/Taxodiaceae	**(16 species)**	
Giant sequoia *Sequoiadendron giganteum* (E)	Up to 330 feet (100 m) high and 28 feet (8.6 m) across; the world's largest living thing.	*California*
Redwood *Sequoia sempervirens* (E)	The world's tallest tree, up to 360 feet (110 m) high with thick, spongy bark.	*California*
Yew/Taxaceae	**(20 species)**	
Yew *Taxus baccata* (E)	Long-lived tree with very durable timber; seeds in fleshy pink cups.	*Europe, W. Asia, and N. Africa*
FLOWERING TREES (ANGIOSPERMS): Dicotyledons		
Magnolia/Magnoliaceae	**(c. 230 species)**	
Magnolia *Magnolia* (c. 35 species) (D and E)	Small decorative trees with cup-shaped or starlike flowers.	*Americas and E. Asia*
Yellow poplar *Liriodendron tulipifera* (D)	Tall tree with tulip-shaped, greenish flowers.	*Americas*
Cistus/Cistaceae	**(c. 165 species)**	
Cistus *Cistus* (c. 20 species) (E)	Aromatic shrubs with pink or white flowers.	*Mainly Mediterranean*
Plane/Platanaceae	**(10 species)**	
London planetree *Platanus* x *acerifolia* (D)	Tall, pollution-tolerant tree, much planted in towns and on roadsides; hybrid of the American and oriental planes.	*Europe*
Elm/Ulmaceae	**(c. 2,000 species)**	
American elm *Ulmus americana* (D)	Tall timber tree and common American street tree.	*North America*
English elm *Ulmus procera* (D)	Tall timber tree with a crown of domed heads; common in hedgerows.	*Europe*
Wych elm *Ulmus glabra* (D)	Tall, many-branched tree; pollution-tolerant and common in towns.	*Europe and W. Asia*
Fig/Moraceae	**(c. 3,000 species)**	
Banyan *Ficus benghalensis* (E)	A fig with numerous roots growing down from its spreading branches.	*India*

Ginkgo
Maidenhair tree

Monkey puzzle
Monkey puzzle tree

Pine
Norway spruce

Redwood
Redwood

Plane
London planetree

Family/Name	Notable features	Original home
Casuarina/Casuarinaceae	**(c. 65 species)**	
Casuarina *Casuarina* (c. 45 species) (E)	Trees and shrubs with slender, green twigs; often called oaks in Australia.	*Australia and S.E. Asia*
Beech/Fagaceae	**(c. 900 species)**	
Coast live oak *Quercus agrifolia* (E)	Sturdy tree once covering huge areas of S.W. United States.	*North America*
Cork oak *Quercus suber* (E)	Spongy outer bark is stripped every few years to provide cork.	*Mediterranean*
English oak *Quercus robur* (D)	Sturdy, much-branched timber tree with stalked acorns.	*Europe*
European beech *Fagus sylvatica* (D)	Tall, smooth-barked timber tree; copper beech is a purple-leaved cultivar.	*Europe*
Northern red oak *Quercus rubra* (D)	Fast-growing ornamental; large spiky leaves are deep red in fall.	*North America*
Sweet chestnut *Castanea sativa* (D)	Tall tree with spirally patterned bark and edible nuts.	*S. Europe*
Birch/Betulaceae	**(c. 100 species)**	
Alder *Alnus* (c. 35 species) (D)	Trees with catkins and seeds in woody cones; usually by water.	*Europe and Asia*
European white birch *Betula pendula* (D)	Slender tree with silvery bark; timber used for plywood.	*Europe and Asia*
Paper birch *Betula papyrifera* (D)	Timber tree with smooth bark used for making canoes.	*North America*
Hornbeam/Carpinaceae	**(c. 50 species)**	
European hornbeam *Carpinus betulus* (D)	Tree with one of the hardest timbers—once used for wheel hubs.	*Europe*
Hazel/Corylaceae	**(15 species)**	
Common hazel *Corylus avellana* (D)	Small tree or shrub used for hurdle making; cultivars produce edible cobnuts.	*Europe and W. Asia*
Walnut/Juglandaceae	**(c. 50 species)**	
Black walnut *Juglans nigra* (D)	Tall, elegant tree often planted on roadsides; nuts of poor quality.	*North America*
Common walnut *Juglans regia* (D)	Broad-crowned tree widely grown for its nuts and fine timber.	*S.E. Europe, S. Asia*
Hickory *Carya* (c. 20 species) (D)	Tall timber trees; some, such as pecan, have edible nuts.	*North America*
Bougainvillea/Nyctaginaceae	**(c. 300 species of trees, shrubs, and herbs)**	
Bougainvillea *Bougainvillea* (c. 18 species) (D)	Decorative climbing shrubs whose tiny flowers are surrounded by colorful petallike bracts; many cultivars.	*South America*
Cactus/Cactaceae	**(c. 2,000 species)**	
▲ Saguaro *Cereus giganteus* (E)	Branching, treelike cactus up to 40 feet (12 m) high; now in rapid decline.	*North American desert*
Tea/Theaceae	**(c. 500 species)**	
Common camellia *Camellia japonica* (E)	Small shrub with glossy leaves, grown for its roselike flowers.	*Japan*
Tea *Camellia sinensis* (E)	Small tree whose young shoots are dried to produce more than two million tons of tea every year; grown mainly in S. and E. Asia and E. Africa.	*S.E. Asia*
Willow/Salicaceae	**(c. 530 species)**	
Basket willow *Salix viminalis* (D)	Shrubby willow whose slender branches are used for basket making.	*Europe*
Lombardy poplar *Populus nigra* var *italica* (D)	Tall columnar form of black poplar widely grown as a windbreak.	*Europe*
Pussy willow *Salix discolor* (D)	Straggly tree with strongly scented, golden male catkins in spring.	*Europe and W. Asia*
Quaking aspen *Populus tremuloides* (D)	Poplar whose thin-stalked leaves tremble in the lightest breeze.	*Europe and N. Asia*
Weeping willow *Salix babylonica* (D)	Many-branched tree with long, hanging twigs; usually near water.	*China*
Heather/Ericaceae	**(c. 3,000 species)**	
Common rhododendron *Rhododendron ponticum* (E)	Large, pink-flowered shrub common in woods, parks, and gardens.	*Europe*
Heather or ling *Calluna vulgaris* (E)	Low-growing shrub of acid heaths and moors; main food of the grouse.	*Europe*
Strawberry tree *Arbutus unedo* (E)	Small tree with red berries vaguely resembling wild strawberries.	*S. and S.W. Europe*
Ebony/Ebenaceae	**(c. 500 species)**	
Ebony *Diospyros ebenum* (D)	A tree with very dark, heavy timber; name is also given to other trees with similar timber.	*Sri Lanka*
Bombax/Bombacaceae	**(c. 180 species)**	
Balsa *Ochroma lagopus* (E)	Very quick growing tree producing the lightest of all timber.	*Tropical Americas*
Baobab *Adansonia digitata* (D)	Tree whose broad, soft trunk yields useful fibers; edible fruits.	*Dry African tropics*
Kapok tree *Ceiba pentandra* (D)	Tree cultivated for the light, water-repellent fibers—kapok—around its seeds.	*Tropical Americas*
Cacao/Sterculiaceae	**(c. 700 species)**	
Cacao tree *Theobroma cacao* (E)	Slender tree with oval pods on its trunk; now grown mainly in W. Africa; the seeds are roasted to produce cocoa and chocolate.	*Tropical Americas*
Cola tree *Cola* (c. 50 species) (E)	Slender trees whose seeds (kola nuts) contain useful stimulants.	*Africa*
Linden/Tiliaceae	**(c. 400 species)**	
Common lime *Tilia* x *vulgaris* (D)	Sturdy tree with slender shoots at the base; planted in parks and on roadsides; hybrid between small-leaved and large-leaved lindens.	*Europe*
Box/Buxaceae	**(c. 100 species)**	
Box *Buxus sempervirens* (E)	Small tree or shrub with good timber; often used for garden hedges.	*Europe and N. Africa*

Beech
Northern red oak

Birch
European white birch

Walnut
Common walnut

Willow
Weeping willow

Heather
Strawberry tree

Family/Name	Notable features	*Original home*
Spurge/Euphorbiaceae	**(*c.* 5,000 species of trees, shrubs, and herbs)**	
Candlenut tree *Aleurites moluccana* (E)	Tree whose oil-rich nuts are strung together and used as candles.	*Tropical Asia*
Poinsettia *Euphorbia pulcherrima* (D)	Widely grown ornamental shrub with brilliant scarlet bracts and tiny flowers.	*Tropical Americas*
Rubber tree *Hevea brasiliensis* (D)	Slender tree grown mainly in S.E. Asia; rubber derived from its latex.	*Brazil*
Rose/Rosaceae	**(More than 3,000 species of trees, shrubs, and herbs)**	
European mountain-ash *Sorbus aucuparia* (D)	Hardy tree with white flowers and red fruits; tolerant of pollution.	*Europe*
Oneseed hawthorn *Crataegus monogyna* (D)	A tough spiny tree; common hedging plant; also called may and quickthorn.	*Europe and W. Asia*
Rose *Rosa* (*c.* 250 species) (D)	Prickly shrubs and climbers with scented flowers; more than 5,000 cultivars.	*N. Hemisphere*
Sweet cherry *Prunus avium* (D)	A useful timber tree and the ancestor of the sweet cherry.	*Europe and W. Asia*
Acacia or Wattle/Mimosaceae	**(*c.* 2,000 species of trees, shrubs, and herbs)**	
Silver wattle *Acacia dealbata* (E)	Good timber tree with abundant tannin and attractive yellow flowers.	*S. Australia*
Legume/Leguminosae	**(More than 12,000 species)**	
Black locust *Robinia pseudoacacia* (D)	Spiny tree with strongly scented white flowers; short lived but grows rapidly.	*North America*
Honey mesquite *Prosopis glandulosa* (E)	Many-branched desert tree; roots can go down 100 feet (30 m) to reach water.	*North American deserts*
Pea/Fabaceae	**(More than 17,000 species)**	
Broom *Sarothamnus scoparius* (E)	Dense, yellow-flowered shrub; cultivars are abundant in parks and gardens.	*Europe*
Common laburnum *Laburnum anagyroides* (D)	Ornamental tree with long sprays of yellow flowers; very poisonous.	*European mountains*
Flame tree *Delonix regia* (D)	Decorative tree with flame-red flowers; widely grown in tropics.	*Madagascar*
Gorse or furze *Ulex europaeus* (E)	Dense, spiny shrub; yellow flowers have a sickly scent.	*W. Europe*
Judas tree *Cercis siliquastrum* (D)	Decorative tree; pink flowers sprout from the trunk and branches.	*Mediterranean*
Wisteria *Wisteria sinensis* (D)	Decorative climber with sprays of lilac flowers; many cultivars.	*China*
Mangrove/Rhizophoraceae	**(*c.* 120 species)**	
Red mangrove *Rhizophora mangle* (E)	Dense shrub in coastal swamps; tangled, basketlike roots build up land.	*Tropics*
Brazil nut/Lecythidaceae	**(*c.* 325 species)**	
Brazil nut *Bertholletia excelsa* (E)	Tall forest tree with edible seeds in heavy, woody, ball-like fruits.	*South America*
Cannonball tree *Couroupita guianensis* (E)	Inedible fruits resemble rusty cannonballs; good timber.	*South America*
Myrtle/Myrtaceae	**(*c.* 3,400 species)**	
Cajuput tree *Melaleuca leucadendron* (E)	Timber tree with thick spongy bark; leaves yield a medicinal oil.	*Australia, S.E. Asia*
Cider gum *Eucalyptus gunnii* (E)	Very hardy timber tree with rounded leaves; widely cultivated.	*Tasmania*
Mountain ash *Eucalyptus regnans* (E)	One of the tallest flowering trees, often more than 300 feet (100 m) high. [NB Mountain ash also refers to group of trees in rose family, *above.*]	*Australia*
Red river gum *Eucalyptus camaldulensis* (E)	Important timber tree growing mainly by rivers; widely cultivated.	*Australia*
Ribbon gum *Eucalyptus viminalis* (E)	One of the "stringy-bark" gums that shed their bark in long strips.	*Australia*
Snow gum *Eucalyptus pauciflora* (E)	Very hardy tree, withstanding long periods of frost and snow.	*Australian mountains*
Willowherb/Onagraceae	**(*c.* 650 species)**	
Fuchsia *Fuchsia* (*c.* 100 species) (D)	Ornamental shrubs with pendulous flowers, often pollinated by birds.	*Americas and Pacific*
Cashew/Anacardiaceae	**(*c.* 600 species)**	
Christmas-berry *Schinus terebinthifolia* (E)	Delicate tree with bright red berries; also called Brazilian pepper.	*South America*
Poison ivy *Rhus toxicodendron* (D)	Climbing shrub containing chemicals that cause severe skin rashes.	*North America*
Staghorn sumac *Rhus typhina* (D)	Decorative shrub with hairy twigs and flame-red fall colors.	*E. North America*
Turpentine tree *Pistacia terebinthus* (D)	Slender tree with coral-red fruits in fall; resin once used for turpentine.	*Mediterranean*
Quassia/Simaroubaceae	**(*c.* 120 species)**	
Ailanthus *Ailanthus altissima* (D)	Common town and park tree; compound leaves are bronze at first.	*China*
Mahogany/Meliaceae	**(*c.* 1,400 species)**	
Mahogany *Swietenia mahogani* (E)	Valuable timber tree, now rare through overexploitation.	*Tropical Americas*
Horsechestnut/Hippocastanaceae	**(15 species)**	
Buckeye *Aesculus* (13 species) (D)	Group of trees whose seeds resemble big eyes.	*North America, Europe*
Horsechestnut *Aesculus hippocastanum* (D)	Broad tree with sticky buds.	*S.E. Europe*
Maple/Aceraceae	**(*c.* 200 species)**	
Field maple *Acer campestre* (D)	Attractive hedgerow tree; leaves pink at first and golden in fall.	*Europe and W. Asia*
Planetree maple *Acer pseudoplatanus* (D)	Tall, with useful pale timber; spreads quickly by dispersing winged fruits.	*S. and C. Europe*
Sugar maple *Acer saccharum* (D)	Tall timber tree, also yielding maple syrup; magnificent fall colors.	*North America*
Coca/Erythroxylaceae	**(*c.* 250 species)**	
Coca tree *Erythroxylum* (E)	Small tree or shrub whose leaves yield cocaine.	*Andes*
Dogwood/Cornaceae	**(*c.* 110 species of trees, shrubs and herbs)**	
Flowering dogwood *Cornus florida* (D)	Common flowering tree; has four white bracts beneath small greenish flowers.	*North America*

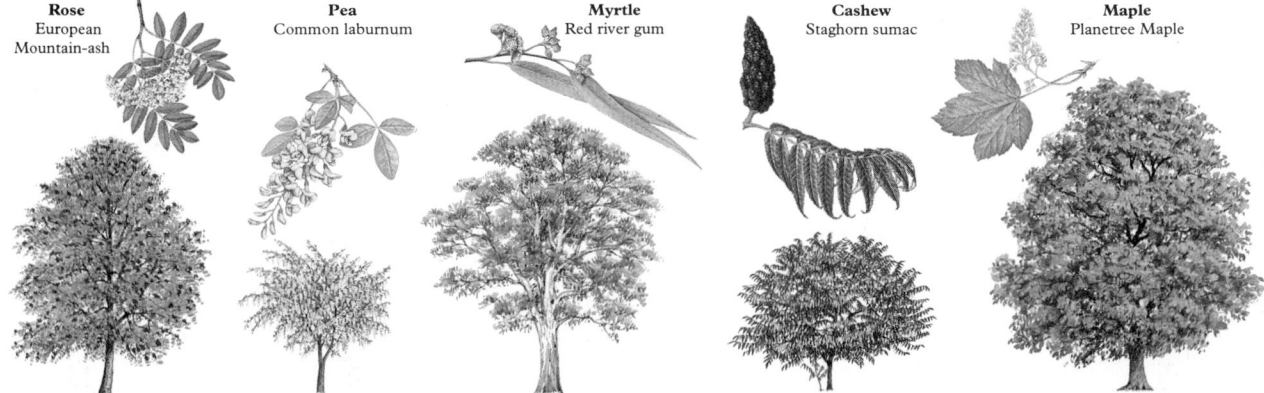

Rose
European
Mountain-ash

Pea
Common laburnum

Myrtle
Red river gum

Cashew
Staghorn sumac

Maple
Planetree Maple

Family/Name	Notable features	Original home
Ginseng/Araliaceae	(*c.* 700 species, mostly tropical)	
Ivy *Hedera helix* (E)	Woody climber, clinging to supports with small roots on the stems; not parasitic, although competes with trees for water and minerals.	Europe and W. Asia
Holly/Aquifoliaceae	(*c.* 400 species)	
English holly *Ilex aquifolium* (E)	Prickly tree or hedgerow shrub; plants are either male or female, the red berries forming only on female plants; useful pale timber.	S. and W. Europe and S.W. Asia
Olive/Oleaceae	(*c.* 600 species)	
Common ash *Fraxinus excelsior* (D)	Tall tree yielding light, strong timber ideal for sports equipment.	Europe and W. Asia
Forsythia *Forsythia* (7 species) (D)	Ornamental shrubs clothed with yellow flowers before the leaves open.	S.E. Europe, E. Asia
Lilac *Syringa vulgaris* (D)	Small ornamental tree widely grown for its fragrant flowers.	S.E. Europe
Manna ash *Fraxinus ornus* (D)	Ornamental tree with white flowers; produces an edible gum (manna).	S.C. Europe, W. Asia
Olive *Olea europaea* (E)	Small, long-living tree cultivated since classical times for its oil-rich fruits.	Mediterranean
Winter jasmine *Jasminum nudiflorum* (D)	Slender, decorative shrub with fragrant yellow flowers in winter.	China
Protea/Proteaceae	(*c.* 1,000 species)	
Banksia *Banksia* (*c.* 50 species) (E)	Shrubs and trees with brushlike spikes of yellow or orange flowers.	Australia
Macadamia *Macadamia tetraphylla* (E)	Small tree whose edible nuts yield an oil used in cosmetics.	Australia
Honeysuckle/Caprifoliaceae	(*c.* 450 species, mostly trees and shrubs, but some herbs)	
Common honeysuckle *Lonicera periclymenum* (D)	Twining woody climber with fragrant, trumpet-shaped flowers; often damages young trees in plantations.	Europe
Elder/Sambucaceae	(40 species)	
Elder *Sambucus nigra* (D)	Scruffy shrub or small tree; berries often used for jam and wine.	Europe and W. Asia
Periwinkle/Apocynaceae	(*c.* 1,500 species, mostly climbing shrubs)	
Frangipani *Plumeria rubra* (E)	Small tree widely grown for its fragrant white or pink flowers.	Tropical Americas
Oleander *Nerium oleander* (E)	Short, upright shrub widely grown for its pink or white flowers.	Mediterranean
Bedstraw/Rubiaceae	(*c.* 7,000 species of trees, shrubs, and herbs)	
Coffee *Coffea arabica* (E)	Small tree with berries in which coffee beans develop; provides about 75% of the world's coffee; the rest comes mainly from *Coffea canephora*.	Ethiopia
Buddleia/Buddlejaceae	(*c.* 150 species)	
Buddleia *Buddleja davidii* (D)	Vigorous shrub; purple flowers famous for attracting butterflies.	China
Catalpa/Bignoniaceae	(*c.* 650 species of trees, shrubs, and climbers)	
Calabash tree *Crescentia cujete* (E)	Forest tree producing woody, gourdlike fruits used as containers.	Tropical Americas
Indian bean tree *Catalpa bignonioides* (D)	Ornamental tree with white flowers and long, beanlike fruits.	North America
Jacaranda *Jacaranda mimosifolia* (D)	Common street tree in warm areas; blue flowers and feathery leaves.	Argentina
Verbena/Verbenaceae	(*c.* 3,000 species of trees, shrubs, and herbs)	
Teak *Tectona grandis* (D)	Tall tree yielding strong, oily, insect-resistant timber.	S.E. Asia

FLOWERING TREES (ANGIOSPERMS): Monocotyledons

Lily/Liliaceae	(*c.* 3,500 species, mostly herbaceous)	
Aloe *Aloe* (*c.* 300 species) (E)	Spikes of reddish flowers and rosettes of thick, spiny leaves.	Africa and Arabia
▲Joshua-tree *Yucca brevifolia* (E)	Hardy, long-lived tree with swordlike leaves at the ends of the few branches.	North American deserts
Grass tree/Xanthorrhoeaceae	(*c.* 70 species, all in Australasian region)	
Grass tree *Xanthorrhoea fulva* (E)	Tufts of grasslike leaves and candlelike flower-spikes on a short, dark trunk.	Australia
Agave/Agavaceae	(*c.* 700 species)	
Agave *Agave* (*c.* 300 species) (E)	Short with large and often spiky leaves; some species yield sisal fibers; widely planted in the Mediterranean.	Americas (warm)
Cabbage tree *Cordyline australis* (E)	Sturdy branches end in cabbagelike tufts of long, pointed leaves.	New Zealand
Dragon tree *Dracaena draco* (E)	Umbrella-like crown of sturdy branches, topped by rosettes of narrow leaves; trunk exudes red resin called dragon's blood.	Canary Islands
Bamboo/Bambusaceae	(*c.* 850 species)	
Bamboo (*c.* 45 genera) (E)	Relatives of the grasses, up to 100 feet (30 m) high, with hollow stems (canes).	Tropics, especially Asia
Palm/Palmae	(*c.* 2,780 species: unbranched stems, leaves usually only at top)	
Oil palm *Elaeis guineensis* (E)	Widely cultivated; oil from the fruit is used to make soap and for industrial purposes, oil from the seed is used for margarine and other foodstuffs.	Tropical W. Africa
Raffia palm *Raphia* (*c.* 20 species) (E)	Leaves are world's largest—up to 80 feet (25 m) long; leaf fibers make raffia.	Africa
Rattan palm *Calamus* (*c.* 370 species) (E)	Climbing palms with stems up to 600 feet (180 m) long; source of good cane.	S.E. Asia

Holly
English holly

Olive
Olive

Catalpa
Indian bean tree

Agave
Joshua tree

Grass tree
Grass tree

FOOD PLANTS

The fruit and vegetables that we eat contain starch, sugar, and other foodstuffs that the plants have stored up for their own use. Botanically speaking, fruits are formed from the pollinated flowers of plants. They always contain seeds. The term vegetable is generally used in a looser way, often simply referring to plants eaten with the main course of the meal. This can cause some confusion. Cucumbers, summer squash, peppers, and tomatoes are commonly considered vegetables, although to the botanist they are in fact fruits (Vegetables, *below*).

Fruits—true and false

A true fruit is derived solely from the carpel or carpels of a flower after pollination. Some fruits are juicy, but many others are dry when they are ripe and they split open to release their seeds. Pea and bean pods are examples, although we eat some of them before they are ripe.

Botanists split juicy fruits into several groups. Berries generally have many seeds embedded in the soft flesh. Grapes, gooseberries, and citrus fruits are familiar examples. Drupes or stone fruits normally have a fleshy outer layer surrounding a pit, which contains a seed. Plums, peaches, and cherries are drupes, and so are coconuts, although their flesh is not as juicy.

False fruits come from more than just the carpels of the flower. Apples and pears, technically known as pomes, consist largely of the receptacle or flower stalk, which swells up around the seeds. Strawberries are also swollen receptacles. The little pips on the surface are the true fruits—nuts enclosing the seeds.

Fruit

Most juicy fruits are rich in sugar and therefore quite sweet when they are ripe. Some also store starch and oils. These food reserves are not consumed by the plants themselves but serve to attract animals that eat the flesh and scatter the seeds.

Most commercial fruits are obtained from trees and shrubs, although some important ones, such as strawberries and pineapples, come from herbaceous plants. A few fruits are still gathered mainly from the wild, but the majority are now cultivated in plantations or orchards and, as with the vegetables, many are now larger and tastier than their ancestral forms. With the availability of fast, modern transportation, people living in temperate regions are now able to enjoy many fresh tropical fruits that were once impossible to obtain.

Temperate
Cherry — Pear
Grape — Lime — Apple

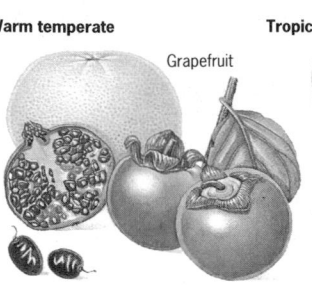

Warm temperate
Grapefruit
Olive — Pomegranate — Persimmon

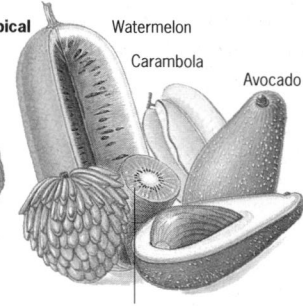

Tropical — Watermelon
Carambola
Avocado
Cherimoya — Kiwi fruit

Vegetables

Our vegetables all contain stored food. Cultivated crops have much larger food stores than their wild ancestors and often bear little resemblance to them.

Many vegetables are biennials, storing food during their first year ready to flower and set seed in the following year—but we harvest them before they can use it.

There are eight different parts of the plant that are eaten (*below*). Bulbs consist of fleshy leaves that surround a short stem. Fruits are the seed enclosures, together with the seeds. Therefore, while individual peas are seeds, peas eaten with the pod—such as green beans—are fruits. Tubers are swollen underground stems.

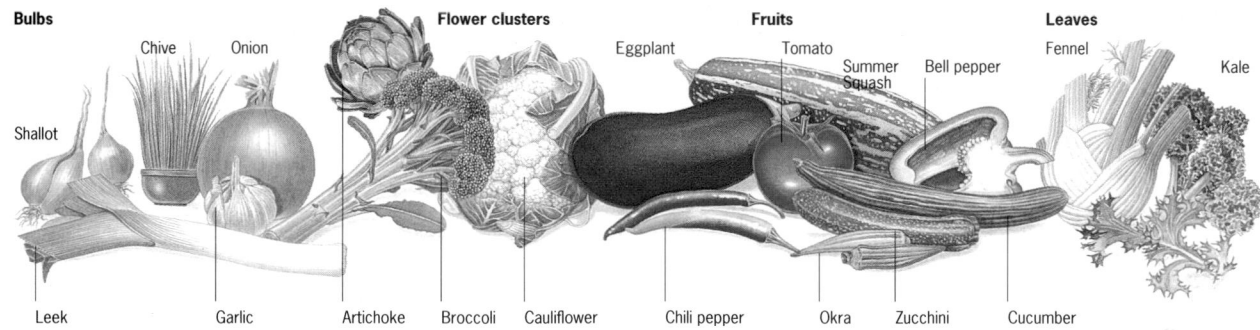

Bulbs
Chive — Onion
Shallot
Leek — Garlic — Artichoke

Flower clusters
Broccoli — Cauliflower

Fruits
Eggplant — Tomato
Summer Squash — Bell pepper
Chili pepper — Okra — Zucchini — Cucumber

Leaves
Fennel — Kale

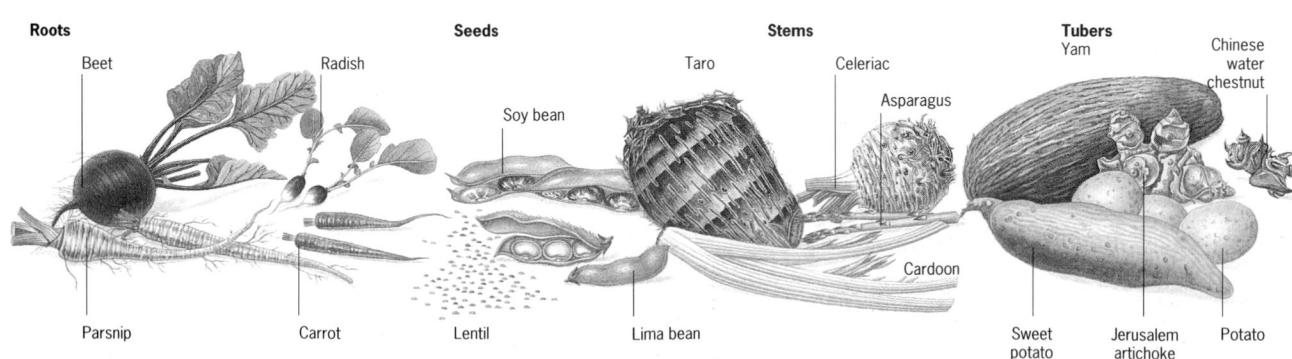

Roots
Beet — Radish
Parsnip — Carrot

Seeds
Soy bean
Lentil — Lima bean

Stems
Taro — Celeriac
Asparagus
Cardoon

Tubers
Yam — Chinese water chestnut
Sweet potato — Jerusalem artichoke — Potato

FOOD PLANTS

Family/Name	Parts eaten	Growth form	Original home
FRUIT AND VEGETABLES			
Custard apple/Annonaceae			
Cherimoya *Anona cherimolia*	Many-seeded fruit.	Small evergreen tree	*Tropical Americas*
Custard apple *Annona squamosa*	Many-seeded fruit with custardlike flesh.	Small evergreen tree	*Central America*
Bay/Lauraceae			
Avocado *Persea americana*	Fruit with a high fat and protein content.	Small evergreen tree	*Central America*
Fig/Moraceae			
Black mulberry *Morus nigra*	Fruit, often used for jam.	Rugged deciduous tree	*W. Asia*
Breadfruit *Artocarpus altilis*	Starch-filled fruit, usually eaten roasted.	Large tree, up to 100 feet (30 m) high	*Pacific islands*
Fig *Ficus carica*	Fruit, eaten fresh or dried.	Small deciduous tree	*W. Asia*
Jackfruit *Artocarpus integrifolia*	Starch-filled fruit up to 165 lb. (30 kg), eaten cooked or raw.	Large evergreen tree	*Tropical Asia*
Dock/Polygonaceae			
Rhubarb *Rheum rhaponticum*	Leafstalks, cooked as "fruit"; oxalic acid in leaves is poisonous.	Herbaceous perennial	*Central Asia*
Sorrel *Rumex acetosa*	Leaves, used in salads or cooked like spinach.	Herbaceous perennial	*N. Hemisphere*
Beet/Chenopodiaceae			
Beet *Beta vulgaris*	Red, sugar-rich root.	Herbaceous biennial	*Eurasia*
Spinach *Spinacea oleracea*	Leaves, cooked as green vegetable and eaten raw in salads.	Annual herb	*Mediterranean*
Spinach beet *Beta vulgaris*	Leaves and leafstalks, cooked as vegetables; chard is a variety with particularly thick, fleshy white stalks.	Herbaceous biennial	*Eurasia*
Sugar beet *Beta vulgaris*	Large sugar-filled root; now yields nearly half the world's sugar.	Leafy biennial	*European coasts*
Mangosteen/Clusiaceae			
Mangosteen *Garcinia mangostana*	Fruit, with tough purplish rind and a sweet white pulp.	Evergreen tree	*S.E. Asia*
Gourd/Cucurbitaceae			
Chayote *Sechium edule*	Leaves, roots, and gourdlike fruits, all used as vegetables.	Perennial climber	*Central America*
Cucumber *Cucumis sativus*	Fruit, usually eaten raw in salads.	Trailing or climbing annual	*S. Asia*
Melon *Cucumis melo*	Sugar-rich fruit, with many varieties.	Trailing annual	*Africa*
Pumpkin *Cucurbita pepo*	Fruit, eaten as vegetable and in pumpkin pie; same species as the summer squash, but with rounded fruits.	Trailing annual	*Central America*
Summer squash *Cucurbita pepo*	Fruit, cooked as vegetable.	Trailing annual	*Central America*
Watermelon *Citrullus vulgaris*	Large fruit with sweet, watery flesh.	Climbing annual	*Africa*
Zucchini *Cucurbita pepo*	Fruit, cooked as vegetable; a squash variety eaten when young.	Trailing or climbing annual	*Central America*
Cabbage/Brassicaceae			
Broccoli *Brassica oleracea*	Unopened flower heads; many varieties.	Herbaceous biennial	*Europe*
Brussels sprout *Brassica oleracea*	Large buds densely packed on the stem.	Herbaceous biennial	*Europe*
Cabbage *Brassica oleracea*	Leaves, usually packed into a dense head; many varieties including red cabbage and savoy.	Herbaceous biennial	*Europe*
Cauliflower *Brassica oleracea*	Densely packed, unopened flower heads.	Herbaceous biennial	*Europe*
Chinese cabbage *Brassica chinensis*	Loose leaves, eaten cooked or raw; also called pak-choi.	Herbaceous biennial	*E. Asia*
Kale *Brassica oleracea*	Leaves; hardy brassicas for winter use.	Herbaceous biennial	*Europe*
Kohlrabi *Brassica oleracea*	Ball-shaped swollen stem; green or purple.	Herbaceous biennial	*Europe*
Radish *Raphanus sativus*	Root, usually eaten raw in salads.	Annual herb	*Unknown*
Rutabaga *Brassica napus*	Root and stem; believed to be hybrid of turnip and cabbage.	Herbaceous biennial	*Europe*
Turnip *Brassica rapa*	Root, but leaves also cooked as "greens."	Herbaceous biennial	*Europe*
Watercress *Nasturtium officinale*	Leaves and stems, eaten raw; high in minerals and vitamins.	Herbaceous perennial	*Europe*
Kiwi fruit/Actinidiaceae			
Kiwi fruit *Actinidia chinensis*	Many-seeded fruit; brown-skinned with green flesh; also called Chinese gooseberry.	Climbing shrub	*E. Asia*
Ebony/Ebenaceae			
Persimmon *Diospyros* (several species)	Tomato-like fruits, also called date plums, eaten raw or cooked; three cultivated species.	Deciduous tree	*North America, E. Asia*
Sapodilla/Sapotaceae			
Sapodilla *Achras zapota*	Sugar-rich, pulpy fruits; the tree's latex also yields chicle gum, used in chewing gum.	Evergreen tree	*Central America*
Mallow/Malvaceae			
Okra *Hibiscus esculentus*	Unripe podlike fruits, eaten cooked or raw.	Herbaceous annual	*Tropical Africa*
Spurge/Euphorbiaceae			
Cassava *Manihot esculenta*	Starch-filled tuberous roots; also called manioc; source of tapioca.	Small shrub	*South and Central America*

Custard apple
Custard apple

Fig
Fig

Gourd
Watermelon

Mangosteen
Mangosteen

Cabbage
Kohlrabi

Kiwi fruit
Kiwi fruit

Spurge
Cassava

Mallow
Okra

Dock
Rhubarb

Beet
Sugar beet

Family/Name	Parts eaten	Growth form	Original home
Papaya/Caricaceae			
Papaya *Carica papaya*	Succulent, many-seeded fruit clustered on trunk.	Small evergreen tree	*Tropical Americas*
Gooseberry/Grossulariaceae			
Blackcurrant *Ribes nigrum*	Small black fruits, rich in vitamin C.	Deciduous woodland shrub	*Eurasia*
Gooseberry *Ribes grossularia*	Hairy, green, yellow, or reddish berries.	Spiny deciduous shrub	*Europe*
Redcurrant *Ribes rubrum*	Small red or white fruits (berries).	Deciduous shrub	*W. Europe*
Rose/Rosaceae			
Almond *Prunus dulcis*	Seed, much used in confectionery.	Small deciduous tree	*W. Europe, N. Africa*
Apple *Malus pumila*	Fruit; the most important temperate fruit with hundreds of varieties descended from crab apple.	Deciduous tree	*Europe*
Apricot *Prunus armeniaca*	Fruit; stone fruit with slightly furry skin; seeds like almonds.	Deciduous tree	*C. and E. Asia*
Blackberry *Rubus fruticosus*	Fruit; a cluster of drupes or stone fruits; many wild varieties and cultivars with differing flavors.	Prickly climbing shrub	*Eurasia*
Cherry, sour *Prunus cerasus*	Bitter-tasting fruit, used for liqueurs; includes morello cherry.	Deciduous tree	*W. Asia*
Cherry, sweet *Prunus avium*	Fruit; varieties descended from wild cherry or gean.	Tall deciduous tree	*W. Asia*
Cloudberry *Rubus chamaemorus*	Fruit resembling a golden blackberry; prized in Scandinavia.	Short herbaceous perennial	*Northern areas*
Damson *Prunus damascena*	Fruit; small, dark, oval plum, usually eaten cooked or in jams.	Deciduous tree	*Europe*
Greengage *Prunus italica*	Fruit; sweet, greenish yellow plum.	Deciduous tree	*W. Asia*
Loquat *Eriobotrya japonica*	Small, yellow, pear-shaped fruit, eaten fresh, cooked, or in jams.	Evergreen tree	*E. Asia*
Medlar *Mespilus germanica*	Fruit; usually eaten when overripe.	Deciduous tree, often spiny	*Europe*
Nectarine *Prunus nectarina*	Fruit; with smooth stone and skin; hybrid of peach and plum.	Deciduous tree	*Europe*
Peach *Prunus persica*	Fruit; velvety skin and a rough stone.	Deciduous tree	*E. Asia*
Pear *Pyrus communis*	Fruit; many dessert and cooking varieties.	Deciduous tree	*Europe*
Plum *Prunus domestica*	Fruit; numerous varieties, all descendants of hybrid of blackthorn and cherry plum.	Deciduous tree	*W. Asia*
Quince *Cydonia vulgaris*	Pear-shaped fruit, used mainly in preserves.	Small deciduous tree	*W. Asia*
Raspberry *Rubus idaeus*	Fruit; red or yellow with many drupes, like blackberry.	Deciduous shrub	*Eurasia*
Strawberry *Fragaria ananassa*	Fruit; cultivated forms descended from hybrids of two American species.	Creeping herbaceous perennial	*Americas*
Tamarind/Leguminosae			
Tamarind *Tamarindus indica*	Pulp from seed pods, eaten fresh or used dried as seasoning.	Deciduous tree	*India*
Pea/Fabaceae			
Broad or fava bean *Vicia faba*	Seeds, cooked as vegetables; an early cultivated vegetable.	Hardy herbaceous annual	*Europe*
Chickpea *Cicer arietinum*	Protein-rich seeds; main Indian pulse crop.	Herbaceous annual	*W. Asia*
Haricot bean *Phaseolus vulgaris*	Ripe seeds, usually dried and cooked in various ways; many varieties include flageolet and borlotti beans.	Tender herbaceous annual	*South America*
Kidney bean *Phaseolus vulgaris*	Unripe seeds and pods.	Tender herbaceous annual	*South America*
Lentil *Lens culinaris*	Seeds, dried for use in soups and stews.	Herbaceous annual	*Mediterranean*
Pea *Pisum sativum*	Seeds, usually picked unripe for use as vegetables, but sometimes gathered ripe and then dried.	Herbaceous annual	*Middle East*
Peanut *Arachis hypogaea*	Seeds, eaten cooked or raw; also a major source of edible oil.	Herbaceous annual; pods maturing underground	*South America*
Scarlet runner *Phaseolus coccineus*	Unripe seeds and pods.	Tender herbaceous climber	*South America*
Soybean *Glycine max*	Seeds, used fresh or dried; also a major source of oil.	Bushy herbaceous annual	*S.W. Asia*
Pomegranate/Punicaceae			
Pomegranate *Punica granatum*	Juicy flesh surrounding the many seeds in the orange-skinned fruit; best used to make refreshing drinks.	Deciduous shrub with bright-red flowers	*W. Asia*
Myrtle/Myrtaceae			
Guava *Psidium guajava*	Many-seeded fruit; rich in vitamin C; often canned or made into jams and soft drinks.	Small evergreen tree	*Tropical Americas*
Cashew/Anacardiaceae			
Cashew *Anacardium occidentale*	Seed; rich in protein and fat; roasted and eaten as a snack.	Evergreen tree	*Tropical Americas*
Mango *Mangifera indica*	Large, juicy fruits; weighing up to 1.5 lb. (0.7 kg).	Large evergreen tree	*S.E. Asia*
Pistachio nut *Pistacia vera*	Green-fleshed seed; used in snacks, confectionery, ice cream.	Deciduous tree	*W. Asia*
Citrus/Rutaceae			
Clementine *Citrus reticulata*	Fruit; probably hybrid of orange and tangerine.	Small evergreen tree	*Unknown*
Grapefruit *Citrus paradisi*	Fruit, eaten fresh or canned; probably a hybrid of sweet orange and pomelo.	Evergreen tree	*Central America*
Kumquat *Fortunella* (many species)	Acidic fruits; like small oranges, used mainly in preserves.	Cold-hardy evergreen tree	*E. Asia*
Lemon *Citrus limon*	Acidic, yellow fruit; characteristic oval shape.	Evergreen tree	*S.E. Asia*
Lime *Citrus aurantifolia*	Small, acidic, green fruit, used mainly for its juice.	Small evergreen tree	*Probably India*
Mandarin	A variety of the tangerine.		

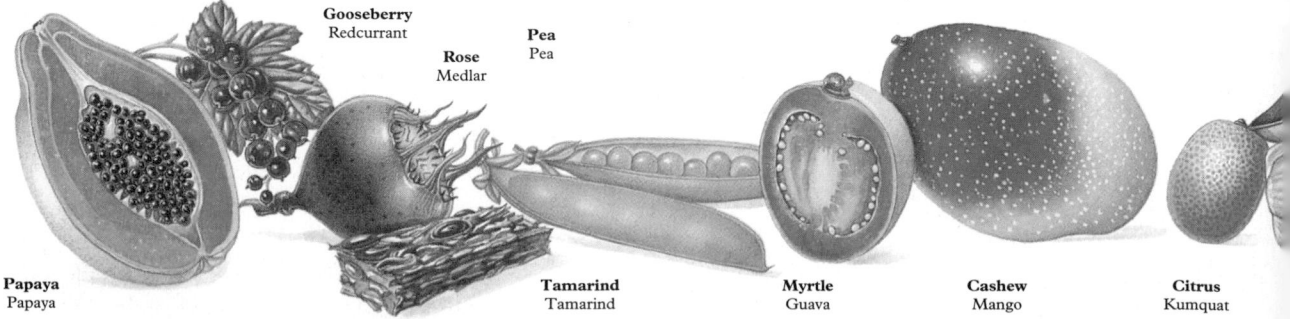

Papaya
Papaya

Gooseberry
Redcurrant

Rose
Medlar

Pea
Pea

Tamarind
Tamarind

Myrtle
Guava

Cashew
Mango

Citrus
Kumquat

Family/Name	Parts eaten	Growth form	Original home
Satsuma	A variety of the tangerine.	Small evergreen tree	*Far East*
Shaddock *Citrus grandis*	Oval, rough-skinned, yellow fruit; the largest of all citrus species; also called pomelo; an ancestor of the grapefruit.	Large-leaved evergreen tree	*S.E. Asia*
Sour orange *Citrus aurantium*	Bitter fruit, used mainly for marmalade.	Small evergreen tree	*S.W. Asia*
Sweet orange *Citrus sinensis*	Juicy fruit; tree has deliciously scented flowers.	Evergreen	*China*
Tangelo	Any hybrid between tangerine and grapefruit.		
Tangerine *Citrus reticulata*	Fruit; like small oranges, but very sweet with "loose" skin.	Small evergreen tree	*Far East*
Ugli	Fruit; a rough-skinned hybrid of tangerine and grapefruit.	Evergreen tree	*Unknown*
Lychee/Sapindaceae			
Lychee *Litchi chinensis*	Plum-sized fruit, with warty skin and sweet, juicy pulp around a large seed.	Evergreen tree	*China*
Carrot/Apiaceae			
Carrot *Daucus carota*	Sugar-filled roots, rich in vitamin C.	Herbaceous biennial	*Europe*
Celeriac *Apium graveolns*	Globular stem base, eaten raw or cooked; a variety of celery.	Herbaceous biennial	*Europe*
Celery *Apium graveolns*	Succulent leafstalks, eaten raw or cooked.	Herbaceous biennial	*Eurasia*
Florentine fennel *Foeniculum vulgare* var *dulce*	Swollen leaf bases, which form a sort of bulb; a variety of normal fennel (Carrot, *p. 113*).	Herbaceous perennial	*S. Europe*
Parsnip *Pastinaca sativa*	Sweet, starch-filled roots.	Herbaceous biennial	*Europe*
Grape/Vitaceae			
Grape *Vitis vinifera*	Juicy berries; hundreds of cultivars; some eaten, most used in wine making.	Climbing shrub	*Europe*
Bindweed/Convolvulaceae			
Sweet potato *Ipomoea batatas*	Sweet, starch-rich underground tubers.	Sprawling perennial	*South America*
Potato/Solanaceae			
Bell pepper *Capsicum annuum*	Fruit, eaten raw or cooked; dried to form paprika powder.	Herbaceous annual	*Tropical Americas*
Eggplant *Solanum melongena*	Fruit, cooked as vegetable.	Herbaceous perennial	*Tropical Asia*
Potato *Solanum tuberosum*	Starch-rich underground tubers.	Tender herbaceous perennial	*South America*
Tomato *Lycopersicon esculentum*	Fruit (a berry), mainly eaten raw in salads.	Herbaceous perennial but treated as annual in gardens	*South America*
Daisy/Asteraceae			
Artichoke *Cynara scolymus*	Fleshy scales around flower heads are cooked.	Thistlelike perennial	*Mediterranean*
Chicory *Cichorium intybus*	Young leaves eaten in salad; root extract is used as coffee substitute or enhancer.	Herbaceous perennial	*Eurasia*
Endive *Cichorium endivia*	Leaves (slightly bitter), used in salads.	Annual or biennial herb	*Asia*
Jerusalem artichoke *Helianthus tuberosus*	Sweet, knobbly, underground tuber.	Herbaceous perennial with sunflower-like flowers	*North America*
Lettuce *Lactuca sativa*	Leaves, used raw in salads; contain little nourishment but rich in vitamin A; many varieties.	Herbaceous annual	*Mediterranean*
Salsify *Tragopogon porrifolius*	Root, cooked as vegetable or used in soups; also called the vegetable oyster.	Herbaceous biennial	*S. Europe*
Lily/Liliaceae			
Asparagus *Asparagus officinalis*	Young shoots, cooked as vegetable.	Herbaceous perennial	*Europe*
Leek *Allium ampeloprasum*	Leaf bases, which form an elongated bulb.	Herbaceous biennial	*Europe*
Onion *Allium cepa*	Bulbs; fleshy scales are rich in sugar.	Herbaceous biennial	*Probably W. Asia*
Yam/Dioscoreaceae			
Yam *Dioscorea* (several species)	Underground tubers, often very large, cooked in various ways.	Herbaceous perennial	*Tropics*
Banana/Musaceae			
Banana *Musa*	Fruit; rich in sugar and starch; eaten raw or cooked; cultivated forms are all seedless hybrids.	Small "trees" growing from underground rhizomes; each trunk flowers just once	*S.E. Asia*
Bromeliad/Bromeliaceae			
Pineapple *Ananas comosus*	Sugar-rich fruit; sitting close to the ground on a leaf cluster.	Herbaceous perennial	*South America*
Grass/Poaceae			
Sugarcane *Saccharum officinarum*	Sugar stored in canelike stems.	Tall perennial—up to 20 feet (6 m) high	*Tropical Asia*
Palm/Arecaceae			
Coconut *Cocos nucifera*	Seed; sweet flesh (meat) eaten fresh or used in confectionery, but most goes for oil.	Tall, unbranched tree with huge, feathery leaves	*Tropical coasts*
Date *Phoenix dactylifera*	Fruit; rich in sugar and usually dried; borne in huge clusters.	Tall, rough-trunked desert tree with fruit at the top	*N. Africa and Middle East*
Sago *Metroxylon sagu*	Starch-rich pith from center of trunk; cooked in various ways.	Short-lived tree	*S.E. Asia*

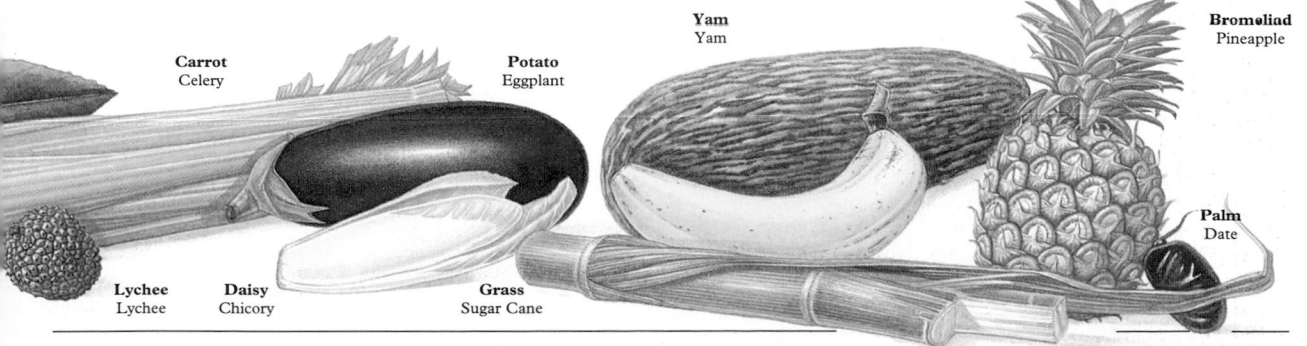

Yam
Yam

Carrot
Celery

Potato
Eggplant

Bromeliad
Pineapple

Palm
Date

Lychee
Lychee

Daisy
Chicory

Grass
Sugar Cane

CEREALS

Cereals are tall annual grasses, bred for their large, starch-filled seeds. They are the staple diets for most of the world's people and are grown on about 75 percent of the world's farmland. Each species has many strains or varieties, each adapted for particular climatic conditions.

Family/Name	Grain form	Major uses	Original home
Grass/Poaceae			
Barley *Hordeum*	Dense ears	Animal feed and malting for beer production.	*W. Asia*
Bulrush millet *Pennisetum glaucum*	Cylindrical spikes of brown or white grain	Major food in drought-affected countries, the crushed grain being cooked like porridge.	*Africa*
Common millet *Panicum miliaceum*	Brushlike heads	Cooked like porridge or used for bread making; commonly sold as birdseed in Britain.	*Africa and Asia*
Corn or maize *Zea mays*	Large ears (cobs) enclosed in a leafy husk	Eaten as vegetable or as cereal (cornflakes), but large quantities go to be made into animal feed or to provide corn oil; unknown in the wild.	*Probably Mexico*
Finger millet *Eleusine coracana*	Several fingerlike spikes	Eaten like porridge or made into bread; a hardy, drought-resistant plant.	*Africa and India*
Foxtail millet *Setaria italica*	Thick spike, like a fox tail	Human food and also grown for hay.	*Asia*
Japanese millet *Echinochloa frumentacea*	Cluster of small ears	Eaten like porridge in many warm countries; a forage crop in North America.	*Asia*
Oats *Avena sativa*	Much-branched head	Animal food, but also for porridge and other breakfast foods; tolerates rain well and most common in northern areas.	*W. Asia*
Rice *Oryza sativa*	Branched, brushlike heads	Grain cooked and eaten without crushing; grown mostly in paddy fields, but dry-land strains also exist.	*E. Asia*
Rye *Secale cereale*	Dense ears	Much used for crackers and black bread in C. Europe; hardier than other cereals and grown mainly in the north.	*Asia*
Sorghum *Sorghum bicolor*	Clusters of small ears	Feeds both people and livestock in semiarid regions.	*Africa*
Wheat *Triticum aestivum* and *Triticum durum*	Dense ears	*Triticum aestivum* is bread wheat. *Triticum durum* is macaroni wheat, providing most of the flour for pasta. Major cereal of temperate regions; about 400 million tons grown each year.	*S.W. Asia*

HERBS AND SPICES

In culinary terms, herbs are those plants whose leaves are used to add flavor to various meals. Spices differ from herbs in that they usually come from different parts of the plants and are normally used in a ground or powdered form. Medicinal herbs are those plants that contain drugs. Many of today's medicines are still extracted from plants or based on synthetic compounds similar to those found in plants.

Family/Name	Parts used and purpose	Growth form	Original home
Nutmeg/Myristicaceae			
Nutmeg *Myristica fragrans*	Seed, ground to form spice used for pumpkin pie and other sweet dishes; the spice mace comes from the same plant.	Evergreen tree	*Indonesia*
Bay/Lauraceae			
Bay *Laurus nobilis*	Leaf, highly aromatic and used for flavoring stews.	Evergreen tree	*Mediterranean*
Cinnamon *Cinnamomum zeylanicum*	Bark, ground to form spice used in sweet dishes; bark used in mulled wine.	Evergreen tree	*India*
Pepper/Piperaceae			
Black pepper *Piper nigrum*	Dried fruits are ground to produce the well-known condiment.	Climbing plant	*India*
Poppy/Papaveraceae			
Opium poppy *Papaver somniferum*	Latex from unripe seed capsule yields morphine, the most effective of all natural painkillers; also yields codeine.	Annual herb	*Asia*
Witch hazel/Hamamelidaceae			
Witch hazel *Hamamelis virginiana*	Leaves and bark yield an antiseptic and anti-inflammatory agent.	Deciduous tree	*North America*
Caper/Capparidaceae			
Caper *Capparis spinosa*	Pickled flower buds are used as a spice to flavor sauces.	Sprawling shrub	*Europe*
Cabbage/Brassicaceae			
Horseradish *Armoracia rusticana*	Root is crushed or minced to make horseradish sauce.	Perennial herb	*Europe*
Mustard *Brassica nigra* (black) and *Sinapis alba* (white)	Seeds yield mustard flour, from which the condiments are made; leaves are high in vitamins A, B, and C.	Annual herb	*Europe*
Spurge/Euphorbiaceae			
Castor oil *Ricinus communis*	Oil from the seeds is used as a purgative and also as a lubricant; the rest of the plant is very poisonous; often grown as ornamental bush.	Small tree	*Africa; common in India, Brazil*
Rose/Rosaceae			
Salad burnet *Sanguisorba minor*	Leaves, tasting mildly of cucumber, are used in salads.	Perennial herb	*Europe*
Pea/Fabaceae			
Licorice *Glycyrrhiza glabra*	Roots and rhizomes yield licorice used in cough medicines, confectionery, and toothpastes.	Perennial herb	*Europe*

Grass
Corn

Grass
Rice

Grass
Wheat

Pepper
Black pepper

Witch hazel
Witch hazel

Family/Name	Parts used and purpose	Growth form	*Original home*
Eucalyptus/Myrtaceae			
Allspice *Pimenta dioica*	Unripe fruits possessing the tastes of several other spices.	Evergreen tree	*West Indies*
Cloves *Eugenia caryophyllus*	Dried flower buds are used to flavor a variety of dishes.	Evergreen tree	*Indonesia*
Carrot/Apiaceae			
Angelica *Angelica archangelica*	All parts are used; roots contribute to gin and seeds to vermouth; crystallized leafstalks used in confectionery.	Biennial	*Europe*
Aniseed *Pimpinella anisum*	Fruits used to flavor confectionery and alcoholic drinks.	Small annual	*Asia*
Caraway *Carum carvi*	Fruits, usually called seeds, used to flavor bread and cakes.	Biennial	*Eurasia*
Chervil *Anthriscus cerefolium*	Curly leaves used in salads and stews; much used in Indian cooking.	Annual	*Asia*
Coriander or cilantro *Coriandrum sativum*	Dried fruits used in curries and also in indigestion remedies; fresh leaves. used in salds, dips, and soups.	Annual	*W. Asia*
Cumin *Cuminum cyminum*	Fruit adds the slightly dry taste to some curries.	Annual	*Mediterranean*
Dill *Anethum graveolans*	Fruit and young leaves used in pickles and sauces; used fresh in salads and dips; oil from the plant is used to relieve colic in babies.	Fine-leaved annual	*Mediterranean*
Fennel *Foeniculum vulgare*	Fine leaves used in soups and sauces; oil from the seed used in edible products.	Tall perennial	*Europe*
Parsley *Petroselinum crispum*	Leaves, often densely curled, used to flavor or garnish hot and cold dishes.	Biennial or perennial	*Europe*
Sweet cicely *Myrrhis odorata*	Leaves used in salads, cooked as vegetable, or used to sweeten rhubarb.	Perennial herb	*Europe*
Potato/Solanaceae			
Chili *Capsicum frutescens*	Fruit and seeds with very hot taste used to add "spice" to curries and other dishes; powdered to make cayenne pepper.	Annual	*South America*
Deadly nightshade *Atropa belladonna*	Leaves yield atropine and other medicinal drugs; a very poisonous plant.	Perennial	*Eurasia*
Henbane *Hyoscyamus niger*	Leaves and young shoots yield drugs with calming effects; a smelly and very poisonous plant.	Perennial	*Eurasia*
Paprika	*See* Bell pepper, (Potato, *p. 111*).		
Snapdragon/Scrophulariaceae			
Foxglove *Digitalis purpurea*	Leaves contain digitalis, an important drug for circulatory problems.	Biennial	*Europe*
Mint/Lamiaceae			
Basil *Ocimum basilicum*	Strongly scented leaves used in soups and stews.	Annual	*Tropics*
Lavender *Lavandula vera*	Healing oils long used medicinally and now in aromatherapy.	Shrub	*Mediterranean*
Lemon balm or Melissa *Melissa officinalis*	Lemon-scented leaves used in herbal teas for fevers and indigestion; also used to make wine.	Perennial herb	*S. Eurasia and N. Africa*
Marjoram *Oreganum*	Leaves of several species flavor stews and many other dishes.	Perennial herb	*Mediterranean*
Mint *Mentha*	Leaves and oils of several species flavor a wide range of foods from roast lamb to candy and chewing gum, toothpaste, and indigestion remedies.	Perennial herb	*Europe*
Rosemary *Rosmarinus officinalis*	Leaves used for flavoring meat, especially roast lamb; fragrant oils used in eau de cologne and other scents.	Evergreen shrub	*Mediterranean*
Sage *Salvia officinalis*	Strongly scented leaves used in cooking.	Shrub	*Mediterranean*
Thyme *Thymus vulgaris*	Leaves and stems; very popular for flavoring meat dishes; also has anti-septic properties and used in cold remedies.	Perennial dwarf shrub	*Mediterranean*
Daisy/Asteraceae			
Chamomile *Anthemis nobilis*	Strongly scented leaves and stems make soothing herbal tea.	Annual	*Europe*
Feverfew *Tanacetum parthenium*	Highly aromatic leaves said to relieve headaches and fever.	Perennial	*Europe*
Tansy *Tanacetum vulgare*	Leaves once boiled to make stimulating "tonic"; old remedy for "worms."	Perennial	*Eurasia*
Tarragon *Artemisia dracunculus*	Leaves used in tartar sauce and other sauces and relishes.	Perennial	*S. Europe*
Wormwood *Artemisia absinthium*	Flower buds flavor absinthe and vermouth; once used in small doses to treat digestive ailments.	Perennial herb	*Europe*
Onion/Alliaceae			
Chives *Allium schoenoprasum*	Chopped leaves are added to many hot and cold dishes.	Perennial	*N. Hemisphere*
Garlic *Allium sativum*	Bulb, composed of several sections called cloves; flavors many foods.	Perennial	*Asia*
Iris/Iridaceae			
Saffron *Crocus sativus*	Styles of the flower, used as a spice and a yellow dye; the most expensive spice, each style having to be picked by hand. Turmeric (*below*) is used as a cheap substitute for saffron in some places.	Purple-flowered corm	*W. Asia*
Ginger/Zingiberaceae			
Cardamom *Elettaria cardamomum*	Small, black-seeded fruits; dried and used mainly in curries.	Perennial herb	*India*
Ginger *Zingiber officinale*	Pungent underground rhizomes; used in curries, candy, and ginger beer.	Perennial herb	*S. Asia*
Turmeric *Curcuma longa*	Underground rhizomes, ground to a yellow powder; adds pungency and color to curries; also used to dye cloth.	Perennial herb	*S. Asia*
Orchid/Orchidaceae			
Vanilla *Vanilla planifolia*	Partly fermented seed pods yield vanillin used in perfumes and confection-ery; world's second most expensive spice, but now made artificially.	Climbing herb	*Tropical Americas*

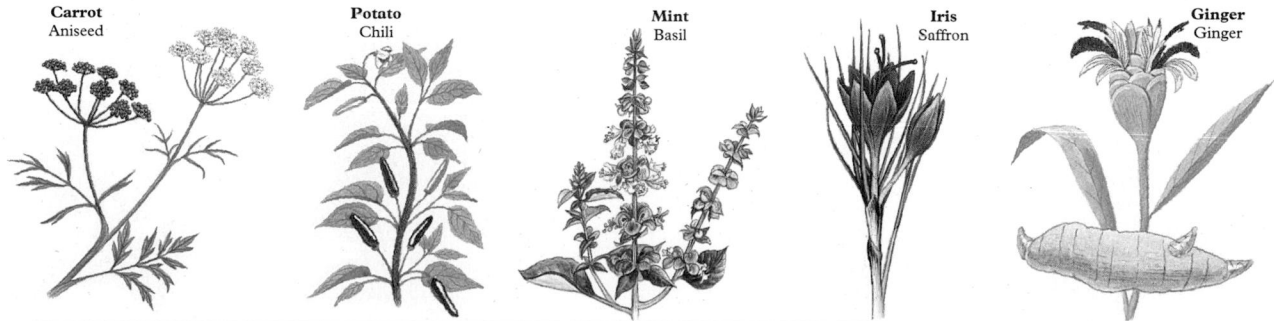

Carrot
Aniseed

Potato
Chili

Mint
Basil

Iris
Saffron

Ginger
Ginger

STRATEGIES FOR SURVIVAL

Scientists have described and named more than a million different species of animals, every one of which is unique in details of both its physical structure and its behavior. Some living in the same area may overlap in their use of a shared environment. In times of hardship, however, such as food shortages in winter or dry seasons, or the stress of breeding and rearing young, each has its own way of coping that excludes all others.

The first stratagem for survival is specialization. Each animal in its own niche is an unassailable specialist. Should the environment change, the specialist may lose out, but in stable habitats the specialist is the winner.

Camouflage

At the end of their lives, almost all animals are eaten by other organisms, but all aim to delay this fate as long as possible. Various mechanisms are used to help them escape from predators or, on the other hand, to enable hunters to catch their prey. One of the most important of these is camouflage, needed by all but burrowing creatures and the very largest of land animals.

The most basic form of camouflage is countershading. Here the back of an animal is more intensely colored than the underside. Light falling from above shadows the paler area, making the color appear uniform. Experiments show that predators faced with countershaded prey find them far more difficult to see than those without this form of camouflage.

Countershading is often augmented with disruptive coloration. Many creatures are patterned with spots and stripes that make them nearly invisible in their background. Disruptive shapes formed by spines or flaps of tissue may add a further degree of camouflage. For instance, the sea dragon of Australian waters is so decorated with flaps of skin that it is almost indistinguishable from the seaweed among which it lives. In some cases, disruptive shape may become an imitation of a particular environment; leaf and stick insects are spectacular examples. Other creatures, such as wasps or ladybugs, are brightly colored to warn predators that they are well protected with stings or chemicals that taste unpleasant.

Venom

Among flesh-eating animals, the use of venom is a method of subduing prey that cuts across taxonomic boundaries. Generally, venomous animals are small, slow moving, or fragile. The delicate tentacles of a Portuguese man-of-war, for instance, deliver paralyzing stings. Were it not for this, it would be thrashed to pieces by the struggles of its prey. With a poisonous bite, near-sighted spiders

Stick insects are exceptionally well camouflaged against green leaves.

prevent insects escaping. Snakes such as vipers or cobras use venom to still fast-moving small mammals.

While each venom is chemically slightly different, almost all have a dual function. The first is to act on the nervous system of the prey, paralyzing it and preventing its escape. The second function is digestive: venoms contain proteolytic enzymes that break down animal tissue. A spider has no need to chew its food: after a while it merely sucks up a largely predigested meal. The mouse eaten by a venomous snake is at least partly digested by the injected poison.

A jumping spider leaps onto a fly.

Migration

In order for the species, and not just individuals, to survive, animals must reproduce. Strategies for successful breeding are widely varied, but many species—including insects and some other invertebrates, fishes, mammals, and birds—make long journeys from wintering or feeding grounds to places suitable for rearing young. These regular journeys are called migrations.

Birds are, to most people, the most obvious migrants. Their travels usually take them north in spring and south again

Birds such as starlings gather together before migrating in flocks.

Hibernation

Animals have many ways of surviving harsh weather when, because of heat and drought or low temperatures, the water and food supplies fall. Some simply move to where food is still abundant. The lives of some African herbivores are a continuous migration following food supplies. Many other animals go into a state of torpor, which is referred to as hibernation in cold conditions or estivation in hot, dry climates.

Cold-blooded animals, such as insects, amphibians, and reptiles, hibernate without any great physical changes. They find a place where they will be safe from predators and where the temperature will not fall below freezing. As their surroundings cool, their bodily activities drop to a level where they are using little energy to stay alive.

No large mammals hibernate truly, but many small species, including some insectivores, bats, and rodents, do. They must make enormous physiological changes in order to survive, perhaps for months, without water or food. To conserve energy, their body temperature drops by many degrees, their heartbeat and blood circulation are reduced to very low levels, and their breathing almost stops. Hummingbirds are able to drop into a torpid state when not in flight; nestling swifts may do so if food is not available; but the only bird known to hibernate fully is the common poorwill, and even it has periods of torpidity lasting only days.

Black bears spend large parts of the winter in semihibernation.

in fall. The northern landmasses have a far greater area than the southern ones, so adequate breeding territories may be set up or, for seabirds, nest sites found near to food-rich waters. Also, the long hours of daylight of the northern summer give more time for feeding hungry young than would be possible in short, tropical days.

Migration routes were probably established at the end of the Pleistocene period, and each species follows its own pattern of movements, led mysteriously but certainly by landmarks, the stars and planets, and even by the earth's magnetic field. Some young birds learn their migration route from their parents. Others, such as young cuckoos, have no such guidance. Flying alone, they have only their innate knowledge of direction and distance to take them to their winter home, a strategy that gives them a chance to survive to be among the next year's breeding population.

Finding food

Food is central to an animal's survival. Most eat plants, for among living things the bulk of vegetation vastly exceeds the biomass of animals. Among these plant feeders, most are specialists—more than 100 different species of insect, for example, may depend on one tree. They vary, however, in their needs for leaves, pollen, bark, wood, or roots, and their different times of feeding. Larger animals are usually less selective, but there are exceptions —such as the three-toed sloth, which feeds only on the tender shoots and leaves of *Cecropia*.

One feeding stratagem that has proved highly successful for large plant-eating mammals is chewing the cud. Cud chewers take in food quickly and pass it directly to a holding compartment of the stomach. Later the food is returned to the mouth for complete mastication. When it is swallowed for a second time it enters another part of the stomach where digestion begins. Normally plant feeders are exposed to predators while gathering food, but a cud chewer can find itself a safe, sheltered place for the lengthy process of mastication. The success of this stratagem can be seen in a comparison of medium-sized plant feeders: 6 species of horselike animals and 2 tapirs do not chew the cud, whereas 40 species of deer and more than 110 species of cattle, sheep, and antelope are all cud chewers.

INVERTEBRATES

The invertebrates are animals with no backbone. Some have no skeleton at all, but many have external skeletons or shells that give them a rigid shape and provide anchorage for their muscles. There are about 30 major groups or phyla of invertebrates, although the great majority of species belong to just two phyla—the Mollusca and the Arthropoda (*pp. 118–21*). The latter includes the insects, spiders, crustaceans, and several other groups, all of which have segmented bodies and jointed legs. The majority of invertebrates are quite small, but examples of the largest—the giant squid—are known to have been as much as 49 feet (15 m) long and possibly well over a ton in weight, which is considerably more than most vertebrates.

Anatomy of a wasp

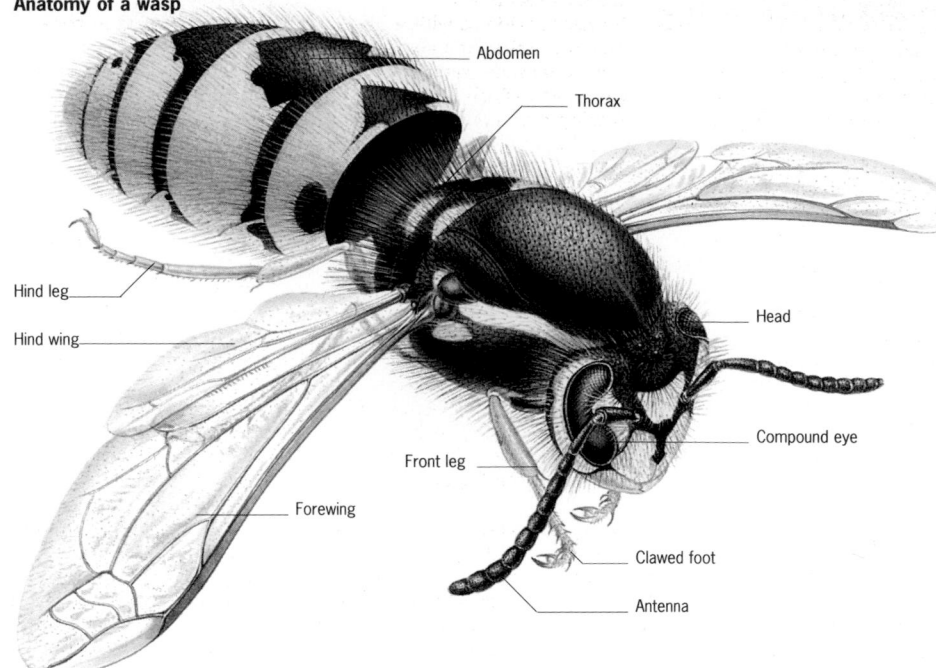

Abdomen

Thorax

Head

Compound eye

Clawed foot

Antenna

Forewing

Front leg

Hind wing

Hind leg

Mollusks

Mollusks are soft-bodied animals with no sign of segmentation. Most have chalky shells. There are more than 60,000 species, three-fourths of which are slugs and snails. Bivalves, such as cockles and mussels, and the squids and their relatives make up most of the rest.

Crustaceans

The crustaceans include animals as diverse as lobsters, barnacles, and water fleas. All have hard outer skeletons impregnated with lime and several pairs of legs. Most of the 30,000 or so species are marine, but many live in freshwater and woodlice live on land.

Insects

The insects are the only type of invertebrates to have wings, although they are not all winged. Adults have three main body sections and three pairs of legs. More than one million species are known, living in almost every habitat, although there are only a very few that live in the sea.

Spiders

Spiders belong to the class of arthropods known as arachnids. They have two main body sections and four pairs of legs. All are carnivorous and kill their prey—usually insects—with venom (*opposite Dangerous Spiders*). Many species snare their prey with extremely intricate silken webs.

Insect life cycles

Insects hatching from their eggs rarely look much like the adults: they often have different feeding habits and never have wings. The change from young to adult form is called metamorphosis and it takes place in one of two ways.

A young grasshopper has the same general shape as an adult grasshopper, and it grows up gradually. Like all insects, it has to change its skin several times because its outer coat does not grow and cannot stretch very much. The youngster becomes more like the adult and its wings get larger at each skin change, or molt, until it reaches maturity. Young insects growing up like this are called nymphs. Dragonflies, earwigs, and true bugs all grow up in the same way.

Butterflies and moths follow a very different life history. Their young stages of development take the form of leaf-eating larvae or caterpillars with no sign of wings. At each molt they simply become bigger larvae, but at the final molt they turn into pupae or chrysalises, and it is inside the pupa that the change to the nectar-feeding adult takes place. Bees, flies, and beetles all grow up in this way.

Butterfly or moth?

Butterflies and moths belong to the order Lepidoptera. The name means "scale-wings" and refers to the minuscule scales that clothe the creatures' wings. These scales are responsible for producing the characteristic colors and patterns of the wings.

The butterflies make up just two of the 22 superfamilies in the order, and there is no single feature that can be used to distinguish all butterflies from all moths. The division is simply one of convenience, with little scientific basis. It is probably based on the fact that almost all butterflies fly by day and most moths fly at night, although there are many day-flying moths. A significant number of languages make no distinction at all between the two groups. In practice, the antennae or feelers provide the best clues to distinguishing butterflies from moths; butterfly antennae almost all end in little clubs, but very few moth antennae have clubs. On the whole, moth antennae tend to be hairlike or slightly feathery.

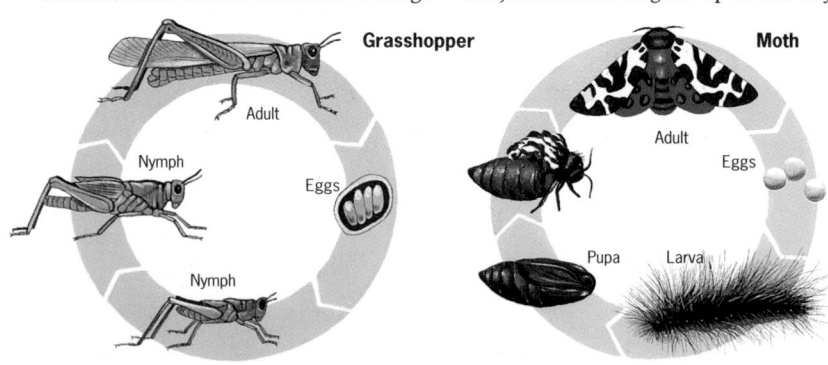

Grasshopper

Adult

Nymph

Eggs

Nymph

Moth

Adult

Eggs

Pupa

Larva

Insects as friends

Vital pollinators

Insects play a vital role in pollinating many of our crops and ensuring that they produce fruit and seed. They are especially important for apples and other fruit crops, and they also pollinate many of our garden flowers. Almost any flower-visiting insect can carry out pollination (*p. 95*), but the bees are by far the most important because they concentrate on one kind of flower at a time. Other insects visit flowers at random, and much of the pollen they carry ends up in the wrong kind of flower and is wasted.

Insect products

Insects provide us with a surprising number of commercially important materials. Cochineal, which is widely employed as a red food dye, and shellac, used in varnishes and polishes, are both obtained from scale insects. The honeybee supplies us not only with honey but also with beeswax for polishes. Silk, most of which is produced by the silk moth *Bombyx mori* in a process that was for centuries a closely guarded Chinese secret, is one of the finest natural fibers in existence and has long been valued for fine clothes because of its shiny appearance and light weight.

Natural pesticides

The role of ladybugs in controlling aphids is well known, but there are many other pest-killing insects. Gardeners can now control whiteflies and other greenhouse pests by buying a supply of minute parasitic insects that attack and kill the pests. The big advantage of these biological control agents is that they leave no harmful residues on the crops.

Insects can also be used to control weeds. For example, the larvae of a South American moth called *Cactoblastis* successfully rid Australia of the introduced prickly pear cactus.

Insects as human food

Locusts have always been eaten in Africa and other warm areas. Fried in butter after removal of their wings and legs, they are said to be very tasty and nutritious. Honeypot ants, which are full of stored honey, are eaten by many desert dwellers. Witchetty grubs, eagerly sought by Australian Aborigines, are wood-boring caterpillars. Many beetle grubs, including the meal-worms often used to feed birds and other pets, are also widely enjoyed by indigenous peoples, among whom they are considered highly desirable food, especially when fried.

Insects as foes

Millions of tons of food and other materials are destroyed by insects each year, and we spend huge amounts of money fighting these pests.

Aphids damage many crops by sucking out the sap and also by spreading disease-causing viruses. The Japanese beetle, introduced in the United States in the early 1900s, wrecks the foliage and fruit of many plants. Colorado potato beetles and cabbage white caterpillars destroy potato and cabbage crops, while boll weevils destroy cotton. Grain weevils and many other beetles attack grain in the fields and in storage after harvesting. Termites and other wood-boring insects damage our houses and furniture, and clothes moth larvae chew holes in fabrics.

Many bloodsucking insects carry diseases that are harmful to people and livestock: mosquitoes carry malaria and yellow fever, African tsetse flies carry sleeping sickness and the cattle disease nagana, and fleas carry Bubonic plague. Houseflies do not suck blood, but their liking for dung and carrion as well as food in the kitchen means that they carry and transfer numerous germs. Greenbottles and some other flies lay their eggs on sheep, and the resulting grubs burrow into the animals' flesh—a condition that is known as sheep strike.

Cabbage white butterfly   **Mosquito**   **Housefly**

Grain weevil   **Japanese beetle**   **Colorado beetle**

DANGEROUS SPIDERS

Almost all spiders possess venom, which they inject into their prey through sharp, hollow fangs. Few spiders are able to pierce human skin, but about 30 species—out of a total of about 40,000—can cause severe illness or even death if they bite people. Spiders are not usually aggressive, however, and have rarely been known to bite unless they are provoked.

The most notorious spider is North America's black widow (*Latrodectus mactans*). Although its fangs are very short, it manages to get them through the skin to inject a venom which is, volume for volume, about 15 times more poisonous than rattlesnake venom. The spider injects a much smaller amount than a rattlesnake, but it causes severe pain and nausea and has resulted in many deaths over the centuries. The closely related red widow (*Latrodectus bishopi*) inhabits the sand-pine scrub of southeast Florida. Similar spiders are found in southern Europe as well as in most other warm areas of the world.

The brown recluse (or violin) spider (*Loxosceles reclusa*), found in the southern United States, injects a venom that destroys blood and other tissues. It has caused some deaths. The Sydney funnel-web (*Atrax robustus*) is Australia's deadliest spider and is particularly dangerous because it often makes its home in gardens. The most deadly South American spider is the wandering spider (*Phoneutria*)—an aggressive hunter that has been known to kill children. It occasionally turns up elsewhere, having traveled in crates of bananas. Its fangs are more than 1/6 inch (4 mm) long, but the longest fangs—up to 1/2 inch (12 mm) long—belong to the tarantulas. Luckily, the U.S. types do not have particularly strong venom.

Antivenins are now available to treat victims of most of the dangerous spiders. Provided they are given quickly, they should result in almost immediate recovery.

Sydney funnel-web   **Brown recluse spider**   **Black widow**   **Red widow**   **Wandering spider**

INVERTEBRATES

For mollusks, lengths given are normally maximum shell lengths, but (b) indicates body length; for spiders, lengths are body lengths, although legs may be much longer. Measurements are in inches, followed by centimeters in parentheses.

Class/Name	Length	Notable features	Range and habitat
MOLLUSKS: Phylum Mollusca			
Slugs and snails/Gastropoda		**(c. 50,000 species)**	
Abalone *Haliotis* (several species)	<11⁴/₅(30)	Feed on seaweed; mainly in coastal waters; collected for food and for the pearly shells.	*Warm seas worldwide*
Common limpet *Patella vulgata*	<2¹/₆(5.5)	Feeds on seaweed in intertidal zone; conical shell pulled tightly down on rocks when tide is out.	*Worldwide*
Common periwinkle *Littorina littorea*	<1(2.5)	Feeds on seaweed; thick, dull brown shell.	*N. Atlantic and adjacent seas; rocky shores*
Conch *Strombus* (several species)	<13(33)	Feed on seaweed; shells with a broad "wing," often used as trumpets.	*Tropical seas*
Cone shell *Conus* (c. 600 species)	<9(23)	Feed on fish and mollusks, killed by poison darts; some species dangerous to humans; beautiful shells much sought by collectors.	*Warm seas worldwide*
Cowrie (c. 150 species in several genera)	<4(10)	Feed on sea anemones and other small creatures; shiny, chinalike shells were once used as money.	*Warm seas worldwide*
Giant African snail *Achatina fulica*	<5⁹/₁₀(15)	Vegetarian; a serious agricultural pest; lays hard-shelled eggs as big as those of a thrush.	*Originally Africa, now tropical Asia and Pacific*
Great gray slug *Limax maximus*	<7⁹/₁₀(20) (b)	Mainly feeds on fungi and rotting matter; mottled gray and brown; common in gardens; mates in midair, hanging from a rope of slime.	*Europe*
Great ramshorn snail *Planorbarius corneus*	<1¹/₅(3)	Vegetarian, often browsing on algae; shell forms a flat spiral; body has bright red blood.	*Europe; still and slow-moving freshwater*
Roman snail *Helix pomatia*	<2(5)	Vegetarian; often a pest, but cultivated for food in some areas.	*C. and S. Europe; lime soils*
Sea butterfly (c. 100 species in several genera)	<2(5)	Carnivorous, eating a variety of small marine creatures; with or without shells, they swim by flapping winglike extensions of the foot.	*Oceans worldwide; most common in warm waters*
Slipper limpet *Crepidula fornicata*	<2¹/₃(6)	Strains food particles from the water; slipperlike shells cling together in chains; a serious pest in oyster and mussel farms, settling on the shells and cutting off their food supplies.	*Originally North America, now common on coasts of Europe*
Waved whelk *Buccinum undatum*	<4³/₄(12)	Carnivorous, feeding on living and dead animals; large numbers are collected for human consumption.	*N. Atlantic and neighboring seas*
Bivalves/Lamellibranchia		**(c. 8,000 species)**	
Blue mussel *Mytilus edulis*	<4¹/₃(11)	Bluish shell clings to rocks with tough threads; farmed on a large scale for human consumption, especially in S. Europe.	*Coasts of Europe and eastern North America*
Common cockle *Cardium edule*	<2(5)	Burrows in sand and mud near low-tide level; important food for fish and wading birds.	*European coasts*
Great scallop *Pecten maximus*	<5⁹/₁₀(15)	Strongly ribbed, eared shells with one valve flatter than the other; lives freely on seabed and swims by opening and closing its valves.	*European coasts; usually below low-tide level*
Oyster *Ostrea edulis*	<5⁹/₁₀(15)	Trough-shaped lower valve cemented to stones, with flat upper valve sitting on it like a lid; large numbers farmed for human consumption.	*Coasts of Europe and Africa*
Piddock *Pholas dactylus*	<4³/₄(12)	Uses rasplike shell to bore into soft rocks and wood, making an inescapable tomb; sucks in water and food through long siphons.	*Coasts of Europe and eastern North America*
Pod razor-shell *Ensis siliqua*	<7⁹/₁₀(20)	Long, straight shell, shaped like a straight razor, is open at both ends; burrows in sand.	*European coasts*
Squids and octopuses/Cephalopoda		**(c. 750 species)**	
Blue-ringed octopus *Hapalochlaena maculosa*	4(10) (span)	The most dangerous species, despite its size; the only octopus whose venom is known to have killed people.	*Australian coasts*
Common cuttlefish *Sepia officinalis*	<11⁴/₅(30)	Eats shrimp and other crustaceans, caught with tentacles; lives on seabed; flat, oval body can change color; cuttlebone is the internal shell.	*Coastal waters of Atlantic and neighboring seas*
Common Atlantic octopus *Octopus vulgaris*	<118 (300) (span)	Eats small fish and crustaceans, killed by a poisonous bite; not dangerous to people.	*Atlantic and Mediterranean coastal waters*
Common squid *Loligo vulgaris*	<19³/₄(50)	Eats fish, crustaceans, and smaller squids; cylindrical body with a triangular fin at the rear; deep pink in life, fading to gray after death.	*Atlantic and Mediterranean coastal waters*
Giant squid *Architeuthis princeps*	<59(1,500)	Largest invertebrate, although tentacles account for more than half its length; eats fish, seals and small whales; main food of the sperm whale.	*Oceans worldwide*
CRUSTACEANS: Phylum Arthropoda			
Crustacea		**(c. 30,000 species)**	
Acorn barnacle *Semibalanus balanoides*	<³/₅(1.5) (diam.)	Cemented to intertidal rocks; the shell opens when the tide is in and the animal combs food particles from the water with its legs.	*Worldwide*
Common lobster *Homarus vulgaris*	<27³/₅(70)	Scavenger; lives on rocky coasts down to depths of about 100 feet (30 m); bluish black in life; now rare in many places through overfishing.	*European coasts*
Common prawn *Palaemon serratus*	<4(10)	Scavenger; almost transparent in life; differs from shrimp in its serrated rostrum.	*European coasts; usually stony or rocky shores*
Common shrimp *Crangon crangon*	<2³/₄(7)	Eats other small animals, living or dead; common on sand and mud, much used for human consumption; front legs stout and clawed.	*Coasts of Europe and eastern North America*

Slugs and snails
Conch

Slugs and snails
Great gray slug

Squids and octopuses
Common octopus

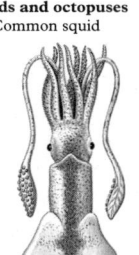

Squids and octopuses
Common squid

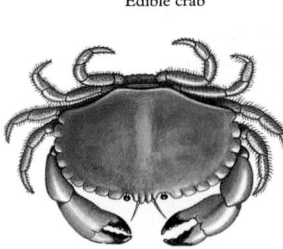

Crustacea
Edible crab

Class/Name	Length	Notable features	Range and habitat
Edible crab *Cancer pagurus*	$<7^{9}/_{10}(20)$	Scavenger; inhabiting rocky coasts to depths of about 164 feet (50 m); widely caught for human consumption.	*Eastern N. Atlantic and neighboring seas*
Fiddler crab *Uca* (many species)	$<1^{1}/_{5}(3)$	Scavengers; male has one big, colorful claw, often much bigger than the rest of his body, which he waves to attract females.	*Seashores and mangrove swamps*
Hermit crab (several species and genera)	$<5^{9}/_{10}(15)$	Scavengers; elongated, soft-bodied crabs using empty seashells as portable homes.	*Worldwide; mainly in coastal waters*
Krill *Euphausia superba*	$<2(5)$	Planktonic shrimplike animal; the main food of the whalebone whales and many other animals in the southern oceans.	*Mainly the southern oceans*
Noble crayfish *Astacus astacus*	$<5^{9}/_{10}(15)$	Shallow, well aerated streams, feeding on other animals, living or dead; reared in large numbers for human consumption, especially in France.	*Europe*
Norway lobster *Nephrops norvegicus*	$<9^{4}/_{5}(25)$	A spiny scavenger living on sandy and muddy seabeds at depths of 100–650 feet (30–200 m); marketed as scampi.	*European seas*
Robber crab *Birgus latro*	$<17^{3}/_{4}(45)$	Related to hermit crab, although not living in discarded shells; terrestrial scavenger feeding mainly on carrion; often climbs trees.	*Islands and coasts of Indian and Pacific oceans*
Spiny lobster *Panuliris vulgaris*	$<17^{3}/_{4}(45)$	Very spiny, with stout antennae much longer than the body; no pincers; feeds on mollusks; a popular food; also known as crayfish.	*Mediterranean and Atlantic; rocky coasts*
Water flea *Daphnia* (many species)	$<^{1}/_{5}(0.5)$	Reddish brown or greenish, abundant in muddy ponds and other freshwater; swims by waving long antennae; a major food of small fish and much used, living or dried, to feed aquarium fish.	*Worldwide; freshwater*
Wood louse (many genera and species)	$<1(2.5)$	Scavengers, feeding mainly on decaying plant material; the only major group of terrestrial crustaceans, but still confined to damp places; also called sow bugs and pill bugs.	*Worldwide*

SPIDERS: Phylum Arthropoda

Arachnida		**(More than 40,000 species)**	
Black widow *Latrodectus mactans*	$<^{2}/_{3}(1.6)$	Black with red markings beneath; although not aggressive, is dangerous as bite can be deadly if not cured with antivenin; female sometimes eats male after mating.	*Most warm parts of the world, including S. Europe*
Bola spider (several species and genera)	$<^{3}/_{5}(1.5)$	Catches moths by whirling a single thread of silk with a blob of sticky gum on the end.	*N. and S. America, Africa, Australia and Oceania*
Crab spider (*c.* 3,000 species in numerous genera)	$<^{3}/_{4}(2)$	Mostly squat, crablike spiders that lie in wait for prey—often in flowers—and grab it with their long front legs.	*Worldwide*
Fishing spider *Dolomedes* (*c.* 100 species)	$<1(2.5)$	Hunting spiders that lurk at the edge of pools or on floating objects, picking up vibrations of prey (insects and small fish) and streaking after them.	*Worldwide*
Funnel-web spider *Atrax* (3 species)	$<2(5)$	Among the deadliest spiders, although antivenins are now available for treating bites; inhabit tubular webs in the ground or among rocks.	*Australia*
Garden spider *Araneus diadematus*	$<^{1}/_{2}(1.2)$	Black to ginger, with a white cross on the back; makes orb-webs up to 20 inches (50 cm) across on fences and vegetation; not only in gardens.	*N. Hemisphere*
Gladiator spider *Dinopis* (several species)	$<1(2.5)$	Slender spiders with enormous eyes; make sticky webs which they throw at passing prey, usually at night.	*Warm regions and some cooler parts of North America and Australia*
House spider *Tegenaria* (*c.* 90 species)	$<^{3}/_{4}(2)$	Long-legged, fast-running spiders often seen running over floors at night; make scruffy triangular webs in neglected corners; harmless.	*Mostly N. Hemisphere*
Jumping spider (*c.* 4,000 species in many genera)	$<^{3}/_{5}(1.5)$	Large-eyed, day-active spiders that leap onto their prey; often brilliantly colored.	*Worldwide*
Money spider (many species and genera)	$<^{1}/_{4}(0.6)$	Believed to bring wealth or good fortune, perhaps because of the silvery appearance of their little hammocklike webs that cover grassland and glisten with dew on fall mornings.	*Worldwide, but most common in cooler areas of N. Hemisphere*
Orb weaver (*c.* 2,500 species in many genera)	$<1^{1}/_{5}(3)$	Makers of the familiar wheel-shaped webs, up to a $3^{1}/_{3}$ feet (1 m) or more in diameter; mostly brown, but some are very colorful; not dangerous.	*Worldwide*
Spitting spider *Scytodes thoracica*	$^{1}/_{4}(0.6)$	Catches small insects by spitting strands of sticky, venom-coated gum at them.	*Worldwide; normally only in buildings*
Tarantula (*c.* 800 species in several genera)	$<11(25)$	Stout-bodied, hairy hunting spiders, often in trees, where they sometimes capture nestling birds; venom not usually dangerous to people, but the hairs may cause a painful rash. Not to be confused with European tarantula, a type of wolf spider whose bite was believed to be curable only by performing a frantic dance called the tarantella.	*Warmer parts of the Americas and southern Africa*
Trapdoor spider (*c.* 700 species in several genera)	$<1^{1}/_{5}(3)$	Live in burrows closed by hinged lids of silk and debris; spiders lie in wait under the lid and grab passing prey.	*Most warm parts of the world, including S. Europe*
Water spider *Argyroneta aquatica*	$<^{3}/_{5}(1.5)$	The world's only truly aquatic spider, living in an air-filled, thimble-shaped web fixed to water plants; darts out to catch passing prey.	*Eurasia; in ponds and slow-moving streams*
Wolf spider (*c.* 2,500 species in many genera)	$<1^{1}/_{5}(3)$	Large-eyed hunting spiders, mostly ground-living; some chase their prey at speed; generally harmless but some of the larger species have dangerous bites. Includes the European tarantula.	*Worldwide, but most common in cooler parts of N. Hemisphere*
Zebra spider *Salticus scenicus*	$<^{1}/_{4}(0.6)$	Black and white jumping spider, commonly hunting on rocks and walls, especially those covered with lichen.	*N. Hemisphere; often in and around houses*

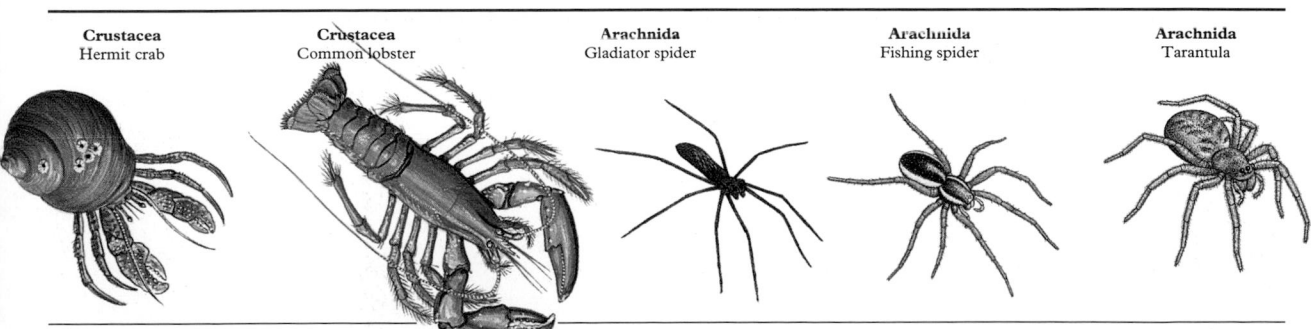

| **Crustacea** Hermit crab | **Crustacea** Common lobster | **Arachnida** Gladiator spider | **Arachnida** Fishing spider | **Arachnida** Tarantula |

INSECTS: Phylum Arthropoda

Sizes given are normally body lengths, but (w) indicates wingspan. Measurements are in inches, followed by millimeters in parentheses.
[▲ = endangered species]

Order/Name	Size	Notable features	Range
Bristletails/Thysanura		**(c. 600 species)**	
Silverfish *Lepisma saccharina*	0.4 (10)	Wingless scavenger of starchy foods in houses.	*Worldwide*
Mayflies/Ephemeroptera		**(c. 2,500 species)**	
	0.6 (16)	Flimsy insects with 2 or 3 long "tails"; grow up in water and have a very short adult life, often only a few hours.	*Worldwide*
Dragonflies/Odonata		**(c. 5,000 species)**	
	< 0.8 –5 (20–130)	Long-bodied insects, with gauzy wings spanning up to 6 inches (150 mm); most fly rapidly and catch insects in midair; grow up in water.	*Worldwide*
Crickets and grasshoppers/Orthoptera		**(c. 23,000 species)**	
Desert locust *Schistocerca gregaria*	3.3 (85)	Herbivorous; swarms periodically destroy crops in Africa.	*Africa and S. Asia*
House cricket *Acheta domestica*	< 0.8 (20)	Scavenger in houses and garbage piles.	*Worldwide*
Katydid/bush cricket (thousands of species)	< 6 (150)	Omnivorous or insect-eating; like grasshoppers but with very long antennae.	*Worldwide, apart from coldest areas*
Migratory locust *Locusta migratoria*	< 2 (50)	Herbivorous; swarm in Africa but solitary in Europe.	*Africa and S. Europe*
Walkingsticks and leaf insects/Phasmatodea		**(c. 2,500 species, mostly tropical)**	
Leaf insect (c. 50 species)	< 3.5 (90)	Very flat, leaflike, green or brown herbivores.	*S.E. Asia,*
Walkingstick (over 2,400 species)	< 14 (350)	Herbivorous; sticklike green or brown bodies with or without wings; often kept as a pet.	*North America Warm areas*
Earwigs/Dermaptera		**(c. 1,300 species)**	
	< 1 (30)	Slender, brownish insects, with or without wings and always with prominent pincers at the rear. Most are omnivorous scavengers.	*Originally Africa, now worldwide*
Cockroaches/Blattodea		**(c. 3,500 species)**	
American cockroach *Periplaneta americana*	1.5 (40)	Scavenger, living outside (if warm) or in buildings; chestnut brown.	*Worldwide*
Mantids/Mantodea		**(c. 1,800 species)**	
Praying mantis *Mantis religiosa*	< 3(75)	Catches other insects with spiky front legs.	*All warm areas*
Termites/Isoptera		**(More than 2,000 species)**	
	< 1(22)	Small and antlike, with or without wings; colonies in mounds of earth, in dead wood or underground; many are timber pests.	*Mostly tropical*
True bugs/Hemiptera		**(More than 40,000 species)**	
Bed bug *Cimex lectularius*	0.2 (5)	Bloodsucking; hides by day and feeds at night, often attacking people in their beds.	*Worldwide*
Common water strider *Gerris remigis*	0.4 (10)	Skims across the surface of still water and catches other insects.	*N. Hemisphere*
Meadow spittlebug *Philaenus spumarius*	0.2 (6)	Sap-sucker; young stages live in froth, often called cuckoo-spit.	*N. Hemisphere*
Cicadas and kin/Homoptera		**(c. 45,000 species)**	
Aphid (numerous species)	< 0.2 (5)	Sap-sucking insects, with or without wings; many are serious pests on ornamental plants.	*Worldwide*
Cicada (numerous species)	< 1.5 (40) (w)	Sap-sucking; males make loud, shrill sounds; young stages live underground on roots, one American species taking 17 years to mature.	*Worldwide, mainly in warm climates*
Thrips/Thysanoptera		**(More than 4,700 species)**	
		Tiny winged or wingless herbivorous insects, many of which grow up in crops and cause much damage; they fly in huge numbers in sultry weather in summer.	*Worldwide*
Net-veined insects/Neuroptera		**(More than 4,000 species)**	
Antlion *Myrmeleon formicarius*	3.5 (90) (w)	Larvae make pits in sandy soil and feed on insects trapped in them.	*Eurasia*
Green lacewing (several genera and many species)	< 0.2 (5)	Predators of aphids and other small insects in a wide range of habitats; delicate green wings.	*Worldwide*
Scorpionflies and kin/Mecoptera		**(c. 400 species)**	
		Scavenging insects in which the male abdomen is usually turned up like a scorpion's tail, although they are harmless.	*Worldwide*
Butterflies and moths/Lepidoptera		**(c. 150,000 species)**	
Butterflies (c. 18,000 species)			
Birdwing butterfly (several genera and species)	< 12 (300) (w)	Tropical forests; they include the world's largest butterflies; many are becoming rare through collecting and loss of habitat.	*S.E. Asia and N. Australia*
Cabbage white butterfly *Pieris brassicae*	< 3 (70) (w)	Flowery places; caterpillar is a pest of cabbages and other brassicas.	*Eurasia, N. Africa*
Fritillary butterfly (many genera and species)	< 3 (80) (w)	Mostly orange with black spots above and silvery spots below; live in woods and open spaces including Arctic tundra.	*Mostly N. Hemisphere*
Monarch butterfly *Danaus plexippus*	< 4(100) (w)	Orange with black markings; a great migrant; it hibernates in huge swarms in Mexico and southern U.S.A.	*Mostly Pacific area and North America*
Skipper butterfly (many genera and species)	< 3 (80) (w)	Mostly small brown or orange grassland insects with darting flight.	*Worldwide*

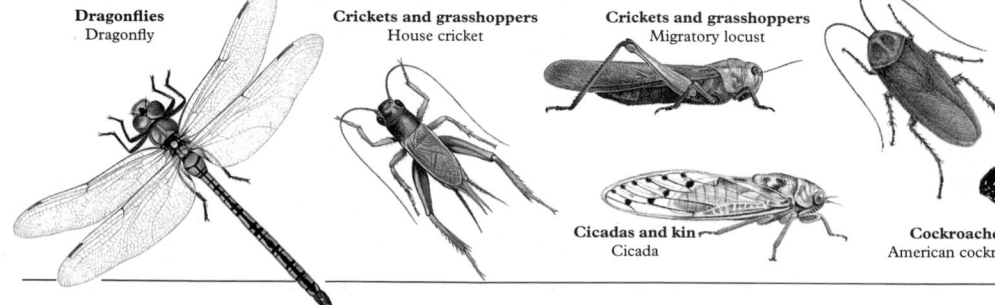

Dragonflies
Dragonfly

Crickets and grasshoppers
House cricket

Crickets and grasshoppers
Migratory locust

Butterflies and moths
Monarch butterfly

Cicadas and kin
Cicada

Cockroaches
American cockroach

Order/Name	Size	Notable features	Range
Swallowtail butterfly (many genera and species)	<5 (120) (w)	Large, usually colorful and with prominent "tails" on hindwings; many becoming rare through collecting and loss of habitat.	*Worldwide, but mostly tropical*
Moths (c. 132,000 species)			
Clothes moth (several species)	<3/5(15) (w)	Small, often shiny moths whose caterpillars damage woolen fabrics; live mainly in buildings.	*Worldwide*
Death's head hawkmoth *Acherontia atropos*	<5 (135) (w)	Sturdy moth with a skull-like pattern on its thorax; larvae on potato and related plants.	*Africa and Eurasia*
Hummingbird hawkmoth *Macroglossum stellatarum*	<2(60) (w)	Day-flying, producing loud hum as it hovers in front of flowers to feed; larvae on bedstraw.	*Eurasia*
Pine processionary moth *Thaumetopoea pityocampa*	<1.5 (40) (w)	Grayish moth whose larvae live in silken tents on pine trees and go out to feed in long processions at night; a serious forest pest.	*S. and C. Europe*
Silk moth *Bombyx mori*	<2 (60) (w)	Cream-colored moth bred for the fine silk obtained from its cocoon—more than 3/5 mile (1 km) from a single cocoon; larvae eat mulberry leaves; all cultured moths flightless.	*Native of China; now unknown in the wild*
Smoky moth *Zygaena* (many species)	<1.5 (40) (w)	Slow, night- and day-flying moths, protected by foul-tasting body fluids and gaudy black and red colors.	*Eurasia and N. Africa*
Tiger moth (many genera and species)	<4 (100) (w)	Mostly brightly colored and hairy, with foul-tasting body fluids.	*Worldwide*
True flies/Diptera		**(c. 90,000 species, a few without wings)**	
Crane fly (many genera and species)	<1.5 (35) (w)	Slender, long-legged flies, often resting with wings outstretched; larvae of many damage crop roots.	*Worldwide*
House fly *Musca domestica*	0.25 (7)	Abundant on farms and garbage dumps; becoming less common in houses; breeds in dung and other decaying matter and carries germs.	*Worldwide*
Hover fly (many genera and species)	<1.5 (40)	Many have amazing hovering ability; adults feed on pollen and nectar; many are black and yellow mimics of bees and wasps.	*Worldwide*
Mosquito (many genera and species)	<0.5 (15)	Females are bloodsuckers; spread malaria and other diseases.	*Worldwide*
Tsetse fly *Glossina* (c. 20 species)	0.5 (10)	Bloodsuckers, spreading human sleeping sickness and cattle diseases.	*Tropical Africa*
Fleas/Siphonaptera		**(c. 16,000 species)**	
		Wingless, bloodsucking parasites feeding on birds and mammals. Long hind legs enable them to jump many times their own lengths. The maggotlike larvae are not parasitic.	*Worldwide*
Bees, wasps, and ants/Hymenoptera		**(More than 120,000 species)**	
Ant weaver *Oecophylla* (several species)	0.5 (10)	Nest made from leaves, joined by sticky silk produced by the grubs.	*E. Hemisphere tropics*
Honeypot ant *Myrmecocystus*	1 (20)	Some workers gorge themselves with sugar-rich food and become living honeypots from which other ants can feed.	*Deserts across the world*
Army ant (several genera and species)	<1.5 (40)	Live in mobile colonies, some of more than a million ants; kill any animal unable to get out of their way; workers much smaller than 1 1/2-inch (40 mm) queen; African species often called driver ants.	*Tropics*
Bumblebee *Bombus* (many species)	<1.2 (35)	Plump, hairy bees living in annual colonies; only mated queen survives winter to start new colonies in spring.	*Worldwide, except Australia*
European hornet *Vespa crabro*	<1.2 (35)	Large brown and yellow wasp, nesting in hollow trees and feeding young on other insects.	*Eurasia and now North America*
Honey bee *Apis mellifera*	<1 (20)	Less hairy than bumble bee; lives in permanent colonies, sometimes in hollow trees but mostly in artificial hives; stores honey for winter.	*Worldwide (probably native of S.E. Asia)*
Ichneumon (thousands of genera and species)	<2 (50)	Parasites, mostly laying their eggs in young stages of other insects; the young grow inside their hosts and gradually kill them.	*Worldwide*
Sawfly (numerous families)	<2 (50)	Named after the sawlike ovipositor of most females, used to cut slits in plants before laying eggs there; larvae all vegetarians.	*Worldwide*
Beetles/Coleoptera		**(More than 350,000 species, front wings usually form casing over body)**	
Carrion beetle *Nicrophorus* (several species)	<1 (25)	Often orange and black; beetles work in pairs to bury small dead animals, near which they then lay their eggs.	*Worldwide*
Click beetle or wireworm (many genera and species)	<1.5 (40)	Bullet-shaped beetles which flick into the air to turn over—making a loud click; larvae, called wireworms, damage crop roots.	*Worldwide*
Colorado potato beetle *Leptinotarsa decemlineata*	0.4 (10)	Black-and-yellow adults and pink grubs both seriously damage potato crops.	*North America and now Europe*
Deathwatch beetle *Xestobium rufovillosum*	2.7 (7)	Tunneling larvae do immense damage to old building timbers; adults tap wood as mating call; also on dead trees.	*N. Hemisphere*
Furniture beetle or woodworm *Anobium punctatum*	0.2 (5)	Larvae, known as woodworm, tunnel in dead wood and cause much damage to furniture and building timbers.	*Worldwide*
Glowworm *Lampyris noctiluca*	0.6 (15)	Wingless female glows with greenish light to attract males flying overhead; feeds on snails.	*Europe*
Goliath beetle *Goliathus* (several species)	<6 (150)	World's heaviest beetles, up to 3 1/2 ounces (100 g); feed on fruit.	*Africa*
Ladybug (c. 3,500 species in many genera)	0.4 (10)	Aphid-eating habits make them friends of gardeners; most are red or yellow, with various spot patterns.	*Worldwide*
Scarab beetle *Scarabaeus* (many species)	<1.2 (30)	Dung feeding—some form the dung into balls and roll it around before burying it; also known as tumblebugs; introduced into Australia to deal with sheep and cattle dung.	*Most warm parts of the world*
Stag beetle *Lucanus cervus*	2 (50)	Males have huge antlerlike jaws, with which they wrestle rivals.	*Eurasia*
Stored-grain billbug *Sitophilus granarius*	0.1 (3)	A serious pest, breeding in and destroying all kinds of stored grain.	*Worldwide*

Butterflies and moths
Death's head hawkmoth

Bees, wasps, and ants
Arid lands honey ant

Beetles
Click beetle

Beetles
Goliath beetle

Bees, wasps, and ants
Honey bee

Bees, wasps, and ants
Ichneumon

FISH

Fish were the first backboned animals to appear—about 500 million years ago. There are about 22,000 living species—more than all the other vertebrates together. They are all aquatic creatures, bearing a number of fins and usually covered with scales. Side-to-side movements of body and tail drive the fish through the water, while the paired fins on the sides or the belly help with steering and braking. Fish include carnivores, herbivores, and omnivores: many are scavengers and some are parasites. Most fish take their oxygen directly from the water through their gills. Some fish give birth to active young, but most lay eggs. With a few exceptions, such as sea horses and sticklebacks, there is no parental care: most species simply shed their eggs and abandon them, but the huge numbers produced ensure that at least a few survive.

Four classes of fish

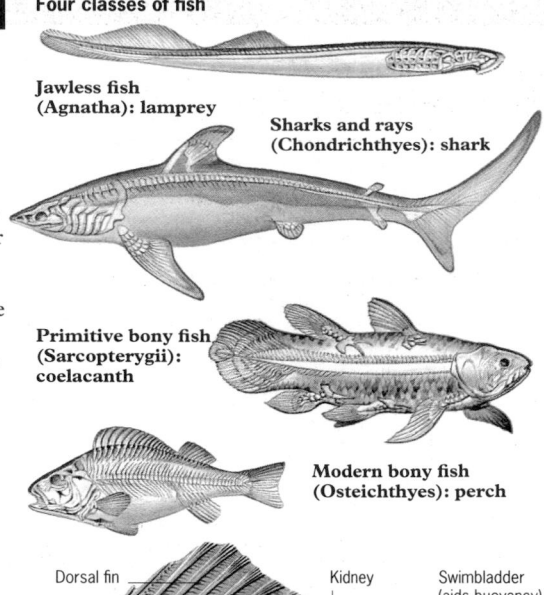

Jawless fish
(Agnatha): lamprey

Sharks and rays
(Chondrichthyes): shark

Primitive bony fish
(Sarcopterygii):
coelacanth

Modern bony fish
(Osteichthyes): perch

Fish classes

Fish are divided into two main groups: jawless and jawed. The jawless fish (Agnatha) are limited to lampreys and hagfish. They have scaleless bodies and cartilage skeletons, and they feed by rasping flesh from other fish using teeth on either their mouths or tongues.

Jawed fish, which make up the vast majority of fish, can be divided into three classes. Sharks and rays (Chondrichthyes) have skeletons of cartilage and their gills open through slits on each side. The primitive bony fish (Sarcopterygii) have bony skeletons and are related to fish living more than 400 million years ago. The most numerous class is the modern bony fish (Osteichthyes). The modern bony fish differ from the primitive bony fish in that they do not have a fleshy lobe at the base of each fin.

Anatomy of a bony fish

Dorsal fin — Kidney — Swimbladder (aids buoyancy)

Spinal cord

Gill (covered by operculum) — Brain

Nostril

Mouth

Muscle

Caudal (tail) fin

Gill opening

Anal fin

Esophagus Heart Liver Pectoral fin Stomach Intestine Pelvic fin Ovary Anus Urogenital opening (outlet from kidneys and ovary)

Gills

Gills are dense clusters of blood-filled filaments attached to the bony gill arches. Each filament has many extensions called lamellae. Water entering the mouth is pumped over the gills, where oxygen passes into the blood.

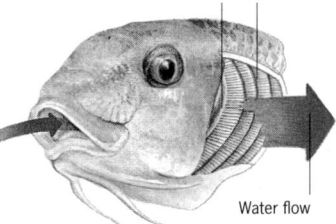

Gill arch Gills

Water flow

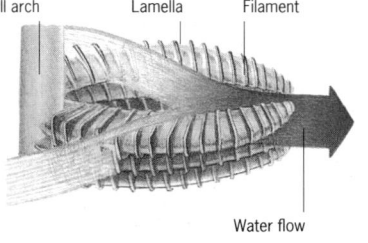

Gill arch Lamella Filament

Water flow

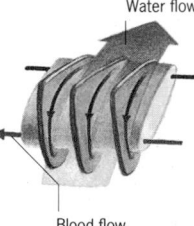

Water flow

Blood flow

Electricity and light

Several fish, including the electric eel (*right*) and the electric ray, can store electric charges in certain muscles and then discharge them to kill prey. Electricity can also be used for navigation. Some deep-sea fish, such as the hatchet fish (*far right*), produce light to attract prey or mates in the pitch-black water.

FISH

Measurements are in inches, followed by centimeters in parentheses. [f = freshwater; m = marine]

Order/Name	Length	Food and habits	Range and habitat
JAWLESS FISH: Lampreys and hagfish, Class Agnatha (c. 50 species)			
Hagfish *Myxine* (several species)	<25 (60)	Bore into dead or dying fish with teeth on their tongue.	*Worldwide*
Sea lamprey (f/m)	25–30	Microscopic organisms in rivers when young, then goes to sea to feed	*N. Atlantic and*
Petromyzon marinus	(60–75)	on other fish; returns to rivers to spawn and die.	*associated rivers*
JAWED FISH: Sharks and rays, Class Chondrichthyes (c. 800 species)			
Sharks/Lamniformes		**(More than 350 species)**	
Basking shark (m)	470 (1,200)	Harmless surface feeder, straining plankton from the water with its	*Atlantic and*
Cetorhinus maximus		enormous gills.	*Mediterranean*
Carpet shark (m)	125 (320)	Grabs passing fish and crustaceans as it lies, well camouflaged, on the	*Australian coastal*
Orectolobidae		seabed; flatter than most sharks.	*waters*
Common thresher shark (m)	<235 (600)	Mackerel and other shoaling fish, hunting in packs and rounding up prey	*Worldwide; apart from*
Alopias vulpinus		with long, whiplike tails.	*the coldest seas*
Hammerhead shark (m)	<275 (700)	Mainly fish; head hammer-shaped with eyes and nostrils at the ends;	*N. Atlantic coastal*
Sphyrna (5 species)		aggressive and dangerous.	*waters*
Porbeagle shark (m)	<140 (350)	Mainly shoaling fish, such as herring and mackerel; fast and frightening,	*Worldwide; in warm*
Lamna nasus		but not dangerous.	*seas*
Spiny dogfish (m)	<40 (100)	Fish, crustaceans, and mollusks; eggs laid in horny cases—"mermaids'	*N. Atlantic and*
Squalus acanthias		purses"—attached to seaweed.	*Mediterranean*
Tiger shark (m)	<210 (540)	Fish and squid; most common of the big sharks and one of the most	*Worldwide; in warm*
Galeocerdo cuvieri		dangerous; often attacks swimmers.	*seas, often near coast*
Whale shark (m)	<591 (1,500)	Plankton and small fish; the world's largest fish, with a mouth more than	*Worldwide; Tropical*
Rhincodon typus		5 feet (1.5 m) wide; despite its size, it seems docile and harmless to people.	*seas*
White shark (m)	<235 (600)	Fish and squid; popularly known as the "Great White," the most dangerous	*Worldwide; in tropical*
Carcharodon carcharias		shark, with more known attacks on people than any other; up to 3 tons.	*and temperate seas*
Skates and rays/Rajiformes		**(More than 400 species)**	
Atlantic manta (m)	<235 (600)	Small fish scooped into mouth with two "horns"; swims by flapping its huge	*Tropical and sub-*
Manta birostris		triangular fins—up to 32 feet (10 m) across—and can glide through the air.	*tropical seas*
Electric ray (m)	<60 (150)	Bottom-living fish and crustaceans, often electrocuted by being wrapped	*Warm and temperate*
Torpedo (c. 30 species)		up in fins; larger species can generate 200 volts—enough to stun a person.	*seas; mainly coastal*
Little skate (m)	<25 (60)	Bottom-living fish and other animals; eggs in horny cases or "mermaids	*Warm seas worldwide;*
Raja erinacea		purses;" An important food fish.	*mainly coastal*
Sawfish (m)	<395 (1000)	Shoaling fish and other marine animals; named after the bladelike snout,	*Atlantic coasts of*
Pristis (6 species)		which carries sharp teeth on each side.	*N. America*
Stingray (m)	<100 (250)	Mollusks and other bottom-living animals; tail, armed with a venomous	*Worldwide; in shallow*
Dasyatis (several species)		spine, is used for defense and causes painful injuries and some human deaths.	*seas*
Thornback ray (m)	<45 (120)	Crustaceans and other bottom dwellers; upper surface of tail and body has	*Coasts of Europe and*
Raja clavata		numerous thornlike scales.	*N. Africa*
JAWED FISH: Primitive bony fish, Class Sarcopterygii (7 species)			
Coelacanth (m) *Latimeria chalumnae*	60 (150)	Survivor of a group thought extinct; rediscovered in 1938.	*Indian Ocean*
Lungfish (f)	<80 (200)	Snails and other aquatic animals; breathe with simple lungs as well as gills;	*Tropical rivers*
(6 species in 3 families)		some can survive in mud when rivers dry up in summer.	
JAWED FISH: Modern bony fish, Class Osteichthyes (More than 20,000 species)			
Sturgeons and paddlefishes/Acipenseriformes		**(c. 28 species)**	
Sturgeon (f/m)	<355 (900)	Fish and other bottom dwellers; spends most of its life at sea, but spawns in	*N. Hemisphere*
(c. 26 species in several genera)		rivers where young spend up to two years; the eggs are eaten as caviar.	
Bowfins/Amiiformes		**(1 species)**	
Bowfin (f)	<35 (90)	Aquatic animals and carrion; lives in still and slow water, gulping air into	*Rivers and lakes of*
Amia calva		swim bladder to augment its oxygen; male makes nest and guards young.	*North America*
Gars/Semionotiformes		**(8 species)**	
Alligator gar (f)	<140 (350)	Fish and other aquatic animals, often lying in wait and then striking	*North America; mainly*
Lepisosteus spatula		with long, toothy snout.	*along Mississippi River*
Tarpons/Elopiformes		**(12 species)**	
Tarpon (f/m)	<95 (240)	Fish; powerful and fast swimming, giving good sport to anglers; in sea	*Warm Atlantic coastal*
Megalops atlanticus		and freshwater; has to gulp air.	*areas; adjacent rivers*
Eels/Anguilliformes		**(More than 500 species)**	
Conger eel (m) *Conger oceanicus*	<120 (300)	Fish, cuttlefish, and crustaceans; leaflike young feed on plankton.	*N. Atlantic*
American eel (f/m)	<40 (100)	Small fish, frogs, and invertebrates; famous for its migrations: spawns in	*Atlantic and rivers of*
Anguilla rostrata		Sargasso Sea in W. Atlantic; young (elvers) make their way to rivers, where	*North America*
		they spend several years before returning to Sargasso Sea to spawn and die.	
Moray eel (m)	<120 (300)	Fish, other animals, and carrion; sharp teeth, some like snake fangs, can	*Warm seas; especially*
(c. 120 species in several genera)		inflict severe injuries on unwary divers; many species brightly colored.	*around coral reefs*

Sharks
Carpet shark

Sharks
Hammerhead shark

Gars
Alligator gar

Rays
Stingray

Sturgeons and paddlefish
Sturgeon

Order/Name	Length	Food and habits	Range and habitat
Herringlike fishes/Clupeiformes		**(More than 400 species)**	
Anchovy (m) *Engraulis encrasiolus*	<8 (20)	Fish eggs and plankton; pelagic, in huge shoals; major food of many seabirds; widely used for human food.	*Tropical and temperate seas*
Atlantic herring (m) *Clupea harengus*	<18 (45)	Planktonic animals; once in huge shoals, with 2–3 million tons caught each year; now much reduced in many areas through overfishing but still very important as human food; kipper is smoked herring.	*N. Atlantic, including North Sea and Baltic Sea*
Pilchard (m) *Sardina pilchardus*	<10 (25)	Fish eggs and planktonic animals; a shoaling fish, known as a sardine when young; an important food fish.	*Coastal waters of Europe and N. Africa*
Sprat (m) *Sprattus sprattus*	<6 (15)	Animal plankton; a shoaling fish forming a major part of the food of many larger species.	*European coasts; especially in north*
Mooneyes/Osteoglossiformes		**(c. 20 species)**	
Arapaima (f) *Arapaima gigas*	<180 (460)	Omnivorous, but principally other fish; a cylindrical, pikelike fish with a bony tongue; gulps air into its lunglike swim bladder; one of the largest freshwater fishes; flesh prized by Native Americans.	*Rivers of tropical South America*
Salmon and trout/Salmoniformes		**(c. 1,000 species)**	
Atlantic salmon (f/m) *Salmo salar*	<60 (150)	Crustaceans and small fish; strongly migratory, spending early stages in rivers and then going to sea; always returns to the river of its birth to spawn; a valuable food fish, now farmed in large numbers.	*N. Atlantic and adjacent rivers*
Rainbow trout (f/m) *Salmo gairdneri*	<10 (25)	Small fish, other aquatic animals; the best-known true trout native to North America, and introduced widely throughout the world; highly prized as game fish; blackspots on upper body and tail with reddish band along each side.	*Freshwater trout: N. America, Eurasia*
Northern pike (f) *Esox lucius*	<60 (150)	Fish, including other pike, with occasional water birds and mammals; lies in wait in vegetation and streaks out to capture prey.	*N. Hemisphere; lakes and slow-moving rivers*
Minnowlike fishes/Cypriniformes		**(c. 3,500 species)**	
Carp (f) *Cyprinus carpio*	<40 (100)	Insects and other small aquatic animals in still and slow-moving water; a valuable food fish, now reared in many countries; many races exist.	*Asia; reached Europe c. 2,000 years ago*
Electric eel (f) *Electrophorus electricus*	<80 (200)	Fish and amphibians, stunned by powerful shocks—up to 550 volts; lives in murky water and uses mild electric discharges for navigation.	*Tropical Americas; in lakes and slow rivers*
Goldfish (f) *Carassius auratus*	<18 (45)	Aquatic insects and small crustaceans; young fish are brown and gray, like the wild form; domesticated for centuries and now has many strange forms.	*Originally E. Asia, but now in ponds and streams in many places*
Minnow (f) *Phoxinus phoxinus*	<4 (10)	Small aquatic animals; in shoals in shallow lakes and upper reaches of rivers; major food of larger fish.	*N. Eurasia*
Piranha (f) *Serrasalmus* (several species)	<16 (40)	Mostly fish but also other animals unlucky enough to get too close; usually live in shoals; victims rapidly carved up with razor-sharp teeth.	*Rivers of tropical South America*
Roach (f) *Rutilus rutilus*	<16 (40)	Omnivorous, often browsing on algae and other vegetation in lakes and slow-moving rivers; one of the most common freshwater fish.	*Eurasia*
Catfishes/Siluriformes		**(More than 2,500 species)**	
Catfish (f/m) (more than 2,000 species in c. 30 families)	<120 (300)	Mostly carnivorous; all have whiskerlike barbels around the mouth; some gather food while swimming upside down at the surface.	*Worldwide; in both fresh- and saltwater*
Codfishes/Gadiformes		**(c. 800 species)**	
Atlantic cod (m) *Gadus morhua*	<80 (200)	Other fish and a wide range of invertebrates; one of the most important food fishes, but it has declined alarmingly through overfishing.	*N. Atlantic and Arctic oceans*
Haddock (m) *Melanogrammus aeglefinus*	<40 (100)	Bottom-living invertebrates and young fish; an important food fish but declining in numbers.	*N. Atlantic and Arctic oceans*
Hake (m) *Merluccius merluccius*	<40 (100)	Other fish, especially herring and other shoaling species, caught near the surface at night; a major food fish, especially in southern Europe.	*Mediterranean and N.W. Europe*
Whiting (m) *Merlangius merlangus*	<28 (70)	Crustaceans and small fish, usually caught on or near the seabed; an important food fish; commonly caught by anglers fishing from the shore.	*European coastal waters*
Frogfishes/Lophiiformes		**(c. 210 species)**	
Anglerfish (m) *Lophius piscatorius*	<67 (170)	Other fish, which the sedentary, bottom-living angler attracts by waving a "fishing rod"—a much modified fin—with a flaglike lure above its mouth.	*Mediterranean and N.E. Atlantic*
Silversides/Atheriniformes		**(c. 200 species)**	
Flying fish (m) *Exocoetidae* (several genera and species)	<20 (50)	Planktonic animals; periodically leap into the air and glide on 2 or 4 big, winglike fins—probably when chased by larger fish; often land on boats.	*Tropical and sub-tropical seas*
Guppy (f) *Lebistes reticulatus*	<2 (5)	Aquatic insects and small crustaceans; popular for freshwater aquaria because of male's bright colors and once known as rainbow fish; much used to control malaria-carrying mosquitos.	*Tropical lakes and rivers*
Sticklebacks/Gasterosteiformes		**(c. 220 species)**	
Three-spined stickleback (f/m) *Gasterosteus aculeatus*	<4 (10)	Small crustaceans and insects, and young fish; three sharp spines on back; male, with red belly in breeding season, builds nest and guards eggs.	*N. Hemisphere; fresh- and saltwater*
Pipefishes and seahorses/Syngnathiformes		**(c. 175 species)**	
Pipefish (m) (c. 150 species in several genera)	<24 (60)	Plankton, sucked in through a tubular snout; very slender fish, usually adopting a vertical stance among seaweed; males carry the eggs.	*Coasts of tropical and temperate regions*
Seahorse (m) *Hippocampus* (c. 20 species)	<8 (20)	Plankton, sucked up by tubular snout on a horselike head; anchors itself to seaweed with prehensile tail; males carry the eggs in a belly pouch.	*Coasts of temperate and tropical regions*

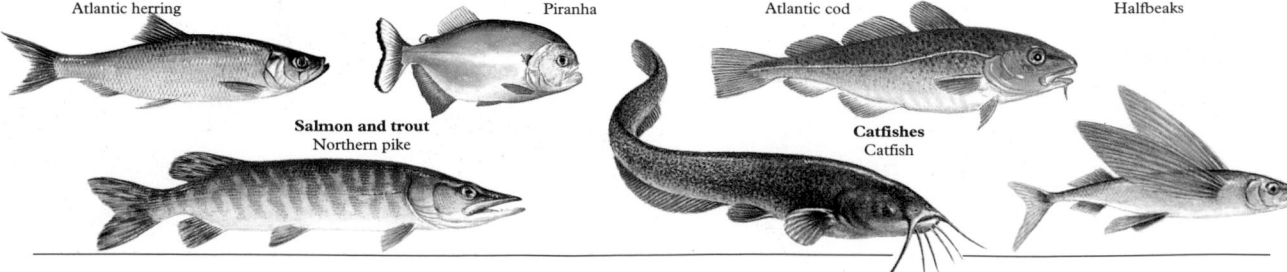

Herringlike fishes
Atlantic herring

Minnowlike fishes
Piranha

Codfishes
Atlantic cod

Silversides
Halfbeaks

Salmon and trout
Northern pike

Catfishes
Catfish

Order/Name	Length	Food and habits	Range and habitat
Scorpion fish/Scorpaeniformes		**(More than 1,000 species)**	
Stonefish (m) *Synanceja verrucosa*	<24 (60)	Fish, gulped into cavernous mouth; an ugly fish, resembling a lump of rock lying on the seabed, with venomous spines on the back.	*Indo-Pacific coasts*
Vermilion rockfish (m) *Sebastes miniatus*	<35 (85)	Fish and small animals; found singly or in small schools; popular sport fish; dorsal and anal spines can cause painful injuries, though not as venomous as some of its smaller relatives.	*Pacific coast*
Zebra fish (m) *Pterois volitans*	<12 (30)	Shrimp and other small animals, swept up by feathery fins; beautifully striped, but fins hide venomous spines; one of a large group called scorpion fish; also known as lionfish and turkeyfish.	*Coastal waters of tropical Asia; found mainly on coral reefs*
Perchlike fishes/Perciformes		**(More than 6,000 species)**	
Angelfish (f) *Pterophyllum scalare*	<6 (15)	Small crustaceans and insects; elegant stripes and trailing fins make it popular for aquariums.	*Tropical Americas*
Archer fish (f/m) *Toxotes joculatrix*	<12 (30)	Insects, shot from overhanging vegetation with a stream of water droplets fired from the mouth; mainly in coastal mangrove swamps.	*S.E. Asia and N. Australia*
Atlantic mackerel (m) *Scomber scombrus*	<20 (50)	Small fish, including herring, and plankton; an important food fish; often in large pelagic shoals.	*N .Atlantic and adjacent seas*
Barracuda (m) *Sphyraena* (c. 20 species)	<107 270)	Fish; among the most voracious hunters, armed with formidable teeth; the larger ones can be dangerous to people; flesh is excellent to eat.	*Most warm seas*
Blenny (f/m) *Blenniidae* (hundreds of species in several families)	<12 (30)	Carnivorous and herbivorous species, mostly marine and living on seabed; common in rock pools; differ from gobies in the single, long dorsal fin.	*Worldwide; mainly in coastal waters*
Goby (f/m) *Gobiidae* (c. 700 species in several genera)	<12 (30)	Carnivorous; pelvic fins form a suction cup to grip rocks; include the smallest fish—*Pandaka pygmaea*, only 1/2 inch (1.3 cm) long.	*Worldwide; mainly in coastal waters*
Marlin (m) *Makaira* (several species)	<160 (400)	Mackerel and other surface-dwelling fish and squid, killed with blow from spearlike beak; probably the fastest fish, with speeds above 50 mph (80 kph).	*Most warm seas*
Mudskipper (m) *Periophthalmus* (many species in several genera)	<12 (30)	Algae and small animals; air breathers that scamper over mud at low tide, using front fins as simple legs; some even climb trees with suckerlike pelvic fins.	*Tropical coasts and mangrove swamps of Asia, Africa, Pacific*
Parrotfish (m) *Scaridae* (many species in several genera)	<40 (100)	Seaweed and coral, nipped off with the sharp, parrotlike beak that gives the fish their name; often browsing in groups, many are brilliantly colored.	*Tropical seas; mainly around coral reefs*
Perch (f) *Perca flavescens*	<12 (30)	Small fish and other aquatic animals; good edible flesh and commercially fished in some areas.	*North America; lakes, rivers*
Pilot fish (m) *Naucrates ductor*	<25 (60)	Small fish and perhaps scraps dropped by the sharks and whales they accompany; once thought to guide the larger animals, but they probably associate just to "catch a ride" in the fast-moving water around them.	*Coasts of Americas*
Remora (m) *Remora* (8 species)	<25 (60)	Small fish; catches rides on larger fish, attaching themselves by a powerful sucker on top of the head; they are tied to ropes and used to catch turtles.	*Mainly tropical seas*
Sailfish (m) *Istiophorus platypterus*	<155 (400)	Fish and squid, stunned or impaled with spearlike upper jaw; related to marlin and named for huge, saillike dorsal fin; can reach 50 mph (80kph).	*All tropical seas*
Sandeel (m) *Ammodytidae* (c. 12 species in several genera)	<12 (30)	Small crustaceans, worms, and fish eggs; very slim, burrowing in sand when disturbed; main food of puffin.	*Mainly coastal waters of N. Hemisphere*
Striped bass(f/m) *Morone saxatilis*	<22 (56)	Small fish and other aquatic animals; native to the Atlantic but also found in freshwater coastal regions because of damming of inland waters in which they breed; caught commercially and for sport.	*Coastal and inland N. America*
Striped mullet (m) *Mugil cephalus*	<25 (60)	Bottom-living animals, largest of all mullet species; good food fish.	*Coasts*
Swordfish (m) *Xiphias gladius*	<180 (450)	Other fish, stunned by long, swordlike beak; a fast-swimming, popular game fish with good edible flesh.	*Most tropical and temperate seas*
Tuna (m) *Thunnus thynnus* (Bluefin)	<160 (400)	Shoaling fish often hunted in groups; oil-rich flesh is a popular food, fresh or canned.	*Tropical and temperate seas*
Weever fish (m) *Trachinus* (4 species)	<18 (45)	Bottom-living animals; lies half-buried in sand by day, and venomous spines cause painful injury if trodden on.	*Coasts of Europe and N.W. Africa*
Flatfishes/Pleuronectiformes		**(c. 500 species)**	
Atlantic halibut (m) *Hippoglossus hippoglossus*	<160 (400)	Fish and a wide range of bottom-living invertebrates; largest of the flatfish and an important food fish.	*Coasts of N. Atlantic and N. Pacific*
Dab (m) *Limanda limanda*	<16 (40)	Bottom-living invertebrates, including sea urchins; widely eaten, but less popular than plaice.	*European coasts; especially North Sea*
Sole (m) *Solea solea*	<25 (60)	Bivalves and other bottom-living animals; mainly nocturnal; excellent flesh, marketed as Dover sole.	*Mediterranean and coasts of N.W. Europe*
Summer flounder (m) *Paralichthys dentatus*	<20 (50)	Bottom-living invertebrates and small fish; a popular game fish; also known as fluke or plaice.	*Atlantic coasts; often in estuaries*
Turbot (m) *Scophthalmus maximus*	<40 (100)	Sandeels and other bottom-living fish; a valuable food fish; introduced to New Zealand.	*European coasts, including Black Sea*
Winter flounder (m) *Pseudopleurnectes Americanus*	<20 (50)	Shrimp and small fish; important food fish; also known as blackback.	*Atlantic coasts; often in estuaries*
Triggerfishes, puffers, and others/Tetrodontiformes		**(c. 320 species)**	
Porcupine fish (m) *Diodon* (several species)	<18 (45)	Mollusks and coral, crushed by powerful beaklike teeth; inflate body with water when alarmed and erect long spines to form impenetrable ball.	*All tropical seas*
Pufferfish (f/m) *Tetraodontidae* (several species and genera)	<18 (45)	Mollusks and coral, crushed with beaklike teeth; inflate body when alarmed; some contain deadly poisons in parts of their bodies, but eaten in Japan (as fugu) after removal of poisonous parts.	*Tropical seas, mainly around coral reefs; also in African rivers*

Perchlike fishes
Red mullet

Perchlike fishes
Sailfish

Tigerfishes and filefishes
Pufferfish

Perchlike fishes
Archer fish

Perchlike fishes
Angelfish

Flatfishes
Flounder

AMPHIBIANS

The amphibians were the first backboned animals to try out life on land, but even then they had to return to the water to breed—just like most of today's amphibians. They evolved from a group of air-breathing fish whose fins became transformed into legs capable of supporting their bodies. With lengths of 13 feet (4 m) or more, some of these early amphibians were very much larger than their present-day descendants.

Amphibians feed mainly on insects and other invertebrates, although the larger species also eat small vertebrates. Most frogs and toads catch their prey with a long sticky tongue, which is flicked out at high speed. The lungs are not very efficient and much of the animals' oxygen is obtained through the thin skin, which is well supplied with blood vessels. The thin skin restricts the amphibians to damp habitats.

Amphibian orders

The amphibians are divided into numerous orders, but only three of these have living members. The Gymnophiona contains the wormlike caecilians of tropical areas. The Urodela contains the tailed amphibians—the newts and the more terrestrial salamanders. The Anura contains the frogs and toads, which are tailless and mostly adapted for jumping. In some parts of the world, including the United States, the name *frog* is applied to amphibians with smooth skins, while *toad* is applied to those with warty, often drier skins.

Amphibian development

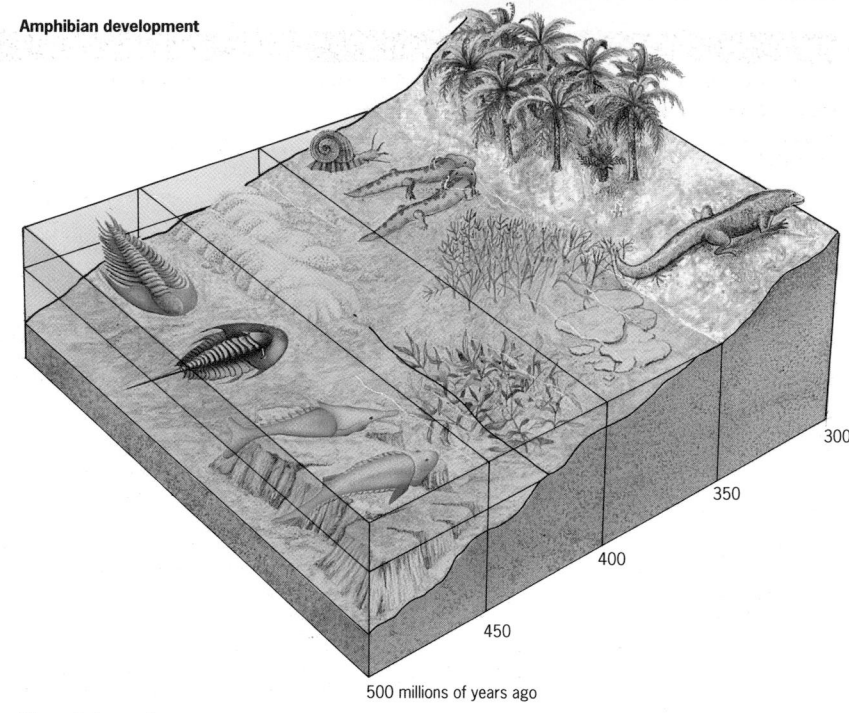

300
350
400
450
500 millions of years ago

Three living orders

Gymnophiona: caecilian

Anura: midwife toad

Urodela: marbled newt

Anatomy of a frog

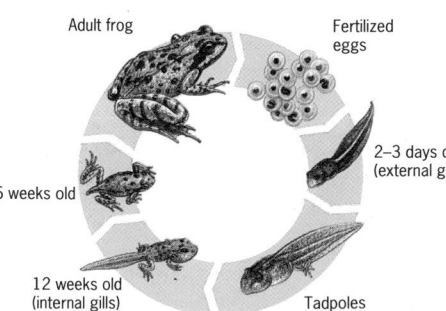

Testis   Liver   Heart

Tongue

Bladder   Intestines   Stomach   Kidney   Lungs

The life cycle

Most frogs and toads lay eggs in water and pass through an aquatic, gill-breathing tadpole stage as they grow up. Newts have a similar life history, although they lay eggs singly and their tadpoles have external gills throughout their lives. Some salamanders give birth to active young,

Adult frog   Fertilized eggs

2–3 days old (external gills)

16 weeks old

12 weeks old (internal gills)   Tadpoles

Life cycle of a typical frog

either well-developed tadpoles or miniature adults. Some frog and toad eggs produce miniature adults, thus avoiding the need to return to water to breed.

AMPHIBIANS

Lengths given are total body lengths, including the tail when present. Measurements are in inches, followed by centimeters in parentheses.

Order/Name	Length	Special features	Range and habitat
Newts and salamanders/Urodela	**(c. 300 species)**		
Axolotl *Ambystoma mexicanum*	<$7^1/_{10}$(18)	An aquatic salamander retaining its gills and larval appearance throughout life.	Mexico; a few freshwater lakes
Fire salamander *Salamandra salamandra*	<10(25)	Largely terrestrial, giving birth to well-developed tadpoles; black-and-yellow pattern warns of poisonous secretions.	Europe, N. Africa, and W. Asia; damp montane woods
Hellbender *Cryptobranchus alleganiensis*	<$29^2/_3$ (75)	A salamander; breathes through wrinkled skin as well as with gills and lungs.	E. North America; fast rivers and streams
Mudpuppy *Necturus maculosus*	<$23^2/_3$(60)	Retains external gills and larval appearance throughout life.	North America; weedy ponds, rivers
Olm *Proteus anguinus*	<10(25)	Retains external gills and larval appearance throughout life.	S.E. Europe; only in lakes and streams in caves
Smooth newt *Triturus vulgaris*	<$4^1/_3$(11)	Largely terrestrial outside breeding season, often far from water.	Europe, apart from S.W., and W. Asia; often in gardens
Warty or great crested newt *Triturus cristatus*	<$6^1/_3$(16)	Stays in water for much of the summer; rough-skinned; breeding male has spiky crest.	W. Eurasia, except Iberia; various habitats near water
Frogs and toads/Anura	**(c. 4,000 species)**		
African clawed toad *Xenopus laevis*	<$4^3/_4$(12)	Eats carrion as well as live prey, gathered with front feet; tongueless; rarely leaves the water; used in pregnancy testing—urine from pregnant women causes toad to discharge eggs.	S. Africa; swamps, ponds, and streams
Poison-arrow frog (c. 100 species in 4 genera)	<2(5)	Vivid colors warn of highly poisonous secretions, traditionally used to poison arrows; males carry eggs until they hatch.	Tropical Americas; usually forests
Bullfrog *Rana catesbeiana*	<$7^9/_{10}$(20)	One of the largest frogs, catching food in and out of water; even eats small alligators; rarely moves far from water.	North America and Britain; in and around ponds and marshes
Grass frog *Rana temporaria*	<4(10)	Usually hibernates in mud at bottom of ponds; most common frog over most of Europe.	Europe, but not in south
European toad *Bufo bufo*	<6(15)	Rough skinned and more likely to walk than to jump; travels long distances to and from ponds.	Eurasia and N. Africa; many habitats
Edible frog *Rana esculenta*	<$4^3/_4$(12)	More aquatic than grass frog, but no more edible than any other species; male has balloonlike vocal sac at each corner of mouth.	Europe; especially around lakes and marshes
Fire-bellied toad *Bombina bombina*	<2(5)	Food grabbed by the jaws in or out of water; disk-shaped tongue cannot be shot out; largely aquatic; red belly scares predators.	E. Europe; lowland marshes and other shallow water
Gliding frog *Rhacophorus* (several species)	<$4^3/_4$(12)	Tree-living frogs; large webbed feet act like parachutes, enabling the frogs to glide from tree to tree; eggs laid in foam on leaves.	Tropical Asia
Goliath frog *Rana goliath*	<$13^3/_4$(35)	World's largest frog, about $3^1/_3$ feet (1 m) long with legs outstretched.	Tropical Africa; forest rivers
Marine or cane toad *Bufo marinus*	<10(25)	Skin exudes strong poison; introduced to Queensland in Australia to control sugarcane beetle, it spread rapidly and damaged fauna.	South and Central America, Australia, and many Pacific islands
Mediterranean tree frog *Hyla meridionalis*	<2(5)	Male utters deep, loud croaks from large balloonlike throat pouch at night.	S. Europe and N. Africa; marshes and damp scrub
Midwife toad *Alytes obstetricans*	<2(5)	Largely nocturnal, with piping call; male carries eggs on back legs; often far from water.	W. Europe ; many habitats
Mouth-brooding frog *Rhinoderma darwinii*	$1^1/_5$(3)	Males carry the eggs in their vocal sacs and tiny frogs eventually hatch out.	S. South America; living on forest floor
Natterjack toad *Bufo calamita*	<4(10)	Nocturnal with very loud voice; runs when disturbed.	Europe; ponds, marshes, sea
Spadefoot toad *Pelobatidae* (several genera and species)	<4(10)	Burrowing toads with small, spadelike blade on hind legs; some live in deserts, their egg and tadpole stages being completed rapidly during the wet season before the pools dry up.	N. Hemisphere; many habitats
Suriname toad *Pipa pipa*	4(10)	Eats carrion as well as live prey, gathered with front feet; tongueless; very flat, rarely leaving the water; eggs carried in pits on female's back, from which miniature frogs emerge.	N.E. South America

Newts and salamanders   Mudpuppy   Fire salamander   Smooth newt   Warty newt

Axolotl

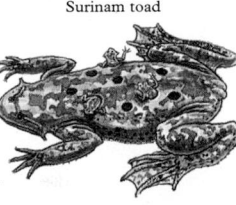

Poison-arrow frog   Bullfrog   Gliding frog   Spadefoot toad   Surinam toad

REPTILES

The reptiles came into being about 300 million years ago, descending from some kind of amphibian ancestor that gained a scaly, waterproof skin and the ability to lay shelled eggs that could survive on land. Most living reptiles still lay eggs, although some give birth to active young. They live on land, in freshwater, and in the sea, and between them they eat almost every kind of food. There are about 6,000 living species, of which some 3,000 are lizards and 2,700 are snakes. Turtles, tortoises, crocodiles, and alligators make up the rest of the class.

Anatomy of a typical lizard

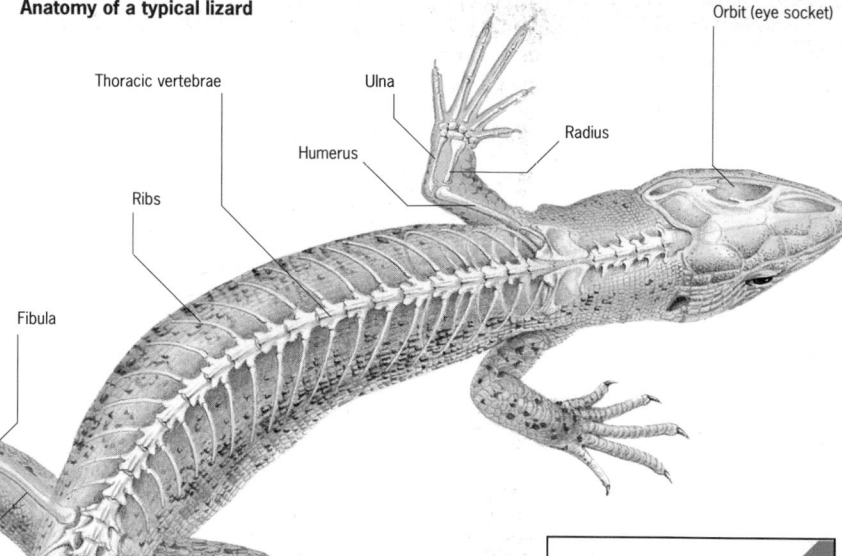

Thoracic vertebrae

Ulna

Humerus

Radius

Ribs

Orbit (eye socket)

Fibula

Phalanges

Tibia

Femur

Caudal (tail) vertebrae

Tuatara—a living fossil

The lizardlike tuatara (*right*) is the only living member of a lineage more ancient than the dinosaurs, but it has hardly changed since its relatives died out more than 200 million years ago. It lives only on a few islands off New Zealand, having been exterminated elsewhere in the country by introduced predators.

Adjusting temperature

Reptiles are said to be cold-blooded because they have no internal mechanism for maintaining a constant temperature like birds and mammals. Many, however, can adjust their body temperatures by varying their behavior. They bask in the morning sun to warm up (*right*), hide away in the midday heat, and then come out again in the evening.

Heat lost

Heat gained

Fangs and venom

Venomous snakes inject their venom with fangs. These are enlarged teeth at either the front or the back of the mouth. The venom is produced in glands in the roof of the mouth. Rattlesnakes and vipers have very long fangs that are folded back along the roof of the mouth when not in use. The longest fangs, up to 2 inches (5 cm) long, belong to Africa's gaboon viper. Snakes can swallow prey much fatter than their own bodies because they dislocate their jaws to give an enormous gape (*right*). Furthermore, the ligaments stretched between bones are extremely elastic. Using their teeth like ratchets, they gradually work their jaws forward to engulf the prey.

Snake dislocates jaw to swallow prey

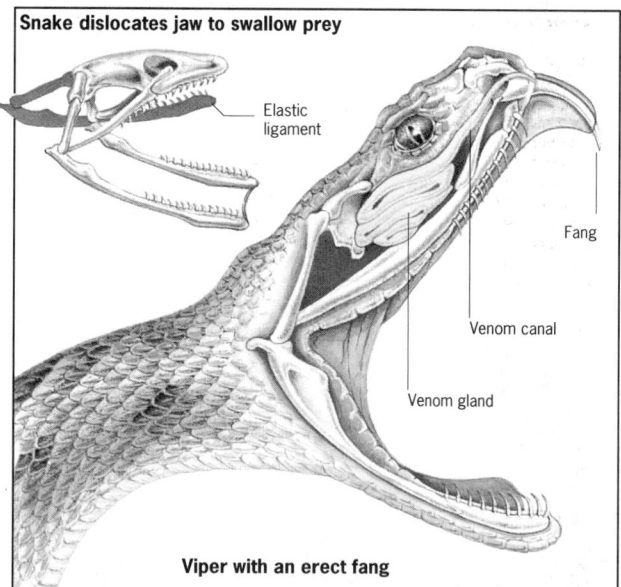

Elastic ligament

Fang

Venom canal

Venom gland

Viper with an erect fang

Dangerous snakes

Only a few venomous snakes are really dangerous to humans, but the most poisonous ones are not necessarily the most dangerous because they may be timid or not live in places where they come into contact with people. In terms of the numbers of people killed, the most dangerous snakes are probably the Indian cobra and the saw-scaled viper. Both kill thousands of people in India and Southeast Asia each year, although exact figures are impossible to obtain. The puff adder is probably the most dangerous of the African snakes, while the western diamondback rattlesnake kills more people than any other North American snake.

REPTILES

Measurements are in inches, followed by centimeters in parentheses. [▲ = Endangered species]

Order/Name	Length	Food and major features	Range and habitat
Turtles and tortoises/Chelonia		**(c. 215 species)**	
Giant tortoise *Testudo gigantea* and *T. elephantopus*	<59(150)	Vegetarian; living more than 100 years and reaching weights of more than 550 pounds (250 kg).	*Aldabra Isles and Galápagos Islands*
Leatherback turtle *Dermochelys coriacea*	<87(220)	Mainly jellyfish; no true shell, just a thick, leathery covering; largest living turtle.	*All warm seas*
▲ Loggerhead turtle *Caretta caretta*	<43½(110)	Jellyfish; becoming rare through disturbance of breeding beaches.	*All warm seas*
Painted turtle *Chrysemys picta*	<7(18)	Aquatic plants and animals; named for its bright red and yellow stripes; a popular pet.	*North America; ponds and sluggish streams*
Snapping turtle *Chelydra serpentina*	<20(50)	Omnivorous, but mainly fish and other animals, grabbed with a quick lunge of the powerful jaws.	*North America; muddy ponds and rivers*
Crocodiles and alligators/Crocodilia		**(c. 25 species)**	
American alligator *Alligator mississippiensis*	<237(600)	Fish, birds, and mammals; blunter snout than crocodiles, with lower teeth hidden when mouth shut.	*S.–E. U.S.A.; swamps and rivers*
Estuarine crocodile *Crocodilus porosus*	<316(800)	Fish, birds, and mammals; largest and most dangerous species, weighing 1,500 pounds (700 kg) or more.	*Australia and Southeast Asia; coastal waters*
Gharial *Gavialis gangeticus*	<237(600)	Fish, caught in very long, slender snout armed with numerous small and more or less uniform teeth.	*Northern India; large rivers*
Lizards/Squamata		**(c. 3,000 species)**	
Chameleon *Chamaeleontidae* (c. 85 species in several genera)	<24(60)	Insects, caught with long, sticky tongue; slow-moving tree dwellers with prehensile tails; can change color to match different habitats.	*Africa, especially Madagascar, and S. Eurasia*
Frilled lizard *Chlamydosaurus kingi*	<40(100)	Insects, spiders, and small mammals; opens mouth and spreads an umbrella-like frill around throat when alarmed, thus looking fierce.	*Australia and New Guinea; dry, scrubby places*
Gecko *Gekkonidae* (c. 400 species in several genera)	<12(30)	Insects and spiders; adhesive toe pads enable them to climb smooth surfaces and even run across ceilings.	*All warm areas; many habitats*
Gila monster *Heloderma suspectum*	<24(60)	Eggs and young birds and rodents; one of only two poisonous lizards, it can be dangerous to humans.	*North American deserts*
Komodo dragon *Varanus komodoensis*	<142(360)	Mainly carrion, but kills mammals as big as pigs; the biggest of all lizards, but surprisingly fast.	*Komodo and other islands of Indonesia; forests*
Monitor *Varanus* (c. 24 species)	<142(360)	Other animals and carrion; all large, heavily built lizards, including the Komodo dragon (*above*).	*All warm parts of "Old World"; many habitats*
Oscellated lizard *Lacerta lepida*	10(25)	Mainly insects, but also birds' eggs, small vertebrates, and fruit; sun-loving lizard with large head.	*S. Europe; dry habitats, especially vineyards*
Slowworm *Anguis fragilis*	<20(50)	Mostly slugs and snails; a legless lizard most active after rain; most often found under logs and stones.	*W. Eurasia and N. Africa; damp, overgrown areas*
Wall lizard *Podarcis muralis*	<10(25)	Insects and spiders; most common lizard around houses in Europe; mainly brown or gray with variable pattern; basks on walls.	*S. and C. Europe; rocky places*
Snakes/Squamata		**(c. 2,700 species)**	
Adder *Vipera berus*	<35½(90)	Mostly small mammals; venomous, but rarely harmful to humans; the only snake breeding north of Arctic Circle.	*Eurasia; wide range of habitats*
Anaconda *Eunectes murinus*	<316(800)	Pigs, deer, and other large mammals, and some fish; a constrictor; probably the world's heaviest snake.	*Amazon basin; swamps and slow-moving rivers*
Asp *Vipera aspis*	<29½(75)	Small mammals and lizards; venomous and dangerous to humans.	*S. and C. Europe*
Boa *Boa constrictor*	<198(500)	Birds, lizards, and small mammals; a slow-moving constrictor unlikely to harm human adults.	*Tropical South America; forests, rarely in water*
Boomslang *Dispholidus typus*	<79(200)	Birds and other small vertebrates; a very agile, very poisonous tree-dwelling snake with back fangs.	*Tropical Africa*
Cobra *Naja* (several species)	<99(250)	Birds and small mammals; very venomous; rear up and spread the neck region (hood) when alarmed; snakecharmer's snake; sacred in India.	*Africa and S. Asia; many habitats, including gardens*
Coral snake (many species)	<51(130)	Snakes and small vertebrates; strikingly colored with bands of red, yellow, and black; some species very poisonous.	*Americas, tropics and subtropics*
Egg-eating snake *Dasypeltis* (5 species)	<40(100)	Eggs, engulfed in the mouth before being opened with sawlike teeth in the throat; nonvenomous.	*Africa; mostly wooded habitats*
Gaboon viper *Bitis gabonica*	<79(200)	Ground-living vertebrates; the longest fangs of any snake.	*Africa; tropical forest floors*
Grass snake *Natrix natrix*	<79(200)	Mostly frogs and toads; nonpoisonous, grabbing prey with its teeth and swallowing it alive; swims well.	*Eurasia and N. Africa; mostly damp habitats*
King cobra *Ophiophagus hannah*	<217(550)	Snakes; largest venomous snake; very poisonous, but rarely bites people.	*S.E. Asia; many habitats*
Krait *Bungarus* (several species)	<59(150)	Mostly other snakes; rarely bite people, but extremely poisonous.	*Asia; variety of habitats*
Python *Python* (several species)	<395(1000)	Animals, including antelopes; constrict with no venom; *P. reticulatus*, the reticulated python of S.E. Asia, is the longest snake.	*Africa and S.E. Asia; both wet and dry habitats*
Rattlesnake *Crotalus and sistrurus* (several species)	<95(240)	Small mammals, detected by their body heat with heat-sensitive pits on the face; very poisonous; rattle on the tail formed from old scales.	*North America; mostly in open country*
Taipan *Oxyuranus scutellatus*	<119(300)	Mammals and birds; highly venomous, but rarely comes into contact with people.	*N.E. Australia; dense forest*

Snakes
Coral snake

Snakes
Taipan

Lizards
Slow-worm

Crocodiles and alligators
American alligator

Lizards
Komodo dragon

Turtles and tortoises
Snapping turtle

Lizards
Gecko

BIRDS

Birds evolved from reptilian ancestors about 140–150 million years ago. The earliest known bird is the *Archaeopteryx*, several fossils of which have been found in Germany. About the size of a pigeon, *Archaeopteryx* had many reptilian features, including toothed jaws and a lizardlike tail, but it also had feathers and was undoubtedly a bird. Birds are the only animals with feathers, which clearly evolved from reptilian scales. As well as aiding birds in flight, feathers help them to maintain their bodies at a constant high temperature.

There are more than 9,000 living bird species, and they have adapted to virtually every kind of food available, from nectar and plankton to carrion. Although most live in the tropics, the group has invaded all habitats, including the sea, and some live in the coldest places on earth.

Feather structure

Each feather has a horny shaft, a rachis (**1**), and numerous branches, or barbs (**2**). The barbs of the outer feathers are linked together by hooked branches, barbules (**3**). The wingtip feathers are primary or flight feathers; those nearer the body are secondary feathers.

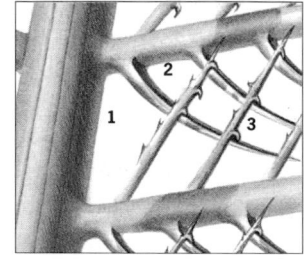

Bill types

Modern birds have no teeth, and with their front legs turned into wings, their bills or beaks have to collect and process their food. The bill of each species is admirably suited to its diet.

The hawk: hooked beak to tear apart prey.

The pelican: pouch-like bill to scoop up fish.

The duck: saw-like teeth to hold slippery catch.

The woodpecker: chisel-like bill to break bark.

The cardinal: strong, stout bill to open seeds.

The kingfisher: long, sharp beak to snatch fish.

Anatomy of an eagle

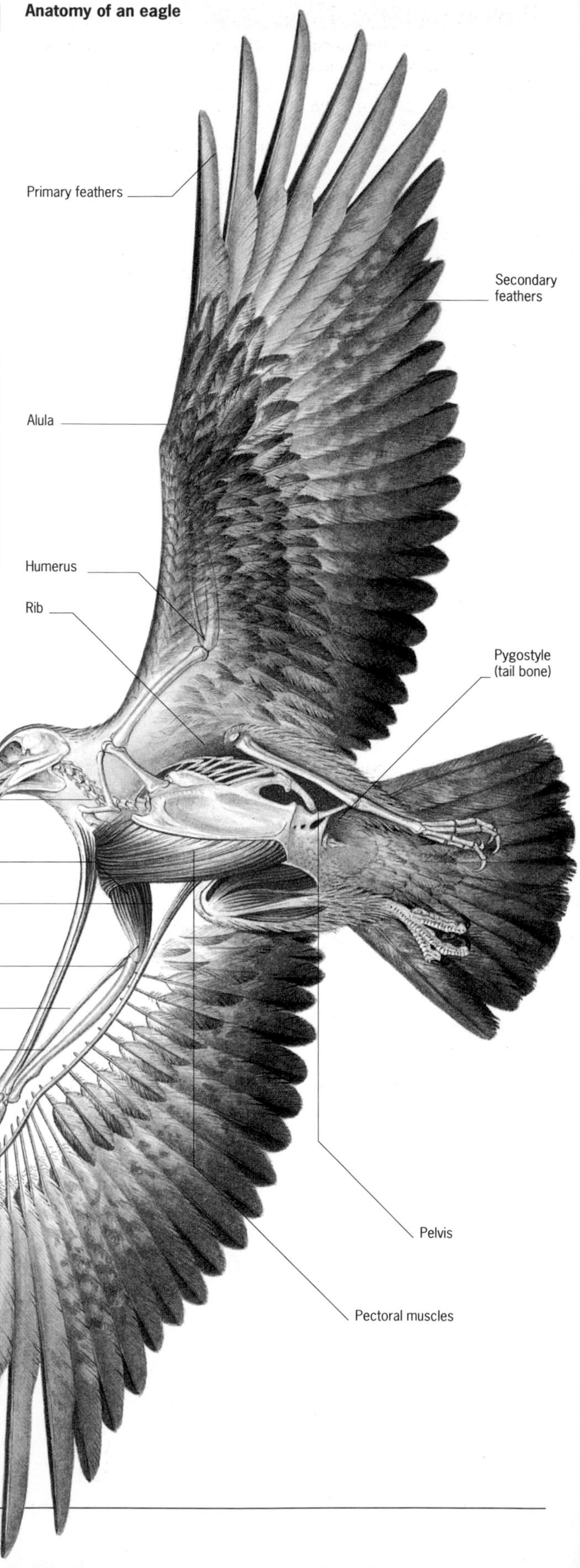

Primary feathers

Secondary feathers

Alula

Humerus

Rib

Clavicle (collar bone)

Biceps

Triceps

Elbow

Radius

Ulna

Metacarpals

Phalanges

Pygostyle (tail bone)

Pelvis

Pectoral muscles

Birds as pets

Millions of birds—from huge eagle owls to tiny waxbills and zebra finches—are kept as pets, usually in cages that are too small for them. Many species are kept for their bright colors, some for their songs, and some for their ability to mimic human voices. Cockatoos, macaws, parakeets, and other members of the parrot family are well-known mimics, but the mynah birds are probably the best of all. They can master many words and even string them together in sentences, but obviously do not understand what they are saying; they simply have an innate urge and ability to copy what they hear. The canary, a member of the finch family, is one of the best of the real songsters.

Many caged birds are bred in captivity but, despite legislation to protect the rarer species, millions of wild birds are still caught each year for the pet trade. Most of them come from the tropics and are then transported across the world in poor conditions. It has been estimated that for every bird reaching a pet store four have died on the way. More than 80 members of the parrot family are in danger of extinction, largely because of the pet trade.

Record holders

Highest flier Ruppell's griffon—a vulture—has been measured at about 7 miles above sea level.

Farthest migrator The Arctic tern travels up to 22,400 miles each year, flying from the Arctic to the Antarctic and back again.

Fastest fliers The peregrine falcon can dive through the air at speeds up to 112 mph. The fastest bird in level flight is probably the eider duck, which can reach about 50 mph.

Smallest bird The bee hummingbird of Cuba is under 2.4 inches long and weighs 0.1 ounces.

Greatest wingspan The wandering albatross can reach 12 feet.

Heaviest flying bird The great bustard and the kori bustard both weigh up to 40 pounds, with swans not far behind at about 35 pounds.

Deepest diver The emperor penguin can reach a depth of 870 feet. The great northern diver can dive to about 262 feet—deeper than any other flying bird.

Most abundant Africa's red-billed quelea is the most numerous wild bird, with an estimated population of about 1½ billion. The domestic chicken is the most abundant of all birds, numbering more than 4 billion.

Most feathers The greatest number of feathers—25,216—actually counted on a bird was on a swan.

Canary

Budgerigar

Love birds

Mynah

Senegalese parrot

Arctic tern

Peregrine falcon

Bee hummingbird

Great bustard

Emperor penguin

Flightless birds

Many birds have lost the power of flight during their evolution. The ostrich—the world's largest living bird—grew too big to fly. However, its size and speed—up to 50 mph (80 kph) in short bursts—give it plenty of protection. Rheas in South America, emus in Australia, and cassowaries in New Guinea have evolved in similar ways and have all come to look alike, although they are not closely related. Birds living on islands with no mammalian predators often became flightless. The kiwi of New Zealand is a familiar example. Some of these birds died out when humans introduced cats and other mammals, and many more are now in danger of extinction. Penguins cannot fly in the air, but they use their powerful wings as flippers to "fly" underwater.

Rhea   Ostrich

Emu

Cassowary

Kiwi

Penguin

BIRDS (Class Aves)

Sizes given are normally lengths, from the bill tip to tail tip, but measurements given in italics are heights. Measurements are in inches, followed by centimeters in parentheses. [▲ = endangered species]

Order/Name	Size	Food; habitat; habits	Range
Ostriches/Struthioniformes		**(1 species)**	
Ostrich *Struthio camelus*	98½ (250)	Omnivorous; dry grassland; flightless but fast running; the largest living bird; farmed for meat in some areas.	*Africa, mainly S. and E.*
Rheas/Rheiformes		**(2 species)**	
Greater rhea *Rhea americana*	51 (130)	Omnivorous; grassland; flightless; largest American bird; populations much reduced by hunting and spread of agriculture.	*South America, especially Argentinian pampas*
Emus and cassowaries/Casuariiformes (4 species)			
Double-wattled cassowary *Casuarius casuarius*	71 (180)	Omnivorous; tropical forest; flightless, with powerful legs and horny "helmet" on head.	*New Guinea and N. Australia*
Emu *Dromaius novaehollandiae*	63 (160)	Mainly vegetarian, with some insect food; bush and open grassland; flightless; an agricultural pest in some regions.	*Australia*
Kiwis/Apterygiformes		**(3 species)**	
Brown kiwi *Apteryx australis*	27½ (70)	Largely insectivorous, but also eats worms and fruit; forests; flightless and nocturnal, using its long beak to probe for food.	*New Zealand*
Penguins/Sphenisciformes		**(18 species)**	
Adélie penguin *Pygoscelis adeliae*	27½ (70)	Fish; breeds on rocky shores in summer, but oceanic at other times.	*Antarctic*
Emperor penguin *Aptenodytes forsteri*	45 (115)	Fish; largest and most southerly penguin; breeds on sea ice in winter, otherwise oceanic.	*Antarctic*
Galápagos penguin *Spheniscus mendiculus*	20 (50)	Fish; cool coastal waters; often nests in caves; most northerly penguin, living around the equator.	*Galápagos Islands*
Little penguin *Eudyptula minor*	16 (40)	Fish; coastal waters; nests in caves or burrows; the smallest penguin, also called fairy penguin.	*New Zealand and S. Australia*
Loons/Gaviiformes		**(4 species)**	
Red-throated loon *Gavia stellata*	<27½ (70)	Fish; ducklike in shape but with pointed bill; breeds on fresh water but winters on coasts; powerful swimmer, diving from surface for food.	*N. Hemisphere: breeding in far north, flies south*
Grebes/Podicipediformes		**(20 species)**	
Great-crested grebe *Podiceps cristatus*	20 (50)	Fish and other aquatic animals; fresh water but often on coasts in winter; named for black and chestnut head feathers in breeding season.	*Temperate regions world-wide, but not Americas*
Fulmars and albatrosses/Procellariiformes (c. 110 species)			
Manx shearwater *Puffinus puffinus*	20 (50)	Fish and squids; oceanic, gliding very close to the waves; breeds in burrows on coastal cliffs, usually coming ashore only at night.	*S. Atlantic; flies to N. Atlantic to breed*
Northern fulmar *Fulmarus glacialis*	<53 (135)	Fish, including offal jettisoned by fishing boats; oceanic but breeds on rocky coasts.	*Arctic, N. Pacific, and N. Atlantic oceans*
Wandering albatross *Diomedea exulans*	15 (38)	Fish and squid; oceanic, coming to land only to breed; wingspan up to 12 feet (3.65 m), greatest of any bird; average lifespan 30 years.	*Southern oceans*
Gannets and pelicans/Pelecaniformes (c. 60 species)			
Brown pelican *Pelecanus occidentalis*	>55 (140)	Fish, caught by plunging into water from a height of several yards; coastal waters.	*North and South America*
Great cormorant *Phalacrocorax carbo*	<40 (100)	Fish; coastal and fresh water; dives for food and can stay submerged for more than a minute; nests on cliffs and in trees.	*Almost worldwide, but not South America*
Great frigatebird *Fregata minor*	40 (100)	Fish and squids; oceanic but cannot swim and rarely lands on water; food snatched from surface or stolen from other birds; nests in trees on islands.	*Tropical and subtropical, especially Indo-Pacific*
Great white pelican *Pelecanus onocrotalus*	<69 (175)	Fish; lakes and slow-moving rivers; lives in large colonies, often working with others to drive fish into shallow water; pouched bill.	*Africa, Asia, and S. Europe*
Northern gannet *Morus bassanus*	35½ (90)	Fish, caught by diving into sea from a height; oceanic but nests in huge colonies on remote cliffs and islands; often feeds in large flocks.	*N. Atlantic*
Red-footed booby *Sula sula*	31½ (80)	Fish; oceanic but nests in trees; plumage white or brown, but with bright-red feet.	*Tropical seas*
Herons and storks/Ciconiiformes		**(c. 120 species)**	
Cattle egret *Bubulcus ibis*	20 (50)	Insects and other small animals, including ticks and other cattle pests; marshes and grassland, including farmland; follows grazing herds.	*Warmer parts of the world, including S. Europe*
Gray heron *Ardea cinerea*	<40 (100)	Mainly fish and frogs; fresh water, often on coast in winter; nests in trees.	*Eurasia and Africa*
Greater flamingo *Phoenicopterus ruber*	55 (140)	Small crustaceans, sieved from water through the comblike edges of the bill; lakes and marshes, mainly in coastal areas.	*Africa, S. Europe, Asia, South America , West Indies*
Sacred ibis *Threskiornis aethiopica*	29½ (75)	Fish, frogs, and other small animals; marshes and other shallow water; venerated by ancient Egyptians, although now extinct in Egypt.	*Middle East and Africa south of Sahara*
Spoonbill *Platalea leucorodia*	<35½ (90)	Small aquatic crustaceans, caught by sweeping spoon-shaped bill through water; marshes and other shallow fresh or brackish water.	*S. Eurasia and N. Africa*
Whale-headed stork *Balaeniceps rex*	47 (120)	Large fish and even young crocodiles, caught in huge, shoe-shaped bill; wetlands.	*Tropical Africa*

Loons
Red-throated loon

Fulmars and albatrosses
Wandering albatross

Gannets and pelicans
Great white pelican

Herons and storks
Greater flamingo

Herons and storks
Gray heron

Herons and storks
Spoonbill

Order/Name	Size	Food; habitat; habits	Range
White stork *Ciconia ciconia*	<45(115)	Frogs, insects, and other small animals; mainly wetlands, usually near human settlements; often nests on houses.	*Eurasia and Africa*

Ducks, geese, and swans/Anseriformes *(c. 150 species)*

Order/Name	Size	Food; habitat; habits	Range
Black swan *Cygnus atratus*	<55(140)	Vegetarian, feeding on land or in water; wetlands, both fresh and brackish.	*Australia and New Zealand*
Brant *Branta bernicla*	24(60)	Vegetarian, grazing on land or eating eelgrass in sea; breeds on Arctic tundra but winters on coasts farther south; head completely black.	*Arctic and N. Atlantic*
Canada goose *Branta canadensis*	<43(110)	Vegetarian, often a pest in parks; lakes and marshes and surrounding grassland.	*Arctic and North America; introduced to Europe*
Common eider *Somateria mollissima*	<27½(70)	Aquatic invertebrates; coastal waters and estuaries; female's down feathers, used to line nest, are collected for stuffing comforters and coats.	*Arctic and N. temperate regions*
Mallard *Anas platyrhynchos*	25½(65)	Omnivorous, feeding on land and in water; fresh and coastal waters; ancestor of domestic duck.	*N. Hemisphere; introduced to Australia and Oceania*
Mute swan *Cygnus olor*	59(150)	Aquatic vegetation; lowland fresh water, sometimes on coast; one of the heaviest flying birds, weighing up to 40 pounds (18 kg).	*Temperate Eurasia, but introduced to other regions*

Birds of prey/Falconiformes *(c. 290 species)*

Order/Name	Size	Food; habitat; habits	Range
Andean condor *Vultur gryphus*	43(110)	Carrion, sometimes killing weak or wounded animals; mountains; largest bird of prey, with wingspan over 10 feet (3 m).	*Andes*
▲ Bald eagle *Haliaeetus leucocephalus*	<37½(95)	Fish, birds, and small mammals; open country; white feathers on head resemble bald head; national bird of U.S.A.; rare because of hunting and pollution.	*North America*
Bearded vulture *Gypaetus barbatus*	43(110)	Skin and bones of carcasses, often smashing bones on rocks to get at marrow; mountains; also known as the lammergeier.	*Africa and S. Eurasia*
Eurasian buzzard *Buteo buteo*	21½(55)	Small mammals and carrion; open country and light woodland; spends much time high in the air.	*Eurasia*
Eurasian kestrel *Falco tinnunculus*	14(35)	Small mammals, birds, and insects; open country and also towns; hovers for long periods while looking for prey on ground; common on roadsides.	*Africa and Eurasia*
Golden eagle *Aquila chrysaetos*	<39(100)	Rabbits and other mammals and large birds; mountains, moors, and open forest.	*N. Hemisphere*
Griffon vulture *Gyps fulvus*	39(100)	Carrion; open country, mainly in upland areas; gathers around carcasses in flocks.	*S. Eurasia and N. Africa*
Harpy eagle *Harpia harpyja*	<43(110)	Birds and mammals, including monkeys, usually plucked from treetops; tropical forests.	*Tropical Americas*
Harrier circus (10 species)	<24(60)	Small mammals, birds, and amphibians; open country, including wetlands; quarter the ground at low level while searching for prey.	*Worldwide*
King vulture *Sarcorhamphus papa*	29½(75)	Carrion, including dead and dying fish; tropical forest; one of the most colorful birds of prey.	*Tropical Americas*
Northern goshawk *Accipiter gentilis*	<25½(65)	Birds and mammals, including game birds and rabbits; woodland; fast-flying and very agile.	*Cooler parts of N. Hemisphere*
Northern sparrowhawk *Accipiter nisus*	<16(40)	Birds, usually caught in flight, and occasional small mammals; woodland; very fast and agile.	*Eurasia and N. Africa*
Osprey *Pandion haliaetus*	22(55)	Fish, scooped from the water by strong, scaly feet; coasts and inland waters.	*Worldwide*
▲ Peregrine falcon *Falco peregrinus*	<20(50)	Birds, especially pigeons, usually caught in midair in spectacular high-speed dives; mainly coastal and upland areas; nests on cliff faces.	*Almost worldwide*
Secretary bird *Sagittarius serpentarius*	<59(150)	Snakes, small birds, and mammals and insects; grassland; named for long, black head feathers, said to resemble secretaries with quill pens behind their ears.	*Africa*
Turkey vulture *Cathartes aura*	<31½(80)	Carrion; wide range of habitat from desert to forest.	*Throughout the Americas*
White-tailed eagle *Haliaeetus albicilla*	<75(190)	Fish and water birds, often snatched from water surface, and small mammals and carrion; coasts and inland waters.	*Greenland and N. Eurasia*

Game birds/Galliformes *(c. 275 species)*

Order/Name	Size	Food; habitat; habits	Range
Capercaillie *Tetrao urogallus*	<33½(85)	Pine seeds and needles (winter) and berries (summer and fall); coniferous forest; a turkeylike bird, largest of the grouse family.	*N. Europe*
Common quail *Coturnix coturnix*	8(20)	Seeds and insects; open grassland and heaths; Europe's only migratory game bird.	*Eurasia and Africa*
Gray partridge *Perdix perdix*	12(30)	Seeds, leaves, and insects; open grassland and farmland.	*Europe*
▲ Great curassow *Crax rubra*	37½(95)	Leaves and fruit; forest; red or black; rare because of hunting and loss of habitat.	*Tropical Americas*
▲ Greater prairie chicken *Tympanuchus cupido*	<20(50)	Mainly vegetarian, but eats some insects; open grassland; becoming rare in face of spread of agriculture.	*North American prairies*
Helmeted guinea fowl *Numida meleagris*	22(55)	Mainly vegetarian; savanna grassland; named for horny crest on its colorful head.	*Native of E. Africa, but domesticated worldwide*
▲ Mallee fowl *Leipoa ocellata*	24(60)	Omnivorous; eucalyptus scrub (mallee); eggs are laid in a mound of rotting leaf litter, which produces warmth necessary for incubation.	*Southern Australia*
Peafowl *Pavo cristatus*	<87(220)	Omnivorous; open woodland with streams and dense undergrowth; famous for the male's shimmering fan used in his courtship display.	*Native of India, now in parks worldwide*
Red jungle fowl *Gallus gallus*	<31½(80)	Mainly seeds and insects; open woodland with dense undergrowth; ancestor of domestic chicken.	*S.E. Asia*
Ring-necked pheasant *Phasianus colchicus*	<35½(90)	Omnivorous; open woodland and farmland; many races, differing in male coloration; raised for shooting in many countries.	*Native of S. Asia, but now almost worldwide*
Rock ptarmigan *Lagopus mutus*	14(35)	Vegetarian; mountains, moorland, and tundra, turning white for winter.	*Arctic, Scotland, and Alps*

Herons and storks
White stork

Ducks, geese, and swans
Black swan

Birds of prey
Bald eagle

Birds of prey
Northern goshawk

Birds of prey
Eurasian kestrel

Game birds
Red-necked pheasant

Order/Name	Size	Food; habitat; habits	Range
Wild turkey *Meleagris gallopavo*	<47(120)	Omnivorous; open forest and scrub, roosting in trees at night; wild birds much slimmer than domestic descendants.	*Native of North America, but introduced to many areas*
Willow ptarmigan *Lagopus lagopus*	<16½(42)	Heather shoots and seeds; moorland; a race of willow grouse, but does not go white for winter.	*Only British Isles*

Cranes, rails, and bustards/Gruiformes (*c.* 190 species)

Common moorhen *Gallinula chloropus*	14(35)	Aquatic plants and insects; ponds, streams, marshes, and surrounding grassland; red forehead.	*Worldwide, apart from Australasia*
▲ Eurasian coot *Fulica atra*	18(45)	Aquatic plants and insects; fresh water of all kinds; white forehead distinguishes it from moorhen.	*Eurasia and Australasia*
Great bustard *Otis tarda*	<41(105)	Omnivorous; open grassland, including farmland; flying bird, male weighs up to 40 pounds (18 kg).	*N. Africa, Spain, and Eurasian steppes*
▲ Whooping crane *Grus americana*	51(130)	Omnivorous; wetlands, breeding in boggy places in summer and wintering on coastal marshes; one of the world's most endangered birds.	*Breeds in Canada; winters in Gulf of Mexico*

Waders, gulls, and auks/Charadriiformes (*c.* 340 species)

Arctic tern *Sterna paradisaea*	14(35)	Fish, usually snatched from surface; oceanic, nesting mainly on shingle beaches; greatest migrants, breeding in the north and flying to edge of Antarctic pack ice.	*Oceans worldwide*
Atlantic puffin *Fratercula arctica*	12(30)	Fish, especially sand eels, caught in the colorful bill while "flying" underwater; oceanic, nesting in burrows on remote cliffs.	*N. Atlantic and Arctic*
Avocet *Recurvirostra avosetta*	18(45)	Aquatic invertebrates, caught by sweeping upturned bill through water; mud and freshwater marshes; coastal winters.	*N. Europe and W. Asia; mainly in Africa*
Common murre *Uria aalge*	16(40)	Fish and other marine animals; oceanic, nesting on coastal cliffs; single egg laid on bare ledge.	*N. Eurasia and North America*
Common snipe *Gallinago gallinago*	10(25)	Invertebrates, pulled from muddy ground by long bill; inland and coastal marshes.	*Eurasia and North America*
Eurasian curlew *Numenius arquata*	<24(60)	Worms and other invertebrates, plucked from mud with long, curved bill; damp grassland and moors, wintering mainly on coasts.	*Eurasia and Africa; northern birds fly south for winter*
Great skua *Catharacta skua*	<25½(65)	Mainly fish, often stolen from other seabirds by piratical chasing; tundra and coasts.	*Arctic and N. Atlantic*
Gull *Larus* (*c.* 40 species)	<31½(80)	Many pluck fish from sea; some are predators of other seabirds; mainly coastal, but many gulls live inland, feeding at garbage dumps and on farmland.	*Cool regions, except Antarctic*
Lily trotter (8 species in 6 genera)	<12(30)	Aquatic plants and animals; lakes and slow rivers with lots of floating vegetation; walk on leaves, spreading weight with very long toes.	*Tropics and E. Australia*
Northern lapwing *Vanellus vanellus*	12(30)	Insects and other invertebrates; marshes, rough grassland, and farmland; also called peewit for its call; northern birds move south for winter.	*Eurasia*
Oystercatcher *Haematopus ostralegus*	18(45)	Cockles and mussels—not oysters—opened with long bill; seashores and inland marshes.	*Eurasia and, in winter, Africa*
Plover (many genera)	<14(35)	Invertebrates; seashores, tundra, and marshes; short-billed waders.	*Worldwide*
Razorbill *Alca torda*	16(40)	Fish and other marine animals; oceanic, nesting in cliff crevices.	*N. Atlantic and (winter only) Mediterranean*
Skimmer *Rynchops* (3 species)	<20(50)	Small fish and other aquatic animals, caught by skimming over surface and dipping lower half of bill in water; coastal and inland waters.	*Tropics*

Pigeons and doves/Columbiformes (*c.* 300 species)

Collared dove *Streptopelia decaocto*	<14(35)	Seeds; towns, gardens, and farmland; a pest in and around grain stores; confined to S.W. Asia until 1900s, now spread to Europe and North America.	*Eurasia and North America*
Rock dove/city pigeon *Columba livia*	16(40)	Seeds and other starchy matter—scavenged in urban habitats; descendants of domesticated rock doves that have escaped captivity over the centuries.	*Worldwide*
Wood pigeon *Columba palumbus*	12(30)	Seeds and leaves; woodland and neighboring farmland; serious pest to cereals and brassicas.	*Eurasia and N. Africa*

Parrots/Psittaciformes (*c.* 340 species)

Parakeet *Melopsittacus undulatus*	6(16)	Seeds; grassland, scrub, and open woodland, rarely far from water; often in huge flocks; wild birds always green, but domesticated ones come in many colors.	*Native of Australia*
Gray parrot *Psittacus erithacus*	<20(50)	Fruits and seeds; tropical forest and savanna; a popular cage bird adept at copying human voices.	*Tropical Africa*
▲ Kakapo *Strigops habroptilus*	24(60)	Omnivorous; woodland; flightless and nocturnal—often called owl parrot—it has almost been wiped out by introduced mammals.	*New Zealand*
Kea *Nestor notabilis*	18(45)	Omnivorous, with a liking for fruit and carrion; said to attack injured sheep with sharply hooked bill; upland forests.	*New Zealand (South Island)*
▲ Macaw (17 species in 3 genera)	<39(100)	Vegetarian, feeding mostly on fruits and seeds; tropical forests; long-tailed parrots, with striking colors; in demand as pets with the result that several species are now endangered.	*Tropical Americas*
Sulfur-crested cockatoo *Cacatua galerita*	12(30)	Fruit, seeds, and insects; forest and savanna; agricultural pest in some areas, but also a popular cage bird.	*New Guinea, Australia, and Pacific*

Cuckoos and relatives/Cuculiformes (*c.* 160 species)

Common cuckoo *Cuculus canorus*	12(30)	Hairy caterpillars; woods and open country, including farmland; famed for male's heralding call of cook-coo and female's habit of laying eggs in other birds' nests.	*Eurasia in summer; Africa in winter*
Greater roadrunner *Geococcyx californianus*	<24(60)	Small animals, including young rattlesnakes; scrub and open country; named for habit of running alongside stagecoaches to grab animals disturbed by wheels.	*S. North America*

Game birds	Waders, gulls, and auks	Waders, gulls, and auks	Waders, gulls, and auks	Cuckoos and relatives
Wild turkey	Avocet	Atlantic puffin	Common snipe	Greater roadrunner

Order/Name	Size	Food; habitat; habits	*Range*
Owls/Strigiformes		**(c. 160 species)**	
Barn owl *Tyto alba*	14(35)	Small rodents and some birds; farmland and other open country.	*Worldwide*
Burrowing owl *Athene cunicularia*	<10(25)	Insects and small mammals; deserts and other open country; nests in burrows; often diurnal.	*North and South America*
Eagle owl *Bubo bubo*	>29½(75)	Birds and mammals, including hares, rabbits, and young deer; upland forests.	*Eurasia and N. Africa*
Snowy owl *Nyctea scandiaca*	<25½(65)	Small birds and mammals, especially lemmings; tundra and neighboring moorland.	*Arctic tundra*
Tawny owl *Strix aluco*	16(40)	Small mammals and birds; wooded areas, including parks and churchyards.	*Eurasia and N. Africa*
Nightjars/Caprimulgiformes		**(c. 100 species)**	
European nightjar *Caprimulgus europaeus*	<12(30)	Insects, caught on the wing at night in the wide, gaping mouth; heaths and open woodland.	*Breeds in Eurasia; winters in Africa*
Tawny frogmouth *Podargus strigoides*	<20(50)	Small animals, including insects, frogs, and mice, snatched from ground at night; open woodland and urban areas.	*Australia*
Whippoorwill *Caprimulgus vociferus*	10(25)	Insects, caught on the wing at night in the wide, gaping mouth; woodland; named for its unusual call, repeated several times.	*Breeds in North America; winters in Central America*
Hummingbirds and swifts/Apodiformes		**(c. 430 species)**	
Bee hummingbird *Calypte helenae*	24(60)	Nectar; woods and gardens; the smallest of all birds with a body little over $2/5$ inch (1cm) long and weighing only $1/14$ ounce (2 g).	*Cuba*
Swift *Apus apus*	6(15)	Insects, caught on the wing; the most aerial of all land birds, it speeds through the air; lands only to nest and rear young—often in buildings.	*Breeds in Eurasia; migrates to tropical Africa for winter*
Kingfishers and relatives/Coraciiformes		**(c. 200 species)**	
European bee-eater *Merops apiaster*	10(25)	Bees, including large bumblebees and other large insects, caught in midair or plucked from vegetation; lightly wooded areas including orchards and farmland.	*Breeds in Eurasia; winters in tropical Africa*
▲ Great Indian hornbill *Buceros bicornis*	<47(120)	Mainly fruit, plucked from branches with the large but very light bill; tropical forest; becoming rare through forest clearance.	*India and S.E. Asia*
Hoopoe *Upupa epops*	10(25)	Insects, usually caught on ground; wooded areas, including parks, orchards, and gardens.	*Eurasia and Africa; always winters in tropics*
Kingfisher *Alcedo atthis*	6(15)	Fish, caught in spectacular dives from a perch; clear streams and canals.	*Eurasia, S.E. Asia, and N. Africa*
Kookaburra *Dacelo novaeguineae*	<18(45)	Invertebrates and small vertebrates; open woodland and urban areas; also called laughing jackass and alarm bird because of its laughlike call at daybreak.	*Australia and New Guinea*
Woodpeckers and relatives/Piciformes		**(c. 380 species)**	
Green woodpecker *Picus viridis*	8(20)	Ants and other insects, and some seeds; open woodland, parks, and large gardens; spends most of its time foraging on the ground.	*W. Eurasia*
Honeyguide *Indicator indicator*	24(60)	Bee grubs and honeycomb; open woodland and savanna; on finding a bees' nest it attracts attention of ratel (honey badger), which opens the nest.	*Tropical Africa*
▲ Ivory-billed woodpecker *Campephilus principalis*	<8(20)	Insect grubs, dug from trees; mature forest; one of the largest woodpeckers and one of the rarest birds, threatened by forest clearance.	*Cuba*
Sapsucker *Sphyrapicus* (4 species)	12(30)	Tree sap, obtained by drilling small holes in bark, together with insects attracted to the sap; woodland and orchards.	*North and Central America*
Toco toucan *Ramphastos toco*	20(50)	Fruit, gathered with long but very light bill; open woodland, plantations, and villages; largest of the toucans, with bill up to 8 inches (20 cm).	*Tropical South America*
Perching birds/Passeriformes		**(c. 5,400 species)**	
American robin *Turdus migratorius*	10(25)	Worms and other invertebrates and fruit; woods, parks, and gardens; largest North American thrush.	*North America*
Barn swallow *Hirundo rustica*	7(18)	Insects, caught in midair; open habitats, especially around human habitation.	*Breeds in N. Hemisphere; winters in S. Hemisphere*
Bird of paradise (42 species in several genera)	<53(135)	Mainly fruit and insects; mostly rain forest, but often in villages; famed for magnificent plumage of males, displayed in elaborate courtship rituals.	*New Guinea and N. Australia*
Black-billed magpie *Pica pica*	18(45)	Omnivorous, often taking other birds' eggs; woods, farms, and gardens.	*Eurasia and North America*
Black-capped chickadee *Parus atricapillus*	5(13)	Insects and seeds; woodland, often visiting gardens in winter; most common American tit.	*North America*
Black currawong *Strepera fuliginosa*	20(50)	Omnivorous; from woodland to open country, often a pest in orchards; demands food at picnic sites with its beady, yellow eyes and menacingly large bill.	*Tasmania*
Blue jay *Cyanocsitta cristata*	12(30)	Mainly seeds, nuts, and insects; wooded areas, including parks and gardens; noisy.	*North America*
Bluethroat *Luscinia svecica*	6(15)	Insects; tundra, birch scrub, mountains, and coastal heaths; many races.	*Eurasia and Africa*
Blue tit *Parus caeruleus*	4(11)	Insects and seeds; wooded habitats, common garden visitors in winter.	*Eurasia and N. Africa*
Bohemian waxwing *Bombycilla garrulus*	8(20)	Fruit and insects; woodland, sometimes seen in town parks and gardens in winter; named for waxlike red blobs on wings.	*Eurasia and North America; moving south for winter*
Bowerbird (18 species in several genera)	<14(35)	Mainly fruit and insects; rain forest and other wooded areas; males make courtship bowers, decorated with flowers and other bright objects.	*New Guinea and Australia*
Brown-headed cowbird *Molothrus ater*	6(16)	Seeds and insects; open areas, farms and villages; lays its eggs in other birds' nests.	*North America*
Canary *Serinus canaria*	5(12)	Seeds; woods, gardens, and open areas; wild birds browner than cage varieties.	*Canary Islands and Azores*
Carrion crow *Corvus corone*	<20(50)	Omnivorous; farmland, parks, and open country with some trees; jet black or with gray shoulders and underparts (hooded crow).	*Eurasia; black form only in W. Europe*

Owls Burrowing owl	**Nightjars** Whippoorwill	**Kingfishers and relatives** European bee-eater	**Kingfishers and relatives** Hoopoe	**Woodpeckers and relatives** Toco toucan	**Perching birds** American robin	**Perching birds** Bluethroat

Order/Name	Size	Food; habitat; habits	Range
Chaffinch *Fringilla coelebs*	6(15)	Seeds; woods, farmland, parks, and gardens; one of Europe's most common birds.	*Eurasia*
Common or garden bulbul *Pycnonotus barbatus*	8(20)	Fruit and buds; open woodland, orchards, and gardens; one of the most common birds in towns and villages in N. Africa.	*N. and C. Africa*
Common mynah *Acridotheres tristis*	8½(22)	Insects and fruit; open country, farms, and town parks; damage to fruit crops often outweighs its usefulness in controlling insect pests.	*Native of S. Asia, but introduced to many areas*
Common raven *Corvus corax*	25½(65)	Carrion, also kills small animals; mountains, tundra, and coasts; largest crow.	*Eurasia, North America, and N. Africa*
Common treecreeper *Certhia familiaris*	5(12)	Insects, mostly collected from bark as it works its way up tree trunks; woodlands.	*Eurasia*
Dipper *Cinclus cinclus*	8(20)	Freshwater shrimp and other aquatic animals; fast-flowing streams, usually in hilly areas; walks or "flies" underwater to find food.	*Eurasia*
Eurasian jackdaw *Corvus monedula*	13(33)	Omnivorous, often scavenging on garbage dumps; woods, farms, towns, and coasts; smallest European crow, recognized by gray neck.	*Eurasia*
Eurasian nuthatch *Sitta europaea*	5(12)	Insects, seeds, and nuts; woodland; wedges nuts in bark crevices and hammers them open.	*Eurasia*
Eurasian skylark *Alauda arvensis*	7(18)	Seeds and insects; moors and fields, well away from trees; sings while hovering high in sky.	*Eurasia; introduced to Australia and New Zealand*
European blackbird *Turdus merula*	10(25)	Omnivorous, but especially fruit and worms; everywhere apart from tundra and mountaintops; very common in gardens, even in urban areas.	*Eurasia and N. Africa; now Australia and New Zealand*
European robin *Erithacus rubecula*	6(15)	Insects and spiders, with seeds in winter; all but the most open habitats; very common in towns.	*Eurasia*
European starling *Sturnus vulgaris*	8(20)	Insects, fruit, and seeds; open woodland, town parks, gardens, and coasts; roosts in huge flocks in winter; one of the most common birds in Europe.	*Native of W. Eurasia, but now worldwide*
Hill mynah *Gracula religiosa*	12(30)	Fruit, nectar, small animals; woodland; excellent mimic, widely kept as cage bird.	*India and S.E. Asia*
House martin *Delichon urbica*	5(13)	Insects, caught on the wing; mainly towns and villages, nesting on houses and other buildings.	*Eurasia; European birds fly to Africa for winter*
House sparrow *Passer domesticus*	6(15)	Seeds and some insects; farms, towns, and villages; feeds largely on discarded scraps in urban areas; a pest in granaries.	*Originally Eurasia and Africa, but now worldwide*
Jay *Garrulus glandarius*	13(33)	Insects and nuts, especially acorns; woods and parks; a noisy bird.	*Eurasia*
Long-tailed tit *Aegithalos caudatus*	6(15)	Insects and seeds; woods and hedges; forages in flocks; tail longer than body.	*Eurasia*
Nightingale *Luscinia megarhynchos*	6(16)	Insects and some fruit; wooded areas; famous for its fine song, produced day and night.	*Breeds in Eurasia; winters in Africa*
Northern mockingbird *Mimus polyglottos*	<11(28)	Fruit and invertebrates; open country and town parks; an expert mimic, often singing at night.	*North America and Caribbean*
Oxpecker *Buphagus* (2 species)	7(18)	Ticks and bloodsucking insects, usually plucked from skins of large grazing animals; savanna.	*Africa*
Red-billed quelea *Quelea quelea*	5(12)	Seeds; light woodland, savanna, and farmland; lives in huge colonies and causes immense damage to cereal crops; said to be the most destructive bird in the world.	*Africa*
Red crossbill *Loxia curvirostra*	6(16)	Conifer seeds, extracted from cones with the crossed tips of bill; coniferous forest and sometimes in parks; breeds in winter.	*Eurasia, N. Africa, and North America*
Red-winged blackbird *Agelaius phoeniceus*	8(20)	Insects; wetlands and farmland, often in huge flocks; possibly North America's most common land bird.	*North and Central America*
Rook *Corvus frugilegus*	18(45)	Omnivorous; farmland and other open country with trees; nests colonially in treetops; bare gray face patch distinguishes from carrion crow.	*W. Eurasia*
Rufous hornero *Furnarius rufus*	8(20)	Worms and insects; open and lightly wooded country; nest, made of mud and straw, resembles a baker's oven; sometimes called ovenbird.	*South America*
Shrike (c. 70 species in several genera)	< 12(30)	Insects and small vertebrates; woodlands and open country; some known as butcher birds because they impale prey on thorns until needed.	*Mostly Africa; some in Eurasia and North America*
Snow bunting (c. 70 species in several genera)	6(16)	Seeds, buds, and insects; Arctic tundra and mountains; on coasts in winter; some winter as far south as N. Africa and central California.	*Arctic, America, and Eurasia*
Song thrush (c. 70 species in several genera)	9(23)	Invertebrates and fruit; woodland, orchards, parks, and gardens; breaks snail shells on stones to get at the flesh.	*Eurasia; introduced to Australia and New Zealand*
Spotted flycatcher *Muscicapa striata*	6(15)	Insects, almost always caught on the wing; open woodland, parks, and gardens; darts out to catch prey and usually returns to the same perch.	*Eurasia and Africa, migrating south for winter*
Superb blue-wren *Malurus cyaneus*	5½(14)	Ground-living invertebrates; woodlands, parks, and gardens, with patches of dense undergrowth.	*S.E. Australia*
Superb lyrebird *Menura novaehollandiae*	<3⅓(1)	Insects and other invertebrates; woodland; one of the largest perching birds, named for the male's delicate, lyre-shaped tail.	*S.E. Australia*
Tailorbird *Orthotomus sutorius*	< 6(15)	Insects and spiders; woodland and gardens; nest made by sewing leaves together with plant fibers or spider silk.	*India and S.E. Asia*
Weaverbird (several genera and species)	<8(20)	Seeds and insects; savanna, light woodland, and farmland near villages; nests made by weaving grasses and other plants, each species having its own design.	*Africa and S. Asia*
White wagtail *Motacilla alba*	7(18)	Insects and other small invertebrates; farms, parks, gardens, and other open habitats, often near water; constantly moves its long tail.	*Eurasia; with many birds wintering in N. Africa*
Winter wren *Troglodytes troglodytes*	3(8)	Insects and spiders; almost any habitat, from woodland to windswept coasts; common in gardens; the only true wren in the Eastern Hemisphere.	*Eurasia, N. Africa, and North America*
Yellowhammer *Emberiza citrinella*	6(16)	Seeds and insects; farmland and other open country; male head largely bright yellow.	*Eurasia*

Perching birds
Red crossbill

Perching birds
Northern mockingbird

Perching birds
Winter wren

Perching birds
Shrike

Perching birds
Spotted flycatcher

Perching birds
Bohemian waxwing

MAMMALS

Mammals are generally considered to be the most advanced group of animals: this is the class that contains humans and the apes. All mammals have relatively large brains and a greater capacity for learning than most other animals. They are the dominant animals in almost every habitat and, thanks to their ability to maintain their bodies at a constant high temperature, they have been able to spread to all parts of the world.

Temperature maintenance is aided by a coat of hair or fur. Hair is found on all mammals, although it is reduced to a few scattered bristles in whales, elephants, and other large land mammals.

The most fundamental attribute of mammals is the possession of milk or mammary glands by the females. The milk is used to feed the young for a varying period of time and so there is always a certain amount of parental care.

Unlike that of a reptile, the lower jaw of a mammal consists of a single bone, the dentary, on each side. This is of great help to paleontologists in identifying fossil skeletons.

Mammals first appeared on the earth about 200 million years ago, the descendants of some small insect-eating reptiles, but they did not come to prominence until the extinction of the dinosaurs about 65 million years ago. When the dinosaurs disappeared, mammals were able to investigate many different ways of life and evolve in different directions. Since then thousands of species have come and gone—many of them weird experimental forms such as the shovel-lipped elephant and the giant *Baluchitherium*. The latter looked like a cross between a rhinoceros and a giraffe and, with a weight of perhaps 30 tons, was the largest of all known land mammals. Today, however, there are only about 4,100 mammalian species.

Anatomy of a large mammal

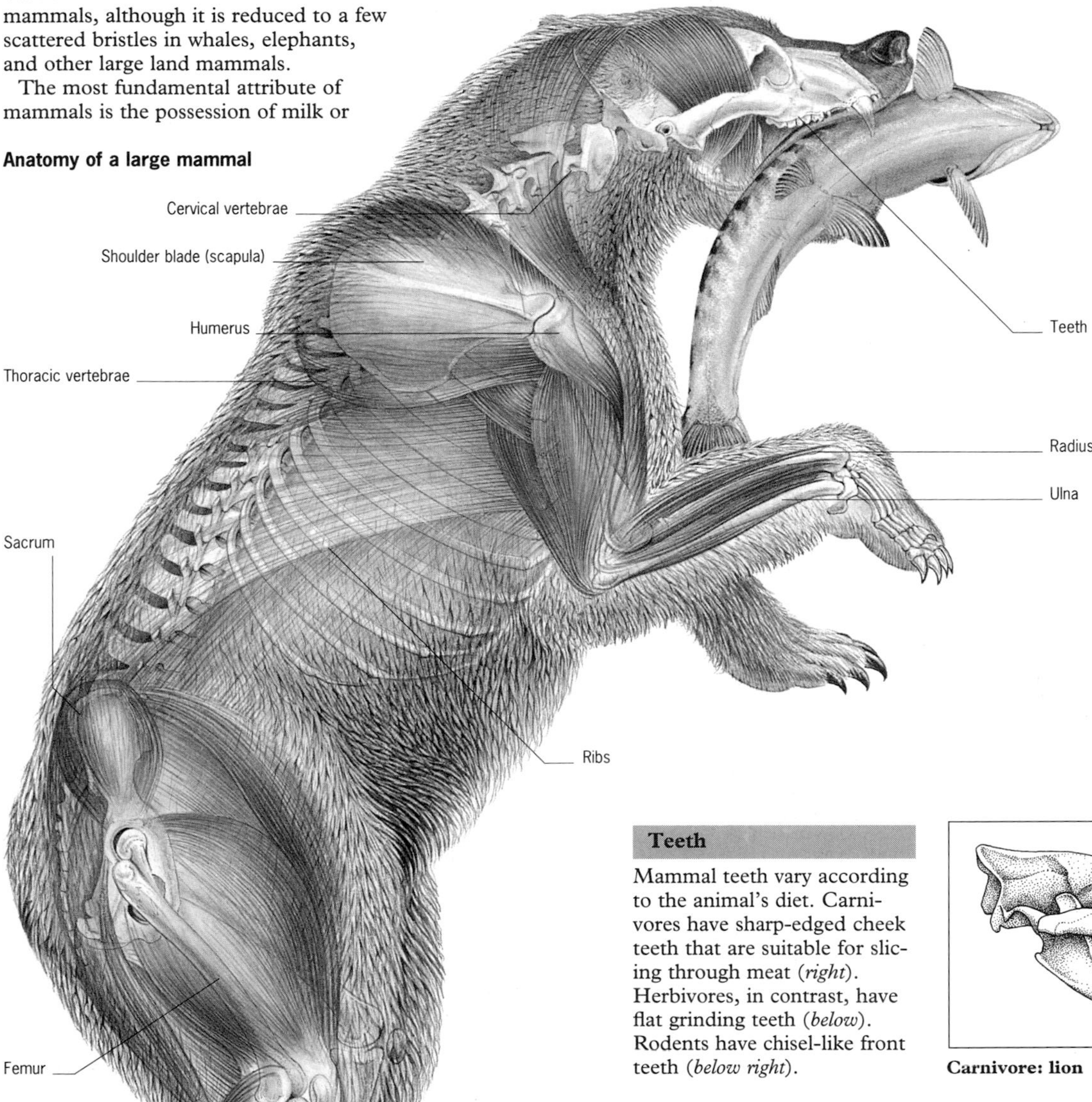

Cervical vertebrae · Shoulder blade (scapula) · Humerus · Thoracic vertebrae · Sacrum · Femur · Ribs · Tibia · Fibula · Teeth · Radius · Ulna

Teeth

Mammal teeth vary according to the animal's diet. Carnivores have sharp-edged cheek teeth that are suitable for slicing through meat (*right*). Herbivores, in contrast, have flat grinding teeth (*below*). Rodents have chisel-like front teeth (*below right*).

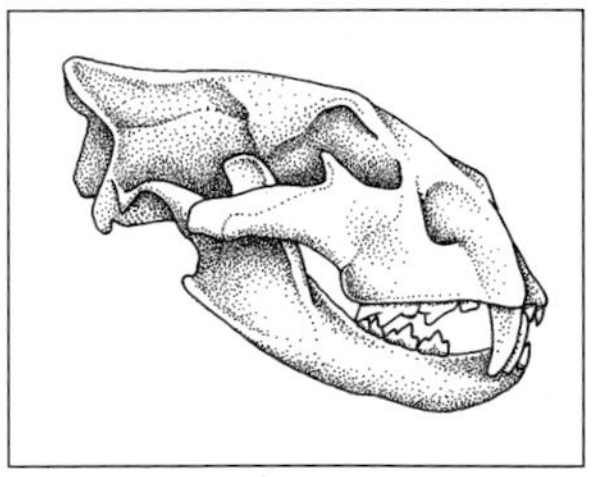

Carnivore: lion

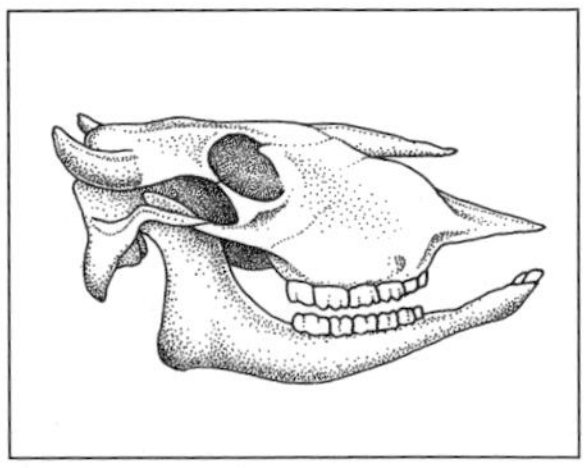

Herbivore: bison

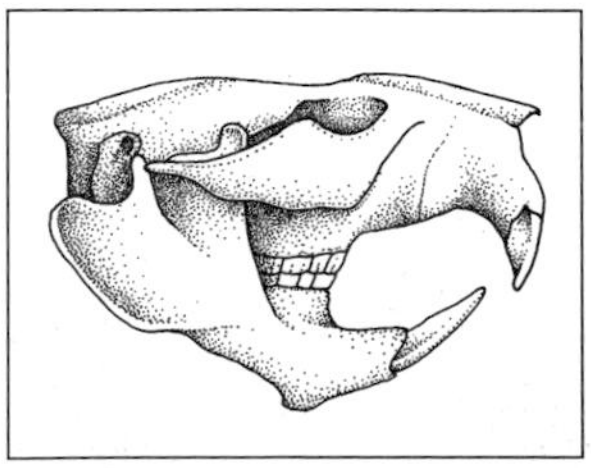

Rodent: beaver

Eggs and pouches

In terms of reproductive behavior, mammals fall into three groups—the egg layers, the pouched mammals, and the placentals. The egg layers, or monotremes, show several reptilian features and are represented only by the platypus and the echidnas (*p. 139*). The pouched mammals, or marsupials, are confined mainly to Australia and New Guinea. They are born at a very early stage—the newborn red kangaroo is about the size of a lima bean—and continue their development while feeding on milk in a pouch on the mother's body.

Placentals, which make up the vast majority of living mammals, give birth to their young at a much later stage of development. While inside the mother's body the offspring are nourished by the placenta, through which food and oxygen pass from the mother's bloodstream to the fetal bloodstream. Many placental babies are so well developed by the time of birth that they can run around almost as soon as they are born.

Airborne and aquatic mammals

Most mammals are firmly based on the ground or in the trees. Some can glide from tree to tree on outstretched flaps of skin, but only the bats can really fly. Their wings are supported on long fingers and run along the sides of the body to take in the back legs and tail as well. They are nocturnal and find their way by echolocation—sending out high-pitched sounds and listening for the echoes coming back from nearby objects. They can even pick up the echoes from flying insects, which enables them to change course to catch them.

Many mammals live in water, but most have to return to land to breed. Only the whales and the sea cows (*p. 142*) are fully adapted for life in the water. Their front limbs form flippers and their tails form lobelike flukes. Hind limbs are absent, apart from some skeletal remains inside the body. The animals mate and give birth in water, and the only thing that indicates a terrestrial origin is that they still breathe air.

Record breakers

Largest The blue whale, up to 98 feet (30 m) long and weighing up to 150 tons, is the largest known mammal. The largest existing land mammal is the male African elephant, standing up to 11 feet (3.3 m) at the shoulder and weighing up to 7 tons.
Tallest The giraffe stands up to 18 feet (5.5 m) high.
Smallest The pygmy white-toothed shrew, also called the Etruscan shrew, has a body only about 2 inches (5 cm) long and weighs up to 0.2 ounces (5.5 g). Some bats weigh even less.
Fastest on land The cheetah can reach 62 mph (100 km/h), but only in short bursts. The pronghorn (*p. 143*) can maintain speeds of 31 mph (50 km/h) for several miles.
Most prolific breeder A North American meadow mouse produced 17 litters in a single year (4–9 babies/litter).
Most widespread Humans are the most widely distributed mammal, closely followed by the house mouse, which has accompanied people to all parts of the world.

Domestic mammals

Humans have domesticated many mammal species for both work and pleasure and have also created many different new breeds. Small mammals, especially rodents such as mice, gerbils, hamsters, and guinea pigs, make excellent pets for children. Among slightly larger animals, cats and rabbits make good pets.

Guinea pig

Short-haired cat

Long-haired cat

Dogs

Dogs were the first animals to be domesticated, probably more than 10,000 years ago. Their ancestors were almost certainly a race of small wolves in southwest Asia. There are now well over 400 recognized breeds of dogs, including a wide range of working and sporting dogs as well as the more familiar pets.

Sporting dog: foxhound

Working dog: husky

Pet: poodle

Horses

Horses were first domesticated more than 4,000 years ago, when at least two breeds of wild horses—the tarpan and Przewalski's horse—roamed the steppes of central Asia. One or both of these may have contributed to the domestic horse. Many breeds of horse now exist, from tiny Shetland ponies to large racehorses and draft farm animals.

Dutch draft horse　　**Akhal-tere**　　**Saddlebred**　　**Shetland pony**

MAMMALS

Measurements are generally approximate head and body lengths without any tail, but measurements given in italics are heights. Measurements are in inches, followed by centimeters in parentheses. [▲ = endangered species]

Order/Name	Length	Food and habitat	Original home
Egg-laying mammals/Monotremata		**(6 species)**	
Echidna (spiny anteater) *Tachyglossus aculeatus*	16 (40)	Termites and ants, picked up with long tongue; woodland and open country, burrowing quickly with short legs; single egg and baby carried in pouch.	*Australia and New Guinea*
Platypus *Ornithorhynchus anatinus*	18 (45)	Aquatic invertebrates, grabbed with ducklike muzzle; rivers, laying soft-shelled eggs in burrows in banks.	*E. and S. Australia*
Pouched mammals/Marsupialia		**(c. 240 species)**	
Bandicoot (c. 20 species in several genera)	<20 (50)	Insects, worms, and some plants; all habitats; some damage gardens by digging for food; long-snouted, ratlike animals, some now rare through hunting for skins and competition from introduced animals.	*Australia*
Brushtail possum *Trichosurus vulpecula*	24 (60)	Largely vegetarian; great climber with a prehensile tail, living anywhere with trees; damages gardens and orchards; Australia's most common marsupial.	*Australia; introduced to New Zealand, where it is a serious pest*
Great gray kangaroo *Macropus major*	<83 (210)	Mainly a browser in open woodland; tail, up to 3½ feet (1.2 m) long, used for balance and steering when leaping.	*E. Australia*
Koala *Phascolarctos cinereus*	24 (60)	Eucalyptus leaves, living almost entirely in the trees; declining, largely through loss of habitat.	*E. Australia*
Phalanger (several genera and species)	<25½ (65)	Larger species vegetarian, smaller ones eat insects and nectar; tree living, many with prehensile tails—the marsupial equivalent of monkeys.	*Australia and New Guinea*
Red kangaroo *Macropus rufus*	<83 (210)	Grazes in huge groups (mobs) on open plains; like great gray kangaroo but browner; competes with sheep and cattle, and numbers have to be controlled.	*Australia*
Tasmanian devil *Sarcophilus harrisii*	24 (60)	Mammals and birds, including carrion; doglike, living mainly in woods.	*Tasmania*
Virginia opossum *Didelphis marsupialis*	24 (60)	Omnivorous; an expert climber with long, prehensile tail; wooded areas, often near human habitation.	*North and South America*
Wallaby (several genera and species)	<40 (100)	Vegetarians in forested and open habitats; essentially small kangaroos; feral red-necked wallabies (*Macropus rufogriseus*) in parts of Britain.	*Australia and New Guinea*
Wombat *Vombatus hirsutus*	<51 (130)	Nocturnal grazer; a stocky, bearlike animal found in all grassy areas; often kept as a pet.	*S.E. Australia and Tasmania*
Insectivores/Insectivora		**(c. 345 species)**	
Common mole *Talpa europaea*	<6 (16)	Earthworms, slugs, and insect larvae; spends most of its life tunneling in soil in woods and grassland, including cultivated areas.	*Europe and N.W. Asia*
Shrew (c. 170 species in many genera)	<6 (15)	Worms, insects, and other invertebrates, living or dead; may eat their own weight of food each day; all habitats, several species living in fresh water; mouselike but with much longer snouts.	*Worldwide, except for Australia and Oceania and polar regions*
Western hedgehog *Erinaceus europaeus*	<10½ (27)	Invertebrates and small vertebrates, with some carrion; woodland, hedges, and gardens; has about 6,000 spines, which are modified hairs.	*W. Europe*
Bats/Chiroptera		**(c. 950 species)**	
Fruit bat (c. 170 species in several genera)	<12(30)	Fruit and nectar, mainly in forested areas; largest species, with wingspans up to 5 feet (1.5 m), foxlike face; damage plantations.	*Eastern Hemisphere tropics*
Vampire bat *Desmodus rotundus*	<3½(9)	Blood; nocturnal, attacking sleeping mammals with razor-sharp teeth; cattle and horses are main victims, but people occasionally bitten; can carry rabies.	*South and Central America*
Monkeys and apes/Primates		**(c. 180 species)**	
▲ Aye-aye *Daubentonia madagascariensis*	16(40)	Insects and fruit, often pulling insects from rotting wood with wirelike middle finger; a nocturnal, forest-dwelling lemur.	*Madagascar*
Baboon (6 species in 2 genera)	<40(100)	Omnivorous; doglike monkeys of the savanna and dry, rocky areas; live in well-structured societies.	*Africa and Arabia*
Bushbaby *Galago senegalensis*	<8(20)	Insects, flowers, and fruit; forest and scrub; agile nocturnal climbers, with call like crying human baby.	*Africa; south of Sahara*
Capuchin monkey *Cebus* (several species)	<18(45)	Fruit and insects in tropical forest; agile tree dwellers with prehensile tails, rarely coming to ground other than to drink; the organ-grinder's monkey.	*South and Central America*
Chimpanzee *Pan troglodytes*	<59(150)	Omnivorous, but mainly fruit; forest-dwelling ape, in family groups; probably humans' nearest living relative.	*Tropical Africa*
Colobus monkey *Colobus* (3 species)	<24(60)	Mainly leaves, in dense forest; several races, some with long, white hair on the head and shoulders.	*Tropical Africa*
Gibbon *Hylobates* (6 species)	<40(100)	Fruit, leaves, and insects; forest-dwelling, swinging through the trees with their arms; very noisy when meeting neighboring groups.	*Southeast Asia*
▲ Gorilla *Gorilla gorilla*	<79(200)	Vegetarian, eating mainly leaves; tropical forest, in family groups; largest ape, but its reputation for ferocity is undeserved; threatened by hunting.	*Tropical Africa*
Howler monkey *Alouatta* (5 species)	<24(60)	Vegetarian, especially fruit; howl and bark in small troops in the forest; can be heard nearly 3 miles (5 km) away; largest Western Hemisphere monkey.	*South and Central America*
▲ Lemur (several genera and species, includes aye-aye, *above*)	<40(100)	Omnivorous and mainly arboreal; long-tailed and foxy-faced; only distantly related to the monkeys; most are declining through habitat loss.	*Madagascar*

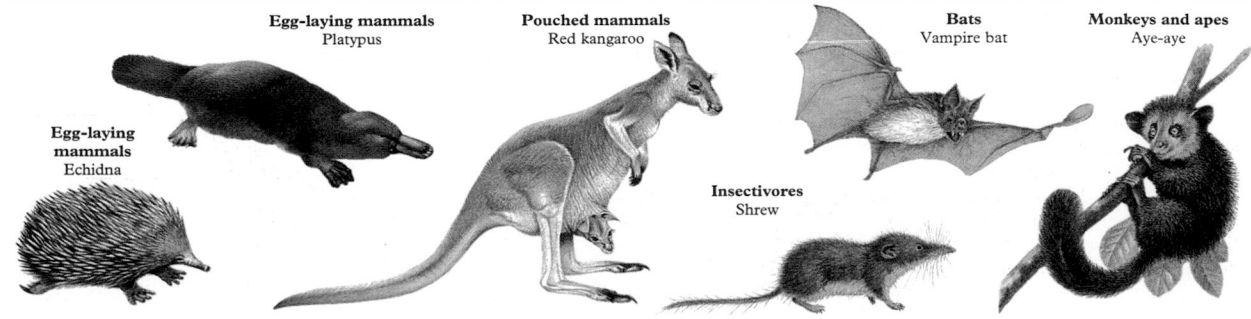

Egg-laying mammals
Platypus

Egg-laying mammals
Echidna

Pouched mammals
Red kangaroo

Insectivores
Shrew

Bats
Vampire bat

Monkeys and apes
Aye-aye

Order/Name	Length	Food and habitat	Original home
Macaque *Macaca* (several species)	<24(60)	Omnivorous in forests and open country, including mountains; often with long tails, but some are tailless; the most common monkeys of Asia; Barbary "ape" of Gibraltar is a macaque.	*S. Asia, Japan, and N. Africa*
Mandrill *Mandrillus sphinx*	<33½(85)	Largely vegetarian in tropical forest; a ground-living, baboonlike monkey famous for the colorful face and rear end of the male.	*W. Africa*
Marmoset (several genera and species)	<10(25)	Insects and fruit; tree-living, with sharp, pointed sickle-shaped nails; pygmy marmoset, only 5 inches (13 cm) long without tail, is smallest monkey.	*South and Central America*
▲ Orangutan *Pongo pygmaeus*	<53(135)	Mainly fruit; tropical forest, staying mainly in the trees; a wonderful climber swinging from legs as well as arms; threatened by hunting and habitat loss.	*Indonesia*
Rhesus monkey *Macaca mulatta*	24(60)	Fruit and insects; wooded country and open hillsides, often common around human habitation; sacred to Hindus, and large troops often overrun villages.	*N. India and adjacent countries*
Spider monkey *Ateles paniscus*	<25½(65)	Fruit, collected high in the trees; slender with long legs and prehensile tail generally longer than body.	*South and Central America*
Tarsier *Tarsius* (3 species)	<10(25)	Insects, lizards, and other small animals; arboreal in dense lowland forest; tail twice as long as body.	*Indonesia and Philippines*
Anteaters, armadillos, and sloths/Edentata		**(c. 30 species)**	
Giant anteater *Myrmecophaga tridactyla*	47(120)	Ants and termites, opening nests with huge claws and licking up insects with long tongue; wooded country and open plains; huge furry tail as long as body.	*South and Central America*
Nine-banded armadillo *Dasypus novemcinctus*	<24(60)	Insects and other invertebrates; dry grassland and semidesert; mainly nocturnal; sleeps in deep burrows.	*North and South America*
Three-toed sloth *Bradypus tridactylus*	20(50)	Leaves and fruit; arboreal, hanging upside down from its hooklike claws—three on each foot.	*South and Central America; tropical forest*
Pangolins/Pholidota		**(7 species)**	
Pangolin or scaly anteater *Manis* (7 species)	<29½(75)	Termites and ants, gathered with long tongue; forests and open country; some climb trees with long prehensile tail; covered in overlapping scales.	*Africa and S.E. Asia*
Aardvark/Tubulidentata		**(1 species)**	
Aardvark *Orycteropus afer*	<79(200)	Termites, opening nests with powerful claws and mopping up insects with long tongue; savanna.	*S. and E. Africa*
Rodents/Rodentia		**(c. 1,700 species)**	
Beaver *Castor* (2 species)	<35½(90)	Grass, twigs, leaves, and bark; river valleys in wooded country; dam streams to make nesting ponds; Canadian and European beavers almost identical.	*North America, Europe, and W. Asia*
Black-tailed prairie dog *Cynomys ludovicianus*	12(30)	Grass and other vegetation; gregarious, in burrow systems ("towns"); covered huge areas of prairies, but numbers now much reduced; a ground squirrel.	*C. and W. North America*
Brown rat *Rattus norvegicus*	<12(30)	Omnivorous; rarely far from human habitation, and a serious pest.	*Probably Asia*
Capybara *Hydrochoerus hydrochaeris*	<47(120)	Aquatic and waterside plants; swamps and rivers; piglike and the largest rodent; runs and swims wells.	*South America*
▲ Chinchilla *Chinchilla laniger*	10(25)	Vegetation on dry mountain slopes; hunted for its fine fur and now rare.	*Andes*
Chipmunk (c. 18 species in 2 genera)	<7(18)	Fruit and seeds, fungi, and small animals; deciduous woodland, scrub, and grassland; ground-living squirrels with striped fur.	*North America and E. Asia*
Coypu *Myocastor coypus*	<25½(65)	Aquatic and waterside vegetation, often damaging crops; marshes and rivers; damages banks with its burrows; bred in many areas for meat and fur (nutria).	*South America*
Crested porcupine *Hystrix cristata*	<31½(80)	Vegetation of all kinds and some carrion; woodland and scrub, sometimes on cultivated land; tail and rear end carry quills up to 16 inches (40 cm) long.	*N. Africa and Italy*
Dormouse *Muscardinus avellanarius*	<3½(9)	Hazelnuts and other fruits, with some insects; deciduous woodland with plenty of undergrowth; small ears and bushy tail distinguish from true mice.	*Europe and W. Asia*
European red squirrel *Sciurus vulgaris*	<9½(24)	Seeds, fruit, bark, and fungi; conifer seeds extracted by gnawing away cone scales; coniferous and mixed forest.	*Eurasia*
Golden hamster *Mesocricetus auratus*	<6(15)	Seeds, roots, and other plant material, with occasional insects; dry grasslands; a popular pet now bred in many color varieties.	*Syria*
Gray squirrel *Sciurus carolinensis*	<12(30)	Omnivorous, but mainly plant matter; deciduous and mixed woodland, parks, and gardens; damages trees.	*E. North America, U.K., S. Africa*
Guinea pig *Cavia porcellus*	<12(30)	Vegetarian in grasslands; long used for food in its native home, but now best known as a docile pet.	*N. South America*
Harvest mouse *Micromys minutus*	<3(8)	Fruit and seeds, especially grain, with insects and buds in spring; grassland and reedbeds, making ball-shaped nest; climbs with long, prehensile tail.	*Eurasia*
House mouse *Mus musculus*	<4(10)	Omnivorous; rarely far from human habitation, causing immense damage to stored grain and other materials.	*Originally C. Asia, but now worldwide*
Jerboa (several genera and species)	<6(15)	Seeds and scattered desert vegetation; tail is longer than body and used as rudder while leaping on long back legs like miniature kangaroos.	*N. Africa and Asia*
Mongolian gerbil or jird *Meriones unguiculatus*	4(10)	Seeds, grass, and roots; open grassland; docile and easily handled, it has been a popular pet since 1960s.	*C. Asia*
Norway lemming *Lemmus lemmus*	<6(15)	Grass, moss, and other low-growing plants; tundra and surrounding birch scrub; famous for "suicide runs"—mass searches for new feeding grounds when food supplies are overutilized; many die trying to cross rivers and seas.	*Scandinavia*
Plains pocket gopher *Geomys bursarius*	10(25)	Vegetarian, mainly roots and bulbs; an active burrower under grassy plains; named for fur-lined cheek pouches in which it carries food.	*North America*

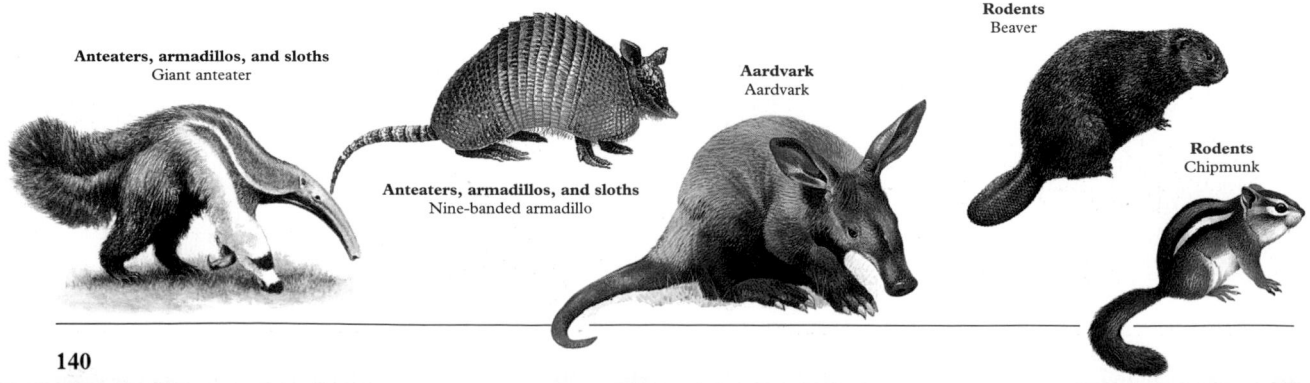

Anteaters, armadillos, and sloths
Giant anteater

Anteaters, armadillos, and sloths
Nine-banded armadillo

Aardvark
Aardvark

Rodents
Beaver

Rodents
Chipmunk

Order/Name	Length	Food and habitat	Original home
Porcupine *Erethizon dorsatum*	<35½(90)	Bark, buds, and leaves in deciduous forests; arboreal and often called tree porcupine; long fur conceals short, barbed spines.	*North America*
Rabbits and hares/Lagomorpha		**(c. 60 species)**	
Brown hare *Lepus europaeus*	<27½(70)	Grass, including cereals, and low-growing plants in open country; larger than rabbit, but best distinguished by black-tipped ears and bounding gait.	*Eurasia*
Rabbit *Orictolagus cuniculus*	<19½(50)	Grass and other vegetation; deciduous woods and all kinds of open country; a serious agricultural pest, whose introduction to Australia has been described as an expensive mistake.	*Europe and N. Africa; introduced into Australia*
Cats, dogs, and other meat eaters/Carnivora		**(c. 240 species)**	
Badger *Taxidea taxus*	24(60)	Rodents and other small vertebrates, insects, and carrion; open grassland, living in burrows.	*North America*
Bobcat *Felis rufus*	<29½(75)	Mammals and birds, including domestic poultry; wide variety of habitats.	*North and Central America*
Cape hunting dog *Lycaon pictus*	<43½(110)	Antelope and other game, hunted in packs on the savanna; not closely related to other dogs.	*Africa*
Cat *Felis catus*	<24(60)	Meat and fish; probably descended from both the Eurasian and African races of wildcat and now existing in many varieties and colors.	*Worldwide*
Cheetah *Acinonyx jubatus*	59(150)	Small mammals, including gazelles, and birds; savanna; a long-legged cat; fastest land animal, reaching 50–70 mph (80–112 kph) in short bursts.	*Africa and S. Asia*
Coyote or prairie wolf *Canis latrans*	35½(90)	Omnivorous; an opportunist feeder, but eating mainly small mammals and carrion; mainly open plains, but also in built-up areas where it scavenges from garbage cans; has spread widely in 1900s.	*North and Central America*
Dingo *Canis dingo*	40(100)	Birds, mammals, and insects in many habitats; a yellowish-brown dog introduced by the Aborigines at least 8,000 years ago and now completely wild; responsible for the loss of many marsupial species; sometimes regarded as the same species as the dog, *Canis familiaris* (*below*).	*Australia*
Dog *Canis familiaris*	8–40 (20–100)	Carnivorous; the first animal to be domesticated; descended from the wolf and now with more than 400 breeds.	*Worldwide*
Ermine *Mustela erminea*	<12(30)	Mostly rabbits and rodents; woods and open country, including farmland; turns white for winter in northern regions, but always keeps black tail tip.	*Eurasia, North America, N. Africa*
European badger *Meles meles*	<31½(80)	Omnivorous, with a particular liking for earthworms; deciduous woods, especially mixed with farmland; lives in family groups in large burrows called setts; like North American badger but with more obvious head stripes.	*Eurasia*
▲ Giant panda *Ailuropoda melanoleuca*	<71(180)	Bamboo shoots and occasional small animals, including fish; upland bamboo forests; rare because of hunting, but now protected; recent studies suggest it belongs to bear family and not raccoon family as once thought.	*S.W. China*
Golden jackal *Canis aureus*	40(100)	Omnivorous, taking carrion and garbage, and various small animals; dry, open country and farms, usually in small family groups; much like small wolf.	*Africa, Middle East, and S.E. Europe*
Gray wolf *Canis lupus*	<59(150)	Wide range of animals, including deer and carrion; most habitats, but now mainly in more remote forests and mountains and on tundra; populations much reduced by hunting; at risk in Europe.	*N. Hemisphere*
▲ Grizzly bear *Ursus arctos*	110(280)	Omnivorous; forests and mountains; a large race of brown bear, sometimes treated as separate species—*Ursus horribilis*; rare because of hunting.	*W. North America, mainly in the north*
Jaguar *Panthera onca*	63(160)	A wide range of terrestrial and freshwater animals, including capybaras and alligators; dense forest, usually near water; largest American cat.	*South and Central America*
Least weasel *Mustela nivalis*	<8(20)	Mostly rodents, with some small birds and their eggs; all habitats with some vegetation; very like stoat, but smaller and lacks black tail tip; turns white for winter in colder areas.	*Eurasia, N. Africa, and North America*
Leopard *Panthera pardus*	59(150)	Wide range of animals, including dogs and antelope; forest and country; prey often carried into trees for storage; black forms known as panthers.	*Africa and S. Asia*
Red (lesser) panda *Ailurus fulgens*	24(60)	Fruit, leaves; arboreal in montane forests; catlike member of raccoon family.	*Himalayan foothills*
Lion *Panthera leo*	<71(180)	Zebra, gnu, and other grazers; savanna, living in well-organized prides of up to about 20 animals; numbers much reduced in last 100 years, but still common in many reserves, especially in E. Africa.	*Africa and India, but Indian race very rare*
Lynx *Felis lynx*	51(130)	Hares, rodents, small deer, and birds; mature forest, usually in uplands; a heavily built, long-legged cat.	*Eurasia and North America*
Mongoose (*c.* 50 species in several genera)	<25½(65)	Wide range of small vertebrates, including snakes, and invertebrates, including scorpions; some also eat eggs; many habitats, some largely aquatic.	*Africa, S. Europe ,and S.E. Asia*
Otter (*c.* 19 species in 5 genera)	48(120)	Fish and other aquatic animals; rivers, marshes, and coastal waters; European otter at risk from pollution.	*Worldwide; apart from Australia and Oceania*
▲ Polar bear *Ursus maritimus*	<99(250)	Seals, with occasional seabirds, and some fruit in summer; pack ice and adjacent coasts; protected.	*Arctic*
Puma *Felis concolor*	<59(150)	Small deer and other mammals; mountains, grassland, desert, and forest; a powerful cat but somewhat cowardly and unlikely to attack people.	*North/South America; mainly in mountains*
Raccoon *Procyon lotor*	20(50)	Omnivorous, but mainly aquatic animals; wooded areas with ponds and streams, but now equally at home in urban habitats, scavenging at garbage cans and often causing damage by getting into houses; a good climber.	*North and Central America*

Golden jackal

Raccoon

Red (lesser) panda

Cats, dogs, and
other meateaters
Bobcat

Mongoose

Order/Name	Length	Food and habitat	Original home
Ratel *Mellivora capensis*	29½(75)	Small animals, living or dead; light woodland; likes bee grubs and is often led to nests by the honey guide (*p. 135*); also called honey badger.	*Africa and S. Asia*
Red fox *Vulpes vulpes*	<35½(90)	Small animals of all kinds, including carrion; in all habitats; well established in many urban areas, living in parks and cemeteries and scavenging in garbage cans; the world's most common carnivore.	*N. Hemisphere*
Skunk (7 species in 3 genera)	<21½(55)	Rodents and other small animals; woods and open country; bold black-and-white pattern warns of nauseous fluid fired from anal glands when attacked.	*North and South America*
Spotted hyena *Crocuta crocuta*	<59(150)	Antelopes and other savanna animals; regularly takes carrion and often shares lions' kills or even drives lions away; powerful bone-crushing jaws.	*South and E. Africa*
▲ Tiger *Panthera tigris*	<118(300)	Deer and other mammals, including buffalo; forests and grassland, especially near swamps and rivers; usually avoids humans, but occasionally attacks and eats them; facing extinction through hunting and loss of habitat.	*India and E. Asia, including southern Siberia*
Wildcat *Felis silvestris*	<27½(70)	Mainly rodents and birds, with some fish; deciduous woods, especially the margins, and young plantations; very like domestic tabby, but stouter and with clearly ringed tail; interbreeds with domestic cats.	*Eurasia (mainly S.), N. Africa, Scotland*
▲ Wolverine *Gulo gulo*	<40(100)	Omnivorous, including carrion; may attack animals much larger than itself; tundra and forest; also called glutton; at risk from hunting in some areas.	*N. Eurasia and North America*
Seals/Pinnipedia		**(33 species)**	
California sea lion *Zalophus californianus*	<95(240)	Fish and other marine animals; coastal waters; one of the eared seals and more agile out of water than true seals; learns tricks easily—a great zoo and circus favorite.	*Pacific North America, Japan, and Galápagos Islands*
Elephant seal *Mirounga* (2 similar species)	<237(6)	Fish and squid; oceanic but breed on beaches like all pinnipeds; males much bigger than females, with inflatable snout responsible for the name.	*Sub-Antarctic (1 sp.), Pacific North America*
Ringed seal *Phoca hispida*	<67(170)	Small fish and crustaceans; on or near pack ice; the most common seal in Arctic waters; smallest of the true seals, differing from eared seals in having no ear flap; much less agile on land than sea lions.	*Throughout the Arctic, but rare in European waters*
Walrus *Odobenus rosmarus*	<138(350)	Mollusks, other invertebrates, dug from seabed with tusks up to 24 inches (60 cm)long; lives in large herds, often basking on remote, rocky beaches.	*Arctic pack ice; rarely far from land*
Whales/Cetacea		**(76 species)**	
▲ Blue whale *Balaenoptera musculus*	<1185 (3,000)	Krill, strained from water with baleen plates; eats up to 4 tons per day; weighs up to 150 tons and is largest living animal; almost wiped out by whaling, but now protected; breeds in subtropics.	*All oceans, but most common in S. Hemisphere*
▲ Gray whale *Eschrictius robustus*	<592(1,500)	Crustaceans and small fish, strained from water; almost wiped out by whaling, but recovering slowly; migrates between Arctic and tropics.	*Pacific*
Harbor porpoise *Phocoena phocoena*	<75(190)	Fish (mainly herring), cuttlefish, and crustaceans; estuaries and other coastal waters; smaller than dolphins, with smaller dorsal fin and no beak.	*N. Hemisphere*
▲ Hump-backed whale *Megaptera novaeangliae*	<711(1,800)	Crustaceans and small fish, strained from water with baleen plates; much reduced by whaling.	*Worldwide; mainly in coastal waters*
Killer whale *Orcinus orca*	<375(950)	Seals, penguins, fish, squid, and smaller whales; usually hunts in groups (pods); a toothed whale.	*Worldwide; mainly in coastal waters*
Narwhal *Monodon monoceros*	<217(550)	Fish, squid, and crustaceans; always near pack ice; male has single tusk up to 10 feet (3 m) long—the only functional tooth it has; female toothless.	*Arctic seas*
Pacific bottle-nosed dolphin *Tursiops truncatus*	<158(400)	Fish and some cuttlefish; mainly coastal waters; named for its narrow snout; often in dolphinaria.	*Atlantic and Mediterranean*
Sperm whale *Physeter macrocephalus*	<790(2,000)	Mainly squid, often caught at great depths; largest toothed whale; huge head yields spermaceti wax used in cosmetics and medicinal products, but hunting now strictly controlled.	*Worldwide; in open oceans*
Elephants/Proboscidea		**(2 species)**	
African elephant *Loxodonta africana*	<138(3,500)	Vegetation, including fruits, twigs, and leaves of trees; savanna; largest land animal, weighing up to 6 tons; flatter back and larger ears than Indian elephant and less easily tamed and trained.	*Africa*
Indian or Asiatic elephant *Elephas maximus*	<118(300)	Vegetation of all kinds; dense forest; weighs up to 4 tons, with convex back; widely domesticated for forestry work.	*India and S.E. Asia*
Sea cows/Sirenia		**(4 species)**	
Dugong *Dugong dugon*	<99(250)	Sea grasses, in estuaries, and other coastal waters; never leaves the water; tail broad and whalelike.	*Coasts of Indian and Pacific oceans*
Manatee *Trichecus* (3 species)	<109(275)	Aquatic vegetation in rivers and coastal waters; never leaves the water; tail rounded; probably the origin of the mermaid legend.	*Caribbean and Atlantic coasts of Africa and tropical Americas*
Horses and rhinoceroses/Perissodactyla		**(16 species)**	
▲ Black rhinoceros *Diceros bicornis*	148(375)	A browser, gathering leaves and twigs with its hooked muzzle; savanna; actually gray; endangered by hunting.	*Africa*
▲ Indian rhinoceros *Rhinoceros unicornis*	<178(450)	Browses on shrubs and long grass; forest and grassland; single-horned, unlike African rhinos.	*N. India*

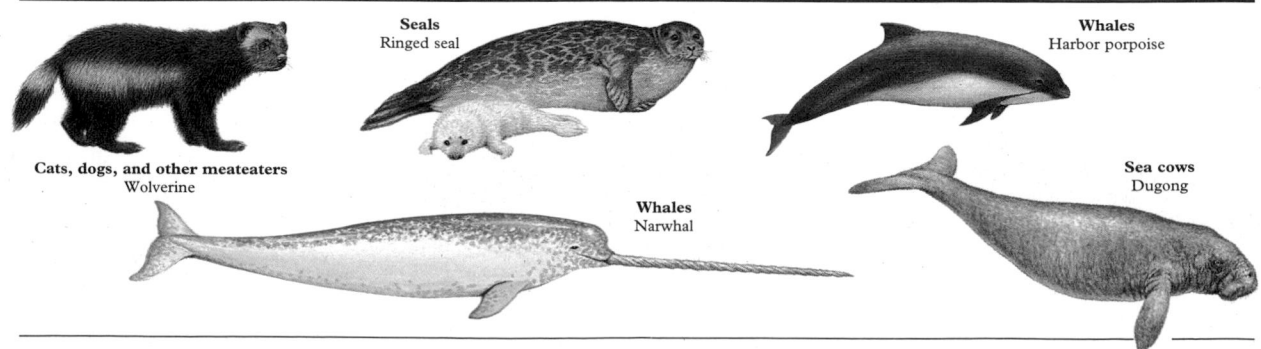

Seals
Ringed seal

Whales
Harbor porpoise

Cats, dogs, and other meateaters
Wolverine

Whales
Narwhal

Sea cows
Dugong

Order/Name	Length	Food and habitat	Original home
▲ Przewalski's horse *Equus caballus przewalskii*	<59(150)	Grazer on open plains; the last surviving wild horse, but no longer truly wild; all known animals in zoos and reserves, where numbers are being built up in the hope of returning the animal to its native steppes.	*C. Asia; last known on the Mongolian steppes*
Tapir *Tapirus* (4 species)	<91(230)	Aquatic vegetation and low-growing plants in thick forest; piglike with long snouts.	*S.E. Asia (1 sp.) and South America*
▲ White rhinoceros *Ceratothesium simus*	<178(450)	Grazes on open plains; actually gray, "white" being a corruption of "wide," referring to wide muzzle.	*Africa*
Zebra *Equus* (3 species)	<59(150)	Grazing relatives of the horse; grassland; black-and-white striped, each species having its own pattern.	*S. and E. Africa*

Cloven-hoofed mammals/Artiodactyla   **(c. 190 species)**

Order/Name	Length	Food and habitat	Original home
African buffalo *Syncerus caffer*	134(340)	Grazer and browser of savanna and tropical forest; lives in large herds; aggressive and dangerous when attacked.	*Africa south of Sahara*
Antelope (many genera and species)	<12–79 (30–200)	Grazers and browsers in cattle family; both sexes normally with horns, often coiled but never branched.	*Africa and Asia*
Arabian camel *Camelus dromedarius*	119(300)	Vegetarian in desert regions; the one-humped camel, up to 6¹/₂ feet (2 m) high at the shoulder; no longer exists as a wild animal; dromedary is a domesticated form specially bred for riding.	*N. Africa and Arabia; introduced to India and Australia*
Bactrian camel *Camelus bactrianus*	119(300)	Vegetarian in desert regions; the two-humped camel a little shorter than Arabian camel but stockier and hairier; a few wild ones in Gobi Desert.	*C. Asia*
Bison *Bison bison*	<130(330)	Grazer, open plains; up to 6¹/₂ feet (2 m) high and 3,300 pounds (1,500 kg); reduced from millions to few hundred in 1800s, now protected.	*North America*
Caribou *Rangifer tarandus*	<87(220)	Grazer on tundra, moving south to forests for winter; both sexes have antlers; wild in North America, but European animals now all herded for meat, skins, milk, and transportation.	*Most Arctic regions*
▲ Chamois *Rupicapra rupicapra*	48(120)	Grazer on mountain slopes, moving down to forests in winter; skin once used for soft leather (chamois).	*Mountains of Eurasia*
Deer (many genera and species)	<24–99 (60–250)	Grazers and browsers; have bony antlers that fall and are replaced each year; normally only male have antlers; many species reared in parks all over world.	*Eurasia, North/South America, and Africa*
Duiker (several genera and species)	<35¹/₂(90)	Grazers in thick forest; small antelopes, mostly with spikelike horns.	*Africa*
Eland *Taurotragus oryx*	<79(200)	Browser in savanna and light woodland; largest of the antelopes; long hunted for meat and populations now much reduced; most live in reserves.	*Africa, mostly south of Sahara*
Gazelle *Gazella* (several species)	<40(100)	Grazers and browsers of desert and grassland; small antelopes with erect horns and black-and-white faces.	*Africa and W. and C. Asia*
Giraffe *Giraffa camelopardalis*	<213(540)	Browser of savanna trees; tallest of all living animals; several races with different coat patterns.	*Africa*
Gnu or wildebeest *Connochaetes taurinus*	<83(210)	Grazer on savanna; lives in huge migratory herds; has mane and tail like those of horse.	*Africa*
Hippopotamus *Hippopotamus amphibius*	<166(420)	Grass and other riverside vegetation, including crops; lives mostly in water and comes out to feed at night; weighs up to 4 tons; related to pigs.	*Tropical Africa*
Ibex *Capra* (several species)	<48(120)	Grazers on mountain slopes, above the tree line for most of the year; wild goats with long curved horns.	*Mountains of Asia and S. Europe*
Impala *Aepyceros melampus*	<40(100)	Grazer of savanna and scrub, usually near water; a gregarious antelope with amazing jumping powers.	*Africa*
Llama *Lama glama*	<71(180)	Vegetarian, mainly grazing; unknown in the wild, this humpless relative of the camel has been used as a beast of burden for more than 4,000 years; also provides meat and wool; ancestor probably the guanaco.	*Andes*
Moose *Alces alces*	<99(250)	Aquatic plants, grass, shoots, and bark of trees; woods and adjacent open country, especially near water; the largest deer; called elk in Europe.	*N. Eurasia and North America*
Mouflon *Ovis orientalis*	51(130)	Grazer and browser in montane woods and meadows; smallest wild sheep, reared for game in some areas.	*S.W. Asia, Corsica, and Sardinia*
Mountain goat *Oreamnos americanus*	<59(150)	Vegetarian in rugged, mountainous country; above tree line in summer, lower in winter; mainly in reserves.	*Rockies, from Montana northward*
Mountain sheep *Ovis canadensis*	40(100)	Grazer on mountain slopes; also eats roots and fungi and nibbles young conifer shoots; males fight by ramming with their huge curved horns.	*Rocky Mountains*
Musk–ox *Ovibos moschatus*	59(150)	Grazer on Arctic tundra, even in winter; protected by thick, shaggy coat, impervious to cold and damp; cattle family, but not closely related to cattle.	*Canada, Greenland; introduced to Norway*
▲ Okapi *Okapia johnstoni*	<79(200)	Vegetarian, grazing in the tropical forest; threatened by habitat destruction.	*C. Africa*
Pronghorn *Antilocapra americana*	<53(135)	Grazing on dry grassland and scrub; resembles antelopes but has branched horns; millions once roamed the prairies, but numbers much reduced today.	*North America*
Springbok *Antidorcas marsupialis*	30(75)	Grazer on open plains; named because of its ability to leap vertically as much as 10 feet (3 m) from standing position.	*Southern Africa*
▲ Vicuna *Lama vicugna*	59(150)	Grazer on mountain slopes above 11,500 feet (3,500 m); a slender member of camel family, yielding the finest wool.	*Andes*
Water or Indian buffalo *Bubalus bubalis*	<71(180)	Tall grasses and other vegetation; forest edges, especially in marshy areas; docile and used as beast of burden in many countries, including Italy; protein-rich milk used for mozzarella cheese.	*India and S.E. Asia*
Yak *Poephagus grunniens*	<75(190)	Grazer in rugged mountains up to 19,500 feet (6,000 m); powers of endurance make it ideal beast of burden, especially in mountains.	*Tibet*

Horses and rhinoceroses
Tapir

Cloven-hoofed mammals
Ibex

Cloven-hoofed mammals
Muskox

Cloven-hoofed mammals
Pronghorn

Cloven-hoofed mammals
Mountain goat

BIODIVERSITY

Each living thing is unique, different in detail from all others. However, individuals may be grouped into kinds or species, which are defined as assemblies of organisms that in nature are capable of interbreeding freely but are unable to breed with any other species.

The exact number of species of plants and animals is unknown, and more are being discovered all the time. To date, more than a million species of animals and a quarter of a million species of plants have been described and named. Estimates vary as to how many remain to be recognized. A few researchers suggest up to 30 million, but most biologists believe that about eight million are so far unknown. The figure might be raised by recent findings that the deep sea, hitherto thought to be sparsely inhabited, could contain up to two million new species.

This huge diversity of living things has come about because each, within its environment, occupies a niche that is different from all of the others. The differences may often be slight, but no two creatures or plants can make identical demands on their habitat. Recent work has shown that in a species-rich environment the use of the sun's energy is more efficient than in a species-poor habitat. Within an environment, species are largely interdependent. If a species should be lost rapidly, there is likely to be a knock-on effect as other plants and animals feel the consequences. The pattern of life in the whole area is then changed and probably impoverished.

NUMBERS OF HUMANS AND ANIMALS

From the time when human beings first began to grow crops and live in settled communities, their numbers increased fairly steadily until about 1700. Shortly after this, the Industrial Revolution led to a doubling of the population in about 100 years. In 1800, the world's population was around one billion. By 1990, the numbers had risen to more than five billion, and by the year 2000, another billion people will be looking for shelter and food somewhere on the earth.

One species cannot increase explosively without affecting all the others. Since about 1700, at least 300 species of vertebrates have become extinct. Nowadays we can observe in detail most creatures that are being lost, and the estimate is between 50 and 100 species a day. If the present trend continues, at least one-fourth of all living things will have disappeared before the human population levels out, probably in the middle of the twenty-first century.

Number of recorded animal and plant extinctions since 1600 by region

Region	Extinctions Animals	Extinctions Plants	Region	Extinctions Animals	Extinctions Plants
Africa	4	50	Pacific Ocean islands	169	118
Asia	13	26	Indian Ocean islands	75	36
Australia and Oceania	40	185	Atlantic Ocean islands	42	9
Europe and C.I.S.	6	35	Southern Ocean islands		
North America			and Antarctica	7	1
and Caribbean	120	127			
South America	2	19			
Total	**185**	**442**		**293**	**254**

Extinctions since 1600 by taxa

Animal	Extinctions	Percentage of taxon
Corals	354	0.4
Mollusks	191	0.2
Crustaceans	4	0.01
Insects	61	0.005
Fish	29	0.1
Amphibians	2	0.07
Reptiles	23	0.4
Birds	116	1.2
Mammals	59	1.3
Total	**486**	**0.04**

Current threatened species by taxa

Taxon	Species	Percentage threatened
Mollusks	354	0.4
Crustaceans	126	3
Insects	873	2
Fish	452	2
Amphibians	59	2
Reptiles	167	3
Birds	1,029	11
Mammals	505	11
Total	**3,565**	**0.3**

DOMESTICATED ANIMALS

When an animal species is domesticated, it is changed in many ways from its wild ancestors. It might become bigger, stronger, and more fecund than the ancestral form. Remaining wild animals are regarded as weeds to be eradicated, for if they breed with the tamed stock, the young may well be intractable and may have characteristics that have been bred out over generations.

Camel Date of first domestication uncertain, perhaps by 4000 B.C. Dromedary (one-humped camel) unknown as a wild animal. Bactrian camels endangered.

Cat First domesticated before 1500 B.C. Now greatly reduced in the wild.

Cow First domesticated about 4000 B.C. The wild ancestor, the aurochs, became extinct before A.D.1630.

Donkey First domesticated about 3500 B.C. Now extinct over almost all of its former range. Remaining wild asses endangered.

Goat First domesticated about 7000 B.C. Now found wild only in the most remote mountainous areas.

Horse First domesticated about 3500 B.C. Now extinct in the wild; several hundred Przewalski's horses survive in zoos around the world.

Pig First domesticated about 7000 B.C. Almost the only domestic animal surviving in significant numbers in the wild.

Sheep First domesticated about 8000–7000 B.C. In Europe reduced to wild populations in Corsica and Sardinia. Elsewhere found in remote mountain areas.

Wolf The first animal to be domesticated, before 10,000 B.C. Once the most widespread mammal, now reduced to strongholds in remote places. The vulnerable gray wolf is numbered in tens in those western European countries where it survives; the red wolf is endangered in the United States.

Domesticated animals would seem to be in the least danger of extinction. In a world where efficiency of production rules supreme, however, many domestic breeds, slower in growth or less productive in the amounts of meat or milk they provide, have disappeared in recent years. Attempts are now being made to rescue the genetic heritage they represent, for they may be of use in the development of future breeds.

EXTINCTION OF PLANTS

Plant extinctions have followed the same pattern as animal extinctions. Destruction of environment, particularly on isolated islands, has led to the most dramatic losses. On Hawaii, for example, about 300 plant species have become extinct within the past 300 years. On St. Helena, only 20 of more than 100 species of native plants survive, and of these, 15 are in danger of extinction. It is said that on Barbados all native trees were felled within 40 years of European colonization.

Just as an animal species may depend on one plant for survival, the reverse may also be true. For instance, the dodo tree, once abundant in Mauritius, has been reduced to 13 very aged trees since the extinction of the dodo, which ate and dispersed its seeds.

Commercially valuable plants have often been exterminated by over-exploitation. Mauritius ebony and San Fernandez sandalwood are both extinct, examples of felling without provision for regrowth. The wine palm of Dominica, tapped (to make alcohol) in a way that killed it, became extinct in the 1920s.

SOME SPECIES ENDANGERED BY HUMAN ACTIVITY

Species/Name	Habitat	Reasons endangered
Endangered by destruction of habitat		
Aye-aye *Daubentonia madagascarensis*	Madagascar	Deforestation.
Bachman's warbler *Vermivora bachmanii*	North America	Felling of swampland forest; rarest songbird in North America.
Cabot's tragopan *Tragopan caboti*	S.E. China	Loss of forest habitat.
Central Asian cobra *Naja oxiana*	C. Asia, N. India	Loss of natural habitat.
False vampire bat (ghost bat) *Macroderma gigas*	N. and W. tropical Australia	Caves in which they live destroyed by quarrying.
Hook-billed hermit hummingbird *Glaucis dohrnii*	Brazil	Destruction of Amazon rain forest.
Indian elephant *Elephas maximus*	S. and S.E. Asia	Mainly deforestation.
Latifi's viper *Vipera latifi*	Iran	Loss of restricted habitat near Tehran with building of hydroelectric plant.
Maned three-toed sloth *Bradypus torquatus*	Brazil	Destruction of Amazon rain forest.
Tuntong (river terrapin) *Batagur baska*	S.E. Asia	Destruction of nesting habitat by sand removal.

Indian elephant

Endangered by poaching or hunting for food, recreation, or zoo trade		
African hunting dog *Lycaon pictus*	S. and E. Africa	Human persecution; disease.
Amazon manatee *Trichechus inunguis*	Brazil	Hunted for meat.
American crocodile *Crocodylus acutus*	North, South, and Central America	Hunting for recreation and for hides; habitat loss.
Arabian oryx *Oryx leucoryx*	S.E. Saudi Arabia	Traditionally hunted; recently exterminated in the wild through use of Jeeps with high-powered weapons.
Blue whale *Balaenoptera musculus*	All oceans	Hunted for blubber, meat.
Californian condor *Gymnogyps californianus*	California	Like many birds of prey, shot, trapped, and poisoned.
Chinese monal pheasant *Ophophorus lhusii*	W. China	Hunted.
Galápagos tortoises *Testudo elephantopus*	Galápagos Islands	Poached for meat, oil, animal trade, and by disaffected farmers and fishers.
Giant otter *Pteronura brasilensis*	Brazil	Hunted for fur.
Green turtle *Chelonia mydas*	Warm oceans worldwide	Killed for meat and hides; eggs taken. Some killed in fishing nets.
Indigo macaw *Andorhynchus leari*	Brazil	Trapped for aviculture trade.
Javan rhinoceros *Rhinoceros sondaicus*	S.E. Asia	Hunted and poached for horn and supposedly medicinal blood and organs.
Short-tailed albatross *Diomedea albatrus*	Japan	Hunted for feathers; also loss of habitat. Breeds slowly, so recovery slow.
Simien fox *Canis simiensis*	Ethiopia	Hunting; loss of natural food.
Swamp deer *Cervus duvauceli*	N. and C. India, Nepal	Poaching and competition from domestic cattle.

Green turtle

Endangered by pollution and introduced diseases		
Hermit ibis *Geronticus eremita*	S. Europe, N. Africa	Pesticide contamination of eggs; hunting, poaching, and zoo trade.
Junin grebe *Podiceps taczanowskii*	Peru	Pollution of lake habitat by copper mining.
Mediterranean monk seal *Monachus monachus*	W. Atlantic, Mediterranean	Marine pollution; persecution by fishers; disturbance at breeding sites.
Salt marsh harvest mouse *Reithrodontomys raviventris*	California	Water pollution from urban and industrial development.
Whooping crane *Grus americana*	North America	Pollution, destruction, and disturbance of wetlands.

Whooping crane

Rabbit-eared bandicoot (bilby)

Endangered by predation by or competition with introduced species		
Arabian tahr *Hemitragus jayakari*	Oman	Competition with domestic goats.
Fijian banded iguana *Brachylophus fasciatus*	Fiji and Tonga	Predation by introduced mongoose.
Kagu *Rhynochetos jubatus*	New Caledonia	Predation by introduced dogs, cats, pigs, and rats.
Lord Howe woodhen *Gallirallus sylvestris*	Lord Howe Island (Tasman Sea)	Damage to habitat by feral goats and pigs; eggs taken by introduced rats.
Rabbit-eared bandicoot (bilby) *Macrotis lagotis*	Australia	Competition with rabbits for habitat.
Short-necked turtle *Pseudemydura umbrina*	S.W. Australia	Predation by introduced foxes and dogs; habitat destruction for farming; damage by fires.
Takahe *Notornis mantelli*	New Zealand	Competition from introduced deer; attacks by introduced weasels.

HABITATS IN DANGER

Habitat destruction is the greatest threat to plant and animal species worldwide. In some cases, such as felling of tropical forests or draining of wetlands, damage is frequently done under the impression that the environment is being improved for human food production or habitation. In others, lack of understanding of the importance of particular environments in the life cycles of certain species has led to the downfall of those environments. Drainage of mangrove swamps, nurseries for many kinds of fish, falls into this category. Sometimes wetland areas are seen as places where disease-carrying insects breed, so they are drained without thought of their importance to the environment as a whole. Forests are felled because of the value of the wood they contain, regardless of the fact that they act as a water-holding system, without which rivers may run faster in rainy seasons, causing soil erosion in their upper reaches and problems of silting as the river approaches the sea. In some areas, even nonessential human demand is regarded as paramount—for example, the breeding beaches of marine turtles in many parts of the world have been sacrificed to vacation homes and hotels, used by a comparatively small number of wealthy visitors.

Although experience should show that environmental damage often has far-reaching effects not foreseen in the early stages of change, humankind seems in many instances incapable of learning. Political prestige and immediate gain seem to take precedence over sensible land use involving as little change as possible to natural systems.

WETLANDS

The wetland ecosystem—rivers, streams, lakes, ponds, and swamps—is under threat. Currently covering about six percent of the earth's surface, wetlands are shrinking rapidly.

Destruction of wetlands may seem to bring nothing but benefit. Draining a marsh creates fertile land for cultivation and reduces breeding areas for insects such as mosquitoes. Damming a river provides a water supply and may mean a source of power as well.

But many changes to water systems carry seeds of disaster. The Aswan High Dam on the upper Nile, completed in 1963 and fully effective by the 1970s, was intended to regulate the river's flow and provide hydroelectric power. The traditional fertility of the Nile Valley, however, was dependent on more than 100 million tons of silt deposited annually as the river flooded. The silt is now silting up the artificial Lake Nasser, forcing farmers downstream to rely on fertilizers and robbing local brickmakers of raw materials; about 35 percent of Egypt's cultivated land is suffering from salination. Deprived of nutrients, the fish stocks of the eastern Mediterranean are declining, while the Nile Delta is being eroded steadily. Schistosomiasis, a disease common in newly irrigated areas, has spread explosively, causing debilitation and death; in 1990 between five and six million people were affected.

Surviving wetlands are often badly damaged: by engineering projects; by eutrophication, when nutrients flow off the land causing huge growths of weeds that overwhelm other plant life; by pollution from sewage or toxic industrial waste; or by thermal pollution from water used for cooling.

Wetland losses

Brazil/Bolivia/Paraguay World's largest wetland area threatened by plans for navigation system along Paraná and Paraguay rivers, with loss of flood-regulatory effect and reduced biodiversity.
Greece Plans to divert Acheloos River for hydroelectricity would destroy Mesolonghi wetlands, home to threatened species.
Iraq Most of Euphrates River diverted into "Third River" canal; in 1993, drainage works on Tigris River meant no water entered 75 percent of marshes.
Japan Dams for Nagara River will block salmon migration (as in northwest U.S.A. and Canada) and destroy clam habitats.
Kazakhstan/Uzbekistan Aral Sea, once the world's fourth-largest freshwater body, has shrunk by 70 percent since the 1970s as feeder rivers diverted for irrigation.
Thailand In 1992, 100 miles (160 km) of rivers polluted by sugar mill; fish recoveries hindered by dam preventing entry from Mekong River.
Turkey Eregli marshes drying because of two reservoirs and polluted by factory; many wild birds losing breeding grounds.
U.S.A. More than half U.S. wetlands (excluding Alaska and Hawaii) drained in the past 200 years; annual loss now 78 sq. miles (203 km²).
Venezuela Canalizing four tributaries of Orinoco River, for 11,600 sq. miles (30,000 km²) for agriculture, would destroy two national parks and two wildlife refuges.

CORAL REEFS AND MANGROVE SWAMPS

Coral reefs are found where the average annual temperature of the sea does not drop below 70°F (21°C). They are the richest of marine environments, estimated to contain one-third of the world's fish species and up to 500,000 animal species in all. Reef corals can only thrive in shallow water, so they are often close to land and therefore at special risk from human activities. Dangers include pollution; dredging and removal for construction purposes; damage by collection of coral and other invertebrates as tourist trophies; and collection of fish for the aquarist trade, which has already wiped out some species of colorful reef fish.

Mangrove swamps occur in tropical regions where soft sediments are covered with seawater. In cooler areas, salt marshes take their place. Both types of environment are rich in species. Mangrove swamps are the nurseries for many kinds of open-water tropical fish; salt marshes are the feeding grounds for the world's migrating waders and waterfowl. Yet both environments are regarded with disfavor by the majority of humankind, and there has been greater destruction of mangrove swamps than of any other habitat type. Currently about 64,000 sq. miles (165,000 km²) of mangrove forest remain, but almost all are under threat—largely from pollution, which in some cases causes harmful mutations, and from expansion of farming.

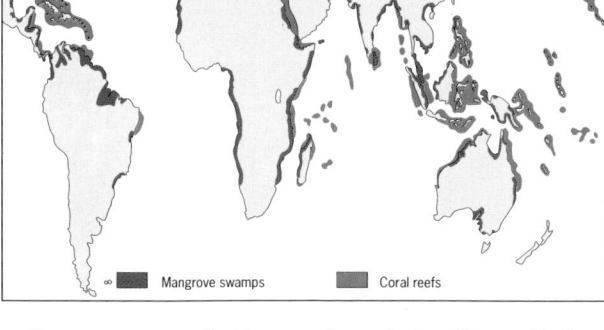

Mangrove swamps   Coral reefs

Coral and mangrove losses

Australia Great Barrier Reef periodically devastated by spread of crown-of-thorns starfish, probably due to overcollecting of Triton shell, which preys on early stages of starfish.
S./S.E. Asia, Africa Half mangroves lost, mainly to saltwater ponds for shrimp and fish. In Vietnam, world's largest mangrove forest being cleared for tiger-shrimp farms.
U.S.A. Coral smothered in Kanehoe Bay, Hawaii, due to silting caused by upstream deforestation.

Other threats to coral include overcollecting of all species for tourist trade, oil and gas production, and military use of reef areas.

FORESTS

At one time, bands of forest stretched around the world. The coniferous forests of the Eurasian and North American taiga thinned out to the north into tundra and southward thickened into broad-leaved forests. Near the equator were dense tropical forests. But with the spread of humans, the picture changed.

In lowland temperate areas, such as much of Europe, the loss of forest cover has not been disastrous, although animal species have been reduced. But in upland areas where trees have been taken for firewood or logging, the soil is often washed away down steep slopes. In regions of heavy rainfall like Scotland, this can result in a "wet desert," where few species can survive. Increasingly, especially in Europe and North America, clear-felled areas are replanted. This replaces trees but does not replace biological diversity, particularly of animals. Meanwhile, taiga forest in northern Asia is being destroyed on a huge scale.

Tropical forests, however, are most under threat. These now occupy only about six percent of the earth's surface, but they include almost half of all growing wood and are thought to contain 70–90 percent of all living species, many of which are still unknown and have great potential value medicinally. Forests have traditionally been used for slash-and-burn agriculture, small patches being cleared and cultivated for a few years and then returned to jungle. But population pressure now means that even this use jeopardizes the forest environment.

Clearing for farmland replaces the huge diversity of the forest with monoculture, or very few species of plants, while the majority of animals dependent on the original forest disappear with the trees. In South America, much of the cleared forest is used for cattle ranching, but the forest soils are low in fertility and the ranching has to be on an extensive, wasteful scale.

Elsewhere, mining for gold and other minerals has caused serious pollution of rivers, while demand for hardwood timber is such that forest is felled on a huge scale, and in some areas timber poachers even fly into conservation areas to cut ancient trees.

Annual world consumption of wood is about 120 million cu. feet (3.4 million m³): 55 percent from broad-leaved trees and 45 percent from conifers; about 77,000 sq. miles (200,000 km²) of broad-leafed and coniferous forest are cut each year. About half is used for fuel for industry.

Tropical forest losses

More than half the world's tropical forests have been destroyed in the past 50 years. Between 1950 and 1975, more than 463,000 sq. miles (1.2 million km²) disappeared, and in 1975–89 another 3,886,000 sq. miles (1.5 million km²). On current trends, a further 772,000 sq. miles (2 million km²) will have vanished by the year 2000. This destruction has led to a huge increase in the amount of carbon dioxide in the atmosphere, while forest soil is degraded and eroded, causing rivers to silt up and flood. The following data are 1991 FAO (United Nations Food and Agriculture Organization) estimates for 87 tropical countries.

	Forest area 1990 (mi.²)	Annual forest loss 1981–90 (mi.²)	Rate of forest loss 1981–90 (%)
Latin America			
Tropical South America	2,815,800	26,200	0.8
C. America, incl. Mexico	245,200	5,400	1.8
Caribbean	181,800	800	0.4
	3,242,800	32,400	0.9
Africa			
C. Africa	831,700	5,800	0.6
Tropical southern Africa	796,500	4,200	0.5
E. Sahelian Africa	329,300	2,700	0.8
W. Africa	167,600	4,600	2.1
W. Sahelian Africa	146,700	1,500	0.9
Insular Africa	45,200	800	1.2
	2,317,000	19,600	0.8
Asia			
Insular S.E. Asia	536,300	7,000	1.2
Continental S.E. Asia	269,100	5,000	1.6
S. Asia	255,600	1,500	0.6
	1,061,000	13,500	1.2
Total	6,620,800	65,500	0.9

THE SPREAD OF DESERTS

About 35 percent of the earth's land surface is now classified as arid or semiarid. Every year this area is increased by about 81,000 sq. miles (210,000 km²), predominantly as a result of human activity. As well as deforestation for commerical purposes, population pressures mean that forests and marginal land are cleared and plowed or used for livestock; both these new farmlands and existing agricultural areas are cultivated more intensively than they can sustain and may become desertified. In some regions, poor irrigation practices cause salination and depletion of the soil's nurients so the soil is sterilized and cannot support any agriculture, while elsewhere overgrazing destroys vegetation and topsoil.

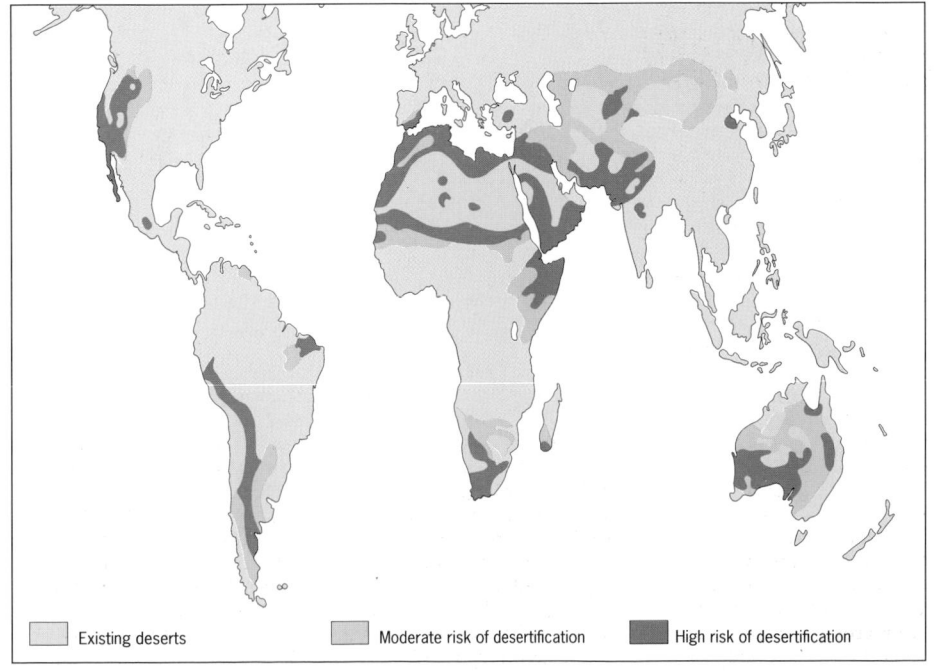

Existing deserts · Moderate risk of desertification · High risk of desertification

WORLD CONSERVATION STRATEGY

Plants and animals are unaware of political boundaries: conservation must be based on worldwide strategies. The World Conservation Strategy, launched in 1980 by IUCN (International Union for Conservation of Nature and Natural Resources), WWF (World Wildlife Fund), and UNEP (United Nations Environment Program), said that conservation of three factors was needed: (1) life-support cycles, water, soil, and air; (2) species of plants and animals; and (3) genetic diversity. This became the basis of conservation policies in more than 50 countries.

In 1991, IUCN, WWF, and UNEP launched Caring for the Earth, an updated policy document setting targets and suggesting some methods of approach. In 1992, the Earth Summit in Rio de Janiero, Brazil was attended by many heads of governments, who pledged to implement much of Caring for the Earth; its strategies were largely embodied in the Biodiversity Convention (although this was not signed by the U.S.A.). Many of those good intentions have since been watered down or bogged down, but the ideas survive and a number are gradually being implemented with a world system of biosphere reserves and heritage sites.

CONSERVATION BODIES

The public concept of conservation originated during the 1800s. Until then, land appeared limitless and resources many: people believed they had a right to use the environment as they wished. But with the Industrial Revolution, populations began to rocket, and predictions of ecological doom followed.

In 1872, land was set aside to establish Yellowstone National Park. Conservationists had become alarmed at the destruction of natural habitats for plants and wildlife. At the same time a federal agency was set up to administer Yellowstone and subsequent national parks. Federal, state, and local government now play an important role in conservation.

Many people trace the start of the whole ecological movement to the establishment of the Sierra Club in 1892. It set the pattern for organizations that reflected concern about wilderness protection, conservation of the environment, and appreciation of complex ecosystems. Such conservation bodies now operate in nearly every country: some tackle broad, global concerns; others focus on conservation in a particular region or of certain species.

Antarctic and Southern Ocean Coalition 707 D St. S.E, Washington, D.C. 20003.
Aim: To protect the Antarctic and maintain it as global commons, science preserve, and wildlife sanctuary.

Australia Conservation Foundation 340 Gore St., Fitzroy, Victoria 3065.
Aim: To conserve resources of land, air, water. To influence decision makers and oppose major environmental degradation.

Appalachian Mountain Club 5 Joy St., Boston, MA 02108
Aim: To promote conservation and responsible recreation. Encourages land and river protection, educational and youth programs, and trail building and maintenance.

Caribbean Conservation Corporation P.O. Box 2866, Gainesville, FL 32602
Aim: To conserve sea turtles and other coastal and marine life of the Caribbean. Promotes protection of natural areas, research, education, and training.

Conservation International 1015 18th St. NW, Suite 1000, Washington, D.C. 20036
Aim: To create and manage ecosystems reserves and act as a catalyst for conservation action in Latin America.

Defenders of Wildlife 1244 19th St. NW, Washington, D.C. 20036
Aim: To protect biological diversity and endangered species.

Ducks Unlimited 1 Waterfowl Way, Memphis, TN 38120
Aim: To fulfill the needs of North American waterfowl through their annual cycle by protecting, restoring, and managing important wetlands and uplands.

Earth Share 3400 International Drive NW, Suite 2K, Washington, D.C. 20008
Aim: Fundraising federation of 39 non-profit environmental and conservation organizations operating payroll-deduction campaigns across the United States.

Earthwatch P.O. Box 403, Watertown, MA 02272
Aim: To match scientists and interested amateurs in ecological field experiments worldwide.

Fauna and Flora Preservation Society 1 Kensington Gore, London SW7 2AR, England.
Aim: To ensure conservation of habitats, flora, and fauna worldwide. Involves public and decision makers in conservation.

Friends of the Earth International P.O. Box 19199, NL-1000 GD Amsterdam, The Netherlands.
Aim: To promote and change policies on the environment through public education and lobbying. Campaigns nationally and locally. Promotes policies that do not harm the environment, including energy conservation and pesticide restrictions.

Greenpeace International Keizersgracht 176, NL-1016 DW Amsterdam, The Netherlands.

Aim: To campaign against abuse of natural world. Lobbies and takes direct action against deliberate killing of wildlife, toxic and radioactive pollution, air pollution, acid rain, loss of ozone layer, nuclear testing, and nuclear weapons.

International Primate Protection League P.O. Box 766, Summerville, SC 29484
Aim: To protect primates worldwide. Investigates traffic in endangered species.

International Whaling Commission The Red House, 135 Station Rd, Histon, Cambridge CB4 4NP, England.
Aim: To conserve whales throughout the world and regulate the whaling industry. Reviews conservation measures; compiles statistics; encourages, coordinates, and funds research into humane killing.

National Audubon Society 700 Broadway, New York, NY 10003
Aim: To preserve and protect wildlife and its habitat through education, research, sanctuary management, litigation, lobbying, and disseminating information.

Rainforest Action Network 301 Broadway, Suite A, San Francisco, CA 94133
Aim: To protect and conserve rain forests by direct action, public pressure, research, and support of economic alternatives.

Sea Shepherd Conservation Society 1314 Second St., Santa Monica, CA 90401
Aim: To conserve and protect wildlife, mainly marine mammals. Direct action against drift-net fishing and tuna vessels that kill dolphins, whales, and seals.

Sierra Club 730 Polk St., San Francisco, CA 94109
Aim: To influence public policy decisions. Encourages responsible uses of world's ecosystems with publications, education, and outings.

World Conservation Union (was IUCN) Avenue du Mont Blanc, CH-1196, Gland, Switzerland
Aim: International leadership for conservation and management of living resources. Research; technical support to conservation treaties, e.g. CITES. Manages World Conservation Monitoring Centres at Cambridge and Kew, England, for information on threatened species.

World Wide Fund for Nature (was World Wildlife Fund) Avenue du Mont Blanc, CH-1196, Gland, Switzerland
Aim: To conserve flora, fauna, and natural environments; promote public awareness; establish and fund projects; stop illegal trade in animals and animal products. Education; work with governments, businesses, conservation groups.

CONVENTION ON INTERNATIONAL TRADE IN ENDANGERED SPECIES (CITES)

Many treaties aimed at protecting animals have been signed since 1900. Most important is CITES, which since 1973 has had 122 signatories. These countries agree to prohibit international trade in about 600 rare species of plants and animals and to require licenses from the country of origin for many more. Trade in many mammal skins, ivory, and turtle shells is banned by CITES signatories.

Unfortunately, illegal trade in wildlife is big business, and some countries turn a blind eye to a source of much-needed cash. In some cases, customs officers cannot distinguish between protected and nonprotected species; in others, a species or subspecies that is protected in one area is exported illegally to a place where it may be harvested, and then re-exported with false documentation. Better methods of recognizing animals from a particular place are gradually leading to improvement, but there is still far to go.

Some traffic in protected species detected in 1993

Ivory

May 546 elephant tusks and 2,122 hippo teeth impounded from two businessmen in Tanzania. **May–June** Two shipments of ivory en route from Malawi to Taiwan seized in Britain. **September** Container of ivory headed to Taiwan recovered from Durban harbor by South African Endangered Species Protection Unit working with Taiwanese and Zambian authorities. **September** Ivory blocks from Zaire seized by customs officers in Belgium on the way to Singapore.

Primates

September Three gibbons and two baby orangutans seized by Taiwanese police in raid on suspected drug dealers. **November** Customs officers in Greece seize two young chimpanzees, dressed in clothes and used as props by a photographer previously charged with illegal possession of three chimpanzees.

Birds

March French officials seize parrots of five species held illegally by a trader, along with 250 goldfinches, protected in France. Four red-fronted macaws en route for Russia seized at Montevideo airport. **November** Bird breeder fined in Adelaide for smuggling four mustached parrots into Australia from Thailand. Two game dealers in New Zealand fined for possession of 15 New Zealand pigeons, a bird in danger of extinction because of well-organized poaching. **November** Shipment of almost 1.9 million tree sparrows, weighing 33 tons, seized in Rotterdam, en route to Italy from China. European legislation prohibits import of these birds.

Big cats

January Five people arrested in Japan for possessing four Amur tiger skins, apparently obtained from a Russian sailor who said more were available. **August** Delhi police seize eight tiger skins, 624 lbs. (283 kg) of tiger bones, 60 leopard skins, and 164 other mammal skins. **September** 73 leopard skins, 42 lbs. (19 kg) of tiger bones, and 158 other mammal skins seized by customs officers in Nepal.

Reptiles

January Customs officers at Heathrow Airport, London, seize a shipment of 788 reptiles and amphibians illegally imported from Ghana. **July** U.S. customs officers in Los Angeles arrest a Taiwanese carrying 16 snakes in sacks attached to his arms and legs, with another 34 in his luggage. **June** Bulgarian forestry officials seize and return to the wild 72 tortoises of two species taken illegally. **July** 3,000 snakeskins heading for Iran seized at Delhi airport. **August** 4,621 skins of cobra, viper, and rat snake seized at Delhi airport from two Syrians bound for Damascus.

Plants

January Collector arrested at Bangkok Airport trying to smuggle out 232 wild lady's slipper orchids. **February** Customs officers at Orly Airport, Paris, seize 390 cacti from a group returning from Mexico. Shipment of 1,490 cacti from Peru seized in Sicily. **March** 367 wild lady's slipper orchids confiscated in Hong Kong. Another Hong Kong collector convicted for the fifth time, this time for possession of 86 wild orchids. **July** 1,630 lbs. (740 kg) of medicinal *Nardostachys grandiflora* seized at Delhi airport. India bans export of all wild-grown medicinal plants.

ZOOS

A visit to the zoo has been standard family entertainment for more than a century. But today the sight of bored animals cooped up in inadequate space is distasteful to many people, and zoos are undergoing a crisis of identity. Traditionally, they have been consumers of the wild: animals living singly, traumatized by crowds of visitors, rarely live long. Although there are still appalling animal prisons, in recent years many zoos have improved markedly.

The first move was toward creating living museums with an educational function. Along with this has come concern that the animals should not merely survive but should thrive in conditions as close as possible to their natural life. Animals kept with this aim usually live in natural groups and often breed successfully. The idea of giving animals more space and confining humans to cars gave rise to safari parks, but unless they are well run, these can be as squalid as old-fashioned zoos.

Since the 1960s, some zoos have taken on another role, that of an ark for beleaguered species. In many zoos captive breeding is keeping species from extinction. Stud books are kept, and to prevent inbreeding animals may be transported from one zoo to another. In some cases, captive breeding has built up sufficient stocks for some animals to be returned, with careful safeguards, to wild habitats from which they had been exterminated.

Captive breeding successes

Worldwide, many hundreds of species are being bred in zoos. These are just a few.

Arabian oryx In 1962, three caught in the wild and others donated by zoos were sent to Phoenix, Arizona, where the present population was built up. Some have been returned to Oman and Saudi Arabia.

Black-footed ferrets One of the world's rarest mammals. Some bred in captivity and released in 1991. First wild breeding in 1992.

Californian condor In 1987, world population was 27 birds. Some were captured and bred in captivity. Now there are 75 birds: 66 in captivity, the others released.

Hawaiian goose or nene In 1950, fewer than 50 left in wild. Three were sent to England, where a large flock was built up. Now many kept in waterfowl collections and reestablished in Hawaii.

Père David's deer. Extinct in the wild. Two animals were smuggled from park of the Imperial Palace in Beijing to build up a herd in England. Now in many zoos, and some have been returned to China.

Peregrine falcon Became very rare due to hunting and pesticide pollution. In 1970, Cornell University Laboratory of Ornithology began to breed peregrines and has released many into the wild.

Przewalski's horse Extinct in the wild, but kept in many zoos. Some to be returned to the Gobi Desert in 1994.

NATIONAL PARKS

Yellowstone National Park in Wyoming was the world's first national park and has become a model for others to follow. Geographical surveys in 1870–71 led to the suggestion that this unique area of hot springs, geysers, mud volcanoes, and waterfalls should be obtained by the government for the use and enjoyment of the people and persuaded Congress to pass a bill establishing a national park. At first there were no guidelines or funds for its management, but in 1916 the National Parks Service was established. Yellowstone and the 51 other U.S. national parks that followed it are now closely managed, with trails, accommodation, information centers, and nature activities; Yellowstone alone receives more than two million visitors each year.

National parks have now been set up in most countries of the world. They are funded by federal government and are often larger than reserves run by local government or private conservation organizations. Unlike some nature reserves, from which people are excluded, in general national parks set out to attract visitors, who are often especially drawn by their dramatic, unspoiled scenery.

The concept of what a national park should be has changed with time and varies in different parts of the world. In the past, in many major parks such as Kruger (in South Africa) and Yellowstone, the policy was to give visitors a chance to see large numbers of herbivores. To this end, predators were ruthlessly exterminated. Today, they are recognized and protected as being part of the balance of numbers of different species. At present, some parks are total conservation areas; others pay their way by allowing tourists to hunt rarities in the park. Unfortunately, in many places conservation is underfunded and parks are understaffed, so surviving plants and animals become a target for poachers. International efforts are, however, being made to support conservation.

By the late 1980s, there were more than 3,000 national parks and wildlife reserves scattered around the world. Altogether they covered at that time approximately 1.5 million sq. mi. (4 million km²).

Heron Island, Great Barrier Reef.

Mineral deposits at Minerva Terrace, Mammoth Hot Springs, Yellowstone.

Asiatic lions, Gir (Gujarat, India).

Phu Rua (Loei, Thailand).

Elephants near Mt. Kilimanjaro.

Some national parks and nature reserves

Name	Country	Area sq. mi.(km²)	Special features
Altos de Campana	Panama	19(48)	Great variety of plant zones.
Amazonia	Brazil	3,837(9,940)	Rain forest.
Badlands	U.S.A.	380(985)	Prehistoric fossils; dramatically eroded hills.
Banff	Canada	2,563(6,640)	Spectacular glacial scenery; hot springs.
Beinn Eighe	U.K.	19(48)	Original Scottish pine forest.
Bialowieski	Poland	20(53)	Largest remnant of primeval forest; European bison.
Burren	Ireland	6(15)	Limestone pavement with remarkable plants.
Camargue	France	51(131)	Wetland; many rare birds, especially flamingoes.
Canaima	Venezuela	11,580(30,000)	World's highest waterfall, Angel Falls.
Canyonlands	U.S.A.	527(1,365)	Deep gorges, colorful rock, spectacular landforms.
Carlsbad Caverns	U.S.A.	52(134)	Huge limestone caves with millions of bats.
Carnarvon	Australia	104(270)	Bush-tailed rock wallabies; aboriginal cave paintings.
Chitwan	Nepal	360(932)	Royal Bengal tigers, gharials, Gangetic dolphins.
Corbett	India	201(520)	Indian tigers, gharials, muggers.
Dartmoor	U.K.	368(954)	Wild ponies.
Death Valley	U.S.A.	3,230(8,368)	Lowest point in W. Hemisphere; unique flora, fauna.
Doñana	Spain	196(507)	Wetland; rare birds and mammals; Spanish lynx.
Everglades	U.S.A.	2,289(5,929)	Swamp, mangrove; subtropical wildlife refuge.
Etosha	Namibia	8,596(22,270)	Swampland and bush; rare and abundant wildlife.
Fiordland	New Zealand	4,852(12,570)	Kiwis, keas, wekas, takahe, kakapo.
Fuji-Hakone-Izu	Japan	476(1,232)	Mt. Fuji; varied animal and plant life.
Galápagos Islands	Ecuador	2,678(6,937)	Giant iguanas, giant tortoises.
Gemsbok	Botswana	9,382(24,305)	Desert, grassland; lions and large herds of game.
Gir	India	545(1,412)	Asiatic lions.
Glacier	U.S.A.	1,583(4,102)	Virgin coniferous forest; glaciers.
Gran Paradiso	Italy	271(702)	Alpine scenery; chamois, ibex.
Grand Canyon	U.S.A.	1,866(4,834)	Mile-deep canyon, colorful walls; many life zones.
Great Smoky Mountains	U.S.A.	808(2,094)	Varied wildlife including wild turkey, black bear.
Hardangervidda	Norway	1,321(3,422)	Plateau of ancient rock; large wild reindeer herd.
Hawaii Volcanoes	U.S.A.	355(920)	Active volcanoes, rare plants and animals.
Heron Island	Australia	0.07(0.17)	Part of Great Barrier Reef; corals, invertebrates, fish.
Hoge Veluwe	Netherlands	21(54)	Largely stabilized dunes; wet and dry heath.
Iguazu/Iguaçú	Argentina/Brazil	2,663(6,900)	Iguazu/Iguaçú Falls.
Ixtacihuatl-Popocatépetl	Mexico	99(257)	Snowcapped volcanoes.
Kafue	Zambia	8,646(22,400)	Numerous animals and birds; black rhinoceros refuge.
Kakadu	Australia	2,316(6,000)	Aboriginal rock art; crocodiles, waterbirds.
Kaziranga	India	166(430)	Indian one-horned rhinoceros, swamp deer.
Khao Yai	Thailand	837(2,169)	Large caves and waterfalls; many bird species.
Kilimanjaro	Tanzania	292(756)	Africa's highest peak, Mt. Kilimanjaro; colobus monkeys.
Kinabalu	Malaysia	291(754)	Orchids; S.E. Asia's highest peak, Mt. Kinabalu.
Kosciusko	Australia	2,497(6,469)	Australia's highest peak, Mt. Kosciusko; mountain pygmy possum.
Kruger	South Africa	7,521(19,485)	Animals and birds: rare white rhinoceros.
Lainzer Tiergarten	Austria	10(25)	Ancient forest and meadow; wild boar, deer, mouflon.
Lake District	U.K.	885(2,292)	Lake and mountain scenery.
Los Glaciares	Argentina/Chile	625(1,618)	Glacial landforms.
Manu	Peru	5,917(15,328)	Small mammals, birds; Amazon/Andean ecosystems.
Mercantour	France	565(1,465)	Alpine scenery and flora.
Mount Apo	Philippines	281(728)	Volcanoes; monkey-eating eagles.
Mount Cook	New Zealand	270(699)	New Zealand's highest peak, Mt. Cook.
Mount Olympus	Greece	15(40)	Mt. Olympus; maquis and forest; wild mountain goats.
Muddus	Sweden	190(493)	Glaciated area with forest and tundra; Lapp pasture.
Namib Desert/Naukluft	Namibia	9,032(23,400)	Only true desert in southern Africa.
Ngorongoro	Tanzania	3200(8,292)	Huge volcanic crater.
Olympic	U.S.A.	1,433(3,712)	Rugged peaks, glaciers, dense forest; elk.
Petrified Forest	U.S.A.	146(379)	Tree trunks millions of years old; colorful sands.
Pfälzerwald	Germany	692(1,793)	Forest; European bison, mouflon, mountain goats.
Phu Rua	Thailand	46(120)	Mountain forest zones from tropical to pine.
Redwood	U.S.A.	171(442)	Virgin redwood stand; elk.
Royal	Australia	58(150)	World's second-oldest national park (1879).
Ruwenzori	Uganda	764(1,978)	Hippopotamuses, chimpanzees, baboons, colobuses.
Sagarmatha	Nepal	443(1,148)	Mt. Everest; impeyan pheasant, Himalayan tahr.
Sarek	Sweden	760(1,970)	Lapland; herds of reindeer.
Serengeti	Tanzania	5,699(14,763)	Huge animal migrations at start of dry season.
Snowdonia	U.K.	827(2,142)	Glaciated mountain scenery; varied flora and fauna.
Swiss	Switzerland	65(169)	Alpine forests and flora; reintroduced ibex.
Tatra	Czech Republic/Poland	275(712)	Bears, lynxes, marmots; mountain scenery.
Tikal	Guatemala	222(574)	Mayan ruins; rain forest animals.
Toubkal	Morocco	139(360)	Barbary apes, porcupines, hyenas, bald ibis.
Tsavo	Kenya	8,033(20,812)	Vast range of wildlife.
Ujung-Kulon	Indonesia	303(786)	Low-relief forest; Javan tiger, Javan rhinoceros.
Uluru	Australia	512(1,326)	Desert; Uluru (Ayers Rock) and the Olgas.
Victoria Falls	Zimbabwe/Zambia	73(190)	Spectacular waterfall.
Virunga	Zaire	3,011(7,800)	Mountain gorillas; active volcanoes.
Waterton Lakes	Canada	203(526)	Varied flora and fauna.
Waza	Cameroon	656(1,700)	Giraffes, elephants, ostriches, waterbuck.
Wolong	China	772(2,000)	Giant pandas; also golden langurs, snow leopards.
Wood Buffalo	Canada	17,293(44,800)	Refuge for American bison, whooping crane.
Yellowstone	U.S.A.	3,471(8,991)	World's greatest geyser area; bears, deer, elk, bison.
Yosemite	U.S.A.	119(308)	High waterfalls; varied flora and fauna; giant sequoias.

PROMINENT PEOPLE

ADAMS, Roy Chapman (1884–1960) U.S. naturalist and explorer. Led many scientific expeditions and wrote and lectured extensively on central and eastern Asia. His many discoveries include the first known dinosaur eggs and fossil remains of giant land mammals.

AUDUBON, John James (1785–1851) Haitian-born U.S. ornithologist and bird artist. His *Birds of America* (1827–38), comprises plates of 1,065 birds in life size. The National Audubon Society was founded (1866) in his honor.

BAILEY, Liberty Hyde (1858–1954) U.S. horticulturalist and botanist. Coined the term "cultivar" and edited *Standard Cyclopedia of Horticulture* (1914–17).

BAIRD, Spencer Fullerton (1823–87) U.S. zoologist. Author of five-volume *History of North American Birds* (1875–84); he developed the "Baird School" of accurate ornithological description. Also contributed to studies of mammals, fish, and plants.

BANKS, Sir Joseph (1743–1820) British botanist. Accompanied James Cook's expedition around world in *Endeavour* (1768–71), collecting many previously unknown plants. President of the Royal Society (1778–1819).

BARTRAM, John (1796–1873) U.S. botanist. Traveled widely in eastern North America, gathering specimens for his Philadelphia garden. Exchanged bulbs and seeds with European species to create many hybrids.

BEADLE, George Wells (1903–89) U.S. geneticist. Showed that genes affect heredity by determining the enzyme structure. His work, in effect creating the study of biochemical genetics, earned him the Nobel Prize in 1958.

BEEBE, Charles William (1877–1962) U.S. naturalist and explorer. Curator of ornithology for New York Zoological Society. Explored ocean depths to almost 3,280 feet (1,000 m).

BUFFON, George-Louis Leclerc, Comte de (1707–88) French naturalist. Proposed a greater age for earth than stated in book of *Genesis* and hinted at theory of evolution.

BURBANK, Luther (1849–1926) U.S. horticulturist. Developed Burbank potato and new breeds of fruits and flowers.

CARSON, Rachel Louise (1907–64) U.S. naturalist and science writer. Her *The Sea Around Us* (1951) warned of increasing danger of marine pollution, and *Silent Spring* (1962) directed public concern to the use of synthetic pesticides and their effect on food chains.

COUSTEAU, Jacques-Yves (b. 1910) French oceanographer. He popularized marine life conservation through the television series *The Undersea World of Jacques Cousteau.*

CUVIER, Georges (Léopold Chrétien Frédéric Dagobert) (1769–1832) French anatomist. Created natural system of animal classification and linked paleontology to comparative anatomy.

DARWIN, Charles Robert (1809–82) British naturalist. Originator (with Alfred WALLACE) of the theory of evolution by natural selection. Discoveries made while traveling on *HMS Beagle*'s around-the-world scientific survey (1831–36) led to *The Origin of Species by Means of Natural Selection* (1859).

DAWKINS, Richard (b. 1941) British ethologist and author of *The Selfish Gene* (1976), *The Blind Watchmaker* (1988).

DOBZHANSKY, Theodosius (1900–75) U.S.–Ukrainian geneticist and author. Using mathematics and experimentation, he challenged the notion that mutation-related genetic changes occur rarely and slowly. He integrated his genetic theories with studies on human evolution.

FRISCH, Karl von (1886–1982) Austrian ethologist and zoologist. Showed that bees communicate using coded dances.

GOODALL, Jane (b. 1934) British zoologist. Best known for studying chimpanzees in Africa (1960).

GRAY, Asa (1810–88) U.S. botanist and taxonomist. Author of textbooks popularizing botany, including *Flora of North America* (1838–43), cowritten with John Torrey (1796–1873). Discovered and classified many new species.

HAECKEL, Ernst Heinrich Philipp August (1834–1919) German naturalist. One of the first to sketch the genealogical tree of animals.

HARDY, Sir Alister Clavering (1896–1985) British marine biologist. Invented the continuous plankton recorder, which permits detailed study of surface life in oceans.

HUXLEY, Thomas Henry (1825–95) British biologist. Foremost scientific supporter of Charles DARWIN's theory of evolution by natural selection.

KORNBERG, Arthur (b. 1918) U.S. biochemist. Won 1958 Nobel Prize for discovering how DNA molecules are duplicated in the bacterial cell.

LAMARCK, Jean (Baptiste Pierre Antoine de Monet) Chevalier de (1744–1829) French naturalist and pre-Darwinian evolutionist. His *Philosophie Zoologique* (1809) proposes that acquired characteristics can be inherited.

LEDERBERG, Joshua (b. 1925) U.S. geneticist. Winner of 1958 Nobel Prize. Mixed strands of bacterium to produce "crossbreed" strains; showed how certain viruses can carry bacterial genes.

LEEUWENHOEK, Anton van (1632–1723) Dutch scientist. Made discoveries related to the circulation of blood and blood corpuscles and spermatozoa.

LINNAEUS, Carolus (Carl von Linné) (1707–78) Swedish naturalist and physician. Introduced modern binomial nomenclature of generic and specific names for animals and plants. The Linnaean Society was founded in London in his honor (1788).

LORENZ, Konrad Zacharias (1903–89) Austrian zoologist and ethologist. Founded ethological school of animal behavior with Nikolaas TINBERGEN in 1930s; chiefly known for his observations on imprinting in young birds.

McCLINTOCK, Barbara (1902–92) U.S. plant geneticist. Discovered genes that could control other genes and move on the chromosome (1951).

MENDEL, Gregor Johann (1822–84) Austrian biologist, botanist, and priest. Known as the founder of genetics: discovered that a parent plant hands down only one gene of each pair to offspring.

MORGAN, Thomas Hunt (1866–1945) U.S. geneticist. His experiments with *Drosophila* fruit flies led him to establish that heredity is determined by genes.

MORRIS, Desmond John (b. 1928) English zoologist, ethologist, writer. His *Naked Ape* (1967) analyzes behavior of human beings when viewed as animals.

MUIR, John (1838–1914) Scottish–U.S. naturalist. Argued for protection of forests; his efforts led to the establishment of Sequoia and Yosemite national parks (1890) and of the first 13 U.S. national forests (1897).

MULLER, Herman Joseph (1890–1967) U.S. geneticist. Won 1946 Nobel Prize for demonstrating that X rays striking living cells can cause mutations and hereditary changes. Campaigned to reduce human exposure to radiation.

PETERSON, Roger Tory (b. 1908) U.S. ornithologist and wildlife artist whose books, such as *A Field Guide to Birds* (1934) and the "Peterson Field Guide Series," stimulated public interest in birds in the United States and Europe.

PINCHOT, Gifford (1865–1946) U.S. forester and conservationist. First chief of U.S. Forest Service (1905); set up school of forestry at Yale University.

RAY, John (1628–1705) British naturalist. Originated the basic principles of plant classification into cryptograms, monocotyledons, and dicotyledons.

ROTHSCHILD, Lionel Walter (Baron Rothschild of Tring) (1868–1937) British zoologist. Assembled largest collection of dead animals by one person.

ROTHSCHILD, Miriam Louisa (b. 1908) British naturalist and conservationist. Proved that fleas transmit myxomatosis, the infectious viral disease of rabbits.

TANSLEY, Sir Arthur George (1871–1955) British botanist. A pioneer ecologist; author of *Practical Plant Ecology* (1923) and *The British Islands and their Vegetation.*

TINBERGEN, Nikolaas (1907–88) Dutch ethologist. Analyzed social behavior of certain animals as an evolutionary process relevant to human behavior.

WALLACE, Alfred Russel (1823–1913) Welsh naturalist. Promulgated theory of natural selection. Traveled in Amazon basin and Malay archipelago and contributed much to scientific foundations of zoogeography.

TERMS

Acquired character Modification of an organ during the lifetime of an individual due to use or disuse, as opposed to inheritance from a previous generation.

Adaptation In zoology, any structural, physiological, or behavioral characteristic that fits an organism to its environment.

Algae Simple plants containing CHLOROPHYLL but without roots, stems, or leaves, which live in aquatic conditions.

Anaerobic Living in the absence of oxygen. Anaerobic respiration is the liberation of energy which does not require the presence of oxygen.

Annual A plant that flowers and dies within a year from germination.

Axil The upper angle between the leaf and stem, or branch and trunk.

Bast Tissue in plants that circulates food materials.

Benthos Collectively, immobile animal and plant life living on the sea bottom.

Biennial A plant that needs two growing seasons: it makes and stores food during the first one, and flowers and dies during the second one.

Biogenesis Formation of living organisms from their ancestors and of minute CELL structures from their predecessors.

Bioluminescence The production of light by living organisms, for example glowworms, some deep-sea fish, some bacteria, and some fungi.

Bract Leaf that bears a flower in its AXIL.

Cambium Actively dividing cells that supply the BAST.

Cell In biology, the unit from which plants and animals are composed.

Cellulose A carbohydrate forming the chief component of CELL walls in plants and in wood.

Chlorophyll Green pigment in plants and algae involved in PHOTOSYNTHESIS.

Chloroplast A CHLOROPHYLL-bearing PLASTID.

Chromosome Rodlike structures found in the NUCLEUS of a CELL, which perform an important role in cell division and transmission of hereditary features.

Clone Organisms or CELLs derived from a single progenitor (i.e. with an almost identical GENOTYPE).

Cultivar A "cultivated variety."

Dimorphism In biology, the condition of having two different forms, such as animals that show marked differences between male and female (sexual dimorphism), and colonial animals in which the members of the colony are of two different kinds.

DNA, deoxyribonucleic acid Within a CHROMOSOME, this carries the genetic material of an organism, directing production of RNA. Usually, two strands of DNA form a double helix, the strands running in opposite directions.

Dominant Describes a GENE which shows its effect in those individuals who received it from only one parent. Also describes an inherited feature due to a dominant gene.

Drupe A fleshy fruit with one or more seeds, each surrounded by a stony layer.

Ecosystem Conceptual view of a plant and animal community, emphasizing the interactions between living and non-living parts and the flow of materials and energy between these parts.

Epiphyte A plant that grows on another plant but, unlike a PARASITE, does not derive subsistence from it.

Ethology The study of animal behavior.

Evolution Changes in genetic composition of a population during successive generations; the gradual development of more complex organisms.

Fossil The relic or trace of some plant or animal which has been preserved by natural processes in rocks.

Gene One of the units of DNA arranged in linear fashion on the CHROMOSOMEs, responsible for passing on specific features from parents to offspring.

Genetic code The system by which GENES pass on instructions that ensure transmission of features inherited from previous generations.

Genetic engineering Manipulation of the GENOME by the modification or elimination of certain GENEs, and the mass production of useful substances (e.g. insulin) by the transplanting of genes.

Genome The full set of CHROMOSOMEs of an individual; the total number of GENES in such a set.

Genotype The genetic constitution of an individual; a group of individuals all with the same genetic constitution.

Gestation In mammals, the act of retaining and nourishing the young in the uterus; pregnancy.

Herbaceous A soft and green plant organ, or a plant without persistent woody tissues above ground.

Hybrid In biology, the offspring of a cross between two different strains, varieties, races, or species.

Imprinting In biology, an aspect of learning in some species, through which attachment to the major parental figure develops and social preferences become restricted to their own species.

Mutation A genetic change that can be transmitted to offspring as an inheritable divergence from previous generations.

Natural selection An evolutionary theory which postulates the survival of the best-adapted forms of a species.

Nucleus In biology, the compartment in a CELL bounded by a double membrane and containing the genomic DNA.

Organic Said of the compounds of carbon. These compounds are far more numerous than those of other elements and are the basis of living matter.

Orthogenesis The evolution of organisms systematically in definite directions and not accidentally in many directions; determinate variation.

Osmosis The diffusion of liquid from a more dilute solution to a more concentrated one, through the semipermeable membrane that separates them.

Ovipositor In fish, the tube extending from the genital aperture; in female insects, the egg-laying organ.

Paleontology The study of FOSSILs.

Parasite An organism that derives subsistence from another without rendering it any service in return.

Perennial A plant that lives for more than two years.

Phosphorescence In biology, the emission of light, usually (in animals) with little production of heat, as in glow-worms.

Photosynthesis The use of energy from light to drive chemical reactions, notably the building-up of complex compounds by the CHLOROPHYLL of plants.

Plankton Animals and plants floating in water, rather than attached to or crawling on the bottom; especially organisms with weak powers of motion.

Plasma The bounding membrane of CELLs that controls the interaction of cells with their environment.

Plastid Membrane-bound structure in plants or algae, outside the NUCLEUS but inside the CELL wall.

Polymorphism (1) The presence in a population of two or more forms of a particular GENE. (2) The occurrence of different structural forms at different stages of the life cycle of the individual.

Recessive GENE that shows its effect only in individuals who received it from both parents. Also describes an inheritable feature due to a recessive gene.

Recombination Reassortment of GENEs or inheritable features in combinations different from those of the parents.

Respiration Breathing: the exchange of oxygen and carbon dioxide between organism and environment.

Rhizome Underground stem bearing leafy shoots.

RNA, ribonucleic acid Nucleic acid containing ribose, which carries out DNA's instructions for making proteins, transferring information from the GENOME to the protein-synthetic machinery of the CELL.

Saprophyte A plant that feeds on dead organic matter.

Scavenger In biology, an animal that feeds on garbage or carrion.

Sex determination In many organisms (including vertebrates) sex is determined by a particular combination of CHROMOSOMEs. In mammals, the female's chromosomes are designated XX and the male's XY.

Spathe A large, often colored, BRACT.

Spore A single-cell asexual reproductive body, sometimes extended to other reproductive bodies.

Stoma A pore in a leaf or stem allowing RESPIRATION; *pl.* stomata.

Symbiosis Mutually beneficial partnership between organisms of different kinds, especially such an association where one lives within the other.

SKELETON AND MUSCLES

The adult human body is supported by a skeleton containing 206 bones. This bony framework also serves to protect delicate organs, such as the brain, heart, and lungs. At its core is the spine, which supports the head and ribs. The arms and legs are connected to this central axis by the shoulder and hips. The skeleton is moved by about 640 skeletal muscles attached to bones by tendons and ligaments. On receipt of signals from the nervous system, muscles contract, or shorten, causing bones to move.

Bone

Although heavier than most tissue, bone combines strength with relative lightness. Compact bone (1) forms a strong layer around lighter spongy bone (2) filled with marrow. Haversian canals (3) enclose nerves and blood vessels and run through compact bone, providing nutrients (4). A thin membrane (periosteum) covers bone.

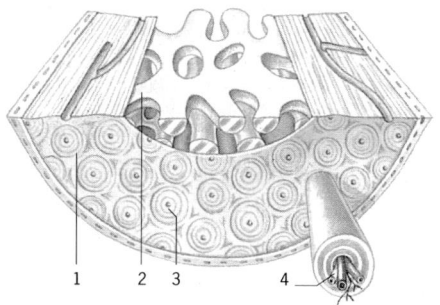

1   2   3   4

Joints

Where two bones meet there is a joint. In some cases, such as where the skull bones meet, the joint does not move, but in most cases joints are freely movable and are classified according to the type of movement they permit. Pivot joints, such as between the upper two neck vertebrae, allow rotational movement—in this instance a headshake for "no." Hinge joints, in the elbow and knee, allow bending in just one plane—backward and forward. Saddle and gliding joints in the hand produce the movements shown by the wrist and thumb. The ball-and-socket joints of the hip and shoulder allow movement in all planes. Joints are held together by tough straps called ligaments.

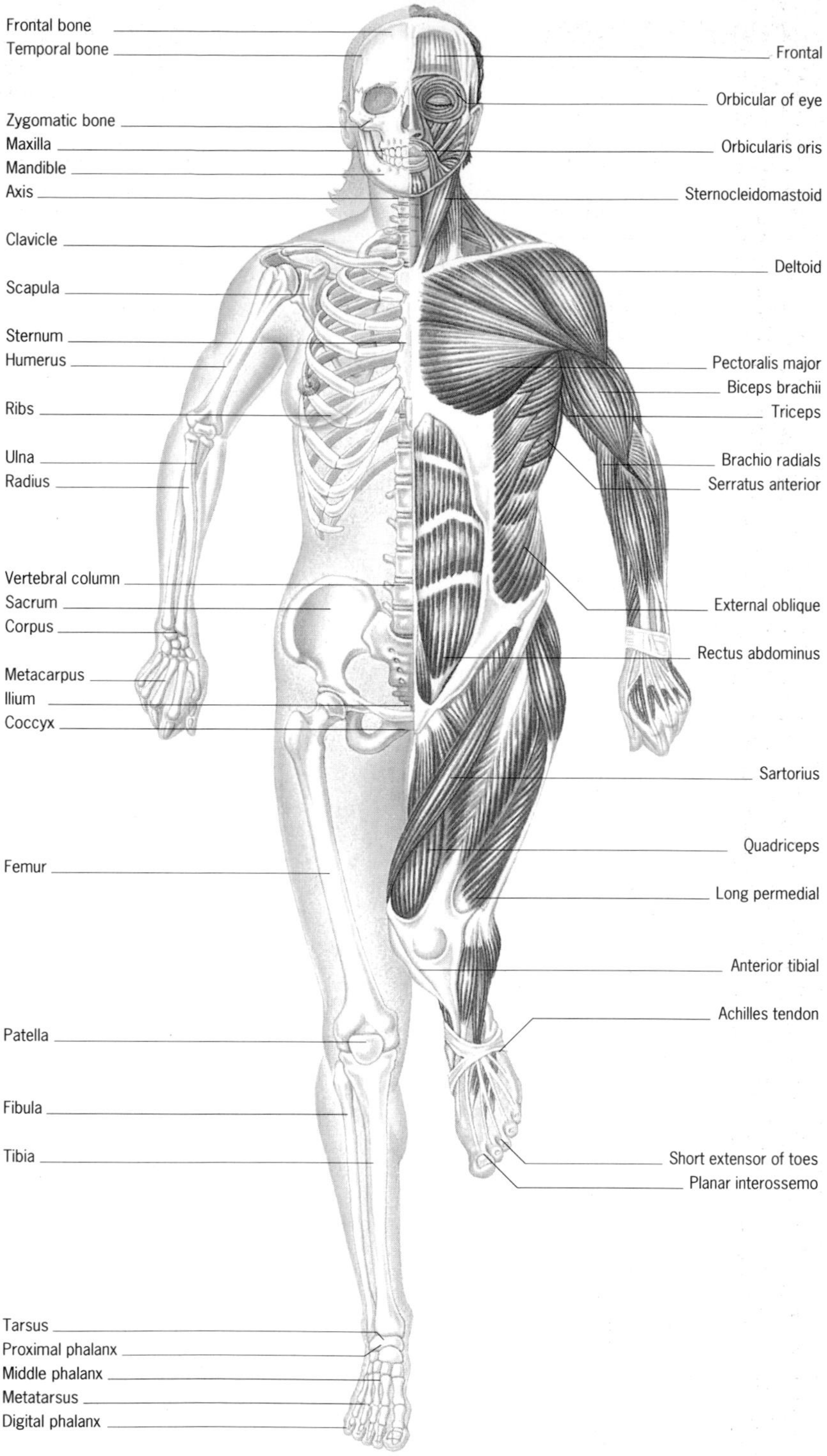

Frontal bone
Temporal bone
Zygomatic bone
Maxilla
Mandible
Axis
Clavicle
Scapula
Sternum
Humerus
Ribs
Ulna
Radius
Vertebral column
Sacrum
Corpus
Metacarpus
Ilium
Coccyx
Femur
Patella
Fibula
Tibia
Tarsus
Proximal phalanx
Middle phalanx
Metatarsus
Digital phalanx

Frontal
Orbicular of eye
Orbicularis oris
Sternocleidomastoid
Deltoid
Pectoralis major
Biceps brachii
Triceps
Brachio radials
Serratus anterior
External oblique
Rectus abdominus
Sartorius
Quadriceps
Long permedial
Anterior tibial
Achilles tendon
Short extensor of toes
Planar interossemo

Pivot joint

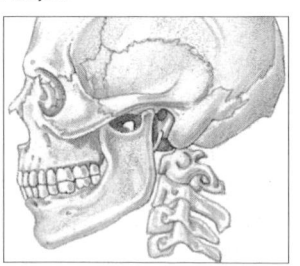

Hinge joint

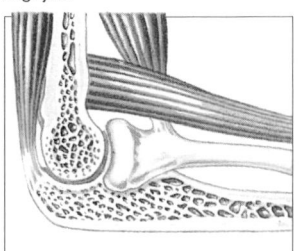

Saddle and gliding joints

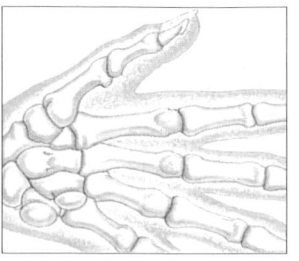

Ball and socket joint

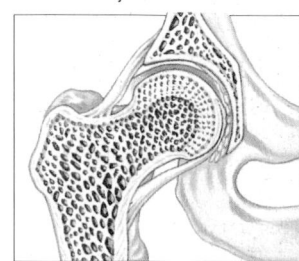

Back pain

The spine is a flexible column which supports the head and trunk and is held upright in its S-shaped curve by muscles and ligaments. It consists of 33 bones, or vertebrae. Between each pair of vertebrae is a cushioning disk. Back pain is caused by many factors, including bad posture, lifting heavy objects, and obesity. This may result in spondylolysis (1), where a damaged ver-

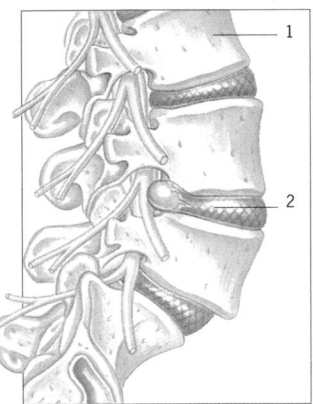

tebra slips over the one beneath it, or disk prolapse (slipped disk) (2), where an intervertebral disk ruptures, pressing on a nerve. Treatments for back problems include physiotherapy, chiropractic, acupuncture, Alexander technique, shiatsu, and osteopathy.

Sports injuries

Muscle strain (1) Pain, tenderness, swelling, and sometimes muscular spasms caused by stretching or tearing of muscle fibers. Common among athletes.
Shinsplints (2) Pain in sides and front of lower leg caused by muscle tears, or muscle or tendon inflammation. Common among runners.
Stress fracture (3) Broken bone resulting from repeated jarring. Common in runners who wear uncushioned shoes.
Torn cartilage (4) Commonly, damage to knee cartilage caused by twisting of leg.
Torn ligaments (5) Tearing of tissue holding joint together. Torn knee ligaments common among football players.
Torn tendon (6) Disconnects a muscle from the bone it moves. Normally caused by sudden, strong contraction of muscles.

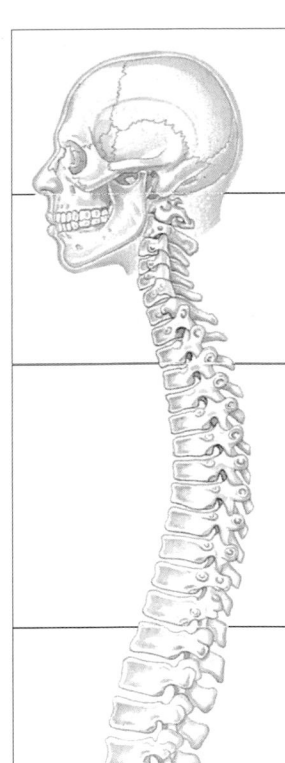

Fractures

A fracture is a break in a bone. Fractures are usually caused by an injury, such as a fall, that suddenly applies more force to a bone than it is able to withstand. Fractures are more common among the elderly, whose bones are more fragile. An X-ray examination reveals whether or not a bone is broken and which type of fracture has taken place. There are two main types of

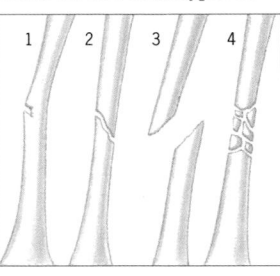

fracture: simple fractures (2), where the broken ends of the bone remain more or less in position beneath the skin; and compound fractures (3), where bone ends project through the skin. There are also various patterns of fracture. Greenstick fractures (1), in which the bone is not completely broken but is twisted, are relatively common in children. In comminuted fractures (4) the bone is shattered into numerous pieces.

Malfunctions

Achondroplasia Inherited condition, sometimes called dwarfism, where long bones do not grow normally, causing short stature.
Ankylosis Fusion of joint following disease or injury, causing its total immobility.
Arthritis Joint inflammation, with various causes, resulting in swelling, stiffness, pain, and possibly deformity.
Bunion Painful, sometimes inflamed, fluid-filled pad over joint at base of big toe.
Bursitis Inflammation of fluid-filled pad around a joint, causing pain and swelling. Often caused by prolonged pressure on elbow or knee joints ("tennis elbow").
Cramp Painful muscle spasm caused by prolonged over-contraction of a muscle.
Dislocation Displacement of two bones in a joint, often the shoulder or elbow.
Frozen shoulder Severe pain, stiffness, and limitation of movement caused by shoulder joint inflammation.
Gout Pain and swelling in a single joint, often in the big toe, caused by crystal deposits.
Muscular dystrophy Inherited disease causing wasting away of muscles, most common in boys.
Osteoarthritis Most common form of arthritis, resulting from wear and tear on joints, affecting spine, hips, hands, knees, and feet.
Osteoporosis Loss of the protein framework from bones, usually in later life, causing them to fracture easily. More common in women.
Repetitive strain injury Pain and stiffness caused by overuse of a part of the body, commonly finger and wrist joints in keyboard operators.
Rheumatism Any disorder causing stiffness or pain in joints or muscles.
Rheumatoid arthritis Severe form of arthritis caused by the body's immune system attacking its own tissues, commonly affecting fingers, wrists, knees, and ankles.
Sprain Tear of ligaments holding joint together, caused by sudden overstretching. Common cause is "twisting" the ankle.
Tendinitis Inflammation of tendon caused by injury or overuse.

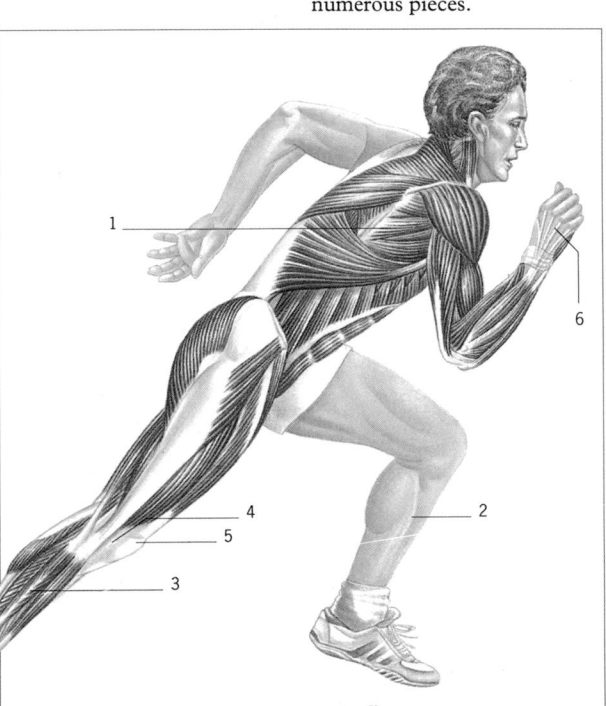

THE NERVOUS SYSTEM

The nervous system—brain, spinal cord, and nerves—controls and coordinates all body activities. The brain (*right*) is the control center. The cerebrum, divided into left and right hemispheres, processes incoming information and is responsible for thought, memory, sensation, and actions. Other parts include the corpus callosum, linking the two hemispheres; the thalamus, which processes incoming signals; the hypothalamus, which controls functions like temperature regulation; the cerebellum, which coordinates complex movements; and the medulla oblongata, which regulates heart and breathing rates.

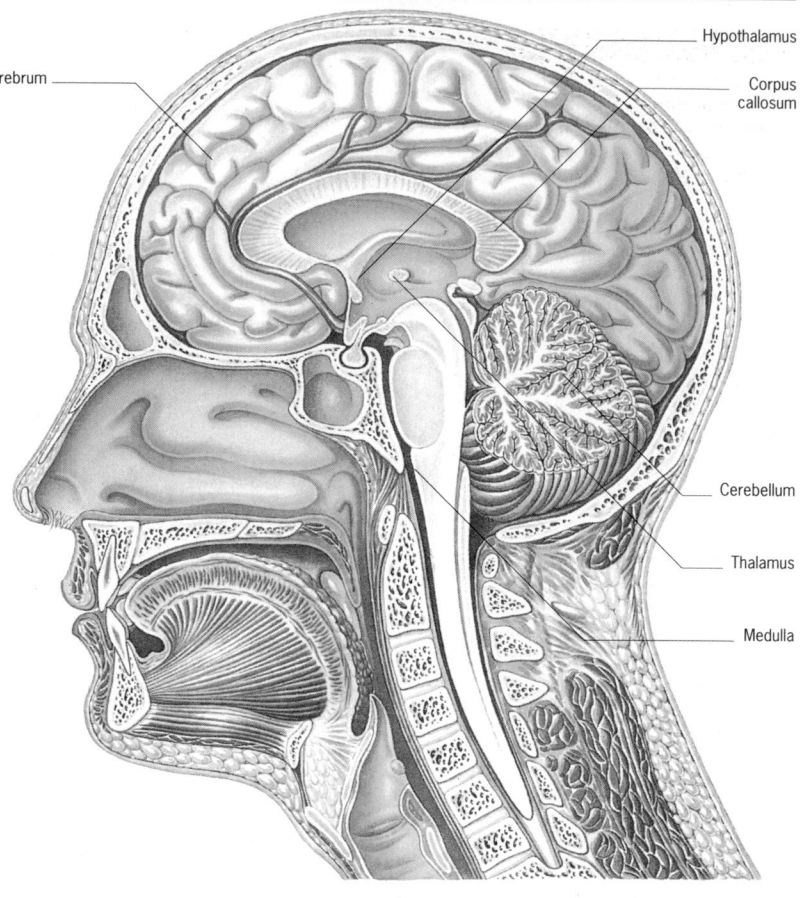

Cerebrum

Hypothalamus

Corpus callosum

Cerebellum

Thalamus

Medulla

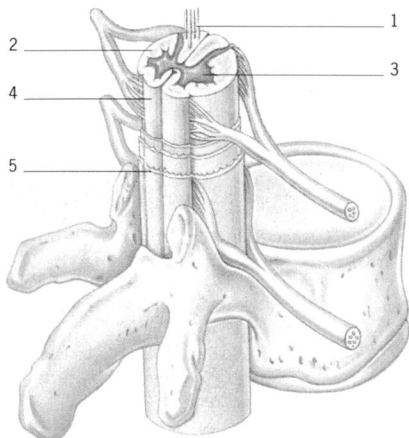

The spinal cord (*above*) links the brain to the rest of the nervous system through the spinal nerves (1). The spine is surrounded by three layers of protective membranes, comprising the dura mater (2), the arachnoid (3), and the pia mater (4), and runs through a tunnel formed by the adjacent vertebrae (5).

Reflex actions

A reflex is a rapid, predictable, involuntary response, such as automatically pulling your hand away from a flame (*below*). Reflexes are routed directly through the spinal cord instead of via the brain. The heat stimulates a pain sensor (1), which sends impulses along a sensory neurone to the spinal cord (2). Here an association neurone relays them to a motor neurone (3), which transmits them to an arm muscle, which contracts and moves the finger away (4). Meanwhile, a message passes to the brain, which registers pain after the finger has been moved.

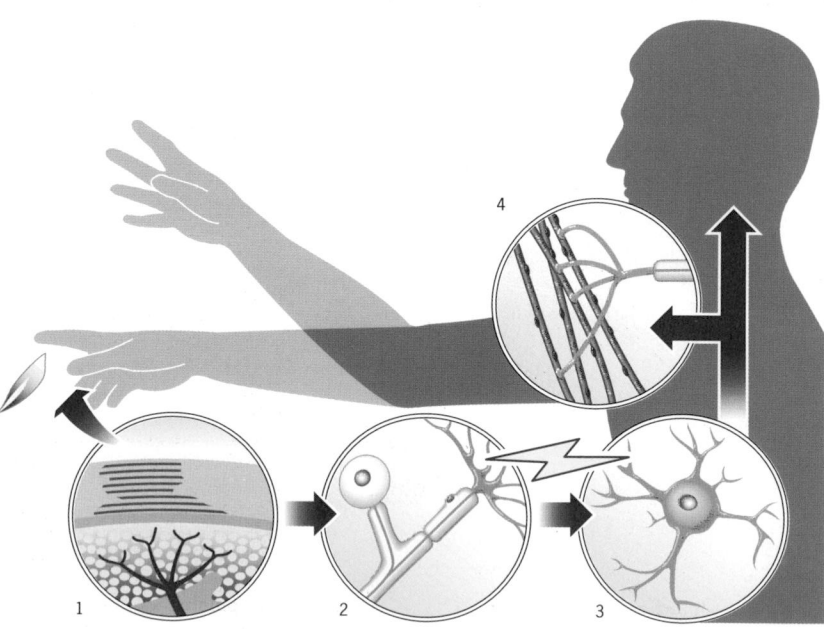

Malfunctions

Hemiplegia Paralysis of one side of the body caused by damage to the motor area of the opposite side of the brain.

Migraine Severe headache accompanied by nausea, vomiting, and light sensitivity.

Motor neurone disease Degeneration of nerves in the central nervous system that causes muscle wasting and usually death.

Multiple sclerosis Progressive disease of the central nervous system which destroys the protective covering of nerve fibers, causing numbness and muscle weakness.

Neuralgia Pain caused by inflammation or irritation of a nerve.

Paraplegia Paralysis or weakness of both legs and lower trunk caused by damage to the lower part of the spinal cord.

Quadriplegia Paralysis of the limbs and trunk caused by damage to the spinal cord in the lower neck region.

Spina bifida Defect in which part of the spinal cord of a newborn child is exposed because some vertebrae fail to develop.

Stroke *See* Malfunctions *p. 158.*

SENSORS

To be aware of and react to its surroundings, the body needs to monitor constantly all changes occurring around it. This job is carried out by its sensors. Stimulated by changes in the external environment, sensors transmit a constant stream of impulses along sensory nerves to the brain, where they are processed. The most widely distributed sensors are those found in the skin that detect touch, pressure, pain, heat, and cold. The other sensors— which provide the senses of sight, hearing, smell, and taste —are all located in the head. Special sensory receptors for each sense are localized in the eyes, ears, nose, and tongue.

Eyes

The eyes, which contain 70 percent of the body's sensory receptors, send information about changing light patterns to the brain along a million nerve fibers. Light enters the eye through, and is focused by, the cornea. The amount of light entering is regulated by the iris, the colored part of the eye, which controls pupil size. Fine focusing by the lens produces a sharp, upside-down image on the retina at the back of the eye. Impulses from the retina are relayed by the optic nerve to the visual cortex at the back of the brain. Here the sensory input is analyzed to create images of the outside world.

Ears

Sound travels through the air in the form of waves, like ripples in a pond. Guided into the ear by the shell-like pinna, they hit the eardrum at the end of the ear canal and make it vibrate. This causes the three tiny bones of the middle ear to vibrate and push the oval window in and out, setting up vibrations in the fluid-filled inner ear. These stimulate sensory hair cells in the coiled cochlea, which send impulses along the vestibulo-cochlear nerve to the temporal lobe of the brain to be interpreted as sounds. The cochlea can distinguish between high- and low-pitched sounds as well as loud and soft sounds.

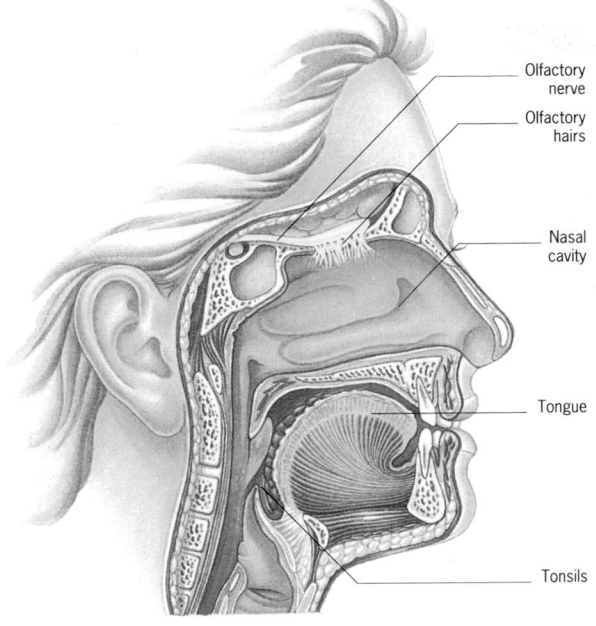

Olfactory nerve
Olfactory hairs
Nasal cavity
Tongue
Tonsils

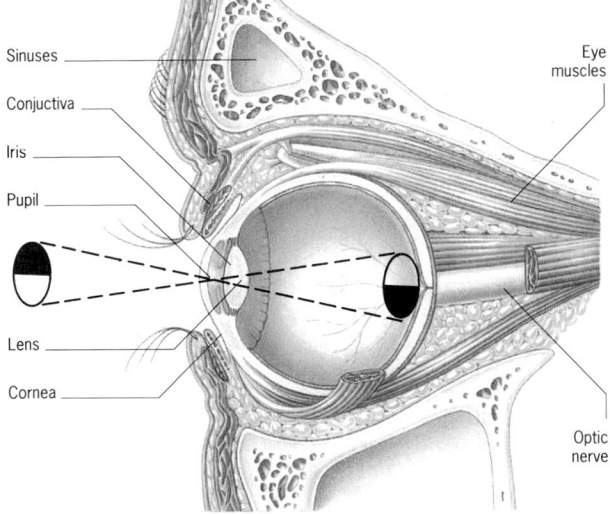

Sinuses
Conjuctiva
Iris
Pupil
Lens
Cornea
Eye muscles
Optic nerve

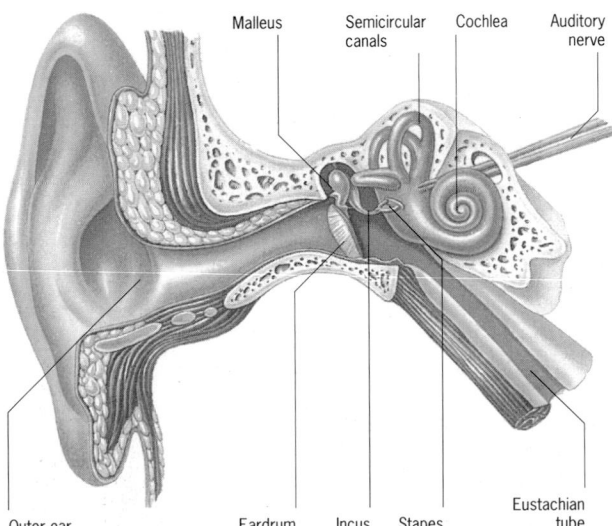

Malleus
Semicircular canals
Cochlea
Auditory nerve
Outer ear
Eardrum
Incus
Stapes
Eustachian tube

Tongue and nose

These provide linked senses of taste and smell, enabling us to discriminate between chemical stimuli, enjoying the pleasurable and avoiding the poisonous. The tongue is covered by small bumps or papillae, in the sides of which are groups of sensory cells called taste buds. These distinguish among four basic tastes— sweet, sour, bitter, and salty— and send the information to the brain. The smell sensor is in the olfactory epithelium— the lining of the upper nasal cavity. Here 25 million microscopic receptors detect inhaled odor molecules and send information to the brain. They can distinguish more than 10,000 different smells.

Malfunctions

Anosmia Loss of sense of smell caused by brain injury.
Astigmatism Irregular curvature of the cornea causing blurred vision.
Cataract Clouding of the eye's lens causing blurring of vision and loss of detail.
Color blindness Inherited defect of retina's color receptor cells, resulting in inability to distinguish between certain colors, usually red and green.
Conjunctivitis Inflammation of the conjunctiva causing discomfort and redness of eye.
Detached retina Separation of the retina from the back of the eye causing blindness if not treated promptly.
Glaucoma High pressure of fluid in eyeball causing loss of vision if not treated.
Glue ear Buildup of fluid in the middle ear causing deafness, usually in children.
Hypermetropia Also called farsightedness; inability to see near objects clearly because the eyeball is too short for normal focusing.
Myopia Also called nearsightedness; inability to see distant objects clearly because the eyeball is too long.
Otitis media Middle ear inflammation, common in children, causing earache.
Tinnitus Continuous ringing or buzzing in the ear.
Vertigo Disturbance of semicircular canals of the inner ear, producing an impression that a person's surroundings are spinning around.

BLOOD COMPOSITION

Blood is a liquid tissue that functions as a transport medium and a defense system. It consists of a mixture of blood cells floating in a watery medium called plasma. Blood cells make up around 45 percent of blood volume. Most are red blood cells that give blood its color; the rest are white blood cells and platelets. Plasma, which makes up the remaining 55 percent, is a straw-colored liquid consisting of 95 percent water with salts, proteins, and other dissolved substances.

Blood functions

Oxygen transport Red blood cells carry oxygen from the lungs to all body cells. Oxygen is picked up by hemoglobin, the red pigment that fills red blood cells.
Defense against infection Two types of white blood cells—neutrophils and monocytes—seek out and engulf any invading bacteria or viruses. A third type, lymphocytes, releases killer chemicals called antibodies that target specific disease-causing organisms.
Clotting Platelets are cell fragments that clump together at wound sites and release chemicals that cause blood to clot.
Waste transportation Plasma carries carbon dioxide from tissues to the lungs, where it is exhaled, and metabolic wastes from the liver to the kidneys, where it enters the urine.
Food transportation After being absorbed by the small intestine, digested food is carried in blood plasma to the liver for processing and then to all body cells.
Hormone transportation Hormones are "chemical messengers" carried in blood plasma from source to target tissue.

Blood groups

Each person belongs to one of four blood groups: A, B, AB, or O. Blood groups are determined by molecular markers or antigens on the outside of red blood cells. Those with A antigens are group A; those with B antigens group B; those with A and B antigens group AB; and those with no antigens group O. Blood transfusions should only be carried out if the blood groups match. If they do not, blood cells may stick together and block the recipient's blood vessels. Blood types are further categorized according to the presence or absence, irrespective of blood group, of the rhesus antigen (rhesus positive or negative, respectively).

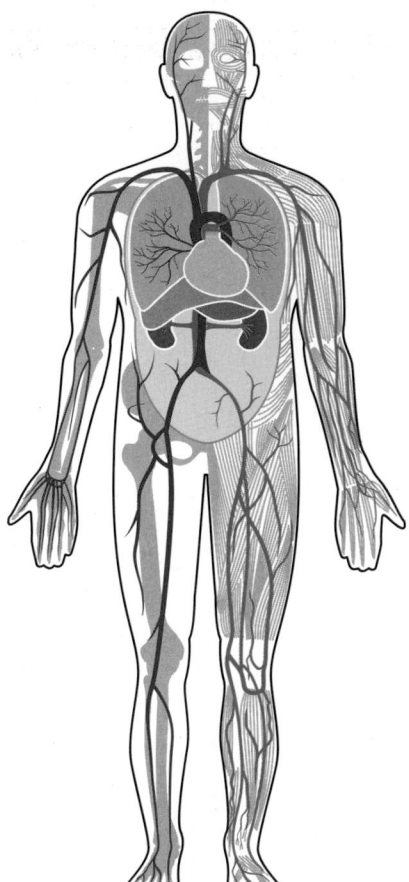

Circulation

The circulatory system carries blood to all parts of the body. At its core is the heart, a muscular pump responsible for pushing blood along the system of blood vessels that distribute it. There are two types of blood vessels. Arteries (red, left) carry oxygen-rich blood from the heart to all body tissues. Veins (blue, left) carry oxygen-poor blood in the reverse direction from the tissues to the heart. Linking arteries and veins is a massive system of microscopic capillaries that deliver oxygen and food to the tissues and remove their wastes.

The heart is divided into unconnected right and left halves, each side with a small upper chamber or atrium and a larger thick-walled lower chamber or ventricle. Oxygen-poor blood enters the right atrium through the vena cava—the large vessel into which all veins empty—and is forced into the right ventricle, which pumps it along the pulmonary artery to the lungs. Here it picks up oxygen and returns along the pulmonary vein, through the left atrium, and into the left ventricle, which pumps it out through the main artery, the aorta, which splits into smaller arteries that supply all parts of the body. Heart muscle is fatigue resistant, beating between 60–80 times per minute, nonstop, for a lifetime. Any interruption to normal functioning can prove fatal as it deprives the vital organs—especially the brain—of their essential oxygen.

Malfunctions

Anemia Tiredness and paleness caused by decreased level of oxygen-carrying red blood cells in the blood.
Aneurysm Bulging of the wall of an artery weakened by disease or injury. If a major artery bursts it is usually fatal.
Atherosclerosis Narrowing of artery walls by fatty deposits or atheromas, which slow or stop blood flow. In coronary arteries this causes heart attacks; in brain arteries it causes strokes.
Hemophilia Inherited condition in which blood fails to clot properly, causing sufferers, usually male, to have recurrent bleeding.
Hemorrhoids Varicose veins in the anus causing pain and bleeding on defecation.
Hypertension Constant high blood pressure leading to increased chances of stroke or heart attack.
Phlebitis Inflammation of a vein.
Septicemia Blood poisoning, often fatal, caused by toxins released into the blood by multiplying bacteria.
Sickle-cell anemia Inherited condition, found mainly in people of West African origin, in which abnormal red blood cells result in long-term anemia.
Stroke Damage to the brain through interruption of its blood supply. Body

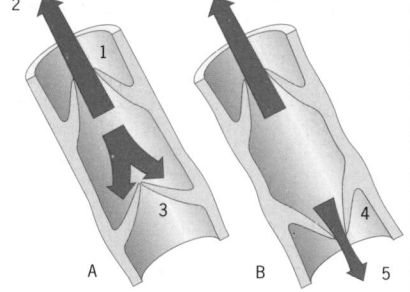

functions controlled by the damaged area are impaired.
Thrombosis Formation of a blood clot inside a blood vessel preventing blood reaching an organ. In arteries supplying the heart this can cause a heart attack.
Varicose veins Swollen or twisted veins, commonly bulging from the legs. Normal veins (A) have valves (1) that ensure that blood flows toward the heart (2) and stop it from draining backward by closing firmly (3). In varicose veins (B) the valves (4) are swollen and leaky so that blood flows backward (5) and accumulates. Varicose veins are more common in women and in people who spend long hours standing.

Heart malfunctions

Angina Gripping chest pain caused by reduced oxygen supply to heart muscle *(below)* as a result of blood flow impaired by coronary artery disease.
Coronary artery disease Damage to the heart caused by narrowing or blockage of the coronary arteries *(inset)*.
Coronary thrombosis Blockage by a blood clot of coronary artery already damaged by coronary artery disease, causing a heart attack.
Heart attack or myocardial infarction Sudden death of part of the heart, usually as a result of coronary thrombosis, commonly fatal.

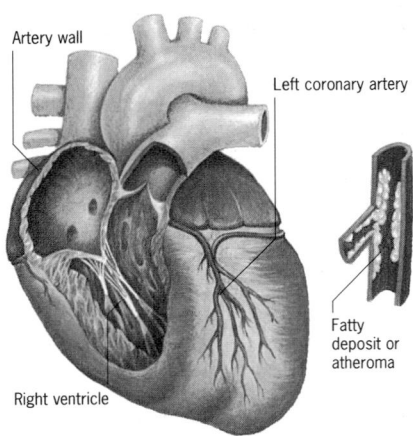

Artery wall
Left coronary artery
Fatty deposit or atheroma
Right ventricle

RESPIRATORY SYSTEM

The body's billions of cells need a non-stop supply of oxygen in order to release the energy from food that keeps them alive. This process has a poisonous by-product, carbon dioxide, which must be removed from the body. Oxygen is obtained from the air through the respiratory system. Air enters the body through the nose and mouth, then passes down the throat and through the larynx into the trachea or windpipe. The trachea splits into two bronchi, which enter the lungs and divide into smaller and smaller bronchioles. The smallest of these, which are thinner than hairs, end in tiny air bags or alveoli, of which there are around 600 million in the lungs. The surface area they provide for exchange of oxygen and carbon dioxide is equivalent to that of a tennis court. Inside the alveoli, oxygen moves from the air into the blood, while carbon dioxide is exhaled.

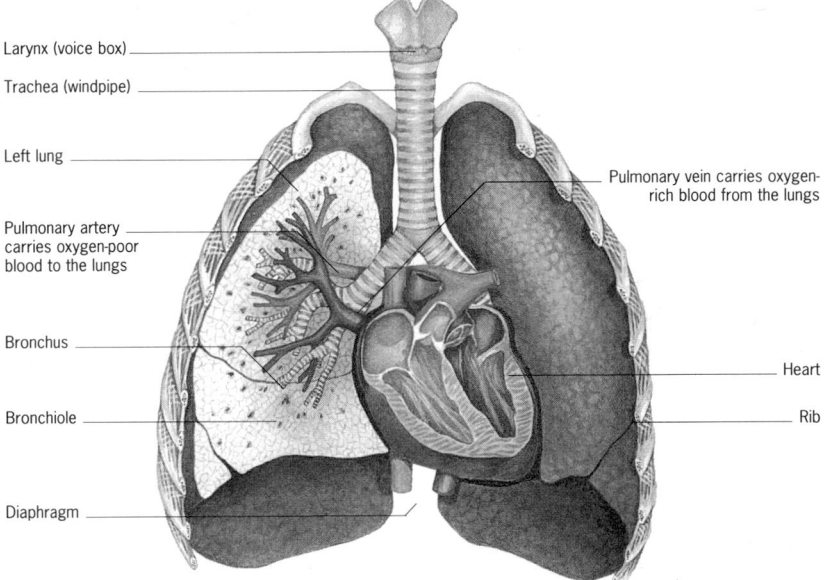

Larynx (voice box)
Trachea (windpipe)
Left lung
Pulmonary artery carries oxygen-poor blood to the lungs
Bronchus
Bronchiole
Diaphragm
Pulmonary vein carries oxygen-rich blood from the lungs
Heart
Rib

Coronary artery disease worldwide

Coronary artery disease leading to a heart attack causes one-third of all deaths in the United States and is the most common cause of death in most industrialized countries. Other developed countries such as Japan and Italy, and countries in the developing world, have much lower rates *(below)*. Of the risk factors—smoking, high blood pressure, a diet high in saturated fats, obesity, and lack of exercise—eating fatty food is believed to be the crux in the Western world, where nevertheless heartattack deaths have decreased recently, mainly because of health education, reduction in smoking, and improved medical care. But rates are increasing in some developing countries as they adopt more western lifestyles.

Deaths per 100,000 of population from coronary heart disease

Country	1970–74 Men	1970–74 Women	1980–84 Men	1980–84 Women
Australia	309	143	215	98
Costa Rica	76	57	100	70
Finland	314	115	238	100
Hong Kong	55	30	57	33
Italy	124	66	109	49
Japan	49	28	41	22
U.K.	259	109	239	99
Uruguay	188	106	131	64
U.S.A.	316	156	205	98

Breathing

Breathing, or ventilation, takes place to maintain a constant intake of fresh air (which contains 21 percent oxygen) to the lungs and to remove stale air (which contains 16 percent oxygen). Breathing is produced by the action of the intercostal muscles, between the ribs, and the diaphragm, a sheet of muscle that separates the chest and abdominal cavities. Contraction of the intercostal muscles pulls the ribs upward and outward, while that of the diaphragm flattens them. The result is to decrease pressure in the chest by increasing its volume, so that air is sucked into the airways supplying the lungs through the mouth and nose. When the intercostal muscles and diaphragm relax, the ribs move downward and inward and the diaphragm is pushed upward, resulting in an increase of pressure inside the chest, which forces air out of the lungs into the atmosphere.

This process of breathing is controlled by the medulla oblongata at the base of the brain. Normally the breathing rate is around 16 times per minute, with about 30 cu. inches (500 cm³) of air transferred. During exercise, however, breathing rate can increase to 25 times per minute, and the amount taken in with each breath to 180 cu. inches (3,000 cm³), to satisfy the body's increased demands for oxygen.

Malfunctions

Alveolitis Inflammation of the lungs' air sacs, often due to spore or dust allergy, causing breathing problems or coughing on exertion. For example, farmer's lung is caused by moldy hay spores.
Asbestosis Scarring of lungs resulting from inhalation of asbestos fibers causing breathlessness and, eventually, death.
Asthma Severe, possibly fatal, attack of breathlessness as a result of narrowing of airways in the lungs commonly caused by an allergic reaction to air particles, such as pollen, by exercise, or by stress.
Bronchitis Inflammation of the bronchi, which link the lungs and trachea, causing a cough with thick phlegm. More common in those who smoke or live in areas with air pollution.
Emphysema Severe breathlessness resulting from irreversible damage to the lungs' air sacs from smoking.
Hemothorax Accumulation of blood between lungs and ribs due to chest injury, causing pain and breathlessness.
Pneumoconiosis Severe lung damage in miners resulting from scarring of the air sacs caused by inhalation of coal dust.
Pneumothorax Chest pain and breathlessness caused by presence of air in the space between the lungs and ribs.
Pulmonary edema Severe breathlessness caused by fluid in the lungs.

DIGESTIVE SYSTEM

The body needs food to provide its energy and the raw materials for growth and repair. The body cannot use the food we eat, however, until it has been processed by the digestive system. That processing is carried out along the alimentary canal, essentially a tube more than 26 feet (8 m) in length. This runs between the mouth, where food is taken in, and the anus, where waste material is ejected. In between, food is broken down into simple molecules by special chemicals called enzymes. These simple molecules are then absorbed into the bloodstream so that they can be used by the body.

Teeth

Firmly fixed in the jaws by their roots, all teeth have the same basic structure. The central pulp cavity (1) contains a nerve ending, for sensitivity, and a blood vessel, to provide food and oxygen. Surrounding this is the bonelike dentine (2), which is covered on the top by white enamel (3), the hardest substance in the body. Tooth problems include: tooth decay or caries (4), where enamel is eroded by acid produced by bacteria; abscesses, where bacteria invading as a result of decay form a painful, pus-filled sac (5) around the tooth's root; and gingivitis, where bacteria create plaque (6) at the base of a tooth and inflame the gum.

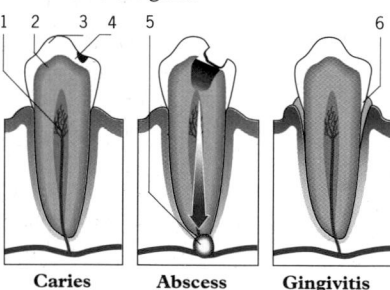

Caries   Abscess   Gingivitis

The alimentary canal

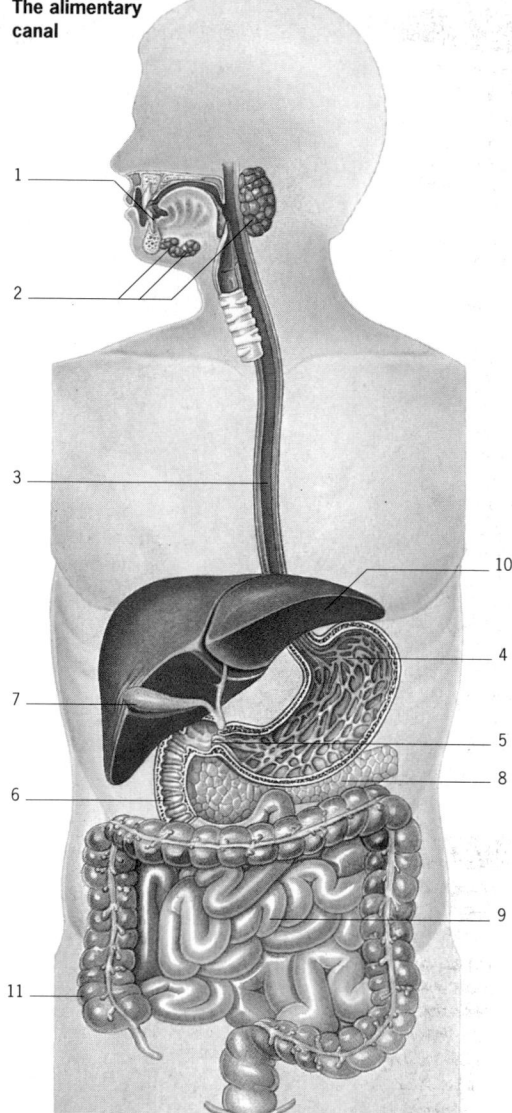

How the system works

1. Teeth Chop and grind up food into small pieces so it can be swallowed easily.

2. Salivary glands Squirt saliva into the mouth to soften crushed food and lubricate it with slimy mucus.

The tongue mixes the food with saliva, then pushes it to the back of the throat for swallowing.

3. Esophagus Carries food from throat to stomach.

4. Stomach Food is liquefied by the stomach juices and muscle action, and stored.

5. Pyloric sphincter Seals off the lower end of the stomach, but opens periodically to allow food to enter the duodenum.

6. Duodenum Here, in the first section of the small intestine, the main part of digestion begins.

7. Gallbladder Bile stored here is released into the duodenum to help digest fats.

8. Pancreas Releases a number of enzymes into the duodenum to aid digestion.

9. Ileum Digestion is completed here in the final part of the small intestine. Simple food molecules are absorbed into the bloodstream across the wall of the intestine and are carried to the liver.

10. Liver Food is stored or processed here.

11. Colon As indigestible food passes along the colon, water is absorbed back into the body.

12. Rectum Waste is stored here before being pushed out of the body through the anus.

The liver's digestive role

The liver, among its many other functions, plays an important part in processing food. Newly absorbed food arrives from the small intestine along the hepatic portal vein. Inside the liver, some food is stored, some is dispatched to other parts of the body, and some is made into other substances. The liver also manufactures bile, which helps digestion in the duodenum, removes drugs and poisons, and generates heat to keep the body warm.

Passage of food through the liver

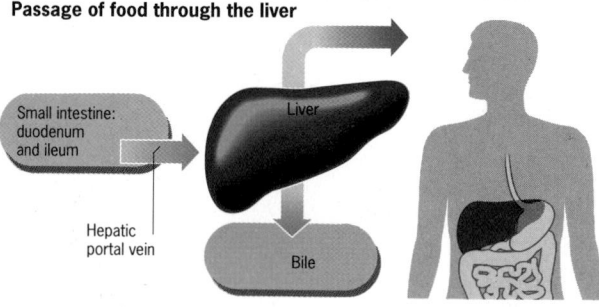

Small intestine: duodenum and ileum

Hepatic portal vein

Liver

Bile

Malfunctions

Appendicitis Inflammation of the appendix causing acute abdominal pain, necessitating its removal.

Cirrhosis Serious, possibly fatal, liver damage caused by internal scarring resulting from heavy drinking or hepatitis.

Constipation Irregular, often painful, passing of dry feces.

Diarrhea Passing very watery feces, often as a result of food poisoning or water contamination.

Dysentery Production of bloody diarrhea as a result of severe intestinal infection.

Gallstones Solid lumps in the gallbladder that cause pain.

Gastroenteritis Any inflammation of the stomach or intestines causing diarrhea and vomiting.

Hepatitis Liver inflammation caused by viral infection.

Indigestion Discomfort in the stomach area caused by eating too much or too quickly.

Irritable bowel syndrome Irregular bouts of abdominal pain, diarrhea, or constipation without known cause.

Pernicious anemia Type of anemia—lack of red blood cells—caused by failure of intestine to absorb vitamin B_{12} (*p. 171*).

Ulcers Open sores on inner lining of the intestine, especially the stomach, duodenum, and ileum, caused by acid gastric juices. Now often treated with antibiotics.

GLANDS AND HORMONES

The hormonal, or endocrine, system works in tandem with the nervous system to control body activities. The hormonal communications system that exerts this control consists of a network of endocrine glands. These glands release 20 different hormones, or chemical messengers, each of which affects particular glands or tissues in other parts of the body. Hormones are carried to their target tissues by the bloodstream. By attaching themselves to the cells' membranes in the target tissues, the hormones pass on their instructions.

Whereas the nervous system communicates rapidly using impulses transmitted along nerves, hormonal communication is slower and its results longer lasting. The most important of the endocrine glands is the pituitary gland, which is situated just below the brain. It secretes eight hormones. The pituitary gland itself is controlled by part of the brain called the hypothalamus. The effects of pituitary and other hormones are shown in the table below.

Endocrine glands (*right*)
1 Pituitary; **2** Pineal;
3 Thyroid and parathyroid;
4 Adrenals; **5** Pancreas;
6 Ovaries; **7** Testes;

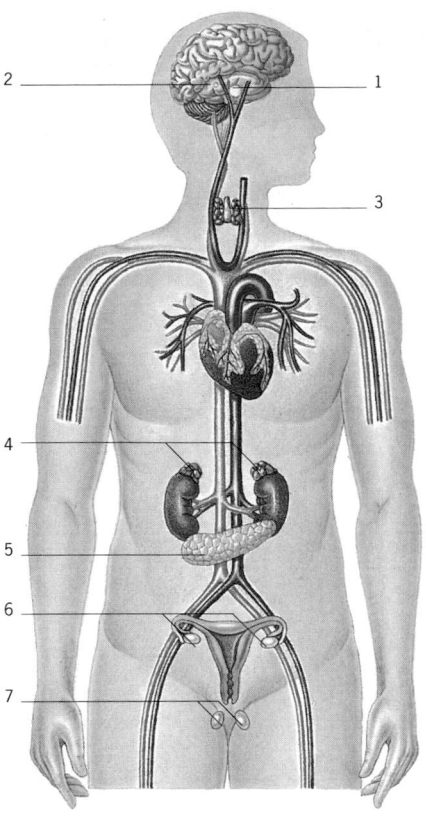

Malfunctions

Cushing's syndrome Overproduction of hormones by adrenal glands, causing a red "moon face," obesity, and humped back. Treated by removal of the glands.
Diabetes mellitus Normally, blood glucose levels are kept relatively constant by the hormone insulin. Where diabetes mellitus occurs, the pancreas secretes insufficient or no insulin. Blood glucose levels then remain dangerously high, requiring regular injections of insulin and controlled intake of carbohydrates.
Hyperthyroidism Overproduction of thyroid hormones, causing increased metabolic rate, irregular heartbeat, excessive sweating, and weight loss. It is treated by drugs or partial removal of the thyroid.
Hypothyroidism Underproduction of thyroid hormones, causing weight gain, tiredness, and hair loss. It may be caused by lack of dietary iodine and can be treated with synthetic hormones.
Pituitary dwarfism Lack of pituitary growth hormone during childhood producing short stature. It can be treated with growth hormone injections.
Pituitary gigantism Oversecretion of pituitary growth hormone during childhood causing excessive growth. It is commonly caused by a pituitary tumor, which can be removed.

The major hormones

Gland	Hormone	Target	Function
Pituitary	ACTH (Adrenocorticotrophic hormone)	Adrenal glands	*Stimulates production of adrenal steroid hormones.*
	ADH (Antidiuretic hormone)	Kidneys	*Reduces urine production to maintain water balance.*
	FSH (Follicle-stimulating hormone)	Ovaries and testes	*Female: stimulates follicle growth and estrogen production. Male: stimulates sperm production.*
	Growth hormone	Bone and muscle	*Stimulates growth and metabolism.*
	LH (Luteinizing hormone)	Ovaries and testes	*Female: triggers ovulation and progesterone production. Male: stimulates testosterone production.*
	Oxytocin	Uterus and breasts	*Stimulates contraction of uterus during labor and milk release in breastfeeding.*
	Prolactin	Breasts	*Stimulates milk production.*
	TSH (Thyroid-stimulating hormone)	Thyroid gland	*Stimulates production and release of thyroid hormones.*
Pineal	Melatonin	Hypothalamus	See *Seasonal affective disorder*, right.
Thyroid	Thyroid hormones	Most cells	*Increase metabolic rate; affect growth.*
	Calcitonin	Bone and kidneys	*Decreases calcium levels in the blood.*
Parathyroid	Parathormone	Bone, kidneys, and intestine	*Increases calcium levels in the blood.*
Adrenals	Adrenaline and noradrenaline	Heart, muscles, and blood vessels	*Increase heart rate, metabolic rate, and blood flow to muscles.*
	Aldosterone	Kidneys	*Controls excretion of sodium in urine.*
	Androgens	Ovaries/testes	*Affect sex drive.*
	Hydrocortisone	All tissues	*Affects metabolism; decreases stress.*
Pancreas	Insulin and glucagon	Liver, muscles, and adipose tissue	*Control level of glucose in the blood.*
Ovaries	Estrogen and progesterone	Uterus, reproductive system, and other tissues	*Affect development of female secondary sexual characteristics and sex organs; control menstrual cycle.*
Testes	Testosterone	Reproductive system and other tissues	*Affects development of male secondary sexual characteristics and sex organs.*

Anabolic steroids

Anabolic steroids are drugs that mimic the male hormone testosterone and have a protein-building effect. They are prescribed by physicians to help repair muscles following injury, but are also widely abused by athletes and bodybuilders to improve their strength and muscle bulk. Although there are increases in muscle weight and strength, anabolic steroids can cause, in men, liver damage, shriveled testicles, impotence, and, in the long term, heart problems. Men may also suffer from violent mood swings. Women steroid abusers develop male characteristics, such as a deeper voice. Despite attempts to stamp out steroid abuse, its use is still widespread.

Seasonal affective disorder

Seasonal affective disorder (SAD) is the term used to describe the tiredness and depression that often afflicts people during the dark winter months. It is the result of the secretion of the hormone melatonin, which is inhibited by the light but stimulated by the darkness in winter. This seasonal change in melatonin levels affects the body processes that show rhythmic changes—such as body temperature, sleep, and appetite. SAD symptoms can be alleviated with phototherapy—treatment with bright lights for about two hours each day. Long-distance flying also disturbs the melatonin balance, producing tiredness and disorientation (jet lag).

HUMAN REPRODUCTION

The reproductive systems produce the sex cells that fuse during fertilization to produce a baby. Mature men produce millions of tiny sex cells called spermatozoa, or sperm, every day. Women, in the years between puberty and the menopause, release an ovum, or egg, each month from their ovaries. Conception occurs when an ovum, released by the woman, is fertilized by one of the millions of sperm released by the man during ejaculation in sexual intercourse. The fertilized ovum develops into a baby inside the uterus.

The male reproductive system is closely associated with the urinary system. The bladder (1) stores urine, releasing it to the outside along the urethra (2), the tube inside the penis (3) that also carries sperm during ejaculation. Sperm are made inside the testes (4) and stored in coiled tubes called the epididymides (5) until, during ejaculation, they are carried to the penis along the sperm duct or vas deferens (6). The prostate gland (7), which is located where the sperm ducts

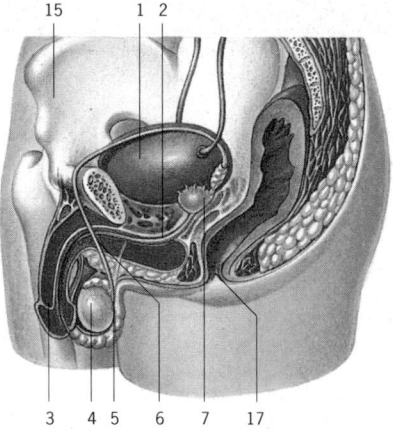

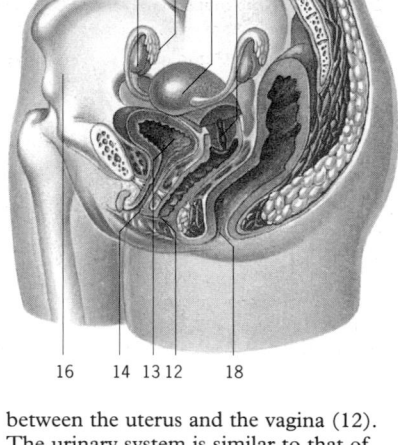

and urethra join, releases semen, the milky medium in which sperm are ejaculated from the penis.

Within the female reproductive system, a single sex cell, or ovum, is released each month from one of the ovaries (8). It travels along the fallopian tube (9) to the uterus (10). The neck of the uterus, or cervix (11), forms a narrow opening

between the uterus and the vagina (12). The urinary system is similar to that of the male, but the bladder (13) empties along a urethra (14) that is separated from the reproductive system.

Both male and female systems are protected within the pelvis (15, 16) and are in close proximity to the anus (17, 18), the lower opening of the digestive system.

Contraception

Contraception aims to prevent a sperm from reaching and/or fertilizing an ovum. The effectiveness of all methods—including so-called natural methods, such as the rhythm method and withdrawal, and various contraceptive devices (whose effectiveness is shown in parentheses) depend largely on how carefully they are used. The intrauterine device or IUD (98 per-

cent) fits inside the uterus and stops a fertilized egg from implanting. The diaphragm (98 percent) fits over the cervix and stops sperm from entering the uterus. The condom (98 percent) fits over the erect penis and traps sperm. The oral contraceptive or pill (99.8 percent) contains hormones that stop the ovary from releasing an ovum each month. Other newer methods include hormonal implants and "morning after" pills.

Sterilization

This is a permanent method of contraception that requires minor surgery. Male sterilization, or vasectomy, involves cutting and tying the sperm ducts to stop sperm leaving the testes. Female sterilization involves cutting or tying the fallopian tubes to prevent ova reaching the uterus. Sterilization is normally 100 percent effective and irreversible.

Coil (IUD)   **Diaphragm**

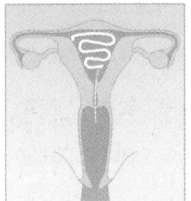 

Sponge   **Condom (female)**

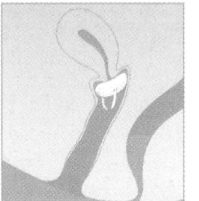 

Sterilization   **Vasectomy**

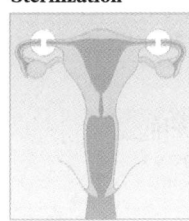 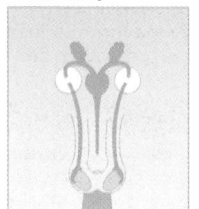

The menstrual cycle

This is the process whereby the female reproductive system prepares itself each month for possible pregnancy. The cycle is controlled by hormones whose levels vary during the month (*right*). Follicle-stimulating hormone (FSH) and luteinizing hormone (LH) released by the pituitary gland in midcycle cause a follicle inside one ovary to swell (1) and burst to release its ovum (2) at ovulation. The hormones also stimulate the ovaries to release estrogen and progesterone, which cause the uterine lining to thicken (3), ready to receive a fertilized egg. If the ovum is not fertilized, progesterone and estrogen levels fall and uterine lining and blood are shed (4) through the vagina, marking the end of the cycle. A complete cycle normally takes about a month.

The most fertile part of the month is the time of ovulation, around days 11–17; menstruation occurs around days 28–5.

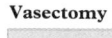

Days of cycle

| 1 | 2 | 3 | 4 | 5 | 6 | 7 | 8 | 9 | 10 | 11 | 12 | 13 | 14 | 15 | 16 | 17 | 18 | 19 | 20 | 21 | 22 | 23 | 24 | 25 | 26 | 27 | 28 |

LH

FSH

Estrogen

Progesterone

Diagnostic tests used during pregnancy

In addition to the routine tests carried out to check the health of the woman during pregnancy—physical examination, blood tests, and urine tests—there are a number of optional procedures that may be used to check the health of the baby.

Test	Time taken	Method	Purpose	Disadvantages
Chorionic villus sampling (C.V.S.)	6–8 weeks	Small sample of tissue that develops into the placenta is removed by inserting a tube in the uterus through the cervix and is sent for genetic analysis.	To detect genetic abnormalities such as Down's syndrome. If an abnormality is detected the woman may decide to terminate the pregnancy.	There is a small risk of harming the fetus and a greater chance (2%) of miscarriage than by using amniocentesis.
Doppler ultrasound scan	After 12 weeks	High-intensity sound waves, directed into the abdomen, produce an image of the fetus on a monitor.	To check movement of the fetus, including blood flow, to monitor the heartbeat to ensure it is normal, to check growth, age and position of fetus, presence of twins, and for abnormalities.	None—the test is believed to be harmless.
Amniocentesis	14–18 weeks	A needle is inserted into the uterus through the abdomen wall and a sample of fluid containing fetal cells is taken and sent for analysis.	To check for abnormalities such as Down's syndrome and spina bifida.	There is a risk of miscarriage in 1% of women. The results from amniocentesis may be too late to terminate the pregnancy.
Alpha-fetoprotein (AFP)	15–18 weeks	Blood sample taken from the woman.	Increased levels of alpha-fetoprotein in the blood can indicate abnormalities such as spina bifida.	Raised levels of AFP may be caused by the presence of twins. Further tests are required.
Fetal blood sampling	After 18 weeks	Needle inserted into uterus to take blood from umbilical cord.	To test for abnormalities indicated by other scans.	Slightly more risk of miscarriage than for amniocentesis.

Fetal milestones

12 weeks The fetus is 3.5 inches (9 cm) long and a human shape. Internal organs have formed, as have fingers and toes. Fetus can make a fist, swallow, and frown.
20 weeks 10 inches (25 cm) long, the fetus has fully formed arms and legs, and the woman can feel fetus moving. Teeth and hair are growing.
28 weeks 14.6 inches (37 cm) long, the fetus lies head down.

Sex determination

Sex is determined by two of the 46 chromosomes found in every body cell. Females have two X chromosomes; males have one X and one Y chromosome. Each sperm and egg only carries one sex chromosome (*below*). An egg fertilized by an X-carrying sperm will produce a baby girl; fertilization by a Y-carrying sperm results in a baby boy.

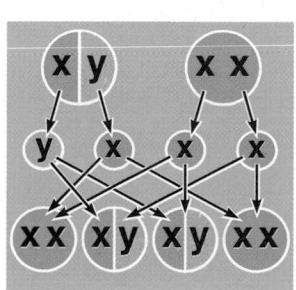

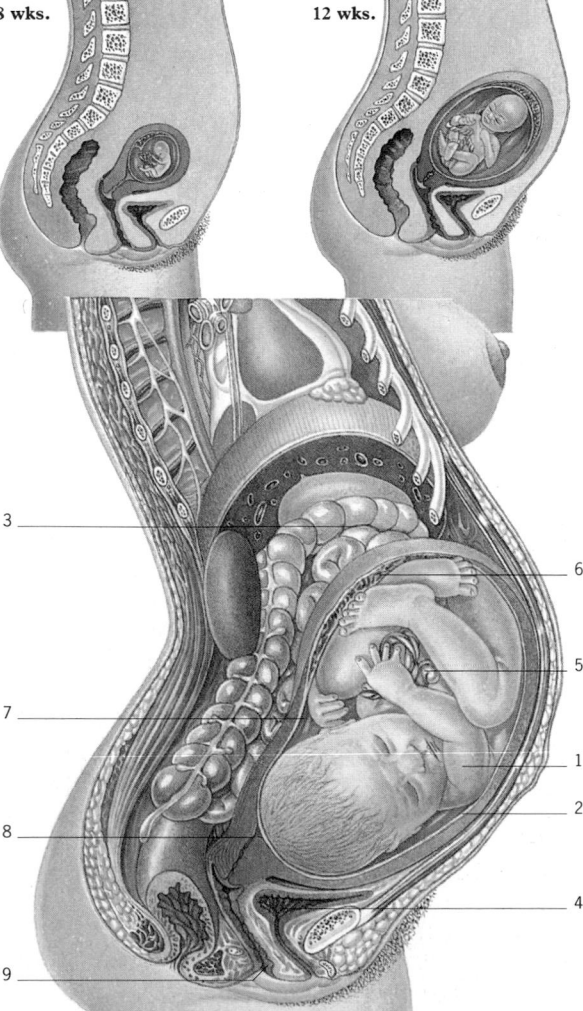

8 wks. 12 wks. 28 wks.

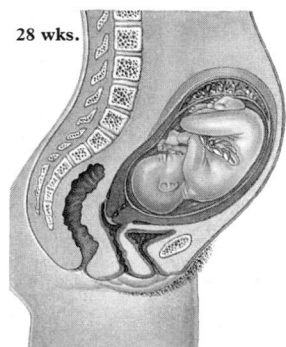

Pregnancy

This is the time during which a baby develops in the uterus. It begins when the fertilized egg implants in the lining of the uterus and ends with birth around 40 weeks later. At 38 weeks (*left*) the fetus (1) lies protected within the uterus (2), displacing other abdominal organs such as the intestines (3) and bladder (4). The fetus receives food and oxygen and has its wastes removed along the umbilical cord (5), which links it indirectly to its mother's blood supply through the placenta (6). The amniotic fluid (7) that surrounds the fetus cushions it against knocks. When the time comes for birth, the cervix (8) opens, the vagina (9) expands, and the uterine wall contracts to push the baby and placenta out.

Problems with reproductive organs

Below are some common problems associated with the reproductive organs.

Amenorrhea Absence of menstrual periods caused by hormonal imbalance, stress, or anorexia nervosa.

Cesarean section Surgical delivery that may be performed if the woman and/or fetus are threatened. This involves making an incision into the lower abdomen to remove the fetus from the uterus.

Dysmenorrhea Pain during a menstrual period caused by hormonal changes. Common in young women.

Ectopic pregnancy The fertilized egg implants in the fallopian tube, causing great pain as it develops. The embryo must be removed surgically.

Endometriosis Fragments of the uterine lining become embedded in other body parts, causing cysts and maybe sterility.

Impotence Inability of males to achieve or maintain an erection during sexual intercourse. It may have a physical or psychological cause or be the result of taking drugs or alcohol.

Ovarian cyst Fluid-filled growth, normally not cancerous, inside an ovary.

Pelvic inflammatory disease (PID) Infection of female reproductive organs that may follow abortion or infection with a sexually transmitted disease.

Sexually transmitted disease (STD) Disease generally transmitted between sexual partners as a result of contact between their sex organs. STDs include AIDS, chlamydia, genital herpes, genital warts, gonorrhea, nonspecific urethritis, pubic lice, syphilis, and trichomoniasis (*pp. 176–79*).

Vaginal tearing This may occur at the entrance to the vagina during childbirth. The doctor may attempt to avoid this by performing an episiotomy, an incision between vaginal opening and anus.

Infertility treatment

Infertility is the inability to produce children. Any couple who has attempted unsuccessfully to conceive by having unprotected sexual intercourse during the woman's most fertile times is deemed to have a fertility problem. Around 17 percent of couples require specialist treatment for infertility; of those 30 percent result from male infertility, 30 percent from female infertility, and 40 percent from infertility of both partners.

Male infertility can be caused by abnormal sperm production resulting in a low sperm count; blockage of the sperm ducts; or failure to ejaculate sperm into the vagina. Treatment of male fertility can involve changes in life-style, such as reducing alcohol intake; hormonal therapy; or surgery to unblock sperm ducts. If the male produces no sperm, the couple might consider artificial insemination (*right*) using sperm from a donor male.

Female infertility can be caused by a failure to release ova from the ovaries; blocked or damaged fallopian tubes; abnormalities of the uterus that prevent the fertilized ovum from implanting; problems with the cervix that block the entry of sperm into the uterus; or the production of antibodies by the woman that destroy sperm before they can fertilize an ovum. As with male infertility, female infertility may be untreatable. However, a number of treatments are now available.

Fertility drugs These are used to stimulate the ovaries to release ova.

Artificial insemination If intercourse is not possible, or the cervix is abnormal, the male's sperm are introduced into the uterus through a syringe.

Microsurgery This fine surgical technique is used to repair damaged fallopian tubes so that ova can travel normally from ovaries to uterus.

In vitro fertilization (IVF) If the fallopian tubes are blocked, ova are removed surgically from a woman's ovaries and fertilized by her partner's sperm in a culture dish. After two days the eggs are examined to see if they have been fertilized and are developing into embryos. If they are, several embryos are placed in the woman's uterus. This treatment has a success rate of 15–20 percent.

Gamete intrafallopian transfer (GIFT) A woman is treated with fertility drugs to stimulate her ovaries to produce ova. Ova are sucked from the ovaries through a needle, mixed with her partner's sperm, and are then injected into her fallopian tube. GIFT can only be used if the fallopian tubes are normal.

URINARY SYSTEM

The urinary system removes waste products, such as urea, as well as excess water and salts from the body. The renal arteries (1) carry 3,000 pints (1,700 l) of blood to the two kidneys (2) each day. Blood is filtered by fine tubules in the cortex (3) and medulla (4) of each kidney to produce around 2.6 pints (1.5 l) of urine, which is a solution of salts and wastes. After being filtered, blood low in wastes and containing the correct balance of water and salts returns to the circulation along the renal veins (5). Urine travels down the ureters (6) to the bladder, a muscular bag clamped at its lower end by a ring of muscle called a sphincter (7). The sphincter is under voluntary control and is released as necessary when the bladder becomes full. Urine flows out of the body along the urethra (8).

Malfunctions

Cystitis Inflammation of the inside of the bladder, more common in women than in men. Usually caused by bacterial infection, often by bacteria transferred from anus to urethra; its main symptom is a frequent need to pass urine.

Enlarged prostate Increase in size of the prostate gland, commonly found in men over 50, obstructing the urine flow along the urethra.

Enuresis Medical term for bedwetting. Common in up to 10 percent of five-year-olds. Usually caused by delayed learning of bladder control.

Incontinence Inability to control urination as a result of either injury or old age.

Kidney stones (calculi) Solid particles up to 1 inch (2.5 cm) wide that form inside the kidney from chemicals in urine. Kidney stones (*below*) can be small, or "staghorn" stones that fill the center of

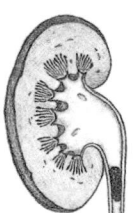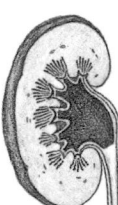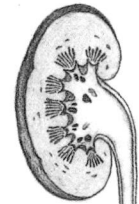

Ureter stone   Staghorn stone   Small stone

the kidney, or large stones that block the urethra. Kidney stones cause pain and difficulty in passing urine. Small stones might pass out naturally; larger ones can be disintegrated by ultrasound.

Pyelonephritis Kidney inflammation caused by bacterial infection.

Renal failure Reduced ability of the kidney to filter the blood, leading to build-up of waste products. The problem can be treated either by kidney dialysis or by transplant.

Urethritis Inflammation of the urethra resulting in pain during urination. Usually caused by infectious microorganisms.

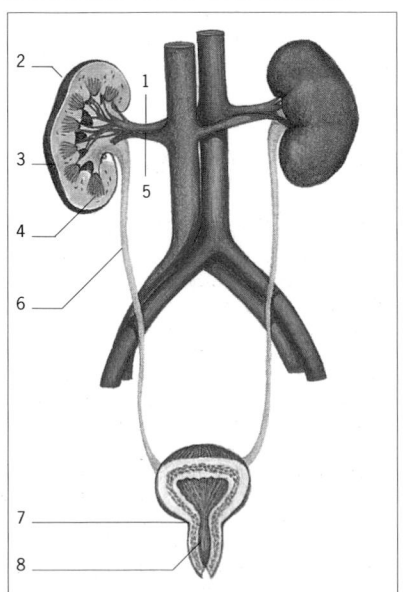

SKIN AND HAIR

Skin, the body's largest organ, has two layers. The outer epidermis provides a waterproof, germproof covering for the body that also protects against the harmful effects of sunlight. It consists mainly of dead, flattened cells filled with hard-wearing keratin. As the epidermis is worn away these cells are replaced from below.

The inner dermis contains touch sensors; sweat glands and blood capillaries, which help regulate body temperature; and sebaceous glands, which release oily sebum onto the skin's surface to keep it waterproof and flexible. There are also more than three million hair follicles from which hairs grow. Most of the hair is dead, filled with tough keratin. Only the base of the hair is alive, with cells that divide to push the hair out of the follicle. Underneath the dermis is a layer of fat for insulation.

Epidermis

Sensory cells

Dermis

Sweat gland

Fat cell

Hair

Sebaceous gland

Muscle

Nerve end

Artery

Vein

Baldness

Scalp hair is constantly falling out and being replaced. If this process is disrupted, it can cause baldness or alopecia. The most common form of baldness, male pattern baldness, is inherited. In affected individuals, the male hormone testosterone inhibits hair growth in parts of the scalp, with the result that lost hair is not replaced. Hair is lost from the temples and crown until the top of the head is covered only with fine "peach fuzz" hair. The only guaranteed cure for this type of baldness is castration, which removes the source of the testosterone. Recently, however, scientists discovered accidentally that minoxidil, a drug used to treat high blood pressure, causes hair regrowth in some balding men—although it was found that for continued growth minoxidil had to be rubbed into the scalp daily.

Body temperature

Skin plays an important role in maintaining the body's temperature in the range 97°F to 100°F regardless of the external temperature. If the body is too hot—during exercise or in hot surroundings—sweat glands (1) release sweat onto the skin's surface; as sweat evaporates the body is cooled. Skin capillaries (2) widen, allowing heat to escape from the increased blood flow. If the body is too cold, sweating stops and the skin capillaries (3) narrow, decreasing blood flow to reduce heat loss. Hair erector muscles (4) may pull the hair upward and produce goosebumps.

Skin color

Human skin color ranges from pale pink to dark brown. The pink tinge is the result of red blood flowing through skin capillaries. Skin darkness is produced by the brown pigment melanin released by melanocytes, cells in the basal layer of the epidermis. Melanin protects underlying skin cells against the harmful, potentially cancer-causing effects of ultraviolet light in sunlight. Dark-skinned people, who live in or originated from sunny climates, produce more melanin than light-skinned people. Melanin production is stimulated by exposure to sunlight, causing what we know as a suntan.

Nails

Nails (1) cover and protect the fingertips and help to pick up objects. They are made of the same dead material as hair. Nails lengthen from their roots (2) and grow about 0.04 inch (1 mm) a week. The cuticle (3) is the tight fold of skin that covers the root of the nail, where growth takes place.

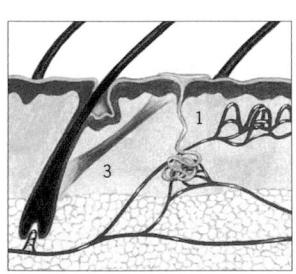

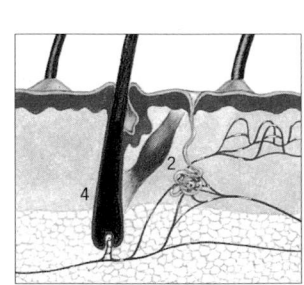

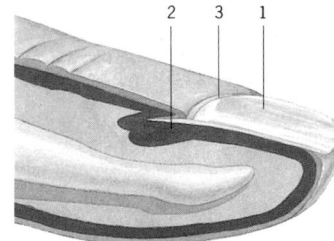

The skin as a sensor

The skin is as much a sensory organ as the eyes or the ears. Millions of microscopic sensors in the dermis respond to outside stimuli by firing impulses which travel along nerve fibers to the brain and help it to make sense of the surroundings. There are five types of sensors in the skin that respond to light touch, pressure, pain, heat, and cold. Their distribution is uneven. For example, the high concentration of light-touch receptors in the fingertips gives them enhanced tactile sensitivity. Sensors also alert the body to the presence of dangerous stimuli such as burning flames or sharp objects.

Malfunctions

Acne Blockage of hair follicles by sebum from infected sebaceous glands, causing inflamed spots on the skin's surface.
Albinism Inherited condition in which affected person lacks the pigment melanin that gives color to hair and skin.
Birthmark A pigmented skin blemish that is present from birth. They range from moles to large "port-wine stains."
Dermatitis Skin inflammation resulting from allergy or other causes.
Eczema Skin inflammation that causes itching and blisters. May result from an allergic response or be inherited.
Prickly heat Itchy skin rash of tiny red spots, associated with profuse sweating, arising in hot conditions.
Psoriasis Disease in which skin becomes inflamed and covered with silvery scales; extensive psoriasis causes discomfort.
Sunburn Skin inflammation caused by overexposure to sunlight. Repeated over-exposure increases the risk of skin cancer.
Urticaria Often caused by a food allergy, the condition causes itchy, inflamed weals on the skin. Also known as hives.
Vitiligo Condition, most obvious in dark-skinned people, in which patches of skin lose their color.

INTRODUCTION

The human mind is the totality of all conscious and unconscious mental processes that have occurred or are occurring in the brain. Mind disorders, from mild emotional disorders to severe illness, are studied and treated in various ways.

Psychology The scientific study of the mind and behavior. Psychology involves research into feelings, intelligence, learning, memory, perception, personality development, speech, and thought. Psychologists may also diagnose and treat mental, behavioral, or emotional problems through psychotherapy although, since they lack medical qualifications, they cannot prescribe drugs. Clinical psychologists hold a Ph.D. in psychology or a similar professional qualification.

Psychotherapy The use of psychological methods to treat mental, behavioral, or emotional problems such as neuroses and personality disorders. Treatment is based on the relationship between sufferer and psychotherapist. Following the framework of the type of therapy used (*right*), they talk about symptoms and problems in an attempt to find a solution.

Psychiatry A branch of medicine concerned with research into and the prevention, diagnosis, and treatment of mental illnesses. Psychiatry sees mental disorders as medical conditions. Psychiatrists are medically qualified and may use psychotherapeutic drugs to treat patients.

Psychotherapeutic drugs Used in the treatment of mental disorders, these can be very effective in the long- and short-term alleviation of symptoms, although some carry risk of dependence.

TYPES OF PSYCHOTHERAPY

Therapy	Focus	Treatment
Behavior	Modify unwanted aspects of an individual's behavior by substituting desirable responses for maladaptive ones.	Usually short-term therapy used to treat specific conditions including phobias such as agoraphobia.
Cognitive	Identify stressful situations that produce an individual's emotional symptoms.	Therapist gets individual to self-monitor by relating symptoms to stressful situations in order to change behavior in these situations.
Gestalt	Develop awareness of the whole personality by reenacting unresolved conflicts and by analysis of how one is feeling and behaving at the moment.	Takes place in a group setting but with therapist working with one patient at a time. Acting out dreams or conflicts in order to enhance awareness. Long-term analysis with one or two sessions each week.
Humanist/existential client-centered	Emphasize an individual's natural potential for growth and self-fulfillment.	Therapist does not interpret or modify individuals' behavior but instead empowers individuals to find solutions by exploring their own thoughts and feelings.
Hypnotherapy	Suggest behavioral change by setting reality aside and making use of imagery.	Therapist modifies behavior by making direct suggestions under hypnosis. Used to combat smoking, phobias, and psychosomatic illnesses.
Psychoanalytic	Make individual aware of how the past influences the present and how actions in the present can be used to correct the harmful effects of the past.	Therapist uses free association and analysis of dreams or early life experiences in order to boost individual's self-esteem and feelings of competence.
Reality	Clarify patient's values in order to evaluate current behavior and future plans and compel individual to accept responsibility.	Therapist helps patient develop awareness of the possible results of various courses of action, one of which the patient then follows.
Rational-emotive	Substitute realistic ideas for certain irrational ones—such as "I must be admired by everyone"—in order to produce emotional changes.	Therapist attempts to persuade the individual to adopt a more rational attitude by using a direct approach to dismantle or contradict his/her ideas.
Transactional	Empower individual to interpret his or her behavior accurately.	Therapist analyzes communications between individuals in a group, exposing destructive interactions or games.

PSYCHOTHERAPEUTIC DRUGS

Drug class	Reasons for use	Drug names	How they work	Possible risks
Antianxiety drugs	To reduce feelings of tension, nervousness, and anxiety if they interfere with a person's ability to cope with everyday life.	**Benzodiazepines:** alprazolam, chlordiazepoxide, diazepam, oxazepam **Beta-blockers:** nadolol, oxprenolol, pindolol, propranolol (*See also p. 183*)	Depress action of the central nervous system, promoting drowsiness and relaxation. Block nerve endings, stopping release of neurotransmitters, so reducing tremors, palpitations, and sweating.	Drug dependence and severe withdrawal symptoms; dizziness, drowsiness, impaired concentration. Breathing difficulties, cold hands and feet, tiredness, reduced capacity for strenuous exercise.
Antidepressant drugs	To treat serious depression by stimulating the nervous system to elevate the mood of a depressed individual.	**Selective serotonin reuptake inhibitors (SSRIs):** fluroxetine (Prozac), paroxetine (Seroxat), fluroamine (Faverin) **Tricyclics:** amitriptyline, clomipramine, dothiepin, imipramine, mianserin, trazodone **Monoamine oxidase inhibitors (MAOIs):** isocarboxazid, phenelzine, tranylcypromine	Elevate level of the neurotransmitter serotonin, so stimulating brain cell activity; also used in the treatment of the eating disorder bulimia nervosa (*p. 173*). Both tricyclics and MAOIs elevate the levels of two neurotransmitters—serotonin and noradrenalin—in the brain, so stimulating brain cell activity.	Nausea, nervousness, (rarely) weight loss, insomnia, headache; known as the "cleanest" of the antidepressants, SSRIs are favored for having relatively few side effects. Weight gain, blurred vision, dry mouth, dizziness, drowsiness, constipation, overdose may cause coma or even death. MAOIs can cause dangerously high blood pressure if taken with food containing tyramine: red wine, beer, cheese, pickles.
Antipsychotic drugs (major tranquillizers)	To treat abnormal behavior shown by patients with psychotic disorders involving loss of contact with reality, particularly schizophrenia.	**Phenothiazines:** chlorpromazine, fluophenazine, perphenazine, thioridazine, trifluoperazine **Butyrophenones:** haloperidol	Antipsychotic drugs block the action of the neurotransmitter dopamine, so inhibiting nerve activity in the brain.	Blurred vision, dry mouth, urine retention, drowsiness, lethargy, jerky movements of the mouth and face, involuntary movements of the limbs.
Other drugs	To treat manic depression.	**Lithium**	Acts on brain neurotransmitters to reduce extreme mood swings.	Dry mouth; overdose may cause blurred vision, twitching, vomiting.

DISORDERS OF THE MIND

Agnosia Difficulty in identifying familiar objects, caused by damage to the brain.

Alzheimer's disease Organic brain disorder characterized by increasing impairment of mental function because of nerve cell degeneration in the brain. Most common form of DEMENTIA.

Amnesia Dissociative disorder in which a person "loses" his or her memory and cannot recall any personal history.

Antisocial personality disorder Personality disorder in which a person fails to conform to accepted standards of behavior. Previously included people classified as "sociopaths" or "psychopaths."

Anxiety disorders Disorders with anxiety as the main symptom, including phobias, obsessive-compulsive behavior, and post-traumatic stress disorder.

Aphasia Organic brain disorder that affects ability to speak, write, and read.

Autism Disorder in which a child is absorbed in fantasy to the exclusion of reality and cannot relate to people.

Automatism State in which a person carries out actions without being aware of what he or she is doing.

Coma State of unconsciousness, often caused by head injury or medical trauma, in which a person does not respond to external stimuli.

Creutzfeldt-Jacob disease Organic brain disorder causing progressive dementia, then death, resulting from viral degeneration of the brain.

Delusional disorder Characterized by the sufferer having a fixed irrational idea, or delusion, not shared by others.

Dementia Organic brain disorder with a number of causes, which produces progressive decline in mental ability, affecting ten percent of people over 65.

Depression MOOD DISORDER characterized by loss of interest in life and feelings of sadness and hopelessness.

Dissociative disorders Disorders where one particular mental function becomes cut off from the rest of the mind because of emotional problems.

Dyslexia Reading difficulty experienced by child with normal intelligence.

Epilepsy Temporary disturbance of brain function characterized by seizures, or fits, caused by abnormal electrical activity in the brain.

Factitious disorders Disorders whose symptoms are identical to true illnesses but which are invented by the patient in order to get attention.

Hypochondriasis SOMATOFORM DISORDER characterized by a person's unrealistic belief that he or she has a serious disease despite a doctor's reassurance.

Impulse control disorders Disorders characterized by an inability to resist certain, often illegal, acts because they produce relief of tension or pleasure.

Kleptomania Impulse control disorder in which a person compulsively steals

objects he or she does not want or need.

Mania Disorder characterized by an abnormally high level of activity, irresponsible behavior, and a feeling of elation. The sufferer may also experience delusions of grandeur.

Manic-depressive illness Mood disorder characterized by mood swings from deep depression to great elation.

Mood disorders Disturbance where a person may be excessively depressed or happy, or alternate between these states.

Multiple personality DISSOCIATIVE DISORDER in which two or more distinct personalities exist within one individual.

Munchausen syndrome FACTITIOUS DISORDER in which a person's plausible invention of physical symptoms results in frequent hospitalization and even unnecessary operations.

Narcissistic personality disorder PERSONALITY DISORDER in which a person has a constant need for praise and an exaggerated sense of self-importance.

Neurosis Psychiatric disorder in which a person cannot cope with conflicts or anxieties and develops symptoms, such as depression, that distress him or her.

Obsessive-compulsive behaviors Anxiety disorders in which sufferers carry out repetitive acts (compulsions) because they are made anxious by persistent ideas (obsessions). Common compulsions include repetitive handwashing and checking (e.g. of locks).

Organic brain disorder Disturbance of brain function, either permanent or temporary, caused by degenerative disease, stroke, tumor, or drugs, and not of psychiatric origin.

Paranoia Delusional disorder where a person may feel he or she is being persecuted or have delusions of grandeur. Paranoia is accompanied by feelings of excessive suspicion and hostility.

Parkinson's disease Trembling, slow, unbalanced movements and depression caused by damage to brain cells.

Pathological gambling Impulse control disorder in which a person is unable to stop gambling, resulting in social or personal problems.

Personality disorders Long-standing disorders characterized by an inability to adapt to change or learn from experience, resulting in anxiety or depression.

Phobias Anxiety disorders resulting from an irrational need to avoid particular objects or situations (*right*).

Post-traumatic stress disorder Anxiety disorder that begins after a frightening or stressful event such as a disaster, violence, or war. Symptoms include disturbed sleep, recurring memories, guilt, and depression.

Psychoactive substance use disorder Behavior altered by excessive use of drugs such as amphetamines, barbiturates, alcohol, or cocaine (*p. 184*).

Psychosexual disorders Disturbances of sexual function resulting from various psychological problems.

Psychosis Severe disorder in which a person is out of touch with reality, with impaired thinking and emotions.

Psychosomatic disorders Physical disorders, such as asthma and headache, made worse by psychological factors.

Pyromania IMPULSE CONTROL DISORDER in which a person persistently succumbs to an urge to start fires.

Schizophrenia Group of psychotic disorders characterized by loss of contact with reality; disturbances in thinking, perception, and emotional reaction; and bizarre behavior. Hallucinations, in the form of voices and delusions, are usual.

Seizure or fit Uncontrolled electrical activity in the brain that may cause loss of consciousness. Recurrent seizures occur in epilepsy.

Sleep disorders *See* Sleep disorders, (p. 168).

Somatoform disorders Mental disorders with physical symptoms but without any organic basis, for instance hypochondriasis.

Tourette's syndrome Disorder in which the sufferer makes involuntary barks, grunts, and muscular jerks, and may have episodes of uncontrollable use of foul language.

Common phobias	
Fear of	**Phobia**
Animals	Zoophobia
Birds	Ornithophobia
Blood	Hematophobia
Blushing	Ereuthophobia
Cats	Ailurophobia
Closed spaces	Claustrophobia
Corpses	Necrophobia
Crowds	Demophobia
Darkness	Achluophobia
Dawn	Eosophobia
Death	Thanatophobia
Disease	Nosophobia
Dogs	Cynophobia
Everything	Pantophobia
Failure	Kakoraphiaphobia
Fears	Phobophobia
Fire	Pyrophobia
Flood	Antlophobia
Fur	Doraphobia
God	Theophobia
Heights	Acrophobia
Insanity	Lyssophobia
Insects	Entomophobia
Light	Photophobia
Men	Androphobia
Mice	Musophobia
Needles	Belonephobia
Newness	Neophobia
Open spaces	Agoraphobia
Responsibility	Hypegiaphobia
Sleep	Hypnophobia
Smothering	Pnigerophobia
Snakes	Ophidiophobia
Spiders	Arachnophobia
Stings	Cnidophobia
Strangers	Xenophobia
Thirteen	Triskaidekaphobia
Thunder	Brontophobia
Touch	Haphephobia
Travel	Hodophobia
Water	Hydrophobia
Wind	Anemophobia
Women	Gynophobia
Work	Ergasiophobia
Worms	Helminthophobia

WHAT IS SLEEP?

Sleep is a state of altered consciousness and not a "turning off" of the brain. Although sleep appears to be the opposite of wakefulness, the two states have a lot in common. Thinking and memory are active in both states, and a sleeping person is sensitive to external stimuli, as evinced by the immediate response of sleeping parents to their crying baby. Studies of sleep deprivation have shown that sleep is a fundamental need that humans cannot do without. The brain needs periods of sleep in order to rest, repair itself, and process information received during periods of wakefulness.

Sleep patterns

The brain produces electrical impulses or brain waves that can be detected using electroencephalography (EEG). Studies using EEG from the 1950s onward showed from the patterns of brain waves that sleep can be divided into two distinct states which alternate in cycles of around 90 minutes throughout the sleep period. The chart (below) shows how a sleeper passes repeatedly through these two states, about every 90 minutes, during an eight-hour sleep period.

The first state is nonrapid eye movement (NREM) sleep, which takes up about 80 percent of the sleep period. During NREM sleep, the sleeper becomes relaxed and drifts into deeper and deeper sleep. The depth of NREM sleep is measured in four stages of progressively greater depth. Stage 4 is the "deepest," when body metabolism is lowest and brain activity least. Dreaming does not occur during NREM sleep.

After 60–90 minutes, the second stage of sleep begins. The brain becomes more active, with wave patterns resembling those of an awake person; temperature and blood flow increase; and the eyes move around beneath the closed eyelids, giving this sleeping state its name of rapid eye movement (REM) sleep. Dreaming takes place during REM sleep.

The first REM period lasts for about 5–10 minutes but, as the chart shows, the length of REM periods increases as sleep

continues. Deep NREM sleep is believed to be the time when the brain rests and repairs itself; REM sleep is when the brain analyzes the day's events and sorts out emotional problems. Some researchers believe REM sleep not to be sleep at all but a third state of existence in addition to sleep and wakefulness.

Duration of sleep

Sleep occupies around one-third of a person's life, although the hours we sleep decrease as we age. A one-year-old child sleeps for about 14 hours each day, while a five-year-old needs around 12 hours. About 90 percent of adults sleep for 6–9 hours per night, with most people sleeping 7.5–8 hours. Less than 6 hours' sleep a night generally leads to daytime sleepiness. Elderly people tend to sleep less at night but doze during the day.

Dreams

Dreams are the result of mental activity during REM sleep. They are believed to represent the processing of all the thoughts and stimuli that have occurred to a person during the day. They may also form part of the process whereby short-term memories are assimilated into long-term memory storage. Many psychiatrists believe that dream analysis can reveal emotional conflicts.

Sleep disorders

Sleep disorders can disrupt normal daytime functioning or cause sleepiness.
Insomnia Difficulty in falling, or staying, asleep. Around 30 percent of adults suffer from insomnia at some time in their lives. The main cause is stress, although other causes include lack of exercise and misuse of drugs. Research indicates that insomniacs actually sleep more than they think but wake more often than normal. Remedies include reducing stress levels; having more exercise; developing a regular sleeping routine; and avoiding coffee late at night. Sleep-inducing drugs are only prescribed if these remedies fail.
Jet lag Disruption of normal body rhythms caused by long-distance flying

across time zones. The normal sleeping cycle is disrupted and the sufferer wants to sleep during the day and stays awake at night. Other symptoms include tiredness and reduced mental ability. Adjustment occurs within a few days.
Narcolepsy Difficulty in staying awake during the day. Characterized by sudden uncontrollable episodes of sleeping that occur several times a day. They may last for seconds or, in severe cases, up to an hour. Sufferers may also experience sleep paralysis. Narcolepsy happens when the sufferer goes into an REM state during the day; he or she may lose muscle control, collapse, and suffer hallucinations.
Nightmares Frightening, vivid dreams experienced during REM sleep. The sleeper awakens with a clear memory of the nightmare. Nightmares are common, especially in children and in adults who have suffered traumatic experiences.
Night terror Sudden waking up with a feeling of fear, experienced mainly by children, during NREM sleep. The child usually wakes screaming, drowsy, and confused but soon falls back to sleep and retains no memory of the event.
Sleep apnea Periods when a person stops breathing for ten seconds or more during sleep. It can be caused by throat muscles being too relaxed or by the brain failing to send out a "breathe" instruction. Sufferers are not aware of the condition but feel sleepy and underperform the next day. In older sufferers the condition can be serious, resulting in high blood pressure, heart attacks, or stroke.
Sleep deprivation Lack of the normal amount of sleep usually enforced as a form of torture. Causes drowsiness, lack of concentration, and hallucinations.
Sleep paralysis Frightening sensation, sometimes accompanied by hallucinations, caused by a temporary inability to move the body at the point of falling asleep or waking up. Occurs most often in people with narcolepsy.
Sleepwalking Characterized by getting out of bed while still asleep and walking around (during NREM sleep). A sleepwalking individual should not be woken but should be guided back to bed.

Sleep-inducing drugs

These drugs are prescribed for people with persistent insomnia affecting everyday life. They depress the part of the brain that keeps you awake, inducing a period of sleep that has more light sleep (NREM stages 1 and 2) but less deep (NREM stages 3 and 4) and dream (REM) sleep. These drugs are useful in establishing a sleep pattern when all else has failed, but long term they can cause addiction so need to be used with care. Sleep-inducing drugs include:
Chloral hydrate; Nitrazepam; Chlormethiazole; Promethazine; Dichloralphenazone; Temazepam; Flurazepam; Triazolam.

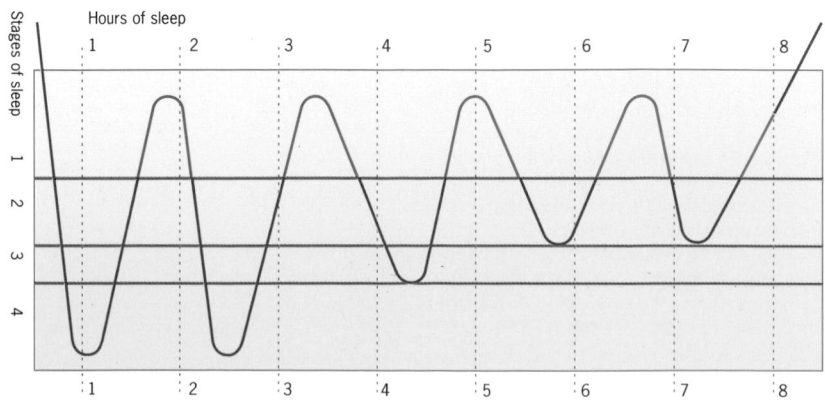

FOOD COMPOSITION

Food is a complex mixture of nutrients required by the body to provide it with energy and the materials needed for the growth and repair of cells, tissues, and organs. Nutrients are divided into two main groups: macronutrients and micronutrients.

Macronutrients, which are needed in large quantities by the body, include carbohydrates, fats, and proteins. They are broken down into simple molecules by the digestive system (p, 161). These simple molecules are absorbed into the body: some are broken down further to release energy; others are reassembled into large molecules often used for structural purposes.

- Carbohydrates supply the energy needed to fuel metabolism —all the life processes going on inside body cells.
- Fats, like carbohydrates, act as an energy store as well as providing insulating fat tissue and are a vital part of the membrane of the body's cells.
- Proteins are broken down during digestion into simpler molecules called amino acids. These form the building blocks of new proteins that are used to build and maintain the tissues, and they also make the enzymes that control the processes of metabolism.

Micronutrients, only required in very small quantities by the body, are vitamins and minerals (pp. 170-71).

Fiber and **water** are the two remaining components of food. Fiber is tough, indigestible material found in plant foods. It encourages the expulsion of feces—undigested food and waste— and is thought to protect against certain diseases including bowel cancer. Health authorities currently encourage people to increase their fiber intake by eating more fruit and vegetables.

Water makes up around 60 percent of body weight, although this varies widely according to age and lifestyle. Because it is lost in biochemical processes as well as by sweating, breathing out, and in urine and feces, water must be replaced. All foods contain water, especially fruits such as oranges and cucumbers.

The human diet needs to be balanced (below) to provide sufficient protein and energy—without too much fat, especially saturated fat. A balanced, varied diet should also provide all the vitamins, minerals, and fiber needed for a healthy life.

Recommended balance of macronutrients

Nutrient	Main sources	Balance
Carbohydrates	Fruits, vegetables, cereals, rice, bread, pasta, potatoes.	58%
Fats		max. 30%
Saturated:	Meat, dairy products, coconut oil.	*(max. 10%)*
Unsaturated and polyunsaturated:	Oily fish, walnuts, corn, vegetable oils.	*(max. 20%)*
Proteins	Meat, poultry, cereals, legumes, fish, milk, cheese, eggs, bread.	12%

Composition of selected foods

[Cals. = kilocalories; Prot. = protein; Carbs. = carbohydrates.] Approximate values given are for 100 g of the food named.

Food	Cals.	Prot. (g)	Carbs. (g)	Fat (g)	Fiber (g)	Food	Cals.	Prot. (g)	Carbs. (g)	Fat (g)	Fiber (g)
almonds	564	19	20	54	15	lamb chop, boned, broiled	353	24	0	29	0
apples	38	trace	15	trace	2	leeks, cooked	25	1	7	0	4
apricots, raw	25	1	13	trace	2	lentils, cooked	106	8	19	trace	4
asparagus, cooked	18	2	4	trace	1	lettuce, raw	12	1	3	trace	1
avocados	221	2	6	16	2	liver, cooked	254	20	6	13	0
bacon, broiled	308	16	2	27	0	lobster, cooked	119	20	trace	3	0
bananas	85	1	22	trace	2	mackerel, cooked	188	25	0	11	0
beans, dried white, cooked	118	8	21	7	25	margarine	730	trace	1	80	0
beans, green, cooked	25	2	5	trace	4	melon, honeydew	21	1	5	trace	1
beef, broiled	218	30	0	12	0	milk, cow's, skim	36	4	5	trace	0
beets, cooked	43	1	7	trace	2	milk, cow's, whole	65	4	5	4	0
blackberries, raw	29	1	13	1	7	mushrooms, raw	14	3	4	trace	2
blackcurrants	29	2	14	trace	9	mussels, cooked	86	17	0	1	0
brazil nuts, raw	618	14	11	67	9	nectarines	64	1	17	trace	2
bread, white	232	10	58	2	3	oatmeal, cooked	399	2	10	1	7
bread, wholewheat	216	10	55	3	9	oil, vegetable	900	0	0	100	0
broccoli, cooked	26	3	5	trace	4	onions, raw	38	2	9	trace	1
brussels sprouts, cooked	18	4	6	trace	3	oranges, raw	49	1	12	trace	2
butter, salted	740	1	trace	82	0	parsnip, cooked	50	1	17	trace	4
cabbage, raw	25	2	5	trace	3	pasta, dry	353	12	71	2	4
carrots, cooked	20	1	5	trace	3	peaches, raw	38	1	8	trace	1
carrots, raw	25	1	6	trace	3	peanuts, fresh	571	26	19	48	8
cauliflower, cooked	22	2	4	trace	2	pears, raw	61	1	15	trace	2
celery, raw	36	1	2	trace	2	peas, fresh, cooked	54	5	4	trace	5
cheese, Cheddar	414	25	2	32	0	pepper, red, raw	20	1	7	trace	1
cheese, cottage	96	17	2	4	0	pineapple, raw	46	trace	14	trace	1
cheese, Edam	314	30	trace	23	0	pork chop, boned, broiled	328	28	0	24	0
cherries	70	1	17	trace	1	potato chips	517	6	40	37	11
chicken, meat only, roast	142	19	0	4	0	potatoes, baked in skin	86	3	21	trace	2
chocolate bar, plain	510	4	63	29	0	potatoes, boiled in skin	75	2	17	trace	2
cod, cooked	94	19	0	1	0	prunes, raw	136	1	77	trace	14
cookies, chocolate chip	512	5	60	30	*	raisins	246	3	77	trace	7
corn (on the cob)	91	3	21	1	5	raspberries, raw	25	1	14	1	7
crab, cooked	129	18	1	5	0	rice, brown, cooked	129	3	26	1	1
cream, heavy	446	2	3	48	0	rutabaga, cooked	18	1	4	trace	3
cucumber, raw	15	1	3	trace	trace	salmon, cooked	196	20	0	13	0
dates	214	2	73	1	7	shrimp, cooked	107	18	0	1	0
eggplant, cooked	14	1	4	trace	2	spinach, cooked	23	3	4	trace	6
egg, boiled	163	13	1	12	0	strawberries, raw	37	1	8	1	2
figs, dried	214	4	69	1	19	sugar	394	0	100	0	0
flour, white	350	9	80	1	4	tomatoes, raw	14	1	5	trace	1
graham crackers	393	7	71	7	*	tuna, canned in brine	118	28	0	1	0
grapefruit	41	1	11	trace	trace	turkey, meat only, roast	140	36	0	3	0
grapes	69	1	16	1	1	walnuts	525	15	16	64	5
haddock, cooked	96	19	0	1	0	watermelon	21	trace	5	trace	0
ham, lean	168	22	0	5	0	yogurt, whole milk	62	3	5	3	0
honey	289	trace	82	0	0	zucchini, cooked	14	1	3	trace	1
jam	261	1	79	trace	1						

VITAMINS AND MINERALS

Vitamins and minerals are substances, required in small amounts, that are essential for the normal, healthy functioning of the body—normal growth and development, energy production, body maintenance, and general well-being and vitality.

Vitamins are a diverse group of organic substances that cannot be manufactured by the body—except for vitamin D (which is produced in the skin when it is exposed to sunlight) and niacin (made in the body from the amino acid tryptophan)—and must, therefore, be obtained from food. Absence of one or more vitamins from the diet will, in time, lead to well-defined deficiency diseases such as scurvy, beriberi, or osteomalacia. The 13 major vitamins, each of which is found in many different foods, are divided into two groups. Fat-soluble vitamins—A, D, E, and K—are found in fat- or oil-containing foods and are stored in the liver so that daily intake of these vitamins is not really essential. In fact, excessive consumption of fat-soluble vitamins, usually by taking too many vitamin tablets, can be harmful. Deficiency of fat-soluble vitamins is usually caused by disorders that stop the intestine absorbing fats efficiently. Water-soluble vitamins—the B-complex vitamins and vitamin C—are not stored in the body (apart from vitamin B12). To avoid deficiency, therefore, foods containing water-soluble vitamins should be eaten each day to keep supplies at a healthy level. Because water-soluble vitamins are destroyed by prolonged cooking, processing, and storage, fresh or lightly cooked foods make the best sources.

Minerals are simple chemical elements that cannot be made by the body but must be present in the diet to maintain good health. There are 20 minerals known to be essential in small amounts, in addition to carbon, oxygen, hydrogen, and nitrogen, which are needed in large amounts to construct the body's framework. Some, including calcium, phosphorus, sodium, chlorine, potassium, and sulfur, are called macrominerals because they are found in significant amounts in the body. More than 100 mg of each macromineral is needed in the diet daily. The other minerals required by the body are called trace minerals, or microminerals, because they are needed only in minute amounts. As with vitamins, absence of certain minerals—especially calcium and iron—will cause deficiency symptoms. Deficiencies of the other minerals are rare, however, unless an individual eats a very restricted diet or always eats processed foods. Vitamin and mineral supplements are not normally required provided the diet includes a wide range of fresh foods. However, a doctor or dietician may recommend vitamin and/or mineral supplements for certain individuals—such as pregnant or breastfeeding women, young children, or individuals suffering from malnutrition—to satisfy the extra demands of their bodies.

VITAMINS: sources, functions, and symptoms of deficiency

R.D.A.* = Recommended daily amount for adults; mg = milligrams (thousandths of a gram); mcg = micrograms (millionths of a gram)

Vitamin	Chemical name	R.D.A.*	Sources	Functions	Deficiency symptoms
Fat-soluble vitamins					
A	Retinol (from animal sources) and carotene (from plant sources); carotene is converted to vitamin A in the body	0.8–1 mg	Deep green and yellow vegetables, especially carrots, orange-yellow fruits, liver, fish liver oils, egg yolk, dairy products, fortified margarine.	Required for normal vision, especially in dim light; bone and tooth formation; normal growth; protecting urinary, digestive, and respiratory systems against infection.	Night blindness; dryness of conjunctiva, clouding of cornea; dry rough skin and skin sores; stunted growth (in children); reduced resistance to infection.
D	Calciferols (several forms)	5–10 mcg	Oily fish, cod liver oil, liver, egg yolk, fortified dairy products, and margarine; also formed in skin by action of ultraviolet rays in sunlight.	Required for strong bones and teeth; blood clotting; normal nerve and muscle function.	Weakened bone: rickets in children, osteomalacia in adults; poor muscle tone; restlessness and irritability.
E	Tocopherols (especially alpha-tocopherol)	8–10 mg	Vegetable oils, egg yolks, wholegrain cereals, wheat germ, nuts, leafy green vegetables, dried beans.	Protects cell membranes (so slowing aging); needed in formation and protection of red blood cells.	Very rare. Possibly anemia caused by destruction of red blood cells.
K	Phytomenadione (vitamin K1); menaquinone (vitamin K2)	60–90 mcg	Vitamin K1 from leafy green vegetables (especially cabbage) cauliflower, broccoli, potatoes, wheat germ, pork, liver, egg yolk, cheese; vitamin K2 made in the gut by bacteria.	Essential for formation of substances that cause blood clotting in the liver.	Very rare. Nosebleeds and other bleeding because of reduced inability to clot; easy bruising.
Water-soluble vitamins					
B complex *(some B vitamins do not have a designated vitamin number)*:					
B1	Thiamine	1–1.4 mg	Wholegrain cereals, brown rice, wheat germ, wholewheat bread, beans, nuts, eggs, liver, fish, milk.	Helps release energy from carbohydrates; essential for nerve and muscle function, including heart muscle.	Loss of appetite, nausea, tiredness, depression, irritability, memory loss; in severe cases, beriberi and eventual death.
B2	Riboflavin	1.2–1.6 mg	Wholegrain cereals, green leafy vegetables, yeast extract, peas and beans, liver, meat, poultry, eggs, milk, cheese, yogurt.	Helps release energy from carbohydrates, proteins, and fats; helps maintain healthy skin and mucous membranes.	Cracked lips, soreness of mouth and tongue, dermatitis, hair loss, light sensitivity, blurred vision, trembling, dizziness.
	Niacin, or nicotinic acid	13–18 mg	Baked wholegrain cereals, peas and beans, nuts, especially peanuts, dried fruits, yeast extract, liver, meat, poultry, eggs, fish.	Helps release energy from glucose and fats; essential for manufacture of sex hormones, maintenance of healthy skin, and nervous and digestive systems.	Rare. Loss of appetite, weight loss, nausea, diarrhea, depression; in severe cases, pellagra: dermatitis, dementia, and even death.
	Pantothenic acid	4–7 mg	Most foods, especially wholegrain cereals, wheat germ, green vegetables, peas, beans, yeast extract, peanuts, liver; also made by gut bacteria.	Helps release energy from carbohydrates and fats; essential for manufacture of sex hormones, healthy skin, hair, and nervous system.	Very rare. Fatigue, loss of appetite, headache, cramps, abdominal pain, increased susceptibility to infections and allergies.

Vitamin	Chemical name	R.D.A.*	Sources	Functions	Deficiency symptoms
B6	Pyridoxine	2 mg	Most foods, especially whole-grain cereals, wheat germ, bananas, potatoes, beans, liver, poultry, meat; also made by gut bacteria.	Essential for carbohydrate, protein, and fat metabolism, production of antibodies against infection, red blood cell production, and for healthy skin.	Rare. Skin problems, cracked lips, anemia, weakness, irritability, depression.
	Biotin	30–200 mcg	Most foods, especially oats, wheat germ, nuts, beans, liver, egg yolk; also made by gut bacteria.	Essential in fat and carbohydrate metabolism and in excretion of waste and from protein breakdown.	Very rare. Loss of appetite, sore tongue, muscle pains, depression, hair loss, eczema.
	Folic acid	400 mcg	Deep green vegetables, fruits, wholewheat bread, nuts, peas, beans, yeast extract, liver, eggs.	Involved in manufacture of DNA, red blood cells, and normal functioning of nervous system.	Anemia, sore tongue and mouth; poor growth in children. May occur during breastfeeding or pregnancy.
B12	Cyanocobalamin	3 mcg	Animal foods, especially liver, meat, poultry, fish, eggs, dairy products (except butter); also traces in yeast extract.	Important in formation of new cells, including red blood cells, and in the normal functioning of the nervous system.	Pernicious anemia, loss of appetite, tiredness; in severe cases, damage to nervous system causing numbness.
C	Ascorbic acid	60 mg (100 mg for smokers)	Vegetables and fruits (best raw) especially peppers, potatoes, broccoli, citrus fruits, blackcurrants, tomatoes.	Essential for growth and healthy bones, teeth, gums, and blood vessels; helps resistance to infection, wound healing, and iron absorption.	Rare. General aches and pains, nosebleeds, swollen gums; in severe cases, scurvy, bleeding gums, loose teeth, anemia.

MINERALS: sources, functions, and symptoms of deficiency

Mineral	R.D.A.*	Sources	Functions	Deficiency symptoms
Macrominerals				
Calcium	800–1,200 mg	Hard water, legumes, nuts, green vegetables, soybean products, dairy products, fish whose bones are eaten (e.g. sardines), eggs.	Needed for growth and maintenance of bones and teeth, muscle contraction, transmission of nerve impulses, normal heart action, and blood clotting.	Rare, usually caused by deficiency in vitamin D, which facilitates uptake of calcium from the intestine. Symptoms include weakened bones, rickets in children, osteomalacia in adults.
Chlorine	None laid down (2,000–3,000 mg in normal diet)	All foods, table salt.	Important constituent, with sodium, of blood and other body fluids.	Muscle cramps (following severe diarrhea and vomiting).
Magnesium	300–350 mg	Wholegrain cereals, wholewheat bread, nuts, legumes, green vegetables, meat, milk, fish.	Needed for bones and dentition and for normal nerve and muscle operation.	Muscle cramps and tremors, irregular heart beat, loss of appetite, nausea, anxiety, weakness.
Phosphorus	800–1,200 mg	Wholegrain cereals, wholewheat bread, legumes, nuts, meat, poultry, fish, eggs, dairy products.	Needed for healthy bones and teeth, normal nerve and muscle activity, making DNA, and energy conversion and storage in cells.	Very rare.
Potassium	None laid down (2,500 mg in normal diet)	All foods, especially wholegrain cereals, vegetables, fruits, meat, dairy products.	Component of fluid inside cells; essential for muscle contraction and nerve impulse conduction.	Muscle weakness, heart abnormalities.
Sodium	None laid down (2,500 mg in normal diet)	Most foods, table salt.	Important constituent of blood and other body fluids; essential for muscle contraction and nerve impulse conduction.	Rare. Muscle cramps, convulsions, kidney failure (following severe diarrhea and vomiting).
Sulfur	None laid down (1,200 mg in normal diet)	Protein-rich foods: pulses, meat, eggs, milk.	Essential constituent of many proteins, such as insulin.	Not known.
Trace minerals				
Chromium	50–200 mcg	Wholegrain cereals, wholewheat bread, nuts, fruits, meat, liver, yeast.	Essential for normal metabolism of carbohydrates.	Not known.
Cobalt	None laid down	Meat, liver, kidney, eggs.	Needed for red blood cells.	Pernicious anemia.
Copper	2–3 mg	Wholegrain cereals, wholewheat bread, nuts, legumes, meat, liver, poultry, fish, shellfish.	Needed for red blood cell formation and functioning of some enzymes.	Very rare. Anemia, lack of white blood cells, changes in hair color.
Fluorine	1.5–4 mg	Fluoridated water, tea, fish whose bones are eaten (e.g. sardines).	Needed for healthy bones and teeth; helps prevent tooth decay.	Tooth decay.
Iodine	150 mcg	Iodized table salt, wholegrain cereals, wholewheat bread, seaweed, fish, shellfish, milk.	Essential for production of thyroid hormones that control growth and metabolic rate.	Decreased metabolic rate, lethargy, fatigue, increased weight, goiter; in children, cretinism.
Iron	18 mg (females) 10 mg (males)	Wholegrain cereals, wholewheat bread, nuts, dried fruits, meat, liver, egg yolk, shellfish.	Constituent of hemoglobin, the oxygen-carrying molecules in red blood cells.	Anemia, tiredness, gastrointestinal problems.
Manganese	2.5 mg	Wholegrain cereals, vegetables, nuts, legumes.	Essential for activity of many enzymes.	Rare. Decreased growth rate, bone deformities.
Molybdenum	150–500 mcg	Buckwheat, barley, legumes, liver.	Constituent of several enzymes.	Very rare.
Selenium	50–200 mcg	Wholegrain cereals, wholewheat bread, meat, liver, shellfish.	Needed for healthy liver function and as an antioxidant.	Very rare. Anemia.
Zinc	15 mg	Wholegrain cereals, wholewheat bread, legumes, meat, liver, yeast, milk, eggs, fish, shellfish.	Constituent of several enzymes; needed for growth, wound healing, sperm production.	Slow wound healing, impaired mental, physical, and sexual development, loss of taste and smell.

A HEALTHY DIET

The food that we eat provides us with the energy to power all our body activities, the materials for the growth and repair of body tissues, and the vital chemicals essential for the metabolic reactions that take place in all cells. To be healthy, a diet should:

- consist of a wide variety of natural foods that provide a balance of carbohydrates, fats, proteins, vitamins, minerals, and fiber (*p. 169-71*);
- supply the body with sufficient energy to meet its needs;
- include only low levels of foods, such as those containing saturated fats, that increase the risk of developing diet-related diseases, for instance coronary artery disease.

Energy requirements

Each person has a certain requirement (*below*) for energy, depending on age and the amount of activity (or other forms of energy consumption, such as breastfeeding) involved in her or his daily life. Energy is derived from energy-rich foods such as carbohydrates and, to a lesser extent, fats. A diet that results in taking in more energy than the body requires in those conditions leads to obesity, while insufficient energy intake leads to weight loss (*p. 174*).

Average daily energy requirements

CHILDREN		
Age	Energy used per day	
	cals	kJ
0–3 months	550	2,300
3–6 months	760	3,200
6–9 months	905	3,800
9–12 months	1,000	4,200
8 years	2,095	8,800
15 years female	2,285	9,600
15 years male	3,000	12,600
ADULT FEMALES		
Age	Energy used per day	
	cals	kJ
18–55 years		
Inactive	1,900	7,980
Active	2,150	9,030
Very active	2,500	10,500
Pregnant	2,380	10,000
Breastfeeding	2,690	11,300
Over 56 years		
Inactive	1,700	7,140
Active	2,000	8,400
ADULT MALES		
Age	Energy used per day	
	cals	kJ
18–35 years		
Inactive	2,500	10,500
Active	3,000	12,600
Very active	3,500	14,700
36–55 years		
Inactive	2,400	10,080
Active	2,800	11,760
Very active	3,400	14,280
Over 56 years		
Inactive	2,200	9,240
Active	2,500	10,500

cals = calories; kJ = kilojoules

Measuring energy

Many food products these days include on their labels an indication of how much energy they contain. Energy content has been traditionally measured in calories. One calorie is the amount of heat energy needed to raise the temperature of 1 gram of water by 1°C. In practice, the calorie is too small a unit to represent energy values on food labels—most food items would contain many thousands of calories—and the kilocalorie (1,000 calories) is used instead. The term Calorie (with a capital C) is sometimes used to represent kilocalories. Although Calorie is a familiar term to most people, the standard unit for measuring energy is, in fact, the joule. One calorie equals 4.2 joules. As with calories, energy content is usually given in kilojoules or thousands of joules. In addition to measuring the energy content of food, Calories and kilojoules are used to measure how much energy the body requires each day and how much energy is required for particular activities.

Energy expenditure

During exercise, energy consumption by the body increases. The amount of energy consumed depends on the age, sex, size, and fitness of the individual and on how vigorous the exercise is. This table shows the approximate energy used by a person of average size and fitness carrying out certain activities over a one-hour period.

Activity	Energy used per hour	
	kcals	kJ
Badminton	340	1,428
Bike riding	660	2,772
Climbing stairs	620	2,604
Football	540	2,268
Gardening, heavy	420	1,764
Gardening, light	270	1,134
Golf	270	1,134
Gymnastics	420	1,764
Housework	270	1,134
Jogging	630	2,646
Resting in bed	60	252
Soccer	540	2,268
Squash	600	2,520
Standing	120	504
Swimming	720	3,024
Tennis	480	2,016
Walking, brisk	300	1,260
Walking, easy	180	756

kcals = kilocalories; kJ = kilojoules

Diet and heart disease

Fats in foods are divided into saturated fats—found mainly in meat and dairy products—and unsaturated fats—found in fish and vegetable oils. Research has established a link between the high level of saturated fats consumed in the United States and northern Europe and the incidence of coronary heart disease, leading to death from heart attacks (*p. 159*). Coronary artery disease is caused by the buildup of obstructions called atheromas that contain cholesterol. A high saturat-ed-fat intake increases blood cholesterol level, so encouraging atheroma formation. A form of unsaturated fat, polyunsaturated fatty acid, found in fish oils and some vegetable oils, decreases blood cholesterol level and reduces the blood's tendency to clot and cause a heart attack. In addition, people with diets high in slow-release carbohydrates (such as potatoes, pasta, and rice), high in fiber, but low in fats are much less likely to suffer from heart disease.

Types of fat

This table shows the relative amounts of saturated and unsaturated (monounsaturated and polyunsaturated) fats in butter and some commonly used oils.

Food	Sat. %	Mono. %	Poly. %
Butter	60	32	3
Coconut oil	85	7	2
Corn oil	16	29	49
Olive oil	14	70	11
Peanut oil	20	45	35
Safflower oil	9.5	13.5	78
Sunflower oil	13	32	50

Dietary recommendations to protect the heart

- Eat less fat, especially saturated fats.
- Avoid sugary and processed foods.
- Avoid obesity.
- Eat plenty of fiber-rich foods.
- Cut down on salt—too much salt can increase your blood pressure.

Diet and cancer

Studies have indicated a strong link between diet and the chances of developing certain cancers. Cancers of the colon, rectum, and stomach may be up to 90 percent diet dependent, and diet may be responsible for up to 35 percent of all cancers in Western countries. For example, there appears to be a close correlation between levels of fat consumption and incidence of breast cancer. In Japan, fat provides 22 percent of energy requirements in the diet and the death rate from breast cancer is 4 per 100,000 people; in the United States, fat provides 40 percent of energy requirements and the death rate is 24 per 100,000 people. Dietary components linked to cancers include:

- excessive alcohol—cancers of the bowel, liver, mouth, esophagus, stomach, and throat, especially in smokers;
- fatty and low-fiber foods—breast and bowel cancers;
- pickled foods—stomach cancer;
- salt-cured meat and fish, nitrate-cured meat—throat and stomach cancers.

Dietary recommendations to reduce cancer risks

1 Eat foods rich in fiber daily.
2 Eat fresh fruit and vegetables daily.
3 Eat less fat.
4 Consume alcohol only in moderation.
5 Eat fewer smoked and salted foods.
6 Keep weight at recommended level.

IDEAL WEIGHT

The human body is much more likely to be healthy and efficient and to look good if it is maintained at the correct weight. Optimum weight depends on the age, sex, and physique or build of the individual. There are two ways of determining whether your weight is within the correct range. One is to use a height/weight chart (*below right*): by finding the point where your height and weight intersect, you can see whether you are in general terms underweight, overweight, or within the correct weight range. The second technique is to calculate your Body Mass Index (B.M.I.). This is explained below.

Measuring your B.M.I.

Body Mass Index (B.M.I.) gives an accurate measure of obesity. In order to determine your B.M.I. you need to find out your height in meters and weight in kilograms. If you know your height in feet and inches, or weight in pounds, they can be converted using the following formulae:

$$\text{Height in meters} = \frac{\text{height in inches}}{39.37}$$

$$\text{Weight in kilos} = \frac{\text{weight in pounds}}{2.2}$$

$$\text{B.M.I.} = \frac{\text{weight(kg)}}{\text{height(m)} \times \text{height(m)}}$$

B.M.I. values:
Less than 18—underweight
18 to 25—in the ideal weight range
25 to 30—overweight
Over 30—obese; endangering health

Obesity

This is a condition in which the body has too much fat. Someone is considered to be obese if his or her weight is 20 percent over the ideal maximum, or if his or her B.M.I. is greater than 30. Around 30 percent of people in Western countries are overweight and around five percent of them are obese. Long-term obesity is a serious threat to health. It increases significantly the chances of developing high blood pressure, coronary artery disease, stroke, adult-onset diabetes mellitus, certain cancers, osteoarthritis, back pain, and varicose veins. Obese patients are advised, under medical supervision, to lose weight using a calorie-reduced diet and increased aerobic exercise.

Anorexia nervosa

Anorexia nervosa is an eating disorder found mainly among teenage girls and young women, although it is occasionally found in males. In fact, one in a hundred young women suffers from the condition, increasing to one in twenty in those young women, such as dancers and models, who are especially concerned with their body image. Anorexia may be a phobia about being fat or a symptom of mental illness. Whatever its cause, however, anorexia is a serious illness in which the individual starves herself and may die. She not only loses her appetite but, more seriously, fails to have a normal perception of the size and shape of her body—she thinks she is fat even when she is far below her normal weight. The main features of anorexia are as follows: excessive weight loss, overactivity, secretive and defensive behavior, being exceptionally choosy about food, obsessive exercising, tiredness, always feeling cold, induced vomiting, use of laxatives, thinning of hair on head, appearance of lanugo, dry skin, and cessation of menstrual periods (amenorrhea). Anorexics require medical treatment and counseling.

Bulimia nervosa

Like anorexia, bulimia is an eating disorder found most commonly among younger women, often those who have had anorexia. Bulimics crave food but fear becoming fat. They indulge in binge eating by consuming vast amounts of food and then induce vomiting and use laxatives. This constant bingeing and vomiting can cause severe medical problems. Sufferers from bulimia require the same medical care as anorexics.

Optimum weight according to height

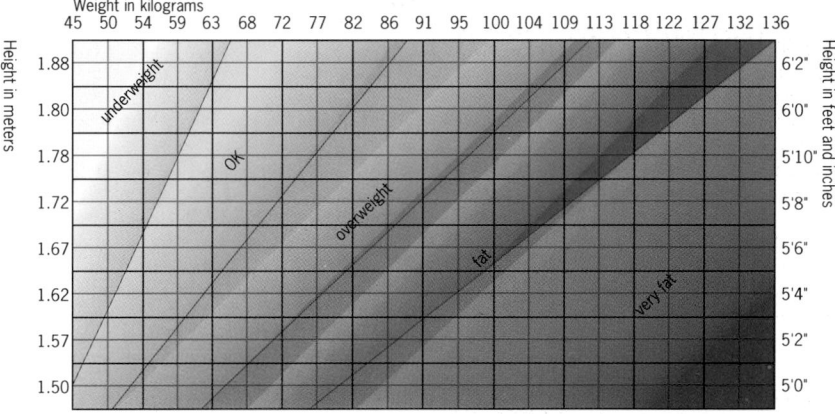

FOOD POISONING

This refers to illnesses caused by eating food contaminated by certain microorganisms or the toxins (poisons) they produce. Worldwide, the incidence of food poisoning is on the increase. This is probably due to the growing use of convenience foods, such as precooked meals, and the consumption of fast foods, which are easily subject to contamination by the people who make and serve them.

Types of food poisoning

Causative organism	Source of infection	Symptoms	Onset time
Bacillus cereus (B)	Spores in raw rice	Diarrhea and vomiting	2 to 14 hours
Campylobacter fetus (B)	Chicken, beef, water, or milk contaminated by feces	Diarrhea, abdominal pain, fever	1 to 4 days
Clostridium botulinum (botulism) (B)	Food contaminated with bacterial toxin	Nausea, vomiting, double vision; usually fatal	8 to 36 hours
Clostridium perfringens (B)	Meat or vegetables contaminated by feces	Abdominal cramps	6 to 12 hours
Entamoeba histolytica (amoebic dysentery) (P)	Food or water contaminated by feces	Severe diarrhea and fever	Up to several years
Listeria monocytogenes (listeriosis) (B)	Infected chicken, pâté, and soft cheeses	Flulike symptoms; can be fatal in elderly and babies	7 to 30 days
Norwalk virus (V)	Contaminated shellfish	Diarrhea and vomiting	2 days
Rotavirus (V)	Food or water contaminated by feces	Diarrhea and vomiting	1 to 2 days
Salmonella (B)	Undercooked infected poultry or eggs	Diarrhea, abdominal pain, vomiting, fever	1 to 2 days
Shigella (dysentery) (B)	Fecal contamination of food by hands or flies	Severe diarrhea and dehydration	1 to 2 days
Staphylococcus (toxin-forming strains) (B)	Food contaminated by contact with wounds	Vomiting	1 to 6 hours

(B) = bacteria; (V) = virus; (P) = protist

DIETS AND DIETING

The word "diet" is commonly used these days to describe an eating regime followed by someone in order for him or her to lose weight, even though in its correct usage the word simply describes what we eat each day (see p. 169 for description of the balanced diet). A diet designed for weight loss is better described as a reducing diet, and there are many of these to choose from. As the percentage of overweight and obese (p. 173) children and adults in the Western world steadily increases—a result of increased inactivity and increased consumption of junk food —so new reducing diets, and books on weight loss, become available in order to commercially exploit fatness. However, most of these diets (some examples are shown below) are not effective because they fail to promote long-term weight loss and in fact may well cause the dieter to end up fatter and heavier than when he or she started.

Being overweight will of course affect an individual's health, and reducing body weight will help to reduce those health risks. But to be healthy, a diet designed to reduce body weight needs to be in tune with the body's physiology.

An effective diet should promote the loss of fatty, or adipose, tissue from the body so that its overall fat content is reduced. To do this successfully, the dieter should eat a well-balanced, high-carbohydrate, high-fiber, low-fat diet with an energy content of between 1,200 and 1,500 calories per day, combining this with regular exercise. This should cause a weight loss of 1–2 lb. (0.45–0.9 kg) per week, that weight loss being mainly in the form of fat. At the same time, exercise will build up muscle tissue which, pound for pound, consumes far more energy than fat does, as well as increasing metabolic rate, the rate at which the body "burns" carbohydrates and fat to release energy. Once the desired weight has been reached—and the body's fat content has

been reduced to within safe limits—then the dieter can gradually increase his or her calorie consumption while maintaining the same balance of foods, in order to maintain that weight for life.

Foods that can be consumed in this kind of low-calorie diet are shown (above) as Type A and Type B foods—Type C foods should be avoided as much as possible. Fat-containing Type B foods, such as meat, should be eaten in moderation; all kinds of fruit and fresh vegetables can and should be eaten freely.

Other weight loss diets (below) put the body in a defensive stance. Because its calorie intake has been severely reduced, the body reduces its metabolic rate to conserve its fat energy reserves and actually "burns" lean muscle tissue in order to provide energy. When the diet stops, the body diverts as much spare food energy as possible to build up its fat reserves in case another calorie "famine" happens —and in consequence the dieter regains lost weight and ends up with more fat than before.

CHOOSING FOODS FOR A LOW-CALORIE DIET

TYPE A FOODS
Vegetarian foods
Cereals (unsweetened)
Fruits—all except avocados

Vegetables—all, including potatoes
Vegetable protein, e.g. tofu
Wholewheat bread

Meat, fish, and dairy foods
Chicken and other poultry (not duck) with skin removed
Cod, haddock, and other nonoily fish
Mussels and other shellfish
Salmon (if canned, in brine or water)
Skim milk
Tuna (if canned, in brine or water)
Yogurt (plain, low fat)

TYPE B FOODS
Vegetarian foods
Dried fruit
Margarine, polyunsaturated
Nuts, except peanuts
Pasta, especially wholewheat
Legumes, such as beans and lentils
Rice, especially wholegrain
Vegetable oils

Meat, fish, and dairy foods
Beef, lean cuts
Eggs
Lamb, lean cuts
Oily fish such as herring or mackerel
Pork, lean cuts
Sardines (if canned, in brine)

TYPE C FOODS
Meat, fish, dairy foods
Bacon
Beef, fatty cuts
Butter
Cheeses, apart from low fat
Duck
Fish, fried
Ice cream
Lamb, fatty cuts
Mayonnaise
Milk, full fat
Pâté
Pork, fatty cuts
Salami
Sausages

Convenience foods
Hamburgers
Cakes
Chocolate
Cookies
French fries
Potato chips

Dieting tips

- Alcohol—reduce intake to a minimum.
- Convenience foods—avoid if possible because many contain "hidden" fats.
- Exercise regularly, at least three times a week.
- Fat—remove it from meat, and remove fatty skin from poultry.
- Frying food—avoid if possible; bake, broil, microwave, or steam instead.
- Mayonnaise or rich sauces—avoid them.
- Overeating—try to work out why you do it in order to identify times when you may eat to relieve boredom or depression.
- Plan meals for the next day the night before, or early in the morning, to avoid impulse eating (of high-calorie foods).
- Regular eating—do not miss meals but try to eat 3–5 small meals each day.
- Second helpings—avoid them.
- Smaller plate—use one to make smaller helpings look larger than they really are.
- Snacking—avoid it and try to eat at main mealtimes; eat raw fruit or vegetables if very hungry between meals.
- Table—try to sit at one when eating; eating in front of the television may encourage you to eat more and faster.
- Take more time when eating—chew well.

COMMON TYPES OF WEIGHT LOSS DIET

Weight loss diet	Component foods	Benefits and problems	Effectiveness
• Liquid diets	Commercially produced high-protein, low-calorie meals in a glass.	Often providing fewer than 800 calories per day, these diets cause weight loss but this will include loss of lean muscle tissue.	Dangerous if continued for long periods. When the diet stops, the dieter usually regains all lost weight.
• Low-carbohydrate, high-protein diets	Low in carbohydrate foods such as potatoes, but with limited amounts of high-protein foods such as meat.	Cause weight loss through loss of lean muscle tissue and fluid, but the body's fat content stays the same.	After stopping this diet the dieter may end up fatter than before as the weight returns. The high-protein fat content of the diet makes it potentially dangerous.
• Low-fat, high-carbohydrate, high-fiber, balanced diets	Diet which contains a wide range of high-fiber, high-carbohydrate, low-fat, fresh foods.	This is the type of diet which, providing it is nutritionally balanced and contains sufficient but not excessive calories, will cause weight loss—especially if combined with exercise.	If this type of diet can be maintained after the desired weight loss has been achieved, the dieter will have a good chance of not regaining the lost fat tissue.
• Single-item or single-category diets	A diet consisting, for example, of just fruit, or a single fruit, such as grapes.	Will cause weight loss, through loss of both lean muscle and fat tissue, if boredom and hunger do not intervene first. May cause nutritional deficiencies and diarrhea.	Ineffective, as any weight lost is regained when the diet stops.

DISEASES

Diseases are abnormalities in the structure or function of the body, apart from those caused by physical injury such as a fracture. Diseases can be infectious or non-infectious. An infectious disease is caused by a specific microorganism such as a virus or bacterium (*pp. 88–89*). A non-infectious disease is not caused by disease-causing microorganisms and cannot be passed from one person to another.

INFECTIOUS DISEASES

Infections arise when disease-causing microorganisms penetrate the body's physical defenses—such as the skin—and enter the bloodstream and the tissues. Their route of entry can be by inhalation of infected droplets, ingestion of contaminated food or water, entry through broken skin, skin-to-skin contact, injection by needle or other sharp object, sexual contact, insect bites, or by transmission from mother to fetus.

Once inside the body, microorganisms multiply, and the body eventually responds to the infection by producing symptoms, such as fever, that can be used to diagnose the disease. The time between infection and the appearance of symptoms is known as the incubation period, and it can last from a few hours to several years. During the incubation period, the infected person may pass the infection on to other people. In most cases, the body's immune system (*p. 181*) acts to destroy the invading microorganism before it can do harm. Most disease signs and symptoms—such as spots in measles—are indicators of the battle between the microorganism and the body's immune system.

In rare cases, the infection may be so virulent (harmful) that it kills the patient before the immune system has time to fight back. Before the 1900s, infectious diseases were a major cause of death in the world. In developed countries today, deaths from infectious disease have been dramatically reduced, and noninfectious diseases such as cancers and heart disease have taken over as major killers. This reduction has been achieved by better public health and sanitation; the use of antibiotics and other antimicrobial drugs; and the use of vaccines. There is no room for complacency, however, since "old" diseases such as TB and malaria are again on the increase; some bacteria are now resistant to drugs; many viral conditions are untreatable; and "new" diseases such as AIDS (*p. 176*) are appearing. Disease-causing organisms include viruses, which are nonliving infectious agents; single-celled organisms including bacteria, chlamydiae, rickettsiae, fungi, and protists; and multicellular organisms such as parasitic worms.

Viral infections

Viruses (*below*) consist of genetic material surrounded by a protein coat and cause diseases such as measles, mumps, and rabies. Viruses have to invade host cells to reproduce (1). They lose their outer protein coat (2) and use the host cell's DNA to replicate their genetic material (3). A protein coat is constructed around the rebuilt genetic material (4), and newly formed viruses burst out of the host cell (5) or exit in an "envelope" (6) and invade other host cells to multiply further.

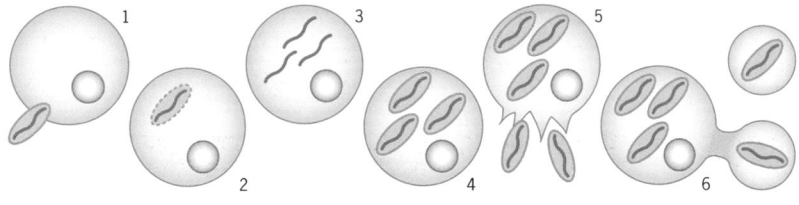

NONINFECTIOUS DISEASES

Noninfectious diseases are now the major cause of death in the developed world. The reason for this is that many infectious diseases are now treatable with drugs. Also, the incidence of non-infectious diseases increases with age, and average life expectancy is increasing.

Noninfectious diseases include circulatory diseases (including heart attacks and strokes), in which blood vessels to the heart or brain become blocked; cancers (*right*); diabetes mellitus, which is the body's inability to control blood-sugar levels; nervous system diseases (such as motor neurone disease); respiratory system diseases (such as bronchitis and emphysema); digestive system diseases (such as cirrhosis of the liver and peptic ulcers); kidney diseases (such as nephritis); and allergies (*above right*).

On average, infectious diseases are responsible for just five deaths per 100,000 of the population per year in the developed world, as compared with nearly 1,000 deaths per 100,000 caused by major noninfectious diseases.

Allergies

Sometimes the immune system overreacts to a particular substance (an allergen), producing an allergy. This may result from eating certain foods, inhaling particles, or exposure of the skin to chemicals. Common allergies include asthma, hay fever, urticaria, food allergies, and contact dermatitis. Treatments include taking antihistamine drugs and avoiding allergens. In cases of anaphylactic shock, the body reacts so violently to an allergen, such as a bee sting, that without treatment the patient could die.

Cancer

The body's tissue cells constantly divide and replace themselves. Sometimes "rogue" cells divide out of control to produce an abnormal tissue growth or malignant tumor. Diseases involving these tumors are called cancers. If untreated, cancer cells spread from the tumor via the bloodstream to other parts of the body, where they produce secondary tumors. Eventually, cancer cells overwhelm the body and the patient dies. The risk of developing a cancer may be inherited, or it may be increased by smoking, drinking alcohol, or exposure to chemicals. Cancer affects around 25 percent of people in the Western world at some point in their lives and is the second most common cause of death after heart disease.

Cancer cells intrude between normal cells.

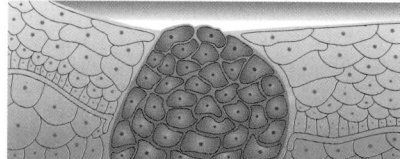

Cancers worldwide

Different types of cancer do not occur with the same frequency worldwide. This uneven distribution points to the involvement of environmental factors—such as food intake, smoking, or exposure to ultraviolet light—as causes of cancer. For example, stomach cancer in Japan and Chile is believed to be related to diets high in salted and pickled food.

Type	High-incidence areas
Bladder	Connecticut
Breast	British Columbia, Canada
Colon	Connecticut
Cervix	Colombia
Esophagus	N. Iran; N. France; E. China
Larynx	Brazil
Liver	Mozambique
Lung	U.K.; southern U.S.A.
Mouth	Bombay, India
Ovary	Denmark
Prostate	U.S.A. (African-Americans)
Rectum	Denmark
Skin	Queensland, Australia
Stomach	Japan; Chile
Throat	Bombay, India
Uterine	California

INFECTIOUS DISEASES

Name	Infective agent	Mode of transmission	Incubation	Symptoms	Treatment
Diseases caused by viruses					
Acquired Immune Deficiency Syndrome (AIDS)	Human immuno-deficiency virus (HIV)	Sexual contact, sharing hypodermic needles, mother to baby, blood transfusions.	Variable, usually several years	Fever, lethargy, weight loss, diarrhea, lymph node enlargement, short-ness of breath, viral and fungal infections; fatal.	Treatment of opportunistic infections, but ultimately incurable
Bronchiolitis (babies, young children)	Respiratory syncitial virus	Airborne droplets.	1 to 3 days	Cough, rapid breathing, and fever.	If severe, hos-pital treatment
Chicken pox (varicella)	*Varicella zoster* virus	Airborne droplets; direct contact.	11 to 21 days	Fever, headaches, sore throat, lethargy, rash.	Relieve symptoms
Cold sores	*Herpes simplex* Type 1	Direct contact.	Variable; virus remains dormant then reappears	During outbreaks, blisters and sores appear on affected areas then disappear.	Relieve symptoms; if serious, antiviral drugs
Common cold (coryza)	Many rhino-viruses and coronaviruses	Airborne droplets; hand-to-hand contact.	1 to 3 days	Runny or blocked nose, sneezing, sore throat, chills, muscle aches.	Relieve symptoms
Dengue or breakbone fever	B group of arboviruses	Bite from *Aedes aegypti*, mosquito carrying virus.	5 to 8 days	Fever, severe joint and muscle pains, headache.	Painkillers
Ebola disease (viral hemorrhagic fever)	Filovirus (thread virus)	Person-to-person contact.	7 to 14 days	Severe headache, fever, diarrhea, vomiting, severe internal bleeding; usually fatal.	Relieve symptoms; inject anti-bodies from blood of survivors
Encephalitis	*Herpes simplex* Type 1; others	Virus from another infection affects the brain.	Variable	Headache, fever, confusion, hallucinations, disturbances of speech and behavior, coma.	Antiviral drugs
Food poisoning (viral)	1. Norwalk virus 2. Rotavirus	Contaminated shellfish. Food or water contaminated by feces.	2 days 1 to 2 days	Diarrhea and vomiting. Diarrhea, vomiting, and dehydration. Young children most at risk.	Fluids Relieve symptoms; fluids
Genital herpes	*Herpes simplex* Type 2	Sexual contact.	1 week; usually recurrent outbreaks	During outbreaks, blisters on genitals burst, leaving painful sores.	Antiviral drugs; relieve symptoms
Hepatitis (viral)	Hepatitis A virus	Food or water contaminated by feces.	3 to 6 weeks	Mild flulike symptoms.	Relieve symptoms
	Hepatitis B virus	Sexual contact, sharing syringes, transfusions.	A few weeks to several months	As hepatitis A; or flulike symptoms, vomiting, jaundice, aching muscles; may be fatal.	Relieve symptoms
Infectious mono-nucleosis	Epstein-Barr virus	Via saliva of infected person.	1 to 6 weeks	Sore throat, fever, swollen glands, lethargy. rest, fluids	Relieve symptoms;
Influenza (flu)	Type A, B, or C influenza viruses	Airborne droplets.	1 to 3 days	Fever, sweating, chills, headache, sore throat, muscle aches, cough.	Relieve symptoms; fluids
Laryngitis	Common cold viruses	Airborne droplets.	1 to 3 days	Hoarseness, sore throat, dry cough, loss of voice.	Relieve symptoms
Lassa fever	Arenavirus	Airborne droplets of infected rat's urine.	3 to 17 days	Fever, sore throat, muscle aches, headache, severe diarrhea; may be fatal.	Antiviral drugs and serum
Marburg disease (green monkey disease)	Filovirus (thread virus)	Infection of blood through scratch or bite	4 to 9 days	High temperature, diarrhea, vomiting, rash, severe internal bleeding, usually fatal.	Relieve symptoms; survivors need prolonged convalescence
Measles	Paramyxovirus	Airborne droplets.	7 to 14 days	Fever, severe cold symptoms, red rash.	Relieve symptoms
Meningitis (viral)	Various viruses	Various methods.	Variable	Flulike symptoms including fever, headache.	Relieve symptoms
Mumps	Paramyxovirus	Airborne droplets.	2 to 3 weeks	Swelling of parotid glands, pain at angle of jaw, fever.	Relieve symptoms
Pharyngitis (sore throat)	Viral infection: part of a cold or influenza (*see* Strep throat *p. 178*)	Airborne droplets.	3 to 5 days	Sore throat, pain on swallowing, slight fever, *swollen neck glands.*	Relieve symptoms
Pneumonia (viral)	Various viruses	Airborne droplets.	Variable	Cough, fever.	Relieve symptoms
Poliomyelitis (polio)	3 types of polio viruses	Airborne droplets, hand-to-mouth infection from feces.	Minor: 3 to 5 days; major: 7 to 14 days	Minor: fever, sore throat, vomiting, headache. Major: fever, severe headache, stiffness of neck and muscles, possible paralysis.	Relieve symptoms
Rabies	Rhabdovirus	Bite or lick by infected animal.	10 days to 8 months	Fever, headache, dis-orientation, hydrophobia, seizures, coma, usually fatal.	Antirabies globulin (preventive)

Name	Infective agent	Mode of transmission	Incubation	Symptoms	Treatment
Rubella (German measles)	Togavirus	Airborne droplets.	17 to 21 days	Fever, rash.	Relieve symptoms
Shingles (Herpes zoster)	*Varicella zoster*	Viruses remaining dormant after chicken pox infection become active.	Variable	Painful rash of encrusting blisters commonly on skin over ribs.	Antiviral and analgesic drugs
Smallpox	Variola minor or major viruses	Now eradicated worldwide.	12 days	Fever, rash developing into pus-filled blisters; often fatal.	No treatment
Tonsillitis	Infection with cold viruses or other agents (*see* Strep throat *p. 178*)	Airborne droplets.	1 to 3 days	Sore throat, red enlarged tonsils, difficulty in swallowing, fever, foul-smelling breath.	Relieve symptoms; possibly antibiotics
Warts (genital)	Papillomavirus	Sexual contact.	Up to 18 months	Soft, cauliflower-shaped warts on penis and around entrance to vagina and anus.	Podophyllin; cryosurgery
Warts (plantar–verrucas)	Papillomavirus	Walking on contaminated communal wet floors.	Variable	Hard, rough-surfaced area on sole of foot; causes discomfort on walking.	Cutting out; cryosurgery
Yellow fever	Togavirus	Bites by mosquitoes carrying virus.	3 to 6 days	Fever, severe headache, pain in neck, back, and legs, jaundice, kidney failure; may be fatal.	Relieve symptoms

Diseases caused by mycoplasmas

Name	Infective agent	Mode of transmission	Incubation	Symptoms	Treatment
Nongonococcal urethritis	*Mycoplasma genitalium*	Sexual contact.	2 to 3 weeks	Pain on urination; discharge.	Antibiotics
Pneumonia	*Mycoplasma pneumoniae*	Droplet inhalation.	1 to 3 weeks	Cough, raised temperature.	Antibiotics

Diseases caused by chlamydiae

Name	Infective agent	Mode of transmission	Incubation	Symptoms	Treatment
Nonspecific urethritis	*Chlamydia trachomatis*	Sexual contact.	2 to 3 weeks	Pain on urination; discharge.	Antibiotics
Psittacosis	*Chlamydia psittaci*	Inhalation of dust from infected bird droppings.	1 to 3 weeks	Fever, flulike symptoms, breathing difficulties.	Antibiotics
Trachoma	*Chlamydia trachomatis*	Direct contact; poor personal hygiene.	5 days	Conjunctivitis, dislike of light, opacity of cornea, possible blindness.	Antibiotics

Diseases caused by rickettsiae

Name	Infective agent	Mode of transmission	Incubation	Symptoms	Treatment
Q fever	*Coxiella burnetti*	Inhalation of dust from contaminated sheep and cattle feces.	7 to 14 days	Fever, severe headache, chest pains, cough; later pneumonia, possibly hepatitis; rarely fatal.	Antibiotics
Rocky Mountain spotted fever	*Rickettsi rickettsi*	Bites by ticks carrying *rickettsiae.*	Not known	Fever, rash of spots that spread over body, enlarge, darken, and bleed.	Antibiotics
Typhus (epidemic)	*Rickettsia prowazekii*	Bites by body lice carrying *rickettsiae.*	7 days	Fever, severe headache, muscle pains, rash, delirium; may be fatal.	Antibiotics

Diseases caused by bacteria

Name	Infective agent	Mode of transmission	Incubation	Symptoms	Treatment
Anthrax	*Bacillus anthracis*	Entry of spores from infected animal materials.	1 to 3 days	Large skin blister with swelling of tissues; may be fatal.	Antibiotics
Botulism	*Clostridium botulinum*	Eating improperly preserved food contaminated with the bacterial toxin.	Toxin takes effect within 8 to 36 hours	Nausea, vomiting, double vision, difficulty speaking or swallowing; usually fatal.	Antitoxin
Brucellosis	*Brucella abortus*	From cattle, pigs, or goats.	3 to 6 days	Fever, drenching sweats.	Antibiotics
Cholera	*Vibrio cholerae*	Contaminated water or food.	1 to 5 days	Severe diarrhea and dehydration; may be fatal.	Fluids, antibiotics
Conjunctivitis	Staphylococci, other bacteria, or by viruses	Hand-to-eye contact.	Variable	Itching, irritation, and redness of eye; pus discharge may occur.	Antibiotics
Cystitis	Intestinal bacteria	Bacteria transferred to female urethra from intestine via anus.	Variable	Stinging pain on passing urine, frequent urge to pass urine.	Plenty of fluids; if severe, antibiotics
Diphtheria	*Cornyebacterium diphtheriae*	Airborne droplets or by direct contact.	4 to 6 days	Fever, gray membrane over throat; in serious cases bacterial toxin can damage heart.	Antibiotics and antitoxin
Dysentery (bacterial)	*Shigella*	Food or water contaminated by feces or by direct contact.	1 to 2 days	Severe diarrhea and dehydration.	Fluids; antibiotics if severe
Food poisoning (bacterial—*see* botulism, listeriosis, *and* dysentery)	1. *Campylobacter*	Food or water contaminated by feces.	1 to 4 days	Diarrhea, abdominal pain, fever.	Fluids; antibiotics if severe
	2. *Salmonella*	Undercooked infected poultry or eggs, or contaminated food.	1 to 2 days	Diarrhea, abdominal pain, vomiting, fever.	Fluids; antibiotics if severe
	3. *Bacillus cereus*	Bacterial spores, found in uncooked rice, survive boiling and release toxins if rice is not refrigerated.	2 to 14 hours	Diarrhea, abdominal pains, vomiting.	Fluids; antibiotics if severe

Name	Infective agent	Mode of transmission	Incubation	Symptoms	Treatment
	4. Staphylococcal bacteria	Food contaminated by contact with wounds or sores in the skin.	1 to 6 hours	Vomiting.	Fluids; anti-biotics if severe
	5. *Clostridium perfrigens*	Contaminated meat, poultry, or vegetables.	6 to 12 hours	Abdominal cramps, vomiting.	Fluids; anti-biotics if severe
Gastroenteritis	Various bacteria (and viruses)	Contaminated food or water.	Variable	Stomach and intestinal inflammation causing vomiting and diarrhea; gastroenteritis is a general term for various diseases.	*See* cholera, dysentery, food poisoning, *and* typhoid
Gonorrhea	*Neisseria gonorrhoeae*	Sexual contact; mother to baby.	2 to 10 days	Male: pain on urination, discharge. Female: no symptoms or vaginal discharge.	Antibiotics
Hansen's disease (leprosy)	*Mycobacterium leprae*	Airborne droplets over prolonged period; not highly contagious.	3 to 5 years	Insensitive light patches on skin; nerve damage causing loss of sensation.	Antibacterial drugs
Legionnaires' disease	*Legionella pneumophila*	Airborne droplets of contaminated water from air conditioners or showers.	1 to 7 days	Headache, muscle pain, dry cough, pneumonia, delirium; may be fatal.	Antibiotics
Leptospirosis (Weil's disease)	Spirochaete bacterium	Contact with urine of rats carrying bacteria.	1 to 3 weeks	Fever, chills, intense headache, skin rash.	Antibiotics
Listeriosis	*Listeria monocytogenes*	Eating soft cheeses, precooked foods, prepared salads, undercooked meat.	1 to 2 days	Fever, aches, pains, sore throat, diarrhea; can cause miscarriages and be fatal for the elderly and newborn children.	Antibiotics
Lyme disease	*Borrelia burgdorferi*	Bites by deer ticks carrying bacteria.	Few days	Red dot appears at site of tick bite; fever, headache, lethargy, joint pains; if untreated will continue.	Antibiotics; anti-inflamm-atory drugs in later stages
Meningitis (bacterial)	*Neisseria meningitidis*, others	Bacteria carried by blood-stream from infection elsewhere in body.	1 day to 3 weeks	Severe headache, fever, stiff neck, dislike of light, vomiting; may be fatal.	Antibiotics
Middle ear infection (otitis media)	Bacteria, or viruses, causing upper respiratory tract infections.	Infection spreads into ear from respiratory tract along eustachian tube.	Variable	Severe earache, fever, deafness, ringing in the ear.	Antibiotics and analgesic drugs
Osteomyelitis	*Staphylococcus aureus*	Bacteria carried to bone from skin wound or in-fection elsewhere in body.	1 to 10 days	Fever, severe pain, and tenderness in infected bone.	Antibiotics
Peritonitis	Gut bacteria such as *Escherichia coli*	Perforation of gut allowing bacteria to escape into peritoneal cavity.	Variable	Fever, severe abdominal pain, vomiting, bloating, shock, dehydration.	Surgery; antibiotics
Plague (bubonic)	*Yersinia pestis*	Bites by rat fleas carrying bacteria.	2 to 5 days	Fever, headaches, swollen lymph glands; may be fatal.	Antibiotics
Pneumonia (bronchopneumonia)	*Haemophilus influenzae*; others	Airborne droplets.	1 to 3 weeks	Fever, cough, green or yellow sputum.	Antibiotics
Pneumonia (lobar)	*Streptococcus pneumoniae*	Airborne droplets.	1 to 3 weeks	Fever, cough, painful breathing, brown sputum.	Antibiotics;
Pyelonephritis	Various bacteria	Intestinal bacteria spread from anus to ureter via urethra (*see also* cystitis p. 177)	Variable	Kidney inflammation causing fever, chills, back pain.	Antibiotics
Scarlet fever	Hemolytic *Streptococcus*	Airborne droplets.	2 to 4 days	Sore throat, headache, fever, red skin rash.	Antibiotics
Strep throat	Streptococci	Airborne droplets.	2 to 4 days	Sore throat, fever, enlarged lymph nodes.	Antibiotics
Syphilis	*Trepanema pallidum*	Sexual contact; mother to baby.	First symptoms appear after 3 to 4 weeks	1. At 3 to 4 weeks: ulcer on genitals or other sites 2. At 6 to 12 weeks: rash, headaches, fever, fatigue 3. At 10 to 25 years: tissue destruction, brain damage.	Antibiotics in early stages
Tetanus	*Clostridium tetani*	Wound infected by bacteria from soil.	2 days to several weeks	Lockjaw, fixed smile, muscle spasms affecting breathing; may be fatal.	Antitoxin
Toxic shock syndrome	*Staphylococcus aureus*	Growth of *S. aureus* and release of its toxins in the vagina, caused by prolonged use of tampons.	Variable	Fever, diarrhea, rash, vomiting, headache, muscle pains, dizziness, shock; rarely fatal.	Antibiotics
Tuberculosis (TB)	*Mycobacterium tuberculosis*	Airborne droplets; drink-ing infected cow's milk.	Several weeks to several years	Cough with bloodstained sputum, weight loss, chest pain, fever; may be fatal.	Antibiotics
Typhoid	*Salmonella typhi*	Food or water contaminated by feces.	7 to 14 days	Headache, abdominal discomfort, fever, diarrhea; may be fatal.	Antibiotics
Ulcers (peptic)	*Helicobacter pylori*	Source unknown; may infect more than 60% of people over 65.	Variable; may live in stomach without causing any symptoms.	Burning pain in abdomen, loss of appetite, nausea, belching; in severe cases, vomiting of blood, black feces.	Antibiotics

Name	Infective agent	Mode of transmission	Incubation	Symptoms	Treatment
Whooping cough (pertussis)	*Bordetella pertussis*	Airborne droplets.	1 to 3 weeks	Severe, persistent coughing followed by a characteristic "whoop."	Antibiotics in early stages

Diseases caused by fungi

Name	Infective agent	Mode of transmission	Incubation	Symptoms	Treatment
Aspergillosis	*Aspergillus* sp.	Inhalation of spores.	Variable	Causes coughing up of blood in people with damaged lungs; infection may be fatal if immune system is impaired.	Antifungal drugs
Athlete's foot (Tinea pedis)	Dermatophyte fungi	Spores picked up on feet from damp or wet floors.	Variable	Itchy, sore skin between toes that may crack.	Antifungal powder
Candidiasis	*Candida albicans*	Changing conditions inside vagina; sexual contact.	Variable	Female: white vaginal discharge, vaginal irritation. Male: penis tip inflamed.	Antifungal drugs
Meningitis (fungal)	*Cryptococcus neoformans*	Fungal spores inhaled from pigeon droppings.	Variable	Headache, stiff neck, dislike of light.	Antifungal drugs
Ringworm (Tinea capitis or corporis)	Dermatophyte fungi	Direct contact.	Variable	Ring-shaped, scaly patches on skin of head or body.	Antifungal drugs
Sporotrichosis iodide	*Sporothrix schenckii*	From plants into the blood through skin wounds.	Variable	Ulcers and nodules under the skin; common in gardeners.	Potassium solution; anti-fungal drugs

Diseases caused by protists

Name	Infective agent	Mode of transmission	Incubation	Symptoms	Treatment
Amoebiasis (amoebic dysentery)	*Entamoeba histolytica*	Food or water contaminated by feces.	Up to several years	Severe diarrhea, fever.	Antiprotozoal drugs
Chagas' disease	*Trypanosoma cruzi*	Assassin bug droppings deposited on skin contain parasites which enter blood through scratches.	Weeks	Fever and swelling of lymph nodes. Long-term infection may affect heart.	Nifurtimox
Giardiasis	*Giardia lamblia*	Food or water contaminated by feces; sexual contact.	3 to 40 days	Foul-smelling diarrhea, abdominal cramps, loss of appetite, nausea.	Antiprotozoal drugs
Leishmaniasis (Kala-azar)	*Leishmania*	Bites by sand flies carrying parasite.	Usually 1 to 2 months	Fever, spleen enlargement, anemia, skin darkening; may be fatal.	Various drugs
Malaria	*Plasmodium falciparum, P. vivax*, others	Bites by anopheline mosquitoes carrying parasite.	10 to 40 days	Severe episodic fever and chills, sweating, fatigue, headache; may be fatal.	Antimalarial drugs
Sleeping sickness (trypanosomiasis)	1. *Trypanosoma brucei gambiense*	Bites by tsetse fly carrying parasite.	1. Weeks or months	Fever, enlarged lymph nodes, headaches, lassitude, coma, death.	Antiprotozoal drugs
	2. *T. brucei rhodesiense*	Bites by tsetse fly carrying parasite.	2. 7 to 14 days	Severe fever, lassitude coma, death.	Antiprotozoal drugs
Toxoplasmosis	*Toxoplasma gondii*	Eating undercooked meat or food contaminated by cat feces; mother to fetus.	Few days	Fever; may cause miscarriage or infant defects.	Pyrimethamine and a sulfonamide drug
Trichomoniasis	*Trichomonas vaginalis*	Sexual contact; indirectly from infected towels.	Variable; may be present in vagina without symptoms	Inflammation of vagina, offensive yellow discharge; in men may cause non-specific urethritis.	Antiprotozoal drugs

Diseases caused by parasitic worms

Name	Infective agent	Mode of transmission	Incubation	Symptoms	Treatment
Bilharzia (schistosomiasis)	Flukes of species *Schistosoma*	Waterborne larvae penetrate bather's skin.	Depends on life-span of parasite	Fever, muscle aches, abdominal pains.	Anthelminthic drugs
Elephantiasis	Various species of filarial roundworms	Larvae injected into bloodstream by mosquitoes.	Variable	Blockage of lymphatic system by worms produces massive fleshy swellings of arms, legs, and, in males, the scrotum.	Diethyl-carbamazine
Hookworm	*Ancylostoma duodenale* or *Necator americanus*	Larvae are taken in with contaminated food or penetrate the skin.	Few weeks	Abdominal discomfort; heavy infestation causes anemia because the worms feed on blood in the intestine.	Anthelminthic drugs
River blindness (onchocerciasis)	*Onchocerca volvulus*	Bites by *Simulium* flies carrying worm larvae.	Worms mature in 2 to 4 months	Nodules in skin; larvae entering eyes may cause blindness.	Diethyl-carbamazine
Roundworm (ascariasis)	*Ascaris lumbricoides*	Food contaminated by feces containing eggs.	Few weeks	Nausea, abdominal pain; in severe cases, anemia, malnutrition.	Anthelminthic drugs
Tapeworm infestation	Commonly beef, pork, or fish tapeworms	Food infested with tapeworm larvae.	Few weeks	Few symptoms in people with good diets; detached segments appear from anus or in feces.	Anthelminthic drugs
Threadworm (pinworm)	*Enterobius vermicularis*	Children transfer eggs from anus to mouth.	Few weeks	Itching in anal region.	Anthelminthic drugs
Toxocariasis	*Toxocara canis*	Children ingest eggs from soil contaminated with dog feces.	Few weeks	Mild fever; in severe cases pneumonia, seizures, and, possibly, blindness.	Anthelminthic drugs
Trichinosis	*Trichinella spiralis*	Eating undercooked pork containing worm larvae.	1 week	Diarrhea, vomiting, fever, muscle pains; rarely fatal.	Anthelminthic drugs

SCREENING AND DIAGNOSIS

These target specific age groups or those considered at risk because a close family member has had a particular disease.

Screening tests

Blood cholesterol test To check for high cholesterol levels—a risk factor for heart disease.

Blood pressure measurement To check for high blood pressure—a major contributor to heart disease.

Colon examination To look for signs of rectal cancer in high-risk patients.

Eye examination To look for glaucoma by checking for high pressure of fluids inside the eyeball.

Mammogram Breast X-ray to check for breast cancer. The American Cancer Society recommends annual mammograms for women over 50 and every one or two years for women between the ages of 40 and 50.

Pap smear Detects abnormal cells in the cervix that may indicate cancer.

Diagnostic techniques

Angiography X-ray imaging to check for blockages or diseases in blood vessels.

Biochemical analysis Chemical tests on samples of blood, urine, and other bodily fluids to assess body function.

Biopsy Removal of a tissue sample by needle, scrape, or surgery. Used to check if tumors are malignant or benign.

CAT scanning Use of computer-enhanced X-rays to detect a variety of lesions, especially in the brain and trunk.

Endoscopy Use of an endoscope to look inside the body (p. 189).

MRI A huge cylindrical magnet around the patient and a computer produce a three-dimensional view inside the body. Used to examine brain and spinal cord.

PET scanning Produces colored images that indicate metabolic activity in tissues. Used to diagnose brain disorders.

Radionuclide scanning X-rays are enhanced by radiation emitted from radioactive chemicals swallowed by the patient. Used to detect cancers.

WARNING SIGNS

Everyone should be aware of the warning signs that *might* indicate serious illness.

Warning signs for cancer
- unexplained weight loss
- sudden change in a wart or mole
- sore that fails to heal
- persistent hoarseness or cough
- difficulty in swallowing
- a lump, especially in the breast or testes
- bleeding from the anus on defecation
- recurrent diarrhea *and* constipation
- difficulty in urinating

Warning signs for heart disease
- breathlessness when lying down
- tight chest pain spreading down arms

BREAST SELF-EXAMINATION

Breast cancer is the most common cancer in women. It affects up to 1 woman in 10 in the U.S.A. and 1 in 20 in the U.K. Women more at risk are those who:
- started their periods early (before 12)
- had a late menopause (after 50)
- have had no children
- had their first child in their thirties
- have grandmothers, mothers, or sisters with breast cancer.

Women should examine their breasts monthly for changes indicative of early breast cancer. Warning signs include a lump, tenderness, or a discharge from the nipple. These should be reported to your doctor immediately. If breast cancer is detected early, the chances of a cure are good. Four out of five lumps discovered by breast self-examination are benign and not caused by cancer.

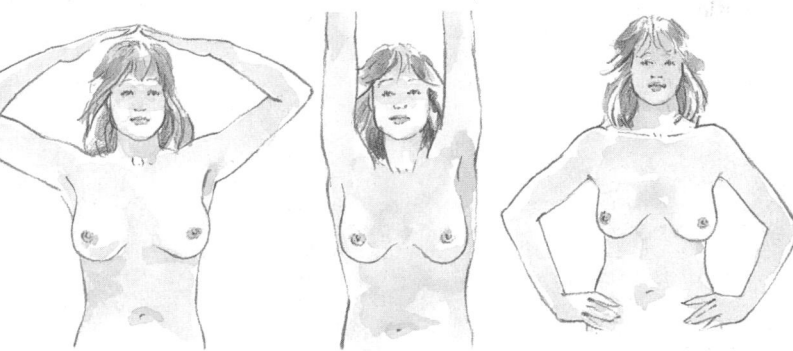

Visual examination
Put your hands at your sides. Examine both of your breasts for lumps, comparing this visual check with previous ones.

In front of a mirror, put your hands over your head. Look at the size, shape, and color of your breasts; note any differences between them; check nipples for changes.

Clasp your hands under your chin while flexing your chest muscles. Then bend forward to examine your breasts while they are hanging. Look for any dimples or puckering.

Manual examination
Bear in mind that breasts are naturally lumpy because they contain milk-producing glands, and these may swell at certain times of the menstrual cycle. This is why breast self-examination should take place at the same time each month, 7–10 days after your period. It should also include an examination along the collarbone and into the armbone.

Lie down with a folded towel or pillow under your right shoulder. Keep

1

your right arm by your side and use the closed fingers of your left hand to examine your right breast. Use the fat pads of three middle fingers to work clockwise around the outside of your breast, feeling firmly but gently for any lumps or swellings. Now bend your arm and raise it above your head to stretch your breast tissue. Examine the inner parts of your breast and nipple.

Examine your left breast with your right hand in the same way.

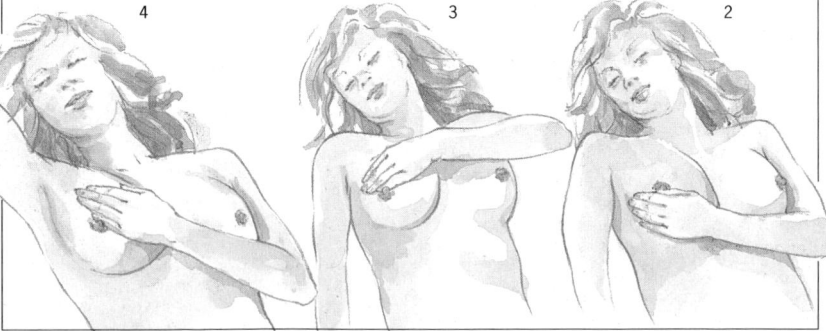

4   3   2

IMMUNE SYSTEM

The human body is constantly under attack from microorganisms such as viruses, bacteria, microscopic fungi, and protozoa (Infectious diseases, *pp. 176-179*). Allowed to invade and multiply inside the body, these would eventually kill it. To protect itself, the body has a range of defense mechanisms controlled by the immune system.

The immune system works in two ways. The innate, or inborn, immune system consists of physical barriers to infection (such as skin) and chemical barriers (such as mucus in the nose, which traps microorganisms). If bacteria get past these barriers they meet white blood cells called phagocytes, which circulate in the bloodstream and roam through the tissues, engulfing and destroying the microbes. A mass invasion of a tissue by microorganisms causes the release of chemicals such as histamine, which produces inflammation and acts as a "beacon" attracting phagocytes to the site of infection.

The innate immune system is fast acting, but it cannot protect the body against all disease-causing microorganisms. It is complemented by a second line of defense called the acquired immune system. Acquired immunity develops as we get older and are exposed to more disease-causing microorganisms. The adaptive immune system protects the body by recognizing specific invaders and acting to immobilize or destroy them. It retains a memory of the first exposure to a microorganism so that if the body is invaded again by the same virus or bacterium, the acquired immune system reacts more vigorously, and more rapidly, to destroy the invader. It also targets abnormal body cells, such as cancer cells.

The functional units of the acquired immune system are white blood cells called lymphocytes. There are two types: B-lymphocytes and T-lymphocytes, found in the bloodstream and in lymph nodes. B-lymphocytes manufacture and release chemicals called antibodies which disable and can destroy foreign microorganisms. Each antibody is custom-built to tackle a specific microorganism: for example, an invasion by the measles virus will cause a release of antimeasles antibodies. When the body is first exposed to a particular microorganism, it takes around 10 days for the B-lymphocytes to get to peak antibody production, in which time signs and symptoms of the disease may develop and the person may suffer a little or a lot. In the case of an invasion by a particularly virulent disease, such as bubonic plague, the microorganism usually gains the upper hand and kills the victim before the antibody response has reached its peak. Reexposed to the same microorganism, whether for the second or 92nd time, special memory cells trigger B-lymphocytes to release antibodies, but this time production of these killer chemicals reaches a peak after just two days. This gives the disease no time to develop any signs or symptoms, explaining why most people rarely suffer a repeat infection by diseases such as measles. Some T-lymphocytes are killer cells that attach themselves to the microorganisms and abnormal cells and destroy them directly. If the immune system is weakened—as it is when infected by the human immunodeficiency virus that causes AIDS—the body is invaded by opportunistic infections that eventually kill the patient.

IMMUNIZATION

While immunity is being acquired a person develops symptoms of the disease. But some infections can be prevented by allowing the body to acquire active immunity artificially. This is achieved by introducing into the body a vaccine made from dead or weakened microorganisms that can no longer cause the disease itself. When injected into the skin or bloodstream (or, as in the case of polio vaccine, swallowed) they stimulate B-lymphocytes to produce antibodies but no significant disease symptoms. And if, or when, the body encounters the real disease-causing microorganism, it is protected against infection because the memory cells immediately produce antibodies. Booster shots may be needed later to ensure that active immunity is still effective. Vaccines are available against many formerly dangerous diseases, including polio, measles, and diphtheria. Immunization programs for children (*above*) have virtually eliminated most common childhood diseases and confer immunity into adult life. But vaccination is advised for travelers to countries where they may contract diseases not previously encountered.

Sometimes antibodies themselves, from external sources, are injected to provide protection without stimulating the immune system. This is called artificial passive immunity; it provides instant protection where a disease might kill before the person's active immune system kicks in. Examples are gamma globulin, given against hepatitis; an antitoxin to treat tetanus; and antirabies injections.

Immunization schedule for children up to age 16

Age	Vaccine	How given
Birth	Hepatitis B	Injection
1–2 months	Hepatitis B	Injection
2 months	Diphtheria, whooping cough (pertussis), tetanus	Combined DPT injection
	Polio	By mouth
	Hib	Injection
4 months	Diphtheria, whooping cough (pertussis), tetanus	Combined DPT injection
	Polio	By mouth
	Hib	Injection
6 months	Diphtheria, whooping cough (pertussis), tetanus	Combined DPT injection
	Hib	Injection
6–18 months	Hepatitis B	Injection
	Hib	Injection
	Measles, mumps, rubella (German measles)	Combined MMR injection
	Diphtheria, whooping cough (pertussis), tetanus	Combined DPT injection
	Polio	By mouth
4–6 years	Diphtheria, whooping cough (pertussis), tetanus	Combined DPT injection
	Polio	By mouth
11–12	Measles, mumps, rubella (German measles)	Combined MMR injection
14–16	Tetanus, diphtheria booster	Combined injection

Travel immunization

Immunization is recommended for travelers of all ages who are visiting countries where there is a chance of contracting serious or potentially fatal diseases. Travelers should check which immunizations are required for their destination(s). They should also check with a doctor which diseases they may need protection against well in advance of travel. For entry into some countries, travelers may need certificates to show they have been immunized.

Recommended immunization for foreign travel

Disease	Area where immunization needed	Effective for	
Cholera	Immunization no longer recommended by WHO, but some countries still require evidence of vaccination. Check with embassy prior to travel.	6 months	[M]
Hepatitis A	Countries with poor hygiene and sanitation.	1 or 10 years	[M]
Meningococcal meningitis	For areas recommended by your doctor.	3–5 years	[H]
Polio	For all areas, if not immunized in childhood.	10 years	[H]
Rabies	Vaccine not recommended as routine.	1–3 years	[H]
Tetanus	For all areas, if no recent booster injection.	10 years	[H]
Tuberculosis	For areas recommended by your doctor.	over 15 years	[H]
Typhoid fever	Countries with poor hygiene and sanitation.	10 years	[M]
Yellow fever	Some African and South American countries.	10 years	[H]

[M] = provides moderate level of protection; [H] = provides high level of protection
Immunization is generally not effective after the periods indicated, and travelers should ask their doctor for a booster injection if they are visiting a country where they may be at risk.

ALTERNATIVE MEDICINE

Traditional medicine is largely mechanistic, treating the body as a machine with separate parts to be treated separately. Alternative, or complementary, medicine treats the body holistically, dealing with the whole body in its environment. In the past, alternative methods, many of them ancient, have been ignored by physicians. Today, however, certain types of alternative medicine are used increasingly to complement traditional methods.

Acupressure Ancient Chinese and Japanese healing massage using fingertip pressure on pain-relieving points around the body. These pressure points lie along the meridians (invisible body channels) used in ACUPUNCTURE. Acupressure balances the flow of Qi (or Chi), the energy flowing through the meridians.

Acupuncture Treatment of illness by sticking special needles into one or more of 2,000 specific points that lie along invisible channels called meridians. This ancient Chinese therapy is believed to control the flow of Qi, the energy flowing along the meridians. Used in the treatment of arthritis, allergy, back pain, and many other disorders.

Alexander technique A method used to retrain the body's movements, positions, and posture during all activities including sitting or reading. The method, which must be learned from qualified teachers, is believed to encourage good mental and physical health and resistance to stress by promoting harmony between mind and body.

Aromatherapy Use of concentrated plant oils—such as bergamot, eucalyptus, or rosemary—to treat conditions including stress, headaches, and arthritis. Extracts, or essential oils, are massaged into the skin by aromatherapists; they can also be inhaled or added to baths in minute quantities.

Art therapy Use of drawing and painting to encourage patients to explore and resolve deep-seated fears and emotions that they find difficult to express in words. Used to treat addiction, alcoholism, anorexia, and other conditions.

Aura therapy An aura is said to be a magnetic field surrounding the body, visible to aura practitioners as lines of light. Aura therapy involves analysis of the aura, which is said to be indicative of a person's health, and balancing or recharging it to treat health problems.

Autogenics Relaxation therapy used to reduce and control stress and fatigue. It is based on six taught mental exercises, which are repeated, sitting or lying down, two or three times a day.

Autosuggestion Form of self-HYPNOTHERAPY which empties the mind by the repetition of positive phrases that enhance well-being, relieve pain, and treat addictions and phobias.

Bach remedies Use of wildflower preparations—chosen according to an individual's particular personality and emotional state—to treat physical and psychological disorders.

Biochemic tissue salts Use of 12 mineral salts to cure disorders by restoring the natural salt balance within the body.

Chiropractic Manipulation of the spine and other joints to relieve musculoskeletal pain, especially of the back and neck.

Cranial osteopathy Manipulation of the bones of the skull and face to correct pressure changes to the brain and nerves in order to treat conditions such as migraine and neuralgia.

Dance movement therapy Use of body movement to express deep feelings too difficult to explain in words. Used to treat depression and anxiety as well as more serious mental illnesses.

Feldenkrais method Technique of teaching people how to improve the way they move by learning how they are moving. The aim is to move with maximum efficiency and minimum movement. Believed to reduce risk of injury in people involved in movement, such as dancers or athletes.

Herbal medicine Use of herbs to treat illnesses, a practice that dates back thousands of years.

Homeopathy Treatment of an illness using dilute doses of substances that imitate the symptoms of the illness (treating like with like). The aim is to restore the body's natural balance by boosting its healing powers.

Hydrotherapy Use of water to stimulate the body's ability to heal itself, based on the fact that water is essential for life. Treatment includes hot and cold baths and the steam baths found at spas and health farms.

Hypnotherapy Use of suggestion under hypnosis to treat conditions including stress, phobias, and addiction to tobacco and alcohol.

Iridology Diagnosis of disorders achieved by studying the patterns on the irises of the eyes. Iridologists believe that each section of the iris indicates the condition of a specific part of the body.

Kinesiology Monitoring of muscle strength and tone, using gentle finger pressure, to indicate how the whole body is working. Based on belief that muscle groups are linked to particular body organs. If imbalances are found, gentle massage is applied to pressure points to restore normal energy flow to muscles and their organs.

Macrobiotics Dietary regime based on Chinese philosophy of yin (flexible and cool) and yang (strong and hot), balancing the two elements to complement an individual's nature and lifestyle. Believed to improve health and resistance to disease.

Massage Ancient therapy whereby one person uses hands and fingers to stroke, press, and knead the body of another person who is lying horizontally. It is used to relax mind and body and reduce tension, as well as to treat disorders such as back pain.

Meditation Achieving a tranquil mental state, without the use of drugs, to reduce tension, decrease blood pressure, and regain confidence when stressed. This technique enables individuals to calm their bodies by controlling their thoughts. The meditative state is reached by focusing on a neutral thought while breathing in a controlled way.

Moxibustion A form of ACUPUNCTURE. Burning moxa wool is placed on the head of an inserted acupuncture needle to heat it. Alternatively, the burning moxa is held above the acupuncture point to warm the skin. Both methods are used to relieve pain after operations and for arthritis.

Naturopathy Using natural cures to seek the underlying cause of illnesses rather than merely alleviating the symptoms. Naturopaths treat patients as whole individuals, taking into account their emotions and lifestyles. Evidently effective against stress and anxiety as well as degenerative diseases such as emphysema and arthritis.

Osteopathy Diagnosis and treatment of disorders of the bones, joints, muscles, tendons, and nerves. Commonly used to treat back and neck problems, tension headaches, and sports injuries. Based on the concept that the musculoskeletal system plays a key role in the body's health. Osteopaths assess the damage, then manipulate the affected area.

Reflexology Treatment of disorders by massaging the feet. Reflexologists relate different zones of the feet to different organs. By massaging a particular foot region, they treat a particular organ by releasing blocks in energy channels.

Rolfing Massage of muscles and connective tissues in order to improve body posture and thereby improve the health of the whole body.

Shiatsu Ancient Japanese finger massage which, like ACUPRESSURE, involves the application of pressure to points lying along the body's meridians in order to control the energy flow (Qi). Used in the treatment of many conditions including migraine, back pain, stress, and digestive problems.

T'ai-chi Ch'uan Technique whereby people focus on their body and emotions by performing slow, circular, dancelike movements. T'ai-chi is believed to remedy imbalances in the movement of the body's natural energy, Qi, so improving a person's well-being.

Yoga System of physical, mental, and spiritual training designed to make the body more relaxed and more flexible. It involves adopting a series of postures while maintaining an inner calm of concentrated awareness. Yoga is used to help pain, especially back pain, stress, and many other conditions.

TYPES OF DRUGS

This list includes drugs that are commonly prescribed in the United States and other countries of the developed world. They are grouped according to their usage and listed by their generic names, not by brand names.

Anabolic steroids
Used to help muscle repair following injury. Abused by some bodybuilders and athletes to improve their physique.
nandrolone; stanozolol.

Analgesic drugs
Pain-relieving drugs. Nonopiod analgesics are used for mild pain; opiod analgesics for severe pain.
- **Nonopiod analgesics**
aspirin; paracetamol; benorylate; nefopam; sodium salicylate.
- **Narcotic analgesics**
buprenorphine; dihydrocodeine; codeine; morphine; dextro-propoxyphene; pentazocine; diamorphine; pethidine.

Antacid drugs
Neutralize stomach acids, relieving heartburn, peptic ulcers, and other gastric complaints.
aluminum hydroxide; magnesium carbonate; magnesium trisilicate; sodium bicarbonate.

Anthelminthic drugs
Kill parasitic worms such as tapeworms, pinworms, and roundworms.
bephenium; piperazine; mebendazole; pyrantel; niclosamide; thiabendazole.

Antibacterial drugs (antibiotics)
Used to treat bacterial infections.
amoxycillin; gentamicin; ampicillin; minocycline; cefaclor;; cephradine; oxytetracycline; cephalexin; phenoxymethyl penicillin; doxycycline; benzlypenicillin; erythromycin; streptomycin; flucloxacillin; tetracycline.

Anticancer drugs
Used to treat certain cancers. Some are cytotoxic, which means they kill cancer cells; others (marked *) are similar to sex hormones or hormone antagonists and, although not curative, may provide palliation of symptoms.
aminoglutethimide*; lomustine; chlorambucil; medroxy-cyclophosphamide; progesterone*; doxorubicin; megestrol*; ethinyloestradiol*; methotrexate; etoposide; procarbazine; fluorouracil; stilboestrol*; tamoxifen*.

Antimuscarinic drugs
These block the transmission of impulses along parts of the nervous system. Used to treat asthma, irritable bowel syndrome, Parkinson's disease, and other conditions.
atropine; hyoscine; ipratropium; benzhexol; orphenadrine; dicyclomine.

Anticoagulant drugs
These are used both to prevent and treat strokes or heart attacks by stopping the abnormal formation of blood clots.
heparin; warfarin; phenindione.

Antidiarrheal drugs
Used to make feces more bulky or to slow down gut motility.
codeine; kaolin; co-phenotrope; loperamide.

Antiemetic drugs
Used to treat vomiting and nausea.
chlorpromazine; metoclopramide; cinnarizine; prochlorperazine; dimenhydrinate; promethazine; hyoscine; thiethylperazine.

Antifungal drugs
Used to treat fungal infections including candidiasis, ringworm, and athlete's foot.
amphotericin B; ketoconazole; clotrimazole; miconazole; econazole; nystatin; flucytosine; tolnaftate; griseofulvin.

Antihistamine drugs
Used to treat allergic reactions such as hay fever and urticaria.
astemizole; promethazine; azatadine; terfenadine; chlorpheniramine; trimeprazine; triprolidine.

Antihypertensive drugs
Used to treat high blood pressure to reduce the risk of heart failure or stroke.
atenolol; hydrochlorothiazide; captopril; methyldopa; clonidine; minoxidil; chlorthalidone; nifedipine; cyclopenthiazide; oxprenolol; diltiazem; prazosin; enalapril; propanolol; hydralazine; verapamil.

Antirheumatic drugs
Used to treat rheumatoid arthritis.
azathioprine; gold; chlorambucil; penicillamine; chloroquine; prednisolone; dexamethasone.

Antispasmodic drugs
Used to control spasms in the wall of the bladder (causing irritable bladder) or intestine (causing irritable bowel syndrome).
dicyclomine; peppermint oil; hyoscine.

Antiviral drugs
Used to treat infections caused by viruses.
acyclovir; inosine pranobex; amantadine; zidovudine; idoxuridine.

Beta-blocker drugs
Used to reduce heart rate in treating anxiety, high blood pressure, and angina.
acebutolol; oxprenolol; atenolol; pindolol; metoprolol; propanolol; nadolol.

Bronchodilator drugs
Widen the airways to the lungs. Used to treat asthma and bronchitis.
aminophylline; rimiterol; fenoterol; salbutamol; terbutaline; pirbuterol; theophylline; reproterol.

Calcium channel blocker drugs
Used to treat irregular heartbeat, high blood pressure, and angina by reducing the work load of the heart.
diltiazem; verapamil; nifedipine.

Corticosteroid drugs
A wide range of uses including the treatment of rheumatoid arthritis, eczema, asthma, and Crohn's disease.
beclomethasone; fludrocortisone; betamethasone; hydrocortisone; cortisone; prednisolone; dexamethasone; prednisone.

Diuretic drugs
Used to treat high blood pressure and edema (fluid retention) by increasing the amount of water lost from the body in urine.
amiloride; cyclopenthiazide; bendrofluazide; frusemide; bumetanide; spironolactone; chlorothiazide; triamterene; chlorthalidone.

Hypoglycemic drugs (oral)
Used to lower levels of glucose in the blood to normal levels in patients with one form of diabetes (type 2).
chlorpropamide; glipizide; glibenclamide; tolazamide; gliclazide; tolbutamide.

Immunosuppressant drugs
Used to suppress activity of the immune system so that it does not cause the rejection of a recently transplanted organ.
antilymphocyte immunoglobulin; cyclosporin; methotrexate; azathioprine; prednisolone; chlorambucil; cyclophosphamide.

NSAID (nonsteroidal anti-inflammatory drugs)
Used to relieve pain and inflammation of joints in patients suffering from arthritis.
diclofenac; indomethacin; diflunisal; ketoprofen; fenbufen; mefenamic acid; fenoprofen; naproxen; flurbiprofen; piroxicam; ibuprofen.

Oral contraceptive drugs
Used by women to prevent conception by stopping the release of eggs from the ovaries or thickening the mucus to block entry of sperm into the uterus.
ethinyloestradiol; mestranol; gestodene; norethisterone; levonorgestrel.

Thrombolytic drugs
Used to dissolve blood clots in cases of heart attack or stroke.
anistreplase; streptokinase. *See also* Psychotherapeutic drugs.

DRUGS, ALCOHOL, TOBACCO

Drugs are chemicals that can change the functioning of one or more human body organs or alter the progress of a disease. Many drugs—such as antibiotics, anti-inflammatory drugs, and diuretics—are prescribed by doctors as medication. Some drugs—such as alcohol, nicotine, cocaine, and heroin—are used, legally or illegally, for pleasurable purposes.

Legal drugs

Alcohol This is a depressant drug that in small doses lowers inhibitions and tensions (*below*). Long-term use can lead to alcohol dependence, which has a deleterious effect on sufferers and their families.
Nicotine The active ingredient of tobacco smoke, nicotine (*below*), is a highly addictive drug that stimulates the nervous system. It causes harm by increasing the heart rate but decreasing the diameter of blood vessels, so increasing blood pressure, a contributory factor in heart disease. In addition, tobacco smoke contains a number of cancer-causing agents.

Illegal drugs

These are drugs that are controlled by legislation but are nevertheless available illegally from drug dealers. Some of them —such as barbiturates—are standard prescription drugs, while others—such as L.S.D.—are manufactured specifically for drug users. The use of many of these illegal drugs (*below*) can lead to dependence and possibly even death.

Alcohol consumption and deaths from liver cirrhosis

Country	Deaths[1]	Consumption[2]
Australia	8	2.5
England/Wales	4	2.0
France	34	4.8
Germany	19	2.9
Norway	5	1.3
U.S.A.	10	2.6

[1] Deaths from cirrhosis of the liver per 100,000 population per year
[2] Gallons of pure alcohol consumed per person per year

Safe limits for alcohol

If kept within the bounds of moderation, drinking is unlikely to harm health. In fact, research has shown that people who drink one or two glasses of red wine per day may live longer. The recommended maximum weekly intake of alcohol is as follows:
Men 21 units   *Women* 14 units
One unit of alcohol is equivalent to a medium-sized glass of beer, ale or stout; or a glass of wine, red or white; or a measure of liquors such as whiskey, gin, vodka, or brandy.

Effects of alcohol in a social drinker[1]

Concentration (mg alcohol per 100 ml blood)[2]	Effects
30–50	Drinker feels a reduction in tensions and inhibitions, becomes more confident and talkative, and develops a feeling of well-being.
50–150	Drinker may behave or speak irresponsibly, doing or saying things he or she will regret later. Thoughts lack clarity.
150–250	Drinker is confused and unsteady, and speech is slurred. Behavior may become unpredictable with signs of aggression.
250–400	Drinker feels very confused and disoriented, finds it difficult to stand upright, and eventually lapses into coma.
400–500	At this level, alcohol may depress the nervous system sufficiently to stop breathing and cause death.

[1] Heavy drinkers are much more tolerant of alcohol and so do not show these effects until they have attained a higher concentration of blood alcohol.
[2] As a guide, a man with a body weight of 155 lb. would have a blood alcohol level of 50 mg/100 ml after drinking three bottles of beer (or equivalent) during a two-hour session.

ALCOHOL AND TOBACCO

Type	Name	How taken	Major effects	Hazards associated with abuse
Depressants	Ethanol—"alcohol": wine, whiskey, etc.	Taken orally	Small amounts produce feeling of well-being and reduced inhibitions; larger amounts depress lower brain centers, impairing motor co-ordination (*table above*).	Short-term: unconsciousness, coma, death; prolonged abuse: dependence, tolerance, cancers of the alimentary canal, cirrhosis of the liver, brain damage.
Stimulants	Nicotine (from tobacco)	Inhaled when tobacco is smoked	Stimulates the sympathetic nervous system, increasing heart rate; psychologically reduces tension.	Dependence, tolerance; increased risk of cancers, including lung cancer, heart disease, bronchitis, emphysema.

COMMON ILLEGAL DRUGS

Type	Name	How taken	Major effects	Hazards associated with abuse
Depressants	Barbiturates— "downers": amytal, nembutal, seconal	Taken orally or injected	Euphoria, tiredness, reduction in anxiety, slurred speech, slowed breathing and heart rate, confusion.	Dependence and tolerance; combination with alcohol may cause death.
Narcotic analgesics	Heroin	Sniffed, smoked, or injected	Euphoria, reduction in pain, slurred speech, tiredness, loss of self-control, mood swings.	Dependence, tolerance; risk of overdose or poisoning if heroin is impure; risk of HIV or hepatitis from needle sharing.
Psychedelics/ hallucinogens	Cannabis	Smoked or taken in food or tea	Euphoria, altered perception of time and sensory phenomena, hunger.	Long-term use may cause paranoia and anxiety in vulnerable users.
	Lysergic acid diethylamide (L.S.D.)	Taken orally	Distortion of auditory and visual imagery, hallucinations, increased/distorted feelings of sensory awareness, unpredictable behavior.	Paranoia, flashbacks—recurrence of hallucinatory events without taking drug, possible long-term psychological damage.
Solvents	Various adhesives, cleaning fluid	Sniffed	Confusion, feeling of well-being, giddiness.	Death when breathing or heart stops; brain, liver, kidney damage.
Stimulants	Amphetamines— "uppers": benzedrine, dexedrine, methedrine	Taken orally, sniffed, injected, or smoked	Feeling of self-confidence, hyper-activity, excitement, restlessness, racing pulse; followed by depression.	Dependence, tolerance, paranoia, violent behavior, weight loss, hallucinations; death from overdose.
	Cocaine	Sniffed, smoked, or injected	Temporary feeling of euphoria and self-confidence, appetite loss, increased heart rate; followed by anxiety, agitation, depression.	Long-term use may cause mental impairment, hallucinations, damage to nasal passages; risk of seizures or death from overdose.
	Crack cocaine	Smoked	Intense feelings of power and euphoria last for 5 minutes, followed by a "crash" and a deep craving for another crack "hit."	Paranoia, violent behavior, suicidal feelings, loss of sex drive, loss of normal moral standards, possible death from heart attack.
	M.D.M.A.—"Ecstasy"	Taken orally	Mood elevation, increased energy, euphoria.	Severe dehydration, slight possibility of sudden death.

PRINCIPLES OF FIRST AID

First aid is the immediate treatment given to someone who has an injury or has suffered a sudden illness, before professional medical care can be given by paramedics, nurses, or doctors. In cases of serious injury, or illnesses such as heart attacks, first aid can make the difference between life and death. Giving effective first aid requires training. The basic aims are to preserve a casualty's life; to take measures to prevent his or her condition from worsening; to protect a casualty from suffering any further harm; and to help a casualty's recovery by providing immediate treatment and ensuring that he or she sees a doctor as soon as possible. If a patient is unconscious, the first aider should follow the ABC procedure (*right*).

The ABC of life support

Follow this procedure in an emergency if someone is not breathing. **A** Open the airway (the route to the lungs) by tilting the head back and lifting the chin. **B** Check if the casualty is breathing. If not, use artificial respiration to breathe your air into the casualty's lungs. **C** Check the pulse to feel if the heart is beating. If not, begin chest compressions (*below*) to pump blood artificially through the body. At the same time you, or another first aider, should use artificial respiration to get oxygen into the blood. This will ensure that all body cells, especially in the brain, continue to receive a supply of oxygen until heartbeat and breathing can be restarted —deprivation for three or four minutes will cause permanent damage.

Basic procedures

Assessing the situation Obtain as much information as quickly as possible. Make sure that both you and the casualty are not in any danger.
Immediate steps to preserve life Any casualty who is breathing but unconscious should be moved into the recovery position (*below*). For unconscious casualties who are not breathing or have no pulse, follow the ABC of life support.
Summoning assistance Phone for help from appropriate agencies—ambulance, fire, or police—as soon as possible, or get someone else to call them.
Diagnosis and treatment Identify signs and symptoms that will enable you to make a diagnosis and relieve pain and anxiety until medical attention arrives.

Artificial respiration

If someone stops breathing, artificial respiration should be given immediately. (1) Tilt the casualty's head back, pinch his nose, take a deep breath, and blow into his mouth until you can see his chest rising. (2) Lift your head and listen for air to come out, then continue at the rate of 12 breaths per minute until he starts to breathe on his own. (3) If mouth-to-mouth respiration is impossible, put your mouth over his nose and blow in the same way.

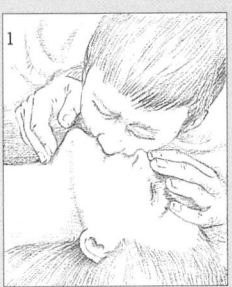
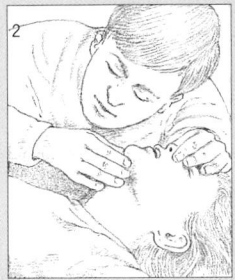

Chest compression

If the heart stops beating, chest compression maintains circulation. (1) Locate where the ribs meet with two fingers, then slide the heel of your other hand down the chest to meet them. (2) Remove the fingers and place the heel of that hand on top of the other, and link the fingers. (3) Lean over the casualty and push down on the breastbone, then release. Repeat at a rate of 80 compressions per minute, stopping every 15 compressions to give two breaths of artificial respiration (*above*).

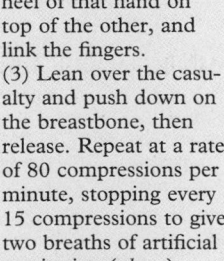
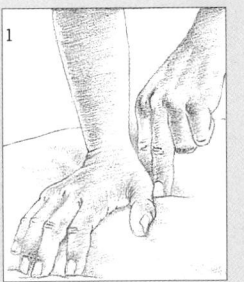
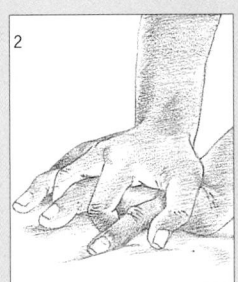
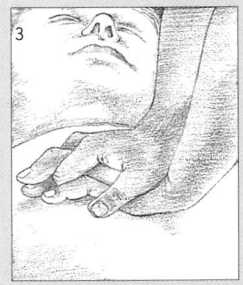

Recovery position

A casualty who is breathing but unconscious should be placed in the recovery position (*right*) unless there are possible injuries to the neck or spine. This keeps the airway open to allow breathing and reduces the risk of dying by inhaling vomit. The casualty should be moved as follows. First tilt the head back to open the airway. Then lay the arm farthest from you across the chest (1). Cross the legs at the ankle (2), and roll the patient over, pulling him toward you by the clothing on the far hip. Support him or her by bending the uppermost leg (3) and arm (4).

Choking

Choking happens when a person's airway—the windpipe and throat—becomes blocked, preventing breathing. The most common cause is food "going down the wrong way," and coughing usually clears the obstruction. If it does not, prompt action is necessary. If blows between the shoulder blades fail, use the abdominal thrust or Heimlich maneuver (*right*). By pulling your grasped hands quickly inward and upward, squeeze the chest and force the obstruction out of the airway.

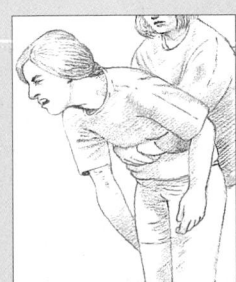

Choking babies

If a baby chokes, support her over your arm with your hand holding her jaw, so that the head is lower than the trunk. Slap her gently between the shoulder blades until the obstruction is coughed up. Avoid abdominal thrusts.

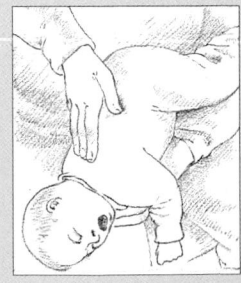

WOUND TREATMENT

Wounds that involve bleeding require immediate treatment to minimize blood loss and to prevent germs entering through open wounds. Most wounds are minor but still require prompt treatment to ensure rapid healing.

There are three main types of wound. Cuts are openings in the skin; they may be clean incisions made by a sharp object or rough tears made by a rougher object. Puncture wounds are produced when the skin is penetrated by a sharp implement such as a knife. Abrasions are caused by scraping the skin against a rough surface, removing the outer epidermal layer; there is little bleeding but the wound may easily become infected.

Minor wounds

Before treating minor cuts, puncture wounds, or abrasions, wash your hands. Dirty wounds should be washed under a faucet and then dried with clean, sterile material. If the wound is still bleeding, press down on the wound with a clean cloth until bleeding ceases. After drying the wound, cover it with a sterile dressing. If a wound becomes infected, seek medical help immediately.

Deep cuts

If the wound is severe, seek medical help as soon as possible and lay the casualty down. Look for embedded objects in the wound (*below*). If there are no embedded objects, put a sterile dressing or clean cloth over it and apply pressure directly to control bleeding (1). If possible, raise and support the affected body part above the level of the heart to reduce blood flow. Put another dressing on top of the first one (2) and bandage them firmly in place. If blood soaks through do not remove them but add another bandage.

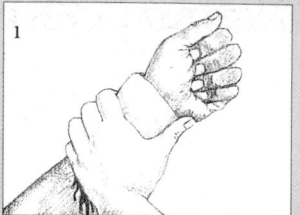
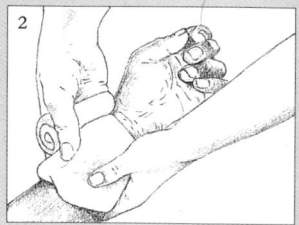

Embedded objects

Do not remove objects embedded in the skin. (1) Press either side of the wound to stop bleeding. (2) Cover with gauze to stop germs entering. (3), (4) Bandage above and below and send the casualty to a hospital.

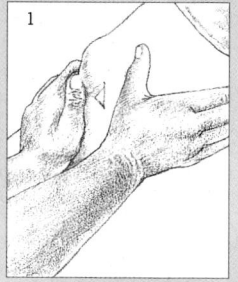

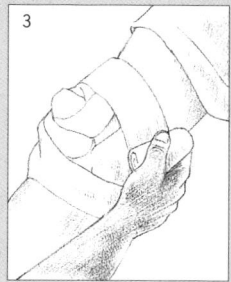
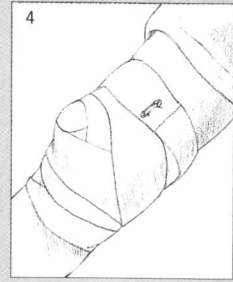

Nosebleeds

These occur if blood vessels in the nose rupture after sneezing, blowing, or being hit on the nose. Sit down, lean forward, and pinch the lower part of the nose for ten minutes. If bleeding continues, seek help.

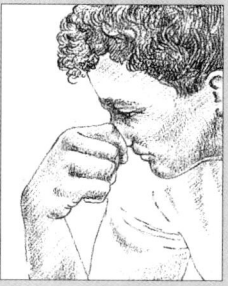

Scalp wounds

These may bleed profusely and look worse than they are. (1) Press a clean dressing over the wound and (2) bandage it in place. It may indicate a deeper skull injury, so the casualty should be taken to a hospital.

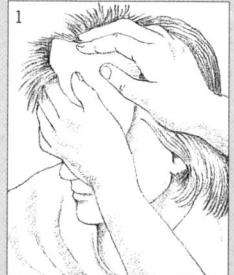
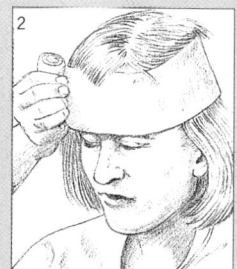

BURNS AND SCALDS

Skin provides a waterproof, germproof covering for the body. If the skin is damaged, the body risks dehydration and infection. Burns and scalds are damage to skin cells that result from exposure to high temperatures. Even brief exposure to temperatures above 120°F (50°C) will cause some damage. Burns are caused by a wide variety of agents, including dry heat (such as flames or friction burns), electricity (from high-voltage cables or lightning), intense cold (from liquid gases or frostbite), chemicals (corrosive industrial and domestic chemicals), and radiation (sunlight or radioactive sources). Scalds are caused by hot liquids or vapors such as steam.

Some general first-aid principles apply to all burns. Never burst any blisters; never apply butter, oils, lotions, or antiseptics; never use fluffy materials to dress burns; never use adhesive dressings.

First-degree burns

These are superficial, affecting only the outer layer of skin. Examples are burns caused by brief contact with hot objects, mild sunburn, or splashing with hot liquids. The skin reddens, but if treated promptly usually recovers rapidly, although the top layer of skin may peel off later. *First aid*: immediately put the affected area under cold running water or apply a cold compress until the pain decreases. Remove watches, rings, or bracelets in case of swelling. Cover the burn with a sterile, lint-free dressing to prevent infection.

Second-degree burns

These cause injury to both the epidermis (the outer layer of the skin) and part of the dermis (the inner layer), resulting in pain and swelling. Common causes are severe sunburn and short-term contact with flames. The skin appears raw and may blister, but healing is generally good unless burns are extensive. *First aid*: as with first-degree burns, and also seek medical attention.

Third-degree burns

These damage all layers of the skin and tissues beneath it. They commonly result from fire or lengthy contact with hot liquids or materials. The skin looks charred and smells burned. Treatment is needed immediately and must be followed by specialist treatment to avoid scarring. *First aid*: lay the casualty down and smother any flames with a coat or blanket. Summon medical help. Pour cold water on the burn and check the patient is breathing—if not, follow the ABC of life support. Remove burned clothing unless it is sticking to the burn. Cover the burn with a sterile, lint-free dressing.

BONE INJURIES

There are two major types of bone injuries. Fractures occur when a bone is broken or split either by direct force, such as a heavy blow, or by indirect force where, for example, the force of falling with arms outstretched is transmitted up the arms to break the collarbone. Fractures may be open, where the broken bone protrudes through the skin and is exposed to infection from outside, or closed, where the skin remains intact.

The second type of bone injury is dislocation, where a bone is pulled out of its joint.

Confronted with a closed fracture of, say, the arm or leg, the first aider should aim to immobilize the site of injury and summon medical help. Injuries to the upper limb are normally supported and immobilized by the use of a sling, and those to lower limbs by bandaging the legs together. With open fractures, the first aider should also attempt to stop blood flow and minimize the risk of infection by covering the wound with a sterile bandage. With shoulder dislocation, the arm should be supported in a sling and the casualty taken to a hospital for further treatment.

Triangular bandage

These bandages can be improvised by taking a piece of fabric around 3 feet (1 m) square and folding it in half, or they can be bought in sterile packs. Open (1), the triangular bandage can be used as a sling to support upper limb injuries or to dress head injuries. A broad-fold bandage is produced by folding the point to the base (2), then folding the bandage in half again (3). This can be used to immobilize both upper and lower limbs and to hold extensive dressings in position over wounds. By folding the broad-fold bandage in half again, a narrow-fold bandage is produced that can be used for immobilizing feet and ankles.

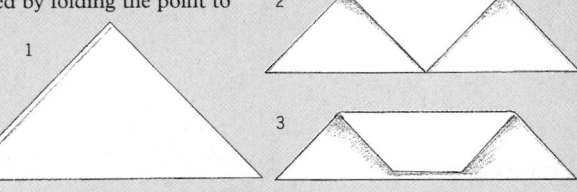

Collarbone

This links the shoulder blade and breastbone and is often broken during a fall. (1) Support the arm on the injured side, then (2) immobilize that arm using an elevated sling, with a broad-fold bandage around the chest.

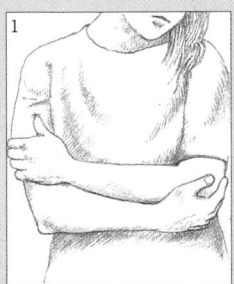
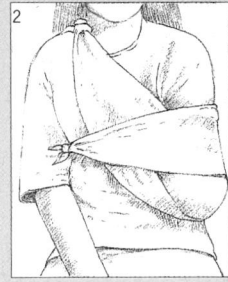

Ribs

Ribs can be fractured by a crushing blow or during a fall. Sit the patient comfortably by supporting the arm on the injured side in an elevation sling (*right*), with the body leaning backward and toward the injured side.

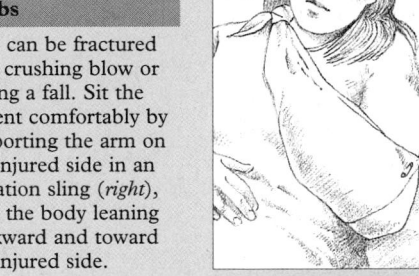

Upper arm

Elderly people often fracture the upper arm if they fall. (1) Put soft padding between the arm and chest and (2) support the arm in a sling. (3) Immobilize it with a broad-fold bandage over the sling tied across the chest.

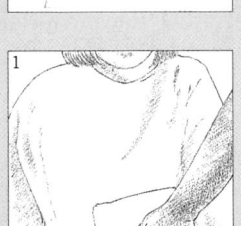

Hand or fingers

If any of the small bones of the hand or fingers are injured by a fall or crushing, the arm must be elevated and immobilized using an elevation sling (*below left*) to reduce swelling in the hand and blood loss from wounds.

Slings

A sling supports the arm. (1) Position a triangular bandage behind the arm, its point at the elbow and one end over the shoulder. (2) Bring the other end up to the neck and tie on the injured side. (3) Pin the point at the front.

Elevation sling

This immobilizes the arm and shoulder. (1) Support the arm across the chest and drape the triangular bandage across it. (2) Tuck the base of the bandage under the arm and (3) bring the lower end across the back and tie them at the shoulder.

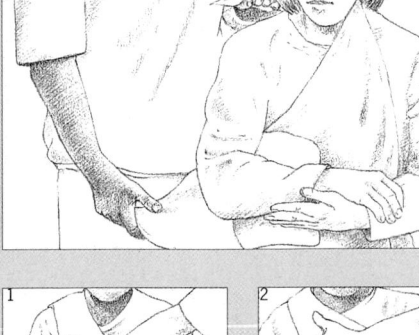
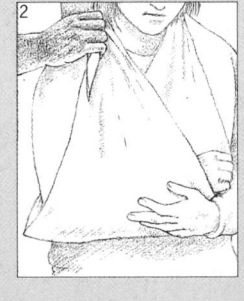

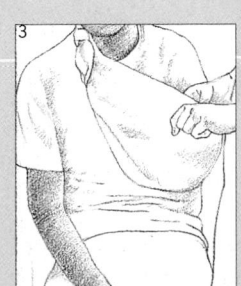

Emergency sling

In the absence of a bandage or piece of cloth, a sling to support the upper limb can be improvised using a belt or tie running under the arm and tied behind the neck; or by folding the hem of a jacket upward and securing it with a pin.

Fractures of lower limbs and pelvis

Fractures of the thigh bone may be caused by falls from heights or car accidents; the elderly also suffer fractures of the hip joint. The thigh bone is the largest in the body, and its fracture may cause tissue damage and severe bleeding. The first aider must immobilize the limb and get the casualty to a hospital. A thigh fracture may be indicated by inability to walk, unusual position of knee and foot, or slight shortening of the thigh. Summon medical assistance immediately and lay the casualty down. (1) Gently straighten the limb and (2) place broad-fold bandages under both legs (p. 187). (3) Pad between the legs and tie the bandages over the uninjured leg above and below the injury. Keep the casualty warm and, if possible, calm; watch for signs of shock.

Fractures of the pelvis are usually caused by crushing. Treatment is much the same as for thigh fractures except that the legs should not be tied together.

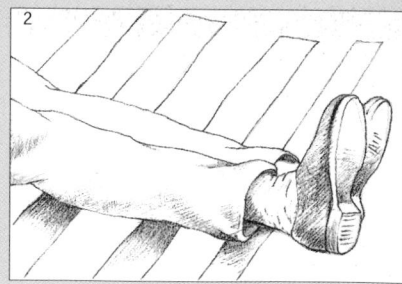
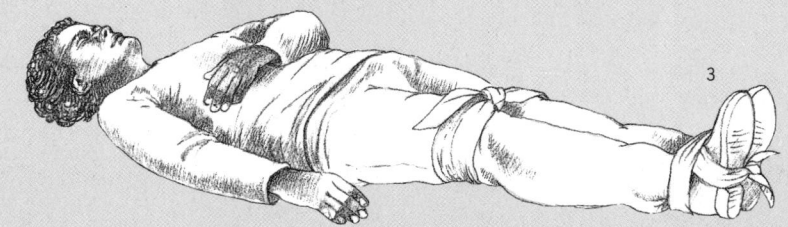

POISONS

These are substances that if taken into the body can cause damage, either temporary or permanent. They might be swallowed, inhaled through nose and mouth, absorbed through the skin or eye, or injected, causing effects ranging from nausea to death. If you suspect someone has swallowed poison, summon medical assistance immediately. Do not try to make the casualty vomit; this may cause further complications. If the casualty is unconscious, move her into the recovery position; give artificial respiration if breathing ceases. Look around for any evidence of what the casualty may have swallowed, and keep any vomited material to give to medical staff. Similar treatment should be applied in cases of alcohol poisoning and poisoning caused by ingesting poisonous plants.

STINGS

Most stings in temperate climates are caused by bees, wasps, and, more rarely, hornets. Generally, stings are painful but not dangerous. First aid can relieve the inflammation or swelling. Some insects, usually bees, leave their sting in the skin, and this must be removed using tweezers. When doing so, be careful not to grasp the sac at the end of the sting as this will inject more poison and increase pain. Apply a cold compress to reduce the swelling. A few people are allergic to stings and develop a life-threatening reaction called anaphylactic shock, requiring immediate medical attention. Signs include difficulty with breathing, anxiety, swelling around the lips and eyes, and, possibly, unconsciousness. If necessary, give artificial respiration, and always summon medical help immediately.

HEATSTROKE

The body has an intricate mechanism that ensures its core temperature stays at around 98.6°F (37°C) whatever the external temperature. However, prolonged exposure to high temperature, especially in very humid conditions, may cause the mechanism to break down. This results in heatstroke, and without immediate treatment the casualty will die. Heatstroke is indicated by hot, flushed, and dry skin, head-ache, lack of sweating, confusion, high pulse rate, and a body temperature above 104°F (40°C). Summon medical assistance immediately, move the casualty to a cool position. Remove the casualty's clothes and wrap him in a wet sheet (which should be kept wet) or sponge him constantly with cold water. Continue treatment until body temperature has dropped to 100°F (38°C) or medical help arrives.

SPLINTERS

These are small pieces of wood, metal, or glass that become embedded in the skin. They may cause pain or localized inflammation and should be removed to minimize risk of infection. The first aider should first wash and dry the area around the splinter. If it is protruding from the skin, it should be pulled out using tweezers sterilized by passing them through a flame. If it is just below the skin, sterilize a needle and use it gently to loosen the skin until the end of the splinter is exposed, then remove it with tweezers. Once the splinter has been removed, the wound should be squeezed to encourage bleeding to remove any debris and germs, then washed and dried and a sterile dressing applied. If a splinter is difficult to remove or deeply embedded, or if the wound becomes infected, the casualty should be referred to a doctor.

FIRST AID KIT

A well-equipped first aid kit should contain the following:

1-inch (2.5-cm) bandages; 2-inch (5-cm) bandages (for holding dressings and supporting joints and splints); cotton balls (for cleaning wounds and applying antiseptics); absorbent lint (surgical dressings); antihistamine cream (for stings and bites); antiseptic cream (and liquid); antiseptic wipes (for cleaning); disposable gloves; freshwater spray (available from pharmacies) or even bottled water; gauze bandages (for minor cuts and grazes); gauze swabs (for open wounds or septic wounds); respirators (available in sterile packs; for placing over the victim's face to aid noncontact mouth-to-mouth resuscitation); safety pins; scissors; triangular bandages (for multipurpose slings and for securing splinters); tubular gauze bandages and applicators; tweezers (small and large); zinc oxide bandages (for securing dressings).

For large organizations, such as health clubs, the following are also desirable: Roll of bandages (but can sometimes cause skin reaction); foil space suits and blankets; conforming bandages (with Velcro or clips), cotton bandages and crepe bandages—these are all "roller" bandages to hold dressings in place mold to limbs; disinfectant for washing wounds or mopping up blood; elastic bandages (for sprains and twists); splints (adjustable ones available); inflatable splints (foot/ankle- or upper limb-shaped; fasten with zippers or velcro and inflate like a balloon—good for taking X-rays without removing splint).

SURGERY

Some diseases and injuries require treatment by surgery, the direct intervention by a specially qualified doctor, or surgeon, using instruments. Surgery generally involves cutting through the skin to expose part of the body. The surgeon may remove tissues for further investigation to establish a diagnosis (biopsy); remove organs damaged by diseases such as cancer; realign structures displaced by injury, such as severe fractures; transplant tissues or organs, such as kidneys, from a donor; or relieve blockages in blood vessels and other structures.

These surgical procedures are carried out during operations. Minor operations often take place in outpatients' clinics and only require a local anesthetic, one that numbs the part of the body being operated on. Major operations are carried out in the sterile conditions of an operating room (*right*). The patient is normally given a general anesthetic and remains unconscious during the operation.

Most surgeons specialize in treating diseases that affect specific body systems. For example, neurosurgery deals with the nervous system; obstetrics and gynecology deals with the female reproductive system and childbirth; gastrointestinal surgery deals with the digestive system; and plastic surgery deals with repairing damage to the skin or with improving a person's appearance.

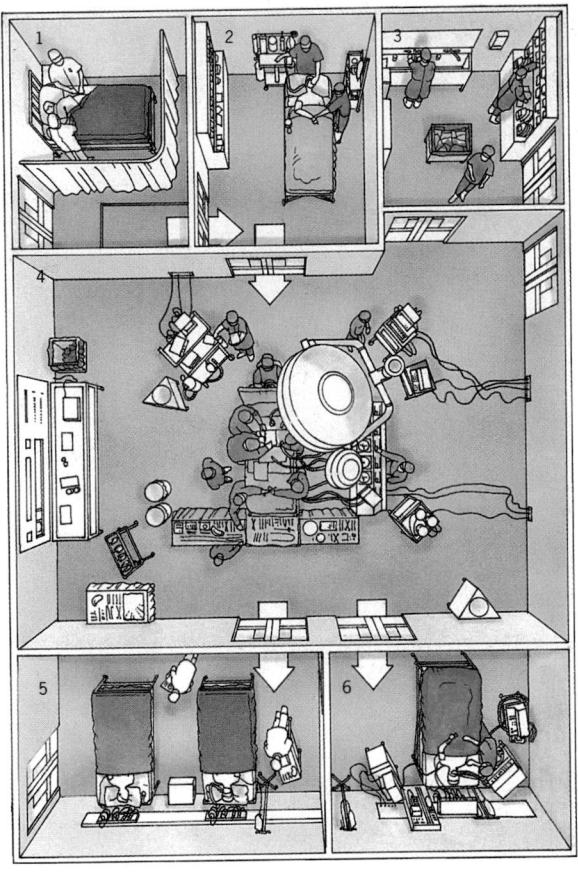

A patient having an operation passes along a "production line" that minimizes risk from the trauma of operation and from infection. Shortly before the operation the patient is given premedication (1) to relieve pain and anxiety. Then the anesthetist administers a general anesthetic (2). The surgeon, other doctors, and nurses "scrub up" (3) to minimize risk of infection. They wear gloves and masks and use sterile instruments. In the operating room (4), the surgeon is assisted by other medical staff. The anesthetist monitors the patient at all times. Afterward the patient is watched in the recovery room (5) until regaining consciousness. Patients whose condition is serious are taken to the ICU (intensive care unit, 6) where their vital signs are closely monitored.

Endoscopy

This is a technique used increasingly that enables doctors to look inside the body for diagnosis—by observation or removing small samples—or for treatment. It uses an endoscope (*below*). The long, flexible tube consists of fiber optics—bundles of plastic fibers that carry light. When the endoscope is inserted, some fiber optics carry light into the body cavity while others carry an image back to the viewing doctor. The endoscope can be introduced through the mouth, anus, or urethra, or through an incision in the skin.
1 Viewer; 2 Steering mechanism;
3 Flexible tube; 4 Tip; 5 Light supply;
6 Optic viewer; 7 Air-water nozzle;
8 Biopsy forceps for taking samples.

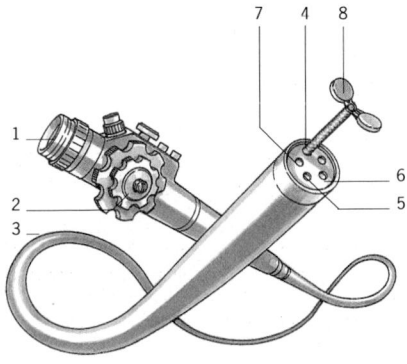

Open-heart surgery

The heart can suffer from diseases just like any other body organ. These include damaged valves, which interfere with normal blood flow through the heart; and coronary artery disease, where the blood vessels that supply the heart muscle with blood become blocked. In the past, surgeons were hampered in attempts to treat heart disease because the heart had to continue beating during an operation or the patient would die. This changed in the 1950s with the development of heart-lung machines to take the role of heart and lungs during an operation.

Now surgeons can perform open-heart surgery, in which the heartbeat is stopped temporarily to enable operation on the heart without great blood loss. During open-heart surgery, the patient is given a general anesthetic, the chest wall is opened by cutting down the breastbone, and the beating heart is exposed. Then the surgeon connects the heart-lung machine to the venae cavae—the large veins that deliver deoxygenated blood to the heart—diverting blood into the machine, where it is warmed, oxygenated, and then pumped back into the aorta, the main artery which carries oxygenated blood to the rest of the body. Once surgery is completed, the heart is restarted, the heart-lung machine connections are removed, and the chest is sewn up.

Keyhole surgery

Also known as minimally invasive surgery, keyhole surgery represents a great advance over traditional surgery, which often involved large incisions. Keyhole surgery is carried out through small incisions in the body. Because damage to the skin and body wall is minimal, the patient does not generally require a long hospital stay to recuperate and may even be treated on an outpatient basis. This means, in theory, that patient turnover is increased and more efficient use can be made of hospital beds.

The development of keyhole surgery has depended on the evolution of new technologies concerned with diagnosis and therapeutics. The new diagnostic tools include ultrasound, CAT (computed tomography) scanning, MRI (magnetic resonance imaging), and PET (positron emission tomography). These enable the surgeon to image body organs and pinpoint possible problems. The major tool in keyhole surgery is the fiber optic endoscope (*left*). Guided by diagnostic scans, the surgeon can make a small incision through the skin and introduce the endoscope to the required site. Looking at the inside of the body down the endoscope, the surgeon steers its tip into position, and can perform surgery or biopsies using small instruments attached to the endoscope's tip.

IMPORTANT DEVELOPMENTS IN MEDICINE

1543 Accurate anatomical drawings of the human body produced by Flemish anatomist Andreas Vesalius.

1545 Basic surgical principles established by French barber-surgeon Ambroise Paré, including a method of ligaturing—tying off blood vessels.

c. 1620 Minute organisms, such as bacteria and protozoa, and blood, muscle, and sperm cells discovered by Dutch draper and naturalist Antoni van Leeuwenhoek using a simple home-made microscope.

1628 Theory that blood circulates around the body, pumped by the heart along blood vessels, published by English physician William Harvey.

1661 Capillaries, the tiny blood vessels linking arteries and veins, discovered by Italian microscopist Marcello Malpighi. This completes the "missing link" in Harvey's 1628 theory of circulation.

1666 Quinine prescribed to treat malaria by British physician Thomas Sydenham: one of the first occasions a specific drug is prescribed to treat a specific disease.

1785 Use of digitalis (from foxglove plants) to treat heart failure described by British physician William Withering.

1796 Vaccination tested scientifically by British doctor Edward Jenner. A young boy vaccinated with the mild disease cowpox proves subsequently to be resistant to deadly smallpox.

1805 Morphine extracted from opium by German pharmacist Friedrich Sertürner and used by physicians to ease pain relief.

1816 Stethoscope, invented by French physician René Laennec, enables doctors to hear the sounds of breathing and the heart clearly.

1842 Ether used as anesthetic in an operation performed by U.S. surgeon Crawford Long.

1843 Theory that infections spread by the unwashed hands of doctors and midwives put forward by U.S. obstetrician Oliver Wendell Holmes.

1844 Nitrous oxide (laughing gas) used as an anesthetic by U.S. dentist Horace Wells when extracting teeth.

1847 Chloroform introduced as an anesthetic by British obstetrician James Simpson.

1850 Germ theory of disease proposed by French bacteriologist Louis Pasteur.

1851 Ophthalmoscope, invented by German scientist Hermann von Helmholtz, enables doctors to look into the interior of the eye.

1853 Chloroform popularized as an anesthetic—Queen Victoria uses it during the birth of Prince Leopold. Hypodermic syringe developed by Alexander Wood of the Edinburgh Medical School to inject solutions directly into the tissues.

1858 Theory that the body's cells arise from one cell—the fertilized ovum— which, in turn, is derived from cells from the two parents, put forward by German pathologist Rudolf Virchow.

1865 Cocaine isolated from leaves of the coca plant—used as a local anesthetic in eye operations in 1883.

1870 Antiseptic surgery pioneered by British surgeon Joseph Lister, a follower of Pasteur's germ theory. He uses a phenol (carbolic acid) spray during operations to help prevent wound infection by bacteria.

1876 Bacteria responsible for anthrax cultured by German doctor Robert Koch.

1895 X rays and X-ray pictures of the body, discovered by German physicist Wilhelm Röentgen, enables doctors to "look" inside the body without cutting it open.

1899 Theory that the malaria parasite is transmitted by mosquitoes is proved, confirming the research of English doctor Ronald Ross. Aspirin, a painkiller based on plant extracts, developed by German scientist Heinrich Dreser.

1900 A, B, AB, and O blood groups discovered by Austrian pathologist Karl Landsteiner, enabling blood transfusions to take place safely.

1906 Electrocardiograph (ECG, or EKG), which measures the electrical activity of the heart, invented by Dutch physiologist Willem Einthoven.

1911 Salvarsan, the first antibacterial drug —used to treat syphilis—discovered by German pharmacologist Paul Ehrlich.

1912 The term "vitamin" coined by Polish-Jewish chemist Casimir Funk.

1921 Isolation of hormone insulin by Canadian physiologists Frederick Banting and Charles Best means that diabetes can be treated.

1924 Existence of brain waves discovered by Hans Berger. This leads to the invention of the electroencephalograph (EEG), an instrument for the study of the waves, five years later.

1928 Penicillin, the first antibiotic—an antibacterial substance produced by a living organism—discovered by British scientist Alexander Fleming.

1932 Transmission electron microscope invented; it magnifies many thousands of times more than the light microscope.

1940 Penicillin developed to treat human bacterial infections by Australian pathologist Howard Florey and German-British biochemist Ernst Chain.

1945 Kidney dialysis machine developed by Dutch surgeon Willem Kolff. Used to treat patients with kidney failure who, previously, would have died.

1951 Coronary artery bypass attempted by surgeon Arthur Vineberg at Royal Victoria Hospital, Montreal, Canada.

1952 First vaccine against polio produced by U.S. doctor Jonas Salk. Amniocentesis—withdrawing amniotic fluid to diagnose abnormalities in a fetus— invented by Briton Douglas Bevis.

1953 Heart–lung machine, allowing the heart to be stopped for surgery while the blood still circulates, used successfully by U.S. surgeon John Gibbon. Structure of DNA discovered by American James Watson and Englishman Francis Crick using research by Rosalind Franklin and Maurice Wilkins.

1954 U.S. bacteriologist John Enders develops first vaccine against measles.

1955 The first successful kidney transplant operation performed by surgeons at Harvard Medical School, Massachusetts. U.S. doctor Albert Sabin develops oral polio vaccine.

1956 Oral contraceptive—the "pill"— developed in the U.S.A. by Gregory Pincus, John Rock, and Carl Djerassi.

1957 Fiber optic endoscopy invented, allowing the inside of the body to be viewed by introducing a flexible tube through the mouth and other orifices.

1959 Librium, the first tranquillizer, introduced by Swiss pharmaceutical company Hoffman-La Roche.

1961 Thermography—mapping the body by the amount of heat each part produces—developed at Middlesex Hospital, London.

1967 Successful human heart transplant performed by surgeon Christiaan Barnard at Groote Schuur Hospital, Cape Town, South Africa.

1972 Computerized axial tomography (CAT) scanner, for viewing the inside of the body in a three-dimensional image, invented by Godfrey Hounsfield of EMI Laboratories, England.

1978 First "test tube" baby—Louise Brown—born in England as a result of in-vitro fertilization (IVF) techniques developed by gynecologist Patrick Steptoe and embryologist Robert Edwards.

1979 World Health Organization (WHO) declares smallpox has been eradicated.

1984 Virus responsible for AIDS (later called HIV) discovered by Luc Montaigner at the Insitut Pasteur, Paris. Genetically engineered human insulin developed by scientists at Genentech, California.

1985 Positron emission tomography (PET) scanner, enabling doctors to see the brain "at work," developed by scientists at the University of California.

mid-1980s Human Genome Project initiated to identify all 100,000 genes in the human cell nucleus.

1986 Gene responsible for Duchenne muscular dystrophy identified by Tony Monaco and Louis Kunkel of Harvard University, Massachusetts.

1987 Transplant of fetal brain tissue into brains of patients with Parkinson's disease performed by research groups in Mexico, the U.S.A., and Europe.

1991 Gene responsible for inheritable form of Alzheimer's disease identified at St. Mary's Hospital, London.

1992 Gene implicated in colon cancer identified by Bert Vogelstein at Johns Hopkins University, Baltimore.

HEALTH CARE

Although good health depends on a number of factors, in general there is a close correlation between the wealth of a country and the health status of its people. In the countries of the developing world, poor living conditions, poverty, and scarce medical resources are all factors contributing to low life expectancies and high death rates among infants and children. A baby girl born in Sierra Leone can expect to live to 43; one born in Japan can expect to reach 80. Access to health care does not necessarily mean that life expectancy is high and mortality rates are low, although increasing immunization of very young children is beginning to have an effect. This is because a major factor determining the health of a nation is its access to clean drinking water and good sanitation. Some 25,000 people die each day through the use of contaminated water; 80 percent of all disease and 30 percent of all deaths in the developing world are linked to dirty water. Diarrhea caused by drinking dirty water kills over 4 million children each year in the developing world; many children suffer repeated bouts of the illness, stunting their growth and preventing them from receiving education. Schistosomiasis is a parasitic disease caught from contaminated water that affects the lives of over 200 million people. Water sanitation is generally far worse in the countryside, where most of the population lives, than in the cities.

Basic health facilities

Percentage of people in developing countries without access to: adequate sanitation (**SAN**), safe drinking water (**WAT**), health services (**HEA**), prenatal care (**PRE**). (Figures for late 1980s.)

Country	SAN	WAT	HEA	PRE	Country	SAN	WAT	HEA	PRE	Country	SAN	WAT	HEA	PRE
AFRICA					Tanzania	22	48	24	2	**ASIA/OCEANIA**				
Algeria	5	23	12	–	Togo	86	65	39	–	Afghanistan	98	87	71	95
Angola	82	72	70	73	Tunisia	54	11	10	40	Bangladesh	96	60	55	–
Benin	90	86	82	73	Uganda	87	84	39	–	Bhutan	–	60	35	97
Botswana	64	23	11	–	Zaire	90	68	74	–	Brunei	20	10	–	0
Burkina Faso	92	65	51	60	Zambia	53	52	25	12	Fiji	–	17	–	3
Burundi	48	77	39	86	Zimbabwe	74	48	29	11	India	92	46	–	55
Cameroon	64	64	59	–						Indonesia	70	67	20	74
C.A.R.	81	84	55	–	**AMERICAS**					Malaysia	25	29	–	34
Chad	86	69	70	–	Argentina	16	33	29	–	Nepal	98	84	–	83
Congo	60	50	17	–	Bahamas	36	41	–	1	Pakistan	81	56	45	74
Côte d'Ivoire	83	80	70	–	Barbados	0	48	–	2	Papua N.G.	79	46	–	46
Egypt	30	10	–	60	Bolivia	77	57	37	–	Philippines	43	35	–	–
Ethiopia	95	58	64	86	Brazil	76	25	–	25	Singapore	15	0	0	5
Gabon	50	50	10	27	Chile	17	15	3	9	South Korea	–	15	7	22
Ghana	74	51	40	12	Colombia	32	9	40	35	Sri Lanka	34	63	7	31
Guinea	88	80	68	–	Costa Rica	24	12	20	46	Thailand	55	30	30	–
Kenya	56	73	–	–	Cuba	69	39	–	–					
Lesotho	88	63	20	60	Dominican R.	73	38	20	–	**MIDDLE EAST**				
Liberia	96	78	61	–	Ecuador	55	41	38	51	Bahrain	0	0	–	15
Libya	30	10	–	24	El Salvador	59	45	44	74	Iran	35	29	22	89
Madagascar	92	79	64	–	Guatemala	64	49	66	–	Iraq	31	20	7	56
Malawi	45	35	20	26	Guyana	10	20	–	0	Israel	5	2	–	15
Mali	79	94	85	–	Haiti	81	67	30	55	Jordan	2	3	3	42
Mauritania	93	63	70	42	Honduras	56	31	27	–	Kuwait	0	0	0	1
Mauritius	3	1	0	10	Jamaica	10	27	10	28	Lebanon	25	2	–	15
Morocco	54	43	30	–	Mexico	44	26	–	–	Oman	40	30	9	21
Mozambique	90	91	61	54	Nicaragua	72	44	17	–	Qatar	65	5	–	5
Niger	91	63	59	53	Panama	34	38	20	34	Saudi Arabia	14	7	3	39
Nigeria	70	64	60	–	Paraguay	16	75	39	35	Syria	30	29	24	79
Senegal	13	56	60	–	Peru	65	48	25	54	U.A.E.	14	0	10	21
Sierra Leone	79	76	–	70	Trinidad and Tobago	1	13	1	10	Yemen	30	–	68	–
Somalia	83	67	73	98	Uruguay	41	17	18	–					
Sudan	95	60	49	80	Venezuela	55	17	–	–					

Immunization availability

Percentage of children in developing countries not fully immunized by one year old (late 1980s).

Country	%	Country	%	Country	%	Country	%	Country	%
AFRICA		Liberia	57	Zaire	54	Mexico	26	Papua N.G.	45
Algeria	29	Libya	38	Zambia	16	Nicaragua	30	Philippines	18
Angola	72	Madagascar	56	Zimbabwe	19	Panama	21	Singapore	5
Benin	65	Malawi	17			Paraguay	35	South Korea	11
Botswana	10	Mali	69	**AMERICAS**		Peru	34	Sri Lanka	21
Burkina Faso	54	Mauritania	55	Argentina	32	Trinidad and Tobago	22	Thailand	21
Burundi	46	Mauritius	16	Bolivia	62	Uruguay	16		
Cameroon	48	Morocco	35	Brazil	32	Venezuela	38	**MIDDLE EAST**	
C.A.R.	67	Mozambique	58	Chile	4			Iran	19
Chad	79	Niger	76	Colombia	15	**ASIA/OCEANIA**		Iraq	16
Congo	24	Nigeria	38	Costa Rica	11	Afghanistan	73	Israel	10
Côte d'Ivoire	63	Senegal	43	Cuba	7	Bangladesh	82	Jordan	29
Egypt	15	Sierra Leone	60	Dominican R.	30	Bhutan	33	Kuwait	49
Ethiopia	82	Somalia	72	Ecuador	38	India	37	Lebanon	12
Gabon	24	Sudan	42	El Salvador	37	Indonesia	29	Oman	10
Ghana	58	Tanzania	14	Guatemala	51	Malaysia	26	Saudi Arabia	12
Guinea	77	Togo	27	Haiti	50	Nepal	29	Syria	37
Kenya	26	Tunisia	12	Honduras	24	Pakistan	35	U.A.E.	27
Lesotho	19	Uganda	48	Jamaica	18			Yemen	50

Measures of national health

Life expectancy for women (**LEW**), life expectancy for men (**LEM**), infant mortality rates per 1,000 live births (**IMR**), and number of doctors per million people (**DMP**) (late 1980s).

Country	LEW	LEM	IMR	DMP	Country	LEW	LEM	IMR	DMP	Country	LEW	LEM	IMR	DMP
AFRICA					**AMERICAS**					Mongolia	66	62	–	2,108
Algeria	64	61	73	380	Argentina	74	67	32	2,506	Myanmar (Burma)	62	58	70	250
Angola	46	43	172	51	Bolivia	55	51	109	577	Nepal	50	52	127	27
Benin	48	45	109	53	Brazil	68	62	62	85	New Zealand	80	72	10	1,747
Botswana	62	56	66	92	Canada	80	73	7	1,883	North Korea	73	66	24	2,060
Burkina Faso	49	46	137	15	Chile	75	68	19	760	Pakistan	57	57	108	331
Burundi	51	47	111	42	Colombia	67	63	46	778	Papua N.G.	55	53	57	76
Cameroon	53	49	93	–	Costa Rica	75	68	19	885	Philippines	65	62	44	138
C.A.R.	47	44	131	34	Cuba	76	72	15	1,813	Saudi Arabia	65	62	70	1,251
Chad	47	44	131	17	Dominican R.	68	64	64	517	Singapore	76	70	9	410
Congo	50	47	72	111	Ecuador	68	63	62	1,082	South Korea	73	66	27	850
Côte d'Ivoire	54	51	95	–	El Salvador	67	58	58	326	Sri Lanka	73	68	32	115
Egypt	62	59	83	183	Guatemala	64	60	58	408	Syria	67	63	47	758
Ethiopia	43	39	153	11	Haiti	56	53	116	147	Thailand	67	63	38	148
Gabon	53	50	102	273	Honduras	66	62	68	583	Tunisia	66	65	58	442
Ghana	56	52	89	58	Jamaica	77	71	18	455	Turkey	66	63	74	741
Guinea	44	41	146	20	Mexico	72	66	46	382	Vietnam	64	61	63	309
Kenya	61	57	71	90	Nicaragua	65	62	61	583					
Lesotho	61	52	99	–	Panama	74	70	23	934	**EUROPE**				
Liberia	56	53	86	–	Paraguay	69	65	42	607	Albania	74	69	–	1,579
Libya	63	59	80	1,232	Peru	63	60	87	856	Austria	78	71	9	3,008
Madagascar	55	52	119	80	Uruguay	74	68	27	1,881	Belgium	78	72	10	3,119
Malawi	48	46	149	34	U.S.A.	79	72	10	2,035	Bulgaria	75	69	15	2,749
Mali	46	42	168	38	Venezuela	73	67	36	1,282	Denmark	78	73	8	2,562
Mauritania	48	44	126	74						Finland	79	71	6	2,237
Mauritius	72	66	22	457	**ASIA/AUSTRALIA AND OCEANIA**					France	80	72	8	2,485
Morocco	63	59	80	205	Afghanistan	42	41	171	151	Germany	78	72	8	2,696
Mozambique	48	45	172	21	Australia	80	73	9	2,215	Greece	78	74	13	2,907
Namibia	58	55	–	–	Bangladesh	50	51	118	143	Hungary	74	67	17	3,279
Niger	46	43	134	24	Cambodia	58	47	127	56	Iceland	80	75	–	2,616
Nigeria	52	49	104	108	China	71	68	31	839	Ireland	77	72	7	1,463
Senegal	47	44	80	45	Hong Kong	79	73	8	906	Italy	79	72	10	4,267
Sierra Leone	43	39	153	66	India	58	58	98	373	Luxembourg	78	71	–	1,800
Somalia	47	43	131	46	Indonesia	57	55	84	95	Netherlands	80	74	8	2,517
South Africa	64	58	71	–	Iran	66	65	61	322	Norway	80	74	8	2,248
Sudan	51	47	107	88	Iraq	65	63	68	547	Poland	76	68	16	1,933
Tanzania	55	51	105	–	Israel	77	74	11	2,415	Portugal	77	70	14	2,534
Togo	55	51	93	70	Japan	81	75	5	1,477	Romania	73	68	22	1,738
Uganda	53	49	102	36	Jordan	68	64	43	751	Russia	74	65	25	4,124
Zaire	54	51	83	–	Kuwait	75	71	19	1,431	Spain	80	74	9	3,547
Zambia	55	52	79	117	Laos	50	47	109	142	Sweden	80	74	6	2,743
Zimbabwe	60	57	71	129	Lebanon	69	65	39	1,397	Switzerland	80	74	7	1,602
					Malaysia	72	68	24	292	U.K.	78	72	9	1,615

Percentage causes of death, 1990

Cause	Developed countries	Developing countries
Cancers	21	7
Childbirth-related	1	10
Heart disease, strokes	53	17
Infectious parasitic diseases	5	45
Injuries, poisoning	7	6
Lung diseases	4	6
Other causes	9	9

AIDS-related deaths worldwide up to late 1994 (WHO figures)

Region	Reported cases	Estimated cases
Africa	348,525	3,183,750
Americas excluding U.S.A.	123,009	438,750
Asia	20,502	258,750
Europe	128,134	180,000
Oceania excluding Australia	5,125	33,750
U.S.A.	399,778	405,000
Total	**1,025,073**	**4,500,000+**

INTERNATIONAL HEALTH ORGANIZATIONS

Organization	Address	Purpose and function
Planned Parenthood Federation of America Inc.	810 Seventh Avenue New York, NY 10019	Development of family-planning services. Funds research into human fertility. Part of worldwide organisation.
International Red Cross and Red Crescent Movement	19 Av. de la Paix, CH-1202, Geneva, Switzerland	Prevention and relief of human suffering during warfare or natural disasters, with humanity, impartiality, neutrality, independence, voluntary service, unity, and universality.
Médecins sans frontières (MSF)	Boulevard Leopold II 209, B-1080 Brussels, Belgium	Sends volunteer doctors and nurses to populations in crisis, through war or disaster; promotes human rights and medical aid.
Save the Children	17 Grove Lane, London SE5 8RD, U.K.	Promotes long-term health and nutrition projects worldwide.
United Nations Children's Fund (UNICEF)	UNICEF House, United Nations Plaza, New York, NY 10017	Helps children and young people, especially in disaster areas and developing countries, with health care and educational services.
United Nations Fund for Drug Abuse Control (UNFDAC)	P.O. Box 500, A-1400 Vienna, Austria	Provides financial and technical assistance to countries with insufficient resources to combat drug abuse.
United Nations Population Fund (UNFPA)	220 E. 42nd Street, 19th Floor, New York, NY 10017	Funds and coordinates population control projects; promotes awareness of social, economic, and environmental consequences of overpopulation.
World Health Organization (WHO)	CH-1211, Geneva, Switzerland	Promotes highest international health standards, controls drug and vaccine standards; sets research guidelines.

PROMINENT PEOPLE

ADLER, Alfred (1870–1937) Austrian psychiatrist. He was a member of the psychoanalytical group that formed around Sigmund FREUD in 1900 in Vienna; main contributions to psychology include the concept of "inferiority complex" and his special treatment of neurosis as the "exploitation of shock."

ALZHEIMER, Alois (1864–1915) German psychiatrist and neuropathologist. He gave a full clinical and pathological description, in 1907, of presenile dementia (Alzheimer's disease); also made contributions to the preparation of microscopical sections of brain tissue.

ANDERSON, Elizabeth Garrett (1836–1917) English physician. She was the first English woman doctor, qualifying as a medical practitioner in 1865; established a dispensary for women in London in 1866, where she instituted medical courses for women.

AXELROD, Julius (b. 1912) U.S. pharmacologist. He discovered the substance that inhibits neural impulses, laying the basis for significant advances in the treatment of disorders such as schizophrenia. Awarded the Nobel Prize in 1970.

BANTING, Sir Frederick Grant (1891–1941) Canadian physiologist. In 1921, working with Charles Best and John Macleod on pancreatic secretions, he discovered the hormone insulin, a remedy for diabetes. Awarded the Nobel Prize in 1923.

BARNARD, Christiaan Neethling (b. 1922) South African surgeon. In December 1967, at Groote Schuur Hospital, Cape Town, South Africa, he performed the first successful human heart transplant.

BEAUMONT, William (1785–1853) U.S. surgeon, noted for giving a firm basis to the physiology of gastric digestion. His work was based on his treatment of a Canadian patient, Alexis St. Martin, who suffered a permanent opening in his stomach resulting from a gunshot wound.

BERNARD, Claude (1813–78) French physiologist founder of experimental physiology. He helped found the principles of homeostasis—the tendency of the internal environment of the body to remain constant despite varying external conditions; his *Introduction to the Study of Experimental Medicine* (1865) is a scientific classic.

BLACKWELL, Elizabeth (1821–1910) British-born U.S. doctor who became the first woman to obtain a Doctor of Medicine (M.D.) degree from an American medical school. After qualifying as a doctor she opened the New York Infirmary for Women and Children, which provided free health care for the poor and training for women who wanted to become doctors.

CHARCOT, Jean Martin (1825–93) French pathologist and neurologist. Sigmund FREUD was among his pupils. He contributed much to the knowledge of chronic and nervous diseases and made important studies of hypnotism.

CRICK, Francis Harry Compton (b. 1916) English molecular biologist. In 1953, he and James Dewey WATSON constructed a molecular model of the complex genetic material DNA: the discovery opened the way for far-reaching research on the genetic code. Awarded the Nobel Prize with Watson and Maurice Wilkins in 1962.

DULBECCO, Renato (b. 1914) Italian-born U.S. biologist. He showed how certain viruses can transform some cells into a cancerous state. Awarded the Nobel Prize in 1975.

EHRLICH, Paul (1854–1915) German bacteriologist. He synthesized Salvarsan as a treatment for syphilis and helped found the science of chemotherapy, in which a compound is formed that seeks out and destroys the disease organism. He also helped found modern hematology by developing techniques for staining blood corpuscles. Awarded the Nobel Prize in 1908.

EIJKMAN, Christiaan (1858–1930) Dutch physician and pathologist. He investigated beriberi in the Dutch East Indies and was the first to produce a dietary deficiency disease experimentally and to propose the concept of "essential food factors," later called vitamins. Awarded the Nobel Prize in 1929.

FLEMING, Sir Alexander (1881–1955) Scottish bacteriologist and the discoverer of penicillin. He became the first to use antityphoid vaccines on human beings and pioneered the use of Salvarsan against syphilis (*see* EHRLICH). In 1928, by the chance exposure of a culture of staphylococci, he noticed a curious mold, penicillin, which he found to have unsurpassed antibiotic powers. Awarded the Nobel Prize in 1945.

FRANKLIN, Rosalind Elsie (1920–58) English X-ray crystallographer. She obtained diffraction photographs of DNA that were of great value to Francis CRICK and James Dewey WATSON in their deduction of the full structure of DNA.

FREUD, Sigmund (1856–1939) Austrian neurologist and founder of psychoanalysis. He developed the technique of conversational "free association" to treat neurosis; he published his seminal work, *Die Traumdeutung* (*The Interpretation of Dreams*) in 1900, arguing that dreams, like neuroses, are disguised manifestations of repressed sexual desires.

GALEN, or **Claudius Galenus** (*c.* 130–*c.* 201) Greek physician, born in Pergamum in Mysia, Asia Minor. He was physician to the emperors Marcus Aurelius, Commodus, and Severus. The work extant under his name consists of 83 genuine treatises and 15 commentaries on HIPPOCRATES; many of Galen's physiological theories were wrong, but until the 1500s he was the standard medical authority.

GALLO, Robert Charles (b. 1937) U.S. physician. As head of the National Institute of Health Tumor Cell Biology Laboratory, Gallo, in 1983, became one of the first scientists to identify the virus —which he called HTLV-3—responsible for AIDS. His attempt to patent a test for the virus was opposed by Luc MONTAGNIER; subsequent resolution of the dispute in 1986 led to the renaming of the virus as HIV (human immunodeficiency virus).

HARVEY, William (1578–1657) English physician. He discovered that blood circulates around the body and published his findings in *Exercitatio Anatomica de Motu Cordis et Sanguinis* (1628); physician to Kings James I and Charles I.

HELMHOLTZ, Hermann von (1821–94) German physiologist and physicist. His physiological works were mainly on the eye, the ear, and the nervous system; he invented an ophthalmoscope (1850) independently of Charles Babbage.

HIPPOCRATES (*c.* 460–377 or 359 B.C.) Greek physician, born on the island of Kos. He is associated with the medical profession's "Hippocratic oath." The so-called Hippocratic corpus is a collection of 72 medical and surgical treatises written over two centuries by his followers, and only one or two can be ascribed to him. He seems to have tried, however, to distinguish medicine from the traditional wisdom and magic of early societies.

JENNER, Edward (1749–1823) English physician, the discoverer of vaccination. In 1775, he became convinced that cowpox could protect against smallpox. In 1796, he vaccinated a boy with lymph from a cowpox vesicle; six weeks later he injected the inoculated boy with smallpox and the boy was able to resist contracting the disease.

JOHNSON, Virginia E. Shelman (b. 1925) U.S. sexologist. She ran, with William MASTERS, a sex program at Washington University School of Medicine (St. Louis) to investigate the psychology and physiology of sexual activity.

JUNG, Carl Gustav (1875–1961) Swiss psychiatrist. After collaborating with Sigmund FREUD in Vienna in the 1900s, he went on to develop his own school of "analytical psychology"; he introduced the concepts of "introvert" and "extrovert" personalities and developed the theory that members of all cultures share in a "collective unconscious."

KINSEY, Alfred Charles (1894–1956) U.S. sexologist and zoologist. One of the first scientists to study human sexual behavior, he founded the Institute for Sex Research at Indiana University in 1942. He published two controversial studies, *Sexual Behavior in the Human Male* (1948, the so-called "Kinsey Report") and *Sexual Behavior in the Human Female* (1953).

KOCH, Robert (1843–1910) German

physician and bacteriologist. He extended PASTEUR'S germ theory by demonstrating the link between specific diseases and the bacteria that cause them. In 1876, he discovered the bacteria that causes anthrax; in 1882, the tuberculosis bacteria; and in 1883, the cholera bacteria. Awarded the Nobel Prize in 1905.

KOLFF, Willem Johan (b. 1911) Dutch-born U.S. physician. He built a rotating-drum artificial kidney in Holland, treating his first patient with it in 1943; he moved to the U.S.A. in 1950 and developed the artificial kidney further.

KREBS, Sir Hans Adolf (1900–81) German-born British biochemist. He discovered the series of chemical reactions known as the urea cycle, in Germany in 1932; after moving to England when the Nazis took power, he worked out the "Krebs cycle," the central energy-generating process of cells. Awarded the Nobel Prize in 1953.

LANDSTEINER, Karl (1868–1943) Austrian-born U.S. pathologist. He discovered the four major human blood groups (A, O, B, AB) in 1901, the M and N groups in 1927, and in 1940, the Rhesus (Rh) factor. Awarded the Nobel Prize in 1930.

LISTER, Joseph, Lord (1827–1912) English surgeon, the founder of antiseptic surgery. In addition to important observations on inflammation and blood coagulation, his great work was the introduction (1867) of antiseptic procedures. This reduced fatal postsurgical infection and encouraged surgeons to develop abdominal and bone surgery.

MALPIGHI, Marcello (1628–94) Italian anatomist. The pioneer in microscopic anatomy, he discovered blood capillary vessels, thus helping vindicate William HARVEY's theories on the circulation of blood; from 1691 he was chief physician to Pope Innocent XII.

MASTERS, William Howell (b. 1915) U.S. gynecologist and sexologist. He began a sex program at Washington University School of Medicine (St. Louis) in 1954, and was joined by Virginia JOHNSON in 1957. Using volunteer subjects under laboratory conditions, they investigated the psychology and physiology of sexual activity.

MAYO, Charles Horace (1865–1939) and **William James** (1861–1939) U.S. surgeons and medical administrators. The brothers began work as surgeons in St. Mary's Hospital in London, founded by their father. In 1900, they established the Mayo Clinic, a cooperative group clinic of surgeons and specialists working in related fields, in Rochester, Minnesota. The Mayo Clinic has since become one of the world's foremost medical research centers.

McCLINTOCK, Barbara (1902–92) U.S. geneticist. In 1951, she discovered genes that could control other genes and move on the chromosome; her ideas were neglected for many years, but in 1983

she was finally awarded the Nobel Prize.

MONTAGNIER, Luc (b. 1932) French virologist. Working in the Viral Oncology Unit of the Pasteur Institute, Paris, Montagnier discovered the virus—which he called LAV—responsible for AIDS in 1983. Conflict arose when the American researcher Robert GALLO also claimed to have discovered the causative virus. In 1986, Montagnier and Gallo finally resolved their differences and the virus was renamed HIV (human immunodeficiency virus).

PASTEUR, Louis (1822–95) French chemist, the founder of modern bacteriology. He proposed the germ theory of disease which explained that microorganisms were responsible for infectious diseases; he showed that it was possible to weaken, or attenuate, the virulence of injurious microorganisms and that the attenuated organisms could be used for immunization; from this he developed vaccinations against anthrax and rabies; he also introduced pasteurization (moderate heating) in order to kill off disease-producing organisms in wine, milk, and other foods.

PAVLOV, Ivan Petrovich (1849–1936) Russian physiologist. He worked on the physiology of circulation and digestion, but is most famous for his study of "conditioned" or acquired reflexes, each associated with some part of the brain cortex—the brain's only function being, in his view, the coupling of neurones to produce reflexes. Awarded the Nobel Prize in 1904.

PIAGET, Jean (1896–1980) Swiss psychologist and pioneer in the study of child intelligence. He is best known for his research on the development of cognitive functions (perception, intelligence, logic).

ROGERS, Carl Ransom (1902–87) U.S. psychotherapist. Originated client-centered, or nondirective, psychotherapy, which attempts to resolve a neurotic person's problems by verbal means; he renounced attempts to talk the patient into accepting any doctrinaire interpretation of his symptoms, the procedure that was practiced by Sigmund FREUD.

Ross, Sir Ronald (1857–1932) British physician, born in India. He discovered that the malaria parasite was transferred by the mosquito; directed the Ross Institute for tropical diseases from 1926. Awarded the Nobel Prize in 1902.

SABIN, Albert (b. 1906–1993) U.S. physician, born in Russia. He spent his career in the forefront of immunology, in particular working on means to combat polio. In 1954, he developed an oral polio vaccine, which helped conquer the disease.

SALK, Jonas Edward (b. 1914) U.S. virologist, best known for creating the first effective vaccine against poliomyelitis in 1953; he became director of the Salk Institute in San Diego, California, in 1963.

SANGER, Frederick (b. 1918) English

biochemist. In the 1940s and 1950s, he devised methods to deduce the sequence of amino acids in the chains of the protein hormone, insulin, for which he won the Nobel Prize in 1958; his later work on RNA and DNA won him a share of the 1980 Nobel Prize. He was the first to win two Nobel prizes for chemistry.

SANGER, Margaret Louise, née Higgins (1883–1966) U.S. nurse and social reformer. In 1914, she published a feminist magazine, *The Woman Rebel*, with advice on contraception. In 1916, she founded the first American birth-control clinic in Brooklyn, New York, for which she was imprisoned.

SCHWANN, Theodor (1810–82) German physiologist. He discovered the enzyme pepsin, investigated muscle contraction, demonstrated the role of microorganisms in putrefaction, and extended cell theory, previously applied to plants, to animal tissues.

SKINNER, Burrhus Frederic (1904–90) U.S. psychologist. The foremost proponent of behaviorism. He invented the "Skinner box," a simple device for training animals (usually rats or pigeons). In education, he developed "programmed learning," which tailors teaching to individual needs and reinforces learning by regular feedback.

SPERRY, Roger Wolcott (b. 1913) U.S. neuroscientist. His experiments in developmental neurobiology helped establish the ways nerve cells come to be "wired up" in the central nervous system; in the 1950s and 1960s, he pioneered the behavioral investigation of "split-brain" animals and humans, arguing that two separate realms of consciousness could coexist under one skull. Awarded the Nobel Prize in 1981.

SPOCK, Benjamin McLane (b. 1903) U.S. pediatrician. He transformed infant care with his book *The Common Sense Book of Baby and Child Care* (1946), which has sold over 30 million copies.

SZENT–GYÖRGYI, Albert von Nagyrapolt (1893–1986) Hungarian-born U.S. biochemist. He discovered actin, isolated vitamin C, and made important studies of biological combustion, muscular contraction, and cellular oxidation. Awarded the Nobel Prize in 1937.

VESALIUS, Andreas (1514–64) Flemish anatomist. One of the first to dissect cadavers. His work *De Humani Corporis Fabrica* (1543), with its descriptions and drawings of bones and the nervous system, repudiated the work of GALEN; condemned by the Galenists, he was sentenced to death by the Inquisition for "body snatching"; the sentence was commuted to a pilgrimage to Jerusalem.

WATSON, James Dewey (b. 1928) U.S. biologist. In 1953, he constructed, with Francis CRICK, a molecular model of DNA at the Cavendish Laboratory in Cambridge, England. Awarded the Nobel Prize with CRICK and Maurice Wilkins in 1962.

TERMS

Abdomen Section of the body between the hips and the THORAX.

Abscess Accumulation of PUS in tissues, such as in the gums, often causing pain.

Allergen Substance, such as pollen, that triggers off an ALLERGY.

Allergy Condition, such as asthma, caused by the IMMUNE SYSTEM over-reacting to contact with an ALLERGEN.

Amino acid One of a group of 20 molecules that form the building blocks of all PROTEINS. Each molecule consists of a carboxyl group and an amino group linked to a variable carbon chain or ring.

Anemia Disorder in which the blood's oxygen-carrying capacity is reduced.

Anesthetic DRUG used to abolish pain during surgery. With a local anesthetic patients remain conscious; under a general anesthetic, the patient is unconscious.

Analgesic DRUG used to relieve pain.

Anorexia nervosa Eating disorder found mainly in young women who see themselves as fat and starve themselves.

Anthelminthic drug DRUG used to kill roundworms and other parasitic worms.

Antibiotic DRUG used to treat infections caused by BACTERIA without harming the infected person.

Antibody PROTEIN released by the LYMPHOCYTES of the IMMUNE SYSTEM that locks onto specific ANTIGENS and helps to destroy invading PATHOGENS.

Antigen Substance foreign to the body, often found on the surface of PATHOGENS, that triggers the IMMUNE SYSTEM to produce ANTIBODIES.

Antiprotozoal drug DRUG used to treat infections caused by PROTISTS.

Antitoxin DRUG containing ANTIBODIES injected into a patient to neutralize TOXINS released by BACTERIA.

Antiviral drug DRUG used to treat infections caused by viruses.

Artery Blood vessel carrying blood away from the heart to the tissues.

Atrium (*pl.* atria) One of the two upper chambers of the heart.

Bacteria (*sing.* bacterium) Microscopic single-celled organisms, some of which—germs—are PATHOGENS.

Benign Describes a TUMOR that does not spread throughout the whole body. *See* MALIGNANT.

Biopsy TISSUE sample taken for examination so a DIAGNOSIS can be made.

Body Mass Index (B.M.I.) Objective estimate of whether body weight is acceptable, calculated by dividing weight in kilograms by height in meters squared. Overweight is defined as, for men, a B.M.I. 27.8 kg/m² or greater; for women, 27.3 kg/m² or greater.

Bulimia nervosa Eating disorder found mainly among young women who indulge in binge eating followed by vomiting in order to avoid weight gain.

Calorie Unit used to measure energy content of food, or energy requirements of an individual. Normally given as kilocalories (kcals or Cals), where 1 kcal = 1,000 calories. *See* KILOJOULE.

Cancer NON-INFECTIOUS DISEASE caused by abnormal tissue growth in the form of a MALIGNANT TUMOR which, left untreated, spreads through the body and kills the individual.

Capillary Small blood vessel which carries blood through the TISSUES linking ARTERIES and VEINS.

Carbohydrates Substances composed of carbon, hydrogen, and oxygen that form the body's main energy supply. There are two groups: sugars and starches.

Carcinogen Substance, such as tobacco smoke, that can cause CANCER.

Chlamydiae Group of PATHOGENS, smaller than BACTERIA.

Cholesterol LIPID that is a normal constituent of body cells. High blood cholesterol increases risk of heart attack.

Communicable Describes an INFECTIOUS DISEASE that can be passed from one person to another.

Conception FERTILIZATION of an ovum by a sperm.

Congenital Describes a disorder present at birth, not necessarily HEREDITARY.

Contagious Describes a COMMUNICABLE DISEASE, such as the common cold, that is passed easily from person to person.

Contraception Method of preventing pregnancy.

Deficiency disease DISEASE caused by lack of VITAMINS or MINERALS in diet.

Diagnosis Identification of a disorder or DISEASE by a doctor examining a patient's SIGNS and SYMPTOMS.

Diaphragm Sheet of MUSCLE that separates the THORAX and ABDOMEN.

Diarrhea Frequent emptying of watery feces from the bowels, a common symptom of many digestive disorders.

Disease Abnormality in body structure or functioning, not caused by a physical injury such as a FRACTURE. INFECTIOUS diseases are caused by PATHOGENS; NON-INFECTIOUS diseases have many causes but are not CONTAGIOUS.

Diurnal rhythm Describes body functions, such as brain activity, that vary on a daily basis.

Drug Chemical substance which, when introduced into the body, may alter the progress of a disease or change the functioning of one or more organs.

Egestion Body's removal through anus of feces consisting of undigested material and gut bacteria. *See* EXCRETION.

Electrocardiogram (ECG or EKG) Record of the heart's electrical impulses; used for DIAGNOSIS of heart DISEASE.

Electroencephalogram (EEG) Record of electrical impulses produced by the brain; used for diagnosis of brain DISEASE and to monitor a patient under general ANESTHETIC.

Embryo Developing child in the uterus between CONCEPTION and eight weeks.

Endocrine gland GLAND that releases HORMONES into the bloodstream.

Endoscope Tubelike optical instrument that allows a doctor to make a DIAGNOSIS by looking inside the body.

Enzyme PROTEIN that acts as a catalyst to control the rate of a specific biochemical reaction. Most enzymes act inside cells although some, such as the digestive enzymes, work outside cells.

Epidermis Outer protective layer of skin, constantly worn away and replaced.

Epithelium Cell layer coating all body surfaces except inside of blood vessels.

Erythrocyte Red blood cell.

Excretion Removal from the body of the waste products of metabolism. Excretory processes include urination and sweating. *See* EGESTION.

Exocrine gland GLAND, such as the salivary gland, that releases its secretions into an organ or onto the body's surface.

Fat (1) Type of lipid usually solid at room temperature. (2) Alternative name for adipose tissue that insulates the body, which in excess causes OBESITY.

Fertilization Fusion of ovum and sperm following sexual intercourse.

Fetus The name given to the developing child in the uterus from the end of the eighth week of pregnancy until birth.

Fracture A break in a bone.

Fungi Group of living organisms, some of which are parasitic in humans, causing diseases such as athlete's foot.

Gamete Sex cell, such as ovum or sperm.

Gland Groups of cells that manufacture substances such as HORMONES or ENZYMES that are useful to the body.

Glucose Sugar that is the main source of energy in the body, the form in which CARBOHYDRATE is carried in the blood.

Heimlich maneuver Technique used in first aid to remove obstruction from throat to prevent choking.

Hepatic Describes something related to the liver, such as the hepatic VEIN, which carries blood away from the liver.

Hereditary Describes a disorder inherited from parents, although not necessarily one that is CONGENITAL.

Holistic Describes a form of medicine that treats the whole person, not just the parts in which symptoms are found.

Hormone Chemical messenger that travels in the bloodstream from the ENDOCRINE GLAND that produces it to the target TISSUE where it has its effect.

Hypertension High blood pressure. Sufferers from hypertension are more likely to suffer heart attacks or strokes.

Immune system Network of nonspecific and specific defenses that protect the body against invading PATHOGENS.

Immunization Medical procedure that primes the body's IMMUNE SYSTEM to be ready to fight specific infections.

Immunodeficiency disorder Weakening of the IMMUNE SYSTEM, inhibiting ability to fight PATHOGENS and TUMORS. Possible causes include the human immunodeficiency virus (HIV) that causes AIDS.

Incubation period Time taken for a disease to develop after a PATHOGEN has invaded the body.

Infant mortality rate A measure of health care determined by the number of children who die during their first year of life for every 1,000 live births.

Infectious Describes a disease that is caused by PATHOGENS.

Infertility Inability to produce offspring either because of failure to produce healthy sperm or eggs, or because EMBRYO cannot develop.

Insomnia Difficulty in falling asleep or staying asleep at night.

In vitro fertilization (IVF) FERTILIZATION of ovum by a sperm in a test tube.

Joint The place where two or more bones meet, enabling the skeleton to move.

Keratin Tough PROTEIN that is the main component of hair, skin, and nails.

Kilojoule Unit of energy used to measure the energy content of food or the energy requirements of an individual; 4.2 kilojoules = 1 kiloCALORIE.

Life expectancy Age to which a person can be expected to live. Generally greater for women than for men.

Ligament Tough tissue that holds together and stabilizes JOINTS.

Lipids Group of substances made up of the elements carbon, hydrogen, and oxygen that include FATS, oils, and CHOLESTEROL. Lipids supply energy and form part of the structure of cells.

Lymphocyte Type of white blood cell that plays a crucial part in the IMMUNE SYSTEM by identifying PATHOGENS and releasing ANTIBODIES.

Macronutrients Foods such as LIPIDS, PROTEINS, and CARBOHYDRATES needed in relatively large amounts in the diet.

Macrophage Type of scavenging cell that roams through TISSUES hunting and ingesting PATHOGENS and dead cells.

Malignant Describes a TUMOR that spreads through the whole body and eventually causes death. The associated disease is a CANCER. *See* BENIGN.

Melanin Brown or black pigment that colors skin and hair.

Menstrual cycle The regular shedding of the lining of the uterus which occurs on an approximately 28-day basis during a woman's reproductive life when she is not pregnant.

Metabolism The sum total of all the chemical processes going on in the cells of the body. The speed of metabolism— the metabolic rate—is usually measured by the heat released by the body.

Micronutrients Foods such as VITAMINS and MINERALS required in only small quantities in the diet.

Microorganism Single-celled organisms visible only with a microscope. Most PATHOGENS are microorganisms.

Mineral One of 20 chemical elements, including iron and calcium, essential for the healthy functioning of the body.

Muscle Tissue capable of contracting and relaxing to create movement.

Mycoplasmas Group of PATHOGENS only slightly larger than VIRUSES.

Myocardial infarction or heart attack. Sudden death of heart muscle caused by the interruption of its blood supply.

Nerve TISSUE consisting of a bundle of NEURONS that carry NERVE IMPULSES to and from the brain and spinal cord.

Nerve impulse The signal that passes along a NEURON caused by electrical changes across its outer membrane.

Neuron A nerve cell. The body's longest cells, neurons transmit nerve impulses.

Neurotransmitter Substance released from a nerve ending on the arrival of a NERVE IMPULSE that transmits the impulse from one NEURON to the next or to a muscle cell.

Noncommunicable Describes an INFECTIOUS DISEASE that cannot be passed from person to person.

Noninfectious Describes DISEASES—such as most cancers or diabetes—that are not caused by PATHOGENS.

Obesity Disorder where the body has too much fat. Usually caused when energy intake exceeds energy used by the body.

Opportunistic infection Disease caused by PATHOGEN that would normally be destroyed by the IMMUNE SYSTEM. Feature of IMMUNODEFICIENCY DISORDERS such as AIDS.

Organ A structure, such as the brain, that consists of various TISSUES working together to perform specific functions.

Ovulation Release of an ovum from the ovary that takes place each month midway through the MENSTRUAL CYCLE.

Parasite Organism that lives and feeds in (such as a tapeworm) or on (such as a pubic louse) another animal's body.

Pathogens Organisms, such as VIRUSES and some BACTERIA, that invade the body and cause disease.

Prognosis Doctor's assessment of the probable course and outcome of a DISEASE based on the DIAGNOSIS.

Proteins Group of substances that each consists of hundreds or thousands of AMINO ACIDS. Some proteins form part of the structure of cells; others are ENZYMES, HORMONES, or ANTIBODIES.

Protists Group of single-celled MICROORGANISMS, some of which cause DISEASES like malaria and sleeping sickness.

Psychotherapy Treatment of mental problems using psychological methods.

Pus Pale fluid containing dead white blood cells and BACTERIA found at the site of an infection.

Rickettsiae Group of PATHOGENS the size of small bacteria that have to invade human cells in order to reproduce.

Seasonal Affective Disorder (SAD) Disorder in which sufferer is depressed in winter but recovers in spring.

Sign An indication of a DISEASE noticed by a doctor rather than the patient.

Sphincter Ring of MUSCLE around a tube (such as the pyloric sphincter) or opening (such as the anal sphincter) that controls inflow or outflow.

Sterilization (1) Treatment of instruments and dressings by heat, chemical, or other means in order to destroy MICROORGANISMS and reduce the risk of infection during surgical procedures. (2) Surgical technique which, by making males or females infertile, acts as a permanent form of CONTRACEPTION.

Stimulant DRUG that increases the activity of the brain, increasing alertness and preventing tiredness.

Stimulus External or internal modification to the body's environment that evokes a response by the body. For example, a sudden bright light causes the pupils to constrict.

Stroke Damage to part of the brain caused by cessation of its blood supply.

Surgery DIAGNOSIS and treatment of a DISEASE or injury by physical intervention, especially using instruments.

Symptom Indication of a DISEASE, such as a sore throat, noticed by a patient.

System Group of organs working together. For example, the mouth, esophagus, stomach, liver, pancreas, and intestines form the digestive system.

Tendon Strong, inelastic cordlike strap that links MUSCLE to bone.

Thorax or chest. Section of the body between the neck and ABDOMEN.

Thrombosis Formation of a blood clot within an intact blood vessel that may lead to its blockage. A common cause of MYOCARDIAL INFARCTION and STROKE.

Tissue Collection of cells of the same type and function, such as MUSCLE cells or NEURONS.

Toxin Poison produced by a living organism, especially pathogenic BACTERIA but also venomous snakes.

Tumor Abnormal TISSUE growth caused by cells dividing faster than normal. May be BENIGN or MALIGNANT.

Twins Type of multiple birth where two children are produced by one pregnancy. Identical twins form when one fertilized ovum divides completely to form two EMBRYOS. Nonidentical twins occur when two ova are released at the same time and fertilized by two sperm.

Ulcer Loss of EPITHELIUM to produce an open sore. Ulcers occur on the skin, in the digestive system, or on the eye.

Urea Poisonous, nitrogen-containing substance produced in the liver as the result of the breakdown of PROTEINS and excreted in URINE.

Urine Liquid produced by the kidneys which contains waste products, such as UREA, and excess water and salts. Urine is excreted through the urethra.

Vein Blood vessel carrying blood toward the heart from the TISSUES.

Ventricle One of the two lower chambers of the heart.

Virus PATHOGEN much smaller than a BACTERIUM that invades human cells and forces them to make copies of itself.

Vitamin One of 13 complex substances all needed in small amounts by the body to ensure normal functioning.

SECTION 3
PEOPLE

Human Origins Timeline

8–4 m.y.a. (million years ago) Emergence of hominid-chimpanzee link, called *Australopithecus ramidus*.

5–2.9 m.y.a. Emergence of earliest hominids, *Australopithecus afarensis*.

3.5–2.5 m.y.a. *Australopithecus africanus*, a biped weighing 60–95 pounds (27–43 kg), in southern and eastern Africa.

2.5 m.y.a. Earliest stone tools in use in Hadar, Ethiopia. (Tool kits are called, after Olduvai Gorge, Tanzania, the Oldowan industry.)

c. 2 m.y.a. *Australopithecus robustus*, a biped weighing 80–126 pounds (36–57 kg), in southern Africa. Representatives of our own genus, *Homo habilis*, at sites such as Koobi Fora (Kenya), and Olduvai Gorge (Tanzania).

c. 1.8 m.y.a. *Australopithecus boisei*, an australopithecine similar to *A. robustus*, in East Africa; these and *A. africanus* coexist with earliest human lineage (*H. habilis*) in what is now the Rift Valley area of Africa.

1.6 m.y.a. *Homo erectus* emerges in East Africa with larger brain than *H. habilis*, and a sophisticated tool kit comprising Acheulian hand axes.

1–1.5 m.y.a. First known use of fire, Swartkrans, S. Africa.

1–0.5 m.y.a. Traces of *H. erectus* appear throughout Africa and in Middle East, Iran, China, Southeast Asia, and southern Europe.

450,000 B.C. Archaic *Homo sapiens* emerges in Africa.

c. 250,000 B.C. *H. erectus* becomes extinct after colonizing from Europe to Indonesia. Different types of *H. sapiens* begin to succeed *H. erectus*.

120,000 B.C. Possible emergence of *Homo sapiens sapiens* in Africa. Recent genetic research of DNA suggests that everyone in the world today has a common source. This idea is known as the "mitochondrial mother."

c. 100,000 B.C. Emergence of Neanderthals (*Homo sapiens neanderthalensis*) in Europe and the Middle East.

60,000 B.C. Neanderthal burial site at Shanidar, Iraq, suggests ritual practices.

c. 55,000 B.C. Humans reach northern Australia, having crossed at least 37 miles (60 km) of open sea.

45,000 B.C. Earliest known rock art (petroglyphs) at Panaramitee, Australia.

45,000–35,000 B.C. *H. sapiens sapiens* spreads throughout Europe. Contacts take place with Neanderthal people.

35,000 B.C. *H. sapiens sapiens* displaces *H. sapiens neanderthalensis*, for reasons still unknown. Development of Paleolithic art in Europe: ivory carvings in Germany, cave paintings in S. France.

25,000 B.C. Animal paintings on rock slabs in southern Africa (Apollo II cave, Namibia).

c. 15,000 B.C. Cave paintings at Lascaux, France.

HUMAN ORIGINS

Scientists believe that humankind shares its origins with australopithecines (southern apes), dating back some four million years. The earliest remains have been found in East Africa, where rich fossil sites are trapped in the sink of the Rift Valley system. In 1974 this region yielded the remarkably complete remains of *Australopithecus afarensis* (southern ape of Afar), better known as "Lucy" after a well-known Beatles song. Lucy was more than three million years old, stood about 4 feet (1.2 m) tall, and walked upright. She was identified as a member of the ancestral stock that later split into two branches, one leading on to *Homo*, while the other developed into two kinds of australopithecine. Datable volcanic ash indicates that two million years ago all three species coexisted together, but whereas the earliest of the *Homo* lineage (*Homo habilis*) evolved into *Homo erectus*, the smaller-brained australopithecines became extinct.

In 1992 scientists discovered bone fragments from the same region suggesting a link between humans and chimpanzees. This was named *Australopithecus ramidus*.

Skeleton of "Lucy," an upstanding australopithecine three million years old.

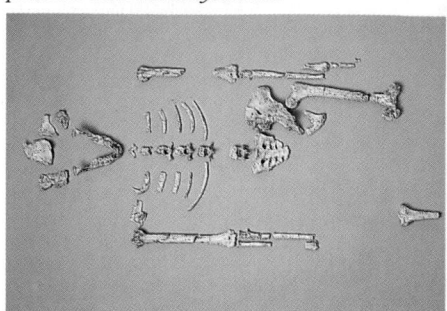

AUSTRALOPITHECUS AND EARLY HOMO

Name	A. afarensis	A. africanus	A. robustus	A. boisei	Homo habilis
Age	5–2.9 mya	3.5–2.5 mya	2–1.3 mya	2.6–1.2 mya	2–1.5 mya
Locality	Ethiopia, Kenya, Tanzania	Taung, Sterkfonten, South Africa	South Africa, Ethiopia, Kenya	Olduvai, Ethiopia	Olduvai, Kenya
Brain size	24 cu. in.	27.5 cu. in.	30.5 cu. in.	30.5 cu. in.	42.7 cu. in.
Weight	77.2 lb.	77.2 lb.	99 lb.	110 lb.	110 lb.
Appearance	Low large face, long arms and short legs, bipedal.	Same as A. afarensis, but braincase more rounded, face more buttressed.	Same as A. africanus, with flatter face, crests for masticatory muscles.	Same as A. africanus, with thick enamel on teeth and more buttressed face.	Rounder braincase, deep, flat face, large teeth. Body parts more like Homo sapiens.

Olduvai Gorge

Five million years ago a lake covered most of the area of Olduvai Gorge in the Serengeti plains, in present-day northern Tanzania. Bones and remains found in the black clay of its ancient shoreline are well preserved by layers of volcanic tuff, making it an excellent site for excavation and dating. Dr. Louis Leakey found the first stone tools at Olduvai Gorge in 1931, and many thousands have been discovered subsequently. Work at the site was continuous and intensified in 1959 when Leakey's wife, Dr. Mary Leakey, discovered an australopithecine skull. By 1971, 72 archaeological sites were being excavated and 34 hominids had been found.

Complete floors of living quarters were exposed at some of the sites. One such living space yielded smashed bones and stone tools with small flakes scattered over a large area. Surrounding them, a ring of larger bones was discovered. Microscope techniques have revealed that the 3,500 mammalian cut bones found were probably brought to the site as a result of scavenging rather than hunting, as cut marks are found over tooth marks.

Olduvai Gorge, Tanzania: strata and fossils.

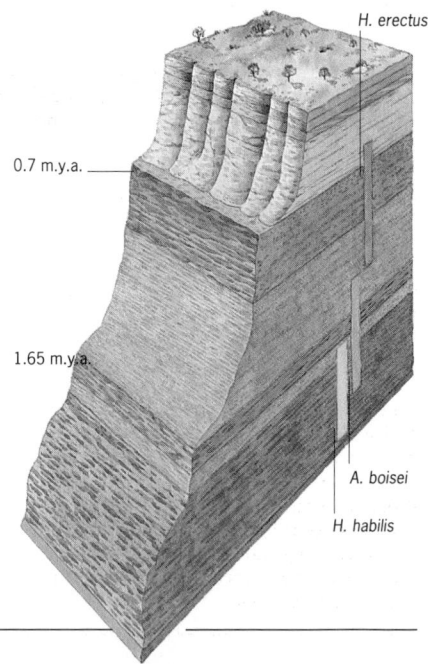

H. erectus

0.7 m.y.a.

1.65 m.y.a.

A. boisei

H. habilis

Homo erectus

Hunting lodge seasonally occupied c. *400,000 B.C. by* H. erectus *nomads.*

A new kind of hominid, *Homo erectus,* appeared in Africa around 1.6 million years ago, between the Pliocene and Pleistocene epochs. Spreading out of Africa into Asia, it survived relatively unchanged for over one million years until replaced by *Homo sapiens.*

The oldest fossils are from Kenya: a cranium found at Koobi Fora in 1975 is 1.6 million years old. Much of the facial skeleton is present, although the lower jaw is missing. Louis Leakey later discovered a large heavy-browed braincase in 1960: known as Hominid 9 from Upper Bed II, it is 1.2 million years old. Another important fossil, nearly the entire skeleton of a 12-year-old male, was found in 1984 on the western side of Lake Turkana.

Just as *Homo erectus* fossils may be easily distinguished from modern humans, so their heavy brows, flexed occiput (back of the head), and different cranial crests and ridges separate them from earlier *Homo* and *Australopithecus* fossils. Most finds consist of skulls and teeth, so descriptions concentrate on these aspects.

Eugene Dubois found the famous Trinil skullcap and femur (1894) in the banks of the Solo River in Java, Indonesia. He named his discovery *Pithecanthropus* (now *Homo*) *erectus*. It was not until the 1920s that more bones were discovered near Beijing in China at the rich site of Zhoukoudian ("Dragon Bone Hill"). The fossils disappeared during World War II, but their casts and photographs have survived.

Information on the lifestyle of *Homo erectus* emerged from excavations at Nice, France (1966), which revealed a site some 400,000 years old. A "hunting lodge" seasonally occupied by nomadic groups, it had a hearth at its center, and traces of ocher pigment found at the site suggest the use of body ornamentation.

MIDDLE AND UPPER PALEOLITHIC

The transition between *Homo sapiens* and *Homo sapiens sapiens* (120,000–40,000 B.C.) was arguably the most important development in human history: it initiated a total restructuring of social relations. An analysis of the transition from Middle to Upper Paleolithic in southwest France shows its striking cultural innovations:
- Stone technology became more varied.
- Bone, ivory, and antlers were shaped for use. The bow and arrow and *atlatl* (throwing stick) were invented.
- Perforated jewelry was worn.
- Hunting became more herd-oriented.
- Population grew in settlement areas; "home base" structures were built.
- Artistic consciousness developed, as illustrated in figurines, wall paintings, rock carvings, and burial techniques.
- Artifact styles developed and trade in exotic items began.

- There was an increase in body size and brain capacity, from 67cu. in. (1,100 cm³) to 85cu. in. (1,400 cm³), and changes in facial structure.

One theory for these dramatic changes proposes that they may have been the result of a new wave of migration from Africa, where tropical conditions had allowed more successful development. (DNA analysis shows that at a certain point humans had a common source: some archaeologists think that this was in southern Africa *c.* 105,000 B.C.) Other theories argue that modern humans evolved independently in different areas, and suggest that the withdrawal of the ice sheet and consequent abundance of food and settlement led to a population explosion. In this scenario, direct evolution followed the relaxing of environmental pressures to selectivity.

Paleolithic cave art

The earliest known Paleolithic "art" (c. 35,000–30,000 B.C.) in Europe comprises small ivory carvings of animals and humans found in caves in southern Germany; later (from 28,000 B.C.) stylized female figurines of fairly consistent form were distributed from southwestern France to southern Russia, and rock art begins to be produced. Some Paleolithic rock engravings have survived in the open air, but most of the art is now restricted to rock shelters and caves, especially in Spain, France, and Italy. Techniques were varied: finger tracings, engravings, hand stencils, clay modeling, bas-relief sculpture, outline drawings, and paintings executed in red and black, brown and yellow. Paint was applied with brushes, pads, and fingertips, or simply sprayed from the mouth.

Much of the art was "public'—readily accessible in the open air, shelters, or shallow caves, but some was produced in deep, inaccessible cave passages, suggesting a religious rather than simply aesthetic function. Early explanations believed it to be a form of shamanistic magic for hunting or fertility, but it is now recognized that its function and meaning are far more complex, probably involving myth, metaphor, and the transmission of social and cultural lore. The work is often naturalistic and executed with great skill.

Nonfigurative (abstract) cave art is open to different interpretations. Suggestions as to what it might represent include protomathematics, hunting tallies, signatures, protowriting, maps, calendars, menstrual records, and moon worship charts. Comparisons have been made between Paleolithic rock art, with its shamanistic associations, and contemporary huntergatherers' art (such as the southern African Koisan), produced under the influences of drugs or meditation.

Cave painting at Lascaux, France, c. *15,000 B.C.*

Migration Timeline

700,000–500,000 B.C. *Homo erectus* appears in Asia.

700,000–300,000 B.C. *H. erectus* colonizes Europe (Germany, Hungary, Italy, France, and Spain).

300,000–200,000 B.C. *Homo sapiens* emerges in Europe.

***c.* 120,000 B.C.** *Homo sapiens sapiens* emerges in Africa.

90,000–100,000 B.C. *H. sapiens* reaches Europe, east Mediterranean and Asia.

55,000–40,000 B.C. Australia is colonized by *H. sapiens sapiens*.

33,000–12,000 years ago *H. sapiens sapiens* crosses Bering land bridge from Siberia to North America; earliest secure date is 12,000 years ago, but several sites in S. America suggest a much earlier colonization.

***c.* 2000 B.C.** Aryans settle in Iran and northern India.

***c.* 1800 B.C.** Indo-Europeans populate Middle East and Aegean area.

***c.* 1300 B.C.** Exodus of the Jews from Egypt and settlement in Palestine.

***c.* 1200-1000 B.C.** Immigrants from Indonesia settle Melanesia, Fiji, Tonga, and Western Samoa, spreading into western Polynesia.

A.D. 400s Germanic peoples (Vandals, Visigoths, Angles, Saxons, Jutes) invade and settle Britain, France, Spain, Turkey, and Italy.

600-1000 Arabs invade and settle north Africa, Spain, Turkey, southern Italy, and southwest Asia.

***c.* 800** First settlers from Polynesia reach Easter Island, later spreading to New Zealand *c.* 850.

1200s Mongols and nomads from central Asia move into Asian borders and Europe; widespread dispersal of Turks over western Asia.

***c.* 1830** First Chinese settlement at Singapore; start of Chinese expansion into Southeast Asia.

1500s Spanish settle Central and South America, particularly Chile, Peru, and Mexico. Portuguese settle Brazil.

1600s English, Dutch, and French expansion into North America. First colonies in Virginia, New England, New Amsterdam (New York), and Quebec. European colonists bring Africans to the Americas as slaves.

1788 First white settlement in Australia with British convicts transported to New South Wales.

1800s Migration of millions from Europe to North America, South Africa, and Australia and Oceania. Chinese emigrate to Siam, Java, Malay peninsula, the Americas, and New South Wales; Indians to West Indies, S. and E. Africa.

1900s Emigration from European countries to U.S.A. up to World War II. After World War II emigration from British colonies to U.K. and U.S.A. Latin American and Asian refugees emigrate to U.S.A.

COLONIZATION OF AUSTRALIA

The colonization of greater Australia (including New Guinea) may have taken place as long as 55,000 years ago. Sundaland (the landmass that in glacial phases joined the Malay peninsula, Sumatra, Java, and Borneo, and parts of the Philippine archipelago) has always been separated by sea from Sahul Land, linking Australia and New Guinea. The area in between, Wallacea, could only have been crossed by sea.

The shortest space for a crossing would have been between Java and Timor, then south to Australia. An indirect but viable route would have been between Kalimantan (Borneo), east through Sulawesi to northwest New Guinea, and then south to Australia. The minimum gap combined with the lowest sea levels is 50–60 miles (80–100 km). The bark dugout canoes of modern Aboriginal Australia are not capable of making even shorter crossings without risking fatality, so it is possible that rafts were constructed out of bamboo, plentiful in Southeast Asia, and the crossings made from there.

In 1969, at Willandra Lakes, New South Wales, the cremated remains of a woman known as Lake Mungo I was discovered and dated to 24,500–26,000 years old—the oldest evidence of cremation in the world. Lake Mungo III, the skeleton of a man, was unearthed at a burial site dating from 28,000– 30,000 years ago. He was found covered in red ocher powder; analysis indicates that he had lived on a diet of mussels, crayfish, perch, emu eggs, wallabies, and wombats.

THE FIRST AMERICANS

When Columbus discovered the New World he was not surprised to find it inhabited; he thought he had landed in India or Japan. Early explorers noted similarities between Egyptian and American cultures, such as pyramids, and some thought that Native Americans were descendants of Ham, one of Noah's sons and supposedly father of the Egyptians.

In 1590, a Spanish Jesuit, José de Acosta, speculated that Native Americans came from Asia. Today it is accepted that the first Americans came from eastern Asia via a land route over the Bering Sea, but debate continues about the date of the first migrations and the way in which these migrants traversed the demanding Arctic environment.

Between 60,000 and 12,000 years ago, world climates cooled, locking up the sea as ice and opening a land bridge across the Bering Strait. The sea level would have been lowered sufficiently to expose a path 900–1,800 miles (1,500–3,000 km) wide, usually referred to as Beringia. Nomadic peoples would have crossed this, following the animals on which they preyed.

Two periods of colonization are possible: 40,000 years ago, following the Mid-Wisconsin Interglacial, and 18,000 years ago after the Late Wisconsin Glaciation. Many believe that it was uninhabited before the so-called Clovis cultures, about 12,000 years ago, but evidence exists for extensive penetration of South America by 11,000 years ago. Some authorities suggest that Monte Verde, Chile, where a human footprint, log foundations, animal skins, and plant remains have been preserved by a peat bog, is even older. This has been dated to 12,000–33,000 years ago.

The Eskimos were the last to enter the Americas before the Europeans, crossing the land bridge to Alaska *c.* 10,000 years ago. Two movements, *c.* 5,000 and *c.* 1,200 years ago, brought Inuit Eskimos to their present home in Greenland and Canada.

Inuit (Eskimo) stone cairn, Hudson Bay, Canada.

Paleolithic rock art from Patagonia, c. 10,000 B. C.

POLYNESIA

It is now believed that most of Polynesia, from the Marianas and Hawaiian Islands in the north to the Solomon Islands, Samoa, and the Society Islands in the south, was progressively colonized from Southeast Asia. However, experimental archaeologists, notably Thor Heyerdahl, showed that it was technically possible that parts of Polynesia could have been reached and settled from America. This was widely dismissed as absurd because the common Peruvian balsa raft was a floating bundle of corkwood which absorbs water easily, although there appeared to be similarities in material culture between coastal South America and Polynesia. Despite much skepticism, Heyerdahl built the *Kon-Tiki* raft and with a crew set sail on April 28, 1947.

After 100 days and 6,900 miles (11,100 km), he reached his destination in the Tuamotu Islands.

Heyerdahl's heroic voyage showed that the settlement of Polynesia could have come from South America. But linguists were able to reconstruct the sequence of routes along which the protolanguages spread from the tongues spoken in the region, demonstrating that there had been only one migration. Contrary to Heyerdahl's belief, this movement of peoples across the Pacific had proceeded from west to east via Melanesia. Archaeologists confirmed this using radiocarbon dating, and their findings are now accepted. Nevertheless, when the first Europeans arrived in the 1500s, some civilizations were more than 1,000 years old.

PREHISTORY AND RACE

Archaeology has sometimes been used to support contemporary social theory, notoriously in cases where notions of national and racial superiority have sought justification for political aims. One example is the German Third Reich's attempt to justify its invasion of Poland by using the idea of archaeological "cultures." By showing that parts of Poland had been Germanic since the Iron Age, the Nazi Reich purported to find evidence in support of its "master race" ideology, documenting the movement of Aryans from an Indo-Germanic base. This fitted in neatly with the Nazi leadership's need to establish evacuation and resettlement points in Poland in the name of the "master race," relegating the more recently arrived Slavs to inferior status.

RACE

Race is of very little biological consequence, focusing as it does on arbitrary factors such as skin and eye color, hair color and form, and body dimensions. The important question regarding race is whether significant genetic variety can be meaningfully categorized into named racial populations.

Geneticists characterize racial groups by the frequency of different genes. They find that, in terms of genes, populations differ by remarkably few percentage points. In fact, variations between populations are small in comparison with often very large variations within populations.

"Gene flow" occurs when genes are transferred between populations; flow is unaffected by environmental factors. Since high mobility has always characterized humankind, gene flow has a homogenizing influence in human evolution, acting to decrease between-population variability and increase within-population variability. Gradients in gene frequency, known as genoclines (or clines), normally occur on a continental basis. Thus gene theories have generally discredited the race concept, and because of the nature of geographical variation in humans it is often said that there are no races, only clines.

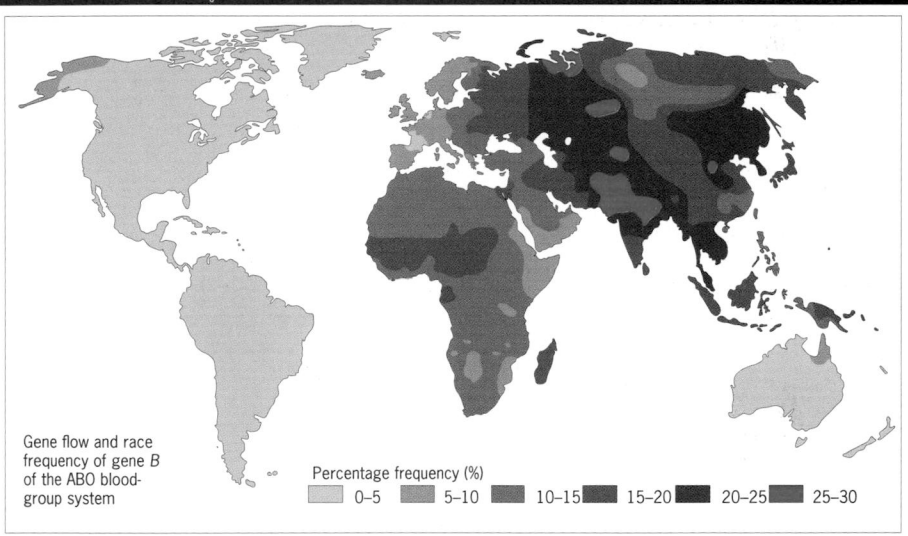

Gene flow and race frequency of gene *B* of the ABO blood-group system

Percentage frequency (%)

| 0–5 | 5–10 | 10–15 | 15–20 | 20–25 | 25–30 |

Distribution of gene B of the ABO blood-group system progressively diminishes in frequency across Eurasia from east to west, possibly indicating a gene flow due to repeated invasions from Asia.

Variation on continental basis

ASIAN (MONGOLOID)
Location
Continental and east Asia including Japan, Taiwan, Philippines, and much of Indonesia. Also Native American peoples (Amerindians), who first came from Asia but differ in the various blood-group frequencies.
Characteristics
Skin of a yellowish or brown hue, straight black hair and eyes, sparse body hair, low noses.
Genes
In east Asia there is a high frequency of the B blood-group gene; in the Americas the B gene was probably lacking before European colonization. The M gene is at high frequency throughout.

AFRICAN (NEGROID)
Location
Related races south of the Sahara desert in Africa.
Characteristics
Heavy pigmentation of the hair, skin, and eyes; helical hair, thick lips, wide noses. Nilotic peoples of Sudan are tall, while South African Bushmen are very short.
Genes
ABO gene frequencies are similar to Europe but S is much rarer. Recent DNA analysis suggests that all contemporary populations are descended from groups emigrating *c.* 50,000 B.C.
Melanesians (Pacific islands) share negroid skin color, but differ in blood-group frequencies.

EUROPEAN (CAUCASOID)
Location
Europe, including north Africa and Near East.
Characteristics
Low skin pigmentation (melanin), high frequency of blue eyes, fair hair, narrow lips and noses.
Genes
High frequency of A genes in the ABO system exceeding 25%. Variation is clinal with most long gradients running from east to west following penetration from Asia: first in the Neolithic, which brought Asian peoples via Atlantic seaboard and Mediterranean, then in the age of migrations (A.D. 300s), and finally with Slav and Turkish invasions of the Balkans.

AUSTRALOID/ POLYNESIAN
Location
Australia and the Pacific; Hawaii to New Zealand, Easter Island to Tuvalu.
Characteristics
Australian Aborigines have robust skulls, heavy jaws, broad, low noses, well-developed bodies, wavy hair. Skin, hair, eyes are heavily pigmented. Polynesians have light skin color.
Genes
ABO genes variable: A in the south, O in the north, and B only in the Bay of Carpentaria. The S gene is absent. The N gene reaches 95% in parts of western Australia. In Polynesians frequencies of blood-group B are low.

PALEOLITHIC TIME

The Russian scholar Boris Frolov noted that some of the marks on Paleolithic Ice Age objects are incised in groups or lines representing multiples of numbers, especially five and seven. Frolov believes these are related to measurement of time. In Malata, Siberia, for example, a piece of ivory from this period was found, marked with a sequence of pockmarks engraved in several spirals. The central spiral had 243 pockmarks in seven turns, while the other two sets comprised 122 pockmarks, totaling 365. At this latitude the number of winter days is 243, while summer consists of 122 days.

SEASONS AND FESTIVALS

Celestial changes have inspired festivals in every culture. Equinox and solstice celebrations mark sowing of seed, growth of crops, and harvest; New Year festivities symbolize "rebirth" of time, giving people the chance to "begin" again.

In the Christian calendar, the 40-day period between Carnival (*right*) and Easter is balanced by the 40-day period between Easter and Ascension, and New Year's Eve falls exactly between Christmas Eve and the Epiphany. In the same way that rites of passage order transitions in a person's life, thus society mirrors the cycles of nature.

Carnival

Carnival has its roots in the cults of Isis and Osiris (Egypt), Saturn (Rome), Attis and Dionysus (Greece), and Cybele (Asia Minor) (Ancient Mystery Cults, *p. 215*). These gods symbolized the onset of fertile springtime after a long, barren winter. New cults and religions had to incorporate earlier carnival traditions into their own rites because of their powerful hold on people, and Christianity is perhaps no exception.

The word "carnival" probably derives from the Latin for "flesh" (*caro*) and "remove" (*levare*), and traditionally precedes the 40 days of fasting and abstinence leading to Easter Sunday. It is a time of ecstatic excess and chaotic frenzy, which the anthropologist J. G. Frazer attempted to link with the old Roman festival of Saturnalia. In this interpretation, the mock-king who is put to death at the end of his reign over the topsy-turvy world (the Golden Age of Saturn) may have associations with the Christian divine sacrifice. The tradition of "king" of the carnival continues in modern festivities, except that he is no longer put to death.

Major carnivals
La Bataille des Fleurs in Nice, France
Carnestolado, Mexico
Carnival of Cologne, Germany
Fasnacht of Basel, Switzerland
Mardi Gras in New Orleans, Rio de
 Janeiro, and Trinidad
Schleicherlaufen of Telfs, Austria

Fasnacht carnival, Tyrol, Austria.

THE MAYAN CALENDAR

Calendar imagery among the Maya is so prominent that some experts believe that they had an obsessive fascination with time rivaling that of present-day humans. They used two calendrical systems, the Long Count and the Calendar Round. The Long Count was perfected in Classical times (A.D. 250–900), and its dates record the number of days that have elapsed since a mythological starting point corresponding to 3114 B.C. in our calendar. In fact, the Maya believed that the world had been created and destroyed at least three times, the last creation having begun on August 13, 3114 B.C., and the next being due on December 24, 2011.

Long Count dates are precise counts of elapsed time based on the 360-day year, which they called a *tun*, divided into 18 months of 20-day *uinals*. The Mayan numbering system is based on 20, not ten, so a year was counted in groups of 20 *tuns*, termed a *katun*, and 20 *katuns*, termed a *baktun*.

A Long Count date is made up of five numbers. The first figure records the *baktun* (400-year span). The second is the *katun* (20-year span), the third a *tun*

(360-day span), the fourth a *uinal* (20-day span) and the last a *kin*, a single day. The oldest recorded date is 8.12.14.8.15 or July 6, A.D. 292, from Stela 29 at Tikal in northern Guatemala.

The Calendar Round simply names the day in two different calendars. The first is the sacred round of 260 days, the *Tzolkin*, composed of 20 day names and 13 numbers. It is pictured as a set of interlocking cogwheels representing

circular time: one with numbers from one to 13, the other with 20 named days, such as *Imix* (day one), *Ik* (day two), *Akbal* (day three), etc. Supplementing this is the *Haab* (also called the Vague Year), a year of 365 days made up of 182-day months, and then a five-day period at the end of the year. It takes 18,950 days, or 52 365-day years, for a combination of these two methods to repeat itself.

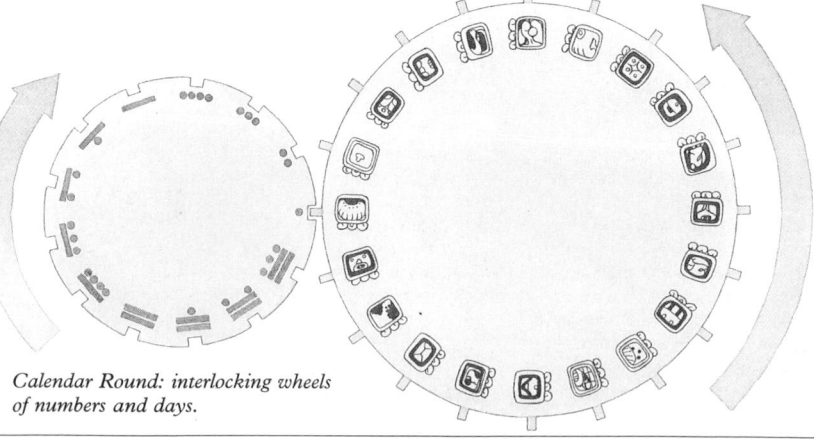

Calendar Round: interlocking wheels of numbers and days.

RITES OF PASSAGE

The major changes in the life cycle of a person's social development are marked by rites of passage—rituals of birth, puberty, marriage, and death. These rituals serve to express the course of social time, indicate changes in personal status, and invoke supernatural aid in bringing them about. The pattern of these rites, analyzed by authorities such as Charles van Gennep, appears to be extraordinarily widespread in societies.

A life transition such as puberty is ritually expressed in three phases: first, the person is removed from the old category (preliminal separation); next, he is isolated from normal social contact and placed in an external, suspended state (liminal transition); and finally, he is ritually re-incorporated into a new place in society (postliminal incorporation).

The disappearance-reappearance sequence indicates a kind of rebirth into each new state, which enables others in the social group to realize that they must establish a new set of relations with the initiate. For example, in rural Italy the pubescent boy is ceremoniously passed through a sapling that has been split in two (reborn) which is then bound up again so that it continues to grow. The boy is considered a young man, and boy and tree mature together.

Death

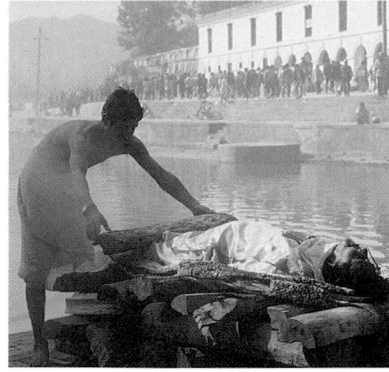

Death: cremation of bodies by the river in Kathmandu, Nepal.

Death is the final and ultimate rite of passage, the last in a long chain of transitions. It is rarely seen as the total eclipse of the person, but more as a transition to another state. The belief that death is not the "end" underlies much of ritual behavior, which attempts to link birth and death and to counter the psychological repugnance of aging (entropy).

Funerary symbolism often focuses on phenomena in nature which repeat themselves in order to disclaim the "reality" of death—asserting that death follows birth as birth follows death in a cycle. Through ritualized ceremonies, presided over by a priest or shaman, both the dead and the living are moved on to new points of orientation.

The corpse (and its physical decay) is normally the focus of the funeral ritual—it is cremated, buried, or, in the case of some Tibetan Buddhists, eaten by vultures. The force that gave the body life is believed to be transformed but not extinguished. Throughout the world, a key principle of most religious dogma proposes the temporary habitation of the body by the soul, suggesting that death is a "passage" or stage of development. The soul may move to a noncorporeal or spirit state, as in the Judeo-Christian tradition, or may be reincarnated, as in the Hindu and Buddhist religions.

At funerals in Berewan, central Borneo, the corpse is first displayed for close relatives on a specially built seat for a couple of days before being placed in a coffin or huge urn. After four to ten days, it is removed for temporary storage in the long house, then placed on a simple wooden platform in the graveyard for eight months to five years. The bones are then transported to their final resting place, which is typically a niche in a richly carved post or a wooden mausoleum.

Birth

In most societies, the individual's experience of pregnancy and childbirth is placed in a larger context which reflects the society's perspective on the creation of life. Rites of passage through these crucial times are subject to community celebration, ritual acknowledgment, and dramatization. In Western society, for instance, the "life-crisis" of birth is turned over to the doctor, who can be viewed as a sort of cultural hero "delivering" the baby.

Elsewhere, childbirth may be seen as polluting. Among the Kaulong of New Britain it is considered dangerous for a pregnant woman to be near adult males, gardens, dwellings, and water sources, and she is physically separated from residential areas.

The pregnant woman is not necessarily the only focus of attention; often the husband assumes the symptoms and behavior of his wife during the pregnancy, delivery and post-partum periods. The rites of passage pattern can be illustrated through the stages of pregnancy:

- During the rites of separation (preliminal phase) the pregnant woman is subject to prenatal care and pollution taboos. Mexican American women believe exposure to cold air, winds, and drafts from air conditioners is dangerous. Hot air is considered equally dangerous; sitting near sun-heated window glass can make one ill. For the Navajo, the pregnant woman's head must not point west, which is associated with death.

- Labor is the rite of transition (liminal phase) during which the woman is often kept physically apart, e.g. in a labor suite or a menstruation hut, as she is "contaminated with holiness," in a vulnerable but "sacred" condition. The common folk position for giving birth is kneeling or squatting, with attendants supporting from behind or pushing on top of the uterus. In Western culture, medication is provided in order to encourage uterine contractions, and the passive "patient" is encouraged to sleep in between.

Melanesians have an elaborate system where the position of the mother-to-be must be arranged according to the day and hour. Mexican women are taught to close their mouths to prevent the uterus from rising up, and Navajo women are forbidden to scream, in order to preserve the secrecy of childbirth.

- The rite of aggregation (postliminal phase) brings the woman back from the "sacred" to the everyday world. The period of convalescence may take from six to 40 days. The end of this final phase is often marked by the baby's first bath, or the woman's first intercourse after childbirth.

Birth: ancient Egyptian temple relief, Denderah.

LANGUAGE FAMILIES

It is estimated that between 5,000 and 10,000 languages are spoken in today's world, although the number is dwindling. Linguists classify these languages into families. The principal language families of the modern world are Indo-European, Afro-Asiatic, Altaic, Finno-Ugric, Sino-Tibetan, Dravidian, and Austro-Asiatic. The Indo-European family was the first to be recognized in this way, when in 1813 the English scholar Thomas Young coined the term to cover a widely spread group of related languages. Surprisingly, these combine many of the languages of India and Iran with European tongues. The German August Schleicher was the first to propose a family tree model for genetic descent (*below*), in 1862.

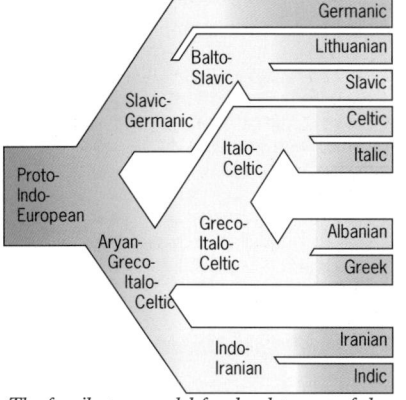

The family tree model for development of the Indo-European languages.

THEORIES FOR LANGUAGE ORIGIN

Theorizing about language origin is for the most part speculative; it can only begin to be a truly scientific study with the invention of written language records. The "ding-dong" theory (also called the "ta-ta" theory as a skeptical reference to the claim that the way the tongue moves while saying the words "ta-ta" reflects the act of waving goodbye) implies there is a mystical correlation between speech and spontaneously produced oral gestures imitating bodily movements. The "bow-wow" theory hypothesizes that speech is an imitation of the sounds occurring in nature. Some words, such as "cuckoo" or "splash," are imitative, or onomatopoeic, but vary from language to language. The "pooh-pooh" theory holds that speech arose because people make instinctive sounds caused, for instance, by pain, surprise, fear, or anger. The main evidence is use of interjections, but no language contains many of these. It is often paired with the "yo-he-ho" theory to the effect that language arose from grunts of physical exertion, and even the "sing-song" theory that language arose from primitive inarticulate chants.

STRUCTURE OF LANGUAGE

The broad distinction in linguistics between the actual practice of speech and its underlying code or language was first clearly drawn by Ferdinand de Saussure (1916). Noam Chomsky in his *Syntactic Structures* (1957) described the distinction between speech and language as a contrast between performance and competence. Performance is the actual "hemming and hawing" of speech behavior; competence is the knowledge of the language, the conceptual code.

Linguistic competence can be seen as one element of "cultural competence." The revolutionary linguistics of the 1960s and 1970s, known as transformative linguistics, took up the challenge of describing, in explicit rules and symbols, how linguistic competence is organized.

It is now recognized that a complex structure underlies the apparent diversity of languages. Dissimilarities between human tongues are superficial, and deep-seated structures determine the shape of all languages, however different certain features seem to be.

Chomsky believes that a universal grammatical system is biologically implanted in the brain. A child knows language but not a particular language. Language is learned in a rapid burst between two and three-and-a-half years of age. This knowledge follows uniform stages of development in which a systematic theory of the language is soon learned, but based on limited, fragmented information.

DIFFERENCES BETWEEN AMERICAN AND BRITISH ENGLISH

Any given language is in a constant state of evolution. Even the same language spoken in two separate places can change in meaning after a very short period of time. American English is in some respects very different from the same language spoken in Britain. This may be for many reasons: the constant influence of foreign languages and cultures on both the United States and Britain, the gradual erosion or evolution of pronunciation, and the influx of new terminology from the scientific and artistic communities. Some common differences in meaning between American and British English are shown (*right*).

American	British
bill	note
candy	sweets
eggplant	aubergine
downtown	city centre
drugstore	chemist's
elevator	lift
fall	autumn
gasoline	petrol
french fries	chips
line	queue
pants	trousers
sidewalk	pavement
suspenders	braces
thumbtack	drawing pin
trash	rubbish
vest	waistcoat
yard	garden
trunk	boot (of car)

Human speech may be a function of the vocal tract. Comparison with a chimpanzee (left) shows modern humans have a larger pharynx (1), and a lower larynx (2), which has been pushed down by the curved skull-base (3). This allows greater modulation of sounds.

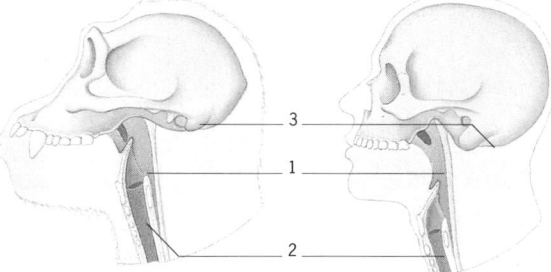

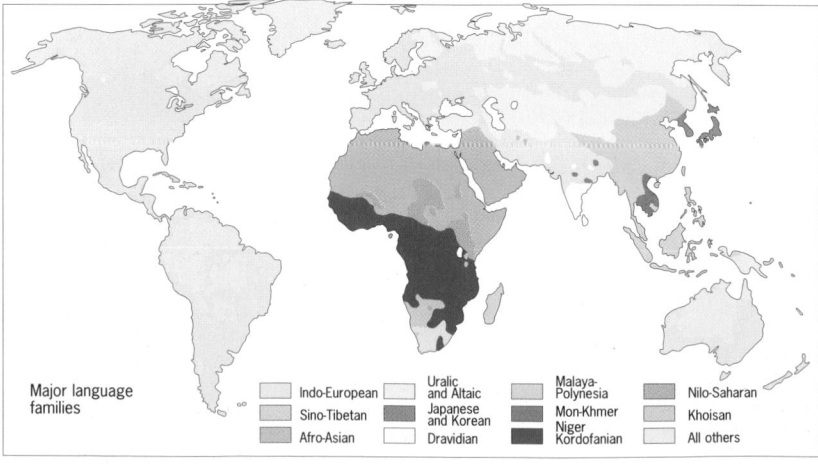

Major language families

Indo-European	Uralic and Altaic
Sino-Tibetan	Japanese and Korean
Afro-Asian	Dravidian

Malaya-Polynesia	Nilo-Saharan
Mon-Khmer	Khoisan
Niger Kordofanian	All others

ENDANGERED LANGUAGES

Over 5,000 languages are known to have existed in the world. Many of these are dead languages, in other words no longer spoken, such as Etruscan, Cretan, Iberian, and Gaulish. During the last 200 years, language death has accelerated, with hundreds becoming extinct. This is true especially of indigenous languages, above all in the Americas and Australia, where the languages of the colonists have obliterated native tongues. Many more look certain to meet the same fate.

Much cultural heritage and irreplaceable knowledge is lost when a language dies. The most serious problem for a language is the influence of an external, more powerful group. Australian Aboriginal and Native American languages have died due to political and cultural pressures, as have many minority languages in China, Africa, the former U.S.S.R., New Guinea (especially Papuan languages), and even in Europe. When a language is replaced by another, the people's linguistic identity survives only in local dialect words and accent.

Nowadays Africa and Asia have the largest number of "living" indigenous languages. However, minority languages are being steadily threatened in many parts of Africa (*below*) by higher-status languages; these include so-called African linguae francae (such as Swahili) and English, which has truly become a "global language."

WRITING

Writing is the single most effective sign system devised by human beings. It is used not only to describe the world, but also to communicate, to organize society as a whole, and to pass on accumulated knowledge to the next generation. Scripts offer a way of expressing abstract concepts by using a permanently coded system. The leaps in communication made possible with the written word make its development more profound, in its way, than the discovery of fire or the wheel. All forms of written information – text, tables, lists, and formulae – can influence and manipulate a people's view of themselves and the world.

Used to store and record information too bulky or too complex to be memorized, writing was developed in many societies as a response to economic pressures caused by intense trade. Writing makes communication possible between diverse groups and over larger geographic areas. However, it can also be socially restrictive, for those in a society who are literate may very easily be able to dominate those who are not.

Literacy is often seen as a prerequisite of civilization. The Incas, however, despite a large trade industry and massive storage facilities for corn payments, did not develop writing. Instead they used a system of knotted ropes or *quipu* to keep their accounts and manage the administration of their large empire.

Writing timeline

8000–7500 B.C. Plain tokens in Middle East.

3350 B.C. Complex tokens in southern Mesopotamia.

3200 B.C. Sumerian cuneiform representing words or syllables.

3050 B.C. Egyptian hieroglyphs, pictographs representing ideas and sounds.

2500 B.C. Indus Valley script.

1650 B.C. Linear A in Crete.

1500 B.C. Old Canaanite alphabet, representing consonants.

1380 B.C. Linear B in Crete and Greece.

1200 B.C. Chinese characters.

1100 B.C. Phoenician script.

1000 B.C. Old Hebrew script. Aramaic script.

740 B.C. Greek script (Crete, Greece, and Asia Minor): Phoenician symbols modified to form Greek alphabet.

700 B.C. Etruscan alphabet, based on Greek.

620 B.C. Roman alphabet, learned from Etruscan.

600 B.C. Zapotec/Mixtec pictographs.

250 B.C. Brahmi alphabet, source of modern Indian alphabets.

A.D. 25 Runes: Germanic, perhaps derived from Etruscan.

200 Ogham, used by Celts of Britain and Ireland.

292 Mayan script.

328 Arabic script.

1500 Easter Island pictographs (Rongo rongo).

African language death

Country	Extinct	Extinct or near extinct	In decline
Angola	1	–	1
Benin	–	–	1
Botswana	1	1	1
Burkina Faso	–	–	1
Cameroon	2	2	2
Chad	1	–	2
Congo	–	1	–
Egypt	1	–	–
Ethiopia	6	1	3
Gabon	–	1	1
Ghana	1	–	1
Côte D'Ivoire	1	–	2
Kenya	8	–	5
Lesotho	1	–	–
Mali	–	1	–
Mauretania	–	1	–
Mozambique	1	1	–
Niger	–	–	1
Nigeria	10	4	13
Senegal	–	–	1
Sierra Leone	1	–	2
South Africa	4	48	–
Sudan	3	3	3
Swaziland	1	–	–
Tanzania	5	1	5
Togo	–	–	1
Uganda	2	1	2
Zaire	4	–	2
Total	**54**	**67**	**49**

Note: It is estimated that 700–2,000 spoken languages exist. A more accurate number is difficult to gauge because the distinction between formal language and dialect may not be clear.

Writing of Middle America

In Mesoamerica (the Central American culture area) 13 different systems of early writing have been distinguished. Forms of writing exist on stelae, and figures, oval altars, and clay pottery. Of these, the hieroglyphic system of the Classical Lowland Maya qualifies as writing in the fullest sense. Closely linked with ceremony, it was used mainly for important matters such as calendars, computation, astronomy, divination and ritual.

In 1954, the British archaeologist Eric Thompson noted that "The hieroglyphic texts of the classical period deal entirely with the passage of time and astronomical matters. They do not appear to treat of individuals at all." The stress was on their accurate calendar and its sophisticated years of 18 months, 20 days, and five unlucky days. This impersonal view was revised in the 1960s, when Tatiana Proskouriakoff observed that the range of dates never exceeded 62 years, a human lifespan, and deciphered real historical sources on the stelae at Piedras Negras, Guatemala. One of these recorded the birth of a king and his enthronement date, thus legitimizing the power of his leadership.

Writing was exclusive: Landa, the famous chronicler of the Spanish conquistadores, noted that not even all the

Stela of Butz Chan, 11th ruler of Copán.

priests were literate. Scribes were the ritual specialists of writing, which was sometimes depicted as a rabbit god, as seen in the iconography on a vase from the 700s. Writing itself was considered a divine gift from Hunabku, son of the creator god, Hzamna. It was also used to legitimize territorial boundaries, like those carved on the stone monuments distinguishing four Mayan cities: Tikal, Calakmul, Palenque, and Copán.

PROMINENT PEOPLE

ALBRIGHT, William Foxwell (1891–1971) U.S. biblical scholar. One of the first academics to apply archaeological and linguistic disciplines to the study of biblical history. His most famous work is *The Archaeology of Palestine and the Bible*. (1932–1935)

BENEDICT, Ruth (1887–1948) U.S. anthropologist. Developed important theories on culture and personality with books such as *Patterns of Culture* (1934) and was an early supporter of cultural relativism.

BETTELHEIM, Bruno (1903–93) U.S. psychiatrist, born in Vienna, Austria. Author of *The Uses of Enchantment: The Meaning and Importance of Fairy Tales* (1976).

BINFORD, Lewis (b. 1930) U.S. archaeologist. Pioneer of anthropologically oriented "processual" school (New Archaeology).

BLOOMFIELD, Leonard (1887–1949) U.S. linguist. Profoundly influenced U.S. studies of linguistics with his work on Algonquian and other languages. His textbook *Language* (1933) remains a classic on college syllabuses.

BOAS, Franz (1858–1942) German-born U.S. anthropologist. Established modern anthropology in the U.S.A.

BREUIL, Abbé Henri Edouard (1877–1961) French prehistorian and archaeologist. In 1901, he discovered Paleolithic cave paintings in the Dordogne, France. His systematic work marked the beginning of the study of Paleolithic art.

CHAMPOLLION, Jean–François (1790–1832) French founder of Egyptology. Known for his work on the Rosetta Stone (trilingual inscription) to decipher hieroglyphics, which provided the key to understanding the ancient Egyptian language.

CHILDE, Vere Gordon (1892–1957) Australian archaeologist. Charted prehistoric development of Europe in terms of its archaeological "cultures."

CHOMSKY, Noam (b. 1928) U.S. linguist and political activist. His *Syntactic Structures* (1957) introduced a new theory of language and began a revolution in linguistics.

CLARK, Grahame (b. 1907) British archaeologist. His *Archaeology and Society* (1939) and *World Prehistory* (1961) pioneered the use of the archaeological record to document the economic and social life of prehistoric communities.

CLARKE, David (1937–76) British archaeologist. His *Analytical Archaeology* (1967) transformed European archaeology in the 1970s.

DART, Raymond (1893–1988) Australian-born South African anatomist. Best known for his discovery of *Australopithecus africanus*.

DURKHEIM, Emile (1858–1917) French sociologist. Regarded as one of the founders of sociology. He believed that sociology should be rigorously objective and scientific.

ELIADE, Mircea (1907–86) Romanian historian and philosopher of comparative religion. A pioneer in the systematic study of world religions.

EVANS, Sir Arthur John (1851–1941) British archaeologist. Excavated Bronze Age city of Knossos, Crete.

EVANS–PRITCHARD, Sir Edward (1902–73) British social anthropologist. His books include *The Nuer* (1940).

FOTES, Meyer (1906–83) South African-born British social anthropologist. Best known for his work on kinship in pre-industrial societies, comparative religion, and ideas of personhood.

FRAZER, Sir James George (1854–1941) Scottish anthropologist, classicist, and folklorist. His major work was *The Golden Bough* (1890, 1911–15), a study in magic and religion that has had an immense influence.

GEERTZ, Clifford (b. 1923) U.S. cultural anthropologist. He advocates an interpretive stance in which cultures are compared to literary texts.

GENNEP, Charles–Arnold van (1873–1957) French ethnographer and folklorist. Known for his work *Les Rites de Passage* (1909), a comparative study of rituals with emphasis on transitions of social status.

GLUCKMAN, Max (1911–75) South African-born British social anthropologist. His works such as *Custom and Conflict in Africa* (1955) put emphasis on the role of conflict in maintaining social cohesion.

HERSKOVITS, Melville (1895–1963) U.S. anthropologist. Overturned many prejudices about African-Americans with his *The Myth of the Negro Past* (1941) and in 1961 founded the first department of African studies at a U.S university (Northwestern).

HEYERDAHL, Thor (b. 1914) Norwegian experimental archaeologist. Sailed across Pacific in balsa-wood raft *Kon-Tiki* to "prove" Easter Island settlement.

JOHANSON, Donald Carl (b. 1943) US paleoanthropologist. His finds of fossil hominids 3–4 million years old in Hadar, Ethiopia, include "Lucy."

LEAKEY FAMILY: Louis (1903–72) Kenyan-born British anthropologist. Discoverer of many early hominid fossil remains in East Africa, he found (1964) the first remains of *H. habilis* (*c.* 2 mya). He and his wife **Mary** (b. 1913) discovered (1959) the skull of australopithecine *Zinjanthropus* (*A. robustus, c.* 1.7 mya*)*. Mary Leakey's discoveries include traces of fossilized hominid footprints (*c.* 3.6 mya) proving that they walked upright. Louis and Mary's son **Richard** (b. 1944), Kenyan anthropologist, made key discoveries in the region, including fossils of *A. boisei* (1969), *H. habilis* (1972), and *H. erectus* (1975).

LÉVI-STRAUSS, Claude (b. 1908) French social anthropologist. Influenced by structural linguistics, he analyzed kinship, ritual, and myth.

LEVY-BRUHL, Lucien (1857–1939) French anthropologist and philosopher, best known for his writing on "primitive mentality."

MALINOWSKI, Bronislaw (1884–1942) Polish-born British anthropologist. Founder of modern social anthropology. His works on the Trobriand islanders of the Pacific set new standards for ethnographic description.

MAUSS, Marcel (1872–1950) French sociologist and anthropologist. His book, *Essai sur le don* (1926), demonstrated the importance of gift exchange in "primitive" social organization.

MEAD, Margaret (1901–78) U.S. anthropologist. Her writings such as *Male and Female* (1949) and *Growth and Culture* (1951) have made anthropology accessible to a wide public.

MONTAGU, Ashley (b. 1905) U.S. anthropologist whose work covers evolution, culture, and child care. Famous for debunking old ideas about race, notably in *Man's Most Dangerous Myth: The Fallacy of Race* (1942).

MORGAN, Lewis (1818–81) U.S. ethnologist. He made extensive investigations into the cultures of Native Americans. His best-known work is *Ancient Society* (1877).

PEYRONEY, Denis (1869–1954) French prehistorian who classified several Upper and Middle Paleolithic periods.

RADCLIFFE-BROWN, Alfred (1881–1955) British anthropologist influenced by Emile DURKHEIM. His books include *The Andaman Islanders* (1922).

RENFREW, (Andrew) Colin (b. 1937) British archaeologist. He excavated in the Cycladic Islands of Greece and wrote many books on cultural change in prehistory, including *Before Civilization* (1973), *Archaeology and Language* (1987), and *Structure and Function in Primitive Society* (1952).

SAHLINS, Marshall David (b. 1930) U.S. cultural anthropologist. Made major contributions in the field of Oceanian anthropology, cultural evolution, and the analysis of symbolism.

SAUSSURE, Ferdinand de (1857–1913) Swiss linguist. He introduced the important dichotomy of *langue* (the system of language) and *parole* (actual speech).

TYLOR, Sir Edward (1832–1917) British anthropologist. His work *Anthropology* (1881) is widely regarded as founding the systematic study of human culture.

VENTRIS, Michael (1922–56) English architect who deciphered Cretan Linear B script.

WHORF, Benjamin (1897–1941) U.S. linguist. He contrasted the language and vocabulary of the North American Hopi Indians with Standard Average European to show how language fundamentally influences people's perception of the world.

TERMS

Acculturation Culture change due to inter-population contact.

Acheulian Stone tool complex used by HOMO ERECTUS, characterized by symmetrically flaked stone hand-axes.

Affinity Relation by marriage.

Alliance System linking kin groups through a rule of prescriptive or recurrent marriage.

Anthropology Study of human beings, especially their society, customs and beliefs. Includes archaeology, social and cultural studies, and LINGUISTICS.

Artifact Any portable object made, modified or used by humans.

Aurignacian Cultural grouping of the European Upper PALAEOLITHIC period, *c.* 33,000–23,000 B.C., named after a cave site at Aurignac, southwest France. First Palaeolithic artworks appear in this period.

Australopithecines Species of HOMINID of the late and early PLIOCENE epochs emerging about five million years ago. One of the australopithecines (*A. afarensis*) was the starting point of human stock, but most survived until about one million years ago, and were contemporary with species of the *Homo* genus.

Bipedal Having two feet and walking upright.

Blood group There are 11 classificatory systems of red blood cells (most famous is the ABO) based on the reaction of the cells with antibodies.

BP Before present (1950).

Bushmen Khoisan speakers of southern Africa: a hunter-gatherer population.

Carbon 14 Dating system based on calculation of the percentage of radiocarbon (which decays at a known rate of 50 percent after 5,730 years) left in a sample. Discovered by W. Libby, it provides a relatively solid chronological framework, especially when taken in conjunction with DENDROCHRONOLOGY.

Cline In population genetics, frequencies of genes change along gradients which are often continental.

Cognate Word or person descended from the same ancestor.

Comparative method Anthropological cross-cultural enquiry of customs and institutions or linguistic assessment of historical relationships between languages.

Cro-Magnon Site in Dordogne, France, giving its name to an Upper PALAEOLITHIC group (*c.* 30,000 B.C.) of nomadic hunters physically identical with modern people.

Culture A society sharing a system of knowledge and unique nonbiological characteristics.

Deep structure In Chomskian transformational LINGUISTICS this is the underlying pattern of a sentence.

Dendrochronology Method of dating by analyzing tree rings. Tree trunk sections reveal a series of rings laid down annually. This provides a recognizable pattern that can be cross-referenced to older trees, giving a sequence covering thousands of years.

Diffusion The spread of customs or technology by cultural contact.

Endogamy Kinship rule requiring marriage to take place within an individual's social and/or territorial group.

Ethnocentrism Viewing other cultures with bias derived from one's own.

Ethnography Analyzing and recording another culture by a process of participant observation called FIELDWORK.

Ethnology Scientific study of different races and cultural traditions, and their relations with each other.

Evolution Development generally accompanied by increasing complexity. Connected to Darwin's concept of natural selection for species survival.

Exogamy Requirement of marriage outside one's kin group.

Fieldwork Partial participation in and close study of a community.

Fossil Mineralized organism or one that has left a cast in other material.

Functionalism Method that seeks the relationships between social institutions rather than causal explanations.

Gene pool All the genes in a breeding population.

Genus Set of closely related species; a biological classification.

Glottochronology Controversial method of assessing the temporal divergence of two languages based on changes of vocabulary.

Hominid Member of the family of PRIMATES to which humans and their closest ancestors belong.

Homo erectus Member of the *Homo* genus. A nomadic hunter, who made so-called hand-axes and discovered fire, *H. erectus* existed from *c.* 1.6 mya until about 300,000–200,000 years ago.

Homo habilis Member of the *Homo* genus preceding HOMO ERECTUS. Discovered in 1964 by Louis Leakey, it is found in conjunction with OLDOWAN industries in eastern Africa.

Homo sapiens Member of the *Homo* genus succeeding HOMO ERECTUS. The human species. It may have appeared about 450,000 years ago, resembling *H. erectus* but with larger brain and smaller jaws and teeth.

Homo sapiens neanderthalensis Member of the *Homo* genus appearing about 100,000 B.C.. It died out around 30,000 B.C..

Homo sapiens sapiens First subspecies of biologically modern humans that has diversified within the last 40,000 years.

Hunter-gatherers Populations that rely exclusively on wild foods hunted and gathered.

Incest taboo Rule prohibiting sex between immediate kin.

Liminal A state between normal categories; a state of transition between different social roles.

Lineage Group claiming descent from a common ancestor.

Linguistics The scientific study of language.

Magdalenian Last Upper PALAEOLITHIC cultural tradition in Europe, 15,000–8,000 B.C., which used both bone and stone tools.

Mousterian Diverse tool industry of the NEANDERTHALS.

Mya Million years ago.

Neanderthal *See HOMO SAPIENS NEANDERTHALENSIS.*

Oldowan An industry of flake and pebble tools, used by HOMINIDS in the Olduvai Gorge, Tanzania.

Palaeolithic (Old Stone Age) Period before 10,000 B.C.; characterized by chipped and flaked tool industries.

Palaeontology Study of extinct life forms through fossil remains.

Phoneme Distinctive unit of sound in LINGUISTICS contrasting with other such units.

Physical anthropology Study of human biological or physical characteristics and their evolution.

Pleistocene First of the two geological epochs of the Quaternary period, *c.* 2,000,000–10,000 B.C..

Pliocene Preceding the PLEISTOCENE; seven to two million years ago.

Pollution The belief that a particular state is ritually contaminating (e.g. menstruation) and needs hedging with proscriptions and TABOOS.

Potassium-argon Dating by measuring percentage of radioactive potassium and argon in rock. Used to date earliest HOMINID environments.

Prehistory Study of culture before the invention of written records.

Primate Order of mammals including humans, apes, prosimians and monkeys.

Ramapithecus A genus of fossil primates living 15–12 mya.

Rite of passage Ritual symbolizing a transition in status.

Stela A free-standing carved stone monument.

Stratification Hierarchical separation of society into classes ranked in power and privilege. Also the laying down of strata or layers one above the other providing a relative chronological sequence whose study is stratigraphy.

Structuralism Identification of underlying structures in LINGUISTICS, especially as they might reflect patterns of behaviour and thought.

Taboo Forbidden especially by sacred, supernatural sanctions.

Tell Near-Eastern term that refers to a mound site formed through successive human occupation.

Universal The opposite of the relative; characteristic of the species in all times and places.

Zhoukoudian Cave site near Beijing where HOMO ERECTUS finds were made in the 1930s.

Timeline

60,000 B.C. Neanderthal people may have practiced ceremonial burial of the dead. (Indicated by Paleolithic remains at Mt. Carmel, Israel.)

c. **20,000 B.C.** Paleolithic cave paintings at European Cro-Magnon sites suggest shamanistic beliefs and practices.

3761 B.C. Traditional date of creation in the Jewish calendar.

3113 B.C. First date in Mayan calendar, related to religious observances.

c. **3,000 B.C.** Neolithic "mother goddess" figurines, associated with forces of nature and cycles of fertility, become widespread with the development of agriculture.

c. **3000–2500 B.C.** In Mesopotamia, major festival celebrates victory of Sumerian god of spring over goddess of chaos.

2773 B.C. First date in the ancient Egyptian calendar.

c. **2750 B.C.** Gilgamesh, legendary king of Uruk, Mesopotamia.

c. **2500 B.C.** Great Pyramid of Cheops (Khufu) built at Giza, Egypt.

PREHISTORIC RELIGIONS

Shamanism Paleolithic cave paintings suggest that shamanism is probably the world's oldest surviving religious tradition, dating from a period when humans lived in nomadic hunter-gatherer communities and needed a close rapport with nature in order to survive. Shamans combine the functions of doctor, future-reader, and priest, using dance, drumming, and psychotropic drugs to enter the world of spirits and enlist their aid. Although especially associated with far northern cultures, vestiges of shamanism are found in most preliterate societies.

Mother goddess Paleolithic "goddess" figurines exist, but the establishment of agriculture (*c.* 8000 B.C.) marked a very widespread worship of a female divinity, identified with nature and fertility, and is typical of the Neolithic age (*c.* 8000–2000 B.C.). Frequently wide-hipped and large-breasted, images of the mother goddess occur in most early agricultural societies, and survived in cults such as the Egyptian Isis or west Asian Cybele.

The Dancing Sorcerer. *Drawing of a Paleolithic cave painting,* c. *20,000 B.C.*

THE GODS OF MESOPOTAMIA

The original inhabitants of Mesopotamia, *c.* 4500 B.C., were the Sumerians, creators of the world's first city-states, whose religious beliefs and mythology pervade the belief systems of their successors, the Akkadians, Babylonians, and Assyrians. The Sumerian creation myth describes the ocean as the beginning of all things. As different regional city-states advanced, their deities overlapped earlier manifestations, often providing alternative names of the same deity.

Ishtar, goddess of love and war, Babylonian version of the Sumerian Innana.

An (Anum) Sumerian sky god. Ancestor god of earthly royalty; city god of Uruk.

Ashur Assyrian Moon and war god.

Enki (Ea) Babylonian god of fresh water; patron of crafts and practical knowledge.

Enlil Sumerian god of the earth. City god of Nippur. Sent a flood from which one man and his family escaped (described in Semitic and Greek flood myths).

Ereshkigal Sumerian goddess of death and queen of the underworld.

Innana (Ishtar) Sumerian fertility goddess and queen of heaven. Goddess of love, whose Babylonian temples were places of sacred prostitution, and goddess of war, especially in her Assyrian form.

Ishkur (Adad) Babylonian god of storms. Known throughout the area of Babylonian influence, his symbols were lightning, held in his hand, and the bull.

Marduk City god of Babylon. Champion of the gods, slayer of the dragon Tiamat.

Nannar (Sin) Sumerian moon god, son of Enlil, he rode across the sky in a ship.

Nergal Babylonian god of the dead. He loved catastrophes, epidemics, and war.

Ninhursaga Sumerian goddess of wildlife and fruitfulness.

Ninurta Sumerian god of farming and war; champion of order.

Nintur Sumerian goddess of childbirth.

Shamash (Utu) Babylonian god of the sun and of justice. Inspirer of the first known written laws, the code of Hammurabi.

Tammuz (Dumuzi) Babylonian god of fertility and rebirth. Husband of Ishtar; every year he died and descended to the underworld until spring.

Tiamat Babylonian goddess of the sea, and primeval dragon of chaos; slain by the champion Marduk.

I CHING

The *I Ching* (Book of Changes) is the world's most ancient divination tool. It consists of combinations of broken lines representing *yin* (female, receptive, negative) and unbroken lines representing *yang* (male, active, positive). The interaction between the complementary forces of *yin* and *yang* underlies all changes in the universe. The mythical ruler Fu Hsi grouped the lines of *yin* and *yang* into eight three-line forms (trigrams), representing every possible situation in heaven and earth, while King Wen (*c.* 1122 B.C.) grouped the eight trigrams into pairs to make 64 hexagrams. These form the central core of the *I Ching*, inspiring Confucius, Lao-tzu, and the whole body of Chinese philosophy. The signs change from one form to another like the natural phenomena that can be observed. By drawing yarrow stalks or throwing coins the seeker can align himself with them.

The eight trigrams of the I Ching, *arranged by the legendary ruler Fu Hsi.*

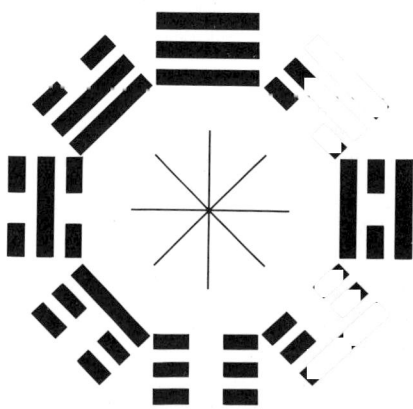

EGYPTIAN GODS

In ancient Egypt, early worship of tribal deities developed into a huge pantheon of local and state gods, many of which represented natural forces to be appeased through worship and sacrifice. The pharaoh (king) was considered the chief priest, responsible for the cult of all the gods, the most important of which was the sun god, Re. The pharaoh was regarded as an incarnation of Horus, son of the mother goddess Isis and Osiris, god of the dead. Just as the sun is reborn with every dawn, so the dead underwent a second birth and were restored to life. The Egyptian preoccupation with the after life is evidenced in their practice of mummifying corpses and building large funerary monuments such as the pyramids. The Egyptian *Book of the Dead*, a collection of incantations and magical formulae, developed from the inscriptions painted around the tomb chambers in the royal pyramids. Thus rites formerly reserved for royalty became available to other social groups. The Egyptian pantheon included (in order of importance):

Re (Ra) Sun god. The most important of the Egyptian deities.

Osiris King and judge of the dead, and god of vegetation and agriculture. Slain by his brother, Set, he was restored to life by his sister-wife, Isis.

Isis Mother goddess; sister, wife, and savior of Osiris. Her worship spread beyond Egypt and she became the center of a popular Greco-Roman mystery cult. Often depicted as a guardian of the dead.

Horus Falcon-headed sun god, associated with pharaohs. Son of Isis and Osiris; he was at constant war with Set.

Hathor Cow-headed goddess of love and fertility. Wife of Horus, sometimes identified with Isis.

Seth Desert sun god and lord of evil, adversary of Osiris and Horus.

Anubis Jackal-headed god of funerals who conducted the souls of the dead to the other world.

Thoth Divine scribe involved in the judgment of souls after death. Portrayed with the head of an ibis or a baboon and associated with learning and magic.

Ptah God of creation, and patron of arts.

Sekhmet Wife of Ptah. Lioness-headed war goddess.

Apis Son of Ptah. Fertility god, incarnate in a series of sacred bulls.

Amun (Amon) Ram-headed god and national deity, later conjoined with Re.

Amun-Re (Amon-Ra) National deity from the New Kingdom.

Mut Vulture goddess wife of Amun-Re.

Khonsou Early moon god and healer, son of Amun and Mut.

Aton (Aten) Creator god, represented as the sun's disk.

Geb Earth god; patron of crops and of healing.

Nut Sky goddess, sister-wife of Geb.

Khepra (Khepii) Early sun god, portrayed as a scarab beetle rolling a ball of dung symbolizing the sun.

Maat Goddess of justice.

Meskhent Goddess of childbirth.

Min God of virility and generation; later guardian of travelers.

Nephthys (Nebhet) "The lady of the castle," goddess of funerals.

Hap River god who sent the annual Nile flood; god of agriculture and prosperity.

Apep (Apophis) Serpent of darkness and enemy of Re.

Bastet Cat-headed hearth goddess, later war goddess.

Sebek Crocodile god of lakes and rivers.

Tauret Hippopotamus goddess, guardian of childbirth and children.

Serapis State god 305–30 B.C., introduced by Ptolemy I in an attempt to link Egyptian and Greek mythology.

Ani's ba *(soul) hovers over his mummified body: papyrus,* c. *1250 B.C.*

c. 2500–2000 B.C. Snake and bull major religious symbols in Crete's Minoan culture. In Egypt, cults of Isis and Osiris promise resurrection from death. Innana worshiped as Assyro-Babylonian goddess of love.

c. 2000 B.C. Jewish patriarch Abraham leaves Ur, Mesopotamia, for Canaan, the "promised land."

c. 2000–1500 B.C. Marduk supreme god in Babylon.

c. 1800 B.C. Layout and orientation of W. European megalithic monuments, e.g. Stonehenge, England, suggest archaeo-astronomical ritual practices.

c. 1750 B.C. Chinese divinatory "oracle bones" (still extant), dating from Shang dynasty; these evolve into *I Ching*.

c. 1570 B.C. Egyptian *Book of the Dead* codifies ideas about afterlife.

c. 1500 B.C. Indo-Aryan Vedic hymns assign different powers to gods of the heavens and the earth. Vedic *Upanishads* form the basis of Hindu philosophy and religion, teaching that God (Brahman) and the individual soul or self (Atman) are identical.

c. 1385 B.C. Egyptian king Akhenaten tries to replace Amun and other ancient gods of Thebes with the sun god, Aton, as single deity.

c. 1300 B.C. Model horse-drawn sun chariot made from bronze indicating solar worship. In use at Trundholm, Denmark.

c. 1250 B.C. After persecution in Egypt, Israelites begin the Exodus, eventually reaching the land of Canaan.

c. 1230 B.C. Moses receives Ten Commandments on Mt. Sinai.

c. 1100 B.C. Oracle of Delphi venerated by Mycenean Greeks.

c. 1020 B.C. After rule of "Judges" elected from the 12 tribes of Israel, Saul becomes king of the Israelites.

c. 1000 B.C. In China, mystical beliefs of Shang dynasty give way to rationalism of Chou dynasty, whose founder, Wen, forms the *I Ching* hexagrams.

c. 900–800 B.C. First Jewish prophets in Palestine; Elijah combats worship of fertility god, Baal. Shrine of Apollo established at Delphi, Greece.

c. 800–700 B.C. Prophets Amos, Hosea, and Isaiah combat abuses in Israel; Isaiah prophesies Messiah.

624 B.C. Birth of Thales of Miletus, Greek philosopher, who believed that water is the primary substance of nature.

611 B.C. Birth of Greek philosopher Anaximander of Miletus, who believed that all things come from one underlying substance, and that humans evolved from fish.

c. 600 B.C. Birth of Lao-tzu in China; his ideas correspond to what is now Taoism. Nazca Indians of Peru make landform representations of birds and animals in desert soil, possibly for purposes of religious ritual.

HINDUISM

 The Hindu religion has preserved, unchanged from Vedic times, the idea that God (Brahman) exists and can be experienced in the depths of one's own being, through the achievement of a transcendent state of consciousness (*samadhi*). The purpose of life is to realize God: "Truth is one," declares the *Rig Veda* (*below*), "Sages call it by various names."

The cycle of birth, death, and rebirth (*samsara*) defines a system of transmigration whereby the effect of deeds (*karma*) in one life influences the next. Yoga (union) is the application of spiritual practices with the object of attaining the union of Atman (the individual self or soul) and Brahman (the supreme self or soul). It consists of various forms:

Karma yoga Union through work by dedicating all actions to the Lord.

Jnana yoga Union through knowledge by introspecting that God alone is "real" and all else "unreal," i.e. transient.

Raja yoga Union through meditation and psychic control.

Bhakti yoga Union through devotion and love of God.

Hindu scriptures

The four *Vedas* (*Rig, Atharva, Sama,* and *Yagur, c.* 1500 B.C.) consist of hymns and rituals, and are accompanied by the 108 extant *Upanishads*, which lay down the fundamental teachings of Hinduism.

The *Smritis* embody the laws formulated by saints and sages. *The Laws of Manu* (*c.* 500 B.C.) deal with human duties and social obligations by caste and class.

The *Puranas* amplify the *Vedas*. They number 18, six devoted to Vishnu, six to Brahma, and six to Shiva. They include the *Bhagavatam*, which is regarded by the Vaishnavas (*right*) as one of the genuinely authoritative scriptures.

The *Tantras* are devoted to Vishnu, Shiva, and Shakti. In the Shakti group, the most popular, God the Mother is seen as not distinct from Shiva or Brahman, but is the power of the absolute. God the Mother has within herself the seeds of creation. At the end of a cycle (*yuga*) she gives birth to a new world and lives within it.

The *Ramayana* is the great epic devoted to Rama, an incarnation of Vishnu embodying *dharma* (right conduct). Rama's rescue of his abducted wife, Sita, aided by his brother Lakshmana and the monkey-god Hanuman, can be read allegorically as the triumph of good action over passion and greed.

The *Mahabharata* describes the conflict between the Pandava clan and the Kaurava clan, and can also be read allegorically. It contains Hinduism's key text, the *Bhagavad Gita*, in which the incarnation Krishna expounds the path of god-realization to his devotee Arjuna.

Worship of the three major deities

Brahman, the One Absolute Reality, becomes Isvara (God) through the assumption of attributes. Isvara has three aspects: Brahma, the creator; Vishnu, the preserver, who incarnates from age to age to restore the balance of the world; and Shiva, the god of destruction and rebirth. These represent the Hindu Trinity, or Trimurti. To this should be added worship of Shakti, the primordial female power of the universe, also called Devi. Worship of God as Mother has attracted some of the greatest Hindu mystics, notably the Bengali saint Sri Ramakrishna in the 1800s.

Shaivism Worship of Shiva. As a great ascetic deity, both destroyer and creator, embodying eternal rest and also ceaseless activity (as Nataraja, Lord of the Dance), Shiva is also called Mahadev—the Great God. His creative power is celebrated in the worship of the phallic *lingam*, one of the most common sacred objects in Indian temples and households.

Vaishnavism Worship of Vishnu is the most popularly practiced of the Hindu faiths, probably because Vishnu has taken on human form from time to time in order to help humankind. There have been nine *avataras* (incarnations) so far, and one more is predicted. Of the nine, it is in the human forms of Rama and Krishna that Vishnu receives most worship. There are many Vaishnava schools, most corresponding to teachings of local religious leaders.

A Shiva lingam, *prime symbol of generation of the Great God Shiva.*

Shaktism Worship of the female "active energy." This may include the destructive aspects of Kali or the gentler attributes of Parvati or Uma. Commonly called simply "Mother," her worship can involve mystic esoteric rituals.

The major Hindu deities

Aditi The Unbounded, goddess of the open sky, mother of all the deities.

Agni God of fire and of sacrifice.

Brahma God of creation.

Ganesha Elephant-headed son of Shiva and Parvati who removes obstacles and is

always invoked before any ceremony.

Hanuman Monkey god, son of Vayu, the wind. Devoted to Vishnu in his incarnation as Rama (*Rambhakta Hanuman*).

Indra God of war, storm, and fertility.

Kali The black goddess, consort (*shakti*) of Shiva.

Lakshmi Goddess of beauty and luck, consort (*shakti*) of Vishnu.

Mitra god of light.

Prajapati Creator of the world and all life-forms.

Rudra God of the jungle, of wild animals, and of water.

Sarasvati Goddess of knowledge and truth, consort (*shakti*) of Brahma.

Sati First wife of Shiva; inaugurated the practice of suttee whereby a widow was required to burn herself alive on her husband's funeral pyre.

Shiva God of destruction and rebirth; the Great God and guru of the gods.

Surya God of the sun.

Varuna God of the waters who also "unties the knots of the heart."

Vayu God of the wind.

Vishnu The Preserver who incarnates for the benefit of humanity.

Universal form of Vishnu: the god's avatar *(incarnation) of Krishna reveals himself.*

JUDAISM

Judaism is usually seen as a "historical" religion, tied intricately to the history and major events of the Jewish people. Its many rituals and ceremonial observations are both a reminder of the continuous presence of God in the life of the believer and a tangible link with events that occured thousands of years ago. The Jewish faith is one of ethical monotheism. Its essence is a relationship with the one God, who created the world, delivered the Israelites from bondage, revealed his law (*Torah*) to them, and chose them to be a light for all humankind.

Jews believe that God made a covenant with Abraham, the founder, an agreement that he and his descendants would be blessed if they remained faithful. This covenant was renewed with Isaac and Jacob (also called Israel), hence the Israelites' title of Chosen People. They were selected to perform special duties and responsibilities, such as establishing a just society and serving only God. In return, they were to receive God's love and protection. God later gave the Israelites the Ten Commandments through their leader Moses.

Judaism has no formal creed but its core is found in the Shema, three passages of the Bible that are read every morning and evening by devout Jews. The first passage is central to Judaism: "Hear, O Israel, the Lord is our God, the Lord is One." Believers seek to love God with their whole being, that love being expressed in practical obedience to the law of God in everyday life. The center for community worship is the local synagogue, operated by the congregation and led by a rabbi of their choice. The synagogue's main feature is the "Ark of the Covenant," which contains the handwritten scrolls of the *Torah*. There is an annual cycle of religious festivals and days of fasting, the first of which is Rosh Hashanah (New Year); Yom Kippur (the Day of Atonement) is the holiest day of the Jewish year.

Jewish scriptures

The Hebrew Bible Called the *Tanakh*, the 24 books of the Hebrew Bible are divided into three parts:
Torah (Pentateuch)
Genesis Creation, covenant between God and Israel.
Exodus Escape from Egypt and entry into the Promised Land.
Leviticus, Numbers, Deuteronomy Rules governing religious and social behavior.
Nevi'im (Prophets)
Joshua The dividing up of the Promised Land.
Judges From Joshua to Samuel.
Samuel From the last judge to King David.
Kings From Solomon to the Captivity.

Isaiah Prophet of a universal God.
Jeremiah The prophet of the heart.
Ezekiel The prophet of the Exile.
12 minor prophets.
Ketubim (Writings)
Psalms The religious songs of Israel.
Proverbs Thoughts on everyday life.
Job The suffering of a just man.
Song of Songs Divine love songs.
Ruth Virtue and compassion.
Lamentations Israel's sadness.
Ecclesiastes The master of wisdom.
Esther The queen of Susa.
Daniel The supremacy of God.
Ezra and Nehemiah The restorers.
Chronicles Rewritten history.
The Talmud Interpretations of and commentaries on the *Torah* by rabbis and teachers of the Law. This includes the *Mishnah,* an oral code of laws covering agriculture, festivals, civil and criminal laws, marriage and divorce, temple sacrifice, dietary laws, and ritual purification; the *Gemara,* commentaries on and elaborations of the Mishnah; the *Midrash,* sermonic exposition and popular interpretation; the *Halakah,* the standard code of Jewish law and ritual; and the *Aggadah,* devoted to legends and stories.
The Cabala (Tradition) With its classic work *Sefer ha-Zohar*, is a medieval document of a mystical nature (*p. 225*). According to the Cabala, God is manifest to the world through ten divine emanations, each of which has esoteric significance.

Laws and customs

Many Jews follow dietary laws laid down in the *Torah*, for instance forbidding the mixing of milk and meat products. Food prepared in accordance with Jewish dietary laws is called kosher. Other rituals include circumcision of (usually infant) males in commemoration of God's covenant with Abraham, and confirmation of teenagers as full members of the community, called Bar Mitzvah (for boys) or Bas Mitzvah (for girls). After a funeral, seven days of deep mourning (*shiva*) are observed.

Thirteen principles of faith

Moses Maimonides (1135–1204) drew up 13 points to defend a faith that he saw as threatened by a shift to rationalism and even atheism. They sum up the most important beliefs of the Jewish religion:

1 That God exists.
2 That God is one alone.
3 That God has no corporeal presence.
4 That God is outside the scope of time.
5 That God alone is to be worshiped.
6 That God informs his prophets.
7 That Moses was the greatest of the prophets.
8 That the *Torah* is the work of God.
9 That the *Torah* cannot change.
10 That God apprehends the thoughts and acts of all people.
11 That those who do good will receive their reward, and those who do evil will receive retribution.
12 That the Messiah will come.
13 That there will be a bodily resurrection of the dead, although only the soul may be eternal.

Torah scrolls of Sephardic Jews of the Middle East, 1600s.

Jewish sects and groups
Pharisees Group within Palestinian Judaism around time of Christ that began traditions of modern rabbinical Judaism.
Essenes Group noted for asceticism and communistic lifestyle (c. 200 B.C.–A.D. 200).
Sephardim Descendants of Jews who lived in Spain and Portugal before 1492, when they were expelled to become refugees in North Africa, Turkey, Italy, and the Middle East.
Ashkenazim Jews of central and east European descent. They developed their own customs, interpretation of the Talmud, music, and language (Yiddish).
Hasidism Movement of Jewish mysticism beginning in Poland, in the 1700s.
Reform Judaism Movement of the early 1800s for the reform of Jewish worship in the light of modern scholarship.
Orthodox Judaism A movement of the 1800s, aimed at preserving traditional values with strict adherence to the *Torah*.
Reconstructionism A movement of the 1900s, holding Judaism to be an evolving religious civilization with standards of conduct established by Jews themselves.
Zionism A secular political movement dedicated to establishing a national homeland in Palestine for the Jews.

A devout Jew prays at the Western Wall in Jerusalem with ram's horn in hand.

Timeline

586 B.C. First Diaspora: Babylonian King Nebuchadnezzar destroys Jerusalem and deports Jews. Birth of Greek philosopher Anaximenes of Miletus, who believed that air is the primary substance of nature.

582 B.C. Greek Delphic oracle's prestige at its height with establishment of Pythian Games.

581 B.C. Birth of Pythagoras of Samos, Greek philosopher and mathematician, who believed in transmigration of souls.

551 B.C. Birth of Confucius in China.

c. 550 B.C. Vardhamana Mahavira founds Jainism in India. Zoroastrianism established in Persia (Iran).

c. 536 B.C. Cyrus the Great, Persian conqueror of Babylon, allows the Jews to return to Palestine and donates funds to rebuild the Temple in Jerusalem.

c. 500 B.C. Prince Siddhartha Gautama, called Buddha, founds Buddhism in India. Heraclitus, Greek philosopher, pronounces that all things are in a state of flux; he believed that fire is the primary substance of nature.

c. 495 B.C. Birth of Empedocles, Greek philosopher, who formulated the theory of four primary elements: earth, air, fire, and water.

c. 490 B.C. Birth of Zeno of Elea, disciple of Parmenides, who denied the reality of time, plurality, and motion.

469 B.C. Birth of Socrates, Greek philosopher and teacher of Plato, who disseminated his ideas.

c. 460 B.C. Birth of Democritus, Greek philosopher, whose theory of atomism held that matter consists of indivisible atoms in a void.

c. 427 B.C. Birth of Plato, Greek philosopher, founder of first philosophy school. In his writings he may have embellished Socrates' philosophy with his own ideas.

ZOROASTRIANISM

Some authorities believe that the dualistic religion called Zoroastrianism was founded before 1000 B.C., and passed on the idea of a struggle between Light and Darkness to some Judaic and Christian traditions. However, the teachings (texts known as the *Avesta*) of the semilegendary Persian sage Zoroaster were current in Persia (modern Iran) from the 600s B.C. until the arrival of Islam. Zoroastrianism held that the one god, Ahura Mazda, is threatened by the spirit of evil Angra Mainyu (identified with the Judaeo-Christian Satan) but will eventually triumph. Zoroastrian rites were performed by priests called magi. Today, the faith barely survives in Iran, but in India it flourishes as Parsiism, with about 150,000 followers.

The mace of Mithra, a symbol of war against the forces of evil.

GREEK PHILOSOPHY

Before the emergence of Socrates (469–399 B.C.) in Athens, the so-called pre-Socratic philosophers of the Greek world (which included Asia Minor, Sicily, and southern Italy) confined themselves to speculations about the natural world and cosmology. Important pre-Socratic philosophers include Zeno of Elea (b. 490 B.C.), whose "paradoxes" challenged notions of plurality and motion; Democritus (c. 460–370 B.C.), whose atomic system assumed an infinite number of randomly combining atoms; and Pythagoras (500s B.C.), who taught the transmigration of souls and the relations between numbers.

Socrates, whose doctrines were recorded by his pupil Plato, was responsible for shifting philosophical interest to ethics and conceptual analysis. Deemed subversive, he was put to death in 399, but Plato, who founded the Academy at

Athens in 387, continued to develop questions raised by Socrates. Indeed, Plato's contribution was so powerful that a British philosopher, A. N. Whitehead, has characterized the subsequent history of Western philosophy as "footnotes to Plato." His doctrines include the theory of knowledge as recollection and, above all, the theory of forms (or "ideas") which contrasts the transient, material world of "particulars" with the timeless, unchanging world of universals or forms.

Aristotle (384–322 B.C.), a pupil and then a teacher at Plato's Academy, explored a vast range of philosophical and scientific subjects. His work exerted an enormous influence on medieval and Islamic philosophy, and indeed on the whole Western intellectual and scientific tradition. The works most widely read today include the *Metaphysics, Politics, Poetics,* and *Nicomachean Ethics.*

CONFUCIANISM

Confucianism is not so much a religion as a moral philosophy, founded by Confucius (K'ung Fu-tzu, "Master K'ung") during the 500s B.C. It invokes *li* (propriety and orderliness) as the ideal state of mind and lifestyle, in which people should know their place and respect others; *li* also embraces *hsiao,* "filial piety." *Ren* (courteous altruism) is the concept whereby the greater good can be fulfilled with no loss of face; *t'ien* (heaven) may have been considered as the abode of providence by Confucius, rather than a supreme being. His ideas for social reform were popular with the people and continue to be influential.

Confucius is believed to have put together the *Five Classics,* texts that are fundamental to Chinese culture. They include an important commentary on the *I Ching (p. 208).* His followers, including Mencius (Meng-tzu), assembled four books after his death.

TAOISM

Whereas Confucianism provides day-to-day rules of conduct, Taoism is concerned with a more spiritual level of being. It is based on writings attributed to a Chinese philosopher of the 500s B.C., Lao-tzu, a contemporary of Confucius. Also called The Way or The Path, Taoism holds that by balancing the flow of *yin* and *yang* energies, which are the basis of all life, humankind can live in harmony with nature which, like water, flows effortlessly and yet can have tremendous effects. The aim is to work with the natural order of things, since trying to change this sets up a resistance and disharmony. Truth is reflected in the clarity of a still and open mind. *Té* (virtue or strength) always exists in the *Tao* (natural law). The essence of Taoism is contained in the *Tao Te Ching* (The Way and its Power).

The Chinese sage Lao-tzu.

A relief of the Buddha from Borobudur, Java (Indonesia), c. A.D. 850.

BUDDHISM

A world religion with roots in ancient Indian thought, Buddhism is based on the teachings of Buddha (Siddhartha Gautama, c. 563–483 B.C.), one of a series of "enlightened" beings. Sharing with Hinduism the doctrine of reincarnation, Buddhism teaches spiritual purity and freedom from human concerns.

The teaching of Buddha is summarized in the Four Noble Truths (*Dhamma*): existence entails unhappiness; unhappiness is caused by attachment to worldly things, which are ephemeral; happiness can be achieved by detachment from material desires; nirvana, a blissful state free from ego, is available to those who follow the Noble Eightfold Way.

The eight "steps" are: right views, right intention, right speech, right conduct, right livelihood, right effort, right awareness or mindfulness, and right meditation or contemplation. Achieving the goal of nirvana, all desires are extinguished and the self is absorbed into the infinite.

Buddhist sects and schools

Of the two main Buddhist traditions, *Theravada* or *Hinayana* Buddhism, found mainly in Sri Lanka, Burma, and Thailand, adheres to the teachings of early Buddhist writings, stressing that liberation is possible only for oneself, by accepting severe discipline. *Mahayana* Buddhism, found in Tibet, Mongolia, China, Korea, and Japan, is more liberal, and introduces the doctrine of the bodhisattva, who postpones his own achievement of nirvana to help others.

Timeline

c. **425–400 B.C.** Hindu epic the *Ramayana* is written down in Sanskrit; the *Torah* (*Pentateuch* or *Five Books of Moses*) takes its present form.

384 B.C. Birth in Macedonia of Aristotle, Greek philosopher, who later studied at Plato's Academy.

371 B.C. Birth of Mencius (Meng-tzu), influential Confucian philosopher.

341 B.C. Birth of Epicurus, Greek philosopher and founder of Epicureanism, an ethically hedonistic philosophy.

336 B.C. Birth of Zeno of Citium, founder of Stoicism, a philosophy that emphasizes parallels between human and cosmic rationality.

335 B.C. Aristotle founds the Lyceum school of philosophy.

306 B.C. Epicurus opens his Garden school of philosophy in Athens.

c. **300 B.C.** Zeno of Citium establishes a philosophical school in the Stoa Poikile ("Painted Colonnade") in Athens, from which the Stoics took their name.

300 B.C. onward Native Americans of the Hopewell culture, based around Ohio, erect massive mounds sculpted in the forms of animals (some still extant), probably for religious ritual purposes.

c. **289 B.C.** Following the death of Mencius in China, his pupils collect his teachings in the *Book of Meng-tzu*.

c. **250 B.C.** Indian king Asoka converts to Buddhism and makes it the state religion. His influence leads to the introduction of Buddhism in Ceylon (Sri Lanka). The *Septuagint*, the Greek version of the Hebrew Old Testament, is produced in Palestine.

c. **175–164 B.C.** Jews in Palestine persecuted by the Syrian ruler Antiochus IV; Temple in Jerusalem desecrated in 168; Judas Maccabaeus expels Syrians and rededicates the temple in 165.

Tibetan Buddhism

Sometimes called Tantric Buddhism or Lamaism, this faith developed its own form and momentum, absorbing some animistic beliefs from earlier cultures.

The *Tantras* are Sanskrit ritual texts said to have been originally transmitted by the Buddha and to have been passed on secretly until the A.D. 400s and 500s, when they emerged in India. The books encourage evocation of various gods, pursuit of magical powers, use of sacred chants (*mantras*) and gestures (*mudras*), and meditation on mystical diagrams (*mandalas*). Tantric Buddhism was introduced into Tibet by the monk Padmasambhava (A.D. 700s), and has recently gained popularity in the West. It includes the *Bardo Thodol*, a guide to the liberation of the spirit after death, which is studied by all Tibetan Buddhists.

Tanka mandala of the "Wheel of Life" held by Mara, the demon tempter.

Zen Buddhism

Zen is a meditative form of Buddhism introduced into Japan by monks returning from China during the 1100s; it adopted elements of Taoism and was very popular. Zen is a Japanese transcription of the Chinese term *ch'an*, which describes sitting meditation in the style of Buddha. Today, Japan has about 10 million Zen Buddhists, divided between the Soto school (introduced in the 1200s by Dogen) and the Rinzai school (introduced by Eisai during the 1100s); the latter seeks spontaneous enlightenment, while Soto teaches a form of meditation in which enlightenment is more gradual. With Zen came the ritualized Japanese tea ceremony and a profound sensitivity toward nature as manifested in the art of Zen gardens, *ikebana* (flower arranging), architecture, painting, pottery, and *haiku* poetry. Zen has been introduced to the West by various Japanese masters and has a growing number of followers.

Timeline

c. **150–100 B.C.** Text of the *Ramayana* standardized.

67 B.C. Cult of Mithras arrives in Rome from Persia (according to Plutarch).

60 B.C. Lucretius, Latin philosophical poet, expounds the Epicurean world-view in *De Rerum Natura*, a six-volume work expounding atomism, the theory that all matter consists of minute individual particles.

42 B.C. Gaius Julius Caesar, whose person was declared sacred in his lifetime, is deified after his death; later Roman emperors assume the godhead even while they are still living.

c. **4 B.C.** Probable date of birth of Jesus Christ in Palestine.

A.D. 29 Probable date of the crucifixion of Jesus Christ.

c. **40** One of the earliest Christian churches erected at Corinth, Greece.

c. **44–49** St. Paul (*c.* 3–*c.* 66) preaches at Antioch before first mission to Cyprus and Galatia (Asia Minor).

c. **60** Buddhism (*p. 213*) reaches China.

64 Christians in Rome persecuted by Nero.

c. **65** The Gospel of Mark, first Christian gospel, appears.

c. **68** Romans destroy Qumran, center of ascetic mystical Jewish sect called Essenes ("Healers"); their writings, the Dead Sea Scrolls, discovered in 1947.

100 Buddhism reaches central Asia.

c. **175** Roman Emperor Marcus Aurelius begins his *Meditations*, the classic exposition of Stoicism.

c. **197** Carthaginian philosopher of the Latin Church, Tertullian, writes *Apologeticum* against Jews and heathens.

c. **200** Indian Buddhist philosopher and ascetic Nagarjuna is major influence on development of Madhamika (middle path) school of Buddhism. Greek philosopher and physician Sextus Empiricus expounds philosophy of agnostic scepticism.

c. **230–45** Origen writes *Eight Books Against Celsus*, the greatest of early Christian apologias.

c. **250** Emperor Decius steps up persecution of Christians; Christian martyrs come to be revered as saints.

c. **250–70** The writings of Plotinus popularize Neoplatonism.

303–13 Final persecution of Christians in Roman Empire under Emperor Diocletian.

305 Antony the Great founds first monastery near Memphis, Egypt.

313 Edict of Milan: Emperor Constantine (the Great) decrees toleration of Christianity throughout Roman Empire.

314 Conference of Arles: first general Council of the Western Christian Church.

c. **325** Eusebius of Caesarea, Father of Church History, writes *Ecclesiastical History* and *Chronicon*, histories of the Christian Church and the world.

GREEK RELIGION

The forebears of the Greeks worshiped a mother goddess, patron of fertility and the harvest. After 2000 B.C., Indo-European Hellenic invaders introduced the sky god Zeus, who was to become the supreme god of classical Greece. The mother cult was absorbed into what became the pantheon of Greek gods. Under the name of Hera ("the lady"), the mother goddess became the consort of Zeus; her other aspects took on other names. Mount Olympus, Greece's highest peak, was revered as the home of the gods (known as the Olympians), where Zeus ruled over all; beyond Olympus, the underworld (the realm of the dead) was ruled by Hades and his consort Persephone.

Major deities

Aphrodite Goddess of love, beauty, and fertility.

Apollo God of prophecy, music, youth, archery, and healing. Patron of the arts.

Ares War god, lover of Aphrodite.

Artemis Virgin goddess of the hunt.

Asclepius God of healing.

Athene Goddess of war and of wisdom, protectress of Athens.

Demeter Corn goddess.

Dionysus God of wine and ecstasy.

Eros Youthful god of love.

Hades God of the underworld.

Hephaestus God of fire and of smiths.

Hera Queen of heaven and wife of Zeus.

Hermes Divine messenger.

Nemesis Goddess of retribution.

Persephone Queen of the underworld, where she spent winters with her husband Hades; she spent summers on earth with her mother Demeter.

Poseidon God of sea and earthquakes.

Zeus Ruler of the gods.

Bronze statue of Poseidon, brother of Zeus and sea god (Athens, 400s B.C.).

Greek heroes Achilles (right) *and Ajax play checkers (Greek vase, 500s B.C.).*

Heroes and legendary figures

Achilles Greek hero of the Trojan War. Invulnerable except for his heel.

Agamemnon Commander of the Greek army in the Trojan War. Killed by his wife Clytemnestra on his return.

Argonauts Band of heroes who sailed with Jason in quest of the Golden Fleece.

Ariadne Cretan princess who helped Theseus. He deserted her, but she became the wife of Dionysus.

Circe Enchantress who transformed Odysseus' men into swine.

Clytemnestra Greek queen who killed her husband Agamemnon. She was killed by her son Orestes.

Daedalus Athenian inventor who worked for King Minos in Crete and constructed the labyrinth. Made wings and undertook a flight to Sicily with his son Icarus.

Deucalion Greek survivor of the flood, with his wife Pyrrha.

Hector Trojan leader slain by Achilles.

Helen Greek daughter of Zeus and most beautiful woman in the world. Taken to Troy by Paris, she was the cause of the Trojan War.

Heracles (Hercules) Greek hero whose achievements included 12 labors carried out for King Eurystheus.

Jason Greek hero who brought back the Golden Fleece from Colchis (Black Sea).

Medea Sorceress of Colchis who helped Jason steal the Golden Fleece.

Midas Phrygian king given power to turn whatever he touched to gold.

Minotaur Cretan monster, half-bull, half-man, who lived in the Labyrinth and was killed by Theseus.

Narcissus Youth who fell in love with his own reflection, slipped into the water, and drowned.

Odysseus (Ulysses) Resourceful Greek warrior in the Trojan War. His ten-year journey home is described in Homer's *Odyssey*.

Oedipus Greek king who unwittingly slew his father and married his mother.

Orestes Greek prince who slew his mother Clytemnestra to revenge his father Agamemnon and was pursued by the Erinnyes.

Orpheus Greek musician who almost rescued his dead wife from the underworld with his music, but lost her when he turned back at the threshold.

Paris Trojan prince who was awarded

Helen as reward for nominating Aphrodite as fairest goddess. His abduction of Helen caused the ruin of Troy.

Perseus Hero whose achievements included slaying the gorgon Medusa. He married Andromeda after saving her from a sea monster.

Psyche Personification of "the soul," usually represented by a butterfly. Beloved of Eros.

Pygmalion King of Cyprus who sculpted the figure of a woman which came to life.

Theseus Greek hero who killed the Minotaur, took power in Athens, and defended Attica against the Amazons, marrying their leader Hippolyta.

Shrines and oracles

Oracles, places where divine advice and prophecy could be purchased, usually through the medium of inspired priests or priestesses, were a feature of the classical world and included sites at Dodona (northern Greece), Dendera (Asia Minor), and Cumae (Italy). The most famous oracle was at Delphi, Greece, situated at the center point or navel (*omphalos*) of the world and sacred to Apollo (who slew the previous deity, the serpent Pytho, taking on its oracular powers).

Other divinities

Titans Pre-Olympian generation of gods, children of Uranus and Gaia, who warred with Zeus and were defeated. They included Atlas, who was made to hold up the heavens; Leto (Latona), mother by Zeus of twins Apollo and Artemis; and Prometheus, bringer of fire to mankind.

Centaurs Creatures that were half-man and half-horse.

Cyclopes One-eyed giants whose leader Polyphemus was blinded by Odysseus.

Erinnyes Furies often euphemistically called **Eumenides** (Kindly Ones). Divine avengers of wrong.

Gorgons Three snake-haired sisters who turned onlookers to stone.

Graces Three daughters of Zeus and Hera; embodied beauty and social accomplishments.

Harpies Three winged bird-women who snatched food from victims' tables.

Moerae (Parcae) The Fates, named Atropos, Clotho, and Lachesis.

Muses Nine goddesses, daughters of Zeus, each with the vocation to promote an area of the arts: Calliope for epic poetry, Clio for history, Erato for lyric poetry and hymns, Euterpe for the flute, Melpomene for tragedy, Polyhymnia for acting and music, Terpsichore for dance, Thalia for comedy, Urania for astronomy.

Nymphs Female spirits associated with natural phenomena: naiads with springs, rivers, and lakes; nereids and oceanids with the sea; dryads with trees.

Satyrs Half-goat and half-human, usually depicted as rural, wild, and lustful. Said to be brothers of the nymphs.

Sirens Demonesses who devoured sailors lured to their island by their song.

GREEK AND ROMAN GODS

Many Greek and Roman gods differed in name only:

Attribute	Greek	Roman
Beauty, love	Aphrodite	Venus
War	Ares	Mars
Hunting	Artemis	Diana
Wisdom	Athene	Minerva
Agriculture	Demeter	Ceres
Wine	Dionysus	Bacchus
Passion	Eros	Cupid
The Earth	Gaia/Ge	Tellus
Underworld/wealth	Hades/Dis	Pluto
Smith god	Hephaestus	Vulcan
Chief goddess	Hera	Juno
Messenger god	Hermes	Mercury
Hearth and home	Hestia	Vesta
The sky	Ouranos	Uranus
Sea/oceans	Poseidon	Neptune
Chief god	Zeus	Jupiter

ROMAN GODS AND HEROES

Roman religion borrowed from several nations but was based on that of Greece. The chief gods were essentially Greek deities under different names (*above*). Alongside these, every household honored its guardian spirits, the *lares* and *penates*; and each individual had his or her own protective spirit, or *genius*. Religious tolerance extended to the worship of foreign gods like the Egyptian Isis and the Persian Mithras. The gods were appeased with sacrifices, the head of each household making offerings on behalf of his family; the emperor acted as high priest (*Pontifex Maximus*) and this led to the deification of the emperor.

Roman deities and heroes

Aeneas Son of Aphrodite and ancestor of the Roman people, Aeneas was a Trojan who escaped the sack of Troy and led a group of survivors to Italy. There he became son-in-law of King Latinus and progenitor of Romulus and Remus.

Bellona War goddess.

Bona Dea "The good goddess," worshiped only by women.

Faunus God of crops and herds.

Flora Goddess of spring and flowers.

Fortuna Goddess of chance and fate.

Janus God of entrances.

Pomona Goddess of fruit trees.

Priapus Fertility god, represented with an erect penis.

Rhea Silvia Vestal Virgin. Vowed to chastity, she was seduced by Mars and gave birth to Romulus and Remus.

Romulus and **Remus** Mythical founders of Rome. Thrown as babies into the Tiber River, they were carried to the Palatine, where they were suckled by a she-wolf, then raised by a shepherd.

Saturn Ancient god of agriculture. His December festival, the Saturnalia, comprised a week of revelry.

Sibyl Prophetess whose prophecies were written on leaves.

Silvanus God of trees and forests. Identified with the Greek god Pan.

Vesta Goddess of hearth and home.

ANCIENT MYSTERY CULTS OF GREECE AND ROME

The mystery cults of the Greco-Roman world were religions to which only initiates were admitted. Their rites were secret and often bloody; most focused on personal survival after death.

The Mysteries of Eleusis A cult of the Athenian state which, very unusually, was open, on payment of a fee, to all Greeks. The Mysteries honored Demeter, goddess of corn, and her daughter Persephone, goddess of the underworld. The rites involved were a well-kept secret.

Dionysian mysteries The followers of Dionysus, god of wine, celebrated his mysteries at orgiastic festivals called Bacchanalia, during which female followers of Dionysus, the Maenads, were said to roam the mountains tearing wild beasts and even men to pieces.

Isis: Egyptian mother goddess in Romanized form spreads the cult.

Orphism Based on poems attributed to the mythical Orpheus, this movement was chiefly concerned with the fate of the soul after death.

Cybelean mysteries The cult of Cybele reached Rome in 204 B.C. Its frenetic rites were based on Cybele's vengeance on her faithless lover Attis, whom she drove to madness, self-castration, and death before they were reunited. During her festival, many devotees castrated themselves.

Mysteries of Isis Cult of the Egyptian mother goddess that spread across the Middle East; in classical times she was a central figure in mystery religions.

Mithraism Mithra was the Persian sun god who slew the primeval bull of darkness. In the first 100 years B.C., he entered the Greco-Roman pantheon as the god Mithras. His worship spread widely across the early Roman Empire, where it developed as a mystery cult, particularly among Roman soldiers, for whom it constituted a secret society.

THE CHRISTIAN FAITH

Christianity is a direct descendant of Judaism (*p. 211*), preserving the Hebrew Bible as its Old Testament. Christians, as their name implies, believe in the devinity of Jesus Christ, who was born in Bethlehem in 4 B.C., was crucified in Jerusalem in A.D 29, but rose from the dead in fulfillment of Old Testament scriptures.

According to Christian theology, Christ was both human and divine in nature, with the miracles he performed and, above all, his resurrection being evidence of his divinity. His life as a man and the message that he preached provide examples for all Christians in their daily lives. His resurrection, according to Christians, is the ultimate message—that death itself had been conquered and that eternal life is available to all who believe in him and strive to follow his teaching.

Christians also hold Christ to be the Son, one of three persons (or manifestations) of the single diety. They believe that Christ now resides with the Father, who sent him, and the Holy Spirit, who reveals God's word through inner grace. Together they comprise the Holy Trinity.

The New Testament is the writings of Christ's deciples. It is an account of the life and death of Christ and an attempt to explain his message. This biblical account, and the message it contains, is a core belief of all Christian denominations, although there is an enormous range in the way Christ is worshiped.

The New Testament

This part of the Bible is solely Christian; originally written in Greek, and standardized in its present form in the 400s.

Gospel According to Matthew (*c.* A.D. 80) Life and work of Jesus from a strictly and historically Jewish standpoint.
Gospel According to Mark (*c.* 63–70) Probably the first, used as a source by Matthew and Luke. It may have been written for non-Jewish audiences.
Gospel According to Luke (*c.* 85) Written from a very literate, Greek standpoint. It continues into the period of the *Acts of the Apostles*, covering the spread of Christianity beyond Palestine.
Gospel According to John (*c.* 90–110) More concerned with doctrine, describing the effect and meaning of Jesus' life from a mystical standpoint.
Acts of the Apostles By Luke; describes beginnings of the Church in Palestine.
The Epistles Letters from Paul and others, outlining points of faith and giving encouragement.
Revelation (The Apocalypse) The author, possibly John the Apostle, covers visions, prophecies, and the triumph of God on the Last Day.

Jesus' 12 apostles

Peter (originally **Symeon** or **Simon**) Fisherman and brother of Andrew. Leader of the apostles (a Greek word meaning those sent forth), and the first to baptize a gentile (non-Jewish) convert. Suffered martyrdom, possibly in Rome. Feast day June 29.
Andrew Brother of Peter. He may have preached in Asia Minor and Scythia, and suffered martyrdom in Achaea (Greece), possibly crucified on an X-shaped cross. Patron saint of Scotland and Russia. Feast day November 30.
James ("the Great") Son of fisherman Zebedee and brother of John. He may have preached in Spain but was executed in Judaea by Herod Agrippa in A.D. 44. According to legend, his remains were spirited away to Santiago de Compostela, in modern Spain, which became center of pilgrimage. Feast day July 25.
John Younger brother of James. Identified with the author of the Apocalypse, he may have lived at Ephesus, dying there at an advanced age.
Philip Possibly a former disciple of John the Baptist and missionary to Asia Minor.

Bartholomew (Nathanael) Possibly a missionary to Armenia.
Matthew (Levi) Former tax collector. Traditionally author of a gospel and missionary to the Hebrews in Judaea, Persia, and Ethiopia. Feast day September 21.
Thomas Didymus ("the Twin") Queried Jesus' resurrection until given proof. Traditionally preached in India. Patron saint of Portugal. Feast day December 21.
James ("the Less") Son of Alphaeus. Mentioned in all the lists of the apostles in the gospels, but nowhere else. Feast day May 3.
Jude (also called **Thaddaeus**) One of "the brethren of the Lord," possibly a brother of St. James "the Just." Traditionally martyred in Persia. Feast day October 28.
Simon the Zealot Political activist; possible missionary to Persia.
Judas Iscariot ("from Kerioth" in the tribe of Judah) Betrayer of Jesus. He is said to have hanged himself in remorse.
Matthias Chosen in place of Judas after his death.

The Christian year

Advent, which begins on the Sunday closest to November 30, is a four-week period of penitence and preparation for the nativity at **Christmas** (December 25). Christmas is celebrated in the Eastern Church at **Epiphany** (January 6), linked with the baptism of Jesus; in the West, Epiphany commemorates him being shown to the three wise men. In the West, the 40-weekday period before Easter, called **Lent**—a time of spiritual self-examination and, traditionally, fasting—begins on **Ash Wednesday** and marks the period of Christ's temptations in the desert. **Good Friday** (marking the crucifixion of Christ) and **Easter** (his resurrection) are followed 40 days later by **Ascension Day**, and ten days after that, by **Pentecost**. During the medieval period many other festivals connected with the Virgin Mary and the various saints were added.

The adoration of the newborn Christ by Persian magi as painted by Dürer (1471–1528).

Christianity before the Reformation

The earliest Christians were Jews who believed that Christ was the Messiah, and his 12 chosen followers formed the nucleus of the Church as a society or communion of believers. Paul, a Jew of the Diaspora, spread the message beyond Palestine, first to other Hellenistic Jews and then to non-Jews (Gentiles). The faith spread through the Greek and Roman world (although frequently persecuted as subversive) and was taken up by the Emperor Constantine in 313.

During the 300s, the Christian Church gradually diverged to form an Eastern (Orthodox) stream, based on Greece and Greek influences, and centered on Constantinople; and a Western (Catholic) stream, based on Rome. The former became the Orthodox Church, a communion of self-governing churches that recognized the primacy of the Patriarch of Constantinople, which included the patriarchates of Alexandria, Antioch, Constantinople, and Jerusalem. The first Orthodox Churches were those of Greece and Georgia; during the 800s, the Bulgarian, Russian, Serbian, and Romanian Orthodox Churches were added. Subsequently, others grew up in Finland, Czechoslovakia, Albania, North America, China, and Japan.

In Rome, the archbishop was accorded an even higher title, that of Father of the Church, or pope (Papa, or some form of the word in almost every European language), and vicar ("representative") of Christ on earth. The Catholic Church of Rome continued to hold sway in northern and western Europe, in central and eastern Europe and the Middle East other Catholic Churches were founded, with the result that there remain some Catholic Churches today which do not recognize the Pope in Rome as their spiritual leader. They include the Ukrainian, Ruthenian, Slovak, Romanian, Armenian,

Crucifixion *by Velázquez (1599-1660).*
Christians believe Christ rose from the dead.

Russian, Belarussian, Hungarian, Albanian, Greek, Syrian, and Ethiopian Catholic Churches, together with the Melkite Church (Middle East), the Chaldaean Church (Iraq), the Maronite Church (Lebanon), the Malabar and Malankarese Churches (India), and the Coptic Catholics of Egypt. Some of these now have large congregations in the United States and Canada.

The Roman Catholics held firm in their own area until the late 1400s and early 1500s, when reformers protested against some of the doctrines and practices that were not part of the original church (*p. 223*). The aim of these Protestants was to bring the church back to the sort of worship that they considered more accurately reflected that of the simple early Christian communities.

Major orders of monks and nuns

Dates of foundation in brackets. RC = Roman Catholic; P = Protestant.
Orders of monks, friars, and hermits
Pachomian monks (318)
Basilian (Orthodox) monks (c. 360)
Augustinian monks (388)
Benedictine (black) monks (529)
Constitutions of Theodore (Orthodox) monks (c. 800)
Cluniac monks (910)
Augustinian canons (c. 1060)
Carthusian monks (1084)
Cistercian (white) monks (1098)
Fontevrault monks (c. 1100)
Premonstratensian (white) canons (1120)
Carmelite (white) friars (c. 1155)
Trinitarian order (1198)
Franciscan (gray) friars (1209)
Dominican (black) friars (1215)
Silvestrine (blue Benedictine) monks (1230)
Augustinian hermits (Black canons, 1256)
Capuchin friars (1525)
Hospitaler friars of St. John of God (1537)
Trappist monks (RC, 1664)
Christian brothers (RC, 1802)
Marist brothers (RC, 1817)
Society of St. John the Evangelist (P, 1866)
Priests of the Sacred Heart (RC, 1878)
The Taizé Community (interdenominational, 1948)
Orders of nuns
Benedictine (529)
Fontevrault (c. 1100)
Beguine (c. 1180)
Poor Clare (Franciscan) nuns (1214)
Carthusian nuns (1229)
Bridgettine nuns (1344)
Carmelite nuns (1452)
Ursuline nuns (1535)
Discalced Carmelite nuns (Barefoot nuns, 1562)
Sisters of Charity of St. Vincent de Paul (RC, 1629)
Society of the Sacred Heart of Jesus (RC, 1800)
Sisters of Mercy (RC, 1827)
Little Sisters of the Poor (RC, 1840)
Nuns of the Community of St. Mary (P, 1865)
Poor Clares of Reparation and Adoration (P, 1922)
Major missionary orders
Theatine Brothers (1524)
Society of Jesus (Jesuits, RC, 1534)
Redemptorists (RC, 1732)
Missionaries of the Sacred Heart of Jesus (RC, 1854)
Salesians of St. John Bosco (RC, 1859)
Society of the Sacred Mission (RC, 1894)
Columban Fathers (RC, 1917)

Patron saints of working people

The ancient tradition of assigning patron saints to specific groups of people has continued into the 1900s.
Accountants Matthew
Architects Thomas the Apostle
Bakers Elizabeth of Hungary, Nicholas
Bankers Matthew
Barbers Cosmas and Damian, Louis
Booksellers John of the Latin Gate
Brewers Augustine of Hippo, Luke
Bricklayers Stephen
Builders Vincent Ferrer
Butchers Antony of Egypt, Luke
Carpenters Joseph
Dentists Apollonia
Doctors Pantaleon, Cosmas and Damian, Luke, Raphael
Farmers George, Isidore the Farmer
Firemen Florian
Fishermen Peter
Grocers Michael

Jewelers Eligius
Laborers Isidore, James, John Bosco
Lawyers Ivo, Genesius, Thomas More
Librarians Jerome
Miners Barbara
Musicians Gregory the Great, Cecilia, Dunstan
Nurses Camillus de Lellis, John of God, Agatha, Raphael
Policemen Michael
Sailors Cuthbert, Brendan, Eulalia, Christopher, Peter Gonzales, Erasmus
Secretaries Genesius
Social workers Louise de Marillac
Soldiers Hadrian, George, Ignatius, Sebastian, Joan of Arc, Martin of Tours
Tailors Homobonus
Tax collectors Matthew
Teachers Gregory the Great, Catherine of Alexandria, John Baptist de la Salle
Undertakers Dismas, Joseph of Arimathea

Timeline

325 Council of Nicea (now Iznik, Turkey) establishes basis of Christian doctrine.

337 Constantine the Great converts to Christianity on his deathbed.

342–43 Papal claims to Church supremacy recognized at Council of Sardica.

c. 350 Christian Church established in Abyssinia (Ethiopia).

c. 370 Buddhism reaches Korea.

c. 386 St. Jerome produces Vulgate, standard Latin translation of the Bible.

391 Emperor Theodosius bans pagan rites throughout Roman Empire and closes temples of the gods.

396 St. Augustine, first great Christian philosopher, becomes Bishop of Hippo, North Africa.

398 John Chrysostom appointed Archbishop of Constantinople.

401 Pope Innocent I claims worldwide supremacy over the Roman Church.

c. 432 St. Patrick begins his mission to Ireland, ordered by Pope Celestine I.

451 Copts break away from the Eastern Church after Council of Chalcedon.

484–519 First schism between Western (Roman) and Eastern (later Orthodox) Christian Churches.

491 Armenian Church breaks away from both Rome and Constantinople.

496 Frankish conversion to Christianity begins with baptism of King Clovis.

c. 520–25 First recorded Buddhist inscriptions (in Indian script) in Indonesian archipelago.

524 Boethius, Roman philosopher and translator of Aristotle, produces *De Consolatione Philosophiae*.

528 Justinian I suppresses Athenian schools of philosophy.

c. 530 Benedict of Nursia founds abbey of Monte Cassino near Naples, Italy. Benedictine Order emphasizes the value of manual labor and educational and artistic activities as well as prayer.

563 St. Columba, of Ireland, begins mission to Scotland; founds monastery on Iona which becomes mother church of Celtic Christianity in Scotland.

c. 570 Birth of prophet Muhammad in Mecca. Beginning of conversion of Spanish Visigoths to Christianity.

c. 585 St. Columba begins mission to Gaul.

587 First Buddhist monastery in Japan.

c. 590 Lombards of northern Italy begin conversion to Christianity.

590 Pope Gregory I begins vital reforms of Roman Church administration and rites.

597 Sent by Gregory I, St. Augustine begins mission to England.

610 Traditional date of first revelation by Allah to Muhammad, who begins to preach the faith of Islam.

622 The Hegira, Muhammad's migration from Mecca to Yathrib (Medina) marks the beginning of the Muslim era.

c. 625 Buddhism established as the religion of Japan. Muhammad begins dictating the Qur'an (Koran).

ISLAM: THE MUSLIM FAITH

A monotheistic faith, one of the world's most widespread religions, Islam means submission to the will of God (Allah). Its adherents, called Muslims, believe that there is one God and Muhammad is his Prophet. The fundamental requirement of Islam is obedience to the command of Allah as laid down in the sacred book, the Qur'an (Koran).

Islam is both a religion and a way of life: most devout Muslims cannot comprehend a faith that does not fundamentally affect their everyday existence. The most important concept of Islam is the *Sharia*, the way of life commanded by God. This includes both doctrine and practice, and is based on the Qur'an and the *Sunna* (way) of the Prophet as recorded in the *Hadith* (tradition).

The five pillars of Islam

Five duties or observances are required of all devout Muslims: to recite the confession of faith (*shahada*); to make an act of worship (*salat*) five times daily at set hours; to fast during *Ramadan*, the holy month when the Qur'an was set down; to give at least one-fortieth of their income as alms (*zakat*) and to donate certain kinds of property to charity; and once in a lifetime to make the pilgrimage (*haj*) to Mecca and fulfill the rites at the Kaaba there (*right*). In addition, gambling, drinking, and eating pork are forbidden.

The five pillars of belief

Five items of faith are firmly held by devout Muslims: that there is but one God; that his messengers are the angels; that there have been many prophets (Adam was the first, Jesus was another, and Muhammad was the last and greatest), but only one message; that there is to be a day of judgment, when humans will be resurrected and assigned to paradise or to hell; and that humankind is responsible for its own actions.

Islamic sects and movements

Sunnis number nearly 90 percent of the world's Muslims and consider that Muhammad's authority descended through the four caliphs who followed him. Their imams are religious leaders and teachers. The Al-Azhar University of Cairo, the intellectual center of Islam, trains students for missionary work.

Shi'ites believe that Muhammad's son-in-law Ali and his descendants constitute the true authority. The line of imams ended during the 800s, and since then the ayatollahs have served as a kind of collective leadership, caretakers of the office until the longed-for appearance of the last imam. With their own law and theology systems, Shi'ites live mainly in Iran (their main center, where Ayatollah Khomeini initiated the Islamic Republic), Iraq, India, and the Middle East.

Ismailis link with the Shias, developing from an underground movement during the 800s. They live in Asia and Africa, and some regard the Aga Khan IV as the 49th imam.

Sufis are the mystics of Islam, coming into existence during the 600s. They developed religious brotherhoods devoted to the idea of mystical union with God, and conflicted with orthodox Islam. The thought of Ibn'Arabi (1165–1240) has dominated Sufi spiritualism.

The word of God: interior of dome, Selimiye Mosque, Edirne, Turkey.

The Qur'an

The Holy Book of Islam, sacred to all Muslims, the Qur'an (Koran) is believed to be the exact and precise word of God, written in heaven and revealed to Muhammad as God's message for all humanity. The words themselves are sacred, and the Qur'an can only be read in the original Arabic, as delivered to Muhammad by the angel Gabriel. To memorize and quote from it is to enter into a kind of communion with ultimate reality, since the earthly book is a copy of the eternal book kept in heaven. It was compiled in full from oral and written sources (from professional memorists and notes taken at the time) shortly after Muhammad's death.

In its traditional form, the Qur'an preserves no chronological sequence of compilation, being arranged instead according

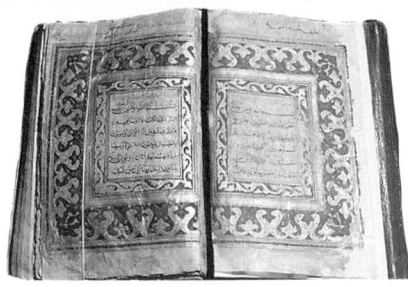

Oldest handwritten Qur'an, by Khawja Shayebh, Bangladesh, 1091.

to the length of each of its 114 *suras* (chapters). As the word of God, it embodies the same authority for every Muslim and makes Islam the "religion of the book."

Mecca and the Kaaba

A shrine situated at the Great Mosque, Mecca, Saudi Arabia, the Kaaba is considered by Muslims to be the most sacred site in Islam. It is a small cube-shaped building, unadorned except for the sacred Black Stone, a meteorite, set into the eastern corner of its walls. Earlier shrines on this spot were important centers of pilgrimage even in pre-Islamic times, but in 630, Muhammad stripped the Kaaba of its pagan decorations and it became the spiritual center of Islam. The stone, or *qibla*, is the focus point to which all Muslims turn when they pray. Pilgrimage to Mecca (known as *haj*) is one of the activities enjoined upon all Muslims.

Holy pilgrims at Mecca, Saudi Arabia.

CELTIC RELIGION

Formerly widespread throughout Europe, the Celts are today confined to northwestern Europe from Brittany to Scotland. A tribal warrior people, they revered the powers of nature and saw gods in natural objects, developing a strong oral tradition that has survived as medieval Irish and Welsh mythological tales. The Celts embraced Christianity early, and the Celtic Church was the first in the British Isles (*c.* A.D. 200).

Aine, An, Ana, Dana Irish mother of the gods, also sun goddess.

Arawn Welsh king of the underworld.

Arianrhod (Aranrhod) Welsh goddess of the sky and of fertility.

Badb Irish war goddess.

Belenos (Belenus) Gaulish pastoral god, patron of order and of medicine.

Bran Hero whose magical, preserved head was buried in London, later to be disinterred by King Arthur.

Brigit (Berecyntia, Briganta) Irish goddess of hearth and home, later merged with St. Brigid/Bridget, Ireland's patron saint (after St. Patrick).

Cernunnos ("horned one") Gaulish early god of nature and wild animals.

Cuchulainn Warrior hero of Ulster.

Donn Irish god of the Underworld.

Dylan Welsh sea deity.

Eithne Irish corn-maiden goddess.

Eriu Goddess of Eire, Erin, Ireland.

Epona ("the mare") Goddess-patroness of horsemen and horsemanship.

Fionn mac Cumhal (Finn Mac Cool) Irish solar demigod.

Gwydion Hero-king of the British Celts, wizard and bard.

Lir (Llyr) Irish Sea god.

Ludd Romano-British river god.

Lugh Irish sun god associated with harvest festival Lughnasa.

Morrigan War goddess.

The Mothers Triple fertility goddess.

Ogmios (Ogma) Club-carrying god of eloquence, credited with inventing the Ogham runic alphabet.

Rhiannon "Great Queen" of the gods, associated with horses.

Taranis Gaulish storm god.

Teutates Revered Gaulish war god.

Tuatha De Danann "People of Dana"; settled Ireland *c.* 1500 B.C. and became divinities. Defeated by the Milesians, they retreated into the mounds (*sidé*).

Celtic horned god, Cernunnos, from the Gundestrup cauldron, Denmark.

Timeline

c. **840–50** Buddhists persecuted in China.

c. **860** Brothers St. Cyril and St. Methodius convert southern Slavs to Christianity; Cyril by tradition the originator of the Slavonic (Cyrillic) alphabet.

c. **940** Christianization of Hungary.

c. **960** Mount Athos, Greece, first becomes a center of monasticism.

c. **965** St. Dunstan orders English clergy to remain celibate. Denmark and Poland become Christian.

980 Birth near Bokhara of Islamic philosopher and physician Avicenna.

c. **987** St. Vladimir I of Kiev first Christian ruler of Russia.

c. **990** Aelfric Grammaticus produces paraphrase of Old Testament in English. Christianity reaches Iceland and Greenland. Spain becomes spiritual center of Judaism.

1003–13 Caliph al-Hakim of Egypt persecutes Christians and Jews, and destroys churches, including Holy Sepulchre, Jerusalem.

1016 Caliph al-Hakim declares himself divine; his followers are forerunners of the Druze of modern Syria and Lebanon.

1022 Synod of Pavia demands celibacy of higher clergy.

c. **1050** Tokolor of Senegal are first Africans south of Sahara to accept Islam.

1054 Final schism between Eastern (Orthodox) and Western (Catholic) Christian Churches.

1073 Pope Gregory VII (St. Hildebrand) elected; greatest advocate of temporal power of medieval papacy.

1079 Birth of Peter Abelard, French philosopher and theologian.

c. **1090** Heretical Muslim sect founded in Persia by Hasan ibn Sabbah who sends out *hashishiyun* ("hashish smokers," or assassins) to kill orthodox Muslims and Christians.

1093 St. Anselm, Italian philosopher, becomes archbishop of Canterbury and later produces *Proslogion*, an attempt to prove the existence of God.

1095 Pope Urban II inspires First Crusade at Council of Clermont; enormous popular response throughout Western Europe.

1096 First Crusade raises more than 30,000 men, led by Godfrey of Bouillon, Raymond of Toulouse, and Bohemund of Taranto; they converge on Constantinople.

1097 Crusaders and Byzantine Greeks defeat Muslims at Nicaea.

1098 Antioch falls to crusaders. Cistercian Order of monks founded at Citeaux, France.

1099 Jerusalem falls to crusaders, who slaughter 40,000 and set fire to mosques and synagogues.

1120 Order of Knights of the Temple (Knights Templar) founded in Jerusalem to guide and protect pilgrims.

NORSE AND GERMANIC RELIGION

Raiders, traders, and settlers from Scandinavia and Denmark, the Norse people conquered and colonized—from the late 700s to around 1050—large parts of Britain, Normandy, and Russia. Information on Viking beliefs and mythology comes mainly from collections compiled in the Middle Ages, of which the *Edda* by Icelander Snorri Sturluson is the most valuable. Norse mythology is heroic and fatalistic, reflecting their harsh society. Envisaged in human form, the warrior gods interacted with the world of mortals in varying degrees. The Norse believed that at the world's end even the gods would be destroyed in their Armageddon: Ragnarok.

Aegir Ocean god, destroyer of ships.

Aesir One (probably the later) of two races of Norse gods, led by Odin.

Balder (Baldur) Son of Odin and Frigg, favorite of the gods, slain through the machinations of Loki.

Freyr ("lord") Fertility god, more earthy than his sister, Freya; associated with crops and the marriage bed.

Freya ("lady") Moon goddess who became goddess of love and fertility; sister of Freyr. She inspired seeresses.

Frigg (Frigga) Teutonic mother goddess adopted as Nordic goddess of fertility and marriage; wife of Odin. She gave her name to Friday.

Heimdall Watchman of the gods and guardian of the Bifrost Bridge between Asgard and the rest of the world. He established social order among mortals.

Hel (Hela) Goddess of death and ruler of Helheim. There she gathered only the souls of those who died shamefully in their beds.

Hermod Messenger god; son of Odin.

Hoder (Hodur) Blind god, tricked by Loki into killing his twin brother Balder with a spear of mistletoe.

Loki Trickster god, a sinister comedian fated to bring about Ragnarok and the catastrophic Twilight of the Gods. He sired two monstrous enemies of the gods, the Fenris wolf and the World Serpent.

Odin (Woden, Wotan) Dominant figure

Thor, deity common to all Germanic peoples, favored humans and opposed the giants.

in Norse legend, chief of the Aesir family of gods. A hooded figure who traded his eye for wisdom and hung for nine days on a gallows to obtain the magic art of runic writing, he was the sinister lord of war and sorcery, and god of the dead. He gifted his followers with elated states of mind, inspiring both poetry and battle rage. He gave his name to Wednesday.

Sif Giantess wife of Thor. Loki burned off her golden hair and was made to replace it with a wig of real gold.

Thor Early thunder god; a mighty, popular brawler with a great ax-hammer that he used to protect gods and men from evil and chaos. A simple, jovial character, he gave his name to Thursday.

Valkyries Divine battle-maidens and messengers of Odin who led souls of slain warriors to Valhalla, hall of the dead.

SCHOLASTICISM AND NEOPLATONISM

Greek philosophy strongly influenced the development of Western thought in the medieval and Renaissance periods. The work of Plato and Aristotle was of primary importance in this evolution.

Scholasticism, a philosophical system based on the writings of the Greek philosopher Aristotle (300s B.C.), and incorporating Arabic and Jewish ideas, that dominated Europe in the medieval period. Translation of Aristotle's work into Latin provided medieval scholars and theologians with new material for reflection and criticism, particularly in relation to the conflict between faith and reason. Thomas Aquinas and Duns Scotus were preeminent in offering a synthesis of Aristotelian philosophy and Christian theology.

Neoplatonism, founded by Plotinus (A.D. 205–270), attempted to combine the doctrines of Plato, Aristotle, the Pythagoreans, and Stoicism. Neoplatonist philosophy was popular with many Christians for centuries after the death of Plotinus, inspiring medieval and Renaissance mystics such as Pico della Mirandola. It taught that from the One (the transcendent Godhead) emanate intelligence or *logos* (which contains the Platonic ideas) and soul (which includes individual souls).

MEDIEVAL LEGEND: THE HOLY GRAIL

A body of medieval legend known as the "Matter of Britain" (in contrast to the "Matter of France," which dealt with the exploits of the Frankish knight Roland and his death at Roncevalles) became universally popular in medieval Europe and has remained an inspiration ever since. This describes the exploits of the British King Arthur and his knights and their quest for the Holy Grail—the cup used by Christ at the Last Supper, and believed to have been brought to Britain by Joseph of Arimathea.

Probably adapting the legend from earlier Celtic sources, medieval European poets established the basic Grail story in the early 1100s, to be further developed by writers such as Chrétien de Troyes (France), Wolfram von Eschenbach (Germany), and Thomas Malory (Britain). The story has proved the inspiration for much later work, including Wagner's operas *Lohengrin* and *Parsifal*, Tennyson's narrative poem *The Idylls of the King*, T. S. Eliot's *The Waste Land*, and T. H. White's *The Once and Future King*, which formed the basis for the popular musical *Camelot*.

Figures of the Grail story include:
Arthur Probably a Romanized Celtic war leader of the 500s, Arthur was king of Britain, with a round table of knights whose exploits became the standard for medieval chivalry.
Galahad A pure, ideal knight, son of Sir Lancelot and Elaine, he alone was able to succeed in the adventures of the Siege Perilous and the Holy Grail.
Lancelot du Lac Despite his near-perfection as a knight, he failed in the quest for the Holy Grail because of his adultery with Arthur's wife Guinevere.

King Arthur's Wedding Feast, 1905, by Arthur Rackham.

Perceval (Parsifal) He nearly succeeded in his quest, but his bashfulness prevented him from asking the right questions of the warden of the Grail castle, and as a result the Fisher King was not healed.
Lohengrin In German legend, the son of Parsifal; he left the temple of the Grail and was carried to Antwerp in a boat drawn by swans; there he saved Princess Elsa of Brabant, but was forced to leave her.

SHINTOISM

Also called "The Way of the Higher Powers," Shintoism is the religion of Japan which reveres ancestors and nature-spirits. The two major Shinto works, *Kojiki* and *Nihongi*, were produced during the early 700s and contain the stories of the gods. A manual of ritual prayers, *Engishiki*, dates from A.D. 927.

Since 1945, when State Shinto was abolished, there have been two major branches.

In **Sect Shinto**, the 13 or more "denominations" may be divided into five categories: traditional Shinto, groups whose main religious fealty is to the monarchy and to veneration of their ancestors; purification sects, which emphasize physical and ritual cleanliness; Confucian sects, which combine elements of the two philosophies; faith-healing sects, which emphasize physical health and respect and care for others by religious ritual; and mountain sects, whose gods are located in sacred mountains.

Folk Shinto believes in the veneration of gods and spirits, many of them specific to a location.

The major Shinto deities include Amaterasu, the sun goddess, whose disk is shown on the Japanese national flag; Tsuki-yomi, the moon god; Susa-no-o, an unruly and disruptive storm god; Hachiman, god of war, guardian of humans, and patron of seafarers; and Inari, god of fertility and the rice harvest.

A torii (Shinto shrine gateway) leading to the Meiji Shrine, Tokyo.

Timeline

1121 Peter Abelard, French theologian condemned as heretic.
1123 First Lateran Council forbids marriage of priests.
1126 Birth of Averroes, Arab philosopher and judge, famous for his commentaries on Aristotle.
1130 "Antipope" Cardinal Pierleone contests election of Pope Innocent II, who flees to France. Birth of Chu Hsi, Chinese philosopher and exponent of Neo-Confucianism that dominates China for the next 800 years.
c. **1146** Cistercian Bernard of Clairvaux preaches Second Crusade.
1147 Second Crusade assembles 500,000 men, led by France's Louis VII and German Conrad III; comes to nothing.
1154 Nicolas Breakspear, first and only English pope, elected as Hadrian IV.
1173 Peter Waldo of Lyons initiates the Waldensian community, devoted to voluntary poverty.
1182 Philip II banishes Jews from France.
1184 Peter Waldo is excommunicated.
1189 Massacre of Jews in England at the coronation of Richard I (Coeur de Lion). Third Crusade begins, led by Frederick Barbarossa of Germany and Richard I.
1190 *Guide for the Perplexed* by Spanish philosopher Maimonides tries to harmonize the thought of Aristotle with Judaism.
1192 Third Crusade ends after Saladin permits free access for Christians to the Holy Sepulchre, Jerusalem.
1208 Pope Innocent III preaches Albigensian crusade against heretics of Albi, S.W. France, and Waldensian crusade against followers of Peter Waldo.
1209 St. Francis of Assisi organizes a brotherhood that will develop into the Franciscan order.
1214 Birth of Roger Bacon, Franciscan philosopher who emphasized the role of experiment and mathematics in science.
1215 Fourth (Great) Lateran Council under Innocent III defines doctrine of Eucharist. Dominican Order founded.
1225 Birth of Thomas Aquinas, Italian scholastic philosopher and theologian.
1228 Francis of Assisi is canonized two years after his death.
c. **1230** Pope Gregory IX gives Dominicans major responsibility for the Inquisition.
1258 Flagellant movement arises in Europe, with public and private self-flagellation to divert divine punishment.
c. **1265** Birth of scholastic theologian Duns Scotus.
c. **1275** Spanish cabalist Moses de Leon compiles *Sefer ha-Zohar*, Jewish mystical work (Kaballah, *p. 225*).
1290 Jews expelled from England.
c. **1295** Mongol rulers of China officially adopt Confucianism.
1306 Jews expelled from France. Christian missions in China.

Timeline

1309 Exile of the papacy to Avignon, France (until 1377).

1349 Jews persecuted in Germany.

1378 Great Schism: rival popes elected in Rome and Avignon (until 1417).

1380 William Wycliffe produces first complete translation of Bible in English.

1402 Bohemian reformer John Huss preaches in Prague; burned at the stake for heresy in 1415.

1419 Death of Tsongkhapa, founder of Gelugpa sect, a powerful order of Tibetan Buddhism.

***c.* 1425** Thomas à Kempis produces his influential *On the Imitation of Christ*.

1440 Platonic Academy founded, Florence, Italy. Nicholas of Cusa, German philosopher, produces *De Docta Ignorantia*, emphasizing limitations of human knowledge.

1453 Ottoman Turks take Constantinople (which they then call Istanbul).

1456 Pope Callistus III condemns Halley's Comet as an agent of the devil.

1469 Birth of Guru Nanak, founder of Sikhism (*right*). Birth of Niccolò Machiavelli, Italian political philosopher who in *Il Principe* advises princes to be cunning and, when necessary, deceitful.

1478 Spanish rulers Ferdinand and Isabella establish the Inquisition, a tribunal for prosecution of heresy directed against Muslims and Jews.

1482 Tomas de Torquemada, Dominican monk, appointed Inquisitor-General of Aragon and Castile in Spain.

1484 Papal bull *Summis Desiderantes* denounces witches and sorcerers.

1489 German Dominican inquisitors Jacob Sprenger and Henricus Institor (Krämer) produce *Malleus Maleficarum* (The Hammer of Witches), which becomes a witch-hunters' manual.

1492 Pico della Mirandola produces *De Ente et Uno*, attempting to reconcile Platonic and Aristotelian ontological doctrines. Jews expelled from Spain.

1497 Jews expelled from Portugal.

1498 Girolamo Savoranola, Italian Dominican religious reformer, is burned at the stake for heresy.

1500 Spanish Inquisitor-General Francisco Jiménez de Cisneros orders forcible mass conversion of Muslims.

1501 The Moravian Brethren, a Bohemian sect, publish the first Protestant hymnbook.

1503 Erasmus produces *Enchiridion Militis Christiani* (Handbook of a Christian Soldier).

1509 Persecution of Jews in Germany opposed by humanist philosopher and cabalist Johann Reuchlin. Erasmus produces *Encomium Moriae* (In Praise of Folly), a satire on church corruption and scholastic philosophy, dedicated to Sir Thomas More.

***c.* 1510** Shi'ism becomes the state religion of Persia.

CENTRAL AND SOUTH AMERICAN RELIGIONS

Chichén Itzá, Mexico: Mayan pyramid with sacred jaguar in foreground.

Europeans arriving in Central and South America during the late 1400s and early 1500s found the inheritors of a succession of societies—Olmecs, Zapotecs, Maya, Aztecs, Toltecs, and Incas—whose subjugation to fierce gods produced a strange blend of primitive and sophisticated culture. These people had not developed wheeled vehicles, but in the service of the gods they evolved writing, astronomy, and advanced mathematics. Their pyramid stone temples in cult centers were so vast that European explorers thought them cities. Their gods demanded not only conventional worship but also human sacrifice—a rite the Aztecs took to extremes. The Maya shifted the emphasis from religious rituals to the calendar developed to schedule them.

Ah Puch Mayan god of death.

Chac Mayan god of rain and agriculture.

Cinteotl Aztec/Toltec god of corn.

Coatlicue ("serpent skirt") Aztec/Toltec earth goddess. The Aztec "flower wars" were fought to obtain prisoners to sacrifice to her.

Ek Chuah ("black war chief") Mayan war god. Bore off the souls of warriors who died in battle; also patron of merchants.

Huitzilopochtli ("blue hummingbird on the left") Aztec chief deity and god of war, demanding human sacrifices.

Hunab Ku Mayan creator god, who three times destroyed the world by flood.

Inti Inca sun god, from whom the ruling dynasty traced its descent.

Itzamna Mayan chief god, lord of day and night, and of medicine. Invented writing; brought fertility to the field.

Ixchel Mayan goddess of birth, fertility, and medicine.

Mictlantecuhtli Aztec/Toltec god of the underworld through which souls pass.

Ometechtli ("dual lord") Aztec hermaphroditic creator god.

Quetzalcoatl ("plumed serpent") Aztec god of the wind.

Tezcatlipoca ("smoking mirror") Aztec sun god of Toltec origin. Alternately kind and cruel; enemy of Quetzalcoatl.

Tlaloc Aztec/Toltec rain god, bringing fertility; demanded child sacrifice.

Tlazolteotl Aztec goddess of love, luxury, and witchcraft.

Viracocha Inca creator god, sun and storm god, bringer of civilization.

Xipe Totec Aztec god of goldsmiths, agriculture, and penitential torture.

Xiuhtecuhtli Aztec/Toltec god of fire, the sun, and volcanoes.

Xochiquetzal ("flower feather") Aztec goddess of flowers and fruits, patron of craftsmen, marriage, and fertility.

Xolotl Aztec god of the night sky.

Yum Kaax Mayan corn deity.

SIKHISM

Sikhism was founded during the early 1500s in Sultanpur, near Amritsar (Punjab province, India) by Guru Nanak. Nanak instituted a monotheistic faith encompassing elements of both the Hindu and Islamic creeds, which could be transmitted to all. Before he died, he appointed a successor, also to have the title guru ("teacher"). There followed a total of ten gurus in a chain of leadership that moved progressively away from Hinduism. This chain ended in 1708 with the death of Gobind Singh, who had named as his successor not a human tutor but the collected scripture of the faith, the *Adi Granth*, thereafter called the *Guru Granth Sahib*. Singh also instituted the Sikh Khalsa Brotherhood and imposed the Sikh "uniform" on the male faithful, the "Five Ks": *kesh* (uncut hair), *kamgha* (a comb), *kara* (a band on the right wrist), *kirpan* (a dagger), and *kachha* (short pants).

Until 1982, Sikhs and Hindus lived in relative harmony, but the desire for an independent Sikh state led to armed conflict in 1984, culminating in an assault by Indian troops on the Sikhs' temple at Amritsar.

The Golden Temple at Amritsar, sacred to the Sikhs.

PROTESTANT REFORMERS

Martin Luther (1483–1546) attacked the papal system, pioneering the Reformation.

The great religious Reformation of Europe in the 1500s resulted in the establishment of Protestantism. A key element was Calvinism, which evolved under the influence of French-born theologian **John (Jean) Calvin**. Influenced by Martin Luther, he traveled around Europe promoting Protestantism. In 1536, he wrote *Christianae Religionis Institutio* (Institutes of the Christian Religion), which became an influential definition of the Reformed faith. He took up residence in Geneva, where he instituted religious and political reforms. Among churches founded on Calvinist principles are the Reformed Churches (especially in the Netherlands) and the Presbyterian Churches. Protestant reformers included:

Martin Luther German theologian and prime mover of the Protestant Reformation. Distressed by the worldliness of many religious authorities, Luther underwent a spiritual crisis that was resolved by his determining that salvation was possible for all by faith alone. In 1517, he attached 95 theses on corrupt practices to the door of the church of Wittenberg castle. Copies were translated from the original Latin, printed, and spread far and wide. German religious authorities originally approved, some accompanying Luther when he traveled to the Diet of Worms in 1521 to argue against his excommunicaton by the pope. Successful, but held in custody, Luther translated the New Testament into German. Later he produced a Reformed mode of church service and liturgy, also in German. Today, Lutheran churches predominate in Germanic Europe.

Huldreich Zwingli Pioneered Reformist ideals in Switzerland in the early 1500s. He also proposed that city councils should be responsible for both the religious and social welfare of their people. His doctrines spread rapidly, and were challenged, not least by Lutherans. His sect became known as the Anabaptists for their emphasis on the cleansing powers of baptism, which for most converts meant a second baptism.

John Huss Bohemian religious reformer who was influenced by the English reformer William Wycliffe (c. 1320–84), spoke out strongly against Roman Catholic authoritarianism. Excommunicated, he continued writing, but was lured into attending the Council of Constance (1414), where he was betrayed into the hands of his enemies and burned at the stake. His followers, known as Hussites, began a reform of Bohemia that eventually gave rise to the Moravian Church.

John Knox Scottish scholar and historian, was a prominent preacher in Henry VIII's (Protestant) England until he fled to Europe in 1553, when the Catholic Mary Tudor ascended the throne. Later he returned to Scotland and, with military help from Elizabeth I of England, established Protestant forms of worship there, based on Calvinism.

Menno Simons Dutch Anabaptist leader who traveled to both North America and Russia. An ex-Catholic priest, he was persecuted by both Catholics and Protestants. Menno founded the Mennonite sect, that also includes the Amish and Hutterites, most of whom now live in North America.

Henry VIII Tudor king who established the Church of England, with himself as head, partly through Reformist zeal, partly in order to annexe the extensive property of the Roman Church in England, and above all in order to be able to remarry without papal consent.

Early English translation of the Bible, Hereford cathedral, England.

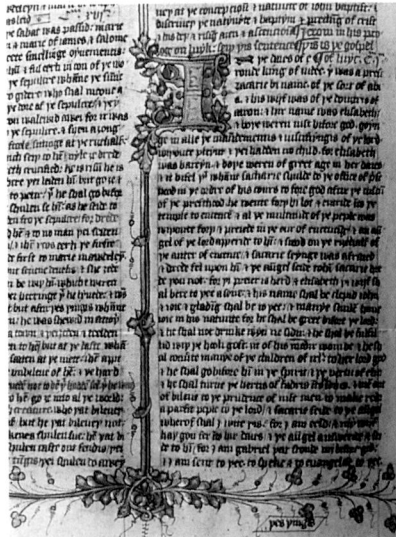

Timeline

1513 Accession of Pope Leo X.

1517 Martin Luther nails "95 theses" to castle church door in Wittenberg, Germany, in protest against corruption: the Reformation begins.

1518 Death of Indian mystic and poet Kabir, venerated by Hindus and Muslims.

1518–25 Haldreich Zwingli in Zurich inaugurates the Reformation in Switzerland.

1519 Luther attacks papal authority in debate with Catholic theologian Johann Mayer von Eck in Leipzig, Germany.

1520 Pope Leo X excommunicates Luther. Anabaptist movement originates in Switzerland, Germany, and the Netherlands.

1521 Diet of Worms: Luther condemned by Holy Roman emperor Charles V and accepts protection of the Elector of Saxony. Leo X awards Henry VIII of England title "Defender of the Faith" for his pro-Catholic sentiments.

1522 Luther produces German translation of the New Testament.

1525 Luther marries ex-nun Katherine von Bora. German Anabaptist Thomas Müntzer sets up short-lived communistic theocratic community at Mulhausen. Capuchin friars founded in Italy, later a force in Counter-Reformation.

1527 Sweden becomes Lutheran.

1528 Austrian Jacob Hutter founds a "community of love" based on Moravian Brethren; John Knox begins Reformation in Scotland.

1529 Protest by Lutherans at Second Diet of Speyer leads to name "Protestants." Persecution of Jews in Hungary.

1530 Protestant doctrine summarized by Luther and Melanchthon in the Augsburg Confession. Protestant princes signing the confession form Schmalkaldic League against Charles V and Catholic allies.

1531 Erasmus publishes complete canon of Aristotle's surviving works. Haldreich Zwingli killed in battle between Swiss Catholics and Protestants.

1534 Ignatius Loyola, with Francis Xavier and other Roman Catholics in Paris, founds Society of Jesus (Jesuits), intended both for missionary activity and to aid the Counter-Reformation. Luther produces German translation of the Old Testament, completing his Bible.

1535 Henry VIII executes Thomas More and John Fisher. Translated by English Protestant Miles Coverdale, first complete English Bible. St. Angela Merici founds the Company of St. Ursula (Ursulines) at Brescia, Italy.

1536 Henry VIII begins dissolution of English monasteries. Denmark and Norway become Lutheran. Calvin's doctrines spread swiftly across Europe.

c. 1537 Dutch Anabaptist Menno Simons founds fundamentalist pacifist sect practicing adult baptism, later known as Mennonites.

Timeline

1541 John Calvin establishes theocratic regime in Geneva, Switzerland.

1542 Jesuit Francis Xavier's mission to Goa, India. Pope Paul III sets up Roman Inquisition in an effort to stem the Reformation.

1543 Pope Paul III promulgates *Index Librorum Prohibitorum* of banned books. Spanish Inquisition burns Protestants.

1545–63 Council of Trent: Ecumenical Catholic Church Council at Trento, Italy, convened to plan the Counter-Reformation and reform Roman Catholic doctrine.

1548 Archbishop Thomas Cranmer produces *The Book of Common Prayer*. Ignatius Loyola produces *Spiritual Exercises*, the guiding rules for Jesuits.

1548–52 Francis Xavier's mission to Japan.

1551 Persecution of Jews in Bavaria.

1553 Queen Mary I returns England to Catholicism; described as "Bloody Mary" for her anti-Protestant policies.

1554 *History of the Acts and Monuments of the Church*, a history of English Protestant martyrs, by John Foxe, published at Strasbourg, France; it appears in England in 1563.

1558 Queen Elizabeth I returns England to Protestantism. John Knox produces *The First Blast of the Trumpet against the Monstrous Regiment of Women*.

1560 Covenanters, Protestants inspired by Knox, gain mastery in Scotland; Church of Scotland ministers draw up *Confession of Faith*, mainly the work of Knox, followed by *First Book of Discipline* in 1561.

1561 Birth of Sir Francis Bacon, first of the great British empiricist philosophers, pioneer of scientific method.

1562 Massacre of Vassy: death of *c.* 1,200 French Huguenots (Protestants) begins the First French War of Religion.

1563 Church of England established by the adoption of the 39 Articles, combining Protestant doctrine with Catholic organization; dissenting groups include Puritans (already so called), Separatists, and Presbyterians. Counter-Reformation in Bavaria and Poland.

1565 Spanish build Catholic church in St. Augustine, Florida—first Christian church in North America.

1566 The "Helvetic Confession" of Swiss theologian Heinrich Bullinger helps reconcile Zwinglians and Lutherans.

1568 Cardinal William Allen founds English College at Douai, France, to train missionaries for reconverting England. Jesuit missionaries welcomed in Japan.

1570 English Queen Elizabeth I excommunicated.

1579 St. John of the Cross, Spanish mystic, writes *Dark Night of the Soul*.

1580 English Jesuits Edmund Campion and Robert Parsons begin mission in England; Campion is captured and

COUNTER-REFORMATION AND THE JESUITS

Stimulated in part by the Reformation, a general movement of reform and missionary activity developed in the Roman Catholic world during the mid-1500s. This included the revival of the monastic movement (Capuchins, 1525; Oratorians, 1575), and especially the creation of the Jesuits (the Society of Jesus). A male religious order founded in 1534 by Spanish-born soldier Saint Ignatius Loyola, the Jesuits soon became firmly established in Europe with their educational work; they also became energetic missionaries to Asia, the Americas, and, later, Africa. One of the first members of the order, Saint Francis Xavier, took Christianity to the Far East. A French Jesuit, Jacques Marquette, was one of the first to explore the Mississippi River in the 1600s. A noncontemplative order, the Society of Jesus has founded many schools, colleges, and universities throughout the world, and continues to be a leading apologist for Roman Catholicism.

Jesuit mission to Japan: frontispiece from a Jesuit book of 1665.

WITCHES AND WITCHCRAFT

Witchcraft, the target of extreme persecution from the Christian Church during the 1400s, 1500s, and 1600s, was probably a form of worship dating back to pre-Christian times, in which the nature worship and fertility rituals found in many preliterate societies were practiced. It was condemned by a papal bull in 1484 and identified as a heretical, satanic religion involving a pact with the devil. Salem, Massachusetts, was the scene of one of the world's most famous witchcraft trials. In 1692, a special court, convened by the governor of Massachusetts, heard the evidence of several girls who claimed that they had been bewitched by a West Indian slave and other Salem women and men. Twenty people were executed before church officials put an end to the hysteria by stopping the trials in late 1692. Accusations spread that witches engaged in black masses, flew, had personal devils as "familiars," and cast malignant spells. It is calculated that more than 300,000 people, most of them women, were executed for "practicing witchcraft."

In the contemporary West, "Wicca" has emerged as a neo-pagan movement, influenced by the work of Gerald Gardner and Margaret Murray. Members of covens meet at "sabbaths" to invoke the mother goddess in her various forms and to "draw down the moon" or draw lunar energy into the magic circle.

Water torture meted out to suspected witches, from a drawing by Pieter Brueghel, 1559.

CHRISTIAN HERESIES

Heresy is defined as false doctrine, or the formal denial of doctrine. The Inquisition was established to root it out. Today, the Christian idea of heresy has been modified and the ultimate sanction is excommunication (withdrawal of the right to Communion). Various heresies have flourished over the centuries.

Adoptionism consisted of two aspects: first came the belief that Jesus was a mortal man "adopted" by God at his baptism (200s), and second the view that Jesus had both human and divine "natures," the human being "adopted" by God (700s).

Docetism (100s) held that Christ on earth was not real, only apparent.

Gnosticism (*c.* 100–400) held that salvation was dependent upon access to secretly revealed knowledge (*gnosis*) about the nature and destiny of the human soul.

Nestorianism (300s and 500s) taught that Jesus' two "natures"—human and divine—were so different as to correspond to two distinct persons.

Monophysitism (400s) taught that Jesus had only one "nature" instead of being both human and divine.

Pelagianism (400s) held that humans are basically good and born in a state of grace, and that God's grace is not therefore essential for godly deeds.

Albingensians (1100s and 1200s), also known as Cathars, lived mainly in France and believed that creation consists of the good and the spiritual (God) contending with evil and the material (Satan) in a world that is basically corrupt.

Arminianism (1600s) implies that God's judgment on the destination of mortals for heaven or hell is preordained even if those in question appear to merit the alternative. This was condemned as encouraging sin and devaluing forgiveness.

Jansenism (1600s and 1700s) implies that the grace of God is necessary not only for salvation, but also for every single godly deed. It was condemned as denying human free will and devaluing redemption by Christ.

Galileo Galilei proved the theories of Copernicus and was tried for heresy.

CABALA

The Cabala (also sometimes Cabbala, Kabbalah), from the Hebrew word meaning "oral tradition," is the mystical aspect of Judaism (*p. 211*). It proposes that the Limitless Light (*Ain Soph Aur*) manifests itself through different *sephiroth,* or spheres, on the Tree of Life. There are ten *sephiroth,* each one of which is an emanation of the divine Godhead. According to the *Sefer ha-Zohar* (Book of Splendor) developed in Spain between about 1260 and 1280, nothing exists unless it participates in divinity, which is the hidden substratum of creation. The vocation of the mystic is to find the elements of the hidden language in which the thoughts of God are revealed.

The Cabala's antecedents can be traced to the teachings of the Neoplatonists and neo-Pythagoreans of the A.D. 200s, and its apogee may belong to the 1200s. However, the tradition influenced Christian mystics such as Paracelsus (1493–1541), Robert Fludd (1574–1637), and Jakob Böhme (1575–1624) through the work of cabalists Isaac Solomon Luria (1534–72) and Hayyim ben Joseph Vital (1543–1620). It went on to inspire Messianic movements in Judaism, including Hasidism, as well as influencing Christian humanists and the Theosophists (*p. 235*) during the late 1800s.

The Tree of Life, its spheres illustrated in detail, as visualized by Christian mystic Robert Fludd (1619).

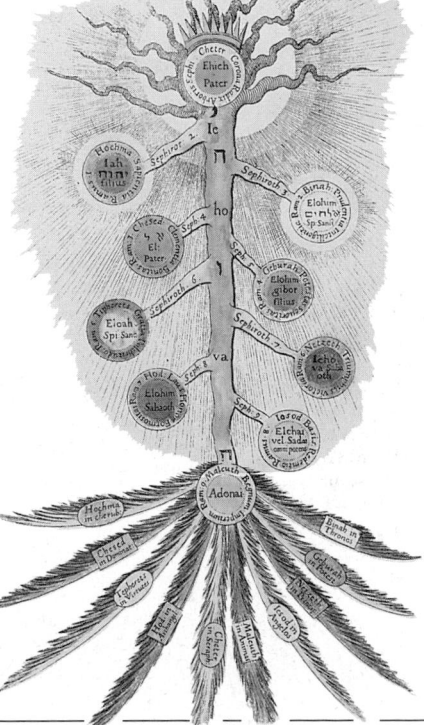

Timeline

hanged in 1581. Charles Borromeo, Italian cardinal and reformer, sets up "Sunday schools" in Milan, Italy.

1582 Death of St. Teresa of Avila, Spanish mystic.

1583 Jesuit Matteo Ricci begins mission in China.

1584 English author Reginald Scot produces *The Discoverie of Witchcraft*, attacking superstition and credulity.

1586 Akbar the Great promotes Din Alahi as universal religion acceptable to Hindus; movement endures until Muslim revival of the 1700s.

1587 Toyotomi Hideyoshi bans Christian missionaries from Japan. Jean Bodin, French philosopher, produces *Colloquium Heptaplomeres*, a plea for religious tolerance.

1588 Death of Sonam Gyatso, third leader of Gelugpa order of Tibetan Buddhism and first to bear the title of Dalai Lama ("Ocean of Wisdom"). Birth of Thomas Hobbes, English philosopher.

1591 Tommaso Campanella, Italian philosopher, produces *Philosophia Sensibus Demonstrata*, a work that is empirical and anti-Scholastic.

1593 Persecution of Christians in Japan.

1594 Richard Hooker, English theologian, produces *Laws of Ecclesiastical Polity*, setting the course of Anglican theology.

1596 Birth of René Descartes, French philosopher.

1597 King James VI of Scotland writes *Demonologie* against witchcraft.

1598 Edict of Nantes grants French Huguenots freedom of worship, with some restrictions; revoked in 1685.

c. **1600** Teachings of Italian Protestant reformers Laelus Socinus and nephew Faustus Socinus give rise to Socinianism, a rationalist anti-Trinitarian movement denying the divinity of Jesus, later to influence Anglican sects from 1600-1800 and the Unitarian movement. Islam becomes dominant religion in much of the Indonesian archipelago.

1600 Giordano Bruno, Italian ex-Dominican philosopher and theologian, burned at the stake for heresy and for supporting Copernican theories. Catholics persecuted in Sweden.

1605 Anti-Catholic legislation increases in England following discovery of plot to blow up the Houses of Parliament.

1608 (St.) Francis de Sales, French Catholic prelate, produces his influential *Introduction to a Devout Life*.

c. **1610–35** Bamberg, Germany, is European center of witch-hunting: some 900 witch trials there during this period.

1611 Publication of the Authorized Version of the Bible in England, the "King James" Bible.

1616 German Protestant theologian

Timeline

Johann Valentin Andreae publishes *The Chemical Wedding of Christian Rosenkreutz*. He is regarded as founder (or reviver) of the Rosicrucian movement.

1617 John Calvin's *Collected Works* posthumously published in Geneva.

1620 Francis Bacon produces *Novum Organum* (New Logic). Puritan Separatists, later called Pilgrim Fathers, arrive in North America on the ship *Mayflower*.

1623 Persecution of Christians in Japan turns into a policy of extermination. Birth of Blaise Pascal, French philosopher.

1624 (Baron) Herbert of Cherbury produces *On Truth*, containing ideas central to English Deism.

1625 St. Vincent de Paul, French priest, founds the Congregation of the Mission (Lazarists, Vincentians) for missionary work among French peasants.

1632 Birth of Baruch Spinoza, Dutch philosopher.

1633 Vincent de Paul and Louise de Marillac found Sisters of Charity, an unenclosed order ministering to the poor. First Baptist Church congregation formed at Southwark, London. Puritan clergyman John Cotton begins to preach in Boston, Massachusetts.

1634 Maryland founded as a Catholic colony with religious tolerance.

1636 Puritan Roger Williams banished from Massachusetts and founds Providence Plantations Colony (Rhode Island) as a pure democracy with religious freedom.

1637 Scottish Presbyterians draw up Covenant to defend their religion. René Descartes produces *Discourse on Method*.

1639 Roger Williams establishes first Baptist Church in North America.

1640 Posthumous publication of *Augustinus*, Dutch theologian Cornelius Otto Jansen's treatise against Jesuits, which proclaims strict predestinarianism. Publication of John Eliot's *Bay Psalm Book*, America's earliest (surviving) printed book.

1641 Descartes produces *Meditations Metaphysiques*, in which he considers whether reality may be a dream, or deception by a demon, and concludes that his awareness proves his existence.

1643 Sir Thomas Browne, English physician, produces *Religio Medici*, a masterpiece of spiritual meditation.

1644 Matthew Hopkins appoints himself England's "Witchfinder General"; within two years around 200 supposed witches are hanged at his instigation. René Descartes produces *Principia Philosophicae*, which includes his famous dictum, "Cogito, ergo sum" ("I think, therefore I am").

1646 Jeremy Taylor, English theologian,

ROSICRUCIANISM

A brotherhood of scholars, alchemists, and esoteric researchers, the Rosicrucian movement arose during the 1600s, when it was claimed, in a pamphlet entitled *The Chemical Wedding of Christian Rosenkreutz*, that Rosenkreutz's tomb, discovered 120 years after his death, was a "summary of the Universe for the living."

During the next two centuries, Rosicrucian societies arose in great numbers, among them Stanislas de Guaïta's Cabalistic Order of the Rose-Cross. Rosicrucianism preached "humility, justice, truth, and chastity" and called on its adepts to "cure all ills." It claimed to be truly Christian and was opposed both to the papacy and Islam.

The Rose Gives Honey to the Bees: *engraving by the Rosicrucian Robert Fludd.*

SHAKERS

The popular name for members of the United Society for Believers in Christ's Second Appearing, the Shakers were founded in England by Ann Lee, who led her followers to America in 1774.

Shakers grew out of a group of French Protestants who had fled to England from their native land to avoid persecution. They formed a sect with some radical Quakers, and their members believed that they received the gift of prophecy through "agitation of the body"; the "agitation" was thereafter formalized into a ritual dance, and the group became known as the Shaking Quakers, or Shakers.

Ann Lee altogether revised the original doctrine. She preached that God had a dual nature, masculine and feminine, that Jesus was a manifestation of the masculine nature, and that she herself was a manifestation of the feminine, and had come to initiate the millennial kingdom.

In the United States, Shakers—who have now virtually disappeared—lived in their own communities, and gained a reputation for excellence in crafts, notably furniture.

THE SOCIETY OF FRIENDS

The Society of Friends, popularly known as the Quakers, is a Christian sect with roots in radical Protestantism. It was founded by George Fox and others in England in the mid-1600s and formally organized in 1667. Persecution led William Penn to establish a Quaker colony in Pennsylvania in 1682.

Friends follow the doctrine of "inner light," rejecting observances associated with other Christians, such as formal ministry, liturgy, and sacraments. Instead, they gather in silence "to wait upon the Lord," except when members feel called to speak out loud in witness or extempore prayer. Men and women share equally in fellowship. The sense of direct dependence on God's spirit is vital to Friends, whose experience of union with God leads to practical good works. They are noted for their financial and commercial probity, their philanthropy, their pacifism, and their involvement in such causes as prison reform and world peace.

Quakers "wait upon the Lord": contemporary engraving.

RELIGION IN COLONIAL AMERICA

The 13 colonies that were to form the United States had begun to show signs of religious diversity even in the early 1600s. These differences were largely regional, reflecting the denominations of Europeans who had settled in different parts of North America. Contributing to this diversity were those Christians and Jews who had fled Europe to escape religious persecution.

The first prominent English settlement in North America, Jamestown, was established by settlers loyal to the established Church of England, or Anglican Church. This set the pattern by which southern colonies, such as Virginia and the Carolinas, came to be settled by "Royalists"—loyal to the English religious and political establishment.

Much of New England, however, was settled by English dissenters. The Puritan movement of the 1560s emphasized prayer, preaching, and Bible reading rather than priestly authority. Their aim, which was resisted by a majority of Anglicans, was to "purify" the Church. One group of Puritans, known as the Pilgrims, broke away from the main Puritan body in the early 1600s. They fled first to the Netherlands and then to North America, where they landed in the *Mayflower* at what is now Plymouth, Massachusetts.

The Puritans are often portrayed as narrow-minded moralists who rejected ordinary human pleasures, but their tenacious insistence on autonomy and self-government served as a basis for later calls for American independence. The Mayflower Compact, signed by the Pilgrims before their Plymouth landfall, was an agreement to form a government and to abide by its rules. Similar English dissenters founded the Massachusetts Bay and Connecticut colonies. The universities of Harvard (1636) and Yale (1701) owe their existence to the Puritans' strong belief in education. New England town meetings,

cited by political scientists as ideals of local democracy, owe their existence to the church meetings of those first Puritans.

Between these two extremes—the Anglican south and the Puritan north—were the "Middle Colonies" where people of different faiths came to live side by side. Some colonies were founded by specific groups—Rhode Island by Baptists, Pennsylvania by Quakers, and Maryland by Roman Catholics—but the founders soon had to deal with settlers of other denominations. New Amsterdam (later to become New York) was notionally Calvinist, but other believers, notably Jews, settled there. Lutherans remained from the short-lived colony of New Sweden (later to become Delaware), and German Lutherans settled Pensylvania in large numbers. Many Presbyterians of Scottish extraction (the "Scotch-Irish") left Ireland to settle along the Appalachians.

Where many of the European immigrants of the 1600s were driven by devout religious conviction, the majority of those arriving in the 1700s were seeking adventure or material gain. Religion played a lesser role in their lives, and their arrival dampened some of the religious fervor in America. Many worshipers believed that the spiritual tone was being set by those who were indifferent to religion.

The "Great Awakening" of the 1730s and 1740s was in reaction to this religious retreat. Beginning in New England, but quickly sweeping through all of the colonies, this Protestant revival spread an evangelizing message with emotional preaching. Denominational—and inter-colonial—differences were played down in favor of the greater message. The Great Awakening coincided with the rise of a new American identity in commerce and the arts, strengthening the awareness of shared American interests that led to the drive for independence.

Puritans Going to Church: a New England scene from the 1600s.

Timeline

produces *The Liberty of Prophesying*, a plea for politico-religious tolerance. John Cotton produces *Spiritual Milk for Babes*. Birth of Gottfried Leibniz, German philosopher. George Fox, English itinerant preacher influenced by the German theosophist and mystic Jakob Böhme, receives divine revelation that inspires him to preach brotherly love: his followers are the Society of Friends.

1648 First documented witch trial in North America: Margaret Jones hanged at Plymouth, Massachusetts. Sabbatai Z'vi, Jewish mystic from Smyrna, self-proclaimed Messiah, wins much support in the Middle East; converts to Islam after arrest in Istanbul in 1666.

1650 Bishop Ussher produces *Annales Veteris et Novi Testamenti*, in which the creation is dated at 4004 B.C.

1651 Hobbes produces *Leviathan*, in which he says that without the social state "the life of man would be solitary, poor, nasty, brutish, and short."

1654 First Jews arrive in New Amsterdam (later New York). Blaise Pascal allies himself with Jansenists at Port-Royal, France.

1655 Oliver Cromwell readmits Jews into England.

1656 Baruch Spinoza expelled from Amsterdam's Jewish community for heresy. Manasseh ben Israel writes *Vindiciae Judaeorum* in response to attacks on the decision to allow the readmission of Jews to England. Blaise Pascal produces *Lettres Provinciales* against the Jesuits. John Bunyan, English writer and preacher, produces *Some Gospel Truths Opened*, an attack on Quakerism.

1661 Joseph Glanvill, English philosopher and clergyman, produces *The Vanity of Dogmatizing*, an attack on Scholastic philosophy and a plea for freedom of thought.

1661–63 John Eliot translates Bible into Native American language Algonquian, to gain converts among the Pequot people: first Bible printed in America.

1662 Jansenists at Port-Royal publish *La Logique, ou L'Art de Penser*, known in English as *Port-Royal Logic*.

1664 Abbot Armand de Rance founds austere Trappist order (Cistercians of the More Strict Observance) of silent monks at the Abbey of La Trappe, Normandy.

1668 William Penn, English Quaker, in *The Sandy Foundation Shaken,* attacks doctrine of the Trinity; imprisoned in the Tower of London.

1674 Nicolas Malebranche, French Cartesian philosopher, produces *De la Recherche de la Vérité*.

1678 John Bunyan publishes *The Pilgrim's Progress*.

1679 Jacques Bossuet, French church-

Timeline

man, produces *Discours sur l'Histoire Universelle,* early philosophy of history.

1682 Some 60,000 French Huguenots are forcibly converted to Catholicism.

1685 Louis XIV of France revokes the Edict of Nantes: Protestant churches closed; all religions other than Catholic banned in France; mass exodus of Huguenots. Last judicial hanging for witchcraft in England. Birth of George Berkeley, Irish philosopher and bishop, exponent of Empiricism; he denied the existence of actual material substance, believing that supposedly material things were in fact collections of "ideas."

1686 Gottfried Leibniz produces *Systema Theologicum,* an ultimately overambitious attempt to reconcile Catholicism and Protestantism through a study of the creeds.

1688 Hermann Busenbaum, German Jesuit theologian, produces *Medulla Theologicae,* a handbook of Jesuit moral philosophy embodying the tenet "the end justifies the means."

1689 Witch mania in Salem, Massachusetts: of around 150 accused from 1689–93, 19 are hanged and four die in jail. Cotton Mather, American clergyman, encourages witch-hunters. Most influential English philosopher, John Locke, produces his two seminal works, *An Essay Concerning Human Understanding* and *Two Treatises of Government*; the former is a classic in the British Empiricist tradition, the latter a defense of constitutional rule and personal liberty; he also publishes *A Letter Concerning Toleration.*

1696 Pierre Bayle, French philosopher, produces *Dictionnaire Historique et Critique,* a sceptical analysis of philosophical and theological arguments.

1699 Guru Gobind Singh, tenth and last guru of Sikhism, institutes the Khalsa, giving the Sikh community a distinctive identity.

1702 Cotton Mather produces *Magnalia Christi Americana,* an ecclesiastical history of New England.

1710 Jansenist nuns expelled from Port-Royal, France; conflict between Jansenists and Jesuits escalates. Bishop Berkeley produces *A Treatise Concerning the Principles of Human Knowledge.* Gottfried Leibniz writes *Théodicée,* arguing that God created the best of all possible worlds out of an infinity of substances.

1711 Birth of David Hume, Scottish philosopher and historian, a great figure in the British Empiricist tradition; an agnostic, he was generally skeptical of all metaphysical claims.

1712 Birth in Geneva of Jean-Jacques Rousseau, political and educational philosopher, who evolved the idea of the noble savage and examined the relationship between morality and environment.

1713 Papal bull *Unigenitus Dei Filius ,*

NATIVE AMERICAN RELIGION

Of the very numerous ethnic groups of Native Americans in North America, most have their own pantheon of supernatural beings, gods, ritual observances, and taboos. The majority traditionally believe in a spirit power, sometimes named as *Wakonda* (Sioux), *Orenda* (Iroquois), *Manitou* (Algonquian), and sometimes centered on certain places or animals. Almost universal is an animistic reverence for the natural world and the sanctity of the land and its components—mountains, rivers, vegetation, even stones—which are seen as imbued with supernatural powers, and are often associated with humanized spirits.

The spirits of animals, birds, and some plants (notably corn and tobacco) are regarded as deities that can represent the *totems* (spiritual guides and guardians) of individual tribes or persons. Some animals, such as the coyote or the raven, have received special reverence as trickster gods and have been honored with their own cults.

Coexistent with this world is the spirit world, which can be attained by means of spiritual disciplines, dance, psychotropic drugs, and certain physical and mental rituals. Most communities have spiritual specialists, shamans or so-called "medicine men," who are able to enter the spirit world in order to gain the advice of the spirits for the benefit of their earthly communities.

The chief Native American groups today are the Navaho, Pueblo, Iroquois, Great Plains, Algonquian, the Pacific Northwest Indians, and the Inuit (Eskimo). Special features of the traditional deities of some of these are:

Navaho Changing Woman, a kind of earth mother who ages as the year progresses, becoming young again each spring. It was she who created all life, from which then sprang First Man and First Woman, who in turn created the universe and humankind.

Pueblo A pantheon of divinities—Cloud

Kwakiutl (Northwest) emblem of the Raven: chief's frontlet.

People, Corn Maidens, Star Spirits, and Dawn Spirits. Enemies who have been killed in war became rainmakers.

Iroquois Orenda, the supreme spirit; Degandawidas (Hiawatha), culture hero, possibly a lawmaker of the 1500s , who united five tribes to form the Iroquois League of Five Nations.

Pacific Northwest The Raven, trickster hero of the Haida (Northwest) people, who created land by flapping his wings, made people from clam shells, and stole a sun and a fire stick from heaven.

Inuit (Eskimo) Sila (Silap Unua) is the supreme being, while Sedna (Nuliajuk, Nerrivik, Arnquagssaq) is the most important, a sea goddess (and god of the dead) who "owns" the sea creatures on whom the Inuit traditionally relied for survival. The passing, after death, to a sky heaven or subterranean hell depends on the type of death and the observance of taboos in life. Shamans play a crucial role in mediating between the natural and the supernatural worlds.

FREEMASONRY

One of the world's largest "fraternal" organizations, Freemasonry is a secret society which developed in its present form in 1717. However, it claims to have a far older background, positing a connection with the biblical architect Hiram whom Solomon brought from Tyre to build the Temple at Jerusalem. The ceremony conferring the degree of master is a reenactment of this. According to the Anderson Constitutions (1723), which represent the organization's central tenets, Freemasons are obliged to be "good men and true, or men of honor and honesty, by whatever denominations or persuasions they may be distinguished, whereby Masonry becomes the center of union, and the means of conciliating true friendship among people that have remained at a perpetual distance."

Freemasonry developed rapidly during the 1700s and was often preferred by rationalists and democrats, although it cannot be reduced to political terms. However, it has often been at odds with the Catholic Church, and its secretive nature has earned the disapproval of some critics, who diminish its altruistic and mystical aspects, and imply that the fraternity works primarily for the benefit of its members. The fact remains that Freemasons annually spend millions of dollars on hospitals, relief works, and scholarships. There are approximately five million Freemasons worldwide, of whom the majority are in the United States.

THE AGE OF REASON

Voltaire presides at a philosophers' dinner: contemporary engraving by Hubert.

The thinkers of the age of reason, which was also known as the Enlightenment, believed in happiness and fulfillment in this world, regarding rational thought rather than faith as the best source of guidance. They were suspicious of all things supernatural, and to them science and scientific method—a systematic and logical approach to the truth—and skepticism toward traditional religion were paramount; the advances of science were translated into a new philosophy and world view. For the most part, European philosophers after René Descartes believed that knowledge is gained through the process of reasoning, while English thinkers, such as John Locke and David Hume, tended towards Empiricism, the belief that knowledge comes from sensory experience.

By the end of the 1700s, France had become the intellectual center of Europe, and it was here that a group including Denis Diderot and François Marie Arouet de Voltaire, known as the *philosophes,* brought the Age of Reason to its climax. Voltaire, although a relentless critic of the established Catholic and Protestant churches, did not wish to deny religion completely, asserting that if a God did not exist, then it would be necessary to invent one.

The most important work of the *philosophes* was the famous French *Encyclopédie,* edited by Diderot. This 28-volume collection expounded the merits of Deism, championed tolerance, denounced superstition, and pronounced the new scientific thought to be supreme.

THE METHODIST CHURCH

Methodism was established as a denomination within the Christian Church by the English cleric, John Wesley, in 1739. The name comes from Wesley's preoccupation with the need for a disciplined and "methodical" approach, but from the beginning the movement displayed an evangelical fervor that drew vast crowds and the disapproval of the Church establishment. His doctrine was nonrevolutionary, however, and some historians have seen it as a counterweight to the political radicalism of the time.

Wesley sent evangelical leaders to the American colonies, where the movement flourished. Separating from the Church of England in 1795, Methodism today numbers about 25 million adherents, nearly two-thirds of whom are in the United States. Worship includes an emphasis on preaching and the singing of hymns.

John Wesley, founder of Methodism.

Timeline

condemning Jansenism, is enforced by Louis XIV, leading to major church-state conflict.

1714 Last witch trial in Russia. Witch trials abolished in Prussia.

1717 Grand Lodge of Freemasons created in London.

1719 Jesuits expelled from Russia.

c. 1722–24 Nicolaus Ludwig, Graf von Zinzendorf, influential German theologian, founds community of Herrnhut, Saxony, for Moravian Brethren driven from Bohemia by persecution.

1724 Birth of Immanuel Kant, German philosopher.

1727 American Philosophical Society founded in Philadelphia.

1729 John and Charles Wesley form the Holy Club ("Oxford Methodists") at Oxford, England.

1730 English Deist, Matthew Tindal writes *Christianity as Old as the Creation,* the Deists' "Bible," which aims to eliminate the supernatural from religion.

1732 Seventh Day Baptists (Ephrata Community) established at Germantown, Pennsylvania.

1733 Corporation for the Propagation of the Gospel in New England founded.

1734 Moravian Brethren establish Moravian Church in North America and begin missionary activity, especially among Native Americans and Inuits. Qur'an (Koran) translated into English. Voltaire publishes *Lettres Philosophiques,* concerned with religious toleration.

1736 Massachusetts makes accusation of witchcraft a criminal offense. English laws against witchcraft repealed.

1737 John Wesley's *Psalms and Hymns* is published in Charleston, South Carolina.

1738 George Whitefield, English Methodist evangelist, follows John Wesley to Georgia in North America, to take part in the "Great Awakening," a religious revival. Pope Clement XII issues bull *In Eminenti* condemning Freemasonry.

1739 John Wesley establishes Methodism as an evangelical movement within the Church of England; founds first Methodist chapel in Bristol. David Hume writes *A Treatise of Human Nature.*

1741 American theologian, Jonathan Edwards publishes *Sinners in the Hands of an Angry God,* the text of a sermon delivered at Enfield, Massachusetts, during the "Great Awakening."

1744 Birth of Johann Gottfried Herder, the German philosopher, critic and poet, who argued that historical periods can be understood only if viewed as products of particular situations.

c. 1745 Muhammad ibn Abd al-Wahhab (1703–92), Arabian religious reformer, gains support of Saud rulers of what is now Saudi Arabia for his Wahhabi movement.

Timeline

1746 Denis Diderot, French philosopher, playwright, and encyclopedist, publishes *Pensées Philosophiques*, influential in the period leading up to the French Revolution.

1747 Emanuel Swedenborg, Swedish scientist and philosopher, abandons scientific activities after visions of Christ and angels; he summarizes his spiritual experiences in *Journal of Dreams*. Julien Offray de La Mettrie, French physician and materialist philosopher, writes *L'Homme Machine*, which puts forward the argument that all psychic phenomena are physically based.

1748 Birth of Jeremy Bentham, English Utilitarian philosopher and legal reformer, who propounded the belief that general good was to be identified with the greatest happiness of the greatest number of people.

***c.* 1750** Baal Shem Tov, Eastern European Jewish leader, founds Hasidism, an ascetic and mystical Jewish movement now established in Europe and the United States as part of Orthodox Judaism.

1751 David Hume produces *An Enquiry Concerning the Principles of Morals*. French encyclopedists, led by Denis Diderot and philosopher Jean le Rond d'Alembert, begin production of the 28-volume *Encyclopédie*, a key work of the Enlightenment characterized by skepticism about religion and tolerant of political liberalism; first two volumes are suppressed (1752) because of their hostility to the clergy.

1752 William Law, English churchman influenced by Böhme, produces *The Way to Divine Knowledge*.

1753 English laws passed permitting naturalization of Jews.

1755 Immanuel Kant publishes his doctoral thesis, *The True Measure of Forces*. Frances Hutcheson, Scots-Irish philosopher, writes *A System of Moral Philosophy*, which develops Shaftesbury's concept of "moral sense."

1758 Claude-Adrien Helvétius, French philosopher, in his *De L'Esprit*, argues that self-interest is the motivating force behind all human actions. Swedenborg publishes *The New Jerusalem*.

1759 Jesuits expelled from Portugal. Voltaire publishes *Candide*, a witty, complex enquiry into the nature of good and evil, satirizing Leibniz's idea of the best of all possible worlds.

1761 Henry Home, Lord Kames, Scottish jurist and philosopher, writes *An Introduction to the Art of Thinking*. American Quakers bar slave traders from their society.

1762 Jean-Jacques Rousseau publishes antimonarchical *Social Contract* ("man is born free yet everywhere is in chains"). France expels Jesuits. Birth of Johann Fichte, German philosopher. Voltaire publishes *Treatise on Tolerance*.

AFRICAN RELIGIONS

Dogon mask of Walu the antelope.

Although most black Africans now profess Christianity or Islam, traditional beliefs endure. The majority have in common a deep belief in the spirit world, whether the spirits venerated are those of ancestors, natural forces, or totem animals. The exceptions to this are the Dogon people of Mali, who trace their deities to a star that has only recently been discovered by Western astronomers.

From the 1500s to the mid-1800s, native West African beliefs, mainly those of the Yoruba and BaKongo, were "exported" via the slave trade. Some melded with the Christianity forced on slaves to form new faiths—among which at least two still have many followers. The Voodoo of Haiti and the Caribbean islands blends African magical lore with Roman Catholicism; the Macumba cults of Brazil unite rites originating from the Yoruba people with both spiritualism and older European cults. This syncretism was the means whereby the enslaved peoples disguised their religion to preserve it.

Major deities of traditional African religions include:

Amma Creator god of the Dogon.
Anansi Spider god of West Africa; a trickster god noted for cleverness.
Chuku Supreme god of the Ibo of eastern Nigeria; a benign creator.
Gu Smith god of the Fon of Dahomey, West Africa; gave mortals the gift of tools.
Imana Supreme god of the Banyarwanda of Rwanda.

Kaang Creator god of the Bushmen of southwestern Africa.
Leza Supreme deity and sky god of the Bantu of southern Africa.
Mawu-Liza Great god of the Fon of Dahomey; hermaphroditic creator deity.
Modimo Zimbabwean creator god. Inaccessible to ordinary mortals, he could be reached only by imperfect beings called Badimo, and by small children, also imperfect because of their age.
Mulungu Sky god of the Nyamwezi of Tanzania.
Nkosazana Fertility goddess of the Zulus of South Africa.
Ogun God of iron, war, and hunters of the Yoruba of Nigeria.
Olorun Supreme god of the Yoruba, ruler of the fates of mortals and judge of their souls after death.
Shango Thunder god, ancestor-deity of the kings of Oyo, West Africa.
Unkulunkulu ("the ancestor") Great spirit of the Zulus.

"Exported" African cults

Agwe Green-eyed, fair-skinned god of the sea and all therein.
Baron Samedi Major member of the Guede, the spirit-gods of death.
Damballa Serpent god, partly identified with St. Patrick.
Erzulie Fair-skinned fertility goddess, partly identified with the Virgin Mary.
Legba Guardian deity of the gate between the worlds of humankind and of the *loa* (gods and spirits); originally Elegua, the Yoruba trickster god.
Loco God of vegetation.
Ogoun (**Ogu**) God of fire and healing, derived from the Yoruba Ogun. His devotees offer him rum, which they set alight to produce his sacred color, red.
Oshun Orisha Goddess of love.
Oshosi Hunter god, identified with St. George.
Shango Thunder god of the Oyo. His worship was syncretized with that of St. Jerome and John the Baptist.
Yemaya Goddess of the sea.

Voodoo pilgrims pray at the Saut d'Eau festival, Haiti.

MYTHS OF THE PACIFIC ISLANDS

In Polynesia and Micronesia, the parents of the principal gods are the primal beings Rangi (or Langi, or Raki), the sky, and Papa, the (female) earth. The forcible separation of these beings by their children created space in which the world could exist, and caused friction between the children-gods, represented as natural disasters on earth. Among the principal gods are:

Luk (Lukunor, Lugeilang, Lukelang) Handsome and creative Micronesian brother-god of Olofat.

Maui Hawaiian trickster demigod, who obtained fire for humankind from the underworld.

Olofat (Yalafath, Iolofath, Yelafaz) Micronesian trickster god whose tricks can refashion the world.

Tane-mahuta Maori god of plants, birds, and insects.

Tangaroa Polynesian god of the oceans and all therein.

Tawhiri-matea Maori god of the winds and the elements.

Tu-matauenga Maori god of war and of man.

In Melanesia, there is no overall pantheon, and it is the elements of mythology (the mythological motifs) that remain more constant than the demigod and legendary figures that feature locally in the stories. Recurrent motifs include the giant associated with death (either his own or his consort's) who causes the growth of taro and tubers; the child who kills an

Maori ancestral carvings at Rotorua, North Island, New Zealand.

ogre; and the man who kills his serpent mother-in-law, to his great loss and misfortune.

Also found among remote tribes are "cargo cults": some tribes afford great reverence to the trappings of the modern Western world ("cargo," especially in the form of supplies and equipment parachuted from an aircraft), regarded as the gifts of deified ancestors or of a Messianic figure who is to rid the world of white dominance. Related closely to ancestor worship, cargo cults have evolved a complex mythology of gods and spirits (sometimes identified with Christian figures).

ABORIGINAL BELIEFS

Where many faiths look to the future, in a life after death, Australian Aboriginal belief looks back to the time of creation, known as the Dreamtime. In that age ancestor spirits such as kangaroo-men and bowerbird-women are said to have lived on earth. They shaped its hills, rocks, waterholes, and trees; created humans;

Dreamtime painting of kangaroo-man.

and taught them how to live on and with the land. So to the Aborigines the entire land is a "temple" in which everyone is an equal inheritor of religious knowledge. The Dreamtime is not only a past event but also organically connected to present-day people and things.

The main figures of this mythology are:

Bagadjimbiri Twin brother creator gods of the Karadjeri (northwest Australia).

Bobbi-Bobbi Snake ancestor-god of the Binbinga (northern Australia); inventor of one kind of boomerang.

Dilga Earth goddess of the Karadjeri.

Manger-kunger-kunja Lizard ancestor-god of the Aranda (central Australia).

Marindi Dingo ancestor-god.

Minawara Kangaroo ancestor-god of the Nambutji (central Australia); inventor, with his brother Multultu, of the spear.

Rainbow Snake (Julunggul) Fertility spirit; both male and female, creator and destroyer; associated with streams and water holes, from which it emerges in the creation story.

Ulanji Snake ancestor-god of the Binbinga (northern Australia), connected with circumcision rituals.

Yurlunyur Ancestor snake god of the Murngin (northern Australia); the rainbow serpent.

Timeline

1763 Touro Synagogue—first in what is now the United States—founded in Newport, Rhode Island.

1764 Publication of Voltaire's *Philosophical Dictionary*, which presents his views on politics, religion, ethics, and metaphysics. Italian economist Cesare Bo'nesana publishes *On Crimes and Punishment*, condemning capital punishment. Russia confiscates church lands.

1766 Catherine the Great of Russia grants freedom of worship.

1767 Moses Mendelssohn, German Jewish philosopher and theologian, writes *Phadon*, which argues for the immortality of the soul.

1769 Edmund Burke, Irish statesman and philosopher, writes *Observations on the Present State of the Nation*.

1770 Birth of Georg Wilhelm Friedrich Hegel, German philosopher, who emphasized the evolutionary nature of the history of thought. Voltaire writes that, "If God did not exist, it would be necessary to invent him."

1773 Pope Clement XIV dissolves the Jesuit order.

1776 Ann Lee founds the United Society for Believers in Christ's Second Appearing (Shakers) settlement at Niskayuna, New York (*p. 226*). Bavarian lawyer Adam Weisshaupt founds Order of Illuminati, a secret society aiming to spread a new religion based on human and divine reason. Final volume of Denis Diderot's *Encyclopédie* is published.

1781 Immanuel Kant publishes his *Critique of Pure Reason*, a seminal work of modern philosophy.

1782 Burning at Glarus, Switzerland, believed to be Europe's last legal execution for witchcraft.

1783 Mendelssohn's *Jerusalem* presents Judaism as the religion of reason.

1784 John Wesley produces the *Deed of Declaration*, the charter of Wesleyan Methodism. First U.S. Methodist denomination established in Baltimore, Maryland. Johann Gottfried Herder, German critic and poet, publishes *Ideas Toward a Philosophy of History*.

1785 William Paley, English theologian, produces *Principles of Moral and Political Philosophy*, expounding a form of Utilitarianism. Immanuel Kant publishes *Groundwork to the Metaphysics of Morals*.

1787 Followers of Emanuel Swedenborg establish the Church of the New Jerusalem in London; Swedenborgianism later spreads worldwide. Antislavery society founded in the U.S.A.

1788 Birth of Arthur Schopenhauer, German philosopher, who distinguished two aspects of the self—the self as represented in perception, and the self that expresses itself in the form of will. Immanuel Kant's *Critique of Practical Reason* expounds the notion of categorical imperatives.

Timeline

1789 John Carroll is installed as the first Roman Catholic bishop in the U.S.A. Protestant Episcopal Church (part of Anglican community) established in the U.S.A.

1791 Bill of Rights establishes freedom of religion as a constitutional right.

1792 Baptist Missionary Society is founded in London. Thomas Paine, English-born American philosopher, publishes *Rights of Man*. Anglo-Irish feminist Mary Wollstonecraft, publishes *Vindication of the Rights of Women*.

1793 Postrevolutionary France abolishes worship of God.

1795 Methodist Church becomes independent of the Church of England.

1800 Church of United Brethren in Christ is founded in the U.S.A.

1803 Birth of Ralph Waldo Emerson, U.S. transcendentalist writer.

1806 Birth of John Stuart Mill, English philosopher, who attempted to reconcile the idea of personal liberty with Utilitarianism.

1807 The American Evangelical Association holds its first convention.

1808 Napoleon abolishes the Inquisition in Spain and Italy.

1811 Most Welsh Protestants leave the Anglican Church in the "Great Schism."

1812 Jews are emancipated in Prussia.

1813 Birth of Søren Kierkegaard, Danish philosopher, whose emphasis on individual existence inspired Existentialism.

1814 Pope Pius VII restores Inquisition and Society of Jesus (Jesuits). The Netherlands abandons slave trade.

1815 Berlin Jews open a "Reform" temple to bring their faith in harmony with the modern world.

1816 American Bible Society established.

1818 Birth of Karl Marx, German social theorist famous for his views on the progressive nature of historical change, an idea with its roots in the work of Hegel.

1819 Unitarianism is founded by Boston Congregationalist pastor William Channing. Arthur Schopenhauer produces *The World as Will and Idea*. Georg Hermes, German Roman Catholic theologian, in his *Philosophical Introduction to Christian Theology* seeks to harmonize Catholic faith with Kantian philosophy.

1820 Spanish Inquisition abolished. Jesuits expelled from Rome. Birth of Herbert Spencer, British philosopher.

1824 American Sunday School Union formed. British reformer Robert Owen advocates women's liberation and progressive education.

1825 Seraphim of Sarov, Russian saint, begins to receive pilgrims as a result of visions.

1827 John Nelson Darby founds evangelical group in Dublin, Ireland which later becomes Plymouth Brethren. U.S. evangelist Alexander Campbell founds Disciples of Christ evangelical group.

SPIRITUALISM

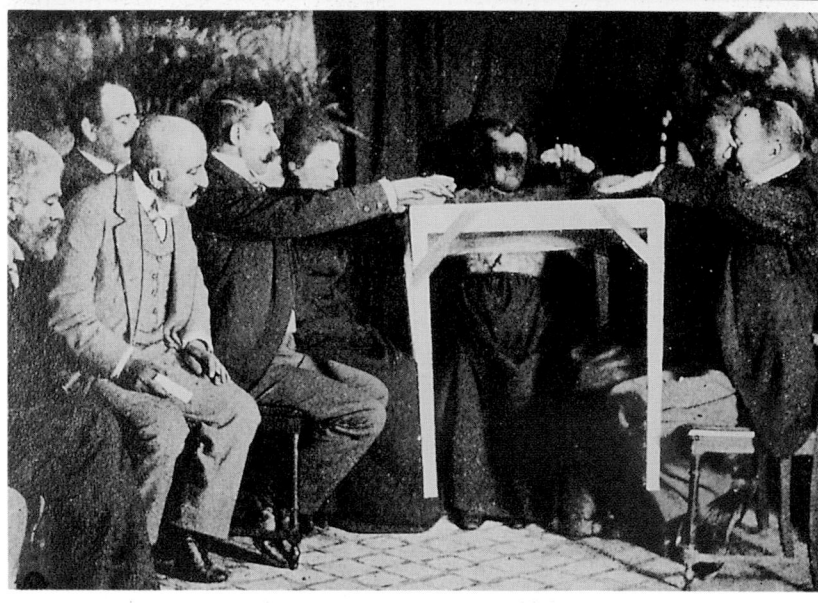

Levitation of a table, Milan, 1892, by medium Eusappia Palladio.

The doctrine of Spiritualism was founded in 1848 by the Frenchman H. L. Rivail (1804–69), who adopted the name Allan Kardec. It involves communication with the spirits of dead people through a medium, or a specially sensitive person. Spiritualism gained many adherents in the late 1800s, including the French author Victor Hugo. Some mediums, such as Daniel Douglas Home, Doris Stokes, and Eusappia Palladio, achieved great fame.

As an organized religion, Spiritualism has been practiced mainly in Europe and the United States. Its adherents believe that communication with the spirits of the dead helps them to understand the laws of God. Spiritualism has many of the trappings associated with churchgoing: a regular (generally weekly) meeting (seance), a sacerdotal medium between this world and the world of spirits, and the certainty of an afterlife.

Spiritualists believe that those who pass over to the Other Side (die) enter a realm of calm and beauty in a spirit state that retains much of their earthly shape. These spirits can watch over the physical world—especially their loved ones remaining there—and they may know enough about the future to be able to warn a person through a medium.

There are several ways of trying to contact the spirit world without the services of a medium, but some claim that these are potentially dangerous. Such methods include the use of a ouija board (or planchette); automatic writing; leaving tape decks on "record" at a preselected place and time; and table rapping.

PLYMOUTH BRETHREN

The Plymouth Brethren is a religious sect founded in 1827 in Dublin, Ireland, by an informal group of young Christian evangelicals. It was the energy of the Church of Ireland clergyman John Nelson Darby, who joined them in 1827, that turned the group into a movement that spread internationally. Meetings began in Plymouth, England (1831), and then throughout the English-speaking world and Europe.

Millenarian in outlook, the beliefs of the Brethren (who do not call themselves "Plymouth Brethren", although that is how they are best known) are simple, with a lifestyle based on the New Testament. They echo the beliefs of Puritans of earlier ages, especially in relation to leisure entertainments. Fully committed to a religious lifestyle, they engage in considerable missionary activities.

JEHOVAH'S WITNESSES

Founded by the American Charles Taze Russell, Jehovah's Witnesses began as a Bible study group in the 1870s researching millenarian prophecies. Previously called the International Bible Students' Association, they adopted the name "Jehovah's Witnesses" in 1931. Much of their funds go on the production of religious literature and their magazine, *The Watchtower*. Jehovah, more often spelled Yahweh in modern Bibles, is a transliteration of the ancient Hebrew personal name of God.

They believe that Christ's Second Coming happened in 1914 and God's Kingdom will shortly be upon us; that this event is more important than nationalities or human loyalties, and that believers thus have only a short time to convert the rest of the world. Bible study is encouraged.

ADVENTISTS

Adventists are members of a Christian religious group who believe that Jesus Christ may return at any moment. They are part of a millenarian tradition, which includes Christadelphians, Jehovah's Witnesses, and Plymouth Brethren, but dates back at least to the early days of the Christian Church and the book of Revelation (the Apocalypse). They believe that the Second Coming will be preceded by a time of destruction and upheaval, with elimination of unwanted elements of the old order.

In 1831, the American Baptist minister William Miller targeted 1843 or 1844 for the Second Coming, and more than 100,000 people assembled for the event. Following the failure of Miller's prediction, a number of his previous supporters formed a group which became the Seventh-Day Adventist Church, with Ellen White (1827–1915) as their prophet. Their name derives from their belief that Saturday, the traditional Jewish sabbath, is the true day of rest and worship. Separatist movements that have derived from the Seventh-Day Adventists include the Davidians.

THE MORMONS

The Church of Jesus Christ of Latter-Day Saints (the Mormons), founded by Joseph Smith, Jr. in 1830, today numbers some 7 million members. Smith had experienced a vision and many visitations by an angel named Moroni who, he claimed, gave him a set of gold plates on which were inscribed a history of an ancient Israelite family's journey from the Mediterranean Sea across the Atlantic, resulting in the foundation of the Native American (Indian) nations. Smith translated these plates and the resultant *Book of Mormon* or *Golden Bible* was deemed a direct divine revelation and regarded as holy scripture together with the Christian Bible. Joseph Smith led his rapidly growing flock first to Kirtland, Ohio, then to Missouri, and finally, following persecution, to Nauvoo, Illinois, which became one of the state's largest cities.

In 1844, public hostility led to the death of Smith and his brother at the hands of a mob, and his successor, Brigham Young, led the persecuted sect to the Valley of the Salt Lake, where they have remained, based in Salt Lake City, since 1847. However, conflict with the federal government persisted until the Mormons abandoned their traditional practice of polygamy in 1890.

Mormons believe that the Trinity is three separate beings; that human beings are, literally, God's children and that they can become gods. They hold that prior to birth, people exist in spirit form with God, and that after death, most people are sent to heaven. They await the coming of a millennium when Jesus Christ will

BABISM AND THE BAHA'I FAITH

Babism is a religious movement founded as an extension of Shi'ite Islam (*p. 218*) by Said Ali Muhammad Shirazi, who in 1844 claimed to be the Bab, an intermediary between the Shi'ites' "hidden" imam and his faithful followers. Within three years his further claim to be the Mahdi ("guided one"), a Messianic figure, led to his imprisonment and then (in 1850) his execution by Shi'ite authorities.

The Baha'i Faith emerged as a revival of Babism in the mid-1850s under the leadership of Mirza Husain Ali Nuri, known as Baha'u'llah ("Glory of God"), a visionary who claimed to be the messenger of God, the promised redeemer of all religions. The Faith thus understands all the great religions of the world to represent parts of a progressive self-revelation of God through various manifestations (such as Abraham, the Buddha, Jesus, and Muhammad); there is an afterlife in the spirit world, but no reincarnation. Because it maintains there is only one religion, the Faith works for the religious, social, economic, and even linguistic unity of all nations.

rule over the world. Key tenets of the sect are that faith in Jesus and his atoning sacrifice must be active—good works are a form of worship; the ready availability of divine revelation; weekly communion; and constant personal morality (including abstinence from alcohol, tea, coffee, and tobacco). A prominent feature of the sect is the promotion of music.

Choir of the Temple Square Tabernacle, Salt Lake City, Utah.

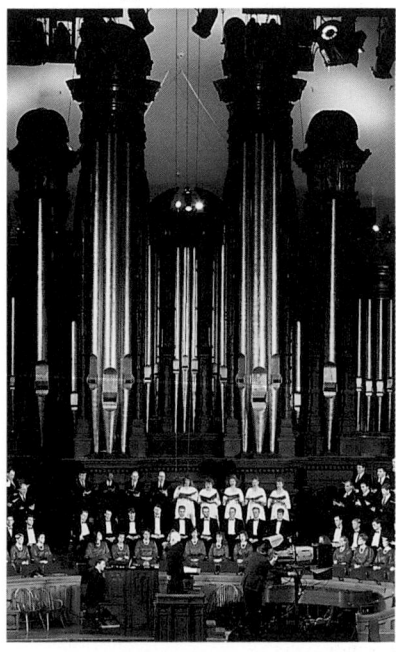

Timeline

1828–29 Passing of the Catholic Emancipation Act allows Roman Catholics and Nonconformists to hold public office in Britain and Ireland.

1830 Joseph Smith, American visionary, founds the Church of Jesus Christ of Latter-Day Saints (Mormons).

1830–42 Auguste Comte, French philosopher, publishes the six volumes of *Cours de Philosophie Positive*, expressing Positivism in a systematic fashion.

1831 William Miller begins Adventist preachings in the U.S.A.

1832 Church of Christ (Disciples) organized in the United States.

1833 Sermon by John Keble marks beginning of Oxford (Tractarian) Movement, seeking to revive high doctrine and ceremonial in the Church of England.

1835 David Friedrich Strauss, German theologian, seeks to prove gospel history a myth with *Leben Jesu* (The Life of Jesus). Birth of Sri Ramakrishna Paramahamsa, Bengali saint and renewer of Hinduism.

1836 Publication of Emerson's *Nature*, which espouses a romantic transcendentalism emphasizing the ideals of self-knowledge and self-reverence.

1837 Friedrich Frobel, German educator, opens the first kindergarten.

1839 Birth of Charles Peirce, American philosopher and physicist, who founded Pragmatism, the view that the practical significance of a concept determines its meaning.

1840 Mormons establish Nauvoo community in Hancock County, Illinois; some 20,000 Mormons in the area by 1843.

1842 Birth of William James, American philosopher and psychologist, who espoused the Pragmatist view that metaphysical debates were either resolvable by appeal to their practical consequences, or trivial.

1843 William Miller, American founder of the Second Adventists, proclaims April 3 to be Doomsday; about 100,000 Millerites gather in New England. Søreu Kierkegaard publishes *Either-Or* and *Fear and Trembling*.

1844 Birth of Friedrich Nietzsche, German philosopher, who saw the will for power as the driving force of all human endeavor. Emerson publishes *Essays*, second series. Kierkegaard writes *The Concept of Anxiety*.

1845 Anti-Catholic Evangelical (all-Protestant) Alliance formed in Britain. John Henry Newman converts to Catholicism. Publication of Friedrich Engels' *The Condition of the Working Classes in England in 1844*.

1846–47 Brigham Young leads Mormons from Nauvoo, Illinois, to Utah, where Salt Lake City is founded.

1847 Russian anarchist Mikhail Bakunin expelled from Paris for antimonarchist views. Karl Marx publishes *Poverty of Philosophy*.

Timeline

1848 Modern Spiritualism begins in the U.S.A. and rapidly expands. Plymouth Brethren splits into Open Brethren and Exclusive Brethren. Marx and Engels produce *The Communist Manifesto*. Mill publishes *Principles of Political Economy*.

1854 Pope Pius IX declares the Immaculate Conception of the Blessed Virgin Mary an article of faith. George Boole, English logician, publishes *An Investigation of the Laws of Thought*.

1855 Herbert Spencer produces *Principles of Psychology*.

1857 "Mormon War" in Utah: troops sent to suppress Mormon polygamists.

1858 Bernadette Soubirious has vision of the Virgin Mary at Lourdes, France. Father Isaac Thomas Hecker, U.S. priest, founds Missionary Priests of St. Paul (Paulist Fathers).

1859 Publication of *On the Origin of Species by Means of Natural Selection* by English naturalist Charles Darwin causes crisis of faith. Konstantin Tischendorf, German scholar, discovers *Codex Sinaiticus* at St. Catherine's monastery, Mt. Sinai. Birth of Edmund Husserl, German philosopher, founder of school of phenomenology.

1863 Ellen Gould White, U.S. visionary, founds Seventh-Day Adventists. Ernest Renan, French historian, publishes *La Vie de Jésus*, attacking supernatural aspects of Christ's ministry. John Stuart Mill publishes *Utilitarianism*.

1864 Pope Pius IX's *Syllabus Errorum* attacks Liberalism, Socialism, and Rationalism.

1865 William Booth, English religious leader, founds the Christian Mission.

1867 Karl Marx publishes the first volume of *Das Kapital*.

1870 First Vatican Council announces the dogma of papal infallibility.

1872 Birth of Bertrand Russell, English philosopher. American Charles Taze Russell founds Jehovah's Witnesses. Jesuits expelled from Germany.

1873 Sikhs' Singh Sabha association formed in Amritsar, India. Birth of G. E. Moore, English Empiricist philosopher who analyzed the moral concept of goodness. Herbert Spencer publishes *The Study of Sociology*.

1875 Theosophical Society founded in New York City by Helen Blavatsky and H. S. Olcott.

1876 Alexander Bain, Scottish philosopher, founds *Mind*, first English journal of philosophy and psychology.

1878 William Booth founds nonsectarian Salvation Army, based on the Christian Mission in London's East End.

1879 Mary Baker Eddy founds the Church of Christ, Scientist in Boston.

1882 Philosopher Henry Sidgwick is co-founder and first president of the British Society for Psychical Research.

1883 Birth of Karl Jaspers, German philosopher, one of the founders of Existentialism.

DARWINISM

The theory of evolution by natural selection, which proposes that environmental pressures act to select better-adapted individuals, was first put forward jointly by Charles Darwin and Alfred Russel Wallace in 1859. The theory gained added credence in the 1900s with discoveries of the genetic origin of variation within species (neo-Darwinism), and is now generally accepted by the great majority of biologists (*p. 91*). Darwinism initially caused dismay among religious people, since it clearly diminishes the role of divine guidance in the universe (although some maintain that God's wisdom and guidance underlie the process of evolution). The idea that life is subject to natural laws guaranteeing the survival of the fittest influenced many later ethical and sociological theories, including those of Karl Marx. It provides the foundation for Evolutionary Humanism, which argues that science, harnessed to human reason, will bring about the goals sought by people and help humanity evolve toward a higher level of achievement.

Darwin satirized in London Sketchbook, *1874.*

MARX AND COMMUNISM

The inspirer of modern Communism, German philosopher and economic theorist Karl Marx described religion as "the opium of the masses." He wrote that, "Philosophers have previously tried to explain the world, our task is to change it." In 1848 he published, in collaboration with Friedrich Engels, the famous *Communist Manifesto* which ends with the words, "The workers have nothing to lose but their chains. They have a world to win. Workers of all lands, unite!"

Marx believed that the proletariat (working class) would be an instrument of revolution that would overthrow the capitalist system, abolishing class distinctions and ending exploitation of the masses. Most social democratic thinkers rejected the revolutionary path, advocating a reformist strategy operating within a constitutional framework, but Communist parties based on Marxist ideology took power in many countries after World War II. With the collapse of Communism in Eastern Europe in the late 1980s and the adoption of market forces systems elsewhere (notably in China), Marxist Communism is no longer a major world force. However, its effect on contemporary values has been massive.

Lenin, Engels, and Marx: a propaganda poster of the late 1800s.

MODERN-DAY CANONIZATION

Saints (Latin *sanctus*, "holy") are those whose religious heroism is formally recognized after death by a Christian Church—although the term is generalized to include non-Christian people. A canonized saint is one whose name has been entered in the canon (register) of saints by the Roman Catholic Church, although it may occur in the Eastern Orthodox Churches (and technically can take place in the Anglican Communion). A process of formal canonization existed in the medieval period, but critical assessment of sainthood was pioneered by Jesuits in the 1600s, and canonization has now become the culmination of an elaborate and drawn-out process.

Probably the best-known of all modern saints is St. Bernadette (1844–79), whose visions at Lourdes, in southwestern France, made its waters the most famous healing center in Christendom. Others include St. Francesca Xavier Cabrini (1850–1917), the first American citizen to be canonized (1946), and, especially, St. Thérèse of Lisieux (1873–97), whose autobiography *Histoire d'une âme*, has inspired countless people and has made Lisieux into a major place of pilgrimage.

St. Bernadette of Lourdes claimed to have received many visions of the Virgin Mary.

PSYCHICAL RESEARCH

Scientific interest in psychical research began in 1882, when the philosopher Henry Sidgwick founded a society for that purpose in Great Britain. In 1884, the American psychologist William James cofounded a similar organization in the United States. Psychical research attempts to provide a basis for the assumption that phenomena such as telepathy, clairvoyance, and other extrasensory perceptions (ESP) exist, and pursues investigations into various claims

of the occurrence of such phenomena.

The work of psychologist J. B. Rhine at Duke University, Durham, N. Carolina, gave impetus to the subject in 1930, when his laboratory-controlled experiments using specially designed cards appeared to establish the phenoma of ESP and telepathy on a statistical basis. Subsequent experiments have failed to convince mainstream scientists, but a vigorous counter-culture continues to exist.

THEOSOPHICAL SOCIETY

Founded in 1875 by Russian-born Helena Petrovna Blavatsky and American philanthropist Henry Steel Olcott, the Theosophical Society has numbered eminent people among its followers. A blend of Hindu and Neoplatonic elements, it proposes that true knowledge comes not through reason but through direct communion of the soul with reality. Although Blavatsky's psychic powers failed to withstand scrutiny by the Society for Psychical Research, the movement helped to revive an interest in Hinduism when Blavatsky and Olcott went to India in 1879. Blavatsky's successor, Annie Besant, became an influential figure in the struggle for Indian independence. The Theosophical Society continues to exercise a certain influence. It has spread worldwide and exists on the fringe of Spiritualism, initiation, and spiritual quest.

Madame Blavatsky, theosophist and author of Isis Unveiled.

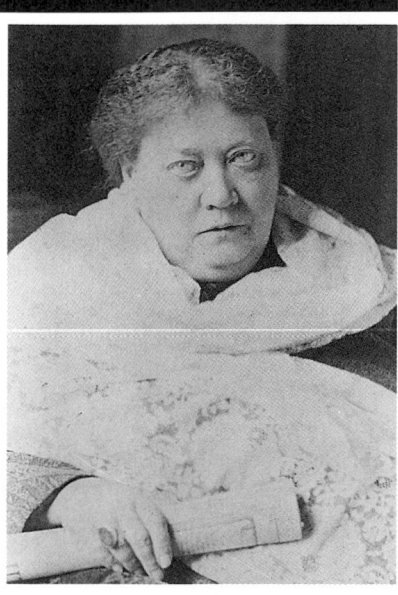

Timeline

1883–92 Friedrich Nietzsche publishes *Also Sprach Zarathustra* (Thus Spake Zarathustra).

1884 Philosopher and psychologist William James is cofounder of the American Society for Psychical Research.

1885 Mormons split into polygamous and monogamous sections.

1886 Nietzsche publishes *Jenseits von Gut und Böse* (Beyond Good and Evil).

1889 Birth of Ludwig Wittgenstein, Austrian-born British philosopher. Henri Bergson, French philosopher, publishes *Time and Freewill*, containing the theory of evolutionary vitalism.

1890 Native American "Messiah War" begun by Paiute shaman Wovoka's claim that the Ghost Dance ceremony will end white oppression. Birth of Rudolf Carnap, German philosopher and member of the Vienna Circle.

1892 Friedrich Ludwig Gottlob Frege, German logician, publishes the paper *Sinn und Bedeutung* (Sense and Reference), in which he makes the distinction between the meaning of a term and the thing to which it refers.

1893 Francis Herbert Bradley, Welsh philosopher, produces *Appearance and Reality*, in which he expounds his metaphysical views. John Dewey, U.S. psychologist, philosopher, and educationist, publishes *School and Society* on the psychology of learning.

1896 Hindu saint Ramana Maharishi teaches at Mt. Arunachala in southern India.

1900 Birth of Gilbert Ryle, English philosopher of language based in Oxford.

1900–01 Edmund Husserl produces *Logische Untersuchungen*.

1901 Pentacostal movement begins in Topeka, Kansas. Rabindranath Tagore, Bengali poet and mystic, founds movement blending Eastern and Western philosophical and educational systems. Birth of Alfred Tarski, Polish logician, whose work on semantics was influential in the philosophy of language.

1902 Birth of Karl Popper, Austrian-born British philosopher of science.

1904 Separation of Church and state in France. Aleister Crowley, British occultist, publishes *The Book of the Law*, a seminal text of modern "magick," influential in the revival of witchcraft and satanic cults.

1905 Birth of Jean-Paul Sartre, French philosopher, novelist, leading Existentialist thinker, and Marxist atheist.

1906 Birth of Kurt Gödel, Austrian-born American mathematician and philosopher who showed that a formal arithmetical system cannot be proved consistent by means of elements from within that system. Albert Schweitzer, German philosopher, theologian, and doctor, publishes *The Quest of the Historical Jesus*, an eschatological interpretation of Christ's role.

Timeline

1908 Birth of Maurice Merleau-Ponty, French philosopher, who attempted a phenomenological description of consciousness.

1910 Bertrand Russell and Alfred North Whitehead produce *Principia Mathematica*.

1912 Rudolph Steiner, Austrian social philosopher, founds the Anthroposophical Society, a mystical system aimed at restoring human capacity for spiritual perception.

1918 Foundation of the Native American Church, based on the "Peyote Road" cult, combining Christian practices with ritual use of the hallucinatory peyote cactus.

1920 Formation of Akali Dal, political wing of Sikhism, in Punjab, India.

1921 Publication of Ludwig Wittgenstein's *Tractatus Logico-Philosophicus*, in which he proposes his "picture" theory of meaning.

1922 Georgi Gurdjieff, Russian mystic, establishes his "Institute for the Harmonious Development of Man" outside Paris.

1923 Martin Buber, Austrian Jewish religious philosopher, publishes *Ich und Du* (I and Thou), the classic expression of his philosophy of dialogue, contrasting mutuality and objective relationships.

c. **1925** The "Vienna Circle" of philosophers is founded.

1927 Martin Heidegger, German philosopher, publishes *Sein und Zeit* (Being and Time), a phenomenological exploration of the structures of human existence.

1930 Rastafarian sect emerges in Jamaica, believing that white religion is a rejection of black culture.

1931 International Bible Students' Association changes its name to Jehovah's Witnesses.

1932 Jacques Maritain, French philosopher, publishes *Les Degrés du Savoir*, in which he applies Aquinas' thought to modern philosophy.

1936 A. J. Ayer, English philosopher, argues in *Language, Truth and Logic* that moral statements are merely expressions of preference.

1937 Persecution of Jews in Germany extends to Christian opponents of Nazism. Buddhist sect Soka Gakkai ("Value Creation Society") formed in Japan, promising that faith will be rewarded with material gains.

1945 State Shinto abolished in Japan.

1946 Jean-Paul Sartre writes *L'Existentialisme est un Humanisme*.

1947 Dead Sea Scrolls discovered at Qumran, Palestine.

1948 World Council of Churches established.

c. **1950–60** Revival of "white witchcraft" in Britain led by Gerald Gardner and Sybil Leek.

1950 Tenzin Gyatso, the 14th Dalai

THE SALVATION ARMY

A Christian organization with a semi-military organizational structure, the Salvation Army today works in more than 85 countries, operating an effective service to provide help for the poor and the needy. Its basic units, the corps community centers, number more than 14,000 around the world.

The organization developed in 1865 from the work of William Booth, a Methodist minister, in the poorer parts of London's East End, where it was known as the Christian Mission until it changed its name to the Salvation Army in 1878. Within a decade the group had spread outside Britain and also became well established in North America.

The Salvation Army numbers many musicians in its ranks, and music is widely used as a way to spread the gospel.

William Booth, Salvation Army founder.

DEAD SEA SCROLLS

Manuscripts hidden by members of the Jewish sect of the Essenes (*p. 211*) at Qumran, near the Dead Sea, were found in desert caves from 1947 onward. Eventually a total of more than 500 documents was discovered, probably concealed when the Romans were closing in to suppress the Jewish revolt in Palestine in A.D. 67–70. Written on leather or papyrus, some were recorded as early as 200 B.C.

Consisting of all the Old Testament books except *Esther*, the Dead Sea Scrolls are almost 1,000 years older than any Old Testament scriptures previously known, and contain some interesting variant readings. But perhaps the most important scrolls are those which describe a Covenant of Love between God and humankind and lay down the rules for the celibate order of Essene monks. Other texts discuss an imminent final battle between the Sons of light and the Sons of darkness. It is thought possible that John the Baptist had close connections with the Essenes, and that Jesus himself maintained friendships with them. The authorities have been slow to release the full texts of the scrolls for general consideration. There has been speculation that some of them are written in a secret code.

THE PENTECOSTAL CHURCHES

Beginning in Topeka, Kansas in 1901, the Pentecostal movement aimed for spiritual renewal within the modern Christian church, inspired by the Holy Spirit as it was on the Day of Pentecost (described in Acts 2). Rejected by their own churches, the new "Pentecostal" bodies spread rapidly, but the segregation tendency of the times led to white and black Pentecostal wings, with the result today that the most popular Pentecostal Churches remain the (white) Churches of God and the Assemblies of God, and the (black) Church of God in Christ.

Pentecostal Churches spread across the world and are particularly strong in Brazil (Assembleias de Deus and Igreja Evangelica Pentecostal) and the Caribbean. In Europe they are associated more with the evangelical wings of Protestant denominations. The Elim Pentecostal Church is particularly concerned with Christian education, and it specializes in training missionaries in northern Europe.

Combining the fervor engendered by the Wesleyan doctrine of "sanctification" with the oral traditions and spirituality of the African-American members, Pentecostalism often has highly charged overtones with the congregation responding at all times. There are more than 22 million Pentecostals worldwide, and the movement has reached established Protestant, Roman Catholic, and Greek Orthodox communities.

Concert at the Temple of Truth, Ministry of Restoration, London.

PSYCHOANALYSIS: FREUD AND JUNG

The work of the Austrian founder of psychoanalysis, Sigmund Freud, has been enormously influential in the history of ideas in the 1900s. His most important contributions include emphasis on the significance of the unconscious mind; dream analysis; the theory that mental disturbance is rooted in early experience; and the view that the analytic therapeutic process can effect explanation, interpretation and eventual change. He was forced into exile by the Nazis in 1938 and died in London.

Freud's early colleague, Carl Gustav Jung, broke away from his mentor because he could not agree with Freud's insistence on the importance of infantile sexuality as the basis of neurosis. Jung's theory is more inclined to religion and mysticism and is based on the idea of the collective unconscious and its archetypes, the psyche as a "self-regulating system,"

Analysts at Clark University, 1909: Freud is seated at left, Jung at right.

and the interpretation of universal symbols in dreams, myth, and art. In his personality theory, Jung contributed the idea of extrovert and introvert.

THE ECUMENICAL MOVEMENT

An impetus for cooperation and unity in the 1900s, at first between many Christian Churches, the ecumenical movement later extended to encompass Churches of different religions.

International Missionary Council
Established 1921, the first Christian interdenominational body to sit in regular conference; most Protestant (including Anglican) and Episcopalian Churches were represented, also a few lesser Orthodox Churches; no official attendance by Roman Catholics.

World Council of Churches
Established August 1948 and incorporated former International Missionary Council; in 1960s, admission of all major Orthodox Churches and some Pentecostal

Churches, so that virtually all Christian Churches except Roman Catholics are represented. It has no ecclesiastical or spiritual authority, but remains an instrument for discussion and for practical cooperation.

Since the 1960s, the Roman Catholic Church has had many discussions on close ecumenical ties with several Christian Churches (notably the Anglican Communion and the Eastern Orthodox Churches). In English-speaking countries it has also become the custom for leaders of most local churches, synagogues, temples, mosques, and citadels to be seen together on public occasions and sometimes even to officiate together at ecumenical devotional services.

RAMAKRISHNA-VIVEKANANDA MOVEMENT

The great Indian mystic and saint Sri Ramakrishna Paramahamsa (1835–86), a priest at the Kali temple of Dakshineswar, near Calcutta, taught the doctrine of God as Mother and affirmed from direct experience that all religions were different paths to the same goal of God-realization. His spiritual power was recognized by leading Bengali intellectuals, of whom the greatest was Swami Vivekananda (Narendranath Dutt). Vivekananda went to the United States in 1893 and introduced Ramakrishna's version of Hinduism throughout the United States and Europe. This work laid the basis of modern Western understanding of yoga, attracting adherents such as the writers Aldous Huxley, Christopher Isherwood, Romain Rolland, etc. The Ramakrishna-Vivekananda Foundation has branches in most countries as well as in India, and serves as the model for most subsequent foundations. Today, its main thrust is alleviation of need in India.

Swami Vivekananda (1863–1902), originator of Western yoga.

Lama, flees Chinese invasion of Tibet. Pope Pius XII proclaims dogma of the bodily assumption of the Blessed Virgin.

1951 W. V. O. Quine, U.S. philosopher, publishes the seminal essay *Two Dogmas of Empiricism*.

1953 Church of Scientology founded in Los Angeles by L. Ron Hubbard. The church, describing itself as "the modern science of mental health" combines therapy with doctrines similar to those of Buddhism.

1954 Korean evangelist Sun Myung Moon founds the Unification Church, whose members come to be known as the Moonies.

1955 Pierre Teilhard de Chardin, French Jesuit theologian, produces *The Phenomenon of Man*.

1957 United Church of Christ established in the U.S.A.

1959 A. J. Ayer publishes *Logical Positivism*.

1962–64 Second (Ecumenical) Vatican Council, convened by Pope John XXIII, liberalizes Roman Catholicism.

1966 Swami Prabhupada (A.C. Bhaktivedanta) founds the International Society for Krishna Consciousness (Hare Krishna) in the U.S.A.

1968 Pope Paul VI reaffirms Vatican opposition to artificial birth control.

1971 The "Jesus Movement" develops in the United States. Mao Zedong launches anti-Confucian campaign in China.

1974 Robert Nozick, American philosopher, publishes *Anarchy, State and Utopia* ("taxation is theft"). U.S evangelist Jim Bakker founds the Praise The Lord television ministry.

1975 Four women are ordained to the Episcopal priesthood in the U.S.A.

1978 Polish Cardinal Karol Wojtyla is elected Pope John Paul II. Mass suicide of members of the People's Temple Church, led by Jim Jones, at Jonestown, Guyana.

1979 Iran becomes an Islamic state. American Jerry Falwell founds the Moral Majority movement with airtime on 300 U.S. television stations.

1983 World Council of Churches holds a historic interdenominational Eucharist.

1984 Sikh leader Sant Jarnail Singh Bhindranwale dies in siege of the Golden Temple, Amritsar, India.

1986 Pope John Paul II visits a synagogue and leads 100 world religious leaders in prayers for peace.

1990 Soviet parliament reverses antireligious legislation of 1929.

1992 General Synod of Church of England approves ordination of women.

1993 Branch Davidian cult community is destroyed by Federal Authorities at Waco, Texas, with many deaths.

1995 Leaders of Aum Shinrikyo, a Japanese cult, are arrested by police following a sarin gas attack on the Tokyo subway.

THE EVANGELICAL MOVEMENT

In its strictest sense, evangelicalism is essentially a Protestant movement that stresses the Reformation doctrine of salvation by faith in Jesus Christ. The emphasis is on the Bible, with the Gospel seen as the only basis for faith. Personal conversion experiences and active home and overseas evangelism and missionary work are stressed, rather than the sacraments or Church traditions. The imminent physical return of Christ, belief in the profound sinfulness of mankind, and substitutionary atonement are evangelical absolutes.

The religious revival of the 1700s and 1800s, which included the Great Awakening in the U.S.A., Pietism in Europe, and Methodist revivalism in Britain, has generally come to be known as the evangelical revival and has had a deep effect on Protestants on both sides of the Atlantic. By the early part of this cen-

tury, divisions had occurred between liberal and fundamentalist wings, but in the 1970s and later, evangelicalism became vigorously fundamentalist, biblically (and often politically) conservative, and anti-ecumenical. More recently, however, there have been cautious moves toward ecumenicalism by some neo-evangelicals who nevertheless remain firmly committed to Protestantism.

Today, the preacher Billy Graham (b. 1918), who comes from a Southern Baptist tradition, leads the largest American Protestant denomination. His worldwide evangelizing crusades have had wide influence and inspired many imitators.

The evangelical movement is organized worldwide by the World Evangelical Fellowship and the Lausanne Committee for World Evangelization.

Billy Graham, world-famous evangelist.

NEW-AGE RELIGIONS

As the end of the millennium approaches, the apparent triumph of scientific rationalism has created a climate of religious "indifferentism" but has failed to satisfy many of the needs previously met by religion. In addition to the upswing in fundamentalism, observable in all the major world religions, the growth of charismatic movements has also been a feature of the late 1900s. Fueled by the "hippy" movement of the 1960s, numerous figures and organizations have emerged, some of whom have enjoyed a certain success while others have proved controversial and even disastrous. Prominent people and organizations include:
Auroville Founded by Sri Aurobindo (1872–1950), this "university center" in Pondicherry, in southern India, attempts to express a "new synthesis" reconciling Western science and Eastern wisdom. From 1926 it was developed by Aurobindo's chief disciple, the French Madame Richard ("Mother"), who died in 1975.
Sathya Sai Foundation Followers of Sathya Sai Baba (b. 1924), a Hindu spiritual leader based in Bangalore, India, number more than 10 million, the majority Indian. He is celebrated for his miracles and manifestations of *vibhuti* (sacred ash).
Scientology Led by Lafayette Ron Hubbard, founder of the study of Dianetics, which claims to increase intellectual ability and self-knowledge by means of a course of lessons.
The Unification Church (the Moonies) Led by the Korean Reverend Sun Myung Moon (b. 1920), this group numbers more than one million and believes that the Second Coming of the Judaeo-Christian Messiah happened in 1920. It emphasizes marriage, and mass weddings are a key feature.
Transcendental Meditation (1959) Leader Maharishi Mahesh Yogi, whose

mainly Western followers meditate twice daily and practice other aspects of Hindu yoga (such as "yogic flying").
The Divine Light Mission Movement led by Guru Maharaj Ji, the "Perfect Master" for this age, and transmitter of the experience of cosmic energy that represents both God and salvation.
The International Society for Krishna Consciousness (Hare Krishna) Founded by A. C. Bhaktivedanta Swami Prabhupada (d. 1989) in 1954, this group follows the precepts of the Hindu saint Chaitanya in advocating ecstatic devotion to Krishna, an austere monastic regime and study of the *Bhagavad Gita*.
Worldwide Church of God Led by Garner Ted Armstrong, radio promulgator of a biblical formula for success and prosperity, and prophet in 1968 of Christ's imminent Second Coming (predicted for dates that have now passed).
Rajneesh Meditation Leader Bhagwan Shree Rajneesh (Osho) (d. 1990), based in Pune, India. Osho emphasized the instinctual and the ascetic, attempting a fusion of Hindu Tantra and Western psychotherapy. He set up a short-lived com-

Hare Krishna devotees in Czech Republic.

munity in Oregon in the 1970s, but was deported from the United States. in 1985.
Dalai Lama (b. 1935) Believed by his followers to be an incarnation of the Bodhisattva Avalokiteshwara, the present Dalai Lama, Tenzin Gyatso, is the 14th incarnation. He left for India after the Chinese invasion of Tibet in 1950 and is regarded as a spiritual leader not only by Tibetans but also by many Westerners. Awarded the Nobel Peace Prize in 1989.

Tenzin Gyatso, Dalai Lama and Nobel Peace Prize winner, visits Estonia.

PROMINENT PEOPLE

ALBERTUS MAGNUS, Saint (c. 1200–80) German scholastic philosopher. A Dominican monk, he tried to harmonize Christian theology and Aristotelian thought.

ANAXAGORAS (500–428 B.C.) Greek philosopher. Believed that matter is infinitely divisible into particles containing a mixture of all qualities.

ANTONY "the Great," Saint (251–356) Egyptian ascetic. Founder of Christian Monachism (monasticism). He sold his possessions and withdrew to the wilderness, where he spent 20 years.

AQUINAS, Thomas, Saint (1225–1274) Italian scholastic philosopher. A Dominican friar, he studied under ALBERTUS MAGNUS. Tried to reconcile ARISTOTLE's scientific Rationalism with Christian doctrines of faith and revelation. His doctrine (Thomism) broadly represents the general teaching of the Catholic Church.

ARISTOTLE (384–322 B.C.) Greek philosopher, born in Macedonia. One of the most influential figures in the history of western thought, he worked at PLATO's Academy in Athens for 20 years and later became tutor to Alexander the Great. In 335 he founded his own school (the Lyceum) in Athens. His work influenced medieval philosophy, Islamic philosophy, and the whole Western intellectual tradition.

AUGUSTINE of Hippo, Saint (Aurelius Augustinus) (354–430) Late Roman theologian, born in North Africa. Greatest of the Latin Church Fathers, he was converted to Christianity after a spiritual crisis in 386. A champion of orthodoxy, he opposed the heresies of MANI and PELAGIUS. His *Confessions* (400) is a classic of world literature, while *The City of God* (412–27) presents human history in terms of conflict between spiritual and temporal.

AVERROES (ibn Rushd) (1126–98) Arab physician and philosopher, born in Spain. Wrote important commentaries on ARISTOTLE that strongly influenced Christian Europe.

AVICENNA (ibn Sina) (980–1037) Arab philosopher and physician, born in Persia. A major interpreter of ARISTOTLE to the Muslim world.

AYER, Sir A(lfred) J(ules) (1910–89) English philosopher. Pupil of RYLE at Oxford. His *Language, Truth and Logic* (1936) forcefully presented the Vienna Circle's antimetaphysical doctrines.

BAAL Shem Tov (Israel ben Eliezer) (1700–60) Ukrainian-born Jewish mystic. Founder of Hasidism.

BACON, Francis, Viscount St. Albans (1561–1626) English philosopher and statesman. Insisted on the importance of experiment in interpreting nature.

BENEDICT of Nursia, Saint (c. 480–c. 547) Italian religious leader. Founder of Western monasticism, he established a monastery at Monte Cassino, near Naples, and composed the rule for Western monasticism.

BENTHAM, Jeremy (1748–1832) English philosopher and jurist. Utilitarian who argued that actions should be decided by the criterion of "the greatest happiness of the greatest number."

BERKELEY, George (1685–1753) Irish Anglican bishop and philosopher. Argued that "to be is to be perceived"—that the contents of the world are "ideas" existing only when perceived by a mind.

BERNARD of Clairvaux, Saint (1090–1153) French theologian. He entered the Cistercian monastery of Citeaux (1113) and founded more than 70 monasteries.

BLAVATSKY, Helena Petrovna (1831–91) Russian-born U.S. Theosophist. Founded the Theosophical Society in New York with Henry Olcott and carried on her work in India.

BOETHIUS (Anicius Manlius Severinus) (480–524) Late Roman philosopher. His translations of ARISTOTLE became standard textbooks in medieval Europe.

BÖHME, JAKOB (1574–1624) German mystic. A shoemaker, he suffered persecution when he tried to express his understanding of the origin of things, especially the existence of evil.

BONIFACE, Saint (680–c. 754) Anglo-Saxon missionary. Major figure in Christianization of Germany.

BRUNO, Giordano (1548–1600) Italian Dominican philosopher and scientist. Propounded pantheistic philosophy of "world-soul."

BUBER, Martin (1878–1965) Austrian-born Israeli philosopher. Reappraised ancient Jewish thought in terms of the modern world.

BURKE, Edmund (1729–97) Irish statesman and philosopher. He opposed the notion of natural rights but supported the concept of social contract.

CALVIN, John (1509–64) French Protestant theologian. Major force in the Reformation, he founded the Presbyterian form of Church government.

CARNAP, Rudolf (1891–1970) German-American philosopher. Leading member of the Vienna Circle.

CHRYSOSTOM, John, Saint (c. 347–407), Syrian doctor of the Church. Early Christianity's greatest orator.

CHU Hsi (1130–1200) Chinese philosopher and leading architect of neo-Confucianism.

COLUMBA, Saint (521–97) Celtic Irish apostle of Christianity in Scotland.

COMTE, Auguste (1798–1857) French philosopher and social theorist. He pioneered the study of society as a science.

CONFUCIUS (K'ung Fu-Tzu) (551–479 B.C.) Chinese philosopher from Lu (modern Shantung province). A great moral teacher who sought to replace the old religious observances with moral values as the basis of social and political order.

CRANMER, Thomas (1489–1556) English prelate. First Protestant archbishop of Canterbury (1533–56). Burned at stake under Queen Mary I.

CROCE, Benedetto (1866–1952) Italian philosopher. Founded historical and philosophical periodical *La Critica*.

CROWLEY, Aleister (1875–1947) English occultist. Self-styled "Great Beast, 666," he led an occultist revival in the 1900s.

DARWIN, Charles (1809–82) English naturalist whose theory of natural selection challenged and subverted existing concepts of divine order.

DE BEAUVOIR, Simone (1908–86) French philosopher. Together with SARTRE, she contributed significantly to the Existentialist movement, and her *The Second Sex* (1953) is regarded as a pioneering feminist text.

DEMOCRITUS (c. 460–370 B.C.) Greek philosopher. Best known for his theory that the world consists of an infinite number of minute particles, or atoms.

DESCARTES, René (1596–1650) French philosopher and mathematician. A key figure in the history of Western thought, he developed a reordering of philosophy into a unified system of truth modeled on mathematics and supported by a rigorous rationalism. The fundamental Cartesian doctrines include the method of systematic doubt and the dualism of mind and matter.

DEWEY, John (1859–1952) American philosopher and educator. Believed that intelligence needed to be stimulated by new experiences and that education should also ensure the moral development of children.

DIDEROT, Denis (1713–84) French encyclopedist. Edited an expanded version of Ephraim Chambers' *Cyclopedia* (1757) with D'Alembert, which became a work of propaganda for the Rationalists of the Enlightenment (1751–76).

DIOGENES of Sinope (c. 410–320 B.C.) Greek philosopher from the Black Sea. Came to Athens and founded the Cynic ("doglike") sect, which advocated self-sufficiency through asceticism and disregard for conventional forms.

DJALAL AD-DIN RUMI (1207–73) Great Sufi mystic, poet, and founder of the "whirling dervish" order. His poetry influenced Goethe and Hegel.

DUNS Scotus (c. 1265–1308) Scottish scholastic philosopher. A member of the Franciscan order, he rivaled AQUINAS as the greatest medieval theologian.

ECKHART, Johannes (Meister Eckhart) (c. 1260–1327) German mystic. He taught a mystical pantheism which influenced later religious mysticism and speculative philosophy.

EDDY, Mary, née **Baker** (1821–1910) American thinker. Founder of Christian Science, she proclaimed the illusory nature of disease.

EDWARDS, Jonathan (1703–58) U.S.

theologian. Foremost theologian of American Puritanism.

ELIOT, John (1604–90) Anglo-American missionary. Known as "Apostle to the Indians" in Massachusetts, he translated the Bible into the Native American tongue.

ENGELS, Friedrich (1820–95) German political philosopher. From 1842 he lived mainly in Manchester, England. Met MARX in 1844 and cowrote *The Communist Manifesto* (1848). With Marx he helped to establish the materialist interpretation of history.

EPICURUS (341–270 B.C.) Greek philosopher. In about 306 B.C. he founded his school in the Garden at Athens, which became a model for Epicurean communities, dedicated to pleasure.

ERASMUS, Desiderius (c. 1466–1536) Dutch priest and scholar. Dedicated to reform, he criticized the clergy but believed in the unity of Christianity, attempting to create a middle ground between Catholics and Protestants.

EUSEBIUS of Caesarea (c. 264–340) Roman Christian theologian, born in Palestine. The "Father of Church History," he recorded the chief events in the Christian Church up to 324.

FICHTE, Johann Gottlieb (1762–1814) German philosopher. Modified KANT's system and proposed the ego as the basic reality, affirming itself in the act of consciousness.

FLUDD, Robert (1574–1637) English mystic and physician. Influenced by PARACELSUS, he developed the idea of man as a microcosm of the world.

FOUCAULT, Michel (1926–84) French philosopher and historian of ideas. Argued that prevailing social attitudes are manipulated by those in power.

FOX, George (1624–91) English religious leader. Founder of the Society of Friends (Quakers), he preached a doctrine of brotherly love.

FRANCIS OF ASSISI, Saint (Giovanni Bernadone) (1181–1226) Italian saint and founder of Franciscan order and Poor Clares (Franciscan order for women). He rejected the idea of property. Canonized in 1228. Famous for his love of nature, he was designated patron saint of ecology in 1980.

FRANCIS XAVIER, Saint (1506–52) Spanish missionary, the "Apostle of the Indies." Went to Goa, India in 1542, and later Ceylon (Sri Lanka) and Japan.

FREGE, Friedrich Ludwig Gottlob (1848–1925) German philosopher. The father of modern mathematical logic and the philosophy of language.

FREUD, Sigmund (1856–1939) Austrian founder of psychoanalysis. His views on the nature of the unconscious have profoundly influenced modern Western thought.

GHAZALI, Abu Hamid Muhammad al– (1058–1111) Islamic philosopher and theologian. Attempted to reconcile Greek philosophy with Muslim dogma.

Michel Foucault, French philosopher.

In 1095 he abandoned academia and became a mendicant Sufi (mystic).

GÖDEL, Kurt (1906–78) Austrian-born U.S. mathematician and logician. "Gödel's theorem" (1931) demonstrated that there can be no proof of the consistency of a formal mathematical system (such as RUSSELL's in *Principia Mathematica*) from within that system.

GRAHAM, Billy (b. 1918) U.S. Evangelist. Ordained as a minister at age 22, he has spent his adult life conducting religious missions in the United States and around the world. He has advised several U.S. presidents, written books, and appeared regularly on television.

GREGORY I, "the Great," Saint (c. 540–604), Late Roman father of the Church and pope (from 590). Reformer and major force of Christianity.

HEGEL, Georg Wilhelm Friedrich (1770–1831) German philosopher. His dialectic proposes that an argument (thesis) generates a counterargument (antithesis), and both are resolved in a synthesis. His philosophy influenced Marxists, Positivists, and Existentialists.

HEIDEGGER, Martin (1889–1976) German philosopher. Classified modes of "being" and examined human modes of existence through participation and involvement in the world of objects.

HERACLITUS (c. 540–460 B.C.) Greek philosopher, born Ephesus, Asia Minor.

HOBBES, Thomas (1588–1679) English political philosopher. His *Leviathan* (1651) conceived the world as a mechanical system, driven by the forces of attraction and repulsion, which also governed human psychology and determined "good" and "evil."

HUME, David (1711–76) Scottish philosopher and historian. Dominant influence on Empiricist philosophers of the 1900s, his *Treatise of Human Nature* (1739–40) extended the Empiricist legacy of LOCKE and BERKELEY.

HUSS (Hus), John (c. 1369–1415) Bohemian religious reformer. An early

voice of the Reformation, he was burned at the stake.

IBN' ARABI (1165–1240) Andalusian Muslim mystic. He is regarded as the greatest of the Sufi mystics.

IGNATIUS LOYOLA, Saint (Inigo Lopez de Recalde) (1491–1556) Spanish soldier. Founder, with St. FRANCIS XAVIER, of Society of Jesus (Jesuits). Sent missionaries to Japan, India, and Brazil.

JAMES, William (1842–1910) U.S. philosopher and psychologist. Describing himself as a "radical Empiricist," he argued that beliefs are true if and because they work.

JANSEN, Cornelius Otto (1585–1638), Dutch theologian. Founder of the Jansenist sect repudiating free will.

JASPERS, Karl (1883–1969) German-born Swiss philosopher. One of the founders of Existentialism.

JEROME, Saint (c. 342–420) Roman scholar. Considered the most learned and eloquent of fathers of the Church. In 385 he led a pilgrimage to the Holy Land and settled in Bethlehem in 386.

KANT, Immanuel (1724–1804) German philosopher. One of the great figures in the history of Western thought, influencing particularly the Idealism of FICHTE, HEGEL, and SCHELLING. His categorical imperative attempted to establish the supreme principle of morality.

KIERKEGAARD, Soren (1813–55) Danish philosopher and religious writer. Pioneer of Existentialism, he reinstated the central importance of the individual and the choices made in forming future selves.

LAO-TZU (500s B.C.) Chinese philosopher, traditionally the founder of Taoism. *Tao Te Ching*, attributed to him, was compiled 300 years after his death.

LEIBNIZ, Gottfried (1647–1716) German mathematician and philosopher. A great Rationalist, he contributed to statistics, logic, and probability theory. He described the world as an infinity of indivisible, immaterial "monads," of which the highest is God.

LOCKE, John (1632–1704) English philosopher. Defended natural rights, individual liberty, and majority rule. His *Essay Concerning Human Reason* (1690) is probably the most important statement of an Empiricist theory of knowledge in the British tradition.

LUTHER, Martin (1483–1546) First and greatest reformer of Christian Church. From 1516 he preached the necessity of theological renewal and taught that salvation can only come as a result of faith in, and union with, the Redeeemer, thus challenging ecclesiastical hierarchy.

MAIMONIDES, Moses (1135–1204) Jewish physician and philosopher, born Cordoba, Spain. He tried to harmonize Aristotelianism and Judaism in *Guide to the Perplexed* (1190).

MANI (Manichaeus) (c. 215–76) Persian religious leader. Founded the heretical sect of Manichaean0ism. In 276 he was crucified by Zoroastrians.

MARX, Karl (1818–83) German economic and political philosopher, father of Communism. Wrote *The Communist Manifesto* (1848, with ENGELS) and *Das Kapital* (1867–95).

MATHER, Cotton (1663-1728) Colonial clergyman and author. Was noted as a fiery preacher and as a major defender of orthodox Puritanism in Boston and throughout New England. Founded Yale University (1701).

MEAD, George Herbert (1863-1931) U.S. philosopher and author. Although known initially for his philosophical work he later became associated with social psychology.

MILL, John Stuart (1806–73) English philosopher and social reformer. A leading exponent of British Empiricism and Utilitarian traditions, he was a campaigner for women's suffrage.

NANAK (Guru Nanak) (1469–1539) Indian religious leader, born near Lahore; founder of Sikhism.

NEURATH, Otto (1882–1945) Austrian philosopher and social theorist. Member of the Vienna Circle.

NEWMAN, John Henry, Cardinal (1801–90) English prelate and theologian. A leading figure in the Oxford Movement before his conversion to Roman Catholicism.

NIETZSCHE, Friedrich (1844–1900) German philosopher. Repudiated Christian and liberal ethics, and democratic ideals. Proposed the idea of the *Übermensch* ("overman") who can create his own law, and the life-affirming "will to power."

PELAGIUS (Morgan) (*c.* 360–*c.* 420) British monk who rejected the doctrine of original sin (Pelagian heresy).

PENN, William (1644–1718) English Quaker reformer and colonialist, founder of Pennsylvania in 1681–82.

PLATO (*c.* 428–*c.* 348 B.C.) Greek philosopher, probably the most important in the history of Western thought. A disciple of SOCRATES, he fled Athens after the latter was executed, returning in 387 to found the Academy, where ARISTOTLE was one of his pupils. His work consists of about 30 philosophical dialogues and a series of letters. The early dialogues feature Socrates as principal character, enquiring into the definition of various moral virtues. The middle dialogues show Socrates expressing more systematic views, which are taken to be Plato's own, including such doctrines as the theory of knowledge as recollection, the immortality of the soul, and the theory of forms (or "ideas") which contrasts the transient world of particulars with the timeless world of universals.

PLOTINUS (*c.* 205–70) Roman Neoplatonist philosopher, born in Egypt. Advocated asceticism and the contemplative life. His writings established the foundations of Neoplatonism, which combined Platonic, Pythagorean,

Bertrand Russell, British philosopher and mathematician.

Aristotelian, and Stoic doctrines.

POPPER, Sir Karl Raimund (1902–94) Austrian-born British philosopher. Rejecting the logical positivism of the Vienna Circle, he stressed the importance of "falsifiability" as a defining factor of true scientific theories, contrasted with "pseudosciences" such as Marxism and psychoanalysis.

PYTHAGORAS (500s B.C.) Greek pre-Socratic philosopher, mystic, and mathematician. In *c.* 530 settled in Crotona, Italy. Believed in transmigration of souls, asceticism, and abstinence.

RAMANUJA (1017–1137) Indian Vaishnavite philosopher. He developed the doctrine of devotion toward a personal god.

ROUSSEAU, Jean-Jacques (1712–78) French political philosopher. Emphasized natural goodness of humans and the corrupting influences of institutionalized life. His *Social Contract* (1762) influenced French revolutionary thought and introduced the slogan "Liberty, Equality, Fraternity."

RUSSELL, Bertrand, 3rd Earl (1872–1970) British philosopher and mathematician. A controversial political figure, he was imprisoned for his pacifist views in 1918 and from 1949 played a leading part in the campaign for nuclear disarmament.

SANKARA (A.D. 700s) Indian philosopher and sage. An itinerant teacher of Hindu *advaita* (nondualistic) doctrine, he affirmed Hinduism's religious and philosophical basis.

SANTAYANA, George (1863-1952) Spanish philosopher and writer, based in the U.S.A. until 1912. Widely traveled and a shrewd observer of human nature, he is remembered for his wide body of work, including books, essays, and aphorisms about language, society, and nationality.

SARTRE, Jean-Paul (1905–80) French philosopher and writer. A disciple of HEIDEGGER, he became the most prominent exponent of Existentialism.

SCHELLING, Friedrich Wilhelm Joseph von (1775–1854) German philosopher.

His view that only in art can the mind become fully aware of itself influenced the Romantic movement.

SCHOPENHAUER, Arthur (1788–1860) German philosopher. His emphasis on the active role of will as a creative but covert and irrational force in human nature strongly influenced NIETZSCHE and FREUD.

SOCRATES (469–399 B.C.) Greek philosopher. One of the three great figures in ancient philosophy, he moved the philosophical agenda from speculation about the natural world to ethics and conceptual analysis. Convicted of "corrupting the youth" by his fellow Athenians, he was sentenced to die by drinking poison.

SPENCER, Herbert (1820–1903) English philosopher. Applied evolutionary theories to ethics and sociology and became an advocate of social Darwinism.

SPINOZA, Baruch (1632–77) Dutch Jewish Rationalist philosopher. Proposed an "infinite substance" that was God or Nature.

TEILHARD De Chardin, Pierre (1881–1955) French theologian and philosopher. His *The Phenomenon of Man* (1940) advanced original proofs for the existence of God.

TERESA OF AVILA, Saint (1515–82) Spanish mystic. After a series of visions she restored the Carmelite order (1562).

TILLICH, Paul (1886–1965), German-born U.S. philosopher and theologian. Attempted to correlate biblical faith with modern philosophical Rationalism.

VOLTAIRE (François Marie Arouet) (1694–1778) French thinker. Embodiment of the Enlightenment, he was imprisoned (1717–18) and exiled (1726–29). Back in France he wrote plays, poetry, historical and scientific treatises, moved to Berlin at the invitation of Frederick the Great (1750–53), and settled near Geneva in 1755, where he wrote the satirical tale *Candide* (1759).

WESLEY, John (1703–91) English founder of Methodism; traveled more than 250,000 mi. (400,000 km) and preached about 40,000 sermons as evangelist in Britain and the U.S.

WITTGENSTEIN, Ludwig (1889–1951) Austrian-born British philosopher. While serving in the Austrian army during World War I he wrote the *Tractatus Logico-philosophicus* (1921) which argues that sentences are pictures of the facts they represent. At Cambridge he wrote *Philosophical Investigations* (1953), which rejects the *Tractatus*, claiming that linguistic meaning is a function of the use to which expressions are put.

ZENO OF CITIUM (334–262 B.C.) Greek philosopher from Cyprus, who attended Plato's Academy before starting his own school of Stoicism.

ZENO OF ELEA (*c.* 490–420 B.C.) Pre-Socratic philosopher from Italy, known for his paradoxes denying the possibility of spatial division of motion.

RELIGIOUS TERMS

Agnosticism Belief that the existence of God can be neither known nor denied.

Animism Belief that plants and natural phenomena have souls (Latin *anima*).

Apocrypha Religious writings not considered sufficiently reliable to merit a place in the Christian scriptures.

Atheism Belief that there is no God.

Atonement Old Testament sacrificial system where the blood of the victim atones for sin; developed in Christianity with the sacrifice of Christ himself.

Baptism Ritual sprinkling of water, or immersion, bringing about purification.

Bodhisattva One destined to become enlightened and a future Buddha, but who postpones entry into nirvana in order to help others.

Catechism Statement of doctrine with key elements explained in question-and-answer format.

Catholic Global body of the Christian Church. May also mean Western (as opposed to ORTHODOX) Church, based on Rome.

Charismatic Movement of renewed spiritual energy and enthusiasm within contemporary religion, especially Christianity (*see* PENTECOSTALISM).

Church Established body with set doctrine, ritual (liturgy), and hierarchy.

Communion (Mass/Eucharist/Lord's Supper) Major Christian Church sacrament commemorating the Last Supper of Jesus before crucifixion, involving ritual consumption of bread and wine.

Cosmogony A theory explaining the origins of the universe.

Covenant Judeo-Christian concept of divine commitment to humanity.

Cult Belief system and the people following such a system.

Deism Belief in a God who stands apart from the world; a strand of religious thought during the 1600s and 1700s.

Dharma Hindu concept of moral law, universal and individual.

Diaspora ("dispersion") Jewish exile from their divinely appointed land.

Dogma Agreed authoritative position on a crucial item of belief.

Dualism Doctrine that puts forward two distinct and irreconcilable principles, for example good and evil or spirit and matter.

Ecumenism Movement seeking unity of divided Churches and denominations within Christianity (*see p. 237*).

Eschatology Doctrine of "last things" (Greek *eschatos*, "last"), specifically concerned with death and judgment.

Eucharist See COMMUNION.

Evangelicalism Commitment to importance of making a personal decision for Christ.

Exorcism Expelling malign spirits from people or places.

Faith healing Cure or alleviation of sickness by calling on supernatural powers.

Fathers of the Church First Christian theologians.

Fatwah Formal legal opinion or decision issued by a Muslim authority.

Friars Mendicant members of Christian orders, such as the Franciscans, working as teachers and ministers.

Fundamentalism Unquestioning faith in traditional teachings, used to describe conservative Protestant movements in the U.S.A. in the 1900s, and extended to cover conservative religious movements in other religions, especially toward the end of the 1900s.

Grace Mercy and favor shown by God to humanity.

Guru Hindu or Sikh spiritual leader.

Holy Spirit Third Person of the Christian Holy Trinity; the term denotes the presence or power of God.

Imam Religious leader of the Sunni Muslims; one of the early leaders of the Shi'ite Muslims.

Immaculate conception Roman Catholic dogma (1854) that the Virgin Mary was conceived free from sin.

Infallibility Roman Catholic doctrine (1871) that authoritative (*ex cathedra*) statements made by the Pope are divinely inspired and therefore free from error.

Jainism Indian religion founded by Vardhamana Mahavira (599–527 B.C.) advocating extreme asceticism as the means to overcome worldly preoccupations and liberate the soul from its KARMA.

Karma Indian belief that actions in one life affect the next incarnation.

Kosher Food prepared according to Jewish law.

Lent Christian period of prayer and abstinence in the 40 weekdays before Easter.

Liturgy Standard form of church service.

Lucifer A name of Satan or the devil.

Magi Priestly clan of Persians.

Mandala In Hinduism or Buddhism, a cosmic diagram used for meditation.

Manichaeism Influential Persian faith founded by Mani (in 240) that believed in a primeval dualistic conflict between light and darkness.

Mantra In Indian religions, word or sound repeated in meditation.

Maronites Syrian Christian community founded by St. Maro (d. 407).

Mass *See* COMMUNION.

Meditation Concentrated thought on some religious or spiritual object.

Menorah Seven-branched candelabrum of Judaism.

Messiah Divinely ordained savior of the Jews; identified by Christians as Jesus Christ.

Millenarianism Belief that the return of Christ will bring a 1,000-year reign of peace preceded by global turmoil.

Moksha Release from the transmigratory cycle of birth and rebirth.

Monasticism System of withdrawal from worldly into spiritual life, with communities subjected to spiritual discipline.

Moravian Brethren Protestant sect founded in Bohemia (1457). Expelled in 1722, they became established in North America in 1734.

Muezzin Islamic mosque official assigned to call the faithful to prayer.

Mullah Islamic teacher or scholar.

Mysticism Pursuit of direct experience or knowledge of God.

Nirvana In Buddhism, ultimate state of spiritual tranquillity following extinction of individual desires.

Om In Hinduism, the eternal word, seed of all knowledge and thought.

Original sin Traditional Christian doctrine that everyone inherits a nature flawed by Adam's original disobedience to God.

Orthodox That which conforms to Church dogma. More specifically, the Eastern Christian Church.

Pantheism Belief that God and the universe are one and the same.

Passover Annual Jewish festival commemorating deliverance of the Israelites from bondage in Egypt.

Pentecost In Judaism *Shabuoth* (Feast of Weeks); for Christians, the day when the Holy Spirit descended upon the apostles.

Pentecostalism Christian renewal movement begun in U.S.A. (1901) emphasizing Bible-based faith with spontaneous worship and evidence of the power of the Holy Spirit.

Pope Bishop of Rome and head of Roman Catholic Church.

Presbyterianism Conciliar form of Church government of Reformed Churches (1500s).

Protestantism Religious movement dating from Luther's protest against the Roman Catholic Church (1516).

Rabbi Teacher of Jewish Law.

Reincarnation Rebirth of an individual in another body after death.

Rosary Sequence of prayers using a string of beads.

Sabbath Day of the week set aside for religious worship and rest, Saturday for Jews and Sunday for most Christians.

Sacrament In Christianity, symbolic ceremony signifying internal spiritual grace.

Sadhu Wandering Hindu holy man.

Sect Religious body separated from main body of believers.

Soul Personal nonphysical self believed to survive after death.

Stigmata Marks appearing on a person's body replicating the wounds of Christ.

Totem Emblem of tribe or family.

Transubstantiation Christian doctrine of consecration of Eucharistic bread and wine to become actual body and blood of Christ.

Unitarianism Religious belief deriving from Anabaptism that claims God to be a singular entity rather than a trinity of Father, Son, and Holy Spirit.

Vision Image communicated supernaturally, especially by God.

Witchcraft Use of magical powers to control objects, events, or people.

PHILOSOPHICAL TERMS

Algorithm A set of predetermined rules which, if applied to a complex problem, will yield a solution or optimal results.

Analytic and synthetic An analytic truth is true by virtue of the meanings of the words used (for example, all bachelors are unmarried men), whereas synthetic truths are true by virtue of particular facts obtaining in the world.

Axiom A statement that forms part of the foundations of a network of arguments: as such it is a premise in some of the arguments but is the conclusion of none.

Causation The relationship between an effect or result and whatever brought it into being. One of the fundamental questions about causality is whether causation is more than just one event following another—that is, whether there is any substance to our intuitive belief that to cause something is to force it into happening.

Consciousness The property of awareness experienced by people when awake. Sometimes consciousness is understood in a narrower sense, to be something we have when we introspect and become aware of our awareness. Exploration of our introspective awareness is known as PHENOMENOLOGY.

Empiricism The collective term for theories of knowledge that involve the claim that all substantive (as opposed to tautological) knowledge derives from, or is grounded in, SENSE EXPERIENCE.

Epistemology The study of the grounds and scope of knowledge; the attempted elucidation of the relationship between the knower and the known.

Ethics The study of human moral values and conduct.

Existentialism A philosophy characterized by emphasis upon the brute fact of our existence, and the ensuing questions about our search for purpose and our responsibility to choose for ourselves.

Free will The ability to think and do what we wish when not restrained, a property that we possess by virtue of having a mind: our various mental states exhibit intentionality, meaning that they are directed toward certain objects in the world, and these states are the causes of our actions.

Intentionality The property of being directed toward some object, just as a desire or a belief is directed toward an aim or object. To say that the dog wants his bone is to attribute intentionality to the dog. There is considerable debate about the relationship between intentionality and CONSCIOUSNESS: both are central to the conception of what it is to have a mind, and yet neither takes obvious precedence over the other.

Logic The systematic study of reasoned argument, or inference, and consequent diagnosis of patterns of incorrect reasoning (fallacies).

Mental and physical Classically, the physical is thought of as solid, and subject to deterministic laws, whereas the mental is seen as the utterly rarefied arena of nondeterministic willful CAUSATION. To have a mind is certainly to exhibit nondeterministic INTENTIONALITY, and physical is as solid as you get, but we should infer from the mess that the philosophy of mind has often gotten into that these conceptions may be misleading. If some group of PREMISES leads us to deny that human beings have FREE WILL, or that our minds cause our actions, then we should very carefully review them.

Metalanguage The medium in which we refer to linguistic items, such as words, phrases, or even entire languages, rather than to the world at large. We can use English words and phrases to refer to English words and phrases, so English can be used as its own metalanguage. If we employ an English word to refer to itself, then we are mentioning it rather than using it (*see* USE AND MENTION).

Metaphysics The study of the broad structure of reality, including inquiry into the relationship between MENTAL AND PHYSICAL, the nature of CAUSATION, the existence and the nature of God, the relationship between a thing and its various properties, and the nature of time and space. Both the boundaries and the EPISTEMOLOGICAL legitimacy of metaphysics are contested.

Ontology The branch of METAPHYSICS concerned with existence; the ultimate categories of existent things (for instance physical objects, minds, numbers); the study of what there is.

Phenomenology A school of philosophy that holds that a certain method of introspection can furnish us with knowledge of the essences of things. Such introspection involves abstracting essences from SENSE EXPERIENCE. Phenomenologists believe that sense experience is not independent of the objects sensed, so sensations are intimately bound up with their objects, the phenomena.

Positivism The view that all genuine knowledge derives from the scientific assessment of our experience. It involves a general hardheadedness about various metaphysical claims, motivated by a broadly Empiricist EPISTEMOLOGY. During the 1900s, the Positivist torch has been carried by the Logical Positivists, who believe that for a sentence to be properly described as "true" or "false," it has to be verifiable by reference to sense experience.

Pragmatism A school of thought, propounded by the U.S. philosophers William James and John Dewey, that assesses the truth of concepts in terms of their practical applications.

Premises In an argument, the statements from which the conclusion is supposed to follow. If an argument is valid, then the truth of the premises guarantees the truth of the conclusion.

Rationalism View proposed by Descartes, Spinoza, and Leibniz that reason is superior to experience as a source of knowledge.

Relativism A broad concept that includes a variety of assaults on the notion of objective knowledge, and on the notion of objective truth. It is often motivated by the observation that values and beliefs vary from culture to culture, and from time to time.

Semantics and semiotics Both these terms pertain to the study of signs and their relationship with what they signify. "Semantics" is used more in formal logic and in the analytical philosophy of language (the study of meaning), whereas "semiotics" is used more in the study of actual communication—although these are not rigid divisions.

Sense experience The sum of the inputs from our various senses. Sense experience is often thought of as formed from various individual sensations—sensations which are independent of the objects that caused them. Such discrete units of experience have been called qualia, sense data, sensa, impressions, and ideas. One problem with such a view is that it is difficult to make sense of the notion of a sensation independently from its object, which tends to undermine the idea that sensations are independent of the objects.

Stoicism A Greek school of philosophy emphasizing similarities between human and cosmic rationality. Founded by Zeno of Citium.

Tautology The term used for a statement which is true because of the way it is formally constructed (*see* ANALYTIC AND SYNTHETIC).

Truth Definitions of truth vary widely. Common answers to the question "When is a sentence true?" include: "When it corresponds to the facts" (a correspondence theory of truth); "When it coheres with other sentences which we believe" (a coherence theory of truth); "When it would be among those believed by the ideal observer" (an epistemic theory of truth); "When it is believed by a group of people" (cultural relativism); and "When believing it leads to succesful action" (a pragmatic approach).

Use and mention A word or phrase is mentioned if we are using it merely to refer to itself (in a METALANGUAGE), and used if we are using it to refer to something in the world.

Utilitarianism The view that, when given a choice, we should choose the option that maximizes overall human happiness. This view effectively renders motives for one's actions morally irrelevant by focusing on the consequences.

Vienna Circle A philosophical discussion group founded in the early 1920s. It became the international focus for Logical Positivism.

POLITICAL DEFINITIONS

Politics is the science of government: it studies and regulates the creation of legislation, as well as defines the role of the individual within society. Each person has a set of individual values which are important to them. When people come together in society, all these different opinions have to be tempered to allow everybody to interact. Politics is essentially the process of cooperation, debate, and interplay necessary to allow society to operate. The degree and emphasis of these rules differ from society to society, depending on what the community is trying to achieve and what is important in that society. All governments exert some influence on the life of the individual, but the scope of governmental influence varies greatly.

Anarchism Rejection of the state and other forms of authority.

Authoritarianism Government not dependent on the consent of society.

Cabinet Advisory body to the president, consisting of the heads of the 13 executive departments of the federal government.

Caucus A meeting of party officials to select candidates, or a meeting of party members in a legislature to plan strategy.

Congress The legislature, comprising the House of Representatives and the Senate.

Civil disobedience Strategy to achieve political goals by refusing to cooperate with a government or its agents.

Civil rights Rights guaranteed by a state to its citizens.

Coalition Arrangement between countries or political parties to pursue a common goal.

Communism Ideology featuring common ownership of property, associated with theories of Karl Marx (*p. 234*).

Conservatism Political beliefs stressing adherence to established authority.

Constitution Principles that determine the way a country may be governed, usually in the form of a written document.

Democracy Rule by the people, usually with decision-making in the hands of popularly elected representatives.

Dictatorship Rule by a single person, or several people (e.g. military dictatorship), unelected and authoritarian in character.

Dissidents People who oppose a regime and may suffer discrimination.

Fascism Nationalistic and authoritarian movement associated with the 1930s.

Federalism Territorial political organization aiming to maintain national unity while permitting regional diversity.

Filibuster The use of obstructive tactics, such as an exceptionally long speech, by a member of a legislature, to prevent the adoption of a measure favored by a majority.

Green Movement opposing ecological and environmental effects caused by technological and economic policies.

House of Representatives The lower house of Congress, in which states are allocated seats according to their population. Members serve two year terms.

Human rights Fundamental rights beyond those prescribed by law.

Imperialism Extension of state power through acquisition of other territories.

Labor union An organization of wage earners for mutual aid and for collective bargaining with employers.

Lame duck An elected official or group continuing in office after election defeat but before a successor's assumption of that office.

Left wing Political position occupied by those with radical and reforming tendencies toward social and political order.

Legislature Institution with power to pass laws.

Liberalism Doctrine that urges freedom of the individual, religion, trade, and economics (*laissez-faire*).

Lobby A group that seeks to influence members of a legislature to vote according to a group's interests.

Nationalism Doctrine that views the nation as the principal unit of political organization.

Nationalization Taking an industry into state ownership.

Pluralism Existence within a society of a variety of groups, limiting the power of any one group.

Pressure group Organization formed to support a particular political interest.

Proletariat In socialist philosophy, term denoting working class.

Proportional representation Voting system ensuring that the representation of voters is in proportion to their numbers.

Racism Ideology alleging inferiority of racial or ethnic groups.

Radicalism Ideology arguing for substantial political and social change.

Referendum Device whereby the electorate can vote on a measure put before it by a government.

Right wing Political position of support for established institutions and opposition to socialist developments.

Sanction Penalty imposed by one state against another, such as denial of trade.

Senate The upper house of Congress, in which each state is allocated two seats. Members serve six-year terms.

States' righter A person who opposes federal intervention in the affairs of separate states, seeing this view as a strict interpretation of the Constitution.

Separatism Demand for separation from territorial and political sovereignty of the state to which the separatists belong.

Socialism Doctrine favoring state intervention to create an egalitarian society.

Terrorism Violent behavior to promote a particular political cause, often aimed at overthrow of the established order.

Totalitarianism System in which political opposition is suppressed and decision-making is highly centralized.

Welfare state System whereby the state assumes responsibility for protecting and promoting its citizens' welfare in areas such as healthcare, employment, pensions, and education.

THE UNITED NATIONS

In the late 1900s, with its highly advanced transportation and communications networks, multinational financial and political organizations, and large-scale movement of people, ideas, and techniques, the world has become an increasingly global community. In this situation, the main organ of international politics is the United Nations (UN). After World War II, the international community recognized its responsibility to guarantee the civil liberties of the peoples of the world, and to work for peace and stability on a global scale. The United Nations Charter was drawn up by the Allied powers in 1945. The Charter lays out the four purposes and seven principles of the UN:

Purposes
1 To preserve world peace and security.
2 To encourage nations to be just in their actions toward each other.
3 To help nations cooperate in solving their problems.
4 To serve as an agency through which nations can work toward these goals.

Principles
1 All members have equal rights.
2 All members must carry out their duties under the Charter.
3 All members agree to the principle of settling their disputes peacefully.
4 Members agree not to use force or the threat of force against other nations, except in self-defense.
5 Members must agree to help the UN in every action it takes in seeking to fulfill the purposes of the Charter.
6 The UN agrees to act on the principle that nonmember states have the same duties as member states to preserve world peace and security.
7 The UN accepts the principle of not interfering in the actions of a member nation within its own borders.

Principal UN institutions

General Assembly
The General Assembly is the UN parliament, and all member nations are represented, each having one vote. It meets annually in New York City in a session that begins on the third Tuesday in September and continues until the year's end. Decisions are made by a simple majority except for "important questions," which require a two-thirds majority.

Security Council
The Security Council has a membership of 15. There are five permanent members: China, France, Russia, the U.K., and the U.S.A. The other ten members are elected for two-year terms by a two-thirds majority vote of the General Assembly.

In its function as a peacekeeping organ, the council may call on the armed forces, and other assistance, from member states.

UNITED NATIONS STRUCTURE

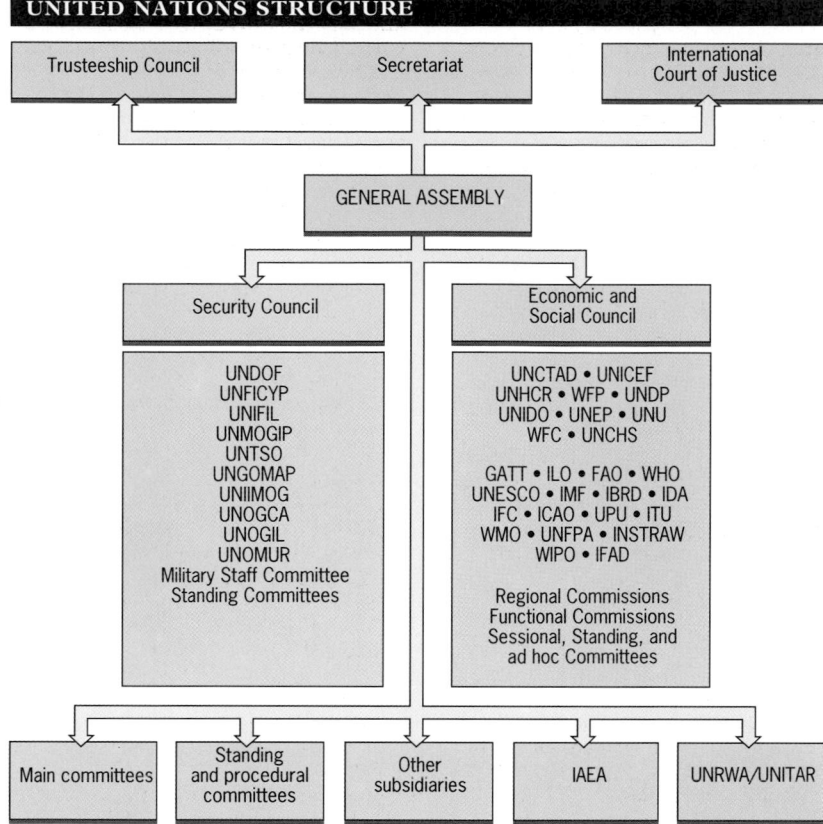

Trusteeship Council | Secretariat | International Court of Justice

GENERAL ASSEMBLY

Security Council
- UNDOF
- UNFICYP
- UNIFIL
- UNMOGIP
- UNTSO
- UNGOMAP
- UNIIMOG
- UNOGCA
- UNOGIL
- UNOMUR
- Military Staff Committee
- Standing Committees

Economic and Social Council
- UNCTAD • UNICEF
- UNHCR • WFP • UNDP
- UNIDO • UNEP • UNU
- WFC • UNCHS

- GATT • ILO • FAO • WHO
- UNESCO • IMF • IBRD • IDA
- IFC • ICAO • UPU • ITU
- WMO • UNFPA • INSTRAW
- WIPO • IFAD

Regional Commissions
Functional Commissions
Sessional, Standing, and
ad hoc Committees

Main committees | Standing and procedural committees | Other subsidiaries | IAEA | UNRWA/UNITAR

Economic and Social Council
The Economic and Social Council monitors economic, social, cultural, educational, and health matters in member states and works to guarantee human rights. It has 54 members, elected by a two-thirds majority vote of the General Assembly.

Trusteeship Council
The Trusteeship Council is responsible for overseeing the administration of the UN Trust Territories. Its members are China, France, Russia, the U.K., and U.S.A.

International Court of Justice
The International Court of Justice is composed of independent judges, elected by the Security Council and the General Assembly to preside over cases of international law. The court's headquarters are in The Hague, Netherlands.

Secretariat
The Secretariat manages the day-to-day running of the various organs of the UN. It consists of the Secretary-General, elected by a majority vote of the General Assembly, various undersecretaries, and a large international staff.

Other agencies

FAO Food and Agriculture Organization.
GATT General Agreement on Tariffs and Trade (this is not officially linked to the UN, but it is generally considered a part of the system).
IAEA International Atomic Energy Agency.
IBRD International Bank for Reconstruction and Development (World Bank).
ICAO International Civil Aviation Organization.
IDA International Development Association.
IFAD International Fund for Agricultural Development.
IFC International Finance Corporation.
ILO International Labor Organization.
IMCO Intergovernmental Maritime Consultative Organization.
IMF International Monetary Fund.
ITU International Telecommunication Union.
UNCHS UN Center for Human Settlements (Habitat).
UNCTAD UN Conference on Trade and Development.
UNDOF UN Disengagement Observer Force.
UNDP UN Development Program.
UNEP UN Environment Program.
UNESCO UN Educational, Scientific, and Cultural Organization.
UNFICYP UN Peacekeeping Force in Cyprus.
UNFPA UN Fund for Population Activities.
UNGOMAP UN Good Offices Mission in Afghanistan and Pakistan.
UNHCR United Nations High Commission for Refugees.
UNICEF UN International Children's Emergency Fund.
UNIDO UN Industrial Development Organization.
UNIFIL UN Interim Force in Lebanon.
UNIIMOG UN Iran-Iraq Military Observer Group.
UNITAR UN Institute for Training and Research.
UNMOGIP UN Military Observer Group in India and Pakistan.
UNOGCA UN Observer Group in Central America.
UNOGIL UN Observation Group in Lebanon.
UNOMUR UN Observer Mission in Uganda-Rwanda.
UNPROFOR UN Protection Force (in former Yugoslavia).
UNRWA UN Relief and Works Agency for Palestine Refugees in the Near East.
UNTSO UN Truce Supervision Organization.
UNU United Nations University.
UPU Universal Postal Union.
WFC World Food Council.
WFP World Food Program.
WHO World Health Organization.
WIPO World Intellectual Property Organization.
INSTRAW International Research and Training Institute for the Advancement of Women.

The UN and Population Growth

Population expansion has become an increasingly important issue since the foundation of the UN. The global population has already reached 6 billion, and it is increasing at a rapid rate. Many of the developing countries have youthful populations, and therefore have a staggering potential for even greater rates of growth.

The effects of these rates of growth are very serious. In a world where resources are so unevenly distributed, overpopulation in many areas has led to poverty and homelessness, and the need for fuel has resulted in the overexploitation of many resources (*p. 444*). It is feared that, at present rates of consumption, many resources will soon be exhausted.

In 1967, in an effort to slow down population growth and thus ease the strain on the economies of many developing nations, the UN founded the Fund for Population Activities (UNFPA). This agency disseminates knowledge about contraceptive techniques and helps to make family planning facilities more widely available.

Secretaries-General of the UN

Date	Name	Nationality
1946–53	Trygve Lie	Norwegian
1953–61	Dag Hammarskjöld	Swedish
1961–71	U Thant	Burmese
1972–81	Kurt Waldheim	Austrian
1982–91	Javier Perez De Cuellar	Peruvian
1992–	Boutros Boutros-Ghali	Egyptian

THE EUROPEAN UNION

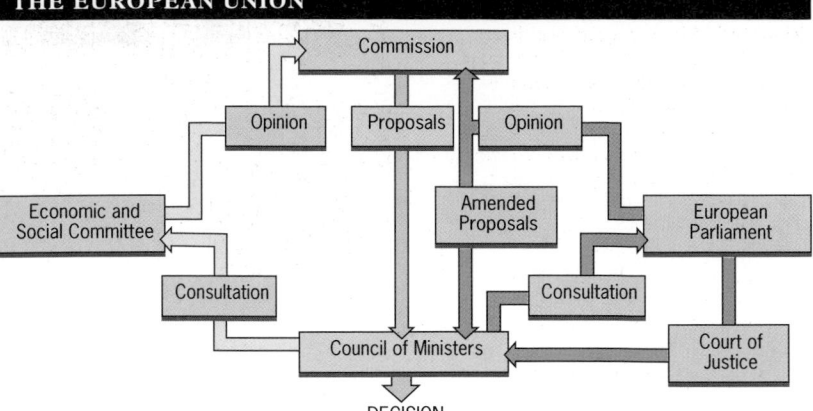

The European Union (EU) took on its present form with the ratification of the Maastricht Treaty in 1993. The EU is a political and economic alliance which currently includes 15 member states: Austria, Belgium, Denmark, Finland, France, Germany, Greece, Ireland, Italy, Luxembourg, the Netherlands, Portugal, Spain, Sweden, and the United Kingdom. Several Eastern European countries hope to join the Union in the near future.

European Commission
The European Commission is one of the main EU bodies. It is headed by a group of 20 commissioners, nominated by member states (two each from France, Germany, Italy, Spain, and the U.K.; one each from other countries) for a four-year renewable term. One member is chosen as president for a two-year term. The Commission's tasks include:
1 Drafting policy.
2 Drafting the Union's budget each year.
3 Liaising with international bodies and states with economic ties with the EU.
4 Managing policies for the community.
5 Ensuring that nation states implement EU laws that have been agreed.
6 Monitoring the "level playing field" in the Union to secure fair competition throughout the EU.

Council of Ministers
The Council of Ministers is composed of ministers from each member state. One of their functions is to deal with proposals made by the Commission. The Council presidency is held for a six-month term by each member in rotation.

Court of Justice
The Court of Justice is the supreme court of the EU and is made up of 15 judges: one from each member state. Legal disputes between the institutions of the EU are settled by the court, as are disputes between member states and institutions of the Union.

Economic and Social Committee (ESC)
The Economic and Social Committee is the official consultative and representative body of economic and social interest groups within the EU.

European Parliament
The European Parliament is made up of 626 members directly elected in their member states. Members sit in their political groupings in the parliament. Part sessions are held in Strasbourg, committee meetings are held in Brussels.
The role of the parliament includes:
1 Scrutinizing EU legislation.
2 Questioning the Council of Ministers and the Commission.
3 Joint responsibility for the EU budget with the Council of Ministers.
4 Ratifying international association and cooperation agreements.

VOTES: COUNCIL OF MINISTERS		MEMBERS OF THE ESC		SEATS IN THE PARLIAMENT	
Austria	4	Austria	12	Austria	21
Belgium	5	Belgium	12	Belgium	25
Denmark	3	Denmark	9	Denmark	16
Finland	3	Finland	9	Finland	16
France	10	France	24	France	87
Germany	10	Germany	24	Germany	99
Greece	5	Greece	12	Greece	25
Ireland	3	Ireland	9	Ireland	15
Italy	10	Italy	24	Italy	87
Luxembourg	2	Luxembourg	6	Luxembourg	6
Netherlands	5	Netherlands	12	Netherlands	31
Portugal	5	Portugal	12	Portugal	25
Spain	8	Spain	21	Spain	64
Sweden	4	Sweden	12	Sweden	22
U.K.	10	U.K.	24	U.K.	87

CIVIL RIGHTS

Civil rights are the freedoms and rights of individuals living within a community. They are guaranteed by laws and customs, and many countries' constitutions include a bill of rights which defines the minimum rights of every citizen. Many civil rights, including universal suffrage, freedom of speech, and freedom of religious belief, were only achieved in some countries after violent conflict. However, thanks to public spirit and the guiding force of a few pioneers, most citizens of democratic countries can expect to have their freedoms assured and to be protected from unfair treatment under the law.

Whether civil rights are written in a constitution or a matter of custom and evolution, they depend on the goodwill and faith of those in power. Oppressive regimes still ignore civil rights and abuse their power. Willing participation and subscription to civil rights is vital to ensure they protect and work effectively.

Both the United Nations and the European Union have declarations on human rights and the UN Universal Declaration of Human Rights is recognized as the benchmark for civil rights.

Timeline of civil rights in the 1900s

1902 Workers and students strike in Italy, Russia, and U.S.A. in demand for recognition of organized unions.
1903 U.K.: Emmeline Pankhurst founds Women's Social and Political Union (WSPU) to fight for female franchise.
1905 Russia: Tsar Nicholas II grants constitution guaranteeing civil liberties, but it is withdrawn within a year.
1906 Finland: women taxpayers over 24 achieve franchise; South Africa: Mahatma Gandhi launches campaign of nonviolent resistance to discrimination.
1908 U.K.: Emmeline Pankhurst imprisoned; Denmark: all taxpayers over 25 achieve suffrage.
1909 U.S.A.: National Association for the Advancement of Colored People (NAACP) founded in New York.
1910 China: slavery abolished.
1911 Japan: Racho Hiratsuka launches feminist movement; U.K.: Trade Disputes Act guarantees the right to strike and to picket peacefully.
1912 South Africa: South African Native Education Association set up (later African National Congress); Austria: election of first woman MP vetoed by Prince Thun of Bohemia.
1913 U.S.A.: National Woman's Party founded by Alice Paul; U.K.: Emmeline Pankhurst sentenced for inciting her supporters to arson; suffragette Emily Davison is killed when she runs in front of the king's horse at the Epsom Derby.
1914 U.S.A.: Colorado state militia kills 21 workers demonstrating for recognition of their union; Turkey: women admitted to universities.

Emmeline Pankhurst at an election rally.

1915 U.S.A.: Ku Klux Klan inaugurated under legal charter in Georgia.

1917 U.S.A.: 15,000 blacks march in silence down Fifth Avenue in New York City to protest against racial violence; Congressional Union for Woman Suffrage pickets the White House.

1918 U.K.: women over 30 and all men over 21 accorded franchise; Commons votes to admit women members.

1919 U.S.A.: Supreme Court formulates a "clear and present danger" test for defining conditions under which the constitutional right of freedom of speech may be abridged; Germany: Spartacist leaders arrested after an insurrection inspired by their party; India: 379 independence activists killed by British army in the Amritsar Massacre; U.K.: royal assent given to Sex Disqualification Removal Bill.

1920 U.S.A.: foundation of American Civil Liberties Union; women get the vote; Switzerland: opening of the International Feminist Congress in Geneva.

1926 South Africa: blacks banned from occupying certain skilled jobs.

1927 U.K.: Trade Disputes Act prohibits sympathy strikes.

1928 Italy: 70 percent of Italians disenfranchised in Mussolini's electoral reforms; U.K.: all women win franchise.

1929 U.S.A.: 2,000-strong lynch mob in Mississippi burns alleged black rapist to death — coroner's jury returns verdict of death "due to unknown causes."

1930 Liberia: U.S.-League of Nations commission reports that slavery still exists in Liberia; India: Mahatma Gandhi begins his campaign of civil disobedience; South Africa: white women achieve suffrage.

1932 U.S.A.: Supreme Court rules that defendants in capital cases in state courts must have adequate legal representation; police open fire on 3,000 demonstrators in Dearborn, Michigan, killing four; U.S.S.R.: Stalin sends troops to Ukraine and the Caucasus to requisition all foodstuffs and blockade railroad lines in crackdown on *kulaks* (rich peasants) resisting collectivization.

1933 U.S.A.: National Labor Board established; Germany: first Nazi concentration camp set up at Dachau.

1935 U.S.S.R.: Stalin decrees children over 12 subject to the same punitive laws as adults; Germany: Nuremberg Laws remove citizenship from Jews.

1936 South Africa: segregation laws passed; U.S.S.R.: Great Purge begins — around 8–10 million opponents of Stalin killed over the next two years.

1937 Albania: Muslim revolt in protest against governmental decree forbidding the wearing of the veil; Germany: Jews evicted from trade and industry, ordered to wear yellow stars of David and barred from public areas; U.S.A.: Henry Ford employs 600 armed thugs to prevent the unionization of workers in his car factories; Supreme Court upholds principle of a minimum wage for women.

1940 U.S.A.: Alien Registration Act requires all immigrants to be fingerprinted and outlaws the advocation of the overthrow of the government.

1941 U.S.A.: President Roosevelt calls for the worldwide protection of the Four Freedoms: freedom of speech and expression, freedom of religion, freedom from want, freedom from fear; Fair Employment Practice Committee founded.

1942 U.S.A.: about 110,000 Japanese-Americans are interned; foundation of Congress of Racial Equality (CORE).

1944 U.S.A.: Supreme Court rules that no American can be denied the right to vote because of color.

1945 France: women achieve suffrage.

1946 Japan and Italy: women achieve suffrage.

1947 Japan: women gain equal status with regard to property and divorce; India: "untouchability" outlawed; U.S.A.: Taft-Hartley Act restricts unions' power to strike and empowers the government to obtain injunctions where strikes "will imperil the national health or safety."

1948 UN: Universal Declaration of Human Rights adopted; U.S.A.: Executive Order 9981 ends racial segregation in armed forces.

1949 Hungary: anti-Communist Cardinal Mindszenty is convicted and sentenced to life imprisonment; U.K.: House of Lords votes to allow women members.

1949-60 *c.* 26.3 million Chinese killed in enforcement of communization.

1950 U.S.A.: McCarran Act introduces severe restrictions against suspected Communists; South Africa: anti-apartheid riots; Korea: UN forces and troops of both sides commit gross human rights violations against POWs and execute many alleged collaborators without trial.

1955 U.S.A.: Supreme Court orders desegregation of all public places; South Africa: legal obstacles to the creation of further apartheid laws are removed.

1956 U.S.A.: Martin Luther King, Jr.'s home in Montgomery bombed; southern congressmen issue a manifesto pledging to use "all lawful means" to disrupt the Supreme Court's desegregation ruling; King leads Montgomery bus boycott following the arrest of Rosa Parks in 1955 for refusing to relinquish her seat to a white passenger; Poland: over 100

King delivers his "I have a dream" speech.

demonstrators killed as Soviet militia suppress riot of workers at Poznan; South Africa: government orders more than 100,000 nonwhites in Johannesburg to leave their homes within a year.

1957 U.S.A.: federal troops sent in to Central High School, Little Rock, Arkansas, when crowds prevent nine black children from entering the school; Civil Rights Commission established; U.K.: Report of the Committee on Homosexual Offences and Prostitution recommends end to punitive laws against homosexual acts between consenting adults in private.

1958 Morocco: women achieve the right to choose their own husbands.

1959 UN: General Assembly votes to condemn racial discrimination; Switzerland: constitutional amendment allowing women to vote in national elections is rejected in referendum.

1960 South Africa: Sharpeville massacre — police open fire on antiapartheid demonstrations in Johannesburg, killing 72; state of emergency imposed and 22,000 people are arrested; African National Congress (ANC) and Pan-African Congress (PAC) are banned.

1962 U.S.A.: riots break out at University of Mississippi when black student James Howard Meredith attempts to take his place.

1963 Martin Luther King Jr., makes his historic "I have a dream" speech in Washington D.C.; more than 200,000 black and white demonstrators march on Washington D.C. in support of civil rights reforms; Congress votes to guarantee women equal pay for equal work; NAACP leader, Medger Evers, murdered in Jackson, Mississippi.

1964 U.S.A.: 75-day filibuster by southern senators to block Civil Rights Bill fails and bill becomes law; three civil rights workers killed by white supremacists discovered in Philadelphia, Mississippi; sit-in at University of California staged by Free Speech Movement ends with 732 arrests; South Africa: Nelson Mandela and seven other civil rights leaders sentenced to life imprisonment for sabotage and subversion; General Laws Amendment Act empowers police to hold suspects for up to six months without reporting their arrests; U.K. (Northern Ireland): foun-

De Klerk congratulates Mandela, 1994

dation of Campaign for Social Justice to fight anti-Catholic discrimination.

1965 U.S.A.: Malcolm X shot dead as he prepares to speak on racial harmony; Martin Luther King, Jr. and 770 supporters arrested at Selma, Alabama during civil rights demonstration; white civil rights leader Viola Liuzzo murdered by four Ku Klux Klansmen near Montgomery; Voting Rights Act becomes law.

1966 U.S.A.: foundation of National Organization for Women; Supreme Court rules that police must advise anyone taken into custody of their rights to council and to remain silent; first black senator elected in Massachusetts.

1967 U.S.A.: Martin Luther King, Jr. calls for a large-scale civil disobedience campaign for civil rights reforms; first black Supreme Court justice sworn in.

1968 U.S.A.: Martin Luther King, Jr. assassinated; Chicago's Mayor Daley gives police a "shoot to kill" order to quell riots following King's death.

1969 U.S.A.: gay rights movement emerges.

1970 U.K.: internment introduced in Northern Ireland.

1971 U.S.A.: Supreme Court reverses 1966 decision and rules that the prosecution may use a defendant's statement in a trial whether or not he or she was advised of his or her rights upon arrest; rioting in Attica Correctional Facility, New York, after inmates discover differences in sentences and parole decisions that appear to have a racial basis.

1972 U.K.: 13 Catholic civil rights marchers shot dead by British soldiers in Northern Ireland (Bloody Sunday).

1975 U.S.A.: American Civil Liberties Union wins compensation for those arrested in antiwar demonstrations in 1971; Age Discrimination Act passed by Congress; Cambodia: Khmer Rouge begins slaughter of intellectuals, political enemies, and peasants, marriage is abolished and all people over the age of ten are put to work in the fields.

1976 China: more than 100,000 political prisoners released; India: government upholds the right to imprison political opponents without trial; South Africa: Soweto Uprising — 176 die when police open fire on protesters against compulsory teaching of Afrikaans in schools.

1978 U.S.A.: Bakke Decision encourages positive discrimination to assist ethnic minorities to get university places.

1979 Iran: women march in Tehran to protest against revocation of the family protection law; U.S.S.R.: many dissidents and Jews allowed to emigrate.

1980 Poland: Solidarity becomes the first independent trade union in the Soviet block; El Salvador: leading human rights activist Archbishop Oscar Arnulfo Romero murdered.

1981 Poland: Solidarity is outlawed.

1983 U.S.A.: congressional committee reports that WWII internment of Japanese-Americans was a "grave injustice" driven by racial prejudice.

1984 Poland: security police murder pro-Solidarity priest Jerzy Popieluszko; Chile: 32,000 alleged leftists arrested and detained for questioning about anti-Pinochet demonstrations.

1985 South Africa: state of emergency declared, giving police almost unlimited power in black townships.

1986 U.S.A.: Supreme Court Rules that states have th eright to outlaw private homosexual acts between consenting adults; Martin Luther King Jr.'s birthday becomes a national holiday; South Africa: "subversive" press reports banned; antiapartheid demonstrations result in abolition of pass laws; U.S.S.R.: several political prisoners released.

1987 U.S.A.: Supreme Court rules that Rotary clubs must admit women.

1988 U.K.: Clause 28 prohibits local government and state schools from in any way promoting homosexuality as an acceptable alternative lifestyle.

1989 U.S.A.: Internment Compensation Act awards $20,000 to each Japanese-American surviving victim of wartime internment; China (Beijing): hundreds of students are killed when troops open fire on prodemocracy demonstration in Tiananmen Square.

1990 U.S.A.: Americans with Disabilities Act outlaws discrimination against disabled people; South Africa: Nelson Mandela released; ANC legalized; Separate Amenities Act repealed; U.S.S.R.: freedom of religious belief restored.

1992 U.S.A.: Supreme Court rules that using as evidence a confession elicited with coercive methods can be "harmless error"; acquittal of policemen charged with beating of unarmed black motorist Rodney King, in 1991, prompts the worst riots in U.S. history; South Africa: all-white referendum votes overwhelmingly in favor of free elections.

1994 South Africa: first free elections bring Mandela to power; U.K.: Criminal Justice Bill removing certain rights and increasing police powers incites large-scale demonstrations.

1995 U.S.A.: slavery is outlawed in Mississippi.

REFUGEES

As a result of wars, revolutions, and persecution of minority groups, the world's refugee population is growing steadily. In 1970, refugees numbered 2.5 million; in 1993 there were an estimated 19 million refugees worldwide.

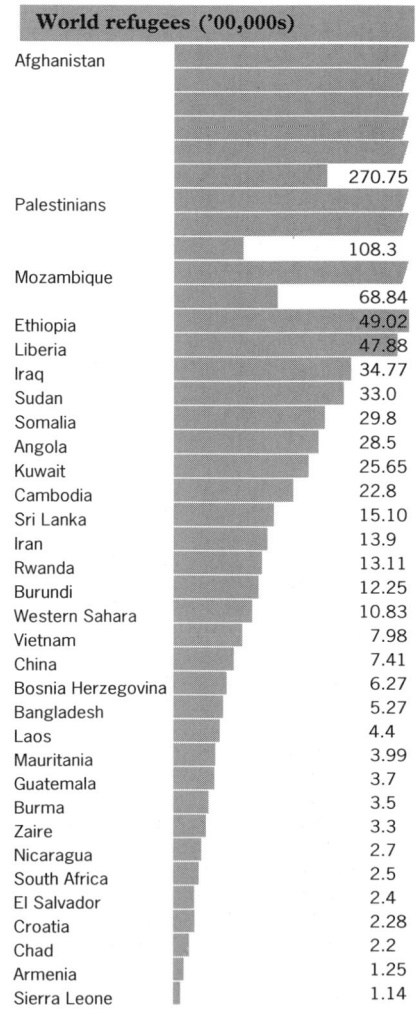

World refugees ('00,000s)	
Afghanistan	
	270.75
Palestinians	
	108.3
Mozambique	
	68.84
Ethiopia	49.02
Liberia	47.88
Iraq	34.77
Sudan	33.0
Somalia	29.8
Angola	28.5
Kuwait	25.65
Cambodia	22.8
Sri Lanka	15.10
Iran	13.9
Rwanda	13.11
Burundi	12.25
Western Sahara	10.83
Vietnam	7.98
China	7.41
Bosnia Herzegovina	6.27
Bangladesh	5.27
Laos	4.4
Mauritania	3.99
Guatemala	3.7
Burma	3.5
Zaire	3.3
Nicaragua	2.7
South Africa	2.5
El Salvador	2.4
Croatia	2.28
Chad	2.2
Armenia	1.25
Sierra Leone	1.14

NOBEL PEACE PRIZE WINNERS

1901 Jean Henri Dunant (Switzerland), founder of Red Cross; Frédéric Passy (France), founder of French Peace Society.

1902 Élie Ducommun (Switzerland), secretary of International Peace Bureau; Charles Albert Gobat (Switzerland), administrator of International Arbitration League.

1903 William R. Cremer (G.B.), founder of International Arbitration League.

1904 Institute of International Law, for studies on laws of neutrality.

1905 Bertha von Suttner (Austria), founder of Austrian Peace Society.

1906 Theodore Roosevelt (U.S.A.), peace negotiator in Russo-Japanese War.

1907 Ernesto T. Moneta (Italy), president of Lombard League for Peace; Louis Renault (France), organizer of peace conferences.

1908 Klas Pontus Arnoldson (Sweden), founder of Swedish Society for Arbitration and Peace; Fredrik Bajer (Denmark), for work with International Peace Bureau.

1909 Auguste M. F. Beernaert (Belgium), for work on Permanent Court of Arbitration; Paul d'Estournelles (France), founder of League of International Conciliation.

1910 International Peace Bureau, organizer of peace conferences.

1911 Tobias M. C. Asser (Netherlands), organizer of international law conferences; Alfred H. Fried (Austria), writer of *Die Friedenswarte*.

1912 Elihu Root (U.S.A.), organizer of Central American Peace Conference.

1913 Henri La Fontaine (Belgium), president of International Peace Bureau.

1914–16 No award.

1917 International Red Cross, for work during World War I.

1918 No award.

1919 Woodrow Wilson (U.S.A.), for work on League of Nations.

1920 Léon Bourgeois (France), president of Council of League of Nations.

1921 Karl Hjalmar Branting (Sweden), for social reforms in Sweden; Christian Louis Lange (Norway), secretary-general of Inter-Parliamentary Union.

1922 Fridtjof Nansen (Norway), for relief work in Russian famine areas.

1923–24 No award.

1925 Sir Austen Chamberlain (U.K.), for work on Locarno Peace Pact; Charles G. Dawes (U.S.A.), originator of plan for payment of German reparations.

1926 Aristide Briand (France), for work on Locarno Peace Pact; Gustav Stresemann (Germany), for work on German reparation agreement.

1927 Ferdinand Buisson (France), president of League of Human Rights; Ludwig Quidde (Germany), for work in international peace congresses.

1928 No award.

1929 Frank Billings Kellogg (U.S.A.), negotiator of Kellogg-Briand Peace Pact.

1930 Nathan Söderblom (Sweden), for writings on and work for peace.

1931 Jane Addams (U.S.A.), for work on Women's International League for Peace and Freedom; Nicholas M. Butler (U.S.A.), for work with Carnegie Endowment for International Peace.

1932 No award.

1933 Sir Norman Angell (U.K.), for work in Royal Institute of International Affairs and League of Nations.

1934 Arthur Henderson (U.K.), chairman of World Disarmament Conference.

1935 Carl von Ossietzky (Germany), for work toward world disarmament.

1936 Carlos Saavedra Lamas (Argentina), peace negotiator between Bolivia and Paraguay in Chaco War.

1937 Sir Edgar Algernon Cecil (U.K.), for work with League of Nations.

1938 Nansen International Office of Refugees, for relief work for refugees.

1939–43 No award.

1944 International Red Cross, for relief work in World War II.

1945 Cordell Hull (U.S.A.), who worked for peace as secretary of state.

1946 John R. Mott (U.S.A.), for YMCA and refugee work; Emily Greene Balch (U.S.A.), who worked with Women's International League for Peace and Freedom.

1948 No award.

1949 John Boyd Orr (U.K.), director FAO.

1950 Ralph J. Bunche (U.S.A.), UN mediator in Palestine.

1951 Léon Jouhaux (France), organizer of labor unions.

1952 Albert Schweitzer (Germany), for humanitarian work in Africa.

1953 George C. Marshall (U.S.A.), pioneer of European Recovery Program.

1954 Office of the United Nations High Commissioner for Refugees, for protection of millions of refugees.

1955–56 No award.

1957 Lester B. Pearson (Canada), organizer of UN force in Egypt.

1958 Dominique Georges Pire (Belgium), for work resettling refugees.

1959 Philip Noel-Baker (U.K.), for work on disarmament and peace.

1960 Albert John Luthuli (South Africa), for peaceful resistance to apartheid.

1961 Dag Hammarskjöld (Sweden), for peace work in the Congo (posthumous).

1962 Linus Pauling (U.S.A.), for work toward ban on nuclear weapons tests.

1963 International Committee of the Red Cross, for humanitarian work.

1964 Martin Luther King, Jr. (U.S.A.), for nonviolent campaign for racial equality.

1965 United Nations International Children's Emergency Fund (UNICEF).

1966–67 No award.

1968 René Cassin (France), for work on human rights.

1969 International Labor Organization, for work to improve labor conditions.

1970 Norman E. Borlaug (U.S.A.), who developed high-yield cereals for Third World countries.

1971 Willy Brandt (Germany), for working toward détente with Communist countries.

1972 No award.

1973 Henry Kissinger (U.S.A.) and Le Duc Tho (North Vietnam), negotiators of cease-fire in Vietnam.

1974 Sean MacBride (Republic of Ireland), for work on human rights in international law; Eisaku Sato (Japan), for work to stop nuclear proliferation.

1975 Andrei Sakharov (U.S.S.R.), for work toward peace.

1976 Mairead Corrigan and Betty Williams (Northern Ireland), organizers of movement against sectarian violence in Northern Ireland.

1977 Amnesty International, for assisting political prisoners.

1978 Menachem Begin (Israel) and Anwar Sadat (Egypt), for attempts to end Arab-Israeli hostilities.

1979 Mother Teresa (Albania), for relief work with the poor in India.

1980 Adolfo Pérez Esquivel (Argentina), for assisting Service for Peace and Justice in Latin America.

1981 Office of the United Nations High Commissioner for Refugees, for protection of Bengali refugees.

1982 Alva R. Myrdal (Sweden) and Alfonso García Robles (Mexico), for helping UN disarmament negotiations.

1983 Lech Walesa (Poland), for improvement of workers' rights.

1984 Bishop Desmond Tutu (South Africa), nonviolent campaigner against apartheid.

1985 International Physicians for the Prevention of Nuclear War, for increasing public awareness of effects of nuclear war.

1986 Elie Wiesel (U.S.A.), for work on the behalf of the victims of racism.

1987 Oscar Arias Sanchez (Costa Rica), for plan to end Central American civil war.

1988 United Nations Peacekeeping Forces, who helped to control conflicts in Middle East and elsewhere.

1989 Tenzin Gyatso, 14th Dalai Lama (Tibet), who sought nonviolent means to end Chinese occupation of Tibet.

1990 Mikhail Gorbachev (U.S.S.R.), who worked to reduce East–West tensions and end the Cold War.

1991 Aung San Suu Kyi (Burma), for leading nonviolent struggle for democracy in Burma (Myanmar).

1992 Rigoberta Menchu (Guatemala), who strove for the establishment of democracy in Guatemala.

1993 Nelson Mandela (South Africa) and F. W. de Clerk (South Africa), for ending apartheid in South Africa.

1994 Yasser Arafat (Palestine), Yitshak Rabin (Israel), and Shimon Peres (Israel), for forging Israeli–Arab peace in the Middle East.

LAWMAKING

All societies need rules to define their members' rights and obligations. Public law does this in terms of the individual's relation to government. Branches of public law overlap but can be subdivided into criminal, constitutional, administrative, and international. Laws are usually the product of compromise and debate within a country's legislature, and often a great deal of time and money is invested to produce the final act or law.

All laws begin life as ideas. These ideas may be for the good of society, or may reflect strong opinions of a section of society. Pressure groups may be formed and petitions organized to gain support for the point of view and to publicize the cause. Evidence of popular support may persuade the group's political representative to back the proposal, and can also increase the validity of the proposal in the eyes of the legislature. When the representative has been approached, if he or she deems it a worthwhile proposal, or if it seems to have significant public support, he or she can work to have the idea submitted to the legislature as a bill.

Once the political representative accepts the concept and tries to promote the idea, compromise and bargaining become important factors. The representative must convince other members of the legislature that the idea is worthy. If pressure groups are effective, the idea will have prominence and a greater chance of success. It has by now evolved into a draft proposal, or bill, which must compete against other bills for discussion time in the legislature. If the bill is successful, it will move through the different procedures and chambers of the legislature. During these phases it may be amended to make it more acceptable to the other political representatives. Finally, the bill emerges from the legislature and becomes an act. Thus an idea becomes law.

COUNTRIES WITHOUT DEATH PENALTY

Africa
Côte d'Ivoire, Mozambique, Namibia

Asia
Cambodia, Nepal, Philippines

Australia and Oceania
Australia, New Zealand, Fiji

Europe
Austria, Belgium, Bulgaria, Czech Republic, Denmark, Finland, France, Germany, Greece (de facto), Hungary, Ireland, Italy, Netherlands, Norway, Portugal, Romania, Slovakia, Spain, Sweden, Switzerland, U.K.

Middle East
Israel

North America
Canada, Costa Rica, Dominican Republic, El Salvador, Honduras, Nicaragua

South America
Argentina, Colombia, Paraguay, Uruguay, Venezuela, Brazil

PASSAGE OF A PUBLIC BILL TO LAW IN THE UNITED KINGDOM

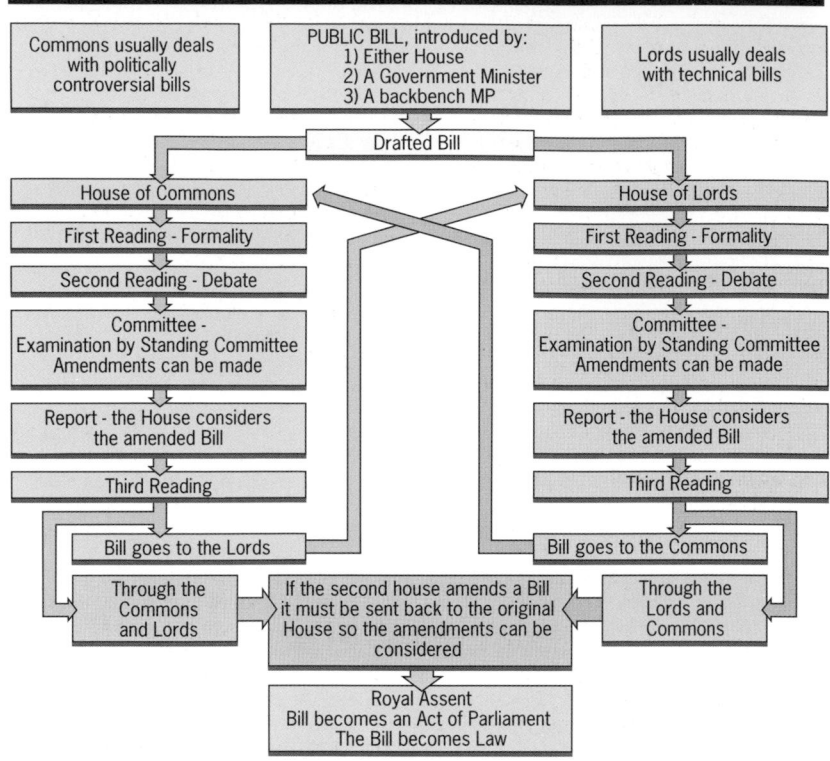

PASSAGE OF A BILL TO LAW IN THE UNITED STATES

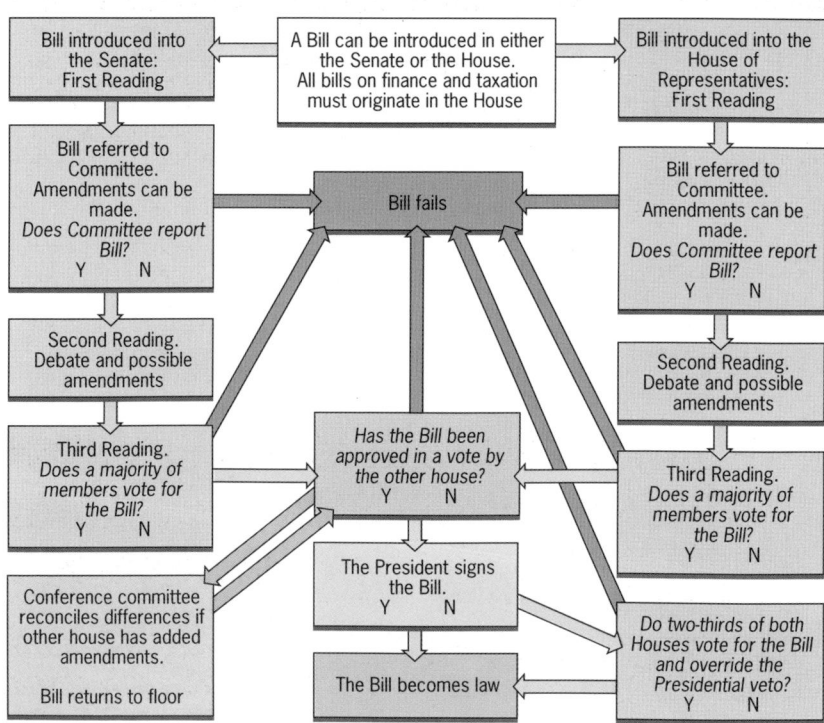

CHECKS AND BALANCES AT WORK

The Constitution establishes the mechanism whereby federal legislation is passed. At its root, the U.S. system relies on a series of "checks and balances," ensuring that no single branch of government (executive, legislative, or judicial) can exercise a monopoly on lawmaking. The founding fathers were familiar with the British system of lawmaking, in which bills are initiated in one of the two houses of parliament (the House of Commons and the House of Lords) and pass through a process of committee scrutiny and separate readings until receiving Royal approval. This system, although offering scope for detailed study of bills and impassioned debate, was fundamentally flawed in the eyes of the framers of the Constitution.

They recoiled at the idea of unelected bodies or individuals (such as the House of Lords and the reigning monarch) having even notional power to influence legislation. Moreover, if these unelected branches deferred to the wishes of their elected counterparts, then a party holding a majority in the House of Commons could force through — or veto — proposed legislation freely. In effect, they foresaw that the House of Commons could become an "elected dictatorship" (in the words of a 20th-century British jurist).

The system of checks and balances adopted by the United States (*above left*) echoes that of Great Britain (*below left*). Bills in each country pass through a similar process of readings, refinements, and debate in both houses. However, the strength of each U.S. element — the House of Representatives, Senate, and president — is underpinned by a popular mandate, so there is no temptation to "rubber stamp" legislation passed by another branch. Also, the U.S. system allows more scope for "cross-party" alliances, often dictated by shared regional concerns.

Recent history has demonstrated the complexity of the U.S. system at work. President Bill Clinton had democratic majorities in both Houses of Congress for the first two years of his presidency. However, his "flagship" piece of legislation — the health care reform package — was defeated after long and sometimes bitter debates. The triumphant Republican takeover of both Houses following the 1994 elections seemed to predict a diminished role for the president in the face of Congressional opposition. But some Republicans soon distanced themselves from supporting the more radical budget-reducing measures, rather than brand themselves as "extremists" at odds with a "reasonable" president.

COURTS IN THE UNITED STATES

The third branch of government outlined by the U.S. Constitution is the judicial branch. The court system in the United States consists of federal and state courts.

Federal Courts
The U.S. Supreme Court, comprising the chief justice of the United States and eight associate justices, is the highest court in the country. Justices are appointed by the president and approved by the Senate. The supreme court hears appeals of cases that were tried in federal courts and the highest state courts. It interprets whether federal, state, and local laws are

constitutional. In this respect it acts as a check and balance to Congress and the president. There are 94 federal district courts as well as regional Courts of Appeal, and courts dealing with specific cases such as international trade, tax, and bankruptcy.

State Courts
State courts are independent of the federal courts. The highest state court is usually called a state supreme court. There are also state appellate courts of general jurisdiction. County and municiple courts also operate within states.

STRUCTURE OF THE COURT SYSTEM IN THE UNITED STATES

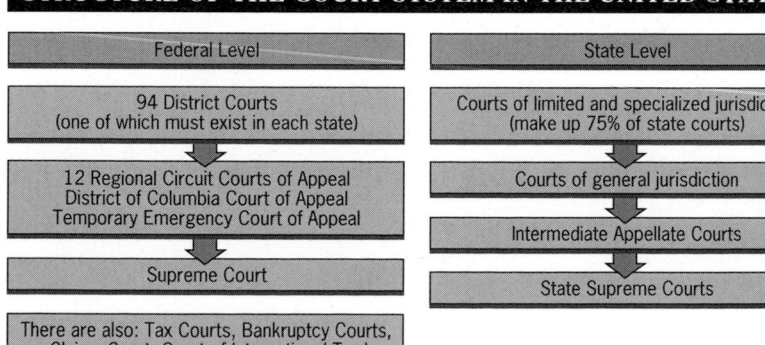

LEGISLATIVE SYSTEMS OF GOVERNMENT

A bicameral political system is one in which there are two chambers in the legislature, whereas a unicameral system has only one chamber. There are 57 countries in the world which operate under the bicameral system and 119 under the unicameral system.

BICAMERAL
Africa
Burkina Faso, Central African Republic, Liberia, Madagascar, Mauritania, Swaziland

Asia
India, Japan, Philippines, Thailand

Australia and Oceania
Australia, Fiji

Europe
Austria, Belgium, Czech Republic, France, Germany, Ireland, Italy, Netherlands, Poland, Romania, Russian Federation, Spain, Switzerland, U.K., Yugoslavia (Serbia and Montenegro)

Middle East
Afghanistan, Jordan

North America
Antigua and Barbuda, Bahamas, Barbados, Belize, Canada, Dominican Republic, Grenada, Haiti, Jamaica, Puerto Rico, St. Lucia, Trinidad and Tobago, U.S.A.

South America
Argentina, Bolivia, Chile, Columbia, Paraguay, Peru, Uruguay, Venezuela

UNICAMERAL
Africa
Algeria, Angola, Benin, Botswana, Burundi, Cameroon, Cape Verde, Chad, Comoros, Congo, Côte d'Ivoire, Djibouti, Equatorial Guinea, Gabon, Gambia, Ghana, Guinea-Bissau, Kenya, Lesotho, Malawi, Mali, Mauritius, Mozambique, Namibia, Nigeria, São Tomé and Principe, Senegal, Seychelles, Sierra Leone, Sudan, Tanzania, Togo, Tunisia, Zaire, Zambia

Asia
Bangladesh, Bhutan, Brunei, Cambodia, China, Indonesia, Kazakhstan, Laos, Nepal, North Korea, Singapore, South Korea, Sri Lanka, Turkmenistan, Uzbekistan, Vietnam

Australia and Oceania
Kiribati, New Zealand, Papua New Guinea, Solomon Islands, Tonga, Tuvalu, Vanuatu, Western Samoa

Europe
Albania, Andorra, Belarus, Bulgaria, Croatia, Cyprus, Denmark, Estonia, Finland, Gibraltar, Greece, Greenland, Hungary, Iceland, Liechtenstein, Lithuania, Luxembourg, Macedonia, Malta, Moldova, Norway, Portugal, San Marino, Slovakia, Slovenia, Sweden, Ukraine

Middle East
Armenia, Azerbaijan, Egypt, Iran, Iraq, Israel, Kuwait, Lebanon, Syria, Turkey, United Arab Emirates, Yemen

North America
Costa Rica, Cuba, El Salvador, Guatemala, Honduras, Nicaragua, Panama, St. Christopher (Kitts) Nevis, St. Vincent and the Grenadines

South America
Ecuador, Guyana, Suriname

CRIME AND THE LAW

Crime is a violation of criminal law which is created to protect members of society from individual acts that might harm them. The purpose of rules and laws within society is to enable individuals to live together. Crimes, such as theft, rape, and murder, that by their very nature are damaging to individuals are viewed as a threat to the fabric of society and are therefore classed as crimes against the state. However, most acts that harm individuals are also violations of civil law and can therefore be brought to trial as civil cases as well as public cases.

Types of crime

Crimes can be classified in a number of ways. For statistical purposes, governments usually divide offenses into crimes against people, crimes against property, and crimes against public order or morality. Sociologists often classify crimes according to the motivation that lies behind them. Therefore we can have economic crimes, political crimes, and crimes of passion. Other divisions are organized crime and white-collar crime.

Crimes are also divided into those that are widely considered to be immoral, and those that the legislature deems to be detrimental to the functioning of society. The first group, which includes murder, rape, and robbery, consists of crimes that are considered serious in all countries and incur heavy penalties, including, in 36 states and in a number of other countries, the death penalty. The second type, which includes violations of tax laws, drug laws, and traffic laws, are called regulatory offences and are generally punished by fines or court orders.

Juvenile delinquency

The age at which a person is deemed to become an adult before the law varies from country to country, but children under the age of 17 are regarded as juveniles in most countries.

Juvenile delinquency is a serious social problem and is increasing in many countries at an alarming rate. It is particularly common in industrialized nations with large cities, and is more likely to occur in societies in which the gap between rich and poor is greatest.

Many efforts have been made to reduce the number of children and adolescents who turn to crime. Statistics show that people who were involved in criminal acts in their youth are likely to continue in that way of life as adults, so it is important to find ways of rehabilitating young offenders. Some institutions offer treatment programs for young offenders, which include work programs, education, and counseling, but as yet this is exceptional and many young offenders receive no help while they are in custody.

MURDERS AND DRUG OFFENCES 1989-90

Country	Murders 1989	Murders 1990	Drug offenses 1989	Drug offenses 1990
Africa				
Botswana	254	NA	1,112	NA
Burundi	334	187	675	333
CAR	49	NA	158	NA
Congo	96	29	60	26
Côte d'Ivoire	393	322	1,004	1,208
Djibouti	53	24	12	7
Gabon	21	22	178	21
Guinea	11	59	19	168
Kenya	902	999	9,543	6,642
Libya	87	101	423	469
Mauritius	28	26	788	943
Rwanda	254	428	785	649
Senegal	NA	NA	68	1,065
Seychelles	5	5	62	55
Swaziland	NA	NA	710	495
Tanzania	1,704	1,485	2,381	1,787
Zimbabwe	1,231	1,788	6,631	6,299
Asia				
Bangladesh	2,364	2,206	215	241
Brunei	5	NA	200	NA
China	19,590	21,214	547	3,670
Indonesia	1,554	1,534	312	364
Japan	1,308	1,238	25,428	22,095
Malaysia	322	NA	7,756	NA
Maldives	4	4	8	8
Myanmar	2,106	2,153	5,876	6,915
Nepal	306	407	251	200
Philippines	19,809	18,277	NA	NA
Singapore	70	44	NA	NA
South Korea	540	633	1,631	2,213
Sri Lanka	8,127	1,985	5,461	12,178
Thailand	5,740	5,334	68,647	8,745
Hong Kong	107	148	5,040	3,604
Oceania				
Fiji	12	32	135	127
Kiribati	3	9	NA	NA
Papua NG	356	289	158	271
Europe				
Austria	156	178	5,110	5,300
Belgium	233	221	3,537	3,014
Bulgaria	NA	NA	360	NA
Cyprus	9	18	78	51
Denmark	262	234	14,161	13,925
Finland	33	30	1,889	2,546
France	2,562	2,526	50,680	56,522
Germany	2,415	2,419	94,000	103,629
Greece	184	1,750	204	1,986
Hungary	306	319	54	42
Ireland	24	29	47	47
Italy	1,583	3,676	30,180	30,691
Luxembourg	44	8	803	751
Malta	26	37	220	180
Monaco	1	NA	60	59
Netherlands	2,339	2,206	4,697	5,897
Norway	96	111	8,139	9,090
Poland	NA	NA	1,071	603
Portugal	417	287	2,010	1,524
Romania	344	789	21	14
Spain	919	963	23,555	20,910
Sweden	618	603	35,163	28,015
Switzerland	148	214	18,780	18,880
U.K.	1,820	1,923	16,444	19,778
Middle East				
Bahrain	NA	2,364	247	215
Egypt	739	859	8,521	7,699
Israel	122	107	8,034	7,803
Jordan	62	NA	115	NA
Qatar	7	11	45	85
Saudi Arabia	103	93	3,039	3,383
Syria	224	188	394	442
Turkey	895	949	1,035	1,014
North and Central America				
Anguilla	1	NA	14	12
Bahamas	93	134	955	1172
Barbados	18	30	510	555
Canada	1,486	NA	67,882	NA
Costa Rica	156	NA	217	NA
Grenada	10	NA	211	NA
Jamaica	439	542	4,086	5,533
St. Vincent and the Grenadines	17	11	352	343
Trinidad and Tobago	128	104	2,361	2921
U.S.A	21,500	23,440	NA	NA
South America				
Argentina	2,720	47	3,831	310
Chile	868	791	1,798	1,663
Paraguay	142	159	129	89

Murders per 100,000 people

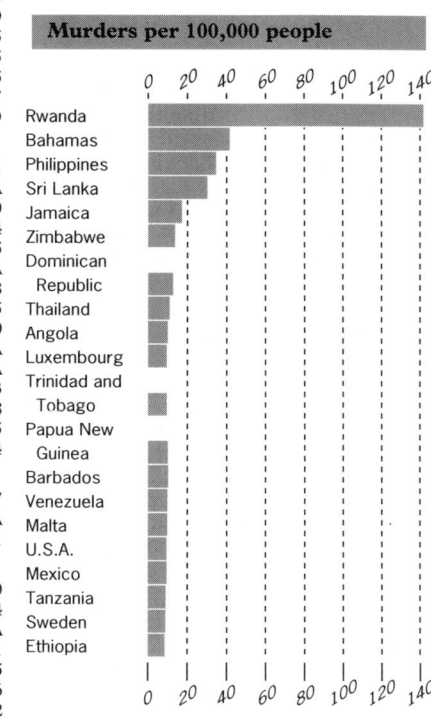

Drug offenses per 100,000 people

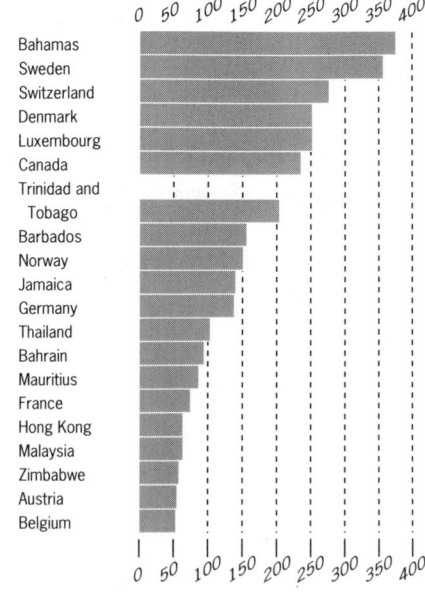

FAMOUS LAW ENFORCEMENT AGENCIES

Bicycle Squad (1895–1934) Specialist U.S. police squad formed to apprehend speeding motorists traveling above the speed limit of 30 mph(48 kph).

Bow Street Runners (1739–1829) A privately employed policing agency that was the forerunner of the London Metropolitan Police force.

Cheka (1917–22) First political police force employed in Russia following the revolution of 1917.

Drug Enforcement Agency The DEA is responsible for enforcing laws relating to the consumption and distribution of illegal narcotics in the U.S.A.

Federal Bureau of Investigation Founded in 1908, the FBI investigates the most serious federal crimes. The agency holds over 50 million finger-prints and 100 million noncriminal files on U.S. Citizens.

GPU (1920s) Soviet secret police, who took over from Cheka in 1922. Officers held sweeping powers of arrest and were immune from regulation and control.

Interpol (International Criminal Police Organization) Data-collecting and information-dispensing agency, founded in 1914, to which almost all national law enforcement agencies belong. Interpol itself is not a law enforcement agency.

OGPU (1924–34) Replacing the U.S.S.R.'s GPU, OGPU focused on political opponents of the Communist system, imprisoning or killing suspects.

Scotland Yard Founded in 1829, the headquarters of the London Metro politan Police is responsible for original law enforcement in greater London area. It often aids investigations in out-lying counties.

Secret Service Agency Founded in 1865, this part of the U.S. Treasury Department is responsible for the pro-tection of the president and Treasury Department, and the apprehension of counterfeiters.

Stasi (1970s–80s) Plainclothes police and security organization serving the Communist regime in East Germany.

FAMOUS LAW ENFORCERS

Abberline, Frederick (1843–1929) Officer in charge of the Jack the Ripper investigation in London.

Anslinger, Harry Jacob (1892–1975) Identified the existence of the Mafia in the U.S.A.

Bertillon, Alphonse (1853–1914) Frenchman generally accredited as the creator of forensic science for establish-ing the first universal identification system.

Bravo-Murillo, Juan Gonzalez (1803–73) Spanish lawyer who founded the first law journal in Spain.

Cherril, Fred (1892–1964) Foremost U.S. expert in fingerprinting.

Dow, Neal (1804–97) Drafted prohibi-tion laws in the U.S.A..

Earp brothers (1870s–80s) Famous law enforcers of the American West who took part in the gunfight at the OK Corral in Tombstone, Arizona, in 1881.

Gonzalez, T.A. (1930s) Pioneered the nitrate test in the U.S.A. to determine if a victim's gunshot wound is self-inflicted or not.

Hoover, John Edgar (1895–72) Controversial head (1924–72) of the FBI who fought organized crime in the 1930s and Communist subversion dur-ing the Cold War.

Lombroso, Cesare (1835–1909) Italian credited as the founder of criminology.

McParland, James (1844–1919) U.S. undercover detective who infiltrated a secret society of Irish subversives, the Molly Maguires, undermining the group.

Ness, Eliot (1902–57) Head of the "untouchables," a special prohibition squad in Chicago during the 1920s. He pursued Al Capone.

Pinkerton, Allan (1819–84) Founder in 1950 of the Pinkerton detective agency, initially to track down famous criminals in Chicago. Today the agency investi-gates fraudulent insurance claims.

Serpico, Francisco Vincent (b. 1936) Uncovered corruption in the New York Police Department.

Vyshinsky, Andrei (1883–1954) Re-nowned for prosecuting cases in the Great Purge trials in the U.S.S.R., 1934–38.

Warren, Charles (1840–1927) Police commissioner while Jack the Ripper was operating in London.

FAMOUS CRIMINALS AND CRIMES

Barker family A gang composed of a mother and her four sons who mur-dered, kidnapped, and robbed through-out the Midwest in the 1930s.

Barrow, Clyde Champion (1909–34) and **Parker, Bonnie** (1910–34) No-torious duo who murdered and robbed throughout the Southwest, 1932–34.

Berkowitz, David (b. 1953) "Son of Sam," mass murderer who terrorized New Yorkers in 1976–77, publicizing his crimes through correspondence with New York City newspapers.

Bonnie and Clyde *See* Barrow.

Brinks robbery Most famous robbery in the U.S.A. in the 1950s. Small-time "underworld" crooks stole a total of $2,775,395.

Bundy, Theodore (1947–89) Murdered between 20 and 40 women throughout the U.S.A. between 1974 and 1978.

Capone, Al(phonse) (1899–1947) An internationally renowned gangster, Capone racketeered, murdered, and robbed in Chicago in the 1920s–30s.

Christie, John (1898–1953) British mass murderer who killed several women between 1943 and the early 1950s.

Crippen, Hawley Harvey (1862–1910) U.S. doctor executed for poisoning his wife. The first murderer to be apprehended by the use of wireless telegraph, which was used to contact the ship on which he made his escape from Britain.

Dahmer, Jeffrey (1958-1995) Murdered at least 18 people in Wiscon-sin, cannibalizing some of their corpses.

Dillinger, John Herbert (b. 1903) Famous gangster, bank robber, and mur-derer in the U.S.A. during the 1930s.

Ellis, Ruth (1926–55) The last woman to be hanged in Britain, having been convicted of the murder of her lover.

Great Train Robbery Sensational rob-bery in Britain in 1963, which netted more than £4,000,000 for the gang who masterminded it. They stopped a train and stole mailbags containing banknotes assigned for shredding.

Gutkind, Johann Agile burglar known as the "human fly" who operated in Berlin during the 1920s.

Haigh, John George (1909–49) Known as the "acid bath murderer," Haigh killed people for their money in Britain during the 1940s and disposed of the corpses in a vat of acid.

Jack the Ripper Britain's most famous unsolved case: six prostitutes were mur-dered and mutilated in London between 1888 and 1891.

Kelly, Edward (Ned) (1855–80) Austra-lia's most famous bushranger, he achie-ved folk hero status in his two-year fight against the authorities (1878-80). After several successful bank raids, his gang was besieged by police at Glenrowan, New South Wales, and Kelly was subse-quently hanged.

Kray, Reginald (b. 1933) **and Kray, Ronald** (1933–95) Controlled orga-nized crime in the East End of London during the 1960s.

Manson, Charles (b. 1934) Leader of a murderous cult and criminal commune in the California in 1969.

Moors murders Myra Hyndley and Ian Brady committed a series of child mur-ders in the Manchester area of Britain in 1963 and 1964.

Nelson, George (1908–34) Infamous gangster known as "Baby-face Nelson," who robbed and murdered in the Midwest during the 1930s.

Nilsen, Dennis (b. 1945) Britain's worst mass murderer to date, Nilsen killed and mutilated the bodies of 15 men in London between 1979 and 1983.

Sutcliffe, Peter William (b. 1946) "The Yorkshire Ripper," as he was known, terrorized Britain during the 1970s, murdering a total of 13 women.

Unabomber Serial killer who has sent explosive devices in the mail to individ-uals involved with computers and tech-nology in the United States.

Zodiac murders Unsolved murders in California in the 1960s and 1970s.

EDUCATION AROUND THE WORLD

In most countries, formal education begins between ages four and seven as primary (or elementary) education. This is usually free and compulsory, and it is at this stage that children learn to read and write as well as how to do basic arithmetic. Pupils may then go on to secondary, and finally higher education. Children in many countries attend nursery school before going on to primary school. In a number of developing countries, a lack of resources means that many children do not even receive a primary education, and secondary and higher education are restricted to the privileged. This is illustrated in the literacy rates of these countries (p. 255). In most countries, apart from Canada and the U.S.A., education is, at least in part, run by the central or federal government.

ENROLLMENT RATIOS BY LEVEL OF EDUCATION

The following table shows the percentage of pupils within the relevant age group enrolled in primary and secondary education throughout the world. Students enrolled in higher education are expressed as a gross ratio, that is, the total number of pupils as a percentage of the population within the relevant age group.

Unless otherwise stated, figures are for 1992 and represent all types of school within the relevant level.

Country	Primary	Secondary	Higher
Africa			
Algeria	90	53	11.8
Benin (1989)	–	45	2.3
Botswana	99	44	5.2
Burkina Faso (1985)	25	4	0.6
Burundi	51	5	–
Cameroon (1989)	76	18	–
Central African Republic (1989)	56	10	1.5
Comoros (1985)	61	–	–
Côte d'Ivoire (1990)	52	12	–
Djibouti	34	-	–
Gambia	56	19	–
Guinea (1989)	26	7	–
Guinea Bissau (1988)	45	–	–
Lesotho	70	17	1.3
Malawi	48	2	–
Mali (1990)	19	5	0.8
Mauritius (1990)	92	47	2.1
Morocco (1990)	57	28	10.2
Mozambique	42	2	0.3
Namibia	81	29	–
Niger (1990)	25	6	–
Rwanda	72	8	–
Senegal	48	12	3.1
Somalia (1985)	8	3	2.3
Swaziland	91	–	0.3
Tanzania (1985)	55	3	0.3
Togo (1989)	73	19	2.6
Tunisia	99	–	10.7
Uganda (1986)	55	10	0.8
Zambia (1988)	81	16	2.2
Asia			
Afghanistan (1986)	19	–	1.7
Bahrain	85	86	19.3
Bangladesh (1990)	69	17	3.8
China (1991)	97	43	1.7
Cyprus (1991)	98	90	14.0
India (1989)	98	39	6.0
Indonesia	97	37	10.1
Iran (1991)	98	–	12.2
Iraq (1988)	94	40	13.8
Japan (1991)	100	97	31.5
Jordan	99	36	19.4
South Korea	100	88	41.6
Kuwait (1991)	45	–	13.8
Laos (1991)	59	15	–
Lebanon (1991)	–	–	27.8
Mongolia (1991)	–	–	15.3
Oman (1991)	82	50	6.2
Pakistan (1989)	40	19	2.8
Qatar (1990)	93	69	28.1
Saudi Arabia (1991)	62	34	13.7
Singapore (1989)	100	71	–
Sri Lanka (1991)	–	–	5.5
Syria	97	44	18.7
Turkey (1991)	100	44	14.8
United Arab Emirates	100	64	10.3
Australia and Oceania			
Australia	98	79	39.6
Fiji	99	56	–
New Zealand	100	85	49.7
Europe			
Austria	91	90	36.5
Belgium (1991)	100	99	–
Bulgaria	80	60	30.0
Denmark (1991)	95	86	37.6
Finland	–	–	57.0
France	100	87	45.6
Greece (1989)	93	87	25.0
Hungary (1991)	86	77	15.3
Ireland (1991)	90	81	37.9
Italy	–	–	33.7
Luxembourg (1986)	–	76	2.4
Malta (1990)	99	80	13.1
Netherlands (1991)	94	79	38.8
Norway	99	95	49.3
Poland	96	78	23.0
Portugal (1991)	100	52	23.4
Romania	78	72	11.9
Spain (1991)	100	88	39.5
Sweden (1991)	100	91	33.8
Switzerland	96	80	30.7
U.K. (1990)	97	80	27.8
Former Yugoslavia (1990)	–	–	17.9
Former U.S.S.R. (1990)	–	–	26.1
North America			
Barbados (1989)	96	80	17.8
Canada	100	93	98.8
Costa Rica	90	39	–
Cuba (1991)	97	67	19.4
Dominican Republic (1986)	73	51	–
El Salvador (1989)	71	15	17.4
Guatemala (1980)	58	13	8.4
Haiti (1990)	26	–	–
Honduras (1986)	91	21	8.9
Jamaica (1990)	100	61	6.0
Mexico	100	48	14.0
Nicaragua (1990)	78	37	9.8
Panama	92	50	21.7
Trinidad and Tobago	89	78	6.7
U.S.A.	98	78	71.7
South America			
Argentina (1987)	–	–	40.8
Bolivia (1990)	81	27	22.2
Brazil (1991)	86	16	11.7
Chile (1991)	87	55	23.3
Colombia (1991)	74	38	14.8
Ecuador (1990)	–	–	20.1
Guyana (1988)	–	20	5.1
Paraguay	98	28	–
Peru (1985)	97	49	24.3
Suriname (1988)	100	45	7.6
Uruguay (1990)	91	–	32
Venezuela (1990)	89	18	29.5

WORLD'S OLDEST UNIVERSITIES

King's College, Cambridge University, England.

Founded	Country	University (present name)
1158	Italy	Bologna
1215	France	Paris
1224	Italy	Naples
1229	France	Toulouse
1249	U.K.	Oxford
1254	Spain	Salamanca
1284	U.K.	Cambridge
1290	Portugal	Coimbra
1293	Spain	Valladolid
1347	Czech Republic	Charles University, Prague
1364	Poland	Jagiellonian University of Cracow
1365	Austria	Vienna
1386	Germany	Rupert Charles University of Heidelberg
1388	Germany	Cologne
1409	Germany	Leipzig
1410	U.K.	St. Andrews
1413	France	Aix, Marseilles
1419	Germany	Rostock
1425	Belgium	Catholic University of Louvain
1432	France	Poitiers
1450	Spain	Barcelona
1451	U.K.	Glasgow
1461	France	Rennes
1477	Sweden	Uppsala
1479	Denmark	Copenhagen
1495	U.K.	Aberdeen
1551	Mexico	Mexico
1551	Peru	San Marcos Lima
1573	Czech Republic	Palacky
1575	Netherlands	Leiden
1582	U.K.	Edinburgh
1592	Ireland	Dublin
1592	Malta	Malta
1595	Slovenia	Ljubljana
1614	Netherlands	Groningen
1625	Mexico	Queretaro
1632	Netherlands	Amsterdam
1635	Hungary	Eotvos Loránd
1636	Netherlands	Utrecht
1636	U.S.A.	Harvard
1640	Finland	Helsinki
1666	Sweden	Lund
1694	Romania	Bucharest
1701	U.S.A.	Yale
1740	U.S.A.	University of Pennsylvania
1742	U.S.A.	Moravian College
1746	U.S.A.	Princeton

WORLD LITERACY RATES

Population expansion and the consequential competition for scarce resources is one of the biggest problems facing the world today. Populations in the developing world are growing at a rapid rate; the reasons for this are complex. One factor that could be important in reducing the rate of population growth is the role of education. Improving the education of the people in the developing countries, including teaching them to read and write, has several knock-on effects. People who have been educated tend to have a greater understanding of economic opportunities, and their outlook becomes less insular. Moreover, people gain a greater understanding of the methods and techniques of birth control, the causes of disease, and the importance of hygiene and clean water.

Literacy rates differ greatly between countries, and are affected by cultural, religious, and ethnic factors. The socio-economic position of women in some societies also has a dramatic effect. The improvement of education and the subsequent benefits rely upon changing the perceptions of the members of a society and encouragement of new attitudes.

Village children attend a rudimentary school at Massangir in Mozambique.

WORLD LITERACY RATES

	Males	Females
Africa		
Algeria	63.0	36.9
Angola	49.0	32.0
Benin	39.8	16.6
Botswana	72.6	69.5
Burkina Faso	20.7	6.1
Burundi	61.0	40.0
Cameroon	70.2	45.0
Cape Verde	55.3	43.4
Central African Republic	58.8	20.4
Chad	42.2	18.0
Comoros	54.2	39.0
Congo	71.4	55.4
Cote d'Ivoire	67.0	40.0
Ethiopia	33.0	16.0
Gambia	35.6	15.1
Ghana	70.0	51.0
Guinea	39.7	17.2
Kenya	80.0	58.0
Lesotho	62.4	84.5
Libya	85.0	50.0
Madagascar	88.0	73.0
Mali	26.0	9.0
Mauritania	47.0	21.0
Morocco	61.0	38.0
Mozambique	44.0	14.0
Namibia	74.2	31.0
Niger	40.0	17.0
Nigeria	62.0	40.0
Rwanda	62.2	31.5
São Tomé and Principe	70.2	42.0
Sierra Leone	31.2	39.1
Somalia	36.0	14.2
South Africa	80.6	75.0
Sudan	36.5	12.0
Swaziland	70.3	65.0
Togo	51.7	31.0
Tunisia	74.0	65.7
Uganda	69.7	35.0
Zaire	84.0	61.0
Zambia	79.3	65.0
Zimbabwe	81.5	60.0
Asia		
Bangladesh	43.3	22.2
Bhutan	31.0	9.0
Brunei	86.5	72.8
China	83.5	68.0
Hong Kong	94.7	96.5
India	63.9	39.4
Indonesia	83.0	65.4
Japan	100.0	100.0

	Males	Females
Laos	52.8	37.6
Macao	93.0	86.0
Malaysia	82.2	63.2
Maldives	92.0	92.0
Mongolia	93.4	85.5
Myanmar (Burma)	89.0	72.0
Nepal	31.9	13.0
Pakistan	47.0	21.0
Philippines	89.9	87.5
Singapore	91.6	84.0
South Korea	97.4	99.0
Sri Lanka	90.8	84.0
Taiwan	95.2	84.6
Thailand	93.2	84.5
Middle East		
Afghanistan	44.0	14.0
Bahrain	81.1	69.0
Egypt	63.0	34.0
Iran	64.0	43.0
Iraq	70.0	49.0
Israel	95.0	88.7
Jordan	89.0	70.0
Kuwait	80.5	73.1
Lebanon	88.0	73.0
Oman	55.0	20.0
Qatar	77.0	72.0
Saudi Arabia	73.0	48.0
Syria	78.0	51.0
Turkey	90.0	71.0
United Arab Emirates	72.7	66.3
Yemen	66.6	26.0
Australia and Oceania		
Australia	100.0	100.0
Fiji	90.2	80.9
New Zealand	100.0	100.0
Papua New Guinea	65.0	38.0
Solomon Islands	62.4	44.9
Tonga	60.0	60.0
Tuvalu	95.5	95.5
Vanuatu	57.3	47.8
Western Samoa	98.5	98.1
Europe		
Albania	79.9	63.1
Austria	100.0	100.0
Bosnia–Herzegovina	94.5	76.7
Cyprus	97.9	91.0
Czech Republic	99.6	99.5
Denmark	100.0	100.0
Finland	100.0	100.0
Germany	100.0	98.7

	Males	Females
Greece	97.3	89.0
Hungary	99.2	98.0
Iceland	100.0	100.0
Ireland	100.0	100.0
Italy	97.9	96.3
Liechtenstein	100.0	100.0
Luxembourg	100.0	100.0
Netherlands	97.0	97.0
Norway	100.0	100.0
Poland	98.0	98.0
Portugal	89.0	82.0
San Marino	98.2	97.7
Slovakia	99.6	99.5
Spain	97.0	93.0
Sweden	100.0	100.0
Switzerland	100.0	100.0
U.K.	100.0	100.0
Yugoslavia	95.5	83.9
(Serbia and Montenegro)		
North America		
Barbados	99.0	99.0
Canada	95.6	95.7
Cayman Islands	97.5	97.6
Costa Rica	92.7	92.6
Cuba	95.0	93.0
Dominican Republic	85.0	82.0
Guatemala	63.0	47.0
Haiti	59.0	47.0
Honduras	76.0	71.0
Jamaica	98.0	99.0
Martinique	91.8	93.2
Mexico	90.0	85.0
Panama	88.0	88.0
Trinidad and Tobago	96.7	93.0
Turks and Caicos Islands	99.0	98.0
U.S.A.	97.0	97.0
South America		
Argentina	95.5	94.4
Bolivia	85.0	71.0
Brazil	82.0	80.0
Chile	95.0	93.8
Ecuador	90.0	86.0
El Salvador	76.0	70.0
French Guiana	82.5	81.3
Guyana	97.1	96.0
Paraguay	92.0	88.0
Suriname	95.0	95.0
Uruguay	97.0	96.0
Venezuela	87.0	90.0

Timeline

1903 Berlin International Monetary Conference: a fixed scale between gold and silver indexed currencies is set.

1927 International Economic Conference takes place in Geneva, Switzerland.

1929 Wall Street Crash (also known as Black Thursday, *p. 363*).

1930 International Economic Conference is held in Geneva, Switzerland, specifically to discuss the Great Depression.

1933 President Roosevelt's New Deal implemented. World Economic Conference opens in London: a plan is drawn up to stabilize currencies, but the conference fails to reach an agreement.

1944 Bretton Woods Conference held in the U.S.A.

1945 International Monetary Fund (IMF) is formed as a UN specialized agency.

1946 World Bank/International Bank for Reconstruction and Development (IBRD) is formed and begins operations. Council of Economic Advisors created as the chief economic advisory body to the U.S. president.

1947 U.S. Marshall Plan aid pumps $12 billion into economies of Western Europe over four years, promoting economic stability.

1948 General Agreement on Tariffs and Trade (GATT) is formed (*p. 259*). Benelux Economic Union Treaty signed.

1949 Comecon is formed as an intergovernmental council between Bulgaria, Czechoslovakia, Hungary, Poland, Romania, and the U.S.S.R. to plan economic development and integration.

1957 Treaty of Rome: the European Economic Community (EEC) is created. Council of Arab Economic Unity is established to promote economic integration of Arab countries. The UN reports that half of the world's population are underfed.

1958 European Atomic Energy Community is created.

1959 Inter-American Development Bank established as a regional development bank to accelerate economic development and integration in Latin America.

1960 Central American Common Market is formed. European Free Trade Association (EFTA) is founded. Organization of Petroleum Exporting Countries (OPEC) is created.

1961 Organization for Economic Cooperation and Development (OECD) is created. Latin American Free Trade Association is established to eliminate regional trade restrictions.

1962 European Community adopts a Common Agricultural Policy (CAP); U.K.'s entry is vetoed.

1968 Arab Fund for Economic and Social Development is formed. Organization for Arab Petroleum Exporting Countries (OAPEC) is created to coordinate petroleum production and economic policies between members.

WHAT IS ECONOMICS?

Economics is the social science concerned with the study of how material resources are managed, the creation and distribution of wealth, and the production and consumption of goods and services. The science of economics is founded on the premise that resources are scarce, and that it is not possible to meet everyone's needs and desires. Its principal concern is therefore to establish how these resources can be most effectively distributed.

Economics is generally divided into two categories. Microeconomics is the study of economic activity on an individual level, whether this means a single company, a specific commodity, or a specific consuming unit and is especially concerned with price levels. Macroeconomics, in contrast, examines economic activity on a national level, and includes the analysis of Gross National Product (GNP), trade policy, inflation, employment levels, exchange rates, economic growth, and forecasting. The principal concern of macroeconomics is to establish how the economy can best be managed to achieve high growth, low inflation, and low unemployment.

Capitalist economies

Most countries have a capitalist economic system. Capitalism is based on the principle of the private ownership of the resources used to produce goods and services; these resources include capital (business premises, equipment, and money), the term from which capitalism is derived. Capitalism, also known as free enterprise, focuses on the individual and promotes a self-help ethic. Individuals are encouraged to carry out their economic activities largely free of government intervention. A capitalist economy functions with very little planning. Individuals and businesses make their own economic decisions, influenced by supply and demand, profit, and competition. Individuals are defined as consumers.

Profit is the main stimulus within the capitalist system. Efficient businesses that target demand and keep costs low can make substantial profits, increase the value of their assets and expand into new areas. Competition among firms helps to maintain efficiency within companies.

Planned economies

In complete contrast to the capitalist system, planned economies work on the principle of government ownership and control of all or most businesses, and most workers are therefore government employees. Government planners decide what and how much should be produced and also fix prices for goods and services. Private ownership generally does exist within a planned economy, but its extent is limited and it is not encouraged.

There are advantages to the planned system. Governments can readily target specific areas for growth, and people and resources can be much more easily transferred to different sectors than within a free-market economy. However, the lack of competition, the driving force of other economic systems, can lead to inefficiency. In recent years, many nations with planned economies have begun to introduce elements of free enterprise in the pursuit of further economic development. All Communist countries have planned economies.

Mixed (semiplanned) economies

These are economies that have elements of government control but mainly adhere to capitalist principles. For the most part, the economy runs in the same way as a capitalist economy, but certain important industries are owned and run by the government. The industries under government control usually include public utilities—gas, electricity, and water—as well as transportation.

Most nations with mixed economies have democratic systems of government. People elect the government and therefore have power to determine how intrusive the government should be in the economy. The political system that follows the principles of mixed economics is known as democratic socialism.

The flow of money and movements of goods and services in a capitalist economy.

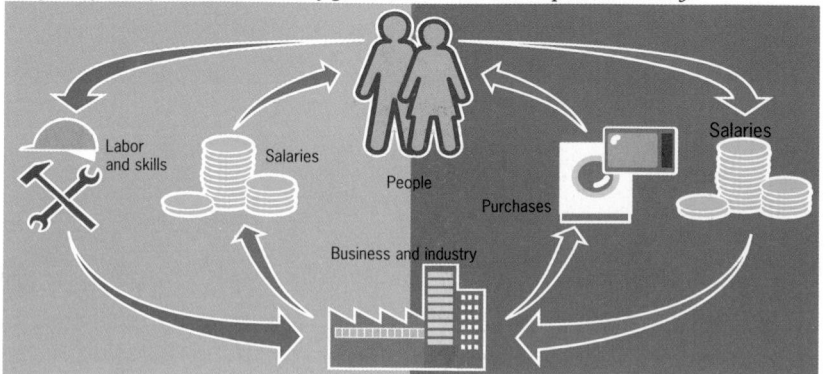

THE G7 COUNTRIES

The Group of Seven (G7) is an association of the seven wealthiest countries in the world: the U.S.A., Japan, Germany, France, the U.K., Italy, and Canada. Since 1975, their heads of government have met once a year to discuss economic and political issues affecting the group. In 1993 and 1994, the Russian Federation was invited to attend the G7 summit.

Imports/exports (Jan.–Sep. 1993)

	Imports ($m)	Exports ($m)
U.S.A.	443,328	341,767
Japan	180,832	270,414
Germany	248,563	270,116
France	149,040	152,051
U.K.	153,082	132,424
Italy	110,441	123,347
Canada	103,146	107,463

Annual growth rate (1985–92)

U.S.A.	2.3%
Japan	4.1%
Germany	2.8%
France	2.5%
U.K.	2.2%
Italy	2.5%
Canada	2.3%

Unemployment (May 1994)

U.S.A.	5.9%
Japan	2.8%
Germany	9.0%
France	10.8%
U.K.	9.4%
Italy	11.3%
Canada (Jan. 1994)	10.7%

INTERNATIONAL AID

International aid is the flow of resources from rich nations to poor nations. Distribution of aid may take place directly from one country to another (bilateral aid), or through an agency, in which case several nations may donate to a number of recipients (multilateral aid). The largest distributor of aid is the World Bank, which in 1992 transferred $49.7 m. Most aid takes the form of capital, equipment, and expertise, which is provided below commercial cost.

Aid is intended for development purposes. It may be used for infrastructural and educational development and cultural reform. Each donor country spends over 50 percent of its contribution on direct bilateral aid, which often has a political cost attached. Recipients may be expected to adopt certain favorable political stances toward the donor, or they may be expected to purchase the donor's industrial products. What at first may appear to be an attempt to reduce inequalities between nations is often corrupted into reciprocal agreements.

The amount of aid provided falls far short of what is required. Many countries fail to deliver the UN aid target of 0.7 percent of GNP. Moreover, aid is often wasted on projects that are overly ambitious or even environmentally destructive. Aid can also be abused by corrupt regimes or reinforce administrations with poor human rights records.

INTERNATIONAL DEBT

International debt is the product of developing countries borrowing to pay for development programs. Finance is provided in the form of loans from the World Bank and from financial organizations in the developed world. These loans have to be paid back, often with interest. The 40 poorest countries in the world can borrow, interest free, from the World Bank. As the World Bank is nonprofit-making, other countries may borrow money at lower rates of interest than those offered by private institutions.

During the 1970s, there was a surplus of capital in the industrialized world, and many private institutions encouraged developing nations to take out loans. OPEC countries also had a glut of capital available. Today, however, developing nations are regarded as bad risks. Many already have high national debts, and political instability is a disincentive to lenders. Commercial institutions still lend to newly industrializing countries, such as Taiwan, Turkey, and Brazil, but other developing nations must depend upon the World Bank for finance.

Many developing countries, Pakistan and Zaire especially, have found their loan repayments difficult to manage. Previous borrowing did not lead to the economic development they had hoped for. This has left many developing nations with loans they cannot pay back and a lack of new investment.

WORLD'S LARGEST RECIPIENTS OF AID

Country	($m)	Country	($ per head)
Egypt	3,538	Netherlands Antilles	485
China	3,065	Israel	404
India	2,435	Suriname	169
Indonesia	2,080	Nicaragua	169
Israel	2,066	Bahrain	133
Philippines	1,738	Papua New Guinea	119
Bangladesh	1,728	Zambia	118
Mozambique	1,393	Albania	117
Tanzania	1,344	Former Yugoslavia	108
Ethiopia	1,301	Mauritania	101
Pakistan	1,169	Jordan	96
Former Yugoslavia	1,148	Namibia	92
Zambia	1,016	Bolivia	90
Morocco	996	Senegal	86
Thailand	789	Fiji	84
Kenya	780	Mozambique	84

WORLD'S LARGEST AID DONORS

Country	($m)	Country	(% of GNP)
U.S.A.	11,709	Norway	1.16
Japan	11,151	Sweden	1.03
France	8,270	Denmark	1.02
Germany	7,572	Kuwait	0.93
Italy	4,122	Netherlands	0.86
U.K.	3,217	France	0.63
Netherlands	2,753	Finland	0.62
Canada	2,515	Saudi Arabia	0.62
Sweden	2,460	Canada	0.46
Spain	1,518	Switzerland	0.46
Denmark	1,392	Belgium	0.39
Norway	1,273	Germany	0.39
Switzerland	1,139	Portugal	0.36
Australia	973	Australia	0.35
Belgium	783	Italy	0.34

COUNTRIES WITH LARGEST FOREIGN DEBT

Country	($m)	Country	($m)
Brazil	121,110	Peru	20,297
Mexico	113,378	Malaysia	19,837
Indonesia	84,385	Chile	19,360
Russia	78,658	Côte d'Ivoire	17,997
India	76,893	Colombia	17,204
China	69,321	Syria	16,513
Argentina	67,569	Former Yugoslavia	16,294
Turkey	54,772	Sudan	16,085
Poland	48,521	Iran	14,166
South Korea	42,999	Bangladesh	13,189
Egypt	40,431	Ecuador	12,280
Thailand	39,424	Bulgaria	12,146
Venezuela	37,193	Nicaragua	11,126
Philippines	32,589	Zaire	10,912
Portugal	32,046	Angola	9,645
Nigeria	30,998	Former Czechoslovakia	9,328
Algeria	26,349	Tunisia	8,476
Pakistan	24,072	Jordan	7,977
Hungary	21,900	Zambia	7,041
Morocco	21,418	Tanzania	6,715

LARGEST FOREIGN DEBT BURDENS

Country	(% of GDP)	Country	(% of GDP)
Nicaragua	822.6	Congo	185.2
Mozambique	583.9	Jordan	179.5
Zambia	386.5	Laos	165.5
Guinea-Bissau	289.6	Madagascar	153.9
Somalia	283.9	Jamaica	153.6
Tanzania	268.4	Angola	140.5
Sudan	220.7	Egypt	116.8
Côte d'Ivoire	207.1	Honduras	114.2
Mauritania	205.6	Panama	111.8
Sierra Leone	202.5	Zaire	111.5

Timeline

1971 The U.S. government ends its two-decade-long trade embargo of China. The U.S. has its first trade deficit since 1888.

1973 World oil crisis: OPEC raises its prices by 70 percent, triggering the worst economic recession since the Great Depression of the 1930s. U.K., Ireland, and Denmark join the EEC.

1974 Economic recession worsens.

1975 OPEC raises its prices by 10 percent, but many countries see the start of economic recovery. First G7 economic summit opens (*p. 257*).

1976 Arab Monetary Fund is created.

1977 China begins to "de-Communize" its economy with free-market programs.

1978 Unemployment rises dramatically throughout the world.

1979 Oil prices increase by 50 percent. The U.S. inflation rate hits 21.5 percent, the highest in the twentieth century. "Most-favored-nation" status granted to China by U.S.A.; U.S. exports to China rise substantially. European Monetary System (EMS) is created. U.S.A., U.K., Germany, and France hold an economic summit.

1981 President Reagan introduces largest tax and budget cuts in U.S. history.

1982 Worldwide recession. Unemployment reaches 10.8 percent in the U.S.A.

1983 U.S. tax and budget cuts, combined with defense spending and widespread stock market speculation, trigger economic boom among industrialized countries.

1985 The U.S. becomes a debtor nation for the first time since 1914. World Bank sets up a fund for Africa. Third Lomé Convention: EEC and 64 states agree greater incentives for investment. Oil glut causes collapse of world oil prices.

1986 The U.S. national debt tops $2 trillion. "Big Bang": City of London (London's financial markets) changes its institutional and regulatory practices. Spain and Portugal join EEC.

1987 Worldwide stock market crash (known as Black Monday). World economic summit in Venice, Italy.

1989 Hyperinflation in many Eastern European countries as Communism collapses.

1990 Deutsche mark comes under pressure on financial markets as the costs of German reunification escalate. Boom ends in U.S.A., France, and U.K.

1991 The Dow Jones Industrial Average closes above 3,000 for the first time.

1992 U.K. withdraws from EMS. Canada, U.S.A., and Mexico sign North American Free Trade Agreement (NAFTA).

1993 EEC becomes the European Union (EU); barriers to trade are eliminated between member states.

ECONOMIC GLOBALIZATION

The board of a transnational company may be truly international.

Over the past 50 years there has been a move toward economic globalization. National boundaries have become increasingly insignificant as barriers to the movement of goods and services, and international trade has become more important than trade within national boundaries. Today, competition in many industries takes place at the international level. This has been made possible by technological advances in communications (*pp. 482–83*) and transportation.

Traditionally, the multinational, or transnational, company was regarded as a stateless firm operating in the international arena. However, the headquarters of these companies remained in their countries of origin, and profits from factories and plants situated in other countries often returned to the companies' bases.

A new type of global firm is beginning to emerge. These firms are not based in one country but are truly international. Shareholders are international, as is the work force. Examples of the new stateless firm include Asea Brown Boveri (ABB), ICI, Philips, and Smithkline Beecham. ABB is the company that has progressed furthest into statelessness in the world. Originally Swedish, it moved its headquarters from Stockholm to Zurich, Switzerland (the geographical center of Europe), its managers are Swedish, Swiss, and German, its business is done in English, and the accounts are kept in U.S. dollars. Also, 50 percent of the shareholders are not Swedish. At present, most internationalized firms are European.

There is still a long way to go before we arrive at true globalization. Many shareholders are still based in the home country of the firm, and many international firms still market and produce goods for specific national markets. It seems unlikely that a great number of products aimed at the global market will be produced, considering the diversity of the planet's cultures, but companies owned by a variety of people in many different nations are sure to become the norm in time.

Advances in telecommunications and computer technology have had a dramatic effect recently, particularly through the expansion of the Internet (*p. 483*). This

WORLD'S TOP 40 BUSINESSES

Name	Location	Sales 1992 $billion
General Motors	U.S.A.	132.8
Exxon	U.S.A.	103.5
Ford Motor	U.S.A.	100.8
Royal Dutch/ Shell Group	U.K./ Netherlands	98.9
Toyota Motor	Japan	79.1
IRI	Italy	67.5
IBM	U.S.A.	65.1
Daimler-Benz	Germany	63.3
General Electric	U.S.A.	62.2
Hitachi	Japan	61.5
British Petroleum	U.K.	59.2
Matsushita Electrical Industrial	Japan	57.5
Mobil	U.S.A.	57.4
Volkswagen	Germany	56.7
Siemens	Germany	51.4
Nissan Motor	Japan	50.2
Philip Morris	U.S.A.	50.2
Samsung	South Korea	49.6
Fiat	Italy	47.9
Unilever	U.K./ Netherlands	44.0
ENI	Italy	40.4
Elf Aquitaine	France	39.7
Nestlé	Switzerland	39.1
Chevron	U.S.A.	38.5
Toshiba	Japan	37.5
E.I. Du Pont de Nemours	U.S.A.	37.4
Texaco	U.S.A.	37.1
Chrysler	U.S.A.	36.9
Renault	France	33.9
Honda Motor	Japan	33.4
Philips Electronics	Netherlands	33.3
Sony	Japan	31.5
Asea Brown Boveri	Sweden/ Switzerland	30.5
Alcatel Alsthom	France	30.5
Boeing	U.S.A.	30.4
Procter & Gamble	U.S.A.	29.9
Hoechst	Germany	29.6
Peugeot	France	29.4
BASF	Germany	28.5
NEC	Japan	28.4

N.B. All these companies obtain at least half of their sales from manufacturing and/or mining. If trading and service companies are included, the Japanese trading corporations Itochu, Sumitomo, Marubeni, Mitsubishi, and Mitsui & Co., along with the U.S.A.'s General Motors, take the top six places. Telecommunications companies such as American Telephone and Telegraph also rank highly.

provides an international computer network that can link businesses directly to customers worldwide, allowing buying and selling via a computer terminal. The Internet already links over 25 million people and membership is increasing rapidly, with over 2,000 businesses joining each month. At present, it is particularly significant for small firms that cannot afford their own international computer networks: the Internet is readily available and comparatively cheap, and thus gives them access to international trade on a scale that allows them to compete with large companies. Despite minor teething problems, the Internet's impact on business is likely to increase.

GENERAL AGREEMENT ON TRADE AND TARIFFS (GATT)

GATT is a multilateral treaty with around 100 contracting parties that works to promote trade among its members. Established in 1948, GATT has become the chief means of international agreement on world trade. GATT member countries meet at least once a year to negotiate the removal of barriers to international trade. There is also a council of representatives that deals with urgent matters between sessions.

WORLD'S TOP 40 BANKS

Name	Location	Capital equity/ reserve 1992/3 $m
Sumitomo Bank	Japan	19,524
Dai-Ichi Kangyo Bank	Japan	17,377
Sanwa Bank	Japan	17,155
Fuji Bank	Japan	17,045
Mitsubishi Bank	Japan	15,982
Sakura Bank	Japan	15,608
Crédit Agricole	France	15,606
Union Bank of Switzerland	Switzerland	12,802
Industrial Bank of Japan	Japan	12,053
HSBC Holdings	U.K.	11,798
Deutsche Bank	Germany	11,303
Crédit Lyonnais	France	10,697
Industrial & Commercial Bank of China	China	10,624
Banque Nationale de Paris	France	10,221
ABN-AMRO Bank	Netherlands	9,531
Long-Term Credit Bank of Japan	Japan	9,433
Tokai Bank	Japan	9,364
Compagnie Financière de Paribas	France	9,316
Bank of China	China	9,216
Asahi Bank	Japan	9,172
Barclays Bank	U.K.	9,014
Bank of Tokyo	Japan	8,977
Swiss Bank Corp.	Switzerland	8,847
Internationale Nederland Group	Netherlands	8,598
BankAmerica Corp.	U.S.A.	8,580
National Westminster Bank	U.K.	8,428
Société Générale	France	7,983
Rabobank Nederland	Netherlands	7,760
Citicorp	U.S.A.	7,752
Mitsubishi Trust & Banking Corporation	Japan	7,508
Chemical Banking Corp.	U.S.A.	7,400
Crédit Suisse	Switzerland	7,384
Sumitomo Trust & Banking	Japan	7,358
Groupe des Caisses d'Epargne Ecureuil	France	7,239
NationsBank	U.S.A.	7,174
Banca di Roma	Italy	6,847
J. P. Morgan & Co.	U.S.A.	6,820
Cariplo	Italy	6,721
People's Construction Bank of China	China	6,380
Dresdner Bank	Germany	6,254

Figures for Japanese banks are for the year to March 1993; figures for all other countries are for the year ending December 1992.

STOCK MARKETS

A stock market or stock exchange is an organized marketplace where securities (that is, stocks, shares, and bonds) are bought and sold by stockbrokers who trade on behalf of their clients. The marketplace is strictly regulated and only members are authorized to trade. Flotation on the stock exchange is an extremely effective way for companies to generate finance for further investment.

The largest stock market in the world is the Tokyo stock exchange, which opened in 1878. Stock markets are compared by volume of trade, the dollar value of the stock traded, the range of financial products marketed, and the number of members entitled to trade. Virtually every industrialized nation in the world now has a stock exchange.

Stock markets can be traced back to 1611 in Amsterdam, the Netherlands, where merchants came together to trade shares in the Dutch East India Company. In 1775, the London stock exchange was formally established after brokers moved from a coffee shop to rooms in Sweeting's Alley. The first organized marketplace in the U.S.A. was the Philadelphia stock market, which opened in 1790. This was quickly followed by Wall Street, New York City, in 1792.

The most advanced exchanges have, by means of new technology, broken out of the physical constraints of the stock-market building. Today, trading is conducted through terminals connected to stock exchange computer systems. The U.S. system is called the National Association of Security Dealers Automatic Quotations System (NASDAQ). The London exchange operates through the Stock Exchange Automated Quotations System (SEAQ). These systems allow brokers to deal over a computer terminal at great speed, with the result that the market now responds to whatever is happening in the world's financial markets at a much swifter pace than ever before.

How a stock market works

1. An investor calls or passes an order with details of the transaction to be implemented to a broker or financial intermediary.
2. The broker or intermediary calls up, through a terminal, the company in which the investor is interested. Companies on the stock market have "pages" on the NASDAQ, the stock exchange computer system.
3. Offers are displayed on the screen from market-makers—people who are authorized to buy and sell shares in the company.
4. The broker calls the dealing desk of the stockbroking firm and asks to buy or sell the shares on behalf of the investor.
5. When a deal is struck, the market-maker enters the transaction into the offer screen of the terminal.
6. Other market-makers take account of the transaction and readjust their subsequent offers accordingly.

Securities are traded on the floor of the Tokyo stock exchange.

World stock markets

Country	Market capitalization 1992 $m	Country	Market capitalization 1992 $m	Country	Market capitalization 1992 $m
U.S.A.	4,757,879	Sweden	76,622	Luxembourg	11,936
Japan	2,399,004	India	65,119	Turkey	9,931
U.K.	838,579	Belgium	64,172	Greece	9,489
France	350,858	Thailand	58,259	Portugal	9,213
Germany	348,138	Singapore	48,818	Kuwait	9,115
Canada	243,018	Brazil	45,261	Pakistan	8,028
Switzerland	195,285	Denmark	39,451	Venezuela	7,600
Hong Kong	172,016	Chile	29,644	Colombia	5,681
Netherlands	171,435	Israel	29,634	Jordan	3,365
South Africa	150,669	Austria	21,750	Jamaica	3,227
Mexico	139,061	Argentina	18,633	Peru	2,630
Australia	135,061	China	18,314	Egypt	2,594
Italy	115,258	Norway	17,821	Morocco	1,876
South Korea	107,448	New Zealand	15,348	Sri Lanka	1,439
Taiwan	101,124	Philippines	13,794	Nigeria	1,243
Spain	98,969	Finland	12,202	Iran	1,157
Malaysia	94,004	Indonesia	12,038		

PROMINENT PEOPLE

ALLAIS, Maurice (b. 1911) French. Awarded the Nobel Prize in 1988, his main contribution was in the reformulation of the theories of general economic equilibrium and the efficient use of resources.

ARROW, Kenneth Joseph (b. 1921) American. His primary field of study is collective decisions based on uncertainty and risk. Awarded the Nobel Prize in 1972 with Sir John Richard HICKS.

BEVERIDGE, William Henry, 1st Baron (1879–1963) British. Director of the London School of Economics (1919–37), he became chairman of an interdepartmental committee (1941–42) from which came the "Beveridge Report,"] a comprehensive plan for social insurance. Noted for his work on unemployment and social security.

BUCHANAN, James McGill (b. 1919) American. Awarded the Nobel Prize in 1986 for his work on theories of public choice.

CHAMBERLAIN, Edward Hastings (1899–1967) American. Turned the attention of economists away from analysis of an industry as a whole to focus on individual firms within that industry.

CLARK, Colin Grant (b. 1905) British. Main field of study is economic growth.

COBDEN, Richard (1804–65) British. The "apostle of free trade," his lectures and speeches contributed to the abolition of the Corn Laws in 1846.

DEBREU, Gerard (b. 1921) French-born American. Awarded the Nobel Prize in 1983 for his work on equilibrium between prices, production, and consumer demand.

FELDSTEIN, Martin (b. 1939) American. Mainly interested in macroeconomic theory.

FRIEDMAN, Milton (b. 1912) American. A leading figure in the "Chicago school" of economics, noted for his monetarist theories. Nobel Prize winner in 1976.

FRISCH, Ragnar Anton (1895–1973) Norwegian. Pioneer of econometrics (the application of statistics to economic planning). Shared the first Nobel Prize with Jan TINBERGEN in 1969.

GALBRAITH, John Kenneth (b. 1908) Canadian-born American. His criticisms of social provision under capitalism have acted as a counterweight to the moneterism of FRIEDMAN.

HAYEK, Friedrich A. von (1899–1992) Austrian-born British. Fields of interest included general economic theory and the history of economic thought. Strongly opposed to Keynesianism. Awarded the Nobel Prize in 1974 with Gunnar MYRDAL.

HICKS, Sir John Richard (1904–89) British. His most notable work was *Value and Capital* (1939) a study of the conflict between business cycle theory and equilibrium theory.

KALDOR, Nicholas, Baron Kaldor of Newnham (1908–86) Hungarian-born British. Advocated expenditure taxes as opposed to income tax.

KANTOROVICH, Leonid Vitaliyevich (1912–86) Russian. Director of Institute of System Studies, Moscow University (1976–85). Shared the Nobel Prize with Tjalling KOOPMANS in 1975.

KEYNES, John Maynard, 1st Baron (1883–1946) British. Pioneer of the theory of full employment. In his great work, *General Theory of Employment, Interest and Money* (1936), he argued that unemployment was not an automatic condition, expounded a new theory of the rate of interest, and set out the principles underlying the flow of income and expenditure. Played a leading part in the establishment of the International Monetary Fund (IMF) in 1945.

KLEIN, Lawrence Robert (b. 1920) American. Economic adviser to President Carter (1976–81), awarded the Nobel Prize in 1980 for his work on forecasting business fluctuations.

KOOPMANS, Tjalling C. (1910–84) Dutch. Greatest achievement was the application of linear programming techniques to transportation problems. Shared the Nobel Prize with Leonid KANTOROVICH in 1975.

KORNAI, Janos (b. 1928) Hungarian. Fields of interest include general economic theory, economic systems, economic growth development, planning theory and policy.

KUZNETS, Simon Smith (1901–85) Russian-born American. Emigrated to the U.S.A. in 1922; his work contained original ideas on economic growth and social change, such as the 20-year "Kuznets cycle" of economic growth. Awarded the Nobel Prize in 1971.

LEWIS, Sir Arthur (b. 1915) West Indian-born British. Awarded the 1979 Nobel Prize with Theodore Schultz for work on economic development in the Third World.

LVEBLEN, Thorstein B, (1857–1929) American. As an economist and social philosopher he scrutinized U.S. social mores, coining the term "conspicuous consumption" and criticizing those who practice it.

MALTHUS, Thomas Robert (1766–1834) British clergyman. In his *Essay on the Principle of Population* (1798), he maintained that population increases faster than the means of subsistence, and therefore called for action to reduce the birthrate.

MARX, Karl (1818–83) German. Major economist and founder of international Communism. His *Das Kapital* (Vol. I, 1867) developed his theories of surplus value, class conflict, and the exploitation,of the working class. He predicted that capitalism would be superseded by socialism, and that the state would ultimately "wither away."

MILL, James (1773–1836) British. Developed the economic aspect of Utilitarianism and wrote the first English-language textbook of economics.

MODIGLIANI, Franco (b. 1918) Italian-born American. Main field of interest is general economic theory. Awarded the Nobel Prize in 1985.

MORISHIMA, Michio (b. 1923) Japanese. Fields of interest include general equilibrium theory, history of economic thought, and capitalist economies.

MYRDAL, Gunnar (1898–1987) Swedish. Main achievement was the design of economic development models. Awarded the Nobel Prize with Friedrich HAYEK in 1974.

RICARDO, David (1772–1823) British. Succeeded Adam SMITH as the major influence in British economics throughout the 1800s.

ROBINSON, Joan Violet, née **Maurice** (1903–83) British. Economic theorist and leader of the Cambridge school which developed macroeconomic theories of growth and distribution based on the work of KEYNES.

ROSTOW, Walt (b. 1916) American. Adviser to president Kennedy and president Johnson. Noted for his theory of five stages of economic growth.

SAMUELSON, Paul (b. 1915) American. General economic theorist and educator, whose text books on economics are used in most U.S. colleges and universities. Received the Nobel Prize in 1970.

SCHUMPETER, Joseph Alois (1883–1950) Austrian. Believed that the key to economic growth lies in innovation, risk-taking, and technological advance.

SIMON, Herbert Alexander (b. 1916) American. Awarded the Nobel Prize in 1978 for pioneering work on the decision-making process within commercial organizations.

SMITH, Adam (1723–90) British. Often regarded as the founder of modern economics. His views on free trade and a self-regulating economy are summed up in *The Wealth of Nations* (1776).

SOLOW, Robert Merton (b. 1924) Awarded the Nobel Prize in 1987 for his study of factors permitting growth and increased welfare.

STONE, Sir Richard (1913–91) Studied at Cambridge University under J. M. KEYNES. Developed complex models upon which world standardized national income reports are based. Awarded the Nobel Prize in 1984.

TINBERGEN, Jan (b. 1903) Dutch. Specialities include economic development and econometric and statistical methods. Awarded the Nobel Prize with Ragnar Anton FRISCH in 1969.

TOBIN, James (b. 1918) American. Awarded the Nobel Prize in 1981 for his "portfolio selection theory" of investment practices.

VANEK, Jaroslav (b. 1930) Czech. Specialist in international economics and labor relations.

TERMS

Balance of payments The difference between a country's income and outgoings over a given period of time.

Black market An "unofficial market" in a product that is either in short supply or prohibited by law.

Bond A certificate issued by the government or a company that promises to pay back money borrowed with interest; used to raise long-term finance.

Boom An expansionary phase in a trade cycle where production, consumption, and employment are high.

Capital goods Goods purchased to be used in production.

Cartel Agreement among firms that dominate a market. Price and output may be agreed to maximize profits and exclude new competitors.

Conglomerate A company that is made up of a holding firm and subsidiary companies. Usually the product of mergers or takeovers.

Consumer goods Goods produced and purchased for final use.

Cost of living The cost of goods and services required to attain a reasonable standard of living.

Cost-push inflation INFLATION as a result of increases in production costs.

Currency Monetary unit in use in a specific country, such as the U.S. dollar, the French franc, or the Spanish peso.

Deficit financing Strategic overspending of public funds by a government in order to pump money into a depressed economy and create new jobs. This is financed by borrowing.

Deflation A reduction in the amount of money available in a country resulting in lower levels of economic activity, industrial output, employment, and decreasing prices. The opposite of INFLATION.

Demand-pull inflation INFLATION caused by excess demand, such as during a BOOM.

Depression An extended SLUMP.

Deregulation Removal of protective controls from business activities in order to promote competition.

Devaluation Reduction in the value of a currency.

Dividend Share in a company's profit enjoyed by shareholders.

Dow Jones Industrial Average Statistic showing the average share price and percentage change of 30 major U.S. companies.

European Currency Unit (ECU) The unit of currency used by the European Union to settle payment imbalances between members. Also used to value intra-EU government transactions.

European Monetary System (EMS) System set up in 1979 by members of the EEC with the aim of stabilizing and harmonizing European currencies.

Exchange Rate Mechanism (ERM) System that regulates currency exchange rates in the EUROPEAN MONETARY SYSTEM. Exchange rates are allowed to fluctuate within narrow bands only, based on the EUROPEAN CURRENCY UNIT rate.

Financial Times index (FT index) Statistic showing the daily movement of 30 major British companies on the London stock exchange.

Fiscal drag The effect of INFLATION on tax revenues. If tax allowances are not kept in line with inflation, individuals pay relatively high amounts of tax, thereby reducing net incomes and, in turn, demand for goods and services.

Fiscal policy Government policy related to raising revenue through taxation, public-sector borrowing, and government expenditure.

Flotation The launching of a commercial company with a sale of shares in order to raise money.

Free trade area A loose grouping of countries within which tariffs and barriers to trade are removed. Each country retains its own commercial policy outside the area.

Gross domestic product (GDP) The value of all goods and services produced within a country's boundaries over a given period, including foreign-owned operations within the country.

Gross national product (GNP) The value of all goods and services produced by firms owned by nationals of that country, even if they are based abroad.

Hyperinflation Dramatic and uncontrollable increase in prices, usually accompanied by political instability.

Import control Controls limiting number of imports entering a country, such as import quotas and TARIFFS.

Incomes policy Government policy of controlling salary increases as a way of curbing INFLATION.

Inflation Rate at which prices are increasing.

Invisible trade In a BALANCE OF PAYMENTS account, invisible trade is the import and export of services rather than products.

Labor Human resources available for use in the process of production.

Laissez-faire A government policy of nonintervention in economic activities characteristic of free-market economies.

Limited (liability) company Company owned by shareholders whose responsibility for its debts is limited to the value of their investment.

Monetarism Regulation of an economy by controlling the amount of money in circulation in the belief that if MONEY SUPPLY rises above the rate of economic growth, prices will rise, leading to INFLATION. A major influence on U.S. and U.K. economics in the 1980s.

Money supply The amount of money in circulation at a given time including bills, coins, and bank deposits used for everyday payments.

Monopoly A situation whereby a commodity or service is supplied by only one agent.

National debt The money borrowed by a government and not yet repaid.

National income The total of all income earned in a country over a given period.

Nationalization The process of bringing an industry under state ownership.

Newly industrialized country (NIC) A country that has recently shown a dramatic rise in manufacturing and export-led economic growth.

Oligopoly Situation where the majority of a market is controlled by a few large companies who may therefore exert considerable influence on that market.

Privatization The sale of state-owned industries to private investors.

Productive resources Components or elements used in production, including natural resources, technology, the work force, and capital.

Productivity Rate and efficiency of work in industrial production, usually measured as output per person.

Profit-sharing Agreement whereby employees receive a fixed share of a company's profits.

Public-sector borrowing requirement (PSBR) The amount of money needed by a government to cover any deficit in its expenditure.

Recession A period of decreased business activity, sometimes defined as a situation where GROSS DOMESTIC PRODUCT declines for two successive quarters.

Retail price index Monthly index of the retail prices of certain goods, taken as an indicator of the COST OF LIVING.

Slump A serious and sometimes long-term decline in a economic growth.

Stagflation State where high INFLATION is accompanied by stagnating or declining output and rising unemployment, often triggered by a sharp increase in costs of raw materials and/or labor.

Stocks and shares Investment holdings (securities) in private or public undertakings.

Supply and demand A fundamental approach to economic theory that analyzes and compares the supply of goods with their demand.

Supply-side Economic approach based on the theory that supply creates demand and resting on the supposition that the most effective way of increasing output is through the removal of tax disincentives to induce people to work harder and leaving more money available for investment.

Tariff Tax or duty levied on imported or exported goods.

Taxation The means by which governments raise money to finance their activities. Taxation may be direct, such as income tax, or indirect, such as taxes levied on goods for sale.

Trade cycle The pattern of changing levels of activity in an economy over a given period of time, including BOOMS, RECESSIONS, and SLUMPS.

OLYMPIC GAMES

The modern Olympic Games were the brainchild of Frenchman Baron Pierre de Coubertin in the late 1800s and were first staged in 1896, in Athens. Since then they have been held every four years, barring world wars, and have grown into a magnificent festival of sport in which most of the world's nations take part. Each four-year period is known as an Olympiad, which has a number whether or not the games take place.

GROWTH OF MODERN GAMES

Year	City	Countries	Sports	Competitors M	F
1896	Athens	13	9	311	–
1900	Paris	22	17	1319	11
1904	St. Louis	13	14	617	8
1906	Athens	20	11	877	7
1908	London	22	21	2013	43
1912	Stockholm	28	14	2490	57
1916	*Canceled during World War I*				
1920	Antwerp	29	22	2618	74
1924	Paris	44	18	2956	136
1928	Amsterdam	46	15	2724	290
1932	Los Angeles	37	15	1281	127
1936	Berlin	49	20	3738	328
1940	*Canceled during World War II*				
1944	*Canceled during World War II*				
1948	London	59	18	3714	385
1952	Helsinki	69	17	4407	518
1956	Melbourne	67	17	2958	384
1960	Rome	83	17	4738	610
1964	Tokyo	94	19	4457	683
1968	Mexico City	112	18	4750	781
1972	Munich	124	21	6077	1070
1976	Montreal	92	21	4834	1251
1980	Moscow	81	21	4238	1088
1984	Los Angeles	140	21	5458	1620
1988	Seoul	159	23	6279	2186
1992	Barcelona	169	28	6659	2710

OLYMPIC MILESTONES

776 B.C. First record of ancient Olympic Games.

A.D. 393 Games prohibited by decree of Emperor Theodosius I.

1896 First modern Olympic Games held in Athens.

1900 First women competitors.

1908 Length of marathon event standardized.

1920 Introduction of the Olympic oath.

1924 First separate Winter Olympics.

1928 Introduction of the ceremonial lighting of the Olympic flame. Women compete in athletics events for first time.

1936 Introduction of torch relay.

1968 African-American athletes stage "Black Power" protest on victory stand.

1972 Palestinian terrorists kill 11 members of Israeli Olympic team.

1976 Political boycott sees withdrawal of 22 countries, mainly from the African continent. Costs of staging games proves financial disaster for the city of Montreal.

1980 Soviet invasion of Afghanistan in 1979 precipitated major boycott, including U.S.A., West Germany, and Japan.

1984 Last-minute boycott by U.S.S.R. and other eastern bloc countries. Sponsorship by private corporations helps to make Games considerable financial success.

1988 Only six nations (including Cuba) back North Korean boycott of Games in Seoul. Ben Johnson (Canada), 100m gold-medalist, disqualified for failing drug test.

The opening ceremony of the Olympic Games held in Barcelona in 1992.

Organization

The Olympic Games are controlled by the International Olympic Committee (IOC), a self-perpetuating body that awards the Games to a city. The host city is responsible for the provision of facilities and the organization of the games, which take place at various venues, some of them outside the city. Competitors take part in more than 20 sports, each under the auspices of the world-governing body for that sport. Nations do not compete for an overall prize, although the media tend to publish ranking tables based on the number of gold (1st place), silver (2nd), and bronze (3rd) medals won.

Qualification

In most individual sports and events, a country is allowed to enter at least one competitor and as many as three if they pass a predetermined standard (time, distance, etc.). In team sports and events, normally only one entry per country is permitted, and in some there is a pre-Olympic qualifying competition in order to reduce the number of participating teams to a set requirement.

Amateurism

The Games were originally strictly amateur in concept, and no athlete is paid for competing or for winning. But in recent times the rules in most amateur sports have been relaxed so that sponsorship (state or commercial) and prize money won in other competitions do not debar Olympic participation.

OLYMPIC RECORDS

Most gold medals
Men 10 Ray Ewry (U.S.A.) Athletics (1900–08)
  9 Paavo Nurmi (Finland) Athletics (1920–28)
Women 9 Larissa Latynina (U.S.S.R.) Gymnastics (1956–64)

Most medals
Women 18 Larissa Latynina (U.S.S.R.) Gymnastics (1956–64)
Men 15 Nikolai Andrianov (U.S.S.R.) Gymnastics (1972–80)

Most gold medals in one Games
Men 7 Mark Spitz (U.S.A.) Swimming (1972)
Women 6 Kristin Otto (G.D.R.) Swimming (1988)

Most medals in one Games
Men 8 Aleksandr Dityatin (U.S.S.R.) Gymnastics (1980)
Women 7 Maria Gorokhovskaya (U.S.S.R.) Gymnastics (1952)

Most gold medals in one event
Men 4 Paul Elvström (Denmark) Yachting, Monotype (1948–60)
  Al Oerter (U.S.A.) Discus (1956–68)

Women 3 Dawn Fraser (Australia) Swimming 100m Freestyle (1956–64)
  Larissa Latynina (U.S.S.R.)** Gym Floor Exercises (1956–64)
*All for the now-defunct Standing Jumps and includes two in the Intercalated Games (1906).
**Includes one shared gold.

WINTER OLYMPIC GAMES

Ice-skating events were included in the 1908 Summer Olympics and again in 1920, when there was also an ice hockey tournament. The first separate Winter Olympics, also under the aegis of the IOC, were staged in 1924, three months before the summer Games. The Summer and Winter Olympics were held in the same year until 1994, when the Winter Olympics were staged at Lillehammer just two years after the previous winter Games at Albertville so that they now alternate with the summer Games two years out of step. Games are numbered successively, with no reference to the Olympiad number retained by the summer Games.

GROWTH OF WINTER GAMES

Year	City	Countries	Sports	Competitors	
				M	F
1924	Chamonix	16	5	281	13
1928	St. Moritz	25	6	468	27
1932	Lake Placid	17	5	274	32
1936	Garmisch	28	6	675	80
1942	*Canceled during World War II*				
1948	St. Moritz	28	7	636	77
1952	Oslo	22	6	623	109
1956	Cortina	32	6	687	132
1960	Squaw Valley	30	5	521	144
1964	Innsbruck	36	7	893	200
1968	Grenoble	37	7	1065	228
1972	Sapporo	35	7	1015	217
1976	Innsbruck	37	7	900	228
1980	Lake Placid	37	7	833	234
1984	Sarajevo	49	7	1287	223
1988	Calgary	57	7	1113	315
1992	Albertville	64	7	1269	460
1994	Lillehammer	67	7	1215	522

WINTER OLYMPIC RECORDS

Most gold medals
Women 6 Lydia Skoblikova (U.S.S.R.) Speed Skating (1960–64)
Men 5 Clas Thunberg (Finland) Speed Skating (1924–28)
  Eric Heiden (U.S.A.) Speed Skating (1980)

Most gold medals in one Games
Men 5 Eric Heiden (U.S.A.) Speed Skating (1980)
Women 4 Lydia Skoblikova (U.S.S.R.) Speed Skating (1964)

Most gold medals in one event
Men 3 Gillis Grafström (Sweden) Figure Skating (1920–28)
  Ulrich Wehling (G.D.R.) Nordic Combined (1972–80)
Women 3 Sonja Henie (Norway) Figure Skating (1928–36)
  Irina Rodnina (U.S.S.R.) Figure Skating Pairs (1972–80)
  Bonnie Blair (U.S.A.) Speed Skating 500m (1988–94)

Pan American Games

A multisports competition open to nations in North, Central, and South America and first held in 1951 in Buenos Aires, the Pan American Games have been staged at four-year intervals ever since. Competitors from nearly 40 nations take part in more than 30 sports.

Commonwealth Games

First staged as the British Empire Games in Hamilton, Canada, in 1930, this multisports competition has been held every four years, apart from 1942 and 1946.

Asian Games

First staged in New Delhi in 1951, these have been held every four years since 1954. Up to 36 nations and 6,000 competitors take part in more than 25 sports.

World Student Games

First staged in 1963, the World Student Games, also known as the Universiade, are held every two years, normally with ten sports. Winter Universiades are held in the same years as summer meetings.

Paralympics

Parallel Olympics for the disabled are staged in the Olympic city directly after summer and winter games, using the same facilities. A full range of sporting events is held.

Special Olympics

The International Special Olympic Games, alternating between summer and winter every two years, stages Olympic-style events for mentally handicapped athletes from more than 80 countries.

Aamodt of Norway races to third place in the supergiant slalom at Lillehammer in 1994.

SOCCER

A rough kind of soccer was played in the streets of London in the 1300s when it was banned by royal decree because of the disturbance it caused. The first rules of the game as we know it today were drawn up at Cambridge University in 1846. The game became known as "association football" to distinguish it from rugby and other forms of the sport that developed from it, and it is referred to as "football" in most countries except the United States.

Played professionally in most parts of the world, soccer has never become a major professional sport in the United States. However, it is extremely popular in elementary and high schools, with more than two million players nationwide.

Rules

Soccer is played 11-a-side, with two substitutes allowed, only one of whom may be for the goalkeeper. Only the goalkeeper may handle the ball, and then only inside the penalty area. The object is to score goals, the team with the higher number of goals being the winner.

A game is played over two periods of 45 minutes, with two further 15-minute periods of extra time in certain elimination competitions if the scores are even. Players propel the ball with feet, head, and any other part of the body except the hands and arms. A certain amount of physical contact is permitted.

A player is offside and concedes an indirect free kick to the opposition if he or she is in the opponent's half when a teammate plays the ball and if the player either touches it or is deemed to be interfering with play or seeking to gain an advantage, unless there are at least two opponents even with or between the player and the opponents' goal line, or the teammate playing the ball is nearer the opponent's goal line.

Field of play

The dimensions of the playing field (*top right*) for international matches are 120 x 80 yards (110 x 73 m) maximum and 110 x 70 yards (100 x 64 m) minimum.

Equipment

The ball is round, 9 inches (22.5 cm) in diameter. The goalkeeper often wears gloves and a different color from the rest of the team. Most players wear the team color with identifying number, shoes, shirt, shorts, socks, and shinguards.

Control

Soccer is controlled by a referee, helped by two linesmen patrolling the touch lines and using a flag to signal to the referee.

Governing bodies

The world governing body for soccer is the Fédération Internationale de Football

Romario of Brazil challenges Albertini of Italy in the final of the 1994 World Cup.

Association (F.I.F.A.), founded in 1904 and with headquarters in Zurich, Switzerland. It is responsible, through the International Football Association Board, for the upkeep of the laws of the game and recognizes six continental groupings: A.F.C. (Asia), C.A.F. (Africa), C.O.N.C.A.C.A.F. (North America and the Caribbean), C.O.N.M.E.B.O.L. (South America), O.F.C. (Oceania), and U.E.F.A. (Europe). Some 180 countries are affiliated directly to F.I.F.A.

International competition

The chief international tournament is the World Cup, held every four years. Only the defending champions and the host country have automatic entry. The rest of the 32 countries (from 1998) must qualify through regional competitions held over the previous two seasons. The final rounds are staged over about a month at several venues, the first round played in groups and the last 16 on a knockout basis. F.I.F.A. also organizes international competitions for various age groups.

Most continental groupings stage their own competitions. The European Championships, for example, are held every four years (between World Cups).

International club competition

Most continents also stage competitions between the leading clubs of their member countries. The chief competitions are the League Champions Cup, formerly the European Cup (inaugurated 1955–56); the European Cup-Winners Cup (1960–61); the U.E.F.A. Cup (1956–58); and the South American Cup (Copa

Libertadores, 1960). A World Club Championship, between the winners of the European and South American cups, and first staged in 1960, has never won the prestige its title suggests and has been played only intermittently since 1974.

WORLD CUP FINALS

Year	Winners		Runners-up	
1930	Uruguay	4	Argentina	2
1934	Italy	2	Czechoslovakia	1
1938	Italy	4	Hungary	2
1950*	Uruguay	2	Brazil	1
1954	West Germany	3	Hungary	2
1958	Brazil	5	Sweden	2
1962	Brazil	3	Czechoslovakia	1
1966	England	4	West Germany	2
1970	Brazil	4	Italy	1
1974	West Germany	2	Netherlands	1
1978	Argentina	3	Netherlands	1
1982	Italy	3	West Germany	1
1986	Argentina	3	West Germany	2
1990	West Germany	1	Argentina	0
1994	Brazil	0	Italy	0

(Brazil won 3–2 on penalties)
*Deciding match of final pool.

WORLD CUP RECORDS

Most wins: 4 Brazil (1958, 1962, 1970, 1994)
Most appearances: 15 Brazil (all, 1930–94)
Most appearances in final: 6 West Germany
Highest score: 10 Hungary (10–1 v. El Salvador, 1982)
Most goals: 14 Gerd Müller, West Germany (10 in 1970, 4 in 1974)
Most in one tournament: 13 Just Fontaine, France (1958)
Most in one match: 5 Oleg Salenko, Russia (v. Cameroon, 1994)
Most in final: 3 Geoff Hurst, England (1966)
Highest attendance: 200,000 Maracaña Stadium, Rio de Janeiro (Brazil v. Uruguay, 1950)

N.F.L. RECORDS

Leading Lifetime Rushers

Player	Years	Attempts	Yards	Average
Walter Payton	13	3838	16,726	4.4
Eric Dickerson	10	2970	13,168	4.4
Tony Dorsett	12	2936	12,739	4.3
Jim Brown	9	2359	12,312	5.2
Franco Harris	13	2949	12,120	4.1
John Riggins	14	2916	11,352	3.9
O.J. Simpson*	11	2404	11,236	4.7
Ottis Anderson	14	2562	10,273	4.0
Earl Campbell	8	2187	9407	4.3
Jim Taylor	10	1941	8597	4.4

*Includes years in A.F.L.

Most Yards Gained, Season: 2105, Eric Dickerson, Los Angeles Rams, 1984.
Most Yards Gained, Game: 275, Walter Payton, Chicago Bears (Nov. 20, 1977).
Most Touchdowns Rushing, Career: 110, Walter Payton, Chicago Bears, 1975–87.

Leading Lifetime Passers (Total Yards)

Player	Years	Attempts	Completions	Yards
Fran Tarkenton	18	6467	3686	47,003
Dan Fouts	15	5604	3294	43,040
Dan Marino	10	5284	3128	39,502
Joe Montana	13	4600	2929	35,124
Ken O'Brien	9	3465	2039	34,386
Ken Anderson	16	4475	2654	32,838
Sonny Jurgensen	18	4262	2433	32,224
Warren Moon	9	4026	2329	30,200
Dave Krieg	13	3989	2326	29,247
Len Dawson*	19	3741	2136	28,711

*Includes years in A.F.L.

Most Yards Gained, Season: 5084, Dan Marino, Miami Dolphins, 1984.
Most Yards Gained, Game: 554, Norm Van Brocklin, L.A. Rams, Sept. 18, 1951.
Most Touchdowns Passing, Career: 342, Fran Tarkenton, Minnesota Vikings (1961–66), N.Y. Giants (1967–71), Minnesota Vikings (1972–78).

CANADIAN FOOTBALL

Rugby was the preeminent fall sport played in Canada during the mid-1800s. The Canadian Rugby Union was formed in the 1860s, fostering games between Canadian and American schools. Elements of the American game—such as the forward pass and running interference—crept into the Canadian game, with 1891 seen as the date that Canadian football emerged as a sport in its own right.

Scoring

Canadian football now is a much closer relative of American football than it is of rugby. The essential differences include the number of players (12—backfield player on offense, linebacker on defense) and the number of downs for offensive teams (three). A punt or kickoff into the end zone must be advanced beyond the goal line or the kicking team is awarded 1 point.

Competition

The Canadian Football League, for professional teams, was established in 1958. It is composed of nine teams playing in two conferences. There are four teams in the Eastern Conference and five in the Western Conference. Teams play for the Grey Cup, originally the trophy awarded to the champions of the Canadian Rugby Union.

The Super Bowl

The two N.F.L. Conference champions play each other in late January in the Super Bowl, the last game in the N.F.L. season. Each year's Super Bowl is designated by a Roman numeral. Super Bowl I was played in 1967 between the N.F.L. and A.F.L. champions. After the A.F.L. was absorbed into the N.F.L. in 1970 the Super Bowl adopted its present format.

The first Super Bowls took their cue from the major Bowl games of college football (see right) and were staged in stadiums in Los Angeles, New Orleans, Miami, and other cities in the South. The advent of covered all-weather domes, however, has led to Super Bowls being staged in the Silverdome (Pontiac, Michigan) and the Metrodome (Minneapolis, Minnesota). Competition to host the Super Bowl is intense as the event brings in millions of dollars to the host city. The Super Bowl's huge popularity is demonstrated by the fact that Super Bowl broadcasts account for 12 of the 30 all-time top television broadcasts.

College football

The game of football is nurtured by competition at college and university level. College football is governed by the National Collegiate Athletic Association (N.C.A.A.). Many college teams play in stadiums holding more than the average N.F.L. stadium. Success on the football field is sometimes the best way to enrich endowments—gifts from nostalgic alumni flow in after a particularly successful season. The promise of full scholarships lures many promising high school players.

Most colleges and universities play other teams in the same conference, or group of teams. The Ivy League, synonymous with academic achievement, is also the name of the sports conference in which these colleges and universities play. The "powerhouses" of college football, however, are the big universities of the Midwest (playing in the Big Eight and Big Ten Conferences) and the South (playing in the Southeastern and Southwestern Conferences).

BOWL GAMES

Conference champions, and other highly ranked college teams, are invited to play in the "Bowl" games at the end of the football season—usually on or around New Year's Day. The oldest Major Bowl game was in 1902, when Michigan beat Stanford 49–0 in the Rose Bowl in Pasadena, California. The second Rose Bowl was in 1916, and the Rose Bowl has been an annual fixture since then. Other Bowl games have developed, usually in southern cities. Occasionally the Bowl games will act as unofficial "playoffs" to help sports writers determine the final rankings of football teams in a given season. Some of these Bowls are listed below:

Name of Bowl	Site	Name of Bowl	Site
Orange Bowl	Miami, Florida	Copper Bowl	Tucson, Arizona
Sugar Bowl	New Orleans, Louisiana	Independence Bowl	Shreveport, Louisiana
Fiesta Bowl	Tempe, Arizona	Citrus Bowl	Orlando, Florida
Hall of Fame Bowl	Tampa, Florida	Peach Bowl	Atlanta, Georgia
John Hancock Bowl	El Paso, Texas	Holiday Bowl	San Diego, California
Cotton Bowl	Dallas, Texas		
Liberty Bowl	Memphis, Tennessee	Aloha Bowl	Honolulu, Hawaii
		Blockbuster Bowl	Miami, Florida
Freedom Bowl	Anaheim, California	Las Vegas Bowl	Las Vegas, Nevada

FOOTBALL

Football evolved from association and rugby football. The landmark event in the history of the game was the visit of the rugby-playing McGill University (Montreal) to soccer-playing Harvard in 1874: the first match was played under the rules of one game, the second match under those of the other. The game evolved into an 11-a-side game in 1876 and underwent drastic rule changes in 1906, including the introduction of the forward pass. The game flourished in the universities, and the first Rose Bowl game, between leading colleges, was staged in 1902. A professional association formed in 1920, becoming the National Football League (N.F.L.) in 1922.

Many people view football as the national sport. College games, professional games, and the Super Bowl regularly attract millions of television viewers.

Rules

The team in possession, the offense, has four plays, called downs, to advance the ball 10 yards by running with it or passing it. Success, in four or fewer downs,

SUPER BOWL

Year	Winner		Runners-up		Venue
1967	Green Bay Packers	35	Kansas City Chiefs	10	Los Angeles Coliseum
1968	Green Bay Packers	33	Oakland Raiders	14	Orange Bowl, Miami
1969	New York Jets	16	Baltimore Colts	7	Orange Bowl, Miami
1970	Kansas City Chiefs	23	Minnesota Vikings	7	Tulane Stadium, New Orleans
1971	Baltimore Colts	16	Dallas Cowboys	13	Orange Bowl, Miami
1972	Dallas Cowboys	24	Miami Dolphins	3	Tulane Stadium, New Orleans
1973	Miami Dolphins	14	Washington Redskins	7	Los Angeles Coliseum
1974	Miami Dolphins	24	Minnesota Vikings	7	Rice Stadium, Houston
1975	Pittsburgh Steelers	16	Minnesota Vikings	6	Tulane Stadium, New Orleans
1976	Pittsburgh Steelers	21	Dallas Cowboys	17	Orange Bowl, Miami
1977	Oakland Raiders	32	Minnesota Vikings	14	Rose Bowl, Pasadena
1978	Dallas Cowboys	27	Denver Broncos	10	Superdome, New Orleans
1979	Pittsburgh Steelers	35	Dallas Cowboys	31	Orange Bowl, Miami
1980	Pittsburgh Steelers	31	Los Angeles Rams	19	Rose Bowl, Pasadena
1981	Oakland Raiders	27	Philadelphia Eagles	10	Superdome, New Orleans
1982	San Francisco 49ers	26	Cincinnati Bengals	21	Silverdome, Pontiac
1983	Washington Redskins	27	Miami Dolphins	17	Rose Bowl, Pasadena
1984	Los Angeles Raiders	38	Washington Redskins	9	Tampa Stadium
1985	San Francisco 49ers	38	Miami Dolphins	16	Stanford Stadium, Palo Alto
1986	Chicago Bears	46	New England Patriots	10	Superdome, New Orleans
1987	New York Giants	39	Denver Broncos	20	Rose Bowl, Pasadena
1988	Washington Redskins	42	Denver Broncos	10	San Diego Stadium
1989	San Francisco 49ers	20	Cincinnati Bengals	16	Joe Robbie Stadium, Miami
1990	San Francisco 49ers	55	Denver Broncos	10	Superdome, New Orleans
1991	New York Giants	20	Buffalo Bills	19	Tampa Stadium
1992	Washington Redskins	37	Buffalo Bills	24	Metrodome, Minneapolis
1993	Dallas Cowboys	52	Buffalo Bills	17	Rose Bowl, Pasadena
1994	Dallas Cowboys	30	Buffalo Bills	13	Georgia Dome, Atlanta
1995	San Francisco 49ers	49	San Diego Chargers	26	Joe Robbie Stadium, Miami

gives them another first down, or series of plays. If they fail, possession passes to the opposition. Professional teams have up to 45 players with separate squads for offense, defense, and kicking; any number of substitutions may be made during the game. There are seven officials—referee, umpire, head linesman, line judge, back judge, side judge, and field judge.

Scoring

Points are scored by taking the ball into the opposition end zone, or catching a pass in it, for a touchdown, worth 6 points, plus 1 extra point for a successful kicking conversion or 2 points for a running or passing conversion; kicking the ball between the goalposts for a field goal (3 points); and tackling a player in his own end zone for a safety (2 points).

Competition

The N.F.L. comprises the National Football Conference (N.F.C.) and the American Football Conference (A.F.C.), each having 15 teams. The A.F.C. was formed in 1970 after the N.F.L. absorbed the American Football League (A.F.L.), which had existed from 1960 to 1969. The N.F.C. and A.F.C. are both divided into Eastern, Central, and Western divisions. The top two teams in each division, along with two "wild card teams," go into post-season playoffs to decide the two Conference champions.

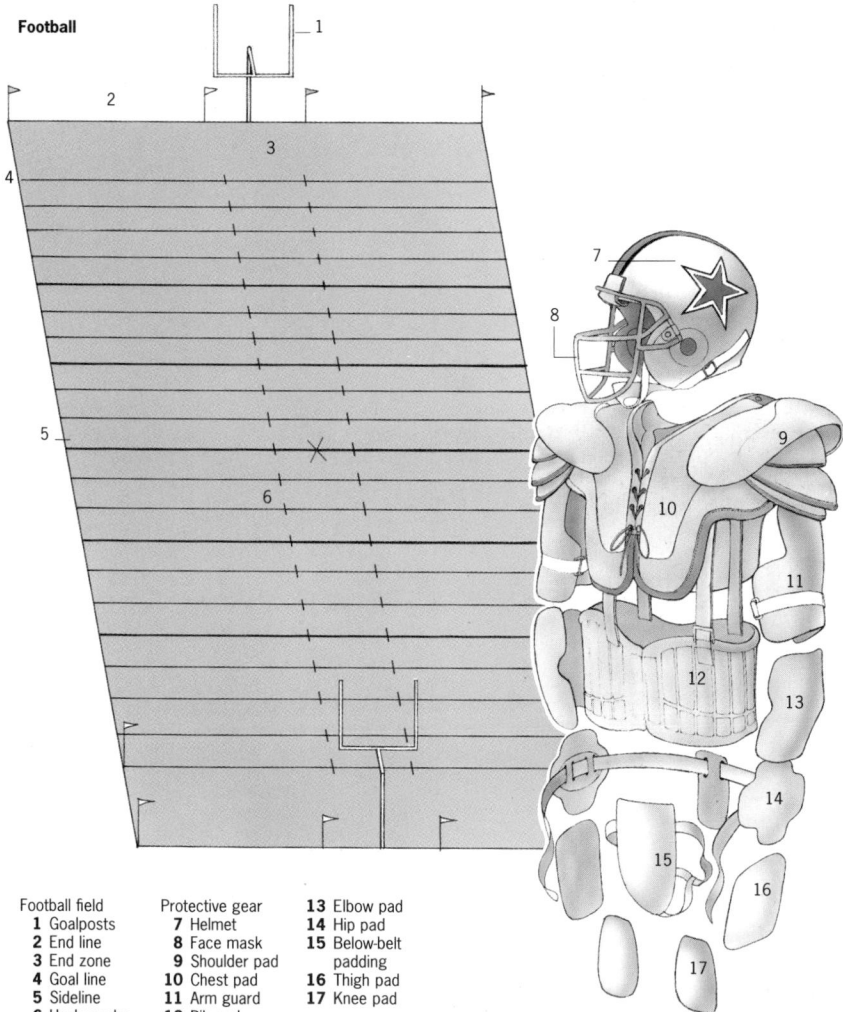

Football

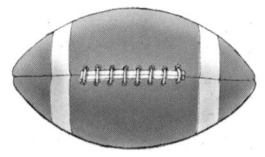

Football field
1 Goalposts
2 End line
3 End zone
4 Goal line
5 Sideline
6 Hash marks

Protective gear
7 Helmet
8 Face mask
9 Shoulder pad
10 Chest pad
11 Arm guard
12 Rib pad

13 Elbow pad
14 Hip pad
15 Below-belt padding
16 Thigh pad
17 Knee pad

AUSTRALIAN RULES FOOTBALL

This is a game played by teams of 18 players on a huge oval field whose dimensions are 148–202 yards (135–185 m) by 120–170 yards (110–155 m). Players may kick, palm, or punch the oval ball, but not throw it. In a technique called hand-balling, they hold the ball in one hand and bat it with the other. Players may also run with the ball provided they bounce it or touch it on the ground approximately every 11 yards (10 m).

Scoring

A goal is worth 6 points and is scored with a clean kick between the tall goal-posts. A behind (1 point) is scored if the ball touches a goalpost or passes between a goalpost and the shorter behind post that flanks it.

Competition

Australian Rules developed from rugby and Irish Gaelic football in the 1840s. Most of the leading clubs of the Australian Football League are in the Melbourne district. The Grand Final, played annually since 1897, is staged at the Melbourne Cricket Ground.

RUGBY

Rugby began its development out of association football at Rugby School in England, when a boy, William Webb Ellis, picked the ball up—which was not permissible at the time—and ran with it toward his opponents' goal instead of kicking it. This was in 1823, but it was 20 years before the first rugby club was formed at Guy's Hospital in London. The Rugby Football Union was founded in 1871, and teams were fixed at 15 players in 1875. The breakaway Northern Rugby Football Union was formed in 1895 to enable players to receive payments for playing the game. This became fully professional in 1898. Teams were reduced to 13 in 1906, and the Northern Union became known as the Rugby League in 1922. Rugby Union remained a largely amateur sport.

Rugby Union

The game is played in two 40-minute halves, and is controlled by a referee with the help of two touch judges. Players may handle the oval ball, run with it, pass it, and kick it, but may not propel it forward with the hands. A player may tackle an opponent and bring him or her down only when holding the ball.

Scoring

Points are scored by carrying the ball over the opposition goal line and touching it down (a try) or by kicking it over the crossbar (a goal). A try is worth 5 points. Converting—that is, scoring a goal from a resultant place kick—scores an extra 2 points. A goal scored from a penalty kick is worth 3 points, as is a drop goal, scored during open play by dropping the ball from the hands and kicking it after it touches the ground.

Competition

The traditional strongholds of Rugby Union are the British Isles, France, South Africa, Australia, and New Zealand. An International Championship was started in 1884 by England, Ireland (who play as a combined side to this day despite the 1920 partition), Scotland, and Wales. This became a Five-Nations Tournament in 1910 when a French team was added to the annual competition. Rugby tours began in 1888. The British teams usually tour abroad as a combined side, called the British Lions, but foreign touring sides visiting Britain play them as the four individual national teams.

The World Cup

First-class status has been accorded to many more nations with the inauguration of the World Cup in 1987, which is contested every four years. The first World Cup was held in Australia and New Zealand, with New Zealand beating France 29–9 in the finals. The 1991 World Cup was held in Britain and France, with Australia beating England 12–6 in the finals. There has also been a women's Rugby World Cup competition since 1990.

Rugby League

Rugby League has a smaller in-goal area and there are some other minor differences in markings. The players' positions are also similar, except that there are six forwards instead of eight. An individual feature of Rugby League is the tackle and play-the-ball rule, in which a tackled player who retains possession of the ball must be immediately released and may then kick or heel the ball. Five consecutive play-the-balls are allowed to a side, but the ball must be conceded to the opposition after a sixth tackle.

Scoring

A try is worth 3 points, a conversion and penalty goal 2 points each, and a drop goal 1 point. The strongholds of Rugby League are England, where the professional game is played mainly in the north, and Australia. A World Cup was inaugurated in 1954 and has gone through several formats and been staged at irregular intervals. The contenders are Australia, Britain, New Zealand, France, and latterly Papua New Guinea.

Players' jersey numbers denote their positions. Forwards: front row—1 loose-head prop, 2 hooker, 3 tight-head prop; second row—4 and 5 lock forwards, 6 and 7 flankers; 8 number eight. Halves: 9 scrum-half, 10 fly-half. Backs: three-quarters—11 and 14 wingers, 12 and 13 centers; 15 full back.

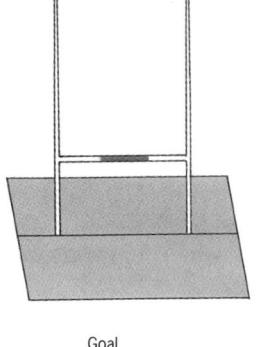

Goal

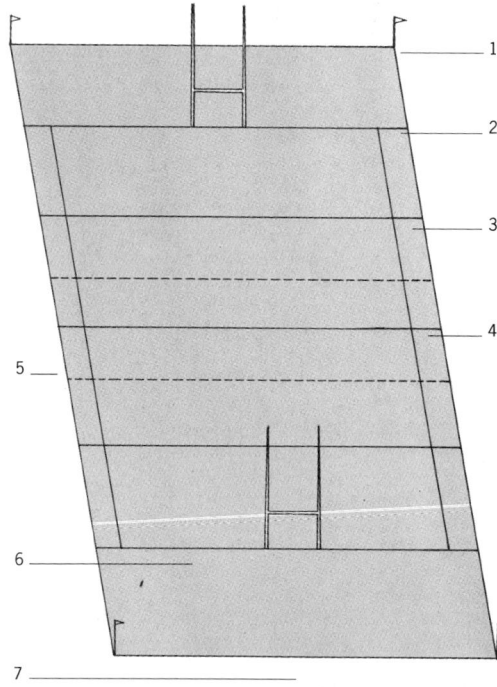

1 Dead-ball line
2 Goal line
3 22-yard line
4 Halfway line
5 Touchline
6 In-goal area
7 Touch-in goal

BASEBALL

Baseball is believed to have developed from English games such as cricket and rounders. The first rules were drawn up in 1845 by Alexander Joy Cartwright, and the first formalized game was played in 1846 in New Jersey. The National League was formed in 1876, the American League in 1900, and the World Series began in 1903.

Rules

Baseball is played by teams of nine players each on a square infield, the diamond, with a large outfield. At one point of the diamond is home plate, where the batter stands, and at the other points are first, second, and third bases. The pitcher throws the ball from a mound in the center of the diamond. To score a run, the batter must progress around the bases to reach home plate; this may be done with one hit or on hits of succeeding batters.

Scoring and dismissal

There are nine innings, each side having nine turns at bat while the other fields. The fielding side must get three batters out to close an inning and take their next turn at bat. Substitutes are allowed at any time, but a substituted player may not return (except, in some competitions, the pitcher), and the substitute must take his or her place in the batting order. A batter who hits the ball into fair territory must drop the bat and run, at least to first base. Any other batter already on a base may run, too, and must run to avoid two batters on one base. Every batter who reaches home plate scores a run. To strike a player out, the pitcher must throw the ball over the plate and within the strike zone (batter's shoulders to knees). A strike is also called if the batter swings and misses or hits a foul (foul line). A batter is also out if the ball is hit into fair territory and is caught. A runner is out if he or she is tagged by a fielder holding the ball or if the fielder, with a foot on the base, catches the ball before the runner reaches the base. More than one player may be put out in the same play. If the batter does not swing at a pitch outside the strike zone, a ball is called. The batter is out after three strikes (but cannot foul on the third strike). If four balls are called, the batter "walks"—automatically moves to first base.

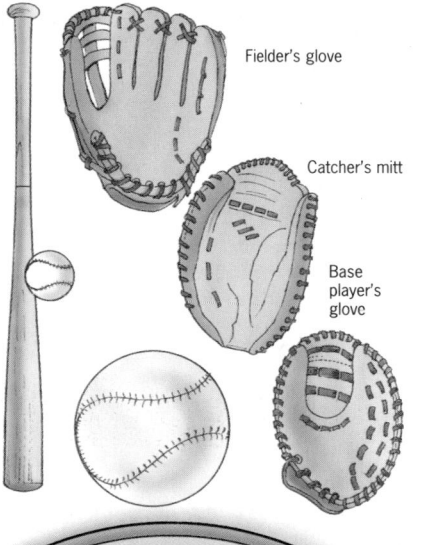

Fielder's glove

Catcher's mitt

Base player's glove

Competition

The World Series, contested only by professional U.S. and Canadian teams, adopted its current best-of-seven format in 1905. It was 1992 before a Canadian team, the Toronto Blue Jays, won it, and they did it again in 1993. Baseball spread to other countries, especially Japan and Cuba, but with no professional international competition. A World Amateur Championship was instituted in 1938, run by the International Baseball Association. It has been dominated by Cuba. Baseball first appeared in the Olympics as a medal sport in 1992, with Cuba winning the gold medal.

World Series

First held in 1903, the World Series takes place each October. Professional baseball's leading event, it consists of the best of seven end-of-season matches between the winners of the National League (N.L.) and the American League (A.L.).

Recent winners

1982 St. Louis Cardinals (N.L.)
1983 Baltimore Orioles (A.L.)
1984 Detroit Tigers (A.L.)
1985 Kansas City Royals (A.L.)
1986 New York Mets (N.L.)
1987 Minnesota Twins (A.L.)
1988 Los Angeles Dodgers (N.L.)
1989 Oakland Athletics (A.L.)
1990 Cincinnati Reds (N.L.)
1991 Minnesota Twins (A.L.)
1992 Toronto Blue Jays (A.L.)
1993 Toronto Blue Jays (A.L.)
1994 No World Series held because of strike
Most wins: (22), New York Yankees, 1923, 1927–28, 1932, 1936–39, 1941, 1943, 1947, 1949–53, 1956, 1958, 1961–62, 1977–78.

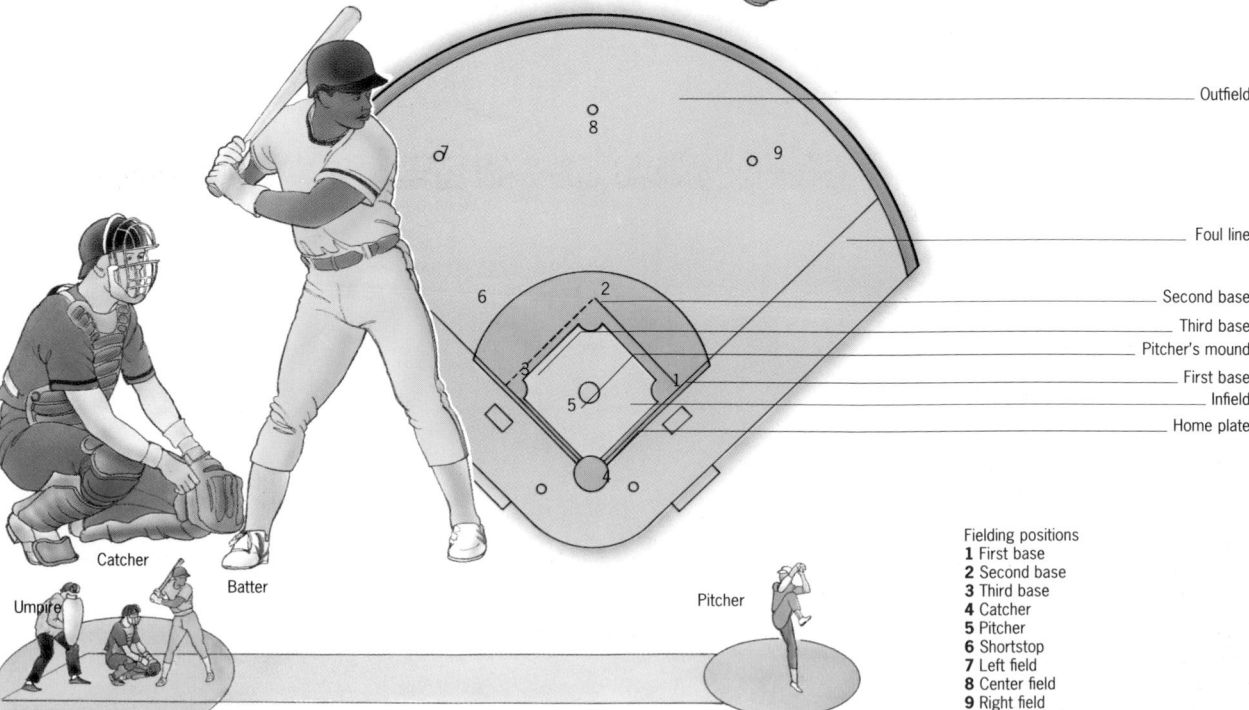

Outfield

Foul line

Second base
Third base
Pitcher's mound
First base
Infield
Home plate

Catcher

Batter

Umpire

Pitcher

Fielding positions
1 First base
2 Second base
3 Third base
4 Catcher
5 Pitcher
6 Shortstop
7 Left field
8 Center field
9 Right field

Expansion and Realignment

The transfer of franchises from city to city (usually taking the team name with the franchise) has been a feature of both the National and American leagues since World War II. In most cases the transfers have opened up the game to cities in the Midwest and West. New Yorkers still regret the transfer of the Giants (to San Francisco) and the Dodgers (to Los Angeles) in the 1950s. Other teams have gone through more than one change of city. The Philadelphia Athletics became the Kansas City Athletics before becoming the Oakland Athletics (or A's). The Boston Braves spent more than a decade as the Milwaukee Braves before settling in Atlanta.

During the same period new franchises were granted, increasing the size of both leagues. Some of these "expansion" teams include the Houston Astros, San Diego Padres, Seattle Mariners, and New York Mets. Professional baseball also crossed the border into Canada at this time, with the creation of the Montreal Expos and Toronto Blue Jays.

The increased number of teams, along with the extra coast-to-coast travel it entailed, led to the establishment of East and West divisions in both leagues in 1969. Best-of-seven elimination series (between divisional winners) preceded the World Series under this new setup. The process was taken a stage further with a three-division alignment (East, Central, and West) for both leagues. The 1995 season, whose opening was delayed by the players' strike, is the first to see the new divisional playoffs, which now resemble those of the N.F.L. Four teams in each league will make these playoffs—the three division winners and a "wild card" team (not a division winner) with the best won-loss record. The new system therefore adds an extra stage of playoffs to precede the World Series.

The new three-divisional alignment is outlined in the panel (right).

Major awards

Baseball has always thrived on statistics and the impassioned arguments in the "hot stove league" (so called because fans traditionally gathered around the winter stove to debate the previous season). The end of each season sees a number of players honored for their performances. Two of these awards—Most Valuable Player and Rookie of the Year—are chosen by the Baseball Writers' Association to recognize achievement in batting or pitching. Other post-season awards are more specific. The Sporting News Golden Glove Awards go to the best Major League fielders at each position; Cy Young Awards honor the best pitcher in each league.

The Hall of Fame, in Cooperstown, New York, was established in 1934. Apart from its intention of displaying baseball memorabilia, the Hall of Fame annually inducts a select few players. Information on their careers goes on display, and players have the satisfaction of having achieved the sport's highest honor. Players become eligible for election five years after their professional playing careers have ended.

Little League

Little League Baseball is an organized league for baseball players between the ages of 6 and 18. There are Little Leagues in more than 30 countries around the world, with nearly 3 million young people playing the game. Girls have been allowed on Little league teams since 1974, and a division for handi-capped players was established in 1989.

The principle behind Little League, like that of other youth organizations, is to encourage teamwork and sportsmanship along with developing the skills of the game itself.

Little League was formed in 1939 in Williamsport, Pennsylvania, and each year a Little League World Series is held there for players between the ages of 8 and 12. This tournament lives up to its "international" name far more than its Major League counterpart. Since 1983 only one U.S. team (from Trumbull, Connecticut) has won the Little League World Series. Taiwan is the foreign country that has produced the most winning teams—17 since it first entered the competition in 1969.

DIVISIONAL REALIGNMENT

National League

East	Central	West
Atlanta Braves	Chicago Cubs	Colorado Rockies
Florida Marlins	Cincinnati Reds	Los Angeles Dodgers
Montreal Expos	Houston Astros	San Diego Padres
New York Mets	Pittsburgh Pirates	San Francisco Giants
Philadelphia Phillies	St. Louis Cardinals	

American League

East	Central	West
Baltimore Orioles	Chicago White Sox	California Angels
Boston Red Sox	Cleveland Indians	Oakland Athletics
Detroit Tigers	Kansas City Royals	Seattle Mariners
New York Yankees	Milwaukee Brewers	Texas Rangers
Toronto Blue Jays	Minnesota Twins	

BASEBALL STADIUMS: FACTS AND FIGURES

Category	Stadium	Team	Details
Longest H.R. distance (R.F.)	Mile High Stadium	Colorado	370 ft.
Shortest H.R. distance (R.F.)	Fenway Park	Boston	302 ft.
Longest H.R. distance (C.F.)	Mile High Stadium	Colorado	423 ft.
Shortest H.R. distance (C.F.)	Fenway Park	Boston	390 ft
Longest H.R. distance (L.F.)	Wrigley Field	Chicago (N.L.)	370 ft.
Shortest H.R. distance (L.F.)	Fenway Park	Boston	315 ft.
	Milwaukee County Stadium	Milwaukee	315 ft.

ALL-TIME MAJOR LEAGUE LEADERS

Batting

Most Games, Career: Pete Rose, Cincinnati Reds—3,562.
Most Hits, Career: Pete Rose, Cincinnati Reds—4,256.
Most Home Runs, Season: Roger Maris, New York Yankees—61 (1961).
Most Home Runs, Career: Hank Aaron, Milwaukee (Atlanta) Braves—755.
Most Runs Batted In, Season: Hack Wilson, Chicago Cubs—190 (1930).
Most Runs Batted In, Career: Hank Aaron, Milwaukee (Atlanta) Braves—2,297.
Highest Batting Average, Season: Rogers Hornsby, St. Louis Cardinals—.424 (1924).
Highest Batting Average, Career: Ty Cobb, Detroit Tigers—.367.
Most Stolen Bases, Season: Rickey Henderson, Toronto Blue Jays—130 (1982).
Most Stolen Bases, Career: Rickey Henderson, Toronto Blue Jays—1,095.

Pitching

Most Wins, Career: Cy Young, Boston Red Sox—511.
Lowest Earned-Run Average, Season: Dwight Gooden, New York Mets—1.53 (1985).
Most No-Hit Games, Career: Nolan Ryan, California Angels, Houston Astros, Texas Rangers—7.
Most Shutouts, Season: Grover Cleveland Alexander—16 (1916).
Most Shutouts, Career: Walter Johnson, Washington Senators—110.
Most Strikeouts, Career: Nolan Ryan, California Angels, Houston Astros, Texas Rangers—5,714.

CRICKET

Cricket as an organized sport can be traced back to the late 1600s in the south of England. It was played long before then, probably as far back as 1300, but its early development is obscure. The first known laws were drawn up in 1744, when it was played with a curved bat and two stumps, and bowling was underarm.

Rules

Cricket is played by 11 players on each team. Each side has two innings to score runs. A wicket consisting of three stumps is placed at each end of a grassy pitch 22 yards (20 m) long. The batting side provides one batsman at each wicket, and when ten batsmen are out the inning is closed. The object of the fielding side is to bowl the batting side out for as few runs as possible. Any member of the fielding side may bowl. Bowling is carried out in overs constituting six balls from one end of the field. Overs are bowled alternately from each end, and no bowler may bowl two consecutive overs. The game is controlled by two umpires.

Scoring

A run is scored when a batsman hits the ball with the bat and both batsmen cross to opposite ends of the pitch without being dismissed. Any number of runs may be scored from a single hit by running between the wickets. A hit over the boundary (marked by a rope, white line, or fence) is worth 4 runs, or 6 if it goes over without first touching the ground; boundaries do not need to be run.

Dismissals

There are several ways in which a batsman may be ruled "out": he or she may be bowled, if the ball breaks the wicket (at least one bail must be dislodged); caught, if the ball is cleanly caught by a fielder off the bat or glove before it touches the ground; leg before wicket (l.b.w.), when any part of a batsman's body, prevents the ball hitting the wicket.

Competition

To be recognized as first-class, a cricket match must have two innings a side, whether it is played over three, four, or five days. Since the early 1960s however, limited-overs cricket, in which each side has only one innings with a maximum of between 40 and 60 overs, has flourished. Such matches are scheduled to be completed within a day, but they sometimes overrun as a result of bad weather. Countries play one-day (limited-overs) international matches as well as full international (Test) matches.

Test cricket

The Test-playing countries are: England (first Test in 1877), Australia (1877), South Africa (1889), West Indies (1928), New Zealand (1931), India (1932), Pakistan (1954), Sri Lanka (1982), and Zimbabwe (1992). Test cricket is too unwieldy for more than two countries to take part in competitions, and it takes the form of series of matches (usually three to six) played by a touring side in another country.

ICE HOCKEY

Deriving from a game called "bandy," a type of hockey played in northern Europe from the early 1800s on fields of ice or packed snow, ice hockey dates from 1860, when British soldiers, playing on the frozen harbor in Kingston, Ontario, used a puck instead of a ball. This new game caught on in Canada. McGill University formed the first club in 1880. The International Ice Hockey Federation was founded in England in 1908, and the first world championships were held in 1920, when ice hockey also became an Olympic sport. Women's world championships were first held in 1990.

Rules

Ice hockey is played six-a-side on an enclosed rink. It is a fast game, with players skates traveling at 33 mph (48kph) and a hard-driven puck at more than 103 mph (160kph). There is considerable physical

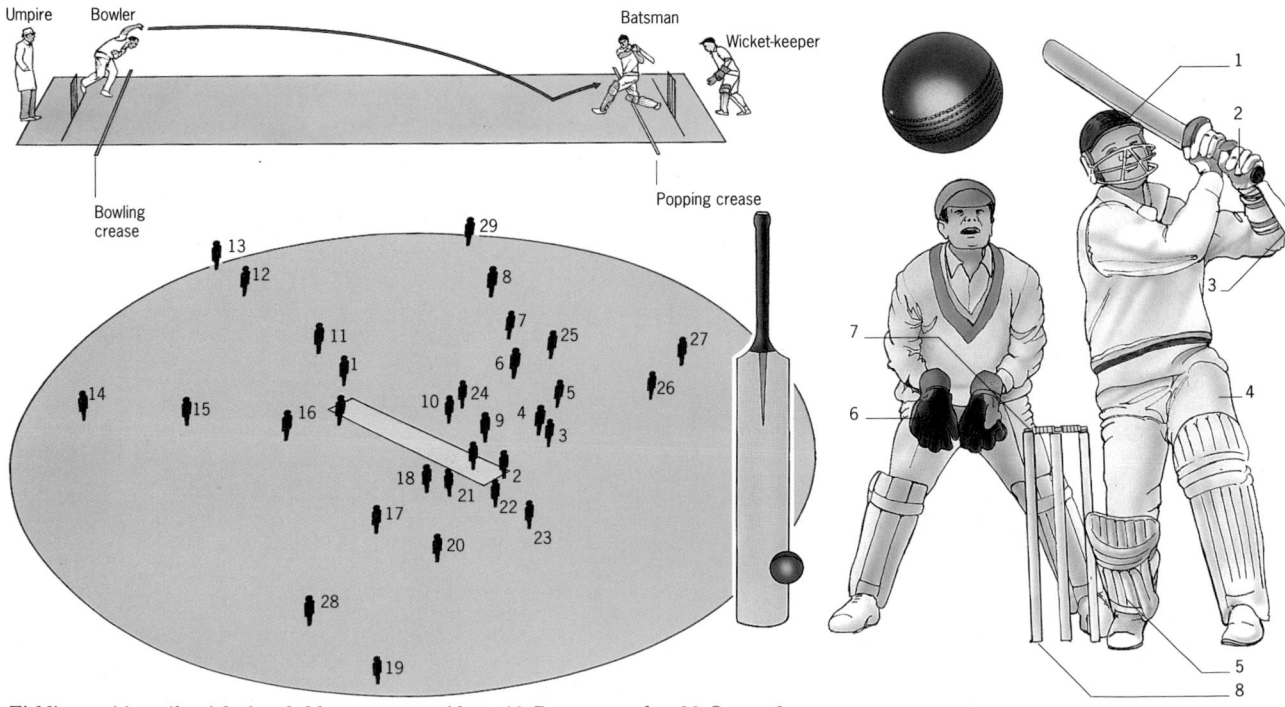

Fielding positions (for right-handed batsman): 1 Bowler; 2 Wicket-keeper; 3 First slip; 4 Second slip; 5 Gully; 6 Point; 7 Cover point; 8 Extra cover; 9 Silly point; 10 Silly mid-off; 11 Mid-off; 12 Deep mid-off; 13 Long off; 14 Long on; 15 Deep mid-on; 16 Mid-on; 17 Mid-wicket; 18 Silly mid-on; 19 Deep square-leg; 20 Square-leg; 21 Forward short-leg; 22 Backward short-leg; 23 Leg slip; 24 Short extra cover; 25 Backward point; 26 Short third man; 27 Third man; 28 Deep mid-wicket; 29 Deep extra cover.

1 Protective helmet
2 Batting gloves
3 Arm pad
4 Thigh pad
5 Leg pads
6 Wicket-keeping glove
7 Bails
8 Stumps

contact, and players may be sent to cool off in the penalty box, or "sin bin," for two, five, or ten minutes. Substitutes may be made at any time, but players serving penalties may not be substituted. A game lasts for three periods of 20 minutes, and the clock stops whenever play stops. The object is to score goals by propelling the puck into the opposition goal cage. The rink is divided into three zones, and a player must not precede the puck into the attacking zone. A player may stop the puck in the air with an open hand, but only the goalkeeper may catch the puck. Players may kick or push the puck along the ice with a hand, but not to pass the puck or to score.

Competition

The National Hockey League (N.H.L.) comprises 24 professional teams in the United States and Canada. The league is divided into two conferences of 12 teams, and each conference in turn consists of two divisions of six teams each. Teams play 84 games in the regular season running from October to April.

The top four teams in each division enter best-of-seven game playoffs. Divisional champions play each other in another best-of-seven series to become the conference champions. These last two teams play for the Stanley Cup, also decided over the best of seven games.

STANLEY CUP CHAMPIONS

Year	Team
1994	New York Rangers
1993	Montreal Canadiens
1992	Pittsburgh Penguins
1991	Pittsburgh Penguins
1990	Edmonton Oilers
1989	Calgary Flames
1988	Edmonton Oilers
1987	Edmonton Oilers
1986	Montreal Canadiens
1985	Edmonton Oilers
1984	Edmonton Oilers

FIELD HOCKEY

Games played with a ball and hooked sticks have been known since ancient times, but the game known today as "field hockey" originated in England in the 1880s; the Hockey Association (founded in 1886) drew up the first set of rules. The International Hockey Board was established in Britain in 1900.

Rules

Field hockey is played by teams of 11. It is controlled by two umpires and played for two halves of 35 minutes. The players strike the traditionally white ball with hooked sticks.

Goals may be scored only from within the shooting, or striking, circle. Players may not play the ball above shoulder height, and only the goalkeeper, inside the shooting circle, may handle the ball or use the feet (or pads) to propel the ball. Field hockey laws are similar to those of soccer, with offsides, free-hits, penalty strokes, and corners.

LACROSSE

Lacrosse developed from a ritualistic game played by North American Indians and taken up in the 1700s by French travelers who, likened the sticks to a bishop's staff—*la crosse*.

Three major versions of lacrosse are played. All involve carrying a ball in a net on the end of a stick, passing it to teammates, and shooting for a goal.

Rules

Men's lacrosse is ten-a-side with, at international level, nine substitutes allowed. There are four 15-minute periods, and the game is controlled by three referees. The field measures 110 x 60 yards (100 x 55 m), with 6-foot (1.8-m) square goals set 79 yards (72 m) apart.

Women's lacrosse is 12-a-side with unlimited substitution under certain conditions, and is played in two 25-minute halves. There are no field boundaries, and the goals are 101 yards (92 m) apart.

Box lacrosse is six-a-side, usually played indoors on a small area bounded by a fence. World championships were first held in 1967.

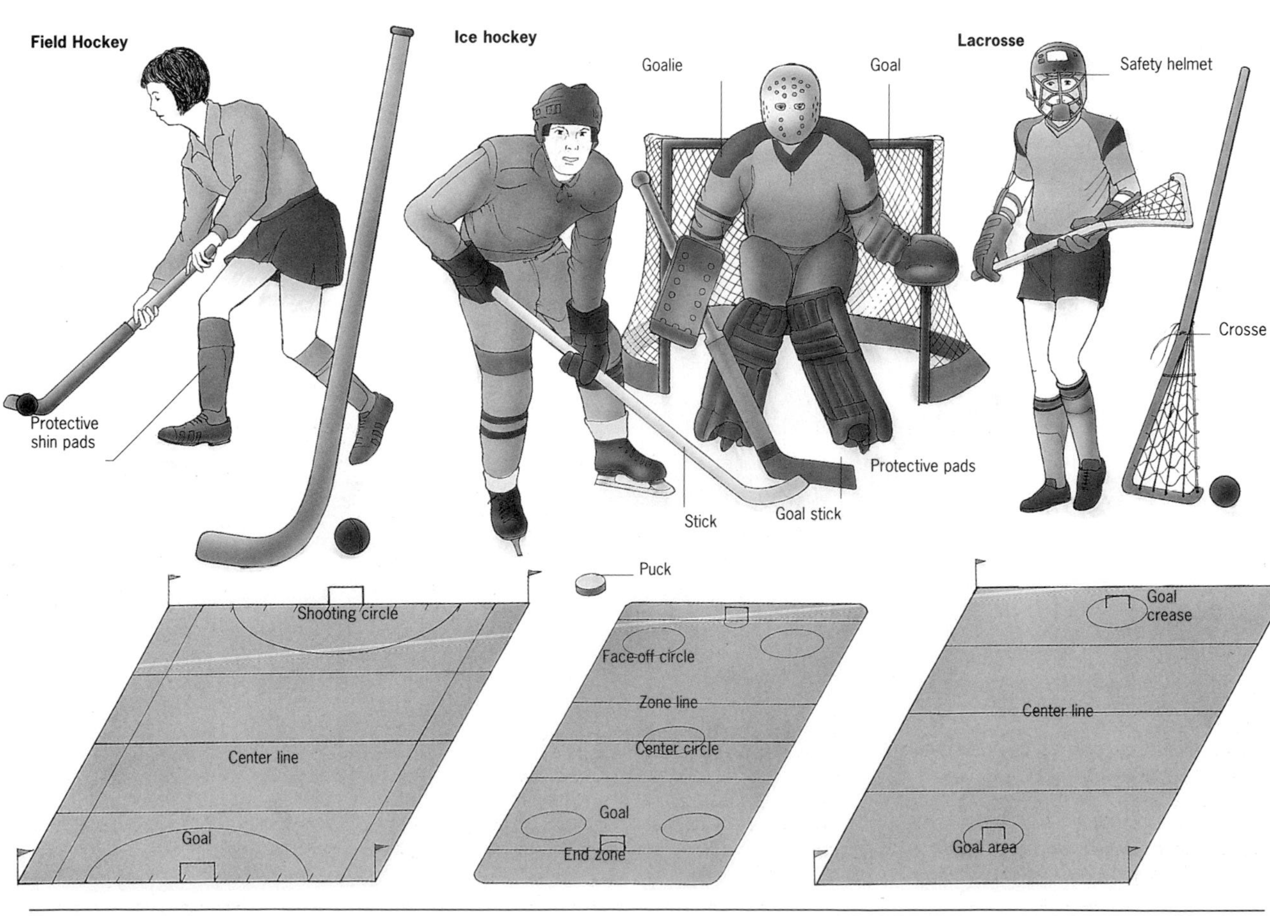

Field Hockey

Protective shin pads

Shooting circle

Center line

Goal

Ice hockey

Goalie

Goal

Stick

Goal stick

Protective pads

Puck

Face-off circle

Zone line

Center circle

Goal

End zone

Lacrosse

Safety helmet

Crosse

Goal crease

Center line

Goal area

TENNIS

The forerunners of racket sports go back to France in the 1100s, but the modern game of lawn tennis developed in Britain in the 1860s. In 1873, Major Walter Wingfield of North Wales published a book of rules for a game he called sphairistike (*sphaira* being Greek for ball), which had an hourglass-shaped court. The game caught on in several versions until the All England Croquet Club, Wimbledon, drew up rules. The Wimbledon Championships began in 1877 with men's singles. Tennis went "open" in 1968.

Rules

The object of tennis is to score points by hitting the ball into court over the net so that your opponent cannot return it into your court. The ball may be struck before it has bounced or after one bounce.

Scoring

Tennis is played in sets, usually the best of three, although some major men's tournaments are the best of five. A set is won by the first player or doubles team to win six games, with a lead of at least two. The points in a game go from love (0) to 15, 30, 40, and game. If the score reaches 40–40, it is called deuce; one or the other must gain a lead of 2 points to win the game. After deuce, the player to win the next point has "advantage" and can win the game on the next point; otherwise the score returns to deuce. Players serve alternate games, changing ends when the number of games in a set is odd.

Tiebreaker

In most competitions, when a set reaches the score 6–6, a tiebreaker is played. This is a game with special scoring: the winner is the first to reach 7 points with a lead of at least 2. The set score is given as 7–6.

Competition

The four "Grand Slam" Championship tournaments are Wimbledon (inaugurated in 1877 and played on grass), U.S. Open (1891, acrylic cement), French Open (1891, red clay), and Australian Open (1905, synthetic hardcourt), each of which has men's and women's singles, and men's, women's, and mixed doubles. The world ranking system is based on achievements in major events. Tennis was an Olympic sport up to 1924, and it returned to the Games in 1988.

The chief team events are elimination competitions for nations: the Davis Cup for men (1900) and the Federation Cup for women (1963). In the Davis Cup, each competition is the best of five matches, comprising two pairs of singles and one doubles played over three days, and is contested in the country of one of the two participants. The Federation Cup is played in one venue over a few days, and each competition is the best of three (two singles and a doubles).

Records

Grand Slam (all four events) in one year
Men
   Donald Budge (U.S.A.) 1938
   Rod Laver (Australia) 1962, 1969
Women
   Maureen Connolly (U.S.A.) 1953
   Margaret Court (Australia) 1970
   Martina Navratilova (U.S.A.) 1983–84
   Steffi Graf (Germany) 1988

Most Wimbledon singles titles*
Men
   5 Bjorn Borg (Sweden) 1976–80
Women
   9 Martina Navratilova (Czechoslovakia 2, U.S.A. 7) 1978–79, 1982–87, 1990

Most Grand Slam singles titles
Men
   12 Roy Emerson (Australia) Australian 6, French 2, Wimbledon 2, U.S. 2
Women
   24 Margaret Court (Australia) Australian 11, French 5, Wimbledon 3, U.S. 5

*Since 1922.

SQUASH

"Squash rackets" was first played at Harrow School, in England, in the 1800s as a smaller version of the game of rackets and with a softer ball. By 1886 it had become a game in its own right. It went on to become popular in the U.S.A., where the American Squash Rackets Association was founded in 1907 and where the game developed with slightly different rules: doubles was also played. The British Open, founded in 1930, was regarded as the unofficial world championship until the World Amateur Championship was instituted in 1967. Squash went "open" and the first World Open Championship was held in 1976.

Rules

Squash is played on an enclosed court, the boundaries of which are marked on each wall. After the service, each player hits the ball alternately. A player must play the ball before it has bounced twice, and the ball must hit the front wall, below the out-of-court line and above the tin, or "telltale," either directly or after hitting one or more of the other walls. The scoring varies according to the competition. Matches are usually the best of five sets, which are either 15-up, with both players able to score, or the traditional 9-up, with only the server scoring.

Records

Most World Open wins
Men: 6 Jahangir Khan (Pakistan)
Women: 5 Susan Devoy (New Zealand)

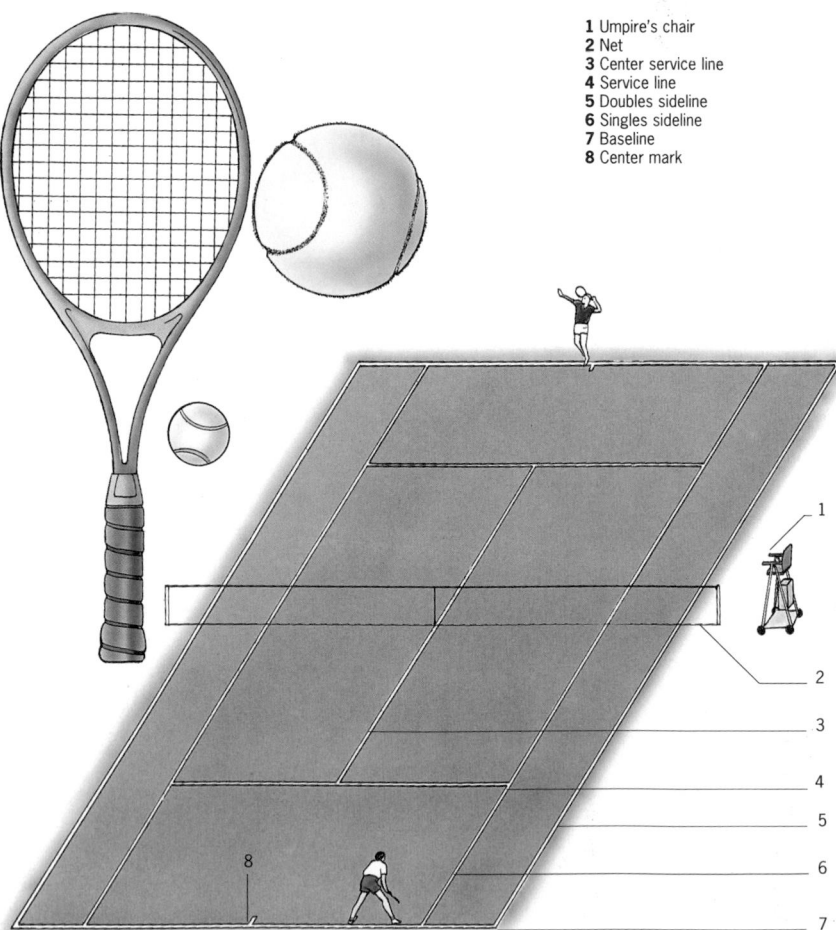

1 Umpire's chair
2 Net
3 Center service line
4 Service line
5 Doubles sideline
6 Singles sideline
7 Baseline
8 Center mark

BADMINTON

Badminton derives from the old children's game of battledore and shuttlecock, its name coming from the country home of the Duke of Beaufort, where guests played it in the 1870s. The rules were fixed by British officers in India in 1877. The International Badminton Federation was founded in 1934.

Rules

Badminton is played singles or doubles by hitting a shuttlecock over a high net into the opposition court. The shuttle must always be played before it touches the floor. Matches are usually the best of three sets, which are 15-up for men, 11-up for women. Only the server can score.

Competition

The All-England Championships, first held in 1899, were the leading event until World Championships began in 1977. World team events, the Thomas Cup (1949) for men and the Uber Cup (1957) for women, are now staged biennially.

Records

Most world team titles
Thomas Cup: 9 Indonesia
Uber Cup: 5 Japan, China
Most U.S. singles titles
Men: 7 David Freeman
Women: 12 Judy Hashman

TABLE TENNIS

Table tennis—originally called Ping-Pong—evolved as an indoor game in the late 1800s, when a variety of improvised rackets were used to bat a cork or rubber ball across the dining-room table. Later, a celluloid ball from the United States, pioneered by James Gibb, revived interest in the game. The International Table Tennis Federation was founded in 1926.

Rules

Table tennis is played singles or doubles. The object is to score points by hitting the ball over the net and into your opponent's half of the table, so that they cannot return it. Games are 21-up and matches are usually the best of three or five games. The ball must not be volleyed—it must bounce on your court before you hit it. When serving, you play the ball onto your own court to bounce over the net into your opponent's. Each player or side serves for 5 points at a time. In doubles, partners play alternate strokes.

Competition

World championships and a men's team event, the Swaythling Cup, have been contested since 1926, and a women's team event, the Corbillon Cup, since 1934, biennially since 1957. Table tennis became an Olympic sport in 1988. Central Europe was the stronghold until the mid-1950s, when the Japanese revolutionized the game with their sponge bats and "penholder" grip. The Chinese began to dominate in the 1960s, challenged seriously only by Swedish men.

Records

Most world titles (singles)
Men: 5 Viktor Barna (Hungary)
Women: 6 Angelica Rozeanu (Romania)
Swaythling Cup: 12 Hungary
Corbillon Cup: 10 China

Other racket sports

Rackets

Rackets in its present form developed during the 1800s, after being played for at least 100 years against the walls of the debtors' prisons of London, where the inmates found they had insufficient room to play real tennis (*below*). Today's courts, which are mainly confined to the United States and the U.K., are about three times the size of those for squash. The floor is of stone and the walls hard enough to stand battering with the hard ball, which is hit with tremendous force.

Racquetball

Racquetball is like squash but is played on larger courts with a short-handled racket. It developed from handball and a game called paddleball, and boasted more than ten million players in the United States in the early 1990s. By then more than 30 countries belonged to the International Racquetball Federation (founded in 1969). World championships are held biennially, with singles, doubles, and team events.

Real tennis

The forerunner of all racket sports, which itself developed from *jeu de paume* in 11th-century France, real tennis is played on a curious court with sloping roofs and open galleries along one side and at the ends. It is played with lopsided rackets and hard balls: the few courts in the world are chiefly in the United States, Britain, France, and Australia. It has the oldest of all world championships, the men's singles, held on a challenge basis since *c.* 1740. There are now women's singles and doubles held biennially.

Jai alai

Fastest of all ball games, jai alai is played on a huge three-walled court (177 feet/54 m long) by players who use a curved, basketlike scoop called a *cesta* to catch and throw a small goatskin-covered ball called a *pelota*. Jai alai originated in the Basque region of Spain.

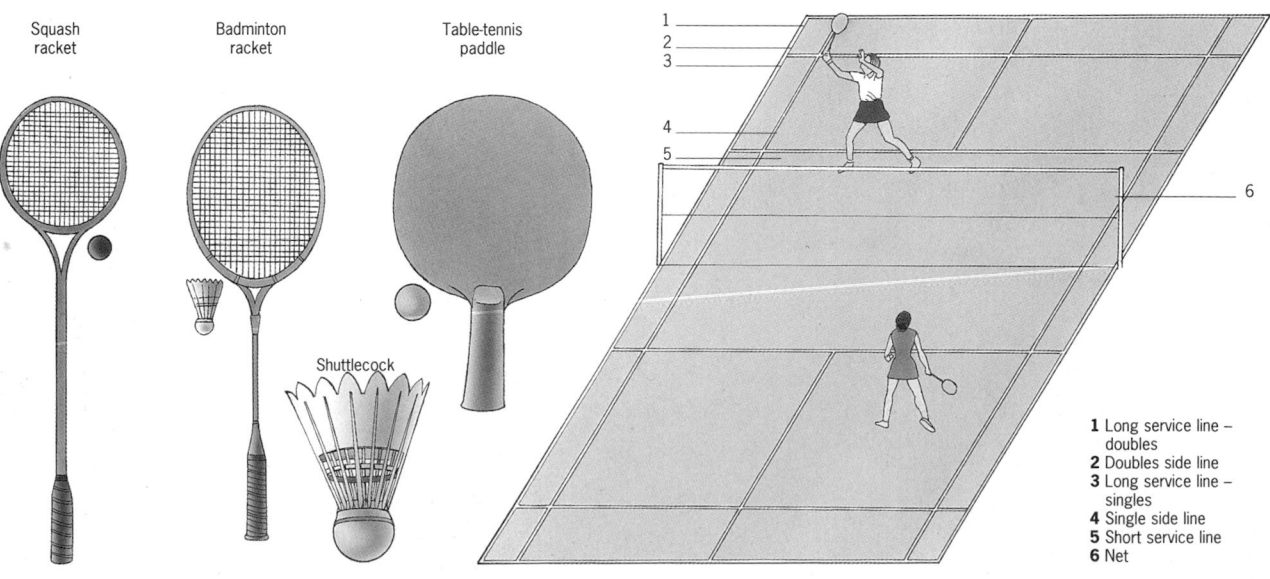

Squash racket
Badminton racket
Table-tennis paddle
Shuttlecock

1 Long service line – doubles
2 Doubles side line
3 Long service line – singles
4 Single side line
5 Short service line
6 Net

BASKETBALL

The game was invented in 1891 by Canadian-born physical-education instructor Dr. James Naismith in an effort to keep students at the Springfield Y.M.C.A. in Massachusetts occupied in the winter. Basketball now claims more participants worldwide than any other team sport. The world ruling body, the Fédération Internationale de Basketball Amateur, was formed in 1932, and basketball became an Olympic sport in 1936 for men and 1976 for women. The world championships were first staged in 1950 (1953 for women). A professional league was established in the U.S.A. as early as 1898, and the National Basketball Association (N.B.A.), formed in 1949, attracts the best players in the world.

Rules
Basketball is played between two teams of five players and five substitutes. The object is to score points by throwing the ball into the opposing team's basket. Players move the ball around the court by passing or dribbling and shooting, using only their hands to play the ball. Dribbling is bouncing or patting the ball on the floor with one hand, taking any number of steps, but a player must not stop and then start again. Running while holding the ball is not permitted, but a player may carry the ball for one step or pivot on one foot. Basketball is a non-contact sport, and fouls and rough play are penalized. A player committing five personal fouls (six in the N.B.A.) is sent off the court for the remainder of the game. The game is controlled by a referee and an umpire. They are assisted by one or two timekeepers and one or two scorekeepers.

Scoring
Baskets may be scored from any part of the court and are worth 3 points from outside the three-point arc, 2 from inside it, and 1 from a free throw, taken from the free-throw line.

Time limits
The amateur game is played in two halves of 20 minutes, N.B.A. professional games in four quarters of 12 minutes. The clock stops when the ball goes out of play. A number of time limits help to keep play moving. A team gaining possession in their half of the court must bring the ball into the front court within ten seconds (and may not then take the ball back into their back court) and must make an attempt at the basket within 30 seconds of gaining possession (24 seconds in the N.B.A.), or they lose possession of the ball. Attacking players may not remain in the restricted area between their opponents' end line and the free-throw line for more than three seconds while their team is in possession.

Michael Jordan of the Chicago Bulls on the attack during the 1993 N.B.A. season.

Competition
The 27-team N.B.A. is divided into two conferences (Eastern and Western). The Eastern Division is in turn divided into the Atlantic and Central divisions, and the Western is divided into the Midwest and Pacific divisions. Teams play an 82-game season running from September through May. Eight teams from each conference qualify for postseason playoffs. Playoff qualifications depend on final standings within a division as well as overall won-loss record.

The first round of the playoffs, eliminating four teams from each conference, is played on a best-of-five basis. The next two rounds, leading to the two conference winners, are the best-of-seven games. The two conference champions face each other to determine the N.B.A. Championship (also best of seven).

The premier college postseason tournament, organized by the National Collegiate Athletic Association (N.C.A.A.), features the 64 leading teams from the East, Midwest, Southeast, and West. The N.C.A.A. Basketball Tournament is played as a series of elimination games until the winner is decided.

Basketball is played at international lev-

Basketball court
1 Backboard
2 Basket
3 Center circle
4 Sideline
5 Free-throw line
6 End line

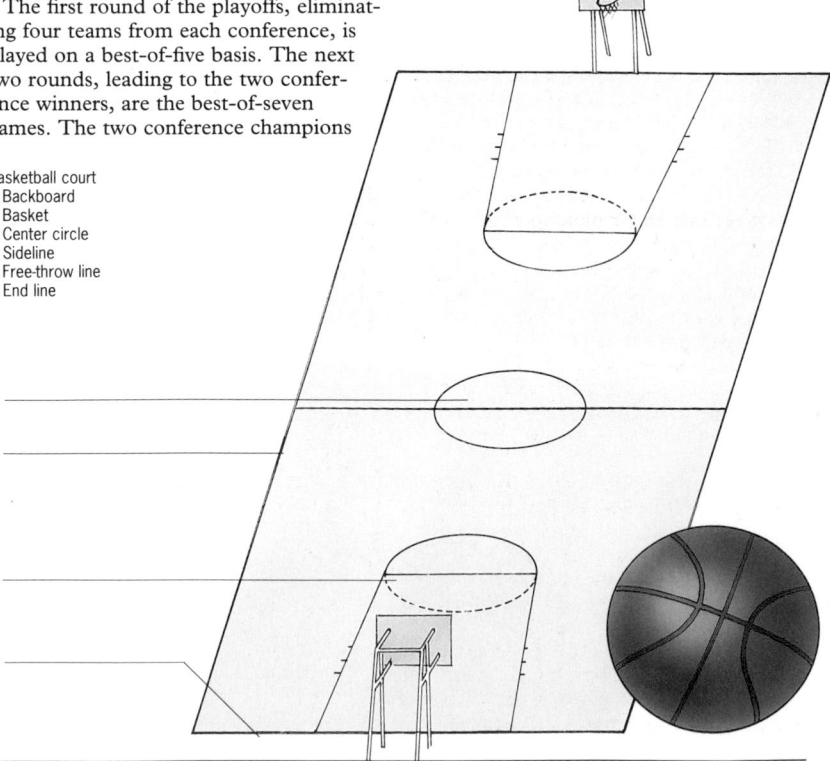

els, with the Olympics being the most important contest. The United States won every Olympic gold medal until 1972, when the Soviet Union beat the United States in the last second. The United States did not dominate the Olympics again until a relaxation of amateur rulings allowed (professional) N.B.A. stars to play. This "Dream Team," in effect an N.B.A. All-Star team, won the Olympic gold medal in Barcelona in 1992.

Professional leagues also exist in Europe, and American players mix with the best local talent in Italy, Israel, and Spain. An annual European Championship (at team rather than national level) was established for men's teams in 1958 and for women's teams in 1959.

RECENT N.B.A. CHAMPIONS

Year	Team
1994	Houston Rockets
1993	Chicago Bulls
1992	Chicago Bulls
1991	Chicago Bulls
1990	Detroit Pistons
1989	Detroit Pistons
1988	Los Angeles Lakers
1987	Los Angeles Lakers
1986	Boston Celtics
1985	Los Angeles Lakers

VOLLEYBALL

A U.S. Y.M.C.A. physical-training instructor, William G. Morgan, invented volleyball in 1895 as a game for out-of-shape businessmen. It was introduced to the Far East by U.S. missionaries in the early 1900s, and to Europe by U.S. servicemen in World War I. Originally for any number of players, volleyball became standardized with six players per team in 1918, and eventually was played by women as well as men. The International Volleyball Federation was founded in 1947 with world championships following in 1949 for men and 1952 for women, and it became an Olympic sport in 1964. Beach volleyball, a variation of the game with two players on each team, originated in California in the 1940s and now has a strong following as a professional sport, with world championships (first held in 1976) and a governing body, the Association of Volleyball Professionals, founded in 1981.

Rules

The object is to score points by playing the ball over the high net into the opposing team's court so that they cannot return it. After the service, from behind the court, each side may hit the ball three times before returning it across the net, the usual tactic being to set the ball up for a smash, or spike, into the opposing team's court on the third hit.

The ball is usually played with hands or arms but may be played with any part of

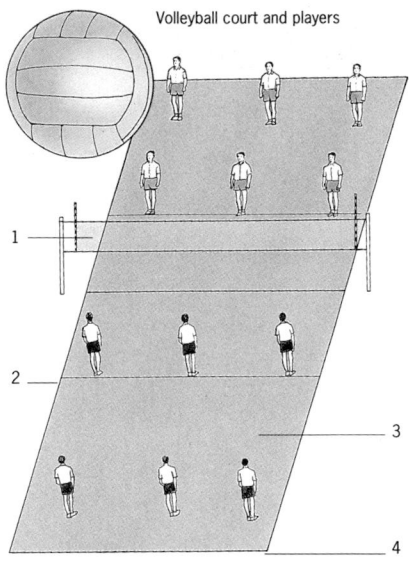

Volleyball court and players

1 Net 2 Attack line 3 Service area
4 Back line

the body from the waist upward. Only the serving team can score points, and, when it loses a rally, service passes to the other team. At each service, the players line up with three at the back and three at the front, and every time they regain service they must rotate their formation clockwise, each moving around by one position, although during a rally they may move about the court. But the three backcourt players may only play a ball from the attack area into their opponent's court when it is below net height. The first team to score 15 points wins the game, and championship matches are the best of five games.

Competition

The most successful nations in the Olympics and the quadrennial world championships, in both men's and women's competition, have been the U.S.S.R. and, chiefly in the women's competition, Japan and China.

TEAM HANDBALL

An indoor game played by teams of seven players on a court 131 x 66 feet (40 x 20 m), team handball is like soccer played with the hands. It also resembles basketball in tactics, but the object is to throw the ball into a goal 6.66 feet (2 m) high.

An outdoor sport first played in Germany in 1895, it appeared in the 1936 Olympics in its 11-a-side form. The International Handball Federation was formed in 1946, and the indoor game soon became predominant. It was reintroduced in the 1972 Olympics for men, and in 1976 for women. There are also world championships and a European Cup for clubs. It is sometimes played outdoors, when it may be called "field team handball" to distinguish it from the indoor court game.

HANDBALL

There is group of individual rather than team sports in which a small ball is played with a gloved hand on a court bounded by between one and four walls. Handball, which is thought to have originated in Ireland, is still popular there and in the U.S.A. and Australia. In tactics and scoring it resembles squash.

The beach volleyball world championship in 1994 at Hermosa Beach, California.

TRACK AND FIELD EVENTS

Track and field athletics have always been the cornerstone of the Olympic Games, and this was true of the ancient Greek Olympics, too. The first recorded games took place in 776 B.C. with just one event, a sprint race, but there is evidence of organized running as a religious ritual as far back as 3800 B.C. in ancient Egypt.

Modern athletics has its roots in 19th-century England, specifically the "public" schools and Oxford and Cambridge universities. The sport developed from the first meeting of Oxford and Cambridge in 1864, leading to the first English national championships in 1866. The first U.S. amateur meet, sponsored by the New York Athletic club, was held in 1868. Athletics spread worldwide with the first modern Olympics in 1896. The International Amateur Athletic Federation was founded in 1912 and kept the sport predominantly amateur. The Olympics served as the world championships for athletics until, in 1983, the first separate championships were held, quadrennially at first and then biennially from 1993. The governing bodies in the United States are The Athletic Congress (T.A.C.), National Collegiate Athletic Association (N.C.A.A.), and National Association of Intercollegiate Athletics (N.A.I.A.). In Canada it is the Canadian Track and Field Association (C.T.F.A.).

Track events

Running events, except for the marathon, take place on a standard 440 yard (400 m) track. Shorter events are run in lanes. Runners are allowed to use starting blocks and spiked running shoes. Modern tracks have an "all-weather" surface, usually made from a special rubber compound. Races are run counterclockwise. There are also indoor meetings, usually with a 220 yard (200 m) track. The starter fires a gun to start a race, after the commands "To your marks" and "Set." Most races have a staggered start so that the runners drawn on the outside are not at a disadvantage. The starting pistol is connected electronically with the photofinish equipment, which produces a continuous photograph of the finish line and timing to 1/100th of a second.

Sprints

The recognized sprints are the 100m, 200m, and 400m, all run in lanes throughout, with the last two employing staggered starts and the 100m run on a straight course. The staggered start ensures that all runners travel the same distance. The disadvantage of a draw in the outside lanes, in which the runner cannot see opponents on the inside until the finishing straight, is compensated for by the greater difficulty experienced in running tight bends. A good start is essential, and runners often try to anticipate the gun. If this happens, the runner "jumps the gun"—makes a false start—and the runners are recalled. A runner held responsible for more than one false start is disqualified from the race.

The 100m is the blue-ribbon event of sprinting; the world record holder is considered the fastest man or woman.

Middle-distance races

The longest track-racing distance is 10,000m, which is 25 laps. The 800m has a staggered start and is run in lanes for about 100m, to the start of the back straight, at which point the runners may break for the inside. Longer races are not run in lanes. The start is staggered along a curved line. The standard middle-distance races in world championships and Olympic Games are 800m, 1,500m, 5,000m, and 10,000m for men; 800m, 1,500m, 3,000m, and 10,000m for women. Official world records, for both men and women, are recognized for 800m, 1,000m, 1,500m, 2,000m, 3,000m, 5,000m, and 10,000m, as well as the mile (1,609m), the classic four-lap race still run at certain meetings. Tactics and judgment of pace are important in middle-distance running; runners need to conserve enough energy for an all-out effort at the finish. In the longer races, stamina is an essential requirement.

Marathon

The marathon is the classic long-distance race and is staged at all major championships for both men and women. It is run over 26 mi. 385 yd. (42.195 km), a distance first set at the 1908 Olympics. It starts and finishes on the track in the Olympic stadium, with a there-and-back

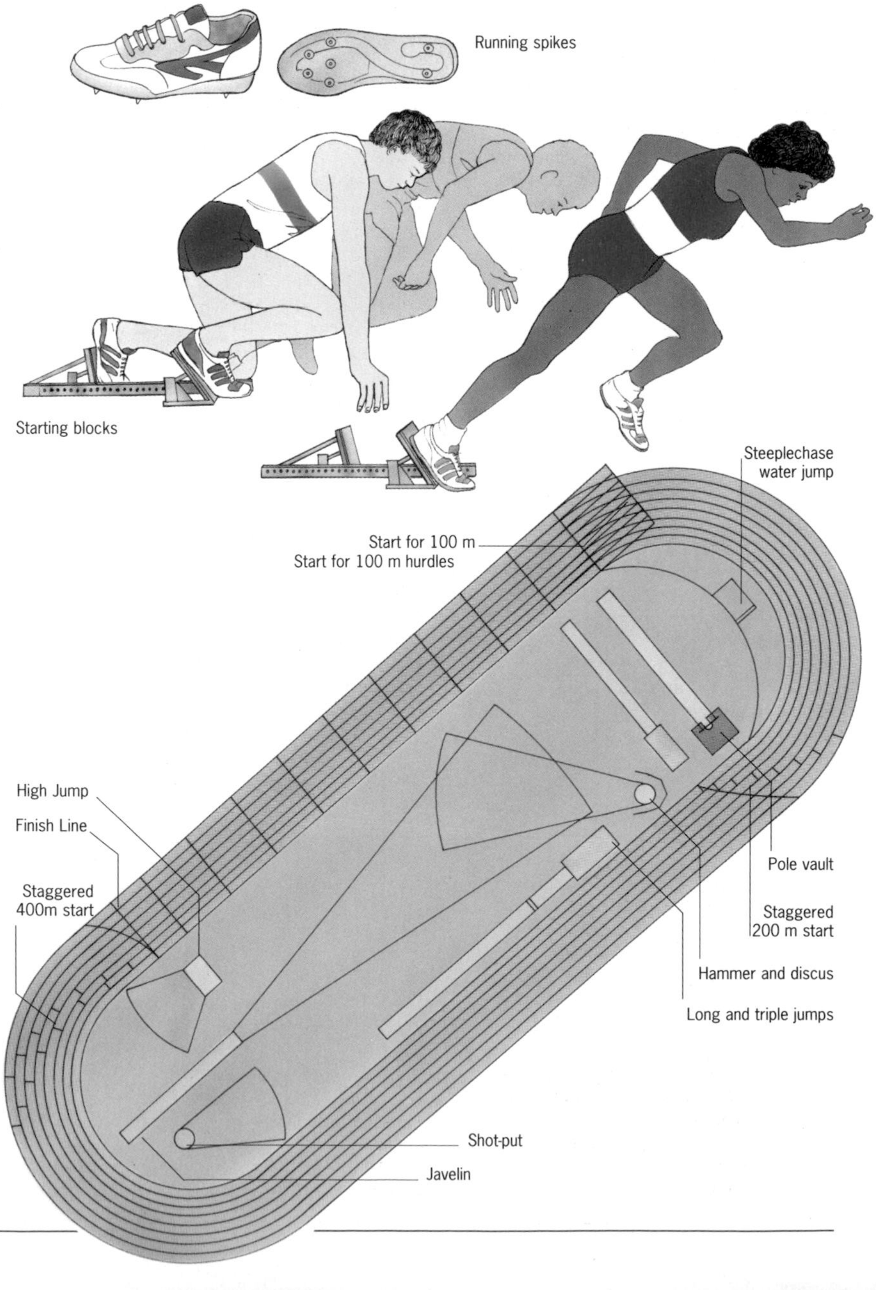

Running spikes

Starting blocks

Start for 100 m
Start for 100 m hurdles

Steeplechase
water jump

High Jump

Finish Line

Staggered
400m start

Pole vault

Staggered
200 m start

Hammer and discus

Long and triple jumps

Shot-put

Javelin

Mary Onyali of Nigeria is one of the new generation of African sprinters.

road course including varying gradients. Refreshment stations along the route help athletes avoid dehydration. Other marathons take place on road routes from place to place, usually in major cities; some attract thousands of entrants. These "mass" marathons often combine separate men's and women's races, and sometimes a paraplegic race. Because of the difference in marathon courses, there are no official world records, only world best times. Ultramarathon races, some lasting as long as six days, attract many track veterans.

Hurdle races

The standard "obstacle" races are the 110m and 400m hurdles and 3,000m steeplechase for men, and the 100m and 400m hurdles for women. The shorter, or "high," hurdles are run on a straight track, the 400m around a standard lap with a staggered start. All races have ten hurdles in each lane: the heights of the hurdles are 42 inches (106.7 cm) and 36 inches (91.4 cm) respectively for the men's 110m and 400m events, and 33 inches (83.8 cm) and 30 inches (76.2 cm) for the women's. Runners may knock hurdles down without penalty. The 3,000m steeplechase is run over 7 1/2 laps of the track. Steeplechasers race over fixed hurdles, four of them plus one water jump on each lap after the first half lap. Runners may place a foot on the hurdles, which are 36 inches (91.4 cm) high and straddle the three inside lanes, but this is not good technique, except for the water jump, which is 12 feet (3.66 m) from the barrier to the edge of the water and is offset inside the track.

Relay races

The standard relays, usually staged at the end of major championships, are the 4 x 100m and 4 x 400m for both men and women, run with staggered starts around the track. The shorter event is run completely in lanes. In the 4 x 400m athletes may break lanes when the second runner reaches the back straight. The baton must be handed over within a specific 20m takeover zone. Relay racing was invented in the United States, where special relay meetings are held over several distances.

Walking

The standard walking events are 20km and 50km for men, and 5km and 10km for women. Like the marathon, they are road races that start and finish in the stadium, but world records are recognized. Walking is plagued with controversy because the rules governing technique are difficult to apply: at least part of a foot must always be in contact with the ground, and the leg of each foot must be momentarily straight as the foot touches the ground.

Cross-country running

Run over set courses through open countryside, fields, and woods, cross-country is a fall and winter sport, with its own individual and team world championships. These grew from the International Championships for the four British countries first held in 1903, and became official in 1973. Men race over 12km (juniors 8km), women over 6km (juniors 4km). The men's events have been dominated by competitors from Kenya since 1986.

Orienteering

A sport invented in Sweden in 1918, orienteering involves cross-country running over a course in which the fastest routes to various control points are found with the help of a map and a special compass. The International Orienteering Federation was founded in 1961, and there are now biennial world championships, for both men and women, which were first held in 1968. The rugged landscape of Scandinavia makes it a natural center of the sport and a strong contender in competition.

The field events, comprising jumping and throwing disciplines, take place mainly on the field inside the track. In the long jump, triple jump, and the four throws—shot, discus, hammer, and javelin—competitors have a number of attempts to achieve their best distance. In the high jump and pole vault, the bar is raised for each round, and competitors continue to jump until they record three successive failures. The competitor with the highest jump is the winner. In the event of a tie, the winner is the one with the fewest failures at the last height cleared, and if still tied, the one with the fewest failures overall. This is called a countback. The field events demand the perfection of technique designed to produce an explosive effort. The runways on throwing events have the same surface as the track. The throwing circles have concrete surfaces. Women compete in all the events except the pole vault and hammer throw.

Jumping for distance

In the long and triple jumps, competitors get at least three attempts, six in the more important meetings. They use the runway to build up speed before launching themselves into the jump from a take-off board, the farther edge of which is the take-off line. Just behind the line is a strip of modeling clay used to detect foul jumps. The landing area is a smoothly raked sandpit, and the jump is measured optically from the take-off line to the nearest impression made by the jumper in the sand, be it with foot, hand, or any other part of the body. In the triple jump—which was formerly known as the hop, step, and jump—the first stage is a hop in that the jumper must take off and land on the same foot. The second stage is a step, landing on the other foot, and in the third stage the jumper lands on both feet in the pit.

Jumping for height

High jumping was revolutionized in 1968 when the American Dick Fosbury won the Olympic title with a new style of jumping, head first and clearing the bar with his back before lifting his legs clear. This technique, known as the "Fosbury flop," is now used by all leading high-jumpers. The only rules governing high jumping limit the thickness of soles to 0.5 inches (13 mm) and require the jumper to take off from one foot. Most advances in pole vaulting have resulted from improved equipment. A vaulter needs to translate horizontal speed developed on the runway to upward motion by planting the pole in a special box on the ground under the bar and levering himself up. Modern fiberglass poles are strong and flexible, enabling the vaulter to do this more efficiently. In both high jumping and pole vaulting, an air mattress is used in the landing area to prevent injury.

Throwing events

The four throwing events all require different specialized techniques and speed of arm and foot as well as brute strength. The javelin throw is measured from the scratch line marking the end of the runway to where the point of the javelin first hits the ground (it does not have to stick in the ground). The other throws are measured from the front edge of the throwing circle to where the implement first hits the ground. All throws must land in marked sectors. The discus and hammer circles are shielded by cages, because the implements sometimes shoot off at dangerous angles as the thrower spins around. In most big competitions, there is a qualifying competition in which each thrower has three trials and a final round in which as many as 12 competitors have six throws each.

Decathlon and heptathlon

All-around track-and-field ability is tested by two-day challenges. Men contest the ten-event decathlon: 100m run, long jump, shot-put, high jump, 400m run (1st day); 110m hurdles, discus, pole vault, javelin, 1,500m run (2nd day). Women used to compete in a pentathlon, but that was extended to a seven-event heptathlon: 100m hurdles, high jump, shot-put, 200m run (1st day); long jump, javelin, 800m run (2nd day). Athletes score points for time or distance in each event according to standard tables.

Modern pentathlon

A sport of military origin, the modern pentathlon was created for the 1912 Olympics, and its five disciplines have remained unchanged: riding (show jumping), fencing, pistol shooting, swimming, and running. In the hope of retaining its Olympic place, the five-day competition was recently reduced to one day, turning it into an almost continuous contest.

Points are awarded according to success against an agreed standard in each sport. The last to take place is cross-country running, in which the start is staggered according to the points held by each competitor. The first across the finishing line in the cross-country event wins the entire competition. World championships began in 1949, when a team event was also introduced. Women, who run and swim over shorter distances than men, entered the world scene in 1978.

Triathlon

The original "Ironman" challenge was formalized in Hawaii in 1978 with a 2.4 mi. (3.8 km) swim, a 112 mi. (180 km) cycle race, and a full marathon. It will enter the Olympics in 1996 with distances of 0.9 mi. (1.5 km), 25 mi. (40 km), and 6.2 mi. (10km) respectively.

Competition

The United States has always been the leading track-and-field nation overall,

High jump

Run up

Landing area

Pole vault

Pole may be of any length or diameter

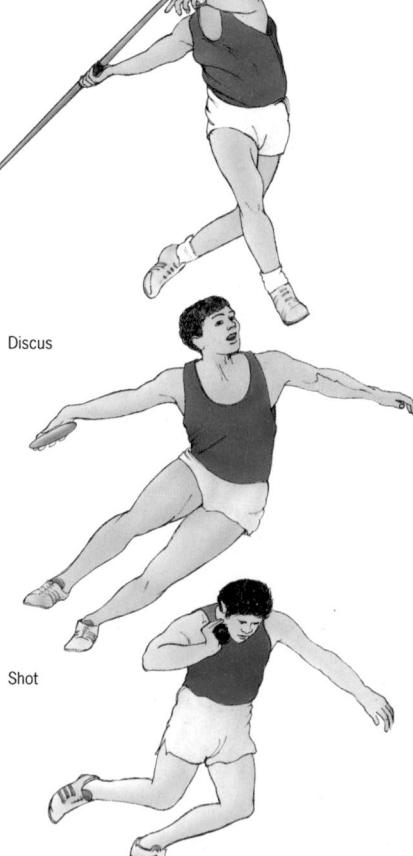

Javelin

Discus

Shot

especially in men's events. Finland has produced great men's middle-distance runners and javelin throwers. Britain has also had outstanding middle-distance runners, but this is a field now dominated by Kenya. Other African nations—including Algeria, Ethiopia, and Morocco—have emerged to challenge the best on the track, and China is fast becoming a new force to be reckoned with in women's middle- and long-distance running.

Indoor athletics

Certain events are contested at indoor meetings, chiefly out of season, and there are various championships. Records are separate from those of outdoor events. The banked, sprung, wooden tracks are usually 220 yards (200 m) per lap, and the straight sprints and hurdles are over 55 or 66 yards (50 or 60 m). All jumping events are staged, but the shot is the only throw. There is sometimes a men's heptathlon and a women's pentathlon.

GYMNASTICS

After its birth in ancient Greece, gymnastics was revived in the late 1700s. In 1811 a German schoolteacher, Friedrich Ludwig Jahn, opened a *Turnverein*—an open-air gymnasium—and he invented several of today's pieces of apparatus. The International Gymnastics Federation was founded in 1891, and gymnastics events were held in the first modern Olympics, in 1896. It has flourished as a sport, and the classic events, with both men and women taking part, have been joined in the Olympics by rhythmic gym-

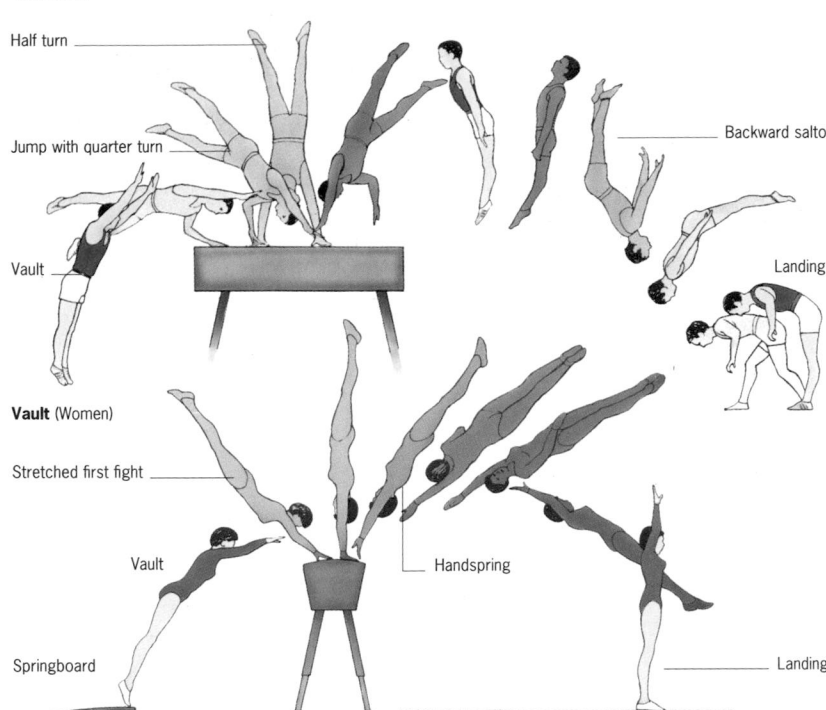

Vault (men)

Half turn

Jump with quarter turn

Vault

Backward salto

Landing

Vault (Women)

Stretched first fight

Vault

Handspring

Springboard

Landing

nastics, performed by women and calling for supreme skill and artistry. Sports acrobatics, yet another discipline, is akin to the tumbling and acrobatics performed by entertainers since ancient times.

Classic gymnastics
The classic events are, for men and boys, floor exercise, high bar, parallel bars, pommel horse, rings, and vault (length-wise); and for women and girls, floor exercise (to music), beam, asymmetric (uneven) bars, and vault (across). In competition, gymnasts are marked out of ten by a panel of judges. In major events, there are team competitions and medals for winners on each apparatus and for the overall gymnastic champions.

Rhythmic gymnastics
In rhythmic gymnastics, the competitors use portable hand apparatus and perform to music. They use balletic dance steps and movements, while twirling, throwing, catching, rolling, bouncing, or swinging their apparatus. The five individual exercises are ribbon, hoop, rope, ball, and clubs, and there are group exercises in which six gymnasts perform with two different types of apparatus. As in classic gymnastics, competitors are marked by a panel of judges.

Sports acrobatics
Apart from the mat, there is no apparatus in sports acrobatics, which includes solo (tumbling), pairs, and group events. In the tumbling events, for men or women, competitors perform a sequence of somersaults and springs on a straight 82-foot

(25-m) sprung track. In the other events —the men's, women's, and mixed pairs, the women's trio, and the men's fours— there are supports, balances, throws, and somersaults. Competitors are marked by a panel of judges.

Competition
All the current men's gymnastics events were included in the 1896 Olympics except the overall (combined) event (1900) and the floor exercise (1932). The women's events were first staged in the 1952 Games, and rhythmic gymnastics in 1984. The first world championships were staged in 1903 (1934 for women) and are now held every two years. The strongholds of classical gymnastics have been Russia in both men's and women's; Japan and latterly China in men's; and Romania, the former Czechoslovakia, and other eastern European countries in women's. Russia and Bulgaria have also excelled in rhythmic gymnastics. The United States has recently joined the top nations.

Trampolining
The modern trampoline was invented by George Nissen in the U.S.A. in 1936. World championships were first held in 1964. Competitors perform routines that include twists, somersaults, and pikes while bouncing up to 66 feet (20 m). Both sexes compete in individual events, as well as trampolining and tumbling in synchronized pairs using two trampolines.

WEIGHTLIFTING
There are records of lifting weights as a test of strength in ancient civilizations. In modern times, a world championship was held in London in 1891, and weightlifting featured in the first modern Olympics, in 1896, with both one- and two-handed lifts. Since 1928 all recognized lifts have been two-handed, and now there are only two standard lifts—the snatch and the clean and jerk (or simply jerk). The sport is governed by the International Weightlifting Federation, founded in 1920. Regular world championships have been held for women since 1987. New body-weight categories were introduced in 1993, ten for men ranging from 119 lb. (54 kg) to more than 238 lb. (108 kg), and nine for women from 101 lb. (46 kg) to more than 183 lb. (83 kg).

Rules
In the snatch, the lifter crouches to grasp the barbell with both hands and then raises it above the head in one continuous movement. In the clean and jerk, the lifter brings the bar up to the shoulders in one movement (the clean), and may rest the bar on collarbone, chest, or fully bent arms. Then comes the jerk part, in which the bar is lifted to arm's length over the head. In both snatch and jerk, the lifter must stand still with arms and legs locked until the three judges press their buttons for either a "good lift" (white light) or "no lift" (red). Two white lights are needed for a good lift.

Weightlifting is a battle of tactics as well as of strength and skill. Lifters have only three attempts in each style. They draw lots for order of lifting and must plan which weights to attempt. The bar is nor-mally increased in multiples of 5.51 lb. (2.5 kg), and once a weight has been lift-ed by a competitor, no one can go back to a lighter weight. However, a lifter who fails at a particular weight may save his or her next attempt for a heavier one. Com-petitors' positions are determined by the aggregate of their best lifts in the two styles. Russia and Bulgaria dominate men's weightlifting; China is the best in women's. Powerlifting is a variant of the sport using different rules and techniques.

Weightlifting

Clean and jerk

BOXING

Boxing is a major world sport in that the leading exponents earn more than any other sports figures, sometimes fighting for "purses" of several million dollars. At the top level, however, professional boxing has no single world governing body, and there are now four "world champions" at each fighting weight. As a result, many title fights are contrived: that is they are arranged by promoters and the managers of fighters to bring in the maximum gate money and television revenue, with no regard to the merits or otherwise of the challenger. Amateur boxing is almost another sport; it is tightly regulated, and both Olympic and world championship tournaments are staged.

Development

Pugilism spread from ancient Greece and Rome to the rest of Europe. Modern boxing originated in during the 1600s in England in the village fairgrounds, with "Prize Ring" rules first drawn up in 1743 by the bare-knuckle champion fighter Jack Broughton. The modern sport was born in 1867, when a new set of rules was drawn up by John Graham Chambers of the Amateur Athletic Club in London and sponsored by the Marquess of Queensberry. The Queensberry Rules, which made gloves mandatory, eliminated all foul holds and blows, introduced points scoring, and limited the duration of rounds to three minutes, have governed the sport ever since.

Boxing caught on in the U.S.A., and the first heavyweight championship fight with gloves was that between John L. Sullivan and James J. Corbett in New Orleans in 1892. The U.S. National Boxing Association was formed in 1920 and became the World Boxing Association (W.B.A.) in 1962. Other regulatory organizations—the World Boxing Council (W.B.C., 1963), the International Boxing Federation (I.B.F., 1983), and the World Boxing Organization (W.B.O., 1988)—have since sprung up, each sponsoring its own world championships at the various weights. Attempts have been made from time to time to organize women's boxing internationally, so far without success.

Rules

The maximum dimensions of the ring are 20 sq. ft./6.1m², the minimum 14 sq. ft./4.3m² for professionals and 16 sq. ft./4.9m² for amateurs. Professional title fights take place over twelve rounds, but other contests have as few as six rounds. Amateur fights are three rounds. Rounds last three minutes, except in some novice contests, with one-minute breaks between rounds. A referee controls the fight from within the ring and, in professional boxing, may be one of the three judges; amateur boxing has five separate judges. Bouts may be won by a knockout (K.O.),

WEIGHTS (W.B.C. NAMES)	
	lb. (kg)
Heavyweight	No limit
Cruiserweight	
(Junior Heavyweight*)	190 (86.2)
Light Heavyweight	175 (79.4)
Super Middleweight	168 (76.2)
Middleweight	160 (72.6)
Super Welterweight	
(Junior Middleweight**)	154 (69.9)
Welterweight	147 (66.7)
Super Lightweight	
(Junior Welterweight**)	140 (63.5)
Lightweight	135 (61.2)
Super Featherweight	
(Junior Lightweight**)	130 (59)
Featherweight	126 (57.2)
Super Bantamweight	
(Junior Featherweight**)	122 (55.3)
Bantamweight	118 (53.5)
Super Flyweight	
(Junior Bantamweight**)	115 (52.2)
Flyweight	112 (50.8)
Light Flyweight	
(Junior Flyweight**)	108 (49)
Straw-weight	
(Mini Flyweight**)	105 (47.6)

*W.B.O.; **W.B.A., I.B.F., W.B.O.

when one boxer is on the canvas for ten seconds and thus "counted out," or by a stoppage by the referee, a retirement, a disqualification, or a points decision. Judges award points for landing blows with the knuckle part of the closed glove on target areas of body and face, and for

other boxing skills. The winner of a round receives ten points and the loser proportionately fewer, but verdicts are given by the majority of judges, not the total of points. Amateur boxing has a different points system, which is based on a positive count for punches correctly landed and the loss of points for breaking the rules. Amateurs wear a vest and a protective headguard when fighting.

Competition

American fighters have dominated boxing at most weights, especially the heavier categories. But at bantamweight and lower, boxers from Mexico and the Far East have enjoyed considerable success. Although there have been great champions at other weights, it is the heavyweight championship that carries the most kudos internationally and by which the sport earns its popularity and exposure. The American Joe Louis was heavyweight champion for 11 years and 252 days (1937–49), a record at any weight, and his 27 title fights and 26 title-fight wins are also records. Rocky Marciano (U.S.A.) was the only unbeaten world champion at any weight with 49 wins out of 49 (1947–55). Most Olympic heavyweight champions turn professional, but the Cuban Teofilo Stevenson remained amateur and won a record three Olympic heavyweight gold medals (1972–80).

Boxing

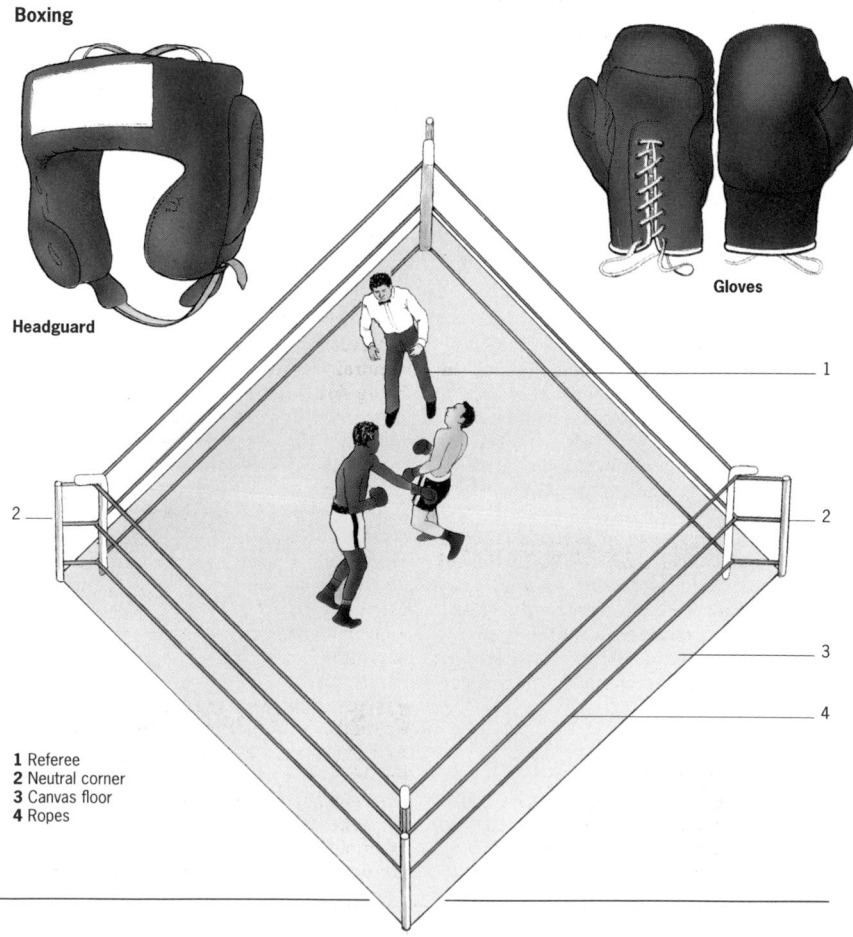

Headguard

Gloves

1 Referee
2 Neutral corner
3 Canvas floor
4 Ropes

WRESTLING

One of the world's oldest sports, wrestling is depicted in wall drawings from 6,000 years ago and played a prominent part in the ancient Greek Olympics. The Romans adapted it, and this Greco-Roman style survived. It was included in the first modern Olympics in 1896. A similar style, freestyle—or catch-as-catch-can—was introduced in the 1904 Games. The difference between the two styles is that use of the legs and holds below the waist are not allowed in Greco-Roman. Both are still Olympic sports, and official world championships have been held annually since the early 1950s. (The International Amateur Wrestling Association was founded in 1912.) Professional wrestling is not regarded as a sport, more a staged entertainment.

Rules
Tournament bouts are fought on a mat inside a 30 ft./9m diameter contest area and controlled and adjudicated by a referee on the mat and a mat chairman (chief official), another judge, and a time-keeper. The wrestlers wear a one-piece jersey, one red and one blue. Bouts last five minutes, unless they are decided earlier, such as by a fall, and are scored by a complex system of points which may be carried over to succeeding rounds. There are ten weight categories, running from light flyweight (106 lb./48kg) to super-heavyweight (more than 220 lb./100kg).

Other wrestling sports
Of the many other variations of wrestling that have developed around the world, the best known is sumo, the indigenous wrestling of Japan. Steeped in the rituals of Shinto, sumo is said to have started more than 2,000 years ago as a fight to the death. The participants routinely weigh as much as 350 lb./160kg: the heaviest, the Hawaiian Konishiki, weighed 550 lb./250kg and was the first non-Japanese to gain international recognition. Sumo is a form of belt wrestling in which the wrestler grabs hold of his opponent's belt and tries to throw him to the ground or push him out of the ring. The fights are mostly ceremony, with rarely more than a few seconds' action.

MARTIAL ARTS

The martial arts are fighting skills that have developed in the Far East over hundreds of years, often bound up with religion. Unknown until the 1950s in the West, judo and karate especially are now popular sports.

Judo
Judo, meaning the "gentle way," grew from the ancient Japanese martial art of jujitsu, based on the ability to turn an opponent's strength and weight against him or her. The International Judo Federation was founded in 1951, and the first world championships were held in 1956. When these were won in 1961 by the Dutch giant Anton Geesink, the Japanese had to acknowledge that weight was a factor, and weight divisions were introduced. Judo became an Olympic sport in 1964 (1992 for women). At world and Olympic championships, weight categories range from more than 209 lb./95kg to under 132 lb./60kg for men, and more than 159 lb./72kg to under 106 lb./48kg for women. Bouts take place on a contest mat, the contestants, or judoki, performing in bare feet, trousers, and a light, loose-fitting jacket tied by a belt, the color of which indicates the judoka's grade. These run through the junior kyu grades, from a white beginner's belt to yellow, orange, green, blue, and brown, to the advanced senior dan grades with their black belts. Bouts may last for three to twenty minutes and are won outright by an ippon, worth ten points, for a perfect throw, or by an accumulation of lesser points-scoring throws.

Karate
Meaning "empty hands," karate derived from kung fu and the fighting arts of Okinawa, where it was developed during the 1500s to resist the invading Japanese. The modern sport evolved in the 1920s as a style called Shotokan. Blows may be delivered with hand or foot, but the more dangerous ones are banned. World championships were first held in 1970. There are now weight categories, and women began to compete in 1980. The Japanese have been overtaken by Britain in the men's events and France in the women's.

Other martial arts
Aikido The "way of harmony," aikido evolved from jujitsu and uses only defensive techniques.
Kendo Japanese sword-fighting in which contestants use bamboo weapons, wear face masks and body protection, and observe the traditional ceremonies of the samurai warriors.
Kung fu A group of Chinese martial arts, meaning "good effort," used to improve health and achieve a life of harmony as well as for self-defense.
Tae kwon do Korean form of unarmed combat similar to karate and meaning "the way of kick and punch." World championships were first held in 1973 (1987 for women), and tae kwon do came into the Olympics in 1988. South Koreans dominate the event, though the American challenge is strong.

FENCING

Fencing as combat practice dates from the Middle Ages. Three weapons are now used—the épée, saber, and foil. Fencing was included in the first modern Olympics (1896), and the world governing body, the Fédération Internationale d'Escrime, was founded in 1913. The European épée championships entered the Olympics in 1936. World championships for women's foil were instituted in 1929 and for épée in 1989. Italy, France, and the former U.S.S.R. are the dominant countries in the sport, with Hungary excelling at saber and in the women's events.

Rules
The object in fencing is to touch your opponent with your sword on the target area to register a hit. Judges determine hits, and are assisted by electronic scoring in épée and foil, the fencers being wired up. Only the point of the weapon may be used in épée and foil, but with saber the edge of the blade also counts.

Fencing

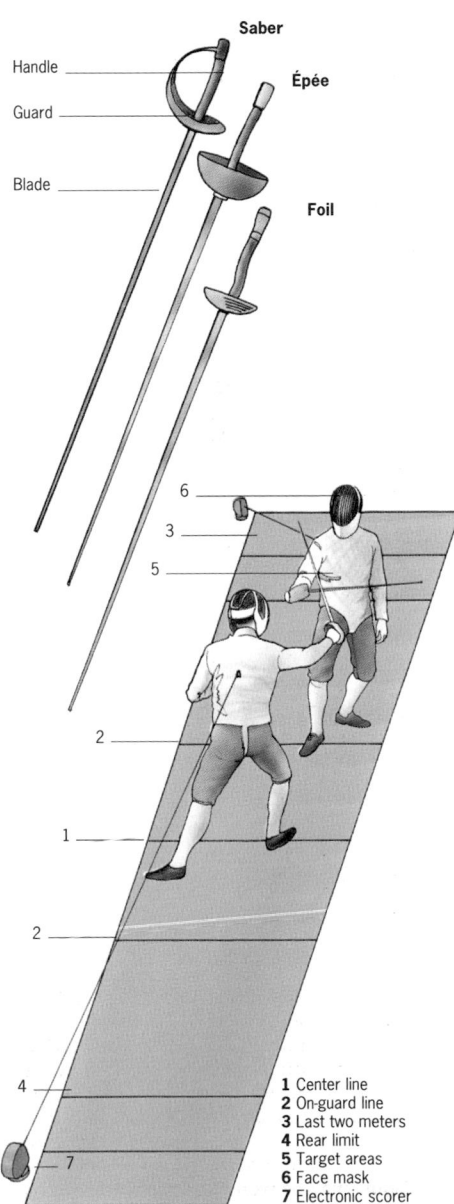

Saber
Handle
Guard
Blade
Épée
Foil

1 Center line
2 On-guard line
3 Last two meters
4 Rear limit
5 Target areas
6 Face mask
7 Electronic scorer

SWIMMING

There were swimming races in Japan 2,000 years ago, but in Europe a fear of spreading disease held swimming back until the 19th century. Swimming events were included in the first modern Olympics in 1896 in Athens, where they took place in a cold, choppy sea, and it was not until 1948 that Olympic swimming events were held indoors. The Fédération Internationale de Natation Amateur was set up in 1908 to govern not only swimming but also diving and water polo. Separate world championships were introduced in 1973. Subaqua swimming led to the sport of underwater hockey (known in Britain as "octopush"), where a weighted puck is pushed over the floor of the pool. It was created in South Africa in the 1960s and now has world championships biennially.

Strokes and events

The four competition strokes in swimming are front crawl (used for freestyle races), backstroke, breaststroke, and butterfly. There are no restrictions in freestyle, but the mechanics of the other strokes and the turns are strictly regulated. Freestyle races in major championships are over 50m, 100m, 200m, 400m, and 1,500m for men, with the 800m instead of the 1,500m for women. In the other three strokes, both men and women race over 100m and 200m. There are medley races for both men and women, over 200m and 400m, in which each stroke is swum for 50m and 100m, respectively, the order being butterfly, backstroke, breaststroke, and freestyle. Relay races include 4 x 100m and, for men, 4 x 200m, as well as a medley 4 x 100m relay in which the order of strokes is backstroke, breaststroke, butterfly, and freestyle.

Competition

The standard long-course events take place in Olympic-size pools, which measure approximately 54 ²/₃ yards (50m) and which have eight lanes, each 8 feet 2 inches (2.3m) wide. There are also short-course competitions, with 82-feet (25m) lengths. Competitors dive in from starting blocks, except for the backstroke, which is started in the pool, and are timed to 1/1,000th of a second by touching electronic pads at the finish. Swimmers must keep in their own lanes, marked with ropes on the surface. Flags hang over the pool to let backstrokers know when they are within 5m of a turn or the finish.

The U.S.A. has always been the leading swimming nation in Olympic and world championships. Australia, Hungary, and the former East Germany have also produced many outstanding swimmers. Mark Spitz (U.S.A.) won a record nine Olympic gold medals (1968–72) and a record seven in one Games (1972), all in world record times—the 100m and 200m freestyle and butterfly, and the three relays. Kristin Otto (East Germany) won six gold medals in the 1988 Olympics—the 50m and 100m freestyle, 100m backstroke, 100m butterfly, and the two relays. Dawn Fraser (Australia) is the only swimmer to win the same title in three consecutive Games—the 100m freestyle in 1956–64.

Diving

The first national diving championships were held in Scotland in 1889. Highboard, or platform, diving for men was included in the 1904 Olympics and springboard in 1908; women's diving followed in 1912 and 1920, respectively. World championships have been held since 1973. U.S. divers have a long record of success in major competition. Greg Louganis won a record four Olympic golds, both events in 1984 and again in 1988, and five world titles. U.S. women, once also supreme, with Pat McCormick winning four Olympic gold medals (1952–56), have had less success since the 1960s, and China has dominated women's diving since the mid-1980s.

Rules

Highboard diving takes place off a static board 33 feet (10m) above the water surface; springboard is from springy boards approximately 10 feet (3m) above and 3 feet 3 inches (1m) high. There are forward, backward, reverse, and inward dives, and, from the highboard, divers may start with an armstand on the edge of the board. Dives include twists and positions such as tucks and pikes. In each competitive event, divers must do a number of required and optional dives, usually about ten in all. Each dive is marked by a panel of from three to seven judges, depending on the status of the competition, who give points out of 10. The highest and lowest marks are discarded, and the others are added up and multiplied by the degree of difficulty allocated to the dive. Divers' points for each dive are aggregated to give their final score.

The competitor with the fastest entry time is assigned the lane on the right of the center line. Slower swimmers are assigned lanes alternately to the left and right, with the slowest swimmers on the outside. If entry times are a true indication of form, the swimmers will spread out into a spearhead formation. Lanes are 8 feet 2 inches (2.3m) wide.

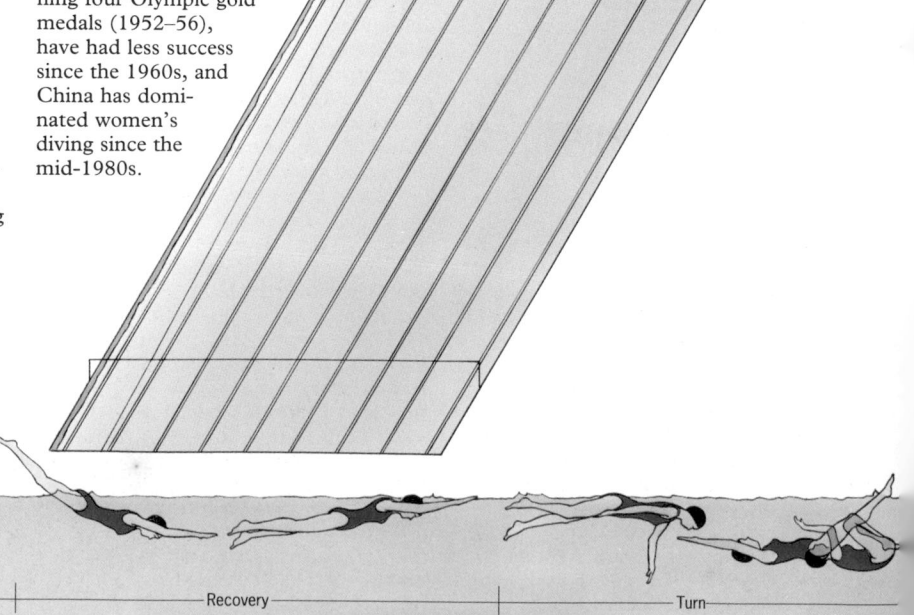

Dive — Recovery — Turn

Water polo

A seven-a-side team sport with rules established in Britain in the 1870s, water polo was first included in the Olympics in 1900. The first, irregular, world championships were in 1973. Hungary has been the most successful nation for men since the 1930s, challenged by the former U.S.S.R., the former Yugoslavia, and Italy. Women's world championships were first held in 1986, with the Netherlands as the leading nation for women.

Rules

The playing area for internationals is 33 yards (30m) long by 22 yards (20m), with goals approximately 10 feet (3m) wide and 3 feet (0.9m) above the water. There are four periods of seven minutes. A team has six substitutes, who may enter the game after a goal is scored. Players may play the ball with hand in or out of the water, but only the goalkeeper may use both hands simultaneously.

Synchronized swimming

Aptly described as "water ballet," "synchro" is a women's sport and derives from the "scientific swimming" of the late 19th century, which consisted of various tricks and stunts. The first national championships took place in the U.S.A. in 1945. World championships were first held in 1973, and synchro became an Olympic sport in 1984. The U.S.A. and Canada provide the leading exponents.

Rules

Swimmers perform under or on the water, matching artistic movements— stunts (acrobatic moves) and routines (stunts combined with strokes)—with music. Judges award points for execution and style, grading stunts according to degree of difficulty. There are three events—solo, duet, and team (between four and eight swimmers).

Long-distance swimming

A lonely sport in which people often take on the elements rather than opponents, long-distance swimming is a test of endurance. There are many recognized swims, ranging from the 8-mile (13km) Strait of Gibraltar to the 80 4/5-mile (130km) Suez Canal. But the ambition of most long-distance swimmers is to conquer the English Channel, between England and France, a distance of 21 miles (34km) at its shortest but made longer and more difficult by currents and tides. Channel swimming as a sport goes back to the 19th century, and the first to complete the course was a British Merchant Navy captain, Matthew Webb, in 1875. It took him 21hr 45min, and he covered about 38 miles (61km). The first woman to swim the Channel was Gertrude Ederle (U.S.A.), who broke the

existing men's record in 1926 with 14hr 39min. Another American woman, Penny Dean, set an official all-comers' record of 7hr 40min in 1978. The first double crossing was made in 1961, by Antonio Abertondo (Argentina), whose 43hr 10min included a four-minute rest, and in 1981 Jon Erikson (U.S.A.) made a nonstop three-way crossing in 38hr 27min. In one swim in 1987, Philip Rush (New Zealand) set new records for the double and triple crossings of 16hr 10min and 28hr 21min respectively.

Surfing

British sailors first saw Hawaiian Islanders surfing more than 200 years ago, but it did not become competitive until the 1950s, with the first world amateur championships held in 1964 and professional in 1970. Surfers paddle out to sea and are judged—for style, grace, and timing—on their "ride" back on the waves. The best surfing beaches are in Australia, California, and Hawaii, home of the most successful professional surfers. Body-surfing, without a board, is also practiced, especially in Australia.

Water skiing

Water skiing developed as a sport in the U.S.A. in the 1920s. The World Water Ski Union was founded in 1946, and the now-biennial world championships, instituted in 1949 for both men and women, are usually dominated by U.S.A.

Events

The competitor in tournament water skiing is towed behind a motorboat at a constant speed of 36mph (58km/h) or 34mph (55km/h) for women. There are three disciplines. Slalom is done on one ski; the skier negotiates a series of buoys, six on each run, while crossing the boat's wake. The rope is shortened for each pass until a buoy is missed or the skier falls. Jumping is performed on two skis. The skier is towed over a ramp; the longest jump wins. Tricks requires the skier to perform maneuvers before the judges during two 20-second passes. Similar contests are held for barefoot skiers. In races, skiers are towed as fast as they can stand. Events are staged on sea, rivers, or lakes.

A slalom course is 283 yards (259m) long. The first set of buoys is 29 yards (27m) from the start. The rest are at 75 yards (68m), 119 yards (109m), 165 yards (150m), 209 yards (191m), and 255 yards (232m), with another at 29 yards (27m) from the exit gate. The outer buoy lies 12 1/2 yards (11.5m) from the center line.

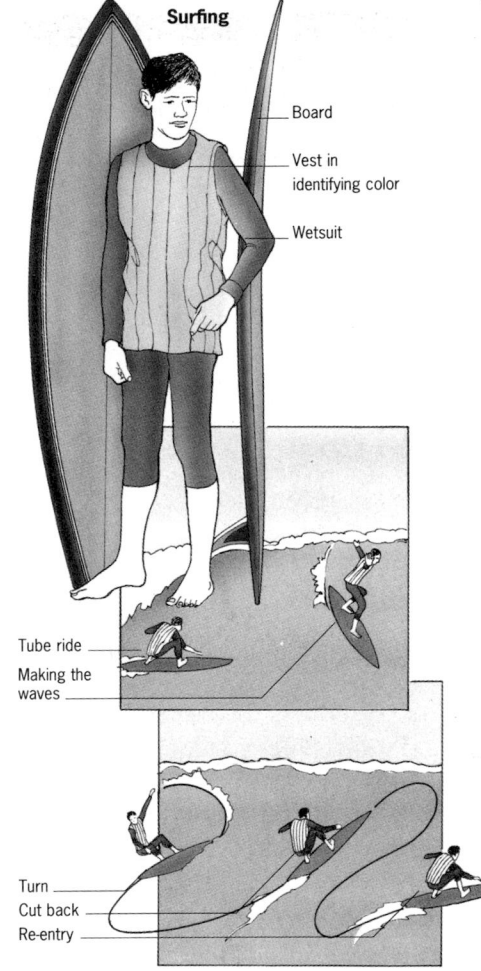

Surfing

Board

Vest in identifying color

Wetsuit

Tube ride

Making the waves

Turn

Cut back

Re-entry

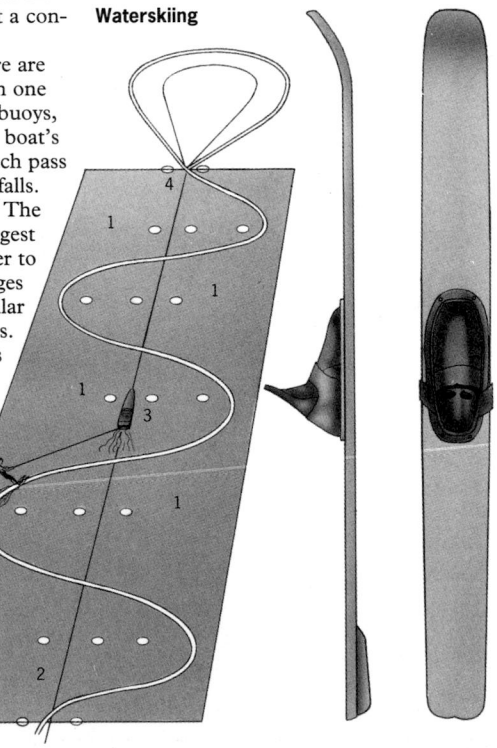

Waterskiing

Boardsailing

Sailboard

Yacht racing

Tornado

Flying Dutchman

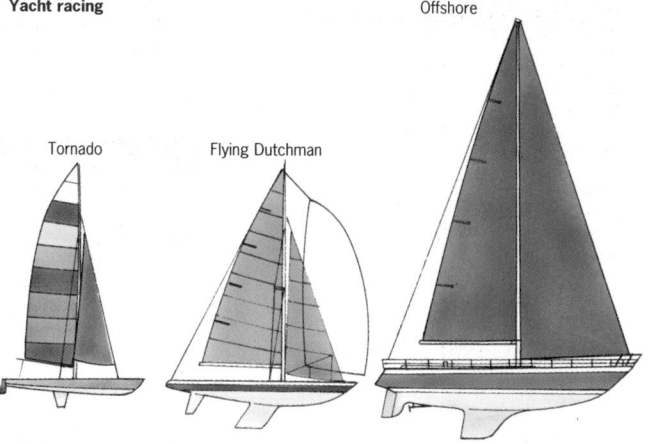

Offshore

YACHT RACING

Competitive sailing began in 1661, when King Charles II of England challenged his brother to a race on the Thames. The prestigious America's Cup began in 1851, when the U.S. schooner *America* beat Britain's best in a race around the Isle of Wight. The New York Yacht Club put the trophy up for challenge, the first taking place in 1870. After another 24 challenges and 113 years, an Australian yacht wrested the America's Cup temporarily from the U.S.A. Yacht racing became an Olympic sport in 1896. An International Yacht Racing Union exists but it does not regulate all major competitions.

Rules

Classes range from one-person dinghies to oceangoing yachts with crews of 20 or more. Detailed design rules govern each class, covering construction, rig, and sail area. Olympic and major one-design events are raced over a triangular course marked by buoys. There are usually seven races (of which six count), with yachts receiving 0 for 1st place, 3 points for 2nd, 5.7 3rd, and then 8 (4th), 10 (5th), 11.7 (6th), and place-plus-6 points thereafter.

Competition

The British home of the sport is Cowes, on the Isle of Wight, where the week-long regatta is a major highlight of the yacht-racing year, especially in uneven years when the Admiral's Cup is held. This is a contest for nations, each entering three boats. Points are scored in six races, inshore and offshore, culminating with the Fastnet race, over 606 mi. (975 km), first staged in 1925. There are also races for boats of different classes, run on a handicap basis. Paul Elvström of Denmark won the single-handed class in four successive Olympics (1948–60), the first such record in any Olympic sport.

Long-distance races

The quadrennial Single-handed Transatlantic Race was first held in 1960, when Sir Francis Chichester (U.K.) sailed *Gypsy Moth III* to victory in just over 40 days. This time was reduced to a little over ten days by the late 1980s as trimarans took over. The longest regular race is the Whitbread Around the World Race, first held in 1973–74, which begins and ends in Southampton, U.K. A handicap race, it is staged every four years.

Boardsailing

The sailboard was invented by 12-year-old Peter Chilvers in 1958. Sail, mast, and "wishbone" boom are connected to the board by a universal joint. World championships began in 1973. It became a yachting event (Windglider class) in the 1984 Olympics (1992 for women).

CANOEING

Canoeing evolved from a pastime into a competitive sport in the 1860s. Canoe clubs in the United States, Britain, and France began organizing unofficial races. Canoeing's popularity increased in the early 1900s with the introduction of the folding canoe. The International Canoe Federation was founded in 1924, and canoeing became an Olympic sport in 1936. Whitewater racing originated in the mountains of Austria and Germany in the 1930s with slalom, and its first world championships were held in 1949, followed by wild-water racing in 1959. Slalom events on artificial courses were held at the 1972 and 1992 Olympics.

Rules and races

Canadian canoes use a single-bladed paddle; kayaks use a double blade. Olympic "sprint" events are held over 500m for men and women, and 1,000m for men. In slalom, competitors have to negotiate "gates," paddling between sets of poles hanging down into the water on a winding and rocky course, containing drops and rapids. Wild-water races are longer, but without gates. Canoe marathons are held on rivers over 3–125 mi. (5–200 km).

POWER BOATING

The Union Internationale Motonautique classes are organized according to engine capacity. Formula One circuit powerboats run on aviation fuel, develop 300 HP and can accelerate from 0 to 100 mph (160 kph) in 4.2 sec. World championships are decided by points in a series of races. Hovercraft powered by motorcycle engines are raced on circuits over land and water.

Formula One powerboat racing.

ROWING

Rowing as a sport began in 1839, when the Henley Regatta was first held along a stretch of the Thames River west of London. Rowing became an Olympic sport in 1900 (officially 1908). World championships began in 1962. Events include single, double, and quadruple sculls, coxed and coxless pairs, coxed and coxless fours, and eights.

Rules

Courses, usually on rivers or lakes, are usually straight. In sculling, each rower has two oars; in rowing (pairs, fours, and eights), each has one. The women's quadruple is the only sculling event with a cox; eights always have a cox to steer. In coxless boats, rowers work the rudder with their feet. Major championships race over 2,000 m.

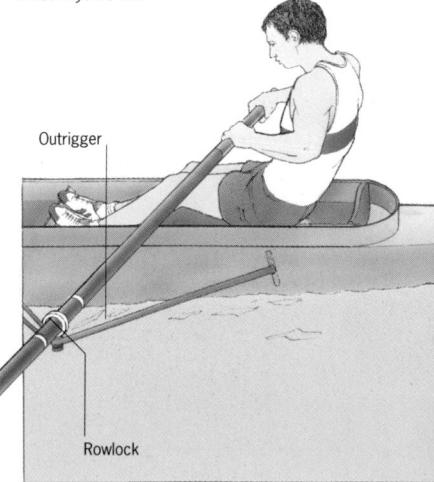

Outrigger

Oar

Rowlock

TENPIN BOWLING

Skittle games (with nine pins) emerged in Europe in the Middle Ages. Ninepins was banned in the U.S.A. in the 1840s when it attracted gamblers, so an extra pin was added, creating a different game that was not covered by the legislation. The American Bowling Congress (A.B.C.), founded in 1895, became the ruling body and standardized the rules. The now quadrennial amateur world championships were first held in 1923. There are singles, doubles, trios, and fives. The game is played worldwide.

Rules

The bowling ball, made of composition rubber or plastic, is 8.5 inches (21.6 cm) in diameter with fingerholes for gripping. The pins are plastic-coated maple and stand 14.9 inches (38.1 cm).

A game consists of ten frames. Players bowl two balls in each frame, unless they knock down all ten pins with their first—a strike. Knocking down all ten with two balls is called a spare. A strike is worth the pins scored with the next two bowls in addition to the ten pins; a spare earns the score of the next bowl plus the ten. A spare or strike in the tenth frame earns an extra ball or two balls to complete the bonus. The maximum score for a frame is 30; for a game 300.

Competition

Bowling is a popular professional sport, with regular televised tournaments and lucrative prizes. Tournaments are organized by the A.B.C., often in conjunction with the Professional Bowlers Association (P.B.A.). The leading organization for women bowlers is the Women's International Bowling Congress. An organization for both men and women bowlers is the Bowling Proprietors' Association of America (B.P.A.A.).

Variations

There are some locally popular variations of bowling, including duckpin bowling (using smaller pins than with traditional tenpin bowling), candlepin bowling (using narrower, cylinder-shaped pins), and lawn bowling.

Most sanctioned 300 games

Men

Bob Learn, Jr., Erie, PA	43
Mike Whalin, Cincinnati, OH	41
Jim Johnson, Jr., Wilmington, DE	38
Ron Woolet, Louisville, KY	33
John Wilcox, Jr., Shavertown, PA	32

Women

Jeanne Maiden-Naccarato, Tacoma, WA	20
Vicki Fischel, Wheat Ridge, CO	15
Aleta Sill, Dearborn, MI	14
Tish Johnson, Panorama City, CA	13
Leanne Barrette, Youkon, OK	12

ARCHERY

One of the first organized sports, archery was revived in England in 1781 and included in early Olympics (1900–08, 1920), returning in 1972. The Fédération Internationale de Tir à l'Arc (F.I.T.A.) was founded in 1931, when world championships began.

Rules

Bows, usually of fiberglass, have stabilizers, but optical sighting devices are not permitted. The target has five colored rings—white, black, blue, red, and yellow (called gold)—each with an inner and outer. Scores range from 1 for the outer white to 10 for the inner gold, the bull's-eye. Archers fire 36 arrows from 30 m, 50 m, 70 m, and 90 m (men), or 30 m, 50 m, 60 m, and 70 m (women). Major competitions are held over two rounds.

SHOOTING

Target shooting began during the 1400s in Switzerland. Pistol and rifle events were included in the first Olympics in 1896, clay-pigeon shooting in 1900. Separate women's target shooting events were introduced in 1984. The International Shooting Union was founded in 1907.

Events

The men's Olympic events are: free pistol (60 shots at 50 m); rapid-fire pistol (60 at 25 m); small-bore rifle and prone (60 at 50 m); small-bore rifle and three positions (40 each kneeling, standing, and prone at 50 m); running game target (60 at 50 m); air rifle (60 at 10 m); and air pistol (60 at 10 m). Women's events are sport pistol (60 at 25 m); air rifle (40 at 10 m); air pistol (40 at 10 m); small-bore rifle and three positions (20 each at 50 m). A bull's-eye scores 10. In clay-pigeon

shooting, double-barrelled shotguns are fired at saucer-shaped targets, 4.3 inches (11 cm) across. In trap shooting, targets are sprung from ground level; in skeet, from a high and low tower.

CUE SPORTS

Cue sports are played on a table with balls and a tapered stick called a cue. Billiards originated during the 1400s in France. Pool developed in the U.S.A. from 1500s' Spanish billiards and a later English version. World professional championships were first held in 1870. Snooker was invented in India by the British in 1875.

English billiards

The standard table is 12 x 6 ft. 1 1/2 in. (3.7 x 1.86 m) and has six pockets. There are a red ball and two white cue balls (one with a spot). Opponents each play one cue ball. Pocketing or going in off the red scores 3 points, off the white 2. Hitting both red and white is worth 2. Players continue until they fail to score.

Pool

The most prestigious of pool's many variations is 14:1, in which players must nominate the ball and the target pocket. Each pocketed ball counts as 1 point; the first player to score 150 points is the winner. Pool tables measure a maximum 10 x 5 ft. (3 x 1.5 m).

Snooker

The white cue ball is used by both players, and there are 15 reds (worth 1 point), a yellow (2), green (3), brown (4), blue (5), pink (6), and black (7). Players must pot a red before a color, continuing until they fail to score. Potted reds stay off the table; colors return to their starting spot. When there are no reds left, colors must be potted in ascending value.

Snooker

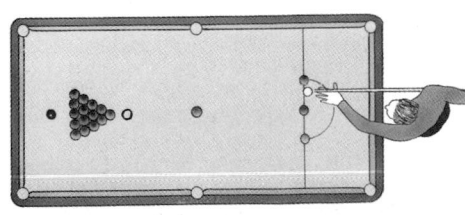

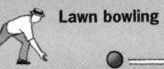

Tenpin bowling

Lawn bowling

EQUESTRIAN SPORTS

Dressage traces its origins to horsemanship exercises taught during the 1500s in the academies in France and Italy, while eventing is a development of military endurance riding. Show jumping began with the Royal Dublin Horse Show in 1868 and the founding of the Société Hippique Française in 1865. It appeared in the 1900 Olympics in Paris. Eventing, known then as "the military" and restricted to army officers, made its first Olympic appearance in 1912, along with dressage. The Fédération Equestre Internationale was founded in 1921 to coordinate equestrian sport. The first World Equestrian Games were held in Stockholm in 1990, combining the world championships of show jumping, three-day eventing, and dressage as well as the lesser-known disciplines of carriage driving, endurance riding, and vaulting. Men and women now compete with each other on the same terms in equestrian events.

Horse racing

There is evidence of horse racing in ancient Egypt, and the sport was introduced in the Greek Olympics in 648 B.C. Modern horse racing has its origins in England, where King Henry I bought an Arabian stallion in 1110. The first organized public race took place in 1174 at a horse fair at London. All today's racehorses are descended on the male side from three stallions brought to England in the early 1700s—Byerly Turk, Darley Arabian, and Godolphin Barb. The first steeplechase is thought to have taken place in 1752, in Ireland.

Rules and racing

Race distances are still measured by the imperial mile and furlongs (one-eighth of a mile). Racing is divided into flat racing and jumping. Flat racing is for two-year-olds plus, over distances mostly from five furlongs (1 km) to $1^1/_2$ mi. (2.4 km), but some races are over more than two miles. In jumping, there are hurdle races for three-year-olds plus (2 to 3 mi.) and steeplechases for four-year-olds plus (2 to about $4^1/_2$ mi.). In handicap races, horses carry weight based on their past form. Jockeys weigh in and out with their saddles, which have pockets to hold lead weights. In nonhandicaps, a weight-for-age scale gives younger horses allowances in all-age races, and fillies and mares receive allowances when racing against male horses. Apprentice jockeys also receive allowances. The owners' colors are worn by their jockeys, and the "nationality" of a winner depends on where it is trained.

The pinnacle of U.S. horse racing is to achieve the Triple Crown by winning the three premier classic races for three-year-olds—the Kentucky Derby, Preakness, and Belmont Stakes.

Horse racing in Hong Kong.

Major races

The strongholds of horse racing and breeding are the U.S.A., Britain, Ireland, and France; most major races are held in these countries.

Race (first run)		Distance
U.S. classics (3-year-olds)		
Kentucky Derby (1875)	Churchill Downs	1 mi. 2 f.
Preakness Stakes (1873)	Pimlico, Baltimore	1 mi. $1^1/_2$ f.
Belmont Stakes (1867)	New York	1 mi. 4 f.
English classics		
Derby (1780, 3-year-olds)	Epsom	1 mi. 4 f.
Oaks (1779, fillies)	Epsom	1 mi. 4 f.
2,000 Guineas (1809)	Newmarket	1 mi.
1,000 Guineas (1814, fillies)	Newmarket	1 mi.
St. Leger (1776)	Doncaster	1 mi. 6 f. 127 yd.
Irish classics		
Irish Derby (1866, 3-year-olds)	The Curragh	1 mi. 4 f.
French classics		
Prix de l'Arc de Triomphe (1920)	Longchamps	2,400 m
Australian classics		
Melbourne Cup (h/cap, 1861)	Flemington	1 mi. 1,739 yd.
Jumps (English)		
Grand National (h/cap, 1839)	Aintree	4 mi. 4 f.
Cheltenham Gold Cup (1924)	Cheltenham	3 mi. 2 f.
Champion Hurdle (1927)	Cheltenham	2 mi.

Harness racing

A racing sport in which horses pull drivers around an oval track in light, two-wheeled carriages called sulkies, harness racing is of two types—pacing and trotting—according to the gait adopted by the horses. There were trotting races in the Netherlands in the 1600s, and Dutch settlers took the sport to North America, where the first trotting race on a track was staged in New York in 1823. Strongholds of the sport include the U.S.A., Australia, New Zealand, France, the Netherlands, and Italy. Races are usually run over a mile (1.6 km). Major races such as the Hambletonian in the U.S.A. and the Inter-Dominion Championship in Australia and New Zealand offer huge sums in prize money and attract heavy gambling.

Show jumping

Show jumping is staged on specially built courses with fences designed to resemble cross-country obstacles such as gates, walls, and rails, and sometimes a water jump. Penalty faults are incurred for knocking down fences and other errors, and final positions are determined by the fewest faults. A "brick" or rail dislodged or a foot in the water jump earns four faults. A refusal incurs three faults, a second refusal six, a third results in elimination, as does taking jumps out of sequence. A fall is penalized by eight faults. Exceeding a time allowance, where applicable, incurs a quarter fault per second. Some competitions are determined on the aggregate faults of more than one round. If riders finish equal first, there is a jump-off against the clock.

Dressage

Eventing

Polo

Harness racing

Competition

Olympic show jumping comprises an individual and a team event, both with two rounds. The team medals are determined by adding the three best scores from four riders. In the quadrennial world championships (first held in 1953), the four finalists jump four rounds, with their own and each other's mounts. There is also a team event, first held in 1978. Teams of four contest the annual Nations Cup, decided over meetings held in several countries. The leading countries in show jumping events are the U.S.A., Britain, France, and Germany.

Dressage

In dressage competitions, the riders take their horses through a series of precise halts, paces, and movements to demonstrate the degree of communication and understanding between human and animal. International dressage is judged by a jury of five who award marks for execution of the movements in the 66 x 22 yd. (60 x 20 m) sand arena. German riders have dominated dressage team events. Since the 1970s, women have ridden off with most of the top honors.

Eventing

The three-day event (trials) involves riding the same horse, on separate days, in first a dressage test, then a four-phase endurance competition, and finally a show-jumping test. Penalty marks for the three elements are combined to determine placings. The chief element, on the second day, is for speed and endurance, and consists of a 10–13 mi. (16–20 km) road and tracks test to be completed in 73–90 minutes and performed at a trot or slow canter; a steeplechase, with nine or ten fences, taking 4½–5 minutes; another road and tracks; and finally up to 5 mi. (8 km) of cross-country jumping, with 28–32 obstacles, to be completed in 13–14 minutes. A less exacting form of the discipline is the one-day event.

Competition

In addition to the Olympic three-day event and the quadrennial world championships, the chief international events are the annual horse trials at Badminton and Burghley, both in England. British riders have an outstanding record in eventing, particularly in the world and European championships. And women riders more than hold their own against men at the level of international competition.

Polo

Polo has its origins in horseback sports of India and Persia played thousands of years ago. The British developed the game in India in the 1860s and brought it back to England, where the Hurlingham Club drew up a set of rules in 1875. The game was played in the U.S.A. in 1876, but Argentina later emerged as the stronghold of polo.

Polo is played between two teams of four on a 300 x 200 yd. (275 x 183 m) grass field, the largest of any sport. The goalposts, at each end of the field, are 24 feet (7.3 m) apart, and the object is to hit a small white ball (3¼ inches/8 cm in diameter) with a mallet into the opposition goal. The game is divided into seven-minute periods called chukkas. There are eight in a full game and the horses, or polo ponies, may be changed after every chukka. Britain and Argentina were most successful when polo was staged in the Olympics, the last time in 1936. The U.S.A. won the first world championships in 1989, beating Britain in the final.

World championships

World show-jumping championships were first held in 1953 (for men) and 1965 (for women); since 1978 men and women have competed together on equal terms. The team show-jumping competition was introduced in 1978. Three-day event and dressage championships were introduced in 1966. All three competitions are now held every four years. The combined international championships were renamed in 1990, and are now known as the World Equestrian Games.

Show jumping (men)

1953	Francisco Goyoago (Spain)
1954	Hans-Günter Winkler (West Germany)
1955	Hans-Günter Winkler (West Germany)
1956	Raimondo D'Inzeo (Italy)
1960	Raimondo D'Inzeo (Italy)
1966	Pierre d'Oriola (France)
1970	David Broome (U.K.)
1974	Hartwig Steenken (West Germany)

Show jumping (women)

1965	Marion Coakes (U.K.)
1970	Janou Lefèbvre (France)
1974	Janou Tissot (Lefèbvre) (France)

Show jumping (individual)

1978	Gerd Wiltfang (West Germany)
1982	Norbert Koof (West Germany)
1986	Gail Greenough (Canada)
1990	Eric Navet (France)
1994	Franke Sloothaak (Germany)

Show jumping (team)

1978	U.K.
1982	France
1986	U.S.A.
1990	France
1994	Germany

Three-day event (individual)

1966	Carlow Moratorio (Argentina)
1970	Mary Gordon-Watson (U.K.)
1974	Bruce Davidson (U.S.A.)
1978	Bruce Davidson (U.S.A.)
1982	Lucinda Green (U.K.)
1986	Virginia Leng (U.K.)
1990	Blyth Tait (New Zealand)
1994	Vaughan Jefferies (New Zealand)

Three-day event (team)

1966	Ireland
1970	U.K.
1974	U.S.A.
1978	Canada
1982	U.K.
1986	U.K.
1990	New Zealand
1994	U.K.

Dressage (individual)

1966	Josef Neckermann (West Germany)
1970	Yeleene Petouchkova (U.S.S.R.)
1974	Reiner Klimke (West Germany)
1978	Christine Stükelberger (Switzerland)
1982	Reiner Klimke (West Germany)
1986	Anne Grethe Jensen (Denmark)
1990	Nicole Uphoft (West Germany)
1994	Anky van Grunsven (Netherlands)

Dressage (team)

1966	West Germany
1970	U.S.S.R.
1974	West Germany
1978	West Germany
1982	West Germany
1986	West Germany
1990	West Germany
1994	Germany

SKIING

Primitive skis were used in Scandinavia more than 4,000 years ago, and the earliest known ski race took place in Norway in 1767. Modern skiing divides into Nordic and Alpine; predictably, the former has been dominated by the Scandinavian countries, while the Alpine countries excel at their brand of skiing.

Alpine ski racing

British visitors to the Alps in the late 1800s invented this sport, and in 1903 they founded the Ski Club of Great Britain and organized the first race in Adelboden, Switzerland. Sir Arnold Lunn invented the slalom in 1922. The modern Fédération Internationale de Ski (F.I.S.) was founded in 1924, and Alpine ski-racing world championships began in 1931, annually before World War II and biennially after. The sport entered the Winter Olympics in 1936, and the first World Alpine Ski Cup was held in 1967.

Rules and races

Alpine ski racing takes place on downhill courses, the skiers starting separately and placed according to their times. In downhill, the object is to take the quickest route down the set course. In slalom (or special slalom), giant slalom, and super giant slalom, skiers have to negotiate "gates" marked by pairs of flagpoles on their way down. There are 55–75 gates for men and 40–60 for women in slalom races. Giant and super giant slalom are held on progressively longer courses with greater vertical drops, and the gates are fewer and wider. The slalom and giant slalom events are decided on the aggregate time of two runs.

Freestyle skiing

This sport, also known as "hot-dogging," evolved in the U.S.A. The first competition was held in New Hampshire in 1966. Freestyle was recognized by the F.I.S. in 1979. World Cup series began in 1980 and world championships in 1986, with Olympic recognition in 1992. There are three disciplines. Aerials are acrobatic jumps judged on height, distance, execution, precision, and landing. The moguls event requires high-speed turns and two aerial maneuvers on a heavily bumped course against the clock. Ballet is performed to music on smooth slopes and is judged on grace and skill.

Nordic skiing

Nordic skiing comprises cross-country racing and ski-jumping. Modern Nordic ski racing dates back to the invention of ski bindings in the 1880s; the Norwegian explorer Fridtjef Nansen's epic Greenland trek on skis in 1888 captured public imagination. Racing, jumping, and

a combined event were included in the first Winter Olympics in 1924, with official world championships in 1931.

Rules and races

Races are run against the clock, with competitors starting at 30-second intervals. Major competitions are held on machine-made parallel tracks; skiers must give way if caught up with. There are freestyle events and classical, in which skiers must use a diagonal stride. Men race over 10 km and 30 km classical, and 15 km, 50 km, and a 4 x 10 km relay freestyle; women in 5 km and 15 km classical, and 10 km, 30 km, and 4 x 5 km freestyle. Nordic skiers use lightweight skis, shorter than for Alpine racing but with longer ski poles. Ski jumpers do not use poles. There are two jumps of different heights, for men only, and points are awarded for style and distance, then totaled for the two jumps. In combined Nordic events, jumping results determine cross-country starting order; competitors are handicapped 10 seconds for each 1.5 points they are behind the lead jumper.

Biathlon

A combination of cross-country skiing and rifle shooting, biathlon has military origins in 1700s' Norway, where the first modern competition was held in 1912. World championships were started in 1958 (1984 for women), and Olympic recognition was gained in 1960 (1992 for women). Biathletes ski with small-bore rifles strapped to their backs and make stops to shoot at targets, five rounds at 50 m. Competitors must ski a penalty loop of 150 m for every miss; the first home is the winner. Men's events are over 10 and 20 km with a 4 x 7.5 km relay, women's over 7.5 km, 15 km, and 3 x 7.5 km.

SLED RACING

Tobogganing races were first held in Switzerland in the 1880s, and bobsleds (bobsleighs) were invented by British enthusiasts, who lashed two toboggans together for more speed. A special bobsled run was constructed in St. Moritz in 1902, and the first world and

Four-person bobsled team in action.

Olympic championships were held in 1924 in Chamonix, France. Women do not compete in major bobsled events. The skeleton toboggan, ridden head-first in a prone position, is used for the Cresta Run in St. Moritz. It is an Olympic event only when the Winter Games are held there, so far in 1928 and 1948. Luge sleds are lighter and are ridden in a sitting or lying position, feet first. The first luge world championships were held in 1953, and luge became an Olympic sport in 1964.

Rules and races

Bobsleds slide on metal runners and are steered by the driver, who operates cords connected to the front runners. They have brakes, which may not be used during a run. There are four- and two-person bobsleds, and placings are determined on the total time for four runs. The luge has no steering or brakes, the sliders using legs and shoulders to guide the sleds. Men compete in two-seater and single luge, women just in single. In the Olympics, singles are decided on four runs, two-seaters on two.

bobsled

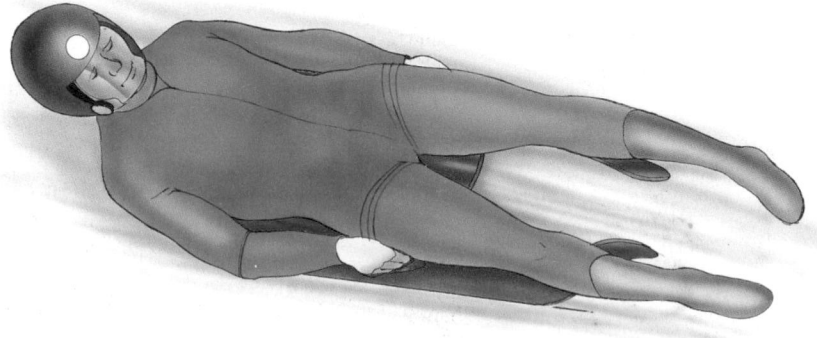

ICE SKATING

The first offical world championships in speed skating were staged in Amsterdam in 1893. The artistic side of skating developed in Britain. The first ice club was opened in Edinburgh in 1742, and the first artificial ice rink was built at the London Glaciarium in 1876. Annual world championships were instituted for men in St. Petersburg in 1896, for women in 1906, and for pairs in 1908. Men's, women's, and pairs skating appeared in the 1908 Summer Olympics; speed skating in 1924, the short-track version in 1992. Ice dancing dates from the 1930s; the first official world championships were from 1952, and Olympic recognition came in 1976.

Skating competitions have had a broad spectrum of winners, with the U.S.A. strong in both men's and women's figure skating. Norway, Finland, and the Netherlands have been strong in the men's speed skating. Canada and Japan have reigned in short-track, with South Korea emerging as a power in the 1990s.

Figure skating

The figure skate has a grooved blade with two edges, and movements are performed on one or other of these. In singles and pairs competition, a short program with eight required moves counts for a third of the marks, a freestyle program for two-thirds. Each program receives two sets of scores from the judges—one for technical merit, the other for artistic impression, both marked out of a maximum of six. There are nine judges, and the best and worst marks are discarded each time. But the final positions depend on placements (1, 2, 3, etc.) from the judges rather than the actual marks. In ice dancing there are two compulsory dances: an original set-pattern dance and a free dance counting for half the score. Dance differs from pairs in that movements must conform to accepted dance patterns, and lifts, jumps, and separate movements are restricted.

Speed skating

The standard, mechanically frozen outdoor track is 440 yd. (400 m) around, and races range from 500 m to 10,000 m. Skaters race in pairs, in lanes with a changeover zone for switching lanes each lap, and are placed according to time. Short-track racing is held on 122-yd. (111-m) indoor circuits, with races from 500 m to 5,000 m and no lanes. Elimination heats are used to progress the fastest four (in shorter races) or six skaters to the final.

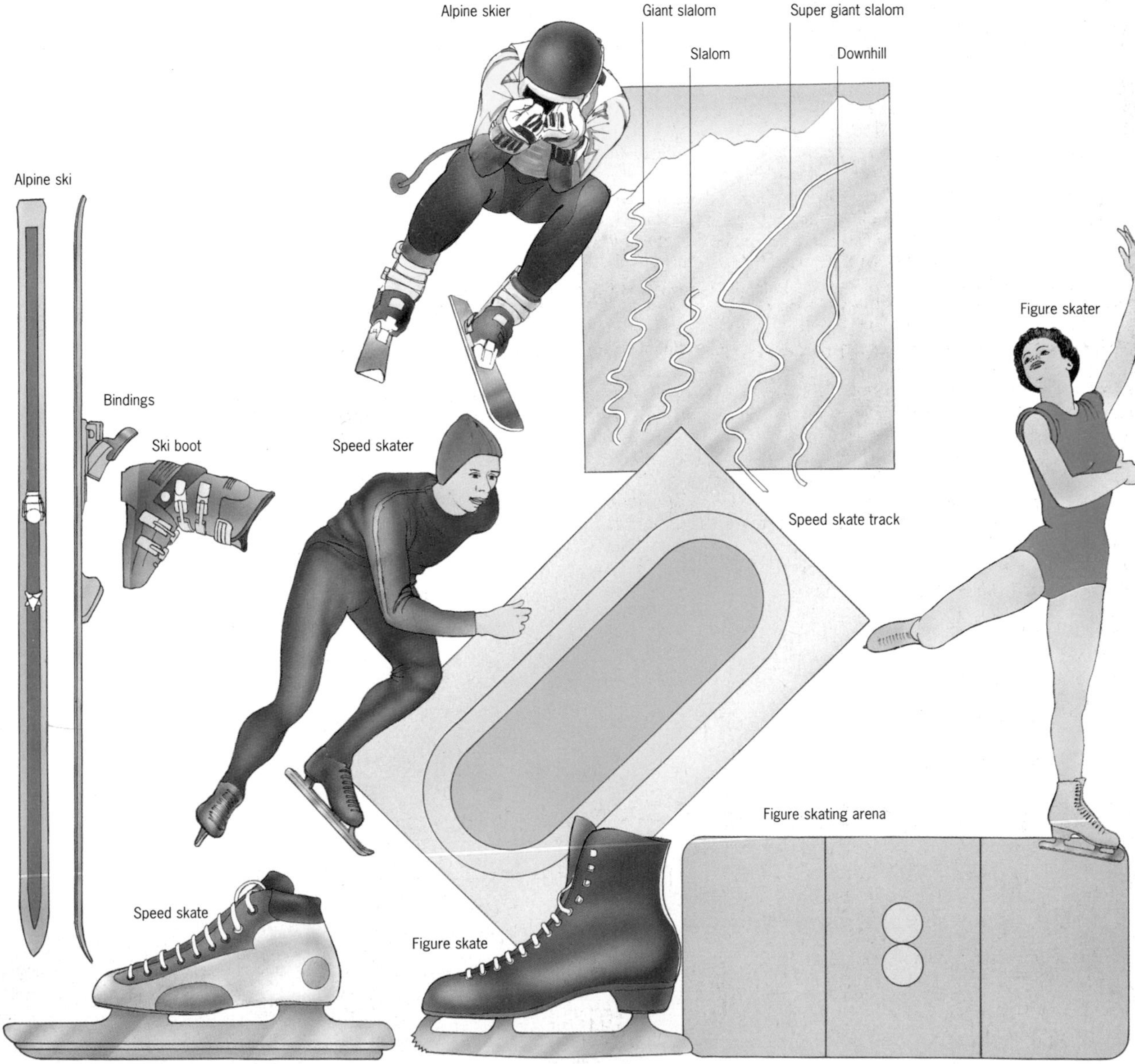

Alpine skier

Giant slalom

Super giant slalom

Slalom

Downhill

Alpine ski

Figure skater

Bindings

Ski boot

Speed skater

Speed skate track

Figure skating arena

Speed skate

Figure skate

MOTOR SPORTS

German engineer Karl Benz designed the first car in the 1880s, and the first organized motor race took place on the roads of France in 1895. The first Grand Prix was held in Le Mans, France, in 1906. The Fédération Internationale de l'Automobile (F.I.A.), the ruling body for motor sports, instituted the World Drivers' Championship in 1950 and the Constructors' Championship in 1958.

IndyCar racing

IndyCar racing has evolved over decades into its current structure of 16 races on a variety of tracks, mostly in the U.S.A. but some in Canada and Australia. The cars are heavy and their engines, which run on methanol fuel, are designed to handle the different demands of tracks ranging from high-speed banked ovals to twisting road circuits with tight corners and fast straights. The first 12 places earn 20, 16, 14, 12, 10, 8, 6, 5, 4, 3, 2, and 1 point respectively, with 1 point for pole position and one for leading for most laps. The distance ranges from 162 mi. (260 km) to the 500 mi. (805 km) of the Indianapolis and Marlboro superspeedways. Circuits range from 1–4 mi. (1.6–6.4 km).

Formula One racing

Formula One cars are light one-seater, open-wheeled vehicles with a monocoque (one-piece) chassis and a body fitting over it. Wide, smooth tires called slicks (not used in wet conditions) ensure good grip, and airfoils provide downward force to help keep the car on the track. Sets of regulations, called formulas, control the engine power and design of racing cars. The top class is Formula One, which has 16 Grand Prix races a season, held in different countries. The drivers' and constructors' championships are decided by points, 10 for 1st place, 6 for 2nd, 4 for 3rd, 3 for 4th, 2 for 5th, and 1 for 6th. More than 20 cars take part in a Grand Prix; lap times in practice sessions determine positions on the starting grid. Grands Prix are held on twisting circuits with laps varying from just over 2 mi. (3 km) to nearly 4.3 mi. (7 km). The total distance for most Grands Prix is a little over 186 mi. (300 km).

Sports car racing

Sports cars are two-seaters with bodywork that covers the wheels. A world sports car championship for manufacturers incorporating a series of races was held, on and off, from 1953 to 1992, and for drivers from 1981 to 1992. The most famous sports car race is the Le Mans 24-Hour Grand Prix d'Endurance. Two or three drivers take turns at the wheel, with numerous pit stops. The winning car averages more than 155 mph (250kph) over the 8.5-mi. (13.6-km) circuit.

Drag racing

Specially built dragsters race in pairs on a straight quarter-mile (402-m) drag strip. Drag racing began in California around 1930, when enthusiasts began to test their modified cars on dry lake beds. "Hot-rodding" developed in the 1940s, and to get this dangerous pastime off the streets, unused airstrips were converted for the purpose. The first organized drag meeting took place in 1948 near Santa Barbara, California. Men and women compete on equal terms, and women have had outstanding success; Shirley Muldowney was the first racer to win the world championship three times (1977, 1980, 1982).

Rules

Competitions are usually run on a knockout basis. The fastest cars are the streamlined, tapering top-fuelers, with airfoils, lightweight front wheels, slicks at the back, and engine behind the driver, run on a type of rocket fuel. The next class is funny cars, which look deceptively like sedans but have a fiberglass body. They have the same engines as top-fuelers, but mounted in front of the driver. They are only marginally slower. Record time for a quarter-mile is below 5 sec., with finishing speed over 300 mph (485kph).

Stock car racing

The sport of racing mainstream production (stock) cars developed after World War II, quickly becoming popular in the South and then elsewhere in the United States. The automobiles driven in the races still resemble those on sale in car showrooms, but alterations to the engines and gutting of the interiors allow them to reach speeds of over 200 mph (320 kph). Chassis and bodywork is specially strengthened to withstand high-speed impact. Cars race within inches of each other in order to benefit from the slipstream effect, thereby saving fuel.

Rules

The National Association for Stock Car Auto Racing (N.A.S.C.A.R.) organizes 23 major races each year in a season running from February through September. Most circuits are oval shaped, and some have banked corners. The most important race is the Daytona 500, held in Daytona Beach, Florida. Drivers earn ranking points for high finishes in each race. The driver with the most points at the end of the season wins the Winston Cup. Dale Earnhardt has been the top points earner, becoming Winston Cup champion six times from 1980 to 1993.

Rally driving

The first long rally took place in 1907, from Beijing to Paris, a distance of some 7500 mi. (12,000 km), that was completed in two months. The Monte Carlo Rally was first staged in 1911 to attract visitors in winter. It became an annual event in the 1920s with cars converging on Monaco from all parts of Europe. Other international rallies were established, such as the R.A.C. Rally in Britain (1927), recognized by the F.I.A. in 1951, and the Safari Rally in Kenya (1954), and world championships were instituted, for cars (1968), male drivers (1977), codrivers (1981), and female drivers (1990).

Rally rules

Cars must be mass-production models, but may be strengthened. Driver and navigator wear crash helmets, the navigator reading from notes covering every bend, corner, and change of road surface. Cars start at 1- or 2-minute intervals on each section of the course, and incur time penalties for arriving late at checkpoints or for changing parts. Final positions are determined by penalties.

Formula One car

IndyCar

Other motor sports

Autograss A type of oval racing (*below*) of British origin run on improvised flat grass or dirt tracks, with classes for Saloons (sedans) and for Specials—open-wheeled, rear-engined vehicles.

Karting High-speed go-karts (100cc or 250cc) racing on circuits of various lengths.

Midget car racing High-speed oval racing (*below*) using small cars with open cockpit, rear airfoil, and rear slicks.

Off-road racing Racing off metaled roads, specifically desert races of the U.S.A. and Mexico, staged on rough country over as much as 1,000 mi. (1,600 km), vehicles ranging from dune buggies to pick-up trucks and even motorcycles.

Oval racing Racing on small oval circuits, up to about 880–1,750 yd. (800–1,600 m) in the U.S.A., 440 yd. (400 m) in Europe, with many classes, most permitting contact between cars.

Rallycross TV-oriented sport invented in Britain in 1967: sedan-type cars race around a course of sharply changing surfaces, from tarmac to chalk, grass, and mud. No more than ten cars in one race.

"Saloon" car racing European sport where "saloon" (sedan), also known as touring, cars compete on racing circuits, with classes for production models and modified cars.

Land Speed Record

The first driver to hold the Land Speed Record (L.S.R.) was Frenchman Gaston de Chasseloup-Laubat, who drove an electric car at 39 mph (63kph) in 1898. The British dominated from the 1920s, with Malcolm Campbell, Henry Segrave, George Eyston, John Cobb, and Campbell's son Donald, until the F.I.A. changed the rules in 1964 to accept jet-propelled cars, when U.S. drivers Art Arfons and Craig Breedlove took over. But in 1983 British driver Richard Noble became the first to break the 1,000 kph barrier with an average speed of 1,019 kph (633 mph) in his jet-engined Thrust 2 on the Black Rock desert in Nevada. Record attempts must be made over either a flying kilometer or mile, taking the average of two runs made in opposite directions.

MOTORCYCLE SPORTS

The German engineer Gottlieb Daimler invented the first motorcycle in 1886. The early racing machines were production motorcycles. A world ruling body, now the Fédération Internationale Motorcycliste, was formed in 1904. Tourist Trophy races on the Isle of Man in Britain began in 1907. The first world championships were staged in 1949 over a series of Grands Prix for 125cc, 250cc, 350cc, 500cc, and sidecar classes.

Grand Prix racing

Grands Prix are held in various countries during the season, with several classes at each meeting; 15, 12, 10, 8, 6, 5, 4, 3, 2, and 1 point respectively are allotted for the first ten places. Current Grand Prix classes are for 500cc, 250cc, 125cc, 80cc, and bikes with sidecars.

Motocross

Also known as scrambling, motocross races comprise several laps of a rough, hilly, cross-country course. The strong, light bikes have chunky tires for better grip on loose surfaces, with the engine mounted well clear of the ground. Motocross began in Surrey in 1924. World championships were inaugurated in 1957 and are held annually for several classes including sidecar.

Speedway

Speedway may have begun in the U.S.A. or in Australia, where a race was staged in 1923 at an agricultural show in New South Wales. World championships were first held in 1936 (individual), with team competitions added in 1960 and pairs in 1968. Strongholds are the U.S.A., Britain, Scandinavia, and Australia and Oceania. Racing takes place over four laps of an oval cinder track, normally 330–440 yd. (300m–400 m) around. There are four riders in each heat, the first three places gaining 3, 2, and 1 point respectively. In individual world championships, 16 riders each take part in five of the twenty heats. The lightweight bikes have chunky tires, no brakes or gearbox, and a small fuel tank.

Other motorcycle sports

Enduro Endurance test for bike and rider over as much as 250 mi. (400 km) of rough terrain. Major components may not be replaced; riders are penalized for exceeding times between checkpoints.

Ice speedway Northern European sport, using bikes with spiked wheels, with its own world championships since 1966.

Trials riding Riding in difficult terrain, including boulders, loose rocks, fast-flowing water, mud, and steep climbs, began as a sport in the early 1900s. Trials are staged over a few miles to six-day events covering as much as 1,000 mi. (1,600 km). Riders tackle sections, often at a snail's pace, and are penalized for putting a foot down (1 point) or stopping (5 points). World trials-riding championships have been held since 1975.

CYCLE RACING

The first cycle race took place in Paris in 1868 over 1,312 yd. (1,200 m). World championships were first held in 1893, in Chicago, with a sprint and a 62-mi. (100-km) motor-paced race. Track and road racing were part of the 1896 Olympics. The world governing body, the Union Cycliste Internationale, was founded in 1900, and the three-week multistage Tour de France, which covers some 2,500 mi. (4,000 km), began in 1903.

Track racing

Sprint is a head-to-head race, with riders jockeying for position on the banked track before an all-out sprint for the line. Pursuit (4,400 yd./4,000 m), individual and team, where riders start on opposite sides of the track, is decided on time or if one rider or team catches their opponents. There are also points races, with points scored for crossing the line first on each lap, and double points at the finish.

Cyclo-cross

Racing on a cross-country circuit, including sections where bikes must be carried. This has developed into mountain bike racing. Courses include rocks, ditches, drops, even flights of stairs. World championships are held for both sexes.

Grand Prix bike

Motocross bike

Pursuit cycle

GOLF

The earliest record of golf is a decree of King James II of Scotland in 1457 banning the sport because it was interfering with archery practice. The world's governing body, the Royal and Ancient Golf Club, founded in 1754, established the St. Andrews game of 18 holes. The first British Open Golf Championship was held in Prestwick in 1860. The United States Golf Association was founded in 1894. The first U.S. Open was held in 1895, the U.S. P.G.A. (Professional Golfers' Association) Championship in 1916, and the U.S. Masters in 1934. Meanwhile, the great amateur championships had been instituted, the British in 1885 and the American in 1895. The Ladies' British Open Amateur Championship began in 1893. The Ladies' (initially Women's) Professional Golf Association (L.P.G.A.) was set up in the U.S.A. in 1944, and the first U.S. Women's Open was played in 1946. In 1989, the World Golf Association was established to reacquire Olympic status for the game.

Rules

The object of the game is to hit a white ball (1.68 in./42.67 mm in diameter) into a series of 18 holes between 110 and 550 yd. (100 and 500 m) from the starting point, or tee, in as few strokes as possible. Most competitions are based on strokeplay, and the top events consist of four rounds, usually played on consecutive days, the winner being the player with the lowest score. Another form is matchplay, in which players compete head-to-head over 18 or 36 holes, winning, losing, or halving each hole until one player leads by more holes than there are remaining.

Equipment

A golfer may take a maximum of 14 clubs on a round. An average club golfer would not need as many, taking probably two woods, four irons, a wedge, and a putter. The woods are the "longest" clubs—that is, they send the ball farthest. They have large heads made of wood, light metal, or plastic, and are used from the tee or on long fairways. Irons have heads of steel or other metals and shorter shafts. They are more accurate than woods and are used for shorter shots. They are numbered, as are woods, depending on the angle, or loft, of the club face. The higher numbers have greater loft, sending the ball higher but over a shorter distance. The loftiest club is the 10 iron, or wedge, and is used for lifting the ball out of sand. The putter is used on the greens. Putters come in all shapes and sizes but have flat heads in order to keep the ball on the ground.

Competition

Golf is predominantly an individual sport, although there are important team competitions between countries. The British Open, the U.S. Open, the P.G.A., and the Masters are highlights of the European and U.S. tours, in which regular strokeplay tournaments offer huge sums of prize money to successful golfers. They are played at different venues each year except for the U.S. Masters, whose permanent home is the Augusta National course in Georgia.

The only individual matchplay tournament of any significance is the World Matchplay Championship (first staged in 1964) held annually in Wentworth, England, in which 12 of the world's best golfers are invited to take part in a knockout competition.

The most keenly fought team tournament is the biennial Ryder Cup. Instituted in 1927 as a match between the U.S.A. and Britain, it was broadened to include all Europe in 1979, and the U.S.A.'s virtual domination of the trophy was broken in 1985 by British and Spanish players particularly. The present format is 28 matches, including foursomes, fourballs, and singles.

The annual World Cup was begun in 1953 to accommodate players from all countries and is a strokeplay tournament for teams of two, which produces an individual winner as well as a top country. The world's leading individuals, however, are still judged primarily by their success in the majors, by the money they win, and by the Sony World Rankings, introduced in 1986. Amateur golf is not as important as it was in earlier days, but the U.S. Amateur (inaugurated in 1895) and the British Amateur (1885), both matchplay knockout tournaments, are still prestigious events. The biennial Walker Cup (1922) is a match between amateurs of the U.S.A. and the British Isles.

Women's golf

Women's golf has flourished in the U.S.A. for many years, but there is now a strong European tour, too. There are four tournaments in the U.S.A. regarded as majors: the U.S. Women's Open (first held in 1946), L.P.G.A. Championship (1955), Nabisco Dinah Shore (1983), and Du Maurier Classic (1979). The British Women's Open (1976) is the leading tournament on the European tour. The U.S.A. meets the British Isles in the biennial Curtis Cup (1932) and Europe in the biennial Solheim Cup (1990).

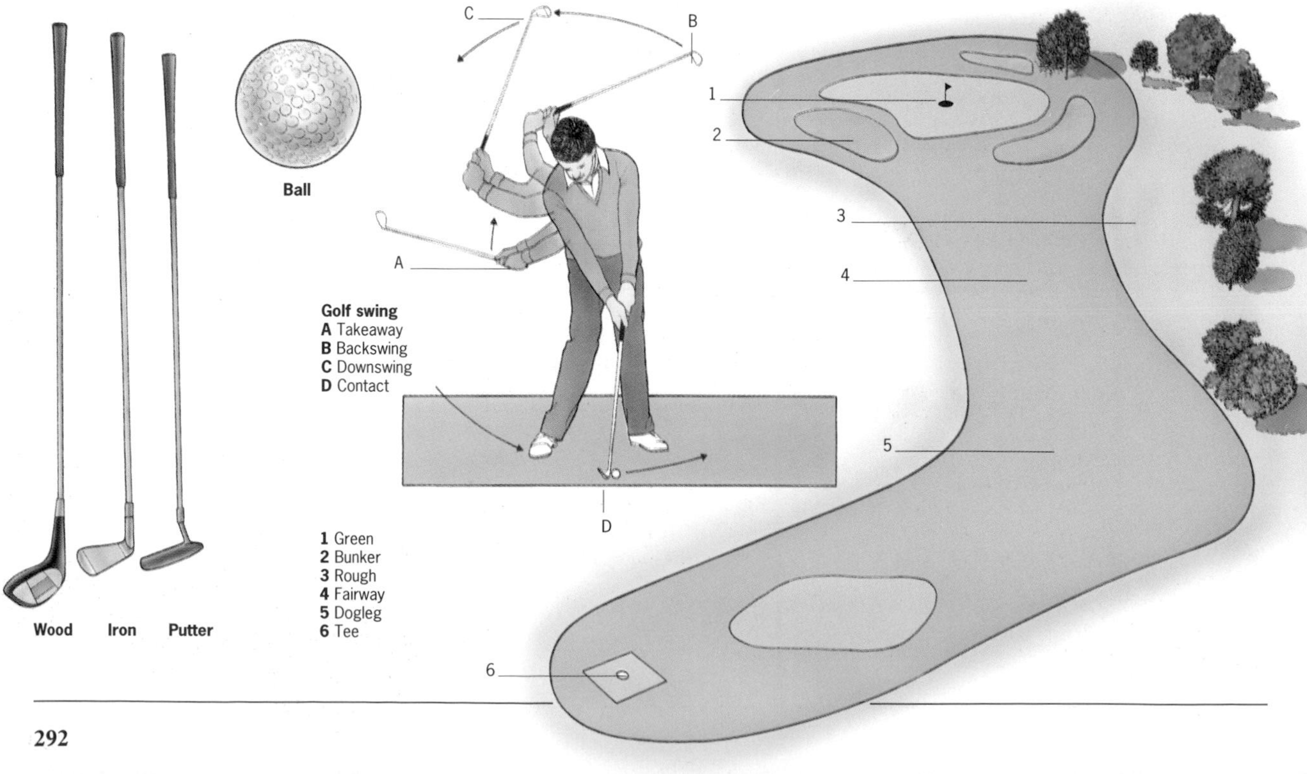

Ball

Golf swing
A Takeaway
B Backswing
C Downswing
D Contact

1 Green
2 Bunker
3 Rough
4 Fairway
5 Dogleg
6 Tee

Wood   Iron   Putter

Records

Lowest four-round total

British Open	268	Tom Watson 1977
U.S. Open	272	Jack Nicklaus 1980
U.S. PGA	271	Bobby Nicklaus 1965
U.S. Masters	271	Jack Nicklaus 1965
	271	Raymond Floyd 1976

Lowest single round

British Open	63	Mark Hayes (U.K.) 1977
	63	Isao Aoki (Japan) 1980
	63	Greg Norman (Australia) 1986
	63	Paul Broadhurst (U.K.) 1990
	63	Jodie Mudd (U.S.A.) 1991
	63	Nick Faldo (U.K.) 1993
	63	William Stewart (U.S.A.) 1993
U.S. Open	63	Johnny Miller (U.S.A.) 1973
	63	Tom Weiskopf (U.S.A.) 1980
	63	Jack Nicklaus (U.S.A.) 1980
U.S. PGA	63	Bruce Crampton (Australia) 1975
	63	Raymond Floyd (U.S.A.) 1982
	63	Gary Player (South Africa) 1984
U.S. Masters	63	Nick Price (South Africa) 1986

Oldest winners (age in years)

British Open	46	Tom Morris Snr. 1867
U.S. Open	43	Raymond Floyd 1986
U.S. P.G.A.	48	Julius Boros 1968
U.S. Masters	46	Jack Nicklaus 1986

Youngest winners (age in years)

British Open	17	Tom Morris Jnr. 1868
U.S. Open	19	John McDermott 1911
U.S. P.G.A.	20	Gene Sarazen 1922
U.S. Masters	23	Severiano Ballesteros 1980

Most wins

	British	U.S.P.G.A.	Masters	
Jack Nicklaus	3	4	5	6
Walter Hagen	4	2	5	-
Ben Hogan	1	4	2	2
Gary Player	3	1	2	3
Tom Watson	5	1	-	2
Harry Vardon	6	1	-	-
Bobby Jones	3	4	-	-
Gene Sarazen*	1	2	3	1
Sam Snead	1	-	3	3
Arnold Palmer	2	1	-	4

*When he won the Masters in 1935 Gene Sarazen became the first man to have won all four majors.

ANGLING

There are almost as many types of angling as there are fish, but fishing can broadly be grouped into two types: game fishing and sea fishing.

Game fishing

Angling for game fish is a sport practiced worldwide. The term "game fish" generally refers to members of the salmon, trout, and char families in most of the world, as well as pike, catfish, and bass in the U.S.A. Although most game fish naturally occur in the northern hemisphere, some species of trout have also been introduced into Africa, India, Australia, and South America, where game fishing has become popular.

Big-game fishing from a powerboat.

Trout are almost always caught by fly fishing. Dry flies resemble insects that rest on the surface film of the water; wet flies penetrate the water and look more like tiny fish and aquatic insects.

Fly fishing is rarely static: the fly is continually cast out, worked slowly back, and recast. Rods are 7–10 ft. (2–3.5 m) long, with a heavy line, known as the shooting head, designed to make the rod bend and catapult the line and fly across the water. The fly is attached to a fine nylon thread, 6–9 ft. (2–3 m) long, tied to the end of the shooting head. The experienced angler can cast flies with precision to trout 65 ft. (20 m) away. Annual tournaments are held in the U.S.A. and the Netherlands.

Sea fishing

Sea fish can be caught from a beach, rocky outcrop, pier, or boat. Fishing is usually confined to the shallower, warmer areas of the continental shelf, and international sea fishing events take place over the summer months. Commonly caught sea fish include bass, jewelfish, cod, conger eels, and some sharks.

Big-game fishing is usually confined to tropical waters where the fish are bigger and generally more ferocious. Quarry include blue, black, and striped marlin, sailfish, tuna, and various sharks, as well as smaller, hard-fighting fish such as tarpon and barracuda. The primary method for big-game fishing is trolling, in which live bait or artificial lures are drawn through the water behind a slow-moving boat. Sonar equipment is often used to locate the fish. Anglers are strapped into a "fighting chair," bolted to the deck of the boat. The butt of the rod is inserted into a "butt pad" strapped around the angler's waist or to the chair, allowing greater leverage when fighting large, powerful fish.

The International Game Fish Association (I.G.F.A.) certifies records (*see right*).

I.G.F.A. world records

Species	Weight	Angler
Saltwater fish		
Striped bass	78 lb., 8 oz.	Albert McReynolds (Atlantic City, NJ: 1982)
Bluefish	31 lb., 12 oz.	James M. Hussey (Hatteras Inlet, NC: 1972)
Atlantic cod	98 lb., 12 oz.	Alphone Bielevich (Isle of Shoals, NH: 1969)
White shark	2,664 lb.	Alfred Dean (Australia: 1959)
Bluefin tuna	1,496 lb.	Ken Fraser (Nova Scotia: 1979)
Freshwater fish		
Large-mouth bass	22 lb., 4 oz.	George W. Perry (Montgomery Lake, GA: 1932)
Atlantic salmon	79 lb., 2 oz	Henrik Henriksen (Norway: 1928)
Rainbow trout	42 lb., 2 oz.	David Robert White (Bell Island, AK: 1970)
Walleye	25 lb.	Mabry Harper (Old Hickory Lake, TN: 1960)

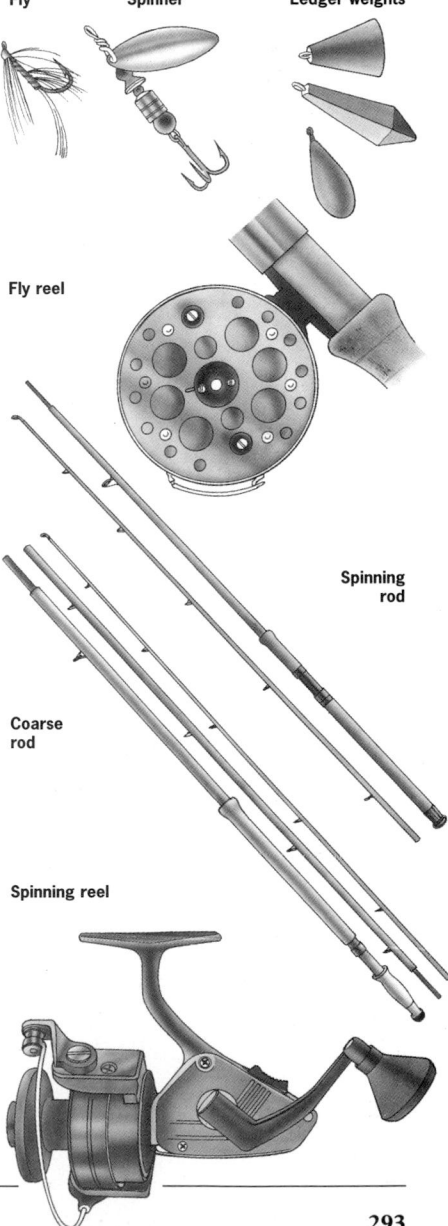

Fly Spinner Ledger weights

Fly reel

Spinning rod

Coarse rod

Spinning reel

BOARD AND TABLE GAMES

Many board games are very old. Weigi, the forerunner of go, was played in China more than 3,500 years ago. The race game pachisi has been played for thousands of years. Many board games depend on the use of dice, and primitive dice have been found in Egyptian tombs and ancient South American burial sites.

Chess

The game of chess is thought to have evolved in India more than 1,000 years ago. The pieces in use today are at least 500 years old, and the game was popular in the Middle Ages. The world's first international tournament was held in London in 1851, and the first officially recognized world championship in 1886. The world governing body, the Fédération Internationale des Echecs (F.I.D.E.), was founded in 1924. A women's world championship was established in 1927. The now biennial world team events called Olympiads were also introduced in 1927, and a separate team competition for women began in 1957. The breakaway Professional Chess Association was formed in 1993.

Rules

A chessboard has 64 light and dark squares with 16 light and 16 dark pieces, always referred to as black and white. The starting positions and names of the pieces are shown in the diagram. Each player has a white square at bottom right, and the queen starts on a square of its own color. The numbers and letters along the sides are used in chess notation. Players make alternate moves; the game always begins with white moving. A play-

er moving a piece onto a square occupied by an opponent's piece captures that piece, removing it from the board. The object is to maneuver the opposing king into a position from which it cannot escape, thus winning the game.

When the king is threatened the opposing player calls "check." The king must then be moved or the threatening piece taken. If it cannot be moved or the threat removed, the king is "checkmated" and the game is over. If the king is not in check but the player cannot make a legal move without placing it in check, the game is drawn.

Moves

Pawn (1) Only up the board on the same file, or row one or two squares on first move, one square thereafter, but capturing only one square diagonally forward.
Rook (2) Any number of unblocked squares along a file.
Knight (3) An L-shaped move, two squares in one direction and one at right angles, ignoring any pieces en route.
Bishop (4) Any number of unblocked squares diagonally; a bishop starting on black cannot move onto a white square.
Queen (5) Combining the moves of rook and bishop, the queen is the most powerful piece, moving any number of unblocked squares in any direction.
King (6) One square only in any direction, but not into check.
Castling A special move, which a player may make only once, in which the king is moved two squares to the left or right toward a rook on its starting square and the rook is placed on the square the king passed over. This may not be done if the rook or king has been moved previously, if there is a piece between them, or if the king or any of the squares it passes over is under attack.
En passant A pawn making a two-square first move may be captured in passing, as if it had moved only one square, by an enemy pawn on the fifth rank.
Queening a pawn A pawn that reaches the eighth rank may be promoted to any major piece, the choice usually being a queen (a player may have two or more queens at the same time).

Competition

The world championship is organized on a challenge basis.

F.I.D.E. stages preliminary rounds every two or three years to find a challenger, who plays the reigning champion in a 12-match contest.

World championships

World champions have been recognized since 1886. The first international tournament was held in London in 1851 and was won by Adolf Anderssen (Germany). The first women's champion was recog-

Postwar champions (Men)

1948–57	Mikhail Botvinnik (U.S.S.R.)
1957–58	Vassiliy Smyslov (U.S.S.R.)
1958–60	Mikhail Botvinnik (U.S.S.R.)
1960–61	Mikhail Tal (U.S.S.R.)
1961–63	Mikhail Botvinnik (U.S.S.R.)
1963–69	Tigran Petrosian (U.S.S.R.)
1969–72	Boris Spassky (U.S.S.R.)
1972–75	Bobby Fischer (U.S.A.)
1975–85	Anatoly Karpov (U.S.S.R.)
1985–93	Gary Kasparov (U.S.S.R.)*
1994–	Anatoly Karpov (Russia)

Champions (Women)

1927–44	Vera Menchik–Stevenson (U.K.)
1950–53	Lyudmila Rudenko (U.S.S.R.)
1953–56	Elizaveta Bykova (U.S.S.R.)
1956–58	Olga Rubtsova (U.S.S.R.)
1958–62	Elizaveta Bykova (U.S.S.R.)
1962–78	Nona Gaprindashvili (U.S.S.R.)
1978–91	Maya Chiburdanidze (U.S.S.R.)
1991–	Xie Jun (China)

* In 1993, Gary Kasparov broke away from F.I.D.E. with Nigel Short to form the Professional Chess Association, and was stripped of his title. Kasparov beat Short for the P.C.A. World Championship title in 1993.

nized in 1927. Players from the U.S.S.R., and now its former states, have dominated world chess for nearly 50 years. The highest rank a player can reach is Grandmaster, attained by earning an Elo rating (listed twice yearly by F.I.D.E.) of 2,500.

Checkers

A game for two played on a chessboard, checkers was popular in Europe during the 1500s and is thought to have derived from similar games played in the ancient world.

Each player has 12 pieces which are thick disks made of wood or plastic and all the same shape. Play takes place only on the black squares, and at the start the pieces are arranged on the three rows nearest to the players, with a black square at bottom left. Black always starts, and the players move alternately. The pieces must be moved diagonally up the board, one square at a time. If an opponent's piece is in the way and has an empty black square behind it, a player may capture that piece by jumping over it into the empty square, and then remove it from the board. More than one enemy piece may be captured by a piece in the same move, provided there is a space behind each piece taken. A player is forced to make a capture if one is available (often there is a choice of captures). If a piece reaches the back line of the opponent's side, it is crowned and becomes a king—a spare piece of the same color is placed on top of it. Kings may move and capture in any direction, diagonally up or down the board. The object of the game is to capture all your opponent's pieces, or to block any remaining pieces so that your opponent cannot move.

There are many variations of checkers, with different starting positions, different moves, and even with a 100-square board and 20 pieces each.

2 3 4 5 6

1

Backgammon

A strategic game for two, played with counters and dice, backgammon originated thousands of years ago in the Mediterranean area, where similar games were played in ancient Greece and Rome.

The board is divided into an inner table and an outer table by a raised section called the bar. The players set out their pieces, called men, on the long triangles called points (*below*). One has white, the other red (or black). The men move in opposite directions, and the object is to get all your men into your own inner table, and then remove them from the board, called bearing off. The men are moved according to throws of the dice, and always in the direction from your opponent's inner table around the board toward your own inner table.

Each player has two dice and makes alternate throws. A player throwing a 4 and a 3, for example, may move one man 4 points and another 3, or one man 4 and 3 (or 3 and 4) in two moves. A double, say 5 and 5, entitles the thrower to double the scores, using any combination of 5 + 5 + 5 + 5 in moving one, two, three, or four men. The important rule is that you can land a man on any point that is not occupied by two or more of your opponent's men. If you move a man onto a point with just one enemy man on it, called a blot, you make a hit and can remove that man to the bar. A player with a man, or men, on the bar must

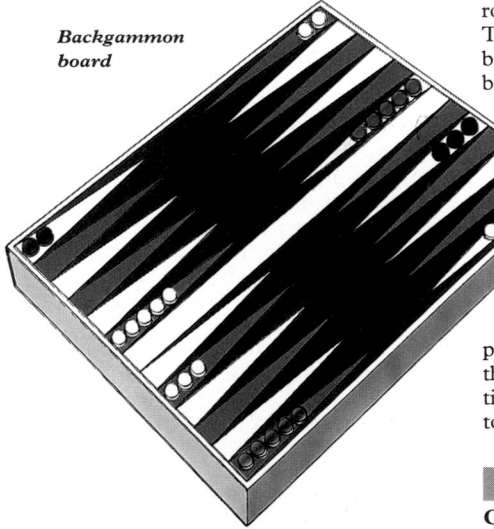

Backgammon board

move them (starting from the beginning of the enemy's inner table) before moving any other men.

Backgammon is not only played for amusement: it is also a gambling game. If you bear off all your men before your opponent has borne off any, you win by a gammon, or 2 points, or by a backgammon (3 points) if your opponent still has at least one man on your inner table or on the bar. There is also a doubling cube the players may use to increase the stakes during the game.

Dominoes

A game for two to four players, dominoes probably originated in China and was taken to Europe during the 1300s. It is a simple game that can be learned in a few minutes, but it calls for considerable strategy in order to play skillfully.

There are 28 dominoes, which are tiles usually made of plastic or wood, each divided into two sections. Each section has from 0 to 6 spots on it, and no two dominoes are the same. In the most popular version of the game, the dominoes are turned face down and mixed up before the players draw seven each (two players) or five each (three or four players). Those remaining are called the boneyard. Players take it in turns to place a domino face up on the table, making a chain of dominoes. A domino may be played if it has a half matching a number at one end of the chain. A player with no matching domino must draw from the boneyard until finding one that matches. When there are none left, players who cannot match miss their turn. The winner is the first player with no dominoes left (called going out), or, if no one goes out, the one with the fewest total spots left.

Mah-Jongg®

A Chinese tile game dating back to the 1800s, Mah-Jongg® evolved from a card game and has some of the features of the rummy games. The name means "sparrows"—birds of mythical intelligence. There are 136 tiles (sometimes 144) of bamboo, wood, bone, or plastic, 108 belonging to three suits—dots (circles), bams (bamboos), and craks (characters). These are numbered 1 to 9 and there are four of each. There are four tiles each of the north, east, south, and west winds, four each of the red, green, and white dragons, and often four flowers and four seasons. The game may be played by two to six people, but usually four play. It spread to the West after World War I, and a variation developed in the U.S.A. that is easier to learn and score.

Other board games

Clue® The board is divided into "rooms," and the players, who are each dealt a few person, place, and implement cards, must find out the facts concerning a murder. They must identify the murderer, implement used, and scene of the crime, which are determined by cards seen by no one and hidden in an envelope at the start of the game. Detective work is done by deduction, arranging meetings, and questioning.

Go The national game of Japan, go was first played in China around 650 B.C. It is a tactical game, played on a board with

19 lines across and 19 up and down, making 361 points on which the stones (counters) are played. Each of the two players has a supply of stones, similar to checkers pieces, and take turns to fill up the board with the intention of surrounding their opponent's pieces, or army. Go is easy to learn but calls for a strategy on a par with chess. There is a handicapping system to equalize playing skills.

Monopoly® This is a board game for two or more players; the aim is to acquire property. Players throw two dice to move a token each around a board which has hotels, houses, stations, and utility companies on it. These can be bought, built upon, mortgaged, etc., and rent must be paid (using Monopoly money) when landed on by a nonowner. The game ends when all but one player are bankrupt. The game was first based on Atlantic City, but there are now a number of national and international versions.

Scrabble® This word game is played on a special board for two to four players. Points are scored by placing letter tiles of different values crossword-fashion to form interlocking words; each player has a hand of seven tiles until none remain. Scores can be doubled or tripled by making use of premium squares on the board.

Trivial Pursuit® In this board game players make progress by giving correct answers to general knowledge questions—on art and literature, entertainment, geography, history, science, and sports—which are found on special cards.

Roulette

Roulette is a casino game played with ball and spinning wheel, which is divided into 36 alternately red and black segments numbered 1 to 36 and a green 0, but not in numerical order. Bets are placed on where the ball will come to rest, and they can take several forms. Roulette emerged in France during the early 1800s, and is particularly associated with Monte Carlo. It is not as popular in American casinos, where the wheel has two zeros, 0 and 00, which doubles the house edge.

Bets are made by placing gambling chips on a betting layout. The odds for bets are 35–1 on a single number (straight), 17–1 on two numbers (split), 11–1 on three numbers (street), 8–1 on four numbers (square or corner), 5–1 on six numbers (line bet), 2–1 on dozens (1–12, 13–24, or 25–36) and columns, and even money on red or black, odd or even, and high (19–36) or low (1–18). In the United States, evens bets are lost when one of the zeros comes up, giving the house a high all-around edge of 5.3 percent. With the French wheel, used in European casinos, even bets are either held "in prison" to await the next spin or half the stake is returned (*le partage*). The house edge for the French wheel is 1.35 percent for even-money bets and 2.7 percent for others.

CARD GAMES

Card games may have originated in India as a derivative of chess, although there is some evidence that they were played in ancient China and Egypt. They were taken to Europe from the Middle East by the crusaders. The current design used for playing cards originated in France during the 1300s, although there are several games that can be played with tarot cards, which have many more symbolic face cards.

Bridge

A card game developed from whist, bridge is thought to have originated in either Greece or India. The version almost universally played today is contract bridge, played by two pairs of players. Scoring uses a chart designed in 1925 by U.S. inventor Harold Stirling Vanderbilt, based on tricks (rounds of play won) successfully contracted for. Worldwide popularity led to world team championships (Bermuda Bowl), first held in 1951 and now biennial. The World Bridge Federation was founded in 1958.

Rules

Bridge is played with a full pack of 52 cards by four players (two pairs of partners), who are dealt, one at a time, 13 cards each. All aspects of bridge move clockwise—the alternation of the dealer after every hand, the deal, the bidding, and the play. A hand of bridge is divided into two distinct parts—the bidding and the play—calling for two separate skills. The highest bidders contract to play the hand with a particular trump suit (or no trumps) and make a certain number of tricks. A contract of one heart signifies making seven tricks (6 + 1) with hearts as trumps; a contract of four spades, ten tricks (6 + 4) in spades. The suits, in ascending order of importance, are clubs, diamonds, hearts, spades, and no trumps. So the bidding range runs from one club to seven no trumps (13 tricks). There are also doubles of a contract (for double points) and redoubles of doubles (for quadruple points), which may be interjected as bids.

Scoring

Making a contract entitles the successful partnership to a number of points "above the line," 20 for clubs (two clubs bid and made is worth 40, for example) and diamonds, 30 for hearts and spades, and 40 for the first no trump and 30 for succeeding no trumps. The object is to "make game" by scoring 100 points (not necessarily in one hand). A partnership that has made game is known as "vulnerable," and two games wins the rubber. Points are scored "under the line" for making game, for defeating a contract, for making overtricks (more tricks than contracted

for), and for bidding and making a slam—a small slam is 12 tricks (a contract of six diamonds, for example); a grand slam is 13. At the end of each rubber, the points, above and below the line, are totaled to find the winning partnership, and a few coins might change hands (the winners of the rubber are not necessarily the winners on points).

Bidding

Bidding is a mixture of natural bids, showing strength in particular suits, and conventional bids, which have a special meaning. Partners must always explain their bidding system, and any special bids, to opponents if required. Secret conventions are not allowed.

Play

When the bidding is finished, after three "no bids," or passes, the member of the successful bidding partnership who bid the contract suit first is "declarer"; the other member is "dummy." The player to the left of declarer makes the opening lead, to the first trick, and then dummy's hand is spread face up on the table, dummy taking no part in the play.

Competition

Bridge is a social game usually played with a small stake. It may be converted into a team game—and the luck of the deal largely eliminated—by playing it as duplicate bridge. In this system, which is used in international competition, the same hands are played at different tables, so that two pairs from a team play opposite hands of the same deal. Italy and the U.S.A. have had by far the greatest success in the world team championship; Italy and France have shared the honors in the quadrennial world team Olympiad for the Vanderbilt Trophy, first contested in 1960. In women's bridge, the U.S.A. has consistently enjoyed success, with Britain its strongest challenger.

Poker

A card game for two to seven or more players, poker is played for low or high stakes, but the betting is an integral part of it. Poker is highly skillful, the art being to deceive one's opponents, disguising the strength or potential of one's hand, chiefly in the betting, maximizing the profit from good hands, and sometimes bluffing one's opponents out of their good hands. Poker originated in the U.S.A. in the mid-1800s and has gripped the public imagination ever since. The basic game is draw poker. Each player is dealt five cards face down, there is a round of betting, the players may discard a number of cards in exchange for new ones from the unused pack, and then there is the final round of betting. The hands in descending order are:

Hand	Example	Explanation
Straight flush	QH JH 10H 9H 8H	Consecutive cards in same suit
Fours	7S 7H 7D 7C JC	Four cards of one denomination
Full house	3H 3C 3S AC AD	A three and a pair
Flush	KD 10D 7D 5D 2D	All cards same suit
Straight	9C 8D 7D 6S 5H	Consecutive cards in any suit
Threes	5H 5S 5C QC 3D	Three cards of same denomination
Two pairs	AC AS 8H 8S KC	Two pairs of same denominations
Pair	4H 4S JC 9S 5H	Two of same denomination
High card	KH JH 7S 4H 2C	No matching cards

Value of hands

In games where there are wild cards, five of a kind is another possible hand, and this beats a straight flush. If two or more players have flushes or straights, the high-

Blackjack—or vingt-et-un—is a popular card game in casinos.

Omar Sharif in a bridge championship.

est card determines the winner; if those are equal, the next highest, etc. The highest denomination determines the value of fours, threes, and pairs (A-A-A beats K-K-K, for example); with full houses the value of the three is decisive; and with two pairs, the value of the higher pair is decisive, but if both pairs are equal, the odd card is decisive.

Betting

Cards are dealt and bets made in a clockwise direction. Sometimes each player puts an ante (in chips or money) into the pot (kitty) before the betting starts. The first player may open (make the first bet), pass (if allowed), or fold (throw in). After the pot is opened, succeeding players may fold, call (match the previous bet), or raise (increase the bet). According to predetermined rules, the betting stops when it has gone around a certain number of times, reaches a set limit, there are no further raises, or only one player is left, in which case that player wins the pot. This prevails for the round of betting after the draw, too. When there are no further raises in the last round of betting, there is a showdown, in which the highest hand wins the pot.

Variations

There are countless variations of poker, many of them including wild cards (nominating cards to count as anything). The most widely played form of poker is stud, in which some cards are dealt face up. In seven-card stud, for example, players receive two cards face down and one face up before the first round of betting, then three more face up and one face down, after each card of which there is another round of betting. In lowball, played either draw or stud, the lowest hand wins. The best hand under most lowball rules is A-2-3-4-6 not of the same suit (A-2-3-4-5 would be the lowest straight), the ace being counted as a one.

Blackjack

Based on the card game pontoon, or twenty-one, blackjack offers the casino gambler considerable choice in the play and, with best play, the least advantage, or edge, to the house. The dealer, or croupier, stands behind a table usually with betting places for up to seven players and, after the players have placed their bets, deals out two cards, one at a time, to each player. The object of the game is to get nearer to a total of 21, without exceeding it, than the dealer.

Cards have their face value, with picture cards counting as 10 and aces as 1 or 11 at the player's discretion. After receiving two cards, a player may "stand" (not draw a further card), "hit" (draw one or more further cards), "double down" (double the stake, but receive only one more card), or, if the cards are the same denomination, split them and treat them as separate hands with separate bets (split aces may receive only one more card each). A player who goes over 21 is bust and the stake is lost. The dealer, whose play is automatic, must draw to a total of 16 or under and must stand on a total of 17 or over. If the dealer's total exceeds that of a player, the player's stake is lost; if it is the same, the result is a standoff; if it is less, the player receives even money, or odds of 3–2 for a blackjack—21 comprising an ace and a 10 or picture card. (Blackjacks are not valid with split aces, counting as just 21, and beaten by a dealer's blackjack.) The house advantage is gained as a result of winning losing stakes from players who have gone bust before the dealer's hand is played.

The rules of blackjack vary from one country to another, but with optimum play, which is quite complex, the bettor can reduce the house edge to less than one percent.

Other card and dice games

Baccarat This is a high-stakes casino card game: the most popular versions are baccarat banque and Nevada baccarat (or punto banco), in which bank plays against players; in another, chemin de fer, all players take turns to hold the bank: the object is to assemble, with either two or three cards, a points value of 9. Picture cards and the ten count 0; ace counts 1; other cards have their face value. If the total is a double figure then the first figure is ignored: for example, a total of 18 would count as 8. Baccarat is thought to have been introduced into France from Italy during the reign of Charles VIII.

Canasta Similar to rummy, canasta is played by partners using two packs, including four jokers. Cards are picked up and discarded; the object is to collect "melds"—sets of the same denomination. All have points value, but jokers and deuces (2s) are "wild" (can take any value). Melds must have at least two nat-

ural cards and no more than three wild cards. A seven-card meld is a canasta and earns bonus points. Canasta originated in Uruguay in the 1940s, the name deriving from the Spanish word *canasta* (meaning "basket"), which probably refers to the tray where cards were discarded.

Craps This casino dice game was adapted in the early 1800s from the old English game of hazard. Throwing two dice, a player immediately loses with 2, 3, or 12 but wins with 7 or 11. With an initial throw of a point—a 4, 5, 6, 8, 9, or 10—the player continues throwing and wins if the point is made again before a 7 is rolled. On a casino craps table, there are a variety of side bets. The house edge is about 1.4 percent on certain basic bets but considerably higher on most of the side bets.

Rummy This is a domestic card game, possibly derived from Mah-Jongg®, in which cards are picked up and discarded with the object of forming melds of three or four of a kind, or three or more of the same suit in sequence. A 52-card deck is used, and six, seven, or ten cards are dealt according to the number of players—two to six can play. A variation, and the most popular gambling game for small or high stakes, is gin rummy (mainly for two players), in which melds may be laid face upwards and can be added to by any player during the game. Points are obtained for each card melded according to face value (face cards = 10) and deducted according to cards remaining in hand when one player wins the game by going gin (disposing of all his or her cards) or knocking (going out with unmatched cards totaling ten or less).

Solo A card game for four players, solo is a form of whist, similar to bridge. Cards are dealt 3-3-3-3-1: the suit of the last card is trumps. Players bid to make certain contracts, in order of ascending precedence: prop and cop (temporary partnership between any two players to make eight tricks), solo (five tricks), misère (no tricks in no-trump play), abundance (nine tricks, nominating trumps), royal abundance (nine in trumps as dealt), misère ouverte (no tricks, with cards face up), and abundance declarée (13 tricks in no trumps).

Whist A nongambling card game, whist developed in the 1700s from a game called triumph and is played by four people in pairs, each player receiving 13 cards. The last card, which is dealt to the dealer, is turned up and its suit is trumps. The object is to win more tricks, or rounds, than the opposing partnership (partners sit opposite each other). A trick consists of one card played in turn by each player (clockwise). The suit of the first card must be followed. A player who cannot follow may discard from another suit or play a trump, which beats any card of the other suits. The winner of each trick plays the first card of the next.

HOBBIES AND PASTIMES

Abseiling
Descending a steep incline by means of a rope; used in mountaineering, but now recognized as a pursuit in itself.

Aerobics
System of exercises designed to increase oxygen consumption and speed blood circulation, thereby increasing fitness.

Ballooning *See* Hot-air ballooning.

Batik
Ancient Indonesian folk art of fabric design using a basic wax-resist technique: warm wax is painted onto light-colored fabric, according to a chosen design, and then dipped into a solution of dye and water—only unwaxed fabric takes dye.

Bell ringing or campanology
Ringing church bells. There are two popular forms: change ringing (pulling ropes by hand) and carillon (using a keyboard connected to a clapper of bells).

Bird-watching or ornithology
Study and observation of birds in their natural habitat. It may involve recording details concerning anatomy, behavior, song, and flight patterns.

Bowling
Term for a number of games, each involving rolling a ball toward a target. Played professionally as a team sport, or for recreation in teams or individually. Played indoors, the ball is rolled down a lane, with a gutter on either side, toward ten pins with the aim of knocking down all pins. Other versions are ninepins, skittles—a British game in which the pins are much smaller than those used in tenpin bowling and are replaced manually—and boules, a French game similar to lawn bowling, with metal boules tossed at a small target ball.

Brass rubbing
Duplicating designs on ornamental brass plate, as found in churches. The brass is covered with paper and then rubbed over with crayons or chalk until an impression is produced.

Bullfighting
National sport in Spain, where it is called *corrida de toros* and the leading matadors are national heroes. Picadors are sent into the ring to weaken the bull before the matador enters to make the final killing.

Bungee jumping
Daredevil sport of leaping from river-crossing bridges on the end of a strong elastic (bungee) rope, common in the U.S.A., Australia, and New Zealand.

Butterfly collecting
Keeping preserved butterflies, having either caught them in their natural environment or bought them. The insects are identified and mounted, usually in a glass display unit.

Caber tossing
Throwing a 12–18-foot (3–4 m) tree trunk or caber, often practiced in Highland Games gatherings in Scotland.

Calligraphy
Penmanship, or handwriting at its most

Boules–the French version of bowls.

formal. A major art form in many countries of East Asia and in Arabic-speaking lands. Special pen nibs, brushes, ink, and paper are usually required.

Campanology *See* Bell ringing.

Candle making
Producing candles by repeatedly dipping a prepared wick into wax, pouring wax over a wick, or pouring wax into molds.

Climbing
Generally refers to scaling anything from a 50-foot (15 m) wall to an assault on the Himalayas, with or without oxygen and mechanical aids. As well as the physical aspect, climbing also involves psychological thrills. Wall-climbing is now a competitive international sport.

Coin collecting *See* Numismatics.

Cookery
Preparing and cooking food. It may involve production of exotic and specialty dishes and creation of new recipes.

Cribbage
A card game that goes back to England in the 1600s, cribbage is played by two to four people with a 52-card deck and a peg board used for scoring. The most popular game is six-card cribbage, played by two people.

Crochet
Making textile items by means of a special hook to loop yarn in a variety of

Physical demands of mountain climbing.

stitches according to a pattern.

Croquet
A lawn game in which players use mallets to hit colored balls through hoops. It is thought to have come from France during the 1100s, but the game as we know it developed in England in the 1860s. It is played either singles or doubles, and women compete on equal terms with men. The MacRobertson International Shield was instituted in 1925, with Britain the most successful country, and the first singles world championships were staged in 1989.

Curling
Often described as "bowls on ice," curling developed in Scotland, where the Grand Caledonian Curling Club, forerunner of the International Curling Foundation, was founded in 1838. The game was taken to Canada, which has become its stronghold. World championships were introduced in 1959 (1979 for women), and curling has been included as a demonstration sport in the Winter Olympics. The object is to slide heavy curling stones as close as possible to a target or "tee." The stones are propelled by means of a handle, which may be twisted to make them curl around.

Dancing
Moving to music, alone or with others, dancing has evolved in most cultures, often originally as part of religious ritual.
Ballroom A dance form developed during the early 1900s, revealing strong influence of ragtime and syncopated rhythms producing the foxtrot, quickstep, and tango, but also incorporating a slower version of the German waltz and later Latin American dances such as the cha-cha-cha, paso doble, rumba, and samba.
Break Athletic street style which involves spinning on the back and head.
Reel A form of stepping dance originating in Scotland and performed to bagpipes. The Virginia reel is an example that is performed in the U.S.A.
Disco Popular form of dance originating in the 1960s. Accompanying music is often loud, with a rhythmic beat.
Jazz A form of modern dance performed to jazz rhythms.
Morris English traditional dance using stamping and hopping. Performers, some wearing bells, carry a stick, handkerchief, or garland and dance to an accordion.
Ballet Classical dance form relying on balance and five foot positions.
Tap Dance relying on rhythmically complex footwork, partly improvised, using foot, heel, and toe beats.
Folk Traditional dance form for groups of male and female dancers in even numbers; includes square dancing.

Darts
The design of the modern board dates from 1896. Professional world championships were instituted in 1978. The dartboard sectors are numbered from 1 to 20, with a central bull's eye worth 50 (inner part) or 25 (outer). The sectors

have strips worth double or triple. Players take turns to throw three darts at the board, maintaining a distance of 7.8 feet (2.4 m). The players start with 501, subtracting their score after each turn until one of them reaches zero, finishing on a double (or inner bull).

Dressmaking
Pastime undertaken often to make low-cost clothes, using a paper pattern and fabric, but also a creative hobby lending itself to sophisticated fashion design.

Electronic and computer games
Games programmed and controlled by a small microprocessor. Most are connected to a visual display unit (V.D.U.) and are known as video games. Many have war themes, others simulate sports, and some board games are available in electronic form. All are operated by using either a computer keyboard or a joystick plugged into a home computer. Larger versions are produced for use in amusement arcades. Among the most popular types are platform games—where the player controls an electronic protagonist who moves from level to level, avoiding obstacles and enemies and collecting rewards—and simulations, where the player is put in control of a notional airplane, spaceship, car, or motorcycle.

Embroidery
Ornamentation of fabric with decorative stitching, embroidery dates from very early times. It became highly developed, e.g. for rich garments and furnishings, including church vestments, in the Middle East, India, and Europe; one example is the Bayeux tapestry depicting the Norman Conquest of Britain in 1066.

Falconry or hawking
Sport in which birds of prey are trained to hunt animals and other birds. Long-winged falcons, such as the peregrine, are used in open country and swoop on their prey from a great height. Short-winged birds, or accipiters, perch on the falconer's gloved fist or the branch of a tree until they can see their prey, then rely on speed to catch their quarry. These birds are usually kept hooded when not hunting.

Fox hunting
Mounted blood sport involving chasing and killing a wild fox with foxhounds. It developed in Britain during the late 1600s; since 1949, there has been a movement to ban the sport.

Gardening
The type of garden depends not only on the gardener's tastes and space available, but also on soil type and fertility, climate, air pollution, and shelter from wind and sun. Some special garden types are:
Espalier Technique involving training trees over a lattice of wood against a wall.
Herb garden Usually includes shrubs as well as herbs, mostly perennial.
Japanese-style garden Maximum use is made of evergreen plants. Features include stone lanterns, walkways, streams and waterfalls, and occasional stones.

Ballooning above the English landscape.

The bonsai technique, associated with Japanese style, involves dwarfing plants by shallow planting in containers, starvation, and the pruning of roots and shoots.
Rock garden Artificial or natural mound of soil and rock fragments for growing rock plants, usually flowering plants, hardy perennials, and dwarf trees.
Water garden Plants arranged in and around natural or artificial pools and streams, e.g. water lilies, marsh marigolds.
Wildflower garden Often includes marsh or bog plants as well as forest-floor wildflowers; usually requires rich, acid soil.

Gliding
Enjoyed by many as a recreation, gliding is also an international sport, with world championships since 1937. Major competitions last several days and involve tasks requiring accuracy over a set course and achievements of speed and distance. Graded by wingspan, gliders are launched by an aircraft tow or a ground winch.

Hang gliding
The pilot is suspended in a harness beneath a wing of light material stretched on a metal frame. The pilot launches the hang glider by running from the top of a suitable slope and steers by exerting pressure on the frame. Although a large percentage of activity is recreational, world

Long wings enable a glider to fly.

championships have been held since 1975, with notable success for pilots (of both sexes) from the U.K. and Australia.

Horseback riding
Involves acquiring specialized skills to control the horse while seated on its back. Commands are signaled by hand, leg, and voice instruction, sometimes reinforced by use of whip and spurs.

Horseshoes
Outdoor game in which a horseshoe is thrown at a peg. Popular in the England of the 1300s, and still played there as quoits using a metal ring.

Hot-air ballooning
Piloting or being carried as a passenger by hot-air balloon, with burners providing bursts of heat when necessary.

Ikebana
Formal Japanese style of flower arrangement, involving the selection of a few blooms or leaves placed in careful relationship to one another.

Jewelry making
Making earrings, bracelets, and necklaces from a variety of materials, including clay, papier maché, and beads.

Kite flying
Flying a light frame covered with paper, cloth, or plastic at the end of a length of string, usually requiring windy conditions. Kites can be brightly colored and various shapes; the simplest kite has only one string, but with two strings, one on each side and held in each hand, a kite can be more easily controlled from the ground and made to do complicated loops and dives in the air.

Knitting
Ancient craft used for making fabric, in which loops of yarn are linked together using two or more hand-held needles. Machines are now used to produce complex knitted garments, but they cannot create all the intricate designs produced by skilled hand knitters.

Lace making
Most popular method (especially in Europe) of lace making is bobbin or pillow lace. As many as 1,000 bobbins are wound with thread and hung on pins which are inserted, according to design, into small holes on a piece of stiff paper attached to a pillow, cushion, or styrofoam base. The bobbins are then looped, braided, and twisted following a pattern.

Macramé
Method of making a type of coarse lace by knotting and braiding; used to make decorative fringed borders for costumes as well as furnishings.

Model making
Mainly the construction of cars, ships, trains, and airplanes by gluing together preshaped plastic or wooden parts from specialized kits.

Numismatics
Studying and collecting coins, notes, and other similar objects, e.g. medals. Dates from the Italian Renaissance; collectors in the 1600s were the first to catalog their collections.

Origami
Making model animals or other objects by folding sheets of paper, with minimum use of scissors or other implements; originated in Japan during the 900s.

Paintball
Simulation of military combat involving firing paint pellets which splatter on contact with clothing to indicate a hit. It is played by two or more teams and is popular in the U.S.A. and Europe.

Panelology
Carving thin, wooden panels which may be either framed or lodged between other upright and cross pieces, usually stretched across the surface of a wall. Pictures are often painted onto these panels. Most effective results are achieved on panels that are made from chestnut, oak, or white poplar.

Paragliding
Being towed through the air while wearing an adapted parachute, then gliding back to the ground.

Philately
Collecting stamps. One of the world's most popular hobbies, it often involves documentation in special books or albums. The first philatelist is said to have been John Tomlinson, who started collecting the day after the issue of the first postage stamp, the penny black, in Britain in 1840.

Pigeon breeding
Breeding pigeons to exhibit or race, popular in the U.S.A., U.K., and France.

Pigeon racing
Pigeons are taken from their loft and released at a starting point that may be hundreds of miles away; their homing instinct takes them back to their loft, where a special clock times their arrival, thus establishing the fastest pigeon.

Pottery
Forming clay objects by shaping moist clay, then drying it, usually by firing in a kiln or oven. Shaping by hand may be aided by using a potter's wheel, on which a lump of clay is rotated so that symmetrical cylindrical objects, such as vases and bowls, can be made. Molding involves either pressing soft clay into a mold and allowing it to dry or, in slip molding, pouring liquid clay, or slip, into a mold that absorbs the moisture. Shaped or molded objects can be decorated by etching and painted with a color glaze.

Quilting
Making quilts (to be used as bed covers or wall hangings), which are two layers of fabric with batting in between, stitched together using decorative designs. The top layer is often made up of pieces of different fabrics arranged in a pattern (patchwork). It originated as a method of recycling old and worn fabrics, and traditionally can be done alone or in a group, or quilting bee.

Rodeo
Competitive riding and cattle-handling skills, derived from cowboy ranching practices in the 1800s. Events include

The excitement of whitewater rafting.

bronco riding with and without a saddle (where the rider must stay on a bucking wild horse for a set time, holding on with only one hand), bull riding, steer wrestling, and calf and team roping.

Rounders
Outdoor bat-and-ball game, one of the origins of baseball. Teams comprise nine players. The ball is bowled from the center of the field. Once the batter has hit it, he or she must run around the outside of four posts without being caught.

Scuba diving
Underwater swimming with the aid of a scuba (self-contained underwater breathing apparatus) or aqualung. It was first developed in 1942 by Jacques Cousteau and Emil Gagnan. Equipment consists of air tank(s), face mask, air regulator, depth gauge, weight belt, and buoyancy compensator. The diver uses his or her legs to propel, wearing large fins or flippers.

Shuffleboard
Deck game played aboard ship. Large wooden disks, usually around 6 inches (15 cm) in diameter, are pushed along the deck with long-handled drivers.

Skateboarding
Riding on a single flexible board, longer and wider than the foot, fixed with four

small wheels on the underside. Speeds of more than 62 mph (100 kph) are possible, and difficult jumps are performed.

Skin diving and snorkeling
Underwater swimming, popularized in the 1930s, using goggles or face mask, flippers, and (in snorkeling) short breathing tube or snorkel.

Skydiving or freefall parachuting
Jumping from an aircraft and falling without opening the parachute until reaching a height of 2000 feet (600 m). Sky divers often perform stunts or hold hands in formation while freefalling.

Softball
A seven-inning version of baseball, started in 1887 and standardized in 1923, softball is played with a softer, larger ball (approx. 12 inches/30 cm circumference) which is pitched underhand. There are two versions: fast pitch and slow pitch (10 players on each team). There are fast-pitch world championships for women (instituted 1965) and men (1966).

Spelunking
Exploration and study of caves and other natural underground features, originally to survey extent, physical history and structure, and natural history of subterranean formations. Scientifically known as speleology. When it is practiced as a hobby, participants descend through an access point and follow the course of underground rivers or streams.

Spinning
Converting fibers into yarn, originally using distaff and later the spinning wheel, and now often using methods such as friction and rotor spinning.

Stamp collecting *See* Philately.

Tapestry
Creation of decorative textiles, originally handwoven, with colored designs, made by passing colored threads among fixed warp threads. Oriental in origin, tapestry is used for wall hangings, furniture, and floor coverings.

Tug-of-war
Two teams of eight pull against each other on a thick rope. It figured in the Olympics 1900–20. There have been world championships since 1975. Competitions are graded by team weight.

Video games *See* Electronic games.

Weaving
Ancient fabric-producing craft in which warp (lengthwise) and weft (crosswise) threads are interlaced on looms.

Whitewater rafting
An exhilarating outdoor sport, in which a crew of people guide a raft down a fast-flowing river.

Yoga
In Indian religious tradition, any of various physical and contemplative techniques designed to free a person's "superior" conscious element from involvement with the "inferior" material world. Importance of physical exercises and positions and breathing-control is stressed in promoting physical and mental well-being.

PROMINENT PEOPLE

AARON, Henry ("Hank") (b. 1943) U.S. baseball player, born in Mobile, Alabama, and one of the greatest batters ever. Hit Major League record 755 home runs and led National League in home runs four times. He set almost every batting record in his 23-season career with the Milwaukee Braves and Milwaukee Brewers.

AGASSI, Andre (b. 1970) U.S. tennis player. A flamboyant style has made him the heartthrob of the courts, and his charismatic tennis has won him Wimbledon (1992), the U.S. Open (1994), then the U.S. Davis Cup on two occasions (1990, 1992) and the Australian Open (1995).

ALI, Muhammad (b. 1942) U.S. boxer, formerly called Cassius Clay, born in Louisville, Kentucky. He won the Olympic light-heavyweight title in 1960, before turning professional. He defeated Sonny Liston for the world heavyweight title in 1964. He joined the Black Muslim sect in 1964 and changed his name to Muhammad Ali. He lost the title to Joe Frazier in 1971, but defeated him in 1974. Ali beat George Foreman, then lost to Leon Spinks, but regained the title in a rematch in 1978. He retired in 1981.

ASHE, Arthur (1943–93) U.S. tennis player. Won U.S. Open (1968) and Wimbledon (1975) with analytical play that took the sting out of more powerful players. Influenced growth of the sport's popularity among African Americans.

BALLESTEROS, Severiano (b. 1957) Spanish golfer. He inspired a new generation of golfers with three wins in the British Open (1979, 1984, 1988) and two in the U.S. Masters (1980, 1983) as well as influential successes for Europe against the U.S.A. in the Ryder Cup.

BANNISTER, Sir Roger (b. 1929) British athlete. The first man to run a mile in under 4 min. when he clocked 3 min. 59.4 sec. at Oxford on May 6, 1954.

BECKER, Boris (b. 1967) German tennis player. Youngest ever Wimbledon men's singles winner when he took the title in 1985 at age 17, as well as the first unseeded winner. He successfully defended his title in 1986 and won it for a third time in 1989.

BERG, Patty (b. 1918) U.S. golfer. Her phenomenal career included more than 80 tournament victories, earning her the A.P. "Woman Athlete of the Year" award three times.

BIONDI, Matt (b. 1965) U.S. swimmer. Won eleven Olympic medals, eight of them gold, between 1984 and 1992; and eleven world championship medals, five of them gold, including seven in the 1986 world championships.

BIRD, Larry (b. 1956) U.S. basketball player. Boston Celtics forward who formed the nucleus of a successful team. N.B.A.'s M.V.P. 1984–86 and playoff M.V.P. 1984, 1986.

BORG, Bjorn (b. 1956) Swedish tennis player. He set a modern Wimbledon record with five consecutive men's singles titles (1976–80); his game is characterized by exaggerated topspin forehands and two-handed backhands from the baseline. Won six French singles and put Sweden on the tennis map.

BUBKA, Sergei (b. 1963) Ukrainian pole vaulter. By far the greatest performer this discipline has ever seen. Has broken the world record at least 16 times and won every world championship between 1983 and 1993.

CHAMBERLAIN, Wilton (b. 1936) U.S. basketball player. "Wilt the Stilt" (Philadelphia) broke all scoring records in his N.B.A. career: highest single game score (100 points), most in a season (4,029 in 1962), and most in a career (31,419).

CHRISTIE, Linford (b. 1960) British athlete. He became the world's top sprinter in his thirties, with 100m gold medals in the 1992 Olympics and 1993 world championships, and has continued since to dominate the European and Commonwealth titles.

COBB, Tyrus ("Ty") (1886–1961) U.S. baseball player. Most successful batter in history, with 4,191 hits, 2,245 runs, and a career average of .367 for Detroit and Philadelphia.

COE, Sebastian (b. 1956) British middle-distance athlete. He set nine world records (1979–81), the 800m mark of 1 min. 41.73 sec. still standing in the 1990s, and became the first runner to win the Olympic 1,500m twice (1980, 1984).

COMANECI, Nadia (b. 1961) Romanian gymnast. At 15, youngest to win an Olympic title, with gold medal in bars, beam, and overall. First to receive a "perfect" mark of 10, which she did six times in the Montreal Olympics (1976).

CONNOLLY, Maureen (1934–69) U.S. tennis player. First woman to complete Grand Slam (1963). Won U.S. Open at 16 and thereafter lost only four singles in three years before retiring after a riding accident. She was never beaten at Wimbledon (1952–54).

CONNORS, Jimmy (b. 1952) U.S. tennis player. Left-hander who ranked no. 1 for a record 159 consecutive weeks 1974–77. Won five U.S. Opens between 1974 and 1983, and Wimbledon in 1974 and 1982.

CORDERO, Angel (b. 1942) U.S. jockey. A natural in the saddle, Cordero was the leading money winner three times (1976, 1982, 1983) and rode three Kentucky Derby winners.

COURT, Margaret (née Smith) (b. 1942) Australian tennis player. Completed the singles Grand Slam in 1970 and won Wimbledon three times (1963, 1965, 1970). Won more titles (singles and doubles) in Grand Slam tournaments than any other player, including 13 French, 21 Australian, and 22 U.S.

CURRY, John (1950–94) British ice skater. European, world, and Olympic figure-skating champion in the 1975–76 season, after which he turned professional. He introduced to the sport a level of balletic skill and choreography that had never before been seen.

DEAN, Christopher (b. 1958) British ice skater. With partner Jayne TORVILL, he won the world ice-dancing championship in four consecutive years (1981–84) and the Olympic title in 1984. In the world tournament that year they received an unprecedented 29 "perfect" marks of 6.0.

DiMAGGIO, Joe (b. 1914) U.S. baseball player. One of the greatest fielders of the game, he achieved a record with New York Yankees by batting safely at least once in 56 consecutive games in 1941. Three times named most valuable player of the year. More widely known for his marriage to Marilyn Monroe.

EVERT, Chris (b. 1954) U.S. tennis player. Reached 34 Grand Slam singles finals between 1973 and 1988, winning 18 (including Wimbledon in 1974, 1976, and 1981, and the U.S. Open in 1975–78, 1980, and 1982).

FALDO, Nick (b. 1957) British golfer. Winner of three British Opens (1987, 1990, 1992) and two U.S. Masters (1989, 1990); ranked world No. 1 in the early 1990s.

FANGIO, Juan Manuel (b. 1911) Argentinian racing driver. Winner of a record five world championships (1951, 1954–57).

FOSBURY, Dick (b. 1947) U.S. high jumper. Fosbury revolutionized the discipline of the high jump by introducing the backward approach to the bar (the "Fosbury Flip") that is now the norm in high jumping. Won the Olympic gold medal in 1968.

GEHRIG, Lou (1903–41) U.S. baseball player. As first baseman on the New York Yankees he played a record 2,130 consecutive games and was voted M.V.P. in 1936 before being stricken with amyotrophic lateral sclerosis (now known as "Lou Gehrig's Disease").

GRAF, Steffi (b. 1969) German tennis player. She won Grand Slam and Olympic gold medal in 1988 at 19, and continued to win major singles and rank no. 1 for most of the early 1990s.

GRETZKY, Wayne (b. 1961) Canadian hockey player. Acknowledged by many as the greatest hockey player of all time. He and the Edmonton Oilers dominated the 1980s. Scored record 92 goals, 212 assists (1982), and was named M.V.P. 1980–87, 1989.

GRIFFITH JOYNER, Florence (b. 1959) U.S. track and field athlete. Dominated the sprints at the 1988 Olympics, setting Olympic records at the 100m and 200m and winning a third gold medal as part of the 4 x 100m relay team.

GUNNELL, Sally (b. 1966) British athlete.

Has dominated 400m hurdles since winning 1992 Olympic title and 1993 world championships in a world-record time of 52.74 sec.

HEIDEN, Eric (b. 1958) U.S. ice skater. Made history in 1980 Olympics by winning every speed-skating gold medal (five distances from 500m to 10,000m) and setting an Olympic record in each event. Three times overall world champion (1977–79).

HORNSBY, Rogers (1896–1963) U.S. baseball player. As second baseman on the St. Louis Cardinals, Hornsby compiled glittering career statistics, batting a record .426 (1924), leading the National League in batting (1920–25), and winning the Triple Crown twice.

HUNT Geoffrey (b. 1947) Australian squash player. Dominated world squash in the 1970s, winning four World Open, eight British Open, and three world amateur titles.

JOHNSON, Earvin (b. 1959) U.S. basketball player. Named athlete of the decade by a U.S. magazine in 1990, "Magic" Johnson helped Los Angeles Lakers to nine National Basketball Association finals and five wins in 12 years. Member of U.S. so-called "Dream Team" in 1992 Olympics.

JORDAN, Michael (b. 1963) U.S. basketball player. Biggest name in the game, said to earn $40 million a year. He drove Chicago Bulls to a third successive N.B.A. championship in 1993. Member of U.S. so-called "Dream Team" in 1992 Olympics.

JOYNER-KERSEE, Jackie (b. 1962) U.S. track and field athlete. Multitalented sportswoman who won the Olympic gold medal for the heptathlon twice (1988, 1992).

KHAN, Jahangir (b. 1963) Pakistani squash player. Most prodigious of a family of champions, Jahangir won the world title at the age of 17 and five times thereafter, and the British Open 10 times. For more than five years remained undefeated in any tournament.

KILLY, Jean-Claude (b. 1943) French alpine skier. Won all three Olympic gold medals in 1968 and was overall world champion 1966–68 and overall World Cup champion 1967–68.

KING, Billie Jean (b. 1943) U.S. tennis player. Won 20 Wimbledon titles between 1961 and 1979, including six singles and four U.S. Open singles. Highly influential in development of women's game across the world.

KORBUT, Olga (b. 1955) Soviet gymnast. Captured the public imagination and advanced her sport in the 1972 Olympics with charismatic displays that won her gold medals on beam and floor at 17.

LATYNINA, Larissa (b. 1935) Russian gymnast. Won more Olympic medals than any other competitor in any sport: nine gold, five silver, four bronze from games of 1956, 1960, 1964.

LAVER, Rod (b. 1938) Australian tennis

Billie Jean King at Wimbledon in 1982.

player. Powerful left-hander, the only man to win two Grand Slams, in 1962, before turning pro and in 1969 after tennis went "open" the previous year.

LENGLEN, Suzanne (1899–1938) French tennis player and legendary personality. Won Wimbledon singles and doubles every year she entered (1919–23, 1925), and lost only one match in amateur lawn tennis between 1919 and 1926.

LEWIS, Carl (b. 1961) U.S. athlete. Winner of eight Olympic track and field gold medals, unrivaled in modern times; won 100m, 200m, long jump, and 4 x 100m relay golds in 1984, 100m and long jump in 1988, and long jump and relay in 1992; won world championship 100m for third time in 1991 in world record 9.86 sec., and long jump in 1983 and 1987.

LOPEZ, Nancy (b. 1957) U.S. golfer. Raised profile of women's golf (L.P.G.A.) while amassing career winnings of more than $3.5 million.

LOUGANIS, Greg (b. 1960) U.S. highboard diver. The most successful diver in history, he won five world and four Olympic gold medals between 1978 and 1988. At the 1982 world championships he was the first diver ever to be awarded maximum points by all seven judges.

LOUIS, Joe (1914–81) U.S. boxer, known as the "Brown Bomber." Universally popular fighter who held the world heavyweight title for a record 11 years 8 months (1937–49) against 25 challengers.

MANSELL, Nigel (b. 1954) British racing driver. Winner of World Drivers' Championship in 1992 in a Williams-Renault, including a record nine Grands Prix; became the first "rookie" to win the IndyCar World Series in 1993.

MARADONA, Diego (b. 1960) Argentinian soccer player. Left-footed midfielder with a magical touch who captained his country to World Cup success in 1986 and was rated the world's most gifted player; suspended for 15 months after being arrested for possession of cocaine.

MARCIANO, Rocky (1923–69) U.S. boxer. World heavyweight champion (1952– 56) whose all-action, "roughhouse" style won him a pro record of 49 fights undefeated; died in a plane crash.

MAYS, Willie (b. 1931) U.S. baseball player. Popular center fielder for the New York (then San Francisco) Giants who was a feared slugger. He hit a career total of 660 home runs and was voted M.V.P. twice.

McENROE, John (1959) U.S. tennis player. Gifted left-hander known as much for his on-court tantrums as his brilliant all-round game; ended Bjorn Borg's Wimbledon singles domination in 1981, won it twice more (1983, 1984), won four U.S. Opens (1979–81, 1984), and was world no. 1 (1981–84) and also world's best doubles player.

McKAY, Heather (b. 1941) Australian squash player. The greatest female competitor in the history of the game, she lost only twice in a 22-year career (1959–80). She won 16 British Opens, 14 consecutive Australian amateur titles, and the first two World Open titles.

MERCKX, Eddie (b. 1945) Belgian cyclist. Most successful of all road racers, he won the Tour de France five times in six years (1969–72, 1974) and the Tour of Italy five times. He recorded altogether an unprecedented 39 wins in the European classic road races and tours.

MONTANA, Joe (b. 1956) U.S. football player. Most celebrated quarterback of all time, he helped San Francisco 49ers to four Super Bowl victories between 1982 and 1990, and was three times voted Super Bowl M.V.P.

MUSIAL, Stan (b. 1920) U.S. baseball player. Stan "The Man" Musial was a successful St. Louis Cardinals hitter who won seven National League batting titles and was named M.V.P. three times.

NAMATH, Joe (b. 1943) U.S. football player. Quarterback who overcame chronic knee ailments to lead the New York Jets to Super Bowl title (1969).

NAVRATILOVA, Martina (b. 1956) Czech-born U.S. tennis player. Won a record nine Wimbledon singles and reigned supreme in the 1980s; a left-hander with a powerful serve-and-volley game, she won nine other Grand Slam singles titles and 37 doubles, amassing record prize money in 18 years at the top.

NICKLAUS, Jack (b. 1940) U.S. golfer. Arguably the greatest golfer ever, winning 18 majors between 1962 and 1986, including three British Opens and a record six U.S. Masters.

NURMI, Paavo (1897–1973) Finnish athlete. Peerless at middle and long distances, breaking more than 20 world records and uniquely winning 12 Olympic medals, nine gold, and three silver. In 1924 Games won 1,500m and 5,000m finals within 90 min.

OERTER, Al (b. 1936) U.S. discus thrower. No other competitor has yet won the one gold medal of his discipline in four successive Olympics—1956, 1960, 1964, 1968.

ORR, Bobby (b. 1948) Canadian hockey player. As an outstanding defenseman for Boston Bruins, he won the Norris

Trophy (for N.H.L.'s best defenseman) 8 times and led the N.H.L. in scoring twice.

OWENS, Jesse (1913–80) U.S. athlete. Hero of the 1936 Olympics when his four gold medals—100m, 200m, long jump, and sprint relay—embarrassed the Nazi hosts' theories of white Aryan supremacy; enjoyed unrivaled record-breaking at domestic meeting in 1935, setting five world records and equaling another in 45 min.

PALMER, Arnold (b. 1929) U.S. golfer, born in Latrobe, Pennsylvania. He enjoyed cult following in 1960s, adulated on the course by "Arnie's Army" and winning seven majors as he saw golf become a major world sport; became the first golfer to earn $1 million. Palmer won the U.S. Masters four times, the British Open twice, and the U.S. Open once.

PAYTON, Walter (b. 1954) U.S. football player. As running back for the Chicago Bears, he amassed a career total of 16,726 yards rushing. Led N.F.C. in rushing 1976–80.

PELÉ (b. 1940) Brazilian soccer player. Regarded by many as the finest player of all time; born Edson Arantes do Nascimento, he was only 17 when he scored twice in the 1958 World Cup final; he went on to score 77 goals in 92 games for Brazil, help them win three World Cups, and amass 1,281 goals in 1,363 games.

PERRY, Fred (1909–95) British tennis player. Winner of three consecutive Wimbledon singles (1934–36) before turning pro, having also won three U.S. titles and helped England win four Davis Cups (1933–36); world table tennis champion in 1929; still a shrewd tennis commentator well into his eighties.

PINCAY, Laffit, Jr. (b. 1946) Panamanian jockey. Won more than $170 million in a career lasting from 1964 to 1992, including six seasons as leading money winner.

PLAYER, Gary (b. 1935) South African golfer. First player in modern times to win all four classics, he totaled nine majors in a 20-year career at the top. He won the British Open three times, the U.S. Masters twice, the U.S. Open once, and the U.S. PGA title twice.

REDGRAVE, Steve (b. 1962) British rower. Unequaled in rowing history, winner of gold medals in three successive Olympics (1984, 1988, 1992) and five world championship titles since 1986.

RICE, Jerry (b. 1962) U.S. football player. Recognized as the indispensable partner to quarterback Joe Montana in four San Francisco Super Bowl victories. He equaled the N.F.L. wide receiver record of seven consecutive seasons, gaining more than 1,000 yards.

ROBINSON, Jack Roosevelt (Jackie) (1919–1972) was the first African-American to play baseball in the major leagues. Born in Cairo, Georgia, he attended the University of California. There he starred in baseball, football,

The great Pelé of Brazil.

basketball, and track. After college, Robinson played in baseball's minor leagues. In 1947, Robinson joined the Brooklyn Dodgers as a second baseman and was named the National League's rookie of the year. During his ten years with the Dodgers, they won six pennants and one World Series. He was elected to the National Baseball Hall of Fame in 1962.

ROBINSON, Sugar Ray (1920–89) U.S. boxer. Widely acknowledged as the greatest boxer of all time, he was middleweight champion five times and also held the welterweight title.

RUTH, George Herman "Babe" (1895–1948) U.S. baseball player. Started as a pitcher but became the most famous batter of all time; joined New York Yankees in 1920 and revolutionized the game with his sensational left-handed hitting; record 714 home runs in career, including landmark 60 in 1927. In 1936 he was elected to the National Baseball Hall of Fame.

SAMPRAS, Pete (b. 1971) U.S. tennis player. World leader since winning Wimbledon 1993–94, U.S. Open 1993 (also 1990), and Australian Open 1994.

SELES, Monica (b. 1973) Serbian tennis player. Left-hander who won French Open at 16 with powerful double-handed play on both sides, and then won seven Grand Slam titles, but not Wimbledon; rose to world no. 1 before being injured with lasting effects in a courtside stabbing by a fanatical admirer of her rival, Steffi GRAF.

SENNA, Ayrton (1959–94) Brazilian racing driver. Deeply committed competitor who won 41 Grand Prix races and three world championships between 1985 and 1994, when he died after an accident in the San Marino Grand Prix.

SPITZ, Mark (b. 1950) U.S. swimmer. Won record seven gold medals in 1972 Olympics, for 100m and 200m in both freestyle and butterfly and three relays—all in world-record times.

STENMARK, Ingemar (b. 1956) Swedish alpine skier. He was a slalom specialist who won two Olympic and three world titles 1978–82, and was the first Scandinavian to win the world cup.

THOMPSON, Daley (b. 1958) British ath-

lete. He dominated the decathlon event, winning the Olympic title in 1980 and 1984 and the world championship in 1983.

THORPE, Jim (1888–1953) U.S. all-round sportsman. His decathlon and pentathlon wins in the 1912 Olympics were nullified for a minor infringement of amateur status; he played major-league baseball and in the 1920s became star U.S. football player; Olympic medals and records restored posthumously in 1982.

TORVILL, Jayne (b. 1957) British ice-skater. With partner Christopher DEAN, she won the world ice-dancing championship in four consecutive years (1981–84) and the Olympic title in 1984. In the world tournament that year they received an unprecedented 29 "perfect" marks of 6.0.

TYSON, Mike (b. 1965) U.S. boxer. Youngest ever world heavyweight champion at age 20, made nine successful defenses before outside influences set his career on a downward path; lost title to James "Buster" Douglas in 1990; was found guilty of rape in 1992 and jailed for six years. He was released in 1995, promising a return to the ring.

UNSER, Al (b. 1939) U.S. race car driver. Most successful member of a famous racing family, he was the four-time winner of the Indianapolis 500 (1970, 1971, 1978, 1987) and twice IndyCar champion (1970, 1983).

WEISSMULLER, Johnny (1904–84) U.S. swimmer. Won five Olympic gold medals (1924–28), set 24 world records, and was the first man to break 1 min. for 100m and 5min for 400m. From 1932 became the most famous of Hollywood's Tarzans.

WHITWORTH, Kathy (b. 1939) U.S. golfer. Was L.P.G.A. leading money winner over eight seasons and helped raise the profile of women's golf by becoming the first woman to win more than $300,000.

WILKIE, David (b. 1954) British swimmer. Outstanding breaststroker who won one Olympic gold medal (1976, 200m) and three world, two European, and two Commonwealth golds in six years. Also set three world records.

ZAHARIAS, Mildred "Babe" (née Didrikson) (1914–56) U.S. all-rounder. Phenomenal athlete who at age 16 broke the world javelin record, and at 18 won Olympic gold medals at javelin and 80m hurdles (world record), and silver in high jump (equaled world record). Then turned to golf, winning amateur championships and three times the U.S. Open.

ZATOPEK, Emil (b. 1922) Czech athlete. Arguably the greatest long-distance runner of any age; between 1948 and 1954 he set 18 world records at nine distances from 5,000m to 30,000m and won four Olympic gold medals, including the unique treble in 1952 of 5,000m, 10,000m, and marathon.

Timeline

c. **8000 B.C.** Jericho, in Jordan Valley, is one of the earliest fortified cities.

c. **4000 B.C.** Egyptian warriors carry shields for protection against missiles.

c. **2700 B.C.** Sailing warships and galleys used in Mediterranean naval conflicts.

c. **2500 B.C.** Mesopotamian warriors use maces, axes, metal-tipped thrusting spears; wear leather armor, bronze helmets; use battlewagons drawn by asses.

c. **2300 B.C.** Sling and javelin in use.

c. **1900 B.C.** Bronze weapons in Europe.

c. **1485 B.C.** At Megiddo, Egyptian two-wheeled chariots drawn by two horses carry driver (with a large shield), and fighter with composite bow and javelin.

c. **1400 B.C.** The sword in use in Greece.

c. **1200 B.C.** Iron weapons in Middle East.

c. **700 B.C.** Assyrian warriors wear iron scale armor, carry long iron swords, and use four-man chariots, wheeled battering rams; mounted archers and slingers form cavalry units.

c. **600 B.C.** War elephants used in India.

c. **500 B.C.** Athenian trireme warship in use.

c. **400 B.C.** Chinese use crossbow. Torsion catapults in use in West.

c. **300 B.C.** Chain mail, perhaps developed by Celtic warriors.

c. **250 B.C.** Roman galleys mount artillery, including ballista and catapult.

c. **214 B.C.** Emperor Shih Huang Ti orders construction of Great Wall of China.

c. **130 B.C.** Parthian cataphracts in use.

c. **A.D. 450** Metal stirrup, giving cavalry a secure seat, appears on Asian steppes.

c. **600** Cataphract archers are the mainstay of Roman and Byzantine armies.

c. **650** Byzantine warships use Greek fire.

c. **850** Early motte and bailey castles.

c. **900** Samurai class emerges in Japan. Nailed horseshoes in N. Eurasia.

1045 Earliest-known formula for gunpowder published in China.

c. **1100** Trebuchet and crossbow in West.

c. **1150** Western warships gain maneuverability from stern-post rudders. Longbow developed in Wales.

1232 War rockets recorded in China.

c. **1300** Concentric castles, which were the strongest type, built in England under Edward I. In China and Arabia early artillery pieces (copper-lined bamboo tubes) in use.

1346 First certain use of cannon, by English against French at Crécy, France.

c. **1380** Ribauldequin developed.

c. **1400** Matchlock arms under development; trigger mechanism appears.

1406 English warship *Christopher of the Tower* is purpose-built to mount guns.

c. **1420** Count Jan Žižka develops "field artillery," the wagenburg. His Hussite troops fire long arms from the shoulder.

1453 Muslim gunners develop mortar in siege of Constantinople.

c. **1460** Bronze guns cast in France. Harquebus appears. European gun-

DECISIVE BATTLES TO 1815

Megiddo, Palestine, 1479 B.C.: first well-recorded battle. Egyptians under Tuthmosis III defeat armies of Prince of Kadesh and open road for northern expansion.

Marathon, Greece, 490 B.C.: Athenians and Plataeans defeat Persian invaders.

Salamis, Greece, 480 B.C.: Athenian navy (360 triremes; Themistocles) crushes Persian fleet (*c.* 600 galleys; Xerxes).

Arbela-Gaugamela (now Iraq), 331 B.C.: Macedonians (47,000; Alexander) shatter Persians (*c.* 250,000; Darius III), making Alexander master of Asia.

Teutoberg Forest (now Germany), A.D. 9: German tribesmen annihilate smaller Roman army (three legions, 19,500; Publius Quintilius Varus), halting Roman conquest of Germany.

Châlons-sur-Marne, France, 451: Roman-Visigothic army checks European advance of Huns (*c.* 40,000; Attila).

Tours, France, 732: Franks (*c.* 30,000; Charles Martel) defeat Saracens (*c.* 80,000; Abd-ar-Rahman) and halt Muslim advance into western Europe.

Hastings, England, 1066: Norman invaders (*c.* 9,000; Duke William of Normandy) defeat Saxons (*c.* 10,000; King Harold II), bringing England under Norman rule.

Agincourt, France, 1415: Hundred Years' War (1338 - 1453). English (5,700; King Henry V) rout French (25,000; Charles d'Albret) and open way for conquest of Normandy.

Orléans, France, 1428–29: French led by Joan of Arc relieve garrison (5,400; Count Jean of Dunois) and force Anglo-Burgundians (5,500; Earls of Salisbury and Suffolk) to raise siege, turning war in France's favor.

Constantinople (Istanbul), Turkey, 1453: Byzantine garrison (8,900; Constantine IX) overwhelmed by Ottoman Turks (50,000; Mehmet II) after bombardment; first great event determined by artillery.

Pavia, Italy, 1525: German pikemen and Spanish arquebusiers of Charles V's army (23,000; Ferdinando Francesco d'Avalos) defeat French army of *Gendarmerie* (heavy cavalry) together with Swiss and German

Battle of Yorktown, October 14, 1781.

mercenaries (28,000; François I), giving Spain control of Italy.

Lepanto, Greece, 1571: Christian Holy League (208 ships; Don John of Austria) defeats Ottoman Turks (230 ships; Ali Pasha) in last great battle of galleys.

Spanish Armada, English Channel, 1588: English fleet (6,000 men; 34 warships, 163 auxiliaries; Lord Howard of Effingham, Francis Drake, John Hawkins, Martin Frobisher) drives off invasion force (28,500 men; 20 galleons, 52 smaller warships, 58 auxiliaries; Duke of Medina-Sidonia).

Breitenfeld, Germany, 1631: Thirty Years' War (1618-1648). Swedish-Saxon armies (40,000; Gustav II Adolf) defeat Hapsburg and Catholic League forces (32,000; Tilly), ensuring survival of German Protestantism.

Blenheim, Germany, 1704: War of the Spanish Succession (1701-1713). English and Imperial allies (52,000; Marlborough and Eugene) defeat Franco-Bavarian force (56,000; Tallard), saving Vienna.

Poltava, Ukraine, 1709: Russian army (40,000; Peter the Great) crushes Swedish and Cossack army (30,000; Charles XII). The victory ensures Russia's position as a dominant power in eastern Europe.

Plassey, India, 1757: Seven Years' War. British East India Company's army (3,000; Clive) defeats Indo-French force (*c.* 60,000; Siraj-ud-Daula, Nawab of Bengal), securing Bengal and initiating British Indian Empire.

Yorktown, Virginia, 1781: American Revolution (1775 -81). British army (7,500; General Cornwallis) surrounded by American (8,850; Washington) and French forces (7,000; Rochambeau), with French naval support, British surrender, ensuring American independence.

Valmy, France, 1792: French Revolutionary War. French forces (36,000; Dumouriez and Kellerman) halt advance on Paris by Prussians (*c.* 34,000; Frederick William IV and Duke of Brunswick), securing future of revolutionary government.

Austerlitz (now Czech Republic), 1805: Napoleonic Wars. French (73,000; 139 guns; Napoleon I) crush Russian-Austrian armies (85,000; 278 guns; Tsar Alexander I of Russia, Emperor François II), winning control in western Germany and ending Holy Roman empire.

Trafalgar, southwest Spain, 1805: Napoleonic Wars. British fleet (27 ships; Nelson) shatters Franco-Spanish fleet (33 ships; Admiral Villeneuve) and ends Napoleon's plans for invasion of England.

Waterloo, now Belgium, 1815: Napoleonic Wars. Anglo-Dutch army (68,000; 156 guns; Wellington), reinforced at critical time by Prussians (31,000; Field Marshal von Blücher), defeat French (72,000; 246 guns; Napoleon I) and end Napoleonic Wars.

MILITARY TERMS TO 1800

Ballista ("Scorpion") A large, spring-operated, crossbow-type weapon.

Bayonet A knife fixed to end of barrel of long arm; plug, ring, and socket bayonets.

Carronade ("Smasher") Short-barreled, short-ranged cannon firing a very heavy ball; principally a naval weapon.

Cataphract Heavy cavalryman; both man and horse are armored.

Catapult Torsion weapon (i.e. powered by stretched and twisted ropes or sinews) for hurling missiles.

Chain mail Protective clothing made by "knitting" together small metal rings. A mail shirt had up to 30,000 rings.

Composite bow A deeply curved stave made of wood, horn, and animal sinew glued together in layers.

Concentric castle Massive central tower (donjon or keep) surrounded by two or more rings of walls with round towers and machicolations (weapon platforms).

Condottiere Leader of mercenary force ("free company") in medieval Italy.

Crossbow Bow placed crosswise on stock, with crank to pull back bow, and trigger to release arrows. Of greater range and penetration than longbow, but much slower firing.

Flintlock Firearm in which priming is ignited by device striking flint on steel to make sparks; it replaced matchlock.

Galley Oared warship; most carried sails to hoist when wind favorable.

Greek fire Compound of naphtha, sulfur, and saltpeter that burns in water; hurled in pots from catapults or projected from bellows-like "flame-throwers."

Harquebus First significant long arm, a heavy Matchlock originating in Spain.

Heliograph Battlefield communication system in which coded messages were flashed by sunlight reflected off angled mirrors.

"Leather guns" Light, mobile field artillery pieces; 3-pounders with cast copper barrels supported by leather binding.

Longbow A near straight, c. 6 ft. (1.83 m) stave of elm or yew, it fired accurately to c. 240 yd. (220 m). A skilled archer could fire 6-12 arrows per minute.

Matchlock Early firearm; powder in priming-pan, which will ignite main charge, lit by length of slow-burning fuse.

Mortar Artillery piece designed to lob missiles, e.g. over walls during siege.

Motte and bailey Early castle form; motte, earth mound typically 46 ft. (14 m) high, 59 ft. (18 m) diameter, is surrounded by bailey, palisaded enclosure.

Musket From the 1500s to the 1800s, generic name for long arms.

Phalanx Solid fighting formation of spearmen, sometimes up to 80 ranks wide and 16 ranks deep; with sarissa, 15 ft. (4.6 m) spear, the points of first 45 ranks projected; phalanx advanced at run.

Ribauldequin Early "machine gun"; light cart mounting a battery of small guns with common fuse to fire in volleys.

Samurai Japanese warrior caste employed as bodyguards by noblemen.

Shrapnel shell Explosive artillery shell packed with musket balls.

Tercio or "Spanish square," a Spanish infantry formation; square of pikemen with squares of musketeers at each corner.

Trebuchet (or mangonel) Medieval variation of catapult; instead of torsion, a counter-weight of up to 10 tons.

Trireme Galley with three banks of oars. Athenian trireme c. 130 ft. (40 m) long, 15 ft. (4.6 m) beam.

Wagenburg ("Wagon Fort") Battlefield mobile fort of four-wheeled wagons linked together; with gunners and cannon.

Wheel lock Sophisticated flintlock with a wound spring; very reliable.

Timeline

smiths make experimental pistols.

c. **1485** Leonardo da Vinci sketches multibarreled "machine guns," "armored car," and "helicopter."

c. **1500** Combination of arquebusiers and pikemen in tercio makes infantry more effective than cavalry.

c. **1510–20** Germany use wheel lock firearms.

1537 Italian Niccolò Fontana (Tartaglia) founds science of ballistics.

1539 Earliest type of flintlock recorded.

1540 Spain introduces convoy system as antipiracy measure in Atlantic.

c. **1545** Musket in use in Spain.

c. **1570** French surgeon Ambroise Paré improves treatment of wounds.

1585 Floating mines detonated by clockwork used by Dutch at Antwerp.

1588 Dutch make first use of explosive artillery shells.

c. **1595** German *Reiter*, pistol-armed horsemen who advance in successive ranks, signal new role for cavalry.

c. **1598** Koreans use an iron-armored warship in battle with Japanese.

c. **1620** Gustav II Adolf introduces "leather guns." Dutch-born British inventor Cornelis Drebbel credited with building first working submarine, powered by 12 oarsmen with air supply in bladders.

1647 French army adopts plug bayonet. First naval flag code in use in English navy.

1674 Trench mortar introduced by Dutch inventor Menno van Coehoorn.

1684 English scientist Robert Hooke invents heliograph.

c. **1700** Ring and socket bayonets in use.

1718 English inventor James Puckle patents a single-barreled, hand-cranked, flintlock "machine gun," fed from a nine-round magazine.

1769 French engineer Nicolas Cugnot builds first self-propelled vehicle, a steam-driven artillery carriage. Austrian dragoons issued with breechloading muskets, perhaps the first breechloaders in military service.

1776 *Turtle*, a one-man submersible powered by hand-crank, designed by U.S. inventor David Bushnell.

1779 British navy introduces the short-barreled carronade.

1784 British General Henry Shrapnel invents "shrapnel" shell.

1794 French general ascends in observation balloon at battle of Fleurus. Publication of treatise on *Gunshot Wounds* by Scottish surgeon John Hunter advances military medicine.

1796 Larrey introduces field hospitals, trained medical teams and "one-horse flying ambulances" to battlefield.

1797 First parachute descent.

1799 Indian leader Haidar Ali bombards the British army with metal rockets. British scientist Sir William Congreve designs explosive and incendiary rocket

Krak des Chevaliers, Syria: impregnable medieval defenses.

Timeline

missiles.

1800 U.S. inventor Eli Whitney sets up "production line" to make muskets with interchangeable parts.

1801 Design of *Nautilus*, iron "submarine torpedo boat," manually propelled, with conning tower.

1807 Percussion lock produced.

1812 Design of breechloading rifle firing self-contained (i.e. all-in-one) cartridge.

1814 Launch of *Demologos*, first steam-driven warship, at New York.

1818 First true revolver made, five-shot flintlock with manually operated turning cylinder.

1828 "Needlegun" invented (*see* 1848).

1836 Colt patents percussion revolver with five-chamber cylinder that revolves automatically (*see* 1847). Screw-propellers patented, and adopted by major navies within ten years.

1843 Colt designs a sea mine remotely fired by submerged electric cable.

1847 First revolver in general service. Nitroglycerine discovered.

1848 First breechloading rifle in general service. Prussian army adopts Dreyse needlegun.

1849 Conical, pointed, expanding bullet invented, thus improving range and accuracy. Guncotton invented.

***c.* 1854** Armstrong initiates breechloading artillery pieces with barrels "built-up" from coils of wroughtiron for greater strength.

1855 Field-service electric telegraph used by British Royal Engineers in the Crimea. First floating contact mines in use; laid by Russians in Baltic Sea during the Crimean War.

1856 Invention of the steel converter facilitates mass arms production.

1858–59 French navy's *La Gloire*, steam frigate, is first iron-clad warship.

1859 Italian War of Independence sees first significant use of railways for military deployment; first aerial photography from reconnaissance balloons.

1860 Effective repeater rifle designed; lever-action, with seven-round tubular magazine in butt.

1862 Ericsson builds *Monitor*, first warship with revolving gun turret, for U.S. navy; first combat between iron-clads when *Monitor* engages CSS *Virginia* on March 9, 1862. American Richard Gatling (1818–1903) patents ten-barreled machine gun, firing 400 rounds per minute.

1863 TNT first made.

1864 Semisubmersible "submarine" CSS *Hunley* sinks USS *Housatonic* with spar-torpedo; fused charge on bow-mounted pole.

1866 Locomotive torpedo developed; adopted by Austria in 1868. Swede Alfred Nobel (1833–96) invents dynamite.

1868 First bolt-action, magazine rifle in service, Swiss army's Vetterl-Vitali 10 mm with 11-round tube magazine.

DECISIVE BATTLES OF MODERN WARFARE

Gettysburg, Pennsylvania, U.S.A., 1863: American Civil War (1861-65). Union Army of the Potomac (88,000; General George Meade) repulses invasion of north by Confederate Army of Northern Virginia (75,000; Lee). Turning point of American Civil War.

Kôniggrâtz, Sadowa (Hradic Kràlovè, now Czech Republic), 1866: Austro-Prussian War. Prussians (278,000; Prince Frederick Charles and Moltke), with needlegun, gain total victory over Austrians (271,000; Field Marshal Ludwig von Benedek) and move closer to establishment of German empire.

Sedan, France, 1870: Franco-Prussian War. Prussians (200,000; 744 guns; Moltke) destroy French (120,000; 564 guns; Marshal MacMahon). French Second empire falls.

Tsushima Strait, Japan–Korea, 1905: Russo-Japanese War (1904-05). Japanese fleet (4 battleships, 8 cruisers; Admiral Togo) destroys Russian 2nd Pacific Squadron (8 battleships, 9 cruisers; Admiral Rozhdestvenski). Japanese sea supremacy ends Russian hope of land victory.

Marne River, France, 1914: World War I (1914-1918). French (*c.* 1,000,000; Field Marshal Joseph Joffre) and British Expeditionary Force (*c.* 80,000; Field Marshal Sir John French) stems German advance and prevents capture of Paris.

Tannenberg, Poland, 1914: World War I. German Eighth Army (300,000; 818 guns; Generals von Hindenburg and Ludendorff) annihilates Russian Second Army (300,000; 620 guns; General Alexander Samsonov) and ends Russian invasion of East Prussia.

Jutland, North Sea, 1916: World War I. British Grand Fleet (28 dreadnought battleships, 9 battlecruisers; Admiral Jellicoe) engages German High Seas Fleet (16 dreadnoughts, 6 older battleships, 5 battlecruisers; Admiral Scheer). British sustain heavier loss, but German navy never again seek major engagement.

Battle of Britain, 1940: air campaign over southern England, World War II (1939-45). On August 13, German Luftwaffe deploy *c.* 2,500 combat aircraft to destroy Royal Air Force (*c.* 800 fighters) and win air supremacy for invasion of Britain. By September 15, Luftwaffe losE *c.* 1,880 planes, 2,660 aircrew; RAF Fighter Command losE 1,020 planes, 537 pilots. Germans abandon invasion plans in October.

Pearl Harbor, Oahu Island, Hawaii, 1941: World War II. Japanese First Air Fleet (8 aircraft carriers, 360 planes; Admiral Nagumo) makes surprise attack on base of U.S. Pacific Fleet. U.S.A. loses 4 battleships, 3 light cruisers, 3 destroyers, 261 aircraft, *c.* 4,000 casualties. Japanese lose 29 aircraft, 5 midget submarines. U.S.A. enters World War II.

Midway, Pacific, 1942: World War II. U.S. Pacific Fleet (3 aircraft carriers, 250

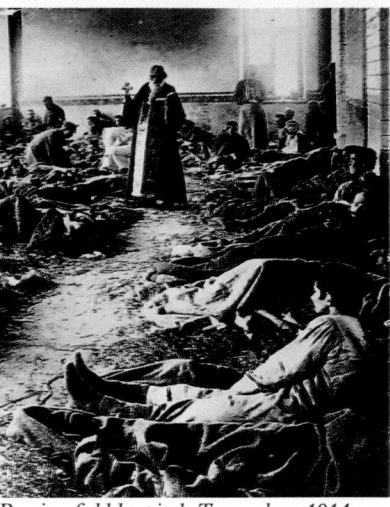

Russian field hospital, Tannenberg 1914.

planes; 73 other warships; Admiral Nimitz) intercepts Japanese Combined Fleet (6 carriers, 280 aircraft, 156 other warships; 51,000 men; Admiral Yamamoto). Japanese lose 4 heavy carriers, 275 aircraft; fail to take Midway, stepping-stone to Hawaii and Australia. Turning point of Pacific War.

Stalingrad (now Volgograd), Russia, 1942–43: World War II. In climactic battle of six months' combat, Soviet 62nd Red Army (300,000; General Chuikov) destroys German Sixth Army (230,000; Field Marshal Paulus). Turning point of war on eastern front.

El Alamein, second battle (October 23–November 4), Egypt, 1942: World War II. British Eighth Army (200,000; 1,029 tanks; Montgomery) ends German threat to Suez Canal by defeat of German Panzerarmee Afrika (104,000; 489 tanks; Rommel).

Ardennes ("Battle of the Bulge"), east Belgium–Luxembourg, 1944–45: World War II. U.S. First and Third Armies (400,000; 1,100 tanks; Eisenhower) stop thrust by German Sixth SS Panzerarmee, Fifth Panzerarmee, Seventh Army (250,000; 1,000 tanks; Field Marshal von Rundstedt), ending final German attempt to stem Allied invasion of Europe.

Dien Bien Phu, Vietnam–Laos border, 1954: French War in Indochina. After three-month siege, communist Viet Minh forces (50,000 combat troops; 48 heavy guns; Giap) force surrender of French garrison (16,000; 28 heavy guns; General de Castries), marking end of French colonial rule in Indochina.

Persian Gulf War, Kuwait and Iraq, 1991: UN Allied forces (490,000 ground troops; 3,400 tanks; 2,500 combat aircraft and helicopters; Schwarzkopf) attack Iraqi forces (550,000 troops; 4,200 tanks; 700 combat aircraft and helicopters). Allies lose *c.* 600 killed, wounded, or missing; Iraq loses *c.* 100,000 killed or wounded.

MILITARY TERMS FROM 1800 TO THE PRESENT

ASDIC/SONAR Methods of sound detection of submerged submarines.

Assault rifle Self-loading rifle, giving greater firepower; best known example is the AK47 rifle.

Atomic bomb Early nuclear weapon. In first A-bomb, conventional explosive drove together elements of uranium 235 to produce neutron chain reaction.

Ballistic missile Rocket-boosted missile that flies on an elliptic trajectory, governed by gravity after the boost cuts out; usually carries nuclear warhead and used against fixed targets.

Ballistite Smokeless propellant made by action of nitroglycerine on guncotton.

Barbed wire Used in fortification, beginning in Spanish-American War, 1898, giving much-strengthened defence, contributing to static trench warfare of World War I.

Blitzkrieg ("Lightning War") Attack combining tanks and aircraft in swift advance that avoids frontal attack and isolates pockets of resistance while striking at enemy's rear areas.

Cordite Smokeless (later also made flashless) propellant in form of cord.

Cruise missile Computer-guided missile which may be launched from the ground, aircraft, submarines, or warships.

Dreadnought "All-big-gun" battleship; generic term from first of kind, HMS *Dreadnought* (1906), which revolutionized naval design, tactics, and strategy.

Guided missile Self-propelled missile whose course may be varied in flight; a computer-guided, pilotless aircraft; may carry nuclear or conventional warhead and often used against moving targets.

Guncotton Propellant made from cotton and nitric acid; alternative to gunpowder.

Holland submarine First submersible to constitute viable weapon of war. Holland VIII (adopted by U.S. navy in 1900; British Royal Navy, 1901) set pattern; gasoline engine for surface running; electric engine for submerged running.

Nuclear-armed Tomahawk cruise missile.

Hydrogen bomb Condensation of hydrogen nuclei to helium nuclei releases thermonuclear energy; more power than an ATOMIC BOMB.

Laser Light Amplification by Stimulated Emission of Radiation; an intensified light beam that transmits large amounts of energy long distances; used in range-finding and for targeting missiles.

Locomotive torpedo Steerable, self-propelled missile that runs underwater.

Maxim gun First viable self-loading machine gun; belt-fed with brass-cased ballistite cartridges, water-cooled, fired *c.* 500 rounds per minute.

Napalm Flammable "jelly" in gasoline, used in incendiary bombs and flame-throwers.

Needlegun Named from its long firing-pin, this was the first effective bolt-action breechloading rifle.

Percussion lock Percussion lock gave faster, less "flashy" detonation than flint-lock by using fulminates (compounds of metallic salts) to detonate propellant charge.

Radar Radio Detection And Ranging; radio waves are broadcast and the returning echoes scanned to measure distance and bearing of reflecting object; now many applications such as navigation, reconnaissance and surveillance (AWACS, *p. 308*), acquisition and tracking, missile guidance.

Self-loading Firearm in which the energy produced by firing a cartridge is used to eject spent round and chamber, and fire another. Also called "semiautomatic"; an "automatic" arm is one which goes on firing as long as the trigger is depressed and the ammunition supply lasts.

"Seventy-five" French quick-firing 75 mm field gun, firing fixed round (shell and cartridge in one piece) and with hydraulic buffer to absorb recoil.

TNT Trinitrotoluene, explosive filling for artillery shells and bombs, in general use from *c.* 1902.

Timeline

1871 First antiaircraft gun, the German Krupp 37mm Ballonkanone; deployed against French balloonists carrying dispatches.

1873 Machine designed to make barbed wire, patented by American Lucien Smith in 1867.

c. **1875** Alfred Nobel invents ballistite; cordite invented.

1877 Purpose-built torpedo boat, HMS *Lightning*, with swiveling tubes for locomotive torpedoes.

1879 First rifle with box magazine is patented.

1883 Maxim gun perfected; adopted by British army in 1888.

1885 First use of electric telegraph in battle at Tofrek, Sudan: British commander telegraphs base *c.* 6 mi.(10 km) away.

1893 Design of first self-loading ("automatic") pistol, 8-shot arm; model for famous Luger Parabellum of 1898.

1897 French "seventy-five" is a landmark in development of field artillery.

1900 Holland submarine is first to constitute viable weapon of war. Demonstration of gas-operated flame-thrower; first used in war in 1915.

1903 First mechanized army units formed, French Corps d'Automobilistes Militaire, British 77/78 Companies, Army Service Corps.

1904 First armored car in service. Austrian army's 35hp Daimler Panzerwagen, with Maxim gun in revolving turret.

1906 *Dreadnought* battleship built.

1908 Dirigibles adapted for bombing operations.

1910 First purpose-designed fighting aircraft, Voisin biplane with machine gun; initiation of BE 2 two-seater reconnaissance and bombing biplane.

1911–12 Italo-Turkish War, Libya: Italian aviators make first day and night bombing raids, photoreconnaissance flights and propaganda leaflet drop; first pilot killed in action (by ground fire); also first battlefield use of motor trucks, motor ambulances and armored cars.

1914 Sikorsky builds first heavy bomber, four-engined Il'ya Mouromets; operational with Russian Imperial forces in 1915–17. First "aircraft carrier" in action, Japanese seaplane carrier *Wakamiya*.

1915 First strategic bombing offensive, raids by Zeppelin dirigibles on Britain. First gas warfare, xylyl-bromide ("tear gas") used by Germans against Russians.

1916 First tanks in action, British Mark I tanks attack on Somme front on September 15. First submachine gun, design of Bergmann Maschinen Pistole 18 begins; operational 1918. French physicist Paul Langevin (1872–1946) initiates development of ASDIC/Sonar.

1917 First guided missile, automatically-piloted biplane "Bug" SSM, carrying 300 lb. (136kg) explosive.

SOME MODERN WEAPONS AND WEAPONS SYSTEMS

AK-47 Russian Avtomat Kalashnikova assault rifle, introduced 1946. Simple, sturdy, reliable; basic model fires 600rpm from "banana" clip holding 30 x 7.62 mm rounds.

ALBM Air-Launched Ballistic Missile.

ALCM Air-Launched Cruise Missile.

ASM Air-to-Surface Missile.

ATGM Anti-Tank Guided Missile.

AWACS Airborne Warning And Control System. Used by aircraft carrying long-range surveillance and detection radar, with C3 (Command, Communication, Control) facilities to direct friendly aircraft.

Copperhead U.S. Martin-Marietta M712 Cannon-Launched Guided Projectile (CLGP) and smart (laser-homing) projectile. Fired from a 155 mm gun; max. range 10 mi. (16km).

Harrier McDonnell Douglas/BAe Harrier II; Vertical/ShortTakeoff and Landing (V/STOL) jump jet fighter and attack aircraft.

ICBM Intercontinental Ballistic Missile. Max. range 6,000 mi. (10,000 km).

IRBM Intermediate-Range Ballistic Missile. Range 2,000-6,000 mi. (3,340–10,000 km).

MIRV Mulitiple Independently-Targeted Reentry Vehicle. ICBM system where warheads (min. 10) each have own guidance systems.

MLRS Multiple-Launch Rocket System. U.S. self-propelled multiple (12-round) launcher for 8.94 in. (227 mm) rockets mounted on M987 tracked vehicle; each rocket (range *c.* 19 mi. [30 km]) disperses 644 bomblets over 0.4 mi.^{2} (1km^2) area.

MRBM Medium-Range Ballistic Missile. Range 1,000–2,000 mi. (1,670–3,340 km)

Neutron bomb Popular name for Enhanced Radiation Weapon (ERW). Low-powered nuclear explosion emits intense short-wave radiation affecting people rather than material.

Patriot (MIM-104) U.S. advanced mobile battlefield SAM system. Phased array radar allows target detection at several hundred miles; 8 launchers, each with 4 missiles guided by Track-via-Missile (TVM) using anti-jamming facility; range *c.* 44 mi. (70 km).

Pioneer Israeli RPV. Transmits TV images over *c.* 119 mi. (190 km).

RPV Remotely Piloted Vehicle. Small unpiloted aircraft with TV/infra-red sensors for reconnaissance.

SAM Surface-to-Air Missile.

SCUD NATO codename for Russian SS-1 SRBM. Iraqi Scud-B ("Al Husayn") carries *c.* 1,100 lb. (500 kg) payload to range *c.* 400 mi. (650 km).

SLBM Submarine-Launched Ballistic Missile.

Smart weapons Bombs, shells, or missiles that achieve pinpoint accuracy through guidance systems such as TV, laser, or TERCOM.

SRAM Short Range Attack Missile.

SRBM Short Range Ballistic Missile, range less than 1,000 mi. (1,670 km).

SSM Surface to Surface Missile.

Stealth Popular name for technologies enabling aircraft, missiles, or ships to avoid detection visually or by RADAR, SONAR, or infra-red sensors.

Strategic Defense Initiative (Star Wars) Proposed system of orbiting space stations using Directed Energy Weapons against incoming missiles.

TERCOM Terrain Contour Matching Guidance system. Onboard radar receives ground-mapping data and updates course.

Tomahawk General Dynamics AGM/BGM-109 long-range TERCOM-guided cruise missile. Fired from ground, air, submarines, and surface ships; warhead 1,000 lb. (454 kg), max. range 345 mi. (576 km), max. speed 550 mph (919 km/h).

TOW Tube-Launched, Optically-Tracked, Wire-Guided ATGM. Fired from ground tripod, vehicle, or attack helicopter, carries 13 lb. (5.9 kg) warhead, max. range 2,743 yd. (3000 m), speed 625 mph (1,003 km/h), penetrating 31.5 in. (800 mm) of armor.

The sophisticated technology of the Stealth fighter makes it almost undetectable—even by radar.

Timeline

1871 First antiaircraft gun, the German Krupp 37mm Ballonkanone; deployed against French balloonists carrying dispatches.

1873 Machine designed to make barbed wire, patented by American Lucien Smith in 1867.

***c.* 1875** Alfred Nobel invents ballistite; cordite invented.

1877 Purpose-built torpedo boat, HMS *Lightning*, with swiveling tubes for locomotive torpedoes.

1879 First rifle with box magazine is patented.

1883 Maxim gun perfected; adopted by British army in 1888.

1885 First use of electric telegraph in battle at Tofrek, Sudan: British commander telegraphs base *c.* 6 mi.(10 km) away.

1893 Design of first self-loading ("automatic") pistol, 8-shot arm; model for famous Luger Parabellum of 1898.

1897 French "seventy-five" is a landmark in development of field artillery.

1900 Holland submarine is first to constitute viable weapon of war. Demonstration of gas-operated flamethrower; first used in war in 1915.

1903 First mechanized army units formed, French Corps d'Automobilistes Militaire, British 77/78 Companies, Army Service Corps.

1904 First armored car in service. Austrian army's 35hp Daimler Panzerwagen, with Maxim gun in revolving turret.

1906 *Dreadnought* battleship built.

1908 Dirigibles adapted for bombing operations.

1910 First purpose-designed fighting aircraft, Voisin biplane with machine gun; initiation of BE 2 two-seater reconnaissance and bombing biplane.

1911–12 Italo-Turkish War, Libya: Italian aviators make first day and night bombing raids, photoreconnaissance flights and propaganda leaflet drop; first pilot killed in action (by ground fire); also first battlefield use of motor trucks, motor ambulances and armored cars.

1914 Sikorsky builds first heavy bomber, four-engined Il'ya Mouromets; operational with Russian Imperial forces in 1915–17. First "aircraft carrier" in action, Japanese seaplane carrier *Wakamiya*.

1915 First strategic bombing offensive, raids by Zeppelin dirigibles on Britain. First gas warfare, xylyl-bromide ("tear gas") used by Germans against Russians.

1916 First tanks in action, British Mark I tanks attack on Somme front on September 15. First submachine gun, design of Bergmann Maschinen Pistole 18 begins; operational 1918. French physicist Paul Langevin (1872–1946) initiates development of ASDIC/Sonar.

1917 First guided missile, automatically-piloted biplane "Bug" SSM, carrying 300 lb. (136kg) explosive.

COMMISSIONED RANKS

Commissioned Ranks: army

U.S.A.	United Kingdom	France	Germany
General of the Army	Field Marshal		
General	General	Général d'Armée	General
Lieutenant General	Lieutenant General	Général de Corps d'Armée	Generalleutnant
Major General	Major General	Général de Division	General major
Brigadier General	Brigadier	Général de Brigade	Brigadegeneral
Colonel	Colonel	Colonel	Oberst
Lieutenant Colonel	Lieutenant Colonel	Lieutenant Colonel	Oberstleutnant
Major	Major	Commandant	Major
Captain	Captain	Capitaine	Hauptmann
First Lieutenant	Lieutenant	Lieutenant	Oberleutnant
	Second Lieutenant	Sous Lieutenant	Leutnant

Commissioned Ranks: navy

U.S.A.	United Kingdom	France	Germany
Fleet Admiral	Admiral of the Fleet	Amiral	Admiral
Admiral	Admiral	Vice Amiral d'Escadre	
Vice Admiral	Vice Admiral	Vice Amiral	Vizeadmiral
Rear Admiral	Rear Admiral	Contre Amiral	Konteradmiral
Commodore	Commodore Admiral	Admiral	Flotillenadmiral
Captain	Captain RN	Capitaine de Vaisseau	Kapitän zur See
Commander	Commander	Capitaine de Frégate	Fregattenkapitän
Lieutenant Commander	Lieutenant Commander	Capitaine de Corvette	Korvettenkapitän
		Lieutenant de Vaisseau	Kapitänleutnant
Lieutenant	Lieutenant	Enseigne de Vaisseau de 1ère classe	Oberleutnant zur See
Lieutenant Junior Grade	Sub Lieutenant	Enseigne de Vaisseau de 2ème classe	Leutnant zur See
Acting Sub Lieutenant			

Commisioned Ranks: air force

U.S.A.	United Kingdom	France	Germany
General of the Air Force	Marshal of the Royal Air Force		
General	Air Chief Marshal	Général d'Armée Aérienne	General
Lieutenant General	Air Marshal	Général de Corps Aérienne	Generalleutnant
Major General	Air Vice Marshal	Général de Division Aérienne	Generalmajor
Brigadier General	Air Commodore	Général de Brigade Aérienne	Brigadegeneral
Colonel	Group Captain	Colonel	Oberst
Lieutenant Colonel	Wing Commander	Lieutenant Colonel	Oberstleutnant
Major	Squadron Leader	Commandant	Major
Captain	Flight Lieutenant	Capitaine	Hauptmann
First Lieutenant	Flying Officer	Lieutenant	Leutnant
	Pilot Officer	Sous Lieutenant	Oberfahnrich

1918 French Renault FT-17 is first tank to have fully rotatable turret. HMS *Argus* is the first true aircraft carrier, with full unobstructed flight deck.

1927 First parachute troops, men of Italian army, make mass practice drop.

1931 First paratroop assault: Soviet troops drop against insurgents.

1935 Radar advances by Robert Watson-Watt. U.S. Boeing B-17 Flying Fortress is first "self-defending" bomber. French-designed Breguet-Dorand Gyroplane Laboratoire is first helicopter with military potential.

1936 First major airlift of troops and materials, German and Italian planes carry 13,000 men of General Franco's Army of Africa from Morocco to Spain.

1937 First jet aircraft engine built.

1938 First ship with radar, HMS *Rodney*.

1939 First jet aircraft to fly, German Heinkel He 178; first liquid-propellant rocket aircraft, Heinkel He 176. In U.S.A., Sikorsky designs R-4 helicopter; first in service use (1942: U.S. Army Air Corps); first to land on ship (1943); first to see active service (1944). Britain erects chain of air-warning radar stations around coastline.

1940 Plasma used in blood transfusions on battlefield. Napalm developed. Lethal "nerve gases" developed by German scientists, Tabun, Sarin, and Soman (*see* 1984).

PROMINENT PEOPLE

ALEXANDER THE GREAT (356–323 B.C.) Macedonian Greek ruler and military genius. Destroyed Persian empire (331 B.C.), invaded India (326 B.C.), and brought about Greek domination of the ancient world.

ARMSTRONG, William George (1810–1900) English artillery designer and industrialist. Head of Vickers-Armstrong arms manufacturers.

ATTILA THE HUN (406–53) Hunnish king who extended his territory from the Rhine to the Chinese frontier. Defeated Roman emperor Theodosius (447), attacked Gaul but was defeated (451), invaded Italy (452).

BELISARIUS (505–65) Byzantine strategist. His victories briefly reunited Eastern and Western Roman empires.

BOLÍVAR, Simón (1783–1830) South American revolutionary leader. Defeated Spanish in Venezuela (1821), took Ecuador (1822), drove Spanish from Peru (1824).

CAESAR, (Gaius) Julius (c. 100–44 B.C.) Roman general and statesman. Defeated Gallic tribes of Helvetii, Belgae, Nervii, Veneti (58–56 B.C.), invaded Britain (55, 54 B.C.), destroyed Gauls (52 B.C.); defeated Roman rival Pompey (48 B.C.) and Pompey's generals (46, 45 B.C.).

CARNOT, Lazare (1753–1823) French revolutionary leader. Strategist in Revolutionary Wars.

CHARLES MARTEL ("the Hammer") (c. 688–741) Frankish ruler and progenitor of Carolingian dynasty. Defeated Moors (732) and drove Saracens out of Burgundy (737).

CLAUSEWITZ, Karl von (1780–1831) Prussian soldier. His book *On War* (1833) greatly influenced strategists.

COLT, Samuel (1814–62) U.S. inventor of percussion revolver and pioneer of assembly-line arms production.

CYRUS THE GREAT (d. 529 B.C.) Founder of Persian empire. Captured Babylon (539 B.C.), Lydia (546 B.C.), conquered from Mediterranean to Hindu Kush.

DAYAN, Moshe (1915–81) Israeli general. Masterminded victory in Six-Day War (1967).

DÖNITZ, Karl (1891–1980) German naval commander. Developed "wolf pack" tactics in German U-boat (submarine) campaign, World War II.

EISENHOWER, Dwight D. (1890–1969) U.S. general. Supreme commander of Allied cross-Channel invasion of Europe in World War II (1944) and of NATO land forces (1950).

EUGENE OF SAVOY, Prince (1663–1736) Austrian general. Ended Turkish power in Hungary (1716–18).

FOCH, Ferdinand (1851–1929) French general. As General-in-Chief, 1918, led Allied armies to victory in World War I.

GERONIMO (Goyathlay) (1829–1909) Native American leader. Led Chiricahua Apache rising (1885–86).

GIAP, Vo Nguyen (b. 1912) Vietnamese general. Created People's Army and led it in successful campaigns against French (1954) and Americans (1973).

GRANT, Ulysses Simpson (1822–85) American Civil War commander. Captured Vicksburg (1863), took Richmond (1865), effectively ending war. U.S. president 1869–77.

GUDERIAN, Heinz (1888–1954) German soldier. Major practitioner of blitzkrieg armored warfare in World War II.

GUSTAV II ADOLF (1594–1632) Swedish king and commander. Successfully warred against Russia (1613–17) and Poland (1621–29). Led Protestants in Thirty Years' War (1618–48), defeating Wallenstein at Lützen (1632).

HUNYADY, János Corvinus (c. 1387–1456) Hungarian warrior. Helped to stem Turkish invasion (1456).

JOAN OF ARC (c. 1412–31) French patriot. Defeated English occupying army (1429); captured Compiègne (1430). Sold to English and burnt at stake.

LAWRENCE, T(homas) E(dward) (1888–1935) Anglo-Irish soldier known as "Lawrence of Arabia". Joined Arab Revolt against Turks (1916) and assisted in defeat of Turks in World War I.

LEE, Robert E(dward) (1807–70) Commander of Confederate forces in American Civil War. Inflicted notable defeats on the Union before his eventual surrender (1865).

MACARTHUR, Douglas (1880–1964) U.S. World War II commander in Far East, recapturing Philippine archipelago from Japanese (1945). Commanded UN forces in Korea (1950).

MARLBOROUGH, John Churchill, 1st Duke of (1650–1722) English soldier. His victories in War of Spanish Succession (1702–13), notably Blenheim (1704), established his reputation as a great general.

MAURICE OF NASSAU, Prince (1567–1625) Dutch soldier. His victories against the Spanish led to recognition of the Dutch republic (1608). Founded first true military academy.

MOLTKE, Helmuth Count von (1800–91) Prussian soldier. He reorganized the Prussian army, which crushed Denmark (1863–64), Austria (1866) and France (1870–71).

MONTGOMERY, Bernard Law, 1st Viscount of Alamein (1887–1976) English soldier. In World War II he commanded Allied forces in successful North African, Italian and Normandy-Germany campaigns.

NAPOLEON I (Napoleon Bonaparte) (1769–1821) French ruler and military genius. His victories in Italy against Austria (1796) led to French acquisition of Lombardy and Belgium (1797). In 1799 he seized power in France and defeated Austria (Marengo, 1800). Renewing war with England, Russia and Austria (1802) he won victories over Austria (1805), Prussia (1806) and Russia (1807). Fearing an alliance with England he invaded Russia, but was forced to retreat. Further victories over the allied armies in 1813 were followed by defeat at Leipzig, and the invasion of France. He was finally defeated at Waterloo (1815).

NELSON, Horatio (1758–1805) English naval commander. Defeated Napoleon's fleet off Egypt (1798) and prevented France's northward expansion (Copenhagen, 1801). Victory over French and Spanish fleets at Trafalgar (1805) ensured British supremacy.

PATTON, George Smith (1885–1945) U.S. World War II commander. Led U.S. 7th Army across France and Germany (1944–45).

PERSHING, John Joseph (1860–1948) U.S. commander of American Expeditionary Force in Europe, World War II.

ROMMEL, Erwin (1891–1944) German World War II general. Initially a successful commander of the Afrika Korps, he was defeated at El Alamein (1942).

SALADIN (Salah al-Din al-Ayyubi) (1137–93) Muslim warrior. Seized Egypt (1171) and conquered Mesopotamia (1174). Defeated crusaders at Hattin (1187) but was defeated by a much larger army at Acre (1191).

SARGON OF AKKAD (fl. 230 B.C.) Sumerian ruler. Perhaps first war leader to create a "professional" standing army.

SHAKA (c. 1787–1828) Zulu leader whose military skills established Zulu kingdom.

SUN TZU (fl. 500 B.C.) Chinese general and theorist. *The Art of War*, earliest known work on strategy, is still studied and greatly influenced Mao Zedong.

TAMERLANE (Timur) (1336–1404) Turkic conqueror. Defeated Central Asian kingdoms (1360–70), Persia (1392–96) and northern India (1398). Occupied Baghdad and Damascus (1401) and destroyed Ottoman forces (1402). Died while leading a campaign against the Chinese.

VAUBAN, Sébastien le Prestre de (1633–1707) French engineer. Revolutionized siege warfare and fortress construction.

WELLINGTON, Arthur Wellesley, 1st Duke of (1769–1852) Irish soldier and statesman. Showed early promise with victories in India (1797). During the Peninsular War (1808–14) gained victories at Talavera (1809), Salamanca (1812) and Toulouse (1814). Defeated French at Waterloo (1815).

YAMASHITA, Tomoyuki (1885–1946) Japanese World War II soldier. Took Malaya and Singapore in lightning campaign (1941–42).

ZHUKOV, Georgi (1896–1974) Russian soldier. Supreme Soviet general of World War II, lifting the siege of Moscow with successful counter-offensive at Stalingrad (1943). Took Berlin (1945).

ZISKA, John (c. 1370–1424) Bohemian Hussite leader. Pioneered field artillery with *wagenburg* (wagon fort).

SECTION 4
HISTORY

5000 B.C. – 2000 B.C.

CRADLES OF CIVILIZATION

Fertile soils enabled the first civilizations (city cultures) to emerge in the valleys of the Tigris-Euphrates, Nile, Indus, and Huang He (Yellow). By 3000 B.C. in Sumeria (1) powerful city-states existed, writing had developed, and the wheel had been invented. Egypt (2) was united under one king, *c.* 3000 B.C. By 2500 B.C. the Indus cities (3) boasted drainage systems and populations in excess of *c.* 35,000. In China (4), jade was being carved by 3000 B.C.

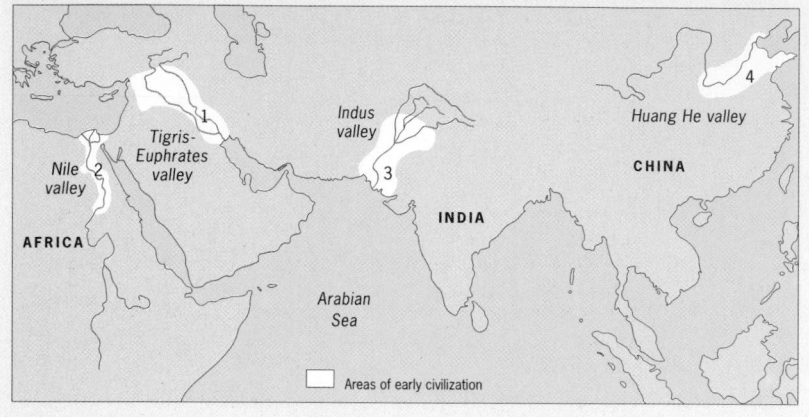

Areas of early civilization

EUROPE

c. **5000** Rising sea level severs last land bridge between Britain and mainland Europe.

c. **3200** First houses built at Skara Brae in Orkney, Scotland.

c. **3000** Cycladic and early Minoan cultures develop in Crete and other islands; trade with Egypt, Levant, and Anatolia. Settlers at Windmill Hill, Wiltshire, England. Weaving loom introduced into Europe from Middle East. Wild horses domesticated in Ukraine region.

c. **2750–2000** On Malta and Gozo construction of megalithic temples and excavation of hypogeum (underground rock temple).

c. **2700** Stonehenge (first stage) constructed, England (*opposite*).

c. **2500** Metal working spreads through Europe. Norway rock carving shows skiing practiced.

c. **2100-1400** Development of Minoan civilization in Crete; Linear A and Linear B scripts.

c. **2000** Bronze Age begins in Europe. Minoans start building palace at Knossos. Stonehenge (second stage) begins in England; megalithic culture in western Europe.

MIDDLE EAST

c. **5000** First Sumerian village settlements in fertile plain between Tigris and Euphrates rivers (Mesopotamia).

c. **4500** Metalworking begins in Sumer and Egypt.

4236 First date in ancient Egyptian calendar.

c. **4000–3500** White painted pottery produced in Egypt.

c. **4000–3500** First towns founded in Sumer, including Ur, Eridu, and Lagash (*left*). First use of potter's wheel.

c. **3800** Earliest known map (on clay tablet) shows Euphrates River in Sumer.

c. **3760** Early use of bronze in Egypt and Sumer.

c. **3500** In Mesopotamia, flax grown for making linen; irrigation canals dug.Two kingdoms of Upper Egypt and Lower Egypt flourish.

c. **3200** Sumerians grow barley, make wine and beer, devise first known system of writing and first written civil law code (*below left*).

c. **3100** Pharaoh Menes unites the kingdoms of Upper and Lower Egypt, founding Ist dynasty; irrigation systems developed, ox-drawn plows invented; first harps and flutes made.

c. **3000** Elamite civilization in Iran. Troy a city-state. Bronze Age begins in Anatolia. First iron objects are made in Mesopotamia; Sumerians first use wheels on vehicles.

c. **2800–2400** City-states of Sumer at zenith.

2772 Egypt introduces 365-day calendar.

c. **2700** Foundation of Old Kingdom of Egypt, from the IIIrd to the VIth dynasties (to 2200 B.C.). First (step) pyramid built for Pharaoh Zoser. First mummies embalmed.

c. **2600** Khufu (Cheops) builds Great Pyramid at Giza (*opposite*) *c.* 2550. The Great Sphinx also built.

THE FIRST WRITING

By the end of the fourth millennium B.C., the Sumerians of southern Mesopotamia were using the earliest known form of writing. The first script in use was pictographic: items were represented by simplified drawings, and a sign scratched beside each pictograph denoted the numbers of items listed. Eventually, the system became more complex with the result that pictographs could express sounds. By around 2500 B.C., scribes were using styluses with triangular tips, which they pressed into the clay to give a neat wedge-shaped, or cuneiform, script.

Sumerian writing: from images to signs.

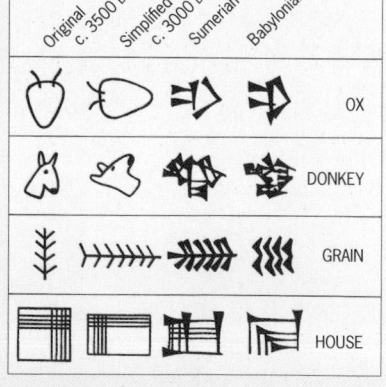

	Original *c.* 3500 BC	Simplified *c.* 3000 BC	Sumerian	Babylonian	
					OX
					DONKEY
					GRAIN
					HOUSE

		5000 B.C.	4500	4000
	RELIGION AND PHILOSOPHY	Earth goddess fertility cults		Hebrew date of creation
	SCIENCE AND TECHNOLOGY			Egypt: copper smelted
	LITERATURE AND MUSIC			Sumer: drum and reed-pipe music
	ART AND ARCHITECTURE			Egyptian cosmetics

PHARAOHS AND PYRAMIDS

The pyramids, huge structures built along the Nile Valley as tombs for the pharaohs, protected the body of the pharaoh as well as the precious funerary goods which, according to belief, he would take with him to the afterlife. The golden age of pyramid building occurred during the IVth Dynasty of the Old Kingdom period of Egyptian history, when the three pyramids at Giza, near Cairo, were raised. Largest of these was the Great Pyramid of Cheops.

The Great Pyramid, c. 2550 B.C.

Dates (B.C.)	Periods
c. 3100–2700	Early Dynastic
c. 2700–2180	Old Kingdom
c. 2180–2000	First Intermediate
c. 2000–1786	Middle Kingdom
c. 1786–1554	Second Intermediate
c. 1554–1070	New Kingdom
c. 1070–712	Third Intermediate
c. 712–332	Late

Dates (B.C.)	Principal pharaohs
c. 3100–3080	Menes (Aha)
c. 2630–2611	Zoser (Djoser)
c. 2551–2411	Cheops (Khufu)
c. 2061–2010	Mentuhotep I
c. 2010–1998	Mentuhotep II
1640–1532	Hyksos kings in north
1555–1550	Kamose reunites in Egypt
1550–1070	Amenhotep I–III
	Tuthmosis I–IV
	Queen Hatshepsut
	Akhenaten (Amenhotep IV)
	Tutankhamen
	Ramses I–XI
945–924	Sheshonq I
770–712	Rule of Nubians
664–610	Psammetichus I
525–404	Rule of Persians
380–362	Nectanebo I
343–332	Rule of Persians

STONEHENGE

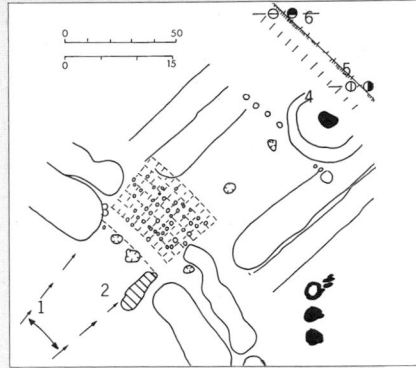

Stonehenge's astronomical alignments.

1 Range of vision from center
2 Slaughter Stone
3 Main entrance
4 Heel Stone
5 Midsummer sunrise
6 Maximum winter moonrise

This impressive stone circle features a series of massive trilithons (16 ft./5 m) —two stones capped by a third. Stonehenge may have been used for rituals. The fact that its axis is aligned with the midsummer sunrise suggests that it may have been laid out in accordance with specific movements of the sun, moon, and other celestial bodies.

c. **2360** Sargon the Great of Akkad begins conquest of Sumer and founds the world's first great empire (to 2180 B.C.).
c. **2200** Semites from Arabia migrate to Mesopotamia and set up Babylonian and Assyrian kingdoms.
c. **2100** Empire of Ur in Mesopotamia (to 2000 B.C.); construction of ziggurat. Hebrew patriarch Abraham migrates from Ur.
c. **2030** Decline of Sumer.
c. **2000** Indo-European Hittites invade Asia Minor (*p. 315*). Construction of Babylon. Start of the Middle Kingdom, covering the XIth and XIIth dynasties (to 1786 B.C.). Considered the golden age of Egyptian art and literature.

ASIA

c. **5000** Yang Shao establish farm com-munities on Huang He River, China.
c. **4000–3500** Colored pottery from Russia reaches China.
c. **4000** Yang Shao rice farming culture.
c. **3500** Copper tools in Thailand.
2697 Huang-ti, "Yellow Emperor" of China.
c. **2500** Metalworking at Indus Valley, India: founding of major civilization.
c. **2350** Yao dynasty in China.
c. **2200** Jomon culture in Japan.
c. **2250** Yu-shun emperor of China.
c. **2205** Hsia dynasty in China.
c. **2000** Invasion of Indus Valley by Aryans from north.

AFRICA

c. **5000** New Stone Age people work pol-ished stone. Development of civiliza-tions at Faiyûm and Nubia in Nile Valley. Agriculture spreads southward.
3400–2000 Egypt controls Nubia.
c. **3000** Lake Chad begins to dry up; the Sahara Desert begins to form.
c. **2000** Bantu migrations east and south from west Africa. Trading centers grow into cities in N. Africa.

THE AMERICAS

c. **5000** Mexico: Cultivation of corn (maize) and beans in Central America.
c. **3500** Potatoes grown in South America.
3372 First date in Mayan calendar.
c. **3500** Agriculture develops in Tehuacan Valley, Mexico. First pottery in Mexico. Villages and towns on coast of Peru.
c. **2000** Cotton cultivated in Peru.

AUSTRALIA AND OCEANIA

c. **5000** Boomerang used in Australia.

	3500	3000	2500	2000 B.C.
	Sumer: temples erected to gods		Egypt: king associated with falcon god Horus	
Sumer: wheeled vehicles	Sumer: kilns in use	China: plow in use / Ecuador: Valdivian pottery	Sumer: horse-drawn chariots / India: cotton grown	
Sumer: pictographic script		Sumer: cuneiform script	Egypt: hieroglyphic script / Indus Valley: script	Egypt: pyramid texts / China: script
Fine pottery from Sumer	Europe: megalithic architecture	Sumer: terracotta statuettes / Egyptian pyramids	Aegean: cycladic art / Indus Valley: corbeled arches, elaborate town planning	Sumerian ziggurats: Temple of Ur

2000 B.C. – 1000 B.C.

EUROPE

c. **1700–1400** Minoan Crete dominates the Aegean Sea region *(below)*.

c. **1650–1100** Mycenaean civilization in Greece *(p. 315)*.

c. **1600** Mycenaeans trade by sea throughout the Mediterranean.

c. **1550** Third phase of Stonehenge, England, completed.

c. **1500** Minoan–Mycenaean rivalry.

c. **1400** Mycenaeans occupy Crete.

c. **1300** Cultivation of olives in central Greece. First Celts appear in upper Danube area.

c. **1100** Invasion of Mediterranean by "Sea People," Indo-Europeans from farther north. Collapse of Hittite Empire.

c. **1150–1100** Growth of Phoenician maritime power.

c. **1100–1050** Collapse of Mycenaean power, possibly because iron-using Dorian people destroy Mycenaean citadels.

c. **1000** Mycenaean Greeks establish colonies in Aegean and Asia Minor.

MIDDLE EAST

1991 Middle Kingdom of Egypt: capital moved to Memphis.

c. **1950** Sesostris I of Egypt invades Canaan (modern Palestine). End of Mesopotamian empire of Ur.

c. **1830** First Babylonian Empire takes over city-states of Mesopotamia.

c. **1750–1500** Old Kingdom of the Hittites in Asia Minor.

c. **1728–1686** Hammurabi the Great of Babylon produces code of laws.

c. **1700** Hittites invade Syria.

c. **1640** Hyksos invaders conquer Egypt, founding XVth dynasty.

c. **1595** Hittites conquer Babylon.

c. **1550** New Kingdom (to *c.* 1070 B.C.) in Egypt *(below)*; Hyksos expelled.

c. **1504–1492** Thebes replaces Memphis as Egyptian capital. Temple of Amun at Karnak begun. Tuthmosis I extends Egypt to its greatest limits, to Palestine, Syria, and S. along the Nile into Kush (Nubia).

c. **1473** Tuthmosis III of Egypt reconquers Palestine.

c. **1500** Hittites control all of Asia Minor.

c. **1430–1100** New Kingdom of the Hittites.

c. **1391–79** Hittites reconquer Asia Minor and make Mitanni subjects.

c. **1375–55** Amenhotep III builds Temple of Luxor and Colossi of Memnon.

c. **1366** Increasing power of Assyria in Mesopotamia.

c. **1353–35** Amenhotep IV (Akhenaten) initiates sun worship in Egypt.

EGYPT: THE NEW KINGDOM

During the New Kingdom period (*c.* 1550–1070 B.C.), Egypt entered an age of great military expansion coupled with fine artistic achievement. Vast tracts of land were controlled, from Nubia in the south to the Euphrates River in the east. The great temples of Karnak and Luxor at Thebes and the famous rock-cut temple at Abu Simbel were built. This was also the time of Amenhotep IV, who, as Akhenaten, instituted his own "heretical" solar cult.

XVIIIth dynasty (1550–1307)	XIXth dynasty (1307–1196)
Ahmosis	Ramses I
Amenhotep I	Sethos I
Tuthmosis I	Ramses II
Tuthmosis II	Merneptah
Tuthmosis III	Sethos II
Hatshepsut	Amenmesses
Amenhotep II	Siptah
Tuthmosis IV	Twosre
Amenhotep III	
Amenhotep IV	**XXth dynasty (1196–1070)**
Smenkhkare	Sethnakhte
Tutankhamen	Ramses III–XI
Aya	
Horemheb	

MINOAN CRETE

The Minoan civilization, centered on the island of Crete, was named by the British archaeologist Sir Arthur Evans after the legendary Cretan king Minos. It is the earliest civilization in Europe. From about 2000 to 1400 B.C., the Minoans controlled the Aegean Sea with their navies. During this period, palaces were built on Crete at Knossos, Malia, Phaistos, and elsewhere. Rebuilt in about 1700 after an earthquake, Knossos was a maze of corridors and rooms and twice the size of any other palace. Its complex layout and the discovery of bull motifs, including a mural showing youths somersaulting backward over a bull, perhaps reflect the legend of the Minotaur—a hybrid monster, half-man, half-bull, kept by the legendary King Minos. Excavations of the palace by Evans during the early years of the 1900s have shown that the Minoans enjoyed a sophisticated life-style. Walls were adorned with colorful

The Queen's Room, palace of Knossos, was built c. 1500 B.C.

frescoes showing, for example, dolphins, other marine life, and ritual processions. Artisans made exquisite gold jewelry, and the palace was equipped with an excellent drainage system. Cretan palaces, apart from Knossos, were destroyed in about

1450B.C., an event perhaps linked with the massive volcanic eruption of the nearby island of Thera. Knossos was repaired soon after and then occupied by Mycenaean invaders from mainland Greece, who, for the next 300 years, dominated the Aegean world.

	2000 B.C.	1900	1800	1700	1600
RELIGION AND PHILOSOPHY		Canaanite religion develops in Palestine		Babylon: law code devised by Hammurabi	Minoan snake and bull worship
SCIENCE AND TECHNOLOGY	Egyptian invention of waterwheel (shaduf)			Mesopotamia: "lost wax" method of bronze casting	Minoan ship design improves shipbuilding
LITERATURE AND MUSIC		Babylonian epic of creation			First known Phoenician inscriptions
ART AND ARCHITECTURE					Minoan golden age

c. **1333-23** Tutankhamen restores the traditional Egyptian god Amun to prominence.

c. **1309-1291** Sethos I begins reconquest of lands in Palestine and Syria.

c. **1308** Assyrian expansion under Adadnirari I.

c. **1307** Ramses I founds XIXth dynasty in Egypt.

c. **1290** Accession of Ramses II (the Great) of Egypt. Construction of great rock temples of Abu Simbel in Egypt. Phoenician port of Sidon flourishes. Medes and Persians invade Iran.

c. **1285** Battle between Egyptians and Hittites at Kadesh in Palestine: both sides claim victory.

c. **1283** Peace between Egypt and the Hittites.

c. **1200** Traditional date for Exodus from Egypt of Israelites under Moses.

1194 Ramses III becomes pharaoh.

c. **1190-70** Asia Minor and Egypt invaded by "Sea People," Indo-Europeans from Europe; invaders are only just defeated by Egypt by armies of Ramses III.

1188 Ramses III becomes pharaoh. XXth dynasty founded.

c. **1175** Shalmaneser I becomes ruler of Assyria and extends its conquests.

c. **1170** Growing power of newly independent Phoenician cities, especially Tyre on E. Mediterranean coast.

c. **1131** Israelites in Canaan (Palestine).

c. **1115** Nebuchadnezzar I of Babylon repels Assyrian attacks.

1100–900 Assyria unable to maintain itself.

c. **1093–935** Babylonia overrun by Aramaeans.

c. **1080–950** Egypt divided into upper and lower kingdoms.

1070 New kingdom in Egypt ends with death of Ramses XI.

c. **1050** Philistines pressure Israel.

c. **1050** Saul, king of Israel, leads successful revolt against Philistines.

c. **1010** David succeeds Saul, captures Jerusalem, and makes it capital.

ASIA

1766 Shang dynasty, centered on Huang He Valley, founded in China (to 1112).

c. **1700** Decline and collapse of Indus civilization.

c. **1600** Aryan invaders enter N. India. Chinese Shang dynasty develops

THE HITTITES

In the course of the second millennium B.C., a people known as the Hittites emerged as a great power in the Near East. From their capital of Hattusas in central Asia Minor (modern Turkey), Hittite kings ruled an empire that fluctuated in size over hundreds of years. It reached its zenith in about 1350 B.C., then eventually collapsed toward the end of the 1200s. The Hittites were able soldiers and fought the famous battle of Kadesh against the Egyptians in about 1285, with both sides claiming victory. They were also renowned for their ability to work iron. Excavations at Hattusas (modern Boghazkoy) have unearthed writing tablets that show that the Hittite language belongs to the Indo-European linguistic family and may be one of the oldest of the group.

A Hittite rock carving shows a lion hunt.

bronze vessels, chariots, and writing system.

c. **1400** Iron Age in India and W. Asia.

c. **1122** Emperor Wu Wang founds Chou dynasty in China (to 256 B.C.).

c. **1000–950** The Western Chou dynasty establishes its capital at Hao in the Wei Valley, China.

AFRICA

c. **1500** Growth of Sahara Desert separates northern Africa from rest of continent. Horses and chariots on trade routes across Sahara.

c. **1000** Kingdom of Kush develops in the middle Nile Valley (to A.D. 350).

THE MYCENAEANS

From about 1600 to 1100 B.C., the Greek mainland was dominated by the Mycenaeans, a Bronze Age people named after the powerful city of Mycenae in the Greek Peloponnese. The Mycenaeans were a warrior people. According to legend, it was the Mycenaean king Agamemnon who led the Greek forces against the city of Troy in Asia Minor. But the Mycenaeans were not only military specialists. Metalwork flourished, as shown by the magnificent gold goblets, death masks, and other items excavated at Mycenae by Heinrich Schliemann. Also impressive were pottery, frescoes, and jewelry, which all show the influence of Minoan Crete (*opposite*). Mycenaean civilization

c. **1000** Iron mining and manufacture in Western Africa.

THE AMERICAS

c. **1504–1450** Stone temples built in Mexico.

c. **1100** Height of Olmec civilization in Mexico.

c. **1000** Chavín and Paracas cultures in South America.

AUSTRALIA AND OCEANIA

c. **1800** First settlers arrive in islands of Micronesia.

c. **1300** First settlers arrive in Tonga, Fiji, and Samoa.

Golden death mask of a Mycenaean king

ended in about 1100 for reasons that are still not understood. There may have been an internal disturbance or an invasion by a people who came to be known as the Dorians, or perhaps it was a combination of both.

1500	1400	1300	1200	1100	1000 B.C.
	Solar worship of Aten in Egypt	Sanskrit Vedas in India	Moses reasserts monotheism	Worship of Zeus, Apollo, and Hermes in Greece	Chinese philosophy begins to develop
Egypt: glass bottles and glazed beads	Egyptian water clock		Hittite ironsmiths spread knowledge	Mesopotamia: iron plowshares	
Egyptian love songs composed		Silver trumpets buried with Tutankhamen	Vedas written in Sanskrit	Minstrels at Assyrian court	Reed organ developed in China
Revival of Mesopotamian art	Egypt: Great Temple of Karnak	Tomb of Tutankhamen	Rock temple of Abu Simbel built by Ramses II		Chinese wall painting begins; Mexico: Olmec culture

1000 B.C. – 300 B.C.

EUROPE

c. 900–800 Phoenician colonies in Sicily and Spain including Utica.

c. 900–400 Etruscan civilization in N. Italy.

814 Traditional foundation date for Carthage.

c. 800–500 Growth of Greek city-states, such as Athens and Sparta.

753 Traditional foundation date of Rome.

716 Sparta begins conquest of Messenia.

c. 700–500 Greeks found new city-states in Mediterranean, Sicily, S. Italy, and Black Sea (*opposite*).

c. 650–500 Tyrants (self-made dictators) rule many Greek city-states.

594 Solon of Athens reforms laws and defines citizenship.

546 Cyrus of Persia overruns Asia Minor and founds the Persian Empire.

534 Tarquinius Superbus last king of Rome (to 510), and Etruscan domination ends.

509 Foundation of Roman Republic.

508 Cleisthenes reforms constitution of Athens and reintroduces democratic government.

499–94 Darius I of Persia crushes Greek city-states in Asia Minor.

496 Romans defeat Latins at Lake Regillus.

494 Plebeians in Rome win political rights with the establishment of the tribunate.

490 Persian invasion of Greece defeated at Marathon (*opposite*).

480 Persian invasion of Greece: Xerxes I defeated in sea battle at Salamis.

479 Final defeat of Persians and their expulsion from Greece.

459–446 War between Athens and Sparta.

c. 450. Celtic La Tène culture develops in C. and N. Europe.

431 Peloponnesian War between Athens and Sparta begins.

430 Outbreak of plague in Athens.

413 Failure of Athenian attack on Sicily.

404 Peloponnesian War ends with Spartans victorious.

399 Trial and condemnation of Athenian philosopher Socrates.

390 Gauls sack Rome but fail to capture the Capitol.

353 Philip II of Macedonia invades Greece.

338 Philip defeats Greeks at Chaeronea.

336 Assassination of Philip; his son, Alexander III (the Great), crushes revolts by Greek cities.

SOLOMON'S TEMPLE

When Solomon became king of Israel in about 965, he set about building a temple in Jerusalem, which became the great spiritual center of the country. The Temple consisted of three principal areas: the outer court, the inner holy place, and, most sacred of all, the Holy of Holies. Here stood the ark of the covenant, the holy treasure of the Israelites, which housed the stone tablets on which the Ten Commandments were inscribed. Destroyed in about 586 by the Babylonians, the temple was rebuilt about 70 years later by Jews returning from exile. King Herod the Great added to the structure in 19 B.C. But it was finally razed by the Romans in A.D. 70.

334–23 Alexander destroys Persian Empire (*opposite*), begins consolidation of Greek world and Hellenistic age.

323 Death of Alexander. Empire is divided among Macedonian generals Antipater, Seleucus, Antigonus, Ptolemy, and Lysimachus.

321 Defeat of Roman army by Samnites at Caudine Forks.

301 Antigonus I killed. Seleucus rules Syria; Ptolemy rules Palestine.

MIDDLE EAST

c. 1000 David captures Jerusalem.

965 David succeeded by Solomon (*above*).

957 Dedication of Temple at Jerusalem.

925 Death of Solomon. Kingdom is split into Judah in south, Israel in north.

883 Assyrian king Ashurnazirpal extends empire to Mediterranean.

854 Assyria attacks Palestine.

722 Sargon II of Assyria captures Samaria and Israel.

712–698 Ethiopian kings rule over Egypt (to 681 B.C.)—the XXVth dynasty. Judah comes under Babylonian rule.

710 Assyrians destroy Chaldean Babylonia.

709 Assyrians led by Sennacherib destroy Babylon.

663 Ashurbanipal, king of Assyria, sacks Thebes in Egypt.

650 Scythian and Cimmerian raiders sweep through Syria and Palestine.

612 Medes, Babylonians, and Scythians destroy Nineveh.

609 End of Assyrian Empire.

605 Judah comes under Babylonian rule.

587 Nebuchadnezzar captures Jerusalem.

580 Nebuchadnezzar begins Hanging Gardens of Babylon (*p. 321*).

550 Cyrus II (the Great) of Persia conquers Media.

539 Cyrus conquers Babylonia and makes Judah and Phoenicia into Persian provinces.

538 Edict of Cyrus allows some Jewish exiles to return to Judah.

525 Cambyses of Persia conquers Egypt.

519 Darius I of Persia divides empire, extending from the Danube to the Indus, into ten satrapies (provinces).

516 Work is resumed on Solomon's Temple in Jerusalem.

513 Darius begins palace of Persepolis.

	1000 B.C.	900	800
RELIGION AND PHILOSOPHY	India: Vedas composed		
SCIENCE AND TECHNOLOGY			Assyrian mass production of iron tools
LITERATURE AND MUSIC			Homer's *Iliad* and *Odyssey*
ART AND ARCHITECTURE		Solomon's Temple built in Jerusalem	

GREEK COLONIZATION

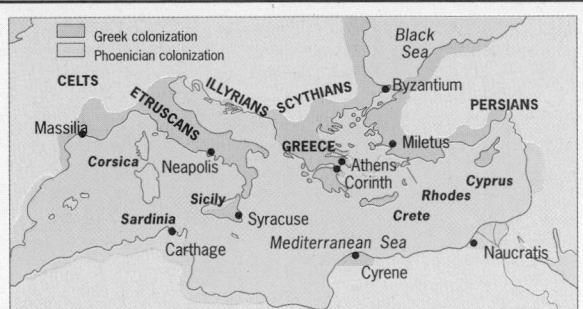

A shortage of arable land at home and increased trade inspired people to settle elsewhere. Between 750 and 500 B.C., many Greek colonists set off to found new cities. In the west, the Greeks arrived in Sicily, southern Italy, and France, where they founded Syracuse, Neapolis (Naples), Massilia (Marseilles), and other cities. The Greeks also colonized the coasts of Asia Minor and the Black Sea. The new settlements usually maintained legal and cultural links with their parent cities.

ALEXANDER THE GREAT

Enthroned as king of Macedonia at the age of 20, Alexander the Great went on to become one of the world's finest commanders. When he died in 323, at the age of only 32, his empire stretched from Illyria in the west to Kashmir in the east.

356 Birth of Alexander.
334 Defeats Persians at Granicus.
333 Persian king Darius III defeated at Issus.
332 Besieges Tyre and enters Egypt.
331 Darius routed at Gaugamela.
326 Alexander defeats Indian king. Army mutinies.
323 Alexander falls ill and dies at Babylon.

Alexander destroyed the Persian army at Issus, capturing Darius's wife and mother.

404 Persians driven out of Egypt.
387 Artaxerxes II of Persia captures Greek cities in Asia Minor.
338 Artaxerxes III is assassinated; succeeded by Darius III.
334 Alexander the Great, king of Macedonia, begins campaign against Persia (*right*).
331 Alexander conquers Egypt and founds Alexandria.
326 Alexander reaches India.

312 Seleucus controls Syria, Babylon, Media, Susiana.

ASIA

***c.* 800–550** Aryans expand their territory in India; development of caste system.
771–256 Nomadic attacks on China; capital moved to Luoyang; start of Eastern Chou dynasty.
755 Solar eclipse sets first verified date in Chinese history.

***c.* 600** Civilizations develop along the Ganges River valley.
551 Birth of Chinese philosopher K'ung Fu-tzu (Confucius) (*p. 212*).
***c.* 500** Indians colonize Sri Lanka.
485 Buddha dies.
481–221 Era of the Warring States in China.
317–16 Alexander the Great invades India.
311 Mauryan dynasty, India (to 184 B.C.).

AFRICA

***c.* 900** Kush becomes independent of Egypt.
***c.* 750** Kushite army defeats Egyptians.
***c.* 600** Expansion of Carthage.
***c.* 500** Bantu-speaking peoples spread in E. Africa. Nok culture established in N. Nigeria.
***c.* 480–400** Carthage dominates W. Mediterranean and takes Sicily.
450 Copper industry flourishes in Mauritania.
400 Iron smelting begins.

THE AMERICAS

***c.* 850–100** Chavín culture flourishes on Peruvian coast.
***c.* 800** Olmecs build earliest American pyramid at La Venta, Mexico.
***c.* 301** Mayan culture, Central America.

PERSIAN WARS

The wars between Persia and the Greek city-states in the early fifth century B.C. had an inestimable effect on the course of western civilization. In 490 B.C., the Persian king, Darius, sent a force to punish Athens, but the Persians were defeated at Marathon. Ten years later, a vast Persian force under Xerxes invaded Greece. Despite their inferior numbers, the Greek allies outfought the enemy, destroying the Persians on sea and land.

490 Marathon: the Persians are beaten by the Athenian infantry.
480 Thermopylae: 300 Spartans put up a valiant stand against Xerxes's forces but are finally outflanked and killed.
480 Salamis: a naval battle in which

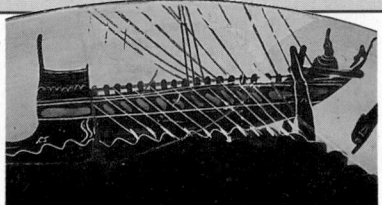

The trireme gave Greece sea mastery.

Athenian ships destroy the Persian fleet.
479 Plataea: A combined Greek army under the Spartan general Pausanias routs the Persians.
479 Mycale: Greek ships defeat the Persian navy off Asia Minor.

	700	600	500	400	300 B.C.
		Lao Tze develops Taoism	Jainism in India	Buddhism founded in India	Socrates attacks Greek sophists	Plato establishes Academy in Athens	Aristotle formulates empirical philosophy
	Greek silver coins in usage		Anaximander produces first map of known world	Pythagoras develops theories	Chinese cast iron appears	Aristotle's work on elements	Euclid's *Elements* of geometry
	Hesiod's *Theogony*	Babylonia: scale theory developed	Greece: Aesop's fables	Herodotus's history of Greek–Persian Wars	Classical Greek tragedy		India: Bhagavad Gita written
	Assyria: Sargon's Palace at Khorsabad	Babylon rebuilt with Ishtar Gate	Etruscan tomb frescoes	Persia: palace of Darius	Athens: Parthenon built	Praxiteles leading sculptor of Greek late classical period	

The classical heritage

Of all the ancient civilizations that have contributed to modern Western culture, classical Greece and Rome stand preeminent. Although they had their dark sides—institutionalized slavery, gladiatorial games, the lowly status of women—these cultures have had a profound influence on Western politics, religion, language and literature,

> *"Mighty indeed are our empire's marks and monuments which we have left. Future generations will marvel at us, as the present marvels at us now."*
> Athenian statesman Pericles
> *c.* 495–429 B.C.

arts, sciences, and many other areas of life. In literature, Greek poets and dramatists such as Homer, Aeschylus, and Sophocles have inspired writers through the ages, from

Dante to T. S. Eliot. Greek thinkers, especially Plato and Aristotle, laid the foundations of Western philosophy. And great municipal buildings around the world, such as the Jefferson Memorial in Washington, D.C. and the British Museum in London, have facades and structures derived from Greek temples. By about the middle of the 100s B.C., Greece had become part of the Roman Empire. The Romans, a militaristic, pragmatic people, readily absorbed Greek culture. But their Latin language, feats of engineering, legal system, and genius for administration, as well as the eventual adoption of Christianity as the official imperial religion, have also made important contributions to Western civilization.

A bronze statue depicts a Greek athlete, stripped for the race.

The Olympic Games

The Greeks' cultural legacy not only included affairs of the mind and spirit but also matters of the body. Athletics played an important part in religious festivals and also acted as valuable training for soldiers. The great sporting occasion of the Greek world—as it is in modern times—was the Olympic festival, which was held every four years at Olympia in the Peloponnese from at least 776 B.C. Here, at a site sacred to Zeus, contestants from Greek cities on the mainland and abroad took part in various sporting events, which evolved over time. At a stadium that held some 40,000 spectators, the five-day festival included footracing, the pentathlon (wrestling, long jump, running, throwing the discus, and throwing the javelin), and boxing. Chariot-racing was eventually included, as was the "pancration," which was a brutal, no-holds-barred mixture of wrestling and boxing. Winners were given the prize of an olive wreath and were also rewarded by their cities. The religious importance of the festival declined after Rome's conquest of Greece, and the Olympic Games were abolished by Emperor Theodosius in A.D. 394. About 1,500 years later, however, they were revived by Baron Pierre de Coubertin (following the rediscovery of the Olympia stadium in 1875). The modern Olympic Games have been held since 1896 and have become one of the world's most important sports events (*p. 262*).

Timetable
480 B.C. – A.D. 476

480 B.C. Athenian victory over the Persian Armada at Salamis inaugurates period of Athens's naval supremacy.
479 Spartan-led victory over Persian army at Plataea liberates Greece.
478 Temple of Apollo built at Delphi.
460 Temple of Zeus built at Olympia.
460 Pericles begins his career as dominant figure in Athenian politics.
447 Construction of the Parthenon begins on the Athenian Acropolis.
429 Sophocles's play *Oedipus Rex* is performed in Athens.
407 Plato becomes Socrates's pupil in Athens.
399 Socrates is found guilty of "corrupting the youth" of Athens. He is forced to commit suicide.
385 Plato opens his academy in Athens.
343 Aristotle becomes tutor to the young Alexander the Great.
335–23 Aristotle writes major works, including *Nicomachean Ethics* and *Politics*.
330 Alexander's conquests spread Greek culture over the known world.
323 Euclid writes *The Elements,* the standard work on geometry until the end of the 1800s.
312 The Via Appia built by road engineers in Rome.
289 Coinage is introduced in Rome.
283 The great library at Alexandria is enlarged by Ptolemy II.
264 First gladiatorial combats in Rome.
c. 240 Eratosthenes of Cyrene proposes a heliocentric earth and accurately estimates the earth's circumference.
104 Marius makes radical changes to the Roman army.
47 Fire destroys the great library of Alexandria.
30–19 Virgil, Rome's greatest poet, writes the *Aeneid,* a national epic of ancient Rome, honoring Augustus (Octavian).
27 Octavian becomes Augustus, emperor of Rome. Beginning of the 200-year Pax Romana (Roman Peace).
A.D. 80 The Roman Colosseum, seating nearly 90,000 people, is built.
138 Antoninus Pius becomes emperor, initiating a long period of prosperity.
212 All freeborn subjects in the empire receive Roman citizenship.
286 Emperor Diocletian splits the empire into self-governing units.
303 Diocletian initiates persecution of the Christians.
313 Constantine the Great grants freedom of worship to Christians.
325 Constantine summons a council of Christian bishops at Nicaea.
330 Constantine moves the Roman capital to Constantinople.
410 Visigoths sack and loot Rome.
476 Last Roman emperor of the West, Romulus Augustulus, is deposed by Germanic chieftain Odoacer. Eastern empire continues until 1453.

City-states and politics

A Roman mosaic illustrates the school of Plato at Athens, cradle of the classical world.

For much of its history, ancient Greece was not unified politically but comprised self-governing city-states, such as Athens, Sparta, and Corinth. Each city, or *polis*, was fiercely independent and framed its own laws and policies. In comparison with modern cities, the *polis* was small. Athens, for example, at the height of its power in the mid-400s B.C., had a population of about 250,000. Of these, only about 40,000 were full citizens—that is free, adult males, both of whose parents were also citizens. Greek citizens were much more directly involved in politics— literally the affairs of the *polis*—than their modern counterparts. And the merits of various forms of government were keenly discussed, especially by Plato and Aristotle, the founders of political theory. The main systems in the Greek world were monarchy, aristocracy, tyranny, oligarchy (rule by the few), and democracy. Although democracy was practiced in Athens and is popularly believed to be the Greeks' greatest gift to modern civilization, in fact it differed from modern democratic constitutions in various ways. And Plato, himself an Athenian, disapproved of it. In *The Republic*, Plato says a state should be run not by the people but by "philosopher kings."

The Delphic oracle

Arguably the holiest shrine in ancient Greece, Delphi was the home of the most famous oracle of antiquity. Pilgrims from all over Greece and farther abroad made their way to this sacred site, set on a mountainside overlooking a deep gorge, to consult the priestess of Apollo. Questions concerning matters such as religion, marriage, and money were written down on tablets. They were then handed to the priestess, or Pythia, who sat on a tripod (a three-legged stand) above a fissure in the rock inside the temple of Apollo. Entering a medium like trance, the Pythia uttered a stream of seemingly incoherent speech, which was interpreted

Pompeii

In A.D. 79, the eruption of Mount Vesuvius, near modern Naples, destroyed the small Roman city of Pompeii and the nearby town of Herculaneum with a deluge of volcanic ash and mud. A vivid eyewitness account of the disaster is given by Pliny the Younger in his letters. About 1,700 years after the event, Pompeii was rediscovered; and excavations since then have continued to unearth a time capsule of Roman urban life. The city was situated at the mouth of the Sarnus River on the Bay of Naples. Luxurious private houses with colonnaded gardens and walls adorned with intricate mosaics and painted murals indicate the wealth of some of Pompeii's citizens. The city also boasted two theaters, an amphitheater, three public baths, a brothel, and various temples. Like other Roman towns, Pompeii had a town council of 80 to 100 men, who held office for life. Two executive magistrates were elected annually, and surviving graffiti show that the elections inspired keen partisanship among the townspeople.

The Villa of the Mysteries *at Pompeii shows a boy reading a sacred text guided by a woman with a scroll and a writing stylus.*

Town plan of Pompeii

1. Temple of Venus
2. Forum baths
3. Forum
4. House of Vettii
5. Bakery of Modestus
6. Central baths
7. Temple of Isis
8. Theaters
9. Palaestra
10. Amphitheater

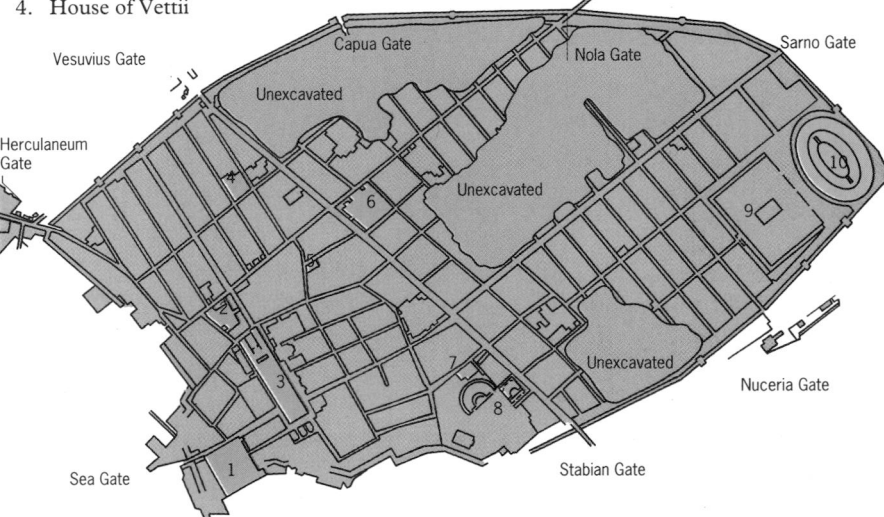

by a priest. The priest then wrote down the answers in verse form on tablets, which he gave to the questioners. The Delphic oracle gained a reputation for its truthfulness and influenced Greek politics and economics as well as religion. Its advice was sought by all the Greek city-states, yet many of its pronouncements were ambiguous. Croesus, king of Lydia (560–546 B.C.), for example, was told that if he attacked the Persians he would destroy a great empire. He did, but it was his own empire that was destroyed, not that of the Persians.

The ruins of the Delphic oracle.

300 B.C. – A.D. 500

EUROPE

298–90 B.C. Romans conquer central Italy.

279 Celtic armies reach Greece (Delphi) and Asia Minor (Galatia).

275–70 Capture of Tarentum gives Rome control of Italy.

264–41 First Punic War between Rome and Carthage.

241 Rome wins Sicily and annexes Corsica and Sardinia a few years later.

218–01 Second Punic War: Hannibal invades Italy across Alps.

216 Hannibal wins victory at Cannae.

212 Rome captures Syracuse.

202 Scipio defeats Hannibal at Zama, Africa. Rome wins Spain.

150–46 Third Punic War.

148–46 Rome annexes Macedonia.

146 Rome destroys Carthage.

122 Gracchus colonizes parts of Italy.

102 Marius defeats Cimbri and Teutones at Aquae Sextiae (Aix-en-Provence, France).

90–88 Civil war in Rome between forces of Sulla and Marius.

82–79 Dictatorship of Sulla.

73–71 Spartacus's slave revolt crushed.

67–66 Pompey adds Asia Minor, Syria, and Palestine to Roman Empire.

60 Caesar, Pompey, and Crassus form First Triumvirate (three-man rule).

58–51 Caesar's Gallic wars.

55 Caesar conquers northern Gaul.

53 Crassus is killed fighting Parthians.

52 Pompey appointed sole consul in Rome.

51 Gaul subdued by Caesar.

49 Caesar crosses Rubicon River with army into Italy; Pompey flees to Greece.

48 Caesar defeats Pompey at Pharsalus. Pompey assassinated in Egypt.

45 Caesar becomes sole ruler (consul).

44 Caesar assassinated.

43 Second Triumvirate: Octavian, Mark Antony, Marcus Lepidus.

42 Triumvirate defeats Caesar's assassins at Philippi.

37 Triumvirate is renewed for five years.

31 Octavian defeats Mark Antony and Cleopatra at sea battle of Actium.

27 Octavian given title Augustus and becomes first emperor (to A.D. 14).

A.D. 4–37 Tiberius reigns.

9 Roman legions under Varus destroyed by Arminius in Germany.

43 Romans invade Britain.

61 Boudicca leads revolt against Romans.

64 Nero makes Christians the scapegoats after fire destroys most of Rome.

68 Civil war in Rome.

THE ROMAN EMPIRE

The Roman Empire reached its greatest extent during the early 100s A.D. Divided up into provinces, the empire stretched from Britain to the Middle East, and from Germany to Egypt. Latin and, in the East, Greek were widely spoken, and this, along with a common currency and an extensive network of roads, helped trade to flourish and bring prosperity to many parts of the empire. It has been said that Rome gave to the world a longer period of peace than history, both before the 200-year Pax Romana and since, has seen.

The Roman military

The success of Rome in carving out and maintaining one of the world's great empires owed much to the discipline, training, and fighting skills of its soldiers. Marius (157–86 B.C.) created a professional army of volunteers, accepted from all classes of Roman life

69 Vespasian becomes emperor and founds Flavian dynasty.

98 Trajan becomes emperor.

101–16 Trajan increases empire to its greatest extent.

122–26 Hadrian's Wall constructed.

259 Shapur I of Persia captures and kills Roman emperor Valerian.

268 Goths sack Athens, Corinth, and Sparta.

286 Emperor Diocletian divides empire, ruling East while Maximian rules West.

303 Diocletian persecutes Christians.

306 Constantine I (the Great) becomes emperor, begins a struggle for power, consolidating his empire by 312.

313 Constantine tolerates Christianity.

324 Constantine defeats Licinius in the East and consolidates the empire.

330 Constantinople capital of empire.

361–63 Emperor Julian revives paganism.

369 Theodosius expels Picts and Scots from Britain.

370 Huns from Asia invade Europe.

378 Valens, emperor in East, is defeated and killed by Goths at Adrianople.

397 Stilicho, Vandal leader of Roman forces, drives Visigoths out of Greece.

401–17 Pope Innocent I claims universal jurisdiction over Roman Church.

406 Vandals overrun Gaul.

407 Last Roman troops leave Britain.

409 Vandals take part of Spain.

410 Goths under Alaric sack Rome.

c. 425 Huns settle in Pannonia (Hungary).

449 Jutes conquer Kent in Britain.

451 Attila the Hun fails Gaul invasion.

452 Attila invades northern Italy.

455 Gaiseric and Vandals sack Rome.

476 Goths depose Romulus Augustulus; end of Western empire.

484 Beginning of split between churches of Rome and Constantinople.

486 Clovis, Frankish king, consolidates his power in N. Gaul.

488 Ostrogoths begin conquest of Italy.

c. 500 Angles and Saxons invade England.

MIDDLE EAST

c. 290 B.C. Ptolemy Soter founds library at Alexandria.

c. 280 The Pharos (lighthouse) of Alexandria constructed (*right*).

c. 230 Attalus defeats Galatians (Celts) and takes title of king of Pergamum in Asia Minor.

217 Ptolemy IV, king of Egypt, defeats Seleucid king Antiochus III.

		300 B.C.	200	100	A.D. 1
	RELIGION AND PHILOSOPHY	Stoic philosophy develops in Greece		Wu Ti establishes Confucianism as an official philosophical school	Jesus Christ born in Judea
	SCIENCE AND TECHNOLOGY		Crossbow invented in China	Rome: water mills	Roman engineering: piping and heating
	LITERATURE AND MUSIC	Ramayana, Indian epic, composed	Alexandria: hydraulic water-powered organ		Rome: Virgil writes *Aeneid* / Horace writes *Odes* / Ovid writes *Metamorphoses*
	ART AND ARCHITECTURE	Aegean: Colossus of Rhodes constructed		Aegean: Venus de Milo created	Roman sculpture reaches its highest excellence

192–89 Rome defeats Antiochus III.

167 Antiochus IV persecutes Jews.

133 Attalus III of Pergamum dies, bequeathing kingdom to Rome.

111 Mithridates VI becomes king of Pontus (N. Turkey).

88 Mithridates attacks Romans in Asia.

66–63 Pompey defeats Mithridates.

63 Pompey annexes Syria and Judea and forms Roman provinces of Pontus and Bithynia.

53 Parthian victory at Carrhae (Turkey) destroys seven Roman legions.

51 Cleopatra becomes last queen of Egypt.

31–30 Octavian defeats Mark Antony and Cleopatra, who commit suicide.

***c*.4** Probable birth of Jesus Christ (*p. 216*).

A.D. 29 Jesus Christ crucified.

66–73 Jewish revolt against the Romans.

70 Titus destroys Jerusalem. First Diaspora (dispersion) of Jews.

116 Roman Empire extends to the Persian Gulf.

132–35 Jewish revolt against Romans.

135 Jewish revolt crushed; Second Diaspora.

161 Parthians capture Armenia and invade Syria.

166 Romans defeat Parthians.

260 Shapur I of Persia defeats Romans.

301 Christianity established in Armenia.

350 Persians capture Armenia.

440 Huns conquer Sogdiana and Bactriana.

ASIA

269–232 B.C. Asoka's Mauryan Empire unites C. and N. India.

221–06 Chíin dynasty unites China.

214 Under Shin Huang Ti, "First Emperor," the Great Wall of China is built.

202 Lui Pang founds earlier Han dynasty in China (to A.D. 9).

184 Sunga dynasty founded in India.

140 Wu Ti, "Martial Emperor," expands Chinese Empire to Manchuria, Korea, and South China.

130 Menander, Greek general of Bactria, founds Gandhara culture.

110 Munda kings reign in Deccan.

108 Wu Ti conquers Korea.

***c*. 60** Chinese extend into Central Asia.

A.D. 28 Later Han dynasty in China.

***c*. 30** Kushan Empire develops around Kabul (Afghanistan).

58 Buddhism introduced to China.

74 China trades silk to Roman Empire.

220 Han dynasty in China falls.

SEVEN WONDERS OF THE WORLD

During the last few hundred years B.C., various writers drew up lists of the greatest known monuments of history. In time, the Seven Wonders became established as:

The Pyramids of Giza (*c*. 2600 B.C.).

The Hanging Gardens of Babylon (580 B.C.).

The Temple of Artemis at Ephesus (550 B.C.).

The Statue of Zeus at Olympia (by Pheidias, *c*. 435 B.C.).

The Colossus of Rhodes (by Chares, *c*. 300 B.C.).

The Pharos (lighthouse) of Alexandria (architect Sostratos, *c*. 280 B.C.).

The Mausoleum (tomb of Mausolus) at Halicarnassus (*c*. 353 B.C.).

A relief from the tomb of Mausolus shows a battle between Greeks and Amazons.

230 Sujin, first known ruler of Japan.

265 China reunited under W. Chíin dynasty.

320–35 Gupta dynasty in India.

484 White Huns dominate N. India.

AFRICA

149–46 B.C. Romans destroy Carthage.

A.D. 100–300 Aksumite hegemony. Occupation of Yemen.

***c*. 350** Christianity reaches Ethiopia.

429–535 Vandal kingdom in N. Africa.

THE AMERICAS

300 B.C. – A.D. 50 Murals indicate wealth and social structure established in Central American communities.

100 B.C. Teotihuacán begins its growth in Mexico.

***c*. 250** Maya Classic period begins.

A.D. 100–200 Pyramid of the Sun.

EUROPE

507 Franks under Clovis conquer Visigoths in southern France.

534 Franks conquer Burgundy.

535–54 Byzantine forces under Belisarius

PRINCIPAL EMPERORS OF ROME

27 B.C. – A.D. 14	Augustus	284–305	Diocletian (East)
14–37	Tiberius	286–305	Maximian (West)
37–41	Caligula	305–306	Constantius I
41–54	Claudius	306–337	Constantine I
54–68	Nero	337–340	Constantine II
69–79	Vespasian	337–350	Constans
79–81	Titus	337–361	Constantius II
81–96	Domitian	361–363	Julian
96–98	Nerva	364–375	Valentinian I (West)
98–117	Trajan	364–378	Valens (East)
117–138	Hadrian	375–383	Gratian (West)
138–161	Antoninus Pius	379–395	Theodosius I
161–169	Lucius Verus	395–408	Arcadius (East)
169–180	Marcus Aurelius	395–423	Honorius (West)
180–192	Commodus	408–450	Theodosius II (East)
193–211	Septimius Severus	410–421	Constantius III (West)
211–217	Caracalla	425–455	Valentinian III (West)
218–222	Elagabalus	475–476	Romulus Augustulus (West)
222–235	Severus Alexander		

	100	200	300	400	A.D. 500
	Pauline version of Christianity	Buddhism reaches China	Nicene Creed adopted at first Council of Christian Church	Saint Patrick's conversion of Ireland	
	China: paper invented	Hadrian's Wall — Ptolemy's geography and astronomy	Abacus in use in China — N. Europe: clinker-built boats developed		
		Tacitus writes *Histories*		Saint Augustine writes his *Confessions*	
	Rome: arch of Titus	Rome: Trajan's column	Palace of Diocletian at Split (Croatia)	Rome: old church of St. Peter	

500–999

conquer most of Italy.

554 Byzantine armies conquer S.E. Spain.

562 Avar Khanate in Hungary.

568 Lombardy founded by Alcuin.

597 Augustine brings Christianity to Anglo-Saxons.

648 Arabs conquer Cyprus.

675 Bulgars settle south of Danube.

687 Thuringia in Germany becomes part of Frankish kingdom.

711 Moors invade Spain.

732 Frankish ruler Charles Martel halts Moors at Poitiers.

756 Umayyad emirate at Cordoba, Spain. Papal States formed in Italy.

759 Moors defeated at Narbonne.

771 Charlemagne becomes sole king of Franks (*opposite*).

788 Charlemagne annexes Bavaria.

790s Viking raids in Britain and Ireland.

800 Charlemagne crowned Holy Roman Emperor.

826–27 Arabs conquer Crete and Sicily.

c. 835 Major Viking raids in England.

838 Arabs settle in southern Italy.

843 Frankish Empire divided up under the Treaty of Verdun.

c. 850 Swedish Vikings (Varangians) in Russia.

862 Varangian Rurik founds Novgorod.

866 Danes establish N. British kingdom.

869 Arabs capture Malta.

870 Bulgars adopt Eastern Orthodox religion.

874 Norse Vikings settle in Iceland.

878 Alfred (the Great) defeats Danes.

879 Pope and Constantinople patriarch excommunicate each other.

880 Byzantine emperor Basil recovers Italy from Arabs.

889 Magyars invade Hungarian plain.

900 Alfonso III of Castile begins reconquest from Moors.

906 Magyars begin invading Germany.

911 Franks grant Normandy to Viking Rollo (later baptized Robert).

950 Otto I, king of Germany, conquers Bohemia.

955 Battle of Lechfeld: Otto I ends westward advance of Magyars.

962 Pope John XII crowns Otto emperor in Rome.

966 Mieszko I first ruler of Poland.

987 Hugh Capet elected king of France.

988 Vladimir of Kiev introduces Eastern Orthodox religion.

997 Stephen I first king of Hungary.

BARBARIAN INVASIONS

Until the early 400s, the so-called folk wanderings across Europe of various Germanic peoples were held in check by the still-strong Roman frontier extending along the Rhine and Danube rivers. The floodgates, so to speak, opened in 406, when the Rhine frontier was breached: by 410 Rome had been sacked. During the centuries that followed, Germanic tribes gradually occupied the territories of the Western Roman Empire. In Britain, the Germanic takeover was comparatively slow in the face of opposition from shrinking Celtic kingdoms. In Gaul, the Frankish invasion of 486 resulted in a large kingdom under Clovis, the first important Germanic ruler to adopt Christianity. The Vandals briefly carved out territory in N. Africa, and later became pirates. For a while the armies of the Byzantine (Eastern Roman) Empire, under their brilliant commander Belisarius, managed to contain the Lombards and Ostrogoths in southern Italy and fought inconclusively with the Visigoths in Spain. Eventually, the Roman Empire in the west was lost, but in the east it was to continue for almost 1,000 years, when its capital of Constantinople was finally taken by the Ottoman Turks.

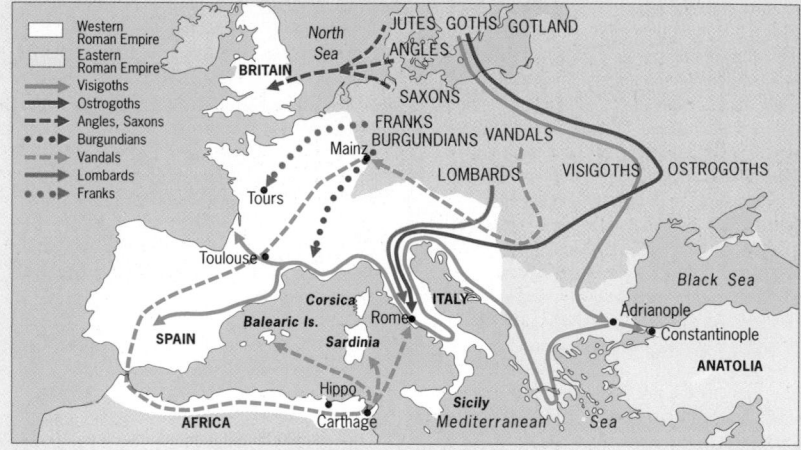

The map shows the principal incursions by "Barbarian peoples" into the Roman Empire.

MIDDLE EAST

524–32 War between Byzantine Empire and Persians.

529 Justinian issues Code of Civil Laws.

570 Muhammad, founder of Islam, born in Mecca (*p. 218*).

572–628 Persians dominate Arabia.

622 The Hegira, Muhammad's flight from Mecca to Medina.

632 Death of Muhammad; father-in-law, Abu Bakr, elected caliph (successor).

634 Omar I, second caliph: Islamic holy war against Persians.

635–42 Omar conquers Syria, Palestine, Persia, and Egypt.

655 Arabs defeat Byzantine fleet.

661–750 Umayyad dynasty in Islam.

673–78 Arabs besiege Constantinople.

685–705 Caliph Abdalmalik unifies Arab Empire; gains control of N. Africa.

691 Dome of the Rock completed in Jerusalem.

716–17 Arabs besiege Constantinople.

750 Abbasids overthrow Umayyads and seize caliphate with capital at Baghdad.

969 Fatimids of Tunisia conquer Egypt.

ASIA

534–50 Eastern Wei dynasty in China.

535 Gupta Empire in India collapses.

550–77 Northern Ch'i dynasty in China.

552 Buddhism introduced into Japan.

562 Japanese power ends in Korea.

589 China united under Sui dynasty.

605–10 Chinese build Grand Canal.

607–8 Great Wall of China rebuilt.

	500	550	600	650	700
RELIGION AND PHILOSOPHY	St. Benedict establishes Monte Cassino monastery	Buddhism introduced into Japan	Muhammad receives call to proclaim Allah	Babylonian Jewish Talmud finalized	Islam reaches India (Spain 715)
SCIENCE AND TECHNOLOGY	Silk production begins in Byzantium		Windmills in use in Persia		Swords developed in Burgundy
LITERATURE AND MUSIC	Boethius translates Aristotelian logic	Harps with twelve strings developed in Europe		Koran is written · Caedmon first English poet	Venerable Bede writes *History*
ART AND ARCHITECTURE		Hagia Sophia cathedral in Constantinople built	Great chalice of Antioch made	Sutton Hoo burial ship	Dome of the Rock built in Jerusalem

THE CELTS

The Celtic peoples, who introduced Europe to the use of iron during the brilliant La Tène period of their culture (c. 500 B.C. – c. A.D. 100), combined technological enterprise with spiritual and artistic sophistication. During their pre-Christian phase, when the Druids exercised both priestly and royal functions, they had no written language. By the time they adopted Christianity, during the 400s and 500s, the Celts principally inhabited Brittany and the British Isles.

A celtic bull's-head cauldron handle.

618–907 Tang dynasty in China.
645 Taika edict of reform in Japan
663 Japanese withdraw from Korea.
668 Korea reunited under kingdom of Silla (to 935).
710 Nara becomes capital of Japan.
712 Muslims establish new state in Sind.
425–1018 Gurjara-Pratihara dynasty in N. India.
751 Arabs defeat Chinese at Samarkand.
c. **802** Khmer dynasty at Cambodia.
907 End of Chinese Tang dynasty followed by civil war (to 960). Mongols begin to take Inner Mongolia and parts of N. China (completed 1126).
935–1392 Koryo period in Korea.
939 Civil wars in Japan.
960–1279 Sung dynasty in China.
998 Mahmud of Ghazni founds empire in N. India and E. Afghanistan (to 1030).

AFRICA

534 Byzantines under Belisarius conquer Vandal kingdom of N. Africa.
c. **569** Nubian kingdom of Makuria (Sudan) converted to Christianity.
641 Arabs begin conquest of N. Africa.
c. **690** State of Gao founded near Niger.
c. **700** Bantu cross Limpopo River.
700 Arabs capture Tunis.
702 Arabs occupy Ethiopian ports.
707 Muslims capture Tangier.
c. **800s** Trans-Sahara trade between W. and N. Africa.

CHARLEMAGNE

Charlemagne inherited the Frankish kingdom in 771 and within 30 years had conquered an empire stretching from Poland to the Pyrenees. The Lombards succumbed quickly (773–74), but the Saxons were beaten only after many years of ruthless attacks. An invasion of Muslim Spain in 778 was unsuccessful. Bavaria fell in 788 and thereafter the rich empire of the Avars. On Christmas Day in 800, Charlemagne was crowned "Holy Roman Emperor" in Rome, a conscious revival of the old Roman Empire. Scholars from all over Christian Europe were attracted to his court at Aachen (Aix-la-Chapelle). On his death in 814, the empire passed to his only surviving son, but with no law of primogeniture, it was later partitioned among his three grandsons.

The coronation of Charlemagne depicted on the sarcophagus in Aachen Cathedral.

c. **900** Hausa kingdom of Daura founded in N. Nigeria.
909 Fatimid dynasty proclaimed in Tunisia (to 1171).
920–1050 Golden age of Ghana Empire.
c. **980** Arab seafarers trade along coast of eastern Africa.

THE AMERICAS

c. **600–1000** Rise of Aymara Indians in Bolivia.
c. **700s** Temple Mound culture in North America.

ARAB EXPANSION

Muhammad's flight from Mecca to Medina in 622 marked the foundation of Islam. After his death in 632, the newly united tribes of Arabia established a huge empire in the Middle East and the Mediterranean region. They took Damascus, which became the first seat of the caliphate, in 636, and Jerusalem two years later. Mesopotamia and Persia were overrun and the Sassanid dynasty toppled in 642. The Byzantine Empire lost its wheat-growing provinces, though the city itself withstood an Arab siege in 673–78, and Europe was cut off from the east. Egypt was wrested from the Byzantines in 640, and the whole of North Africa eventually fell to Arabs. Sicily was overrun during the 800s, and

The interior of the mosque at Cordoba was erected by the Umayyad emirate.

N. African Berbers overthrew the Visigothic kings in Spain in 711. The emirate of Cordoba was founded by an Umayyad exile in 756.

c. **950** Yucatan invaded by Toltecs.
c. **985** Viking explorer Eric the Red leads expedition to land he names Greenland.

AUSTRALIA AND OCEANIA

c. **950** Polynesian peoples start to settle North Island of New Zealand.

	750	800	850	900	950	999
	Buddhism state religion in Japan	Development of Sufi mysticism in Islam				
	Gunpowder invented in China	Printing with blocks developed in Japan		Cotton and silk manufacture introduced into Spain	Alembics, distilling instruments, developed in Arabia	
	Anglo-Saxon epic *Beowulf* written			Anglo-Saxon *Chronicle* begun by Alfred the Great		
		Great mosque at Cordoba	Java: great stupa of Borobudur	Samarra: spiral minaret of Malwiyya Mosque	Imperial academy of painting in China	

1000–99

THE VIKINGS

The Norse seafarers who plundered Europe in the 800s and 900s were pirate-traders who delivered furs, timber, and slaves (chiefly Slavs, hence the word "slave") to Byzantium in exchange for gold. Their routes ran through Russia and as far south as Seville and Pisa. Where they settled, as in parts of England and northern France, they demanded tribute, or Danegeld.

793 Sacking of Lindisfarne begins European raids.

***c.* 850–62** Vikings found Kiev and Novgorod.

***c.* 850–75** Vikings discover Iceland and begin to colonize Shetlands and Orkneys.

878 Danish rule in N. and E. England (Danelaw) accepted by King Alfred.

911 Charles III of France cedes northwestern lands to Norse leader Rollo.

980 Vladimir unites Kiev and Novgorod princedoms to form Kievan Rus.

***c.* 1000** Vikings reach North America.

1014 Brian Boru ends Viking threat to Ireland.

1016 Canute assumes the throne of England.

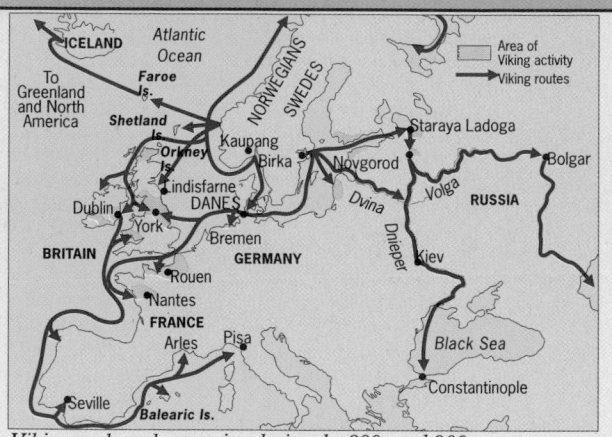

Viking trade and expansion during the 800s and 900s.

EUROPE

1000 Battle of Svolder: Sweyn Forkbeard of Denmark kills Olaf of Norway; Norway becomes Danish.

1013 Sweyn invades England and overthrows Ethelred II, who flees.

1014 English recall Ethelred II as king on death of Sweyn.

1015 Sweyn's son, Canute, king of Denmark, invades England; war between Saxons and Danes.

1016 Canute becomes king of England; he divides England into four earldoms: Wessex, Mercia, East Anglia, and Northumbria.

1028 Canute conquers Norway.

1032 Kingdom of Burgundy absorbed into German Empire.

1035 Danish Empire splits on death of Canute; his illegitimate son, Harold Harefoot, rules England as Harold I; Harthacanute becomes king of Denmark. William, illegitimate son of Robert, becomes duke of Normandy.

1040 Macbeth kills Duncan in battle at Elgin; Macbeth becomes king of Scots.

1042 Edward the Confessor, son of Ethelred II, becomes king of England; real power in hands of Earl Godwin of Wessex and his sons.

1051 Earl Godwin exiled for opposing king (to 1052); returns with fleet and wins back power.

1052 Edward the Confessor founds Westminster Abbey, London.

1053 Death of Godwin; his son, Harold, succeeds him as Earl of Wessex.

1057 Battle of Lumphanan: Malcolm Canmore defeats and kills Macbeth.

1058 Malcolm becomes king of Scots. Boleslaw the Bold becomes king of Poland; conquers Upper Slovakia.

1060–61 Norman leader, Robert Guiscard, conquers extreme south of Italy and N.E. corner of Sicily.

1063 Harold and his brother Tostig (earl of Northumbria) subdue Wales.

1064 Harold shipwrecked in Normandy; swears solemn oath to support William of Normandy's claim to English throne.

1065 Northumbria rebels against Tostig.

1066 Harold of Wessex succeeds Edward the Confessor as king of England. Tostig joins forces with Harold Hardrada of

RULERS OF ENGLAND AND GREAT BRITAIN

England							
802–39	Egbert	1016–35	Canute	1327–77	Edward III	1660–85	Charles II
839–58	Ethelwulf	1035–40	Harold I Harefoot	1377–99	Richard II	1685–88	James II
858–60	Ethelbald	1040–42	Harthacanute	1399–1413	Henry IV	1689–94	Mary II (jointly)
860–65	Ethelbert	1042–66	Edward the	1413–22	Henry V	1689–1702	Wiliam III (jointly)
866–71	Ethelred I		Confessor	1422–61	Henry VI	**Great Britain**	
871–99	Alfred the Great	1066	Harold II	1461–83	Edward IV	1702–14	Anne
899–924	Edward the Elder	1066–87	William I, the	1483	Edward V	1714–27	George I
924–39	Athelstan		Conqueror	1483–85	Richard III	1727–60	George II
939–46	Edmund	1087–1100	William II	1485–1509	Henry VII	1760–1820	George III
946–55	Edred	1100–35	Henry I	1509–47	Henry VIII	1820–30	George IV
955–59	Edwy	1135–54	Stephen	1547–53	Edward VI	1830–37	William IV
959–75	Edgar	1154–89	Henry II	1553–58	Mary I	1837–1901	Victoria
975–78	Edward the Martyr	1189–99	Richard I	1558–1603	Elizabeth I	1901–10	Edward VII
978–1016	Ethelred II, the	1199–1216	John	1603–25	James I	1910–36	George V
	Unready	1216–72	Henry III	1625–49	Charles I	1936	Edward VIII
1016	Edmund Ironside	1272–1307	Edward I	1649–58	Oliver Cromwell	1936–52	George VI
		1307–27	Edward II	1658–59	Richard Cromwell	1952–	Elizabeth II

		1000	1010	1020	1030	1040
	RELIGION AND PHILOSOPHY		Islam: Avicenna writes *The Book of Healing*	Council of Pavia forbids clerical marriage	Buddhism established in Tibet	
	SCIENCE AND TECHNOLOGY	Islam: Al-Biruni analyzes structure of flowers		Islam: Alhazen writes *Optical Thesaurus*	Botanical texts published in China	China: movable type invented
	LITERATURE AND MUSIC	Japanese novel *The Tale of Genji*		Guido d'Arezzo invents music notation	Sung period in Chinese literature	Ou Yang Hsiu writes Confucian history
	ART AND ARCHITECTURE	Mexico: Chichen Itza		India: temple of Shiva at Tanjore		

Norway to invade England: Harold defeats them both at Stamford Bridge. Battle of Hastings: William of Normandy invades England, defeats and kills Harold, and is crowned king.

1069 William subdues north of England.

1070 Hereward the Wake begins Saxon revolt in eastern England.

1072 William invades Scotland; receives submission of Hereward the Wake. Malcolm invades Northumbria.

1075 Dispute between Holy Roman Emperor Henry IV and Pope Gregory VII as to who appoints bishops.

1076 Pope dethrones and excommunicates emperor.

1077 Emperor Henry IV does penance to Pope Gregory at Canossa.

1080 Henry IV again excommunicated and deposed by Gregory.

1083 Henry IV attacks Rome.

1084 Robert Guiscard, Duke of Apulia, forces Henry IV to retreat to Germany.

1085 Alfonso captures Toledo in Spain from Moors.

1086 Almoravids come to aid of Moors and defeat Christians at az-Zallaqah.

1086 Domesday Book completed; feudal system established in England (*above right*).

1092 Almoravids impose their rule on most of Muslim part of Spain.

1093 Death of Malcolm III of Scotland. Brother, Donald Bane, becomes king.

1094 El Cid (Rodrigo Díaz de Vivar), Spanish national hero, takes Valencia.

1096 First Crusade begins (*p. 328*).

1097 Malcolm's second son, Edgar, king of Scotland after defeat of Donald Bane.

MIDDLE EAST

1017 In Egypt, Caliph al-Hakim declares himself divine and founds Druze sect.

1055 Seljuk Turks take Baghdad.

1071 Seljuks defeat Byzantines at Manzikert and take control of Asia Minor.

1075 Seljuk leader, Malik Shah, conquers Syria and Palestine.

1090 Hasan ibn Sabbah founds Assassin sect in Persia.

1096–99 First Crusade (*p. 328*).

ASIA

c. 1000–1100 Fujiwara hold power in Japan; development of samurai class.

1017 Cholas of S. India invade Ceylon (Sri Lanka).

1018 Mahmud of Ghazni pillages sacred

EUROPEAN FEUDALISM

Feudalism, the name for the military and social system that prevailed in most of Europe in the Early Middle Ages, had its source in the king's need to be supplied with armored knights for battle. Horses and armor were expensive, and in return for them the king granted landed estates (fiefs or feuds) to the great of the land. The king vowed to defend his vassals and they swore allegiance to him. They also parceled out their lands to lesser vassals under the same terms. Feudalism enshrined the notion of mutual rights and obligations between lord and tenant, although the indentured serfs or villeins, who worked the land, were excluded.

A feudal community was often defended by its lord, living in a nearby keep or castle.

city of Muttra, India.

1021 Chola empire of S. India reaches maximum extent with Bengal.

1068–85 Shen Tsung, emperor of China: his minister, Wang Anshi, carries through radical reforms.

AFRICA

c. 1000 Kingdom of Ghana reaches height of power (*below*). Founding of Kanem Empire in northern Nigeria.

c. 1040s Tokolor of Senegal first people south of Sahara to adopt Islam.

1048 Zirids of Tunisia revert to orthodox (Sunni) Islam, repudiating suzerainty of caliphs of Cairo.

1054–1150 Almoravids (fundamentalist

Berber Muslim sect) control Morocco.

1052 Zirids of Tunisia forced to abandon interior to Bedouin tribes.

1058 Abdallah ben Yassim begins Arab conquest of W. Africa.

1062 Yusuf ben Tashfin, leader of Almoravids, founds city of Marrakesh, Morocco.

1076–c. 1090s Almoravids occupy Ghana (to 1087).

THE AMERICAS

c. 1000 Arawak culture in Caribbean destroyed by Caribs from S. America. Chimú state formed in Peru (to 1476).

c. 1003 Viking Leif Ericsson journeys down North American coast.

EARLY AFRICAN KINGDOMS

The first African kingdom to enter the Iron Age was Kush, whose heyday lasted from the 600s B.C. until its conquest by Axum in the mid-A.D. 300s Ghana, the greatest early medieval kingdom of sub-Saharan Africa, rose to prominence in the 700s on profits gained from the trade in slaves, salt, and gold. Ghana's wealth provoked invasion by Almoravid Berbers in the 1000s and, later, by a people from Takrur (now Senegal), whose attacks in 1230 marked the collapse of the kingdom.

Early African states ranged from Kush in Sudan to Songhai in W. Africa.

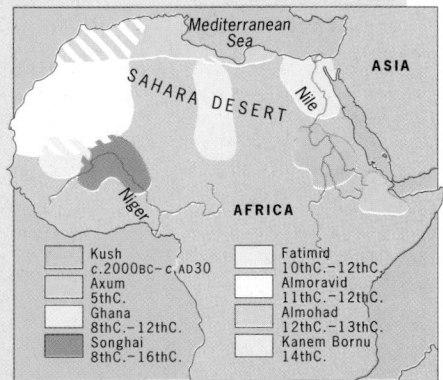

Kush c.2000BC–c.AD30	Fatimid 10thC.–12thC.	
Axum 5thC.	Almoravid 11thC.–12thC.	
Ghana 8thC.–12thC.	Almohad 12thC.–13thC.	
Songhai 8thC.–16thC.	Kanem Bornu 14thC.	

1050	1060	1070	1080	1090	1099
	Schism between Greek church and papacy		*Dictatus Papae* allows popes to depose emperors		
			China: magnetic compass	Chinese medical texts written	
		Omar Khayyam writes *The Rubaiyat*	Troubadours set poems to music	*Chanson de Roland* composed	
Japan: Byodo-in Temple example of Fujiwara culture		France: Romanesque architecture	France: Bayeux tapestry		

The medieval Christian Church

By the end of the 900s most of Europe had adopted Christianity. In place of a disintegrated empire there arose the idea of a Christian world united by faith, a universal Christendom. To be a member of society was to be a Christian; not to be a Christian was to be outside society, a pagan or a heretic, deserving of death at the hands of the Inquisition. At the apex of this Christian social order was the papacy; then came the bishops, abbots, and monks. But increasingly, all encompassing Christendom was challenged by the power of the Holy Roman emperors and by the dawning notion of the national monarchy.

> "... those who were drawn into the monastic movement ... discerning little hope of improvement through human agencies ... withdrew from the darkness and turmoil around them into the tranquil light of the Christian paradise."
>
> H. A. L. Fisher,
> *A History of Europe*

In this medieval painting, nuns in a convent refectory are listening to readings from the scriptures.

Monasticism

Monasticism, which began in the deserts of Egypt in the 200s, was the highest expression of holiness in medieval Europe. Its greatest early figure was St. Benedict, the 6th-century Italian founder of the monastic rule that came to be the model for Western monasticism. The early monks lived in independent, self-governing houses, cut off from the world. The devotional life, away from the cares of the temporal world, was enshrined in self-denying vows, like those of chastity and poverty, and the austere rules that governed the hourly activities of a monk.

Later orders, such as the Dominicans, Franciscans, Carmelites, and Augustinians, allowed their mendicant friars to travel outside the cloistered walls of the monastery. In the "Dark Ages" that fell upon Europe after the decline of Rome and the Arab conquest of much of the Mediterranean world, Europe became a poor backwater, surviving on a subsistence agriculture; and the self-sufficient monastic cell, with its economy of corn, wine, and oil, spread the arts of agriculture and carried the seeds of economic and intellectual regeneration.

LEADING CHRISTIAN RELIGIOUS ORDERS		
Popular Name	**Founder**	**Date**
Monastic	St. Pachomius	300s
Brotherhood	Basil, Theodore, and Athanasios	1000s
Benedictines	St. Benedict	529
Carthusians	St. Bruno	1084
Cistercians	St. Robert of Molesme	1098
Augustinian Canons	St. Augustine	1100s
Carmelites	St. Berthold	1100s
Franciscans	St. Francis of Assisi	1209
Dominicans	St. Dominic	1215
Jesuits	St. Ignatius Loyola	1534
Capuchins	Friar Matteo di Bassi	1529
Ursulines	St. Angela Merici	1535
Sisters of Charity	Sts. Vincent de Paul and Louise de Marillac	1633

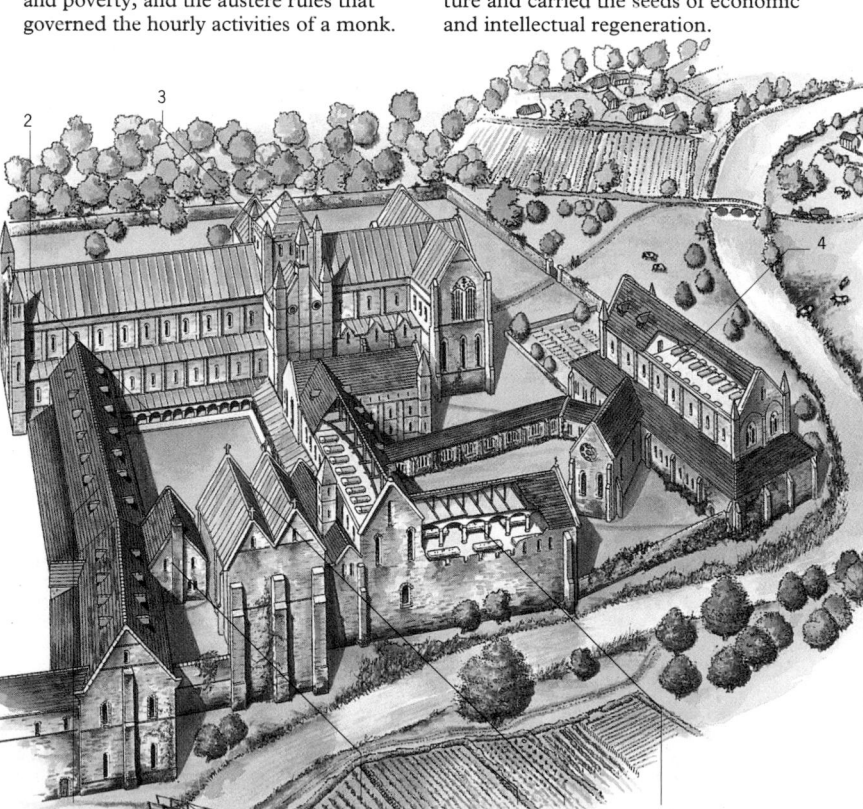

A Cistercian abbey in the early Middle Ages. The Cistercians (who took their name from Cîteaux in France) built abbeys in the countryside or on wasteland, where they could grow crops and keep livestock.

1. Lay brothers' refectory and dormitory
2. Cloisters
3. Abbey church
4. Infirmary
5. Monks' refectory
6. Monks' dormitory
7. Kitchen garden
8. Abbot's house

Timetable

c. 410 Monasteries founded at Marseilles and Lerins.

c. 413–26 St. Augustine writes *The City of God*.

451 Council of Chalcedon defines Christ as having both human and divine natures in one person.

496 Clovis, king of the Franks, converted to Christianity.

c. 529 St. Benedict founds monastery at Cassino and formulates his rule.

597 Augustine, first archbishop of Canterbury, begins conversion of England.

664 Synod of Whitby accepts Roman authority in English Church.

c. 718 Christian kingdom established in the Asturias.

726 Imperial edict banning worship of images widens gulf between eastern and western Churches.

909 Burgundian abbey founded at Cluny.

c. 987 Vladimir of Kievan Rus baptized into the eastern Church.

c. 1000 Sweden, Bohemia, Hungary, and Poland become Christian states.

1054 Schism between eastern and western Churches sealed when Pope Leo IX excommunicates the eastern patriarch for "unorthodox" practices.

1075 Papacy bans lay investiture of bishops and abbots (*right*).

1076 Investiture controversy flares up: Emperor Henry IV and German bishops defy Pope Gregory VII and are excommunicated.

1077 Henry IV makes peace with the papacy at Canossa.

1084 Carthusian order founded by Bruno at the Grande Chartreuse.

1098 Cistercian order founded at Cîteaux, near Dijon, by Robert of Molesme.

1115 Second Cistercian house founded by St. Bernard at Clairvaux.

1122 Concordat of Worms settles investiture controversy.

1147 Alfonso Henriques drives Islamic Moors from Lisbon.

1208–29 Dominicans lead Albigensian Crusade against Cathar heretics of southern France.

1216 Papacy gives approval to Order of Dominicans.

1232 Gregory IX establishes Inquisition at Toulouse.

1302 Pope Boniface VIII defines papal power in bull, *Unam Sanctam*.

1309–77 Papacy enters its "Babylonian Captivity" as French popes make Avignon their seat of residence.

1378 Great Schism in western Church begins.

1382 English reformer John Wycliffe has writings condemned.

1414–17 Council of Constance ends papal schism.

1415 Bohemian reformer, John Huss, burned at stake.

1479 Spanish Inquisition established to rout out Jewish and Muslim minorities.

Empire and papacy: the investiture controversy

A long-brewing quarrel between the Holy Roman Empire (Germany, Burgundy, and Italy) and the papacy came to a head in the late 1000s. In 1075, Pope Gregory VII issued a ban on the investiture, or nomination, of bishops and abbots to appointments in the Church by secular, or lay, rulers. The ban was resisted by the Holy Roman emperor, Henry IV, who was supported by the bishops of Germany. A synod of the German clergy "deposed" the pope in 1076; Gregory's answer was to excommunicate Henry and to release the subjects of the empire from obedience to him. In the next year, Henry pleaded for forgiveness and was absolved. Peace, however, was short-lived. In 1080, Henry was again excommunicated, and in 1084 his army occupied Rome and drove Gregory into exile, replacing him with the antipope, Clement VII. The investiture quarrel itself was brought to an end by the Concordat of Worms in 1122; but the general contest between a spiritual head and a temporal head for ascendancy in Christendom continued until the Reformation (*p. 338*).

Pope Gregory VII: a detail from a painting in the Vatican Palace.

Pilgrims

Believers who make pilgrimages to a religious shrine have been a feature of many cultures. In medieval times, Christians from all over Europe were willing to travel for months and even years to visit the places in Palestine associated with Jesus Christ. Other Christian pilgrimage centers included Santiago de Compostela in Spain, where the body of St. James was buried, and Rome, where saints Peter and Paul had lived and died. To journey to these sites, European pilgrims were willing to put up with almost any degree of hardship and danger.

A medieval manuscript depicts pilgrims giving alms to the poor (right).

Pilgrimage routes in medieval Europe; many led to Santiago de Compostela in Spain (below).

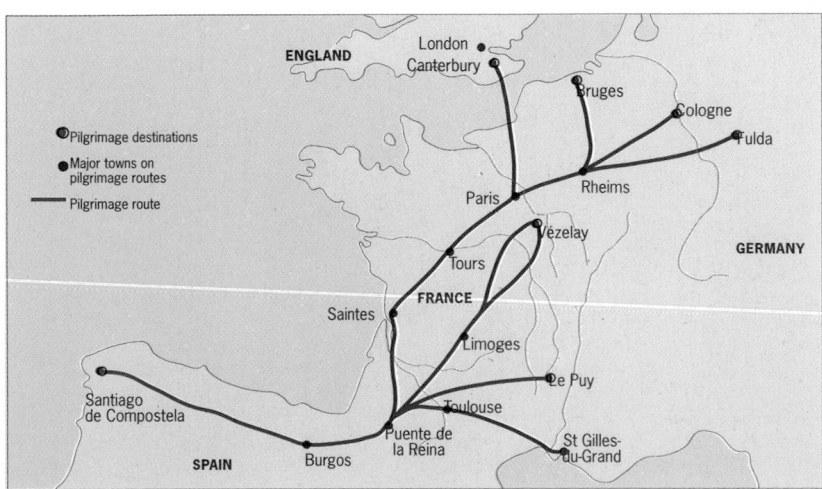

1100–99

EUROPE

1106 Henry I of England defeats his brother Robert, duke of Normandy, at Tinchebrai: Robert captive for life.

1109–13 War between England and France.

1111 Holy Roman Emperor Henry V forces Pope Paschal II to acknowledge power of emperor.

1114 Matilda (Maud), daughter of King Henry I of England, marries Emperor Henry V.

1115 St. Bernard founds Abbey of Clairvaux, France.

1120 William, heir of Henry I of England, drowns in the *White Ship*.

1122 Concordat of Worms: conference of German princes ends dispute between pope and emperor over appoinment of bishops.

1128 Empress Matilda, widow of Emperor Henry V, marries Geoffrey, count of Anjou, nicknamed "Plantagenet."

1135 Stephen of Blois seizes English crown on death of Henry I; civil war breaks out.

1138 Battle of the Standard: defeat of David I of Scotland, fighting on behalf of Matilda in English civil war.

1139 Matilda lands in England from France. Division of Russian state into independent principalities.

1140 Power of Doge of Venice is transferred to a Great Council.

1141 Battle of Lincoln: Matilda captures Stephen and reigns as queen; she is driven out by popular rising, and Stephen is restored as king.

1143 Alfonso Henriques, count of Portugal, becomes king of Portugal (to 1185) and makes Portugal independent of Spain.

1146–72 Almohades conquer Moorish Spain.

c. **1150–1200** Rise of city-states in northern Italy (*p. 336*).

1152 Marriage of Louis VII and Eleanor of Aquitaine annulled on grounds of blood relationship; Eleanor marries Henry of Anjou, son of Matilda, allying Aquitaine to his lands of Anjou and Normandy.

1153 Henry of Anjou invades England

and forces Stephen to make him heir to English throne.

1154 Henry of Anjou becomes King Henry II (to 1189); also rules more than half of France.

1155 Pope Adrian IV grants Henry II right to rule Ireland.

1158 Bologna University founded (*opposite*).

1159 Henry II demands scutage, payment in cash instead of military service.

1162 Thomas à Becket appointed archbishop of Canterbury; quarrels with Henry II over Church's rights.

1170 Becket murdered by four knights at Canterbury. Normans from England invade Ireland under command of Strongbow.

1171 Henry II defeats Strongbow and annexes Ireland.

1173 Rebellion of Henry's eldest sons, Henry, Richard, and Geoffrey, supported by mother, Eleanor of Aquitaine.

1174 Coast of Finland settled by Swedes.

1182 French monarch Philippe II banishes Jews from France.

1190 Holy Roman emperor, Frederick

THE CRUSADES

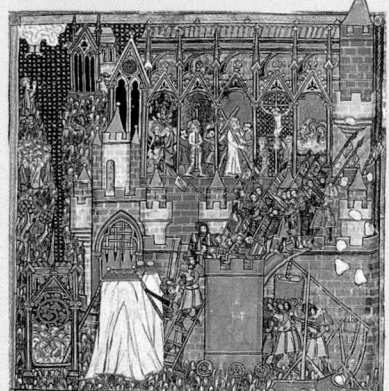

A mid-1300s depiction of Crusaders capturing Jerusalem during the First Crusade.

In 1095, Pope Urban II called for a "holy war" to recover the Holy Land from the Muslims. The First Crusade regained Jerusalem, Antioch, Tripoli, and Edessa, but success was short-lived. Eight crusades and 200 years later, the Holy Land remained in Arab hands.

1096–99 First Crusade: Frankish army recapture Jerusalem.

1147–49 Second Crusade: preached by Bernard of Clairvaux; ends in failure.

1189–92 Third Crusade: led by Richard I of England, Philippe II of France, and Emperor Frederick I; ends in temporary truce.

1202–4 Fourth Crusade: fiasco in which Venetian Crusaders ransack Christian center of Constantinople.

1212 Children's Crusade: thousands of children, led by a mystic French peasant boy, die or are sold into slavery before they ever reach Palestine.

1217–22 Fifth Crusade: Crusaders' attempt to conquer Egypt fails.

1228–29 Sixth Crusade: Emperor Frederick Barbarossa secures truce and surrender of holy places.

1248–54 Seventh Crusade: Louis IX (St. Louis) of France fails to take Egypt.

1270 Eighth Crusade: cut short by the death of Louis IX.

1270–72 Ninth Crusade: led by future Edward I of England; limited success with negotiated truce.

CHIVALRY

By the 1400s, jousting contests had replaced tournaments as popular social events.

Chivalry, a knight's code of behavior, was a fusion of Christian and military ideals that evolved during the 1100s and 1200s. According to the code, the ideal knight was pious, honorable, brave, and loyal. Away from the battlefield, the code of chivalry was extended to participation in tournaments (in which large numbers of knights fought each other), or jousts (a combat between two knights). By the 1400s, jousting had given way to tilting in tournaments—at which two knights charged each other equipped with a blunted lance.

		1100	1110	1120	1130	1140
	RELIGION AND PHILOSOPHY			Theologian Peter Abelard condemned		Bernard of Clairvaux opposes rational scholasticism
	SCIENCE AND TECHNOLOGY	Chinese invent multicolor printing		Italy: alcohol distilled from wine		
	LITERATURE AND MUSIC			Hindi epic *Prithyi Rah Raso*	Three- and four-part polyphony begins	
	ART AND ARCHITECTURE	Stained-glass windows in Europe		Li Chieh writes treatise on Sung architecture		Mature Gothic style at St. Denis Cathedral, France

Barbarossa, drowned in Turkey on way to join Third Crusade in Palestine.

1192 Richard I of England captured by enemy Duke Leopold of Austria; Leopold hands Richard over to Emperor Henry VI, who demands ransom.

1194 Emperor Henry VI conquers Sicily. Richard I ransomed and returns to England.

1197 Civil war follows death of Henry VI in Germany.

1198 Bohemia becomes a kingdom.

MIDDLE EAST

1113 Founding of Order of Knights of St. John in Jerusalem formally acknowledged by papacy.

1119 Hugues de Payens founds Order of Knights Templar.

1147–49 The Second Crusade.

1167 Almaric, king of Jerusalem, captures Cairo.

1168 Arabs recapture Cairo.

1169 Saladin (Salah al-Din Yusuf ibn-Ayyub) becomes vizier of Egypt (to 1193); sultan from 1174.

1174 Saladin conquers Syria.

1177 Baldwin IV of Jerusalem defeats Saladin at Mont Gisard.

1179 Saladin besieges Tyre; truce agreed between Baldwin IV and Saladin.

1187 Saladin captures Jerusalem.

1189–92 Third Crusade.

1193 Saladin dies and is succeeded by Al Aziz Imad al-Din (to 1198).

ASIA

1113 Work starts on temple of Angkor Wat, Cambodia.

1126 Sung dynasty loses control of northern China after invasion of Juchen horsemen.

1150 Temple at Angkor Wat completed by Suryavaraman II.

1156–85 Civil wars between rival clans in Japan.

1161 Battle of Ts'ai-shih: Chinese first use explosives in battle.

1185–1333 Kamakura period in Japan.

c. 1190 Mongol leader, Temujin, begins to create empire in eastern Asia.

1192 Minamoto Yoritomo establishes first shogunate of Japan, usurping power of the emperor (*below*).

1193 Muslims, under Muhammad of Ghur (Mu'izz-ud-din), capture Bihar and Bengal in India.

AFRICA

c. 1100s Growth of kingdom of Ife, a holy city in S.W. Nigeria.

c. 1130 Almohad dynasty, founded by preacher Ibn Tumart, begins rule of Morocco.

1147–1212 Almohad Empire under Abd-el-Mumin controls N. Africa from western Sahara to Egyptian borders.

1196–1464 Marimid dynasty in Morocco founded at Fez.

THE AMERICAS

c. 1150 Toltec Empire, Mexico, ends after being overrun by nomadic tribes.

1189 Last recorded Viking visit to North America.

c. 1191 Second era of Mayan civilization begins in Central America.

AUSTRALIA AND OCEANIA

c. 1100 Islands of the central Pacific colonized by Polynesians.

EUROPE'S FIRST UNIVERSITIES

A professor and his students at Bologna, in Italy, Europe's first university.

By the 1100s, monastic schools were no longer the centers of scholarship that they had been. Alongside the urban regeneration of Europe went an intellectual awakening, sometimes called the "12th-century renaissance," that spawned the foundation of Europe's first universities.

1158 Bologna	**1224** Naples
1200 Paris	**1254** Salamanca
1214 Oxford	**1347** Prague
1220 Montpellier	**1365** Vienna

MEDIEVAL JAPAN

During the Nara period, 710–94, Japan became an aristocratic culture under the emperor, with Buddhism a powerful force. The move of the capital to Heian (Kyoto) in 794 signified an attempt to strengthen imperial authority against Buddhist interference, but by 858 the powerful Fujiwara family had gained total dominance over the emperor. In the Heian period, 794–1185, Japan threw off Chinese influence, and new Buddhist sects, more Japanese in spirit, were founded. Aristocrats assembled vast estates with private armies; a warrior class, the samurai, emerged. A samurai family, the Taira, gained control of the government in 1160, but they were overthrown in 1185 by rivals, the Minamoto. The Minamoto established the first of the military governorships, or shogunates, which were to rule Japan until 1868. The Kamakura period, an age of spiritual revival, ended when the Ashikaga gained the shogunate in 1338.

One of the first samurai battles took place during civil war-torn Japan of the 1150s.

1150	1160	1170	1180	1190	1199
	Spain: Averroes writes on Aristotle		Neo-Confucianism emerges in China	Zen Buddhism in Japan	
	Jewish doctor Maimonides at Saladin's court	Cast iron first produced in Europe		Averroes school of scientific thought in Europe	Fibonacci writes first Western textbook on algebra
			Chretien de Troyes's prose romance *Conte del Graal*		
			Cambodia: Angkor Wat constructed		High Gothic style at Chartres Cathedral

1200–99

EUROPE'S EXPANDING TRADE

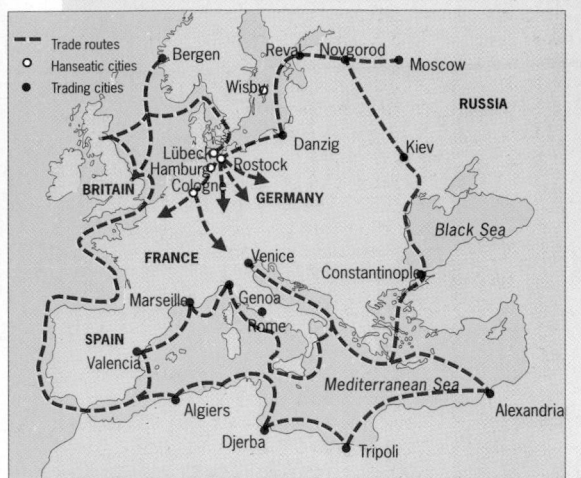

Trade routes
○ Hanseatic cities
● Trading cities

Major towns of the Hanseatic League, c. 1400.

The Hanseatic League was a confederation of German merchant guilds, or hanse, begun in *c.* 1241 to foster and protect international trade. The League—which was a symbol of Europe's economic revival from the "Dark Ages"—had a near-monopoly over the Baltic and North Sea trade routes. At its peak, in the mid-1300s, about 100 towns were League members. It then swiftly declined in the face of competition from the English and Dutch.

MERCHANT AND CRAFT GUILDS

Guilds, or professional associations of merchants and of craftsmen, emerged in Europe in the 1000s and proliferated during the "urban renaissance" of the next two centuries. Craft guilds regulated product standards, terms of sale, and labor conditions; the powerful guilds of rich merchant traders were in many places almost identical with town government.

The coats-of-arms of two medieval French guilds: the roofers (left) and the tailors.

EUROPE

1203–14 Philippe II of France seizes Normandy, Anjou, Maine, and Brittany from England.

1207 King John of England refuses to recognize appointment of Stephen Langton as archbishop of Canterbury by Pope Innocent III.

1209–28 Crusades against Albigensians, a heretical set from southern France.

1209 Innocent III excommunicates King John for attacks on Church property.

1210 Innocent III excommunicates Emperor Otto IV.

1212 Children's Crusade: 30,000 children from France and Germany set off for Palestine: thousands die of disease or are sold into slavery (*p. 328*). Venice conquers Crete. Christian kings defeat Almohades in Spain.

1213 King John makes peace with pope, making England and Ireland papal fiefs.

1215 Magna Carta: English barons force King John to agree to charter of rights for barons, clergy, and commoners.

1224–27 Anglo-French War.

1227 Germans defeat Danes at Bornhoued: Holstein ceded to German Empire.

1233 Teutonic Knights invade Prussia.

1236 Ferdinand III of Castile captures Córdoba from Moors.

1236–40 Volga Bulgars conquered by Mongols. Mongols conquer Russia.

1240 Battle of Neva: Alexander Nevski, prince of Novgorod, defeats Swedes. Mongols capture Moscow and Kiev.

1241 Mongols invade Poland, Hungary, and Austria; they withdraw from Europe following death of Ogedei Khan.

1241 Batu establishes Mongol khanate of Kipchak, known as "Golden Horde" (*opposite*). Alexander Nevski defeats Teutonic Knights on frozen Lake Peipus.

***c.* 1241** Hanseatic League formed in Germany (*above*).

1245 Synod of Lyon declares Emperor Frederick II deposed.

1247–50 War in Italy between Emperor Frederick II and papal allies.

1248 Moors lose Seville to Ferdinand of Castile.

1249 Moors expelled from Portugal.

1256–73 Interregnum in Holy Roman Empire: political anarchy in Germany.

1261 Byzantine emperor, Michael VIII Palaeologus, recovers Constantinople. Greenland conquered by Norway.

1262–64 Iceland comes under Norwegian rule.

1263 Haakon of Norway defeated by Scots; cedes Hebrides.

1264 Battle of Lewes: Simon de Montfort leader of rebel English barons captures Henry III.

1265 Henry III's son, Edward I, kills Simon de Montfort at Evesham.

1266 Norway cedes Isle of Man to Scotland. Charles of Anjou claims Sicilian crown after defeating Manfred at Benevento.

1268–71 Papacy vacant.

1277 Edward I of England embarks on conquest of Wales.

1278 Holy Roman emperor, Rudolf I, kills Ottakar of Bohemia at Marchfeld.

1282 "Sicilian Vespers": massacre of French in Sicily; Charles of Anjou overthrown.

1282 Edward I of England defeats and kills Llewellyn, prince of Wales; English conquest of Wales complete. Teutonic Order completes subjection of Prussia.

1290 Jews expelled from England.

1291 Pact of Rutli: three Swiss cantons declare independence from Hapsburg Empire.

1293 Sweden conquers Karelia.

1296 Edward I deposes John Balliol from Scottish throne; Scottish coronation throne moved from Scone to Westminster. Conflict between Philippe IV of France and Pope Boniface VIII over papal powers in France (to 1303).

1297 Battle of Cambuskenneth: Scottish patriot, William Wallace, defeats English. Geonese defeat Venetians at sea battle of Curzola.

1298 Edward I defeats Wallace at Falkirk. German barons depose Adolf of Nassau and elect Albert I (to 1308).

		1200	1210	1220	1230	1240
	RELIGION AND PHILOSOPHY		European universities		Franciscan and Dominican orders established	
	SCIENCE AND TECHNOLOGY	Europe: wheelbarrow in use		China develops shrapnel bombs		
	LITERATURE AND MUSIC	Icelandic *Edda* by Snorri Sturluson	German minnesinger tradition			
	ART AND ARCHITECTURE	Europe: many cathedrals built				

MIDDLE EAST
1202–4 Fourth Crusade (*p. 328*).
1217–22 Fifth Crusade (*p. 328*).
1218 Mongols (*below*) under Genghis Khan conquer Persia.
1228–29 Sixth Crusade (*p. 328*).
1243 Egyptians capture Jerusalem from Christians.
1248–70 Seventh and Eighth Crusades (*p. 328*): Saracens ransom Louis IX of France (St. Louis) at Mansourah, Egypt.
1258 Mongols capture Baghdad and end Abbasid caliphate.
1260 Mongols defeated by Mamluks of Egypt in Palestine.
1268 Mamluks take Antioch, held by the Christians.
1291 Mamluks capture Acre, last Crusader stronghold in Palestine.

ASIA
1200s Islam arrives in Sumatra; begins to spread through East Indies.
1206 Temujin proclaimed Genghis Khan (*below*). Dynasty of Islamic sultanate of Delhi in India, known as "slave dynasty" (to 1290).

1219 Hojo clan rules Japan (to 1333), following overthrow of Minamoto family.
c. 1220 Khmer rulers overthrown in Siam (Thailand); founding of first Thai kingdom.
1234 Mongols annex Chin Empire of N. China.
1260 Kublai, Mongol leader, elected khan by his army at Shan-tu, China; founds Yuan dynasty (to 1368).
1264 Kublai Khan moves China's capital to Khanbaliq (now Beijing).
1271–95 Venetian traveler Marco Polo travels widely in Kublai Khan's Mongol Empire.
1274 First Mongol invasion of Japan.
1281 Second Mongol invasion of Japan; Mongol fleet scattered by *kamikaze* ("divine wind").
1287 Mongols invade Burma (to 1301).
1290 Turkish leader, Firuz, founds Khalji dynasty (to 1320) in Delhi, India.
1293 First Christian missionaries in China.
1295–1307 Temur Oljaitu (Ch'eng Tsung) last effective ruler of Yuan dynasty.

AFRICA
c. 1200–1400 Great Zimbabwe Empire in S.E. Africa (*below*).
c. 1200 Christian kingdoms in Sudan conquered by Muslims.
1235–55 Suidiata, Keita King of Mali.
1236 Almohad Empire begins to disintegrate; Hafsids of Tunis declare independence.
1240 Empire of Ghana incorporated into kingdom of Mali (*p. 333*).
1280s Arabs trading with Zimbabwe discover Comoros and Madagascar.

THE AMERICAS
c. 1200–50 Foundation of Aztec Empire in Mexico (*p. 334*).
1200 Hunac Ceel revolts against Mayas of Chichén ltzá; sets up capital at Mayapán.
c. 1220 Manco Capac founds Inca ruling dynasty in Peru (*p. 334*).
c. 1250 Inca capital founded at Cuzco.

AUSTRALIA AND OCEANIA
c. 1200 Tahitians arrive in Hawaii and win control over earlier settlers.

THE MONGOL EMPIRE

The great Mongol nomad-warriors were among the most ruthless ever known. The invasion of China alone may have cost 30 million lives. The Mongols established one of the largest empires in history, with territory stretching from China in the east to Russia in the west. The empire broke up after the death of Timur in 1405, by which time the Mongols in China had been assimilated and lost their Mongol identity.
1213 Genghis Khan leads Mongol tribes over Great Wall of China.
1218 Having conquered most of China, Mongols sweep west in great arc through Turkestan, Persia, and S. Russia.
1236 Establishment of Mongol khanate of Golden Horde brings era of Kievan Rus to end.
1260 Kublai Khan completes conquest of China; Yuan dynasty founded.
1368 "Red Turbans" drive Mongols from Peking, and Ming era begins.
1384–1405 Timur (Tamerlane) extends Mongol rule briefly to Persia and even more briefly to Delhi (1398–99).

Timur's sacking of Isfahan in 1387—a graphic example of how the Mongols pillaged the lands they conquered.

GREAT ZIMBABWE

Spurred by the gold trade, Zimbabwe began its rise to prominence under the Shona kingship of the late 1200s and 1300s in *c.* 1000. As in other parts of sub-Saharan Africa at that time, stone building began in the 1100s and reached maturity with the erection of the vast royal capital, temple complex, and burial site at Great Zimbabwe in *c.* 1300.

The structures that once dominated the city of Great Zimbabwe were made of granite slabs, fitted together with mortar.

1250	1260	1270	1280	1290	1299
	Aquinas influences Catholic theology		Roger Bacon pioneers scientific experimentation	Duns Scotus scholastic philosopher	
First cannons used by Moors			Commercial fishing widespread in Baltic	First spectacles with convex lenses	Gunpowder for artillery in Europe	Italy: watermarks used in papermaking
Motet introduced as new musical form	Chinese opera developed	Turkey: Sufi Rumi writes mystic poetry	France: *Roman de la Rose*		
Spain: León Cathedral	Nicola Pisano at Pisa	Padua: Giotto frescoes		China: new impetus in landscape painting	Africa: Benin bronzes cast by "lost wax" method

1300–99

EUROPE

1301 Edward I of England invests son, Edward, as first prince of Wales.

1302 Defeat of French at Courtrai saves Flemish from French occupation.

1309 Papacy moves from Rome to Avignon (to 1377).

1312 Order of Knights Templar abolished for malpractices.

1314 Robert Bruce declares Scotland independent after defeating English at Bannockburn. Louis IV, king of Germany, conducts civil war with his rival, Frederick of Austria.

1333 Edward III of England invades Scotland.

1337 Beginning of a series of conflicts between France and England known as the Hundred Years' War (*below*).

c. 1340 Zenith of Moorish civilization in Granada, Spain.

1345 Ottoman Turks cross the Bosporus into Europe.

1346 English defeat French at Crécy.

1347 Black Death reaches Cyprus and Italy from Asia (*below right*). English capture Calais from French.

1348–49 Black Death reaches France, England, and Germany.

1350 Black Death reaches Russia, Poland, Scandinavia, and Scotland; by now 25 million have died from Black Death in Europe and millions more have died in China, India, and Persia.

1356 English defeat French at Poitiers.

1358 The Jacquerie, revolt by peasants in N.E. France, brutally suppressed by Dauphin, Charles, and his nobles.

1367 In Moscow the Kremlin (meaning "citadel") is rebuilt in stone.

1369 Ottoman Turks begin conquest of Bulgaria (completed 1372).

1370 Peace of Stralsund establishes power of Hanseatic League, with right to veto Danish kings.

1371 Robert II of Scotland becomes first Stuart monarch (to 1390).

1371–75 Ottoman Turks defeat Serbs and conquer Macedonia.

1378 Great Schism (to 1417): rival popes elected: Urban VI, pope at Rome; Clement VII, antipope at Avignon.

1381 Peasants' Revolt in England led by Wat Tyler, resulting from discontent generated by the imposition of three oppressive poll taxes between 1377 and 1381; Venice wins "Hundred Years' War" against Genoa.

1386 Union formed between Lithuania and Poland.

1397 Union of Kalmar unites Norway, Denmark, and Sweden under one king.

1399 After death of John of Gaunt, his

THE HUNDRED YEARS' WAR

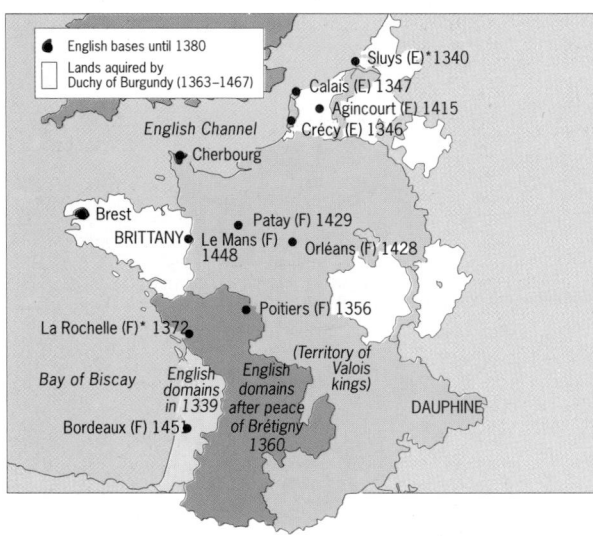

Legend:
- ● English bases until 1380
- ☐ Lands aquired by Duchy of Burgundy (1363–1467)

Sluys (E) *1340
Calais (E) 1347
Agincourt (E) 1415
Crécy (E) 1346
English Channel
Cherbourg
Brest
BRITTANY
Patay (F) 1429
Le Mans (F) 1448
Orléans (F) 1428
Poitiers (F) 1356
La Rochelle (F) * 1372
(Territory of Valois kings)
Bay of Biscay
English domains in 1339
English domains after peace of Brétigny 1360
DAUPHINE
Bordeaux (F) 145

(E) English victory (F) French victory * Naval battle

The Hundred Years' War was a series of Anglo-French conflicts that continued for more than a century. A key cause was the sovereignty of Guienne (Gascony), which had come to Henry II of England on his marriage to Eleanor of Aquitaine in 1152.

As dukes of Gascony, the English kings increasingly resented having to pay homage to the French king for their continental possessions. A more immediate cause of the war was a dispute over the French crown. The English king, Edward

III, had a claim to the throne from his mother Isabella, daughter of Philippe IV of France; but on the death of Philippe's son in 1328, Edward's claim was ignored in favor of that of Philippe's nephew, Philippe VI. War finally broke out after Philippe VI's confiscation of Edward's French possessions in 1337.

1337–60 After naval and land victories, Edward III secures large parts of France under the treaty of Brétigny.

1360–96 French gradually recapture most of lost French territory.

1415–22 Henry V revives English claim to French throne; defeats French at Agincourt. Dies in 1422, leaving a baby son as heir.

1422–53 After initial victories, the English lose conquered territory to French forces under Joan of Arc. By 1453, the English lose all French possessions, except Calais (lost in 1558) and the Channel Islands.

THE BLACK DEATH

The Black Death was an epidemic of bubonic plague that killed up to half of Europe's population in the mid-1300s. Its name came from the spots of blood which turned black under the skin. The outbreak started in Asia and spread along the trade routes to the West, carried by fleas on infected rats. One effect of the plague was a shortage of labor that put the peasantry in a strong bargaining position for better wages. This led to peasant uprisings in countries such as France and England.

Flagellants atone for the Black Death.

		1300	1310	1320	1330	1340
	RELIGION AND PHILOSOPHY	Corvino forms first Christian missions in China	Papacy moves to Avignon (1309)		William of Ockham, English philosopher, attacks Aquinas	Flagellant movement arises in response to Black Death
	SCIENCE AND TECHNOLOGY	Gunpowder used for artillery in Europe		Chaulmoogra oil used in China to treat leprosy	Spinning wheel illustrated in Luttrell psalter	Black Death reduces population
	LITERATURE AND MUSIC	Manuscript of Marco Polo's travels in Asia and China	Dante Alighieri's *Divine Comedy* (begun 1307)	Italy: Petrarch sonnets Persia: Háfiz mystic poet	*Sir Gawain and the Green Knight*, anonymous allegory epic	
	ART AND ARCHITECTURE	Giotto paints Padua frescoes	Duccio paints Sienna "Maesta"			Japanese Muromachi scroll paintings

son, Henry Bolingbroke, invades England; deposes Richard II and becomes Henry IV.

MIDDLE EAST

1301 Osman, founder of the Ottoman Turks (*p. 337*), defeats Byzantines.
1326 Ottoman Turks capture Bursa, Asia Minor.
1361 Turks make Adrianople their capital.
1390 Turks complete conquest of Asia Minor.
1391 First siege of Constantinople by Turks (to 1397).
1392–93 Mongol ruler Timur captures Baghdad and invades Mesopotamia (now Iraq).
1396 20,000 European knights defeated by Turks at Nicopolis. Turks conquer Bulgaria.
1397 Turks invade Greece.

ASIA

1320 Tughluk dynasty in Delhi, India (to 1413), founded by the Turk Ghidyas-ud-din Tughluk.
1333 Japanese emperor Daigo II overthrows Hojo family of shoguns and sets up a period of personal rule.
1336 Daigo II exiled; Ashikaga family rule Japan as shoguns (to 1568).
1339–1400 Civil war between *daimyo* (feudal lords) and their samurai armies (to 1392).
1350–1400 Ayuthia succeeds the Sukhothai kingdom; Siamese destroy Khmer kingdom and unite Siam.
1353 Foundation of kingdom of Lanxang in Laos.
1363 Mongol ruler Timur begins conquest of Asia (*p. 331*).
1368 Rebellion by Chu Yuan-chang overthrows Yuan (Mongol) dynasty in China; founds Ming dynasty (*right*).
1369 Korea submits to Ming dynasty. Timur becomes king of Samarkand.
1369 Timur becomes ruler of Turkestan.
1384 Timur conquers Persia.
1388 Chinese drive Mongols out of their capital, Karakorum.
1391 Timur defeats Golden Horde (Mongols) and again in 1395.
1392 Yi Song-gye founds the Yi dynasty in Korea; provides country with long period of political and social stability (to 1910).
1398 Timur invades kingdom of Delhi; about 100,000 prisoners massacred.

THE MALI EMPIRE

The breakup of the W. African empire of Ghana and the collapse of Almohad power in Morocco in the 1100s left a power vacuum in the western Sahel. Under Sundiata, king of Kangaba, a new Mande empire, that of Mali, began to rise *c.* 1235. Its rulers became Muslims, and the most famous of them, Mansa "emperor" Musa, visited Cairo and Mecca in 1324. He distributed so much gold that its price was depressed in Europe. The traveler Ibn Battuta visited Mali in 1352–53. He gave a detailed account of the court and wrote admiringly of the crime-free roads, the productive farming, and rich trade of the empire. Timbuktu, already an established trade center, became a center of Islamic culture and learning. With its capital at Niani, Mali stretched from the Atlantic to the Niger, but central authority declined in the 1400s, to be replaced by the still greater empire of Songhai.

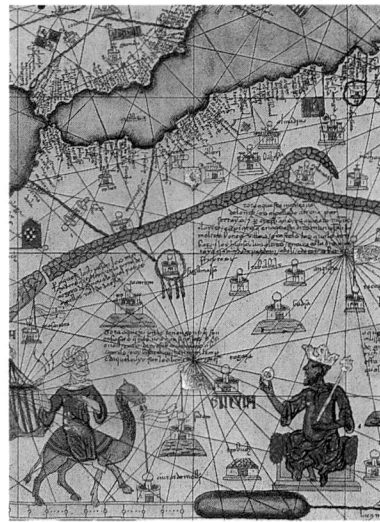

In a Catalan atlas of 1375 Mansa Musa sits in his W. African empire.

AFRICA

c. **1300** Emergence of Benin Empire in Nigeria.
c. **1300** Search for Prester John (legendary Christian priest and king) in western Ethiopia.
1312–37 Mali Empire at its zenith (*above*).

THE MING DYNASTY

In 1368, the humbly born Chu Yuan-Chang led a peasant rebellion that drove the alien and decadent Yuan (Mongol) dynasty from Peking and made him the first emperor of the Ming dynasty. At their height, the autocratic Ming emperors ruled an empire reaching from Burma to Korea. Peace and economic expansion encouraged intellectual and cultural life. Ceramics were particularly fine, and Peking was rebuilt in lavish style by the third Ming emperor, Yung Lo (1403–24), who sent the admiral Cheng Ho on voyages to E. Africa and secured tribute from Japan and S.E. Asia. The dynasty finally collapsed before another foreign invasion, by the Manchus, who established the Qing dynasty in 1644.

AMERICAS AND AUSTRALIA AND OCEANIA

c. **1300** Incas begin period of expansion in Peru.
c. **1350** Second wave of Maori arrive in New Zealand from Marquesas Islands.
1325 Traditional foundation date of Tenochtitlán (now Mexico City) by Aztecs (*p. 334*).

A Ming leys jar.

1350	1360	1370	1380	1390	1399
Sufis, mystics of Islam, spread into India, Malaya, and Africa		John Wycliffe, religious leader, founds Lollards		Ibn Khaldun, Islamic scholar, formulates his "science of culture"	
	Iron cannons in use in Germany	Lock gates on Dutch canal		Weight-driven clocks appear in Europe (Salisbury Cathedral)	Observatories built by Arab astronomers
Italian Boccaccio writes *Decameron*	William Langland writes *Piers Plowman*			The Nō (Noh) play emerges in Japan. Geoffrey Chaucer writes the *Canterbury Tales*	
New papal seat at Avignon attracts Italian painters to France	Potters of Ming dynasty discover underglaze painting		English perpendicular style at Canterbury Cathedral	Timur's mausoleums constructed at Samarkand	

Pre-Columbian America

The first agricultural revolution—the transition from a hunter-gatherer economy to an agrarian way of life—began in the Western Hemisphere at about the same time as it did in Mesopotamia. But the first sedentary communities did not make their appearance until the middle of the second millennium B.C. Hence what we call "civiliza-tion"—a settled society with some leisure time and a division of labor—was also delayed. The only literate culture to develop before the arrival of the Spanish at the beginning of the 1500s was that of the Mayans. The history of pre-Columbian America is, even so, rich in social and political development, in monumental architecture, in religious ceremonial, and in warfare and empire building.

> "... peacefully, safely
> sun, shine on and illumine
> the Incas, the people, the servants
> whom you have shepherded
> guard them from sickness and suffering
> in peace, in safety"
>
> Inca prayer in worship of Viracocha

Temple of the Warriors Mayan rain god in Chichén Itzá, Mexico c. 1300.

By the time Europeans arrived in Central America, the Mayans had developed a highly complex culture, the centerpieces of which were great cities in which steeply stepped pyramids, temples, and palaces were situated in ceremonial plazas (left).

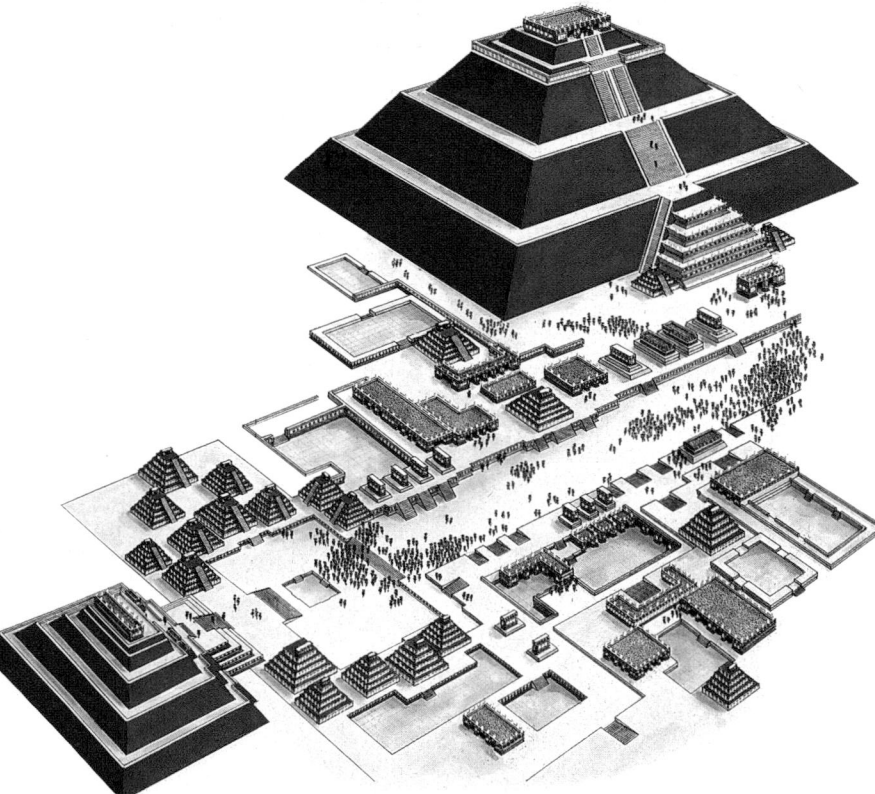

Mesoamerican cultures

Mesoamerica, south of the Rio Grande, gave rise to four great cultures: in succession that of the Olmecs, who rose to prominence in the centuries before the birth of Christ, the Mayans, the Toltecs, and the Aztecs. All four peoples inhabited the fertile lands around the Gulf of Mexico and depended upon a rich harvest of corn and root crops to support a work force that was able to construct huge ceremonial sites and produce splendid decorative works of art, especially pottery. All four peoples were polytheistic in religion and sun worshipers. Although the Olmecs introduced hieroglyphics and the calendar to America, only the Mayans developed a true form of ideographic writing. The Mayans' monumental buildings were erected without metal tools; the first metal-working culture in America was the Toltec. Both the Toltecs and the Aztecs were renowned warriors, driven to conquer further and further afield in their search for wealth; but they were empire builders, not colonizers, who demanded tribute from the people they defeated. For the Aztecs, conquest had another essential purpose: to supply human beings for the hundreds of blood sacrifices offered daily to the sun-god at their magnificent capital, Tenochtitlán.

The Incas of Peru

The briefest of all the great pre-Columbian empires was that of the Incas. First heard of in the 1100s, they established their capital at Cuzco, high in the Peruvian Andes, early in the 1300s, but they entered into their expansionist phase only after Pachacuti came to the throne c. 1438. By 1500, the Incas ran an empire (with a superb network of roads and tunnels, partly inherited from the defeated Chimu people, partly built by conscript labor) that stretched from Quito in the north to the south of Santiago in Chile and covered nearly 400,000 sq. mi. (1,036,000km²). The Incas had no writing, but they developed a remarkable form of communication and information storage called quipu, which was a system based on color-coded and knotted yarn. Oppressive taxation was a feature of the Incas' highly centralized administration under the divine emperor, believed to be descended from the sun-god. The subjects of tyrannical rulers, like the Aztecs and to an extent the Incas, looked upon Pizarro and the Spanish *conquistadores* (conquerors) of the early 1500s almost as liberators.

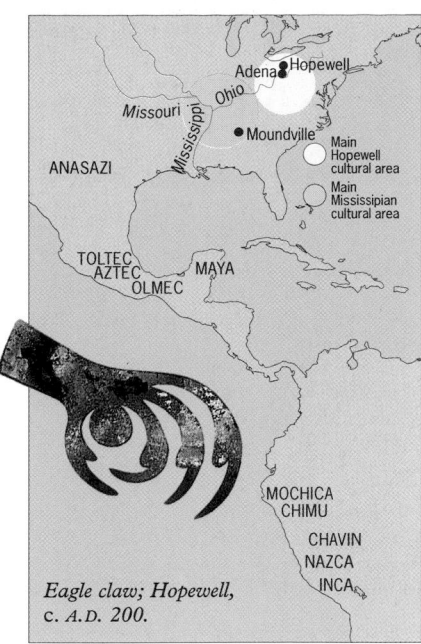

Eagle claw; Hopewell, c. A.D. 200.

Ancient peoples of the Americas.

Timetable

c. 40,000–c. 10,000 B.C. Hunters cross landlink from Russia to Alaska.

c. 10,000 B.C. Melting of ice cap isolates American continent.

c. 9000 B.C. Evidence points to cave-dwelling hunters in southernmost part of South America.

c. 8500 B.C. Agricultural revolution comes to the Andes in South America and spreads to Mexico.

c. 5500–c. 4000 B.C. Ancestors of alpaca and llama domesticated.

c. 2600 B.C. First temple sites appear, in coastal Peru.

c. 1200 B.C. –c. 300 B.C. Olmecs build first great Mexican civilization.

c. 1000 B.C. –c. 300 B.C. Chavin culture flourishes in Andes.

c. 1000 B.C. Hunter-gatherers of S.W. North America take up agriculture.

c. 1000 B.C. –c. 300 B.C. Adena people dominate eastern North America.

c. 300 B.C. Hohokam, Mogollon, and Anasazi cultures, S.W. North America.

c. 100 B.C. –c. A.D. 500 Hopewell culture succeeds Adena.

c. 250 B.C. – c. A.D. 450 Nazca people dominate southern Peru; Moche people erect huge buildings in northern Peru.

c. A.D. 300– c.850 Mayan civilization of Central America develops literacy.

c. 500–c. 1000 Tiahuanaco and Huari empires dominate the Andes basin.

c. 700 Mound-building Mississippian culture rises in Mississippi Valley.

c. 800 Chimu people emerge as a power in northern Peru.

c. 950 Toltecs rise to prominence in place of collapsed Mayan Empire.

c. 1000 Vikings explore N.E. coast of America.

c. 1200 Incas, under Manco Capac, settle in Andean Valley near Cuzco.

c. 1325 Aztecs settle in the central Valley of Mexico.

c. 1440–76 Incas carry out destruction of Chimu Empire.

1492 Columbus makes landfall on the Bahamas and sights Haiti and Cuba.

1521 Aztec resistance to Spanish conquest comes to an end.

1533 Inca Empire falls to Pizarro.

North American cultures

The three prehistoric cultures of eastern North America—the Adena, the Hopewell, and the Mississippian—shared a distinctive trademark: they were all mound builders. Mounds seem to have served both a general ceremonial, sacred function and a more specific purpose as burial sites. The Mississippians built earthen mounds as foundation platforms for wooden temples, mausoleums, and dwelling places. The Adena and the Hopewell (whose eras lasted from 1000 B.C. to 300 B.C. and from 100 B.C. to A.D. 500 respectively) left behind carved pipeheads—some in human, some in animal form—for ceremonial smoking. The last

of the three cultures, the Mississippian, had disappeared by 1400. In southwestern North America, west of the Rockies, lived a number of agricultural peoples who cultivated crops imported from Mexico—corn, squash, and beans—after c. 1000 B.C. The most notable of them—the Hohokam, Mogollon, and Anasazi—occupied the region between 300 B.C. and A.D. 1400. The most impressive remainder of their cultures is the collection of around 100 Anasazi villages, which consist of multistory rock dwellings built into the cliffs at Chaco Canyon in New Mexico. The best known, Pueblo Bonito, had about 800 rooms.

Carving of a panther and a bird of prey; shell gorget, Mississippian culture, c. A.D. 1000.

The Anasazi, who probably built these cliff dwellings at Mesa Verde, Colorado, in the 1200s, used the rocky overhang as protection against other tribes; the dwellings were abandoned c. 1300, possibly because of drought.

1400–99

EUROPE

1400 Richard II of England murdered. Owen Glendower of Wales rebels against English; he is defeated in 1405.

1409 Council of Pisa attempts to resolve Great Schism; declares rival popes deposed and elects a third.

1410 Poles and Lithuanians defeat Teutonic Knights at battle of Tannenberg. Civil war in France between Orléanists and Burgundians.

1415 Hundred Years' War (*p. 332*): battle of Agincourt.

1417 End of Great Schism: Council of Constance elects Martin V as only pope.

1429 Hundred Years' War: Charles VII crowned king of France.

1431 Hundred Years' War: Joan of Arc burned at Rouen; Henry VI of England crowned king of France.

1434 Cosimo de Medici becomes de facto ruler of Florence, establishing dynasty that lasts until 1737.

1438 Hapsburgs inherit imperial crown.

1450–51 Hundred Years' War: English lose Cherbourg and Gascony.

1453 English cease attempts to conquer France; end of Hundred Years' War. Ottomans take Constantinople.

1455–85 Wars of the Roses: civil war in England between houses of York and Lancaster over succession to throne.

1456 Ottoman Turks conquer Athens.

1459 Ottoman Turks conquer Serbia.

1460 James II of Scotland killed when English besiege Roxburgh Castle.

1461 Wars of the Roses: Edward, Duke of York, defeats Lancastrians; crowned Edward IV after Henry VI flees.

1463–79 War between Ottoman Turks and Venice.

1466 Peace of Thorn: Poland gains western Prussia from Teutonic Knights.

1470 Earl of Warwick defeats Edward IV and restores Henry VI to throne.

1471 Battle of Barnet: Edward IV kills

Warwick; Henry VI dies, probably murdered, in Tower of London.

1474–77 War between Charles the Bold of Burgundy and Swiss Confederation instigated by Louis XI of France; after Charles's death at Nancy, Burgundy annexed to French crown.

1478 Spanish Inquisition established by Queen Isabella of Castile and husband, Ferdinand. Ivan III of Moscow conquers Novgorod. Matthias of Hungary gains Lusatia, Moravia, and Silesia. Ottomans conquer Albania.

1479 Union of Spain when Queen Isabella of Castile's husband, Ferdinand, inherits throne of Aragon.

1480 Ivan III (the Great) of Moscow defeats Golden Horde at battle of Oka. Ottomans besiege Rhodes, held by Knights of St. John.

1483 After death of Edward IV of England, Edward V and brother Richard imprisoned and murdered by

THE RENAISSANCE

The Renaissance, which began in the 1300s with the rebirth of classical Greek and Roman learning in Italy, grew out of a blossoming of painting, sculpture, and architecture into an explosion of European energy and curiosity in all fields. The closing of eastern trade routes after Constantinople fell to the Ottoman Turks in 1453 shifted the economic focus north from the Mediterranean, spurred the rise of protocapitalist merchant-bankers, and ushered in a search for new Atlantic trade routes and the great age of maritime exploration. A revived interest in humankind and the natural world for their own sakes marked the birth of modern science: the anatomist Vesalius forced open a debate against the Church on human dissection, and Copernicus's heliocentric theory of the solar system, reviving Greek ideas, challenged the cosmology of the Church.

Europe found a new confidence and optimism as the waning of the Middle Ages sounded the knell of medieval, feudal Christendom.

c. **1455** Mazarin Bible printed by Gutenberg's revolutionary machine using movable type.

1495–98 Leonardo paints *The Last Supper*.

1512 Michelangelo completes

painting of Sistine Chapel in Rome.

1513 Machiavelli's *The Prince* outlines political theory shorn of religion.

1536 Henry VIII of England appoints Hans Holbein his court painter.

1543 Vesalius's *Fabric of the Human Body* and Copernicus's *Revolution of the Heavenly Spheres* published.

A Renaissance condottiere *(soldier of fortune) as depicted in a fresco from the 1300s by Guidoriccio da Fogliano in Siena.*

THE ITALIAN CITY-STATES

The great city-states of Italy—Venice, Florence, Milan, Naples, and Rome—whose merchants had grown rich from trade in the Mediterranean, provided the capital for lavish patronage of the arts. The rulers of the independent city-states vied with one another for cultural prestige. Rival centers of commerce and artistic creativity in northern Europe—such as Antwerp and Bruges—rose to prominence in the 1500s.

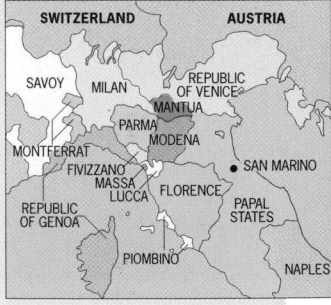

The city-states of north Italy.

	1400	1410	1420	1430	1440
RELIGION AND PHILOSOPHY		Islam: Ibn Khaldun "science of culture"	Bohemia: John Huss sets up Hussites	Thomas a Kempis writes *Imitation of Christ*	
SCIENCE AND TECHNOLOGY		Drift nets introduced by Dutch			Portugal: Henry the Navigator develops sailing technology
LITERATURE AND MUSIC		Europe: miracle plays widespread			India: Chandidas writes *Song of Krishna*
ART AND ARCHITECTURE	International Gothic style flourishes		Brunelleschi in Italy	Masaccio frescoes	Flemish painting flourishes Donatello's *David*

uncle, Richard of Gloucester; Richard crowned Richard III.

1485 Battle of Bosworth Field: Henry Tudor defeats and kills Richard III; crowned Henry VII. Matthias of Hungary captures Vienna; Hungary most powerful state in central Europe.

1486 Henry VII of England marries Elizabeth of York, thus uniting houses of York and Lancaster and ending Wars of the Roses.

1492 Granada, last Moorish emirate in Spain, surrenders to Ferdinand and Isabella. Jews expelled from Spain, Sicily, and Sardinia.

1494 Charles VIII of France invades Italy in pursuit of claim to throne of Naples. French drive Medici from Florence. Irish Parliament made subservient to English Parliament.

1495 Charles VIII of France enters Naples; Holy League—Milan, Venice, Maximilian I, Pope Alexander VI, and Ferdinand V—forces him to withdraw.

1499 After inheriting French throne, Louis XII conquers Milan.

MIDDLE EAST

1400 Timur captures Baghdad.

1402 Timur invades Asia Minor; defeats Sultan Bayazid and Ottoman army in battle of Ankara.

ASIA

1405 Death of Timur; his empire disintegrates (*p. 331*).

1403–04 Emperor Yongle extends empire; Beijing new capital of China.

1432 Khmer city of Angkor, Cambodia, abandoned for Phnom Penh; Khmer Empire declines.

1467 Start of civil war in Japan between feudal lords; lasts more than 100 years.

1446–71 Annamese conquest of Champa (part of Vietnam).

1498 Portuguese navigator Vasco da Gama first European to find sea route to India (*p. 340*).

AFRICA

c. **1400** Kanem-Bornu Empire dominates Nigeria and Chad. Rise of Mossi states in modern Burkina Faso.

1415 Henry the Navigator of Portugal captures Ceuta, N. Africa.

c. **1440–81** Ewuare the Great, *oba* (king) of Benin, institutes reforms, introduces hereditary succession, and conquers

THE OTTOMAN EMPIRE

The Ottomans were an obscure Turkish people named after Osman, who created a small principality in Anatolia *c.* 1300. They built an empire that lasted more than 600 years; conquests in the 1400s and 1500s made it the largest empire in the world. Under Mehmed II, who restored Ottoman power after the defeat inflicted by Timur (Tamerlane) in 1402, they conquered Constantinople (1453), the Christian bastion that had resisted Muslim attacks since the 600s, finally obliterating the Byzantine Empire. Under later sultans, conquest accelerated, spearheaded by the janissaries, an elite corps of young Christians. Suleiman the Magnificent controlled the eastern Mediterranean, and overran Hungary. The battle of Lepanto (1571) broke Ottoman sea power, and the Siege of Vienna (1683) halted expansion.

The Ottoman Empire 1300–1600.

Yoruba to west and Lower Niger to east.

1441 Portuguese explore Guinea-Bissau.

1448 Portuguese build first European fort on African coast at Arguin (Mauritania).

c. **1450–1550** Rise of Kongo and Ndongo kingdoms in Angola and Zaïre.

c. **1450** Sultanate of Agadès (modern Niger) becomes powerful.

1460 Portuguese explore west coast of Africa as far as Sierra Leone.

1464 Sonni Ali becomes ruler of Songhai in W. Africa, making it independent of Mali Empire (*p. 339*).

1468 Sonni Ali captures Timbuktu.

1471 Portuguese take Arabian Tangier.

1482–84 Portuguese explorer Diego Cão reaches the Congo River and establishes settlements on Gold Coast.

1488 Portuguese navigator Bartolomeu Dias first European to go around Cape of Good Hope (*p. 340*).

1493–1528 Songhai Empire reaches greatest extent under Askia Muhammad.

1497–99 Portuguese commander Vasco da Gama sails to and from India; period of greatest Portuguese exploratory effort.

THE AMERICAS

c. **1400–1500** Aztec Empire covers most of modern Mexico.

1438 Pachacutec establishes Inca Empire in Peru.

1441 Sack of Mayapán; several smaller Maya states formed.

c. **1476–50** Incas conquer Chimú in northern Peru.

1460 End of Mayan civilization in Mexico.

1463 Sapa Inca emperor wages war against Lupaca and Colla tribes; Quechua, Inca language, established.

1470 Chimú Empire (now Ecuador) overrun by Inca leader, Topa.

1471 Topa becomes Inca emperor; starts program of road building to connect all parts of empire with capital, Cuzco.

1480 Incas conquer Bolivia.

1485 Incas conquer N. and C. Chile, S. coast of Peru, and N.W. Argentina.

1492–93 Christopher Columbus crosses Atlantic and reaches Bahamas, Cuba, Haiti (*p. 340*), and Hispaniola.

1493–96 Columbus explores Puerto Rico, Dominica, and Jamaica.

1494 Columbus establishes Spanish colony on island of Hispaniola. Treaty of Tordesillas: Spain and Portugal agree to divide New World. Huayna Capac becomes Inca emperor; founds second capital at Quito.

1497 John Cabot (*p. 340*) rediscovers Newfoundland and explores coast south to Delaware.

1498 On third voyage, Columbus reaches Trinidad and coast of South America. Huayna Capac extends Inca Empire into present-day Colombia.

1499 Italian Amerigo Vespucci (*p. 340*) explores N.E. coast of South America.

AUSTRALIA AND OCEANIA

c. **1400s** Indonesian traders visit Australia's north coast.

	1450	1460	1470	1480	1490	1499
	First printed Bible	Indian mystic Kabir		Spanish Inquisition established	*Malleus Maleficarum* initiates witchcraft persecution	
					First modern globe made in Nuremberg	Europe: dissection of corpses
	France: Villon writes *Ballad of a Hanged Man*	Scottish poetry: Henryson, Dunbar	Sir Thomas Malory writes *Morte d'Arthur*			Europe: keyboard instruments widespread
				Italy: Mantegna, Botticelli, Bellini		Leonardo's *Last Supper*; Michelangelo's *Pieta*

1500–49

EUROPE

1500 Louis XII of France and Ferdinand of Spain agree to divide kingdom of Naples under the treaty of Granada (effected 1501).

1501–03 Russia and Poland at war; Russia gains Lithuania and border territories.

1502–03 War breaks out between French and Spanish in Naples; French defeated at battles of Cerignola and Garigliano.

1505 Treaty of Blois; France keeps Milan but cedes Naples to Spain.

1508–10 League of Cambrai; the Holy Roman Empire, France, Spain, and the papacy become allies against Venice.

1509 Henry VII of England dies and is succeeded by his son Henry VIII (until 1547).

1510–14 Papacy, Spain, and Venice form Holy League to drive French from Italy.

1512 Swiss join Holy League and drive French from Milan. Russia and Poland at war (to 1522).

1513 Battle of Flodden Field; James IV of Scotland killed by English. Battle of Novara: French are defeated and driven from Italy.

1514 Peasants' Revolt in Hungary.

1515 Battle of Marignano; French defeat the Swiss and regain Milan.

1516 Treaty of Noyon between France and Spain; France gives up claim to Naples. Treaty of Freiburg: peace between French and Swiss.

1517 Reformation (*right*) begins when Martin Luther nails 95 theses to church door at Wittenberg, Germany, in protest against the sale by the Church of indulgences to raise money for a new St. Peter's in Rome.

1520 Field of the Cloth of Gold: François I of France meets Henry VIII of England but fails to gain his support against Charles V, the Holy Roman emperor; Henry makes a treaty with Charles instead. Christian II of Denmark and Norway defeats Swedes at Lake Asunden.

1520–23 Gustavus Vasa leads Swedish revolt against Danes; voted Gustavus I.

1521 Henry VIII of England made "Defender of the Faith" by Pope Leo X for his opposition to Luther. Ottoman Turks take Belgrade.

1522 Charles V drives French from Genoa and Milan. Ottoman Turks take Rhodes from Knights of St. John. Knights' Revolt in Germany (to 1524).

1524 Peasants' Revolt in Germany (to 1525).

1525 Battle of Pavia: defeat of French and Swiss by Germans and Spanish; François I of France captured.

1526 Battle of Mohacs: Ottomans defeat and kill Hungarian king; Ferdinand Hapsburg crowned king of Hungary, making Austria nucleus of an empire.

1527 Sack of Rome by Spanish and German troops; Pope Clement VII captured. Sweden becomes Lutheran.

1529 Henry VIII of England divorces Catherine of Aragon; begins to cut ties with Church of Rome. Peace of Cambrai between France and Spain: France renounces claims to Italy. Turks unsuccessfully besiege Vienna.

1530 Knights of St. John established on Malta by Charles V. His army forces Florence to readmit Medicis.

1531 Civil war in Switzerland between Catholic and Protestant cantons; after Protestant defeat, it is agreed that each canton can choose own faith.

1532 Sir Thomas More, English lord chancellor, resigns over question of Henry VIII's divorce; Thomas Cranmer becomes archbishop of Canterbury.

1533 Henry VIII marries Anne Boleyn and is excommunicated by Pope Clement VII.

1534 Ignatius Loyola founds Society of Jesus (Jesuits) in Spain. Henry VIII is declared supreme head of the Church in England under the Act of Supremacy.

1535 Henry VIII executes Sir Thomas More for refusing to take oath of supremacy. Milan comes under Spanish control. War between France and Spain (to 1538).

1536 Act of Union joins England to Wales; dissolution of monasteries starts (to 1540). France invades Savoy and Piedmont; forms alliance with Ottoman Turks. Denmark becomes Lutheran.

1541 Beginning of "Counter-Reformation" (*below*). John Knox brings Reformation to Scotland. Ottomans conquer Hungary.

1542 Battle of Solway Moss: James V of Scotland killed; daughter, Mary, becomes queen of Scots (to 1567); she is only a baby so her French mother, Mary of Guise, rules as regent.

1544 Henry VIII of England and Charles V of Spain invade France; Treaty of Crespy between France and Spain.

1547 Charles V defeats German Protestant princes at Muhlberg. Ivan IV

THE REFORMATION

The convulsion of European society known as the Reformation was led by the antipapal reformers Luther and Calvin. Its religious core was a belief that salvation lay in the individual's personal relationship with God. That idea

The spread of Protestantism to France resulted in religious wars and incidents such as the St. Bartholomew's Day Massacre of the Huguenots in Paris, 1572.

was greatly assisted by the invention of movable type, which brought the Bible directly into ordinary people's lives. But the effects went far beyond the division of the Christian Church into Protestant and Roman wings. The war against the papacy fostered national feeling and was the crucible in which the modern division of Europe into sovereign national states—Protestant such as England and the Netherlands, and Roman Catholic such as France and Spain—was forged.

1517 Luther challenges papal authority.

1521 Charles V outlaws Luther at Worms.

1530 Confession of Augsburg fails to bring religious peace in Germany.

1534 Act of Supremacy severs English Church from Rome.

1541 Calvin subjects Geneva to a Puritan theocracy. Council of Trent sets Counter-Reformation in motion.

1555 Peace of Augsburg brings German religious wars to an end.

		1500	1505	1510	1515	1520
	RELIGION AND PHILOSOPHY			Machiavelli writes *The Prince*		Nanak founds Sikhism
	SCIENCE AND TECHNOLOGY	Coach developed in Hungary		Sunflowers introduced in Europe	Coffee introduced in Europe	Chocolate introduced in Europe
	LITERATURE AND MUSIC			Italy: development of *Commedia dell'arte*		
	ART AND ARCHITECTURE			Michelangelo's Sistine Chapel; Leonardo's *Mona Lisa*		Grünewald's Isenheim altarpiece

(the Terrible) becomes first crowned czar of Russia (*p. 344*).

MIDDLE EAST

1501 Shah Ismail founds Safavid dynasty in Persia (now Iran) (to 1736).
1513 War between Ottoman (*p. 337*) and Safavid empires.
1514 War between Ottomans and Persia; Persians defeated at battle of Chaldiran.
1516–17 In war between Ottoman Empire and Egypt Ottomans capture Cairo: end of Mameluk Empire; Syria and Egypt added to Ottoman Empire.
1534 Ottoman Turks capture Baghdad and Mesopotamia (now Iraq).

ASIA

1504 Babur rules Kabul in Afghanistan.
1510 Portuguese seize Goa.
1516 European traders and missionaries given access to China.
1525–26 Babur of Afghanistan invades India and defeats sultan of Delhi; founds Mogul Empire (*p.343*).
1533 North Vietnam splits into Tongking and Annam.
1539 Central kingdom of Toungoo in Burma conquers Mon kingdom of Pegu.
1542–52 Portuguese Jesuit missionary, Francis Xavier, arrives in Japan.

AFRICA

c. **1500** Portuguese slave bases established on coast of W. Africa.
1505 Songhai invade Mali Empire.
1509 Spanish capture Oran and Mers el Kebar in N. Africa.
1516 Corsair (pirate) bases in N. Africa accept authority of Ottoman Turks.
1518 Founding of Barbary states of Algiers and Tunis.
1531 Portuguese establish trading posts in Mozambique.
1545 Turks occupy Ethiopia.

NORTH AMERICA

1505 Juan de Bermúdez discovers Bermuda.
1507 The New World named America after Amerigo Vespucci.
1508–11 Spaniard Juan Ponce de Léon conquers Puerto Rico.
1511 Spaniard Diego de Velázquez invades Cuba.
1513 Ponce de León discovers Florida.
1519–21 Hernán Cortés conquers Mexico; end of Aztec Empire (*above*).

THE SPANISH EMPIRE

The Spanish and Portuguese conquest of Central and South America destroyed proud cultures—notably the Aztec and the Inca—and provided the silver to sustain Spain's supremacy in Europe in the 1500s. The whole region remained subject to European rule until the liberation movements of the 1800s.
1494 Treaty of Tordesillas divides New World into Spanish and Portuguese spheres.
1515 Velazquez captures Cuba for Spain.
1521 Cortés defeats Montezuma and takes Aztec Mexico for Spain.
1532 Portugal founds first European settlement in Brazil at São Vicente.
1533 Pizarro vanquishes the Incas and makes Peru Spanish.

The Spanish conquerors often treated the Native Americans with extreme cruelty.

1522–39 Cortés's conquest of northern Central America.
1524 Verrazano sails from North Carolina to Newfoundland; Gomez sails from Novia Scotia to Florida.
1535–36 French explorer Jacques Cartier navigates St. Lawrence River; claims Canada for France.
1541 Spaniard Hernando de Soto reaches Mississippi River.

SOUTH AMERICA

1501 Portuguese captain Gonçalo Coelho explores Brazilian coast.
1502 First African slaves arrive in New World (*p. 349*). On fourth voyage, Columbus reaches Nicaragua.
1520 Portuguese Ferdinand Magellan finds entry to Pacific Ocean (*p. 340*).
1521–35 Spanish colonize Venezuela.
1525–32 Civil war in Inca Empire between brothers Huascar in south and Atahualpa in north; Huascar defeated.
1530 Portuguese begin to colonize Brazil.
1532–34 Francisco Pizarro leads expedition from Panama that conquers Peru.
1535 Spaniard Diego de Almagro sets out from Peru to explore Chile.
1545–49 Spanish discover major silver mines at Potosi, Peru.

AFRICAN MEDIEVAL EMPIRES

During the Middle Ages, a succession of states and empires rose and fell in west Africa, based largely on the growing trans-Sahara trade in gold, salt, and luxury goods and strengthened by the spread of Islam throughout the Sahel region. The largest of these empires was that of Songhai, whose armies under Sonni Ali began to capture outlying parts of the Mali Empire in the late 1400s. By *c.* 1520, Songhai rule, centered in Gao on the Niger, had entirely superseded Mali and stretched from the Gambia in the west to Hausaland in the east. Attacks from Morocco, eager to control the gold trade, began in 1590

A Benin bronze of an oba (king).

and presaged the collapse of the Songhai state. Among other important medieval kingdoms, where prosperity encouraged the arts, were Benin, famous for its bronze sculptures, Kanem-Bornu, and, later, the Yoruba kingdom of Oyo.

	1525	1530	1535	1540	1545	1549
		Luther, Calvin start Reformation	Henry VIII takes over English Church			Council of Trent begins Counter-Reformation
		Coal mines open in Liege and Newcastle		Copernicus proposes sun-centered universe		
		Italian epic *Orlando Furioso* published	Meistersang minstrel song popular in Germany		Lute popular in Europe	
			Mannerist painting in Italy			

The Age of Exploration

The fall of Constantinople to the Ottoman Turks in 1453 closed off the land trade routes from Europe to the East. The result was an economic shift away from the Mediterranean toward the Atlantic nations of Europe. The next 50 years saw an explosion of maritime exploration (a splendid manifestation of Renaissance energy and curiosity) as the European monarchies sought to find a sea route to the "Indies." Accidental discoveries were the fruit of this endeavor: the West Indies by Columbus, cod-rich Newfoundland by Cabot, and, above all, the rich silver and gold mines of South America. That influx of precious metal from the New World underpinned Spain's position as the most powerful European nation in the 1500s. It also produced that century's great price rise and helped to promote the early development of European capitalism.

"It is proper to call it a New World. Men of old said . . . there was no land south of the Equator. But this last voyage of mine has proved them wrong, since in southern regions I have found a country more thickly inhabited by people and animals than our Europe or Asia or Africa."

Amerigo Vespucci (1507)

Early compass

Backstaff

Astrolabe

Navigators used the backstaff and astrolabe for calculating latitude.

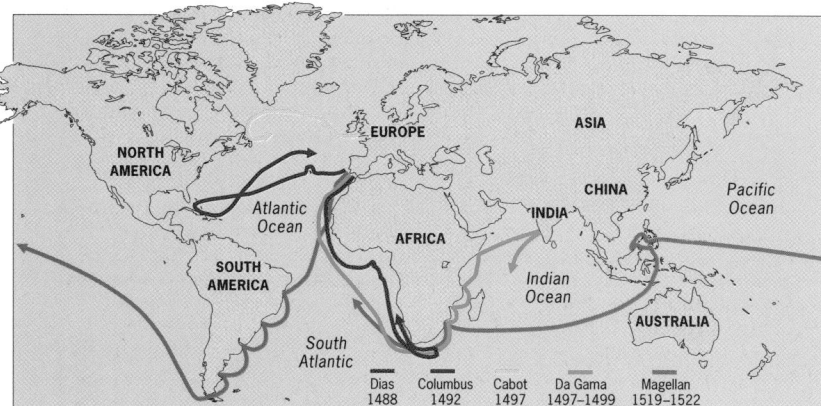

Leading voyages of exploration and discovery, 1480s to 1520s.

Improvements in ships and navigation

Overseas exploration and expansion would have been almost impossible without the advances made in the scientific study of geography and astronomy, leading to accurate navigation and improvements in ship construction. Schools of professional hydrographers had existed from the 1200s in Italian and Catalan ports, but their beautiful charts owed little to science. In 1462, however, the first recorded observation of latitude from the altitude of the Pole Star was made by a Portuguese ship. In 1478, an almanac containing tables of the sun's declination (for calculating latitude in the southern seas) was compiled in Portugal; a few years later these tables were incorporated in the first practical manual of navigation to be published, *O Regiment odo Astrolabo*. As great an innovation was the charting of Atlantic winds and currents. In a remarkably short time—between 1488 and 1500—the elliptical routes to India around the tip of Africa and to the Caribbean were discovered by Bartolomeu Dias, Vasco da Gama, and Christopher Columbus. European ships had carried compasses since the 1200s; by Henry the Navigator's time they were greatly improved (*above*). The Atlantic explorers also carried with them improved astrolabes (*above*), which had been in use since ancient times, and quadrants, which were new devices for measuring angles. From the Arabs the Portuguese and Spanish borrowed the lateen caravel (*opposite*), which became their preferred ocean-going ship. But they altered it by breaking up the canvas area of the sail (adding a topsail and combining a square and lateen rig in one vessel) to improve ease of handling, giving it three masts instead of two, and grafting its general design onto the square-rigged construction common to European ships at the time. However, Columbus's flagship, the *Santa María*, was a *nao*, a larger ship than a caravel.

TRAILBLAZERS OF THE AGE OF EXPLORATION

1487–88 Bartolomeu Dias
Portuguese. First European to round Cape of Good Hope.

1492–1504 Christopher Columbus
Genoese. "Discoverer" of New World; made four voyages to West Indies and Caribbean for Spain.

1497–98 John Cabot
Genoese. Rediscovered Newfoundland, first settled by Norsemen in the 1000s.

1497–99 Vasco da Gama
Portuguese. First European to reach India by sea.

1500–01 Pedro Alvares Cabral
Portuguese. Reached Brazil 1500; sailed around Africa to India 1501.

1513 Vasco Nuñez de Balboa
Spanish. First European to sight Pacific Ocean.

1519–22 Ferdinand Magellan
Portuguese. Led first circumnavigation of the world.

1526 Sebastian Cabot
Son of John Cabot. Explored South American coast for Spain.

1535 Jacques Cartier
French. Sailed up St. Lawrence River. Founded French Empire in America.

1535–37 Diego de Almagro
Spanish. Crossed Andes into Chile.

1539–42 Fernando de Soto
Spanish. Explored Florida. First European to cross Mississippi River.

1540–42 Francisco de Coronado
Spanish. Explored American southwest; discovered Grand Canyon.

1541 Francisco de Orellana
Spanish. Crossed Andes from Pacific; descended Amazon River.

1577–80 Sir Francis Drake
English. First Englishman to circumnavigate the world.

1 Foremast; 2 Main mast; 3 Mizzenmast; 4 Counter mizzen; 5 Poop deck;
6 Tiller; 7 Compass; 8 Provisions; 9 Cabins; 10 Ballast; 11 Water; 12 Bilge pump;
13 Sail locker; 14 Powder room; 15 Windlass; 16 Cook

A caravel was the type of ship used by Portuguese and Spanish explorers of the 1500s.

European trade and the New World

Before the age of exploration, European merchants rarely ventured beyond Mediterranean ports, where in dealings with Arab traders they bought slaves and gold from W. Africa and spices, ivory, and silk from the East. Now they began to establish direct contact with the producers of those commodities. More dramatically, they found new markets for export and new products for import in the New World. Transatlantic trade introduced a host of new products, chiefly plants. Four of the crops most widely grown in the world today are of American origin: corn, potatoes, sweet potatoes, and cassava. Potatoes have become a staple ingredient

in the northern European diet; corn is a worldwide fodder as well as food crop, especially in Africa; and W. Africa is a large consumer of cassava. The peanut is also native to the New World, as are tobacco, chocolate, and cocaine. Chocolate became a popular drink in Europe in the mid-1600s. Sugar from the West Indies was, after precious metals, the principal export from the New World, and it was paid for chiefly with African slaves. Export opportunities also increased; manufactured goods from Europe found a market across the Atlantic, especially clothing, weapons, glass, and paper.

New World crops, such as tobacco, quickly became popular throughout Europe.

1550–99

EUROPE

1552 War between Charles V of Spain and Henri II of France; France seizes Metz, Toulon, and Verdun.

1553 On death of Edward VI, Lady Jane Grey reigns as queen of England for nine days; Mary Tudor becomes Mary I of England; marries Philip, heir to Spanish throne (1554).

1555 England returns to Roman Catholicism: Protestants persecuted and about 300 burned at stake. Peace of Augsburg: Lutheran states in Germany granted freedom of worship.

1556 Charles V abdicates: Spanish crown and colonies go to son, Philip; office of emperor and Hapsburg lands go to brother, Ferdinand.

1557 Battle of St. Quentin: Spanish forces in Netherlands defeat French.

1558 England loses Calais, last English possession in France. With ascent of Elizabeth I to English throne, Catholic legislation repealed in England.

1559 Treaty of Câteau-Cambrésis between France and Spain: France gives up almost all conquests; Spain controls most of Italy. Sweden takes Estonia.

1561 Madrid becomes capital of Spain.

1562 Start of religious wars in France between Huguenots and Catholic League. Hugh O'Neill leads unsuccessful Irish rebellion against English.

1564 Peace of Troyes ends war between England and France. Ivan the Terrible attacks power of Russian nobles.

1565 Ottomans besiege Malta, but are defeated by Knights of St. John.

1566–1648 Rebellion in Netherlands against Spanish rule (*below right*).

1567 Murder of Darnley, husband of Mary, Queen of Scots, probably by Earl of Bothwell; Mary marries Bothwell, is forced to abdicate, and takes refuge in England (1568); infant son, James VI, declared king of Scotland.

1569 Diet of Lublin merges Poland and Lithuania.

1570 Peace of St. Germain-en-Laye: Huguenots given conditional freedom of worship. Czar Ivan IV razes Novgorod. Ottomans invade Cyprus (to 1572).

1571 Battle of Lepanto: Spanish-Venetian fleet defeats Ottomans.

1572 Massacre of St. Bartholomew: more than 20,000 Huguenots killed in Paris.

1576 Pacification of Ghent: Netherlands provinces unite to drive out Spanish. Protestantism forbidden in France.

1578 Duke of Parma subdues southern provinces of Netherlands (now Belgium).

1579 Northern provinces of Netherlands form Union of Utrecht to fight Spain.

1580 Philip II of Spain claims throne of Portugal.

1581 Union of Utrecht declares itself Dutch republic and elects William of Orange as ruler. Poland invades Russia.

1582 Gregorian calendar introduced into Roman Catholic countries.

1584 William of Orange, father of Dutch republic, murdered. Alliance of Bern, Geneva, and Zurich against Roman Catholic cantons of Switzerland.

1585 "War of the Three Henrys" in France, involving Henri III of France, Henri of Navarre, and Henri of Guise. Reestablishment of Spanish rule over southern provinces of Netherlands.

1587 Elizabeth I orders execution of Mary, Queen of Scots. England at war with Spain; Drake destroys Spanish fleet at Cadiz.

EUROPEAN DRAMA

Interest in the classical world in Renaissance Italy led to the revival of classical plays. Modern drama grew from that tradition: Ludovico Ariosto (1474–1533) translated Latin comedies and wrote his own in the vernacular. Neoclassicism and humanist teaching inhibited the growth of popular drama in Italy, despite the growth of the commedia dell'arte, and in France, but not in England. The disappearance of the old religious drama—"mystery" plays—in England preceded the great age of Elizabethan drama and William Shakespeare (1564–1616). In Spain, too, neoclassicism was less powerful, but religious drama survived to fertilize the golden age of Lope de Vega and Calderon. In France the reassertion of classicism during the 1600s led to the dramatic success of Corneille, Racine, and Molière.

A view of the Thames in London in 1647; Shakespeare's Globe Theatre (rebuilt in 1614) is wrongly labeled "beere bayting."

THE WINNING OF DUTCH INDEPENDENCE

The Netherlands' prolonged but successful rebellion against Spain and the mighty Hapsburgs was the first modern national revolution in Europe. It was also a triumph for militant Calvinism against Roman Catholicism and the Counter-Reformation.

1566 Northern provinces under William the Silent (later William of Orange) begin revolt against Spain.

1573 Dutch open their dikes, forcing Spanish to abandon siege of Leiden.

1576 Pacification of Ghent unites all 17 Netherlands provinces against Spain; Alessandro Farnese's armies soon recover south (modern Belgium) for Spain.

1579–81 Seven northern provinces of Netherlands form Union of Utrecht and declare independence.

1609 Spain agrees to truce; ends with start of Thirty Years' War in 1618.

1648 Treaty of Westphalia formally recognizes an independent Dutch republic.

	1550	1555	1560	1565	1570
RELIGION AND PHILOSOPHY		Holy Roman Empire acknowledges Lutheranism	39 Articles establish Church of England		
SCIENCE AND TECHNOLOGY			First use of Mercator's projection		Potato introduced to Europe from South America
LITERATURE AND MUSIC	Rabelais completes *Pantagruel*		Japan: development of musical forms		
ART AND ARCHITECTURE	Italy: Palladio designs Villa Rotunda		Spanish colonial style: Mexico cathedral	India: Mogul miniatures	

1588 English fleet and bad storms destroy Spanish Armada.

1589 Murder of Henri III of France ends Valois line; Protestant Henri of Navarre becomes first Bourbon ruler of France, as Henri IV.

1593–1606 War between Austria and Ottoman Empire.

1595 Treaty of Teusina between Sweden and Russia: Sweden gains Estonia.

1597 Dutch defeat Spanish army at Turnhout. Second Spanish Armada leaves for England but is forced to scatter by bad weather. Second Irish rebellion is led by Hugh O'Neill (until 1601, when it is ended by English).

1598 Edict of Nantes ends civil wars in France by giving Huguenots equal political rights with Roman Catholics. Beginning of "Time of Troubles" in Russia: period of social and political unrest (to 1613).

1599 Irish rebels defeat English army led by Earl of Essex.

MIDDLE EAST

1590 Peace between Ottoman Turks and Persian Safavid Empire.

1598 Abbas I drives Uzbek Turks out of Persia.

ASIA

1550–1700 Wars between unified Burmese state and Siam (Thailand).

1558 Kingdom of Annam (Vietnam) splits into two after rebellion.

1567 Japanese warrior, Oda Nobunaga, deposes Shogun from Kyoto and establishes strong rule.

1576 Mogul emperor Akbar completes annexation of N. India (*right*).

1579 Portuguese set up trading colonies in Bengal, India.

1582–84 Civil War in Japan; Nobunaga commits suicide; Hideyoshi succeeds.

1585–90 Hideyoshi destroys power of feudal lords and unifies Japan.

1592–93 Hideyoshi invades Korea, but withdraws under pressure from Chinese.

1595 Dutch colonization of East Indies begins.

1598 Second Japanese invasion of Korea ends with Hideyoshi's death; Tokugawa shogunate established.

AFRICA

1553 Beginning of Sharifian dynasties in Morocco.

1571 Bornu Empire in Nigeria reaches greatest extent.

1572 Spanish recapture Tunis from Ottoman Turks.

1574 Ottomans regain Tunis from Spain. Portuguese colonize Angola.

1578 Sebastian of Portugal invades Morocco but is killed, and his troops defeated at battle of Alcazar.

1591 Songhai Empire (modern Mali) destroyed by Spanish and Portuguese mercenaries in service of Morocco.

1595 First Dutch settlement in Guinea.

NORTH AMERICA

1565 Pedro Menendez de Aviles founds colony at St. Augustine, Florida.

1576–78 English explorer Martin Frobisher explores N. Atlantic and discovers Baffin Island off the N. Canadian coast.

1583 Humphrey Gilbert claims Newfoundland for England.

1584 Sir Walter Raleigh names Virginia after Elizabeth I, the "Virgin Queen."

SOUTH AMERICA

1554 Portuguese found São Paulo, Brazil.

1567 Portuguese found Rio de Janeiro, Brazil.

1572 Túpac Amaru, last ruler of the Incas, executed at Cuzco.

1592 Englishman John David discovers Falkland Islands.

ARMS AND ARMOR

The steel suit of armor worn by medieval European knights reached its highest level of development in the early 1500s, despite the development of guns. The manufacture of guns was in fact first recorded at Ghent in 1314, with siege cannon in use by *c.* 1340 and grapeshot and canister a century later. Mobile field artillery appeared *c.* 1475. But early guns were largely ineffective, and some armor—helmet and cuirass—was still worn by infantry in the 1600s. (Armor in which fiber replaces the steel cuirass is still worn.) The first effective small arms followed the invention of the matchlock in the 1500s. The wheel lock, in use before 1550, gave greater speed and accuracy. Too fragile for infantry, the cavalry were better served by the flintlock.

An early 17th-century matchlock musket.

The more sophisticated wheel lock pistol.

THE MOGUL EMPIRE

Miniature of the founders of the Mogul dynasty, including Babur and Timur.

The Moguls were a Muslim dynasty of Mongol ancestry in India, founded in 1526 when Babur overthrew the Delhi sultanate. His conquests were consolidated by his grandson Akbar, a ruler renowned for tolerance and wise government. Mogul art and architecture are among the world's great cultural achievements; the Taj Mahal, built by Akbar's grandson Shah Jahan, is the best-known example. Later emperors were less capable and became puppets of the British. The last was deposed in 1858. Mogul culture, however, continues to influence Indian life.

	1575	1580	1585	1590	1595	1599
				Jacobus Arminius leads Arminianism		France: Edict of Nantes grants freedom to Protestants
	Italy:Tasso's *Jerusalemme Liberata* and *Aminta*			Brahe and Kepler extend Copernican theory		
		English drama: Marlowe, Kyd, Sidney		Shakespeare: 20 plays written by 1600		
		Monoyama style at Azuchi castle, Japan		El Greco painting in Spain		Caravaggio's *Doubting Thomas*

1600–49

THE CZARS OF RUSSIA

Russia emerged as a power by defeating the Tatars in 1380. In 1472, Ivan the Great took the title of czar, but the first crowned czar was Ivan the Terrible in 1547. The monarchy ended when Nicholas II abdicated.

Ivan the Terrible with his son, whom he murdered in 1581.

Czars and Tsarinas

1462–1505	Ivan III (the Great)
1505–33	Vasily III
1533–84	Ivan IV (the Terrible)
1584–98	Fydor I
1598–1605	Boris Godunov
1605	Fydor II
1605–06	Dmitri
1606–10	Vasily (IV) Shuiski
1610–13	(Interregnum)
1613–45	Michael Romanov
1645–76	Alexis
1676–82	Fydor III
1682–96	Ivan V and Peter I (the Great)
1696–1725	Peter I (the Great)
1725–27	Catherine I
1727–30	Peter II
1730–40	Anna
1740–41	Ivan VI
1741–62	Elizabeth
1762	Peter III
1762–96	Catherine II (the Great)
1796–1801	Paul I
1801–25	Alexander I
1825–55	Nicholas I
1855–81	Alexander II
1881–94	Alexander III
1894–1917	Nicholas II

THE ENGLISH CIVIL WAR

Religious wars in Europe had ended, but a new type of conflict, between governor and governed, was presaged by civil war in England. Charles I's attempt to govern without Parliament collapsed because of Parliament's control of tax revenue and Charles's need for money. His attempt to arrest five recalcitrant M.P.s led to war in 1642. The war had a religious element: The Royalists, or "Cavaliers," represented Anglicanism, and Parliament, or the "Roundheads," represented the Church's puritan wing. Parliament allowed Oliver Cromwell to form a "New Model Army." His victories at Marston Moor (1644) and Naseby (1645) resulted in Charles's capture, but he escaped in 1647 and secured Scottish support. The Scots were defeated and Charles was executed. Parliamentary government proved equally contentious, and Cromwell assumed supreme power as lord protector in 1653. He died in 1659, and Charles II was crowned king in 1660.

The execution of Charles I.

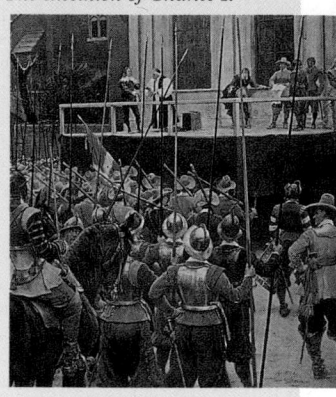

EUROPE

1603 James VI of Scotland becomes James I of England, the first Stuart king of England.

1604 Peace between England and Spain.

1605 Gunpowder Plot to blow up English Parliament discovered.

1606 Treaty of Zsitva-Torok between Turks and Austrians: Austria abandons Transylvania.

1608 Protestant Union formed in Germany, led by Frederick IV.

1609 Twelve Years' Truce ends fighting between United Provinces and Spain; ensures virtual independence of the Netherlands. Catholic League, led by Maximilian of Bavaria, formed in opposition to Protestant Union.

1610 Henri IV of France assassinated; succeeded by Louis XIII.

1611 Plantation of Ulster: English and Scottish Protestant colonists settle in Northern Ireland. Ottoman Turks invade Hungary.

1614 Estates General summoned in France to curb nobility, last such meeting until 1789 (*p. 350*).

1617 Treaty of Stolbovo ends war between Russia and Sweden.

1618 "Defenestration of Prague": Bohemians claiming independence throw two Austrian officials from window in Prague Castle; sparks the Thirty Years' War (*opposite*).

1622 Spain occupies Valtelline pass; war with France follows.

1627 Seige of Huguenots at La Rochelle by France's chief minister, Cardinal Richelieu; attempt by English to relieve La Rochelle fails.

1628 Huguenots surrender at La Rochelle, losing all political power. Petition of Rights: Charles I forced to accept English Parliament's Petition of Rights in return for financial grants.

1629 Charles I dissolves Parliament; it does not meet again until 1640.

1640 Portugal wins independence from Spain.

1641 Catholic revolt in Ireland; massacre of Protestants in Ulster.

1642–48 Civil war in England (*above*).

1643 Battle of Rocroi: France defeats Spain. Sweden at war with Denmark over Baltic supremacy (to 1645).

1648 Revolt of Fronde against Louis XIV of France (suppressed 1653). Oliver Cromwell suppresses Catholic rebellion in Ireland. Serfdom established by law in Russia.

MIDDLE EAST

1602–18 Holy War between Persia, under Shah Abbas I, and Ottoman Turkey.

1603 Persians defeat Turks at Tabriz.

1638 Ottoman Turks conquer Baghdad.

ASIA

1600 British East India Company formed.

1602 Dutch East India Company formed.

1603 Tokugawa Ieyasu appointed Shogun of Japan.

1604 French East India Company formed. Russians begin settlement of Siberia.

1611 Dutch merchants permitted to trade with Japanese.

1615 Tribes in northern China combine to form military organizations, later called *Manchus*. Dutch seize Moluccas (Spice Islands) from Portuguese.

1616 Manchu army invades China.

1619 Dutch East India Company makes Batavia (now Jakarta) its headquarters.

1622–24 Execution of European Christian

	1600	1605	1610	1615	1620
RELIGION AND PHILOSOPHY		Tung-lin Academy revives Confucianism in China			England: Bacon develops scientific method
SCIENCE AND TECHNOLOGY			Telescope invented	Galileo discovers moons of Jupiter	
LITERATURE AND MUSIC	Shakespeare's great tragedies	Cervantes's *Don Quixote*			Monteverdi composes *Orfeo*
ART AND ARCHITECTURE	India: high point of Mogul culture				Baroque style in Europe

THE THIRTY YEARS' WAR

Fought mostly on German soil, the war of the Protestant powers (the German princedoms, England, Holland, Scandinavia) and their ally, France, against the Hapsburg Empire and Spain was an affair of territorial ambition, dynastic interests, and religion. Its effect was to stop the Hapsurgs making Germany a centralized, Catholic, absolute monarchy.

1618 Bohemian revolt against Austrian (Hapsburg) rule sparks off war.

1623 Initial Hapsburg successes capped by victory at Stadtlohn.

1627 Wallenstein and Tilly lead Imperial armies to crushing victory over Danes.

1630 Sweden enters war.

1632 Gustavus Adolphus leads Protestant powers to victory at Lutzen.

1635 France enters war. Desire for peace leads to Peace of Prague, bringing German war to an end.

1648 Treaty of Westphalia ends conflict and brings period of toleration.

---

missionaries in Japan reaches its height.

1629 Mogul emperor Shah Jahan orders building of the Taj Mahal in memory of his wife Mumtaz-i-Mahal.

1635 Dutch occupy Formosa (Taiwan).

1637 English merchants establish base at (Guangzhou) Canton, China.

1638 Series of decrees closes Japan to foreigners.

1644 Ming dynasty collapses in China; Manchus establish Qing dynasty.

AFRICA

c. **1600s** Height of Oyo kingdom, Nigeria.

c. **1600–***c.* **1800** Kingdom of Gondar in Ethiopia.

1614 French explorer Paul Imbert reaches Timbuktu.

1626 First French settlements on Madagascar.

1637 French establish fort of Saint-Louis in Senegal.

NORTH AMERICA

1603 Samuel de Champlain explores St. Lawrence River.

1604 French settle Nova Scotia.

1605 Spanish found Santa Fe, New Mexico.

1607 English colony of Virginia founded at Jamestown (*p. 347*). Henry Hudson begins voyage to eastern Greenland and Hudson River.

1608 De Champlain founds Quebec.

1612 Dutch merchants begin fur-trading on Manhattan Island. Settlers plant tobacco in Virginia.

1619 African slaves begin to arrive in Virginia to work on first tobacco plantations.

1620 Pilgrims sign Mayflower Compact, first instrument of self-government in colonies.

1623 Dutch begin trading on Hudson River.

1626 Dutch found New Amsterdam (New York). English settle Barbados.

1635 French establish settlement in Martinique and Guadeloupe.

1636 Harvard College founded in Cambridge, Massachusetts.

1641 French set up trading posts in Michigan.

1642 French found Montreal.

1646 English occupy Bahamas.

SOUTH AMERICA

1616 Dutch navigator Willem Schouten rounds Cape Horn.

1630 Dutch colonists invade Brazil.

AUSTRALIA AND OCEANIA

1606 Willem Jansz first European to sight Australia.

1642 Abel Tasman sights Van Diemen's Land (now Tasmania) and New Zealand.

TRADE IN SOUTHEAST ASIA

Maritime exploration opened up E. Asia to European trade. The demand for spices and other luxury goods led to the founding and development of ports and, ultimately, empires.

1511 Albuquerque conquers Malacca for Portugal.

1512–13 Portuguese traders first visit Moluccas, or Spice Islands.

1600 British East India Company founded.

1602 Dutch East India Company founded.

1684 Pepper-rich sultanate of Bantam comes under Dutch control.

THE SCIENTIFIC REVOLUTION

Scientist Isaac Newton as portrayed by William Blake, c. 1800.

The advance in scientific inquiry that began in the Renaissance reached a peak in the 1600s. René Descartes postulated a theoretical basis for the new science, and Francis Bacon confirmed the importance of empirical observations. Vasalius explained human anatomy, Harvey described the circulation of blood, van Leeuwenhoek discovered microscopic organisms, and Leibniz invented calculus. Efforts to understand the nature and workings of the universe culminated in Isaac Newton's *Principia Mathematica* (1687), which demonstrated the three laws of motion and the law of universal gravitation. Religious authority still hindered free thought, especially in Roman Catholic countries, but learned societies devoted to scientific inquiry were founded in England and Prussia.

Robert Clive of the British East India Co. being granted the right to collect revenues.

1625	1630	1635	1640	1645	1649
	Galileo founder of modern science condemned by inquisition		France: Jansenism founded	Descartes founder of modern philosophy	
	Circulation of blood discovered by Harvey		Galileo proposes heliocentric theory	Pascal invents adding machine	
English metaphysical poets: Herbert, Donne	French classicism: Poussin		Italy: Bel Canto		
			High point of Dutch art: Rembrandt, Vermeer, Hals	India: Taj Mahal completed	Japan: koto becomes national instrument

1650–99

EUROPE

1650 Charles Stuart lands in Scotland and is proclaimed Charles II. Second revolt of Fronde suppressed in France.

1651 Charles II invades England with Scots army; defeated at Worcester.

1652 Anglo-Dutch War (to 1654). Spain intervenes in Fronde revolt against Louis XIV of France (to 1653).

1653 Oliver Cromwell becomes lord protector of England (*p. 344*).

1655 Sweden declares war on Poland.

1656 Battle of Warsaw: Swedish victory; Russia, Denmark, and Holy Roman Empire declare war on Sweden. Turks routed by Venetians off Dardanelles.

1659 Treaty of the Pyrenees between France and Spain: settles borders and confirms supremacy of France over Spain. Elector Frederick William drives Swedish out of Prussia.

1660 Charles II restored to English throne (*p. 344*). Treaty of Copenhagen: Denmark surrenders territory to Sweden.

1661 Louis XIV of France becomes absolute monarch (*right*). Treaty of Kardis: Russia and Sweden restore all conquests to each other. Turkey and Holy Roman Empire at war (to 1664).

1663 Ottoman Turks invade Transylvania and Hungary.

1664 Battle of St. Gotthard: Austrians defeat Turks; Treaty of Vasvar between Holy Roman Empire and Turkey.

1665 Great Plague in London. Second Anglo-Dutch War (to 1667).

1666 Great Fire of London.

1667 Peace of Breda ends war among England, France, and the Netherlands. Treaty of Andrussovo: Russia gains Smolensk and E. Ukraine from Poland.

1668 Triple Alliance of England, Sweden, and the Netherlands against France. Treaty of Lisbon: Spain recognizes Portugal's independence.

1669 Venice surrenders Candia (Crete) to Ottoman Turks.

1671 Turks declare war on Poland.

1672 France declares war on the Netherlands (to 1674) and invades southern Netherlands. William of Orange appointed *stadholder* of the Netherlands. Third Anglo-Dutch War (to 1674). Poland and Turkey at war for control of Ukraine (to 1676).

1673 Test Act excludes Roman Catholics and Non-Conformists from holding

LOUIS XIV

The reign of the "Sun King," Louis XIV, was the longest (1643–1715) and grandest in French history. Taking over the government in 1661, Louis exercised unchallenged personal power from amid a large and sycophantic court. Until *c.* 1685, when Louis revoked the Edict of Nantes and ended toleration of the Huguenots (Protestants), France prospered, but its territorial ambitions, especially against the Netherlands, provoked international hostility. A series of wars drained French resources and led finally to humiliation in the Peace of Utrecht (1713).

The Palace of Versailles, built by Louis XIV in 1662, from a painting of 1722.

public office in England. Holy Roman Empire declares war on France in defence of Dutch.

1676 Treaty of Zuravno: Turkey gains Polish Ukraine.

1677 William of Orange marries Mary, heir to the English throne. Russia and Turkey at war (to 1681).

1678 "Popish Plot" in England: Titus Oates falsely alleges Catholic plot to murder Charles II. Treaty of Nijmegen ends Franco-Dutch War.

1679 Act of habeas corpus in England forbids imprisonment without trial.

1681 Treaty of Radzin: Russia gains most of Turkish Ukraine.

PETER THE GREAT

Peter the Great bequeathed Westernization and expansionism to Russia. From edicts banning beards and traditional Muscovite dress to thorough reforms of the army, civil service, and education, he impregnated Russia with Western European ideas and practices. By his military success he gained the Baltic provinces, enabling Russia to replace Sweden as the great northern power in Europe.

1697–98 Peter travels in Germany, Holland, and England.

1699 Reforms begin to enlarge and professionalize the army.

1701 Founding of School of Navigation and Mathematics begins a program of "Westernization."

1703 Peter builds a new capital, St. Petersburg, the design of which is

Peter the Great's drive for modernization included compulsory removal of beards

based on Western, neoclassical lines.

1721 Treaty of Nystad: Russian victory over Sweden. Peter I proclaimed emperor of all Russians; Church brought under czarist control.

		1650	1655	1660	1665	1670
	RELIGION AND PHILOSOPHY	England: egalitarian movements—Levelers, Quakers	Hobbes writes *Leviathan*		Royal Society founded in England	
	SCIENCE AND TECHNOLOGY	Air pump developed		Huygens invents pendulum clock	Boyle's law of physics	Leibniz devises calculating machine
	LITERATURE AND MUSIC		Netherlands: Vondel's *Lucifer*	Germany: Grimmelshausen's *Simplicissimus*	Milton's *Paradise Lost*	Racine's *Andromaque*
	ART AND ARCHITECTURE	Velazquez at Spanish court			Palace of Versailles	Dutch landscape painting

1683–99 Turkey at war with Austria.

1683 Seige of Vienna by Turks: city relieved by German and Polish troops.

1684 Holy League formed by Pope Innocent XI: Venice, Austria, and Poland united against Turkey.

1686 League of Augsburg formed by Holy Roman Empire, Spain, Sweden, Saxony, Bavaria, and Palatinate against Louis XIV.

1687 James II of England issues Declaration of Liberty of Conscience: extends toleration of all religions. Venetians bombard Athens. Battle of Mohacs: Turks defeated by Austrians.

1688 England's "Glorious Revolution": William of Orange invited to save England from Roman Catholicism; James II flees to France. Austria captures Belgrade from Turks. War of the League of Augsburg (to 1697); France invades Palatinate. Bill of Rights establishes constitutional monarchy in England; William III (William of Orange) and Mary II become joint monarchs of England and Scotland.

1690 Battle of the Boyne: William III defeats exiled James II in Ireland. Turks retake Belgrade from Austrians.

1691 Austrians win decisive victory over Turks at Szalankemen.

1692 Battle of La Hogue: Anglo-Dutch fleet defeats French fleet. Massacre of Clan Macdonald by Campbells at Glencoe, Scotland, on pretext of disloyalty to English crown.

1696 Peter the Great of Russia takes port of Azov from Turks.

1697 Treaty of Ryswick: France returns Spanish conquests.

1699 Under the Treaty of Karlowitz, Austria receives Hungary from Turkey, Venice gains Morea and much of Dalmatia, and Poland receives Podolia and Turkish Ukraine.

ASIA

1661 Chinese under Koxinga seize Formosa (Taiwan) from Dutch.

1663 French missionaries enter Vietnam.

1674 Moguls defeated by Maratha kingdom (*p.343*) in W. central India.

1676–78 Sikh uprising against Mogul rulers in India.

1677 Dutch extend possessions in Java.

1690 English establish trading settlement at Calcutta, India.

1697 Manchus conquer W. Mongolia.

AFRICA

1652 Dutch East India Company founds colony at Cape of Good Hope.

1660 Rise of Bambara kingdoms on Upper Niger.

1662 Battle of Ambuila: Portuguese destroy Kongo kingdom. Portuguese cede Tangier to England.

1686 French annex Madagascar.

1689 Osei Tutu founds Asante Empire in W. Africa (*p. 349*).

NORTH AMERICA

1655 English seize Jamaica from Spain.

1663 French colonies join as Province of New France with capital at Quebec.

1664 English seize New Amsterdam from Dutch, renaming it New York.

1670 Hudson's Bay Company founded.

1673 French explorers Marquette and Joliet sail down Mississippi to Arkansas.

1675–76 King Philip's War: New England settlers fight Wampanoags (*below*).

1680 Portuguese establish colony at Sacramento, California.

1681 Englishman William Penn granted charter to found Pennsylvania.

1682 French explorer La Salle claims Mississippi Valley for France.

1686 English establish Dominion of New England.

1692 Witchcraft trials take place in Salem, Massachusetts.

1693 College of William and Mary founded in Williamsburg, Virginia.

1697 Spanish lose Haiti to French.

1699–1702 French colonize Louisiana.

SOUTH AMERICA

1654 Portuguese drive out last Dutch colonists from Brazil.

AUSTRALIA AND OCEANIA

1699 English explorer William Dampier explores west coast of Australia and Pacific; names one island New Britain.

COLONIAL NEW ENGLAND

In 1621, having survived their first winter, the *Mayflower* Puritans celebrated their freedom from religious persecution in the Old World by sitting down to their first Thanksgiving dinner with the local Wampanoags. Although the government they subsequently formed gave voting rights only to members of the Puritan church, it stands, alongside the Virginia Assembly, as one of the twin foundation stones of American representative democracy.

1607 First permanent English colony in the New World founded at Jamestown, Virginia.

1619 Virginia Assembly first meets.

1620 Puritans land at Plymouth Rock, Massachusetts.

1630 Massachusetts Bay Company sends 1,000 settlers to found Boston.

1651 English Navigation Act restricts New England trade to raw materials in English ships.

1675–76 New England Confederation (Massachusetts, Plymouth Colony, Connecticut, New Haven) breaks power of local Wampanoags.

1684 Massachusetts charter revoked and royal control from London reasserted.

The 13 British colonies, 1763.

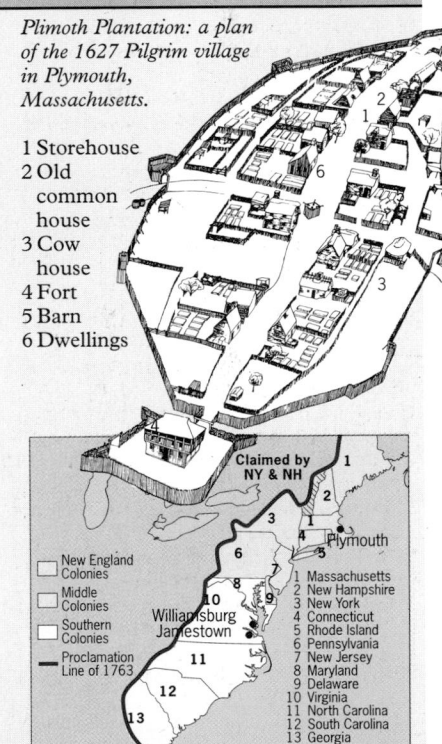

Plimoth Plantation: a plan of the 1627 Pilgrim village in Plymouth, Massachusetts.

1 Storehouse
2 Old common house
3 Cow house
4 Fort
5 Barn
6 Dwellings

Claimed by NY & NH

New England Colonies
Middle Colonies
Southern Colonies
Proclamation Line of 1763

Williamsburg
Jamestown

Plymouth

1 Massachusetts
2 New Hampshire
3 New York
4 Connecticut
5 Rhode Island
6 Pennsylvania
7 New Jersey
8 Maryland
9 Delaware
10 Virginia
11 North Carolina
12 South Carolina
13 Georgia

1675	1680	1685	1690	1695	1699
Spinoza's *Ethics*	Bossuet upholds Absolutism		Locke's empiricist *Essay concerning Human Understanding*		
		Newton's *Principia*	Huygens develops wave theory of light	Savery invents practical steam engine	
	Bunyan writes *Pilgrim's Progress*	Japan: Basho composes haiku poetry	Scarlatti composes cantatas / Purcell composes *Dido and Aeneas*		
Wren builds St. Paul's Cathedral, London	Claude's landscape paintings				

1700–49

THE AGE OF REASON

The intellectual developments in 18th-century Europe, known as the Age of Reason or the Enlightenment, represented the rise of secularism and the extension of rational, scientific methods to every aspect of life and thought. The leaders were the French *philosophes*, such as Voltaire, who admired the comparative freedom of political life in England. They saw themselves as the heirs of 17th-century thinkers like Bacon, Descartes, Newton, and John Locke, who influenced Rousseau's *Social Contract* (1762), advocating government that obeyed the "general will." Montesquieu propounded equality before the law, and the intrepid Diderot spent years producing the great *Encyclopédie* in the teeth of government opposition. The advocacy of civil liberties such as free speech and the enthusiasm for popular education threatened ecclesiastical authority and absolutist government, but some reforming monarchs, "enlightened despots" like Joseph II of Austria and Frederick II of Prussia, a friend of Voltaire, adopted Enlightenment ideas. In economics, the concern for freedom led to the laissez-faire doctrines of the Physiocrats and Adam Smith's *Wealth of Nations* (1776). Enlightenment ideas also liberated scientific research, with results such as the discovery of oxygen.

François Voltaire was the embodiment of French "enlightenment." In his writings he was scathing of political and religious narrow-mindedness.

In 1735, von Linné produced a system for naming and classifying plants and animals.

EUROPE

1700–21 Great Northern War: rivalry between Russia and Sweden for supremacy in Baltic; battle of Narva: Russia defeated by Sweden.

1701 War of the Spanish Succession (until 1714): Grand Alliance formed among England, the Netherlands, Holy Roman Empire, and German states against France. Sweden invades Poland.

1703 Hungarian revolt against Austria (to 1711). St. Petersburg founded by Peter the Great of Russia *(p. 346)*.

1704 War of Spanish Succession: allied force under Marlborough and Prince Eugène defeats French and Bavarians at Blenheim.

1706 War of Spanish Succession: French defeated by Marlborough at Ramillies; French defeated by Prince Eugène at Turin.

1707 Act of Union unites England and Scotland under name of Great Britain. War of Spanish Succession: at Almanza, Union Castille and Aragon allies defeated by Spain.

1708 War of Spanish Succession: British and Austrian troops defeat French at Oudenarde.

1709 War of Spanish Succession: French defeated at Malplaquet. Peter the Great defeats Swedish army at Poltava.

1710–11 Russia at war with Turkey.

1713 Peace of Utrecht; Britain gains Gibraltar and Minorca and territory in North America; Philip V of Spain gives up claim to French throne and loses Spanish lands in Europe.

1714 Russians conquer Finland after winning battle of Storkyro. France cedes Spanish Netherlands to Austria. Treaties of Rastatt and Baden; end of War of Spanish Succession.

1715–16 Jacobite uprising in Scotland in support of claim to the throne of James Edward Stuart ("the Old Pretender").

1717 Spain seizes Sardinia from Austria.

1718–20 Quadruple Alliance of Austria, Britain, France, and Netherlands against Spain. Treaty of Passarowitz ends war between Turkey and Austria.

1720 Collapse of John Law's Mississippi Company in France leads to French national bankruptcy. "South Sea Bubble": South Sea Company fails in England, causing financial panic.

1725 Treaty of Vienna between Austria and Spain. Treaty of Hanover: alliance of Britain, France, Prussia, Sweden, Denmark, and the Netherlands.

1727–29 War between England and France against Spain.

1731 Vienna Treaty between Britain, Holland, Spain, and the Holy Roman Empire; Russia, Prussia, and Holy Roman Empire also agree to fight together against Poland.

1733–35 War of Polish Succession: conflict between France and Spain and Austria and Russia.

1734 France invades Lorraine.

1736 Russia and Austria at war with Turkey.

1738 Treaty of Vienna ends War of Polish Succession; Lorraine ceded to France.

1739 War of Jenkins' Ear between Britain and Spain (to 1741). Turks advance toward Belgrade in Serbia; Treaty of Belgrade ends Austro-Russian war against Turkey.

1740 War of Austrian Succession (to 1748) caused by rival claims of Bavaria, Spain, and Saxony to Austrian throne; war starts after Frederick the Great of Prussia invades Silesia.

1741 Sweden and Russia at war (to 1743). Alliance among France, Bavaria, Spain, Saxony, and Prussia.

	1700	1705	1710	1715	1720
RELIGION AND PHILOSOPHY		Rise of Deism, or Natural Religion	Bishop Berkeley's *Principles of Human Knowledge*		
SCIENCE AND TECHNOLOGY	Jethro Tull develops seed drill	Halley correctly predicts comet		Fahrenheit invents mercury thermometer	
LITERATURE AND MUSIC	c. 1700 Italy: concerto developed by Corelli		Italy: pianoforte invented	English journalism: *Tatler*, *Spectator* founded	Defoe writes *Robinson Crusoe*
ART AND ARCHITECTURE		France: Rococo style introduced			

THE AFRICAN SLAVE TRADE

For nearly four centuries, Western powers traded in African slaves to supply the labor for their plantations. At least 15 million slaves were carried to the New World. Many millions more died in the "coffin ships" that transported them. It was not until the 1700s that the movement to abolish slavery began.

1441 First African slaves taken to Europe by Portuguese.
1501 African slaves taken to Americas.
1619 First black slaves taken to Virginia.
1808 Importing of slaves outlawed in U.S.A., though it continues illegally.
1833 British Empire abolishes slavery.
1865 Slavery abolished in U.S.A. by Thirteenth Amendment.

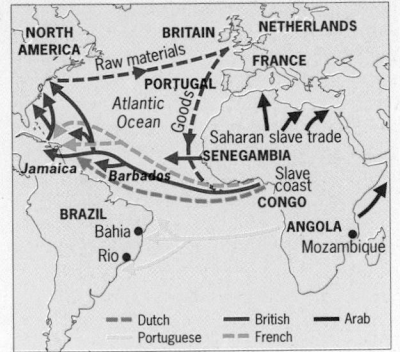

The international slave trade between Africa, Europe, and the Americas.

1712–55 Growth of Bambara kingdoms of upper Niger.
1714 Tripolitania (western province of Libya) wins independence from Ottoman Empire.
1715 Dutch leave Mauritius; French take control.
1723 British Africa Company acquires land in Gambia.
c. **1750** Asante Empire in W. Africa at its most powerful (*below*).

NORTH AMERICA

1713 Under Treaty of Utrecht ending War of Spanish Succession, France cedes Newfoundland, Nova Scotia, and Hudson Bay territory to Britain.
1714–16 War between French and Native Americans in New France.
1717 Collegiate School of America expands and reforms at Yale University in Connecticut.
1720 Spanish troops invade Texas.
1728 Danish navigator Vitus Bering explores northern seas between Siberia and Alaska.
1733 Foundation of Georgia, last of the Thirteen Colonies.
1735 European settlers begin westward expansion: French colony established at Vincennes, Indiana.
1742 Russians cross the Bering Strait and explore Alaska.
1740–48 King George's War between Britain and France over control of North America.
1745 British capture Louisburg in Canada.

SOUTH AMERICA

1747 Venezuela becomes separate province within Spanish Empire.

1742 Treaty of Berlin between Austria and Prussia.
1744 Frederick the Great of Prussia invades Bohemia; driven out by Austrian and Saxon forces.
1745 The "Forty-Five" Jacobite rebellion in England and Scotland led by Charles Edward Stuart ("the Young Pretender"). Austria, Saxony, Britain, and the Netherlands ally against Prussia. War of Austrian Succession: French defeat British at Fontenoy; Treaty of Dresden between Russia and Austria.
1746 Battle of Culloden: Jacobites defeated by English.
1748 Treaty of Aix-la-Chapelle ends War of Austrian Succession: Prussia keeps Silesia and emerges as major power.

MIDDLE EAST

1724 Russians and Turks divide conquered Persian (Iranian) lands.
1725 Shah Ashraf of Afghanistan takes control of Persia.
1726 Persian armies defeat Turks.
1730–36 War between Turkey and Persia.
1737–38 Nadir Shah, ruler of Persia, conquers Afghanistan.

ASIA AND AUSTRALIA AND OCEANIA

1707 Death of Aurangzeb leads to disintegration of Mogul Empire (p. 343).
1715 China conquers Mongolia and east Turkestan.
1720 China conquers Tibet. In Japan, government removes ban on European books, but Christianity still outlawed.

1722 Dutch navigator Jacob Roggeveen discovers Samoa and Easter Island.
1724 State of Hyderabad, India, achieves independence from Moguls.
1727 Russia and China agree on borders.
1729 Opium smoking banned in China.
1730 Marathas become preeminent in India. Emperor Yung Cheng begins to abolish slavery in China.
1732–33 Famine in Japan.
1739 Nadir Shah's troops sack Delhi, capital of Mogul India.
1738 Nadir Shah of Persia invades northern India.
1747 Nadir Shah assassinated.

AFRICA

1705 Turkish authority overthrown in Tunis, N. Africa.
1710 Algeria in N. Africa becomes self-governing part of Ottoman Empire.

THE ASANTE

In the late 1600s, a number of states arose in W. Africa, beyond the coastal kingdoms. The Akan-speaking Asante (Ashanti) rose to prominence in the Gold Coast region after *c.* 1730. The state captured the interior trade and dealt with Dutch slave traders on the coast. It survived until British annexation in 1901. Farther east lay the Yoruba Empire of Oyo, which was overwhelmed by the Muslim Fulani in the early 1800s. A new kingdom, Dahomey, grew between Oyo and Asante and prospered on the slave trade until *c.* 1850. It was conquered by the French in 1893.

An Asante mounted warrior used as a gold weight.

1725	1730	1735	1740	1745	1749
Ba'al Shem Tov founds Hasidism in Poland		Voltaire writes empiricist *Lettres philosophiques*	Hume writes *Treatise on Human Nature*	John Wesley founds Methodist movement		Islam: foundation of puritanical Wahhabi movement
Harrison develops navigational chronometer			John Kay invents the flying shuttle		Celsius devises temperature scale	
Italy: Vivaldi composes *Four Seasons*	Swift publishes *Gulliver's Travels*	France: Prevost writes *Manon Lescaut*	Bach composes *Mass in B Minor*		Pope writes *The Dunciad*	Richardson writes *Tom Jones*
	Venice: Tiepolo, Canaletto		France: Boucher, Chardin		Japan: Utamaro develops *ukio-e* style	Chinese art and design fashionable in Europe

1750–99

THE FRENCH REVOLUTION

The storming of the Bastille, July 14, 1789.

The French Revolution, which began with hopes of "liberty, equality, and fraternity," abolished feudalism and the monarchy before descending into the Terror. It ended in a long, unsuccessful war for French hegemony in Europe. But it bequeathed modern ideas of nationalism and the struggle for national freedom and democracy in many countries throughout the world.

1789 Louis XVI calls a meeting of the Estates General at Versailles with a double representation of the middle classes as the Third Estate. Bastille falls.

1793 Louis XVI and Marie Antoinette beheaded: ensuing Terror kills 14,000 "enemies of the republic."

1799 Napoleon overthrows the Directory and assumes personal rule; in 1804 he proclaims himself emperor.

1810 Napoleon's new criminal code.

EUROPE

1756 Seven Years' War (to 1763) caused by colonial rivalry between France and Britain and by rivalry between Austria and Prussia. Treaty of Westminster: alliance between Britain and Prussia. Treaty of Versailles: alliance between France and Austria.

1757 Russia joins alliance with France and Austria; battle of Rossbach and Leuthen: Prussia defeats French and Austrian armies.

1758 Battle of Zorndorf: Russia defeats Prussia; halts invasion.

1762 Britain declares war on Spain.

1768 Turkey declares war on Russia.

1772 First partition of Poland between Russia, Prussia, and Austria.

1773 Peasant uprising in Russia led by Cossack Pugachev (suppressed 1775).

1774 Treaty of Kutchuk Kainjardi between Russia and Turkey: Russia gains Black Sea ports.

1780 Riots against Roman Catholics in London ("the Gordon Riots").

1783 Russia annexes Crimea.

1785 League of German Princes formed by Frederick II of Prussia against Joseph II of Austria.

1789 Start of French Revolution (*above*). Belgium becomes republic. Austrian Netherlands (Belgium) declare independence; France declared a republic.

1792 France declares war on Austria and Prussia; battle of Valmy: French defeat Prussians. Treaty of Jassy between Russia and Turkey. Denmark first nation to abolish slave trade (*p. 349*).

1793 Revolutionary France declares war on Britain, Spain, and the Dutch republic. Execution of Louis XVI. Second partition of Poland between Russia and Prussia.

1794 Dutch republic invaded and Dutch fleet captured by France (1795); French occupy the Netherlands (to 1795). France abolishes slavery in its colonies.

1795 Treaty of Basle between France and Prussia; Spain also makes peace with France. Remainder of Poland divided among Russia, Prussia, and Austria.

1796 Napoleon Bonaparte (*p. 354*) leads French army; conquers most of Italy.

1797 Battle of Cape St. Vincent: British navy defeats Franco-Spanish fleet. Treaty of Campo Formio: Austria makes peace with France.

1798 Napoleon captures Rome and establishes Roman republic; English fleet under Nelson defeats French fleet in battle of Nile (Abukir Bay); French invade Switzerland: Helvetic republic set up. Rebellion at Vinegar Hill, Ireland, by United Irishmen.

1799 Coalition of Britain, Austria, Russia, Portugal, Naples, and Ottoman Empire against France; battles of Zurich, Trebbia, Novi: French driven out of Italy; Napoleon overthrows Directory and sets up Consulate (to 1804).

ASIA

1751 British defeat French at Arcot, India. China conquers Tibet.

1755 Alaungpaya founds Konbaung dynasty in Burma; series of wars with Siam (Thailand) begins.

1756 "Black Hole of Calcutta": 120 Britons die after capture by Nawab Siraj-ud Daulah of Bengal.

1757 Battle of Plassy: Clive defeats Nawab of Bengal and French army.

1761 British capture French fort at Pondicherry; French lose power in India.

1767 Burma overthrows Ayuthia kingdom and occupies Siam.

1770 Burma repels Chinese invasion. Burmese expelled from Siam.

1773 Warren Hastings appointed first governor-general of India.

1775–82 War between British and Marathas in India.

1782 Rama I founds new dynasty in Siam; capital is Bangkok.

1784 Britain makes peace with Tipu Sultan, sultan of Mysore.

1785 Russia founds whaling base in Aleutian Islands, near Japan.

1787 Famine causes rice riots in Japan.

1792 China invades Nepal.

1796 British conquer Ceylon (Sri Lanka) from Dutch.

1797 American ships trade with Japan (to 1809) on behalf of Dutch; end of Japanese isolation.

1799 Tipu Sultan, last ruler of Mysore, killed fighting British; British control extends over most of southern India.

AFRICA

1776 Fulani overthrow Denianke dynasty in W. Africa.

1787 Britain sets up colony in Sierra Leone, W. Africa.

c. 1790 Buganda kingdom expands frontiers. Luanda kingdom at height.

1795 British take Cape of Good Hope.

1798 Napoleon invades Egypt.

1799 Discovery of Rosetta Stone enables Egyptian hieroglyphic writing to be translated by scholars.

NORTH AMERICA

1753 French troops from Canada invade Ohio Valley.

1755–63 French and Indian War.

1759 British capture Quebec; French general, Marquis de Montcalm, and

		1750	1755	1760	1765	1770
	RELIGION AND PHILOSOPHY	France: vol. 1 of *Encyclopédie*, edited by Diderot		France: Rousseau writes *Social Contract*	Germany: Mendelssohn begins Reform Judaism	Germany: Herder, forerunner of Romanticism
	SCIENCE AND TECHNOLOGY	America: Franklin proves lightning is electricity		Watt builds steam engine	Hargreaves's spinning jenny	Italy: Galvani discovers current electricity
	LITERATURE AND MUSIC	Austria: Haydn develops symphony			Walpole writes Gothic *Castle of Otranto*	
	ART AND ARCHITECTURE	Italy: neoclassicism develops following archaeological discoveries	Russia: winter palace constructed in St. Petersburg			Royal Academy of Art founded by Joshua Reynolds

British general, James Wolfe, killed.
1763 Peace of Paris gives Canada to Britain. Native American uprising against British settlers led by Ottawa chief, Pontiac, crushed. Britain gains Grenada from France.
1765 Stamp Act passed by British Parliament imposes tax in American colonies on newspapers, playing cards, pamphlets, and legal documents.
1767 Townshend Acts: tax imposed on various imports into North America. Mason-Dixon line established between Pennsylvania and Maryland, separating slave colonies and free colonies.
1774 First Continental Congress meets in Philadelphia to protest against British actions. Quebec Act secures Canada's loyalty to Britain, guarantees Roman Catholicism to French Canadians, and halts westward expansion.
1775–83 American Revolution (right); ended by Treaty of Paris.
1776 Second Continental Congress issues Declaration of Independence.
1781–89 Articles of Confederation establish loose federation of U.S. states.
1787 Constitutional convention of U.S. states meets in Philadelphia; federal system of government agreed on and New York declared federal capital.
1788 U.S. Constitution ratified by New Hampshire.
1789 George Washington becomes first U.S. president. Bill of Rights: first ten Amendments to U.S. Constitution.

THE AMERICAN REVOLUTION

The colonies' revolt against British rule, resting on a people's "inalienable right" to "life, liberty, and the pursuit of happiness," tore a hole in the British Empire. The imposition of taxes by Britain on imports into the colonies resulted in an increasingly acrimonious dispute, culminating in the Boston Tea Party in 1774, when cargo was emptied into Boston harbor to avoid payment of tax. The first shots in the American Revolution were fired at Lexington and Concord in 1775. The British surrendered at Yorktown in 1781, and U.S. independence was recognized in 1783. Anglo-American trade expanded rapidly, but diplomatic relations remained sour.

Important battles of the American Revolution.

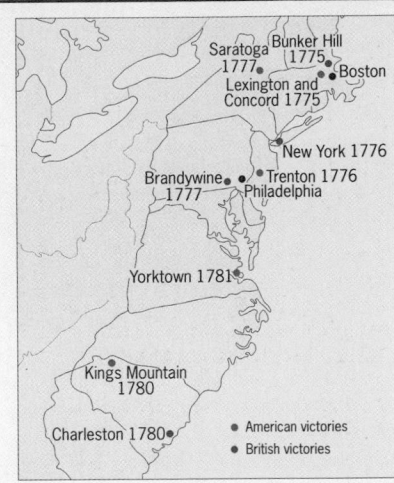

1790 George Vancouver explores Pacific coast.
1791 Constitutions Act divides Canada into British and French-speaking territories. Slave rebellion in French colony of Haiti led by Toussaint L'Ouverture.
1794 U.S. navy founded.
1796 George Washington refuses third term of presidency.
1797 John Adams becomes president. British take Trinidad from Spanish.
1798 Spanish found Los Angeles.

SOUTH AMERICA
1780–81 Peruvian Indians, led by Inca Tupac Amara, in unsuccessful rebellion against Spanish rulers.

AUSTRALIA AND OCEANIA
1768–71 First voyage of British navigator Captain James Cook (below).
1772–75 Second voyage of James Cook.
1789 Mutiny on *Bounty*; mutineers settle on Pitcairn Island in South Pacific.
1793 First free settlers arrive in Australia.

COLONIAL AUSTRALIA

Cook discovered New South Wales during his around-the-world voyage in 1770 and claimed Australia for Britain. The "First Fleet" under Captain Arthur Phillip arrived in 1788. It carried more than 1,000 people, three-fourths of them convicts, and included nearly 200 women, 13 children, and stores for two years. Cook had recommended Botany Bay, but Port Jackson proved more suitable. In spite of severe hardship, the colony survived, more convicts were sent, and the first free settlers arrived in 1793. Although sheep raising began in the 1790s, in the early years New South Wales depended on fishing and whaling for revenue. The social differences between the motley British colonists and the Aborigines precluded understanding or cooperation. Violent clashes were common, and many Aborigines died from European diseases. Others were driven from their hunting grounds into the inhospitable bush. The Tasmanian Aborigines became extinct within a century.

In this painting by Samuel Calvert, Captain Cook takes possession of the Australian continent on behalf of the British crown.

1775	1780	1785	1790	1795	1799
Adam Smith writes *Wealth of Nations*	Germany: Kant's *Critique of Pure Reason*		Tom Paine writes *Rights of Man*	Mary Wollstonecraft writes *Vindication of Rights of Women*	
	France: Montgolfiers in first piloted balloon flight	Cartwright invents power loom	America: Whitney invents cotton gin	France: metric system adopted	
Germany: Goethe leads *Sturm und Drang* movement	Austria: Mozart in Vienna	Beaumarchais writes *Barber of Seville*	Boswell's *Life of Johnson*	*Lyrical Ballads* by Wordsworth and Coleridge begin Romanticism	
	France: David's neoclassical *Oath of the Horatii*		France: revolutionary art of David's *Death of Marat*		

The Agricultural and Industrial revolutions

The Industrial Revolution, which began in the 1700s, developed in Britain first because freedom from wars meant that the British people were generally prosperous and had the money to buy manufactured

"Manchester streets may be irregular . . . its smoke may be dense and its mud ultra-muddy . . . but not all or any of these things can prevent the image of a great city . . . foremost in the grand march of improvement, a grand incarnation of progress."

British periodical (1858)

goods. This settled state saw a rise in population, which put pressure on the supply of fuel. As the forests of England declined, so the age of charcoal came to an end. The new fuel to power developing industry was provided by coal, powering the steam engine, which brought about a revolution in the social and economic order of the Western world.

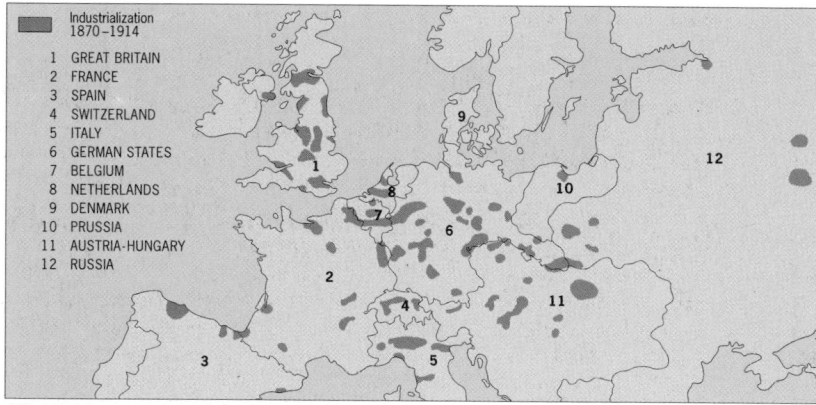

Industrialization 1870–1914

1 GREAT BRITAIN
2 FRANCE
3 SPAIN
4 SWITZERLAND
5 ITALY
6 GERMAN STATES
7 BELGIUM
8 NETHERLANDS
9 DENMARK
10 PRUSSIA
11 AUSTRIA-HUNGARY
12 RUSSIA

Worldwide expansion of the Industrial Revolution.

The Agricultural Revolution

The precondition of Great Britain's industrial revolution was a great increase in agricultural productivity. Industrialization was possible only because the countryside could release workers for industrial production while still producing enough to feed an expanding population. The "agricultural revolution" of the 1700s was stimulated partly by new agricultural implements, like Tull's seed drill, partly by improved drainage and more efficient crop rotation, and partly by the enclosure of two million acres of hitherto unworked land. But the revolution was also accompanied by the emergence of larger and larger estates with a peculiarly English rural social structure—landlords, capitalist tenants, and wage laborers—that facilitated the growth of capitalist farming.

Among the new agricultural aids of the 1700s was Crosskill's patent roller.

Timetable 1700–1840

1701 Jethro Tull's seed drill provides technical basis for constant tillage.

1705 Thomas Newcomen invents the atmospheric steam engine.

1709 Abraham Derby produces coke and uses it to smelt iron ore.

1730 Rotherman's triangular plow patented: it facilitates widespread use of Tull's seed drill.

1733 John Kay's flying shuttle doubles a weaver's productivity, exposing severe shortages of spinners in Britain and sparking the Industrial Revolution.

1754 Henry Cort invents iron-rolling process; establishes a mill in Fareham, England.

1762 At Carron Ironworks in Scotland, cast iron converted into malleable iron for first time.

1764 James Hargreaves's spinning jenny multiplies most spinners' productivity 16-fold.

1765 James Watt's improvements to Newcomen's steam engine provide an economical alternative to the water-wheel.

1769 Richard Arkwright's water frame lays basis of revolution in cotton manufacture: powered by water, later by steam, it spells the doom of domestic industry and produces cotton yarn strong enough to be both warp and weft, so eliminating dependence on linen.

1775 John Wilkinson invents precise hole-boring machine.

1776 Watt and Boulton produce their first commercial steam engine.

1779 Samuel Crompton's mule combines principles of the jenny and the water frame to produce finer yarn. First cast-iron bridge built at Coalbrookdale, Shropshire, England (*opposite*).

1784 Cort invents puddling process for manufacture of wrought iron. Scottish millwright Andrew Meikle invents threshing machine.

1785 Edmund Cartwright's power loom introduced: it revolutionizes cotton industry in England.

1792 British engineer Thomas Maudsley develops first machine tools.

1793 American Eli Whitney's cotton gin mechanizes reaping and brings great reductions in the price of raw cotton.

1803 John Horrocks, a British machine manufacturer, builds all-metal loom.

1804 British engineer Richard Trevithick builds first successful steam locomotive.

1807 American inventor Robert Fulton builds first commercially successful steamboat.

1816 Briton John MacAdam originates crushed-stone (macadam) roads.

1825 Stockton-Darlington railway in N.E. England is first line to carry passengers.

1831 American Cyrus McCormick's reaper enables one person to do the work of five.

1839 American inventor Charles Goodyear pioneers vulcanized rubber.

The cotton gin removed seeds and impurities from cotton fibers.

King Cotton

The textile industry in the north of England was the catalyst of industrialization. Much of the cotton was imported from the United States, where Eli Whitney's cotton gin revived slavery in the south and increased cotton output. The machines developed by British inventors increased productivity and required less skilled labor than manual processes; greater mechanization also led to the increase in large factories, drawing workers into the rapidly expanding towns of the north. Factory life led to social problems of overcrowding, poor sanitation, and child labor. Between 1820 and 1850, profits from cotton manufacturing rose by 50 percent; wages rose hardly at all. The effects of the Industrial Revolution were worldwide, bringing a population explosion and improvement in living conditions for many, but also a host of problems.

Urbanization

Prior to the massive industrialization that took place in the 1700s and 1800s, the vast majority of people lived in small rural communities. Cities were few and, in 1790, the first decennial census of the United States revealed that the average number of people living in a town was just 8,400. In 1800, London was the only city in the world with a population of more than one million. One hundred years later, nine other cities had populations in excess of one million. The growth of urban areas in the 1800s was phenomenal, as people left the land in search of employment in the growing industrial sector. In the latter half of the century, the world's urban population increased by nearly 300%.

Overcrowding and poor sanitation were serious problems for city dwellers in the 1800s, but ultimately urbanization meant a huge rise in both quality of life and life expectancy.

The railroad and the age of iron

In 1830, England had the world's only railroad lines operating steam locomotives: the Stockton-Darlington, opened in 1825, and the Liverpool-Manchester, opened in 1830. In 1828, the first U.S. passenger railroad, the Baltimore & Ohio, was begun. France built its first line, Saint-Etienne to Lyons, in 1832; Germany opened its first in 1835. In 1836, Belgium became the first nation to operate a state-owned railroad system. In the United States, the first transcontinental railroad was completed in 1869, linking Nebraska and California.

Rail transportation changed people's lives, opened unseen prospects, and widened markets. It also, with steamships and engineering generally, stimulated the growth of the iron industry and the arrival of steel. Throughout the second iron phase of the Industrial Revolution, Great Britain remained ahead of its rivals Germany and France. The United States was a net importer of iron and steel from Britain for many years, but its industries expanded rapidly, and by the 1900s it was the world's leading industrial power.

World population and world urban population 1800–1950			
Year	Total population (millions)	Urban population (millions)	% urban
1800	906	27.2	3.0
1850	1,171	74.9	6.4
1900	1,608	218.7	13.6
1950	2,400	716.7	29.9
(Urban population indicates number of people living in towns with populations of more than 5,000.)			

Ironworks such as those at Coalbrookdale, Shropshire, made Britain the world's leading iron producer in the late 1700s and early 1800s.

1800–49

THE NAPOLEONIC WARS

Europe during the Napoleonic age.

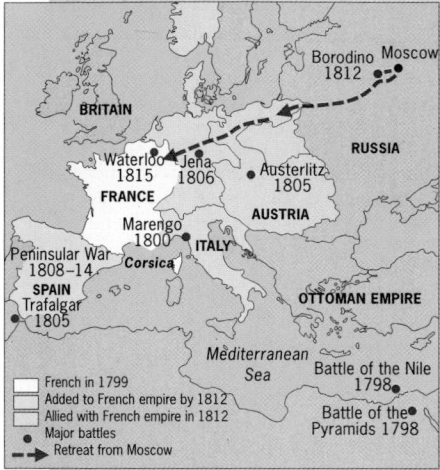

British cartoon by Cruikshank depicting the French retreat from Moscow in 1812.

By 1797, after five years of revolutionary wars, Napoleon's *grande armée* had carried all before it, and Britain stood alone against France. In 1802, British prime minister William Pitt made peace with Napoleon. After the great French victories of 1805–06, Britain again stood alone. Economic warfare followed, Napoleon's continental blockade being answered by Britain's attempt to control Atlantic shipping. In 1812, the tide turned against France. Yet more wars ended with France having made no permanent gains and the Bourbon monarchy restored.

1797 France conquers the Netherlands, Belgium, the Rhineland, Switzerland, and northern Italy.

1798 Nelson defeats French navy at Battle of the Nile.

1802 Peace of Amiens ends fighting until 1805.

1804 Napoleon crowns himself emperor.

1805–07 French victories at Austerlitz (1805) and Jena (1806) drive Austria, Prussia, and Russia out of war (until 1813).

1809–12 Wellington's victory in Peninsular Campaign secures Spanish and Portuguese national integrity.

1812 Russia invaded, but terrible weather conditions force the *grande armée* back from Moscow.

1814 Allies enter Paris and Napoleon abdicates; he goes into exile.

1815 Battle of Waterloo ends the wars.

British fleets under Codrington.

1830 July Revolution in Paris: Charles X overthrown; Louis Philippe becomes "citizen king." Revolution in Belgium against Dutch rule. Protocol of London proclaims Greece an independent kingdom.

1831 Belgium wins independence from Netherlands.

1832 First Reform Act passed in Britain gives vote to middle-class men.

1834 Carlist wars in Spain (to 1839). Tolpuddle martyrs transported.

1838–48 Chartist movement in Britain demands votes for all adult males.

1842 Chartist riots in Staffordshire and Lancashire.

1845–51 Irish potato famine (*opposite*).

1846 Growth of anti-British movement in Ireland. Repeal of Corn Laws in Britain.

1848 "Year of Revolutions" in Europe: revolutions in Paris, Milan, Naples, Venice, Rome, Berlin, Vienna, Prague, and Budapest. Louis Philippe abdicates French throne; *Communist Manifesto* published by German socialists Karl Marx and Friedrich Engels (*p. 234*).

MIDDLE EAST

1805 Mehemet Ali appointed pasha of Egypt by Selim III, sultan of Turkey.

1811 Ruling Mamluk's dynasty of Egypt brought down by Mehemet Ali.

1820–21 Egyptian conquest of Sudan.

1831 Syria conquered by Egypt.

1839 British occupy Aden. Mehemet Ali defeats Ottoman Turks in Syria.

1840 Britain, Russia, Prussia, and Austria form alliance against Mehemet Ali.

1841 Mehemet Ali becomes hereditary viceroy of the Sudan.

ASIA AND AUSTRALIA AND OCEANIA

1803–18 Marathas fight against growing power of Britain in India.

1803 Settlers begin to arrive in Tasmania.

1815 Britain gains Ceylon (now Sri Lanka).

1819 Singapore founded by British. Kashmir conquered by Sikhs.

1824 Britain gains Assam. First Anglo-Burmese War (to 1826).

1825–30 Dutch defeat Javanese anti-colonial forces.

1839 First Opium War between Britain and China (to 1842). Britain and Afghanistan at war (to 1842).

1840 Treaty of Waitangi: New Zealand becomes British colony.

EUROPE

1800 Act of Union unites Great Britain and Ireland to form United Kingdom.

1804 Napoleon crowned emperor (*above*).

1806 Nelson dies at Trafalgar, having defeated the French/Spanish fleets. Napoleon dissolves Holy Roman Empire; replaces it with Confederation of the Rhine. Turkey at war with Russia and Britain (to 1812).

1807 Slave trade abolished in British Empire (*p. 349*).

1808 Russia invades Finland. France occupies Spain.

1810 France annexes Holland.

1815 Napoleon returns from exile to rule for a hundred days before being defeated at Waterloo; Louis XVIII restored as

king. Congress of Vienna: settlement of postwar Europe; Austrian and Prussian monarchies restored. Kingdom of the Netherlands unites Belgium and Holland. France ends slave trade.

1819 Peterloo massacre at Manchester.

1820 Revolutions in Italy, Portugal, and Spain.

1821 War of Greek Independence against Ottoman Empire (to 1828).

1823 Spanish revolution crushed.

1825 Failure of "Decembrist" conspiracy in Russia against czar. Egyptian forces invade Greece.

1826 Turks capture Missolonghi from Greeks.

1827 Battle of Navarino: Egyptian fleet destroyed by French, Russian, and

	1800	1805	1810	1815	1820
RELIGION AND PHILOSOPHY		Germany: Hegel writes *Phenomenology of Mind*			Germany: Schopenhauer writes *The World as Will and Idea*
SCIENCE AND TECHNOLOGY	Italy: Volta invents battery	France: Lamarck coins word "biology"	Gas lighting introduced in Europe · Dalton proposes atomic theory	Single wire telegraph invented	
LITERATURE AND MUSIC		Germany: Schiller's *William Tell* urges political freedom	Germany: Goethe's *Faust, Part 1*	Beethoven extends symphonic form · Italy: Rossini's *Barber of Seville* · Byron writes *Don Juan*	
ART AND ARCHITECTURE		France: Ingres paints *Napoleon as Emperor*		Spain: Goya's *Disasters of War* · France: Gericault's *Raft of the Medusa*	

1841 Sultan of Brunei grants Sarawak to British. Japan begins reforms (to 1843).

1842 Treaty of Nanking ends First Opium War; China cedes Hong Kong Island to Britain. French occupy Tahiti. British withdraw from Kabul, Afghanistan.

1845 Anglo-Sikh wars in India (to 1848). Britain annexes the Punjab. Anglo-Maori Wars in New Zealand (to 1872).

AFRICA

1801 Islamic kingdom of Sokoto founded. Third Xhosa War between Xhosa and colonial forces.

1802 Cape Colony in South Africa restored to Dutch.

1804 Uthman dan Fodio conquers Hausa states in W. Africa and creates large empire in Mali.

1806 Britain seizes control of Cape Colony from Dutch.

1807 Sierra Leone and Gambia become British colonies.

1810 Shaka founds Zulu Empire in southern Africa.

1821 Gold Coast (Ghana) becomes British colony.

1822 Liberia founded as colony for freed U.S. slaves (independent 1847).

1824 War between British and Asante (to 1827) in Gold Coast.

1830 Algeria becomes French colony.

1835–38 Great Trek: 10,000 Boers (Dutch) settlers in Cape Colony trek northward where they found Natal.

1838 Boers defeat Zulus at battle of Blood River.

1839 France annexes part of Gabon.

1843 Britain annexes Natal.

1846–53 Xhosa resist expansion of Dutch and British in Cape Colony.

NORTH AMERICA

1801 Thomas Jefferson inaugurated as president in the new federal capital of Washington, D.C.

1801–04 Slave revolt led by Toussaint L'Ouverture eventually gains Haiti independence from France.

1803 "Louisiana Purchase" from France doubles size of U.S.A.

1804–06 Lewis and Clark expedition explores new U.S. territory and reaches Pacific.

1808 Importation of slaves made illegal.

1812–14 Britain and U.S.A. at war over shipping and territory.

1813 Mexico declares independence from Spain.

1814 British burn Washington D.C.; Treaty of Ghent ends Anglo-American war.

1818 Canadian–U.S. border fixed along 49th parallel; both countries occupy Oregon. Spain cedes Florida to U.S.A.

1820 Missouri Compromise: admission of Maine (1820) as free state and Missouri (1821) as slave state; slavery banned from all states north of Missouri.

1821 First U.S. public high school founded in Massachusetts.

SOUTH AMERICAN INDEPENDENCE

The torch of liberation was carried by nationalist leaders José de San Martin and Simón Bolivar. By the mid-1820s, the New World empires of Spain and Portugal had nearly disappeared. In 1823, President Monroe issued his famous doctrine that the United States would interpret further European interference in the Western Hemisphere as a threat to American security.

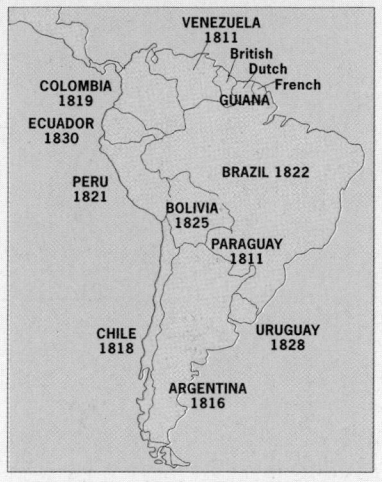

Dates of South American independence.

1823 Monroe Doctrine warns European powers not to interfere in U.S. politics.

1829–37 Ninety-four treaties force Native American tribes to surrender their lands.

1833 Oberlin College, Ohio, becomes first coeducational college.

1836 Battles of Alamo and San Jacinto: Texas wins independence from Mexico.

1838 Cherokees' "Trail of Tears": forced relocation to Oklahoma.

1839 Rebellions in Upper and Lower Canada.

1840 Union Act unites Upper and Lower Canada.

1842 Webster-Ashburton Treaty settles U.S.–Canadian border dispute.

1846 Oregon Treaty settles western border of U.S.A. and Canada. U.S.–Mexican war starts.

1848 U.S.–Mexican war ends. U.S.A. gains California and New Mexico. Start of Californian gold rush. First women's rights convention, Seneca Falls, NY.

IRELAND IN THE 1800s

Ireland's population increased rapidly during the first decades of the 1800s. Many people lived in poverty, dependent on their potato crop both for food and a meager income. The disease that hit the potato crop in 1845–47, causing its failure, therefore had devastating consequences. The resulting famine cost perhaps a million lives and resulted in the emigration of about two million Irish people, chiefly to the United States. It also dealt a blow to the efforts of Irish patriots to secure the repeal of the legislative union between Great Britain and Ireland.

1798 Wolfe Tone leads Irish revolt against British rule.

1801 Act of Union unites Irish and British parliaments.

A funeral during the Irish famine.

1843 Daniel O'Connell heads campaign for the repeal of the Union.

1845–51 Potato famine devastates Ireland and provides British prime minister Robert Peel with the opportunity to repeal the Corn Laws.

1848 Irish repeal movement collapses in the year of European revolutions.

1825	1830	1835	1840	1845	1850
	Joseph Smith founds Mormonism	America: Emerson develops transcendentalism	France: Comte's writings initiate sociology	Iran: Bahai religion founded	Marx and Engels write *Communist Manifesto*
Stevenson's locomotive runs between Stockton and Darlington	Faraday discovers electric generator	America: Colt patents first repeating firearm	Brunel's *Great Western* introduces transatlantic steam service	Ether first used as anesthetic	
Schubert's *Unfinished Symphony*	America: Cooper's *Last of the Mohicans*	France: Berlioz's *Symphonie Fantastique* Stendahl publishes *le rouge et le noir*	Chopin works in Paris	Lermontov writes *A Hero of Our Times*	Balzac's *Comédie Humaine* series	Hawthorne writes *The Scarlet Letter*
France: Delacroix's *Massacre at Chios*		Japan: Hokusai's *Thirty Six Views of Mount Fuji*	Gothic revival style: British Houses of Parliament	Turner's *Rain, Steam and Speed*	Pre-Raphaelite Brotherhood founded	

1850–99

THE EUROPEAN EMPIRES

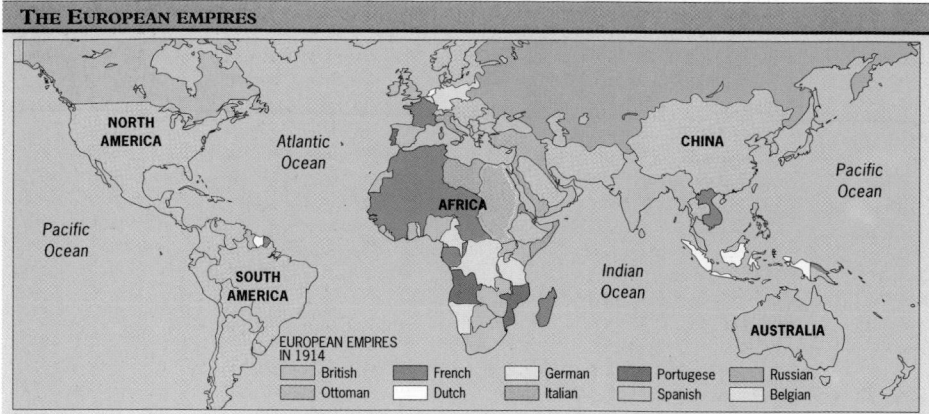

EUROPEAN EMPIRES IN 1914

British	French	German	Portugese	Russian
Ottoman	Dutch	Italian	Spanish	Belgian

The industrialized nations of Europe in the 1800s needed a large supply of raw materials for new factories. Much of Africa and Asia had both materials and cheap labor in abundance, so many European nations sought to establish new colonies during the 1800s. By 1900, European empires covered much of the world, with the most territory being controlled by Britain, France, and Germany.

EUROPE

1850 German Confederation restored under Austrian leadership at Frankfurt.

1854–56 Crimean War: Britain, France, and Turkey defeat Russia.

1858 Irish (Fenian) Republican Brotherhood set up in Dublin and U.S.A. to work for Irish republic.

1859 France and Sardinia at war with Austria; Austrians defeated; Piedmont gains Lombardo–Venetia.

1860 First Italian national parliament at Turin. Giuseppe Garibaldi and his "Thousand Redshirts" conquer Naples and Sicily.

1861 Italy (except for Rome and Venice) united as one kingdom. Serfdom in Russia abolished by Alexander II.

1864 Prussia and Austria take Schleswig-Holstein from Denmark.

1866 German Confederation is dissolved, leading to Austro-Prussian War (Seven Weeks' War); Austria defeated.

1867 North German Confederation formed under Prussian leadership. Dual kingdom of Austria-Hungary founded.

1870 Franco-Prussian War (to 1871): Prussians besiege Paris. Kingdom of Italy annexes Papal States.

1871 Rome becomes capital of Italy. German Empire declared. Franco-Prussian War: Paris surrenders after gruelling siege; Paris Commune set up in opposition to peace terms is crushed; Alsace-Lorraine ceded to Germany.

1877–78 Russo-Turkish War over the Balkans.

1879 Austria-Hungary and Germany form Dual Alliance (to 1918). Irish Land League formed.

1882 Italy joins Germany and Austria-Hungary in Triple Alliance (to 1914).

1886 British Parliament rejects Irish Home Rule Bill.

1893 Independent Labour Party founded in Britain by socialist Keir Hardie.

1894 French officer Alfred Dreyfus convicted of treason and deported.

1897–98 Greece and Turkey at war in Macedonia.

1899 Permanent Court of Arbitration set up at the Hague: aims to settle international disputes peacefully.

MIDDLE EAST

1856–57 Persian invasion of Afghanistan leads to war with Britain.

1869 Opening of Suez Canal.

1876 Britain and France assume joint control of Egypt's finances.

1882 British bombard Alexandria and occupy Cairo to suppress nationalists; leads to French withdrawal from Egypt.

ASIA

1850–64 Taiping Rebellion: revolt in China against the Manchu dynasty.

1853 U.S. naval officer Matthew Perry compels Japan to open ports for trade with U.S.A.

1856–60 Second Opium War between China and Britain.

1857–58 Indian Mutiny: rebellion of sepoys in Bengal army.

1858 Indian Mutiny: Lucknow relieved; Indian Mutiny ends. India Act: government of India passes to British crown from East India Company.

1860 British and French occupy Peking (Beijing); end of Opium wars.

1862 Cochin-China (Cambodia) becomes French protectorate.

1868 Meiji Restoration (to 1912) ends Tokugawa shogunate in Japan.

1876 Korea opened to Japanese trade.

1877 Samurais defeated in Satsuma Rebellion in Japan.

1878–80 Second Anglo-Afghan War; Britain gains control of Afghan affairs.

1884 War between China and France (to 1885) over Annam (Vietnam).

1885 Third Anglo-Burmese War (to 1886); Britain annexes Upper Burma. France gains protectorate of Annam and Tonkin (Indochina). Indian National Congress founded in India.

1887 China recognizes Portuguese possession of Macao. French complete union of Indochina.

1894-95 War between Japan and China over Korea.

1895 Treaty of Shimonoseki: Japan gains Formosa (Taiwan); China recognizes Korea's independence.

1898 Britain gains Hong Kong colony on 99-year lease.

AFRICA

1852 Sands River Convention: Britain agrees to Transvaal becoming independent Boer republic.

1853 Scottish explorer Livingstone begins crossing of African continent.

1854 Orange Free State set up in South Africa. France occupies Senegal. Quinine successful against malaria.

1868 British expedition sent to Ethiopia.

		1850	1855	1860	1865	1870
	RELIGION AND PHILOSOPHY		Thoreau's transcendentalism in *Walden*	Mill's *Utilitarianism*	Marx writes *Das Kapital*	Papal infallibility proclaimed
	SCIENCE AND TECHNOLOGY	U.S.A.: Singer develops the sewing machine	Parkes invents celluloid, first plastic material	Darwin writes *Origin of Species*	Austria: Mendel founds genetics	France: Pasteur founds bacteriology Lister introduces antiseptic surgery
	LITERATURE AND MUSIC	Melville's *Moby Dick* Stowe's *Uncle Tom's Cabin*	Whitman's *Leaves of Grass* Poems by Arnold, Browning	Flaubert's *Madame Bovary*	Tolstoy's *War and Peace* Dostoyevsky's *Crime and Punishment*	Alcott's *Little Women*
	ART AND ARCHITECTURE	France: Realist Courbet's *Stone-breakers*	France: Haussmann begins town planning of Paris	France: Salon des Refusés exhibits work by Manet, Pissarro, Cézanne		

1869 Tunisia controlled by Britain, France, and Italy.

1871 American explorer Stanley meets Livingstone at Lake Tanganyika.

1873 Second Asante War in W. Africa; Asante defeated by British (in 1874).

1874 Britain establishes colony of Gold Coast (Ghana).

1876 Last Xhosa War against Europeans (to 1879).

1877 Britain annexes South African Republic of Transvaal.

1879 Zulu War: Zulus defeat British at Isandhlwana but are crushed at Ulundi.

1880 Boer revolt against British in South Africa.

1881 "Scramble for Africa": rival European nations seek new colonies. French establish protectorate in Tunis. Battle of Majuba Hill: Boers defeat British; Transvaal self-government restored.

1882–85 Anti-Egyptian revolt in Sudan led by Muslim leader Mahdi Mohammad Ahmad.

1884 Berlin Conference decides colonial divisions in Africa.

1885 Britain establishes protectorate over southern Nigeria and Bechuanaland. German East Africa established.

1887 Ethiopia becomes Italian protectorate.

1889 British empire-builder Cecil Rhodes founds British South Africa Company.

1892 French occupy Dahomey (Benin).

1893 War between Matabele and British. Ivory Coast becomes French colony.

1895 British South African Company's territory named Rhodesia.

1896 Anglo-Egyptian force begins reconquest of Sudan. Italy recognizes Ethiopian independence. Final Anglo-Asante War: Asante defeated.

1898 Battle of Omdurman: Anglo-Egyptian force defeats Sudan rebels.

1899 Boer War between Boers and British in South Africa (to 1902); Boers besiege Mafeking, Kimberley, and Ladysmith.

North and Central America

c. 1850–90 Wars between U.S. army and Native American tribes.

1853 Gadsden Purchase: U.S.A. buys land from Mexico.

1857 Civil war in Mexico.

1858 Lincoln–Douglas debates in Illinois.

1860 South Carolina secedes from U.S.A.

1861 Abraham Lincoln inaugurated president; Confederate States of America formed by South Carolina and ten other southern states (later joined by four more states); civil war in America (to 1865) between the Union (northern states) and Confederates (seceded southern states) (*right*).

1863 Emancipation Proclamation in U.S.A. Gettysburg Address: Lincoln expresses democratic ideals. French occupy Mexico City.

1864 French install Archduke Maximilian of Austria as emperor of Mexico.

1865 American Civil War ends; Lincoln assassinated; Thirteenth Amendment abolishes slavery; Bureau of Freed Slaves set up; Ku Klux Klan founded.

1865–67 Reconstruction reintegrates former Confederate states.

1867 Russia sells Alaska to U.S.A. Confederation of Canada established. France withdraws from Mexico.

1868–78 Ten Years' War: Cuba attempts to gain independence from Spain.

1869 Union Pacific Railroad completed in U.S.A. State of Wyoming first to grant women's suffrage. Red River Rebellion: Canadian settlers resist British rule.

1876 Battle of Little Bighorn: Custer's forces killed by Sioux and Cheyenne.

1881 President Garfield assassinated.

1890 Massacre of Sioux Indians by U.S. cavalry at Wounded Knee.

1898 Spanish-American War: Cuba gains independence; Spain cedes Puerto Rico, Guam, and Philippines to U.S.A.

South America

1865–70 Paraguayan War: Paraguay fights Brazil, Uruguay, and Argentina.

1879–84 War of the Pacific: Chile defeats Peru and Bolivia.

1888 Slavery abolished in Brazil.

1889 Brazil becomes a republic.

Australia and Oceania

1851 Gold rush in Australia.

1852 New Zealand granted constitution.

1853 Van Diemen's Land renamed Tasmania.

1860–70 Second Maori War in New Zealand.

1861 Gold rush in New Zealand.

1867 End of transportation of convicts from Britain to Australia.

1881 Peace declared between Maoris and New Zealand settlers.

1893 Women granted vote in New Zealand (first nation to do so).

THE AMERICAN CIVIL WAR

Many contributing factors caused the conflict between the northern (Union) and southern states (Confederacy) that resulted in the latter's secession: these included sectional rivalry, the moral campaign of the abolitionists of slavery, and especially federal control versus states' rights. The war began when Confederate troops attacked Fort Sumter, South Carolina, in April 1861. By 1864, the superior strength of the Union began to tell. Short of soldiers, money, food, and weapons, the Confederate commanders were forced to surrender in April 1865. The seceding southern states were eventually readmitted to the Union, and slavery was abolished.

Battle	Result
1861	
Bull Run (1st)	North defeated.
1862	
Fort Donelson	Northern victory.
Seven Days	Richmond saved from capture; Northern forces retreat.
Bull Run (2nd)	South regains most of Virginia.
Antietam	Confederate retreat.
Fredericksburg	Bad defeat for North.
1863	
Chancellorsville	Southern victory.
Gettysburg	Northern victory marks turning point in war.
Vicksburg	Gives North control of the Mississippi River.
Chattanooga	Northern win; splits Confederacy in two.
1864	
Petersburg	Trench warfare pins North down.
Mobile Bay	North closes key Southern port.
Nashville	North ends Southern resistance in west.

Union troops take Fort Fisher, 1865.

1875	1880	1885	1890	1895	1899
Ramakrishna revives Hinduism U.S.A.: Mme. Blavatsky formulates theosophy	U.S.A.: Baker Eddy founds Christian Science	Charles Russell founds Jehovah's Witnesses			
	Bell invents telephone	Edison invents electric light bulb	Maxim gun invented	Germany: Benz develops automobile	France: Lumières develop cinema
Eliot's Middlemarch	Ibsen's A Doll's House	James's Portrait of a Lady	Twain's Adventures of Huckleberry Finn	Kipling's Plain Tales from the Hills	Hardy's Tess of the D'Urbervilles Wilde's The Picture of Dorian Gray	Chekhov's Seagull	Chopin's The Awakening
France: Monet's Impression, Sunrise gives name to Impressionism		Cezanne paints L'Estaque	Eiffel Tower constructed Statue of Liberty dedicated	Art nouveau develops in Europe	Austria: Klimt a leading member of Vienna Secession

The making of the United States

American life changed dramatically during the decades following the Civil War (1861–65). In fewer than 40 years the population more than doubled (from 31 to 76 million people, of whom 15 million were immigrants). As with other newly industrialized countries, a period of intense economic growth saw a great movement of people from rural areas to the cities.

"How astounded I have been by the amazing changes I have seen around me on every side [since1849] . . . changes physical, changes in the amount of land subdued and peopled, changes in the rise of vast new cities . . . changes in the graces and amenities of life."

Charles Dickens
American Notes (1868)

Although these demographic changes caused new social and political problems, not least the widening gap between the rich and poor, the era also coincided with a new confidence in American culture and way of life. This optimism was underpinned by the United States' vast supply of raw materials, its genius for converting those raw materials into industrial products, its ready-made transportation system of internal waterways (supplemented by the new railroads), and its plentiful supply of cheap labor from immigration.

The railroads played a leading part in the opening up of the American West.

Settling a continent

By 1850, the white population had begun to stretch across the entire continent. The European traders had been followed by convoys of covered wagons carrying settlers across the plains and over the Rockies. Between 1865 and 1900, the United States consolidated its borders and settled its remaining territory. In 1890, the Bureau of Census declared that a frontier no longer existed.

1852 Wells Fargo service founded.
1853 U.S.A. acquires parts of New Mexico and Arizona. New York–Chicago rail connection established.
1859 Colorado gold rush.
1861 Cross-country telegraph completed.
1862 Homestead Act: cheap land offered to settlers.
1867 Gold discovered in Wyoming.
1869 First transcontinental railroad completed.
1874–75 Gold rush in Black Hills of S. Dakota.
1878 Lincoln County War: feud between rival cattlemen.
1881 Tombstone, Arizona, founded.
1889 Oklahoma Territory opened to non-Indian settlement.

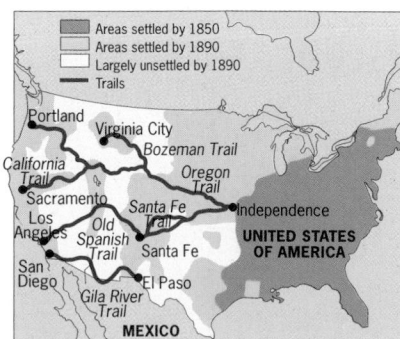

Areas settled by 1850
Areas settled by 1890
Largely unsettled by 1890
Trails

Portland
Virginia City
Bozeman Trail
California Trail
Oregon Trail
Sacramento
Santa Fe Trail
Los Angeles
Old Spanish Trail
Independence
San Diego
Santa Fe
UNITED STATES OF AMERICA
El Paso
Gila River Trail
MEXICO

Expansion of settled areas by 1890.

Timetable 1850–1900

1850 Population of U.S.A.: 23 million (3.2 million African-American slaves). Between 1850 and 1860, 424,000 people emigrate from Britain and 914,000 from Ireland to U.S.A.
1851 The *New York Times* first appears.
1853 Samuel Colt revolutionizes manufacture of small arms.
1855 First train crosses Mississippi River.
1857 Dred Scott decision upholds slavery.
1858 National Association of Baseball Players organized.
1859 First U.S. oil well drilled, Titusville, PA. Samuel Smiles publishes *Self-Help*, a manual on how to succeed in life.
1861 Outbreak of Civil War (*p. 357*). Passport system introduced.
1862 President Lincoln introduces first legal U.S. paper money (Greenbacks).
1865 Slavery abolished. Railroad sleeping cars designed by George M. Pullman.
1866 Atlantic cable laid. National Labor Union (craft unions) established.
1867 Horatio Alger publishes first in series of edifying stories.
1868 First professional baseball club, the Cincinnati Red Stockings, founded.
1869 Women's suffrage law passed in Territory of Wyoming. U.S. National Prohibition Party founded in Chicago. Princeton and Rutgers play first intercollegiate football game in New Jersey.
1870 John D. Rockefeller founds Standard Oil Company.
1871 The Great Fire in Chicago.
1872 First national park established at Yellowstone, Wyoming.
1874 First U.S. zoo opens in Philadelphia. Mark Twain publishes *Tom Sawyer*.
1876 World Exhibition in Philadelphia. National Baseball League founded.
1877 Railroad strike: first major industrial dispute. First public telephones appear.
1878 First commercial telephone exchange opens in New Haven, CT. First bicycles in U.S.A. manufactured.
1879 First successful "five and dime" opens in Lancaster, Pennsylvania.
1880 New York streets first lit by electricity. Canned fruit and meat available.
1881 President Garfield assassinated.
1882 Edison designs first hydroelectric plant, in Appleton, Wisconsin.
1883 W. F. Cody ("Buffalo Bill") organizes his "Wild West Show." Brooklyn Bridge is opened.
1885 Golf introduced by John M. Fox.
1886 American Federation of Labor founded. Haymarket Riot in Chicago (after bitter labor battles): 11 dead.
1888 George Eastman perfects "Kodak" box camera.
1889 Oklahoma open to settlement: 2 million acres claimed within 24 hours.
1890 Sherman Antitrust Act passed to curb monopolies.
1892 Ellis Island opens.
1893 Henry Ford builds his first car.
1895 First professional football game played in Latrobe, Pennsylvania.

The Native Americans

As the United States grew and prospered, Native Americans were powerless to prevent the destruction of their population, cultures, and economies. Between the first contact with Europeans and 1900, the Native American population was reduced from more than 1 million to only a few hundred thousand through European diseases, the imposition of white culture, and warfare. As more Europeans moved west, Native American resistance to the settlers increased. Most of the "Indian wars" were actually skirmishes between a local tribe and the settlers usurping their land. Throughout the conflict, the Native Americans were at a serious material and numerical disadvantage, and they lacked the cohesion to repel the influx of well-supplied, determined settlers.

An influx of peoples

Economic change, population surplus, and famine sent millions of Europeans to North America, and particularly to the United States, where scarcity of labor and unused land provided economic opportunity. At first, immigrants came predominantly from northern and western Europe; later, from the 1890s on, the majority were Russian Jews and the subject nationalities of the Austro-Hungarian Empire, as well as Poles and Italians. For most immigrants arriving in the United States at the end of the 1800s, the first glimpse of their new home was the giant Statue of Liberty overlooking New York Harbor. The 151-foot (46-m) statue was a gift from the French people for the United States Centennial of 1876, although only the torch was completed in time. Inscribed on a tablet on the pedestal is the poem by Emma Lazarus that includes the celebrated lines: "Give me your tired, your poor, your huddled masses yearning to breathe free."

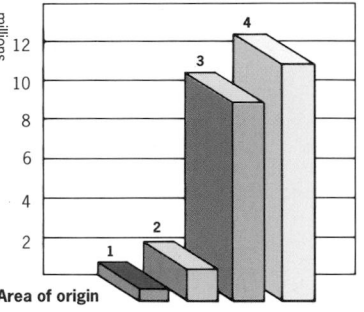

millions

Area of origin

1 Asia, Africa and Oceania
2 North and South America
3 Northern and Western Europe
4 Southern and Eastern Europe

The "battle" of Wounded Knee was in fact a massacre of defenseless Sioux by U.S. troops.

Immigrants arriving in New York hail the Statue of Liberty.

THE INDIAN WARS OF 1850–1900

The Sioux Wars (1854–90)
Minnesota 1862: Hundreds of settlers massacred in Sioux uprising.
Wyoming 1868: Red Cloud forces government to give up three forts.
Montana 1876: Crazy Horse defeats Crook at battle of Rosebud.
S. Dakota 1876: Crazy Horse and Sitting Bull defeat Custer at battle of Little Bighorn.
N. Dakota 1890: Soldiers massacre 153 Sioux, battle of Wounded Knee.
The Southern Plains (1860–79)
Colorado 1864: Sand Creek Massacre: U.S. army kills peaceful Cheyenne and Arapaho.
Missouri 1874: Red River War: General Sheridan wins campaign after 14 battles.
The Nez Percé War (1877)
Montana 1877: Chief Joseph leads his people in 800 mi. (500 km) retreat while trying to reach Canada.
Navaho Conflicts (1846–64)
Arizona 1863-64: Navaho defeated by troops led by Kit Carson.
Apache Warfare (1861–1900)
Arizona 1886: Apache chief Geronimo leads one of last major uprisings against U.S. government.

The Home Insurance Co. building, Chicago: the first skyscraper, 1885 (demolished 1931).

The new technology

The second half of the 1800s saw technological advances undreamed of even by observers such as Charles Dickens. U.S. inventors not only played a key part in the communications revolution but were also involved in the technological changes that resulted from the new construction materials and techniques. These in turn led to a specifically American phenomenon: the skyscraper. Important 19th-century U.S. inventions included:
1846 Sewing machine (Howe)
1853 Safety elevator (Otis)
1862 Machine gun (Gatling)
1867 Typewriter (Sholes, Glidden, Soulé)
1868 Air brake (Westinghouse)
1873 Barbed wire (Glidden)
1876 Telephone (Bell)
1877 Phonograph (Edison)
1879 Incandescent light (Edison)
1882 Electric flatiron (Seely)
1884 Fountain pen (Waterman)
1892 Zipper (Judson)

1900–18

EUROPE

1900 German Navy Act leads to massive increase in sea power; starts arms race with Britain.

1904 *Entente Cordiale* reached between Britain and France.

1905 "Bloody Sunday": troops fire on workers in St. Petersburg, Russia, resulting in a general strike and, ultimately, revolution (*opposite*); October Manifesto issued by Czar Nicholas grants constitution. Union of Sweden and Norway ends; Prince Carl of Denmark chosen by independent Norway and becomes King Haakon VII. Irish nationalist society, Sinn Féin, formed by Arthur Griffiths.

1906 French officer Alfred Dreyfus declared innocent of treason on retrial. First Russian Duma (parliament) meets but is dissolved.

1907 Second Hague Peace Conference: Britain fails to secure arms limitation from Germany. Anglo-Russian *Entente*; triple *entente* between Britain, France, and Russia. Second Duma dismissed in Russia; third lasts until 1912.

1908 Proclamation of annexation of Bosnia and Herzegovina by Austria.

1910 Revolution in Portugal; republic proclaimed.

1912 First Balkan War (to 1913): Bulgaria, Greece, Serbia, and Montenegro unite against Turkey. Fourth Russian Duma (to 1916). British ocean liner *Titanic* sinks, on maiden voyage with the loss of 1,513 lives.

1913 Ulster Volunteers form to oppose proposed Home Rule legislation in Ireland. First Balkan War ends; new state of Albania created. Second Balkan War: Serbia, Greece, Romania, and Turkey unite against Bulgaria; war caused by Serbian claims to Macedonia; Bulgaria defeated; Balkan states again partitioned.

1914 Archduke Franz Ferdinand of Austria assassinated in Sarajevo by Serbian student; World War I (to 1918) (*below*): Germany invades Belgium; battle of the Marne: Allies halt German advance on Paris; battle of Ypres: Germans fail to reach English Channel ports. Irish Home Rule Act provides for separate parliament in Ireland (*opposite*).

1915 World War I: Germany begins submarine blockade of Britain. Allied forces land in Gallipoli, Turkey, but fail to gain Dardanelles; Italy joins Allied Powers, Bulgaria joins Central Powers; western front: second battle of Ypres; battles of Nueve Chapelle, Artois, Champagne, Loos: British and French offensive fails. Warsaw, Poland, and Lithuania fall to Germany.

1916 World War I: western front: battle of the Somme: British offensive; more than one million killed. Portugal and Romania join war against Germany and Austria. Easter Rising in Ireland.

1917 World War I: third battle of Ypres (Passchendaele); Germans resume campaign. Russian Revolution (*opposite*).

1918 World War I: Russia and Germany sign Treaty of Brest-Litovsk; Russia withdraws from war; second battle of the Marne: last major German offensive fails. Revolution in Germany: Austria-Hungary and Germany surrender; Germany signs Armistice; World War I ends. President Wilson's fourteen points for peace outlined. Russian czar, Nicholas II, and family murdered. Civil war in Russia (to 1921). Civil war in Ireland (to 1923). Women over 30 given vote in Britain. World influenza epidemic (to 1920) kills millions.

WORLD WAR I

The causes of World War I were diverse and complex. The conflict arose from the following:
– colonial and trade rivalry among the major powers throughout the world
– secret diplomacy that caused universal distrust among nations
– a clash of interests between Germany and Russia in the Balkans and elsewhere and between Austria and Serbia in the Balkans
– the French desire to regain Alsace-Lorraine and wipe out disgrace of 1870
– a prewar system of alliances that was designed to give security yet pitted nations against one another.

Troops went off in high spirits to fight the war that would be "over in six weeks." Four years of grim trench warfare shocked Europe by the extent of the casualties for so little apparent reward. The chief legacy of the war was the emergence of new nation states following the collapse of the Ottoman and Austro-Hungarian empires.

1914 Archduke Franz-Ferdinand assassinated in Sarajevo; Austria-Hungary declares war on Serbia and begins general conflict; Germany joins Austria in war against Russia; trench war settles in on western front.

1915 *SS Lusitania* sunk by German torpedoes; Allies retreat from Gallipoli.

1916 German assault on Verdun meets heroic French resistance; only naval battle with German and British fleets at Jutland; battle of the Somme begins.

1917 Third Battle of Ypres, bogged down in the mud, achieves nothing; entry of U.S.A. aids Allies' progress.

1918 Second battle of the Marne forces Germany's surrender; armistice signed on November 11.

1919 Treaty of Versailles takes industrial heartlands from Germany and imposes heavy reparations.

1919–23 Treaties establish new nations: Finland, Lithuania, Estonia, Latvia, Czechoslovakia, Yugoslavia, Lebanon, Syria, Iraq, Transjordan, and Palestine.

Australian signalers crossing a communications trench in France, 1917.

World War I battlefronts.

	1900	1903	1906
RELIGION AND PHILOSOPHY	Austria: Freud publishes *Interpretation of Dreams* — Pentecostal movement begins	Max Weber combats historical materialism	France: Bergson publishes *Creative Evolution*
SCIENCE AND TECHNOLOGY	Marconi transmits radio signals across Atlantic	Wright brothers fly their aircraft in North Carolina	Third law of thermodynamics
LITERATURE AND MUSIC	Conrad writes *Lord Jim* Baum writes *The Wizard of Oz* — America: ragtime jazz develops	Russia: Chekhov's *Three Sisters* — Ireland: Celtic Renaissance	U.S.A.: first Ziegfeld Follies staged
ART AND ARCHITECTURE	Picasso begins his blue period	Great Train Robbery, pioneering movie, produced	Cubist painters Leger, Gris, and Picasso

MIDDLE EAST

1902 Turks agree to Baghdad railroad, linking Germany to Persian Gulf.

1906 Liberal revolution in Persia; Shah Nasir ud-Din grants constitution.

1908 Revolution in Turkey led by Young Turk movement. Successful counter-revolution by the shah in Persia, supported by Russia.

1914 Mesopotamian Campaign to protect oil supply begins.

1916–18 Grand Sharif Ali ibn Hussein of Mecca leads Arab revolt against Turks.

1917 Balfour Declaration: Britain pledges support for Jewish homeland in Palestine. World War I: British capture Baghdad and Jerusalem from Turkey.

ASIA

1900 Boxer Rebellion: Nationalist forces (Boxers) in China besiege foreign legations in Peking (Beijing); rebellion suppressed by international forces.

1901 Russia occupies Manchuria.

1902 Anglo-Japanese alliance formed.

1904 Japan and Russia at war.

1905 Japan defeats Russia at battles of Mukden and Tsushima; Treaty of Portsmouth ends Russo-Japanese war.

1910 Japan annexes Korea.

1911–12 Sun Yat-sen leads Chinese revolution and overthrows Manchu dynasty; republic established (*p. 362*).

AFRICA

1900 Second Boer War (to 1902).

1906 Algeciras Conference discusses Moroccan crisis between Germany and France; French rights recognized.

1907 Mahatma Gandhi leads civil disobedience campaign in South Africa in support of Indian rights.

1908 Belgium takes over Congo Free State; changes name to Belgian Congo.

1910 Union of South Africa is an independent dominion in British Empire.

1911 Agadir crisis: Germany sends gunboat to Morocco but withdraws claim. Italy occupies Tripoli; war with Turkey.

1912 African National Congress (ANC) formed in South Africa. Treaty of Ouchy ends Italo-Turkish war: Tripoli ceded to Italy.

1914 World War I: South Africa enters war against Central Powers.

NORTH AND CENTRAL AMERICA

1901 President McKinley assassinated.

THE RUSSIAN REVOLUTION

The first Russian Revolution, sparked off by disasters in the Japanese war in 1905, drew concessions from the czar, including an elected Duma (parliament). Some concessions were later withdrawn and, after new military defeats, revolution erupted again in March 1917. It resulted in the abdication of the czar and the establishment of a Western-type, liberal, republican regime. This was in turn overthrown in November (October in the Old Style calendar) by the Bolsheviks, a small, tightly organized, hard-line Marxist group led by Lenin. More coup d'état than revolution, it was bloodless. Plenty of blood was spilled, however, in the

Petrograd (St. Petersburg) in 1917.

ensuing civil war (1918–21). The Red Army, led by Trotsky, defeated the counterrevolutionary White Russians and established the Soviet Union under Bolshevik leadership.

1902 Republic declared in Cuba, gaining independence from Spain.

1903 Panama achieves independence from Colombia. American explorer Robert Peary reaches North Pole.

1906 Earthquake and fire devastate San Francisco.

1909 National Conference on the Negro (leading to the NAACP) convened.

1910 Mexican revolution begins.

1911 Mexican President Diaz overthrown; period of disorder follows.

1914 World War I: Canada enters war against Germans. Panama Canal opens; controlled by U.S.A.

1916 U.S. troops land in Haiti.

1917 U.S.A. declares war on Germany; Americans join Allies on western front.

SOUTH AMERICA

1902 British, German, and Italian warships seize Venezuelan navy to enforce debt payment.

AUSTRALIA AND OCEANIA

1901 Commonwealth of Australia established.

1907 Dominion of New Zealand established.

1911 Norwegian Roald Amundsen reaches South Pole.

1914–18 Australia and New Zealand enter World War I against Central Powers; German territories occupied: Western Samoa by New Zealand, Nauru by Australia, Micronesia and the Marshall Islands by Japan.

IRISH INDEPENDENCE

Irish home rule, a form of regional self-government within the U.K., was finally gained in 1914 but was destroyed by war and Sinn Féin's insistence on full separation. The war between the IRA and the British forces, with their auxiliaries, the Black and Tans, left a legacy of bitterness.

1873 Home Rule League founded in Dublin.

1886 Home Rule bill defeated.

1905 Sinn Féin ("Ourselves Alone") founded in Dublin.

1914 Home Rule bill passed; postponed on account of World War I.

1916 Easter Rising suppressed; rebel leaders executed.

1918–23 Civil war in Ireland.

1921 Irish Free State created by Anglo-Irish treaty.

1923 Attempt to bring the 6 counties of Ulster within new Irish republic.

Fighting in Dublin in 1922.

1909	1912	1915	1918
	Edmund Husserl founds phenomenology	Bertrand Russell, British analytical philosopher	Lenin writes *State and Revolution* · Carl Jung develops theory of collective unconscious
Henry Ford introduces Model T	Rutherford's theory of atomic physics	Niels Bohr's theory of atomic physics · Germany: Einstein publishes general theory of relativity	
	Stravinsky composes ballet music *The Fire Bird*	Ezra Pound works on his *Cantos* · France: Proust publishes first part of *A la recherche du temps perdu*	English war poets including Owen and Sassoon · Carl Sandburg publishes *Chicago Poems*
Fauvist painters Matisse, Duft, and Derain	Germany: Expressionist painters Kandinsky and Klee	U.S.A.: Chaplin makes his first film	Switzerland: Dadaist Duchamp exhibits *Fountain* (a urinal)

1919–38

EUROPE

1919 Peace conference begins in Paris; founds League of Nations. Treaty of Versailles: Germany loses colonies and Alsace-Lorraine and has to pay reparations. Treaty of Saint-Germain: ends Hapsburg monarchy; independence of Czechoslovakia, Poland, Yugoslavia, and Hungary. Rebellion in Ireland led by Sinn Féin (p. 361); Irish Republican Army (IRA) formed. Weimar Constitution adopted in Germany. First woman M.P. in Britain, Lady Astor.

1920 Civil war in Ireland; Northern Ireland accepts Home Rule Act; two Irish parliaments, in Belfast and Dublin. Russia and Poland at war (to 1921). Treaty of Sèvres between Allies and Turkey opposed by Turkish Nationalists led by Mustafa Kemal (later Atatürk) Fascist movement founded in Italy (below).

1921 Irish Free State established; IRA continues opposition. Greece attacks Turkey, defying League of Nations, but is finally defeated (1922).

1922 Fascist march on Rome; King Victor Emmanuel III invites Benito Mussolini to be prime minister. Union of Soviet Socialist Republics (U.S.S.R.) estab-lished with Lenin as leader. Civil war in Ireland between Free Staters and Republicans (to 1923). Sultan of Turkey deposed by Mustafa Kemal.

1923 French and Belgian troops occupy Ruhr district in western Germany after Germany fails to pay reparations; Adolf Hitler, founder of National Socialist (Nazi) Party in Germany (below), attempts to overthrow government. Turkey declared republic. Mussolini creates Fascist state in Italy.

1924 First Labour government in Britain under Ramsey Macdonald. Lenin dies in Russia; Joseph Stalin succeeds him.

1925 Locarno Conference: great powers agree to put disputes to arbitration. Mussolini bans all non-Fascist parties in Italy. French troops evacuate Ruhr.

1926 General Strike in Britain. Army in Portugal overthrows government.

1927 German economy collapses on "Black Friday."

1928 Joseph Stalin introduces first Five-Year Plan to develop heavy industry and collective farms in U.S.S.R. Kellogg Briand Pact signed denouncing war.

1929 Young Plan reassesses German repa-ration payments. Lateran Treaties rec-ognize sovereignty of Vatican City.

1930 Allied troops leave Germany.

1931 King Alfonso XIII of Spain flees country; republic is proclaimed (opposite).

1933 Adolf Hitler appointed chancellor of Germany; burning of German *Reichstag* (parliament); Germany withdraws from League of Nations; National Socialists (NAZIS) gain control of Germany. U.S.S.R. Communist Party purged by Stalin.

1934 Balkan Pact formed among Turkey, Greece, Romania, and Yugoslavia. German plebiscite votes for Hitler as führer; "Night of the Long Knives" as S.S. troops purge party of Hitler's rivals. Soviet Union joins League of Nations.

1935 Hitler renounces Treaty of Versailles; announces policy of rearm-ament; Nuremberg Laws classify Jews as second-class citizens (p.365).

1936 German troops reoccupy Rhineland. Military revolt led by General Franco against Spanish Republican government begins Spanish Civil War (to 1939) (opposite): Italy and Germany support Falange rebels; U.S.S.R. sends aid to Republicans. Agreement between Italy

CHINESE REVOLUTION

Karl Marx theorized that Communist revolutions would occur in industrial societies. China, like Russia before it, proved that they were more likely in preindustrial societies. Chinese Communists led by Mao Zedong eventually gained power by winning the confidence of the peasantry.

1911 Manchu dynasty overthrown; China becomes republic.

1928 Chinese Nationalists (Kuomintang) take Shanghai; war with Communists begins.

1934–35 Mao Zedong and followers make "Long March" from Kiangsi to Yen-an in north, a distance of 6,000 mi. (9,660 km).

1937 Japan takes control of N. China; Nationalists and Communists join to fight Japanese.

1949 Communists crush last Nationalist resistance; Mao Zedong becomes chairman of the People's Republic of China; Nationalists dri-ven to Formosa (Taiwan).

THE RISE OF FASCISM

Fascism—a form of extreme, antidemo-cratic nationalism involving total gov-ernmental control—arose from social and economic discontent after World War I and dissatisfaction with the Versailles settlement of 1919. In Italy, victory had brought no economic improvement and few territorial gains: Benito Mussolini founded the original fascist movement in 1921 and had acquired near-dictatorial power by 1922. In Germany, the racist National Socialist (Nazi) party, employing intimi-dation and violence and gaining popular support as a result of the Depression, came to power in 1933. Its leader, Adolf Hitler, abolished the constitution and assumed dictatorial powers. Hitler and Mussolini helped the fascist Falange to power in Spain, and Hitler's policy of national aggrandizement led to the out-break of World War II.

A soldier prevents business at a Jewish shop in Nazi Germany.

	1919	1922	1925
RELIGION AND PHILOSOPHY	France: Joan of Arc canonized	Austria: Wittgenstein's *Tractatus Logico-Philosophicus*	
SCIENCE AND TECHNOLOGY	Alcock and Brown make first transatlantic flight	Radio broadcasting begins in U.S.A.	U.S.A.: Birdseye develops frozen foods
LITERATURE AND MUSIC	Sherwood Anderson's *Winesburg, Ohio*	Edith Wharton's *The Age of Innocence*	Joyce publishes *Ulysses*	Germany: Mann's *The Magic Mountain* Austria: Kafka's *The Trial*
ART AND ARCHITECTURE	Germany: Bauhaus school of architecture by Walter Gropius	Lloyd Wright builds antiearthquake Imperial Hotel in Tokyo	France: Surrealism founded	Germany: Lang directs *Metropolis*

SPANISH CIVIL WAR

The Spanish Nationalists' war on parliamentary democracy was assisted by Fascist Italy and Nazi Germany. The Western democracies did nothing to intervene.

1923 Miguel Rivera's coup establishes dictatorship.

1930–31 Fall of Rivera heralds proclamation of Second Republic.

1936 Republicans win general election; Franco leads civil war.

1937 Nationalists control south and west, Republicans north and east.

1938 Franco breaks through in north and in Catalonia, cutting off Republican territory.

1939 Civil war ends; Franco becomes dictator (to 1975).

A Falangist poster.

and Germany: Rome-Axis pact set up.

1937 German planes bomb Basque town of Guernica, Spain. Britain continues appeasement of Hitler.

1938 German troops invade Austria; Hitler declares *Anschluss*, union of Austria with Germany. Munich Pact signed by Hitler, Mussolini, British Prime Minister Chamberlain, and French Premier Daladier; gives Czech Sudetenland to Germany. Riots in Germany against Jews during *Kristallnacht* ("night of broken glass").

MIDDLE EAST

1920 Palestine established as Jewish state under British administration.

1922 Egypt declared independent from British and French influence.

1929 First major conflict between Jews and Arabs in Palestine.

1932 Saudi Arabia established.

1936 Anglo-Egyptian Treaty restricts British to Suez Canal zone for 20 years.

ASIA

1919 Indian leader Mahatma Gandhi begins campaign of passive resistance to British rule; Amritsar massacre: British troops fire on nationalist rioters.

1921 Communist Party founded in China.

1924 Chinese government set up at Guangzhou (Canton) under Sun Yat-sen; includes Communist members.

1925 Chiang Kai-shek becomes leader of Chinese Nationalist Party (Kuominteng).

1928 Chiang Kai-shek purges Communists; becomes president and sets up government at Nanking (Nanjing). Civil war between Communists and Nationalists (to 1937).

1930 Gandhi leads protest against British; Civil disobedience movement in India (to 1934) demands independence.

1931 Chinese Communists set up rival government in Jiangxi. Mukden Incident: Japanese occupy Manchuria.

1932 Japanese set up puppet state of Manchukuo in Manchuria. Indian Congress declared illegal.

1934–35 Mao Zedong leads Chinese Communists on the "Long March."

1935 Britain separates Burma from India; Burma given partial self-government.

1937 Japan invades China; captures Shanghai and Peking (Beijing).

1938 Japan wins victories over Chinese.

AFRICA

1925-26 Arab uprising in Morocco; crushed by France and Spain.

1935 Italian forces invade Ethiopia; League of Nations' intervention fails.

1936 Italy annexes Ethiopia (Abyssinia).

NORTH AMERICA

1919 Prohibition in the U.S.A. (to 1933).

1920 U.S. women given right to vote. First licensed radio broadcasting begins.

1921 U.S. government follows policy of isolationism; refuses to join League of Nations. Washington Conference agrees to Pacific Treaty on naval armaments among Britain, France, Japan, and U.S.A. Radicals Sacco and Vanzetti convicted of murder in controversial trial (executed in 1927). Nationwide revival of Ku Klux Klan violence.

1925 John Scopes found guilty of teaching evolution in Tennessee high school.

1927 American pilot Charles Lindbergh makes first solo transatlantic flight.

1929 U.S. stock market collapses, leading to worldwide economic depression *(below)*.

1932 American Amelia Earhart becomes first woman to fly solo across Atlantic.

1933 U.S. president Franklin D. Roosevelt launches "New Deal" policy to help U.S.A. out of the Depression *(below)*.

1935 U.S. Social Security Act passed.

1935–39 U.S. Neutrality Acts prevents U.S. involvement in affairs of other nations.

1938 Child labor outlawed in U.S.A.

SOUTH AMERICA

1930 Dictatorships set up in Argentina and Brazil.

1932–35 Paraguay defeats Bolivia in war over Chaco region.

AUSTRALIA AND OCEANIA

1920 Australia and Japan assigned former German colonies as a mandate by the League of Nations.

1926 Canberra becomes Australian capital.

1928 Australian pilot Charles Kingsford Smith makes first crossing of Pacific.

1929 American explorer Richard Byrd flies over South Pole.

1930 English pilot Amy Johnson flies solo to Australia.

THE DEPRESSION

A fall in international wheat prices in 1928–29 heralded the Great Depression, which was precipitated by a collapse of prices on Wall Street (the New York stock exchange) on "Black Thursday," October 24, 1929. Fortunes were lost, output slumped while prices fell, and unemployment in indutrial countries rose to around 25 percent in the early 1930s. In the United States President Franklin Roosevelt combated the Depression by vigorous state action in his "New Deal" (1933).

A 1930s breadline in New York.

	1928		1931		1934		1938
	Germany: Heidegger develops existentialism	Austria: Vienna circle of philosophers formulates logical positivism	U.S.A.: Dewey publishes *Philosophy and Civilization*		India: Gandhi organizes *satyagraha* (truth force)	Keynes writes *The General Theory*	
	Alexander Fleming discovers penicillin	U.S.A.: Hubble identifies red shift of galaxies	Wallace Carothers invents nylon			Radar invented by Robert Watson-Watt	
		D. H Lawrence writes *Lady Chatterly's Lover*	Pearl Buck's *The Good Earth*	F. Scott Fitzgerald's *Tender is the Night*	Faulkner's *Light in August*	Prokofiev writes *Peter and the Wolf*	Zora Neale Hurston's *Their Eyes Were Watching God*
		Salvador Dali, leading exponent of Surrealism	Le Corbusier designs Villa Savoye			Georg Grosz anti-Nazi expressionist artist	Picasso paints *Guernica*

World War II

World War II is usually said to have begun in September 1939 with the German invasion of Poland, but for the Japanese and Chinese it began in 1931 and for the Americans in 1941. Its origins, in Europe, lay in the harsh conditions imposed on Germany by the Treaty of Versailles in 1919, the democracies' failure to enforce the treaty, and the Nazis' desire for European expansion. The consequent breakdown of collective security enabled the Nazis to attack, just as the Japanese were invading China. Until the fall of 1942, German armies carried all before them. The great turning point may be seen to be the heroic Soviet resistance to the Nazis at Stalingrad. Thereafter, the combined powers of the United States, the U.S.S.R., and Britain meant that Germany's defeat was only a question of time.

"The most shocking fact about war is that its victims and its instruments are individual human beings, and that these individual human beings are concerned by their monstrous conventions of politics to murder or be murdered in quarrels not their own."

Aldous Huxley, *The Olive Tree*

> ### CAUSES FOR GERMANY'S DEFEAT IN WORLD WAR II
> 1. Battle of Britain ensured continued freedom of Britain from Nazi occupation.
> 2. Attack of Russia and Japan on U.S.A. created new powerful alliance against Axis powers.
> 3. Naval and air power gradually turned in favor of Allies.
> 4. Germany not equipped to fight long war against industrial powers of U.S.A., Russia, and Britain.
> 5. Early defeat of Italy was a liability to Hitler; German forces had to be deployed to prop up Italian regime.
> 6. Persecution of some of Germany's most brilliant scientists enabled U.S.A. to produce first atomic bomb; had Hitler gained it first, he may have retrieved the situation.
> 7. Hitler's increasing control of military affairs was fatal for Germany.

World War II casualties

During World War I, approximately ten million members of the armed forces died in action; World War II, however, took far more lives and inflicted much more destruction than any other conflict before or since. The Soviet Union alone lost 7.5 million men, killed or missing, a reflection of the fact that by far the fiercest fighting of the war occurred on the eastern front. The United States and Britain suffered the fewest battle deaths of the major powers. World War II was, indeed, "total war": the number of civilians who lost their lives from disease, bombing, and enemy fire, added to those who died working as slave laborers, or in concentration and extermination camps, exceeded 40 million, but precise figures are difficult to calculate as many records were lost during the war.

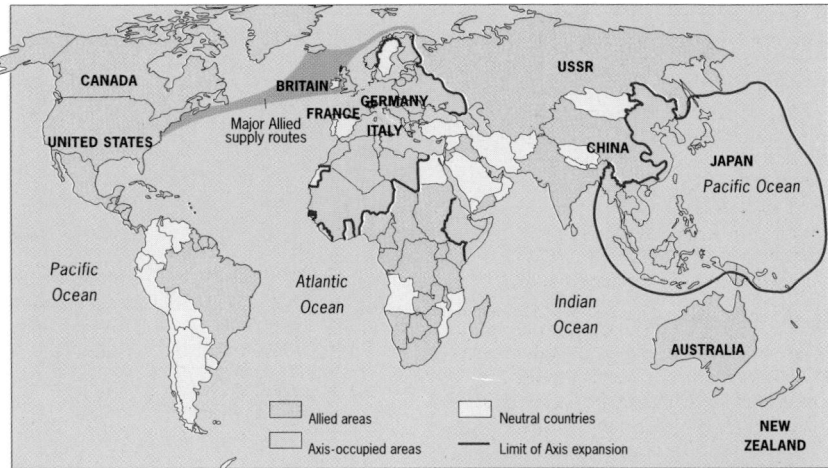

Country	Wartime Pop.	Forces Peak	Forces Killed/ Missing	Forces Wounded	Civilians Killed/Missing
Australia	7.1m	680,000	34,000	181,000	100
Belgium	8.1m	800,000	10,000	15,000	90,000
Bulgaria	6.7m	450,000	19,000	22,000	N.A.
Canada	11.4m	780,000	43,000	53,000	N.A.
China	541m	5m	1.5m	2m	20m
Czechoslovakia	15.2m	180,000	7,000	8,000	310,000
Finland	3.9m	250,000	79,000	50,000	11,000
France	41.9m	5m	245,000	390,000	173,000
Germany*	79.4m	10m	3.5m	2m	2m
Greece	7.2m	150,000	17,000	47,000	391,000
Hungary	14m	350,000	147,000	N.A.	280,000
India	388.8m	2.4m	48,000	65,000	N.A.
Italy**	45.4m	4.5m	380,000	225,000	180,000
Japan**	73.1m	6m	2.6m	326,000	953,000
Netherlands	9m	500,000	14,000	2,000	242,000
New Zealand	1.7m	157,000	12,000	16,000	N.A.
Norway	3m	25,000	5,000	400	8,000
Poland	35m	1m	600,000	530,000	6m
Romania	20m	600,000	73,000	49,000	465,000
South Africa	10.7m	140,000	9,000	15,000	N.A.
U.K.***	47.8m	4.7m	420,000	377,000	70,000
U.S.A.	132m	16.4m	292,000	675,000	N.A.
U.S.S.R.	193m	20m	13.6m	5m	7.7m
Yugoslavia	16.3m	3.7m	305,000	425,000	1.4m

*Figures include Austria.** Figures include colonies and mandated territories.*** Figures for killed and wounded include colonies other than India. N.A. = not available.

Russian civilians trying to survive in the ruins of Stalingrad, 1942.

Timetable 1931–45

1931–32 Japan seizes Manchuria and part of Mongolia.

1935 League of Nations fails to stop Italy from annexing Ethiopia.

1936 Hitler reoccupies the Rhineland.

1937 Nanking falls as the Japanese begin full-scale invasion of China; Chinese civilians raped and massacred.

1938 Hitler declares Anschluss, union of Germany and Austria; Munich Pact transfers Czech Sudetenland to Germany.

1939 Hitler signs nonaggression pact with the U.S.S.R.; Germany invades Poland and annexes Danzig on September 1, and World War II begins in Europe. Poland partitioned between Germany and U.S.S.R. Russo-Finnish war (to 1940).

1940 German blitzkrieg fells Denmark, Norway, Belgium, the Netherlands, and France; 335,490 Allied troops evacuated from Dunkirk; Italy joins war against Britain and France; battle of Britain ends with British victory; Germany launches bombing blitz against Britain.

1941 Roosevelt signs Lend-Lease agreement with Britain; Germans invade U.S.S.R. in June; Roosevelt and Churchill issue statement of war aims in Atlantic Charter; Japan's bombing of Pearl Harbor in December brings U.S.A. into the war. Germany invades Greece and Yugoslavia; Japan invades Philippines and takes Hong Kong.

1942 Japan captures Manila, Singapore, Rangoon, Mandalay, Burma, and Philippines; Germans take over unoccupied France (Vichy). U.S.A. defeats Japanese navy at battle of Midway Island; Allies suffer heavy losses at Dieppe, but Montgomery commands British victory over German army led by Rommel at El Alamein in N. Africa.

1943 German invasion of U.S.S.R. ends in defeat at Stanlingrad in January. At Casablanca conference Churchill and Roosevelt demand Germany's "unconditional surrender." Massacre of Jews in Warsaw Ghetto; Allies invade Italy and begin around-the-clock bombing of Germany.

1944 Allies enter Rome; Normandy landings on D-Day, June 6, begin liberation of occupied Europe; Allies liberate Paris and Brussels; at battle of Leyte Gulf Japanese fleet defeated by Americans; failure of Allied airborne landings at Arnhem; German counteroffensive: the battle of the Bulge in the Ardennes is last German offensive in the west.

1945 Mussolini killed by Italian underground movement. Yalta Conference agrees to division of postwar Germany among France, Britain, U.S.A., and U.S.S.R.; Berlin falls to the Allies in April and Hitler commits suicide; Japan surrenders in August after atom bombs dropped by U.S.A. on Hiroshima and Nagasaki. United Nations founded in San Francisco (p. 244–45).

Jews arriving at the Auschwitz death camp.

The Holocaust

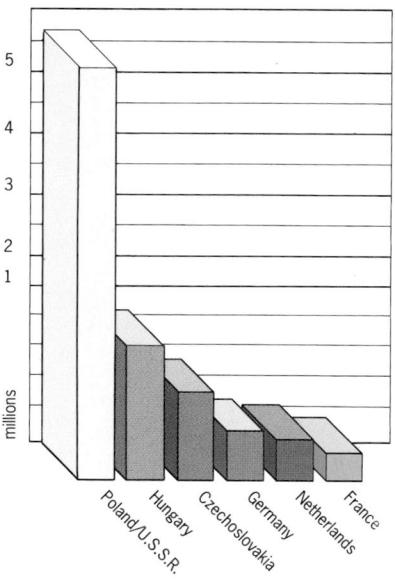

The figures above are taken from the Encyclopedia Judaica.

During World War II, the Holocaust—meaning widespread destruction—killed about two-thirds of the Jews in Europe. The persecution of the Jews in Germany started as soon as Hitler came to power in 1933. This inititally took the form of punitive laws and terror tactics that deprived Jews of their rights and livelihoods. After the Nazi conquest of mainland Europe, Jewish persecution included forced labor and, eventually, mass deportation and imprisonment and death in concentration camps. The number of Jews murdered by the Nazis between 1941 and 1945, as part of the "Final Solution," is indeterminate, but certainly it was about six million. Much of the killing took place in death camps such as Auschwitz and Dachau.

Civilian workers

Unlike previous wars, World War II affected the lives of the civilians at home in the fighting nations as much as the troops on the frontline. In many European and Asian countries men, women, and children suffered hardship, illness, and even death and witnessed the destruction of their homes and disruption of their daily lives on an unprecedented scale.

Although civilians in countries far from the battlefield suffered from shortages of food and goods, the main change to their daily lives was their involvement in the war effort. Millions of women joined their countries' labor force, filling the jobs in factories and on the land that had previously been held by the men who had gone to war. In the United States, the women who worked in defense plants were celebrated in the song "Rosie the Riveter"; in Britain there were the "landgirls".

"Rosie the Riveter" by Norman Rockwell: a Saturday Evening Post cover of 1943.

1946–67

EUROPE

1946 Nuremberg Trials: Nazi leaders sentenced for war crimes by international court. Republic of Hungary proclaimed.

1947 Marshall Plan program of aid for Europe introduced by U.S.A. (to 1951).

1948 Communist coup in Czechoslovakia; People's Republic formed. U.S.S.R. blockades West Berlin; zone supplied by airlift (until 1949).

1949 North Atlantic Treaty Organization (NATO) formed. Germany divided. COMECON (Council for Mutual Economic Assistance) founded by U.S.S.R. and Communist states.

1952 Bonn Convention ends occupation of West Germany.

1954 Unrest in Cyprus and Greece over *enosis* (union of Cyprus and Greece).

1955 West Germany admitted to NATO. Warsaw Pact: Eastern European defense treaty signed by communist nations.

1956 Anti-Soviet uprising in Hungary crushed by Soviet troops.

1957 Treaty of Rome establishes European Economic Community (the Common Market). U.S.S.R. launches *Sputnik 1*, first artificial satellite.

1961 East Germany tightens borders: Berlin Wall built. Soviet cosmonaut Yuri Gagarin first human in space.

1963 Nuclear test ban treaty signed by Soviet Union, U.S.A., and Britain.

1964 Fighting between Greece and Turkey in Cyprus: UN troops sent in.

1967 Military coup in Greece. EEC becomes European Community (EC).

MIDDLE EAST

1947 Partition of Palestine into Arab and Jewish states agreed on by United Nations; Arabs reject proposals.

1948 State of Israel declared; war between Israel and Arab League (*below right*).

1949 Arab-Israeli armistice: Jerusalem partitioned between Israel and Jordan.

1950 Anglo-Egyptian dispute over future of Sudan and Suez begins.

1953 Military coup in Egypt: monarchy ends and republic established.

1956 Egypt nationalizes Suez Canal; Israel invades Egypt over denied use of canal; Anglo-French forces occupy canal zone; UN calls for cease-fire and sends troops.

1957 Suez Canal reopened to shipping.

1961 Organization of Petroleum Exporting Countries (OPEC) formed.

1964 Palestine Liberation Organization (PLO) formed.

1967 Six-Day War between Israel and Arab states; Israel occupies Sinai Desert, Jerusalem, and West Bank of the Jordan River; cease-fire arranged by UN.

ASIA

1946–54 Civil war in Indochina between Vietnamese Nationalists, led by Ho Chi Minh, and French.

1947 India gains independence; two

THE COLD WAR

Nikita Khrushchev (USSR) and J.F. Kennedy (USA) in confrontation, depicted in a contemporary cartoon.

Spheres of influence in Europe after 1945.

Before the end of World War II, rivalry over "spheres of interest" signaled the conflict that was to develop between two ideologically hostile blocs: the U.S.S.R. with its satellites and the U.S.A. with its allies, who in 1949 formed NATO. Soviet expansionist policy prompted the Truman Doctrine, promising U.S. aid to countries threatened with a Communist takeover. Although intended as a universal statement, the Truman Doctrine came to epitomize U.S. policy during the Cold War. The conflict never developed into direct, open warfare, but the opposing ideologies featured in Third World disputes, notably in Korea (1950–53). The nuclear capabilities of each side helped to prevent all-out war over crises such as the Soviet blockade of West Berlin (1948), the suppression of the Hungarian rising (1956), and the discovery of Soviet nuclear missiles in Cuba (1962). The Nuclear Test Ban treaty of 1963 led to a period of détente.

THE ARAB–ISRAELI CONFLICT

The partition of Palestine was approved by the UN in 1947 despite Arab opposition. When the state of Israel was proclaimed (1948), the Arab nations attacked but were defeated. Their hostility, augmented by the plight of Palestinian refugees, remained undiminished. In the Six-Day War of 1967, Israel was again victorious and occupied the Gaza Strip, much of Sinai, the Golan Heights, and the West Bank.

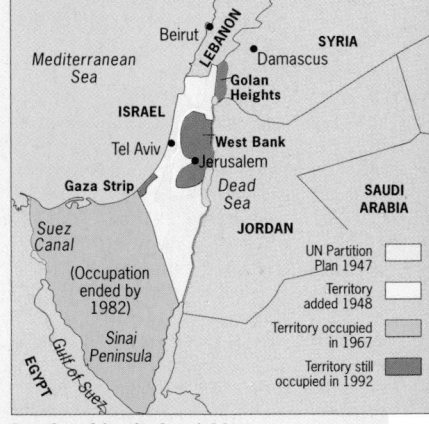

Israel and its Arab neighbors.

	1939	1946	1949	1952
RELIGION AND PHILOSOPHY	Popper writes *The Open Society and its Enemies*	Israel: Dead Sea scrolls discovered		Buber writes *The Hassidic Message*
SCIENCE AND TECHNOLOGY				Hydrogen bomb tested by U.S.A.
LITERATURE AND MUSIC		W. H. Auden wins Pulitzer poetry prize	Orwell writes *1984* / Salinger writes *Catcher in the Rye*	
ART AND ARCHITECTURE		Abstract Expressionism develops, including painters Pollock and Rothko	Le Corbusier designs Chandigarh, capital of Punjab	

dominions created—India (Hindu) and Pakistan (Muslim); dispute between India and Pakistan over Kashmir, which is ceded to India. Indonesia gains independence from Dutch.
1948 Indian leader Mahatma Gandhi assassinated in Delhi. China split by conflict between Communists and Nationalists. Korea divides into Republic of Korea (South Korea) and People's Republic of Korea (North Korea).
1949 Mao Zedong establishes Communist regime in China. France recognizes independent Vietnam and Cambodia.
1950 U.S.S.R. and China sign 30-year friendship treaty. Korean War (to 1953) between North Korea, supported by China, and South Korea, supported by the UN.
1951 Chinese Communists occupy Tibet.
1953 Korean War ends. French occupy North Vietnam; Vietminh invade Laos.
1954 French finally defeated by Vietminh; Vietnam divided: North under Communist government of Ho Chi Minh, South supported by U.S.A.
1959 Uprising in Tibet; Dalai Lama escapes to India; China crushes revolt.
1962 U.S.A. supports South Vietnamese government against Communists. Border clashes between India and China.
1963 South Vietnamese government toppled. North Vietnam attacks U.S. navy.
1964 U.S. attack on North Vietnam.
1965 U.S.A. undertakes regular bombing raids on North Vietnam; first American marines land in South Vietnam. India and Pakistan go to war over Kashmir.
1966 Cultural Revolution in China (to 1976); Red Guards formed. Australian troops join U.S.A. in Vietnam.

AFRICA
1949 Apartheid adopted in South Africa.
1952 Mau Mau (secret organization of Kikuyu tribespeople) begins terrorist activities against British rule in Kenya.
1956 France recognizes independence of Morocco, Sudan, and Tunisia.
1960 Seventeen colonies in Africa gain independence; in newly independent Congo war breaks out as Katanga province, Tshombe, secedes. Sharpeville Massacre in South Africa.
1962 Algeria gains independence from France after eight-year war.
1963 Organization of African Unity (OAU) formed by independent African

THE VIETNAM WAR
When the Japanese withdrew from Vietnam in 1945, French colonial rule was restored, but Ho Chi Minh proclaimed a Communist-dominated republic of Vietminh, which resisted the French and forced them out. Vietnam was divided into North, under Ho, and South, under a U.S.-backed regime which proved highly unpopular. It was soon threatened by the Vietcong, a Communist-led guerilla group. The United States, already supplying military "advisers" to the South, stepped up support. North Vietnamese forces invaded, and a brutal war ensued. Well televised, the war became highly unpopular in the United States which, despite its firepower, did not win. U.S. forces were gradually withdrawn, from 1969–73; by 1975 the whole country was in Communist hands.

A South Vietnamese soldier rides past a ruined church during the Vietnam War.

states. Kenya gains independence.
1964 Malawi (formerly Nyasaland) and Zambia (formerly Northern Rhodesia) gain independence. Tanzania gains independence. White government of Rhodesia makes unilateral declaration of independence (UDI) from Britain.
1966 UN imposes economic sanctions on Rhodesia. South African prime minister, Hendrik Verwoerd, assassinated.
1967 Civil war in Nigeria: Biafra region proclaimed republic (to 1970).

NORTH AMERICA
1947 Truman Doctrine: U.S. foreign policy aimed at restricting the expansion of Communism (The Cold War, *opposite*).
1950 Harry Truman authorizes hydrogen bomb production. Puerto Rican nationalists try to assassinate Truman.
1950–54 American senator Joseph McCarthy heads inquiry into "un-American (Communist) activities."
1954 U.S. Supreme Court rules that racial segregation in public schools is unlawful.
1958 Government in Cuba overthrown; Fidel Castro becomes premier.
1958 Alaska becomes U.S. state.
1959 Hawaii becomes U.S. state. St. Lawrence Seaway opened.
1960 John F. Kennedy becomes youngest U.S. president. U-2 "spy" plane shot down in Soviet Union, raising Cold

War tensions.
1961 Bay of Pigs Cuban exiles' invasion of Cuba fails.
1962 Confrontation between U.S.A. and U.S.S.R. over missiles based in Cuba; U.S.S.R. agrees to withdraw. John Glenn becomes first American to orbit earth. Rachel Carson's *Silent Spring* launches environmentalist movement.
1963 President Kennedy assassinated in Dallas Texas. Supreme Court rules against laws requiring prayer in schools.
1964 U.S. Civil Rights Act passed.
1965 U.S. troops sent to Dominican Republic during civil war.
1966 Anti-Vietnam War protests and race riots in many cities. Medicare, medical funding for senior citizens, introduced.
1967 Mass anti-Vietnam War demonstrations in U.S.A. and Europe.

SOUTH AMERICA
1946 Juan Perón elected president of Argentina, helped by wife, Evita.
1955 Armed rebellion and general strike in Argentina: President Perón exiled.

AUSTRALASIA
1946 U.S. atomic tests carried out at Bikini and Eniwetok atolls.
1951 ANZUS security treaty signed by Australia, New Zealand, and U.S.A.
1960 International agreement to reserve Antarctica for scientific research.

1955	1958	1961	1964	1967
America: King organizes civil rights movement	Chomsky writes *Syntactic Structures*	Claude Levi-Strauss develops structuralism	Pope John XXIII initiates Ecumenical Movement	Foucault writes on history of ideas
Oral contraception developed	Nuclear power first generated	U.S.S.R. launches satellite *Sputnik 1*	U.S.A.: scientists develop laser	Crick and Watson determine molecular structure of DNA	First heart transplant
Nabokov writes *Lolita*	Presley launches rock 'n' roll music	Kerouac publishes *On the Road* Bernstein composes *West Side Story*	U.S.A.: Heller's *Catch-22*		Marquez writes *One Hundred Years of Solitude*
	Kinetic art develops, including Alexander Calder	France: New Wave cinema, Trauffaut, Godard		U.S.A.: Pop art; Rauschenberg, Johns, Warho.	

A world transformed

The second half of the 1900s has been overshadowed by the threat of mass destruction and the awareness that the world's ecology is at the mercy of human beings. The population explosion and the deepening of poverty in vast stretches of the globe have added to the sense of human society in crisis.

"Mankind has become so much one family that we cannot insure our own prosperity except by insuring that of everyone else. If you wish to be happy yourself, you must resign yourself to seeing others also happy."

Bertrand Russell
The New York Times Magazine

That is nothing new in history. And against the anxieties can be set sources for optimism: the aggressive grasp for freedom and respect by minorities and the underrepresented, whether blacks, women, or homosexuals; the strides forward in medicine; and, for all the difficulties it brings in its wake, the revolution in computer technology and international telecommunications. We have also been made aware that environmental pollution has become a serious problem and that we need to reduce pollution levels immediately.

A Bosnian soldier kneels by a freshly dug Muslim grave during the Balkan conflict.

Nationalism in Europe

An aftereffect of the collapse of the Soviet Union was the rise of the darker side of nationalism, both in Russia itself and in other European countries. Racial hatred, the persecution of previously tolerated minorities, and the desire for military conquest—all these negative aspects of nationalism became apparent in the Balkan conflict that developed following the death of Marshal Tito in 1980.

1991–92 Civil war erupts in Balkans after Croatia, Slovenia, and Bosnia declare independence from Yugoslavia; within months Bosnia loses about 70 percent of its territory to Serbia and about 20 percent to Croatia; Serbian forces open concentration camps and impose "ethnic cleansing"; reports of atrocities on both sides of conflict.

1992–93 Thousands of Germans march in protest after neo-Nazis attack Gypsies, Turkish families, and Jewish monuments and buildings.

1993 Croatia and Serbia propose settlement entailing partition of Bosnia into three ethnic republics. Russian parliamentary elections boost Liberal Democratic Party, led by extreme nationalist Vladimir Zhirinovsky.

Environmental pollution

Among the most serious global problems is the widespread pollution of soil, water, and air and the destruction of the earth's natural resources such as the rain forests and many species of animal and plant life.

1984 Poisonous gas leak from pesticide plant in Bhopal, India, kills more than 2,000.

1986 Explosion at nuclear power plant at Chernobyl, Ukraine, releases radioactive debris into atmosphere. Thousands of fish killed in the Rhine River by the release of toxic chemicals resulting from a fire at a chemical storage warehouse near Basel, Switzerland.

1988 Virus devastates seal population in eastern North Atlantic; epidemic believed to be caused by pollutants.

1989 Ecological disaster when tanker *Exxon Valdez* spills 11 million gallons of crude oil off Alaska coast; livelihood of many local people destroyed and thousands of fish, seabirds, and sea mammals die.

Cleaning up the Alaskan coast after the Exxon Valdez *oil spill of 1989.*

Timetable

1960 First oral contraceptives are marketed. Ceylon: Sirimavo Bandaranaike world's first woman prime minister.

1962 Telstar (television satellite) launched by U.S.A.

1966 French scientists define death as brain inactivity as opposed to heart stoppage. LSD made illegal.

1967 Direct dialing from New York to London and Paris becomes possible.

1968 Vatican publishes *Humanae Vitae,* prohibiting artificial contraceptive use. Albania becomes first completely atheist state. Gay men and police clash in Stonewall riots in New York.

1969 U.S. astronauts land on the moon.

1970 New York State introduces abortion on demand. Divorce becomes legal in Italy under certain circumstances.

1971 Referendum in Switzerland approves the introduction of female suffrage. Fiberoptic endoscopes developed.

1972 U.S. Supreme Court rules that death penalty contrary to constitution. In Japan, Sony launches *Betamax* videocassette recorder.

1973 U.S. Supreme Court rules first-trimester abortions legal (*Roe v. Wade*).

1976 In U.S.A. relatives of the terminally ill allowed to authorize removal of life-support equipment. U.S. Supreme Court reendorses constitutionality of death penalty. Concorde begins regular transatlantic service.

1977 Episcopal Church in U.S.A. ordains first women priests. International Lesbian and Gay Association founded.

1979 U.S. surgeon-general confirms that smoking causes cancer. CAT scans provide images of human body. Nuclear reactor accident at Three Mile Island.

1980 Sony's Walkman launched.

1981 TGV (*Train à Grand Vitesse*) goes into operation in France *(p. 471)*. Death penalty abolished in France.

1982 Equal Rights Amendment defeated.

1983 CD players go on sale. In Iran, Ayatollah Khomeini declares Islam a "religion of the sword"; religious fundamentalism increases in Arab world.

1985 In South Africa, mixed marriages celebrated for first time.

1986 First heart, lung, and liver transplant performed in U.K.

1987 World population passes five billion. Suspect convicted of murder in U.K. using genetic fingerprinting.

1988 Abortion-inducing drug RU486 marketed in France.

1989 In Poland, independent trade union Solidarity legalized. Fall of Communist ideology in Eastern Europe *(p. 371)*.

1990 First human gene experiment. Amnesty International lobbies for men and women imprisoned because of their sexual preferences. Nelson Mandela released from prison in South Africa.

1992 In Brazil, UN Conference Convention signed on prevention of climate change and preservation of biodiversity.

African-American civil rights

Troops sent in by President Eisenhower guard black students attending Little Rock Central High School in Arkansas under a federal court order of 1957.

Abraham Lincoln freed the black slaves of America in 1863, but not until after 1945 did a black civil rights movement arise to demand an end to discrimination in education, housing, jobs, and voting rights. The 1963 Freedom March on Washington, D.C., when civil rights leader Martin Luther King, Jr. gave his famous "I have a dream" speech, was the high point of the nonviolent campaign for racial equality in the U.S.A. Beside King there arose the militant Black Muslin and Black Panther movements, which rejected passive disobedience and preached forceful resistance to white rule.

1954 Supreme Court decision makes segregated schools unconstitutional.

1955 Martin Luther King, Jr. organizes Alabama bus boycott after Rosa Parks refuses to give her seat to a white rider.

1957 President Eisenhower sends troops to Little Rock, Arkansas, to enforce desegregation in schools; King founds Southern Christian Leadership Conference.

1964 Civil Rights Act makes all public segregation illegal and fosters black electoral registration. King awarded Nobel Peace Prize.

1965 Federal Act outlaws racial discrimination in housing.

1965–67 Black riots break out in cities across U.S.A.

1968 King assassinated in Memphis.

1975 Thirty states sign the Human Rights agreement.

Medicine and physiology

Thanks to better living conditions and continually improving medicine, life expectancy in industrialized countries has rapidly increased in the past hundred years or so. In Germany, it has doubled for both men and women. Polio, smallpox, typhoid, cholera, whooping cough, and diptheria have been virtually eradicated in the developed world. But even in the West, the development of hitherto unknown diseases such as AIDS (Acquired Immune Deficiency Syndrome) and uncertainty about continuing treatment with antibiotics cast a shadow over the future, while in the developing nations, the eternal enemies of good health—malnutrition, unsanitary conditions, and inadequate medical services—continue to prevail.

1945 Penicillin becomes widely available; first trials for fluoridating water take place in the U.S.A.

1949 Linus Pauling discovers cause of sickle-cell anemia in a molecular error in hemoglobin.

1952 George (later Christine) Jorgensen undergoes first sex-change operation in Copenhagen.

1953 Francis Crick and James Watson (winners of the Nobel Prize in Medicine and Physiology 1962) discover the structure of DNA; Jonas Salk tests polio vaccine successfully.

1955 Gregory Pincus reports successful trials of an oral contraceptive for women.

1967 Christian Barnard performs first heart transplant in Cape Town, South Africa; Alick Isaacs and colleagues discover the antiviral protein interferon.

1963 Valium introduced in U.S.A.

1969 First in vitro fertilization of a human egg achieved in U.K.

1976 Bacterial infection, Legionnaires' disease, discovered in Philadelphia.

1977 Lassa fever identified as a viral infection in Germany.

1978 First "test-tube" baby born in England.

1980 UN claims that smallpox has been eradicated throughout the world.

1981 First cases of AIDS reported in New York.

1982 First permanent artificial heart given to patient in Salt Lake City.

1984 HIV identified in France and U.S.A.

False-color transmission electron micrograph of the particles of a virus causing AIDS.

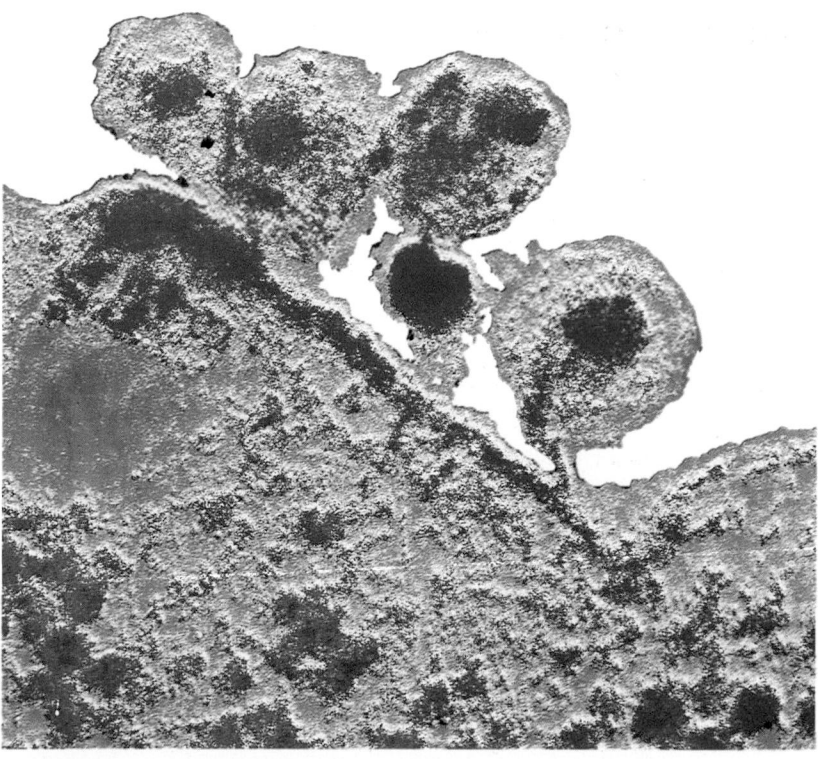

1968–94

NEW NATIONS

Membership of the United Nations increased from 51 in 1945, when it was founded, to 184 in 1994. Many of the new members were former colonies of European powers. Later entrants included states of the former Soviet Union. The ten largest countries formed since 1945 are listed below:

Nigerian troops carrying out UN duties.

Country	Date of Independence	Area
India	August 15, 1947	1,222,396 sq. mi./3,166,829km²
Kazakhstan	December 25, 1991	1,049,150 sq. mi./2,717,300km²
Zaire	January 27, 1960	905,366 sq. mi./2,344,900km²
Indonesia	December 27, 1949	740,905 sq. mi./1,919,443km²
Nigeria	October 1, 1960	356,576 sq. mi./923,773km²
Pakistan	August 14, 1947	307,295 sq. mi./796,100km²
Ukraine	August 24, 1991	233,089 sq. mi./603,700km²
Turkmenistan	October 27, 1991	188,406 sq. mi./488,100km²
Uzbekistan	December 25, 1991	172,741 sq. mi./447,400km²
Malaysia	September 16, 1963	127,287 sq. mi./329,759km²

EUROPE

1968 U.S.S.R. invades Czechoslovakia. Student and worker demonstrations in Paris lead to clashes with police.
1969 British troops sent to Northern Ireland to quell riots.
1972 Arab terrorists kill 11 Israeli athletes at Munich Olympics. Northern Ireland Catholics killed by British troops on "Bloody Sunday"; Britain imposes direct rule over Northern Ireland.
1973 IRA terrorist campaign in Britain.
1974 Greek Turkish conflict in Cyprus; Turks occupy north of island.
1975 Spanish dictator Francisco Franco dies; Juan Carlos becomes king.
1979 Margaret Thatcher first British woman prime minister (to 1990).
1980 Polish Solidarity trade union, led by Lech Walesa, confronts Communist government. After death of President Tito, Yugoslav government faces demands for regional independence.
1981 IRA hunger strikes in Northern Ireland; death of Bobby Sands.
1985–91 Soviet president Mikhail Gorbachev introduces major reforms.
1986 Nuclear accident at Chernobyl power plant near Kiev in Ukraine results in large leak of radiation.

1987 U.S.A. and U.S.S.R. agree to eliminate medium-range nuclear weapons.
1989 Poland holds first partially free elections for 45 years; Solidarity wins many seats. Communist rule ends in East Germany; Berlin Wall demolished. U.S.S.R. announces end of Cold War. Revolution in Romania: President Ceaucescu shot. Communist rule ends in Bulgaria, Hungary, Czechoslovakia.
1990 East and West Germany reunite. Lithuanians call for independence.
1991 Hard-line Communists attempt coup in U.S.S.R.; resistance led by Yeltsin; Gorbachev resigns and U.S.S.R. is officially dissolved; Yeltsin elected president. Civil war in Balkans as Slovenia and Croatia fight for independence.
1992–93 Civil war continues in Balkans as Serbia tries to maintain federation.
1992 Czech and Slovak republics become separate states.
1993 Armed uprising in Russia against Yeltsin fails; 60 killed in Moscow.
1994 IRA calls cease-fire.

MIDDLE EAST

1970 Civil war in Jordan between government troops and Palestinian guerrillas.
1973 Yom Kippur War (October War):

Egypt and Syria attack Israel. Cease-fire imposed after five weeks of fighting. World energy crisis after Arab oil producers stop supplies to West.
1976–90 Civil war in Lebanon.
1977 President Sadat of Egypt and Prime Minister Begin of Israel exchange visits; negotiations on peace terms begin.
1979 Israel and Egypt sign peace treaty in Washington. Islamic revolution in Iran: Shah forced into exile; return of exiled religious leader Ayatollah Khomeini.
1980–88 War between Iran and Iraq.
1981 President Sadat assassinated.
1982 Israel invades Lebanon.
1988 Israel occupies Gaza Strip.
1990 Iraq invades Kuwait. North and South Yemen unite.
1991 Persian Gulf War: U.S.A.-led coalition forces Iraq to pull out of Kuwait.
1994 Jericho and Gaza come under Palestinian administration.

ASIA

1968 Tet Offensive: Vietcong launch major offensive in Vietnam.
1970 U.S.A. invades Cambodia.
1971 Vietnam War: fighting spreads to Laos; U.S.A. bombs North Vietnam. China joins UN and Taiwan (Formosa) is expelled. Bangladesh (formerly East Pakistan) becomes independent.
1973 U.S.A. withdraws from Vietnam.
1975 South Vietnam surrenders to North Vietnam; end of Vietnam War.
1976 Pol Pot comes to power in Cambodia; many civilians massacred.
1978 Vietnam invades Cambodia. U.S.A. agrees to diplomatic relations with China and ends those with Taiwan.
1979 U.S.S.R. invades Afghanistan.
1984 President Indira Gandhi of India assassinated.
1986 Overthrow of President Marcos of the Philippines.
1987 Vietnam promises to withdraw forces from Cambodia.
1989 Prodemocracy student demonstrations in Tiananmen Square, Beijing, China, crushed by government troops. Last Soviet troops leave Afghanistan.
1990 Fighting flares up between Soviet republics of Armenia and Azerbaijan.
1993 Former prime minister Benazir Bhutto reelected in Pakistan.

AFRICA

1974 Communists depose Emperor Haile

		1968	1971	1974	1977
	RELIGION AND PHILOSOPHY		Environmentalists predict depletion of natural resources	International Women's Year	U.S.A.: Episcopal Church agrees to ordination of women
	SCIENCE AND TECHNOLOGY	First moon landing		Soviet spacecraft lands on Venus	England: first test-tube baby
	LITERATURE AND MUSIC	Beckett receives Nobel Prize	Germaine Greer's *The Female Eunuch*	Synthesizer introduced	Star Wars: special effects breakthrough
	ART AND ARCHITECTURE		U.S.A.: conceptual art popular	The Pompidou Center built in Paris	

Selassie in Ethiopia.

1976 Riots in black townships in South Africa (*below*). Angola: outbreak of civil war; success of Communist forces.

1977–91 Civil war and famine in Ethiopia.

1980 Rhodesia becomes independent as Zimbabwe.

1986 U.S.A. bombs Libya in retaliation for its support of anti-American terrorists. In South Africa, political rivals ANC and Inkatha clash.

1993 Violence in Burundi and Rwanda after death of both countries' presidents; hundreds of thousands die in fighting between Hutus and Tutsis; millions flee, sparking refugee crisis.

1994 First free elections in South Africa.

NORTH AMERICA

1968 Martin Luther King, Jr. and Senator Robert Kennedy assassinated. Antiwar demonstrations disrupt Democratic National Convention in Chicago.

1969 American astronauts land on moon.

1974 Watergate scandal: President Nixon resigns. Nicaraguan civil war (to 1979).

1977 President Carter pardons Vietnam War draft evaders. Neutron bomb tested.

1978 Sandinista rebels fight against U.S.-backed government in Nicaragua.

1979 Sandinistas win Nicaraguan civil war in. Carter and Brezhnev sign arms limitation treaty. Nuclear accident at Three Mile Island. U.S. citizens taken hostage in Tehran (released in 1981).

1981 Illnesses resulting from the AIDS virus first recognized in New York. Sandra Day O'Connor approved as first woman Supreme Court Justice.

EASTERN EUROPEAN REVOLUTIONS

One consequence of the collapse of the U.S.S.R. and the almost unresisted fall of Communism in the Eastern Bloc as nations gained independence was the re-emergence of fierce nationalist rivalries in Eastern Europe.

1985 Mikhail Gorbachev's rise to power in U.S.S.R. ushers in *glasnost* and *perestroika*.

1989 June: "Solidarity" wins election landslide and Poland gets a non-Communist government. Sept.: Hungary opens border to Austria, East Germans flee to the West. Nov.: East German and Czech Communist governments resign; Berlin Wall comes down. Dec.: demonstrations force Ceausescu from power in Romania.

1990 Communist Party abolishes its leading role in U.S.S.R. constitution; East and West Germany reunite.

1991 U.S.S.R. dissolves; Yugoslavia collapses into civil war.

1994 Fighting in former Soviet republic of Chechnya when Russian troops sent to quell independence effort.

Berliners standing on the Berlin Wall the day after its demolition began in 1989.

1983 U.S.A. invades Grenada in Caribbean to stop army taking control.

1986 *Challenger* space shuttle explodes, killing all seven aboard. "Iran-gate" scandal in Washington. First observance of Martin Luther King, Jr. Day in U.S.A. (Jan. 20).

1989 U.S.A. invades Panama.

1991 Haiti's President Aristide ousted in bloody coup lead by General Cédras.

1992 Los Angeles riots kill 52, cause $1 billion damages.

1993 Canada's first woman prime minister, Conservative Kim Campbell, ousted from office after Liberals win elections.

1994 U.S. troops restore President Aristide to power in Haiti.

SOUTH AMERICA

1970 Marxist Salvador Allende becomes president of Chile.

1973 Military coup in Chile overthrows and kills Allende.

1982 Argentina invades Falkland Islands; British task force reoccupies islands.

1983 Democratic elections in Argentina.

1990 Chile and Brazil hold free elections and return to civilian government.

1992 Earth Summit in Rio de Janeiro on world environmental concerns.

AUSTRALIA AND OCEANIA

1972 Labour Party victories in Australia and New Zealand lead to changes.

1975 Australian prime minister Gough Whitlam dismissed by governor general.

1985 France continues nuclear tests in Pacific; alleged sabotage of Greenpeace ship, *Rainbow Warrior,* by French. South Pacific Forum draws up Nuclear Free Zone Treaty.

1987 Scientists confirm existence of a hole in the ozone layer above Antarctica.

SOUTH AFRICA

Nelson Mandela salutes supporters after his release in 1990 after 27 years' imprisonment.

South Africa was the last bastion of imperialist, white-minority rule in Africa. The release of Nelson Mandela from prison in 1990 signaled its end.

1949 South Africans classed as white, black, or colored; Group Areas Act legalizes segregation (apartheid).

1960 Sixty-seven black protesters killed by police at Sharpeville.

1962–90 Nelson Mandela imprisoned.

1976 Black rioters killed at Soweto.

1994 African National Congress (ANC) wins election; Mandela becomes president.

1980	1983	1986	1989	1992	1994–95
John Paul II first non-Italian pope for 450 years		Desmond Tutu first black archbishop of Cape Town		Deconstructionist philosopher Derrida achieves fame	Church of England agrees to ordination of women
U.S.A.: illnesses caused by AIDS virus recognized	U.S. space shuttle *Columbia* reused	U.S.S.R.: accident at Chernobyl nuclear reactor		Channel Tunnel constructed	
	Bob Geldof organizes Live Aid pop concert	Tom Wolfe writes *Bonfire of the Vanities*	Salmon Rushdie writes *Satanic Verses*		
		Van Gogh's *Irises* sold for $53,900,000	Glass pyramid added to the Louvre		

PROMINENT PEOPLE

BANCROFT, George (1800–91) U.S. historian. His major work was the monumental *History of the United States* (1834–40, 1852–74).

BEARD, Charles Austin (1874–1948) U.S. historian. With wife, **Mary Ritter Beard** (1876–1958), wrote *The Rise of American Civilization* (1927) and the influential *A Basic History of the United States* (1944).

BEDE, the Venerable, St. (c. 673–735) Anglo-Saxon scholar, theologian and historian. His greatest work was the *Ecclesiastical History of the English People* (731), the single most valuable source for early English history.

BLOCH, Marc (1886–1944) French historian. Major works include *La Société féodale* (1939), a memoir of France in 1939–40, *Strange Defeat* and the unfinished *The Historian's Craft*.

BREASTED, James Henry (1865–1935) U.S. archaeologist and historian. Set up Oriental Institute in Chicago (1919) which researched the Middle East.

BROOKS, Van Wyck (1886–1963) U.S. historian. Used critical analysis of literature to widen the historical understanding of New England. Awarded 1937 Pulitzer Prize for *The Flowering of New England*.

BURNS, James McGregor (b. 1917) U.S. historian and political adviser. Uses privileged access to several presidential administrations to produce biographies such as Pulitzer-Prize-winning *Roosevelt: The Soldier of Freedom* (1971).

CARLYLE, Thomas (1795–1881) Scottish historian and essayist. Best-known work a history of *The French Revolution* (1837); most ambitious work, six-volume *History of Frederick the Great* (1858–65).

CARTER, Howard (1874–1939) English Egyptologist. Excavated in Egypt's Valley of the Kings (1906–23); discovered several pharaonic tombs, including the virtually intact tomb of Tutankhamun.

CATTON, Bruce (1899–1978) U.S. historian. His many books about the American Civil War include *A Stillness at Appomattox* (1954 Pulitzer Prize).

CHANNING, Edward (1856–1931) U.S. historian. One of the first historians to synthesis a thoroughgoing history of the United States. Awarded Pulitzer Prize (1926) for his six-volume *A History of the United States*.

CHILDE, Vere Gordon (1892–1957) Australian archaeologist. Wrote influential *The Dawn of European Civilization* (1925), arguing that the earliest ancestors of human beings came from Egypt.

DE VOTO, Bernard (1897–1955) U.S. editor and historian of western frontier. Won 1948 Pulitzer Prize for *Across the Wide Missouri*.

DU BOIS, William Edward Burghardt (1868–1963) African-American historian and sociologist. Cofounder of National Association for the Advancement of Colored People (NAACP) in 1909; works included *Color and Democracy* (1945).

EVANS, Sir Arthur John (1851–1941) English archaeologist. Between 1899 and 1935 excavated Cretan city of Knossos, discovering remains of a civilization which he named (1904) "Minoan" after Cretan king, Minos.

GIBBON, Edward (1737–94) English historian. Wrote *The History of the Decline and Fall of the Roman Empire* (1776–88).

HERODOTUS (c. 485–425 B.C.) Greek historian and traveler, often called "the father of history." Best known for books on the rise of the Persian Empire and on the wars between Persia and Greece.

IBN KHALDUN (1332–1406) Arab historian and politician. Wrote influential *Maqaddimah (Introduction to History)*, outlining a cyclical theory of history.

JOHANSON, Donald Carl (b. 1943) U.S. paleoanthropologist. Made spectacular finds of fossil hominids three to four million years old at Hadar, Ethiopia (1972–77); included "Lucy," a half-complete early hominid belonging to the so-called "First Family;" wrote *Lucy: The Beginnings of Humankind* (1981).

KENYON, Dame Kathleen Mary (1906–78) English archaeologist of biblical sites. Books include *Digging Up Jericho* (1957), *Archaeology in the Holy Land* (1965), *Digging up Jerusalem* (1974).

LEAKEY, Louis Seymour Bazett (1903–72) African-born British archaeologist and physical anthropologist. His greatest discoveries were of early hominid fossils and took place at Olduvai Gorge in east Africa, where, together with wife **Mary Leakey** (b. 1913), he unearthed the skull of *Australopithecus robustus*; also found remains of *Homo habilis*. Son **Richard Leakey** (b. 1944), also an anthropologist, made the important discoveries of *Australopithecus boisei* (1969), *Homo*

Traveler and historian Francis Parkman.

habilis (1972) and *Homo erectus* (1975).

LE ROY LADURIE, Emmanuel Bernard (b. 1929) French historian. Works include *Montaillou, village occiton de 1294 à 1324* (1975), a study of a medieval village.

LIVY (Titus Livius) (59 B.C.–A.D. 17) Roman historian. His *Annals of the Roman People* is a history of Rome from its foundation to the death of Nero Claudius Drusus in 9 B.C.

MACAULAY, Thomas Babington (1800–59) English historian and statesman. Celebrated for *History of England from the Accession of James II* (1848–61).

MAHAN, Alfred Thayer (1840–1914) U.S. historian and naval officer. Expert in the field of naval and maritime history. Wrote *The Influence of Sea Power upon History* (1890).

MICHELET, Jules (1798–1874) French historian. His greatest works were the *Histoire de France* (1833–67) and *Histoire de la révolution* (1847–53).

MORISON, Samuel Eliot (1887–1976) U.S. naval historian who himself had reached the rank of Admiral. Wide-ranging series of scholarly — yet popular — books include *John Paul Jones: A Sailor's Biography* (1959) *and History of the American People* (1965).

PARKMAN, Francis (1823–93) U.S. historian. Authority on history of French dominion in America; works include *The Oregon Trail* (1849) and *Pioneers of France in the New World* (1865).

PETRIE, Sir (William Matthew) Flinders (1853–1942) English archaeologist. Surveyed Stonehenge, England (1874–77). He turned to the study of Egyptology, the Middle East, and, finally, to Palestine.

PIRENNE, Henri (1862–1935) Belgian historian. Developed expertise in history of medieval town, culminating in *Medieval Cities* (1925); also wrote seven-volume *History of Belgium* (1900–32).

PLUTARCH (Greek **Ploutarchos**) (c. 46–c. 120) Greek historian and essayist. Famous for *Parallel Lives of Illustrious Greeks and Romans*, a major source for Shakespeare's Roman plays.

PRESCOTT, William (1796–1859) U.S. historian. Specialist in Pre-Columbian and colonial history of Latin America; *The Conquest of Peru* (1836).

RANKE, Leopold von (1795–1886) German historian. Works include *History of the Popes* (1834–36), and *History of the Reformation in Germany* (1839–47).

SCHLIEMANN, Heinrich (1822–90) German businessman and archaeologist. Excavated sites of Mycenae (1876), Troy (1871–90) and other ancient cities referred to in Homer's *Iliad*.

SPENGLER, Oswald (1880–1936) German historian. His book *The Decline of the West* (1926–29) was much admired by the Nazis.

STEPHENS, John Lloyd (1805–52) U.S. traveler and archaeologist, founder of field of Mayan archaeology. Explored Mesoamerica (1839–42), rediscovering cities of Copan, Quirigua, Palenque, Uxmal, and Chichen Itza.

SUETONIUS (Gaius Suetonius Tranquillus) (*c.* 69–140) Roman biographer and antiquarian. Best-known work *Lives of the First Twelve Caesars.*

TACITUS, Publius or **Gaius Cornelius** (*c.* 55–120) Roman historian. Works describe Germany and Britain under Roman Empire, including *Annals,* Roman history from Tiberius to Nero (14–68) and *Historiae,* covering reigns of Galba, Otho, and Vitellius.

TAINE, Hippolyte Adolphe (1828–93) French historian and philosopher. Greatest work, *Les Origines de la France contemporaine* (1875–94), is an attack on the motives of the French Revolution.

TAYLOR, Alan John Percivale (1906–90) English historian. Major works include *The Struggle for Mastery in Europe 1848–1918* (1954), his revisionist *Origins of the Second World War* (1961), and *English History 1914–1945* (1965).

THIERS, (Louis) Adolphe (1797–1877) French politician and historian. Works include massive *Histoire de la révolution française* (1823–27) and *L'Histoire du consulat et de l'empire* (1845–62).

THUCYDIDES (*c.* 460–*c.* 400 B.C.) Athenian historian. His *History of the Peloponnesian War* covers 21 of the war's 28 years.

TREVELYAN, George Macaulay (1876–1962) English historian. Best known for *History of England* (1926) and *England under Queen Anne* (1930–34).

TUCHMAN, Barbara (1912–89) U.S. historian. Won Pulitzer Prizes for *The Guns of August* (1962) and *Stilwell and the American Experience in China (1911–1945)* (1971); works also include *A Distant Mirror: the Calamitous Fourteenth Century* (1978).

TURNER, Frederick Jackson (1861–1932) U.S. historian. Asserted that American democracy derived from the country's frontier experience; works include *The Frontier in American History* (1920) and *The Significance of Sections in American History* (1932 Pulitzer Prize).

WHEELER, Sir (Robert Eric) Mortimer (1890–1976) English archaeologist. Carried out notable excavations at Verulamium (St. Albans) and Maiden Castle in England, and sites at Mohenjo-daro and Harappa in India.

WINCKELMAN, Johann Joachim (1717–68) German archaeologist and art historian. His masterpiece, *Geschichte der Kunst des Altertums* (1764), is a history of Greek culture and art.

WOOLLEY, Sir (Charles) Leonard (1880–1960) English archaeologist. He directed important excavations at Ur in Mesopotamia (1922–34).

XENOPHON (*c.* 427–355 B.C.) Athenian historian and soldier. Works include *Hellenica,* a history of Greece, and *Cyropaedia,* a life of CYRUS the Great.

PEOPLE IN HISTORY

ADAMS, John (1735–1826) U.S. politician and second president. Helped draft Declaration of Independence (1776); vice-president under WASHINGTON (1789–96). President (1796–1800), defeated by JEFFERSON.

ADAMS, Samuel (1722–1830) U.S. patriot. Eloquent political firebrand who organized the Sons of Liberty and masterminded the Boston Tea Party (1773); signed Declaration of Independence (1776); later became govenor of Massachusetts.

ADENAUER, Konrad (1876–1967) German politician. Imprisoned by Nazis (1933, 1944); founder of Christian Democratic Union (1945–66); chancellor of Federal Republic of Germany (1949–63); promoted West Germany's place in NATO.

AKBAR "the Great" (1542–1605) Mughal emperor of India (1556–1605); grandson of BABUR; expanded empire in N.C. India to include Afghanistan and all of N. India; reign saw toleration toward non-Muslims and a flowering of Mughal culture.

ALARIC I (*c.* 370–410) Visigoth king. First served Emperor Theodosius, then rebelled against Roman rule; his sacking of Rome (410) marks beginning of end of Western Roman Empire.

ALEXANDER "the Great" (356–323 B.C.) King of Macedonia (336–323 B.C.). Educated by Aristotle; one of the greatest generals of all time, he undertook the widest conquest in ancient times; at his death he ruled an empire stretching from Greece to Indus valley. Died of fever when about to invade Arabia.

ALEXANDER I (1777–1825) Tsar of Russia (1801–25). Early years of reign marked by promise of liberal constitutional reforms; after series of military defeats by French, forced to conclude Treaty of Tilsit with NAPOLEON (1807); at Congress of Vienna (1814–15) laid claim to Poland; increased political reactionism during last years of reign.

ALEXANDER II (1818–81) Tsar of Russia (1855–81). Liberal reformer, who abolished serfdom (1861) and reformed Russia's local government and judicial system; assassinated by terrorists.

ALLENDE, (Gossens) Salvador (1908–73) Chilean politician. Helped found Chilean Socialist Party (1933); became the world's first democratically elected Marxist president (1970); killed during military coup.

ARAFAT, Yasser (Mohammed Abed Ar'ouf Arafat) (b. 1929) leader of the Palestinian Liberation Organization (PLO) since 1971. In 1988 he persuaded the majority of his PLO colleagues to formally recognize the state of Israel. In 1994, the agreement between the Israelis and the Palestinians led to his Nobel Peace Prize.

ARNOLD, Benedict (1741–1801) U.S.

Atatürk, leader of Turkey in the 1920s–30s.

general and traitor. His plot to surrender West Point to British in American Revolution (1780) failed; escaped from colonial lines and fought for British; died in England.

ASOKA (*c.* 264–238 B.C.) Ruler of Mauryan dynasty in N India (*c.* 269–*c.* 238 B.C.). Empire included most of India and Afghanistan; renounced warfare after converting to Buddhism.

ASSURBANIPAL (600s B.C.) King of Assyria (668–627 B.C.). Last of great Assyrian kings; completed Assyrian conquest of Egypt (669–662 B.C.); overran Babylon (652 B.C.).

ATAHUALPA (*c.* 1500–33) Last ruler of the Incas (1525–33). Defeated brother and coruler Huáscar (1530); murdered by Spanish conquistadores.

ATATÜRK, Kemal (Mustafa Kemal) (1881–1938) Turkish general and statesman. Led nationalist rebellion against post-World War I division of Turkey; president (1923–38); launched program of social and political reform; took name of Atatürk ("Father of the Turks").

ATTILA (*c.* 406–453) King of Huns (434–453). Ravaged divided Roman Empire, invading Gaul (451); defeated near Châlons-sur-Marne by combined Roman, Frankish, and Visigoth forces; invaded Italy, but forced to retreat.

ATTLEE Clement (1883–1967) British politician. Deputy prime minister in CHURCHILL's war cabinet (1942–45); as prime minister (1945–51) he carried through program of nationalization and social welfare, including introduction of National Health Service (1948); his government granted independence to India (1947) and Burma (1948).

AUGUSTUS or **Octavian (Gaius Octavius)** (63 B.C.–A.D. 14) Founder of Roman Empire. Great-nephew of and heir to Julius CAESAR; gained power in Rome after Caesar's assassination; defeated MARK ANTONY and CLEOPATRA at battle of Actium (31 B.C.); Senate voted him Augustus ("sacred") in 27

B.C.; first Roman emperor (27 B.C.–A.D. 14); as absolute monarch he made Rome prosperous after a century of civil war.

BABUR (Zahiruddin Muhammad) (*c.* 1483–1530) Founder of Mughal (Mongol) Empire. Descendant of GENGHIS KHAN and TIMUR; ruler of Kabul, Afghanistan (1504); conquered nearly all N. India (1525–56); initiated Mughal policy of toleration toward non-Muslims.

BAKUNIN, Mikhail (1814–76) Russian anarchist and revolutionary. Exiled to Siberia after revolutions of 1848–49; failed in attempt to win leadership of First International from MARX (1868), and expelled from movement (1872) for militant views; continued to promote nihilist creed and violent revolution.

BANDARANAIKE, Sirimavo (b. 1916) Sri Lankan politician. Widow of S.W.R.D. Bandaranaike (assassinated 1959); became first woman prime minister in world (1960–65, 1970–77); stripped of her civil rights (1980); relinquished leadership of SLFP (Sri Lanka Freedom Party) to son, Anura.

BARTON, Clara (1821–1912) U.S. humanitarian. Was clerk in U.S. Patent Office; set up organization to send food supplies to wounded Civil War soldiers (1861); established American Red Cross (1881) after seeing the work done by the Red Cross in Switzerland.

BEGIN, Menachem (1913–92) Israeli statesman and prime minister (1977–84). Active member of Zionist movement, especially during Arab-Israeli War (1967), but hardline policies changed during meetings with Anwar SADAT, Egyptian president, leading to peace treaty and sharing of Nobel Peace Prize (1978).

BEN-GURION, David (1886–1973) Israeli statesman. Born in Poland but emigrated to Palestine (1906); helped organize Jewish Legion in World War I; became leader of Mapai (Labor) Party (1930); first prime minister of Israel (1948–53 and 1955–63).

BHUTTO, Benazir (b. 1953) Pakistani politician. Put under house arrest (1977–84) by General Zia ul-Haq, who executed her father, Zulfikar Ali BHUTTO; leader of Pakistan People's Party (1984) while in exile in England; returned to Pakistan (1986); elected prime minister (1988–90 and 1993–).

BHUTTO, Zulfikar Ali (1928–79) Pakistani politician. Joined Pakistani cabinet (1958) as minister of commerce; foreign minister (1963); founded Pakistan's People's Party (1967); after secession (1971) of East Pakistan (now Bangladesh), became president (1971–73) and prime minister (1973–77); after 1977 elections, army under General Zia ul-Haq seized control; Bhutto tried for corruption and murder; executed (1978).

BISMARCK, Prince Otto von (1815–98)

The capture of John Brown after his raid on Harper's Ferry, 1859.

Prusso-German statesman, known as the "Iron Chancellor." Enlarged Prussian army; led German states in war: against Denmark (1864); in the Seven Weeks' War against Austria (1866); and in Franco-Prussian War (1870–71). After Prussian king, Wilhelm I, crowned emperor of German Second Empire, became chancellor (1871–90); created Triple Alliance with Austria and Italy (1881–1914); forced to resign by WILHELM II (1890).

BOABDIL (Abu Abdallah Muhammad) (d. *c.* 1533) Last Moorish king in Europe. Ruled as Muhammad XI, king of Granada (1482–83, 1486–92); driven out by FERDINAND and ISABELLA.

BOLÍVAR, Simón (1783–1830) South American revolutionary leader, known as "the Liberator." Born Venezuela; involved in South American uprisings from 1812; led armies that liberated modern Bolivia, Colombia, Ecuador, Peru, and Venezuela from Spanish rule; president of Republic of Colombia (1819–30).

BOONE, Daniel (1734–1820) U.S. frontiersman. Explored Kentucky (1769–73); blazed the "Wilderness Road," his route through the Cumberland Gap, used by American settlers traveling west.

BORGIA: Spanish-Italian noble family: **Alfonso** (1378–1458), as Pope Callistus III (1455–58), and nephew **Rodrigo** (*c.* 1431–1503), as Pope Alexander VI (1492–1503), endeavored to break power of Italian princes; apportioned New World between Spain and Portugal; **Rodrigo** fathered **Cesare** (*c.* 1475–1507) and **Lucrezia** (1480–1519). Cesare was outstanding soldier and administrator. Lucrezia established court of artists and men of letters after marriage to Duke of Ferrara.

BOURBON, House of Royal family of France. Founded by **Robert of Clermont** (1256–1317); **Antoine de Bourbon** (1518–62) became king of

Navarre; on death of last Valois king Antoine's son became king of France as HENRI IV (ruled 1589–1610); his direct descendants ruled France (except 1792–1814) until 1830.

BRANDT, Willy (b. **Karl Herbert Frahm**) (1913–92) German politician. As anti-Nazi fled to Norway (1933); returned to Germany 1945; mayor of West Berlin (1957–66); chancellor of Federal Republic of Germany (1969–74); success in restoring relations with E. Europe brought Nobel Peace Prize (1971)

BREZHNEV, Leonid Ilyich (1906–82) Russian politician. Chairman of the Presidium of Supreme Soviet (1960–64); general secretary of Communist Party of Soviet Union (1964–82); his period in power saw the establishment of the Soviet Union as both a military and a political superpower.

BROWN, John (1800–59) U.S. militant abolitionist. Organized several anti-slavery enterprises; hanged after leading raid on U.S. arsenal at Harper's Ferry, Virginia (1859).

BUDDHA (Gautama Siddhartha) (*c.* 563–*c.* 483 B.C.) Founder of Buddhism. Son of rajah of Sakya tribe, which ruled in Kapilavastu, Nepal. Aged *c.* 30 left court, wife, and all earthly ambitions for ascetic's life; after six years saw contemplative life as a perfect way to self-enlightenment. Taught for the next 40 years, gaining many disciples, and died in Kusinagara in Oudh, India.

BUFFALO BILL (b. William Cody) (1846–1917) U.S. showman. Army scout in Sioux wars; nickname earned after killing 5,000 buffalo in 18 months for a contract; from 1883 toured world with his Wild West Show.

BUNCHE, Ralph (Johnson) (1904–71) U.S. diplomat. First African-American division head in U.S. Department of State; negotiated armistice between Israel and Arab neighbors (1949); won Nobel Peace Prize (1950); UN undersecretary for Special Political Affairs (1957–71).

BURKE, Edmund (1729–97) Irish-born British politician and political philosopher. Supported American colonists; opposed French Revolution; exposed injustices in India and instigated trial of Warren HASTINGS.

BURR, Aaron (1756–1836) U.S. politician. Vice President (1801-1805) renowned for his volatile temper; killed rival Alexander HAMILTON in duel (1804); acquitted of treason (1807) after being accused of plotting to take over lands acquired in Louisiana Purchase.

BUSH, George (b. 1924) U.S. politician and 41st president. Elected for two terms in U.S. House of Representatives (1967–71); U.S. ambassador to UN (1971–73); chairman of Republican National Committee (1973–74); U.S. envoy to China (1974–75); head of CIA (1976–77); vice-president (1981–89);

elected 41st president (1989–93); during presidency Allies defeated Iraq in Gulf War (1991).

CAESAR, (Gaius) Julius (100–44 B.C.) Roman statesman and general. Joined with Crassus and POMPEY in First Triumvirate (60 B.C.); conquered Gaul and invaded Britain; ordered by senate to disband army, but crossed Rubicon River and invaded Italy; dictator from 49 B.C.; assassinated by political rivals; orator and writer, who wrote masterly accounts of Gallic wars and the Roman civil war.

CALHOUN, John C. (1782–1850) U.S. politician. Served as vice president (1825-1833); later became senator for South Carolina (1835); prominent spokesman for states' rights and Southern causes, including the admission of slave states to the Union.

CALIGULA, (Gaius Caesar) (A.D. 12–41) Roman emperor. Succeeded great uncle Tiberius as emperor (37–41); mentally unstable and cruel; finally assassinated.

CANUTE (or **Cnut**) (c. 994–1035) King of England (1016), Denmark (1018), and Norway (1028). Successfully challenged Ethelred the Unready and Edmund II for English throne; reign saw firm government, justice, and peace.

CARTER, James Earl ("Jimmy") (b. 1924) U.S. politician and 39th president. Democratic governor of Georgia (1970–74); president (1977–81); main achievement was the treaty between Israel and Egypt (Camp David Accord, 1979); administration ended in difficulties over Iran hostage crisis (1980).

CASANOVA DE SEINFELT, Giovanni Jacopo (1725–98) Italian adventurer. Worked and traveled throughout Europe; wrote scandalous memoirs about his amatory escapades.

CASEMENT, Sir Roger David (1864–1916) Irish nationalist. Worked as British consul in Africa and Brazil; arrested (1916) on landing in Ireland from German submarine to head Sinn Féin rebellion; hanged by British for high treason.

CASTRO, Fidel (b. 1927) Cuban revolutionary. Led revolution in Cuba that overthrew dictator Batista (1956–59); prime minister (1959–); president (1976–); put through far-reaching reforms; overthrew U.S. economic dominance; dependence on Soviet aid led to missile crisis of 1962; collapse of U.S.S.R. in 1980s isolated his regime.

CATHERINE DE' MEDICI (1519–89) Italian-born queen of Henri II of France and mother of three kings of France. Regent for Charles IX (1560–63); implicated in St. Bartholomew's Day Massacre (1572).

CATHERINE II "the Great" (1729–96) German-born empress of Russia. Deposed mad husband, Tsar Peter III; empress of Russia (1762–96); strengthened power of nobility; extended serfdom; captured Crimea, Black Sea, coast

Fidel Castro, Cuban revolutionary leader.

and much of Poland.

CAVOUR, Conte di Camillo Benso (1810–61) Piedmontese statesman. Premier of Sardinia (1852–59); architect of Italian unification under Victor Emmanuel II in 1861.

CETEWAYO (c. 1826–84) King of the Zulu (1872–79). Beat British regiment at Isandhlwana, but defeated at Ulundi (1879); exiled, then restored by British as ruler of central Zululand until driven out by anti-royalist faction.

CHAMBERLAIN: family of British politicians. **Joseph** (1836–1914) was Liberal colonial secretary. **Sir Austen** (1863–1937), eldest son of Joseph; Conservative foreign secretary (1924–29); Nobel Peace Prize (1925). **Neville** (1869–1940), second son of Joseph; Conservative prime minister (1937–40); followed appeasement policy toward Nazis at Munich (1938); forced to resign 1940.

CHAMPLAIN, Samuel de (c. 1567–1635) French navigator and governor of New France. Traveled to North America (1603), exploring coast (1604–07) and founding Quebec (1608); governor of New France (1612); governor of Quebec (from 1633).

CHANDRAGUPTA (Vikramaditya) (c. 380–c. 415) Indian emperor; grandfather of ASOKA; extended control over neighboring Gujurat, Saurashtra, and Malwa; during reign cultural development of ancient India reached climax.

CHARLEMAGNE (742–814) King of the Franks (771–84) and Holy Roman emperor (800–14). Defeated Saxons (772) and Lombards (773–74); fought Arabs in Spain and took control of most of Christian Europe; crowned emperor by Pope Leo III (800); court was center of intellectual and artistic renaissance.

CHARLES I (1600–49) King of England, Scotland, and Ireland (1625–49). Marriage to Henrietta Maria, a Catholic French princess, disliked; tried to rule without parliament (1629–40); growing need for money led to unpopular eco-

nomic policies, but parliament revolted against unjust taxation; defeated in English civil wars (1642–48), put on trial, convicted of treason, and publicly beheaded.

CHARLES V (1500–58) Holy Roman emperor (1519–56) and, as Charles I, king of Spain (1516–56). Greatest of HAPSBURG emperors; rivalry with FRANÇOIS I of France led to four wars, but left him in control of disputed territories in Italy and Netherlands; sought to restore unity of faith during Protestant Reformation; tried to halt advance of Ottoman Turks under SULEYMAN I; renounced crown in 1556.

CHARLES XII (1682–1718) King of Sweden (1697–1718). Led armies to victory in Northern wars (1700–21) against alliance of Denmark, Russia, and Saxony; defeated by Russians at Poltava (1709); continued struggle against coalition but shot dead in battle.

CHARLES MARTEL (c. 688–741) Frankish ruler of Austrasia (714–741). Halted Muslim expansion in W. Europe at battle of Poitiers (732); established as effective leader of much of Gaul, although never crowned; grandfather of CHARLEMAGNE.

CHIANG KAI-SHEK (Jiang Jieshu) (1887–1975) Chinese revolutionary leader. Joined government of SUN YAT SEN (1918); after Sun's death (1925), began long civil war with Communists (1927–49); head of Nationalist government at Nanjing (1928); resisted Japanese invasion (1937–45); defeated by Communists and retreated to Taiwan (1949); presided over beginnings of Taiwan's "economic miracle."

CHURCHILL, Sir Winston Leonard Spencer (1874–1965) British politician and author. Newspaper correspondent in second Boer War; Conservative MP 1900; joined Liberal Party 1904; first lord of the admiralty (1911–15, 1939–40); rejoined Conservative Party (1929); prime minister of coalition government during World War II (1940–45); prime minister again (1951–5); also painter and writer (won Nobel Prize for Literature 1953); honorary U.S. citizenship conferred 1963.

CICERO, Marcus Tullius (106–43 B.C.) Roman orator, politician, and philosopher. Opposed Julius CAESAR; delivered famous series of speeches against MARK ANTONY defending the republic (43 B.C.); murdered on orders of Octavian (AUGUSTUS).

CLARK, William (1770–1838) U.S. explorer. Joint leader with Meriwether LEWIS, of the expedition (1804-1806) to study the lands acquired under the Louisiana Purchase (1803).

CLAUDIUS (10 B.C.–A.D. 54) Roman emperor (A.D. 41–54). Nephew of Emperor Tiberius; became emperor by accident in chaos following murder of CALIGULA; able and progressive ruler; extended empire by sending armies to

Britain, Mauretania, and Thrace; poisoned by fourth wife, Agrippina.

CLAY, Henry (1777–1852) U.S. politician. Failed three times to be elected president but made his mark in Congress representing Kentucky; devised Missouri Compromise (1820) which preserved balance of free and slave states; his Compromise of 1850 postponed Southern secession.

CLEMENCEAU, Georges Eugène Benjamin (1841–1929) French politician, called "the Tiger." Elected to national assembly 1871; led campaign to rehabilitate DREYFUS; prime minister (1906–09, 1917–20); opposed Woodrow WILSON at Paris Peace Conference (1919), believing Treaty of Versailles gave inadequate protection to France from future German attack.

CLEOPATRA VII (69–30 B.C.) Queen of Egypt (51–48 B.C., 47–30 B.C.). Of Macedonian origin; ruled jointly with brother, Ptolemy; mistress of Julius CAESAR (49–44 B.C.), who supported her against Ptolemy; married MARK ANTONY (36 B.C.); committed suicide after she and Antony defeated by Octavian (AUGUSTUS) at Actium (31 B.C.); subject of works by Plutarch, Shakespeare, and George Bernard Shaw.

CLINTON, William ("Bill") (b. 1946) U.S. politician and 42nd president. Five terms as Democratic governor of Arkansas (1979–81, 1983–92); elected president in 1992, ending 12-year Republican hold on presidency.

CLIVE, Robert (1725–74) British soldier and administrator. Joined British East India Company (1743); took part in campaigns against French; victory at battle of Plassey (1757) gave British control of India; governor of Bengal (1764–67); censured for misgovernment; committed suicide in London.

COLLINS, Michael (1890–1922) Irish politician and Sinn Féin leader. With Arthur Griffiths, negotiated treaty with Britain that set up Irish Free State (1921); commander-in-chief of government forces in Irish civil war, during which he was killed.

COLUMBUS, Christopher (1451–1506) Genoese navigator. Discovered the Bahamas, Cuba, and other West Indian islands (1492) while seeking westward route to Indies; voyages were sponsored by FERDINAND and ISABELLA of Spain, and included a landing on lowlands of South America (1498).

CONFUCIUS (K'ung Fu-Tsu) (551–479 B.C.) Chinese philosopher (*p. 239*).

CONSTANTINE I "the Great" (*c.* 285–337) Roman emperor (306–337). Defeated Maxentius and became emperor of the West (312); defeated Licinius and became emperor of the East (324); first emperor to promote Christianity; Edict of Milan (313) brought toleration of Christians throughout empire; built capital of Constantinople.

COOK, James (1728–79) British naval

George Armstrong Custer.

officer and navigator. Explored Pacific, charting coasts of New Zealand and Australia; named Botany Bay, Australia (1770); surveyed Newfoundland coast; murdered in Hawaii.

COOLIDGE, Calvin (1872–1933) U.S. politician and 30th president (1923–29). Son of a farmer, he became a lawyer and governor of Massachusetts (1919–20); won acclaim for breaking the Boston police strike. His term as president was marked by prosperity.

CORNWALLIS, Charles (1738–1805) British general. British military leader during the American Revolution; masterminded British victory at Brandywine (1777) but surrendered at Yorktown (1781), in effect ending the war.

CORTÉS, Hernán (1485–1547) Spanish conquistador. Conquered Mexico (1519–21) with force of only 500 men; marched on Aztec capital, Tenochtitlán, killing king, MONTEZUMA II; governor of New Spain (1522–30).

CRAZY HORSE (c. 1840–1877) Oglala Sioux chief who took part in the defeat of General CUSTER at the battle of Little Big Horn. Described by a U.S. army officer as "one of the great soldiers of his day and generation."

CROCKETT, Davy (David) (1786–1836) U.S. frontiersman. Elected to U.S. House of Representatives from Tennessee (1827–31, 1833–35); died fighting for Texas at battle of Alamo.

CROESUS (d. 546 B.C.) Last king of Lydia in Asia Minor (560–546 B.C.). Extended his kingdom eastward from the Aegean to the Halys River (Asia Minor); his conquests and mines made his wealth legendary; defeated and imprisoned by CYRUS II of Persia.

CROMWELL, Oliver (1599–1658) English soldier and statesman. Fought on Parliamentary side in English civil wars; as second-in-command to Fairfax reorganized New Model Army; leading voice in demanding CHARLES I's execution (1649); suppressed Irish rebellion (1649–50) and Scottish royalists (1650–51); dissolved Rump Parliament (1653); refused crown; established protectorate and became lord protector of England (1653–58).

CUSTER, George Armstrong (1839–76)

U.S. army officer. Cavalry commander in American Civil War; led seventh cavalry in campaigns against Indian tribes of the Great Plains; killed with over 200 of his men at battle of Little Bighorn by combined force of Sioux and Cheyenne.

CYRUS II "the Great" (d. 529 B.C.) Founder of Achaemenid Persian Empire. Defeated Medes (549 B.C.); king of Persia (548 B.C.); took Lydia (*c.* 546 B.C.) and Babylon (539 B.C.); empire ran from Mediterranean to Hindu Kush; policy of religious toleration; placed Jews in power in Palestine.

DA GAMA, Vasco (*c.* 1469–1524) Portuguese navigator. First European to discover sea route to India by sailing around Cape of Good Hope, up coast of Africa, and across Indian Ocean (1497).

DALAI LAMA (Tenzin Gyatso) (b. 1935) Spiritual and temporal head of Tibet. Designated the 14th Dalai Lama in 1937. Forced into permanent exile in India (1959) after the Chinese invasion of Tibet. Awarded the 1989 Nobel Peace Prize for his commitment to the nonviolent liberation of his homeland.

DANTON, Georges Jacques (1759–94) French revolutionary politician. Minister of justice (1792); voted for death of LOUIS XVI (1793); came to dominate Committee of Public Safety; advocated relaxation of Reign of Terror; lost leadership of Revolutionary Tribunal to ROBESPIERRE; guillotined.

DARIUS I "the Great" (548–486 B.C.) Achaemenid king of Persia (521–486 B.C.). Noted for administrative reforms, military conquests (Thrace and Macedonia), and religious toleration; defeated by Athenians at battle of Marathon (490 B.C.); consolidated Persian power in E. continued CYRUS II's policy of restoring Jewish state.

DAVIS, Jefferson (1808–89) U.S. politician. Entered U.S. House of Representatives for Mississippi (1845); secretary of war (1853–57); in Senate (1847–51, 1857–61) led States' Rights Party and supported slavery; president of the Confederacy during Civil War (1861–65); imprisoned for two years; included in amnesty of 1868.

DE GAULLE, Charles André Joseph Marie (1890–1970) French general and politician. Colonel in French army at start of World War II; opposed French-German Armistice (1940); fled to England and organized Free French Forces; head of provisional government (1944–46); Algerian crisis led to recall from retirement (1958) as last prime minister of Fourth Republic; drew up constitution for Fifth Republic (1958) and became first president (1959–69); negotiated end of Algerian War (1962); developed French nuclear deterrent and removed France from NATO (1966); resigned on losing referendum on constitutional reform (1969).

DE KLERK, F(rederick) W(illem) (b. 1936) South African politician.

National Party leader in Transvaal (1982–89); president (1989–94); won referendum supporting negotiations with ANC (1989); with MANDELA joint winner of Nobel Peace Prize 1993; vice-president under Mandela (1994–).

DENG XIAOPING (Teng Hsiao-P'ing) (b. 1904) Chinese politician, dominant figure in Chinese politics since death of MAO TSE-TUNG. Secretary-general of Chinese Communist Party (1954); purged during Cultural Revolution (1966); leader of Chinese Communist Party since 1978.

DE VALÉRA, Eamon (1882–1975) Irish politician, born in U.S.A. Imprisoned for part in Easter Uprising (1916); leader of Sinn Féin (1917–26); president of Dáil Eireann (1926); founder of Fíanna Fáil (1926); prime minister (1932–48, 1951–54, 1957–9); established Irish Free State as Eire; president of Republic of Ireland (1959–73).

DISRAELI, Benjamin (1st Earl of Beaconsfield) (1804–81) British politician. Author of *Coningsby* and *Sibyl*; Conservative prime minister (1868, 1874–80); bought half ownership in Suez Canal for Britain (1875); rival of GLADSTONE; friend of Queen VICTORIA.

DOUGLASS, Frederick (1817–1895) African-American civil rights leader. Born a slave, he was taught to read and write by his mistress then continued his education secretly; escaped to the North (1838) to become a leader of the Abolitionist movement; acted as adviser to President LINCOLN; later held several jobs in U.S. government.

DRAKE, Sir Francis (c. 1540–96) English seaman and explorer. Plundered Spanish settlements in West Indies; destroyed a Spanish fleet at Cádiz (1577); circumnavigated the globe (1577–80); fought against Spanish Armada (1588); died of dysentery on voyage to Spanish West Indies.

DREYFUS, Alfred (1859–1935) French Jewish army officer. Officer on general staff of French army, falsely accused (1893–94) of giving defence secrets to Germans; court-martialed and transported to Devil's Island, French Guinea; efforts to free him deeply divided French political and intellectual world; acquitted (1906) after two more trials; innocence proved in 1930.

DUBČEK, Alexander (1921–92) Czechoslovak politician. First secretary of Communist Party (1968); his far-reaching reforms during "Prague spring" led to occupation of Czechoslovakia by Warsaw Pact forces; following popular uprising (1989), became chairman of new federal assembly; died after car crash.

DULLES, John Foster (1888–1959) U.S. politician. Advised at Charter Conference of United Nations (1945); U.S. delegate to UN general assembly (1945–49); secretary of state in EISENHOWER administration (1953–59);

Alexander Dubček and well-wishers in 1968.

known chiefly for aggressive anti-communist policies.

DUVALIER, François ("Papa Doc") (1907–71) Haitian politician. Held power from 1957 until his death; autocratic regime saw creation of civilian militia known as Tonton Macoutes and the exile of many Haitians.

EDWARD I (1239–1307) King of England (1272–1307). In two devastating campaigns (1276–77, 1282–83) annexed N.W. Wales; ensured permanence of conquests by building series of castles; led long, unsuccessful campaign to conquer Scotland.

EDWARD III (1312–77) King of England (1327–77). Made attempts to wrest Scottish throne from David II, whom he defeated at battle of Halidon Hill (1333); reign dominated by Hundred Years' War, during which he won major victory at Crécy (1346).

EISENHOWER, Dwight David ("Ike") (1890–1969) U.S. general and 34th president. Commanded Allied forces in French North Africa landings (1942); supreme commander of Allied expeditionary force in 1944 invasion of Europe; supreme commander of NATO forces in Europe (1950); won presidential election as Republican candidate in 1952; reelected (1956); administration negotiated truce in Korean War (1953), and continued U.S. efforts to contain Communism.

ELIZABETH I (1533–1603) Queen of England (1558–1603). Daughter of HENRY VIII and Anne Boleyn; never married but used possibility of marriage as diplomatic tool; made peace with France and Scotland; imprisoned and executed MARY Queen of Scots (1587); persecuted Catholics in 1580s and 1590s; navy defeated Spanish Armada (1588); reign saw England become important European power with expansion overseas and flowering of the arts.

ELIZABETH II (b. 1926) Queen of the United Kingdom (1952–) and head of Commonwealth of Nations. Daughter of George VI; has traveled extensively, especially in the Commonwealth, and done much to reduce the distance between monarch and people.

FAWKES, Guy (1570–1606) English con-spirator. Member of Gunpowder Plot to blow up Parliament (1605); caught red-handed, tried, and executed.

FAYSAL I (1885–1933) King of Iraq (1921–33). Together with T. E. LAWRENCE, led Arab revolt against Turkish rule (1916); after peace installed as king of Iraq by British; ability to unite diverse interests made him leader of Arab nationalism.

FERDINAND II "the Catholic" (1452–1516) King of Aragon and Castile as Ferdinand V (1479–1516), king of Sicily as Ferdinand II and of Naples as Ferdinand III (1503–16). Married ISABELLA of Castile (1469) and ruled jointly with her until her death; introduced the Inquisition (1478–80); expelled the Jews (1492); took Naples from French (1503); under his rule Spain gained imperial influence following discovery of America.

FOX, Charles James (1749–1806) British politician. Whig MP at 19; enemy of GEORGE III and PITT "the Younger;" foreign secretary in 1782, 1783, and 1806; supported American independence and French Revolution; advocated independence for Ireland, enlargement of franchise, and parliamentary reform; championed anti-slavery bill (passed 1807).

FRANCO (Bahamonde), Francisco (1892–1975) Spanish general and dictator. Joined conspiracy against Popular Front government (1936); in ensuing civil war became Generalissimo of the rebel forces and chief of Nationalist state; after leading Nationalists to victory (1939) became head of state (*El Caudillo*) and dictator; provided Germany with logistical and intelligence support during World War II; declared Spain a monarchy with himself as regent (1947); named Juan Carlos as his successor (1969).

FRANÇOIS I (1494–1547) King of France (1515–47). Failed in bid to be elected Holy Roman emperor (1519); planned alliance with HENRY VIII against successful candidate, CHARLES V, failed to occur at Field of the Cloth of Gold (1520); rivalry with Charles V led to series of wars (1521–26, 1528–29, 1536–38, 1542–44); after capture at Pavia in first war (1525) was forced to give up territorial claims in Italy to gain freedom; patron of the arts and learning.

FRANKLIN, Benjamin (1706–90) U.S. politician, author, and scientist. Deputy postmaster-general for the Colonies (1753); began research that proved electricity and lightning are identical (1748); helped draw up Declaration of Independence (1776); negotiated Britain's recognition of U.S. independence (1783); U.S. minister in Paris; member of Federal Constitutional Convention (1787).

FREDERICK I "Barbarossa" (c. 1123–90) German king and Holy Roman emperor. Reign was continuous struggle against unruly vassals at home, city republics of Lombardy and papacy; asserted feudal superiority over Poland, Hungary, Denmark, and Burgundy; drowned while leading Third Crusade against SALADIN.

FREDERICK II "the Great" (1712–86) King of Prussia (1740–86). His exploits in War of Austrian Succession (1740–48) and Seven Years' War (1756–63) made Prussia strongest military power in Europe; involved in first partition of Poland (1772); promoted important legal and social reforms; renowned patron of the arts.

GANDHI, Indira (Priyadarshini) (1917–84) Indian politician. Daughter of NEHRU; prime minister (1966–77, 1980–84); after conviction for election malpractices declared state of emergency (1975–77); elected prime minister again; assassinated by Sikh extremists, who were members of her bodyguard.

GANDHI, Mohandas Karamchand ("Mahatma") (1869–1948) Indian nationalist leader. Spent 21 years in South Africa agitating for equal rights for Indians there; supported Indian Home Rule movement; leader of Indian National Congress (1920), advocating policy of nonviolent civil disobedience; jailed several times by British; major figure in postwar negotiation that led to India's independence (1947); murdered by Hindu fanatic.

GARIBALDI, Giuseppe (1807–82) Italian revolutionary, soldier, and politician. Hero of the Risorgimento; invited by CAVOUR to defeat Austrians in N. Italy (1859); set sail from Genoa with 1,000 volunteers ("Redshirts") to assist anti-BOURBON rebellion in Sicily; seized control of the island (1860) and crossed to mainland, conquering Naples, capital of the Two Sicilies, before handing it over to VICTOR EMMANUEL II; twice tried unsuccessfully to seize Rome (1862 and 1867); member of Italian parliament (1874).

GENGHIS KHAN (c. 1162–1227) Mongol conqueror. Changed name of Temujin to Genghis Khan ("ruler of all men"); after uniting Mongol tribes, conquered them (1213–24). Empire stretched from Black Sea to the Pacific, including N. China, Turkistan, and Afghanistan; also raided Persia and E. Europe.

GEORGE III (1738–1820) King of Great Britain and Ireland, and king of Hanover (1815–1820). With prime minister, Lord North, shared blame for loss of American colonies; suffered from porphyria, a disease that causes mental derangement; illness brought about regency of Prince of Wales (later George IV) from 1811.

GERONIMO (c. 1829–1909) Native American warrior. A Chiricahua Apache chief; after massacre of family by Mexican soldiers, led numerous raiding parties in Mexico and Arizona in 1880s; finally surrendered 1886.

Mikhail Gorbachev, president of the U.S.S.R.

GLADSTONE, William Ewart (1809–98) British politician. Entered parliament as Conservative (1832); leader of Liberal Party (1867); prime minister (1868–74, 1880–85, 1886, 1892–94); tried but failed to secure Home Rule for Ireland.

GLENDOWER, Owen (c. 1354–c. 1416) Welsh national leader. Rebelled against Henry IV of England (1401); proclaimed Prince of Wales and established separate Welsh parliament.

GOEBBELS, Joseph Paul (1897–1945) German Nazi politician. Political radical and anti-Semite; became enthusiastic suporter of HITLER; led Nazi Party (from 1926); as head of Ministry of Public Enlightenment and Propaganda (1933–45) was powerful exponent of Nazi philosophy; killed his six children and committed suicide with wife in Hitler's Berlin bunker.

GOERING, Hermann Wilhelm (1893–1946) German Nazi politician. Air ace in World War I; joined Nazi Party (1922); president of Reichstag (1932); air minister (1933); founded Gestapo (1933); took charge of Luftwaffe (1935); directed German economy (1940–43); in World War II responsible for initiating total air war; influence waned with drug dependency; sentenced to death at Nuremberg Trials but committed suicide.

GORBACHEV, Mikhail (b. 1931) Russian politician. General secretary of the Communist Party (1985–91); first and last executive president of U.S.S.R. (1990); launched program of reform (*perestroika*); allowed greater degree of civil liberty under policy of *glasnost*; ended Soviet occupation of Afghanistan (1989); accepted withdrawal of Soviet troops from Eastern Europe, and reunification of Germany; following unsuccessful coup against him (1991) lost power to Boris YELTSIN; resigned from presidency later the same year.

GRANT, Ulysses S(impson) (1822–85) U.S. general and 18th president

(1869–77). Supreme commander of Union forces in Civil War; won victories during Vicksburg campaign (1862–63) and Wilderness campaign (1864); successful Republican candidate for president (1868); reelected (1872); administration marred by scandal.

GREGORY VII, St. (Ildebrando) (c. 1020–85) Italian Pope (1073–85). Attempts to change secularized condition of Church resulted in conflict with German emperor Henry IV; he excommunicated Henry, who then appointed antipope, Clement III (1080); after siege, forced out of Rome (1084); died in exile.

GUEVARA, Che (Ernesto) (1928–67) Argentine revolutionary leader. Played important part in Cuban revolution (1956–59); held government posts under CASTRO; guerrilla leader in South America (1965); executed by government troops in Bolivia; inspiration to left-wing groups in South America.

GUSTAVUS II Adolphus (1594–1632) King of Sweden (1611–32). Intervened on Protestant side (1630–32) in Thirty Years' War; made sweep through Germany, turning tide against Catholic forces; won decisive victory at Breitenfeld (1631); killed during Swedish victory at Lützen.

HAPSBURG (or Habsburg) Ruling house of Austria from 1452-1918. Founded by Albert, Count of Hapsburg (d. 1240); held crown of Holy Roman Empire with few interruptions from 1273; members included CHARLES V, Maria Theresa, MARIE ANTOINETTE.

HAILE SELASSIE I (Prince Ras Tafari Makonnen) (1892–1975) Emperor of Ethiopia (1930–36, 1941–74). Driven out when Italians occupied Ethiopia (1936); restored by British (1941); deposed (1974) after economic crisis and mutiny by army.

HAMILTON, Alexander (1755 or 1757–1804) U.S. politician. Fought in American Revolution; WASHINGTON's aide-de-camp (1777–1804); as secretary of treasury (1789–95) restored U.S. finances; founder of Federalist Party; killed in duel with rival Aaron Burr.

HAMMURABI (1700s B.C.) Amorite king of Babylon (c. 1792–1750 B.C.). Best known for Code of Laws, whose legal provisions had a strong influence on other Middle Eastern civilizations.

HANCOCK, John (1737–1793) U.S. patriot and leader of the American Revolution. As president of the Continental Congress became the first to sign the Declaration of Independence (1776).

HANNIBAL (247–182 B.C.) Carthaginian general and statesman. In Second Punic War (218–202 B.C.) defeated Gauls and crossed the Alps in face of almost insuperable obstacles; won victory against Romans at Cannae (216 B.C.) but could not take Rome; beaten at Zama (202 B.C.); made peace (201 B.C.); committed suicide to avoid capture by the Romans.

HARUN AL-RASCHID (766–809) Caliph of Baghdad (786–809), ruler of Middle East and N. Africa. Under his rule Baghdad reached its height as a cultural center.

HAVEL, Vaclav (b. 1936) Czechoslovak dramatist and politician. As a founder of Charter 77 was imprisoned and had his plays banned by Communist government; during revolution of 1989 elected president; president of Czech Republic (1993–).

HENRI IV (Henri of Navarre) (1553–1610) First BOURBON king of France (1589–1610). Leader of Huguenot Party (1569); spared after St. Bartholomew's Day Massacre (1572); resumed command of army in opposition to Catholic Holy League (1576); after murder of Henri III, he succeeded to throne; became Catholic (1593) to unify country; assassinated by religious fanatic.

HENRY VIII (1491–1547) King of England (1509–47). Broke with Church of Rome in order to divorce first wife, Catherine of Aragon; later marriages were to Anne Boleyn, Jane Seymour, Anne of Cleves, Catherine Howard, and Catherine Parr; became sole head of Church of England (1534).

HENRY, Patrick (1736–1799) U.S. legislator. Impassioned supporter of the cause of American Independence; elected to Virginia legislature (1765); led outcry against Britain's Stamp Act (1773).

HESS, Rudolf (1894–1987) German Nazi politician. Hitler's deputy as party leader; on eve of Germany's attack on U.S.S.R., flew to Scotland to plead cause of Anglo-German peace (1941); sentenced to life imprisonment at Nuremberg Trials (1946).

HIMMLER, Heinrich (1900–45) German Nazi politician. Head of SS (1929); took over secret police (Gestapo) in Prussia (1934); chief of police (1936); initiated systematic liquidation of Jews; minister of interior (1943); committed suicide after capture by Allies.

HINDENBURG, Paul von (1847–1934) German general and president. Recalled from retirement in World War I; won victories against Russians (1914–15); president of German Republic (1925); reelected to block HITLER's candidacy (1932), but appointed Hitler as chancellor (1933).

HIROHITO (1901–89) Emperor of Japan (1926–89). Reign marked by militarization and aggressive wars against China (1931–02, 1937–45) and the Allies (1941–45); under U.S. occupation, renounced mythical divinity and most of powers (1946).

HITLER, Adolf (1889–1945) German dictator and leader of Nazi Party. Born in Austria; corporal in World War I; leader of extreme right-wing Nationalist Socialist (Nazi) Party (1920); attempted to overthrow Bavarian government

The death of Joan of Arc in 1431.

(1923); served term of imprisonment, during which he wrote political testament *Mein Kampf* (1925); party won parliamentary elections (1930, 1932); chancellor of Germany (1933); suspended constitution, silenced all opposition, openly rearmed country; established Rome-Berlin "Axis" with MUSSOLINI (1936); pursued aggressive foreign policy which culminated in World War II (1939–45); extended war with invasion of U.S.S.R. (1941); available evidence suggests committed suicide in Berlin bunker with wife, Eva Braun.

HO CHI MINH (1892–1969) Vietnamese revolutionary leader. Founder member of French Communist Party; led Viet Minh independence movement from 1941; directed successful military operation against French (1946–54); prime minister (1954–55) and president (1954–69) of North Vietnam.

HOOVER, Herbert Clark (1874–1964) U.S. politician and 31st president (1929–33). Republican candidate 1928, beating "Al" Smith. Opposition to governmental assistance for the unemployed after slump of 1929 made him unpopular. Lost presidency to F. D. ROOSEVELT (1932).

HOUSTON, Sam(uel) (1793–1863) U.S. soldier and politician. Beat Mexican army at San Jacinto and won Texan independence (1836); president of Texas republic (1836–38, 1841–44); U.S. senator (1846–49); governor of Texas (1859–61); deposed for refusing to swear allegiance to the Confederate states (1861).

HUSSEIN, Saddam (b. 1937) Iraqi dictator. Attempted to assassinate head of state, General Kassem, in 1959. Involved in 1968 revolution, setting up Revolutionary Command Council (RCC). Became chairman of RCC and state president 1979. Waged bitter war against Iran (1980–88). Invaded Kuwait (1990) but repulsed by U.S.-led multinational force. Remains in power.

INNOCENT III (Lotario de' Conti di Segni) (1160–1216) Italian pope (1198–1216). Pontificate regarded as high point of papal supremacy; asserted right to choose between two rivals for imperial crown in Germany, and had

Emperor Otto IV deposed (1210); excommuniated King JOHN of England (1212); promoted Fourth Crusade (1202–04).

ISABELLA I "the Catholic" (1451–1504) Queen of Castile (1474–1504). Married FERDINAND of Aragon with whom she ruled jointly; during reign Inquisition was introduced (1478–80) and Jews expelled (1492); sponsored voyage of COLUMBUS to New World (1492).

IVAN IV "the Terrible" (1530–84) Grand Prince of Moscow (1533–84). First prince to assume title of tsar; conquered Kazan (1552) and Astrakhan (1557); expanded into Siberia; death of wife, Anastasia (1560), affected mental balance; embarked on reign of terror directed principally at feudal aristocracy (boyars); killed eldest son, Ivan (1581).

JACKSON, Andrew ("Old Hickory") (1767–1845) U.S. politician and seventh president. In war of 1812 given command of the South; famous for defense of New Orleans (1814–15); president 1829–37.

JACKSON, "Stonewall" (Thomas Jonathan) (1824–1863) Confederate general during the Civil War. Received his nickname after his steadfast defense at the first Battle of Bull Run (1862); captured 13,000 Union troops at Harper's Ferry (1862); died during Battle of Chancellorsville (1863).

JEFFERSON, Thomas (1743–1826) U.S. politician and third president. As delegate to Second Continental Congress (1775), drafted Declaration of Independence; governor of Virginia (1779–81); minister to France (1785–89); secretary of state (1790–93); vice-president (1797–1801); president 1801–09; presidency included Louisiana Purchase (1803) and Embargo Act (1807).

JESUS CHRIST (*c.* 4 B.C.–*c.* A.D. 29) Founder of Christianity, born in Bethlehem, Judaea to Mary and Joseph, a carpenter. Aged *c.* 30, baptized by his cousin, John; undertook two missionary journeys through Galilee, but apparent flouting of traditional religious practices and revolutionary Sermon on the Mount incensed strict Jewish establishment; sought refuge with disciples in Gentile (non-Jewish) territories; return to Jerusalem, betrayed by disciple Judas Iscariot and condemned to death by Sanhedrin (Jewish supreme court); after confirmation of the sentence by Pontius Pilate, Roman procurator, was crucified and buried the same day.

JINNAH, Muhammad Ali (1876–1948) Indian Muslim politician and founder of Pakistan. Member of Indian National Congress (1906); advocated Hindu-Muslim unity, but after 1934 advocated separate state of Pakistan; forced Congress to agree to partition of India (1947); first governor-general of Pakistan (1947–48).

JOAN OF ARC, St. (Jeanne d'Arc) (*c.* 1412–31) French patriot and martyr.

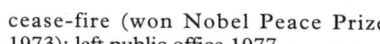

At 13 heard voices of saints telling her to rescue France from English domination; taken to dauphin and eventually allowed to lead army that lifted siege of Orléans and forced English to retreat (1429); other victories turned tide of Hundred Years' War; captured and sold to English by Burgundians; put on trial for heresy and sorcery, and burned at stake; canonized 1920.

JOHN ("John Lackland") (1167–1216) King of England (1199–1216). Tried to seize crown during brother, Richard I's, captivity in Germany (1193–4); had nephew, Prince Arthur, murdered (1203); excommunicated by INNOCENT III for refusal to receive Stephen Langton as archbishop of Canterbury; his oppressive government led to demands by barons for constitutional reform in 1215 (the Magna Carta).

JOHN III SOBIESKI (1629–96) King of Poland (1674–96). Raised Turkish siege of Vienna (1683); formed Holy League against Turks with Pope, Emperor Leopold I, and Venice (1684); death triggered end of Polish independence.

JOHNSON, Lyndon Baines ("L.B.J.") (1908–73) U.S. politician and 36th president. Democratic senator for Texas (1948–61); vice-president (1961–63); after assassination of John KENNEDY sworn in as president; elected to office (1964); his administration (1963–69) passed Civil Rights Act of 1964, Voting Rights Act of 1965, and Great Society program; escalation of Vietnam War led to his growing unpopularity; he did not seek reelection in 1968.

JUSTINIAN I "the Great" (c. 482–565) Byzantine emperor (527–65). Presided over most brilliant period of late Roman Empire; strongly influenced by wife, Theodora; his generals recovered N. Africa, Spain, and Italy from barbarians; carried out codification of Roman law.

KELLER, Helen (1880–1968) U.S. author and lecturer. Became deaf and blind when 19 months old; learned to speak and read Braille; graduated from Radcliffe (1904); inspired millions with a lifelong series of books and lectures about overcoming handicaps.

KENNEDY, John F(itzgerald) (1917–63) U.S. politician and 35th president. Elected to House of Representatives as Democratic senator for Massachusetts (1952–60); president (1960–63), the first Catholic and youngest person to be elected president; induced U.S.S.R. to withdraw missiles from Cuba (1962); domestic policies called for federal desegregation in education, and civil rights reform; assassinated in Dallas, Texas; Warren Commission concluded he was killed by Lee Harvey Oswald.

KENNEDY, Robert Francis (1925–68) U.S. politician. Attorney-general during presidency of brother John KENNEDY; Democratic senator for New York (1964); assassinated by Sirhan Sirhan in California while running for president.

Martin Luther King Jr. addresses followers in Montgomery, 1965.

KENYATTA, Jomo (Kamau Ngengi) (1891–1978) Kenyan nationalist and politician. Country's main spokesman for anticolonial movement; detained during Mau Mau uprising (1953–61); after independence became prime minister (1963); president of new republic (1964); led Kenya into period of economic growth and tribal harmony.

KERENSKY, Alexander (1881–1970) Russian revolutionary. Member of Third and Fourth Dumas; a moderate socialist, in 1917 Revolution he became minister of justice, then minister of war, then prime minister in provisional government; swept from power by Bolsheviks; settled in U.S.A. in 1940.

KHOMEINI, Ayatollah Ruhollah (1900–89) Iranian religious and political leader. Opposed to Shah's pro-Western regime; after collapse of Shah's government (1979), returned from exile to become virtual head of state; under his leadership Iran underwent "Islamic Revolution;" waged war against Iraq (1980–88); issued *fatwa* on Salman Rushdie for *The Satanic Verses* (1989).

KHRUSHCHEV, Nikita Sergeyevich (1894–1971) Soviet politician. On death of STALIN (1953), became first secretary; denounced Stalinism and "personality cult" at 20th Communist Party Congress (1956); crushed Hungarian uprising (1956); failed to install missiles in Cuba (1962); deposed (1964).

KING, Martin Luther Jr. (1929–68) U.S. civil rights leader. Helped found Southern Christian Leadership Council (SCLC) as base in struggle for racial equality; mobilized black community to challenge segregation laws in South through nonviolent demonstrations; his voter registration drive in Alabama led to passage of Voting Rights Act (1965); assassinated in Memphis, Tennessee, by James Earl Ray.

KISSINGER, Henry (b. 1923) U.S. politician. Family emigrated from Germany to escape Nazis; NIXON's adviser on national security affairs in negotiations to end Vietnam War; secretary of state (1973–77); diplomacy during Arab-Israeli War of 1973 helped bring about

cease-fire (won Nobel Peace Prize 1973); left public office 1977.

KUBLAI KHAN (1214–94) Mongol emperor of China (1279–94). Grandson of GENGHIS KHAN; conquered Sung dynasty in China (1279); defeated in campaigns against Japan, and in Southeast Asia; made Buddhism state religion; established capital at Cambaluc (modern Beijing), where court visited by Marco Polo.

LAFAYETTE, Marie Joseph, Marquis de (1757–1834) French soldier and revolutionary. Fought in America against British during American Revolution (1777–79, 1780–82); made major-general by Congress and became friend of WASHINGTON; in National Assembly of 1789 presented draft Declaration of the Rights of Man based on Declaration of Independence; active in French Revolution, but hated by Jacobins for his moderation; sat in Chamber of Deputies (1818–24); radical leader of opposition (1825–30); commanded national guard in July Revolution of 1830 that dethroned BOURBONS.

LAURIER, Sir Wilfred (1841–1919) Canadian politician. Leader of Liberal Party (1887–1911); first French Canadian and Roman Catholic to be prime minister of Canada (1896–1911); firm supporter of self-government for Canada; in home policy an advocate of compromise and free trade with U.S.A.

LAWRENCE, T(homas) E(dward) ("Lawrence of Arabia") (1888–1935) British soldier and Arabist. Worked as archaeologist in Middle East; joined British military intelligence (1914); appointed British liaison officer to Arab revolt led by FAISAL I (1916); his account of the Arab revolt, *The Seven Pillars of Wisdom* (1926), is a classic of war literature.

LEE, Robert E(dward) (1807–70) Military adviser to Jefferson DAVIS. Commander of Confederate forces in the Civil War (1861–65). A great general, he won many famous victories over Union forces before he surrendered at Appomattox Court house (1865).

LENIN, Vladimir Ilyich (V.I. Ulyanov) (1870–1924) Russian Marxist revolutionary and political leader. Imprisoned and exiled to Siberia for revolutionary activities in 1890s; leader of Bolshevik Party (1903); following February Revolution in 1917, returned to Petrograd from Zurich; initiated Bolshevik revolution of October 1917; head of first Soviet government and ruled as virtual dictator; made peace with Germany (1918); defeated Whites in Russian Civil War (1918–21); body lies in mausoleum in Red Square.

LEWIS, Meriwether (1774–1809) U.S. explorer. Together with fellow army officer William CLARK led a party of 44 to explore (1804-1806) the vast area acquired under the Louisiana Purchase; followed president JEFFERSON's commission to find the source of the Missouri River, to report on the tribes living there, and to study the natural history of the region.

Lincoln, Abraham (1809–65) U.S. politician and 16th president. Joined new Republican Party (1856); spoke against extension of slavery; elected president on platform of hostility to slavery expansion (1860); during American Civil War moved to free slaves by issuing Emancipation Proclamation (1863); preserving Union remained main war aim, as expressed in Gettysburg Address (1863); reelected after Union victory (1864); shot at Fords Theatre, Washington D.C.

Lindbergh, Charles Augustus (1902–1974) U.S. aviator and author. First pilot to make solo flight across the Atlantic (1927) in his plane The Spirit of St. Louis. Feted as hero upon landing in Paris and on his return to New York.

Livingstone, David (1813–73) Scottish missionary and explorer. Medical missionary in Bechuanaland (1841–52); crossed Kalahari desert and traveled down Zambezi River seeking sources of Congo (Zaïre) and Nile rivers; discovered Victoria Falls (1855); feared lost, but found by Henry Stanley (1871).

Lloyd-George David (1st Earl of Dwyfor), (1863–1945) British politician. Liberal MP for Caernarvon Boroughs (1890–1945); coalition prime minister (1916–22); conceded Irish Free State (1921); following division of Liberal Party, led group of Independent Liberal MPs (1931); opposed appeasement policy before World War II.

Louis IX, St. (1214–70) King of France (1226–70). Compelled Henry III of England to acknowledge French suzerainty in Guyenne (1259); led Seventh Crusade (1248–54); defeated in Egypt, taken prisoner and ransomed; embarked on Eighth Crusade (1270), but died of plague at Tunis.

Louis XIV (Louis the Great or The Sun King) (1638–1715) King of France (1643–1715), the greatest monarch of his age. Maintained system of absolute rule; despite military successes in early years of reign, aggressive foreign policy led to War of the Grand Alliance (1688–97) and War of the Spanish Succession (1701–14); defeats in these wars left France deeply in debt; persecution of Huguenots in 1680s, culminating in the Revocation of the Edict of Nantes (1685), saw thousands of Huguenots flee France; reign marked cultural ascendancy of France within Europe, symbolized by his palace at Versailles.

Louis XVI (1754–93) King of France (1774–93). Married Austrian archduchess, Marie Antoinette (1770); failed to support ministers who tried to reform country's financial and social structures; to avert economic crisis summoned Estates General (1789); French Revolution began after refused demands

Rosa Luxemburg.

for sweeping reforms; attempted flight with royal family to Austria (1791); tried before national convention and guillotined in Paris.

Louis-Philippe (1773–1850) King of France (1830–48), known as the "Citizen King." Son of Duke of Orléans; during French Revolution entered national guard; placed on throne after abdication of Charles X (1830); political corruption and economic depression caused discontent; when Paris mob rose (1848), abdicated and escaped to England.

Luther, Martin (1483–1546) German religious reformer and principal initiator of Protestantism. Ordained priest (1507); career as reformer began after visit to Rome (1510–11) and his protestation at selling of indulgences to raise money for the Church; drew up 95 theses on indulgences (1517), which he pinned to church door at Wittenberg; publicly burned papal bull issued against him; called to defend doctrines before Diet of Worms (1521), but was excommunicated by pope; retired to Wittenberg; his translation of the Bible is a landmark in German literature.

Luxemburg, Rosa (1871–1919) German left-wing revolutionary.

Mao Zedong in a Chinese poster of 1949.

Founded the Polish Social Democratic party. She wrote tracts like *Sozialreform oder Revolution.* Spent most of World War I in prison. Was murdered after her release in 1919.

MacArthur, Douglas (1880–1964) U.S. general. Commander of U.S. forces in Pacific during World War II; forced to retreat from Philippines (1942), promising "I shall return," began series of "island-hopping" advances which led to Japanese surrender. Commanded U.N. forces in Korea (1950) but recalled by Truman when he proposed using atomic weapons.

Macbeth (c. 1005–57) King of Scotland (1040–57), the subject of Shakespeare's play *Macbeth.* Overthrew and killed Duncan I near Elgin (1040); despite bad Shakespearian image, seems to have ruled wisely; killed by Malcolm III, son of Duncan, at Lumphanan.

Macdonald, John Alexander (1815–91) Scottish-born Canadian politician. Leader of Conservative Party and joint premier (1856); prime minister (1857–58, 1864); played important role in bringing about confederation of Canada; formed first government of new dominion (1867); Pacific Scandal brought down government (1873), but he regained premiership (1878–91); during second term Canadian Pacific Railway completed (1885).

Macmillan, (Maurice) Harold (1st Earl of Stockton) (1894–1986) British politician. Conservative M.P. (1924); critic of appeasement before World War II; prime minister (1957–63); popular during period of economic boom, but resigned after political setbacks.

Magellan, Ferdinand (1480–1521) Portuguese navigator. Organized voyage with five ships to Moluccas by western route (1519); forcing way through Magellan Strait, entered Pacific (1520); killed in skirmish in Philippines; remaining ship and 18 men completed first voyage around world.

Malcolm X (1925–65) U.S. black leader. Born Malcom Little, he took name of "X" to symbolize stolen identities of slaves; leading spokesman for Black Muslims in 1950s; extreme oratory criticized by moderate civil rights leaders; suspended by leader, Elijah Muhammad (1963); founded Organization for Afro-American Unity; announced conversion to orthodox Islam, and put forward belief in brotherhood between blacks and whites; assassinated by Black Muslims.

Mandela, Nelson Rolihlahla (b. 1918) South African nationalist leader. Practiced law before joining African National Congress (ANC) (1944) and founding Congress Youth League; campaigned for free, multiracial, democratic society in South Africa; "banned" (1956–61); sentenced to life imprisonment (1964) for leadership of ANC; released on de Klerk's orders (1990);

elected deputy president of ANC (1990) and president of ANC (1991); elected first black president of South Africa (1994–).

MAO ZEDONG (Mao Tse-tung) (1893–1976) Chinese political leader. Founding member of Chinese Communist Party (CCP) (1921); after Communists broke with Nationalists (1927), helped create Red Army; leader of Long March (1934–35) to new base in N. China; his guerrilla forces resisted Japanese in Sino-Japanese War and defeated Nationalist forces of CHIANG KAI-SHEK; chairman of CCP and president of the People's Republic of China (1949–59); launched Great Leap Forward (1958) in attempt to encourage economic development; initiated Cultural Revolution (1966), an attempt to radicalize the country; influential outside China as a revolutionary figure.

MARAT, Jean Paul (1743–93) French revolutionary politician. His articles against those in power instrumental in overthrow of French monarchy (1792); elected to national convention, where advocated radical reforms; became locked in struggle with Girondists; assassinated by Girondist supporter.

MARIE ANTOINETTE (Josèphe Jeanne) (1755–93) Queen consort of France (1774–93). Daughter of Maria Theresa and Emperor Francis I of Austria; married dauphin (later LOUIS XVI) (1770); aroused criticism for extravagance and opposition to reform; attitude from outbreak of French Revolution helped alienate monarchy from the people; with Louis tried (1791) to escape to Austria, but was apprehended and imprisoned; after king's execution, arraigned before Revolutionary Tribunal and guillotined.

MARK ANTONY (Marcus Antonius) (c. 83–30 B.C.) Roman soldier and politician, known from Shakespeare's plays *Julius Caesar* and *Antony and Cleopatra*. Served with CAESAR in Gaul (53–50 B.C.), and governed Italy while Caesar was in Africa; as consul tried in vain to have Caesar made emperor (44 B.C.); after Caesar's assassination, formed alliance with Octavian (AUGUSTUS) and Lepidus as member of Second Triumvirate; agreed to rule Asia; began affair with CLEOPATRA (41 B.C.); donation (34 B.C.) to her children of parts of Roman Empire helped cause civil war; defeated with Cleopatra at Actium (31 B.C.); they both committed suicide.

MARX, Karl (Heinrich) (1818–83) German founder of modern international communism. Moved to Paris (1843), where he met closest collaborator Friedrich Engels; in Brussels (1845) he and Engels wrote *Communist Manifesto* for the Communist League (1848); expelled from Brussels, settled in London (1849); studied economics, and wrote first volume of major work, *Das Kapital* (1867).

MARY, Queen of Scots (1542–87)

Golda Meir as Israeli Minister of Labor, 1952.

Queen of Scotland (1542–67) and queen consort of France (1559–60). Daughter of James V of Scotland; married dauphin of France (later François II) (1558); widowed at 18 and returned to Scotland; married cousin, Henry Stuart, Lord Darnley (1565); gave birth to son (future James VI of Scotland and I of England); after Darnley's murder (1567), married chief suspect, the Earl of Bothwell; uprising of Scottish lords resulted in military defeat and abdication (1567); fled to England, where kept prisoner by ELIZABETH I; her presence in England stimulated numerous Catholic plots; after Babington conspiracy (1586), brought to trial and executed for treason.

MASARYK, Jan (1886–1948) Czech politician. Son of Tomás MASARYK; helped establish state of Czechoslovakia; foreign minister in Czechoslovakian government from end of World War II to Communist takeover (1945–8); either murdered or committed suicide.

MASARYK, Tomás (1850–1937) Czech politician. Deputy in Czech and Austrian imperial parliaments off and on after 1891; after 1914, traveled widely to win support for independent state of Czechoslovakia; became first president (1918); regularly reelected until retirement (1935).

MATA HARI (Margaretha Gertruida Zelle) (1876–1917) Alleged Dutch spy. Dancer in France (1905); had several lovers in high military and governmental positions (on both sides before and during World War I); found guilty of spying for Germans; shot in Paris.

MATHER, Cotton (1663–1728) U.S. clergyman. He published 382 books. His *Memorable Providences relating to Witchcraft and Possessions* (1685) did much to incite witch-hunts.

MAXIMILIAN (Ferdinand Maximilian Joseph) (1832–67) Emperor of Mexico (1864–67). Brother of Emperor Joseph Francis I; supported by French, accept-

ed offer of crown of Mexico (1863); when French troops under U.S. pressure withdrew from Mexico, refused to abdicate; tried by court-martial, and shot in civil war.

MAZZINI, Giuseppe (1805–72) Italian patriot and key figure of Italian Risorgimento. Exiled to France (1833), where founded Young Italy movement; took part in several abortive insurrections, including revolution of Milan (1848); helped organize Roman republic of 1849; after its defeat, fled to exile in England.

McCARTHY, Joseph Raymond (1909–57) U.S. politician. Republican senator from Wisconsin (1947–57); as chairman of Senate Permanent Subcommittee on Investigations (1953) he made unsubstantiated accusations that Communists had infiltrated State Department; term "McCarthyism" became synonymous with witch-hunt that gripped U.S.A. in early 1950s; power declined after censure by President EISENHOWER and the Senate (1954).

MEDICI Family that made its wealth through banking and ruled Florence (1434–94) without holding formal office. Founder **Giovanni de' Medici** (1360–1429), wealthy merchant. Sons **Cosimo** (1389–1464), banker, statesman, and philanthropist (founded Europe's first public library); and **Lorenzo "the Magnificent"** (1449–92), patron of literature and art; who made Florence leading state in Italy. **CATHERINE DE' MEDICI** (1519–89), daughter of Lorenzo. **Marie de' Medici** (1573– 1642) married HENRI IV of France; after his death, acted as regent (1610–17) to son, Louis XIII.

MEIR, Golda (1898–1978) Israeli politician. Emigrated from Russia to U.S.A. aged eight; married and settled in Palestine (1921); as prime minister (1969–74) efforts for peace in Middle East halted by Arab-Israeli War of 1973.

MENZIES, Robert Gordon (1894–1978) Australian politician. Prime minister 1939–41; Leader of the Opposition 1943–49; prime minister again 1949–66; during ministry, led Australia into Southeast Asia Treaty Organization (SEATO), and the Anzus Pact.

METTERNICH, Klemens (Wenzel Nepomuk Lothar), Prince of (1773–1859) Austrian politician. Foreign minister (1809); negotiated marriage between NAPOLEON I and Marie Louise; played prominent part in Congress of Vienna (1814–15); while chancellor (1821–48) suppressed liberal and nationalist movements; forced to flee after 1848 revolution.

MITTERRAND, François (Maurice Marie) (b. 1916) French politician. Elected deputy in French National Assembly (1946); held office in all governments of Fourth Republic; leader of Socialist Party (1971); stood unsuccessfully as Socialist candidate in presidential elections of 1965 and 1974; became president of France 1981, then re-elected for second seven-year term in 1988. Retired in 1995.

MONROE, James (1758–1831) U.S. politician and fifth president. Served in War of Independence; governor of Virginia (1799–1802); president (1817–25); administration agreed Missouri Compromise (1820), acquired Florida (1821), and set forth principles of Monroe Doctrine (1823).

MONTEZUMA II (1466–1520) Last Aztec emperor of Mexico (1502–20). A distinguished warrior and legislator; died at Tenochtitlán during Spanish conquest.

MORE, Sir Thomas (1478–1535) English statesman and humanist scholar. Wrote *Utopia* in 1516. Under HENRY VIII became lord chancellor (1529–32), but opposed Henry's break with Rome; on refusing to recognize Henry as head of English Church, was imprisoned and beheaded; canonized in 1935.

MUHAMMAD (*c.* 570–632) Arab prophet, and founder of Islam, born in Mecca. Soon after 600 began to receive revelations of the word Allah, the "one and only God"; reduced to poverty after death of wife and uncle, he and his small band of devotees were saved by invitation from people in Yathrib; migration there (Hegira) marks beginning of Muslim era, and Yathrib's name was changed to Medina ("city of prophet"); repelled Meccan siege of Medina (629), which recognized him as chief and prophet; by 630 controlled Arabia; his tomb at Medina is venerated throughout Islam.

MUSSOLINI, Benito (1883–1945) Italian politician and dictator (*Il Duce*). Founded National Fascist Party (1919); took power after Fascist "march on Rome" (1922); ended parliamentary government (1928); annexed Ethiopia (1936) and Albania (1939); made alliance ("Axis") with HITLER (1936); in World War II military involvement in Greece and N. Africa a failure; imprisoned just before Allied invasion of Italy (1943), but rescued by German troops; after German collapse, captured and shot by partisans.

NAPOLEON I (Napoleon Bonaparte) (1769–1821) French general and emperor (1804–15). Born in Corsica; married Josephine Beauharnais (1796); commander of French army in Italy, where won important victories against Austrians (1796–97); attacked British in Egypt, entering Cairo, and defeated Turks; assumed power as first consul or dictator after coup d'état of 18th Brumaire (1799); routed Austrians at Marengo (1800), and made peace with Austria and Britain; reformed French legal system with Code Napoléon (1804); crowned himself emperor (1804), and proclaimed himself king of Italy (1805); fought Third Coalition (Britain, Austria, and Russia), winning

Napoleon at the battle of Jena, 1806.

victories at Ulm and Austerlitz (1805) over Austria and Russia; defeated Prussia at Jena and Auerstäde (1806), and Russia at Friedland (1807); sent armies to Spain and Portugal, resulting in unsuccessful Peninsular War (1808–14); divorced Josephine (1809) and married Archduchess Marie Louise of Austria, who had son (1811); defeated Russians at Borodino and entered Moscow (1812), but forced to retreat; victories over allied armies at Lützen, Bautzen and Dresden (1813); defeated by allied force at Leipzig (1813); after invasion of France, forced to abdicate (1814); brief exile on Elba; returned to France and ruled for Hundred Days (1815); defeated in Waterloo campaign (1815) by British and Prussians; died in exile on St. Helena.

NASSER, Gamal Abd al- (1918–70) Egyptian politician. Involved in military coup against King Farouk (1952); prime minister (1954–56); president (1956–70); instituted far-reaching land reforms and building of Aswan Dam; nationalized Suez Canal, which led to Israeli invasion of Sinai and intervention of Anglo-French forces (1956).

NEHRU, Jawaharlal ("Pandit") (1889–1964) Indian politician. Joined Indian Congress Committee (1918) and became follower of GANDHI; president of Indian National Congress (1929); after independence, India's first prime minister (1947–64); introduced policy of industrialization, reorganized states on linguistic basis and brought dispute with Pakistan over Kashmir to peaceful, though not final, solution.

NELSON, Horatio (1758–1805) British admiral. Played part in defeat of French and Spanish fleets at Cape St Vincent (1797); destroyed French fleet at battle of the Nile (1798); began liaison with Emma, Lady Hamilton, which lasted until his death; defeated Danes at battle of Copenhagen (1801); defeated combined French and Spanish fleets at battle of Trafalgar (1805), but was mortally

wounded.

NERO (Nero Claudius Caesar) (A.D. 37–68) Roman emperor (A.D. 54–68). Mother, Agrippina, persuaded husband CLAUDIUS to adopt him; murdered Agrippina (59) and wife Octavia (62); neglected affairs of state and corruption set in; despite blaming Christians, widely held responsible for Great Fire of Rome (64); toppled from power by army and forced to commit suicide.

NICHOLAS II (1868–1918) Last tsar of Russia (1895–1917). Reign saw Russia's defeat in Russo-Japanese War (1904–05) and inadequate social change which helped to accelerate Russian revolution of 1905; failure to concede any real power to Duma (1906) and incompetence as commander of army in World War I helped to precipitate Russian Revolution of 1917; forced to abdicate (1917); imprisoned, and later murdered with his family by Bolshevik guards.

NIGHTINGALE, Florence (1820–1910) English nurse, considered founder of modern nursing. National heroine after organized unit of women nurses in Crimean War (1854).

NIXON, Richard M(ilhous) (1913–1994) U.S. politician and 37th president. Republican senator (1950); vice-president under EISENHOWER for two terms (1953–61); lost 1960 presidential election to KENNEDY; during presidency (1968–74) sought to bring end to Vietnam War (cease-fire agreed 1973), but only after U.S. invasion of Cambodia and Laos, and saturation bombing of N. Vietnam; diplomatic successes with China and U.S.S.R.; re-elected (1972); resigned under threat of impeachment for his involvement in cover-up of Watergate burglary (1974).

NKRUMAH, Kwame (1909–72) Ghanaian politician. Founded Convention People's Party (1949); prime minister (1952–57), continuing in that post on independence (1957); president after Ghana became republic (1960) ousted by military coup (1966).

O'CONNELL, Daniel (1775–1847) Irish political leader. Election as MP for County Clare precipitated crisis in WELLINGTON's government, which eventually granted Catholic Emancipation (1829); founded Repeal Association (1840); imprisoned on charges of sedition (1844); in conflict with "Young Ireland" movement (1846); left Ireland and died in Genoa.

O'CONNOR, Sandra Day (b. 1930) U.S. jurist. Worked as lawyer for U.S. Army and later set up private practice in Arizona; became judge of the Arizona Court of Appeals (1979); became female Supreme Court Justice (1981) after unanimous approval by Senate.

O'HIGGINS, Bernardo (1778–1842) Chilean revolutionary. Played major role in Chilean struggle for independence; became first leader ("supreme dictator") of new Chilean state (1817); reforms

aroused antagonism among aristocracy, Church, and business community; deposed (1823); lived in exile in Peru.

OTTO I "the Great" (912–73) German king (936–73) and Holy Roman emperor (962–73). Often considered founder of Holy Roman Empire; brought tribal duchies under control of monarchy and made Church main instrument of royal government; prevented Hungarian invasion by victory at Lechfeld (955); re-established imperial rule in Italy; reign also noted for flowering of culture.

PAHLAVI, Mohammed Reza (1919–80) Shah of Persia (1941–79). Reign marked by social reforms, but during 1970s economic situation deteriorated, social inequalities worsened and protest at Western-style "decadence" grew among religious fundamentalists; having lost control of situation, left country (1979); died in exile in Egypt.

PANKHURST, Emmeline (1857–1928) English suffragette. Founded the Women's Franchise League (1889) and, with her daughter Christabel, the Women's Social and Political Union (1903), which fought for women's suffrage with extreme militancy. Frequently imprisoned and underwent hunger strikes for the cause.

PARNELL, Charles Stewart (1846–91) Irish politician. Became MP (1875), supporting Irish Home Rule; gained great popularity in Ireland by use of obstructive parliamentary tactics; elected president of Irish National Land League (1878); allied with Liberals in support of GLADSTONE's Home Rule bill (1886); forced to retire as leader of Irish nationalists (1890) after being cited in divorce case.

PATTON, George Smith (1885–1945) U.S. general. Successful World War II commander who championed the use of tanks. Led U.S. armies through North Africa, Italy, and then France after D-Day landings (1944).

PEEL, Sir Robert (1788–1850) British politician. As Conservative home secretary (1822–27, 1828–30) carried through Catholic Emancipation Act (1829) and reorganized London police force ("Peelers" or "Bobbies"); as prime minister (1834–35, 1841–46), second ministry concentrated on economic reforms; his decision to repeal Corn Laws (1846) split Conservative Party and forced his resignation.

PERICLES (c. 495–429 B.C.) Athenian politician and general. As leader of Athens (461 B.C.) fostered development of Athenian democracy; hostility to Sparta brought about Peloponnesian War (431 B.C.); associated with leading philosophers and artists of the time; responsible for construction of Parthenon and other buildings of Athenian Acropolis; died of plague.

PERÓN, Juan (Domingo) (1895–1974) Argentinian soldier and president. Took leading part in army coup of 1943;

Peter the Great.

gained widespread support through social reforms and became president (1946–55); his support declined after the death of his popular wife, **Eva Péron** (1919–52); deposed by the military and exiled (1955); recalled and re-elected (1973).

PERRY, Matthew Galbraith (1794–1858) U.S. naval officer. Led naval expedition (1852–54) to Japan that forced it to open diplomatic negotiations with U.S.A. and grant first trading rights with western powers.

PERSHING, John Joseph (1860–1948) U.S. general. Began military career fighting Apaches; fought in Spanish-American War (1898); led U.S. troops against Mexican revolutionary leader Pancho Villa (1916); led 2 million U.S. troops of the American Expeditionary Forces during World War 1 (1917-1918).

PÉTAIN, (Henri) Philippe (1856–1951) French soldier and politician. National hero during World War I for defense of Verdun (1916); made commander-in-chief (1917) and marshall of France (1918); negotiated armistice with Germany after collapse of France (1940); chief of state with Vichy government; tried for treason (1945); death sentence commuted to life imprisonment.

PETER I "the Great" (1672–1725) Tsar (1682–1721) and emperor (1721–25) of Russia. As tsar, embarked on series of reforms, many based on W. European models; fought major wars with Ottoman Empire, Persia, and Sweden (Northern War of 1700–21); established Russia as major power, including maritime exit on Baltic coast, where he built new capital, St. Petersburg; son, Alexei, died under torture (1718).

PHILIP II (1527–98) King of Spain (1556–98) and (as Philip I) king of Portugal (1580–98). Only son of CHARLES V; four marriages included Mary I of England (1554–58); inherited HAPSBURG possessions in Italy, the Netherlands, Spain, and New World; as champion of Counter-Reformation tried to destroy heretics and infidels alike; sought to crush Protestantism in Low Countries, England, and France; despite

curbing sea power of Ottoman Empire at battle of Lepanto (1571) and conquering Portugal (1580), defeat of Spanish Armada (1588) by English and continuing revolt of Netherlands saw relative failure of foreign policy.

PITT "the Younger," William (1759–1806) British politician. Became prime minister in 1783 (until 1801), aged only 24; carried through important administrative and financial reforms, but liberal policies ended with French revolutionary wars (from 1792); negotiated coalitions against France (1793 and 1798); obtained union of Great Britain and Ireland (1800), but failed to win Catholic Emancipation and resigned (1801); resumed office (1804), but heavy drinking contributed to early death.

PIUS XII (Eugenio Pacelli) (1876–1958) Pope (1939–58). During World War II tried to alleviate suffering of prisoners of war and displaced persons, but criticized for not speaking against persecution of Jews; proclaimed excommunication of Italian Catholics who joined Communist Party (1949).

PIZARRO, Francisco (c. 1478–1541) Spanish conquistador. Served with expedition that discovered the Pacific (1513); began exploring coasts of Ecuador and Peru (1524); conquered Incas, killing their king, ATAHUALPA (1533); founded Lima (1535) and other cities in Peru; assassinated in Lima.

PLANTAGENET DYNASTY Royal dynasty in England from Henry II to Richard II (1154–1399), then continued by two rival houses of Lancaster and York until 1485; dynasty so-called because allegedly Henry II's father, Geoffrey of Anjou, wore broom (Old French *plante genêt*) in his cap; members included EDWARD I, EDWARD III, and JOHN.

POL POT (Saloth Sar) (b. 1926) Cambodian Communist. Became prime minister (1976), and introduced brutal Communist regime which resulted in the death of over two million people. Officially retired as military leader in 1985, but still remains an influential, feared figure in the movement.

POMPEY "the Great" (Gnaeus Pompeius Magnus) (106–48 B.C.) Roman politician and general. Settlement of the East (63 B.C.) established pattern of Roman administration for over a century; driven into alliance with enemy Julius CAESAR in First Triumvirate (60 B.C.); became sole consul (52 B.C.), but precipitated civil war crisis in 49 B.C.; defeated by Caesar at battle of Pharsalus (48 B.C.); assassinated in Egypt.

RALEIGH (or Ralegh), Walter (1552–1618) English courtier, navigator and author. Favorite of ELIZABETH I and rival of Earl of Essex; first expedition to Americas (1584) ended in tragedy with "lost colony" of Roanoke Island, Virginia; convicted of treason and imprisoned in Tower of London, where he wrote *History of the World* (1614); after release from imprisonment (1616), made unsuccessful expedition to the Orinoco; on return, executed under original sentence for treason; as well as history, he wrote poetry, essays, and philosophical treatises.

RASPUTIN, Grigory (1871–1916) Russian holy man. Gained confidence of NICHOLAS II and Empress Alexandra by apparent ability to control bleeding of hemophiliac tsarevitch; created public scandal through combination of immoral way of life and influence over royal family; virtually ruled Russia with empress when Nicholas commanded army during World War I; murdered by group of aristocrats.

REAGAN, Ronald (Wilson) (b. 1911) U.S. politician and 40th president. Began career as radio sports announcer and film actor; president of Screen Actors Guild (1947–52, 1959); originally a Democrat, but registered as Republican 1962; governor of California for two terms (1967–75); campaigned unsuccessfully for presidential nomination (1968, 1976); elected president (1980); elected for second term (1984); during his presidency he negotiated major accord with the Soviet Union on strategic nuclear arms reduction.

REVERE, Paul (1735–1818) U.S. patriot. Followed trade as silversmith and printer; one of party that destroyed tea in Boston Harbor (1773); on 18 April 1775, the night before the battles of Lexington and Concord, rode from Boston to Lexington rousing minutemen as he went; his ride was the subject of a poem by Longfellow.

RICHELIEU, Armand Jean du Plessis, Cardinal and Duke of (1585–1642) French politician. As chief minister under Louis XIII he was the effective ruler of France (1624–42); twin aims were to secure obedience to BOURBON monarchy within France and enhance French prestige abroad; principal achievement was to check HAPSBURG power, ultimately by sending armies into Spanish Netherlands, Alsace, Lorraine, and Roussillon.

ROBESPIERRE, Maximilien François Marie Isidore de (1758–94) French revolutionary leader, called "the Incorruptible." Elected to estates-general (1789) and national convention (1792); leader of Jacobins in their struggle with Girondins; member of Committee of Public Safety (1793), and dominated French politics for three months; supported Reign of Terror (1793–94) and cult of Supreme Being; arrested and guillotined on orders of Revolutionary Tribunal.

ROMANOV DYNASTY Second (and last) Russian royal dynasty (1613–1917). First Romanov tsar, **Mikhail**, was elected, but dynasty soon ruled as absolute autocrats; dynasty ended with abdica-

Theodore Roosevelt (center) *leads his Rough Riders during the Spanish American War.*

tion of NICHOLAS II (1917); members included PETER I, CATHERINE II, ALEXANDER I, ALEXANDER II.

ROOSEVELT, (Anna) Eleanor (1884–1962) U.S. humanitarian and diplomat. Niece of Theodore ROOSEVELT and wife of Franklin D. ROOSEVELT; became active in politics during husband's illness from polio; assistant director of the Office of Civilian Defense (1941); U.S. delegate to UN Assembly (1945–53, 1961); chairman of the UN Human Rights Commission (1947–51); U.S. representative at the UN General Assembly (1946–52).

ROOSEVELT, Franklin, D(elano) ("F.D.R.") (1882–1945) U.S. politician and 32nd president. Only president to be elected three times. Democratic candidate for vice-president (1920); stricken with polio (1921); governor of New York (1929–33); during first "hundred days" of presidency (1933–45) bombarded economic crisis with New Deal for national recovery (1933); strove to avoid U.S. involvement at start of World War II; provided economic resources to Allies in form of "lend-lease" agreement; brought U.S.A. into war after Japan's attack on Pearl Harbor (1941); met Churchill and Stalin at Tehran Conference (1943) and Yalta

Anwar Sadat, president of Egypt (1970–81).

Conference (1945) to formulate postwar plans including UN; died three weeks before German surrender.

ROOSEVELT, Theodore ("Teddy") (1858–1919) U.S. politician and 26th president. In Spanish American War raised volunteer cavalry known as Rough Riders (1898); governor of New York (1898–1900); vice-president (1900); president on assassination of president McKinley (1901); reelected 1904; during presidency (1901–09) strengthened U.S. navy, initiated construction of Panama Canal, introduced "Square Deal" policy; Nobel Peace Prize (1906) for mediation in Russo-Japanese War (1904–05); split Republican Party by running for president as third-party Progressive; lost election to WILSON.

SADAT, Anwar (1918–81) Egyptian political leader. Had strong anti-Communist views; became president in 1970 after death of NASSER; also temporary prime minister and military governor-general during the fourth Arab-Israeli war. He jointly won the 1978 Nobel Peace Prize with BEGIN for seeking peaceful treaty. Assassinated by Muslim extremists.

SAKHAROV, Andrei (1921–89) Russian physicist and dissident. Played critical role in developing Soviet hydrogen bomb; began to oppose nuclear testing in late 1950s; awarded Nobel Peace Prize (1975); criticism and harassment in Russia caused exile to Gorky as leading dissident (1980); restored to favor by GORBACHEV (1987); elected to Congress of People's Deputies (1989).

SALADIN (Salah al-Din al-Ayyubi) (1137–93) Sultan of Egypt and Syria, founder of Ayyubid dynasty (1169–93) and leader of Muslims against crusaders in Palestine. Proclaimed himself sultan (1147); reduced Mesopotamia and received homage of Seljuk princes of Asia Minor; in wars with Christians, won victory near Tiberias (1187), which led to capture of Jerusalem and Acre; in Third Crusade (1191), defeated by Christians at Acre and Arsuf.

SAN MARTIN, José de (1778–1850) Argentine soldier and politician. Played major role in winning independence from Spain for Argentina, Chile and Peru; led army across Andes into Chile (1817), defeating Spanish at Chacubuco (1817) and Maipú (1818); captured Lima and became protector of Peru (1821); resigned (1822) after failure to reach agreement with BOLÍVAR over future of Peru; died in exile in France.

SITTING BULL (c. 1834–90) Native American warrior. Chief of Dakota Sioux; a leader in Sioux War of 1876–77; with CRAZY HORSE, led Sioux and Cheyenne in battle of Little Bighorn against U.S. cavalry under CUSTER (1876); escaped to Canada, but surrendered in 1881; toured in BUFFALO BILL's Wild West Show; killed during army

action to suppress "ghost dance" religious movement.

SMUTS, Jan (Christian) (1870–1950) South African general and politician. Fought in second Boer War (1899–1902); entered House of Assembly (1907); held several cabinet posts; led campaigns against Germans in S.W. Africa and Tanganyika; member of Imperial War Cabinet in World War I; prime minister (1919–24 and 1939–1948).

STALIN, Joseph (Iosif Vissarionovich Dzhugashvili) (1879–1953) Georgian Marxist revolutionary and dictator of U.S.S.R. As leading Bolshevik, played active role in October Revolution (1917); after LENIN's death (1924), gradually isolated and disgraced political rivals, notably TROTSKY; launched campaign for collectivization of agriculture, and first five-year plan for forced industrialization of economy (1928); between 1934 and 1938 inaugurated mass purge of party, government, armed forces, and intelligentsia; signed Non-Aggression Pact with HITLER (1939); after German invasion (1941), took title, as war leader, of Generalissimus; achieved Soviet military and political control over postwar E. and C. Europe; during postwar years conducted foreign policies that contributed to Cold War between U.S.S.R. and West.

STANLEY, Sir Henry Morton (1841–1904) American-British explorer and journalist. Sent by *New York Herald* to Africa to find LIVINGSTONE (1871); explored lakes Victoria and Tanganyika (1874); won territorial concessions which led to Belgian control of Congo Free State (now Zaïre).

STUART, House of Scottish royal family. Commenced with **Robert II** (1371–90); succeeded to English throne with **James VI** (of Scotland) and **I** (of England) in 1603; ended with death of **Queen Anne** (1714), although pretenders laid claim to throne and invaded Britain in support of their claims as late as 1745; members included MARY, Queen of Scots, CHARLES I, WILLIAM III.

SUKARNO, Ahmed (1902–70) Indonesian statesman and first president of Indonesia. Formed Indonesia National Party (1927); imprisoned by Dutch (1929–31); lived in exile until 1942; Nationalist leader during Japanese occupation; president at independence (1945); abortive coup (1965) led to takeover by army; powers devolved to General Suharto; finally retired 1968.

SÜLEYMAN I "the Magnificent" (1494–1566) Ottoman sultan (1520–66). Added to dominions, by conquest, Belgrade, Budapest, Rhodes, Tabriz, Baghdad, Aden, and Algiers; fleets dominated Mediterranean, although failed to capture Malta (1565); great patron of arts and architecture.

SUN YAT SEN (Sun Zhongshan/Sun Yixian) (1866–1925) Chinese politician. Founder and leader of China's

Mother Teresa and young child in Calcutta.

Nationalist Party, the Kuomintang (or Guomindang) (1912); after outbreak of civil war (1913), set up separate government at Guangzhou (Canton); at the time of his death, he was widely accepted as true leader of China.

TALLEYRAND (-Perigord), Charles Maurice de (1754–1838) French politician. As foreign minister under the Directory (1797–1807) helped consolidate NAPOLEON I's position as consul (1802) and emperor (1804); leader of anti-Napoleonic faction after 1807; foreign minister under Louis XVIII (1815).

TAMERLANE (Timur) (1336–1405) Tatar conqueror. Ascended to throne of Samarkand (1369); in series of wars subdued nearly all Persia (1392–96), Georgia and the Tatar Empire, and conquered all states between the Indus and lower Ganges (1398); won Damascus and Syria from Mamluks of Egypt, then defeated Turks at Ankara (1402).

THATCHER, Margaret (Hilda) (b. 1925) British politician. Elected MP (1959); minister of education (1970–74); leader of Conservative Party (1975–90), first woman party leader in British politics; prime minister 1979–90; her government privatized several nationalized industries and made professional services, such as healthcare and education, more responsive to market forces; popularity waned and anti-European statements caused division within Conservatives; resigned after losing leadership contest (1990).

THERESA, Mother (b. 1910) Roman Catholic nun and missionary to India. Received the 1979 Nobel Peace Prize for her outstanding efforts to relieve human suffering.

TOUSSAINT L'OUVERTURE (François Dominique Toussaint) (1746–1803) Haitian black revolutionary leader. Freed from slavery (1777); joined black insurgents (1791); drove out British and Spanish expeditions, and conquered San Domingo (1801); seized by the French (1802) and died in a French prison.

TRAJAN (Marcus Ulpius Trajanus) (c. 53–117) Roman emperor (A.D.

98–117). First emperor after AUGUSTUS to expand Roman Empire significantly; brought Dacia (Romania) under Roman control, and conquered Parthia (Khurasan); launched ambitious building program, especially in Rome.

TROTSKY, Leon (Lev Davidovich Bronstein) (1879–1940) Russian revolutionary. Exiled to Siberia (1898); escaped and joined LENIN in London (1902); returned to Russia and joined Bolsheviks (1917); played major part in October Revolution; organized Red Army in Russian Civil War (1918–20); ousted from Communist Party by STALIN after Lenin's death (1924); expelled from U.S.S.R. (1929); found asylum in Mexico, where assassinated.

TRUDEAU, Pierre (b. 1919) Canadian politician. Prime minister (1968–79, 1980–84); term in office saw terrorist crisis in Quebec (1970), federal victory during Quebec referendum (1980) and Constitution Act of 1982; resigned as leader of Liberal Party in 1984.

TRUMAN, Harry S. (1884–1972) U.S. politician and 33rd president. Vice-president (1944); president on Franklin ROOSEVELT's death (1945); elected in surprise victory over Thomas E. Dewey (1948); as president (1945–53) ordered dropping of first atomic bomb on Japan; developed Marshall Plan to rebuild Europe after World War II, and created NATO (1949); sent U.S. troops to South Korea (1950).

TRUTH, Sojourner (Isabella) (1797–1883) U.S. abolitionist. Born a slave in New York state, becoming free when New York outlawed slavery (1828). Became famous as a preacher across all of the Northeast, with the simple message that Christian love and slavery were incompatible. Traveled to Washington D.C. to receive endorsement of President LINCOLN (1864)

TUBMAN, Harriet (c. 1820–1913) U.S. abolitionist. Escaped from slavery in Maryland (1849); freed over 300 slaves through underground railroad escape route; Northern spy and scout during American Civil War.

TUDOR, House of Welsh family that ruled England from 1485 to 1603. Founder **Owen Tudor** (d. 1461); his grandson became **Henry VII** after overthrowing **Richard III** (1485); Henry's descendants included HENRY VIII, Edward VII, Mary I, ELIZABETH I.

VALOIS Dynasty that ruled France from the accession of **Philippe VI** (1328) to the death of **Henri III** (1589). Last three Valois kings – **François II, Charles IX,** and **Henri III** – were all childless; succeeded by BOURBON dynasty.

VICTOR EMMANUEL II (1820–78) King of Sardinia (1849–61) and king of Italy (1861–78). Went to war in alliance with France to drive Austria out of N. Italy (1859); led in wars of Risorgimento (1859–70), aided by CAVOUR; crowned first king of Italy (1861); ruled as constitutional monarch.

VICTORIA (1819–1901) Queen of Great Britain (1837–1901) and empress of India (1876–1901). Only child of GEORGE III's son, Edward; married Prince Albert of Saxe-Coburg-Gotha (1840) and had four sons and five daughters; marriages of children had important diplomatic and dynastic implications in European history; her reign was the longest in English history.

VILLA, Pancho (Francisco) (1877–1923) Mexican revolutionary. Military commander in Mexican Revolution (began 1910); in struggle for control of revolution he and ZAPATA were defeated (1915); after shooting of U.S. citizens in Mexico and U.S. border towns (1916), escaped from U.S. punitive force; pardoned (1920), but assassinated three years later.

WALESA, Lech (b. 1943) Polish trade unionist and politician. Gdansk shipyard worker; leader of independent trade union Solidarity, which challenged Polish government's policies (1980); detained by authorities when martial law declared (1981); released (1982); awarded Nobel Peace Prize 1983; largely responsible for negotiations which led to Solidarity effectively forming the first non-Communist government (1989), became president of Poland (1990–).

WALPOLE, Sir Robert (1676–1745) English politician. Dominated British political life (1721–42); usually described as first British prime minister.

WASHINGTON, Booker Taliaferro (1856–1915) U.S. educationalist and reformer. Born a slave in Virginia; began working his way through college (1872), qualifying as a teacher; became head of Tuskegee Institute, school for blacks in Alabama (1881), building it into a center of excellence.

WASHINGTON, George (1732–99) U.S. general and first president. Fought in French and Indian War (1754–63); represented Virginia in First (1774) and Second (1775) Continental Congresses; in American Revolution made commander-in-chief of Continental forces (1775); following early reverses, defeated British at Trenton (1776) and Princeton (1777); held army together through winter 1777–78 at Valley Forge; forced surrender of British at Yorktown (1781); presided over Constitutional Convention (1787); became first president (1787–97).

WEBSTER, Daniel(1782–1852) U.S. statesman. Elected U.S. Representative (1812) to begin distinguished careeer in the House and Senate; strongly supported the Union and the supremecy of the federal government over the individual interests of states.

WEIZMANN, Chaim (Azriel) (1874–1952) Israeli politician and scientist. Born in Russia, became British citizen

Queen Victoria and family in 1846.

(1910); helped secure Balfour Declaration (1917); president of World Zionist Organization (1920–30, 1935–46), and Jewish Agency (from 1929); played major role in establishment of state of Israel (1948); first president of Israel (1949–52).

WELLINGTON, Arthur Wellesley (1st Duke of) (1769–1852) British general and politician. Born in Ireland; in India (1796–1805) helped defeat Tippoo Sahib and Mahratta chiefs; became MP (1806) and Irish Secretary (1807); commander in Peninsular War (1809–11), driving French out of Spain and Portugal; defeated NAPOLEON at battle of Waterloo (1815); prime minister (1828–30).

WHITLAM, (Edward) Gough (b. 1916) Australian politician. Australian Labor administration (1972–75) noted for radicalism, ending conscription, withdrawing Australian troops from Vietnam War, recognizing Communist China, relaxing restrictions on nonwhite immigrants; controversially dismissed by governor-general (1975); lost subsequent election; retired from politics (1977).

WILHELM II (1859–1941) German

Lech Walesa addressing striking textile workers in Zyrardow, Poland, in 1981.

emperor and king of Prussia (1888–1918). Grandson of Queen VICTORIA; dismissal of BISMARCK (1890) began long period of personal rule; intensive rearmament policy and support of Austria contributed to the start of World War I in Europe in 1914; only figurehead during World War I; forced to abdicate after German defeat (1918).

WILLIAM I "the Conqueror" (c. 1028–87) Duke of Normandy and first Norman king of England (1066–87). Illegitimate son of Duke Robert of Normandy; cousin, Edward the Confessor, probably named him as future king of England (1051); invaded England when Harold Godwin took throne as Harold II (1066); defeated and killed Harold at battle of Hastings (1066); as king conquered rest of England, replaced Anglo-Saxon ruling class with Normans, and ordered Domesday Book (1085–86).

WILLIAM III "of Orange" (1650–1702) Stadholder of United Provinces (1672–1702) and king of England, Scotland and Ireland (1689–1702). Married cousin Mary, daughter of future James II of England; invited by James's opponents to land in England, forcing James to flee country; ruled England jointly with Mary; defeated James at battle of the Boyne (1690); successfully led armies in War of Grand Alliance against France (1689–97); accepted Bill of Rights (1689), which reduced royal power.

WILSON, (Thomas) Woodrow (1856–1924) U.S. politician and 28th president. Democratic governor of New Jersey (1911–13); served two terms as president (1913–21); sought to keep U.S.A. out of World War I, but was compelled to enter war in 1917; championed idea of League of Nations (1919); Nobel Peace Prize (1919).

YELTSIN, Boris Nicolayevich (b. 1931) Russian politician. Appointed Moscow party chief by GORBACHEV (1985); elected to CPSU Politburo (1986); downgraded to lowly administrative post (1988); elected to New Congress of People's Deputies (1989); in 1991 took open stand that foiled anti-Gorbachev coup; elected president of Russian Federation (1991–).

ZAPATA, Emiliano (1879–1919) Mexican revolutionary. Led army of Indians at onset of Mexican Revolution (1910); largely responsible for toppling dictatorship of Porfirio Díaz; subsequently fought Carranza government with aim of gaining land for his people; killed by an emissary of Carranza.

ZHOU ENLAI (1898–1976) Chinese Communist leader. A founder of the Chinese Communist Party; participated in Long March with MAO ZEDONG (1934–5); foreign minister of People's Republic of China (1949–58); prime minister (1949–76).

EUROPEAN ROYAL FAMILIES DESCENDED FROM QUEEN VICTORIA

Asterisks denote the same person occurring more than once in the tree.

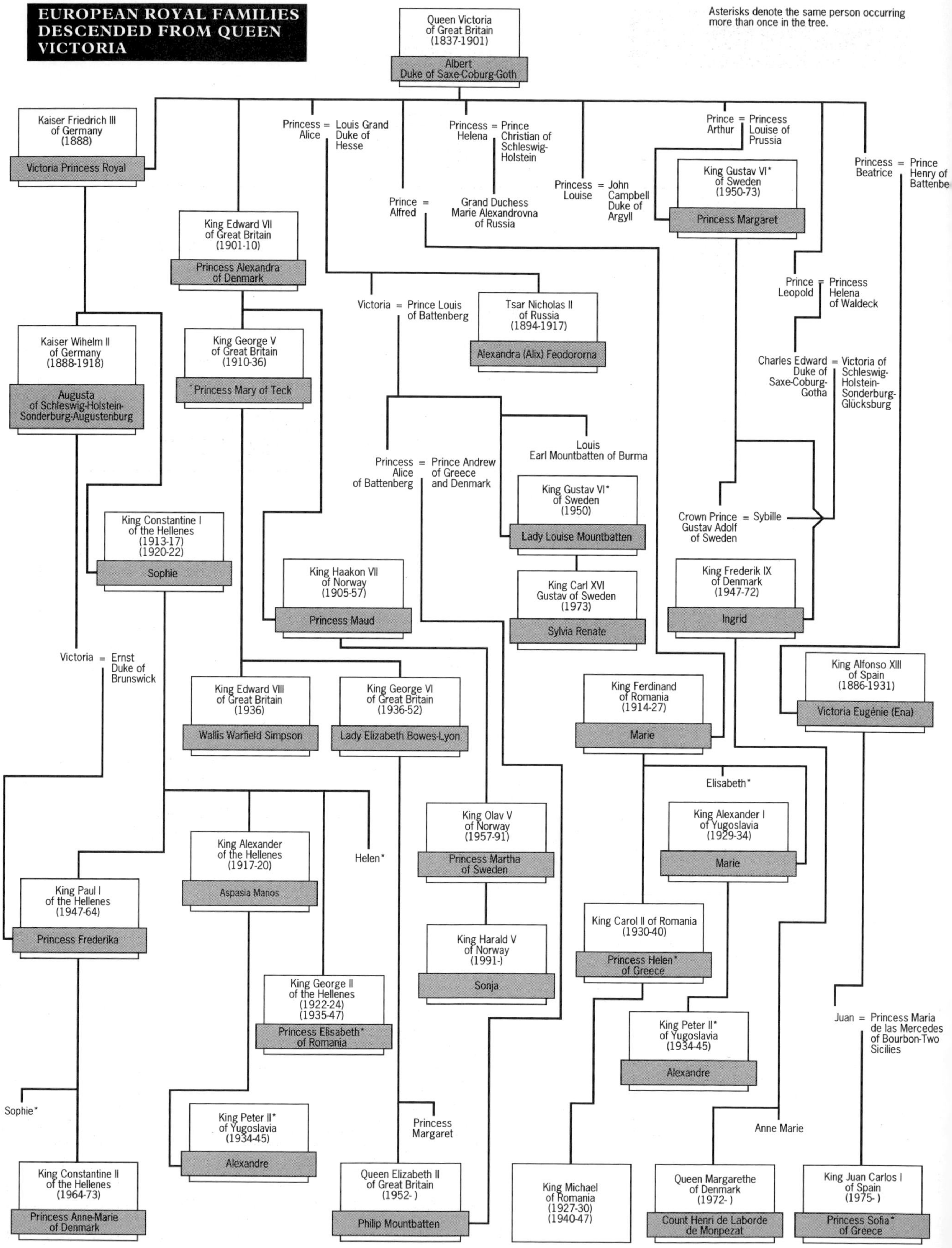

Queen Victoria of Great Britain (1837-1901)
Albert Duke of Saxe-Coburg-Goth

Kaiser Friedrich III of Germany (1888)
Victoria Princess Royal

Princess Alice = Louis Grand Duke of Hesse

Princess Helena = Prince Christian of Schleswig-Holstein

Princess Louise = John Campbell Duke of Argyll

Prince Arthur = Princess Louise of Prussia

King Gustav VI* of Sweden (1950-73)
Princess Margaret

Princess Beatrice = Prince Henry of Battenbe

Prince Alfred = Grand Duchess Marie Alexandrovna of Russia

King Edward VII of Great Britain (1901-10)
Princess Alexandra of Denmark

Victoria = Prince Louis of Battenberg

Tsar Nicholas II of Russia (1894-1917)
Alexandra (Alix) Feodororna

Prince Leopold = Princess Helena of Waldeck

Kaiser Wihelm II of Germany (1888-1918)
Augusta of Schleswig-Holstein-Sonderburg-Augustenburg

King George V of Great Britain (1910-36)
Princess Mary of Teck

Charles Edward = Victoria of Schleswig-Holstein-Sonderburg-Glücksburg
Duke of Saxe-Coburg-Gotha

Princess Alice of Battenberg = Prince Andrew of Greece and Denmark

Louis Earl Mountbatten of Burma

King Gustav VI* of Sweden (1950)
Lady Louise Mountbatten

Crown Prince Gustav Adolf of Sweden = Sybille

King Constantine I of the Hellenes (1913-17) (1920-22)
Sophie

King Haakon VII of Norway (1905-57)
Princess Maud

King Carl XVI Gustav of Sweden (1973)
Sylvia Renate

King Frederik IX of Denmark (1947-72)
Ingrid

Victoria = Ernst Duke of Brunswick

King Edward VIII of Great Britain (1936)
Wallis Warfield Simpson

King George VI of Great Britain (1936-52)
Lady Elizabeth Bowes-Lyon

King Ferdinand of Romania (1914-27)
Marie

King Alfonso XIII of Spain (1886-1931)
Victoria Eugénie (Ena)

Elisabeth*

King Olav V of Norway (1957-91)
Princess Martha of Sweden

King Alexander I of Yugoslavia (1929-34)
Marie

Helen*

King Alexander of the Hellenes (1917-20)
Aspasia Manos

King Paul I of the Hellenes (1947-64)
Princess Frederika

King Harald V of Norway (1991-)
Sonja

King Carol II of Romania (1930-40)
Princess Helen* of Greece

King George II of the Hellenes (1922-24) (1935-47)
Princess Elisabeth* of Romania

King Peter II* of Yugoslavia (1934-45)
Alexandre

Juan = Princess Maria de las Mercedes of Bourbon-Two Sicilies

Sophie*

King Peter II* of Yugoslavia (1934-45)
Alexandre

Anne Marie

King Constantine II of the Hellenes (1964-73)
Princess Anne-Marie of Denmark

Princess Margaret

Queen Elizabeth II of Great Britain (1952-)
Philip Mountbatten

King Michael of Romania (1927-30) (1940-47)

Queen Margarethe of Denmark (1972-)
Count Henri de Laborde de Monpezat

King Juan Carlos I of Spain (1975-)
Princess Sofia* of Greece

HAPSBURGS, BOURBONS, & THRONES OF SPAIN, FRANCE, & HOLY ROMAN EMPIRE

1 denotes first marriage, 2 second marriage, 3 third marriage
HRE Holy Roman Emperor

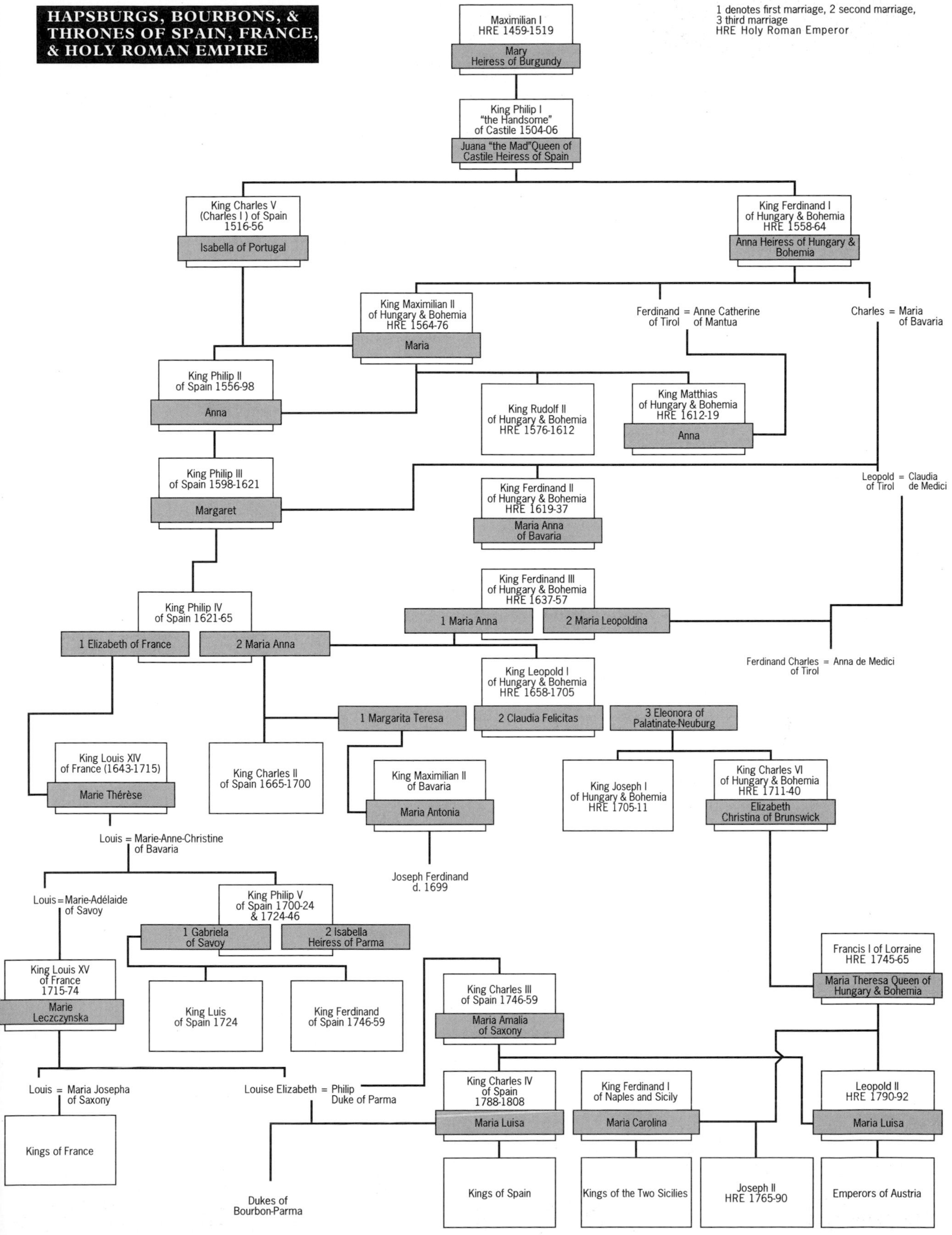

Maximilian I HRE 1459-1519
Mary Heiress of Burgundy

King Philip I "the Handsome" of Castile 1504-06
Juana "the Mad" Queen of Castile Heiress of Spain

King Charles V (Charles I) of Spain 1516-56
Isabella of Portugal

King Ferdinand I of Hungary & Bohemia HRE 1558-64
Anna Heiress of Hungary & Bohemia

King Maximilian II of Hungary & Bohemia HRE 1564-76
Maria

Ferdinand = Anne Catherine of Tirol of Mantua

Charles = Maria of Bavaria

King Philip II of Spain 1556-98
Anna

King Rudolf II of Hungary & Bohemia HRE 1576-1612

King Matthias of Hungary & Bohemia HRE 1612-19
Anna

King Philip III of Spain 1598-1621
Margaret

King Ferdinand II of Hungary & Bohemia HRE 1619-37
Maria Anna of Bavaria

Leopold = Claudia of Tirol de Medici

King Ferdinand III of Hungary & Bohemia HRE 1637-57
1 Maria Anna   2 Maria Leopoldina

Ferdinand Charles = Anna de Medici of Tirol

King Philip IV of Spain 1621-65
1 Elizabeth of France   2 Maria Anna

King Leopold I of Hungary & Bohemia HRE 1658-1705
1 Margarita Teresa   2 Claudia Felicitas   3 Eleonora of Palatinate-Neuburg

King Louis XIV of France (1643-1715)
Marie Thérèse

King Charles II of Spain 1665-1700

King Maximilian II of Bavaria
Maria Antonia

King Joseph I of Hungary & Bohemia HRE 1705-11

King Charles VI of Hungary & Bohemia HRE 1711-40
Elizabeth Christina of Brunswick

Louis = Marie-Anne-Christine of Bavaria

Joseph Ferdinand d. 1699

Louis = Marie-Adélaide of Savoy

King Philip V of Spain 1700-24 & 1724-46
1 Gabriela of Savoy   2 Isabella Heiress of Parma

Francis I of Lorraine HRE 1745-65
Maria Theresa Queen of Hungary & Bohemia

King Louis XV of France 1715-74
Marie Leczczynska

King Luis of Spain 1724

King Ferdinand of Spain 1746-59

King Charles III of Spain 1746-59
Maria Amalia of Saxony

Louis = Maria Josepha of Saxony

Louise Elizabeth = Philip Duke of Parma

King Charles IV of Spain 1788-1808
Maria Luisa

King Ferdinand I of Naples and Sicily
Maria Carolina

Leopold II HRE 1790-92
Maria Luisa

Kings of France

Dukes of Bourbon-Parma

Kings of Spain

Kings of the Two Sicilies

Joseph II HRE 1765-90

Emperors of Austria

POLITICAL LEADERS

AUSTRALIA

Co. Country; *Free* Free Trade; *Lab.* Labor; *Lib.* Liberal; *Nat.* Nationalist; *Nat. Lab.* National Labor; *Prot.* Protectionist; *Un.* United

PRIME MINISTER

1901–1903	Edmund Barton *Prot.*
1903–1904	Alfred Deakin *Prot.*
1904	John C. Watson *Lab.*
1904–1905	George H. Reid *Free.*
1905–1908	Alfred Deakin *Prot.*
1908–1909	Andrew Fisher *Lab.*
1909–1910	Alfred Deakin *Prot.*
1910–1913	Andrew Fisher *Lab.*
1913–1914	Joseph Cook *Lib.*
1914–1915	Andrew Fisher *Lab.*
1915–1917	William M. Hughes *Nat. Lab.*
1917–1923	William M. Hughes *Nat.*
1923–1929	Stanley M. Bruce *Nat.*
1929–1932	James Scullin *Lab.*
1932–1939	Joseph A. Lyons *Un.*
1939	Earle Page *Co.*
1939–1941	Robert G. Menzies *Un.*
1941	Arthur Fadden *Co.*
1941–1945	John Curtin *Lab.*
1945	Francis M. Forde *Lab.*
1945–1949	Ben Chifley *Lab.*
1949–1966	Robert G. Menzies *Lib.*
1966–1967	Harold E. Holt *Lib.*
1967–1968	John McEwen *Co.*
1968–1971	John G. Gorton *Lib.*
1971–1972	William McMahon *Lib.*
1972–1975	Gough Whitlam *Lab.*
1975–1983	Malcolm Fraser *Lib.*
1983–1991	Robert Hawke *Lab.*
1991–	Paul Keating *Lab.*

CANADA

Con. Conservative; *Lib.* Liberal; *Un.* Unionist; *Coal.* Coalition

PRIME MINISTER

1867–1873	John A. MacDonald *Con.*
1873–1878	Alexander Mackenzie *Lib.*
1878–1891	John A. MacDonald *Con.*
1891–1892	John J. C. Abbot *Con.*
1892–1894	John S. D. Thompson *Con.*
1894–1896	Mackenzie Bowell *Con.*
1896	Charles Tupper *Con.*
1896–1911	Wilfrid Laurier *Lib.*
1911–1920	Robert L. Borden *Un.*
1920–1921	Arthur Meighen *Coal.*
1921–1926	W. L. Mackenzie King *Lib.*
1926	Arthur Meighen *Un.*
1926–1930	W. L. Mackenzie King *Lib.*
1930–1935	Richard B. Bennett *Con.*
1935–1948	W. L. Mackenzie King *Lib.*
1948–1957	Louis S. St Laurent *Lib.*
1957–1963	John Diefenbaker *Con.*
1963–1968	Lester B. Pearson *Lib.*
1968–1979	Pierre E. Trudeau *Lib.*
1979–1980	Joseph Clark *Con.*
1980–1984	Pierre E. Trudeau *Lib.*
1984	John N. Turner *Lib.*
1984–1993	Brian Mulroney *Con.*
1993	Kim Campbell *Con.*
1993–	Jean Chrétien *Lib.*

CHINA

PRESIDENT

1912	Sun Yat Sen
1912–1916	Yüan Shih-k'ai
1916–1917	Li Yuan-hung
1917–1918	Feng Kuo-chang
1918–1922	Hsü Shih-ch'ang
1921–1925	Sun Yat Sen (*Canton Admin.*)
1922–1923	Li Yuan-hung
1923–1924	Ts'ao K'un
1924–1926	Tuan Ch'i-jui
1926–1927	*Civil Disorder*
1927–1928	Chang Tso-lin
1928–1931	Chiang Kai-shek
1931–1932	Ch'eng Ming-hsu (*Acting*)
1932–1943	Lin Sen
1940–1944	Wang Ching-wei (*in Japanese-occupied territory*)
1943–1949	Chiang Kai-shek
1945–1949	*Civil War*
1949	Li Tsung-jen
1993–	Jiang Zemin

People's Republic of China

1949–1959	Mao Zedong (Mao Tse-tung)
1959–1968	Liu Shaoqi
1968–1975	Dong Biwu
1975–1976	Zhu De
1976–1978	Sung Qingling
1978–1983	Ye Jianying
1983–1988	Li Xiannian (Li Hsien-nien)
1988–	Yang Shangkun

Communist Party

CHAIRMAN

1935–1976	Mao Zedong (Mao Tse-tung)
1976–1981	Hua Guofeng
1981–1982	Hu Yaobang

GENERAL SECRETARY

1982–1987	Hu Yaobang
1987–1989	Zhao Ziyang (Chao Tzuyang)
1989–	Jiang Zemin

FRANCE

PRIME MINISTER

1815	Duc de Talleyrand-Périgord
1815–1818	Duc de Richlieu
1818–1819	Jean Joseph, Marquis Dessolles
1819–1820	Duc Élie Decazes
1820–1821	Duc de Richlieu
1821–1828	Comte de Villèle
1828–1829	Vicomte de Martignac
1829–1830	Auguste, Prince de Polignac
1830–1831	Jacques Lafitte
1831–1832	Casimir Périer
1832–1834	Nicolas Soult
1834	Etienne, Comte Gérard
1834	Duc de Bassano
1834–1835	Duc de Trévise
1835–1836	Achille, Duc de Broglie
1836	Adolphe Thiers
1836–1839	Louis, Comte Molé
1839–1840	Nicolas Soult
1840	Adolphe Thiers
1840–1847	Nicolas Soult
1847–1848	François Guizot
1848	Jacques Dupont de L'Eure
1848	Louis-Eugène Cavaignac

1848–1849	Odilon Barrot
1849–1870	*No Prime Minister*

Third Republic

1870–1871	Bordeaux Administration
1871–1873	Louis Adolphe Thiers
1873–1874	Maurice de Mac-Mahon
1874–1875	Ernest Louis Courtot de Cissey
1875–1876	Louis Buffet
1876	Jules Dufaure
1876–1877	Jules Simon
1877	Albert, Duc de Broglie
1877	Gaetan de Grimaudet de Rochebouët
1877–1879	Jules Dufaure
1879	William H. Waddington
1879–1880	Louis de Freycinet
1880–1881	Jules Ferry
1881–1882	Léon Gambetta
1882	Louis de Freycinet
1882–1883	Eugène Duclerc
1883	Armand Fallières
1883–1885	Jules Ferry
1885–1886	Henri Brisson
1886	Louis de Freycinet
1886–1887	René Goblet
1887	Maurice Rouvier
1887–1888	Pierre Tirard
1888–1889	Charles Floquet
1889–1890	Pierre Tirard
1890–1892	Louis de Freycinet
1892	Émile Loubet
1892–1893	Alexandre Ribot
1893	Charles Dupuy
1893–1894	Jean Casimir-Périer
1894–1895	Charles Dupuy
1895	Alexandre Ribot
1895–1896	Léon Bourgeois
1896–1898	Jules Méline
1898	Henri Brisson
1898–1899	Charles Dupuy
1899–1902	Pierre Waldeck-Rousseau
1902–1905	Emile Combes
1905–1906	Maurice Rouvier
1906	Jean Sarrien
1906–1909	Georges Clemenceau
1909–1911	Aristide Briand
1911	Ernest Monis
1911–1912	Joseph Caillaux
1912–1913	Raymond Poincaré
1913	Aristide Briand
1913	Jean Louis Barthou
1913–1914	Gaston Doumergue
1914	Alexandre Ribot
1914–1915	René Viviani
1915–1917	Aristide Briand
1917	Alexandre Ribot
1917	Paul Painlevé
1917–1920	Georges Clemenceau
1920	Alexandre Millerand
1920–1921	Georges Leygues
1921–1922	Aristide Briand
1922–1924	Raymond Poincaré
1924	Frédéric François-Marsal
1924–1925	Édouard Herriot
1925	Paul Painlevé
1925–1926	Aristide Briand
1926	Édouard Herriot
1926–1929	Raymond Poincaré
1929	Aristide Briand
1929–1930	André Tardieu

1930	Camille Chautemps
1930	André Tardieu
1930–1931	Théodore Steeg
1931–1932	Pierre Laval
1932	André Tardieu
1932	Édouard Herriot
1932–1933	Joseph Paul-Boncour
1933	Édouard Daladier
1933	Albert Sarrault
1933–1934	Camille Chautemps
1934	Édouard Daladier
1934	Gaston Doumergue
1934–1935	Pierre Étienne Flandin
1935	Fernand Bouisson
1935–1936	Pierre Laval
1936	Albert Sarrault
1936–1937	Léon Blum
1937–1938	Camille Chautemps
1938	Léon Blum
1938–1940	Édouard Daladier
1940	Paul Reynaud
1940	Philippe Pétain

Vichy Government

1940–1944	Philippe Pétain

Provisional Government of the French Republic

1944–1946	Charles de Gaulle
1946	Félix Gouin
1946	Georges Bidault

Fourth Republic

1946–1947	Léon Blum
1947	Paul Ramadier
1947–1948	Robert Schuman
1948	André Marie
1948	Robert Schuman
1948–1949	Henri Queuille
1949–1950	Georges Bidault
1950	Henri Queuille
1950–1951	René Pleven
1951	Henri Queuille
1951–1952	René Pleven
1952	Edgar Faure
1952–1953	Antoine Pinay
1953	René Mayer
1953–1954	Joseph Laniel
1954–1955	Pierre Mendès-France
1955–1956	Edgar Faure
1956–1957	Guy Mollet
1957	Maurice Bourgès-Maunoury
1957–1958	Félix Gaillard
1958	Pierre Pflimin
1958–1959	Charles de Gaulle

Fifth Republic

1959–1962	Michel Debré
1962–1968	Georges Pompidou
1968–1969	Maurice Couve de Murville
1969–1972	Jacques Chaban Delmas
1972–1974	Pierre Mesmer
1974–1976	Jacques Chirac
1976–1981	Raymond Barre
1981–1984	Pierre Mauroy
1984–1986	Laurent Fabius
1986–1988	Jacques Chirac
1988–1991	Michel Rocard
1991–1992	Edith Cresson
1992–1993	Pierre Bérégovoy
1993–	Edouard Balladur

PRESIDENT
Third Republic

1870–1871	*Commune*
1871–1873	Louis Adolphe Thiers
1873–1879	Marie Edmé de MacMahon
1879–1887	Jules Grévy
1887–1894	Sadi Carnot
1894–1895	Jean Paul Casimir-Périer
1895–1899	François Félix Faure
1899–1906	Émile Loubet
1906–1913	Armand Fallières
1913–1920	Raymond Poincaré
1920	Paul Deschanel
1920–1924	Alexandre Millerand
1924–1931	Gaston Doumergue
1931–1932	Paul Doumer
1932–1940	Albert Lebrun
1940–1945	*German occupation*
1945–1947	*No President*

Fourth Republic

1947–1954	Vincent Auriol
1954–1958	René Coty

Fifth Republic

1958–1969	Charles de Gaulle
1969–1974	Georges Pompidou
1974–1981	Valéry Giscard D'Estaing
1981–1995	François Mitterrand
1995–	Jacques Chirac

GERMANY

CHANCELLOR

1871–1890	Otto von Bismarck
1890–1894	Georg Leo, Graf von Caprivi
1894–1900	Chlodwic, Fürst zu Hohenlohe-Schillingfürst
1900–1909	Bernard, Prince von Bülow
1909–1917	Theobald von Bethmann Hollweg
1917–1918	Georg von Herfling
1918	Prince Max of Baden
1918	Friedrich Ebert
1919–1920	Philipp Scheidemann
1920	Hermann Müller
1920–1921	Konstantin Fehrenbach
1921–1922	Karl Joseph Wirth
1922–1923	Wilhelm Cuno
1923	Gustav Stresemann
1923–1925	Wilhelm Marx
1925–1926	Hans Luther
1926–1928	Wilhelm Marx
1928–1929	Hermann Müller
1929–1932	Heinrich Brüning
1932–1933	Franz von Papen
1933	Adolf Hitler

CHANCELLOR AND FÜHRER

1934–45	Adolf Hitler
1945	Karl Dönitz

German Democratic Republic (East Germany)
PRESIDENT

1949–1960	Wilhelm Pieck

CHAIRMAN OF THE COUNCIL OF STATE

1960–1973	Walter Ulbricht
1973–1976	Willi Stoph
1976–1989	Erich Honecker
1989	Egon Krenz

1989–1990	Gregor Gysi

PREMIER

1949–1964	Otto Grotewohl
1964–1973	Willi Stoph
1973–1976	Horst Sindermann
1976–1989	Willi Stoph
1989–1990	Hans Modrow
1990–	Lothar de Maizière

German Federal Republic (until 1990 West Germany)
PRESIDENT

1949–1959	Theodor Heuss
1959–1969	Heinrich Lübke
1969–1974	Gustav Heinemann
1974–1979	Walter Scheel
1979–1984	Karl Carstens
1984–1990	Richard, Baron von Weizsäcker

CHANCELLOR

1949–1963	Konrad Adenauer
1963–1966	Ludwig Erhard
1966–1969	Kurt Georg Kiesinger
1969–1974	Willy Brandt
1974–1982	Helmut Schmidt
1982–	Helmut Kohl

INDIA

PRESIDENT

1950–1962	Rajendra Prasad
1962–1967	Sarvepalli Radhakrishnan
1967–1969	Zakir Husain
1969	Varahagiri Venkatagiri (*Acting*)
1969	Mohammed Hidayatullah (*Acting*)
1969–1974	Varahagiri Venkatagiri
1974–1977	Fakhruddin Ali Ahmed
1977	B. D. Jatti (*Acting*)
1977–1982	Neelam Sanjiva Reddy
1982–1987	Giani Zail Singh
1987–	Ramaswami Venkataraman

PRIME MINISTER

1947–1964	Jawaharlal Nehru
1964	Gulzari Lal Nanda (*Acting*)
1964–1966	Lal Bahadur Shastri
1966	Gulzari Lal Nanda (*Acting*)
1966–1977	Indira Gandhi
1977–1979	Morarji Desai
1979–1980	Charan Singh
1980–1984	Indira Gandhi
1984–1989	Rajiv Gandhi
1989–1990	Vishwanath Pratap Singh
1990–1991	Chandra Shekhar
1991–	P. V. Narasimha Rao

SOVIET UNION

PRESIDENT

1917	Lev Kamenev
1917–1919	Yakov Sverdlov
1919–1946	Mikhail Kalinin
1946–1953	Nikolai Shvernik
1953–1960	Klimenti Voroshilov
1960–1964	Leonid Brezhnev
1964–1965	Anastas Mikoyan
1965–1977	Nikolai Podgorny
1977–1982	Leonid Brezhnev
1982–1983	Vasily Kuznetsov (*Acting*)
1983–1984	Yuri Andropov

1984	Vasily Kuznetsov (*Acting*)
1984–1985	Konstantin Chernenko
1985	Vasily Kuznetsov (*Acting*)
1985–1988	Andrei Gromyko
1988–1991	Mikhail Gorbachev (*Executive president from 1990*)

Russian Federation (from 1991)
PRESIDENT

1991–	Boris Yeltsin

UNITED KINGDOM

Coal. Coalition; *Con.* Conservative; *Lab.* Labour; *Lib.* Liberal; *Nat.* National Coalition

PRIME MINISTER

1721–1742	Sir Robert Walpole *Whig*
1742–1743	Earl of Wilmington *Whig*
1743–1754	Henry Pelham *Whig*
1754–1756	Duke of Newcastle *Whig*
1756–1757	Duke of Devonshire *Whig*
1757–1762	Duke of Newcastle *Whig*
1762–1763	Earl of Bute *Tory*
1763–1765	George Grenville *Whig*
1765–1766	Marquis of Rockingham *Whig*
1766–1767	William Pitt the Elder *Whig*
1767–1770	Duke of Grafton *Whig*
1770–1782	Lord North *Tory*
1782	Marquis of Rockingham *Whig*
1782–1783	Earl of Shelburne *Whig*
1783	Duke of Portland *Coal.*
1783–1801	William Pitt the Younger *Tory*
1801–1804	Henry Addington *Tory*
1804–1806	William Pitt, the Younger *Tory*
1806–1807	Lord Grenville *Coal*
1807–1809	Duke of Portland *Coal.*
1809–1812	Spencer Perceval *Tory*
1812–1827	Earl of Liverpool *Tory*
1827	George Canning *Tory*
1827–1828	Earl of Ripon *Tory*
1828–1830	Duke of Wellington *Tory*
1830–1834	Earl Grey *Whig*
1834	Viscount Melbourne *Whig*
1834–1835	Sir Robert Peel *Con.*
1835–1841	Viscount Melbourne *Whig*
1841–1846	Sir Robert Peel *Con.*
1846–1852	Lord John Russell *Whig.*
1852	Earl of Derby *Con.*
1852–1855	Earl of Aberdeen *Coal.*
1855–1858	Viscount Palmerston *Whig.*
1858–1859	Earl of Derby *Con.*
1859–1865	Viscount Palmerston *Whig–Lib.*
1865–1866	Lord John Russell *Whig–Lib.*
1866–1868	Earl of Derby *Con.*
1868	Benjamin Disraeli *Con.*
1868–1874	William Gladstone *Lib.*
1874–1880	Benjamin Disraeli *Con.*
1880–1885	William Gladstone *Lib.*
1885–1886	Marquess of Salisbury *Con.*
1886	William Gladstone *Lib.*
1886–1892	Marquess of Salisbury *Con.*
1892–1894	William Gladstone *Lib.*
1894–1895	Earl of Rosebery *Lib.*
1895–1902	Marquess of Salisbury *Con.*
1902–1905	Arthur Balfour *Con.*
1905–1908	Sir Henry Campbell-Bannerman *Lib.*
1908–1915	Herbert Asquith *Lib.*
1915–1916	Herbert Asquith *Nat.*
1916–1922	David Lloyd-George *Nat*

1922–1923	Andrew Bonar Law *Con.*
1923–1924	Stanley Baldwin *Con.*
1924	Ramsay MacDonald *Lab.*
1924–1929	Stanley Baldwin *Con.*
1929–1931	Ramsay MacDonald *Lab.*
1931–1935	Ramsay MacDonald *Nat.*
1935–1937	Stanley Baldwin *Nat.*
1937–1940	Neville Chamberlain *Nat.*
1940–1945	Winston Churchill *Coal.*
1945–1951	Clement Attlee *Lab.*
1951–1955	Sir Winston Churchill *Con.*
1955–1957	Sir Anthony Eden *Con.*
1957–1963	Harold Macmillan *Con.*
1963–1964	Sir Alec Douglas-Home *Con.*
1964–1970	Harold Wilson *Lab.*
1970–1974	Edward Heath *Con.*
1974–1976	Harold Wilson *Lab.*
1976–1979	James Callaghan *Lab.*
1979–1990	Margaret Thatcher *Con.*
1990–	John Major *Con.*

UNITED STATES

Dem. Democrat; *Fed.* Federalist; *Nat.* National Union; *Rep.* Republican

PRESIDENT
Vice-president in parentheses

1789–1797	George Washington *Fed.* (John Adams)
1797–1801	John Adams *Fed.* (Thomas Jefferson)
1801–1809	Thomas Jefferson *Dem.-Rep.* (Aaron Burr, 1801–1805) (George Clinton, 1805–1809)
1809–1817	James Madison *Dem.-Rep.* (George Clinton, 1809–1812) (*No vice-president 1812–1813*) (Elbridge Gerry, 1813–1814) (*No vice-president 1814–1817*)
1817–1825	James Monroe *Dem.-Rep.* (Daniel D. Tompkins)
1825–1829	John Quincy Adams *Dem.-Rep.* (John Calhoun, 1829–1832)
1829–1837	Andrew Jackson *Dem.* (John Calhoun, 1829–1832) (*No vice-president 1832–1833*) (Martin Van Buren, 1833–1837)
1837–1841	Martin Van Buren *Dem.* (Richard M. Johnson)
1841	William Harrison *Whig* (John Tyler)
1841–1845	John Tyler *Whig* (*No vice-president 1841–1845*)
1845–1849	James K. Polk *Dem.* (George M. Dallas)
1849–1850	Zachary Taylor *Whig* (Millard Fillmore)
1850–1853	Millard Fillmore *Whig* (*No vice-president*)
1853–1857	Franklin Pierce *Dem.* (William R. King) (*No vice-president 1853–1857*)
1857–1861	James Buchanan *Dem.* (John C. Breckinridge)
1861–1865	Abraham Lincoln *Rep.* (Hannibal Hamlin, 1861–1865) (Andrew Johnson, 1865)
1865–1869	Andrew Johnson *Dem.-Nat.* (*No vice-president*)
1869–1877	Ulysses S. Grant *Rep.*

	(Schuyler Colfax, 1869–1873) (Henry Wilson, 1873–1875) (*No vice-president 1875*)
1877–1881	Rutherford B. Hayes *Rep.* (William A. Wheeler)
1881	James A. Garfield *Rep.* (Chester A. Arthur)
1881–1885	Chester A. Arthur *Rep.* (*No vice-president*)
1885–1889	Grover Cleveland *Dem.* (Thomas A. Hendricks, 1885) (*No vice-president 1885–1889*)
1889–1893	Benjamin Harrison *Rep.* (Levi P. Morton)
1893–1897	Grover Cleveland *Dem.* (Adlai E. Stevenson)
1897–1901	William McKinley *Rep.* (Garret A. Hobart, 1897–99) (*No vice-president 1899–1901*) (Theodore Roosevelt, 1901)
1901–1909	Theodore Roosevelt *Rep.* (*No vice-president 1901–1905*) (Charles W. Fairbanks, 1905–1909)
1909–1913	William H. Taft *Rep.* (James S. Sherman, 1909–1912) (*No vice-president 1912–1913*)
1913–1921	Woodrow Wilson *Dem.* (Thomas R. Marshall)
1921–1923	Warren G. Harding *Rep.* (Calvin Coolidge)
1923–1929	Calvin Coolidge *Rep.* (*No vice-president 1923–1925*) (Charles G. Dawes, 1925–1929)
1929–1933	Herbert C. Hoover *Rep.* (Charles Curtis)
1933–1945	Franklin D. Roosevelt *Dem.* (John N. Garner, 1933–1941) (Henry A. Wallace, 1941–1945) (Harry S. Truman, 1945)
1945–1953	Harry S. Truman *Dem.* (*No vice-president 1945–1949*) (Alben W. Barkley, 1949–1953)
1953–1961	Dwight D. Eisenhower *Rep.* (Richard M. Nixon)
1961–1963	John F. Kennedy *Dem.* (Lyndon B. Johnson)
1963–1969	Lyndon B. Johnson *Dem.* (*No vice-president 1963–1965*) (Hubert H. Humphrey, 1965–1969)
1969–1974	Richard M. Nixon *Rep.* (Spiro T. Agnew, 1969–1973) (*No vice-president Oct-Dec 1973*) (Gerald R. Ford, 1973–1974)
1974–1977	Gerald R. Ford *Rep.* (*No vice pres. Aug–Dec 1974*) (Nelson A. Rockefeller, 1974–1977)
1977–1981	Jimmy Carter *Dem.* (Walter F. Mondale)
1981–1989	Ronald W. Reagan *Rep.* (George H. W. Bush)
1989–1992	George H. W. Bush *Rep.* (Dan Quayle)
1992–	Bill Clinton *Dem.* (Albert Gore, Jr.)

SECTION 5
SCIENCE AND TECHNOLOGY

INTRODUCTION

Science embraces many topics including physics, chemistry, mathematics, agronomy, and the geology and mineralogy of the earth's resources—the subjects covered in this section. Technology deals with the various applications of science—in this case, as well as to engineering and manufacturing, to transportation, communications, and the media. The fields of astronomy, earth sciences, and life sciences are dealt with elsewhere (*pp. 10-41, 42-86,* and *88-196* respectively).

The key developments in physics and chemistry are introduced chronologically, linked to timelines cataloging major discoveries that run through the section.

The timelines extend from the early ideas of ancient Greek natural philosophers and alchemists, to the discovery of quarks and transuranic elements. Scientists who have made a major contribution to the advancement of science over the centuries are profiled and, finally, scientific terms are explained.

The section on mathematics explores the idea of numbers and progresses through the various branches of mathematics to the advent of today's powerful computers.

A chapter on food and agriculture describes agricultural land use worldwide and the application of science to crop cultivation, animal husbandry, and food processing. Humankind needs resources of all kinds for its everyday activities.

Supplies of nonreplaceable fossil fuels such as coal, oil, and gas are limited, and other energy resources are either controversial or have not yet been widely applied. Mineral resources are similarly finite, and no story of resource exploitation is complete without due consideration of conservation and recycling.

There are two major areas of the practical application of science to modern living. One is summarized under transportation and communications—the ways in which people, goods, and information are moved around the world. The other main area, technology and engineering, includes all the manufacturing techniques that go into providing a huge range of machines, mechanisms, and structures, from safety pins to suspension bridges.

Transparent side glazing, (1) to keep out the weather without reducing visibility, is made from clear plastics such as polycarbonates or polymethyl methacrylate.

The driver's seat (2) is molded out of a thermoplastic material such as A.B.S., upholstered with polyurethane foam, and covered with P.V.C. resembling leather.

Diesel fuel, or D.E.R.V., is made in an oil refinery by the fractionation (distillation) of crude oil. It is the fraction that boils in the region of 390–660°F (200–350°C).

The windshield (3) is made of safety glass, which is heat treated so that in the event of an impact it shatters into many tiny granular pieces—not dangerous splinters.

Mild steel is still the favored material for the body panels (4) of most vehicles because it is relatively cheap and can easily be pressed into the shapes required.

Tires (5) are produced using synthetic rubber, a polymer of the organic chemicals known as dienes. The rubber is made harder by vulcanization using sulfur.

Gears and drive shafts (6) are manufactured from special alloys such as manganese steels, which are difficult to work but are extremely hard and wear resistant.

Lubricating oil is also a product of the oil refinery. It is specially formulated to remain fluid even when very cold, and it may also contain anticorrosion additives.

Aluminum, or even magnesium, alloys are increasingly being used to make engine blocks (7) because they have only one-third of the weight of similar steel blocks.

To prevent frost damage in very cold weather, the water in the tractor's cooling system (8) contains an antifreeze, commonly based on the chemical ethylene glycol.

AREAS OF PHYSICAL SCIENCE

Acoustics The science of mechanical waves, particularly sound waves, including their production and propagation.

Aerodynamics The part of FLUID MECHANICS that deals with the dynamics of gases, particularly the study of forces acting on objects such as missiles or aircraft in motion in air.

Aerology The branch of science dealing with the study of the free atmosphere.

Aeronautics All activities concerned with the motion of objects in air.

Aerothermodynamics The branch of THERMODYNAMICS that deals with the heating effects associated with the dynamics of a gas, e.g. the effects on the air flowing over a space vehicle during reentry into the earth's atmosphere.

Algebra The branch of MATHEMATICS that uses symbols to represent unknown variable quantities. The unknowns are usually determined by solving equations containing them.

Analytical chemistry The branch of CHEMISTRY in which the composition of a chemical sample is determined. It is, in turn, divided into QUALITATIVE ANALYSIS and QUANTITATIVE ANALYSIS.

Astrometry The branch of ASTRONOMY concerned with measuring the exact positions of celestial objects (in the celestial sphere).

Astronautics The study of space flight.

Astronomy The study of all scientific aspects of celestial objects and the universe as a whole.

Astrophysics The branch of ASTRONOMY that applies the laws of PHYSICS to the study of interstellar matter, stars, and galaxies, in particular their origin, composition, evolution, and characteristics.

Autonomics The study of self-regulating systems for process control with the aim of optimizing performance.

Ballistics The study of the dynamics of the path taken by an object moving under the influence of a gravitational field, such as a missile.

Biochemistry The branch of CHEMISTRY concerned with living organisms in terms of their composition and biochemical reactions.

Biophysics The application of PHYSICS to the study of biological processes and other phenomena.

Biotechnology The use of organisms or their components in industrial and commercial processing and, with the aid of genetic manipulation, in the creation of other materials.

Calculus A system of MATHEMATICS in which variable quantities are considered to be made up of an infinite number of small parts. In differential calculus, the value of a continuously varying quantity can be determined (at a particular point) by finding its derivative (i.e. by differentiating it). In integral calculus, values can be found by totaling infinitely small values between a pair of limits in the technique known as integration.

Cartography The science of making maps, either using surveys, aerial or satellite photographs, or, increasingly, computer techniques.

Celestial mechanics The branch of ASTROPHYSICS that studies the forces acting between celestial objects and how those objects move.

Chemical engineering A branch of ENGINEERING concerned with the design and construction of plant and machinery for industrial chemical processes.

Chemistry The study of the properties, structure, and composition of substances and the reactions that occur between substances.

Chromatics The science of color as effected by phenomena that are determined by wavelength.

Classical physics The science of PHYSICS up to the end of the 1800s, when it was largely replaced by QUANTUM THEORY and relativity theory.

Climatology The study of climates.

Computing The use of computers in MATHEMATICS and STATISTICS.

Condensed-matter physics The branch of PHYSICS that studies amorphous solids, crystalline solids, and liquids.

Cosmology The study of the universe on the largest scales of space and time, particularly with regard to theories about its origin, nature, structure, and evolution.

Cryogenics The study of materials at low temperatures, in particular their physical properties, and of methods of obtaining such temperatures.

Crystallography The study of the formation, structure, and properties of crystals.

Cybernetics The study of control and communications in complex electronic systems and the comparison of these systems with biological systems.

Dynamics The branch of applied MATHEMATICS that studies the ways in which forces produce motion.

Electrochemistry The branch of CHEMISTRY concerned with the reactions of ions in solution or in a molten state, particularly during electrolysis and in electrolytic cells (batteries).

Electrodynamics The study of electric charges in motion and their accompanying electric and magnetic fields.

Electromagnetism The study of the properties of and relationships between electricity and magnetism.

Electrometallurgy The science that investigates the use of electricity in the winning and refining of metals and their applications to electroplating and electroforming.

Electronics The branch of PHYSICS that studies the behavior of electrons in a vacuum, in gases, and in semiconducting materials.

Electron optics The study of beams of electrons, particularly their use in electron microscopes and cathode-ray tubes.

Electrostatics The part of the science of electricity that deals with phenomena associated with electric charges substantially at rest.

Energetics The abstract study of the energy relations associated with physical and chemical changes.

Engineering The application of scientific principles to the design, construction, and maintenance of machinery and structures.

Fluid dynamics The part of FLUID MECHANICS that studies forces and pressures acting on fluids (gases and liquids) in motion.

Fluidics The science of liquid flow in tubes, which simulates the flow of electrons in conductors and plasmas and which can be used in place of electronic systems in certain applications such as the control of instruments.

Fluid mechanics The branch of PHYSICS that deals with the properties of moving and stationary fluids (gases and liquids). It embraces FLUID DYNAMICS and FLUID STATICS.

Fluid statics The part of FLUID MECHANICS that is concerned with the forces and pressures acting on fluids (gases and liquids) at rest.

Geochemistry The study of the composition of the earth, particularly with regard to the distribution of chemical elements.

Geochronology The branch of GEOLOGY concerned with the dating of events in the history of the earth.

Geodesy The branch of science that deals with the mapping and surveying of the surface of the earth.

Geology The study of the origin, evolution, structure, and composition of the planet earth. It increasingly involves the use of chemical, physical, and mathematical sciences.

Geomagnetism The branch of PHYSICS that studies the earth's magnetism, its origins, and variable behavior.

Geometry The branch of MATHEMATICS concerned with the properties and measurement of, and relationships among, points, lines, curves, and surfaces.

Geophysics The study of the physical properties of the earth and the physical processes acting upon it. It includes SEISMOLOGY and METEOROLOGY.

Horology The science of time measurement, or the construction of timepieces.

Hydraulics The area of science relating to the flow of fluids (gases and liquids).

Hydrodynamics The branch of FLUID MECHANICS that studies the motion produced in incompressible liquids by the application of forces.

Hydrogeology The study of the geological aspects of the earth's water.

Hydrography The study of the conditions of the earth's oceans, rivers, and lakes, particularly with the aim of publishing maps and charts.

Hydrology The study of the distribution and use of water resources, including

the various forms of precipitation, on the earth's surface.

Hydrostatics The branch of FLUID MECHANICS that studies the effects of forces on liquids at rest.

Inorganic chemistry The division of CHEMISTRY concerned with all compounds other than those of carbon (but including the oxides of carbon and carbonates).

Kinematics The branch of applied MATHEMATICS that studies the way in which the velocities and accelerations of the various parts of a moving system are interrelated.

Kinetics The study of the rates at which chemical reactions (including biological processes) proceed; or of the effects of forces on the motions of bodies.

Limnology The scientific study of lakes.

Lithology The study and classification of rocks, particularly sedimentary rocks.

Logic The system and principles of reasoning, using MATHEMATICS, as employed by computers.

Magnetochemistry The branch of PHYSICAL CHEMISTRY that deals with the magnetic properties of molecules, particularly in coordination compounds.

Magnetohydrodynamics (M.H.D.) The study of the motions of an electrically conducting fluid (plasma) in the presence of a magnetic field.

Magnetostatics The study of steady-state magnetic fields.

Mathematics In its broadest sense, the study of the logical consequences of sets of axioms. Pure mathematics includes those branches studied for their own sake or their relationships with other branches. The most important of these are ALGEBRA, analysis, CALCULUS, and TOPOLOGY. Applied mathematics is the application of these principles to other branches of science and commerce, such as economics or STATISTICS.

Mechanics The study of the behavior and motion of matter under the influence of forces. It includes DYNAMICS, KINEMATICS, and STATICS.

Metallography The study of the structure and composition of metals and their alloys.

Metallurgy The science that applies CHEMISTRY and PHYSICS to the extraction and manufacture of metals and their alloys, to the measurement of their properties, and to their uses in engineering and manufacturing.

Meteorology The study of the earth's atmosphere and its relationship with weather processes.

Metrology The science of measurement, especially as it applies to units of measurement and their definitions.

Microelectronics The design and manufacture of small electronic circuits, particularly integrated circuits for computer microprocessors.

Mineralogy The branch of GEOLOGY that deals with the occurrence and composition of minerals.

Nuclear physics The branch of PHYSICS that deals with atoms, subatomic particles and their properties and interactions, and the generation of nuclear power (fission or fusion).

Nucleonics The branch of PHYSICS that deals with the applications of nuclear power.

Oceanography The scientific study of oceans, including the geological, chemical, physical, and biological processes that affect them.

Optics The branch of PHYSICS that studies light. Physical optics deals with the nature of light, its production and propagation, diffraction, and interference. Geometric optics is concerned with the behavior of light in terms of reflection and refraction, and includes the design of optical instruments.

Organic chemistry The division of CHEMISTRY concerned with compounds of carbon (excluding the oxides of carbon and carbonates).

Pedology The study of soil.

Petrology The study of rocks, including their origins, evolution, formation, and mineral composition.

Photochemistry The branch of CHEMISTRY that deals with reactions initiated by light or ultraviolet radiation.

Physical chemistry The branch of chemistry that deals with the physical properties of substances and how they determine chemical structure, properties, and reactions.

Physics The study of electrical, luminescent, mechanical, magnetic, radioactive, and thermal phenomena and how they interact with matter to produce changes of form or energy state (but without any change in chemical composition), with energy, or with each other.

Physiography The scientific study of the surface features of the earth and the effects of the interrelationships between air, water, and land.

Planetology The study of the origins, composition, and distribution of matter in the planets of the solar system.

Qualitative analysis The branch of ANALYTICAL CHEMISTRY devoted to determining the composition of an unknown compound or compounds.

Quantitative analysis The branch of ANALYTICAL CHEMISTRY concerned with determining the proportions of known components of a substance.

Quantum electrodynamics The study of the ways in which the various forms of electromagnetic radiation interact with charged particles.

Quantum mechanics A branch of MECHANICS concerned with explaining the behavior of atoms and molecules in terms of QUANTUM THEORY.

Quantum theory The branch of PHYSICS concerned with the relationship between energy and subatomic matter and with the behavior of elementary particles.

Radio astronomy The study of radio waves emitted by celestial objects such as pulsars, quasars, and radio galaxies.

Radiology The study of the origin and effects of ionizing or penetrating non-ionizing radiations such as X rays.

Rheology The branch of PHYSICS that studies the deformation and flow of matter, including the effects of elasticity, viscosity, and plasticity.

Robotics The study of the design and use of robots, particularly their application in manufacturing and related processes.

Seismology The branch of GEOLOGY concerned with the study of earthquakes.

Solid-state physics The study of the physical properties of solids, in particular the electrical conduction of semiconductors, superconductivity, and photoconductivity.

Sonics A general term for the study of mechanical vibrations in matter, also known as ACOUSTICS.

Spectroscopy The study of methods of producing and analyzing spectra, with applications in ASTRONOMY, CHEMISTRY, and PHYSICS.

Statics The branch of applied MATHEMATICS that deals with the way in which forces combine with each other, often to achieve equilibrium. This formerly included the study of gravitational attraction, which is now generally regarded as a separate subject.

Statistical mechanics The branch of PHYSICS that employs statistical methods to analyze submicroscopic particles in order to account for the behavior of macroscopic systems.

Statistics The branch of MATHEMATICS that deals with the collection and analysis of numerical data.

Stratigraphy The study of stratified rocks in the earth's crust, particularly their formation, structure, and arrangement into chronological groups.

Superaerodynamics The study of AERODYNAMICS at low air densities, which occur at altitudes greater than 100,000 feet (30,000 meters).

Tectonics The branch of GEOLOGY concerned with the study of the major structural features of the earth's crust.

Thermionics The study of the processes involved in the emission of electrons from hot objects.

Thermodynamics The branch of PHYSICS that studies the interconversion and heat content of various forms of energy, particularly mechanical energy; the study of ways in which energy can be made to do work.

Topology The branch of MATHEMATICS that studies those properties of shapes and space that remain unchanged by bending, stretching, or molding.

Ultrasonics The branch of PHYSICS concerned with the study and application of pressure waves that have frequencies above the threshold of human hearing (20,000Hz).

Wave mechanics see QUANTUM MECHANICS.

SI units

Basic unit	Symbol	Quantity	Standard
meter	m	length	Distance light travels in vacuum in 1/299792458 of a second
kilogram	kg	mass	Mass of the international prototype kilogram, a cylinder of platinum-iridium alloy (kept at Sèvres, France)
second	s	time	Time taken for 9192631770 resonance vibrations of an atom of caesium-133
kelvin	K	temperature	1/273.16 of the temperature of the triple point of water
ampere	A	electric current	Current that produces a force of 2×10^7 newtons per meter between two parallel conductors of infinite length and negligible cross section placed a meter apart in vacuum
mole	mol	amount of substance	Amount of substance that contains as many atoms (or molecules, ions, or subatomic particles) as 12 grams of carbon 12 has atoms
candela	cd	luminous intensity	Luminous intensity of a source that emits monochromatic light of frequency 540×1012 hertz of radiant intensity 1/683 watt per steradian in a given direction

Supplementary units

Basic unit	Symbol	Quantity	Standard
radian	rad	plane angle	Angle subtended at the center of a circle by an arc whose length is the radius of the circle
steradian	sr	solid angle	Solid angle subtended at the center of a sphere by a part of the surface whose area is equal to the square of the radius of the sphere

Derived units

Basic unit	Symbol	Quantity	Standard
becquerel	Bq	radioactivity	Activity of a quantity of a radioisotope in which 1 nucleus decays every second (on average)
coulomb	C	electric charge	Charge that is carried by a current of 1 ampere flowing for 1 second
farad	F	electric capacitance	Capacitance that holds a charge of 1 coulomb when it is charged by a potential difference of 1 volt
gray	Gy	absorbed dose	Dosage of ionizing radiation corresponding to 1 joule of energy per kilogram
henry	H	inductance	Mutual inductance in a closed circuit in which an electromotive force of 1 volt is produced by a current that varies at 1 ampere per second
hertz	Hz	frequency	Frequency of 1 cycle per second
joule	J	energy	Work done when a force of 1 newton moves its point of application 1 meter in its direction of application
lumen	lm	luminous flux	Amount of light emitted per unit solid angle by a source of 1 candela intensity
lux	lx	illuminance	Amount of light that illuminates 1 square meter with a flux of 1 lumen
newton	N	force	Force that gives a mass of 1 kilogram an acceleration of 1 m/s²
ohm	Ω	electric resistance	Resistance of a conductor across which a potential of 1 volt produces a current of 1 ampere
pascal	Pa	pressure	Pressure exerted when a force of 1 newton acts on an area of 1m²
siemens	S	electric conductance	Conductance of a material or circuit component that has a resistance of 1 ohm
sievert	Sv	dose equivalent	Radiation dosage equal to 1 joule of radiant energy per kilogram
tesla	T	magnetic flux density	Flux density (or magnetic induction) of 1 weber of magnetic flux per square meter
volt	V	electric potential difference	Potential difference across a conductor in which a constant current of 1 ampere dissipates 1 watt of power
watt	W	power	Amount of power equal to a rate of energy transfer of (or of doing work at) 1 joule per second
weber	Wb	magnetic flux	Amount of magnetic flux that, decaying to zero in 1 second, induces an electromotive force of 1 volt in a circuit of one turn

Physical constants

Constant	Symbol	Value (SI units)	Constant	Symbol	Value (SI units)
Acceleration of free fall	g	9.80665 m s⁻²	Gravitational constant	G	6.670×10^{-11} Nm² kg⁻²
Avogadro's number	N	$6.02214 \times 10^{22} \times 10^{23}$mol⁻¹	Magnetic constant (permeability of free space)	$\{\mu\}o$	$4\{pi\} \times 10^{-7}$ Js²C⁻² m⁻¹
Bohr magnetron	$\{\mu\}B$	9.2732×10^{-24} J T⁻¹			
Boltzman constant	k	1.38054×10^{-23} J K⁻¹	Mass unit	u	1.66043×10^{-27} kg
Electric constant (permittivity of free space)	$\{\epsilon\}_0$	8.854×10^{-12} J⁻¹C² m⁻¹	Neutron rest mass	m_n	1.67492×10^{-27} kg
			Planck constant	h	6.62559×10^{-34} J s
Electron charge	e	1.60210×10^{-19} C	Proton rest mass	m_p	1.67252×10^{-27} kg
Electron charge/ mass ratio	e/m_e	1.758796×10^{11} C kg⁻¹	Rydberg constant	R^p	1.097373×10^7 m⁻¹
Electron radius	re	2.81777×10^{-15} m	Speed of light	c	2.997925×10^8 m s⁻¹
Electron rest mass	m_e	9.10908×10^{-31} kg	Standard atmosphere		101325 N m⁻²
Faraday constant	F	9.64870×10^4 C mol⁻¹	Stefan-Boltzmann constant	σ	5.6697×10^{-8} W m⁻² K⁻⁴
Gas constant	R_0	8.31434 J K⁻¹ mol⁻¹			

Metric prefixes

Prefix	Symbol	Multiple
atto-	a	x 10⁻¹⁸
femto-	f	x 10⁻¹⁵
pico-	p	x 10⁻¹²
nano-	n	x 10⁻⁹
micro-	μ	x 10⁻⁶
milli-	m	x 10⁻³
centi-	c	x 10⁻²
deci-	d	x 10⁻¹
deca-	da	x 10
hecto-	h	x 10²
kilo-	k	x 10³
mega-	M	x 10⁶
giga-	G	x 10⁹
tera-	T	x 10¹²
peta-	P	x 10¹⁵
exa-	E	x 10¹⁸

Mathematical signs and symbols

+	plus; positive; underestimate
−	minus; negative; overestimate
±	plus or minus; positive or negative; degree of accuracy
∓	minus or plus; negative or positive
×	multiplies (6 x 4)
•	multiplies (6·4); scalar product of two vectors (A·B)
÷	divided by (6 ÷ 4)
/	divided by; ratio of (6/4)
=	equals
≠ ≠	not equal to
≡	identical with
≢, ≠	not identical with
:	ratio of (6:4); scalar product of two tensors (Y:Z)
: :	proportionately equals (1 : 2 : : 2 : 4)
≈	approximately equal to; equivalent to; similar to
>	greater than
≫	much greater than
≯	not greater than
<	less than
≪	much less than
≮	not less than
≥,≧,≥	equal to or greater than
≤,≦,≤	equal to or less than
∝	directly proportional to
—	vinculum: division ($\overline{a-b}$)
∞	infinity
→	approaches the limit
√	square root
∛, ∜	cube root, fourth root, etc.
!	factorial (4! = 4 x 3 x 2 x 1)
%	percent
'	prime; minute(s) of arc; foot/feet
"	double prime; second(s) of arc; inch(es)
∩	arc of circle
°	degree of arc
∠,∠ˢ	angle(s)
≌	equiangular
⊥	perpendicular
∥	parallel
≅	congruent to
∴	therefore
∵	because
m	measured by
Δ	increment
Σ	summation
Π	product
∫	integral sign
∇	del: differential operator
∩	intersection
∪	union

Timeline

c. **450 B.C.** Empedocles proposes the four-element theory of matter.

c. **400 B.C.** Democritus proposes his theory that matter is made up of atoms.

c. **330 B.C.** Pytheas postulates that tides are caused by the moon.

c. **230 B.C.** Archimedes formulates his principle (*right*).

A.D. 132 Zhang Heng invents a seismograph to record earthquake shock waves.

c. **1010** Alhazen makes a parabolic mirror and explains how lenses work.

c. **1100** Chinese invent and use a magnetic compass (Magnets, *right*).

1491 Leonardo da Vinci first describes capillary action.

1544 Georg Hartmann observes magnetic dip (the alignment of a compass needle, mounted vertically).

1590 Zacharias Janssen invents the compound microscope.

1593 Galileo Galilei invents a thermometer.

1600 William Gilbert describes the earth's magnetism (*right*).

1604 Galileo discovers the uniform acceleration due to gravity (*p. 399*). Johannes Kepler states inverse square law for light (light intensity varies inversely with the square of the distance from its source).

1608 Hans Lippershey makes the first refracting telescope.

1609 Galileo makes his first telescope (*p. 399*).

1610 Johannes Kepler proposes his first two laws of planetary motion (adding the third law in 1619).

1611 Marco de Dominis explains how a rainbow forms (Solar spectrum, *right*).

1612 Sanctorius (Santorio Santorio) constructs a clinical thermometer.

1621 Willebrod Snell (Snellius) formulates the law of refraction of light.

1638 Galileo publishes the results of his research on motion.

1644 Evangelista Torricelli invents the mercury barometer.

1647 Blaise Pascal publishes the results of his study on the effects of vacuums.

1648 Blaise Pascal proposes law concerning equal pressures throughout a liquid.

1650 Otto von Guericke invents a vacuum pump.

1654 Otto Von Guericke demonstrates the existence of atmospheric pressure.

1662 Robert Boyle proposes a law relating the volume and pressure of an ideal gas.

1665 Isaac Newton completes his work on gravitation and calculus (*p. 399*). Francesco Grimaldi's works on the diffraction of light are published posthumously. Robert Hooke proposes the wave theory of light.

1666 Isaac Newton discovers the solar spectrum (*p. 399*).

1668 Isaac Newton constructs a reflecting telescope (Lenses and mirrors, (*p. 399*). John Wallis proposes the law of conservation of momentum.

Physics

Physics is the major science that studies matter and energy and how they interact. The properties of matter include three chief phases (gases, liquids, and solids), how they are structured, and how they behave under various conditions of temperature and pressure. This area encompasses such related topics as fluid flow, viscosity, elasticity, and the strengths of materials. The latter introduce forces treated in statics and dynamics—which, in turn, lead to the concept of work.

Performing work requires the expenditure of energy; not just mechanical energy but perhaps heat, light, electricity, and even sound and magnetism. Light is just one part of a whole range of wave phenomena that makes up the electromagnetic spectrum: radio waves, microwaves, infrared radiation, visible light, ultraviolet radiation, X rays, and gamma rays. All these topics are subject to natural laws—the laws of physics.

Archimedes' principle

According to legend, the king of Syracuse asked Archimedes to find out whether or not a crown he had been given was made of pure gold. Archimedes knew that he had to find the crown's density (mass divided by volume). The density of pure gold was known, and known to be greater than that of any cheaper alloy. He could easily weigh the crown, and he found its volume by submerging it in water and measuring the volume of water displaced. Archimedes' breakthrough was to realize that the weight of water displaced was equal to upthrust acting on the submerged object. If the object floats (i.e. is less dense than the liquid), the weight of liquid displaced equals the weight of the object—a relationship now known as Archimedes' principle.

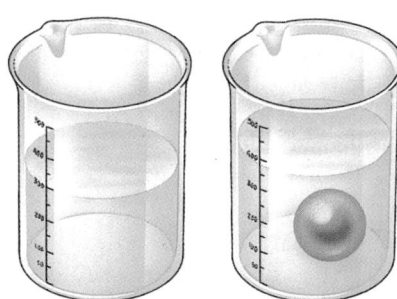

The weight of water displaced by a submerged object equals the upthrust acting upon it.

Magnets

In the 1100s, the Chinese found pieces of naturally magnetic iron ore, later called lodestone (meaning leadstone), which always pointed north when hung from a thread. Used originally for divination, these natural magnets were soon used by sailors as primitive compasses. Later, magnets were made of soft iron bars by aligning them north–south and stroking

them with another magnet. A compass needle points north because the Earth itself behaves as if it had a large bar magnet along its axis—an observation first made by English geophysicist William Gilbert (1544–1603) in 1600.

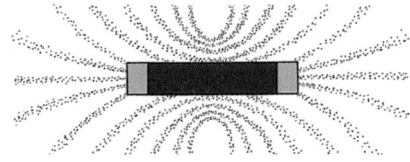

The lines of force in a magnetic field extend from pole to pole.

Surrounding every magnet there is a magnetic field, an area in which the field exerts a force on any other magnetic object. A magnetic field can be plotted by sprinkling iron filings on a sheet of paper held over a magnet. Iron and a few other metals, such as nickel and cobalt, become magnetized in a magnetic field because all the tiny molecular magnets within its structure align in the same direction.

The parts of a magnet where the field appears to come from or go to are called its poles. There are two kinds: north poles (to which a compass needle is attracted) and south poles. Unlike poles attract each other, whereas two similar poles repel each other. Furthermore, the force of attraction between two dissimilar poles is proportional to the product of their magnitudes and inversely proportional to the square of their distance apart. This is an example of an inverse square law.

Solar spectrum

When light from the sun is passed through a triangular glass prism, it is split into the colors of the rainbow—a spectrum. The experiment was first performed by Isaac NEWTON in 1666. The splitting of light in this way is called dispersion, and a similar effect takes place in a rainbow. Light from the sun enters a raindrop, is dispersed, and then is reflected from the back of the drop toward the ground.

Each of the different colors represents a different wavelength of light in the range 740 nanometers (red) to 390nm (violet). White light is a mixture of all wavelengths. This can be demonstrated by taking the three primary colors of light—red, blue, and green—and shining them together onto a plain surface, where they combine to form white light.

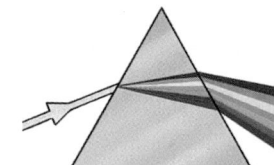

A prism splits white light into the colors of the spectrum.

Galileo

One of the greatest scientists of all time, Galileo Galilei was born in Pisa, Italy. It was while watching chandeliers swinging in the cathedral there that he realized how a pendulum could be used to measure time. He went on to propose that all objects, light or heavy, fall at the same speed (ignoring the effect of air resistance), though there is probably no truth to the story that he proved his point by dropping a feather and a cannonball from the top of the Leaning Tower of Pisa. In optics, Galileo perfected a refracting telescope, with which he discovered the four moons of Jupiter in 1610 *(p. 21)*. He also deduced correctly that the earth's moon shines by reflected sunlight. Later in life he was imprisoned by the Inquisition for championing the Copernican theory that the sun (not the earth) is at the center of the solar system *(p. 18)*.

Lenses and mirrors

Galileo and Issac Newton shared an interest in the study of optics. Both scientists worked with lenses, and Newton also found applications for curved mirrors. They showed that light rays passing through a convex (positive) lens are brought to a focus and that such a lens magnifies objects. Passing though a concave (negative) lens, light rays diverge and objects appear smaller.

Focal length (F), Twice focal length (2F)

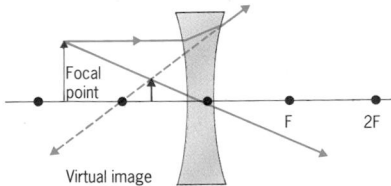

A concave lens makes light rays diverge.

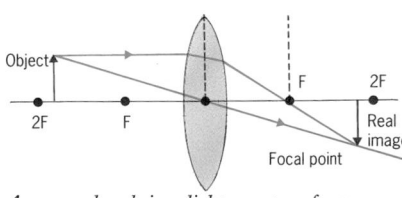

A convex lens brings light rays to a focus.

Similar effects occur with curved mirrors: a convex (outwardly curved) mirror produces a reduced image, as in a car's rearview mirror, whereas the effect of a concave (inwardly curved) mirror depends on how close the object is to the mirror. Close up, an enlarged image results, as with a shaving mirror.

Galileo used lenses to make an astronomical telescope; Newton made telescopes using curved mirrors instead of lenses. Mirrors could be made larger (and were lighter) than lenses, thus enabling bigger telescopes to be constructed.

Newton

Isaac NEWTON was born in Woolsthorpe, England, and by the time he graduated from Cambridge University in 1665, he had already worked out the principles of calculus. A year or so later, after reputedly seeing an apple fall, he formulated the law of gravitation. He deduced that there is a force of attraction between any two objects, and that this force is proportional to the product of the objects' masses and inversely proportional to the square of the distance between them. This was the first formulation of an inverse square law, a fundamental law of physics in which the magnitude of a physical quantity varies inversely with the square of the distance from its source.

Newton then went on to study light. He proved that it is impossible to make a simple single lens that does not suffer from chromatic aberration because each color (wavelength) is brought to a slightly different focus. This led him to develop reflecting astronomical telescopes (using mirrors instead of lenses *pp. 12-13*).

His greatest contributions, however, were in mathematics, and these achievements were gathered together in his monumental work *Principia Mathematica*.

Franklin and electricity

Benjamin Franklin (1706–90) was a notable U.S. statesman who helped draft the Declaration of Independence. But he was also a keen amateur scientist and inventor. Beginning in 1746, he made a series of famous (and extremely dangerous) experiments with electricity by flying a kite in a thunderstorm. A metal key attached to the kite string became electrically charged, demonstrating that lightning and electricity are the same thing. He also demonstrated that there is positive and negative (static) electricity and proposed the use of lightning rods—metal rods earthed to the ground—to discharge the electric field, thus protecting buildings from lightning strikes.

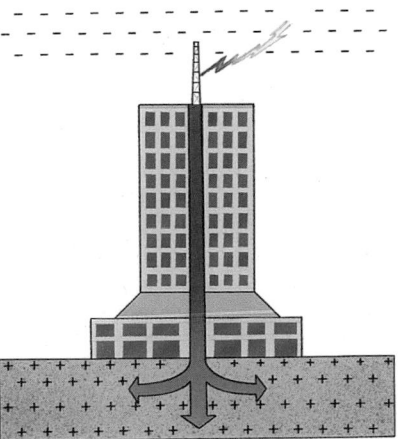

A lightning rod brings an electric charge to earth.

Timeline

1672 Guillaume Cassegrain designs a reflecting telescope.

1675 Isaac Newton proposes that light consists of a stream of particles.

1676 Ole Römer determines the speed of light. Edmé Marriotte independently formulates Boyle's law (Gas laws, *p.400*).

1678 Christiaan Huygens explains the wave theory of light.

1679 Robert Hooke proposes a law of elasticity (stress is proportional to strain).

1687 Isaac Newton formalizes his laws of gravitation and motion *(left)*. Guillaume Amontons invents a hygrometer (for measuring humidity).

1699 Guillaume Amontons investigates the effect of temperature on the volumes of gases.

1702 Guillaume Amontons makes a constant-volume gas thermometer.

1704 Isaac Newton publishes his theories of optics *(left)*.

1705 Francis Hauksbee proves that sound will not travel in a vacuum.

1709 Gabriel Fahrenheit makes an alcohol thermometer. Francis Hauksbee describes capillarity (the rise of liquid up a narrow tube).

1714 Gabriel Fahrenheit makes a mercury thermometer.

1721 John Hadley designs a high-quality reflecting telescope.

1724 Gabriel Fahrenheit describes the supercooling of water.

1729 James Bradley discovers the aberration of light.

1742 Anders Celsius devises the centigrade temperature scale.

1744 Pierre Maupertuis formulates the principle of least action.

1746 Pieter van Musschenbroek invents the Leyden jar (for storing an electric charge).

1747 Jean Nollet constructs an electrometer (for measuring difference of electric potential).

1752 Benjamin Franklin shows that lightning is a form of electricity *(left)*.

1757 Joseph Black proposes the theory of latent heat.

1758 John Dollond makes the first achromatic lenses.

1760 Daniel Bernoulli postulates an inverse square law for the force between electric charges.

1761 Joseph Black measures the latent heat of freezing of water.

1765 Henry Cavendish proposes the theory of specific heat.

1768 Antoine Baumé invents a hydrometer (for measuring the density of liquids).

1772 Johan Wilcke determines the latent heat of ice.

1777 Charles de Coulomb invents the torsion balance.

1781 Antoine Lavoisier formulates the law of conservation of mass. Johan Wilcke proposes the concept of specific heat.

Timeline

1783 Horace de Saussure constructs a hair hygrometer.

1784 George Atwood determines the acceleration of an object in free-fall.

1785 Charles de Coulomb formulates his law regarding the force between two unlike electric charges (Static electricity, *right*).

1786 Abraham Bennet invents the gold-leaf electroscope (for detecting an electric charge).

1787 Jacques Charles states his law linking volume and temperature of a fixed mass of gas when at constant pressure (Gas laws, *right*).

1788 Charles Blagden formulates his law regarding the depression of the freezing point of solutions. Joseph Lagrange puts forward his theories of mechanics.

1791 Pierre Prévost formulates his theory of heat exchange.

1794 Daniel Rutherford constructs a maximum-minimum thermometer.

1798 Henry Cavendish determines the mass and density of the earth. Count Rumford (Benjamin Thompson) studies friction-generated heat.

1800 Alessandro Volta constructs his voltaic pile for storing electric current (*right*). William Nicholson discovers electrolysis. William Herschel discovers infrared radiation. Johann Ritter invents process of electroplating.

1801 John Dalton formulates his law concerning the partial pressures of gases (Gas laws, *right*). William Henry postulates his law on the solubility of gases. Johann Ritter describes ultraviolet electromagnetic radiation.

1802 Johann Ritter makes a dry battery.

1803 John Dalton proposes his atomic theory of matter. Thomas Young demonstrates the interference of light (thus proving Robert Hooke's wave theory of light proposed in 1665).

1808 Etienne Malus describes the polarization of light.

1811 Amedeo Avogadro proposes his hypothesis (Gas laws, *right*). Dominique Arago discovers the optical activity of quartz.

1813 David Brewster proposes his law of the polarization of light.

1814 Joseph von Fraunhofer discovers the lines in the sun's spectrum now known as Fraunhofer lines.

1815 Jean Biot discovers the circular polarization of light.

1817 David Brewster invents the kaleidoscope.

1819 N. Clément and C. Désormes measure the specific heats of gases.

1820 Hans Oersted discovers electromagnetism (*p. 401*). Dominique Arago, André Ampère, and Michael Faraday also independently describe electromagnetism. Johann Schweigger invents the galvanometer (for detecting a small electric current).

Static electricity

Static electricity is, as its name implies, electricity that does not normally move. It manifests itself as an accumulated electric charge—positive or negative—on a material, which can be an insulator or a conductor. An unbalanced charge arises when electrons are removed from or added to the atoms of the material. For example, a plastic comb pulled through the hair several times soon acquires a static charge which is sufficient to attract small pieces of paper, in much the same way that a magnet attracts small pieces of iron. As in magnetism, unlike electric charges (a positive and a negative) attract, whereas like charges (both positive or both negative) repel.

The force resembles magnetism—and gravitation—in another important way. The equation for its magnitude is an inverse square law. Known as Coulomb's law, it states that the force of attraction between two unlike electric charges is proportional to the product of the charges and inversely proportional to the distance between them. This relationship was first worked out by the French physicist Charles de Coulomb, and the modern SI unit of electric charge is named after him.

Gas laws

Gases were among the forms of matter eagerly studied by early physicists because of their three interconnected properties of volume, pressure, and temperature. Increase the pressure on a gas and its volume gets less. But increase its temperature and its volume increases. These observations were formalized by the Irish physicist Robert Boyle in 1662 and, independently, by the Frenchman Jacques Charles (1746–1823) in 1787. Boyle's law states that, at a given temperature, the pressure of a gas is inversely proportional to its volume (pV = constant). Charles's law—which is also known as Gay-Lussac's law, after another French physicist who made the same observations—formulates that, at constant pressure, a fixed mass of gas expands by a constant fraction (about $1/273$) of its volume at 0°C for each degree Celsius rise in its temperature (i.e. V/T = constant). The two laws are combined in the universal gas equation $pV = nRT$, in which n is the amount of gas and R is the gas constant.

English chemist John Dalton also worked with gases but, as a chemist, he was usually dealing with mixtures. How much pressure, for example, does each component gas exert in such a mixture? Dalton answered this question with his law of partial pressures, which states that in a mixture of gases, each gas exerts the same pressure that it would if it alone occupied the total volume.

The final major contribution to the properties of gases was provided by another physicist, Italian Amedeo Avogadro. In 1811, he proposed, as a hypothesis only, that equal volumes of all gases contain the same number of molecules. This relationship turned out to have major implications in physics and chemistry and, slightly rephrased, is now known as Avogadro's law.

Volta and batteries

At the beginning of the 1600s the main interest of Italian scientist Alessandro Volta was investigating how muscles contract. During his research, he hung the legs of recently killed frogs on iron nails. When he brought a copper wire up to them, the legs twitched (because the muscles had been stimulated). He realized that the combination of iron and copper, with the frog's salty tissue fluids, had generated a force —electricity—that had made the animal's muscles contract.

He went on to build a stack of alternate copper and zinc or silver disks separated by pieces of cloth or leather saturated in brine (salt solution). This voltaic pile, as it came to be known, was the first battery and for many years was the standard direct-current source for electrical experiments. Ever since, batteries have relied on a pair of dissimilar electrodes separated by a salty electrolyte.

1. Halving the volume of a gas doubles its pressure (at constant temperature).
2. Doubling the temperature doubles the volume (at constant pressure).
3. Doubling the temperature doubles the pressure (at constant volume).

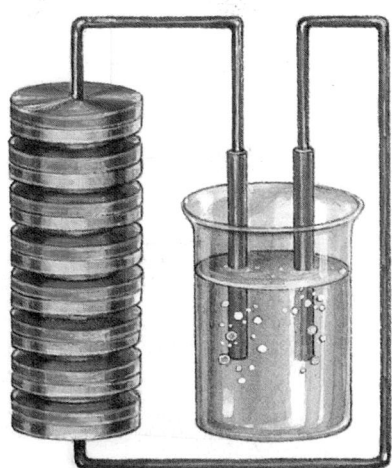

The voltaic pile was the first electric battery.

Electromagnetism

As physicists became increasingly aware of the existence of electric and magnetic fields, several experimenters discovered situations in which the two demonstrably coexisted. One key experiment was carried out in 1820 by Danish physicist Hans Christian Oersted (1777–1851), who noticed that a compass needle was deflected when an electric current passed along a nearby wire. He deduced that the wire had an associated magnetic field generated by the flowing current. He had discovered electromagnetism. In the same year, Frenchman André Ampère and Britain's Michael Faraday made similar discoveries, but it was Faraday who was first to apply the idea to electric motors and generators.

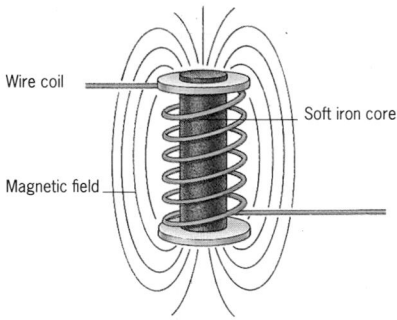

Current flowing through a coil makes it behave like a magnet.

A few years later, William Sturgeon (1783–1850) wound insulated copper wire around an iron bar and passed a current through the wire to create a powerful electromagnet. He went on to invent the moving-coil galvanometer (for detecting and measuring electric currents) and various electromagnetic machines.

Faraday, motors, and dynamos

Michael Faraday was an influential (but initially part-time) physicist and chemist who began as assistant to Humphry Davy at London's Royal Institution, where he began lectures for young people.

His major contribution to physics was the discovery in 1821 of electromagnetic

Faraday constructed the first dynamo.

induction. When the magnetic field cutting a circuit changes (perhaps because the circuit moves in the field), a current is induced in the circuit. Conversely, when a current passes through a circuit, such as a coil in a magnetic field, the circuit moves and the coil can be made to rotate. These two principles are fundamental to the dynamo and the electric motor.

Faraday combined his interests in physics and chemistry when he formulated his laws of electrolysis, which quantify the amounts of electricity needed to release elements at electrodes in an electrolytic cell.

Faraday's laws of electromagnetic induction state: (1) An electromotive force (voltage) is induced in a circuit whenever the magnetic field linking it changes; (2) The size of the induced e.m.f. is proportional to the rate of change of the magnetic field linking the circuit.

Faraday's laws of electrolysis state: (1) The amount of chemical decomposition that takes place during electrolysis is proportional to the electric current passed; (2) The amounts of substances liberated are proportional to their chemical equivalent weights.

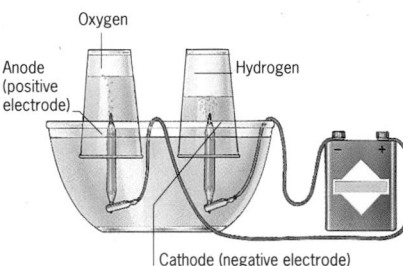

Electrolysis splits water into its constituent elements—oxygen and hydrogen.

Ohm's law

By the 1820s, physicists had ways of producing and detecting electric currents and of measuring voltages. They had also begun to quantify resistance—the property of a conductor that makes it resist the passage of an electric current. These parameters were finally brought together in 1827, when the German physicist Georg Ohm (1778–1842) formulated a law that interrelates the three: the voltage (V) across a conductor is equal to the product of the current flowing through it (I) and its resistance (R): $V = IR$. The unit of resistance is the ohm, and it is the oldest unit still in use in physics today.

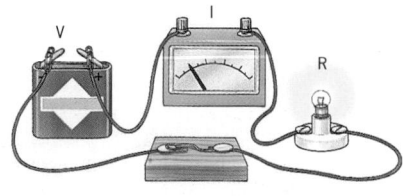

Ohm's law relates voltage, current, and resistance by the equation $V = IR$.

Timeline

1821 Michael Faraday discovers the principle of the electric motor (*left*).
1822 Thomas Seebeck discovers thermoelectricity.
1824 Nicolas Carnot founds thermodynamics by studying heat engines.
1825 André Ampère formulates his law relating to magnetic induction (the strength of a magnetic field) in an electric circuit. William Sturgeon constructs an electromagnet (*left*). Leopoldo Nobili invents the astatic galvanometer.
1827 Georg Ohm proposes his law linking voltage, current, and resistance (*left*). André Ampère puts forward a mathematical theory of electrodynamics.
1828 William Nicol invents an optical prism.
1829 Thomas Graham proposes his law relating to gaseous diffusion. Joseph Henry constructs a practical electric motor. Leopoldo Nobili constructs a thermopile (a device for measuring heat radiation).
1830 Joseph Lister produces an achromatic lens for the microscope.
1831 Michael Faraday invents a dynamo (*left*).
1832 Joseph Henry describes self-induction (whereby an electric current induces a second current).
1834 Jean Peltier describes the thermoelectric effect of passing an electric current between unlike metals to cause a change in temperature. Heinrich Lenz formulates his law concerning the direction of an induced electric current.
1835 Gaspard de Coriolis describes the effect explaining the deflection of a body moving relative to the earth as a result of the earth's rotation. Joseph Henry invents the electric relay (enabling a current to travel a long distance).
1836 William Sturgeon invents a moving-coil galvanometer (Electromagnetism, *left*). John Daniell invents a battery (Daniell cell). William Sturgeon invents the commutator (for reversing the flow of electric current) for electric motors.
1838 Michael Faraday discovers fluorescence of electric discharges in gases at low pressure.
1842 Christian Doppler observes the change in wavelength of an approaching source of vibration (Doppler effect). Julius von Mayer formulates the principle of the law of conservation of energy.
1843 Charles Wheatstone devises the Wheatstone bridge (for measuring electrical resistance). James Joule determines the mechanical equivalent of heat (Kinetic theory, *p. 402*).
1845 Michael Faraday discovers the effect of a magnetic field on the polarization of light (Faraday effect) and hence all electromagnetic waves. Gustav Kirchhoff formulates his laws concerning currents and voltages in electric circuits. Zygmunt von Wroblewski liquefies hydrogen.

Timeline

1847 Lambert Babo formulates his law concerning the depression of vapor pressure of solutions. Hermann von Helmholtz develops the law of conservation of energy. Lord Kelvin (William Thomson) proposes his theory of electrostatic fields.

1848 James Joule develops the kinetic theory of gases (*right*). Lord Kelvin devises the absolute temperature scale: -273°C becomes absolute zero.

1849 Hippolyte Fizeau determines the speed of light.

1850 Hippolyte Fizeau and Jean Foucault provide experimental proof of the wave theory of light (*see 1803*). Rudolf Clausius formulates the second law of thermodynamics.

1851 Jean Foucault demonstrates the rotation of the earth. George Stokes devises his formula describing how a small object falls through a fluid.

1852 Lord Kelvin formalizes the law of conservation of energy. James Joule and Lord Kelvin explain the temperature fall of an expanding gas. Jean Foucault invents the gyroscope (a device containing a spinning body mounted so that its orientation is not affected by movement of the device).

1853 William Rankine introduces the concept of potential energy (stored energy) (Energy, *right*).

1855 Heinrich Geissler invents the mercury vacuum pump, with which he makes a discharge tube.

1859 Gaston Planté makes a storage battery (secondary cell).

1860 Thomas Graham describes colloids.

1864 James Clerk Maxwell mathematically describes electromagnetic waves.

1865 Rudolf Clausius introduces the concept of entropy (disorder in a system, resulting in the unavailability of energy for doing work).

1866 August Kundt devises a method of measuring the speed of sound. Georges Leclanché invents the dry cell battery.

1869 Thomas Andrews succeeds in liquefying gases. John Tyndall discovers the scattering of light by a colloidal solution (known as the Tyndall effect).

1872 James Dewar invents the vacuum flask (Moving heat, *p.403*). Ernst Abbe invents a condenser lens for microscopes. Emile Amagat studies gases at high pressures.

1873 Johannes Van der Waals formulates his gas equation.

1874 Karl Braun uses crystals as rectifiers (for converting AC to DC).

1875 William Crookes invents the radiometer (for the detection of radiant energy).

1876 Eugen Goldstein introduces the term "cathode ray," referring to a beam of electrodes.

1877 Louis Calletet liquefies oxygen.

1879 Joseph Stefan proposes his law of heat radiation.

Energy

A physicist defines energy as the capacity to do work. For example, if a heavy weight is hauled up by a rope or chain and then allowed to fall, the falling weight can do work—as it does in an old-fashioned grandfather clock. The raised weight has energy by virtue of its position or state; it has potential energy. Other examples include the energy in the water stored behind a dam (released when the water is allowed to flow through pipes to turn turbines) or stored in a compressed spring (such as an archer's bow before it fires an arrow toward its target).

It is a basic principle of physics that energy can neither be created nor destroyed. Therefore the moving water or flying arrow in the above examples must retain energy. It is called kinetic energy— the energy of movement—and is equal to $1/2\, mv^2$, where m is the mass of a moving object and v is its velocity. This expression explains why a high-speed road crash is so much more destructive than a slow-speed one: because the vehicle's velocity is squared in the formula. For instance, a 1-ton (2,000-lb.) car traveling at 12mph has a kinetic energy of about 200,000 joules. But at a speed of 62mph, the vehicle's kinetic energy increases to 5,000,000 joules.

The other forms of energy studied in physics include heat energy and sound, although as both of these depend on the vibration (that is, the movement) of atoms or molecules they can be regarded as types of kinetic energy. Similarly, chemical, electrical, gravitational, and nuclear energy all depend on the position or state of objects and can therefore be considered as forms of potential energy.

Kinetic theory

In the middle of the 1800s, British physicist James Joule was studying heat as a form of energy. By measuring the rise in temperature of a mass of water after turning a paddle wheel in it, he calculated the mechanical equivalent of heat (as about 4.2 joules per calorie: it has a value of 1 in SI units because all forms of energy are measured in joules).

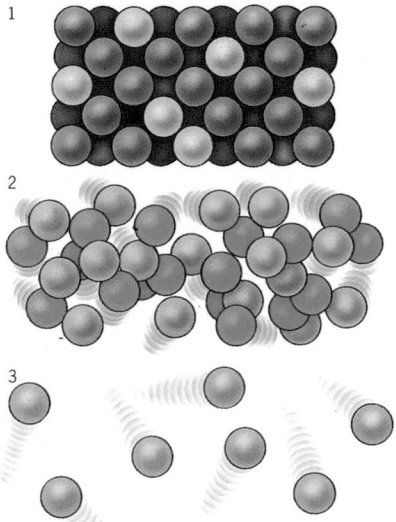

Kinetic theory explains the differences between solids (1), liquids (2), and gases (3) in terms of moving molecules.

He also accounted for pressure in a gas by postulating that it is caused by the millions of collisions of rapidly moving gas atoms or molecules with the walls of the container. He conceived of a gas as a

A turbogenerator converts the energy of flowing water into electrical energy.

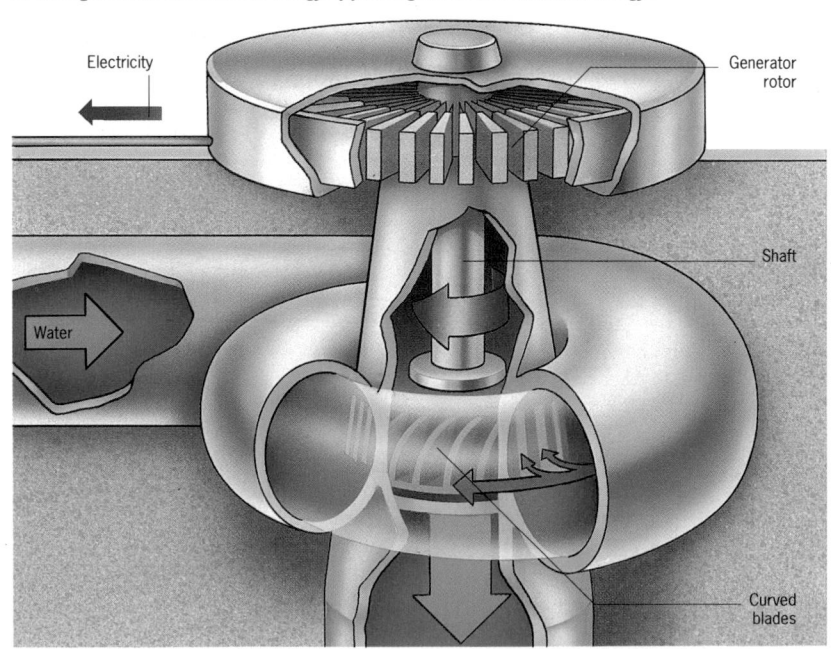

Electricity

Water

Generator rotor

Shaft

Curved blades

collection of freely moving molecules. That is why a gas always fills its container.

But if a gas, such as water vapor, is cooled sufficiently, it condenses to form a liquid. In a liquid, although the molecules are still moving, they remain below the surface and the liquid takes on the shape of the container below the liquid surface. If water is cooled even further, it freezes: that is, it condenses to form a solid (ice). In the solid state, the molecules are more or less fixed in their positions in a crystal lattice, although they do vibrate slightly.

Moving heat

Heat can travel in three ways: by conduction, convection, or radiation. If an iron bar is heated at one end, heat travels along the bar by means of conduction. The rapidly vibrating "hot" atoms jostle their neighbors, making them vibrate and thereby pass on the heat energy.

In convection, the heated material actually moves. Hot air near the ground, for example, becomes less dense and rises, carrying heat with it. Cooler air moves in to take its place, causing a circular convection of air. Finally, when we hold our hands near a hot object, such as a fire, we can feel the heat, which reaches our hands by means of radiation.

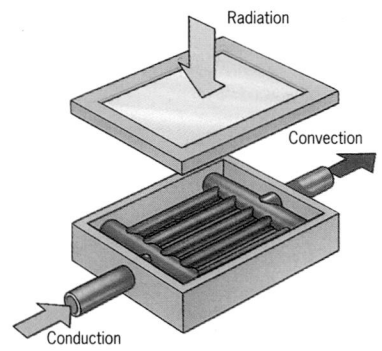

Within a solar power collector, energy radiated from the sun is transferred via conduction and convection.

A vacuum flask prevents heat movement by virtually eliminating conduction, convection and radiation.

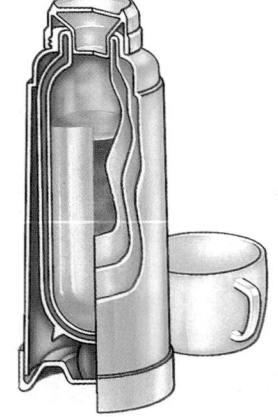

The vacuum flask, invented by James Dewar (1842–1923) in 1872, is designed to prevent heat loss (or gain) by the contents by virtually eliminating conduction, convection, and radiation. An insulating material prevents heat traveling by conduction; a vacuum between the vessel's two walls prevents convection; and silvering on the glass vessel prevents radiation.

Discovery of the electron

By the end of the 1800s, physicists had no doubt that matter consists of atoms, which many thought resembled tiny, indivisible solid marbles. Then in 1897, British physicist J. J. Thomson carried out experiments with cathode rays, which travel across a vacuum from a hot, negatively charged cathode to a nearby positive anode. He showed that the rays were actually particles originating in the atoms of metal in the cathode. The particles, called electrons, turned out to be negatively charged and have a mass of about $1/1800$ of a single hydrogen atom. Electrons are also the fundamental charges in static electricity.

Discovery of the nucleus

At the turn of the twentieth century, physicist Ernest Rutherford began studying radioactivity (discovered in 1896 by Henri Becquerel). He found that there were two main types of rays involved—positively charged alpha particles and negatively charged beta particles.

Beta particles turned out to be the same as electrons, but alpha particles were energetic enough to penetrate thin films of metal. Rutherford suggested an experiment in which alpha particles were fired at gold foil: unexpectedly, some of them were deflected through large angles. He deduced that the gold atoms had a positively charged core, or nucleus. He also showed that one particular nucleus—that of hydrogen—is a component of all other atoms. He called this subatomic particle the proton; it has a positive charge.

Finally, in 1932, James Chadwick discovered the third basic subatomic particle, the neutron, which also resides in the atomic nucleus. The simple picture of the atom was complete.

An atom's positively charged nucleus is surrounded by orbiting electrons.

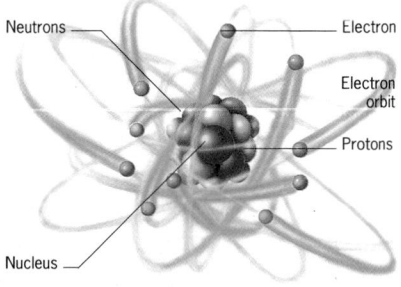

Neutrons

Electron

Electron orbit

Protons

Nucleus

Timeline

1902 Oliver Heaviside and Arthur Kennelly describe an atmospheric layer that reflects radio waves (later termed the ionosphere). Philipp Lenard experiments with cathode rays.

1903 Ernest Rutherford and Frederick Soddy propose the existence of the radioactive decay series. Richard Zsigmondy develops the ultramicroscope.

1904 Hendrik Lorentz and George Fitzgerald propose the contraction of objects approaching the speed of light (later explained in mathematical terms by Einstein). John Fleming invents the diode tube (allowing electrons to flow in one direction only, Controlling electron flow, *right*). Charles Barkla demonstrates the polarization of X rays.

1905 Ernest Rutherford and Frederick Soddy demonstrate nuclear transmutation. Albert Einstein proposes the theory of special relativity (*p. 405*).

1906 Walther Nernst formulates the third law of thermodynamics. Lee de Forest invents the triode tube (Controlling electron flow, *right*). Theodore Lyman describes lines in the ultraviolet region of the hydrogen spectrum (known as the Lyman series).

1907 Pierre Weiss introduces the domain theory of magnetism (an explanation of magnetic behavior).

1908 Heike Kamerlingh-Onnes liquefies helium.

1909 Robert Millikan determines the charge on an electron.

1911 Charles Wilson invents the cloud chamber (thus proving the ionizing properties of radioactive emission). Ernest Rutherford proposes the nuclear model of the atom (based on E. Marsden's experiments of the scattering of alpha particles by gold foil). Heike Kamerlingh-Onnes discovers superconductivity. Victor Hess discovers cosmic rays. Albert Einstein predicts the effect of gravity on light (Relativity, *p. 405*).

1912 Max von Laue demonstrates the diffraction of X rays. William Bragg formulates his law of X-ray diffraction. Peter Debye proposes his theory of specific heats (of solids).

1913 Niels Bohr elaborates on the quantum theory of atoms and their spectra (*p. 405*). Frederick Soddy introduces the term "isotope" (Weighing atoms, *p.405*). Hans Geiger invents the Geiger counter (for detecting ionized particles). Johannes Stark discovers that spectral lines are doubled in an electric field. Kasimir Fajans quantifies radioactive decay products. Henry Moseley introduces the concept of atomic numbers.

1914 Ernest Rutherford discovers the proton (positively charged particle of mass within the atomic nucleus; Discovery of the nucleus, *p.403*).

1915 William Bragg invents the X-ray spectrometer.

Quantum theory

As ideas of atomic structure continued to develop, scientists tried to apply this new-found knowledge to other physical phenomena. One insight into atomic structure and behavior is the light emitted by atoms when they are heated to incandescence. For a gaseous atom, such as hydrogen, light is emitted when an electric current passes through a discharge tube containing hydrogen at very low pressure in a near vacuum.

When studied through a spectrometer, which splits light into its various wavelengths, the hydrogen spectrum is revealed as a series of lines of different colors (*p. 412*), not as a continuous spectrum like that of the sun. It is as if hydrogen can emit only a few colors but not the whole range. To account for this, in 1900, German physicist Max Planck suggested that light—and other forms of energy—is not emitted from atoms as a continuous stream but in discrete "packets," which he called quanta.

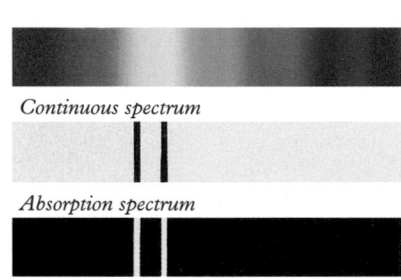

Continuous spectrum

Absorption spectrum

Emission spectrum

Furthermore, each quantum of light (a light quantum is known as a photon) reveals something about the behavior of electrons orbiting the atom concerned. The electrons are restricted to certain energy levels. When energy—in the form of electricity or heat—is supplied to an atom, some of its electrons are elevated to higher energy levels; in modern terminology they are "excited." But when the stimulating energy supply is removed, those same electrons "jump" back down to their original energy levels. As they do so, they emit their excess energy as photons (quanta) of light.

The new quantum theory was embraced by Danish physicist Niels Bohr, who in 1913 proposed that the various energy levels of an atom's electrons correspond

An electron emits a photon of light when it jumps to a lower orbit.

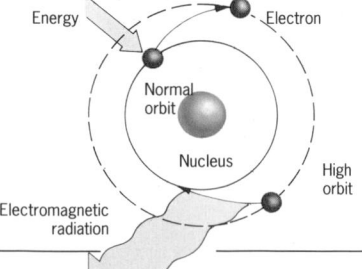

to a series of permitted concentric orbits around the nucleus of the atom. Quanta of energy are involved when electrons move between orbits.

Controlling electron flow

The cathode-ray tube was the key to the discovery of the electron. A cathode ray is a stream of electrons flowing between a cathode and an anode inside an evacuated glass tube. A stream of electrons constitutes an electric current, so controlling cathode rays provides a means of controlling electric current.

The first person to make this association was British scientist John Fleming (1849–1945), who invented the diode tube in 1904. In effect a miniature cathode-ray tube, the diode had a heated cathode (which produced a stream of electrons by thermionic emission) and an anode, which collected the electrons. The

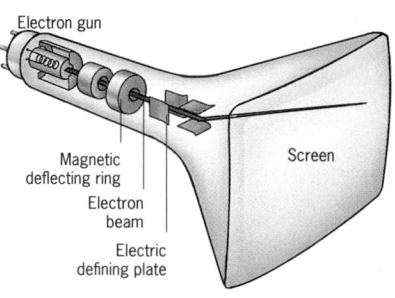

An electron beam scans the face of a cathode-ray tube.

tube permitted electrons to flow only in that one direction (cathode to anode) and soon came to be used as a rectifier, converting alternating current (AC) into direct current (DC).

Then in 1906, a U.S. inventor, Lee De Forest (1873–1961), added a third grid-shaped electrode to the tube to make a triode. The grid permitted electrons to pass through on their way from the cathode to the anode, but applying an external voltage to the grid controlled the number of electrons allowed through. Indeed, the voltage on the grid could increase the number of electrons, so amplifying the current at the cathode. The triode became the basis of the electronic amplifier, soon to be a critical component in the development of radio broadcasting, a position it retained for 40 years until the invention of the transistor.

Relativity

While experimental physicists such as Thomson and Rutherford were unraveling the structure of the atom, and Fleming and De Forest were finding practical applications for the new findings, theoretical physicists were trying to combine all the new knowledge in a way that applied to the whole of science. In particular, it seemed that there had to be some com-

mon ground between quantum theory and the classical mechanics of Newton and his contemporaries.

Then came Albert Einstein. His totally new outlook was presented first in his special theory of relativity (1905), in which he proposed the concept of a space–time continuum that allowed a merging of the previous points of view. In particular, it emphasized the fundamental significance of the velocity of light (which is given the symbol c in physics). Einstein showed that for objects traveling at speeds approaching that of light, strange phenomena such as shrinkage in size and increase in mass can be expected. The increase in mass m of an object is a measure of the energy imparted to it, as expressed in the famous equation $E = mc^2$. This equation was later to be proved dramatically by its ability to predict the power unleashed by a nuclear explosion, in which the small amount of mass that "disappears" appears as huge amounts of energy released from the event.

Eleven years later, in 1916, Einstein proposed his general theory of relativity, which revolved around the fact that acceleration and gravitational force cannot be distinguished. Einstein saw the universe as a four-dimensional continuum of space and time in which any mass curves space to create a gravitational field.

Weighing atoms

One of the ways experimenters distinguished between various kinds of subatomic particles was to observe how they behaved in a magnetic field. Elec-trons, (negative) were deflected to one side; protons (positive) were deflected the other way; and neutrons (neutral) passed through the magnetic field unaffected.

British physicist Francis Aston (1877–1945) saw other applications of this phenomenon. He took a mixture of charged particles—all with the same charge but different masses—and fired them between the poles of a magnet. The apparatus resulting from these experiments, called a mass spectrograph, sorted the particles according to their mass. When he ionized a single element, such as neon, to produce positively charged ions, he found that the spectrum revealed ions

A mass spectrometer identifies atoms by separating their ions.

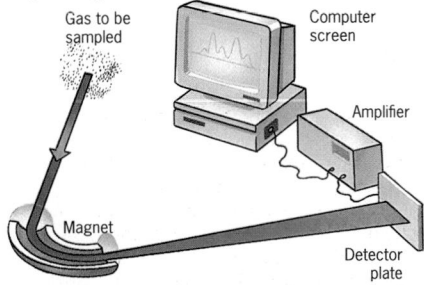

of two different masses. He had in fact discovered that neon has two isotopes

Isotopes are forms of an element whose atoms have the same number of electrons and protons (and so their chemical identity is the same) but different numbers of neutrons in their atomic nuclei (so their masses are different). Isotopes became especially important when it was realized that the radioactivity of heavy elements, such as uranium, depends on the composition of the isotope concerned.

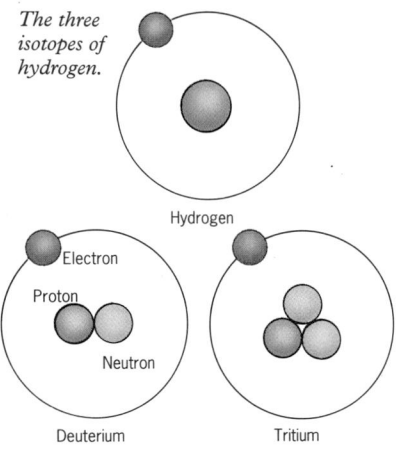

The three isotopes of hydrogen.

Smashing atoms

Natural radioactive disintegration involves the splitting of atoms as particles are emitted from their nuclei. In 1932, two British physicists, John Cockroft (1897–1967) and Ernest Walton (b. 1903), used a large electric field to accelerate charged particles—protons—so that they smashed into atoms like bullets. In this way, they artificially split atoms of the light metallic element lithium.

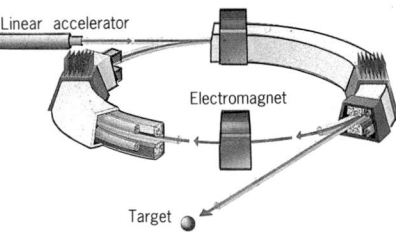

In a circular accelerator, a cyclotron, particles get faster and faster before being deflected.

Since that time, larger atom smashers, such as the circular particle accelerators or cyclotrons first constructed in the United States by Ernest Lawrence (1901–58) in the late 1930s, have produced artificial radioactive elements and ultimately a whole series of new elements that are heavier than uranium. The largest of these, such as the synchrocyclotron at C.E.R.N. (the Centre Européen de Recherche Nucléaire) in Europe and the giant synchrotron at the Fermi National Accelerator Laboratory in Illinois, work at energies measured in billions of electron volts.

Timeline

1916 Albert Einstein proposes the general theory of relativity (Relativity, *p.404 left*). Arnold Sommerfeld proposes that electron orbits are elliptical. Robert Millikan confirms the mathematics of quantum theory. Peter Debye develops powder X-ray crystallography.

1919 Francis Aston constructs the mass spectrograph (Weighing atoms, *left*). Arthur Eddington demonstrates the bending of light by the sun's gravity (as predicted by general relativity).

1921 Otto Hahn clarifies the theory of isotopes (atoms that can exist in different mass forms). Johannes Brönsted and György Hevesy separate isotopes.

1922 Niels Bohr awarded Nobel Prize for his proposal that electrons orbit atomic nuclei (Quantum theory, *p.404*).

1923 Arthur Compton explains the scattering of X rays by electrons (known as the Compton effect).

1924 Wolfgang Pauli formulates the exclusion principle of electrons. Louis de Broglie proposes the wave-particle duality of the electron leading to an explanation of the dual nature of light. Edward Appleton locates the Heaviside-Kennelly layer (*see 1902*).

1925 Erwin Schrödinger introduces wave mechanics. Pierre Auger discovers the Auger effect of electron emission. Samuel Goudsmit and George Uhlenbeck propose that electrons spin. Werner Heisenberg and Niels Bohr develop quantum mechanics.

1926 Albert Michelson accurately measures the speed of light.

1927 Werner Heisenberg proposes his uncertainty principle. Clinton Davisson and George Thomson independently demonstrate electron diffraction. Eugene Wigner introduces the concept of parity in nuclear reactions.

1928 Hans Geiger and Walther Müller invent the Geiger-Müller counter (a device for measuring radioactivity). Chandrasekhara Raman discovers the scattering of light by molecules (known as the Raman effect).

1929 Walther Bothe shows that cosmic rays are particles. George Gamow proposes the "liquid drop" model of the atomic nucleus.

1930 Wolfgang Pauli proposes the existence of the neutrino (Ultimate particles, *p.407*). Paul Dirac introduces the concept of antimatter.

1931 Harold Urey prepares heavy water (deuterium oxide). Robert Van de Graaff devises a high-voltage electrostatic generator.

1932 James Chadwick discovers the neutron (a neutral atomic particle within the nucleus and of same mass·as a proton; Discovery of the nucleus, *p.403*). John Cockcroft and Ernest Walton build a particle accelerator (Smashing atoms, *left*). Ernest Lawrence builds a cyclotron (Smashing atoms, *left*).

Timeline

1933 Carl Anderson and Robert Millikan discover the positron. Enrico Fermi explains beta decay and proposes the existence of the weak interaction force (in atoms). Ernst Ruska proposes the concept of a transmission electron microscope. Robert Van de Graaff invents the high-voltage electrostatic generator.

1934 Pavel Cherenkov discovers light emitted by the passage of high-speed particles (known as Cherenkov radiation). Irène and Frédéric Joliot-Curie produce artificial radioactivity (by the addition of neutrons to the atom). Enrico Fermi recognizes the significance of slow neutrons in nuclear fission.

1935 Hideki Yukawa predicts the existence of the meson (subatomic particle).

1936 Erwin Mueller invents the field-emission microscope.

1937 Peter Kapitza discovers superfluidity (of helium). Carl Anderson discovers the muon (subatomic particle).

1938 Otto Hahn achieves nuclear fission (*right*). Fritz Zernike invents the phase contrast microscope.

1939 Vladimir Zworykin builds the electron microscope.

1940 Maurice Goldhaber discovers that beryllium acts as a moderator (in nuclear fission reactions).

1942 Enrico Fermi *et al.* achieve a nuclear fission chain reaction (Nuclear fission, *right*). Hannes Alfvén proposes that there are hydromagnetic waves in plasmas.

1944 Vladimir Veksler builds a synchrocyclotron.

1945 L. Jánossy investigates cosmic rays.

1946 Felix Bloch and Edward Purcell independently develop nuclear magnetic resonance (N.M.R.) spectroscopy. Abraham Pais introduces the term "lepton" for light subatomic particles.

1947 Cecil Powell *et al.* discover the pion (subatomic particle). Willard Libby introduces carbon dating (a method of dating remains by measuring the amount of radioactive carbon 14 present). John Bardeen, Walter Brattain, and William Shockley invent the point-contact transistor.

1948 Richard Feynman, Julian Schwinger, and Sinichiro Tomonaga propose the theory of quantum electrodynamics. William Shockley invents the junction transistor. Dennis Gabor develops the concept of holography.

1950 Albert Einstein proposes a unified field theory. Aage Bohr and Ben Mottelson propose that an atomic nucleus has structure.

1951 Walter Zinn constructs the first breeder nuclear reactor. Erwin Mueller develops the field-ion microscope.

1952 Donald Glaser invents the bubble chamber.

1953 Murray Gell-Mann introduces the property of strangeness for subatomic particles (unexplained rate of decay).

Electron microscope

One of the great achievements of physics, which greatly benefited other areas of science such as biology and medicine, came with the development of powerful optical microscopes. But no matter how well lenses are made, there is a limit to the magnifying power of such a microscope imposed by the wavelength of light used to illuminate the object being studied.

Then in 1939, the Russian-born U.S. physicist Vladimir Zworykin (1889–1982) built a microscope using a different kind of radiation. He used beams of electrons instead of light, with electromagnets instead of lenses to focus them. The greatly magnified image—of objects as small as a millionth of a millimeter across—is formed on a screen or picked up by a television camera.

The electron microscope also demonstrates another important principle of 20th-century physics. A beam of electrons had already been shown to be a stream of subatomic particles. But in the microscope they behave as if they are waves, just like a beam of light. This confirmed the wave-particle duality of such particles, as first proposed in 1923 by French physicist Louis de Broglie (1892-1987).

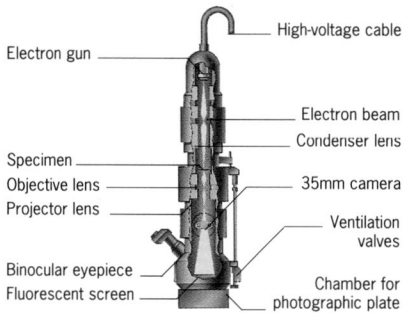

An electron microscope uses a beam of electrons to form a highly magnified image.

Nuclear fission

Einstein's famous $E = mc^2$ equation shows that a small amount of mass can theoretically be converted into large amounts of energy. The first realization of how this might be achieved came when physicists added up the masses of the particles before and after an atom of uranium splits to form two lighter atoms. Even taking into account the masses of all subatomic particles involved, there is still some mass apparently "missing" from the products. That matter should appear as energy.

That prediction was confirmed in 1945 when U.S. scientists detonated the first atomic bomb in New Mexico. Even earlier, other physicists had worked on controlled nuclear fission, as the process was called. When a nucleus of a uranium isotope of mass 235 (U-235) absorbs a low-energy neutron, the nucleus becomes unstable and splits into two fragments, releasing on average three more neutrons

and energy. If these three neutrons are slowed down to reduce their energy, by means of a substance such as heavy water or graphite known as a moderator, they go on to split three more U-235 nuclei. The process then accelerates as a chain reaction, with the release of large amounts of heat energy. The heat can be used to make steam to drive turbines. The reaction can be stopped using control rods of a substance such as boron or cadmium, which absorbs the free neutrons and prevents fission continuing.

Uranium atoms are split in a thermal nuclear reactor. The heat energy released is used to produce steam to drive electricity generators.

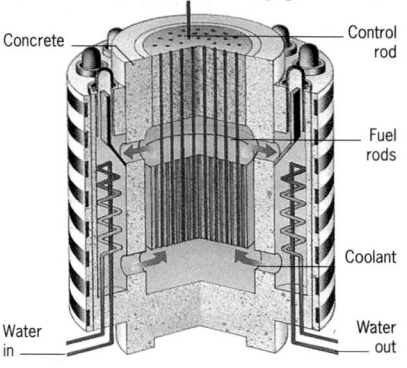

Semiconductors

One of the triumphs of kinetic theory and atomic theory is their ability to explain nearly all physical properties of matter, such as why some materials are good conductors of heat and electricity and others are not (they are insulators). There is an intermediate class of substances, known as semiconductors, that are better at conducting electricity than insulators but not as good as conductors such as copper. These semiconductors have turned out to have far-reaching applications to electronics.

A pure semiconductor, such as the element silicon, is a fairly poor conductor of electricity. But if very small amounts of impurities are incorporated into its crystal structure, its electrical properties change

Silicon is a semiconducting material used in the integrated circuits of computers.

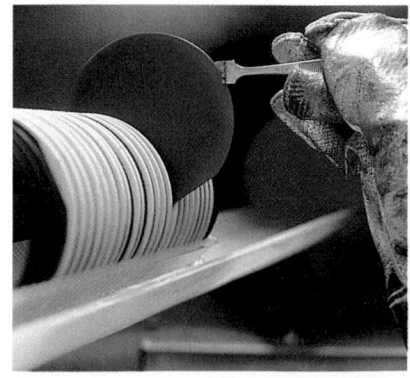

markedly. It might conduct for example, but in one direction only, so it acts like a diode. A different impurity allows it to conduct only in the other direction.

A combination of different types of semiconductors makes a transistor, a device that can be used like a triode tube to make amplifiers and other electronic circuits. But unlike a tube, a transistor does not use any power (a tube uses power to heat its cathode) and can be made microscopically small, so that hundreds of such devices can now be incorporated on a chip of silicon measuring only a few millimeters across.

Ultimate particles

The original elementary particles—the first to be discovered—were the electron (a lepton) and the proton and neutron (both of which are baryons). Throughout the mid-1900s, various other subatomic particles were discovered. These included other leptons—the muon, tauon, and neutrino—and their respective antiparticles. For example, the antielectron—termed a positron—has a positive rather than a negative charge.

What rapidly became an extremely confused picture was finally resolved in 1964, when Murray Gell-Mann (b. 1929) in the United States proposed the existence of the most fundamental particle of all—the quark. According to current theory, there are six types of quarks (and six antiquarks). The types are distinguished by their "flavor," which is defined as up (u), down (d), charmed (c), strange (s), top (t)—which is questionable—or bottom (b). (In the table below antiquarks are distinguished by underlining.) Quarks between them make up all other subatomic particles (baryons and mesons).

Elementary particles

Type	Particle	Quark content
Gauge bosons	photon	
	W-plus/minus	
	Z-zero	
Leptons	neutrino	
	electron	
	muon	
	tauon	
Baryons	proton	uud
	neutron	udd
	lambda	uds
	sigma-plus	uus
	sigma-zero	uds
	sigma-minus	dds
	xi-zero	uss
	xi-minus	dss
	omega-minus	sss
	lambda-plus	udc
Mesons	pi-plus/minus	u$\underline{d}$, $\underline{u}$d
	pi-zero	u$\underline{u}$, d$\underline{d}$
	K-plus/minus	u$\underline{s}$, $\underline{s}$u
	K-zero	d$\underline{s}$
	eta-zero	u$\underline{u}$, d$\underline{d}$, s$\underline{s}$
	D-plus/minus	c$\underline{d}$, d$\underline{c}$
	D-zero	c$\underline{u}$
	B-plus/minus	u$\underline{b}$, b$\underline{u}$
	B-zero	d$\underline{b}$

Lasers and holography

Most light is a mixture of wavelengths (colors) and is incoherent (that is, the waves are not in step with each other). A laser produces light that is monochromatic—of only a single wavelength—and coherent—all the waves are exactly in step. The term laser stands for **l**ight **a**mplification by **s**timulated **e**mission of **r**adiation: atoms emit photons of light when some electrons jump down to lower energy levels. In a simple laser, atoms in a crystal of synthetic ruby are stimulated by pulsed flashes of bright white light from a flash tube coiled around the ruby. Mirrors at each end of the crystal reflect the light back and forth, and energy builds up and eventually emerges as a laser beam.

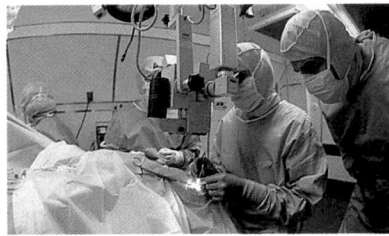

Surgeons use lasers to remove diseased tissue.

To produce a hologram, a beam of laser light is split in two. One half of the beam is reflected onto a photographic plate, while the other half illuminates an object before being reflected onto the plate. The two half-beams arrive at the plate out of step. They produce an interference pattern of light and dark circular fringes which, when viewed using laser light, presents a three-dimensional image of the original object.

Superconductivity

Some materials, particularly metals, take on unusual properties at low temperatures. They lose all electrical resistance, for example, becoming superconductors. If they are incorporated into a circuit and a source of current is introduced, the current continues to flow around the circuit even after the source has been removed.

An explanation of the phenomenon was given in 1956 by U.S. physicist Leon Cooper (b. 1930). In a metallic conductor at ordinary temperatures, the current is carried by electrons moving through the positive charges on the metal's crystal lattice. Electrostatic repulsion between electrons and lattice hinders the electrons' movement, thus accounting for the metal's electrical resistance. In a superconductor, however, the electrons travel in couples (called Cooper pairs) whose momentum—and hence movement—is unimpeded by the lattice. Research continues to make superconduct at relatively high temperatures (-300°F/-150°C). Such superconductors are used to construct powerful electromagnets.

Timeline

c. 400 B.C. Democritus proposes that matter is made up of atoms.

c. A.D. 180 The first writings on alchemy appear (in Egypt).

c. 400 Alexandrian scholars first use the word "chemistry."

c. 750 The alchemist Geber makes acetic acid (ethanoic acid) from vinegar and nitric acid (from saltpeter).

c. 890 Arab chemists make alcohol (by distilling wine).

c. 1000 Chinese invent gunpowder.

c. 1300 "False Geber" describes the preparation of sulfuric acid.

c. 1310 Raymond Lully of Majorca discovers ammonia gas.

1597 Andreas Libavius describes the preparation of hydrochloric acid (from salt and sulfuric acid).

1625 Johann Glauber discovers Glauber's salt (sodium sulfate).

1649 Schröder discovers the toxic element arsenic.

1661 Robert Boyle defines an element— a substance containing only one type of atom which cannot be chemically broken down into anything simpler.

1669 Hennig Brand discovers yellow phosphorus (in urine).

1695 Nehemiah Grew isolates Epsom salts (magnesium sulfate).

1697 Georg Stahl introduces the phlogiston theory of combustion (Combustion, *p.409*).

1702 Wilhelm Homberg makes boric acid (from borax).

1735 Georg Brandt discovers the magnetic metal cobalt.

1736 Henri Duhamel distinguishes between the salts of sodium and potassium.

1746 John Roebuck introduces the lead-chamber process (for manufacturing sulfuric acid).

1751 Axel Cronstedt discovers the metal nickel.

1756 Joseph Black discovers carbon dioxide (Composition of air, *right*).

1765 Carl Scheele discovers the highly toxic prussic acid (Scheele, *right*).

1766 Henry Cavendish identifies hydrogen ("inflammable air").

1771 Carl Scheele discovers (but fails to isolate) fluorine, one of the most reactive elements (*see 1886*).

1772 Daniel Rutherford discovers nitrogen (Composition of air, *right*). Antoine Lavoisier begins his experiments on combustion (Combustion, *p.409*).

1774 Johan Gahn discovers the metal manganese. Joseph Priestley discovers oxygen (Composition of air, *right*). Carl Scheele discovers chlorine and formic acid (methanoic acid).

1775 Joseph Priestley rediscovers hydrochloric and sulfuric acids.

1776 Carl Scheele and Torbern Bergman independently discover the organic compound urea.

1778 Alessandro Volta discovers the flammable gas methane.

Chemistry

Chemistry is the study of the elements, how they react with each other to form compounds, and how compounds interact. Because all matter is made up of elements, chemistry is therefore the study of matter, particularly how it is formed and the ways in which it can be changed.

All matter is composed of atoms. In any particular element, all the atoms are the same, but they are different from the atoms of another element. An atom consists of a central nucleus, composed of protons and neutrons, surrounded by shells of electrons. The identity of an atom—and therefore an element—depends on the number of protons in its nucleus, a quantity known as its atomic number. The atomic numbers of all the elements are given in the table on p. 411. The way an element behaves chemically depends on the arrangement of electrons in its shells, particularly the outermost ones.

When atoms combine they form molecules. Again, in any particular pure substance, all the molecules are the same. When different elements combine they form compounds. Chemists represent elements and compounds by formulae, which indicate the ratio of atoms present. For example, water has the chemical formula H_2O; its molecules consist of two atoms of hydrogen (H) combined with one atom of oxygen (O). Reactions are represented by equations. For instance, the reaction between hydrogen and oxygen to form water is written:

$$2H_2 + O_2 \longrightarrow 2H_2O$$

This tells us that two molecules of hydrogen combine with one molecule of oxygen to produce two molecules of water. The equation is balanced: it shows an equal number of atoms on each side.

There are two major branches of chemistry: organic chemistry, which is concerned with the thousands of compounds of carbon; and inorganic chemistry, which deals with all the other elements and their compounds. The exception to this is that the oxides of carbon (such as carbon monoxide, CO, and carbon dioxide, CO_2), bicarbonates (hydrogen carbonates), and carbonates (salts of carbonic acid, which is carbon dioxide dissolved in water) are included in inorganic chemistry.

The alchemists

Chemistry had its beginnings in China and Egypt in the 200s B.C. After a long period of decline in science, chemistry was revived in Arabia with the work of the alchemists in the 700s A.D. They cloaked their experiments in mysticism and spent much time seeking the philosopher's stone, a magical substance that was supposed to turn base metals such as lead into gold—a process they termed transmutation. They also sought the elixir of life, which was supposed to confer immortality. Twentieth-century physicists have finally achieved transmutation of elements, but the elixir of life remains beyond our reach.

The Art of the Alchemist *as depicted in a print* from the 1500s.

Scheele

Carl Wilhelm Scheele was a Swedish chemist who made many discoveries, although not all of them came immediately to the attention of other chemists. He made the first preparations of many acids, including benzoic, citric, gallic, hydrofluoric, oxalic, and tartaric acids. He discovered that air consists mainly of two gases, one that supports combustion and one that does not. He isolated chlorine and oxygen and prepared glycerine, hydrogen sulfide, and hydrocyanic (prussic) acid. The mineral pigment copper arsenite was named Scheele's Green after him.

Composition of air

The British chemist Joseph Priestley was a Presbyterian minister by profession and at first experimented in chemistry only as a hobby. He contributed greatly to the study of gases, his most celebrated discovery being that of oxygen in 1774, three years before it was found independently by Carl Scheele. Priestley showed that oxygen makes up about one-fifth of air— previously thought to be a gas itself—and supports combustion.

The composition of dry air.

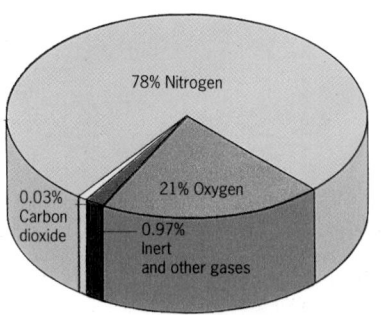

78% Nitrogen

21% Oxygen

0.03% Carbon dioxide

0.97% Inert and other gases

The other four-fifths of air consist mostly of nitrogen, which had been discovered in 1772 by the Scottish physician Daniel Rutherford (1749–1819). He originally called the gas "noxious air" and was able to distinguish it from carbon dioxide, another gas that occurs in variable amounts in air. This gas was discovered by another Scottish chemist and doctor, Joseph Black (1728–99), in 1756; he had christened it "fixed air" and showed that it could be made from limestone (calcium carbonate). Black also made a contribution to physics, developing the concept of latent heat (the heat needed to change the state of a solid to that of a liquid, or of a liquid to a gas).

Another scientist who studied gases at about this time was the British chemist Henry Cavendish (1731–1810). In 1766, he discovered hydrogen, and in 1781, he showed that air consists mainly of a mixture of nitrogen and oxygen. Two years later he confirmed that the atmosphere—sampled at various locations—always has the same composition.

Industrial chemicals

By the turn of the 1700s, chemistry was applied more to industrial processes. Many of these centered on the textile industry, which used a great deal of soap and required a reliable method of bleaching cloth. A key substance for soap and glass making is soda (sodium carbonate). In about 1780, the French government offered a substantial prize to anybody who could invent a process for making it cheaply. Nicolas Leblanc (1742–1806) devised a method of making soda from brine (salt solution) and carbon dioxide, but he never received his prize.

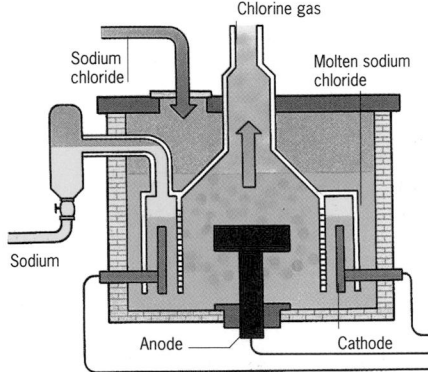

Chlorine gas

Sodium chloride

Molten sodium chloride

Sodium

Anode   Cathode

The Solvay process for manufacturing sodium carbonate.

Two years later, another French chemist, Claude Berthollet (1748–1822), produced a successful bleach called *eau de Javel*, made by dissolving chlorine in water or a dilute alkali. This was used throughout the textile industry until it was superseded by bleaching powder, invented by Scottish chemist Charles Tennant (1768–1838) in 1799.

Common chemicals

Many chemicals have common names. This table lists some of them, with their chemical names and formulae.

Substance	Chemical	Formula
Baking soda	Sodium hydrogen carbonate	$NaHCO_3$
Blue vitriol	Copper(II) sulfate	$CuSO_4$
Blackboard chalk	Calcium sulfate	$CaSO_3$
Caustic soda	Sodium hydroxide	$NaOH$
Common salt	Sodium chloride	$NaCl$
Epsom salts	Magnesium sulfate	$MgSO_4$
Glauber's salt	Sodium sulfate	Na_2SO_4
Lime	Calcium oxide	CaO
Magnesia	Magnesium oxide	MgO
Mineral chalk	Calcium carbonate	$CaCO_3$
Sal soda	Sodium carbonate	Na_2CO_3
Saltpeter	Potassium nitrate	KNO_3
Smelling salts	Ammonium carbonate	$(NH_4)_2CO_3$
Vinegar	Ethanoic acid	C_2H_5COOH

Combustion

Combustion puzzled chemists for many years. In 1669, Johann Becher (1635–82) suggested that all combustibles contain a substance, later called phlogiston, that was released when they burned. A metal, for example, was considered to be made up of a powdery calx and phlogiston. When the metal was strongly heated, the phlogiston was set free and the calx remained. When heated with charcoal, the calx absorbed phlogiston released by the burning charcoal and turned back into a metal.

The matter was finally sorted out by the French chemist Antoine Lavoisier, who carried out a series of experiments in the late 1700s and disproved the phlogiston hypothesis once and for all. His careful weighings proved that metals (and other substances) increased in mass after burning. He went on to show that during combustion a metal combines with oxygen (from the air) to form a calx, which he properly called an oxide.

Atomic theory

John Dalton was a British scientist whose interests spanned natural history, medicine, meteorology, and chemistry. He studied various mixtures of gases, formulating Dalton's law of partial pressures. His greatest contribution to science, however, was to propose that all elements are made up of indivisible atoms and that atoms combine to form chemical compounds. He devised a set of symbols for the elements and showed that these symbols could be combined to represent substances containing them.

Timeline

1781 Henry Cavendish determines the composition of air (Composition of air, *p.408, left*). Antoine Lavoisier proposes the law of conservation of mass.

1782 Franz Joseph Müller von Reichenstein discovers the metal tellurium (later named by Klaproth).

1783 Henry Cavendish combines hydrogen and oxygen to form water, confirming its composition. Don Fausto and Don Juan d'Elhuyar discover the heavy metal tungsten. Carl Scheele discovers glycerine (glycerol), an organic compound that is partly an alcohol and partly a sugar. Nicolas Leblanc invents a process for manufacturing sodium carbonate (soda), an important ingredient in glassmaking (Industrial chemicals, *left*).

1784 Carl Scheele discovers citric acid, the acidic component of citrus fruits.

1785 Claude Berthollet produces a bleach (Industrial chemicals, *left*).

1789 Antoine Lavoisier correctly explains combustion (Combustion, *left*). Martin Klaproth discovers the metallic elements uranium and zirconium.

1791 William Gregor discovers the metal titanium (named by Klaproth in 1795).

1796 J.T. Lowitz prepares pure ethyl alcohol (ethanol).

1797 Louis Vauquelin discovers the metal chromium.

1798 Louis Vauquelin discovers (but fails to isolate) the light metal beryllium (*see 1828*).

1799 Joseph Proust proposes that the elements in a compound always combine in definite proportions by mass. Charles Tennant invents bleaching powder (Industrial chemicals, *left*).

1800 William Nicholson demonstrates electrolysis of water, showing how an electric current can bring about a chemical reaction.

1801 William Henry proposes his law concerning the solubility of gases. Charles Hatchett discovers the metal niobium (which he calls columbium). Andrès del Rio discovers the metal vanadium, but is persuaded it is a form of chromium (*see 1830*).

1802 Anders Ekeberg discovers the metal tantalum. John Dalton devises the first table of atomic weights (relative atomic masses).

1803 John Dalton proposes his atomic theory that all elements are composed of indivisible atoms (Atomic theory, *left*). Jöns Berzelius and Wilhelm Hisinger discover the metal cerium. Smithson Tennant discovers the hard metals iridium and osmium.

1804 William Wollaston discovers the precious metals palladium and rhodium.

1807 Jöns Berzelius distinguishes between organic and inorganic substances. Humphry Davy isolates the alkali metals potassium and sodium, using electrolysis (*p. 420*).

Timeline

1808 Joseph Gay-Lussac proposes his law of combining volumes of gases. Humphry Davy isolates the five elements barium, boron, calcium, magnesium, and strontium (Element hunter, *right*).

1811 Amadeo Avogadro proposes his hypothesis, later to become Avogadro's law (Gas laws, *p. 400*). Bernard Courtois discovers the heavy nonmetallic element iodine. Jöns Berzelius devises a system of chemical symbols that has remained largely unchanged to this day.

1815 William Prout proposes his hypothesis that all elements have integral atomic weights.

1816 Humphry Davy discovers that platinum is a good catalyst for accelerating chemical reactions.

1817 Friedrich Strohmeyer discovers the toxic metal cadmium. Johan Arfvedson discovers (but fails to isolate) the alkali metal lithium (*see 1818*). Jöns Berzelius discovers the metalloid selenium, now much used in photocells and semiconductors.

1818 Jöns Berzelius isolates the alkali metal lithium. Louis Thénard discovers hydrogen peroxide, a powerful oxidizing agent and bleach.

1819 Pierre Dulong and Alexis Petit formulate their law on the constancy of atomic heat capacities. John Kidd isolates the aromatic organic compound naphthalene (from coal tar). Eilhardt Mitscherlich proposes his law of isomorphism.

1824 Jöns Berzelius isolates the metalloid element silicon (now used as the basis of microprocessor chips) and the metal zirconium.

1825 Michael Faraday isolates the aromatic hydrocarbon benzene (from whale oil), the basic compound of aromatic organic chemistry. Antoine Balard discovers the liquid nonmetallic element bromine.

1826 Henri Dutrochet studies osmosis and proposes the laws governing it. Otto Unverdorben isolates the aromatic organic compound aniline (by distilling indigo), an important base for the manufacture of organic compounds such as dyes and drugs.

1827 Friedrich Wöhler isolates pure aluminum. John Walker invents friction matches.

1828 Friedrich Wöhler isolates the metal beryllium (originally called glucinium) and synthesizes an organic compound from an inorganic one (Organic organization, *right*). Jöns Berzelius discovers the metal thorium, whose oxide was to become important as the incandescent substance in gas mantles.

1829 Johann Döbereiner proposes his law of triads (of elements with similar properties).

1830 Nils Sefström rediscovers (and names) vanadium (*see 1801*).

Element hunter

The British chemist Humphry Davy took up chemistry in 1797. He experimented on himself, testing the effects of breathing various gases (which nearly killed him), and described the anesthetic effect of inhaling nitrous oxide (laughing gas). He became a lecturer at London's Royal Institution in 1801. He proposed that most alkalis and "earths" consist of a metal combined with oxygen, and in 1807, he began using electric current to decompose them. From molten potash (potassium hydroxide) and caustic soda (sodium hydroxide) he extracted the alkali metals potassium and sodium, and he went on to isolate the alkaline earth elements barium, calcium, magnesium, and strontium. In 1815, he investigated fire damp (methane) in coal mines and invented the miner's safety lamp that bears his name. A year later Davy discovered the catalytic properties of platinum.

Early Davy safety lamps.

Organic organization

Before 1828, chemists thought that organic compounds (those of carbon) could be made only by and from living organisms. Then in that year, the German chemist Friedrich Wöhler heated the inorganic compound ammonium cyanate, NH_4CNO, and discovered that he had prepared the organic compound urea (carbamide), $(NH_2)2CO$. This discovery revolutionized thinking about organic chemistry, which from then on began to take on a systematic form.

One large organic group is hydrocarbons, which are compounds of hydrogen and carbon only. The simplest aliphatic hydrocarbons (so called because early ones were extracted from fats) are called alkanes (paraffins), alkenes (olefins), and alkynes (acetylenes). These three form a homologous series, with the general group formulae given by C_nH_{2n+2}, C_nH_n, and C_nH_{2n-2}. The names and individual formulae of the first few members of these series are as follows:

Alkanes

methane	CH_4
ethane	C_2H_6
propane	C_3H_8
butane	C_4H_{10}
pentane	C_5H_{12}
hexane	C_6H_{14}

Alkenes

ethene (ethylene)	C_2H_4
propene (propylene)	C_3H_6
butene (butylene)	C_4H_8
pentene (pentylene)	C_5H_{10}
hexene (hexylene)	C_6H_{12}

Alkynes

ethyne (acetylene)	C_2H_2
propyne (methyl acetylene)	C_3H_4
butyne (ethyl acetylene)	C_4H_6

Ethyne (acetylene), the simplest alkyne, was one of Friedrich Wöhler's many discoveries in organic chemistry.

Contact process

Sulfuric acid is one of the most important industrial chemicals. At one time, the wealth of an industrial nation could be measured in terms of the amount of this acid it consumed. Britain alone produces more than 12,000 tons a day.

Originally, the large-scale manufacture of sulfuric acid used the chamber process, so called because the reaction "vessels" consisted of large lead chambers. Lead was used because it is not corroded by sulfuric acid, being protected early in the acid-making process by the development of a layer of insoluble lead sulfate. The chamber process involved reactions between sulfur dioxide, air, and nitrogen oxides.

In 1831, P. Philips devised a new method of manufacturing sulfuric acid called the contact process (because the reacting gases were held in contact with a catalyst). Sulfur dioxide (SO_2) is made by roasting sulfur or pyrites (an iron sulfide mineral) in dry air. Then, with a catalyst of vanadium pentoxide (V_2O_5), the dioxide reacts to form sulfur trioxide (SO_3). This gas is dissolved in concentrated sulfuric acid to form oleum ($H_2S_2O_7$), which is carefully reacted with water to form sulfuric acid (H_2SO_4).

The contact process for manufacturing sulfuric acid.

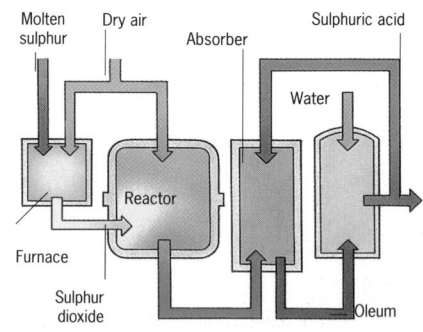

Allotropes

Some elements exist in different forms with markedly different physical properties (although their chemical properties may be similar). An example is the element carbon, which exists in two familiar forms—called allotropes—graphite and diamond. Graphite is a soft black substance used as a lubricant and in the "lead" of pencils. Diamond is crystalline and the hardest known natural substance.

The difference in appearance and properties is due to the arrangement of the carbon atoms in each allotrope. In graphite, the atoms form planes of joined hexagonal rings. The planes easily slide over each other, giving graphite its lubricant properties. In diamond, on the other hand, the atoms are bonded to each other tetrahedrally to form huge macromolecular crystals. Cutting a diamond involves breaking millions of chemical bonds,

which is why diamond is so hard. A third class of carbon allotropes, called fullerenes, has been discovered recently.

Other elements that form allotropes include oxygen, phosphorus, and tin. Oxygen's allotropes are ordinary gaseous oxygen (O_2), with two atoms in each molecule, and the triatomic gas ozone (O_3). Ozone occurs in the upper atmosphere, where it filters out harmful ultraviolet radiation from the sun.

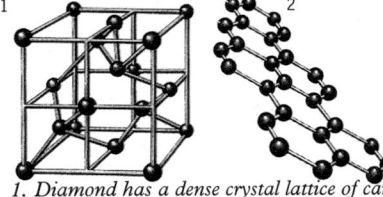

1. Diamond has a dense crystal lattice of carbon atoms. 2. In graphite, the carbon atoms are arranged in sheets.

Chemical elements

Name	Symbol	At. no.	R.a.m.	Name	Symbol	At. no.	R.a.m.
actinium	Ac	89	(227)	mercury	Hg	80	200.59
aluminum	Al	13	26.9815	molybdenum	Mo	42	95.94
americium	Am	95	(243)	neodymium	Nd	60	144.24
antimony	Sb	51	121.75	neon	Ne	10	20.179
argon	Ar	18	39.948	neptunium	Np	93	(237)
arsenic	As	33	74.9216	nickel	Ni	28	58.71
astatine	At	85	(210)	niobium	Nb	41	92.9064
barium	Ba	56	137.34	nitrogen	N	7	14.0067
berkelium	Bk	97	(247)	nobelium	No	102	(255)
beryllium	Be	4	9.0122	osmium	Os	76	190.2
bismuth	Bi	83	208.9806	oxygen	O	8	15.9994
boron	B	5	10.81	palladium	Pd	46	106.4
bromine	Br	35	79.904	phosphorus	P	15	30.9738
cadmium	Cd	48	112.40	platinum	Pt	78	195.09
calcium	Ca	20	40.08	plutonium	Pu	94	(244)
californium	Cf	98	(251)	polonium	Po	84	(209)
carbon	C	6	12.001	potassium	K	19	39.102
cerium	Ce	58	140.12	praseodymium	Pr	59	140.9077
cesium	Cs	55	132.9055	promethium	Pm	61	(145)
chlorine	Cl	17	35.453	protactinium	Pa	91	231.0359
chromium	Cr	24	51.996	radium	Ra	88	226.0254
cobalt	Co	27	58.9332	radon	Rn	86	(222)
copper	Cu	29	63.546	rhenium	Re	75	186.20
curium	Cm	96	(247)	rhodium	Rh	45	102.9055
dysprosium	Dy	66	162.50	rubidium	Rb	37	85.4678
einsteinium	Es	99	(254)	ruthenium	Ru	44	101.07
erbium	Er	68	167.26	rutherfordium	Rf	104	-
europium	Eu	63	151.96	samarium	Sm	62	150.35
fermium	Fm	100	(257)	scandium	Sc	21	44.9559
fluorine	F	9	18.9984	selenium	Se	34	78.96
francium	Fr	87	(223)	silicon	Si	14	28.086
gadolinium	Gd	64	157.25	silver	Ag	47	107.868
gallium	Ga	31	69.72	sodium	Na	11	22.9898
germanium	Ge	32	72.59	strontium	Sr	38	87.62
gold	Au	79	196.9665	sulfur	S	16	32.06
hafnium	Hf	72	178.49	tantalum	Ta	73	180.9479
hahnium	Ha	105	-	technetium	Tc	43	(99)
helium	He	2	4.0026	tellurium	Te	52	127.60
holmium	Ho	67	164.9303	terbium	Tb	65	158.9254
hydrogen	H	1	1.0080	thallium	Tl	81	204.39
indium	In	49	114.82	thorium	Th	90	232.0381
iodine	I	53	126.904	thulium	Tm	69	168.9342
iridium	Ir	77	192.22	tin	Sn	50	118.69
iron	Fe	26	55.847	titanium	Ti	22	47.90
krypton	Kr	36	83.80	tungsten	W	74	183.85
lanthanum	La	57	138.9055	uranium	U	92	238.029
lawrencium	Lr	103	(257)	vanadium	V	23	50.9414
lead	Pb	82	207.19	xenon	Xe	54	131.3
lithium	Li	3	6.941	ytterbium	Yb	70	173.04
lutetium	Lu	71	174.97	yttrium	Y	39	88.9059
magnesium	Mg	12	24.305	zinc	Zn	30	65.38
manganese	Mn	25	54.9380	zirconium	Zr	40	91.22
mendelevium	Md	101	(258)				

* Numbers in parentheses are the masses of the most stable isotope of a radioactive element.

Timeline

1831 P. Philips invents the contact process for manufacturing sulfuric acid (Contact process, *p. 410*). Justus von Liebig and Samuel Guthrie independently discover chloroform (chloromethane).

1833 Michael Faraday formulates the laws of electrolysis.

1834 Friedlieb Runge discovers carbolic acid (phenol), later (1865) used by Joseph Lister to pioneer antiseptic surgery. Justus von Liebig makes melamine, later used in thermosetting plastics (Plastics, *p. 417*).

1835 Jean Dumas and Eugène Péligot make methyl alcohol (methanol), the simplest alcohol.

1836 William Gossage devises an improved process for manufacturing an alkali (sodium carbonate). Edmund Davy prepares acetylene gas (from potassium carbide and water).

1837 Charles Gerhardt discovers quinoline, a heterocyclic compound (having a ring containing atoms other than carbon).

1838 Victor Regnault produces P.V.C. (polyvinyl chloride), which later becomes important in the production of plastics (Plastics, *p. 417*).

1839 J. Simon produces polystyrene, the first synthetic polymer.

1840 Germain Hess postulates his law of constant heat summation in a reaction. Christian Schönbein discovers ozone, an allotrope of oxygen present in the upper atmosphere and important in the blocking of harmful ultraviolet radiation (Allotropes, *left*).

1841 Jöns Berzelius discovers allotropy of carbon (Allotropes, *left*).

1843 Alexander Parkes patents a process for the vulcanization of rubber by cooling latex (Rubber, *p. 414*).

1844 Charles Goodyear invents the sulfur process for the vulcanization of rubber (Rubber, *p. 414*).

1845 Anton von Schrötter discovers red phosphorus and uses it to develop the safety match. Adolphe Kolbe synthesizes acetic acid (ethanoic acid) from inorganic reactants.

1846 Ascanio Sobrero prepares the high explosive nitroglycerine (glyceryl trinitrate). Christian Schönbein prepares the propellant explosive guncotton (nitrocellulose/cellulose trinitrate).

1848 Louis Pasteur shows that optical activity is a property of asymmetrical molecules and discovers isomerism (of tartaric acid).

1850 Thomas Graham discovers dialysis and classifies substances into crystalloids and colloids. Rubber-based adhesives are introduced.

1852 Edward Frankland proposes his theory of valence to explain the combining power of various chemical elements. Abraham Gesner discovers kerosene (paraffin).

Timeline

1855 Henry Bessemer invents his converter for the manufacture of steel. Robert Bunsen invents the Bunsen burner to heat substances to incandescence so that their spectra can be studied (Spectral evidence, *right*). Henri Sainte-Claire Deville devises a process for the large-scale production of aluminum. Alexander Parkes invents celluloid (Celluloid, *p. 413*). Charles Wurtz devises his synthesis (for making long-chain hydrocarbons).

1856 William Perkin produces the first aniline dye (Chemical colors, *right*).

1858 Fredrich Kekulé Von Stradonitz proposes his theory of carbon bonding. Stanislao Cannizaro introduces the concept of the molecule and distinguishes between atomic and molecular weights.

1860 Robert Bunsen discovers the alkali metal cesium (Spectral evidence, *right*).

1861 Robert Bunsen and Gustav Kirchhoff discover the alkali metal rubidium (Spectral evidence, *right*). William Crookes discovers thallium (Spectral evidence, *right*). Ernest Solvay devises the ammonia-soda process for manufacturing sodium carbonate (Industrial chemicals, *p. 409*).

1862 Anders Angström discovers hydrogen in the sun's spectrum.

1863 Johann von Baeyer makes the first barbiturates.

1864 Cato Guldberg and Peter Waage postulate the law of mass action. John Newlands proposes his law of octaves (Patterns and periods, *p. 413*). William Siemens and Pierre Martin develop the open-hearth process for the manufacture of steel.

1865 Friedrich Kekulé Von Stradonitz describes the hexagonal cyclic structure of benzene. Jean Louvain produces the first modern table of atomic weights.

1867 Alfred Nobel invents dynamite.

1868 Pierre Janssen and Joseph Lockyer discover helium in the sun's spectrum. Henry Deacon invents a process for making chlorine (by catalytic oxidation of hydrogen chloride).

1869 Dmitri Mendeleyev publishes his Periodic Table (Patterns and periods, *p. 413*).

1870 Julius Lothar Meyer publishes his periodic classification (of elements).

1873 Josiah Gibbs proposes a theory of chemical thermodynamics.

1874 Jacobus Van't Hoff proposes the tetrahedral structure of carbon bonds in organic compounds.

1875 Paul Lecoq de Boisbaudran discovers the light metal gallium.

1876 Josiah Gibbs devises the phase rule, relating the phases, components, and degrees of freedom of a chemical system.

1877 Charles Friedel and James Crafts discover a synthesis reaction (using a catalyst to join organic ring compounds).

Spectral evidence

One of the most familiar pieces of chemical apparatus is the Bunsen burner, routinely used to heat test tubes and other containers. But when it was invented in 1855 by the German chemist Robert Bunsen (1811–99), he was not trying to provide a general heat source. The burner, which can produce an extremely hot flame by mixing air with the incoming fuel gas, is designed to heat substances to incandescence. When elements get this hot, they emit light of a characteristic color, which can be used to identify them in an analytical procedure. For example, sodium compounds produce an intense yellow flame, whereas strontium compounds give a bright red one.

In 1859, Bunsen, with Gustav Kirchhoff, took the technique a stage further and looked at hot flames with a spectroscope. This reveals the presence of elements as

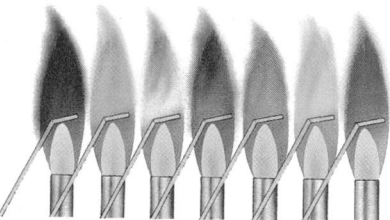
Elements are identified by color.

an emission spectrum consisting of one or more colored lines. Within a couple of years the two scientists found new lines and correctly deduced that they had found new elements. A prominent blue line found in 1860 revealed the presence of the alkali metal cesium, and in 1861, rubidium showed up as a new red spectral line. In Britain, William Crookes (1832–1919) had adopted Bunsen's technique and, also in 1861, discovered thallium by a light-green line in the spectrum.

Later, in 1868, British astronomer Joseph Lockyer (1836–1920) gave the name helium to a new line discovered in the spectrum of the sun, 27 years before William Ramsay discovered the new element on earth. Spectral analysis had thus become a powerful tool, and not only for chemists. Astronomers today can turn their spectroscopes toward far more distant stellar objects, learning much about their chemical composition and physical properties from spectral analysis.

Chemical colors

Until the mid-1800s, the production of dyes, mostly from plants, was a long-established industry worldwide. Indigo, madder, and henna, for example, were produced in large quantities. Then in 1856, an 18-year-old British chemist named William Perkin (1838–1907),

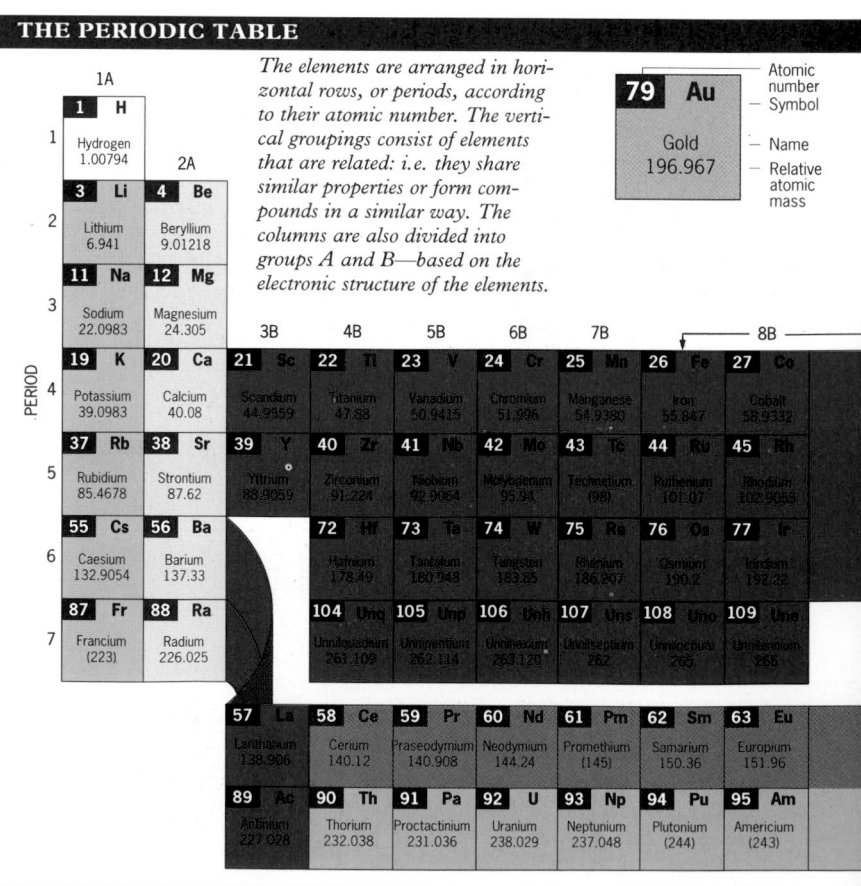

THE PERIODIC TABLE

The elements are arranged in horizontal rows, or periods, according to their atomic number. The vertical groupings consist of elements that are related: i.e. they share similar properties or form compounds in a similar way. The columns are also divided into groups A and B—based on the electronic structure of the elements.

79	Au
Gold	196.967

Atomic number
Symbol
Name
Relative atomic mass

Mauvine was the first aniline dye.

while trying to synthesize the antimalarial drug quinine from aniline, accidentally discovered a whole new class of synthetic dyes. The first was called mauvine, after its color, and soon many other aniline dyes followed, establishing a whole new chemical industry. The indigo trade collapsed, and the British Parliament had to enact special legislation to enable Perkin, still under 21, to patent his discovery.

Celluloid

The traditional material for making piano keys—and billiard balls—is ivory. Even in the 1850s, it was a rare commodity. Then, in 1855, British chemist Alexander Parkes (1813–90) invented a new material. It was made from a mixture of cellulose trinitrate (nitrocellu-

lose) and camphor, and Parkes called it celluloid. It was highly inflammable; in fact, in 1846 Christian Schönbein (1799–1868) had first prepared nitrocellulose for use as a propellant explosive for rifle cartridges. Parkes' material was the first plastic, and it could be melted (carefully) and molded or extruded to make a variety of useful articles, including the transparent plastic sheeting that became the base of the first photographic film.

Patterns and periods

Throughout the 1800s, chemists discovered new elements. They measured their physical properties, particularly atomic weights (now called relative atomic masses), and carried out various experiments

Dmitri Mendeleyev was the first to arrange all known chemical elements in tabular form.

Periodic Table

				Ti = 50	Th = 118?	? = 180
				V = 51	Zr = 90	Ta = 182
				Cr = 52	Nb = 94	W = 186
				Mn = 55	Mo = 96	Pt = 197
				Fe = 56	Rh = 104,4	
				Ni=Co=59C	Bu = 104,4	Ir = 198
H = 1	Be = 9,4	Mg = 24	Cu = 63,4	Pl = 106,6	Os = 199	
	B = 11	Al = 27,4	Zn = 65,2	Ag = 108	Hg = 200	
	C = 12	Si = 28	? = 68	Cd = 112		
	N = 14	P = 31	? = 72	Ur = 116	Au = 197?	
	O = 16	S = 32	As = 75	Sn = 118		
	F = 19	Cl = 35,5	Se = 79,4	Sb = 122	Bi = 210	
Li = 7	Na = 23	K = 39	Br = 80	Te = 128?		
		Ca = 40	Rb = 85,4	I = 127		
		? = 45	Sr = 87,6	Cs = 133	Tl = 204	
		?Er= 56	Ce = 92	Ba = 137	Pb = 207	
		?Yt= 60	La = 94			
		?In = 75,6	Di = 95			

Eka-silicon	Es
(as predicted by Mendeleyev in 1871)	
Atomic weight	72
Atomic volume	13
Specific gravity	5.5
Dirty gray element forming white oxide	EsO_2

Germanium	Ge
(as discovered by Winkler in 1886)	
Atomic weight	72.3
Atomic volume	13.2
Specific gravity	5.47
Grayish-white element forming white oxide	GeO_2

to determine their chemical properties. Gradually they noticed groups of elements with similar properties. For example, in 1864 in Britain, John Newlands (1837–98) noticed that if the elements were listed in order of ascending atomic weight, every eighth element resembled the other elements in the eight places before or after it.

Then in 1869, Russian chemist Dmitri Mendeleyev (1834–1907) plotted all the known elements in the form of a table, in which (as revised) there was a gradation in properties across the horizontal periods and marked chemical similarity among elements that occupied the same vertical group. Mendeleyev even had the courage to leave gaps to make the table work and to predict that the gaps represented "missing" elements that had yet to be discovered. Two of these, gallium and germanium (Mendeleycv had called them eka-aluminum and eka-silicon), were discovered within a few years and turned out to have almost exactly the properties he had predicted.

The modern Periodic Table is plotted in terms of increasing atomic number (not atomic weight) because we now know that the gradation in chemical properties is due to the gradual filling of electron shells around the atoms' nuclei. A few places before the end of the table is the element mendelevium, after the scientist who devised the system.

Periodic Table chart

Alkali metals	Actinide series
Alkaline earth metals	Other metals
Transition metals	Nonmetals
Lanthanide metals	Noble gases

		3A	4A	5A	6A	7A	8A
							2 He Helium 4.00260
		5 B Boron 10.81	**6 C** Carbon 12.011	**7 N** Nitrogen 14.0067	**8 O** Oxygen 15.9994	**9 F** Fluorine 18.9984	**10 Ne** Neon 20.179
1B	**2B**	**13 Al** Aluminium 26.9815	**14 Si** Silicon 28.0855	**15 P** Phosphorous 30.9738	**16 S** Sulphur 32.06	**17 Cl** Chlorine 35.453	**18 Ar** Argon 39.948
28 Ni Nickel 58.69	**29 Cu** Copper 63.546	**30 Zn** Zinc 65.39	**31 Ga** Gallium 69.72	**32 Ge** Germanium 72.59	**33 As** Arsenic 74.9216	**34 Se** Selenium 78.96	**35 Br** Bromine 79.904	**36 Kr** Krypton 83.80
46 Pd Palladium 106.42	**47 Ag** Silver 107.868	**48 Cd** Cadmium 112.41	**49 In** Indium 114.82	**50 Sn** Tin 118.71	**51 Sb** Antimony 121.75	**52 Te** Tellurium 127.60	**53 I** Iodine 126.905	**54 Xe** Xenon 131.29
78 Pt Platinum 195.08	**79 Au** Gold 196.967	**80 Hg** Mercury 200.59	**81 Ti** Thallium 204.383	**82 Pb** Lead 207.2	**83 Bi** Bismuth 208.980	**84 Po** Polonium (209)	**85 At** Astatine (210)	**86 Rn** Radon (222)

64 Gd Gadolinium 157.25	**65 Tb** Terbium 158.925	**66 Dy** Dysprosium 162.50	**67 Ho** Holmium 164.9304	**68 Er** Erbium 167.26	**69 Tm** Thulium 168.934	**70 Yb** Ytterbium 173.04	**71 Lu** Lutetium 174.967
96 Cm Curium (247)	**97 Bk** Berkelium (247)	**98 Cf** Californium (251)	**99 Es** Eisneinium (252)	**100 Fm** Fermium (257)	**101 Md** Mendelevium (257)	**102 No** Nobelium (259)	**103 Lr** Lawrencium (260)

Timeline

1883 Johann Kjeldhal devises a method of analyzing nitrogen in organic compounds.

1884 Henry le Chatelier proposes his principle (about chemical equilibria). Svante Arrhenius proposes his theory concerning the dissociation of aqueous electrolytes into ions. Hilaire Chardonnet invents rayon (Artificial silk, *right*). William Tilden prepares synthetic rubber (Rubber, *right*).

1886 Henri Moissan isolates the reactive, toxic element fluorine (*see 1771*). Clemens Winkler discovers the semimetallic element germanium, later much used in semiconductors. Charles Hall and Paul Héroult independently devise an electrolytic process for the commercial extraction of aluminum (Chemical coincidences, *right*).

1889 Frederick Abel and James Dewar invent cordite (a propellant explosive). Vladimir Markovnikov makes ring compounds that have carbon rings with seven atoms.

1891 Edward Acheson devises a method of manufacturing the abrasive carborundum (silicon carbide).

1892 Edward Bevan and Charles Cross devise the viscose process (Artificial silk, *right*).

1894 William Ramsay and Lord Rayleigh discover the inert gas argon (Inert gases, *p. 415*). Hermann Frasch devises his process for extracting sulfur (Sulfur mining, *p. 415*). Hamilton Castner and Carl Kellner independently devise an electrolytic method of extracting sodium from brine.

1895 William Ramsay and William Crookes discover helium (Inert gases, *p. 415*).

1897 Paul Sabatier uses catalysts to hydrogenate unsaturated organic compounds.

1898 William Ramsay and Morris Travers discover the inert gases krypton, neon, and xenon (Inert gases, *p. 415*). Marie Curie discovers radium and polonium (Radioactive elements, *p. 415*).

1899 André Debierne discovers actinium (Radioactive elements, *p. 415*).

1900 Ernst Dorn discovers radon (Radioactive elements, *p. 415*). Moses Gomberg prepares the first organic free radical.

1901 Victor Grignard introduces organic magnesium halides (known as Grignard reagents) to organic synthesis.

1902 William Pope makes optically active inorganic compounds. Wilhelm Ostwald invents a process for making nitric acid from ammonia (by catalytic oxidation).

1904 Frederick Kipping discovers silicones (polymers containing no carbon). Kristian Birkland and Samuel Eyde begin commercial fixation of nitrogen using high-voltage sparks (Acid from air, *p. 415*).

1906 Mikhail Tswett develops paper chromatography.

Artificial silk

After Alexander Parkes' invention of celluloid (celluloid, *p. 413*), the next attempt by chemists to make a plastic also involved modified cellulose. This time the incentive was to find a substitute for silk, an expensive fabric dependent on moth caterpillars for its production. The first successful product was rayon, invented in 1884 by the French chemist Hilaire Chardonnet (1839–1924).

There are currently two processes for making rayon. In the acetate process, devised by Chardonnet, cellulose from cotton or wood pulp is first converted to cellulose ethanoate (acetate) and dissolved in a solvent. The sticky solution is forced into the air through fine nozzles, called spinnerets, where the solvent evaporates to leave filaments of acetate rayon. In the viscose process, developed in 1892 by Edward Bevan (1856–1921) and Charles Cross (1855–1935), the cellulose is dissolved in carbon disulfide and sodium hydroxide to make a viscous solution of cellulose xanthate. This is forced through spinnerets into a bath of sulfuric acid, which decomposes the xanthate to leave filaments of cellulose, or viscose rayon.

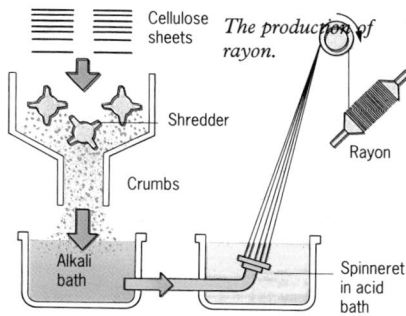

Cellulose sheets / Shredder / Crumbs / Alkali bath / Spinneret in acid bath / Rayon

The production of rayon.

Rubber

Cellulose, the starting material for rayon (*above*), is a natural polymer. Another such useful polymer is rubber, now of great importance for making vehicle tires.

Natural rubber—renowned for its elastic properties—is derived from the sap of the rubber tree, which is tapped off and allowed to harden before it is processed. The chemical structure of rubber is based on the organic compound isoprene (2-methylbuta-1,3-diene), a 5-carbon molecule with two double bonds. In 1884, British organic chemist William Tilden (1842–1926) succeeded in synthesizing isoprene, from which artificial rubber could be made. Subsequently, several other monomers were used to make rubber, such as butadiene and chlorobutadiene (which produces the chemical-resistant neoprene).

Like natural rubber, synthetic rubbers are soft and elastic with good waterproofing and insulating properties but little wear resistance. Natural rubber was first modified in 1844 by U.S. inventor Charles Goodyear (1800–60), who heated natural rubber with sulfur in a process that became known as vulcanizing. Chemically, the process forges sulfur bridges between the long polymer molecules of rubber, reducing its elasticity while greatly increasing its hardness. Synthetic rubbers are good imitations of the natural material, and they too can be vulcanized using sulfur or sulfur compounds to improve their durability.

Chemical coincidences

Aluminum was discovered in 1827 by German chemist Friedrich Wöhler. The new metal proved to be light, fairly resistant to corrosion, and, in its alloys, extremely strong for its weight. But it was so difficult to produce from its compounds that it remained an expensive chemical curiosity.

Then in 1886, Charles Hall in the United States and, working independently, Paul Héroult in France devised a feasible commercial method of extracting aluminum. Both chemists were born in 1863, and both came up with the same solution to the problem. Bauxite, a mineral form of aluminum oxide, is purified and mixed with cryolite (aluminum fluoride), and the mixture is then heated in carbon-lined cells until it melts; the fluoride lowers the melting point, but even so temperatures of 1562°F (850°C) are needed. Graphite anodes are lowered into the cell, and a large direct electric current is passed through the molten electrolyte. Molten aluminum collects in the bottom of the cell from which it can be tapped off.

Commercial method of extracting aluminum.

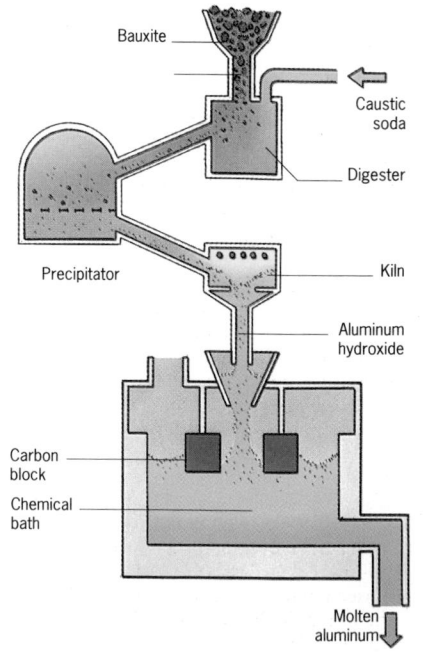

Bauxite / Caustic soda / Digester / Precipitator / Kiln / Aluminum hydroxide / Carbon block / Chemical bath / Molten aluminum

The final coincidence occurred in 1914, when both inventors died. This method of aluminum production is named the Hall-Héroult process after both men.

Inert gases

Toward the end of the 1800s, the Periodic Table (*p. 412-13*) was looking fairly complete, with eight groups of elements in ordered array. Then came a series of discoveries that created a whole new group of elements. In 1894, William Ramsay and Lord Rayleigh discovered the gas argon (comprising nearly 1 percent of air); in 1895, Ramsay and William Crookes discovered helium (previously observed in the spectrum of the sun); in 1898, Ramsay and Morris Travers (1872–1961) found another trio of gases in air—krypton, neon, and xenon; finally, in 1900, Ernst Dorn completed the set with his discovery of the gas radon.

The six new elements were assigned to Group 0, tacked on the end of the Periodic Table. None of the discoverers could persuade any of the gases to react chemically with anything, and so they were called noble gases. Today the term rare or inert gases is preferred because a few compounds of a couple of them have been prepared.

Radioactive elements

While the British chemists were hunting down the inert gases (*above*), in France, Marie Curie (1867–1934) and her husband Pierre (1859–1906) were seeking new radioactive elements in the uranium ore pitchblende. In 1898, they isolated radium and polonium (named after Mme. Curie's native Poland). A year later, André Debierne (1874–1949) discovered another radioactive element, actinium, and in 1900, Ernst Dorn (1848–1916) discovered radon—a gaseous decay product of radium and the last of the inert gases.

Sulfur mining

With the growth of the chemical industry, sulfuric acid became an increasingly important substance (Contact process, *p. 410*). The starting material for its manufacture is sulfur, which as rock sulfur can be mined near the surface in certain parts of the world. It was known that large deposits of sulfur also exist at deeper levels; in particular in Texas and Louisiana not far from the important oil-bearing strata of these states. The problem was how to get the sulfur out. The solution was provided by German-born U.S. chemist Hermann Frasch (1851–1914), who went after sulfur in much the same way that others prospected for oil.

The start of the Frasch process involves drilling a hole down to the sulfur beds. Three concentric pipes are lowered down the borehole. Superheated steam passed down the outermost pipe melts the sulfur.

Compressed air passed down the central pipe forms a froth, and pressure pushes it up the third pipe to the surface, where it runs into molds and hardens.

The Frasch process for extracting sulfur.

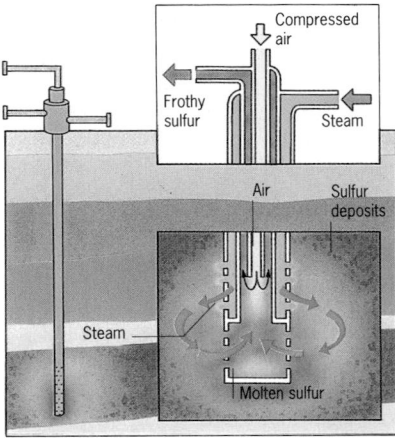

Acid from air

Second only to sulfuric acid as an industrial chemical is nitric acid. At the beginning of the 1900s, chemists turned their attention to finding commercial methods of production. The most attractive starting material is nitrogen—freely available in air but renowned for its reluctance to react chemically. One solution was to make ammonia (Ammonia from air and water, *p. 416*) first, but in Norway scientists were developing another solution.

Chemists had noticed that air contains nitrogen oxides after a thunderstorm. The lightning flash—an electrical discharge—provides enough energy to oxidize nitrogen in the air. In 1904, using readily available and cheap hydroelectricity, Norwegian chemists Kristian Birkeland (1867–1913) and Samuel Eyde (1866–1940) passed air through a high-voltage electric arc. The nitrogen oxide formed was dissolved in water to make nitric acid. The acid was then used to make fertilizers and explosives.

The production of TNT uses an acid mixture.

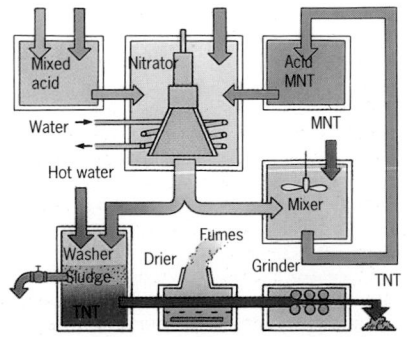

Timeline

1934 Paul Harteck and Mark Oliphant isolate the hydrogen isotope tritium. Arnold Beckman makes the first pH meter (for measuring the acidity of solutions).

1935 Wallace Carothers invents nylon.

1937 Emilo Segrè makes the radioactive element technetium (originally masurium), the first artificial element. Robert Thomas and William Sparks develop butyl rubber.

1939 Marguerite Perey discovers the radioactive alkali metal francium. Paul Müller synthesizes DDT for use as an insecticide.

1940 Emilio Segrè *et al.* discover the radioactive element astatine. Philip Abelson and Edwin McMillan make neptunium, the first synthetic element heavier than uranium. Martin Kamen and S. Ruben discover the carbon 14 radioisotope.

1941 Glenn Seaborg and Edwin McMillan synthesize plutonium.

1944 Glenn Seaborg *et al.* discover the transuranium elements americium and curium. Archer Martin and Richard Synge develop paper chromatography.

1949 Dorothy Hodgkin determines the structure of penicillin (using an electronic computer).

1950 Glenn Seaborg *et al.* discover the transuranium element californium.

1952 E. Fischer determines the "sandwich" structure of ferrocene. Glenn Seaborg *et al.* discover the transuranium element einsteinium.

1953 Karl Ziegler introduces a catalyst that combines monomers into polymers.

1954 Giulio Natta develops polypropylene. Marc Grégoir invents the nonstick frying pan (using P.T.F.E., or Teflon).

1955 Percy Bridgman produces the first synthetic diamonds.

1958 The Certas company introduces epoxy resin adhesives.

1961 Albert Ghiorso *et al.* synthesize the transuranium element lawrencium.

1962 Neil Bartlett makes the first compound of an inert gas (xenon platinum hexafluoride).

1964 The Reeves company introduces acrylic paints.

1977 Alan Heeger and Alan MacDiarmid develop electrically conductive plastics.

1980 M.T.B.E. (methyl-tert-butyl ether) is introduced as a lead-free antiknock additive for gasoline.

1985 Harold Kroto and David Walton discover a third class of carbon allotropes, called fullerenes, which are almost spherical molecules and are also known as buckminsterfullerenes.

1987 Ovchinnikov *et al.* develop magnetic polymers.

1989 G. Winter produces biodegradable pesticides (from antibodies).

1992 Rebek *et al.* develop synthetic self-replicating molecules that mimic several characteristics of living systems.

Ammonia from air and water

By the early 1900s, several European nations, including Germany, had become aware of their dependence on mineral resources from elsewhere in the world. Nitric acid, needed to manufacture artificial fertilizers and explosives, was made from potassium or sodium nitrates, known as niter or saltpeter, much of which was imported from South America (and called Chile saltpeter). If Germany's ports were blockaded in time of war, how could it get its essential nitrates? Nitric acid can also be made fairly easily from ammonia, but it requires plentiful supplies of ammonia. In 1907, however, German chemist Fritz Haber developed a process for manufacturing ammonia from nitrogen gas (obtained from liquid air) and hydrogen (from water gas, a mixture of hydrogen and carbon monoxide made by passing steam over red-hot coke).

The chemical reaction to synthesize ammonia is deceptively simple on paper:

$$N_2 + 3H_2 \longrightarrow 2NH_3$$

To make the reaction go in the required direction, however, Haber had to use a high temperature—about 850°F (450°C), high pressure (about 250 atmospheres), and a catalyst, usually iron with metal oxide promoters. The process is still used today, except that synthesis gas (made by reforming natural gas) has replaced water gas as the source of hydrogen.

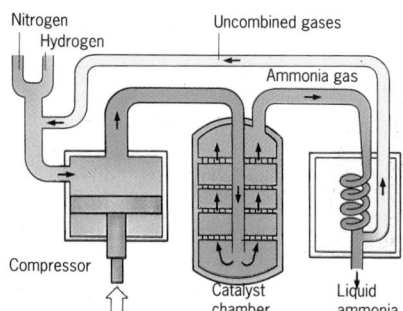

The Haber process for making ammonia.

Chemical bonding

One spin-off of the emerging knowledge about the structure of atoms and molecules was a greater understanding of the nature of chemical bonding—the forces that hold atoms together in a molecule. Once again, the key player in this phenomenon is the electron—the tiny, negatively charged subatomic particle that occupies shells surrounding an atom's positively charged nucleus.

Chemists now recognize three chief types of chemical bonding. In ionic bonding, as two atoms come together an electron abandons one to take up residence with the other. The result is a pair of ions, and the resulting bond is known as ionic (or electrovalent) bonding. For example, sodium has a single electron in its outer

shell, whereas chlorine has seven electrons in its outer shell. When the two atoms react to form sodium chloride (common salt), an electron moves from sodium to chlorine, creating a sodium ion (Na^+) and a chloride ion (Cl^-). Sodium chloride crystals consist of a lattice of sodium and chloride ions, held together by their electrostatic charges (like charges attract).

Sodium chloride molecules are held together by ionic bonds.

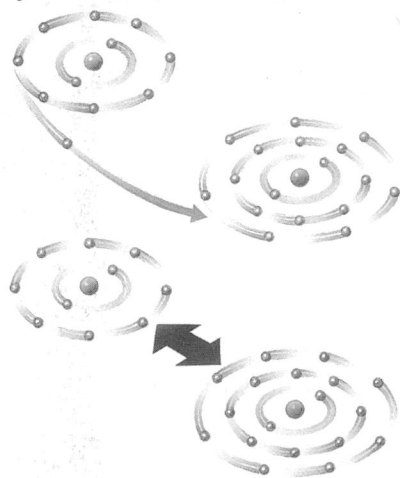

In covalent bonding—as occurs in water, methane, and nearly all other organic compounds—there is no transfer of electrons. Instead, each of the combining atoms contributes one electron to the bond that holds them together. Electrons are therefore shared.

Carbon dioxide molecules are held together by covalent bonds.

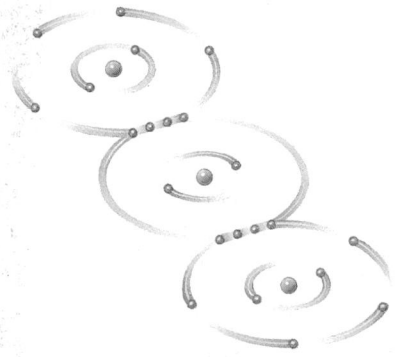

There is a third type of chemical bonding, a special form of covalent bonding in which both bonding electrons are contributed by one of the atoms involved. Called dative—or coordinate—bonding, it occurs most frequently with variable-valence metals when they form complexes (coordination compounds) with groups of ions or organic residues. Nickel carbonyl $[Ni(CO)_4]$ is an example in which the nickel atom contributes eight electrons to form four dative bonds with carbon monoxide molecules.

Plastics

Plastics are polymers, and early attempts at making polymers were based on the imitation of natural ones to produce celluloid (Plastic piano keys, *p. 413*), rayon, and synthetic rubber (Rubber, *p. 414*). Polymers consist of repeating units of one or two simple molecules called monomers. Polymerization makes the monomers join together—which is not always easy—and results in two main types of plastics.

Thermosetting plastics can be molded when they are first formed, after which they go hard and cannot be remelted. The first of this type was Bakelite, invented in 1908 by Belgian-born U.S. chemist Leo Baekeland (1863–1944). While trying to make photographic printing paper, he reacted methanal (formaldehyde) with phenol (carbolic acid) and obtained a resinous substance that hardened on heating. More recent thermosetters include nylon, polycarbonates, urea-formaldehyde, and melamine-formaldehyde plastics.

The second major type of plastic is known as thermoplastic because it can be repeatedly melted on heating. The group includes polyethene (polyethylene), polyvinyl chloride (P.V.C.), polystyrene, polytetrafluoroethene (Teflon), and polymethylmethacrilate (Plexiglas). Many of these plastics are available as solids, sheets, and foams, and they can be extruded or molded to nearly any shape.

A recent development in plastics technology is the production of plastics that conduct electricity. Such materials have revolutionized the electronics industry and have an increasingly wide application elsewhere in manufacturing.

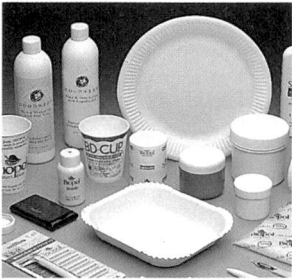

Polycarbonates are heat resistant, do not stain, and are ideal for microwave containers (above).

Toughness and transparency make polycarbonates an ideal material for riot shields (below).

A photocopier (bottom) *contains plastic that conducts electricity in the presence of light.*

Plastics for use in the human body, such as a replacement hip joint (above), *have to be biocompatible so they are not rejected by the human immune system.*

Plastic earphones (above) *can generate an electric field when pressure is applied.*

Plastic limbs (left) *must be light, durable, and easily molded.*

Carbon-fiber reinforced plastic has replaced metal in helicopter rotor blades (below).

PROMINENT PEOPLE

AMPÈRE, André Marie (1775–1836): French mathematician and physicist who laid the foundations of electrodynamics. His name is given to the SI unit of electric current.

APPLETON, Edward Victor (1892–1965): British physicist who investigated radio waves. He discovered an atmospheric layer of electrically charges particles, important in radio communications; he received the 1947 Nobel Prize in Physics.

ARCHIMEDES (*c.* 287–212 B.C.): ancient Greek mathematician and physicist who devised geometric techniques for determining volumes and areas. His inventions include the Archimedean screw, which is still used today for raising water, and his work laid the foundations of mechanics and statics.

ARRHENIUS, Svante (1859–1927): Swedish physical chemist who explained the dissociation of electrolytes in solution. He received the 1903 Nobel Prize in Chemistry.

AVOGADRO, Amedeo (1776–1856): Italian physicist who formulated a hypothesis concerning the properties of equal volumes of gases.

BECQUEREL, Antoine Henri (1852–1908): French physicist who discovered radioactivity. He shared the 1903 Nobel Prize in Physics.

BERZELIUS, Jöns Jakob (1779–1848): Swedish chemist who determined atomic weights and introduced symbols for the chemical elements. He discovered several elements.

BOHR, Niels Henrik (1885–1962): Danish physicist who greatly extended the theory of atomic structure and quantum theory. He received the 1922 Nobel Prize in Physics.

BOLTZMANN, Ludwig Eduard (1844–1906): Austrian physicist who established the kinetic theory of gases and the principle of distribution of gas molecular energies (Boltzmann's law).

BOYLE, Robert (1627–91): Irish physicist and chemist who deduced the inverse square law as it relates to the temperature and pressure of gases (Boyle's law).

CHADWICK, James (1891–1974): British physicist who studied radioactivity and confirmed the existence of the neutron (as postulated by Ernest RUTHERFORD in 1920).

COULOMB, Charles Augustin de (1736–1806): French physicist who experimented with friction and invented the torsion balance for measuring the forces of magnetic and electrostatic attraction. His name is given to the SI unit of electric charge.

CURIE, Marie (1867–1934): Polish-born French physicist who studied radioactivity and discovered radium and polonium. She shared the 1903 Nobel Prize in Physics.

CURIE, Pierre (1859–1906): French physicist and chemist who carried out research into radioactive elements.

DALTON, John (1766–1844): English chemist who formulated a law of partial pressures of gases and devised an atomic theory distinguishing between elements and compounds.

DAVY, Humphry (1778–1829): English chemist who experimented with gases. He first isolated many metals using electrolysis, and devised the miner's safety lamp named after him.

DIRAC, Paul Adrien (1902–84): British mathematical physicist who worked on quantum mechanics and published a mathematical formulation of EINSTEIN'S theory of relativity. He shared the 1933 Nobel Prize in Physics.

DOPPLER, Johann Christian (1803–53): Austrian physicist who in 1842 explained the change in frequency of light and sound waves when there is relative movement between the source of light or sound and the observer.

EINSTEIN, Albert (1879–1955): German-Swiss–born U.S. mathematical physicist who devised the special and general theories of relativity. He also discovered the photoelectric effect and was awarded the 1921 Nobel Prize in Physics.

FAHRENHEIT, Gabriel (1686–1736): German physicist who devised the alcohol-in-glass and later the mercury thermometer.

FARADAY, Michael (1791–1867): English physicist and chemist who discovered electromagnetic induction, the laws of electrolysis, and the rotation of polarized light by a magnetic field. He also discovered benzene.

FERMI, Enrico (1901–54): Italian-born U.S. physicist who first split atomic nuclei. He received the 1938 Nobel Prize in Physics.

FEYNMAN, Richard (1918–88): U.S. physicist who made advances in the field of theoretical quantum electrodynamics. He shared the 1965 Nobel Prize in Physics.

FISCHER, Emil (1852–1919): German chemist who synthesized sugars and various enzymes. His work laid the foundations of biochemistry. He received the 1902 Nobel Prize in Chemistry.

FOUCAULT, Jean Bernard (1819–68): French physicist who determined the speed of light and established that light travels faster in air than in water. He also showed that the earth rotates on its axis.

GALILEI, Galileo (1564–1642): Italian scientist who studied the period of a pendulum and the motion of falling bodies. He developed the telescope, discovered the moons of Jupiter, and propounded the Copernican view of the solar system.

GAUSS, Karl Friedrich (1777–1855): German physicist and mathematician who studied the earth's magnetism and devised a mathematical theory of optics.

GEIGER, Hans Wilhelm (1882–1945): German physicist who investigated beta-ray radioactivity and, with Walther Müller, devised the Geiger counter to measure it.

GIBBS, Josiah (1839–1903): U.S. chemist and theoretical physicist who developed a mathematical approach to thermodynamics, formulating the phase rule.

GRIGNARD, Victor (1871–1935): French chemist who discovered organometallic compounds (Grignard reagents), which became important in organic synthesis. He shared the 1912 Nobel Prize in Chemistry.

HABER, Fritz (1868–1934): German chemist who devised an industrial process for synthesizing ammonia. He also researched into electrochemistry. He received the 1918 Nobel Prize in Chemistry.

HAWORTH, Norman (1883–1950): British organic chemist who first synthesized a vitamin (vitamin C), for which he shared the 1933 Nobel Prize in Chemistry.

HEISENBERG, Werner (1901–76): German theoretical physicist who developed quantum mechanics and the uncertainty principle. He received the 1932 Nobel Prize in Physics.

HELMHOLTZ, Hermann von (1821–94): German physicist who studied fluid dynamics, vibrating systems, spectra, and current flow in electrolytic cells.

HERTZ, Heinrich (1857–94): German physicist who confirmed James Clerk MAXWELL'S predictions of invisible electromagnetic waves (radio waves).

HODGKIN, Dorothy (b. 1910): British biochemist who analyzed complex organic molecules. She received the 1964 Nobel Prize in Chemistry.

HOFMANN, August Wilhelm (1818–92): German chemist who studied the extraction and exploitation of coal tar derivatives, discovering aniline and formaldehyde.

HOOKE, Robert (1635–1703): English physicist and chemist who formulated a law of elasticity and constructed a Gregorian reflecting telescope.

HUYGENS, Christiaan (1629–95): Dutch physicist who made a pendulum clock, discovered polarization and the laws relating to colliding objects, and championed the wave theory of light.

JOULE, James Prescott (1818–89): British physicist who proved experimentally that heat is a form of energy and established the mechanical equivalent of heat (which became the basis of the principle of conservation of energy). His name is given to the SI unit of energy and work.

KELVIN, William Thomson, 1st Lord (1824–1907): Irish-born Scottish physicist who solved important problems in electrostatics and proposed the absolute temperature scale and the second law of thermodynamics. His name is given to the SI unit of temperature.

KEKULÉ, August von (1829–96): German chemist who described the

structure of benzene and explained carbon bonding.

KIRCHHOFF, Gustav Robert (1824–87): German physicist who carried out important research into electricity, heat, optics, and spectroscopy.

LANGMUIR, Irving (1881–1957): U.S. scientist who studied surface chemistry and devised the mercury vapor pump. He received the 1932 Nobel Prize in Chemistry.

LAVOISIER, Antoine (1743–94): French chemist who correctly explained the phenomenon of combustion. He showed that water is a compound consisting of hydrogen and oxygen.

LIEBIG, Justus von (1803–73): German chemist who discovered chloroform and chloral and was a pioneer in the study of agricultural chemistry.

LORENTZ, Hendrik Antoon (1853–1928): Dutch physicist who predicted that near the speed of light an object's length would be slightly less (later part of relativity theory).

MACH, Ernst (1838–1916): Austrian physicist who experimented with projectiles and the flow of gases. He devised a system of speed measurement (Mach numbers).

MARTIN, Archer John (b. 1910): British biochemist who, with Richard Synge, developed paper chromatography. Both men shared the 1952 Nobel Prize in Chemistry.

MAXWELL, James Clerk (1831–79): Scottish physicist who formulated a mathematical theory of electromagnetism and identified light as electromagnetic radiation.

MENDELEYEV, Dmitri (1834–1907): Russian chemist who devised the Periodic Table of elements.

MICHELSON, Albert (1852–1931): German-born U.S. physicist who carried out the famous Michelson-Morley experiment confirming the nonexistence of the ether that was thought to permeate space. He also worked in optics. He received the 1907 Nobel Prize in Physics.

MILLIKAN, Robert (1868–1953): U.S. physicist who determined the charge on the electron and did important work on cosmic rays. He received the 1923 Nobel Prize in Physics.

NERNST, Hermann (1864–1941): German physical chemist who proposed the third law of thermodynamics. He received the 1920 Nobel Prize in Chemistry.

NEWTON, Isaac (1642–1727): English scientist whose enormous contributions to physics and mathematics include the principles of calculus, the law of gravity, three laws of motion, the corpuscular theory of light, studies of light and optics, and the development of a reflecting telescope.

NOBEL, Alfred (1833–96): Swedish industrial chemist who invented dynamite. He left his accumulated wealth to endow the Nobel Prizes.

OSTWALD, Wilhelm (1853–1932): German chemist who devised an industrial process for making nitric acid. He received the 1909 Nobel Prize in Chemistry.

PASTEUR, Louis (1822–95): French chemist who discovered the optical activity of substances whose molecules contain asymmetric carbon atoms. He invented pasteurization and devised vaccines and pioneered their use in immunization.

PAULI, Wolfgang (1900–58): Austrian-born U.S. physicist who formulated the exclusion principle of electrons and predicted the existence of the neutrino. He received the 1945 Nobel Prize in Physics.

PAULING, Linus (b. 1901) U.S. chemist who discovered the helical structure of proteins and produced fundamental work on chemical bonding. He received the 1954 Nobel Prize in Chemistry.

PLANCK, Max Karl Ernst (1858–1947): German physicist who researched thermodynamics and black body radiation, leading to his formulation of quantum theory. He received the 1918 Nobel Prize in Physics.

PORTER, George (b. 1920): British chemist who studied fast chemical reactions. He shared the 1967 Nobel Prize in Chemistry.

PRIESTLEY, Joseph (1733–1804): English chemist who identified oxygen (independently of Antoine LAVOISIER).

RAMSAY, William (1852–1916): Scottish chemist who discovered the inert gases. He received the 1904 Nobel Prize in Chemistry.

RAOULT, François (1830–1901): French chemist who formulated a law relating to the freezing points and vapor pressures of solutions.

RAYLEIGH, John Strutt, 3rd Lord (1842–1919): British physicist who researched vibratory motion, sound, and the wave theory of light. With William RAMSAY he discovered argon. He received the 1904 Nobel Prize in Physics.

RÖNTGEN, Wilhelm (1845–1923): German physicist who discovered X rays and did important work on the heat conductivity of crystals and the specific heat of gases. He received the 1901 Nobel Prize in Physics.

RUTHERFORD, Ernest (1871–1937): New Zealand-born British physicist whose work led to the discovery of the atomic nucleus. From his studies, he predicted the existence of the neutron in the nucleus and received the Nobel Prize in Chemistry in 1908.

SCHEELE, Carl (1742–86): Swedish chemist who discovered or prepared many substances and proposed that air consists of one inert and one active gas.

SCHRÖDINGER, Erwin (1887–1961): Austrian physicist who applied wave mechanics to atoms. He received the 1933 Nobel Prize in Physics.

SEABORG, Glenn (b. 1912): U.S. chemist who, with coworkers, discovered many transuranic elements. He received the 1951 Nobel Prize in Chemistry.

SODDY, Frederick (1877–1956): British physical chemist who pioneered studies of radioactivity and coined the term isotope. He received the 1921 Nobel Prize in Chemistry.

SÖRENSEN, Sören Peter (1868–1939): Danish biochemist who devised the pH scale for measuring acidity.

SVEDBERG, Theodor (1884–1971): Swedish chemist who revolutionized chemical analysis. He received the 1926 Nobel Prize in Chemistry.

THOMSON, Joseph John (1856–1940): British physicist who studied the nature of cathode rays and the conduction of electricity by gases, which led to his revolutionary discoveries of the electron and of isotopes. He received the 1906 Nobel Prize in Physics.

TISELIUS, Arne (1902–71): Swedish chemist who developed electrophoresis as an analytical technique. He received the 1948 Nobel Prize in Chemistry.

UREY, Harold (1893–1981): U.S. chemist who isolated heavy water and discovered deuterium. He received the 1934 Nobel Prize in Chemistry.

VAN DE GRAAFF, Robert (1901–67): U.S. physicist who built a high-voltage electrostatic generator, later used as a particle accelerator in atomic physics.

VAN DER WAALS, Johannes (1837–1923): Dutch physicist who formulated an equation relating to the states of gases. He received the 1910 Nobel Prize in Physics.

VAN'T HOFF, Jacobus (1852–1911): Dutch chemist who founded stereochemistry, and studied osmotic pressure and asymmetry in carbon atoms. In 1901 he received the first Nobel Prize in Chemistry.

VOLTA, Alessandro (1745–1827): Italian physicist who invented the electric battery (voltaic pile) and first electrolyzed water. His name is given to the SI unit of electric potential difference.

WINKLER, Clemens (1838–1904): German chemist who in 1866 discovered germanium.

WÖHLER, Friedrich (1800–82): German chemist who was the first to synthesize an organic compound from an inorganic one. He devised methods of extracting metals from their ores.

YOUNG, Thomas (1773–1829): English physicist who explained the phenomenon of interference, thus proving the wave theory of light.

ZIEGLER, Karl (1898–1973): German organic chemist who devised catalysts for polymerizing ethene to make polymers. He shared the 1963 Nobel Prize in Chemistry.

TERMS

Aberration A defect in an image produced by a lens or curved mirror. That formed by a lens often has colored fringes (chromatic aberration).

Absolute zero Theoretically, the lowest possible temperature, -523.67°F (-273.15°C/0 kelvin). ATOMS have no KINETIC ENERGY at this temperature.

AC *see* ALTERNATING CURRENT.

Acceleration The rate of change of VELOCITY of a moving object.

Acid rain Rain that is unnaturally acidic because of the presence of (mainly) sulfuric and nitric ACIDS, derived from atmospheric pollutants.

Acid A substance that, in general, (1) dissolves in water with the formation of hydrogen IONS; (2) dissolves METALS with the liberation of hydrogen gas; or (3) tends to lose a PROTON and accept an ELECTRON. An acid has a pH VALUE less than 7.

Aliphatic compound ORGANIC COMPOUND whose ATOMS are linked in an open chain structure.

Alkali A substance that dissolves in water with the formation of hydroxyl IONS and has a pH VALUE greater than 7.

Allotropy The existence of two or more forms of an ELEMENT in one phase of matter (GAS, LIQUID, or SOLID), called allotropes.

Alloy A MIXTURE of METALS, or of a metal and a nonmetal, in which the metal is the major component.

Alpha particle The NUCLEUS of a helium ATOM, emitted by radioactive ELEMENTs, consisting of two PROTONs and two NEUTRONs.

Alternating current (AC) An electric CURRENT whose flow rapidly alternates in direction.

Amorphous Noncrystalline.

A.m.u. *see* ATOMIC MASS UNIT.

Anion A negative ION.

Anode A positively charged ELECTRODE.

Antimatter *see* ANTIPARTICLE.

Antiparticle A particle with the same MASS as its corresponding particle but opposite values of other properties such as CHARGE. Antiparticles make up antimatter.

Aromatic compound ORGANIC COMPOUND whose ATOMS are linked in a ring structure, especially BENZENE rings.

Atom The smallest particle of an ELEMENT that can take part in a chemical reaction. It consists of a central, positively charged NUCLEUS, surrounded by shells of orbiting, negatively charged ELECTRONs.

Atomic mass unit (a.m.u) One-twelfth of the MASS of a neutral ATOM of the most abundant isotope of carbon (equal to 1.660×10^{-27}kg).

Atomic number The number of PROTONs in the NUCLEUS of an ATOM. An ELEMENT's atomic number is unique to each and responsible for its chemical identity.

Background radiation Ionizing RADIATION from natural sources such as rocks, soil, and the atmosphere.

Base A substance that reacts chemically with an ACID to form a SALT and water.

Benzene Simplest AROMATIC hydrocarbon whose MOLECULE consists of a hexagonal ring of carbon ATOMS, each with an attached hydrogen atom.

Beta decay A type of radioactive disintegration in which the NUCLEUS of an ATOM emits an ELECTRON or POSITRON.

Beta particle ELECTRON or POSITRON emitted by the NUCLEUS of a radioactive ISOTOPE.

Carbon dating Method of estimating the age of an ORGANIC material from the amount of radioactive carbon 14 it contains.

Catalysis The acceleration or retardation of a chemical reaction by a substance (catalyst) that undergoes no permanent chemical change itself.

Cathode A negatively charged ELECTRODE.

Cation A positively charged ION.

Celsius scale A temperature scale on which the freezing point of water is 0°C and its boiling point is 100°C (at normal pressure). Formerly the centigrade scale.

Charge Quantity of electricity, being either positive or negative.

Chip Common name for an INTEGRATED CIRCUIT.

Colloid A mixture in which there are two or more phases, with the dispersed phase distributed evenly in the continuous phase. Examples include a sol (SOLID particles dispersed in a LIQUID), an emulsion (a liquid dispersed in another liquid), and an aerosol (a liquid or solid particles dispersed in a GAS).

Compound A substance consisting of two or more ELEMENTs in chemical combination in definite proportions.

Conductor A material that readily carries heat or electricity.

Convection The transfer of heat in a fluid by movement of the fluid itself. Warmer fluid tends to rise, while cooler fluid descends.

Coriolis effect The effect whereby an object moving relative to the earth is deflected from its path (as viewed from earth) due to the earth's rotation.

Cosmic rays Highly penetrating rays from interstellar space, consisting of ELECTRONS, PROTONS, and POSITRONS.

Cracking The breaking down of hydrocarbons into lighter ones, using heat, pressure, or catalysts.

Current Flow of electric CHARGE in a SOLID, LIQUID, or GAS.

DC *see* DIRECT CURRENT.

Diffraction The bending of light or sound waves at the edge of an obstruction. ELECTRONS can also be diffracted.

Diffusion The mixing of substances by the random motion of particles.

Dimorphism The existence of a substance in two different physical (for example, crystalline) forms.

Direct current (DC) An electric CURRENT that flows in one direction only.

Dispersion The separation of visible (white) light into its various wavelengths (colors) as it passes between media of different optical density.

Doppler effect The apparent change of frequency of light or sound because of the relative motion of the source and the observer.

Elasticity The property of a material that makes it return to its original shape after a deforming FORCE has been removed.

Electric field A region in which FORCES are exerted on any electric CHARGE that is present.

Electrode A CONDUCTOR along which electric CURRENT passes into or out of an electrolytic cell or gas discharge tube.

Electrolysis A chemical change brought about by the passage of a direct CURRENT through an electrolyte (solution or molten SALT). The current is carried between a pair of ELECTRODEs by IONS.

Electromagnetic spectrum A spectrum of ELECTROMAGNETIC WAVES that ranges from gamma rays (at the shortest wavelength end), X rays, and ultraviolet radiation through visible light to infrared radiation, microwaves, and radio waves at the longest wavelength end.

Electromagnetic wave A wave that consists of two mutually perpendicular transverse waves of ELECTRIC and MAGNETIC FIELD. In a vacuum such waves move at 186,000 miles (300,000 km) per second.

Electromagnetism Combination of an ELECTRIC FIELD and a MAGNETIC FIELD, and how they interact with electric CHARGES.

Electron A subatomic particle with a negative electric CHARGE and a MASS approximately 1/1,800 that of a hydrogen ATOM.

Element A substance, composed of ATOMS, which cannot be split into simpler substances by normal chemical means. It is characterized by its ATOMIC NUMBER.

Energy The capacity for doing work.

Fahrenheit scale A temperature scale on which the freezing point of water is 32°F and its boiling point is 212°F.

Field theory An attempt to link all physical FORCES into a single unified system.

Fission The spontaneous or induced splitting of a heavy atomic NUCLEUS, with the release of nuclear ENERGY.

Fluid A substance (GAS or LIQUID) that takes the shape of all or part of the vessel containing it.

Force An agency that changes the MOMENTUM of a body. Forces occur in equal and opposite pairs.

Fusion The formation of a new atomic NUCLEUS by combining two lighter ones, with the release of nuclear ENERGY.

Gamma radiation *see* ELECTROMAGNETIC SPECTRUM.

Gas State of matter that can expand indefinitely to fill a container.

Gravitation A FORCE of attraction between MASSes.

Gravitational waves Waves, produced by accelerating MASSes, that move through a gravitational field. They have yet to be directly observed.

Gyroscope An apparatus in which a heavy flywheel rotates at high speed, resisting change of direction of axis.

Inert gases Describing the ELEMENTs helium, neon, argon, krypton, xenon, and radon, so called because they take part in practically no chemical reactions.

Inertia The property of an object, proportional to its MASS, that opposes any change in its motion.

Infrared radiation *see* ELECTROMAGNETIC SPECTRUM.

Inorganic compound Any chemical COMPOUND not containing carbon.

Insulator A material that is a poor CONDUCTOR of heat or electricity.

Integrated circuit Miniature electronic circuit produced within a single crystal of a SEMICONDUCTOR.

Ion Any ATOM or MOLECULE that has acquired an electric CHARGE through gaining or losing one or more ELECTRONs.

Ionization The formation of IONs from ATOMs or MOLECULEs by adding or removing ELECTRONs.

Isomerism The existence of two or more chemical COMPOUNDs with the same molecular composition (and MASS) but different structure and, often, chemical properties.

Isotope One of a set of chemically identical forms of an ELEMENT that differ in the number of NEUTRONs in their nuclei.

Kelvin scale A temperature scale on which absolute zero is assigned the value 0K and the temperature interval is the same as the CELSIUS SCALE.

Kinetic energy The ENERGY possessed by an object by virtue of its motion.

Latent heat The heat exchange that occurs when a substance changes state, but which does not produce a change in temperature.

Liquid A state of matter that, without changing volume, takes up the shape of the lower part of a container.

Magnetic field A field of FORCE that exists around a magnet or a current-carrying CONDUCTOR.

Mass The amount of matter in an object.

Mesomerism Simultaneous existence of a COMPOUND in two different structural forms.

Metal An ELEMENT or ALLOY that is a good CONDUCTOR of heat and electricity. Most metals dissolve in an ACID to produce hydrogen and a SALT.

Metalloid ELEMENT whose properties are intermediate between those of a METAL and a nonmetal.

Microwave radiation *see* ELECTROMAGNETIC SPECTRUM.

Mixture More than one ELEMENT or COMPOUND together, but not chemically combined.

Molecule An ATOM or combination of atoms that is capable of independent existence and has properties characteristic of the substance of which it is the basic unit.

Momentum The product of MASS and VELOCITY of a moving object.

Monomer *see* POLYMER.

Neutrino A subatomic particle.

Neutron An uncharged subatomic particle, of about the same mass as a PROTON.

Noble gases *see* INERT GASES.

Nuclear fission *see* FISSION.

Nuclear fusion *see* FUSION.

Nucleon A PROTON or NEUTRON.

Nucleus The central part of an ATOM in which most of its MASS resides. It is made up of PROTONs and NEUTRONs.

Organic compound Chemical COMPOUND containing carbon.

Oxidation The addition of oxygen to, or removal of hydrogen from, a COMPOUND.

Periodic Table An arrangement of the chemical ELEMENTs into periods (rows) and groups (columns), in which each element has an ATOMIC NUMBER that is one larger than its predecessor.

Photoelectric effect A phenomenon in which PROTONs of radiant ENERGY are absorbed by ELECTRONs, giving them enough energy to escape from a surface.

Photon A quantum of radiant ENERGY such as light.

pH value Technically, for a solution, the negative logarithm of the hydrogen ION concentration; a measure of acidity or alkalinity.

Plasma A high-temperature gaseous discharge with no overall CHARGE.

Polarization In physics, the nonrandom orientation of the ELECTRIC and MAGNETIC FIELDs of ELECTROMAGNETIC WAVES. In chemistry, the separation of the positive and negative parts of a MOLECULE by an external agent.

Polymer A macromolecule made up of one or more much smaller repeating units (MONOMERs).

Positron A subatomic particle.

Potential energy The ENERGY possessed by an object by virtue of its position, state, or shape.

Proton A positively charged subatomic particle of about the same MASS as a NEUTRON; the NUCLEUS of a hydrogen ATOM.

Quantum theory A theory that assumes that the emission and absorption of ENERGY is not continuous but occurs in small "packets" or quanta.

Quark A fundamental subatomic particle.

Radiation The dissemination of ENERGY from a source, such as heat or ELECTROMAGNETIC WAVES. Also applies to emitted particles such as ALPHA and BETA PARTICLES.

Radical A group of ATOMs in a MOLECULE that retains its identity during chemical changes that affect the rest of the molecule.

Radioactivity The spontaneous disintegration of certain heavy elements, with the emission of ALPHA or BETA PARTICLES or GAMMA RADIATION.

Radio waves *see* ELECTROMAGNETIC SPECTRUM.

Rare gases *see* INERT GASES.

Reduction The addition of hydrogen to, or removal of oxygen from, a COMPOUND.

Refraction The bending of light waves as they pass from one transparent medium to another of different density.

Relative atomic mass (atomic weight) MASS of ATOMs in an ELEMENT on a scale on which 1 unit equals 1.660×10^{-27}kg.

Relative molecular mass (molecular weight) Combined RELATIVE ATOMIC MASSes of all the ATOMs in a MOLECULE.

Relativity The special theory postulating that all motion is relative and the speed of light is constant for all observers; the general theory showing the equivalence of acceleration and gravitation.

Salt A chemical COMPOUND formed, together with water, when an ACID reacts with a BASE. A salt is also formed, usually together with hydrogen, when a METAL dissolves in an acid.

Semiconductor A material, such as silicon, whose conductivity is intermediate between those of a CONDUCTOR and a nonconductor (insulator).

SI (Système International d'Unités) System of coherent metric units used throughout science.

Silicon chip *see* INTEGRATED CIRCUIT.

Solid A state of matter that has a definite shape, which it resists having changed.

Solubility The quantity of a substance (solute) that dissolves in a solvent to form a solution.

Specific heat The property of a material defining the amount of heat required to raise a unit MASS of the material by a unit temperature.

Superconductivity The property of some substances at low temperatures of having negligible electrical resistance.

Thermonuclear energy ENERGY released by FUSION.

Torsion A twisting force exerted on any material.

Transuranic elements Elements beyond uranium in the PERIODIC TABLE.

Ultraviolet radiation *see* ELECTROMAGNETIC SPECTRUM.

Uncertainty principle The principle stating that there is a fundamental limit to the precision with which a particle's position and MOMENTUM can simultaneously be known.

Unified field theory *see* FIELD THEORY.

Valence (valency) Measure of the combining power of an ELEMENT, ION, or RADICAL.

Velocity The distance traveled by a moving object in a particular direction divided by the time taken.

X-ray radiation *see* ELECTROMAGNETIC SPECTRUM.

INTRODUCTION

Mathematics and computing use numbers to count things and to perform calculations. Numbers can be used for counting whole numbers of things, and then, with a knowledge of fractions, measuring things that do not add up to a whole number.

Applying various rules to numbers enables us to do calculations. The calculation often applies the rules of multiplication, and requires a knowledge of how to manipulate fractions. A computer engineer calls such a set of rules an algorithm – a set of detailed instructions that tell a computer how to perform a certain task.

Numbers and counting

People have always needed to count. Farmers use to keep a record of the number of goats in a field by cutting notches on a stick. This method of counting – called a tally – was common in many parts of the world. To make counting the notches easier, they were probably grouped, say in 5s. A mathematician would say that the farmer was counting to the base 5.

Today the best-known number system is the decimal system, which uses the base 10. Its numbers (digits) are 0, 1, 2, 3, 4, 5, 6, 7, 8 and 9. The next number, 10, is the base of the system. In fact, in any number system, the base is the number represented by 10. For example, the binary system, as used by computers, has only two numbers (digits), 0 and 1. Its sequence of numbers, after 0, begins 1, 10 (representing decimal 2, the base), 11, 100, 101, 110, and so on. Computers also use numbers expressed to the base 16, termed the hexadecimal system.

Four number systems

Roman	Decimal	Binary	Hex.
I	1	1	1
II	2	10	2
III	3	11	3
IV	4	100	4
V	5	101	5
VI	6	110	6
VII	7	111	7
VIII	8	1000	8
IX	9	1001	9
X	10	1010	A
XI	11	1011	B
XII	12	1100	C
XIII	13	1101	D
XIV	14	1110	E
XV	15	1111	F
XVI	16	10000	10
XVII	17	10001	11
XVIII	18	10010	12
XIX	19	10011	13
XX	20	10100	14

Roman numerals also use the letters L (50), C (100), D (500) and M (1000). In each of the above systems, the number 45 is written XLV, 45, 101101 and 2D.

MEASURING

The practice of measurement necessitates the use of a measuring device – such as a ruler – and a set of units in which to express the measurement. Lengths and distances are expressed using linear measure, such as centimetres (cm), metres (m) and kilometres (km) or, using the imperial system, in inches (in), feet (ft) and miles (mi).

Measurement of the areas of shapes and volumes of forms (*below*) requires dimensional theory in the form of formulae based on fundamental lengths.

Area has the dimensions length x length and is measured using square units, such as square metres (m²). Volume has the dimensions length x length x length and is measured in cubic units, such as cubic metres (m³). Another dimensional fundamental is mass which is expressed in units such as grams (g).

The Greek letter π is used in some of the formulae below: this represents the ratio of the circumference of a circle to its diameter, and is approximately equal to 3.14159.

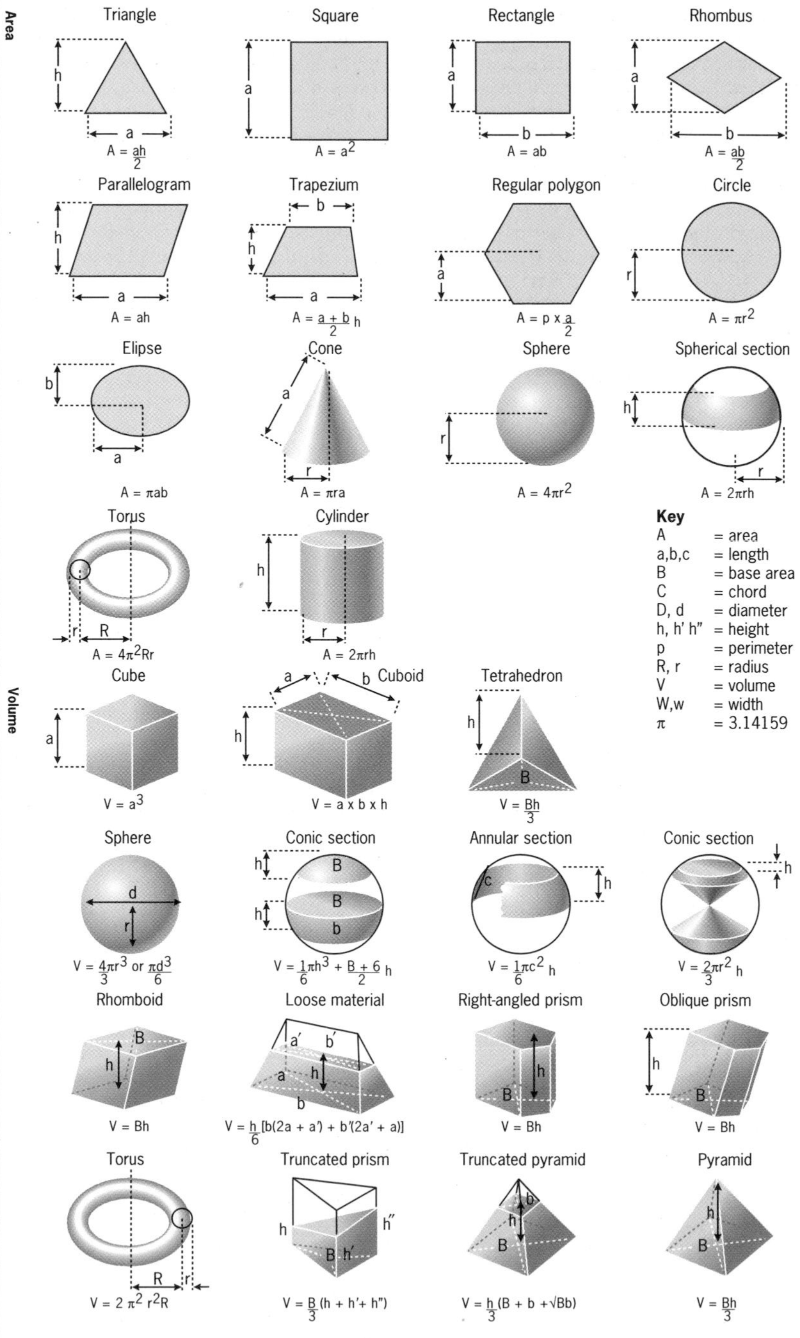

Area

Triangle
$A = \frac{ah}{2}$

Square
$A = a^2$

Rectangle
$A = ab$

Rhombus
$A = \frac{ab}{2}$

Parallelogram
$A = ah$

Trapezium
$A = \frac{a + b}{2} h$

Regular polygon
$A = p \times \frac{a}{2}$

Circle
$A = \pi r^2$

Elipse
$A = \pi ab$

Cone
$A = \pi ra$

Sphere
$A = 4\pi r^2$

Spherical section
$A = 2\pi rh$

Torus
$A = 4\pi^2 Rr$

Cylinder
$A = 2\pi rh$

Key

A	= area
a,b,c	= length
B	= base area
C	= chord
D, d	= diameter
h, h' h"	= height
p	= perimeter
R, r	= radius
V	= volume
W,w	= width
π	= 3.14159

Volume

Cube
$V = a^3$

Cuboid
$V = a \times b \times h$

Tetrahedron
$V = \frac{Bh}{3}$

Sphere
$V = \frac{4\pi r^3}{3}$ or $\frac{\pi d^3}{6}$

Conic section
$V = \frac{1}{6}\pi h^3 + \frac{B + 6}{2} h$

Annular section
$V = \frac{1}{6}\pi c^2 h$

Conic section
$V = \frac{2\pi r^2}{3} h$

Rhomboid
$V = Bh$

Loose material
$V = \frac{h}{6} [b(2a + a') + b'(2a' + a)]$

Right-angled prism
$V = Bh$

Oblique prism
$V = Bh$

Torus
$V = 2\pi^2 r^2 R$

Truncated prism
$V = \frac{B}{3} (h + h' + h")$

Truncated pyramid
$V = \frac{h}{3} (B + b + \sqrt{Bb})$

Pyramid
$V = \frac{Bh}{3}$

Fractions

Any usable number system has to be able to cope with non-whole numbers – that is, fractions. Everyday notation in fractions is based on the idea of parts of a whole. We use such terms as a half ($1/2$), three-quarters ($3/4$) and two-thirds ($2/3$): such fractions are called common, or vulgar, fractions. The number above the line is termed the numerator; that below the line is the denominator. If the denominator is larger than the numerator (that is, if the fraction is less than 1), the fraction is also known as a proper fraction.

To multiply two fractions we multiply one numerator by the other, and one denominator by the other, and write the product of the numerators over the product of the denominators. Thus $1/2$ x $1/4$ (that is, a half of a quarter) = (1 x 1)/(2 x 4) = $1/8$. To divide one fraction by another, one of them should be inverted and then the two fractions multiplied. For example, $1/8 \div 1/4 = 1/8$ x $4/1 = 4/8 = 1/2$.

To add or subtract fractions, they must have the same denominator. If necessary, one or both fractions should be re-expressed so they share a common denominator. So, $1/2 + 1/3$ is rewritten as $3/6 + 2/6$, and then added, giving $5/6$.

In decimal notation, fractions of numbers are expressed as tenths, hundredths, thousandths and so on (below). For example, $1/2$ can also be expressed as $5/10$, which in decimal notation is written as 0.5; the fractional number $4 3/8$ becomes 4.375. The advantage of expressing fractions in decimal notation is that they can be manipulated – that is, multiplied, divided, added or subtracted – using the rules of ordinary arithmetic.

Fractions can also be written in binary, using a point system. For example, 1001.01 = $9 1/2$ (because .01 in binary represents (0 x $1/2$) + (1 x $1/4$) = $1/4$). Yet another system of expressing fractions, common in business and banking, is as percentages (below), which are fractions expressed as hundreds. Thus 25 percent can be expressed as $25/100$, which = $1/4$.

Comparing fractions

Common	Percentage	Decimal
$1/2$	50.0%	0.5
$1/3$	33.33%	0.333
$1/4$	25.0%	0.25
$1/5$	20.0%	0.2
$1/6$	16.66%	0.166
$1/8$	12.5%	0.125
$1/10$	10.0%	0.1
$2/3$	66.66%	0.666
$3/4$	75.0%	0.75
$3/5$	60.0%	0.6
$4/5$	80.0%	0.8
$3/8$	37.5%	0.375
$5/8$	62.5%	0.625
$7/8$	87.5%	0.875
$3/10$	30.0%	0.3
$7/10$	70.0%	0.7
$9/10$	90.0%	0.9

Angles and triangles

Measuring angles requires special units. For general use, angles are measured in degrees, written with the symbol °. A complete turn, or a full circle, contains 360°; thus a quarter turn – a right angle – is 90°, and a half turn is 180°. For precise measurement, a degree can be divided into 60 minutes (written using the symbol ') and each minute can be further subdivided into 60 seconds ("). For certain mathematical and scientific purposes, angles are measured in radians. In a full circle, there are 2π (approximately 6.283) radians: a radian therefore equals 57.296°.

We measure the angles of a triangle in degrees. A special type of triangle, called a right-angled triangle because one of its angles is 90°, gave rise to a branch of mathematics called trigonometry (literally, "triangle measuring"). This deals with the relationships, or ratios, between the sides and angles of a right-angled triangle.

To describe these trigonometrical ratios, and the properties of the angles determined by these ratios, we need certain nomenclature (below). The side opposite the angle θ is called the "opposite"; the

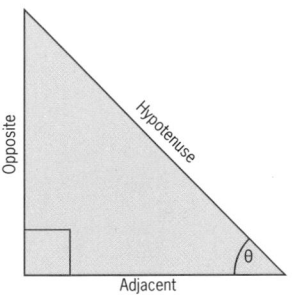

shorter of the sides next to the angle is termed the "adjacent"; and the longest side of a right-angled triangle is known as the "hypotenuse".

The ratio of the opposite side to the hypotenuse (that is, the opposite divided by the hypotenuse) is called the sine of the angle θ (and is usually written sin θ, where θ is the angle in degrees); the ratio of the adjacent to the hypotenuse is termed the cosine of the angle (cos θ); and, finally, the ratio of the opposite to the adjacent is called the tangent of the angle (tan θ).

The sine of an angle of 0° is 0. The value of sine increases gradually with the size of the angle until it equals 1 when the angle equals 90°. The converse is true of cosines: the cosine of 0° is 1, and that of 90° is 0. The tangent of 0° is also 0, but that of 90° is infinitely large, and is written as ∞ (the symbol for infinity). The way in which the value of sine varies with angle – called a sine curve (top right) – is of fundamental importance in many branches of physics, such as the study of periodic motion (like that of a pendulum) and alternating current electricity.

Sine curve

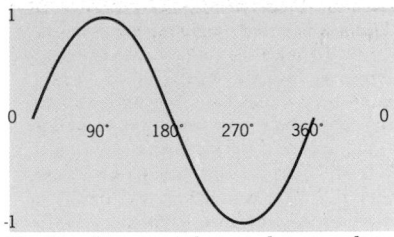

The sine of any angle has a value somewhere between -1 and 1. The sines of 0° and multiples of 180° equal 0.

Cosine curve

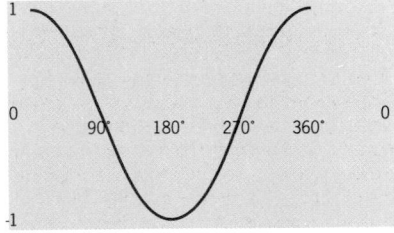

The graph of cosine against angle has the same shape as the sine curve, but begins at 1 for an angle of 0°.

Tangent curve

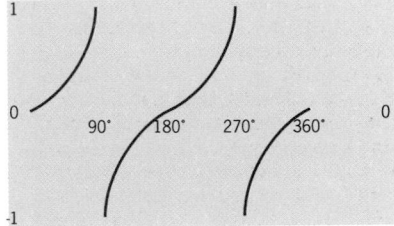

Tangents plotted against angle create a discontinuous curve with values between plus infinity and minus infinity.

The sides of a right-angled triangle are also related by an important geometrical concept known as Pythagoras' theorem (below). This states that the square of the hypotenuse (ABED) is equal to the sum of the squares of the other two sides (ACHK plus CBFG). Euclid was one of many who proved the theorem in a complex sequence of statements relating the areas outlined by red dotted lines and the squares of the triangle's sides.

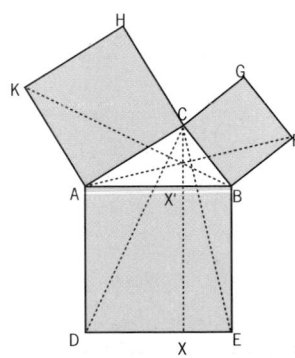

Kinds of numbers

Numbers such as 2, 5 and 11 are known as integers or whole numbers. They are also termed rational numbers, because they can be expressed as a ratio of two integers – that is, as a fraction. An irrational number, on the other hand, cannot be expressed as a whole-number fraction, that is, it cannot be defined as an exact number. Examples include π and $\sqrt{2}$.

All rational and irrational numbers, positive or negative, are also real numbers. A real number is any number that can be represented by a point on the number line (*right*). Imaginary numbers are based on i, which is equal to $\sqrt{-1}$. The imaginary number axis runs at right angles to the real numbers, and takes the form $a + bi$, in which a and b are real. Complex number J, for example, is $-4 -5i$, and G is $5+3i$. Complex numbers have applications in physics, particularly in the theory of alternating electric currents.

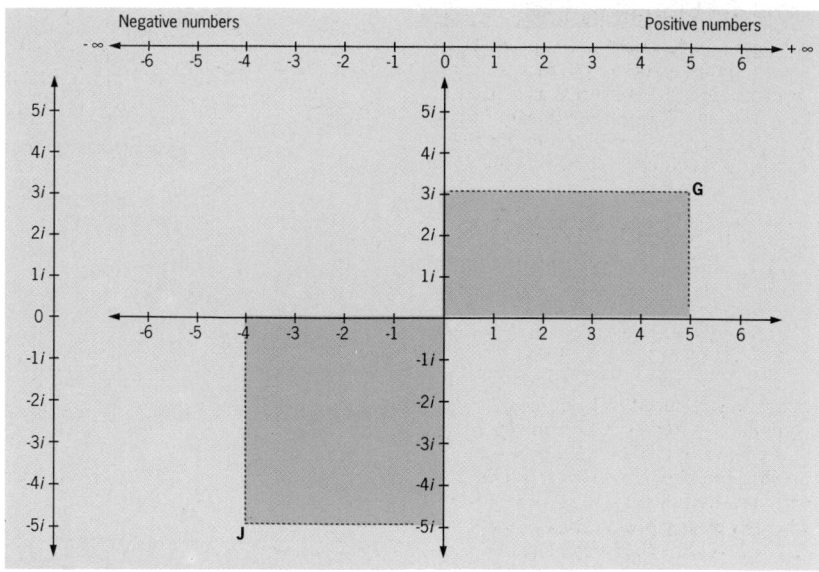

Unknown numbers

Arithmetic supplies mathematics with all the techniques it needs to deal with things that can be counted or measured: it deals with known numbers. But what if the value of a number is not known? This is the province of algebra, which deals with unknown quantities that are represented by letters in equations.

If you add 7 and then subtract 2 from a certain number and the answer is 11, what is the number? If you call the number x, the question can then be written as an equation:

$$x + 7 - 2 = 11$$

In solving an equation, whatever is performed on one side should be performed on the other in order for the equation to be valid. If 7 is subtracted and 2 added to each side, then

$$x = 11 - 7 + 2$$
So $\qquad x = 6.$

An unknown quantity does not have to have a fixed value, but can vary in terms of another unknown depending on a fixed relationship between them shown by an equation (in this case called a function). For example, the function $y = 2x + 3$ tells you that there is a whole range of values of y for a similar range of values of x. As x varies through a range of definable values – say from -3 through -2, -1, 0, +1 and 2 to 3 – the function would reveal that y has the corresponding values -3, -1, 1, 3, 5, 7 and 9.

Sometimes the values of an unknown (such as x) are expressed in terms of x to the power 2 (x^2), which is known as a quadratic function: if x is raised to the power 3, it is a cubic function. There are algebraic techniques to solve such functions. There are also techniques to find the values of two different "unknowns", as long as there are two functions that simultaneously (but in a different relationship) define the pair.

Changing quantities

Calculus is a branch of mathematics that lets you look at continuously varying quantities. If, for example, an object travels 50 kilometres in 60 minutes, its average speed is 50km/h. But in the first couple of seconds after it started it might have been going much faster (like a bullet) or much slower (like a car) than this average. Algebra provides a function (an equation) that defines the relationship between the variable quantities, and calculus offers the means of determining the values of the variable quantities.

Calculus has two major techniques: differentiation and integration. Differentiation gives the derivative of a function. If the function is $y = f(x)$, the derivative is $dy/dx = f'(x)$, which represents the rate at which the value of y changes as the value of x changes. So, using the example above, if y in the function $y = f(x)$ represents the distance a car travels in time x, dy/dx is the speed at which the car is travelling at any moment.

The two main rules for carrying out differentiation are that the derivative of Ax^n is nAx^{n-1} (where A is a number and n is the power to which x is raised), and the derivative of a constant is 0. For example, in the equation

$$y = x^3 + 4x^2 - 2x + 5,$$
$$dy/dx = 3x^2 + 8x - 2.$$

If dy/dx is positive, y will be increasing as x increases (A in the diagram *below*); if dy/dx is negative, y will be decreasing as x increases (C *below*). In fact, the value of dy/dx represents the slope or gradient of the graph of y plotted against x for any particular pair of values of x and y. But what happens if dy/dx is 0? It means that y is not changing at all. If the graph has a maximum (like the brow of a hill – B *below*) or a minimum (like a valley – D *below*), its slope at those points will be zero. The maximum and minimum values of x and y can therefore be found by setting dy/dx equal to 0.

Integration is the opposite of differentiation. It can be used, for example, to find the area under a curve between certain values (called limits) of x. It is equivalent to cutting the area into a huge number of very thin strips, and adding up the areas of all the strips.

If a graph, represented by a function of x and y, is rotated about one of the axes, it generates a surface that encloses a volume (known as a volume of revolution). Using integration, it is possible to calculate the values of such volumes, a useful technique in solving problems in engineering and other technologies.

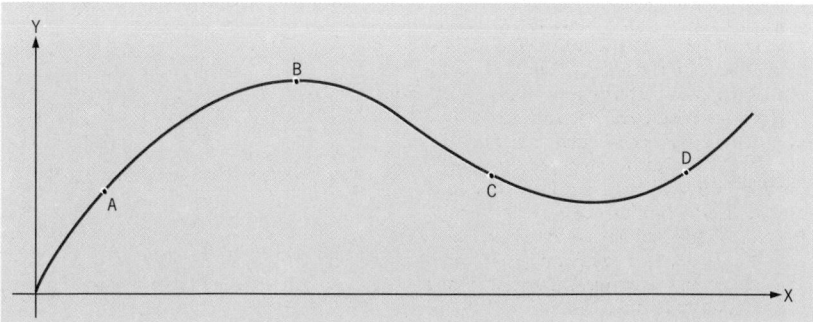

Coordinate geometry

An algebraic function can be plotted on a piece of graph paper to produce a curve (a straight line is also regarded as a "curve" in this sense). This is the subject of co-ordinate (or analytical) geometry, where algebra and geometry come together. Graphs are plotted using a pair of axes at right angles, termed the y-axis (vertical) and x-axis (horizontal). Each point on a curve has a pair of values, one of x and one of y, called its coordinates. They are written as (x, y) and generally known as Cartesian coordinates (after the French mathematician René Descartes).

The simplest curve, and simplest function, is a straight line. It has the general equation $y = mx + c$, where m is the slope of the line and c is the value of y where the line cuts the y-axis. Two straight lines with different slopes must intersect somewhere in the x y plane. The point of intersection could be found by plotting the lines on paper. But it can also be found using straightforward algebra. At the point of intersection (and only there) the two equations are true for the same values of x and y – they constitute a pair of simultaneous equations. Solving the equations gives the coordinates of the point without having to plot the lines.

Other types of equations represent different kinds of curves. Equations of the general type $y = ax^2 + b$ are parabolas (*above right*); those of the form $xy = c$ are hyperbolas (*below right*). Others represent circles, ellipses, sine curves and so on.

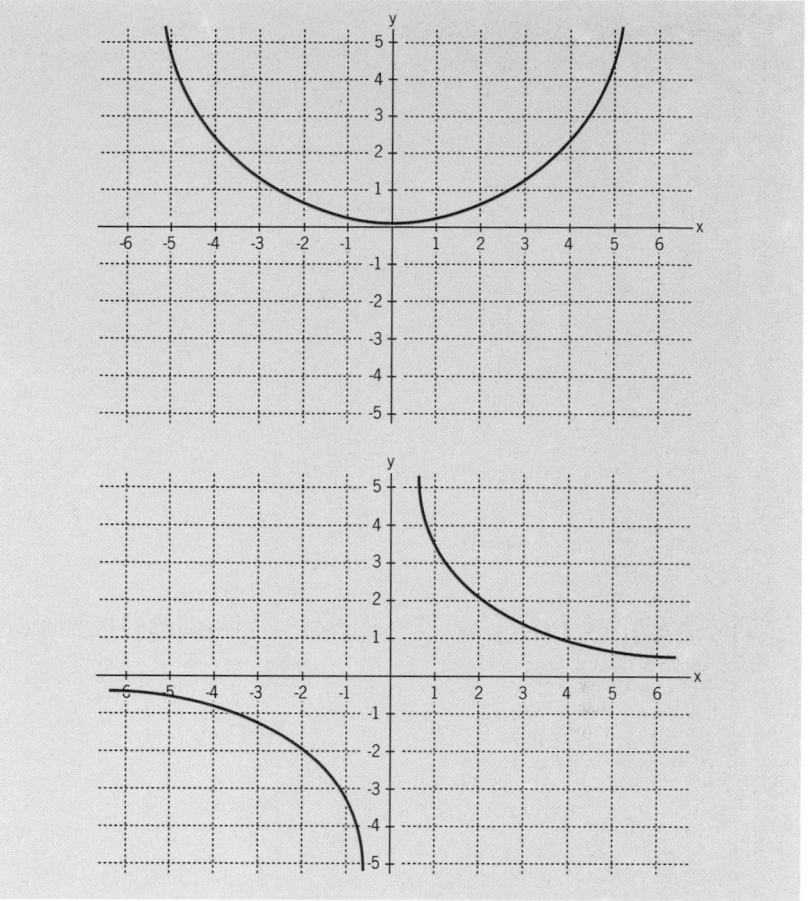

Organization or chaos

Apparently complex and irregular geometric shapes are often composed of progressively smaller-shaped versions of the original. Such patterns occur in nature; each one of the myriad different forms adopted by snowflakes is based on the same principle.

A mathematical curve or shape that mimics such shapes is called a fractal, and is produced by repeated subdivision of a basic shape. Regular, or geometric, fractals consist of large and small shapes that are identical apart from their size. A Koch snowflake (*left*) is built up by replacing each side of a triangle with a line containing another triangle - called a generator. Each side is then replaced with another generator, and so on for as many generations as required. Scientists use fractals to represent the regular features of complex concepts in their studies of such phenomena as weather patterns.

Some seemingly chaotic and fragmentary natural patterns – such as the distribution of galaxies or the apparent random motion of microscopic particles suspended in a fluid – can also be studied using fractals. These are random fractals, however: the larger and smaller constituent structures are mathematically related but their details may differ.

Odds and probabilities

When a coin is tossed, the odds that it will land "heads" uppermost are evens: that is to say, the coin is just as likely to land "heads" as it is "tails". Similarly, the odds that a particular number will be uppermost when a dice is rolled are 1 in 6. Mathematicians would use the term probability rather than odds in these examples: probabilities are easier to manipulate in calculating the odds of something happening. Every event has a probability of between 0 and 1. The value 0 corresponds to an impossibility (for example, the probability that I shall live for ever), and a probability of 1 corresponds to a certainty (the probability that I shall eventually die). The probability of landing a "head" (or "tail") with a coin is 0.5, because either option is equally possible.

The probability of throwing a six with a single dice is 1 in 6; that is 1/6, which is equal to 0.1667. The probability of throwing a four, or any other number, is the same. But what is the probability of throwing two sixes at the same time using two dice? The answer to this is found simply by multiplying the individual probabilities of each dice, in this case 0.1667 x 0.1667, which equals 0.02779. (In terms of odds, this represents 1/6 x 1/6; that is, 1 in 36).

Timeline

c. 500 BC The abacus is in use (in China).

1617 John Napier devises "Napier's bones", rods for multiplication.

1621 William Oughtred invents the slide-rule.

1641 Blaise Pascal devises an adding machine.

1832 Charles Babbage constructs his "analytical engine", a mechanical computer.

1876 Lord Kelvin (William Thomson) shows that machines can be programmed to solve problems.

1885 Dorr Felt makes his Comptometer, a key-operated adding machine.

1888 William Burroughs invents an adding machine.

1889 Dorr Felt fits his Comptometer with an integral printer.

1890 Herman Hollerith devises an electrically-driven, punched-card system.

1892 William Burroughs markets an adding machine with a printer.

1893 A four-function calculator is marketed.

1896 Herman Hollerith founds the company that later becomes IBM (International Business Machines).

1925 Vannevar Bush *et al* design an analog computer for solving differential equations.

1936 Konrad Zuse uses electric relays to build a primitive digital computer.

1937 John Atanasoff designs an electronic computer for solving linear equations.

1938 T. Ross makes a machine that finds its way through mazes (and learns "by experience", using feedback). Konrad Zuse builds a binary calculating machine (Z1).

1941 Konrad Zuse makes a computer (Z2) using electric relays and punched paper tape.

1942 The ABC (Atanasoff-Berry Computer), a punched-card version of Atanasoff's machine (*see 1937*), works intermittently.

1943 Alan Turing *et al* develop the first all-electronic (using valves) calculating machine (the Colossus).

1944 Howard Aiken *et al* build the second electronic computer (Automatic Sequence Controlled Calculator), which uses punched cards and valves.

1945 John Eckert and John Mauchley develop ENIAC (Electronic Numerical Integrator And Computer), the first true stored-program computer.

1946 John Von Neumann initiates computer research at Princeton.

1948 The Mark I prototype stored-program electronic computer begins operation at Manchester University.

1949 Cambridge University's EDSAC (Electronic Delay Storage Automatic Computer) begins operation.

1951 John Eckert and John Mauchley build UNIVAC I, the first commercially available electronic computer, which uses magnetic tape storage.

Handling data

Much of science and technology involves making observations and assembling facts, or data. A collection of data is of little value on its own; it has to be interpreted and valid conclusions drawn from it. For example, simple questioning might reveal that the ages of seven people in a room are 13, 14, 21, 34, 36, 36 and 59. There are various statistical conclusions that can be drawn from this simple collection of data. For example, what is the average age? A mathematician would first ask what kind of average do you want? The mean (or arithmetic mean) is obtained by adding all the ages and dividing by the number of people; this gives 30.43 as the mean age.

Another type of average is called the root mean square (r.m.s.) value. It is obtained by adding together the squares of each value, dividing by the number of values, and taking the square root of the answer. In the above example, the r.m.s. value is $\sqrt{8035/7} = 33.88$.

Yet another type of average is a median, which is the middle value of a set of values in order: there is an equal probability that any value will be larger or smaller than the median. In the example, the median is 34. (If there are an even number of values, the median is the mean of the middle two.)

The mode of a set of values is the one that occurs most frequently. In the example, the mode is 36. (There can be more than one mode in a large set of values.) So what is the average age of the people in the room? It is 30.43, 33.85, 34 or 36, depending on how you define average.

Presenting data

Data can be presented in various ways. In the example (*above*), the "raw" data was initially presented as a list (of peoples' ages). Data can also be plotted as a bar chart, as points on a graph or as a series of symbols in a pictogram. Many people think that such presentations are more immediate – which is why they are often used as a means of reporting information in the media – although the "picture" can be distorted by the choice of axes in the case of graphs.

Monthly rainfall figures, for example, can be presented in a variety of ways, (*below* and *above right*).The bar chart gives

Graph

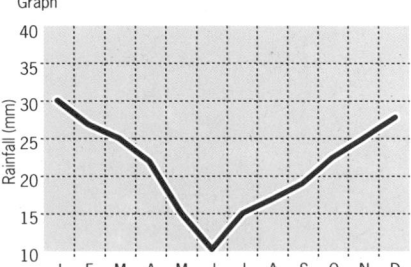

Bar chart

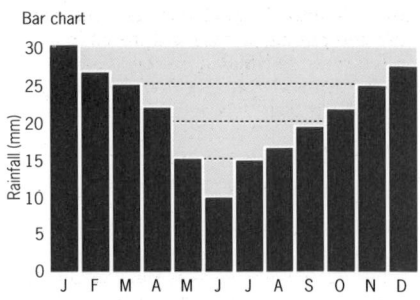

Pictogram

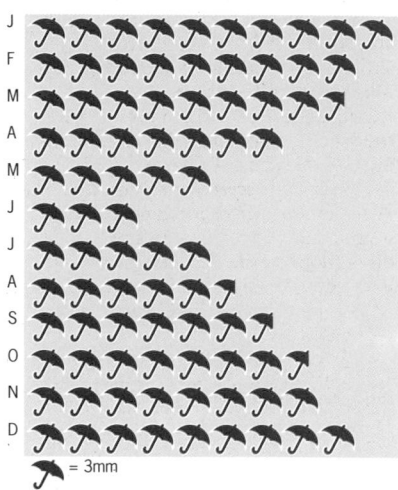

 = 3mm

the best picture. It is immediately obvious from this that June is the driest month, but even so there are 10mm/0.4in of rain during that period. The graph presents the same data, but because the vertical axis begins at 10mm (and not zero) it conveys the impression that there is virtually no rain in June. The pictogram with its umbrella symbols gives the impression of a dry summer while making the actual rainfall figures difficult to calculate.

Machines for dealing with data

Since the time of Blaise Pascal and Charles Babbage, scientists and inventors have devised machines for taking the labour (and inaccuracies) out of "doing sums". By the 1970s, electronic tills and calculating machines were common. But they had to be instructed to perform a particular function every time they were used. A much more useful machine was one that could be given – and remember – a whole series of instructions (a program), carry them out on inputted data, and then output the results. That is what a computer does, and that is why it is much more than a mere calculating machine.

A computer program is written in a chosen programming language, and consists of numbers, letters and symbols. With a digital computer, the data must also be inputted as alphanumeric (letter or number) symbols. Together with the program, the data is converted by the machine into binary characters (Numbers and computing, *p. 422*) and stored in a memory, from which it can be accessed.

Programmed operations on the data are carried out by the computer's central processing unit (CPU). The operations include various arithmetical procedures (done by the arithmetic unit) and logical steps that may include making decisions about data-derived calculations. Data and instructions may be inputted to a computer in various ways, such as via a keyboard (resembling a typewriter), a light pen (which "draws" on a television-type screen) or a mouse (which rolls on the desk to move an indicator or cursor to symbols on the computer screen). Programs are usually inputted by means of magnetic disk or tape.

Output devices – which present the results of a computer's data processing – include the visual display unit (VDU), a television-type screen which is also known as a monitor. More permanent versions of output can be provided on small magnetic disks (floppy disks) or, using a printer, as hard copy. Graphic information – illustrations such as graphs and charts – can also be printed out.

Digital and analog

A digital computer is basically a clever calculating machine. Data is provided as, or converted into, binary numbers that the machine can manipulate. The items of input information are necessarily discrete – that is, separate sets of numbers. An analog computer, on the other hand, deals with a continuously varying input (usually presented as a varying voltage from some sort of sensing device). It is therefore more like a measuring machine. Engineers use an analog-to-digital converter (ADC) to enable digital computers to deal with analog information – just as a thermometer, spring-driven watch or speedometer (all analog devices) can be modified to give a digital output.

Coupling computers

An individual computer used by one person is called a personal computer (PC) or work station. Such individual machines can share facilities and resources if they are joined together in a network. The joining is done with cables or telephone lines, forming what is termed a local area network (LAN).

Machines with only a limited amount of hard disk (storage) space may be connected through a network to a powerful computer called a file server, which stores all the files for all the members of the network. Users can also send messages to each other using electronic mail (E-mail). This is the main function of the worldwide system called Internet, which is virtually a network of networks interconnected through machines known as gateways. Its members can also access, in seconds, files from another participating member anywhere in the world.

Computer networking systems

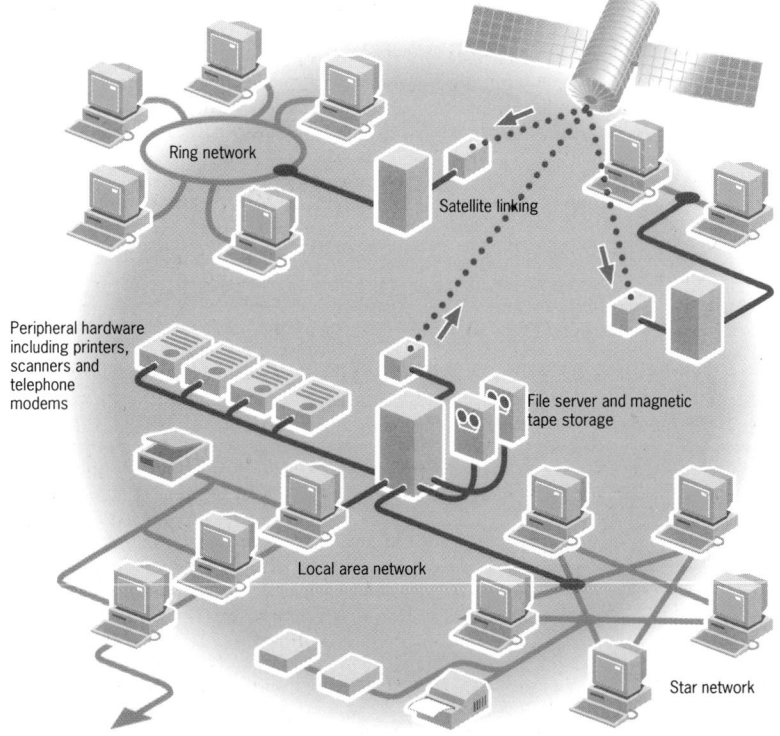

Ring network

Satellite linking

Peripheral hardware including printers, scanners and telephone modems

File server and magnetic tape storage

Local area network

Star network

PROMINENT PEOPLE

ABEL, Niels (1802–1829) Norwegian mathematician who studied groups and infinite series.

ARCHIMEDES (*c.* 287–212 BC) Ancient Greek mathematician and physicist who devised geometric techniques for determining curves, surfaces, volumes and areas, and who founded mechanics and statics.

ARGAND, Jean-Robert (1768–1822) Swiss mathematician who worked with complex numbers and devised a method of representing them graphically as points (Argand diagram).

BABBAGE, Charles (1791–1871) English mathematician who designed two mechanical calculators, one of which could be simply programmed.

BANACH, Stefan (1892–1945) Polish mathematician who founded functional analysis (the study of functions in terms of the linear spaces defining them).

BERNOULLI, Jakob (1654–1705) Swiss mathematician and physicist who made many studies in algebra and geometry.

BIRKHOFF, George (1884–1944) US mathematician who applied analysis to dynamics and developed a relativity theory of gravity (independently of Albert Einstein).

BOOLE, George (1815–1864) British mathematician who worked on differential equations, analytical transformations and a method of solving logical problems using mathematical symbols, now known as Boolean algebra.

CANTOR, Georg (1845–1918) Russian-born German mathematician who founded set theory and worked in topology and number theory.

CAUCHY, Augustin (1789–1857) French mathematician who developed the theory of functions of complex variables and established the basis of modern analysis.

CAYLEY, Arthur (1821–1895) British mathematician and prolific author who worked on theories of matrices and multidimensional geometry.

DE MOIVRE, Abraham (1667–1754) French mathematician who worked mainly on probability theory.

DE MORGAN, Augustus (1806–1871) British mathematician who made contributions to mathematical induction and algebra.

DESARGUES, Gérard (1593–1662) French mathematician who was a founder of modern projective geometry.

DESCARTES, René (1596–1650) French mathematician and philosopher who devised coordinate (analytical) geometry, employing a system of Cartesian coordinates (named after him).

DIRICHLET, Peter (1805–1859) French-born German mathematician who studied functions and made significant progress in complex analysis, number theory and mechanics.

EUCLID (*fl.* 300 BC) Ancient Greek mathematician who was the founder of classical geometry, summarized in 13 books entitled *Elements*, which are still studied today.

EULER, Leonhard (1707–1783) Swiss mathematician who published many books and papers on mathematical topics, which included important work on calculus.

FERMAT, Pierre de (1601–1665) French mathematician who founded modern number theory, coordinate geometry (independently of DESCARTES) and probability theory (independently of PASCAL).

FIBONACCI, Leonardo (*c.* 1170–1250) Italian mathematician who contributed to algebra and number theory, and introduced the Arabic (decimal) number system to Europe.

FOURIER, Jean Baptiste (1768–1830) French mathematician who introduced the expansion of functions in trigonometrical series (Fourier series), and developed a theorem concerning the roots of algebraic equations.

FREGE, Friedrich Gottlob (1848–1925) German mathematician and philosopher who in 1879 founded symbolic mathematical logic.

GALOIS, Evariste (1811–1832) French mathematician who worked on the theories of equations, functions and numbers, and founded group theory.

GAUSS, Karl Friedrich (1777–1855) German mathematician and physicist who in 1801 published a significant work on the theory of numbers; he also pioneered mathematical optics.

GREGORY, James (1638–1675) Scottish mathematician who first distinguished between convergent and divergent series and studied power series, and anticipated NEWTON's work on calculus.

HAMILTON, William (1805–1865) Irish mathematician and theoretical physicist who invented quaternions (generalized four-term complex numbers).

HERMITE, Charles (1822–1901) French mathematician who developed the theory of functions.

HILBERT, David (1862–1943) German mathematician who did important work on general geometry and mathematics, and spurred the introduction of computability theory.

JACOBI, Karl (1804–1851) German mathematician who in 1829 discovered elliptical functions, and worked on number theory and differential equations.

JORDAN, Marie-Ennemond (1832–1922) French mathematician whose wide interests included algebra, functions, topology and group theory.

KLEIN, Christian (1849–1925) German mathematician who studied elliptical functions and tried to unify geometry using group theory.

LAGRANGE, Joseph (1736–1813) French mathematician who worked on the calculus of variations and applied higher mathematics to the study of mechanics and dynamics.

LAPLACE, Pierre (1749–1827) French mathematician and physicist who is best known for applying mathematics to the resolution of astronomical problems, particularly planetary motions.

LEGENDRE, Adrien-Marie (1752–1833) French mathematician who worked on elliptical functions and in 1806 invented the method of least squares (to fit a curve to a series of points).

LEIBNIZ, Gottfried (1646–1716) German mathematician who developed calculus at about the same time as Isaac NEWTON. He also invented a calculating machine.

LOBACHEVSKI, Nikolai (1793–1856) Russian mathematician who invented non-Euclidean geometry.

MACLAURIN, Colin (1698–1746) Scottish mathematician and physicist who worked on series and analysis, and developed the mathematics of NEWTON.

MINKOWSKI, Hermann (1864–1909) Russian-born German/Swiss mathematician who developed the theory of four-dimensional space-time, the foundation of relativity.

MOBIUS, August (1790–1868) German mathematician who worked mainly in geometry and topology, inventing the Mobius strip (a one-sided continuous surface).

NEWTON, Isaac (1642–1727) English mathematician and physicist who invented calculus (at about the same time as Gottfried LEIBNIZ). His scientific thoughts and discoveries were explained in his monumental work *Principia Mathematica* (1687).

PASCAL, Blaise (1623–1662) French mathematician and physicist who invented a calculating machine and pioneered work on probability (independently of Pierre de FERMAT). The SI unit of pressure and a computer programming language are named after him.

POINCARÉ, Jules Henri (1854–1912) French mathematician who contributed to nearly all branches of mathematics, particularly probability and topology.

POISSON, Siméon (1781–1840) French mathematician who applied mathematics to physics (particularly electricity and magnetism).

PYTHAGORAS (6thC. BC) Ancient Greek mathematician whose discoveries included the ratios of musical intervals, relations of numbers and the relationship between the sides of a right-angled triangle (Pythagoras' theorem).

TAYLOR, Brook (1685–1731) English mathematician and philosopher who pioneered calculus, although his work remained unpublished at the time.

TURING, Alan (1912–1954) British mathematician and logician who constructed some of the first digital computers and invented the theoretical Turing machine to test the computability of mathematical problems.

COMPUTING TERMS

Access To connect to a remote computer DATABASE, usually by using a MODEM.

Address The location (represented by a number) of a value stored in a computer's MEMORY.

ALGOL ALGOrithmic Language, a mathematically oriented computer programming LANGUAGE.

Algorithm A set of rules given to a computer for it to carry out a calculation.

Alphanumeric A character that is either a letter or a number.

Analog A representation of numerical or physical quantities by means of a physical variable (such as a voltage).

ASCII American Standard Code for Information Interchange, a system of codes used by most computers to represent numbers, letters and punctuation marks.

Assembler A computer PROGRAM that translates an ASSEMBLY LANGUAGE into MACHINE LANGUAGE.

Assembly language A computer LANGUAGE that uses symbols as well as words, and that is more difficult to use than a HIGH-LEVEL LANGUAGE.

Backup A copy of a PROGRAM or FILE, made in case the original is lost.

Base The number represented by 10 (that is one-zero) in any number system. In the decimal number system the base is 10; in binary it is 2; and in hexadecimal it is 16.

BASIC Beginner's All-purpose Symbolic Instruction Code, a computer programming LANGUAGE using readable words.

Baud rate The rate at which signals are sent along transmission lines: 1 baud equals one signal (BIT) per second.

Binary A number system with the base 2, using the digits 0 and 1. It can be represented by off and on pulses of electricity (as in a computer).

Bit Binary DigIT: a numeral in BINARY notation – that is, a 0 or 1.

Bug An error in computer SOFTWARE or HARDWARE, causing it to fail.

Byte A space in a computer's MEMORY occupied by one character, usually made up of 8 BITS.

Cardinal number A counting number, such as 1, 2, 3, 4 and so on.

CD ROM Compact Disc ROM (Read Only Memory), a DISK system for holding information and games, with audio and video if required.

COBOL COmmon Business Oriented Language, a computer programming LANGUAGE designed for business and commercial use.

Compiler A computer PROGRAM that translates a HIGH-LEVEL LANGUAGE into MACHINE LANGUAGE.

Cursor A highlighted area on a computer screen that indicates the character or block of text being worked on.

Data General term for the information inputted to, processed by or outputted by a computer.

Database A collection of DATA stored in a computer for retrieval as it is required. Information may be added or updated at any time.

Debug To remove BUGS from computer SOFTWARE.

Decimal A number to the BASE 10.

Default The DRIVE or PROGRAM a computer automatically enters if it receives no other command.

Digit Any of the numbers from 1 to 9.

Digital Describing measurements made (or displayed) using DIGITS.

Disk The most commonly used means of storing computer DATA. A hard disk is often fixed inside the machine; a floppy disk can generally be removed.

Drive The part of a computer that holds a DISK, writing to it and reading from it.

Field A set of characters treated as a whole; the recording area on a computer DISK used for a particular type of DATA.

File A collection of DATA, or the contents of a document, as stored in a computer MEMORY or on DISK.

File-name A collection of (permitted) characters by which a computer OPERATING SYSTEM recognizes a FILE.

Formating The electronic marking of a computer DISK so that it will accept DATA.

FORTRAN FORmula TRANslation, a computer programming LANGUAGE for scientific use.

Fractal A type of mathematical curve (graphic), usually generated by a computer, that appears equally complex no matter how much it is enlarged.

Gate A small circuit that accepts a number of inputs and produces an output that is a logical combination of them.

Graphics Pictures or diagrams on a computer screen or PRINT-OUT, as opposed to text.

Hard copy A PRINT-OUT of a document held in a computer.

Hardware The physical working parts of a computer system.

High-level language A computer LANGUAGE that allows a user to write instructions in everyday words.

Internet A computer NETWORK that extends throughout the world, linking local area networks through gateways.

Language A defined set of characters for communicating with a computer.

Machine language The LANGUAGE of BINARY numbers – representing codes and symbols – with which a computer works.

Mainframe A powerful computer that can be used by many people simultaneously, and which stores large amounts of information.

Memory the part of a computer in which DATA and PROGRAMS are stored.

Microprocessor A miniature electronic circuit on a silicon chip, one or several of which form the processing unit of a computer and hold some MEMORY.

Modem MOdulator-DEModulator, a device that enables computers to communicate with each other via telephone lines.

Monitor A cathode-ray tube similar to a television receiver, on which DATA is displayed. Also called a VDU (Visual Display Unit).

Mouse A small pointing device which, when rolled along a desktop, causes a pointer to move on a computer screen.

MS-DOS MicroSoft Disk Operating System, used by commercial MICROPROCESSORS.

Network A group of computers linked together so that they can share resources.

Operating system A type of SOFTWARE that controls the operation of a computer system.

Personal computer (PC) A desktop or laptop computer designed for general-purpose use.

Pixel A picture element, the smallest unit of a computer display. Pixels combine to produce images.

Port An outlet that allows a computer to be connected to other equipment.

Printer A machine that produces the output from a computer.

Print-out The printed output from a computer.

Program The sequence of instructions that tells a computer how to perform a particular task.

RAM Random Access Memory, the computer MEMORY in which PROGRAMS and DATA are held ready for processing. Its contents are normally lost when the machine is switched off.

ROM Read Only Memory, the permanent programs or instructions retained in a computer's MEMORY even when the machine is switched off.

Simulation The imitation of a situation on a computer, usually by means of a mathematical model, to project and analyse what is likely to occur under various conditions.

Software PROGRAMS, usually available on DISK, for instructing a computer what to do.

Spreadsheet A computer PROGRAM that displays DATA in a regular array of cells, in which information can be altered and manipulated.

VDU See MONITOR.

Virus A PROGRAM introduced into a computer's OPERATING SYSTEM that may be designed to damage the system by deleting, changing or otherwise modifying information. A virus may replicate itself and "infect" other systems in a NETWORK.

Window A small section of a computer screen that has a separate display from the main section.

Word processor A computer PROGRAM designed to store and edit text inputted by means of a keyboard; a computer dedicated to this task alone.

WYSIWYG What You See Is What You Get, describing a computer screen that displays exactly what is keyed in.

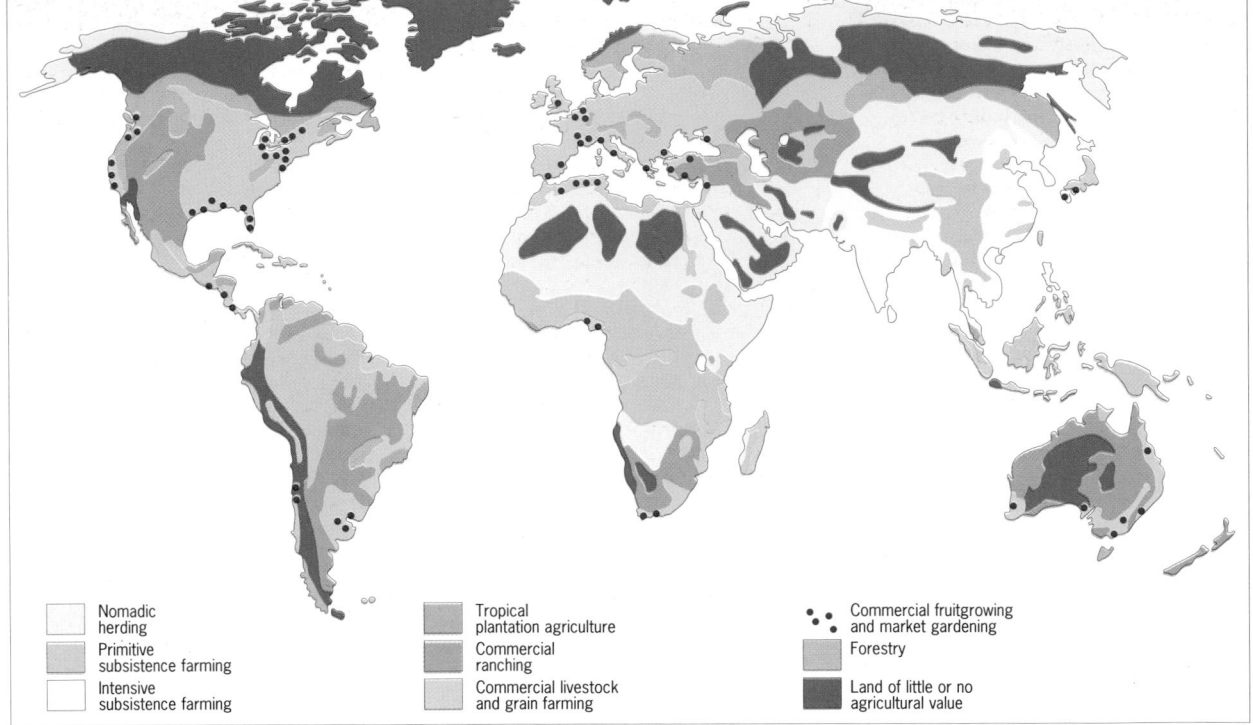

Nomadic herding

Primitive subsistence farming

Intensive subsistence farming

Tropical plantation agriculture

Commercial ranching

Commercial livestock and grain farming

Commercial fruitgrowing and market gardening

Forestry

Land of little or no agricultural value

Timeline

***c.* 9000 B.C.** Sheep and goats domesticated in Afghanistan and Iran.

***c.* 8500 B.C.** Emmer wheat (*Triticum dicoccum*) and barley cultivated in Israel.

***c.* 8000 B.C.** Beans cultivated in Peru. Rice farmed in Indochina.

***c.* 7500 B.C.** Ancient Egyptians begin annual flooding of the Nile Valley for agricultural purposes.

***c.* 7000 B.C.** Einkorn wheat (*Triticum monococcum*) cultivated in Syria and durum wheat (*Triticum durum*) in Turkey. Sugarcane grown in New Guinea. Bananas, coconuts, and yams cultivated in Indonesia.

***c.* 6500 B.C.** Pigs and water buffalo domesticated in China. Chickens kept for eggs and food in parts of S. Asia.

***c.* 6000 B.C.** Flax grown in S.W. Asia. Cattle domesticated in S.E. Turkey. Beans, corn, squash, and peppers farmed in Mexico.

***c.* 5500 B.C.** Millet and peaches farmed in China.

***c.* 5000 B.C.** Alpacas and llamas domesticated in Peru.

***c.* 4500 B.C.** Date palms grown in India. Avocados and cotton (*Gossypium hirsutum* species) cultivated in Mexico. Horses domesticated in Russia.

***c.* 4000 B.C.** Grapes grown for wine in Turkistan. Oil palms cultivated in Sudan.

***c.* 3500 B.C.** Olives grown in Crete. Zebu cattle domesticated in Thailand. Beer brewed in Mesopotamia.

***c.* 3200 B.C.** Cotton (*Gossypium barbadense*) cultivated in South America.

DEVELOPMENT OF AGRICULTURE

Agriculture began in the Middle East more than 10,000 years ago with the cultivation of cereal crops and domestication of sheep and goats for milk, meat, and wool. The establishment of human settlements followed, except for nomadic herders who followed the natural migrations of their flocks. People in lakeside and coastal settlements turned to fishing as a source of food.

The progress of agriculture was aided by various technical innovations, such as plows and harnesses for oxen and horses to pull them. Later inventions included drilling machines (for sowing seed) and reapers, then steam tractors, and finally diesel tractors and combine harvesters. Mechanization made farming a much less labor-intensive industry (*p.441*), releasing workers to supply factories and staff service industries. The biological sciences have also played their part in modernizing farming —first through selective breeding of farm plants and animals, and more recently by genetically engineering new strains of plants or animals that give higher yields, resist disease better, or tolerate extremes of climate.

World fisheries

Most commercial fisheries operate in the open sea, and mainly in the Northern Hemisphere, although there are also fisheries on some large lakes and estuaries. Sometimes simple fishing methods are used, such as rod and line or harpoon, but more often fish are caught in nets by a variety of methods such as drifting, trawling, and seining.

The greatest tonnages landed are of herrings and sardines in northern waters, and of anchovies in the southern seas, although anchovy catches have plummeted in recent years because of overfishing and habitat disturbance. Cod, haddock, tuna, mackerel, and salmon are also taken in large quantities. Crustaceans such as crabs and lobsters, and mollusks such as squid and various types of shellfish, are further important food sources. The largest fish catches come from the seas between Japan and the Philippines. Whaling, banned by international agreement, is still practiced clandestinely by some nations.

Fish farming, in which fish are intensively fed in estuarine or freshwater "ponds," has provided a new source of food. In parts of Asia it is carried out in waterlogged rice paddies, which serve a double function by simultaneously producing a crop of rice.

World fish catches

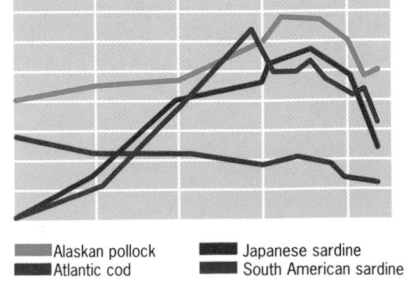

Alaskan pollock

Atlantic cod

Japanese sardine

South American sardine

Cereal crops

Cereals are the most important source of food for humankind—and for farm animals. All the common cereals are derived from species of grass, including barley, corn, oats, rice, rye, and wheat.

Barley (*Hordeum vulgare*) grows best in the cooler climates of the Northern Hemisphere. It is usually sown in the fall (winter barley), although it may also be sown in the spring (spring barley) in very northerly latitudes. Barley is used mainly as animal feed or for brewing (*p. 435*). In northern India it is ground into flour for making chapati, an unleavened bread.

Corn (*Zea mays*) is generally regarded as a semitropical crop, mostly associated with southern and central North America. But new strains are increasingly being grown in Europe, often as a fodder crop or for silage. Sweeter varieties are used for cornmeal and as a vegetable for human consumption. Corn is also made into popcorn, breakfast cereal (cornflakes), and vegetable oil for cooking.

Oats (*Avena sativa*) need a temperate climate with high rainfall. They are grown principally to feed animals and for making hay; only about one-tenth of production goes for human food (oatmeal).

Rice (*Oryza sativa*) is the main food crop of Asia. In lowland areas and on terraced mountainsides, it is grown in wet rice paddies. On higher or drier land, it is grown like other cereal crops on dry soil. The grain may be fermented to make the alcoholic drink saké, popular in Japan.

Rye (*Secale cereale*) is grown mainly in northern Europe. It is used to make hay, to feed stock, to make black bread or rye bread, and as a base for making alcoholic drinks such as whiskey and vodka.

Wheat (*Tricum aestivum*) is the most widely grown crop, although it does not yield as well as rice. Canada, China, Russia, and the United States are the principal producers. High-protein "hard" wheats are ground for flour to make bread; "soft" wheat flour is used to make cookies and cakes. Like barley, the crop is sown as either winter wheat or spring wheat, depending on climate. Durum wheat is ground to make semolina for making pasta.

Root crops

By far the most important root crop is the potato (*Solanum tuberosum*), grown throughout Eurasia and North America. It is a tuber that matures as "early" or "main crop" depending on the variety.

Other common tuber crops are the sweet potato (*Ipomoea batatas*) of Central America and the Pacific islands and the yam (*Dioscorea* species) of the tropics.

Starchy-rooted food plants include arrowroot (*Maranta arundinacea*), grown in swampy tropical areas, and cassava or manioc (*Manihot utilissima*), whose roots are ground to make a flour that is a staple food in parts of South America.

Among other root crops grown for food are carrots (*Daucus carrota*), parsnips (*Pastanaca sativa*), and rutabagas (*Brassica rapa*) in temperate regions. Beets (*Beta sativa*) for sugar manufacture are grown in cooler regions. Radishes (*Raphanus sativus*) are grown as a pungent relish for use in salads.

Green vegetables and pulses

The most important green vegetables belong to the cabbage (*Brassica*) genus. They include cabbages, broccoli, brussels sprouts, cauliflower, and rape (*Brassica napus*), grown as a fodder plant or to produce vegetable oil. Chard (*Beta cicla*), chicory (*Cichorium intybus*), endive (*Cichorium endivia*), lettuce (*Lactuca sativa*), and spinach (*Spinacia oleracea*) are grown as green vegetables or for salads.

Legumes include broad beans (*Vicia* species), peas (*Pisum* species), and various kinds of string beans (*Phaseolus*), many of which can be dried, canned, or frozen. The high-protein soybean (*Glycine max*) is grown as a food in the tropics of eastern Asia. It is also used to make soy sauce, tofu, and vegetable oil.

Fruits and nuts

Fruits are the widest variety of foods available today. It is convenient to regard fruits in two major categories: those generally grown in temperate regions, and those from the tropics and subtropics.

Many temperate fruit trees are members of the rose family; they include apricots, apples, cherries, peaches, pears, and plums. These are grown throughout Europe, North America, South Africa, and Australia. Cider of various types is made from apples (*p. 435*).

In the warmer parts of these regions citrus fruits, such as grapefruit, limes, lemons, oranges, and tangerines (and their hybrids), are grown. Many are produced principally for making fruit juice. Grapes are also grown in warmer regions for wine-making (*p. 435–37*), although some are dried to make raisins. Olives are grown in the Mediterranean region, mainly for their oil. Other smaller fruits include berries, such as blackberries, cranberries, gooseberries, raspberries, blueberries, and strawberries, many of which are used for preserves.

Melons in their many varieties—including cantaloupe, honeydew melon, winter melon, and watermelon—continue to rise in popularity. Another important temperate fruit is the tomato, grown mainly for use raw in salads and cooked in sauces; its juice is also widely drunk.

The most popular tropical fruits are bananas and pineapples. Starchy plantain bananas are a staple food in the West Indies. Figs have been grown since Roman times, and more recent exotic exports from the tropics include mangoes, papayas, and kiwifruits (also called Chinese gooseberries).

The largest of the "nuts," the coconut, is an important tropical crop; its succulent flesh is dried for export. True nuts include almonds (the Mediterranean), Brazil nuts (South America), cashews and pecans (North America), and chestnuts, hazelnuts, and walnuts (Europe). Some of these yield edible oils.

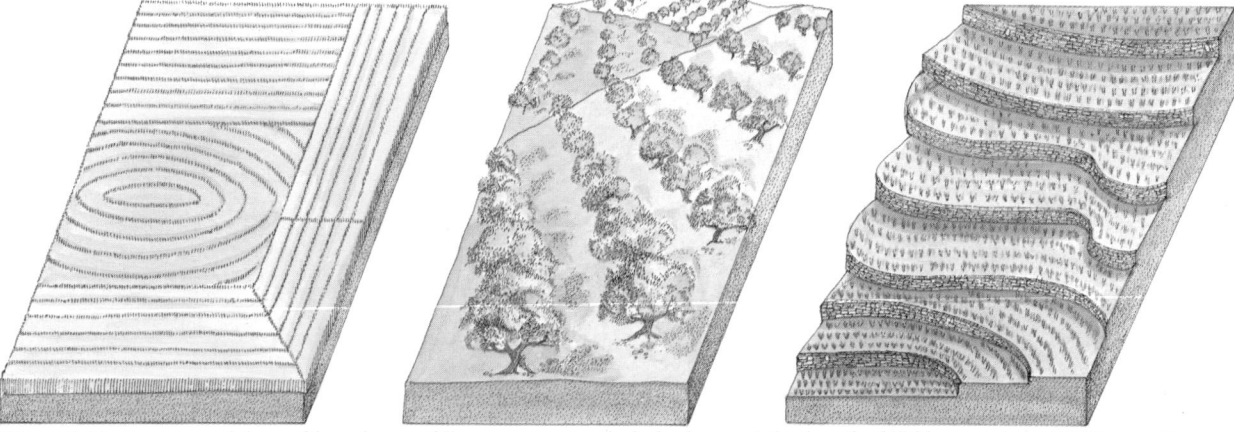

Wheat fields cover more of the earth's surface than any other food crop.

Olive groves are particularly characteristic of the Mediterranean region.

On hillsides, wet rice cultivation can be practiced using constructed terraces.

Timeline

c. 3000 B.C. Donkeys domesticated in Israel and the Nile Valley, elephants in India, and camels in Arabia. Ancient Egyptians and Mesopotamians use ox-drawn plows and large-scale irrigation systems.

c. 2900 B.C. Cotton grown in India (*right*).

c. 2700 B.C. Silkworms cultured for silk in China.

c. 2500 B.C. Potatoes domesticated in Andean South America. Breadfruit cultivated in S.E. Asia. Yaks domesticated in Tibet. Peanuts grown in Central America.

c. 2200 B.C. Ancient Egyptians domesticate ducks and geese for food.

c. 2000 B.C. Guinea pigs domesticated (for food) in Peru.

c. 1950 B.C. "Stick" plows (with no plowshare) used in Mesopotamia. Asian rice (*Oryza sativa*) grown in rice paddies in S.E. Asia.

c. 1900 B.C. Alfalfa cultivated in Egypt as fodder for farm animals.

c. 1750 B.C. Cloves imported into Syria from S.E. Asia.

c. 1700 B.C. Sunflowers cultivated in North America, to be stored as a winter food supply.

c. 1600 B.C. Mesopotamians invent the plowshare.

c. 1550 B.C. Bronze plows in use in Vietnam.

c. 1500 B.C. Soybeans cultivated in Manchuria; they are introduced to China about 300 years later.

c. 1450 B.C. Chinese develop brewing; alcoholic drinks are distilled in other parts of Asia.

c. 1400 B.C. Cassava (manioc) is cultivated in South America.

c. 1100 B.C. Mesopotamians introduce iron plowshares.

c. 1000 B.C. Oats grown in central Europe.

c. 500 B.C. Reindeer domesticated in Asia. Chinese begin "modern" farming practices such as manuring and hoeing weeds, with crops planted in rows. Sorghum, millet domesticated in Sudan.

c. 450 B.C. Chopsticks become common in China and soon spread across Asia.

c. 300 B.C. Turkeys domesticated in Mexico. African rice (*Sativa glaberrima*) cultivated in the Niger Delta.

290 B.C. Chinese develop a chest harness to enable horses to pull plows.

250 B.C. Thai farmers begin to use domesticated water buffalo to pull plows in rice paddies; the practice soon spreads in S.E. Asia.

200 B.C. Ox-powered waterwheels used for irrigation.

125 B.C. Chinese farmers begin to grow wine grapes imported from the West.

100 B.C. Waterwheels used to drive mills for grinding corn in Albania. First specialized breed of dairy cattle, the Holstein, produced by farmers in what is now the Netherlands.

PLANT RESOURCES

As well as providing food, plants are of use to people in many ways. Even so, much of their potential—for instance, medicinal properties of some tropical rain forest plants—remains to be investigated.

Rubber

Natural rubber remains an important crop, even though for many applications it has been superseded by various kinds of synthetic polymers. The rubber tree (*Hevea brasiliensis*) is native to South America but has been introduced into other tropical regions as a plantation crop, particularly in the Malay peninsula.

Raw rubber is a white or yellow latex that occurs in the tree's bark. The tree is tapped by means of diagonal cuts, and the latex is allowed to ooze into a collecting cup. It is then coagulated with acid and pressed into bales for shipment. The properties of natural rubber are much improved by the process of vulcanization (Rubber, *p. 414*), invented in the United States in 1839.

Cotton

Cotton (*Gossypium* species) is the world's most important fiber crop, a position it has held since it was first cultivated in China, Egypt, and India nearly 5,000 years ago. The fibers cover the seed capsules, or bolls, of the plants and are removed by a process called ginning.

Cotton needs a long, warm growing season, so it is still grown in its original locations and in the southern U.S.A., where the main variety is *Gossypium hirsutum*.

As well as being a textile fiber, cotton is a source of cellulose (for cotton batting and for making rayon), and the crushed seeds yield valuable cottonseed oil.

Other fiber crops

Vegetable fibers can also be removed from leaves and stems of plants. Flax (*Linum usitatissimum*) is a blue-flowered plant that grows in temperate regions. Its long stems are soaked in water ("retting") to loosen the bast fibers, which are then separated by beating and rolling. Hemp (*Cannabis* species) and jute (*Corchorus* species) are processed in a similar way. Flax fibers are fine and flexible and are woven to make linen. Crushed flax seeds yield linseed oil, used in making paint, putty, and varnish. Jute and hemp fibers are much coarser and are used to make sacking and ropes; hemp seeds also yield oil. Another coarse fiber is coir, made from coconut husks and used for making matting. Kapok, also from seed fibers, is much finer and is used for heat insulation, stuffing winter clothing, and pillows.

Fibers derived from leaves, such as abaca (from the plant *Musa textilis*), henequen (from *Agave fourcroydes*), and sisal (from *Agave sisalana*), are generally coarse and short. They are used as brush bristles or made into rope and twine.

Cotton is used for cotton thread, jute and hemp for rope and sacking, and flax for linen.

Linen Rope Flax

Cotton

Jute

Sacking Cotton thread Hemp

World forestry

Communities have cut down trees for fuel and timber since the emergence of humankind (*p. 444*). The temperate areas of northern Europe, for example, including most of Britain and the land around the Mediterranean, were once covered with mixed hardwood forests. More recently, the tropical forests have come under attack, both for timber and to clear land for stock-raising to meet the increasing world demand for meat.

Sometimes the results are disastrous. Tree roots bind the soil together and

without them rain runs rapidly off the ground and washes the soil away, leaving a barren wasteland. Meanwhile the loss of habitats is causing the extinction of many animal species (*pp. 144–45*).

On the positive side, many northern countries have replanted large forests of quick-growing conifers, which are selectively felled (and then replanted) to provide wood for building and for making particleboard and pulp for paper. Selective cutting can also be successfully used in tropical forests, although the gaps created take a long time to fill naturally and there is risk of damage to the ecosystem.

LIVESTOCK

Cattle

Modern domestic cattle include the European species (*Bos taurus*) and the Asian domesticated zebu (*Bos indicus*). The European type is a domesticated version of the wild aurochs (*Bos primigenius*), which had been hunted to extinction by the early 1600s. Other cattle domesticated and farmed in mountainous parts of Asia include the gaur (*Bos gaurus*) and the yak (*Bos grunniens*). In many parts of Africa, local people keep herds of semiwild Ankole cattle.

Cattle are farmed for cow's milk and meat and, in parts of Africa, for blood. In Asia and parts of Africa they are not kept for milk—the adults' digestive systems lack the enzyme necessary to digest lactose (milk sugar). After the cattle are slaughtered, their hides provide leather and the bones, horns, and hooves are used for making gelatin, glue, and bonemeal fertilizer.

Young females, before they have borne a calf, are called heifers; the males or bulls, when castrated and fattened for meat, are known as steers.

There are many different breeds of cattle. Some, such as the Ayrshire and the Jersey, have been developed to produce high yields of milk (*p. 434*); others, such as the Hereford, are bred for their yield of lean meat. A few breeds—like the black-and-white Holstein—are dual-purpose, providing both milk and meat.

Pigs

Wild pigs (genus *Sus*) show a much wider variety of types than the forerunners of any other kind of farm animal. The European wild boar (*Sus scrofa*) probably gave rise to the pig farmstock of the West. Pigs are farmed for their meat, the many meat products derived from them, and their hides, which are used to make fine leather. Important breeds include the large white (or Yorkshire) and the black Berkshire; the Landrace types are bred for bacon.

Lean pig meat—pork—is a prime meat. The best cuts are from the hams (hind legs). These are often cured using salt or brine and possibly by smoking over a fire made from chips of hardwood. Fattier

Merino sheep   **Corriedale sheep**   **Pygmy goat**

Ayrshire cow   **Hereford bull**

Black Berkshire pig   **Large white pig**   **Friesian cow**

cuts are made into various kinds of sausages, and congealed pig's blood is the principal ingredient used for making blood sausage. Hooves (or "trotters") may be eaten or converted into gelatin; pork fat is rendered into lard; and pigs' bristles are used for brushes.

Sheep and goats

Sheep (genus *Ovis*) are raised for their wool and meat. They are farmed in vast numbers in Australia, New Zealand, India, and the Middle East. There are also many smaller sheep farms in the hilly districts of northern European countries, where the animals are raised mainly for meat. Sheep are slaughtered young and their meat sold as lamb (meat from older animals is mutton).

The finest wool comes from Merinos and the French breed called the Rambouillet. The hides of the hardy Karakul sheep of Central Asia are marketed as the short, curly "fur" that is known as Persian lamb. The British Lincoln, on the other hand, has extremely long wool but is usually crossed with other breeds in order to increase the size of the animal for meat.

Unlike sheep, which have solid horns, goats (genus *Capra*) have hollow horns and are more hardy, living in cold mountainous areas or dry regions throughout the world. Males, or billy goats, are distinguished from females, known as nanny

goats, by a characteristic beard beneath the chin. The wild goat, or bezoar (*Capra aegagrus*), of the Middle East probably gave rise to the domestic species (*Capra hircus*), which is farmed for milk and meat. Mohair is the long, shiny wool of the Angora goat (*Capra angorensis*).

Poultry and eggs

Various birds have been domesticated for their meat and eggs and, sometimes, their feathers. The main examples are chickens, ducks, geese, and turkeys, although semiwild birds such as pheasants and pigeons are also included in this category.

The domestic chicken was probably bred from the Asian jungle fowl (*Gallus gallus*), a small, shy ground-dwelling member of the pheasant family. Today chickens are largely raised commercially in high-density "factories" with automatic feeding and control of the environment. Using such methods, farmers can produce broiler chickens, ready for market, in eight to ten weeks. More than 3 billion chickens are raised on U.S. farms, and billions of eggs are also produced. A hen begins to lay eggs at about 20 weeks and lays 240–250 eggs during a working life of about one year. The birds are then usually slaughtered for meat.

The much larger turkey came originally from Central America, where its wild ancestor (*Meleagris gallopavo*) can still be found. Even wild birds can weigh as much as 22 lb. (10 kg), and domestic birds, such as the Black Norfolk, can weigh more than twice as much. In much of the Western world, turkey is traditionally eaten at Christmas and, in the United States, at Thanksgiving.

Ducks are eaten worldwide, and geese are especially popular in continental Europe; both are birds of the family Anatidae. The white Aylesbury duck is one of the heaviest, while Embden, Toulouse, and Strasbourg are among the best-known geese bred for their meat or, after overfeeding, for their livers—which in France are made into pâté de fois gras. Both ducks and geese are also often reared for their eggs.

Rhode Island red chicken

Black Norfolk turkey

Aylesbury duck

Toulouse duck

Timeline

A.D. 60 Roman emperor Nero bans the import of pepper from India because of its cost to the economy.

80 Chinese inventors make a chain pump for lifting water for irrigation.

90 Chinese invent a fanlike machine for winnowing grain.

100 Chinese farmers begin to cultivate tea. They also make insecticide from dried chrysanthemum flowers (pyrethrum).

110 Chinese develop a multitube seed drill.

530 Chinese invent a water-powered machine for shaking and sifting flour.

552 Byzantines try silk production using insects smuggled out of China.

600 Windmills used to grind grain in Iran.

1000 Arabs introduce lemon plants to Sicily and Spain; iron used to make plowshares.

1100 Italians distill wine to make brandy.

1191 Tea imported into Japan from China.

1280 The Hanseatic League Baltic fisheries net huge catches (13,000 tons of herring in one year).

1350 Shogun bans tea drinking in Japan.

1400 Wild coffee harvested to make a beverage in Ethiopia.

1410 Dutch fishermen introduce drift nets (and use salt to preserve the catch).

1450 Coffee exported from the Arabian port of Mocha.

1484 Spaniard Pedro de Vera introduces sugarcane to the Canary Islands and builds their first refinery, a cane-grinding mill.

1500 German merchants import spices from the East Indies by sea.

1514 Pineapples imported into Europe.

1517 Coffee imported into Europe.

1519 Hernándo Cortés introduces Spanish horses into North America.

1520 Portuguese import orange trees from China. Spanish import chocolate from Mexico. Turkeys and corn imported into Europe from the Americas.

1525 Belgian hops introduced into Britain.

1532 Cultivation of sugarcane begins in Brazil.

1548 Pepper plants (capsicum) from Africa first grown in Britain.

1550 Spanish begin to import tobacco.

1560 Frenchman Jean Nicot introduces tobacco plants into W. Europe.

1565 Potatoes introduced into Spain from South America. John Hawkins introduces tobacco and sweet potatoes into his native England.

1566 Camillo Torello patents a seed drill, the first in Europe.

1573 Sugarcane refinery built in Germany.

1580 Italians begin importing coffee for drinking from Turkey.

1596 Tomatoes introduced into England.

ANIMAL PRODUCTS

Dairy products

On all but the smallest dairy farms, cattle are milked by machines, which withdraw milk from the cows' udders using a pulsating partial vacuum. After cooling, the milk is taken by road or rail tankers to large depots for processing. Milk for human consumption is pasteurized by prolonged heating and then rapid cooling. The resulting nutritious liquid contains carbohydrates (sugars), fats, and proteins, as well as the minerals calcium and phosphorus and vitamins A, C, and D.

Milk can then be subjected to a number of other processes. It may be skimmed to remove most of the fat or even rendered almost totally fat-free. It may be dried or "powdered" by evaporation. Milk removed in the middle of this process is described as "evaporated" (if unsweetened) or "condensed" (if extra sugar is added). It may also be homogenized, to prevent the fat from separating on standing, or completely sterilized (usually by irradiation) to produce milk with a shelf life of several months.

Alternatively, milk is used to make cream, butter, and cheese. Cream is the fatty part of milk, removed during skimming, and may be lightly churned to produce thicker "heavy" cream. Prolonged churning converts it to butter; the residual liquid is called buttermilk.

Adding a curdling agent (such as rennet) to milk separates it into semisolid curds and watery whey. The curds are put into molds and enzyme action gradually converts the curds into cheese. Hard cheeses such as cheddar and Parmesan improve with keeping; soft cheeses for immediate use include Edam and, after ripening, Brie and Camembert. Molds are included in cheese-making to produce blue cheeses such as Gorgonzola and Stilton. If the cheese is sterilized, the product is processed cheese. Cheeses are also made from goat's or sheep's milk, especially in Mediterranean countries.

Skimmed cow's milk is more commonly used than goat's milk for making yogurt. The milk is warmed and allowed to ferment by the action of bacteria. The creamy, slightly sour product of this process is "natural" yogurt, which may then have fruit or flavoring added to it.

In the Middle East and in northern Asian countries, goat's milk is widely drunk or used for yogurt, soured milk drinks, or cheese. In the Himalayas, yak milk is used.

Angora goat   Kashmir goat   Alpaca

Wool and hair

The chief animal fibers used for making yarn and cloth are sheep's wool and hair from camels and goats. Short fibers are spun into yarn and made into a soft cloth, which may be dyed before or after weaving; the softest cloth is made from lambswool. Long fibers are aligned by combing and spun into worsted yarn for making tougher fabrics such as gabardine.

Goat's hair is made into fabrics such as cashmere (from the Kashmir goat) and mohair (from the Angora goat). The silky wool of the alpaca—a llamalike South American animal—may be blended with sheep's wool to make high-quality cloth. Camel hair is woven into a light cloth with good heat insulation properties, hence its use for coats.

Fur and leather

People have made clothing out of fur since prehistoric times. Beavers, foxes, and rabbits were hunted for their fur, and the most highly prized chinchilla, mink, and sable were bred on farms as well as being trapped in the wild. Seals were also hunted for their fur, and exotic species—particularly the big cats—were also exploited. However, overhunting and a rising body of opinion against such exploitation of animals have made natural fur clothing unpopular in many countries. Today, polymer chemists can produce synthetic fabrics with all the looks and thermal properties of real fur.

Leather is the preserved skin or hide of an animal, made tough and flexible by tanning. In this process, the hide is first scraped or treated with chemicals to remove the hair, then degreased and soaked—for up to a month—in a solution of tannin. Alternatively, light leather can be made much more quickly by soaking in chromium salts. The cured leather may be dyed or buffed to produce suede. It may be embossed or "tooled" to incorporate a permanent design. Leather is still used for saddles, horse harnesses, and high-quality upholstery, shoes, and handbags, although for most other purposes it has been replaced by synthetic materials.

BEVERAGES

Tea, coffee, and cocoa

Tea is the most widely drunk beverage. It is made from the dried evergreen leaves of the subtropical tea plant (*Camellia sinensis*), which originated in China. It is now an important plantation crop in many Asian countries, particularly China, India, and Sri Lanka. The young leaves are usually picked by hand, passed through rollers to remove juices, and allowed to ferment in a humid atmosphere. Fermentation is arrested by drying the leaves over a fire, when they acquire their brown or black color. Unfermented green tea is also available. The maté, or Paraguay tea, drunk in South America is made from the leaves of a holly plant (*Ilex paraguayensis*).

Coffee "beans" are the seeds from the red berrylike fruits of the evergreen coffee tree. Coffee trees need a moist, hot climate and are grown in tropical regions throughout the world. Most coffee comes from the Arabian species (*Coffea arabica*), although Congo coffee (*Coffea robusta*) and Liberian coffee (*Coffea liberica*) are also grown commercially, mainly for making "instant" coffee.

The ripe berries are picked and the seeds extracted by machines; the leftover seed pulp is used as fertilizer. The beans are washed and dried, traditionally in the sun, and the skins are removed. Beans may be sold in this form or roasted before sale. Roasted beans are ground immediately before use, or they are converted into instant coffee by powdering or by freeze-drying strong liquid coffee. Like tea, coffee contains the stimulant caffeine, although decaffeinated versions are also increasingly available.

Cocoa is a chocolate drink made from the powdered, dried seeds ("beans") of the cacao tree (*Theobroma cacao*), a tropical plant that originated in South America. The tree bears its seed pods on its trunk and branches. These are collected and split open, and the pulp containing 30–40 seeds per pod is removed. After being left to ferment for about a week, the seeds are dried in a kiln or in the sun. To make cocoa and chocolate, the seeds are roasted, the hulls removed, and the kernels ground to produce liquid cocoa butter. This, in turn, is dried and milled to make cocoa powder.

Wine

Wine-making begins when grapes are crushed in a press (or, traditionally, by being trodden) to produce grape juice, called must. The juice is transferred to a fermenting vat and yeast may be added; extra yeast is not always necessary because of the presence of natural wine yeast on grape skins.

Fermentation converts the sugar in the juice (mostly fructose) into alcohol and carbon dioxide gas. The grape skins are removed in making white wine; for red wines the skins are left in the fermentation vat; and for rosé wines the skins are removed after fermentation begins. Fermentation is halted to make sweet wines; dry wines result if fermentation is allowed to go to completion. Sparkling wines result from secondary fermentation after bottling. Fortified wines such as Madeira, port, and sherry have brandy added.

Beer and "hard" cider

Like wine-making, the brewing of beer relies on a fermentation process. In this case, the source of sugar is a grain, usually barley. The grain is soaked in water and then spread out to germinate, when natu-ral enzymes convert some of the grain's starch into sugar. As soon as this happens, the germinated barley—now known as malt—is roasted and dried in kilns. Other kilns or oast houses are used to dry hops, which are another ingredient in beer making.

At the brewery, the malt is crushed and "mashed" with hot water to produce a liquid called wort. The wort is boiled with hops and, if necessary, extra sugar, then cooled and transferred into an open fermenting vat to which brewer's yeast is added. For beer, the yeast falls to the bottom of the vat during fermentation, which generally takes about a week. The stronger ales are made with top-fermenting yeasts. Newly brewed beer is allowed to mature in tanks before being "packaged" for sale in wooden or metal barrels (kegs), bottles, and cans. Most bottled and canned beers have extra carbon dioxide added to make them effervescent.

In parts of Europe, "hard" cider is an alcoholic drink made by fermenting apple juice, a process more akin to wine-making than brewing. Cider-making is quicker than either, except when a high-alcohol brew is being made. As with wines, the flavor of cider depends on the choice of fruit and the sugar and gas content.

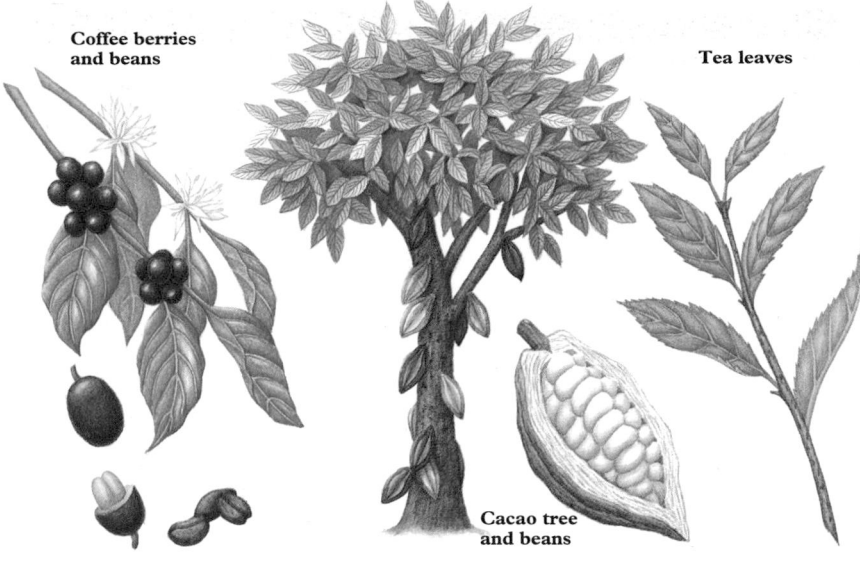
Coffee berries and beans
Tea leaves
Cacao tree and beans

Mechanical harvesting at a cider apple orchard in England.

THE WORLD OF WINE

Grapes are high in sugar with plenty of wild yeast on their skins, and they have a natural tendency to ferment: the yeasts react with the sugars to form alcohol. Wine-making was already a craft by the time of the ancient Egyptians, and the Romans took their love of wine wherever they conquered. It was not until the 1600s, however, that certain French wine makers began to apply rigorous standards—in order to get higher prices for their wine—and the age of fine wine was born. Today more than 40 billion bottles a year are being made in more than 50 countries.

The importance of climate

The grapevine grows in temperate regions of the world between latitudes 30° and 50° north and south of the equator, where long, warm summers ripen the fruit and cool winters allow the vine to rest. The vine is harmed by excessive heat and extreme cold. It also needs about 30 inches (75 cm) of rain a year, most of it in winter and spring.

The natural limits of latitude are extended by conditions in specific areas: for example, the warm Gulf Stream allows grapes to be grown in England, while cool polar airstreams allow the vine to grow nearer the equator in South America. Grapes can also be grown at higher altitudes in hotter regions.

Within the natural parameters, microclimates and topography influence the choice of vineyard site. In northern Europe the best vineyards are on south-facing slopes with maximum exposure to the sun; the shelter afforded by a range of hills may protect them from rain and severe cold; a lake or large river can moderate temperature, while flowing water hinders frost. A slope also means well-drained soil: good-quality wine seldom comes from flat land, or valley bottoms, where water collects and frosts may be severe; the tops of hills are also avoided, because of exposure to strong wind.

The vintage

In any winegrowing region, the weather in a particular year can determine the quantity, quality, and longevity of the wine. Short periods of winter frost benefit the plant by killing pests, but frosts in late spring can be disastrous to the tender buds. Heavy rain, when the grapes are ready for harvest, can seriously damage the fruit, or cause it to rot. A long, warm, dry summer, just before the grapes are picked, generally indicates a good vintage.

The better the vintage, and the better the wine, the longer it will last compared to other wines from the same region made from similar grape varieties. Good red Bordeaux improves in the bottle for 15–50 years, as can the finest sweet white Sauternes. Less expensive wines in these styles are best drunk after 5–15 years.

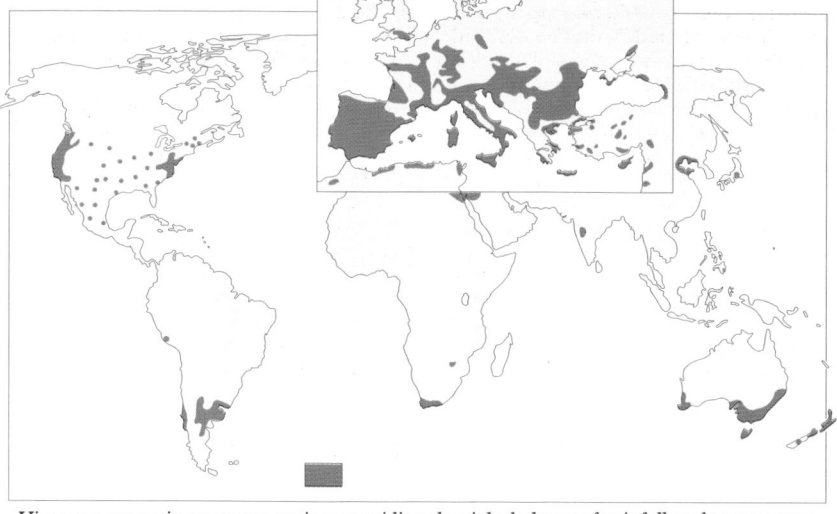

Vines are grown in temperate regions providing the right balance of rainfall and temperature.

European vineyards

Steeped in tradition, the wine names and laws of Europe's old-established vineyards are not always easy to understand. Wines may be named after a large region, smaller district, a village, or an individual vineyard; others are known by the name of the estate or producer; some are named after a grape or wine style.

Wines are aged in upright barriques *at Château Margaux in the Médoc.*

FRANCE About 30 percent of French wines are subject to strict Appellation Contrôlée (A.C.) laws, which set out the location and method of manufacture of each wine. Less strictly controlled are many *vins de pays*, or country wines.

Bordeaux wines are known by the names of châteaux, the estates where they are produced. The main areas for fine red wine are Médoc, Graves, St.-Emilion, and Pomerol; dry whites are made in Graves and Entre-deux-Mers; some of the world's greatest sweet wines come from Sauternes and Barsac in the Graves.

Burgundy's vineyards are divided into hundreds of tiny parcels of land: the best are the Grands crus, which have their own A.C.s; next best are the Premiers crus; then wines named after communes. Some are red, some white; all are dry. Chablis, which is variable in quality, is

the best known of the Burgundy whites. Immediately south of Burgundy, the Côte Chalonnaise and Mâcon regions produce similar reds and whites. South of Mâcon, Beaujolais is known for its fresh reds, for drinking within two years of the vintage.

The **Loire Valley** is a diverse region, producing mainly fresh light wines: Muscadet (white) comes from near the coast; going inland, Anjou, Saumur, and Touraine offer whites, reds, and rosés; Touraine is also the home of Vouvray, a great sweet white wine, and of crisp white Sancerre and Pouilly Fumé.

Champagne has set the world standard for sparkling wine, usually white, sometimes pink; the wines are known by the names of the producers.

Alsace wines, unusually in France, are described by grape variety. Nearly all are dry whites, from grapes such as Riesling, Gewürztraminer, Sylvaner, Pinot Blanc, and Pinot Gris.

The **Rhône's** wines include many good-value Côtes du Rhône reds (and some whites), as well as some strong, long-lived—and expensive—reds such as Hermitage and Châteauneuf-du-Pape.

Other well-known names include sweet white Monbazillac, heavy red Cahors, and Madiran from southwest France; **Provence** and the **Midi** (Languedoc-Roussillon) produce everyday rosés and reds such as Corbières, Minervois, Fitou, and Côtes du Roussillon.

ITALY has an even greater variety of wines than France; most are named after their place of origin, sometimes linked to the name of the grape. Wine is made in all but the most mountainous areas.

Piedmont, in the northwest, has the powerful, long-lived red Barolo and Barbaresco (made from Nebbiolo grapes); only slightly less robust are the wines made from Barbera grapes (e.g. Barbera d'Asti); lighter reds are made from Dolcetto grapes (e.g. Dolcetto d'Alba). The town of Asti is famous for sweet sparkling whites. **Veneto**, in the northeast, uses various local grapes for white Soave, light red Bardolino, and red Valpolicella, made in a variety of styles.

In central Italy, **Emilia-Romagna** produces Lambrusco—slightly sparkling, sweet or dry, low-alcohol red wine. Italy's most famous wine is red Chianti, from **Tuscany**, which is also home to the expensive, long-lived red Brunello di Montalcino and many other fine reds, such as Vino Nobile di Montepulciano.

Other central regions, such as **Umbria**, **Marche**, and **Lazio**, are best known for light whites: Orvieto (sweet and dry), Verdicchio dei Castelli di Jesi (dry), and Frascati (usually dry). Southern Italy, Sicily, and Sardinia produce all styles. Sicily's brown, fortified Marsala, which is usually sweet, is known worldwide.

SPAIN has long been synonymous with sherry, the fortified wine from Jerez in the south. It is made in a variety of styles,

Picking Chardonnay grapes in a traditional Burgundy vineyard.

from the crisp, dry fino and manzanilla to the rich sweet cream sherries; amontillado and the fuller flavored oloroso may be made dry or sweet. Spain's finest quality wine is the robust red Rioja: other regions producing fine wines, both red and white, include Navarra, Ribera del Duero, Rueda, Galicia, and Penedès.

PORTUGAL, like Spain, produces a huge amount of everyday red and white wine for local consumption. The best-known names are Dao, which can improve in the bottle for many years, and Vino Verde, which is best drunk very young. Portugal's international reputation rests on the fortified wines port and Madeira.

GERMANY The best wines produced in Germany's cool northern climate are the fresh, fruity whites made from the Riesling grape. They are usually low in alcohol and often medium-sweet, although *trocken* (dry) is increasingly seen on labels. Some of the finest wines are the rare and intensely sweet Beerenauslesen and Trockenbeerenauslesen.

It is difficult to distinguish the best German wines because wine law defines quality by the ripeness of the grape: in theory any vineyard can produce quality wine. The top level is Qualitätswein mit Prädikat (QmP)—or quality wine with distinction. These wines are distinguished

by the degree of ripeness: they are Kabinett, Spätlese, Auslese, Beerenauslese, and Trockenbeerenauslese and carry the name of the grape.

The name of the producer may be prominent on the label. Quality wine will always state the region of origin, or Anbaugebiet, of which there are 13, the best known being Mosel-Saar-Ruwer, Rheingau, Rheinhessen, Rheinpfalz (or Pfalz), and Nahe. A district within a region is known as a Bereich; within the Bereich are hundreds of Grosslagen (collective vineyard sites) and thousands of Einzellagen (individual vineyards), the names of which may be linked to a village name.

New World vineyards

Wine makers outside Europe and the Mediterranean have no traditions of vine growing and are much freer to choose which varieties to grow. Many wines made in North America and Australia used to be given the names of well-known European wines, such as Burgundy or Champagne, in order to give the consumer an idea of the wine style. Today consumers recognize New World wines mainly by grape variety.

U.S.A. California produces 90 percent of all U.S. wine in an enormous range of styles, but particularly dry whites made from Chardonnay and dry reds from Cabernet Sauvignon and Zinfandel. The best-known zones are around the San Francisco Bay area, especially Napa Valley and Sonoma County.

AUSTRALIA Wines made in Australia's hot climate tend to have powerful, fruity flavors, although the range is vast: there are many dry reds made from Cabernet Sauvignon, Shiraz (Syrah), and blends of the two, and dry whites from Chardonnay and Sémillon. The Barossa Valley is perhaps the best-known area.

NEW ZEALAND The cool climate produces mainly crisp white wines: Sauvignon Blanc can be superb, as can Chardonnay and Riesling. Marlborough, Hawkes Bay, and Gisborne are the largest wine-producing areas.

SOUTH AFRICA Historically known for dessert wines, South Africa also makes wine from all the major grapes and spe-

New World mechanized harvesting—of Pinot Noir in California.

cializes in dry whites made from Steen (Chenin Blanc) and Colombard and reds from Cinsaut and Pinotage.

SOUTH AMERICA Argentina produces huge amounts of everyday wine; Chile and Argentina also make some fine wines, both red and white, from the major grapes. Some of Argentina's best reds are made from Malbec.

Grape varieties

There are several thousand varieties of *Vitis vinifera,* the native European vine. Other species, such as *Vitis labrusca,* are native to North America and Asia. Certain varieties are ideally suited to the microclimate and soil type of specific locations. Given different conditions, sites, or vinification, a variety will produce wine with different characteristics.

Chardonnay   Syrah

Sauvignon Blanc

Cabernet Sauvignon

Red-wine grapes
Cabernet Sauvignon The basis of most red Bordeaux; adaptable, grown worldwide.

Merlot Used in Bordeaux; in many soft, fruity wines for drinking young.

Pinot Noir Traditional grape of Burgundy; difficult to grow, an irresistible challenge to wine makers.

Syrah Foremost grape of the hot Rhône Valley; particularly at home in Australia, where it is known as Shiraz.

White-wine grapes
Chardonnay Used in Burgundy and Champagne; versatile, grown worldwide.

Sauvignon Blanc Used in Bordeaux and Sancerre; makes excellent wine in New Zealand and California.

Sémillon Used in Bordeaux whites; particularly good in Australia's Hunter Valley region.

Riesling The classic German grape; makes dry and sweet white wines.

FOOD AROUND THE WORLD

Food is one of man's most basic requirements. We need food to provide the energy for our bodily functions. With the establishment of communities and the development of farming, people began to look for ways to vary their diet. Thus food became more than a necessity for life, it became a pleasure. The need to produce, preserve, and process food was also responsible for some of man's earliest technological achievements.

Modern transportation and communications networks have left few areas of the developed world without knowledge of and access to foods from all around the globe, although the import of "exotic" foods has existed since the Romans began to trade gold and silver for pepper, cinnamon, and many other spices from Asia. When Columbus chanced upon the Americas, he established trading patterns that shaped the food of the world as we know it today: Indian corn is now a staple in Africa and widely used in Europe and Asia; potatoes, which originated in South America, are an important part of northern European cooking; and Mediterranean cuisine is unimaginable without tomatoes and peppers. Many other foodstuffs that originated in the Americas have also been adopted far from their birthplace. However, trade worked both ways, and many European foods and cooking methods have become common in the Americas.

Europe

The countries of Europe, with their temperate climate and long-established trading relations, have enjoyed a varied diet throughout much of their history. Several items, such as pork, olive oil, and grain are common to many countries.

The Moors brought rice to Spain and Portugal, as well as saffron and other spices, almonds, citrus fruits, and a love of sweet things. Both countries were great trading nations and exotic foods often appeared in the Iberian Peninsula before anywhere else in Europe.

The geography of France accounts for its famously varied food. The south once felt Greek, Roman, and Arab influences, and today, Provence's sun-drenched cuisine is abundant with fruit, vegetables, and fish. The mountains of the southwest, center, and east—with their more limited resources—have substantial winter dishes, many of which are based on potatoes, beans, and cabbage, with flavors varied by specially raised duck and goose. Shellfish are still abundant on the Atlantic coast, with its well-known oyster farms. Normandy's maritime climate has fostered a rich dairying tradition, with many dishes—especially fish and pork—bathed in butter and cream. Artois, French Flanders, and Picardy look north for inspiration, with a tradition of beer-brewing and herring from the North Sea.

Trading in the floating market, Bangkok, Thailand.

Wheat for bread, olives for oil, and grapes for wine have long been the mainstay of the Mediterranean countries. The sea provides a good fish catch and, although much of the land is ill-suited to cattle, there is plenty of meat, milk, and cheese from sheep and goats. Herbs, such as rosemary, thyme, and oregano, pervade the foods. Cooking methods remain simple in Greece, with spit-roast meats, charcoal grills, and stews cooked long and slow in a baker's oven. Italy's regions have their own zealously guarded traditions. The Venetians were great travelers and acquired sophisticated culinary arts. Italy has a clear north-south divide. Regions south of Rome are poorer and more reliant on simple sustenance, leaving the more elaborate dishes to the prosperous north. Wheat is grown throughout Italy, with a hard variety, durum wheat, being used to make pasta. Rice, grown in the plains around the Po River, goes into the many variations of risotto.

Vienna, the capital of Austria, was a center of culture and wealth in the 1700s and 1800s, and gained a reputation for cakes, rich breads, chocolate, and cream-based sauces, enriching a basic cuisine of more sustaining foods which included goose and pork, boiled beef, noodles and dumplings, cabbage and root vegetables. Much of northern, central, and eastern

Europe experiences cold winters, when food is scarce. Root vegetables such as potatoes, turnips, kohlrabi, radishes, and beets are less perishable than other vegetables, and therefore form the basis of many traditional dishes in these parts of Europe, as does cabbage, which is easily preserved by salting or pickling sauerkraut.

Asia

The technique of growing rice in flooded fields to take advantage of seasonal rain was learned some 4,000 years ago in the islands and peninsulas of Southeast Asia. Rice was introduced to southern China in around 2000 B.C., and its consumption soon led to the invention of the wok, in which food chopped into small pieces is cooked quickly over a fierce heat. Steaming food over rice as it boils is another widely used technique.

Northern China is less suited to rice cultivation, and remains faithful to its original staples: wheat (used for noodles and steamed buns), millet, sorghum, and barley. Frequent invasions from the west introduced a taste for lamb and mutton as well as cooking techniques such as spit-roasting, barbecuing, and the Mongolian hotpot, in which food is cooked by dipping it into a pot of broth boiling over a charcoal burner. As in

Europe, most peasant families in China and southern Asia managed to keep a pig and also supplemented their rice diet with fish such as carp and eel, frogs, snakes, and small mammals such as rats and dogs, which are still eaten today.

Another major source of protein throughout Asia is the versatile soybean, grown in southern China for more than 2,000 years, which can be simmered and reduced to make bean curd, fermented to make a flavorsome paste and sauce, and germinated to produce beansprouts.

Japan's long coastline means that fish and seaweed are central to the national cuisine, and the humid maritime climate allows the production of abundant fruit and vegetables. Again, the staple cereal is rice. The Japanese interpretation of Buddhism gave rise to much of the ritual surrounding the serving and presentation of food, and there is a strong emphasis on keeping food as close to nature as possible, so actual cooking is limited.

In the hot climates of southern India, Thailand, Malaysia, and Indonesia it was found that rich spices caused perspiration which cooled the body, and the chili pepper, introduced from Central America, was a welcome addition to a cuisine based on rice, tropical fruits and vegetables, and fish.

India's many regions vary enormously. The Hindus of the south are largely vegetarian and, despite poor land, have developed an inventive and highly spiced cuisine based on lentils, other legumes, and rice, which is boiled or made into flour for pancakes. The west coast has a long history of Christian settlers who appreciated the many varieties of seafood available. The staple food of the north is wheat, often eaten in the form of chapati bread. The Mughals brought with them the Muslim religion and a cuisine based on meat (beef and lamb), enhanced by rich cream and yogurt sauces, thickened with nuts and flavored with more subtle herbs and spices than those of the south, such as cumin, coriander, and saffron. Their pilaus and biryanis are rich and complex rice dishes, often topped with almonds or raisins.

The fertile crescent of the Middle East, stretching from Israel to the Persian Gulf, was home to many early civilizations who farmed wheat, barley, and millet, and domesticated chickens, as well as sheep, goats, pigs, and buffalo. Everyday meals were based on cereals with onions, leeks, garlic, legumes, cucumbers, and lettuce, often supplemented by fish and game.

Persia (now Iran), between Asia and the Mediterranean, was ideally placed to develop a rich cuisine, often using fruit, vegetables, and meat in intriguing combinations, such as in *faisinjan* (lamb, duck, or chicken with walnuts and pomegranates). Orange-flower water and rosewater were used to flavor sweet dishes, and yogurt went into soups and sauces.

Drying parboiled rice in Madaripur district, Bangladesh.

Africa

The countries of north Africa share with other Mediterranean countries the benefits of an amenable climate and early civilization. Morocco, Algeria, and Tunisia were converted to Islam in 788, and the Muslims brought with them a taste for meat and poultry with fruit, as in the *tajines* of lamb, chicken, and pigeons cooked with dried fruit.

Parts of central Africa were originally colonized for their spices, and European influences are still felt in many former colonies. Fish resources are limited and game was once traditional, but increasing poverty and stricter game laws have put an end to hunting game. Millet and sorghum were the only cereals that grew well until corn was introduced from America to provide food for slaveships.

The earliest traditions in white South African cooking date from the 1600s, when Dutch settlers colonized the Cape as a stopover en route to the spice islands of the East. Farm laborers and domestic staff were imported from Indonesia and Malaysia and brought with them a taste for spices such as cinnamon as well as chilies, garlic, and cloves, and created dishes such as *bredie* (braised spiced meat and vegetables).

Americas

Europeans arriving in the Caribbean and Central America found a long-established tradition of growing corn, beans, pumpkins, and squash. These staples, with many varieties of peppers and tomatoes, plus avocados and potatoes, still form the basis of many Latin American dishes. However, today's diet generally features more familiar meat (especially beef in Argentina) than the dogs and guinea pigs that used to be bred for the table.

African influences that came with slaves brought to work on Caribbean and Central American sugar plantations are still felt in the cuisines of these areas.

Rice was taken to South Carolina in 1685 and formed the basis of two distinct cuisines in Louisiana: Cajun, which uses freshwater fish, sausages, and ham with fiery spices, and Creole, a more sophisticated cuisine developed in New Orleans with foods imported from Europe.

When settlers moved west across North America in the 1800s, their food was basic, with a strong emphasis on beef cooked simply over an open fire.

The first settlers in Québec, Canada, were farmers and fishermen from northwest France, and eastern Canadian cooking still shows a strong French influence. They had to adapt their diet to the long, cold winters and created sustaining meals often using fish and shellfish, for example in chowders. As they moved inland, the settlers trapped moose, elk, caribou, and beaver for meat as well as for skins. Native nuts, berries, such as cranberries and blueberries, and fiddlehead fern shoots remain popular.

Australia and Oceania

The first British settlers in Australia and New Zealand imported a wide range of livestock, grains, fruit, and vegetables from all over the world that flourished in the favorable climate. The food has its origins in plain British cooking, but long, hot summers encourage picnicking and barbecuing, and tropical fruits are readily available. Wheat is the staple grain. A lot of meat (beef in Australia, lamb in New Zealand) is eaten, as well as fish and shellfish around the coasts.

Food and religion

Many of the world's religions have rules about the preparation of food, and certain foods are often forbidden. These rules may influence the diet of large numbers of people. For example, pork is not eaten by either Muslims or Jews, and both these religions have rules about how meat must be killed in order to be *kosher* (in Judaism) or *halal* (in Islam). Hinduism has many vegetarian sects, so Indian cooking relies heavily on vegetables. Most Buddhists and some Christian sects are also vegetarian.

Edible offerings placed at the toes of the Buddha at Indra Viharn, Thailand.

Timeline

1609 Dutch East India Company begins shipping tea from China to Europe.

1612 British colonists begin cultivating tobacco in Virginia.

1620 Farmers begin draining the marshy fens in Lincolnshire, England (using Dutch-style wind pumps) to produce fertile land for crops.

1621 German farmers begin to cultivate potatoes.

1627 The aurochs (a wild ox that gave rise to domestic cattle) becomes extinct.

1650 People in Britain begin drinking tea.

1657 Drinking chocolate introduced into Britain.

1701 Englishman Jethro Tull invents a mechanical seed drill.

1724 Paul Dudley produces cross-fertilized cereals.

1727 Coffee first cultivated in Brazil.

1735 Frenchman Charles de la Condamine discovers the rubber tree in South America.

1736 British import caoutchouc ("India rubber") from South America.

1747 German Andreas Marggraf finds sugar in beets, founding Europe's beet industry.

1750 Englishman Robert Bakewell uses selective breeding to produce improved strains of sheep and other farm animals.

1765 Italian Lazzaro Spallanzani proposes hermetically sealing foods.

1788 Scotsman Andrew Meikle invents the threshing machine.

1793 American Eli Whitney invents the cotton gin.

1795 Frenchman Nicolas Appert experiments with sterile canning and bottling of food; method perfected in 1809.

1797 John MacArthur introduces merino sheep to his native Australia.

1800 Jute (for making ropes) cultivated in India.

1804 Thaer improves crop rotation farming (originally proposed 50 years earlier by Englishman Charles Townshend).

1820 European farmers start using natural fertilizers (guano).

1831 American Cyrus McCormick invents his reaping machine, patenting an improved version in 1834 *(p. 441)*.

1836 Combine harvester developed in the U.S.A.

1837 American John Deere makes plows with curved steel moldboards.

1839 American Charles Goodyear invents vulcanization for strengthening rubber.

1840 Frenchman Jean-Baptiste Boussingault discovers the significance for plants of nitrates in soil; German Justus Liebig explains how artificial fertilizers can improve crops.

1842 Samuel Dana discovers the role of phosphates in manure fertilizer.

1847 Henry Sorby explains the functions of phosphorus and sulfur in the growth of crop plants. Evaporated milk first manufactured. Justus Liebig produces concentrated meat extracts.

FARMING

Harvesting wheat in the United States.

Farms vary in size from small family concerns occupying only a few acres to huge corporations covering many square miles of land. They also differ in activities: an arable farmer concentrates on growing crops, others breed and raise livestock, and some run mixed farms. There may be further specialization within these categories—for example, a farm may consist entirely of orchards with fruit trees, or a hill farm may be devoted purely to raising sheep.

In poorer countries, the chief activity may be subsistence farming, with villagers producing just enough for their own needs. Once there is any surplus, it can be taken to market and sold. Or the farmer may grow some cash crops, produced entirely for market. In the former Soviet Union, small peasant farms within a community were collectivized, and profits from the collective farms were shared by the people who worked them. In Western industrialized countries, many farmers belong to cooperatives. Much of the farming activity is incorporated into agribusiness, which includes the processing of agricultural products as well as the marketing of them. It also encompasses the manufacture and sale of agricultural machinery. As a result, a comparatively small number of workers effectively feed an entire nation. For example, in the United States only about three percent of the working population is employed on farms (compared with 90 percent 200 years ago), and yet these workers produce more food than the country can use.

Intensive farming, also sometimes called factory farming, uses a controlled indoor environment to raise a single type of livestock, such as calves, pigs, or poultry. The special buildings housing the animals have controlled temperature, ventilation, and light levels. Feeding is regulated for optimum growth, sometimes supplemented by growth hormones. Antibiotics may also be administered to the animals to reduce the risk of infection in the crowded conditions. The buildings also have to have facilities for removal of the large amounts of manure and urine produced by the animals.

A totally different approach is adopted in organic farming, which may be described as nonintensive and which does not use artificial fertilizers or pesticides. The farmer may, however, use natural manure and techniques such as crop rotation to maintain the fertility of the soil. Nitrogen fertilizers can be introduced by including a leguminous crop, such as beans or alfalfa, in the system (these plants have root nodules that fix nitrogen from the air and turn it into chemicals that can be absorbed by the roots of plants). Despite all these techniques, the yields are lower on organic farms and the produce consequently more expensive in the supermarket.

Farm machinery

Ever since the invention of the wooden plow in prehistoric times, farmers have increasingly turned to machines to reduce the amount of human labor needed. At first, the early machines were pulled by draft animals such as horses or oxen. Even so, great progress was made. A horse-drawn reaper invented in the United States in 1831 revolutionized the cutting of grain. It had a pair of multipointed, overlapping, horizontal blades that oscillated sideways like a long row of scissors.

The next advance came with the elimination of the draft animals. Steam tractors—some with caterpillar tracks—were built to pull plows, or a pair of traction engines on each side of a field dragged a large reversible plow from side to side using steel cables. Belt drives from such engines were also used to power threshing machines and bailers.

The invention of the internal combustion engine—first the gasoline engine and then the diesel—gave rise to the type of tractors in use today. Using rotary drives and hydraulic "take-offs" at the front and rear, a whole range of ancillary machinery can be coupled to the tractor and increase its versatility. The modern descendant of the reaper is the self-powered combine harvester. It cuts the grain, threshes it to separate the grain from the straw (the chaff is blown away), gathers the straw into bales, and delivers the grain into a trailer towed alongside. The process is controlled by one worker, who drives the combine.

Various other machines are used for sowing seed and planting. Drills bury seed (such as those of cereal crops, root vegetables, and crops like peas and beans) at a particular depth in rows. Cultivators can later pass along the rows of young plants to hoe any weeds. For very large areas of grain, grass, or clover, machines randomly spread the seed on the surface of the tilled soil. Other planters mechanize the backbreaking task of setting out rows of vegetables such as brassicas or cereals such as rice.

At the end of the growing season, crops other than cereals also have to be harvested. There are machines for lifting potatoes or beets, for gathering pea plants to get them to the freezers within hours of picking, and even for picking fruit from orchard trees. Most of the latter resemble an upturned umbrella surrounding the tree, which is shaken so that the fruit falls into the "umbrella." Prime fruit, however, is still largely harvested by hand to preserve quality.

Origins of farm animals

Today's breeds of farm animals have been developed over thousands of years from their wild, undomesticated ancestors. It is thought that sheep and goats were the first farm animals to be domesticated, in about 9000 B.C. in what is today Afghanistan and Iran. By selectively breeding from their best animals, farmers over the centuries have developed the wide range of breeds seen today (*p. 433*). Cattle have been farmed for meat and milk since Neolithic times (about 4000 B.C. in Europe), and the ancient Egyptians were using oxen for pulling plows in about 3000 B.C. Even familiar breeds such as the Holstein were already established 2,000 years ago. Major improvements in cattle came in the 1700s with the selective breeding experiments of English agriculturists such as Robert Bakewell.

Pigs were first domesticated in China and parts of S.E. Asia in about 6500 B.C. but were not used as farm animals in Europe until the domestication of the wild boar about 3,000 years later. Again selective breeding and occasional cross-breeding have produced the wide range of modern breeds.

Today, techniques such as artificial insemination and embryo implantation mean that offspring of the very best animals can be raised almost anywhere in the world, without the original parent animals having to move from their home farms. In some countries, state authorities maintain stud farms from which semen from prime male animals is sent to inseminate females throughout the country. Semen may also be frozen and stored, so that a bull, for example, can go on siring offspring long after it is dead.

The latest developmental experiments involve genetic engineering, also called recombinant DNA technology, in which a gene for a desirable characteristic in one animal is spliced into the DNA of another, which then retains that characteristic. It may be possible in this way to develop new breeds that resist disease or drought, mature faster, or produce more wool, milk, eggs, or whatever is required.

Chemicals on the farm

For healthy growth, crop plants require the key substances of nitrogen, phosphorus, and potassium, as well as traces of other minerals. Chemicals removed from the soil by plants have to be replaced by fertilizers. Natural fertilizers, such as manure, can be used, but most modern farms use artificial fertilizers to supply the necessary plant nutrients.

The compound fertilizer called NPK (nitrogen, phosphorus, potassium), in the form of powder or granules, can be mechanically spread on the soil. Liquid fertilizers are also used. But they need to be used carefully so they do not run off into streams and rivers, where they can ultimately kill plant and animal life.

Farmers also use a range of chemicals to combat pests, either weeds (using herbicides) or insects (using insecticides). There are two main types of herbicides. Some are total, in that they kill all plants they come into contact with, and so are only used by farmers to get rid of weeds and other plants before plowing. More frequently used are selective herbicides, such as 2,4-D, which are designed to kill specific plants and can be sprayed on growing crops to remove weeds without damaging the crop itself. They are applied through nozzles on a boom carried by a tractor or, for large areas, may be sprayed from low-flying light aircraft.

Insecticides are also applied by spraying a liquid or by dusting a powder. Contact insecticides kill all insects they come into contact with, including useful insects such as bees and ladybugs, and so they must be used with care—for instance, by spraying in the evening when bees are not active. Also some synthetic organic insecticides, such as DDT, do not break down easily and so they can accumulate in the food chain: for example, birds eat poisoned insects and predators eat the birds. Because of this, DDT has been banned for agricultural use in many countries.

Other insecticides (stomach poisons) kill only if they are eaten by insects. More selective are systemic insecticides, such as certain organophosphates, which are absorbed by plants and kill only insects that feed on the plants. Also, organophosphates break down fairly rapidly into nonpoisonous substances.

Nitrogen, the most essential fertilizer, constantly circulates between air, plants, animals, and soil. Microorganisms are key agents in this transfer.

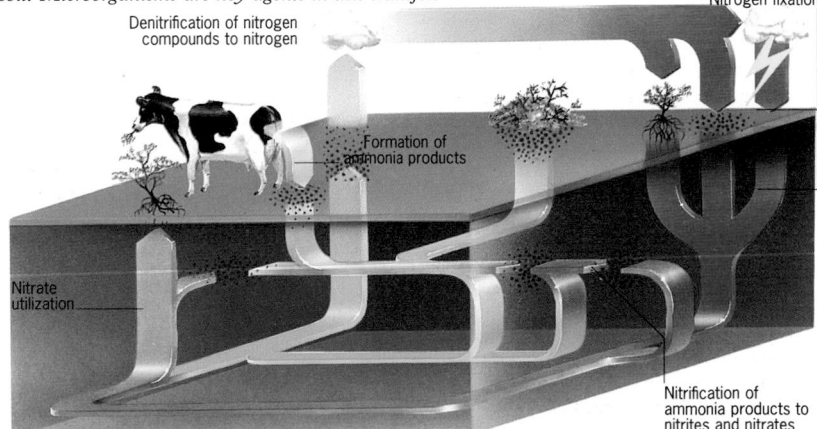

Timeline

1849 American Luther Burbank develops new varieties of fruit.

1852 Potassium sulfate used as an artificial fertilizer in Germany.

1864 Frenchman Louis Pasteur develops pasteurization process (for wine).

1874 H. Solomon develops a method of food canning using pressure cookers.

1880 Canned meat and fruit goes on general sale in stores (previously supplied exclusively to the military).

1896 First selective weed killers used in France.

1906 Frenchman Jacques-Arsène d'Arsonval invents freeze-drying as a method of preserving food (*right*).

1908 U.S. Holt Company develops a tractor with caterpillar tracks.

1910 U.S. Holt Company develops a gasoline-driven combine harvester.

1924 Insecticides in widespread use.

1925 American Clarence Birdseye develops commercial quick-freezing process for preserving foods.

1927 Crop-spraying (with insecticidal "dust") from aircraft introduced in Canada.

1934 Ships with refrigerated holds introduced for carrying cargoes of meat.

1937 Instant coffee marketed in U.S.A.

1939 Precooked frozen foods go on sale in the U.S.A. In Switzerland, Paul Muller discovers the insecticidal properties of DDT.

1944 Artificial fertilizers in general use.

1967 U.S. agricultural scientists use gamma rays to kill insects on wheat and other foods.

1968 A U.S. company uses gamma rays to sterilize bacon and potatoes.

1972 U.S. government places restrictions on use of DDT (because of its effects on insect-eating birds).

1973 Calves produced using frozen embryos. Americans Herbert Boyer and Stanley Cohen pioneer genetic engineering.

1984 American Steen Willadsen clones sheep.

1986 American Biologics company markets a vaccine (against herpes in pigs) made from a cloned virus.

PRESERVING FOOD

There are various ways of preventing food from spoiling, from simple pickling to sophisticated freeze-drying. In pickling, the food—fruit, vegetables, or fish—is soaked in a liquid and sealed in jars. The traditional liquids are brine (strong salt solution) or vinegar for nonsweet foods. Vegetables and fruits may be mixed and stewed with vinegar to make relishes. Fruit may also be preserved by pickling it in an alcoholic liquor or in syrup (sugar solution).

Other traditional preservation methods include drying and smoking. Fish or meat (known as pemmican when prepared according to North American Indian tradition) may be cut into strips and hung in the sun to dry slowly. Fruits, particularly grapes, plums, and apricots, can also be dried—grapes become raisins, and plums turn into prunes. Drying is a form of dehydration, as is smoking. To create a smoked product, meat, fish, or cheese is hung on racks for 24 hours or so in a box or room over smoldering sawdust or hardwood chips. Herring, salmon, trout, mackerel, haddock, and cod are popular smoked fish. Ham and various kinds of sausages may also be smoked; smoking over a fuel such as peat—found in Ireland, for instance—can create a very distinctive flavor. Smoking coats the surface of the food with chemicals that restrict both decomposition and growth of bacteria and molds. Some liquid or semiliquid foods are preserved by dehydration. The process is used to make powdered versions of such products as soups, eggs, and mashed potatoes, which are reconstituted by adding hot water.

Canning was developed by the Frenchman Nicolas François Appert at the beginning of the 1800s, using first glass jars and later steel cans. He sealed the food in the container, then cooked it for several hours in boiling water. Today, most food is cooked quickly before being canned. The purpose of canning is to destroy organisms that cause food to go bad and then keep them away from the food. Pasteurization—which is prolonged heating at more than 140°F (60°C)—is

Sausages being smoked in a German smokehouse.

used to kill any bacteria in liquids such as milk and wine. Germs can also be killed by irradiation (usually with gamma rays), and as long as the food is then hermetically sealed it will keep for months. "Long-life" milk has often been irradiated in this way.

Refrigeration to below 39°F (4°C) prolongs the time for which food may be kept. But for long-term storage it has to be rapidly frozen (slow freezing causes large crystals of ice to form in the food, which destroy its texture when it is defrosted). An allied process is that of freeze-drying, in which a quick-frozen food is placed in a vacuum so that the water (in the form of ice) sublimes out of the food. The process is used for vegetables such as peas and for making "instant" coffee powder. The food does not have to be kept frozen, just sealed, and it is then reconstituted by adding boiling water.

Alternatively, preservative chemicals can be added to food to prevent it from spoiling. Such chemicals may include antioxidants (Food additives, *below*) and various kinds of salts.

Food additives

Various substances are added to commercially processed foods to change their color, prolong shelf life (preservatives and antioxidants), maintain texture (emulsifiers and stabilizers), prevent food from clumping together (anticaking agents), enhance flavor, or improve appearance (glazing agents). Some additives are harmless, but others have been known to have bad side effects in many people, especially in children. The Food and Drug Administration (FDA) is responsible for enforcing standards for the food industry, including safety of additives and honesty in labeling.

Additives likely to cause negative reaction

Name	Source	Function	Name	Source	Function
Amaranth	synthetic "coal tar" dye and azo dye	purplish red	Brown FK	synthetic mix of six azo dyes, sodium chloride and/or sodium sulfate	brown
Benzoic acid	berries, fruits, vegetables; chemical synthesis	antifungal and antibacterial preservative	Brown HT	synthetic "coal tar" dye and azo dye	brown
Black PN	synthetic "coal tar" dye and azo dye	black	Butylated hydroxyanisole	mixture of 2- and 3-tert-butyl-4-methoxyphenol	antioxidant
Brilliant blue FCF	synthetic "coal tar" dye	blue, green hues (with tartrazine)	Butylated hydroxytoluene	synthetic	antioxidant

Name	Source	Function
Calcium hydrogen sulfite	calcium salt of sulfurous acid	preservative; firming; used for washing beer casks
Calcium sulfite	calcium salt of sulfurous acid	preservative; firming; disinfectant
Caramel color	sugar	brown to black
Carbon black	animal charcoal; activated charcoal; laboratory preparation	black
Carboxymethyl cellulose, sodium salt	cellulose	thickening; texture modifier; stabilizer; moisture; migration controller; gelling; bulking; prevents crystal growth and syneresis; decreases fat absorption; foam stabilizer
Carmoisine	synthetic azo dye	red
Carrageenan	red seaweed (*Chondrus crispus* and *Gigartina*)	stabilizer; thickener; suspending and gelling; texture modifier
Chlorine	naturally occurring gas (earth's crust, seawater)	flour bleaching; drinking water
Chlorine dioxide	synthetic preparation	bleaching; improving; oxidizing; water purifying; bactericide and antiseptic
Cochineal	pregnant scale insects (*Dactilopius coccus*)	red
Erythrosine	disodium salt of 2, 4, 5, 7 tetraiodofluorescein; synthetic "coal tar" dye	cherry pink to red
Formic acid	ants	preservative (prohibited in U.K.)
Guanosine 5'(disodium phosphate)	sodium salt of 5' guanylic acid (synthetic preparation)	flavor enhancer
Hexamine	formaldehyde and ammonia	antimicrobial preservative
Indigo carmine	synthetic "coal tar" dye	blue; diagnostic
Inosine 5'-(disodium phosphate)	disodium salt of inosinic acid (meat extract and dried sardines)	flavor enhancer
Mannitol	coniferous trees; seaweed; manna ash (*Fraxinus ornus*); hydrogenation of invert sugar	texturizing; dietary supplement; humectant; sweetener; anticaking; antisticking
Monosodium glutamate	sodium salt of glutamic acid	flavor enhancer
Patent blue V	synthetic "coal tar" dye	dark bluish violet; diagnostic
Polyoxyethylene (8) stearate	stearate and ethylene oxide mixture	emulsifier; stabilizer
Polyoxyethylene (40) stearate	stearate and ethylene oxide mixture	emulsifier; makes bread "feel fresh"
Poncean 4R	synthetic "coal tar" dye and azo dye	red
Potassium bromate	synthetic preparation	flour maturing or improving; used to make beer
Potassium ferrocyanide	coal gas purification by-product	anticaking; metals removal in wine making ("blue finings")
Potassium metabisulfite	sodium salt of sulfurous acid	antimicrobial preservative; antibrowning
Quinoline	synthetic "coal tar" dye	dull yellow to greenish yellow
Red 2G	synthetic "coal tar" dye and azo dye	red
Refined microcrystalline wax	petroleum	chewing gum ingredient; polishing and release; stiffening; tablet coating
Sodium ferrocyanide	synthetic manufacture	anticaking; crystal modifier
Sodium hydrogen sulfite	sodium salt of sulfurous acid	preservative for alcoholic beverages
Sodium metabisulfite	sodium salt of sulfurous acid	antimicrobial preservative; antioxidant (commercially manufactured); bleaching
Sodium 5'-ribonucleotide	disodium guanylate and disodium inosinate mixture	flavor enhancer
Sodium sulfite	sodium salt of sulfurous acid	antimicrobial preservative; sterilizer; prevents discoloration
Sorbitan monolaurate	sorbitol and lauric acid	emulsifier; stabilizer; antifoaming
Sorbitol derivatives	sorbitol and ethylene oxide	emulsifier; stabilizer; dispersing; preserves moistness; prevents oil leaking
Sorbitol syrup	Mountain ash (*Sorbus aucuparia*) fruits, cherries, pears, plums, apples; seaweed, other algae	sweetening; glycerol substitute; retards crystallization; masks saccharin; texturizing; humectant; stabilizer
Sulfur dioxide	natural; chemical production by combustion of sulfur or gypsum	preservative; bleaching; improving; stabilizer; antioxidant; used in beer and wine–making
Sulfuric acid	commercial preparation by "contact" or "chamber" process	acid; for consistent quality in beer
Sunset Yellow FCF	synthetic "coal tar" dye and azo dye	yellow
Talc	naturally occurring mineral	release; anticaking; chewing gum component; filtering aid; dusting powder
Tartrazine	synthetic, an azo dye	yellow
Various benzoates	benzoic acid	antifungal and antibacterial or antimicrobial preservative
Various gallates	ester of gallic acid	antioxidant
Various nitrates	nitrous acid or sodium nitrate	preservative; curing; some prevent growth of *Clostridium botulinum*
Various phenols	synthetic	antibacterial and antifungal
Various phosphates	salts of phosphoric acids	buffer; sequestrant; emulsifier; raising; color; improver; chelating; stabilizer; texturizer
Yellow 2G	synthetic "coal tar" dye	yellow and azo dye

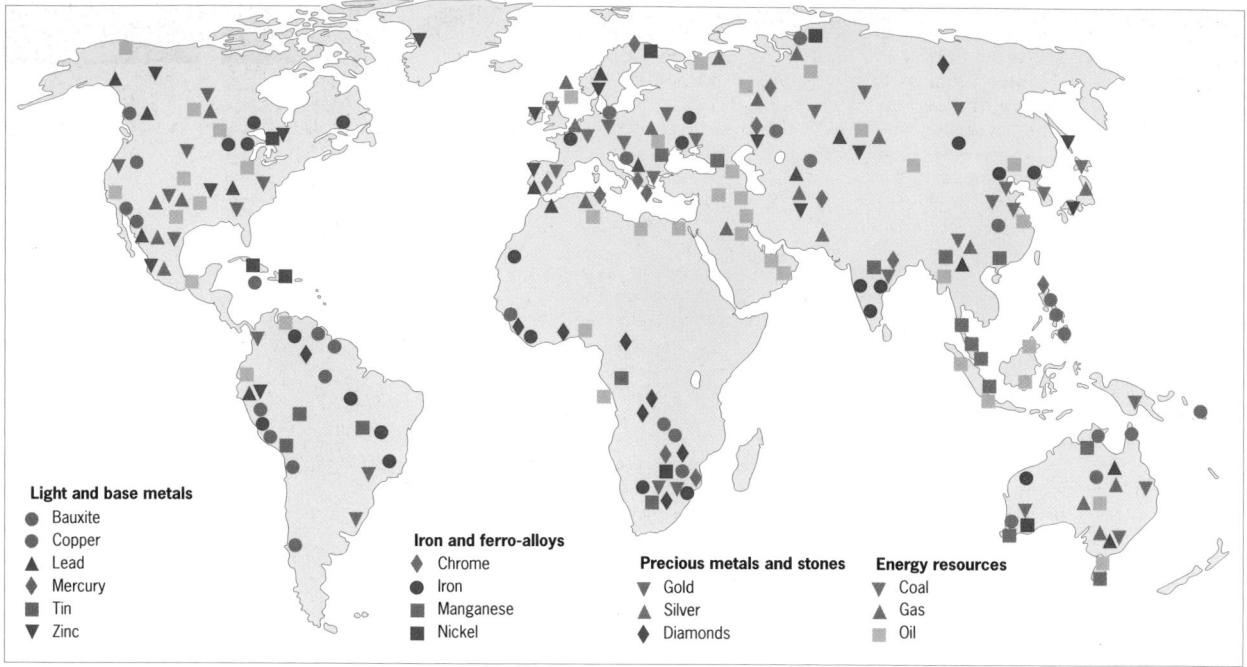

World distribution of metals, diamonds, and energy resources.

RESOURCES AND ENERGY

Since the advent of humankind and the growth of civilization, people have been exploiting the resources of the earth. At first they cut down trees for fuel and for building materials for boats, ships, and shelter. Wood is still a major resource, and it has the advantage of being renewable. Forests can be replanted and, in time, the timber that was consumed is replaced. This policy fails, however, if—as now—trees are felled faster than they can be replaced and if the felling is so wholesale that in the process ecosystems are lost before the forest can recover.

Early pressure on the world's forests was to some extent relieved with the exploitation of fossil fuels. The first of these was coal, the fuel that powered the Industrial Revolution by feeding steam engines and locomotives. Oil (*p. 446*) as crude oil or petroleum, was exploited from the end of the 1800s—just in time for the invention of the internal combustion engine. Soon gasoline and diesel engines replaced steam as the motive power for transportation. More recently, natural gas has provided a fuel for homes and industry and a starting material for the petrochemical industry.

But, unlike timber, fossil fuels are not renewable. Reserves are finite, and at some point in the future—estimates as to exactly when vary widely among experts—we shall run out of fossil fuels. People will have to turn to alternative forms of energy. Nuclear power (*p. 447*) from fission reactors is available but is unpopular in many quarters because of the risk of accident and the considerable problems entailed in decommissioning

nuclear power plants and in disposing of nuclear waste. Wind power (*p. 449*) has been used in the past, but usually when human energy requirements were very much smaller than they are now. Hydroelectric power, derived from the force of falling water (*p. 449*), is now widely used where conditions are appropriate. Harnessing the power of tides is another possible alternative, and its potential is currently being examined.

More promising in the long term is the power of nuclear fusion. (Nuclear fission, as used in today's reactors, involves splitting heavy elements such as uranium. Nuclear fusion, in contrast, is the joining together of light elements such as hydrogen. Both types of reaction produce large amounts of heat energy.) Still at the experimental stage, fusion uses a cheap, nonpolluting "fuel"—hydrogen—and produces no harmful waste products.

Comparative energy consumption					
	Coal equivalent		Oil equivalent		Electricity
	Total	Kg per capita	Total	Kg per capita	generation
	('000 tons)		('000 tons)		(million kwh)
Country					
Algeria	26,767	1,044	18,737	731	17,345
Australia	126,984	7,321	88,889	5,125	156,883
Brazil	121,178	799	84,825	560	234,366
Canada	299,484	11,095	209,638	7,766	507,913
Chile	15,825	1,182	11,077	827	19,961
China	933,020	811	653,114	568	677,550
Greenland	257	4,589	180	3,214	215
India	273,314	317	191,320	222	309,370
Japan	589,599	4,754	412,719	3,328	888,086
Kuwait	4,094	1,963	2,866	1,374	9,100
Libya	20,377	4,328	14,264	3,030	19,500
New Zealand	18,517	5,304	12,710	3,713	29,556
Poland	121,317	3,167	84,922	2,217	134,696
Russia	1,867,297	6,425	1,307,108	4,491	1,712,900
South Africa	107,436	2,431	75,205	1,701	169,645
Suriname	808	1,879	566	1,316	1,400
Turkey	59,213	1,036	41,449	725	60,338
U.K.	309,253	5,353	216,477	3,747	322,133
U.S.A.	2,757,794	10,921	1,930,456	7,645	3,079,085
Region					
Africa	268,591	406	188,013	284	324,972
America, North	3,277,952	7,628	2,294,567	5,339	3,777,707
America, South	323,901	1,082	226,730	758	464,944
Asia	2,742,217	859	1,919,552	601	2,711,562
Europe	2,336,913	4,650	1,635,839	3,255	2,850,580
Oceania	148,996	5,496	10,429	3,847	191,415
World	10,965,874	2,029	7,676,112	1,420	12,034,080

Minerals

Early humans also exploited various minerals. Flint was the basic material of the first toolmakers. Other types of stone were used for building. Small, brightly colored crystals were valued for their rarity. These included precious stones, such as ruby and emerald, as well as semiprecious stones (not quite as rare) like amethyst and onyx.

People also discovered chunks of gold, silver, and even copper, which they fashioned into ornaments and tools. Next came the discovery of ores of tin, which when alloyed with copper produced bronze, a much harder metal. Finally the Hittites discovered how to smelt iron, and the Bronze Age was succeeded by the Iron Age.

These early developments illustrate the two main types of minerals still exploited today. Nonmetallic minerals (pp. 451-53)— minerals not employed just for their metal content (if any)—include clays, silica, and silicates, and various types of sand, gravel, and stone. Rock-forming minerals—more the subject of geology—are not usually included in this category.

The other main type of mineral is exploited for its metal content and is usually termed ore (pp. 450-51). Apart from the few metals—referred to above—found in the free state or "native," all those found in ores exist in chemical combination with other elements. They have to be extracted by smelting or refining, and the usefulness of an ore depends on the cost of getting it out of the ground and on the subsequent yield of the required metal. This in turn depends on the technology of the extraction process. As metals become more scarce, or technology improves, ores that were once uneconomic are now being exploited. Like fossil fuels, metallic minerals are also nonrenewable, but many metals can be used again (p. 454). Many communities have collection points where scrap metals can be left, such as aluminum, for recycling.

Lignite (brown coal) mining near Cologne, Germany.

COAL

Coal is the third most important fossil fuel, after oil and natural gas. But although its consumption has declined in recent years, this trend will almost certainly be reversed as reserves of the other fuels begin to run out in the next century.

Coal consists mostly of carbon, derived from the remains of plants that sank in swamps and were then overlaid with rock. The major deposits were laid down in the Carboniferous period, between about 360 million and 290 million years ago. The effect of pressure—in the absence of oxygen, which is needed for normal decomposition—gradually turned the plant debris into coal.

There are various types of coal, categorized in terms of their carbon content. The best (90 percent carbon) hard coal is known as anthracite. Bituminous coal generally has a lower calorific value and contains about 3–14 percent water. Coal leaves ash when it burns. Lignite, or brown coal, is the poorest of all, containing as much as 43 percent water. The precursor of lignite is peat, which occurs near the surface in swampy areas. It can be dug up and dried to provide a cheap, though inefficient and smoky, fuel.

Coal mining

Coal occurs underground in seams varying in thickness from about 1 inch (2.5cm) to 80 feet (25 m). Deposits at or near the surface can be extracted by strip mining where overlying matter is stripped away and the coal is dug out mechanically.

Deeper deposits are reached by sinking shafts down to the coal seams. Tunnels are made into the seams, with roofs supported by pit props, and machines with rotary cutters dig out the coal. Conveyor belts or diesel or electric cars carry the coal to the foot of the shaft, and it is lifted to the surface.

Apart from collapsing tunnels, the main dangers faced by coal miners are gases. Methane—a highly inflammable gas called "firedamp" by miners—forms an explosive mixture with air, which is why there are stringent precautions to prevent sparks in coal mines. Methane burning in a limited supply of oxygen (air) forms carbon monoxide ("after damp"), which is highly poisonous. Today, special monitors detect any dangerous gases.

Coal has many applications. If it is heated in the absence of air, it changes into coke—which is almost pure carbon and is used in the smelting of iron ore and other metals. The coking process also produces coal tar, a dark, sticky liquid rich in aromatic chemicals and formerly a major source of benzene, phenol, and other chemicals. Coal can even be made into gasoline. In the process called hydrogenation, coal is combined with hydrogen gas to produce an oil, which can then be distilled in order to make various liquid hydrocarbon fuels.

Coal cutting using a modern shearer in Yorkshire, England.

Coal production

Region	Annual production ('000 tons)	Reserves (million tons)
Africa	183,146	144,461
America, North	873,331	758,301
America, South	34,060	28,278
Asia	1,421,150	1,569,715
Europe	360,019	473,243
Oceania	167,139	51,785
Russia	413,979	388,211
World	3,452,824	3,413,994

OIL AND NATURAL GAS

Two-thirds of the energy currently used in the world is derived from oil and natural gas. Oil—also known as crude oil or, technically, petroleum—is a sticky liquid found in underground deposits. Its color and composition vary, depending on where it is found. Like coal, it is an organic substance rich in carbon but is thought to be derived from dead animal organisms such as plankton rather than from plants. Millions of dead planktonic animals sank to the seabed, were overlaid by later deposits, and compacted. In the absence of oxygen, anaerobic bacteria acted on the organic remains; this, together with pressure, converted them into oil and natural gas.

Petroleum may occur in oil shales and tar sands—porous rocks from which oil is extracted by heating. There are also tar pits containing thick crude oil called bitumen, long used as a fuel and water-proofing material for boats.

Oil and natural gas consist of a mixture of hydrocarbons—liquids in the case of oil and gases such as methane and ethane in natural gas. Most crude oils contain about 85 percent carbon (the rest is combined hydrogen). Natural gas has a little carbon dioxide, nitrogen, and helium.

Oil is carried by pipeline across Alaska.

OIL PRODUCTION AND CONSUMPTION

Region	Production	Consumption
	(million metric tons)	
Africa	272.5	47.0
Asia and Russia	548.6	500.4
Australia, Oceania & S.E. Asia	84.0	374.2
Caribbean and South America	221.9	147.8
Middle East	1077.5	69.7
North America	623.8	904.6
W. Europe	22.6	699.2

OIL PRODUCTION

Country	Million barrels*
China	982
Iraq	978
Mexico	923
Saudi Arabia	1,719
Russia	4,554
U.S.	2,981
U.K.	867
*1 barrel = 42 gallons	

GAS PRODUCTION

Country	Million m³
Algeria	44,174
Canada	96,419
Indonesia	35,396
Netherlands	80,590
Romania	35,991
Russia	648,681
U.K.	45,760
U.S.	486,992

Extracting gas and oil

Underground oil and gas deposits are reached by drilling. Diamond-tipped rotary drills bore through the rock, and the center of the drill pipe and borehole are filled with liquid mud. This lubricates the drill, carries away fragments of rock that may otherwise jam the drill, and contains gas pressure to prevent a blowout of gas or a "gusher" of liquid oil.

Oil under pressure rises to the surface, where it flows through a set of pressure-reducing valves to storage tanks or pipelines. If the oil is not under pressure it may be pumped to the surface, using a beam engine called a "nodding donkey." If pipelines cannot be used, oil is transported by rail, or by sea in oil tankers. At about 1.2 miles (2 km) long, some supertankers are the largest ships in the world, carrying up to 450,000 tons of oil. If such a tanker is damaged or sunk, widespread pollution could result.

Many gas deposits occur under the beds of shallow seas and are extracted using off-shore drilling rigs. Some oil is also drilled far offshore. The rigs stand on legs that reach the seabed and have helicopter landing pads and accommodation for the hundreds of people who work on them. The gas is carried by pipes to the shore, where it is stored in tanks or fed into pipelines. Some gas is liquefied under pressure and used as LPG (liquid petroleum gas) to power car engines.

Oil refining

Crude oil is processed at an oil refinery. The chief technique, which separates the oil into its main components, is fractional distillation, or fractionation. The crude oil is heated to vaporize it and passed into the bottom of a tower. Different fractions—hydrocarbons of different boiling points—condense out at different levels up the tower and are led off. Gases such as methane pass out of the top of the tower. The next most volatile hydrocarbons, such as pentane, condense a little farther down; they are made into gasoline. The next fraction is kerosene (jet engine fuel), then diesel fuel and heating oil. Thick lubricating oils, waxes, and bitumen are led off near the bottom of the fractionating tower. Some of the heavier fractions can be converted into gasoline by a process called cracking, using heat or a catalyst. Oil refinery products are important raw materials for the petrochemical industry.

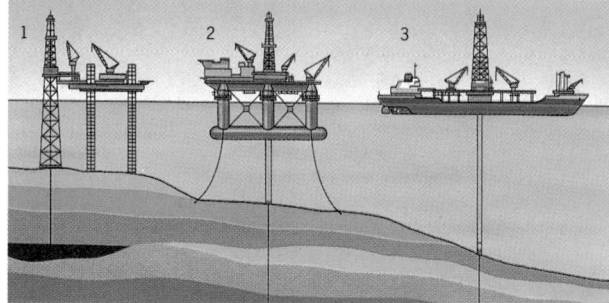

In shallow seas, oil rigs are able to stand on the seabed (1); in deep water, however, semisubmersible rigs (2) are tethered or oil is drilled directly from ships (3).

MAJOR OIL SPILLS

Year	Location	Vessel/oil well	Metric tons	Cause
1967	U.K.	Torrey Canyon	123,624	grounding
1972	Gulf of Oman	Sea Star	115,000	collision
1976	Spain	Urquiola	91,120	grounding
1977	Hawaiian Islands	Hawaiian Patriot	100,980	fire
1978	France	Amoco Cadiz	221,408	grounding
1979	West Indies	Atlantic Empress	257,040	collision
	Turkey	Independenta	94,703	collision
	Gulf of Mexico	Ixtoc 1 oil well	571,200	blowout
1980	Greece	Irenes Serenade	81,600	fire
1983	South Africa	Castillo De Bellver	239,360	fire
	Persian Gulf	Nowruz oil field	700,000	blowout
1988	Canada	Odyssey	136,000	fire
1989	Alaska	Exxon Valdez	39,375	grounding
	Canary Islands	Khark V	76,160	explosion
1991	Italy	Haven	100,000	fire
	Persian Gulf	Kuwaiti oil wells	340,000	war
1992	Spain	Aegean Sea	80,000	fire
1993	U.K.	Braer	84,000	breakup

NUCLEAR POWER

Nuclear power is the power of the atom. There are two possibilities: heavy atoms may be split into smaller fragments in the process called nuclear fission, or light atoms may be joined together to form heavier ones in nuclear fusion. Both reactions release large amounts of heat energy. Fission is the process that takes place in an atomic bomb and in today's nuclear reactors; fusion takes place in a hydrogen bomb and is the process by which stars (such as the sun) produce heat and light. The purpose of a nuclear fission reactor is to control the reaction that runs away in an atomic explosion. The key material—termed the fuel—is usually an isotope of uranium called U-235. (It has an atomic mass of 235; uranium has another, more common isotope of mass 238, but this will not undergo fission.) The U-235 is usually in the form of its oxide and shaped into thin rods encased in a protective sheath of another metal.

The fission process is triggered off by an incoming neutron. This is absorbed by a U-235 nucleus, which becomes unstable and splits into two smaller nuclei with the release of two or three more neutrons. Each of these can cause fission of further uranium nuclei, and the process can escalate into what is termed a chain reaction.

To control the chain reaction, a nuclear reactor has two other main features. Control rods are made of materials, such as boron or cadmium, that readily absorb neutrons. They are moved into or out of the reactor core to control the number of neutrons available for fission and prevent a runaway chain reaction.

The neutrons produced by each fission have high energy—they are called fast neutrons. But the fission process requires lower energy slow neutrons. For this reason, the fuel rods are surrounded by a substance (such as graphite or heavy water) called a moderator. It slows down the neutrons as they collide with its atoms. The whole core is surrounded by a containment vessel made of steel and thick concrete.

Finally the heat of the nuclear reaction has to be taken from the reactor core and, at a power plant, used to boil water into steam to drive turbines. The heat is removed by a fluid—a liquid such as water under pressure or a gas such as carbon dioxide—known as a coolant.

In a type of reactor called a breeder reactor, the U-235 fuel rods are surrounded by a blanket of U-238. When this isotope absorbs neutrons it is converted into the highly toxic metal plutonium, which is itself a fissile material that can be used to build reactors (or bombs). As a result, more fissile material is produced than is consumed—hence the term "breeder." In this type of reactor the coolant is liquid sodium.

PRODUCTION OF ELECTRICITY

		Total (million kwh)	Nuclear (million kwh)	(% of total)
Country	France	454,702	331,340	72.9
	Japan	888,086	213,460	24.0
	Russia	1,712,900	212,000	12.4
	U.K.	322,133	70,543	21.9
	U.S.A.	3,079,085	612,565	19.9
Region	Africa	324,972	4,200	1.3
	America, North	3,777,707	700,524	18.5
	America, South	464,944	9,213	2.0
	Asia	2,711,562	310,856	11.5
	Europe	2,850,580	841,212	29.5
	Oceania	191,415	0	0
World		12,034,080	2,078,005	17.3

Nuclear waste

Eventually the U-235 fuel becomes used up and has to be replaced. Spent fuel rods are taken to a reprocessing plant, where they are separated into component metals (which often include plutonium) and recycled through an enrichment plant so that they can be made into new fuel rods.

But when an old nuclear power plant is decommissioned, its spent fuel and much of the reactor structures are highly radioactive—and present a significant problem of disposal. One of the major difficulties arises because many of the radioactive elements remain radioactive for a very long time—it takes 4.5 billion years for the activity of U-238 to fall to half its initial value. Various solutions have been proposed, such as encasing the material in ceramic or concrete and storing it in deep underground repositories, but as yet no answer has proved ideal. Less radioactive material is stored in large "ponds" of water until its activity has fallen to safe levels.

ACCIDENTS IN NUCLEAR POWER STATIONS

1957	Windscale, Sellafield, Cumbria, U.K.	Fuel in plutonium production reactor overheated, igniting graphite and three tons of uranium. Workers on site received up to five times maximum permissible radioactivity; local villagers received ten times permitted lifetime dose.
1957–58	Chelyabinsk-40, Kasli, Russia	Chemical explosion (supposedly) at plutonium plant contaminated much of the Urals and may have caused hundreds of human casualties. True cause and effect not known.
1961	SL-1 reactor, Idaho Falls, Idaho	Central control rod withdrawn manually and too quickly. Three men died. Most radioactivity contained at the plant.
1972	Wurgassen reactor, Kassel, West Germany	Accidental opening of a valve led to discharge of 35,000 feet[3] (1,000 m[3]) of radioactive water into Weser River.
1973–79	Windscale, Sellafield, Cumbria, U.K.	Incidents at reprocessing plants, including release of radioactive gas (1973), contaminating skin and lungs of 35 staff.
1979	Three Mile Island, Pennsylvania	Equipment malfunction and human error led to meltdown of reactor core and release of radioactive gas. Local residents suffered radiation sickness and cancer death rates rose.
1981	Cap Le Hague, Normandy, France	Spent-fuel dry-waste silo caught fire, exposing workers to 38 times maximum permissible level of radioactivity.
1986	Gore, Oklahoma,	Accident at uranium reprocessing plant. A cylinder of uranium hexafluoride burst, releasing radioactive gas. One person died, 100 treated for breathing difficulties.
1986	Chernobyl, Ukraine	Nuclear reactor exploded, releasing radioactive cloud over Europe. Thirty-one firemen and workers killed, mostly from severe radiation burns. Worldwide, deaths from Chernobyl-induced cancers expected to be about 40,000.
1991	Rhopsodie, Cadarache, France	Explosion at old experimental fast reactor killed one engineer and seriously injured four others.
1992	Mihama, Japan	Pipe broke and leaked radioactive steam.
1993	Tomsk, Siberia, Russia	Explosion at reprocessing plant started fire, releasing 700 feet[3] (20 m[3]) of radioactive material, radioactive gas cloud.

Fusion reactors

Many of the problems associated with fission reactors—possible leakage of radioactive materials and the disposal of waste—would not apply to a reactor that made use of nuclear fusion. The "fuel" would be an isotope or isotopes of hydrogen, and the product of the reaction would be the inert gas helium. The hydrogen isotope deuterium, the favored candidate as "fuel" for nuclear fusion, occurs as 0.015 percent of all natural hydrogen, which is abundantly available in water (H_2O). Scientists in the United States, Britain, and Russia are experimenting with controlled fusion reactions.

Thermonuclear fusion requires an extremely high temperature—millions of degrees. At such a temperature, the reacting gases would be in the form of a plasma. This is a fourth state of matter in which the gas is totally ionized with the electrons and atomic nuclei entirely separate. A plasma cannot be contained in any ordinary vessel, and current experiments use magnetic fields for "holding" the plasma.

ELECTRICITY

Most of the energy used in the world is derived from fossil fuels or nuclear sources, but the most common form in which it is supplied to homes, offices, and industry is as electric power. Electricity generation is inefficient, but the convenience of this nonpolluting form of power far outweighs this disadvantage.

Electricity is produced by generators called alternators. These are electromagnetic machines that rotate at high speeds. In a large power plant, the rotary drive comes from steam turbines, and the combination of turbine and generator is known as a turbo-alternator. Smaller power plants and standby generators may use kerosene-burning gas turbine engines for their rotary power.

The steam to drive steam turbines is produced by boiling water—which requires a source of heat. In a thermal power station, the heat comes from burning a fossil fuel such as coal, oil, or natural gas. The overall efficiency is about 40 percent. In a nuclear power plant, the heat comes from the core of a nuclear reactor (overall efficiency 30 percent). The turbines usually have three stages, with turbine blades of increasing diameter, using high-pressure, medium-pressure, and lastly low-pressure steam; the same steam passes from one stage to the next. Characteristic features of a thermal power plant are large concrete cooling towers in which the spent steam is condensed back to water to be recycled to the boilers.

A different type of turbine is employed in hydroelectric power plants. In these, a stream of fast-flowing water—usually from behind a dam—turns water turbines, which are coupled to alternators. There are also a few tidal power plant, in which the flow of seawater in and out of an estuary is used to turn turbines.

Distributing electricity

Power plant generators produce alternating current at about 25,000 volts. Such a voltage would require very thick wires to carry it, so the voltage is increased by a step-up transformer to 400,000 volts or higher. The high-voltage current is distributed via the national grid by underground (and sometimes undersea) cables or overhead wires to substations, where step-down transformers reduce the voltage to that required by industry (33,000 or 11,000 volts) or homes and offices (usually 110 volts). Circuit breakers protect the system from current surges and lightning strikes.

In some countries national grid connects all its power plants. As a result, power can be switched from an area with low demand to another where the demand is exceptionally high. In Britain, for example, the national grid is linked to that in France, so that each country can sell electricity to the other, to meet peak demands. The current is usually three-phase, carried by four conductors (three phase wires and one neutral); it is delivered to homes as single-phase along two wires (live and neutral).

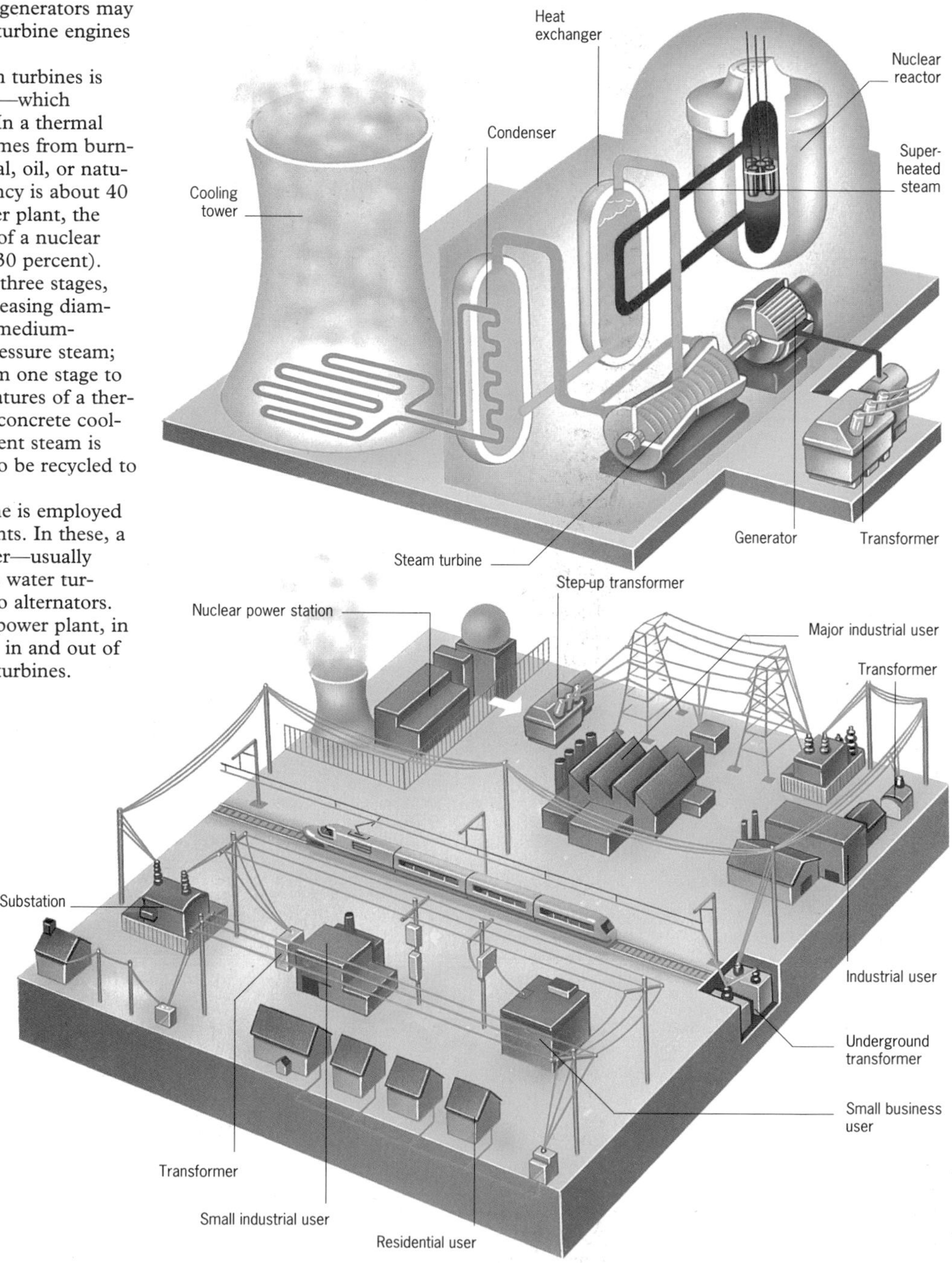

Electricity distribution from nuclear power station (top) *through substations to users.*

ALTERNATIVE ENERGY

Industrialized nations rely heavily on fossil fuels as their principal source of energy. But there is not an infinite supply of such fuels, nor are they renewable, and so one day they will run out. This unpalatable fact has spurred on the search for other sources of energy. Power from nuclear fission is already one alternative, but it has potential problems, particularly with regard to the disposal of nuclear waste. Thermonuclear power (from nuclear fusion) is an attractive possibility, but so far it has progressed only to the experimental stage.

What other sources are there? There are ways to use the light and heat of the sun; wind power can make a contribution; ocean waves "carry" energy that could be harnessed; and the heat inside the earth itself (geothermal energy) could be made available. There are also schemes to return to plants as a source of fuel—because plants are renewable.

Solar power

Light from the sun can be converted directly into electricity by a photovoltaic cell, commonly called a photocell. Modern cells consist of two thin slices of semiconductor material (n-type and p-type). When light shines on the arrangement, electrons diffuse across the junction between the semiconductors and are collected by a conductor on each side. Photocells do not work at night, of course. More important, the process is only 20 percent efficient: electricity produced in this way costs ten times as much as that from other sources. This is probably why photovoltaic cells are reserved for powering pocket calculators and instruments in spacecraft and satellites.

The heat of the sun can be focused by a large array of mirrors to give an absolutely clean source of heat—a solar furnace—or to boil water to drive steam turbo-alternators. Solar panels are passive devices containing water that is heated by the sun's rays, often part of a domestic hot-water system in countries where sunshine is plentiful.

Wind power

Differential heating of air results in atmospheric winds, which in turn create winds that blow across the earth's surface. Windmills for grinding corn or driving pumps (for land drainage) have been used for centuries, and all ships were wind powered until the middle of the 1800s. Today's windmills have variable-pitch propeller blades (usually about 170 feet/52 m across) which drive electric generators. A hydraulic system keeps the blades turned toward the wind. Up to 100 mills may be sited near each other in a "wind farm" and can generate up to 30 megawatts of electricity.

La Rance dam in Brittany, France, houses a tidal power plant.

Water power

The water turbines for generating electricity below hydroelectric dams are the modern equivalent of the waterwheel, which has been used as a source of power for hundreds of years. In a pumped storage scheme, electricity produced at off-peak times is used to pump water to a high-level reservoir, from which it is later released to drive the turbines.

Ocean tides are another possible source of power. A dam across the mouth of the Rance River in France, built in 1966, has a series of sluices and water turbines. When the tide is coming in, the sluices are open and the flow of water upstream

A geothermal plant produces energy at Walora in New Zealand.

Geothermal energy

Within the earth's crust, the temperature rises by about 77°F (25°C) with each kilometer of depth. As a result, 2.5 miles (4 km) below the surface, the rocks are hot enough to boil water. A geothermal power plant takes advantage of this characteristic: cold water is pumped down a borehole into porous or fissured rock, and the steam generated is allowed to pass up another hole. The steam drives a turbo-alternator, and spent steam is condensed and recycled down again. In countries such as Iceland and New Zealand there are natural hot springs that can be used as energy sources.

turns the turbines (to generate electricity). At high tide the sluices are closed, trapping the tidal water behind the dam. After the tide has ebbed, the sluices are opened, and the outflowing water again turns the turbines (which are reversible).

Attempts have also been made to harness the power of ocean waves. One design consists of a series of rocking floats that are pear shaped in section. The floats are anchored across the direction of the waves, and when they rock they drive a small air turbine. Another experimental scheme to harness wave power employs a large float at the head of a rapidly narrowing coastal channel. An inrushing wave lifts the float, which falls as soon as the wave recedes. The up-and-down motion of the float generates power.

The water at the ocean surface is much warmer than deep water—at a depth of 3,300 feet (1,000 m) it is 77°F (25°C) cooler than at the surface. This temperature difference could be made to generate power. In one design, the cold water is pumped up to the surface, where it is used to condense ammonia gas into a liquid. Warm surface water evaporates the liquid back to a gas, which circulates to drive a turbine. The principle is similar to that of a refrigerator working in reverse.

Plant power

There are various ways of getting power from plants—apart from burning them to produce heat. If vegetation (such as kitchen waste), packed into a suitable container, is acted on by bacteria in the absence of air (by anaerobic fermentation), methane gas is produced. Such biogas generators are popular in China and some developing countries. The compost that remains makes good fertilizer.

In another process, sugar from plants—or made from plant starch—is fermented to produce alcohol (ethanol), which is then mixed with gasoline to produce "gasohol" for powering cars. Brazil leads in this technology and also practices mixing palm oil with diesel fuel for commercial vehicles and farm tractors.

METALLIC MINERALS

Minerals that contain relatively high concentrations of metals, and from which the metal can be economically extracted, are called ores. With a very few exceptions (such as gold), nearly all metals in use today are refined from ores.

The major commercial metals are aluminum, chromium, copper, iron, magnesium, manganese, nickel, tin, and zinc. Aluminum occurs as the clayey mineral bauxite (mainly aluminum oxide), and major producers are Australia, Guinea, and Jamaica. The metal is extracted by electrolysis of the molten oxide (mixed with cryolite as a flux).

Chromite is the major ore of chromium. It is a spinel mineral consisting of mixed oxides of chromium and iron, hence its alternative name chrome iron ore. It is mined in Turkey, South Africa, and Russia.

Copper occurs in several ores, chief of which are azurite (basic copper carbonate), chalcopyrite (mixed copper and iron sulfides), cuprite (cuprous oxide), and malachite (basic copper carbonate). Called *cuprum* by the Romans (after their name for the island of Cyprus), the metal has been used for thousands of years, either on its own or alloyed with tin (making bronze) or zinc (making brass). The ores are found in many countries, particularly Canada, Chile, the United States, and Zambia. Copper is extracted by smelting and purified by electrolysis of one of its salts in solution.

Iron, the major component of steel and therefore still the world's most important metal, occurs mainly as oxides (in hematite, limonite, and magnetite) and sulfides (pyrite). Siderite (ferrous carbonate) is also mined as an iron ore. Iron ore is mixed with coke and limestone for smelting in a blast furnace, producing pig iron.

Magnesium is extracted by electrolysis of its molten chloride salt, which is prepared from carnallite (mixed magnesium and potassium chlorides), dolomite (mixed magnesium and calcium carbonates), or magnesite (magnesium carbonate). It also occurs in seawater. The metal is used for making lightweight alloys.

Manganese ores include pyrolusite (manganese dioxide) and rhodochrosite (manganese carbonate). Another source of manganese is nodules found on parts of the ocean floor. They contain about 24 percent manganese, in addition to other metals. Manganese is obtained from the oxide by a vigorus reaction using magnesium or aluminum, or it may be produced, deliberately mixed with iron, in an electric furnace; the resulting ferromanganese alloy is used in making special steels.

The mineral pentlandite (nickel-iron sulfide) is the principal ore of nickel, mined mainly in Canada. Other ores include garnierite (a complex silicate of nickel and magnesium) and pyrrhoite (also a nickel-iron sulfide). In the extraction process, the ores are roasted to form nickel oxide, which is then reduced using carbon monoxide (to form nickel carbonyl, which decomposes to pure nickel at high temperatures).

Tin occurs as its oxide in the mineral cassiterite, from which it is extracted by smelting with carbon. Zinc also occurs as its oxide (in zincite) and as the carbonate (smithsonite) and sulfide (sphalerite), which is found in many countries. The nonoxide ores are roasted to form zinc oxide, which is smelted with coke at high temperatures.

Major metallic minerals

Alumina Aluminum oxide, as in the mineral bauxite, from which the metal is extracted by electrolysis.

Argentite A mineral form of silver sulfide, used as a source of silver.

Azurite Bright-blue hydrated basic copper carbonate in mineral form, an ore of copper, formerly used as a pigment and semiprecious stone.

Barytes Also called heavy spar, a mineral form of barium sulfate, used for making other barium salts.

Bauxite A mineral form of alumina (aluminum oxide) and the chief ore of aluminum.

Calamine See Smithsonite.

Cassiterite A mineral form of tin (stannic) oxide, the chief ore of tin.

Chalcopyrite Also called copper pyrites, a gold-colored mineral consisting of copper and iron sulfides, the main copper ore.

Chromite Also known as chrome iron ore, a mineral that consists of a mixture of the oxides of chromium and iron, used as the main source of chromium.

Cinnabar A mineral form of mercury sulfide, used as the red pigment vermilion and as a source of mercury.

Common salt See Halite.

Copper pyrites See Chalcopyrite.

Cryolite The mineral sodium aluminum fluoride, used as a flux in the electrolytic extraction of aluminum from bauxite.

Cuprite A mineral form of copper (cuprous) oxide, used as a source of copper.

Dolomite A mineral that consists of a mixture of calcium and magnesium carbonates; a source of magnesium.

Epsomite Also called Epsom salts, a mineral form of magnesium sulfate with many uses in medicine and the chemical industry.

Fluorite Also known as fluorspar, a mineral form of calcium fluoride, used as a flux in iron smelting and in making glass and ceramics.

Fluorspar Another name for fluorite.

Fool's gold See Pyrite.

Galena A mineral form of lead sulfide, the principal source of lead.

Gold panning by the Indus River, Pakistan.

Hematite A mineral form of iron (ferric) oxide, a principal ore of iron. A gray crystalline form is used as a semiprecious stone.

Halite Also called rock salt, a mineral form of sodium chloride (common salt), with many uses in the chemical industry.

Heavy spar See Barytes.

Hydromagnesite A mineral form of basic magnesium carbonate, used for making magnesium oxide (magnesia).

Ilmenite A mineral that consists of oxide of iron and titanium, often found concentrated in dark beach sands, the principal ore of titanium.

Iron pyrites See Pyrite.

Kainite A mineral consisting of a mixture of magnesium sulfate and potassium chloride, used in the chemical industry.

Kalinite A mineral form of aluminum potassium sulfate, of the same composition as alum, used as a mordant in dyeing and in tanning leather.

Kieserite A mineral form of magnesium sulfate. See also Epsomite.

Laterite A tropical clay consisting mainly of a mixture of oxides of iron (ferric) and aluminum oxide.

Limonite A mineral that consists mainly of hydroxides and oxides of iron but is not a major source of iron. It is used as a pigment.

Lodestone See Magnetite.

Magnesite A mineral form of magnesium carbonate, used as a refractory for lining furnaces and for making magnesia (magnesium oxide).

Magnetite Also known as lodestone, a magnetic mineral form of black iron oxide, used as a source of the metal and in the manufacture of ceramics.

Malachite A bright-green mineral

consisting of a mixture of copper carbonate and hydroxide, used as an ore of copper and as a semiprecious stone for making ornaments.

Natron Mineral form of sodium carbonate, found on the beds of dried-out soda lakes, used in the chemical industry and for glassmaking.

Nesquehonite A mineral form of magnesium carbonate. *See also* Magnesite.

Ocher A clayey mineral rich in iron (ferric) oxide, used as a yellow to brown pigment.

Orpiment A yellow mineral form of arsenic sulfide.

Pentlandite A lustrous bronze-colored mineral consisting of mixed iron and nickel sulfides; the principal ore of nickel.

Pitchblende Also called uraninite, a black mineral form of uranium oxide and the principal ore of uranium.

Pyrite Also called iron pyrites or fool's gold (because of its deceptive color), a mineral form of iron (ferrous) sulfide, mined as a source of sulfur (for sulfuric acid) rather than as an ore of iron.

Pyrolusite A mineral form of manganese dioxide, used as a source of manganese.

Realgar A bright-red mineral form of arsenic (arsenous) sulfide, often associated with orpiment.

Rhodochrosite A pink mineral form of manganese carbonate, a minor ore of manganese.

Rock salt *See* Halite.

Rutile A brown mineral form of titanium dioxide, used as a source of titanium.

Scheelite A mineral form of calcium tungstate, an important ore of tungsten.

Siderite An important iron ore consisting of a brown or green mineral form of iron (ferrous) carbonate, sometimes also

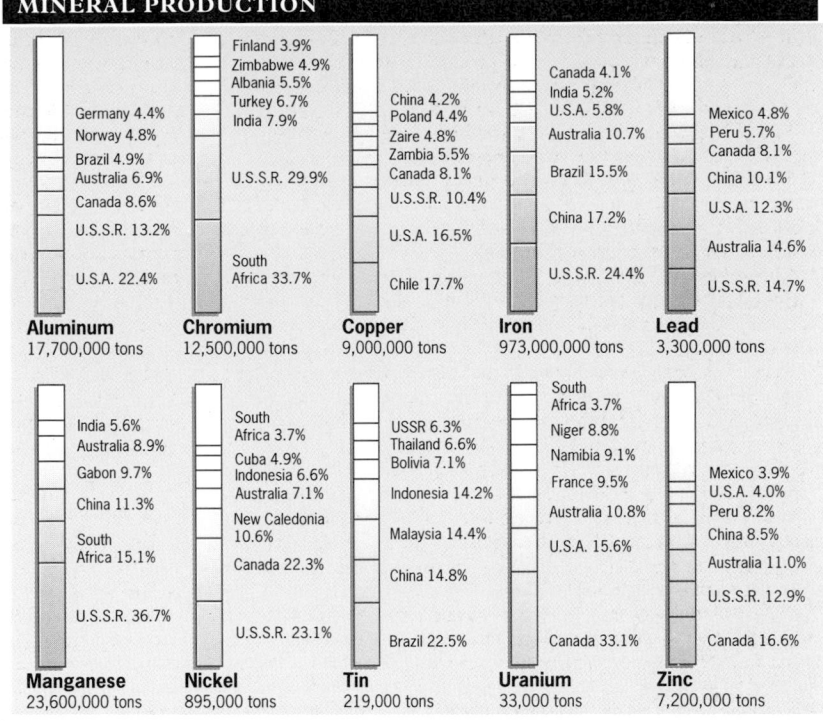

MINERAL PRODUCTION

Aluminum 17,700,000 tons
- Germany 4.4%
- Norway 4.8%
- Brazil 4.9%
- Australia 6.9%
- Canada 8.6%
- U.S.S.R. 13.2%
- U.S.A. 22.4%

Chromium 12,500,000 tons
- Finland 3.9%
- Zimbabwe 4.9%
- Albania 5.5%
- Turkey 6.7%
- India 7.9%
- U.S.S.R. 29.9%
- South Africa 33.7%

Copper 9,000,000 tons
- China 4.2%
- Poland 4.4%
- Zaire 4.8%
- Zambia 5.5%
- Canada 8.1%
- U.S.S.R. 10.4%
- U.S.A. 16.5%
- Chile 17.7%

Iron 973,000,000 tons
- Canada 4.1%
- India 5.2%
- U.S.A. 5.8%
- Australia 10.7%
- Brazil 15.5%
- China 17.2%
- U.S.S.R. 24.4%

Lead 3,300,000 tons
- Mexico 4.8%
- Peru 5.7%
- Canada 8.1%
- China 10.1%
- U.S.A. 12.3%
- Australia 14.6%
- U.S.S.R. 14.7%

Manganese 23,600,000 tons
- India 5.6%
- Australia 8.9%
- Gabon 9.7%
- China 11.3%
- South Africa 15.1%
- U.S.S.R. 36.7%

Nickel 895,000 tons
- South Africa 3.7%
- Cuba 4.9%
- Indonesia 6.6%
- Australia 7.1%
- New Caledonia 10.6%
- Canada 22.3%
- U.S.S.R. 23.1%

Tin 219,000 tons
- USSR 6.3%
- Thailand 6.6%
- Bolivia 7.1%
- Indonesia 14.2%
- Malaysia 14.4%
- China 14.8%
- Brazil 22.5%

Uranium 33,000 tons
- South Africa 3.7%
- Niger 8.8%
- Namibia 9.1%
- France 9.5%
- Australia 10.8%
- U.S.A. 15.6%
- Canada 33.1%

Zinc 7,200,000 tons
- Mexico 3.9%
- U.S.A. 4.0%
- Peru 8.2%
- China 8.5%
- Australia 11.0%
- U.S.S.R. 12.9%
- Canada 16.6%

containing magnesium or manganese.

Smithsonite Sometimes known as calamine, a mineral form of zinc carbonate.

Spartalite *See* Zincite.

Sphalerite Also called zinc blende, a brown mineral form of zinc sulfide and the main ore of zinc.

Stibnite A mineral form of antimony sulfide, which is the chief source of the metalloid element antimony.

Strontianite A mineral form of strontium carbonate.

Uraninite *See* Pitchblende.

Wolframite Also known as Wolfram, a mixed iron-manganese tungstate, and an important ore of tungsten.

Zinc blende *See* Sphalerite.

Zincite Also called spartalite, a deep orange-red mineral form of zinc manganese oxide, one of the chief ores of zinc.

NONMETALLIC MINERALS

Nonmetallic minerals are those which are not exploited for their metal content, even if they do contain metals. They include clays, stone, various salts, useful substances such as gypsum, and even a few elements (such as sulfur and carbon in the form of graphite). Precious and semiprecious stones are also classified as nonmetallic minerals.

Clays are soft, fine-grained, moldable deposits that are waterproof when wet. They vary from fine white China clay (kaolin), used for making porcelain, to coarser materials used for making bricks and tiles. Other clay minerals are used as fillers in paper and plastics manufacturing or as insulating materials. Some clays are roasted (usually with lime) to make cement.

At the other end of the hardness scale are minerals based on quartz (silica, or silicon dioxide), such as flint. Sand is also composed of silica crystals. Other silicate minerals include asbestos and mica, which are exploited for their fireproof and insulating properties. Talc is exceptional in that it is a soft silicate mineral.

Most stone is quarried for use as a building material or for roads. Chalk and limestone consist mainly of calcium carbonate (derived from the shells of sea creatures), which in mineral forms, such as calcite, can be roasted to make quicklime (calcium oxide). Calcium phosphate (apatite) is a rocky mineral used as a fertilizer, and gypsum (calcium sulfate) is roasted to make plaster.

The most common salt is sodium chloride (the mineral halite, or rock salt), which occurs in underground deposits and dried-up salt lakes as well as in seawater. Potassium salts such as carnallite (potassium-magnesium chloride) and sylvite (potassium chloride) are valued as fertilizers.

Major nonmetallic minerals

Alabaster A compact, fine-grained form of gypsum (calcium sulfate), used for making ornaments.

Amphibole Any member of a large group of silicate minerals which include asbestos and jade.

Apatite A mineral form of calcium phosphate, used for making fertilizers and as the main source of phosphorus.

Asbestos A fibrous form of various amphibole silicate minerals, valued for its heat and electrical resistance. Exposure to certain types of asbestos dust is associated with lung diseases and cancers.

Bentonite A type of clay derived from volcanic rock, used as a filler in making paper.

Calcite A crystalline, mineral form of calcium carbonate that occurs commonly in many minerals (such as limestone and marble).

Carnallite A mineral consisting of a mixture of potassium and magnesium chlorides, used as a fertilizer.

Chalcedony A form of the mineral quartz (silicon dioxide).

Chert Another name for flint.

China clay *See* Kaolin.

Clay A fine-grained mineral deposit characterized by being plastic and waterproof (while wet). Its main use is in making bricks, pottery, and other ceramics. *See also* Kaolin.

Corundum An extremely hard mineral form of aluminum oxide, used as an abrasive. *See also* Major precious and semiprecious stones.

Diatomite Also known as diatomaceous earth, a finely powdered form of the silica mineral kieselguhr, which is used as an abrasive.

Emery An extremely hard, impure form of the mineral corundum (aluminim oxide), used as an abrasive.

Feldspar Any member of a group of common silicate minerals containing aluminum, calcium, potassium, and sodium. It is used in the ceramics industry to make glazes and porcelain.

Flint Also known as chert, a hard, crystalline form of quartz (silicon dioxide), used as an abrasive.

French chalk *See* Talc.

Fuller's earth A clayey mineral, mostly montmorillonite, used to decolorize fats and oils.

Graphite A soft, mineral form of carbon, used as an abrasive, as a moderator in nuclear reactors, and for making pencil leads.

Gravel A naturally occurring aggregate consisting of small pebbles, often associated with sand.

Gypsum A soft, mineral form of calcium sulfate, used for making cement and plaster. Dehydrated by heating, it forms plaster of paris.

Kaolin Also called China clay, a soft white mineral form of kaolinite (aluminum silicate), much used to make ceramics and in the manufacture of rubber, paint, and paper.

Keiselguhr A mineral form of silica (silicon dioxide) derived from the skeletons of diatoms, used in fireproof cements and as an absorbent in making dynamite. *See also* Diatomite.

Limestone A sedimentary rock consisting mainly of calcium carbonate, used as a mineral for building stone, in iron

Marble quarry, Greece.

smelting, and for making lime (calcium oxide).

Marble A mineral form of calcium carbonate, used as an ornamental material (especially when polished) in architecture and sculpture.

Meerschaum A fine-grained clayey mineral form of magnesium silicate, used for making ornaments and the bowls of smoking pipes.

Mica A silicate mineral that has a layered structure and is easily split into thin flakes, used as an electrical insulator and dielectric (in capacitors).

Montmorillonite The principal clay mineral in fuller's earth.

Mother-of-pearl *See* Nacre.

Muscovite A mineral form of potassium aluminosilicate, the most important component of mica and used in its own right as an insulating material.

Nacre Also called mother-of-pearl, a type of calcium carbonate that forms the

iridescent layer inside a mollusk's shell, used for making buttons and ornamental objects.

Niter *See* Saltpeter.

Olivine A silicate mineral containing magnesium and iron.

Plaster of Paris *See* Gypsum.

Quartz A mineral form of silicon dioxide (silica), the most common mineral. A colorless type, called rock crystal, is used for making ornaments; colored crystalline forms include various gemstones (such as agate, amethyst, and jasper). Quartz itself is used in making glass and ceramics.

Saltpeter Also called niter, naturally occurring potassium nitrate, a component of gunpowder and a useful chemical (for example in fertilizers).

Sand A granular sediment consisting of rounded grains of quartz (silicon dioxide). Beach sands may also contain some salt; coral sands are composed of calcium carbonate, which is derived from broken-down coral fragments.

Sandstone A sedimentary rock consisting of consolidated sand (quartz grains) bound together with calcium carbonate, clay, or iron oxide. It is used as a building stone.

Silica A hard, high-melting-point mineral form of silicon dioxide, the chief component of flint, quartz, and sand. Some colored varieties are used as semiprecious stones, including agate, amethyst, carnelian, jasper, and onyx.

Silicate A compound containing the silicon-oxygen unit SiO_4, common on its own or in combination with metals in many minerals.

Slate A metamorphic rocky mineral derived from fine sediments (such as mudstones) and characterized by its property of splitting into thin sheets, used for roofing.

Soapstone A soft rock consisting mainly

Marble is used to striking effect in the bell tower of Florence Cathedral, begun in 1334 on the basis of a design by Giotto that was amended as work proceeded.

of talc (magnesium silicate), which is easily carved and so used for making ornaments, etc.

Steatite *See* Soapstone.

Sulfur One of the very few nonmetallic elements that occurs native (i.e. as a free element: carbon, in the form of diamond and graphite, is another example). Sulfur may be mined or extracted from underground using superheated water and compressed air (this is known as the Frasch process). It has many uses, the

chief of which is in the manufacture of sulfuric acid.

Sylvite A mineral form of potassium chloride, used as a fertilizer.

Talc Also known as French chalk, a soft white or greenish mineral form of magnesium silicate, used in talcum powder and in making ceramics, cosmetics, and paints.

Tincal A mineral form of borax (sodium borate), used as a flux in smelting and in making glass and ceramics. It is also the

starting material for many other boron compounds.

Vermiculite A clay mineral (a mixed silicate of aluminum, iron, and magnesium), used as an insulating material, in making plaster, and as a "soilless" medium for growing plants (hydroponics).

Zeolite A hydrated aluminosilicate mineral from which water is easily removed by heating, used for making molecular sieves and ion-exchange water softeners.

PRECIOUS AND SEMIPRECIOUS STONES

The most valuable gemstones are rubies, emeralds, diamonds, and sapphires. Ruby and sapphire are made of the extremely hard mineral corundum (aluminum oxide); emerald is a form of beryl (a silicate mineral containing aluminum and beryllium). The best rubies and sapphires come from Myanmar (Burma), Sri Lanka, and Thailand; emeralds come from Colombia and South Africa. All three stones can also be synthesized.

Diamond is pure crystalline carbon and the hardest naturally occurring substance. It is formed by the action of great heat and pressure on "pipes" of the mineral kimberlite below the earth's crust. The kimberlite rises toward the surface along fissures in

the crust. The mineral was named after Kimberley in South Africa, still a center of diamond mining. Other producing countries include Australia, Tanzania, Russia (Siberia), and the United States. In Brazil and India, diamonds can be found in alluvial deposits containing weathered kimberlite.

Pearls are unusual "stones" in that they are organic in origin, being produced from the iridescent substance nacre (calcium carbonate) which an oyster secretes to cover a grain of sand within its shell.

There is a wide range of semiprecious stones, from agate to zircon, and their compositions are described below.

Major precious and semiprecious stones

Agate An extremely hard, banded form of the silica mineral chalcedony (silicon dioxide), used for making knife-edge bearings and ornaments and as a semiprecious stone.

Amethyst A form of quartz (silicon dioxide), colored purple by impurities such as iron oxide and used as a gemstone.

Aquamarine A form of the mineral beryl (beryllium aluminum silicate), colored greenish blue by impurities and used as a gemstone.

Beryl The mineral beryllium aluminum silicate, used as a source of the element beryllium. Impurities give it various colors, the greenish blue (aquamarine) and green (emerald) forms being used as gemstones.

Carnelian A red or reddish-brown form of the mineral chalcedony (silicon dioxide), used as a semiprecious stone.

Chalcedony A form of the mineral quartz (silicon dioxide), some types of which (such as agate, carnelian, jasper, and onyx) are used as semiprecious stones.

Citrine A yellow, crystalline type of quartz, used as a semiprecious stone.

Corundum A hard mineral form of aluminum oxide. Colored forms include the precious stones ruby and sapphire.

Diamond A crystalline, mineral form of carbon, the hardest naturally occurring substance. It is used as a gemstone and, if not of gem quality, as an abrasive and for cutting tools.

Emerald A green type of beryl (beryllium aluminum silicate), valued as a gemstone.

Garnet A silicate mineral used as an abrasive or, if colored, as a semiprecious stone.

Lapis lazuli on a Sumerian standard.

Hematite A mineral form of iron (ferric) oxide, a principal ore of iron. A gray crystalline form is used as a semiprecious stone.

Jade A hard mineral, either a rare sodium aluminum silicate or a more common amphibole, used as a semiprecious stone and for making ornaments.

Jasper A red or reddish-brown form of the mineral chalcedony (silicon dioxide), which owes its color to the presence of iron impurities; used as a semiprecious stone.

Jet A type of very hard coal that can be cut and polished to make jewelry.

Lapis lazuli A deep-blue form of the mineral lazurite (sodium aluminum silicate with some sulfur), the original source of the pigment ultramarine and used as a semiprecious stone and to make ornaments.

Olivine A silicate mineral containing magnesium and iron, a green form of which is the semiprecious stone peridot.

Onyx An extremely hard, banded form of the mineral chalcedony, used for making jewelry and ornaments.

Opal An amorphous (noncrystalline),

hydrated form of the mineral silica (silicon dioxide) whose layered structure makes it reflect iridescent colors.

Pearl A shiny, usually spherical, accretion of nacre (calcium carbonate) on a grain of foreign material, which sometimes forms within the shells of mollusks such as oysters.

Peridot A semiprecious stone that is a form of the mineral olivine.

Ruby A form of the mineral corundum (aluminum oxide) colored red by chromium impurities and highly valued as a gemstone. Rubies not of gem quality are used as bearings in watches.

Sapphire A form of the mineral corundum (aluminum oxide) colored—typically blue—by impurities and valued as a gemstone. Sapphires not of gem quality are used for making styluses for record players.

Spinel A hard, glassy mineral form of aluminum magnesium oxide, used as a semiprecious stone when pink or transparent. The substitution of other metals for the aluminum or for the magnesium results in other types of spinels, such as chromite (chromium) and magnetite (iron), which are important metal ores.

Topaz A type of hard, crystalline aluminosilicate mineral containing fluorine, which varies in color from yellow to brown or sometimes blue and is used as a semiprecious stone.

Tourmaline Any member of a group of crystalline, complex aluminum borosilicate minerals of various colors, used as semiprecious stones.

Turquoise A hard, blue mineral form of copper aluminum phosphate, valued as a semiprecious stone.

Zircon A hard mineral form of zirconium silicate, the chief source of the metal zirconium. Colorless zircons are cut, polished, and used as imitation diamonds.

CONSERVING RESOURCES

The world does not have an inexhaustible supply of fossil fuels and minerals. Reserves of ores of aluminum, magnesium, and iron are greater than those of other metals, although some (mercury and tin, for example) are in short supply already. And there are larger stocks of coal than of oil and natural gas.

Scientists estimate—at current rates of consumption—that there is enough aluminum in the world to last until about 2220, enough iron until 2160, nickel until 2060, and copper until 2035. The remaining stocks of lead, mercury, tin, and zinc are expected to run out as soon as 2015.

One way of dealing with this problem is to conserve what resources remain and to seek alternative materials and sources of energy for those that will soon run out. But materials and energy (which is expended on extraction or fabrication) are inextricably linked. For example, plastics can replace metals in many applications. But many plastics are made from chemicals derived from oil and consume large amounts of energy during their manufacture. Similarly, as high-grade ores run out, attention turns to

low-grade ones considered until now to be unsuitable. It takes far more energy, however, to mine large quantities of low-grade ores and to extract the metals from them. It might be better to use alternative, renewable resources (such as timber) instead of the nonrenewable ones.

Some materials that were formerly merely thrown away after use can be collected and used again. Metals (particularly aluminum and steel), glass, paper, and plastics can all be recycled in this way. Each year, 30 percent of the aluminum and 50 percent of the steel produced worldwide is derived from scrap. Empty bottles are sorted by color and added to raw materials in making new glass. Paper can be pulped and added to the wood pulp used in papermaking. There are even ways of removing ink from the paper pulp so that it does not affect the color of the finished product.

Many communities have centers where people can take their recyclable garbage for collection. "Bottle banks" and containers for aluminum cans, waste paper, and cloth are now widely available. Some garages will accept old car batteries—or even pay a small

Recycling plastic bottle tops in the Netherlands.

price for them—so that the lead they contain can be recycled. Old cars themselves are good sources of reusable parts and materials, particularly those made from steel.

If plastics can be sorted into their individual types, they can be returned to the melting pot. But such sorting is difficult; an alternative approach—pyrolysis—involves heating the plastics in the absence of air. This produces a mixture of mainly hydrocarbon vapors which can be condensed and separated into combustible gases, liquid fuels, oils, and tar (in much the same way as crude oil is fractionated). Other forms of waste can be incinerated: the heat produced in the process can subsequently be used as an energy source.

The most systematic method of recycling domestic waste is to use a materials recovery plant or facility (MRF, *left*). Mixed waste (1), containing steel (mainly food cans), paper, plastics, aluminum, and glass—but no organic matter—enters the facility on a conveyor belt (2). It passes under an electromagnet (3), which removes any steel objects (4), and onto a second conveyor made of chains (5). There powerful fans (6) on

one side blow the paper into wire receptacles (7). Only the glass (8) is heavy enough to fall between the chains; it is then sorted by hand into colors—clear (9), green (10), or brown (11). At the end of the belt is a magnetized drum (12) where aluminum (13) falls into a separate hopper while plastic (14) continues along another belt. Organic waste is incinerated to provide heat; composted to make plant fertilizer; or acted on by anaerobic bacteria to produce methane gas, which is also usable as a fuel. Each year in the United States alone, 12 million tons of domestic waste are treated in about 3,000 recycling centers.

Incineration remains the most common way of dealing with waste. Denmark and Sweden, for example, convert more than half their burnable waste into heat energy, which is then often used in the generation of electricity.

MRFs are expensive to construct but generally profitable. An alternative approach is to get households to pre-sort their waste into major categories: metals (ferrous and aluminum), paper, plastics, and glass. Municipal or other authorized collectors then pick up the separated waste.

Materials recovery facility

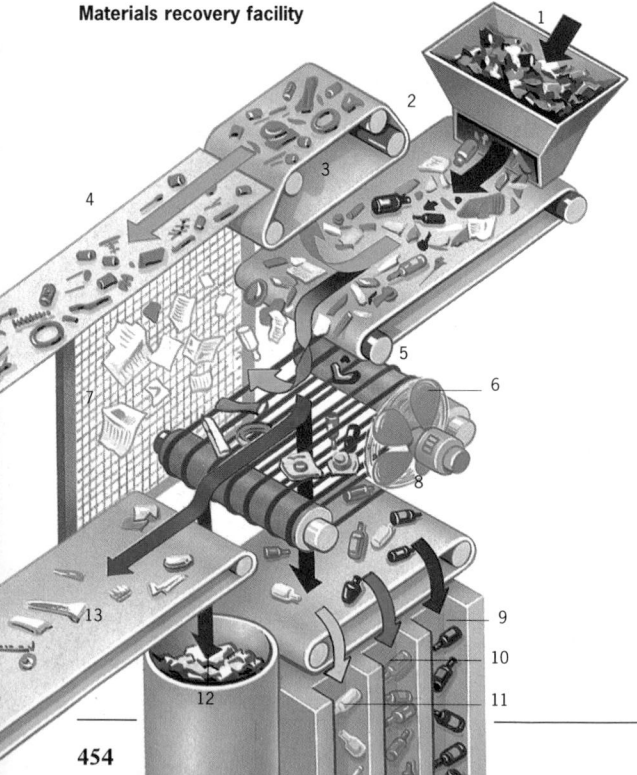

TERMS

Anthracite The hardest and highest grade type of coal (with up to 98 percent carbon content). When it burns, it produces little smoke or ash.

Argentiferous Describing a MINERAL or ORE that contains silver.

Auriferous Describing a MINERAL or ORE that contains gold.

Biogas Methane, used as a fuel, produced by the action of bacteria on rotting vegetation.

Bitumen See TAR.

Breeder reactor A type of NUCLEAR REACTOR that produces more fuel (fissile material such as plutonium) than it consumes.

Brown coal Another name for LIGNITE.

Chain reaction In NUCLEAR FISSION, a fission reaction that is self-sustaining because enough neutrons are produced.

Charcoal Porous form of carbon produced by heating organic material (such as wood or bones) in the absence of air. Wood charcoal is used as a fuel; animal (bone) charcoal to absorb gases or clarify liquids (as in sugar refining).

Coal Black MINERAL consisting mainly of carbon, formed from plant remains by pressure underground (in the absence of air). It is used as a fuel, for making COAL GAS and COKE, and as a source of organic chemicals. See also ANTHRACITE; LIGNITE; PEAT.

Coal gas A fuel gas, consisting mainly of carbon monoxide, hydrogen, and methane, made by heating COAL in the absence of air. COKE is a by-product.

Coal tar A black, sticky liquid obtained by heating COAL in the absence of air. It is the source of many organic chemicals, particularly compounds of benzene.

Coke A black solid, containing 85 percent carbon, made by heating COAL in a limited supply of air. It is used in smelting metals from their ores (particularly iron) and as a smokeless fuel.

Control rod A rod of neutron-absorbing material that is moved into or out of the core of a NUCLEAR REACTOR to control the rate of NUCLEAR FISSION.

Coolant The heat exchange medium in a NUCLEAR REACTOR which circulates through the hot core to carry heat to boil water (to drive turbines). It may be a gas (carbon dioxide) or liquid (water or molten sodium).

Critical mass The smallest mass of a FISSILE element that will allow a sustained CHAIN REACTION to take place.

Crude oil See PETROLEUM.

DERV The abbreviation of diesel engine road vehicle. See DIESEL OIL.

Diesel oil Also called DERV, a liquid fuel obtained by refining PETROLEUM and used in diesel engines. Chemically, it is a mixture of alkanes in the boiling range 390–660°F (200–350°C).

Fast neutron A high-energy neutron produced during NUCLEAR FISSION.

Fissile Describing a substance capable of undergoing NUCLEAR FISSION.

Fractionation Fractional distillation as applied to PETROLEUM (CRUDE OIL) to separate it into its various components (GASOLINE, DIESEL OIL, heating oil).

Fuel element Also called fuel rod, a length of encased FISSILE material in the core of a NUCLEAR REACTOR.

Fuel oil Any of the heavier oils produced during the FRACTIONATION (distillation) of CRUDE OIL, used for domestic heating and for industrial furnaces and boilers.

Gas See COAL GAS; NATURAL GAS; PRODUCER GAS; REFINERY GAS.

Gas-cooled reactor Type of NUCLEAR REACTOR in which the COOLANT is a gas, such as carbon dioxide.

Gasohol A mixture of alcohol and GASOLINE, used as a fuel for car engines.

Gas oil A heavy oil obtained by the FRACTIONATION (distillation) of CRUDE OIL, used as a FUEL OIL.

Gasoline Liquid fuel, obtained by refining PETROLEUM, used mainly for internal combustion engines. Chemically, it consists of a mixture of alkanes from pentane to decane.

Geothermal energy Energy derived from the heat of rocks several miles below ground.

Heavy water Deuterium oxide: water (H_2O) in which the hydrogen atoms have been replaced by hydrogen's isotope deuterium. It is used in some NUCLEAR REACTORS as a MODERATOR.

Lignite Also called BROWN COAL, a soft, moisture-containing form of COAL intermediate between PEAT and bituminous coal in carbon content.

Magnox A type of NUCLEAR REACTOR, formerly favored in Britain and France, in which the uranium fuel rods are encased in an alloy of magnesium.

Mineral A naturally occurring, usually rocky and crystalline substance of more or less fixed chemical composition, extracted from the ground for its properties or composition.

Moderator A substance that slows down FAST NEUTRONS in NUCLEAR FISSION so they can take part in a CHAIN REACTION.

Natural gas A naturally occurring mixture of gases (hydrocarbons), often associated with deposits of PETROLEUM, extracted and used as a fuel gas.

Nuclear fission The splitting of an atomic nucleus into two similar fragments as a result of capture of a slow neutron. Much heat energy is released.

Nuclear fusion The combination of light atomic nuclei to form a heavier nucleus, releasing large amounts of energy.

Nuclear reactor An assembly containing FISSILE fuel rods in which NUCLEAR FISSION occurs by CHAIN REACTION.

Nuclear waste Radioactive by-products of the mining and extraction of nuclear fuels, or of the use of such fuels in NUCLEAR REACTORS.

Oil sand See TAR SAND.

Oil shale A carbon-containing sedimentary rock, which on heating yields PETROLEUM, often in the form of TAR.

Ore A mineral containing a metal or metals from which the metal(s) can economically be extracted.

Peat A black or brown fibrous substance formed on the ground by decomposition of plant remains. Dried peat is used as fuel or made into CHARCOAL; undried it is used in composts and as an insulating material. If buried and compressed, in time it is converted into LIGNITE and, eventually, COAL.

Petroleum Also called CRUDE OIL, a MINERAL oil consisting of a mixture of hydrocarbons which can be separated to provide liquid fuels, TAR, and waxes.

Photovoltaic cell See SOLAR CELL.

Plasma A highly ionized GAS, the form in which hydrogen and its isotopes exist in THERMONUCLEAR REACTORS.

Pressure water reactor Type of NUCLEAR REACTOR in which the COOLANT is water maintained at high pressure (so that it does not boil).

Producer gas A fuel gas consisting of a mixture of carbon monoxide and nitrogen, made by passing air over red-hot carbon (such as COKE).

Reactor See GAS-COOLED REACTOR; MAGNOX; NUCLEAR REACTOR; PRESSURE WATER REACTOR; THERMONUCLEAR REACTOR.

Refinery gas A fuel gas consisting of a mixture of light hydrocarbons (methane to propane), made by the FRACTIONATION of PETROLEUM (CRUDE OIL).

Slow neutron Also called a THERMAL NEUTRON, a low-energy neutron that can take part in a nuclear CHAIN REACTION.

Solar cell A device for converting the energy of sunlight into electricity, usually using a pair of semiconductors.

Solar furnace An array of mirrors that focus the sun's heat in one place.

Steam reforming A method of converting methane from NATURAL GAS into carbon monoxide and hydrogen (similar to WATER GAS).

Tar A blackish, sticky liquid obtained by heating COAL in the absence of air or by the FRACTIONATION of CRUDE OIL (when the product is often called BITUMEN). It is used for road surfaces and as a raw material in the organic chemical industry. See also COAL TAR.

Tar sand A porous rock (such as sandstone) that contains PETROLEUMlike hydrocarbons, which can be extracted by heating.

Thermal neutron See SLOW NEUTRON.

Thermonuclear reactor A REACTOR that makes use of NUCLEAR FUSION to produce heat energy. Still experimental.

Turbo-alternator Also called a turbogenerator, a combination of a steam turbine and an alternator for generating electricity at a power station.

Water gas A fuel gas consisting of a mixture of carbon monoxide and hydrogen, made by passing steam over red-hot carbon (COKE).

Timeline

c. 7000 B.C Fired pottery is made in Iran.

c. 6000 B.C Bricks are made in Palestine.

c. 3500 B.C Copper smelting begins in Egypt and bronze alloys are made in Mesopotamia.

c. 3000 B.C Glass and bronze are first used (in Egypt).

c. 1400 B.C Iron artifacts are used by the Hittites.

c. 600 B.C Sundials are used in China.

522 B.C Eupalinus of Megara constructs a 6 mi. (1 km) tunnel on the island of Samos, Greece.

c. 500 B.C The abacus is invented in China.

c. 300 B.C Cast iron is invented in China.

c. 200 B.C Archimedes' screw is in use.

c. 190 B.C Concrete is first used (in Italy).

c. 100 B.C A piston bellows (for use in metalworking) is invented in China.

c. 60 B.C Hero of Alexandria constructs a simple steam turbine.

A.D. 532 Isidore of Miletus builds Hagia Sophia in Constantinople; its dome is the first to be supported by pendentives.

c. 600 Windmills in use in Syria.

610s Great Stone Bridge built over Chiao Shui River in China, the first example of a segmental arch bridge.

725 Buddhist monk I-Xing builds a water clock that ticks.

1175 Old London Bridge and the bridge at Avignon, France, are built.

1280s The first cannons are made (in China).

1290s Rope-cable (suspension) bridges are built by South American Indians.

1327 China's Grand Canal is completed; it is 1,100 mi. (1,770 km) long.

1340s First form of blast furnace developed in Belgium.

1380s Weight-driven clocks are in use.

1430 Hollow-post windmills are invented in Holland.

1502 Peter Henlein makes the first spring-driven watch.

1520 J. Kotter makes a muzzle-loading rifle. Jakob the Czech invents the fusee (for controlling a clock mainspring).

1540 Christoph Schurer makes blue glass using cobalt.

1551 Leonard Digges invents the theodolite.

1570 Andrea Palladio builds the first (timber) truss girder bridge.

1581 Galileo demonstrates that a pendulum's period (of oscillation) depends on its length.

1589 William Lee invents a knitting machine (for making stockings).

1617 John Napier devises "Napier's bones" (which employ logarithms).

1622 William Oughtred invents the slide-rule.

1631 Pierre Vernier makes an accurate measuring caliper.

1636 William Gascoigne invents the micrometer gauge.

1642 Blaise Pascal builds a calculating machine.

EARLY TECHNOLOGY

Modern technology has developed as a consequence of the Industrial Revolution (*pp. 35-53*), which began in Britain in the middle of the 1700s and rapidly spread throughout the developed world. It provided the materials and motive power that made modern machinery possible. Before then, people devised and built machines of various kinds but had to depend on wind, water, or muscle power (human or animal) to drive them.

However, early technological endeavor flourished in the field of observation and measurement. The development of the telescope and microscope made possible the scientific breakthroughs of the 1500s and 1600s. Time measurement has always been a preoccupation and clocks represent one of the earliest forms of applied technology.

MEASURING TIME

Early devices for measuring time included shadow clocks, graduated candles or oil lamps, sundials, and sand in an hourglass. The first mechanical clock was probably the Egyptian *clepsydra*, a water clock in which a rising float turned a pointer on a dial by a rack-and-pinion mechanism.

In the early 1500s, German clockmakers were producing spring-driven portable clocks and, soon afterward, watches. In 1583 Galileo proposed using a pendulum to regulate a clock's mechanism, and in 1657 the Dutch physicist Christiaan Huygens made a successful pendulum clock. A year later, the British scientist Robert Hooke invented the hairspring, initially used in watch escapements.

Further developments included special alloys or combinations of metals that prevented pendulums and hairsprings from changing length as temperatures varied.

Clocks remained spring-powered for more than two centuries until the development of the synchronous electric motor, whose speed is accurately controlled by the frequency of the alternating current in the mains electricity supply. Pendulum motion can also be accurately controlled by an electromagnet.

In theory, any regular oscillation can be used to keep time. When a quartz crystal is connected in an alternating current circuit, it vibrates at a regular frequency which can be used in a clock or watch.

Quartz crystals can also be stimulated by oscillations created when atoms are made to vibrate in an alternating electric field. A clock using vibrating ammonia atoms was made in the U.S.A. in 1948, and the first atomic clock, employing cesium atoms, was constructed in Britain in 1955. Atomic clocks are accurate to a small fraction of a second a year.

ENGINES

A major breakthrough came with the invention of an engine that could drive machines and provide what seemed to be a limitless source of power. The steam engine took the energy of a fuel (such as wood or coal) in the form of heat which was used to boil water thus creating steam. The pressure of the steam given off was the force that drove the parts of the engine and made it work.

A steam engine is a form of external combustion engine—because the fuel is burned outside the engine. Toward the end of the 1800s, engineers began experimenting with internal combustion engines, in which the fuel is burned inside the engine. First using gas, then gasoline and finally diesel oil, these engines gradually superseded the steam engine for smaller vehicles and made possible the cars and trucks that fill our roads today.

Boulton and Watts' double-action steam engine, 1784.

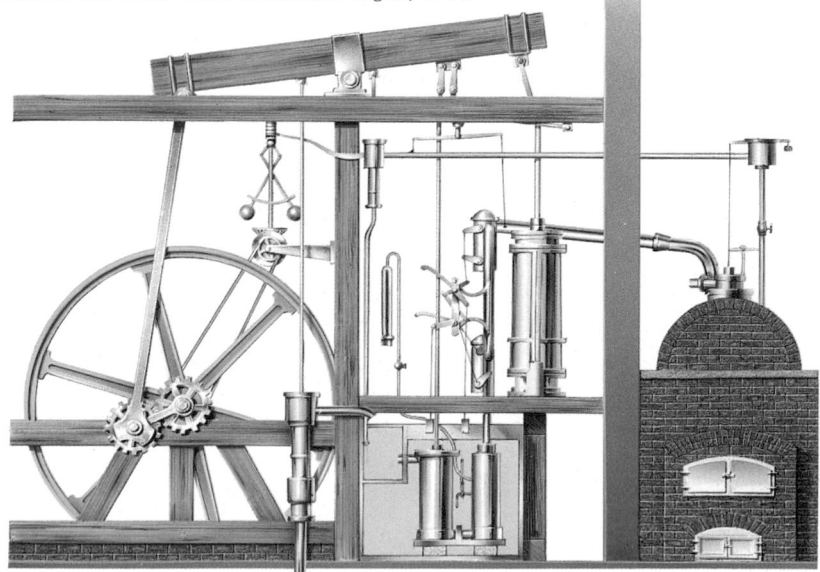

Both the conventional steam engine and the original internal combustion engines relied on the to-and-fro motion of pistons in cylinders; they are termed reciprocating engines. In the 1880s, the British engineer and inventor Charles Parsons devised a totally different type of steam engine that used rotary motion. Called a steam turbine, it used high-pressure steam to turn the fanlike blades of a turbine, in a way combining the principles of the old windmill and water wheel.

Then in the late 1930s, inventors in Britain and Germany began to build turbines that used the pressure of hot gases from burning petroleum fuels to turn their blades. Called a gas turbine, or jet engine, this type of engine was first used to power aircraft. From it developed the turboprop (with a propeller) and the turbofan, the standard engines on today's civil aircraft. Gas turbines are also used in helicopters and railway locomotives.

Reciprocating steam engines

The steam engine was born of the necessity of finding a powerful pump to remove water from deep mines. The first of these was invented in 1712 by the British engineer Thomas Newcomen. Steam from a boiler forced a vertical piston to the top of a cylinder—the piston was linked to the rocking horizontal beam of the pump. Cold water was then sprayed into the cylinder, condensing the steam and forming a vacuum which "sucked" the piston back down the cylinder. The cycle was then repeated.

The great improvement James Watt made 50 years later was to convert the used steam back to water in a separate condenser, so that the working cylinder could remain hot all the time. Soon Watt's engines were powering machines for making textiles and working metals,

A prototype of the Maclaren F1 (right), which applies the technology developed on the Grand Prix racing circuit to a car intended for road use. It is powered by a six-liter V12 engine (below).

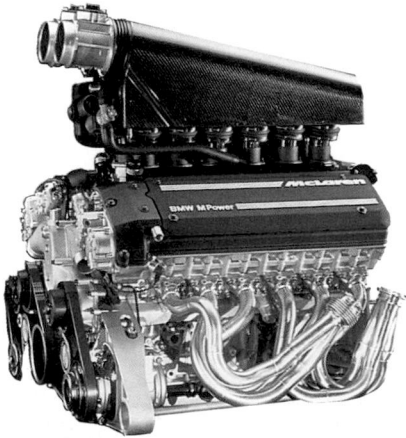

The four-stroke cycle

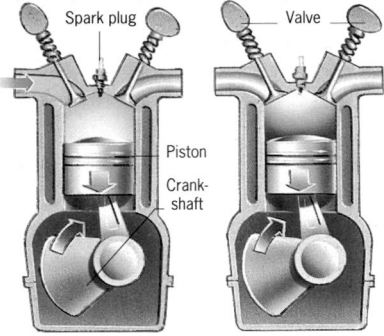
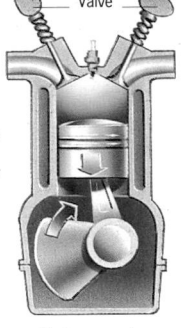

Spark plug — Valve

Piston

Crank-shaft

Induction   **Compression**

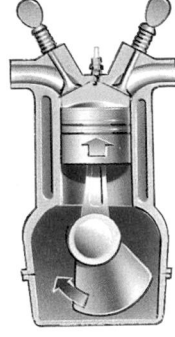
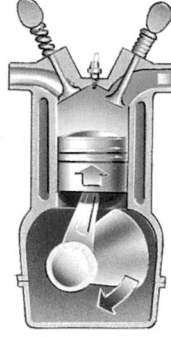

Power   **Exhaust**

and the Industrial Revolution had arrived. His engines were later employed in steam locomotives—initiated by George Stephenson—and later still in farm machines and road vehicles.

Internal combustion engines

The German engineer Nikolaus Otto made the first successful internal combustion engine in 1876. It used fuel in gaseous form and operated by means of

the motion of pistons in cylinders in a four-stroke cycle. This is the principle on which modern internal combustion engines are based (*left*).

The first stroke, called induction, draws a mixture of air and fuel into the cylinder as the piston descends. On the second, compression, stroke, the ascending piston compresses the fuel. An electrical spark then ignites the fuel, and the expanding gases produced force the piston down again on the power stroke. Finally, on the fourth or exhaust stroke, the piston rises again to expel the exhaust gases from the cylinder. The entry and exit of the air and fuel is controlled by valves at the top of the piston. The pistons are connected to the crankshaft and their motion up and down turns the crankshaft, thus providing the power to move the vehicle.

Internal combustion engines use a mixture of gasoline and air – turned into a gas or vapor by a carburetor – as the working fuel. Modern engines use gasoline/fuel injection which delivers a precise amount of fuel to the cylinder for ignition. They commonly have four, six or even more cylinders. On older engines, the valves are actuated by rods driven by the crankshaft. Most modern engines have separate overhead camshafts to actuate the valves.

A different design of gasoline engine, popular for chain saws and lawnmowers, uses a two-stroke cycle. The piston functions also as a valve of the engine as it moves up and down a cylinder that has two side openings, known as ports. On the first upstroke, the piston rises, uncovering an inlet port and compressing the fuel/air mixture already contained in the cylinder. A spark plug then ignites the fuel, producing gases which force the piston down again. On its way, it uncovers an exhaust port (to let out the exhaust gases). Most two-stroke engines are air-cooled.

Timeline

1650 Otto von Guericke makes a vacuum pump.

1657 Christiaan Huygens makes a pendulum clock.

1658 Robert Hooke invents the hairspring (for a watch's balance wheel).

1660 Otto von Guericke forecasts weather using a barometer. Robert Hooke invents the anchor escapement (for clocks).

1671 Gottfried Leibniz makes a calculating machine (for division and multiplication).

1675 Anton van Leeuwenhoek makes a (single-lens) microscope.

1676 Robert Hooke invents the universal joint.

1679 Denis Papin invents the pressure cooker.

1698 Papin makes a working model of a steam engine. Thomas Savery constructs a high-pressure steam pump.

1701 Jethro Tull in England invents the machine drill for planting seeds.

1707 Papin constructs an atmospheric steam engine.

1709 Abraham Darby smelts iron using coke (instead of charcoal).

1712 Thomas Newcomen builds a piston-operated atmospheric steam engine.

1713 René de Réaumur makes glass fiber.

1716 Edmund Halley makes a diving bell with an air supply.

1718 Henry Beighton makes a self-working valve gear (for steam engines). James Puckle invents a (flintlock) machine gun (military terms, *p. 309*).

1720 De Réaumur devises the cupola furnace (for iron smelting).

1721 George Graham invents a mercury pendulum for clocks (compensating for changes in length with temperature).

1733 John Kay invents the flying shuttle for use in weaving.

1735 John Harrison invents the chronometer.

1738 Charles de Labelye invents the caisson (for building bridge piers below water level).

1740 Benjamin Huntsman introduces the crucible method of making steel.

1749 Philip Vaughan invents radial ball bearings.

1758 Jedediah Strutt invents a knitting machine for hosiery.

1759 John Smeaton builds a lighthouse (the Eddystone) using hydraulic cement.

1764 James Hargreaves invents the spinning jenny. James Watt invents a steam engine with a separate condenser.

1765 John Smeaton constructs a cylinder-boring machine.

1769 Richard Arkwright invents the spinning frame.

1774 John Wilkinson invents a boring machine (initially for making cannons and later for boring cylinders for steam engines).

1778 Joseph Bramah invents a practical water closet.

A massive diesel excavator used in strip mining.

Diesel engines

In 1892 the German engineer Rudolf Diesel discovered that certain fuels, which are slightly less volatile than gasoline, ignite by the action of high compression alone—there is no need for a spark plug. Called a compression-ignition engine or, more popularly, a diesel engine, this type also employs a four-stroke cycle.

On the first, induction, stroke, air is drawn through a valve into the cylinder as the piston descends. Then on the upward, compression, stroke, the air is heated and compressed, and liquid fuel injected into the cylinder. The fuel burns, producing gases which force down the piston on the power stroke. Finally the piston rises on the exhaust stroke as the exhaust valve opens to let the gases out of the cylinder.

Diesel engines need no carburetor; instead there is a pump to inject the correct quantity of fuel into the cylinders on the compression stroke. They are favored for buses, trucks, tractors, and earth-moving machinery. Large, slow-revving diesels are used as marine engines to power boats and ships.

Gas-turbine engines

A gas-turbine engine consists basically of a cylindrical tube with a single shaft along its center. Rotating blades at the front compress air entering the engine, and the compressed air passes back to a combustion chamber into which liquid fuel (usually kerosene) is sprayed. The fuel/air mixture burns at high temperature, and the hot gases produced turn the blades of a turbine at the rear of the engine. The gases then leave the rear of the engine at high speed, providing thrust. A turbofan engine (*below*), as used on large civil aircraft, has an extra set of blades at the front which compress additional air and pass it round the combustion chamber into the tailpipe for extra thrust.

Turbofan engine

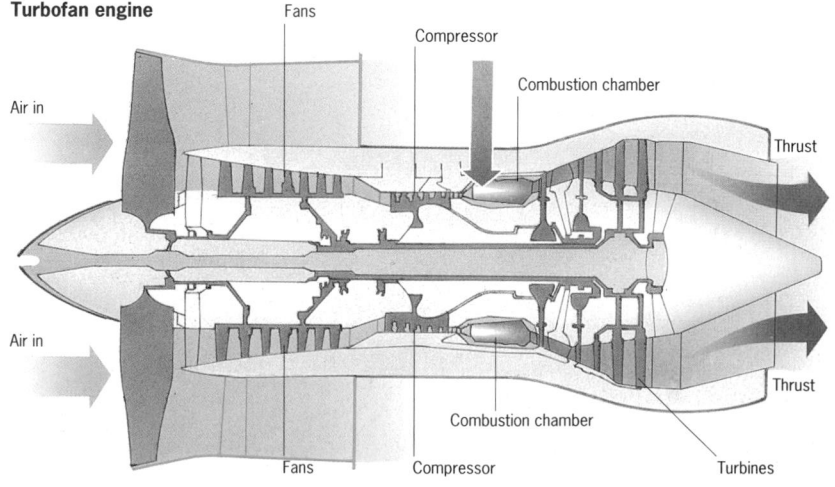

Fans · Compressor · Combustion chamber · Thrust · Air in · Air in · Fans · Compressor · Combustion chamber · Turbines · Thrust

ROADS

Soon after the advent of wheeled vehicles, carts and the animals that pulled them established earthen tracks across the countryside. But cart wheels soon cut up an earth surface, and in wet weather the tracks became seas of mud. In cities some of the tracks were paved with stone, becoming true roads. The Romans established paved roads between the major cities in their extensive empire. For example, the Appian Way ran between Rome and the naval base at Brindisi in southeastern Italy. The Romans built their roads by compacting the earthen roadbed, which was covered with small stones set in sand and lime mortar. Slabs of cut masonry were laid on top to provide the actual road surface, which had raised curb stones along each edge, parallel to a drainage ditch. Often the road was raised slightly above the surrounding land, also as an aid to drainage. So good was Roman road construction that sections survive today.

The same principles—a compacted foundation and a rainproof surface—were adopted during the second half of the 1700s by the French road engineer Pierre Trésaguet. He made a foundation of large stones rammed into the earth, which he covered with a layer of compacted medium-sized stones. The actual road surface consisted of small stones rammed into position. An overall curve, or camber, to the surface ensured good drainage.

The British engineer John McAdam also adopted a camber to his compacted earth footing, covering it with two layers of stones and topped off with small stones that were soon crushed to a smooth surface. To prevent breakup and improve drainage, he later incorporated tar into the surface, producing tarmacadam (Tarmac), which is used on roads and airport runways today.

Most modern roads are made of concrete. A base layer of crushed stones or clinker is covered by a weak concrete mix and topped off with fine concrete. The surface may be covered with tar. For very heavy traffic such as that on highways, the lower concrete layer may be reinforced with steel mesh. For speed and consistency, new expressways are built using a concrete-paving machine, which moves along while slowly laying a strip of ready-mixed concrete and vibrating it so that it compacts. Steel matting is laid in place and a second paver lays the top coat of fine concrete. Road traffic is increasing much faster than roads can be built to accommodate it. The U.S. Interstate Highway System, inaugurated in 1956, is still expanding, although at a slower rate than in the 1960s. In Europe, maintaining and upgrading existing roads takes priority over new building. New roads are expensive and in some countries there is very little space for expansion.

The national highway systems of Western Europe link up to form a network enabling the motorist to travel with relative ease from northern Denmark to southern Spain.

Freeway construction in Los Angeles, after the earthquake of 1992.

Timeline

1779 Samuel Crompton invents the spinning mule. Abraham Darby III builds the first iron bridge (over the River Severn at Coalbrookdale).

1782 James Watt patents a double-acting steam engine.

1783 Henry Cort invents a rolling mill for metals.

1784 Joseph Bramah invents an "unpickable" lock. Henry Cort develops the puddling method of making wrought iron.

1785 Edmund Cartwright invents the power-loom.

1786 Ezekiel Reed invents a nail-making machine.

1789 Samuel Slater developes first U.S. textile mill in Pawtachet, Rhode Island. James Watt invents the governor (a device for controlling the speed of steam engines). The first steam-powered cotton factory opens in Manchester, England.

1790 T. Saint invents an industrial sewing machine.

1791 John Barber builds a gas-turbine engine (p.458).

1792 William Murdock invents gas lighting.

1793 Eli Whitney invents the cotton gin for separating cotton seeds from fiber.

1795 Joseph Bramah invents the hydraulic press.

1796 Joseph Montgolfier invents the hydraulic ram (for pumping water into a reservoir).

1797 Henry Maudslay invents the screw-cutting lathe.

1799 William Murdock invents the slide valve (for steam engines).

1800 Richard Trevithick builds the first high-pressure steam engine.

1804 Frederick Winsor contructs an oven for making coal gas.

1808 Humphry Davy makes an electric arc lamp.

1812 Samuel Pauli invents the cartridge (for breech-loading firearms).

1815 Humphry Davy invents the miner's safety lamp. Marc Brunel invents a boot-making machine and a tunneling shield (boring machine for making tunnels).

1816 George Manby invents a fire extinguisher (containing compressed air and water). Robert Stirling designs a closed-cycle external combustion engine.

1823 Charles Macintosh invents a waterproof fabric.

1824 Joseph Aspdin invents Portland cement.

1825 Thomas Drummond and Goldsworth Gurney invent limelight (to illuminate theater stages). John Appolt develops a retort for making coal gas.

1826 Thomas Telford builds a suspension (road) bridge over the Menai Strait between Wales and Angelsey.

1827 Benoît Fourneyron constructs the first practical water turbine.

1828 J. Nielson invents the blast furnace.

DAMS

Dams are built to regulate the flow of water, to control flooding, to provide irrigation, or to drive hydroelectric power stations. They date from the time of the ancient Egyptians, 5,000 years ago, when the pharaoh Menes built an earthen dam on the Nile River.

Earth dams are still built today. Also called embankment dams, they are constructed by excavating a large trench down to the bedrock, which holds a compacted clay core in place. Soil is then banked against the core on each side. The side facing upstream is covered in gravel, on which rocks and stones are bedded to prevent water scouring away the earth. The other side of the dam and the top are seeded with grass to hold the earth in place and prevent erosion by rain. Alternatively, an embankment dam may be constructed entirely of rock and rubble faced with bitumen, like a road surface.

Most modern dams (*right*) are made of concrete which may be reinforced or prestressed by internal, vertical steel cables (making a vertical cantilever dam). An arch dam is held in place mainly by its own enormous weight. A cupola dam is also arched, but its sides are curved vertically for extra strength. A buttress dam is supported by walls or buttresses.

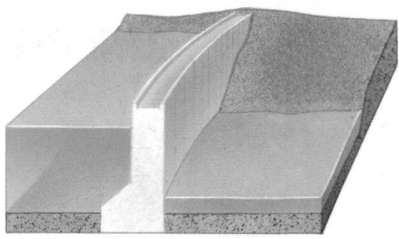

Arch dam.

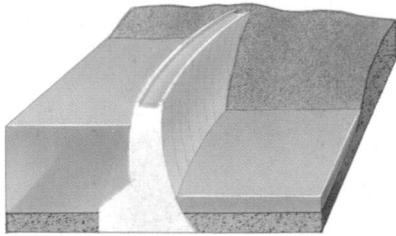

Cupola dam.

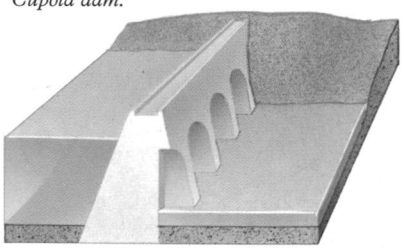

Buttress dam.

WORLD'S HIGHEST DAMS

Name	River and location	Height (ft.)	Name	River and location	Height (ft.)
Rogun	Vakhsh, Tajikistan	1,100	Sayansk	Yenisey, Russia	774
Nurek	Vakhsh, Tajikistan	1,010	Hoover	Colorado, U.S.A.	725
Grand Dixence	Dixence, Switzerland	935	Itaipú	Paraná, border of Brazil and Paraguay	620
Inguri	Inguri, Russia	892	Atatürk	Euphrates, Turkey	604
Chicoasen	Grijalva, Mexico	863	Grand Coulee	Columbia, U.S.A.	551
Vaiont	Vaiont, Italy	860	Kariba	Zambezi, border of Zambia and Zimbabwe	420
Kiev	Dneiper, Ukraine	840			
Guavio	Guaviare, Colombia	804			
Mica	Columbia, Canada	800	Bratsk	Angara, Russia	410
Mauvoisin	Drance de Bagnes, Switzerland	777	Aswan High	Nile, Egypt	364

Dam on Jackson Lake, Wyoming.

TUNNELS

The earliest tunnels were probably constructed for purposes of irrigation, and the Romans used tunnels to connect the aqueducts carrying water supply. The first major tunnel for carrying traffic was not built until the 1670s, when a 520 ft. (158 m) tunnel was blasted through a rocky hill near Beziers, France, to carry part of the Canal du Midi (*p. 469*). Tunnel building increased rapidly with the age of rail. The task was made easier in 1818 when Marc Brunel invented the tunneling shield, held in place at the digging face by jacks. As work progressed, the shield was moved forward and the tunnel behind it lined with bricks or masonry.

Many early railway tunnels, particularly in cities, were made by digging a large trench and roofing it over, a method known as cut and cover. A similar method—known as immersed tube—can be used underwater. Precast concrete tunnel sections are laid in a trench, and the water and mud pumped out. Other hand- and machine-dug methods of tunneling include drill and blast, used particularly in regions of hard rock. Explosives are packed into a series of small holes drilled in the tunnel face and detonated. The New Austrian Tunneling Method (NATM) uses sprayed concrete (shortcrete) to line a tunnel once it is excavated.

Automatic tunneling machines can be used in soft or hard rocks. They have a rotating drilling head with a long conveyor belt to carry back the excavated material. A tunnel boring machine (*below*) of the kind used in the construction of the Channel Tunnel (*top, right*)—opened in 1994—was up to 28 ft. (8.5 m) in diameter with a service train some 850 ft. (260 m) long. The alignment and performance of the cutting head were determined and monitored by laser and computer technology.

A freight car and car shuttle at the French portal of the Channel Tunnel.

WORLD'S LONGEST TUNNELS

Name	Location	Length (mi.)	Date	Name	Location	Length (mi.)	Date
Seikan	Japan	33	1988	Arlberg	Austria	6	1884
Channel	U.K.-France	31	1994	Kvineshei	Norway	6	1943
Dai-shimizu	Japan	14	1979	Moffat	U.S.A.	6	1928
Simplon I	Switz.-Italy	12	1906	Santa Lucia	Italy	6	1977
Simplon II	Switz.-Italy	12	1922	Bigo	Japan	6	1975
Gt. Appenine	Italy	12	1934	Rimutaka	N. Zealand	6	1955
Kanmon	Japan	12	1975	Ricken	Switz.	6	1910
Rokko	Japan	10	1972	Connaught	Canada	5	1916
Hokuriku	Japan	9	1962	Grenchenberg	Switz.	5	1915
Lötschberg	Switz.	9	1913	Karawanken	Aust.-Yugo.	5	1906
Mt. MacDonald	Canada	9	1989	Kobe	Japan	5	1971
Rogers Pass	Canada	9	1988	New Tunna	Japan	5	1964
St. Gotthard	Switz.	9	1882	Otira	N. Zealand	5	1923
Aki	Japan	8	1975	Haegebostad	Norway	5	1943
Cascade	U.S.A.	8	1929	Hoosac	U.S.A.	5	1876
Flathead	U.S.A.	8	1970	Lower			
Fréjus	France-Italy	8	1871	Hauenstein	Switz.	5	1916
Shin-shimizu	Japan	8	1961	Ronco	Italy	5	1889
Keijo	Japan	7	1970	Tauem	Austria	5	1909
Lierasen	Norway	7	1973	Box	U.K.	2	1841
London and				Detroit River	U.S.A.	1	1910
Southwark	U.K.	7	1890	Kilsby Ridge	U.K.	1	1838

Tunnel boring machine (T.B.M.)

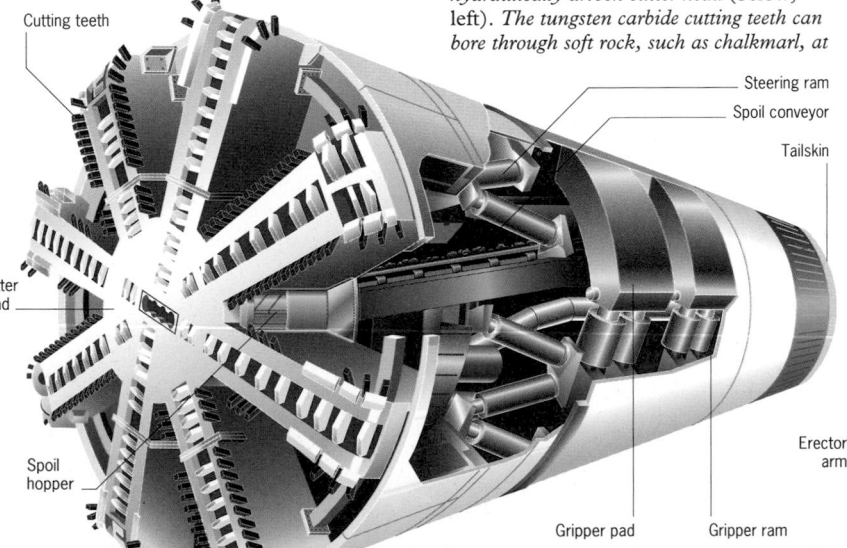

Cutting teeth

Cutter head

Spoil hopper

Gripper pad

Gripper ram

Steering ram

Spoil conveyor

Tailskin

Modern automatic tunneling methods use a hydraulically driven cutter head (below, left). The tungsten carbide cutting teeth can bore through soft rock, such as chalkmarl, at a rate of up to 3,300ft. (1,000 m) a month. The tailskin is immediately followed by a segment erector (cross-section, below) which places the lining segments in position.

Segment erector

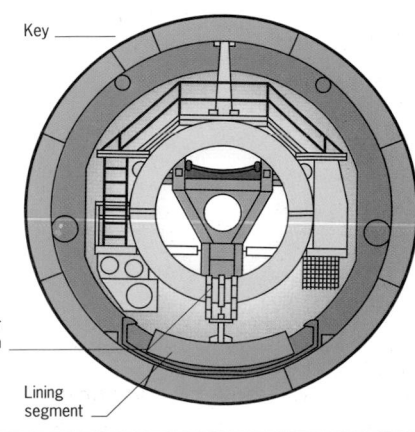

Key

Erector arm

Lining segment

Timeline

1829 Joseph Henry constructs a practical electric motor.

1830 Charles Sauria makes phosphorus matches. Andrew Ure invents the bimetallic strip thermostat. Joseph Whitworth introduces standard screw threads. Barthelemy Thimonnier patents a sewing machine.

1831 Cyrus McCormick develops the first mechanical reaper. Michael Faraday constructs a dynamo.

1832 Hippolyte Pixii makes an electro-magnetic generator.

1835 Joseph Henry patents the electric relay.

1836 Samuel Colt manufactures a revolver from interchangeable parts. James Nasmyth makes a metal-shaping machine. The combine harvester comes into use in the U.S.A.

1839 Nasmyth invents the steam hammer. Isaac Babbitt produces a metal alloy for making bearings (Babbitt metal). William Grove designs a (hydrogen-oxygen) fuel cell.

1840 Alexander Bain makes an electric clock.

1843 Joseph Fowle invents a pneumatic drill.

1844 Charles Goodyear patents the sulfur process for the vulcanization of rubber (*p. 414*).

1845 Edward Chrimes invents the ball-valve (for cisterns). Robert Stephenson builds the high-level bridge at Newcastle upon Tyne in the north of England, using bow-string girders.

1846 Elias Howe invents the modern sewing machine.

1847 Charles Ellet builds a suspension bridge over the Ohio River.

1848 Gold discovered in California, leading to new mines and methods.

1849 Walter Hunt invents the safety pin. Joseph Monier invents reinforced concrete.

1850 Robert Stephenson builds the box-girder railway bridge over the Menai Strait, Wales.

1851 Joseph Paxton builds the Crystal Palace in London; it is made from pre-fabricated parts.

1852 Jean Foucault invents the gyroscope.

1853 Pierre Carpentier invents corrugated iron.

1854 William Hampson introduces a method of producing liquid air in bulk.

1855 Henry Bessemer invents his convert-er (for making steel). James Harrison invents a compression refrigerator.

1858 H. Smith invents a washing machine. The Foreland Lighthouse (in Kent, U.K.) is fitted with electric arc lights.

1859 First drilled oil well begins operating in Pennsylvania. Gaston Planté makes an accumulator (storage battery). Jean Lenoir constructs a (gas-burning) inter-nal combustion engine.

BRIDGES

The earliest "dry" river crossings were probably made on logs or boats coupled together to make a pontoon bridge. Small spans could be made from a single long block of stone, as in the clapper bridges in Cornwall and Devon, England. Ravines were crossed by bridges made of ropes or vines, and crude rope suspension bridges are still built by people in regions such as South America and the Himalayas.

The Romans built bridges of timber or masonry. The first bridge to span the Tiber River in Rome was probably built as early as the 600s B.C. Like the 1,377 ft. (420 m) bridge across the Rhine River constructed in 50 B.C., it was made entire-ly of timber. In 62 B.C. Roman engineers built the Pons Fabricus in Rome, with two 78 ft. (24 m) semicircular stone arch-es. Now called the Ponte Quattro Capi, the bridge still stands today. The Romans are also famous for building aqueducts to carry a water supply, often with many arches crossing a valley like a modern viaduct. The Pont du Gard at Nîmes, France, and the aqueduct at Segovia, Spain (*right*), are still standing.

As with road building, it was the French who next advanced the building of bridges. Best known is the Pont d'Avig-non over the River Rhône. It had 21 stone arches and was constructed in 1177 by an

The Roman aqueduct in Segovia, Spain.

order of monks. By 1716, there was an official corps of engineers for designing and building bridges and roads in France.

The first bridge to be made of iron was built in 1779 across the River Severn at Coalbrookdale in England. The compo-nents of the bridge were cast by the iron-master Abraham Darby III. Cast iron was replaced by wrought iron to make the chains for the suspension bridge across the Menai Strait linking Wales and

Types of bridges

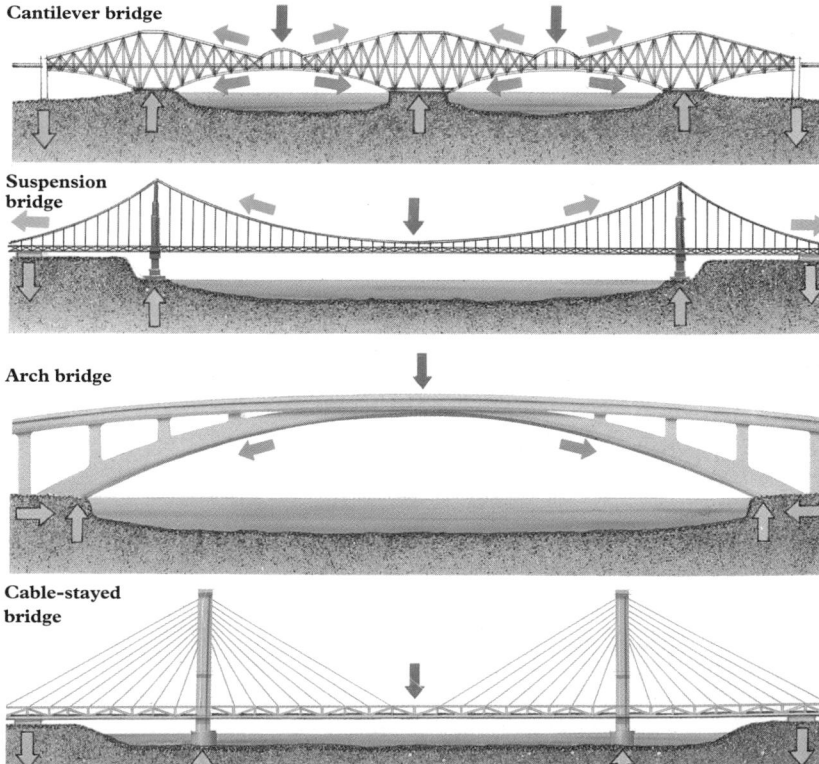

Cantilever bridge

Suspension bridge

Arch bridge

Cable-stayed bridge

Load   Support   Tension   Compression

Switzerland's Ganter Bridge has cantilevers and cable-stays embedded in prestressed concrete.

Anglesey. With a span of 584 ft. (178 m), it was constructed in 1826 by Thomas Telford. The bridge is still in regular use. Twenty-four years later a parallel railway bridge across the strait was built by Robert Stephenson. Called the Britannia Tubular Bridge, it consisted of a wrought iron tube lined with timber. For longer spans, steel arches became standard, such as James Eads' bridge over the Mississippi River at St. Louis, built in 1874.

Most long modern bridges are suspension bridges, with cables built of many strands of steel and road or rail decks made of concrete. For shorter spans, a box girder construction (also in concrete) is favored.

Runners crossing the Verrazano Narrows suspension bridge during the 1994 New York Marathon.

WORLD'S LONGEST BRIDGES

Name	Location	Length (ft.)	Date
Humber[1]	U.K.	4,626	1981
Verrazano Narrows	U.S.A.	4,259	1964
Golden Gate	U.S.A.	4,200	1937
Mackinac	U.S.A.	3,800	1957
Bosphorus II	Turkey	3,576	1988
Bosphorus	Turkey	3,524	1973
George Washington	U.S.A.	3,500	1931
Bendorf	Germany	3,380	1965
Salazar	Portugal	3,327	1966
Firth of Forth	U.K.	3,300	1964
Severn	U.K.	3,241	1966
Rainbow	Japan	3,012	1993
Yokohama Bay	Japan	2,865	1989
Tacoma Narrows II	U.S.A.	2,802	1950
Kincardine	U.K.	2,697	1936
Transbay	U.S.A.	2,313	1933
Ambassador	U.S.A.	1,850	1929
Benjamin Franklin	U.S.A.	1,752	1926
New River Gorge[2]	U.S.A.	1,700	1977
Bayonne	U.S.A.	1,653	1932
Sydney Harbour	Australia	1,650	1932
Delaware River	U.S.A.	1,644	1974
Cooper River	U.S.A.	1,601	1989
Brooklyn	U.S.A.	1,594	1883
Greater New Orleans	U.S.A.	1,575	1958
Lions Gate	Canada	1,552	1938
Alex Fraser[3]	Canada	1,526	1986
Chao Phraya	Thailand	1,476	1989
Astoria	U.S.A.	1,233	1966
Port Mann	Canada	1,200	1964
Duisburg	Germany	1,148	1970
Thatcher Ferry	Panama	1,129	1962
Lower Yarra	Australia	1,102	1970
Trois-Rivières	Canada	1,102	1962
Cincinnati	U.S.A.	1,089	1867
Kniebrücke	Germany	1,050	1969
Wheeling	U.S.A.	1,010	1849
Erskine	U.K.	1,000	1970
Gladesville	Australia	1,000	1964

[1] Longest suspension bridge
[2] Longest arch bridge
[3] Longest cable-stay bridge

DOMES AND TOWERS

The urge to build high and wide has always driven engineers and architects, but until the invention of new building materials such as cast iron, reinforced concrete, steel, aluminum, Plexiglas, high-tensile fabric, and modern plastics, their dreams have remained earthbound by the limitations of brick and masonry. Even so, early efforts to span wide spaces or reach for the sky were impressive. It was anonymous Roman engineers who built the Pantheon in 118–108 B.C., using the newly invented building material called concrete. The Pantheon dome is 142 ft. (43 m) high and spans an interior diameter of exactly the same dimension; it was unsurpassed until the 1800s.

Dome technology leaped forward when the Byzantine engineers commissioned to build Hagia Sophia in Constantinople in 537 devised the pendentive, a triangular vaulted segment which enabled them to build a dome over a square or rectangular base, rather than as a continuation of a cylindrical base. Later refinements on the dome endeavored to make it both larger and lighter; the Renaissance architect Filippo Brunelleschi (*p. 534*) designed the double-shelled dome of Florence cathedral (1418–36). In 1710, Sir Christopher Wren's innovative design for the dome of St. Paul's cathedral, London, featured an inner brick cone and an outer shell of lead-clad timber.

When new materials and mass production techniques became available during the 1800s, they made it possible for engineers to design structures that enclosed large spaces and build them quickly and easily. The great glass and iron edifice of the Crystal Palace, erected to celebrate London's Great Exhibition in

Currently the highest freestanding tower in the world, the CN (radio) tower dominates the skyline of Toronto.

1851, was assembled from prefabricated sections in just 17 weeks. Today, domes and wide-span roofs cover exposition halls, shopping malls, transportation terminals and sports stadia; the Louisiana Superdome, finished in 1975, has a steel roof 680 ft. (207 m) in diameter.

Domes took another direction in the hands of Buckminster Fuller, deviser of the geodesic dome, in which a huge space can be enclosed in a comparatively light structure made up of triangular aluminum panels mounted on a steel framework.

The architects of the 1900s were quick to see how the properties of concrete and steel could liberate them from conventional building styles. Danish architect Otto von Spreckelsen built the extraordinary concrete structure of La Grande Arche de la Défense in Paris.

The new materials also made it possible to build high. There had been lighthouses and campaniles (bell-towers) before, but in 1889, Gustave Eiffel built his tower in Paris using prefabricated iron and steel components. For 40 years, it was the tallest structure in the world. The highest free-standing tower today is the CN tower in Toronto, Canada, a slender lance of prestressed concrete and reinforced steel 1,815 ft. (553 m) high.

L'Arche de la Défense in Paris, built in 1989, contains art galleries and a conference center.

SKYSCRAPERS

Skyscrapers originated in the U.S.A. in the second half of the 1800s, largely because of the invention in 1852 of the passenger safety elevator by the American engineer Elisha Otis. Many of the first skyscrapers were constructed in Chicago, during its major rebuilding program after the disastrous fire of 1871. As iron and then steel replaced masonry as the main constructional material, buildings could be made taller and taller. The tallest to date is the Sears Roebuck Tower in Chicago, rising 1,454 ft. (443 m) above street level.

The usual method of skyscraper construction is to build a lattice of steel girders, then add the floors and walls, generally by cladding (so-called curtain walling). Alternatively the skeleton of the building is made from reinforced or prestressed concrete. In a novel method known as the lift-slab system, tall reinforced concrete columns are erected first, surrounded by vertical steel rods. The floors are cast, one after the other, in a stack at ground level. Then hydraulic jacks at the tops of the steel rods raise the floors, one at a time, into position, where they are secured. As a result, the top floor is fixed first, so the building could be said to be constructed from the top downward.

Most of the world's very tall buildings are in the U.S.A., where the skyscraper was first conceived.

Chrysler Building, New York 1,046 feet

Library Tower, Los Angeles 1,018 feet

Bank of China, Hong Kong 1,033 feet (excluding masts)

John Hancock Tower, Boston 1,476 feet

Empire State Building, New York 1,250 feet

World Trade Center, New York 1,710 feet

Sears Tower, Chicago 1,454 feet

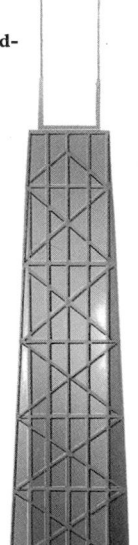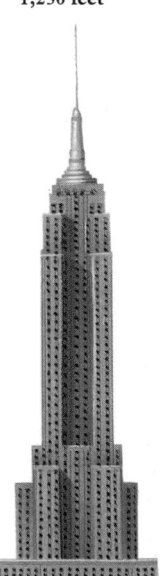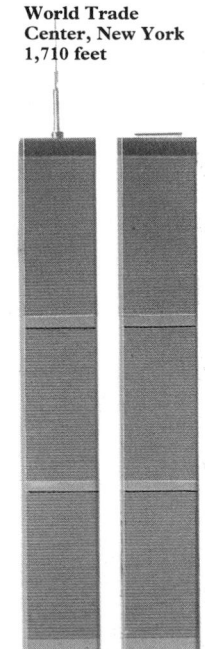

MANUFACTURING

The history of manufacturing is as old as the history of civilized humankind. Originally, in village communities, people with special skills used them to make things for other people—either for money or for barter. The Industrial Revolution sprang from the development of machines that could outproduce the cottage workers, especially those who wove cloth. Mechanized looms—with the spinning machines to supply them with yarn—replaced the outworkers, with the labor concentrated in factories (originally called mills, after their counterparts, the water-powered mills for grinding corn). Soon steam power became available to drive the new manufacturing industries, and migration from the country to the new towns and cities followed as laborers sought work in the new factories.

Even in the factories, many of the products remained what we would now term "one-shots": each product—be it a spoke-shave or a gun—was made by one craftsman to a slightly variable design.

Then in the U.S.A. toward the end of the 1700s, several manufacturers realized that goods could be made and sold more cheaply if their component parts were interchangeable (so that if a part failed it could immediately be replaced by an identical part already manufactured). Furthermore, the manufacturing process could be streamlined by adopting what became known as mass production techniques, which combined the idea of inter-changeable parts with assemblyline methods. Instead of one worker carrying out all the procedures to manufacture a single product, an assembly line has several workers who each perform one task on the item being manufactured as it travels along a conveyor belt.

The idea of mass production was pioneered in Britain by Marc Brunel who, beginning in 1803, devised a series of machines for making pulley blocks for the

The early Ford production line where the Model T was manufactured.

sailing ships of the British Royal Navy. In 1835 in the U.S.A., Samuel Colt (1814–62) introduced interchangeable parts for the revolvers manufactured at his armory in Hartford, Connecticut. But the real pioneer of modern assembly–line methods for mass production was the car manufacturer Henry Ford, who introduced the technique at his Highland Park factory in Detroit, Michigan, in 1913.

Technology on the factory floor

Today most aspects of the manufacturing process in a wide variety of industries are computer controlled. The principle of the assembly line has been retained but the repetitive tasks are now carried out by electronic machines that are popularly known as robots. Robots are used extensively in the car industry as well as in manufacturing processes that demand sterile or dust-free conditions, such as pharmaceutical manufacture. Computer control is also applied to machine tools for making components and running the handling equipment that feeds them onto the production line. Stock control, distribution, and administration systems within many industries, too, are controlled by computer technology.

Robotics on the Detroit production line.

Timeline

1862 Richard Gatling invents the machine gun. Joseph Brown makes a universal milling machine (for cutting metal).

1865 Linus Yale invents the cylinder lock.

1866 Robert Whitehead invents the self-propelled torpedo.

1867 Alfred Nobel invents dynamite. George Babcock and Stephen Wilcox develop the water-tube boiler (for steam engines).

1868 George Leclanché invents the zinc-carbon battery (Leclanché cell). A. Hills invents a lawnmower. Charles Gould invents the stapler. Germain Sommeiller completes the first major railway tunnel (through Mont Cenis in the Alps).

1869 John Wesley Hyatt invents celluloid.

1871 Ives McGaffrey constructs a (steam-powered) vacuum cleaner.

1872 James Dewar invents the vacuum bottle (Moving heat, *p. 403*).

1874 James Eads builds the first steel arch bridge, at St. Louis, MO.

1876 Karl von Linde constructs a refrigerator. Nikolaus Otto invents a four-stroke internal combustion (gas) engine. Anatole Mallet invents the compound steam engine. Melville Bissel invents a mechanical carpet sweeper.

1878 Dugald Clerk invents the two-stroke (internal combustion) engine.

1879 Joseph Swan invents a carbon-filament incandescent lamp. Thomas Bouch builds the ill-fated Tay Bridge (Scotland), which collapses the same year. James Ritty invents a cash register. James Lee invents a magazine (for holding rifle cartridges).

1882 Hiram Maxim develops his machine gun. Henry Seeley patents an electric flatiron. Attempts to construct a tunnel under the English Channel are abandoned for political reasons.

1883 John Roebling's Brooklyn Bridge opens in New York City (the first with steel suspension cables). Percival Everitt constructs a vending machine.

1884 Charles Parsons invents the multi-stage steam turbine.

1885 William Stanley invents the transformer. Carl Auer invents the gas mantle. Karl Benz and Gottlieb Daimler develop an internal combustion engine. The first skyscraper is built in Chicago.

1886 Nikola Tesla constructs an AC electric motor.

1887 Edward Butler invents the float-feed carburetor (for gasoline engines). W. Leigh Burton patents an electric heater.

1888 Nikola Tesla invents an AC induction motor.

1889 Gustave Eiffel's tower is built in Paris. Louis Glass invents a jukebox (coin-operated phonograph). W.A. Cockran invents an automatic dishwasher.

1891 Dugald Clerk introduces super-chargers (for gasoline engines).

Timeline

1892 Whitcomb Judson invents the zipper. William Burroughs patents his cash register. Rudolf Diesel invents the compression-ignition (Diesel) engine (*p. 458*). François Hennebique develops pre-stressed concrete.

1895 King Gillette invents the safety razor. Wilhelm Fein makes the first portable electric drill.

1897 Charles Parsons builds a steam turbine for boats (*p. 469*). Konstantin Tsiolkovsky constructs the first wind tunnel (for testing aircraft design).

1900 Thomas Edison invents the nickel-iron (alkali) accumulator. Johann Vaaler invents the paper clip.

1901 Hubert Booth invents an electric vacuum cleaner. Peter Hewitt invents the mercury vapor lamp. George Abraham invents the snap fastener.

1902 First Aswan Dam over the Nile is completed (by B. Baker). James Ransome patents his lawnmower.

1904 Julius Elster makes a practical photocell. Leon Guillet develops stainless steel but finds no immediate application for it.

1906 The Zuider Zee drainage scheme is begun in the Netherlands.

1908 William Hoover introduces electric vacuum cleaners. Leo Baekeland invents bakelite.

1909 The first electric toaster is manufactured in the U.S.A.

1910 Georges Claude invents neon lighting. B. Ljundstrom builds a high-pressure steam turbine.

1911 Isaac Lewis patents a machine gun.

1912 Henry Ford develops first moving assembly line. V. Kaplan designs a turbine for low–pressure water flow. Sidney Russell invents the prototype electric blanket.

1913 William Coolidge invents the (hot-cathode) X-ray tube. Hans Geiger invents a radiation detector, named the Geiger counter.

1915 Irving Langmuir invents the gas-filled tungsten filament lamp. Fokker aircraft are fitted with an interrupter gear (to allow a machine gun to fire between the rotating blades of the propeller). Corning Glass Works, in the U.S.A., develops heat-resistant glass for cooking. Paul Langevin invents sonar.

1917 Clarence Birdseye invents a process for preserving food by deep-freezing it.

1918 John Browning patents his self-loading (automatic) rifle.

1920 John Thompson patents his submachine (Tommy) gun.

1922 The world's largest hydroelectric power station, at Queenston near Niagara in Canada, begins operation. LaPlante-Choate Company introduces the bulldozer in the U.S.A.

1923 The first continuous steel strip mill begins operation.

1926 Erik Rotheim invents the aerosol (spray can). Robert Goddard launches the first liquid-fuel rocket; it soars to a

THE ELECTRONICS INDUSTRY

Computers are the latest and arguably the most important products of an industry that more than any other typifies technological progress during the 20th century. The science of electronics is, formally, concerned with the behavior of electricity in a vacuum, in gases, and in solid-state devices made from semiconductors. It originated with the invention in 1904 of the diode (two-electrode tube, also known as a thermionic tube or vacuum tube) by the British physicist John Fleming. The diode's first important use was as a detector in early radio receivers.

Two years later the American radio pioneer Lee De Forest added a third electrode to the diode to make the first triode. This tube can be used to amplify small electric currents, and for the next 40 years it was one of the key components in electronic circuits, particularly those used in radio and, later, television (*p. 481*). Large industries were established in Europe and North America to meet the domestic demand created by broadcast radio and TV. There were also many military applications for electronics, spurred on by World War II.

Tubes were used in the first computers, built toward the end of World War II. But these early machines needed thousands of tubes, which required a lot of power (tubes contain an electrically heated cathode to produce a stream of electrons), and the tubes themselves were not sufficiently reliable for the machines using them to function for more than a few minutes without breaking down. The required breakthrough came in 1947, when scientists working at the U.S. Bell Telephone Laboratories invented the transistor. This semiconductor device requires no power and can be used to replace the triode; semiconductor diodes were invented at about the same time.

Now electronic circuits could be made smaller (even early transistors were only about a hundredth the size of their tube equivalents). Tube circuits were assembled on a metal chassis and the components wired together using soldered joints. Transistor circuits made use of printed circuits, in which the conductors are strips of thin copper produced by etching the metal adhering to a plastic board. The new technique was soon applied to all the products of the electronics industry.

The advent of integrated circuits in the late 1950s and early 1960s allowed even more compact miniaturization. In this technique, all the required circuit components are produced by a combination of metal deposition and etching on a single slice of semiconductor — the now ubiquitous silicon chip. The device that benefited most was the computer, particularly the small personal computers (PCs) (*p. 427*) that are so popular — today there are more computers than cars.

Computer applications

There are very few manufacturing or service industries that do not use computers in some way or other. Originally valued for their speed and accuracy at performing mathematical calculations ("number crunching"), computers were first used by the military and then for accounting and banking. The ability of the machines to handle vast amounts of data, and if necessary compare it with a built-in mathematical model, enabled them to be applied to weather forecasting (*p. 78*) and stock market dealing (*p. 259*). Similar applications

Operation Control at the Goddard Space Center, where the flight path of the space shuttle is controlled by computer.

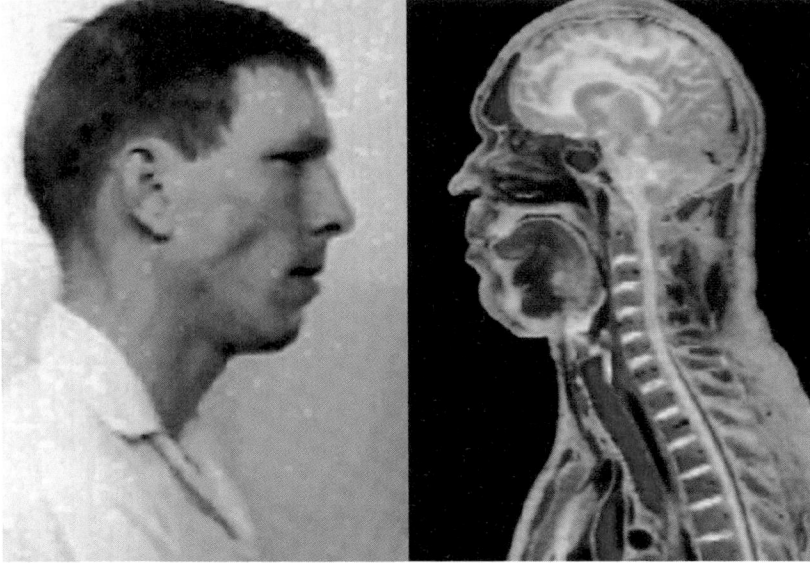

Executed murderer J. P. Jernigan became the first man in cyberspace when his frozen cadaver was dissected into 1 mm slices to be photographed and digitally stored as a medical study aid.

can be found in medical practice and air traffic control, and in control systems for power generation and in the chemical industry. Computers are used in the leisure and travel industries to make theater and airline reservations, in the printing industry (for typesetting and page make-up) and by police forces.

In communications, computers are applied to information retrieval and message switching for telephone systems and in the international network of the information superhighway (*pp. 482-83*).

Among later applications came the use of computers in design, known as CAD (computer-aided design). Computer techniques are used by architects and industri-al designers to produce images and then plans for new products without the laborious (and costly) procedure of making models. In the car industry, for example, manufacturers can design a new car and then "crash" the design (a computer model) to test its strength and other features in accidents.

Another important application of computer-generated video graphics is in machines for training civilian and military aircrew. Pilots can learn how to fly a supersonic strike aircraft without risk to themselves or the machine. The technology is also used by the leisure industry for games or, at its most developed, as a virtual reality experience.

In car manufacture, CAD software helps to design the prototype and can then be integrated with production machinery to make a computer-aided manufacturing (CAD/CAM) system.

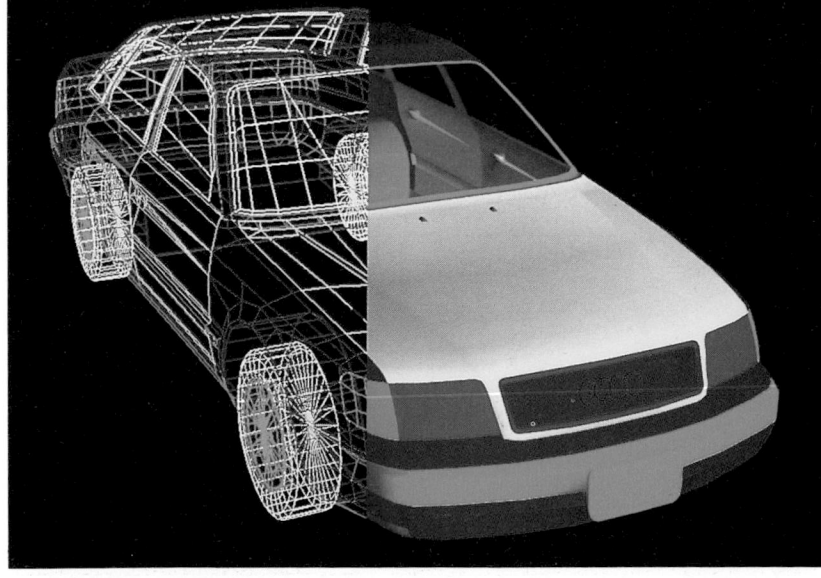

Timeline

height of 184 ft. (56 m).

1927 S. Junghans invents continuous casting for nonferrous metals. Holland Tunnel, the first road tunnel linking New York and New Jersey, opens. Charles Strite invents an electric toaster.

1928 J. W. Horton and W. A. Marrison invent the quartz clock. Joseph Schick invents the electric shaver. Richard Drew invents Scotch tape. A. Refell *et al* build a working robot.

1929 Felix Wankel patents rotary engine.

1930 Barnes Wallis develops geodetic construction.

1931 Owens Illinois Glass company begins the industrial manufacture of glass fiber. The tallest building in the world at the time, the Empire State Building in New York, is completed.

1932 The Zuider Zee drainage scheme is completed in the Netherlands. Sydney Harbour Bridge is opened.

1936 Boulder Dam (Colorado River) becomes operational.

1937 San Francisco's Golden Gate Bridge is opened.

1940 Donald Bailey invents the portable Bailey Bridge for the military.

1941 Grand Coulee Dam, Washington, becomes operational.

1942 Max Muller develops a turboprop aircraft engine for Junkers, Germany. Jacques Cousteau and E. Gagnan design the aqualung.

1945 Percy Spenser invents the microwave oven.

1948 George de Mestral invents Velcro for use by the armed forces. An atomic clock is constructed with ammonia atoms.

1953 Charles Townes develops the maser (Microwave Amplification by Stimulated Emission of Radiation). Friction welding is invented in the U.S.S.R.

1955 Cesium atomic clock is constructed in Britain.

1960 Theodore Maiman develops the ruby laser.

1962 General Motors begins using the first industrial robots. Carbon fiber is developed in Britain.

1964 The Verrazano Narrows Bridge opens in New York.

1967 The Krasnoyarsk hydroelectric dam, the world's largest, is completed in Siberia. A tidal power station opens on the Rance River in France.

1968 The Aswan High Dam is completed in Egypt.

1974 Holographic electron microscope is developed in the U.S.A..

1975 Tokamak thermonuclear power station is opened in the U.S.S.R.

1984 The Thames Flood Barrier, the world's largest, opens in London.

1988 The Seikan railway tunnel, the longest under the sea, opens between Japan's Hokkaido and Honshu islands.

1994 The Channel Tunnel opens, linking Britain with mainland Europe.

Timeline

c. 4000 B.C. Sailing ships are used in Mesopotamia. Writing (*p. 478*) is introduced in Mesopotamia (*right*).

c. 3200 B.C. The (solid disk) wheel is invented in Mesopotamia (*right*).

c. 2000 B.C. Spoked wheels come into use.

312 B.C. Romans construct the Appian Way (road) between Capua and Rome.

c. A.D. 100 Writing paper is first manufactured in China.

984 Ch'iao Wei-Yo invents the canal lock in China.

c. 1000 The camera obscura is invented in Arabia.

c. 1040 Movable type (made of ceramic) is used in China.

c. 1100 Magnetic compass in general use in China.

1370s Locks are built on Dutch canals.

1400s Three-masted ships are built.

1403 Metal type is used for printing in Korea.

1440s Johannes Gutenberg invents the printing press.

1474 William Caxton prints books in English.

1477 Intaglio printing (*p. 479*), using engraved metal plates, is introduced.

1492 Graphite (lead) is used for pencils.

1494 A papermill is built in England.

1500 Leonardo da Vinci designs an (impractical) helicopter.

1573 Humphry Cole invents the ship's log for measuring speed through the water.

1605 Abraham Verkoevan prints the first newspaper in Antwerp.

1620 Cornelius van Drebbel builds a submarine.

1642 The Briare Canal opens in France between the Loire and Seine rivers. Ludwig van Siegen invents the mezzotint process (for printing halftones).

1666 Pierre Riquet builds the Canal du Midi across France between the Mediterranean and the Atlantic.

1676 Robert Hooke invents the universal joint.

1710 Jacob Le Blon invents three-color printing.

1716 Edmund Halley makes a divingbell with an air supply.

1725 William Ged invents a stereotype process for printing. Johann Schulze discovers the light-sensitive properties of silver nitrate used in photography.

1735 John Harrison invents the chronometer.

1759 James Brindley builds a canal on an aqueduct.

1768 Jean le Prince invents the aquatint engraving process.

1770 Nicolas Cugnot builds a three-wheeled steam-powered gun carriage.

1775 David Bushnell builds a submarine.

1783 Jean Pilétre makes the first flight in a hot-air balloon built by Jacques and Joseph Montgolfier. Jacques Charles makes the first ascent in a manned hydrogen balloon.

TRANSPORTATION

Transportation is concerned with the application of technology and engineering to move people and goods. Communications deals with the movement and dissemination of information. Early peoples could get from place to place only by walking; later they learned to domesticate animals such as horses and camels, which they could ride. By 3500 B.C. the ancient Sumerians had developed land sledges which were pulled by draft animals. In North America, the Inuit (Eskimos) used dogs to pull sleds over snow and ice, and farther south, Plains Indians developed the *travois*, a long A-shaped leather-covered frame that was dragged behind a horse or a dog to carry loads.

A camel train crosses China's Taklimakan Desert, following the old Silk Route.

THE WHEEL

The first major breakthrough in the development of land transport, came with the invention of the wheel. Most historians agree that the original application was as a potter's wheel for shaping wet clay to make pots and beakers, and there are Persian wheel-made jars dating from 4000 B.C. By 3200 B.C., the Mesopotamians had adapted the solid wheel—made by fixing three shaped planks together—for simple, unsteerable carts, which could be drawn by draft animals such as oxen.

Spoked wheels came into use by about 2000 B.C., and two centuries later the Hittites were fitting them to their war chariots. Horse-drawn chariots were also in use in Egypt at about this time.

The Romans made extensive use of wheeled vehicles and built fine roads to permit speedy travel between towns (*p. 459*). Gradually carriages were developed with springs (first made of wood or leather, later of metal) and a steerable front axle. Wheels were made larger to even out the ride over bumpy roads, which were very poor after the roads of the former Roman empire had fallen into disrepair. A 17th-century stagecoach, for example, rarely exceeded 30 mi.(50 km) a day; a century later mail-coach schedules assumed speeds of 10 mph (16 kph).

The long-awaited road improvements came at the beginning of the 1800s with the work of the Scottish engineer John McAdam. The inventions of the automobile and the pneumatic tire were still nearly a century away, and so for another 100 years the carriage, hansom cab, and horse-drawn omnibus remained the main forms of road transportation.

WATER TRANSPORTATION

Long before the invention of the wheel, people traveled by water. At first they merely used floating logs, then they built rafts of several logs or bundles of reeds bound together, or made dugout canoes by hollowing half a treetrunk. Reed boats were in use in places as far apart as Egypt and South America. Tree bark or animal skins stretched over a wooden frame, as in the Welsh coracle, was an alternative form of construction.

The use of these primitive craft also spawned the invention of the oar, which by Egyptian times was being used also as a rudder for steering. The motive power was human muscle.

As early as 4000 B.C. came the development of the sail (in Mesopotamia), and by 2000 B.C. the Egyptians had ships with a single square sail that traveled upstream along the Nile River. They returned downstream, against the prevailing wind, using the current, with the sail furled. The Romans also had square-rigged ships with one or two sails. These were difficult to sail against the wind, a problem largely overcome by the fore-and-aft rig using a lateen sail, introduced in about A.D. 300 by Arab sailors on their dhows. The idea did not reach the Vikings, who were still using square-rigged vessels 600 years later.

Sumerian solid-wheeled war chariots (c. 2000 B.C.).

Canals

Early Chinese engineers built canals for carrying boats—the Grand Canal was begun in 485 B.C. and by the time of its completion in A.D. 1283 was 1,106 mi. (1,780 km) long. Simple single-gate locks, resembling a dam with an opening that allowed the passage of a boat, were first used from about 500 B.C., also in China. Two-gate locks of the modern type were developed in Europe in the late 1400s.

The first important canal in Europe was the 175 mi.(250km) Canal du Midi, completed in 1681, which crossed France linking the Mediterranean Sea to the Atlantic Ocean. Britain's first man-made waterway was the Bridgewater Canal from Worsley to Manchester, completed in 1761 and the first in a 2,485 mi.(4,000 km) system of canals that transported raw materials and manufactured goods throughout Britain. Some were contour canals, which followed the natural contours of the land and did not require large engineering works. A more direct route could be obtained by building locks (to vary the height of the canal), with tunnels and aqueducts to cross hills and valleys.

Toward the end of the canal era, steam-driven boats became available. But steam engines also powered locomotives and gave rise to the railroad age, which finally saw the demise of small inland waterways in Europe. Canals carrying seagoing ships, however, have continued to play an important part in world freight transportation. The Netherlands moves over 57 percent of its freight by canal, and barge traffic is increasing on the Rhine. The Rhine-Maine-Danube canal links 2,200 mi.(3,500 km) of waterway from Rotterdam to the Black Sea.

North America has many miles of canals. One of the finest feats of canal engineering is the St. Lawrence Seaway (completed in 1959), which extends for 2,320 mi.(3,830 km) to link all the Great Lakes with the Atlantic Ocean (below).

The Great Lakes canal system.

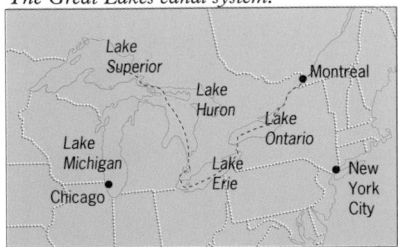

Clipper ships were the fastest way to move cargo in the 1800s.

The age of sail

Europeans did not start building ships with several masts until the 1200s, after reports of multimasted Chinese vessels reached the west. Three masts (fore, main, and mizzen) soon became a common pattern, with square sails on the masts and triangular fore-and-aft sails between them.

By the middle of the 1800s, the fastest sailing ships were the clippers (*above*) which sailed from Britain and the U.S.A. to China and Australia. The ships' wooden hulls were often clad in copper, to deter boring marine worms. Later developments included composite hulls, with iron ribs and wooden planking, and then all-steel hulls. The number of masts also increased, and multimasted steel barks became the common cargo vessels of the late 1800s.

Modern propulsive power

The rise of the steam engine saw the decline of sail for seagoing ships. At first iron-hulled ships retained some sails as a means of auxiliary power. The steam engine powered the ship, using first paddle wheels and then one or more screw propellers. Isambard Brunel had anticipated this trend with his steam-and-sail screw-propelled *Great Britain*, was launched as a transatlantic passenger liner in 1843. By the early 1900s, steam had almost totally replaced sail.

At the review of the British navy's fleet in 1897, the British inventor Charles Parsons had amazed the watching admiralty by charging between the lines of iron-clad warships in his steam-turbine-driven boat *Turbinia* at speeds of up to 20 knots (23 mph or 37 kph). By 1907, with the launch of the *Mauritania*, steam-turbine ships were crossing the Atlantic at speeds of 27 knots (30mph or 50km/h). Oil became the preferred boiler fuel.

By the middle of the century, the luxury liner—except for cruise ships—was in decline because of the rise of air transportation. For cargo vessels, the cheaper (and simpler) marine diesel engine became the usual form of propulsion. Steam turbines are still retained for some fast bulk carriers and container ships, and there are a few nonnaval vessels that use nuclear power to produce the steam for turbines.

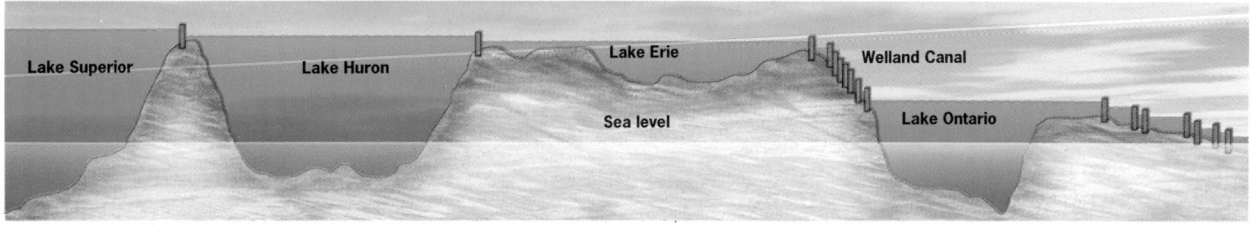

Timeline

1784 William Murdock builds a model steam-powered carriage.

1785 Jean Blanchard crosses the English Channel in a balloon.

1786 Lionel Lukin builds an "unsinkable" lifeboat.

1787 John Fitch builds a steamboat.

1789 James Watt invents the governor for controlling the speed of steam engines. Oliver Evans patents a steam-powered road vehicle.

c. **1790** Firmin Didot invents a method of making stereotypes (*Printing Newspapers p. 450-51*). Comte Mede de Sirrac invents a bicycle (without pedals).

1795 Nicholas Conté makes colored pencils.

1798 Louis Robert makes a machine for producing paper (from wood pulp) in a continuous roll. Aloys Senefelder invents lithography (*p. 479*). Robert Fulton builds a submarine.

1800 Thomas Wedgewood and Humphry Davy produce (unfixed) photographic images using silver salts.

1801 Richard Trevithick builds a steam-powered carriage.

1804 Trevithick builds a steam railroad locomotive. Francisco Salva makes a multiwire electric telegraph.

1806 Ralph Wedgwood invents carbon paper.

1808 Trevithick builds a circular demonstration railroad (in London).

1810 Friedrich König invents a steam-powered printing press.

1814 George Stephenson builds his first steam railroad locomotive (*Blücher*).

1815 John McAdam invents paved roads.

c. **1816** Baron Karl von Drais invents a bicycle with a steering bar (the draisine).

1821 The first iron-hulled merchant ship (*Aaron Manby*) is built.

1822 William Church invents a typesetting machine. Joseph Nicéphore Niepce takes the first photograph (on metal).

1823 Francis Ronalds devises an electric telegraph.

1825 The Stockton-Darlington Railway opens in the north of England (the first passenger railroad). George Cayley invents the caterpillar track.

1827 Stanislaus Baudry introduces the first (horse-drawn) buses.

1828 Onésiphore Pecquer invents differential gears.

1829 George Shillibeer introduces horse-drawn buses to London streets.

1830 The South Carolina Railroad—the first in the U.S.A.—opens. The Rainhill (near Liverpool, England) locomotive trials are won by Stephenson's *Rocket*.

1831 Charles Wheatstone and William Fothergill make an electric telegraph.

1832 Wheatstone invents the stereoscope.

1833 Karl Gauss and Wilhelm Weber build an electric telegraph. The *Royal William* becomes the first steamship to cross the Atlantic Ocean entirely under its own power.

Ferries and freighters

In addition to cruise liners, the major passenger-carrying vessels today are ferries linking neighboring countries and islands. Some also carry cars and trucks and are therefore effectively freight carriers. Roll-on-roll-off (roro) vessels have been developed for speedy loading and unloading, although a series of accidents in the 1980s and 1990s has raised questions about their seaworthiness.

Cargo-only vessels range from the general purpose tramp, so called because such vessels originally "tramped" from port to port seeking cargoes, to huge bulk carriers and supertankers. Today tramps are more likely to be chartered to convey a single cargo, perhaps to a port where larger vessels cannot dock. Since the mid-1950s, the size of oil tankers has increased tenfold (to about 500,000 tons). A number of accidents resulting in severe oil pollution (*p. 446*) have given rise to demands that supertankers be redesigned to make them less vulnerable if they run aground or are involved in collisions.

Keeping a cargo vessel in dock and unloading and loading it is expensive (because of harbor charges). A much quicker turnround can be achieved by using container vessels. The cargo is packed in metal containers, which can be rapidly handled by dockside cranes and placed on railroad cars or container trucks for distribution on land. A computer system is used to ensure that containers are loaded onto the ship in the correct order for unloading at various ports.

Large ships are difficult to maneuver in the confined space of a harbor. This task is therefore taken over by tugs, powerful small vessels that nudge the large ship into position. Tugs are also used to assist vessels in trouble and to tow barges out of rivers and estuaries.

Hovercraft and hydrofoils

One of the reasons why ships—particularly large ones—require such powerful engines is that moving them through the water involves overcoming the frictional drag of the water as it passes around the hull. Refinements of hull design and improvements in propellers have gradually reduced this problem, but one of the best solutions is to have less of the hull—or, at best, none at all—in the water.

An air-cushion vehicle, or hovercraft, overcomes the problem of drag by providing a cushion of air under the hull, with a flexible "curtain" around it to prevent the air from escaping. Craft of this type were invented by the British engineer Christopher Cockerell in the late 1950s, and the first experimental hovercraft, the SR-N1, had a large fan to provide air to the cushion as well as an airstream to the steering vanes or rudders.

Hovercraft can operate in shallow water, on marshes or on land. Small one-man machines can travel on lakes and reed beds in remote areas, while large cross-channel vessels operate as a form of high-speed car ferry.

A hydrofoil is a waterborne vehicle that makes use of the same principle that enables a fixed-wing aircraft to fly (*p. 477*). Although the detailed geometry varies between different systems, in essence a hydrofoil has one or more "wings" supported on struts under the hull. As the craft moves forward (driven by propellers), the "wings" create lift that raises the hull until, in some designs, it is completely out of the water. The craft speeds along on stilts, with only the supporting wings in the water; there is no drag at all on the hull. The angle of the wings is adjusted by servomechanisms under the control of an autopilot. At low speeds, a hydrofoil handles like a conventional boat.

A container ship in Hong Kong harbor.

The Réseau *is the latest generation of TGV and runs throughout the French network.*

RAILROADS

The well-known history of the railroads parallels the development of the steam engine (*p. 457*) by pioneers such as Denis Papin, James Watt, and Richard Trevithick. Although there had been previous experimental road vehicles and boats using steam power, the railroad age really began with Trevithick's locomotive of 1804 and George Stephenson's *Blücher* of 1814. The Stockton-Darlington Railway opened for passengers in 1825, and in the same year engineer John Stevens built America's first steam locomotive (which did not work). In Britain, Stephenson asserted his authority when his *Rocket* won the Rainhill trials in 1830 and became the motive power for the new Liverpool-Manchester Railway.

Many historians date the beginning of the Industrial Revolution from the rise of steam power and the building of the first railroads. Transcontinental railroads opened up the interiors of the U.S.A. and Canada, and linked farming regions of India and South America with distant ports. In Europe, steam railroads took over from the canals, and by the beginning of the 1900s there were 100-ton locomotives capable of pulling trains at up to 95 mph (150 kph).

Electrification and diesel

Steam reigned supreme on the railroads for more than 100 years. It was even used for light railroads and streetcars running through city streets. Its first rival was electric traction, using direct-current (DC) motors in locomotives or mounted on the cars. In places with cheap hydroelectricity, such as Scandinavia and Switzerland,

electric railroads became the norm, usually using a system in which high-voltage alternating current (AC) was supplied via overhead wires. The transformer was mounted on the locomotive itself. DC traction also became popular for streetcars and underground railroads (shunned in the days of steam locomotives). By the 1860s the sections of passenger railroads around cities were starting to become important, and some lines were taken through the inner areas by tunnel, providing the first underground railroads. By the end of the century, urban railroads were being developed to serve the burgeoning suburbs (*p. 473*).

Later electric railroads used DC to drive the motor via an alternator. Today's high-speed trains, such as the Japanese Shinkansen (known as the "bullet train") of 1964 and the French TGV (*Train à Grande Vitesse*) of 1981, employ electric traction to attain normal operating speeds up to 162 mph (260 kph). But both systems run on specially laid track; attempts in Britain and elsewhere to design high-speed trains to run on existing tracks had to be abandoned. The electric Eurostar service through the Channel Tunnel between London and Paris or Brussels, inaugurated in 1994, can cruise at 196 mph (300 kph) on suitable track.

Railroad electrification still tends to be reserved for prime high-speed routes or dense commuter networks. The demise of steam saw the introduction of another form of railroad traction—diesel power. Diesel locomotives are much more cost-effective than their steam counterparts (up to 45 percent efficiency compared to 8 percent for steam) and they do not need to carry large volumes of water. They are also easier to maintain.

Timeline

1835 John Ericsson, in the U.S.A., and Francis Smith, in Britain, independently invent the screw propeller (for use in ships).

1837 Steam streetcars begin operation in New York City. William Cooke and Charles Wheatstone construct a five-wire electric telegraph. Godfrey Engelmann invents chromolithography (for color printing). Louis Daguerre invents the daguerreotype photographic process.

1838 Samuel Morse invents a single-wire telegraph and the Morse code (*p. 482*). The London-Birmingham Railway opens.

1839 William Fox Talbot invents the calotype photographic process (using paper negatives) and takes photographs using a camera. Kirkpatrick Macmillan invents the modern pedal-driven bicycle.

1843 The *Great Britain*, the first iron-hulled propeller-driven steamship, crosses the Atlantic Ocean.

1847 Richard Hoe invents the rotary printing press (*p. 482*).

1848 The Illinois-Michigan Canal is opened, linking the Great Lakes to the Mississippi River.

1850 Francis Galton invents a teleprinter.

1851 Frederick Archer invents wet glass (collodion) photographic plates. A cross-Channel submarine telegraph cable is laid (between Dover in Britain and Calais in France).

1852 Elisha Otis invents the safety passenger elevator. Henri Giffard builds a (steam-powered) dirigible.

1853 George Caley builds a man-carrying glider.

1854 J. Ross Ward invents the (cork) life-jacket.

1855 David Hughes invents a printing telegraph. Alphonse Poitevin invents the collotype printing process.

1859 Jean Lenoir constructs a (gas) internal combustion engine.

1863 The first underground Railroad (steam-powered) opens in London.

1865 William Bullock builds the first web-fed rotary printing press.

1866 The first successful transatlantic submarine telegraph cable is laid (by Brunel's ship *Great Eastern*). Wilhelm Ritter constructs a cable car.

1867 George Westinghouse invents the air brake (for railroad vehicles). Heinrich Gerber builds a balanced cantilever bridge over the Main River at Hassfurt in Germany.

1868 Christopher Scholes invents a typewriter. J. P. Knight designs traffic lights.

1869 Ernest and Pierre Michaux construct a (steam-powered) motorcycle. Ferdinand de Lesseps completes the Suez Canal. Thomas Edison invents the tickertape machine. The transcontinental railroad across the U.S.A. is completed.

1872 George Pullman introduces sleeping cars on trains. Thomas Edison patents an electric typewriter.

Timeline

1873 Cablecars begin operation in San Francisco. Bromide paper is introduced (for making photographic prints).

1874 Alexander Graham Bell constructs a multiple telegraph.

1876 Bell patents the telephone. Nikolaus Otto invents a four-stroke internal combustion (gas) engine (*p. 457*). H. J. Lawson invents the safety bicycle.

1877 Thomas Edison invents the phonograph.

1878 David Hughes coins the term microphone for his improved sound-sensitive device.

1881 The first electric streetcars run in Berlin, Germany.

1883 Gottlieb Daimler builds a motorboat. Sydney-Melbourne Railway opens.

1884 Charles Parsons invents the multistage steam turbine. Ottmar Mergenthaler invents the linotype machine (*p. 479*). Paul Nipkow patents a rotating-disk optical scanning system. Lewis Waterman patents his design for a fountain pen.

1885 Karl Benz and Gottlieb Daimler develop an internal combustion (gasoline) engine and build the first motorcycles and cars using it. Charles Tainter invents the dictaphone. George Eastman markets (paper) rollfilm.

1886 Edward Butler builds a motorcycle with a two-cylinder water-cooled engine. Frederick Ives develops a halftone engraving process (for printing). Clement Ader builds an (unmanned) steam-powered airplane.

1887 Emil Berliner invents the gramophone. Tolbert Lanston invents the monotype process.

1888 Edward Butler invents the spray carburetor (for motorcycle engines). John Dunlop invents the pneumatic tire (for bicycles). George Eastman markets a hand-held box camera.

1889 Alman Strowger builds the first automatic telephone exchange. Anatole Mallet builds an articulated steam locomotive. Eastman introduces rollfilm on transparent celluloid instead of paper.

1890 London's first underground railroad opens.

1891 Gabriel Lippman invents a color photography process. Thomas Edison and William Dickson introduce the kinetoscope (cinecamera/projector).

1892 Rudolf Diesel invents the compression-ignition engine (Freight, *p. 476*). René Levasser builds a car with pneumatic tires.

1894 Oliver Lodge invents the coherer (for detecting radio waves). Guglielmo Marconi develops radio communications. Jesse Reno makes an escalator.

1895 David Schwartz constructs a rigid airship. Auguste and Louis Lumière demonstrate cinematography. Karl Klic invents photogravure printing. The first X-ray photographs are taken.

1896 Lee De Forest produces film with an optical soundtrack.

Diesel power

Small diesels such as shunters and diesel railcars use a hydraulic clutch mechanism to transfer the drive from the engine to the wheels—like a bus or truck. Most larger locomotives are diesel-electric. The diesel engine drives a generator to produce electricity to turn electric motors, often mounted on the carriage axles. In countries such as Brazil and South Africa, trains carrying as much as 20,000 tons of mineral ore are pulled by two or three powerful diesel-electric locomotives. In some areas, mostly in France and the U.S.A., intercity trains have locomotives with gas-turbine (jet) engines.

High-speed trains (max. of. speed)

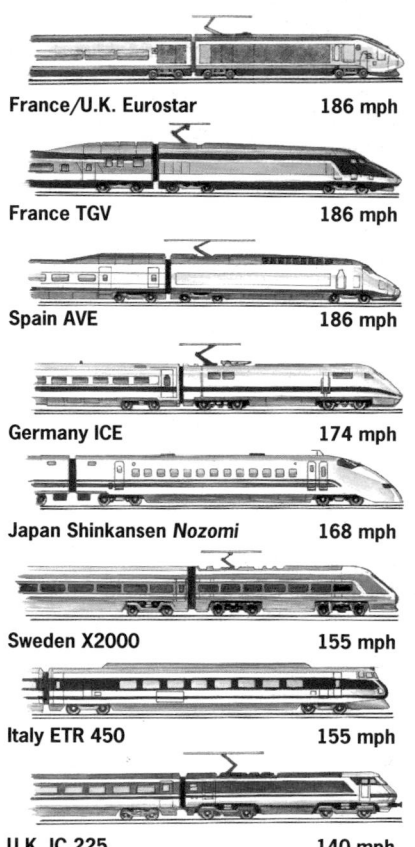

France/U.K. Eurostar	186 mph
France TGV	186 mph
Spain AVE	186 mph
Germany ICE	174 mph
Japan Shinkansen *Nozomi*	168 mph
Sweden X2000	155 mph
Italy ETR 450	155 mph
U.K. IC 225	140 mph

Linear motors

A different form of electric railroad traction uses linear motors, which are particularly suited to monorail systems. A series of electric coils mounted under the locomotive or train generate a traveling electromagnetic field, which interacts with a conductor on the track to propel the train.

If electromagnets on the train interact with certain currents in the conductor, a force is generated that lifts the train clear of the track—the system known as magnetic levitation or maglev. The result, a silent, pollution-free form of rail transportation that never wears out the track, is ideal for use in inner cities.

URBAN TRANSPORTATION

With the advance of the Industrial Revolution, people moved away from the land to go and work in mills and factories. As a result, towns and cities became larger, and people needed public transportation to get to and from work.

Streetcars

The first form of mass urban transportation was the streetcar. It originated in the United States in the 1860s. Streetcars run through city streets on rails laid flush with the road surface, which can also carry other traffic.

Streetcars were drawn by horses for 40 to 50 years. Later steam cars appeared, pulled by small locomotives with their wheels and driving motion hidden behind protective "skirts." But steam traction was noisy and smelly, and the locomotives had to make frequent stops to refuel and take on more water.

The solution—as on some railroads—was the electric streetcar . There were various forms of pickup for the vehicles to collect electricity. Many cars used overhead wires, with a sprung pole that ran under the wire, a sprung bow-shaped pickup or a pantograph to make contact with the wire. Current picked up from the overhead wire was returned through the running rails to complete the circuit.

To prevent the cost (and unsightliness) of overhead wires, some streetcar companies adopted a system in which the current was collected by sliding contacts running in a conduit below the center of the track. An underground pickup was also used by cablecars, such as those that have run on the hilly streets of San Francisco since 1873. The underground conduit housed a steel cable that was hauled along by winding engines. To move off, the cablecar driver depressed a lever which clamped the vehicle onto the moving cable. To stop, he unclamped the car and used its brakes. Cablecars were also used in Edinburgh (U.K.), Melbourne (Australia), and Wellington (New Zealand).

Nearly all cities in Britain and the United States got rid of their streetcars with the advent of buses. They remained, however, in many European cities, which still have long, articulated Streetcars. Recently, streetcar systems have been reintroduced into some cities as an alternative to air-polluting buses.

Trolleybuses

A spinoff of the streetcar not constrained by rails in the road is the trolleybus. This is an electrically driven public-service vehicle, which collects its current by means of a trolley running on parallel overhead wires but has steerable rubber-tired wheels like those of a motor bus. As a result, it can overtake other slower or stationary vehicles and, if necessary, travel for a while on battery power away from the overhead power supply. The vehicles are silent and non-polluting, but were originally uneconomic compared to diesel buses. Since the recognition of the polluting effects of buses in confined city streets, trolleybuses are again being considered as urban transportation vehicles.

Buses

Just as the truck increased the capacity of the car to carry freight, the bus increased its capacity to carry people. But the complete history of the bus predates that of the car by at least 60 years. Horse-drawn "carriages" with multiple seating originated in Paris in the mid-1850s. By the end of the decade, the British coach builder George Shillibeer had introduced an omnibus service capable of carrying up to 20 passengers at a time between the City of London and Paddington (site of a major railroad terminus). Soon an open upper deck was added to his buses (to increase carrying capacity—but charged at only half-fare). New York City acquired its first horse-drawn buses shortly after London.

There was a brief time when operators experimented with steam buses, but these soon gave way to gasoline-engined buses (originated by Karl Benz in 1895). The flexibility of a public-service vehicle not constrained by rails or overhead wires gradually led, in many cities, to the decline of the streetcar and the trolleybus. And as with trucks, the introduction of reliable diesel engines greatly improved the efficiency of this form of transportation.

Today, in the U.K. for instance, large double-decker buses are uneconomical on many underutilized routes. Where single-deckers are still too big, operators have turned to minibuses. Diesel buses also contribute to atmospheric pollution in towns and cities. For this reason, there is increasing interest in reintroducing electric streetcars in places that had previously abandoned this form of public transportation.

Subways and metros

With the rapid expansion of major cities in the late 1800s, short-distance passenger railroads were built to provide convenient mass transportation. The first "underground," in London, opened in 1890, was completely underground, like most systems; but some also included elevated sections, like the New York subway and the Paris metro. The word metro comes from the French *chemin de fer métropolitain*, meaning metropolitan railroad. Early lines, and some later ones, were often woven between the foundations of buildings. This required tight curves, so trains consisted of several short cars. Cars were also narrower, and sometimes lower, than on mainline railroads, reducing tunnel sizes and hence tunneling costs.

The subway in Washington, D.C.

Since the 1890s, almost all subway trains have been powered by electric motors, fitted to some (occasionally most) cars, and driven by low-voltage current collected from a third rail alongside the track. Trains operate as multiple units, with all motors controlled by the driver in the front cab. Most subways consist of separate lines, with no through-running between them: passengers can change between lines at the main interchange stations.

In the 1920s and 1930s most existing subways were extended outward into expanding new suburban areas, and some new systems were started by city authorities to serve expanding conurbations. Suburban extensions were often partly on the surface.

Over the last 30 years, existing subways have been extended, and new systems have been started. A few of these, such as the Bay Area Rapid Transit (BART) in San Francisco, have aimed to provide a high-quality travel environment. In contrast, some rapidly developing cities, such as Hong Kong, have built high-capacity subways. Today there are approximately 80 subway systems in the world.

The technology applied has been constantly improved over time to increase efficiency, safety, and attractiveness. By the 1970s, the running of trains on several lines was controlled by a central computer system, with signals transmitted through cables laid along the tracks. Some fully automated lines have since been developed, such as the Docklands Light Railway in east London and Skytrain in Vancouver, Canada. Electronic control of traction current for driving and braking has replaced banks of resistors. Cars are now built from aluminum instead of steel, to reduce weight, and hence provide more carrying capacity for lower power.

Timeline

1897 Charles Parsons builds a steam-turbine-powered vessel (*Turbinia*) (*p. 469*). Karl Braun invents the cathode-ray tube (later used in televisions).

1898 Valdemar Poulsen invents the (wire) tape recorder.

1900 The first zeppelin flies (designed by Ferdinand Graf Zeppelin). The Paris Métro (subway) opens.

1901 Guglielmo Marconi makes the first transatlantic radio transmissions. Ferdinand Braun uses a crystal detector in a radio receiver. The first front-wheel-drive car is constructed in France.

1902 Reginald Fessenden introduces radio telephony. Robert Bosch invents the spark plug. Wilhelm Schmidt invents the steam superheater (for railroad locomotives). Valdemar Poulson develops an arc transmitter (of radio waves). Louis Renault invents drum brakes for cars. The first transpacific telegraph cable is laid (between Canada and New Zealand/Australia). The Berlin underground railroad opens.

1903 Orville and Wilbur Wright invent the airplane (*p. 477*). The Lumière brothers devise the first three-color photographic process. William Siemens builds an electric railroad locomotive. The first four-wheel-drive car is manufactured (in the Netherlands).

1904 The New York subway opens. The first escalator is demonstrated (in Paris). The caterpillar tractor is developed (in the U.S.A.). The Michelin company introduce pneumatic car tires with raised flat treads. John Fleming invents the diode (rectifying) tube. Emile Berliner introduces disks for phonograph records (instead of cylinders). The Trans-Siberian Railway (Moscow to Vladivostok) opens.

1905 Almon Strowger invents the dial telephone. Gasoline-driven taxicabs run in Paris. Gasoline-driven buses run in London. Double-sided phonograph records are first marketed. The electrification of London's underground railroad is completed. Nonshatter safety glass (Triplex) is introduced for car windshields.

1906 Lee De Forest invents the triode (amplifying) tube. Reginald Fessenden begins commercial AM broadcasting (of speech and music). Wratten & Wainwright company introduces panchromatic photographic plates (sensitive to light of all colors).

1907 Arthur Korn invents a facsimile machine. Louis and Jacques Breguet build a helicopter. The SS *Lusitania* and SS *Mauritania* (both 31,000 tons) are launched; *Lusitania* makes a record crossing of the Atlantic Ocean (in 5 days, 45 minutes). Pierre Cornu builds a vertical takeoff helicopter (unsuccessful). The Lumière company introduces a single-emulsion (transparency) color film.

Timeline

1908 Henry Ford introduces the Model T car (*p. 475*). A. Campbell-Swinton describes a method of electronic scanning for capturing images.

1909 Louis Blériot flies a single winged aircraft across the English Channel.

1910 Hermann Fottinger invents an automatic gearbox (for cars). H. Frahm invents an antirolling mechanism for ships.

1911 Elmer Sperry invents the gyrocompass. Ferdinand Braun and A. Campbell-Swinton propose using a cathode-ray tube for image scanning.

1912 Reginald Fessenden develops the heterodyne radio receiver. The first diesel locomotive runs in Germany. Diesel power is introduced for ocean-going ships with the launch of the *Selandia* in Denmark. The SS *Titanic* sinks in the North Atlantic after hitting an iceberg on her maiden voyage. (The wreck was found in 1980 and extensively photographed in 1985.)

1914 The Panama Canal opens. Edwin Armstrong invents a positive-feedback radio receiver. G. Gauthier builds the first motoscooter. Edward Kleinschmidt invents a telex machine. Alfred Benesch invents automatic traffic lights, which are first installed in Detroit, Michigan, in 1919.

1915 Hugo Junkers builds the first all-metal cantilever-wing aircraft.

1916 Paul Langevin constructs a kind of sonar for detecting icebergs. Frederick Kolster develops a radio direction finder. Dodge Company markets the first all-steel-bodied cars.

1917 E.C. Wente invents the condenser microphone. The Trans-Australian Railway is completed (including the longest straight track—298 mi. [480 km]—in the world).

1918 Alexander Bell builds a high-speed hydrofoil boat (*p. 480*). Anti-Submarine Detection Committee (ASDIC) detectors are used to detect submarines and mines (by Britain).

1919 Edwin Armstrong invents the superheterodyne radio receiver. John Alcock and Arthur Whitten Brown fly nonstop across the Atlantic Ocean (in a modified Handley Page twin-engined biplane bomber). The first commercial air service begins (between London and Paris). The Citroën Type A, the first mass-produced car in Europe, is launched.

1920 Handley Page Company fits radio finders to their transportation aircraft. The HMV company introduces an autochanger for disc gramophones.

1921 Albert Hull invents the magnetron valve (for generating microwaves). Duesenberg Company constructs cars with hydraulic brakes. W. Cady introduces crystal detectors for radio receivers (used with a "cat's whisker" in crystal sets).

INTEGRATED SYSTEMS

The term "integrated transportation" applies primarily to public transportation. It involves complete coordination, so that buses, streetcars, subways, and local trains all link together as one network. All routes and timetables must be coordinated, and the network should have one fare, and ticketing system. Good interchange is essential, so that travelers can transfer between routes and systems easily at stations and main stops.

In Lille, France, two automated subway lines form the axis of the integrated public transportation network. The VAL (*Véhicule Automatique Léger*) system has driverless trains which operate very frequently; the stations have glass screens and doors that open only when the train doors have shut (like an elevator). The two lines intersect at the central railroad station, where they connect with modernized streetcars serving two adjacent towns. One VAL line is currently being extended. Other areas are served by bus routes, which connect with the subway and streetcars at stations. Parking lots at the city's edge make it easy for travelers from outside to park and ride the VAL or streetcars.

Bay Area Rapid Transit, San Francisco.

In Utrecht, Netherlands, fast streetcars (the *Sneltram*) run from the central station, downtown, through newer parts of the city to outlying suburbs. Two new lines are planned, one to run across the city. Other areas are served by frequent bus services, also radiating from the central station, which are helped by dedicated bus lanes and traffic signals that give the buses priority. There is a frequent service on local railroad lines, and Utrecht is an important interchange for intercity and trans-European railroad lines. The *strippenkaart* (single ticket) system provides efficient through-tickets on buses, streetcars, and trains, and is valid throughout the Netherlands. Traffic flow on the main roads in the city is closely managed, while a dense network of bicycle lanes and traffic-calming measures on all residential roads means that walking and cycling are safe and pleasant.

Integrated traffic systems offer a solution to urban transportation problems such as pollution, congestion, safety, and ease of movement. Integration is most easily achieved in those countries where the political will to provide a functioning public service is present and where cities have effective planning powers.

The automated VAL train (left) *serves the integrated transportation system of the French industrial town of Lille* (below).

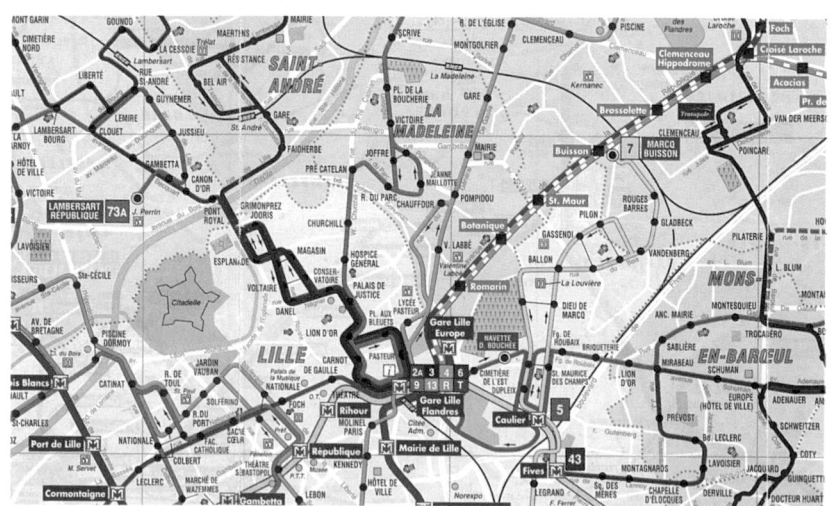

PERSONAL TRANSPORTATION

Once small, more-or-less reliable, steam engines became available, several inventors tried fitting them as power units to make a self-propelled road vehicle. As early as 1770, the French engineer Nicolas Cugnot constructed a steam-driven three-wheeled gun carriage, and in Britain, William Murdock (1780s), Richard Trevithick (1801), and Thomas Hancock (early 1800s) built steam-powered carriages. Steam cars (and trucks) were even manufactured in the early 1900s, as were cars driven by battery-powered electric motors. In 1906, an American, Stanley Steamer, set a world land–speed record of 128 mph (205 kph). The car is now the most popular form of transportation: in the United States, 56 percent of the population owns a car.

Cars

The real development of the car had to wait for the invention of the internal combustion engine, by the German engineer Nikolaus Otto in 1876 (p. 457). Running first on gas and then on gasoline (a refinement introduced by Gottlieb Daimler in 1883), this engine and its descendants have powered cars for more than 100 years. In 1885, Daimler built his first, three-wheeled car, and the following year he had a four-wheeled machine, as did his fellow German Karl Benz. By 1891, the French firm of Panhard and Levassor was marketing gasoline-engined cars with the engine mounted at the front, driving the rear wheels through a gearbox and propeller shaft—a layout that was to become standard for at least 50 years.

Although there were continual improvements in the design of engines, steering, suspension, and brakes—many first tried and tested on the track in the emerging sport of car racing—the revolution came with the introduction of new manufacturing methods. The popularity of the car, particularly in the United States, demanded mass production. In 1904, the U.S. company Oldsmobile produced 100 cars a week, assembled out of interchangeable parts manufactured by several other companies. In 1908, Henry Ford introduced a new technique—the assembly line—when he began manufacture of the famous Model T. Other companies, in the United States and Europe, followed suit to meet an ever-increasing market for cars.

Two significant innovations occurred in the 1930s. In 1934, the French company Citroën introduced the 15CV or Traction Avant, the first mass-produced front-wheel drive car. In the same year, Ferdinand Porsche in Germany designed the Volkswagen "Beetle" with an air-cooled, rear-mounted engine. Today most small cars have front-wheel drive, although few have persisted with air-cooled engines. There have also been two

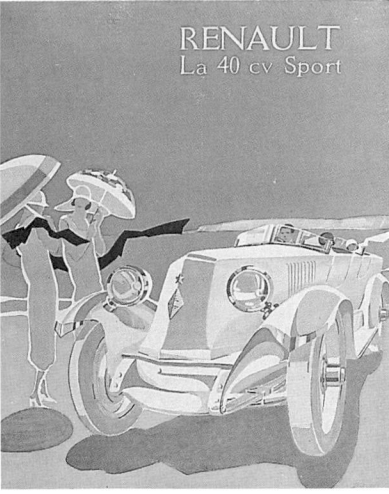

The motor car soon became fashionable.

major developments in construction methods. Early cars were built on a chassis—a rigid frame on which were mounted the engine, gearbox, transmission, and axles. The body was built up, panel by panel, on the chassis. Since the 1950s, most cars have been made with a boxlike monocoque body (no chassis) to which the other parts are attached. This method of construction is ideal for the latest innovation—the use of computer-controlled robots to do the assembly work.

Bicycles and motorbikes

The ultimate original "personal" transportation is the bicycle—doubled in capacity by the tandem, the bicycle made for two. Both machines still rely on human muscle power, and so it is not surprising that with the advent of the small internal combustion engine, inventors tried motorizing the bicycle. Even before the advent of the car, the French brothers Michaux had in 1869 fitted a small single-cylinder steam engine to a "bone-shaker" velocipede. Sixteen years later Gottlieb Daimler attached an air-cooled gasoline engine to a bicycle, while at about the same time the British engineer Edward Butler built a three-wheeled motor tricycle powered by a water-cooled engine. Butler also invented a spray carburetor for motorcycle engines. The first commercial machine was the De Dion Bouton motor tricycle of 1895, with a top speed of 25 mph (40 kph).

Throughout the first half of the 1900s, developments in motorcycles paralleled those in cars, with bigger engines, and better brakes and suspensions. Four-stroke engines were offered as alternatives to two-stroke units, although smaller two-strokes continue to be made because of their simplicity and economy. Other small bikes include mopeds and motor scooters, an Italian development of the 1960s currently enjoying a return to popularity.

SOCIAL IMPLICATIONS

Motor transportation—personal cars and motorcycles, commercial trucks and buses—has revolutionized 20th-century life in westernized countries. Today the world's roads carry nearly a billion vehicles, mainly cars, each of them consuming irreplaceable oil-derived fuel and contributing to atmospheric pollution. There are three obvious ways of tackling this problem: use alternative fuels, prevent cars from causing pollution, or do away with cars altogether.

Alternative "cleaner" fuels for internal combustion engines include gasohol (an alcohol/gasoline mixture) and hydrogen. Hydrogen could be carried as a refrigerated liquid and burned as a gas to produce—as the only product of combustion—water vapor.

Hydrogen-burning engines would obviously prevent atmospheric pollution. At present, the main approach is to use catalytic converters to "clean" the exhausts of gasoline- or diesel-burning engines. These devices convert carbon monoxide, nitrogen oxides, and unburned hydrocarbons (in the exhaust) to the less polluting gases ammonia and carbon dioxide.

Alternatively, cars that do not use internal combustion engines do not emit pollutants. A candidate for this role is the electric car, running either off batteries (which are heavy and have to be recharged regularly) or employing fuel cells—"batteries" that generate electricity directly from fuels such as hydrogen or alcohol. Both types of vehicle are still in the experimental stage.

Could the car be eliminated altogether? For personal travel in rural areas this would be extremely difficult in most countries unless there were a complete change in policy regarding public transportation. But in towns and cities it is theoretically possible to provide comprehensive rapid-transportation systems—ideally using electric vehicles—which would make private cars unnecessary. Underground railroads, monorails, streetcars, trolleybuses, and even moving walkways could all contribute to such a system.

Smog smothers Los Angeles.

Timeline

1922 Reginald Fessenden develops an echo-sounder for detecting submarines. H. Kalmus develops Technicolor for full-color cinefilms.

1923 Vladimir Zworykin invents the iconoscope television camera tube (*p. 482*). Juan de la Cierva invents the autogyro. The Benz company begins manufacturing diesel-engined trucks.

1924 Donald Douglas makes an around-the-world flight (in 15 days). The *autostrada* between Milan and Varese in Italy—the world's first expresssway—is opened. Edward Appleston demonstrates that short-wave radio transmission penetrates the ionosphere.

1925 John Logie Baird demonstrates television (using mechanical scanning). Oskar Barnack introduces the Leica camera.

1926 Robert Goddard launches the first successful liquid-fuel rocket (*p. 31*).

1927 Charles Lindbergh makes the first nonstop solo transatlantic flight. Telegraph and Telephone Company demonstrates a videophone. Ford Motor Company introduces the Model A.

1928 The first transatlantic passenger flight is made (by a German airship). John Logie Baird achieves a transatlantic television transmission. Vladimir Zworykin is granted a patent for a color television system.

1929 Fritz Pfleumer introduces plastic magnetic tape for audio recording. Synchromesh gearboxes introduced in their vehicles by Cadillac. Robert Davis invents the decompression chamber (intended initially for divers). The Kodak company introduces a 16mm color cinefilm.

1930 Barnes Wallis develops geodetic construction, later used in constructing aircraft fuselages. Hermann Oberth tests a gasoline-fuelled rocket.

1931 Harold Edgerton invents electronic flash (for photography). Wiley Post and Harold Gatty fly around the world in 8 days, 15 hours, and 51 minutes including stops for refueling. The first teleprinter exchange begins operation (in London).

1932 Auguste Piccard makes a balloon ascent into the stratosphere (over 52,493 ft.[16,000 m]). RCA Company demonstrates a television receiver that uses a cathode-ray tube.

1933 Edwin Armstrong patents frequency modulation (FM) radio transmission. Alan Blumlein pioneers stereophonic sound recording. Wiley Post makes the first solo around-the-world flight (in 7 days, 18 hours, and 49 minutes). The Boeing 247, the first modern airliner, is introduced into service.

1934 Citroën Company manufactures cars with a monocoque construction (combined body and chassis). Percy Shaw invents "cat's eyes" (reflectors in the road surface).

FREIGHT

In 1896 Gottlieb Daimler built the first truck, by enlarging the basic format of the car. But in 1892 his compatriot Rudolf Diesel had invented a different kind of internal combustion engine—the compression-ignition engine (so called because the high pressure of compressing the fuel makes it ignite so that, unlike a gasoline engine, the diesel engine does not need spark plugs). Soon diesel-engined trucks took over the local carriage of goods and freight, although railroads still handled long-distance transportation of bulk goods.

The further development of the truck paralleled that of the car, with bigger engines and better engineering giving rise to larger and larger trucks. To increase carrying capacity, trucks were made to tow trailers. Then, to simplify the transfer of loads without the need for unloading, engineers designed articulated trucks. These have a detachable tractor unit (the towing vehicle) that hooks onto a trailer with an axle or axles only at its rear end. Today's giant articulated trucks carry freight long distances and have largely replaced rail freight for point-to-point loads. Roll-on-roll-off ferries (*p. 470*) allow these vehicles to cross water and reach places not directly served by through roads. In countries such as Australia, where goods have to be carried very long distances, huge trucks couple up to compete with rail freight services. The largest road freight carriers are to be found in the United States: the so-called tractor-trailers, which have 18 wheels.

Intermodal systems

Since the beginning of the 1990s, more and more freight has been carried by road. For journeys under 300 mi.(500 km), transportation by rail is not economically viable except for bulk aggregates such as sand or gravel, or where a company rents out stretches of track and uses its own rollingstock. All freight is delivered to or collected from its end point by road, as rail cannot serve specific locations. However, convoys of heavy diesel-powered trucks pollute the atmosphere, dam-

A "road train" powering across Australia.

Comparative freight transportation

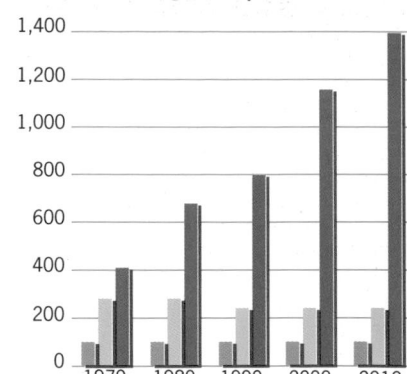

Road freight is predicted to expand to almost five times its 1970 market share by the next century; figures are given in billion tons per km and are for EU countries only.

age road structure, clog the road network, and are a major contributory factor to the rising road accident figures. In Europe particularly, where the roads are already overloaded, a new system is needed.

The solution favored by the European Union, and supported by various directives, is intermodal freight. This extends the principle of containerization used in seaborne freight to an integrated railroad system. Mainline railroads linking Europe's major ports (including the U.K. via the Channel Tunnel) carry the freight over long distances and deliver it to intermodal terminals known as "freight villages." From here it is picked up and delivered by truck. The system is built around a transferable freight unit called a "swapbody," developed in the U.S.A. A similar system using semitrailers is already in place. Loaded trailers, complete with wheels, are craned onto flatbed rail trucks for the long-haul section of the journey. This is a limited and cumbersome system; the swapbody method would be more efficient. Although it accounts for about 80 percent of road/rail traffic, its success depends on the establishment of a common standard size for the freight unit.

AIRCRAFT

Flight in a heavier-than-air machine was first achieved in the 1890s by the German Otto Lilienthal. He made many flights in unpowered gliders. The first powered flight in a heavier-than-air machine came in December 1903, when the American Wright brothers' flimsy biplane (the *Flier*) took off from the sands at Kitty Hawk, North Carolina. Both Lilienthal and the Wrights realized that the secret of flight lies in the physical principle of lift, which in turn depends on the curved cross-sectional shape of the wing. As the plane moves forward, air has to travel farther over the upper curved surface than it does past the lower surface. This results in higher pressure below the wing than above, creating "lift" that supports the aircraft in the air.

Aircraft development

The first single-winged aircraft (monoplane) was built by the Frenchman Louis Blériot, who in 1909 made the first air crossing of the English Channel. World War I led to rapid advances in aircraft design; biplanes became the norm, with all-metal structures instead of the wood and fabric employed previously.

A pioneer among these was the Junkers G23, a three-engined transport plane with a corrugated aluminum "skin." The U.S. equivalent, dating from 1935, was the ubiquitous Douglas DC-3 "Dakota," a two-engined transport/passenger plane with retractable landing-gear.

World War II saw another rapid advance in the development of military aircraft, which by the end of hostilities had jet engines that propelled them at speeds approaching that of sound. The jet engine—properly termed a gas turbine—was developed in Britain from 1937 by Frank Whittle. Germany also produced jet engines, and by 1939 had an experimental jet fighter (the Heinkel 178), followed in 1942 by the twin-engined Messerschmidt Me262. After the war the new engines were applied to civil aircraft, the first jet airliner being the De Havilland Comet, which entered service in

1952. As aircraft became larger, noisy pure jets were replaced by turbofan engines, characterized by a large multi-bladed fan at the front. Small aircraft use turboprops, in which a gas-turbine engine drives a conventional propeller through a set of gears. By the 1970s, long-distance air travel was dominated by wide-bodied planes with turbofan engines (*Gas-turbine engines, p. 458*), pioneered by the Boeing 747 of 1969.

On December 31, 1968, the world's first supersonic aircraft, the Tupelov TU44 (from the then Soviet Union) entered service as a cargo plane. The following year (March 2, 1969) Concorde, the BAC/Aerospatiale supersonic aircraft, made its maiden flight. In 1976 it became the first passenger-carrying supersonic aircraft with capacity for 100 passengers.

Over the last two decades, interest in commercially viable supersonic flight has waned. Instead, the aerospace industry has concentrated on carrying large numbers of people nonstop over long distances. The airbus, a product of an Anglo-Franco-German consortium, was designed to fulfill this brief. It is a wide-bodied two-engined jet and much of its success derives from developments in computer and fuel technology. With only two engines, there is more space in the wings to store fuel. The fuel itself has been specially formulated to produce a high-density fuel that can go farther on less. This means that the airbus can carry enough fuel to travel nonstop long-distance between the hemispheres.

Development in computer technology has given the aerospace industry a sophisticated extension of the automatic pilot ("George") used in previous aircraft. It is called the fly-by-wire system, and uses three on-board computers, all doing the same job but programmed with different software so that failure of one computer will not jeopardize the plane. The computers fly the aircraft and, if traveling to an international airport equipped with ILS (Instrument Landing System), can hook up with computers on the ground to land safely in conditions of bad visibility. If there is no ILS system, the human pilot takes over the controls.

Helicopters at San Diego airport, California, wait to make short-haul trips ferrying business passengers to skyscraper helipads.

Rotating wings

Even while designers of fixed-wing aircraft were making rapid advances, other engineers were experimenting with a different method of flying. They reasoned that a rapidly rotating horizontal propeller (with an airfoil cross-section) would act like a rotating wing and produce the required lift. The first successful machine of this type was the autogyro, built by the Spanish engineer Juan de la Cierva in 1923. It had a fuselage and conventional powered propeller (for take-off), but no wings. Instead, a large horizontal "propeller" was mounted above the cockpit. This rotor was unpowered, and "freewheeled" as the aircraft moved forward, providing the necessary lift.

The helicopter, which has a powered rotor, was pioneered by the Russian-American inventor Igor Sikorsky. It was the first heavier-than-air machine that could take off vertically. By tilting the rotor, the pilot can make a helicopter rise, descend, go forward, go backward, or hover. The turning motion of the machine's engine causes torque, which tends also to rotate the cabin. This effect is overcome by a small vertical propeller on a boom at the tail of the aircraft. The effect is absent in twin-rotor helicopters (because they rotate in opposite directions) or in jet helicopters in which the thrust is applied at the rotor blade tips.

As well as many military applications, helicopters are used for rapid passenger transportation, between islands or between an offshore oil rig or an airport and downtown. They are employed industrially as flying cranes to lift and transport heavy loads, and by emergency services as air ambulances or for rescuing people from the sea or inaccessible places.

The Boeing 767-336, a wide-bodied two-engine jet used for long-haul, nonstop flights.

Timeline

1935 Robert Watson-Watt invents radar. The Douglas DC-3 (Dakota) makes its maiden flight, as does the Boeing B-17 bomber (Flying Fortress). Kodak Company introduces Kodachrome (transparency) color film. The first section of *autobahn* (motorway), between Frankfurt and Darmstadt, opens in Germany.

1936 First train ferry service across the English Channel. The *Wupperthal*, the first diesel-electric ship, is launched. Jean Batten flies solo from Britain to New Zealand (in 11 days and 56 minutes). Ihagee Company introduces the Kine Exacta, the first single-lens reflex 35mm camera. Mercedes introduces the first diesel-engined production car (the 260D). The Supermarine Spitfire fighter makes its maiden flight.

1937 Werner von Braun and colleagues begin testing German military rockets at Peenemünde. Frank Whittle develops the first practical jet (gas-turbine) engine. Chester Carlson invents xerography (dry photocopying). Automatic transmission introduced for cars by Chrysler. Lockheed Company introduces the XC-35, the first fully pressurized aircraft.

1938 Ferdinand Porsche reveals the prototype Volkswagen (VW) "Beetle." Laszlo Biro patents the ballpoint pen. The British *Mallard* sets the all-time record for steam railway traction at 126mph (203km/h). SS *Queen Elizabeth* is launched, becoming the largest liner afloat.

1939 Igor Sikorsky builds the first helicopter for mass production. The first (military) jet aircraft, the Heinkel-178, is tested (in Germany). The Heinkel-176 rocket-powered fighter aircraft first flies (in Germany). Pan American Airways introduces the first transatlantic passenger service. William Heubner invents a photocomposing machine.

1940 The first expressway in the U.S.A., the Pennsylvania Turnpike (across the Appalachian Mountains) opens. The four-wheel-drive Jeep (from GP meaning general purpose) is adopted by the U.S. army. The Plan Position Indicator (PPI) radar screen is introduced.

1942 The Messerschmidt Me262 jet fighter begins flight testing. Kodak Company introduces Kodacolor color print film.

1943 Herbert Wagner designs an air-to-air missile.

1947 John Bardeen, Walter Brattain and William Shockley invent the point-contact transistor. Edwin Land invents the Polaroid camera. Charles "Chuck" Yeager makes the first supersonic flight in a Bell XI rocket-powered aircraft, at more than 597mph (960 km/h). Goodyear Company introduces tubeless tires (for cars). Holgar Toftoy builds a two-stage rocket.

WRITING

The beginning of communications came with the invention of writing. The first "alphabets," used in the ancient Middle East and in Central America, consisted of pictograms, in which each "word" was a picture of an object. The pictogram gave way to the hieroglyph, a stylized "picture" whose resemblance to an actual object became less and less obvious. Hieroglyphics were used by the ancient Egyptians in about 3000 B.C. and by some of the early people of Central America. The characters were usually produced using ink or paint and a brush.

At about the same time the Sumerians invented a form of writing known today as cuneiform (from the Latin *cuneus*, wedge). It was produced by pressing a wedge-ended stylus or "pen," probably made from a reed, into a tablet of wet clay. The clay could be fired to make a permanent record. Repeated messages were made as raised characters on a fired clay cylinder, which was rolled across wet clay to produce all the symbols at once.

Other forms of alphabet gradually emerged, such as Arabic, Greek, Hebrew, and Cyrillic (Russian); the alphabet used today for languages originating from western Europe, including English, is based on the Roman alphabet. These alphabets are phonetic: each letter represents a vocal sound or phoneme. In syllabary alphabets, each "letter" represents a syllable, as in Chinese characters, Japanese *kana* and *devanagari*, the main alphabet in India.

Writing implements

A brush, which gives subtle variations of line thickness, is the traditional writing implement for Chinese and Japanese. An early implement for other languages was the quill pen, made from a bird's wing-feather cut to a point. Pens with steel nibs were in use by the 1800s; from them developed the fountain pen, invented by Lewis Waterman in 1844. The hollow body of the pen contained a rubber tube of ink connected to the nib. The next major advance was the invention of the ballpoint pen by the Hungarian Laszlo Biro in 1938. The body contains a tube of thick ink and the "nib" is a small metal ball that leaves an ink line as it rolls across paper. More recent developments have been felt-tip and fiber-tip pens, which use a thin quick-drying ink that flows easily through the porous tip.

Sticks of charcoal have been used for writing and drawing for thousands of years. The pencil dates from the 1490s. Original pencils had a lead made of pure graphite. The leads in modern pencils are made from a mixture of fine clay and graphite; hardness is controlled by varying the amount of clay. Colored pencils were invented by the French chemist Nicholas Conté in 1795, and artists' crayons are still sometimes known as contés.

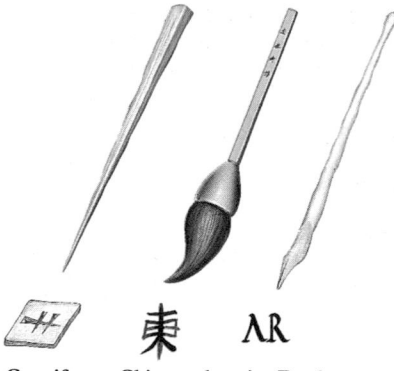

Cuneiform stylus **Chinese sheep's hair brush** **Reed pen**

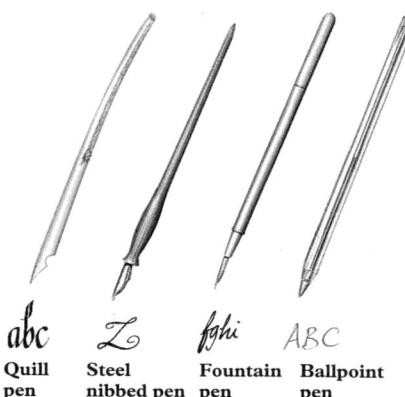

Quill pen **Steel nibbed pen** **Fountain pen** **Ballpoint pen**

Writing implements through the ages, from the Sumerian stylus to the ballpoint pen.

PRINTING

By the 800s, Chinese artists were making blocks to print designs on cloth and paper. (Printing on paper in the west originated in woodcuts of the early 1300s). An illustration, or page of type, was carved in mirror image into a block of wood, with the lines or characters in relief. The block was then inked and placed in contact with paper in a press.

Carving a page at a time was a laborious process. This difficulty was overcome with the invention in China around 1045 of movable, reusable type, with each letter on its own small block. Then in Korea in the 1400s, printers cast the first metal movable type. Independently in Germany at the same time, Johannes Gutenberg began printing with movable type. By 1474, William Caxton was printing books in London in English rather than Latin.

Relief (letterpress) printing
The method of printing from inked raised type—termed relief printing, or letterpress—remained the norm for many years. The original printing presses would today be described as flatbed. In a letterpress (relief) flatbed press, the frame (forme) holding the type is locked onto a horizontal table, inked by a roller, and paper is laid on the inked type and pressed into

contact by a second roller. As the paper is usually in sheets, the machine is known as a sheet-feed flatbed press. Gravure and litho plates may also be printed using such a press.

Planographic printing (lithography)

In planographic printing, the printing and non-printing areas of the printing plate are both flat (unlike relief printing). The method was developed from the artist's technique of lithography (literally "stone drawing"). The artist would draw a design using wax crayons on a flat piece of limestone, which was then wetted and a greasy ink spread over it. The ink adhered only to the wax, and was repelled by the wet areas. A mirror image of the design could then be transferred (printed) onto a piece of paper pressed on the stone.

The method was first adopted in printing for reproducing music scores. Today metal plates—usually aluminum—are used instead of stone. The type-matter is set (by any of several methods) and produced as a sheet of film. The film is used in a photographic process to transfer the type image to the aluminum plate, which has areas that will hold ink (printing areas) and ones that will repel it (non-printing areas). The thin plate can, if necessary, be curved to fit a rotary press.

Intaglio (gravure) printing

Intaglio is the reverse of relief printing—the design is cut into a polished printing plate. After inking, the plate is wiped, leaving ink only in the incised design. Paper is then laid on the plate and squeezed in a press, so that ink is transferred to the paper. In the first applications of this method, the design was cut by hand into a plate of steel or copper, and the resulting prints known as engravings. In a later method, the plate was covered with wax and the design scratched through it. The plate was then immersed in acid, which etched the design into the metal. After removal of the wax, the plate was inked and printed, the results being known as etchings. The modern intaglio process is called photogravure, because the design—often a half-tone illustration—is applied to the plate photographically before the etching process produces a printing plate with many small pits (cells) that hold the ink.

Typesetting

The metal type still had to be cast letter by letter and then set (assembled) by hand. In 1822 American William Church invented a machine for setting type. Then in 1884 Ottmar Mergenthaler, a German working in the U.S., created a machine for casting a line of type at a time. Called a Linotype machine, it held a supply of brass molds (matrices) which it assembled into correct order before casting molten type-metal into them. A compositor working at a typewriter-like keyboard instructed the machine which letters to cast. A

The printworks of the Financial Times, *London.*

much faster machine controlled by a pre-punched paper tape was developed in 1897. Called a Monotype machine, it cast characters one at a time at a rate of three a second.

With the widespread introduction of lithography, inventors turned their attention to methods of producing type-matter directly on film (for plate-making), rather than having to typeset it conventionally and photograph the assembled text. Early photocomposition machines employed a rotatable disk which had negative images of characters around its edge. Computer-generated punched-paper or magnetic tape controlled the rotation of the disk, switching a lamp on and off to project the required characters onto film. In modern computer-controlled typesetting systems, the characters are presented on a monitor as they are typed on the computer's keyboard, and a disk produced by the computer is used to make film from which litho plates are created.

Reproducing illustrations

In relief printing, illustrations made up of lines are converted into copper or zinc line blocks by a photo-etching process. To make a suitable relief printing block, the image is photographed through a grid of close-spaced parallel lines. This converts the image into "half-tone" dots—large dots in dark areas and small ones in pale areas. A negative of the image is then used in an etching process, to produce a printing block with raised dots of varying size. In printing, the dots hold the ink, which is transferred to the paper. Similar techniques are used to produce planographic plates (line or half-tone) for litho printing.

Color images are normally printed using four plates and four different (transparent) inks: yellow, red (magenta), blue (cyan) and black. Four halftone films are made by exposing the image through yellow, magenta, cyan, and neutral filters. The films can be used to make a set of four relief (letterpress), planographic (litho), or intaglio (gravure) printing plates. Each plate is printed consecutively, one on top of the other, using the four different inks.

Rotary presses

In a rotary press, the printing plate (relief, litho, or gravure) is curved round a rotating cylinder, which is inked by other rollers in contact with it. Paper passes between the inked roller and a second, pressure roller. Usually, the paper is fed through the press as an unbroken length off a reel, termed a web, which is cut into sheets as it emerges from the press. For multi-color printing, a rotary press has to have sets of reels for each ink.

Lithography on a rotary press is the most versatile type of printing, but the litho plates wear out rapidly. This problem is overcome in an offset press, in which the inked image on the plate is transferred (offset) onto a rubber or plastic roller which prints onto the paper.

Printing newspapers

A method of making duplicate printing plates (stereotypes) from assembled type was invented by the French printer Firmin Didot in 1790, and perfected by the Englishman Charles Stanhope ten years later. A mold of the set type was made using plaster of Paris, and molten type-metal poured into the mold to make a single-piece copy of the whole page. The English printer Edwin Cowper invented a method of curving stereotype plates for use on a rotary press in 1816.

Power-operated rotary presses were widely used for printing newspapers by the mid-1800s. In 1845 a French printing firm patented a method of curving the stereotype moulds (now called flongs), so that the type cast from them was already curved for the rotary press. In a later process, the flong was made electrically conductive (with graphite) and copper was electroplated onto it to produce an electrotype for printing.

Today most national, and larger regional newspapers, are typeset directly into computer typesetting systems by journalists rather than compositors. The text is keyed into position on the page layout, made up to finished page on a computer screen, and transferred to the regional printing works through dedicated telephone or fiber-optic lines.

Timeline

1948 William Shockley invents the junction transistor. Peter Goldmark invents the long-playing phonograph record. The Vickers Viscount, the first turbo-prop airliner, makes its maiden flight. Michelin Company introduces radial-ply tires. Edwin Land develops Polaroid printing.

1949 Boeing Superfortress makes first nonstop around-the-world flight. Multi-stage rockets are tested in the U.S.A.

1950 Commercial color television broadcasting begins in the U.S.A. Rover Company builds the first gas-turbine car. Chrysler Company introduces power-assisted steering for cars. The Videcon television camera tube is introduced in the U.S.A.

1951 3–D films are first shown in cinemas. Deutsche Grammophon Company markets the first 33 rpm long-playing records.

1952 The first commercial jet aircraft (De Havilland Comet) enters service. The SS *United States* crosses the Atlantic in record time—3 days, 10 hours, and 40 minutes.

1953 The first hovercraft (the SRN1) is built (in Britain) (*p. 470*).

1954 Grumman Company develops a swing-wing airplane. The first nuclear-powered submarine, *Nautilus*, is launched by the U.S.A.

1955 Narinder Kapany first demonstrates fiber optics.

1956 Bell Telephone Company introduces the videophone. A. Poniatoff demonstrates the first videotape recorder.

1958 The nuclear-powered icebreaker *Lenin* (built in the U.S.S.R.) and the nuclear-powered merchant ship *Savannah* (built in the U.S.A.) are launched. Stereo recordings become available. The Boeing 707, the first U.S. jet airliner, enters service. French engineers design diesel locomotives that cruise at 85 mph (140 kph).

1959 The Austin/Morris Mini car (designed by Alec Issigonis) goes on sale. The first commercial Xerox photocopier is marketed. Sony Company markets the first portable television.

1960 Echo 1 (radio reflector balloon satellite) is launched by the U.S.A. The U.S. nuclear submarine *Triton* circumnavigates the world underwater.

1961 Silicon chip is patented in the U.S.A.

1962 Television satellite Telstar is put into orbit by the U.S.A.

1963 The first Wankel-engined car is produced in Japan. Philips Company introduces audio cassette tapes.

1964 Geostationary satellite radio links come into use. Container cargo ships are introduced. Japanese Shinkansen high-speed train enters service.

1965 Early Bird (the first commercial communications satellite) is launched by the U.S.A. Computer typesetting is introduced in Germany.

PHOTOGRAPHY

Photography (meaning "writing with light") involves a series of processes in which chemical reactions are brought about by the energy of light. The image-forming reaction makes use of salts of the metal silver; called halides, they include silver chloride, bromide, and iodide. These insoluble salts are incorporated into an emulsion (originally made using gelatine), which is coated onto transparent plastic film or paper and allowed to dry. When the film is exposed in a camera, light causes subtle changes to the silver salts so that when the exposed film is later immersed in a developer (a chemical reducing agent, such as hydroquinone), the silver ions are converted into minute grains of metallic silver. Immersion in a second solution, called a fixer (such as sodium thiosulfate, or hypo), dissolves away any unaffected silver salts. The result, after washing, is a negative. Areas that received a lot of light have a lot of silver grains and appear black; areas unaffected by light are represented by clear film.

A positive photograph is made from the negative by putting the negative in contact with (or using an enlarger to project its image onto) an emulsion-coated, photosensitive paper.

Color photography

Color photography did not become readily available for the amateur until the introduction of Kodachrome film (originally for cinecameras) in the late 1920s.

Transparency film has three layers of emulsion, sensitive to blue, green, and red light. After exposure it is developed to produce a black-and-white negative in each layer. The film is then exposed to light and color developed. Finally the silver is bleached out to leave a set of three dye images in which the colors combine.

With color negative film, the first development creates the dyes in the three emulsion layers. The film is then bleached, resulting in an image in which the colors appear as their complements: yellow is represented by blue and red by cyan (blue-green). A true color image is produced by making a print on color-sensitive paper (which is developed by a similar process).

Edinburgh photographed by satellite camera.

Kodak brought photography to the masses.

How a camera works

Every camera, no matter what type, has a lens to focus an upside-down image of a scene onto film held at the rear of the camera. The lens can usually be moved in and out (by rotating it on a screw thread) to bring the image into exact focus. Light is allowed to reach the film by opening the shutter, which may be a briefly opened hole behind the lens, or resemble a roller blind with a slit that runs rapidly next to the film (a focal plane shutter). The amount of light entering the camera depends on the size of the aperture (a hole behind the lens), usually controlled by an adjustable iris diaphragm. The amount of light reaching the film is determined by the correct combination of shutter speed and aperture size.

The early plate camera was essentially a wooden box, with a plate holder at the back and a lens at the front. The lens could be racked in and out to focus the image on the plate. Eastman's Kodak cameras were much the same, but a roll film holder replaced the plate. Eastman also introduced a simple viewfinder.

A much more exact view of what the camera "sees" is provided by a reflex camera, in which a mirror inside the camera diverts the image onto a ground glass screen. The mirror is folded away before the exposure is made. A similar principle is used in a twin-lens reflex camera, which has one lens for the reflex viewfinder and one "taking" lens.

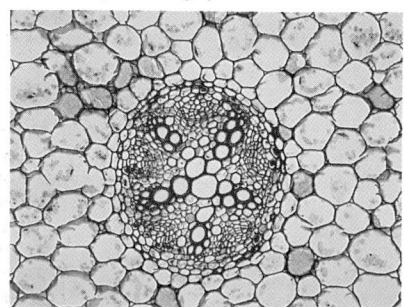

A buttercup root magnified 50 times.

RADIO

Radio waves are a form of electromagnetic radiation (as are light and X-rays). Their nature was first described by the British physicist James Clerk Maxwell in 1873, but it was not until 1887 that the German physicist Heinrich Hertz began experimenting with radio waves. Hertz generated the waves by a high-voltage spark between two spherical electrodes.

In 1894, the British physicist Oliver Lodge developed the coherer, a glass tube containing iron filings, which became magnetized and clumped together ("cohered") with the arrival of radio waves. Karl Ferdinand Braun devised a crystal detector—nicknamed the cat's whisker—which was the basis of early crystal set receivers.

In the U.S.A. in 1902, Reginald Fessenden sent voice messages by radio. In 1904, John Fleming invented the diode tube and two years later, Lee De Forest invented the triode—the basis of the electronic amplifier. These inventions made it possible to broadcast voices. Commercial radio broadcasts began in 1906.

How radio works

A radio transmitter is never "off," even when there is silence between spoken words or sections of music. It continuously broadcasts a radio signal called a carrier wave. The sound to be broadcast, converted to a varying voltage by a microphone, modulates the carrier wave.

Every wave has an amplitude (the height from the average level to each peak) and a frequency (the number of waves passing in one second). In amplitude modulation (AM), the sound signal modulates the amplitude of the carrier wave; the frequency remains constant. In frequency modulation (FM), it is the carrier wave's frequency that is modulated (and the amplitude remains unchanged). FM requires very high frequencies, and so is sometimes termed VHF radio. AM broadcasts can travel long distances, even around the world, but suffer from interference and poor sound quality. FM transmission can travel only between points that are in line-of-sight of each other (so a national FM station needs many transmitters). But FM suffers from little interference and provides excellent sound quality.

At the radio receiver, the modulated carrier wave is picked up by an antenna. Special circuits remove the higher-frequency carrier signal, leaving the required sound signal to be amplified and drive a loudspeaker.

By international agreement, the whole range of radio signals from ultrahigh frequency (UHF) to long wave is divided into bands, reserved for specific purposes (such as television, radio broadcasting, and emergency services). The bands themselves are again divided into channels so that transmissions do not overlap within the same geographical region.

TELEVISION

Television is an extension of radio—indeed the sound signal is transmitted in exactly the same way. To transmit pictures, they must be converted to a varying electrical signal that can be used to modulate a carrier wave (as the sound signal does). A television camera makes this necessary conversion.

The key to a TV camera is the picture tube, originally in the form of an image orthicon or iconoscope (invented by Vladimir Zworykin in 1923), later replaced by photoconductive tubes and charge-coupled devices (in domestic camcorders). The picture tube emits electrons from a mosaic or photoconductive layer in proportion to the amount of light falling on it, and this pattern of charges is scanned by an electron beam to produce a varying electric current. It is this current that is amplified and passed to the transmitter to modulate a carrier wave (of ultra high frequency). A color TV camera has three picture tubes, one each for three primary colors (red, green, and blue), into which the incoming light is split by a system of mirrors and colored filters.

At a TV receiver, the incoming signal (picked up by an antenna) is demodulated and, if color, decoded to produce three color signals. Sound is processed as in a radio receiver. The amplified color signals pass to three electron guns at the rear of a cathode-ray tube (originally developed by Karl Ferdinand Braun, inventor also of the cat's whisker—Radio, *left*). Magnetic fields at right angles make the three electron beams scan the inside face of the tube (the "screen"), where they make red, green, and blue phosphor dots or stripes glow with color and build up pictures at a rate of 30 a second.

Most modern TV systems produce pictures made up of 525 (in the United States) or 625 horizontal lines (in most other parts of the world). High-definition television (HDTV), using 1,125 lines, is currently under development. "Flat screen" TV is also at development stage.

News captured live can be electronically transmitted back to base anywhere in the world.

VIDEO

Within the circuitry of a television camera or receiver, the "pictures" actually exist as a varying electric current. Known as the video signal, this current can be recorded on magnetic tape (as can the sound, or audio signal). A video recorder works in much the same way as an audio tape recorder except that the tape is much wider (to hold more information) and it moves much faster. Also, the recording head rotates in such a way as to make the magnetized stripe zigzag on the tape—another way of packing more signal into the available space. As with most audio tapes, the videotape is housed in a plastic cassette—hence the term VCR (Video Cassette Recorder).

On playback, a similar head "reads" the magnetic stripe and reconverts it into the video signal, which is fed into the antenna socket of a TV receiver. Video signals can be recorded directly from a TV camera or camcorder, or from broadcast TV using a television receiver. The tape can be erased and used over and over again.

Video signals—which are normally continually varying, or analog, signals—can also be digitized and recorded (like sound) on a compact disc. In a variant known as CD-ROM (Compact Disc—Read Only Memory), the disk is "read" by a computer and may allow the viewer to interact with the images using a computer keyboard or mouse.

Timeline

1966 Fuel injection is introduced for car engines in Britain. Japanese scientists develop laser radar.

1967 R. M. Dolby invents his noise-reduction system for sound recording.

1968 The first supersonic commercial airliner flies (in the U.S.S.R.).

1969 The supersonic Concorde airliner makes its maiden flight.

1970 Boeing 747 "Jumbo" airliner enters transatlantic service.

1971 The Japanese supertanker *Nisseki Maru* (372,400 tons) is launched, becoming the world's largest ship.

1973 BBC television introduces teletext.

1974 A Lockheed SR-71 Blackbird flies across the Atlantic in 1 hour, 56 minutes at speeds over 2,000 mph (3,200 kph).

1976 The Canon AE-1, the first camera with a microprocessor-controlled exposure system, is launched.

1977 Television signals are transmitted along optical fibers in the U.S.A.

1979 The first satellite television service is opened (in Canada). Sony Company launches the Walkman personal stereo cassette player.

1980 The first compact discs (CDs) are produced (in both Japan and the Netherlands).

1981 The NASA Space Shuttle *Columbia* is first launched from the ground (and later that year is reused). The French high-speed *Train à Grand Vitesse* (TGV), the fastest in the world at the time, enters service.

1984 Optical disks are introduced (for data storage).

1985 American engineers send 300,000 simultaneous telephone signals along a single optical fiber.

1986 Richard Rutan and Jeana Yeager fly the aircraft *Voyager* nonstop around the world (in nine days) without refueling.

1987 A glass fiber optic communications cable is laid across the Atlantic Ocean.

1988 Lead-free gasoline is introduced throughout the European Community. The catamaran *Jet Services 5* breaks the record for the fastest transatlantic crossing under sail.

1989 An exhibition of solar-powered cars is held in West Germany.

1989 Double-decker trains are introduced in the U.S.A., Austria, and Australia.

1990 A new world speed rail record is set at 320 mph (515 kph) by the TGV.

1991 The A-340 Airbus makes its maiden nonstop flight from London to Sydney. The Swedish X2000 tilt train is tested in Switzerland and the U.S.A. Los Angeles and Stockholm reintroduce streetcars.

1993 New York City Metropolitian Transportation Authority provides the first Braille subway map. Freight trains between Rotterdam and Milan are computer-controlled via satellite. In Hong Kong, world's longest escalator system (2,625 ft.[800 m]) opens, comprising 20 escalators and three moving sidewalks.

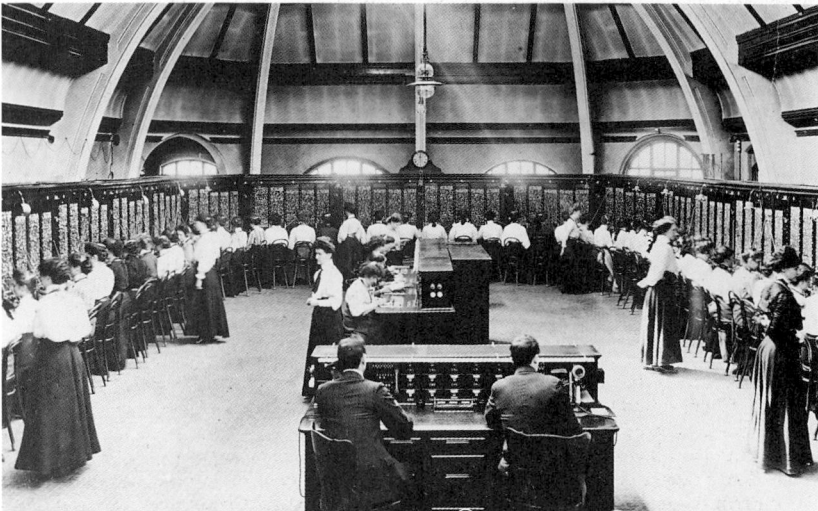

A telephone switchboard in the early 1900s.

TELECOMMUNICATIONS

For thousands of years, the range of instantaneous communication was limited to how far a person could shout. But people can see farther than they can hear, and so "optical telegraphs" developed, using visible signals representing letters or words. One of the simplest systems employs flag signals, once used between ships at sea. A further development was flag semaphore, in which the sender held two flags at various angles to the body to represent the letters of the alphabet.

Long-distance information

A method of carrying coded messages farther than the line-of-sight distance had to wait for the development of a source of electricity—the voltaic cell. Messages could then be sent along wires as pulses of electric current. In 1816, the Englishman Francis Ronalds made a single-wire telegraph that relied on disks carrying letters around their rims (one at each end of the wire) rotated in synchrony by clockwork motors. The arrival of the signal was indicated by an electroscope. In about 1820, the American physicist Joseph Henry improved on this crude device by making an electromagnetic sounder, similar in design to an electric bell.

The first commercial telegraphs, used by railroad companies, were installed by two British physicists, William Cooke and Charles Wheatstone, in the late 1830s. Theirs was a five-line telegraph, and the letter being sent was indicated by the alignment of magnets pointing to the letter on a grid. At about the same time, the American Samuel Morse built a single-wire telegraph that used a "key" (an on-off switch) to tap out coded pulses. But Morse's major contribution was devising a standard code of combinations of short and long electric pulses—dots and dashes—to represent letters and numbers.

A different code was devised in France by Emile Baudot. It consisted of combinations of five on or off electric pulses of equal length, and in this respect resembled the binary code used today by computers. Indeed, the modern unit of modem message speed is called the baud after the French pioneer. In 1892, Baudot devised a method of multiplexing—of sending six messages simultaneously along a single wire.

Baudot's code was the basis for the teleprinter or telex, which uses a five-unit code, sending up to 26 simultaneous messages at a rate of a dozen characters a second (about 100 words a minute). Teleprinters were used in the 1920s and were superseded in the 1930s by the telex, which remained in use as worldwide means of instant communication for several decades. Such machines have now largely been replaced by the fax (facsimile transmission) or modem in which computers transmit data to each other. Both systems are based on telephony.

The fax was an idea that agitated the minds of inventors as early as the 1800s; the principle was first demonstrated by Scottish inventor Alexander McHinery. In the newspaper offices of the 1930s, an early form of fax was used to send photographs "down the line" using radio waves. Now telephone lines are used. A fax works by electronically scanning a page, converting the image into electrical signals and sending them through the telephone system to a machine at the other end where they are decoded.

A modem is a link through which one computer can communicate with another using telephone lines. Both computers need to have a modem, which encodes or decodes the message, changing it from digital (computer language) to analog (telephone message signal). If the computers are linked in an ISDN (Integrated Services Digital Network) line, the message can be sent much more quickly.

Telephony

The invention of the telephone is a chapter of coincidences. On the same day in 1876, the Scottish professor Alexander Graham Bell, living in Hartford, Connecticut, and Elisha Gray in Chicago applied for a patent for an electric telephone. Bell beat Gray by a few hours and he was granted a patent in the following year.

Then in 1877, the American inventor Thomas Edison made the first carbon microphone. The same type of microphone was invented independently a year later by David Hughes. The heart of the device is a cylinder of compressed carbon granules, connected to the center of a diaphragm. When sound waves strike the diaphragm it vibrates, compressing the granules and altering their electrical resistance. The changes in resistance vary a DC current to create a voltage that varies in step with the sound signal. It is this signal that passes along the telephone line, to work an electromagnetic earpiece (another vibrating diaphragm).

The first telephone exchanges—to interconnect callers—were opened in the United States and Britain in 1878 and 1879. As exchanges got bigger, they required more and more operators to plug and unplug wires to carry out the switching. Then in 1892, an automatic exchange was opened in Indiana, using a rotating electromechanical selector switch invented by Almon Strowger three years earlier. It was replaced by the so-called crossbar switch in the 1920s, which has since been replaced by all-electronic telephone exchanges that have no moving parts, operating like minicomputers.

For 60 years every telephone transmission required a pair of wires to carry it. Trunk telephone cables contained hundreds of wire pairs, and the connections at each end provided a challenge for any electrician. Even so, telephone cables of this type were laid under oceans to interconnect continents, although they had to incorporate amplifiers (called repeaters) every few miles to boost the signal, which weakened with distance.

In 1936, British telephone engineers installed the first coaxial cable, consisting of a central conductor insulated from a second cylindrical conductor concentric with it. By using carrier waves of different frequencies (*p. 000*), the new cable could carry 12 telephone messages simultaneously. Band width (carrying capacity) was steadily improved and submarine coaxial cables laid—although repeaters were still required every so often.

Since the 1980s, coaxial cables have been gradually replaced by fiber optic cables. Fiber optic technology, a development from the branch of physics called fiber optics (*p. 000*), has revolutionized the telecommunications industry. It has allowed light (usually from a laser) to replace electrical pulses as the message carrier. Optical fibers are glass or plastic

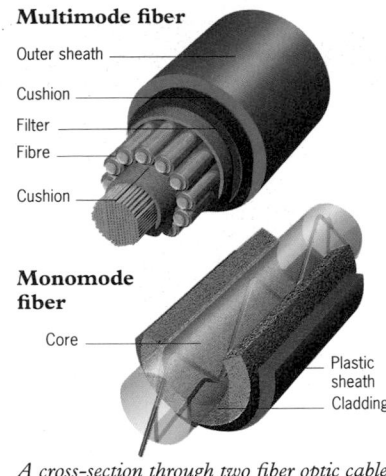

Multimode fiber

Outer sheath
Cushion
Filter
Fibre
Cushion

Monomode fiber

Core
Plastic sheath
Cladding

A cross-section through two fiber optic cables. Multimode fibers have thick glass cores which carry several light messages at once over short distances. Monomode fibers have narrow cores to carry one light message only over long distances.

fibers encased in a light-tight cladding. Light beamed in at one end of the fiber passes through the glass tube and emerges at the other end undiffused. To pass on a message, laser light is sent in a code of extremely rapid on-off flashes which are decoded at the other end of the fiber.

Fiber optic cables have several advantages; they are not subject to electrical disturbance, they can carry much more information than traditional cable, and the message does not need to be amplified or boosted on its journey. As the fiber optic system is digital (rather than analog) (*p. 427*) more and more telephone exchanges are becoming digital as traditional cables are being replaced.

Another development is the use of microwave radio links (*p. 000*) to transmit signals over line-of-sight distances. A cellular phone or mobile phone uses this system. Local radio transmitters distributed throughout a city or area beam out a low-level microwave signal and a computer switches the phone handset over to the

nearest beam as the user moves around within that area. Using a satellite, microwaves can also carry telephone messages across continents.

With the advent of fax and computer data transmission, telephone "lines" (cables and microwave links) have taken on a new importance. In particular, they form part of local and international networks that link computers.

The Internet

The Internet began in the 1960s as an experiment conducted by the Department of Defense. It was designed to be a self-protecting information exchange that would carry on functioning even if parts of it were knocked out in some unspecified disaster. Academics and researchers would be able to access each other's machines and transfer documents and files electronically. There were no fixed, predictable routes that could be sabotaged; groups of computers were linked to each other in various configurations all with equal access. Software was developed to make sure that the right connections were made in this database.

At first, the Internet was only available to academics and computer experts who could write their own programs. During the 1980s, as computers gradually began to dominate the workplace and personal computers became affordable, more people began to join the Internet on a variety of levels. The range of information available expanded hugely. Special search tools and software were developed to help people find their way around what has become a vast system.

By far the most popular and easy-to-access service on the Internet at the moment is e-mail (electronic mail) which calls for a computer, a modem, a phone line, and the minimum of software.

Until 1995, the Internet was a democratic collective overseen by the U.S. government-funded NSF (National Science Foundation); in that year it passed into commercial hands.

Cyberia Café, in London, where, for a small fee, customers can tap into the Internet.

PROMINENT PEOPLE

ARKWRIGHT, Richard (1732–92) British inventor who in 1769 created the spinning frame (for spinning cotton yarn). In 1771 he set up a factory with Jedediah Strutt (the inventor of a stocking-making machine in 1758), and 20 years later was one of the first to introduce steam engines to drive machinery in his textile factory in Nottingham.

AUSTIN, Herbert (1866–1941) British engineer who in 1895 designed a three-wheeler car for the Wolsley company, before founding Austin Motors in 1905.

BABCOCK, George (1832–93) U.S. engineer who in 1867, with Stephen Wilcox, invented the water-tube boiler for steam engines.

BELL, Alexander Graham (1847–1922) British-born U.S. inventor, in 1876, of the telephone.

BENZ, Karl Friedrich (1844–1929) German engineer who in 1885, with Gottlieb Daimler, designed an early two-stroke gasoline engine, which they incorporated into a three-wheeler car.

BESSEMER, Henry (1813–98) British engineer who in 1855 invented a process for making steel from molten pig iron by blowing compressed air through it (in a Bessemer converter).

BRAMAH, Joseph (1748–1814) British inventor whose achievements included a water closet (1778), a safety ("unpickable") lock (1784), the hydraulic press (1795) and a banknote-printing machine (1806).

BRAUN, Ferdinand (1850–1918) German physicist who in 1897 invented the cathode-ray tube.

BROWN, Joseph (1810–76) U.S. engineer who devised several precision instruments for use in manufacturing. In 1862 he invented a universal milling machine for shaping metal.

BRUNEL, Marc (1769–1849) French-born British engineer who pioneered production-line manufacture with his machines for making pulley blocks (1806) and boots (1815), both for the British navy. In about 1825 he invented the tunnel shield, for driving tunnels through soft ground.

BRUNEL, Isambard Kingdom (1806–59) British engineer whose many feats included the steamships *Great Western* (1838), *Great Britain* (1845) and *Great Eastern* (1858), Hungerford Bridge over the Thames River in London (1845) and Clifton Suspension Bridge in Bristol (1864). From 1833 onward he was chief engineer of the Great Western Railway.

CLERK, Dugald (1854–1932) British engineer who in 1878 invented the two-stroke internal combustion engine (known at the time as the Clerk cycle gas engine). In 1891 he developed superchargers for gasoline engines.

COLT, Samuel (1814–62) U.S. inventor who revolutionized manufacture in 1836 when he set up a factory for making pistols (of his own design) from interchangeable parts.

CORT, Henry (1740–1800) British ironmaster who invented a steel-rolling mill in 1783 and a year later devised the puddling process for making wrought iron from pig iron (heating it with iron oxide to oxidize the carbon).

COUSTEAU, Jacques (b. 1910) French underwater explorer who in 1942 invented the aqualung.

CROMPTON, Samuel (1753–1827) British textile worker who in 1779 invented the spinning mule, which made much finer yarn than James HARGREAVES' machine.

DAGUERRE, Louis (1789–1851) French photographer who invented the daguerrotype process.

DAIMLER, Gottlieb (1834–1900) *See* Karl Friedrich BENZ.

DAVY, Humphry (1778–1829) British chemist who, as well as discovering several chemical elements, invented the electric arc lamp (1808) and the miner's safety lamp (1815).

DE LESSEPS, Ferdinand (1805–94) French engineer who built the Suez Canal (1859–69).

DIESEL, Rudolf (1858–1913) German engineer who in 1892 invented the compression-ignition engine.

DREBBEL, Cornelius van (1572–1634) Dutch engineer who worked in England from 1604 and in 1620 invented a crude submarine.

DUNLOP, John (1840–1921) Scottish veterinary surgeon, who in 1888 invented the pneumatic tire (for bicycles). In the following year he founded the Dunlop Rubber company.

DU PONT NEMOURS, Eleuthere (1771–1834) French-born U.S. industrial chemist who emigrated to the U.S.A. in 1802. He began his career by manufacturing gunpowder and enlarged the business into one of the world's largest chemical concerns.

EASTMAN, George (1854–1932) American inventor of roll-film (1885) and the Kodak box camera (1888).

EDISON, Thomas (1847–1931) U.S. inventor. Most of his early inventions concerned telegraphy. He also invented the carbon granule microphone, a cinematograph, the nickel-iron accumulator, an incandescent electric lamp (independently of Joseph SWAN) and, in 1877, the cylinder phonograph.

EIFFEL, Gustave (1832–1923) French engineer best known for his design for the Eiffel Tower in Paris (completed in 1889). He also constructed the internal framework of the Statue of Liberty (1886) in New York.

ELSTER, Julius (1854–1920) German physicist who in 1904, with Hans Geitel (1855–1923), constructed the first photocell (to be used for converting light into electricity).

EVANS, Oliver (1755–1819) U.S. inventor of a high-pressure steam engine used for a road vehicle (1789) and a dredging machine (1804).

FITCH, John (1743–98) U.S. inventor who built his first steamboat in 1787 and for several years had exclusive rights to run his boats in several of the American states.

FORD, Henry (1863–1947) U.S. engineer who built his first car in 1893, and in 1903 founded the Ford Motor company, in which he pioneered the techniques of the production line.

FOURNEYRON, Benoit (1802–67) French engineer who in 1827 invented the first successful water turbine.

GED, William (1690–1749) British printer who in 1725 invented a method of casting stereotypes.

GIFFARD, Henri (1825–82) French engineer who in 1852 built a steam-powered, steerable airship.

GILLETTE, King (1855–1932) U.S. inventor and champion of industrial welfare who in 1895 patented the safety razor.

HALLEY, Edmund (1656–1742) British scientist, best known as an astronomer (Halley's Comet is named after him), who in 1716 invented a diving-bell with an independent air supply.

HARGREAVES, James (1720–78) British textile worker who in 1764 invented the spinning jenny (a spinning frame with several spindles).

HARRISON, John (1693–1776) British inventor best known for making the first chronometer (1735), which enabled navigators to determine longitude accurately at sea.

HENNEBIQUE, François (1842–1921) French engineer who in 1892 developed prestressed concrete.

HOOKE, Robert (1635–1703) British scientist who made various discoveries in the fields of chemistry and physics. He worked out the principle of the steam engine, and in 1658 invented a pendulum clock. A year later he devised the hairspring for watch mechanisms, and in 1660 invented the anchor escapement for clocks. He also constructed the first Gregorian or reflecting telescope.

HOOVER, William (1849–1932) U.S. inventor of the electric vacuum cleaner and founder in 1908 of the Electric Suction Sweeper company.

HOWE, Elias (1819–67) U.S. inventor who in 1846 patented the modern type of sewing machine.

HUNT, Walter (1796–1859) U.S. inventor who in 1849 patented the safety pin. He also invented the eye-pointed needle and interlocked stitch for sewing machines.

HUYGENS, Christiaan (1629–95) Dutch mathematician and physicist who in 1657 made the first reliable pendulum clock.

KAY, John (1704-80) British engineer who in 1733 invented the flying shuttle, greatly increasing the speed of looms.

KÖNIG, Friedrich (1774–1833) German printer who in 1810 invented a steam-

driven press and a year later constructed a powered rotary press for printing newspapers.

LANGMUIR, Irving (1881–1957) U.S. scientist who in 1915 invented the gas-filled tungsten filament lamp. He won the Nobel Prize for Chemistry in 1932.

LE BLON, Jacob (1670–1741) French artist who in 1720 devised a process to print engravings in color.

LEEUWENHOEK, Anton van (1632–1723) Dutch optician who ground his own lenses and in 1675 used one to make the first microscope.

LENOIR, Jean (1822–1900) French engineer who in 1859 constructed the first internal combustion engine (which used gas as a fuel).

LUKIN, Lionel (1742–1834) British coachbuilder who in 1786 invented an unsinkable boat (kept buoyant with cork and hollow spaces).

LUMIÈRE, Auguste (1862–1954) and **Louis** (1864–1948) French brothers who developed cinematography, beginning in the 1890s.

MACINTOSH, Charles (1766–1843) British chemist who in 1823 patented a method of waterproofing cloth using rubber (a method first devised in 1818 by James Syme).

MALLET, Anatole (1837–1919) Swiss locomotive engineer who in 1876 invented a compound steam engine. He also invented the type of powerful articulated steam locomotive that bears his name.

MARCONI, Guglielmo (1874–1937) Italian inventor who, from 1894, developed radio as a means of communication. He made his first trans-Atlantic transmission in 1901.

MAUDSLEY, Henry (1771–1831) British engineer who in 1800 invented a lathe for accurately cutting screw threads.

MCADAM, John (1756–1836) British road surveyor who in 1815 invented the "macadamizing" method of surfacing roads (with tar and gravel).

MONIER, Joseph (1823–1906) French engineer who in 1849 invented reinforced concrete (with internal iron rods for strengthening).

MONTGOLFIER, Joseph (1740–1810) French engineer who in 1796 invented the hydraulic ram (for raising water). In 1783, together with his brother **Jacques** (1745–99), he built the first passenger-carrying hot-air balloon.

MORSE, Samuel (1791–1872) U.S. artist who in 1838 invented a single-wire telegraph and devised the telegraph code that bears his name.

MURDOCK, William (1754–1839) British engineer who in 1792 invented a method of lighting using coal gas, which he made by the distillation of coal.

NAPIER, John (1550–1617) Scottish mathematician who in 1613 invented logarithms, leading three years later to "Napier's bones" as a calculating aid.

NEWCOMEN, Thomas (1663–1729) British engineer who made an atmospheric steam engine in 1698, and by 1712 had fitted it with a piston so that it acted as a pumping engine to remove water from coal and tin mines.

NIEPCE, Joseph Nicéphore (1765–1833) French chemist who in 1822 became one of the first inventors of a successful photographic process.

NOBEL, Alfred (1833–96) Swedish chemist who invented dynamite, by absorbing nitroglycerine into the earthy mineral kiselguhr (diatomite). He bequeathed $9 million of his fortune to set up the annual Nobel prizes.

NUFFIELD, William (1877–1963) British engineer who by 1910 was building Morris Oxford cars at Cowley, Oxford, becoming the first British manufacturer to introduce production-line techniques.

OTIS, Elisha (1811–61) U.S. engineer who in 1852 invented the safety passenger elevator and then in 1861 a steam-driven elevator.

OTTO, Nikolaus (1832–91) German engineer who in 1876 made the first four-stroke internal combustion engine (which used gas as a fuel).

PAPIN, Denis (1647–1712) French physicist who in 1681 made a steam condensing pump and as early as 1698 had made a steam engine.

PARSONS, Charles (1854–1931) British engineer who in 1884 invented the compound steam turbine, fitting it in a ship, the *Turbinia*, in 1897.

RIQUET, Pierre (1604–80) French engineer who in 1666 began construction of the Canal du Midi.

ROLLS, Charles (1877–1910) British engineer who in 1902 founded the Rolls company to make luxury cars. He later went into partnership with Henry Royce to make Rolls Royce cars.

SENEFELDER, Aloys (1771–1834) German printer who in 1798 invented lithography (planographic printing). By 1826 he was using a three-color lithographic process.

SIEGEN, Ludwig von (1609–c. 1676) German engraver who invented the process for making mezzotints (which provide a half-tone effect).

SINGER, Isaac (1811–75) U.S. engineer who invented and (from 1852) manufactured sewing machines that used an interlocked chain stitch and a needle (with the eye at the pointed end) invented by Walter HUNT.

SMEATON, John (1724–94) British engineer who designed the third Eddystone lighthouse (in the English Channel), which was built in 1759 using hydraulic cement – which sets under water.

STEPHENSON, George (1781–1848) British railroad engineer who is usually credited with inventing the steam locomotive (in 1814). He constructed the Stockton-Darlington Railway (opened in 1825) and the Liverpool-Manchester Railway (1830).

STEPHENSON, Robert (1803–59) British engineer who worked on railroads with his father **George**, and went on (1847–59) to design and build bridges in various countries.

SWAN, Joseph (1828–1914) British scientist who invented dry plates (1871) and bromide paper (1879) for use in photography. Also, in 1879, he invented (and subsequently patented) a carbon-filament incandescent electric lamp shortly before Thomas EDISON.

SYMINGTON, William (1763–1831) British engineer who in 1788 and 1801 built steam paddleboats.

TALBOT, William Fox (1800–77) British pioneer photographer who in 1839 first made paper negatives and prints.

TELFORD, Thomas (1757–1834) British engineer who built the Caledonian Canal (1803–23), the Menai suspension bridge (1825) and London's St. Katherine's Dock (1826–28).

THIMONNIER, Barthelemy (1793–1859) French tailor who in 1830 became the first of many to invent a sewing machine.

THOMSON, Robert (1822–73) British inventor who in 1845 of a pneumatic tire for carriages. *See also* John DUNLOP.

TREVITHICK, Richard (1771–1833) British engineer who built a steam-powered carriage (1801) and a steam locomotive (1804), as well as stationary steam engines; he demonstrated a small steam railroad in London in 1808.

VERNIER, Pierre (c. 1580–1637) French mathematician who in 1631 invented the Vernier scale for making accurate measurements in engineering.

WALLIS, Barnes (1887–1979) British engineer who designed the R-100 airship (1929) and bouncing bombs that were used in attacks on German dams during World War II.

WATT, James (1736–1819) British engineer who is generally credited with inventing the steam engine. In 1764 he made a steam engine with a separate external condenser (in NEWCOMEN's earlier engine the steam was condensed in the cylinder). He made a double-acting steam engine in 1782, and in 1789 he invented a governor for controlling the speed of such engines.

WESTINGHOUSE, George (1846–1914) U.S. railroad engineer who in 1867 invented the air brake for rolling stock.

WHEATSTONE, Charles (1802–75) British physicist who from 1837, with William Cooke (1806–79), invented electric telegraphs.

WHITWORTH, Joseph (1803–87) British engineer and inventor who in 1830 devised the series of standard screw threads that bears his name.

WILCOX, Stephen (1832–93) *See* George BABCOCK.

WILKINSON, John (1728–1808) British iron founder who in 1774 invented a machine for accurately boring cylinders (required for the new steam engines).

YALE, Linus (1821–68) U.S. locksmith who in 1865 invented the type of cylinder lock that still bears his name.

TECHNICAL TERMS

AC Alternating current. Electric current that reverses the direction of its flow regularly. Each completed return is a cycle; the number of cycles a second denotes the current's frequency. Most household appliances run on AC. *See also* DC.

Accelerator Pedal that controls the speed of a PETROL or DIESEL ENGINE.

Ahead In front of the BOW of a ship or boat.

Alternator Electric generator that produces alternating current.

Aileron A movable control surface at the rear of an airplane's wing that enables the pilot to roll the aircraft.

Air brake Brake worked by a PISTON driven by compressed air which is supplied to the brake cylinder from reservoirs connected to it.

Aft Toward the rear of a boat or ship.

Alphabet A set of letters used in writing and printing (from alpha and beta, the first two letters of the Greek alphabet).

Anode Positive electrode; the terminal through which electrons leave a system; works with a negative CATHODE.

Aperture Opening of variable size made by a camera's IRIS DIAPHRAGM. Together with the chosen SHUTTER speed, it controls the amount of light reaching the film.

Arc lamp Lamp that produces light by means of an arc of electricity across a gap between two conductors, usually carbon rods. Light is produced when the rods become white hot.

Arrester Trackside device on a railroad that slows or stops shunted vehicles.

Biplane Aircraft with two fixed parallel wings separated by struts.

Bitumen A mixture of carbon and hydrogen. Mineral pitch and asphalt are forms of bitumen.

Blast furnace Rapid burning furnace whose fuel is fanned by a current of air under pressure.

Bow or **bows** Front of a boat or ship.

Bowsprit A long projection from the BOW of a boat or ship that supports rigging and possibly a JIB or SPRITSAIL.

Brake car A railroad car marshaled at the rear of a FREIGHT TRAIN. It is manned by a conductor and contains a screw brake.

Buffers Sprung metal "studs" at the ends of a railroad vehicle to absorb the shocks of minor collisions in shunting.

Buffer stop A set of BUFFERS mounted at the end of a length of railroad track.

Cablegram A telegram sent along an undersea cable.

CAD Computer-aided design. A method of building three-dimensional models of a building, car, structure, etc. and testing its advantages and limitations on screen rather than in the real world.

Carburetor A device on a GASOLINE ENGINE that mixes the correct proportion of gasoline vapor and air and passes it to the CYLINDERS for ignition.

Caisson Cylindrical or rectangular box structure used as an underwater foundation. Caissons are constructed on land and then sunk underwater to support piers, jetties, or bridges.

Cantilever A structural beam that is supported at one end and free at the other.

Cast iron Iron mixed with carbon. It is brittle, hard, absorbs shocks, and does not change shape when heated.

Catenary An arrangement of posts and suspension wires that hold an electric railroad's overhead electricity supply wire horizontal.

Cathode Negative electrode; the terminal through which electrons enter a system.

Chair A U-shaped metal casting that holds rails to a TIE on a railroad track.

Charcoal Graphitic carbon residue of burned wood.

Choke A flap valve on a CARBURETOR that controls the amount of air entering.

Chronometer Marine clock mounted on gimbals so that it keeps level at sea.

Classification Sorting railroad vehicles into the correct order to make up a train.

Coil An induction coil associated with a GASOLINE ENGINE, which produces the high-voltage electricity for the SPARK PLUGS.

Compression-ignition engine Another name for a DIESEL ENGINE.

Concrete Mixture of cement, sand, gravel, crushed stones, and water.

Coupling A hooking device for joining railroad vehicles to a locomotive or to each other.

Crankshaft Shaft in a reciprocal engine (such as a steam engine or INTERNAL COMBUSTION ENGINE) that converts the up-and-down or side-to-side motion of PISTONS into rotary motion.

Crow's nest A look-out position near the top of a ship's mast.

Cuneiform Sumerian wedged-shaped writing (from 3000 B.C.) impressed in wet clay tablets with a stylus.

Cylinder The "tube" in a steam or INTERNAL COMBUSTION ENGINE in which the PISTON moves back and forth.

DC Direct current. Electrical current that flows one way only. *See also* AC.

Developer A solution of chemical reducing agent (such as hydroquinone) which, on an exposed photographic film (or paper), converts silver halide salts affected by light into microscopic grains of metallic silver. *See also* FIXER.

Diaphragm *See* IRIS DIAPHRAGM.

Diesel engine An INTERNAL COMBUSTION ENGINE, commonly in buses, trucks, and marine vessels, in which pressure alone ignites the fuel-air mixture (that is, it has no SPARK PLUGS).

Differential gear Gearing system that makes it possible for wheels on the same vehicle to go at different speeds, when cornering, for example.

Diode A VACUUM TUBE with two electrodes, used to change AC to DC.

Displacement The weight of water (in tons) displaced by a floating vessel.

Distributor A rotary switch on a GASOLINE ENGINE that directs high-voltage electricity to each of the SPARK PLUGS in correct sequence.

Double-heading The practice of using two locomotives to pull one train.

Draft The amount of a ship's hull below the waterline—that is, the minimum depth of water in which it will float.

Drag An aerodynamic force that resists motion and slows a plane or vehicle down. Shape influences drag, so planes and cars are designed to offer as little resistance as possible to air.

Duplex system A method of sending two telephone messages simultaneously in opposite directions along the same cable.

Dynamo Electric generator which converts mechanical energy into electricity.

Electromagnet Temporary magnet formed when electrical current flows through wires wrapped round a piece of iron.

Electrotype A copy of engravings and/or type matter made by an electroplating process and used in a printing press.

Elevator A control surface at the rear of an airplane's TAILPLANE that enables the pilot to alter the pitch of the aircraft (allowing it to climb or descend).

Engraving A metal plate engraved for printing, or an illustration printed from such a plate.

Escapement In clocks, a curved piece of metal with hooks at each end that regulates the descent of the clock's weight or pendulum.

Exposure The time for which a camera's SHUTTER is open when taking a photograph. *See also* TIME EXPOSURE.

Fanbelt A belt around a pulley driven by the drive shaft of an INTERNAL COMBUSTION ENGINE that, via another pulley, rotates a cooling fan and drives the DYNAMO or ALTERNATOR.

Fin The vertical surface above the TAILPLANE of an airplane; its movable rear part is the RUDDER.

Firebox The part of a steam railroad locomotive in which fuel (usually coal or oil) is burned to heat water in the boiler.

Firetube One of many tubes that pass through the boiler of a steam railroad locomotive. Hot gases from the FIREBOX passing along the firetubes boil the water surrounding them.

Fishplate A metal plate that is bolted to rails to join them end-to-end on a railroad track. Also named joint bars.

Fixer A solution of a chemical (such as sodium thiosulphate, or hypo) which, after an exposed photographic film (or paper) has been developed, dissolves away any silver halide salts that have not been affected by light during exposure. *See also* DEVELOPER.

Flap A movable surface at the rear edge of an airplane's wing that increases lift during takeoff (and DRAG during landing).

Flatbed press A type of printing press in which the inked type matter is in a flat

plane and the paper is pressed against it. *See also* ROTARY PRESS.

Flywheel Heavy wheel attached to a rotating shaft in an engine to moderate fluctuations in power. The inertia of the flywheel, which is heaviest at its rim, evens out the variable thrust.

F-number A number that indicates the size of the APERTURE of a LENS, equal to its FOCAL LENGTH divided by the diameter of the aperture. Large apertures have small f-numbers, and vice versa.

Focal length Distance from the back of a LENS to the point at which an image is in focus. For photographs that best reproduce what the eye sees, the focal length should be approximately equal to the diagonal dimension of the photograph.

Focal plane shutter A type of camera SHUTTER that acts (close to the film plane) like a window blind with a slit in it. As the slit moves (usually rapidly) past the film, it allows light through to expose the image.

Focus To adjust a LENS, by moving it slightly farther from or nearer to the film plane, so that the image is clear and sharp in the viewfinder and on the film.

Footplate The part of a railroad locomotive on which the crew work.

Foremast Mast at the front of a ship.

Foresail The lowermost sail on the FOREMAST.

Freight train A railroad train of cars or tankers for carrying freight.

Frog An X-shaped casting that allows rails to "cross" at points on a railway track.

Fuselage The main body of an aircraft (excluding the wings, TAILPLANE, and FIN).

Gasoline engine An INTERNAL COMBUSTION ENGINE, as in most cars, that uses gasoline (mixed with air) as fuel. The fuel is ignited by means of SPARK PLUGS.

Gauge Width of a railroad track, measured between inside edges of the rails.

Geodesic dome Sphere constructed of many polygonal facets made of struts or flat sections so that the stresses are distributed about the whole structure.

Governor Mechanical device that controls engine speed by regulating the fuel supply.

Hairspring Device in spring clocks to regulate the balance wheel that drives the clock. The balance wheel must turn one way and then the other to keep the wheels in the clock turning uniformly. The hairspring pushes the balance wheel back when it has completed its forward movement.

Halftone A printed illustration in which the picture is made up of tiny dots. In a black-and-white halftone, the varying sizes of the dots gives an impression of different shades of gray. Colored images can also be printed as halftones (using four sets of dots in the colors cyan, magenta, yellow, and black).

Hieroglyphics A type of "picture writing," especially as used by the ancient Egyptians.

Hydroelectricity Electricity produced from turbines driven by fast-flowing or falling water.

Hydraulic Describing any device in which liquid is used to transfer force. Pressure in a liquid is transmitted uniformly in all directions (Pascal's law, 1650) and so pressure applied to liquid at one end of a tube will be felt where the liquid meets an obstruction at the other end of the tube. Hydraulic jacks work on this principle.

Image The upside-down picture focused onto the film (or onto a picture tube) when a camera's SHUTTER is open.

Intaglio A method of printing in which a design is cut into a metal plate. Ink stays in the cutaway part when the rest of the plate is wiped clean, and can then be transferred to paper.

Internal combustion engine An engine in which the fuel (mixed with air) is burned inside the engine, such as a GASOLINE ENGINE, DIESEL ENGINE, or gas-turbine engine.

Iris diaphragm Arrangement of thin, overlapping plates of very thin metal that form an APERTURE behind a camera's LENS. Rotating the plates alters the size of the aperture.

Jib On a sailing vessel, a triangular sail between the FOREMAST and BOWSPRIT.

Keel The main structural member running lengthwise along the bottom of a ship's hull.

Knot Unit of speed used by planes and ships, equal to one nautical mile per hour (1.15 mph or 1.85 kph).

Laser An acronym formed from Light Amplification by Stimulated Emission of Radiation. A device that amplifies an input of light, producing a narrow, intense monochromatic beam.

Lateen On a sailing vessel, a triangular sail suspended from a sloping YARD attached to a mast.

Leaf shutter A type of camera SHUTTER that consists of two or more thin, sprung metal plates that rapidly open and close to allow light to reach the film and expose the IMAGE.

Lens One or more specially shaped pieces of glass that FOCUS an IMAGE onto the film or picture tube in a camera.

Lift The aerodynamic force that keeps planes in the sky. It is produced when the air pressure is greater underneath the wing than on top. This happens because air rushing over the curve of a wing's surface moves faster than air passing the straight section underneath. Pressure decreases with speed, and so the wing has more pressure underneath it, forcing it upward.

Light engine A railroad locomotive traveling without pulling a train.

Lithography A type of PLANOGRAPHIC PRINTING.

Loading gauge The maximum permitted height of a railroad vehicle, and the suspended frame that defines that height.

Load line *See* PLIMSOLL LINE.

Lock On a waterway, an enclosure with gates that can be closed so that the water level can be raised or lowered (by pump) to join one waterway to another. Sometimes a series of locks is needed to join waterways on very different levels.

Logogram A symbol that represents a complete word or phrase (such as $, meaning dollar).

Mainmast The mast second from the front; the middle mast on a three-masted vessel.

Mainsail The lowermost sail on the MAINMAST.

Modem A portmanteau word from modulator/demodulator. A device to convert signals from one code to another.

Multiplex system A method of sending several telephone messages simultaneously along the same cable.

Negative In photography, an IMAGE produced on film after development. With black-and-white film, light tones appear dark and dark tones appear light. With color print film, the colors appear as their complementaries.

Pantograph A framework on the roof of an electric train or locomotive for collecting electricity from an overhead wire.

Photocell Another name for a photoelectric cell, which has a light-sensitive cathode ray producing electrons at one end and a negative electrode to collect them at the other.

Photogravure A form of INTAGLIO printing using a plate made photographically.

Pictograph A "picture" that represents an object in any of the earliest systems of writing. *See also* HIEROGLYPHICS.

Piston A cylindrical part that moves to and fro in a hollow cylinder, used in engines and pumps.

Planographic printing A method of printing from a flat surface on which the design (or type matter) is in a greasy medium. The ink clings to the greasy part and can be transferred to paper.

Plexiglass Trade name for acrylic plastic.

Plimsoll line Also called a load line, a set of lines on the side of a (usually ocean-going) ship's hull that indicate the waterline if the vessel is correctly loaded.

Pneumatic Any device driven by or using compressed air.

Pontoon Bridge constructed from floating units; the word comes from the old French *ponton*: flat-bottomed boat.

Precast concrete Concrete cast into a form and transported to a construction site rather than poured in situ.

Prestressed concrete Concrete that is cast around steel cables held under tension by hydraulic jacks. When the concrete has set, the steel cables are released and compress the concrete.

Radio telephony A method of sending telephone messages by radio. *See* TELEPHONY.

Rake The slope from the vertical of a ship's masts, smokestack, or STERN.

Rebus A mixture of pictures and words,

in which the pictures represent syllables or words.

Reflex camera A camera with an internal mirror or mirrors that reflect light entering the LENS onto a viewing screen (usually in a viewfinder).

Reinforced concrete Concrete cast around rigid steel rods to make it stronger.

Relief printing A method of printing from an inked design (or type) which is raised above the background.

Revolver Multishot pistol with a revolving cylinder to transport the bullets quickly to the chamber.

Robot Mechanical device designed to carry out repetitive tasks. The word derives from the Czech verb *robota*, to labor.

Rotary press A type of printing press in which the inked type matter is on a rotating cylinder, kept in contact with the paper.

Rudder The vertical control surface at the rear of a boat or ship, by means of which it is steered. The term is also used for the vertical control surface at the rear of the fin of an aircraft, which serves a similar purpose.

Runes Letters of an alphabet used in northern Europe before A.D. 1000.

Safety valve A device on a steam engine or locomotive that allows steam to escape if its pressure exceeds a preset safe value.

Semaphore A method of signaling that uses two flags or mechanical arms, held in various positions to represent letters or numbers.

Semiconductor A material used in electronics that can conduct electricity better than an insulator (glass, ceramics) but not as well as a conductor (copper). Silicon is a semiconductor.

Servomechanism Automatic device designed to correct performance when it detects an error or deviation from the norm. Used to adjust velocity and position in planes and hydrofoils.

Sheet A rope or cable attached to the end of a YARD on a sailing vessel for controlling the angle of the sail to the mast.

Shoe A steel collector on an electric train or locomotive for picking up electricity from a third rail.

Shutter The part of a camera that opens and closes (usually rapidly) to allow light to reach the film and make an exposure.

Siding A branch railroad track for holding stationary vehicles.

Skyscraper Originally, the triangular sky sail on a clipper ship; then applied to anything extremely tall; now exclusively refers to very tall buildings.

Slide rule Device made up of three separate graduated scales that can slide against each other to make complex calculations (logarithms, square roots, etc.). Mostly used by engineers and architects, but now largely superseded by the electronic calculator.

Smelting Method of extracting metal from ore by heating it beyond its melting point, usually with coke.

Smokebox An area at the front of a steam railroad locomotive from which smoke (from burning fuel) passes up the smokestack. Exhaust steam from the cylinders escapes by the same route, creating a draft that pulls hot gases through the FIRETUBES.

Solar power Conversion of the sun's radiation (50 percent visible light, 45 percent infrared radiation, and the rest ultraviolet radiation) into heat or electrical energy.

Sonar An acronym formed from Sound Navigation and Ranging. It uses sound waves bounced from distant objects to tell how far away they are.

Spark plug Device that produces a high-voltage electric spark to ignite the fuel-air mixture in the CYLINDERS of a GASOLINE ENGINE.

Spinning jenny Spinning machine which used a wheel to drive a band linked to several shuttles. It revolutionized what had been a cottage industry.

Spritsail On a sailing vessel, a square sail on a YARD suspended from the BOWSPRIT.

Square-rigged Describing a mast or sailing vessel on which the sails are square, on YARDS attached to the masts.

Stainless steel Alloy of steel with chromium, iron, carbon, and manganese that resists rust. It may also contain molybdenum, titanium, sulphur, selenium, or nickel, depending on how it is to be used.

Standard gauge In most of North America and Europe, the common railroad track GAUGE of 4 ft. 8½ in. (1.44 m).

Stereotype A copy of assembled type matter (possibly with illustrations) which is made with the aid of a mold.

Stern The rear of a boat or ship.

Stylus Originally, a wedge-shaped tool for impressing CUNEIFORM characters into clay tablets. Also the crystal pickup on the arm of a record player.

Supercharger In a car engine, an air compressor that supplies extra air to the CYLINDERS, so encouraging more fuel to burn and the vehicle to go faster.

Switches A set of movable rails on a railroad, laid where trains need to switch from one track to anoter.

Syllabary A set of symbols that represent spoken syllables, as in Japanese writing.

Tailplane The horizontal surface of an airplane's tail, bearing the ELEVATORS.

Tank engine A railroad locomotive that has tanks for carrying its supply of water, so does not need to have a TENDER.

Telegraphy Any method of sending messages, as electric pulses, along wires.

Telephony Sending of voice messages, as varying electric currents, along wires.

Telephoto lens Sometimes also called a long LENS, a lens whose FOCAL LENGTH is more than the normal length for a par-

ticular camera. It produces an IMAGE larger than that of the normal lens.

Tender A vehicle attached immediately behind a steam railroad locomotive, which carries water and fuel (usually coal or oil).

Throttle A flap valve in a CARBURETOR that controls the amount of fuel-air mixture passing to the GASOLINE ENGINE. The term is also applied to the ACCELERATOR pedal (which controls the throttle).

Thrust Force exerted by one part of a structure on another, or the driving force developed by a propellor (or engine).

Tie A wood or concrete support to which the rails of a railroad track are attached.

Time exposure A long EXPOSURE, necessary in very poor lighting, during which a camera's SHUTTER is kept open. The camera must be kept perfectly still, preferably on a TRIPOD.

Transparency A positive color photograph—that is, one in which the colors are true-to-life and which can be viewed by holding it to the light or by projection.

Transistor Electronic device using SEMICONDUCTORS to control electrical flow. Transistors can amplify the current, change its frequency, or switch it on or off.

Tripod A three-legged stand on which a camera can be mounted to keep it still when taking photographs. Most types have collapsible telescopic legs.

Triode A VACUUM TUBE with three electrodes used to amplify weak signals.

Undercarriage The landing wheels of an aircraft, usually retracted during flight.

Vacuum brake Type of brake for railroad vehicles which is held off by very low air pressure (vacuum). If the vacuum fails, air enters the system and immediately applies the brakes.

Vacuum tube A now superseded device developed to control electric current. Vacuum tubes could only work with almost all the air removed from them. Current flowing into them was modified by a DIODE or TRIODE.

Viewfinder The part of a camera that the photographer looks through to see what will be included on the photograph (and with some types, to see whether or not the IMAGE is in focus).

Vulcanization Heating rubber with sulfur until it combines to form a tough material suitable for car tires, etc.

Welded rail Railroad track made continuous by welding together shorter lengths. Diagonal expansion joints allow for expansion and contraction with varying temperatures.

Wide-angle lens Sometimes also called a short LENS, a lens whose FOCAL LENGTH is less than the normal length for a particular camera. It includes a wider view than the normal lens.

Yard On a sailing vessel, a generally horizontal spar, pivoted to a mast, from which a sail is suspended.

SECTION 6
ARTS AND CULTURE

Timeline

c. 2000 B.C. Anon., *Epic of Gilgamesh*, Sumerian creation story.

c. 1500 B.C. Anon., Indo-Aryan, *Rig Veda*.

c. 760 B.C. Hesiod, Greek poet, *Theogony* and *Works and Days*. Homer, Greek epic poet, *Iliad* and *Odyssey* (Epic poetry *right*). Anon., Chinese, *Book of Songs*. Anon., Hebrew, *Song of Solomon*.

700–600 B.C. Greek lyric poets Alcaeus, Archilochus, Sappho (Lyric poetry *p. 494*).

c. 550 B.C. Aesop, Greek fabulist.

c. 500 B.C. Pindar, Greek poet, *Triumphal Odes*. Anon., *Mahabharata*, Indian epic.

458 B.C. Aeschylus (*right, below*), Greek tragic dramatist, *Oresteia* trilogy.

443 B.C. Sophocles (*right, below*), Greek tragic dramatist, *Antigone*.

431 B.C. Euripides (*right, below*), Greek tragic dramatist, *Medea*.

423 B.C. Aristophanes (*right, below*), Greek comic dramatist, *Clouds*.

c. 290 B.C. Theocritus, Greek poet.

167 Terence (Publius Terentius Āfer), Roman comic dramatist, *Andria*.

c. 60 B.C. Gaius Valerius Catullus, Roman poet, love poems.

19 B.C. Horace (Quintus Horatius Flaccus), Roman poet and satirist, *Odes*. Virgil (Publius Vergilius Maro), Roman poet, *Aeneid* (*right, above*).

2 B.C. Ovid (Publius Ovidius Naso), Roman poet, *Ars Amatoria*.

c. A.D. 100 Juvenal (Decimus Junius Juvenalis), Roman satirist.

c. 150 Lucius Apuleius, Roman novelist, *Golden Ass*.

c. 400 Kálidása, Indian dramatist, *Sákuntala*.

c. 550 Taliesin, Welsh poet, *Book of Taliesin*.

c. 600 Antara ibn Shaddad, Arab poet, *Divan*.

c. 650 Aneirin, Welsh poet, *Gododdin*. Caedmon, first known English poet.

c. 700 Anon., *Beowulf*, Old English epic poem. Filiad (Irish bardic class), *Ulaid*, cycle on hero Cuchulainn.

c. 730 Bhavabhuti (Sri-Kantha), Indian dramatist.

c. 740 Li Po and Tu Fu, Chinese poets.

795 Cynewulf, Anglo-Saxon poet.

c. 800 Abu Nuwas, Arab poet, originator of *Arabian Nights*.

c. 840 Abu Tammâm, Arab poet, *Hamâsa*.

868 Oldest known printed book, the *Diamond Sutra*, China.

890 Anon., *Cantilène de Ste.-Eulalie*, earliest French poem. Anon., *The Story of the Bamboo-Gatherer*, Japanese narrative.

c. 965 Roswitha of Gandersheim, first German woman poet.

c. 995 Anon., *Battle of Maldon*, Anglo-Saxon war poem.

c. 1000 Sei Shonagon, Japanese woman court diarist, *The Pillow Book*.

1008 Firdausi, Persian poet, *Book of Kings*.

c. 1015 Murasaki Shikibu, Japanese

EPIC POETRY

Often with origins in oral, preliterate tradition, epics are continuous narrative poems recounting the heroic actions of historical or legendary characters. Examples include:

Epic of Gilgamesh (c. 2000 B.C.), story of Sumerian founder hero, anon.

Iliad (c. 800–700 B.C.), epic of the Trojan War (c. 1250 B.C.), and *Odyssey*, wanderings of Greek hero Odysseus, attributed to Homer.

Mahabharata (c. 500 B.C.), Indian epic of war between Pandava and Kaurava families (c. 1200 B.C.), anon. Also includes *Bhagavad Gita* (Hinduism, *p. 210*).

Ramayana (c. 350 B.C.), story of Lord Rama, attrib. to Indian poet Valmiki.

Aeneid (19 B.C.), story of Aeneas, founder hero of Rome, Virgil.

Beowulf (c. A.D. 700), Old English epic of eponymous Nordic warrior, anon.

Song of Roland (c. 1050–1100), French epic about the Charlemagne era, anon.

Poema de mio Cid (c. 1140), deeds of Spanish national hero Rodrigo Diaz de Vivar, "El Cid," anon.

Nibelungenlied (c. 1200), Middle High German story of Siegfried, anon.

Divine Comedy (c. 1307–21), Italian poet Dante Alighieri.

The Lusiads (1572), exploits of Vasco da Gama, Portuguese poet Luiz Vaz de Camões (Camöens).

The Faerie Queene (1590–96), allegorical knightly adventures, Elizabethan poet Edmund Spenser.

Paradise Lost (1667), the Fall of Man, English poet John Milton.

The Prelude (1798–1805), the growth of a poet's mind, English poet William Wordsworth.

The Song of Hiawatha (1855), Native American stories; U.S. poet Henry Wadsworth Longfellow.

The Mahabharata*: Arjuna, leader of the Pandavas, battles with Kaurava champion Karna.*

CLASSICAL GREEK DRAMA

Greek drama evolved from an annual festival honoring Dionysus, the god of wine, with sung choruses. In the 500s B.C., Thespis supposedly founded "modern" drama by extending the choral performance with an actor who delivered speeches.

Western notions of theatrical space stem from the physical nature of these performances, in which the chorus acted from an *orchestra* (dancing place), set against the backdrop of the *skene* (scene), which was surrounded by a semicircular *theatron* (seeing-place) capable (in Athens) of seating some 27,000 spectators.

Tragedy:

Aeschylus (c. 525–456 B.C.) introduced the idea of divine will shaping the course of events. Seven of his 60 plays are extant, including *Prometheus Bound* and his trilogy the *Oresteia*, which includes the great *Agamemnon*.

Sophocles (c. 496–405 B.C.) introduced the notion of human will, working with or against the divine will. Eight of c.100 works survive, including *Electra*, *Antigone*, and *Oedipus Rex I*.

Euripides (c. 480–406 B.C.) developed the turning point, or *peripeteia*, making it more abrupt and striking. Of c. 80 plays, 18 survive, including *Medea*, *Electra*, and *The Bacchae*.

Comedy:

Aristophanes (c. 448–388 B.C.), writer of "Old Comedy," a blend of religious ceremony, satire, and political criticism: 11 of c. 55 plays extant, including *Clouds*, *Wasps* (before c. 425), and *Lysistrata* (411; Athenian women withold sexual favors to stop male militarism).

Menander (c. 343–291 B.C.), writer of "New Comedy," which introduced representations of contemporary life and the theme of romantic love. Only one of his comedies (*Dyskolos*) has survived.

MYSTERY, MORALITY, AND PASSION PLAYS

Mystery play: Martyrdom of St. Apollonia painted *by Johan Fouquet.*

Mystery (miracle) plays, based on bible stories or saints' lives, evolved in the 1100s from Latin playlets performed in church on feast days. Moving to the vernacular, they were performed outdoors, on wheeled stages, by laymen. Some regions developed their own play cycles. They were later augmented by Morality plays, teaching moral lessons through personified vices and virtues, and Passion plays, portraying Christ's crucifixion. Examples include:

Mystère d'Adam (c. 1150–1200), Anglo-Norman Mystery play: anon.
The Harrowing of Hell (c. 1250–1300), earliest surviving English Mystery play: anon.
Chester Cycle (c. 1327), 25 plays thought to be the earliest English Mystery cycle: anon.
The Castle of Perseverance (c. 1400–25): English Morality play: anon.
Le Mans Passion (c. 1450), French Mystery play: Arnoul Greban.
Elckerlijk (c. 1495), Dutch source of the play *Everyman*: Petrus Dorlandus.
Everyman (c. 1500), best-known English Morality play: anon.
La Condemnation de Banquet (c. 1500), French secular Morality play: Nicolas de la Chesnaye.
Oberammergau Passion Play (1634), a Bavarian Mystery play celebrating the town's deliverance from plague; still performed every ten years.

COURTLY POETRY: TROUBADOURS AND SINGERS

The concept of courtly love (romantic love seen as an ennobling force) developed in southern France during the early 1100s, forming the basis of a new aristocratic tradition of lyric poetry and romance. The tradition appears to have been influenced by the poetry of Ovid and ancient Arab writers. As a literary movement, courtly love flourished in Provence and northern France, supported by royal patronage. From around 1100 to 1400 the troubadours and *trouvères* of France, including Guillaume de Poitou (1070–1150), Marcabru (d. 1150), and Bertrand de Born (1140–1215), traveled far afield, spreading the movement across Europe. Their counterparts in Germany were the minnesingers, including Walther von der Vogelweide (1172–1230) and Tannhäuser (1205–70).

Courtly love also inspired verse romancers like Chrétien de Troyes and Guillaume de Lorris (*Roman de la Rose*, c. 1225). The German poet Heinrich Frauenlob von Meissen (1250–1318) created a new, more erudite style of lyric. His successors, the meistersingers, formed guilds to control subject matter and versification. Dante's *La Vita Nuova* (1292), which tells of his youthful passion for Beatrice, represents the culmination of the influence of this tradition.

Courtly figures in the Castle Grounds: *a painting by the Limbourg brothers, Flemish miniaturists, from the* Très Riches Heures, *the Duc de Berry's illuminated manuscript from the 1400s.*

Timeline

1528 Baldassare Castiglione, Italian courtier and writer, *The Courtier*.

1531–33 François Rabelais, French satirist, *Gargantua*.

1552 Étienne Jodelle, French dramatist, *Cléopatre captive*, first French tragedy.

1557 Anon., England, *The Sack-Full of Newes*, the first English play to be censored.

1560 Hsu Wei, *Ching P'Ing Mei*, first Chinese novel. Thomas Sackville, 1st Earl of Dorset, and Thomas Norton, English dramatists, *Ferrex and Porrex* (*Gorboduc*).

1564 Birth of William Shakespeare.

1586 Japanese *Kabuki* theater develops.

1587 Christopher Marlowe, English dramatist, *Tamburlaine*.

1588 Marlowe, *Dr. Faustus*.

c. **1589** Thomas Kyd, English dramatist, *The Spanish Tragedy*.

1590 Edmund Spenser, English poet, begins *The Faerie Queen*. William Shakespeare becoming known as a dramatist.

c. **1595** John Donne, English poet, begins *Satires and Elegies* (publ. after 1611).

1598 Ben Jonson, English dramatist, *Every Man in his Humour*. Lope Félix de Vega Carpio, Spanish dramatist and poet, *La Dragoneta*.

1599 Shakespeare and comrades build Globe Theatre in London.

1600 François de Malherbe, French poet, *Ode à Marie de Médicis*.

1605 Miguel de Cervantes Saavedra, Spanish novelist, publishes first part of *Don Quixote* (second part in 1615).

1606 Ben Jonson, *Volpone*.

1607 Francis Beaumont and John Fletcher, English dramatists, *The Knight of the Burning Pestle*.

1608 John Webster, English dramatist, *The White Divel*.

c. **1612** Don Luis de Argote y Góngora, Spanish lyric poet, *Polifemo*. Webster, *The Duchess of Malfi*.

1616 Death of Shakespeare.

1626 Francisco Gómez de Quevedo y Villegas, Spanish novelist and poet, *Vida del Buscón Pablos* (or *Gran Tacaño*).

1632 Vega Carpio, *Dorotea*.

1633 John Ford, English dramatist, *'Tis Pity She's a Whore*.

1636 Pierre Corneille, French dramatist, *Le Cid*.

1637 John Milton, English poet, *Lycidas*.

1639 Corneille, *Horace*. Andreas Gryphius (Greif), German poet, *Sunday and Holiday Sonnets*.

1650 Henry Vaughan, Welsh poet, *Silex Scintillans*.

1654 Joost van den Vondel, Dutch dramatist, *Lucifer*.

1660 John Dryden, English poet, *Astrea Redux*.

1664 Molière, French dramatist, *Tartuffe*.

1665 Jean de La Fontaine, French poet, *Tales and News in Verse*.

PASTORAL POETRY

Pastoral literature provides an escape from everyday hardship through depictions of the pleasures of rural life.

Pastoral eclogue concentrates on the essential glories of a static Golden Age, while the georgic mode includes realistic details of rustic labor and agricultural practice. These terms were forged by Virgil, who drew on the work of Theocritus, the earliest author to idealize rural pleasures. During the 1600s and 1700s, pastorals described the pleasures of the gentleman's country seat. However, pastoral waned as a literary form with the onset of Romanticism, which advocated the high moral and spiritual experience to be gained through communion with nature.

Theocritus (*c.* 310–250 B.C.), Greek: *Bucolics*; "idylls," cameos of rural bliss.

Virgil (70–19 B.C.), Roman: *Eclogues*, modeled on Theocritus; *Georgics* (29 B.C.), on farming.

Jacopo Sannazaro (*c.* 1458–1530), Italian: *Arcadia* (1504), the lives and loves of shepherdesses in Arcadia, a rural paradise.

Torquato Tasso (1554–95), Italian: *Aminta* (1581), transl. into English 1596.

Giovanni Battista Guarini (1538–1612), Italian: *Il Pastor Fido* (1590).

Edmund Spenser (*c.* 1552–99), English: *The Shepheardes Calender* (1579).

William Shakespeare (1564–1616), English: *As You Like It* (1599–1600), a dramatic pastoral.

John Milton (1608–74), English: *Comus* (1634), a masque (drama with music and dance).

Alexander Pope (1688–1744), English: *The Pastorals* (1709), early poems.

John Greenleaf Whittier (1807–92), American: *Snow-Bound: A Winter Idyll* (1866).

Sheep-tending in May: a pastoral image from the Anglo-Saxon Calendar.

THE WORKS OF WILLIAM SHAKESPEARE

William Shakespeare (1564–1616), English playwright and poet, ranks as the greatest English dramatist by reason of his range (from broad comedy to profound tragedy), his depth of meaning, and the beauty and virtuosity of his blank verse. He has inspired complex works of criticism by writers such as Johnson, Coleridge, Goethe, and T. S. Eliot.

Shakespeare's plays have been translated and performed worldwide. His extraordinary output continues to offer artistic and interpretative challenges. The collected plays were published in the First Folio edition in 1623.

Complete works:

1590–91: *The Two Gentlemen of Verona* (comedy).

1592: *Henry VI Part One* (history).

1592: *Henry VI Part Two* (history).

1592: *Henry VI Part Three* (history).

1592: *Titus Andronicus* (tragedy).

1592–93: *Richard III* (history).

1592–98: *Sonnets* (poems).

1593: *The Taming of the Shrew* (comedy).

1593: *Venus and Adonis* (poem).

1594: *The Rape of Lucrece* (poem).

1594: *The Comedy of Errors* (comedy).

1594–95: *Love's Labour's Lost* (comedy).

1595: *Richard II* (history/tragedy).

1595: *Romeo and Juliet* (tragedy).

1595: *A Midsummer Night's Dream* (comedy).

1596: *King John* (history).

1596–97: *The Merchant of Venice* (comedy).

1596–97: *Henry IV Part One* (history).

1597–98: *Henry IV Part Two* (history).

1598: *Much Ado About Nothing* (dark comedy).

1598–99: *Henry V* (history).

1599: *Julius Caesar* (Roman).

1599–1600: *As You Like It* (comedy).

1600: *The Merry Wives of Windsor* (comedy).

1600–01: *Hamlet, Prince of Denmark* (tragedy).

1601: *The Phoenix and the Turtle* (poem).

1601: *Twelfth Night* or *What You Will* (comedy).

1602: *Troilus and Cressida* (history).

1603: *Measure for Measure* (dark comedy).

1603–04: *Othello* (tragedy).

1604–05: *All's Well That Ends Well* (dark comedy).

1605: *Timon of Athens* (romantic drama).

1605–06: *The Tragedy of King Lear* (tragedy).

1606: *Macbeth* (tragedy).

1606: *Antony and Cleopatra* (tragedy).

1607: *Pericles* (romance).

1608: *Coriolanus* (Roman).

1609: *The Winter's Tale* (romance).

1610: *Cymbeline* (comedy).

1611: *The Tempest* (comedy).

1613: *Henry VIII* (history).

THE SONNET

A sonnet (Italian "little song") is a 14-line poem. Its rhyme scheme varies. Best-known forms are the Italian (Petrarchan), an octave (eight lines) followed by a sestet (six lines); and the English (Shakespearean), three quatrains (four lines) followed by a couplet. Probably invented in Sicily in the early 1200s, the sonnet was largely confined to Italy until the 1500s, when the rest of Europe adopted this verse form. Often amatory, it has attracted many poets:

Francesco Petrarch (1304–74), Italian poet: *Le Rime* (1366).

Juan Boscán de Almugáver (c. 1490–1542) established the sonnet in Spain.

Thomas Wyatt (1503–42), first English sonneteer.

Pierre de Ronsard (1524–85), French poet: *Amours* (1552–53).

Edmund Spenser (c. 1552–99), English poet: *Amoretti* (1594).

William Shakespeare (1564–1616), English playwright and poet: *Sonnets* (c.1592–98).

John Donne (c. 1572–1631), English poet: *Songs and Sonnets* (c. 1600).

John Milton (1608–74), English poet and essayist: *On His Blindness* (1645).

William Wordsworth (1770–1850), English poet: *Upon Westminster Bridge* (1802).

John Keats (1795–1821), English poet: *On First Looking into Chapman's Homer* (1817).

Elizabeth Barrett Browning (1806–61), English poet: *Sonnets from the Portuguese*.

Dante Gabriel Rossetti (1828–82), English poet: *The House of Life* (1881).

George Meredith (1828–1909), English poet and novelist: *Modern Love* (1862).

José María de Heredia (1845–1905), French poet: *Les Trophées* (1893).

Rainer Maria Rilke (1875–1926), Austrian poet: *Sonnets to Orpheus* (1923).

THE ENLIGHTENMENT

The term describes an intellectual movement rooted in Europe of the 1700s, when man was supremely confident in his ability to articulate an empirical understanding of the world. The German philosopher Kant (1724–1804) coined the term, and the French provided the Enlightenment's most impressive monument in the form of *L'Encyclopédie*, a dictionary of universal knowledge published between 1751 and 1776 in 35 volumes under the editorship of Diderot, with contributions from the leading intellectuals of his age: Voltaire, Montesquieu, Rousseau, and Buffon. Many writers were inspired by the educational and scientific ideas of the Enlightenment, seeing the potential of literature to reach a wide readership, and it is no accident that this period witnessed the growth of literary realism and the rise of the novel.

François Voltaire (1694–1778), French writer, genius of the Enlightenment: *Candide* (1759).

Samuel Johnson (1709–1804), English writer: *Dictionary* (1755), the product of nine years' individual labor.

David Hume (1711–76), Scottish philosopher: *Dialogues Concerning Natural Religion* (1779).

Denis Diderot (1713–84), French philosopher and man of letters. He assumed editorship of *L'Encyclopédie* in 1746.

Edward Gibbon (1737–94), English historian: *The History of the Decline and Fall of the Roman Empire* (1776–88). *Encyclopaedia Britannica* (1768–71), issued by a "Society of Gentlemen in Scotland," edited by **William Smellie**, later Director of the Society of Antiquities.

Voltaire's bust presides over an assembly of Enlightenment leaders (contemporary painting).

Timeline

1763 Christopher Smart, English poet, *A Song to David*.

1766 Oliver Goldsmith, Irish dramatist, poet and novelist, *The Vicar of Wakefield*, novel.

1768 Sterne, *A Sentimental Journey through France and Italy*.

1770 Goldsmith, *The Deserted Village*.

1772 Pierre Amboise François Choderlos de Laclos, French novelist, *Les Liaisons dangereuses*.

1773 Johann Wolfgang von Goethe, German poet and dramatist, *Götz von Berlichingen*. Goldsmith, *She Stoops to Conquer*. Friedrich Gottlieb Klopstock, German poet, *Messiah*.

1774 Goethe, *The Sorrows of Young Werther*.

1775 Pierre Augustin Caron de Beaumarchais, French dramatist, *The Barber of Seville*. Richard Brinsley Sheridan, Irish dramatist, *The Rivals*.

1777 Sheridan, *The School for Scandal*.

1778 Fanny Burney, English novelist and diarist, *Evelina*. Voltaire, *Irène*.

1779 Lessing, *Nathan the Wise*.

1781 Johann von Schiller, German dramatist and poet, *The Robbers*.

1782 William Cowper, English poet, *Poems*.

1783 William Blake, English poet, *Poetical Sketches*. George Crabbe, English poet, *The Village*.

1784 Beaumarchais, *The Marriage of Figaro*.

1785 Cowper, *The Task*.

1787 Goethe, *Iphigenie auf Tauris*. Schiller, *Don Carlos*.

1789 Jean Jacques Rousseau, French philospher, *Confessions*.

1790 Robert Burns, Scottish poet, *Tam o'Shanter*.

1793 Johann Paul Friedrich Richter, German novelist, *The Invisible Lodge*.

1794 Blake, *Songs of Experience*.

1796 Burney, *Camilla*. Goethe, *Wilhelm Meister's Apprenticeship*.

1797 Samuel Taylor Coleridge, English poet, *Kubla Khan* (publ. 1816). Ann Radcliffe, English novelist, *The Italian*.

1798 Coleridge, *The Rime of the Ancient Mariner*.

1799 Johann Christian Friedrich Hölderlin, German poet and novelist, *Hyperion*. Novalis (Friedrich von Hardenberg), German poet, *Heinrich von Ofterdingen*. Schiller, *Wallenstein*.

1800 Novalis, *To the Night*. Schiller, *Mary Stuart*. Maria Edgeworth, Irish novelist, *Castle Rackrent*.

1802 Anne Louise Germaine Necker, Madame de Staël, French writer, *Delphine*.

1804 Schiller, *William Tell*.

1805 William Wordsworth, English poet, *The Prelude*.

1807 George Gordon, Lord Byron, English poet, *Hours of Idleness*. Staël, *Corinne*. Wordsworth, *Ode on Intimations of Immortality*.

ROMANTICISM

The Romantic movement (*c.* 1780–1840), often categorized as a reaction to the Enlightenment, was politically inspired by revolutions in America and France and popular uprisings elsewhere. The movement was marked by a new intuition for the power of natural landscape and the aesthetic principle of "organic form" (as in Wordsworth's *Prelude*). Liberated imagination was important, as were new valuations of the irrational, the unconscious, and the legendary. Romantic poets cultivated a sense of special genius and access to "original" feeling, in a revolt against classical form and human moderation. Important contributions to the movement include:

Jean Jacques Rousseau (1712–78), French philosopher: *Julie, ou La Nouvelle Héloïse* (1761), a tutor's love for his young pupil.

Johann Wolfgang von Goethe (1749–1832), German poet, novelist, and dramatist: *The Sorrows of Young Werther* (1774), semiautobiographical novel.

Johann von Schiller (1759–1805), German dramatist: *The Robbers* (1781), exploring liberty and authoritarianism.

William Wordsworth (1770–1850) and **Samuel Taylor Coleridge** (1772–1834), English poets: *Lyrical Ballads* (1798), basis of British Romanticism.

Lord Byron (1788–1824), English poet: *Childe Harold's Pilgrimage* (1812).

Percy Bysshe Shelley (1792–1822), English poet: *Ode to the West Wind* (1819), *Defence of Poetry* (1821).

John Keats (1795–1821), English poet: *Lamia, The Eve of St. Agnes and other Poems* (1820).

A scene from Coleridge's Rime of the Ancient Mariner *by Gustave Doré.*

LYRIC POETRY

Derived from the Greek word *lyrikos*, meaning "for the lyre," Europe's oldest surviving lyric poetry comes from ancient Greece and probably began with choral song. The tradition of popular song among Germanic tribes contributed to lyric poetry's subsequent development in the West. In England the genre reached perfection in Elizabethan songbooks. It has grown to be associated with simple, direct expression of personal feeling, while retaining a strong sense of rhythm. Examples of lyric poetry include:

Archilochus of Paros (714–676 B.C.), Greek: the first known lyric poet.

Sappho (650 B.C.), Greek: love lyrics to female friends on the island of Lesbos.

Gaius Valerius Catullus (*c.* 87–57 B.C.), Roman: love poems to his mistress.

Horace (Quintus Horatius Flaccus) (65–8 B.C.), Roman: *Epodes, Odes*.

Po Chu–i (A.D. 772–846), Chinese: *Songs of Ch'in* (808–10).

Robert Herrick (1591–1674), English: *Hesperides* (1648).

Johann Wolfgang von Goethe (1749–1832), German: *West-östliche Diwan* (1819).

William Blake (1757–1827), English: *Songs of Innocence* (1789).

Samuel Taylor Coleridge (1772–1834), English: *Poems on Various Subjects*; (with Wordsworth) *Lyrical Ballads* (1798).

Percy Bysshe Shelley (1792–1822), English: *Ode to the West Wind* (1819).

Giacomo Leopardi (1798–1837), Italian: *I Canti* (1831).

Alfred de Musset (1810–57), French: *Les Nuits* (1835–37).

Juan Rameón Jiménez (1881–1958), Spanish: *Baladas de primavera* (1910).

Boris Pasternak (1890–1960), Russian: *My Sister, Life* (1922).

e. e. cummings (1894–1962), American: *Tulips and Chimneys* (1923).

W. H. Auden (1907–73), English: *The Sea and the Mirror* (1944).

"The Divine Image," an etching by Blake from his Songs of Innocence.

BIOGRAPHY AND AUTOBIOGRAPHY

Biography's main concern may be to convey a sense of a person's character, but it also offers the reader access to historical and political issues seen through an individual's experience. There is a strong element of gossip, reflected in today's ever-growing commercial market for both biography and autobiography. However, the roots of the genre lie in the earliest didactic and religious writings. Landmarks of the form include:

Plutarch (A.D. 46–120), Greek: *Parallel Lives*, comparison of pairs of Greek and Roman characters.

St. Augustine (354–430), Latin religious teacher: *Confessions*, a record of his spiritual development with details of his early life in Roman North Africa.

Benvenuto Cellini (1500–71), Italian goldsmith and sculptor: *Autobiography*.

Giorgio Vasari (1511–74), Italian painter: *Lives of the Most Excellent Architects, Painters and Sculptors*.

James Boswell (1740–95), Scottish writer: *The Life of Samuel Johnson* (1791).

Mary Hays (1760–1843), English feminist: *Female Biography* (1803), catalogue of female pioneers in arts and sciences.

Frederick Douglass (1817–95), American abolitionist: *Narrative of the Life of Frederick Douglass, an American Slave* (1845); *My Bondage and My Freedom* (1855).

Edmund Gosse (1845–1928), English writer: *Father and Son* (1907), his father's story.

Maxim Gorky (1868–1936), Russian novelist: *Childhood* (1913–14), *My Universities* (1923), autobiographies.

Lytton Strachey (1880–1932), English biographer: *Eminent Victorians* (1918).

Richard Ellmen (1918–1987), American biographer: *James Joyce, Oscar Wilde* (1958).

Maya Angelou (b. 1928), American writer and black activist: *I Know Why the Caged Bird Sings* (1970), first volume of autobiography.

GOTHIC, HORROR, AND FANTASY

The modern "horror" story stems from the "Gothic" tales of the supernatural that became popular in Britain in the later 1700s. Writers participated in a revival of medieval art and literature, setting their tales in haunted castles, dilapidated ruins, and wild landscapes. Fantasy blends elements of the fairy tale, Gothic, science fiction, and sometimes horror. Noted writers in this genre include:

Horace Walpole (1717–97), English novelist and essayist: *The Castle of Otranto* (1764) set the fashion for Gothic romances.

William Beckford (1760–1844), English novelist and travel writer: *Vathek, an Arabian Tale* (1786).

Ann Radcliffe (1764–1823), English novelist: *The Mysteries of Udolpho* (1794).

James Hogg (1770–1835), Scottish poet and novelist: *Private Memoirs and Confessions of a Justified Sinner* (1824).

Matthew Lewis (1775–1818), English novelist: *Ambrosio or The Monk* (1796).

Mary Shelley (1797–1851), English novelist: *Frankenstein or The Modern Prometheus* (1818); Gothic science fiction.

Edgar Allan Poe (1809–49), U.S. writer and poet: *Tales of the Grotesque and Arabesque* (1840).

Bram Stoker (1847–1912), Irish novelist and story writer: *Dracula* (1897).

Robert Louis Stevenson (1850–94), Scottish novelist: *The Strange Case of Dr. Jekyll and Mr. Hyde* (1886).

M. R. James (1862–1936), English scholar: *Ghost Stories of an Antiquary* (1904).

Edgar Rice Burroughs (1875–1950), U.S. novelist: *Tarzan of the Apes* (1914).

H. P. Lovecraft (1890–1937), U.S. short-story writer and poet: *Shadow over Innsmouth* (1936).

J. R. R. Tolkien (1892–1973), English author and scholar: *The Lord of the Rings* (3 vols, 1954–55).

Mervyn Peake (1911–68), English novelist and poet: *Gormenghast* trilogy (1946–59).

Stephen King (b. 1947), American novelist and short-story writer: *Carrie* (1974), *The Shining* (1977).

Terry Pratchett (b. 1948), English novelist: *The Colour of Magic* (1983) and other "Discworld" fantasies.

Frankenstein: Hollywood's 1931 interpretation of Mary Shelley's novel.

Timeline

1835 Théophile Gautier, French poet and novelist, *Mademoiselle de Maupin*. Georg Büchner, German dramatist, *Danton's Death*.

1836 Charles Dickens, English novelist, *Sketches by Boz*, *Pickwick Papers*. Nikolai Gogol, Russian novelist and dramatist, *The Government Inspector*. Antonio García Gutiérrez, Spanish poet and playwright, *El Trovador*.

1837 Dickens, *Oliver Twist*.

1838 Poe, *The Narrative of Arthur Gordon Pym* (unfinished novel).

1839 Mikhail Lermontov, Russian novelist, *A Hero of Our Time*. Stendhal, *La Chartreuse de Parme*.

1840 Prosper Mérimée, French novelist, *Colomba*.

1842 Micolai Gogol, *Dead Souls*. Thomas Babington Macaulay, English historian, *Lays of Ancient Rome*.

1843 Dickens, *A Christmas Carol*. James R. Lowell, U.S. poet and essayist, *Poems*.

1844 Alexandre Dumas (Dumas père), French novelist, *The Three Musketeers*, *The Count of Monte Cristo*.

1846 Fyodor Dostoyevsky, Russian novelist, *Poor Folk*. George Sand, *La Mare au diable*.

1847 Charlotte Brontë, English novelist, *Jane Eyre*. Emily Brontë, *Wuthering Heights*. Mérimée, *Carmen*. Thackeray, *Vanity Fair*.

1848 Alexandre Dumas (Dumas fils), *La Dame aux Camélias*. Mrs. Elizabeth Gaskell, English novelist, *Mary Barton*.

1849 Dickens, *David Copperfield*.

1850 Nathaniel Hawthorne, U.S. novelist, *The Scarlet Letter*. Tennyson, *In Memoriam*. Thackeray, *Pendennis*.

1851 George Borrow, English travel writer, *Lavengro*. Hawthorne, *The House of the Seven Gables*. Herman Melville, U.S. novelist, *Moby Dick*.

1852 Dickens, *Bleak House*. Gérard de Nerval, French writer, *Contes et facéties*. Harriet Beecher Stowe, U.S. propagandist, *Uncle Tom's Cabin*.

1853 Matthew Arnold, English poet, *The Scholar-Gypsy*. C. Brontë, *Villette*.

1854 Charles Kingsley, English novelist, *Westward Ho!* Nerval, *Les Filles du feu*. Henry David Thoreau, U.S. essayist, *Walden* or *Life in the Woods*.

1855 Robert Browning, English poet, *Dramatic Romances and Lyrics*. Gaskell, *North and South*. Henry Wadsworth Longfellow, U.S. poet, *The Song of Hiawatha*. Anthony Trollope, English novelist, *The Warden*. Ivan Turgenev, Russian novelist, *A Month in the Country*. Walt Whitman, U.S. poet, *Leaves of Grass* (compl. 1889).

1856 Gustave Flaubert, French novelist, *Madame Bovary*.

1857 Borrow, *The Romany Rye*. Elizabeth Barrett Browning, English poet, *Aurora Leigh*. Trollope, *Barchester Towers*. Charles Baudelaire, French poet, *Les Fleurs du Mal*.

NOVELS

Fiction has been produced from the earliest times, but the branch of literature known as the novel is usually considered to have emerged during the 1700s. It has been defined as an invented prose narrative, of volume length or more, with a plot and characters which, in most cases, could occur in real life. A reading list of novels would include most of the following works:

Robinson Crusoe (1719), Daniel Defoe, English.

Pamela (1740), Samuel Richardson, English.

The History of Tom Jones (1749), Henry Fielding, English.

The Life and Opinions of Tristram Shandy (1760), Laurence Sterne, Irish.

Pride and Prejudice (1813), Jane Austen, English.

The Last of the Mohicans (1826), James Fenimore Cooper, American.

Le Rouge et le noir (1830), Stendhal, French.

Le Père Goriot (1834), Honoré de Balzac, French.

Dead Souls (1842), Nikolai Gogol, Russian.

Vanity Fair (1847), William Thackeray, English.

Jane Eyre (1847), Charlotte Brontë, English.

Wuthering Heights (1847), Emily Brontë, English.

Moby Dick (1851) Herman Melville, American.

Bleak House (1852), Charles Dickens, English.

Madame Bovary (1856), Gustave Flaubert, French.

Fathers and Sons (1862), Ivan Turgenev, Russian.

Crime and Punishment (1866), Fyodor Dostoyevsky, Russian.

War and Peace (1863–69), Leo Tolstoy, Russian.

Middlemarch (1872), George Eliot, English.

The Portrait of a Lady (1880), Henry James, American.

Adventures of Huckleberry Finn (1884), Mark Twain, American.

Germinal (1885), Emile Zola, French.

The Mayor of Casterbridge (1886), Thomas Hardy, English.

Sister Carrie (1900), Theodore Dreiser, American.

Nostromo (1904), Joseph Conrad, Polish-born English.

The House of Mirth (1905), Edith Wharton, American.

Howards End (1910), E. M. Forster, English.

À la recherche du temps perdu (1913–27), Marcel Proust, French.

Women in Love (1920), D. H. Lawrence, English.

Ulysses (1922), James Joyce, Irish.

The Magic Mountain (1924), Thomas Mann, German.

The Great Gatsby (1925), F. Scott Fitzgerald, American.

The Castle (1926), Franz Kafka, German.

Steppenwolf (1927), Hermann Hesse, German.

To the Lighthouse (1927), Virginia Woolf, English.

The Sound and the Fury (1929), William Faulkner, American.

A Farewell to Arms (1929), Ernest Hemingway, American.

Tropic of Cancer (1934), Henry Miller, American.

Goodbye to Berlin (1939), Christopher Isherwood, English.

The Grapes of Wrath (1940), John Steinbeck, American.

The Power and the Glory (1940), Graham Greene, English.

Native Son (1940), Richard Wright, American.

Malone Dies (1951), Samuel Beckett, Irish.

The Catcher in the Rye (1951), J. D. Salinger, American.

The Adventures of Augie March (1953), Saul Bellow, American.

Go Tell it on the Mountain (1953), James Baldwin, American.

The Lord of the Flies (1954), William Golding, English.

Lolita (1955), Vladimir Nabokov, Russian-born American.

Doctor Zhivago (1957), Boris Pasternak, Russian.

Gimpel the Fool (1957), Isaac Bashevis Singer, Polish-born American.

On the Road (1957), Jack Kerouac, American.

The Bell (1958), Iris Murdoch, English.

Naked Lunch (1959), William S. Burroughs, American.

The Tin Drum (1959), Günter Grass, German.

The Man-Eater of Malgudi (1961), R.K. Narayan, Indian.

The Confessions of Nat Turner (1967), William Styron, American.

One Hundred Years of Solitude (1967), Gabriel García Màrquez, Colombian.

Cancer Ward (1968), Alexander Solzhenitsyn, Russian.

Couples (1968), John Updike, American.

Portnoy's Complaint (1969), Philip Roth, American.

Slaughterhouse-Five (1969), Kurt Vonnegut, Jr., American.

Group Portrait with Lady (1971), Heinrich Böll, German.

Gravity's Rainbow (1973), Thomas Pynchon, American.

Aunt Julia and the Scriptwriter (1977), Mario Vargas Llosa, Peruvian.

Lanark (1981), Alasdair Gray, Scottish.

Midnight's Children (1981), Salman Rushdie, Indian-born English.

Ironweed (1984), William Kennedy, American.

The Unbearable Lightness of Being (1984), Milan Kundera, Czech.

DIARISTS AND ESSAYISTS

While being a profoundly intimate, private form, diaries can also provide invaluable eyewitness accounts of history's great events. The essay, "attempt" or "trial," was a term first coined by Montaigne, master of the form.

Michel de Montaigne (1533–92), French essayist: *Essais* (1572–80, 1588).

Francis Bacon (1561–1626), English philosopher: *Essays* (1597–1625).

Samuel Pepys (1633–1703), English diarist: *Diary* (1660–69).

William Byrd (1674–1744) U.S. tobacco planter, socialite, and diarist: *The London Diary (1717–21)*, publ. 1958.

Fanny (Frances) Burney (1752–1840), English novelist and diarist: *Diaries and Letters* (posth. publ. 1846).

Madame de Staël (1766–1817), French novelist: *De la littérature* (1800).

William Hazlitt (1778–1830), English essayist: *Plain Speaker* (1826).

Ralph Waldo Emerson (1803–82), U.S. transcendentalist poet and essayist: *Essays* (1841, 1844).

Oliver Wendell Holmes (1809–94), U.S. academic and essayist: *Autocrat of the Breakfast Table* (1857-1858).

Henry David Thoreau (1817–62), U.S. transcendentalist writer: *Walden* (1854).

Edmond (1822–96) and **Jules** (1830–70) **de Goncourt**, French diarists: *Journal des Goncourts* (9 vols, 1887–96).

Francis Kilvert (1840–79), English clergyman: *Diary* (publ. 1970)

George Orwell (1903–50), novelist and essayist: *Inside the Whale* (1940).

Gore Vidal (b. 1925), U.S. novelist: *Collected Essays* (1993).

Anne Frank (1929–45), German Jewish schoolgirl: *Diary*, (1942–44).

Susan Sontag (b. 1933), U.S. critic: *Against Interpretation* (1966).

Frontispiece of Walden, *Thoreau's account of a two-year experiment in self-sufficiency.*

WALDEN.

By HENRY D. THOREAU,
AUTHOR OF "A WEEK ON THE CONCORD AND MERRIMACK RIVERS."

I do not propose to write an ode to dejection, but to brag as lustily as chanticleer in the morning, standing on his roost, f rely to wake my neighbors up. — Page 8

BOSTON:
HOUGHTON, MIFFLIN AND COMPANY.
The Riverside Press, Cambridge
1881.

THE LITERATURE OF TRAVEL

During medieval and Renaissance times merchants wrote down tales of their journeys. As curiosity about the world developed, explorers sent reports of their adventures home. By the 1700s, the "Grand Tour" of Europe had become an obligatory part of young gentlemen's education. Travel writing retains its attraction, although nowadays it is more sociological than geographical.

Pausanias (c. A.D. 160–80), Greek geographer: *Itinerary*, the earliest surviving guidebook, a ten-volume work that provides much of our knowledge of the myths and monuments of ancient Greece.

Marco Polo (1254–1324), Venetian traveler: *Divisament dou Monde* (1298), the major source of information on Asia during the Renaissance.

Ibn Battutah (1304–68), Arab traveler and geographer: *Rihla* (Journey), records some of his travels in the Muslim world, India, China, and Sumatra.

Richard Hakluyt (1552–1616), English diplomat and traveler: *Divers Voyages Touching the Discoverie of America* (1582), achievements of British navigators.

James Boswell (1740–95), Scottish writer: *Journal of a Tour of the Hebrides* (1785), accompanying Samuel Johnson.

Mary Wollstonecraft (1759–97), Anglo-Irish feminist and novelist: *A Short Residence in Sweden* (1796).

Alexis de Tocqueville (1805–59), French historian: *Journeys to England and Ireland* (c. 1837–57).

Isabella Bird (1831–1904), English traveller: *A Lady's Life in the Rocky Mountains* (1879).

Charles Doughty (1843–1926), English poet: *Travels in Arabia Deserta* (1888).

Henry James (1843–1916), U.S. writer: *Portraits of Places* (1883).

Lafcadio Hearn (1850–1904), U.S.-Irish journalist: *Glimpses of Unfamiliar Japan* (1894).

Robert Louis Stevenson (1850–94), Scottish novelist: *Travels with a Donkey in the Cevennes* (1879).

Mary Kingsley (1862–1900), English traveler: *Travels in West Africa* (1897).

Wilfred Thesiger (b. 1910), English explorer: *Arabian Sands* (1959).

Eric Newby (b. 1919), English writer: *A Short Walk in the Hindu Kush* (1958).

Colin Thubron (b. 1939), English writer: *Behind the Wall* (1987).

Paul Theroux (b. 1941), U.S. writer: *The Great Railway Bazaar* (1975).

Stevenson's Travels with a Donkey in the Cevennes, *illustrated by Walter Crane.*

Timeline

1876 Benito Pérez Galdós, Spanish novelist, *Doña Perfecta*. Gerard Manley Hopkins, English poet, *The Wreck of the "Deutschland."* Stéphane Mallarmé, French poet, *L'Après-midi d'un faune.* Mark Twain, U.S. novelist and essayist, *The Adventures of Tom Sawyer.*

1878 Thomas Hardy, *Return of the Native.* Henry James, U.S. novelist, *The Europeans.*

1879 Henrik Ibsen, *A Doll's House.* George Meredith, English novelist, *The Egoist.*

1880 Dostoyevsky, *The Brothers Karamazov.* Lew Wallace, U.S. general and novelist, *Ben Hur.*

1881 Gustave Flaubert, *Bouvard et Pécuchet* (posth.). Anatole France, French novelist, *Le Crime de Sylvestre Bonnard.* Henry James, *Portrait of a Lady.* Paul Verlaine, *Sagesse.*

1883 Auguste Villiers de L'Isle Adam, French writer, *Contes cruels.*

1884 Joris Huysmans, French novelist, *À rebours.* Ibsen, *The Wild Duck.* Twain, *The Adventures of Huckleberry Finn.*

1885 Guy de Maupassant, French novelist, *Bel-Ami.* Meredith, *Diana of the Crossways.*

1886 Thomas Hardy, *The Mayor of Casterbridge.* James, *The Bostonians.* Arthur Rimbaud, *Illuminations.* Robert Louis Stevenson, English novelist, *Kidnapped.*

1888 Rudyard Kipling, English novelist, *Plain Tales from the Hills.*

1888 August Strindberg, Swedish dramatist, *Miss Julie.*

1890 Emily Dickinson, U.S. poet, *Poems* (posth.). Ibsen, *Hedda Gabler.*

1891 George Gissing, English novelist, *New Grub Street.* Thomas Hardy, *Tess of the D'Urbervilles.* Joris Huysmans, *Là-bas.* Oscar Wilde, Irish novelist and dramatist, *The Picture of Dorian Gray.*

1892 Henrik Ibsen, *The Master Builder.* Oscar Wilde, *Lady Windermere's Fan.*

1894 Sir Arthur Conan Doyle, Scottish novelist, *The Memoirs of Sherlock Holmes.* George Bernard Shaw, Irish dramatist, *Arms and the Man.*

1895 Anton Chekhov, Russian dramatist, *The Seagull.* Hardy, *Jude the Obscure.* Wilde, *The Importance of Being Earnest.* W. B. Yeats, Irish poet, *Poems.*

1896 A. E. Housman, English poet, *A Shropshire Lad.*

1897 Edmond Rostand, French poet and playwright, *Cyrano de Bergerac.*

1898 Thomas Hardy, *Wessex Poems.* Henry James, *The Turn of the Screw.*

1899 Stèphane Mallarmé, *Poésies.*

1900 Anton Chekhov, *Uncle Vanya.* Joseph Conrad (Jozef Korzeniowski), Polish-born English novelist, *Lord Jim.*

1901 August Strindberg, *The Dance of Death.* Rudyard Kipling, *Kim.*

1902 Arnold Bennett, English novelist, *Anna of the Five Towns.* Anton Chekhov, *Three Sisters.* Joseph Conrad,

HUMOR AND SATIRE

The purpose of humorous writing is self-evidently to amuse, whereas satire (invented in classical Rome), ridicules its subject. It may be very effective, as with Voltaire's *Candide* (1759), which helped to precipitate the French Revolution. Some important works include:

Satires:

Satires (c. 100–128): Juvenal, Roman creator of the term.

Pantagruel (1532), *Gargantua* (1534): François Rabelais, French humanist.

The Rape of the Lock (1712), *The Dunciad* (1728): Alexander Pope, English poet.

Gulliver's Travels (1726), *A Modest Proposal* (1729)—that the starving Irish should eat their children: Jonathan Swift, Anglo-Irish clergyman.

Decline and Fall (1928), *A Handful of Dust* (1934): Evelyn Waugh, English novelist.

Humor:

A Book of Nonsense (1846): Edward Lear, English artist and traveler.

The Diary of A Nobody (1892): George and Weedon Grossmith, English.

A Christmas Garland (1912): Max Beerbohm, English comic writer.

The Inimitable Jeeves (1923): P. G. Wodehouse, English. Considered by many the master of the comic form.

Hard Lines (1931): Ogden Nash, American light versifier.

Guys and Dolls (1932): Damon Runyon, American journalist.

At Swim-Two-Birds (1939): Flann O'Brien, Irish journalist and novelist.

Gulliver's Travels, a French edition of 1884, illustrated by V. Poirson.

CHILDREN'S LITERATURE

Before c. 1700, children's books were generally grim, godly works of moral instruction or collections of legends. Children's writing evolved as a more imaginative genre with the creation of fairy tales such as those of Charles Perrault (1628–1703), France; Jakob and Wilhelm Grimm (1827–87), Germany; and Hans Christian Andersen (1805–75), Denmark. Since the 1950s, the publishing of fiction for children has been a vast industry. Key works include:

The Water Babies (1863), Charles Kingsley, English.

Alice's Adventures in Wonderland (1865), Lewis Carroll, English.

Little Women (1868), Louisa M. Alcott, American.

Tom Sawyer (1876), Mark Twain, American.

Pinocchio (1880), Carlo Collodi, Italian.

Treasure Island (1883), Robert Louis Stevenson, Scottish.

Nights with Uncle Remus (1883), Joel Chandler Harris, American.

The Jungle Book (1894), Rudyard Kipling, English.

The Wonderful Wizard of Oz (1900), L. Frank Baum, American.

The Tale of Peter Rabbit (1900), Beatrix Potter, English.

Peter Pan (1904), J. M. Barrie, Scottish.

The Wind in the Willows (1908), Kenneth Grahame, Scottish.

Winnie-the-Pooh (1926), A. A. Milne, English.

Babar the Elephant (1931), Jean de Brunhoff, French.

Chronicles of Narnia (1950–56), C. S. Lewis, English.

The Cat in the Hat (1957), Dr. Seuss, American.

Where the Wild Things Are (1963), Maurice Sendak, American.

Charlie and the Chocolate Factory (1964), Roald Dahl, English.

Hans Christian Andersen's Wild Swans, *illustrated by the Irish artist Harry Clarke.*

THE SHORT STORY AND NOVELLA

Short stories made their first appearance on Egyptian papyri. Supernatural and historical short stories were perfected by Chinese authors of the Tang period (618–907). The form reached its peak during the 1800s in Russia, Europe, and the United States. It is generally accepted that a short story runs to about 2,500–10,000 words; a long short story is over 10,000 words; a novella, 20,000 or more words. Masterpieces of the form include:

Decameron (1348–53), Giovanni Boccaccio, Italian.
Contes drolatiques (1833), Honoré de Balzac, French.
Mosses from an Old Manse (1846), Nathaniel Hawthorne, American.
Boule de suif (1880), Guy de Maupassant, French.
Motley Stories (1886), Anton Chekhov, Russian.
Plain Tales from the Hills (1888), Rudyard Kipling, English.
Tales of Soldiers and Civilians (1891), Ambrose Bierce, American.
Cabbages and Kings (1904), O. Henry, American.
Dubliners (1914), James Joyce, Irish.
Winesburg, Ohio (1919), Sherwood Anderson, American.
The Garden Party (1920), Katherine Mansfield, New Zealander.
Red Cavalry (1926), Isaac Babel, Russian.
Bones of Contention (1936), Frank O'Connor, Irish.
Collected Stories (1956), V. S. Pritchett, English.
Everything That Rises Must Converge (1965), Flannery O'Connor, American.
Marriages and Infidelities (1972), Joyce Carol Oates, American.
Will You Please Be Quiet, Please? (1976), Raymond Carver, American.
The Collected Stories (1979), John Cheever, American.

HISTORICAL AND WAR NOVELS

The historical novel often contains both historical and fictional characters and events, and attempts to offer an accurate impression of previous ways of life. It may also provide the author with the necessary distance to assess political problems relevant to his or her own time. Today the form, sometimes known as the "bodice-ripper," is enormously popular at the lower end of the market and sells by the thousands. War novels share many features with historical novels, but concentrate on military activities and their effects on humankind. Major works include:

Simplicissimus (1669): Johann von Grimmelshausen, German novelist.
La Princesse de Clèves (1678): Comtesse de la Fayette. Thought to be the first example of the historical novel form.
Waverley (1814): Sir Walter Scott, Scottish novelist who emphatically established the historical form.
The Betrothed (1825-27): Alessandro Manzoni, Italian novelist and poet. Considered one of the greatest Italian novels.
Le Rouge et le Noir (1830): Stendhal, French novelist. Remarkable for its political and psychological dimensions.
A Tale of Two Cities (1859): Charles Dickens, English novelist. Paris and London at the time of the French Revolution (modeled on historian Carlyle's *The French Revolution*).
The Cloister and the Hearth (1861): Charles Reade, English novelist. Life in the 1400s.
War and Peace (1863–69): Leo Tolstoy, Russian novelist. Russian society during the Napoleonic Wars of the early 1800s.
The Red Badge of Courage (1895): Stephen Crane, U.S. novelist and poet. Set in the Civil War.

The Scarlet Pimpernel (1905): Baroness Orczy (Mrs. Montague Barstow), Hungarian-born English novelist. Courageous Englishmen rescue French aristocrats from the terrors of the French Revolution.
All Quiet on the Western Front (1929): Erich Maria Remarque, German (later American) novelist. The classic novel of World War I.
I Claudius (1934): Robert Graves, English novelist and poet. Set in imperial Rome.
Regency Buck (1935): Georgette Heyer, English historical and detective novelist. First of a number of historical romances set in the Regency period. Pioneer of the "bodice-ripper."
Gone with the Wind (1936): Margaret Mitchell, U.S. novelist. Novel during the Civil War and Reconstruction that became a famous film.
The Happy Return (1937): C. S. Forester, English novelist. First of the "Hornblower" novels about naval warfare in the Napoleonic era.
The Naked and the Dead (1948): Norman Mailer, American novelist. Pacific campaign of World War II.
The Cruel Sea (1951): Nicholas Monsarrat, English novelist: the Battle of the Atlantic during World War II.
Andersonville (1956): MacKinlay Kantor, American novelist. Life around a Civil War prisoner-of-war camp..
The Leopard (1958): Giuseppe Tomasi di Lampedusa, Italian novelist. Sicily in the later 1800s.
The King Must Die (1958), *The Bull from the Sea* (1962): Mary Renault, English novelist. Ancient Greece.
Burr (1973) and other novels: Gore Vidal, U.S. novelist and essayist. American political life.

Timeline

Heart of Darkness. André Gide, French novelist, *The Immoralist*. Maxim Gorky, Russian novelist, *The Lower Depths*.
1903 Samuel Butler, *The Way of All Flesh* (posth.). R. W. Emerson, *Complete Works* (posth.). G. R. Gissing, *The Private Papers of Henry Ryecroft*. Jack London, U.S. novelist, *Call of the Wild*. G. B. Shaw, *Man and Superman*.
1904 Anton Chekhov, *The Cherry Orchard*. Conrad, *Nostromo*. Henry James, *The Golden Bowl*. John Millington Synge, Irish dramatist, *Riders to the Sea*.
1906 John Galsworthy, English novelist, *The Man of Property*.
1907 Joseph Conrad, *The Secret Agent*. Synge, *The Playboy of the Western World*. Jacinto Benavente, Spanish playwright, *Los intereses credos*.
1908 E. M. Forster, English novelist, *A Room with a View*.
1909 Count Maurice Maeterlinck, Belgian dramatist, *The Blue Bird*. Andrei Bely, Russian novelist, *The Silver Dove*.
1910 E. M. Forster, *Howards End*. H. G. Wells, English novelist, *The History of Mr. Polly*.
1911 Max Beerbohm, English essayist and novelist, *Zuleika Dobson*. Saki (H. H. Munro), English novelist and short-story writer, *The Chronicles of Clovis*.
1912 Anna Ahkmatova, Russian poet, *Evening*. Thomas Mann, German novelist, *Death in Venice*. Saki, *The Unbearable Bassington*. Rabindranath Tagore, Indian poet, *A Handful of Songs*.
1913 Guillaume Apollinaire, French poet, *Alcools*. Bely, *Petersburg*. Alain-Fournier,

Gone With the Wind: Clark Gable and Vivien Leigh in the 1939 Hollywood version.

Timeline

French novelist, *Le Grand Meaulnes*. D. H. Lawrence, English novelist, *Sons and Lovers*. Marcel Proust, French novelist, *À la recherche du temps perdu* (compl. 1927). G. B. Shaw, *Pygmalion*.

1914 Robert Frost, U.S. poet, *North of Boston*. James Joyce, Irish novelist and short-story writer, *Dubliners*, *A Portrait of the Artist as a Young Man* (compl. 1915). Tagore, *Chitra*.

1915 Rupert Brooke, English poet, *1914 and Other Poems*. Ford Madox Ford, English novelist, *The Good Soldier*. Lawrence, *The Rainbow*. W. Somerset Maugham, English novelist, *Of Human Bondage*.

1916 Henri Barbusse, French novelist, *Under Fire*. Franz Kafka, Austrian novelist, *Metamorphosis*. Carl Sandburg, U.S. Poet, *Chicago Poems*.

1917 T. S. Eliot, English poet, *Prufrock and Other Observations*. Knut Hamsun, Norwegian novelist, *Growth of the Soil*. Ezra Pound, U.S. poet and critic of poets, *The Cantos* (first of a series compl. in 1959).

1918 Sherwood Anderson, U.S. novelist, *Winesburg, Ohio*. Apollinaire, *Calligrammes*. Hopkins, *Poems* (posth.).

1919 Ronald Firbank, English novelist, *Valmouth*. Maugham, *The Moon and Sixpence*.

1920 Colette, *Chéri*. Lawrence, *Women in Love*. Sinclair Lewis, U.S. novelist, *Main Street*. Wilfrid Owen, English poet, *Poems* (posth.). Edith Wharton, U.S. novelist, *The Age of Innocence*.

1921 Aldous Huxley, English novelist, *Crome Yellow*. Luigi Pirandello, Italian dramatist, *Six Characters in Search of an Author*.

1922 T. S. Eliot, *The Waste Land*. A. E. Housman, *Last Poems*. Joyce, *Ulysses*. Sinclair Lewis, *Babbitt*.

1923 Rainer-Maria Rilke, Austrian poet, *Duino Elegies*. Wallace Stevens, U.S. poet, *Harmonium*.

1924 Ford Maddox Ford, *Parade's End* (compl. 1928). E. M. Forster, *A Passage to India*. Thomas Mann, *The Magic Mountain*. Pablo Neruda, Chilean poet, *Twenty Love Poems and a Song of Despair*. Sean O'Casey, Irish dramatist, *Juno and the Paycock*. Eugene O'Neill, U.S. dramatist, *Desire under the Elms*. Saint-John Perse, French poet, *Anabase*. Shaw, *Saint Joan*.

1925 Noel Coward, English dramatist, *Hay Fever*. John Dos Passos, U.S. novelist, *Manhattan Transfer*. F. Scott Fitzgerald, U.S. novelist, *The Great Gatsby*. Gide, *The Counterfeiters*. Kafka, *The Trial* (posth.). Eugenio Montale, Italian novelist, *Ossi di Seppia*. Virginia Woolf, English novelist, *Mrs. Dalloway*.

1926 Jean Cocteau, French poet and dramatist, *Orphée*. Kafka, *The Castle* (posth.). Marianne Moore, U.S. poet, *The Pangolin and Other Verse*.

1927 Hermann Hesse, German novelist,

SCIENCE FICTION

Science fiction (SF) has as its subjects real or imaginary techno-scientific developments and environmental changes, which may have far-reaching consequences. The boundary between science fiction and fantasy is often indefinable. Among the writers most influential in the development of the genre are:

Jules Verne (1828–1905), French: *20,000 Leagues Under the Sea* (1870).

H. G. Wells (1866–1946), English: *The War of the Worlds* (1898).

Evgeny Zamyatin (1884–1937), Russian: *We* (1920–21).

Aldous Huxley (1894–1963), English: *Brave New World* (1932).

Arthur C. Clarke (b. 1917), English: *2001: A Space Odyssey* (1968).

Isaac Asimov (1920–92), Russian-born American who coined the term "robotics": *I, Robot* (1950).

Ray Bradbury (b. 1920), American: *The Martian Chronicles* (1950).

Philip K. Dick (1928–82), American: *The Man in the High Castle* (1959).

J. G. Ballard (b. 1930), English: *The Drowned World* (1962).

William Gibson (b. 1948), Canadian: *Neuromancer* (1984). A landmark "cyberpunk" novel.

Title page of a volume combining two novels by the French science-fiction writer Jules Verne, who initiated this highly popular form as we know it today.

DETECTIVE AND ESPIONAGE LITERATURE

As a genre the detective story dates from the 1850s, along with the adventure novel or "thriller." The classic "whodunnit" offers the reader a puzzle to solve. More recent developments are the "private eye," "police procedural," and espionage novels. Important works include:

The Mystery of Marie Roget (1845), often called the first modern detective story: Edgar Allan Poe, American.

The Moonstone (1868), first English detective story: Wilkie Collins, English.

A Study in Scarlet (1887), debut of "Sherlock Holmes": Arthur Conan Doyle, Scottish.

The Innocence of Father Brown (1911), detective novel: G. K. Chesterton, English.

The Thirty-nine Steps (1915), espionage thriller: John Buchan, Scottish.

The Mysterious Affair at Styles (1920), classic English detective novel: Agatha Christie, English.

Whose Body? (1923), detective novel: Dorothy L. Sayers, English.

The Maltese Falcon (1930), private eye novel: Dashiell Hammett, American.

M. Gallet Deceased (1931), first "Inspector Maigret" novel: Georges Simenon, Belgian.

The Big Sleep (1939), introducing private eye Philip Marlowe: Raymond Chandler, American.

Casino Royale (1953), debut of "James Bond, 007": Ian Fleming, English.

The Spy Who Came in From The Cold (1963) espionage: John Le Carré, English.

Blood on the Moon (1984), thriller: James Ellroy, American.

A Taste for Death (1986), detective novel: P. D. James, English.

The Silence of the Lambs (1990), thriller: Thomas Harris, American.

Cover of a novel featuring private eye Philip Marlowe (1939).

PSEUDONYMS

Many writers have used pen names for a variety of reasons. In the following cases, the writer's pseudonym (given first) has become far better known than his or her real name:

AE: George William Russell (1867–1935), Irish poet.

Anna Akhmatova: Anna Andreeyevna Gorenko (1888–1966), Russian poet.

Guillaume Apollinaire: Wilhelm Apollinaris Kostrowitzky (1880–1918), French poet.

Lewis Carroll: Rev. Charles Lutwidge Dodgson (1832–98), British children's writer.

Isak Dinesen: Baroness Karen Blixen (1885–1962), Danish novelist and story writer.

George Eliot: Mary Ann (Marian) Evans (1819–80), British novelist.

Ford Madox Ford: Ford Hermann Hueffer (1873–1939), British novelist.

Maxim Gorky: Aleksei Maksimovich Peshkov (1868–1936), Russian writer.

O. Henry: William Sidney Porter (1862–

George Eliot (Mary Ann Evans), aged 46.

1910), U.S. short-story writer.

John Le Carré: David Cornwell (b. 1931), British spy novelist.

Ed McBain and **Evan Hunter**: Salvatore A. Lombino (b. 1926), U.S. crime writer (as McBain) and novelist (as Hunter).

Hugh MacDiarmid: Christopher Grieve (1892–1978), Scottish poet.

Yukio Mishima: Hiraoka Kimitake (1925–70), Japanese novelist.

Molière: Jean Baptiste Poquelin (1622–73), French playwright.

Alberto Moravia: Alberto Pincherle (1907–90), Italian novelist.

Pablo Neruda: Ricardo Reyes (1904–73), Chilean poet.

George Orwell: Eric Blair (1903–59), British novelist and essayist.

Ouida: Marie Louise de la Ramée (1839–1908), British novelist.

Ellery Queen: Frederic Dannay (1905–82) and Manfred B. Lee (1905–71), U.S. writers.

Mary Renault: Eileen Challans (1905–83), British novelist.

Jean Rhys: Gwen Williams (1894–1979), British novelist.

Françoise Sagan: Françoise Quoirez (b. 1935), French novelist.

George Sand: Amandine Aurore Lucie Dupin (1804–76), French novelist.

Saki: Hector Hugh Munro (1870–1916), British novelist and story writer.

Ignazio Silone: Secondo Tranquilli (1900–78), Italian novelist.

Mickey Spillane: Frank Morrison (b. 1918), U.S. crime writer.

Stendhal: Henri Marie Beyle (1783–1842), French novelist.

Tom Stoppard: Thomas Straussler (b. 1937), Czech-born British playwright.

Mark Twain: Samuel Langhorne Clemens (1835–1910), U.S. novelist and humorist.

EROTICA

Erotica, or sexually oriented literature, is distinguished from pornography by its aesthetic value. Many great writers have produced erotica, often only for private circulation, among them Voltaire, Tennyson, and Swinburne. Well-known erotic works include:

Ovid (43 B.C.–A.D. 17), Roman: *Ars Amatoria* (The Art of Love) (*c.* A.D. 8).

Giovanni Boccaccio (1313–75), Italian, *The Decameron* (1348–53).

Pietro Aretino (1492–1557), Italian: *Sonetti Lussuriosi*, obscene sonnets, long circulated with accompanying engravings.

Anaïs Nin (1903–77), French-born American: *Delta of Venus* (1969), *Journals* (1966–83), candid and explicit accounts of some of the leading avant-garde Parisians

Thomas Nashe (1567–1601), English: *The Merie Ballad of Nashe, His Dildo*, a long, obscene poem dating from 1601.

John Cleland (1709–89), English novelist: *Fanny Hill: Memoirs of a Woman of*

Pleasure (1748–49), not openly published unexpurgated until 1963.

Denis Diderot (1713–84), French man of letters: *Indiscreet Toys* (1749).

Robert Burns (1759–96), Scottish poet: *The Merry Muses of Caledonia*, a collection of bawdy verse that was not openly published unexpurgated until 1965.

Comte (called **Marquis**) **de Sade** (1740–1814), French novelist from whose name comes the word sadism: *Les 120 Journées de Sodome* (1784), *Justine ou Les Malheurs de la Vertu* (1791).

D. H. Lawrence (1885–1930), English novelist and poet: *Lady Chatterley's Lover* (1928). Its publication unexpurgated in Britain in 1963 is said to have signaled the onset of the "permissive society."

Henry Miller (1891–1980), American novelist: *The Rosy Crucifixion* trilogy (1949–60).

Pauline Réage (pseud.), French: *The Story of O* (1970), a classic of masochism.

Timeline

1944 Jean Anouilh, French dramatist, *Antigone*. T. S. Eliot, *Four Quartets*. Tennessee Williams, U.S. dramatist, *The Glass Menagerie*.

1945 S. Maugham, *The Razor's Edge*. Nancy Mitford, English novelist, *The Pursuit of Love*. George Orwell, English essayist and novelist, *Animal Farm*. Eveleyn Waugh, English novelist, *Brideshead Revisited*. H. Hesse, *The Glass Bead Game*.

1946 Elizabeth Bishop, U.S. poet, *North and South*. Nikos Kazantzakis, Greek novelist, *Zorba the Greek*. Robert Lowell, U.S. poet, *Lord Weary's Castle*. Eugene O'Neill, *The Iceman Cometh*. Dylan Thomas, Welsh poet, *Deaths and Entrances*.

1947 Malcolm Lowry, English novelist, *Under the Volcano*. Primo Levi, Italian writer, *If This is a Man*. Thomas Mann, *Doctor Faustus*. Tenessee Williams, *A Streetcar Named Desire*.

1948 A. Camus, *La Peste*. Truman Capote, U.S. novelist, *Other Voices, Other Rooms*. W. Faulkner, *Intruder in the Dust*. Eugène Ionesco, French-Romanian dramatist, *The Bald Prima Donna*. Norman Mailer, U.S. novelist, *The Naked and the Dead*.

1949 Simone de Beauvoir, French novelist and essayist, *The Second Sex*. Heinrich Böll, German novelist, *The Train was on Time*. Paul Bowles, U.S. novelist, *The Sheltering Sky*. Orwell, *1984*. Arthur Miller, U.S. dramatist, *Death of a Salesman*.

1950 T. S. Eliot, *The Cocktail Party*. Isaac Bashevis Singer, U.S. novelist, *The Family Moskat*.

1951 Mulk Raj Anand, Indian novelist, *Seven Summers*. Anthony Powell, English novelist, *A Dance to the Music of Time* (12-novel sequence, compl. 1975). J. D. Salinger, U.S. novelist, *The Catcher in the Rye*. William Styron, U.S. novelist, *Lie Down in Darkness*.

1952 John Steinbeck, *East of Eden*.

1953 Jorge Luis Borges, Argentinian short-story writer, *Labyrinths*. L. P. Hartley, English novelist, *The Go-Between*. William Inge, U.S. dramatist, *Picnic*. Theodore Roethke, U.S. poet, *The Waking*.

1954 Kingsley Amis, English novelist, *Lucky Jim*. William Golding, English novelist, *The Lord of the Flies*. Simone De Beauvoir, *The Mandarins*. Iris Murdoch, Anglo-Irish novelist, *Under the Net*. Stevens, *Collected Poems*.

1955 Samuel Beckett, Irish dramatist and novelist, *Waiting for Godot*. G. Greene, *The Quiet American*. Vladimir Nabokov, U.S. novelist, *Lolita*. J. R. R. Tolkein, *The Lord of the Rings*.

1956 J. Genet, *The Balcony*. Allen Ginsberg, U.S. poet, *Howl and Other Poems*. John Osborne, English dramatist, *Look Back in Anger*.

1957 A. Camus, *La Chute*. Laurence Durrell, English novelist, *Alexandria Quartet* (compl. 1960). Jack Kerouac, U.S. novelist, *On the Road*. Boris

MAJOR LIBRARIES OF THE WORLD

Each library is shown with its name, location, date of foundation, and the approximate number of books (not including periodicals, manuscripts, etc.) held there in 1994.

Library of Congress, Washington, D.C.; 1800; 27,000,000.
British Library, London; 1753 (independent from 1973); 18,000,000.
Harvard University Library, Cambridge, MA; 1638; 12,200,000.
State V. I. Lenin Library, Moscow; 1862 (as Rumyantsev Library); 11,800,000.
New York Public Library, New York, NY; 1895; 10,000,000 (reference only).
Yale University Library, New Haven, CT; 1701; 10,000,000.
Biblioteca Academiei Romane, Bucharest; 1867; 9,400,000.
Bibliothèque Nationale, Paris; 1480; 9,000,000.
M. E. Saltykov-Shchedrin State Public Library, St. Petersburg; 1795; 8,000,000.
University of Illinois, Urbana, IL; 1867; 8,000,000.

New York Public Library, the largest city library in the United States.

NOBEL PRIZE FOR LITERATURE

Awarded annually since 1901 to the writer whom the Swedish Academy of Arts judges to have contributed most to the common good; it is currently worth around $200,000.

1901 R. Sully-Prudhomme, French poet.
1902 T. Mommsen, German historian.
1903 Björnstjerne Björnson, Norwegian novelist, poet, and dramatist.
1904 Frédéric Mistral, French Provençal poet; José Echegaray y Eizaguirre, Spanish dramatist.
1905 Henryk Sienkiewicz, Polish novelist.
1906 Giosuè Carducci, Italian poet.
1907 Rudyard Kipling, English novelist.
1908 Rudolf Christoph Eucken, German philosopher.
1909 Selma Lagerlöf, Swedish novelist.
1910 Paul von Heyse, German poet, novelist, and dramatist.
1911 Maurice Maeterlinck, Belgian dramatist.
1912 Gerhart Hauptmann, German dramatist.
1913 Rabindranath Tagore, Indian poet.
1914 No award.
1915 Romain Rolland, French novelist.
1916 Verner von Heidenstam, Swedish poet and novelist.
1917 Karl Gjellerup, Danish poet and novelist; Henrik Pontoppidan, Danish novelist and short-story writer.
1918 No award.
1919 Carl Spitteler, Swiss poet, essayist and short-story writer.
1920 Knut Hamsun, Norwegian novelist.
1921 Anatole France, French novelist.
1922 Jacinto Benavente, Spanish dramatist.
1923 William Butler Yeats, Irish poet.

1924 W. Reymont, Polish novelist.
1925 G. B. Shaw, Irish dramatist.
1926 Grazia Deledda, Italian novelist.
1927 Henri Bergson, French philosopher.
1928 Sigrid Undset, Norwegian novelist.
1929 Thomas Mann, German novelist.
1930 Sinclair Lewis, U.S. novelist.
1931 Erik Axel Karlfeldt, Swedish poet.
1932 John Galsworthy, English novelist.
1933 Ivan Bunin, Russian poet, novelist and short-story writer.
1934 Luigi Pirandello, Italian dramatist.
1935 No award.
1936 Eugene O'Neill, U.S. dramatist.
1937 R. M. du Gard, French novelist.
1938 Pearl S. Buck, U.S. novelist.
1939 Frans Sillanpää, Finnish novelist.
1940–43 No award.
1944 Johannes V. Jensen, Danish novelist.
1945 Gabriela Mistral, Chilean poet.
1946 Hermann Hesse, Swiss poet and novelist.
1947 André Gide, French novelist.
1948 T. S. Eliot, British-American poet.
1949 William Faulkner, U.S. novelist (award delayed until 1950).
1950 Bertrand Russell, English philosopher.
1951 Pär Lagerkvist, Swedish novelist.
1952 François Mauriac, French novelist.
1953 Sir Winston Churchill, English statesman and historian.
1954 Ernest Hemingway, U.S. novelist.
1955 Halldór Laxness, Icelandic novelist.
1956 Juan Ramón Jiménez, Spanish poet.
1957 Albert Camus, French novelist.
1958 Boris Pasternak, Russian novelist (declined).
1959 Salvatore Quasimodo, Italian poet.

THE PULITZER PRIZE FOR FICTION

This prize of $1,000, worth far more in terms of increased sales, is awarded annually for distinguished fiction, preferably dealing with American life, published in book form during the year by an American writer. Winners since 1960 are:

1960 Allen Drury, *Advise and Consent*.
1961 Harper Lee, *To Kill a Mockingbird*.
1962 Edwin O'Connor, *The Edge of Sadness*.
1963 William Faulkner, *The Reivers*.
1964 No award.
1965 Shirley Ann Grau, *The Keepers of the House*.
1966 Katherine Anne Porter, *Collected Stories*.
1967 Bernard Malamud, *The Fixer*.
1968 William Styron, *The Confessions of Nat Turner*.
1969 N. Scott Momaday, *House Made of Dawn*.
1970 Jean Stafford, *Collected Stories*.
1971 No award.
1972 Wallace Earle Stegner, *Angle of Repose*.
1973 Eudora Welty, *The Optimist's Daughter*.

1974 No award.
1975 Michael Shaara, *The Killer Angels*.
1976 Saul Bellow, *Humboldt's Gift*.
1977 No award.
1978 James A. McPherson, *Elbow Room*.
1979 John Cheever, *The Stories of John Cheever*.
1980 Norman Mailer, *The Executioner's Song*.
1981 John Kennedy Toole, *A Confederacy of Dunces*.
1982 John Updike, *Rabbit is Rich*.
1983 Alice Walker, *The Color Purple*.
1984 William Kennedy, *Ironweed*.
1985 Alison Lurie, *Foreign Affairs*.
1986 Larry McMurtry, *Lonesome Dove*.
1987 Peter Taylor, *A Summons to Memphis*.
1988 Toni Morrison, *Beloved*.
1989 Anne Tyler, *Breathing Lessons*.
1990 Oscar Hijuelos, *The Mambo Kings Play Songs of Love*.
1991 John Updike, *Rabbit at Rest*.
1992 Jane Smiley, *A Thousand Acres*.
1993 Robert Olen Butler, *A Good Scent from a Strange Mountain*.
1994 E. Annie Proulx, *The Shipping News*.

1960 Saint-John Perse, French poet.
1961 Ivo Andric, Yugoslavian novelist.
1962 John Steinbeck, U.S. novelist.
1963 George Seferis, Greek poet.
1964 Jean-Paul Sartre, French philosopher (declined).
1965 Mikhail Sholokov, Russian novelist.
1966 Shmuel Yosef Agnon, Israeli novelist and short-story writer; Nelly Sachs, German-born Israeli poet and dramatist.
1967 Miguel Angel Asturias, Guatemalan novelist.
1968 Yasunari Kawabata, Japanese novelist.
1969 Samuel Beckett, Irish dramatist and novelist.
1970 Alexander Solzhenitsyn, Russian novelist.
1971 Pablo Neruda, Chilean poet.
1972 Heinrich Böll, German novelist and dramatist.
1973 Patrick White, Australian novelist.
1974 Eyvind Johnson, Swedish novelist; Harry Edmund Martinson, Swedish poet, novelist, and dramatist.
1975 Eugenio Montale, Italian poet.
1976 Saul Bellow, U.S. novelist.
1977 Vicente Aleixandre, Spanish poet.
1978 Isaac Bashevis Singer, Polish-born American novelist and short-story writer (Yiddish).
1979 Odysseus Elytis, Greek poet.
1980 Czeslaw Milosz, Polish-American poet, novelist, and critic.
1981 Elias Canetti, Bulgarian-British novelist, essayist, and playwright.
1982 Gabriel García Márquez, Colombian novelist.
1983 William Golding, English novelist.

1984 Jaroslav Seifert, Czech poet.
1985 Claude Simon, French novelist.
1986 Wole Soyinka, Nigerian playwright, poet, and novelist.
1987 Joseph Brodsky, Russian-born U.S. poet.
1988 Naguib Mahfouz, Egyptian novelist.
1989 Camilo José Cela, Spanish novelist.
1990 Octavio Paz, Mexican poet.
1991 Nadine Gordimer, South African novelist.
1992 Derek Walcott, Santa Lucian poet.
1993 Toni Morrison, U.S. novelist.
1994 Kenzaburo Oe, Japanese novelist and short-story writer.

Toni Morrison receives the 1993 award.

Timeline

Pasternak, Russian novelist, *Doctor Zhivago*. Octavio Paz, Mexican poet and novelist, *Sun Stone*. Stevie Smith, English poet, *Not Waving but Drowning*.
1958 Chinua Achebe, Nigerian novelist, *Things Fall Apart*. Beckett, *Endgame*. Capote, *Breakfast at Tiffany's*. Harold Pinter, English dramatist, *The Birthday Party*.
1959 William S. Burroughs, U.S. novelist, *Naked Lunch*. Günther Grass, German novelist, *The Tin Drum*. Philip Roth, U.S. novelist, *Goodbye Columbus*.
1960 Anouilh, *Becket*. Ionesco, *Rhinoceros*. Olivia Manning, English novelist, *The Balkan Trilogy* (completed 1965). Edna O'Brien, Irish novelist, *The Country Girls*. Sylvia Plath, U.S. poet, *The Colossus*. John Updike, U.S. novelist, *Rabbit, Run*.
1961 Joseph Heller, U.S. novelist, *Catch-22*. V. S. Naipaul, Trinidadian novelist, *A House for Mr. Biswas*. White, *Riders in the Chariot*.
1962 Edward Albee, U.S. dramatist, *Who's Afraid of Virginia Woolf?* Anthony Burgess, English novelist, *A Clockwork Orange*. Friedrich Dürrenmatt, Swiss dramatist, *The Physicists*. Doris Lessing, English novelist, *The Golden Notebook*. Alexander Solzhenitsyn, Russian novelist, *One Day in the Life of Ivan Denisovich*.
1963 Akhmatova, *Requiem*. Plath, *The Bell Jar*. Thomas Pynchon, U.S. novelist, *V*.
1964 Philip Larkin, English poet, *The Whitsun Weddings*. Lowell, *For the Union Dead*. A. Miller, *After the Fall*. Joe Orton, English dramatist, *Entertaining Mr Sloane*.
1965 James Baldwin, U.S. novelist, *Another Country*. Edward Bond, English dramatist, *Saved*. N. Mailer, *An American Dream*. Yukio Mishima, *The Sea of Fertility* (novel sequence, compl. 1970). Orton, *Loot*. H. Pinter, *The Homecoming*.
1966 Bernard Malamud, U.S. novelist, *The Fixer*. Jean Rhys, English novelist, *Wide Sargasso Sea*. Paul Scott, *The Raj Quartet* (four novels, compl. 1975). Tom Stoppard, English dramatist, *Rosencrantz and Guildenstern are Dead*.
1967 Angela Carter, English novelist, *The Magic Toyshop*. Gabriel García Márquez, Colombian novelist, *One Hundred Years of Solitude*. Styron, *The Confessions of Nat Turner*. Gore Vidal, U.S. novelist, *Washington, DC*.
1968 Marianne Moore, *The Complete Poems*. Roethke, *Collected Poems* (post.). Solzhenitsyn, *Cancer Ward*. Vidal, *Myra Breckinridge*.
1969 Margaret Atwood, Canadian novelist, *The Edible Woman*.
1970 Dario Fo, Italian dramatist, *Accidental Death of an Anarchist*. Toni Morrison, U.S. novelist, *The Bluest Eye*.
1971 Mordecai Richler, Canadian novelist, *St. Urbain's Horseman*. Solzhenitsyn, *August 1914*.

Timeline

1972 Italo Calvino, Italian novelist, *Invisible Cities*. Don DeLillo, U.S. novelist, *End Zone*. Thomas Keneally, Australian novelist, *The Chant of Jimmy Blacksmith*. Amos Oz, Israeli novelist, *My Michael*.

1973 Alan Ayckbourn, English dramatist, *Absurd Person Singular*. Pynchon, *Gravity's Rainbow*. Singer, *A Crown of Feathers*.

1974 Böll, *The Lost Honour of Katharina Blum*. André Brink, South African novelist, *Looking on Darkness*.

1975 E.L. Doctorow, U.S. novelist, *Ragtime*. David Mamet, U.S. dramatist, *American Buffalo*.

1977 Mario Vargas Llosa, Peruvian novelist, *Aunt Julia and the Scriptwriter*. Colleen McCullough, Australian novelist, *The Thorn Birds*.

1978 John Irving, U.S. novelist, *The World According to Garp*.

1979 Milan Kundera, Czech novelist, *The Book of Laughter and Forgetting*. Naipaul, *A Bend in the River*. Styron, *Sophie's Choice*.

1980 Burgess, *Earthly Powers*. Umberto Eco, Italian novelist, *The Name of the Rose*. Golding, *Rites of Passage*.

1981 Burroughs, *Cities of the Red Night*. Alasdair Gray, Scottish novelist, *Lanark*. Molly Keane, Irish novelist, *Good Behaviour*. Salman Rushdie, Indian-born English novelist, *Midnight's Children*.

1982 Plath, *Collected Poems* (posth.). Alice Walker, US novelist, *The Color Purple*.

1983 J.M. Coetzee, South African novelist, *The Life and Times of Michael K*.

1984 J.G. Ballard, English novelist, *Empire of the Sun*. Carter, *Nights at the Circus*. Heller, *God Knows*. Kundera, *The Unbearable Lightness of Being*.

1985 Peter Carey, Australian novelist, *Illywhacker*. DeLillo, *White Noise*. Brian Moore, Irish novelist, *Black Robe*. Roth, *Zuckerman Bound*.

1986 Atwood, *The Handmaid's Tale*.

1987 Maya Angelou, U.S. novelist, *And Still I Rise*. Ian McEwan, English novelist, *The Child in Time*.

1988 Raymond Carver, U.S. short-story writer, *Where I'm Calling From*. Eco, *Foucault's Pendulum*. Rushdie, *The Satanic Verses*. Tom Wolfe, U.S. essayist and novelist, *The Bonfire of the Vanities*.

1989 Kazuo Ishiguro, Japanese-born English novelist, *The Remains of the Day*.

1990 Martin Amis, English novelist, *London Fields*. Angelou, *I Shall Not Be Moved*. Larry McMurtry, U.S. novelist, *Buffalo Girls*.

1991 Carter, *Wise Children*. Kundera, *Immortality*.

1992 Mamet, *Oleanna*.

1993 Atwood, *The Robber Bride*.

1994 Albee, *Three Tall Women*. Vargas Llosa, *A Fish in the Water*. A. Miller, *Broken Glass*.

THE PULITZER PRIZE FOR FICTION

The Pulitzer Prizes were endowed by Joseph Pulitzer (1847–1911), publisher of the *New York World*, in a bequest to Columbia University. The prizes, worth $3,000, honor work in 20 categories of journalism and letters, along with a prize for music. They are awarded annually by the president of Columbia on the recommendation of the Pulitzer Prize Board. The Pulitzer Prize for fiction is seen as the highest accolade for American writers. It is awarded for fiction in book form by an American author, preferably for work dealing with American life. Winners to date are:

1918 Ernest Poole. *His Family*.
1919 Booth Tarkington. *The Magnificent Andersons*.
1921 Edith Wharton. *The Age of Innocence*.
1922 Booth Tarkington. *Alice Adams*.
1923 Willa Cather. *One of Ours*.
1924 Margaret Wilson. *The Able McLaughlins*.
1925 Edna Ferber. *So Big*.
1926 Sinclair Lewis. *Arrowsmith*. (refused prize)
1927 Louise Bromfield. *Early Autumn*.
1928 Thornton Wilder. *The Bridge of San Luis Rey*.
1929 Julia M. Peterkin. *Scarlet Sister Mary*.
1930 Oliver LaFarge. *Laughing Boy*.
1931 Margaret Ayer Barnes. *Years of Grace*.
1932 Pearl S. Buck. *The Good Earth*.
1933 T. S. Stribling. *The Store*.
1934 Caroline Miller. *Lamb in His Bosom*.
1935 Josephine W. Johnson. *Now in November*.
1936 Harold L. Davis. *Honey in the Horn*.
1937 Margaret Mitchell. *Gone With the Wind*.
1938 John P. Marquand. *The Late George Apley*.
1939 Marjorie Kinnan Rawlings. *The Yearling*.
1940 John Steinbeck. *The Grapes of Wrath*.
1942 Ellen Glasgow. *In This Our Life*.
1943 Upton Sinclair. *Dragon's Teeth*.
1944 Martin Flavin. *Journey in the Dark*.
1945 John Hersey. *A Bell for Adano*.
1947 Robert Penn Warren. *All the King's Men*.
1948 James A. Michener. *Tales of the South Pacific*.

1949 James Gold Cozzens. *Guard of Honor*.
1950 A. B. Guthrie, Jr. *The Way West*.
1951 Conrad Richter. *The Town*.
1952 Herman Wouk. *The Cain Mutiny*.
1953 Ernest Hemingway. *The Old Man and the Sea*.
1955 Wiliam Faulkner. *A Fable*.
1956 MacKinlay Cantor. *Andersonville*.
1958 James Agee. *A Death in the Family*.
1959 Robert Lewis Taylor. *The Travel of Jamie McPheeters*.
1960 Allen Drury. *Advise and Consent*.
1961 Harper Lee. *To Kill a Mockingbird*.
1962 Edwin O'Connor. *The Edge of Sadness*.
1963 Wiliam Faulkner. *The Reivers*.
1965 Shirley Ann Grau. *The Keepers of the House*.
1966 Katherine Anne Porter. *The Stories of Katherine Anne Porter*.
1967 Bernard Malamud. *The Fixer*.
1968 William Styron. *The Confessions of Nat Turner*.
1969 N. Scott Momaday. *House Made of Dawn*.
1970 Jean Stafford. *Collected Stories*.
1972 Wallace Stegner. *Angle of Repose*.
1973 Eudora Welty. *The Optimist's Daughter*.
1975 Michael Shaara. *The Killer Angels*.
1976 Saul Bellow. *Humboldt's Gift*.
1978 James Alan McPherson. *Elbow Room*.
1979 John Cheever. *The Stories of John Cheever*.
1980 Norman Mailer. *The Executioner's Song*.
1981 John Kennedy Toole. *A Confederacy of Dunces*.
1982 John Updike. *Rabbit is Rich*.
1983 Alice Walker. *The Color Purple*.
1984 William Kennedy. *Ironweed*.
1985 Alison Lurie. *Foreign Affairs*.
1986 Larry McMurty. *Lonesome Dove*.
1987 Peter Taylor. *A Summons to Memphis*.
1988 Toni Morrison. *Beloved*.
1989 Anne Tyler. *Breathing Lessons*.
1990 Oscar Hijuelos. *The Mambo Kings Play Songs of Love*.
1991 John Updike. *Rabbit at Rest*.
1992 Jane Smiley. *A Thousand Acres*.
1993 Robert Olen Butler. *A Good Scent from a Strange Mountain*.
1994 E. Annie Proulx. *The Shipping News*.

THE PULITZER PRIZE FOR AMERICAN POETRY

1980 Donald Justice. *Selected Poems*.
1981 James Schuyler. *The Morning of the Poem*.
1982 Sylvia Plath. *The Collected Poems*.
1983 Gallway Kinnell. *Selected Poems*.
1984 Mary Oliver. *American Primitive*.
1985 Carolyn Kizer. *Yin*.
1986 Henry Taylor. *The Flying Change*.
1987 Rita Dove. *Thomas and Beulah*.
1988 William Meridith. *Partial Accounts: New and Collected Poems*.
1989 Richard Wilbur. *New and Collected Poems*.
1990 Charles Simic. *The World Doesn't End*.
1991 Mona van Duyn. *Near Changes*.
1992 James Tate. *Selected Poems*.
1993 Louise Glück. *The Wild Iris*.
1994 Yusef Komunyakaa. *Neon Vernacular*.

PROMINENT PEOPLE

AESCHYLUS (525–456 B.C.) Ancient Greek tragedian, known as the father of Greek tragedy. *Oresteia* trilogy.

ALBEE, Edward (b. 1928) U.S. playwright. *Who's Afraid of Virginia Woolf?*

ANDERSEN, Hans Christian (1805–75) Danish author, famous for fairy tales. *The Emperor's New Clothes, The Ugly Duckling, The Snow Queen.*

ANDERSON, Sherwood (1876–1941) U.S. short-story writer. *Winesberg, Ohio.*

ANGELOU, Maya (b. 1928) African-American writer who read her poem "On the Pulse of the Morning" at President Clinton's Inauguration.

ANOUILH, Jean (1910–87) French playwright. *Thieves' Carnival, Antigone, The Lark, Becket.*

ARNOLD, Matthew (1822–88) English poet and critic. *The Scholar-Gypsy, Culture and Anarchy.*

ATWOOD, Margaret (Eleanor) (b. 1939) Canadian novelist, poet, and story writer. *The Edible Woman, Surfacing, The Handmaid's Tale.*

AUDEN, W(ystan H)ugh (1907–73) Anglo-American poet, essayist, and critic. The "Poet of the Thirties." *Look, Stranger!, The Shield of Achilles.*

AUSTEN, Jane (1775–1817) English novelist noted for dry humor and witty elegance. *Sense and Sensibility, Pride and Prejudice, Emma.*

BABEL, Isaac (1894–1941) Russian short-story writer, exiled and died in Siberia. *Odessa Tales, Red Cavalry.*

BALDWIN, James Arthur (1924–87) African-American novelist. *Go Tell it on the Mountain, Another Country.*

BALZAC, Honoré de (1799–1850) French novelist, an early master of Realism. *La Comédie humaine, Les Paysans.*

BAUDELAIRE, Charles (Pierre) (1821–67) French Symbolist poet and critic. *Les Fleurs du mal, Les Paradis artificiels.*

BECKETT, Samuel (1906–89) Irish experimental novelist and dramatist. *Molloy* trilogy, *Waiting for Godot.*

BELLOW, Saul (b. 1915) Canadian-born realist U.S. novelist. *Herzog, Humboldt's Gift.*

BISHOP, Elizabeth (1911–79) U.S. poet. *North and South, A Cold Spring.*

BLAKE, William (1757–1827) English poet, painter, engraver, and mystic. *Songs of Innocence, Songs of Experience.*

BOCCACCIO, Giovanni (1313–75) Italian writer and diplomat. *Decameron.*

BÖLL, Heinrich Theodor (1917–85) German novelist of life during the Nazi regime. *The Unguarded House, The Bread of our Early Years.*

BORGES, Jorge Luis (1899–1986) Argentinian poet and short-story writer. of intricate and fantasy-woven stories. *Labyrinths, The Aleph.*

BRECHT, Bertolt (1898–1956) German Marxist playwright. *Threepenny Opera, Mother Courage and Her Children, The Good Woman of Sezuan, Galileo.*

BRONTË sisters English novelists. **Anne** (1820–49): *Agnes Grey,* **Charlotte** (1816–55): *Jane Eyre,* **Emily** (1818–48): *Wuthering Heights.*

BROWNING, Elizabeth Barrett (1806–61) English poet. *Aurora Leigh, Sonnets from the Portuguese.*

BROWNING, Robert (1812–89) English Victorian poet. Master of dramatic monologue. *The Ring and the Book.*

BULGAKOV, Mikhail (1891–1940) Russian novelist and playwright. *The White Guard, The Master and Margarita.*

BURNS, Robert (1759–96) Scottish poet. *Tam o' Shanter, Auld Lang Syne.*

BUTLER, Samuel (1835–1902) English satirist. *The Way of All Flesh.*

BYRON, Lord (1788–1824) English poet. *Childe Harold's Pilgrimage, Don Juan.*

CALVINO, Italo (1923–85) Italian "fantastic" novelist and short-story writer. *Invisible Cities.*

CAMUS, ALBERT (1913–60) French Existentialist novelist and playwright. *L'Etranger, La Peste.*

CATHER, Willa (1876–1947) U.S. novelist. *My Antonia, One of Ours.*

CÉLINE, Louis–Ferdinand (1894–1961) French novelist. *Journey to the End of the Night.*

CERVANTES Saavedra, Miguel de (1547–1616) Spanish novelist. *Don Quixote de la Mancha.*

CHAUCER, Geoffrey (c. 1343–1400) English poet, first great English writer. *The Canterbury Tales.*

CHEKHOV, Anton (1860–1904) Russian short-story writer and influential playwright. *Uncle Vanya, The Three Sisters, The Cherry Orchard.*

COCTEAU, Jean (1889–1963) French novelist, poet, and playwright. *Les Enfants terribles, La Belle et la bête.*

COLERIDGE, Samuel Taylor (1772–1834) English Romantic poet and critic. *The Rime of the Ancient Mariner, Biographia Literaria.*

COLETTE, Sidonie-Gabrielle (1873–1954) French novelist. *Claudine, Chéri, Gigi.*

CONRAD, Joseph (1857–1924) Polish-born British novelist. *Heart of Darkness, Lord Jim, Nostromo.*

COOPER, James Fenimore (1789–1851) U.S. novelist famous for tales of action in 18th-c. America. *The Last of the Mohicans.*

CORNEILLE, Pierre (1606–84) French playwright. Father of French tragedy. *Horace, Le Cid.*

COWARD, Noel (1899–1973) English playwright. *Blithe Spirit, Hay Fever.*

CUMMINGS, e. e. (1894–1962) U.S. poet who fluted rules of traditional poetry. *Tulips and Chimneys.*

DANTE ALIGHIERI (1265–1321) Greatest Italian poet. Said to have "made the Italian language." *Divine Comedy.*

DE BEAUVOIR, Simone (1908–86) French novelist and feminist. *The Second Sex, Memoirs of a Dutiful Daughter.*

DEFOE, Daniel (1660–1731) English novelist and pamphleteer. *Robinson Crusoe, Moll Flanders.*

DE QUINCEY, Thomas (1785–1859) English essayist, critic and novelist. *Confessions of an English Opium-eater.*

DICKENS, Charles (1812–70) Possibly the greatest English novelist. *Oliver Twist, Great Expectations, A Christmas Carol, Nicholas Nickleby, Dombey and Son, David Copperfield, A Tale of Two Cities, Hard Times.*

DICKINSON, Emily (1830–86) U.S. poet. *Poems, The Single Hound, Bolts of Melody.*

DIDEROT, Denis (1713–84) French writer. Editor of the *Encyclopédie,* key work of the French Enlightenment.

DONNE, John (1572–1631) English poet. Master of religious and love poetry. *Songs and Sonnets, Divine Poems.*

DOS PASSOS, John (1896–1970) U.S. novelist and playwright. *U.S.A.* trilogy: *42nd Parallel, 1919, The Big Money.*

DOSTOYEVSKY, Fyodor (1821–81) Profoundly influential Russian novelist, second only to Tolstoy. *Crime and Punishment, The Brothers Karamazov.*

DOVE, Rita (b. 1952) First African-American U.S. Poet Laureate.

DURRELL, Lawrence (1912–90) English novelist and poet. *Alexandria Quartet.*

DÜRRENMATT, Friedrich (1921–90) Swiss playwright and novelist. *The Marriage of Mr. Mississippi.*

ECO, Umberto (b. 1929) Italian novelist concerned with semiotics. *The Name of the Rose, Foucault's Pendulum.*

ELIOT, George (Marian Evans) (1819–80) One of the greatest English novelists. *Adam Bede, The Mill on the Floss, Middlemarch.*

ELIOT, T(homas) S(tearns) (1888–1965) American-born Modernist British poet, playwright, and critic. *The Waste Land, Murder in the Cathedral, Four Quartets.*

ELLISON, Ralph (b. 1914) African-American novelist. *Invisible Man.*

EMERSON, Ralph Waldo (1803–82) U.S. transcendentalist poet and essayist. *Representative Men, English Traits.*

EURIPIDES (480 or 484–406 B.C.) Greek dramatist. *Medea, Hecuba, Bacchae.*

FAULKNER, William (1897–1962) U.S. novelist. Regarded as one of the modern masters of the novel. *The Sound and the Fury, Absalom, Absalom!*

FIELDING, Henry (1707–54) English picaresque novelist, a founder of the novel form. *The History of Tom Jones, Amelia.*

FITZGERALD, F(rancis) Scott (1896–1940) U.S. novelist and leading writer of the American "Jazz Age." *The Great Gatsby, Tender is the Night.*

FLAUBERT, Gustave (1821–80) French novelist and short-story writer. Master of language and form. *Madame Bovary, Salammbo, The Temptation of St. Anthony.*

FORSTER, E(dward) M(organ) (1879–1970) English novelist and short-story writer who explored the pre-1914 middle-class ethos. *A Room with a View, Howards End, A Passage to India.*

FROST, Robert (1874–1963) U.S. poet. *A Boy's Will, North of Boston.*

GENET, Jean (1910–86) French play-

wright and chronicler of the underworld. *Our Lady of the Flowers, Thief's Journal.*

GIDE, ANDRÉ (1869–1951) French novelist. *The Immoralist, The Pastoral Symphony, The Counterfeiters.*

GINSBERG, Allen (b. 1926) U.S. poet of the "Beat" movement. *Howl, Kaddish and Other Poems.*

GOETHE, Johann Wolfgang von (1749–1832) German poet, playwright, novelist, and scientist. One of the most important and influential writers of modern European literature. *Faust, Willhelm Meister's Apprenticeship.*

GOGOL, Nikolai (Vasilievich) (1809–1852) Russian novelist and playwright. A master of the grotesque. *The Government Inspector, Dead Souls.*

GOLDING, William Gerald (b. 1911–93) English novelist. *The Lord of the Flies.*

GOLDSMITH, Oliver (1728–74) Irish playwright, novelist, and poet. *The Vicar of Wakefield, She Stoops to Conquer.*

GRASS, Günter (Wilhelm) (b. 1927) German novelist, playwright and poet. Possibly Germany's greatest living novelist. *The Tin Drum, Cat and Mouse.*

GRAY, Thomas (1716–71) English poet. *Elegy Written in a Country Churchyard.*

GREENE, Graham (1904–91) English novelist. Known for serious novels and lighter "entertainments." *Brighton Rock, The Third Man, Our Man in Havana.*

HAMSUN, Knut (1859–1952) Norwegian novelist. *Hunger, Growth of the Soil.*

HARDY, Thomas (1840–1928) English novelist, poet, and playwright. *Far From the Madding Crowd, The Mayor of Casterbridge, Tess of the D'Urbervilles.*

HAWTHORNE, Nathaniel (1804–64) U.S. novelist and short-story writer. *The Scarlet Letter, The House of the Seven Gables.*

HEMINGWAY, Ernest (1899–1961) Influential much-imitated U.S. novelist and short-story writer. *A Farewell to Arms, For Whom the Bell Tolls, The Old Man and the Sea.*

HERBERT, George (1593–1633) English metaphysical poet. *The Temple, Sacred Poems and Secret Ejaculations.*

HESSE, Hermann (1877–1962) German-born Swiss mystical novelist. *Steppenwolf, The Glass Bead Game.*

HOMER (700s B.C.) Greek epic poet. *Iliad, Odyssey.*

HOPKINS, Gerard Manley (1844–89) English poet, priest, largely unknown in his lifetime. *The Windhover, Pied Beauty.*

HUGO, VICTOR MARIE (1802-85) French poet, playwright, and novelist. Led the Romantic movement in French literature. *The Hunchback of Notre Dame, Les Misérables.*

HUXLEY, Aldous (1894–1963) English novelist and essayist. *Brave New World, Eyeless in Gaza.*

IBSEN, Henrik (1828–1906) Norwegian playwright, founder of modern prose drama. *Peer Gynt, A Doll's House, Hedda Gabler.*

IONESCO, Eugène (1912–1994) Romanian-born French "Absurdist"

Wordsworth, seated (left), *with Southey and Coleridge. Washington Irving is behind.*

playwright. *The Bald Prima Donna, The Rhinoceros.*

IRVING, Washington (1783–1859) U.S. short-story writer and essayist. *The Sketch Book* (containing *Rip Van Winkle* and *The Legend of Sleepy Hollow*).

JAMES, Henry (1843–1916) U.S. novelist and playwright. Master of the psychological novel who has profoundly influenced 20th-century novelists. *The Bostonians, Portrait of a Lady, The Ambassadors.*

JOHNSON, Samuel (1709–84) English writer, critic, and lexicographer. *Dictionary of the English Language, A Journey to the Western Isles of Scotland.*

JONSON, Ben (1572–1637) English dramatist. *Volpone, The Alchemist.*

JOYCE, James (1882–1941) Irish novelist and short-story writer. Revolutionized the novel form through his exploration of language and development of the "stream of consciousness" method. *Dubliners, Ulysses, Finnegans Wake.*

KAFKA, Franz (1883–1924) Czech-born Austrian novelist and short-story writer. Nightmare visions of the modern world. *The Trial, America.*

KEATS, John (1795–1821) English Romantic poet. *Lamia, Ode to a Nightingale, The Eve of St. Agnes.*

KIPLING, Rudyard (1865–1936) Indian-born English novelist, poet, and short-story writer. *The Jungle Book, Kim, Just So Stories.*

KUNDERA, Milan (b. 1929) Czech-born French novelist and short-story writer. *The Joke, Immortality, The Unbearable Lightness of Being.*

LACLOS, Pierre Ambroise François Choderlos de (1741–1803) French novelist. *Les Liaisons dangereuses.*

LARKIN, Philip (Arthur) (1922–85) English poet, most influential of 1970s–80s. *The Whitsun Weddings, High Windows.*

LAWRENCE, D(avid) H(erbert) (1885–1930) Influential English novelist. Concerned with complicated male-female relationships. *Sons and Lovers, The Rainbow, Women in Love, Lady Chatterley's Lover.*

LERMONTOV, Mikhail Yurevich (1814–41) Russian novelist and poet. *A Hero of our Time, The Demon.*

LESSING, Doris (b. 1919) English novelist. *The Golden Notebook.*

LEVI, Primo (1919–87) Italian novelist, autobiographer, and scientist. Chronicler of Auschwitz. *The Periodic Table, If This is a Man.*

LEWIS, Sinclair (1885–1951) U.S. novelist who was a shrewd social observer. *Babbitt, Arrowsmith, Main Street.*

LLOSA, Mario Vargas (b. 1936) Peruvian novelist and politician. *The Time of the Hero, Aunt Julia and the Scriptwriter.*

LONDON, Jack (1876–1916) U.S. novelist, journalist, and man of action. *Call of the Wild.*

LONGFELLOW, Henry Wadsworth (1807–82) U.S. poet. *Hiawatha.*

LORCA, Federico García (1899–1936) Spanish poet and playwright. *Blood Wedding, The House of Bernarda Alba.*

LOWELL, James Russell (1819–1891) U.S. poet and editor. *The Biglow Papers.*

LOWELL, Robert (1917–77) U.S. poet. *For the Union Dead, Life Studies.*

MacNEICE, Louis (1907–63) Irish poet. *Blind Fireworks, Solstices.*

MANN, Thomas (1875–1955) Humanistic German novelist and short-story writer. *Death in Venice, Buddenbrooks.*

MARLOWE, Christopher (1564–93) English playwright and poet. *Tamburlaine the Great, The Tragical History of Dr. Faustus, Edward II.*

MÁRQUEZ, Gabriel García (b. 1928) Colombian novelist. Master of "magical reality." *One Hundred Years of Solitude, Chronicle of a Death Foretold.*

MAUGHAM, W(illiam) Somerset (1874–1965) English realist novelist, playwright, and short-story writer. *Of Human Bondage, The Moon and Sixpence.*

MAUPASSANT, Guy de (1850–93) French novelist and one of the greatest short-story writers. *Boule de suif, La Maison tellier, La Peur, Bel-Ami.*

MELVILLE, Herman (1819–91) U.S. epic novelist and poet. *Moby Dick, Billy Budd.*

MILLER, Henry (1891–1980) U.S. novelist known for sexual themes. *Tropic of Cancer, The Colossus of Maroussi.*

MILLER, Arthur (b. 1915) U.S. playwright of international renown. *Death of a Salesman, View from the Bridge.*

MILTON, John (1608–74) One of the greatest English poets. *Paradise Lost, Paradise Regained, Samson Agonistes.*

MISHIMA, Yukio (Hiraoka Kimitake) (1925–70) Japanese writer. *Confessions of a Mask, Sea of Fertility.*

MOLIÈRE (Jean-Baptiste Poquelin) (1622–73) Greatest French comic playwright. *Le Misanthrope, Tartuffe.*

MONTAIGNE, Michel Eyquem de (1533–92) French essayist. *Apologie de Raymon Sebond, Essais.*

MOORE, Marianne (1887–1972) African-American poet. *Poems, Predilections.*

MORRISON, Toni (b. 1931) U.S. novelist. *Tar Baby, Beloved.*

NABOKOV, Vladimir (1899–1977) Russian-born U.S. novelist. *Pale Fire, Lolita.*

NAIPAUL, V(idiadhar) S(urajprasad)

(b. 1932) Trinidadian novelist. *A House for Mr. Biswas, A Bend in the River.*

NERUDA, Pablo (1904–73) Chilean poet. *Twenty Love Poems and a Song of Despair, Canto General.*

O'NEILL, Eugene (1888–1953) U.S. playwright recognized as a giant of 20th-century drama. *Long Day's Journey into Night, Anna Christie.*

ORWELL, George (Eric Arthur Blair) (1903–50) English novelist and essayist. *Animal Farm, 1984.*

OVID (Publius Ovidius Naso) (43 B.C.–A.D.17) Roman poet. *Medea, Ars Amatoria, Metamorphoses.*

OWEN, Wilfred (Edward Salter) (1893–1918) English poet. *Anthem for Doomed Youth.*

PASTERNAK, Boris Leonidovich (1890–1960) Russian novelist. *Dr. Zhivago.*

PETRARCH, Francesco Petrarca (1304–74) Italian poet. Inventor of Petrarchan sonnet form. *Africa, Canzoniere.*

PINDAR (Pindaros) (c. 522 B.C.–c. 440 B.C.) Greek lyric poet, famed for his odes. *Epinikia.*

PINTER, Harold (b. 1930) English absurdist playwright. *The Birthday Party, The Caretaker.*

PIRANDELLO, Luigi (1867–1936) Italian playwright, novelist. *Six Characters in Search of an Author.*

PLATH, Sylvia (1932–63) U.S. tragic poet. *Ariel, The Bell Jar.*

POE, Edgar Allan (1809–49) U.S. poet and short-story writer of the macabre. *The Raven, The Murders in the Rue Morgue.*

POUND, Ezra Loomis (1885–1972) Controversial U.S. poet and critic. *Homage to Sextus Propertius, Cantos.*

PRÉVOST, Abbé (1697–1763) French novelist. *Manon Lescaut.*

PROUST, Marcel (1871–1922) French novelist. Regarded as one of the greatest writers of the 20th century for his seven-part novel *À la recherche du temps perdu* (Remembrance of Things Past).

PUSHKIN, Alexander (Sergeyevich) (1799–1837) Russian poet and playwright. *Eugene Onegin, Boris Godunov.*

RABELAIS, François (1494–1553) French satirist and comic writer. *Gargantua, Pantagruel.*

RACINE, Jean (1639–99) Great French classical playwright. *Andromaque, Phèdre.*

RICHARDSON, Samuel (1689–1761) Early English novelist. *Pamela, Clarissa.*

RILKE, Rainer Maria (1875–1926) Austrian lyric poet. *Sonnets to Orpheus, Duino Elegies.*

RIMBAUD, (Jean Nicolas) Arthur (1854–91) French poet. *Le Bateau ivre.*

ROTH, Philip (Milton) (b. 1933) U.S. novelist and short-story writer. *Portnoy's Complaint.*

RUSHDIE, (Ahmad) Salman (b. 1947) British "magic realist" novelist. *Midnight's Children, The Satanic Verses.*

SAINT-EXUPÉRY, Antoine de (1900–44) French novelist and aviator. *Le Petit Prince.*

SALINGER, J(erome) D(avid) (b. 1919)

John Updike.

U.S. novelist and short-story writer. *The Catcher in the Rye, Franny and Zooey.*

SANDBURG, Carl (1878–1967) U.S. poet. *Chicago Poems, The People, Yes, Smoke and Steel.*

SARTRE, Jean-Paul (1905–80) French existentialist philosopher, playwright, and novelist. *Nausea, No Exit.*

SCHILLER, Johann Christoph Friedrich von (1759–1805) German playwright and poet. *Wallenstein.*

SCOTT, Sir Walter (1771–1832) Scottish novelist and poet on historical themes. the *Waverley* novels.

SHAKESPEARE, William (1564–1616) Possibly the greatest English poet and playwright. *Romeo and Juliet, Hamlet, A Midsummer Night's Dream.*

SHAW, George Bernard (1856–1950) Irish playwright and novelist. *Man and Superman, Pygmalion.*

SHELLEY, Percy Bysshe (1792–1822) English Romantic poet. *Prometheus Unbound, The Triumph of Life.*

SHERIDAN, Richard Brinsley (1751–1816) Irish playwright. *The Rivals, The School for Scandal.*

SINCLAIR, Upton (1878–1968) U.S. novelist and exposer of scandal and social ills. *The Jungle.*

SINGER, Isaac Bashevis (1804–1991) Polish-born U.S. novelist and short-story writer most of whose works were translated from Yiddish. *The Magician of Lublin.*

SOLZHENITSYN, Alexander Isayevich (b. 1918) Russian novelist and historian. *One Day in the Life of Ivan Denisovich, The First Circle, Cancer Ward, August, 1914, The Gulag Archipelago.*

SOPHOCLES (c. 496–406 B.C.) Athenian tragedian. *Electra, Oedipus Rex.*

SPENSER, Edmund (c. 1552–99) English Elizabethan poet. *The Faerie Queene.*

STEIN, Gertrude (1891–1980) U.S. modernist writer and poet. *Three Lives.*

STEINBECK, John (1902–68) U.S. novelist. *The Grapes of Wrath, Of Mice and Men, East of Eden.*

STERNE, Laurence (1713–68) Irish comic novelist. *The Life and Opinions of Tristram Shandy.*

STEVENS, Wallace (1879–1955) U.S. poet. *Ideas of Order.*

STEVENSON, Robert Louis (1850–94) Scottish novelist and traveler. *Kidnapped,*

The Strange Case of Dr. Jekyll and Mr. Hyde.

STRINDBERG, (Johan) August (1849–1912) Swedish playwright. *The Red Room, The People of Hemsö.*

SWIFT, Jonathan (1667–1745) Anglo-Irish poet and satirist. *Gulliver's Travels, A Modest Proposal.*

SWINBURNE, Algernon Charles (1837–1909) Hedonistic English poet. *Poems and Ballads, Songs Before Sunrise.*

SYNGE, J(ohn) M(illington) (1871–1909) Irish playwright. *Riders to the Sea, The Playboy of the Western World.*

TENNYSON, Alfred, Lord (1809–92) English Victorian poet. *In Memoriam, Idylls of the King.*

THACKERAY, William Makepeace (1811–63) English Victorian novelist. *Vanity Fair, Henry Esmond.*

THOREAU, Henry David (1817–62) U.S. essayist and poet. *Walden.*

TOLSTOY, Count Leo Nikolayevich (1828–1910) Possibly the greatest Russian novelist. *War and Peace, Anna Karenina.*

TROLLOPE, Anthony (1815–82) English novelist. *Barchester Towers, Phineas Finn.*

TURGENEV, Ivan Sergeyevich (1818–83) Russian novelist. *Fathers and Sons.*

TWAIN, Mark (Samuel Langhorne Clemens) (1835–1910) U.S. novelist and satirist. *Huckleberry Finn, Tom Sawyer.*

UPDIKE, John Hoyer (b. 1932) U.S. novelist, poet and critic. *Couples, The Witches of Eastwick.*

VERLAINE, Paul (1844–96) French poet. *Fêtes galantes, Sagesse.*

VIRGIL (Publius Vergilius Maro) (70–19 B.C.) Roman poet. *Aeneid.*

VONNEGUT, Kurt, Jr. (b. 1922) U.S. novelist. *Slaughterhouse-Five.*

WAUGH, Evelyn Arthur St. John (1903–66) English satirical novelist. *Scoop, Decline and Fall.*

WHARTON, Edith (Newbold) (1861–1937) U.S. novelist. *The Age of Innocence.*

WHITE, Patrick (1912–90) Australian novelist. *The Tree of Man.*

WHITMAN, Walt (1819–92) U.S. poet. *Leaves of Grass.*

WILDE, Oscar (1854–1900) Irish playwright, novelist, and wit. *The Picture of Dorian Gray, Lady Windermere's Fan, A Woman of No Importance, The Importance of Being Earnest.*

WILLIAMS, Tennessee (1911–83) U.S. playwright. *A Streetcar Named Desire, Suddenly Last Summer.*

WOOLF, Virginia (1882–1941) English novelist. *Mrs. Dalloway, The Waves, A Room of One's Own.*

WORDSWORTH, William (1770–1850) English poet. *Tintern Abbey, The Prelude.*

WRIGHT, Richard (1908–1960) African-American novelist. *Native Son, Black Boy.*

YEATS, W(illiam) B(utler) (1865–1939) Irish poet and playwright. One of the greatest poets of the 1900s. *Collected Poems, Countess Cathleen.*

ZOLA, Emile (1840–1902) French Realist novelist. *Nana, La Bête humaine.*

Timeline

c. 3200 B.C. First ritualistic religious dramas are performed in Egypt.

c. 600 B.C. Greek theater originates in choral rites (dithyrambs) of Dionysus.

c. 500–400 B.C. Golden age of Greek drama, exemplified by the tragedies of Aeschylus (*Oresteia* trilogy), Sophocles (*Oedipus Rex*), and Euripides (*The Bacchae*), and the comedies of Aristophanes (*Lysistrata, The Frogs*).

c. 320 B.C. Amphitheater at Epidauros, Greece, is built, seating more than 13,000 people.

c. 300–100 B.C. Roman theater mounts plays by Plautus (*Asinaria*) and Terence (*The Mother-in-Law*). In India the epic *Ramayana* is put on stage.

c. 250 B.C. Gladiatorial combat becomes popular in Rome.

A.D. 80 The Colosseum, Rome, opens for the performance of games, mock battles, and spectacles (*right*).

c. 1000–1300 European drama originates in "Miracle" and "Mystery" plays (*p. 491*).

c. 1200 First appearance of court jesters in Europe (*p. 509*).

c. 1350 *Noh* drama develops in Japan.

c. 1400 French actors' guild performs religious dramas to paying audiences.

c. 1500 Masques (elaborate musical and dramatic performances) take place at European courts.

c. 1530 Italian *commedia dell'arte* companies begin to tour Europe (*p. 509*).

1548 Actors' guild sets up France's first permanent theater in Paris.

1576 James Burbage, British actor, builds The Theatre, London, Britain's first purpose-built playhouse.

c. 1580 Beginning of *Kabuki,* Japanese popular theater, combining music, dance, and mime.

1583 Edward Alleyn emerges as one of the first notable actors in Britain.

c. 1585–1615 English drama flourishes with works by Marlowe, Shakespeare (*p. 492*), Kyd, Jonson, Tourneur, Fletcher, and Webster.

1597 British actor Richard Burbage heads companies at London's Blackfriars Theatre and Globe Theatre (opened in 1599), in partnership with William Shakespeare and actors John Heminges and Henry Condell.

c. 1610 Golden age of Spanish drama begins with works by Lope De Vega and Calderón.

c. 1640 French theater flourishes with classical works by Corneille and Racine and comedies by Molière.

1660 Professional actresses first appear on the British stage.

1661 Lincoln's Inn Fields Theatre, London, is first to have proscenium arch and scenery that is "set" and "struck."

1680 Comédie-Française, French national theater, is formed by amalgamation of Molière's company with Hôtel de Bourgogne and Théatre du Marais.

GREEK AND ROMAN

All theater derives from religious ritual. In its earliest form, the *drama* (Greek "action, performance") was an integral part of religious ceremony, celebrating and placating the gods on whom all life depended. It was also entertainment.

In ancient Egypt the Abydos passion play, depicting the life-and-death struggle of the god Osiris and his brother Seth, was performed for almost 4,000 years until A.D. 400. In Greece the populace honored Dionysus, the "raging" god of fertility, in rites and ceremonies inspired by the cult of the Maenads, women who marked the god's death and rebirth with the slaughter of a goat—and much drinking; Dionysus (the Roman Bacchus) was also the god of the vine.

At first, performers consisted of one actor and chorus, but by the 400s B.C. true theater had emerged with the plays of Aeschylus, Sophocles, Euripides, and the comic dramatist Aristophanes.

The Roman theater took its inspiration from the Greek; Plautus, Terence, Seneca, and others borrowed liberally from Greek models for their plays which, like the Greek, were performed in open-air amphitheaters. The less refined

Roman audiences preferred spectacle to theater; Juvenal (d. A.D. 140) complained that they found a tightrope walker more uplifting than a drama. The more violent, grotesque, and horrific elements of Greek drama were stressed, with masks and costumes to heighten the excitement.

The Colosseum (A.D. 80), Rome's largest theater, staged chariot races, mock naval battles, gladiatorial contests, battles between men and beasts, beasts and beasts, and the setting of voracious animals upon defenseless victims. These reflected Roman taste in the imperial era.

Classical masks of comedy and tragedy.

EASTERN THEATER

Eastern theater, with its complexity of gesture, speech, and action, owes much to India and its parent language, Sanskrit, whose great epic poems such as the *Ramayana* were enacted (*c.* 300 B.C.). The cultural debt of a vanished Hindu Empire in Southeast Asia remains in Balinese temple dances and in the lion dances of China and Japan.

Kalidasa (400s A.D.) was the greatest Indian playwright: *Abhijnana-Sakuntala* was his most important work. At this time, gesture and dress became enhanced as audiences, speaking local dialects, ceased to understand Sanskrit.

The complex and stylized Chinese theater evolved during the Middle Ages from ancient origins into regional forms, with the *Yuan* plays of the north (in which actors and actresses played both sexes) and later the *K'un Ch'u* of the south, which gained a national popularity.

Dance and drama in Japan have a continuous history. *Nō* (*Noh*), the classical theater, was refined by Zeami (1363–1443). Chikamatsu (1653–1725), Japan's greatest playwright, blended *Bunraku* puppets plays with *Kabuki*, an offshoot of *Nō*, to provide Japanese theater with a repository of tradition.

Ramayana: Huge puppets enact the great Hindu epic.

MEDIEVAL AND RENAISSANCE

Medieval drama (like Greek drama before it) drew on religion for its inspiration. Making use of the liturgy and traditions of the church, it consisted at first of simple tableaux performed by local people.

From these early "Mysteries" and "Moralities" emerged the comedies and tragedies of Elizabethan times.

Permanent theaters became a feature of great cities. The Italian Sebastiano Serlio (1475–1554) designed perspective stage sets for the French court in Paris, and Giovanni Battista Aleotti (1546–1636) set the final style for the modern theater with the Teatro Farnese in Parma, Italy. In London, the Globe—Shakespeare's "Wooden O"—was built, burned down, rebuilt, and demolished (1599–1644).

The Elizabethan Globe Theatre, Southwark, London.

COMMEDIA DELL'ARTE

In the 1500s there developed in Italy the boisterous style of drama known as *commedia dell'arte*. This was a popular form of theater, as opposed to the literary drama of the court. Performed by professional actors who improvised the dialogue as they went along, it typically featured the story of Harlequin (the clown), Columbina (the girl), and Pantalone (the old man). *Commedia dell'arte* toured Italy and Europe, and its mix of acrobatics, dance, and mime lived on in pantomimes and Punch and Judy shows long after the form itself had ended.

In Paris, the "great sorcerer" Giacomo Torelli (1608–78) introduced stage machinery with moving clouds and airborne deities to mount the plays of Corneille, Molière, and Racine.

A commedia dell'arte figure (Italy, 1500s).

DEVELOPMENT OF DRAMA

The 1700s and 1800s were dominated by great actor-managers. David Garrick (1717–79) brought Shakespeare back to life; John Philip Kemble (1757–1823) shared the stage with his sister Sarah Siddons; and Edmund Kean (c. 1787–1833) drank himself to death after dominating the Regency stage.

Henry Irving (1838–1905) was the last of the great Victorian actor-managers, whose role has been continued in recent times by Donald Wolfit and Laurence Olivier, the latter making a successful transition from stage to movie set with *Henry V* and *Hamlet*.

In the first years of the 1900s, paying audiences were flocking to see the new marvel of movies, featuring subjects that the public has never tired of: science fiction (*Le Voyage dans la Lune*, 1902) and the first Western to be made (*The Great Train Robbery*, 1903, *p. 511*).

Meanwhile, early developments were occurring in the technology that was to become television with Nipkow's scanning disk (1884) and Crookes' cathode ray tube (1878). In 1897, the German

Images of Shakespearean characters, 1700s.

Ferdinand Braun modified Crookes' tube to produce the forerunner of the modern TV picture tube.

Timeline

1717 Drury Lane, London, stages the first British pantomime.

c. **1718** Charles Stagg and wife Mary, British actors, appear at Williamsburg, Virginia, a newly opened playhouse which is probably the first in North America.

1737 Britain's Stage Licensing Act decrees all plays must be approved for performance by Lord Chamberlain.

1741 David Garrick makes London debut as Shakespeare's *Richard III*.

1747 David Garrick becomes manager at Drury Lane; his reforms include the introduction of concealed stage lighting; the removal of all audience seating from the stage; and relocating the orchestra from the gallery to front stalls.

c. **1770** Emergence of the Comedy of Manners in England with works by Richard Brinsley Sheridan and Oliver Goldsmith.

1775 Sarah Siddons makes her Drury Lane debut.

c. **1780** German theater flourishes with works by Goethe, Schiller, and others, introducing Romantic *Sturm und Drang* (storm and stress) drama.

1783 John Philip Kemble, brother of Sarah Siddons, makes Drury Lane debut.

1788 Sweden's Royal Dramatic Theater established at Stockholm.

1789 *The Recruiting Officer* by George Farquhar, played by convicts, marks the first theatrical performance in Australia.

c. **1800** Punch and Judy handpuppet show, modeled on characters from *commedia dell'arte*, takes its modern form.

1814 Edmund Kean, British actor who brings new physicality to roles, makes London debut as Shylock in the *Merchant of Venice*.

c. **1830** Romantic revolution begins in French theater with works by Victor Hugo.

1834 Junius Brutus Booth makes U.S. debut.

1864 Edwin Booth appears in 100 consecutive performances as Hamlet, New York City.

1871 Henry Irving (*left*) achieves stardom in melodrama *The Bells* at Lyceum Theatre, London.

1872 French actress Sarah Bernhardt becomes famous as the queen in *Ruy Blas*. Eleonora Duse makes debut, aged 14, as Juliet.

1877 The French "praxinoscope" projects successive images onto screen, prefiguring the cinema.

1878 Sir William Crookes, British scientist, invents Crookes tube that produces cathode rays, forerunner of television.

1878 Henry Irving is appointed actor-manager of the Lyceum Theatre, London; his long partnership with Dame Ellen Terry begins with her playing Ophelia to his Hamlet.

Timeline

1884 Paul Nipkow (1860–1940), German engineer, invents Nipkow scanning disk, used in early TV development. First performance of *The Wild Duck* by Henrik Ibsen, Norwegian dramatist, who revolutionized European drama with his realism and concern for social issues. Ibsen's plays include *Pillars of Society* (1877), *A Doll's House* (1879), *An Enemy of the People* (1882), *The Wild Duck* (1884), *Hedda Gabler* (1890), and *The Master Builder* (1892).

1887 *Ivanov*, first full-length play by Anton Chekhov, Russian dramatist. Chekhov's plays include *The Seagull* (1896), *Uncle Vanya* (1900), *The Three Sisters* (1901), and *The Cherry Orchard* (1904). Louis Aimé Augustin Le Prince, French inventor, first produces series of images on perforated film.

1888 *Miss Julie*, by August Strindberg, Swedish dramatist.

1889 William Friese-Greene, British inventor, develops sequential projection of still slides. George Eastman, U.S. inventor, develops celluloid film.

1891 Thomas Edison, U.S. inventor, develops Kinetograph camera and Kinetograph viewer, and begins to use 35mm film.

1892 *Widowers' Houses,* by Irish dramatist George Bernard Shaw, marks the beginning of a prolific output, including *Mrs. Warren's Profession* (1893), *Arms and the Man* (1894), *Candida* (1897), *The Devil's Disciple* (1897), *Man and Superman* (1903), *Major Barbara* (1905), *The Doctor's Dilemma* (1906), *Caesar and Cleopatra* (1907), *Pygmalion* (1914; adapted as the musical *My Fair Lady,* 1956), *Heartbreak House* (1919), and *Saint Joan* (1924).

1893 *Pelléas et Mélisande* by Belgian dramatist Maurice Maeterlinck. Thomas Edison establishes revolving "film studio" at West Orange, New Jersey.

1894 Kinetoscope parlors open in U.S.A.

1895 *The Importance of Being Earnest*, by Irish dramatist Oscar Wilde. Auguste and Louis Lumière, French chemists, invent the Cinematograph, the first true cinécamera and projector system.

1896 French dramatist Alfred Jarry writes pioneering Absurdist play *Ubu Roi* (aged 16). Thomas Edison develops Vitascope projection system. French film pioneers Charles and Emile Pathé experiment with sound system of synchronized gramophone disks.

1897 Ferdinand Braun, German physicist, produces forerunner of TV receiver picture tube. Russian actor-producer Konstantin Stanislavsky founds Moscow Arts Theater.

1902 Méliès makes *Le Voyage dans la Lune.* Irish poet and dramatist William Butler Yeats writes *Cathleen ni Houlihan* with Irish dramatist Lady Gregory.

1904 Yeats and Lady Gregory found Abbey Theater, Dublin.

THEATER: 19TH AND 20TH CENTURIES

Moscow Arts Theatre production of Chekhov's Uncle Vanya.

The histrionics of theater in the 1800s yielded in the last decades to the social consciousness and realism of Norwegian Henrik Ibsen, the father of modern theater. Anton Chekhov, a Russian dramatist, brought compassion to realism, while Ibsen's fellow Scandinavian August Strindberg explored the darker aspects of the human condition, laying the groundwork for Expressionism—in plays such as the Czech Karel Capek's *R.U.R.*, a "robot play" (1921).

In Italy, Luigi Pirandello broke new ground with *Six Characters in Search of an Author* (1921), and in Germany Carl Zuckmayer targeted militarism with *The Captain of Köpenick* (1931). His Marxist compatriot Bertolt Brecht pilloried bourgeois attitudes, beginning with *The Threepenny Opera* (1928), famous for its music by Kurt Weill. In France, the outstanding French dramatist of the interwar years was Jean Giraudoux, whose plays protested against war and greed. Giraudoux influenced the more popular Jean Anouilh.

In England the Anglo-Irish George Bernard Shaw drew on Ibsen's work, adding Irish wit, while Ireland itself saw a dramatic revival with plays by J. M. Synge and Sean O'Casey. In America, a playwright of international stature emerged with Eugene O'Neill, who wrote a dozen or more plays in the 1920s and 1930s.

THEATER: WORLD WAR II AND AFTER

The theater in World War II flourished as far as possible. Bertolt Brecht, a fugitive from Hitler, used his alienation effect brilliantly in the antimilitaristic epic *Mother Courage* (1941); Jean-Paul Sartre's *Les Mouches* (1943) was a coded call to arms against the occupying power; Noel Coward lightened the blackout with com-edies like *Blithe Spirit* (1941). In the United States, Arthur Miller's, *All My Sons* (1947) was a comment on war profiteering.

Miller and his contemporary Tennessee Williams enriched postwar theater in the United States; Miller's *Death of a Salesman* (1949) and *A View from the Bridge* (1955), and Williams' *The Glass Menagerie* (1943) and *A Streetcar Named Desire* (1948), were critical and popular successes.

In Europe, Irishman Samuel Beckett, wrote *En attendant Godot* (*Waiting for Godot,* 1952), which proved to be the most influential of modern plays. With *Fin de partie* (*Endgame,* 1957) and *Krapp's Last Tape* (1958), *Godot* is the outstanding example of the Theater of the Absurd, which flourished in Paris, with the work of Eugène Ionesco (*The Bald Prima Donna,* 1950; *La Leçon,* 1951) and Jean Genet (*Le Balcon* 1957).

John Osborne changed the direction of British theater in the late 1950s with his social dramas *Look Back in Anger* (1956)

Williams' A Streetcar Named Desire.

and *The Entertainer* (1957). In the United States Edward Albee's *Who's Afraid of Virginia Woolf* (1962) had echoes of Strindberg, while Harold Pinter's *The Caretaker* (1958) and later plays gave an English context to the Theater of the Absurd. The urban dramas of Neil Simon (*The Odd Couple,* 1965; *The Sunshine Boys,* 1972) were lifted by wit, while David Mamet's *Oleanna* (1992) is a cruel account of America's obsession with sexual politics.

FILM: HOLLYWOOD AND WESTERNS

Hollywood and the film industry in the 1900s were born when a group of producers set up shop in the Los Angeles suburb before World War I. Reliable sunlight and wide-open spaces nearby were ideal for early filmmaking and for the genre that has lasted from the earliest days to the present–the Western. Primitive studio lots, open to the skies, sprang up to create a legend and a dream world for the huddled masses. The Western movie is one of the truly American art forms. Drawn from the recent history of a young country, it combines the spectacle of dramatic landscape with the eternal struggle between "good" and "evil": the white stetson versus the black sombrero; the Colt and Winchester versus the bow and arrow.

The Great Train Robbery (1903), the first Western, established the genre which, over the great years of movies, provided box-office hits together with a steady stream of matinée and second-feature films that made household names of their stars. *Butch Cassidy and the Sundance Kid* (1969) pursued *The Great Train Robbery* theme but added a feeling of nemesis overtaking its heroes, played by Paul Newman and Robert Redford.

The Western was at its traditional best

John Wayne and Claire Trevor starred in John Ford's classic Stagecoach.

in the films of director John Ford, notably those starring John Wayne, the archetypal "Westerner", (*Stagecoach*, 1939; *She Wore a Yellow Ribbon*, 1949; *The Searchers*, 1956).

Over the years, many stars appeared in Hollywood Westerns (Stewart, Fonda, Brando, Lancaster, Douglas); another, Clint Eastwood starred in the TV *Rawhide* series before making his name in "spaghetti" Westerns—shoestring productions directed by Italians with heavily dubbed supporting casts. Eastwood went on to success as actor-director winning a Best Director Oscar (1993).

MUSICALS

The arrival of sound in Hollywood brought the first talkie and the first musical, *The Jazz Singer* (1927) starring Al Jolson. A flood of musical extravaganzas dominated Hollywood output in the 1930s, provided pure escapism during World War II, and continued for another 20 years after.

Productions in the 1930s were largely "backstage" stories of which the *Broadway Melody* series (1929, 1936, 1937, 1940) was typical. The most influential figure was U.S. choreographer and director Busby Berkeley, whose sparkling song and dance direction remains a cinematic marvel to this day.

Musicals created a new generation of stars, often in pairs–Ruby Keeler and Dick Powell, Fred Astaire and Ginger

Rogers, Jeanette MacDonald and Nelson Eddy, Bob Hope and Bing Crosby, Judy Garland and Mickey Rooney. Garland (1922–69) went on to make one of the most famous of all films, *The Wizard of Oz* (1939). Wartime morale boosters included *Yankee Doodle Dandy* (1942) with casts in uniforms.

The postwar years brought new musicals that have remained evergreen; Gene Kelly's *On the Town* (1949), *An American in Paris* (1951), and *Singin' in the Rain* (1952) set new standards in the art of choreography on film. Other classics include *Oklahoma!* (1955), *South Pacific* (1958), *West Side Story* (1961), *My Fair Lady* (1964), and *The Sound of Music* (1965), one of the most popular films ever to emerge from Hollywood.

The Wizard of Oz has lost none of its appeal after 50 years of repeated screening.

Timeline

All films mentioned in this timeline were made in the U.S.A. unless otherwise stated.

1905 The "Nickelodeon" in Pittsburgh, Pennsylvania, shows both live and filmed entertainment.

1906 George Smith, British inventor, patents Kinemacolor, the first color film.

1907 *The Ghost Sonata*, play by Swedish dramatist August Strindberg. *The Playboy of the Western World*, play by Irish dramatist J. M. Synge. Lumière brothers develop a color photography process. U.S. filmmakers begin to work in Hollywood, California (*left*).

1908 D. W. Griffith, U.S. filmmaker, screens *For the Love of Gold*.

1912 Mack Sennett, U.S. film director, forms Keystone Company, famed for short, slapstick comedies.

1913 U.S. film producers Cecil B. De Mille, Jesse Lasky, and Samuel Goldwyn select Hollywood for making *The Squaw Man*.

1914 London's Old Vic Shakespeare Company opens.

1915 D. W. Griffith makes *The Birth of a Nation*.

1916 D. W. Griffith's *Intolerance* stars Lillian Gish.

1919 *Such is Life*, play by German dramatist Frank Wedekind. Robert Wiene directs *The Cabinet of Dr. Caligari*.

1920 *The Emperor Jones*, play by U.S. dramatist Eugene O'Neill, probably America's greatest playwright. His other works include *The Hairy Ape* (1922), *Desire Under the Elms* (1924), *The Great God Brown* (1926), *Mourning Becomes Electra* (1931), *The Iceman Cometh* (1939), and *Long Day's Journey into Night* (1941).

1921 *Six Characters in Search of an Author*, play by Italian dramatist Luigi Pirandello. Rex Ingram directs *The Four Horsemen of the Apocalypse*, starring Rudolph Valentino.

1922 John Barrymore makes 101 consecutive appearances as Hamlet in New York city. U.S. documentary filmmaker Robert Flaherty makes *Nanook of the North*. Fritz Lang directs *Dr. Mabuse* (Germany). Frederick W. Murnau directs *Nosferatu* (Germany).

1923 Harold Lloyd, U.S. comedy actor, stars in *Safety Last*. The German Tri-Ergon sound system and Phonofilm system of Lee De Forest, U.S. inventor, lead to sound being photographically recorded on film.

1924 *Juno and the Paycock*, by Irish dramatist Sean O'Casey at Dublin's Abbey Theater. Lon Chaney stars in the film *The Hunchback of Notre Dame*. DeMille produces *The Ten Commandments*.

1925 *Hay Fever*, play by British dramatist Noel Coward. Sergei Eisenstein directs *The Battleship Potemkin* (Russian Epics, *p. 514*). Charlie Chaplin directs and stars in *The Gold Rush*.

Timeline

1926 *Don Juan*, first film with synchronized music and effects, stars John Barrymore.

1927 *The Jazz Singer*, first full-length talking picture, stars U.S. singer Al Jolson.

1928 *Siegfried*, play by French dramatist Jean Giraudoux. *The Threepenny Opera*, with words by German dramatist Bertolt Brecht and music by Kurt Weill. *Steamboat Willie*, first synchronized sound cartoon by U.S. animator Walt Disney (*right*), introduces Mickey Mouse. *Un Chien Andalou*, Surrealist film, directed by Spaniard Luis Buñuel in collaboration with Salvador Dalí.

1929 *The Passion of Joan of Arc* by Danish director Carl Theodor Dreyer. *Blackmail* (U.K.) by Alfred Hitchcock. *The Blue Angel* (Germany) by Josef von Sternberg, with Marlene Dietrich.

1930 *L'Age d'Or* (France) by Luis Buñuel. *Sous les Toits de Paris* (France) by René Clair. *Little Caesar*, first major gangster movie, by Mervyn LeRoy, with Edward G. Robinson. *All Quiet on the Western Front* by Lewis Milestone (*p. 514*).

1931 *The Captain from Köpenick*, play by German dramatist Carl Zuckmayer. Charlie Chaplin (*right*) directs and stars in *City Lights*. James Whale's *Frankenstein* stars Boris Karloff.

1932 *Grand Hotel* by Edmund Goulding, with Greta Garbo, Joan Crawford, John and Lionel Barrymore. *A nous la liberté* (France) by René Clair. *Scarface* by Howard Hawks, with Paul Muni. Sir Alexander Korda, Hungarian-British producer, makes *The Private Life of Henry VIII* (U.K.), with Charles Laughton.

1933 *Blood Wedding*, play by Spanish dramatist and poet Federico Garcia Lorca. *King Kong* by Ernest Schoedsack, stars Fay Wray. *Flying Down to Rio* establishes partnership of U.S. dancers Fred Astaire and Ginger Rogers. *César* (France) by Marcel Pagnol, stars Raimu and Pierre Fresnay. Jean Vigo directs *Zero de Conduite* (France). *Testament of Dr. Mabuse* (Germany) by Fritz Lang.

1934 *It Happened One Night* by Frank Capra. Shirley Temple (b. 1928) is child star in *Stand Up and Cheer* and *Little Miss Marker*.

1935 *Murder in the Cathedral*, play by Anglo-American poet T. S. Eliot. Fred Astaire and Ginger Rogers star in *Top Hat*. Jean Renoir directs *Le Crime de Monsieur Lange* (France).

1936 *French Without Tears*, play by English dramatist Terence Rattigan. *Mr. Deeds Goes To Town* by Frank Capra, with Gary Cooper. Charlie Chaplin directs and stars in *Modern Times*. *Pépé le Moko* (France) by Julien Duvivier, with Jean Gabin. The BBC offers regular public television service in the London area, using the Baird system.

FILM FUN AND ANIMATION

Charlie Chaplin was the first of the cinema clowns and, like other early stars of the comic genre, began his career in music hall, or vaudeville. The many films of his younger contemporary Buster Keaton have lasted equally as well as those of Chaplin.

Unlike Chaplin or Keaton, W. C. Fields (William Claude Dukenfield) had to await the arrival of talkies for his genius to flower on the screen. Bottle-nosed, cantankerous, and misogynistic, Fields was as eccentric in real life as in his films.

The Marx Brothers, notably Groucho, Harpo, and Chico, dominated Hollywood "team" comedy with *Animal Crackers* (1928) and *Monkey Business* (1932), *A Night at the Opera* and *A Day at the Races* (1937), *At the Circus* (1939), *Go West* (1940), *The Big Store* (1941), and *A Night in Casablanca* (1946). However, the "Road" films of Bob Hope and Bing Crosby covered 20 years, and their influence is evident in the films of director and actor Woody Allen.

In Europe, the language barrier was overcome by the rubber-faced film comedian Fernandel and the storlike mime of Jacques Tati. Peter Sellers, British comedian, gained international success in films such as *Dr. Strangelove* (1964).

Among animators, Walt Disney stands supreme. Disney began with the simple cartoon creation of Mickey Mouse in 1928, but within ten years he was producing the full-length feature films that were to make his name a legend; *Snow White and the Seven Dwarfs* (1937) set the standard for subsequent feature-length animation films. It was followed by *Pinocchio* (1939) and *Fantasia* (1940), with music performed by the Philadelphia Orchestra, conducted by Leopold Stokowski. *Dumbo* (1941) and *Bambi* (1942) came next, followed by *Cinderella* (1950), *Alice in Wonderland* (1951), *Peter Pan* (1953), *Lady and the Tramp* (1956), *The Sleeping Beauty* (1959), and *One Hundred and One Dalmatians* (1961).

Jim Henson (1937–90) was not an animator but a puppeteer, whose TV creations—known as Muppets because they represent a cross between marionettes and puppets—were first seen in 1959. In 1969, he launched *Sesame Street*, a series that playfully educated preschool children, while *The Muppet Show* (1976–81), featuring Kermit the Frog and Miss Piggy, enjoyed huge popularity.

Prickly, eccentric W. C. Fields wrote his own screenplays as Otis J. Criblecobis.

SCIENCE FICTION

The movies' pioneer monster King Kong (1933) was as moving as it was terrifying.

Science fiction looks to the laboratory at one end of the spectrum and outer space at the other; the addition of special effects creates fantasy, often spilling over into horror. The English writer H. G. Wells (1866–1946), an accurate prophet of scientific trends, provided the inspiration for many early sci-fi films and later remakes including *The Invisible Man* (1933), *The War of the Worlds* (1953), and *The Time Machine* (1960).

R. L. Stevenson's *Dr. Jekyll and Mr. Hyde* (1931) saw horror emerge from the laboratory to public acclaim; best of all perhaps was *Frankenstein* (1931) directed by James Whale and starring Boris Karloff.

Space fiction finds its origins in the earliest of films, Méliès' *Voyage to the Moon* (1902), and climaxes with Stanley Kubrick's *2001: A Space Odyssey* (1968) and George Lucas' *Star Wars* (1977).

The primitive effects which made *King Kong* (1933) one of the greatest of films have moved on; Steven Spielberg's *Jurassic Park* (1993) is its direct heir.

FILM A CLEF

Citizen Kane (1941), regarded by many filmmakers and critics alike as the greatest movie ever made, was a *film à clef*— that is, one based on a true story or character. Welles' masterpiece was modeled on Randolph Hearst, the U.S. newspaper tycoon, and was damned by his newspapers. *All the King's Men* (1949) fictionalized the life and death of Huey Long, a U.S. politican corrupted by power; Charlie Chaplin's *The Great Dictator* (1940) was inescapably Adolf Hitler; and *The Carpetbaggers* (1964) told the story of Howard Hughes, aviator, industrialist, and Hollywood tycoon.

Orson Welles' Citizen Kane was a stylistic landmark in the developing art of cinema.

FILM NOIR

Film Noir, "black film," is the title given to a style of film whose story is often set in the gloomier, more threatening milieux of (usually) a city. Early examples are the French *Le Jour se lève* (1939), in which a criminal, trapped by the police, kills himself; and *Quai des brumes* (1938), in which an army deserter dies after rescuing a girl from criminals.

The label is attached to a number of late 1940s and 1950s Hollywood productions: outstanding are *Double Indemnity* (1944), starring Barbara Stanwyck, Fred MacMurray (b. 1907) and Edward G. Robinson (1893–1973) in which a wife conspires with an insurance agent to murder her husband; and *The Killers* (1946), in which a petty criminal awaits the arrival of two men sent to kill him. *The Killers* was the first starring role in movies for Burt Lancaster.

Double Indemnity was the first important film to be taken from a novel by Raymond Chandler (1888–1959). Many others followed, all in the *film noir* genre; *The Big Sleep* (1946) and *Farewell My Lovely* (remade in 1975) featured the honest private eye Philip Marlowe. The constant theme of the private detective involved deeply with his clients and end-ing in murder was successfully used once again in *Chinatown* (1974). It starred (but was not directed by) John Huston, also an outstanding screenwriter and director.

Jean Gabin in Carné's Quai des brumes.

NEOREALISM

From the rubble of World War II, Roberto Rossellini drew *Rome—Open City* (1945), an almost documentary melodrama about the efforts of Italian resistance workers in Rome during the last days of the German occupation.

He followed it the following year with *Paisà*, also with the war as its theme. The two films set a new cinematic style called Neorealism in which there is a strong sense of improvisation, using living locations and unknown actors. A later classic of the genre was Vittorio de Sica's *The Bicycle Thief* (1948).

Stark neorealism in The Bicycle Thief.

Timeline

1937 *Le Voyageur sans Bagage*, play by Jean Anouilh. Walt Disney produces *Snow White and the Seven Dwarfs*. *Camille* by George Cukor, with Greta Garbo. *La Grande Illusion* (France) by Jean Renoir, with Jean Gabin (War Films, *p.514*).

1938 *Our Town*, play by U.S. dramatist Thornton Wilder. Errol Flynn, Australian-U.S. actor, stars in *The Adventures of Robin Hood*. Bette Davis stars in *Jezebel* by William Wyler. Eisenstein directs *Alexander Nevsky* (Soviet Union). *La Sauvage*, play by French dramatist Jean Anouilh.

1939 *Gone With the Wind*, greatest box-office earner of all time, stars Clark Gable and Vivien Leigh. Greta Garbo stars in *Ninotchka* by Ernst Lubitsch, German-U.S. director. *The Wizard of Oz* stars Judy Garland. *Golden Boy*, play by U.S. dramatist Clifford Odets.

1940 Charlie Chaplin directs and stars in *The Great Dictator*. Walt Disney produces *Fantasia*. John Ford directs *The Grapes of Wrath*, with Henry Fonda. Alfred Hitchcock directs *Rebecca* (U.K.), with Laurence Olivier. Columbia Broadcasting System (CBS), demonstrates color TV system developed by Peter Carl Goldmark, U.S. physicist.

1941 *Blithe Spirit*, play by Noel Coward. Orson Welles directs and stars in *Citizen Kane*, often voted "best film" by critics and fans (Film à Clef, *left*).

1942 Michael Curtiz, Hungarian-U.S. director, makes *Casablanca*. Luchino Visconti directs *Ossessione* (Italy) a landmark of neorealism.

1943 *Les Mouches*, play by French Existentialist dramatist Jean-Paul Sartre (*p. 510*). Michael Powell and Emeric Pressburger make *The Life and Death of Colonel Blimp* (U.K.).

1944 *Antigone*, play by Jean Anouilh. *The Madwoman of Chaillot*, play by Jean Giraudoux. *Huis clos* (*In Camera*), play by Jean-Paul Sartre. *Gaslight* by George Cukor, with French actor Charles Boyer. Vincente Minnelli directs *Meet Me in St. Louis*, with Judy Garland.

1945 *The Glass Menagerie*, play by U.S. dramatist Tennessee Williams. Other plays by Williams include *A Streetcar named Desire* (1947), *Cat on a Hot Tin Roof* (1955), and *Sweet Bird of Youth* (1959). Marcel Carné directs *Les Enfants du Paradis* (France), with Arletty and Jean-Louis Barrault. Roberto Rossellini's *Rome—Open City* (Italy). David Lean's *Brief Encounter* (U.K.) stars Trevor Howard. Wilder's *The Lost Weekend* stars Ray Milland.

1946 David Lean directs *Great Expectations* (U.K.), with John Mills. Powell and Pressburger film *A Matter of Life and Death* (U.K.), with David Niven. Jean Cocteau films *La Belle et la Bête* (France). Roberto Rossellini directs *Paisà* (Italy). Carol Reed directs *Odd Man Out* (U.K.), with James Mason.

Timeline

1947 *All My Sons*, play by U.S. dramatist Arthur Miller. *L'invitation au Château (Ring Around the Moon)*, play by Jean Anouilh.

1948 Laurence Olivier directs and stars in *Hamlet* (U.K.). Vittorio de Sica directs *The Bicycle Thief* (Italy). Powell and Pressburger make *The Red Shoes* (U.K.).

1949 *Death of a Salesman*, play by Arthur Miller. *All the King's Men* by Robert Rossen, with Broderick Crawford. George Cukor directs *Adam's Rib*, starring long-term partners Spencer Tracy and Katharine Hepburn. Reed directs *The Third Man* (U.K.), with Trevor Howard, Orson Welles. *Kind Hearts and Coronets* (U.K.) by Robert Hamer, with Alec Guinness playing eight roles.

1950 *All About Eve* by Joseph Mankiewicz, with Bette Davis. *Sunset Boulevard* by Billy Wilder, with Gloria Swanson. Robert Bresson directs *Diary of a Country Priest* (France). Jean-Pierre Melville directs *Les Enfants Terribles* (France).

1951 John Huston directs *The African Queen*, with Bogart and Hepburn. Akira Kurosawa directs *Rashomon* (Japan). Hitchcock directs *Strangers on a Train*.

1952 *Waiting For Godot*, play written by Irish dramatist Samuel Beckett. Chaplin directs and stars in *Limelight*. *Viva Zapata!* by Elia Kazan, with Marlon Brando. Jacques Tati directs and stars in *Mr. Hulot's Holiday* (France).

1953 Wide-screen Cinemascope and stereophonic sound are introduced. Montgomery Clift, Deborah Kerr, and Burt Lancaster star in Zinnemann's *From Here to Eternity*. *Ugetsu Monogatari* (Japan) by Kenji Mizoguchi. *The Wages of Fear* (France) by Henri-Georges Clouzot.

1954 *A Star is Born* by Cukor, with Garland. Brando stars in Kazan's *On the Waterfront*. Federico Fellini directs *La Strada* (Italy), with Anthony Quinn. *Seven Samurai* (Japan) by Kurosawa.

1955 *A View From The Bridge*, play by Arthur Miller. James Stewart stars in *The Man from Laramie*. James Dean stars in Nicolas Ray's *Rebel Without a Cause*. Ingmar Bergman directs *Smiles of a Summer Night* (Sweden). Satyajit Ray's *Pather Panchali* puts Indian cinema on the map. Laurence Olivier directs and stars in *Richard III* (U.K.).

1956 *Look Back in Anger*, play by British dramatist John Osborne. *Le Balcon*, play by French dramatist Jean Genet. *Giant* stars James Dean, Rock Hudson, and Elizabeth Taylor.

1957 John Osborne's play *The Entertainer*. Samuel Beckett's play *Endgame*. Ingmar Bergman's *The Seventh Seal* (Sweden), with Max Von Sydow. Alexander Mackendrick directs *Sweet Smell of Success*, with Tony Curtis and Burt Lancaster. *Twelve Angry Men* by Sidney Lumet, with Henry Fonda.

RUSSIAN EPICS

Eisenstein's Odessa Steps sequence from The Battleship Potemkin *(1925).*

Historical epics are the stuff of Russian films. Recognizing the potential of the film as propaganda, the Bolsheviks encouraged filmmakers to create tributes to their country's heroes. From this came some of the world's greatest films and a director of giant stature, Sergei Eisenstein, who drew on the revolution for his first masterwork, *The Battleship Potemkin* (1925). The "Odessa Steps" sequence, in which innocents are massacred, set standards of camerawork which were to influence all later filmmaking.

Although he drew on recent events for his earliest films, Eisenstein was to turn to his country's vivid, violent history for later masterpieces. *Alexander Nevsky* (1938) culminates in the defeat on a frozen lake of the Teutonic knights; his last great work was the huge *Ivan the Terrible*, made in two parts (1942–46).

War and Peace (1967) is a later film in the best heroic traditions of Eisenstein. Lasting 8½ hours and directed by Sergei Bondarchuk it is a faithful adaptation of Tolstoy's novel, with battle scenes (Borodino) of which Eisenstein would have been proud.

WAR FILMS

Lewis Milestone's epic *All Quiet on the Western Front* (1930) was an early Academy Award winner, setting a standard for war films to follow but rarely approach. It told the story of a group of young German recruits thrown into the nightmare pit of World War I trench warfare. Few films contain a moment more piteous than when the young soldier is shot as he reaches out to touch a butterfly on the parapet. Jean Renoir's *La Grande Illusion* (1937), although lacking gory battle scenes, is considered a definitive statement on the futility of war.

War films made during World War II and in following years tended to celebrate heroes and their deeds (such as RAF pilot Douglas Bader) and provided stars like John Wayne with macho film roles.

The advent of TV, with live hard-news footage of bloody conflict, made the conventional war film appear spurious, not to say vainglorious, although (after a decent pause) the campaign in Vietnam brought a rush of films about it.

The Deer Hunter (1978) opened the assault, followed by *Apocalypse Now* (1979), inspired it is said by Conrad's *Heart of Darkness* and featuring an almost invisible performance by Marlon Brando. Australia's *The Odd Angry Shot* (1979) gave an uncomplicated and honest account of Vietnam action, and a new milestone was reached with Oliver Stone's *Platoon* (1986) for which Stone earned an Academy Award.

Oliver Stone came close to the ugly truth of the Vietnam War in Platoon.

NOUVELLE VAGUE

A brief but influential period in French film—the late 1950s, early 1960s—was known as *Nouvelle Vague* (New Wave), describing the work of a group of young directors who scorned the conventions (as they saw them) of filmmaking.

The first, *Le Beau Serge* (*Bitter Reunion*, 1958), was directed by Claude Chabrol (b. 1930), soon to be followed by *Les Quatre Cent Coups* (*The 400 Blows*, 1959), directed by François Truffaut (1932–84) and *A Bout de souffle* (*Breathless*, 1960), directed by Jean-Luc Godard (b. 1930). The work of all three was characterized by a youthful spontaneity and unique freshness.

Talent and modest budgets underpinned New Wave films like A Bout de souffle.

ACADEMY AWARD-WINNING FILMS (OSCARS)

1927–28	*Wings* William Wellman
1928–29	*Broadway Melody* Harry Beaumont
1929–30	*All Quiet on the Western Front* Lewis Milestone
1930–31	*Cimarron* Wesley Ruggles
1931–32	*Grand Hotel* Edmund Goulding
1932–33	*Cavalcade* Frank Lloyd
1934	*It Happened One Night* Frank Capra
1935	*Mutiny on the Bounty* Frank Lloyd
1936	*The Great Ziegfeld* Robert Z. Leonard
1937	*The Life of Emile Zola* William Dieterle
1938	*You Can't Take It With You* Frank Capra
1939	*Gone With the Wind* Victor Fleming
1940	*Rebecca* Alfred Hitchcock
1941	*How Green Was My Valley* John Ford
1942	*Mrs. Miniver* William Wyler
1943	*Casablanca* Michael Curtiz
1944	*Going My Way* Leo McCarey
1945	*The Lost Weekend* Billy Wilder
1946	*The Best Years of Our Lives* William Wyler
1947	*Gentleman's Agreement* Elia Kazan
1948	*Hamlet* Laurence Olivier
1949	*All the King's Men* Robert Rossen
1950	*All About Eve* Joseph L. Mankiewicz
1951	*An American in Paris* Vincente Minnelli
1952	*The Greatest Show on Earth* Cecil B. DeMille
1953	*From Here to Eternity* Fred Zinnemann
1954	*On the Waterfront* Elia Kazan
1955	*Marty* Delbert Mann
1956	*Around the World in Eighty Days* Michael Anderson
1957	*Bridge on the River Kwai* David Lean
1958	*Gigi* Vincente Minnelli
1959	*Ben Hur* William Wyler
1960	*The Apartment* Billy Wilder
1961	*West Side Story* Robert Wise/Jerome Robbins
1962	*Lawrence of Arabia* David Lean
1963	*Tom Jones* Tony Richardson
1964	*My Fair Lady* George Cukor
1965	*The Sound of Music* Robert Wise
1966	*A Man for All Seasons* Fred Zinnemann
1967	*In the Heat of the Night* Norman Jewison
1968	*Oliver!* Carol Reed
1969	*Midnight Cowboy* John Schlesinger
1970	*Patton* Franklin J. Schaffner
1971	*The French Connection* William Friedkin
1972	*The Godfather* Francis Ford Coppola
1973	*The Sting* George Roy Hill
1974	*The Godfather, Part II* Francis Ford Coppola
1975	*One Flew Over the Cuckoo's Nest* Milos Forman
1976	*Rocky* John G. Avildsen
1977	*Annie Hall* Woody Allen
1978	*The Deer Hunter* Michael Cimino
1979	*Kramer vs Kramer* Robert Bento
1980	*Ordinary People* Robert Redford
1981	*Chariots of Fire* Hugh Hudson
1982	*Gandhi* Richard Attenborough
1983	*Terms of Endearment* James L. Brooks
1984	*Amadeus* Milos Forman
1985	*Out of Africa* Sydney Pollack
1986	*Platoon* Oliver Stone
1987	*The Last Emperor* Bernardo Bertolucci
1988	*Rain Man* Barry Levinson
1989	*Driving Miss Daisy* Bruce Beresford
1990	*Dances with Wolves* Kevin Costner
1991	*The Silence of the Lambs* John Demme
1992	*Unforgiven* Clint Eastwood
1993	*Schindler's List* Steven Spielberg
1994	*Forrest Gump* Robert Zemeckis

Timeline

1958 *The Hostage,* play by Irish dramatist Brendan Behan. Hitchcock's *Vertigo.* Arthur Penn's *The Left-Handed Gun. Touch of Evil* by Orson Welles. Andrzej Wajda's *Ashes and Diamonds* (Poland).

1959 Otto Preminger's *Anatomy of a Murder,* with James Stewart. Billy Wilder's *Some Like it Hot,* with Tony Curtis, Jack Lemmon and Marilyn Monroe. William Wyler's *Ben Hur* stars Charlton Heston. French New Wave films (*left*) include Alain Resnais' *Hiroshima mon Amour,* François Truffaut's *Les Quatre Cents Coups;* Claude Chabrol's *Les Cousins.*

1960 *The Caretaker,* play by Harold Pinter English dramatist. Alfred Hitchcock's *Psycho* stars Janet Leigh and Anthony Perkins. Billy Wilder's *The Apartment,* with Jack Lemmon and Shirley MacLaine. Fellini's *La Dolce Vita* (Italy), with Marcello Mastroianni. Luchino Visconti's *Rocco and his Brothers* (Italy); Jean-Luc Godard's *A Bout de souffle* (*Breathless*), with Jean-Paul Belmondo.

1961 Robert Rossen's *The Hustler* stars Paul Newman. John Huston's *The Misfits* stars Montgomery Clift, Clark Gable and Marilyn Monroe. Francesco Rosi directs *Salvatore Giuliano* (Italy). François Truffaut's *Jules et Jim* (France) stars Jeanne Moreau.

1962 *Who's Afraid of Virginia Woolf?,* play by U.S. dramatist Edward Albee. First broadcast of *The Tonight Show,* U.S. TV talk show hosted by Johnny Carson.

1963 *Barefoot in the Park,* play by U.S. dramatist Neil Simon. Stanley Kubrick directs *Dr. Strangelove,* with Peter Sellers. Fellini's *8½* (Italy) stars Marcello Mastroianni. Visconti's *The Leopard* (Italy). Tony Richardson's *Tom Jones* (U.K.) stars Albert Finney.

1964 *Entertaining Mr. Sloane,* play by English dramatist Joe Orton. *Mary Poppins,* with Julie Andrews.

1965 Milos Forman's *A Blonde in Love* (Czechoslovakia). Godard's *Pierrot le Fou* (France). Lean's *Dr. Zhivago* (U.K.).

1966 *Rosencrantz and Guildenstern are Dead,* play by Czech-born English dramatist Tom Stoppard.

1967 Mike Nichols' *The Graduate* stars Dustin Hoffman. Arthur Penn's *Bonnie and Clyde* with Warren Beatty and Faye Dunaway. Losey's *Accident* (U.K.).

1968 Stanley Kubrick's *2001: A Space Odyssey.* Jack Lemon and Walter Matthau star in *The Odd Couple.* Roman Polanski's *Rosemary's Baby.*

1969 *Butch Cassidy and the Sundance Kid* stars Paul Newman and Robert Redford. Dennis Hopper's *Easy Rider* stars Jack Nicholson and Peter Fonda. Sam Peckinpah's *The Wild Bunch.* John Schlesinger's *Midnight Cowboy,* with Dustin Hoffman. Visconti's *The Damned* (Italy). *Monty Python's Flying*

Timeline

Circus (U.K.), TV comedy series. John Wayne stars in *True Grit*.

1970 Robert Altman directs *M*A*S*H*, with Donald Sutherland and Elliot Gould. Stanley Kubrick's *A Clockwork Orange*. *Straw Dogs* by Sam Peckinpah.

1972 Francis Ford Coppola directs *The Godfather* with Brando and Al Pacino. Liza Minelli stars in Bob Fosse's *Cabaret*. Bertolucci's *Last Tango in Paris* stars Brando. Buñuel's *The Discreet Charm of the Bourgeoisie* (France).

1973 Martin Scorsese's *Mean Streets*. Woody Allen's *Sleeper*. François Truffaut's *Day for Night* (France).

1974 Mel Brooks' *Young Frankenstein*. Francis Ford Coppola's *The Godfather, Part II*. Roman Polanski's *Chinatown*. Rainer Werner Fassbinder's *Fear Eats the Soul* (Germany).

1975 Milos Forman's *One Flew Over the Cuckoo's Nest* stars Jack Nicholson. Robert Altman's *Nashville*. Steven Spielberg's *Jaws*.

1976 National Theater, London, opens. Oshima's *Ai No Corrida* (*In the Realm of the Senses*, Japan). Scorsese's *Taxi Driver* with De Niro and Jodie Foster. Sylvester Stallone stars in *Rocky*. *American Buffalo*, play by David Mamet.

1977 *Star Wars* by George Lucas. Woody Allen's *Annie Hall*.

1978 Michael Cimino's *The Deer Hunter* stars De Niro and Meryl Streep. Soap opera *Dallas* begins on U.S. TV.

1979 Coppola directs *Apocalypse Now*. Woody Allen's *Manhattan*. *Christ Stopped at Eboli* (Italy) by Rosi.

1980 Cimino's *Heaven's Gate*. Scorsese's *Raging Bull* stars De Niro.

1981 *Chariots of Fire* (U.K.) by Hudson, with John Gielgud. Steven Spielberg's *Raiders of the Lost Ark*.

1982 Steven Spielberg's *E.T.* Dustin Hoffman stars in *Tootsie*.

1984 Arnold Schwarzenegger in *The Terminator*. *Ghostbusters* by Ivan Reitman. *Paris, Texas* by Wim Wenders.

1985 Madonna stars in *Desperately Seeking Susan*. John Huston directs *Prizzi's Honor*.

1986 David Lynch's *Blue Velvet*.

1987 Michael Douglas in *Wall Street*.

1988 Robert Zemeckis directs *Who Framed Roger Rabbit?*

1989 *Batman* with Michael Keaton, Kim Basinger, and Jack Nicholson.

1990 Warren Beatty's *Dick Tracy*. Scorsese's *Goodfellas*. Lynch's *Wild at Heart*. Bertolucci's *The Sheltering Sky*.

1991 Scorsese's *Cape Fear*. Jonathan Demme's *The Silence of the Lambs*.

1992 Spike Lee's *Malcolm X*. Clint Eastwood's *Unforgiven*.

1993 Altman's *Short Cuts*. Spielberg's *Jurassic Park* and *Schindler's List*. James Ivory's *The Remains of the Day*.

1994 Disney studio's *The Lion King*. Zemeckis's *Forrest Gump*. Mike Newell's *Four Weddings and a Funeral* (U.K.).

TELEVISION

The development and lightning growth of television during the 1950s and 1960s were a nightmare for Hollywood and movie producers generally. Thirty years later, each medium had become dependent upon the other.

Filmmakers found a new market for their work after general cinema release (or box-office failure), and a source of inspiration in successful TV shows. TV has also proved invaluable for the promotion of conventional big-budget films through film clips, trailers, and star interviews. Films too poor for release were unloaded onto TV, to be followed by the TV movie made especially for the medium. Satellite TV channels devoted

Upstairs, Downstairs: the cast assembles.

entirely to film have added to an apparently insatiable demand.

Comedy and drama programs made purely for TV have been built largely around the series concept. *I Love Lucy* (1951–55, and sequels), starring Lucille Ball, was among the first programs to bridge the "live" broadcast/prerecorded format. Much later the *Bill Cosby Show* gave belated recognition to black performers.

Peyton Place (1964–69) was the first U.S. prime-time "soap" (originally dramatic series on U.S. radio, sponsored by soap manufacturers), drawing its inspiration, if not its theme, from the success of the British *Coronation Street* (1960–), whose integrity has depended upon its resistance to updating to fit contemporary, "socially aware" themes.

The most successful drama series of the 1970s—if not of all time—the British *Upstairs, Downstairs* (1970–75) was watched by more than 300 million viewers in 50 countries and was twice voted Best Series by the American National Academy of TV Arts. Its story of a family and its servants in a grand London house before and during World War I contrasted sharply with that of *Dallas* (1978–91), a story of sex and sharp practice among Texas oilmen. *Dallas* began as a miniseries, but the infinite variety of villainies of its central figure, J. R. Ewing, played by Larry Hagman, ensured a long life and

Stalwarts of Star Trek*: Kirk and Spock of the starship* Enterprise.

a large following for the series.

The small screen proved an ideal medium to portray travel through time and space with the creation of *Doctor Who* (1963–), a British children's program with an adult cult following. The Doctor, a "time lord," underwent a series of successful metamorphoses to keep the show going over subsequent decades.

As successful, and conceived on an altogether more lavish scale, *Star Trek* (1966–69), with its "international" crew aboard the starship *Enterprise*, transferred successfully to the big screen.

Westerns (such as *Rawhide*,1958–65, and *Bonanza*, 1959–73) were among pioneering "saddlesoaps." Crime and police work were permanently popular (*Z Cars*, 1962–78, *Hill Street Blues*, 1980–86), while crime and fantasy were successfully combined in *Batman* (1965–67), later filmed for the movies.

New ground was broken in Germany with an honest and unembroidered saga of village life in *Heimat*, (*Homeland*, 1984). Spanning the history of a small Hunsruck community over two world wars, it employed the unusual device of

Das Boot: claustrophobia captured on the small screen.

having the village simpleton as chorus. Germany also achieved critical success with its film/TV series *Das Boot*, (*The Boat*) in 1981, a tense, claustrophobic story of a U-boat during the World War II Battle of the Atlantic.

TV in Britain has also proved a fine vehicle for the dramatic masterpieces of Dennis Potter and the satire of Alan Bennett. Neither requires the elaborate technology on which much of modern cinematography has come to depend.

PROMINENT PEOPLE

Dramatists are listed on (pp. 505-7).

ALLEN, Woody (b. 1935) U.S. actor, director: *Annie Hall* (1977), *Manhattan* (1979), *Husbands and Wives* (1992).

ALTMAN, Robert (b. 1925) U.S. director; *Nashville* (1975), *The Player* (1992).

ANTONIONI, Michelangelo (b. 1912) Italian director: *L'Avventura* (1960), *Blow-up* (1966), *Zabriskie Point* (1970).

ASHCROFT, Dame Peggy (1907–91) British actress: *Romeo and Juliet* (stage, 1935), *Quiet Wedding* (1940), *A Passage to India* (1984), *Jewel in the Crown* (TV, 1984).

ASTAIRE, Fred (1899–1987) U.S. dancer, actor: *Top Hat* (1935), *Easter Parade* (1948).

ATTENBOROUGH, Sir Richard (b. 1923) British actor, director: *Brighton Rock* (stage, 1947), *Gandhi* (dir., 1982).

BARDOT, Brigitte (b. 1934) French actress: *And God Created Woman* (1956), *Le Mépris* (1963), *Viva Maria!* (1965).

BARRAULT, Jean-Louis (1910–94) French actor: *Les Enfants du paradis* (1944). Head of Théâtre de France (1959).

BARRYMORE family U.S. actors: **Ethel** (1879–1959), *Rasputin and the Empress* (1933); brother **John** (1882–1942), *Don Juan* (1926), *Twentieth Century* (1934); brother **Lionel** (1878–1954), *It's a Wonderful Life* (1946).

BEATTY, Warren (b. 1937) U.S. actor, director: *Splendor in the Grass* (1961), *Bonnie and Clyde* (1967), *Shampoo* (1975), *Reds* (dir., 1981); brother of Shirley MACLAINE.

BELMONDO, Jean-Paul (1933–94) French actor: *Borsalino* (1970), *Stavisky* (1974).

BERGMAN, Ingmar (b. 1918) Swedish director: *Persona* (1966), *Cries and Whispers* (1972), *Autumn Sonata* (1978), *Fanny and Alexander* (1983).

BERGMAN, Ingrid (1915–82) Swedish actress: *Casablanca* (1943), *Stromboli* (1949), *Autumn Sonata* (1978).

BERKELEY, Busby (1895–1976) U.S. director: *Whoopee* (1930), *Dames* (1934), *Babes in Arms* (1939).

BERNHARDT, Sarah (1845–1923) French stage actress: first "superstar": *Phèdre* (1877), *Hamlet's Duel* (film, 1900).

BERTOLUCCI, Bernardo (b. 1940) Italian director: *Last Tango in Paris* (1972), *The Last Emperor* (1987).

BOGARDE, Sir Dirk (b. 1921) British actor: *The Blue Lamp* (1949), *A Tale of Two Cities* (1958), *Death in Venice* (1971).

BOGART, Humphrey (1899–1957) U.S. actor: *The Petrified Forest* (1936), *Casablanca* (1943), *The Big Sleep* (1946).

BOORMAN, John (b. 1933) British director: *Point Blank* (1967), *Deliverance* (1972), *Excalibur* (1981), *Hope and Glory* (1987).

BRANDO, Marlon (b. 1924), U.S. actor: *A Streetcar Named Desire* (stage, 1947; film 1951), *On the Waterfront* (1954)

Guys and Dolls (1955), *Last Tango in Paris* (1972), *A Dry White Season* (1989).

BRESSON, Robert (b. 1907) French director: *Un Condamné à mort s'est echappé* (1956), *Pickpocket* (1959).

BROOK, Sir Peter (b. 1925) British director: *Marat/Sade* (stage, 1964; film, 1967), *The Mahabharata* (stage 1988; film 1989).

BUÑUEL, Luis (1900–83) Spanish director: *Belle de Jour* (1967), *Tristana* (1970), *That Obscure Object of Desire* (1977).

BURTON, Richard (1925–84) British actor: *Look Back in Anger* (1959), *Cleopatra* (1963), *Who's Afraid of Virginia Woolf?* (1966).

CAGNEY, James (1899–1986) U.S. actor: *The Roaring Twenties* (1939), *Yankee Doodle Dandy* (1942), *Mister Roberts* (1955).

CAPRA, Frank (1897–1991) Italian-U.S. director: *Why We Fight* (World War II documentaries, 1942–44), *It's a Wonderful Life* (1946).

CARNÉ, Marcel (b. 1909) French director: *Les Enfants du paradis* (1945).

CHAPLIN, Sir Charles (Charlie) (1889–1977) Anglo-U.S. actor, director: *The Kid* (1921), *Modern Times* (1936), *Monsieur Verdoux* (1947).

CIMINO, Michael (b. 1943) U.S. director: *Thunderbolt and Lightfoot* (1974), *The Deer Hunter* (1978), *The Sicilian* (1987).

CLIFT, Montgomery (1920–66) U.S. actor: *A Place in the Sun* (1951), *Freud* (1962).

COCTEAU, Jean (1889–1963) French director: *Le Sang d'un poète* (1930), *La Belle et la Bête* (1946), *Orphée* (1950).

CONNERY, Sean (b. 1930) Scottish actor: seven *James Bond* films, *The Hill* (1965), *The Name of the Rose* (1986).

COOPER, Gary (1901–61) U.S. actor: *Sergeant York* (1941), *High Noon* (1952).

COPPOLA, Francis Ford (b. 1939) U.S. director: *The Godfather* (1972), *The Conversation* (1974), *Apocalypse Now* (1979), *Bram Stoker's Dracula* (1992).

COSTNER, Kevin (b. 1955) U.S. actor, director: *The Untouchables* (1987), *Dances with Wolves* (1989), *Robin Hood: Prince of Thieves* (1991), *The Bodyguard* (1992), *A Perfect World* (1993).

CRAWFORD, Joan (1904–77) U.S. actress: *Mildred Pierce* (1945), *Whatever Happened to Baby Jane?* (1962).

CRUISE, Tom (b. 1962) U.S. actor: *Top Gun* (1986), *Rain Man* (1988), *Born on the Fourth of July* (1989), *Interview with the Vampire* (1994).

CUKOR, George (1899–1983) U.S. director: *The Philadelphia Story* (1940), *Gaslight* (1944), *A Star is Born* (1954).

DAVIS, Bette (1908–89) U.S. actress: *Of Human Bondage* (1934), *Dark Victory* (1939), *The Little Foxes* (1941).

DEAN, James (1931–55) U.S. actor: *Rebel without a Cause* (1955), *East of Eden* (1955), *Giant* (1956).

DEMILLE, Cecil B(lount) (1881–1959) U.S. producer and director, noted for spectaculars: *The Greatest Show on Earth*

(1952), *The Ten Commandments* (Cinemascope remake, 1956).

DEMME, Jonathan (b. 1944) U.S. director: *Citizens' Band* (1977), *Melvin and Howard* (1980), *The Silence of the Lambs* (1991).

DENEUVE, Catherine (b. 1943) French actress: *Les Parapluies de Cherbourg* (1964), *Repulsion* (1965), *Belle de Jour* (1967), *Tristana* (1970).

DE NIRO, Robert (b. 1943) U.S. actor: *Taxi Driver* (1976), *The Deer Hunter* (1978), *Raging Bull* (1980), *The Untouchables* (1987), *Goodfellas* (1990), *Cape Fear* (1991).

DEPARDIEU, Gérard (b. 1948) French actor: *The Return of Martin Guerre* (1982), *Jean de Florette* (1986), *Cyrano de Bergerac*; *Green Card* (1990).

DE SICA, Vittorio (1902–74) Italian director, actor: *Umberto D* (1952), *Madame de...* (1953).

DIETRICH, Marlene (1901–92) German-U.S. actress: *Morocco* (1930), *Shanghai Express* (1932), *A Foreign Affair* (1948).

DISNEY, Walt(er Elias) (1901–66) U.S. animator and executive: Disney studio-productions include: *Pinocchio* (1940), *Dumbo* (1941), *Bambi* (1942), *Peter Pan* (1953), *Mary Poppins* (1964).

DOUGLAS family U.S. actors: **Kirk** (b. 1916): *Champion* (1949), *Lust for Life* (1956), *Paths of Glory* (1957); son **Michael** (b. 1944): *The Streets of San Francisco* (TV, 1972–77), *Wall Street* (1987), *Falling Down* (1993).

DREYER, Carl Theodor (1889–1968) Danish director: *Vampyr* (1932), *Day of Wrath* (1943), *Ordet* (The Word 1955).

DUSE, Eleonora (1859–1924) Italian actress, outstanding in plays of Ibsen and d'Annunzio.

EASTWOOD, Clint (b. 1930) U.S. actor, director: *The Good, the Bad, and the Ugly* (1966), *Dirty Harry* (1971), *The Outlaw Josey Wales* (dir., 1975), *Bird* (dir., 1988) *Unforgiven* (dir., 1992).

EISENSTEIN, Sergei (1898–1948) Russian director: *Strike* (1925), *October* (1928), *Ivan the Terrible* (Pts. I, II; 1945–46).

FAIRBANKS family U.S. actors: **Douglas, Sr.** (1883–1939): *The Mark of Zorro* (1920), *Robin Hood* (1922); son **Douglas, Jr.** (b. 1909): *The Prisoner of Zenda* (1937).

FASSBINDER, Rainer Werner (1946-82) German director: *The Bitter Tears of Petra von Kant* (1972).

FELLINI, Federico (1920–93) Italian director: *I Vitelloni* (1953), *La Strada* (1954), *La Dolce Vita* (1960), *Fred and Ginger* (1987).

FIELDS, W. C. (1879–1946) Anglo-U.S. actor: *Never Give a Sucker an Even Break* (1941).

FINNEY, Albert (b. 1936) British actor: *Saturday Night and Sunday Morning* (1960), *Tom Jones* (1963).

FLYNN, Errol (1909-59) Australian-U.S. actor: *Captain Blood* (1935), *The Sea Hawk* (1940).

FONDA family U.S. actors: **Henry**

(1905–82): *Young Mr. Lincoln* (1939), *The Grapes of Wrath* (1940), *On Golden Pond* (1981); daughter **Jane** (b. 1937): *Barbarella* (1968), *Klute* (1971), *Stanley and Iris* (1989); son **Peter** (b. 1939): *Easy Rider* (1969); daughter of Peter, **Bridget** (b. 1964): *Scandal* (1989).

FORD, Harrison (b. 1942) U.S. actor: *American Graffiti* (1973), three *Indiana Jones* films (1981–89), *Witness* (1985), *The Fugitive* (1993).

FORD, John (1895–1973) U.S. director: *The Quiet Man* (1952), *The Man Who Shot Liberty Valance* (1962).

FORMAN, Milos (b. 1932) Czech—U.S. director: *The Fireman's Ball* (1967), *Amadeus* (1984), *Valmont* (1989).

FOSTER, Jodie (b. 1962) U.S. actress, director: *Taxi Driver* (1976), *The Accused* (1988), *The Silence of the Lambs* (1991), *Little Man Tate* (dir., 1991).

GABLE, Clark (1901–60) U.S. actor: *It Happened One Night* (1934), *Gone with the Wind* (1939), *The Misfits* (1961).

GARBO, Greta (1905–90) Swedish-U.S. actress: *Flesh and the Devil* (1927), *Anna Christie* (1930), *Queen Christina* (1933).

GARRICK, David (1717–79) British actor: greatest of his time; dramatist, manager; introduced more naturalistic acting style.

GIELGUD, Sir John (b. 1904) British actor; leading Shakespearean stage roles: *The Good Companions* (1933), *Arthur* (1981), *Prospero's Books* (1991).

GISH, Lillian (1896–1993) U.S. actress: *Birth of a Nation* (1915), *The Wind* (1928), *The Whales of August* (1987).

GODARD, Jean-Luc (b. 1930) French New Wave director: *A Bout de souffle* (1960), *Weekend* (1968).

GRANT, Cary (1904–86) Anglo-U.S. actor: *Arsenic and Old Lace* (1944), *North by Northwest* (1959).

GRIFFITH, D(avid) W(ark) (1875–1948) U.S. director: *The Lonedale Operator* (1911), *Birth of a Nation* (1915), *Way Down East* (1920), *The Sorrows of Satan* (1926).

GUINNESS, Sir Alec (b. 1914) British actor: *The Bridge on the River Kwai* (1957), *Star Wars* (1977), *Smiley's People* (TV, 1981), *Little Dorrit* (1987).

HALL, Sir Peter (b. 1930) British stage and film director: director, Royal Shakespeare Company, 1957–68; National Theater, 1973–88; *Work Is a Four-Letter Word* (1968).

HARRISON, Sir Rex (1908–90) British actor: *Blithe Spirit* (1945), *Cleopatra* (1963), *Dr. Doolittle* (1967).

HAWKS, Howard (1896–1977) U.S. director: *The Big Sleep* (1946).

HAYES, Helen (1900–1993) U.S. actress: *Arrowsmith* (1931), *A Farewell to Arms* (1932), *Airport* (1969).

HEPBURN, Audrey (1929–93) British actress: *Roman Holiday* (1953), *Breakfast at Tiffany's* (1961), *My Fair Lady* (1964).

HEPBURN, Katharine (b. 1907) U.S. actress: *Morning Glory* (1933), *The African Queen* (1951), *The Lion in Winter*

(1968), *On Golden Pond* (1981).

HERZOG, Werner (b. 1942) German director: *The Mystery of Kaspar Hauser* (1975), *Fitzcarraldo* (1982).

HESTON, Charlton (b. 1923) U.S. actor, director: *The Ten Commandments* (1956), *The Agony and the Ecstasy* (1965), *Antony and Cleopatra* (1972).

HITCHCOCK, Sir Alfred (1899–1980) Anglo-U.S. director: *The Thirty-Nine Steps* (1935), *The Lady Vanishes* (1938), *Rear Window* (1954), *Psycho* (1960), *The Birds* (1963), *Frenzy* (1972).

HOFFMAN, Dustin (b. 1937) U.S. actor: *The Graduate* (1967), *Midnight Cowboy* (1969), *Tootsie* (1982), *Rain Man* (1988).

HOPKINS, Anthony (b. 1937) British actor: *The Lion in Winter* (1968), *Equus* (stage, 1974), *The Bunker* (TV, 1981), *The Silence of the Lambs* (1991), *The Remains of the Day* (1993).

HOWARD, Trevor (1916–88) British actor: *The Heart of the Matter* (1953), *Mutiny on the Bounty* (1962).

HUSTON family U.S. actors and directors: **Walter** (1884–1950): *Dodsworth* (1936), *The Devil and Daniel Webster* (1941); son **John** (1906–87) U.S. actor, director: *The Maltese Falcon* (1941), *Key Largo* (1948), *Prizzi's Honor* (1985), granddaughter **Anjelica** (b. 1952) Irish—U.S. actress: *Prizzi's Honor* (1985); *The Grifters* (1990), *Lonesome Dove* (TV 1992).

IRVING, Sir (John) Henry (Brodribb) (1838–1905) British actor-manager: dominant figure of Victorian theater.

JANNINGS, Emil (1884–1950) Swiss-German actor: *The Way of All Flesh* (1927), *The Last Command* (1928), *Ohm Krüger* (1941).

KAZAN, Elia (b. 1909), Greek-U.S. director: *Gentleman's Agreement* (1947), *A Streetcar Named Desire* (1951), *On the Waterfront* (1954), *East of Eden* (1955).

KEATON, Buster (1895–1966) U.S. actor, director: *Our Hospitality* (1923), *The Navigator* (1924), *The General* (1927), *The Railrodder* (1965).

KELLY, Gene (b. 1912) U.S. actor, dancer, director: *For Me and My Gal* (1942), *Singin' in the Rain* (1952), *It's Always Fair Weather* (1955).

KEMBLE family British actors: **John** (1757–1823): noted for Shakespearian roles; **Frances** (Fanny) (1809–93): her Juliet debut (1829) caused a sensation.

KUBRICK, Stanley (b. 1928) U.S. director: *Paths of Glory* (1957), *Spartacus* (1960), *A Clockwork Orange* (1971), *Full Metal Jacket* (1987).

KUROSAWA, Akira (b. 1910) Japanese director: *Yojimbo* (1961), *Kagemusha* (1980), *Ran* (1985).

LANCASTER, Burt (1913–94) U.S. actor: *The Killers* (1946), *Elmer Gantry* (1960), *Birdman of Alcatraz* (1962), *Atlantic City* (1981), *Local Hero* (1983).

LANG, Fritz (1890–1976) Austrian-U.S. director: *Metropolis* (1927), *Rancho Notorious* (1952).

LAUGHTON, Charles (1899–1962) Anglo-U.S. actor, director: *Mutiny on the Bounty* (1935), *The Hunchback of Notre Dame* (1939), *The Night of the Hunter* (dir., 1955).

LAUREL, Stan (1890–1965) Anglo-U.S. actor, and **HARDY, Oliver** (1892–1957) U.S. actor: comedy duo; *Putting Pants on Philip* (1927), *Big Business* (1929), *The Music Box* (1932), *Way Out West* (1937).

LEAN, Sir David (1908–91) British director: *Bridge on the River Kwai* (1957), *Lawrence of Arabia* (1962).

LEIGH, Vivien (1913–67) British actress: *Gone With the Wind* (1939), *A Streetcar Named Desire* (1951), *Ship of Fools* (1965).

LITTLEWOOD, Joan (b. 1914) British stage director, founder of Theater Union (1936), Theater Workshop (1945): *A Taste of Honey* (1958), *Oh, What a Lovely War!* (1963).

LUBITSCH, Ernst (1892–1947) German-U.S. director: *Trouble in Paradise* (1932), *Heaven Can Wait* (1943).

LYNCH, David (b. 1946) U.S. director: *Eraserhead* (1977), *Blue Velvet* (1986), *Twin Peaks* (TV series, 1989).

MACLAINE, Shirley (b. 1934) U.S. actress: *Sweet Charity* (1969), *Terms of Endearment* (1983).

MALLE, Louis (b. 1932) French director: *Zazie dans le métro* (1960), *Lacombe Lucien* (1973), *Atlantic City* (1981), *Au Revoir les Enfants* (1987).

MANKIEWICZ, Joseph (1909–93) U.S. director: *All About Eve* (1950), *Julius Caesar* (1953), *Guys and Dolls* (1955).

MARVIN, Lee (1924–87) U.S. actor: *Cat Ballou* (1965), *Point Blank* (1967), *Paint Your Wagon* (1969), *Prime Cut* (1972).

MARX brothers U.S. comedy team: **Chico** (1886–1961), **Harpo** (1888–1964), **Groucho** (1890–1977), **Gummo** (1893–1977), **Zeppo** (1901–79); *Monkey Business* (1931), *A Night at the Opera* (1935).

MASON, James (1909–84) British actor: *The Desert Fox* (1951), *The Verdict* (1982).

McKELLEN, Sir Ian (b. 1939) British actor: *Macbeth* (stage, 1976), many more Shakespearean roles, *Walter* (TV, 1982), *Scandal* (1989), *Wild at Heart* (1990).

MINNELLI family: **Vincente** (1910-1986) U.S. director: *Father of the Bride* (1950), *An American in Paris* (1951), *Gigi* (1958); daughter **Liza** (b. 1946): U.S. actress: *Cabaret* (1972).

MITCHUM, Robert (b. 1917) U.S. actor: *The Night of the Hunter* (1955), *Farewell My Lovely* (1975).

MONROE, Marilyn (1926–62) U.S. actress: *Gentlemen Prefer Blondes* (1953), *Niagara* (1953), *Bus Stop* (1956), *Some Like It Hot* (1959).

MONTAND, Yves (1921–91) French actor: *Z* (1968), *Jean de Florette* (1986), *Manon des Sources* (1986).

MOREAU, Jeanne (b. 1928) French actress: *La Notte* (1961), *Jules et Jim* (1961), *Diary of a Chambermaid* (1964).

NEWMAN, Paul (b. 1925) U.S. actor, director: *Cat on a Hot Tin Roof* (1958), *The Hustler* (1961), *Hud* (1963), *The Color of Money* (1986).

NICHOLS, Mike (b. 1931) U.S. director: *Who's Afraid of Virginia Woolf?* (1966), *The Graduate* (1967), *Silkwood* (1983).

NICHOLSON, Jack (b. 1937) U.S. actor, director: *Five Easy Pieces* (1970), *Chinatown* (1974), *One Flew Over the Cuckoo's Nest* (1975), *The Shining* (1980), *The Two Jakes* (dir., 1990), *A Few Good Men* (1992).

NIVEN, David (1909–83) British actor: *Around the World in Eighty Days* (1956).

OLIVIER, Lord Laurence (1907–89) British actor, director: *Romeo and Juliet* (stage, 1935), *Wuthering Heights* (1939), *Henry V* (dir., 1944), *Richard III* (dir. 1955), *The Entertainer* (1960).

OPHULS, Max (1902–57) German director: *Letter from an Unknown Woman* (1948), *Lola Montes* (1955).

OSHIMA, Nagisa (b. 1932) Japanese director: *The Sun's Burial* (1960), *The Ceremony* (1971).

PACINO, Al (b. 1940) U.S. actor: *Dog Day Afternoon* (1975), *Sea of Love* (1989), *The Godfather, Part III* (1990).

PARKER, Alan (b. 1944) British director: *Bugsy Malone* (1976), *Birdy* (1985), *Angel Heart* (1987), *The Commitments* (1991).

PASOLINI, Pier Paolo (1922–75) Italian director: *The Gospel According to St. Matthew* (1964), *The Decameron* (1971).

PECKINPAH, Sam (1925–84) U.S. director: *Straw Dogs* (1971), *Cross of Iron* (1977).

PENN, Arthur (b. 1922) U.S. director: *Miracle Worker* (1962), *Alice's Restaurant* (1969).

PICKFORD, Mary (1893–1979) Canadian-U.S. actress: *The Little Teacher* (1909), *Tess of the Storm Country* (1922).

POITIER, Sidney (b. 1924) U.S. actor: *The Blackboard Jungle* (1955), *In the Heat of the Night* (1967).

POLANSKI, Roman (b. 1933) Polish-U.S. director, actor: *Knife in the Water* (1962), *Repulsion* (1965), *Tess* (1979).

POWELL, Michael (1905–90) British director; usually in collaboration with Emeric Pressburger, Hungarian writer (1902–88): *The Red Shoes* (1948).

PREMINGER, Otto (1905–86) Austrian-U.S. director: *The Man with the Golden Arm* (1955), *Exodus* (1960).

RAY, Nicholas (1911–79) U.S. director: *They Live by Night* (1948), *Rebel Without a Cause* (1955).

RAY, Satyajit (1921–92) Indian director: *Unvanquished* (1956), *The World of Apu* (1959), *The Home and the World* (1984).

REDFORD, Robert (b. 1937) U.S. actor, director: *Barefoot in the Park* (1967), *Butch Cassidy and the Sundance Kid* (1969), *The Sting* (1973), *Ordinary People* (dir., 1980), *Quiz Show* (dir. 1994).

REDGRAVE family British actors: Sir **Michael** (1908–85): *Mourning Becomes Electra* (1947), *The Browning Version* (1951); daughter **Vanessa** (b. 1937): *Blow-Up* (1966), *Isadora* (1968), *Julia* (1977), *Howards End* (1992); daughter **Lynn** (b. 1943): *Georgy Girl* (1966), *House Calls* (TV, 1979–81).

REED, Sir Carol (1906–75) British director: *Third Man* (1949), *Our Man in Havanna* (1959), *Oliver!* (1968).

RENOIR, Jean (1894–1979) French director; *La Bête Humaine* (1938), *La Règle du jeu* (1939), *The River* (1950), *Le Déjeuner sur l'herbe* (1959).

RESNAIS, Alain (b. 1922) French director: *Last Year at Marienbad* (1961), *Smoking/No Smoking* (1994).

RICHARDSON, Sir Ralph (1902–83) British actor: *The Fallen Idol* (1948), *The Heiress* (1949), *Greystoke* (1984).

RICHARDSON, Tony (1928–91) British director: *Look Back in Anger* (stage, 1956, film, 1959).

RIEFENSTAHL, Leni (b. 1902) German director: *Triumph of the Will* (1935), documentary of Nazi rally, *Olympia* (1938).

ROBESON, Paul (1898–1976) U.S. actor and singer: *The Emperor Jones* (1932), *Show Boat* (1936), *The Proud Valley* (1940).

ROEG, Nicholas (b. 1928) British director: *Don't Look Now* (1971), *The Man Who Fell to Earth* (1973), *Bad Timing* (1980), *The Witches* (1990).

ROSSELLINI, Roberto (1906–77) Italian director: *Rome–Open City* (1945), *Germany, Year Zero* (1947).

SCOFIELD, Paul (b. 1922) British actor: *A Man for All Seasons* (stage, 1960, film 1966), *Othello* (stage, 1980).

SCORSESE, Martin (b. 1942) U.S. director: *Taxi Driver* (1976), *Raging Bull* (1980), *Cape Fear* (1991), *Age of Innocence* (1993).

SCOTT, Ridley (b. 1937), British director: *Alien* (1979), *Blade Runner* (1982), *Black Rain* (1989), *Thelma and Louise* (1991).

SELLERS, Peter (1925–80) British actor: *I'm Alright Jack* (1959), *Dr. Strangelove* (1964), *The Pink Panther* (1964), *Being There* (1979).

SIDDONS, Sarah (1755–1831) considered Britain's greatest tragic actress.

SIGNORET, Simone (1921–85) French actress: *La Ronde* (1950), *Ship of Fools* (1965), *Madame Rosa* (1977).

SPIELBERG, Steven (b. 1947) U.S. director: *Duel* (TV, 1972), *Jaws* (1975), *Close Encounters of the Third Kind* (1977), *E.T.* (1982), *Schindler's List* (1993), *Jurassic Park* (1993).

STANISLAVSKY, Konstantin Sergeyevich (1863–1938) Russian actor, producer; "method acting" based on his teachings.

STANWYCK, Barbara (1907–90) U.S. actress: *Stella Dallas* (1937), *Walk on the Wild Side* (1962).

STERNBERG, Josef von (1894–1969) Austrian-U.S. director: *The Last Command* (1928), *Morocco* (1930), *Shanghai Express* (1932).

STEWART, James (b. 1908) U.S. actor: *The Philadelphia Story* (1940), *It's a Wonderful Life* (1946), *Rear Window* (1954).

STONE, Oliver (b. 1946) U.S. director: *Salvador* (1983), *Platoon* (1986), *JFK* (1991), *Natural Born Killers* (1994).

STREEP, Meryl (b. 1949) U.S. actress: *The Deer Hunter* (1978), *Kramer vs. Kramer* (1979), *Sophie's Choice* (1982), *Silkwood* (1983).

STREISAND, Barbra (b. 1942) U.S. actress, director: *Funny Girl* (1968), *Hello Dolly* (1969), *Yentl* (dir., 1983).

STROHEIM, Erich von (1885–1957) Austrian—U.S. director, actor: *Foolish Wives* (1922), *Greed* (1925).

TARANTINO, Quentin (b. 1963) U.S. director, writer: *Reservoir Dogs* (1992), *Pulp Fiction* (1994).

TARKOVSKY, Andrei (1932–86) Russian director: *Ivan's Childhood* (1962), *Andrei Roublev* (1966), *Solaris* (1972), *Mirror* (1975), *Stalker* (1979), *Nostalgia* (1983).

TATI, Jacques (1908–82) French actor, director: *Jour de Fête* (1949), *Mon Oncle* (1958).

TAYLOR, Elizabeth (b. 1932) British actress: *National Velvet* (1944), *Butterfield 8* (1960), *Cleopatra* (1962), *Who's Afraid of Virginia Woolf?* (1966).

TRACY, Spencer (1900–67) U.S. actor: *Captains Courageous* (1937), *Guess Who's Coming to Dinner* (1967).

TRUFFAUT, François (1932–84) French director: *Shoot the Pianist* (1960), *Fahrenheit 451* (1966), *The Story of Adèle H* (1975), *The Green Room* (1978).

ULLMANN, Liv (b. 1939) Norwegian actress: *Face to Face* (1976), *Autumn Sonata* (1978).

VALENTINO, Rudolph (1845–1926) Italian—U.S. actor: *The Sheik* (1921), *Blood and Sand* (1922), *The Eagle* (1925).

VISCONTI, Luchino (1906–76) Italian director: *Senso* (1954), *Death in Venice* (1971), *Ludwig* (1972), *L'Innocente* (1976).

WAJDA, Andrzej (b. 1926) Polish director: *Kanal* (1957), *Man of Marble* (1977), *Man of Iron* (1981), *Danton* (1982).

WAYNE, John (1907–79) U.S. actor: *The Alamo* (1960), *True Grit* (1969), *The Shootist* (1976).

WEIR, Peter (b. 1944) Australian director: *Picnic at Hanging Rock* (1975), *Witness* (1985), *Dead Poets Society* (1989).

WELLES, Orson (1915–85) U.S. actor, director: *Citizen Kane* (1941), *The Magnificent Ambersons* (1942), *Lady from Shanghai* (1948), *The Trial* (1962).

WENDERS, Wim (b. 1945) German director: *Kings of the Road* (1976), *Paris, Texas* (1984), *Wings of Desire* (1987).

WEST, Mae (1892–1980) U.S. actress: *I'm No Angel* (1933), *Klondike Annie* (1936), *The Heat's On* (1943).

WILDER, Billy (b. 1906) Austrian-U.S. director: *Double Indemnity* (1944), *The Fortune Cookie* (1966), *Fedora* (1978).

WYLER, William (1902–81) U.S. director: *Wuthering Heights* (1939), *The Little Foxes* (1941), *The Heiress* (1949), *Roman Holiday* (1953), *The Big Country* (1958).

MUSIC DEFINITIONS

Music is the art of making sound in a rhythmically organized, harmonious form, either sung or produced with instruments. Music and dance are perhaps as old as humankind. All the ancient civilizations, such as those of Sumeria, China, and Egypt, used music in religious and other ceremonies. In the West, music is often divided into "classical" and "popular," with the former including symphonies, operas, and ballets, and the latter including folk and country music, jazz, and rock. Some terms from classical music are given below.

Adagio At a slow pace.

Allegro At a fast pace.

Alto High falsetto male voice; or lowest female voice (contralto).

Arpeggio Notes of a chord played in rapid succession.

Bar Metrical division of musical beats bounded by vertical bar lines.

Bass Low voice or part.

Brass instruments Metal instruments sounded by blowing through mouthpiece and altering tension of lips, e.g. trumpet.

Chamber music Music performed by a small group such as a quartet in which each part is played by a single instrument.

Chord Combination of three or more notes played together.

Chorus Main body of singers in choir; or words and music repeated after each stanza of song.

Clef Sign in musical notation that fixes pitch of each note written on the stave.

Concerto Composition for one or more solo instruments and orchestra.

Contralto Lowest female voice.

Counterpoint Two or more melodies combined to form a satisfying harmony.

Crescendo Gradually louder.

Diminuendo Gradually softer.

Flat Conventional sign showing pitch of a note has been lowered by a semitone.

Forte Played or sung loudly.

Fortissimo Played very loud.

Fugue Musical composition in which a theme is introduced in one part and then developed by two or more "voices."

Harmony Combining of sequences of notes or sounds to make musical sense.

Interval Difference in pitch between two notes or tones.

Key Classification of the notes of a scale.

Largo At a slow pace.

Lied German word for "song" (plural lieder).

Major One of the two main scales, with semitones between 3rd and 4th, and 7th and 8th notes.

Melody A tune; or sequence of musical sounds, as distinct from harmony.

Mezzo Half, medium, or moderately.

Minor One of the two main scales. Harmonic minor scales have a semitone between 2nd and 3rd, 5th and 6th, and 7th and 8th notes.

Movement Complete section of a larger work (such as a symphony).

Nocturne A "night-piece," tuneful but sad.

Octave Range of sound, or series of notes, between the 1st note and the 8th note on a major or minor scale, e.g. from C to the C above.

Oratorio Religious musical composition for soloists, chorus, and orchestra.

Orchestra Large group of musicians playing a variety of different instruments as an ensemble, led by a conductor.

Percussion instruments Musical instruments played by striking, e.g. drums, xylophone, etc.

Piano Played or sung softly.

Pitch Highness or lowness in sound of one note compared with another.

Plainsong Unaccompanied vocal melody used in medieval church music.

Presto At a fast pace.

Scale Progression of successive notes, ascending or descending, through one octave or more in order of pitches.

Score Written music showing all parts (vocal and instrumental) of composition on separate staves.

Semitone A halftone; smallest interval commonly used in western music.

Sharp Conventional sign showing that the note referred to has been raised in pitch by a semitone.

Sol-fa Musical notation using letters and syllables instead of notes on a stave.

Sonata Musical piece, in three or more movements, chiefly for a solo instrument.

Soprano Highest female voice.

Stave or **staff** Framework of lines and spaces on which music is usually written.

Stringed instruments Instruments that are played with a bow, or plucked.

Symphony Long orchestral piece of music in several movements.

Tempo Pace or speed of piece of music.

Tenor Highest natural male voice.

Theme Short melody forming the basis of a piece of music and which is developed and repeated with variations.

Tone A sound having a definite pitch.

Woodwind instruments Instruments that are blown and are traditionally, but not always, made of wood, e.g. flute.

MEDIEVAL, RENAISSANCE

Terpsichore, muse of music and dance.

Church music dominated the Middle Ages, becoming more complex as new parts were added to the old single line of plainsong, creating polyphony. An early exponent was the Frenchman Perotin (*c.* 1200), but the greatest was Josquin des Prés, the Flemish master who took his polished polyphony to Italy where it was to inspire the genius of Palestrina. The medieval period also saw the emergence of secular music as art, with the songs of troubadours (Provence) and minnesingers (Germany) (*p. 491*).

Musicians were itinerant. Lassus (1532–94), the Flemish master, worked in Sicily, Rome, and Munich, while English madrigalists like John Bull and John Dowland also traveled widely.

The Reformation (*p. 338*) affected all music. Luther pressed for the mass to be sung in the German vernacular, which led to the glories of the Bach chorale. But it was printing that chiefly allowed the wider dissemination of music and the flowering of the great era of Baroque music. The last great composer of the Renaissance (and the first of the Baroque) was Claudio Monteverdi. As adept in madrigals as in sacred music, he also composed operas, of which *La Favola D'Orfeo* (1607) and *L'Incoronazione di Poppaea* (1642) have survived.

Music and dance flowered in Renaissance Italy as new instruments appeared.

BAROQUE, CLASSICAL

The Baroque era in music (c.1600–1750) began with Italian domination. As a result, musical vocabulary became essentially Italian; *sonata* ("sounded"), *cantata* ("sung"), and *opera* were terms defining the paths that music was to follow.

All music—and civilization—owes a debt to the year 1685, the birth year of Georg Friedrich Handel, Johann Sebastian Bach, and Domenico Scarlatti. Handel and Bach were born near to each other, but never met: Bach remained in Germany, while Handel became a peripatetic virtuoso, settling in England.

Johann Sebastian was not the only musical Bach of Eisenach; his sons Wilhelm Friedemann, Carl Philipp Emanuel, and Johann Christian (the "English Bach") achieved lasting fame. But true greatness belongs to their father, perhaps the most accomplished musician who ever lived.

Bach's reputation, largely provincial, languished for more than a century; not so that of Handel, his direct contemporary. Lionized by the Hanoverian court in London, Handel composed a body of operas and oratorios—the *Messiah* was first performed in Dublin in 1742—which remain firmly in the repertoire.

By the time of Bach's death in 1750, Europe's musical center of gravity had shifted north from Italy to Germany, where Johann Stamitz was laying the foundations of the modern symphony at the court of Mannheim. The Classical age had begun, its heart not in Italy (which was still important) but in Vienna.

Christoph Willibald von Gluck, a German who worked in Vienna, was inspired by Handel, but abandoned conventional form in favor of dramatic impact and simplicity of expression, thus transforming opera with *Orfeo ed Euridice* (1762) and *Alceste* (1767). The Austrian Joseph

The giant of Baroque music, Johann Sebastian Bach.

Haydn, the "father of the symphony," was as prolific as he was popular, with more than 100 symphonies and 80 string quartets to his name. His work brought the Classical era to its peak, and was surpassed only by his protégé and close friend Wolfgang Amadeus Mozart.

A child prodigy, Mozart had written about 200 works by the time he was 18. His first opera, *Apollo et Hyacinthus*, was composed when he was 11, and the last, *The Magic Flute*, in the year of his death. In between were the glories of *Idomeneo*, *Il Seraglio*, *The Marriage of Figaro*, *Così fan tutte*, and *Don Giovanni*. With all this came 27 piano concertos, one of his favorite forms. He died penniless and was buried in an unmarked grave. His *Requiem*, unfinished at his death, is an apt and moving coda to his life.

Classical genius Mozart and his sister, Maria-Anna, at the keyboard with their father Leopold.

Timeline

c. 700 B.C. Earliest recorded music, a Sumerian hymn written in cuneiform. Choral and dramatic music begin to develop in Greece.

c. 530 B.C. Pyathagoras discovers musical intervals and the octave.

A.D. 350 Foundation of Schola Cantorum for church song, Rome.

386 St. Ambrose introduces hymn singing into the Christian church.

c. 750 Gregorian church music flourishes in England, France, and Germany.

855 Polyphonic music begins.

990 Systematic musical notation is developed.

1026 Guido d'Arezzo introduces a form of tonic sol–fa.

c. 1050 Polyphonic song replaces Gregorian chant.

c. 1150 Troubadours flourish in France; minnesingers in Germany (*p. 491*).

1325 First polyphonic mass is performed (Tournai, France).

1360 Clavichord develops. The lute becomes popular.

1465 Printed music appears.

1495 Josquin des Prés (*p. 520*), Flemish composer, becomes choirmaster at Cambrai, France.

1537 First conservatories of music are founded in Naples and Venice.

1551 Giovanni Perluigi da Palestrina, Italian composer, is director of music at the Cappella Giulia, Rome.

1553 The violin is developed.

1563 William Byrd, English composer, becomes organist at Lincoln cathedral.

1600 The recorder becomes popular.

1610 Italian composer Claudio Monteverdi (*p. 520*) writes *Vespers* (choral).

1637 Teatro San Cassiano, Venice, is Europe's first public opera house.

1644 Birth of Antonio Stradivarius, Italian violin maker.

c. 1650 Beginning of modern harmony. Development of the overture.

1661 Louis XIV founds Académie Royale de Danse, Paris.

1663 French horn becomes orchestral instrument.

1664 German composer Heinrich Schütz's *Christmas Oratorio*.

1679 French composer Jean-Baptiste Lully's *Belérophon* (opera). Italian composer Alessandro Scarlatti's *Gli equivoci nel sembiante* (opera).

1689 Henry Purcell's *Dido and Aeneas* (opera).

1709 Italian Bartolommeo Cristofori invents the pianoforte. The clarinet becomes an orchestral instrument.

1712 Italian composer Arcangelo Corelli's *Twelve Concerti Grossi*.

1721 German composer Johann Sebastian Bach's *Brandenburg Concertos*.

1723 Bach (*above, left*) becomes director of music at Leipzig, Germany.

1727 J.S. Bach's *Saint Matthew Passion* (oratorio).

1732 First concerto held in Charleston,

Timeline

South Carolina.

1741 G. F. Handel's *Messiah* (oratorio) (*p. 521*).

1749 J. S. Bach's Mass in B minor.

1750 Bach's *Art of Fugue.*

1759 Austrian composer Franz Joseph Haydn's Symphony No. 1 in D major.

1762 German composer Christoph Gluck's *Orfeo ed Euridice* (opera).

1776 Bolshoi Ballet is established in Moscow.

1780 Haydn's "Toy" Symphony.

1786 Austrian composer Wolfgang Amadeus Mozart's *The Marriage of Figaro* (opera).

1787 Mozart's *Don Giovanni* (opera).

1788 Mozart's Symphony No. 41 ("Jupiter").

1790 Mozart's *Così fan tutte* (opera).

1795 Haydn completes the Twelve London Symphonies.

1798 Haydn's *The Creation* (oratorio).

1803 German composer Ludwig van Beethoven's Symphony No. 3 ("Eroica").

1805 Italian violin virtuoso Nicolo Paganini tours Europe.

1806 Beethoven's Violin Concerto.

1808 Beethoven's Symphony No. 6 ("Pastoral").

1814 Austrian composer Franz Schubert begins production of *lieder* (songs).

1816 Italian composer Gioacchino Rossini's *The Barber of Seville* (opera).

1819 Beethoven Society formed in Portland, Maine (eight years before composer's death).

1821 German composer Carl Maria von Weber's *Der Freischütz* (opera).

1824 Beethoven's Symphony No. 9 ("Choral").

1828 Schubert's Symphony No. 9.

1830 French composer Hector Berlioz's *Symphonie Fantastique* (*right above*).

1833 German composer Felix Mendelssohn's "Italian" Symphony.

1837 Academy of Music Orchestra (first in U.S.) founded in Boston. Hector Berlioz's *Grande Messe des Morts.*

c. 1840 French instrument maker A. F. Debain invents the harmonium.

1841 German composer Robert Schumann's Symphony No. 1. German composer Richard Wagner's *The Flying Dutchman* (opera) (*p. 523*).

1844 Italian composer Giuseppe Verdi's *Ernani* (opera). Mendelssohn's Violin Concerto.

1845 Wagner's *Tannhäuser* (opera).

1846 Mendelssohn's *Elijah* (oratorio).

1848 Wagner's *Lohengrin* (opera).

1849 Hungarian composer Franz Liszt's *Tasso* (symphonic poem).

1851 Verdi's *Rigoletto* (opera) (*p. 523*).

1853 Verdi's *Il Trovatore* (opera).

1854 Berlioz's *The Infant Christ* (oratorio). Liszt's *Les Preludes* (symphonic poem).

1858 French composer Jacques Offenbach's *Orpheus in the Underworld* (light opera).

ROMANTIC

One figure dominates the Romantic era—and all subsequent music: Ludwig van Beethoven. A Rhinelander, Beethoven went to Vienna as a youth, where his ability to improvise on the keyboard impressed Mozart. At 22, he moved to the musical city permanently. The world was in a state of upheaval; the American and French revolutions had broken the old patterns of life, and Napoleon was on the march. The times are reflected best of all by the tempestuous power of Beethoven's music. His symphonies stand unmatched (the 9th, or "Choral," provides the European Union with its anthem); his violin concerto is the finest for the instrument. The "Pathétique" sonata and his first string quartets date from his middle 20s; his last and greatest sonatas and quartets from the last years of his life, when he was totally deaf.

Franz Schubert was Viennese through and through. Dogged by ill health (which resulted in the "Unfinished" Symphony), Schubert wrote more than 600 songs in his short lifetime, chamber music such as *Die Forelle* ("Trout" Quintet), symphonies, and music for the theater.

Beethoven and Schubert heralded the Romantic era; and the musical stage was now to be crowded with an unparalleled cast of composers and virtuosi. A period of less than 20 years saw the births of Schubert (1797), Vincenzo Bellini (1801), Hector Berlioz (1803), Felix Mendelssohn (1809), Frederic Chopin (1810), Robert Schumann (1810), Franz Liszt (1811), Guiseppe Verdi (1813), and Richard Wagner (1813). The Italian virtuoso of the violin, Niccolò Paganini (1782-1840), was stalking the stage, and the operas of Gioacchino Rossini were being performed by this time.

The Romantic era was exemplified by the music of Hector Berlioz. An admirer of Shakespeare and a friend of Hugo, Dumas, and Balzac, Berlioz's forte was music inspired by literary and historical themes—operas (*Les Troyens, Benvenuto Cellini,* among others) and symphonies (*Fantastique, The Corsair, Roméo et Juliette*).

The last great symphonists of the 1800s were Anton Brückner and, above all, Johannes Brahms, whose symphonies and concertos for piano and violin, and variations (on themes of Haydn, the St. Anthony Chorale, and Handel) have the widest musical appeal. His greatest choral work, the *German Requiem,* was first performed in 1869.

Mozart, Beethoven, and all later generations of composers owe an eternal debt to the Italian Bartolommeo Cristofori (1655–1731), the inventor of the pianoforte, most widely used of all instruments. At first, pianos had wooden frames, but the tension on the stringing proved too much. During the 1800s, makers added an iron frame to make the most popular of instruments a difficult thing to shift. Modern stringing exerts a pull of 30 tons, but gives the instrument its great power and sonority.

Chopin, Schumann, and Liszt were virtuosi of the keyboard as well as composers (Schumann's platform career was shortened by a hand injury; his wife Clara took his place in public as one of the most accomplished pianists of her time).

Lionized by society, Liszt composed more than 400 original works and 900 transcriptions.

OPERA

The young Vincenzo Bellini (who died aged 34) composed 11 operas during his brief lifetime. The melodic nature of works such as *I Puritani* and *Norma* were to find perfect interpretation in the 1900s, by the divas Maria Callas and Joan Sutherland.

The genius of the two greatest opera composers of the 1800s, Guiseppe Verdi and Richard Wagner, emerged at almost the same moment—Verdi's *Nabucco* and *I Lombardi* (1842–43), Wagner's *Rienzi* (1840) and *The Flying Dutchman* (1841). The medieval and Renaissance contrast between the "Gothic North" and the "Golden South" had appeared again.

Verdi's were the most popular operas, and between 1844 and 1871 he wrote *Ernani, Il Trovatore, Rigoletto, La Traviata, The Masked Ball, La Forza del Destino, Don Carlos,* and *Aida.*

During the same period, Wagner composed (and wrote) his great "Ring" cycle *Der Ring des Nibelungen* (*Rhein-gold, Walküre, Siegfried,* and *Götterdämmerung*, 1854–74). Verdi lived much longer, writing two of his masterpieces, *Otello* and *Falstaff*, just before his 80th birthday.

In France, and younger than his two great contemporaries, Charles Gounod was enjoying great success with *Faust* (1859), *Romeo and Juliet* (1867), and *Mireille* (1864); the merrier music of Jacques Offenbach, *Orpheus in the Underworld* (1858), *La Belle Hélène* (1864), and *La Vie Parisienne* (1866) became internationally popular. The quieter talents of César Franck, the Franco-Belgian organist, were appreciated only after he died.

Georges Bizet wrote two operas, *The Pearl Fishers* (1863) and *The Fair Maid of Perth* (1867), which received only a modest reception when they were first performed, but neither drew the opprobrium of *Carmen*, written in the year of his death (1875). It was to become one of the most successful of all operas.

Verdi's Aida *was written to celebrate the opening of the Suez Canal in 1871.*

NATIONAL MUSIC

The revolutionary turbulence that dominated the mid-1800s injected a new element of nationalism into the music of many countries, which gave native talent there a special impetus.

In Eastern Europe, its first green shoots appeared with the Russian Mikhail Glinka and his operas, *A Life for the Tsar* (1836) and *Ruslan and Ludmila* (1842). He was the father figure of a group of young composers—Aleksandr Borodin (b. 1833), Mili Balakirev (b. 1837), Modest Mussorgsky (b. 1839), and Nikolai Rimsky-Korsakov (b. 1844) among others. But the greatest composer of czarist Russia, Peter Ilich Tchaikovsky, was not overtly nationalist. He remains the most popular with audiences all over the Western world; little of his work is ignored, and the fantasy overture *Romeo and Juliet* (1880) is among the most frequently performed worldwide of all orchestral compositions.

At the musical heart of Europe, Bohemia was the birthplace of Bedrich Smetana and Antonín Dvořák. Smetana's symphonic poem *Ma Vlast* (My Country) was written in celebration of his homeland. Slavonic themes infuse Dvořák's work, as they did Smetana's, but his symphonic and chamber music was to reach beyond the old world into the new. His Fifth Symphony, called "From the New World," incorporates echoes of African-American music and folk song, and has had important influences upon American classical music.

The distinctively national flavor of Slavonic music found its echo in Scandinavia, with Edvard Grieg's *Peer Gynt* suite (1875), while the Finn Jean Sibelius also found inspiration in national themes. In Spain, Isaac Albéniz created a national style of music with his *Spanish Rhapsody* (1887) and his 12-piece suite *Iberia* (1908).

Timeline

1917 Russian composer Sergei Prokofiev's *Classical Symphony*.

1919 Spanish composer Manuel de Falla's *The Three-Cornered Hat* (ballet).

1922 Hollywood Bowl concerts begin.

1924 French composer Francis Poulenc's *Poèmes de Ronsard* (song cycle). Czech composer Leos Janácek's *The Cunning Little Vixen* (opera).

1925 German composer Alban Berg's *Wozzeck* (opera) (*right*).

1926 U.S. composer Aaron Copland's Concerto for Piano and Orchestra. Igor Stravinsky's *Oedipus Rex* (oratorio).

1928 Ravel's *Boléro* (orchestral suite).

1931 English composer William Walton's *Belshazzar's Feast* (oratorio).

1935 American composer George Gershwin's *Porgy and Bess* (opera).

1937 Russian composer Dmitri Shostakovich's Symphony No. 5.

1939 Copland's *Billy the Kid* (ballet).

1944 Bela Bartók's Violin Concerto.

1945 English composer Benjamin Britten's *Peter Grimes* (opera).

1951 Britten's *Billy Budd* (opera).

1955 English composer Michael Tippet's *The Midsummer Marriage* (opera).

1960 Karlheinz Stockhausen's *Kontakte* (electronic).

1962 American composer Samuel Barber's Piano Concerto No. 1.

1971 Shostakovich's Symphony No. 15.

1976 German composer Hans Werner Henze's *We Come to the River* (opera).

1988 Polish composer Witold Lutoslawski's Piano Concerto.

1989 Tippett's *New Year* (opera).

1992 U.S. composer Philip Glass' *The Voyage* (opera).

RECORDED MUSIC OF THE 1900s

Thomas Edison's invention of the phonograph (1877) took music into domestic life. The first recording stars were singers: the Australian Nellie Melba, followed by Enrico Caruso and Adelina Patti. Among them, they began the lasting popularity of recorded operatic and other arias which was to reach its zenith almost 100 years later with the televised "World Cup" concerts (1990, 1994) of the "three tenors"—Luciano Pavarotti, Placido Domingo, and José Carreras. Their repertoire owed much to the operas of Giacomo Puccini, notably *Manon Lescaut, La Bohème, Tosca, Madame Butterfly,* and the unfinished *Turandot.*

Claude Debussy was the first composer to work directly for recording, but France's mentor was Gabriel Fauré, pupil of Camille Saint-Saëns. Fauré's *Requiem* (1900) is a masterpiece, while Saint-Saëns' *Samson and Delilah* (1877) and *The Carnival of the Animals* (1886) remain popular. Maurice Ravel's *Boléro* (1928) has become one of the most performed pieces of all time. He was influenced, as were Debussy, Darius Milhaud, and Francis Poulenc, by Erik Satie, who was in violent revolt against Wagnerism and orthodoxy in general.

National themes continued to be prominent during the early 1900s, with the British composers Ralph Vaughan Williams and Gustav Holst drawing on their country's folk traditions, while the Hungarians Béla Bartók and Zóltan Kodály made an exhaustive study of their nation's folk music. Meanwhile, the works of Edward Elgar, such as *Enigma Variations* (1899) and *The Dream of Gerontius* (1900), achieved lasting popularity over the years.

In Germany and Austria, new symphonists appeared with Gustav Mahler and Richard Strauss. Strauss' contribution included songs, tone poems and operas such as *Salome* (1905), *Elektra* (1909), and *Der Rosenkavalier* (1911). In contrast, the music of Arnold Schönberg and his disciples Anton Webern and Alban Berg amazed audiences with the innovative dissonance of "12-tone" serialism, conflicting with the eight-tone orthodoxy of the octave.

In Russia, the last Romantic Russian composer, Sergei Rachmaninov, was a virtuoso pianist whose three piano concertos are regularly performed. He taught Igor Stravinsky, who leapt to fame with his ballet scores, *The Firebird* (1910), *Petrushka* (1911), and *Sacre du Printemps* (The Rite of Spring, 1913), composed for Diaghilev's Ballets Russes. Opera and ballet scores such as *The Love for Three Oranges* (1921) and *Romeo and Juliet* (1938) brought fame also to Sergei Prokofiev.

Composers to flourish before and after World War II include Dmitri Shostakovich (Russia); Olivier Messiaen and Pierre Boulez (France); Witold Lutoslawski, Andrej Panufnik, and Krzystof Penderecki (Poland); and the Germans Hans Werner Henze and Karlheinz Stockhausen. In Britain, opera was revived with Benjamin Britten's *Peter Grimes* (1945) and *The Turn of the Screw* (1954). American contributions include works by Charles Ives, Aaron Copland, Samuel Barber, and Leonard Bernstein.

BALLET

Ballet (French *ballet,* diminutive of *bal,* dance) is a classical style of dancing and mime, using set steps and body movements. It was first performed by masked dancers for the nobility and flowered at the court of Louis XIV (*p. 346*). Until 1717, ballet was combined with singing, but in that year John Weaver's *The Loves of Mars and Venus,* performed at Drury Lane, London, refined and reduced the form to dancing and music alone.

The francophile Russian court at St. Petersburg developed the art of ballet during the 1700s, when the Kirov company was founded at the Maryinsky Theater. It was there that, later, Marius Petipa (1818–1910) collaborated with Peter Tchaikovsky on *The Sleeping Beauty.*

During the 1800s, a formalized technique evolved to produce Romantic ballets such as *Les Sylphides* and Russian classics like *Swan Lake.* As the dance became more gymnastic the *maillot* (tights) was introduced; and dancing on point (tiptoe), which was to characterize the classical form, was introduced by the Italian Marie Taglioni (1804–84).

In the early 1900s, ballet was revitalized in the West when the impresario Serge Diaghilev (1872–1929) brought the Ballets Russes to Europe. Under his direction, painters (Bakst, Picasso), composers (Stravinsky, Satie), and the legendary dancers Anna Pavlova (1885–1931) and Vaslav Nijinsky (1890–1950) came together in such classics as Stravinsky's *Petrushka.*

A Ballets Russes dancer, Marie Rambert (1888–1982), established a school in London in 1920; her most famous pupil was Margot Fonteyn (1919–91). Fonteyn's partnership with emigré Russian dancer Rudolf Nureyev after 1962 took the popularity of ballet to new heights.

Meanwhile, in the United States, Isadora Duncan brought a new interpretive spirit to the dance, in turn inspiring her fellow Americans Martha Graham (1894–1991) and Twyla Tharp (b. 1942). The choreographer Jerome Robbins (b. 1918) gave a balletic impulse to stage and film musicals such as *West Side Story* (1957).

The legendary dancer Nijinsky (by Bakst).

POPULAR

Popular music ranges over a broad spectrum and depends above all on accessibility. In the Middle Ages, itinerant troubadours carried songs from town to town and court to court, spreading popular music.

With the birth of modern theater, popular music began to look to the stage for inspiration. Ballads from *The Beggar's Opera* by John Gay (1685–1732) were on everybody's lips in the early 1700s.

The "domestication" of the piano during the 1800s made the drawing room ballad a common form of home entertainment, but the popular composer of the century was Johann Strauss the younger, the "Waltz King" of Vienna. His operetta *Die Fledermaus* (1874) and many waltzes remain in public affection. The Viennese tradition was continued and taken to the United States by Franz Lehár (1870–1948) with *The Merry Widow* (1905). In England, the quality of popular music was lifted from the comic and lugubrious songs of the music hall by the catchy tunes of Arthur Sullivan (1842–1900) from the Savoy Operas (*HMS Pinafore*, 1878, and *The Mikado*, 1885, among others), with librettos by W. S. Gilbert (1836–1911).

During the 1900s music has been dominated by recorded sound. The United States came to achieve similar dominance through "Tin Pan Alley" composers, Broadway and film musicals, big band swing, and jazz.

Irving Berlin (1888–1989) wrote popular songs enjoyed on both sides of the Atlantic during two world wars; Jerome Kern (1885–1945) created the first modern musical, *Showboat*, in 1927. Broadway and Hollywood musicals brought international popularity to the sophisticated songs of Cole Porter (1891–1964), as well as those of George Gershwin (with his brother Ira's lyrics) whose black folk opera *Porgy and Bess* (1935) achieved international operatic status. The most prolific composer of stage and film music was Richard Rodgers (1902–79) with *Oklahoma!* (1943), *The King and I* (1951), *South Pacific* (1949), and *The Sound of Music* (1959). Austrian-born Frederick Loewe (1904–88) brought a European flavor with *Gigi* (1958) and *My Fair Lady* (1956), while Leonard Bernstein's *West Side Story* (1957) featured lyrics by Stephen Sondheim (b. 1930).

During the late 1900s, the tide of American domination of the musical stage has been challenged by Britain's Andrew Lloyd Webber (b. 1948), including *Evita*, (1978), *Cats*, (1981), *The Phantom of the Opera*, (1986).
Ella Fitzgerald sang many Cole Porter hits.

Jazz and Rock Timeline

1899 Scott Joplin's *Maple Leaf Rag* popularizes ragtime, lending inspiration for future jazz piano styles (*p. 526*).
1917 The original Dixieland Jazz Band become the first white band to popularize recorded jazz with *Livery Jazz Blues*.
1923–33 Bessie Smith (*p. 526*) records over 100 songs for Columbia Records.
1925 Alan Lomax discovers bluesman Leadbelly in prison and records his repertoire of black American folk songs.
1926 Louis Armstrong's *Heebie Jeebies* features "scat" singing.
1927–31 Duke Ellington in residence at the Cotton Club, New York City.
1935–39 Ella Fitzgerald stars with a band led by Chick Webb.
1936 Robert Johnson (*p. 526*) records the influential *Cross Road Blues*.
1937 Mahalia Jackson's first recording *God's Gonna Separate the Wheat*.
1938 Sister Rosetta Tharpe appears at the Cotton Club with Cab Calloway band. Robert Johnson dies of poisoning, reputedly by a jealous husband, aged 27.
1940 Jimmy and Tommy Dorsey top the first "Top 10" list compiled by *Billboard* magazine.
1949 Country singer and songwriter Hank Williams performs *Lovesick Blues* at the Grand Ole Opry, in Nashville, to great acclaim. Sidney Bechet's *Les Oignons* repopularizes traditional jazz.
1951 *Three O'Clock in the Morning* launches B. B. King's career (*p. 526*).
1952 Gerry Mulligan forms Quartet, introducing West Coast "cool jazz."
1953 Charlie Parker plays with Dizzy Gillespie at Toronto's Massey Hall.

1955 Bill Haley's *Rock Around the Clock* marks the official birth of rock 'n' roll. John Coltrane plays with the Miles Davis Quintet.
1956 *Heartbreak Hotel* launches Elvis Presley's career (*p. 527*). Johnny Cash's *I Walk the Line* crosses over from country to pop charts.
1957 Buddy Holly makes his television debut with *That'll Be the Day*.
1958 Phil Spector produces records with his distinctive "wall of sound."
1959 Ray Charles' *What'd I Say?*, one of the first soul songs.
1960 Berry Gordy founds the Tamla Motown record label in Detroit.
1963 *Please Please Me* becomes the Beatles' first number one hit (*p. 527*).
1964 The Beatles tour U.S.A. to pandemonium crowds; world premiere of their film *A Hard Day's Night*. Motown Revue tours U.S.A., with the Supremes, Stevie Wonder, and Smokey Robinson.
1965 Bob Dylan is booed off stage at the Newport Folk Festival after going "electric" (*p. 527*). Robert Moog develops the moog synthesizer.
1966 Beach Boys' classic *Pet Sounds*. First rock "supergroup," Cream, is formed.
1967 *Sgt. Pepper's Lonely Hearts Club Band,* most acclaimed Beatles album. Monterey Pop Festival features Jimi Hendrix, Janis Joplin, and Otis Redding.
1969 Woodstock Music and Arts Festival attracts 450,000 fans; artists include Joan Baez, Jimi Hendrix, Sly and the Family Stone, and The Who. *Led Zeppelin II* tops the charts, influencing future heavy metal and hard rock.

1970 Paul McCartney begins proceedings to disband the Beatles. Deaths of Jimi Hendrix and Janis Joplin.
1972 Bob Marley's *Catch a Fire* sparks worldwide interest in reggae music.
1973 Stevie Wonder releases the sociopolitical *Innervisions* album.
1976 The Sex Pistols' *Anarchy in the U.K.* introduces punk rock (*p. 527*).
1978 Bee Gees' *Saturday Night Fever* brings disco to a worldwide audience.
1980 John Lennon is shot dead in New York City. Sugarhill Records launches rap/hip-hop artist Grandmaster Flash.
1981 MTV, the first U.S. television station dedicated to music, is launched.
1982 Grandmaster Flash's *The Message* brings rap music to the charts.
1983 Michael Jackson's *Thriller* is the best-selling album of all time.
1985 Bob Geldof organizes Live Aid concert, raising £50 million for Ethiopian famine. Michael Jackson outbids Paul McCartney for rights to Beatles' songs.
1986 Paul Simon's *Graceland* rouses interest in world music (*p. 527*).
1988 Rave music's "Second Summer of Love." Mandela Day, a benefit concert for South African Nelson Mandela.
1990 MC Hammer becomes first rap artist to win a Grammy award. The House Factory in Manhattan, New York opens, a mecca for house and garage music.
1991 Using sophisticated recording techniques, Natalie Cole records an album of duets with her father, Nat King Cole.
1994 Two festivals celebrate the 25th anniversary of Woodstock.

JAZZ AND BLUES

The roots of jazz lie in African musical traditions merged with European folk and classical styles, with formal, highly syncopated arrangements serving as a base for harmonic and solo improvisation. Jazz began to emerge toward the end of the 1800s in New Orleans, first played by marching bands and dance groups.

Around 1900, the ragtime piano of Scott Joplin encouraged later musicians such as "Fats" Waller to develop the popular "stride" style, as well as influencing the more improvised boogie-woogie piano of Albert Ammons among others.

Trumpeter Louis "Satchmo" Armstrong began playing in marching bands in New Orleans at the age of nine, before moving to Chicago where he backed Bessie Smith in the 1920s. His amazing versatility, range, and tone, combined with his charismatic personality, made him the first internationally acclaimed jazz "great."

Louis Armstrong, known as "Satchmo."

As jazz became more popular, orchestras playing sophisticated arrangements broke new ground. The outstanding bandleader/composer "Duke" Ellington paved the way for musicians like swing maestro Tommy Dorsey to make jazz styles acceptable to white audiences.

Band singers Billie Holiday, Ella Fitzgerald, and Sarah Vaughan became stars in their own right, and in the late 1940s musicians frustrated with strict orchestral arrangements began to develop a more improvised style. The bebop movement, led by saxophonist Charlie Parker and horn player Dizzy Gillespie, broke musical taboos, encouraging free expression. West Coast players Stan Getz and Gerry Mulligan, and pianists Oscar Peterson and Dave Brubeck, became stars in the 1950s–60s, playing smooth, complex jazz. Thelonious Monk, Charles Mingus, and John Coltrane continued to stretch musical boundaries ever further. In the 1970s, trumpeter Miles Davis and pianist Herbie Hancock, influenced by rock musicians such as Jimi Hendrix, experimented with electronic sounds to found the jazz/rock movement.

The blues sprang from the poverty-stricken Mississippi Delta region at the end of the 1800s, and like jazz, its roots lie in West African music, merged with spirituals and work songs. It was performed mainly by itinerant musicians, and different rural areas developed their own styles. W. C. Handy, called "father of the blues," published many traditional songs such as *St. Louis Blues* under his own name. Bessie Smith became the first great blues star, recording over 100 classic songs before 1930.

The legendary guitarist Robert Johnson exemplified country blues, and although he left only a few recordings, his powerful songs such as *Love in Vain* became huge-

"Empress of the blues" Bessie Smith.

ly influential. Huddie "Leadbelly" Ledbetter was a rural blues "shouter" and guitarist; many of his songs, including *Goodnight Irene*, have become standards.

The country style was eclipsed after World War II by the harsher Chicago blues style, and was developed by such artists as Howlin' Wolf and Muddy Waters, with songs like Waters' *Mannish Boy*. B. B. King helped to define the electric blues guitar with classic recordings such as *How Blue Can You Get?*

During the 1960s, blues players finally became popular with white audiences. The Rolling Stones, Fleetwood Mac, and Eric Clapton helped to bring international recognition to blues artists like B. B. King, John Lee Hooker, Albert King, and Buddy Guy.

SOUL

Soul music grew out of the African-American gospel tradition. The spiritual hymn was its base, with its rich harmonies and moving rhythms, and most artists gained their musical training in the churches. Ray Charles, an early soul pioneer, wooed audiences with his gravelly voice and fine piano playing in the late 1950s. Other pioneers include Sam Cooke, whose ballads became a great influence on future artists, and singer Otis Redding, noted for his passionate delivery.

The southern soul sound of the 1960s was exemplified by "Stax" band Booker T and the MGs, with their trademark Hammond organ and choppy guitar riffs, and by Wilson Pickett and Percy Sledge.

"Queen of soul" Aretha Franklin is considered to be the greatest female soul vocalist. The daughter of a famous Baptist preacher, Aretha was tutored as a child by gospel singer Mahalia Jackson,

and elements of gospel remain prevalent in her music. With a voice of great range and subtlety, and a supreme sense of melody, she makes every song her own.

Motown Records in Detroit became the home of Midwestern soul. Diana Ross and the Supremes, Smokey Robinson, the Temptations, and Stevie Wonder all began their careers there. Marvin Gaye's upbeat tunes and seductive love songs, and the lively soul-pop hits of the Jackson Five, topped the charts in the late 1960s.

"Godfather of soul" James Brown practically invented funk with a catalogue of hits. His wild and theatrical stage show made him a huge star, and *Say It Loud, I'm Black and I'm Proud* (1968) became a stirring anthem for the civil rights movement. Sly and the Family Stone, along with George Clinton's Funkadelic and Parliament, paved the way for the emergence of 1970s' disco.

Aretha Franklin, the "queen of soul."

ROCK AND POP

While the rock 'n' roll era was officially launched in 1955 with Bill Haley's *Rock Around the Clock*, it was Elvis Presley who made this largely R&B– (rhythm and blues) based music acceptable to white audiences. Presley rose to stardom with the first of many hits, *Heartbreak Hotel* (1956), and along with the Beatles, he remains one of the two biggest influences on popular culture during the 1900s. Chuck Berry, Fats Domino, Gene Vincent, and Eddie Cochran also pioneered the new genre, while Buddy Holly and the Crickets combined country music with R&B to create their own particular kind of sound.

In the U.K., the Beatles exploded onto the music scene in 1963, heralding the social as well as musical revolution of the 1960s. The compositional genius of songwriters John Lennon and Paul McCartney led them to experiment with

The revolutionary Beatles in 1964.

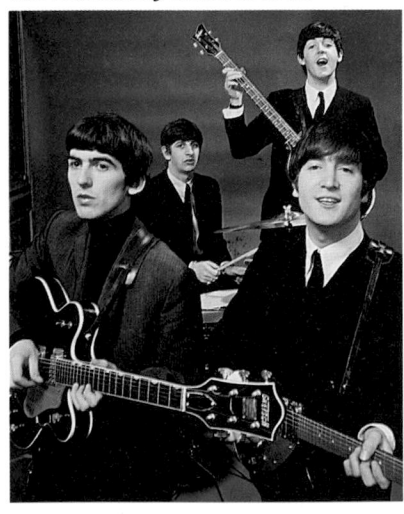

"The king" of rock 'n' roll, Elvis Presley.

musical styles and recording techniques, and along with guitarist George Harrison and drummer Ringo Starr, they released a catalogue of classic songs. *Sgt. Pepper's Lonely Hearts Club Band* (1967) marked the artistic pinnacle of their career. The Rolling Stones represented the "street" face of rock: their music was heavily blues-based, their image overtly sexual. Also blues-influenced were definitive rock guitarists Eric Clapton, Jimmy Page, and Jeff Beck—all members of the Yardbirds. Clapton went on to form the band Cream, and Page to form the hugely successful Led Zeppelin, both of which spawned the heavy metal genre. The "mod" band The Who recorded the first rock-opera, *Tommy* (1969).

Bob Dylan has made a monumental contribution to music; widely hailed as the spokesman of his generation, the poetry and political comment of his lyrics contrasts with his raw vocal style and trademark harmonica playing. He ushered in the era of singer/songwriters like Joan Baez and Joni Mitchell, and after

switching to electric guitar in 1965, inspired the folk-rock genre—from the Byrds and Crosby, Stills, Nash, and Young, to the Celtic strains of Fairport Convention. Jimi Hendrix was an electric guitar virtuoso who took his instrument to new heights. The Beach Boys' *Pet Sounds* (1966) demonstrated composer Brian Wilson's highly innovative approach to arranging and recording.

The 1970s saw the rise of big names such as Led Zeppelin, Pink Floyd, ELO, and "glam" rockers David Bowie and Roxy Music, one of whose members, Brian Eno, went on to become a major figure in experimental music. Punk music shot on to the U.K. scene in 1976, led by the Sex Pistols. Their raw, anarchic sound was a statement against the self-indulgent stadium bands of the time, and their song *Anarchy in the UK* shocked the nation. Among the many punk bands producing energetic, rebellious music, the Damned and the Clash were noteworthy.

During the "new wave" of the 1980s, technology made it possible for musicians to produce music on a very low budget. German art band Kraftwerk were the first to feature a totally electric sound with synthesizers; the Eurythmics mixed techno-pop with psychedelia. The Police topped the charts with their reggae/rock beat, while Talking Heads married unusual lyrics with exotic rhythms, and U2 combined lyricism and social conscience.

In 1983, Michael Jackson became a pop phenomenon with *Thriller*, the biggest-selling album in the world. The multi-talented Prince brought elements of rock, pop, and soul to his funky compositions. In reaction to the computerized music of the "rave" scene, bands like R.E.M. and "grunge" band Nirvana became popular in the 1990s, with a return to the classic rock lineup of guitars, bass, and drums.

WORLD MUSIC

The term "world music" usually refers to the traditional music of non-Western cultures, but it can also include Western-influenced genres as diverse as Israeli pop, Indian Bhangra, and and Irish-Celtic New Age. Indian music became popular in the 1960s after the Beatles "discovered" Ravi Shankar, maestro of the sitar (a plucked stringed instrument).

Reggae from Jamaica, a blend of African rhythms, Afro-Cuban pop, and U.S. soul, reached a world audience in the 1970s, with the music of Toots and the Maytals, Jimmy Cliff, and especially Bob Marley. The music of the Jamaican ghetto took the rock scene by storm; its melodic and rhythmic structures were borrowed by bands like The Police and UB40. Calypso from Trinidad, voodoo from Haiti, and zouk, the creole dance music of the French Antilles, are other West Indian styles, while salsa is an umbrella term for

many Latin American rhythms.

The African continent is rich in musical traditions. Sunny Adé and Fela Kuti helped to popularize Nigerian Juju music, and Salif Keita, the Maninka music of Mali. Guinean Mory Kanté was the first African rock musician to be recognized in Europe with *Yéké Yéké* (1988); talented Senegalese singer Youssou N'dour is a superstar who sings Mbalax music. Roots from Ghana, Soukous from Zaire, and Jit and Mbira from Zimbabwe are other popular styles.

Regional genres in the U.S.A. include Cajun, Zydeco, and Tex-Mex, while Native American tribes each have their own ritual and dance music. South American styles include the tango from Argentina and the panpipe music of the Andes. Haunting gamelan music from Java and Bali is played on tuned percussion—gongs, xylophones, and drums.

Jamaican reggae star Bob Marley.

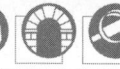

PROMINENT PEOPLE
JAZZ AND ROCK

Titles in italics are those of albums and possibly also singles; quotation marks indicate singles.

ABBA (1973–82) Swedish pop group: *Waterloo* (1974), "Dancing Queen" (1976), *Arrival* (1976).

ARMSTRONG, Louis ("Satchmo") (1901–71) U.S. jazz cornet player, trumpeter, singer: "West End Blues" (1928), "C'est Si Bon" (1951).

BAEZ, Joan (b. 1941) U.S. folksinger, songwriter: "There but for Fortune" (1965), "The Night They Drove Old Dixie Down" (1971).

BASIE, "Count" (William Allen) (1904–84) U.S. jazz bandleader, pianist: "One O'Clock Jump" (1936), *The Atomic Mr. Basie* (1959).

BEACH BOYS, The (1961) U.S. group, with Brian Wilson (b. 1942): "I Get Around" (1964), *Pet Sounds* (1966), "Good Vibrations" (1966).

BEATLES, The (1960–70) U.K. group that revolutionized rock music, with George Harrison (b. 1943), John LENNON, Paul McCARTNEY, and Ringo Starr (b. 1940): *A Hard Day's Night* (1964), *Help!* (1965), *Rubber Soul* (1965), *Sgt. Pepper's Lonely Hearts Club Band* (1967), *The White Album* (1968), *Abbey Road* (1969).

BEIDERBECKE, Bix (1903–31) U.S. jazz cornet player, trumpeter: "Singing the Blues" (1928), "In a Mist" (1928), "Rocking Chair" (1930).

BERRY, Chuck (b. 1926) U.S. singer, songwriter, guitarist: "Maybellene" (1955), "Roll Over Beethoven" (1956), "No Particular Place to Go" (1964).

BOOKER T AND THE MGs (1960s) U.S. R&B band, created the "Stax" sound: *Green Onions* (1962).

BOWIE, David (b. 1947) U.K. singer, songwriter, actor: *Hunky Dory* (1971), *The Rise and Fall of Ziggy Stardust* (1972), *Heroes* (1977), *Let's Dance* (1983).

BROWN, James (b. 1933) U.S. singer, songwriter, soul/funk pioneer: "Papa's Got a Brand New Bag" (1965), "Say it Loud, I'm Black and I'm Proud" (1968).

BRUBECK, Dave (b. 1920) U.S. jazz pianist, bandleader, composer: *Time Out* (1959).

BYRDS, The (1964) U.S. folk-rock group: "Mr. Tambourine Man" (1965), "Eight Miles High" (1966).

CASH, Johnny (b. 1932) U.S. country singer, songwriter: "A Boy Named Sue" (1969), "Folsome Prison Blues" (1968).

CHARLES, Ray (b. 1930) U.S. singer, pianist, composer, soul pioneer: "Georgia on My Mind" (1960), "Hit the Road Jack" (1961).

CLAPTON, Eric (b. 1945) U.K. guitarist, singer, songwriter, formerly with CREAM: "Layla" (1970), "Lay Down Sally" (1977), *Slowhand* (1977).

CLASH, The (1976–85) U.K. punk band: *London Calling* (1979), "Rock the Casbah" (1982), "Should I Stay or Should I Go" (1982).

CLINE, Patsy (1932–63) U.S. country singer: "I Fall to Pieces" (1961), "Crazy" (1961).

COLE, Nat "King" (1917–65) U.S. jazz pianist, singer: "When I Fall in Love" (1957), "Ramblin' Rose" (1962).

COLTRANE, John (1926–67) U.S. jazz saxophonist, composer: *Blue Train* (1958), *Giant Steps* (1960), *A Love Supreme* (1964).

COOKE, Sam (1931–64) U.S. soul pioneer, singer, songwriter: "You Send Me" (1956).

COSTELLO, Elvis (b. 1954) U.K. singer, songwriter, guitarist: *My Aim Is True* (1977), "Oliver's Army" (1979), *Punch the Clock* (1983).

CREAM (1966–68) U.K. rock band, with Eric CLAPTON: *Fresh Cream* (1966), "Strange Brew" (1967), *Wheels on Fire* (1968).

DAVIS, Miles (1926–91) U.S. jazz trumpeter, composer, bandleader, cofounder of bebop (1940s), cool jazz (1950s), jazz-rock (1960s): *Bitches' Brew* (1970), *Kind of Blue* (1959).

DIDDLEY, Bo (b. 1928) U.S. guitarist, singer, songwriter: "Bo Diddley" (1955).

DOMINO, Fats (b. 1929) U.S. R&B singer, pianist: "The Fat Man" (1949), "Ain't That a Shame" (1955).

DOORS, The (1965–72) U.S. rock band, with Jim Morrison (1943–71): "Light My Fire" (1966), *Strange Days* (1967), "Riders on the Storm" (1971).

DORSEY, Tommy (1905–56) U.S. swing bandleader, trombonist: "I'll Never Smile Again" (1940), "Opus No. 1" (1944).

DYLAN, Bob (b. 1941) U.S. folksinger, songwriter: "The Times They Are A-Changin'" (1964), *Blonde on Blonde* (1966), *Blood on the Tracks* (1975).

ELLINGTON, Duke (1899–1974) U.S. jazz bandleader: "Black and Tan Fantasy" (1927), "Creole Love Call" (1927), "The Mooche" (1929), "Mood Indigo" (1930).

EURYTHMICS (1981–89) U.K. rock band, with Dave Stewart (b. 1952) and Annie Lennox (b. 1954): *Sweet Dreams Are Made of This* (1983).

FAIRPORT CONVENTION (1966) U.K. folk and rock group: *Unhalfbricking* (1969).

FITZGERALD, Ella (b. 1918) U.S. jazz singer: "A Tisket a Tasket" (1938), *Gershwin Songbook* (1950).

FLEETWOOD MAC (1967) U.S.–U.K. rock group, with Peter Green (b. 1946): "Albatross" (1968).

FRANKLIN, Aretha (b. 1942) U.S. soul singer, pianist, "queen of soul": "Respect," "Chain of Fools" (1968), "Think" (1968), *Aretha* (1980).

GABRIEL, Peter (b. 1950) U.K. singer, songwriter: *Peter Gabriel* (1980), *So* (1986).

GAYE, Marvin (1938–84) U.S. singer, songwriter: "I Heard It Through the Grapevine" (1968), *What's Goin' On* (1971).

GETZ, Stan (1927–91) U.S. jazz tenor saxophonist: *Focus* (1961), *Stan Getz: Gold* (1977).

GILLESPIE, Dizzy (1917–93) U.S. jazz trumpeter, bandleader, composer, cofounder of bebop: "Groovin' High" (1945), "Night in Tunisia" (1946).

GOODMAN, Benny (1909–86) U.S. bandleader, clarinetist, "king of swing": "King Porter Stomp" (1935), "Why Don't You Do Right?" (1943).

GRANDMASTER FLASH (b. 1958) U.S. hip-hop pioneer: "The Message" (1982), "White Lines (Don't Do It)" (1984).

GRAPPELLI, Stephane (b. 1908) French jazz violinist: "Tiger Rag" (1935), *Tea for Two* (1978, with Yehudi Menuhin).

GRATEFUL DEAD (1965) U.S. band: *American Beauty* (1970), *Live Dead* (1969).

GUTHRIE, Woody (1912–67) U.S. folksinger, songwriter, influenced 1960s folk movement: "This Land Is Your Land" (1935).

GUNS 'N' ROSES (1985) U.S. rock band: "Sweet Child O'Mine" (1989).

HALEY, Bill (1925–81) U.S. rock 'n' roll pioneer, with The Comets: "Shake Rattle and Roll" (1954), "Rock Around the Clock" (1955).

HANDY, W. C. (1873–1958) U.S. composer, "father of the blues": "St. Louis Blues," "Beale Street Blues," "Yellow Dog Blues" (all 1920s-30s).

HAWKINS, Coleman (1901–69) U.S. jazz tenor saxophonist: "Body and Soul" (1939), *High and Mighty Hawk* (1957).

HENDRIX, Jimi (1942–70) U.S. rock guitar virtuoso, singer, songwriter: "Hey Joe" (1966), "Purple Haze" (1967), *Are You Experienced?* (1967).

HOLIDAY, Billie ("Lady Day") (1915–59) U.S. jazz and blues singer: "Strange Fruit" (1949) and "I Cover the Waterfront" (1949).

HOLLY, Buddy (1936–59) U.S. singer, guitarist, songwriter, rock 'n' roll pioneer, with The Crickets: "Peggy Sue" (1957).

HOOKER, John Lee (b. 1917) U.S. blues singer, guitarist: "Boogie Chillen" (1948), "Dimples" (1964), *The Healer* (1989).

JACKSON, Mahalia (1911–72) U.S. gospel singer: "Move On Up a Little Higher" (1947), "Black, Brown, and Beige" (1958, with Duke ELLINGTON).

JACKSON, Michael (b. 1958) U.S. soul singer, formerly with the Jackson Five, soul/electro-funk: *Thriller* (1982), *Bad* (1987).

JOEL, Billy (b. 1949) U.S. singer: "Just the Way You Are" (1978), *52nd Street* (1979).

JOHN, Elton (b. 1947) U.K. singer, songwriter, pianist: "Your Song" (1970) *Tumbleweed Connection* (1971), *Goodbye Yellow Brick Road* (1973).

JOHNSON, Robert (1911–38) U.S. blues singer, guitarist, songwriter: "Love in Vain" (1936), "Terraplane Blues" (1937), "Cross Road Blues" (1937).

JOPLIN, Janis (1943–70) U.S. singer, songwriter: "Piece of My Heart" (1967), *Pearl* (1971).

JOPLIN, Scott (1868–1917) U.S. classical

and popular composer, known as "king of ragtime": "Maple Leaf Rag" (1899).

KANTÉ, Mory (b. 1951) West African singer, guitarist, popularized Maninka country rock: "Yéké Yéké" (1988).

KING, B.B. (b. 1925) U.S. guitarist, singer, songwriter, Chicago blues: *Live at the Regal* (1964), *Blues is King* (1967).

KINKS, The (1964) U.K. rock group, with Ray Davies (b. 1944): "You Really Got Me" (1964), "Waterloo Sunset" (1967).

KRAFTWERK (1970s) German art-rock band, first to use entirely synthesized instruments: *Autobahn* (1974).

LED ZEPPELIN (1968–80) U.K. rock band: influential heavy metal sound: *Led Zeppelin I* (1969), *Untitled* (1971).

LEWIS, Jerry Lee (b. 19435) U.S. pianist and singer: "Whole Lotta Shakin' Goin' On" (1958).

LITTLE RICHARD (b. 1932) U.S. pioneer of rock 'n' roll: "Tutti Frutti" (1957).

LENNON, John (1940–80) U.K. singer, songwriter, guitarist, formerly with The BEATLES: "Give Peace a Chance" (1969), *Imagine* (1971).

MADONNA (Madonna Louise Ciccone) (b. 1958) U.S. singer, songwriter, actress, pop icon: *Like a Virgin* (1984), *Erotica* (1992).

MAKEBA, Miriam S. African-born U.S. singer, introduced African sounds in 1960's.

MARLEY, Bob (1945–81) Jamaican reggae singer, songwriter, guitarist with The Wailers, popularized reggae: "Get Up, Stand Up" (1973), "I Shot the Sheriff" (1973), "No Woman No Cry" (1974).

MARSALIS, Wynton (b. 1961) U.S. jazz and classical trumpeter, bandleader: "Think of One" (1983), *Live at Blues Alley* (1986).

McCARTNEY, Paul (b. 1942) U.K. singer, songwriter, guitarist, formerly with The BEATLES: "Maybe I'm Amazed" (1970), *Ram* (1971), "Mull of Kintyre" (1977).

MICHAEL, George (b. 1963) U.K. singer, songwriter, formerly with Wham!: "Careless Whisper" (1984), *Faith* (1987).

MINGUS, Charlie (1922–79) U.S. jazz bassist, pianist, bandleader, cofounder of West Coast cool jazz: *Tijuana Moods* (1962).

MITCHELL, Joni (b. 1943) U.S. singer, songwriter: "Big Yellow Taxi" (1970), *Blue* (1971), *Night Ride Home* (1991).

MODERN JAZZ QUARTET (1952–74, 1981–) U.S. chamber jazz group, with Milt Jackson (b. 1923) on piano and vibraphone: "Vendome" (1953), *Fontessa* (1956).

MONK, Thelonious (1917–82) U.S. jazz pianist, composer: "Round Midnight" (1947), "Brilliant Corners" (1957), "The Man I Love" (1971).

MORRISON, Van (b. 1945) U.K. singer, songwriter, guitarist: "Baby Please Don't Go" (1964), *Astral Weeks* (1968).

MORTON, Jelly Roll (1890–1941) U.S. jazz composer, pianist: "Mr. Jelly Lord" (1924).

N'DOUR, Youssou (b. 1959) Senegalese singer, leading exponent of Mbalax music: *Inédits 84-85* (1987).

NIRVANA (1988) U.S. grunge band, with Kurt Cobain (1967–94), exemplified the "Seattle sound": *Nevermind* (1991).

PARKER, Charlie ("Bird") (1920–55) U.S. jazz alto saxophonist, bandleader, composer, cofounder of bebop movement: "Koko" (1945), *Quintet of the Year* (1953).

PETERSON, Oscar (b. 1925) Canadian jazz pianist, composer: *Night Train* (1963), *Affinity (1963)*, *My Favorite Instrument (1968)*.

PINE, Courtney (b. 1964) U.K. jazz saxophonist, bandleader, composer: *Journey to the Urge Within* (1986).

PINK FLOYD (1965) U.K. rock group, experimental electric sound: *Dark Side of the Moon* (1973), *Division Bell* (1994).

POLICE, The (1977) U.K. group, reggae influenced, with STING: "Roxanne" (1978), *Regatta de Blanc* (1979), *Synchronicity* (1983).

PRESLEY, Elvis (1935–77) U.S. singer, highly influential pop icon: "Love Me Tender" (1956), "Heartbreak Hotel" (1956), "In the Ghetto" (1969).

PRINCE (Prince Rodgers Nelson) (b. 1960) U.S. singer, songwriter, guitarist: *1999* (1983), *Purple Rain* (1984).

QUEEN (1970) U.K. rock group, with Freddie Mercury (1946–91): *Sheer Heart Attack* (1974), *A Night at the Opera* (1975), *A Day at the Races* (1976).

REDDING, Otis (1941–67) U.S. singer, soul pioneer: "Try a Little Tenderness," "Dock of the Bay" (1967).

REED, Lou (b. 1942) U.S. rock singer, songwriter, guitarist, formerly with VELVET UNDERGROUND; *Transformer* (1972), *Songs for 'Drella* (1990).

REINHARDT, Django (1910–53) Belgian jazz guitarist, composer: "Shine" (1936), "Nuages" (1940).

R.E.M. (1982) U.S. rock group: *Reckoning* (1984), *Automatic for the People* (1993).

ROBINSON, Smokey (b. 1940) U.S. soul singer, songwriter (with The Miracles, 1957–72): "Shop Around" (1961), "Tears of A Clown" (1970).

RODGERS, Jimmy (1897–1933) U.S. country singer, songwriter: "Blue Yodel No. 9" (1928).

ROLLING STONES (1962) U.K. rock band, with Mick Jagger (b. 1943), Keith Richards (b. 1943), Charlie Watts (b. 1941), Bill Wyman (b. 1936), Brian Jones (1942–69) who was replaced by Mick Taylor (b. 1948), then Ron Wood (b. 1947): "Satisfaction" (1965), "Honky Tonk Women" (1969), *Undercover* (1983).

ROSS, Diana (b. 1944) U.S. soul singer, formerly with The Supremes, 1959–69; "Ain't No Mountain High Enough" (1970), "You Are Everything" (1974, with Marvin GAYE).

SEX PISTOLS (1975–78) U.K. punk group: "God Save The Queen" (1977),

Never Mind The Bollocks (1977).

SHAW, Artie (b. 1910) U.S. swing bandleader, clarinetist: "Begin the Beguine" (1938), "Dancing in the Dark" (1941).

SIMON, Paul (b. 1942) U.S. singer, songwriter, guitarist, with Art Garfunkel (b. 1942): *Bookends* (1968), "Bridge Over Troubled Water" (1970); solo: *Graceland* (1986), *Rhythm of the Saints* (1990).

SLY AND THE FAMILY STONE (1969) U.S. soul/funk group: "Dance to the Music" (1968), "Family Affair" (1972).

SMITH, Bessie (1894–1937) U.S. blues singer: *St. Louis Blues* (1924).

SPRINGSTEEN, Bruce (b. 1949) U.S. rock singer, songwriter, guitarist: *Born to Run* (1975), *The River* (1980), *Born in the U.S.A.* (1984).

STING (b. 1951) U.K. singer, songwriter, formerly with The POLICE: *The Dream of the Blue Turtles* (1985), *Ten Summoner's Tales* (1993).

SUN RA (c. 1914–93) U.S. jazz pianist, composer, bandleader: *Heliocentric Worlds of Sun Ra* (1965).

TALKING HEADS (1974) U.S. new wave group: "Psycho Killer" (1977), *Stop Making Sense* (1984), *Naked* (1988).

TEMPTATIONS (1962) U.S. soul group: "Just My Imagination" (1968), "Cloud Nine" (1969).

TURNER, Tina (b. 1938) U.S. soul/pop singer, with Ike Turner (b. 1931): "Nutbush City Limits" (1973); solo: *Private Dancer* (1984).

U2 (1977) Irish group, with Bono (b. 1960), The Edge (b. 1961): *The Joshua Tree* (1987), *Zooropa* (1993).

VAUGHAN, Sarah (1924–90) U.S. jazz singer: "Broken Hearted Melody" (1959).

VELVET UNDERGROUND (1965) U.S. rock group: *The Velvet Underground and Nico* (1967), *White Light, White Heat* (1968).

WALLER, Fats (1904–43) U.S. jazz pianist, composer, singer, bandleader, "stride" master: "Ain't Misbehavin'" (1929).

WATERS, Muddy (1915–83) U.S. singer, songwriter, guitarist: "Rollin' Stone" (1950), "Hoochie Coochie Man" (1953), "Got My Mojo Working" (1957).

WHO, The (1964–89) U.K. mod rock group, with Pete Townsend (b. 1945): *My Generation* (1966), *Who's Next* (1971), *Tommy* (1968).

WILLIAMS, Hank (1923–53) U.S. country singer, songwriter: "Move It On Over" (1947).

WONDER, Stevie (b. 1950) U.S. singer, songwriter, harmonica and keyboard player: "For Once in My Life" (1968), *Innervisions* (1973), *Songs in the Key of Life* (1976).

YOUNG, Neil (b. 1945) Canadian guitarist, singer, songwriter, country–rock pioneer: *Harvest* (1972), *Rust Never Sleeps* (1979).

ZAPPA, Frank (1940–93) U.S. singer, composer, guitarist, bandleader: *Lumpy Gravy* (1967), *Joe's Garage* (1979).

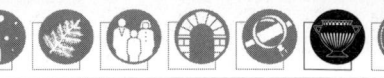

PROMINENT CLASSICAL COMPOSERS

ALBÉNIZ, Isaac (1860–1909) Spanish. *Iberia* (1908).

ALBINONI, Tommaso (1671–1750) Italian. *Sinfonie e Concerti a 5* (1707).

BACH, Johann Sebastian (1685–1750) German. *Brandenburg Concertos* (1721), *The Well-tempered Clavier* (1722), Mass in B minor (1748), Chorales for Organ (1739), *The Musical Offering* (1747), *The Art of Fugue* (1750). Sons **Wilhelm Friedemann** (1710–84) Church cantatas, instrumental pieces; **Carl Philipp Emanuel** (1714–88) *Magnificat, The Israelites in the Wilderness* (oratorio); **Johann Christian** (1735–82) Masses, *Requiem, Te Deum*, operas.

BARBER, Samuel (1910–1981) U.S. *Vanessa* (1958).

BARTÓK, Béla (1881–1945) Hungarian. *The Miraculous Mandarin* (opera 1919), Concerto for Orchestra (1943).

BEETHOVEN, Ludwig van (1770–1827) German. Sonata for Violin and Piano "Kreutzer" (1805), Symphony No. 3 "Eroica" (1803), Piano Sonata No. 23 "Appassionata" (1807), Symphony No. 5 (1807), Violin Concerto (1809), Piano Concerto No. 5 "Emperor" (1811), *Fidelio* (opera, 1814), Symphony No. 7 (1816), Mass in D (*Missa Solemnis*) (1818–23), Symphony No. 9 "Choral" (1824), String Quartet No. 13 with *Grosse Fuge* (1826).

BELLINI, Vincenzo (1801–35) Italian. *La Somnambula* (1831), *Norma* (1831).

BERG, Alban (1885–1935) Austrian. Lulu Symphony (1934), Violin Concerto (1935).

BERLIOZ, Hector (1803–69) French. *Symphonie Fantastique* (1830), *Roméo et Juliette* (dramatic symphony, 1839), *Le Carnaval Romain* (overture, 1844), *Les Troyens* (opera 1858–60).

BERNSTEIN, Leonard (1918–90) U.S. composer and conductor. Jeremiah Symphony (1944), Kaddish Symphony (1961–63).

BIZET, Georges (1838–75) French. Symphony in C major (1855), *L'Arlésienne* (orchestral suite, 1872), *Jeux d'enfants* (piano, 1871), *Carmen* (opera, 1875).

BLOW, John (1649–1708) British. *Venus and Adonis* (masque, 1687), *Begin the Song* (ode for St. Cecilia's Day).

BORODIN, Aleksandr (1833–87) Russian. *In the Steppes of Central Asia* (orchestral suite, 1880), *Prince Igor* (unfinished opera).

BOULEZ, Pierre (b. 1925) French. *Livre pour Quattuor* (1949), *Le Marteau sans Maitre* (1955), Third Piano Sonata (1957).

BRAHMS, Johannes (1833–97) German. Piano Concerto No. 1 (1859), *German Requiem* (1868), Symphony No. 1 (1876), Violin Concerto (1879), Symphony No. 4 (1886), Concerto for Violin and Cello (1887), Clarinet Quintet (1891).

BRITTEN, Benjamin (1913–76) British. *Peter Grimes* (opera, 1945), *The Turn of the Screw* (opera, 1954), *War Requiem* (1962).

BRUCH, Max (1838–1920) German. Violin Concerto (1866).

BRÜCKNER, Anton (1824–96) Austrian. *Te Deum* (1884), Symphony No. 7 (1885).

BULL, John (1562–1628) British madrigalist. *Queen Elizabeth's Pavan*, one of his virginals, may have been the source of the tune of the British national anthem.

BYRD, William (1543–1623) British. *Cantiones Sacrae* (1575), motets (with John BULL and Orlando GIBBONS), *Parthenia* (1611).

CHOPIN, Frédéric (1810–49) Polish. Nocturnes for Piano (1827–46), Etudes for Piano Op. 10 and 25 (1833 and 1837), Ballades for Piano No. 1 (1836), Piano Sonata No. 2 "Funèbre" (1839), Preludes (1839).

COPLAND, Aaron (1900–90) U.S. Symphony for Organ and Orchestra (1927), *A Lincoln Portrait* (orchestral suite, 1942).

CORELLI, Arcangelo (1653–1713) Italian. *Twelve Concerti Grossi* (1682).

COUPERIN, François (1668–1733) French. *Second Book of the Harpsichords* (suites, 1717).

DEBUSSY, Claude (1862–1918) French. *Prélude à l'Après-midi d'un Faune* (1894), *La Mer* (symphonic sketches, 1905), *Jeux* (ballet, 1913), Sonata for Violin and Piano (1917).

DELIUS, Frederick (1862–1934) British. *Sea-drift* (orchestral suite, 1903), *A Song of Summer* (orchestral suite, 1928).

DONIZETTI, Gaetano (1797–1848) Italian. *La Favorita* (opera, 1840), *Don Pasquale* (opera, 1843).

DOWLAND, John (1563–1626) British madrigalist. Pieces for voice accompanied by lute. "Flow my Tears" from *Second Book of Airs* (1600).

DVOŘÁK, Antonín (Leopold) (1841–1904) Czech. *Slavonic Dances* (1878), Symphony No. 9 "From the New World" (1893, alternatively ranked as Symphony No. 5).

ELGAR, Sir Edward (1857–1934) British. *Enigma Variations* (orchestral suite, 1899), *The Dream of Gerontius* (oratorio, 1900), Second Symphony (1911).

FAURÉ, Gabriel (1845–1924) French. Violin and Piano Sonata No. 1 (1876), Quartet for Piano and Strings No. 1 (1884) *Pelléas et Melisande* (orchestral suite, 1898), *Requiem* (choral work, 1900), *Pénélope* (opera, 1913).

FRANCK, César (1822–90) Belgian. *Les Béatitudes* (oratorio, 1879), Symphonic Variations (1885), Violin Sonata (1886).

GERSHWIN, George (1898–1937) U.S. *Rhapsody in Blue* (orchestral suite, 1924), *Porgy and Bess* (opera, 1935).

GIBBONS, Orlando (1583–1625) British. *Madrigals and Motets of 5 Parts: apt for Viols and Voyces* (1612).

GLASS, Philip (b. 1937) U.S. *Einstein on the Beach* (opera, 1976), *Akhnaten* (opera, 1984).

GLUCK, Christoph Willibald von (1714–87) Austro-German. *Orfeo ed Euridice* (opera, 1762), *Alceste* (opera, 1767).

GOUNOD, Charles François (1818–93) French. *Faust* (opera, 1859), *Roméo et Juliette* (opera, 1867).

GRIEG, Edvard (1843–1907) Norwegian. Piano Concerto in A minor (1868), Holberg Suite (orchestral suite, 1884).

HANDEL, Georg Frederick (1685–1759) Anglo-German. *Acis and Galatea* (dramatic oratorio, 1731), *Water Music* (orchestral suite, 1717), *Twelve Concerti Grossi* (1739), *Messiah* (oratorio, 1741).

HAYDN, Franz Joseph (1732–1809) Austrian. Symphony No. 45 "Farewell" (1772), Symphony No. 92 "Oxford" (1789), String Quartet in D minor "The Lark" (1791), Symphony No. 103 "Drumroll" (1795), Trio for Piano, Violin, and Cello (1797), *The Seasons* (oratorio, 1801).

HENZE, Hans Werner (b. 1926) German. *Boulevard Solitude* (opera, 1952), *The English Cat* (opera, 1983).

HINDEMITH, Paul (1895–1963) German. Philharmonic Concerto (1932), *Die Harmonie der Welt* (opera, 1957).

HOLST, Gustav (1874–1934) British. *The Planets* (orchestral suite, 1914–17), Concerto for Two Violins (1929).

IVES, Charles (1874–1954) U.S. String Quartet No. 2 (1913).

JANÁČEK, Leoš (1854–1928) Czech. *The Cunning Little Vixen* (opera, 1924), Sinfonietta (1927).

JOSQUIN des Prés (c. 1440–1521) Franco-Flemish. c. 30 masses, 50 motets, and 70 songs, and represents transition from the musical styles of the later Middle Ages to those of the Renaissance.

LISZT, Franz (1811–86) Hungarian. Piano Sonata in B minor (1853), Hungarian Rhapsodies for Piano (1853, 1885), Faust Symphony (1857), Mephisto-waltz No. 1 (1863).

LUTOSLAWSKI, Witold (b. 1913) Polish. Symphonic Variations (1938), Concerto for Orchestra (1954), Piano Concerto (1988).

MAHLER, Gustav (1860–1911) Czech-Austrian. *Das Lied von der Erde* (song-symphony, 1909), Symphony No. 7 (1905), Symphony No. 9 (1910).

MENDELSSOHN (-Bartholdy), Felix (1809–47) German. *A Midsummer Night's Dream* (overture, 1826), *The Hebrides* (overture, 1830–32), Symphony No. 4 "Italian" (1833), Violin Concerto (1845), *Elijah* (oratorio 1846).

MENOTTI, Gian Carlo (b. 1911) Italian-born U.S. *The Medium* (opera, 1947), *Amahl and the Night Visitors* (opera, 1951).

MESSIAEN, Olivier (1908–92) French. *Quattuor pour la Fin de Temps* (quartet, 1941), *Turangalila Symphony* (1949), *Oiseaux exotiques* (piano and orchestra, 1956).

MILHAUD, DARIUS (1892–1974) French. *Le Boeuf sur le Toit* (ballet, 1919), *Christophe Colomb* (opera, 1928).

MONTEVERDI, Claudio (1567–1643) Italian. *La Favola D' Orfeo* (opera, 1607), *Vespers* (choral, 1610), *L'Incoronazione di Poppaea* (opera, 1642).

MOZART, Wolfgang Amadeus (1756–91) Austrian. Flute and Harp Concerto (1778), Sonata for Piano and Violin (1784), Symphony No. 35 "Haffner" (1784), Piano Sonata No. 14 (1785), Quartet No. 19 "Dissonance" (1785), Piano Concerto No. 20 (1785), Symphony No. 38 "Prague" (1786), *Eine kleine Nachtmusik* (serenade, 1787), *Don Giovanni* (opera, 1787), Symphony No. 41 "Jupiter" (1788), Clarinet Quintet (1789), Clarinet Concerto (1791), *The Magic Flute* (opera, 1791), *Requiem* (choral, 1791).

MUSSORGSKY, Modest (1839–81) Russian. *Night on a Bare Mountain* (symphonic poem, 1867), *Pictures at an Exhibition* (piano suite, 1874).

NIELSEN, Carl (1865–1931) Danish. *Saul and David* (opera, 1902), Symphony No. 2 "The Four Temperaments" (1902).

OFFENBACH, Jacques (1819–80) French. *Orpheus in the Underworld* (1858), *La Vie Parisienne* (1866), *The Tales of Hoffmann* (1880).

PALESTRINA, Giovanni Pierluigi da (1525–94) Italian. major figure of Renaissance music: *Missa Papae Marcelli* (c. 1555–56), more than 90 other masses, 60 motets.

PENDERECKI, Krzystof (b. 1933) Polish. *Threnody for the Victims of Hiroshima* (strings, 1960), *Paradise Lost* (opera, 1978).

POULENC, François (1899–1963) French. *Mass in G* (1937), *Gloria* (1959), *The Dialogues of the Carmelites* (opera, 1957).

PROKOFIEV, Sergei (1891–1953) Russian. Symphony No. 1 "The Classical" (1918), Concerto for Piano and Orchestra No. 3 (1921), *Peter and the Wolf* (voice and orchestra, 1936), *Romeo and Juliet* (ballet, 1938), Piano Sonata No. 7 (1943).

PUCCINI, Giacomo (1858–1924) Italian. *La Bohème* (opera, 1896), *Tosca* (opera, 1900), *Madame Butterfly* (opera, 1904), *Turandot* (opera, 1924).

PURCELL, Henry (1659–95) British. *Dido and Aeneas* (opera, 1689), *The Fairy Queen* (opera, 1692), *Te Deum and Jubilate* (choral, 1694).

RACHMANINOV, Sergei (1873–1943) Russian. Piano Concerto No. 2 (1901), *The Isle of the Dead* (symphonic poem, 1907), Rhapsody on a Theme of Paganini (piano and orchestra, 1934).

RAMEAU, Jean Philippe (1683–1764) French. New Suite of Pieces (harpsichord, 1728), *Les Indes Galants* (opera ballet, 1735), *Castor et Pollux* (opera, 1737).

RAVEL, Maurice (1875–1937) French. String Quartet in F (1903), *Valses Nobles*

et Sentimentales (piano, 1910), *Daphnis et Chloé* (ballet 1912), *Boléro* (orchestral dance, 1928).

RIMSKY-KORSAKOV, Nikolai (1844–1908) Russian. *Russian Easter Festival Overture* (1888), *The Golden Cockerel* (opera, 1907).

ROSSINI, Gioachino (1792–1868) Italian. *The Barber of Seville* (opera, 1816), *Semiramide* (opera, 1823), *William Tell* (opera, 1829), *Stabat Mater* (choral, 1842).

SAINT-SAËNS, Camille (1835–1921) French. *Samson et Dalila* (opera, 1877), *Carnival of the Animals* (piano and chamber orchestra, 1886), Symphony No. 3 "with organ" (1886).

SATIE, Erik (1866–1925) French. *Parade* (ballet, 1917), *Socrate* (four sopranos and chamber orchestra, 1918).

SCARLATTI, Alessandro (1660–1725) Italian. *Tigrane* (opera, 1715) and more than 100 other operas; many keyboard works. Son **Domenico** (1685–1757) c. 600 harpsichord sonatas, his work strongly influencing the development of the sonata form.

SCHÖNBERG Arnold (1874–1951) Austrian. *Verklärte Nacht* (string sextet, 1899), Quartet No. 2 (1908), Five Pieces for Orchestra (1909), Five Pieces for Piano (1923).

SCHUBERT, Franz (1797–1828) Austrian. Famous for more than 600 lieder, including song cycles *Die Schöne Müllerin* (1823) and *Winterreise* (1827): Quintet in A major "Trout" (1819), Symphony No. 8 "Unfinished" (1822), Quartet No. 14 "Death and the Maiden" (1826), Symphony No. 9 "Great" (1828), Piano Trio No. 2 (1828).

SCHUMANN, Robert (1810–56) German. *Kreisleriana* (piano, 1838), Fantasia for Piano (1839), *Dichterliebe* (song cycle 1840), Piano Concerto (1845), Symphony No. 3 "Rhenish" (1851).

SCRIABIN, Alexander (1872–1915) Russian. *Poem of Ecstasy* (symphonic poem, 1907), Piano Sonata No. 10 (1913).

SHOSTAKOVICH, Dmitri (1906–75) Russian. Symphony No. 2 "October" (1927), Symphony No. 5 (1937), Symphony No. 7 "Leningrad" (1941), String Quartet No. 8 (1960).

SIBELIUS, Jean (1865–1957) Finnish. *The Swan of Tuonela* (symphonic poem, 1893), *Finlandia* (symphonic poem, 1900), *Valse Triste* (symphonic poem, 1904). Symphony No. 5 (1919).

SMETANA, Bedrich (1824–84) Czech. *The Bartered Bride* (opera, 1866), *Ma Vlast* (My Country) (symphonic poem, 1879).

STAMITZ, Johann (1717–57) Czech. Numerous symphonies, concertos, and sonatas. Son **Carl Phillip** (1745–1801) German. Many symphonies, including a symphony for double orchestra.

STOCKHAUSEN, Karlheinz (b. 1928) German. *11 Klavierstücke* (for piano, 1952–57), *Gruppen* (for three orchestras, 1958), *Kontakte* (electronic, 1960), *Stimmung* (for voices, 1968).

STRAUSS, Johann (1825–99) Austrian. *The Blue Danube* (1867) and many other waltzes, *Die Fledermaus* (opera, 1874).

STRAUSS, Richard (1864–1949) German. *Till Eulenspiegel* (symphonic poem, 1895), *Also sprach Zarathustra* (symphonic poem, 1896), *Elektra* (opera, 1909), *Der Rosenkavalier* (opera, 1911), *Metamorphosen* (for strings, 1945).

STRAVINSKY, Igor (1882–1971) Russian. *Petrushka* (ballet, 1911), *Sacre du Printemps* (ballet, 1913), *Symphony of Psalms* (choral, 1930), Symphony in C (1940), *The Rake's Progress* (opera, 1951).

TCHAIKOVSKY, Peter Ilich (1840–93) Russian. Piano Concerto No. 1 (1875), *Swan Lake* (ballet, 1876), *Romeo and Juliet* (symphonic poem, 1880), Violin Concerto (1881), *Sleeping Beauty* (1888–89), *The Nutcracker* (ballet, 1892), Symphony No. 6 "Pathétique" (1893).

TIPPETT, Sir Michael (b. 1905) British. *The Midsummer Marriage* (opera, 1955), *The Knot Garden* (opera, 1969).

VARÈSE, Edgar (1883–1965) French-American. *Ionization* (percussion, 1933), *Destiny 21.5* (solo flute, 1936), *Déserts* (orchestra and tapes, 1954).

VAUGHAN WILLIAMS, Ralph (1872–1958) British. *Fantasia on a Theme by Tallis* (symphonic poem, 1909), Symphony No. 6 (1947), *The Pilgrim's Progress* (opera, 1951), Symphony No. 7 "Sinfonia Antarctica" (1952).

VERDI, Giuseppe (1813–1901) Italian. *Nabucco* (opera, 1842), *Macbeth* (opera, 1847), *Rigoletto* (opera, 1851), *Il Trovatore* (1853), *La Traviata* (1853), *La Forza del Destino* (opera, 1862), *Aida* (opera, 1871), *Messa da Requiem* (choral, 1874).

VIVALDI, Antonio (1678–1741) Italian. *The Four Seasons* (violin concerti, 1725), Concerto for Flute and Strings (1730).

WAGNER, Richard (1813–83) German. *Rienzi* (opera, 1840), *The Flying Dutchman* (opera, 1841), *Tannhäuser* (opera, 1845), *Lohengrin* (opera, 1848), *Der Ring des Nibelungen* (opera sequence, 1854–74), *Tristan und Isolde* (opera, 1859), *Die Meistersinger von Nürnberg* (opera, 1867), *Siegfried Idyll* (symphonic poem, 1870).

WALTON, Sir William (1902–83) British. *Belshazzar's Feast* (oratorio, 1931), *Violin Concerto* (1939), *Troilus and Cressida* (opera, 1954).

WEBER, Carl Maria von (1786–1826) German. *Der Freischütz* (opera, 1821), *Oberon* (opera, 1826).

WEBERN, Anton von (1883–1945) Austrian. Five Movements for String Quartet (1909), Concerto for Nine Instruments (1934), *Das Augenlicht* (choral 1935), Variations for Orchestra (1940).

WEILL, Kurt (1900–50) German composer and songwriter: *The Threepenny Opera* (opera, 1928), *The Rise and Fall of the City of Mahagonny* (opera, 1930), *The Seven Deadly Sins* (opera, 1933).

Timeline

c. 2550 B.C. Pyramids at Giza, Egypt: immense royal sepulchral monuments, only surviving example of ancient Seven Wonders of the World (*p. 321*).

c. 1800 B.C. Stonehenge, Wiltshire, U.K., completed: megalithic ceremonial site.

c. 1500 B.C. High point of Minoan culture in Crete, named after Minos, the island's legendary king; remains include palace at Knossos.

c. 1323 B.C. Death of Tutankhamen, whose tomb, discovered in 1922, is the only one of an Egyptian pharaoh to survive almost intact; it contains superb jewelry and decorative arts.

c. 1300 B.C. "Treasury of Atreus" (actually a tomb), Mycenae, Greece: one of the major surviving works of Mycenaean art, named after the dominant city in the Aegean region at the time.

c. 1200 B.C. Chinese artists achieve standards in bronze casting (particularly ritual vessels) that have never been surpassed.

c. 1100–800 B.C. Peak of Olmec art: the first great civilization of ancient Mexico; works include colossal stone heads.

c. 700 B.C. High point of Assyrian culture, covering much of Middle East.

c. 600 B.C. Hanging Gardens of Babylon, one of the Seven Wonders (*p.321*).

447–434 B.C. Parthenon, Athens: regarded as summit of Greek architecture and sculpture of Classical period.

c. 350 B.C. Tholos at Epidaurus, Greece: finest surviving Greek theater.

c. 250 B.C. Great Stupa at Sanchi, India, begun (*see* Buddhist Art and Architecture, *p. 533*).

c. 214 B.C. Great Wall of China begun as defense against Mongolian Huns. It eventually stretched 1,500 miles (2,400 km), the only building project observable from space (most of the present structure dates from A.D. 1400s and 1500s).

c. 150 B.C. Earliest paintings in the Buddhist caves at Ajanta, India (latest paintings there date from *c.* A.D. 700).

c. 20 B.C. Pont du Gard across the Gard River, near Nîmes, France: finest surviving Roman viaduct and aqueduct.

A.D. *c.* 72–80 Colosseum, Rome: largest Roman amphitheater.

c. 100 Pyramid of the Sun, Teotihuacán: immense ritual structure built by pre-Mayan civilization of ancient Mexico.

113 Dedication of Trajan's Column, Rome: monument decorated with the finest example of Roman relief sculpture, a continuous spiral celebrating Emperor Trajan's victories.

c. 118–25 Pantheon, Rome: huge temple to all the gods, the best-preserved major Roman building.

326 Dedication of Old St. Peter's, Rome: huge Early Christian building demolished in 1506 to make way for New St. Peter's.

525 Pulguk-sa temple, Kyongju, Korea, first constructed (rebuilt 700s).

EGYPTIAN ART

No other civilization has endured as long as that of the ancient Egyptians. It covered a period of three millennia, from about 3000 B.C., when the country became unified as a single kingdom, to 30 B.C., when, following the death of Cleopatra, it became a Roman province. The antiquity and continuity of Egyptian culture inspired a sense of awe through succeeding ages. Growing out of such a stable civilization, Egyptian art was in general extremely conservative and was little touched by outside influence.

The Egyptians thought that life was governed by an all-embracing cosmic order covering past, present, and future, and their art has an appropriate sense of immutable grandeur. Artists were regarded as skilled workmen who maintained traditional values, rather than as creative figures who expressed their own personalities (the names of some artists

have survived, but they can rarely be associated with particular works).

Much of the most impressive Egyptian art was created in the service of the pharaoh, particularly to sustain his divinity after his death. The most famous works are the pyramids—royal funerary monuments on an immense scale. Apart from these the most impressive buildings are temples. Painting and sculpture were mainly for decoration of tombs and temples, and figures were shown in static poses, expressing a schematic idea of their essence rather than depicting how they appeared to the eye. Sculpture used a variety of materials, sometimes very hard rock such as granite, which increased the sense of permanence. The applied arts were less inhibited by religion; Egyptian jewelry made lavish use of the country's abundant gold and semiprecious stones, at times becoming quite gaudy.

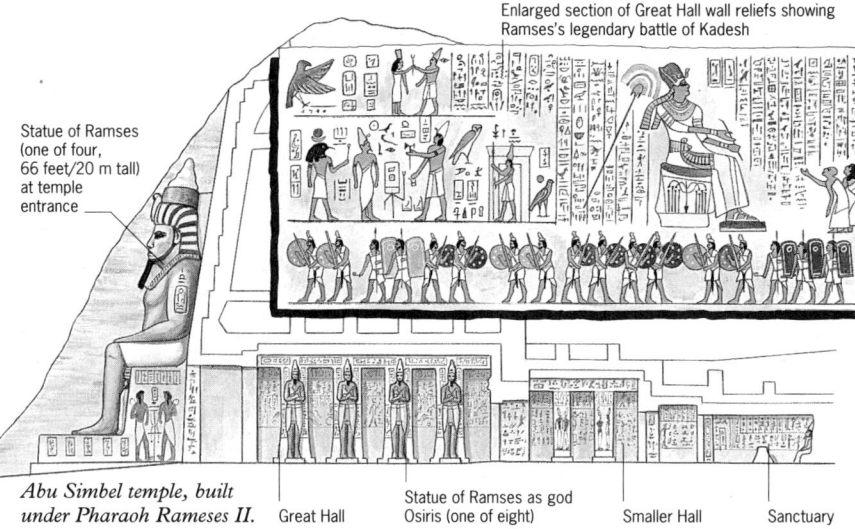

Enlarged section of Great Hall wall reliefs showing Ramses's legendary battle of Kadesh

Statue of Ramses (one of four, 66 feet/20 m tall) at temple entrance

Abu Simbel temple, built under Pharaoh Rameses II. Great Hall | Statue of Ramses as god Osiris (one of eight) | Smaller Hall | Sanctuary

GREEK ART

Greek art is the foundation for much subsequent Western art. Greek painters and sculptors were the first to master naturalistic depiction of the human body, and Greek builders evolved a system of design using various types of column that was regarded as the heart of architecture from the Renaissance to the 1800s.

Nevertheless, very little Greek art was known in the original before the later 1700s (its influence was exerted mainly through Roman copies), and only a very small proportion of the works that the Greeks themselves considered the most important have survived to the present day. Almost all the Greek buildings that survive are temples, most of the painting is on vases (there are some fragments of wall paintings), and although there is a good deal of sculpture, the famous statues that were extolled in the ancient world are known only in copies.

Greek art is usually divided into four phases: the Geometric period (named after a style of vase decoration) in the 800s and 700s B.C.; the Archaic period, from 700 to 480 B.C., (the date of the Persian sack of Athens); the Classical period, from 480 to 323 B.C. (the date of the death of Alexander the Great); and the Hellenistic period, from 323 to 27 B.C., when Augustus became the first Roman emperor (during this period Greece lost its political power, but Greek and "Hellenic" culture spread to other parts of the Mediterranean world and beyond). Greek art reached its greatest harmony and majesty in the Classical period. Athens was the most important artistic center, and the Parthenon (a temple to Athena, the city's patron goddess) is the most celebrated monument of the age. Much of its sculptural decoration is in the British Museum in London.

ISLAMIC ART

The Islamic, or Muslim, religion was founded in Arabia in the early A.D. 600s and spread with astonishing rapidity: within a century it reached as far west as Spain and as far east as India. Not surprisingly, in view of this vast geographical span, there are marked regional variations in Islamic art, but there is also an underlying unity.

The focus of religious life is the mosque: prayers are said facing Mecca (the birthplace of Muhammad, the founder of the religion) and an ornate niche in the appropriate wall indicates the correct direction. A minaret, from which the faithful are called to prayer, is a standard feature, and many mosques also have a dome, symbolizing the heavens. The Dome of the Rock in Jerusalem, built in about 690 B.C., is the earliest surviving monument of Islamic architecture; it was built as a shrine for pilgrims, rather than as a mosque. Like many of the finest Islamic buildings, it has rich decoration in marble and mosaic. By tradition, it was forbidden to represent the human figure in religious art, so the decoration is abstract, sometimes in complex geometrical patterns and sometimes incorporating flowing Arabic script.

The human figure could be represented in secular art, however, and Islamic artists produced superb illuminated manuscripts showing such subjects as hunting scenes and courtly life. Some of the best manuscripts were produced in Persia and for the Mogul dynasty in India, which reached a great cultural peak in the late 1500s and early 1600s. The greatest work in Mogul art is the Taj Mahal, built by Emperor Shah Jahan as a mausoleum for his favorite wife. Sculpture played little part in Islamic art, but there were superb achievements in the applied arts, among them carpets, ceramics, and metalwork.

Moorish decor, incorporating Arabic script, Alhambra Palace, Granada, Spain.

BUDDHIST ART AND ARCHITECTURE

Buddhism was founded in India in the 500s B.C.; eight hindred years later it was made the national religion by the Emperor Asoka. From India it spread over much of Asia, and it is still a major religion in several countries, although it now has comparatively few adherents in India itself.

Early Buddhist art included rock-cut shrines and stupas. The latter monuments, in the form of domelike mounds, either mark a sacred place or enshrine relics of Buddha or some other holy personage. Usually they are surrounded by a railing with four gateways. They were erected all over the Buddhist world, and in some places developed into complex architectural forms, as at Pagan in Myanmar and Borobudur in Indonesia, the largest of all Buddhist temples. Where the stupa came under Chinese architectural influence, it evolved into a pagoda.

Initially Buddha himself was not represented in art (although his presence was sometimes indicated by symbols such as his footprints); he was first shown in human form in about A.D. 100, and thereafter statues of Buddha became characteristic of the religion's art. They range from small bronzes to huge figures cut from living rock; Buddha is usually shown sitting cross-legged in a meditative pose, but in some cases he is standing or, in immense rock sculptures, reclining.

Bodhisattvas are also common in Buddhist art: these are people who, like Buddha, have attained enlightenment but have chosen to help others attain it rather than entering a state of nirvana themselves. In China, Japan, and Korea, the popular forms of Buddhism, such as Zen, tend to focus on achieving enlightenment through meditation. Influenced by vernacular architecture, temples in these countries are closely attuned to nature: many are built of wood, with serene gardens to aid meditation.

Buddha at Kofukuji temple, Nara, Japan.

Timeline

c. 1305 Fresco cycle, Arena Chapel, Padua, Italy, painted by Giotto: major extant work by founder of central tradition of European painting.

1308–11 Duccio paints *Maestà* for Siena cathedral: sumptuous Italian altarpiece.

c. 1325 Founding of Tenochtitlán, capital city of the Aztecs in Mexico.

1338–91 Main period of building of the Alhambra, Granada, Spain: most splendid Islamic Spanish palace.

1395–1406 Claus Sluter sculpts the *Well of Moses*: surviving part of a Calvary group for a Carthusian monastery at Dijon, France; major work by Netherlandish-born Sluter, the outstanding sculptor of his time in northern Europe.

c. 1400 Tamerlane's mausoleum, Samarkand, Central Asia.

1401–24 Lorenzo Ghiberti makes first set of bronze doors for the baptistery, Florence: the most prestigious commission in the city at this time.

1406 Forbidden City, Beijing, begun: greatest palace of the Chinese emperors.

c. 1410 Andrei Rublev, the icon of the Old Testament Trinity: surviving masterpiece by Russian icon painter.

1416 Donatello sculpts *St. George*: early work by the dominant figure in 15th-century Italian sculpture.

1418–36 Brunelleschi builds dome of Florence cathedral: great engineering feat and triumphant symbol of Renaissance Florence *(right)*.

1419 Filippo Brunelleschi begins the Foundling Hospital, Florence, Italy, regarded as first Renaissance building.

1420 Great Temple of the Dragon, Beijing, China.

c. 1425–28 Masaccio paints fresco cycle in the Brancacci chapel, Santa Maria del Carmine, Florence, Italy: major work by chief founder of Renaissance painting *(right)*.

1425–52 Ghiberti creates second set of bronze doors for the baptistery in Florence, more Renaissance in style.

1432 Jan van Eyck completes the *Adoration of the Lamb* altarpiece for Ghent cathedral, Flanders (now Belgium): most famous painting of the Early Netherlandish School.

1443–53 Donatello sculpts *Gattamelata*, Padua, Italy: first life-size equestrian statue to be made since antiquity.

1446 King's College chapel, Cambridge, England begun: masterpiece of the Perpendicular style, a type of late Gothic architecture found only in England.

c. 1454–65 Piero della Francesca paints *The Story of the True Cross,* fresco cycle in San Francesco, Arezzo, Italy: major surviving work of revered Italian painter.

1478–86 Sandro Botticelli's *Primavera* and *The Birth of Venus*: two of the best-loved masterpieces of Renaissance painting, treating mythological subjects on a scale and with a seriousness previously reserved for religious themes.

MEDIEVAL ART

When the concept of the "Middle Ages" came into being, the period between the fall of the Roman Empire and the Renaissance (roughly a thousand years) was regarded as a largely barbaric interlude between two great ages of culture. We now have a more well-informed attitude toward this era and can see that it was remarkably diverse culturally. Even in the early period (sometimes called the Dark Ages because of our lack of detailed knowledge of it), there were great achievements in, for example, manuscript illumination and work with precious stones.

In the later Middle Ages, two great styles successively dominated European art: Romanesque, which prevailed in the 1000s and 1100s; and Gothic, which was born in the mid-1100s in France and spread to many other countries by the end of the century, lasting in some places into the 1500s. The dominant art of these times was architecture. Romanesque buildings have massive solidity, with round arches and often vigorous abstract ornamentation. Gothic architecture uses a more skeletal system of construction: windows became progressively larger until they formed a kind of translucent wall supported by a graceful framework of stone. Most of the great buildings of the Romanesque and Gothic periods are churches; the cathedrals of Durham and

Lady and the Unicorn, *French tapestry*.

Chartres rank among the finest examples of all time.

Large-scale painting and sculpture existed mainly as adjuncts to architecture. The type of "painting" that belongs specifically to the Middle Ages is stained glass *(p551)*, which reached its greatest heights in France in the 1100s.

RENAISSANCE

"Renaissance" means rebirth. The term refers to a revival of the values of the ancient world that began in Italy and spread throughout Europe, affecting various fields of intellectual life *(p336)*, not least the visual arts. It is difficult to put a date on the beginning of the movement, but in the visual arts the formative period was in the early 1400s in Florence, Italy (a city rich from banking and trading).

Architecture is the field in which this can best be seen: classical buildings are clearly distinct from the Gothic of the later Middle Ages. The Florentine Filippo

Florence cathedral: dome by Brunelleschi, bell tower by Giotto.

Brunelleschi was the first architect to work in a style that can be called Renaissance.

Although not so obviously, the sculptor Donatello and the painter Masaccio (friends of Brunelleschi) occupy positions of comparable importance. Donatello was the first sculptor who was attuned to the spirit of ancient sculpture rather than merely borrowing motifs from it. Very little Roman painting had survived, so unlike sculptors, Masaccio could not look directly to Roman models for inspiration; ancient painters, however, were known to value fidelity to nature, and as the first painter to master perspective, Masaccio achieved a momentous advance in naturalism. Brunelleschi, Donatello, and Masaccio were each pioneering work in Renaissance style by 1425.

Florence continued to be the center of Renaissance style throughout the 1400s; a roster of great names (many of them native Florentines, some visitors) worked there in this period, among them Botticelli, Piero della Francesca, and Uccello. In the 1500s, Rome and Venice began to rival Florence. Artistic ideas were spread by the travels of artists to and from Italy (among them Albrecht Dürer and Pieter Brueghel), by the commissioning of works from foreign artists, and (from the later 1400s) by the proliferation of engravings.

HIGH RENAISSANCE

The High Renaissance is a name given to a brief period (c. 1500–20) during which the ideals of the Renaissance are thought to have been given most complete expression in art. Towering over this period are three figures: Leonardo da Vinci, Michelangelo, and Raphael. Their contemporaries regarded them with awe, and together they created the idea of the artist as an inspired genius rather than merely a skilled artisan. Subsequent generations thought they had brought art to a peak of balance and grace that could hardly be surpassed, and their work remained touchstones for centuries.

In architecture, Bramante was a figure of comparable authority. His contemporaries saw his buildings as the first to rival those of the Romans in grandeur.

The most important works of the High Renaissance were created in Florence and above all Rome, notably under the patronage of Pope Julius II. He commissioned Bramante to design the new St. Peter's Church, of which he laid the foundation stone in 1506; Michelangelo to paint the ceiling of the Sistine Chapel (1508–12); and Raphael to decorate a suite in the Vatican (begun 1508). In Florence, Andrea del Sarto and Fra

Leonardo da Vinci, The Adoration of the Magi.

Bartolomeo Della Porta were the leading painters after Leonardo, Raphael, and Michelangelo had left the city, by 1509.

The High Renaissance is sometimes extended to other cities, notably Venice, where the period coincided with the old age of Giovanni Bellini, the brief career of Giorgione, and the early maturity of Titian. Outside Italy, the idea of a High Renaissance has little coherence.

MANNERISM

Many of the terms used as stylistic or period labels in art have a complex history and are employed in a confusing variety of ways. Originally the Italian word "maniera" was used in the mid-1500s as a term of praise, conveying the idea of graceful sophistication. Later, many crit-

Francesco Parmigianino, Madonna with the Long Neck.

ics thought that Italian art of this period marked a sad decline from the High Renaissance, and "Mannerism" came to describe art that was considered artificial, exaggerated, and superficial. The word then extended in meaning to become a general period label for the time between High Renaissance and Baroque styles, roughly 1520–1600, and was applied to art throughout Europe. Today the term generally suggests neither praise nor censure, but writers vary in how they apply it.

Mannerism is usually traced back to the late paintings of Raphael, when he was moving away from the harmonious High Renaissance style to a more complex and emotional one. Younger contemporaries took this further, using elongated figures, strained poses, and sometimes lurid colors. In the hands of masters such as Pontormo and Parmigianino, these traits produced powerful and moving works. In the hands of lesser artists, they degenerated into empty posturing. In sculpture, Mannerism was characterized by elaborate twisting poses; Giambologna was the archetypal master. In architecture, it is often distinguished by playful manipulation of classical conventions, so that certain features seem to have slipped out of their rightful places. Outside Italy, Mannerism flourished mainly in sophisticated courts, notably those of François I of France and Emperor Rudolf II in Prague, but there were also independent figures, such as El Greco in Spain.

Timeline

c. 1495–97 Leonardo da Vinci's mural *The Last Supper,* in the refectory of Santa Maria delle Grazie Monastery, Milan: most famous painting of the time, remarkable for its psychological subtlety and dignified composition.

c. 1500 Inca mountain fortress city of Machu Picchu, Peru, so remote that it was unknown to the Spanish conquistadores and was not discovered until 1911. Peak of court art in the African kingdom of Benin *(p339)*; the finest works are superbly refined, aristocratic bronze heads.

c. 1503 Leonardo da Vinci's *Mona Lisa*: probably the world's most famous painting, bringing a new naturalism of pose and subtlety of expression to portraiture.

1506 New St. Peter's, Rome, begun, with Bramante *(left)* as architect; many other architects worked on this, the largest church in Christendom, before its consecration in 1626.

1508–12 Michelangelo *(left)* paints ceiling of Sistine Chapel in the Vatican, Rome: one of the most revered and influential works in European art.

1511 Raphael *(left)* completes frescoes in Stanza della Segnatura in the Vatican, Rome, first of a series of rooms: among the purest expressions of High Renaissance ideals.

1516–18 Titian paints *Assumption of the Virgin*: huge altarpiece establishing him as the leading painter in Venice.

1526 Giulio Romano begins Palazzo del Te, Mantua, Italy, cited as first Mannerist building.

1528 François I begins rebuilding château at Fontainebleau, which becomes center for Mannerist art in France.

1533 Hans Holbein paints *The Ambassadors*: full-length double portrait by greatest portraitist of Northern Renaissance, painted in England, where he spent much of his career at the court of King Henry VIII.

1546 Michelangelo appointed architect of St. Peter's, Rome; his work includes the dome.

1551 Suleimaniye Mosque, Constantinople, begun; designed by Sinan, most famous Islamic architect.

1555–61 St. Basil's Cathedral, Moscow: multidomed church, picturesque masterpiece of Russian architecture (multicolored paintwork of the exterior added in the 1600s).

1563 Escorial, near Madrid, begun: enormous monastery-palace built for King Philip II of Spain; most important Spanish building of the period, richly decorated with paintings and sculpture.

1565 Pieter Brueghel, *Hunters in the Snow*: most famous work by greatest Dutch painter of the century.

1565–69 Andrea Palladio's Villa Rotunda, near Vicenza, Italy: famous villa designed by one of the most influential architects of all time.

Timeline

1583 Giambologna, *Rape of the Sabine Women*: a high point of Mannerist work, by Flemish-born Italian sculptor based in Florence, Italy.

1586–88 El Greco's *The Burial of Count Orgaz*: altarpiece for S. Tomé, Toledo, Spain, by the famous Cretan-born Spanish painter.

1597–1600 Annibale Carracci paints ceiling of Farnese Gallery, Farnese Palace, Rome: secular fresco cycle, foundation of much Baroque decorative painting.

1599–1602 Caravaggio carries out major commissions for the churches of San Luigi dei Francesi and Santa Maria del Popolo, Rome, which establishes him as most powerful and original Italian painter of his day.

1611–14 Peter Paul Rubens paints *The Raising of the Cross* and *The Descent from the Cross*, two huge altarpieces for churches in Antwerp, Flanders (now Belgium) that establish him as pre-eminent painter in northern Europe.

1616–25 Katsura imperial villa, Kyoto, Japan: masterpiece of Edo period architecture and garden design.

1619–22 Inigo Jones builds Banqueting House, Whitehall, London, bringing pure classical style to England—where Italian influence had previously been superficial.

1630–48 Taj Mahal, Agra, India: architectural masterpiece built as mausoleum for the favorite wife of Shah Jahan, art-loving Islamic Mogul emperor.

1637–41 Francesco Borromini builds church of San Carlo alle Quattro Fontane, Rome: first major independent commission for this original genius of Baroque architecture.

1642 Rembrandt's group portrait *The Night Watch*: most famous work by the Neherlands' greatest painter.

1642–51 François Mansart builds château of Maisons-Lafitte, near Paris: most complete surviving work by great French architect.

1645–52 Gianlorenzo Bernini's Cornaro Chapel in Santa Maria della Vittoria, Rome: archetypal Baroque art, blending architecture, painting, and sculpture (Bernini's marble group *The Ecstasy of St. Theresa*).

1656 Diego Velazquez's group portrait *Las Meninas* (*The Maids of Honor*): most famous work by this great Spanish painter.

1669 Louis XIV of France begins building work at Versailles, transforming it from modest château to the largest palace in Europe; architects are Louis Levau and Jules Hardouin-Mansart.

1672 Kao-t'sen paints *Autumn Landscape*: well-known Chinese indiaink picture.

1675–1710 St. Paul's Cathedral rebuilt by Sir Christopher Wren: greatest English building of the age, part of the rebuilding of London after the Great Fire of 1666.

BAROQUE

The name "Baroque" is applied to the dominant style in European art and architecture of the 1600s and early 1700s. It was originally a term of abuse, suggesting grotesque overelaboration, coined at a time when much 17th-century art was out of critical favor. Now it is used to describe the dynamic style that was born in Rome around 1600 and spread through Europe.

This took root particularly in Catholic countries, the confident style becoming associated with the reinvigorated Catholic Church, which at that time was asserting itself against Protestantism. Baroque inherited movement from Mannerism, which preceded it, and a sense of grandeur and solidity from the art of the High Renaissance. These influences were fused into a fervent style particularly suited to expressing intense religious emotion. Some of the greatest Baroque artists—such as Italian sculptor-architect Bernini and Flemish painter Rubens—were extremely devout Catholics.

However, the sense of lavish eloquence characteristic of Baroque art also lent itself to certain types of secular art. In France, for example, Baroque art reached its greatest height as propaganda for Louis XIV. His enormous palace at Versailles brought together architecture, painting, sculpture, decoration, and landscape gardening to celebrate his royal glory. This combination of various arts to create a "total work of art" was one of the char-

Giovanni Bernini, Ecstasy of St. Theresa, *Santa Maria della Vittoria, Rome.*

acteristics of the period.

Baroque art made comparatively little impact in Britain (where there was a suspicion of anything associated with Catholicism). In the early 1700s, however, there was a short-lived idiosyncratic flourishing of Baroque architecture, particularly in the work of Sir John Vanbrugh and Nicholas Hawksmoor.

DUTCH ART OF THE 1600s

During the 1500s, the Netherlands was ruled by Spain. By 1609, after much bitter fighting, the Netherlands had won its freedom (although this was not officially recognized until 1648). The resulting national pride and self-confidence were expressed in a golden age in Dutch art, which lasted until about 1670. It produced some fine sculpture and architecture but is most remarkable for its painting.

Jan Vermeer, The Cook.

The number of distinguished painters who were working in this small country over such a short period is astonishing. Their work was varied, but much of it dwelt on subjects that celebrated the hard-won peace and prosperity of their country. Landscapes, seascapes (the Netherlands was later to become a great maritime power), domestic scenes, portraits of successful merchants, still lifes of the objects in which they traded—these were the kinds of subjects in which the Dutch painters excelled. There was comparatively little religious painting at this time because most of the Dutch were Protestants and their churches had little decoration.

Whereas in other countries paintings were owned only by the rich and powerful, in the Netherlands they were bought by the middle classes. The cheaper ones were sold at fairs, like any other merchandise.

Among the large number of very good painters were several truly great artists, including the brilliant portraitist Frans Hals; Vermeer, creator of some exquisite domestic scenes; and Rembrandt, the towering genius of Dutch art. Unlike most Dutch painters, he painted virtually every type of subject, although it is as a portraitist and a religious painter that he

ROCOCO

The Rococo style was born in France in about 1700, partly as a development from Baroque art and partly as a reaction against it. In both styles there is richness and complexity of form, but whereas Baroque art is characteristically solid and sometimes somber, Rococo art is much lighter (often intentionally playful) in spirit. The two styles often merge; with many works it is impossible to say dogmatically that they belong to one rather than the other. Initially Rococo was mainly a style of interior decoration; one explanation of the origin of the word is that it comes from "rocaille," a term for fancy rock- and shell-work in grottoes.

The first great Rococo painter was Watteau, and the artists who best sum up the elegant frivolity of the style at its peak are Boucher and Fragonard. From Paris (which by this time had replaced Rome as international capital of the art world), the Rococo style spread throughout Europe, although like the Baroque it was most at home in Catholic countries. In France, tastes began to turn toward Neoclassicism by the 1760s, but in central Europe Rococo flourished until almost the end of the 1700s. Unlike Baroque, Rococo style is usually secular in spirit, but in Austria and southern Germany some churches were decorated in the Rococo manner; the finest are breathtakingly light and exuberant.

NEOCLASSICISM

Neoclassicism was the dominant style in European art and architecture in the late 1700s and early 1800s. The word means "new classicism," and the style was a conscious attempt to revive the spirit and forms of the art of the classical world—ancient Greece and Rome. This was partly a reaction against the frivolity of the Rococo style and partly a response to growing scholarly knowledge of antiquity, stimulated particularly by excavations at Pompeii and Herculaneum, the Roman towns that had been buried by an eruption of Mt. Vesuvius in A.D. 79.

In the early days of Neoclassicism, very little Greek art was known in the original, and Rome was initially the center of the style. Artists spent significant parts of their career in the city. Their work was varied, for although Neoclassicism gener-ally aimed at order and clarity, it embraced many influences from antiquity.

The paintings of Frenchman Jacques-Louis David show Neoclassicism at its most heroic and severe. His work was in tune with the ideals of the French revolution, and he often chose subjects from ancient history in which devotion to the state is put before personal concerns. Other artists were more interested in the decorative aspects of ancient art, and Neoclassicism had enormous influence on the applied arts. In architecture, Neoclassicism culminated in the Greek revival of the 1820s and 1830s, when the grave simplicity of Greek buildings was imitated. The term "federalism" was applied to much American Neoclassical architecture, typified by Charles Bulfinch's State House building in Boston.

Germain Soufflot's Panthéon, Paris, was largely inspired by Greek temples at Paestum, southern Italy.

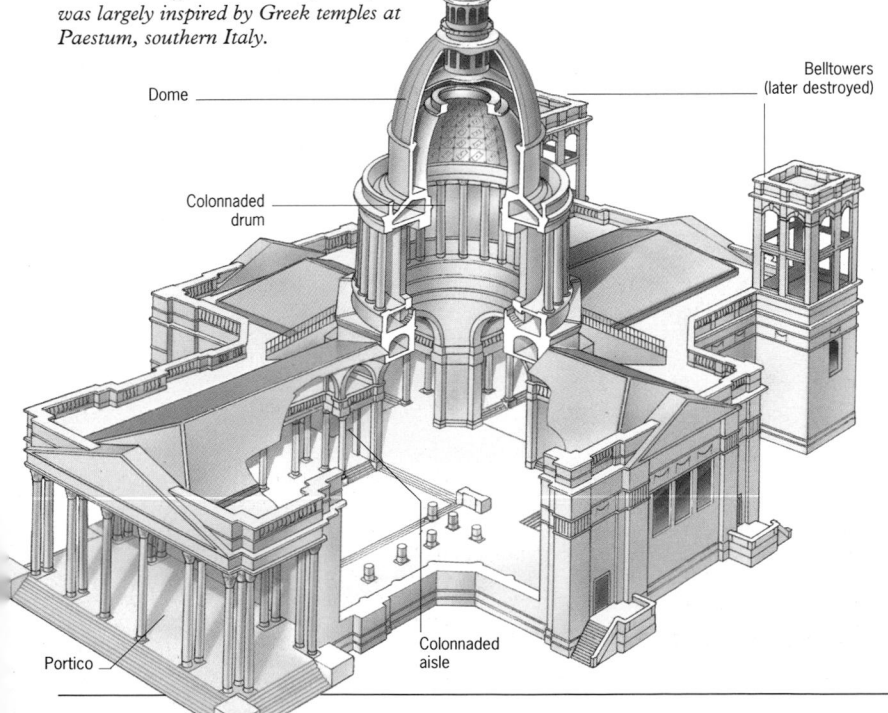

Dome

Colonnaded drum

Portico

Colonnaded aisle

Belltowers (later destroyed)

Timeline

1799 Francisco de Goya publishes *Los Caprichos* (*Caprices*), first of a series of engravings satirizing human folly and cruelty.

1805–18 Benjamin Latrobe builds Catholic cathedral, Baltimore: outstanding work of Neoclassical architecture in U.S.A.

1807 Latrobe completes the south, or House, wing of the U.S. Capitol in Washington, D.C.; construction of the remainder only completed in 1863.

1808 Caspar David Friedrich, *Cross in the Mountains*: one of the first major works by outstanding German Romantic painter.

1819 Théodore Géricault paints *The Raft of the Medusa*: masterpiece of French Romanticism.

1823–29 Katsushika Hokusai's *Thirty-Six Views of Mount Fuji*: celebrated series of color woodblock prints by most revered Japanese artist.

1824 John Constable's *The Hay Wain* (1821) wins a gold medal at the Paris Salon; the most popular of English landscape painters is initially more admired in France than in Britain.

1825–28 Altes Museum, Berlin, Germany, built by Karl Friedrich Schinkel: Neoclassical masterpiece by greatest German architect of the century.

1832 Ando Hiroshige publishes *Fifty-Three Stages of the Tokaido*: series of color woodblock prints by Japan's other great master.

1833–36 François Rude, *La Marseillaise*: relief sculpture on the Arc de Triomphe, Paris, glorifying the French Revolution in Romantic style.

1830s–1840s Hudson River School of Painters, led by Thomas Cole, Thomas Doughty, and Asher Brown Durand, brings a Romantic approach to American landscape painting.

1836–68 Palace of Westminster (Houses of Parliament), London, England, designed by Sir Charles Barry, with detailing by A. W. N. Pugin: one of the most original public buildings of the century, classical but with highly ornate Gothic detailing.

1838 Joseph Mallard William Turner, *The Fighting Temeraire:* popular work by English landscape painter, it shows an old warship being towed to the breaker's yard—a poignant symbol of the age of steam replacing the age of sail.

1848 Foundation of the Pre-Raphaelite Brotherhood, a small group of idealistic young British artists who reject academic conventions and aim to recapture the freshness and sincerity of early Italian painting (before Raphael).

1850 Gustave Courbet shows three large paintings at the Paris Salon that establish him as leader of the Realist movement, treating everyday scenes with a seriousness previously reserved for subjects taken from history, mythology, and religion.

ROMANTICISM

Romanticism was an intellectual trend expressed in all arts in the Western world in the late 1700s and the first half of the 1800s literature and music were just as involved as the visual arts. It was not so much a style as a set of attitudes toward art and life. Romantic artists believed above all in self-expression—the duty of the artist was to be sincere, spontaneous, and original. This outlook stands in contrast to Neoclassicism, in which great importance was placed on respect for the art of the past. Romanticism was to some extent a reaction against Neoclassicism, but the two movements were not incompatible: sometimes a love of the ancient world was tinged with a Romantic nostalgia for a lost golden age; this has been called "Romantic Classicism."

Romanticism flourished in Britain, France, and Germany, but it affected most of Europe and even had adherents among the Hudson River School in New York. Outstanding Romantic artists included Turner in Britain, Delacroix in France, Friedrich in Germany, and Goya in Spain. Typical themes were wild or mysterious landscapes and dramatic scenes from literature (especially Shakespeare) as well as dreams and nightmares, the horrific and the macabre, and extremes of feelings and behavior.

Caspar-David Friedrich, The Wanderer over the Sea of Clouds.

Sculpture and architecture were less suited to this kind of inspiration, but an aspect of Romanticism—love of the medieval world—comes out in Gothic Revival architecture. Imitation of exotic architectural styles, such as Egyptian or Indian, was also a part of Romanticism.

EAST MEETS WEST

Cultural contacts between Europe and the civilizations of Asia go back many centuries. Alexander the Great conquered as far as India in the 300s B.C., introducing Greek influence into Indian sculpture. By the about 100 B.C., Chinese silk had reached the Roman Empire in the hands of Egyptian and Persian merchants traveling the caravan route to China. Trading

Katsushika Hokusai, Kingfisher, Irises, and Pinks.

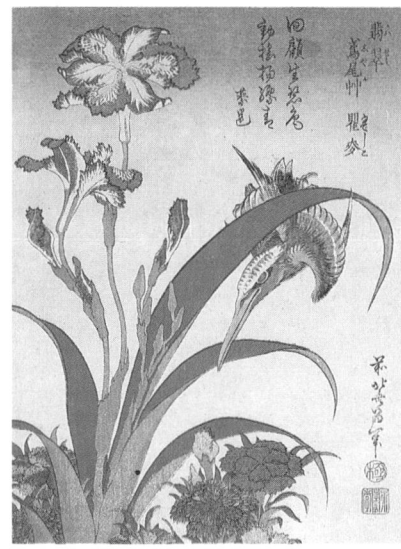

states such as the Venice or the Netherlands naturally had most contact with the East, either by land or by sea. As a result, Dutch paintings, for instance, often show luxury articles from distant lands, notably Chinese porcelain.

By the 1700s there was a fashion in Europe for all things Chinese, known as chinoiserie. This was expressed not only in the decorative arts but also in painting (Watteau painted a series of *Chinese Figures*, now lost) and even architecture (for example Sir William Chambers' pagoda in Kew Gardens, London, 1761–62: Chambers had spent nine years in the Swedish merchant navy, visiting India as well as China). The taste for chinoiserie faded with the dominance of Neoclassicism in the later 1700s, but revived in the Romantic climate of the early 1800s.

Later in the 1800s, a new wave of oriental influence came from Japan. The country had deliberately isolated itself from the rest of the world for two centuries, but in 1854 it began trading with the West. European artists were impressed by Japanese color woodblock prints, so common in Japan that they were sometimes used as ballast in ships. Several of the leading Impressionists and Post-Impressionists (notably van Gogh) were influenced by their boldness and vigor, especially their use of strong, flat color and offbeat angles of view.

IMPRESSIONISM

Impressionism was born in 1874, when a number of French artists who had found it hard to get their work accepted for the official Paris Salon organized a group exhibition of their own. One of the paintings shown there, Monet's *Impression: Sunrise*, was the subject of a sarcastic attack by a critic, and the term "Impressionists" was applied to the group as a whole. Like many such terms, it was coined in mockery, but the painters in the group accepted it as appropriate to their aims and methods.

With Monet, the central figures of the group were Cézanne (*below*), Degas, Manet, Pissarro, Renoir, and Sisley. There were seven more Impressionist exhibitions (the last in 1886), but the group was united by loose ties of friendship rather than by a common policy. Manet never exhibited at any of the exhibitions, and the commitment of the others varied greatly. What they shared was an interest in depicting contemporary life in a fresh and immediate way—conveying the impression of a scene rather than minute detail. Most of them were interested in landscape, but it played very little part in the work of Degas and Manet, who were primarily figure painters.

The bright colors and sketchy brushwork of the Impressionists were at first bewildering or shocking to many people, but the artists overcame initial mockery and most began to prosper in the 1880s (although Sisley was only moderately successful financially). Only Monet, however, was committed to the ideals of Impressionism throughout his career; the others developed in different directions. Impressionism was enormously influential, leading artists all over Europe to look afresh at the world and paint in a freer, livelier, more colorful way.

Paul Cézanne, Peaches and Pears.

POST-IMPRESSIONISM

Post-Impressionism is an umbrella term for a number of trends in French painting that developed in the wake of Impressionism between about 1880 and 1905. Many artists found the work of the Impressionists a liberating influence, but some thought that they had put too much emphasis on depicting momentary appearances and surface effects and had thereby sacrificed deeper meaning.

The four greatest figures of Post-Impressionism illustrate the variety of developments from Impressionism and reactions against it. Paul Cézanne, who said he wanted "to make of Impressionism something solid and enduring, like the art of the museums," was concerned above all with the structure of the things he depicted. Paul Gauguin used color and line decoratively and symbolically rather than naturalistically (he was one of the first artists to be influenced by primitive art, referring to "the abominable error of naturalism"). Vincent van Gogh brought to art a new emotional intensity, using brilliant color and swirling brushstrokes to express what he called "man's terrible passions." Georges Seurat was the founder of Neo-Impressionism, in which the radiant depiction of color associated with Impressionism was given a more rational, scientific basis.

All four of these artists were extremely influential on early 20th-century art throughout Europe. The term "Post-Impressionism" was coined by the British art critic Roger Fry for an exhibition of avant-garde painting (dominated by Cézanne, Gauguin, and van Gogh) that he organized in London in 1910.

Timeline

1851 Sir Joseph Paxton builds Crystal Palace for the Great Exhibition in Hyde Park, London: an enormous glass and iron structure, first example of large-scale prefabrication in building.

1859 Jean-François Millet's *The Angelus*: immensely popular scene of sentimentalized peasant life, probably the most reproduced painting of its time.

1861–74 Charles Garnier builds L'Opéra, Paris: example of the century's most sumptuous architecture, part of the rebuilding of Paris directed by Baron Haussmann for Napoleon III.

1863 Salon des Refuses held in Paris: exhibition of works rejected by the official Salon; although many, including Manet's *Olympia*, are mocked by public and critics, the Salon des Refuses helps to undermine conservative attitudes and encourages artists to organize their own exhibitions.

1874 First Impressionist exhibition held in Paris: start of the most influential movement in 19th-century painting.

1875 Thomas Eakins, *The Gross Clinic*: most celebrated work by the greatest U.S. painter of the 1800s.

1880 Auguste Rodin, greatest sculptor of the age, begins work on *The Gates of Hell*, a vast project for which he creates almost 200 figures but which he never finishes in definitive form.

1884 Antonio Gaudi takes over as architect of the church of Sagrada Familia, Barcelona, Spain, and transforms it from a conventional Gothic Revival building into a bizarrely expressive masterpiece; unfinished at his death in 1926.

1885 Washington Monument dedicated in Washington, D.C.

1886 Final Impressionist exhibition, at which Seurat emerges as the leader of Neo-Impressionism.

1888 Paul Gauguin and Vincent Van Gogh, two of the greatest figures of Post-Impressionism, work together at Arles in southern France. Statue of Liberty dedicated in New York Harbor.

1889 Eiffel Tower, Paris: the tallest structure in the world at the time, built to mark the centenary of the French Revolution; helps to make iron an acceptable material for architecture.

1890s Winslow Homer's landscapes and seascapes of his native Maine combine naturalism with a sensitive treatment of light.

1890–91 Wainwright Building, St. Louis, Missouri, built by Louis Sullivan: outstanding early skyscraper.

1892–93 Victor Horta's Tassel House, Brussels, Belgium: a masterpiece of Art Nouveau architecture and decoration.

1893 Edvard Munch, *The Scream*: original depiction of anguish that helps inspire 20th-century Expressionism.

1895 Exhibition of Paul Cézanne's work in Paris establishes his reputation among the avant-garde.

Timeline

1897 Charles Rennie Mackintosh commences work on Glasgow School of Art: most famous building by this original architect. Augustus St.-Gauden's *Shaw Memorial* confirms him as sculptor of international importance.

***c.* 1900** Hector Guimard designs entrances for several Paris metro stations, featuring some of the finest examples of Art Nouveau metalwork.

1905 Fauvism launched at the Salon d'Automne, Paris: the first of the major avant-garde movements that revolutionized European painting and sculpture. Foundation in Dresden of Die Brücke, important German Expressionist group *(p541)*.

1907 Georges Braque and Pablo Picasso begin to develop Cubism *(right below)*.

1909 Futurism founded: Italian avant-garde movement indebted to Cubist formal analysis but adding a sense of movement and the excitement of machinery; leading Futurists include Giacomo Balla and Umberto Boccioni.

***c.* 1910** Birth of abstract art *(Neo-Plasticism p542)*: Wassily Kandinsky is sometimes credited as first abstract artist, but it is likely that several artists in several countries arrived at abstraction more or less simultaneously.

1910 Critic Roger Fry organizes the first Post-Impressionist exhibition in London; it is attacked by conservative critics but influences many young artists. Fry organizes a second Post-Impressionist exhibition in 1912.

1911 Der Blaue Reiter, German Expressionist group, founded in Munich *(p541)*.

1912 Orphism (or Orphic Cubism) born: French painting movement combining Cubist fragmentation of form with radiant color. Rayonism develops in Russia: its founders, Natalia Goncharova and Mikhail Larionov, call it "a synthesis of Cubism, Futurism, and Orphism."

1913 Armory Show held in New York City (then Chicago and Boston): the most influential exhibition in U.S. art history, showing modern European art on a large scale for the first time. In Russia, Kasimir Malevich begins developing Suprematism, a radically simple style of abstract art; it culminates *c.* 1918 in a white square on a white background.

1914–15 Vorticism comes into being: radical British art movement related to Cubism and Futurism; the central figure is painter Percy Wyndham Lewis; also associated are two major sculptors—American Jacob Epstein and Frenchman Henri Gaudier-Brzeska.

1915 Dada *(p541)* founded in both Zurich, Switzerland, and New York City: perhaps the most disruptive and controversial movement in 20th-century art; although short-lived, it is highly influential, with resonances beyond its time.

PRIMITIVISM

The word "primitive" is used in various ways in the history of art. Broadly, it embraces the art of all societies outside the mainstream of civilization in the Western world and the Orient, even though some of these peoples were and are highly sophisticated in many ways. Pre-Columbian art in Central and South America, Native American art, African art, and Oceanic art are the main areas covered. This kind of "primitive" art tended to find its way to the West as colonial booty and for centuries was valued mainly ethnographically or, in the case of articles made of precious materials, as bullion (as early as 1520, Albrecht Dürer enthused about Aztec treasures from "the new land of gold").

In the late 1800s, however, Paul Gaugin tried to escape "the disease of civilization" by living among the people of Tahiti, and during the early 1900s many avant-garde artists—following his example in spirit if not in body—began looking to "primitive" art as a source of inspiration, a way of finding a sense of vitality and truth that had been polished out of Western painting and sculpture. It was African rather than Polynesian art that had the greatest effect on these artists. Matisse and Picasso were among those who collected African masks, and two of the heads in Picasso's celebrated *Les*

Zambian woodcarving.

Demoiselles d'Avignon (1906–07) clearly derive from such sources. Artists also studied "primitive" works in museums, such as the Musée de l'Homme in Paris and the British Museum in London — where Henry Moore was influenced by Maya sculpture.

CUBISM AND BEYOND

Cubism was the most radical and influential of the avant-garde art movements that revolutionized European painting and sculpture between 1905 and the outbreak of World War I in 1914. It was the creation of two artists working in Paris—the Frenchman Georges Braque and the Spaniard Pablo Picasso, who had settled

Pablo Picasso, Girl Before a Mirror.

there in 1904. They met in 1907 and collaborated closely until the war (during which Braque was severely wounded). Their artistic bond was so close that it is sometimes hard to tell their work apart in this period—they regarded themselves "like mountaineers roped together."

The essence of Cubism was that instead of depicting subjects from a single, fixed viewpoint, the artists broke them up into a multiplicity of facets, so that several different aspects of an object were seen simultaneously. Still life was the most suitable subject for this kind of treatment, but landscape also played an important part in Cubism.

By 1910, so many artists were being influenced by the work of Braque and Picasso that critics were referring to a Cubist school. Among the artists included was Juan Gris, whose paintings introduced a new note of color (Braque's and Picasso's pictures were often virtually monochromatic). Sculptors were also influenced by Cubism—notably the Russian-born Alexander Archipenko, the Lithuanian-born Jacques Lipchitz, and the Frenchman Henri Laurens.

Cubism spawned numerous other movements in various countries. Its resonances continued long after the war, not least in the U.S.A., where Stuart Davis subtly but energetically adapted it to his paintings of specifically American subjects.

DADA AND SURREALISM

Dada and Surrealism were two of the most important movements in Western art (they had an impact in the U.S.A. as well as in Europe) between 1915 and about 1940. They were closely related, each being conceived as a state of mind and way of life rather than a stylistic outlook. Several artists figured in each movement in turn. Both movements were pointedly antirationalist, laying emphasis on incongruous or shocking effects, but a key difference was that Dada was predominantly nihilistic, while Surrealism was much more positive in spirit.

Dada was created in Zurich (in neutral Switzerland) in 1916, arising from the mood of despair and disillusionment created by World War I *(p360)*. Almost simultaneously, and quite independently, another Dada group was formed in New York City. Dada artists used extremes of provocative behavior to shock the public. At an exhibition in Cologne, Germany, in 1920, for example, Max Ernst provided an axe with which spectators were invited to smash the exhibits. By this time Dada was widespread in Europe, but as an organized movement it died by 1922.

Surrealism was founded two years later in Paris. Like Dada, it was a literary as well as an artistic movement, and its founder and chief theorist was the French poet André Breton. Its central feature was

Salvador Dalí, The Ship.

a fascination with the bizarre and the irrational, and its aim was to release the creative powers of the subconscious by rejecting the dominance of reason. The most classic examples are the paintings of Salvador Dalí, which he described as "hand-painted dream photographs."

EXPRESSIONISM

The term "expressionism" denotes the use of distortion and exaggeration for emotional effect. It can be applied to any art that gives primacy to intense subjective feeling, but when it has a capital E it usually refers to a movement in modern European art. This flourished particularly in Germany from about 1905 to the early 1930s (along with all other avant-garde art, it was stamped out by the Nazis from 1933). The Dutch painter van Gogh and the Norwegian painter Munch were major inspirations for the Expressionists—van Gogh for his brilliant color and turbulent brushwork, and Munch (who lived mainly in Germany from 1892 to 1908) for his angst-ridden view of life, based on his traumatic childhood.

Two groups of artists mark the high point of German Expressionism—Die Brücke (The Bridge) and Der Blaue Reiter (The Blue Rider). They lasted from 1905 to 1913 and 1911 to 1914 respectively. The members of Die Brücke (who included Erich Heckel and Ernst Kirchner) used strident color and violently clashing forms. The members of Der Blaue Reiter were varied in their aims but generally more spiritual in outlook. They included Wassily Kandinsky and Paul Klee, and also August Macke and Franz Marc, who both died in battle in World War I.

After the war, German Expressionism took a new slant in a movement called Neue Sachlichkeit (New Objectivity); this stressed social criticism, and its leading masters were two powerful satirists—Otto Dix and George Grosz. There were also several outstanding Expressionists in Austria and Germany not associated with any group; Max Beckmann and Oskar Kokoschka are among the best known.

Ernst Kirchner, Self-Portrait with a Model.

Timeline

1940–42 Henry Moore makes drawings of Londoners sheltering from air raids in subway stations: probably the best known of the many works produced by Official War Artists.

1941 Francis Bacon's *Three Studies for Figures at the Base of a Crucifixion*: shocking, horrific work with which Bacon establishes his reputation as the most controversial painter in Britain.

1942 Edward Hopper paints *Nighthawks*: example of American Scene Painting, a trend in which American artists depict the life around them in a naturalistic, descriptive style.

1942–46 Dealer and collecter Peggy Guggenheim runs the "Art of this Century" gallery in New York City, the main showcase for the early work of the Abstract Expressionists.

1947–52 Le Corbusier designs Unité d'Habitation, Marseilles, France: huge housing block, with stores and other facilities, intended as a self-contained community; influential in its social ideas and its rugged, sculptural style, in which Le Corbusier moves away from International Modernism.

1948 French painter Bernard Buffet and Swiss sculptor Alberto Giacometti have great success with exhibitions in Paris and New York City respectively, and are recognized as leading exponents of a type of "existentialist" art (with emaciated solitary figures) expressing postwar spiritual alienation.

1950 Jackson Pollock paints *Autumn Rhythm* and *Lavender Mist*, two masterpieces of Abstract Expressionism.

1954–58 Ludwig Mies van der Rohe designs Seagram Building, New York City: superb example of Mies's elegance and refinement, regarded by many as the world's most beautiful skyscraper.

1957–73 Sydney Opera House built by Danish architect Jorn Utzon (who won the commission in an international competition): original and spectacular.

1958 Jasper Johns and Robert Rauschenberg have one-person shows in New York City and emerge as leaders of the move away from Abstract Expressionism to more experimental forms.

1958–62 Paul Rudolph's Art and Architecture Building, Yale University: an outstanding example of Brutalism *(p545)*.

1961 "Young Contemporaries" exhibition in London, at which British Pop Art first appears in force; David Hockney, Allen Jones, and Peter Phillips are among the artists represented.

1961–64 Tokyo: spectacularly spacious building designed for the 1964 Olympic Games.

1962 Andy Warhol has sensational success with New York City one-person show and becomes leading figure in American Pop Art *(post-modernism p543)*.

INTERNATIONAL MODERN MOVEMENT

The terms "Modernism" and "Modern Movement" have been applied to a wide range of progressive trends in the arts from about 1900; any art that abandons or questions traditional ideas, subjects, or techniques can be so labeled. In a more restricted sense, the name "International Modern Movement" (sometimes simply "International Modern" or "Modern style") refers to a style that was adopted by many leading architects (in Europe particularly) between the two world wars and remained a major force long after.

Buildings in this style are rationally and clearly designed, with clean lines, predominantly cubic shapes, and a conscious rejection of ornament and historical references. Often the construction uses a steel frame, with the windows arranged in horizontal bands, sometimes forming a kind of transparent skin around the building. Where the windows are less prominent, wall surfaces are often painted white, externally and internally. The leading exponents of the style include Walter Gropius, Le Corbusier, and Ludwig Mies van der Rohe. It also influenced Frank Lloyd Wright, notably in the smooth expanses of concrete he used in Fallingwater, his masterpiece of domestic architecture. These four architects are generally regarded as the greatest of their age, which gives some indication of the impact of International Modern style. Its

Walter Gropius's Bauhaus in Dessau, Germany.

dominance among progressive architects was challenged in the 1950s by a rougher and more expressive style called Brutalism, and in the 1970s by the High Tech style (based on giving visual expression to the constructive and technological aspects of the building) and by Post-Modernism.

NEOPLASTICISM TO NEO–EXPRESSIONISM

Abstract art developed more or less simultaneously in the United States and several European countries around 1910. Many early exponents pursued with almost religious fervor a belief in the potential of art divorced from representation. Of none was this more true than the Dutch painter Piet Mondrian. He believed in a mystical philosophy–religion, Theosophy, and in his austerely geometrical works he tried to express an ideal of universal harmony. He called his style (and theories) Neoplasticism. Mondrian's work was influential on design in general, but in the 1930s figurative art was more popular than abstraction (and abstract art was banned in totalitarian countries such as Hitler's Germany and Stalin's U.S.S.R.).

There was a second great upsurge of abstract art after World War II, building on the huge success of the Abstract Expressionists, who helped New York City to replace Paris as the world capital of avant-garde art. Their work was often very emotional in tone and spontaneous in technique, most famously in the "action paintings" of Jackson Pollock, in which he splashed and dripped paint onto a canvas laid flat on the floor. This kind of work not only inspired imitation, but also caused a reaction in favor of cooler forms of abstraction, notably Minimal art, prominent (particularly in sculpture) in

the 1960s and 1970s, in which forms are extremely simple with a deliberate lack of expressiveness. By the late 1970s, emotionalism had returned in Neo-Expressionism, which is sometimes abstract, sometimes figurative, and sometimes bordering between the two. Neo-Expressionist works go to extremes of aggressive rawness in technique and feeling. Leading exponents included the American painter Julian Schnabel and the German painter Anselm Kiefer.

Piet Mondrian, Composition in Red, Blue, and Yellow.

POST-MODERNISM

Nicholas Grimshaw's international terminal at Waterloo Station, London.

In the 1980s, the term "Post-Modernism" dominated discussions of contemporary art, although its meaning and usefulness are disputed. It seems to have been coined in the 1940s but did not seriously enter cultural debate until the 1970s.

Originally it was applied mainly to architecture, especially in the writings of the critic Charles Jencks, and it is in this field that it has the clearest meaning. Jencks used the term to characterize a reaction against the rational, functionalist style of the International Modern Movement in favor of a more eclectic approach. Post-Modern buildings often incorporate references to past styles, sometimes in the form of what amount to visual jokes, as when an enormous classical pediment is put at the top of a skyscraper. The American architects Robert Venturi and Michael Graves and the British architects Terry Farrell and Piers Gough are regarded as exemplifying this approach.

In other arts, works have been dubbed Post-Modernist if they similarly blend disparate styles and make knowing use of cultural references. The Pop Art of the 1960s, for example, has been retrospectively labeled Post-Modernist because it emphasized style and surface and blurred the traditional distinction between high art and popular culture. In a vaguer sense, the idea of Post-Modernism has been applied to the general state of contemporary Western culture; in a world dominated by the mass media and technology, the argument runs, culture will inevitably become superficial and self-referential.

FEMINIST ART

Feminist art is not simply art made by women but art that explores issues specifically relating to women's identity and experience. It began as a movement in the 1960s, and by the 1970s there was a great deal of collective endeavor among committed feminist artists to combat what they regarded as bias in favor of male artists throughout the art world. This involved reviving the reputations of neglected women artists of the past through books about them and exhibitions of their work, as well as setting up periodicals such as *Feminist Art Journal* (1972) and courses such as the Feminist Art Program at the California Institute of Arts (1971).

The work produced by feminist artists has varied greatly. It has often focused on sexuality—attacking male sexual violence, for example, or reversing long-established stereotypes by presenting erotic male nudes as a subject for female delectation. The best-known feminist artist is probably Judy Chicago, whose sculpture *The Dinner Party* was finished in 1979 and has been seen on tour by large audiences in the United States and elsewhere. In a publicity leaflet for one of these exhibitions it is described as "an open triangular banquet table, 48 feet on each side, with 39 place settings, each representing a woman of achievement in Western civilization. Plates of delicate china rest on elaborate cloth runners of needlework typical of each woman's era. The table rests on the Heritage Floor of porcelain tiles inscribed with the names of 999 other women who have made significant contributions to our cultural development." Chicago wrote a book on the sculpture and has also written *Through the Flower: My Struggle as a Woman Artist* (1975). Other well-known feminist artists include the Americans Miriam Schapiro, whose most characteristic works are large collages that she calls "femmages," and Cindy Sherman, who photographs herself in various "roles."

Judy Chicago, The Dinner Party.

Timeline

1965 Joseph Beuys, *How to Explain Pictures to a Dead Hare*: a work of Performance art (a genre particularly popular in the late 1960s and 1970s) by influential avant-garde artist; in line with the vogue for Conceptual art, Beuys helps to shift emphasis from the objects an artist makes to his or her actions, opinions, and personality. "The Responsive Eye" exhibition at the Museum of Modern Art, New York City, puts Op Art on the map; a work by British painter Bridget Riley is illustrated on the cover of the catalog.

1966 *Equivalent VIII* by American sculptor Carl Andre: typical work of Minimal art *(p542)*, which becomes notorious (the "Tate bricks") in 1976 when there is a public outcry about its purchase by the Tate Gallery, London.

1970 Robert Smithson creates *Spiral Jetty*, Great Salt Lake, Utah: the best-known example of Land art, or Earthworks, a type of work that became popular in the late 1960s, especially in the U.S.A.

1970–73 Sears Tower, Chicago, the world's tallest building, is designed by Skidmore, Owings, and Merrill (SOM), one of the world's best-known corporate architectural firms.

1971–77 Pompidou Center, Paris, built by British architect Richard Rogers and Italian architect Renzo Piano: cultural center, the best-known building in High Tech style *(p545)*; housing the Musée Nationale D'Art Moderne, it is quickly established as a great tourist attraction.

1979 Judy Chicago completes *The Dinner Party*, one of the best-known works of feminist art *(left)*. "A New Spirit in Painting" at the Royal Academy, London: key exhibition in helping to put Neo-Expressionsim *(p542)* on the map.

1980–82 Public Services Building, Portland, Oregon, built by Michael Graves: large and spectacular example of Post-Modernist architecture.

1985 Saatchi Collection opens to the public, London: huge collection of contemporary art owned by advertising millionaire Charles Saatchi; his purchasing power helps to promote the vogue for Neo-Expressionism as well as for the reaction against it—Neo-Geo, which favors cool, impersonal, or sometimes kitsch works (the American Jeff Koons is a leading exponent).

1989 I. M. Pei's Glass Pyramid at the Louvre, Paris: startlingly original new entrance to the famous museum by Chinese-born American architect. Tadao Ando designs Hyogo Prefecture Children's Museum, Japan: ascetic concrete structure in tune with natural surroundings, by maverick Japanese architect.

1991 "Walking in Circles": exhibition in London by Richard Long, avant-garde artist whose work brings together sculpture, Conceptual art, and Land art.

GREAT COLLECTIONS

Austria Kunsthistorisches Museum, Vienna: Brueghel, *The Hunters in the Snow* (1565).

Belgium Musée Royale des Beaux-Arts, Antwerp: van der Weyden, *The Seven Sacraments Altarpiece* (c. 1445–50).

France Louvre, Paris: *Aphrodite of Melos* (*Venus de Milo*) (1st century B.C.); Leonardo da Vinci, *Mona Lisa* (c. 1504). Musée d'Orsay, Paris: Courbet, *The Painter's Studio* (1855).

Germany Alte Pinakothek, Munich: Cranach the Elder, *The Virgin of the Grapes* (c. 1525).
Dahlem Museum Gemäldegalerie, Berlin: Cranach the Elder, *The Fountain of Youth* (1546).

Holland Boymans-van Beuningen Museum, Rotterdam: Bosch, *The Wayfarer* (date uncertain).
Rijksmuseum, Amsterdam: Rembrandt, *The Night Watch* (1642).

Italy Borghese Gallery, Rome: Bernini, *Apollo and Daphne* (sculpture, 1624). Museo di Capodimonte, Naples: Titian, *Pope Paul III and his Nephews* (1546). Uffizi, Florence: Botticelli, *The Birth of Venus* (c. 1486).

Russia Hermitage, St. Petersburg: Rembrandt, *The Return of the Prodigal Son* (c. 1669).

Spain Prado, Madrid: Velázquez, *Las Meninas* (1656); Goya, *Saturn Devouring One of his Sons* (1820–23).

U.K. Courtauld Institute, London: Manet, *A Bar at the Folies-Bergères* (1881–82).

Rembrandt van Rijn, The Night Watch.

National Gallery, London: Piero della Francesca, *The Baptism of Christ* (c. 1450–55).
Tate Gallery, London: Rothko room (1958–59).
Victoria and Albert Museum, London: Hillyard, *Young Man among Roses* (1588).
U.S.A. Art Institute of Chicago: Grant Wood, *American Gothic* (1930).
J. Paul Getty Museum, Malibu, California: Lysippus, *The Getty Victor* (300s B.C.).
Metropolitan Museum of Art, New York

City: Vermeer, *Young Woman with a Water Jug* (c. 1660).
Museum of Fine Arts, Boston: Turner, *Slave Ship* (1840).
Museum of Modern Art, New York: van Gogh, *Starry Night* (1899); Picasso, *Les Demoiselles d'Avignon* (1906–07).
National Gallery of Art, Washington D.C.: Leonardo da Vinci, *Portrait of Ginevra de' Benci* (1476).
Philadelphia Museum of Art: Duchamp, *Bride Stripped Bare by her Bachelors, Even* (1915–23).

PAINTINGS SOLD AT AUCTIONS: RECORD PRICES

$82,500,000 van Gogh, *Portrait of Dr. Gachet*, Christie's, New York City, 1990, Japanese collector.
$78,100,000 Renoir, *Au Moulin de la Galette*, Sotheby's, New York City, 1990, Japanese collector.

$53,900,000 van Gogh, *Irises*, Sotheby's, New York City, 1987, Australian collector (resold 1990 to J. Paul Getty Museum, undisclosed sum).
$51,895,000 Picasso, *Les Noces de Pierette*, Binoche et Godeau, Paris, 1989, Japanese

collector.
$47,850,000 Picasso, *Self-Portrait: Yo Picasso*, Sotheby's, New York City, 1989, anonymous collector.
$40,700,000 Picasso, *Au Lapin Agile*, Sotheby's, New York City, 1989, Walter Annenberg Foundation.
$40,300,000 Van Gogh, *Sunflowers*, Christie's, London, 1987, Japanese company.
$38,900,000 Pontormo, *Portrait of Duke Cosimo I de' Medici*, Christie's, New York City, 1989, J. Paul Getty Museum. Record for an Old Master.
$32,900,000 Picasso, *Acrobate et Jeune Arlequin*, Christie's, London, 1988, Japanese company.
***c.* $28,600,000** Cézanne, *Nature Morte les Grosses Pommes*, Sotheby's, New York City, 1993.

Highest price for work by living artist:
***c.* $20,680,000** Willem De Kooning (Dutch-American painter and sculptor, b. 1904), *Interchange*, Sotheby's, New York City, 1989.

Vincent van Gogh, Irises.

MAJOR ARCHITECTURAL STYLES

Milan cathedral, northern Italian Gothic.

Greek The style characteristic of ancient Greece and its Mediterranean colonies from the 600s B.C., when stone building was revived, to the 1st century B.C., when Greece was absorbed into the Roman Empire. The most important Greek buildings were temples, and the beautifully proportioned columns that became typical of them were immensely influential on Roman architecture and through that on much subsequent European architecture.

Roman The style of the ancient Romans, which spread over their empire, at its peak in the first 400 years A.D.; the Romans took much of the "vocabulary" of classical architecture from the Greeks (particularly the systematic use of columns), but added many features of their own and excelled in the sheer size of their buildings and civil engineering projects.

Byzantine The style of the Byzantine Empire, which flourished from the 300s to 1400s, its capital being Constantinople (originally called Byzantium, now Istanbul). It blends Roman and Eastern influences, and its most typical form is the large domed church, lavishly decorated with mosaics.

Romanesque The style prevailing in most of Europe in the 1000s and 1100s, characterized by massive strength of construction and the use of round-headed arches and windows (as opposed to the pointed arches of the Gothic style that succeeded it).

Gothic The style that succeeded Romanesque throughout Europe, characterized most obviously by the use of pointed arches and also by rib vaults, flying buttresses, and elaborate window tracery. It began in France in the 1140s and flourished in many places into the 1500s, windows generally becoming an increasingly prominent feature.

Renaissance A revival or "rebirth" of the classical art of ancient Rome, beginning in Italy in the early 1400s and spreading over Europe.

Baroque The dominant European style of the 1600s and early 1700s, typically bold and exuberant, using Renaissance forms with a new freedom.

Rococo A style emerging from Baroque in the early 1700s; like Baroque, it made vigorous use of curved forms, but it was lighter and more playful.

Gothic revival A revival of the Gothic style of the Middle Ages, beginning in the 1700s and flourishing in the 1800s, particularly in Britain; buildings of all kinds—civil, commercial, and domestic—as well as churches were built in the style.

Neoclassicism A revival of the styles of ancient Greece and Rome in the late 1700s and early 1800s—often referred to as "federalism" in the United States.

Art Nouveau A deliberately new style, c. 1890–1910, uninfluenced by past art, characterized mainly by undulating plantlike forms (particularly as surface decoration) and colored materials.

International Modern A sleek, functional style that dominated progressive architecture in the 1930s and 1940s.

Brutalism A reaction in the 1950s against the sleek sophistication of the International Modern style, characterized by chunky forms and exposed concrete.

High Tech An approach popular since the 1970s in which architects stress the technological aspects of a building, typically by giving dramatic visual expression to structural elements or services (pipes, air ducts, and so on) that are usually hidden from view.

Post-Modernism A trend, beginning in the 1970s, in which the cool rationalism of International Modern style was abandoned in favor of stylistic eclecticism.

Left: *Gaudi's buildings such as Casa Battlo give Barcelona, Spain a unique Art Nouveau style.*

Below: *Brutalism at its most sympathetic in Lloyd Wright's Fallingwater, Pennsylvania.*

PROMINENT PEOPLE

ADAM, Robert (1728–92) Scottish architect and designer. Prolific in England and Scotland; graceful Neoclassical style. Sometimes collaborated with brother **James** (1730–94). Works include Home House, Portman Square, London (c. 1775).

ALBERTI, Leon Battista (1404–72) Italian Renaissance architect. Influential also as art theorist; wrote on architecture, painting, and sculpture. Works include Santa Maria Novella, Florence, and San Andrea, Mantua.

ANGELICO, Fra (c. 1400–55) Early Renaissance Florentine painter. A Dominican friar (the name by which he is known means "angelic friar") and famous mainly for frescoes in his own friary of San Marco in Florence.

BACON, Francis (1909–92) Anglo-Irish figurative painter. His paintings often show people in a nightmarish state of isolation and despair.

BELLINI, Giovanni (c. 1430–1516) Venetian painter, the major figure in establishing Venice as an artistic center to rival Florence and Rome. Highly inventive, but famous mainly for depictions of the Virgin and Child. His brother **Gentile** (c. 1429–1507) and their father **Jacopo** (c. 1400–70) were also eminent painters.

BENTON, Thomas Hart (1899–1975) U.S. realist painter and muralist; spokesperson for the Regionalist group of U.S. artists in the 1920s and 1930s.

BERNINI, Gian Lorenzo (1598–1680) Italian Baroque sculptor, architect, painter, and designer. Virtual dictator of the arts in Rome for much of his career.

BLAKE, William (1757–1827) English painter, engraver, and poet, one of the most original figures in Romantic art. His work includes illustrations to many of his own poems, as well as subjects from Shakespeare and the Bible.

BONNARD, Pierre (1867–1947) French painter and lithographer. He was the leading exponent of Intimisme, a style in which quiet domestic subjects are depicted in a warm, Impressionist manner.

BORROMINI, Francesco (1599–1667) Italian Baroque architect. Almost all his work, including the churches of San Carlo alle Quattro Fontane (1641) and San Andrea delle Fratte (1653–65), is in Rome. Most of his buildings are small but with rich interplay of vigorous forms.

BOSCH, Hieronymus (c. 1450–1516) Netherlandish painter, famous for bizarre allegorical pictures showing the sins and follies of humans.

BOTTICELLI, Sandro (c. 1445–1510) Renaissance Florentine painter. Known for religious subjects, portraits, and original mythological works in graceful style.

BRAMANTE, Donato (1444–1514) Italian architect (early in his career also a painter). Worked mainly in Milan, then from 1499 in Rome, where he created the High Renaissance style in architecture. Works include Santa Maria delle Grazie, Milan, and the basilica of New St. Peter's, Rome (begun in 1506; subsequently altered by other architects).

BRANCUSI, Constantin (1876–1957) Romanian sculptor, active in Paris from 1904. Often regarded as the greatest sculptor of the 1900s, he pared forms down to radically simplified shapes that approach abstraction.

BRAQUE, Georges (1882–1963) French painter. Developed Cubism with PICASSO, 1907–14. His later career was devoted to subtle variations on his Cubist work.

BRUEGHEL, Pieter the Elder (c. 1520–69) Netherlandish painter, engraver, and draftsman. Painted religious subjects and sympathetic scenes of everyday life. His sons **Pieter the Younger** (1564–1638) and **Jan** (1568–1625) were also distinguished painters.

BRUNELLESCHI, Filippo (1377–1446) Early Renaissance Florentine architect and sculptor. Famous as designer of the dome of Florence cathedral (1420–36), he was also a pioneer of perspective. Other works include San Spirito and San Lorenzo, both in Florence.

CALDER, Alexander (1898–1976) U.S. sculptor, painter, and illustrator of children's books. Early training as an engineer influenced his works and notably his invention of the mobile.

CANALETTO (Giovanni Antonio Canal) (1697–1768) Italian painter, famous for his views of Venice. Much patronized by wealthy English visitors to Italy, he also worked in England for almost a decade.

CARAVAGGIO, Michelangelo Merisi da (1571–1610) Italian painter, active mainly in Rome. The most influential painter of the early 1600s, creator of a powerful, dramatically lit style that spread throughout Europe.

CASSATT, Mary (1844–1926) U.S. painter who settled in Paris in 1868, later becoming a champion—and member—of the Impressionist School of painters. Famous for tender but unsentimental treatment of "mother and child" theme.

CATLIN, George (1796–1872) U.S. self-taught painter whose portrayal of Native American life won great acclaim in Europe.

CÉZANNE, Paul (1839–1906) French Post-Impressionist painter. His subtle analysis of pictorial forms was influential on Cubism.

CHAGALL, Marc (1887–1985) Russian-born painter active mainly in Paris. Painted in a colorful, highly personal Expressionist style, especially scenes from the Bible and Jewish folklore.

CONSTABLE, John (1776–1837) English landscape painter. Slow to achieve success in his lifetime, but later immensely popular.

COPLEY, John Singleton (1738–1815) American painter, also active in England from 1775. Chiefly a portraitist, but also painted lively scenes of contemporary events.

CORREGGIO (Antonio Allegri) (c. 1489–1534) Italian High Renaissance painter, based mainly outside the great art centers. His works include two major church dome paintings in Parma and erotic mythological pictures.

COURBET, Gustave (1819–77) French Realist painter, mainly of figure subjects and landscapes.

CRANACH, Lucas the Elder (1472–1553) German painter and printmaker, renowned for portraits, religious scenes, and erotic female nudes. His son and assistant **Lucas the Younger** (1515–86) skillfully imitated his style.

DALÍ, Salvador (1904–89) Spanish Surrealist painter, sculptor, graphic artist, writer, filmmaker, and eccentric, active in Paris and the U.S.A. as well as his native country. His best work was done before 1940, but his talent for self-publicity sustained his fame.

DAVID, Jacques-Louis (1748–1825) French Neoclassical painter, famous for the heroic severity of his style. His later work became more Romantic in feeling.

DAVIS, Stuart (1894–1964) U.S. painter whose stylized use of labels and commercial packaging has been seen as paving the way for Pop Art.

DEGAS, Edgar (1834–1917) French painter, sculptor, and graphic artist. One of the major Impressionists and a great draftsman of the 1800s.

DE KOONING, Willem (b. 1904) Dutch-born U.S. painter whose "Action Painting" style led to creative association and rivalry with POLLOCK in the 1950s.

DELACROIX, Eugéne (1798–1863) French Romantic painter famous for the color and splendor of his work. He also kept a journal that is a rich source of information on his life and times.

DONATELLO (c. 1386–1466) Florentine Renaissance sculptor, widely considered the greatest sculptor of the 1400s. Versatile, prolific, and powerful in style, he influenced many other artists.

DUCCIO DI BUONINSEGNA (c. 1260–1320) Italian painter, greatest artist of the Sienese School. Famous mainly as the creator of the *Maestà* altarpiece for Siena cathedral.

DUCHAMP, Marcel (1887–1968) French avant-garde artist and art theorist, active mainly in the U.S.A. Created relatively few works but is regarded as one of the central figures in modern art because of the fertility of his ideas, which repudiated the traditional values of art.

DÜRER, Albrecht (1471–1528) German engraver and painter, the major artist of the Northern Renaissance.

ENSOR, James (1860–1949) Belgian painter and engraver. An isolated, eccentric figure but one of the most individual exponents of Expressionism.

EPSTEIN, Sir Jacob (1880–1959) U.S.-born British sculptor. His work was often controversial because of alleged indecen-

cy and his expressive use of distortion.

ERNST, Max (1891–1976) German-born French painter and sculptor. One of the leading figures successively of Dada and Surrealism.

EYCK, Jan van (c. 1390–1441) The most famous painter belonging to the Early Netherlandish School. For centuries regarded as the "inventor" of oil painting. This is now known to be untrue, but he was the first painter to show the potential of the medium, creating glowing color and extraordinarily fine detail.

FRAGONARD, Jean-Honoré (1732–1806) French Rococo painter. Playfully erotic subjects and frothy technique.

FRIEDRICH, Caspar David (1774–1840) German Romantic painter. Produced intensely spiritual landscape paintings.

GAINSBOROUGH, Thomas (1727–88) Popular British portraitist and landscape painter with elegant and vivacious style.

GAUDI, Antonio (1852–1926) Spanish architect of extraordinarily bizarre originality, active mainly in Barcelona. His works, which include Casa Mila (1905–09) and Sagrada Familia (1884 onward), have twisted, voluptuous forms and weird decorative features, such as broken crockery set in plaster.

GAUGIN, Paul (1848–1903) French Post-Impressionist painter. Had little success in his lifetime, but his use of color for decorative and emotional effect had an immense influence on 20th-century art.

GÉRICAULT, Théodore (1791–1824) French Romantic painter, second only to DELACROIX. Work of intense passion.

GHIBERTI, Lorenzo (1378–1455) Florentine sculptor. One of the most important Italian artists of his time. Produced bronze doors for the baptistery of Florence cathedral. Style evolved from Gothic elegance to Renaissance grandeur.

GIAMBOLOGNA (Giovanni Bologna) (1529–1608) Flemish-born Italian Mannerist sculptor, active mainly in Florence. His work is generally characterized by graceful, spiraling forms.

GIORGIONE (c. 1477–1510) Venetian painter. Short-lived, enigmatic, and highly influential, he was the first major artist to specialize in small-scale works for collectors. The poetic mood of his pictures was considered more important than their often obscure subjects.

GIOTTO DI BONDONE (c. 1267–1337) Florentine painter and architect. Regarded as the founder of the central tradition of Western painting because his work—powerfully three-dimensional and intensely human—broke away decisively from medieval stylizations.

GOYA, Francisco de (1746–1828) Spanish painter and graphic artist. Perhaps the most powerful and original European painter of his period. His mature work shows great intensity of feeling and freedom of technique.

GRECO, El (Domenikos Theotokopoulos) (1541–1614) Cretan-born painter who settled in Spain in 1577. His work expresses the religious fervor of his adopted country in an original Mannerist style, with figures elongated into flame-like forms.

GROPIUS, Walter (1883–1969) German-born architect and designer who became a U.S. citizen in 1944. Founder of the Bauhaus (the most influential design school of the 1900s) in 1919. An uncompromising advocate of modern materials and lucidity of design.

GRÜNEWALD, Mathias (c. 1470–1528) German painter. Influenced by some Renaissance ideas, but his work is essentially a culmination of medieval tradition. Painted only religious subjects, most notably the crucifixion, depicted with an unsurpassed anguished intensity.

HALS, Frans (1582/3–1666) Dutch painter. One of the greatest of all portraitists, celebrated for vivacious characterization and vigorous brushwork.

HEPWORTH, Dame Barbara (1903–75) English sculptor. One of the leading pioneers of abstract art in Britain.

HIROSHIGE, Ando (1797–1858) Japanese woodblock print artist. One of the three key figures of the period.

HOCKNEY, David (b. 1937) English painter, graphic artist, photographer, and stage designer. The most famous British artist of his generation. Made an impact as a Pop artist; subsequently worked in a more naturalistic style. A superb draftsman and etcher. Since the 1970s has lived mainly in the U.S.A.

HOGARTH, William (1697–1764) English painter and engraver. The most important British artist of his time, he is said to have freed British art from foreign domination. Invented a novel type of work in which a sequence of pictures tells a contemporary moral tale.

HOKUSAI, Katsushika (1760–1849) Japanese painter and wood engraver. His country's most celebrated artist, renowned for the boldness, fantasy, and wit of his work. Utterly devoted to art and hugely prolific.

HOLBEIN, Hans the Younger (1497–1543) German painter and designer. The greatest portraitist of the Northern Renaissance, active for most of his later career in England, where he was court painter to Henry VIII. His father, **Hans the Elder**, and his brother, **Ambrosius**, were also painters.

HOMER, Winslow (1836-1910) U.S. painter who began as a Civil War illustrator. His mature style blended this eye for accuracy with techniques borrowed from the French Impressionists.

Hopper, Edward (1882–1967) U.S. realist painter whose most famous work conveyed the alienation and loneliness of life in big cities. Also known for a series of evocative landscape paintings.

INGRES, Jean Auguste Dominique (1780–1867) French painter. A leading but highly personal exponent of Neoclassicism. His work has great purity of line (he was a superb draftsman), but is often very sensuous.

JEFFERSON, Thomas (1743–1826) Third U.S. president and a fine architect—not just a talented amateur but a man of vision and originality. He helped to plan the city of Washington, D.C. and the University of Virginia, the first great campus plan.

JOHNS, Jasper (b. 1930) U.S. painter and sculptor. With his friend RAUSCHENBERG, he was one of the leading figures in the American move away from Abstract Expressionism to Pop Art.

JOHNSON, Philip (b. 1906) U.S. architect whose designs, such as the Seagram Building in New York City, created a "wall of glass" outside a building's superstructure.

KANDINSKY, Wassily (1866–1944) Russian-born painter and writer on art, who became a German and then a French citizen. One of the great pioneers of abstract art, influential through his writings as well as his paintings.

KLEE, Paul (1879–1940) German-Swiss painter and graphic artist. One of the best-loved and most prolific figures in 20th-century art. His work moves freely between figuration and abstraction and has a joyful spirit of wit and fantasy.

KLINE, Franz (1910–1962) U.S. painter whose works—inspired by oriental calligraphy and usually limited to black, white, and gray—contributed to the development of Abstract Expressionism.

LATROBE, Benjamin (1764–1820) British-born and the first American professional architect; a fine exponent of Neoclassicism.

LE CORBUSIER (Charles Edouard Jeanneret) (1887–1965) Swiss-born French architect, painter, designer, and writer. Probably the most influential architect of the 1900s. Saw buildings in terms of the problems and potential of industrial society. Works include Salvation Army Hostel, Paris (1929) and Chandigarh, Punjab, India.

LEONARDO DA VINCI (1452–1519) Florentine Renaissance painter, sculptor, architect, engineer, and scientist. The most versatile figure of his time; important principally as a painter, he was the chief creator of the High Renaissance style and enormously influential.

LE VAU, Louis (1612–70) French architect. Less subtle than his contemporary MANSART, but his confident, rhetorical style and efficiency made him the favorite architect of Louis XIV, for whom he worked on the Louvre and Versailles.

LEWIS, (Percy) Wyndham (1884–1957) English painter and writer. The central figure of Vorticism, the first major British art movement to embrace the ideas of abstraction.

LICHTENSTEIN, Roy (b. 1923) U.S. Pop artist whose large works draw inspiration from advertising and comic books. His technique often mimics the coarse screen process of newspaper color printing.

LIPPI, Fra Filippo (c. 1406–69)

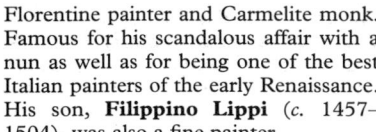

Florentine painter and Carmelite monk. Famous for his scandalous affair with a nun as well as for being one of the best Italian painters of the early Renaissance. His son, **Filippino Lippi** (c. 1457–1504), was also a fine painter.

LUTYENS, Sir Edwin (1869–1944) British architect. His early buildings were mainly country houses in romantic vernacular style; later he concentrated on dignified, classical-style public buildings.

LYSIPPUS (300s B.C.) Greek sculptor. Said to have been long-lived and prolific, but his work is now known only through copies. He seems to have been the most influential sculptor of the Hellenistic period.

MAGRITTE, René (1898–1967) Belgian painter. Perhaps the most popular of the Surrealist painters. His work abounds in bizarre juxtapositions and has a wit that most Surrealists lacked.

MALEVICH, Kasimir (1878–1935) Russian painter, founder (c. 1915) of Suprematism, the most radically pure abstract movement up to that date. His most famous work consists of white squares on a white background.

MANET, Edouard (1832–83) French painter and graphic artist. The freshness of his handling of everyday-life subjects inspired the Impressionists.

MANSART, François (1598–1666) French architect. Master of a grand, lucid, subtly detailed style. An uncompromising perfectionist, he often lost commissions by quarreling with patrons, so he completed few buildings.

MANTEGNA, Andrea (1431–1506) Italian painter and engraver. Active mainly at the court of Mantua. His style owes much to classical antiquity and was highly influential in northern Italy. Brother-in-law of Giovanni and Gentile BELLINI.

MASACCIO (Tommaso di Ser Giovanni) (1401–28). Italian painter. Short lived but immensely important: the first to master perspective and, with BRUNELLESCHI and DONATELLO, one of the founders of the Renaissance.

MATISSE, Henri (1869–1954) French painter, sculptor, graphic artist, and designer. One of the greatest masters of color and line in the history of art.

MICHELANGELO BUONARROTI (1475–1564) Florentine sculptor, painter, architect, draftsman, and poet. One of the greatest Renaissance figures and a chief source of Mannerism. Considered himself a sculptor, but stature just as great as a painter and architect. Spent much of his later career in Rome.

MIES VAN DER ROHE, Ludwig (1886–1969) German-born architect and designer who became a U.S. citizen in 1944. Director of the Bauhaus 1930–33. Elegant, refined works, largely in glass and steel. His buildings include the Seagram Building, New York City (1956–59, with Philip JOHNSON) and the New National Gallery, Berlin (1962–68). Also a distinguished furni-

ture designer.

MIRÓ, Joan (1893–1983) Spanish painter, graphic artist, and designer. A versatile and prolific Surrealist artist.

MODIGLIANI, Amedeo (1884–1920) Italian painter and sculptor, active mainly in Paris. Also famous for his dissolute lifestyle—he was the archetypal bohemian genius.

MONDRIAN, Piet (1872–1944) Dutch painter. A major figure in abstract art. Spent much of his career in Paris but later based in New York City.

MONET, Claude (1840–1926) French Impressionist painter. Regarded as the archetypal Impressionist because he alone remained dedicated to the ideals of the movement throughout his career.

MOORE, Henry (1898–1986) British sculptor. Also renowned as a graphic artist, particularly for his wartime drawings of Londoners taking shelter from air raids in subway stations.

MOSES, Grandma (1860–1961) Self-taught U.S. painter (real name Anna Mary Robertson Moses) whose naive style suited her "old-timey" subject matter of life in her native upstate New York.

MUNCH, Edvard (1863–1944) Norwegian painter and printmaker. Powerful and original artist whose anguished visions of life influenced Expressionism. After he recovered from a nervous breakdown in 1908, his work became more optimistic.

NASH, John (1752–1835) The most prolific and successful British architect of the Regency period, best known for his majestic layout of Regent Street and Regent's Park in London.

NEWMAN, Barnett (1905–70) U.S. painter. One of the leading exponents of Abstract Expressionism.

O'KEEFFE, Georgia (1887–1986) U.S. abstract painter who drew inspiration from the landscapes and natural forms of the New Mexico desert.

PALLADIO, Andrea (1508–80) Italian architect, active mainly around Vicenza and, later, in Venice. Maybe the most influential architect, through his *Four Books of Architecture* (1570) as much as his buildings. His grand but humane classical style was a model throughout Europe and later in the U.S.A.

PEI, I(eoh) M(ing) (b. 1917) Chinese-born U.S. architect. Works include National Gallery of Art, Washington, D.C. (1937–40) and the glass pyramid at the Louvre, Paris (1989).

PHIDIAS (c. 490–430 B.C.) Greek sculptor, the most famous artist of antiquity. Celebrated in his day for two huge gold and ivory statues (of Athena and Zeus). These, like all his own works, have disappeared, but his majestic style can be seen in the sculpture of the Parthenon, Athens, which he supervised.

PICASSO, Pablo (1881–1973) Spanish painter, sculptor, graphic artist, and designer, active mainly in France. Probably the most versatile and prolific

artist of the 1900s.

PIERO DELLA FRANCESCA (c. 1420–92) Italian painter. One of the greatest masters of the Renaissance, famous for the grandeur and lucidity of his compositions and his handling of light and color.

PISANO, Nicola (c. 1225–84) and **Giovanni** (c. 1250–1314) Italian sculptors, father and son, who sometimes collaborated. The greatest sculptors of their day, they broke away from medieval conventions. Works include the pulpit and baptistery of Pisa cathedral and pulpit of Siena cathedral.

PISSARRO, Camille (1830–1903) French Impressionist painter. Mainly a landscape painter. He was a central figure of Impressionism and the only artist to take part in all eight of the Impressionist exhibitions.

POLLOCK, Jackson (1912–56) U.S. painter, the most famous exponent of Abstract Expressionism. The first U.S. painter to become a "star."

POUSSIN, Nicolas (1594–1665) French painter who spent almost all his career in Rome. Painted in a learned, classical style, mainly for private patrons.

PRAXITELES (active mid-300s B.C.) Greek sculptor. After PHIDIAS, the most famous. His work was renowned for its gracefulness.

RAPHAEL (Raffaello Santi) (1483–1520) Italian High Renaissance painter and architect. His style, learned and majestic but also deeply humane, was regarded for centuries as an unsurpassable model. Spent most of his short but prolific career in Rome.

RAUSCHENBERG, Robert (b. 1925) U.S. painter and sculptor. See Jasper JOHNS.

REMBRANDT HARMENSZOON VAN RIJN (1606–69) Dutch painter and etcher. The Netherlands' greatest artist and one of the most revered in the world. Versatile, prolific, and unsurpassed in the emotional depth of his work.

REMINGTON, Frederic (1861–1909) U.S. painter, sculptor, and illustrator. His many works in a prolific career established him as the most famous portayer of the "Old West."

RENOIR, Pierre Auguste (1841–1919) French painter and (late in his career) sculptor. Perhaps the best loved of the Impressionists, known for the joyful spirit of his work, particularly pictures of pretty young women and children.

REYNOLDS, Sir Joshua (1723–92) English painter and writer on art. The first president of the Royal Academy (1768), he was one of the greatest portraitists of his age and a figure of immense authority who raised the status of the artist in Britain.

ROCKWELL, Norman (1894–1978) Extremely popular U.S. painter and illustrator whose works, including many magazine covers, depicted typically American scenes with a good-natured affection.

RODIN, Auguste (1840–1917) French

sculptor and draftsman. The greatest sculptor of his day. After a period when it had lagged behind painting, he brought sculpture to the center of the art world, making it a vehicle for intense personal expression.

ROGERS, Richard (b. 1933) British architect. One of the leading exponents of the High Tech style. Works include Pompidou Centre, Paris (1971–77, with Renzo Piano) and Lloyds Building, London (1979–85).

ROSSETTI, Dante Gabriel (1828–82) English painter and poet of Italian extraction. One of the major figures of Victorian art. Found fame very young as one of the members of the Pre-Raphaelite Brotherhood. Later career devoted mainly to paintings of beautiful, languorous women.

RUBENS, Sir Peter Paul (1577–1640) Flemish painter and designer. The most influential figure in Baroque art in northern Europe. Prolific and energetic, he enjoyed international acclaim, working for several of Europe's greatest rulers. Also a diplomat.

RYDER, Albert Pinkham (1847–1917) U.S. Romantic painter and admirer of Edgar Allan Poe. His works, notably seascapes, conveyed a brooding, visionary quality.

SAARINEN, Eliel (1873–1950) and **Eero** (1910–61) Finnish-born architects, father and son, who settled in the U.S.A. in 1923. Worked in partnership from 1937, but Eero is best known for the buildings he designed after his father's death, in a highly individual sculptural style—such as TWA terminal at John F. Kennedy International Airport, New York City (1956–62).

SAINT-GAUDENS, Augustus (1848–1907) Leading U.S. sculptor of the 1800s who is best represented by his commemorative works, such as the Shaw Memorial in Boston.

SARGENT, John Singer (1856–1925) U.S. portrait painter and watercolorist famous for his virtuoso style. His subjects were often members of high society in London, where he lived from 1884.

SEURAT, Georges (1859–91) French painter. Founder and greatest exponent of Neo-Impressionism.

SHAHN, Ben (1898–1969) U.S. Social Realist painter and muralist who used photographic realism as a vehicle for his radical political ideas.

SIMONE MARTINI (c. 1285–1344) Italian painter. Second only to DUCCIO in the Sienese School. Renowned for the grace of his work.

STUART, Gilbert (1755–1828) U.S. portrait painter who worked in London and Dublin before returning to the United States. Famous for several versions of George Washington, including the version used on the dollar bill.

SULLIVAN, Louis (1856–1924) U.S. architect who is closely linked with the early development of skyscrapers. His

work accentuated their steel-frame construction rather than trying to hide it.

TINTORETTO (Jacopo Robusti) (1518–94) Venetian painter. With VERONESE, the most successful painter in Venice in the generation after TITIAN. Mainly painted religious subjects in an emotional, energetic style, but also a fine portraitist.

TITIAN (Tiziano Veccellio) (c. 1485–1576) The greatest painter of the Venetian School. Equally outstanding in portraits, religious pictures, and mythological works. Revolutionized the use of oil paint with his free and expressive brushwork. Immensely influential.

TOULOUSE-LAUTREC, Henri de (1864–1901) French painter and lithographer. Born into an aristocratic family, but often took his subjects from Parisian lowlife. Led a dissolute life, but was also hard working and dedicated to art. Important as a poster designer as well as a painter.

TURNER, Joseph Mallord William (1775–1851) English painter in oils and watercolor. One of the greatest of all landscape painters. Started with conventional topographical views, but developed a very free personal style.

UCCELLO, Paolo (c. 1396–1475) Florentine painter, one of the best-loved artists of the early Renaissance. Famous for his skill with perspective and for the decorative charm of his work.

UTAMARO, Kitagawa (1753–1806) Japanese woodblock print artist.

VAN DYCK, Sir Anthony (1599–1641) Flemish painter. Great portraitist, renowned for the aristocratic dignity of his work. Spent most of his last decade as court painter to Charles I of England.

van GOGH, Vincent (1853–90) Dutch Post-Impressionist painter. Famous for the emotional intensity of his work. Neglected in his lifetime, but after his suicide became famous and influential.

VASARI, Giorgio (1511–74) Italian painter, architect, and writer. A successful Mannerist artist in his day, but now remembered mainly as a biographer. His *Lives of the Artists* (1550, revised 1568) is the major source of information on Italian Renaissance art and a model for many later biographers.

VELÁZQUEZ, Diego (1599–1660) Spanish painter. Known mainly as a portraitist of unsurpassed depth and subtlety. Court painter to Philip IV in Madrid for most of his life.

VENTURI, Robert (b. 1925) U.S. architect, a leading Post-Modernist. Works include National Gallery Extension, London (1986–91). His book *Complexity and Contradiction in Architecture* (1967) argues against the purity of International Modern style.

VERMEER, Jan (1632–75) Dutch painter, little known in his day but now second only to REMBRANDT in esteem among his Dutch contemporaries. Only about 35 paintings survive, among them serenely

beautiful everyday-life scenes.

VERONESE (Paolo Caliari) (1528–88) Italian painter, born in Verona and active mainly in Venice. There, with TINTORETTO, he was the leading artist after TITIAN's death. Specialized in large pageantlike scenes expressing the material splendor of Venice in its golden age.

VERROCCHIO, Andrea del (c. 1435–88) Florentine sculptor and painter. The greatest Italian sculptor between DONATELLO and MICHELANGELO. Few paintings by him survive, but he taught several important painters, above all LEONARDO DA VINCI.

WARHOL, Andy (1927–87) American painter, printmaker, and filmmaker. The most famous exponent of Pop Art.

WATTEAU, Jean-Antoine (1684–1721) French Rococo painter. Specialized in *fêtes galantes* (romantic outdoor scenes of people flirting and enjoying themselves), painted with great sensitivity.

WEST, Benjamin (1738–1820) American-born painter, based in London. His historical works and portraits upset some conventions but broadly echoed the transition from the Neoclassical to Romantic movements.

WEYDEN, Rogier van der (1399/1400–64) Netherlands painter. Mainly a religious painter, but also a refined portraitist. His style, much more emotional than that of Jan van EYCK, was extremely influential.

WHISTLER, James Abbott McNeill (1834–1903) U.S. painter and etcher, active mainly in England. Subtle painter and one of the greatest etchers. Also famous as a wit, dandy, and controversialist.

WOOD, Grant (1892–1942) U.S. painter who used a detailed style to depict ordinary people in ordinary situations in his native Iowa. His *American Gothic*, a portrait of a farming couple, overcame initial negative reactions to achieve iconic status.

WREN, Sir Christopher (1632–1723) British architect. Originally a brilliant scientist, but turned decisively to architecture after the Great Fire of London (1666) led him to rebuild much of the city. Prolific, versatile, and hard working. Works include Sheldonian Theatre, Oxford (1664) and St. Paul's Cathedral, London (1675–1710).

WRIGHT, Frank Lloyd (1869–1959) U.S. architect and designer. Extremely versatile and imaginative, he believed in "organic" architecture, in which a building should be closely related to its site. His works—both houses and larger commissions—include Fallingwater, Pennsylvania (1937–39) and the Guggenheim Museum, New York City (1942–59).

WYETH, Andrew (b. 1917) U.S. painter, equally inspired by his native Pennsylvania and by his summer home in Maine. His technical facility—and popularity—have divided critics for decades.

Timeline

7000 B.C. First pottery appears in Egypt and Sumeria.

5000–4000 B.C. White painted pottery in Egypt and S.E. Europe. Blue-green glazed beads in Egypt.

4000–3000 B.C. Potter's wheel developed in Mesopotamia. Glazed pottery in Egypt. Valdivian handmade pottery in South America.

3000–2500 B.C. Small faience statuettes in Egypt. Cotton yarns, polychrome pottery at Mohenjo-Daro, Indus Valley. Weaving loom known in Europe. Silk produced in China.

2500–2000 B.C. Black and painted pottery in China. Cotton cultivated in Peru and in Indus Valley.

2000–1500 B.C. Small containers of core-molded opaque glass in Mesopotamia. Pottery with curved designs and animal figures. Fine goldwork and jewelry in Minoan Crete.

1500–1000 B.C. Glassware introduced into Egypt, possibly from W. Asia. Tapestries in Egypt. Elaborate bronze vases, large bronze drums and bells in China. Fine goldwork and jewelry in Mycenaean Greece (Treasury of Atreus).

1000–900 B.C. Geometric art designs on Greek artifacts. Gold vessels and jewelry in N. Europe. Purple fabric dyes from snails in Mediterranean area.

800–700 B.C. Metal sculpture, carpet weaving, embroidery in Asia Minor. Celtic gold and bronze ornaments in Europe. Chavin painted cotton cloth in South America.

600–500 B.C. Attic pottery, black-figure and later red-figure in Greece. Celtic La Tène ornamentation in Europe. Scythian metalwork in Black Sea area.

500–400 B.C. Nok pottery in W. Africa. Classical period of Greek jewelry and pottery. Chinese craftsmen develop lead glazes.

521–486 B.C. The Persepolis palace in Mesopotamia, built by Darius I, borrows decorative ideas from Assyria, Egypt, and Greece: it includes, respectively, bull statues guarding gateways, cavetto-molded doorways, and pleated folds on gowns of numerous rows of bas-relief figures.

300–200 B.C. Felt textiles in C. Asia.

c. **200 B.C.** China exports silk to west.

c. **100 B.C.** Syrians invent glassblowing.

A.D. 450–500 Mochica pottery and textiles in Peru.

550 Draw looms for patterned silk weaving in Egypt.

552 Byzantine emperor Justinian sends missionaries to China and Ceylon to smuggle out silkworms: beginning of European silk industry.

c. **600** Development of goldsmithing in Merovingian France (Gourdon gold chalice). Chinese and Korean craftsmen settle in Japan. Celtic Irish gold and metalwork.

Chinese Shang dynasty bronzes

Bronzesmiths of the Shang dynasty (1766–1112 B.C.) produced magnificent vessels, weapons, and chariot fittings. The bronze vessels in particular are notable for their artistry. Made to contain food or wine for ritual, not everyday use, they are superbly decorated, yet the method used was the laborious one of piece-mold casting, using a clay mold. Not until *c.* 550 B.C., under the Chou dynasty (1126–256 B.C.), did Chinese bronze smiths discover the lost-wax process; in this technique vessels are modeled in wax, covered in clay, and fired, after which the melted wax is replaced with bronze to cast a detailed model.

Shang bronzes come in many forms, from wine buckets and wide-mouthed vases to tripod cooking vessels and animal-form containers. Some vessels are inscribed to commemorate a high-ranking owner's feats or to honor his ancestors, but it was not until the Chou period that lengthy inscriptions became popular. The intricate decoration, predominantly based on animal forms and perhaps intended to aid shamans in communication with the spirit world, ranges from abstract patterns to realistic animal heads. A popular motif

Bronze ritual vase with dragons of the Shang dynasty (1500s–1400s B.C.).

is the *t'ao-t'ieh* monster mask. Human images are rare. The fine bronze bells of this period are also notable. Made without clappers, they resounded when struck with a wooden mallet.

Greek painted pottery

In the late 700s B.C., the Greek vase painters of Corinth adopted the technique of black-figure painting. They painted their designs in black on a red clay ground, incising fine details before firing. White was used for women's faces and limbs.

From 600 B.C., Athens dominated black-figure painting, making greater use of human figures. Vase painters customarily signed their work, and the surviving names reveal that the Athenian monopoly owed much to craftsmen from Egypt, Thrace, and Scythia. The master of Athenian black-figure painting was Exekias, but it was one of his pupils who, by 530 B.C., invented the technique that superseded this style: red-figure painting. Here the design was left in the clay's natural color, with detail added in black paint and the background painted black. Occasionally touches of color, chiefly red and gold, were added. This technique enabled painters to introduce much finer detail, and soon more real-

istic human figures were being depicted. The red-figure style achieved its peak in the 400s, then degenerated. In Athens it faded out around 325 B.C., lingering a little longer in southern Greece.

Left: *Theseus slaying the Minotaur, amphora of 500s.* Below: *Greek warrior arming himself, red-figure cylix of 400s by Epicteus.*

Medieval stained glass

The earliest stained-glass windows, from the 1000s, depict static, monumental figures in simple settings and muted colors. Architectural design in the 1100s resulted in large window spaces, where stained glass could develop to its full glory. Pictorial scenes were painted within medallions, several of which might follow a storyline. The armature (framework) around them evolved into elaborate patterns of lozenges, quatrefoils, circles, and squares.

Some monastic orders, notably the Cistercians, favored a less distracting (and cheaper) grayish glass with simple patterns, known as grisaille. But all over Europe glaziers, inspired by works like the magnificent rose window of Chartres cathedral, vied with each other to produce brilliant colors and designs. They illustrated Bible stories and saints' lives, sometimes with sym-

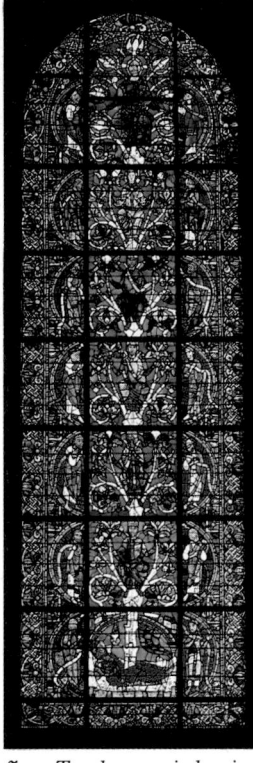

Jesse Tree lancet window in Chartres Cathedral.

bolic imagery, notably the Jesse tree, which depicts the descent of Christ as a tree rooted in the patriarch Jesse's body, with Mary forming its trunk and Christ its flower or fruit. Colors became more vivid as glassmaking technology improved and glass-painting techniques developed. Realistic sketches of animals appear on little panels known as quarries.

By the 1300s, glaziers had evolved a freer style and new techniques, although the Black Death (*p332*) wiped out many individuals and their skills. Glassworkers achieved lighter effects with the growing tastes for line design, white glass, and naturalism. They stained glass with silver nitrate, or flashed (layered) clear and colored glass, cutting the color away in parts to leave clear areas. Sadly, they scrapped much 13th-century glass to make way for their own.

Medieval tapestries

Thought to have been introduced to southern Europe by the Arabs in the 700s, tapestry weaving was a major industry in France and, to a lesser extent, Germany by 1200. Hung on walls as well as covering beds and tables, tapestries served to adorn (and insulate) both grand homes and churches. They also served as prestige symbols on ceremonial occasions and could be rolled up to accompany the nobility on their travels, ensuring the comforts and grandeur of home.

In the late 1300s, Paris was the major center of tapestry manufacture under royal patronage. By this time tapestry was in common use for items from canopies to chair covers and horse blankets. Wealthy noblemen like the dukes of Burgundy commissioned tapestry sets illustrating hunting scenes or incidents from epics and romances. Also popu-

lar were *mille fleurs* ("thousand flowers") designs, with little flowering plants scattered over a dark ground, sometimes accompanied by small birds and animals. The *"Angers Apocalypse,"* one of the oldest surviving tapestries, was made in Paris in the late 1300s. The English occupation of 1418–36 sent the Parisian weavers into flight. Many

joined the tapestry workshops at Arras, which became the new center of production and gave its name to tapestry hangings. After the sack of Arras in 1477, the tapestry weaving industry moved to Tournai in Belgium. Other major centers were Bruges and Brussels, where the famous "Lady with the Unicorn" tapestries were made in the 1500s.

The Angel with the Sickle, *"Angers Apocalypse" tapestry.*

Timeline

c. **625** High point of Byzantine silverwork (plates depicting life of King David, found near Kyrenia, 1902).

630 Cotton introduced in Arab countries.

c. **645** Anglo-Saxon gold and metalwork (Sutton Hoo treasure found in 1939 in a ship burial).

674 Glass windows in English churches.

700 Tapestry weaving established in Peru.

751 Wooden "Gigaku" masks in Japan.

c. **850** Chinese potters develop porcelain.

c. **875** Anglo-Saxon silver (Trewhiddle hoard).

900 Danish crafts (Oseberg wood carvings, sleighs, carts, tools, etc.).

942 Manufacture of linens and woolens in Flanders.

1025–29 Mantled fireplaces develop in W. Europe.

1067 Norman needlewomen begin the Bayeux Tapestry. It is not in fact a tapestry but a work of embroidery.

c. **1120** German monk Theophilus writes *De Diversis Artibus*, treatise on medieval Christian arts and crafts.

1125–29 Earliest stained glass to survive in situ, in Augsburg cathedral, Germany.

c. **1150** York Minster's Jesse window, oldest surviving stained glass in England.

1193 Indigo and brazilwood for dyeing imported from India to Britain.

c. **1200** Engagement rings come into fashion.

1205 Nicolas of Verdun completes jeweled shrine of St. Mary for Tournai cathedral, Belgium.

1227 Japanese potter Toshiro starts porcelain manufacture in Japan.

1292 Venetian glass industry begins.

1315 Lyon silk industry developed by Italian immigrants.

c. **1333** Sienese workshop of Ugolino da Vieri (silver-gilt reliquary with enamel plates for Orvieto cathedral), Italy.

1348 First ordinances for regulation of pewtering in London.

1379 Oldest surviving medieval tapestries (French weaver Nicolas Bataille's *Apocalypse*).

1402 Arras tapestry workshops left, produce tapestry story of St. Piat and Eleuthère in Tournai Cathedral.

c. **1430** Luca della Robbia founds his majolica workshop in Florence.

c. **1450** Gobelin family found cloth-dyeing factory outside Paris, later to become most famous of all tapestry factories.

1482 Paris silversmith, Pierre le Flamand, makes the Burghley Nef (silver-gilt table ornament in form of ship).

c. **1490** "Abraham of Kütahya" blue and white Ottoman ware produced for the court displays painted exotic scrolls and arabesques, revealing a strong Chinese influence.

c. **1500** First manufacture in Europe of faience (Faenza, Italy) and majolica (Majorca).

Timeline

c. **1509** Earliest made wallpaper (surviving today), black-and-white design imitating brocade by English printer Hugo Goes.

1518 Porcelain from E. Asia first imported into Europe.

c. **1542** Medici tapestry factory founded in Florence.

1543 Benvenuto Cellini produces his magnificent salt cellar for François I of France.

c. **1571** Delft introduced to England by potters from Antwerp, Belgium.

1572 Hugues Sambin publishes *Oeuvre de la diversité des termes*, which becomes the sourcebook for 16th-century French cabinetmakers.

1575 First European porcelain (inferior to the Chinese original) produced at Florence.

1578 Faience pottery manufactured at Nevers, France (Conrade brothers).

1589 Rev. William Lee of Cambridge, England, invents first knitting machine.

1601 Henri IV of France takes over Gobelin factory, employing 200 Flemish weavers to make tapestries.

1604 Silk manufacture begins in England.

1609 Tin-enameled ware manufactured at Delft, the Netherlands.

1619 King James I opens Mortlake tapestry works near London, employing Flemish weavers.

1622 Georg Schwanhardt develops method of glass engraving with wheel and diamond.

c. **1630** Barberini tapestry workshop established in Rome.

1644 End of the age of fine Chinese porcelain *(right, above)*.

1645 Wallpaper used as inexpensive substitute for tapestry.

1650 Leather upholstery used for furniture. In Japan, the Kakiemon family of potters introduces the technique of overglaze enamels on porcelain.

1656 Artificial pearls produced in Paris.

1660 First Russian glass factory founded at Izmailovskii, employing Venetian glassblowers.

1672 Fulham pottery, London, founded by John Dwight.

1673 Fine soft-paste porcelain manufactured at Rouen, France.

1676 William Sherwin of England develops fast-dyeing process for calico.

1685 French Huguenots begin silk manufacture in Britain. First porcelain tea services made in France.

1690 Calico printing introduced to England from France.

1693 Grinling Gibbons appointed master carver in England.

1695 James Morley makes brown glaze stoneware in Nottingham, England.

1700 Earliest accurate metalworking lathes in use.

1701 Royal charter granted to weavers of Axminster and Wilton, England, for making carpets.

Ming dynasty porcelain

Developed in China during the Tang dynasty (618–907), porcelain became fashionable during the Ming dynasty (1368–1644). Blue and white ware is best known. At

Cloisonné enamel flask, Ming dynasty, early 1600s.

first traditional flower and animal designs were used, but soon human figures, landscapes, and literary characters appeared. The blue or copper-red monochrome ware of previous dynasties was still made, but polychrome was more popular. This included *Tou-ts'ai*, "dove-tailed colors," in which motifs were drawn in underglaze blue before a first firing and other colors were added for a second firing. In *Wu-ts'ai* ware, motifs are outlined in black or red over the glaze; in *San-ts'ai* ware, brilliant enamels are painted onto fired, unglazed porcelain before refiring at a lower temperature. Some fine white ware was also produced, including statuettes of

Kuan-yin, goddess of mercy, and cups with *an-hua*, "secret decoration," etched with a needlepoint before glazing, so fine as to be visible only when held to the light.

A Judge of Hell, *Ming dynasty, 1500s.*

French Regency furniture

French Regency style arose as a reaction against the formal opulence of Louis XIV style and culminated in the decorative Rococo style. At the Paris court of the regent, elegance was now associated with ease and comfort, without any loss of artistry. Lighter colors were favored for upholstery and general decor.

Under the influence of oriental art, cabinetmakers introduced a flowing, curvilinear style. Chairs and sofas acquired a softer appearance, with gentle curves and delicately carved frames, and were richly upholstered. Ornate chased gilt-bronze appliqué decoration was popular. Cabinetmakers used brilliantly colored

woods for high-quality marquetry, or they gilded or painted any exposed woodwork.

During this period, too, the market for quality furniture spread beyond the court. The Paris craft guilds were kept busy supplying the bourgeoisie with their requirements via newly established dealers. These wares might have been less extravagant, but standards of crafting expertise remained high under the iron control of the guilds. At court level, however, the master of this style was Charles Cressent (1675–1768), from 1719 the Regent's cabinetmaker. It was his development of serpentine curves to the front and sides of bureaus and commodes that gave rise to the double-curved bombé ("swollen") commodes characteristic of Louis XV style. Cressent was also noted for unusual superb metalwork with which he enriched his furniture—from gilded bronze handles shaped like Chinese dragons to female figures at the corners of tables.

French Régence (Regency) chair of the early 1700s.

Wedgwood china

English master potter Josiah Wedgwood was in partnership with Thomas Whieldon from 1754 before starting his own business. His range of wares, the best-known noted below, contributed much to the success of the Staffordshire pottery industry.

Basalt ware Unglazed black stoneware developed c. 1767, painted Greek style in red or white; included "Etruscan" ware.

Cauliflower ware Earthenware in fruit or vegetable shapes, glazed green or yellow; first made in partnership with Whieldon.

Cane ware Tan-colored ware, introduced c. 1775, often resembling bamboo.

Creamware Lightweight, lead-glazed, cream-colored earthenware, developed c. 1760; Wedgwood's first major success.

Jasperware Wedgwood's most famous product, developed 1775: a hard, fine, unglazed stoneware colored (notably "Wedgwood blue") with metallic oxides and decorated with white reliefs.

Lusterware Pottery given a metallic effect by tiny quantities of gold ("copper luster") or platinum ("silver luster"). Lusters might cover the entire piece or only a decorative band.

Pearlware Durable white version of creamware, developed c. 1779.

Pebbleware Pottery made by the mixing together of colored clays, with the end product resembling semiprecious stones

Wedgwood porphyry vase, based on an antique design.

such as the banded translucent agate or serpentine.

Queen's ware Name given to creamware after Josiah Wedgwood's appointment as potter to Queen Charlotte in 1765.

Rosso Antico Unglazed red stoneware ranging from light red to brown.

Thomas Sheraton

English furniture designer and cabinet-maker Thomas Sheraton (1751–1806) gave his name to a major Georgian furniture style, yet no furniture made by him survives. His fame rests on his publications, "intended to exhibit the present taste of furniture, and at the same time to give the workman some assistance in the

A typical Thomas Sheraton office bureau, late 1700s.

manufacturing of it." His designs for elegant, delicate furniture with simple lines and restrained inlay had considerable influence on Regency cabinetmaking. The lightness of his chair designs is further brought out by cane seats, tapered legs, and gently upswept arms. He favored graceful rectilinear lines over curves, abandoning the shield-shaped or oval chairbacks of the Neoclassical period for an upright, rectangular shape. The compact Sheraton style uses material economically and saves on space, with neat, light chairs and tables and portable bookcases. Sheraton valued versatility, designing larger pieces with hidden mechanisms, such as the Harlequin Pembroke Table, which has a concealed nest of small drawers that can be raised above the surface for use.

Sheraton's reputation rests largely on the designs in *The Cabinet-maker and Upholsterer's Drawing Book.* He followed this up with the *Cabinet Dictionary* (1803), explaining a rather arbitrary selection of terms of the trade. His last work was the *Cabinet-maker, Upholsterer and General Artist's Encyclopaedia* (1805), published a year before his death. In this he abandoned the simplicity and elegance of his earlier designs in favor of an eccentric extravagance, but the early Sheraton style always remained popular.

Timeline

c. 1800 Josiah Spode founds his porcelain factory at Stoke-on-Trent, England.

1801 French architects Percier and Fontaine produce their *Recueil des décorations intérieurs*: interior and furniture designs influence development of Empire style.

1803 Thomas Sheraton publishes *Cabinet Dictionary (p. 553)*.

1815 John Doulton founds Doulton Pottery and Porcelain company in London.

1818 The New England Glass Company of East Cambridge, Massachusetts, founded: one of the 19th-century's international glass giants.

1823 Baccarat and other French glass factories begin to produce opaline glass *(p. 556)*.

1825 American cabinetmaker Lambert Hitchcock opens Connecticut factory for the mass production of chairs.

1827 King Ludwig I of Bavaria founds the Munich workshop of the Royal Bavarian Glass Painting Studio, heading Germany's stained-glass revival.

1830 Dawn of lacquered papier-mâché ware industry in Russia.

1836 Austrian glassworks of Johann Loetz Witwe founded.

1842 The firm of Fabergé *(right)*, Russian jewelers and goldsmiths, founded.

1846 U.S. inventor Elias Howe patents a sewing machine.

1850–1920 Arts and Crafts movement *(p. 555)*.

1851 Great Exhibition in London. In the U.S.A., Singer produces the first practical sewing machine (an improved version of Howe's).

1855 First patent for production of rayon by George Audemars.

1865 French silk industry saved when Louis Pasteur cures silkworm disease.

1868 Charles Lock Eastlake publishes *Hints on Household Taste in Furniture, Upholstery and other Details* describing the favored medieval English and Jacobean style; highly influential in England and the U.S.A.

1870 Viennese furniture firm of Michael Thonet, originator of modern bentwood designs, is producing 400,000 pieces annually. Whitby jet-carving industry at its peak, employing 1,400 people.

1873 English stained-glass artist Daniel Cottier opens studios in New York City and Sydney, Australia.

1875 Arthur Lasenby Liberty opens his London shop promoting Arts and Crafts products, and later Art Nouveau *(p. 557)*. Daum brothers found world-famous French glassworks Verrerie de Nancy (now Cristalleries de Nancy).

1876 Norwegian firm of David Andersen founded, working in decorative enamels.

1877 Rhode Island School of Design founded.

Fabergé

Russian goldsmith Carl Fabergé (1846–1920) was perhaps the last exponent of court art in Europe. His firm's skilled artisans produced useful objects such as cigarette cases and scent bottles, miniature hardstone carvings, and, best known today, the jeweled Easter eggs made originally for the Russian imperial family. The English royal family also commissioned works, notably animal carvings and jeweled flowers.

Fabergé's works are characterized by a sensitive attention to color and texture; the use of semiprecious stones like moonstones and peridot; and superb enameling techniques. Fabergé himself commented "Expensive things interest me little if the value is merely in so many diamonds or pearls," and the exquisite artistry of his famous firm's finest works redeems them from accusations of *fin de siècle* decadence.

Jewel-encrusted snail by master craftsman Fabergé.

1842 Firm established by Gustav Petrovich Fabergé in St. Petersburg.

1870 At the age of 24, Carl Fabergé takes control of the firm and begins to develop its international reputation.

1882 The firm exhibits for the first time at the Pan-Russian Exhibition, Moscow, winning a gold medal.

1884 First imperial Easter egg presented by Alexander III to the empress Marie Feodorovna. Alexander grants his royal warrant to the house of Fabergé.

1900 Imperial eggs first exhibited at the Paris Exposition. Fabergé awarded *Légion d'honneur*.

1904 First exhibition of objects by Fabergé in England.

1907 King Edward VII commissions artists from the house of Fabergé to make portrait models of the royal family's favorite animals.

1911 Nicholas II commissions Fabergé to carve miniature hardstone figures of the empress's Cossack bodyguard.

Liberty and Co.

The London department store of Liberty and Co. played a major part in popularizing the Arts and Crafts movement and went on to do the same for Art Nouveau. Its founder, Arthur Lasenby Liberty (1843–1917), began his career in 1862 as manager of an oriental warehouse. In 1875, he opened his own London store, the East India House, one of the first importers of oriental wares and furniture on a commercial basis.

Always quick to respond to changes in taste, during the 1890s he did much to popularize the Arts and Crafts movement, commercializing its ideals with great success. By combining crafting expertise with mass production (often hand-finished), Liberty and Co. brought a broad Arts and Crafts aesthetic to an eager mass market. Liberty was the first of several retailers to commission designs to satisfy the growing demand for "aesthetic" furnishings.

Pendant made for Liberty by Archibald Knox.

While exploiting the benefits of mass production, he encouraged his designers —including Christopher Dresser, Archibald Knox, and Charles Voysey—to experiment. Liberty's insistence on high standards had a major influence on the silk and woolen industries, leading to higher quality fabrics and the introduction of fine dyes. Many Liberty fabric designs, including the famous "Peacock Feather," came from the London-based Silver Studio, which also adapted the designs of William Morris for mass production. Archibald Knox developed the popular Celtic-inspired "Cymric" silver range, introduced in 1899 and joined in 1903 by a "Tudric" pewter range.

Mass-produced, hand-finished furniture was strongly influenced by Charles Mackintosh and other Glasgow designers. The work of Liberty designers gradually moved away from the historical inspiration of the Arts and Crafts movement toward the burgeoning Art Nouveau style. Indeed it was this new movement with which the firm was to become irrevocably identified.

Arts and Crafts movement

The Arts and Crafts movement (1850–1920) originated in Britain as a reaction against industrial mechanization: social change called for an improved unity of art and life. Leading exponents were the multitalented designer-writer William Morris and the outspoken critic John Ruskin, author of *The Seven Lamps of Architecture* (1849).

Augustus Pugin had already pleaded the cause for honesty in design and a return to the Gothic style in *The True Principles of Pointed or Christian Architecture* (1841). Victorian elaborate ornamentation was seen as destroying all natural form. The burgeoning production lines of the Industrial Revolution were destroying the pride of the artisan's role. In 1861, disheartened by soulless, machine-made articles and the counterproductive demarcation of artist and artisan, Morris founded Morris, Marshall, Falkner and Co. to produce stylish hand-fashioned furnishings for the masses—stained glass, textiles, wallpapers, and furniture. The source of inspiration flowed

Earthenware tile-dish by William de Morgan (1839–1917), painted with peacock pattern.

from the fundamental medieval principles of the integration of materials and imaginative crafting. In 1890, Morris founded the Kelmscott Press, and his vision and ideas—by then more formulated—influenced book design and printing.

In 1882, another supporter of the Arts and Crafts movement, Arthur Mackmurdo, founded the Century Guild for British Craftsmen. By 1884, the Homes Arts and Industries Association—a charitable body teaching crafts to rural workers—had been set

up. In the same year, the Arts Workers' Guild was inaugurated as a meeting place for lectures and the exchange of ideas. Its spin-off, the Arts and Crafts Exhibition Society, held its first exhibition in London in 1888. This coincided with the establishment of the Guild of Handicraft by designer Charles Ashbee.

This developing crusade was not restricted to Britain; it had far greater consequences. Important writings such as Owen Jones's *The Grammar of Ornament* (1856) and other exponents' later works and artifacts had an enormous international influence. The Centennial Exhibition, held in 1876 in Philadelphia, introduced the new ethos to the artisans in the United States. In 1887, Candice Wheeler founded the New York Society of Decorative Arts, and in 1888, the friendship between Ashbee and an Austrian architect, Josef Hoffman, led to the establishment of similar artist-artisan workshops in his native country. Gustav Stickley followed suit in Italy in 1902.

Great exhibitions

With the coming of industrialization (p. 353), many governments came to see that economic prosperity could be boosted by promotional exhibitions displaying highlevel design and technical innovations in industry and engineering. The lead was taken by France. After the French Revolution, the national industries that had been under royal patronage went into decline, and to encourage their revival, national exhibitions of French manufacturing were set up in 1797, and from 1839 they became a regular showcase for French industry.

Other countries soon followed France's example, but the 1851 Crystal Palace Exhibition in London was to be the inspiration for the 30 or so international world fairs that were held between 1885 and 1940. Prominent among these were the 1888–89 Paris Exposition Universelle, the World Columbian Exposition in Chicago in 1893, the Exposition Internationale in Brussels in 1897 and in Turin in 1902, and the Louisiana Purchase Exhibition at St. Louis in 1904. The Exposition des Arts Décoratifs et Industriels, held in Paris in 1925, gave a name to the style known as Art Deco (p. 558), though the exhibition was a turning point in the clash between "decorative" and "functional." By 1939 at the

New York World's Fair, mass production had most evidently won the day. National rivalry was always a prominent feature of international exhibitions, no more dramatically evident than in 1937 at the International Exposition in Paris, where the Soviet Union and Germany confronted each other in pavilions on either side of the entrance. Healthy competition, however, led to further innovative ideas.

Exposition Universelle (1888–89) in Paris promoted national design innovations.

Timeline

1885 German immigrant Philip Handel founds Handel and Co. in Connecticut, later the second most important U.S. manufacturer of glass lamps (after Tiffany).

1892 Stained-glass window *The Four Seasons* by Louis Comfort Tiffany and Samuel Bing is exhibited in Paris.

1894 Alphonse Mucha begins to design costumes, jewelry, posters, and stage sets for French actress Sarah Bernhardt.

1896 Publication of German art magazines *Die Jugend* and *Simplicissimus*.

1897 Founding of Austrian art movement the Vienna Sezession *(Art Nouveau, opposite)*.

1898 Mackintosh School of Art founded in Glasgow *(Art Nouveau, opposite)*. Alphonse Mucha's *Combinaisons Ornamentales* and *Documents Décoratifs* design manuals, embodying Art Nouveau typefaces and decorative motifs, inspire printers.

1900 Exhibition of Auguste Rodin sculptures opens at Place de l'Alma, Paris.

1902 Exhibition at the Société Nationale des Beaux-Arts of modern style or Art Nouveau.

1903 Irish stained-glass artist Sarah Purser founds glass workshop An Túr Gloine ("The Tower of Glass") in Dublin, the focus of Irish stained-glass development. Josef Hoffmann founds the Wiener Werkstätte (Vienna Workshop).

1907 German architect Hermann Muthesius founds the Deutscher Werkbund with the intention of improving the aesthetic standard of industrial design.

1908 Belgian chemist Leo Baekeland discovers Bakelite, a synthetic plastic that becomes popular for making jewelry, lamps, and household goods.

1909 René Lalique opens his glassworks. First commercial manufacture of Bakelite signals the dawn of the age of plastic *(p. 417)*.

1911 Charles Sykes creates "Spirit of Ecstasy" car figurehead for Rolls Royce.

1913 Roger Fry founds the Omega Workshops in London for pottery, furniture, fabrics, printing, etc. Lalique stops making jewelry to concentrate on glass.

1914 René Joubert founds the firm of D.I.M. (Décoration Intérieure Moderne), which by 1930 is one of Paris's largest studio galleries.

1915 Alfred Wolmark's window in St. Mary's Church, Slough, England, makes innovative use of abstract design in stained glass.

1916 French artist Jean Luráat begins modern movement in tapestry: reduces color scale and reverts to coarse textures of Middle Ages.

1917 Publication of *De Stijl* magazine, the organ of the Modernist movement in the Netherlands.

Decorative glass

Art glass Highly decorated glass from the late 1800s and 1900s.

Cameo glass Two or more layers of different colored glass, the upper carved in a relief pattern on contrast ground. First used in Egypt and developed in Rome.

Cased glass Two or more layers of different colored glass, the outer (usually paler) partly cut away.

Crackle (or ice) glass A decorative glass with tiny cracks over its surface, developed in Venice in the 1500s.

Cranberry glass A Victorian pink glass.

Favrile glass: Brilliant iridescent glass made by Tiffany from 1893.

Flakestone glass A marbled-effect opaque glass popular in the 1930s.

Marqueterie de verre A technique whereby colored glass details are inlaid into a glass object while it is in a semi-molten state.

Milk (or enamel) glass A white translucent glass opacified with tin oxide.

Millefiori glass Patterned with "a thousand flowers" by embedding into it sections of composite multicolored canes.

Opaline A semiopaque translucent glass of the 1800s, made in pastel colors, sometimes iridescent.

Paté-de-verre ("glass paste") A thick opaque glass, resembling alabaster, made by mixing powdered glass to a paste then molding it to shape. This ancient technique was rediscovered in 1884 and first exploited commercially by the Daum brothers. It was skillfully used by Art Nouveau artists. French paté-de-cristal has a higher lead content and is clear.

Stained-glass window at Nancy medical institution by Jacques Gruber, 1906.

Ruby glass A deep-red glass obtained with the use of gold chloride; first made in the late 1600s.

Silveria glass Glass incorporating glittering fragments of silver foil. An ancient technique revived in the 1890s.

Spatter glass An opaque glass speckled with brightly colored enamel glass.

Vaseline glass A yellowish-green glass (the color created by the use of uranium) popular in the 1800s.

Verre glomis Glass decorated with a layer of engraved gold.

China painters

After 1900, the demand for pretty china —aided by the huge expansion of stores like *Woolworth's*—paved the way for a new generation of talented female china painters. Most women who apprenticed as "paintresses" developed decorative skills, but some also exhibited amazing design and business accomplishments.

In the 1920s, Susie Cooper turned from fashion design to making pottery for A. E. Gray. In 1932, she opened her own company producing painted tableware with brightly colored geometric designs for the mass market. Clarice Cliff started painting pottery in 1912, as a thirteen-year-old factory hand in Staffordshire, England. She studied sculpture at the Royal College of Art, and in 1928 joined the Newport Pottery, where she introduced her "Bizarre" range of tableware. Within a year of a trial run of 720 hand-painted pieces, the whole factory was dedicated to this range. In 1940, she was designated Royal Designer for Industry, the only woman potter to achieve this accolade. Other notable china painters include Charlotte Rhead (1885–1947), who produced platters, jugs, and vases; Jessie Marion King (1876–1949), best-known

for her book illustrations; Daisy Makeig-Jones, who painted "Fairyland Lustre" plaques for Wedgwood; and Ann Macbeth (1875–1948).

"Bizarre" tableware in "House of Bridge" pattern by Clarice Cliff.

Art Nouveau

Art Nouveau (*c.* 1890–1910), though now expressed in terms of a particular style, was essentially a diverse art movement that stemmed from widely differing groups of artists and designers who spurned the constraints of the Arts and Crafts attachment to a medieval and gothic age. Instead they sought to create new designs, featuring curving

Art Nouveau clock with stained-glass longcase designed by Gustave Servrier-Bory.

forms, waves, and tendrils; botanical realism; and symbolist allusions.

Despite evolving from the basic theories of the British Arts and Crafts movement (*p. 555*), the name Art Nouveau came from Samuel Bing's gallery in Paris, the "Maison de l'Art Nouveau." There patrons could view Toulouse-Lautrec posters, René Lalique jewelry, and British textiles and wallpapers designed by Walter Crane and Charles Voysey. In 1883, Arthur H. Mackmurdo was one of the first British furniture and graphic designers to move in a new direction. He used ornate floral motifs, curvilinear furniture structures, and sinuous organic illustration on the cover of his book *Wren's City Churches*.

In 1890, a group of French artists, inspired by Emile Gallé, experimented with complex techniques and avant-garde designs in glassware and furniture. Among the most renowned members of this group were the Daum brothers, Auguste and Antonin; Eugéne Vallin; Jacques Gruber; and Louis Majorelle. Five years later Lalique incorporated his first nude figure in a jewel, and the highly distinctive Tiffany lamps—the name of which became synonymous with the style—made their debut.

By 1898, at an exhibition in Turin, Italian designers like Carlo Zen exhibited Art Nouveau at its most florid. At the same time Josef Hoffmann and other Viennese designers founded the Vienna Sezession, pursuing a far less ornamented style, while the "Glasgow Style," developed by Charles Mackintosh, replaced an earlier use of floral motifs with a more austere and functional design. Issues such as individual artisanship versus mass production, the use of natural forms as a basis of design, and the choice of appropriate ornamentation had been and continued to be subjects for debate among artists and designers, but by the second decade of the 1900s many more issues occupied their thoughts and molded their creativity.

Ceramics and pottery

Since ancient times clay has been used for creating utilitarian and purely ornamental objects. Over the centuries, production has been influenced by the development of a wealth of different techniques and a great variety of methods of decoration. It is generally accepted that ceramic materials fall into three main groups—earthenware, stoneware, and porcelain—each fired at a progressively hotter temperature.

The lowest-fired earthenware is porous, but the application of a vitreous glaze overcomes the problem. Early glazes were made from a mixture of silica and lead oxide. During the Chinese Tang dynasty (A.D. 618–907), some glazed pieces were already being colored with metal oxides. The increased heating of stoneware firing, even when unglazed, makes it almost liquid resistant. Potters in England and Germany developed the strength of this resistance further by adding salt into the kiln, which created a thin but tough glaze. "True" (hard-paste) porcelain developed during the Tang dynasty and was made from China clay and China stone. Superbly modeled and decorated animal and human figures and jars spattered with three-colored glazes were among the works produced.

By the 1600s, Japan, using porcelain in its purest form (translucent and white), produced the famous, beautifully decorated Kakiemon ware. Europe, meanwhile, still concentrated on pottery using the earlier discovered Middle Eastern tin glaze, which pro-

Rocking pot (1956) by American Peter Voulkos.

duced a white surface that was excellent for decoration. Less strong (soft-paste) porcelain was developing in France during the 1600s, but it was the famous Meissen factory in Saxony that independently discovered "true" porcelain in the early 1700s. Kakiemon designs were copied in Europe, and chinoiserie decoration was used on tea services. Later, patronized by the wealthy Madame de Pompadour, the French factory at Sèvres attracted talented artists and influenced porcelain pottery production throughout Europe. In Britain the establishment of creamware, good for mass production, gave rise to the popular Staffordshire potteries. The Wedgwood factory introduced new processes, producing lines such as jasperware and ironstone china. As the 1900s progressed, the Arts and Crafts movement, Art Nouveau, and Art Deco changed the styles and decoration of ceramic pottery and society's attitude to the potter.

Stoneware by English potter Bernard Leach.

Timeline

1919 Walter Gropius founds the Bauhaus German design school at Weimar revolutionizing the teaching of the arts, architecture, and industrial design (p. 559).

1920 René Lalique establishes his own glass factory.

1923 László Moholy-Nagy becomes director of Bauhaus metal workshop.

1924 Marcel Breuer becomes director of the Bauhaus furniture design department.

1925 Art Deco (right) dominates Paris Exposition Internationale des Arts Décoratifs et Industriels Modernes. Gropius moves the Bauhaus from Weimar to Dessau. In France, Daum glassworks introduces range of crystal sculptures.

1929 American manufacturers begin to make aluminum furniture (especially chairs). Le Corbusier exhibits seating with steel frame structures.

1932 Century of Progress Exhibition in Chicago features Streamlining movement. Hoffmann's Wiener Werkstätte closed down as a result of financial difficulties.

1933 Bauhaus closed by Nazis as a "cathedral of socialism" (p. 559).

1935 Alvar Artek establishes firm to distribute his Modernist furniture.

1937 Russel Wright designs phenomenally successful American Modern earthenware china.

1940 Museum of Modern Art, New York City, inaugurates competition for "Organic Design in Home Furnishings": prizewinners include Eero Saarinen and Charles Eames. Italian glassworker Paolo Venini introduces his "handkerchief" vases with latticino decoration.

1942 Beginning of "Utility furniture" in Britain (continues until 1952).

1946 "Britain Can Make It" exhibition. Saarinen begins creating furniture designs for Knoll International.

1947 Finnish craftsman Tapio Wirkkala designs Kanttarelli glassware for the Iittala glassworks.

1948 "Low-Cost Furniture Competition" at the Museum of Modern Art, New York City. Eames designs his prototype chaise with amoeboid seat and distinctive thin legs.

1950 Finnish designer Timo Sarpaneva begins designing glass for Iittala works.

1951 Festival of Britain. At the Milan Triennale exhibition, Scandinavian silverware comes to the fore.

1955 Knoll International starts manufacture of Mies van der Rohe's classic prewar furniture designs.

1956 London Haymarket's Design Centre opens. British silversmith Gerald Benney creates parcel-gilt chalice with 18th-century-style textured surface.

1959 Anni Albers, On Designing. In Germany, Walter Pabst designs the first one-piece plastic table.

Art Deco

Art Deco (c. 1920s–30s) reacted against Art Nouveau's sinuous curves and botanical extravaganza, replacing them with simple, geometrical, streamlined shapes and strong colors. But it shared with Art Nouveau, (p. 557) a concern for fine artistry. Many 1920s designers used materials that would today be frowned upon by conservationists, such as exotic animal skins, ivory, and tortoiseshell. Drawing on influences from such disparate sources as ancient Egypt, Cubism, Futurism, and Functionalism, the Art Deco style ranged between extremes of opulent high-style and practical Moderne.

As early as 1903, the annual French salons of the Société des Artistes Décorateurs began moving away from the influence of Art Nouveau. The 1925 Paris Exposition des Arts Décoratifs et Industriels Modernes is generally seen as the peak of the Art Deco movement and featured top designers such as Emile Ruhlmann, Paul

1920s Art Deco jewelry: Lacloche pendant with platinum, onyx, and pearl.

Follot, Edgar Brandt, René Lalique, Maurice Dufrène, and many others. The Art Deco style was publicized internationally by traveling exhibitions and by large department stores hiring well-known designers to head their creative workshops.

Although designers such as Armand-Albert Rateau and Britain's Eileen Gray and Betty Joel were commissioned by the famous during the 1920s and 1930s for individual, handmade pieces, Art Deco acclaimed the Machine Age, embracing companies that sold well-designed, mass-produced, and less expensive items. In particular, Art Deco encouraged and revived the metalworking industry. Inspired by Le Corbusier and the Bauhaus, metal furniture, gates, grilles, stair railings, and elevator doors in the Art Deco style became fashionable in hotels, theaters, and other buildings.

Lighting and lamps

The introduction of electric light inspired designers to create beautiful lighting fixtures. French Art Nouveau lamps were among the loveliest, although they were not always very functional—many generated more heat than light. Glassworkers like Gallé, the Daum brothers, and Lalique created blown and molded, etched, cased, and hand-painted shades. The Muller brothers produced a range of lamps adorned with bronze snakes, flowers, and foliage. In the United States, Tiffany created sensational mosaic glass shades. High-style Art Deco produced extravagances like Brandt's "La Tentation" standard lamp, a gilt-bronze cobra upreared to hold an etched-glass Daum bowl. Figure lamps supported by chryselephantine sculptures were also popular.

Along more severe lines, Art Deco also yielded the classic Anglepoise (patented in 1937) and Pierre Chareau's "La Religieuse" lamp, which had a mahogany base topped with bronze and alabaster. The 1930s saw Jacques Adnet's wall-mounted neon strip lights, Jean Perzel's cast-metal table lamps, and the first appearance of triangular wall lights. In 1952 another design classic emerged when U.S. sculptor Isamu Noguchi (1904–88) created the Akari Lamp, a spherical paper lamp merging Japanese tradition and modern austerity. The

1960s saw the innovative use of plastic, as in the Boalum table lamp, a flexible hose of translucent plastic housing many small light bulbs, by Livio Castiglioni. And the 1970s saw the popular double-cantilevered Tizio desk lamp by Richard Sapper, exhibited at New York's City's Museum of Modern Art.

Tiffany "lily lamp" (c. 1900) with fabrile glass shades and bronze base.

Twentieth-century chairs

Chair design during the early part of the 1900s was beginning to move away from the excesses of some Art Nouveau pieces and to minimize the more elaborate Art Deco designs. Although still being tempered by certain aspects of the Arts and Crafts movement (*p. 555*), other early influences included Josef Hoffmann's Wiener Werkstätte and Charles Mackintosh's "Glasgow School," with their emphasis on line and geometric forms, and later the elegant simple creations of Eileen Gray. In these early years the paramount trend of chair design came from northern Europe, in particular designs for mass production. Richard Riemerschmid, a German architect, was one of the first to create chairs to be assembled from several pieces. After World War II, U.S. designers such as Eero Saarinen and Charles Eames—having been inspired by the Bauhaus movement and, in particular, Walter Gropius and Marcel Breuer—began working with fiberglass and plastics and using molds to

(Red-blue chair 1918) by Dutch architect Gerrit Rietveld of De Stijl movement.

create functional, light, but sturdy seating. Adapted designs of Robin Day's stacking chair, a single-molded seat on a metal base (1963), can still be seen in function halls today.

Bauhaus

The Bauhaus was a school of architecture and applied arts founded in 1919 in Weimar, Germany. Developing the pioneering activity of William Morris, the Deutsche Werkbund, and Henri van der Velde, its manifesto was illustrated by a woodcut of a German cathedral, considered to be a total work of art. The aims of the school were not only a return to the integrity of the crafts but also the harnessing of technology for the benefit of society through socialist ideals of a collective life.

The school became a renowned center of modern design and a model of art education: its staff included the painters Paul Klee and Wassily Kandinsky. Its revolutionary spirit echoed the political reality of the period—the Armistice, the Russian Revolution, the abortive Communist uprisings in Germany, and the declaration of a republic. The innovative and unifying *Vorkurs* developed by Johannes Itten emphasized the need for creative self-discovery through the exploration of color, texture, and geometric construction. Students were known as apprentices and their education was centered on the workshop—at that time a completely original concept.

Political pressure forced a move to Dessau in 1925, and here the emphasis shifted from individual crafted pieces to products inspired by engineering and intended for the mass market. This was the most influential period of Bauhaus production in the fields of textiles, advertising, and metalwork. Marcel Breuer used tubular steel and leather for furniture, and characteristic is the Wassily chair, named after Wassily Kandinsky, designed in 1925 and produced commercially by Standard Möbel from 1926.

This, along with designs by Mies van der Rohe, became modern classics.

Although architecture had originally been made the core of all activity, an architectural department was not introduced until 1925 under Mies van der Rohe, who became the Bauhaus director in 1930. The radical, unruly "Bolshevik" image of Bauhaus forced a final move to Berlin in September 1932, where it was closed down by the Nazis in April 1933. Ironically, this enabled Bauhaus thinking to reach its greatest influence as a result of the emigration of staff and students. It took deepest root in the United States with the New Bauhaus founded by Moholy-Nagy in Chicago in 1937.

Rug (1927–28) by Gunta Stölzl from the Dessau Bauhaus.

Timeline

1960 Verner Panton designs his classic stacking chair. Revival of Art Nouveau inspired by Museum of Modern Art's survey exhibition. Dawn of International Pop and Op Art styles in interior design.

1962 Toledo Museum of Art hosts the first seminar on contemporary handcrafted glass. U.S. glass designers perfect new formula glass, workable at lower temperatures.

1963 U.S. jeweler David Webb develops middle-range luxury jewelry.

1964 Terence Conran opens his first Habitat shop in England, with avowed intention of bringing good taste to a mass market.

1965 Albers' *On Weaving*. Japanese furniture designer Shiro Kuramata opens his design firm.

1966 Innovative British jeweler Andrew Grima opens his first shop in London. Paco Rabanne launches body jewelry.

1968 Danish jeweler Bent Gabriel Pedersen creates his celebrated fire-gilded silver necklace.

1969 Finnish glass sculptor Oiva Toikka produces Pop colored sculpture *Lollipop Isle*. Foundation of The Glasshouse, London, for commercial promotion of young glass designers. English artist Allen Jones creates fiberglass furniture mounted on fetishistic female figures.

1970 Beginning of British and U.S. revival of fine handcrafted furniture. Grima's novel style, inspired by natural texture and patterns, leads to his nomination as British crown jeweler. Finnish jeweler Bjorn Weckström launches his "Space Silver" bracelets.

1972 International Ceramics exhibition at Victoria and Albert Museum, London, shows studio work by contributors from 38 countries.

1975 The Worshipful Company of Goldsmiths inaugurates "Loot" exhibitions to support young British jewelers.

1978 Dawn of High-Tech interior decoration and furniture.

1979 Silversmith Stuart Devlin opens his London shop. More than 400 international entries at Corning Museum's exhibition "New Glass."

1980 Terry Jones launches a graphic style magazine *i-D*, demonstrating a mixture of typefaces, layered images, multivarious textures, decorative artworks, and innovative photographic representations.

1983 Laura Ashley, in the *Laura Ashley Book of Interior Decoration*, reflects the international success of her floral "country" design style, initially developed in the 1950s.

1989 Keith Haring produces *Ignorance = Fear* poster; his sensational, socially convicted work earns him international acclaim before his untimely death in 1990.

PROMINENT PEOPLE

AARNIO, Eero (b. 1932) Finnish interior and industrial designer; plastic chairs.

ADAM, Robert (1728–92) Scottish architect and furniture designer; neoclassical style.

ALBERS, Anni (b. 1888–1977) German designer. Pioneer in weaving and textile design.

ALBINI, Franco (1905–77) Italian designer and architect; innovative furniture.

ARGY-ROUSSEAU, Gabriel (1885–1953) French Art Deco glass designer.

ASH, Gilbert (1717–85) U.S. cabinetmaker. Most outstanding New York maker of furniture, notably chairs.

ASHBEE, Charles Robert (1863–1942) British Arts and Crafts designer.

BEHRENS, Peter (1868–1940) German architect and industrial designer. Major figure in development of Modernism.

BERAIN, Jean I. (1640–1711) French decorator and designer; influenced later Rococo and chinoiserie styles.

BING, Samuel (1838–1905) German writer and entrepreneur of Art Nouveau.

BOJESON, Kaj (1886–1958) Danish craft designer of silver and wooden products.

BOULLE, André-Charles (1642–1732) French cabinetmaker employed by Louis XIV; noted for tortoiseshell and brass marquetry; still termed Boulle.

BRANDT, Edgar (1880–1960) French metalwork designer.

BRANDT, Marianne (1893–1983) German designer and Bauhaus metalwork instructor.

BREUER, Marcel (1902–81) Hungarian Bauhaus-inspired designer and architect; molded plywood furniture, cantilevered tubular steel chair.

CARDER, Frederick (1863–1963) English glass craftsman-designer. Emigrated to U.S.A. and contributed significantly to Art Nouveau and Art Deco.

CELLINI, Benvenuto (1500–71) Italian goldsmith and sculptor.

CHIPPENDALE, Thomas the Elder (1718–79) Most famous English master cabinetmaker and furniture designer.

CLAIR, Godefroid de (1100s) Leading German goldsmith-enameler; developed champleve enameling.

COOPER, Susie (Susan Vera) (b. 1902) English ceramic designer.

COPER, Hans (1920–81) German-born British studio potter. Worked with Lucie RIE; sculptural thrown vases.

CRESSENT, Charles (1685–1768) French cabinetmaker.

DAUM, Auguste (1853–1909) and **Antonin** (1864–1930) French Art Nouveau glass designers.

DE MORGAN, William Frend (1839–1917) English Pre-Raphelite ceramic artist; best known for tiles.

DOESBURG, Theo van (1883–1931) Dutch architect and designer; major figure in the 1920s De Stijl movement.

DORN, Marion (1900–64) U.S. textile designer; pioneered Modernist rug.

DRESSER, Christopher (1834–1904) British industrial designer.

EAMES, Charles (1907–78) U.S. architect and designer; modern furniture.

FABERGÉ, Peter Carl (1846–1920) Russian jewelry designer; jeweler to the Russian imperial court.

FOLLOT, Paul (1877–1941) French designer whose career spanned transition from Art Nouveau to Art Deco.

FORNASETTI, Piero (1913–88) Italian decorative designer; furniture with *trompe l'oeil* and other patterns.

FOUQUET, Georges (1862–1957) French designer and maker of jewelry in Art Nouveau and Art Deco styles.

FRANCK, Kaj (b. 1911) Finnish glassware and ceramics designer.

FRANK, Josef (1885–1967) Austrian designer of furniture and household products; major figure in Swedish Modern movement.

FRANKL, Paul T. (1887–1958) Austrian furniture designer; 1920s "skyscraper" furniture; later "California Modern."

FRITSCH, Elizabeth (b. 1940) English potter; geometric patterns in colored slips with matt texture.

GAILLARD, Eugene (1862–1933) French designer of Art Nouveau interiors, furniture, and textiles.

GALLÉ, Emile (1846–1904) French glassmaker and furniture designer; a leading figure of the Art Nouveau movement.

GAUDREAU, Antoine-Robert (c. 1680–1751) French cabinetmaker to the court of Louis XV.

GRAY, Eileen (1878–1976) Irish-born, Paris-based furniture and architectural designer; Art Deco/Modernist.

GROPIUS, Walter (1883–1969) German architect; leader of the Bauhaus; major figure in development of Modernism.

GRUBER, Jacques (1871–1936) French designer of Art Nouveau glassware, furniture, and stained glass.

HAMADA, Shoji (1894–1978) Japanese potter, combining traditional technique with modern design concepts.

HEPPLEWHITE, George (d. 1786) Influential English furniture designer and cabinetmaker.

HOFFMANN, Josef (1870–1956) Austrian architect and designer; helped found the Vienna Sezession.

JACOB, Georges (1739–1841) French cabinetmaker; innovative neoclassical.

JENSEN, Georg (1866–1935) Danish silversmith; Arts and Crafts tableware.

JOEL, Betty (b. 1896) British furniture and textile designer.

JOUBERT, Gilles (1689–1775) French cabinetmaker in Louis XV style.

KENT, William (1685–1748) English architect and furniture designer; greatest exponent of Baroque furniture.

KNOX, Archibald (1864–1933) British silver designer; inspired Liberty and Co.'s "Cymric" and "Tudric" lines.

LABINO, Dominick (b. 1910) Leading U.S. glass artist.

LALIQUE, René (1860–1945) French designer of Art Nouveau and Art Deco glass and jewelry.

LA FARGE, John (1835–1910) U.S. stained-glass designer and artist.

LEACH, Bernard (1887–1979) British ceramist; studied pottery in Far East.

LOEWY, Raymond (1893–1986) French-born U.S. industrial designer.

MACKMURDO, Arthur Heygatte (1851–1942) British Arts and Crafts architect and designer; founded Century Guild.

MAJORELLE, Louis (1859–1926) French Art Nouveau cabinetmaker.

MARCKS, Gerhard (b. 1889) German sculptor and potter; worked at the Bauhaus.

MORRIS, William (1834–96) British writer, poet, and designer; leader of the Arts and Crafts movement.

NAHL, Johann August (1710–85) German carver and designer; a leading exponent of German Rococo style.

NICOLAS of Verdun (late 1100s/early 1200s) French goldsmith, enameler, and metalworker.

PHYFE, Duncan (1768–1854) The preeminent U.S. cabinetmaker and furniture maker of the late 1700s/1800s.

PUGIN, Augustus Welby (1812–52) British architect; the leading influence on the English Gothic revival of the 1800s.

RATEAU, Armand-Albert (1882–1938) French Art Deco furniture designer.

REVERE, Paul (1735–1818) U.S. patriot who established himself as a silversmith and engraver. Designed first paper money for Massachusetts.

RIE, Lucie (1902–95) London-based Austrian potter, producing stoneware, glazed earthenware, and porcelain.

RIETVELD, Gerrit Thomas (1888–1965) Dutch designer and architect; member of the De Stijl group.

RUHLMANN, Emile-Jacques (1879–1933) French Art Deco designer.

RUSKIN, John (1819–1900) British social critic whose writings inspired the Arts and Crafts movement.

SHERATON, Thomas (1751–1806) English cabinetmaker and furniture designer.

STICKLEY, Gustav (1857–1942) U.S. writer and furniture designer.

TIFFANY, Louis Comfort (1848–1933) U.S. designer and interior decorator, notably stained glass and art glass.

VOYSEY, Charles Frederick Annesley (1857–1941) British Arts and Crafts architect and designer.

WAGENFELD, Wilhelm (b. 1900) German designer of glass and tableware; associated with the Bauhaus.

WEDGWOOD, Josiah (1730–95) English master potter.

WEGNER, Hans (b. 1914) Leading furniture designer in Danish Modern style.

WHEELER, Candice (1827–1923) U.S. designer of textiles and wallpapers in Arts and Crafts style.

WHIELDON, Thomas (1719–95) English potter working in colored glazes.

ZEN, Carlo (1851–1918) Italian Art Nouveau cabinetmaker.

TERMS

Amoeboid A term used when describing the free-flowing design of an object that is not subject to rigid outlines—much like an amoeba.

Appliqué A shape or MOTIF cut from a particular type of material and attached permanently onto another as a form of decoration.

Artifacts Objects made by humans.

Artisan A term coined from the Latin *artitus* to describe a skilled craftworker.

Baroque A name given to the highly ornate style of art prevailing in Europe during the 1600s and early 1700s. Mainly stemming from the Counter-Reformation in Italy, it exhibits religious, dramatic, and sometimes vulgar theatrical themes and decoration. Carravaggio, Rubens, and Bernini were among its first pioneers.

Bentwood Sheets or rods of plywood, softened and bent by steam to produce curved forms often used in furniture manufacture.

Bone china A form of translucent PORCELAIN that contains bone ash.

Brocade A rich fabric with a raised design, created with additional threads woven into the fabric where the raised pattern is required.

Calico A cotton cloth—bleached or unbleached, plain or printed with simple patterns. First imported from Calicut in India.

Cantilevered chair A U-shaped construction, often made of metal tubing or BENTWOООD.

Chasing The process of ENGRAVING ornamental designs on metalwork.

Chinoiserie Imitation of Chinese art and architecture copied by Europeans. Often "true" Chinese designs were confused with those from Japan and even sometimes India.

Cloisonné A method of applying a metal strip, or "cloisons," to an object to be filled with ENAMEL, or a raised clay ridge designed to be filled with different colored GLAZES, kept separate by cloisons.

Cubism A movement and a style originally invented by Picasso and Braque in the early 1900s. The reality of the artist's subject was treated as though it consisted of more than its immediate appearance, and thus a single piece of work could be created geometrically and presented as viewed from different aspects, or at different times.

Curvilinear Any object bounded by curved lines; seen regularly in works of the Art Nouveau period.

Decorative arts Any of the applied arts, such as fabrics, furniture, ceramics, etc., decorated in an aesthetic way and thus pleasing to the eye as well as being functional.

Delftware TIN-GLAZED POTTERY developed in the Netherlands and Britain.

Earthenware Clay made into objects and fired at about 2,190°F(1,200°C); the simplest form of ceramics.

Embroidery A method of stitching threads directly onto fabrics as a form of decoration.

Enamel Colored, powdered glass fired onto a metal surface.

Engraving A method of carving a design with finely pointed tools onto hard surfaces such as metal and wood.

Faience TIN-GLAZED POTTERY made in France, although name is believed to have come from Faenza, Italy.

Functionalism In its purest sense, it was a movement that began in the mid-1700s as a reaction against ornate decoration for decoration's sake.

Futurism A form of art originating in Italy in the early 1900s, dominated by instinctive reactions to a modern world, such as experience of conflict, change, and speed.

Glaze A hard, shiny, transparent coating applied to POTTERY.

Gothic A style of architecture, seen as early as *c.* 1140, characterized mainly by geometric TRACERY, ribbed constructions, and pointed arches. It declined with the dawning of the Renaissance, but underwent a revival—in buildings, furniture, STAINED GLASS, and gardens in particular—from the early 1700s onward.

Hard-paste porcelain Often known as "true" PORCELAIN and made from easily melted china stone and white china clay. China stone melts at around 2,460°F(1,350°C), and on cooling fuses together the disseminated china-clay particles. China stone, together with a flowing agent such as potash or lime, is used for GLAZING.

Jet A rich black variety of lignite, taking a high polish and capable of being carved. Much used for creating ornaments and jewelry.

Lacquer A waterproof varnish obtained from an oriental tree sap, or the boiled secretions of the lac insect.

Latticino decoration A technique used by Venetian glassmakers (*c.* 1500), consisting of opaque white glass threads set in clear or colored glass and which can be twisted and spiraled to form ornate patterns.

Majolica TIN-GLAZED POTTERY made mainly in Italy.

Marquetry A way of decorating the surfaces of furniture, or objects such as boxes, by applying patterns made from colored VENEERS or exotic and expensive materials such as tortoiseshell, ivory, and precious metals.

Modernism A name encompassing much of the art and architecture of the 1900s that seemed to be "ahead of its time."

Motif A well-defined, obvious, and divisible element in the arrangement of a painting, sculpture, or architectural design of a building.

Papier-mâché Paper soaked with water, to which glue and sometimes sand is added to make a pulp capable of being molded and fired. Usually painted or lacquered to make decorative items.

Parcel-gilt A method of partially gilding gold onto a work of art as a form of decoration. It was also used on objects made from wood.

Plating A term used in metalwork to describe the coating of a cheap metal with a more precious kind, such as gold or silver, for "pecuniary" decorative ornamentation.

Porcelain A translucent, hard type of chinaware made from kaolin and silica, originating in China *c.* 600s.

Pottery A term usually used to describe EARTHENWARE and STONEWARE.

Reliquary A receptacle for relics. Most often for the keeping of ecclesiastical relics—bones or personal items of famous religious persons.

Rococo A lighter, less symmetrical version of the BAROQUE style, making great use of water MOTIFS such as shells and water nymphs and flowery decoration on chinaware, along with asymmetrical scrolls on furniture and paneling.

Romanesque A term used to describe pre-Gothic European art *c.* 700s–1100s In sculpture and painting, forms were linear and displayed emotion and religious fervor excessively .

Rose window A round window with TRACERY of radiating compartments.

Silver gilt Refers to the gilding of silver onto parts or all of an object, often made of another metal, in order to prevent tarnishing.

Soft-paste porcelain Glass is substituted for the china stone that is usually used and can be fired at a lower temperature. The GLAZING material also contains some form of glass.

Stained glass Glass painted with certain pigments fused into its surface.

Stoneware Clay objects fired at a temperature of approximately 2,280°F (1,250°C); hotter than that of EARTHENWARE firing.

Symbolist Any work of art, including literature, that displays or includes one or more symbols to suggest subjective reality.

Tapestry A textile whereby a pattern or picture is formed by weaving colored threads onto a base material. Sometimes a cartoon, or template, is placed beneath the material as a guide, or the design is outlined directly onto the base material to be followed.

Textiles Woven fabrics; fibers, yarns, etc. suitable for weaving into fabrics.

Tin-glazed pottery Early clay EARTHENWARE on which a tin oxide GLAZE produced a suitable surface for decorating.

Tracery Elaborate stonework patterns that ornament walls or are used to fill windows.

Veneers Thin slices of often rare—therefore expensive and precious—woods applied to more widely obtainable and cheaper woods for decorative purposes.

Timeline

1822 Joseph Niépce produces a photograph on metal, said to be world's first.

1829 Louis Daguerre invents photographs using silver salts—daguerreotypes *(right)*.

1839 Daguerre given an annuity by French government and his process made public. Fox Talbot announces his invention of making prints on silver chloride paper.

1840 Viennese mathematician Joseph Petzval invents a portrait lens, reducing exposure time by 90 percent. John Frederick William Herschel discovers sodium thiosulfate as a fixer for silver halides.

1841 Fox Talbot *(right)* patents the calotype (the first process for photographic negatives from which prints could be made).

1843 Robert Adamson and David Hill pioneer Fox Talbot's calotype process for a commission to portray founders of Scottish Free Church.

1844 First book illustrated with photographs: Fox Talbot's *Pencil of Nature*.

1850 Mathew Brady's *The Gallery of Illustrious Americans* published.

1851 Fox Talbot demonstrates high-speed photography. Invention of the wet collodion on glass process. Photographs displayed at the Great Exhibition in London.

1852 The London Society of Arts exhibits 779 photographs.

1855 Roger Fenton goes to the Crimea as the world's first accredited war photographer *(right)*, using special caravan with portable darkroom.

1856–59 Francis Frith produces first traveler's record in photographs seen in Britain based on his travels in Egypt and Near East.

1858 Nadar *(right)* takes first photographs from a balloon.

1860 J. J. E. Mayall photographs Queen Victoria. Mathew Brady takes political campaign photographs of Abraham Lincoln.

1861 Nadar takes underground photographs in Paris using battery-powered arc lights. Thomas Sutton patents the single-lens reflex camera. Physicist James Clerk Maxwell demonstrates the principles of three-color photography.

1865 Mathew Brady and his team photograph the Civil War, capturing its grim horrors *(p. 563)*.

1869 Louis Duclos du Hauron outlines principles of additive and subtractive color separation in *Les Couleurs en Photographie*.

1870 Julia Margaret Cameron *(right above)* uses long lenses for her portraits and experiments with special effects.

1871 Richard Maddox invents the dry photographic plate.

1878 Louis Duclos du Hauron patents new practical photographic methods outlined in *Photographie en Couleur*.

VICTORIAN PORTRAIT PHOTOGRAPHERS

Alice Liddell photographed by Julia Margaret Cameron.

The announcement in 1839 by Louis Daguerre of his photographic method created a sensation, and viewers flocked to his exhibition in Paris. Portrait studios sprang up using daguerreotypes, one-off positives on metal. In the 1840s, these were replaced by Fox Talbot's calotypes, with their high contrasts, sharp definition, and paper negatives.

Gaspard Félix Tournachon, nicknamed Nadar, initially used photography to provide resource material for his work as a caricaturist, but the quality of his work soon attracted the gifted and famous to his Parisian studio. He allowed the qualities of his subjects to speak for themselves, and his portraits of artists and intellectuals have an open, relaxed look.

Julia Margaret Cameron took up photography in 1863 and became an ardent champion of photography as an art form. She immortalized many Victorian celebrities, including Charles Darwin and Alfred Tennyson. Inventive in her handling of lighting, she used blur and soft focus to create bold and beautiful effects.

Photo by Nadar of the French painter and book illustrator Gustave Doré.

EADWEARD MUYBRIDGE

Born in England in 1830, Eadweard Muybridge lived most of his life in California, where he made his initial reputation as a landscape photographer. His interest in movement began when Leland Stanford, a railroad magnate and horse breeder, laid a $25,000 bet that at a certain stage of a horse's full trot, all four legs leave the ground simultaneously. Muybridge took up the challenge and, with Stanford's sponsorship, produced a sequence of pictures proving the claim.

Muybridge's method was ingenious. On one side of a racetrack he hung a white backdrop and along the other he placed a row of cameras at regular intervals. Threads laid across the horse's path, when broken by its run, released the spring shutters of the cameras one by one. Shots two and three clearly reveal all four legs off the ground. The sequence also proved to the art world that the "rocking horse gallop," the traditional artistic depiction of a running horse, was an illusion. As the series shows, all four legs move independently, not in pairs.

Using the slow wet plates of the time for such fast motion shots had proved difficult. The advent of the more sensitive dry plates widened Muybridge's scope, and he embarked on a huge series of movement studies involving other animals and humans, often using several batteries of cameras. These sequences were later collected into large and expensive volumes. Some were also made into slides and projected onto a screen through a zoopraxiscope. This device (patented by Muybridge) flashed images in quick succession, creating the illusion of continuous movement—all before the film projector had been conceived of.

Though not strictly speaking the founder of cinema, Muybridge nevertheless paved the way for the invention of the single, motor-driven film camera.

Galloping horse by Eadweard Muybridge.

WAR PHOTOGRAPHY

Death of a soldier in the Civil War photographed by Mathew Brady.

The earliest combat photographer was Roger Fenton, who went to the Crimea in 1855 as a representative of the British government. Although he was equipped with a special photographic wagon, he was still hampered by the slow photographic processes of the time. His sanitized shots are mostly of quiet arsenals and serene encampments, with none of the action and blood of warfare.

Mathew Brady, along with a team of 20 photographers, shot comprehensive coverage of the Civil War in the 1860s. As with Fenton's photography, there are few action shots but many fascinating studies of battlefields, finishing units, and the aftermath of war, notably by Alexander Gardner (1821–82). These pictures were the first to capture the grim realities of war.

Troops landing in Normandy by Capa.

Miniature cameras revolutionized the whole concept of war photography. The legendary Robert Capa was typical of the modern photojournalist who penetrates with his lightweight equipment as close to the action as a frontline soldier. His famous motto was: "If your pictures aren't good enough, you aren't close enough." Capa brought back memorable pictures of the Spanish Civil War in the 1930s, and waded onto the Normandy beaches with the Allies during World War II, producing a handful of blurred, gritty images of momentous historical impact. He was killed by a land mine a decade later, after having covered several other international combat zones.

Margaret Bourke-White was the first woman to become an official photographer for the U.S. military forces. She covered World War II for *Life* magazine and produced a series of photographs on the siege of Moscow in 1941; she also covered the momentous opening of the concentration camps in Germany in 1945.

Southeast Asia has been one of the most troubled war zones of this century. Bert Hardy, an extremely versatile reportage photographer, returned from the Korean War in 1950 with a series of powerful images of the conflict which *Picture Post*, his employer, felt were too shocking to print. Hardy resigned his job in disgust.

The Vietcong, by Don McCullin.

In the 1960s, U.S. military involvement in Vietnam attracted many photographers, of whom Larry Burrows, Philip Jones Griffiths, and Don McCullin produced outstanding work. Burrows broke new ground by shooting in color. McCullin is the successor of Robert Capa. For 20 years, from 1964, he worked in virtually all the major areas of conflict in the world and returned with eloquent records of the chaos and misery of war.

The spate of uncensored news photos from Vietnam played a large part in altering the attitudes of the American public to the war and set off the protest movement against it. Since then, to the disgust of McCullin himself, only "official" war photographers are likely to be sanctioned: his own application to cover Britain's invasion of the Falklands in the 1980s was summarily rejected.

Timeline

1879 Invention of photogravure process.

1880 Eadweard Muybridge *(p. 562)* invents the zoopraxiscope to show picture sequences, achieving a kind of cinematography. In New York City, first production of photographs in newspapers using the halftone engraving process. Silver bromide emulsion used.

1882 Etienne-Jules Marey invents a camera to take a series of photographs in a second, bringing the advent of the motion picture nearer.

1884 George Eastman invents roll-film.

1887 Eadweard Muybridge's *Animal Locomotion*, studies in photographic motion.

1888 Eastman patents film emulsion set on a transparent celluloid base and produces the Kodak box camera, opening the door to amateur photography.

1889 Jacob August Riis's *How the Other Half Lives*, a photographic study of New York City slum life *(p. 564)*.

1891 First telephoto lens. French doctor Gabriel Lippmann develops interference process of color photography.

1892 Photography popularized by the formation of the Eastman Kodak Co. Founding of The Linked Ring, a British association of photographers seeking artistic creation (which develops into the international Photo-Secession); founder members included Henry Peach Robinson.

1896 Paul Martin's *London by Gaslight*, late-Victorian daily life shot with disguised camera.

1897 Invention of gum-bichromate (or photo-aquatint) process, enabling photographers to alter print image.

1900 George Eastman produces the inexpensive Kodak Brownie camera; also daylight film, loaded in normal light.

1902 American Alfred Stieglitz founds the Photo-Secession group, supporting pictorialism (soft-focus effects in painterly compositions). In Germany, Deckel invents a prototype leaf shutter; Zeiss introduces Tessar lens.

1903 First issue of Stieglitz's *Camera Work*, a 50-part journal.

1904 First telegraphic transmission of photographs from Munich to Nuremberg. Lumière brothers patent autochrome color process.

1905 Stieglitz opens Gallery 291 in New York City to promote photography. Lewis Hine uses photography to expose exploitation of child labor *(p.564)*.

1907 Autochrome color process beginning to be factory produced.

1914 Oskar Barnack designs prototype Leica camera for Leitz.

1920 Charles Sheeler's *Mannahatta*: photographs of skyscrapers.

1922 Man Ray experiments with the photogram (which he called the rayograph), a black-and-white image made by placing objects on sensitized photographic paper (without using a camera).

Timeline

1923 László Moholy-Nagy teaches photography at the Bauhaus *(p. 559)*.

1924 Leitz launches the first 35mm camera, the Leica. Start of European New Objectivity movement; Moholy-Nagy is a leading member.

1929 Rolleiflex produces a twin-lens reflex camera. German photographer August Sander publishes *Faces of Our Times*, planned as first part of massive photographic documentary study of people in the 1900s; sequels barred by Nazi Ministry of Culture.

1930 Ansel Adams's *Taos Pueblo*. Electronic flash invented in U.S.A.

1930–31 Lewis Hine photographs construction of the Empire State Building.

1931 Margaret Bourke-White's *Eyes on Russia*. Spicer-Dufay develops process of natural color photography.

1932 Ansel Adams, Edward Weston, and others found the F64 Group, advocating precise definition in photographs (as a reaction against pictorialism).

1935 Kodachrome transparency film introduced. Walker Evans *(right)* becomes photographer for U.S. Farm Security Administration, documenting farm life in the Depression *(p. 363)*.

1936 *Life* magazine, significant for its photojournalism, published in U.S.A. Bill Brandt's *The English at Home*.

1938 *Picture Post* magazine introduced in Britain. Bill Brandt's *A Night in London*. Walker Evans's *American Photographs*.

1939 Sir Cecil Beaton's *My Royal Past*. Dorothea Lange's *An American Exodus: A Record of Human Erosion*. Berenice Abbott's *Changing New York*.

1940 Ansel Adams establishes photography department of the California School of Fine Arts.

1941 Arthur Rothstein founds American Society of Magazine Photographers. *Life* magazine features Yousuf Karsh's portrait of Winston Churchill.

1942 Kodacolor negative film is introduced. First Pulitzer Prize awarded for spot news photography.

1944 Adams's *Born Free and Equal*.

1945 Adams's *Exposure Record* publishes the zone system of exposure estimation.

1946 Margaret Bourke-White's *Halfway to Freedom*.

1947 Dr. Edwin Land invents the Polaroid Land camera, developing an "instant" photograph in one minute. In England, Dennis Gabor demonstrates the principles of holography. Henri Cartier-Bresson *(right)* holds one-person show at New York's Museum of Modern Art.

1950 Robert Doisneau produces his image *The Kiss* at the Hotel de Ville for *Life* magazine.

1952 Cartier-Bresson's *The Decisive Moment*.

1954 Lennart Nilsson's *Sweden in Profiles*, a collection of portraits. Sir Cecil Beaton's *The Glass of Fashion*.

SOCIAL DOCUMENTARY

Lewis Hine's photograph of young boys working in a Georgia cotton mill.

Providing an authentic record of a scene or event is a unique talent of photography. As early as 1870, John Thomson was pointing his camera at the sights in London's poor areas. In 1889, Jacob Riis, using a detective camera and crude flash equipment, recorded scenes of such squalor and degradation in the slums of New York City that laws were changed. The sociologist Lewis Hine also used photography to bring about social change; among his many indictments of social injustices were shots of Italian immigrant families arriving, bewildered and frightened, off the boats from Ellis Island. His records of children working in mills and factories, like Riis's slum pictures, helped change child labor laws.

Peter Henry Emerson was one of the first photographers to document a community and its way of life *(1889)*. Even in the Victorian era, traditional occupations such as reed gathering were dying out. Emerson's photographs seem romantic today, but they opened up the field for later documentary photographers. At the

Man jumping over a puddle, by Henri Cartier-Bresson.

turn of the century, the American Edward S. Curtis embarked on a 30-year project documenting the Native American tribes of the United States and Canada. He was horrified by the wholesale slaughter of many of these peoples by European settlers and the disintegration of a rich and ancient spiritual culture. His somber, formal studies of chieftains, settlements, and ceremonies form an elegy to a dying race.

Part of Franklin D. Roosevelt's "New Deal" in 1935 was a government-sponsored initiative to investigate rural poverty. Teams of photographers were sent to depressed areas to document the plight of farmers evicted from their smallholdings. One photographer was Walker Evans, whose spare, cool style is especially eloquent in his shots of neighborhoods in shambles with makeshift shacks. Another was Dorothea Lange, whose compassionate pictures of migrant families in overloaded jalopies take on an epic dignity. And in Eastern Europe, in a committed defiance of the Nazis, the Russian Jew Roman Vishniac made poignant undercover records of ghetto life in Warsaw and other locations.

The art of photojournalism in the 1930s owed its rise to the 35mm camera and the development of the picture magazine. The best-known photojournalist was Henri Cartier-Bresson, who trained as a painter and brought to his subjects a sense of compositional balance and intuition for what he termed the "decisive moment." His most celebrated pictures are ironic comments on human comedy.

Focusing a lens on the ills of society can be a lonely and dangerous activity. Eugene Smith, a respected photographer for *Life*, shot a story on a Japanese fishing village threatened by mercury poisoning, but his harrowing photos nearly cost him his life. The Brazilian Sebastio Selgado is committed to capturing manual work in raw production, particularly in the developing world. He takes the viewer close to often lethal working conditions.

MAN RAY

Born in the United States in 1890, Man Ray (real name Emanuel Rudnitsky) moved to Paris in 1921 and remained there the rest of his life. Initially, he was associated with the Dada artists (*p. 541*), and he made an impact with his first exhibition, which displayed his paintings alongside photographs. He regarded himself as primarily a painter, but the possibilities for photography fascinated him and he experimented boldly.

Photograms (prints produced by laying solid or transparent objects on light-sensitive paper) were not his invention, but his rayographs, as he called them, are refined examples of the technique. Likewise, solarization, a method of surrounding an image with a dark outline by deliberately fogging the film, was not his discovery, but he made it a hallmark of his style. Photography was also his living, and his portraits were much in demand. Picasso, Joyce, and other artists and writers posed for him, and he was often commissioned to photograph artists' works.

His photographs of women were witty and daring. *Le Violion d'Ingres*, which features Kiki de Montparnasse, a famous cabaret singer of the time, parodies a famous painting by Ingres. The addition of violin holes painted on the print, together with the violin of the title, neatly emphasize her body's curves, suggesting sexual allure. Man Ray was closely involved with the Surrealist movement;

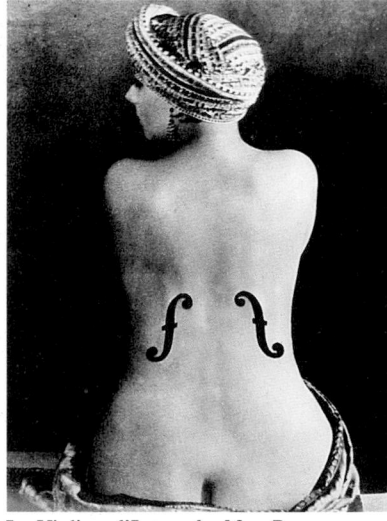

Le Violion d'Ingres *by Man Ray.*

many of his photographs are reminiscent of Surrealist paintings, not only in their sometimes bizarre subjects but also in their teasing sense of mystery. Literalness is often an asset in photography, but Man Ray subverted it to create his own visual world. Nothing is as it seems; fantasy and reality are intertwined and ambiguity remains unresolved. "The streets are full of admirable craftsmen," he once said, "but so few practical dreamers."

THE FUTURE OF PHOTOGRAPHY

New technology is constantly changing the face of photography. The principle of holography, a method of recording three-dimensional (3-D) images, was first suggested in the 1940s, but a pure light source was needed for its application. With the invention of the laser beam in 1960, it became possible to produce a 3-D picture called a hologram. The technique splits a laser beam in two; each beam contains information about the subject which is reconstructed to form an image. Reflection holograms produce an image when ordinary light is passed through them and are used widely as a

fraud deterrent, as on credit cards. Other holograms show scrambled patterns in ordinary light and a synthesized image only when a laser light is projected through them. As well as artistic applications, holography can be used in police work to detect forged documents and paintings, and in architecture to detect structural strain in buildings.

Computer technology has made it possible to manipulate and produce images in dramatic new ways. A photograph can be transferred to digital form using a scanner, a machine that copies visual information and translates it into pixels (single units that make up an image on a computer screen). Photographs can be stored directly onto a computer disk, or film stored on a PhotoCD (compact disc), which can be read by computer.

Once the photograph has been translated into pixels, it can be manipulated in many ways using computer software. Color and resolution can be changed in any or all parts of the photo-image, and special effects that mimic lens filters can be used as postproduction tools in endless permutations. An image may be resized, cropped, or retouched, and can be mixed with artwork and text to create a montage. It can then be printed or used with multimedia software.

Computer image made up of pixels.

Timeline

1955 Kodak introduces Tri-X, a black-and-white 200 ASA film. Henri Cartier-Bresson's *The Europeans*.

1959 German firm Voigtlander invents the zoom lens.

1960 The laser is invented in the U.S.A., making holography (3-D photography) possible. Polaroid introduces Polacolor, a self-processing color film.

1961 Bill Brandt's *Perspective of Nudes*, his most influential photographic collection.

1962 Ernst Haas holds the first one-person show of color photographs. The color Polaroid camera is introduced.

1963 Cibachrome, paper and chemicals for printing directly from transparencies, is made available by Ciba-Geigy.

1964 André Kertész's photographs win belated recognition at a retrospective at the Museum of Modern Art in New York City.

1966 The International Center of Photography opens in New York City. Walker Evans's *Many Are Called*; Bill Brandt's *Shadows of Light*.

1967 *Ett Barn Blir Till* (The Everyday Miracle: A Child is Born), Lennart Nilsson's pioneering film of the human fetus from conception to birth, using special lenses to film inside the body.

1968 First Pulitzer Prize awarded for feature photography.

1969 Photographs taken on the moon by U.S. astronauts (*p. 31*).

1970 Bell Laboratories invents a charge-coupled device to record very faint images (e.g. in astronomy). Diane Arbus's *A Box of Ten Photographs*.

1971 Opening of the Photographers' Gallery, London, and the Photo Archive of the Bibliothéque Nationale, Paris.

1972 Polaroid produces the SX70 system, a single-lens reflex camera with instant prints.

1975 Center for Creative Photography established at University of Arizona. Sir Cecil Beaton's *The Magic Image*.

1980 Ansel Adams sells an original print, *Moonrise: Hernandez*, for $45,000, a record price. Voyager I sends photographs of Saturn back to Earth.

1983 The National Museum of Photography, Film and Television opens in Bradford, England.

1985 The Minolta 7000, the first body-integral autofocus single-lens reflex camera, is introduced.

1988 The electronic camera, storing pictures on magnetic disk instead of film, introduced in Japan.

1990 Kodak introduces PhotoCD to convert 35mm camera pictures (on film) into digital form and store them on compact disc (CD) for viewing on television.

1992 Canon introduces a camera with autofocus controlled by the user's eye.

1993 Man Ray's *Glass Tears*, sold for £122,500 (about $80,000), becomes world's most famous photograph.

Timeline

1845 English costumier Charles Frederick Worth moves to Paris, where his establishment in the Rue de la Paix becomes the center of the fashion world. Worth transforms the role of couturier from tradesperson to aristocrat of taste.

1849 Amelia Bloomer attempts women's dress reform in the U.S.A. with her corsetless "bloomer" outfit.

1904 Paul Poiret *(right)* sets up his Paris fashion house, which becomes a major influence, using fine artists like Raoul Dufy and Sonia Delaunay to give his designs a high profile.

1905 In Paris, Paul Poiret introduces his distinctive loose coats, leading to more fluid day and evening wear.

1908 The "Merry Widow": a large-brimmed hat with lavish trims.

1909 Paris fashion adopts an oriental look (turbans, harem pants) inspired by the stage success of the Ballets Russes. *(p. 524)*

1911 Poiret launches the hobble skirt.

1912 Coco Chanel *(right, below)* opens her first shop in Deauville, France.

1914 Ankles shown for the first time with shorter, "peg-top" skirts.

1915 Cristóbal Balenciaga opens his first dressmaking and tailoring shops in Madrid and Barcelona.

1918 Easy-fitting chemise dress is popularized by Coco Chanel and others.

1922 In Paris, straight-line dresses with no bust and dropped waistline. Norman Hartnell starts his couturier business.

1923 Parisian fashion includes the "cloche" hat.

1925 Cosmetics worn freely by women. "Oxford bags"—wide, flapping trousers —worn by men.

1926 Skirt hems reach a record height, just above the knee.

1927 Coco Chanel's casual daytime look.

1928 Elsa Schiaparelli opens her fashion house in Paris: her imaginative knitwear and "sports" clothes are a hit.

1929 The bias-cut dresses of Vionnet become popular.

1932 Nina Ricci opens her salon.

1934 Alix (Madame Grés) opens her Paris fashion house: immediate success with clinging evening dresses.

1935 Christian Dior creates his first fashion sketches. The padded, built-up shoulder begins to be emphasized. First slacks and shorts worn by women.

1937 Cristóbal Balenciaga moves his dressmaking business to Paris because of the Spanish Civil War: collection of neo-Victorian dresses with rounded bust and shaped waist.

1938 Elsa Schiaparelli's colorful Circus Parade collection.

1939 Platform and wedge-heeled shoes come into vogue.

1945 In the U.S.A., jeans with oversized "sloppy Joe" sweaters are worn by teenage girls and boys. Pierre Balmain opens his French fashion house. Hardy

CHANGING SHAPES

Standards of beauty throughout the world vary enormously. In the West, the fashion for a particular female body shape reflects constantly shifting social climates, which may be seen as focusing popular attention on different erogenous zones.

The "S-bend" corset, worn during the early 1900s before the enfranchisement of women, was a crippling, tightlaced garment which threw the bust forward and made the waist tiny. Desmond Morris, in his book *Bodywatching*, describes how this style embodied an unspoken "bondage" factor—the fragile flesh of the woman trapped in a rigid, curve-defining case. Paul Poiret claimed to have set women free from this confining corset in 1908: his new dress designs fell loosely over the natural figure.

By the 1920s, it had become fashionable for women to look like young boys. Dresses showed straight silhouettes with low waists and no curves. A softer, more fluid line was introduced in the 1930s. The back was appreciated as an erogenous zone, and many evening gowns had backs cut away almost to the buttocks.

Like the patriarchal Victorian era, the postwar 1950s saw the hips and breasts (as fertility symbols) emphasized. Tight bodices allowed the breasts high definition above pinched waists and wide crinoline skirts. The virginal "little girl" of the 1960s followed; her short, shapeless A-line dress eroticized legs.

With more women entering the work force in the 1980s, the accent was on a fitter model of femininity. The use of clinging fabrics like Lycra defined the well-toned body, and muscle became sexy.

A Paul Poiret design of 1913 (below) *shows the fluid lines that freed women from the crippling "S-bend" corset* (above).

COCO CHANEL

Coco Chanel in 1929 wearing one of her own designs—a casual suit made of knit fabric.

Since the mid-1800s, France has led the fashion industry with its haute couture. Coco Chanel, the most prolific of the French couturiers, was a key figure in shaping the modern woman's wardrobe. Born in France in 1883, she was to become one of the top fashion designers of the 1900s. By 1914, she had opened two shops in France which sold hats, blouses, and her simple chemise dress—a single, loose garment designed to be worn without corsets, tied at the waist or hips. Chanel virtually invented sportswear in the 1920s and 1930s by adapting men's designs into comfortable, casual clothes for women. She popularized her creations by wearing them herself, including the cardigan, knit twin sets, sweaters, and yachting pants. The "little black dress," based on the simple lines of the chemise, became an essential wardrobe item. Her line of accessories included bags, belts, scarves, and costume jewelry, and she engaged the help of perfumer Ernest Beaux to create the classic Chanel No. 5. In 1954, at the age of 71, she came out of retirement to create perhaps her most enduring design—the Chanel suit. Simple and beautiful, it is still worn by women the world over.

FASHIONS OF THE 1960s

Fashion began to focus on teenagers for the first time in the early 1960s, and London became the center of a music and fashion explosion. The young designer Mary Quant created bold, colorful, and low-priced clothes that were a huge success. She popularized the miniskirt, which reached an unprecedented 8–9 inches (20–23 cm) above the knee, and her playful designs were in perfect tune with the spirit of the time.

In Paris, André Courrèges launched his "Space Age" look of 1964—stark, futuristic, all-white outfits worn with his much-imitated white kid boots. Paco Rabanne experimented with clothes made from unusual materials, including crinkled paper, metal disks, and chains instead of fabric, and Yves Saint Laurent designed the daring see-through blouse in 1968.

The Beatles (p. 527) popularized Pierre Cardin's suit of 1963, with its collarless jacket and straight-leg trousers. Their psychedelic look parodied military uniforms in bright, primary colors, mixed with tie-dyed garments or Indian tunics and trousers. African designs in vivid prints were adopted by musicians like Sly and the Family Stone, and the natural, bushy Afro hairstyle became popular.

The San Francisco hippie scene at the end of the decade was a fashion blend of flavors: ethnic, historic, psychedelic, and

Rounded collars and striped trousers, shown in this 1967 suit, were popular in the 1960s.

even beatnik styles were interchangeable, usually worn with jangling jewelry and long hair. Elsewhere, the decade ended with a soft, "romantic" look, featuring flower-print cotton and crushed velvet.

Hippies at a 1969 music festival in London wearing elements of ethnic dress styles.

RECYCLED FASHION

In the late 1980s, designer fashions were eclipsed by a more individual, "do-it-yourself" look. Many people purchased clothes from secondhand shops, not only to economize but also to recycle existing fabrics as an ecological statement. Martin Margiela and Comme des Garçons reflected this trend with their "deconstruction" designs—clothes turned inside out with their seams showing, sometimes ripped and torn, and new garments made from recycled clothing. The "grunge" look of the 1990s is an assembly of re-used styles from the past, including 1970s fashions and elements of men's clothing.

"Grunge" style—a hippie skirt and platform shoes worn with a man's army coat.

Timeline

Amies founds his fashion house.

1947 Christian Dior founds his Paris salon: his "New Look" with tight bodice, clinched waist, and long, flowing skirt is an overnight sensation.

1948 Royal College of Art, London, founds a fashion design course.

1949 Elsa Schiaparelli opens her New York City salon.

1950 Emilio Pucci opens his couture house. Dior, Balenciaga, Fath, and Balmain lead the fashion world. Clothes are very constructed and sculptured, emphasizing large breasts and a small waist.

1951 Hubert de Givenchy opens his own salon.

1953 Laura and Bernard Ashley begin manufacturing furnishing materials and wallpapers. Pierre Cardin opens his fashion house in Paris. Christian Dior's "sheath" dress.

1954 Coco Chanel, who had retired in 1939, stages a comeback and promotes her classic style, including the Chanel suit. Elsa Schiaparelli closes her couture business.

1955 Mary Quant opens her first Bazaar boutique in Chelsea, London. Christian Dior invents the "A-line" skirt. Hardy Amies receives royal warrant as dressmaker to Queen Elizabeth II.

1957 Fashion designers favor capes, bulbous, enveloping coats, and "the sack." For casual wear, tapered trousers are worn with colorful Italian silk blouses.

1958 Yves Saint Laurent designs the 1958 Dior collection after Christian Dior's death.

1959 The balloon look becomes popular, including puffball skirts.

1960 "Swinging London" is set to become the world's fashion center. Saint Laurent's "Beat" collection: leather suits and plenty of black.

1961 André Courrèges opens his fashion house.

1962 Yves Saint Laurent launches his own couture house and designs the pea jacket. The Chanel suit and pillbox hat are worn and popularized by Jackie Kennedy. Hardy Amies begins designing men's fashion.

1963 Mary Quant (left) sets up her Ginger Group to market her designs.

1964 André Courrèges introduces the miniskirt. American designer Rudi Gernreich proposes first topless swimsuit.

1965 Courrèges's show of "Clothes of the Future": stark, all-white ensembles. Ossie Clark's "Op Art" designs.

1966 Yves Saint Laurent opens his first Rive Gauche boutique and makes first dresses on "Pop Art" themes.

1967 Ralph Lauren joins Beau Brummel Neckwear and creates the Polo fashion range for men (left, above), later including womenswear. Paco Rabanne decrees "My swimsuits are not for bathing. My dresses are not for sitting in."

Timeline

1968 Laura and Bernard Ashley establish the firm of Laura Ashley, Ltd., with a London store selling interior design products. Calvin Klein sets up his own firm. Martin Margiela's first fashion collection. Ungaro launches his Ungaro Parallele ready-to-wear range. Zandra Rhodes begins to design professionally. Saint Laurent's see-through black chiffon evening dress with ostrich feathers.

1969 "Funky Chic movement" inspired by hippie subculture.

1970 Takada Kenzo opens his shop Jungle Jap to sell his trendsetting clothes.

1971 Issey Miyake's first fashion collection is shown in New York City and in Tokyo.

1972 Giorgio Armani's first menswear collection. The "G-string" becomes fashionable on Saint Tropez beaches.

1975 Giorgio Armani begins to design women's fashion.

1976 In the U.S.A., easy-to-wear clothes: "the effortless look." In Britain, Vivienne Westwood, Miss Mouse, and Zandra Rhodes create the punk look.

1977 Claude Montana's first fashion collection.

1978 American designer Norma Kamali opens OMO shop. British Jasper Conran's first fashion collection.

1979 Paris designer Thierry Mugler's sequinned, skintight body suit with pointed fins hits the news.

1980s The decade of "power dressing" begins. More women in the work force means stylish business suits, usually with big, padded shoulders. Designer labels often displayed on the outside of clothes as status symbols.

1982 Norma Kamali introduces The Package, all-white clothes made from disposable material.

1984 Rifat Ozbek's first fashion collection in London. Karl Lagerfeld's first fashion collection under his own label.

1987 Christian Lacroix opens his Paris fashion house.

1990 Lingerie as outerwear comes into vogue, made popular to a large degree by pop star Madonna.

1991 Jean Muir launches knitwear collection. Return to natural fabrics and natural/synthetic blends.

1992 "Grunge" style enters mainstream fashion: layered bodies and lumberjack shirts with ethnic skirts and heavy, laced boots; 1970s revival style. Helen Storey's "Second Life" collection, featuring recycled clothing.

1993 Crushed velvets, suedes, and chiffons are used for daytime as well as evening garments.

1994 The "gym-slip" and A-line dresses are worn over cap-sleeved T-shirts. Eco-friendly materials like cotton, grown and colored using natural methods, usher in the trend for clothes in all shades of cream and beige.

SIGNIFICANCE OF COLOR

No element of clothing says more about its wearer than color. Choice of color not only reflects the mood of the wearer; it can also affect his or her influence on other people. Psychologists have recognized that each hue has a different effect on human physiology—although the traditional meaning of each color varies from culture to culture. Red, the color of vitality, passion, and aggression, increases the heartbeat, blood pressure, and breathing. In the West, red clothing can denote anger or desire and is usually a sign that the wearer is "ready for action."

Blue tends to have a calming effect on blood pressure and heartbeat and has been used for work clothes for centuries. Blue jeans, which have become almost a uniform for leisure wear, have made blue the most typical color for clothes in the United States. Yellow denotes mental energy, hope, and cheerfulness. Adults wearing yellow and gold shades are likely to be optimistic and extroverted.

Black and white are perhaps the colors

An outfit by Kenzo features bold, extrovert colors: active red and energizing yellow.

Denim blue has become the most common color of clothing for casual wear.

that vary most in significance between cultures. Black can signify death, as in traditional Western mourning clothes, but can also represent sophistication, mystery, and danger. Many people choose black clothing for evening occasions for a look of simple chic. Used for weddings and christenings (and in some societies for mourning), white represents purity and innocence and suggests new beginnings. The secondary colors of purple, orange, and green are less common in clothes and are thought to indicate artistic tendencies if worn frequently.

STREET STYLE

Street style is an alternative way of dressing developed by an individual or a group as a symbol of rebellion or social protest. Often advocated by artists and intellectuals, it can be strongly innovative or merely eccentric.

Parisian postwar bohemians, intellectuals, and beatniks set out to shock by wearing entirely black costumes, including the essential black turtleneck. Because it can exude an air of mystery and danger, black is still a key element of many street styles—from motorcycle gangs with black leather jackets and trousers to Goths with all-black outfits, black-dyed hair, and stark black-and-white makeup.

British punks of the 1970s represent perhaps the most extreme example of street style. In contrast to their hippie predecessors who wore playful clothes and advocated peace and love, punks personified the violence and ugliness they saw in a world of social decay and unemployment. Their black, white, and blood-red outfits were often ripped and smudged, and faces and bodies were pierced with safety pins. Hair was dyed bright,

A group of punks wearing "violated" clothes, London, 1983.

unnatural colors and often glued into threatening spikes; chains and bondage gear were worn as a symbol of protest.

Instead of dictating from the catwalk, some designers in the 1990s have begun to copy the new, emerging street styles, many associated with music trends like hip-hop and rave. Even sadomasochistic fetish wear can be found in the couturier's portfolio, and nothing is thought too outrageous for mainstream fashion.

PROMINENT PEOPLE

ABBOT, Berenice (1898–91) U.S. photographer. Documented New York City.

ADAMS, Ansel (Easton) (1902–84) U.S. photographer. Specialized in capturing the broad landscapes of western U.S.A.

ANSCHÜTZ, Ottomar (1846–1907) German photographer. Pioneer of instantaneous photography.

ARBUS, Diane (1923–71) U.S. photographer. Ironic studies of social poses and deprived classes.

ARMANI, Giorgio (b. 1935) Italian fashion designer. Creator of men's and women's clothes characterized by casual elegance.

ASHLEY, Laura (1925–85) British designer. Introduced "cottage style" interior design products and women's clothing.

ATGET, Eugène (1856–1927) French photographer. Documented urban Paris.

AVEDON, Richard (b. 1923) U.S. photographer. Fashion shots and portraits.

BAILEY, David (b. 1938) British fashion photographer. Portraits expressing the spirit of the 1960s.

BALENCIAGA, Cristóbal (1895–1972) Spanish dressmaker and tailor. Designs of dramatic simplicity and elegance.

BALMAIN, Pierre Alexandre (1914–82) French fashion designer. Noted for his elegant simplicity; also stage costumes.

BEATON, Sir Cecil (Walter Hardy) (1904–80) British photographer. Society and fashion portraits.

BLASS, Bill (b. 1922) U.S. Fashion designer. Noted for his championing of U.S. designers as an alternative to the Milan and Paris "establishment."

BLOOMER, Amelia (1818–94) American advocate of women's clothes reform. Introduced functional trousers, or bloomers, worn under a skirt.

BOURKE-WHITE, Margaret (1904–71) U.S. war photographer. First woman photographer with U.S. armed forces.

BRADY, Mathew (1823–96) U.S. photographer. Documented American Civil War on location with his team.

BRANDT, Bill (1904–83) British photographer. Social records; Blitz scenes; landscapes; nude studies.

BRASSAI (Gyula, Halasz) (1899–1986) Hungarian-born French photographer. Noted for recording the Parisian underworld and nightlife.

CAMERON, Julia Margaret (1815–79) British photographer. Portraits of Victorian celebrities.

CAPA, Robert (André Friedmann) (1913–54) Hungarian-born U.S. war photographer.

CARDIN, Pierre (b. 1922) French fashion designer. Brought haute couture to the mass market.

CARTIER-BRESSON, Henri (b. 1908) French photographer. Recorded underworld and nightlife in Paris with a rigorous aesthetic.

CHANEL, Gabrielle known as **Coco** (1883–1971) French couturier. Designs combined simple elegance with comfort; popularized costume jewelry and the evening scarf; also created Chanel No. 5 perfume with Ernest Beaux.

CONRAN, Jasper (b. 1959) British fashion designer. Known for easy-to-wear, quality clothes with uncluttered lines.

COURRÈGES, André (b. 1923) French fashion designer. Noted for "Space Age" designs, miniskirt, white kid boots, and women's pantsuits.

CUNNINGHAM, Imogen (1883–1976) U.S. photographer. Moved from soft-focus romanticism to sharply defined images.

CURTIS, Edward S. (1868–1952) U.S. photographer. Recorded Native American peoples and their lives.

DAGUERRE, Louis Jacques Mandé (1787–1851) French inventor of the daguerreotype, a photographic image on a copper plate coated with silver.

DE LISI, Ben (b. 1955) British fashion designer. Noted for simple dresses of excellent cut with striking detail.

DE LA RENTA, Oscar (b. 1932) U.S. fashion designer. Noted for opulent, ornately trimmed evening dresses.

DIOR, Christian (1905–57) French fashion designer. Introduced the long-skirted "New Look" of 1947 and the "A-line" and "the Sack" dresses of the late 1950s.

DODGSON, Charles (Lewis Carroll) (1832–98) English pioneer photographer. Mainly shot portraits.

DOISNEAU, Robert (b. 1912) French photographer. Sensitive, witty pictures of Parisians and everyday situations.

DUCLOS DU HAURON, Louis (1837–1920) French developer of new photographic methods.

EAKINS, Thomas (1844–1916) U.S. photographer. Continued MUYBRIDGE's work on studies of figures in motion.

EASTMAN, George (1854–1932) U.S. inventor of rollfilm, the Kodak box camera, and (with Edison) experiments that made possible moving pictures.

EDGERTON, Harold Eugene (1903–90) U.S. engineer. Specialized in high-speed photography.

EISENSTAEDT, Alfred (b. 1898) Polish-born U.S. photographer. Photographer for *Life* magazine.

EMERSON, Peter Henry (1856–1936) Cuban-born British photographer.

EVANS, Walker (1903–75) U.S. social photographer. Recorded rural life in the southern states and people in New York City subways.

FATH, Jaques (1912–54) French fashion designer. Famous for simple, structured, hourglass dress shapes and plunging necklines.

FENTON, Roger (1819–69) British photographer. World's first accredited war photographer.

FRITH, Francis (1822–98) British topographical photographer.

GALLIANO, John (b. 1960) British fashion designer inspired by historical themes.

GAULTIER, Jean-Paul (b. 1952) French fashion designer. Designs inspired by the London street scene.

GERNREICH, Rudy (1925–1985) Austrian-born U.S. fashion designer who was at the forefront of the unisex movement in the 1960s. Introduced the "monokini" (topless swimsuit) in 1964.

GIVENCHY, Hubert James Marcel Taffin de (b. 1927) French fashion designer. Noted for the elegance and quality of his designs and his famous white cotton Bettina blouse.

HAAS, Ernst (1921–86) Austrian photojournalist. Pioneered color photography in the study of nature; worked for *Life* and *Vogue* magazines.

HAMNETT, Katherine (b. 1948) British fashion designer. Draws inspiration from work wear and social issues such as the peace movement.

HARDY, Bert (b. 1913) British photojournalist. Recorded World War II concentration camps and the Korean and Vietnam wars.

HARTNELL, Sir Norman (Bishop) (1901–78) British couturier. Produced costumes for leading actresses, 1940s wartime "utility" dresses and uniforms, and Elizabeth II's wedding and coronation gowns.

HEARTFIELD, John (Helmut Herzfelde) (1891–1968) German photographer who satirized Nazism.

HILL, David Octavius (1802–70) British pioneer in photography. Worked with Robert Adamson on calotypes and early portraits of celebrities.

HINE, Lewis (Wickes) (1874–1940) U.S. documentary photographer. Famous for his poignant studies of Ellis Island immigrants, child labor, and World War I refugees.

HOSKING, Eric (John) (1909–90) British wildlife photographer. Captured British birds on film.

JACKSON, Betty (b. 1940) British fashion designer. Invented the "body" all-in-one garment; stylish yet comfortable and practical clothes for women.

KARAN, Donna (b. 1948) American fashion designer. Smart, casual clothes for the active, working woman.

KARSH, Yousuf (b. 1908) Canadian portrait photographer.

KENZO, Takada (b. 1940) Japanese fashion designer. Oriental and Western influences; trendsetting knitwear.

KERTÉSZ, André (1894–1985) Hungarian-U.S. photographer. Shot photos of World War I and the "human condition" in Paris.

KLEIN, Anne (1921–74) U.S. fashion designer. Women's sportswear.

KLEIN, Calvin Richard (b. 1942) U.S. fashion designer. Understated, sophisticated clothes for both sexes and "designer label" jeans.

KLEIN, Roland (b. 1938) U.K.-based French fashion designer. Menswear designs for the Japanese market.

KOUDELKA, Josef (b. 1938) Czech photographer. Studies of eastern European Romanies and current events.

LACROIX, Christian (b. 1951) French

couturier. Fantasy clothes; puffball skirt, rose-prints, décolleté necklines.

LAGERFELD, Karl (b. 1939) German fashion designer. Noted for meticulous cut, extravagant beading, furs, and knitwear.

LAND, Edwin (1910-1991) U. S. photographer and inventor. Changed the nature of photography with his invention of the Polaroid instant camera.

LANGE, Dorothea (1895–1965) U.S. photographer of rural life in the south and west during the Depression.

LARTIGUE, Jacques-Henri (1894–1986) French photographer whose informal approach elevated the snapshot into a creative art form.

LAUREN, Ralph, originally **Ralph Lifschitz** (b. 1939) American fashion designer. The "prairie look," "frontier fashions," and a U.S. version of the "English look."

LEIBOVITZ, Annie (b. 1950) U.S. photographer. Noted for her elaborately staged celebrity portraits.

LICHFIELD, Patrick, 5th Earl of (b. 1939) English photographer. Travel and publicity shots; royal portraits.

MAINBOCHER, originally **Main Rousseau Bocher** (1890–1976) U.S. fashion designer. Created the Duchess of Windsor's wedding dress.

MAPPLETHORPE, Robert (1946–89) U.S. art photographer. Controversial racial and homoerotic imagery.

MAREY, Etienne Jules (1830–1903) French physiologist. Pioneered scientific cinematography.

MARGIELA, Martin Belgian fashion designer. Noted for "deconstruction" designs from used fabrics and second-hand clothes; some with unpicked seams.

McBEAN, Angus Rowland (1904–90) British photographer. Surrealistic pictures using montage and collage.

McCULLIN, Donald (b. 1935) British war photographer.

MEISELAS, Susan (b. 1948) U.S. war photographer.

MISSONI, Tai Otavio (b. 1921) Italian fashion designer. Innovative knitwear with distinctive colors and patterns.

MIYAKE, Issey (b. 1938) Japanese fashion designer. Noted for almost theatrical styles combining Eastern and Western influences and for fashion sculpture.

MOHOLY-NAGY, Laslo (1895–1946) Hungarian-born U.S. photographer. Member of the Bauhaus school.

MOLYNEUX, Edward Henry (1891–1974) British couturier. Noted for tailored suits with pleated skirts in neutral colors and evening wear.

MONTANA, Claude (b. 1949) French fashion designer. Advocated the broad-shouldered look in the 1980s, black leather outfits, and pants with chains.

MORGENSEN, Erik (b. 1926) Danish fashion designer. Manager of Balmain fashion house after Balmain's death in 1982.

MUGLER, Thierry (b. 1946) French fashion designer. Dress designs influenced by 1940s and 1950s style.

MUIR, Jean Elizabeth (1933–95) British fashion designer. Designs characterized by classic shapes, softness, and fluidity; unique special-occasion clothes.

MUYBRIDGE, Eadweard (1830–1904) British photographer. Pioneered reproduction of movement sequences which led to the motion picture camera.

NADAR (Gaspard-Felix Tournachan) (1820–1910) French portrait photographer and journalist. Pioneered aerial photographs; Victorian celebrity portraits.

NIÉPCE, Nicephore (1765–1833) French doctor. Produced first photograph using a camera obscura.

NILSSON, Lennart (b. 1922) Swedish photographer. Pioneering work on microfilm showing the anatomy of plants and animals.

OLDFIELD, Bruce (b. 1950) British fashion designer. Svelte evening gowns for royalty and screen stars; ready-to-wear.

OZBEK, Rifat (b. 1953) Turkish fashion designer influenced by diverse cultures, including his native land.

PARKINSON, Norman (1913–90) British portrait and fashion photographer.

PATOU, Jean (1880–1936) French fashion designer. Renowned for simple, elegant, and understated clothes in the 1920s.

PENN, Irving (b. 1917) U.S. photographer. Fashion shots, advertising, fine art, and native peoples.

POIRET, Paul (1879–1944) French fashion designer. Started his own fashion house after working for Worth and Doucet in Paris. His exotic oriental-influenced designs were looser and less corseted and showed more of the natural figure than previous styles.

PUCCI, Emilio, Marchese di Barsento (1914–92) Italian fashion designer. Bold patterns and brilliant color.

QUANT, Mary (b. 1934) British fashion designer. Her simple geometric designs and original colors were an essential feature of the "Swinging 60s" era.

RAY, Man (Emanuel Rudnitsky) (1890–1976) U.S. photographer. Noted for surrealist and experimental shots.

RHODES, Zandra (b. 1940) British fashion designer. Noted for exotic designs in chiffons and silks; inventive use of textile prints influenced by many cultures.

RICCI, Nina (1883–1970) Italian fashion designer. Noted for elegant, sophisticated garments in classic styles, popular with older women.

RICHMOND, John (b. 1960) British fashion designer. 1990s street style and trendy clubland designs.

RIIS, Jacob (1849–1914) Danish-born U.S. photographer. Recorded poverty and homelessness in New York City; pioneered the use of the flash.

ROBINSON, Henry Peach (1830–1901) British photographer. Composite scenes using models in painted settings.

RODCHENKO, Alexander M. (1891–1956) Russian photojournalist. Experimented with collage.

ROTHSTEIN, Arthur (b. 1915) U.S. documentary photographer.

SAINT LAURENT, Yves originally **Henri Donat Mathieu** (b. 1936) French fashion designer. Launched a trend for ready-to-wear clothes.

SALGADO, Sebastiao (b. 1943) Brazilian photojournalist. Documents industry in the developing world.

SANDER, August (1876–1964) German documentary photographer.

SCHIAPARELLI, Elsa (1890–1973) Italian-born French fashion designer. Noted for inventive sensational designs of the 1930s in bright colors and traditional fabrics; also outrageous hats.

SHEELER, Charles (1883–1965) U.S. industrial photographer.

SISKIND, Aaron (1903–91) U.S. art photographer.

SMITH, Edwin (1912–71) British architectural and landscape photographer.

SMITH, Eugene W. (1918–78) U.S. photojournalist. Worked for *Newsweek* and *Life* magazines.

SMITH, Paul (b. 1946) British menswear designer. Simple, practical styles.

SNOWDON, Antony Armstrong-Jones, 1st Earl of (b. 1930) English photographer. Specializes in celebrity portraits.

STEICHEN, Edward Jean (1879–1973) U.S. portrait and fashion photographer.

STIEGLITZ, Alfred (1864–1946) U.S. photographer. Developed photography as an art form.

STRAND, Paul (1890–1976) U.S. photographer. Straight photographic style of precision and clarity.

TALBOT, William Henry Fox (1800–77) British photographic pioneer. Inventor of photographic prints on paper, the calotype, and flash photography.

UNGARO, Emanuel Maffeolti (b. 1933) French fashion designer. Specializes in angular styled clothing with sharp, clean lines in his own fabrics.

VALENTINO (b. 1933) Italian fashion designer. Noted for his glamorous and colorful designs with a dramatic yet elegant sensibility.

VERSACE, Gianni (b. 1946) Italian fashion designer. Casually styled clothes in simple shapes and strong colors.

VIONNET, Madeleine (1876–1975) French fashion designer. Called greatest modern couturière; developed the 1930s bias-cut dress; used subtle colors and geometric shapes.

WESTON, Edward (1886–1958) U.S. photographer. Known for his studies of nature, landscape, and the human body.

WESTWOOD, Vivienne (b. 1941) British fashion designer. Inspired in the 1970s by the anarchic punk style of rebellious urban youth; later, by historical dress.

WORTH, Charles Frederick (1825–95) British-born fashion designer whose Paris establishment became the center of the fashion world in the 1800s.

YAMAMOTO, Yohji (b. 1943) Japanese fashion designer. Noted for loose, functional clothes for both sexes.

SECTION 7

INTERNATIONAL WORLD

* Asterisks denote dependent countries
Italics denote areas of special interest

POLITICAL WORLD MAP

The political map of the world changes as countries become independent, secede, or merge. Recent changes to it include the emergence of the states of the former U.S.S.R., the split of Czechoslovakia, the breakup of Yugoslavia, and the independence of Palau. An interesting feature of the last few years has been the increasing power of supranational groupings such as the European Union (*p. 246*) (EU) and OPEC and the decline in power of national governments and the nation state.

EUROPE
1 Ireland
2 United Kingdom
3 Portugal
4 Spain
5 France
6 Belgium
7 Netherlands
8 Luxembourg
9 Germany
10 Denmark
11 Norway
12 Sweden
13 Finland
14 Estonia
15 Latvia
16 Lithuania
17 Poland
18 Belarus
19 Ukraine
20 Moldova
21 Romania
22 Hungary
23 Slovakia
24 Czech Republic
25 Austria
26 Liechtenstein
27 Switzerland
28 Italy
29 Malta
30 Slovenia
31 Croatia
32 Bosnia and Herzegovina
33 Yugoslavia
34 Albania
35 Macedonia
36 Greece
37 Bulgaria
38 San Marino
39 Vatican City
40 Monaco
41 Andorra
42 Gibraltar (U.K.)
43 Iceland

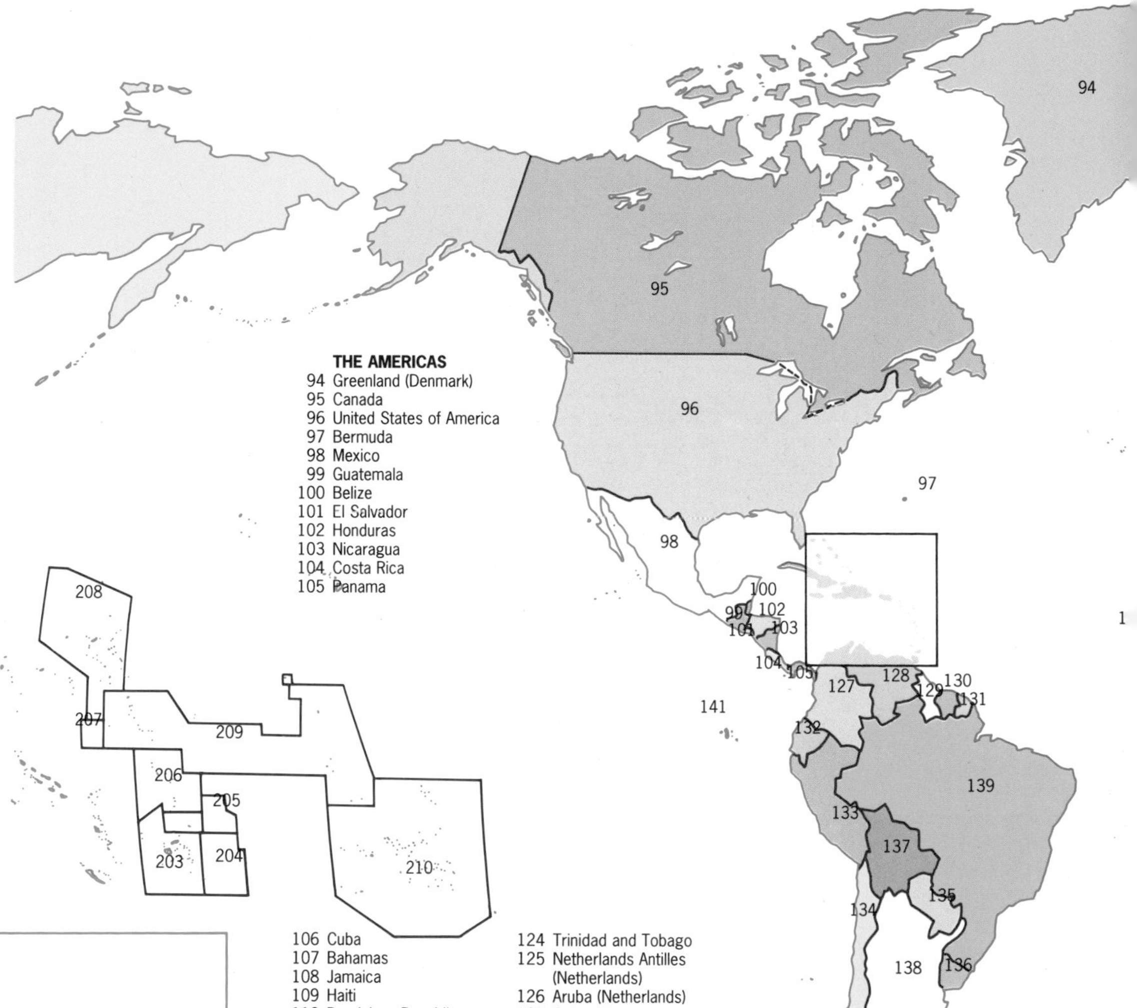

THE AMERICAS
94 Greenland (Denmark)
95 Canada
96 United States of America
97 Bermuda
98 Mexico
99 Guatemala
100 Belize
101 El Salvador
102 Honduras
103 Nicaragua
104 Costa Rica
105 Panama

106 Cuba
107 Bahamas
108 Jamaica
109 Haiti
110 Dominican Republic
111 Puerto Rico (U.S.A.)
112 Virgin Islands (U.S.A./U.K.)
113 Antigua and Barbuda
114 St. Christopher-Nevis
115 Anguilla (U.K.)
116 Montserrat (U.K.)
117 St. Lucia
118 Dominica
119 Guadeloupe (France)
120 Martinique (France)
121 Barbados
122 Grenada
123 St. Vincent and the Grenadines
124 Trinidad and Tobago
125 Netherlands Antilles (Netherlands)
126 Aruba (Netherlands)
127 Colombia
128 Venezuela
129 Guyana
130 Suriname
131 French Guiana (France)
132 Ecuador
133 Peru
134 Chile
135 Paraguay
136 Uruguay
137 Bolivia
138 Argentina
139 Brazil
140 Falkland Islands (U.K.)
141 Galápagos Islands (Ecuador)

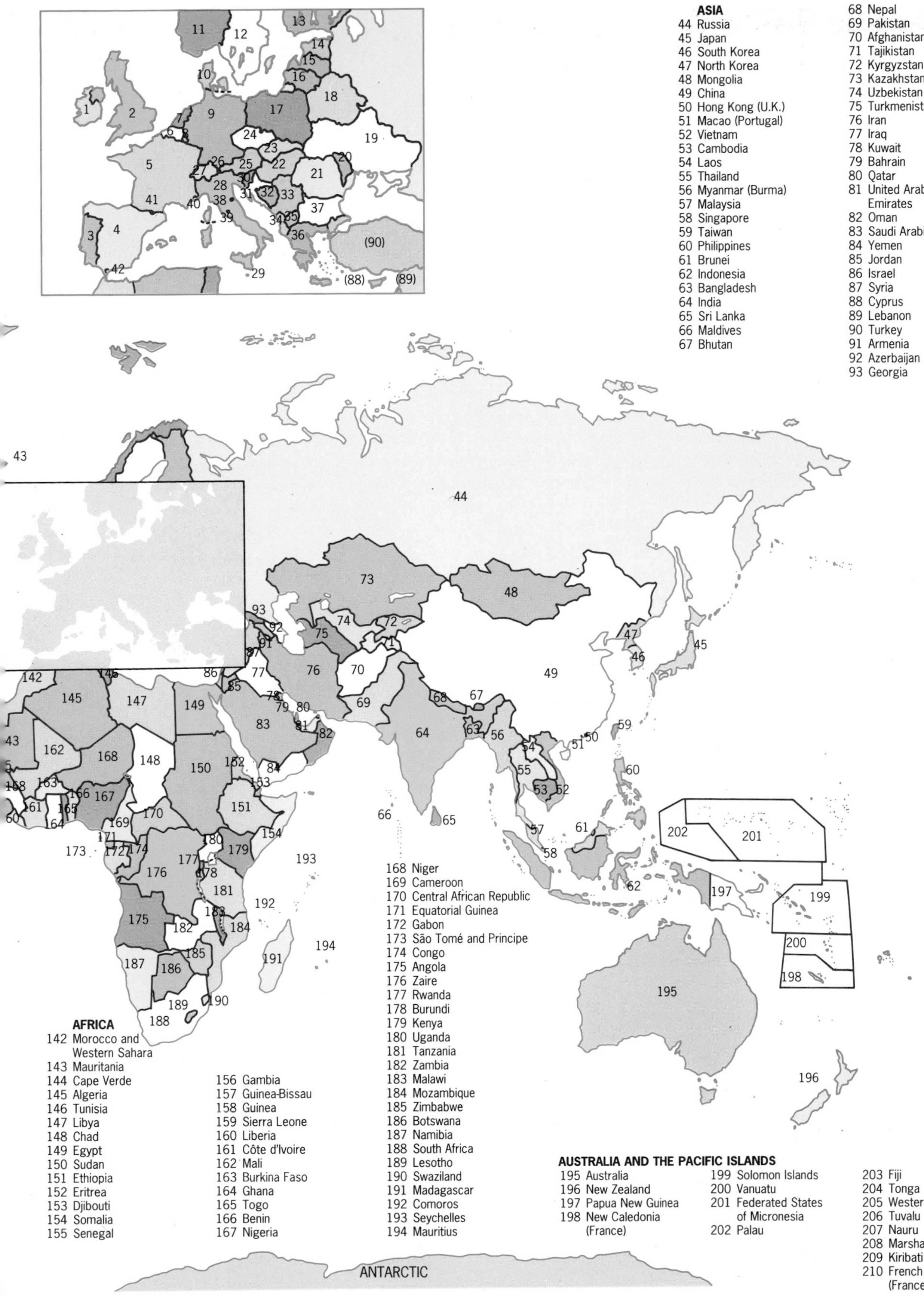

ASIA

44 Russia	68 Nepal
45 Japan	69 Pakistan
46 South Korea	70 Afghanistan
47 North Korea	71 Tajikistan
48 Mongolia	72 Kyrgyzstan
49 China	73 Kazakhstan
50 Hong Kong (U.K.)	74 Uzbekistan
51 Macao (Portugal)	75 Turkmenistan
52 Vietnam	76 Iran
53 Cambodia	77 Iraq
54 Laos	78 Kuwait
55 Thailand	79 Bahrain
56 Myanmar (Burma)	80 Qatar
57 Malaysia	81 United Arab
58 Singapore	Emirates
59 Taiwan	82 Oman
60 Philippines	83 Saudi Arabia
61 Brunei	84 Yemen
62 Indonesia	85 Jordan
63 Bangladesh	86 Israel
64 India	87 Syria
65 Sri Lanka	88 Cyprus
66 Maldives	89 Lebanon
67 Bhutan	90 Turkey
	91 Armenia
	92 Azerbaijan
	93 Georgia

AFRICA

142 Morocco and
Western Sahara
143 Mauritania
144 Cape Verde
145 Algeria
146 Tunisia
147 Libya
148 Chad
149 Egypt
150 Sudan
151 Ethiopia
152 Eritrea
153 Djibouti
154 Somalia
155 Senegal

156 Gambia
157 Guinea-Bissau
158 Guinea
159 Sierra Leone
160 Liberia
161 Côte d'Ivoire
162 Mali
163 Burkina Faso
164 Ghana
165 Togo
166 Benin
167 Nigeria

168 Niger
169 Cameroon
170 Central African Republic
171 Equatorial Guinea
172 Gabon
173 São Tomé and Principe
174 Congo
175 Angola
176 Zaire
177 Rwanda
178 Burundi
179 Kenya
180 Uganda
181 Tanzania
182 Zambia
183 Malawi
184 Mozambique
185 Zimbabwe
186 Botswana
187 Namibia
188 South Africa
189 Lesotho
190 Swaziland
191 Madagascar
192 Comoros
193 Seychelles
194 Mauritius

AUSTRALIA AND THE PACIFIC ISLANDS

195 Australia	199 Solomon Islands	203 Fiji
196 New Zealand	200 Vanuatu	204 Tonga
197 Papua New Guinea	201 Federated States	205 Western Samoa
198 New Caledonia	of Micronesia	206 Tuvalu
(France)	202 Palau	207 Nauru
		208 Marshall Islands
		209 Kiribati
		210 French Polynesia
		(France)

ANTARCTIC

ARCTIC

Area: The Arctic includes parts of Europe, Asia, and North America but has no agreed boundaries.
Resources: The world's best fishing grounds are found in the Arctic region. It is also rich in many valuable minerals including coal, uranium, iron ore, lead, nickel, petroleum, gold, copper, oil, natural gas, and tin.

PHYSICAL FEATURES

Central ocean surrounded by ring of mountainous continental plateaus divided by other oceans. Many regions are permanently ice-covered. **Vegetation:** The 10° Summer Isotherm marks the point beyond which trees do not grow. This area is mostly tundra. South of the treeline, evergreen forests grow. Transitional area has sparse trees, mosses, and lichens. **Climate:** Polar; persistent cold with little seasonal variation; winters characterized by constant darkness, summers by continuous daylight.

PEOPLE

Population: c. 1,000,000. **Languages:** Inuit, Finno-Ural-Altaic, Paleo-Siberian. **Ethnic groups:** Inuit, Lapp, Komi, Tungus, Yakut, Paleo-Siberian.

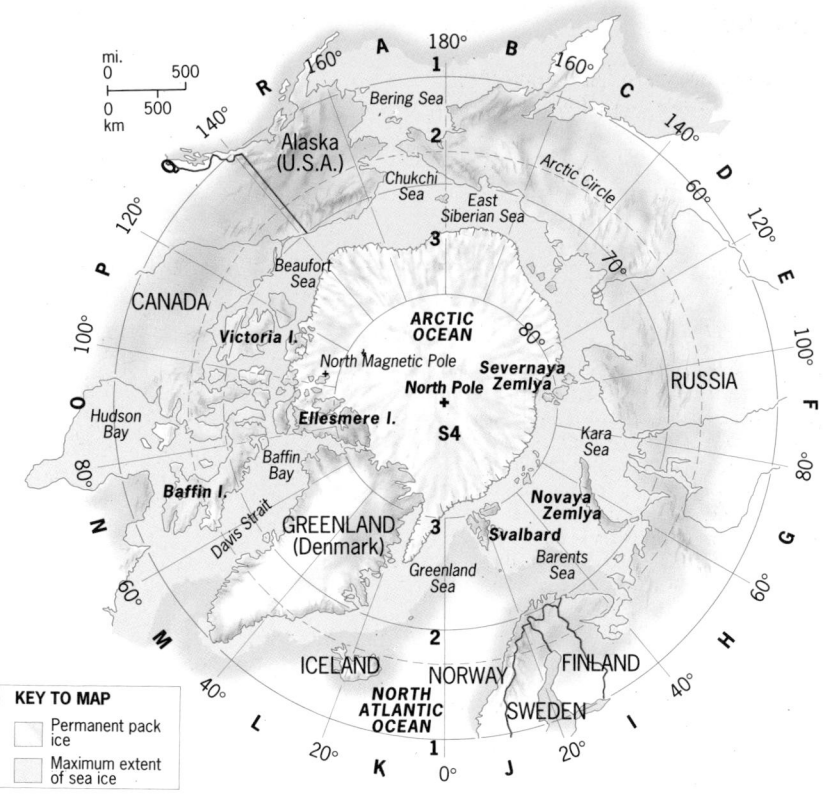

KEY TO MAP
- Permanent pack ice
- Maximum extent of sea ice

GREENLAND

Area: 840,000 sq. mi./2,175,600 km² **Local name:** Grønland/Kalaallit Nunaat. **Currency:** Danish krone. **Capital:** Godthåb. **Physical features:** Flat to gently sloping ice cap with rim of rugged mountains; narrow, ice-free coastal plain. **Climate:** Polar. **Time zone:** GMT –1h(E), –4hr(W). **Political system:** Self-governing province of Denmark. **Head of state:** Queen Margrethe II (from 1972). **Head of government:** Home Rule Chairman Lars Emil Johansen (from 1991). **Main exports:** Fish and fish products, hides and skins, metallic ores and concentrates. **Resources:** Fish, zinc, lead, iron ore, coal, molybdenum, uranium, the only sizable deposits of cryolite in the world.

PEOPLE

Population: 57,000. **Distribution urban/rural:** 77%/23%. **Life expectancy:** 63(m), 69(f). **Languages:** Inuit, Greenlandic, Danish. **Ethnic groups:** Inuit, Greenlandic, Danish. **Religion:** Evangelical Lutheran c. 98%. **Literacy rate:** NA. **Per capita GNP:** $9,000.

KEY DATES

1380   Comes under Danish rule.
1979   Home rule granted.

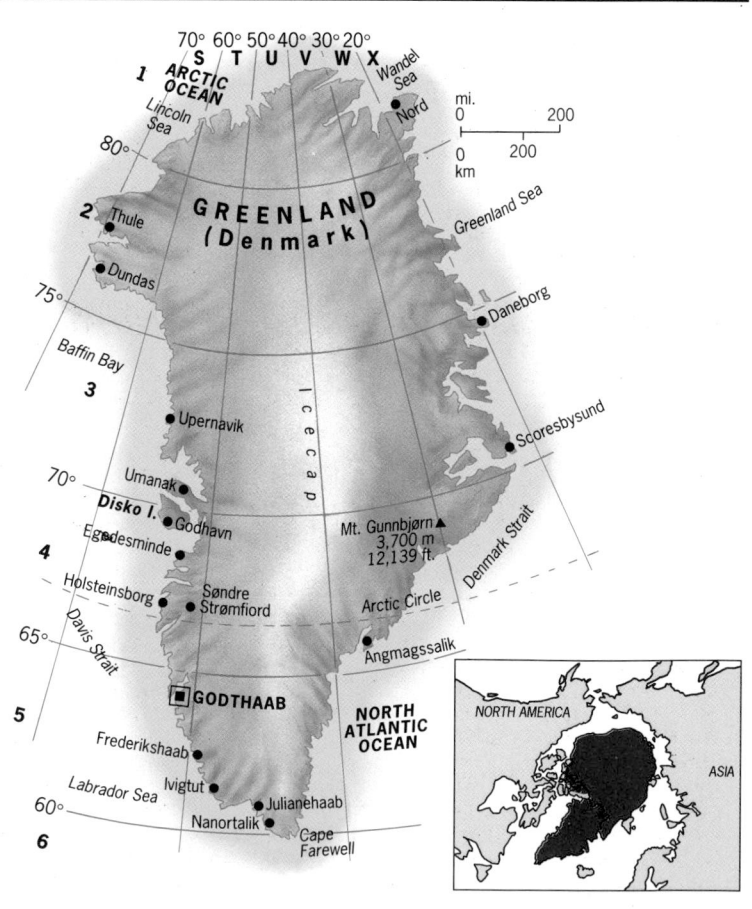

ANTARCTICA

Area: 5,400,000 sq. mi./14,000,000 km² **Resources:** Minerals, krill (below).

PHYSICAL FEATURES

Antarctica is the fifth-largest continent and covers around 9.5% of the world's total land area. The Transantarctic Mountains cross the continent. Antarctica is the highest continent with an average elevation of 7,546 ft./2,300 m above sea level. About 98% of the land is covered in a thick layer of ice and snow. *Vegetation:* Plant life is limited because of the extreme climate, but mosses and lichens can be found around the coast. In 1994, scientists reported an increase in the number of coastal plants, which seems to confirm predictions that the world's climate is getting warmer. *Climate:* Polar; Antarctica is the coldest continent and one of the driest places on earth. Average precipitation is 23 in./60 cm a year and the temperature rarely rises above 32°F (0°C).

PEOPLE

Population: No permanent population; up to 3,000 residents in scientific research stations; increasing numbers of tourists causing environmental damage.

MINERAL RESOURCES

About 175 million years ago, Antarctica was part of the giant continent that geologists call Gondwanaland. The parts of other continents that were adjacent to Antarctica are particularly rich in many minerals including gold, diamonds, copper, and crude oil. Scientists believe that many of these resources are also buried beneath the ice of Antarctica. The natural obstacles to mining in Antarctica are great, and international concern over the

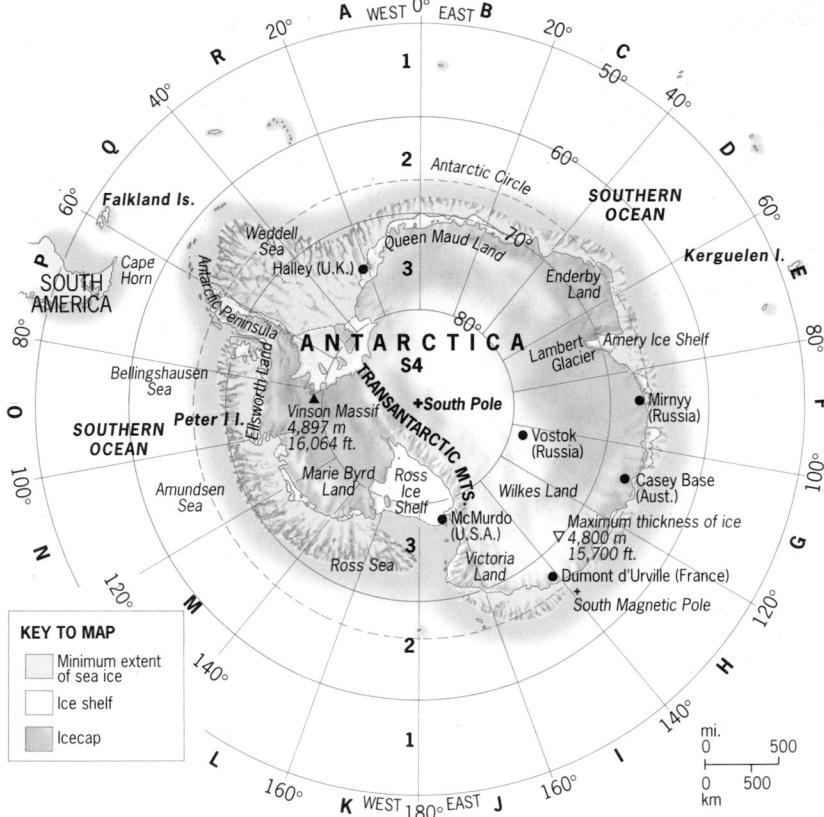

KEY TO MAP

- Minimum extent of sea ice
- Ice shelf
- Icecap

environmental damage that mining could cause has prompted the establishment of laws controlling mineral exploitation.

The snow and ice which constitute the Antarctic ice cap represent around 70 percent of the world's fresh water, and scientists are currently examining the possibility of towing icebergs from Antarctica to desert regions as a source of fresh water.

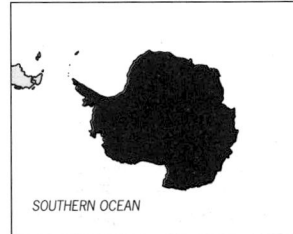

SOUTHERN OCEAN

SCIENTIFIC RESEARCH

When Captain Cook first sailed around Antarctica in 1775, he said "I make bold to declare that the world will derive no benefit from it."

Two centuries later, scientists from more than 20 countries work in over 50 research stations to learn the lessons this unique continent has to teach about meteorology, biology, geology, and many other areas of scientific study.

The Antarctic ice cap is a unique source of information about atmospheric conditions in the past because it contains bubbles of air that have been suspended there for many thousands of years. Being one of the few places on earth that remain relatively untouched by human colonization, this continent can also act as a barometer against which atmospheric changes over other continents can be measured.

Environmental change has been possibly the most important area of Antarctic research since scientists first noticed a hole in the ozone layer above Antarctica. This hole has grown in size each year. Scientists believe that it could even-

tually become larger than the continent itself. They are also worried about global warming and the effect that it could have on the Antarctic. The Antarctic ice cap contains 1,730,000 cu. mi. (7,250,000km³) of ice and snow. If the earth's climate were to warm even slightly, this ice and snow might begin to melt, raising sea levels and engulfing low-lying coastal regions and cities around the world.

Seven countries claim territory in Antarctica: Australia, France, Argentina, Chile, the U.K., New Zealand, and Norway.

KEY DATES

1957–58 International Geophysical Year (IGY): 12 countries set up over 50 scientific research stations in Antarctica.
1959 12 countries sign Antarctic Treaty encouraging exploration and scientific research, and banning military activity and the dumping of toxic waste, as well as suspending acceptance of territorial claims over parts of

the continent and preventing further claims from being made; 27 other countries subsequently sign the treaty.
1966–67 Wildlife conservation areas set up.
1979 Discovery of a hole in the ozone layer above Antarctica.
1980 Conservation of Antarctic Marine Living Resources agreed.
1987 31 countries sign the Montreal Protocol to limit the production of CFCs, believed to damage the ozone layer.
1988 Convention on the Regulation of Antarctic Mineral Resource Activities accords signatories the power of veto over mining on environmental grounds; Environmental Defense Fund charges U.S. scientific bases with polluting the Antarctic environment.
1989 Australia and France withdraw support from 1988 convention.
1991 Antarctic Treaty renewed and expanded to ban mining activity for 50 years.
1995 Munich sea level conference.

EUROPE

Area: 4,031,866 sq. mi./10,442,533 km². **Largest cities:** Moscow, London, Paris, Essen, St. Petersburg, Madrid, Barcelona, Athens, Rome, Berlin, Naples. **Organizations:** European Union (EC), European Free Trade Association (EFTA), Council of Europe, Commonwealth of Independent States (CIS) [also Asia]. **Main products* (and percentage of world output):** Olive oil (84%), wine (69%), rye (44%), barley (43%), motor vehicles (40%), oats (31%), steel (25%). *Excludes Russia.

PHYSICAL FEATURES

Europe is the second smallest of the continents and covers 7% of the earth's land area. It includes W. Russia up to the Ural Mountains (the rest of Russia is in Asia). The continent is dominated by a vast central plain dissected by mountain ranges. **Highest point:** Mount Elbrus (8,1481 ft./5,633 m). **Lowest point:** Shore of the Caspian Sea (–92 ft./–28 m). **Longest river:** Volga. **Largest lake:** Ladoga. **Other features:** Appenines, Alps, Pyrenees, Balkans, Carpathians; Danube, Dnepr, Rhine rivers; Lakes Ladoga, Onega, Vänern. **Vegetation:** Mostly forest in the N.; steppe and other grassland in the central plain; tundra at high altitudes and in the extreme N.

PEOPLE

Population: 704,189,000 (13% of the total world population). **Growth rate:** 0.4%. **Density:** 269/sq. mi.* **Distribution urban/rural:** 73%/27%. **Life expectancy:** 71(m), 78(f). **Languages:** c. 50 Indo-European languages spoken; exceptions are Finnish and Hungarian, which are related, and Euskara (Basque) which is unrelated to any known language. **Ethnic groups**: Most countries dominated by one ethnic group; minority groups include Basque and Lapp; also substantial number of Asians, Arabs, and black Africans in W., often with origins in former European colonies. **Religions:** Mostly Christian; also Jewish, Hindu, Muslim. *Excludes former U.S.S.R.

Arctic Circle

ATLANTIC OCEAN

EUROPE

ASIA

Tropic of Cancer

AFRICA

Equator

KEY
1 Iceland
2 Latvia
3 Lithuania
4 Estonia
5 Finland
6 Sweden
7 Norway
8 Denmark
9 United Kingdom
10 Ireland
11 Netherlands
12 Belgium
13 Luxembourg
14 Monaco
15 France
16 Spain
17 Andorra
18 Portugal
19 Gibraltar (UK)
20 Italy
21 San Marino
22 Vatican City
23 Malta
24 Liechtenstein
25 Switzerland
26 Austria
27 Germany
28 Poland
29 Czech Republic
30 Slovakia
31 Hungary
32 Slovenia
33 Croatia
34 Bosnia and
Herzegovina

35 Macedonia
36 Yugoslavia
37 Albania

38 Greece
39 Romania
40 Moldova
41 Bulgaria
42 Ukraine
43 Belarus
44 Russia

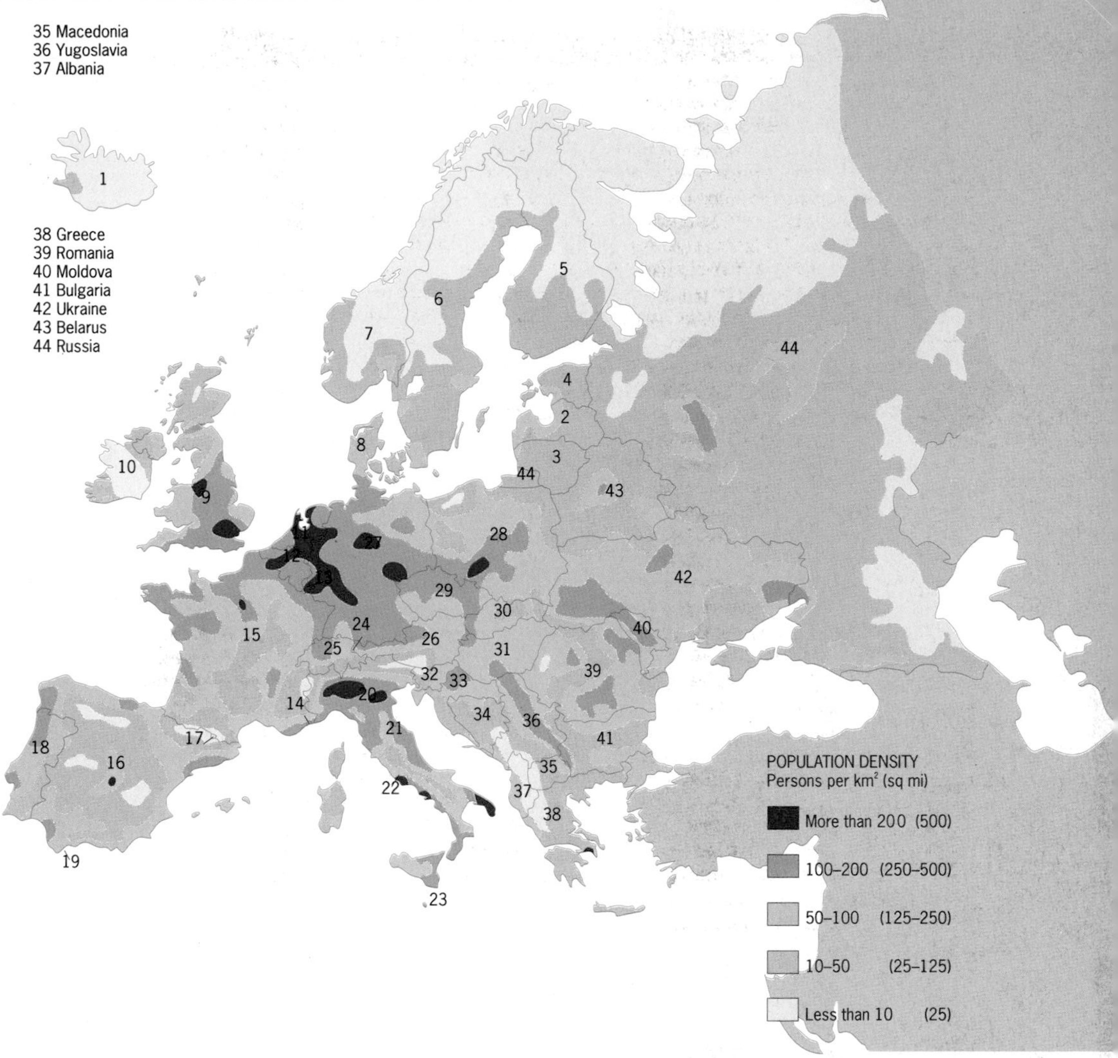

POPULATION DENSITY
Persons per km² (sq mi)

More than 200   (500)

100–200   (250–500)

50–100   (125–250)

10–50   (25–125)

Less than 10   (25)

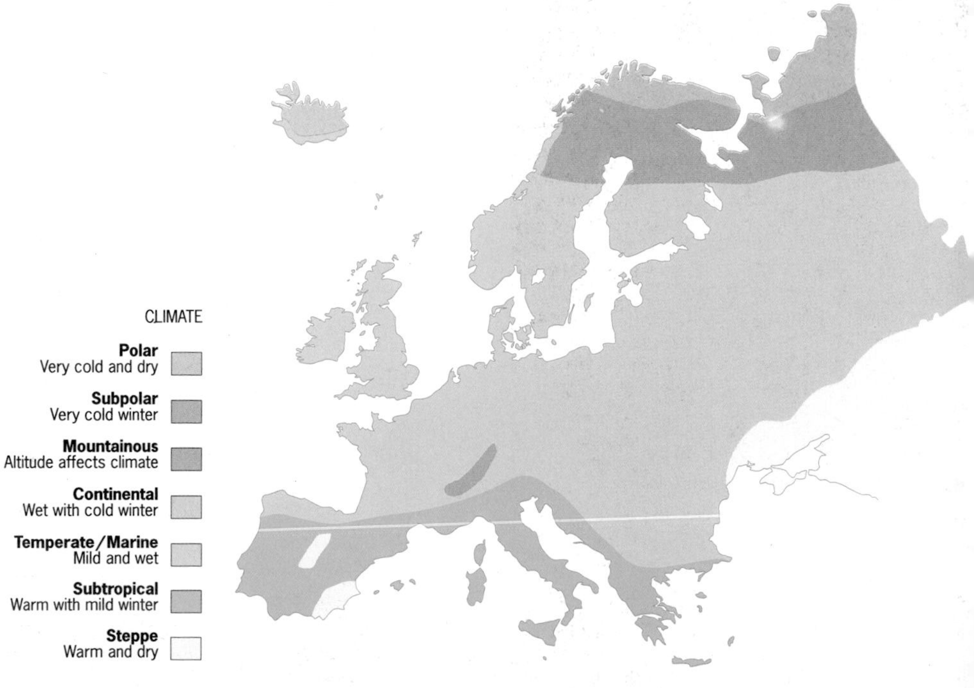

CLIMATE

Polar
Very cold and dry

Subpolar
Very cold winter

Mountainous
Altitude affects climate

Continental
Wet with cold winter

Temperate/Marine
Mild and wet

Subtropical
Warm with mild winter

Steppe
Warm and dry

ICELAND

Area: 39,771 sq. mi./103,000 km². **Local name:** Lýdvelydid ísland. **Currency:** Króna. **Capital:** Reykjavík. **Physical features:** Mostly plateau with mountain peaks and ice-fields. **Climate:** Polar, temperate in S. **Time zone:** GMT. **Political system:** Republic. **Head of state:** Vigdís Finnbogadóttir (from 1980). **Head of government:** David Oddsson (from 1991). **Main exports:** Fish and fish products, metals, diatomite. **Resources:** Fish, hydroelectric and geothermal power, diatomite.

PEOPLE

Population: 263,000. **Distribution urban/rural:** 90%/10%. **Life expectancy:** 76(m), 81(f). **Language:** Icelandic (official). **Ethnic group:** Icelandic 100%. **Religions:** Evangelical Lutheran 96%, other Christian 3%. **Literacy rate:** 100%. **Per capita GDP:** $16,200.

KEY DATES

1380 Iceland comes under Danish rule.
1940 Occupied by British troops.
1944 Independence achieved.
1946 Joins UN.
1949 Joins NATO.
1976 "Cod War" with Great Britain.
1985 Iceland declared nuclear-free zone.

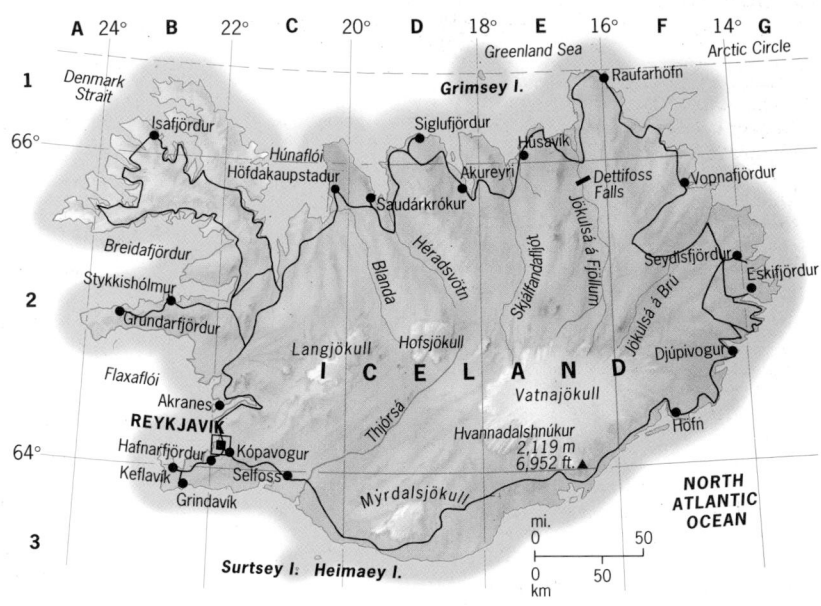

TRAVEL
Visa: None neded by U.S. **Driving permit:** IDP exchanged for temporary local license. **Health and safety:** No inoculations needed. **Tourist features:** Thingvellir, home of the oldest parliament in the world; Lake Mývatn. **National holiday:** June 17 (Anniversary of the Establishment of the Republic).

LATVIA

Area: 24,712 sq. mi./64,000 km². **Local name:** Latvijas Republika. **Currency:** Latss. **Capital:** Riga. **Physical features:** Low, wooded plain. **Climate:** Marine. **Time zone:** GMT +2h. **Political system:** Republic. **Head of state:** Guntis Ulmanis (from 1993). **Head of government:** Valdis Birkavs (from 1993). **Main exports:** Food, chemicals. **Resources:** Amber, peat, dolomite.

PEOPLE

Population: 2,632,000. **Distribution urban/rural:** 71%/29%. **Life expectancy:** 65(m), 75(f). **Languages:** Latvian (official), Lithuanian, Russian. **Ethnic groups:** Latvian 52%, Russian 34%, Belorussian 5%, Ukrainian 3%, Polish 2%. **Religions:** Lutheran, Roman Catholic, Russian Orthodox. **Literacy rate:** NA. **Per capita GDP:** $1,930.

KEY DATES

1940 Latvia becomes part of U.S.S.R.
1988 Foundation of Popular Front.
1989 Opposition parties legalized.
1990 Independence declared.
1991 Full independence achieved; joins UN; Communist Party outlawed.

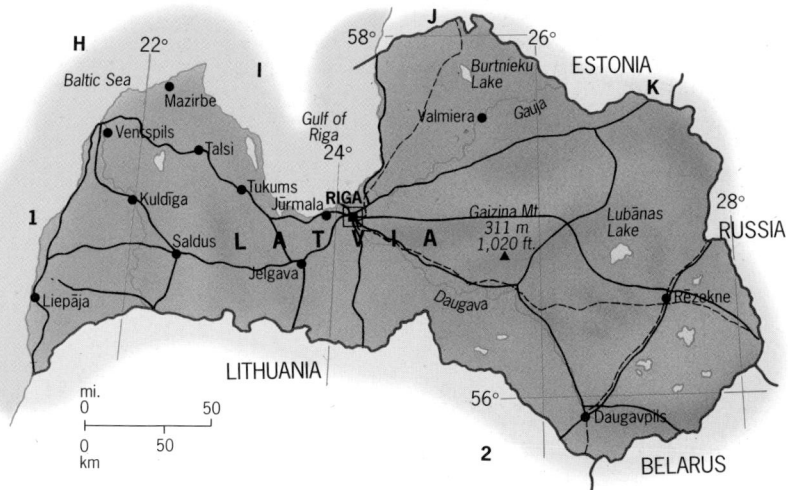

TRAVEL
Visa: None needed by U.S. **Driving permit:** IDP. **Health and safety:** No inoculations needed. **Tourist features:** Western Dvina River; Old Riga; Gauja National Park. **National holiday:** November 18 (Independence Day).

LITHUANIA

Area: 25,098 sq. mi./65,000 km².
Local name: Lietuvos Respublika.
Currency: Litas. *Capital:* Vilnius.
Physical features: Mostly lowland
with hills in W. and S.E. *Climate:*
Marine. *Time zone:* GMT +2h.
Political system: Republic. *Head of
state:* Algirdas Brazauskas (from
1993). *Head of government:* Adol-
fas Slezevicius (from 1993). *Main
exports:* Electronics, petroleum products, chemicals. *Resource:* Peat.

PEOPLE

Population: 3,742,000. *Distribution
urban/rural:* 68%/32%. *Life expectancy:* 66(m), 76(f). *Languages:* Lithuanian
(official), Polish, Russian. *Ethnic groups:*
Lithuanian 80%, Russian 9%, Polish 8%,
Belorussian 2%, other 1%. *Religions:*
Roman Catholic, Lutheran. *Literacy
rate:* NA. *Per capita GNP:* $1,310.

KEY DATES

1940 Lithuania becomes part of U.S.S.R.
1940–52 Guerrilla warfare kills thousands.
1972 Anti-Soviet demonstrations.
1990 Independence declared; U.S.S.R.
imposes economic sanctions.
1991 Soviet troops sent in to put down
independence movement, 15 die; independence achieved; U.S.S.R. dissolved.

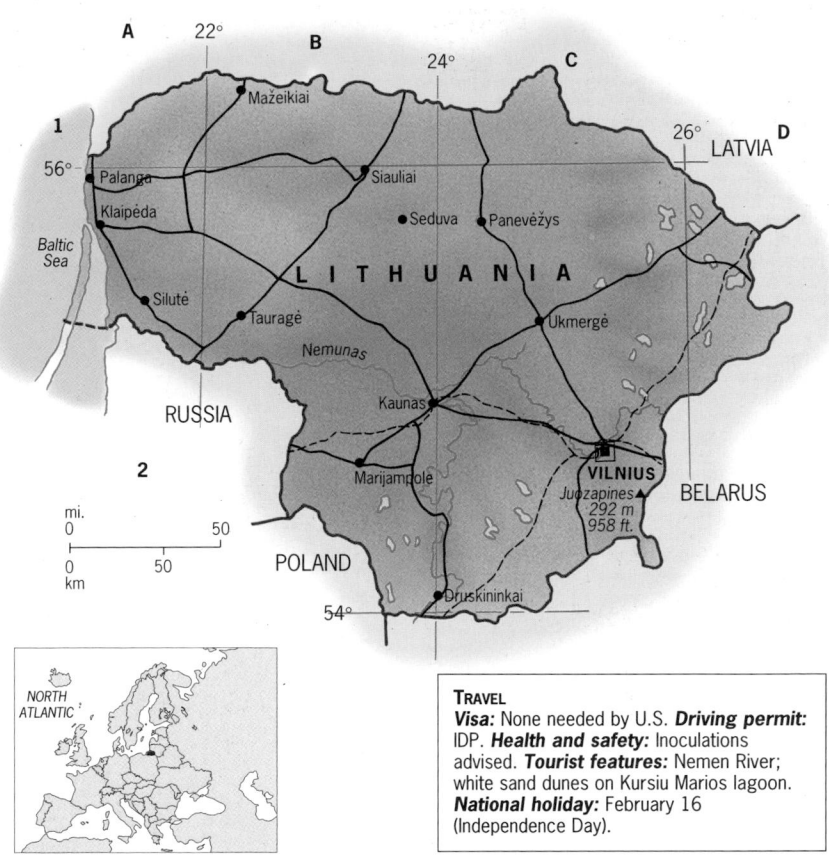

TRAVEL
Visa: None needed by U.S. *Driving permit:*
IDP. *Health and safety:* Inoculations
advised. *Tourist features:* Nemen River;
white sand dunes on Kursiu Marios lagoon.
National holiday: February 16
(Independence Day).

ESTONIA

Area: 17,376 sq. mi./45,000 km².
Local name: Eesti Vabariik.
Currency: Kroon. *Capital:* Tallinn.
Other cities: Tartu, Narva, Kohtla-
Järve, Pärnu. *Physical features:*
Marshy lowlands. *Climate:* Marine.
Time zone: GMT +2h. *Political
system:* Republic. *Head of state:*
Lennart Meri (from 1992). *Head of
government:* Mart Laar (from
1992). *Main exports:* Machinery,
food, chemicals, electricity.
Resources: Shale oil, peat, phospho-
rite, amber.

PEOPLE

Population: 1,542,000. *Distribution
urban/rural:* 72%/28%. *Life expectancy:* 75(m), 74(f). *Languages:* Estonian
(official), Latvian, Lithuanian, Russian.
Ethnic groups: Estonian 62%, Russian
30%, Ukrainian 3%, Belorussian 2%,
Finnish 1%, other 2%. *Religions:*
Lutheran. *Per capita GDP:* $1,310.

KEY DATES

1940 Estonia becomes part of U.S.S.R.
1941 Thousands deported to Siberia.
1941–44 German occupation during WW II.
1940s Guerrilla resistance to Soviet occupation; many deported to Siberia.
1988 Adopts constitution with power of
veto over all legislation from Moscow.
1989 Estonian becomes official language.
1990 Multiparty politics introduced.
1991 Independence achieved; joins UN;
Communist Party outlawed.
1994 Ferry distaster claims 902 lives.

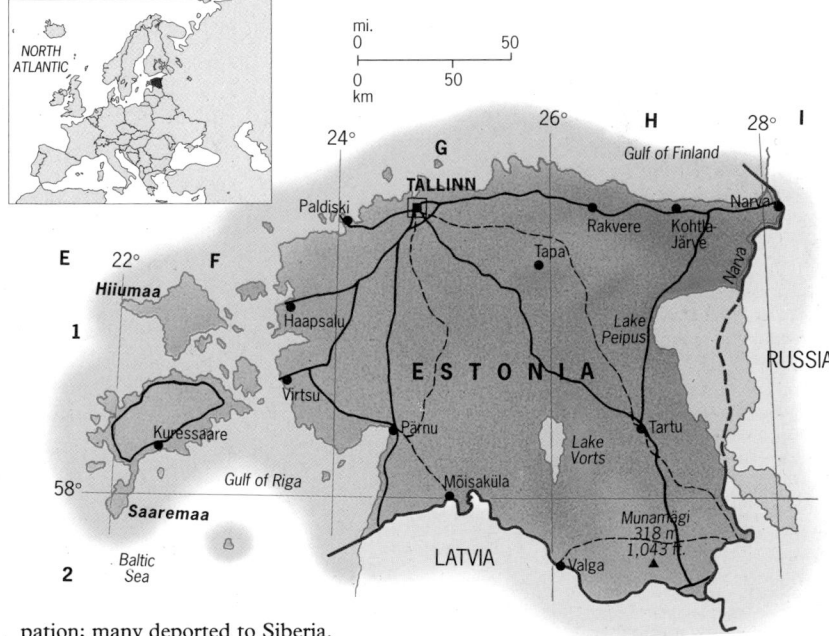

TRAVEL
Visa: None needed by U.S. *Driving permit:*
IDP. *Health and safety:* No inoculations
needed. *Tourist features:* Lake Peipus and
Narva River; Baltic islands. *National
holiday:* February 24 (Independence Day).

FINLAND

Area: 130,128 sq. mi./337,032 km². *Local name:* Suomen Tasavalta. *Currency:* Markka. *Capital:* Helsinki. *Other cities:* Tampere, Turku. *Physical features:* Mostly low forested plains interspersed with low hills and lakes; one-third lies within the Arctic Circle. *Climate:* Subpolar. *Time zone:* GMT +2h. *Political system:* Republic. *Head of state:* Martti Ahtisaari (from 1994). *Head of government:* Esko Aho (from 1991). *Main exports:* Wood, paper and pulp, ships, machinery, clothing, food, vehicles. *Resources:* Wood, copper, zinc, iron ore, silver.

PEOPLE

Population: 5,067,000. *Distribution urban/rural:* 61%/39%. *Life expectancy:* 72(m), 80(f). *Languages:* Finnish 94% and Swedish 6% (both official), small Lapp- and Russian-speaking minorities. *Ethnic groups:* Finnish, Swedish, Lapp, Gypsy, Turkish, Jewish small communities. *Religions:* Evangelical Lutheran 89%, Greek Orthodox 1%, other 1%. *Literacy rate:* 100%. *Per capita GDP:* $16,200.

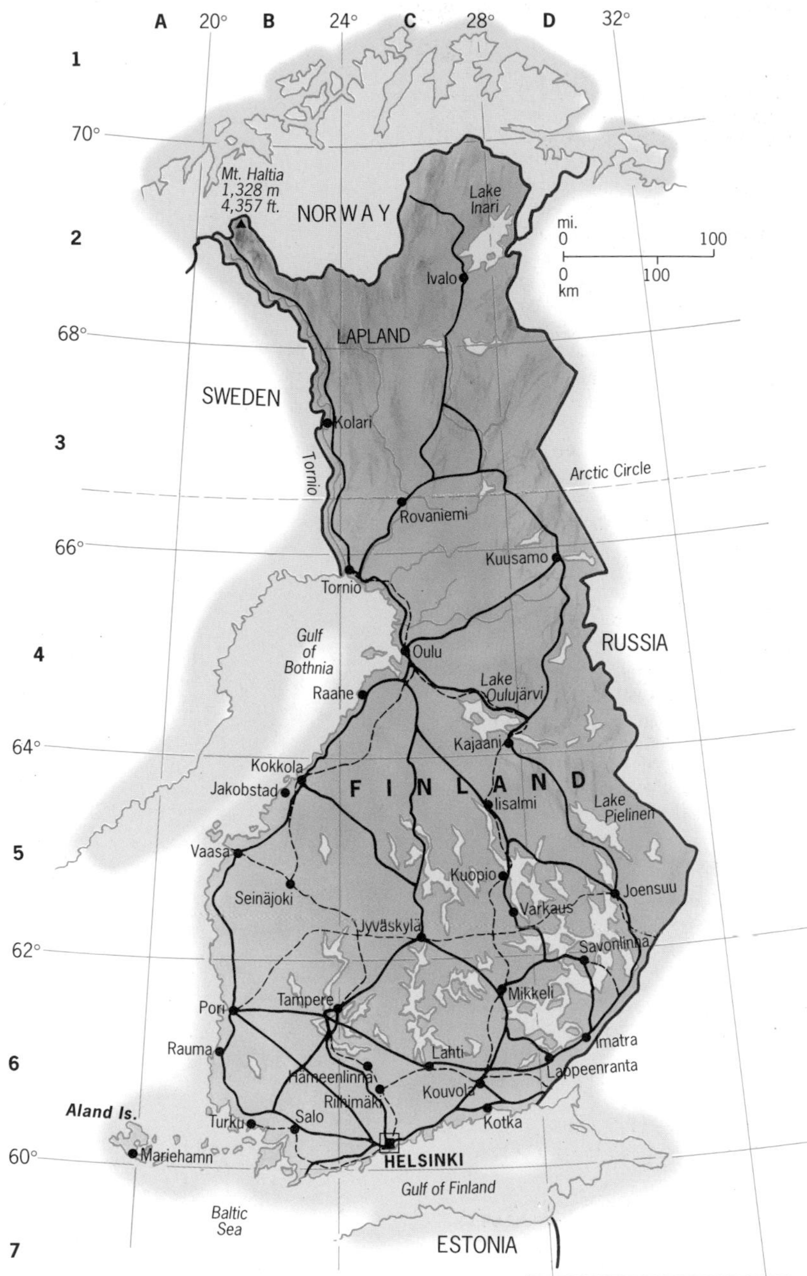

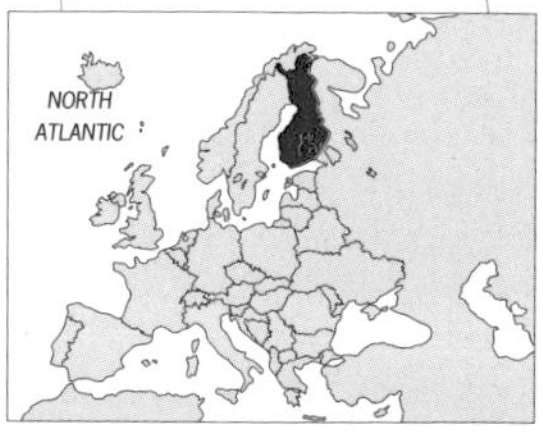

KEY DATES

1100s–1200s Finland comes under Swedish control; Roman Catholicism established as official religion.

c. **1540** Lutheranism becomes the official religion of Finland.

1700–21 Great Northern War: Russia gains control of much Finnish territory.

1809 Finland annexed by Russia.

1899 Czar Nicholas II attempts to quash Finnish nationalism and impose greater control over Finland; Russian becomes the official language.

1903 Finnish constitution suspended.

1905 Six-day general strike in protest against Russian rule; much self-government restored.

1906 First parliamentary elections with universal suffrage.

1918 Civil war between socialists, the Red Guards, and nonsocialists, the White Guards, won by nonsocialists; new republican constitution; Kaarlo J. Ståhlberg becomes first president.

1920 Independence achieved.

1920s Communist Party outlawed.

1932 Nonaggression treaty with U.S.S.R.

1939 Finland declares neutrality in World War II; Winter War: much territory lost to Soviet Union.

1941 Neutrality reaffirmed, but Finland allows Germany to station troops in Finland to attack the Soviet Union; U.S.S.R. begins bombing Finland; U.K. declares war on Finland; Finland declares war on Soviet Union.

1948 Treaty of Friendship, Cooperation, and Mutual Assistance signed with U.S.S.R.; Communist Party legalized.

1955 Finland joins UN; treaty with Soviet Union renewed.

1956 Urho Kekkonen elected president.

1973 Trade treaty with EEC.

1977 Trade agreement signed with U.S.S.R.

1981 President Urho Kekkonen resigns.

1982 Mauno Koivisto elected president.

1987 First Conservative government elected since World War II.

1989 Finland joins Council of Europe.

1992 Finland makes a formal application to join the European Community.

1995 Becomes a member of the EC.

TRAVEL

Visa: None needed by U.S. *Driving permit:* Nat. license. *Health and safety:* No inoculations needed. *Tourist features:* Helvetinkolu (Hell's Chasm); Laukaa; Seitseminen National Park. *National holiday:* December 6 (Independence Day).

SWEDEN

Area: 173,731 sq. mi./449,964 km². ***Local name:*** Konungariket Sverige. ***Currency:*** Krona. ***Capital:*** Stockholm. ***Other large cities:*** Göteborg, Malmö. ***Physical features:*** Mostly flat to gently rolling plains; mountains in W. and N.W. border; several large lakes. ***Climate:*** Marine in S., subpolar in N. ***Time zone:*** GMT +1h. ***Political system:*** Constitutional monarchy. ***Head of state:*** King Carl XVI Gustaf (from 1973). ***Head of government:*** Ingvar Carlssen (from 1994). ***Main exports:*** Machinery, transportation equipment, paper, wood, paperboard, iron and steel, petrochemicals, chemicals. ***Resources:*** Zinc, iron ore, lead, copper, silver, wood, uranium, hydropower potential.

PEOPLE

Population: 8,716,000. ***Distribution urban/rural:*** 85%/15%. ***Life expectancy:*** 75(m), 81(f). ***Languages:*** Swedish; Sami- (Lapp) and Finnish-speaking minorities. ***Ethnic groups:*** Swedish 91%; small minorities of Finns, Lapps, Yugoslavs, Danes, Norwegians, Greeks, Turks. ***Religions:*** Evangelical Lutheran 94%, Roman Catholic 2%, Pentecostal 1%, other 3%. ***Literacy rate:*** 99%. ***Per capita GDP:*** $17,200.

KEY DATES

1397 Sweden unites with Norway and Denmark.

1523 Sweden secedes from union.

1866 Alfred Nobel invents dynamite, with important effect on mining industry.

1909 Constitutional amendments extend voting franchise and introduce proportional representation.

1920 Sweden joins League of Nations.

1939 Proclaims neutrality in World War II.

1946 Sweden joins the UN.

1949 Sweden refuses to join NATO.

1958 Sweden receives financial aid from U.S.A. to help with the construction of a nuclear reactor.

1959 Extension of social welfare services; Sweden founding member of European Free Trade Association (EFTA).

1964–75 Sweden opposes U.S. involvement in Vietnam War and provides asylum for many young U.S. opponents.

1971 New electoral system introduced.

1972–74 Relations with the U.S.A. strained during Vietnam War.

1973 Carl XVI Gustaf becomes king.

1975 New constitution removes remaining powers of king.

1986 Prime Minister Olof Palme assassinated; Ingvar Carlsson elected.

1990 Austerity measures introduced in response to economic problems.

1991 Formal application for EC membership; Carlsson resigns after Social Democrats are defeated in general elections; Conservative government takes office and begins tax and social security reforms and privatization program.

1995 Sweden joins the EC.

TRAVEL
Visa: None needed by U.S. ***Driving permit:*** Nat. license. ***Health and safety:*** No inoculations needed. ***Tourist features:*** Storkyrkan Cathedral; Bosjökloster Castle. ***National holiday:*** June 6 (Day of the Swedish Flag).

NORWAY

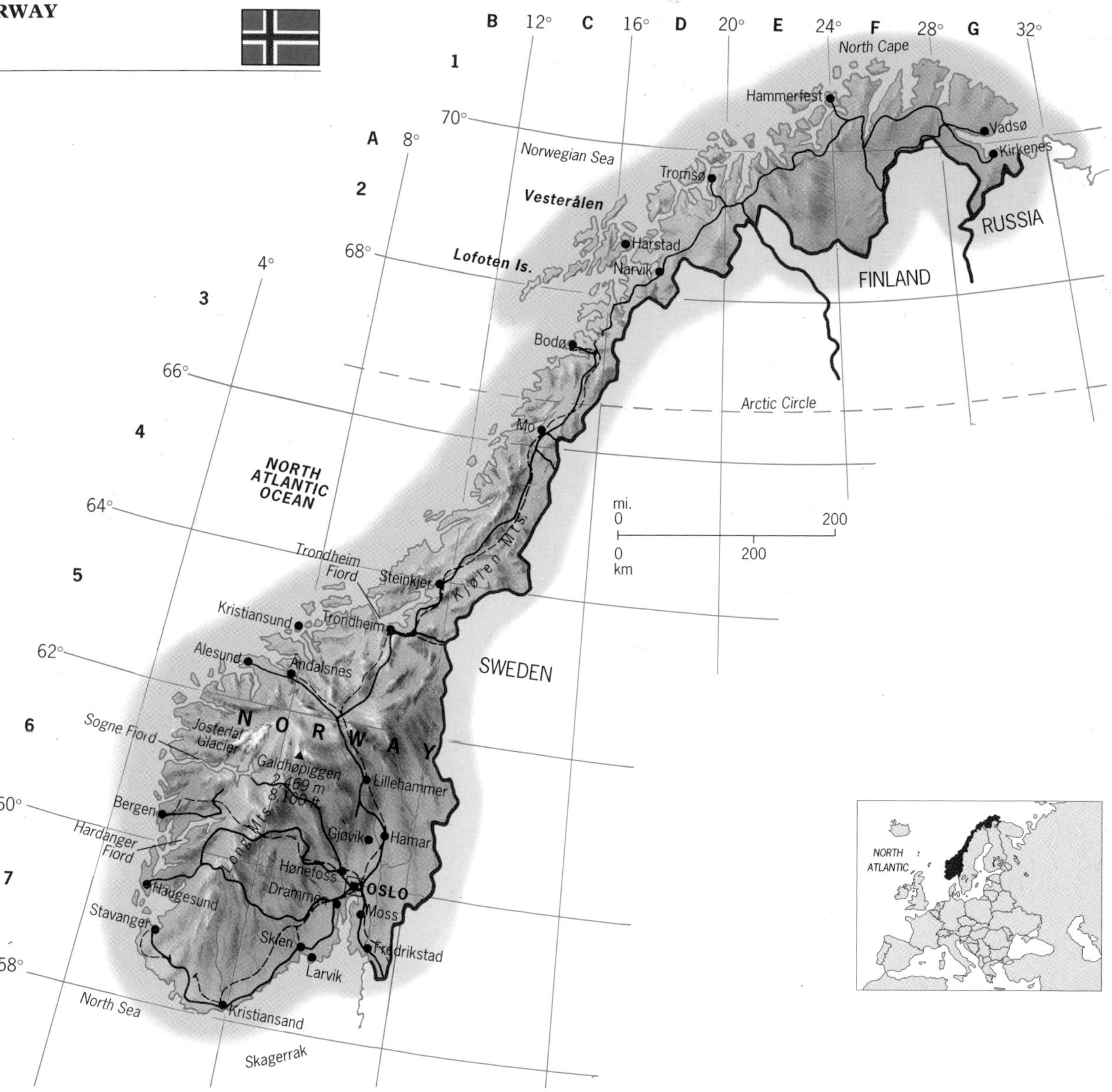

Area: 125,181 sq. mi./324,219 km².
Local name: Kongeriket Norge.
Currency: Norwegian krone.
Capital: Oslo. **Other cities:** Bergen,
Trondheim. **Physical features:** High
plateaus and rugged mountains; highly
indented coast with thousands of
islands. **Climate:** Temperate on
coast; subpolar inland. **Time zone:**
GMT +1h. **Political system:**
Constitutional monarchy. **Head of
state:** King Harald V (from 1991).
Head of government: Gro Harlem
Brundtland (from 1990). **Main
exports:** Oil and oil products, natural
gas, fish, aluminum, ships, paper,
iron. **Resources:** Crude oil, copper,
natural gas, pyrites, nickel, iron ore,
zinc, lead, fish, wood, hydropower.

PEOPLE

Population: 4,312,000. **Distribution
urban/rural:** 75%/25%. **Life expectancy:** 74(m), 81(f). **Languages:**
Norwegian (official); small Lapp- and
Finnish-speaking minorities. **Ethnic
groups:** Germanic; small Lapp minority.
Religions: Evangelical Lutheran (state
religion) 88%, other Christian 4%, other
5%. **Literacy rate:** 99%. **Per capita
GDP:** $17,100.

KEY DATES

1397 Norway comes under Danish rule.
1814 Denmark cedes Norway to Sweden.
1905 Independence achieved.
1940–45 German occupation.
1945 Becomes charter member of UN.
1949 Joins NATO.
1960 Joins European Free Trade
Association (EFTA).

1966 National Insurance Act introduces
extensive social welfare program.
1970s Starts producing petroleum and
natural gas from North Sea oilfields.
1972 Norwegians reject EC membership
treaty in national referendum.
1990 Constitutional amendment allows
women to inherit the throne.
1991 Harald V becomes king.
1992 Norway defies international whaling
ban; formal application to join EC.
1994 Maastricht Treaty (for a stronger
EC) rejected in national referendum.

TRAVEL
Visa: None needed by U.S. **Driving permit:**
Nat. license. **Health and safety:** No inocula-
tions needed. **Tourist features:** Fjords;
Briksdal glacier; Arctic wildlife. **National
holiday:** May 17 (Constitution Day).

DENMARK★

Area: 16,633 sq. mi./43,075 km².
Local name: Kongeriget Danmark.
Currency: Danish krone. *Capital:*
Copenhagen. *Other cities:* Arhus,
Odense. *Physical features:* Flat to
gently rolling plains. *Climate:* Temperate. *Time zone:* GMT +1h. *Political system:* Constitutional monarchy. *Head of state:* Queen Margrethe
II (from 1972). *Head of government:* Poul Nyrup Rasmussen (from
1993). *Main exports:* Meat, machinery, metals, dairy products, transportation equipment, fish, mink pelts,
chemicals, textiles. *Resources:* Crude
oil, natural gas, fish, salt, limestone.

PEOPLE
Population: 5,189,000. *Distribution
urban/rural:* 86%/14%. *Life expectancy:* 72(m), 78(f). *Languages:* Danish,
Faroese; German-speaking minority.

Ethnic groups: Scandinavian, Faroese,
German. *Religions:* Evangelical
Lutheran 91%, other Christian 2%, other
7%. *Literacy rate:* 99%. *Per capita
GDP:* $17,700.

KEY DATES
1397 Denmark unites with Sweden and
Norway.
1523 Sweden secedes from union.
1618–48 Danish-Swedish War.
1700–21 Great Northern War.
1814 Norway ceded to Sweden after
Napoleonic Wars.
1848 Revolt against Danish rule in
Schleswig and Holstein.
1849 First democratic constitution.
1864 War with Austria over Schleswig
and Holstein.
1915 New constitution.
1940–45 German occupation.
1945 Becomes charter member of UN;
accords independence to Iceland.
1948 Faroe Islands accorded home rule.
1949 Becomes member of NATO.
1953 New constitution abolishes upper

house of parliament and allows women
to inherit the throne.
1960 Founding member of European
Free Trade Association (EFTA).
1972 Resigns from EFTA.
1973 Joins EEC.
1979 Grants home rule to Greenland.
1972 Margrethe II becomes first female
head of state in nearly 600 years.
1985 Antinuclear movement grows.
1990 Ferry disaster claims 166 lives.
1991 Maastricht Treaty rejected in
national referendum.
1993 Prime minister resigns; second referendum approves Maastricht Treaty
after modifications.
*Excludes Greenland (p. 574)

TRAVEL
Visa: None needed by U.S. *Driving permit:*
Nat. license. *Health and safety:* No inocula-
tions needed. *Tourist features:* Kronborg
Castle in Helsingør; Tivoli gardens,
Copenhagen; Legoland park. *National
holiday:* April 16 (Birthday of the Queen).

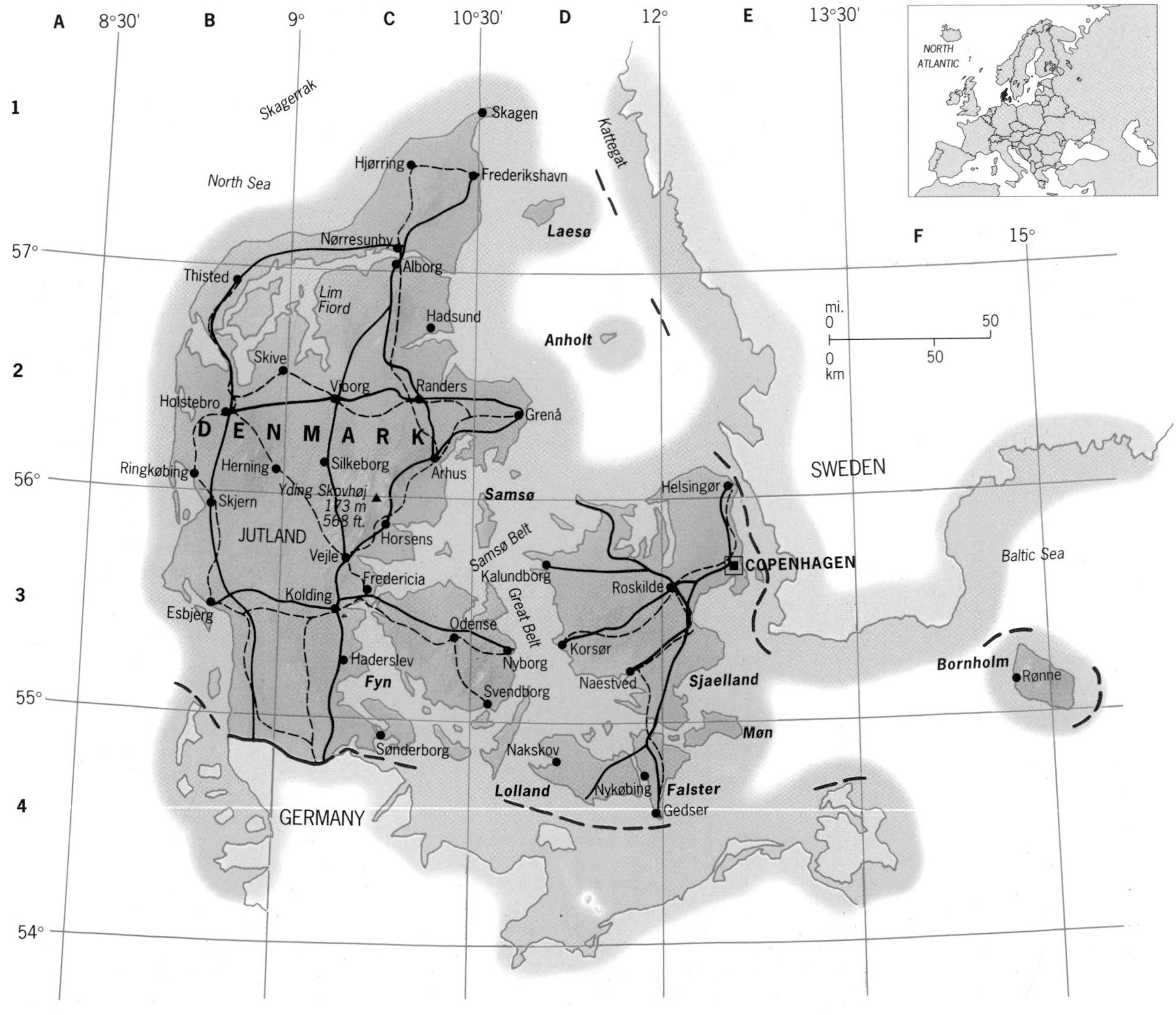

UNITED KINGDOM

Area: 93,620 sq. mi./242,477 km². **Local name:** United Kingdom (U.K.). **Currency:** Pound sterling. **Capital:** London. **Other large cities:** Birmingham, Glasgow, Leeds, Sheffield, Liverpool, Manchester, Edinburgh, Bradford, Belfast, Newcastle-upon-Tyne, Cardiff. **Physical features:** Mostly rugged hills; level to rolling plains in E. and S.E. **Climate:** Temperate. **Time zone:** GMT. **Political system:** Constitutional monarchy. **Head of state:** Queen Elizabeth II (from 1952). **Head of government:** John Major (from 1990). **Main exports:** Manufactured goods, machinery, fuels, chemicals, semifinished goods, transportation equipment. **Resources:** Coal, crude oil, natural gas, tin, limestone, iron ore, salt, clay, chalk, gypsum, lead, silica.

PEOPLE

Population: 57,826,514. **Distribution urban/rural:** 90%/10%. **Life expectancy:** 73(m), 79(f). **Languages:** English, Welsh, small Gaelic-speaking minority. **Ethnic groups:** English 81%, Scottish, 10%, Irish 4%, Welsh 2%, West Indian, Indian, Pakistani, and other 3%. **Religions:** Anglican 63%, Roman Catholic 14%, Presbyterian 4%, Methodist 3%, Baptist 1%, Orthodox 1%, other Christian 6%, Muslim 3%, Sikh 2%, Hindu 1%, Jewish 1%, other 1%. **Literacy rate:** 99%. **Per capita GDP:** $15,900.

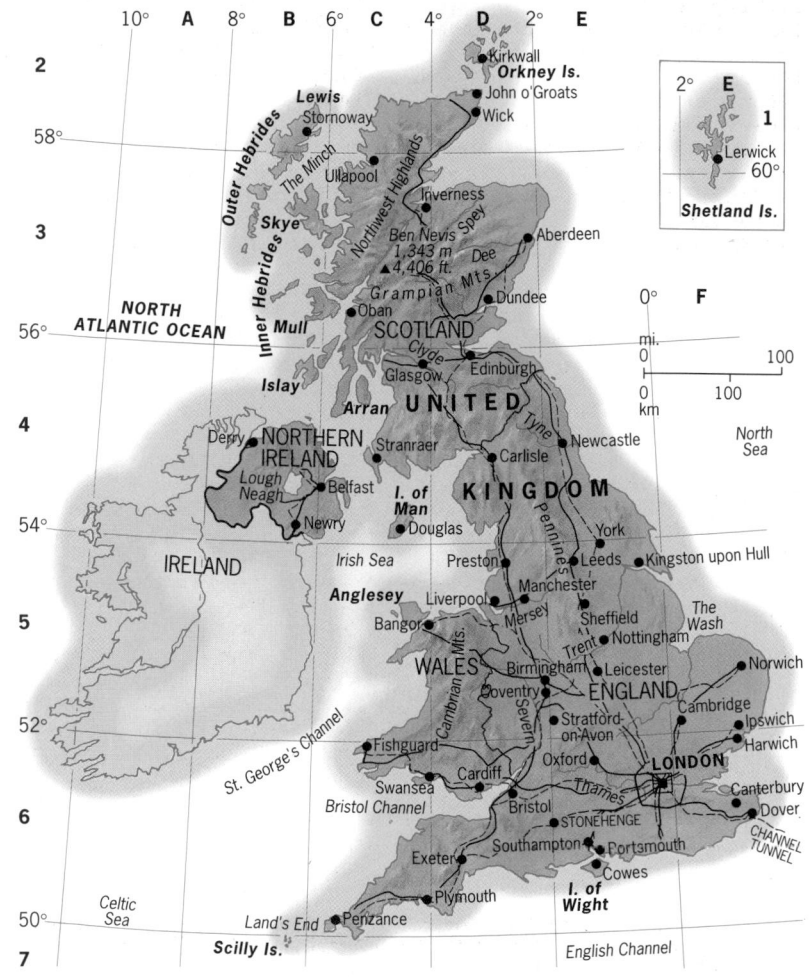

KEY DATES

1700s Start of Industrial Revolution.
1707 Act of Union creates the United Kingdom of Great Britain.
1776 Loss of North American colonies making up U.S.A.
1801 Act of Union creates the United Kingdom of Great Britain and Ireland.
1815 Economic depression; Napoleonic wars end at the Battle of Waterloo.
1819 Peterloo massacre: mass demonstration for social reforms in St. Peter's Square, Manchester, is brutally suppressed by army.
1820s Robert Peel reforms penal code.
1824 Combination Acts forbidding trade unions repealed.
1829 Peel founds Metropolitan Police; Catholic Emancipation Act removes restrictions introduced in the 1600s.
1832 Electoral Reform Act extends voting franchise to most male property owners.
1833–53 Factory Acts improve working conditions; workhouses created.
1833 Slavery abolished throughout the British Empire.
1834 Tolpuddle Martyrs convicted of illegal trade union activities and deported to Australia.

1835 Municipal Corporation Act; Tamworth Manifesto: Tories take the name Conservatives.
1836 Tolpuddle Martyrs pardoned.
1837 Queen Victoria comes to the throne.
1838 Foundation of working-class movement for electoral reform, the Chartists.
1842 Mines Act outlaws underground employment of boys under ten years old and women.
1844 Cooperative movement started by the Rochdale Equitable Pioneers.
1845–46 Potato famine in Ireland.
1846 John Peel repeals Corn Laws, marking the beginning of the decline of British agriculture.
1851 Great Exhibition in London.
1854–56 Crimean War.
1858 Government takes over British East India Company.

1867 Reform Act (also 1884) extends voting franchise to most working men; British North America Act makes Canada a self-governing dominion within the British Empire.
1868 Foundation of Trades Union Congress (TUC).
1870 Education Act funds schools from rates and taxes.
1875 Employers and Workmen Act allows peaceful picketing during strikes.
1899–1902 Boer War.
1900 Foundation of Labor Representation Committee by trade unions and socialist groups.
1904 Entente Cordiale signed with France.
1906 Trade Disputes Act extends rights of trade unions; Liberals elected in general election; Labor Representation

Committee becomes the Labour Party.

1907 Triple Entente is formed.

1908 Old Age Pensions Act grants pension to all people over 70 years old.

1911 Parliament Act reduces power of the House of Lords.

1914–18 World War I.

1918 Treaties of Versailles and Sèvres give Britain control of German colonies in Africa and some Ottoman territories in the Middle East.

1919 War in Ireland.

1920 U.K. joins the League of Nations; Government of Ireland Act incorporates Northern Ireland into the U.K.

1921 Peace treaty ends war in Ireland; creation of Irish Free State.

1924 Ramsay MacDonald forms Britain's first Labour government.

1926 General strike against wage cuts.

1929 The Depression hits Britain.

1931 Unemployment reaches three million; austerity measures introduced.

1936 Edward VIII comes to the throne but abdicates in order to marry U.S. divorced woman, Wallis Simpson; George VI becomes king.

1938 Munich Agreement: Prime Minister Neville Chamberlain reaches agreement with Adolf Hitler and declares "peace in our time."

1939 Outbreak of World War II.

1940 Chamberlain resigns; Winston Churchill becomes prime minister.

1945 Allies defeat Axis powers; Britain joins the UN; Labour wins landslide victory in general election with Clement Attlee as leader; social welfare reforms;

nationalization program begins.

1949 U.K. joins NATO.

1950–53 Britain enters Korean War.

1951 Conservatives return to power with Churchill as prime minister.

1956 Britain and France attack Egypt after Egypt seizes the Suez Canal; international pressure forces British and French to withdraw.

1960 U.K. joins European Free Trade Association (EFTA).

1963 Application to join EEC rejected.

1964 Economic problems; Labour returns to power under Harold Wilson.

1967 Application for EEC membership rejected once more; pound devalued.

1969 Troops sent into Northern Ireland to maintain order.

1970 Conservatives come to power under Edward Heath.

1972 Direct rule imposed on Northern Ireland.

1973 U.K. joins EEC; labor unrest.

1974 Coal strike; three-day week introduced to conserve electricity; Labour wins general election under Wilson.

1976 James Callaghan replaces Wilson as prime minister.

1977 Liberal–Labour pact.

1979 Referendums in Scotland and Wales on devolution are defeated; Margaret Thatcher becomes Britain's first woman prime minister.

1981 Rioting in inner cities.

1982 Unemployment passes three million; Falklands War; foundation of Social Democratic Party (SDP).

1980s Government embarks upon large-

scale privatization program.

1984–85 Mine closures prompt longest coal strike in British history.

1985 Anglo-Irish treaty establishes advisory council for Northern Ireland.

1986 Metropolitan counties abolished.

1987 SDP merges with Liberal Party to form Liberal Democrats; work on Channel Tunnel begins.

1990 Riots in London over poll tax; Thatcher resigns and is replaced by John Major; British troops are sent to the Persian Gulf; Britain joins European Exchange Rate Mechanism (ERM).

1991 Persian Gulf War ends.

1992 Conservative Party wins fourth consecutive general election with reduced majority; John Smith replaces Neil Kinnock as Labour leader; pound devalued and Britain withdraws from ERM; extensive coal mine closure program meets with widespread opposition; Maastricht Treaty on European Union ratified; senior government figures implicated in arms sales to Iraq.

1993 Recession continues; Downing Street Declaration by British and Irish leaders pledges to achieve peace in Northern Ireland.

1994 John Smith dies suddenly and is replaced by Tony Blair; Conservatives defeated in local and European Parliament elections.

1995 "Sleaze" scandals shake public confidence in MPs and Parliament, leading to Nolan Committee on Standards in Public Life; conservatives suffer most definitive defeat in history of local government.

NORTHERN IRELAND

In 1920, the Government of Ireland Act accorded internal self-government to Ireland and incorporated six of Ulster's nine counties into the U.K. A large proportion of Northern Ireland's population are Protestants of English or Scottish descent, and many of these campaigned to keep Northern Ireland part of the U.K. Since partition, Northern Ireland's history has been dominated by violence between Unionist (or Loyalist) and Nationalist groups. In 1969, the situation was so volatile that the British army was sent in to maintain order, but this did not stop the escalation of violence. In the 1970s, the Provisional IRA began a terrorist campaign on the island of Great Britain. In August 1994, the IRA announced a cease-fire, and British and Irish leaders are now looking for ways to ensure lasting peace in Northern Ireland.

KEY DATES

1920 Northern Ireland becomes a self-governing province of the U.K.; rioting in Derry.

1964 Campaign for Social Justice in Northern Ireland founded to oppose discrimination against Catholics.

1968 Catholic civil rights marches repeatedly disrupted by Unionist counter-demonstrations.

1969 IRA splits into Provisional and Official factions; British troops sent to Ulster.

1970 Internment introduced.

1972 Bloody Sunday: 13 Catholics shot dead by British troops during civil rights demonstration in Derry; direct rule imposed.

1973 Catholics boycott referendum on status of Northern Ireland; 57.4% vote for union.

1974 Self-government restored; Protestant workers lead general strike, prompting resignation of the Executive Council of Northern Ireland; direct rule reestablished; Prevention of Terrorism Act proscribes the IRA and accords police the power to detain people "reasonably suspected of terrorist activities."

1979 Lord Mountbatten killed by IRA bomb.

1981 March: imprisoned IRA member Bobby Sands begins hunger strike, demanding political status for IRA prisoners; April: Sands' election to parliament leads to enactment of Representation of the People Act, disqualifying from election prisoners serving terms of more than one year; May: Sands dies.

1982 Seventy-eight-member assembly established, but meetings are boycotted by both Catholic and Protestant members.

1984 IRA hotel bombing during Conservative Party conference in Brighton, England.

1985 Eleven Unionist MPs resign over Anglo-Irish Treaty establishing Northern Ireland advisory council.

1986 Assembly dissolved; Deputy Chief Constable of Greater Manchester, John Stalker, finds

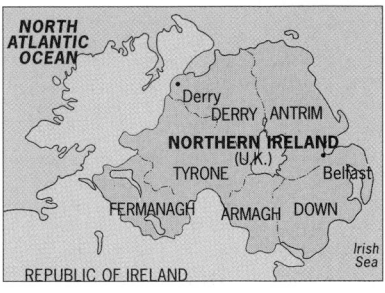

evidence of a "shoot to kill" policy by Royal Ulster Constabulary.

1988 Margaret Thatcher introduces broadcasting ban on Sinn Féin members; three IRA members shot dead in Gibraltar by SAS.

1991 Mortar attack on 10 Downing Street.

1993 Peace rally drawing 15,000 in Dublin; IRA bomb in City of London causes an estimated $600 million in damage and lost revenue; British government acknowledges long-standing contacts with the IRA; Downing Street Declaration provides "framework for peace."

1994 Sinn Féin rejects Downing Street Declaration; cease-fire by IRA and Loyalist paramilitaries.

1995 Britain opens talks with Sinn Féin, framework document for peace debated.

IRELAND

Area: 27,119 sq. mi./70,283 km².
Local name: Poblacht na h'Eireann/
Republic of Ireland. **Currency:** Punt.
Capital: Dublin. **Other city:** Cork.
Physical features: Central plain sur-
rounded by rugged hills. **Climate:**
Temperate. **Time zone:** GMT.
Political system: Republic. **Head of
state:** Mary Robinson (from 1990).
Head of government: John Bruton
(from 1994). **Main exports:**
Livestock, transportation equipment,
food, industrial machinery, chemicals.
Resources: Zinc, lead, natural gas,
oil, barite, copper, gypsum, limestone.

PEOPLE

Population: 3,563,000. **Distribution
urban/rural:** 57%/43%. **Life expectancy:** 72(m), 78(f). **Languages:** Irish,
English (both official). **Ethnic groups:**
Celtic with English minority. **Religions:**
Roman Catholic 93%, Protestant 3%,
other 3%. **Literacy rate:** 98%. **Per
capita GDP:** $11,200.

KEY DATES

1801 Act of Union creates United
Kingdom of Great Britain and Ireland.
1845–46 Potato famine: one million people die and nearly a million emigrate.
1858 James Stephens founds the Irish
Republican Brotherhood in Dublin.
1865 British government arrests members
of the Republican movement.
1867 Republican uprising suppressed.
1870 Home Rule movement founded.
1882 Chief secretary of Ireland, Lord
Frederick Cavendish, and undersecretary, T. H. Burke, are assassinated in
Phoenix Park, Dublin.
1902 Arthur Griffith founds Sinn Féin.
1905 Unionists form provisional government to rule Ulster independently; Irish
Volunteers formed.
1912 Ulster Volunteer Force founded and
imports arms from Germany.
1914 British government passes Home
Rule Bill.
1916 Easter Rising: nationalists seize
Dublin general post office and proclaim
a republic; rebellion suppressed by
British army and 15 leaders executed.
1918 Sinn Féin wins majority of Irish
seats in British parliament and establishes separate Irish parliament (Dáil
Eireann); Irish Volunteers become Irish
Republican Army (IRA).
1919 Dáil declares independent Ireland;
war between IRA and British forces.
1920 Dáil rejects Government of Ireland
Act dividing Ireland; Britain sends auxiliary forces to Ireland.
1921 Truce between British forces and
IRA; Anglo-Irish Treaty establishes
Irish Free State; split within Sinn Féin.
1922 Irish Free State achieves dominion
status; many Sinn Féin leaders refuse to

swear allegiance to British crown and
do not take their seats in dominion government; civil war breaks out.
1926 Breakaway Sinn Féin members
found Fianna Fáil under Eamon de
Valera.
1932 Fianna Fáil wins Irish Free State
general election; British links severed.
1937 Independence achieved as Eire.
1948 External Relations Act repealed,
severing remaining links with U.K.
1949 Ireland leaves Commonwealth and
the Republic of Ireland is declared.
1973 Joins EEC; Fianna Fáil defeated in
election for first time in 40 years.
1977 Fianna Fáil returns to power; Jack
Lynch becomes prime minister.
1979 Lynch resigns; Charles Haughey
becomes prime minister.
1981 Garrett FitzGerald forms coalition
government.
1983 New Ireland Forum established but
rejected by British government.
1985 Treaty with U.K. establishing advisory council for Northern Ireland.
1986 Ulster Unionist protest against
Anglo-Irish Agreement.

1987 Charles Haughey wins election.
1988 Strained relations with U.K. over
extradition decisions.
1990 Mary Robinson becomes president.
1992 Haughey resigns after losing parliamentary majority; Albert Reynolds
becomes Fianna Fáil leader and prime
minister; Maastricht Treaty approved in
national referendum; Reynolds loses
vote of confidence.
1993 Fianna Fáil-Labour coalition
formed; Downing Street Declaration
with U.K. pledges end to violence in
Ulster; peace rally in Dublin.
1994 IRA declares a cease-fire; Reynolds
resigns over appointment of Harry
Whelehan as chief justice minister; John
Bruton becomes prime minister.

TRAVEL
Visa: None needed by U.S. **Driving permit:**
Nat. license. **Health and safety:** No inoculations needed. **Tourist features:** Macgillicud-
dy's Reeks; Wicklow Mountains; Galway Bay
and Aran Islands; Blarney stone. **National
holiday:** March 17 (St. Patrick's day).

NETHERLANDS

Area: 16,034 sq. mi./41,526 km². *Local name:* Koninkrijk der Nederlanden. *Currency:* Guilder. *Capital:* Amsterdam. *Other cities:* Rotterdam, The Hague, Utrecht. *Physical features:* Flat coastal lowland, some reclaimed land (polders). *Climate:* Temperate. *Time zone:* GMT +1h. *Political system:* Constitutional monarchy. *Head of state:* Queen Beatrix Wilhelmina Armgard (from 1980). *Head of government:* Wim Kok (from 1994). *Main exports:* Agricultural products, processed food, electronic equipment, petrochemicals, natural gas. *Resources:* Natural gas, crude oil.

PEOPLE

Population: 15,287,000. *Distribution urban/rural:* 88%/12%. *Life expectancy:* 75(m), 81(f). *Language:* Dutch. *Ethnic groups:* Dutch 96%, Moroccan, Turkish, and other 4%. *Religions:* Roman Catholic 36%, Protestant 27%, none 31%, other 6%. *Literacy rate:* 99%. *Per capita GDP:* $16,600.

KEY DATES

1581 Achieves Independence from Spain.
1600s Becomes a major sea power.
1795–1813 Napoleonic wars: France gains control of the Netherlands; Britain seizes many Dutch colonies.
1814 Constitution written.
1815 Congress of Vienna accords the Netherlands independence from France and control of Belgium.
1830 Belgium and the Netherlands separate after Belgian revolt.
1848 New constitution diminishes the power of the monarchy.
1914–18 The Netherlands remains neutral during World War I.
1932 Zuider Zee project: nearly 800 sq. mi. (2,000 km²) of land reclaimed.
1939 Declares neutrality in World War II.
1940–45 German occupation: 75% of the nation's Jews are killed and around 270,000 Dutch are killed overall.
1945 The Netherlands joins the UN; war breaks out with nationalists in Dutch East Indies (now Indonesia).
1948 Benelux customs union formed with Luxembourg and Belgium; receives financial aid through the European Recovery Program.
1949 The Netherlands gives up all territories in the East Indies except Netherlands New Guinea (now Irian Jaya); becomes a founding member of NATO.
1950 The Netherlands joins European Coal and Steel Community.
1952 The Netherlands joins European Defence Community (EDC).
1953 Dykes broken by storms; around 2,000 people and several hundred thousand cattle are killed in floods.

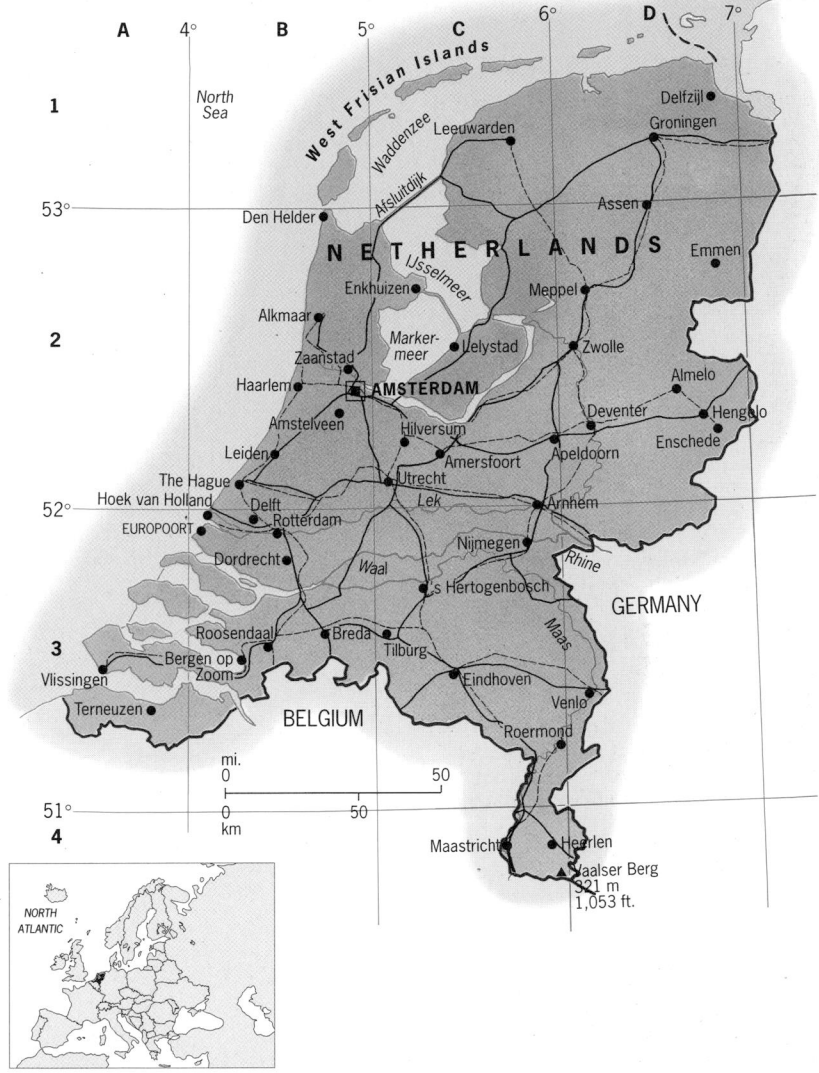

1958 The Netherlands joins the EEC.
1962 Independence granted to Netherlands New Guinea.
1969 Civil unrest in Netherlands Antilles.
1971 Anti-Revolutionary Party leads new coalition government.
1973 Joop den Uyl (Labor Party) becomes premier.
1975 Suriname gains independence; hundreds of thousands of Surinamese immigrants arrive in the Netherlands.
1977 Andreas van Agt (Christian Democrat Party) becomes premier.
1980 Queen Beatrix comes to the throne.
1981 Plans to site cruise missiles on Dutch soil are obstructed by public opposition.
1982 Andreas Van Agt unexpectedly resigns as party leader and premier and is succeeded by Ruud Lubbers (Christian Democrat Party).
1989 Prime minister Ruud Lubbers rejects his old coalition partners, the Liberal Party, and forms a new

alliance with Labour.
1990 Parliament passes one of the most ambitious environmental programs in the world; Schengen Treaty eliminates border controls among France, Belgium, Germany, Luxembourg, and the Netherlands.
1992 Israeli cargo jet crashes into apartment building in Amsterdam, killing 65 people; Maastricht Treaty on European Union ratified.
1993 Relaxation of laws relating to euthanasia.
1994 Wim Kok elected prime minister.
1995 Floods devastate the country.

TRAVEL
Visa: None needed by U.S. *Driving permit:* Nat. license. *Health and safety:* No inoculations needed. *Tourist features:* Canals; Rijksmuseum; Frisian Islands; Van Gogh Museum; Anne Frank's house. *National holiday:* April 30 (Queen's Day).

BELGIUM

Area: 11,788 sq. mi./30,528 km². ***Local name:*** Koninkrijk België/Royaume de Belgique. ***Currency:*** Belgian franc. ***Capital:*** Brussels. ***Other cities:*** Antwerp, Ghent. ***Physical features:*** Flat coastal plains in N.W. rising to rolling hills in S.E. ***Climate:*** Temperate. ***Time zone:*** GMT +1h. ***Political system:*** Constitutional monarchy. ***Head of state:*** King Albert II (from 1993). ***Head of government:*** Jean-Luc Dehaene (from 1992). ***Main exports:*** Iron, steel, textiles, vehicles, diamonds, petroleum products, machinery, chemicals, food. ***Resources:*** Coal, natural gas, oil.

PEOPLE
Population: 10,010,000. ***Distribution***

urban/rural: 96%/4%. ***Life expectancy:*** 73(m), 80(f). ***Languages:*** Flemish (Dutch) 56%, French 32%, German 1%, legally bilingual 11%. ***Ethnic groups:*** Fleming 55%, Walloon 33%, other 12%. ***Religions:*** Roman Catholic 75%, Protestant and other 25%. ***Literacy rate:*** 99%. ***Per capita GDP:*** $17,300.

KEY DATES
1815 Belgium unites with the Netherlands.
1830 Belgium declares independence from the Netherlands.
1914–18 Belgium fights on the Allied side during World War I.
1940–45 Occupied by Germany.
1948 Benelux customs union formed with Luxembourg and the Netherlands.
1950 Joins NATO.
1957 Helps to set up the EEC.
1971 Divided into three cultural communities based on its three languages.

1972 German-speaking cabinet members allowed for the first time.
1980 Violent clashes throughout Belgium over language divisions.
1989 Federal system adopted.
1990 Decentralization of some government functions such as education, industrial development, and local issues to regional councils; abortion legalized; Schengen Treaty relaxes border controls among several EC countries.
1991 Rioting in Brussels as a result of racial tension: immigrants claim to face discrimination in jobs and housing.
1992 Brussels fails in its bid to become the capital of the EC when it is decided that the European Parliament's official seat should remain in Strasbourg.
1993 Belgium officially becomes a federal state with three regions: Flanders, Wallonia, and Brussels; King Baudouin dies and is succeeded by his brother, Prince Albert of Liège.

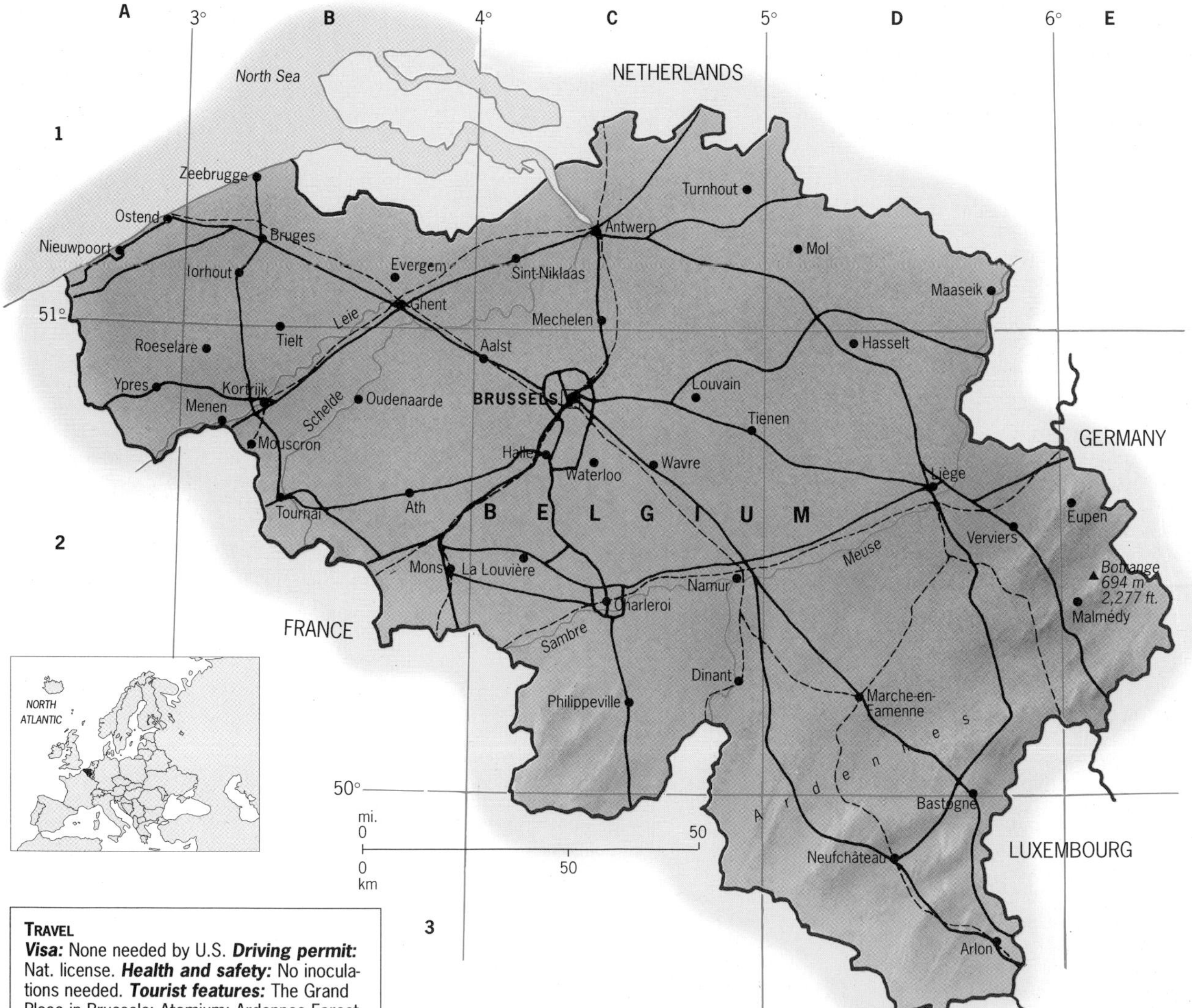

TRAVEL
Visa: None needed by U.S. ***Driving permit:*** Nat. license. ***Health and safety:*** No inoculations needed. ***Tourist features:*** The Grand Place in Brussels; Atomium; Ardennes Forest. ***National holiday:*** July 21 (National Day).

LUXEMBOURG

Area: 999 sq. mi./2,586 km². ***Local name:*** Grand-Duché de Luxembourg. ***Currency:*** Luxembourg franc. ***Capital:*** Luxembourg City. ***Other city:*** Esch-sur-Alzette. ***Physical features:*** Mostly gently undulating plain, slightly mountainous in N. ***Climate:*** Temperate. ***Time zone:*** GMT +1h. ***Political system:*** Constitutional monarchy. ***Head of state:*** Grand Duke Jean (from 1964). ***Head of government:*** Jacques Santer (from 1984). ***Main exports:*** Steel, synthetic textiles, chemicals, glass, machinery, plastics, transportation equipment. ***Resource:*** Iron ore.

PEOPLE

Population: 380,000. ***Distribution urban/rural:*** 91%/9%. ***Life expectancy:*** 73(m), 80(f). ***Languages:*** Letzebuergesch, German, French. ***Ethnic groups:*** Luxembourger 70%, Portuguese, Italian, French, German. ***Religions:*** Roman Catholic 97%, Protestant and Jewish 3%. ***Literacy rate:*** 100%. ***Per capita GDP:*** $20,200.

KEY DATES

1354 Creation of Duchy of Luxembourg.
1684 Comes under French control.
1815 Treaty of Vienna creates Grand Duchy of Luxembourg, to be ruled by the king of the Netherlands.
1830 Rebellion against Dutch rule.
1890 Luxembourg declares independence from the Netherlands.
1914–18 Occupied by Germany during World War I.
1940–45 Occupied by Germany during World War II.
1945 Joins UN.
1948 Benelux customs union formed with Belgium and the Netherlands.
1949 Joins NATO.

1957 Joins EEC.
1964 Grand Duchess Charlotte abdicates in favor of her son, Prince Jean.
1991 European Free Trade Pact signed in Luxembourg.
1992 Maastricht Treaty ratified.

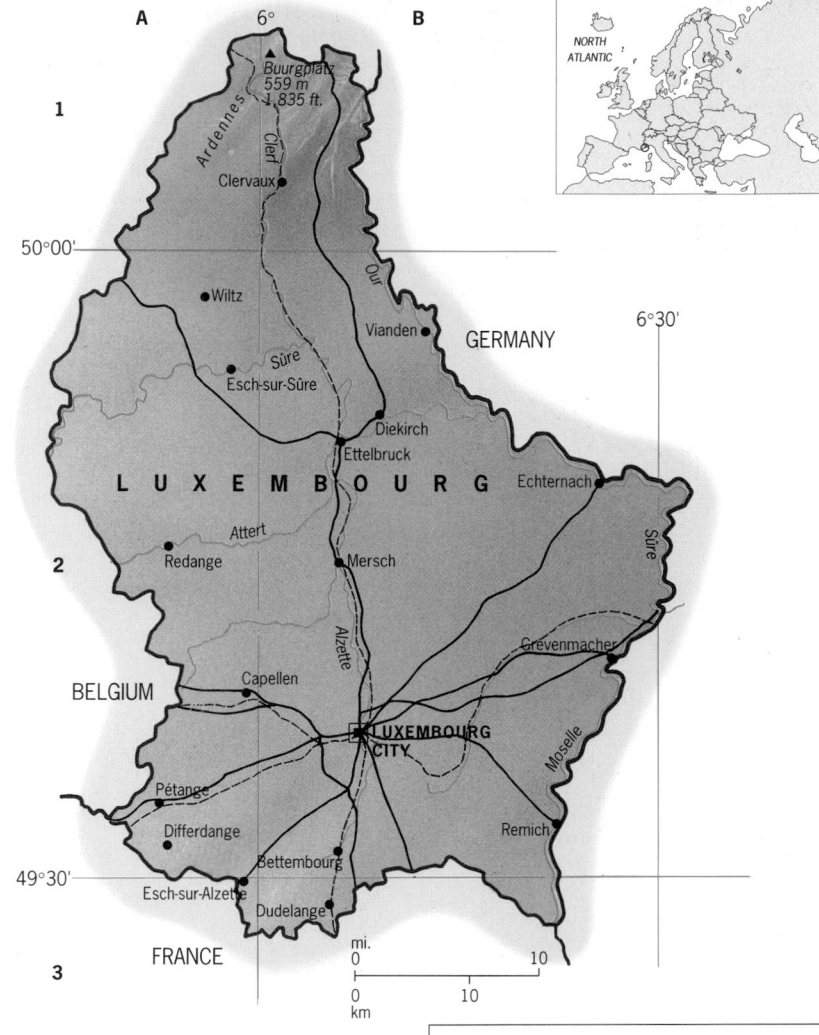

TRAVEL
Visa: None needed by U.S. ***Driving permit:*** Nat. license. ***Health and safety:*** No inoculations needed. ***Tourist features:*** Ruins of Bock fortress; Vianden Castle. ***National holiday:*** June 23 (National Day).

MONACO

Area: 0.7 sq. mi./1.9 km². ***Local name:*** Principauté de Monaco. ***Currency:*** French franc. ***Capital:*** Monaco. ***Other city:*** Monte Carlo. ***Physical features:*** Rugged hills. ***Climate:*** Subtropical. ***Time zone:*** GMT +1h. ***Political system:*** Constitutional monarchy. ***Head of state:*** Prince Rainier III (from 1949). ***Head of government:*** Jacques Dupont (from 1991). ***Main exports:*** Chemicals, pharmaceuticals. ***Resources:*** None.

PEOPLE

Population: 38,000. ***Distribution urban/rural:*** 100% urban. ***Life expectancy:*** 72(m), 80(f). ***Languages:*** French (official), English, Italian, Monégasque. ***Ethnic groups:*** French 47%, Monégasque 16%, Italian 16%. ***Religion:*** Roman Catholic. ***Literacy rate:*** n.a. ***Per capita GDP:*** $16,000.

KEY DATES

1793 Comes under French control.
1815 Independence restored.
1940–45 Occupied by Axis powers.
1993 Joins the UN.

TRAVEL
Visa: None needed by U.S. ***Driving permit:*** Nat. license. ***Health and safety:*** No inoculations needed. ***Tourist features:*** Grand Prix; oceanographic center; casinos. ***National holiday:*** November 19 (National Day).

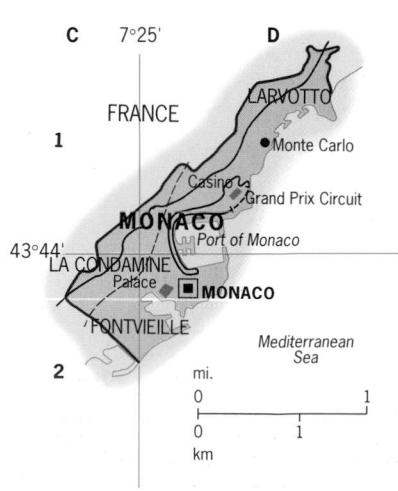

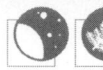

FRANCE

Area: 210,025 sq. mi./543,965 km². *Local name:* République Française. *Currency:* French franc. *Capital:* Paris. *Other cities:* Lyon, Marseille, Lille. *Physical features:* Rolling hills in N., mountainous in S., especially the Pyrenees and Alps. *Climate:* Temperate; subtropical in S. *Time zone:* GMT +1h. *Political system:* Republic. *Head of state:* Jacques Chirac (from 1995). *Head of government:* Edouard Balladur (from 1993). *Main exports:* Machinery and transportation equipment, chemicals, foodstuffs, agricultural products, iron, steel, textiles. *Resources:* Coal, iron ore, bauxite, fish, wood, zinc, potash.

PEOPLE
Population: 57,660,000. *Distribution urban/rural:* 74%/26%. *Life expectancy:* 74(m), 82(f). *Language:* French. *Ethnic groups:* Celtic and Latin with Teutonic, Slavic, N. African, and Basque minorities. *Religions:* Roman Catholic 90%, Protestant 2%, Jewish 1%, Muslim 1%, unaffiliated 6%. *Literacy rate:* 99%. *Per capita GDP:* $18,300.

KEY DATES
1789–99 French Revolution.
1799 Napoleon takes control of France.
1814 Louis XVIII comes to power; Napoleon is exiled to Elba.
1815 Napoleon returns and is defeated at Waterloo; Louis XVIII regains power.
1914–18 French troops fight on Allied side during World War I.
1939 France declares war on Germany.
1940–42 Germany invades and occupies N. France; armistice signed; collaborationist government formed in Vichy; Charles de Gaulle establishes government-in-exile in London.
1942–44 Germany occupies the rest of France; resistance groups formed.
1944 Normandy landings; Charles de Gaulle becomes president.
1946 Constitution rewritten establishing the Fourth Republic; de Gaulle resigns.
1949 France joins NATO.
1954 France withdraws from Indochina after eight years of fighting; war breaks out in French colony of Algeria.
1957 France joins the EEC.
1958 New constitution establishes the Fifth Republic; de Gaulle returns to presidency; French settlers in Algeria rebel against the government.
1962 Algeria achieves independence.
1966 De Gaulle withdraws troops from NATO but remains a political member.
1968 Violent antigovernment demonstrations, initiated by students in Paris, spread rapidly across the country.
1969 De Gaulle resigns after referendum defeat; Georges Pompidou becomes president.

1974 Pompidou dies; Giscard d'Estaing becomes president.
1981 François Mitterand becomes the first socialist president since 1958.
1982 Troops sent to Lebanon to join peacekeeping force.
1983 Terrorist bomb kills 54 French troops in Beirut.
1984 Troops withdrawn from Lebanon.
1987 Work begins on Channel Tunnel.
1990 France supports the U.S.A.'s decision to impose sanctions on Iraq; Prime Minister Michel Rocard's government survives no-confidence vote over new taxes; parliament passes a law to prevent anyone inciting racial hatred from holding public office.
1991 Edith Cresson is elected as France's first woman prime minister; French forces assist the Allies in the Persian Gulf War; race riots in several cities including Paris and Lyon; decline in support for socialist government.
1992 Cresson dismissed as prime minister; Pierre Bérégovoy becomes prime minister; National Front wins record 13% of votes in local elections; referendum endorses the Maastricht Treaty by a majority of just 51%; drivers block roads for 10 days as a protest against new licensing laws.
1993 Conservative parties win parliamentary elections; Edouard Balladur becomes prime minister; Bérégovoy commits suicide following the defeat; Bank Nationale de Paris becomes the first company to be privatized under the new regime; René Bousquet, the former chief of police who cooperated with the Nazis in World War II, assassinated.
1994 First passenger trains go through the Channel Tunnel.

ECONOMY
Industry by sector
Farming France is Europe's leading farming nation. The single most important crop is wheat. Other major crops include barley, oats, flax, beets, fruit, and vegetables. About two-thirds of French farming income comes from meat and dairy products. Dairy cattle and sheep are the chief animals raised, and wine and cheese are important products.
Fishing About 680,000 tons are caught each year. Catches include cod, crabs, lobsters, monkfish, scallops, oysters, mussels, and tuna.
Forestry Forests cover about one-fourth of France. Wood is used to make furniture, timber, and pulp and paper.
Mining Iron ore is France's most important mineral. Bauxite, potash, natural gas, coal, gypsum, salt, sulfur, tungsten, and uranium are also mined.
Manufacturing France is one of the world's leading manufacturing nations, and manufacturing accounts for 34% of the GNP. France is the fourth largest producer of cars in the world after Japan, the U.S.A., and Germany. Railroad equipment is also produced, and France has

the world's fastest trains. Other important products include aircraft, military equipment, electronics (including computers, radios, televisions, and telecommunications equipment), chemicals, iron and steel, industrial machinery, and aluminum. Food processing is also significant. The Paris Basin is France's principal industrial center, but there are factories in towns and cities across the country, and Lyon, Rennes, and Douai are important centers of the vehicle-producing industry.
Services About 60% of workers are employed in service industries and this sector accounts for 62% of the GNP. Community, government, and personal services form the most important area, employing around one-third of all workers. The second most important area is trade, hotels, and restaurants. Tourism makes a substantial contribution to the economy.

NORTH ATLANTIC

A 4°
1
50°
2
Lannion
Ouessant I.
Brest
Morlaix
48°
Quimper
Quimperlé
CARNAC
ATLANTIC OCEAN
Belle-I.
3
46°
mi.
0   100
0   100
km
Bay of Biscay

2° C 0° D CHANNEL TUNNEL 2° E BELGIUM 4° F 6° G 8°

English Channel

Dunkerque
Calais
Boulogne-sur-Mer
Etaples Béthune Lille Roubaix
Lens
Arras Valenciennes
Abbeville Somme
Cap de la Hague Dieppe Amiens St.-Quentin Charleville-Mézières LUX.
Channel Is. (U.K.) Cherbourg Bay of the Seine Le Havre GERMANY
Valognes Rouen Aisne Reims Thionville
Bayeux Caen Seine Creil Marne Châlons-sur-Marne Forbach
Gulf of St.-Malo Granville Evreux St.-Denis Epernay Metz
St.-Malo Versailles PARIS Nancy Strasbourg
Fougères Alençon Chartres Melun St. Dizier St.-Dié Colmar
Rennes F R A N Troyes C E Chaumont Vosges Mts. Rhine
Laval Le Mans Seine Belfort Mulhouse
Orléans Auxerre Dijon Besançon Montbéliard
St.-Nazaire Angers Loire Blois Loire Doubs
Nantes Tours Vierzon SWITZERLAND
Yeu I. Châtellerault Châteauroux Bourges Nevers Chalon Jura Mts. Lake Geneva
La Roche-sur-Yon Poitiers Cher Moulins Mâcon Bourg-en-Bresse
Ré I. Niort Montluçon Saône Chamonix
Oléron I. La Rochelle Vichy Roanne Annecy Mt. Blanc 4,807 m 15,771 ft.
Limoges Clermont-Ferrand Lyon Villeurbanne Chambéry
Cognac Angoulême Tulle Allier St.-Etienne Vienne ALPS ITALY
Périgueux Massif Central Rhône Grenoble
4 Bordeaux Libourne Brive Le Puy Valence
Arcachon Bergerac Dordogne Aurillac
Langon Lot Mende Montélimar MONACO
Agen Garonne Tarn Alès Avignon Nice
44° Montauban Nîmes Arles Aix-en-Provence Cannes
Bayonne Dax Albi Durance St.-Tropez
Biarritz Orthez Toulouse Montpellier Marseille Riviera
Pau Béziers Sète
Tarbes Canal du Midi Toulon
Lourdes Carcassonne Gulf of Lion
5 Pyrenees Foix Narbonne Mediterranean Sea
Perpignan
SPAIN ANDORRA

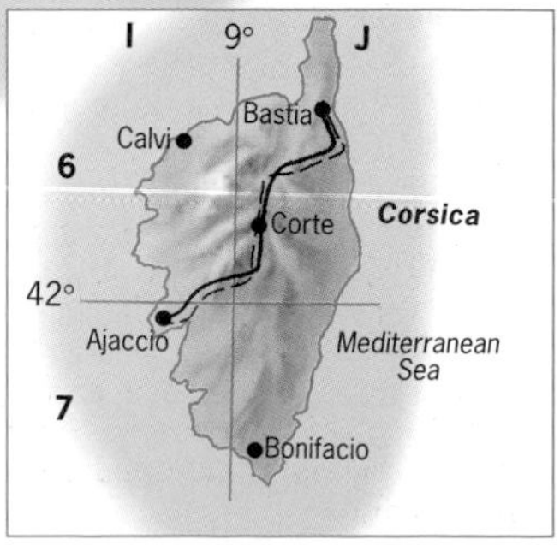

Lascaux

I 9° J
Calvi Bastia
6
Corte *Corsica*
42°
Ajaccio Mediterranean Sea
7
Bonifacio

THE BASQUES

The Basques are a people of the western Pyrenees of N. Spain and the extreme S.W. of France. Their origin is unknown and their language, Euskara, is unrelated to any other known language and is the oldest living language in S.W. Europe. Their culture distinguishes them from the other peoples of Europe, and nationalist feeling is strong. The majority of Basques live in Spain and, while they have never lived under a united government of their own, Spain's Basque population maintained a large degree of autonomy up until Spanish unification in the late 1800s. During the Spanish Civil War, they enjoyed a brief period of independence, but after the victory of the Nationalists under General Franco, the Basque country was reabsorbed into Spain. Since then, the Spanish government has made efforts to suppress Basque cultural identity by banning the language and abolishing traditional laws and privileges, but these efforts have been unsuccessful.

A separatist movement, with strong ecclesiastical support, has surfaced at intervals and has grown in strength since the 1960s, when the militant Euzkada Ta Askatasuna (ETA) began its campaign of terrorism. Concessions made in recent years by the Spanish government have divided ETA into moderates and extremists. In the 1980s, the extremists increased their activities and the situation approached a state of civil war, in spite of energetic, sometimes brutal, efforts by the police to quash it and declining support from moderate Basque nationalists.

KEY DATES
1936 Basque republic of Euzkadi is established.
1937 General Franco abolishes most rights of

the Spanish Basques, including the use of the Basque language; German aircraft bomb Euzkadi town, Guernica.
1947 Widespread demonstrations and strikes against Franco regime.
1951 Ban on Basque language lifted in schools.
1954 ETA founded by radical students.
1968 State of emergency declared; police make mass arrests and employ torture.
1970 Trial of 16 middle-class Basques by military court in Burgos encourages separatism.
1973 ETA terrorists assassinate Spanish prime minister, Carrero Blanco.
1974 Bishop of Bilbao defends Basque rights.
1975 Several Basque militants are executed; General Franco dies.
1976 Special taxation rights granted to two Basque provinces.
1977 Herri Batasuna ("United People") party emerges as political wing of ETA; 75% of Basques vote for parties supporting regional autonomy in local elections.
1980 Government grants limited autonomy to Basque provinces; HB Party gains 17% of vote in regional elections.
1983 Counter terrorist organization, Grupos Antiterroristas de Liberación (GAL), formed.
1984 New antiterrorist laws increase powers of security forces; "social reintegration" offered to former ETA members.
1986 Bombs kill 16 policemen in Madrid; provincial military governor and family killed by bomb in San Sebastian; amnestied ETA member executed by former associates.
1987 Spanish government acknowledges secret ETA contacts; ETA issues apology after killing 21 with Barcelona car bomb.

1989 Government–ETA peace talks in Algeria break down.
1990 Spanish police claim breakthrough after widespread arrests of ETA terrorists; Basque parliament approves self-determination.
1991 Police officers convicted of organizing GAL death squads; government denies intent to reopen ETA contacts.
1992 Moderate Basque parties combine in denouncing ETA terrorism; French capture key ETA leader; weakened ETA proposes truce during Barcelona Olympic Games.
1993 Thousands demonstrate against ETA in chief Basque cities; ETA kidnaps industrialist for ransom; French police seize large ETA arsenal.
1994 Government adopts tougher policy toward ETA after discharge of security chief, Rafael Vera; ETA orders its 600 imprisoned members to go on hunger strike; officials of the Spanish government's interior ministry implicated in organizing GAL.
1995 Spanish prime minister denies government involvement in GAL.

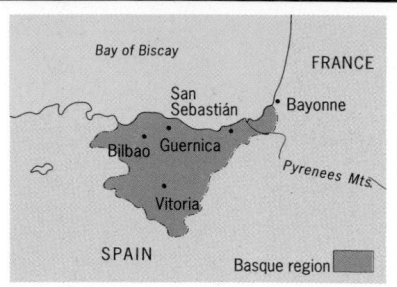

ANDORRA

Area: 175 sq. mi./453 km². **Local name:** Principat d'Andorra. **Currency:** French franc and Spanish peseta. **Capital:** Andorra la Vella. **Physical features:** Rugged mountains dissected by narrow valleys. **Climate:** Temperate. **Time zone:** GMT +1h. **Political system:** Co-principality ruled jointly by Spanish bishop of Seo de Urgel and president of France. **Heads of state:** Jacques Chirac (from 1995) and Mgr. Joan Martí y Alanís (from 1971). **Head of government:** Oscar Ribas Reig (from 1992). **Main exports:** Tobacco, clothing, mineral water; tourism very important. **Resources:** Hydropower, mineral water, wood, iron ore, lead.

PEOPLE
Population: 48,000. **Distribution urban/rural:** n.a. **Life expectancy:** 74(m), 81(f). **Languages:** Catalan (official); French and Castilian also widely used. **Ethnic groups:** Spanish 61%, Andorran 30%, French 6%, other 3%.

Religion: Roman Catholic almost 100%. **Literacy rate:** 99%. **Per capita GDP:** $14,000.

KEY DATES
1278 Franco-Spanish Treaty signed: makes Spanish bishop of Urgel and French count of Foix joint rulers of Andorra.
1933 Andorran youths storm General Council and force electoral reform.
1970 Women achieve suffrage.
1976 First political party, the Democratic Party of Andorra, formed.
1985 Voting age lowered to 18.
1991 Ties with EC formalized.
1992 Prime Minister Oscar Reig resigns and is reelected.
1993 New constitution; first direct elections result in coalition led by Reig.

TRAVEL
Visa: None needed by U.S. **Driving permit:** Nat. license with translation/IDP. **Health and safety:** No inoculations needed. **Tourist features:** Casa dels Valls; wild untamed countryside. **National holiday:** September 8 (Mare de Deu de Meritxell).

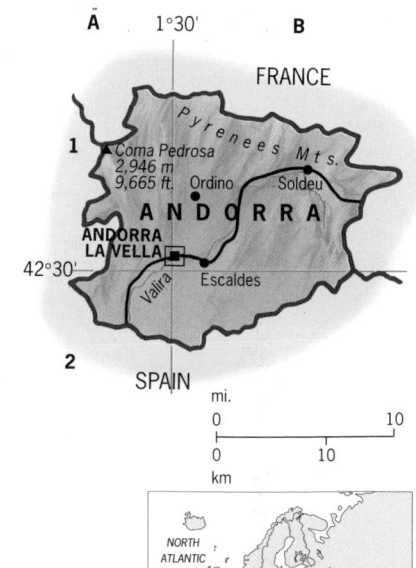

SPAIN

Area: 208,800 sq. mi./504,750 km². **Local name:** España. **Currency:** Peseta. **Capital:** Madrid. **Other cities:** Barcelona, Valencia, Seville. **Physical features:** Central plateau, mountainous in N., coastal plains in S. **Climate:** Temperate in N., subtropical in S. **Time zone:** GMT +1h. **Political system:** Constitutional monarchy. **Head of state:** King Juan Carlos I (from 1975). **Head of government:** Felipe González Márquez (from 1982). **Main exports:** Manufactured goods, vehicles, agricultural products, machinery. **Resources:** Coal, lignite, iron ore, uranium, mercury, pyrites, gypsum, zinc, lead.

PEOPLE

Population: 39,433,942. **Distribution urban/rural:** 79%/21%. **Life expectancy:** 74(m), 81(f). **Languages:** Castilian Spanish (official), second languages include Catalan, Galician, Basque. **Ethnic groups:** Composite of Nordic and Mediterranean types. **Religion:** Roman Catholic 99%. **Literacy rate:** 95%. **Per capita GDP:** $12,400.

KEY DATES

1469–1512 Unification of Spain.
1480 Spanish Inquisition founded to rid Spain of non-Catholics.
1810–25 Most Spanish colonies gain independence.
1936–39 Spanish Civil War between Nationalists led by General Francisco Franco and the Republicans.
1939 Nationalist victory: Franco becomes head of state and government; Fascist party, Falange Española, declared only legal political party.
1945–46 Most countries sever diplomatic relations with Spain.
1947 Franco announces restoration of the monarchy in the event of his death.
1960s–70s Emergence of independence movement in the Basque region.
1975 Death of General Franco: King Juan Carlos I becomes head of state.
1977 First free elections since 1936.
1978 New constitution; Adolfo Suárez (Union of the Democratic Center) becomes prime minister.
1981 Suárez resigns; Leopoldo Calvo Sotelo becomes prime minister; attempted military coup foiled.
1982 Joins NATO; Felipe González of the Socialist Worker Party (PSOE) wins landslide victory in election.
1985 Border with Gibraltar reopened.
1986 Spain joins the EEC.
1988 Joins Western European Union.
1990 Government refuses to accept a truce with the Basque liberation group (ETA) without assurance that there will be no more violence.
1992 Spain hosts Expo '92 and summer Olympics; Maastricht Treaty ratified.
1993 PSOE accused of corruption.

TRAVEL
Visa: None needed by U.S. **Driving permit:** Nat. license with translation/IDP. **Health and safety:** No inoculations needed. **Tourist features:** Barcelona cathedral; Royal Palace, Madrid; the Alhambra. **National holiday:** October 12 (National Day).

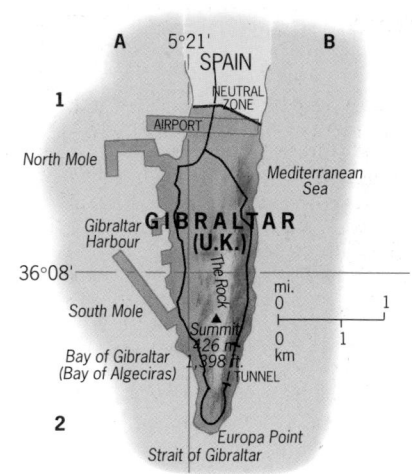

GIBRALTAR

Area: 2.5 sq. mi./6.5 km². *Local name:* Gibraltar. *Currency:* Pound sterling. *Capital:* Gibraltar. *Physical features:* Dominated by Gibraltar Rock (limestone mass) with coastal plains. *Climate:* Subtropical. *Time zone:* GMT +1h. *Political system:* Dependent territory of the U.K. *Head of state:* Queen Elizabeth II (from 1952). *Head of government:* Joseph John Bossano (from 1988). *Main exports:* Mainly reexports: petroleum, manufactured goods. *Resources:* Negligible.

PEOPLE
Population: 28,074. *Distribution*

urban/rural: 100% urban. *Life expectancy:* 72(m), 79(f). *Languages:* English (official), Spanish; Italian and Portuguese are also widely spoken. *Ethnic groups:* Mostly Spanish, English, Italian, Maltese, and Portuguese descent. *Religions:* Roman Catholic 74%, Protestant 11%, Muslim 8%, Jewish 2%, unaffiliated or other 5%. *Literacy rate:* n.a. *Per capita GNP:* $4,600.

PORTUGAL

Area: 35,459 sq. mi./91,831 km². *Local name:* República Portuguesa. *Currency:* Escudo. *Capital:* Lisbon. *Other city:* Oporto. *Physical features:* Mostly mountainous in N., rolling plains in S. *Climate:* Subtropical/temperate. *Time zone:* GMT. *Political system:* Republic. *Head of state:* Dr. Mário Alberto Nobre Lopes Soares (from 1986). *Head of government:* Aníbal Cavaço Silva (from 1985). *Main exports:* Cotton and other textiles, paper, chemicals, wine, wood. *Resources:* Fish, wood, tungsten, iron ore, uranium ore, marble.

PEOPLE
Population: 9,860,000. *Distribution urban/rural:* 34%/66%. *Life expectancy:* 71(m), 78(f). *Language:* Portuguese (official). *Ethnic groups:* Homogeneous Mediterranean stock with small black African minority. *Religions:* Roman Catholic 97%, Protestant denominations 1%, other 2%. *Literacy rate:* 85%. *Per capita GDP:* $8,400.

KEY DATES
1580 Portugal invaded by Spain.
1640 Duke John of Braganza leads revolt against Spanish; independence restored.
1807–21 King João VI flees to Brazil during French occupation.
1811 British army under Wellington drives French troops from Portugal.
1822 Brazil achieves independence.
1908 King Carlos I and his son are assassinated by revolutionaries; Manuel II comes to the throne.
1910 Manuel II is overthrown; Republic of Portugal proclaimed.
1914–18 World War I.
1926 Government overthrown in military coup; civil rights suspended.
1928 António de Oliveira Salazar installed as minister of finance; Salazar assumes dictatorial powers.
1932 Salazar named prime minister.
1959 Joins European Free Trade Association (EFTA).
1961 Colonial conflicts cost thousands of lives and weaken economy.
1968 Salazar suffers a stroke; Marcello Caetano becomes prime minister.
1974 Caetano removed from office in Armed Forces Movement coup; secret police abolished and civil rights restored.
1974–76 Remaining colonies are lost.
1976 New constitution providing for return to civilian government; Mário Soares becomes prime minister in first multiparty elections in over 50 years.
1978 Mário Soares resigns.
1980 Centrist coalition government formed by Francisco Balsemão.
1982 New constitution reduces power of the presidency.
1983 Center-left coalition government formed.
1985 Aníbal Cavaço Silva prime minister.
1986 Soares becomes first civilian president in 60 years; Portugal joins EC.
1988 Joins Western European Union.
1989 Constitutional amendment allows for privatization of major state-owned industries.

TRAVEL
Visa: None needed by U.S. *Driving permit:* IDP. *Health and safety:* No inoculations needed. *Tourist features:* Tua Valley, Fatima (important center for Christian pilgrimage); monastery of Jerónimos; Algarve. *National holiday:* June 10 (Day of Portugal).

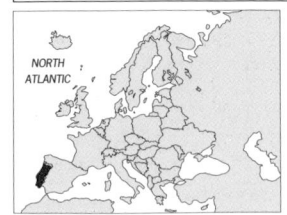

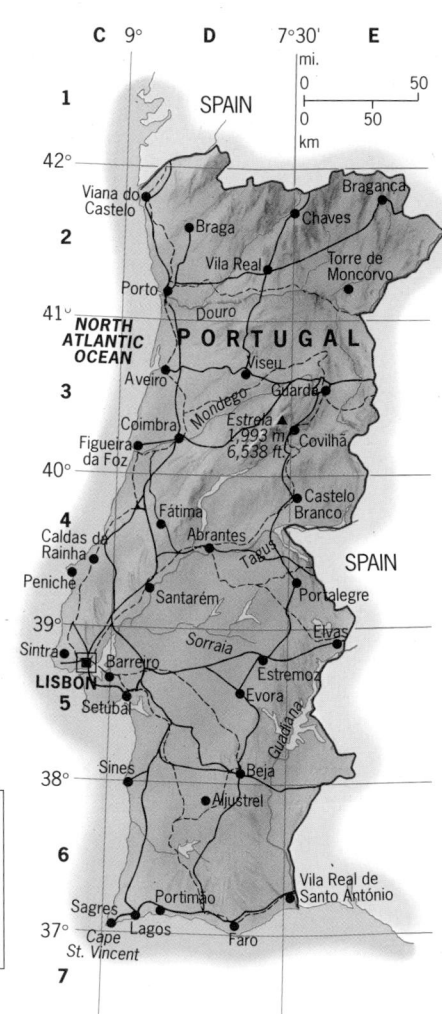

ITALY

Area: 116,332 sq. mi./301,302 km². **Local name:** Repubblica Italiana. **Currency:** Italian lira. **Capital:** Rome. **Other cities:** Milan, Naples. **Physical features:** Mountains and plains. **Climate:** Subtropical, alpine in N. **Time zone:** GMT +1h. **Political system:** Republic. **Head of state:** Oscar Luigi Scalfaro (from 1992). **Head of government:** Lamberto Dini (from 1995). **Main exports:** Wine, fruit, textiles, vehicles. **Resources:** Mercury, potash, marble.

PEOPLE
Population: 57,057,000. **Distribution urban/rural:** 67%/33%. **Life expectancy:** 74(m), 81(f). **Language:** Italian. **Ethnic groups:** Italian; some French, German, Slovene, and Albanian. **Religion:** Roman Catholic. **Literacy rate:** 97%. **Per capita GDP:** $16,700.

KEY DATES
1861 Kingdom of Italy declared.
1922 Fascists march on Rome; Benito Mussolini becomes prime minister and soon establishes himself as dictator.
1936 Alliance formed with Germany.
1940 Italy declares war on Allied powers.
1943 Benito Mussolini overthrown; German troops invade and reinstall him.
1945 Benito Mussolini shot by partisans.
1946 Italy becomes a republic.
1947 New constitution; peace treaty with Allies: Italy loses much territory.
1949 Joins NATO.
1955 Joins UN.
1958 Founding member of the EEC.
1962 Socialists join coalition government.
1969 Economic problems; labor unrest.
1978 Former prime minister Aldo Moro murdered by Communist terrorists.
1982 Gen. Dalla Chiesa, who had fought against the Mafia, is assassinated.
1986 Conviction of 338 Mafia members in Palermo.
1991 Communist Party splits into the Democratic Party of the Left and the Communist Refoundation; Italian troops fight in Persian Gulf War.
1992 Lira devalued and Italy withdraws from the ERM.
1993 Investigation of corruption exposes Mafia links with several politicians; referendum supports ending system of proportional representation.
1994 Elections won by right-wing alliance led by Silvio Berlusconi; Dec.: Berlusconi resigns.
1995 Lamberto Dini leads coalition.

TRAVEL
Visa: None needed by U.S. **Driving permit:** IDP. **Health and safety:** No inoculations needed. **Tourist features:** Tower of Pisa; Florence; Coliseum; Pompeii. **National holiday:** June 2 (Anniversary of the Republic).

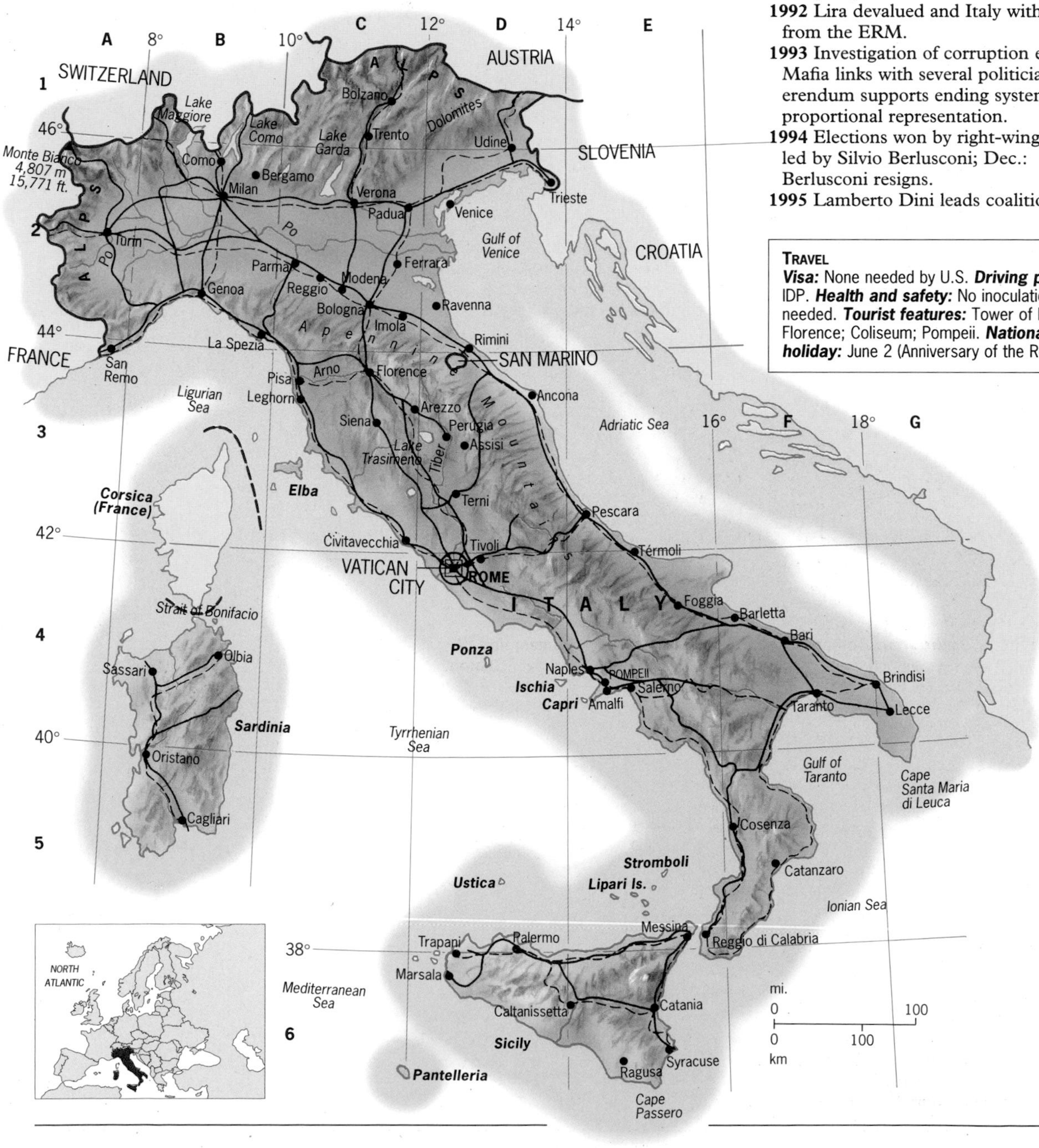

SAN MARINO

Area: 24 sq. mi./61 km². *Local name:* Serenissima Repubblica di San Marino. *Currency:* Italian lira. *Capital:* San Marino. *Physical features:* Rugged mountains. *Climate:* Subtropical. *Time zone:* GMT +1h. *Political system:* Republic. *Joint heads of state:* Cap. Regent Edda Cetcoli and Cap. Regent Mariano Riccardi (from 1991). *Head of government:* Gabriele Gatti (from 1986). *Main exports:* Wine, hides, lime, wood, ceramics, building stone. *Resource:* Building stone.

PEOPLE

Population: 23,000. *Distribution urban/rural:* 91%/9%. *Life expectancy:* 74(m), 79(f). *Language:* Italian. *Ethnic groups:* Sanmarinese, Italian. *Religion:* Roman Catholic. *Literacy rate:* 96%. *Per capita GDP:* $17,000.

KEY DATES

1291 Pope Nicholas IV recognizes San Marino as a sovereign state.

1862 Treaty of friendship signed with the kingdom of Italy; independence recognized under Italy's protection.

1877 Treaty with Italy renewed.

1939–43 San Marino controlled by Fascists during World War II.

1945–57 Governed by coalition of Communists and Socialists.

1957 Christian Democrats take control aided by Communist dissidents.

1973–86 Governed by a succession of left-wing and center-left coalitions.

1986 Formation of Communist and Christian Democrat "grand coalition."

1992 San Marino joins UN.

TRAVEL

Visa: None needed by U.S. *Driving permit:* Some licenses accepted with translation, otherwise IDP. *Health and safety:* No inoculations needed. *Tourist features:* Valloni Palace gallery; San Marino Historical Museum. *National holiday:* September 3 (Anniversary of the Foundation of the Republic).

VATICAN CITY

Area: 0.16 sq. mi./0.4 km². *Local name:* Stato della Cittá del Vaticano. *Currency:* Vatican City lira/Italian lira. *Capital:* Vatican City. *Physical features:* Low hill within Rome, Italy. *Climate:* Subtropical. *Time zone:* GMT +1h. *Political system:* Monarchical-sacerdotal state. *Head of state:* Pope John Paul II (from 1978). *Head of government:* Secretary of State Cardinal Angelo Sodano (from 1990). *Main exports:* n.a. *Resources:* None.

PEOPLE

Population: Approximately 1,000. *Distribution urban/rural:* 100% urban. *Life expectancy:* n.a. *Languages:* Italian, Latin, and various other languages. *Ethnic groups:* Primarily Italian; some Swiss. *Religion:* Roman Catholic. *Literacy rate:* 100%. *Per capita GDP:* n.a.

KEY DATES

1500s St. Peter's Church built over tomb in which St. Peter is said to be buried.

1867 U.S. ban on diplomatic relations with the Vatican comes into effect.

1870 Papal states become part of the kingdom of Italy; Pope Pius IX severs relations with Italian government.

1871 Law passed by Italian government confining papal sovereignty to the Vatican, the Lateran palace, and the villa of Castel Gandolfo.

1929 Lateran Pact signed with Benito Mussolini recognizes the Vatican City as a sovereign state.

1947 Sovereignty confirmed by new Italian constitution.

1978 Cardinal Karol Wojtyla, archbishop of Kraków, Poland, becomes the first non-Italian pope to be elected in more than 400 years.

1984 U.S.A. establishes diplomatic relations with Vatican City.

1985 Concordat signed with Italy ending the Church's influence over Italian state matters.

1993 Formal relations established with Israel.

TRAVEL

Visa: None needed by U.S. *Driving permit:* n.a. *Health and safety:* No inoculations needed. *Tourist features:* Vatican palace; Sistine Chapel. *National holiday:* October 22 (Installation of the Pope).

MALTA

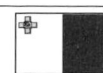

Area: 122 sq. mi./316 km². *Local name:* Repubblika Ta'Malta. *Currency:* Maltese lira. *Capital:* Valletta. *Other city:* Birkirkara. *Physical features:* Flat, rocky plains, coastal cliffs. *Climate:* Subtropical. *Time zone:* GMT +1h. *Political system:* Republic. *Head of state:* Mifsud Bonnici (from 1994). *Head of government:* Edward Fenech Adami (from 1987). *Main exports:* Textiles, machinery, chemicals, food, plastics. *Resources:* Limestone, salt.

PEOPLE

Population: 345,418. *Distribution urban/rural:* n.a. *Life expectancy:* 74(m), 79(f). *Languages:* Maltese and English (both official). *Ethnic groups:* Mixture of Arab, Sicilian, French, Spanish, Italian, English. *Religion:* Roman Catholic 98%. *Literacy rate:* 84%. *Per capita GDP:* $7,000.

KEY DATES

1800 Becomes a British protectorate.
1814 Becomes a British Crown Colony.
1921 Limited self-government achieved.
1930–32 Constitution suspended.
1932 Constitution reestablished.
1933 Constitution suspended again because of Maltese sympathy with Fascist Italy.
1947 New constitution.
1953 NATO's Mediterranean headquarters established in Malta.

1956 Referendum supports integration with U.K.
1958 Constitution suspended; appearance of independence movement.
1964 Independence achieved as a constitutional monarchy.
1974 Malta becomes a republic.
1979 British troops withdraw from Malta.
1990 Malta applies for EC membership.

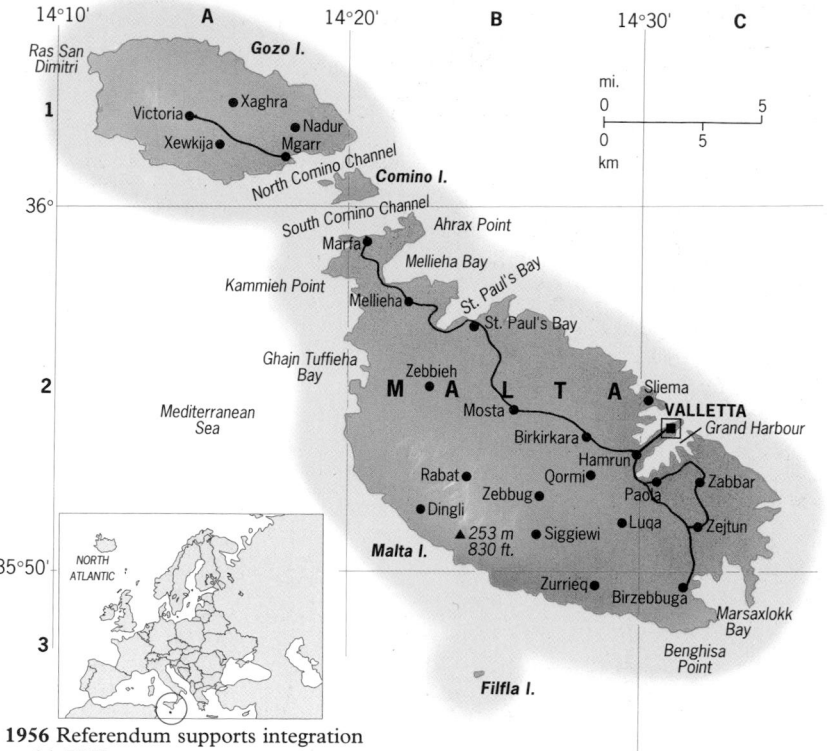

TRAVEL
Visa: None needed by U.S. *Driving permit:* Nat. license. *Health and safety:* No inoculations needed. *Tourist features:* National Museum of Fine Art; Upper Barrakka gardens; Grand Master's Palace. *National holiday:* September 21 (Independence Day).

LIECHTENSTEIN

Area: 62 sq. mi./160 km². *Local name:* Fürstentum Liechtenstein. *Currency:* Swiss franc. *Capital:* Vaduz. *Physical features:* Mostly mountainous. *Climate:* Temperate. *Time zone:* GMT +1h. *Political system:* Constitutional monarchy. *Head of state:* Prince Hans Adam II (from 1989). *Head of government:* Mario Frick (from 1993). *Main exports:* Machinery, dental products, stamps. *Resources:* Hydropower potential.

PEOPLE

Population: 30,000. *Distribution urban/rural:* n.a. *Life expectancy:* 74(m), 81(f). *Languages:* German, Alemannic dialect. *Ethnic groups:* Alemannic 95%, Italian and other 5%. *Religions:* Roman Catholic 87%, Protestant 8%. *Literacy rate:* 99%. *Per capita GDP:* $22,300.

KEY DATES

1342 Becomes a sovereign state.

1815–66 Part of German Confederation.
1921 Swiss currency adopted.
1924 Economic union with Switzerland.
1938 Franz Josef II comes to power.
1984 Women achieve suffrage; Prince Josef II hands over power to his son.
1989 Prince Franz Josef II dies and is succeeded by Prince Hans Adam II.
1990 Liechtenstein joins UN.
1991 Joins European Free Trade Association (EFTA).

TRAVEL
Visa: None needed by U.S. *Driving permit:* Nat. license. *Health and safety:* No inoculations needed. *Tourist features:* National Museum; Malbun Spa, Vaduz Castle. *National holiday:* August 15 (Assumption Day).

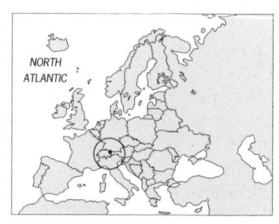

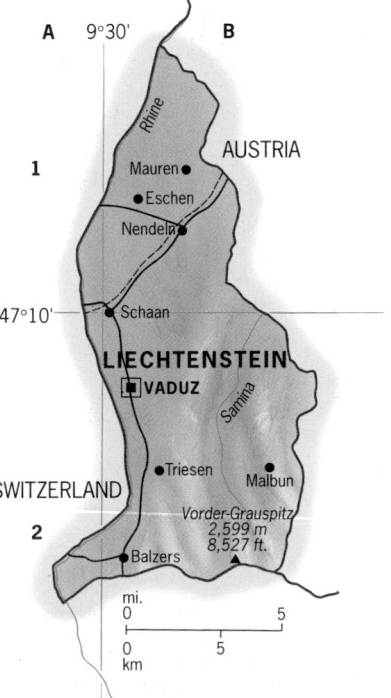

SWITZERLAND

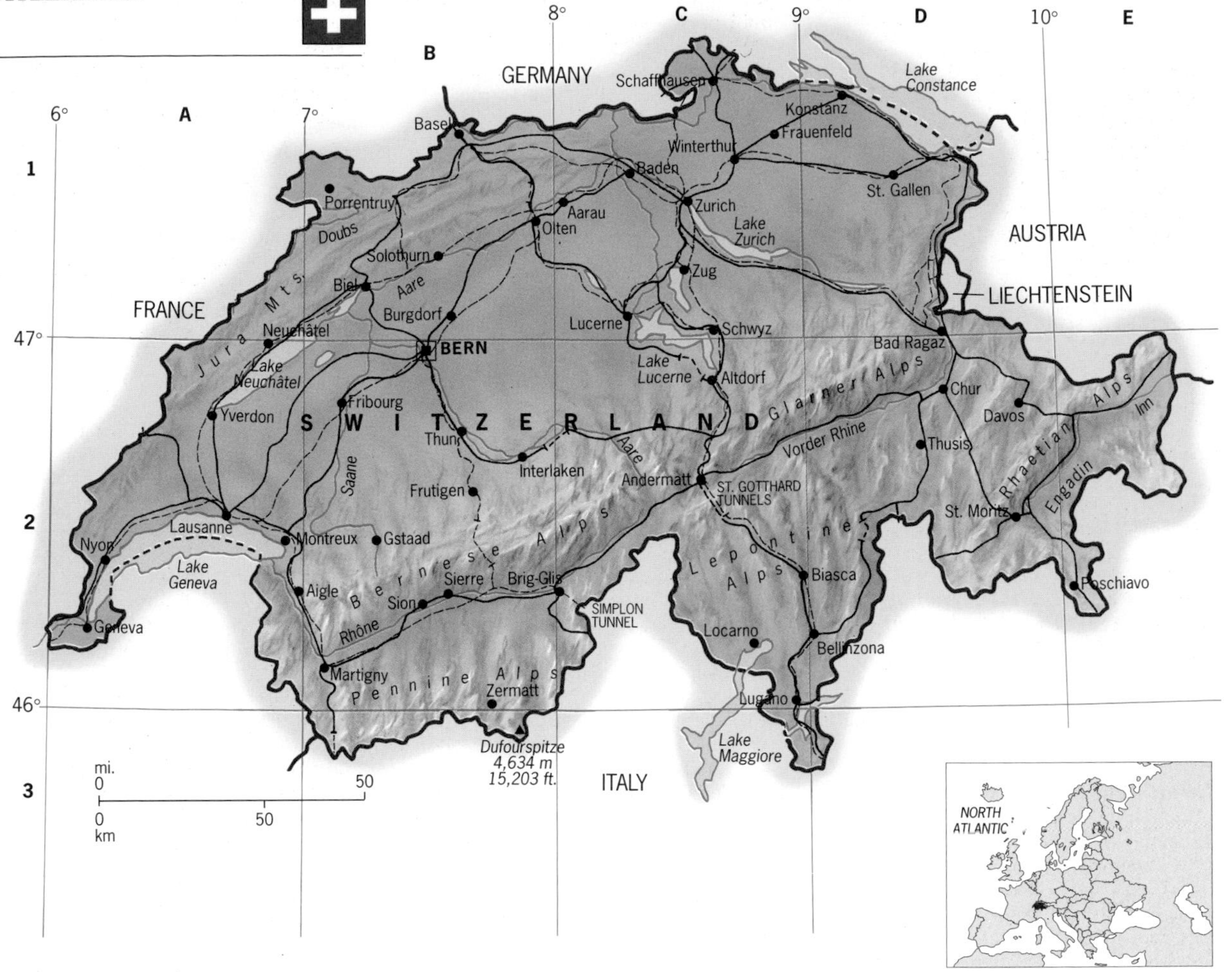

Area: 15,881 sq. mi./41,129 km².
Local name: Schweiz(German)/
Suisse (French)/Svizzera (Romansch).
Currency: Swiss franc. **Capital:**
Bern. **Other cities:** Zürich, Geneva.
Physical features: Mostly mountainous. **Climate:** Temperate, but varies
with altitude. **Time zone:** GMT +1h.
Political system: Federal republic.
Head of state and government:
Otto Stich (from 1994). **Main
exports:** Machinery, precision instruments, metal products, foodstuffs,
pharmaceuticals. **Resources:**
Hydropower potential, wood, salt.

PEOPLE
Population: 6,938,687. **Distribution
urban/rural:** 68%/32%. **Life expectancy:** 76(m), 83(f). **Languages:** German
65%, French 18%, Italian 12%,
Romansch 1%, other 4%. **Ethnic
groups:** German 65%, French 18%,
Italian 10%, Romansch 1%, other 6%.
Religions: Roman Catholic 48%,
Protestant 44%, unaffiliated and other
8%. **Literacy rate:** 99%. **Per capita
GDP:** $21,700.

KEY DATES
1033–1648 Part of Holy Roman Empire.
1798 Under French rule as the Helvetic
Republic.
1815 Independence restored as
Switzerland becomes a confederation by
the Congress of Vienna.
1847 Three-week civil war results in
increased centralization.
1848 New constitution adopted establishing a federal democracy.
1863 Red Cross founded in Geneva by
Jean Henri Dunant.
1874 Principle of the referendum introduced; federal power increases.
1914–18 Switzerland declares its neutrality during World War I.
1920 Geneva becomes the headquarters
of the League of Nations.
1939–45 Switzerland remains neutral in
World War II; up to 100,000 refugees
seek asylum there.
1960 Founding member of European
Free Trade Association (EFTA).
1963 Joins council of Europe
1964 The first motor traffic tunnel
through the Alps is opened.
1971 Women gain the right to vote.
1974 Referendum approves the creation

of a majority French-Roman Catholic
canton (state), Jura, from part of Bern.
1979 Jura becomes the 23rd canton.
1984 Elizabeth Kopp appointed first
female cabinet minister.
1986 Referendum rejects joining the UN.
1989 Abolition of the army rejected in
referendum; government begins investigation of Swiss banks following the revelation of their frequent use in
laundering money; justice minister
Kopp is forced to resign.
1991 Voting age reduced to 18; rightwing parties show increased support in
parliamentary elections.
1992 Closer ties with the EC rejected in
referendum; IMF and World Bank
membership approved in referendum;
René Felber elected president.
1994 Otto Stich becomes president.

TRAVEL
Visa: None. **Driving permit:** Nat. license.
Health and safety: No inoculations needed.
Tourist features: Thermal spas; Augusta
Raurica amphitheater; Roman relics; skiing.
National holiday: August 1 (Founding of the
Swiss Federation).

AUSTRIA

Area: 32,380 sq. mi./83,859 km². *Local name:* Republik Österreich. *Currency:* Schilling. *Capital:* Vienna. *Other cities:* Graz, Salzburg, Linz. *Physical features:* Mountainous in S. and W.; gentle slopes in N. and E. *Climate:* Temperate; cooler at higher altitudes. *Time zone:* GMT +1h. *Political system:* Federal republic. *Head of state:* Thomas Klestil (from 1992). *Head of government:* Franz Vranitzky (from 1986). *Main exports:* Machinery and transportation equipment, iron and steel, wood, textiles, paper products, chemicals, foodstuffs. *Resources:* Iron ore, crude oil, wood, magnesite, aluminum, lead, coal, lignite, copper, hydropower.

PEOPLE

Population: 7,984,000. *Distribution urban/rural:* 54%/46%. *Life expectancy:* 73(m), 80(f). *Language:* German. *Ethnic groups:* German 99%. *Religions:* Roman Catholic 85%, Protestant 6%, other 9%. *Literacy rate:* 99%. *Per capita GDP:* $20,895.

KEY DATES

1867 Dual monarchy of Austria-Hungary established by Emperor Franz Josef.

1914 Assassination of Archduke Franz Ferdinand in Serbia and Austria's subsequent invasion of Serbia lead to the outbreak of World War I.

1918 Austria-Hungary defeated in World War I; Austria becomes a republic; Treaty of St. Germain establishes Austria's boundaries and forbids future unification with Germany.

1920 New constitution drawn up.

1933 Four-day civil war ends with the establishment of the dictatorship of Engelbert Dollfuss.

1934 Dollfuss assassinated by the Nazis after he refuses to unite with Germany.

1938 Austria becomes part of the Third Reich when Hitler announces the *Anschluss* (union with Germany).

1939 Outbreak of World War II.

1943 Moscow Declaration cites the re-establishment of an independent Austria as one of the Allies' principal objectives.

1945 Constitution of 1920 restored under Allied occupation; formation of coalition government by the Socialist Party of Austria (SPO) and Austrian People's Party (OVP).

1951 Austria agrees to Soviet demands for repayment of occupation expenses as a condition of independence.

1951–55 Rapid economic growth.

1955 Allied forces leave Austria; Austrian independence is recognized internationally on condition that it remains permanently neutral; joins the UN.

1960 Joins the European Free Trade Association.

1961 Austria completes war reparation payments to the Soviet Union totaling $150 million.

1966 The OVP forms the first majority government of Austria since World War II under the leadership of Josef Klaus.

1970 First socialist government formed under Bruno Kreisky.

1983 Kreisky resigns as chancellor and is replaced by Fred Sinowatz.

1986 Relations with the international community become strained when Dr. Kurt Waldheim is elected president despite suggestions that he was involved in a number of war crimes; Fred Sinowatz resigns.

1989 Application for EC membership; far-right Freedom Party shows increased support in local elections.

1990 Joins the Pentagonal Association with Czechoslovakia, Hungary, Italy, and Yugoslavia to improve communications among the member countries; Austria allows the U.S.A. to use Austrian airspace in the Persian Gulf War; more controversy surrounds Waldheim when he flies to Iraq and returns with 80 Austrian hostages: his was the only visit by a Western leader to Iraq during the Persian Gulf War.

1991 The EC endorses Austrian membership; large numbers of Eastern European immigrants attempt to enter Western Europe via Austria; Chancellor Franz Vranitzky publicly apologizes for his country's role in the Holocaust; Austria works alongside the EC in attempting to mediate between the warring republics of former Yugoslavia.

1992 International relations improve when Waldheim steps down from the presidency.

1993 The Freedom Party declines in popularity and fails to achieve sufficient support for its anti-immigration "Austria First" petition; diplomatic relations with Israel restored.

1995 Austria joins the EU.

> **TRAVEL**
> *Visa:* None. *Driving permit:* IDP. *Health and safety:* No inoculations needed. *Tourist features:* Vienna; Hohenwerfen Castle; Danube River; skiing. *National holiday:* October 26 (National Day).

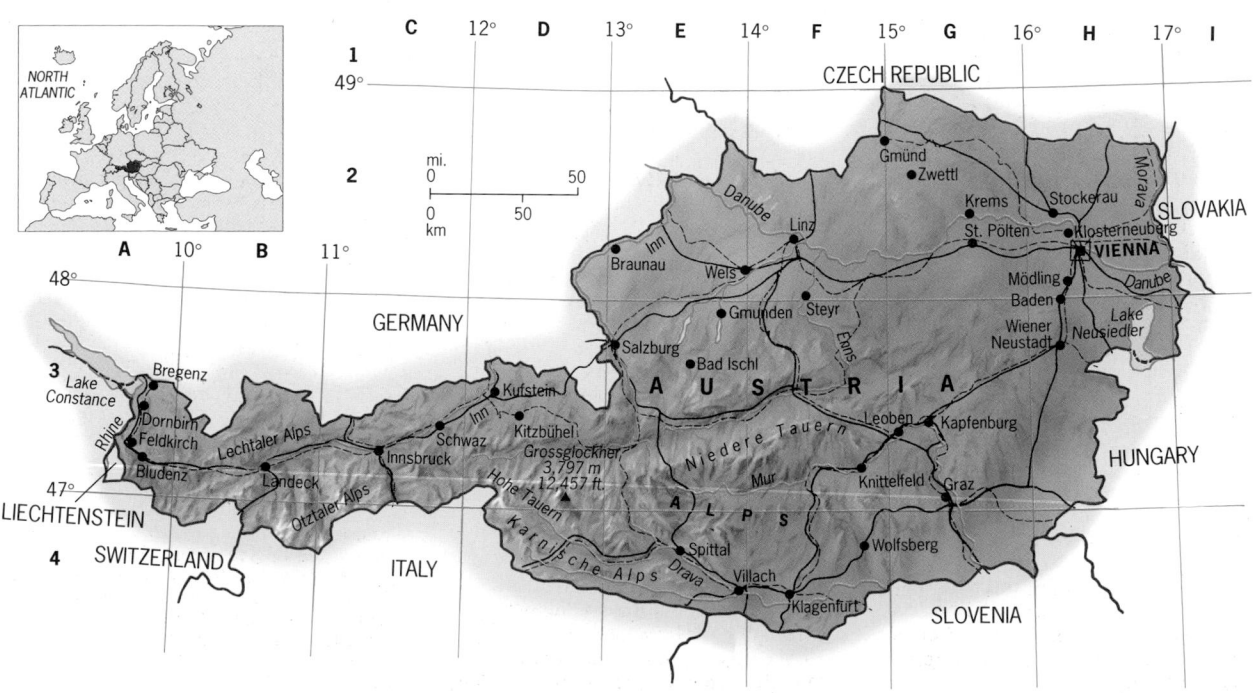

GERMANY

Area: 137,735 sq. mi./356,733 km². *Local name:* Bundesrepublik Deutschland. *Currency:* Deutsche mark. *Capital:* Berlin. *Other cities:* Hamburg, Munich, Cologne, Essen, Frankfurt, Düsseldorf. *Physical features:* Relatively flat in N., mountainous in S. (Alps). *Climate:* Temperate/marine. *Time zone:* GMT +1h. *Political system:* Federal republic. *Head of state:* Roman Herzog (from 1994). *Head of government:* Chancellor Helmut Kohl (from 1982). *Main exports:* Machine tools, machinery, chemicals, motor vehicles, electronics, iron and steel, textiles, wine, lignite, uranium, coal, fertilizers, plastics. *Resources:* Iron ore, coal, potash, wood, lignite, uranium, copper, natural gas, salt.

PEOPLE

Population: 81,187,000. *Distribution urban/rural:* 86%/14%. *Life expectancy:* 73(m), 79(f). *Language:* German. *Ethnic groups:* Primarily German; small Danish and Slavic minorities. *Religions:* Protestant 45%, Roman Catholic 37%, unaffiliated and other 18%. *Literacy rate:* 99%. *Per capita GDP:* $16,700.

KEY DATES

1815 German Confederation founded.
1867 Bismarck founds the Prussian-led North German Confederation.
1870–71 France defeated in Franco-Prussian War; S. German states join Confederation.
1882 Triple Alliance signed with Austria-Hungary and Italy.
1914 Germany joins Austria-Hungary in World War I.
1916 Foundation of revolutionary socialist group, the Spartacists.
1918 Emperor Wilhelm II flees to the Netherlands; republic declared in Berlin; Nov.: armistice agreed.
1919 Spartacist revolt suppressed in Berlin; new constitution creates Weimar Republic; Treaty of Versailles signed; National Socialist (Nazi) Party founded.
1923 Hyperinflation leaves deutsche mark almost valueless; Hitler captured after failed putsch in Munich.
1929 Depression and civil unrest.
1933 Hitler becomes chancellor; many civil liberties suspended; Enabling Act gives Hitler dictatorial power; all Jews removed from government posts.
1934 Nazis murder 200 opponents in "Night of the Long Knives"; Hitler declares himself *der Führer* (the leader) and establishes the Third Reich.
1935 Nuremberg laws forbid intermarriage with Jews.
1936 Alliance with Italy creates Rome-Berlin Axis; anti-Communist pact signed with Japan.
1938 March: Germany begins program of expansion; Nov.: widespread anti-Jewish violence on *Kristallnacht.*
1939 Aug.: Nazi-Soviet pact signed; Sept.: Germany invades Poland; World War II breaks out.
1944 Allies invade German-occupied France; bomb plot against Hitler fails.
1945 Hitler commits suicide; Germany surrenders to Allies and is divided into four occupied zones.
1948 Soviet withdrawal from Allied Control Council exacerbates East-West division; Soviets blockade West Berlin; West Germany receives financial aid under Marshall Plan.
1949 Blockade of West Berlin ends; Soviet zone becomes German Democratic Republic (G.D.R.) under Communist rule; Federal Republic (F.R.G.) founded (West Germany).
1950–55 "Economic miracle" in F.R.G.
1953 Soviet troops suppress East Berlin uprising over increased working hours.
1955 East and West Germany accorded full sovereignty; F.R.G. joins NATO; G.D.R. joins Warsaw Pact.
1957 F.R.G. joins EC.
1961 East German border sealed; construction of Berlin Wall.
1964 G.D.R.: Treaty of Friendship and Mutual Assistance signed with U.S.S.R.
1969 Social Democrats win F.R.G. elections; Willy Brandt becomes chancellor.
1971 Erich Honecker succeeds Walter Ulbricht as Party chief in East Germany.
1972 Basic Treaty normalizes relations between East and West Germany.
1973 G.D.R. and F.R.G. enter UN.
1974 Helmut Schmidt becomes West German chancellor after Brandt resigns over spy scandal; many Western nations open diplomatic relations with G.D.R.
1977 Red Brigade terrorists kill West German business leader.
1982 Schmidt forced to resign after losing vote of no confidence; Helmut Kohl becomes West German chancellor.
1983 Green Party gains parliamentary representation in F.R.G. elections; deployment of U.S. nuclear missiles in F.R.G. provokes popular protests.
1987 Erich Honecker makes official visit to West Germany.
1989 Rising support for far right in local and European elections in G.D.R.; mass East German exodus to West follows unrest and demonstrations; Oct.: Honecker overthrown; Nov.: Berlin Wall demolished; West German Council of Ministers resigns; New Forum movement legalized; reformist Hans Modrow appointed prime minister of G.D.R.; Dec.: Helmut Kohl presents plan for reunification.
1990 March: Christian Democrats win first free elections in G.D.R.; May: economic union; Sept.: Allied powers relinquish remaining rights over Germany in Treaty on the Final Settlement with Respect to Germany; Oct.: Germany reunified under West German constitution; Dec.: Kohl wins majority in first national elections in reunited Germany.
1991 Bundestag votes to move federal capital from Bonn to Berlin; Kohl's popularity declines after tax increases; government inherits East German debt of DM300 billion; unrest in East follows rising crime and unemployment.
1992 Neo-Nazi riots against immigration; popular demonstrations against rising incidence of racial violence.
1993 Severe recession; restrictions on refugee admission introduced.
1994 General election: Kohl remains chancellor with greatly reduced majority; Roman Herzog elected president.

ECONOMY

Before reunification in 1990, West Germany had one of the strongest economies in the world. East Germany, although it was wealthy in comparison to many other Communist nations, was considerably poorer than the Federal Republic. After reunification, the old East Germany suffered severe difficulties in adapting to a free-market economy, and many West Germans believed that the East was an economic burden. Most economists agree, however, that Germany's economy will remain strong after the adjustment has been made.

Industry by sector

Farming Germany imports a large quantity of its food and is self-sufficient only in potatoes. Other crops include barley, oats, rye, and beets. In the central uplands, grapes, hops, and tobacco are grown. Cattle, horses, pigs, poultry, and sheep are raised. Most of Germany's farms are less than 25 acres in size, and the large government-owned farms of former East Germany are being broken up and sold to individuals.
Mining Germany's large mineral reserves include coal, lignite, and iron ore.
Manufacturing Manufacturing is Germany's fastest growing industry. Important products include iron and steel, motor vehicles, agricultural machinery, ships, and tools. Germany is the world's third-largest manufacturer of cars after Japan and the U.S.A. Cement, clothing, chemicals and pharmaceuticals, electrical equipment, processed food, and metals are also important.
Services Service industries account for around 50% of Germany's GDP. The most important are community, government, and personal services. Finance and insurance, trade, transportation, communications, and utilities are also important.

TRAVEL
Visa: None. *Driving permit:* Nat. license/IDP. *Health and safety:* No inoculations needed. *Tourist features:* Neuschwanstein Castle; Black Forest; Olympic stadium, Munich; site of Berlin Wall. *National holiday:* October 3 (Unity Day).

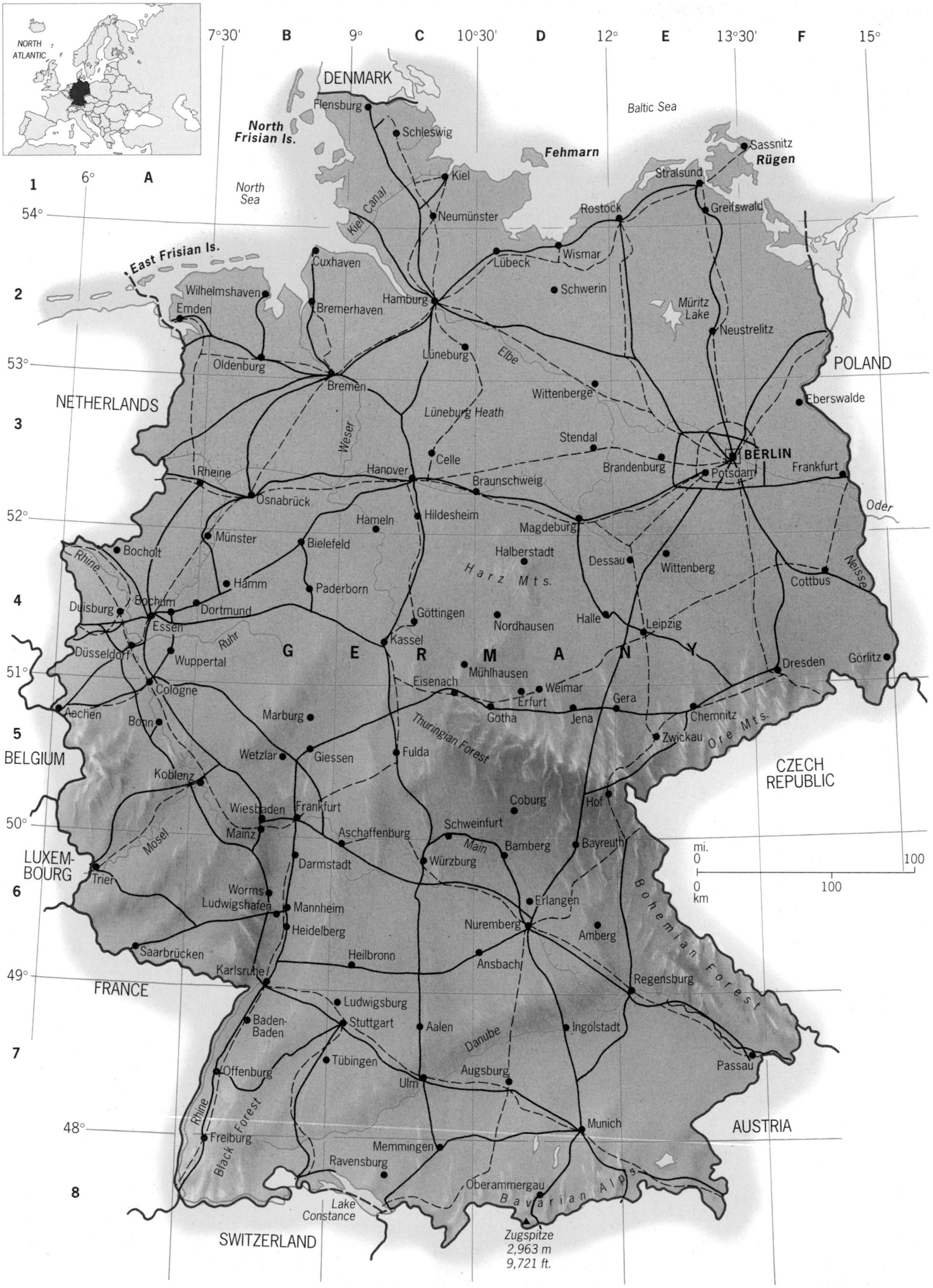

NORTH
ATLANTIC

7°30'　　B　　9°　　C　　10°30'　　D　　12°　　E　　13°30'　　F　　15°

DENMARK

*North
Frisian Is.*

Baltic Sea

Fehmarn

Sassnitz
Rügen

Flensburg
Schleswig

1　　6°　　A

*North
Sea*

54°

Kiel

Stralsund

Neumünster

Rostock

Greifswald

East Frisian Is.

Cuxhaven

Lübeck

Wismar

POLAND

Wilhelmshaven
Emden

Bremerhaven

Hamburg

Schwerin

*Müritz
Lake*

2

Neustrelitz

53°

Oldenburg

Lüneburg

Elbe

Bremen

Wittenberge

Eberswalde

NETHERLANDS

Lüneburg Heath

Stendal

3

Rheine

Hanover

Celle

Brandenburg

BERLIN
Potsdam

Frankfurt

Oder

Osnabrück

Braunschweig

52°

Hameln

Hildesheim

Magdeburg

Rhine

Bocholt

Münster

Bielefeld

Halberstadt

Dessau

Wittenberg

Cottbus

Neisse

Hamm

Paderborn

H a r z   M t s.

4

Duisburg
Bochum

Dortmund

Göttingen

Nordhausen

Halle

Leipzig

Düsseldorf

Essen

Ruhr

Kassel

G　E　R　M　A　N　Y

Dresden

Görlitz

51°

Wuppertal

Eisenach

Mühlhausen

Weimar

Gotha

Erfurt

Jena

Gera

Chemnitz

Ore Mts.

Cologne

Aachen

Bonn

Marburg

Thuringian Forest

Zwickau

5

Wetzlar

Giessen

Fulda

**CZECH
REPUBLIC**

BELGIUM

Koblenz

Coburg

Hof

Bohemian Forest

Wiesbaden
Frankfurt

Schweinfurt

50°

Mainz

Aschaffenburg

Bamberg

Bayreuth

**LUXEM-
BOURG**

Trier

Darmstadt

Würzburg

Main

mi.
0　　　　　100

6

Worms
Ludwigshafen

Mannheim

Erlangen

0　　　100
km

Heidelberg

Amberg

Saarbrücken

Heilbronn

Nuremberg

Karlsruhe

Ansbach

Regensburg

49°

Ludwigsburg

FRANCE

Baden-
Baden

Stuttgart

Aalen

Ingolstadt

Passau

7

Offenburg

Tübingen

Danube

Augsburg

Ulm

AUSTRIA

Munich

48°

Freiburg

Black Forest

Memmingen

Ravensburg

Oberammergau

B a v a r i a n   A l p s

Rhine

8

*Lake
Constance*

SWITZERLAND

▲ Zugspitze
2,963 m
9,721 ft.

POLAND

Area: 120,727 sq. mi./312,683 km². *Local name:* Rezczpospolita Polska. *Currency:* Zloty. Capital: Warsaw. *Other cities:* Lódź, Kraków, Wroclaw, Poznań. *Physical features:* Mostly flat plain, mountains in S. *Climate:* Continental. *Time zone:* GMT +1h. *Political system:* Democratic republic. *Head of state:* Lech Walesa (from 1990). Head of government: Waldemar Pawlak (from 1993). *Main exports:* Machinery, coal, coke, cars, metals, chemicals, fuels. *Resources:* Coal, sulfur, copper, natural gas.

PEOPLE
Population: 37,459,000. *Distribution urban/rural:* 62%/38%. *Life expectancy:* 68(m), 76(f). *Language:* Polish.

Ethnic groups: Polish 98%. *Religions:* Roman Catholic 95%, Russian Orthodox, Protestant, and other 5%. *Literacy rate:* 98%. *Per capita GDP:* $4,300.

KEY DATES
1772–95 Poland partitioned among Prussia, Russia, and Austria.

1918 Independence achieved.

1939 German invasion and occupation; World War II breaks out; government-in-exile set up in Paris.

1941 Polish Communists set up rival government-in-exile in U.S.S.R.

1944 Anti-Nazi revolt in Warsaw; Soviet invasion; foundation of Committee of National Liberation (Communist).

1947 Proclamation of the Communist People's Republic of Poland.

1952 New Soviet-style constitution.

1976 Rioting over price increases.

1980 Thousands of workers strike for reform; emergence of independent trade union, Solidarity.

1981 Martial law imposed; Solidarity suspended and hundreds of union leaders arrested.

1982 Solidarity outlawed.

1983 Martial law ends.

1984 Amnesty for political prisoners.

1988 Solidarity leads strikes and demonstrations; reformist Mieczyslaw F. Rakowski becomes premier.

1989 Solidarity legalized; first open elections in 40 years; Tadeusz Mazowiecki (Solidarity) becomes prime minister; privatization program begun.

1990 Communist Party dissolved; Solidarity splits into two rival groups; Lech Walesa elected president.

TRAVEL
Visa: Not needed by U.S. *Driving permit:* IDP. *Health and safety:* No inoculations needed. *Tourist features:* Tatra Mountains; Kraków; Bialowieza Forest. *National holiday:* May 3 (Constitution Day).

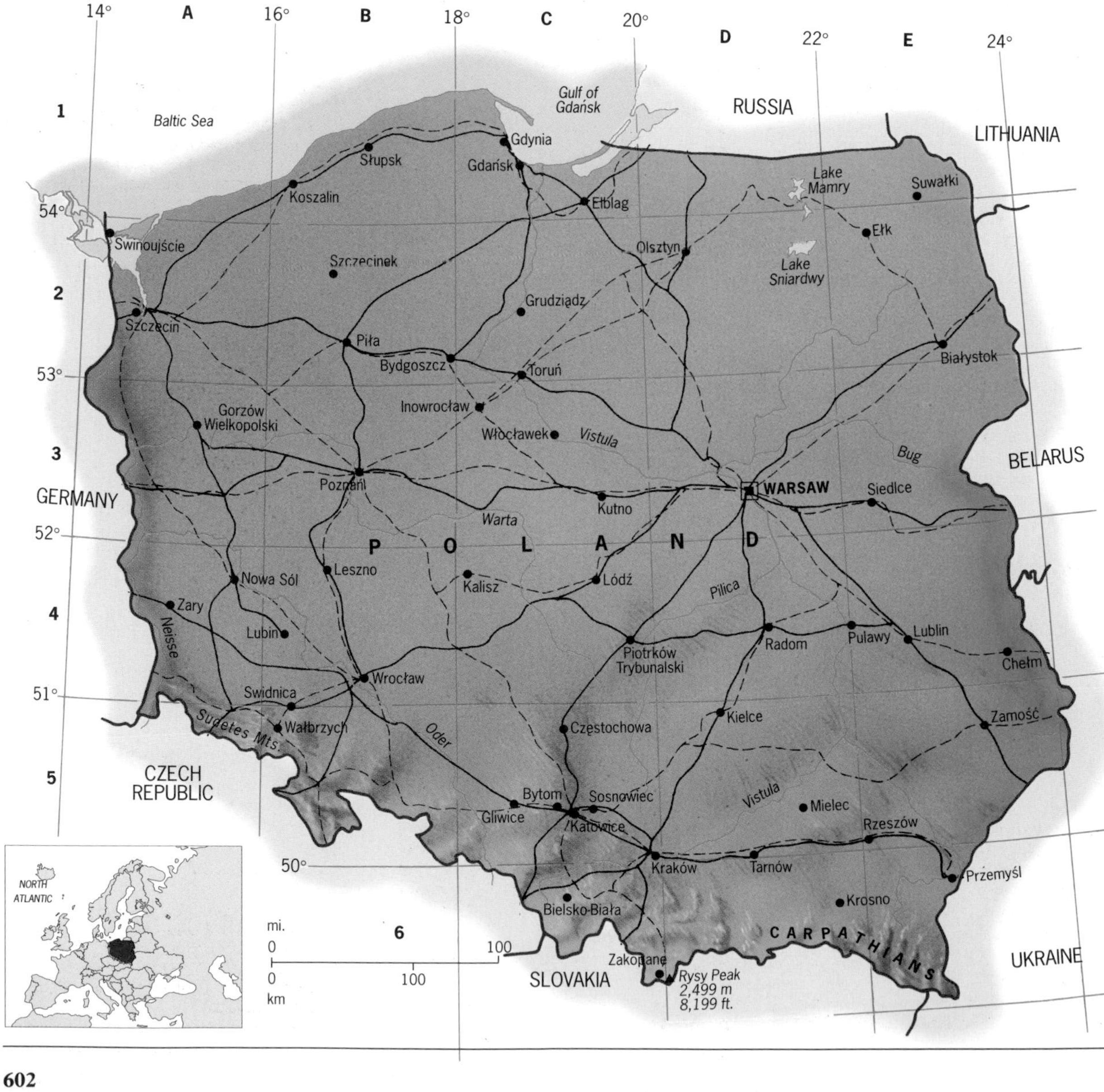

Map

Baltic Sea
RUSSIA
LITHUANIA
Gulf of Gdańsk
Słupsk
Gdynia
Koszalin
Gdańsk
Suwałki
Lake Mamry
Elbląg
Ełk
Swinoujście
Olsztyn
Szczecinek
Lake Sniardwy
Szczecin
Grudziądz
Piła
Białystok
Bydgoszcz
Toruń
GERMANY
Gorzów Wielkopolski
Inowrocław
Włocławek
Vistula
Bug
BELARUS
Poznań
WARSAW
Siedlce
Warta
Kutno
P O L A N D
Nowa Sól
Leszno
Kalisz
Lódź
Pilica
Zary
Lubin
Piotrków Trybunalski
Radom
Pulawy
Lublin
Neisse
Swidnica
Wrocław
Chełm
Sudetes Mts.
Wałbrzych
Oder
Kielce
Zamość
CZECH REPUBLIC
Częstochowa
Bytom
Sosnowiec
Vistula
Mielec
Rzeszów
Gliwice
Katowice
Kraków
Tarnów
Krosno
Przemyśl
Bielsko-Biała
CARPATHIANS
UKRAINE
Zakopane
SLOVAKIA
Rysy Peak 2,499 m 8,199 ft.

NORTH ATLANTIC

mi. 0 100
km 0 100

CZECH REPUBLIC

Area: 30,452 sq. mi./78,864 km². **Local name:** Ceská Republika. **Currency:** Koruna. **Capital:** Prague. **Other cities:** Brno, Ostrava. **Physical features:** Mostly mountainous. **Climate:** Temperate. **Time zone:** GMT +1h. **Political system:** Democratic republic. **Head of state:** Václav Havel (from 1993). **Head of government:** Václav Klaus (from 1993). **Main exports:** Machinery, vehicles, coal, ceramics, iron and steel, chemicals, clothing. **Resources:** Coal, uranium, mercury, tin.

PEOPLE

Population: 10,328,000. **Distribution urban/rural:** 73%/27%. **Life expectancy:** 68(m), 75(f). **Language:** Czech. **Ethnic groups:** Czech 94%, Slovak 6%. **Religions:** Roman Catholic 75%, Protestant, Hussite, Orthodox. **Literacy rate:** 100%. **Per capita GDP:** $2,562.

KEY DATES

1526 Comes under Hapsburg control.
1918 Czechoslovakia becomes an independent state.
1939–45 Occupied by Germany.
1949 Communists gain control.
1968 Troops from neighboring communist countries invade after liberal,

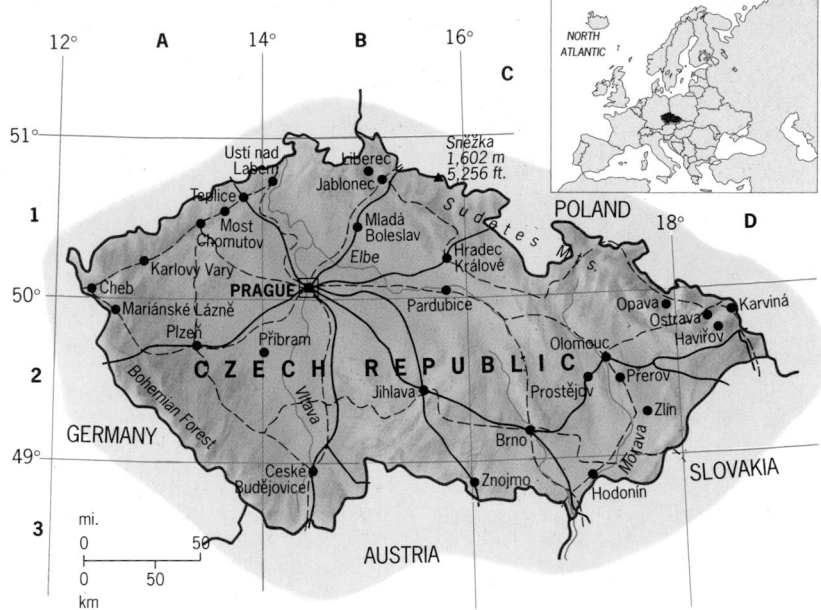

Alexander Dubček, comes to power.
1989 Pro-democracy demonstrations in Prague; political parties legalized and many civil liberties restored.
1990 Multiparty elections.
1992 Creation of separate Czech and Slovak nations agreed.
1993 Czech Republic becomes an independent state; joins the UN.

TRAVEL
Visa: Needed by U.S. **Driving permit:** Nat. license. **Health and safety:** No inoculations needed. **Tourist features:** St. Vitu Cathedral, Prague; 12th-century Premyslid Palace, Olomovc; silver-mining museum, Kutria Hora. **National holiday:** October 28 (Independence Day).

SLOVAKIA

Area: 18,934 sq. mi./49,035 km². **Local name:** Slovenská Republika. **Currency:** Koruna. **Capital:** Bratislava. **Other cities:** Kosice. **Physical features:** Mostly mountainous with fertile river valleys. **Climate:** Temperate. **Time zone:** GMT +1h. **Political system:** Democratic republic. **Head of state:** Michal Kovak (from 1993). **Head of government:** Vladimir Meciar (from 1993). **Main exports:** Steel, metals, petroleum products, armaments, chemicals, textiles, machinery, ceramics, wood, footwear. **Resources:** Coal, copper, lead, iron, zinc, manganese, hydropower.

PEOPLE

Population: 5,318,000. **Distribution urban/rural:** n.a. **Life expectancy:** 68(m), 75(f). **Language:** Slovak. **Ethnic groups:** Slovak 87%, Hungarian 10%. **Religions:** Roman Catholic over 50%, Lutheran Reformist, Orthodox. **Literacy rate:** 100%. **Per capita GDP:** $1,887.

KEY DATES

1526 Comes under Hapsburg control.
1918 Becomes an independent state with-

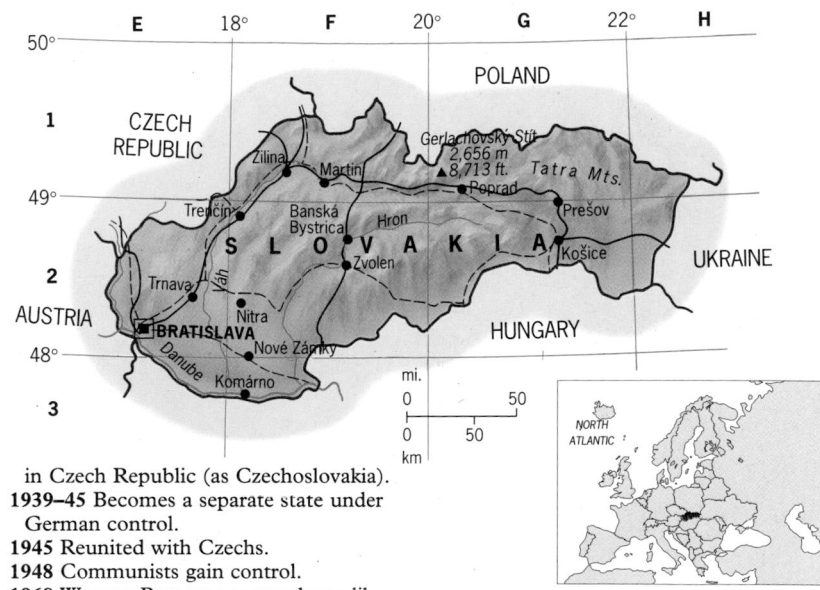

in Czech Republic (as Czechoslovakia).
1939–45 Becomes a separate state under German control.
1945 Reunited with Czechs.
1948 Communists gain control.
1968 Warsaw Pact troops overthrow liberalizing regime of Alexander Dubcek.
1989 Political parties legalized and many civil liberties restored.
1990 Multiparty elections.
1992 Creation of separate Czech and Slovak nations agreed.
1993 Slovak Republic becomes an independent state.

TRAVEL
Visa: None needed by U.S. **Driving permit:** Nat. license. **Health and safety:** No inoculations needed. **Tourist features:** Tatra Mountains; Bojnice Chatêau; Nitra Castle. **National holiday:** September 1 (Day of constitution of Slovakia).

HUNGARY

Area: 35,922 sq. mi./93,030 km².
Local name: Magyar Köztársaság.
Currency: Forint. **Capital:**
Budapest. **Other cities:** Debrecen.
Physical features: Mostly flat to
rolling plains. **Climate:** Temperate.
Time zone: GMT +1h. **Political
system:** Democratic republic. **Head
of state:** Arpád Göncz (from 1990).
Head of government: Gyula Horn
(from 1994). **Main exports:** Food,
vehicles, textiles, chemicals, consumer
goods, metals. **Resources:** Bauxite,
coal, natural gas.

PEOPLE

Population: 10,294,000. **Distribution
urban/rural:** 62%/38%. **Life expectancy:** 66(m), 75(f). **Language:** Hungarian
(Magyar). **Ethnic groups:** Magyar 92%,
Gypsy 3%, German, Slovak, Southern
Slav, Romanian. **Religions:** Roman
Catholic 68%, Calvinist 20%, Lutheran
5%, atheist and other 7%. **Literacy rate:**
99%. **Per capita GDP:** $5,700.

KEY DATES

1867 "Dual Monarchy" agreement with
Austria creates Austria-Hungary.
1914–18 Defeated in World War I.
1918 Independent republic proclaimed.
1919 Communist dictatorship lasting 133
days; Romanian occupation; Hungary
becomes a monarchy again with
Admiral Nicholas Horthy as regent.
1938 Germany accords Hungary some of
the territory lost after World War I.
1939 Hungary proclaims neutrality in
World War II.
1941 Enters war on German side.
1944 German troops invade Hungary and
imprison Nicholas Horthy; Soviet invasion.
1945 Armistice agreement with Allies.
1946 Proclaimed a republic once again.
1947 Communists take over government.
1949 Soviet-style constitution adopted;
joins Comecon.
1953 Imre Nagy becomes premier.
1955 Joins Warsaw Pact; Nagy is accused
of anti-Soviet nationalism and is forced
out of office.
1956 Anti-Soviet rebels stage violent
demonstration and reinstate Nagy as
premier; Nagy promises economic and
political reform but Soviet forces invade
and arrest leaders of revolution; János
Kádár installed as president.
1958 Imre Nagy is convicted of treason
and executed; thousands of his supporters are deported to the U.S.S.R.
1968 Economic reforms.
1970s Relations with the West improve.
1987 Miklós Németh becomes premier.
1989 Communist Party declares that trial
of revolutionary leaders in 1958 was
illegal; new democratic constitution;
opposition parties legalized.
1990 Free elections won by non-
Communist coalition.
1991 Legislation passed to compensate
owners of land and property expropriated under Communist rule; EC association pact signed.
1994 Socialists return to power with
Gyula Horn as prime minister.

TRAVEL
Visa: Not needed by U.S. **Driving permit:**
IDP. **Health and safety:** No inoculations
needed. **Tourist features:** Castle district,
Budapest; Pannonhalma monastery; Bükk
Mountains. **National holiday:** October 23
(commemorates the Hungarian Uprising).

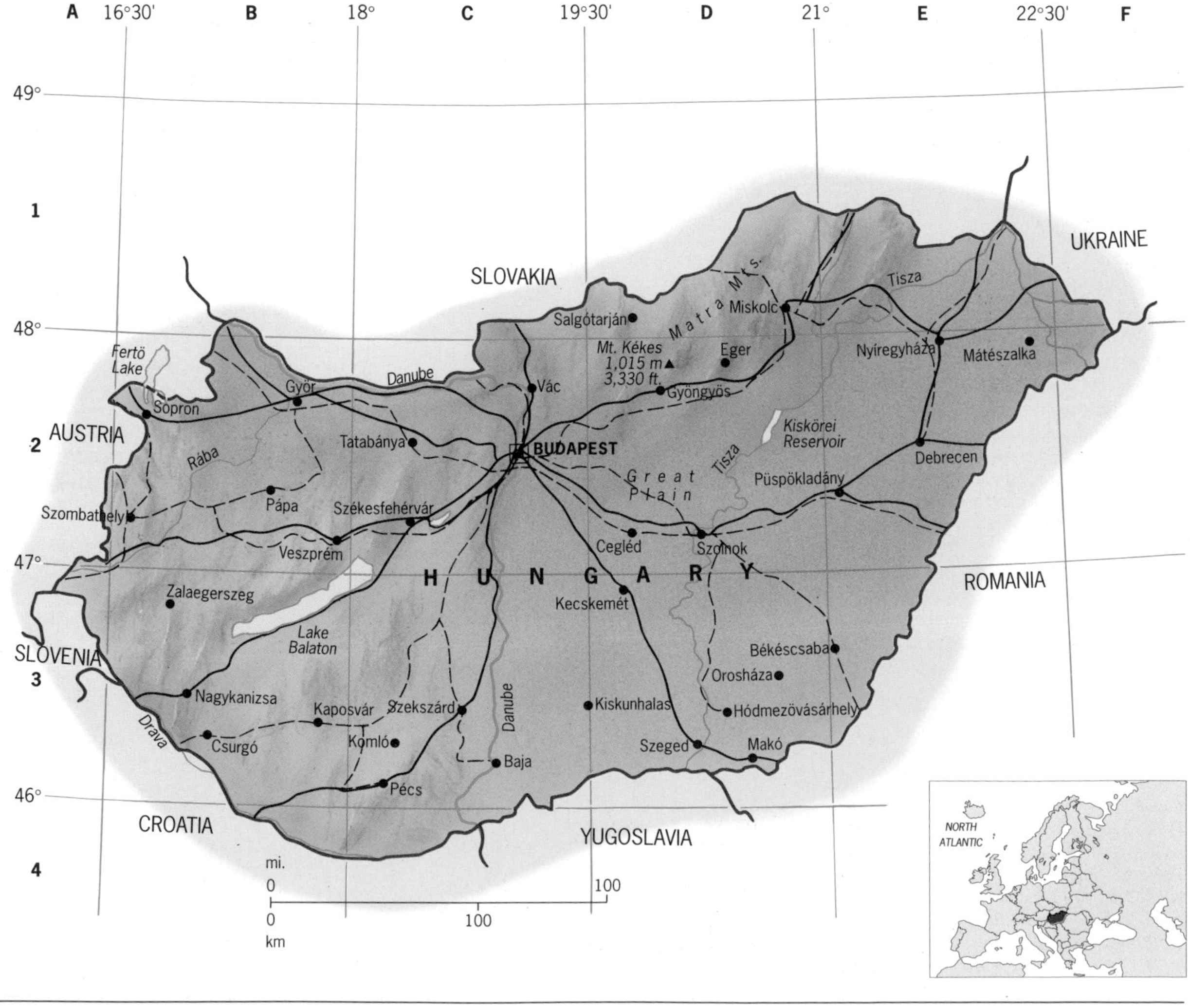

SLOVENIA

Area: 7,820 sq. mi./20,251 km².
Local name: Republica Slovenija.
Currency: Tolar. *Capital:* Ljubljana.
Physical features: Mostly mountain-
ous. *Climate:* Subtropical/temperate.
Time zone: GMT +1h. *Political
system:* Democratic republic. *Head
of state:* Milan Kucan (from 1990).
Head of government: Janez
Drnovsek (from 1992). *Main
exports:* Machinery and transporta-
tion equipment, chemicals, food.
Resources: Lignite coal, lead, zinc.

PEOPLE
Population: 1,990,000. *Distribution
urban/rural:* n.a. *Life expectancy:*
70(m), 78(f). *Languages:* Slovenian,
Serbo-Croatian. *Ethnic groups:* Slovene
91%, Croat 3%, Serb 2%. *Religions:*
Roman Catholic 94%, Orthodox 2%,
Muslim 1%, other 3%. *Literacy rate:*
99%. *Per capita GDP:* $10,700.

KEY DATES
1918 Becomes part of Kingdom of Serbs,
    Croats, and Slovenes (later Yugoslavia).
1941 Invaded by Germany.
1945 Communists come to power.
1972–73 Liberals expelled from Slovenian
    Communist Party.

1990 First free elections won by loose
    coalition of non-Communists, DEMOS.
1991 Independence declared; fighting
    erupts between federal troops and
    nationalists. Cease-fire agreed; DEMOS
    coalition falls apart.
1992 Joins UN.

TRAVEL
Visa: Not needed by U.S. **Driving permit:**
Nat. license. **Health and safety:** No inocula-
tions needed. **Tourist features:** Tivoli Park;
Rožnik hills; wine regions of Podravjc,
Posavje, Primoije. **National holiday:** n.a.

CROATIA

Area: 21,831 sq. mi./56,538 km².
Local name: Republika Hrvatska.
Currency: Croatian dinar. *Capital:*
Zagreb. *Physical features:* Mountainous. *Climate:* Subtropical/tem-
perate. *Time zone:* GMT +1h.
Political system: Democratic republic. *Head of state:* Franjo Tudjman
(from 1990). *Head of government:*
Nikica Valentic (from 1993). *Main
exports:* Clothing, food, machinery,
chemicals. *Resources:* Crude oil,
coal, bauxite.

PEOPLE
Population: 4,773,000. *Distribution
urban/rural:* n.a. *Life expectancy:*
67(m), 74(f). *Language:* Serbo-
Croatian. *Ethnic groups:* Croat 78%,
Serb 12%. *Religions:* Roman Catholic
76%, Orthodox 11%, Muslim. *Literacy
rate:* 97%. *Per capita GDP:* $5,600.

KEY DATES
1918 Becomes part of Kingdom of Serbs,
    Croats, and Slovenes (later Yugoslavia).
1941-45 Separate state under Germans.
1945 Part of Communist Yugoslavia.
1991 Independence; war with Serbs.
1992 Peace accord; joins UN.
1995 Captures Serb enclave of Krajina.

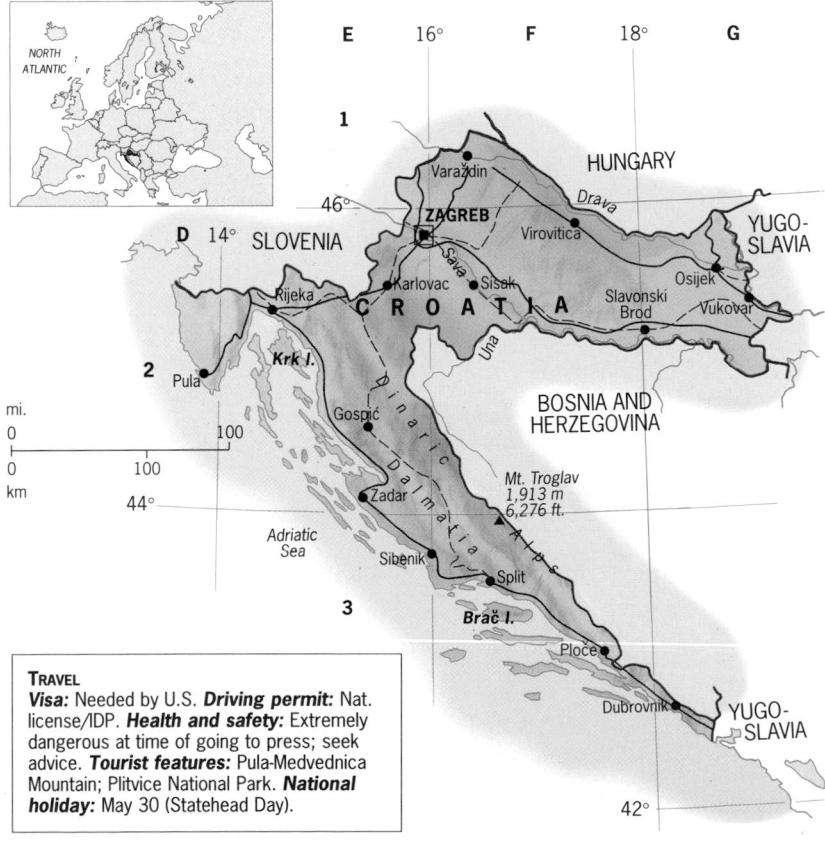

TRAVEL
Visa: Needed by U.S. **Driving permit:** Nat.
license/IDP. **Health and safety:** Extremely
dangerous at time of going to press; seek
advice. **Tourist features:** Pula-Medvednica
Mountain; Plitvice National Park. **National
holiday:** May 30 (Statehead Day).

BOSNIA AND HERZEGOVINA

Area: 19,742 sq. mi./51,129 km². *Local name:* Republika Bosnai Hercegovina. *Currency:* Bosnian dinar. *Capital:* Sarajevo. *Other cities:* Banja Luka, Mostar. *Physical features:* Rugged mountains. *Climate:* Subtropical/temperate. *Time zone:* GMT +1h. *Political system:* Republic. *Head of state:* Alija Izetbegović (from 1990). *Head of government:* Haris Silajdzic (from 1993). *Main exports:* Machinery, furniture, clothing, chemicals. *Resources:* Copper, lead, zinc, gold.

PEOPLE

Population: 4,383,000. *Distribution urban/rural:* n.a. *Life expectancy:* 68(m), 73(f). *Languages:* Serbo-Croatian (official), Bosnian, Croatian, Serbian. *Ethnic groups:* Bosnian 44%, Serb 33%, Croat 17%. *Religions:* Sunni Muslim, Roman Catholic, Serb Orthodox. *Literacy rate:* 86%. *Per capita GDP:* $3,200.

KEY DATES

1918 Ceded to the future Yugoslavia.
1945 Part of Federal People's Republic of Yugoslavia under Tito.
1980 Tito dies; nationalist feeling grows.
1990 Ethnic violence erupts between muslims and serbs.
1991 Serbia reveals plans to annex S.E.
1992 Independence declared against wishes of Serbs; civil war breaks out.
1994 Cease-fire agreed with Serbs.

1995 Cease-fire expires; fighting resumed.

TRAVEL
Visa: n.a. *Driving permit:* IDP. *Health and safety:* Extremely dangerous at time of going to press; seek advice. *Tourist features:* Dinaric Alps; limestone gorges. *National holiday:* n.a.

MACEDONIA

Area: 9,919 sq. mi./25,173 km². *Local name:* Republika Makedonija. *Currency:* Denar. *Capital:* Skopje. *Physical features:* Mostly mountain-ous. *Climate:* Subtropical. *Time zone:* GMT +1h. *Political system:* Democratic republic. *Head of state:* Kiro Gligorov (from 1990). *Head of government:* Branko Crevenkovski (from 1992). *Main exports:* Machin-ery and transportation equipment, food, textiles, chemicals. *Resources:* Chromium, lead, zinc.

PEOPLE

Population: 2,173,000. *Distribution urban/rural:* n.a. *Life expectancy:* 71(m), 75(f). *Languages:* Macedonian, Albanian, Turkish, Serbo-Croatian. *Ethnic groups:* Macedonian 67%, Albanian 21%, Turkish 4%, Serb and other 8%. *Religions:* Eastern Orthodox 59%, Muslim 26%, Catholic 4%, Protestant 1%, unknown 10%. *Literacy rate:* 89%. *Per capita GDP:* $3,110.

KEY DATES

1913 Ancient Macedonia divided among Serbia, Bulgaria, and Greece.
1918 Serbian region becomes part of what is to become Yugoslavia.
1980 Increased nationalist feeling.
1992 Independence declared.
1993 Joins UN.

TRAVEL
Visa: Not needed by U.S. *Driving permit:* IDP. *Health and safety:* Unstable at time of going to press; seek advice. *Tourist features:* Mountain scenery; Lake Ohrid. *National holiday:* n.a.

YUGOSLAVIA

Area: 39,452 sq. mi./102,173 km². *Local name:* Federativna Republika Jugoslavija. *Currency:* Dinar. *Capital:* Belgrade. *Other cities:* Kraljevo, Leskovac, Novi Sad, Nis, Kragujevac. *Physical features:* Fertile plains in N., limestone ranges in E., extremely high shoreline. *Climate:* Continental in N., subtropical in S. *Time zone:* GMT +1h. *Political system:* Republic. *Head of state:* Zoran Lilic (from 1993). *Head of government:* Mirko Marjanovic (from 1994). *Main exports:* Machinery, electrical goods, chemicals, textiles, food, tobacco. *Resources:* Oil, gas, coal, antimony, copper, lead, zinc, nickel, gold, pyrite, chrome.

PEOPLE

Population: 10,485,000. *Distribution urban/rural:* 47%/53%. *Life expectancy:* 69(m), 75(f). *Languages:* Serbo-Croatian (official), Slovenian, Macedonian, Hungarian. *Ethnic groups:* Serbs 63%, Albanians 14%, Montenegrins 6%, Hungarians 4%. *Religions:* Serb Orthodox 65%, Muslim 19%, Roman Catholic 4%, Protestant 1%, other 11%. *Literacy rate:* 89%. *Per capita GDP:* $4,200.

KEY DATES

1918 Kingdom of Serbs, Croats, and Slovenes founded, consisting of Bosnia and Herzegovina, Croatia, Dalmatia, Montenegro, Serbia, and Slovenia.
1929 Name of Yugoslavia adopted.
1941 March: enters World War II with Axis Powers; April: Germany invades.
1941–45 Fighting between partisan groups led by Draja Mikhailovich and Josip Broz (Marshal Tito).
1943 Marshal Tito's Communists liberate Belgrade and begin to govern.
1945 Proclamation of the Federal People's Republic of Yugoslavia under the leadership of Marshal Tito; opponents to Communist government are imprisoned or exiled.
1946 Draja Mikhailovich executed.
1948 Relations with U.S.S.R. severed.
1955 Relations with U.S.S.R. restored.
1971 A 23-member council ("the Presidency") established to head Yugoslav government.
1972 Ethnic violence in Croatia leads to restrictions on political activities.
1974 New constitution reduces the Presidency to nine members.
1980 Tito dies; post as head of collective Presidency and League of Communists to be filled by a rotating system of succession among members; upsurge in nationalist feeling in the republics.
1988 Economic problems create labor unrest; ethnic unrest in Montenegro and Vojvodina; government resigns.

1989 Serb nationalist, Slobodan Milosević, becomes president of Serbian republic; 29 die in Kosovo province riots prompted by Serbian attempt to end autonomous status of Kosovo and Vojvodina; state of emergency imposed; continued economic problems.
1990 First multiparty elections; Communists lose all but Serbia and Montenegro to non-Communist parties; Kosovo's government is dissolved; Alija Izetbegović, a Muslim, is elected president of Bosnia and Herzegovina.
1991 Serbia vetoes the election of a Croat due to become head of the Presidency; Albanians vote for independence in referendum and hold governmental elections; Serbia declares election and referendum illegal; Slovenia and Croatia declare independence; violence breaks out between federal and republican armies; UN imposes arms embargo against Serbia.
1992 Macedonia declares independence; Serbia and Montenegro proclaim a new Federal Republic of Yugoslavia, but it is not recognized externally; Bosnia and Herzegovina admitted to UN; civil war breaks out between nationalists and Bosnian Serbs, backed by Yugoslav National Army; UN imposes oil and trade embargo against Yugoslavia; Western ambassadors leave Belgrade; 100,000 gather in Belgrade to call for resignation of President Milosević; Dobrica Cosic becomes president; Milan Panić becomes prime minister; UN membership suspended; Slobodan Milosević reelected; Milan Panić ousted in vote of no confidence.
1993 Severe economic problems.
1994 Mirko Marjanovic becomes prime minister.

[Map of Yugoslavia showing Hungary, Croatia, Vojvodina, Romania, Bosnia and Herzegovina, Serbia, Bulgaria, Montenegro, Kosovo, Albania, Macedonia, and cities including Subotica, Sombor, Kikinda, Bečej, Novi Sad, Zrenjanin, Ruma, Vršac, Belgrade, Sabac, Smederevo, Valjevo, Kragujevac, Užice, Čačak, Kraljevo, Zaječar, Kruševac, Niš, Novi Pazar, Leskovac, Nikšić, Mitrovica, Peć, Priština, Podgorica, Mt. Daravica, Uroševac, Petrovac, Prizren, Ulcinj. Rivers: Danube, Tisza, Sava, Drina, Tara, Morava. Iron Gate Reservoir, Iron Gate Dam, Lake Scutari, Adriatic Sea, North Atlantic.]

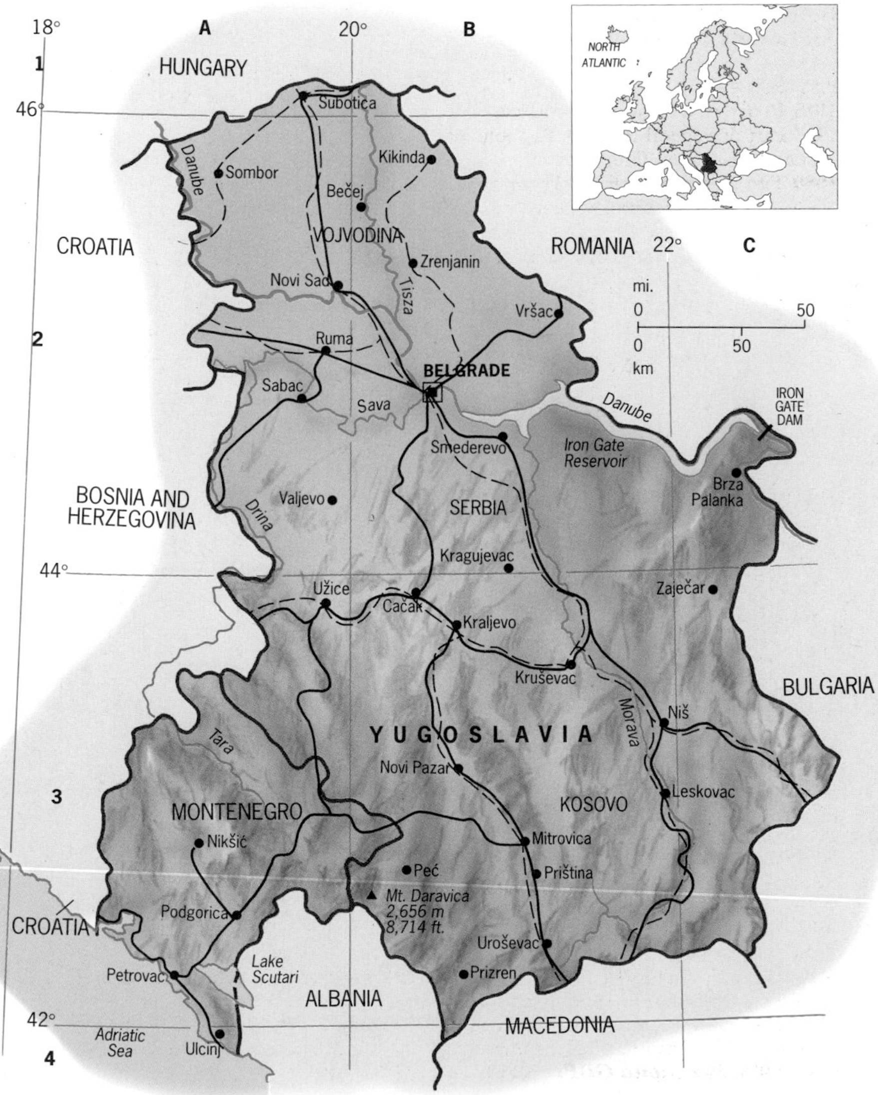

WAR IN FORMER YUGOSLAVIA

Yugoslavia was founded in 1918 as the Kingdom of the Serbs, Croats, and Slovenes. Torn by ethnic disputes, this union of disparate peoples and cultures was already disintegrating when Axis forces occupied the country in 1941, setting up Croatia as a puppet state. After World War II, Yugoslavia was held together under the leadership of Marshal Tito, half Croat, half Slovene, who carefully maintained an ethnic mix within his government. Nationalist tendencies grew stronger as time passed, however, encouraged by economic rivalries and arguments over centralism and the power of the Communist Party. After Tito's death in 1980, the old divisions reopened, exacerbated by a worsening economic decline. In the late 1980s, Serbian nationalists, led by Slobodan Milosević, began trying to absorb the smaller republics and the autonomous provinces. Fearing Serbian domination, other republics opted for independence; civil war broke out, bringing to the forefront many longstanding ethnic hatreds. The cruelest and most intractable disputes have involved Bosnia and Herzegovina, which was inhabited before the war by Muslims, Serbs, and Croats. UN troops have been deployed to protect civilians from starvation and massacre.

KEY DATES
1987 Nationalist Slobodan Milosević becomes chief of Serbian League of Communists.
1989 Slobodan Milosevic´ becomes president of Serbia and Montenegro and begins to strip Kosovo and Vojvodina provinces of their autonomy.

1990 Serbia dissolves Kosovo's government; Slobodan Milosević is reelected in Yugoslavia's first multiparty elections.
1991 May: Serbia blocks the election of Croat as head of "the Presidency"; June: Slovenia and Croatia declare independence; civil war breaks out as Serb-dominated federal forces attack targets in breakaway republics; Sept.: Serbian forces control about one-third of Croatia; UN imposes arms embargo against Serbia and Montenegro; referendum in Macedonia backs independence; Oct.: Bosnia and Herzegovina declare "sovereignty"; EC-sponsored peace plan proposes free association of sovereign states; Dec.: federal president resigns, declaring that Yugoslavia no longer exists.
1992 Jan.: cease-fire ends fighting; March: UN protection force is deployed in Croatia; Bosnian Serbs declare Serbian republic within Bosnia; widespread violence begins between Bosnian Serbs and Muslim-dominated Bosnian government forces; April: new Federal Republic of Yugoslavia (F.R.Y.) proclaimed by Serbia and Montenegro; May: UN imposes economic sanctions on F.R.Y. to discourage support for Bosnian Serbs; Bosnian Serbs lay siege to Sarajevo; presidential election staged by ethnic Albanians in Kosovo is declared illegal by F.R.Y. government; Aug.: discovery of Serb concentration camps in Bosnia and Herzegovina reveals program of "ethnic cleansing"; Sept.: Yugoslavia is suspended from the UN; more than 14,000 UN troops sent to Croatia; Oct.: UN sets up war crimes commission;

fighting breaks out between Muslims and Croats in Bosnia.
1993 April: Vance-Owen peace plan is rejected by Bosnian Serbs despite being accepted by Serbia; May: UN creates supposed "safe areas" in Bosnia and Herzegovina; Croat-Muslim fighting destroys Mostar.
1994 Feb.: Mortar shell kills 70 in Sarajevo market; NATO authorizes air attacks against Serb military installations as requested by UN; March: Bosnian Federation agreed to by Bosnian Croats and Muslims in Washington, D.C.; Serbs attack Bosnian "safe areas"; Croatia signs cease-fire agreement with breakaway Serb republic of Krajina; April: Bosnian Serbs occupy Gorazde "safe area"; June: Bosnian Muslim-Croat federation agrees to a truce with Bosnian Serbs.
1995 Hostilities resume; Croatia takes Serb-held Krrajna; Serbs shell Sarejevo and take UN hostages to prevent NATO air attacks.

ALBANIA

Area: 11,100 sq. mi./28,748 km².
Local name: Republika e Shqipërisë.
Currency: Lek. **Capital:** Tiranë.
Physical features: Mostly mountainous. **Climate:** Mild temperate. **Time zone:** GMT +1h. **Political system:** Democratic republic. **Head of state:** Sali Berisha (from 1992). **Head of government:** Alexander Meksi (from 1992). **Main exports:** Asphalt, oil, chrome, nickel, copper, food. **Resources:** Crude oil, natural gas, coal, chromium, copper.

PEOPLE
Population: 3,338,000. **Distribution urban/rural:** 35%/65%. **Life expectancy:** 71(m), 78(f). **Languages:** Albanian (Tosk), Greek. **Ethnic groups:** Albanian 90%, Greek 8%, other 2%. **Religions:** Muslim 70%, Greek Orthodox 20%, Roman Catholic 10%. **Literacy rate:** 72%. **Per capita GDP:** $820.

KEY DATES
1468 Becomes part of Ottoman Empire.
1912 Independence achieved.
1914–20 Occupied by Italy.
1925 Becomes a republic.

1939 Comes under Italian control.
1946 Becomes Communist republic led by Enver Hoxha.
1949 Joins Comecon.
1961 Relations broken off with U.S.S.R.
1978 Relations severed with China.
1985 Enver Hoxha dies.
1991 First multiparty elections won by Party of Labor of Albania (PLA).
1992 Several former Communist officials charged with corruption; Communist parties banned.
1993 Many refugees cross to Italy.
1994 Closer relations with Turkey.

TRAVEL
Visa: Not needed by U.S. **Driving permit:** IDP. **Health and safety:** Inoculations advised; water unsafe. **Tourist features:** Dinaric Alps; wild boar and wolves. **National holiday:** November 29 (Liberation Day).

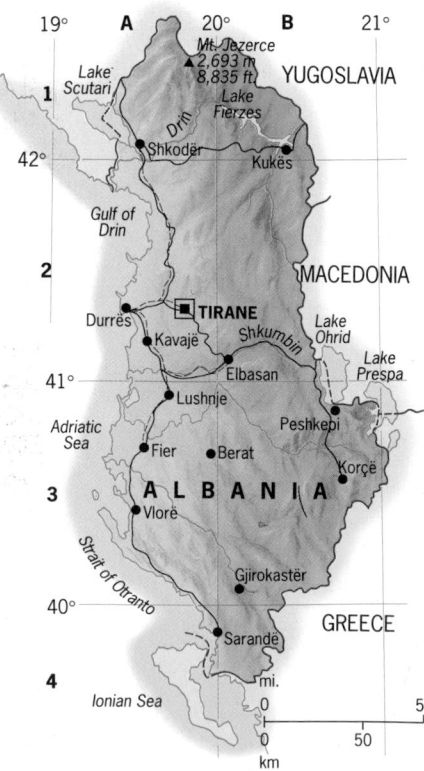

GREECE

Area: 50,953 sq. mi./131,957 km². *Local name:* Elliniki Dimokratia. *Currency:* Drachma. *Capital:* Athens. *Other cities:* Thessaloniki. *Physical features:* Mostly mountainous. *Climate:* Subtropical. *Time zone:* GMT +2h. *Political system:* Republic. *Head of state:* Constantine Karamanlis (from 1990). *Head of government:* Andreas Papandreou (from 1993). *Main exports:* Cement, petroleum products, tobacco, fruit, vegetables, olives, olive oil, textiles. *Resources:* Bauxite, lignite, magnesite, crude oil, marble.

PEOPLE
Population: 10,350,000. *Distribution* *urban/rural:* 63%/37%. *Life expectancy:* 75(m), 81(f). *Language:* Greek. *Ethnic groups:* Greek 98%, Turkish and other 2%. *Religions:* Greek Orthodox 98%, other 2%. *Literacy rate:* 93%. *Per capita GDP:* $7,730.

KEY DATES.
1669 Ottomans gain control of Crete, completing their conquest of Greece.
1829 Independence achieved.
1924 Greece declared a republic.
1941–44 German occupation.
1945 Becomes a founding member of UN.
1946 Communists defeated in civil war with Royalists.
1949 Monarchy reestablished.
1950s Conflict with Turkey over Cyprus.
1952 Joins NATO.
1967 King overthrown in military coup; martial law imposed.
1974 Martial law lifted; restoration of monarchy rejected in referendum.
1981 Joins the EC; Andreas Papandreou (Socialist) elected prime minister.
1989 Political instability; Papandreou charged with embezzlement.
1990 After three elections in one year, a majority government is finally formed.
1992 Papandreou acquitted; Greece objects to international recognition of Macedonia, fearing a claim on Greek territory of the same name.
1993 Papandreou reelected. Greece recognizes Macedonia.

TRAVEL
Visa: Not needed by U.S. *Driving permit:* IDP. *Health and safety:* No inoculations needed. *Tourist features:* Archaeological sites; Corinth Canal; Mount Olympus; the Acropolis. *National holiday:* March 25 (Independence Day).

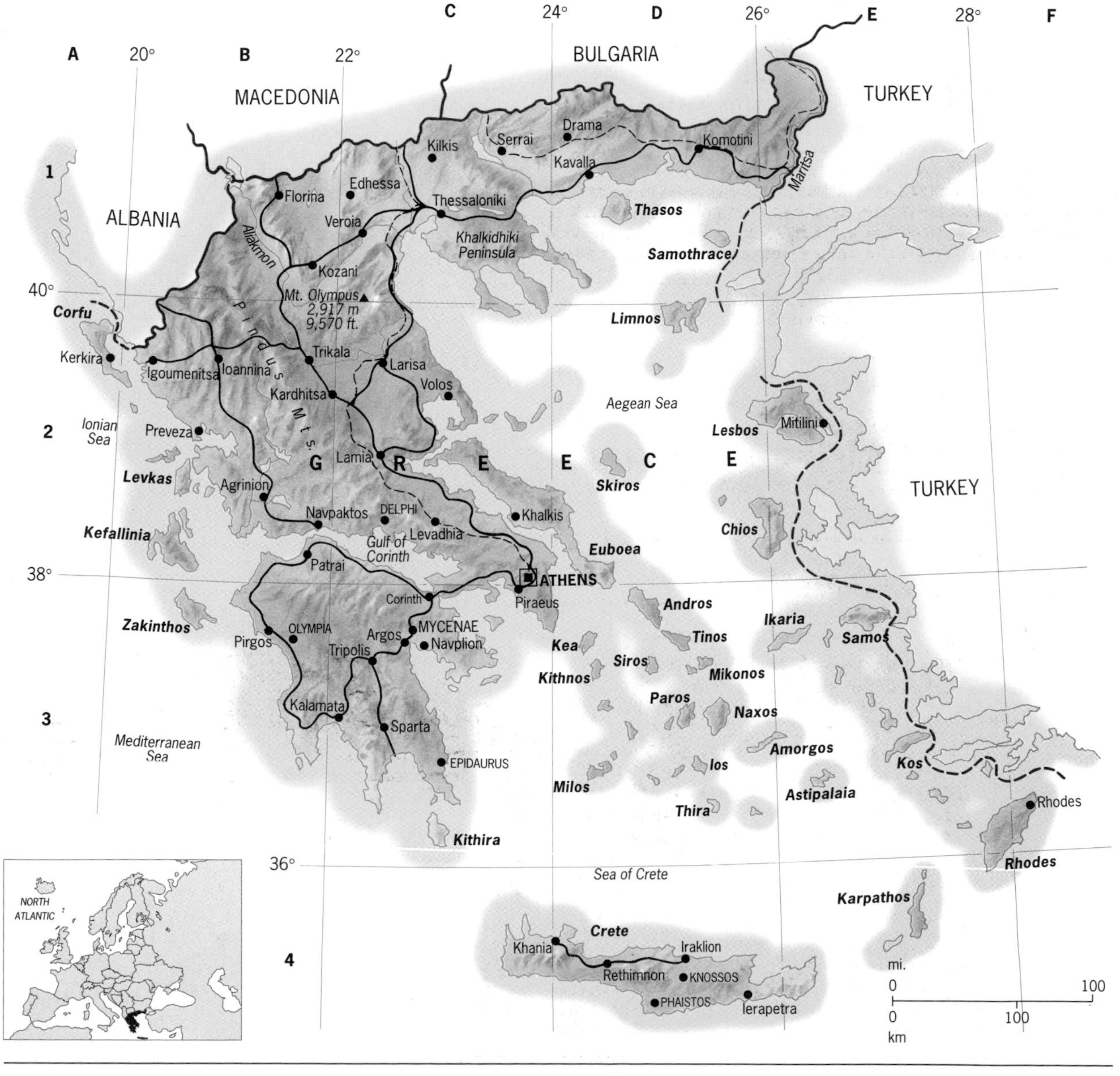

Map

A 20° B 22° C 24° D 26° E 28° F

BULGARIA

TURKEY

MACEDONIA

ALBANIA

Kilkis
Serrai
Drama
Komotini
Edhessa
Kavalla
Florina
Veroia
Thessaloniki
Thasos
Khalkidhiki Peninsula
Samothrace

Aliakmon

Kozani
Mt. Olympus ▲ 2,917 m 9,570 ft.

40°
Corfu
Kerkira
Igoumenitsa
Ioannina
Trikala
Larisa
Volos

Limnos

Lesbos
Mitilini

Pindus Mts.

Kardhitsa
Aegean Sea

Ionian Sea
Preveza

Levkas
Agrinion
Lamia
G R E E C E

Kefallinia
Navpaktos
DELPHI
Levadhia
Khalkis
Gulf of Corinth
Skiros
Chios
TURKEY

Patrai
Euboea

38°
Corinth
ATHENS
Piraeus
Andros
Ikaria
Samos

Zakinthos
OLYMPIA
Argos
MYCENAE
Navplion
Kea
Tinos
Pirgos
Tripolis
Kithnos
Siros
Mikonos

Kalamata
Paros
Naxos
Amorgos
Kos

Sparta
Ios
Astipalaia

Mediterranean Sea
EPIDAURUS
Milos
Thira
Rhodes

Kithira
Rhodes

Karpathos

36°
Sea of Crete

NORTH ATLANTIC

Khania
Crete
Iraklion
Rethimnon
KNOSSOS
PHAISTOS
Ierapetra

mi.
0   100
0   100
km

ROMANIA

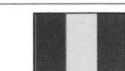

Area: 91,699 sq. mi./237,500 km². *Local name:* Rômania. *Currency:* Leu. *Capital:* Bucharest. *Other cities:* Braşov, Constanţa. *Physical features:* Mountains separated by central plain. *Climate:* Temperate with high precipitation. *Time zone:* GMT +2h. *Political system:* Republic. *Head of state:* Ion Iliescu (from 1990). *Head of government:* Nicolai Vacaroiu (from 1992). *Main exports:* Machinery, petroleum products, oil field equipment, cement, chemicals. *Resources:* Crude oil, wood, natural gas, coal, iron ore, salt.

PEOPLE

Population: 22,755,000. *Distribution urban/rural:* 55%/45%. *Life expectancy:* 68(m), 74(f). *Languages:* Romanian, Hungarian, German. *Ethnic groups:* Romanian 89%, Hungarian 9%, other 2%. *Religions:* Romanian Orthodox 70%, Roman Catholic 6%, Protestant 6%, unaffiliated 15%, Greek Orthodox 3%. *Literacy rate:* 96%. *Per capita GDP:* $3,100.

KEY DATES

1476–1504 Comes under Ottoman rule.
1861 Principalities of Moldavia and Walachia unite as Romania.
1878 Romanian independence from Turkey internationally recognized.
1916 Enters World War I on Allied side.
1920 Romania gains much territory in treaties of St. Germain and Trianon.
1930s Rise of Fascism.
1930 King Carol II becomes dictator.
1939 Nonaggression pact with Germany.
1940 King Carol II abdicates and names Gen. Ion Antonescu as leader; Romania occupied by Germany.
1941 Joins World War II on side of Axis powers.
1944 King Michael overthrows Ion Antonescu and transfers allegiance to Allies; Soviet occupation begins.
1947 Communists force King Michael to abdicate; People's Republic proclaimed.
1948 Soviet-style constitution adopted; Romania joins Comecon.
1952 Second Soviet-style constitution.
1955 Joins Warsaw Pact.
1958 Soviet forces withdraw.
1964 Diplomatic relations established with U.S.A.
1965 New constitution adopted which reduces ties with U.S.S.R.
1974 Nicolae Ceauşescu president.
1977 Earthquake kills 1,500.
1985 Austerity measures introduced.
1987 Workers demonstrate against austerity measures.
1989 Government security forces open fire on antigovernment demonstrations in Timişoara, prompting violent demonstrations throughout Romania; army assists in overthrow of Ceauşescu regime in "Christmas Revolution"; Nicolae Ceauşescu is executed.
1990 Multiparty elections; violent confrontations in Bucharest between pro- and antigovernment demonstrators.
1991 Treaty of cooperation signed with U.S.S.R.; privatization law passed; government resigns following strikes and violent demonstrations; new constitution.

TRAVEL

Visa: Needed by U.S. *Driving permit:* Nat. license/IDP. *Health and safety:* Inoculations advised; water unsafe. *Tourist features:* Carpathians; Black Sea coast; Count Dracula's castle. *National holiday:* December 1 (National Day).

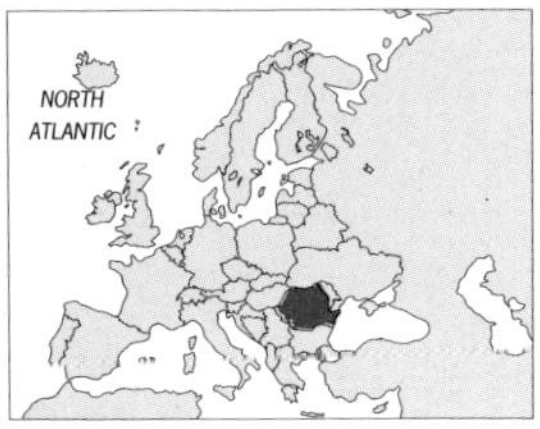

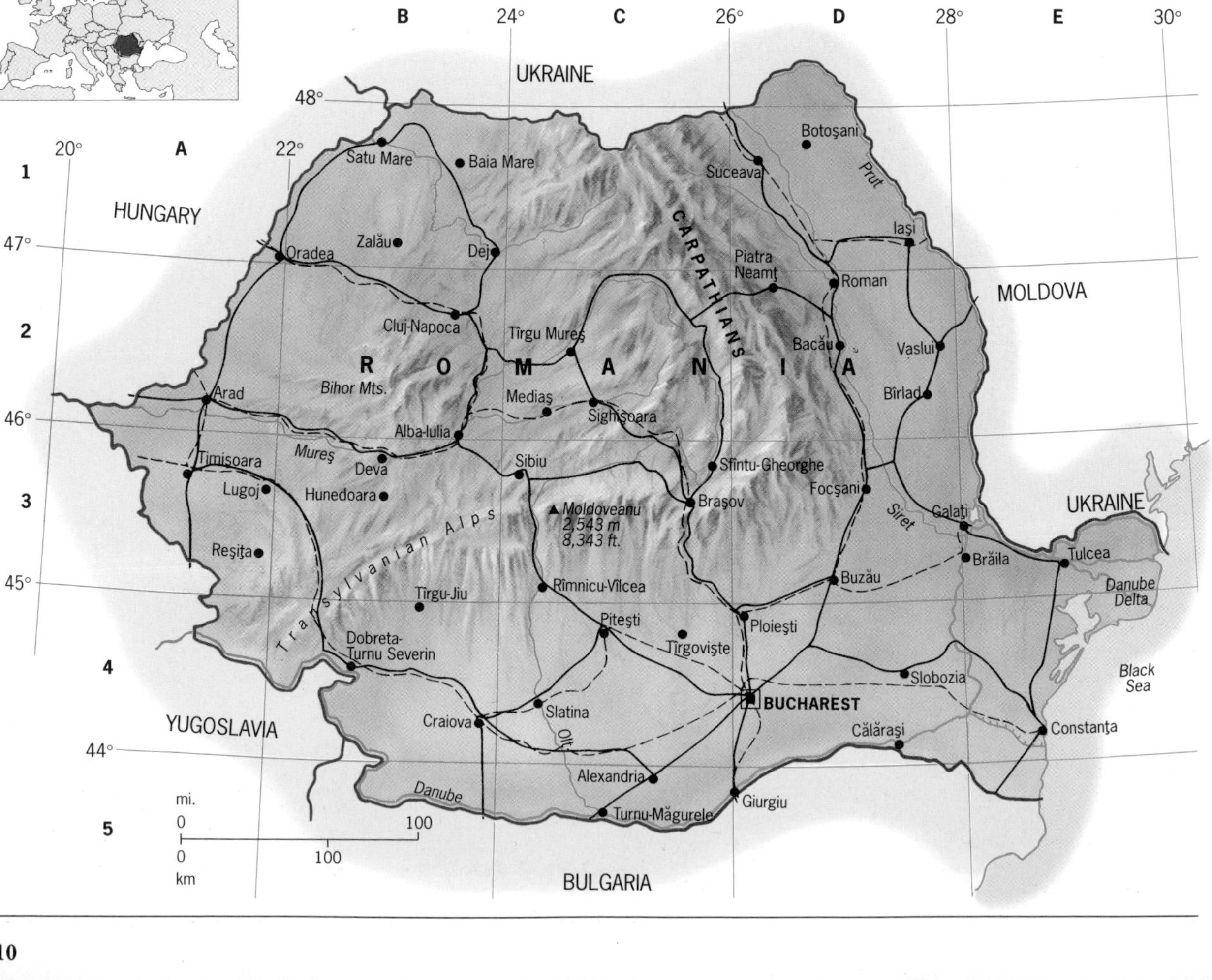

MOLDOVA

Area: 13,013 sq. mi./33,700 km². *Local name:* Republica Moldoveneasca. *Currency:* Leu. *Capital:* Chişinău (Kishinëv). *Physical features:* Gently undulating steppe. *Climate:* Moderate continental. *Time zone:* GMT +2h. *Political system:* Republic. *Head of state:* Mircea Snegur (from 1989). *Head of government:* Andre Sangheli (from 1992). *Main exports:* Chemicals, food, tobacco, textiles, machinery, chemicals. *Resources:* Negligible.

PEOPLE

Population: 4,356,000. *Distribution urban/rural:* 48%/52%. *Life expectancy:* 64(m), 71(f). *Languages:* Moldovan (official), Russian. *Ethnic groups:* Moldovan 65%, Ukrainian 14%, Russian 13%, Gagauz 3%, Jewish 2%, Bulgarian and other 3%. *Religions:* Eastern Orthodox 98%, Jewish 2%. *Literacy rate:* n.a. *Per capita GNP:* $1,260.

KEY DATES

1920 Becomes part of Romania.
1940 Becomes part of Soviet Union.
1990 Name of Moldova adopted.

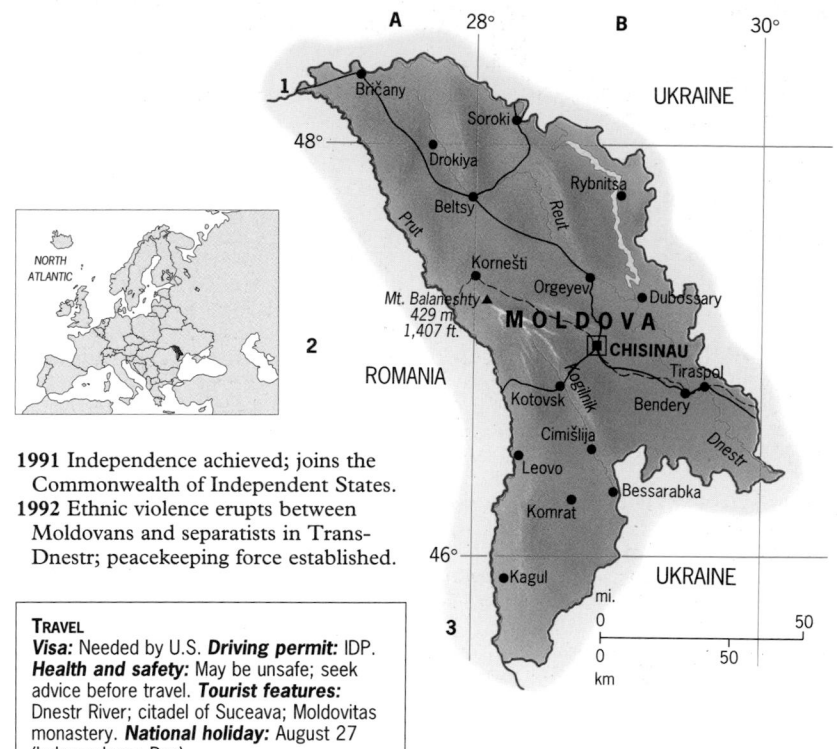

1991 Independence achieved; joins the Commonwealth of Independent States.
1992 Ethnic violence erupts between Moldovans and separatists in Trans-Dnestr; peacekeeping force established.

TRAVEL
Visa: Needed by U.S. *Driving permit:* IDP. *Health and safety:* May be unsafe; seek advice before travel. *Tourist features:* Dnestr River; citadel of Suceava; Moldovitas monastery. *National holiday:* August 27 (Independence Day).

BULGARIA

Area: 42,858 sq. mi./110,994 km². *Local name:* Republika Bulgaria. *Currency:* Lev. *Capital:* Sofia. *Physical features:* Mostly mountainous. *Climate:* Temperate. *Time zone:* GMT +2h. *Political system:* Democratic republic. *Head of state:* Zhelyu Zhelev (from 1990). *Head of government:* Lyuben Berov (from 1992). *Main exports:* Tobacco, machinery, wine, iron and steel, food, nonferrous metals. *Resources:* Bauxite, copper, lead, zinc, coal.

PEOPLE

Population: 8,469,161. *Distribution urban/rural:* 67%/33%. *Life expectancy:* 69(m), 76(f). *Languages:* Bulgarian, local dialects. *Ethnic groups:* Bulgarian 85%, Turkish 9%, Gypsy 3%, Macedonian 3%. *Religions:* Bulgarian Orthodox 85%, Muslim 13%, Jewish, Catholic, and other 2%. *Literacy rate:* 93%. *Per capita GDP:* $4,100.

KEY DATES

1396 Comes under Ottoman rule.
1908 Independence achieved.
1939 Enters World War II on Axis side.
1944 Soviet invasion.
1946 Bulgaria becomes a republic.
1947 Soviet-style constitution adopted.
1971 Todor Zhivkov becomes president.

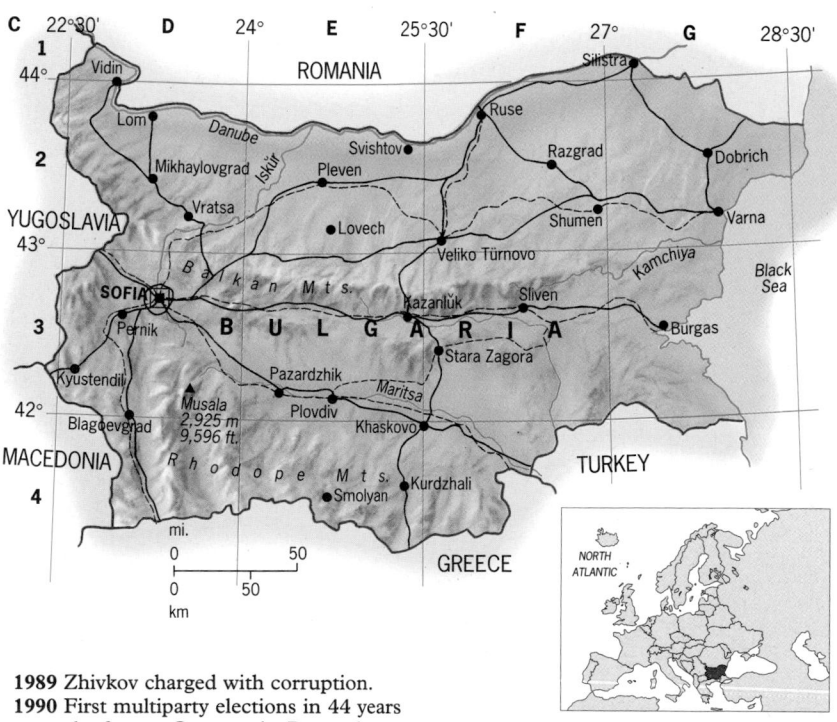

1989 Zhivkov charged with corruption.
1990 First multiparty elections in 44 years won by former Communist Party, the Bulgarian Socialist Party (BSP).
1991 New constitution; BSP defeated in general election; Filip Dimitrov heads minority government.
1992 Dimitrov resigns and is replaced by Lyuben Berov.

TRAVEL
Visa: None needed by U.S. *Driving permit:* Nat. license/IDP. *Health and safety:* No inoculations required. *Tourist features:* Sofia cathedral; Black Sea coast. *National holiday:* March 3 (National Day).

RUSSIA

Area: 6,592,857 sq. mi./17,075,500 km². *Local name:* Rossiiskaya Federatsiya. *Currency:* Ruble. *Capital:* Moscow. *Other cities:* St. Petersburg, Novosibirsk, Novgorod, Samara, Yekaterinburg, Omsk, Chelyabinsk. *Physical features:* Broad plain with low hills W. of Urals; forest and tundra in Siberia; highlands and mountains along S. border. *Climate:* Continental/subpolar. *Time zone:* Ranges from GMT +3h (W) to +11h (E). *Political system:* Federal republic. *Head of state:* Boris Yeltsin (from 1990). *Head of government:* Viktor Cheromyrdin (from 1992). *Main exports:* Petroleum and petroleum products, natural gas, wood and wood products, coal, nonferrous metals, chemicals, paper, machinery. *Resources:* Natural gas, petroleum, coal, manganese, nickel and other metals, salt, zinc, bauxite, wood.

PEOPLE
Population: 148,366,000. *Distribution urban/rural:* 73%/27%. *Life expectancy:* 63(m), 74(f). *Languages:* Russian (official), numerous other languages including Estonian, Latvian, Lithuanian, Ukrainian, Belorussian, Uzbek. *Ethnic groups:* Russian 82%, Tatar 4%, Ukrainian 3%, Chuvash 1%, other 10%. *Religions:* Russian Orthodox 25%, none 60%, other 15%. *Literacy rate:* n.a. *Per capita GNP:* $2,680.

KEY DATES
1547 Ivan IV becomes first czar.
1812 Napoleon fails in attempt to invade Russia.
1853–56 Crimean War.
1861 Serfdom abolished.
1864 Conquest of Caucasus completed.
1885 Control of C. Asia established.
1904–05 Russo-Japanese War.
1905 Troops open fire on protesters at Winter Palace; civil unrest, strikes, and armed risings spread throughout Russia; czar concedes limited reforms; revolutionaries found the Soviet of Workers' Deputies in St. Petersburg.
1907 Russia signs the Triple Entente; Trotsky flees Russia to evade arrest for involvement in the 1905 revolution.
1914 Outbreak of World War I; influence of Grigori Rasputin grows.
1916 Rasputin murdered by nobles.
1917 March: riots lead to collapse of government and abdication of czar Nicholas II; provisional governments formed in Petrograd and throughout Russia; Trotsky returns to Russia; Nov.: Bolsheviks seize power and form new government under Lenin; Dec.: ceasefire with Germany.
1918 Civil war breaks out between Red Army and non-Communist White

Russians who are backed by the Allies; imperial family murdered.
1919 Allied forces withdraw from Russia.
1920 White Russians defeated.
1921 Kronstadt rising crushed; Lenin establishes a "New Economic Policy," tightening state control of the economy.
1922 Treaty of Rapallo begins economic and military cooperation with Germany; U.S.S.R. founded as four-state federation; Stalin becomes secretary-general of Communist Party.
1924 Lenin dies.
1928 First Five-Year Plan for industrial development.
1929 Stalin becomes dictator; Trotsky exiled; beginning of forced agricultural collectivization and persecution of

PACIFIC OCEAN

opponents to Stalin in the Great Purge.
1939 Nazi–Soviet pact; Soviet forces invade E. Poland.
1940 U.S.S.R. annexes Baltic states; Trotsky is assassinated in Mexico.
1941 German invasion.
1943 Germans defeated at Stalingrad.
1945 World War II ends after Soviets capture Berlin; U.S.S.R. joins UN.
1948 Blockade of West Berlin.
1949 Comecon set up for economic cooperation among Communist nations; Moscow tightens control on E. Europe; U.S.S.R. explodes atomic bomb.
1950 Sino-Soviet Alliance.
1953 Stalin dies; Nikita Khrushchev becomes Communist Party secretary.
1955 Geneva summit fails to solve Cold

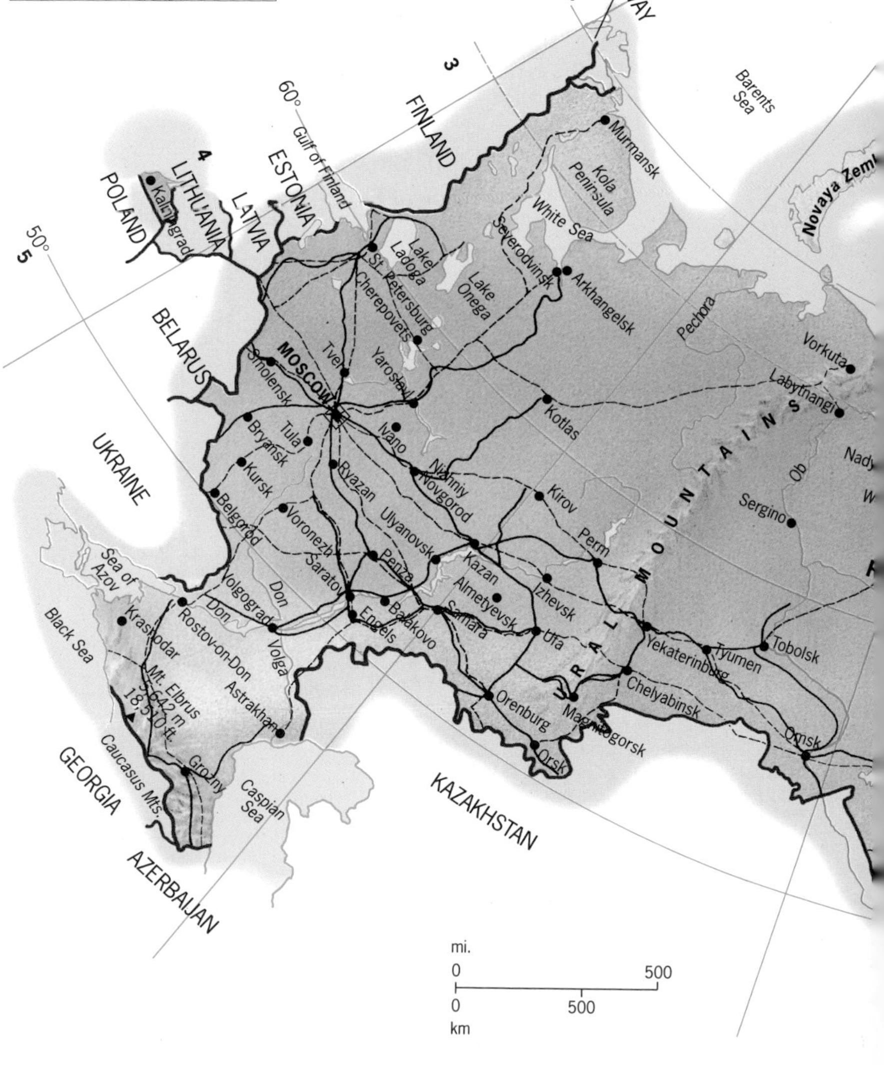

mi.
0   500
0   500
km

War conflicts; Warsaw Pact establishes military alliance of Communist states.

1957 First space satellite launched.

1958 Khrushchev becomes premier.

1960 Trade agreement with Cuba; U.S. spy plane shot down by Soviet missile; Soviet "revisionism" causes rift with Communist China.

1962 Khrushchev defuses world crisis by removing Soviet missiles from Cuba.

1963 Chinese walk out of Moscow talks; telephone "hotline" established between Moscow and Washington D.C.; first Test Ban Treaty signed in Moscow.

1964 Khrushchev ousted and replaced by Leonid Brezhnev as party secretary and Aleksei Kosygin as premier; Brezhnev adopts policy of détente with West.

1968 Liberal reforms in Czechoslovakia prompt invasion by soviet forces.

1969 Border dispute with China.

1972 U.S.S.R. and U.S.A. sign Strategic Arms Limitation Treaty (SALT 1).

1975 U.S.S.R. signs Helsinki Agreement on human rights.

1979 SALT 2 Treaty signed; Soviet forces invade Afghanistan.

1982 Strategic Arms Reduction Talks (START) begin in Geneva; Yuri Andropov succeeds Brezhnev as party chief.

1984 Konstantin Chernenko succeeds Andropov.

1985 Mikhail Gorbachev becomes first secretary and announces new policies of *glasnost* ("openness") and *perestroika*

("reconstruction").

1986 Gorbachev replaces old Brezhnev appointees with reformers.

1987 Baltic states demand autonomy; U.S.A. and U.S.S.R. agree to destroy their intermediate-range missiles.

1988 Conservatives purged as Gorbachev calls for reform; Democratic Union founded in Moscow as party opposed to

---

TRAVEL
Visa: Needed by U.S. **Driving permit:** Nat. license with translation/IDP. **Health and safety:** Inoculations advised. **Tourist features:** Red Square; St. Basil's cathedral; Moscow underground; Lenin's tomb. **National holiday:** n.a.

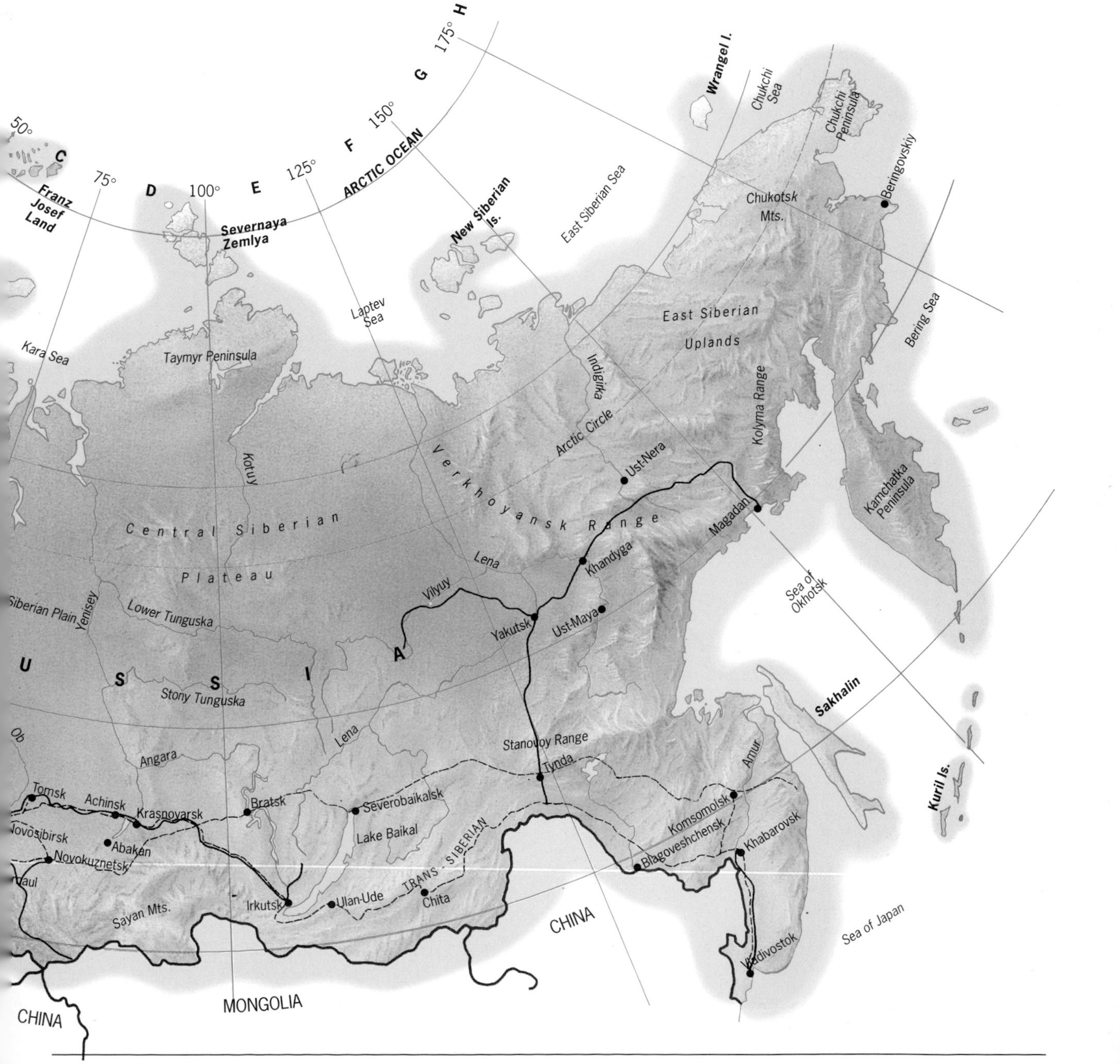

50°
C
Franz Josef Land
D 75°
100°
E 125°
F 150°
G 175°
H
ARCTIC OCEAN
Severnaya Zemlya
New Siberian Is.
Wrangel I.
Chukchi Sea
Chukchi Peninsula
Kara Sea
Taymyr Peninsula
Laptev Sea
East Siberian Sea
Chukotsk Mts.
Beringovskiy
Bering Sea
East Siberian Uplands
West Siberian Plain
Yenisey
Central Siberian Plateau
Lower Tunguska
Katuy
Indigirka
Arctic Circle
Verkhoyansk Range
Ust-Nera
Kolyma Range
Lena
Khandyga
Magadan
Kamchatka Peninsula
Vilyuy
Yakutsk
Ust-Maya
Sea of Okhotsk
U S S I A
Stony Tunguska
Lena
Ob
Angara
Stanovoy Range
Tynda
Sakhalin
Tomsk
Achinsk
Krasnoyarsk
Bratsk
Severobaikalsk
Lake Baikal
Komsomolsk
Amur
Khabarovsk
Kuril Is.
Novosibirsk
Abakan
Novokuznetsk
Ural
Sayan Mts.
Irkutsk
Ulan-Ude
Chita
TRANS - SIBERIAN
Blagoveshchensk
Vladivostok
Sea of Japan
CHINA
CHINA
MONGOLIA

totalitarianism; withdrawal of troops from Afghanistan begins; reductions in Soviet armed forces; czarist flag raised in demonstrations in Leningrad; explosion caused by Urals pipeline leak results in thousands of fatalities.

1989 Communism collapses throughout E. Europe as Soviet control is lifted; Gorbachev and U.S. president George Bush declare end of Cold War.

1990 Boris Yeltsin elected president of Russian Federation; Gorbachev becomes president of U.S.S.R.; all 15 Soviet republics declare sovereignty.

1991 July: sovereignty of Baltic states recognized; Aug.: hardliners' attempted coup against Gorbachev fails; Dec.: Gorbachev resigns as president and the U.S.S.R. is dissolved; the Commonwealth of Independent States (CIS) comes into being; Russia joins UN; economic problems worsen.

1992 Communist Party banned; price controls lifted; widespread demonstrations as living standards plummet; federal treaty signed by all constituent republics except Chechen-Ingush and Tatarstan; growing ethnic conflicts and separatism threaten federation; new constitution; START II arms-reduction agreement signed with U.S.A.

1993 April: Russians endorse Yeltsin's presidency in referendum; Sept.: Yeltsin dissolves parliament; Yeltsin's opponents stage siege in White House; Oct.: violent riots in Moscow; state of emergency imposed; troops storm White House, crushing anti-Yeltsin uprising; Dec.: conservatives gain influence in first Federal Assembly elections; Chechen borders close; referendum approves new Russian constitution.

1994 Jan.: radical reformers resign from cabinet; June: presidential decree increases police powers; Sept.: civil conflict grows in Chechnya; extensive oil pollution reported in Arctic; economic deterioration continues.

1995 Hundreds gather in Red Square to protest against conflict in Chechnya.

ECONOMY

Five-year economic plans under Communism helped Russia's economy to develop speedily, but once it was developed, heavy central controls stifled innovation and impeded further advances.

The government is now working to convert state-owned businesses and property to private ownership and encouraging individuals to start up small businesses. Russia is turning to Western countries and Japan for assistance in modernization and training.

Industry by sector

Farming Russia has a large amount of farmland but faces the problems of a short growing season, inadequate rainfall, and a lack of fertile soil. Furthermore, the inefficient farming systems of the Communist era hindered the development of the farming sector.

In 1992, there were around 50,000 privately run farms and about 25,000 state-run farms, but the private farms constitute only a small proportion of Russia's farmland. The move away from the huge state-run farms of the former U.S.S.R. has proved slow and problematic. To aid transition, new laws have been passed calling for the breakup of such farms, and financial aid is now available to help those farmers wishing to start up on their own.

Major crops include barley, flax, fruit, oats, potatoes, rye, beets, vegetables, and wheat. Many fodder crops are also grown. Livestock breeding is very important; cattle, pigs, and sheep are raised.

Fishing Cod, haddock, herring, and salmon are caught in the Barents Sea and the White Sea. Sturgeon are caught in the Black and Caspian seas, and caviar is a famous Russian delicacy. Russian vessels also fish in inland waterways, the Atlantic and Pacific oceans, and the Baltic and Black seas.

Mining Russia has vast mineral wealth and is a leading producer of asbestos, coal, steel, iron ore, oil, manganese, mercury, nickel, and potash. Gold, diamonds (particularly in Siberia), lead, salt, tin, tungsten, zinc, bauxite, copper, and silver are also important.

Manufacturing A series of five-year plans expanded the former U.S.S.R.'s manufacturing industry until it was second only to the U.S.A. in production. However, many factories and much of the machinery is archaic and in need of modernization. Heavy industry is the most highly developed sector, and tractors and other heavy machinery as well as electrical equipment are produced. The chemical industry produces fibers, fertilizers, petrochemicals, plastics, soda ash, and synthetic resins. The construction materials industry is also important. The consumer goods sector lags behind other areas, and Russia is obliged to import many consumer products.

Service industries In the former U.S.S.R., the service sector was relatively underdeveloped. Most service industry workers were poorly trained and underpaid. Since the collapse of the U.S.S.R., many private individuals have started small service-sector businesses, and this is now a rapidly expanding area, accounting for an estimated 50% of GDP.

CHECHNYA

Chechnya is an autonomous republic in Caucasia, a region in southern Russia. When the Soviet Union collapsed in 1991, some Caucasian republics—notably Armenia, Azerbaijan, and Georgia—declared independence. In December 1994, conflict erupted in the republic of Chechnya when the Chechen president, Dzhokhar Dudayev, threatened to kill 21 captive Russian soldiers. This was a direct challenge to Russian authority. In response, Boris Yeltsin ordered Russian troops into the Chechen capital of Grozny, despite reluctance by some army members to engage in a military operation that would certainly result in many civilian deaths.

Russia is determined to retain control of Chechnya for several reasons. Chechnya provides an important gateway to the oil fields of the Caspian Sea and is also a vital link to the former Soviet republics in the Caucasus. The most important issue at stake is that of Russian unity. The Soviet Union was composed of many republics with diverse peoples and cultures. Many have already gained independence, and nationalism is growing in many more. If Yeltsin is seen to back down in Chechnya, it could set a precedent for the rebellion of other republics and a further breakup of the Russian Federation.

KEY DATES

1859–64 Annexation of the northern Caucasus.

1922 Chechen Autonomous Oblast established.

1936 Becomes part of the Chechen-Ingush Autonomous Soviet Socialist Republic.

1944 Entire population of Chechen-Ingush A.S.S.R. deported to Kazakhstan and Kyrgyzstan, allegedly for collaborating with the Germans; autonomous oblast dissolved.

1960s Chechens and Ingush return to find that their land has been reappropriated to Russians; violent clashes result.

1991 Attempted coup against Mikhail Gorbachev fails; National Congress of the Chechen People seize power; many Soviet Republics secede as the U.S.S.R. breaks up, but President Yeltsin refuses independence for Chechnya; Russian troops deployed in Chechnya but withdrawn shortly afterward.

1992 March: Eighteen autonomous republics

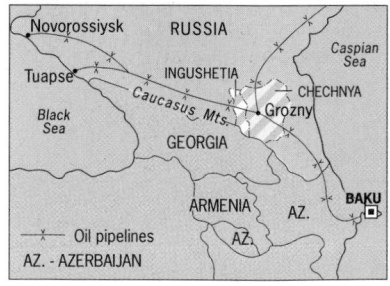

sign Federation Treaty with Russia confirming allegiance to Moscow, but Tartar and Checheno-Ingushetia refuse to sign; Nov.: constitutional amendment establishes Chechnya and Ingushetia as separate republics.

1994 Dec.: Russian jets shell Grozny; other Caucasian republics express solidarity with Chechnya.

1995 Chechen rebels expelled from presidential palace in Grozny; fighting continues; Grozny destroyed; thousands killed.

UKRAINE

Area: 233,107 sq. mi./603,700 km². **Local name:** Ukrayina. **Currency:** Karbovanets. **Capital:** Kiev. **Physical features:** Mostly fertile plains and plateaus. **Climate:** Temperate/continental. **Time zone:** GMT +2h. **Political system:** Democratic republic. **Head of state:** Leonid Kuchma (from 1994). **Head of government:** Vitali Masol (from 1994). **Main exports:** Coal, machinery, metals, chemicals. **Resources:** Iron ore, coal, natural gas and oil.

PEOPLE

Population: 52,179,000. **Distribution urban/rural:** 68%/32%. **Life expectancy:** 65(m), 75(f). **Languages:** Ukrainian, Russian, Romanian, Polish. **Ethnic groups:** Ukrainian 73%, Russian 22%, Jewish 1%. **Religions:** Ukrainian Autonomous Orthodox, Ukrainian Autocephalous Orthodox, Ukrainian Catholic (Uniate), Jewish. **Literacy rate:** n.a. **Per capita GNP:** $2,500.

KEY DATES

1750s Controlled by Russia.
1918 Declares independence from Russia.
1920 Becomes Soviet Socialist Republic.
1991 Independence achieved.

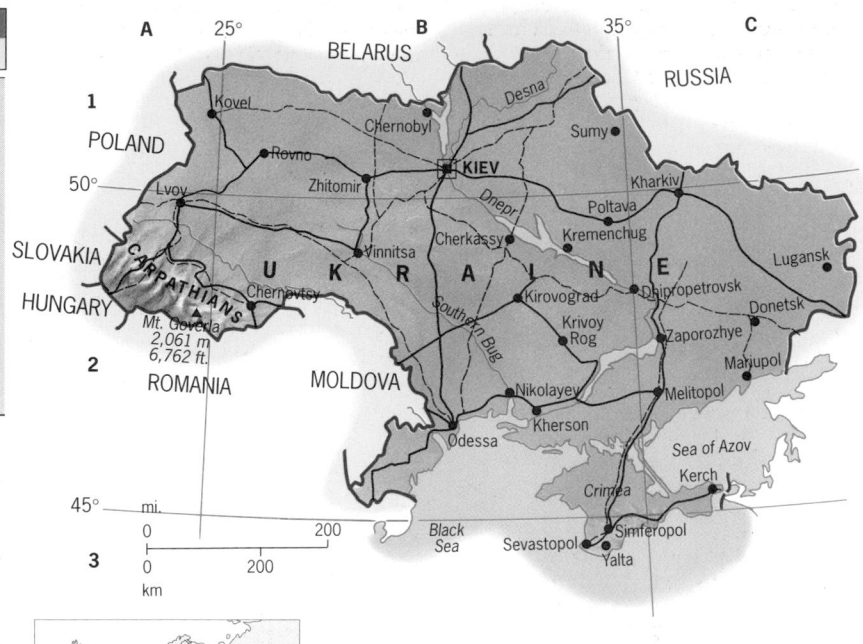

TRAVEL
Visa: Needed by U.S. **Driving permit:** IDP. **Health and safety:** Inoculations advised. **Tourist features:** Askaniya-Nova nature reserve; health spas with mineral springs; Dnieper River. **National holiday:** August 24 (Independence Day).

BELARUS

Area: 80,160 sq. mi./207,600 km². **Local name:** Respublika Belarus. **Currency:** Ruble. **Capital:** Minsk. **Physical features:** Generally flat. **Climate:** Continental/maritime. **Time zone:** GMT +2h. **Political system:** Democratic republic. **Head of state:** Alexander Lukashenko (from 1994). **Head of government:** Mikhail Chygir (from 1994). **Main exports:** Machinery and transportation equipment, chemicals, food, oil, metal goods. **Resource:** Peat.

PEOPLE

Population: 10,346,000. **Distribution urban/rural:** 67%/33%. **Life expectancy:** 66(m), 76(f). **Languages:** Belorussian, Russian. **Ethnic groups:** Belorussian 78%, Russian 13%, Polish 4%, Ukrainian 3%, Jewish 1%, other 1%. **Religion:** Russian Orthodox. **Literacy rate:** n.a. **Per capita GNP:** $2,910.

KEY DATES

1772–95 Annexed by Russia.
1918–19 Brief independence from Russia.
1991 General strike; independence achieved; Commonwealth of Independent States formed in Minsk.
1994 New constitution.

TRAVEL
Visa: Needed by U.S. **Driving permit:** IDP. **Health and safety:** May be unsafe; seek advice. **Tourist features:** Belovezhskaya Pushcha (scenic forest reserve); Brest fortress; Minsk cathedral. **National holiday:** August 24 (National Day).

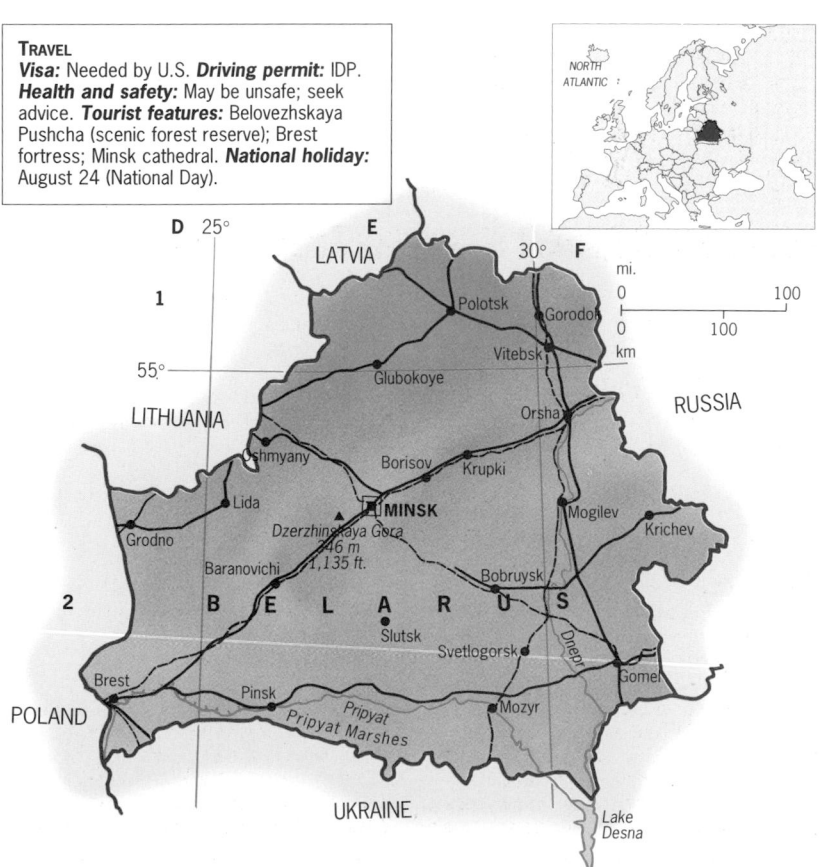

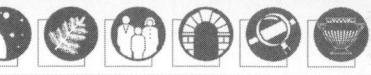

ASIA

Area: 17,005,000 sq. mi./44,043,000 km². **Largest cities:** Tokyo-Yokohama, Seoul, Osaka-Kobe-Kyoto, Bombay, Calcutta, Jakarta, Teheran, Delhi. **Main organizations:** Arab League, Asia-Pacific Economic Cooperation Conference (APEC), Association of South East Asian Nations (ASEAN). **Main products* (and percentage of world output):** Jute (97%), silk (94%), rubber (93%), rice (92%), copra (83%), tea (80%), tungsten (71%), peanuts (67%). *Excludes Russia.

PHYSICAL FEATURES

Asia is the largest continent and covers almost one-third of the earth's land area. The physical geography of the continent is extremely varied and ranges from high mountains to flood plains. **Highest point:** Mount Everest (29,029 ft./8,848 m). **Lowest point:** Shore of the Dead Sea (−1,309 ft./−399 m). **Longest river:** Chang Jiang (Yangtze). **Largest lake:** Caspian Sea (salt). **Other features:** Gobi, Syrian, Taklimakan, and Arabian deserts; Himalayas. **Vegetation:** Very varied, from desert to tropical rain forest.

PEOPLE

Population: 3,234,000,000 (60% of the total world population). **Growth rate:** 2%. **Density:** 306/sq. mi.* **Distribution urban/rural:** 47%/53%. **Life expectancy:** 63(m), 66(f). **Languages:** Many languages and dialects of every language family other than African spoken. The most common is Chinese. **Ethnic groups:** Large number of ethnic groups, and any one country may have a variety of different peoples among its population. The most prevalent ethnic groups include Chinese, Luclians, and Arabs. **Religions:** Asia is the birthplace of all the world's major religions, including Islam, Hinduism, Buddhism, Christianity, Judaism, Taoism, and Shinto. The most commonly practiced religions are Hinduism and Islam; Buddhism is important in Southeast Asia. *Excludes former U.S.S.R.

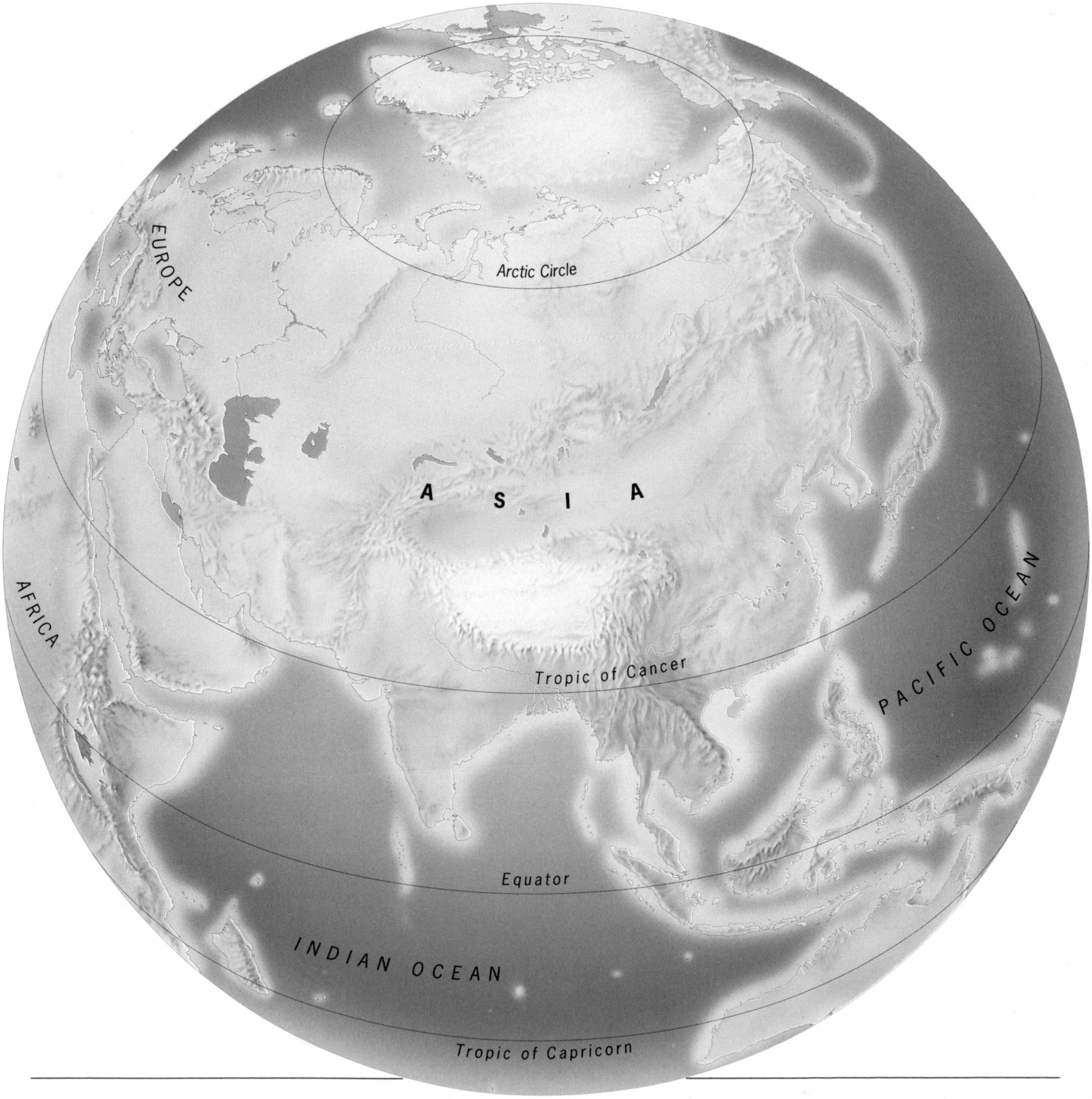

EUROPE

AFRICA

Arctic Circle

A S I A

PACIFIC OCEAN

Tropic of Cancer

Equator

INDIAN OCEAN

Tropic of Capricorn

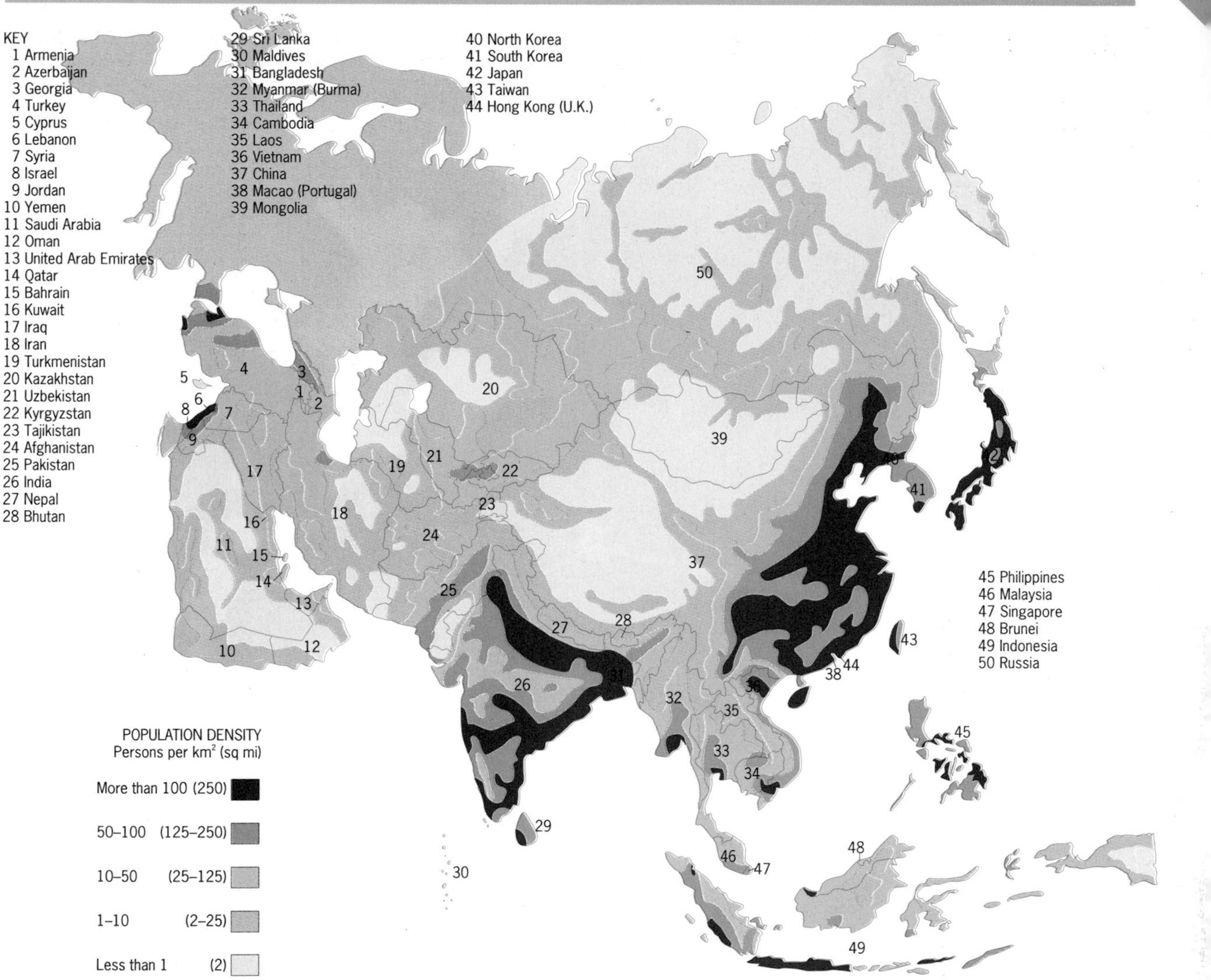

KEY
1 Armenia
2 Azerbaijan
3 Georgia
4 Turkey
5 Cyprus
6 Lebanon
7 Syria
8 Israel
9 Jordan
10 Yemen
11 Saudi Arabia
12 Oman
13 United Arab Emirates
14 Qatar
15 Bahrain
16 Kuwait
17 Iraq
18 Iran
19 Turkmenistan
20 Kazakhstan
21 Uzbekistan
22 Kyrgyzstan
23 Tajikistan
24 Afghanistan
25 Pakistan
26 India
27 Nepal
28 Bhutan

29 Sri Lanka
30 Maldives
31 Bangladesh
32 Myanmar (Burma)
33 Thailand
34 Cambodia
35 Laos
36 Vietnam
37 China
38 Macao (Portugal)
39 Mongolia

40 North Korea
41 South Korea
42 Japan
43 Taiwan
44 Hong Kong (U.K.)

45 Philippines
46 Malaysia
47 Singapore
48 Brunei
49 Indonesia
50 Russia

POPULATION DENSITY
Persons per km² (sq mi)

More than 100 (250)

50–100 (125–250)

10–50 (25–125)

1–10 (2–25)

Less than 1 (2)

Demography

Asia has the highest population of any continent and is also the most densely populated, with an average of 306 people per square mile. Much of the center of the continent is uninhabitable, and most people live along river valleys and around coasts. Many parts of Asia, including Bangladesh, Hong Kong, Singapore, E. China, much of India, Japan, and the Indonesian island of Java, rank among the most densely populated areas on earth. Even rural areas in these countries can be very heavily populated.

About one-third of all Asians and one-fifth of the total world population live in S. Asia, and the population density here is approximately seven times the world average. About 76% of S. Asians live in India, and the city of Bombay has about 127,000 people per square mile, making it one of the most densely populated cities. The majority of Asians (41%), and one-fourth of the world's population, live in E. Asia, and China has a larger population than any other nation in the world.

Climate

Asia's climate covers practically every climatic variation known. Much of the S.E. of the continent has a tropical monsoon climate: rainfall is seasonal and can be very high, causing floods in low-lying regions. However, much of the central part of the continent, along with S.W. Asia, is generally hot and arid, and the Arabian Peninsula sometimes receives no rain at all from one year to the next.

In the polar regions of N. Siberia, the extreme temperatures keep the land frozen all year round. In other parts of N. Asia the winter temperature can reach a low of –40°F.

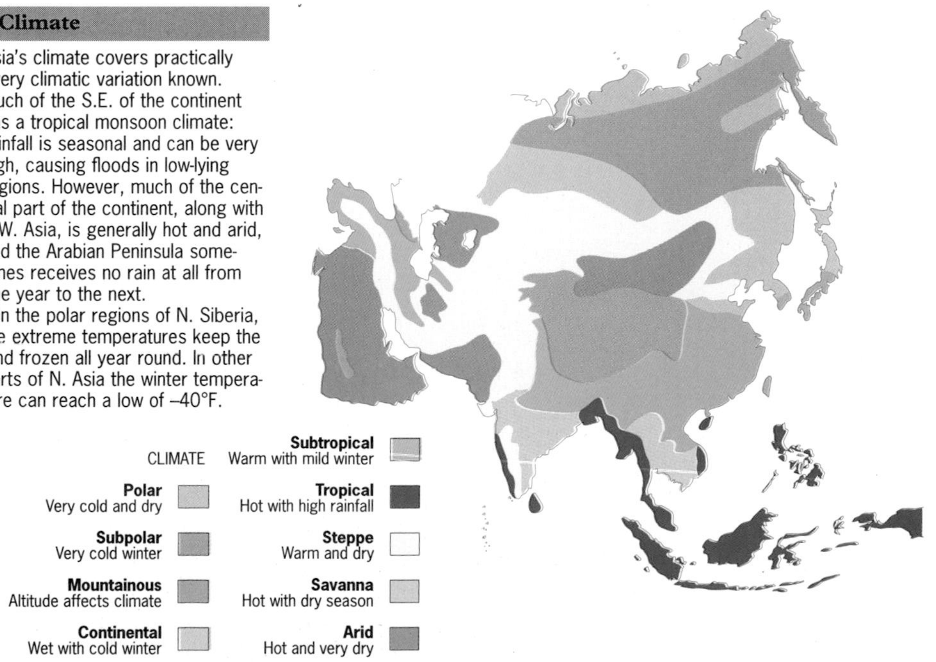

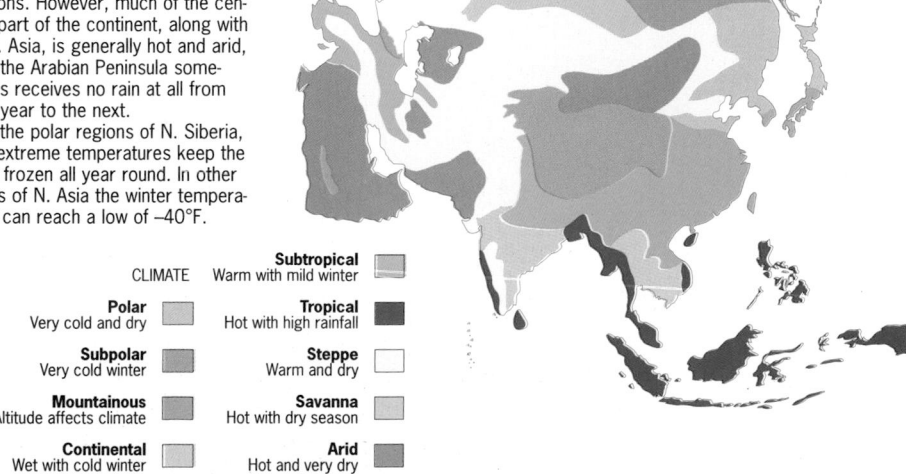

CLIMATE

Polar
Very cold and dry

Subpolar
Very cold winter

Mountainous
Altitude affects climate

Continental
Wet with cold winter

Subtropical
Warm with mild winter

Tropical
Hot with high rainfall

Steppe
Warm and dry

Savanna
Hot with dry season

Arid
Hot and very dry

ARMENIA

Area: 11,506 sq. mi./29,800 km². *Local name:* Haikakan Hanrapetoutioun. *Currency:* Dram (ruble still in use). *Capital:* Yerevan. *Physical features:* High plateau with mountains. *Climate:* Continental. *Time zone:* GMT +2h. *Political system:* Republic. *Head of state:* Levon Akopovich Ter-Petrosyan (from 1991). *Head of government:* Hrand Bagratian (from 1993). *Main exports:* Silk, cotton, food, machinery, nonferrous metals, chemicals. *Resources:* Copper, zinc.

PEOPLE

Population: 3,732,000. *Distribution urban/rural:* 68%/32%. *Life expectancy:* 68(m), 74(f). *Languages:* Armenian (official) 93%, Russian, Kurdish. *Ethnic groups:* Armenian 93%, Russian, Kurdish. *Religion:* Armenian Orthodox. *Literacy rate:* n.a. *Per capita GDP:* n.a.

KEY DATES

1936 Becomes republic within U.S.S.R.
1990s Conflict with Azerbaijan Nagorno-Karabakh enclave.
1991 Independence from U.S.S.R.

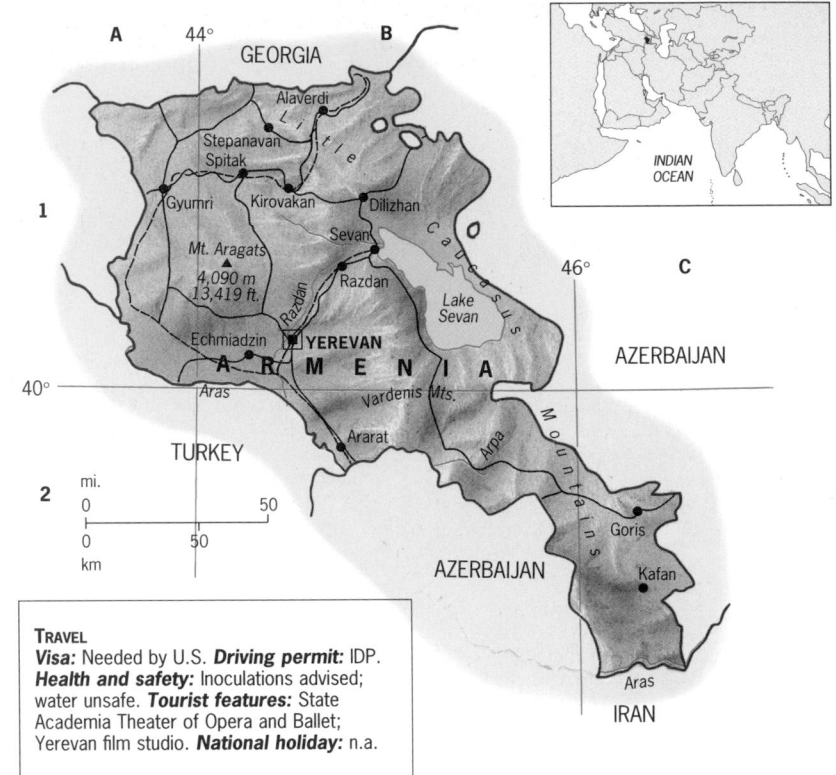

TRAVEL
Visa: Needed by U.S. *Driving permit:* IDP. *Health and safety:* Inoculations advised; water unsafe. *Tourist features:* State Academia Theater of Opera and Ballet; Yerevan film studio. *National holiday:* n.a.

AZERBAIJAN

Area: 33,439 sq. mi./86,600 km². *Local name:* Azerbaijchan Respublikasy. *Currency:* Manat (ruble still in use). *Capital:* Baku. *Other cities:* Sumgait. *Physical features:* Large, flat Kura lowland with mountains to N., Karabakh upland in W. *Climate:* Steppe. *Time zone:* GMT +2h. *Political system:* Republic. *Head of state:* Geidar A. Aliyev (from 1993). *Head of government:* Surat Huseynov (from 1993). *Main exports:* Petroleum, chemicals, textiles, gas, cotton, food. *Resources:* Petroleum, natural gas, iron ore.

PEOPLE

Population: 7,392,000. *Distribution urban/rural:* 54%/46%. *Life expectancy:* 65(m), 73(f). *Languages:* Azeri 82%, Russian 7%, Armenian 5%. *Ethnic groups:* Azeri 82%, Russian 7%, Armenian 5%. *Religions:* Muslim (Shi'ite) 87%, Russian Orthodox 6%, Armenian Orthodox 6%. *Literacy rate:* n.a. *Per capita GDP:* n.a.

KEY DATES

1922 Incorporated into U.S.S.R.
1936 Becomes separate republic.
1990s Conflict with Armenia over Nagorno-Karabakh enclave.

TRAVEL
Visa: Needed by U.S. *Driving permit:* IDP. *Health and safety:* Inoculations advised; water unsafe. *Tourist feature:* Breathtaking mountain scenery. *National holiday:* n.a.

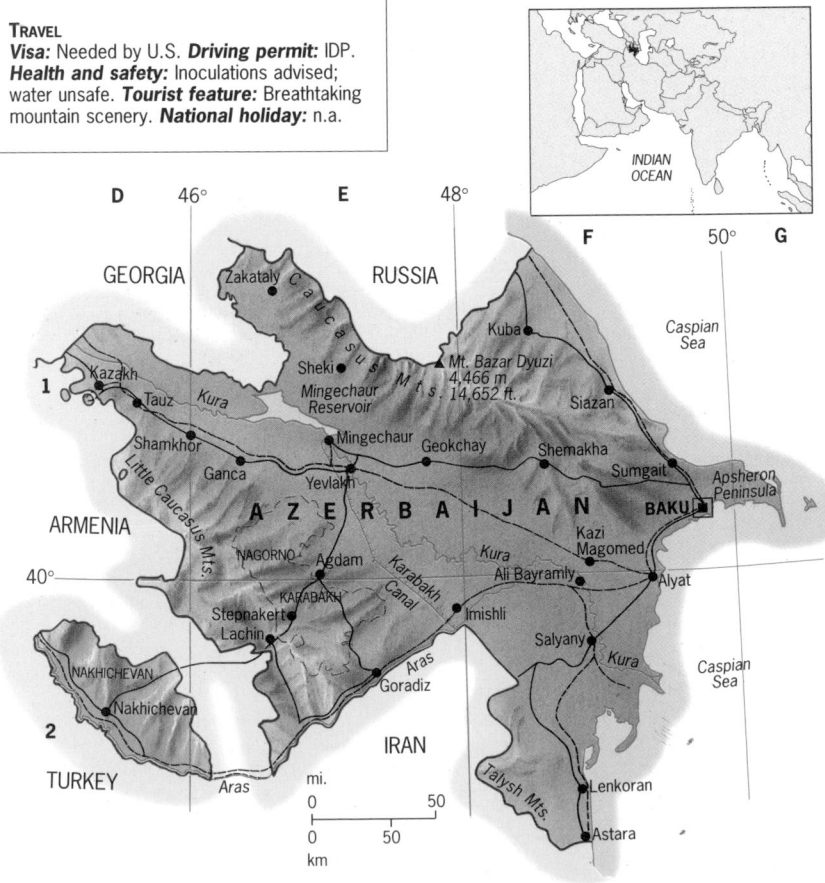

GEORGIA

Area: 26,913 sq. mi./69,700 km². **Local name:** Sakartvelos Respublica. **Currency:** Lari (ruble still in use). **Capital:** Tbilisi. **Other cities:** Kutaisi, Rustavi, Baumi, Sukhumi. **Physical features:** Mainly mountainous. **Climate:** Steppe, altitude affects climate. **Time zone:** GMT +2h. **Political system:** Republic. **Head of state:** Chairman of State Council Eduard Shevardnadze (from 1992). **Head of government:** Otar Patsatsia (from 1993). **Main exports:** Citrus fruits, tea, agricultural products, machinery, chemicals, ferrous and nonferrous metals, textiles. **Resources:** Forest, manganese deposits, iron ore, copper.

PEOPLE
Population: 5,471,000. **Distribution urban/rural:** 56%/44%. **Life expectancy:** 67(m), 75(f). **Languages:** Georgian 71%, Russian 9%, Armenian 7%, Azerbaijani 6%. **Ethnic groups:** Georgian 69%, Armenian 9%, Russian Azeri 5%, Ossetian 3%, Abkhaz 2%. **Religions:** Georgian Orthodox 65%, Muslim 11%, Russian Orthodox 10%, Armenian Orthodox 8%. **Literacy rate:** n.a. **Per capita GDP:** n.a.

KEY DATES
1921 Invasion of Red Army.
1922–36 Part of Transcaucasian Federal Republic with Armenia and Azerbaijan.
1936 Becomes republic within U.S.S.R.
1978 Outbreaks of nationalist violence.
1989 Abkhazians demand secession; interethnic violence in South Ossetia and Abkhazia; state of emergency imposed on Abkhazia.

1990 South Ossetia declares independence and fighting breaks out; non-Communists win free elections; Zviad Gamsakhurdia becomes president; Georgian Communist Party secedes from Communist Party of U.S.S.R.
1991 Independence declared; relations with U.S.S.R. severed; Gamsakhurdia accused of move toward dictatorship; state of emergency declared.
1992 Opposition forces form alternative government; Gamsakhurdia flees to Armenia; Eduard Shevardnadze becomes interim head of state.

TRAVEL
Visa: Needed by U.S. **Driving permit:** IDP. **Health and safety:** Inoculations advised; water unsafe. **Tourist features:** Narikala fortress; resorts and spas on Black Sea. **National holiday:** April 9 (Independence Day).

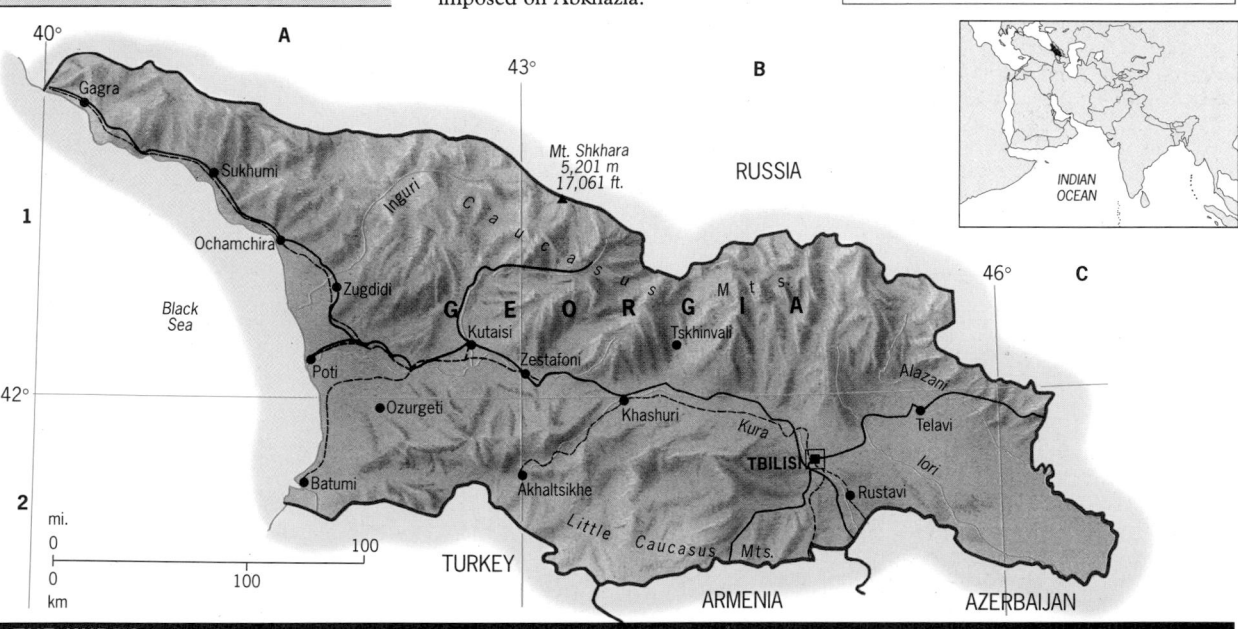

THE KURDS

The Kurds are a tribal people of the mountainous regions of S.W. Asia. The Kurdish homeland is officially only a small province of Iran, although the name Kurdistan is generally applied to an area covering parts of Azerbaijan, Iran, Iraq, Syria, and Turkey that is home to an estimated 20 million Kurds. The Kurds have never had their own government, and their struggle for independence has led to bitter conflicts between them and the governments under which they live, particularly in Iraq and Turkey where they are very sizable minorities.

KEY DATES
1920 Treaty of Sèvres promises an independent Kurdistan, but it is never ratified.
1961–70 Kurdish uprising in Iraq ends with promise of self-rule in 1974.
1974 Renewed fighting when Iraqi government reneges on 1970 agreement.
1979–80 Kurdish rebellions in Iran put down.

1984 Turkish Marxist Kurdish Workers' Party (PKK) launches offensive.
1984–89 Chemical weapon attacks on Kurdish villages in Iraq kill 25,000.
1989 Iraqi army moves hundreds of thousands of Kurds from their homes to create an uninhabited "security zone" on Iranian and Turkish borders; Kurdish guerrillas in Turkey step up their attacks on Turkish army posts.
1990 Separatist protests in Turkey.
1991 Iraqi Kurds rebel; more than one million Kurds flee to Iran and Turkey and thousands die in refugee camps; Allied troops provide relief supplies and create a safety zone in N. Iraq; April: talks between Kurdish rebel leaders and government break down when Saddam orders an economic blockade of the Kurdish region; July: at least 15 Turkish soldiers killed in clashes with Kurdish guerrillas; Aug.: Turkish air force attacks PKK camps.
1992 First free elections in Iraqi protected

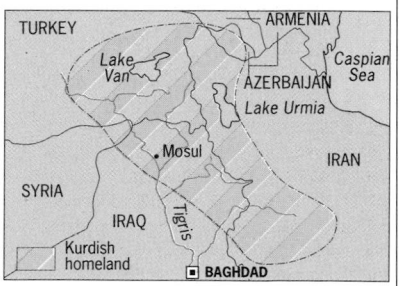

zone; hostilities between Iraqi Kurds and PKK; newly elected Kurdish parliament in protected zone votes to expel the PKK from Iraq.
1993 March: PKK declares a cease-fire; May: cease-fire broken when PKK guerrillas kill 34 Turkish army recruits; hundreds die in ensuing violence; June: Kurds launch attacks against Turkish expatriates in 13 European cities.

TURKEY

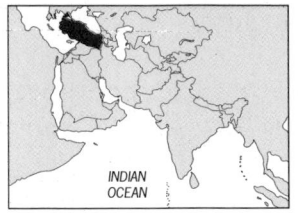

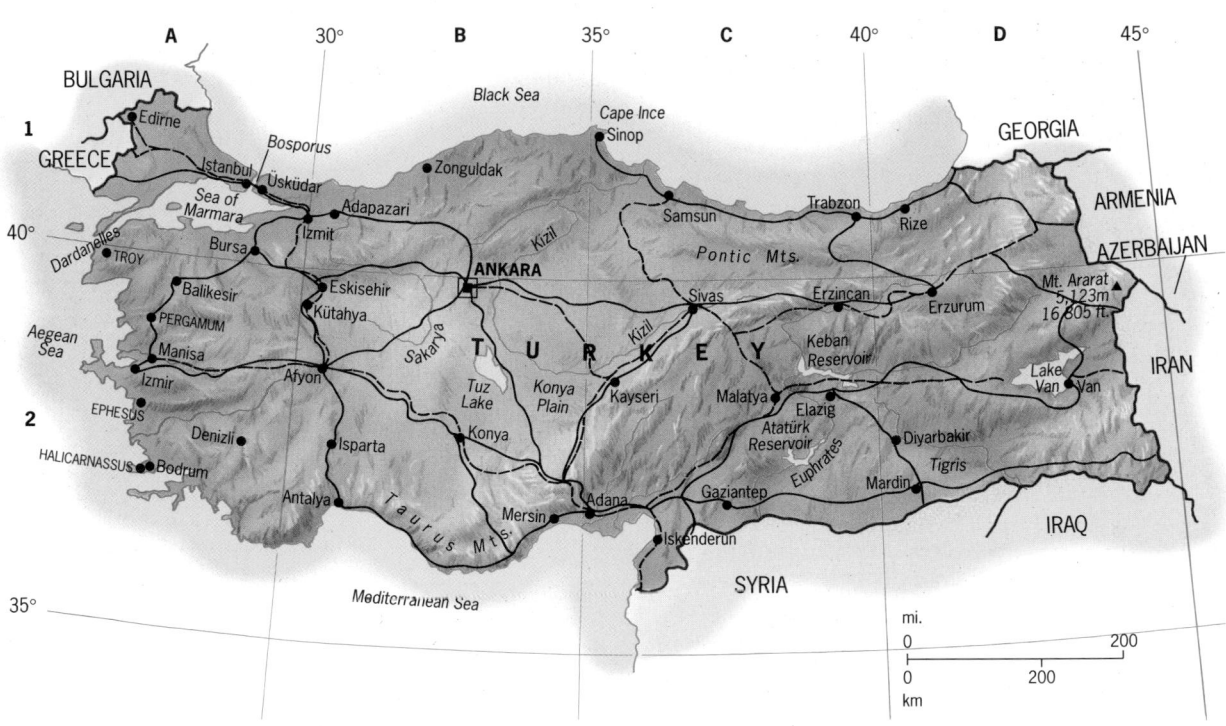

Area: 301,380 sq. mi./780,576 km².
Local name: Turkiye Cumhuriyeti.
Currency: Lira. *Capital:* Ankara.
Other cities: Istanbul, Izmir, Adana.
Physical features: Mostly mountainous with central plateau. *Climate:*
Subtropical/steppe. *Time zone:*
GMT +2h. *Political system:*
Republic. *Head of state:* Süleyman
Demirel (from 1993). *Head of government:* Tansu Ciller (from 1993).
Main exports: Steel, chemicals, cotton, yarn, chromium, plastic, rubber, machinery, fruit, vegetables, tobacco, meat products. *Resources:*
Antimony, coal, chromium, mercury, copper, borate, sulfur, iron ore.

PEOPLE
Population: 58,775,000. *Distribution urban/rural:* 61%/39%. *Life expectancy:* 68(m), 72(f). *Languages:* Turkish (official), Kurdish, Arabic. *Ethnic groups:* Turkish 80%, Kurdish 17%, other 3%. *Religion:* Muslim (mostly Sunni) nearly 100%. *Literacy rate:* 81%. *Per capita GDP:* $3,400.

KEY DATES
1453 Ottomans capture Constantinople.
1700s Beginning of Ottoman decline.
1908 Armed revolt against despotic ruler, Sultan Abdul-Hamid.
1909 Liberal group, the "Young Turks," overthrows Abdul-Hamid and rules through his brother, Muhammad V.
1914 Ottomans join Germans in WWI.
1919 Greek army occupies Izmir; nationalist leader Mustafa Kemal founds opposition government.
1920 Territories lost in Treaty of Sèvres.
1923 Treaty of Lausanne; Turkey proclaimed a republic; Kemal president.
1920s Westernization program; Kemal renamed Atatürk (father of the Turks).
1925 Kurdish revolt put down.
1938 Atatürk dies.
1960 Gen. Cemal Cürsel seizes power and sets up provisional government.
1965 Süleyman Demirel prime minister.
1971 Military forces Demirel to resign.
1974 Turkish troops invade Cyprus; relations with Greece deteriorate.
1975 Demirel returns to office.
1980 Military coup.
1982 New constitution.

1983 Return to civilian rule.
1984 Marxist Kurdish Workers' Party (PKK) launches campaign of violence.
1988 Improved relations with Greece.
1989 Prime minister Turgut Ozal elected president; Yildirim Akbulut prime minister; application to join EC rejected.
1991 Mesut Yilmaz prime minister; 15 soldiers killed and 122 injured in clashes with Kurdish guerrillas; ban on speaking Kurdish language lifted after 66 years, but publishing and broadcasting in Kurdish remain illegal.
1992 Thousands killed in earthquake.
1993 Ozal dies; Demirel succeeds; Tansu Ciller elected Turkey's first woman prime minister; PKK cease-fire broken when guerrillas ambush and kill 34 army recruits.

TRAVEL
Visa: Not needed by U.S. **Driving permit:**
Nat. license for 90 days. **Health and safety:**
Inoculations advised; water unsafe. **Tourist features:** Mount Ararat; archaeological sites including Çatal Hüyük, Ephesus, and Troy.
National holiday: October 29 (Anniversary of the Declaration of the Republic).

CYPRUS

Area: 3,572 sq. mi./9,251 km². ***Local name:*** Kypriaki Dimokratia (Greek); Kibris Cumhuriyeti (Turkish). ***Currency:*** Cyprus pound. ***Capital:*** Nicosia. ***Physical features:*** Central plain with mountains in N. and S. ***Climate:*** Subtropical. ***Time zone:*** GMT +2h. ***Political system:*** Republic. ***Head of state and government:*** Glafcos Clerides (Greek) (from 1993). ***Main exports:*** Citrus fruits, potatoes, grapes, wine, cement, clothing. ***Resources:*** Copper, pyrites, asbestos, gypsum, wood.

PEOPLE

Population: 723,000. ***Distribution urban/rural:*** 53%/47%. ***Life expectancy:*** 74(m), 78(f). ***Languages:*** Greek, Turkish, English. ***Ethnic groups:*** Greek 78%, Turkish 18%, other 4%. ***Religions:*** Greek Orthodox 78%, Muslim 18%, Maronite, Armenian, Apostolic, and other 4%. ***Literacy rate:*** 90%. ***Per capita GDP:*** $4,000.

KEY DATES

1925 Becomes a British Crown Colony.
1960 Independence achieved with Archbishop Makarios as president.

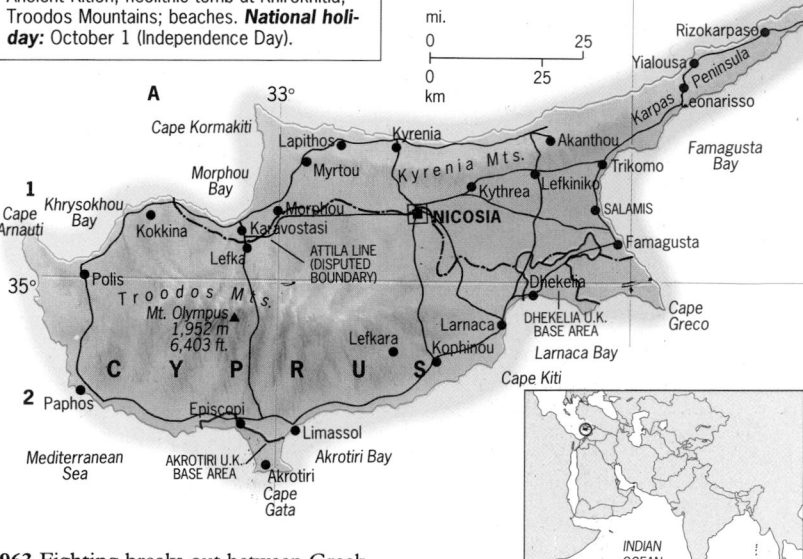

1963 Fighting breaks out between Greek and Turkish Cypriots.
1974 Makarios overthrown; Turkish occupies northern Cyprus; island divided by "Attila Line"; Makarios returns to presidency.
1983 Turkish Cypriots declare N.E. region independent as Turkish Cypriot Federated States, but it is not recognized outside Turkey.

LEBANON

Area: 4,016 sq. mi./10,400 km². ***Local name:*** Al-Jumhouriya al-Lubnaniya. ***Currency:*** Lebanese pound. ***Capital:*** Beirut. ***Physical features:*** Narrow coastal plain; Lebanon and Anti-Lebanon mountains. ***Climate:*** Subtropical. ***Time zone:*** GMT +3h. ***Political system:*** Republic. ***Head of state:*** Ilyas Harawi (from 1989). ***Head of government:*** Rafik al-Hariri (from 1992). ***Main exports:*** Agricultural products, chemicals, textiles, jewelry, metal products. ***Resources:*** Limestone, iron ore, salt.

PEOPLE

Population: 2,838,000. ***Distribution urban/rural:*** 81%/19%. ***Life expectancy:*** 66(m), 71(f). ***Languages:*** Arabic and French (both official), Armenian, English. ***Ethnic groups:*** Arab 95%, Armenian 4%, other 1%. ***Religions:*** Muslim 75%, Christian 25%. ***Literacy rate:*** 80%. ***Per capita GDP:*** $1,400.

KEY DATES

1944 Independence achieved.
1975–76 Civil war between Christians and PLO-Muslim alliance.
1982 Israel drives PLO from south.
1988 Syrian troops enter Beirut.
1991 PLO expelled; disarmament begins.

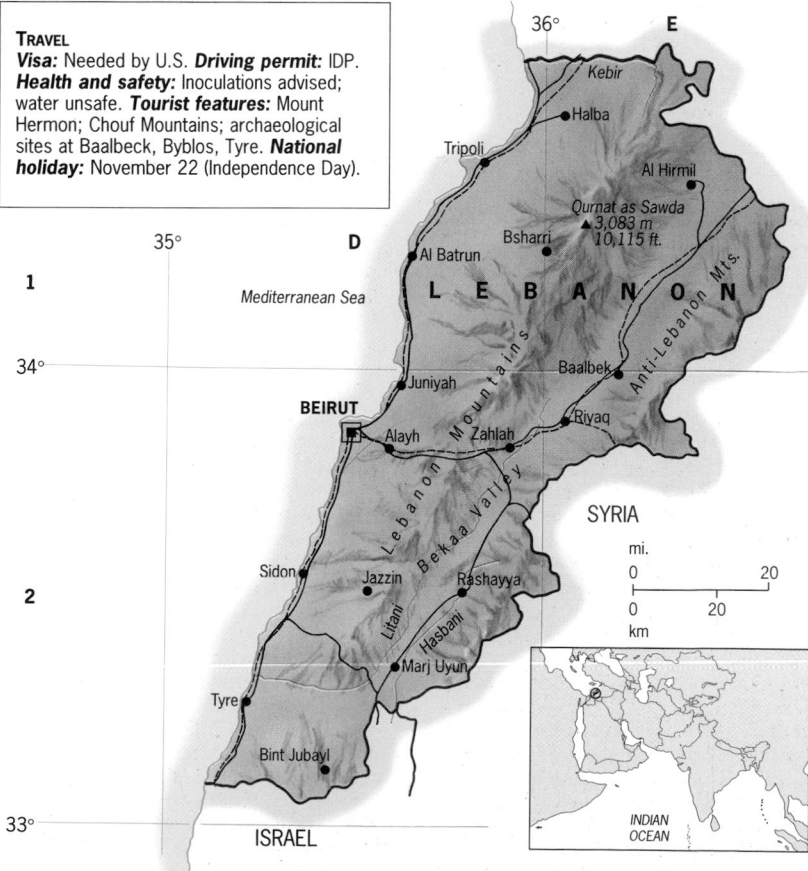

SYRIA

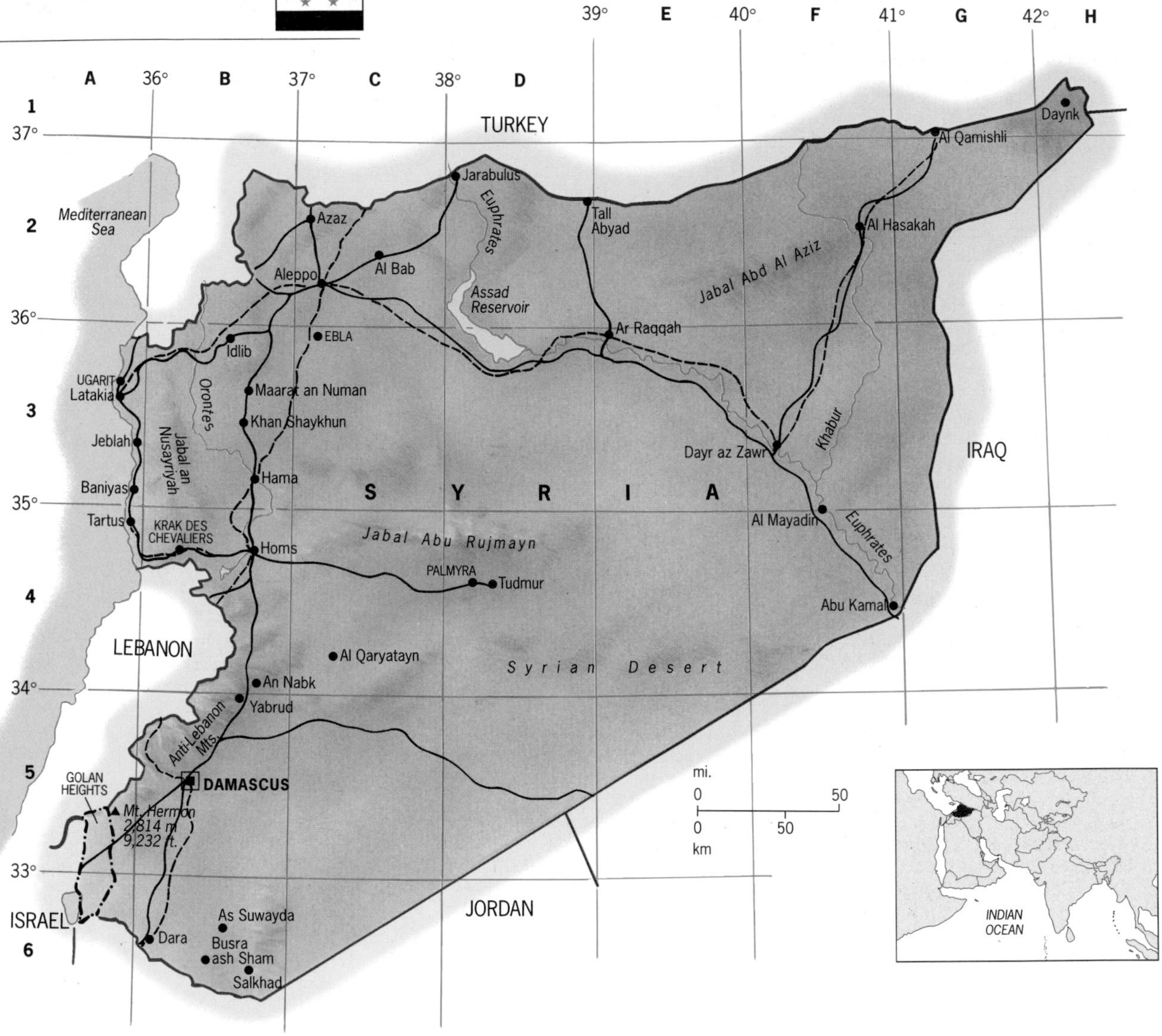

Map of Syria showing cities and geographic features:

TURKEY

Mediterranean Sea

Jarabulus, Azaz, Aleppo, Al Bab, Euphrates, Tall Abyad, Al Qamishli, Daynk, Al Hasakah, Jabal Abd Al Aziz, Assad Reservoir, Ar Raqqah, EBLA, Idlib, UGARIT, Latakia, Maarat an Numan, Khan Shaykhun, Orontes, Jabal an Nusayriyah, Jeblah, Hama, Khabur, Dayr az Zawr, IRAQ, Baniyas, S Y R I A, Tartus, KRAK DES CHEVALIERS, Homs, Jabal Abu Rujmayn, Al Mayadin, Euphrates, PALMYRA, Tudmur, Abu Kamal, LEBANON, Al Qaryatayn, Syrian Desert, An Nabk, Yabrud, Anti-Lebanon Mts., GOLAN HEIGHTS, DAMASCUS, Mt. Hermon 2,814 m 9,232 ft., ISRAEL, As Suwayda, Dara, Busra ash Sham, Salkhad, JORDAN

mi. 0 — 50
km 0 — 50

INDIAN OCEAN

Area: 71,500 sq. mi./185,180 km². **Local name:** Al-Jumhuriyah al-Arabya as-Suriya. **Currency:** Syrian pound. **Capital:** Damascus. **Other cities:** Aleppo, Homs. **Physical features:** Plateau with narrow coastal plain; mountains in S.W. **Climate:** Arid. **Time zone:** GMT +2h. **Political system:** Republic. **Head of state:** Hafez al-Assad (from 1971). **Head of government:** Mahmud Zu'bi (from 1987). **Main exports:** Petroleum, textiles, phosphates. **Resources:** Crude oil, phosphates.

PEOPLE

Population: 13,393,000. **Distribution urban/rural:** 50%/50%. **Life expectancy:** 65(m), 67(f). **Languages:** Arabic (official), Kurdish, Armenian, Aramaic, Circassian. **Ethnic groups:** Arab 90%, Kurdish, Armenian, and other 10%.

Religions: Sunni Muslim 74%, Alawite, Druze, and other Muslim sects 16%, Christian 10%. **Literacy rate:** 64%. **Per capita GDP:** $2,300.

KEY DATES

1516 Becomes part of Ottoman Empire.
1914–18 Syrian troops fight in World War I on Allied side.
1920 League of Nations divides Greater Syria into four states: Syria, Lebanon, Palestine, and Transjordan. France accorded a mandate to manage Syria.
1946 Independence achieved.
1948 Syria and other Arab forces invade Israel; UN-sponsored cease-fire agreed.
1958–61 Federated with Egypt in United Arab Republic (U.A.R.).
1967 Arab nations defeated in Six-Day War with Israel; Syria loses much land to Israel, including the Golan Heights.
1971 Military coup installs Hafez al-Assad as president.

1973–74 Yom Kippur War with Israel.
1976 Syrian troops sent into Lebanon to restore order.
1982 Militant Islamic extremist uprising put down; 5,000 are killed.
1985 Assad secures release of 39 U.S. hostages held in an aircraft hijacked by extremist Shi'ite group, Hezbollah.
1987 Improved relations with U.S.A.; Syria works for release of western hostages held in Lebanon.
1991 Enters Persian Gulf War on Allied side; relations with Britain restored.

TRAVEL
Visa: Needed by U.S. **Driving permit:** IDP preferred. **Health and safety:** Inoculations advised; water safe in cities. **Tourist features:** Crusader castles; Phoenician city sites; ruins of ancient Palmyra. **National holiday:** April 17 (National Day).

ISRAEL

Area: 8,473 sq. mi./21,946 km². *Local name:* Medinat Israel. *Currency:* Shekel. *Capital:* Jerusalem. *Other cities:* Tel Aviv, Haifa. *Physical features:* Desert in S., low coastal plain, central mountains. *Climate:* Arid. *Time zone:* GMT +2h. *Political system:* Republic. *Head of state:* Ezer Weizman (from 1993). *Head of government:* Yitzhak Shamir (from 1992). *Main exports:* Diamonds, fruit, textiles. *Resources:* Copper, phosphates, bromide, potash, sulfur, asphalt.

PEOPLE

Population: 4,516,000. *Distribution urban/rural:* 89%/11%. *Life expectancy:* 76(m), 80(f). *Languages:* Hebrew (official), Arabic. *Ethnic groups:* Jewish 83%, remainder mostly Arab. *Religions:* Jewish 82%, Muslim 14%, Christian 2%, Druze and other 2%. *Literacy rate:* 92%. *Per capita GDP:* $12,000.

KEY DATES

1948 Independent state of Israel declared; fighting with Arab neighbors erupts.
1967 Six-Day War.
1973 Yom Kippur War.
1978 Camp David Accord with Egypt.
1980 Israel and Egypt exchange diplomats for the first time; Jerusalem becomes capital (formerly Tel Aviv).
1982 Israeli troops invade Lebanon.
1987 Palestinian *intifada* (uprising).
1989 Proposed peace plan for Palestine almost brings downfall of government.
1990 Temple Mount killings; discord with U.S.A. over settlement policy.
1993 Peace accord signed with Jordan.
1994 Two Palestinian territories gain self-rule.

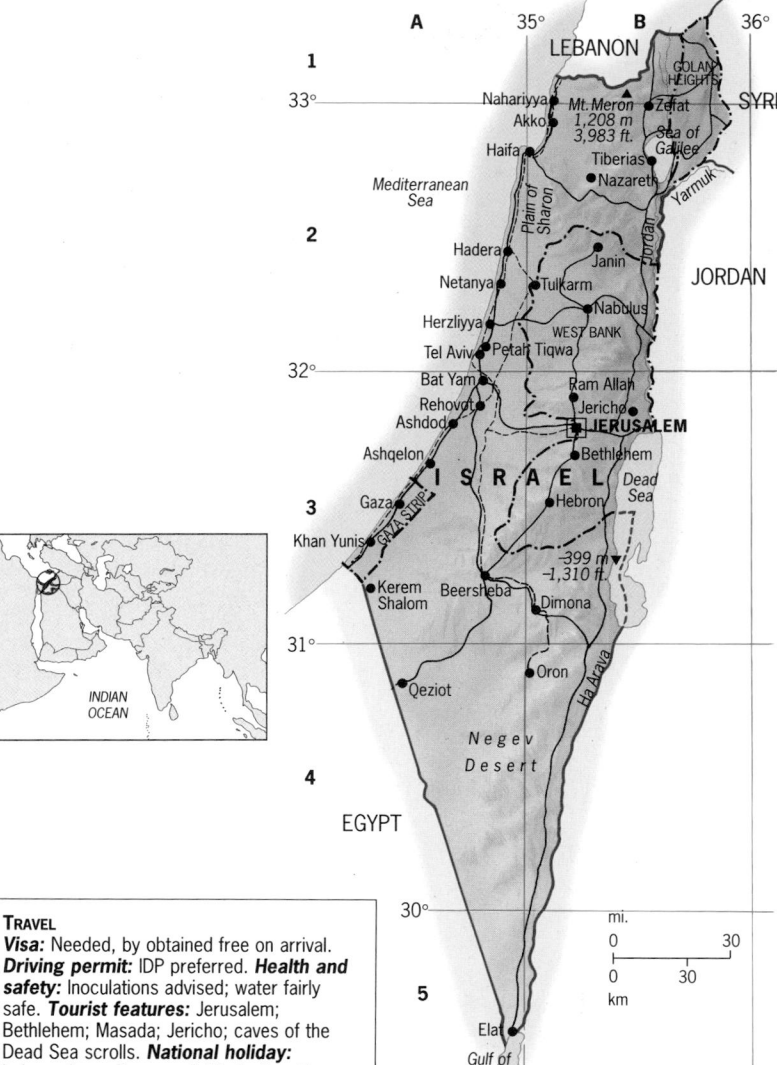

TRAVEL

Visa: Needed, by obtained free on arrival. *Driving permit:* IDP preferred. *Health and safety:* Inoculations advised; water fairly safe. *Tourist features:* Jerusalem; Bethlehem; Masada; Jericho; caves of the Dead Sea scrolls. *National holiday:* Independence Day may fall in April or May.

PALESTINE

Palestine is a territory on the E. shore of the Mediterranean where two of the world's most important religions, Judaism and Christianity, originated. Jerusalem is also a sacred place for Muslims. After WWII the UN attempted to divide Palestine into two independent states, one Jewish and one Arab, but the Arabs did not accept the legitimacy of a Jewish state in Palestine until 1993. This, and Israeli annexation of much of the territory intended for Arab Palestine, has meant that Israel has been at war with its neighbors almost continuously since the 1940s. Both sides have recently shown a willingness to compromise, but the emergence of a new, more militant organization, Hamas, has resulted in increased violence in the occupied territories.

KEY DATES

1917 Balfour Declaration promises Zionists a Palestinian homeland.
1948 Palestine partitioned; Jerusalem put under international control; Israel attacked by neighboring Arab nations; Israel defeats the Arabs and gains control of around half the land designated for the new Arab state, with Egypt and Jordan controlling the remainder.
1956 Israeli forces invade Egypt; UN peace-keeping force installed in occupied territories.
1964 Palestinian Liberation Organization (PLO) founded in Lebanon.
1967 Six-Day War.
1973 Yom Kippur War.
1978 Camp David Accord signed.
1982 Israeli troops drive PLO from S. Lebanon.
1987 Widespread violence breaks out in Palestine; protestors killed by Israeli army.
1988 Jordan severs financial and administrative ties with West Bank; PLO proclaims independent Palestinian state.
1990 Temple Mount killings.
1991 Peace talks open in Madrid; increasing hostility between PLO and Hamas; curfew imposed in occupied territories.
1993 "Declaration of principles" signed by Yasser Arafat PLO and Yitzak Rabin; Israel recognizes PLO as sole representative of the Palestinian people, and PLO recognizes Israel's right to exist.
1994 Gaza Strip and Jericho achieve self-government.

JORDAN

Area: 35,478 sq. mi./91,880 km². **Local name:** Al Mamlaka al Urduniya al Hashemiyah. **Currency:** Jordanian dinar. **Capital:** Amman. **Physical features:** Mostly desert plateau. **Climate:** Arid. **Time zone:** GMT +2h. **Political system:** Constitutional monarchy. **Head of state:** King Hussein Ibn Talal Al Hashemi (from 1952). **Head of government:** Abdul-Salam-al-Mujali (from 1993). **Main exports:** Phosphates, fertilizers, potash. **Resources:** Phosphates.

PEOPLE

Population: 4,440,000. **Distribution urban/rural:** 70%/30%. **Life expectancy:** 70(m), 73(f). **Language:** Arabic. **Ethnic groups:** Arab 98%, Circassian 1%, Armenian 1%. **Religions:** Sunni Muslim 92%, Christian 8%. **Literacy rate:** 80%. **Per capita GDP:** $1,100.

KEY DATES

1517 Becomes part of Ottoman Empire.
1914–18 Arabs join forces with Allies to drive Ottomans from Middle East.
1918 Comes under British rule.
1946 Independence achieved.
1950 Jordan annexes West Bank.
1967 West Bank lost in Six-Day War with Israel; martial law declared.
1989 Martial law lifted; first parliamentary elections held–the first for 22 years.
1990 Thousands of Kuwaitis flee to Jordan from Iraq and Kuwait.
1993 Peace accord with Israel.

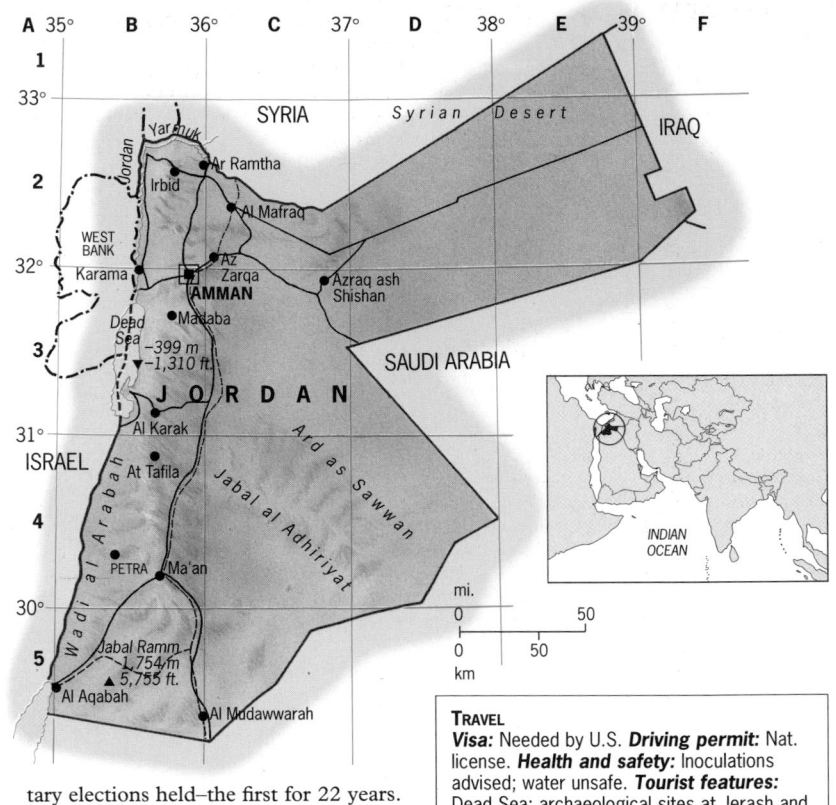

TRAVEL

Visa: Needed by U.S. **Driving permit:** Nat. license. **Health and safety:** Inoculations advised; water unsafe. **Tourist features:** Dead Sea; archaeological sites at Jerash and Petra. **National holiday:** May 25 (Independence Day)

YEMEN

Area: 205,000 sq. mi./531,000 km². **Local name:** Al-Jumhurīyah al-Yamanīyah. **Currency:** Yemeni dinar; riyal. **Capital:** Sana. **Physical features:** Coastal plain rising to interior mountains and desert. **Climate:** Arid. **Time zone:** GMT +3h. **Political system:** Republic. **Head of state:** Ali Abdullah Salen (from 1990). **Head of government:** Mohamed al-Attar (from 1992). **Main exports:** Oil, cotton, coffee. **Resources:** Crude oil, marble.

PEOPLE

Population: 12,302,000. **Distribution urban/rural:** n.a. **Life expectancy:** 49(m), 52(f). **Language:** Arabic. **Ethnic groups:** Arab, some Indian, and Afro-Arab. **Religions:** Muslim, some Christian, and Hindu. **Literacy rate:** 38%. **Per capita GDP:** $545.

KEY DATES

1918 North achieves independence.
1968 South achieves independence.
1971–72 War between the two Yemens.
1978–79 War breaks out again.
1990 The two Yemens formally unite.
1994 Secession of South not recognized.

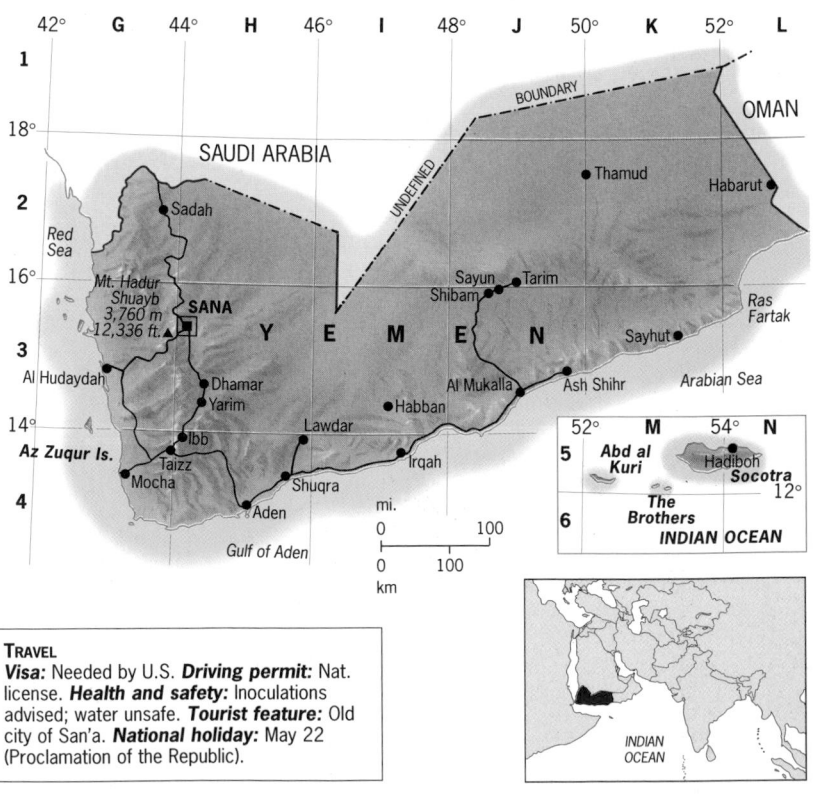

TRAVEL

Visa: Needed by U.S. **Driving permit:** Nat. license. **Health and safety:** Inoculations advised; water unsafe. **Tourist feature:** Old city of San'a. **National holiday:** May 22 (Proclamation of the Republic).

SAUDI ARABIA

Area: 849,400 sq. mi./2,200,000 km². *Local name:* Al-Mamlaka al-'Arabiya as-Sa'udiya. *Currency:* Riyal. *Capital:* Riyadh. *Other cities:* Jiddah, Mecca, Medina. *Physical features:* Mostly (uninhabited) desert. *Climate:* Arid. *Time zone:* GMT +3h. *Political system:* Monarchy. *Head of state and government:* King Fahd bin 'abd al-'aziz Al Sa'ud (from 1982). *Main exports:* Petroleum. *Resources:* Natural gas and oil, iron ore, gold, copper, and silver.

PEOPLE

Population: 17,050,934. *Distribution urban/rural:* 73%/27%. *Life expectancy:* 65(m), 68(f). *Language:* Arabic. *Ethnic groups:* Arab 90%, Afro-Asian and other 10%. *Religion:* Muslim 100%. *Literacy rate:* 62%. *Per capita GDP:* $5,800.

KEY DATES

1932 Kingdom of Saudi Arabia proclaimed.

1973 Saudi Arabia stops exporting oil to countries who support Israel.

1987 400 die in clashes between Iranian pilgrims and Saudi police in Mecca; diplomatic relations with Iran severed.

1990 Saudi oil revenues double as a result of international embargo against Iraq and Kuwait; about 1,420 die in stampede during annual pilgrimage to Mecca.

1991 War with Iraq; religious leaders call for "consultative assembly" to assist in government.

1992 New constitution; "consultative council" formed in move toward representative government.

ECONOMY

Farming Most of Saudi Arabia is desert, and the country has traditionally imported most of its food. Thanks to irrigation projects and massive capital investment, however, farming is developing steadily. Since the late 1980s, Saudi Arabia has become self-sufficient in many important agricultural products including barley, wheat, and dairy produce; about 25% of workers are employed in this sector.

Mining Saudi Arabia's huge oil fields contain about one-fourth of the world's known oil reserves. There are also small, largely unexploited deposits of copper, gold, silver, iron ore, and other minerals.

Manufacturing Petroleum and petroleum products account for 40% of the country's total economic production and 86% of exports, but the oil industry employs only 2% of workers. There are not many manufacturing industries, but some industrial complexes produce petrochemicals, fertilizers, and steel.

TRAVEL
Visa: Needed by U.S. **Driving permit:** Local license required; women not permitted to drive. **Health and safety:** Inoculations advised; water unsafe. **Tourist features:** Nafud Desert in N. and the Rubal Khali (Empty Quarter) in S. **National holiday:** September 23 (Unification of the Kingdom).

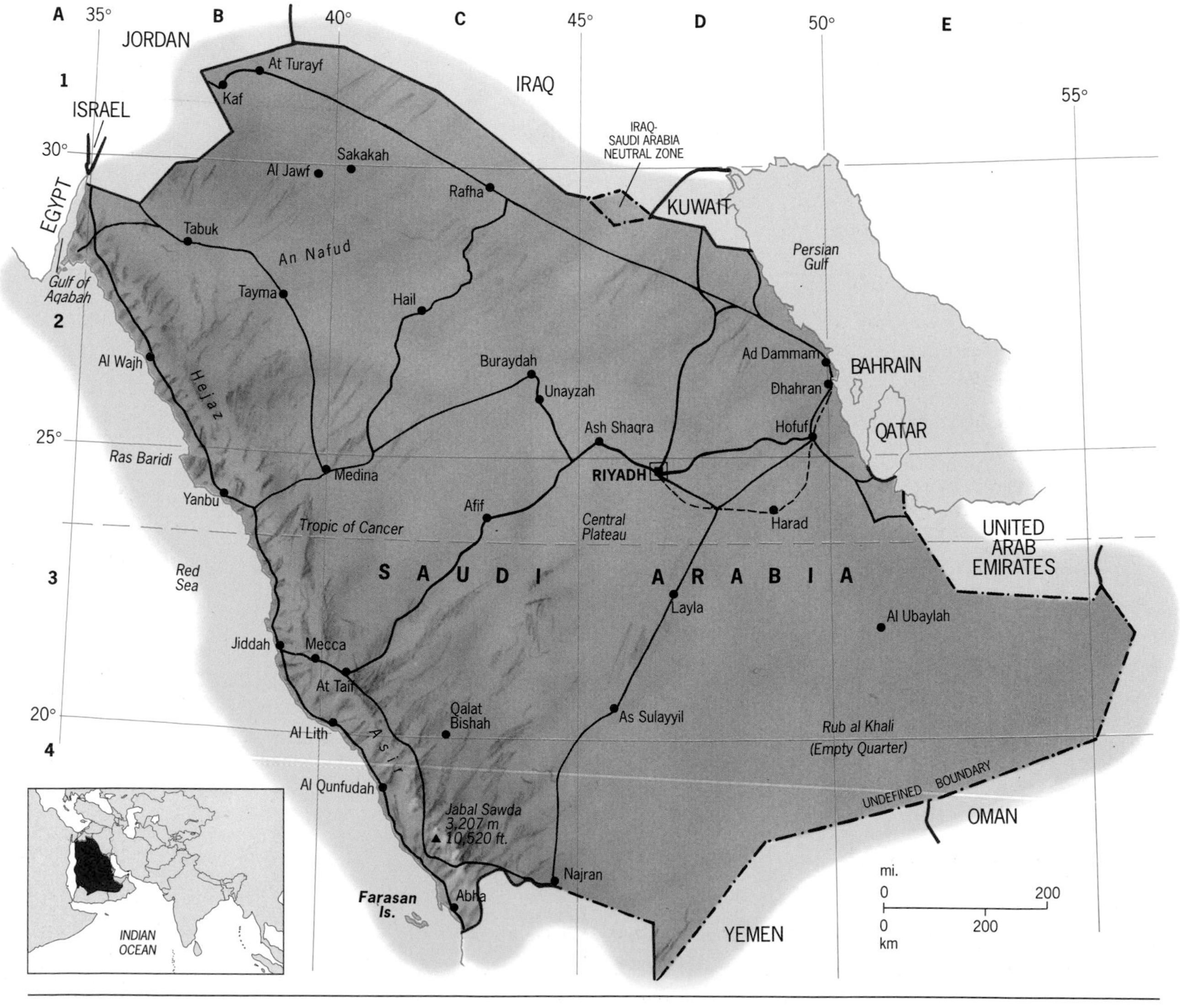

MAP: Saudi Arabia and surrounding region showing grid references A–E and 1–4, with cities including At Turayf, Kaf, Sakakah, Al Jawf, Rafha, Tabuk, Tayma, Hail, Buraydah, Unayzah, Ash Shaqra, Ad Dammam, Dhahran, Hofuf, RIYADH, Harad, Medina, Afif, Yanbu, Al Wajh, Ras Baridi, Jiddah, Mecca, At Taif, Al Lith, Al Qunfudah, Qalat Bishah, Layla, As Sulayyil, Al Ubaylah, Najran, Abha, Farasan Is. Neighboring countries: JORDAN, IRAQ, KUWAIT, BAHRAIN, QATAR, UNITED ARAB EMIRATES, OMAN, YEMEN, ISRAEL, EGYPT. Physical features: An Nafud, Hejaz, Asir, Red Sea, Gulf of Aqabah, Persian Gulf, Central Plateau, Rub al Khali (Empty Quarter), Jabal Sawda 3,207 m/10,520 ft., Tropic of Cancer, IRAQ-SAUDI ARABIA NEUTRAL ZONE.

OMAN

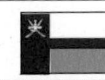

Area: 119,500 sq. mi./309,500 km². *Local name:* Saltanat 'Uman. *Currency:* Rial. *Capital:* Muscat. *Physical features:* Vast desert plain, mountains in N. and S. *Climate:* Arid, monsoonal in S. *Time zone:* GMT +4h. *Political system:* Monarchy. *Head of state and government:* Sultan and Prime Minister Qaboos bin Sa'id Al Sa'id (from 1970). *Main exports:* Petroleum, fish, processed copper. *Resources:* Crude oil, copper, asbestos, marble.

PEOPLE

Population: 1,697,000. *Distribution urban/rural:* 9%/91%. *Life expectancy:* 65(m), 69(f). *Languages:* Arabic, English, Balochi, Urdu. *Ethnic groups:* Arab with small Balochi, Zanzibari, and S. Asian groups. *Religions:* Ibadhi Muslim 75%, Sunni and Shi'ite Muslim, small Hindu minority. *Literacy rate:* n.a. *Per capita GDP:* $6,925.

KEY DATES

1951 Independence from Britain.
1975 Left-wing rebels in S. defeated.
1982 Memorandum of Understanding signed with Britain.
1991 Joins Allies in Persian Gulf War.

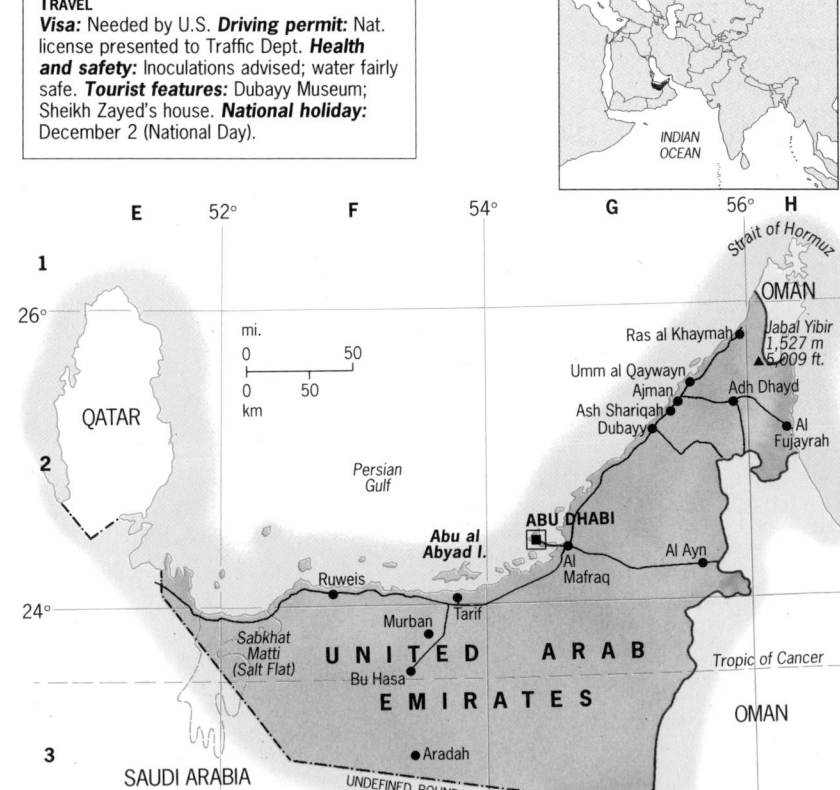

UNITED ARAB EMIRATES

Area: 32,302 sq. mi./83,657 km². *Local name:* Ittihād al-Imarat al-Arabiyah. *Currency:* Dirham. *Capital:* Abu Dhabi. *Other cities:* Dubayy, Al Ayn. *Physical features:* Flat coastal plain, dunes. *Climate:* Arid. *Time zone:* GMT +4h. *Political system:* Monarchy; union of emirates. *Head of state:* Sheikh Zayed bin Sultan al-Nahyan (from 1971). *Head of government:* Sheikh Maktoum bin Rashid al-Maktoum (from 1990). *Main exports:* Natural gas, petroleum. *Resources:* Gas, oil.

PEOPLE

Population: 1,206,000. *Distribution urban/rural:* n.a. *Life expectancy:* 70(m), 74(f). *Languages:* Arabic (official), Persian, English, Hindi, Urdu. *Ethnic groups:* Arab 42%, S. Asian 50%, other 8%; less than 20% of the population are U.A.E. citizens. *Religion:* Muslim 96%, Christian, Hindu. *Literacy rate:* 68%. *Per capita GDP:* $14,100.

KEY DATES

1971 Trucial States gain independence and adopt name United Arab Emirates.
1980s Economic crisis.
1991 Joins Allies in Persian Gulf War.

QATAR

Area: 4,416 sq. mi./11,437 km². **Local name:** Dawlet al-Qatar. **Currency:** Qatari riyal. **Capital:** Doha. **Other cities:** Al Wakrah. **Physical features:** Mostly flat and barren desert. **Climate:** Arid. **Time zone:** GMT +4h. **Political system:** Traditional monarchy. **Head of state and government:** Emir and Prime Minister Khalifa bin Hamad al-Thani (from 1972). **Main exports:** Fertilizers, petroleum products, steel. **Resources:** Crude oil, natural gas, fish.

PEOPLE

Population: 484,387. **Distribution urban/rural:** 90%/10%. **Life expectancy:** 69(m), 74(f). **Languages:** Arabic (official), English widely understood. **Ethnic groups:** Arab 40%, Pakistani 18%, Indian 18%, Iranian 10%, other 14%. **Religion:** Muslim 95%. **Literacy rate:** 76%. **Per capita GDP:** $15,000.

KEY DATES

1872 Becomes part of Ottoman Empire.
1916 Becomes a British protectorate.
1939 Oil discovered in west.
1971 Independence achieved.
1972 Khalifa bin Hamad al-Thani takes power in bloodless coup.
1981 Gulf Cooperation Council formed to unite E. Arabic states in such matters as defense and economic projects.

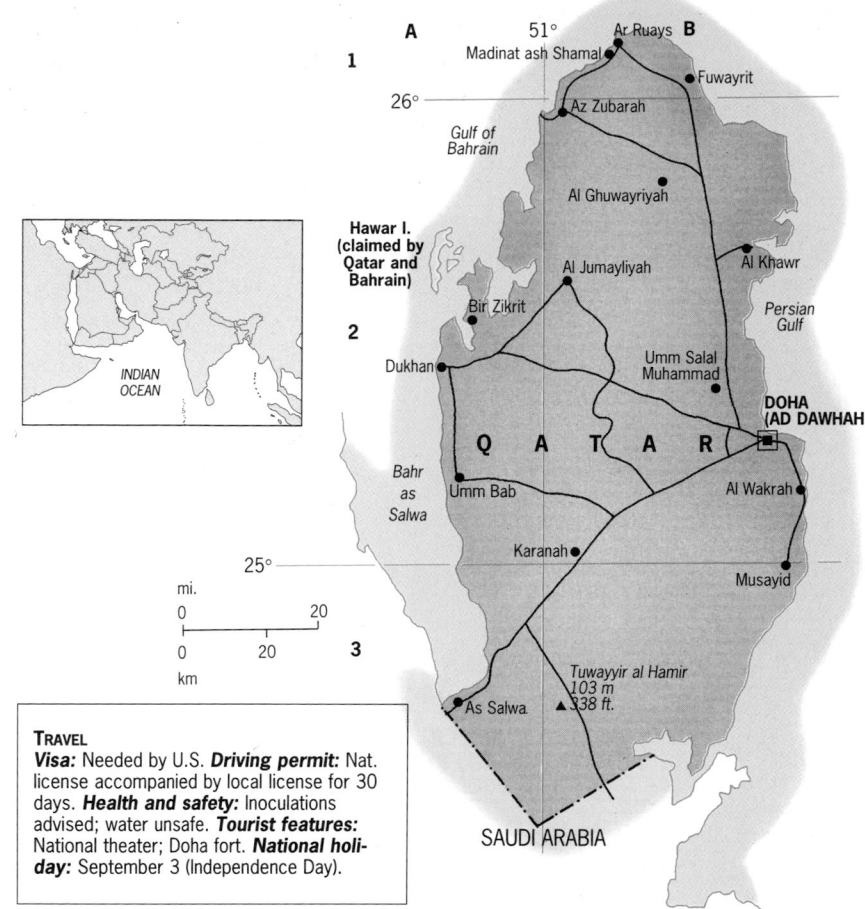

TRAVEL
Visa: Needed by U.S. **Driving permit:** Nat. license accompanied by local license for 30 days. **Health and safety:** Inoculations advised; water unsafe. **Tourist features:** National theater; Doha fort. **National holiday:** September 3 (Independence Day).

BAHRAIN

Area: 266 sq. mi./688 km². **Local name:** Dawlat al-Bahrayn. **Currency:** Bahraini dinar. **Capital:** Manamah. **Physical features:** Mostly low desert plain. **Climate:** Arid. **Time zone:** GMT +4h. **Political system:** Monarchy. **Head of state:** Emir 'isa bin Salman Al Khalifa (from 1961). **Head of government:** Khalifa bin Salman Al Khalifa (from 1970). **Main exports:** Petroleum. **Resources:** Gas; oil.

PEOPLE

Population: 521,000. **Distribution urban/rural:** 82%/18%. **Life expectancy:** 70(m), 75(f). **Languages:** Arabic (official), English widely spoken, Farsi, Urdu. **Ethnic groups:** Bahraini 63%, Asian 13%, other Arab and other 24%. **Religion:** Muslim. **Literacy rate:** 77%. **Per capita GDP:** $7,500.

KEY DATES

1861 Becomes a British protectorate.
1932 Large deposits of oil discovered.
1971 Becomes independent.
1991 Joins Allies in Persian Gulf War.

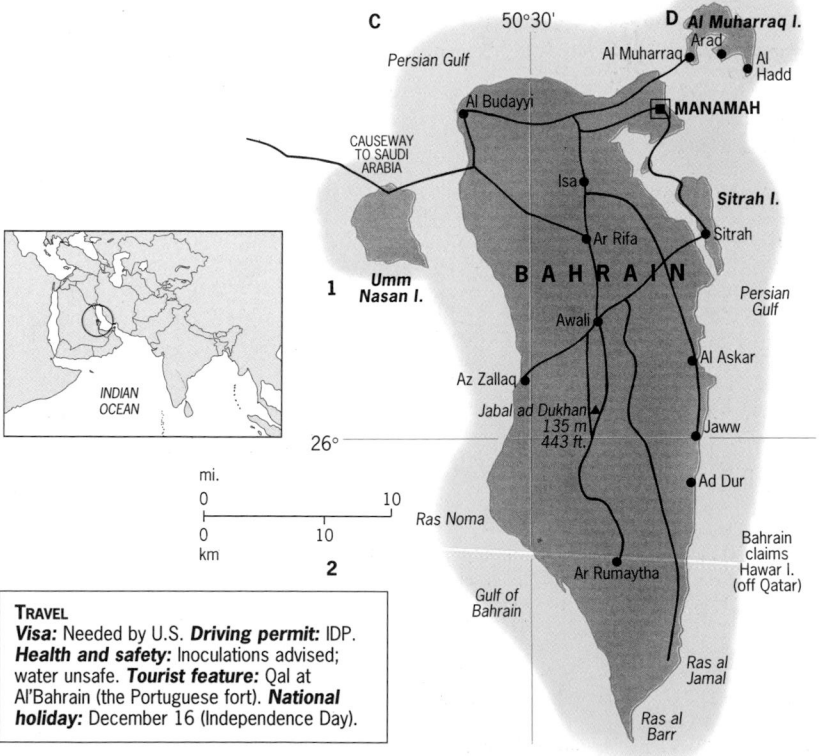

TRAVEL
Visa: Needed by U.S. **Driving permit:** IDP. **Health and safety:** Inoculations advised; water unsafe. **Tourist feature:** Qal at Al'Bahrain (the Portuguese fort). **National holiday:** December 16 (Independence Day).

KUWAIT

Area: 6,880 sq. mi./17,818 km². *Local name:* Sowlat al-Kuwait. *Currency:* Kuwaiti dinar. *Capital:* Kuwait. *Other cities:* As-Salimiyah City, Hawalli. *Physical features:* Flat to undulating desert plain. *Climate:* Arid. *Time zone:* GMT +4h. *Political system:* Nominal constitutional monarchy. *Head of state:* Emir Sheikh Jabir al-Ahmad al-Jabir al-Sabah (from 1977). *Head of government:* Prime Minister and Crown Prince Sa'ud al-'Abdallah al'Salim al'Sabah (from 1978). *Main exports:* Petroleum, natural gas. *Resources:* Petroleum, natural gas.

PEOPLE

Population: 1,433,000. *Distribution urban/rural:* n.a. *Life expectancy:* 72(m), 76(f). *Languages:* Arabic (official), English widely spoken. *Ethnic groups:* Kuwaiti 50%, other Arab 35%, South Asian 9%, Iranian 4%, other 2%. *Religion:* Muslim 85% (Shi'ite 30%, Sunni 45%, other 10%). *Literacy rate:* 74%. *Per capita GDP:* $6,200.

KEY DATES

1756 Comes under Ottoman rule.
1899 Becomes a British protectorate.
1934 Kuwait Oil Company granted concession to drill for oil.
1936 Vast petroleum deposits discovered.
1961 Independence achieved.
1967 Troops sent to Egypt during Middle East crisis.
1973 Kuwaiti troops sent into Yom Kippur War; oil supplies to U.S.A. and other countries supporting Israel cut off.
1983 17 arrested after Shi'ite bombings.
1986 Emir dissolves national assembly after criticism of his policies.

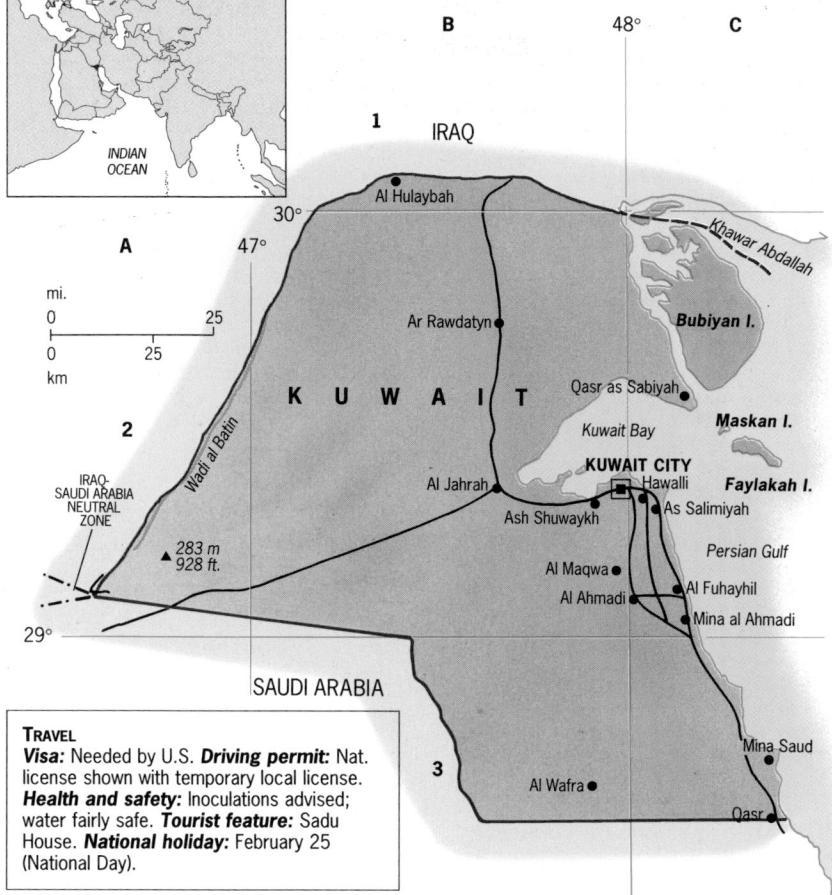

1988 Pro-Iranian Shi'ites hijack aircraft.
1990 Civil unrest; Aug.: Iraqi invasion; emir sets up government in exile in Saudi Arabia.
1991 Feb.: liberated by U.S.-led forces; criticism of undemocratic leadership of Sabah family grows; March: Cabinet resigns; martial law declared.

1992 International pressure forces emir to call first parliamentary elections since 1986; opposition party wins majority.
1993 Severe economic problems; Iraqi incursions into Kuwait forced back by U.S. air strikes.
1994 Iraqi troops prepare for invasion but withdraw in response to U.S. threats.

THE PERSIAN GULF WAR

On August 2, 1990, one day after talks between the two countries broke down, Iraqi president Saddam Hussein ordered his troops into neighboring Kuwait. Iraq accused Kuwait of flooding world oil markets thereby driving prices down and of pumping more than its allocation of oil from the jointly owned Rumaila oil field which lies on the border between the two countries.

Days after the annexation of Kuwait, the UN imposed economic sanctions on Iraq. On November 29, a resolution was passed authorizing the use of military force to expel Iraqi troops from Kuwait, and on January 17, 1991, Allied forces launched air strikes against military targets in Iraq. By April, the war was over.

The Persian Gulf War had several lasting effects. Iraq's economy was left crippled by sanctions, but some oil-producing countries benefited from the increased value of oil. The war was an environmental disaster, with the creation of a massive oil slick in the Persian Gulf and oil-

well fires in Kuwait. Allegiances during the war had a profound effect on diplomatic relations among Arab states, healing old rifts and creating some new ones.

Relations between Iraq and Kuwait have always been uneasy, and the conflict is by no means resolved. In 1994, Iraq invaded Kuwait once more and, although the threat of U.S. military action prompted a speedy retreat, its potential to reinvade remains.

KEY DATES

1990 Aug.: Iraqi forces invade Kuwait; economic sanctions imposed; c. 9,000 westerners taken hostage and moved to strategic sites to act as "human shields"; half of Kuwait's citizens flee; Nov.: UN Security Council passes resolution authorizing use of military force against Iraq; Dec.: hostages released.
1991 Jan.: Allied forces launch air strikes against Iraq; Iraq retaliates by launching scud

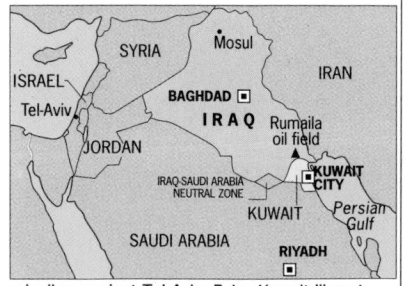

missiles against Tel Aviv; Feb.: Kuwait liberated; April: cease-fire; Security Council approves establishment of UN peacekeeping force; Sep.: Iraqi authorities detain 44 UN inspectors for four days after they find evidence of Iraqi nuclear weapons program.
1994 Saddam Hussein orders his troops into Kuwait once more, but withdraws in response to U.S. threats.

IRAQ

Area: 169,234 sq. mi./438,317 km². *Local name:* Al-Jumhouriya al'Iraqia. *Currency:* Iraqi dinar. *Capital:* Baghdad. *Other cities:* Al Basrah, Mosul. *Physical features:* Desert plains; mountains in N. and E. *Climate:* Arid. *Time zone:* GMT +3h. *Political system:* One-party republic. *Head of state:* Saddam Hussein (from 1979). *Head of government:* Muhammad Hamza al'Zubaydi (from 1991). *Main exports:* Oil (until UN sanctions), dates. *Resources:* Oil, natural gas.

PEOPLE
Population: 19,918,000. *Distribution urban/rural:* 72%/28%. *Life expectancy:* 62(m), 64(f). *Languages:* Arabic (official), Kurdish, Assyrian, Armenian. *Ethnic groups:* Arab 75%, Kurdish 20%, other 5%. *Religion:* Muslim 97% (Shi'ite 63%, Sunni 34%). *Literacy rate:* 60%. *Per capita GDP:* $1,940.

KEY DATES
1920 Britain accorded mandate over Iraq.
1932 Independence achieved.
1961 Kurds request autonomy within Iraq and share of oil revenues from N. Iraq; president refuses and fighting erupts.
1970 Agreement signed with Kurds promising self-rule from 1974.
1974–75 Renewed fighting with Kurds.

1980 Invasion of Iran; war breaks out.
1987–88 Poison gas released in Kurdish villages in retaliation for Kurdish support of Iran during Iran-Iraq War.
1988 Cease-fire with Iran.
1989 Amnesty International charges Saddam with the torture of children.
1990 Iraq invades Kuwait.
1991 Persian Gulf War; Kurdish and Shi'ite uprisings; safety zone set up in N. Iraq to protect Kurds; Iraq agrees to destruction of its biological and chemical weapons and any facilities for production of nuclear weapons.
1992 Allies impose flight ban over S. Iraq to protect Shi'ites.
1993 Iraqi incursions into "no-fly zone" result in Allied bombings.
1994 Attempted Iraqi invasion of Kuwait.

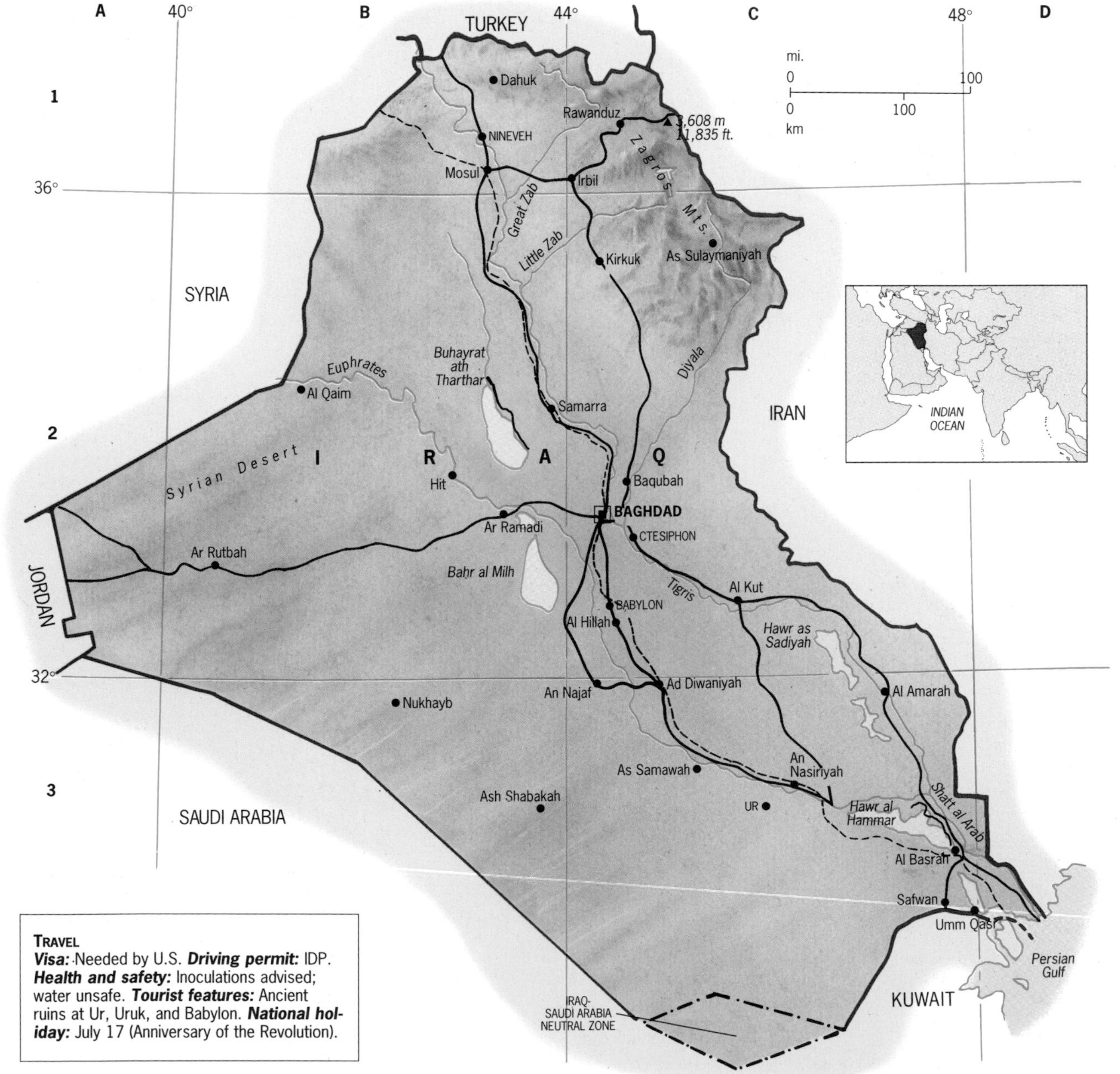

TRAVEL
Visa: Needed by U.S. *Driving permit:* IDP. *Health and safety:* Inoculations advised; water unsafe. *Tourist features:* Ancient ruins at Ur, Uruk, and Babylon. *National holiday:* July 17 (Anniversary of the Revolution).

TURKEY
SYRIA
IRAN
JORDAN
SAUDI ARABIA
KUWAIT

Dahuk
Rawanduz
NINEVEH
Mosul
Irbil
3,608 m 11,835 ft.
Zagros Mts.
Kirkuk
As Sulaymaniyah
Great Zab
Little Zab
Diyala
Euphrates
Al Qaim
Buhayrat ath Tharthar
Samarra
Syrian Desert
Hit
Baqubah
BAGHDAD
CTESIPHON
Ar Ramadi
Ar Rutbah
Bahr al Milh
Tigris
Al Kut
BABYLON
Al Hillah
Hawr as Sadiyah
Al Amarah
Nukhayb
Ad Diwaniyah
An Najaf
As Samawah
An Nasiriyah
Ash Shabakah
UR
Hawr al Hammar
Shatt al Arab
Al Basrah
Safwan
Umm Qasr
Persian Gulf
IRAQ-SAUDI ARABIA NEUTRAL ZONE

INDIAN OCEAN

IRAN

Area: 636,293 sq. mi./1,648,000 km². **Local name:** Jomhori-e-Islami-e-Irân. **Currency:** Rial. **Capital:** Teheran. **Other cities:** Meshed, Isfahan, Tabriz. **Physical features:** Mountainous rim, high central basin with deserts, coastal plains. **Climate:** Mostly arid/steppe. **Time zone:** GMT +3:30h. **Political system:** Theocratic republic. **Head of state:** Ayatollah Ali Hoseini-Khamenei (from 1989). **Head of government:** Ali Akbar Hashemi-Rafsanjani (from 1989). **Main exports:** Petroleum, carpets, fruit, hides. **Resources:** Petroleum, natural gas, coal, chromium, copper, zinc.

PEOPLE

Population: 63,180,000. **Distribution urban/rural:** 55%/45%. **Life expectancy:** 64(m), 66(f). **Languages:** Persian and Persian dialects 58%, Turkic 26%, Kurdish 9%, Luri 2%, Arabic, Turkish, and other 5%. **Ethnic groups:** Persian 51%, Azerbaijani 25%, Kurdish 9%, Gilaki and Mazandarani 8%, Lur 2%, other 5%. **Religions:** Muslim 99% (Shi'ite 95%, Sunni 4%), Zoroastrian, Jewish, and other 1%. **Literacy rate:** 54%. **Per capita GDP:** $1,500.

KEY DATES

1960s "White Revolution": social reforms including land redistribution, education and welfare reforms, and suffrage for women meet with much opposition.
1979 Shah flees following widespread civil unrest; Ayatollah Ruhollah Khomeini declares Islamic Republic of Iran; hundreds of officials of shah's government tried and put to death; many civil freedoms suspended; revolutionaries take hostages at U.S. embassy in Teheran.
1980–90 Iran-Iraq War.
1988 U.S. warship shoots down Iranian passenger airplane in Persian Gulf.
1989 Khomeini dies; Ali Khameini elected ayatollah.
1990 Peace settlement with Iraq; earthquake in N.W. kills estimated 40,000.
1991 Almost one million Kurdish refugees arrive from Iraq.
1992 Moderates win assembly elections.

TRAVEL
Visa: Needed by U.S. **Driving permit:** IDP preferred. **Health and safety:** Inoculations advised; water unsafe. **Tourist features:** Ruins of Persepolis; Mount Demavend. **National holiday:** April 1 (Islamic Republic Day).

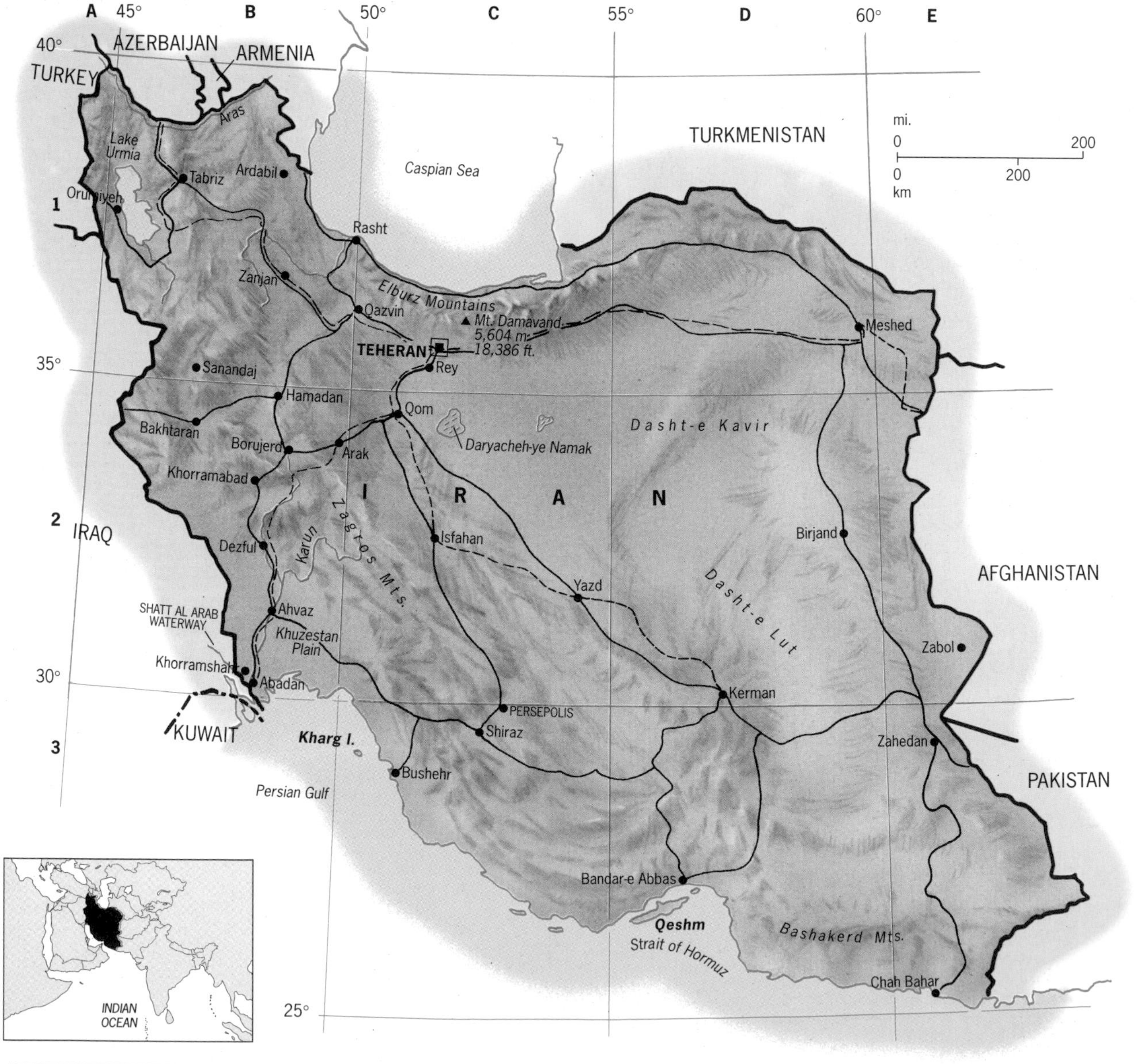

TURKMENISTAN

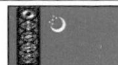

Area: 188,456 sq. mi./488,100 km². *Local name:* Turkmenistan. *Currency:* Manat. *Capital:* Ashkhabad. *Physical features:* Mostly desert. *Climate:* Arid/steppe. *Time zone:* GMT +4h. *Political system:* Republic. *Head of state:* Saparmurad Niyazov (from 1991). *Head of government:* Sakhat Muradov (from 1992). *Main exports:* Gas, oil, chemicals, textiles. *Resources:* Natural gas, oil.

PEOPLE

Population: 3,809,000. *Distribution urban/rural:* n.a. *Life expectancy:* 59(m), 66(f). *Languages:* Turkmen (official), Russian. *Ethnic groups:* Turkmen 72%, Russian 9%, other 19%. *Religions:* Muslim 85%, Eastern Orthodox 10%, other 5%. *Literacy rate:* n.a. *Per capita GDP:* n.a.

KEY DATES

1925 Becomes republic within U.S.S.R.
1991 Aug.: Communist Party leader supports attempted anti-Gorbachev coup; Oct.: declares independence; Dec.: joins Commonwealth of Independent States.
1992 New constitution; admitted into UN; joins Muslim Economic Cooperation Organization.

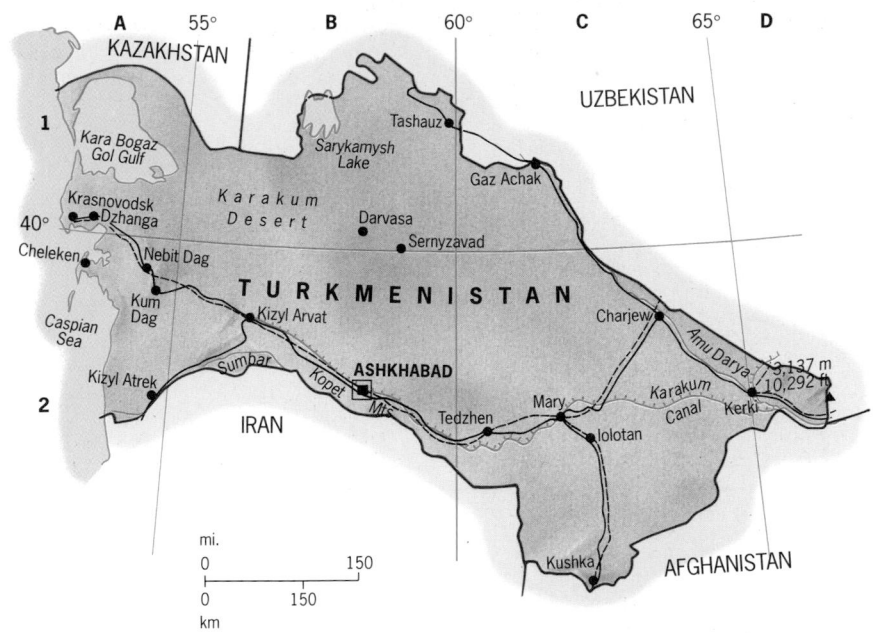

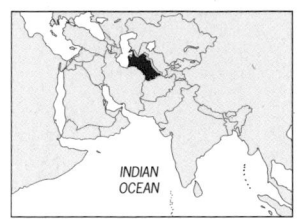

TRAVEL
Visa: Needed by U.S. *Driving permit:* Nat. license. *Health and safety:* Inoculations advised; water unsafe. *Tourist feature:* Altyn Depe, ruined city with a stepped pyramid. *National holiday:* October 27 (Independence Day).

KAZAKHSTAN

Area: 1,049,154 sq. mi./2,717,310 km². *Local name:* Kazak Republikasy. *Currency:* Tenge. *Capital:* Almaty. *Physical features:* Chiefly desert plateaus. *Climate:* Dry continental. *Time zone:* GMT +4h (W), +5h (E). *Political system:* Republic. *Head of state:* Nursultan Nazarbayev (from 1990). *Head of government:* Sergey Tereshchenko (from 1991). *Main exports:* Oil, consumer goods, chemicals, ferrous/nonferrous metals. *Resources:* Petroleum, coal, iron.

PEOPLE

Population: 16,956,000. *Distribution urban/rural:* n.a. *Life expectancy:* 63(m), 72(f). *Languages:* Kazakh, Russian. *Ethnic groups:* Kazakh 40%, Russian 38%, German 6%. *Religions:* Muslim, Russian Orthodox. *Literacy rate:* n.a. *Per capita GNP:* $1,680.

KEY DATES

1936 Joins the U.S.S.R.
1991 Independence declared; Communist Party abolished; joins newly formed Commonwealth of Independent States.
1992 Admitted into UN; trade agreement with U.S.A.

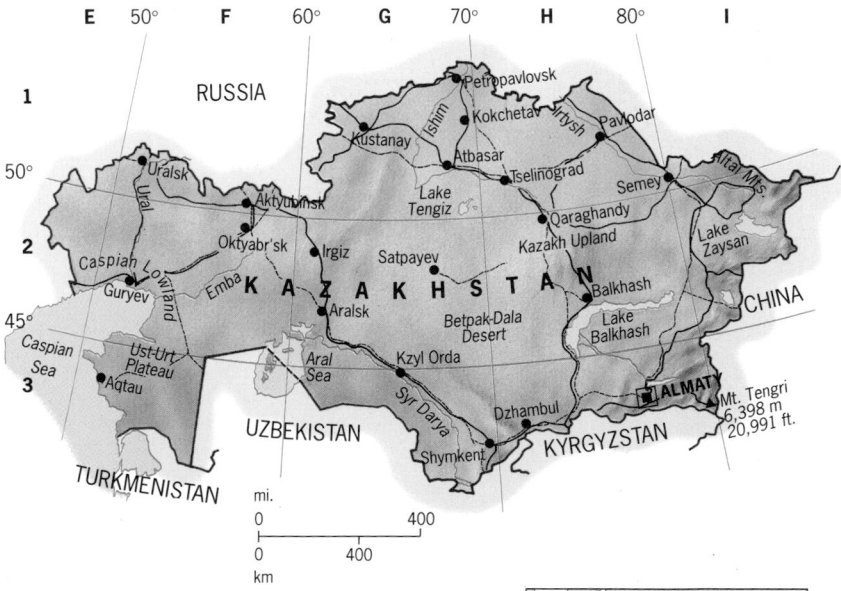

TRAVEL
Visa: Needed by U.S. *Driving permit:* Nat. license. *Health and safety:* Inoculations advised; water unsafe. *Tourist feature:* Space launch site at Tyuratam, near Baikonur. *National holiday:* December 16 (Independence Day).

UZBEKISTAN

Area: 172,741 sq. mi./447,400 km². *Local name:* Ozbekiston Republikasy. *Currency:* Som (ruble still in use). *Capital:* Tashkent. *Physical features:* Mostly desert. *Climate:* Continental. *Time zone:* GMT +5h. *Political system:* Republic. *Head of state:* Islam Karimov (from 1990). *Head of government:* Abdul Hashim Mutalov (from 1991). *Main exports:* Cotton, gold, textiles. *Resources:* Natural gas, petroleum, coal.

PEOPLE
Population: 21,207,000. *Distribution urban/rural:* 40%/60%. *Life expectancy:* 64(m), 70(f). *Languages:* Uzbek, Russian. *Ethnic groups:* Uzbek 71%, Russian 8%, Tajik 5%, other 16%. *Religion:* Muslim 75–80%. *Literacy rate:* n.a. *Per capita GDP:* n.a.

KEY DATES
1925 Becomes part of the U.S.S.R.
1989 70 killed and 850 wounded in riots.
1991 Independence achieved; joins new Commonwealth of Independent States.
1992 Food shortages prompt riots in Tashkent; admitted into UN.
1993 Indo-Uzbek commission meets in Delhi.

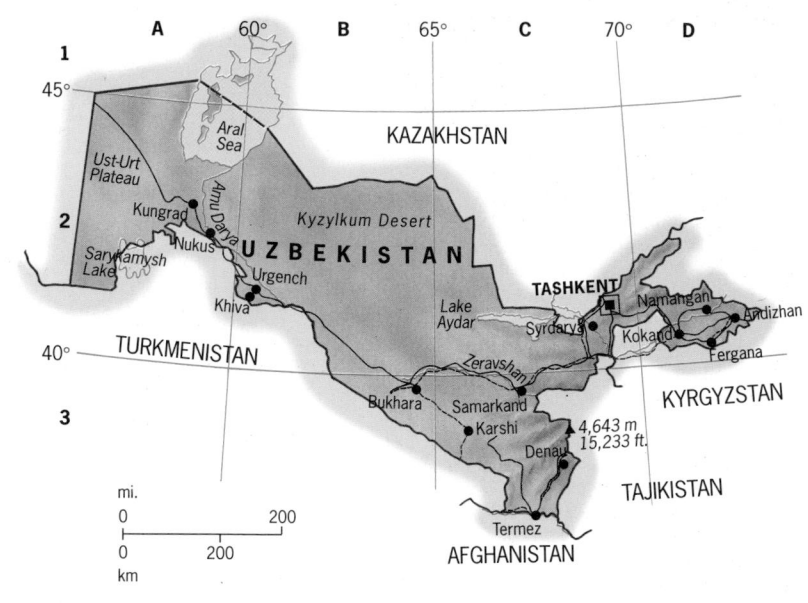

TRAVEL
Visa: Needed by U.S. *Driving permit:* Nat. license. *Health and safety:* Inoculations advised; water unsafe. *Tourist feature:* Fergana Valley in E. *National holiday:* August 31 (Independence Day).

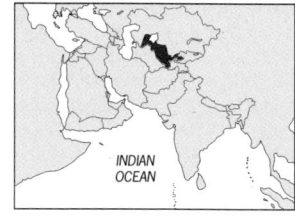

KYRGYZSTAN

Area: 76,647 sq. mi./198,500 km². *Local name:* Kyrgyz Republikasy. *Currency:* Som (ruble still in use). *Capital:* Bishkek. *Physical features:* Mountainous. *Climate:* Steppe, subtropical in S. *Time zone:* GMT +5h. *Political system:* Republic. *Head of state:* Askar Akayev (from 1990). *Head of government:* Apas Jumagulov (from 1993). *Main exports:* Wool, chemicals, cotton. *Resources:* Natural gas, oil.

PEOPLE
Population: 4,528,000. *Distribution urban/rural:* 40%/60%. *Life expectancy:* 66(m), 71(f). *Languages:* Kyrghiz (official), Russian. *Ethnic groups:* Kyrghiz 52%, Russian 21%, Uzbek 13%, other 14%. *Religions:* Muslim (Sunni) 70%, Russian Orthodox. *Literacy rate:* n.a. *Per capita GDP:* n.a.

KEY DATES
1919 Soviet rule established, though violent resistance continues until 1922.
1936 Becomes republic within U.S.S.R.
1990 Government declares that its laws overrule those from the U.S.S.R.; state of emergency declared in Bishkek as a result of ethnic clashes; Askar Akayev chosen as president.
1991 Independence achieved; Communist Party suspends activities; joins Commonwealth of Independent States; economic reform program.

TRAVEL
Visa: Needed by U.S. *Driving permit:* Nat. license. *Health and safety:* Inoculations advised; water unsafe. *Tourist feature:* Tian Shan Mountains. *National holiday:* August 31 (Independence Day).

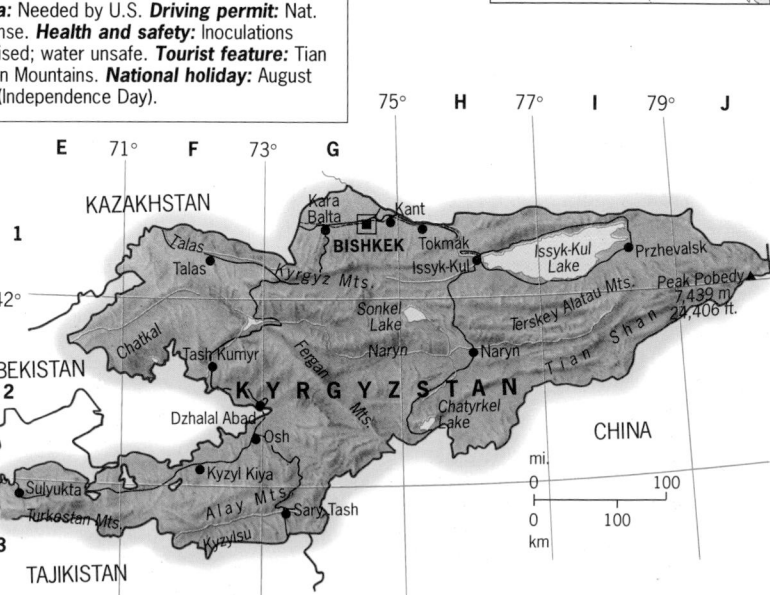

TAJIKISTAN

Area: 52,255 sq. mi./143,100 km². *Local name:* Respubliki i Tojikiston. *Currency:* Ruble. *Capital:* Dushanbe. *Physical features:* Mountainous. *Climate:* Steppe. *Time zone:* GMT +5h. *Political system:* Republic. *Head of state:* Imamali Rakhmanov (from 1992). *Head of government:* Abduljalil Samadov (from 1993). *Main exports:* Aluminum, fruits, textiles. *Resources:* Petroleum, uranium.

PEOPLE

Population: 5,514,000. *Distribution urban/rural:* 31%/69%. *Life expectancy:* 64(m), 70(f). *Languages:* Tajik, Russian. *Ethnic groups:* Tajik 62%, Uzbek 24%, Russian 8%. *Religion:* Muslim 85%. *Literacy rate:* n.a. *Per capita GNP:* $480.

KEY DATES

1929 Becomes part of U.S.S.R.
1991 Independence declared; Tajikistan Communist Party severs links with Moscow and becomes the Socialist Party of Tajikistan; state of emergency declared; joins new Commonwealth of Independent States.
1992 Civil war begins.

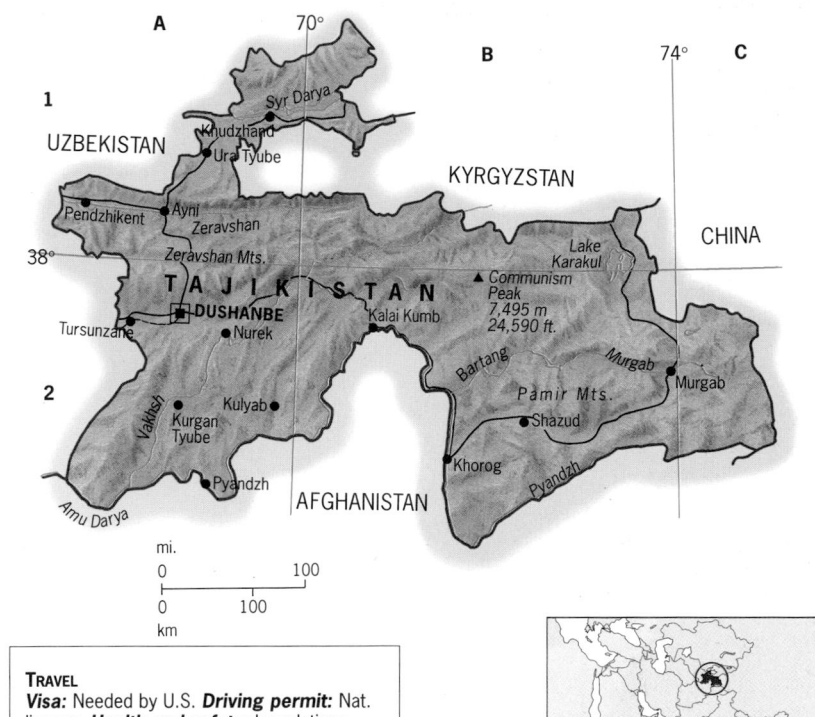

TRAVEL
Visa: Needed by U.S. *Driving permit:* Nat. license. *Health and safety:* Inoculations advised; water unsafe. *Tourist features:* Pamir and Alay mountains. *National holiday:* September 9 (Independence Day).

AFGHANISTAN

Area: 251,772 sq. mi./652,090 km². *Local name:* Jamhuria Afghanistan. *Currency:* Afghani. *Capital:* Kabul. *Physical features:* Rugged mountains. *Climate:* Steppe. *Time zone:* GMT +4:30h. *Political system:* Democracy. *Head of state:* Burhanuddin Rabbani (from 1992). *Head of government:* Gulbuddin Hekmatyar (from 1993). *Main exports:* Gas, fruit, carpets. *Resources:* Natural gas, oil.

PEOPLE

Population: 20,547,000. *Distribution urban/rural:* 20%/80%. *Life expectancy:* 45(m), 43(f). *Languages:* Pashtu, Dari, Uzbek. *Ethnic groups:* Pashtun 38%, Tajik 25%, Hazara 19%, Uzbek 6%. *Religion:* Muslim. *Literacy rate:* 29%. *Per capita GDP:* $200.

KEY DATES

1978 Left-wing rebels take over government; violent demonstrations ensue.
1979 Soviet forces enter Afghanistan.
1989 Soviet troops withdraw; civil war continues; state of emergency declared.
1992 Government overthrown; Islamic law introduced.
1993 Peace accord between rival leaders.

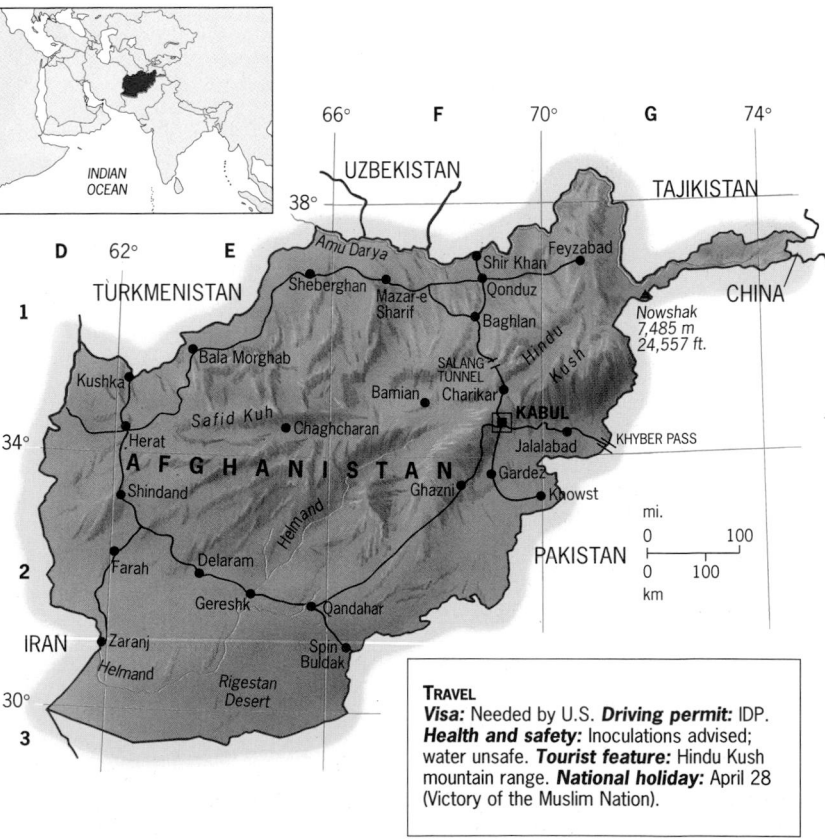

TRAVEL
Visa: Needed by U.S. *Driving permit:* IDP. *Health and safety:* Inoculations advised; water unsafe. *Tourist feature:* Hindu Kush mountain range. *National holiday:* April 28 (Victory of the Muslim Nation).

PAKISTAN

Area: 307,373 sq. mi./796,095 km². *Local name:* Islam-i Jamhuriya-e Pakistan. *Currency:* Pakistani rupee. *Capital:* Islamabad. *Other cities:* Karachi, Lahore. *Physical features:* Chiefly plain; mountains and Baluchistan plateau in W. *Climate:* Mostly arid with hot summers and cool winters; highly variable precipitation. *Time zone:* GMT +5h. *Political system:* Republic. *Head of state:* Farooq Leghari (from 1993). *Head of government:* Benazir Bhutto (from 1993). *Main exports:* Cotton, textiles, clothing, rice. *Resources:* Extensive natural gas reserves, limited reserves of crude oil.

PEOPLE

Population: 122,802,000. *Distribution urban/rural:* 32%/68%. *Life expectancy:* 56(m), 57(f). *Languages:* Urdu, English (official), Punjabi, Sindhi. *Ethnic groups:* Punjabi 66%, Sindhi 13%, Pushtun 9%, Urdu 8%, other 4%. *Religion:* Muslim 97%. *Literacy rate:* 35%. *Per capita GDP:* $380.

KEY DATES

1206 Most of Pakistan becomes part of Muslim Empire, the Sultanate of Delhi.
1526 Mogul Empire established in most of Pakistan, India, and Bangladesh.
1740s Mogul Empire breaks up; British East India Company takes control of much Mogul territory.
1858 British government takes over East India Company and its territories; Muslims are reduced to a minority group within India, and many resent the loss of privileges they enjoyed under Mogul rule.
1875 Muslim leader, Syed Ahmad Khan, begins the Aligarh Movement; foundation of Muhammadan Anglo-Oriental College, offering Western-style education to Muslims, thereby opening doors of civil service and government.
1906 Muslim League founded.
1930s Fearing unfair treatment at hands of Hindu majority should India gain independence from Britain, Muslims call for a separate Islamic nation.
1940 Muslim League's demands for partition are rejected by Britain and Indian National Congress.

1940s Widespread violence between Hindus and Muslims.

1947 Britain and Indian National Congress agree to partition of India; new nation of Pakistan is created comprising East and West Pakistan separated by almost 1,240 mi. (2,000 km) of Indian territory; intense fighting between Hindus and Muslims kills thousands; about ten million people flee from one country to the other.

1947–49 War with India over Kashmir.

1956 Pakistan proclaimed a republic with Maj.-Gen. Iskander Mirza as president; economic development program begins.

1958 Military takes over government with Gen. Ayub Khan as leader; economic reforms.

1965 Renewed fighting with India over Kashmir.

1967 Mangla dam on Jhelum River completed, giving West Pakistan flood control, irrigation, and electric power; work begun on Tarbela dam on Indus River.

1970 Cyclone and tidal wave hits East Pakistan, killing about 266,000; many East Pakistanis charge government with delaying shipment of relief supplies; East Pakistan demands self-government.

1971 March: army sent into East Pakistan to put down antigovernment demonstrations; East Pakistan declares independence as Bangladesh; civil war breaks out; Dec.: India joins war on Bangladeshi side; West Pakistan surrenders in two weeks; President Yahya Khan resigns and is succeeded by Zulfikar Ali Bhutto; more than a million die in conflict.

1972 Pakistan leaves Commonwealth when Britain accords diplomatic recogi-tion to Bangladesh; Bhutto meets with Indian prime minister, Indira Gandhi, who agrees to withdraw Indian troops from Pakistani territory, although Kashmir remains in dispute.

1973 New constitution; Zulfikar Ali Bhutto becomes prime minister; Chaudhri Fazal Elahi becomes president.

1975 Tarbela dam completed.

1977 Bhutto is accused of rigging parliamentary elections and is overthrown in military coup led by Gen. Mohammed Zia ul Haq; constitution suspended and martial law declared.

1978 Chaudhri resigns and Zia declares himself president.

1979 Bhutto convicted of ordering the murder of a political opponent during the last election and is executed.

1980 Islamic court chaired by Muslim scholars is established.

1985 Zia ends martial law and restores many constitutional rights; civilian government elected.

1988 Zia dissolves parliament; Aug.: Zia killed in plane crash; Ghulam Ishaq Khan, leader of Senate, is installed as acting president; Zulfikar Ali Bhutto's daughter, Benazir Bhutto (Pakistan People's Party), elected first woman prime minister in an Islamic nation; Ishaq Khan elected president.

1989 Rejoins Commonwealth of Nations.

1990 Aug.: Ishaq Khan charges Benazir Bhutto's government with corruption, abuse of power, and incompetence and dissolves parliament; Oct.: Islamic Democratic Alliance (IDA) wins majority in parliamentary elections and Nawaz Sharif becomes prime minister; Bhutto charges Sharif with election fraud and misappropriation of funds, though her allegations are not substantiated by the investigation that follows; U.S.A. suspends aid over suspected Pakistani nuclear weapons program.

1991 Bhutto publicizes her accusations against Sharif; economic reform program diminishing state intervention includes privatization of many national industries and causes widespread labor unrest.

1992 Worst floods in Pakistan's history destroy hundreds of villages, kill around 2,000, and leave more than a million homeless; foreign minister acknowledges existence of facilities to build nuclear weapons; Islamic Court passes new laws requiring television actresses to wear the veil and making blasphemy a capital offense; Benazir Bhutto leads demonstrations against Nawaz Sharif in Islamabad; army sent into Sind province to restore order.

1993 Ishaq Khan dismisses Sharif's government, but the Supreme Court rules his actions to be unlawful and Sharif resumes office; Bhutto demands general election; army chief of staff, Gen. Abdul Waheed, forces resignations of both Ishaq Khan and Sharif; Bhutto wins majority in parliamentary elections.

TRAVEL
Visa: Needed by U.S. **Driving permit:** Nat. license. **Health and safety:** Inoculations advised; water unsafe. **Tourist features:** Takht-i-Bahi Buddhist temple; Swat Valley. **National holiday:** August 31 (Independence Day).

KASHMIR

Around two-thirds of Kashmir, in the north of India, is administered by India as the state of Jammu and Kashmir and one-third is administered by Pakistan as Azad (free) Kashmir.

The area has been a source of contention between the two countries since the partition of British India in 1947, and neither country recognizes the other's right to govern. At partition, Kashmir remained independent under the rule of Gulab Singh, but when Pakistan invaded that same year, the Hindu maharajah was forced to accede to the Indian Republic in return for military aid. The UN has tried to arrange a plebiscite to resolve the matter, but India fears that the predominantly Muslim population of the area would vote to join the Islamic state of Pakistan and has not agreed to this solution.

KEY DATES

1820 Gulab Singh becomes maharajah of Kashmir and founds the Dogra dynasty.

1845–46 Anglo-Sikh War: Gulab Singh remains neutral and acts as a mediator between the two sides; he is rewarded by the British in a treaty confirming him as ruler of Kashmir.

1947 British India partitioned into Pakistan and the Republic of India; a large proportion of the Muslim Kashmiris demand accession to Pakistan; the maharajah, Sir Hari Singh, refuses and Pakistan invades; Singh signs the Instrument of Accession to the Indian Union in return for Indian military aid.

1949 Partition followed by a cease-fire, but the UN fails to get Indian approval for a plebiscite; furthermore, the boundaries set down at partition have never been ratified as a formal national boundary.

1965 War between India and Pakistan.

1970 Renewed border fighting.

1972 Simla Accord between India and Pakistan.

1987 Outbreak of guerrilla warfare in Kashmir.

1989 Conflict worsens; India accuses Pakistan of training Kashmiri terrorists.

1990 Riots in Srinagar after police open fire on demonstrators, killing around 50; India imposes central rule on province; Pakistan blames India for assassination of Kashmir's senior Muslim cleric, Mohammad Farooq, and the killing of 47 mourners at his funeral.

1991 May: 14 die when police open fire on mourners at funeral for earlier victims of police brutality; June: police kill a further 18 after a policeman is killed by terrorists.

1992 Fighting breaks out between guerrilla

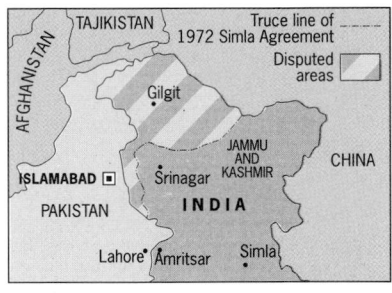

groups in Kashmir; extremist Hindu party, the BJP, marches to Srinagar to raise Indian national flag as a symbol of the party's opposition to separatism; in response to charges of human rights violations, the Indian government agrees to allow Amnesty International to send investigators to Jammu and Kashmir.

1993 Feb. and Oct.: Pakistani troops open fire and kill several members of Jammu and Kashmir Liberation Front as they try to cross cease-fire line from Pakistan to India; Indian security forces besiege militants in Hazrat Bal Mosque in Srinagar.

INDIA

Area: 1,222,332 sq. mi./3,165,596 km². *Local name:* Bharat. *Currency:* Rupee. *Capital:* Delhi. *Other cities:* Calcutta, Bombay, Madras, Bangalore, Hyderabad. *Physical features:* Himalaya Mountains in N.; Deccan Plateau in S.; flat to rolling plain along Ganges River; desert in W. *Climate:* Varies from tropical monsoon in S. to temperate in N. *Time zone:* GMT +5:30h. *Political system:* Federal republic. *Head of state:* Shankar Dayal Sharma (from 1992). *Head of government:* P. V. Narasimha Rao (from 1991). *Main exports:* Textiles, jewelry, chemicals, tea, coffee. *Resources:* Coal, iron ore, manganese, gas, and oil.

PEOPLE

Population: 896,567,000. *Distribution urban/rural:* 28%/72%. *Life expectancy:* 57(m), 58(f). *Languages:* 16 official languages including Hindi (national), English, Bengali, Telugu, Kannada, Oriya, Punjabi, Assamese, Kashmiri, Sindhi, and Sanskrit. *Ethnic groups:* Indo-Aryan groups 72%, Dravidian 25%, Mongoloid and other 3%. *Religions:* Hindu 83%, Muslim 11%, Christian 3%, Sikh 2%, Buddhist and other 1%. *Literacy rate:* 48%. *Per capita GDP:* $350.

KEY DATES

1526 Mogul Empire established.

1600 Foundation of British East India Company.

1740s British East India Company gains control of much Mogul territory.

1858 British government takes over East India Company.

1885 Indian National Congress founded.

1906 Foundation of Muslim League.

1919 Amritsar massacre: Gurkha troops open fire on illegal meeting of independence activists in Amritsar, Punjab.

1920 Mohandas Karamchand ("Mahatma") Gandhi begins his *satyagraha* (nonviolent campaign) with Jawaharlal Nehru against British rule.

1935 Government of India Act secures election of Indians to lawmaking assembly, although Britain retains control of central government and reserves power of veto over all legislation.

1939–45 Indian troops fight on Allied side in desert campaigns during WWII.

1940 Muslim League begins demanding a separate Islamic state.

1942 Congress leadership is arrested and detained until the end of the war.

1943 Requisition of food supplies by the army causes severe famine in Bengal.

1945 Muslims increase demands for partition; widespread riots; India joins UN.

1946 Muslim League's "Direct Action Day" results in many deaths.

1947 India partitioned as independent

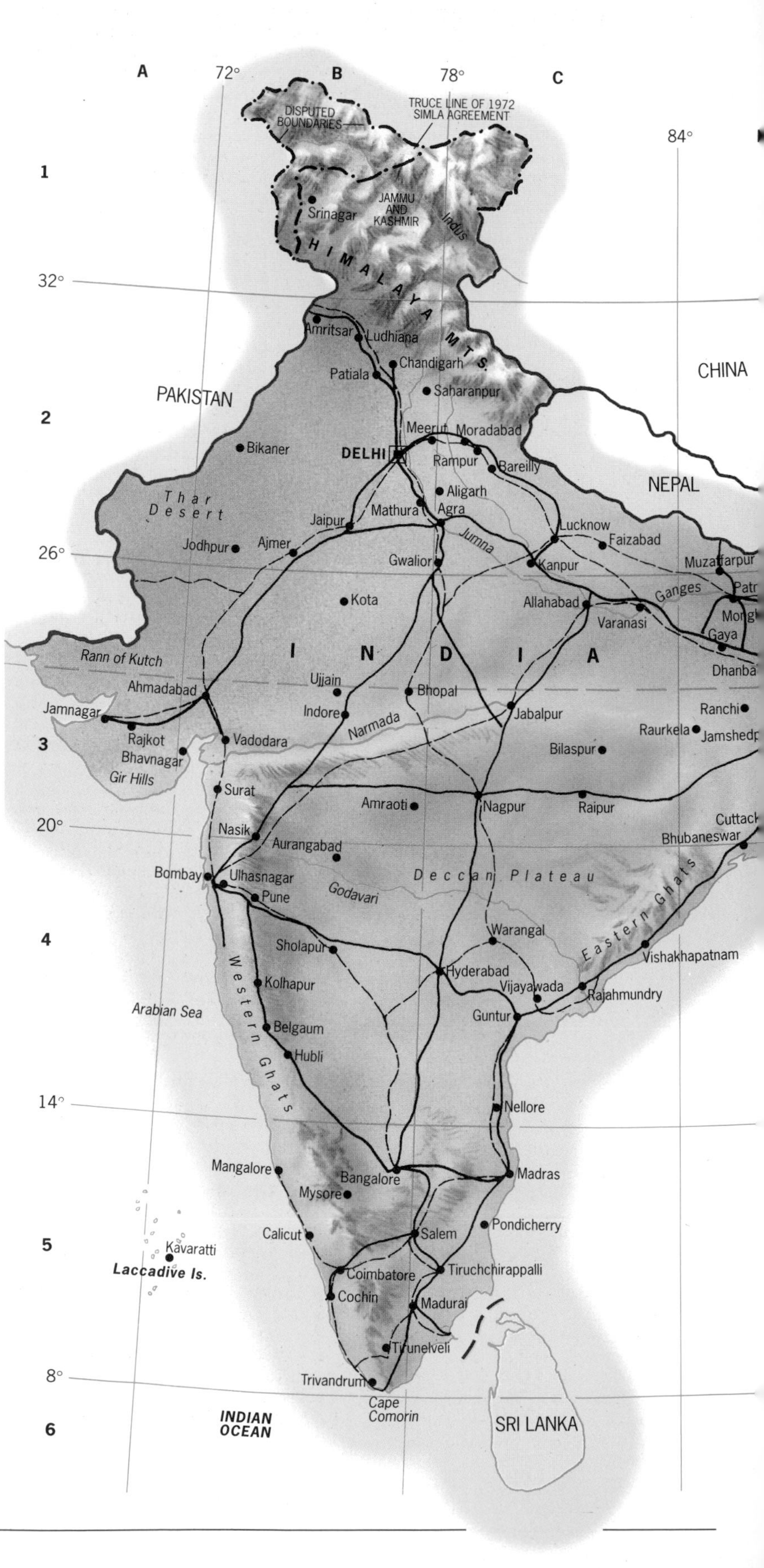

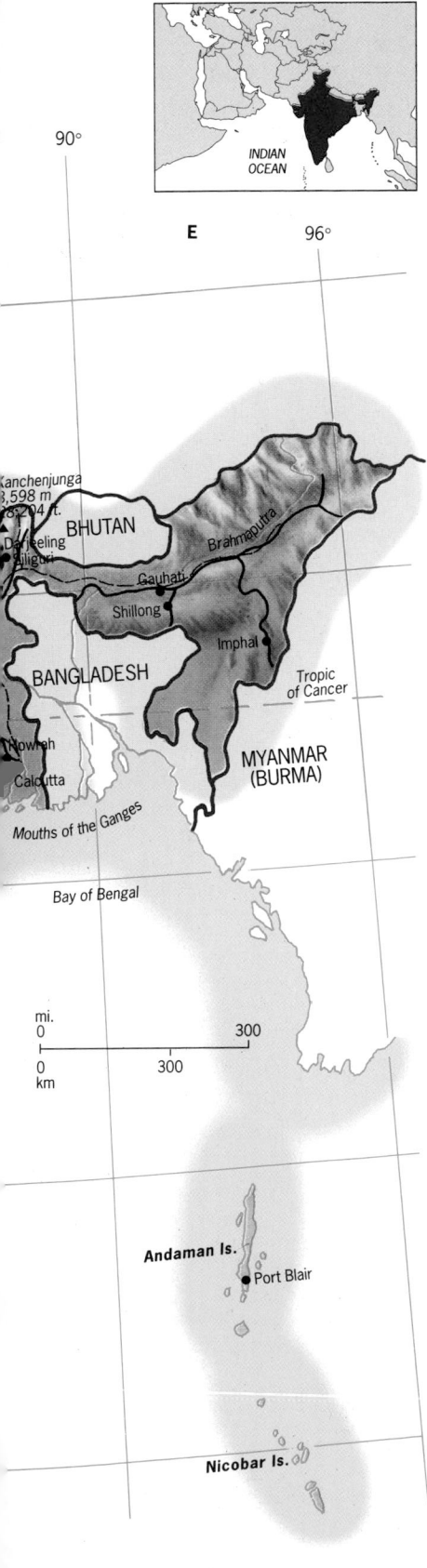

90°

E

96°

Kanchenjunga
8,598 m
28,204 ft.

BHUTAN

Darjeeling
Siliguri

Brahmaputra

Gauhati

Shillong

Imphal

BANGLADESH

Tropic
of Cancer

MYANMAR
(BURMA)

Howrah

Calcutta

Mouths of the Ganges

Bay of Bengal

mi.
0   300

0   300
km

Andaman Is.

Port Blair

Nicobar Is.

nations of India and Pakistan; Nehru becomes prime minister; widespread violence between Hindus and Muslims; Kashmir accedes to India.

1948 Gandhi assassinated; Democratic Republic of India declared.

1949 UN partitions Kashmir.

1962 Border war with China.

1964 Jawaharlal Nehru dies and is succeeded by Lal Bahadur Shastri.

1965 War with Pakistan over Kashmir.

1966 Shastri dies; Nehru's daughter, Indira Gandhi, becomes prime minister.

1971 India intervenes in Pakistani civil war; Gandhi retains power in general election.

1975 Indira Gandhi tried and found guilty of using illegal practices in 1971 election campaign; Gandhi declares state of emergency and passes laws legalizing her actions in 1971.

1977 Morarji Desai prime minister.

1979 Severe economic problems and civil unrest prompt Desai's resignation.

1984 Hundreds die when army attacks Golden Temple in Amritsar, which is being used as a base for Sikh rebels; Indira Gandhi shot dead by Sikh bodyguards; her son Rajiv becomes prime minister; 2,100 die when poison gas escapes from factory in Bhopal.

1987 Outbreak of terrorist activity in Kashmir; Indian troops sent to Sri Lanka to help disarm Tamil guerrillas; central rule imposed on Punjab state.

1989 Government officials implicated in Bofors arms scandal; more than 100 members of parliament resign in protest against corruption; ethnic unrest in Assam and Punjab kills more than 1,200; V. P. Singh prime minister.

1990 Jan.: central rule imposed on Kashmir after riots; April: 32 Punjabi Hindus die in Sikh bombing; Aug.: Assamese separatists gain much territory; Oct.: hundreds die and 100,000 arrested in clashes over mosque at Ayodhya, Uttar Pradesh, an historic Hindu site; V. P. Singh resigns after losing confidence vote; Chandra Shekhar heads military government.

1991 Jan.: diplomatic relations with Israel restored after many years; March: Shekhar resigns; May: Rajiv Gandhi assassinated during election campaign; P. V. Narasimha Rao prime minister.

1992 Jan.: Right-wing Bharatiya Janata Party leader, Murli Manohar Joshi, leads march to Srinagar in protest against concessions made to separatists; several BJP marchers are killed by Sikhs in Punjab; April: markets collapse after Mehta financial scandal is revealed; June: Hindu extremists begin construction of temple at Ayodhya; Dec.: more than 1,000 die in riots following destruction of Ayodhya mosque.

1993 Jan.: renewed violence over mosque at Ayodhya kills a further 500 in Bombay; Feb.: BJP banned from holding a mass rally in Delhi; March: more than 250 die in Bombay bombings; June:

Rao implicated in Mehta scandal; Sept.: major earthquake hits Maharashtra, Karnataka, and Andhra Pradesh, killing nearly 16,000; Oct.: security forces besiege militants in Srinagar mosque; 38 die in violent clashes between security forces and protesters in Kashmir.

1994 Plague epidemic spreads throughout north, claiming many lives.

ECONOMY

India's GDP is high and it is rich in natural resources, but it is a densely populated country and its per capita GDP is low enough to rank it among developing countries. Notwithstanding, India's economy has grown steadily since independence, and the government continues its commitment to industrial growth.

Industry by sector

Farming Farming is one of the most important sectors of the Indian economy. It employs 70% of the workforce and accounts for about one-third of the GDP. India ranks fifth in the world in terms of total farming area: more than half the land is put to agricultural use. A large proportion of this land is used for subsistence farming and half of all farms are less than 1.25 acres in area.

Rice is the single most important crop; India is the world's second largest producer after China. India also grows more than half the world's mangoes and is the greatest producer of cashews, millet, peanuts, legumes, sesame seeds, and tea. It ranks second in production of cauliflower, jute, onions, rice, sorghum, and sugarcane and is a major producer of bananas, coffee, cotton, rubber, and tobacco. There are more cattle and buffalo than in any other country, although cows are sacred in the Hindu religion and are not used for meat.

In the past India had to import much of its food, but improved farming techniques, irrigation, and the use of high-yield grains have all meant that India is now able to fulfill most of its own food needs. To this end, the government sponsors many projects to develop and modernize the farming industry, and there are also government subsidies to encourage farmers to grow food crops.

Fishing Mackerel, sardines, shark, and shrimp are caught at sea, and carp and catfish in the rivers.

Mining The most important mineral resources are iron ore (accounting for 5% of total world output), mica, coal, oil, bauxite, beryllium, chromite, gypsum, limestone, manganese, natural gas, salt, and titanium.

Manufacturing Since independence, successive governments have worked hard to stimulate industrial growth, and industrial production is now six times as great as it was in 1950. In the past 40 years, major iron and steel mills have been built at Bhilai, Bokaro, Durgapur, and Raurkela with financial aid from the

U.S.S.R., Britain, and West Germany. The clothing and textile industries, however, still employ more workers than any other area.

The development of India's manufacturing industry has been hampered by a lack of energy resources; India imports large quantities of oil, and much of the country is without an electricity supply. Cottage industries are very important.

Service industries The wholesale and retail trades, including hotels and restaurants, make up the most important group of service industries. Second most important are community, government, and personal services, such as education and health care, public administration, and national defense. The service industries account for 42% of the GDP.

STATES OF INDIA

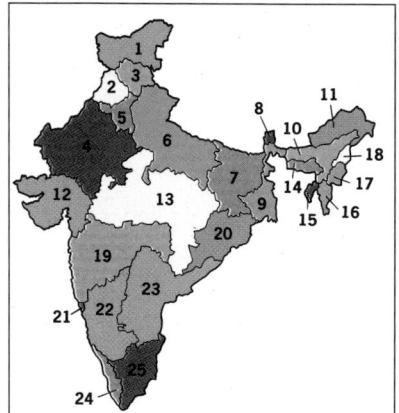

Jammu and Kashmir 1, Punjab 2, Himachal Pradesh 3, Rajasthan 4, Haryana 5, Uttar Pradesh 6, Binar 7, Sikkim 8, West Bengal 9, Assam 10, Arunachal Pradesh 11, Gujarat 12, Madhya Pradesh 13, Meghalaya 14, Tripura 15, Mizoram 16, Manipur 17, Nagaland 18, Maharashtra 19, Orissa 20, Goa 21, Karnataka 22, Andhra Pradesh 23, Kerala 24, Tamil Nadu 25.

(in order of achieving statehood)

ASSAM 1947
Capital: Dispur. *Area:* 30,287 sq. mi./78,438 km². *Population:* 22,400,000. *Principal language:* Assamese. *Religions:* Hindu, Muslim, Christian.

BIHAR 1947
Capital: Patna/Ranchi (summer capital). *Area:* 67,139 sq. mi./173,877 km². *Population:* 86,374,465. *Principal language:* Hindi. *Religions:* Hindu, Muslim, Christian.

JAMMU AND KASHMIR 1947
Capital: Jammu/Srinagar (summer capital). *Area:* 85,806 sq. mi./222,236 km². *Population:* 7,718,700. *Principal languages:* Urdu (official), Kashmiri, Hindi, Dogri, Balti. *Religions:* Muslim, Hindu, Sikh, Buddhist, Christian, Jain.

UTTAR PRADESH Constituted as United Provinces 1947, renamed Uttar Pradesh 1950.
Capital: Lucknow. *Area:* 113,673 sq. mi./294,411 km². *Population:* 139,112,287. *Principal languages:* Hindi (official), Urdu. *Religions:* Hindu, Muslim.

WEST BENGAL 1947
Capital: Calcutta. *Area:* 34,267 sq. mi./88,752 km². *Population:* 68,077,965. *Principal languages:* Bengali, Hindi, Urdu. *Religions:* Hindu, Muslim.

HIMACHAL PRADESH 1948
Capital: Simla. *Area:* 21,495 sq. mi./55,673 km². *Population:* 5,170,877. *Principal languages:* Hindi, Pahari. *Religion:* Hindu.

ORISSA 1948
Capital: Bhubaneswar. *Area:* 60,119 sq. mi./155,707 km². *Population:* 31,659,736. *Principal language:* Oriya (official). *Religion:* Hindu.

MANIPUR 1949
Capital: Imphal. *Area:* 8,621 sq. mi./22,327 km². *Population:* 1,837,149. *Principal languages:* Manipuri, English. *Religions:* Hindu, Christian.

ANDHRA PRADESH 1953
Capital: Hyderabad. *Area:* 106,212 sq. mi./275,068 km². *Population:* 66,500,000. *Principal language:* Telugu. *Religions:* Hindu, Muslim.

KARNATAKA Constituted as Mysore 1956, renamed Karnataka 1973.
Capital: Bangalore. *Area:* 74,051 sq. mi./191,791 km². *Population:* 44,977,201. *Principal languages:* Kannada (official), Telugu, Urdu, Marathi, Tamil, Tulu, Konkani. *Religions:* Hindu, Muslim, Christian, Jain, Buddhist, Sikh.

KERALA 1956
Capital: Trivandrum. *Area:* 15,005 sq. mi./38,863 km². *Population:* 29,098,518. *Principal languages:* Malayalam, Tamil, Kannarda. *Religions:* Hindu, Muslim, Christian, Jain, Sikh.

MADHYA PRADESH 1956
Capital: Bhopal. *Area:* 171,215 sq. mi./443,446 km². *Population:* 66,181,170. *Principal languages:* Hindi (official), Urdu, Marathi, Gujarati. *Religions:* Hindu, Muslim, Christian, Buddhist.

RAJASTHAN 1956
Capital: Jaipur. *Area:* 132,139 sq. mi./342,239 km². *Population:* 44,005,990. *Principal languages:* Rajasthani, Hindi. *Religions:* Hindu, Muslim, Jain.

GUJARAT 1960
Capital: Gandhinagar. *Area:* 75,685 sq. mi./196,024 km². *Population:* 41,309,582. *Principal languages:* Gujarati, Hindi. *Religions:* Hindu, Christian, Jain.

MAHARASHTRA 1960
Capital: Bombay. *Area:* 118,800 sq. mi./307,690 km². *Population:* 78,937,187. *Principal language:* Marathi. *Religions:* Hindu, Muslim, Buddhist, Christian, Jain, Sikh.

TAMIL NADU Constituted as Madras 1960, renamed Tamil Nadu 1968.
Capital: Madras. *Area:* 50,216 sq. mi./130,058 km². *Population:* 55,858,946. *Principal languages:* Tamil (official), Telugu. *Religions:* Hindu, Christian.

NAGALAND 1962
Capital: Kohima. *Area:* 6,401 sq. mi./16,579 km². *Population:* 1,209,546. *Principal languages:* Nagamese, English. *Religions:* Christian, Hindu.

HARYANA 1966
Capital: Chandigarh. *Area:* 17,070 sq. mi./44,212 km². *Population:* 16,463,648. *Principal languages:* Hindi, Urdu, Punjabi. *Religions:* Hindu.

PUNJAB 1966
Capital: Chandigarh. *Area:* 19,445 sq. mi./50,362 km². *Population:* 20,281,969. *Principal languages:* Punjabi (official), Hindi. *Religions:* Sikh, Hindu.

MEGHALAYA 1972
Capital: Shillong. *Area:* 8,660 sq. mi./22,429 km². *Population:* 1,774,778. *Principal languages:* Mon-Khmer languages. *Religions:* Animist, Jain.

MIZORAM 1972
Capital: Aizawl. *Area:* 8,139 sq. mi./21,081 km². *Population:* 689,756. *Principal languages:* Mizo, English. *Religions:* Christian, Buddhist.

TRIPURA 1972
Capital: Agartala. *Area:* 4,049 sq. mi./10,486 km². *Population:* 2,757,205. *Principal languages:* Bengali, Kokbarak (both official), Manipuri, Tripuri. *Religions:* Hindu, Christian.

SIKKIM 1975
Capital: Gangtok. *Area:* 2,740 sq. mi./7,096 km². *Population:* 406,457. *Principal languages:* Sikkimese, Nepali. *Religions:* Buddhist, Hindu (Lamaist).

ARUNACHAL PRADESH 1986
Capital: Itanagar. *Area:* 32,336 sq. mi./83,743 km². *Population:* 864,558. *Principal languages:* Khamti and about 50 other local dialects of Sino- and Burmese-Tibetan origin. *Religions:* Animist, Buddhist, Hindu.

GOA 1987
Capital: Panaji. *Area:* 1,430 sq. mi./3,702 km². *Population:* 1,169,793. *Principal languages:* Konkani (official), English, Hindi, Marathi. *Religions:* Hindu, Christian (Roman Catholic).

TRAVEL
Visa: Needed by U.S. *Driving permit:* IDP. *Health and safety:* Inoculations advised; water unsafe. *Tourist features:* Paintings in mountain caves of Ajanta; Taj Mahal in Agra. *National holiday:* January 26 (Anniversary of the Proclamation of the Republic).

NEPAL

Area: 54,366 sq. mi./140,797 km². *Local name:* Nepal Adhirajya. *Currency:* Nepalese rupee. *Capital:* Kathmandu. *Physical features:* Ganges River plain in S., central hills, Himalayas in N. *Climate:* Varies from extreme cold in N. to tropical in S. *Time zone:* GMT +5:30h. *Political system:* Constitutional monarchy. *Head of state:* King Birendra Bir Bikram Shah Dev (from 1972). *Head of government:* Girija Prasad Koirala (from 1991). *Main exports:* Clothing, carpets, leather goods. *Resources:* Quartz, wood.

PEOPLE

Population: 21,086,000. *Distribution urban/rural:* 8%/92%. *Life expectancy:* 51(m), 51(f). *Languages:* Nepali (official), 20 dialects spoken. *Ethnic groups:* Newar, Indian, Tibetan, Gurung, many smaller groups. *Religions:* Hindu 90%, Buddhist 5%, Muslim 3%, other 2%. *Literacy rate:* 26%. *Per capita GDP:* $165.

KEY DATES

1846 Jung Bahadur seizes power and decrees that a member of his family will be prime minister from this point on.
1951 Revolution restores monarchy.
1960 King outlaws all political parties.
1962 New constitution establishes dictatorial panchayat system.
1979 Violent prodemocracy demonstrations result in referendum; most Nepalese vote to continue as before.
1990 Violent demonstrations bring about the legalization of political parties; new constitution establishes Nepal as a constitutional monarchy.
1991 Democratic elections won by Nepalese Congress Party with Communists finishing second.

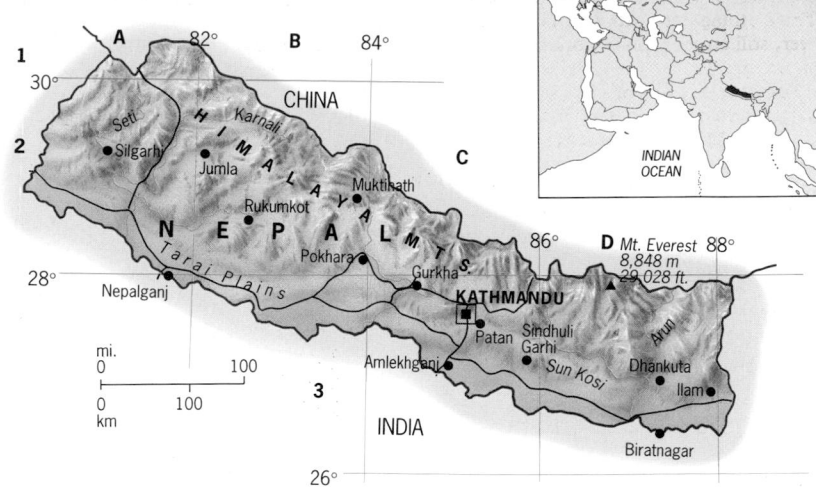

TRAVEL

Visa: Needed by U.S. *Driving permit:* IDP. *Health and safety:* Inoculations advised; water unsafe. *Tourist features:* Lumbini, birthplace of the Buddha; Mount Everest. *National holiday:* December 28 (Birthday of His Majesty the King).

BHUTAN

Area: 17,955 sq. mi./46,500 km². *Local name:* Druk-Yul. *Currency:* Ngultrum. *Capital:* Thimphu. *Physical features:* Mostly mountainous; some river valleys. *Climate:* Varies from tropical in S. to extreme cold in Himalayas. *Time zone:* GMT +5:30h. *Political system:* Monarchy. *Head of state and government:* King Jigme Singye Wangchuck (from 1972). *Main exports:* Spices, wood, gypsum, cement, fruit, coal, rice. *Resources:* Wood, hydropower, gypsum.

PEOPLE

Population: 1,650,000. *Distribution urban/rural:* n.a. *Life expectancy:* 50(m), 49(f). *Languages:* Dzongkha, English, Nepali (all official). *Ethnic groups:* Bhote 60%, ethnic Nepalese 25%, migrant tribes 15%. *Religions:* Buddhist 75%, Hindu 25%. *Literacy rate:* n.a. *Per capita GDP:* $200.

KEY DATES

1907 First hereditary monarch installed.
1910 Anglo-Bhutanese Treaty.
1949 India takes over foreign affairs.
1959 4,000 Tibetan refugees are granted asylum in Bhutan.
1979 Tibetan refugees ordered to take Bhutanese citizenship or leave.
1988 King imposes "code of conduct," enforcing Bhutanese customs.
1990 Nepalese organizations based in India charge Bhutan with human rights violations against Nepalese in Bhutan.

TRAVEL

Visa: Needed by U.S. *Driving permit:* IDP. *Health and safety:* Inoculations advised; water unsafe. *Tourist features:* Gangkar Punsum, one of the world's highest unclimbed peaks. *National holiday:* December 17 (National Day).

SRI LANKA

Area: 25,334 sq. mi./65,610 km². *Local name:* Sri Lanka Prajathanthrika Samajavadi Janarajaya. *Currency:* Sri Lankan rupee. *Capital:* Colombo. *Physical features:* Flat coastal and N. region; mountainous in S. and interior. *Climate:* Tropical. *Time zone:* GMT +5:30h. *Political system:* Republic. *Head of state:* Dingiri Banda Wijetunga (from 1993). *Head of government:* Chandrika Bandaranaike Kumaratunga (from 1994). *Main exports:* Textiles, tea, coconut, rubber. *Resources:* Limestone, graphite, mineral sands, gems.

PEOPLE

Population: 17,619,000. *Distribution urban/rural:* 22%/78%. *Life expectancy:* 69(m), 74(f). *Languages:* Sinhala and Tamil (both official), English. *Ethnic groups:* Sinhalese 74%, Tamil 18%, Moor 7%, other 1%. *Religions:* Buddhist 69%, Hindu 15%, Christian 8%, Muslim 8%. *Literacy rate:* 86%. *Per capita GDP:* $410.

KEY DATES

1802 Becomes a British colony.
1948 Achieves independence.
1983 Tamil guerrilla warfare breaks out; state of emergency imposed.
1991 2,552 Tamil Tigers killed by Sri Lankan army at Elephant Pass.
1993 President Premadasa assassinated.

TRAVEL

Visa: Needed by U.S. *Driving permit:* IDP. *Health and safety:* Inoculations advised; water unsafe. *Tourist features:* Fort at Galle; wildlife at Yala National Park. *National holiday:* February 4 (Independence Day).

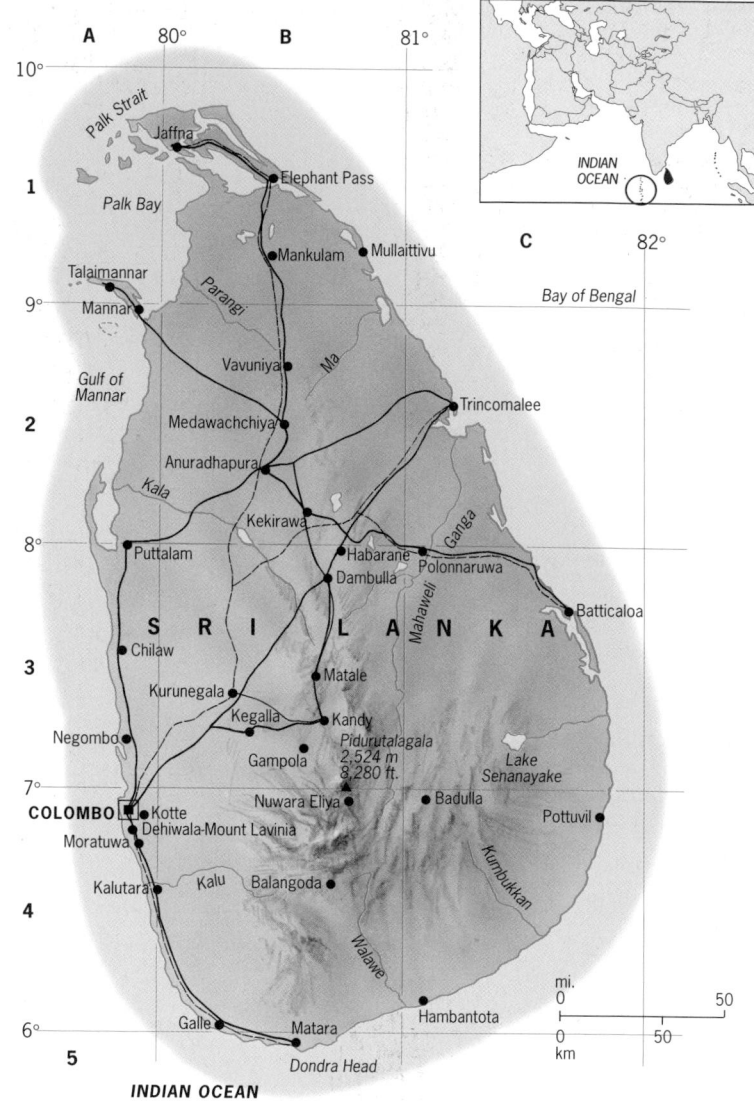

MALDIVES

Area: 115 sq. mi./298 km². *Local name:* Divehi Jumhuriya. *Currency:* Rufiya. *Capital:* Male. *Physical features:* 1,196 coral islands, largely flat. *Climate:* Tropical. *Time zone:* GMT +5:30h. *Political system:* Republic. *Head of state and government:* Maumoon Abdul Gayoom (from 1978). *Main exports:* Fish, clothing. *Resources:* Fish.

PEOPLE

Population: 238,000. *Distribution urban/rural:* 26%/74%. *Life expectancy:* 62(m), 64(f). *Languages:* Divehi (Sinhalese dialect), English widely spoken by government officials. *Ethnic groups:* Sinhalese, Dravidian, Arab, African, Australasian mixture. *Religion:* Sunni Muslim. *Literacy rate:* 92%. *Per capita GDP:* $770.

KEY DATES

1887 Becomes a British protectorate.
1953 Becomes a republic.
1954 Sultan restored.
1965 Full independence achieved.
1968 Sultan deposed; becomes a republic.
1982 Joins Commonwealth of Nations.
1985 Joins South Asian Association for Regional Cooperation (SAARC).
1988 Indian paratroops foil coup attempt.

TRAVEL

Visa: Needed by U.S. *Driving permit:* IDP. *Health and safety:* Inoculations advised; water unsafe. *Tourist features:* Marine life; beaches. *National holiday:* July 26 (Independence Day).

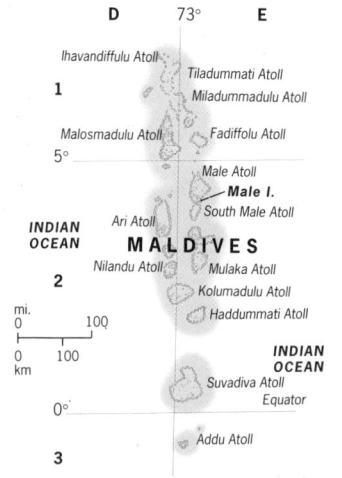

BANGLADESH

Area: 57,299 sq. mi./148,393 km². **Local name:** Gana Prajatantri Bangladesh. **Currency:** Taka. **Capital:** Dhaka. **Other cities:** Chittagong. **Physical features:** Flat alluvial plain; hills in S.E. **Climate:** Tropical, with monsoon. **Time zone:** GMT +5:30h. **Political system:** Republic. **Head of state:** Abdur Rahman Biswas (from 1991). **Head of government:** Khalenda Zia (from 1991). **Main exports:** Jute, clothing. **Resources:** Natural gas, uranium.

PEOPLE

Population: 122,210,000. **Distribution urban/rural:** 24%/76%. **Life expectancy:** 55(m), 54(f). **Languages:** Bangla (official), English widely spoken. **Ethnic groups:** Bengali 98%, Bilhari and tribal less than 2%. **Religions:** Muslim 83%, Hindu 16%, Buddhist, Christian, and other 1%. **Literacy rate:** 35%. **Per capita GDP:** $200.

KEY DATES

1526 Becomes part of Mogul Empire.
1740s British East India Company takes control of much Mogul territory.
1858 Bengal becomes a province of British India.
1906 Foundation of Muslim League.
1947 India partitioned; Eastern Bengal province becomes East Pakistan.
1970 East Pakistan hit by tidal wave and cyclone killing about 266,000; many East Pakistanis charge government with delaying shipments of relief supplies.
1971 March: antigovernment protests; East Pakistan declares independence as Bangladesh; civil war breaks out; Dec.: West Pakistan defeated.
1972 Sheik Mujib prime minister.
1975 Constitutional amendment accords all executive power to president; Mujib becomes president; Mujib killed in coup led by Maj.-Gen. Zia ur-Rahman; martial law declared.
1978 Zia elected president; foundation of Bangladesh Nationalist Party (BNP).
1979 Martial law ends.
1981 Zia killed by army rebels; Vice-President Abdus Sattar president.
1982 Military coup led by Lt.-Gen. H. M. Ershad; martial law declared and political activities outlawed.
1986 Ershad elected president in first multiparty elections since 1979; martial law ended and constitution restored.
1987 State of emergency declared after antigovernment demonstrations.
1988 Islam becomes state religion; state of emergency lifted; monsoon floods kill 2,000 and leave c. 25 million homeless.
1990 Violent antigovernment demonstrations; H. M. Ershad resigns and is arrested and charged with corruption and possession of illegal firearms.
1991 Zia's widow, Khaleda Zia, becomes prime minister; constitutional amendment returns power to prime minister; cyclone and tidal wave kill 138,000.

TRAVEL
Visa: Needed by U.S. **Driving permit:** IDP. **Health and safety:** Inoculations advised; water unsafe. **Tourist feature:** Traditional sculpture and architecture. **National holiday:** March 26 (Independence Day).

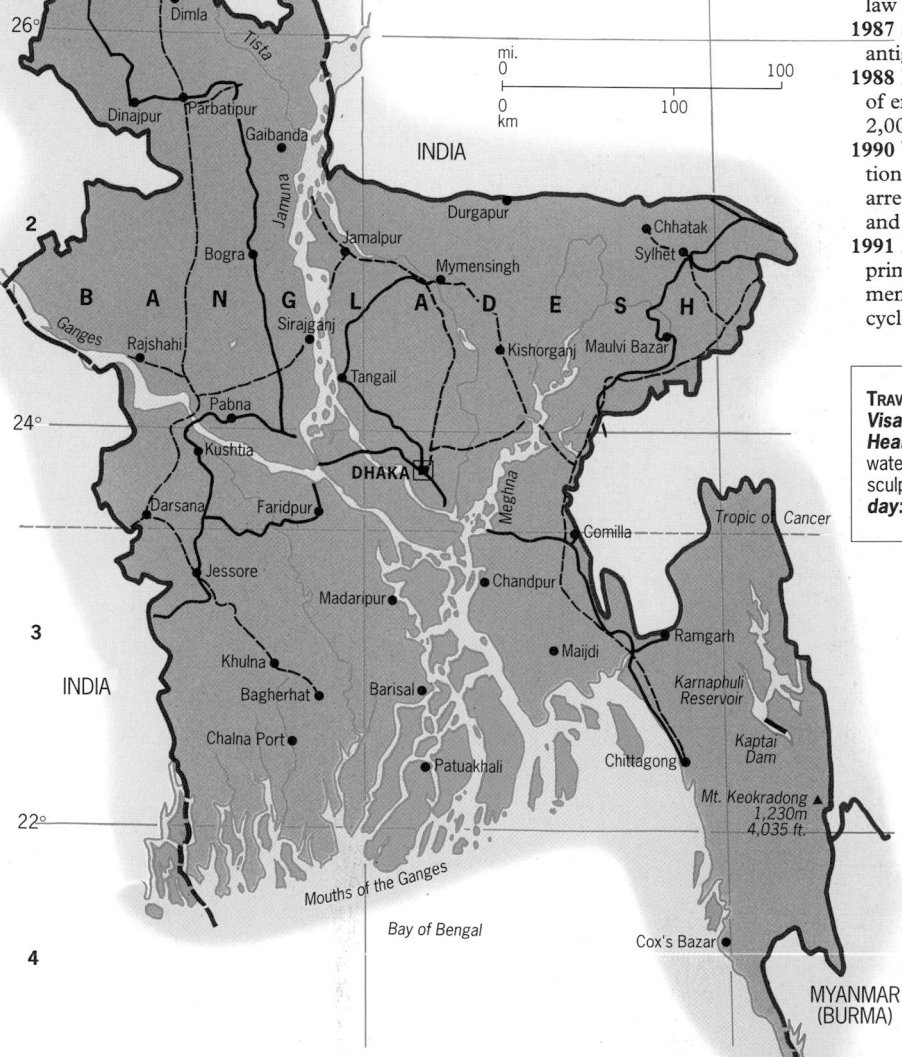

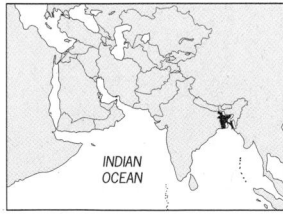

INDIAN OCEAN

MYANMAR (BURMA)

Area: 261,226 sq. mi./676,577 km². *Local name:* Myanmar Naingngandaw. *Currency:* Kyat. *Capital:* Yangon (formerly Rangoon). *Other cities:* Mandalay, Mawlamyine, Pegu. *Physical features:* Central lowlands surrounded by steep, rugged highlands. *Climate:* Tropical, with monsoon. *Time zone:* GMT +6:30h. *Political system:* Military. *Head of state and government:* Chairman of the State Law and Order Restoration Council Gen. Than Shwe (from 1992). *Main exports:* Rice, jute, teak, rubber. *Resources:* Crude oil, wood, tin.

PEOPLE

Population: 35,307,913. *Distribution urban/rural:* 24%/76%. *Life expectancy:* 57(m), 61(f). *Languages:* Myanmar (official), various ethnic languages. *Ethnic groups:* Burman 68%, Shan 9%, Karen 7%, Rakhine 4%, Chinese, Mon, Indian 7%. *Religions:* Buddhist 89%, Christian 4%, Muslim 4%, other 3%. *Literacy rate:* 81%. *Per capita GDP:* $530.

KEY DATES

1885 War with Great Britain; Burma becomes a province of British India.

1935 Separated from India and accorded limited self-government.

1942–45 Occupied by Japanese; emergence of the Anti-Fascist People's Freedom League (AFPFL).

1948 Independence achieved with U Nu (AFPFL) as prime minister.

1958 Fighting between AFPFL factions threatens to escalate into civil war; U Nu asks Gen. U Ne Win to set up temporary military government.

1960 U Nu returns to power.

1962 U Nu overthrown in bloodless coup led by U Ne Win; Burma becomes one-party socialist state; widespread unrest.

1974 New constitution proclaims Socialist Republic of the Union of Burma.

1975 Foundation of opposition National Democratic Front.

1981 U Ne Win resigns and is replaced by U San Yu.

1988 Thousands killed in massive pro-democracy demonstrations; July: U Sein Lwin becomes president but resigns after 17 days; U Maung Maung becomes president; Sep.: military coup establishes State Law and Order Restoration Council (SLORC).

1989 Burma becomes the Union of Myanmar.

1990 National League for Democracy leader, Daw Aung San Suu Kyi, is arrested but still wins landslide victory in multiparty elections; rebel group forms alternative government.

1991 Daw Aung San Suu Kyi wins Nobel Peace Prize for her nonviolent struggle for democracy and human rights but remains under house arrest.

1992 SLORC installs Than Shwe as prime minister; martial law ends.

1993 Constitutional convention agrees to more liberal constitution; cease-fire agreed with rebels.

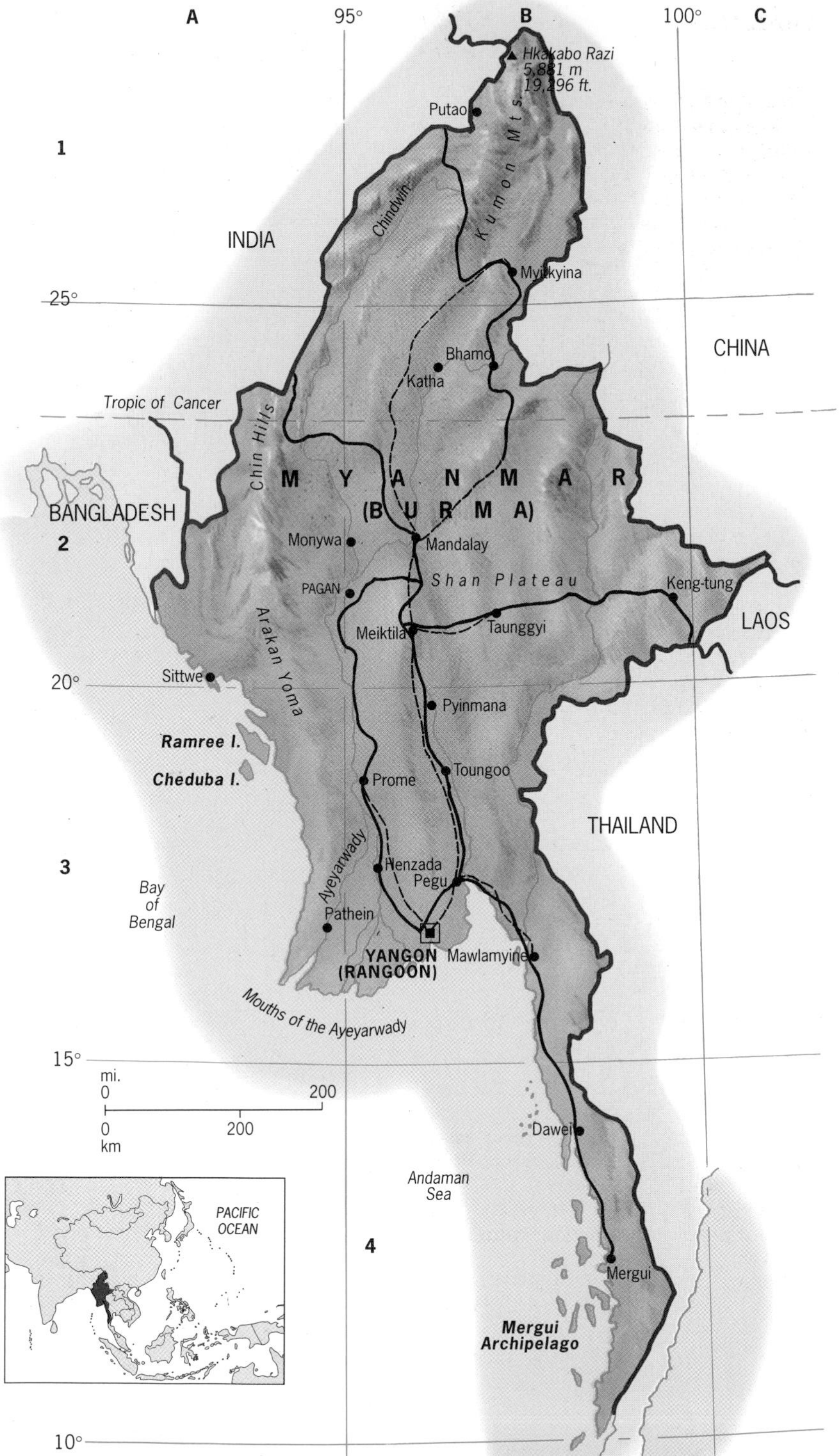

Map

A 95° B 100° C

1

Hkakabo Razi
5,881 m
19,296 ft.

Putao

INDIA

Kumon Mts.

Chindwin

Myitkyina

25°

Bhamo

CHINA

Katha

Tropic of Cancer

Chin Hills

M Y A N M A R
(B U R M A)

Monywa

Mandalay

2

BANGLADESH

PAGAN

Shan Plateau

Keng-tung

Meiktila

Taunggyi

LAOS

20°

Sittwe

Arakan Yoma

Pyinmana

Ramree I.

Cheduba I.

Prome

Toungoo

THAILAND

3

Bay of Bengal

Ayeyarwady

Henzada

Pegu

Pathein

YANGON
(RANGOON)

Mawlamyine

Mouths of the Ayeyarwady

15°

mi.
0   200

0   200
km

Dawei

Andaman Sea

4

PACIFIC OCEAN

Mergui

Mergui Archipelago

10°

TRAVEL

Visa: Needed by U.S. *Driving permit:* IDP. *Health and safety:* Inoculations advised; water unsafe. *Tourist features:* Ruined cities of Pagan and Mingun. *National holiday:* January 4 (Independence Day).

THAILAND

Area: 198,113 sq. mi./513,115 km². *Local name:* Muang Thai/Prathet Thai. *Currency:* Baht. *Capital:* Bangkok. *Other cities:* Chiang Mai, Nakhon Sawan. *Physical features:* Mountainous, with central plain and plateau in E. *Climate:* Tropical. *Time zone:* GMT +7h. *Political system:* Constitutional monarchy. *Head of state:* King Bhumibol Adulyadej (from 1947). *Head of government:* Chuan Leekpai (from 1992). *Main exports:* Machinery, food, textiles, rubber. *Resources:* Tin, rubber, natural gas, tungsten.

PEOPLE

Population: 58,584,000. *Distribution urban/rural:* 20%/80%. *Life expectancy:* 67(m), 71(f). *Languages:* Thai, English also used. *Ethnic groups:* Thai 75%, Chinese 14%, other 11%. *Religions:* Buddhist 95%, Muslim 4%, other 1%. *Literacy rate:* 93%. *Per capita GNP:* $1,630.

KEY DATES

1782 Chakri dynasty established; name changes from Ayutthaya to Siam.

1914–18 Siamese troops fight in World War I on Allied side.

1932 Becomes constitutional monarchy.

1939 Siam renamed Thailand.

1941 Japanese occupation; treaty of alliance signed with Japan.

1942 Declares war on U.S.A. and Britain.

1944 Pro-Japanese government overthrown in coup.

1947 Military coup reinstates wartime leadership in Thailand.

1957 Military seizes power.

1965 Thai troops enter Vietnam War on side of U.S.A.

1967 Joins Association of Southeast Asian Nations (ASEAN) for economic, cultural, and social cooperation.

1973 University students lead revolt against government, forcing return to civilian government.

1976 Conservative groups attack students, killing around 40; military takes control again; thousands arrested.

1980 Gen. Prem Tinsulanonda becomes prime minister.

1988 Prem resigns and is replaced by Chatichai Choonhaven.

1991 Military seizes power; demonstrations against military bias of new constitution.

1992 General election results in five-party coalition led by Gen. Suchinda Kraprayoon; widespread riots; Suchinda flees after army shoots 100 demonstrators; new coalition government led by Chuan Leekpai.

1993 Site chosen for new capital to replace Bangkok by 2010; government troops ambushed by guerrillas in S.

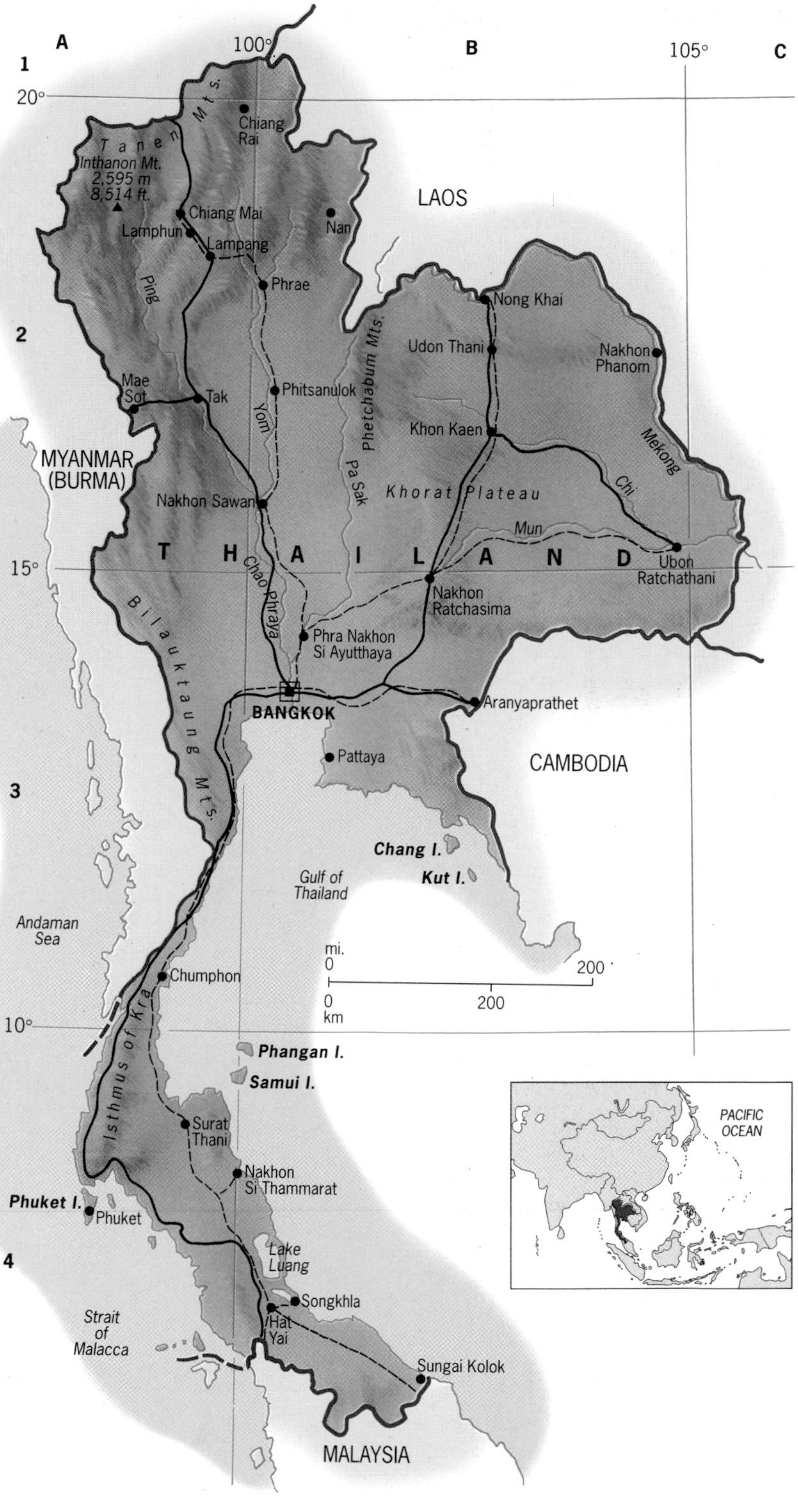

TRAVEL
Visa: Not needed. *Driving permit:* IDP. *Health and safety:* Inoculations advised; water unsafe. *Tourist features:* Buddhist temples throughout Thailand; Bangkok. *National holiday:* December 5 (Birthday of His Majesty the King).

CAMBODIA

Area: 69,898 sq. mi./181,035 km². *Local name:* Roat Kampuchea. *Currency:* Riel. *Capital:* Phnom Penh. *Physical Features:* Mostly low, flat plains. *Climate:* Tropical. *Time zone:* GMT +7h. *Political system:* Constitutional monarchy. *Head of state:* King Norodom Sihanouk (from 1993). *Head of government:* Prince Norodom Ranariddh (from 1993). *Main exports:* Rubber, pepper, rice, wood. *Resources:* Wood, iron ore.

PEOPLE

Population: 9,308,000. *Distribution urban/rural:* 10%/90%. *Life expectancy:* 48(m), 51(f). *Languages:* Khmer (official), French. *Ethnic groups:* Khmer 90%, Chinese 5%. *Religion:* Theravada Buddhist 95%. *Literacy rate:* 35%. *Per capita GDP:* $130.

KEY DATES

1863 Becomes a French protectorate.
1941–45 Occupied by Japan.
1953 Independence achieved.
1970 Prince Norodom Sihanouk overthrown in coup led by Lon Nol; civil war breaks out.
1975 Khmer Rouge led by Pol Pot seizes power.
1976–78 Over 2.5 million people die from

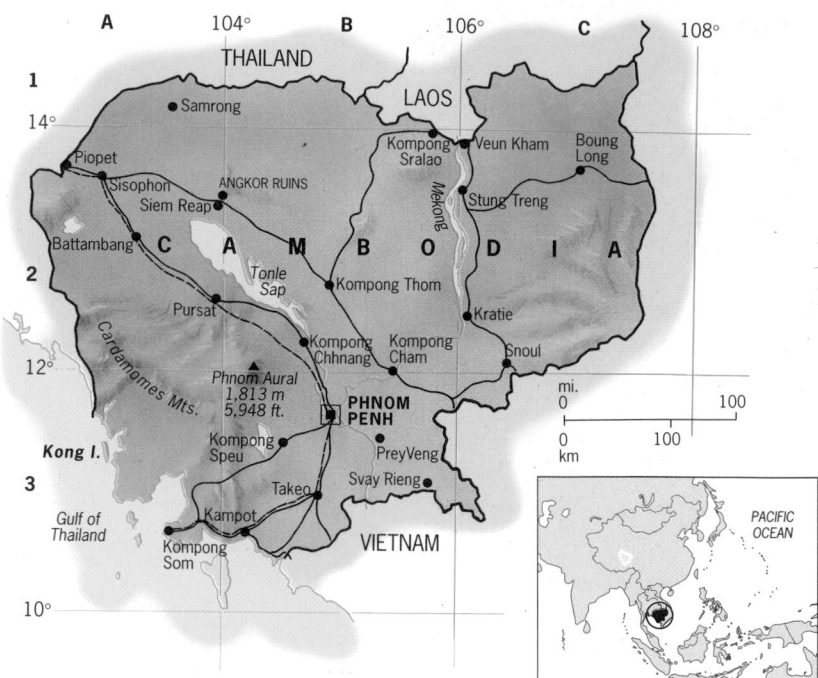

famine and state violence.
1978 Communist rebels and Vietnamese troops overthrow the Khmer Rouge.
1991 Peace treaty provides for UN transitional rule.
1992 Khmer Rouge refuses to disarm.
1993 Moderate coalition wins majority in free elections; fighting continues.

TRAVEL
Visa: Needed by U.S. *Driving permit:* IDP. *Health and safety:* Inoculations advised; water unsafe. *Tourist feature:* Ruined city of Angkor. *National holiday:* January 7 (Liberation Day).

LAOS

Area: 91,428 sq. mi./236,800 km². *Local name:* Saathiaranagroat Prachhathippatay Prachhachhon Lao. *Currency:* Kip. *Capital:* Vientiane. *Physical features:* Mostly rugged mountains. *Climate:* Savanna. *Time zone:* GMT +7h. *Political system:* Communist. *Head of state:* Nouhak Phoumsavan (from 1991). *Head of government:* Gen. Khamtai Siphandon (from 1991). *Main exports:* Electricity, wood products. *Resources:* Wood, hydropower, gypsum, gemstones.

PEOPLE

Population: 4,605,000. *Distribution urban/rural:* 15%/85%. *Life expectancy:* 49(m), 52(f). *Languages:* Lao (official), French, English. *Ethnic groups:* Lao 50%, Kha 15%, Thai 20%, other 15%. *Religions:* Buddhist 85%, animist and other 15%. *Literacy rate:* 84%. *Per capita GDP:* $200.

KEY DATES

1893 Becomes a French protectorate.
1954 Independence achieved.
1960 Capt. Kong Le seizes power; civil

war breaks out soon after.
1962 Coalition government installed.
1963 Renewed fighting.
1971 South Vietnamese troops enter Laos to attack Communist supply routes.
1975 Communists take over government; around 50,000 Vietnamese troops arrive to maintain order.
1989 First assembly elections since Communist takeover.

TRAVEL
Visa: Needed by U.S. *Driving permit:* IDP. *Health and safety:* Inoculations advised; water unsafe. *Tourist features:* Vientiane, Mekong River. *National holiday:* December 2 (Proclamation of the Democratic Republic).

VIETNAM

Area: 127,242 sq. mi./329,556 km². *Local name:* Cong Hoa Xa Hoi Chu Nghia Viet Nam *Currency:* Dong. *Capital:* Hanoi. *Other cities:* Ho Chi Minh City (formerly Saigon), Da Nang, Haiphong. *Physical features:* Delta in S. and N.; central highlands; mountains in extreme N. *Climate:* Tropical in S., tropical monsoon in N. *Time zone:* GMT +7h. *Political system:* Communist. *Head of state:* Le Duc Anh (from 1992). *Head of government:* Vo Van Kiet (from 1991). *Main exports:* Agricultural products, coal, iron, crude petroleum, marine products. *Resources:* Coal, phosphates, manganese, offshore oil deposits.

PEOPLE

Population: 70,902,000. *Distribution urban/rural:* 20%/80%. *Life expectancy:* 63(m), 67(f). *Languages:* Vietnamese (official), French, Chinese, English, Khmer, other languages. *Ethnic groups:* Vietnamese 85%, Chinese 3%, Muong, Thai, Meo, Khmer. *Religions:* Buddhist, Confucian, Taoist, Roman Catholic, animist, Islamic, Protestant. *Literacy rate:* 88%. *Per capita GDP:* $220.

KEY DATES

1883 Comes under French control.

1940–45 Japanese occupation.

1945 Ho Chi Minh proclaims the Democratic Republic of Vietnam.

1946 War breaks out with France.

1949 France forms the State of Vietnam in opposition to Ho Chi Minh's Communist state; many Nationalists support new state.

1954 France defeated at Dien Bien Phu; Geneva Accords temporarily divide Vietnam, with elections planned for 1956 to unite the country.

1955 Ngo Dinh Diem becomes president of South Vietnam and, fearing Communist victory, refuses to hold elections.

1957 Communists in South Vietnam (the Vietcong) begin to rebel against Diem.

1959 North Vietnam orders Vietcong to launch armed offensive against Diem's government.

1962 Diem imposes state of emergency.

1963 Diem killed in military coup.

1964 U.S.A. enters Vietnam War.

1969 Ho Chi Minh dies; Communist Party Politburo takes control of North Vietnam.

1973 Cease-fire agreement; U.S.A. withdraws troops from South Vietnam; North Vietnam soon renews offensive against the South.

1975 Communists capture Saigon.

1976 Vietnam is unified as the Socialist Republic of Vietnam.

1978 Invasion of Cambodia.

1979 Sino-Vietnamese War.

1987–89 More than 10,000 political prisoners are released.

1992 Le Duc Anh elected president.

1994 U.S.A. removes 30-year-old trade embargo against Vietnam.

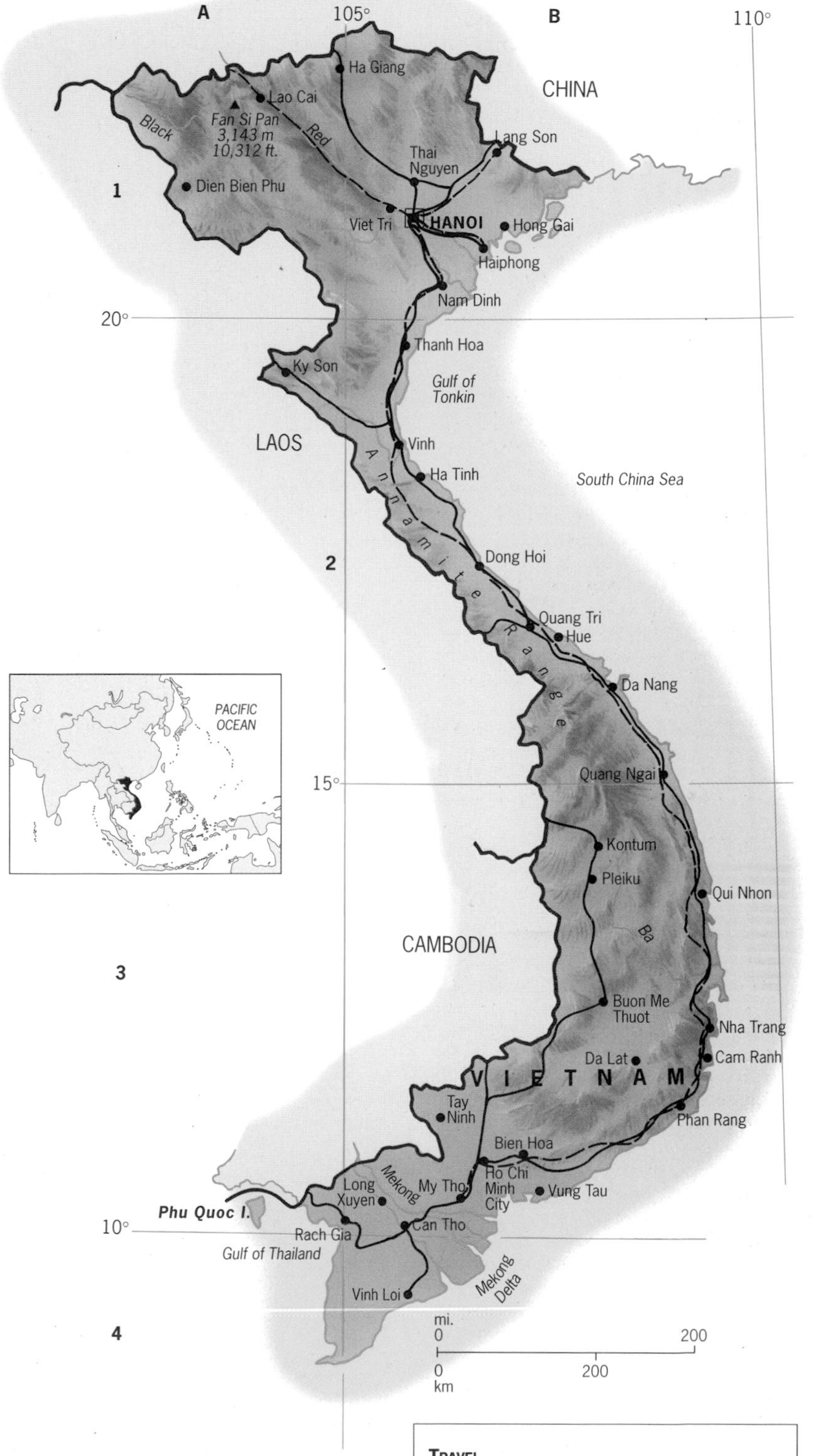

TRAVEL

Visa: Needed by U.S. *Driving permit:* IDP. *Health and safety:* Inoculations advised; water unsafe. *Tourist features:* Hanoi; markets of Ho Chi Minh City. *National holiday:* September 2 (Independence Day).

CHINA

Area: 3,696,100 sq. mi./9,572,900 km². *Local name:* Zhonghua Renmin Gonghe Guo. *Currency:* Yuan. *Capital:* Beijing. *Other cities:* Shenyang, Chongqing, Wuhan, Nanjing, Harbin, Tianjin, Shanghai, Qingdao, Luda, Guangzhou. *Physical features:* Mountainous highlands in N. and S.W.; deserts in N.W.; uplands in N.E. and S.E.; lowlands in E. *Climate:* Extremely varied; from tropical in S. to subpolar in N. *Time zone:* GMT +8h. *Political system:* Communist. *Head of state:* Jiang Zemin (from 1993). *Head of government:* Li Peng (from 1987). *Main exports:* Textiles, telecommunications equipment, tea, coal, ores, cereals, petroleum. *Resources:* Iron ore, coal, crude oil, mercury, tin, tungsten, antimony, other minerals.

PEOPLE

Population: 1,205,181,000.
Distribution urban/rural: 27%/73%.
Life expectancy: 69(m), 72(f).
Languages: Mandarin or Putonghua (Standard Chinese), Yue (Cantonese), Wu (Shanghainese), Minbei (Fuzhou), Minnan (Hokkien-Taiwanese), minority languages. *Ethnic groups:* Han Chinese 93%, also Zhuang, Uygur, Hui, Yi, Tibetan, Miao, Manchu, Mongol, Buyi, Korean. *Religions:* Officially atheist; traditionally Confucian, Taoist, and Buddhist; small Muslim and Christian minorities. *Literacy rate:* 73%. *Per capita GDP:* $330.

KEY DATES

1644 Manchus establish Qing dynasty.
early 1800s Western traders, resenting the large value of Chinese exports in relation to imports, start smuggling opium to China.
1839 Chinese officials seize 20,000 chests of opium from British merchants in Guangzhou; war with Britain.
1842 Opium War ends with Treaty of Nanjing, the first of many "unequal treaties" between China and the West; Britain gains control of Hong Kong.
1844–51 "Unequal treaties" signed with several Western nations; treaties state that any right accorded to one power must also be accorded to the others.
1851–64 Taiping Rebellion: attempt by quasi-religious group, the Taipings, to overthrow the Manchus and establish a Christian dynasty is put down with foreign military aid; millions are killed.
1894–95 Sino-Japanese War.
1899 Xenophobic secret society, the Boxers, begins terrorist offensive against Christian missionaries in N.E.
1899 "Open Door" agreement ensuring U.S. access to Chinese ports.
1900 Boxer Rebellion: quarter of Beijing

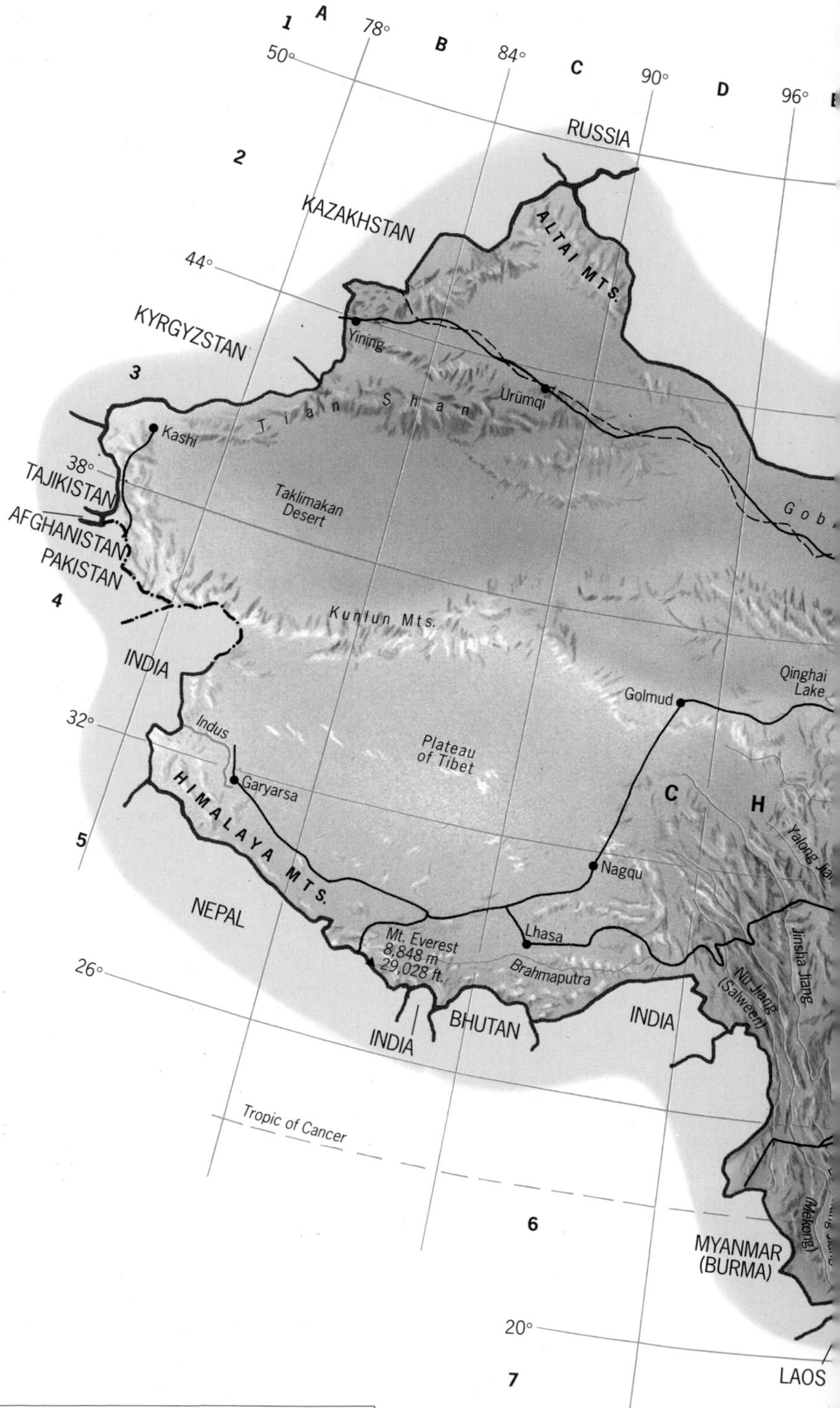

H 120° **I** 126° **J**
G 114° 132° **K**
F 108°
102°

RUSSIA

Greater Hinggan Mts.
Lesser Hinggan Mts.
Amur

MONGOLIA

Hulun Lake

Qiqihar
Jiamusi
Harbin
Jixi

Mongolian Uplands

Changchun
Jilin
Liao
Liaoyuan

Desert

Shenyang
Fushun
Baotou
Hohhot
Zhagjiakou
Jinzhou
Benxi
Jixi
Anshan
NORTH KOREA
BEIJING
Datong
Tangshan
Luda
Yinchuan
Baoding
Tianjin
SOUTH KOREA
THE GREAT WALL
Shijiazhuang
Taiyuan
Qingdao

Huang He (Yellow)

Lanzhou
Jinan
Zibo
Anyang
Yellow Sea
Xinxiang
Zhengzhou
Luoyang
Xuzhou
Grand Canal
Xi'an

N **A**

Central Uplands

Huainan
Nanjing
Suzhou
Hofei
Wuxi
Shanghai
Mianyang
Wuhu
Jiaxing
Nanchong
Wuhan
Hangzhou
Shaoxing
East China Sea
Chengdu
Ningbo

Chang Jiang (Yangtze)

Chongqing
Dongting Lake
Nanchang
Wenzhou
Changsha
Pingxiang
Hengyang
Guiyang
Fuzhou
Guilin
Li Jiang
Taiwan Strait
Liuzhou
Xiamen
TAIWAN
Nanning
Guangzhou
Shantou
Xi Jiang
HONG KONG (U.K.)
VIETNAM
MACAO (Portugal)
Zhanjiang

mi.
0
500

Gulf of Tonkin
Haikou
0
500
km
South China Sea
Yulin
Hainan I.

PACIFIC OCEAN

where foreign legations are located is beseiged; Western forces occupy Beijing.

1901 Peace treaty signed with Western nations; relief forces leave Beijing.

1911 Leaders of the Revolution establish Republic of China in Nanjing.

1912 Emperor Pu Yi gives up throne; Yuan Shih'kai becomes president.

1913 Kuomintang (Nationalist Party) founded by former revolutionaries; unsuccessful coup attempt against Yuan; Nationalist leaders flee to Japan.

1916 Yuan dies; control of central government of N. China diminishes as power moves to warlords.

1917 Sun Yat Sen sets up rival government in Guangzhou supported by warlords.

1919 Students demonstrate in Beijing against Treaty of Versailles, which allows Japan to keep control of Chinese territories seized during World War I.

1921 Communist Party founded.

1922 Washington Naval Conference: Japan agrees to return former German holdings in Shandong to China.

1923 Soviet advisers sent to China to help Nationalists.

1925 Sun Yat Sen dies; Chiang Kai-shek takes over Kuomintang Party.

1926 Chiang Kai-shek leads military expedition to reunify China under Kuomintang rule.

1927 Civil war breaks out.

1928 Nationalists capture Beijing; China united for the first time since 1916.

1931 Communists set up rival government with Mao Zedong as chairman; Japanese forces occupy Manchuria.

1932 Japanese establish puppet state of Manchukuo with Pu Yi as leader.

1933 Nationalists launch massive attack against Communists.

1934 Nationalist troops force Communists out of their bases, and 100,000 begin the "Long March."

1936 Manchurian forces kidnap Chiang; he is released only after agreeing to end civil war and form a united front against Japan.

1937–38 Japanese launch major attack against China and gain much territory.

1941 China joins Allies in World War II.

1946 Civil war breaks out.

1949 Mao proclaims People's Republic of China; Nationalists flee to Taiwan.

1950 Invasion of Tibet.

1953 Economic development program begins; government takes control of all major industries; peasants' landholding amalgamated into cooperatives.

1956 China criticizes U.S.S.R. for policy of "peaceful coexistence" with West.

1958 "Great Leap Forward": economic reforms attempting to achieve "true Communism."

1959–61 Depression and famine.

1962 Border war with India; U.S.S.R. refuses request for military aid.

1962–63 Economic recovery program.

1963 Relations with U.S.S.R. severed.

1966–69 "Great Proletarian Cultural Revolution"; many officials accused of failing to follow Communist principles are removed from their positions; students set up semimilitary organizations called "Red Guards" and demonstrate against counterrevolutionaries and anti-Maoists; frequent eruptions of violence.

1969 Border clashes with U.S.S.R.

1971 Admitted to UN.

1972 U.S. President Nixon visits Beijing; Shanghai Communiqué establishes normal relations with U.S.A.

1975 New constitution; Premier Zhou Enlai introduces "Four Modernizations" program.

1976 Mao and Zhou both die; moderates and radicals fight for power; moderates win and Hua Guofeng becomes premier.

1979 "One-child family scheme" adopted in Sichuan province; later spreads throughout China.

1980 Hua resigns.

1984 Economic reforms diminishing government control over business.

1986 Students demonstrate for increased freedom of speech and democracy.

1988 Li Peng becomes premier; Yang Shangkun becomes state president.

1989 Tiananmen Square massacre: 2,000 students killed when prodemocracy demonstrations are put down by army; international sanctions imposed.

1991 EC and Japan lift sanctions; diplomatic relations with U.S.S.R. restored; relations with Vietnam normalized.

1993 Jiang Zemin becomes president.

ECONOMY

China ranks among the ten leading countries in terms of the total value of goods and services it produces annually. However, like India, the size of China's population means that the per capita GDP is low.

As a Communist country, most important industries are state run; the government rations some foodstuffs, clothing, and other necessities and sets the prices of many goods and services.

Industry by sector

Farming Since the 1950s, farming in China has been collectivized, and farmers have worked cooperatively in communes. In the 1980s, the emphasis on communes began to decline, and many farms are now run by individual farmers. However, state control is still strong, and farmers must give a share of their crop to their collective and must also sell an agreed quota to the state at a fixed price.

Farming is the largest sector in China's economy. It employs 74% of the workforce and accounts for about 44% of the GDP. China is the world's largest producer of cotton, pears, potatoes, rice, and tobacco. Barley, cotton, peanuts, corn, millet, tea, sorghum, and wheat are also important. More pigs are raised in China than in any other country. Cattle, sheep, and goats are also kept.

Mining China is the world's leading producer of tungsten and one of the world's largest producers of coal, antimony, gold, and tin. Since the 1950s, large deposits of petroleum have been discovered, and this is now an important area of mineral production. The government has greatly increased production of iron ore to meet the needs of the growing iron and steel industry, and China is now a leading world producer. Coal, bauxite, lead, manganese, salt, and zinc are also mined.

Manufacturing When the Communists came to power, they began to rebuild China's factories in a bid to make China an important industrial power. They concentrated on developing heavy industries such as metals and machinery, and today China is one of the world's greatest producers of steel. Other important industries are cement, chemicals, and irrigation and transportation equipment. The largest consumer goods industries are textiles and food processing.

Two of the greatest obstacles to the expansion of China's manufacturing industries are outmoded technology and a lack of highly trained technicians. To remedy this, China is now contracting foreign companies to modernize old factories and build new ones, and has begun to expand scientific and technical education in China as well as sending students abroad for extra training.

Tourism Restrictions on travel to China were lifted in the early 1970s, and tourism has since made an increasingly important contribution to the economy. The potential earnings from this industry are enormous, and in 1979 the government launched a five-year plan for the development of tourism.

TIBET (Xizang)

Tibet is an autonomous region of S.W. China covering 471,700 sq. mi./1,221,600 km². It was first conquered by China in the early 1700s, although it enjoyed a large degree of autonomy until the Communists took over. Tibetan nationalism runs high and, as a deeply religious people, Tibetans do not live easily under Communist rule. The Tibetan people practice a form of Buddhism called Lamaism, and before Communists took control of China, monks (or *lamas*) had tremendous influence in Tibet and also owned the farmland. Executive power lay in the hands of the two grand lamas, the Dalai Lama and the Panchen Lama. In the 1960s and 1970s, the Chinese government split up the lamas' estates and distributed the land among the people, and most of Tibet's monasteries were closed or destroyed. Since then, there have been many anti-Chinese uprisings, some very violent, and the Chinese government has used a heavy hand to put them down. In the 1980s, China adopted a more liberal policy toward Tibet. As a result, some monasteries have been allowed to reopen and some other freedoms have been restored, but reform has been slow and the conflict continues.

KEY DATES

1717 China conquers Tibet, although a large degree of autonomy is retained by Tibet.

1911 Tibetans expel the Chinese.

1920s Rivalry between Dalai and Panchen lamas; Panchen Lama flees to China.

1933 Dalai Lama dies; successor chosen.

1937 Panchen Lama dies in China.

1944 New Panchen Lama enthroned in China.

1949 Communists gain control in China.

1950 Chinese forces invade Tibet; Tibet surrenders sovereignty but retains the right to regional self-government; China promises no immediate change in Tibet's political system and guarantees freedom of religious belief.

1956 Formation of Preparatory Committee for the Tibetan Autonomous Region with Dalai Lama as chairman; China tightens hold over Tibet; Nationalist uprisings.

1958 Widespread anti-Communist guerrilla activity prompted by Chinese attempt to establish people's communes in Tibet.

1959 87,000 die in riots in Lhasa; Dalai Lama flees to India and Panchen Lama takes over as head of Preparatory Committee; UN resolution condemns the suppression of human rights in Tibet.

1964 Panchen Lama is removed from his post.

1965 Tibet officially becomes an "Autonomous Region"; Chinese government takes control of press, banks, and food stores, and enforces strict controls on farmers; many monasteries are closed down.

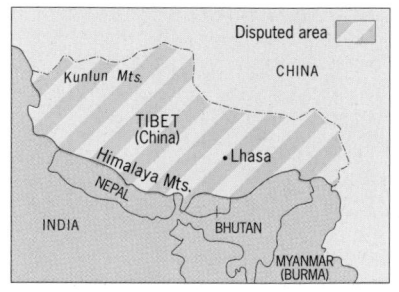

1979 Panchen Lama readmitted to Committee.

1980 Chinese government admits that Tibet has been misgoverned and promises reform; some monasteries are reopened.

1989 Police open fire on demonstrators in Lhasa; China admits to 16 deaths, but many more are reported; martial law imposed; Panchen Lama dies; Dali Lama wins Nobel Peace Prize for nonviolent opposition to Chinese rule in Tibet.

1990 Martial law lifted.

1992 China celebrates the 40th anniversary of the "peaceful liberation of Tibet"; thousands of troops are sent to Lhasa to quell violent anti-Chinese demonstrations.

1993 New taxes and price increases prompt violent demonstrations.

MACAO

Area: 6 sq. mi./16 km². *Currency:* Pataca. *Capital:* Macao. *Physical features:* Generally flat; comprises city of Macao on a peninsula and three small islands. *Climate:* Subtropical. *Time zone:* GMT +8h. *Political system:* Overseas territory of Portugal (Chinese government has the power of veto over any laws concerning Macao, and the territory is due to become a Special Administrative Region of China in December 1999). *Head of state:* Mario Alberto Soares (from 1986). *Head of government:* Gov. Gen. Vasco Joachim Rocha Vieira (from 1991). *Main exports:* Textiles, clothes, toys. *Resources:* Negligible.

PEOPLE
Population: 473,333. *Distribution*

urban/rural: n.a. *Life expectancy:* 78(m), 84(f). *Languages:* Portuguese (official), Cantonese used by virtually the entire population. *Ethnic groups:* Chinese 95%, Portuguese 3%, other 2%. *Religions:* Buddhist 45%, Roman Catholic 7%, Protestant 1%, none 46%, other 1%. *Literacy rate:* 90%. *Per capita GDP:* $6,900.

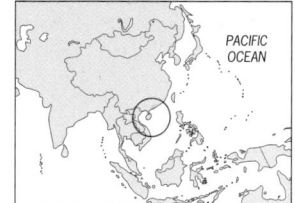

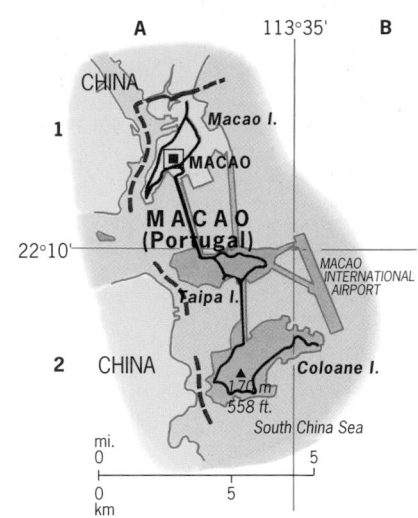

MONGOLIA

Area: 604,826 sq. mi./1,566,500 km². *Local name:* Mongol Uls. *Currency:* Tugrik. *Capital:* Ulan Bator. *Other cities:* Darhan, Choybalsan. *Physical features:* Semidesert and desert plains; mountainous in W. and S.W.; Gobi Desert in S.E. *Climate:* Arid/steppe. *Time zone:* GMT +7h (W), +9h (E). *Political system:* Republic. *Head of state:* Punsalmaagiyn Ochirbat (from 1990). *Head of government:* Puntsagiyn Jasray (from 1992). *Main exports:* Copper, livestock, wool, hides, nonferrous metals, minerals, fuels, raw materials. *Resources:* Oil, coal, copper, molybdenum, tungsten, phosphates, tin, nickel, zinc, wolfram, fluorspar, gold.

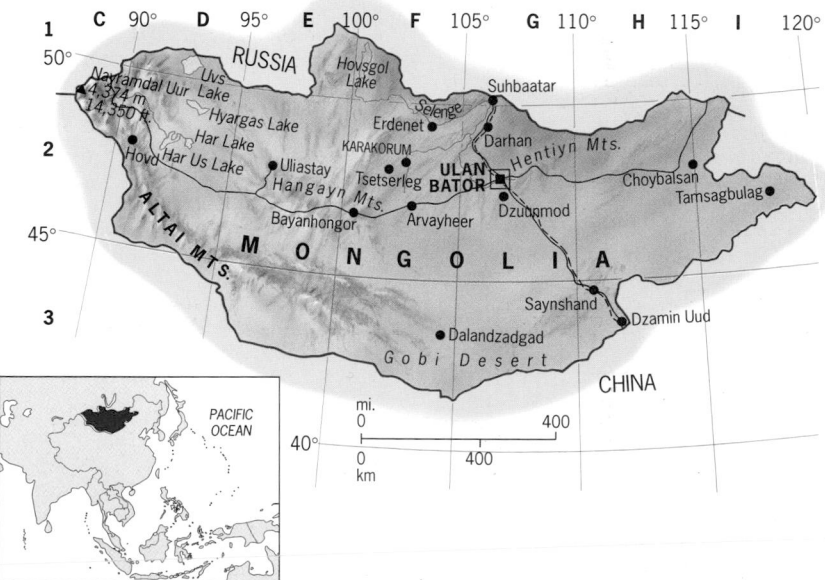

PEOPLE
Population: 2,182,000. *Distribution urban/rural:* 58%/42%. *Life expectancy:* 63(m), 68(f). *Languages:* Khalkha Mongol 90%, Turkic, Russian, Chinese. *Ethnic groups:* Mongol 90%, Kazakh 4%, Chinese 2%, Russian 2%, other 2%. *Religions:* Mainly Tibetan Buddhist; Muslim 4%; religious activity limited under Communist regime. *Literacy rate:* 90%. *Per capita GDP:* $900.

KEY DATES
1206 Genghis Khan proclaimed universal ruler of Mongolia.
1279 Kublai Khan completes conquest of China and founds the Yuan dynasty.
1369 Timur conquers N. India.
1400s Decline of Mongol Empire.
1696 Comes under control of Manchus.
1911 Chinese driven out of Mongolia.

1915 Chinese regain control.
1920 Occupied by anti-Bolshevik Russian forces with Japanese assistance.
1921 Mongolian People's Revolutionary Party (MPRP) regains control from China with Soviet assistance.
1924 People's Republic of Mongolia established.
1946 China recognizes Mongolia's independence.
1961 Joins UN.
1962 Border treaty signed with China.
1966 A 20-year treaty of friendship, co-operation, and mutual assistance signed with U.S.S.R.
1984 Effective leader, Yumjaagiyn Tsedenbal, overthrown and replaced by Jambyn Batmonh.
1985 Friendship treaty with U.S.S.R. renewed.

1989 Soviet forces withdraw.
1990 Prodemocracy demonstrations; MPRP win majority in multiparty elections; Punsalmaagiyn Ochirbat becomes president in free elections.
1991 Large-scale privatization program begun in move toward free market economy; economic problems.
1992 New constitution introduced; economic problems worsen; Puntsagiyn Jasray becomes prime minister.

TRAVEL
Visa: Needed by U.S. *Driving permit:* IDP. *Health and safety:* Inoculations advised; water unsafe. *Tourist features:* Altai and Hangayn mountain ranges, Uvs Lake. *National holiday:* July 13 (Mongolian People's Revolution).

NORTH KOREA

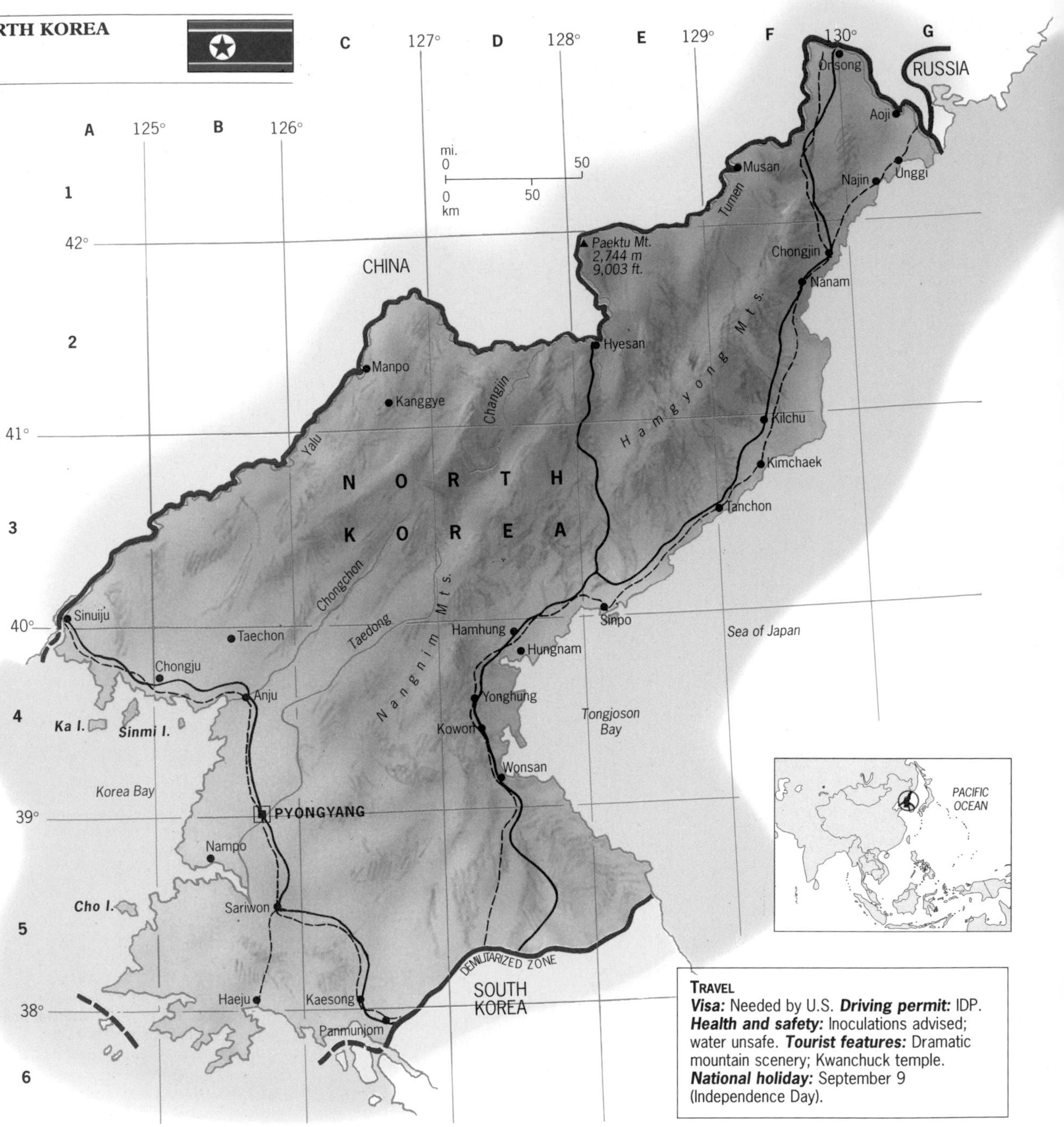
C
127°
D
128°
E
129°
F
130°
G
A
125°
B
126°
RUSSIA
Onsong
Aoji
Musan
Unggi
Najin
Tumen
mi.
0
50
0
50
km
1
42°
Paektu Mt.
2,744 m
9,003 ft.
Chongjin
Nanam
CHINA
2
Hyesan
Manpo
Kanggye
Changjin
Hamgyong Mts.
41°
Yalu
Kilchu
Kimchaek
NORTH
KOREA
3
Tanchon
Chongchon
Nangnim Mts.
Taedong
Sinuiju
40°
Taechon
Hamhung
Sinpo
Sea of Japan
Hungnam
Chongju
Anju
Yonghung
4
Ka I.
Sinmi I.
Kowon
Tongjoson
Bay
Wonsan
Korea Bay
39°
PYONGYANG
PACIFIC
OCEAN
Nampo
Cho I.
Sariwon
5
DEMILITARIZED ZONE
SOUTH
KOREA
Haeju
Kaesong
38°
Panmunjom
6

TRAVEL
Visa: Needed by U.S. ***Driving permit:*** IDP. ***Health and safety:*** Inoculations advised; water unsafe. ***Tourist features:*** Dramatic mountain scenery; Kwanchuck temple. ***National holiday:*** September 9 (Independence Day).

Area: 47,402 sq. mi./122,762 km². ***Local name:*** Chosun Minchu-chui Inmin Konghwa-guk. ***Currency:*** Won. ***Capital:*** Pyongyang. ***Physical features:*** Mostly hills and mountains. ***Climate:*** Subtropical. ***Time zone:*** GMT +9h. ***Political system:*** Communist. ***Head of state:*** Kim Jong Il (from 1994). ***Head of government:*** Kang Song San (from 1992). ***Main exports:*** Coal, iron, copper, metallurgical products. ***Resources:*** Coal, lead, tungsten, zinc, graphite, iron ore, copper, gold.

PEOPLE
Population: 23,054,000. ***Distribution urban/rural:*** 62%/38%. ***Life expectancy:*** 66(m), 72(f). ***Language:*** Korean (official). ***Ethnic group:*** Korean. ***Religions:*** Buddhist and Confucian; small Christian minority; religious activity is restricted by the state and religious groups are government run. ***Literacy rate:*** 99%. ***Per capita GNP:*** $1,100.

KEY DATES
1910 Korea is annexed by Japan.
1945 North Korea occupied by Soviets.
1948 Democratic People's Republic of Korea proclaimed by Kim Il Sung.
1950 North Korean forces invade South Korea.
1953 Armistice agreed to end war.
1961 Friendship treaty signed with China.
1972 Reunification talks begin between the two Koreas.
1980 Talks break down.
1983 North Korean bomb kills 17 South Koreans in Yangon, Burma.
1991 Joins UN; nonaggression treaty signed with South Korea.
1992 Nuclear Safeguards Agreement allows for international inspection of nuclear facilities.
1994 Kim Il Sung dies and is succeeded by his son, Kim Jong Il.

SOUTH KOREA

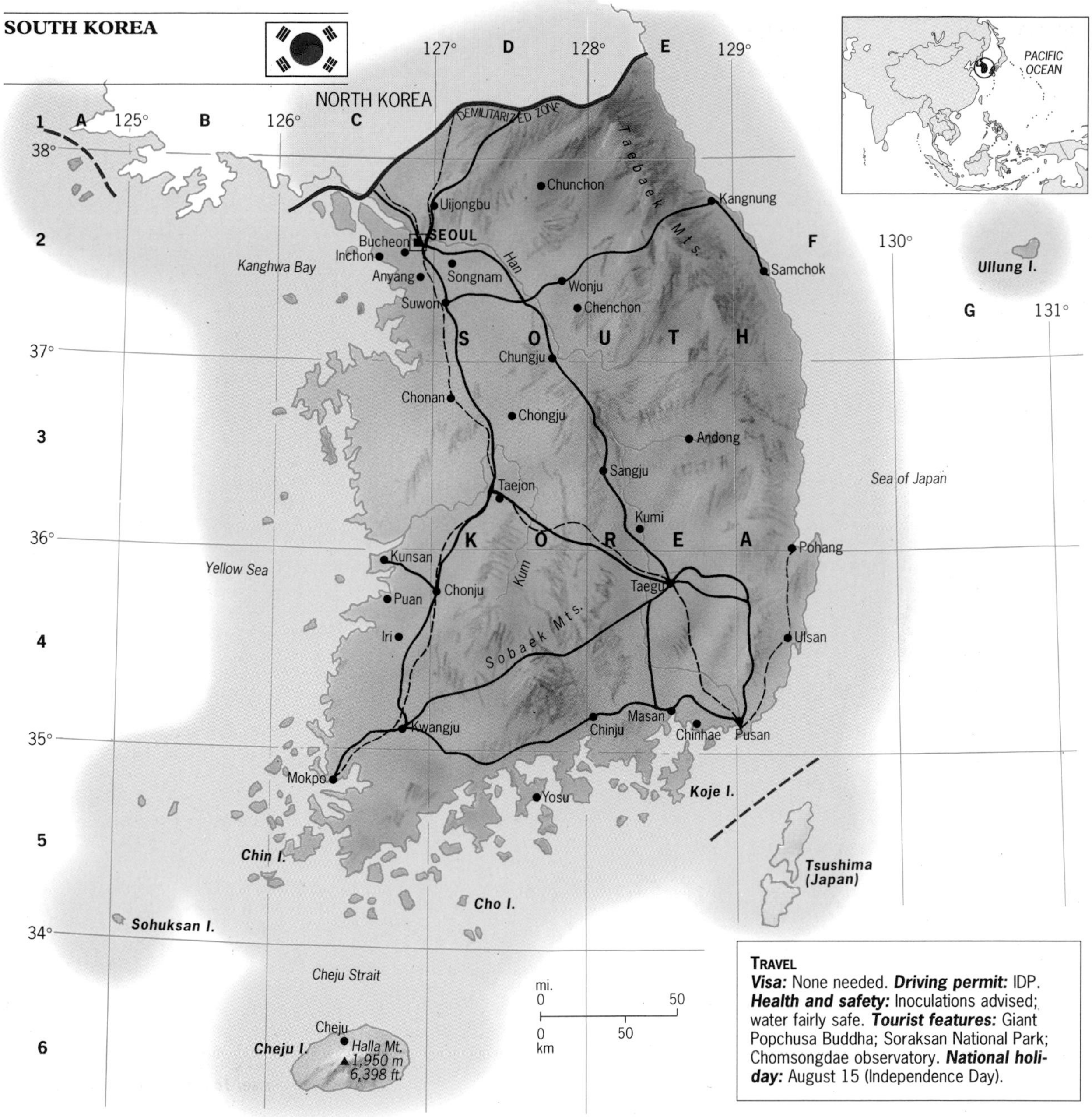

NORTH KOREA

DEMILITARIZED ZONE

Chunchon

Uijongbu

Bucheon **SEOUL**
Inchon
Anyang Songnam
Suwon

Wonju

Chenchon

Taebaek Mts.

Kangnung

Samchok

S O U T H

Chungju

Chonan

Chongju

Andong

Taejon

Sangju

Kumi

K O R E A

Kunsan

Chonju

Puan

Iri

Taegu

Pohang

Ulsan

Sobaek Mts.

Kwangju

Chinju Masan
Chinhae Pusan

Mokpo

Yosu

Koje I.

Chin I.

Cho I.

Sohuksan I.

Tsushima (Japan)

Cheju Strait

Cheju
Cheju I.
Halla Mt.
1,950 m
6,398 ft.

Kanghwa Bay

Yellow Sea

Sea of Japan

Ullung I.

PACIFIC OCEAN

Han

Kum

mi.
0 ———— 50
0 ———— 50
km

Area: 38,333 sq. mi./99,274 km².
Local name: Daehan Minguk.
Currency: Won. *Capital:* Seoul.
Other cities: Pusan, Taegu, Inchon.
Physical features: Mostly mountain-
ous. *Climate:* Tropical. *Time zone:*
GMT +9h. *Political system:*
Emergent democratic republic. *Head
of state:* Kim Young Sam (from
1992). *Head of government:* Lee
Yung Duk (from 1994). *Main
exports:* Textiles, electronics, trans-
portation equipment, steel, chemicals.
Resources: Coal, tungsten, graphite,
molybdenum, lead, hydropower.

PEOPLE
Population: 44,149,199. *Distribution*

urban/rural: 74%/26%. *Life expectancy:* 67(m), 73(f). *Language:* Korean.
Ethnic groups: Korean, small Chinese
minority. *Religions:* Buddhist about
30%, Christian about 25%, Shamanist,
Chondogyo, Confucian. *Literacy rate:*
96%. *Per capita GNP:* $6,300.

KEY DATES
1910 Korea is annexed by Japan.
1945 South Korea occupied by U.S.
forces.
1948 Republic of South Korea proclaimed with Syngman Rhee as leader.
1949 U.S. forces withdraw.
1950 North Korean forces invade.
1953 Armistice agreed with North Korea.
1960 Widespread antigovernment demonstrations; Rhee resigns.

1961 Government ousted in military coup
led by Gen. Park Chung Hee.
1963 Park elected president.
1972 Park assumes dictatorial powers.
1979 Park assassinated; Choi Kyu Hah
becomes president; hundreds die in violent antigovernment demonstrations.
1980 Military leaders led by Gen. Chun
Doo Hwan declare martial law; Choi
resigns and Chun becomes president.
1981 Martial law ends.
1983 Soviet fighter shoots down South
Korean passenger plane, killing 269; 17
South Koreans killed by North Korean
bomb in Burma.
1987 New, more democratic constitution.
1991 Joins UN; violent antigovernment
demonstrations; nonaggression pact
signed with North Korea.

JAPAN

Area: 145,840 sq. mi./377,727 km². *Local name:* Nippon. *Currency:* Yen. *Capital:* Tokyo. *Other cities:* Yokohama, Osaka, Nagoya, Sapporo, Kyoto, Kobe. *Physical features:* Mostly mountainous. *Climate:* Tropical in S., continental in N. *Time zone:* GMT +9h. *Political system:* Constitutional monarchy. *Head of state:* Emperor Akihito (from 1989). *Head of government:* Tomiichi Murayama (from 1994). *Main exports:* Machinery, motor vehicles, electrical goods, ships, iron, steel, chemicals, metals. *Resources:* Fish.

PEOPLE
Population: 124,460,481. *Distribution urban/rural:* 77%/23%. *Life expectancy:* 77(m), 82(f). *Language:* Japanese. *Ethnic groups:* Japanese 99%. *Religions:* Shinto, Buddhist (often combined), Christian; 30% profess a personal religious faith. *Literacy rate:* 99%. *Per capita GDP:* $19,000.

KEY DATES
1185 Yoritomo becomes the first shogun.

1549 Saint Francis Xavier brings Roman Catholicism to Japan.

1600s All missionaries ordered to leave Japan; most remaining Christians are persecuted or killed.

1630s Japan severs links with all other nations and forbids foreign travel.

1854 Treaty signed with U.S.A. establishing diplomatic and trade links.

1858 "Unequal treaties" signed with U.S.A., Britain, France, the Netherlands, and Russia.

1867 Shogun is forced to resign; imperial rule reestablished.

1868 Modernization program includes abolition of samurai in favor of a modern army and navy, large-scale public works agenda, and economic and social reforms.

1889 First constitution establishes two-house parliament, the Diet.

1890s Unequal treaties revised.

1894 War with China over Korea.

1895 Treaty of Shimonoseki: Japan gains control of Taiwan, and Korea is accorded independence, leaving it open to Japanese influence.

1902 Alliance formed with Britain.

1904 War breaks out with Russia.

1905 Peace treaty with Russia accords Japan the Liaodong Peninsula and recognizes Japanese supremacy in Korea.

1910 Japan formally annexes Korea.

1914 World War I: Japan fights on British side and gains much German territory in the Pacific.

1920 Joins the League of Nations.

1920s Rise of political parties.

1930s Worldwide depression hits Japan.

1931 Japanese forces occupy Manchuria.

1932 Prime Minister Tsuyoshi Inukai is assassinated by nationalists.

1933 Japan withdraws from League of Nations over Manchuria.

1936 Three leading government members killed during nationalist army revolt; military leaders establish influence.

1937–38 Further territory gained in war with China.

1940 Japan occupies N. Indochina; accord with Germany and Italy.

1941 Japanese forces enter S. Indochina; U.S.A. imposes economic sanctions; Gen. Hideki Tojo becomes prime minister; Japan bombs U.S. military bases at Pearl Harbor, Guam, Wake Island, and the Philippines.

1942 Battle of the Coral Sea.

1944 Tojo resigns after U.S. attack on Saipan military base.

1945 U.S. submarines block vital supplies to Japan; U.S.A. drops atomic bombs on Hiroshima and Nagasaki; U.S.S.R. declares war on Japan; Japan surrenders, having lost all territory on the Asian mainland and all Pacific island territories; Allied forces occupy Japan; seven leaders executed and 18 others imprisoned for war crimes; Emperor Hirohito renounces claims to divinity.

1946 Allied officials draft new constitution establishing constitutional monarchy; army and navy abolished.

1951 Peace treaty signed with 48 nations in San Francisco; security treaty signed with U.S.A. providing for U.S. military bases in Japan.

1952 Allied forces leave Japan.

1955 Foundation of Liberal Democratic Party (LDP).

1956 Japan joins the UN.

1960 Treaty of Mutual Cooperation and Security with the U.S.A. replaces 1951 accord; prompts anti-U.S.A. riots.

1968 U.S.A. returns Bonin and Volcano islands to Japan.

1972 Ryukyu Islands regained.

1974 Prime minister resigns; economic crisis caused by Arab oil embargo.

1981 Japan agrees to limit car exports to U.S.A., Canada, and West Germany removes some restrictions on imports.

1988 Many LDP leaders implicated in Recruit Company scandal.

1989 Emperor Hirohito dies and is succeeded by his son, Akihito; Prime Minister Takeshita resigns over Recruit scandal and is succeeded by Sosuke Uno; Uno resigns after sex scandal and is succeeded by Toshiki Kaifu.

1991 Küchi Miyazawa replaces Kaifu as prime minister.

1992 More than 200 politicians implicated in Tokyo Sagawa Kyubin Company scandal; Emperor Akihito makes first imperial visit to China.

1995 More than 5,000 people killed in earthquake centered in Kobe area; 12 die and over 5,000 are injured when nerve gas is released in Tokyo subway stations by religious group.

ECONOMY

World War II shattered Japan's economy, but since then it has emerged as one of the greatest economic powers in the world. Japan now has the world's second-largest GDP after the U.S.A.

Industry by sector
Farming Farming accounts for about 3% of the GDP and employs around 9% of the workforce. There is a shortage of cultivable land, but farmers still manage to meet most of the nation's food requirements. This is made possible by the use of irrigation, high-yield varieties, and modern agricultural chemicals and machinery. More than half the farmland is used to grow rice; Japan is a leading rice-producing country. Other important crops include apples, mandarin oranges, pears, eggplant, cabbage, and sweet potatoes. In recent years production of meat and dairy produce has increased in response to increased demand.

Fishing Japan has the world's largest fishing industry with more than 400,000 vessels. Although it employs only 1% of workers, 12 million tons of fish are caught each year. Japan is the world's leading producer of tuna and ranks second to the U.S.A. in the amount of salmon caught. Other products include eels, flatfish, mackerel, sardines, octopus, and shellfish. For many years Japan was a leading whaling nation, but in 1988 it joined an international moratorium on all commercial whaling. Despite a very large catch, Japan has been the world's largest importer of fish since 1978.

Mining Japan has only a small quantity of minerals and depends heavily on imports. It is the world's largest importer of coal, natural gas, and oil, and is only able to meet 20% of its own energy requirements.

Manufacturing Manufacturing is the single most important economic activity in Japan, accounting for around 28% of the GDP and employing about 24% of the workforce. Japan's industrial growth rate is among the highest in the world, and in the 1970s industrial output more than tripled. Japanese factories use the most advanced equipment and processes available, and manufacturers are constantly investing in new technology to maximize production. The most important industry is the production of transportation equipment; Japan produces about eight million cars annually, making it the world's largest car manufacturer. It is the world's most important shipbuilding country. Japan is also a leading producer of iron, steel, and chemicals. One of the fastest-growing industries is the production of machinery, including heavy machines, electrical appliances, and electronic equipment.

Services Service industries account for about 60% of the GDP and employ around 55% of workers.

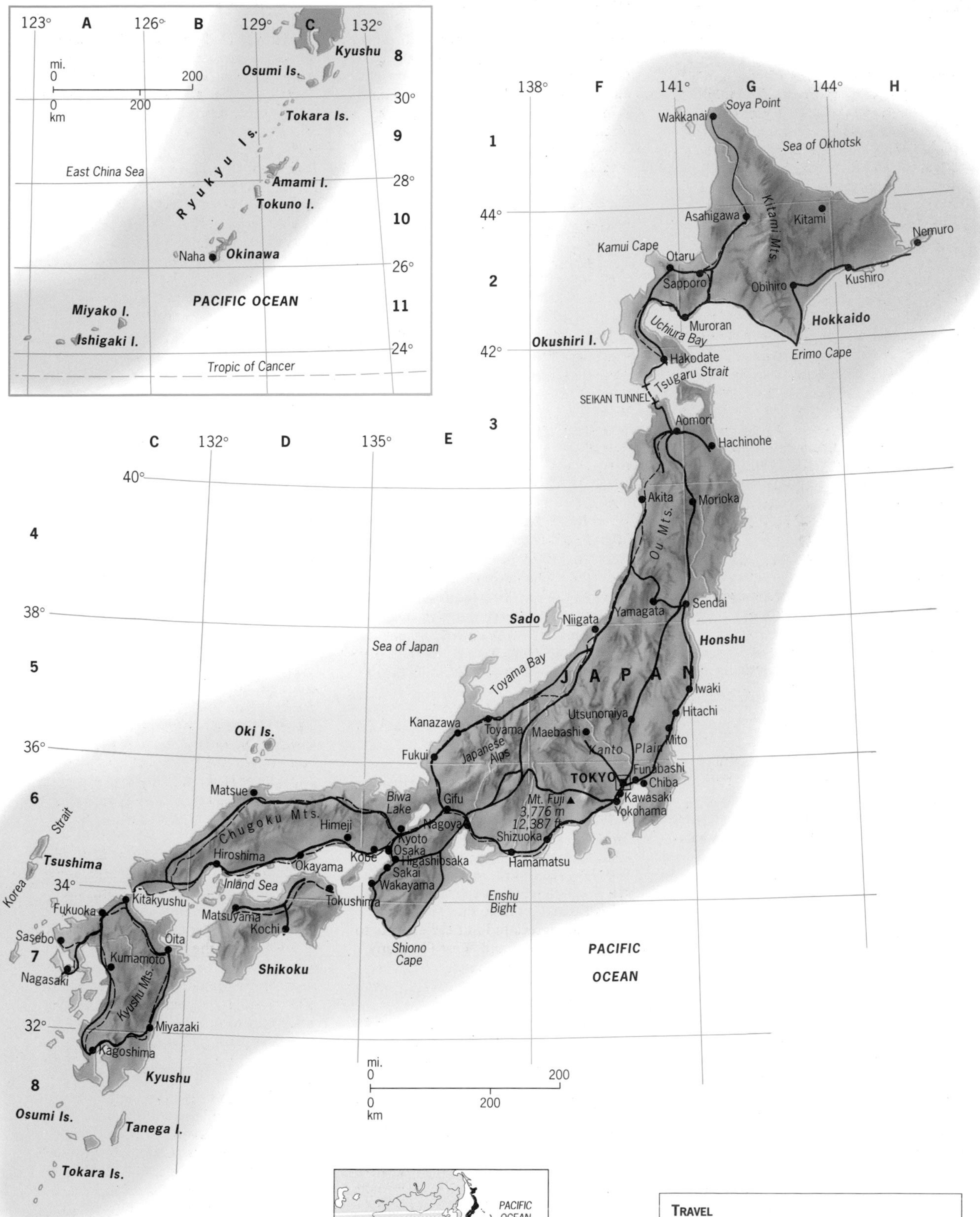

Inset map (Ryukyu Islands)

123° **A** 126° **B** 129° **C** 132°

Kyushu 8

mi.
0   200

0   200
km

Osumi Is.

30° **9**

Tokara Is.

East China Sea

28° **Amami I.**

Tokuno I. 28°

R y u k y u   I s.

10

Naha • **Okinawa** 26°

PACIFIC OCEAN 11

Miyako I.

Ishigaki I. 24°

Tropic of Cancer

Main map

138° **F** 141° **G** 144° **H**

Soya Point
Wakkanai

Sea of Okhotsk

1

44°
Asahigawa • Kitami
Kamui Cape
Otaru
Sapporo • Obihiro • Kushiro
Muroran **Hokkaido**

Okushiri I. 42° Uchiura Bay
Hakodate • Erimo Cape
2

SEIKAN TUNNEL Tsugaru Strait
Aomori
Hachinohe
3

40°

4

Akita • Morioka

Ou Mts.

38° **Sado** Niigata Yamagata • Sendai

Sea of Japan **Honshu**

5 Toyama Bay
J A P A N Iwaki
Kanazawa Hitachi
Utsunomiya
Toyama Maebashi Mito
36° Fukui Japanese Kanto Plain
Oki Is. Alps TOKYO Funabashi
Matsue Biwa Gifu Chiba
Lake Nagoya Mt. Fuji ▲ Kawasaki
6 Chugoku Mts. Himeji Kyoto 3,776 m Yokohama
Hiroshima Kobe Osaka 12,387 ft
Okayama Higashiosaka Shizuoka
Inland Sea Sakai Hamamatsu
Kitakyushu Wakayama
34° Matsuyama Tokushima Enshu
Fukuoka Kochi Bight
Tsushima
Sasebo Oita **Shikoku**
7 Kumamoto Shiono
Nagasaki Cape **PACIFIC**
Kyushu Mts.
32° Miyazaki **OCEAN**
Kagoshima
8 **Kyushu**

Osumi Is.

Tanega I.

Tokara Is.

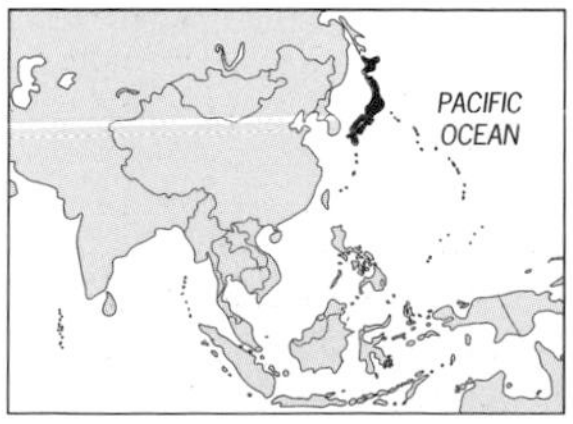

mi.
0   200

0   200
km

Legend/Travel box

TRAVEL
Visa: None needed. *Driving permit:* IDP.
Health and safety: Inoculations advised.
Tourist features: The Great Buddha at
Kamakura; Japanese Alps; Mount Fuji and
Mount Aso. *National holiday:* December 23
(Birthday of the Emperor).

PACIFIC
OCEAN

TAIWAN

Area: 13,970 sq. mi./36,179 km². **Local name:** Chung-hua Min-kuo (Republic of China). **Currency:** New Taiwan dollar. **Capital:** Taipei. **Other cities:** Kaohsiung, Taichung, Tainan. **Physical features:** Mostly mountainous with flat to rolling plains in W. **Climate:** Subtropical in N., tropical in S. **Time zone:** GMT +8h. **Political system:** Emergent democratic republic. **Head of state:** Lee Teng-hui (from 1988). **Head of government:** Lien Chan (from 1993). **Main exports:** Electronics, textiles, machinery, metals and metal products, plastics, vehicles, aircraft. **Resources:** Crude oil, natural gas, coal, limestone, marble, asbestos.

PEOPLE
Population: 20,800,000. **Distribution urban/rural:** 72%/28%. **Life expectancy:** 72(m), 78(f). **Languages:** Mandarin Chinese (official), Taiwanese and Hakka dialects. **Ethnic groups:** Taiwanese 85%, Chinese 14%, other 1%. **Religions:** Mixture of Buddhism, Confucianism, and Taoism 93%, Christian 5%, other 2%. **Literacy rate:** 91%. **Per capita GNP:** $7,380.

KEY DATES
1624 Dutch establish settlement on S.E. coast and name island Formosa.
1683 Becomes part of Chinese empire.
1895 Ceded to Japan; Chinese inhabitants rebel against Japanese rule.
1945 Taiwan is returned to China after Japan's defeat in World War II.
1947 Uprising against Chinese rule.
1949 Communists take control of China; Nationalists (Kuomintang) set up alternative government in Taiwan led by Chiang Kai-shek.
1950 U.S.A. pledges to protect Taiwan from Communist China.
1954 Mutual defense treaty with U.S.A.

1960s Many foreign nations withdraw diplomatic recognition of Taiwan in favor of the People's Republic of China.
1971 U.S.A. backs People's Republic of China's admission to UN; Taiwan is expelled from UN on admission of Communist China.
1972 U.S. military forces withdraw from Taiwan; legislative election.
1975 Chiang Kai-shek dies and is succeeded by his son, Chiang Ching-kuo.
1979 U.S.A. severs diplomatic relations and annuls 1954 security pact, though unofficial relations are continued through nongovernmental agencies.
1986 Foundation of opposition Democratic Progressive Party (DPP).
1987 Martial law is ended after nearly 40 years; press restrictions are lifted;

opposition parties legalized.
1988 Chiang Ching-kuo dies; Lee Teng-hui becomes president.
1991 President Lee Teng-hui declares end to state of civil war with China; Nationalist Party wins majority in first multiparty assembly elections.
1992 Diplomatic relations with South Korea severed.

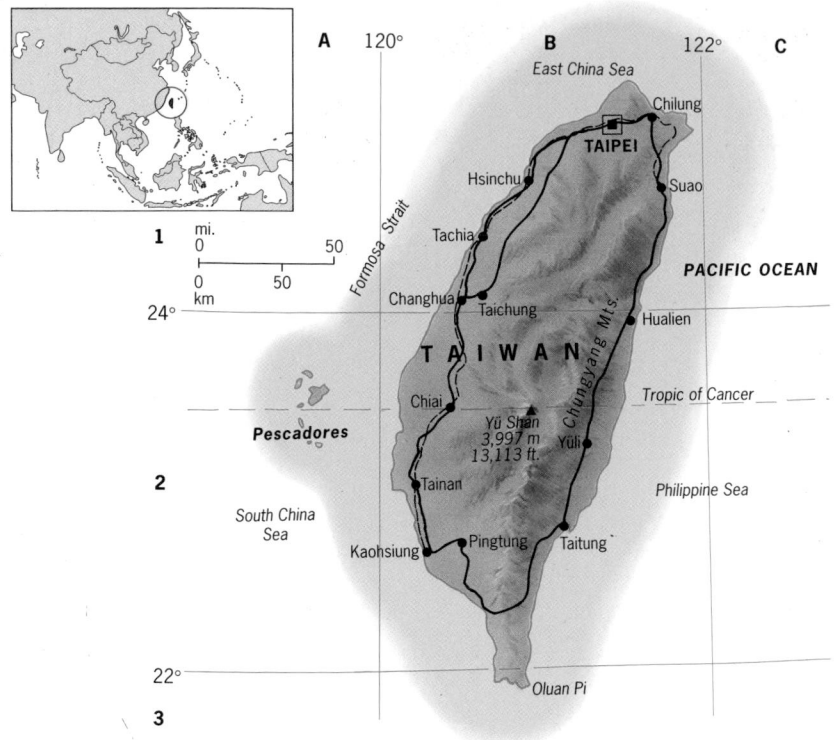

> **TRAVEL**
> **Visa:** Required by U.S. **Driving permit:** Nat. license. **Health and safety:** Inoculations advised; water unsafe. **Tourist features:** Taipei art museum; Mount Morrison. **National holiday:** October 10 (National Day).

HONG KONG

Area: 403 sq. mi./1,045 km². **Local name:** Hong Kong. **Currency:** Hong Kong dollar. **Capital:** Central district, Hong Kong Island. **Physical features:** Hilly to mountainous; lowlands in N. **Climate:** Tropical monsoon. **Time zone:** GMT +8h. **Political system:** Dependent territory of U.K. (due to return to China in 1997). **Head of state:** Queen Elizabeth II (from 1952). **Head of government:** Gov. designate Chris Patten (from 1992). **Main exports:** Clothing, textiles, electrical appliances. **Resources:** Bauxite, coal, natural gas.

PEOPLE
Population: 5,889,095. **Distribution urban/rural:** 100% urban. **Life expectancy:** 76(m), 83(f). **Languages:** Cantonese, English. **Ethnic groups:** Chinese 98%. **Religions:** Indigenous beliefs 90%, Christian 10%. **Literacy rate:** 77%. **Per capita GDP:** $13,800.

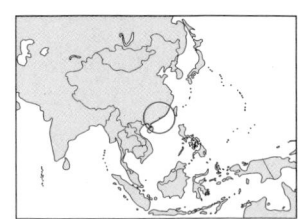

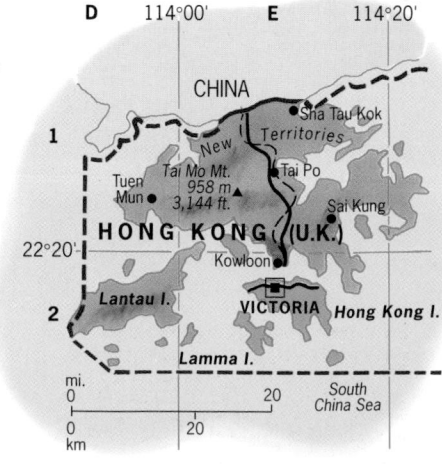

PHILIPPINES

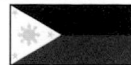

Area: 115,830 sq. mi./300,000 km². ***Local name:*** Republika ng Pilipinas. ***Currency:*** Philippine peso. ***Capital:*** Manila. ***Other cities:*** Quezon City. ***Physical features:*** Mostly mountainous with low coastal plains. ***Climate:*** Tropical. ***Time zone:*** GMT +8h. ***Political system:*** Republic. ***Head of state and government:*** Fidel Ramos (from 1992). ***Main exports:*** Copra and coconut oil, electrical equipment, textiles, furniture. ***Resources:*** Wood, crude oil, nickel, cobalt, silver, gold, copper.

People

Population: 65,649,000. ***Distribution urban/rural:*** 41%/59%. ***Life expectancy:*** 62(m), 68(f). ***Languages:*** Filipino, English (both official), other languages. ***Ethnic groups:*** Malay 96%, Chinese 2%, other 2%. ***Religions:*** Roman Catholic 83%, Protestant 9%, Muslim 5%, Buddhist and other 3%. ***Literacy rate:*** 90%. ***Per capita GNP:*** $720.

Key dates

1565 Comes under Spanish rule.
1898 Ceded to U.S.A. in Treaty of Paris.
1942–45 Occupied by Japan.
1946 Independence achieved.
1965 Ferdinand Marcos president.
1972 Martial law declared in response to widespread guerrilla activity.
1981 Martial law lifted.
1986 Marcos overthrown by People's Power movement.
1987 Attempted right-wing coup fails.
1989 Marcos dies in exile; coup attempt suppressed with U.S. aid; state of emergency imposed.
1991 Hundreds die when Mount Pinatubo erupts.
1992 Fidel Ramos becomes president.

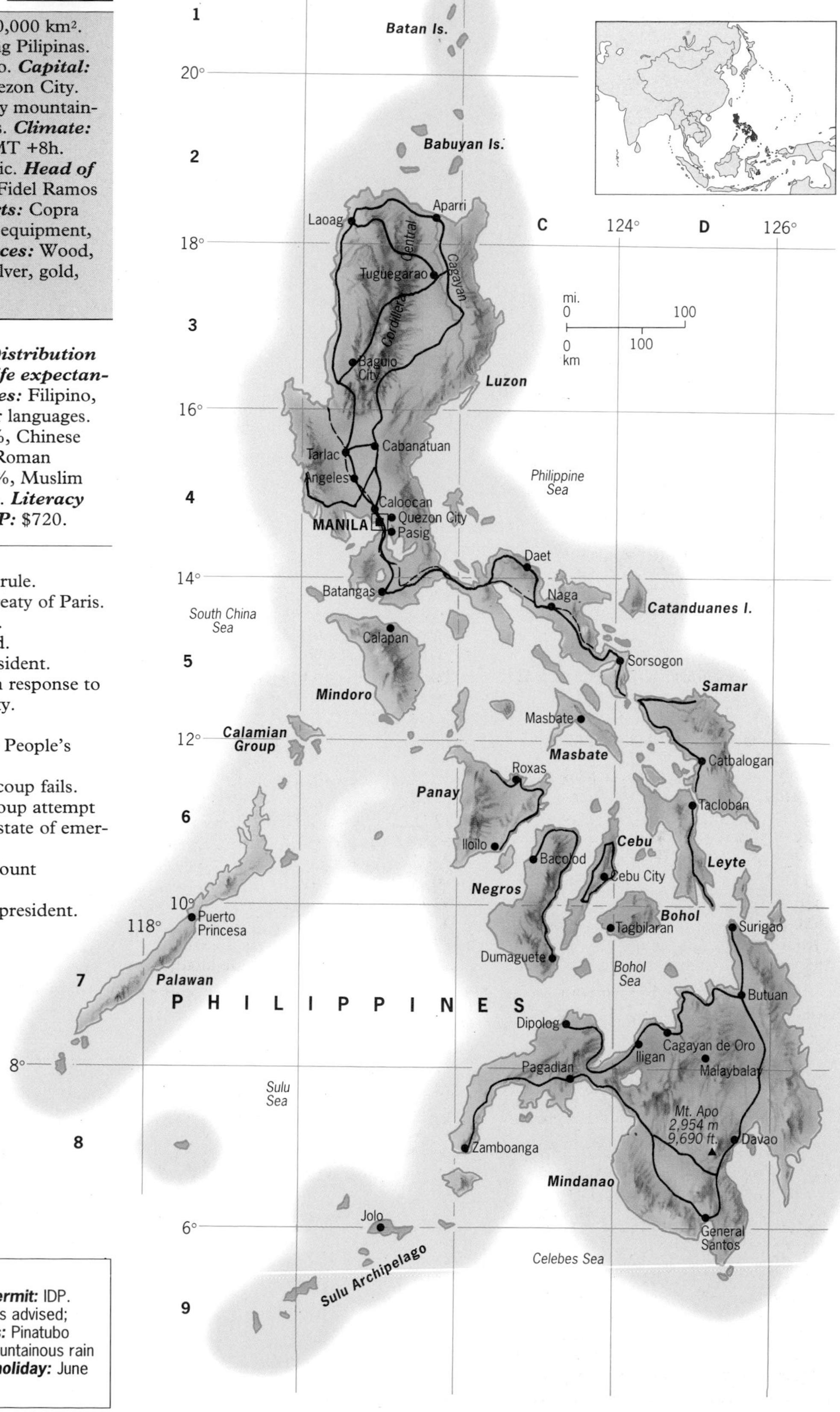
A
120°
B
122°
C
124°
D
126°
1
2
3
4
5
6
7
8
9
20°
18°
16°
14°
12°
10°
8°
6°
118°
Batan Is.
Babuyan Is.
Aparri
Laoag
Central
Cordillera
Cagayan
Tuguegarao
Baguio City
Luzon
Tarlac
Cabanatuan
Angeles
Caloocan
MANILA
Quezon City
Pasig
Philippine Sea
Daet
Batangas
Naga
Catanduanes I.
South China Sea
Calapan
Sorsogon
Mindoro
Samar
Masbate
Masbate
Calamian Group
Catbalogan
Roxas
Panay
Tacloban
Iloilo
Bacolod
Cebu
Cebu City
Leyte
Negros
Bohol
Puerto Princesa
Tagbilaran
Surigao
Dumaguete
Bohol Sea
Palawan
Butuan
P H I L I P P I N E S
Dipolog
Iligan
Cagayan de Oro
Malaybalay
Pagadian
Sulu Sea
Mt. Apo 2,954 m 9,690 ft.
Davao
Zamboanga
Mindanao
Jolo
General Santos
Celebes Sea
Sulu Archipelago
mi.
0
100
0
100
km

Travel

Visa: None needed. ***Driving permit:*** IDP. ***Health and safety:*** Inoculations advised; water unsafe. ***Tourist features:*** Pinatubo Volcano; active volcano and mountainous rain forest on Mindanao. ***National holiday:*** June 12 (Independence Day).

MALAYSIA

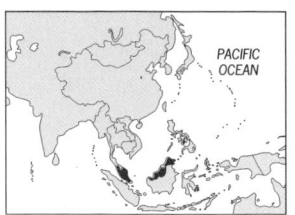

PACIFIC OCEAN

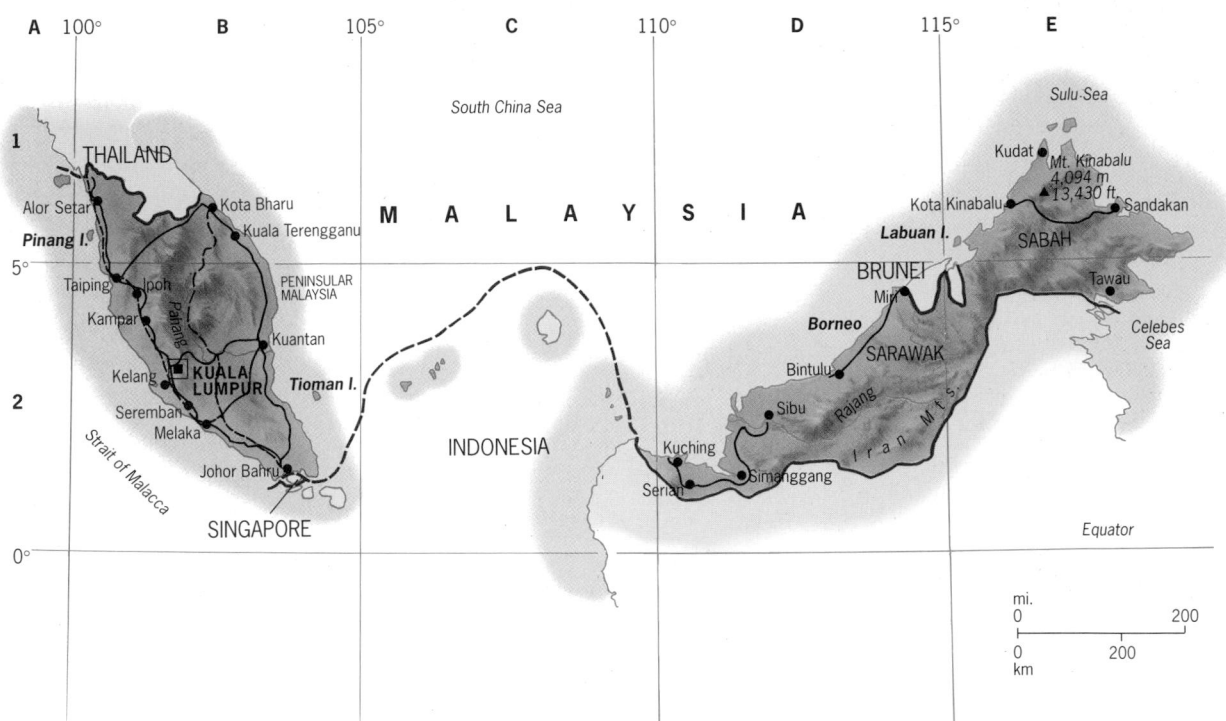

Area: 127,250 sq. mi./329,578 km². **Local name:** Persekutuan Tanah Melaysiu. **Currency:** Malaysian dollar (ringgit). **Capital:** Kuala Lumpur. **Other cities:** Ipoh. **Physical features:** Coastal plains rise to mountainous interior; 75% tropical jungle. **Climate:** Tropical monsoon. **Time zone:** GMT +8h. **Political system:** Constitutional monarchy. **Head of state:** Paramount Ruler Sultan Jaafar bin Abdul Rahman (from 1994). **Head of government:** Datuk Seri Mahathir bin Mohamad (from 1981). **Main exports:** Electrical goods, pineapples, palm oil, rubber, wood, crude petroleum, bauxite. **Resources:** Tin, petroleum, wood, copper, iron ore, bauxite.

PEOPLE
Population: 19,239,000. **Distribution urban/rural:** 38%/62%. **Life expectancy:** 66(m), 71(f). **Languages:** Bahasa Malaysian (official), English, Tamil, Mandarin and Hakka dialects, local dialects. **Ethnic groups:** Malay 59%, Chinese 32%, Indian 9%. **Religions:** Muslim, Christian, Hindu, Confucian, Buddhist, indigenous beliefs. **Literacy rate:** 78%. **Per capita GDP:** $2,670.

KEY DATES
1786 Britain gains control of Malaya.
1800s Many Chinese and Indians arrive in Malaya to work in tin mines.
1867 Becomes a British crown colony.
1930 Foundation of Malayan Communist Party (MCP).
1941–45 Japanese occupation.
1945 Communist terrorist campaign against Japanese.
1945–46 Widespread violence between Malays and Chinese.
1946 Pan-Malayan Congress meets in Kuala Lumpur to oppose proposed Malayan Union; Malayan Union comes into being.
1948 Federation of Malaya Agreement; Communists launch guerrilla offensive; state of emergency imposed.
1952 Alliance Party formed.
1957 Independence achieved.
1960 State of emergency ended.
1961 Joins Association of Southeast Asia (ASA) with Philippines and Thailand.
1963 Sarawak, Sabah, and Singapore unite with Malaya to form Malaysia.
1965 Singapore secedes.
1967 Formation of Association of Southeast Asian Nations (ASEAN) including the Philippines, Thailand, and Indonesia.
1969 Race riots in Kuala Lumpur.
1971 Malaysia supports Communist China's admission to UN.
1972 First ASEAN conference held in Kuala Lumpur.
1973 Diplomatic relations established with North Vietnam, North Korea, and East Germany.
1974 Prime Minister Tun Abdul Razak visits China; Alliance Party joins other political parties to form the Barisan National (National Front).
1987 More than 100 political activists arrested as relations between Malaysia and China worsen.
1991 Economic development program is launched.

SINGAPORE

Area: 248 sq. mi./641 km². ***Local name:*** Hsing-chia p'o Kung-ho Kuo/Republik Singapura/Republic of Singapore. ***Currency:*** Singapore dollar. ***Capital:*** Singapore City. ***Other cities:*** Jurong, Changi. ***Physical features:*** Low and flat rising to gently undulating central plateau; includes 57 small islands. ***Climate:*** Tropical. ***Time zone:*** GMT +8h. ***Political system:*** Republic. ***Head of state:*** Ong Teng Cheong (from 1993). ***Head of government:*** Goh Chok Tong (from 1990). ***Main exports:*** Petroleum products, rubber, electrical goods, machinery. ***Resources:*** Fish.

PEOPLE

Population: 2,874,000. ***Distribution urban/rural:*** 100% urban. ***Life expectancy:*** 73(m), 78(f). ***Languages:*** Chinese, Malay, Tamil, English (all official); Malay (national). ***Ethnic groups:*** Chinese 76%, Malay 15%, Indian 6%, other 3%. ***Religions:*** Buddhist and traditional Chinese beliefs 54%, Muslim 15%, Christian 13%, Hindu 4%, Taoist. ***Literacy rate:*** 88%. ***Per capita GDP:*** $13,900.

KEY DATES

1824 Comes under British control.
1800s Many Chinese and Indian immi-

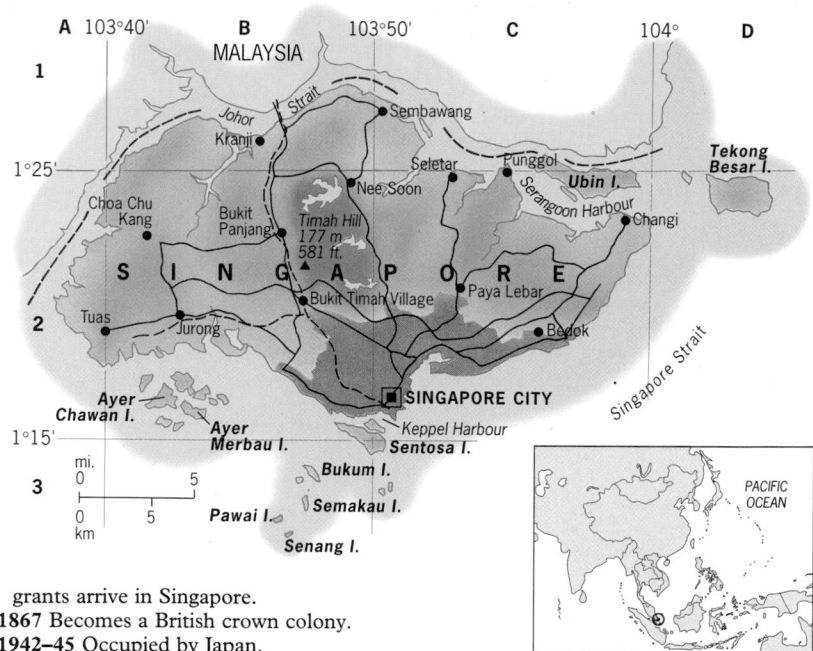

grants arrive in Singapore.
1867 Becomes a British crown colony.
1942–45 Occupied by Japan.
1959 Independence achieved. Lee Kuan Yew becomes prime minister.
1963 Becomes a part of Malaysia.
1964 Riots between Chinese and Malays.
1965 Singapore secedes from Malaysia.
1986 Opposition leader convicted of perjury and barred from election.
1990 Lee Kuan Yew resigns and is replaced by Goh Chok Tong.

TRAVEL
Visa: None needed. ***Driving permit:*** IDP.
Health and safety: Inoculations advised; water safe. ***Tourist features:*** Bukit Timah Nature Reserve; Chettia Temple. ***National holiday:*** August 9 (National Day).

BRUNEI

Area: 2,226 sq. mi./5,765 km². ***Local name:*** Negara Brunei Darussalam. ***Currency:*** Brunei dollar (ringgit). ***Capital:*** Bandar Seri Begawan. ***Physical features:*** Flat coastal plain with mountains in E. ***Climate:*** Tropical. ***Time zone:*** GMT +8h. ***Political system:*** Absolute monarchy. ***Head of state and government:*** Sultan Sir Muda Hassanal Bolkiah Mu'izzadin Waddaulah (from 1967). ***Main exports:*** Natural gas, crude oil, petroleum products. ***Resources:*** Crude oil, natural gas.

PEOPLE

Population: 276,000. ***Distribution urban/rural:*** n.a. ***Life expectancy:*** 69(m), 73(f). ***Languages:*** Malay (official), English, Chinese. ***Ethnic groups:*** Malay 64%, Chinese 20%, other 16%. ***Religions:*** Muslim 63%, Buddhist 14%, Christian 8%, other 15%. ***Literacy rate:*** 77%. ***Per capita GDP:*** $8,800.

KEY DATES

1888 Becomes a British protectorate.
1929 Oil discovered.
1941–45 Japanese occupation.

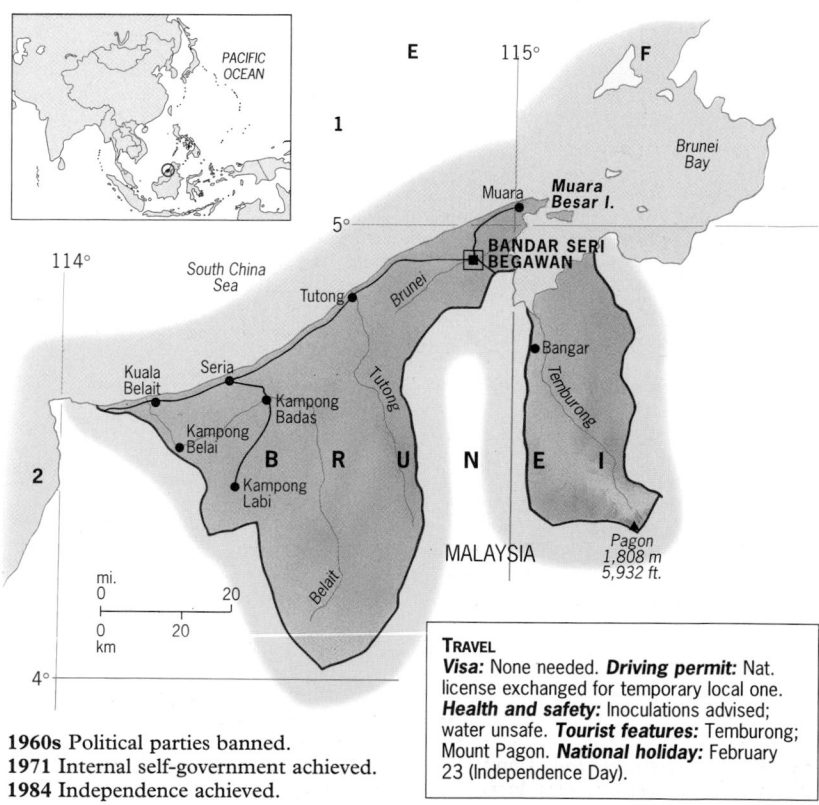

1960s Political parties banned.
1971 Internal self-government achieved.
1984 Independence achieved.

TRAVEL
Visa: None needed. ***Driving permit:*** Nat. license exchanged for temporary local one.
Health and safety: Inoculations advised; water unsafe. ***Tourist features:*** Temburong; Mount Pagon. ***National holiday:*** February 23 (Independence Day).

INDONESIA

Area: 741,097 sq. mi./1,919,443 km². *Local name:* Republik Indonesia. *Currency:* Rupiah. *Capital:* Jakarta. *Other large cities:* Surabaya, Medan, Bandung. *Physical features:* Mostly coastal lowlands. *Climate:* Tropical. *Time zone:* GMT +7h (W), +9h (E). *Political system:* Republic. *Head of state and government:* Gen. T. N. J. Suharto (from 1967). *Main exports:* Petroleum and liquefied natural gas, rubber, wood, coffee, textiles, palm oil. *Resources:* Petroleum, natural gas, tin, nickel, wood, bauxite, copper.

PEOPLE

Population: 189,136,000. *Distribution urban/rural:* 30%/70%. *Life expectancy:* 59(m), 64(f). *Languages:* Bahasa Indonesian (allied to Malay), local dialects including Javanese. *Ethnic groups:* Javanese 45%, Sundanese 14%, Madurese 8%, Malay 8%, other 25%. *Religions:* Muslim 87%, Protestant 6%, Roman Catholic 3%, Hindu 2%, Buddhist and other 2%. *Literacy rate:* 77%. *Per capita GDP:* $630.

KEY DATES

1600s Dutch East India Company begins to control parts of the East Indies.

1799 Dutch government takes control of land administered by Dutch East India Company.

1811–16 British troops occupy Dutch East Indies during Napoleonic wars in Europe.

1824 Treaty between Britain and the Netherlands divides the islands of the East Indies along the Strait of Malacca: Dutch retain control of the Sumatran side (now Indonesia).

1900–30 The 300 states of the East Indies are united as Indonesia under the rule of the Governor General in Batavia (now Jakarta).

1927 Foundation of Indonesian Nationalist Party (PNI) led by Achmed Sukarno.

1942–45 Occupied by Japan.

1945 Independence declared but not recognized by the Netherlands; Achmed Sukarno becomes president.

1949 Indonesian independence recognized by the Netherlands; Dutch retain control of West New Guinea.

1950 First constitution; joins UN.

1956–58 Army deployed in outer islands to put down violent protests against central rule.

1959 Sukarno increases his own power by replacing liberal democracy with "guided democracy."

1963 West New Guinea (now Irian Jaya) ceded by the Netherlands.

1964 Indonesian attempts to invade Malaysia are thwarted by British troops.

1965 Attempted Communist coup is put down by Lt.-Gen. T. N. J. Suharto; hundreds of thousands of people are killed; Communist Party outlawed; Indonesia withdraws from UN as a protest against Malaysia's election to the UN Security Council.

1966 Sukarno delegates emergency powers to Suharto to restore order; Indonesia rejoins UN after agreeing to end confrontations with Malaysia.

1967 Sukarno steps down as president in favor of Suharto; Indonesia joins the Association of Southeast Asian Nations (ASEAN).

1971 Suharto retains power in first parliamentary elections since 1955.

1975 Economic crisis; Indonesia invades East Timor; South Moluccan separatist guerrillas hijack train and besiege Indonesian consulate in Netherlands.

1978 Widespread student demonstrations against Suharto regime; government increases control over the media.

1983 Around 10,000 people killed during government crackdown on crime; UN resolution affirms East Timor's right to independence and demands the withdrawal of Indonesian troops.

1989 Army attacks Muslim separatists in Sumatra, killing 100; economic crisis: foreign creditors offer aid if concessions are made to foreign companies and austerity measures are introduced.

1990 Government media censorship relaxed; independence movements continue activity in Irian Jaya, Sumatra, and East Timor; Indonesian politicians call for a limit on presidential powers; economy benefits from inflated oil and gas prices due to Middle East crisis.

1991 Separatist rebellion in Sumatra crushed by the army; EC charges Indonesia with human rights violations in East Timor; troops open fire on mourners at the funeral of a youth in Dili, East Timor, killing hundreds.

1992 Earthquake and tidal waves kill at least 2,500 and leave millions homeless.

1993 Suharto reelected president, having been nominated (unopposed); government approves formation of an independent national human rights commission; some political prisoners freed.

TRAVEL
Visa: None needed. *Driving permit:* IDP. *Health and safety:* Inoculations advised; water unsafe. *Tourist features:* Kraton; Sam Po Kong Temple; Sunda Kelapa. *National holiday:* August 17 (Independence Day).

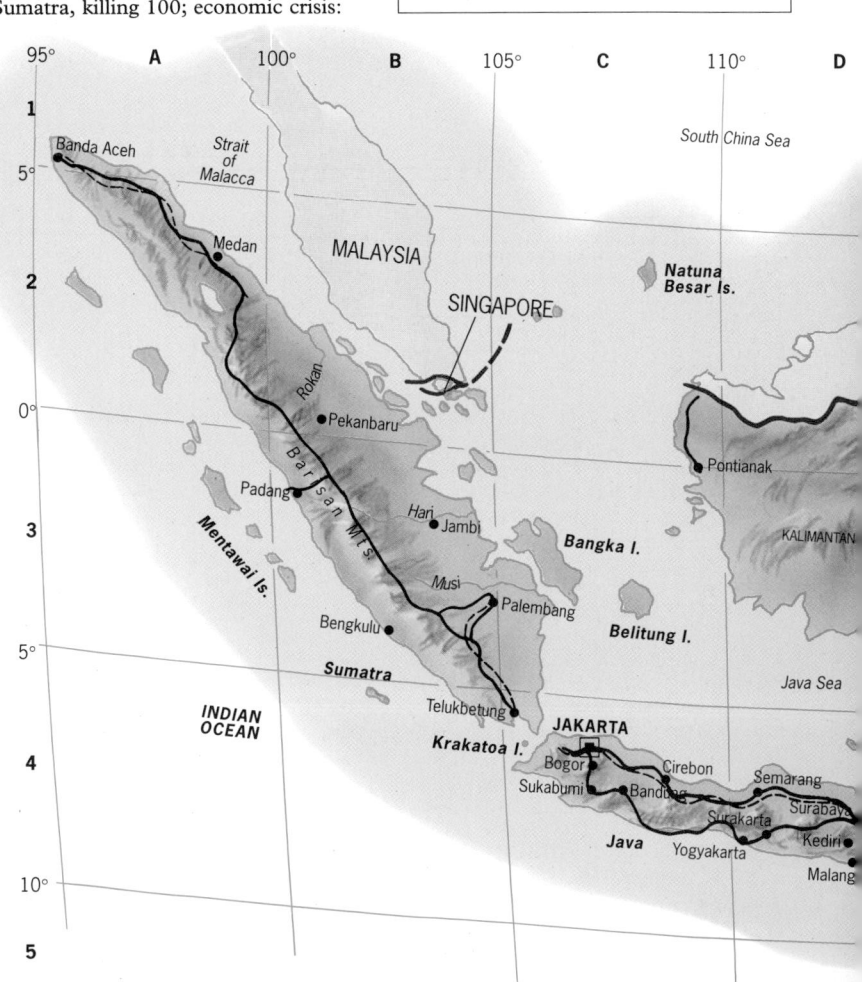

EAST TIMOR

East Timor is part of the Lesser Sunda archipelago to the east of Java. After declaring its independence from Portugal in 1975, the island of East Timor was invaded by Indonesia. The ensuing conflict was particularly brutal. Although Indonesian control of East Timor was not recognized internationally, no action (including sanctions) was taken against it. After the collapse of communism, Western countries were freed from the diplomatic constraints that had made them reluctant to speak out against the actions of the Indonesian government. Three UN resolutions passed since 1992 condemned the actions of Indonesia in East Timor. In spite of this, however, reports of human rights violations continue, and the issue of East Timor remains unresolved.

KEY DATES

1500s First Portuguese settlements established.

1859 First Dutch–Portuguese agreement to establish boundaries between holdings (further agreements signed in 1893, 1898, and 1914); Timor is divided into east and west to be controlled by the Portuguese and Dutch.

1950 Dutch (West) Timor becomes part of the Republic of Indonesia.

1974 FRETLIN (Revolutionary Front of Independent East Timor) founded.

1975 Aug.–Nov.: FRETLIN becomes de facto government and declares East Timor independent; Dec.: East Timor invaded by Indonesia.

1976 Indonesia claims East Timor as a territory, although the UN does not recognize this; guerrilla warfare begins; at least 15% of the population of East Timor is killed in the first five years of the invasion; the Indonesian army uses particularly brutal torture methods.

1979 An Australian journalist publishes first photos of starvation and malnutrition among the people of East Timor.

1988 Partial easing of travel restrictions to East Timor by Indonesian government.

1989 Pope John Paul II visits East Timor and is met by pro-independence demonstrations by students.

1991 Army shoots between 70 and 100 mourners at the funeral of a youth killed by the security forces in Dili, East Timor's capital; subsequently 60 witnesses to the event are assassinated; Indonesia becomes a member of the UN Commission on Human Rights, but little real change is observed in the government's attitude toward the people of East Timor.

1992 In response to international outrage, Indonesia publicly punishes a number of the local army officers responsible for the massacre in Dili; Xanana Gusmao, leader of the resistance movement, is captured by Indonesian army; Indonesia and Portugal resume talks via the UN about the future of East Timor.

1993 U.S. government refuses to allow Jordan to sell U.S.-built fighter planes to Indonesia because of the situation in East Timor; Indonesia claims East Timor wanted to be part of Indonesia to achieve independence from the Portuguese; Indonesian government establishes a National Human Rights Commission, but its powers are limited and the situation is not resolved.

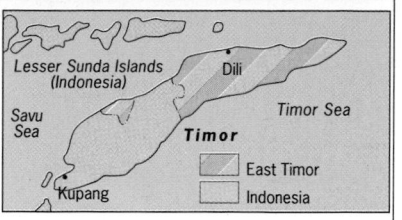

Lesser Sunda Islands (Indonesia) · Dili · Savu Sea · Timor Sea · **Timor** · Kupang · East Timor · Indonesia

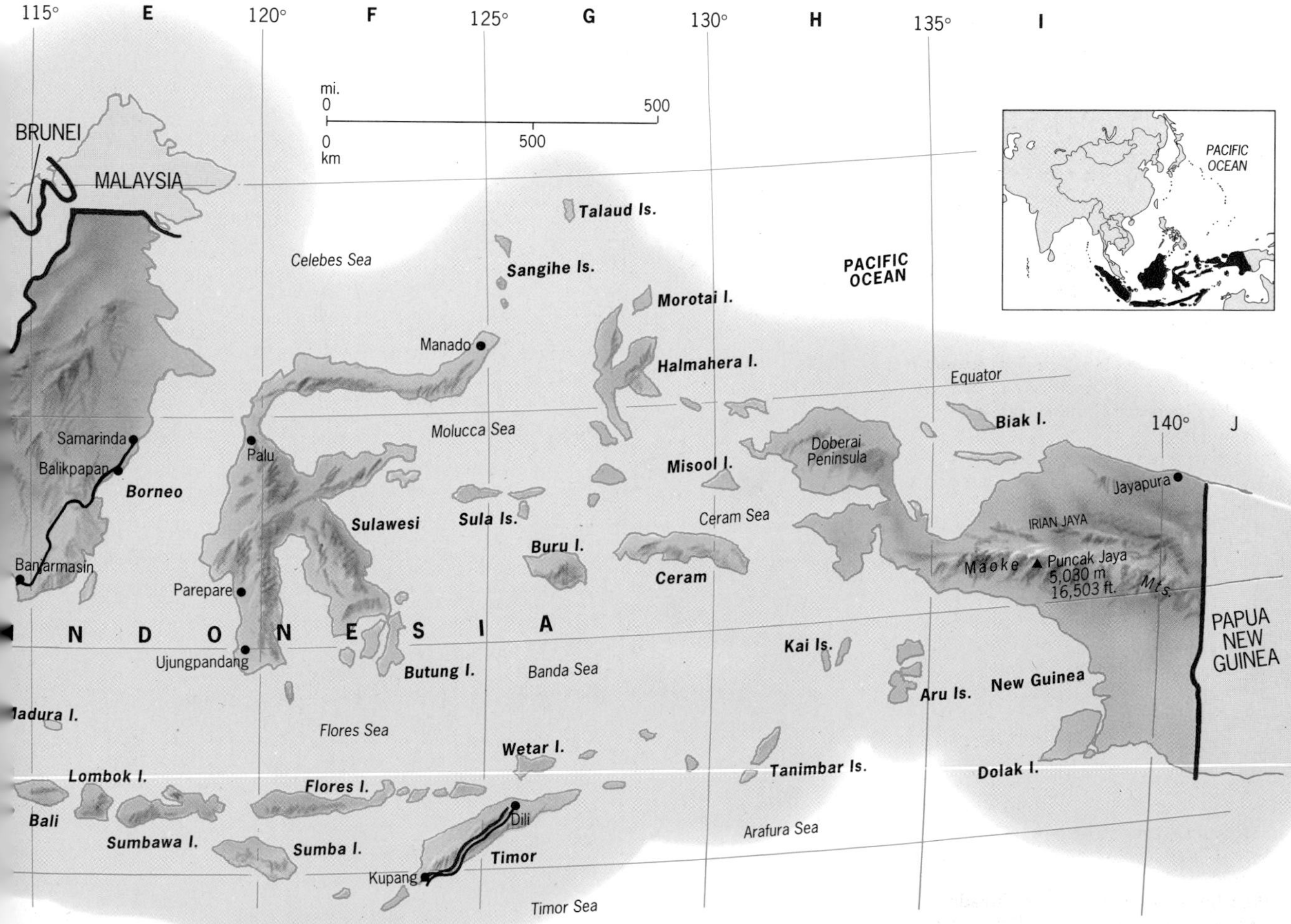

115° **E** 120° **F** 125° **G** 130° **H** 135° **I**

BRUNEI

MALAYSIA

mi.
0 — 500
0 — 500
km

Talaud Is.

Celebes Sea

Sangihe Is.

Morotai I.

Manado

Halmahera I.

PACIFIC OCEAN

Equator

Molucca Sea

Biak I.

140° **J**

Samarinda

Palu

Misool I.

Doberai Peninsula

Jayapura

Balikpapan

Borneo

Sulawesi

Sula Is.

Ceram Sea

IRIAN JAYA

Buru I.

Ceram

Maoke ▲ Puncak Jaya 5,030 m 16,503 ft. *Mts.*

Banjarmasin

Parepare

I N D O N E S I A

Kai Is.

New Guinea

PAPUA NEW GUINEA

Ujungpandang

Butung I.

Banda Sea

Aru Is.

Madura I.

Flores Sea

Wetar I.

Tanimbar Is.

Dolak I.

Lombok I.

Flores I.

Bali

Sumbawa I.

Sumba I.

Dili

Timor

Arafura Sea

Kupang

Timor Sea

PACIFIC OCEAN

AUSTRALIA AND OCEANIA

Area: 3,300,000 sq. mi./8,500,000 km². *Largest cities:* Sydney, Melbourne, Brisbane. *Organizations:* Rarotonga Treaty, South Pacific Bureau for Economic Cooperation (SPEC), South Pacific Commission (SPC), South Pacific Forum (SPF). *Main products (and percentage of world output):* Wool (42%), bauxite (37%), diamonds (36%), lamb (18%), lead (17%), cobalt (17%), gold (17%).

PHYSICAL FEATURES

Australia and Oceania is the smallest continent and covers 6% of the earth's land area. Australia accounts for more than 90% of the continent's area. New Zealand, Papua New Guinea, and up to 30,000 Pacific islands—their exact number is unknown—comprise the rest. The islands of the Pacific fall into two categories: volcanic and coral. The volcanic islands are generally larger than the coral islands and are mostly mountainous, frequently with active volcanoes. Many Pacific islands are uninhabited. *Highest point:* Mount Wilhelm (14,793 ft./4,509 m). *Lowest point:* Lake Eyre (–52 ft./–16 m). *Longest river:* Murray-Darling. *Largest lake:* Lake Eyre. *Other features:* Ayers Rock, Great Barrier Reef, hot springs, volcanic and coral islands, Cape York Peninsula, Gibson Desert, Arnhem Land. *Vegetation:* Ranges from alpine to tropical rain forest to desert scrub (Australia only). Many islands have unique fauna and flora as a result of their isolation.

PEOPLE

Population: 26,000,000 (0.5% of the total world population). *Growth rate:* 2.2%. *Density:* 8.5/sq. mi. *Distribution urban/rural:* 41%/59%. *Life expectancy:* 64(m), 69(f). *Languages:* English, French, Aboriginal, Maori, Melanesian, Micronesian, and Polynesian. *Ethnic groups:* European (chiefly British origin), Melanesian, Polynesian, Micronesian, Aboriginal, Maori. *Religions:* Christian, indigenous beliefs.

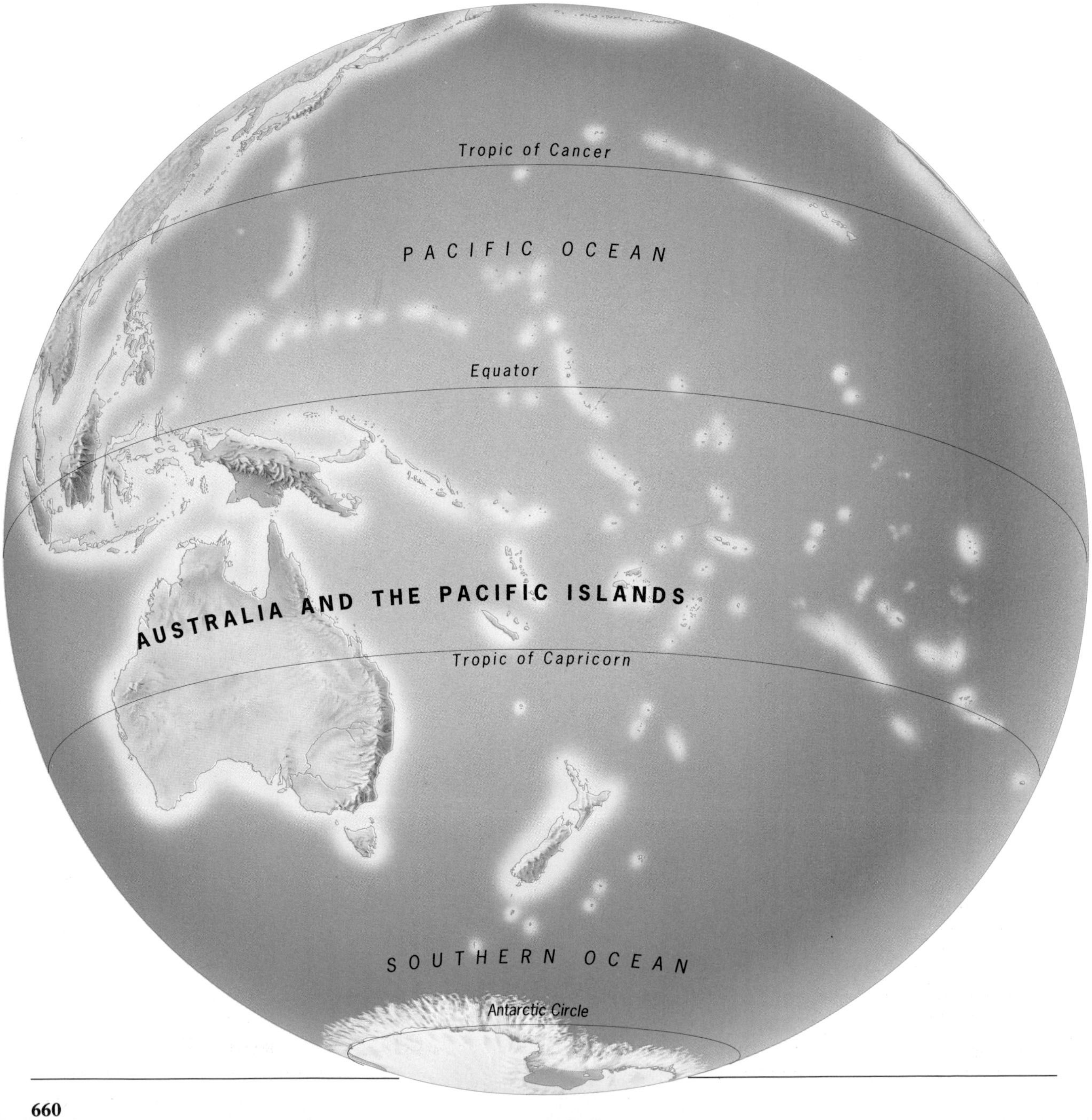

Tropic of Cancer

PACIFIC OCEAN

Equator

AUSTRALIA AND THE PACIFIC ISLANDS

Tropic of Capricorn

SOUTHERN OCEAN

Antarctic Circle

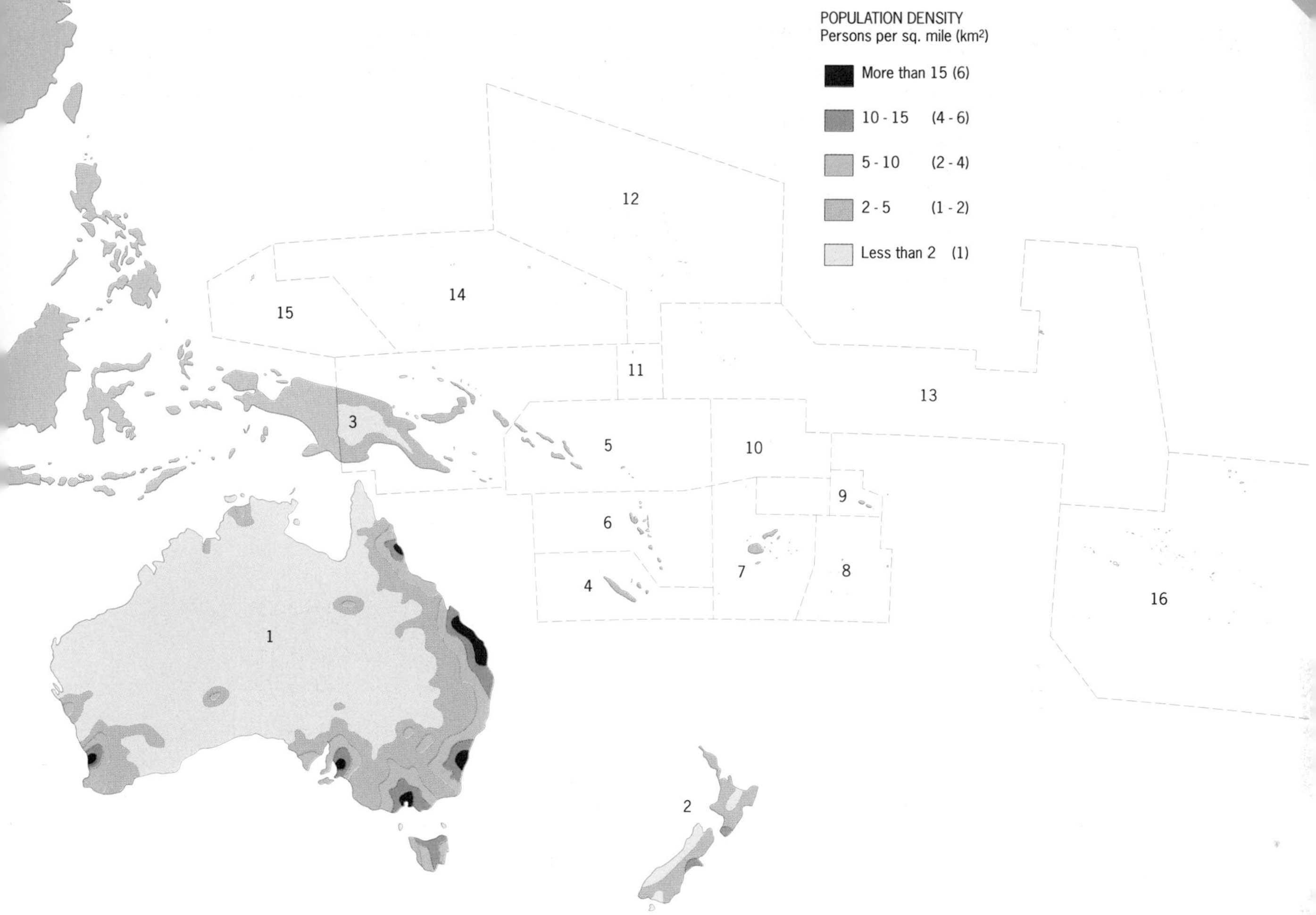

POPULATION DENSITY
Persons per sq. mile (km²)

■	More than 15	(6)
■	10 - 15	(4 - 6)
■	5 - 10	(2 - 4)
■	2 - 5	(1 - 2)
□	Less than 2	(1)

Demography

Sixty-five percent of Australia and Oceania's population lives in Australia. Most of the remainder live in New Zealand and Papua New Guinea. Only a few of the other islands of the area have sizable populations. Some of the smaller islands have fewer than a hundred people, while many others are uninhabited.

The population of Australia itself is very unevenly distributed. Much of the country is desert scrub and barely habitable, and about 80% of the population is concentrated in the S.E. quarter, with most of the rest living around the other coasts.

Australia has always relied heavily on high levels of immigration to build its work force—about 20% of Australians were born abroad. Since the 1970s, the number of people migrating to Australia from New Zealand and Southeast Asia has increased. New Zealand also has a high rate of immigration: 15% of New Zealanders were born abroad.

Australia is a highly urbanized country with only about 13% of Australians living in rural areas. New Zealand's population is also more than 80% urban. The Pacific islanders are predominantly rural dwellers, although urban areas are beginning to grow steadily.

Climate

Pacific islands: Almost all tropical with little seasonal variation in temperature. On most islands precipitation varies greatly from season to season. Typhoons are relatively common.

Australia: Most of the country is arid to semiarid. The climate becomes temperate in the S. and E. Rainfall is generally low and seasonal except for along the E. coast of Queensland, where rainfall is consistently higher.

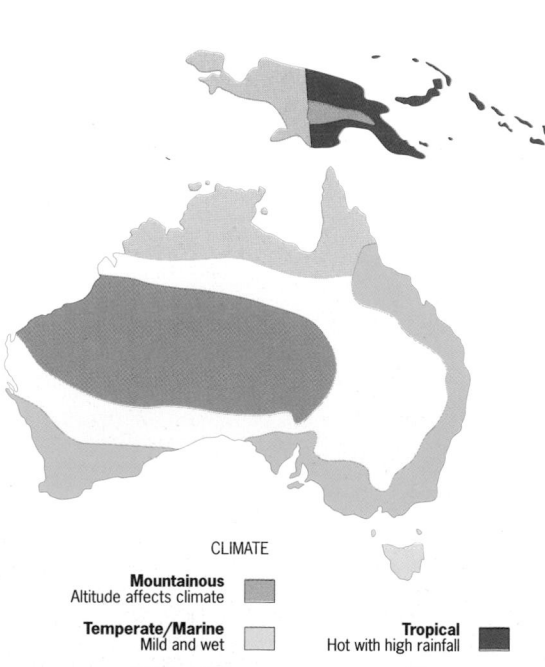

CLIMATE

Mountainous Altitude affects climate		
Temperate/Marine Mild and wet	**Tropical** Hot with high rainfall	**Savanna** Hot with dry season
Sub Tropical Warm with mild winter	**Steppe** Warm and dry	**Arid** Hot and very dry

AUSTRALIA

Area: 2,966,368 sq. mi./7,682,300 km². *Local name:* Commonwealth of Australia. *Currency:* Australian dollar. *Capital:* Canberra. *Other cities:* Sydney, Melbourne, Brisbane, Perth. *Physical features:* Mostly low plateau with deserts; more fertile in S.E. and along coasts. *Climate:* Mostly steppe to arid; tropical in N.; subtropical in S. and E. *Time zone:* GMT ranges from +8h (W) to +11h (E). *Political system:* Constitutional monarchy. *Head of state:* Queen Elizabeth II represented by Gov.-Gen. William Hayden (from 1989). *Head of government:* Paul Keating (from 1991). *Main exports:* Metals, minerals, wool, cereals, meat, manufactured goods. *Resources:* Uranium, bauxite, iron ore, diamonds.

PEOPLE

Population: 17,662,000. *Distribution urban/rural:* 85%/15%. *Life expectancy:* 74(m), 80(f). *Languages:* English, Aboriginal languages. *Ethnic groups:* European 95%, Asian 4%, Aboriginal and other 1%. *Religions:* Anglican 26%, Roman Catholic 26%. *Literacy rate:* 99%. *Per capita GDP:* $16,200.

KEY DATES

1770 James Cook claims E. coast region for Britain, calling it New South Wales.

1788 Britain establishes a penal colony in New South Wales; many convicts die on the voyage to Australia.

1793 First free settlers arrive in Australia.

1820s Wool industry is established.

1825 Van Diemen's Land (Tasmania) colony established.

1829 Colony of Western Australia established. All Australia becomes British dependency.

1830s Immigration of free settlers is encouraged by the British government; introduction of diseases such as smallpox, influenza, measles, and whooping cough kills many Aborigines.

1851 Colony of Victoria established; Australian gold rush follows discovery of gold in New South Wales and Victoria.

1855–60 The first state parliaments are established in Victoria, New South Wales, South Australia, Tasmania, and Queensland.

1870 Transportation of convicts to all parts of Australia is abolished.

1880 Ned Kelly, the notorious bushranger (outlaw), is executed.

1890 State parliament of Western Australia established. Severe economic depression.

1901 Foundation of the Commonwealth of Australia; Canberra becomes capital.

1902 Women achieve suffrage.

1907 Minimum wage introduced.

1914–18 Australian troops fight on Allied side in World War I.

1919 Influenza epidemic kills more Australians than World War I.

1930 Great Depression hits Australia.

1939 Australian troops are sent to Europe and Africa to assist the Allies against Germany in World War II.

1941 Australian troops return to the Pacific to fend off Japanese invasion.

1942 Independence achieved.

1945 World War II ends; Australia encourages immigration to expand the workforce and ethnic base.

1951 ANZUS Pacific Treaty signed with U.S.A. and New Zealand.

1964 Conscription introduced.

1965 Australian troops are sent to fight in the Vietnam War.

1967 Referendum passed giving Aborigines full rights of citizenship.

1970–71 Mass antiwar demonstrations.

1972 Conscription is abolished and Australia pulls its troops out of Vietnam.

1983 Bob Hawke elected prime minister.
1986 Australia Act eliminates remaining British legal power in Australia.
1991 Severe drought in E.; Hawke is defeated in a leadership challenge by Deputy Prime Minister Paul Keating.
1992 Severe economic problems; Oath of allegiance to the British crown abolished; high court declares that Australia was not *terra nullius* (unoccupied) when the Europeans first arrived, which has important implications for Aborigines.
1993 An opinion poll reveals that 62% of Australians are in favor of it becoming a republic; floods in Victoria leave 2,000 homeless; droughts and bushfires ravage eastern Australia.

Economy

Australia is distinguished from other developed countries in that, while most developed economies are founded on the production and export of manufactured goods, Australia's economy depends heavily on primary industries. Many workers are also employed in processing and distributing the goods produced by these industries.

Farming Australia is largely self-sufficient in food and also exports vast quantities of agricultural products. It is the world's leading wool producer with more than 160 million sheep. Beef, wheat, dairy products, fruit, and sugarcane are also very important. Grapes grown in several regions are used in the expanding area of wine production.
Fishing Catches include shellfish, tuna, mullet, and salmon.
Mining Australia is rich in mineral resources, but exploitation has been hindered by the inaccessibility of many deposits. The cost of developing this industry is high, and Australia depends a great deal on foreign investment. Important products include uranium, bauxite, diamonds, manganese, tin, iron ore, lead, coal, and tungsten.
Manufacturing Australian factories are able to supply most of the country's consumer goods, but a large proportion of its producer goods (equipment used for production) must be imported. The most important exports are processed foods, steel, farm products, chemicals, textiles, and light engineering.
Services About 65% of workers are employed in this sector and it represents 61% of the GDP. Tourism is important.

Travel
Visa: Needed by U.S. *Driving permit:* Nat. license. *Health and safety:* No inoculations needed. *Tourist features:* Great Barrier Reef; Cape York Peninsula; Arnhem Land; Ayers Rock; unusual wildlife. *National holiday:* January 26 (Australia Day).

Map

135° F 140° G 145° H 150° I

Arafura Sea
Torres Strait
Cape York
Gulf of Carpentaria
Cape York Peninsula
Coral Sea
Arnhem Land
Groote Eylandt
TERRITORY
Cooktown
PACIFIC OCEAN
Cairns
Tennant Creek
Great Barrier Reef
Townsville
Mount Isa
Hughenden
Mackay
Ranges
Winton
QUEENSLAND
Great Dividing Range
Rockhampton
Alice Springs
Fraser I.
Simpson Desert
Great Artesian Basin
R A L I A
Lake Eyre
-16 m
-52 ft.
Toowoomba
Brisbane
Coober Pedy
Marree
Ipswich
Gold Coast
Lake Torrens
Darling
Coffs Harbour
arcoola
Broken Hill
Woomera
NEW SOUTH WALES
Great Dividing Range
Salisbury
Lachlan
Newcastle
Gosford-Woy Woy
Adelaide
Wagga-Wagga
Sydney
Campbelltown
Wollongong
Kangaroo I.
Murray
Albury-Wodonga
CANBERRA
VICTORIA
Bendigo
AUSTRALIAN CAPITAL TERRITORY
Ballarat
Mt. Kosciusko
2,228 m
7,310 ft.
Melbourne
7
Geelong
King I.
Bass Strait
Flinders I.
40°
Tasman Sea
Launceston
TASMANIA
8
Hobart

NEW ZEALAND

Area: 104,453 sq. mi./270,534 km². **Local name:** Dominion of New Zealand. **Currency:** New Zealand dollar. **Capital:** Wellington. **Other cities:** Auckland, Christchurch. **Physical features:** Mostly mountainous. **Climate:** Subtropical in N., temperate in S., cooler at higher altitudes. **Time zone:** GMT +12h. **Political system:** Constitutional monarchy. **Head of state:** Queen Elizabeth II represented by Gov.-Gen. Dame Catherine Tizard (from 1988). **Head of government:** Jim Bolger (from 1990). **Main exports:** Wool, lamb, mutton, beef, fruit, fish, cheese, manufactured goods, chemicals, wood products. **Resources:** Natural gas, iron ore, coal, wood, gold, limestone.

PEOPLE

Population: 3,471,000. **Distribution urban/rural:** 85%/15%. **Life expectancy:** 72(m), 80(f). **Languages:** English (official), Maori. **Ethnic groups:** European 88%, Maori 9%, Polynesian 3%. **Religions:** Anglican 24%, Presbyterian 18%, Roman Catholic 15%, Methodist 5%, Baptist 2%. **Literacy rate:** 99%. **Per capita GDP:** $14,000.

KEY DATES

1769 Captain Cook claims New Zealand for Britain.

1800s Violent clashes between Europeans and the Maori.

1835 Becomes a British protectorate.

1840 Treaty of Waitangi: many Maori chiefs are persuaded to give up their land in return for British citizenship.

1841 Becomes a British Crown Colony.

1860 Gold rush in Otago (South Island).

1860–72 New Zealand Wars: British troops and Maori warriors clash over Maori territory.

1914–18 New Zealand fights in World War I on Allied side.

1931 Independence achieved within British Commonwealth.

1935 Labour Party comes to power; extensive public works program begins; nationalization of major industries constrains.

1938 Comprehensive social welfare system introduced.

1939–45 New Zealand troops fight in World War II on Allied side.

1949 National Party comes to power; labor unrest.

1951 ANZUS Pacific defense treaty with U.S.A. and Australia; deregistration of trade unions creates labor unrest.

1957 Labour Party returns to power.

1960 National Party wins elections.

1972 Labour Party returns to power led by Norman Kirk.

1974 Maori Land March to Wellington; Wallace Rowling elected prime minister.

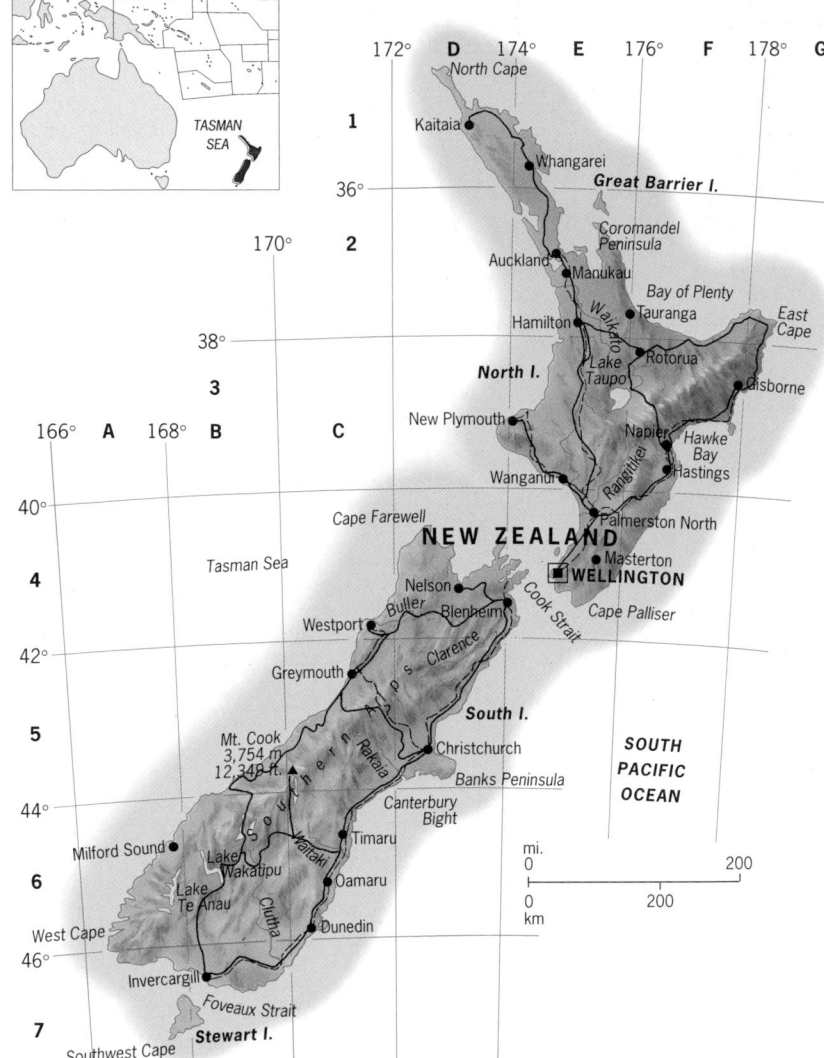

1975 National Party returns to power under Robert Muldoon.

1984 Labour Party returns to power with David Lange as prime minister.

1985 Antinuclear policy banning nuclear-powered and nuclear-armed ships from entering New Zealand's ports strains relations with U.S.A. and France.

1986 U.S.A. withdraws guarantee of New Zealand's security under ANZUS defense treaty.

1987 National Party declares its support for Labour's antinuclear policy; relations with U.S.A. deteriorate.

1988 Free trade agreement with Australia.

1989 Lange resigns over reinstatement of former finance minister Robert O. Douglas to the cabinet; Geoffrey Palmer becomes prime minister.

1990 National Party returns to office led by Jim Bolger; government announces cuts in social welfare spending.

1991 Foundation of new amalgamated Alliance Party; improved relations with U.S.A.; economic problems.

1992 Electoral reform approved in referendum; South Island hit by severe snow storms killing more than one million sheep and lambs and causing damage amounting to an estimated N.Z.$40 million; two mass murders prompt the passing of new regulations controlling the ownership of firearms.

1993 National Party wins election with a majority of one seat; introduction of proportional representation approved in referendum.

TRAVEL
Visa: None needed by U.S. **Driving permit:** Nat. license/IDP. **Health and safety:** No inoculations needed. **Tourist features:** Geysers and hot springs in Rotorua district; Victoria Park markets, in Auckland. **National holiday:** February 6 (Waitangi Day).

PAPUA NEW GUINEA

Area: 178,703 sq. mi./462,840 km². *Local name:* Papua New Guinea. *Currency:* Kina. *Capital:* Port Moresby. *Other cities:* Lae, Rabaul. *Physical features:* Mostly mountainous; coastal lowlands. *Climate:* Tropical. *Time zone:* GMT +10h. *Political system:* Constitutional monarchy. *Head of state:* Queen Elizabeth II represented by Gov.-Gen. Wiwa Korowi (from 1991). *Head of government:* Sir Julian Chan (from 1994). *Main exports:* Copper, gold, coffee. *Resources:* Gold, copper.

PEOPLE

Population: 3,922,000. *Distribution urban/rural:* 13%/87%. *Life expectancy:* 55(m), 56(f). *Languages:* English, pidgin English; Motu is spoken in the Papua region; more than 700 indigenous languages. *Ethnic groups:* Papuan 84%, Melanesian 15%. *Religions:* Protestant 44%, Roman Catholic 34%, indigenous beliefs and other 22%. *Literacy rate:* 52%. *Per capita GDP:* $8,000.

KEY DATES

1884 N.E. New Guinea annexed by Germany; the S.E. of the country comes under British protection.

1920s Gold is discovered.

1921–42 Administered by Australia as a League of Nations mandated territory.

1942–45 Japanese occupation.

1973 Internal self-government achieved.

1975 Independence achieved within British Commonwealth; Michael Somare becomes prime minister.

1980 Julius Chan prime minister.

1982 Michael Somare returns to office.

1985 Somare's leadership challenged by Deputy Prime Minister Paias Wingti; Wingti becomes prime minister.

1988 Paias Wingti loses no-confidence vote; Rabbie Namaliu becomes prime minister; the Bougainville Revolutionary Army (BRA) demands independence and orders the government to pay $12 billion in compensation for damage caused by copper mining on the island.

1989 State of emergency imposed in Bougainville in response to separatist violence in which 30 civilians are killed; copper mines on the island are closed, substantially reducing Papua New Guinea's income.

1990 Violence continues in Bougainville; Rabbie Namaliu orders his army to attack the rebels; more than 100 civilians and soldiers die; May: BRA leaders and the government hold talks and agree to a truce; Aug.: BRA leaders declare Bougainville's independence, although it is not recognized by Papua New Guinea.

1991 Peace agreement with Bougainville separatists is quickly broken by both government and rebel forces; many die in Bougainville because of insufficient medical supplies; economic boom produced by twofold increase in gold production; Deputy Prime Minister Ted Diro resigns after being found guilty on 81 charges of corruption.

1992 Paias Wingti returns to power.

1993 Government regains control of most of Bougainville; Wingti announces plans to develop closer ties with the rest of Asia, especially Indonesia.

1994 Sir Julian Chan prime minister

TRAVEL

Visa: Needed by U.S. *Driving permit:* Nat. license. *Health and safety:* Inoculations advised; water unsafe. *Tourist features:* Madang cultural center; tropical rain forest; unique wildlife. *National holiday:* September 16 (Independence Day).

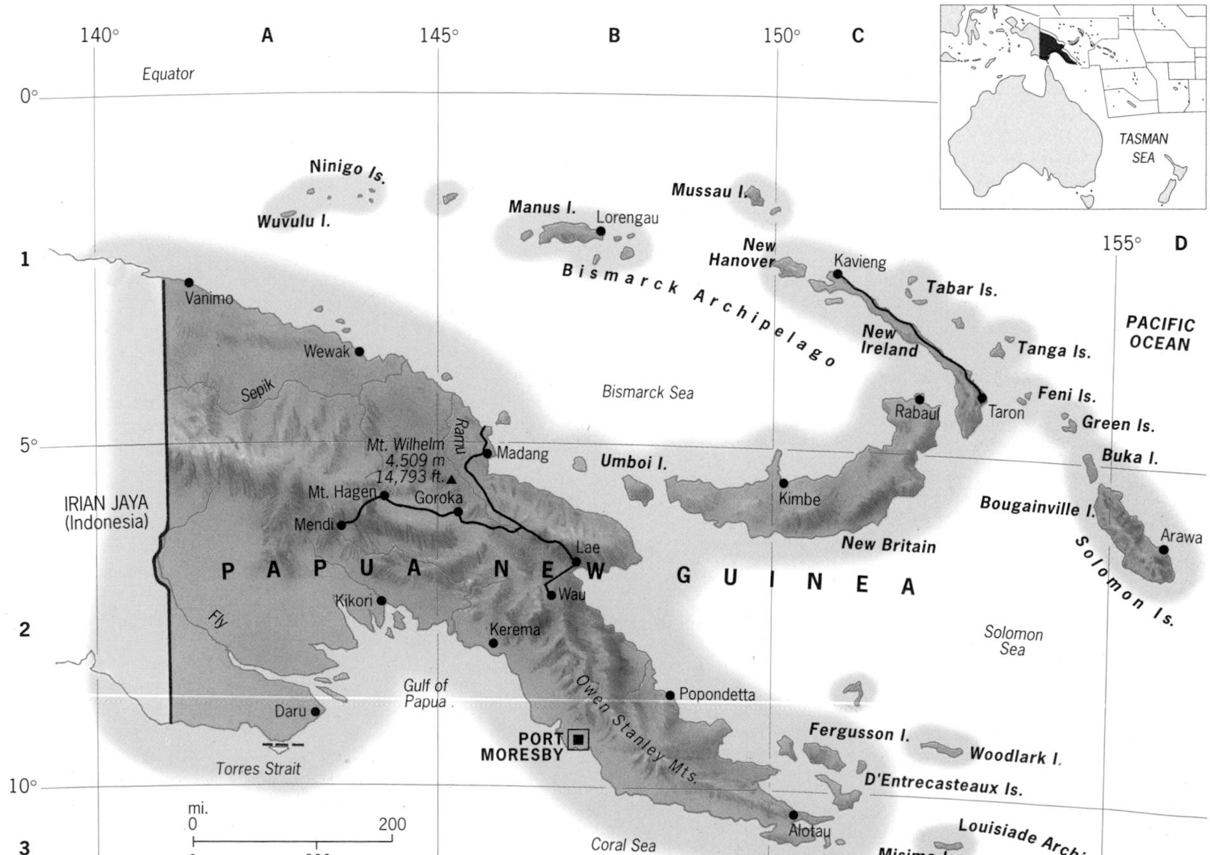

NEW CALEDONIA (Nouvelle Calédonie)

New Caledonia is an overseas territory of France situated in the S.W. Pacific about 1,200 mi. (2,000 km) N.E. of Australia. It consists of one main island, New Caledonia, the Loyalty Islands, the Bélep Islands, the Isle of Pines, and some uninhabited islands. The islands produce about 10% of the world's nickel.

The territory has a population of approximately 170,000 people of varied ethnic origin. About 43% of the population are Kanaks (Melanesians), the original inhabitants of the islands and a people of distinctive culture and traditions. Around 37% are of European (chiefly French) origin, and the remainder are the descendants of indentured laborers who came from Vietnam, Polynesia, and Indonesia to work in the nickel mines.

All the ethnic groups have retained their ancestors' way of life and have chosen not to integrate. In addition, the Melanesians are alarmed by the high proportion of French on the islands and fear that they may soon be outnumbered by Europeans, minimizing their chances of ever achieving independence from France. The result is a bitter conflict that erupted into violence in the 1980s at the cost of hundreds of lives. The French government has scheduled a referendum on independence for 1998, but as a similar referendum in 1987 was boycotted by nationalists, a truly democratic result may be difficult to achieve.

KEY DATES

1774 Captain Cook lands in New Caledonia.
1843 French Catholic mission established at Balade.
1853 Becomes a French possession.
1863 Huge reserves of nickel discovered.
1864–97 Islands of Nou and Pines used as penal colonies.
1870s Nickel rush: immigrants arrive from S.E. Asia and Oceania under indentured labor.
1939 New Caledonia declares support for Free French forces in World War II.
1942 U.S. military base established on island of New Caledonia.
1946 Becomes an overseas territory of France.
1951 Indentured labor system is abolished.
1960s Many former indentured laborers return to their homelands.
1970s Nationalist movement begins to emerge.
1974 General strike in attempt to gain control of nickel mines is defeated.
1981 Leader of Kanak independence movement assassinated; French government promises move toward independence
1980s Nationalism grows among Kanaks; riots between nationalists and ethnic French islanders, who wish to remain linked to France.
1984 French government passes legislation which will allow the Kanaks internal autonomy and self-determination.

1986 New conservative government in France reverses self-rule legislation of 1984.
1987 New Caledonians vote overwhelmingly in referendum to remain under French control, although the voting is boycotted by Kanaks.
1988 The Matignon Accord is passed to avert civil war.
1989 Matignon Accord is severely tested when Jean-Marie Tjibaou, leader of the Socialist National Liberation Front, who had been involved in its creation, is assassinated by militant Kanaks who oppose the agreement.
1998 Second referendum on independence scheduled.

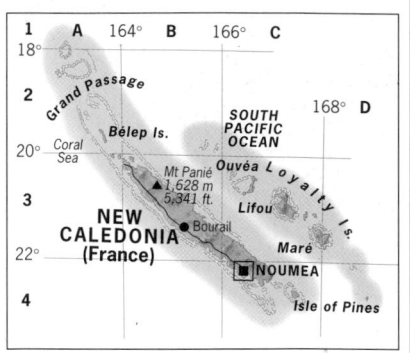

SOLOMON ISLANDS

Area: 10,955 sq. mi./28,370 km². *Local name:* Solomon Islands. *Currency:* Solomon Island dollar. *Capital:* Honiara. *Physical features:* Mostly rugged mountains with some low coral atolls. *Climate:* Tropical monsoon. *Time zone:* GMT +11h. *Political system:* Constitutional monarchy. *Head of state:* Queen Elizabeth II represented by Gov.-Gen. George Lepping (from 1991). *Head of government:* Francis Billy Hilly (from 1993). *Main exports:* Fish products, palm oil, copra, wood, cocoa beans. *Resources:* Fish, wood, gold, bauxite, phosphates.

PEOPLE

Population: 354,000. *Distribution urban/rural:* 13%/87%. *Life expectancy:* 67(m), 72 (f). *Languages:* English (official); about 120 Melanesian languages. *Ethnic groups:* Melanesian 93%, Polynesian 4%, Micronesian 2%, European, Chinese, and other 1%. *Religions:* Anglican 34%, Roman Catholic 19%, Baptist 17%, United (Methodist Presbyterian) 11%, Seventh-Day Adventist 10%, other 9%. *Literacy rate:* 60%. *Per capita GDP:* $600.

KEY DATES

1893 Becomes a British protectorate.
1978 Independence achieved within

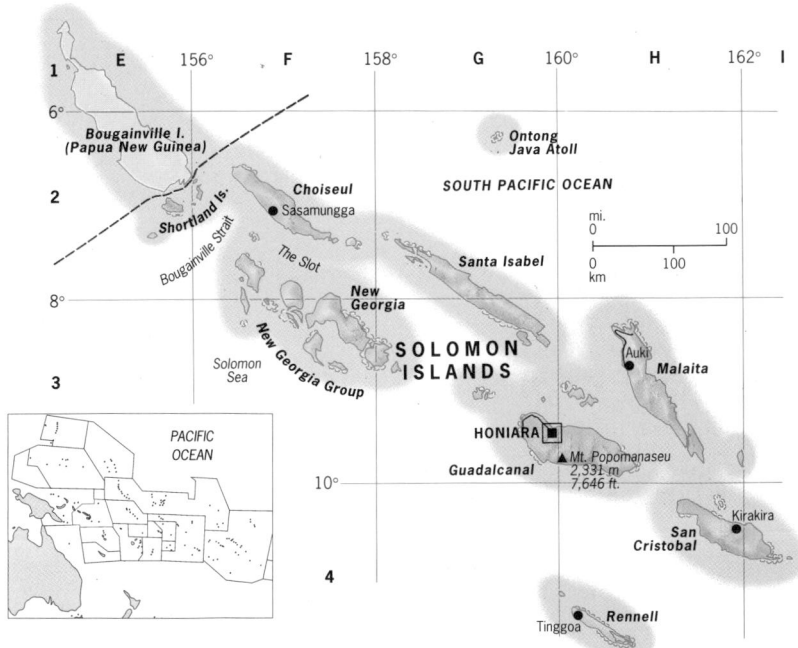

British Commonwealth with Peter Kenilorea as prime minister.
1985 Peter Kenilorea resigns after allegations of corruption.
1988 Joins Spearhead Group with Vanuatu and Papua New Guinea to conserve Melanesian culture and secure independence for New Caledonia.
1993 Francis Billy Hilly prime minister.

TRAVEL

Visa: None needed by U.S. **Driving permit:** Nat. license. **Health and safety:** Inoculations advised; water unsafe. **Tourist features:** Quonset huts; bamboo band musicians; traditional dancing. **National holiday:** July 7 (Independence Day).

VANUATU

Area: 4,707 sq. mi./12,190 km². **Local name:** Ripablik Blong Vanuatu. **Currency:** Vatu. **Capital:** Port-Vila. **Physical features:** Mostly volcanic mountains. **Climate:** Tropical. **Time zone:** GMT +11h. **Political system:** Republic. **Head of state:** Jean-Marie Leye (from 1994). **Head of government:** Maxime Carlot Korman (from 1991). **Main exports:** Copra, fish, coffee, cocoa, beef, wood. **Resources:** Manganese, wood, fish.

PEOPLE

Population: 156,000. **Distribution urban/rural:** n.a. **Life expectancy:** 67(m), 72(f). **Languages:** English, French, Bislama (all official); pidgin English. **Ethnic groups:** Melanesian 94%, French 4%, other 2%. **Religions:** Presbyterian 37%, Anglican 15%, Roman Catholic 15%, indigenous beliefs 8%, Seventh-Day Adventist 6%, Church of Christ 4%, other 15%. **Literacy rate:** 53%. **Per capita GDP:** $900.

KEY DATES

1906 Comes under joint British and French administration.
1975 Representative assembly established.

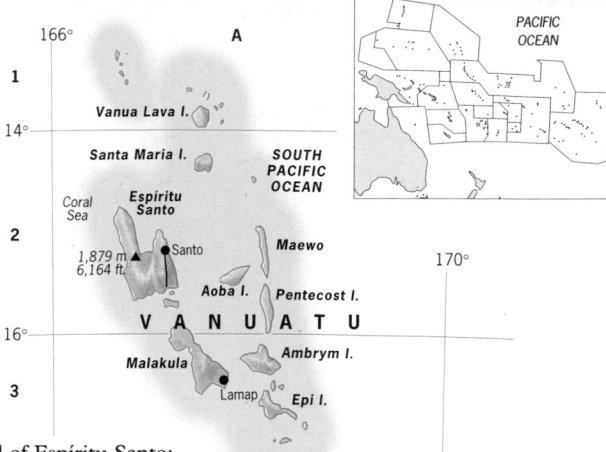

1980 Revolt on island of Espíritu Santo; independence achieved with George Kalkoa (Sokomanu) as president and Father Walter Lini as prime minister.
1988 Sokomanu dismisses Lini and is arrested for treason (later imprisoned).
1992 Cyclones devastate the island.

TRAVEL
Visa: None needed by U.S. **Driving permit:** Nat. license. **Health and safety:** Inoculations advised; water unsafe. **Tourist features:** Cultural center in Efatel; traditional dances. **National holiday:** July 30 (Independence Day).

FIJI

Area: 7,079 sq. mi./18,333 km². **Local name:** Republic of Fiji. **Currency:** Fiji dollar. **Capital:** Suva. **Physical features:** Mostly volcanic mountains, more than 300 islands. **Climate:** Tropical. **Time zone:** GMT +12h. **Political system:** Republic. **Head of state:** Ratu Sir Kamisese Mara (from 1994). **Head of government:** Col. Sitiveni Rabuka (from 1992). **Main exports:** Sugar, coconut oil, ginger, wood, canned fish, gold, clothing, molasses. **Resources:** Wood, fish, gold, copper.

PEOPLE

Population: 747,000. **Distribution urban/rural:** 39%/61%. **Life expectancy:** 67(m), 71(f). **Languages:** English (official), Fijian, Hindi. **Ethnic groups:** Indian 49%, Fijian 46%, European, Chinese, and other 5%. **Religions:** Hindu 38%, Methodist 37%, Roman Catholic 9%, Muslim 8%, other 8%. **Literacy rate:** 86%. **Per capita GDP:** $1,700.

KEY DATES

1874 Becomes a British Crown Colony.
1874–1946 Large-scale immigration of Indians to work on sugar plantations.
1970 Independence achieved.

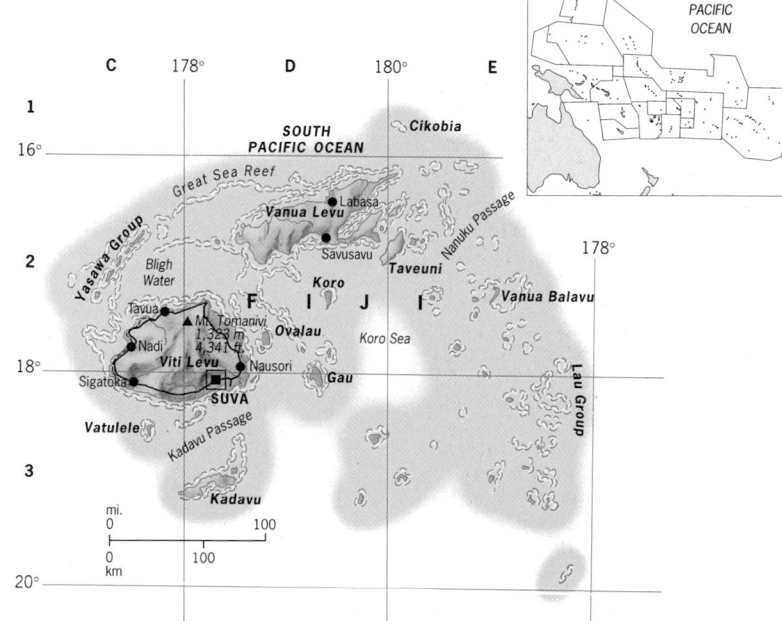

1987 General election results in Indian-dominated government; military coup led by Lt. Col. Sitiveni Rabuka; constitution abolished; Fiji ceases to be a member of the Commonwealth.
1990 New constitution.
1992 Sitiveni Rabuka elected prime minister.

TRAVEL
Visa: None needed by U.S. **Driving permit:** Nat. license. **Health and safety:** Inoculations advised; water unsafe. **Tourist features:** Coral reefs; volcanoes; traditional arts; Colo-i-Suva forest park. **National holiday:** October 10 (Independence Day).

TONGA

Area: 289 sq. mi./748 km². **Local name:** Pule'anga Fakatu'i 'o Tonga. **Currency:** Tongan dollar/pa'anga. **Capital:** Nukualofa. **Physical features:** 170 islands of which 36 are inhabited; actively volcanic in W. **Climate:** Tropical. **Time zone:** GMT +11h. **Political system:** Constitutional monarchy. **Head of state:** King Taufa'ahau Tupou IV (from 1965). **Head of government:** Baron Vaea (from 1991). **Main exports:** Coconut products, bananas, taro, vanilla beans, fruit, fish, copra. **Resources:** Fish.

PEOPLE

Population: 98,000. **Distribution urban/rural:** 29%/71%. **Life expectancy:** 65(m), 70(f). **Languages:** Tongan, English (both official). **Ethnic groups:** Polynesian. **Religions:** Wesleyan 47%, Roman Catholic 14%, Free Church of Tonga 14%, Mormon 9%, Church of Tonga 9%, other 7%. **Literacy rate:** 100%. **Per capita GDP:** $900.

KEY DATES

1800s Christian missionaries arrive from Great Britain.
1845 Islands are united under the rule of King George Tupou I.
1875 First constitution.
1893 Tupou I dies and is succeeded by his great-grandson, George Tupou II.
1900 Becomes a British protectorate.
1918 Queen Salote comes to the throne and works to improve education and welfare services.
1965 King Taufa'ahau Tupou IV comes to the throne.
1970 Independence achieved within the British Commonwealth.
1992 Parliament rejects motion that all M.P.s should be democratically elected.

TRAVEL
Visa: None needed by U.S. **Driving permit:** Nat. license/ IDP exchanged for local license at police station. **Health and safety:** Inoculations advised; water unsafe. **Tourist features:** Yellow Pier; royal palace and tombs. **National holiday:** June 4 (Emancipation Day).

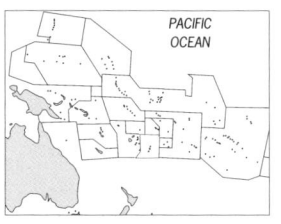

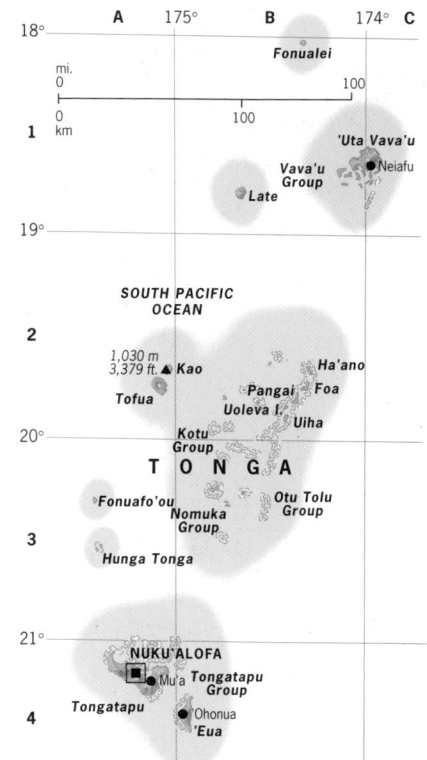

WESTERN SAMOA

Area: 1,093 sq. mi./2,831 km². **Local name:** Malotuto'atasi o Samoa i Sisifo. **Currency:** Talà. **Capital:** Apia. **Physical features:** Narrow coastal plain with volcanic mountains inland. **Climate:** Tropical. **Time zone:** GMT –11h. **Political system:** Constitutional monarchy. **Head of state:** King Malietoa Tanumafili II (from 1962). **Head of government:** Tofilau Eti Alesana (from 1988). **Main exports:** Coconut oil and copra, taro, cocoa, cigarettes, wood. **Resources:** Hardwood, fish.

PEOPLE

Population: 158,000. **Distribution urban/rural:** 21%/79%. **Life expectancy:** 65(m), 70(f). **Languages:** Samoan (Polynesian), English (official). **Ethnic groups:** Samoan 93%, Euronesian, mixed European and Polynesian 3%, other 4%. **Religions:** Protestant 70%, Roman Catholic 20%, other 10%. **Literacy rate:** 97%. **Per capita GDP:** $690.

KEY DATES

1899 Comes under German control.
1914 Occupied by New Zealand.
1920 League of Nations mandate over Western Samoa accorded to New Zealand; influenza epidemic kills one-sixth of the population.
1920s Foundation of Mau movement to oppose New Zealand rule.
1945 Becomes a UN trust territory.
1961 New constitution ratified.
1962 Full independence achieved.
1976 Joins UN.
1990 Universal adult suffrage introduced.

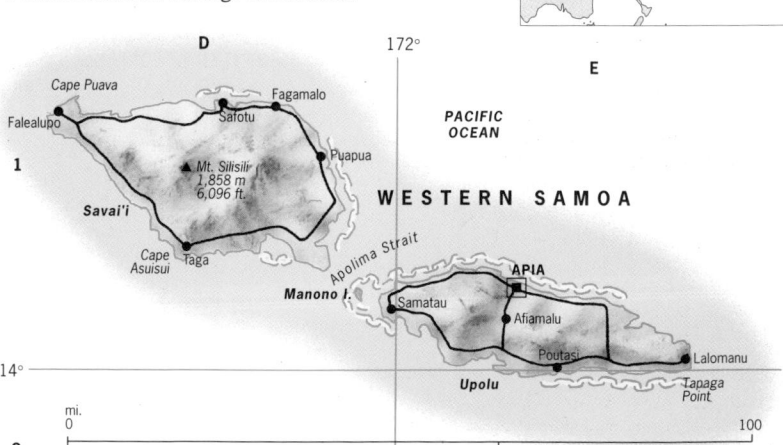

TRAVEL
Visa: None needed by U.S. for 30 days. **Driving permit:** IDP. **Health and safety:** Inoculations advised; water unsafe. **Tourist features:** Lava flows on Savai'i; diving, deep-sea fishing; Robert Louis Stevenson's house. **National holiday:** June 1 (National Day).

TUVALU

Area: 9 sq. mi./24 km². *Local name:* South West Pacific State of Tuvalu. *Currency:* Australian dollar. *Capital:* Funafuti. *Physical features:* Mostly coral atolls. *Climate:* Tropical. *Time zone:* GMT +12h. *Political system:* Constitutional monarchy. *Head of state:* Queen Elizabeth II represented by Gov.-Gen.Toaripi Lauti (from 1990). *Head of government:* Kamuta Laatari (from 1993). *Main exports:* Copra, stamps. *Resource:* Fish.

PEOPLE
Population: 13,000. *Distribution urban/rural:* n.a. *Life expectancy:* 60(m), 63(f). *Languages:* Tuvaluan, English. *Ethnic group:* Polynesian. *Religion:* Church of Tuvalu 97%. *Literacy rate:* 96%. *Per capita GDP:* $711.

KEY DATES
1892 Becomes a British protectorate.
1916 Becomes a British colony as part of Gilbert and Ellice Islands.
1975 Separation of Ellice Islands from Gilbert Islands.
1978 Ellice Islands achieve independence, taking precolonial name of Tuvalu.
1986 Proposal for republican status rejected in referendum.

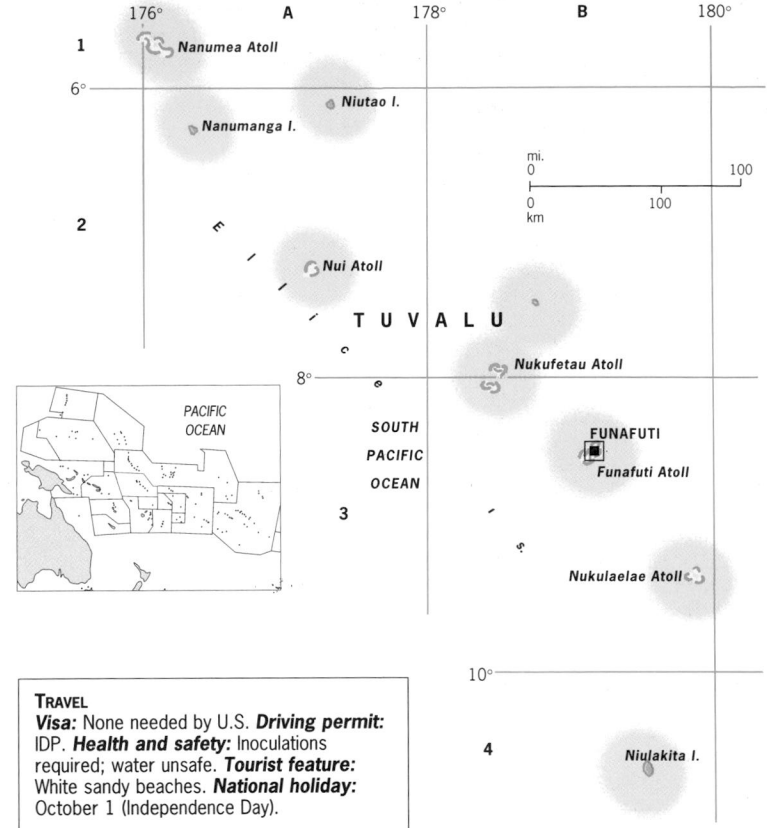

TRAVEL
Visa: None needed by U.S. *Driving permit:* IDP. *Health and safety:* Inoculations required; water unsafe. *Tourist feature:* White sandy beaches. *National holiday:* October 1 (Independence Day).

NAURU

Area: 8 sq. mi./21 km². *Local name:* Naoero. *Currency:* Australian dollar. *Capital:* Yaren. *Physical features:* Phosphate plateau surrounded by sandy beaches. *Climate:* Tropical. *Time zone:* GMT +12h. *Political system:* Republic within British Commonwealth. *Head of state and government:* Bernard Dowiyogo (from 1989). *Main export:* Phosphates. *Resource:* Phosphates.

PEOPLE
Population: 8,100. *Distribution urban/rural:* n.a. *Life expectancy:* 64(m), 69(f). *Languages:* Nauruan (official), English. *Ethnic groups:* Polynesian 84%, Chinese 8%. *Religions:* Protestant 66%, Roman Catholic 33%. *Literacy rate:* 99%. *Per capita GNP:* $10,000.

KEY DATES
1920 Administered by Australia, New Zealand, and U.K. under League of Nations mandate.
1942–45 Occupied by Japan.
1945 Comes under joint Australian, New Zealand, and British administration.
1968 Independence achieved.

1989 Nauru claims compensation from Australia for damage caused by phosphate mining.
1993 Australia agrees to pay A$107 million compensation.

TRAVEL
Visa: Needed by U.S. *Driving permit:* IDP. *Health and safety:* Inoculations advised; water unsafe. *Tourist features:* Underwater caves; deep-sea diving; forest wildlife. *National holiday:* January 31 (Independence Day).

MARSHALL ISLANDS

Area: 70 sq. mi./181 km². *Local name:* Republic of the Marshall Islands. *Currency:* U.S. dollar. *Capital:* Majuro. *Physical features:* Low coral, limestone, and sand islands. *Climate:* Tropical. *Time zone:* GMT +12h. *Political system:* Republic. *Head of state and government:* Amata Kabua (from 1991). *Main exports:* Copra and coconut oil, agricultural produce. *Resources:* Phosphates, seabed minerals.

PEOPLE

Population: 52,000. *Distribution urban/rural:* n.a. *Life expectancy:* 61(m), 64(f). *Languages:* English, Marshallese. *Ethnic group:* Micronesian c. 100%. *Religion:* Protestant. *Literacy rate:* 93%. *Per capita GDP:* $1,500.

KEY DATES

1855 Occupied by Germany.
1914 Comes under Japanese control.
1946–63 Eniwetok and Bikini atolls used for U.S. atomic bomb tests.
1947 Becomes part of UN Pacific Islands Trust Territory under the administration of the U.S.A.
1986 Self-government achieved.
1990 UN trust status ends.
1991 Independence achieved; joins UN.

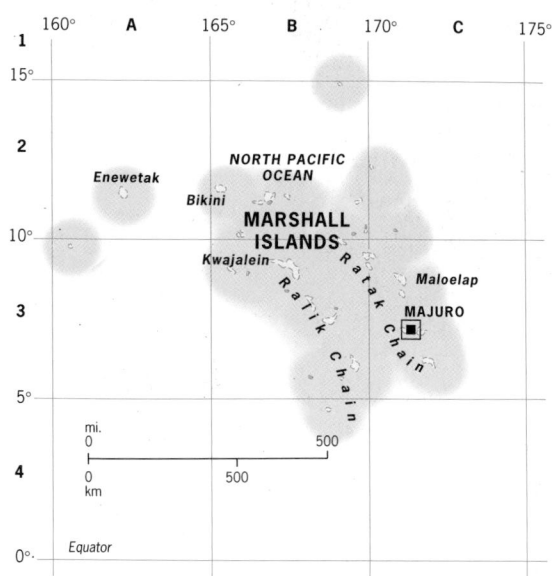

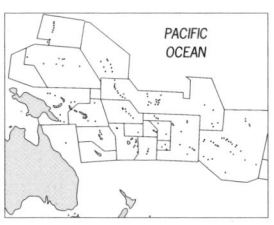

TRAVEL
Visa: Needed by U.S. *Driving permit:* IDP. *Health and safety:* Inoculations advised; water unsafe. *Tourist features:* Tropical flowers; variety of coral life; white sandy beaches. *National holiday:* May 1 (Proclamation of the Republic of the Marshall Islands).

KIRIBATI

Area: 281 sq. mi./728 km². *Local name:* Republic of Kiribati. *Currency:* Australian dollar. *Capital:* Bairiki. *Physical features:* Mostly low-lying coral atolls. *Climate:* Tropical. *Time zone:* GMT +12h. *Political system:* Republic. *Head of state and government:* Teatao Teannaki (from 1991). *Main exports:* Copra, fish. *Resources:* Fish.

PEOPLE

Population: 75,000. *Distribution urban/rural:* n.a. *Life expectancy:* 52(m), 56(f). *Languages:* English (official), Gilbertese. *Ethnic group:* Micronesian. *Religions:* Roman Catholic 48%, Protestant 45%, Seventh-Day Adventist, Baha'i, Church of God, Mormon. *Literacy rate:* 90%. *Per capita GDP:* $430.

KEY DATES

1892 Becomes a British protectorate as part of the Gilbert and Ellice Islands.
1962 Kiritimati used for nuclear tests.
1975 Ellice Islands become Tuvalu.
1977 Gilbert Islands achieve internal self-government.
1979 Gilbert Islands achieve independence as the Republic of Kiribati.
1985 Foundation of first political party, the Christian Democrats.

TRAVEL
Visa: None needed by U.S. *Driving permit:* IDP. *Health and safety:* Inoculations advised; water unsafe. *Tourist features:* World War II relics; Alele museum. *National holiday:* July 12 (Independence Day).

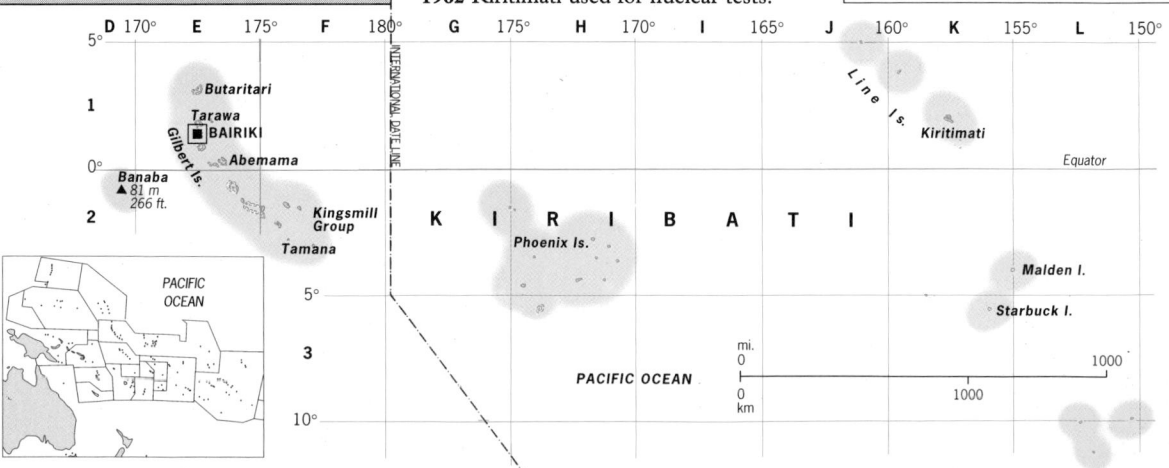

MICRONESIA

Area: 271 sq. mi./701 km². *Local name:* Federated States of Micronesia (FSM). *Currency:* U.S. dollar. *Capital:* Kolonia. *Physical features:* 607 islands of varied geography. *Climate:* Tropical. *Time zone:* GMT +11h. *Political system:* Federal republic. *Head of state and government:* Bailey Olter (from 1991). *Main export:* Copra. *Resources:* Fish, seabed minerals.

PEOPLE

Population: 114,000. *Distribution urban/rural:* n.a. *Life expectancy:* 63(m), 67(f). *Languages:* English (official), Trukese, Pohnpeian, Yapese, Kosrean. *Ethnic groups:* Nine ethnic Polynesian and Micronesian groups. *Religions:* Mainly Roman Catholic and Protestant. *Literacy rate:* 90%. *Per capita GNP:* $1,500.

KEY DATES

1886 Comes under Spanish rule.
1899 Sold by Spain to Germany.
1921–44 Administered by Japan under League of Nations mandate.
1944 Occupied by U.S.A.
1947 Incorporated into the UN Pacific Islands Trust Territory under U.S. administration.
1982 Enters free association with U.S.A.
1990 Independence achieved.
1991 Joins the UN.

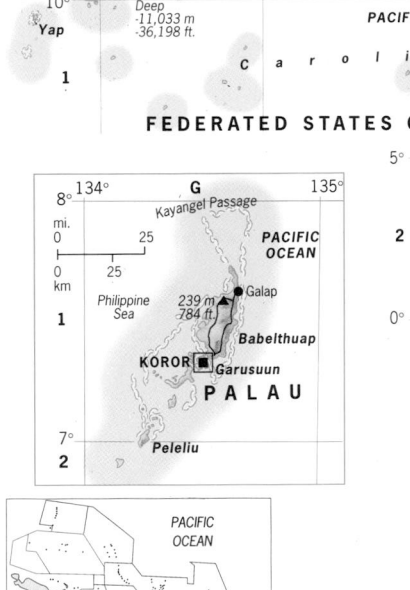

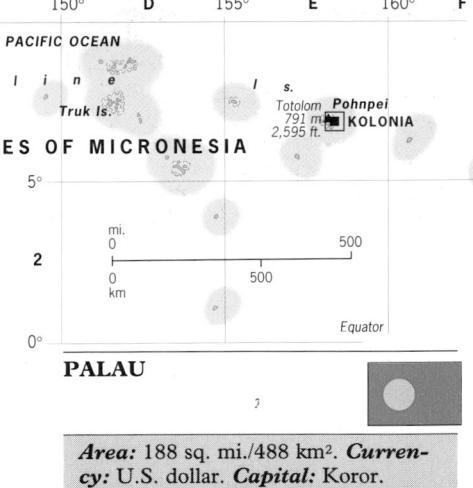

TRAVEL

Visa: None needed by U.S. for stays up to 30 days. **Driving permit:** IDP. **Health and safety:** Inoculations advised; water unsafe. **Tourist features:** Enpine marine park. **National holiday:** May 10 (Independence Day).

PALAU

Area: 188 sq. mi./488 km². *Currency:* U.S. dollar. *Capital:* Koror. *Time zone:* GMT +10h. *Political system:* Republic. *Head of state and government:* Kuniwo Nakamura (from 1992). *Main exports:* Fish, fruit, vegetables. *Resource:* Fish.

PEOPLE

Population: 16,000. *Life expectancy:* n.a. *Languages:* Palauan, English (both official). *Ethnic groups:* Micronesian and Polynesian. *Religion:* Roman Catholic. *Per capita GDP:* n.a.

KEY DATES

1921–44 Under Japanese administration.
1944 Comes under U.S. control.
1994 Independence achieved; application made for UN membership.

FRENCH POLYNESIA

Area: 1,260 sq. mi./3,265 km². *Local name:* Territoire de la Polynésie Française. *Currency:* C.F.P. Franc. *Capital:* Papeete. *Physical features:* 130 islands over five archipelagos varying from rugged high islands to low islands with reefs. *Climate:* Tropical. *Time zone:* GMT +12h. *Political system:* Overseas territory of France. *Head of state:* Jacques Chirac represented by High Commissioner of the Republic Jean Montpezat (from 1987). *Head of government:* Gaston Flosse (from 1991). *Main exports:* Coconut products, cultured pearls, vanilla, shark meat. *Resources:* Wood, fish, cobalt.

PEOPLE

Population: 212,000. *Distribution urban/rural:* n.a. *Life expectancy:* 68(m), 73(f). *Languages:* French and Tahitian (official). *Ethnic groups:* Polynesian 78%, Chinese 12%, French 10%. *Religion:* Protestant 54%, Roman Catholic 30%, other 16%. *Per capita GDP:* $6,000.

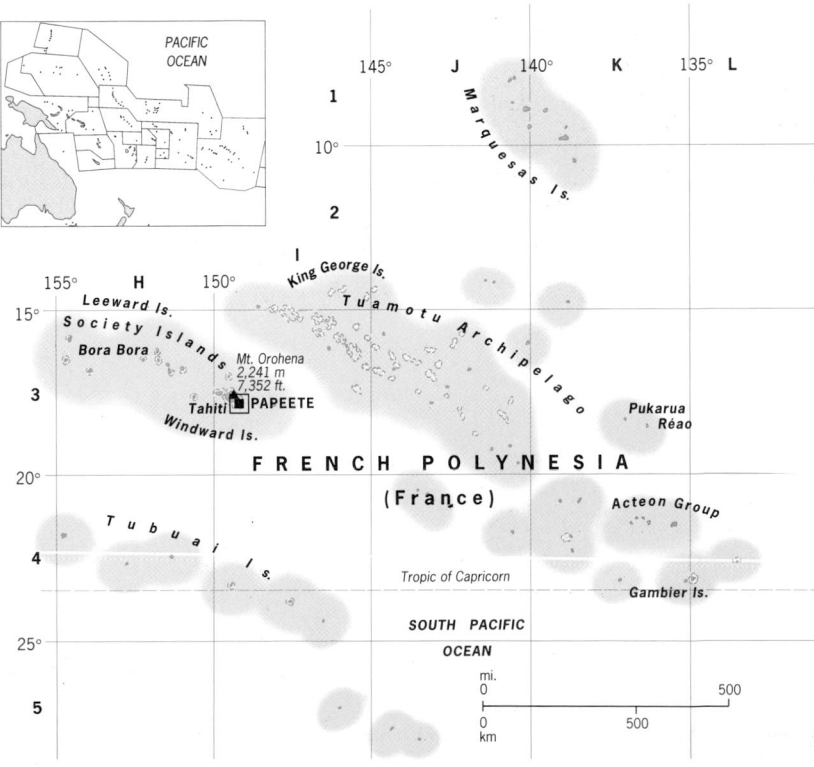

NORTH AMERICA

Area: 9,358,000 sq mi./24,237,000 km² *Largest cities:* Mexico City, New York City, Los Angeles, Chicago, Philadelphia, San Francisco, Miami, Guadalajara, Toronto. *Organizations:* North American Free Trade Agreement (NAFTA), Organización de Estados Centroamericanos (ODECA). *Main products (and percentage of world output):* Wood pulp (53%), corn (44%), silver (39%), natural gas (33%), linseed (32%), potash (32%), salt (29%), beef (26%), nickel (21%).

PHYSICAL FEATURES

North America is the world's third-largest continent and covers about 16% of its land area. The terrain varies widely and includes polar regions, rugged plateaus, mountain ranges, flat plains, and tropical islands. *Highest point:* Mt. McKinley (20,320 ft./6,194 m). *Lowest point:* Death Valley (-282 ft./-86 m). *Longest river:* Mississippi. *Largest lake:* Superior. *Other features:* Rocky Mountains, Great Plains, Grand Canyon, Sierra Madre, Caribbean islands. *Vegetation:* Includes tundra; coniferous; deciduous and pine forest; swamp and sawgrass; savanna; desert; and rain forest.

PEOPLE

Population: 432,000,000 (8% of the total world population). *Growth rate:* 1.6%. *Density:* 47/mi.². *Distribution urban/rural:* 67%/33%. *Life expectancy:* 72(m), 76(f). *Languages:* English, French, Spanish; some Indian and Inuit dialects. *Ethnic groups:* About half of Americans and Canadians are of British or Irish origin; about one-fourth of Canadians have French ancestry; most European Central Americans have Iberian ancestry; blacks comprise 12% of the U.S. population and most Caribbean islanders are descended from black Africans; other Caribbeans are mulatto; most Mexicans and Central Americans are mestizo; also Native Americans and Inuit. *Religions:* Mostly Christian or Jewish; c. 97% of Central Americans are Roman Catholic.

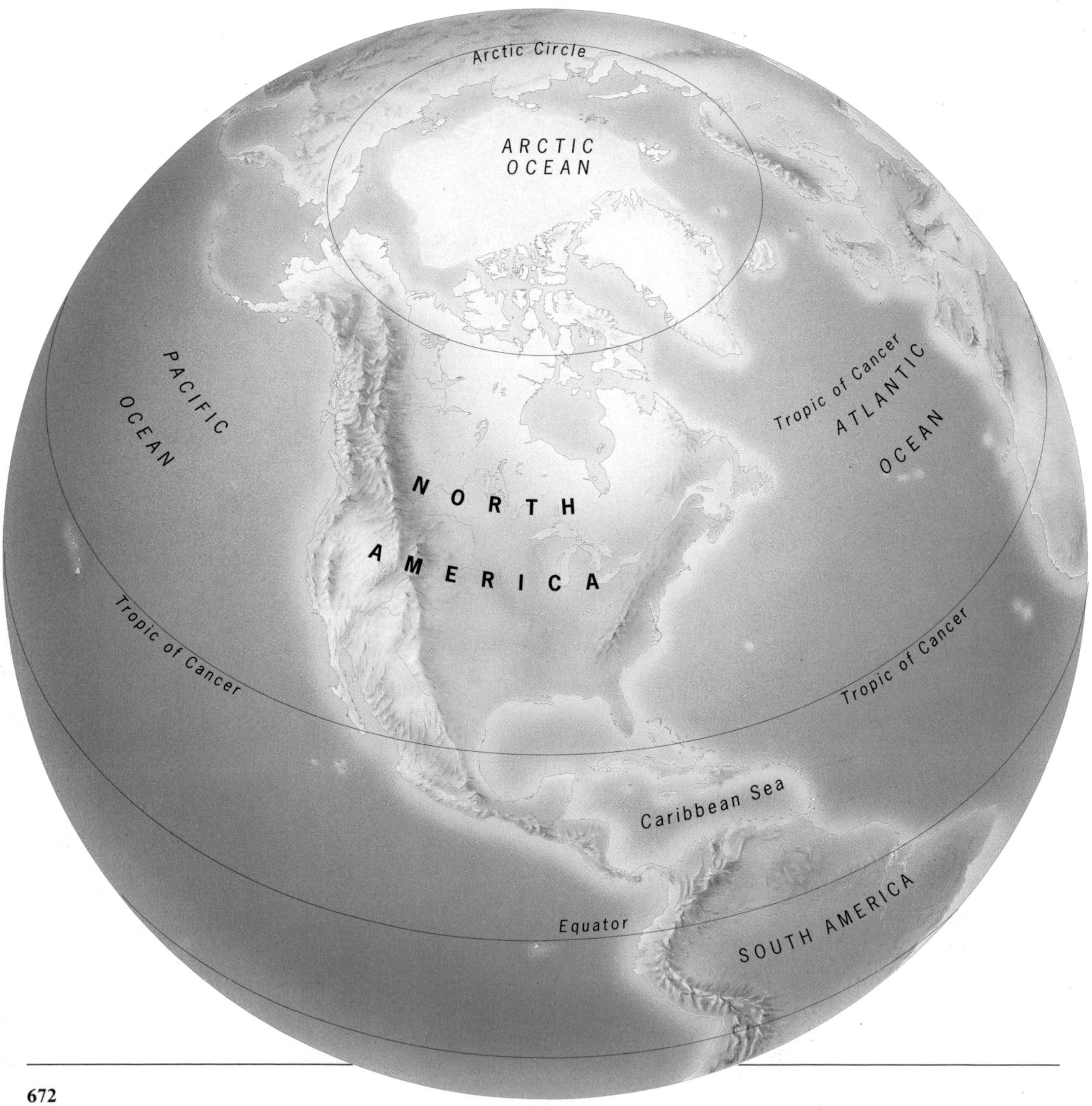

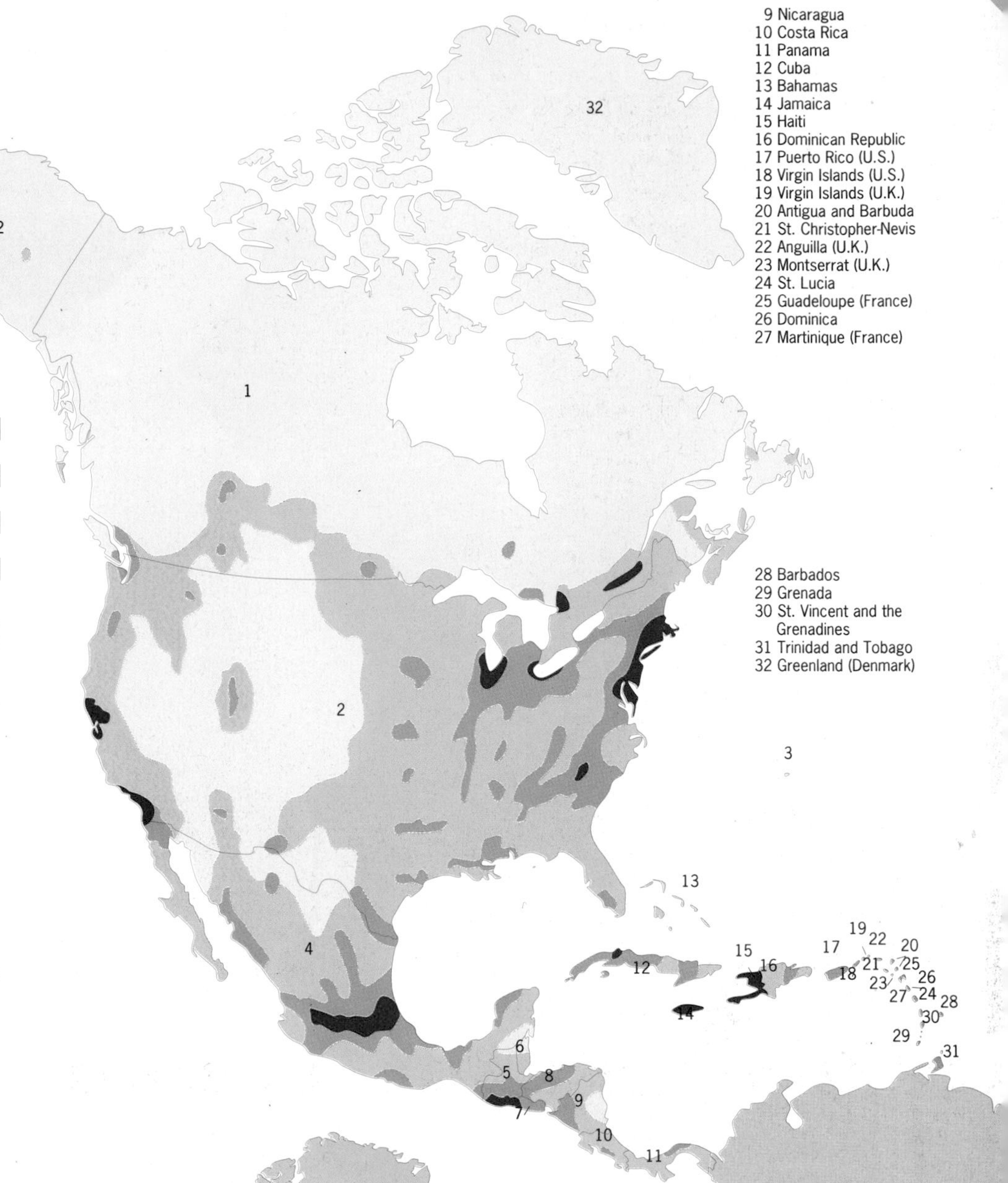

KEY
1 Canada
2 U.S.A.
3 Bermuda
4 Mexico
5 Guatemala
6 Belize
7 El Salvador
8 Honduras

9 Nicaragua
10 Costa Rica
11 Panama
12 Cuba
13 Bahamas
14 Jamaica
15 Haiti
16 Dominican Republic
17 Puerto Rico (U.S.)
18 Virgin Islands (U.S.)
19 Virgin Islands (U.K.)
20 Antigua and Barbuda
21 St. Christopher-Nevis
22 Anguilla (U.K.)
23 Montserrat (U.K.)
24 St. Lucia
25 Guadeloupe (France)
26 Dominica
27 Martinique (France)

POPULATION DENSITY
Persons per km² (sq mi)

More than 40 (100)

20–40   (50–100)

2–20   (5–50)

Less than 2   (5)

28 Barbados
29 Grenada
30 St. Vincent and the
   Grenadines
31 Trinidad and Tobago
32 Greenland (Denmark)

Demography

North America ranks fourth among the continents in terms of population size, although it is very sparsely populated in some areas, particularly in the cold northern part of the continent and the western deserts.

The population of North America is predominantly urban and the continent has many large cities, including the second-largest city in the world, Mexico City. Mexico has a higher proportion of rural dwellers than the other countries.

Many large urban areas are concentrated around the Great Lakes, along the St. Lawrence River and the Atlantic coast of the U.S.A., and on the central plateau of Mexico. Most Canadians live in a relatively narrow strip along the southern border.

The average growth rate of the continent is less than 2%, but Mexico's growth rate is over three times the average of the other countries.

Since 1900, many Central Americans have migrated to the U.S.A., and Hispanics now make up 9% of the U.S. population. Every year many Central Americans risk their lives to enter the U.S.A. illegally in the hope of achieving a better quality of life.

Climate

North America is the only continent that has every type of climate. In the polar region the land is permanently frozen. Even in the subpolar parts the temperature only rises above freezing for a few days in summer. Other areas with little variation are the low-lying regions of the S. and the Caribbean where it is always hot and rainy, and the desert regions of the center and S.W. Most of the rest of the continent is cold in the winter and warm in the summer with moderate precipitation.

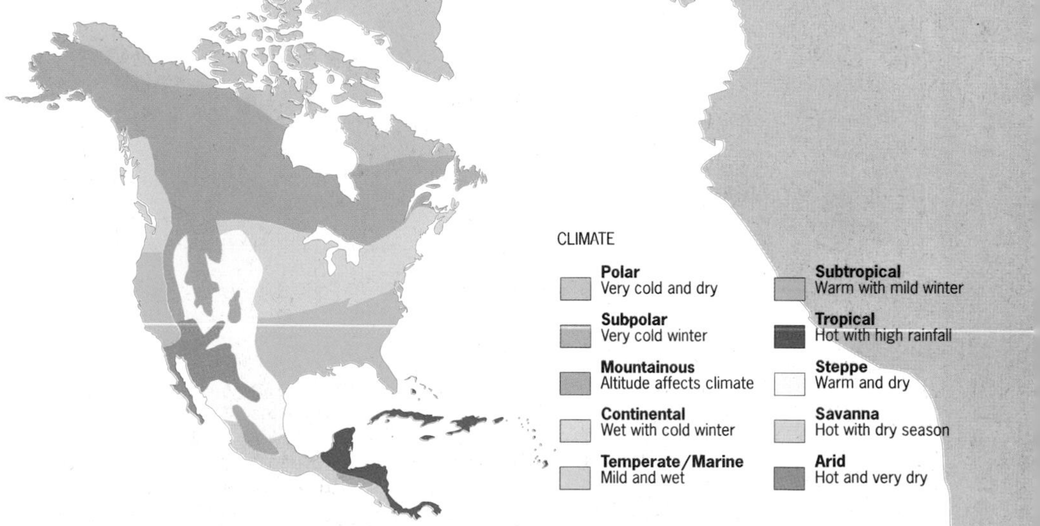

CLIMATE

Polar
Very cold and dry

Subpolar
Very cold winter

Mountainous
Altitude affects climate

Continental
Wet with cold winter

Temperate/Marine
Mild and wet

Subtropical
Warm with mild winter

Tropical
Hot with high rainfall

Steppe
Warm and dry

Savanna
Hot with dry season

Arid
Hot and very dry

CANADA

Area: 3,849,656 sq. mi./9,970,610 km². *Currency:* Canadian dollar. *Capital:* Ottawa. *Other cities:* Toronto, Montreal, Vancouver, Edmonton, Calgary, Winnipeg, Québec, Hamilton, Saskatoon, Halifax. *Physical features:* Mostly plains with mountains in W. and lowlands in S.E. *Climate:* Continental with extremes; polar in N. *Time zones:* GMT –4h (E), –8h (W). *Political system:* Confederation with parliamentary democracy. *Head of state:* Queen Elizabeth II represented by Gov.-Gen. Ramon Hnatyshyn (from 1990). *Head of government:* Jean Chrétien (from 1993). *Main exports:* Newsprint, wood pulp, wood, crude oil, natural gas, aluminum, motor vehicles and parts, telecommunications equipment. *Resources:* Nickel, zinc, copper, gold, lead, molybdenum, potash, silver, fish, wood, wildlife, coal, crude oil, natural gas.

PEOPLE
Population: 28,436,000. *Distribution urban/rural:* 77%/23%. *Life expectancy:* 74(m), 81(f). *Languages:* English, French (both official). *Ethnic groups:* British 45%, French 27%, other European 20%, Native American 1.5%, others 6.5%. *Religions:* Roman Catholic 46%, Protestant 41%. *Literacy rate:* 99%. *Per capita GDP:* $19,400.

KEY DATES
1608 Québec founded by the French.
1663 Colony of New France declared.
1760 British conquer French Canada.
1791 Division into upper and lower Canada.
1812–15 U.S. invasions repulsed.
1837 Revolts in upper and lower Canada.
1841 Upper and lower Canada united.
1848 Canada and Nova Scotia achieve self-government.
1858 Colony of British Columbia established.
1867 Dominion of Canada founded.
1870 Nortwest territories established.
1885 Rebellion of Northwest.
1898 Yukon Territory added.
1931 Statute of Westminster recognizes Canadian independence.
1949 Newfoundland joins Canada.
1970 Québec separatists active.
1980 Québec referendum rejects demand for independence.
1982 Canada Act removes last legal control of Britain over Canadian affairs.
1992 Self-governing Inuit homeland in Northwest Territories approved.
1993 North American Free Trade Agreement with U.S.A. and Mexico ratified. Ruling Conservatives defeated and Jean Chrétien elected prime minister

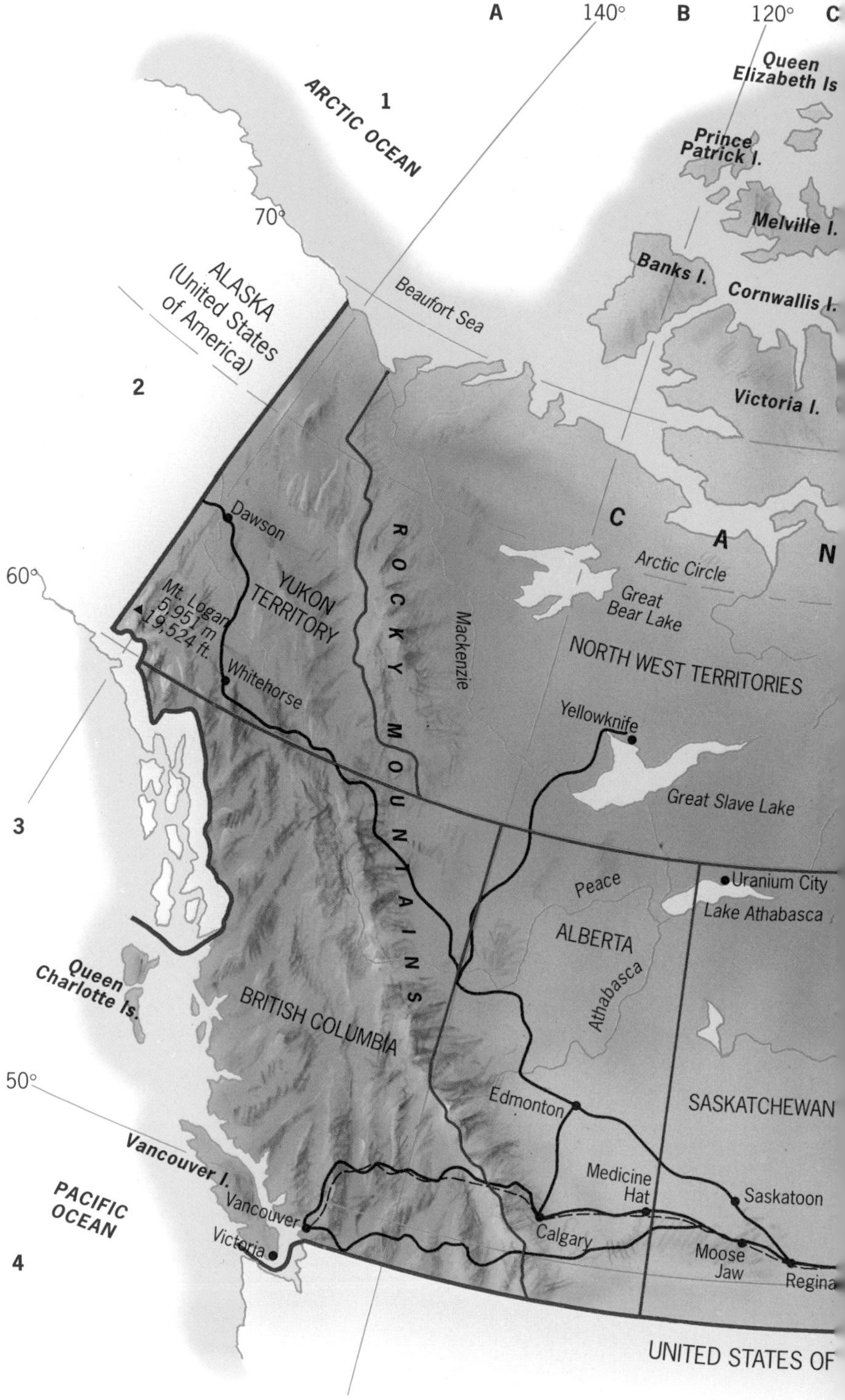

TRAVEL
Visa: None needed by U.S. *Health and safety:* No inoculations needed. *Driving permit:* IDP. *Tourist features:* St. Lawrence Seaway; Great Lakes; Rocky Mountains; Niagara Falls. *National holiday:* July 1 (Canada Day).

Map labels: A 140° B 120° C · ARCTIC OCEAN · 70° · Queen Elizabeth Is · Prince Patrick I. · Melville I. · Banks I. · Cornwallis I. · Beaufort Sea · 1 · ALASKA (United States of America) · 2 · Victoria I. · Dawson · YUKON TERRITORY · ROCKY MOUNTAINS · Mackenzie · C A N · Arctic Circle · Great Bear Lake · NORTH WEST TERRITORIES · Mt. Logan 5,951 m 19,524 ft. · Whitehorse · Yellowknife · 60° · Great Slave Lake · 3 · Uranium City · Lake Athabasca · Peace · ALBERTA · Athabasca · Queen Charlotte Is. · BRITISH COLUMBIA · SASKATCHEWAN · 50° · Vancouver I. · Edmonton · Medicine Hat · Saskatoon · PACIFIC OCEAN · Vancouver · Calgary · Moose Jaw · Regina · Victoria · 4 · UNITED STATES OF

ATLANTIC
OCEAN

PACIFIC
OCEAN

80°

D **E** 60° **F**

Axel
Heiberg I.

Ellesmere I.

Bathurst I.

Devon I.

Baffin Bay

Somerset I.

Bylot I.

Prince of
Wales I.

Baffin I.

Davis Strait

A **D** **A**

Frobisher
Bay

Southampton I.

Hudson Strait

Labrador Sea

Ungava
Bay

mi.
0   500

0   500
km

Ungava
Peninsula

N E W F O U N D L A N D

Hudson Bay

Churchill

Goose Bay

Churchill

St. John's

MANITOBA

QUEBEC

ST. PIERRE
& MIQUELON
(France)

Gulf of St.
Lawrence

James Bay

Lake
Winnipeg

PRINCE
EDWARD I.

Cape Breton I.

ONTARIO

Chicoutimi

Charlottetown

NEW
BRUNSWICK

ATLANTIC OCEAN

Jonquière

Winnipeg

Kapuskasing

Québec

Fredericton

Halifax

St. Lawrence

NOVA
SCOTIA

Thunder Bay

Montréal

St. Lawrence

AMERICA

Lake Superior

Sault Sainte
Marie

Sudbury

Lake Huron **OTTAWA**

Lake Michigan

Toronto

Lake Ontario

Hamilton

Niagara Falls

London

Windsor

Lake Erie

UNITED STATES OF AMERICA

Area: 3,536,278 sq. mi./9,158,960 km². *Currency:* U.S. dollar. *Capital:* Washington D.C. *Other cities:* New York City, Los Angeles, Chicago, Philadelphia, Detroit, San Francisco, Dallas, Seattle, San Diego, San Antonio, Houston, Boston, Baltimore, Phoenix, Indianapolis, Memphis, Honolulu, San José, Miami, New Orleans, Las Vegas. *Physical features:* Range from arctic (Alaska) to tropical (Hawaii); vast central plain with mountains in W., hills and low mountains in E.; Rocky Mountains separate rivers that flow into Pacific from those emptying into Gulf of Mexico; Great Lakes in N.; rivers include Mississippi, Missouri, Hudson, Colorado. *Climate:* Great regional variation: E. coast is generally temperate, although temperatures rise in the S. and Florida is subtropical; the Midwest, Middle Atlantic states, and New England have warm summers and cold winters with high snowfall; the S.W. has arid and semiarid conditions inland and a Mediterranean climate in California; Hawaii has a tropical climate with high temperatures, heavy rainfall, and little seasonal variation; Alaska has a cold maritime climate on the coast and a polar climate in the interior and the N.; normal temperatures in the U.S.A. range from -19°F in Barrow, Alaska, to 91°F in Mobile, Alabama (but temperatures outside this range also occur); precipitation ranges from a yearly average of less than 2 inches at Death Valley, California, to about 460 inches at Mount Waialeale in Hawaii. *Time zone:* range from GMT –5h (E) to –8h (W) in contiguous states (Alaska, GMT –9h; Hawaii, GMT –10h). *Political system:* Federal republic. *Head of state and government:* President Bill Clinton (from 1993). *Main exports:* Aircraft, coal, chemicals, machinery, corn, wheat, cars, aluminum. *Resources:* Coal, copper, lead, molybdenum, uranium, bauxite, gold, iron ore, nickel, silver, tungsten, crude oil, natural gas, wood.

PEOPLE

Population: 258,233,000. *Distribution urban/rural:* 76%/24%. *Life expectancy:* 72(m), 79(f). *Languages:* English, Spanish. *Ethnic groups:* European origin 71%, African origin 12%, Hispanic origin 9%, Asian or Pacific Islander 3%, Native American, Inuit, and Aleut 1%. *Religions:* Protestant 61% (Baptist 21%, Methodist 12%, Lutheran 8%, Presbyterian 4%, Episcopalian 3%, other 13%), Roman Catholic 25%, Jewish 2%, other 5%, none 7%. *Literacy rate:* 97%. *Per capita GDP:* $22,470.

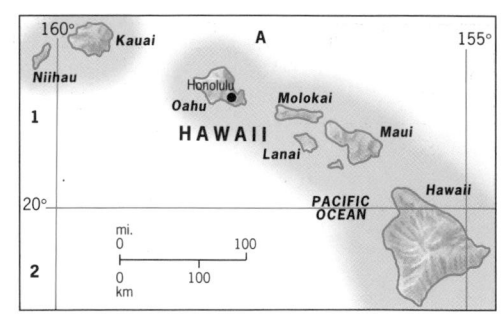

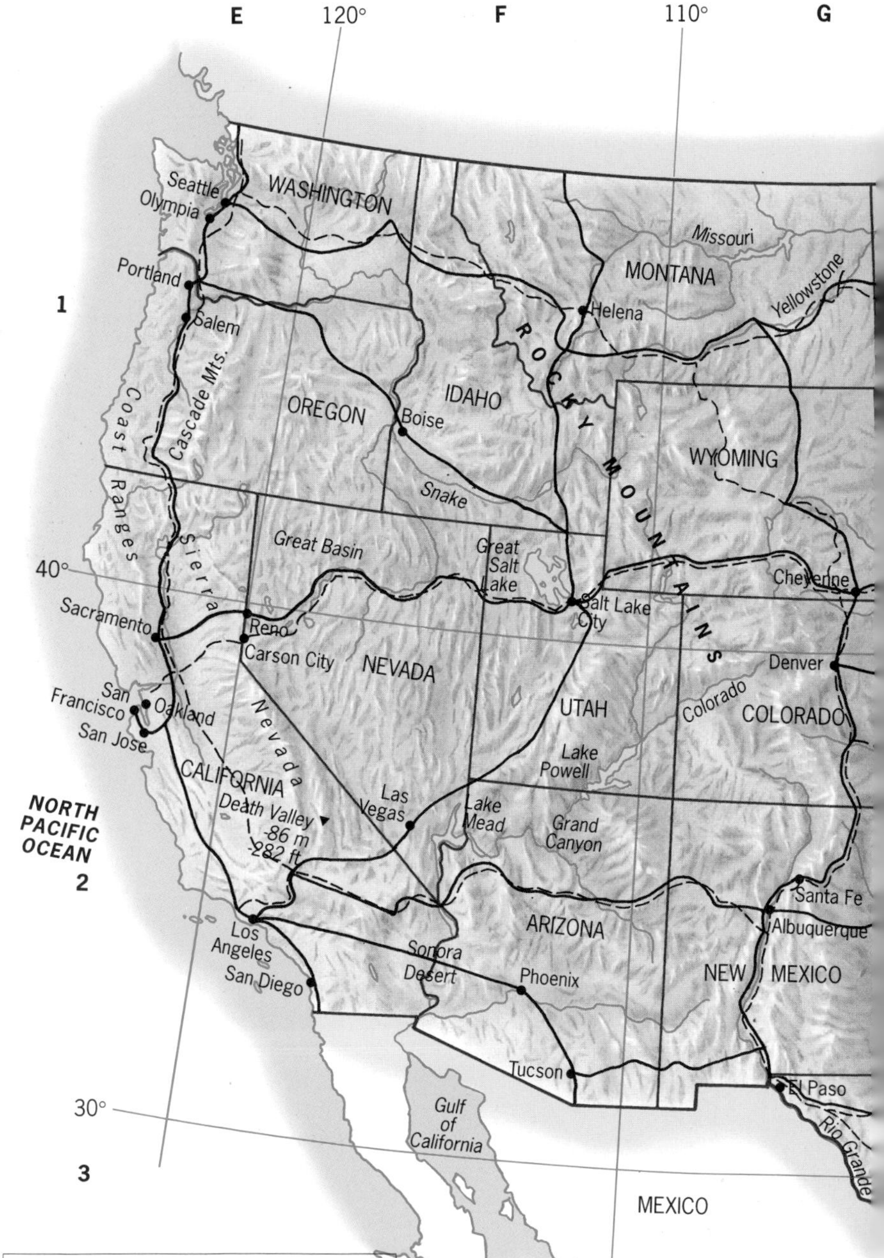

Travel
Tourist features: Disney World (Fl); Grand Canyon (AZ); Statue of Liberty (NY); Yellowstone National Park (WY); **National Holiday:** July 4 (Independence Day).

Alaska Inset

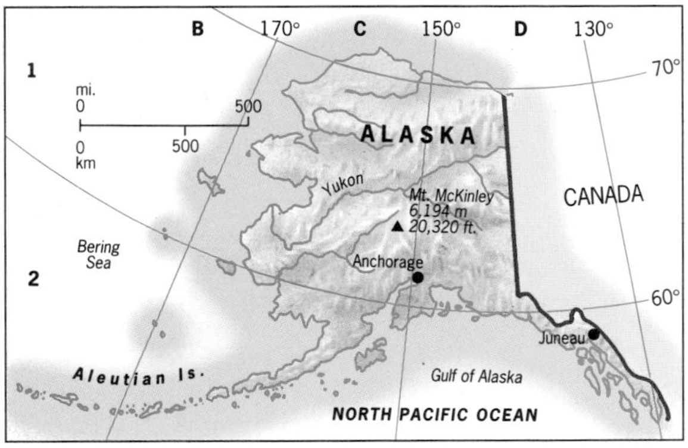

B 170° C 150° D 130°
1
70°

mi.
0 500
0 500
km

ALASKA

Yukon

Mt. McKinley
6,194 m
▲ 20,320 ft.

Anchorage

CANADA

60°

Juneau

Bering
Sea

2

Aleutian Is.

Gulf of Alaska

NORTH PACIFIC OCEAN

Locator Inset

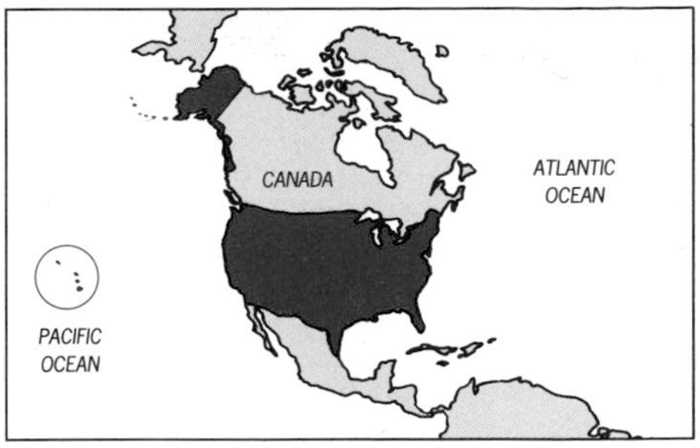

CANADA

ATLANTIC
OCEAN

PACIFIC
OCEAN

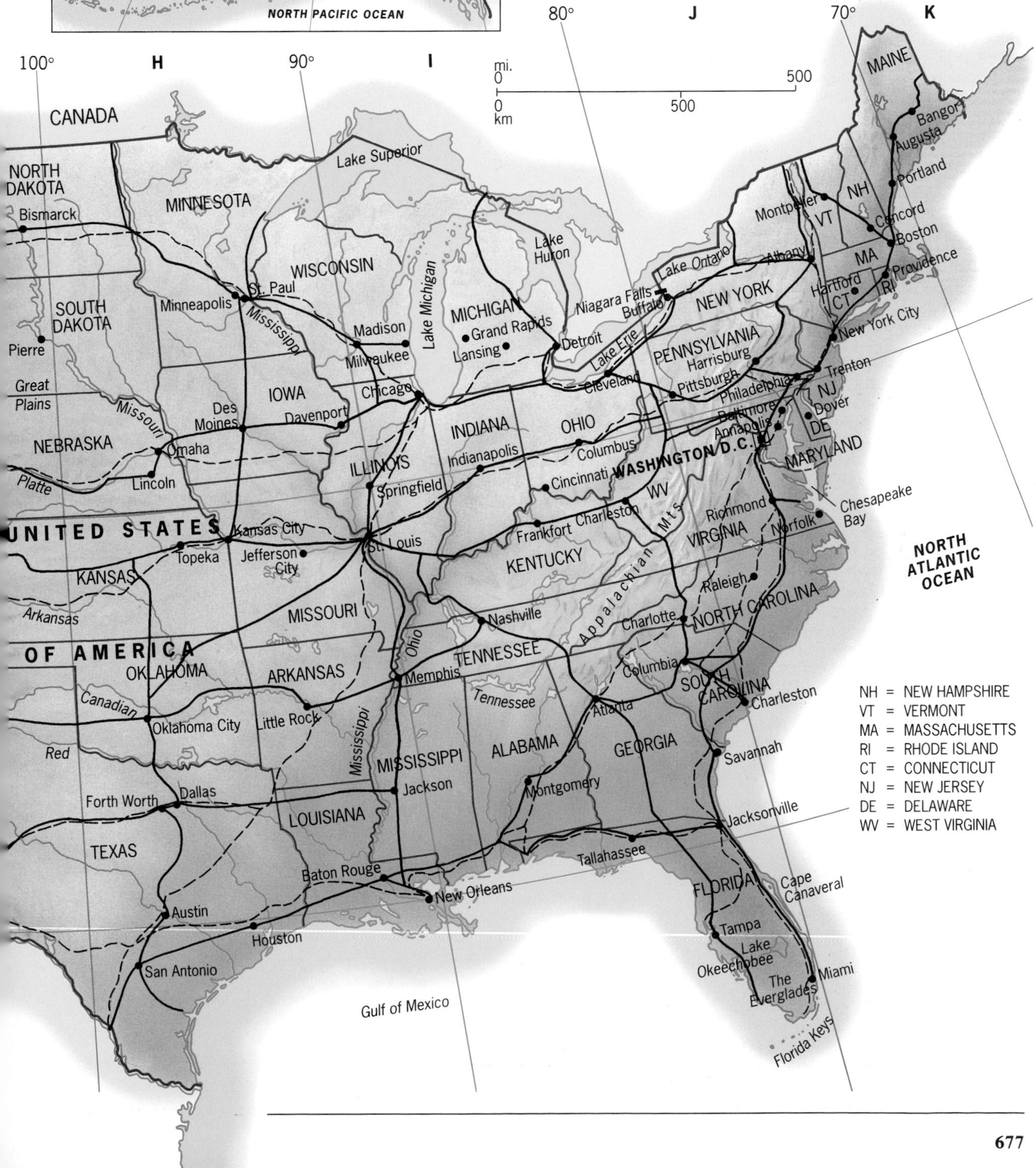

Main Map

80° J 70° K

mi.
0 500
0 500
km

100° H 90° I

CANADA

NORTH
DAKOTA

Bismarck

MINNESOTA

Lake Superior

MAINE

Bangor

Augusta

SOUTH
DAKOTA

Pierre

Great
Plains

Missouri

WISCONSIN

St. Paul

Minneapolis

Madison

Milwaukee

Lake Michigan

Lake
Huron

MICHIGAN

Grand Rapids

Lansing

Detroit

Niagara Falls
Buffalo

Lake Ontario

Lake Erie

Cleveland

NEW YORK

Albany

Montpelier

VT

NH

Concord

Boston

Portland

MA

Hartford
CT

Providence
RI

NEBRASKA

Omaha

Lincoln

Platte

Des
Moines

IOWA

Davenport

Chicago

ILLINOIS

Springfield

INDIANA

Indianapolis

OHIO

Columbus

Cincinnati

PENNSYLVANIA

Harrisburg

Pittsburgh

Philadelphia

Trenton

New York City

NJ

Dover

DE

Baltimore

Annapolis

WASHINGTON D.C.

MARYLAND

Chesapeake
Bay

UNITED STATES

Kansas City

KANSAS

Topeka

Jefferson
City

St. Louis

MISSOURI

Frankfort

Charleston

WV
Mts.

Richmond

Norfolk

VIRGINIA

NORTH
ATLANTIC
OCEAN

Arkansas

KENTUCKY

Nashville

Appalachian

Raleigh

OF AMERICA

OKLAHOMA

Canadian

Red

Oklahoma City

ARKANSAS

Little Rock

Mississippi

Ohio

TENNESSEE

Memphis

Tennessee

NORTH CAROLINA

Charlotte

Columbia

SOUTH
CAROLINA

Charleston

MISSISSIPPI

ALABAMA

GEORGIA

Savannah

Forth Worth

Dallas

TEXAS

LOUISIANA

Jackson

Montgomery

Atlanta

Jacksonville

Austin

Baton Rouge

New Orleans

Houston

Tallahassee

FLORIDA

Cape
Canaveral

San Antonio

Tampa

Lake
Okeechobee

The
Everglades

Miami

Gulf of Mexico

Florida Keys

NH = NEW HAMPSHIRE
VT = VERMONT
MA = MASSACHUSETTS
RI = RHODE ISLAND
CT = CONNECTICUT
NJ = NEW JERSEY
DE = DELAWARE
WV = WEST VIRGINIA

KEY DATES

1492 Christopher Columbus lands in America.

1607 First permanent British settlement.

1767 Townsend Acts levy high duties on tea, paper, lead, and glass.

1770 Boston Massacre—British troops open gunfire on crowd of hecklers; all Townsend duties, apart from those on tea, repealed.

1773 Boston Tea Party—protesters in several ports destroy cargoes of tea.

1775–83 Revolutionary War.

1776 Declaration of Independence. Creation of the United States of America.

1780 British defeated at Yorktown.

1787 Constitution drawn up.

1789 Washington elected first president.

1791 Bill of Rights becomes law.

1803 Louisiana Purchase arranged with France almost doubles size of U.S.A.

1812–14 War with England.

1818 Florida purchased from Spain.

1836 Battle of the Alamo: Texas declares independence from Mexico and applies for annexation to the U.S.A.; independence not recognized by Mexico.

1846–48 Mexican War results in cession to U.S.A. of Arizona, California, Nevada, New Mexico, Texas, Utah, and parts of Colorado and Wyoming.

1848–49 California Gold Rush.

1854 Kansas-Nebraska Act, allowing people of central part of Louisiana Purchase territory to choose whether to become free or slave states, arouses bitter criticism in North; Republican Party founded as antislavery party.

1856 Kansas invaded by abolitionists from New England and applies proslavery forces from Missouri; violence between the two factions begins when abolitionists set up government in Topeka and apply for admission to Union as free state.

1860 Lincoln elected first Republican president, arousing fear for the future of slavery among southerners; 11 southern states secede from the Union.

1861–65 Civil War.

1865 Abolition of slavery; President Lincoln assassinated.

1867 Alaska bought from Russia.

1890 Battle of Wounded Knee, South Dakota, the last major battle with Native American tribes.

1898 War with Spain ends with cession to U.S.A. of Philippines, Puerto Rico, and Guam; annexation of Hawaii.

1917 U.S.A. declares war on Germany.

1919 18th Amendment ratified: Prohibition begins.

1919–21 President Wilson's 14 Points become framework for League of Nations.

1920 19th Amendment ratified: women achieve suffrage.

1920s Economic boom.

1925 Scopes Trial in Tennessee upholds right of states to ban teaching of Darwin's theory of evolution.

1929 Wall Street crash; beginning of Great Depression.

1930 Hawley-Smoot Act raises tariffs; more than 20 nations respond by raising tariffs against the U.S.A.

1932 Franklin D. Roosevelt elected president by overwhelming majority.

1933 National Prohibition ends with 21st Amendment.

1941 Dec. 7: Japanese attack Pearl Harbor; U.S.A. enters World War II.

1945 U.S.A. ends war in the Pacific; Roosevelt dies; atomic bombs dropped on Hiroshima and Nagasaki; Japan surrenders five days later.

1949 U.S.S.R. develops atomic bomb.

1950–53 U.S.A. involved in Korean War.

1954 Supreme Court outlaws compulsory segregation in schools.

1955 Martin Luther King, Jr. emerges as leader in fight against racial discrimination.

1958 First U.S. satellite in orbit.

1961 Abortive invasion of Cuba.

1962 Riots on University of Mississippi campus when black student, James Meredith, tries to enroll.

1963 President John F. Kennedy assassinated; Lyndon B. Johnson assumes the presidency.

1964 Civil Rights Act outlaws discrimination in employment and public accommodations; U.S.A. enters the Vietnam War.

1966 Mississippi becomes last state to repeal statewide Prohibition.

1968 Assassination of Martin Luther King, Jr. precipitates new wave of riots.

1969 Neil Armstrong lands on the moon.

1970 Four students killed by National Guard during demonstrations at Kent State University, Ohio.

1971 Government attempts to prevent publication of "Pentagon Papers," containing details of U.S. participation in Vietnam War; Supreme Court rules in favor.

1973–74 Watergate scandal results in resignation of President Nixon.

1975 U.S.A. withdraws from Vietnam.

1979–80 Iranian hostage crisis.

1980 U.S.A. restricts trade with U.S.S.R. in retaliation for Soviet intervention in Afghanistan.

1983 U.S.A. invades Grenada; relations with U.S.S.R. worsen as President Reagan announces a Strategic Defense Initiative, known as "Star Wars."

1986 Major air strikes against Libya in retaliation for terrorist attacks against Americans; "Irangate" scandal over arms sales to Iran.

1987 U.S.–U.S.S.R. intermediate-range nuclear forces treaty; Wall Street crash.

1988 George Bush elected president.

1989 Bush and Gorbachev declare end to the Cold War; U.S.A. invades Panama.

1991 Allies defeat Iraq in Persian Gulf War; recession hits U.S.A.; April: riots in Los Angeles, killing 52 and causing $1 billion damage.

1993 Inauguration of Bill Clinton.

1994 Democrats lose control of senate in mid-term elections.

1995 Oklahoma City bombing by extremists leaves over 150 dead.

STATES OF THE U.S.A.

N.B.: Each state has two senators. The number of members in the House of Representatives reflects the size of the population of each state.

ALABAMA (AL) 1819
Capital: Montgomery. *Area:* 51,705 sq. mi./133,915 km². *Population:* 4,062,608. *Distribution urban/rural:* 62%/38%. *Representatives:* 7.

ALASKA (AK) 1959
Capital: Juneau. *Area:* 591,004 sq. mi./1,530,700 km². *Population:* 551,947. *Distribution urban/rural:* 64%/36%. *Representatives:* 1.

ARIZONA (AZ) 1912
Capital: Phoenix. *Area:* 114,000 sq. mi./295,260 km². *Population:* 3,677,985. *Distribution urban/rural:* 84%/16%. *Representatives:* 6.

ARKANSAS (AR) 1836
Capital: Little Rock. *Area:* 53,187 sq. mi./137,754 km². *Population:* 2,362,239. *Distribution urban/rural:* 52%/48%. *Representatives:* 4.

CALIFORNIA (CA) 1850
Capital: Sacramento. *Area:* 158,706 sq. mi./411,049 km². *Population:* 29,839,250. *Distribution urban/rural:* 81%/19%. *Representatives:* 52.

COLORADO (CO) 1876
Capital: Denver. *Area:* 104,091 sq. mi./269,595 km². *Population:* 3,307,912. *Distribution urban/rural:* 81%/19%. *Representatives:* 6.

CONNECTICUT (CT) 1788
Capital: Hartford. *Area:* 5,018 sq. mi./12,997 km². *Population:* 3,295,669. *Distribution urban/rural:* 79%/21%. *Representatives:* 6.

DELAWARE (DE) 1787
Capital: Dover. *Area:* 2,044 sq. mi./5,295 km². *Population:* 668,696. *Distribution urban/rural:* 62%/38%. *Representatives:* 1.

FLORIDA (FL) 1845
Capital: Tallahassee. *Area:* 58,664 sq. mi./151,939 km². *Population:* 13,003,362. *Distribution urban/rural:* 84%/16%. *Representatives:* 23.

GEORGIA (GA) 1788
Capital: Atlanta. *Area:* 58,910 sq. mi./152,576 km². *Population:* 6,508,419. *Distribution urban/rural:* 62%/38%. *Representatives:* 11.

HAWAII (HI) 1959
Capital: Honolulu. *Area:* 6,471 sq. mi./16,759 km². *Population:* 1,108,229. *Distribution urban/rural:* 87%/13%. *Representatives:* 2.

IDAHO (ID) 1890
Capital: Boise. *Area:* 83,564 sq.

mi./216,432 km². *Population:* 1,011,986. *Distribution urban/rural:* 54%/46%. *Representatives:* 2.

ILLINOIS (IL) 1818
Capital: Springfield. *Area:* 56,245 sq. mi./145,934 km². *Population:* 11,466,682. *Distribution urban/rural:* 83%/17%. *Representatives:* 20.

INDIANA (IN) 1816
Capital: Indianapolis. *Area:* 36,185 sq. mi./93,720 km². *Population:* 5,564,228. *Distribution urban/rural:* 64%/36%. *Representatives:* 10.

IOWA (IA) 1846
Capital: Des Moines. *Area:* 56,275 sq. mi./145,753 km². *Population:* 2,787,424. *Distribution urban/rural:* 59%/41%. *Representatives:* 5.

KANSAS (KS) 1861
Capital: Topeka. *Area:* 82,277 sq. mi./213,098 km². *Population:* 2,465,600. *Distribution urban/rural:* 67%/33%. *Representatives:* 4.

KENTUCKY (KY) 1792
Capital: Frankfort. *Area:* 40,409 sq. mi./104,660 km². *Population:* 3,698,969. *Distribution urban/rural:* 51%/49%. *Representatives:* 6.

LOUISIANA (LA) 1812
Capital: Baton Rouge. *Area:* 47,752 sq. mi./124,677 km². *Population:* 4,238,216. *Distribution urban/rural:* 69%/31%. *Representatives:* 7.

MAINE (ME) 1820
Capital: Augusta. *Area:* 33,265 sq. mi./86,156 km². *Population:* 1,233,223. *Distribution urban/rural:* 52%/48%. *Representatives:* 2.

MARYLAND (MD) 1788
Capital: Annapolis. *Area:* 10,460 sq. mi./27,092 km². *Population:* 4,535,000. *Distribution urban/rural:* 80%/20%. *Representatives:* 8.

MASSACHUSETTS (MA) 1788
Capital: Boston. *Area:* 8,284 sq. mi./21,456 km². *Population:* 6,029,051. *Distribution urban/rural:* 84%/16%. *Representatives:* 10.

MICHIGAN (MI) 1837
Capital: Lansing. *Area:* 58,527 sq. mi./151,586 km². *Population:* 9,328,784. *Distribution urban/rural:* 71%/29%. *Representatives:* 16.

MINNESOTA (MN) 1858
Capital: St. Paul. *Area:* 84,402 sq. mi./218,661 km². *Population:* 4,337,029. *Distribution urban/rural:* 67%/33%. *Representatives:* 8.

MISSISSIPPI (MS) 1817
Capital: Jackson. *Area:* 47,689 sq. mi./123,515 km². *Population:* 2,586,443. *Distribution urban/rural:* 53%/47%. *Representatives:* 5.

MISSOURI (MO) 1821
Capital: Jefferson City. *Area:* 69,697 sq.

mi./180,516 km². *Population:* 5,137,804. *Distribution urban/rural:* 68%/32%. *Representatives:* 9.

MONTANA (MT) 1889
Capital: Helena. *Area:* 147,046 sq. mi./380,848 km². *Population:* 803,655. *Distribution urban/rural:* 53%/47%. *Representatives:* 1.

NEBRASKA (NE) 1867
Capital: Lincoln. *Area:* 77,355 sq. mi./200,350 km². *Population:* 1,584,617. *Distribution urban/rural:* 63%/37%. *Representatives:* 3.

NEVADA (NV) 1864
Capital: Carson City. *Area:* 110,561 sq. mi./286,352 km². *Population:* 1,206,152. *Distribution urban/rural:* 85%/15%. *Representatives:* 2.

NEW HAMPSHIRE (NH) 1788
Capital: Concord. *Area:* 9,297 sq. mi./24,032 km². *Population:* 1,113,915. *Distribution urban/rural:* 52%/48%. *Representatives:* 2.

NEW JERSEY (NJ) 1787
Capital: Trenton. *Area:* 7,787 sq. mi./20,169 km². *Population:* 7,365,011. *Distribution urban/rural:* 69%/31%. *Representatives:* 13.

NEW MEXICO (NM) 1912
Capital: Santa Fe. *Area:* 121,593 sq. mi./314,295 km². *Population:* 1,521,779. *Distribution urban/rural:* 72%/28%. *Representatives:* 3.

NEW YORK (NY) 1788
Capital: Albany. *Area:* 49,108 sq. mi./127,189 km². *Population:* 17,990,455. *Distribution urban/rural:* 85%/15%. *Representatives:* 31.

NORTH CAROLINA (NC) 1789
Capital: Raleigh. *Area:* 52,669 sq. mi./136,413 km². *Population:* 6,657,630. *Distribution urban/rural:* 48%/52%. *Representatives:* 12.

NORTH DAKOTA (ND) 1889
Capital: Bismarck. *Area:* 70,702 sq. mi./183,119 km². *Population:* 641,364. *Distribution urban/rural:* 51%/49%. *Representatives:* 1.

OHIO (OH) 1803
Capital: Columbus. *Area:* 41,330 sq. mi./107,044 km². *Population:* 10,887,325. *Distribution urban/rural:* 73%/27%. *Representatives:* 19.

OKLAHOMA (OK) 1907
Capital: Oklahoma City. *Area:* 69,956 sq. mi./181,186 km². *Population:* 3,025,495. *Distribution urban/rural:* 67%/33%. *Representatives:* 6.

OREGON (OR) 1859
Capital: Salem. *Area:* 97,073 sq. mi./251,419 km². *Population:* 2,853,733. *Distribution urban/rural:* 68%/32%. *Representatives:* 5.

PENNSYLVANIA (PA) 1787
Capital: Harrisburg. *Area:* 45,308 sq.

mi./117,348 km². *Population:* 11,864,751. *Distribution urban/rural:* 69%/31%. *Representatives:* 21.

RHODE ISLAND (RI) 1790
Capital: Providence. *Area:* 1,212 sq. mi./3,140 km². *Population:* 1,003,464. *Distribution urban/rural:* 87%/13%. *Representatives:* 2.

SOUTH CAROLINA (SC) 1788
Capital: Columbia. *Area:* 31,113 sq. mi./80,582 km². *Population:* 3,505,707. *Distribution urban/rural:* 54%/46%. *Representatives:* 6.

SOUTH DAKOTA (SD) 1889
Capital: Pierre. *Area:* 77,116 sq. mi./199,730 km². *Population:* 699,999. *Distribution urban/rural:* 54%/46%. *Representatives:* 1.

TENNESSEE (TN) 1796
Capital: Nashville. *Area:* 42,114 sq. mi./109,641 km². *Population:* 4,896,641. *Distribution urban/rural:* 60%/40%. *Representatives:* 9.

TEXAS (TX) 1845
Capital: Austin. *Area:* 266,807 sq. mi./691,030 km². *Population:* 18,031,000. *Distribution urban/rural:* 80%/20%. *Representatives:* 30.

UTAH (UT) 1896
Capital: Salt Lake City. *Area:* 84,899 sq. mi./219,889 km². *Population:* 1,727,784. *Distribution urban/rural:* 84%/16%. *Representatives:* 3.

VERMONT (VT) 1791
Capital: Montpelier. *Area:* 9,614 sq. mi./24,900 km². *Population:* 564,964. *Distribution urban/rural:* 34%/66%. *Representatives:* 1.

VIRGINIA (VA) 1788
Capital: Richmond. *Area:* 40,767 sq. mi./105,586 km². *Population:* 6,216,568. *Distribution urban/rural:* 66%/34%. *Representatives:* 11.

WASHINGTON (WA) 1889
Capital: Olympia. *Area:* 68,139 sq. mi./176,479 km². *Population:* 4,887,941. *Distribution urban/rural:* 74%/26%. *Representatives:* 9.

WEST VIRGINIA (WV) 1863
Capital: Charleston. *Area:* 24,231 sq. mi./62,759 km². *Population:* 1,801,625. *Distribution urban/rural:* 64%/36%. *Representatives:* 3.

WISCONSIN (WI) 1848
Capital: Madison. *Area:* 56,143 sq. mi./145,436 km². *Population:* 4,906,745. *Distribution urban/rural:* 54%/36%. *Representatives:* 9.

WYOMING (WY) 1890
Capital: Cheyenne. *Area:* 97,809 sq. mi./253,326 km². *Population:* 453,588. *Distribution urban/rural:* 63%/37%. *Representatives:* 1.

MAIN OUTLYING AREAS

BAKER AND HOWLAND ISLANDS 1856
Status: Unincorporated territory.
Location: c. 1,600mi./2,575km SW of
Hawaii. *Area:* c. 1sq. mi./1.6km².
Population: Uninhabited since 1942.

JARVIS ISLAND 1856
Status: Unincorporated territory.
Location: c. 1,300mi./2,090km S of
Hawaii. *Area:* 1.75sq. mi./4.5km².
Population: Uninhabited since 1942.

JOHNSTON ATOLL 1858
Status: Unincorporated territory.
Location: c. 700mi./1,130km SW of
Hawaii. *Area:* 1.1sq. mi./2.8km².
Population: 1,375 (all U.S. government
personnel).

MIDWAY ISLAND 1867
Status: Unincorporated territory.
Location: 1,150mi./1,850km W-NW of
Hawaii. *Area:* 2sq. mi./5.2km².
Population: Uninhabited Naval Defense
Sea Area.

GUAM 1898
Status: Organized unincorporated territory. *Location:* NW Pacific. *Area:*
209sq. mi./541km². *Capital:* Agaña.
Population: 132,726.

PUERTO RICO 1898
Location: NE Caribbean Sea *(p. 689).*

WAKE ISLAND 1898
Status: Unincorporated possession.
Location: W Pacific Ocean. *Area:* 2.5sq.
mi./6.5km². *Population:* Air Force base;
temporary population of 189 U.S. government employees.

AMERICAN SAMOA 1899
Status: Unorganized unincorporated territory. *Location:* S central Pacific *c.*
2,220mi./3,700km S of Hawaii. *Area:*
77sq. mi./199km². *Capital:* Pago Pago.
Population: 46,638.

U.S. VIRGIN ISLANDS 1917
Location: NE Caribbean Sea *(p. 689).*

KINGMAN REEF 1922
Status: Unincorporated territory.

Location: c. 1,000mi./1,670km S of
Hawaii. *Area:* 47.5sq. mi./123km².
Population: Uninhabited Naval Defense
Sea Area and Airspace Reservation.

NORTHERN MARIANA ISLANDS 1947
Status: Commonwealth. *Location:* Nine
major islands in W central Pacific E of
Philippines and S of Japan. *Area:* 293sq.
mi./759km². *Capital:* Saipon.
Population: 43,345.

ECONOMY

With a huge home market and vast
resources, the U.S.A. has the most powerful economy in the world. It has a major
financial and commodity market in New
York. In many fields, such as civil aviation, the U.S.A. leads the world.

The economy is based on the ethic of
free enterprise, with most decisions being
made by private individuals and companies and a policy of minimal state intervention. Nevertheless, government regulations do exist to ensure that businesses
operate fairly and that working conditions
are safe. The government is also the
nation's largest single buyer of many
goods and services and employs around
20% of the workforce.

Industry by sector
Services In common with most developed nations, the most important sector
in the U.S. economy is the service sector,
which accounts for 72% of the GNP and
in 1990 employed 77% of workers. It is
estimated that, by 2005, four out of five
working Americans will be employed in
the service industries.
Manufacturing Manufacturing accounts
for 19% of the GNP and employs 17% of
workers. The value of U.S. manufactured
goods is greater than that of any other
nation in the world. American factories
produce a very great variety of goods: the
most important products include chemicals, machinery, cars, aircraft, printed
materials, fabricated metal products, scientific instruments, and paper products.
An extensive range of consumer goods is
also produced.

Agriculture, forestry and fishing 2%
of the GNP is accounted for in these areas
which employ 3% of the workforce. The
U.S.A. is the world's leading agricultural
producer and around 16% of world food
exports come from U.S. farms. The single
most important product is beef, but dairy
produce, corn, soy beans, pigs, wheat,
chicken, tobacco, and cotton are also
important. Almost a third of the U.S.A. is
covered by forests which produce timber
and pulp for paper making. The three
fishing grounds of the Atlantic, the Gulf
of Mexico and the Pacific yield the U.S.A.
5.5 million tons of fish a year.
Mining Mining accounts for 2% of the
GNP and employs 1% of the work force.
The U.S.A. is the world's second-largest
producer of petroleum, natural gas, and
coal. Other important minerals are copper, gold, iron ore, silver, and uranium.
Although mining accounts for only a
small proportion of the total output, it is
the key to the growth of other industries.
For example, coal and iron ore are needed
to make steel, which is then used to make
cars, and so on.

North American Free Trade Agreement
On August 12, 1992, the U.S.A., Canada,
and Mexico announced a comprehensive
plan for free trade across North America.
The North American Free Trade
Agreement (NAFTA) was greeted with
enthusiasm by the business community,
but U.S. trade unions feared that it would
send jobs to Mexico where labor costs are
cheaper and environmental regulations
less stringent. The three governments
attempted to quell their anxieties by
adding side agreements to the accord
ensuring that existing labor and environmental laws would be enforced across the
trading bloc. These were signed on 13
and 14 September 1993.

NAFTA brings together 360 million
consumers, creating the largest trading
bloc in the world. It aims to eliminate tariffs within North America and reduce the
value of imports from outside the bloc
within 15 years.

BERMUDA

Area: 19 sq. mi./50 km². *Local
name:* Bermuda. *Currency:* Bermu-
dian dollar. *Capital:* Hamilton.
Physical features: Low hills separat-
ed by fertile depressions. *Climate:*
Subtropical. *Time zone:* GMT −4h.
Political system: Dependent territory
of U.K. *Head of state:* Queen Eliza-
beth II represented by Gov. Lord
David Waddington (from 1992).
Head of government: Premier John
William David Swan (from 1982).
Main exports: Semitropical produce.
Resources: Limestone.

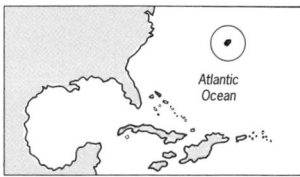

PEOPLE
Population: 60,213. *Distribution
urban/rural:* n.a. *Life expectancy:*
73(m), 77(f). *Language:* English.
Ethnic groups: African origin 61%,
European and other 39%. *Religions:*

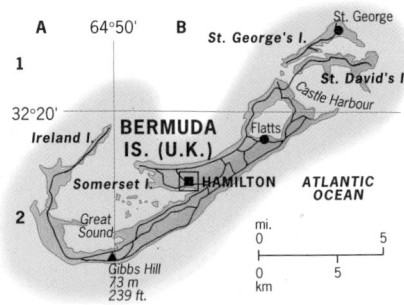

Anglican 37%, Roman Catholic 14%,
African Methodist Episcopal (Zion) 10%,
Methodist 6%, Seventh-Day Adventist
5%, other 28%. *Literacy rate:* 98%. *Per
capita GDP:* $22,400.

MEXICO

Area: 759,530 sq. mi./1,967,183 km². *Local name:* Estados Unidos Mexicanos. *Currency:* Mexican peso. *Capital:* Mexico City. *Other cities:* Guadalajara, Monterrey. *Physical features:* Central plateau between two mountain ranges; coastal lowlands. *Climate:* Tropical in S. and coastal lowlands, cooler and drier in central plateau and mountains. *Time zone:* GMT –6h (E), –8h (W). *Political system:* Federal republic. *Head of state and government:* Ernesto Zedillo (from 1994). *Main exports:* Petroleum, petroleum products, silver, gold, lead, motor vehicles, coffee, cotton. *Resources:* Crude oil, silver, copper, gold, lead, zinc, natural gas, wood.

PEOPLE

Population: 91,261,000. *Distribution urban/rural:* 72%/28%. *Life expectancy:* 69(m), 76(f). *Languages:* Spanish (official), Native American languages. *Ethnic groups:* Mestizo 60%, Native American 29%, European 9%. *Religion:* Roman Catholic 97%. *Literacy rate:* 90%. *Per capita GDP:* $3,200.

KEY DATES

1813 Independence from Spain.
1846–48 Mexican War; much land lost to U.S.A.
1857 War of the Reform between Liberals and Conservatives.
1863 French occupy Mexico City; conservative government installs Archduke Maximilian of Austria as emperor.
1866 Pressure from U.S.A. forces French to leave Mexico; Maximilian is shot.
1876–1911 Dictatorship of Porfirio Diaz.
1911 Francisco Madero president.
1913 Madero killed in military coup; Gen. Victoricao Huerta dictator.
1914 U.S. forces seize Veracruz; Huerta forced to leave Mexico.
1915 Venustiano Carranza president.
1917 Revolutionary constitution brings reforms.
1920 Gen. Alvaro Obregón leads revolt in which Carranza is killed; Obregón elected president.
1928 Obregón assassinated.
1938 Oil workers strike for higher wages; government seizes properties of U.S. and British oil companies.
1942 Mexico joins Allies in World War II.
1952 Women achieve suffrage.
1962 Constitutional amendment empowers government to make businesses share profits with workers.
1970 Luis Echeverria Alvarez becomes president; government tightens controls over foreign-owned businesses.
1974–75 Vast crude oil deposits found.
1976 Economic austerity program; peso devalued twice.
1983–84 Foreign debt and falling oil prices cause severe economic crisis.
1985 Earthquakes; *c.* 7,200 die.
1988 Carlos Salinas de Gortari president; many believe election rigged.
1993 North American Free Trade Agreement with U.S.A. and Canada ratified.
1994 Ernesto Zedillo president.

ECONOMY

Farming Principal food crop is corn; other important crops are bananas, beans, coffee, cotton, oranges, sorghum, sugarcane, and wheat; livestock includes cattle, pigs, sheep, poultry, and horses.
Fishing Sardines, anchovies, shrimp, and tuna are caught.
Mining Silver, gold, copper, and oil.
Manufacturing Petroleum products;

TRAVEL
Visa: None needed by U.S. *Driving permit:* Nat. license/ IDP. *Health and safety:* Check water; inoculations advised. *Tourist features:* Rio Grande; Cancun, Acapulco resorts; Baja California; pre-Columbian archaeological sites, Yucatán Peninsula. *National holiday:* September 16 (Independence Day).

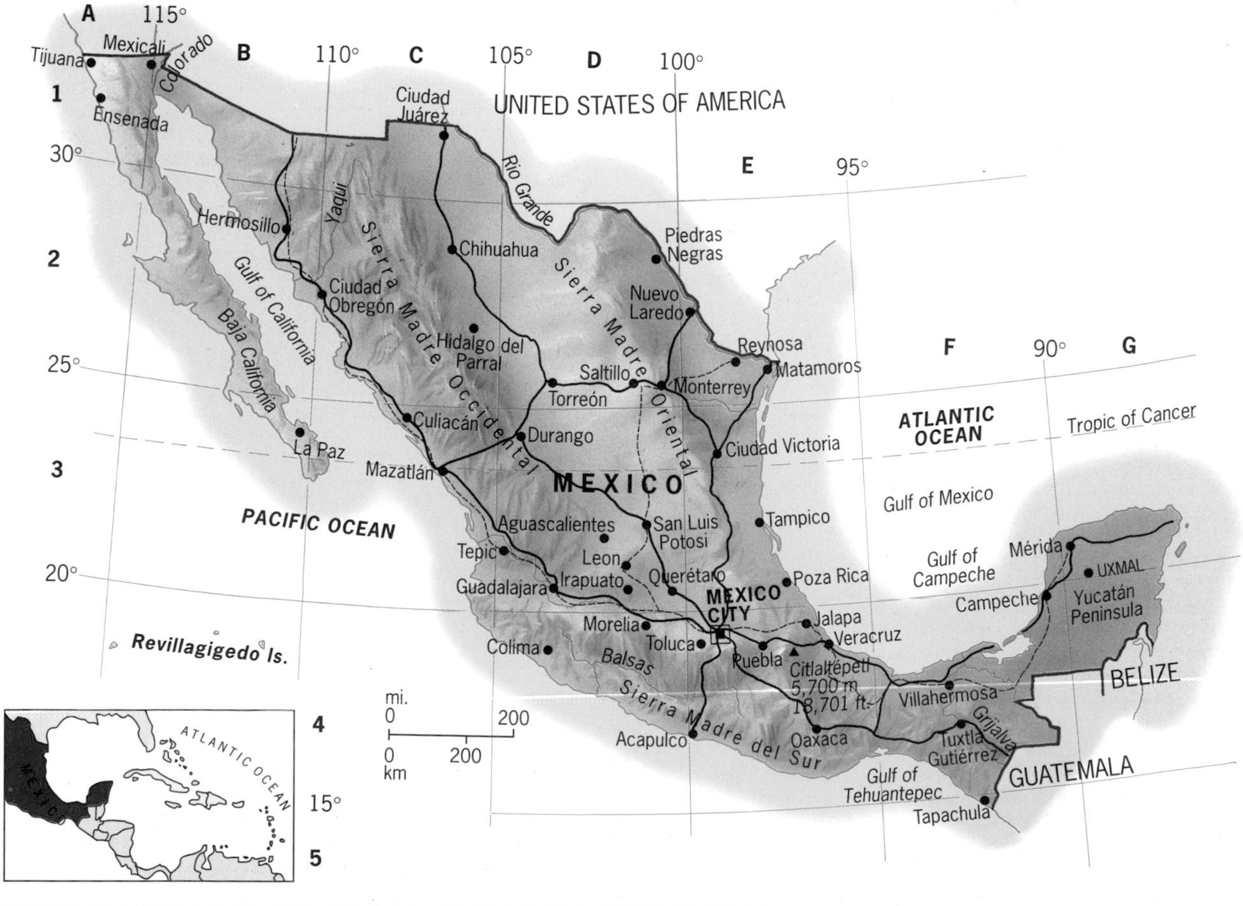

GUATEMALA

Area: 42,045 sq. mi./108,889 km². **Local name:** República de Guatemala. **Currency:** Quetzal. **Capital:** Guatemala City. **Other cities:** Quezaltenango, Puerto Barrios. **Physical features:** Mostly mountainous with narrow coastal plain and rolling limestone plateau. **Climate:** Tropical by coast, temperate in mountains. **Time zone:** GMT –6h. **Political system:** Republic. **Head of state and government:** Ramiro de Leon Carpio (from 1993). **Main exports:** Coffee, sugar, bananas, beef. **Resources:** Crude oil, nickel, fish.

PEOPLE

Population: 10,029,000. **Distribution urban/rural:** 39%/61%. **Life expectancy:** 61(m), 66 (f). **Languages:** Spanish (official), Mayan language. **Ethnic groups:** Maya 55%, Mestizo 44%. **Religion:** Roman Catholic. **Literacy rate:** 55%. **Per capita GDP:** $1,260.

KEY DATES

1821 Independence from Spain.
1954 U.S.-backed coup brings Col. Carlos Castillo to power.
1974 Political violence follows falsified election results.
1981 Antigovernment guerrilla movement grows.
1985 New constitution adopted.
1989 Coup attempt against elected president fails; more than 100,000 killed and 40,000 reported missing since 1980.
1991 Jorge Serrano Elías president.
1993 Military deposes President Serrano; assembly elects Ramiro de León Carpio president.

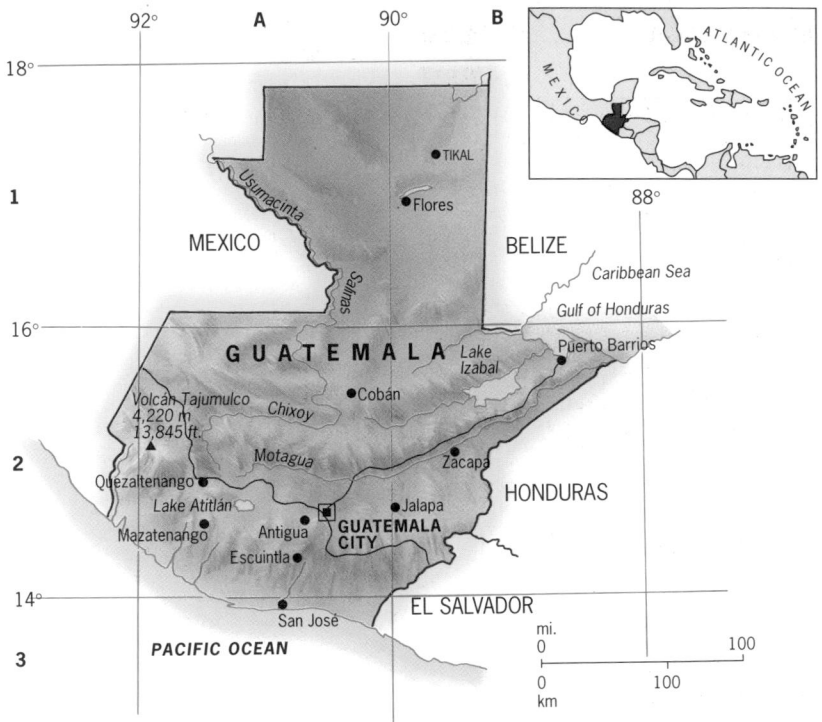

TRAVEL
Visa: Needed by U.S. **Driving permit:** IDP. **Health and safety:** Check water; inoculations advised. **Tourist features:** Mayan archaeological ruins, especially at Tikal. **National holiday:** September 15 (Independence Day).

BELIZE

Area: 8,867 sq. mi./22,965 km². **Currency:** Belize dollar. **Capital:** Belmopan. **Other cities:** Belize City. **Physical features:** Low mountains in S., flat, swampy coastal plain in N., coral reef. **Climate:** Subtropical; rainy season June–Jan. **Time zone:** GMT –6h. **Political system:** Constitutional monarchy. **Head of state:** Queen Elizabeth II represented by Gov.-Gen. Colville Young (1993). **Head of government:** Manuel Esquivel (from 1993). **Main exports:** Sugar, clothing, lobster, shrimp, fish, molasses, citrus fruit, wood and wood products. **Resources:** Wood, fish, arable land potential.

PEOPLE

Population: 205,000. **Distribution urban/rural:** 52%/48%. **Life expectancy:** 67(m), 73 (f). **Languages:** English (official), Spanish, native Creole languages. **Ethnic groups:** Mestizo 43%, Creole 29%, Maya 8%. **Religions:** Roman Catholic 57%, Protestant 28%. **Literacy rate:** 93%. **Per capita GDP:** $1,635.

KEY DATES

1862 Becomes British colony (British Honduras).
1954 Adopts constitution providing for limited self-government.
1964 Granted internal self-government.
1973 British Honduras becomes Belize.
1975 British troops help defend disputed frontier with Guatemala.
1981 Achieves full independence.

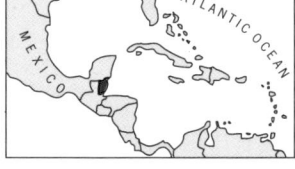

TRAVEL
Visa: None needed by U.S. **Driving permit:** All recognized for 90 days. **Health and safety:** Check water; inoculations advised. **Tourist features:** Second-longest barrier reef in world; Mayan ruins; extensive national parks and reserves. **National holiday:** September 21 (Independence Day).

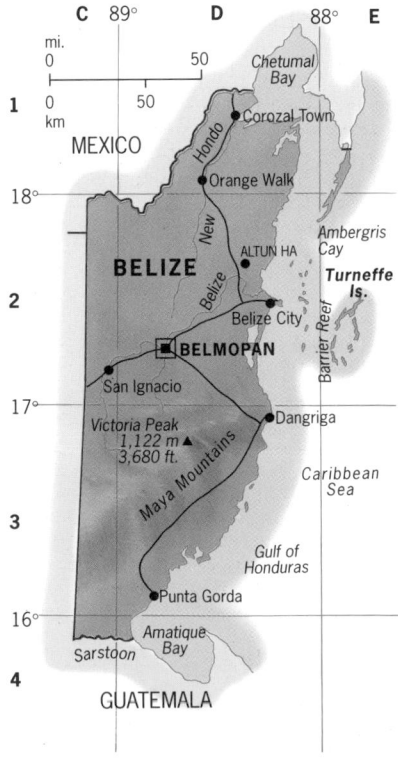

EL SALVADOR

Area: 8,125 sq. mi./21,041 km². *Local name:* República de El Salvador. *Currency:* Salvadoran colón. *Capital:* San Salvador. *Other cities:* Santa Ana, San Miguel. *Physical features:* Narrow coastal plain, mountains in N. and central plateau. *Climate:* Tropical coast, interior steppe. *Time zone:* GMT –6h. *Political system:* Republic. *Head of state and government:* Armando Calderón Sol (from 1994). *Main exports:* Coffee, sugar, corn, cotton, pharmaceuticals. *Resources:* Hydropower, crude oil, geothermal power.

PEOPLE

Population: 5,517,000. *Distribution urban/rural:* 45%/55%. *Life expectancy:* 68(m), 75 (f). *Language:* Spanish. *Ethnic groups:* Mestizo 89%, Indian 10%. *Religion:* Roman Catholic 75%. *Literacy rate:* 75%. *Per capita GDP:* $1,010.

KEY DATES

1821 Achieves independence from Spain.
1931 Military coup.
1969 "Soccer" war with Honduras leaves 2,000 dead; further clashes in 1970 and 1974.
1979 Military coup replaces President Romero with military-civilian junta; start of rebellion by left-wing Farabundo Marti Liberation Front (FMLN).
1991 Government and FMLN sign UN-sponsored peace accord.
1992 Peace accord validated, ending 12 years of civil war; FMLN becomes political party.
1994 Armando Calderón Sol president.

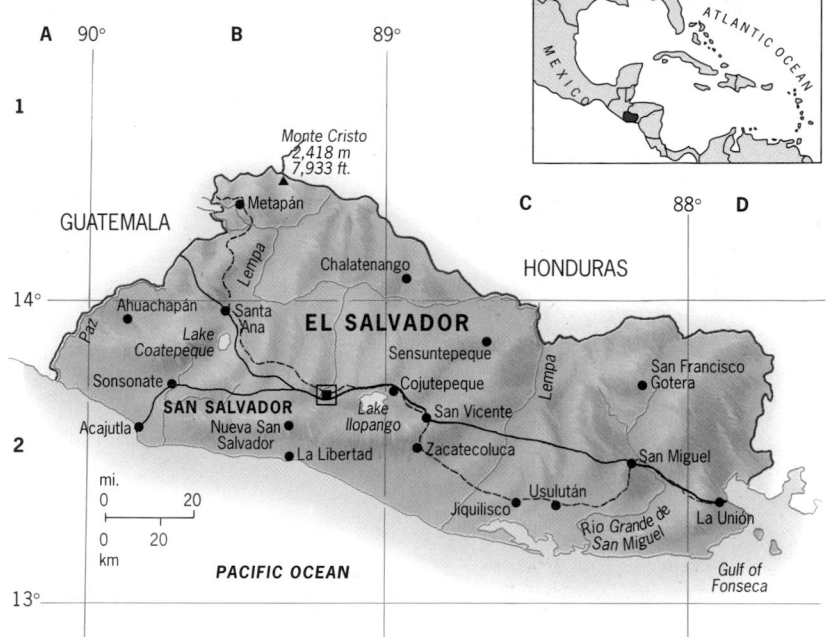

TRAVEL
Visa: Needed by U.S. *Driving permit:* For 30 days from police. *Health and safety:* Check water; inoculations advised. *Tourist features:* Mayan archaeological ruins; many volcanoes. *National holiday:* September 15 (Independence Day).

HONDURAS

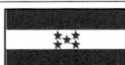

Area: 43,277 sq. mi./112,088 km². *Local name:* República de Honduras. *Currency:* Lempira. *Capital:* Tegucigalpa. *Other cities:* San Pedro Sula, La Ceiba. *Physical features:* Mountainous interior with narrow coastal plains. *Climate:* Subtropical/temperate. *Time zone:* GMT –6 h. *Political system:* Republic. *Head of state and government:* Carlos Roberto Reina (from 1993). *Main exports:* Bananas, coffee, seafood, wood, minerals. *Resources:* Wood, minerals, fish, metals.

PEOPLE

Population: 5,595,000. *Distribution urban/rural:* 41%/59% *Life expectancy:* 65(m), 68(f). *Language:* Spanish (official). *Ethnic groups:* Mestizo 90%, Indian 7%. *Religion:* Roman Catholic 95%. *Literacy rate:* 73%. *Per capita GDP:* $758.

KEY DATES

1821 Independence from Spain.
1980 Civilian government takes power after a century of mostly military rule.

1983 Nicaraguan "contras" operate from Honduras with assistance of U.S.A.
1992 Resolves 130-year-old border dispute with El Salvador.

TRAVEL
Visa: None needed by U.S. *Driving permit:* Nat. license. *Health and safety:* Check water; inoculations advised. *Tourist features:* Mayan ruins at Copan. *National holiday:* September 15 (Independence Day).

NICARAGUA

Area: 50,456 sq. mi./130,682 km². *Local name:* República de Nicaragua. *Currency:* Córdoba. *Capital:* Managua. *Other cities:* León, Granada, Esteli. *Physical features:* Coastal plains rise to central interior mountains. *Climate:* Tropical; rainy season May–Oct. *Time zone:* GMT –6h. *Political system:* Republic. *Head of state and government:* Violeta Barrios de Chamorro (from 1990). *Main exports:* Coffee, cotton, sugar, bananas, seafood, meat, chemicals. *Resources:* Gold, silver, copper, tungsten, lead, zinc, fish, wood.

PEOPLE

Population: 4,265,000. *Distribution urban/rural:* 60%/40%. *Life expectancy:* 61(m), 66(f). *Language:* Spanish. *Ethnic groups:* Mestizo 69%, European 17%, African 9%, Indian 5%. *Religion:* Roman Catholic 88%. *Literacy rate:* 57%. *Per capita GDP:* $425.

KEY DATES

1821 Independence from Spain.
1926–33 Occupation by U.S. Marines.
1936 Gen. Anastasio Somoza becomes president: beginning of Somoza dictatorship.
1962 Sandinista National Liberation Front (FSLN) fights Somoza regime.

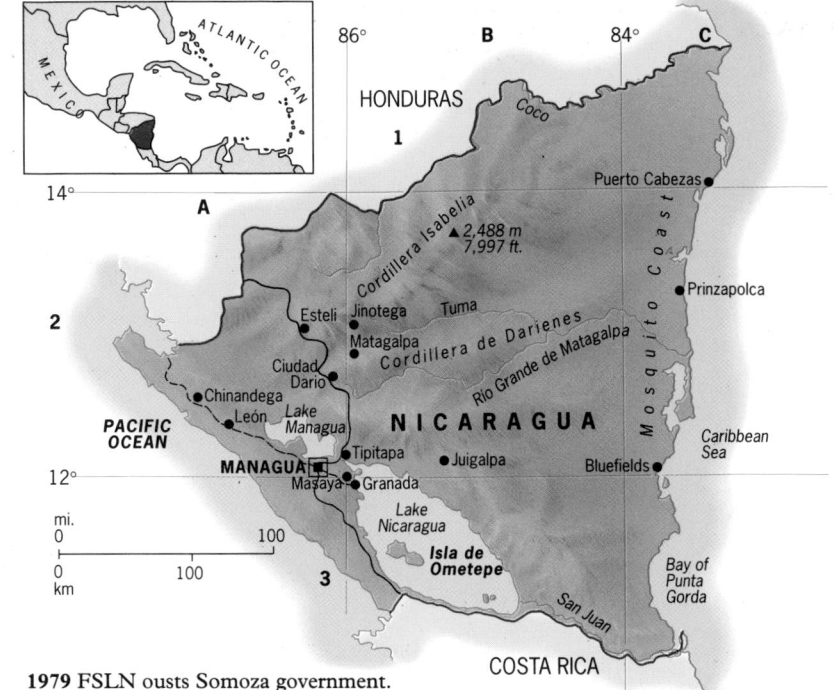

1979 FSLN ousts Somoza government.
1982 Contra guerrillas launch offensive.
1984 U.S.A. mines Nicaraguan harbors; FSLN win democratic elections.
1988 Government holds talks with Contra rebels.
1989 Demobilization of rebels; release of Somoza supporters.
1990 FSLN defeated in elections; Violeta Chamorro becomes president.

TRAVEL
Visa: Needed by U.S. *Driving permit:* Nat. license/ IDP. *Health and safety:* Check water; inoculations advised. *Tourist features:* Mosquito Coast; Fonseca Bay. *National holiday:* September 15 (Independence Day).

COSTA RICA

Area: 19,730 sq. mi./51,100 km². *Local name:* República de Costa Rica. *Currency:* Costa Rican colón. *Capital:* San José. *Other cities:* Limón, Puntarenas. *Physical features:* Coastal plains separated by rugged mountains. *Climate:* Tropical; temperatures vary with altitude; rainy season May–Nov. *Time zone:* GMT –6h. *Political system:* Democratic republic. *Head of state and government:* Rafael Calderón (from 1990). *Main exports:* Coffee, bananas, textiles, sugar, cocoa. *Resources:* Hydropower potential.

PEOPLE

Population: 3,199,000. *Distribution urban/rural:* 50%/50%. *Life expectancy:* 75(m), 79(f). *Language:* Spanish. *Ethnic groups:* Spanish (with Mestizo minority). *Religion:* Roman Catholic 95%. *Literacy rate:* 93%. *Per capita GDP:* $1,900.

KEY DATES

1821 Independence from Spain.
1919 Social reforms under Julio Acosta.

1948–49 Civil war.
1949 New constitution adopted.
1985 U.S.-trained antiguerrilla troops patrol Nicaraguan border.
1987 President Oscar Arias Sánchez wins Nobel Peace Prize for devising Central American peace plan.

TRAVEL
Visa: None needed by U.S. *Driving permit:* Nat. license. *Health and safety:* Inoculations advised; water safe in cities. *Tourist features:* Guayabo pre-Columbian ceremonial site; Poas volcano; national parks. *National holiday:* September 15 (Independence Day).

PANAMA

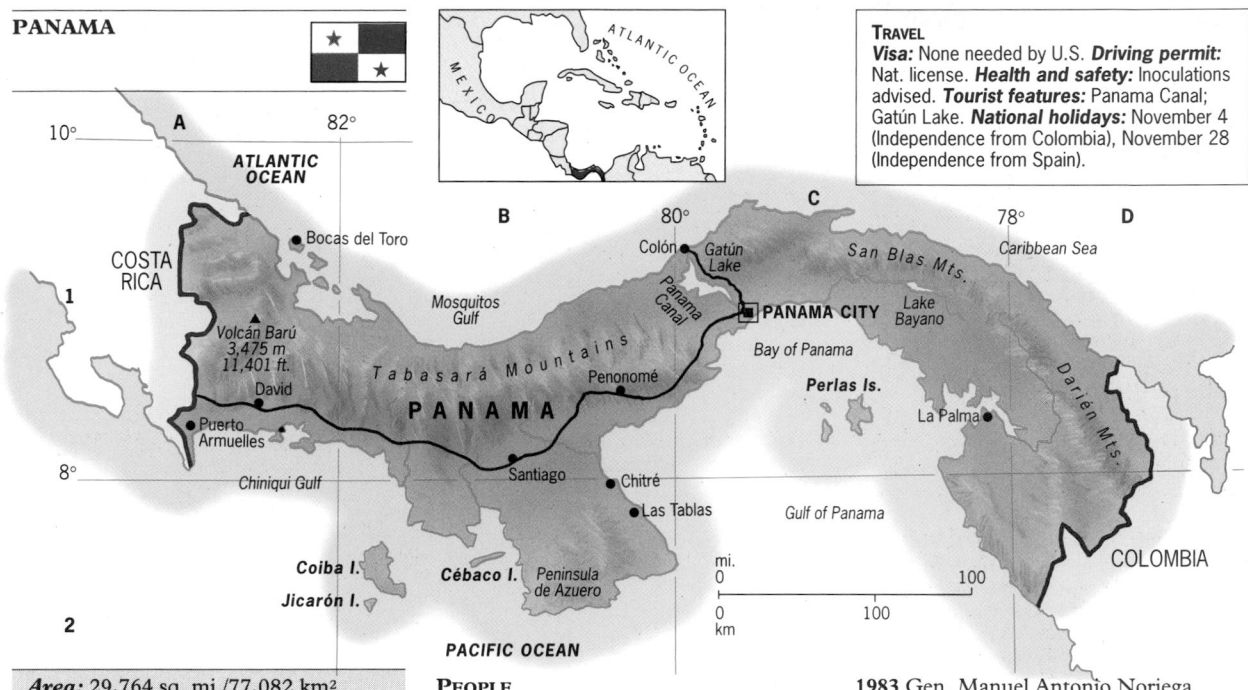

Area: 29,764 sq. mi./77,082 km².
Local name: República de Panamá.
Currency: Balboa. **Capital:** Panama City. **Other city:** Colón. **Physical features:** Interior: mostly steep with rugged mountains and upland plains; coastal areas: plains and rolling hills. **Climate:** Tropical; rainy season May–Jan. **Time zone:** GMT –5h (E), –6h (W). **Political system:** Centralized republic. **Head of state and government:** Guillermo Endara (from 1989). **Main exports:** Bananas, shrimp, sugar, textiles, coffee. **Resources:** Copper, mahogany, forests, shrimp.

PEOPLE

Population: 2,529,902. **Distribution urban/rural:** 53%/47%. **Life expectancy:** 73(m), 77(f). **Languages:** Spanish (official), English. **Ethnic groups:** Mestizo 70%, West Indian 14%, European 10%, Indian 6%. **Religions:** Roman Catholic 93%, Protestant 6%. **Literacy rate:** 87%. **Per capita GDP:** $2,040.

KEY DATES

1821 Independence from Spain.
1903 Gains independence from Colombia with U.S. assistance.
1968–78 Dictatorship of Brig.-Gen. Omar Torrijos Herrera.

1983 Gen. Manuel Antonio Noriega becomes head of military.
1988 Two U.S. federal grand juries indict Noriega on drug trafficking charges; President Eric Arturo Delvalle dismisses Noriega but is ousted by his supporters; U.S.A. imposes economic sanctions; state of emergency declared.
1989 Elections declared invalid by government; attempted coup; assembly declares Noriega head of government; U.S.A. invades Panama; Noriega seeks asylum in Vatican embassy; Guillermo Endara named president.
1990 Noriega surrenders to U.S. officials.
1992 Noriega sentenced to 40 years in prison in U.S.A. for drug trafficking.

PANAMA CANAL ZONE

The Panama Canal Zone is a strip of land across the Isthmus of Panama which extends for 5 mi. (8 km) on either side of the Panama Canal. Apart from Panama City and Colón, the Panama Canal Zone was under U.S. rule between 1903 and 1979. The land was accorded to the U.S.A. in order for it to build, control, and defend the Panama Canal, but conflict arose between the two countries as many of the Panamanians living in the zone resented being governed by a foreign power: violent rebellions were common. The canal zone is due to be returned to Panama at the end of 1999.

KEY DATES

1903 Hay-Bunau-Varilla Treaty between the U.S.A. and Panama gives the U.S.A. construction rights to the Panama Canal and control of the Canal Zone. In return, for an initial payment of $10 million plus $250,000 a year, independence from Colombia is guaranteed.
1914 Panama Canal completed.
1958–59 Riots break out as Panamanians

demand the right to fly their country's flag in the Canal Zone.
1962 Panama and the U.S.A. agree that both flags should fly side by side in selected civilian areas of the zone; the U.S. government grants higher wages to Panamanians working in the Canal Zone who were previously paid less than their U.S. counterparts.
1964 Further riots during which 20 Panamanians and four U.S. citizens are killed; Panama severs diplomatic relations with the U.S.A.; the U.S. government agrees to negotiate a new treaty to replace the 1903 pact, and diplomatic relations are restored.
1977 After much negotiation, two new treaties are signed: one accords Panama territorial jurisdiction of the zone from 1979 and control of the canal itself from December 31, 1999, and the other allows the U.S.A. to retain the right to defend the neutrality of the canal after 1999.
1978 The U.S. Senate approves the treaties of 1977.

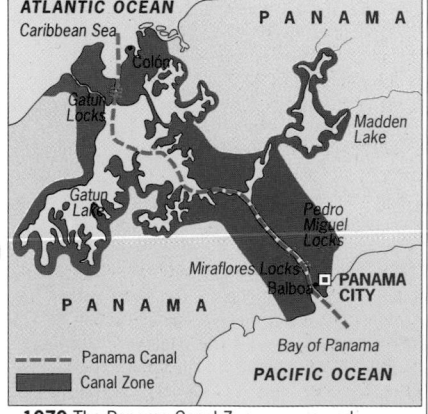

1979 The Panama Canal Zone comes under Panamanian jurisdiction.
1999 Control of the Panama Canal scheduled to return to Panama.

CUBA

Area: 42,806 sq. mi./110,861 km². *Local name:* República de Cuba. *Currency:* Cuban peso. *Capital:* Havana. *Other cities:* Santiago de Cuba, Camagüey, Cienfuegos. *Physical features:* Mostly flat to rolling plains with rugged hills and mountains in the S.E. *Climate:* Tropical with heavy rainfall; rainy season May–Oct. *Time zone:* GMT –5h. *Political system:* Communist state. *Head of state and government:* Fidel Castro Ruz (from 1959). *Main exports:* Sugar, nickel, medical products, shellfish, citrus fruit, refined minerals. *Resources:* Cobalt, chromium, nickel, iron ore, copper, manganese, salt, wood, silica.

PEOPLE

Population: 10,905,000. *Distribution urban/rural:* 72%/28%. *Life expectancy:* 74(m), 79(f). *Language:* Spanish. *Ethnic groups:* Hispanic, African origin. *Religions:* Roman Catholic 42%, none 49%. *Literacy rate:* 99%. *Per capita GNP:* $1,580.

KEY DATES

1492 Christopher Columbus lands in Cuba and claims it for Spain.

1898 U.S.A. defeats Spain in Spanish-American War; Spain gives up all claims to Cuba.

1898–1902 U.S. military government controls Cuba.

1902 Achieves independence; Platt Amendment: provision in new constitution entitles U.S.A. to intervene in Cuban affairs.

1906–09 Second U.S. occupation.

1952 Former president Fulgencio Batista seizes power; harsh dictatorship begins.

1953 Fidel Castro leads unsuccessful coup against Batista.

1956 Second unsuccessful coup by Castro; guerrilla fighting ensues.

1959 Castro overthrows Batista and becomes prime minister; government begins program of sweeping economic and social change.

1960 All U.S. businesses in Cuba appropriated without compensation; U.S.A. breaks off diplomatic relations.

1961 Failure of U.S.-sponsored invasion of Cuba at the Bay of Pigs; Castro announces Cuba is a Communist state following Marxist-Leninist models of economic development.

1962 U.S.A. imposes trade embargo; Soviet nuclear missiles installed in Cuba but removed at U.S. insistence.

1972 Becomes full member of Moscow-based Council for Mutual Economic Assistance (COMECON); adopts new constitution declaring the nation to be a socialist republic.

1976 Castro elected president; new constitution adopted.

1976–81 Involvement in overseas affairs, including the sending of Cuban troops to Africa, especially to Angola.

1983 U.S. invasion of Grenada involves conflict with Cubans working there; 24 die, 700 captured.

1984 Attempt to improve U.S.-Cuban relations by discussing exchange of U.S. prisoners in Cuba for Cuban "undesirables" in the U.S.A.

1988 Cuba signs peace agreement with South Africa and pledges to withdraw from Angola.

1991 Soviet troops withdraw from Cuba; economy suffers badly from demise of Communist bloc.

1993 Epidemic sweeps country, affecting 43,000; later discovered to be due to a vitamin deficiency.

1994 Aug.: Crisis over Cuban "boat refugees"; thousands go to U.S.A., which restricts entry; Sept.: new U.S.-Cuban emigration agreement.

ECONOMY

Farming All major farms are state run, and private farmers have to sell their produce to the state. Sugar cane and tobacco are the chief products. Other crops include bananas, corn, cassava, fruit, coffee, rice, potatoes, and tomatoes. Cattle raising has been encouraged. Pigs, horses, sheep, and goats are also kept.

Fishing Cuba's state-owned fishing fleet is an important revenue source.

Mining Cuba has large nickel reserves, and also deposits of limestone, chromium, copper, and iron.

Manufacturing Textiles, cement, shoes, and clothing are made. Food processing and refining of imported petroleum.

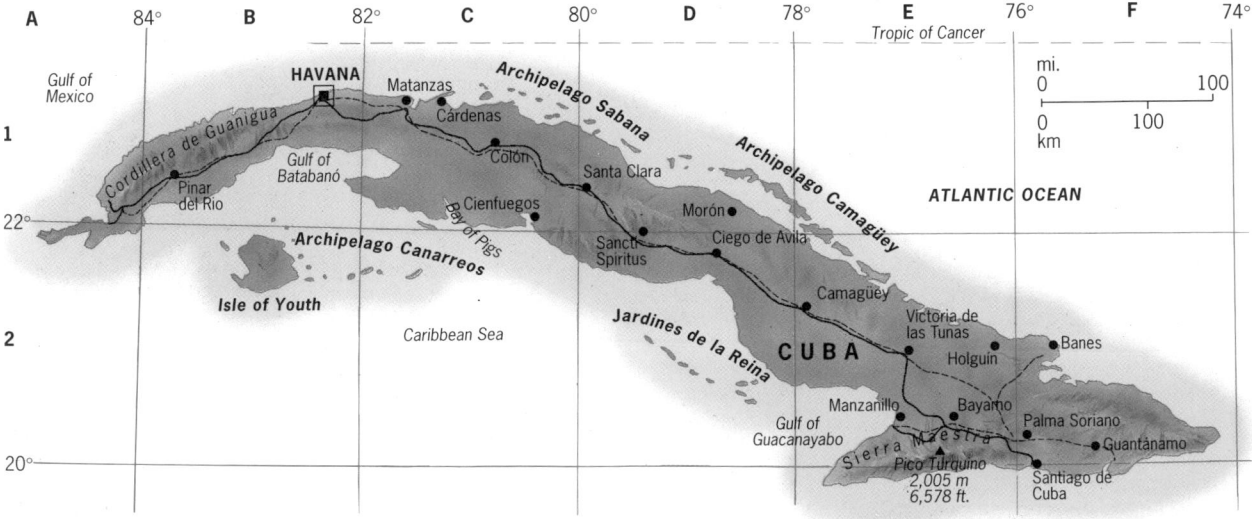

TRAVEL

Visa: Travel not permitted from U.S.A.
Driving permit: Nat. license. *Health and safety:* Check water; inoculations advised.
Tourist features: Beaches; coral islands, and reefs; scuba diving; deep-sea fishing.
National holiday: July 26 (Rebellion Day).

BAHAMAS
TURKS AND CAICOS ISLANDS

Area: 5,353 sq. mi./13,864 km². *Currency:* Bahamian dollar. *Capital:* Nassau. *Other cities:* New Providence, Freeport. *Physical features:* Long, flat coral formations; some low hills. *Climate:* Mild and tropical. *Time zone:* GMT –5h. *Political system:* Constitutional monarchy. *Head of state:* Queen Elizabeth II represented by Gov.-Gen. Sir Clifford Darling (from 1992). *Head of government:* Prime Minister Hubert Ingraham (from 1992). *Main exports:* Mineral fuels, chemicals, food, tobacco, livestock, rum. · *Resources:* Salt, aragonite, wood.

PEOPLE
Population: 269,000. *Distribution urban/rural:* 60%/40%. *Life expectancy:* 69(m), 76(f). *Language:* English. *Ethnic groups:* African origin 85%; British, Canadian, U.S. 15%. *Religions:* Baptist 32%, Anglican 20%, Roman Catholic 19%. *Literacy rate:* 95%. *Per capita GDP:* $9,900.

BAHAMAS KEY DATES
1717 Becomes a British colony.
1964 Britain grants self-government.

1967 First national assembly elections.
1973 Achieves full independence within British Commonwealth.

TURKS AND CAICOS Islands
Area: 166 sq. mi./430 km². *Population:* 12,697. *Political system:* Dependent territory of United Kingdom.

TRAVEL
Visa: None needed by U.S. *Driving permit:* IDP. *Health and safety:* Check water; inoculations advised. *Tourist features:* Scuba diving; deep-sea fishing; Blue Holes of Andros, world's longest and deepest submarine caves; beaches. *National holiday:* July 10 (Independence Day).

JAMAICA
CAYMAN ISLANDS

Area: 4,412 sq. mi./11,425 km². *Currency:* Jamaican dollar. *Capital:* Kingston. *Other cities:* Montego Bay, Spanish Town. *Physical features:* Mountainous with narrow coastal plain. *Climate:* Tropical lowlands, cooler highlands. *Time zone:* GMT –5h. *Political system:* Constitutional monarchy. *Head of state:* Queen Elizabeth II represented by Gov.-Gen. Howard Cooke (from 1991). *Head of government:* P. J. Patterson (from 1992). *Main exports:* Bauxite, aluminum, sugar, fruit, building materials, molasses, rum. *Resources:* Bauxite, gypsum, limestone.

PEOPLE
Population: 2,495,000. *Distribution urban/rural:* 52%/48%. *Life expectancy:* 72(m), 76(f). *Languages:* English (official), Creole. *Ethnic groups:* African 76%, mixed 15%, Asian, European. *Religions:* Protestant 60%, Roman Catholic 5%. *Literacy rate:* 98%. *Per capita GDP:* $1,400.

JAMAICA KEY DATES
1509 Spanish occupy Jamaica.
1655 British capture island.
1944 Limited self-government.
1962 Independence in Commonwealth.
1988 Hurricane Gilbert damages island.

CAYMAN ISLANDS
Area: 100 sq. mi./259 km². *Population:* 29,139. *Political system:* Dependent territory of United Kingdom.

TRAVEL
Visa: Needed by U.S. *Driving permit:* IDP. *Health and safety:* Inoculations advised. *Tourist features:* Waterfall climbing; Blue Mountains; beaches. *National holiday:* August 5 (Independence Day).

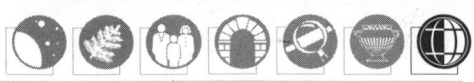

HAITI

Area: 10,715 sq. mi./27,750 km². *Local name:* République d'Haïti. *Currency:* Gourde. *Capital:* Port-au-Prince. *Other cities:* Les Cayes, Cap-Haïtien, Gonaïves. *Physical features:* Mostly rugged mountains. *Climate:* Tropical. *Time zone:* GMT –5h. *Political system:* Republic. *Head of state:* Jean-Bertrand Aristide (from 1994). *Head of government:* Smarck Michel (from 1995). *Main exports:* Light manufactures, coffee. *Resources:* Bauxite.

PEOPLE

Population: 6,903,000. *Distribution urban/rural:* 29%/71%. *Life expectancy:* 53(m), 55(f). *Languages:* French, Creole (both official). *Ethnic groups:* African origin 95%. *Religions:* Catholic 80%, Protestant 10%, Voodoo practiced widely. *Literacy rate:* 53%. *Per capita GDP:* $440.

KEY DATES

1804 Independence from France.
1957 Beginning of dictatorship of "Papa Doc" Duvalier.
1971 Son "Baby Doc" succeeds.
1986 "Baby Doc" Duvalier flees.
1988 Martial law declared.

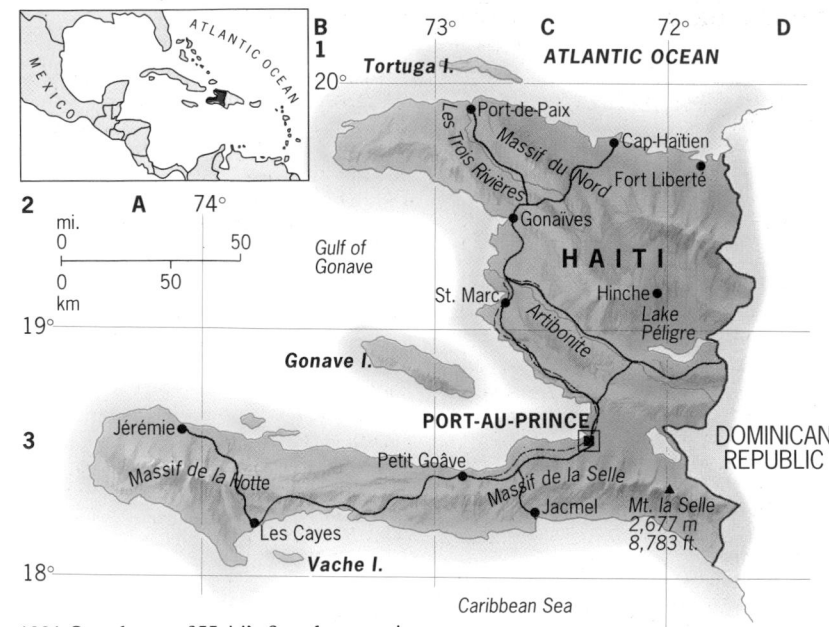

1991 Overthrow of Haiti's first democratically elected president, Jean-Bertrand Aristide, in coup led by Brig.-Gen. Raoul Cedras.
1993 UN embargo to force Aristide's reinstatement fails.
1994 U.S. invasion forces Aristide's return to office; constitutional government restored.

TRAVEL
Visa: Needed by U.S. *Driving permit:* IDP. *Health and safety:* Check water; inoculations advised. *Tourist feature:* La Tortuga Island, former pirate den, off N. coast. *National holiday:* January 1 (Independence Day).

DOMINICAN REPUBLIC

Area: 18,704 sq. mi./48,442 km². *Local name:* República Dominicana. *Currency:* Peso. *Capital:* Santo Domingo. *Other cities:* Santiago, San Pedro de Macoris. *Physical features:* Rugged highlands and mountains interspersed with fertile valleys. *Climate:* Mostly subtropical with heavy rainfall. *Time zone:* GMT –4h. *Political system:* Republic. *Head of state and government:* Joaquín Ricardo Balaguer (from 1986). *Main exports:* Sugar, coffee, molasses, cocoa, gold. *Resources:* Nickel, bauxite, gold, silver.

PEOPLE

Population: 7,608,000. *Distribution urban/rural:* 60%/40%. *Life expectancy:* 66(m), 70(f). *Language:* Spanish. *Ethnic groups:* European 16%, African 11%, mixed 73%. *Religion:* Roman Catholic 95%. *Literacy rate:* 83%. *Per capita GDP:* $950.

KEY DATES

1844 Dominican Republic established.
1930–61 Dictatorship of Rafael Trujillo.
1962 First democratic elections bring Juan Bosch to power.
1963 Bosch overthrown in military coup.

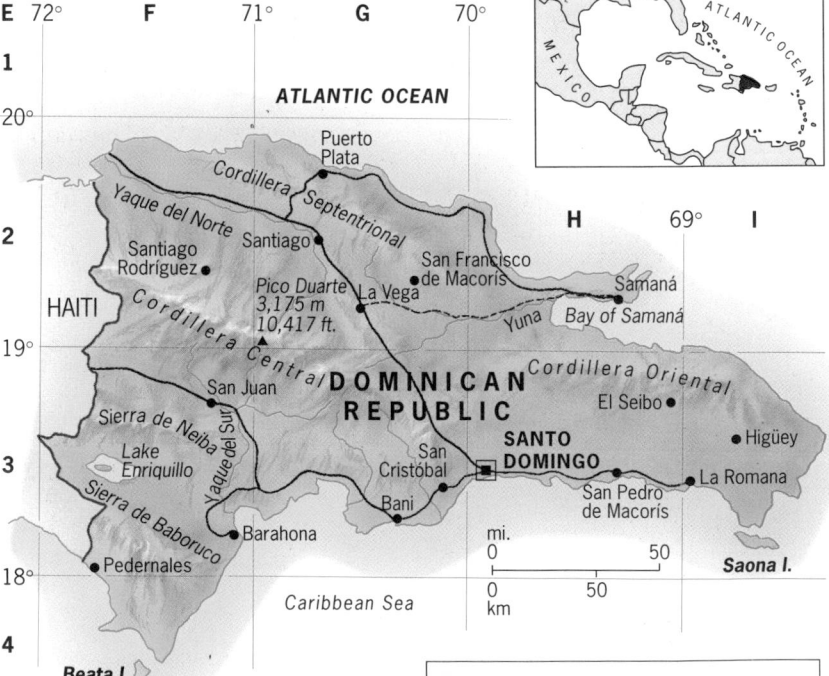

1965 Communist rebels attempt to overthrow military junta; U.S. Marines intervene to restore order.
1966 Constitutional government restored.
1979 Hurricane devastates much of island, killing 2,000.

TRAVEL
Visa: None needed by U.S. *Driving permit:* Nat. license. *Health and safety:* Check water; inoculations advised. *Tourist feature:* Santo Domingo, oldest European city in the Western Hemisphere. *National holiday:* February 27 (Independence Day).

PUERTO RICO

Area: 3,435 sq. mi./8,897 km². *Local name:* Estado Libre Asociado de Puerto Rico. *Currency:* U.S. dollar. *Capital:* San Juan. *Other cities:* Mayaguez, Ponce. *Physical features:* Mostly mountainous with coastal plain in N.; mountains precipitous to sea on W. coast. *Climate:* Tropical with little seasonal variation. *Time zone:* GMT –4h. *Political system:* Commonwealth associated with the U.S.A. *Head of state:* Bill Clinton (from 1993). *Head of government:* Gov. Hernández Colón (from 1988). *Main exports:* Pharmaceuticals, electronic machinery, tuna, rum. *Resources:* Some copper and nickel; crude oil (unexploited).

PEOPLE
Population: 3,620,000. *Distribution urban/rural:* 67%/33%. *Life expectancy:* 70(m), 78(f). *Languages:* Spanish (official), English. *Ethnic groups:* Hispanic 99%. *Religions:* Roman Catholic 85%, Protestant and other 15%. *Literacy rate:* 89%. *Per capita GDP:* $6,600.

KEY DATES
1898 Ceded to the U.S.A. after Spanish-American War.
1917 Puerto Ricans gain U.S. citizenship.
1940s Start of "Operation Bootstrap" to improve economy.
1952 National referendum votes in favor of commonwealth status.
1967 Vote to retain commonwealth status.

TRAVEL
Visa: None needed by U.S. *Driving permit:* IDP. *Health and safety:* Inoculations advised. *Tourist feature:* Camuy caves. *National holiday:* July 25 (Constitution Day).

VIRGIN ISLANDS (U.K.)

Area: 59 sq. mi./153 km². *Currency:* Dollar. *Capital:* Road Town. *Physical features:* Coral islands flat; volcanic islands hilly. *Climate:* Tropical. *Time zone:* GMT –4h. *Political system:* Dependent territory of the U.K. *Head of state:* Queen Elizabeth II represented by Gov.-Gen. P. A. Penfold (from 1991). *Head of government:* H. Lavity Stoutt (from 1986). *Main exports:* Rum, fish, sand, fruits. *Resources:* Negligible.

PEOPLE
Population: 12,555. *Life expectancy:* 71(m), 75(f). *Language:* English. *Ethnic groups:* Afro-Caribbean 90%, European and Asian 10%. *Religions:* Protestant 86%, Roman Catholic 6%, other 8%. *Literacy rate:* 98%. *Per capita GDP:* $10,000.

VIRGIN ISLANDS (U.S.)

Area: 132 sq. mi./342 km². *Currency:* Dollar. *Capital:* Charlotte Amalie. *Physical features:* Hilly to mountainous with little level land. *Climate:* Tropical; rainy season May–Nov. *Time zone:* GMT –4h. *Political system:* Organized, unincorporated territory of the U.S.A. *Head of state and government:* Bill Clinton (from 1993). *Main exports:* Refined petroleum products. *Resources:* Negligible.

PEOPLE
Population: 98,942. *Life expectancy:* 74(m), 77(f). *Languages:* English (official), Spanish, Creole. *Ethnic groups:* Afro-Caribbean 74%, mixed 13%, Puerto Rican 5%, other 8%. *Religions:* Protestant 59%, Roman Catholic 34%, other 7%. *Per capita GDP:* $11,000.

ANTIGUA AND BARBUDA

Area: 170 sq. mi./442 km². *Currency:* E. Caribbean dollar. *Capital:* St. John's. *Physical features:* Limestone and coral islands with volcanic areas. *Climate:* Tropical. *Time zone:* GMT –4h. *Political system:* Constitutional monarchy. *Head of state:* Queen Elizabeth II represented by Gov.-Gen. Sir Wilfred Jacobs (from 1981). *Head of government:* Vere Cornwall Bird (from 1981). *Main exports:* Petroleum products, cotton, sugar, fruit. *Resources:* Negligible.

PEOPLE
Population: 67,000. *Distribution urban/rural:* 32%/68%. *Life expectancy:* 71(m), 75(f). *Language:* English. *Ethnic groups:* Mostly African descent. *Religion:* Anglican. *Literacy rate:* 90%. *Per capita GDP:* $6,500.

KEY DATES
1632 English settlers colonize Antigua.
1967 Becomes Commonwealth state.
1981 Independence from Britain.
1983 Assists U.S. invasion of Grenada.

TRAVEL
Visa: None needed by U.S. *Driving permit:* From police by showing nat. license. *Health and safety:* Inoculations advised. *Tourist feature:* Nelson's Dockyard. *National holiday:* November 1 (Independence Day).

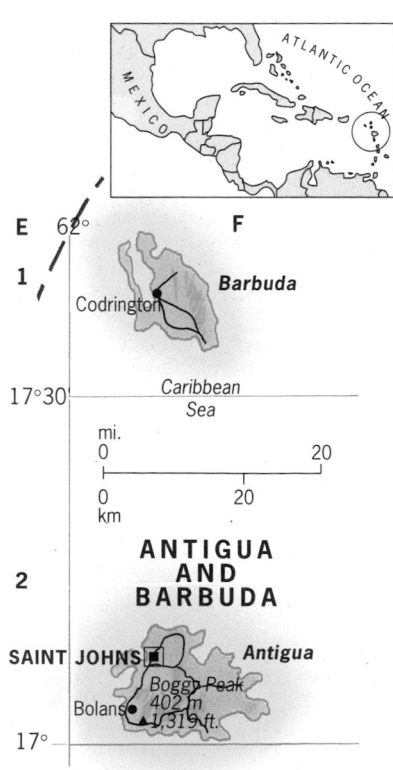

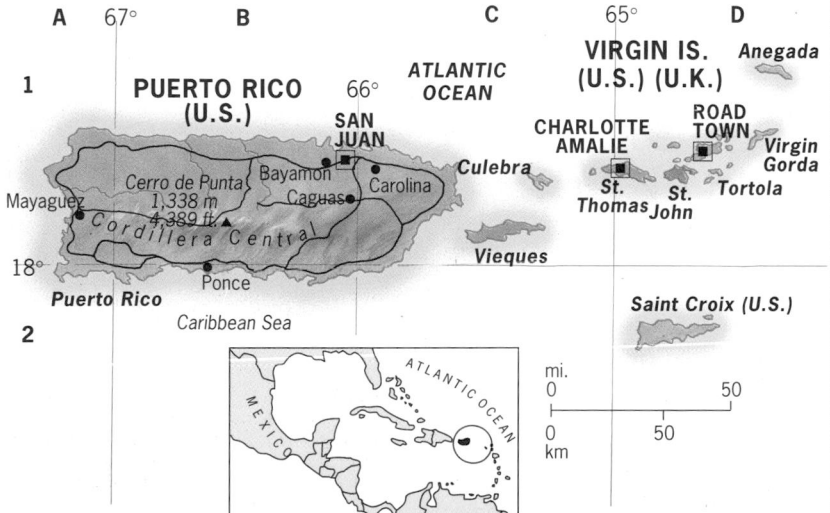

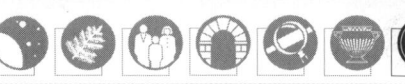

ST. CHRISTOPHER (ST. KITTS) AND NEVIS

Area: 101 sq. mi./261 km². *Currency:* E. Caribbean dollar. *Capital:* Basseterre. *Physical features:* Volcanic with mountainous interior. *Climate:* Moist tropical cooled by sea. *Time zone:* GMT –4h. *Political system:* Constitutional monarchy. *Head of state:* Queen Elizabeth II represented by Gov.-Gen. Sir Clement Arrindell (from 1993). *Head of government:* Kennedy A. Simmonds (from 1980). *Main exports:* Sugar, clothing. *Resources:* Negligible.

PEOPLE

Population: 42,000. *Life expectancy:* 63(m), 69(f). *Language:* English. *Ethnic groups:* Black African 95%. *Religion:* Protestant 76%. *Literacy rate:* 98%. *Per capita GDP:* $3,650.

KEY DATES

1623 First British settlement.
1871–1956 Part of the Leeward Islands Federation.
1958–62 Part of the Federation of the West Indies.
1967 Internal self-government granted.
1983 Independence achieved.

TRAVEL
Visa: None needed by U.S. *Driving permit:* Visitor's license required. *Health and safety:* Inoculations advised. *Tourist features:* Fertile plains on coast; black beaches. *National holiday:* September 19 (Independence Day).

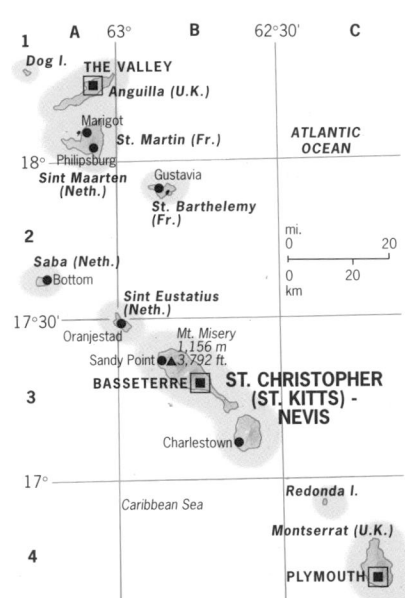

ANGUILLA

Area: 37 sq. mi./96 km². *Currency:* E. Caribbean dollar. *Capital:* The Valley. *Physical features:* Flat and low lying. *Climate:* Tropical. *Time zone:* GMT –4h. *Political system:* Dependent territory of the U.K. *Head of state:* Queen Elizabeth II represented by Gov. Brian Canty (from 1989). *Head of government:* Emile Gumbs (from 1984). *Main exports:* Lobster, salt. *Resources:* Negligible.

PEOPLE (ANGUILLA)

Population: 6,963. *Life expectancy:* 71(m), 77(f). *Language:* English (official). *Ethnic groups:* Black African 94%. *Religions:* Protestant 85%, Roman Catholic 3%, other 12%. *Literacy rate:* 95%. *Per capita GDP:* $3,300.

MONTSERRAT

Area: 38 sq. mi./98 km². *Currency:* E. Caribbean dollar. *Capital:* Plymouth. *Physical features:* Mostly mountainous. *Climate:* Tropical. *Time zone:* GMT –4h. *Political system:* Dependent territory of the U.K. *Head of state:* Queen Elizabeth II represented by Gov. David Taylor (from 1990). *Head of government:* Chief Minister Reuben Meade (from 1991). *Main exports:* Electronics, hot peppers. *Resources:* Negligible.

PEOPLE (MONTSERRAT)

Population: 12,617. *Life expectancy:* 74(m), 78(f). *Language:* English. *Ethnic groups:* Mostly black African. *Religions:* Various Christian denominations. *Literacy rate:* 97%. *Per capita GDP:* $4,500.

ST. LUCIA

Area: 238 sq. mi./616 km². *Currency:* E. Caribbean dollar. *Capital:* Castries. *Physical features:* Volcanic and mountainous. *Climate:* Tropical, moderated by N.E. trade winds; rainy season May–Aug. *Time zone:* GMT –4h. *Political system:* Parliamentary democracy. *Head of state:* Queen Elizabeth II represented by Gov.-Gen. Sir Stanislaus James (from 1988). *Head of government:* Prime Minister John Compton (from 1982). *Main exports:* Bananas, clothing, cocoa, vegetables, fruits, coconuts. *Resources:* Forests, minerals (pumice), geothermal potential.

PEOPLE

Population: 139,000. *Life expectancy:* 70(m), 75(f). *Languages:* English, (official), French patois. *Ethnic groups:* African origin 90%, mixed 6%. *Religions:* Roman Catholic 90%, Protestant 10%. *Literacy rate:* 78%. *Per capita GDP:* $1,930.

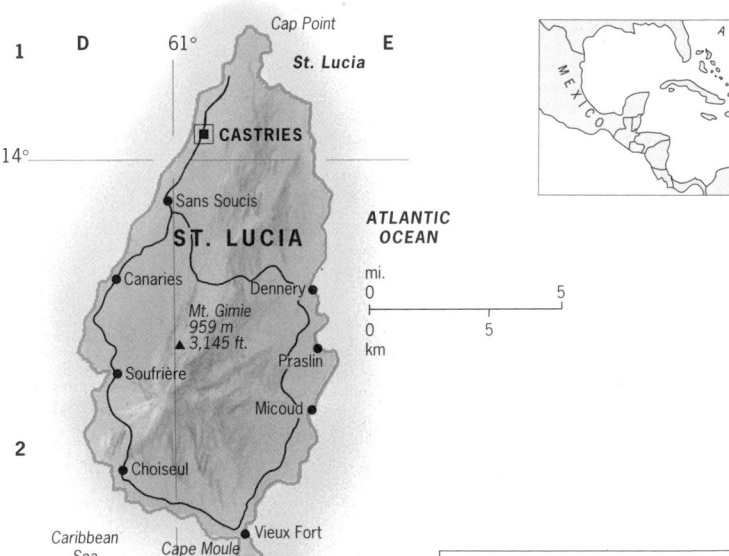

KEY DATES

1814 Becomes British Crown Colony.
1967 Acquires internal self-government.
1979 Independence in Commonwealth.
1991 Integration into Windward Islands confederation proposed.

TRAVEL
Visa: None needed by U.S. *Driving permit:* Visitor's license required. *Health and safety:* Inoculations advised. *Tourist features:* Gros and Petit Pitons. *National holiday:* February 22 (Independence Day).

GUADELOUPE

Area: 687 sq. mi./1,779 km². *Currency:* French franc. *Capital:* Basse-Terre. *Physical features:* Basse-Terre: volcanic origin with interior mountains; Grande-Terre: low limestone formation. *Climate:* Tropical. *Time zone:* GMT –4h. *Political system:* Overseas department of France. *Head of state:* Jaques Chirac (from 1995). *Head of government:* Commissioner of the Republic Jean-Paul Proust (from 1989). *Main exports:* Bananas, sugar, rum. *Resources:* Cultivable land, beaches and climate for tourism.

PEOPLE

Population: 409,132. *Life expectancy:* 74(m), 80(f). *Languages:* French, Creole. *Ethnic groups:* Black or mulatto 90%, white 5%, East Indian, Lebanese, Chinese less than 5%. *Religions:* Roman Catholic 95%, African religions and Hindu 5%. *Literacy rate:* 90%. *Per capita GDP:* $3,300.

DOMINICA

Area: 290 sq. mi./751 km². *Currency:* E. Caribbean dollar. *Capital:* Roseau. *Physical features:* Rugged volcanic mountains. *Climate:* Tropical with heavy rainfall. *Time zone:* GMT –4h. *Political system:* Parliamentary democracy. *Head of state:* Clarence Seignoret (from 1983). *Head of government:* Eugenia Charles (from 1980). *Main exports:* Bananas, coconut, fruit juices, essential oils, soap. *Resources:* Wood.

PEOPLE

Population: 72,000. *Life expectancy:* 74(m), 79(f). *Languages:* English (official), French creole. *Ethnic groups:* Nearly all African or mulatto, Carib Indians. *Religions:* Roman Catholic 77%, Protestant 15%, other or none 8%. *Literacy rate:* 90%. *Per capita GDP:* $2,000.

KEY DATES

1763 Becomes British possession.
1978 Independence from Britain.
1981 Former prime minister Patrick John implicated in plot to overthrow government of Dominica Freedom Party.
1982 John acquitted and released.
1983 Takes leading role in instigation of U.S.-led invasion of Grenada.
1991 Integration into Windward Islands confederation proposed.
1992 Government institutes controversial program offering passports to Far Easterners who agree to invest large sums in the country.

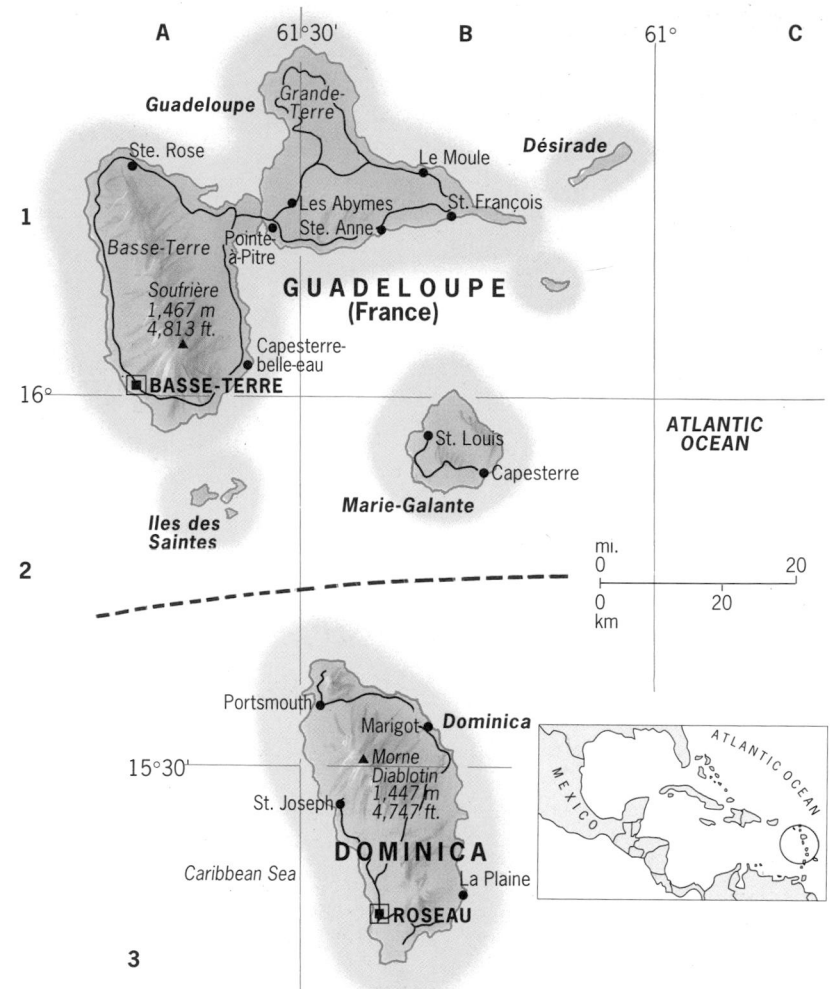

TRAVEL (DOMINICA)
Visa: None needed by U.S. **Driving permit:** Nat. license. **Health and safety:** Check water; inoculations advised. **Tourist features:** Volcanic mountains; Boiling Lake (escaping subterranean gas). **National holiday:** November 3 (Independence Day).

MARTINIQUE

Area: 425 sq. mi./1,102 km². *Currency:* French franc. *Capital:* Fort-de-France. *Physical features:* Mountainous with indented coastline. *Climate:* Tropical, moderated by trade winds. *Time zone:* GMT –4h. *Political system:* Overseas department of France. *Head of state:* Jaques Chirac (from 1995). *Head of government:* Government Commissioner Jean-Claude Roure (from 1989). *Main exports:* Refined petroleum products, bananas, rum, pineapples. *Resources:* Cultivable land, beaches and climate for tourism.

PEOPLE

Population: 371,803. *Life expectancy:* 75(m), 81(f). *Languages:* French, Creole. *Ethnic groups:* African origin and mulatto 90%. *Religions:* Christian 95%, African religions and Hindu 5%. *Literacy rate:* 93%. *Per capita GDP:* $6,000.

BARBADOS

Area: 166 sq. mi./431 km². *Currency:* Barbados dollar. *Capital:* Bridgetown. *Physical features:* Relatively flat; rises gently to central highlands. *Climate:* Tropical with heavy rainfall. *Time zone:* GMT –4h. *Political system:* Parliamentary democracy. *Head of state:* Queen Elizabeth II represented by Gov.-Gen. Dame Nita Barrow (from 1990). *Head of government:* Erskine Sandiford (from 1987). *Main exports:* Sugar and molasses, chemicals, clothing, electrical components, rum, edible oils, margarine. *Resources:* Crude oil, fish, natural gas.

PEOPLE

Population: 260,000. *Distribution urban/rural:* 42%/58%. *Life expectancy:* 70(m), 76(f). *Language:* English. *Ethnic groups:* African 80%, mixed 16%, European descent 4%. *Religions:* Protestant 67%, Roman Catholic 4%. *Literacy rate:* 99%. *Per capita GDP:* $6,500.

KEY DATES

1627 Becomes a British colony; develops a sugar-plantation economy.
1834 Abolition of slavery.

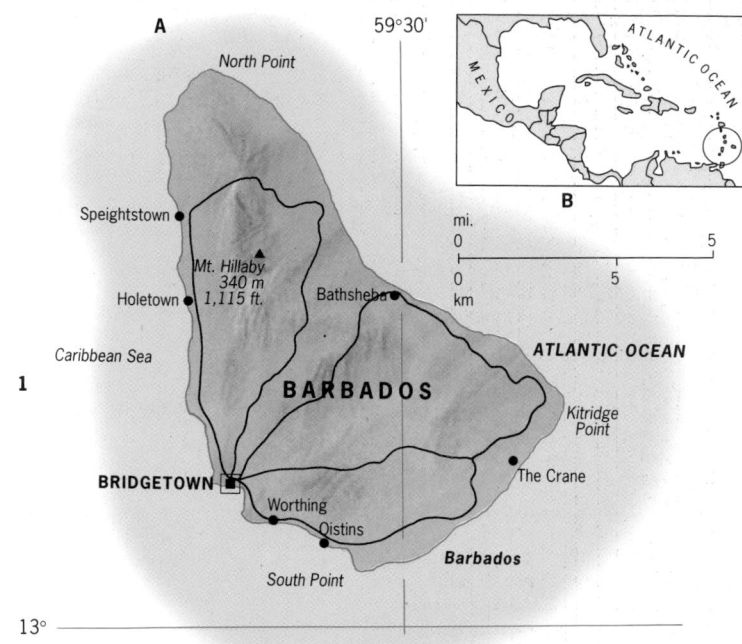

1951 Introduction of universal suffrage.
1966 Achieves full independence within the British Commonwealth.
1972 Diplomatic relations established with Cuba.
1983 Supports U.S. invasion of Grenada.

TRAVEL
Visa: None needed by U.S. *Driving permit:* All recognized for B.D. $30 fee. *Health and safety:* Inoculations advised. *Tourist features:* Capital and chief port of Bridgetown; sandy beaches. *National holiday:* November 30 (Independence Day).

GRENADA

Area: 133 sq. mi./344 km². *Currency:* E. Caribbean dollar. *Capital:* St. George's. *Physical features:* Volcanic with central mountains. *Climate:* Tropical. *Time zone:* GMT –4h. *Political system:* Constitutional monarchy. *Head of state:* Queen Elizabeth II represented by Gov.-Gen. Sir Paul Scoon (from 1978). *Head of government:* Nicholas Braithwaite (from 1990). *Main exports:* Nutmeg, mace, bananas, cocoa beans. *Resources:* Wood, tropical fruit, deep-water harbors.

PEOPLE

Population: 92,000. *Life expectancy:* 69(m), 74(f). *Languages:* English (official), French patois. *Ethnic groups:* African descent 84%. *Religions:* Roman Catholic 64%, Anglican 22%. *Literacy rate:* 98%. *Per capita GDP:* $2,800.

KEY DATES

1783 Becomes a British colony.
1974 Independence from Britain; Eric Gairy prime minister.
1979 Bloodless coup; Maurice Bishop prime minister; constitution suspended; left-wing government set up.
1982 Relations with U.S.A. and Britain

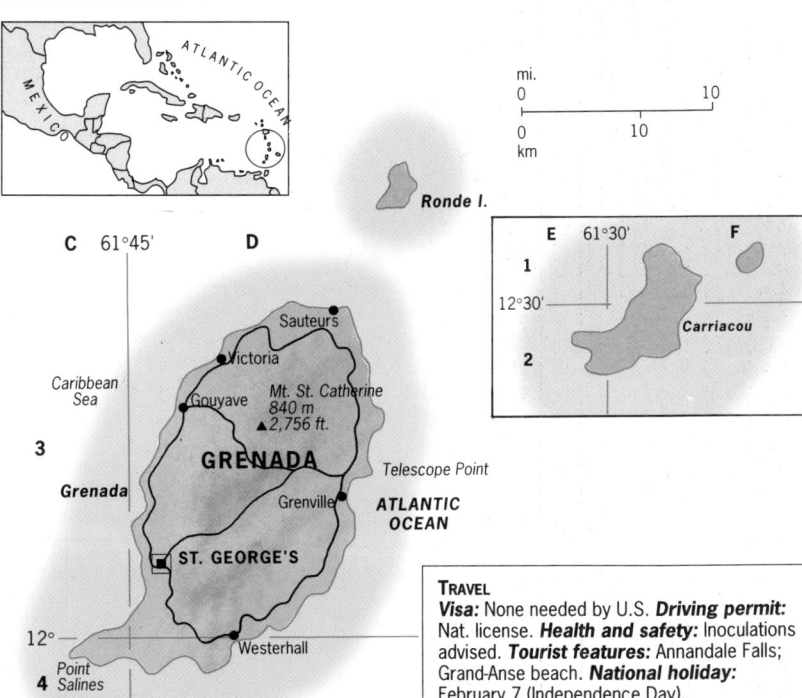

TRAVEL
Visa: None needed by U.S. *Driving permit:* Nat. license. *Health and safety:* Inoculations advised. *Tourist features:* Annandale Falls; Grand-Anse beach. *National holiday:* February 7 (Independence Day).

deteriorate as ties with U.S.S.R. and Cuba are strengthened.
1983 Left-wing opponents overthrow Bishop in military coup; Bishop and three colleagues executed;

Revolutionary Military Council overthrown by U.S. and E. Caribbean military; 1974 constitution reintroduced.
1991 Integration into Windward Islands confederation proposed.

ST. VINCENT AND THE GRENADINES

Area: 150 sq. mi./388 km². *Currency:* E. Caribbean dollar. *Capital:* Kingstown. *Physical features:* Volcanic and mountainous; Mount Soufrière, active volcano on island of St. Vincent. *Climate:* Tropical; rainy season May–Nov. *Time zone:* GMT –4h. *Political system:* Constitutional monarchy. *Head of state:* Queen Elizabeth II represented by Gov.-Gen. David Jack (from 1989). *Head of government:* James Mitchell (from 1984). *Main exports:* Bananas, coconuts, spices, taro plant tubers, arrowroot starch, tennis racquets. *Resources:* Negligible.

PEOPLE

Population: 111,000. *Life expectancy:* 71(m), 74(f). *Languages:* English (official), French patois. *Ethnic groups:* Mostly black African descent, some white, East Indian, Carib Indians. *Religions:* Methodist, Anglican, Roman Catholic. *Literacy rate:* 96%. *Per capita GDP:* $1,300.

KEY DATES

1783 Becomes British crown colony.
1969 Achieves internal self-government.

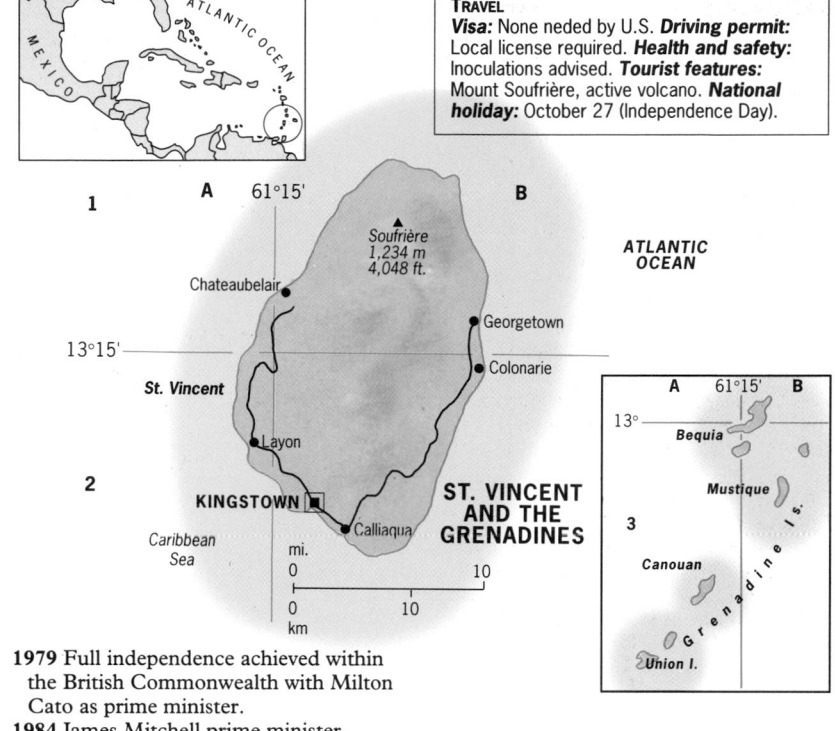

TRAVEL
Visa: None neded by U.S. *Driving permit:* Local license required. *Health and safety:* Inoculations advised. *Tourist features:* Mount Soufrière, active volcano. *National holiday:* October 27 (Independence Day).

1979 Full independence achieved within the British Commonwealth with Milton Cato as prime minister.
1984 James Mitchell prime minister.
1989 Mitchell reelected.
1991 Integration into Windward Islands confederation proposed.

TRINIDAD AND TOBAGO

Area: 1,981 sq. mi./5,130 km². *Currency:* Trinidad and Tobago dollar. *Capital:* Port-of-Spain. *Other cities:* San Fernando. *Physical features:* Mostly plains with some low mountains. *Climate:* Humid and tropical. *Time zone:* GMT –4h. *Political system:* Democratic republic. *Head of state:* Noor Hassanali (from 1987). *Head of government:* Patrick Manning (from 1991). *Main exports:* Petroleum, petrochemicals, rum. *Resources:* Crude oil, natural gas, asphalt.

PEOPLE

Population: 1,260,000. *Life expectancy:* 68(m), 73(f). *Language:* English (official). *Ethnic groups:* African 43%, East Indian 40%, mixed 14%. *Religions:* Roman Catholic 32%, Protestant 29%, Hindu 25%, Muslim 6%. *Literacy rate:* 97%. *Per capita GDP:* $3,600.

KEY DATES

1888 Trinidad and Tobago unite.
1959 Achieves internal self-government.
1962 Achieves independence from Britain within the Commonwealth.
1976 Becomes a republic.
1990 Defeat of attempted coup.

TRAVEL
Visa: None needed by U.S. *Driving permit:* IDP. *Health and safety:* Inoculations advised. *Tourist feature:* Self-renewing asphalt lake. *National holiday:* August 31 (Independence Day).

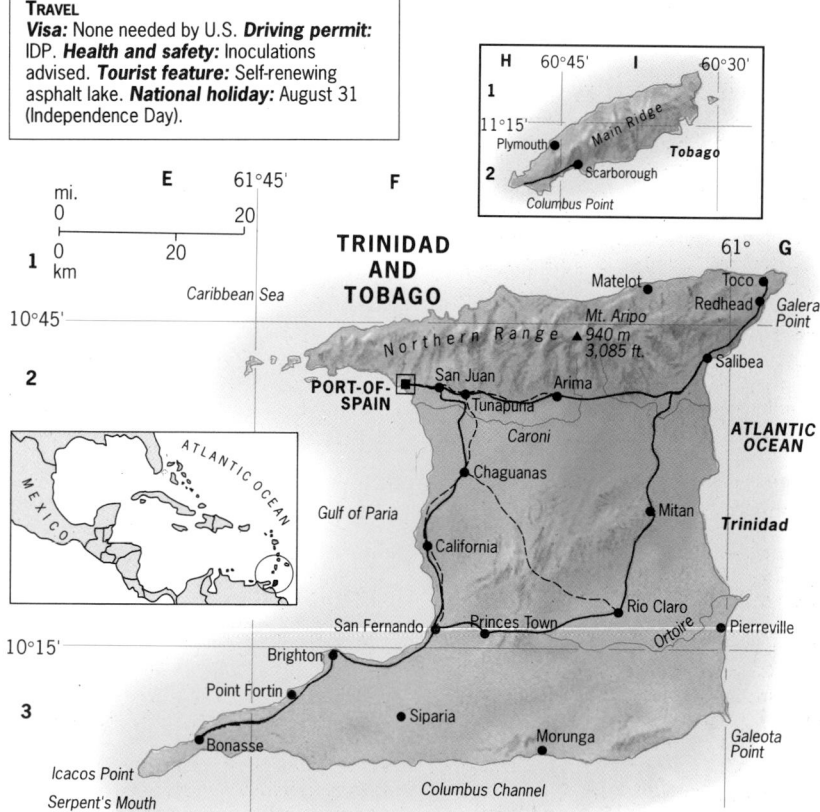

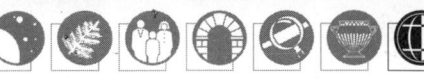

SOUTH AMERICA

Area: 6,875,000 sq. mi./17,806,000 km² **Largest cities:** São Paulo, Rio de Janeiro, Buenos Aires, Lima, Bogotá, Santiago, Belo Horizonte. **Organizations:** Amazon Pact, Grupo Andino, Group of Río, Sistema Económico Latino-Americana (SELA), Associación Latino-Americana le Integración (ALADI), Mercosur. **Main products (and percentage of world output):** Coffee (40%), cocoa (23%), citrus fruit (39%), sugarcane (29%), iron ore (19%), beef (15%).

PHYSICAL FEATURES

South America is the world's fourth-largest continent and covers around 12% of the total land area. The terrain is dominated by chains of high mountains in the W., central plains with rivers rising to rolling mountains in the E. **Highest point:** Aconcagua (22,831 ft./6,959 m). **Lowest point:** Valdés Peninsula (−131 ft./−40 m). **Longest river:** Amazon. **Largest lake:** Maracaibo. **Other features:** Atacama Desert, Paraná, Madeira, São Francisco, Magdalena, Paraguay, Orinoco rivers; Andes Mountains; Angel and Cuquenán waterfalls; Lake Titicaca. **Vegetation:** Tropical rain forests cover most of the interior of the N.; savannas stretch south from the center.

PEOPLE

Population: 302,000,000 (6% of the total world population). **Growth rate:** 2.2%. **Density:** 44/mi.². **Distribution urban/rural:** 67%/33%. **Life expectancy:** 67(m), 73(f). **Languages:** Spanish, Portuguese (Brazil), Dutch (Suriname), French (French Guiana), Amerindian languages, Hindi, Javanese (Suriname and Guyana), various Creole dialects. **Ethnic groups:** Iberian, black African, mestizo, mulatto, Amerindian, small black-Indian minority. **Religions:** Almost entirely Roman Catholic; small minorities practice indigenous (chiefly animist) religions; Hindu and Islam in Suriname and Guyana; 11 million Protestants in Brazil and Chile.

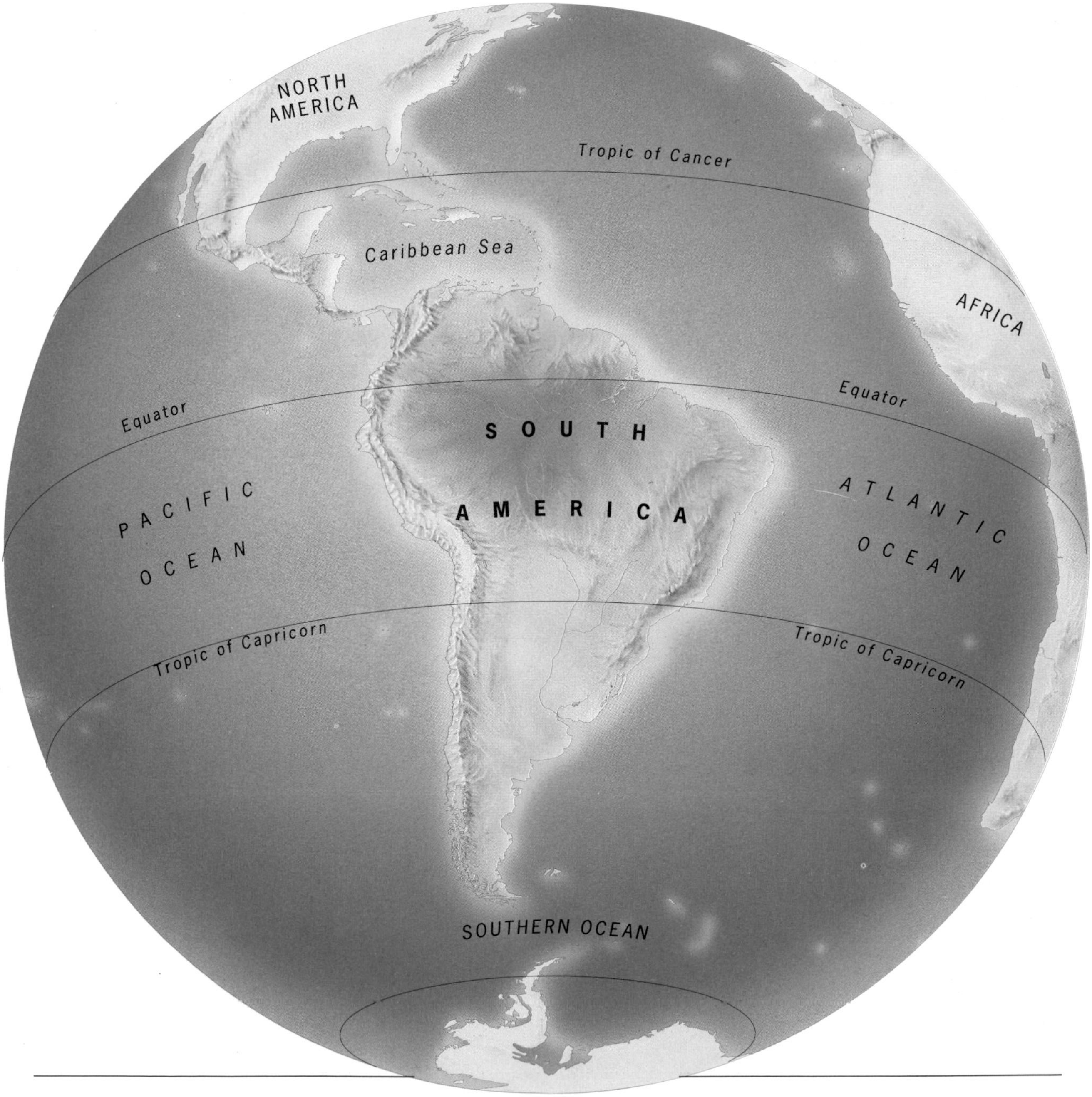

NORTH AMERICA

Tropic of Cancer

Caribbean Sea

AFRICA

Equator

Equator

S O U T H

A M E R I C A

PACIFIC

OCEAN

ATLANTIC

OCEAN

Tropic of Capricorn

Tropic of Capricorn

SOUTHERN OCEAN

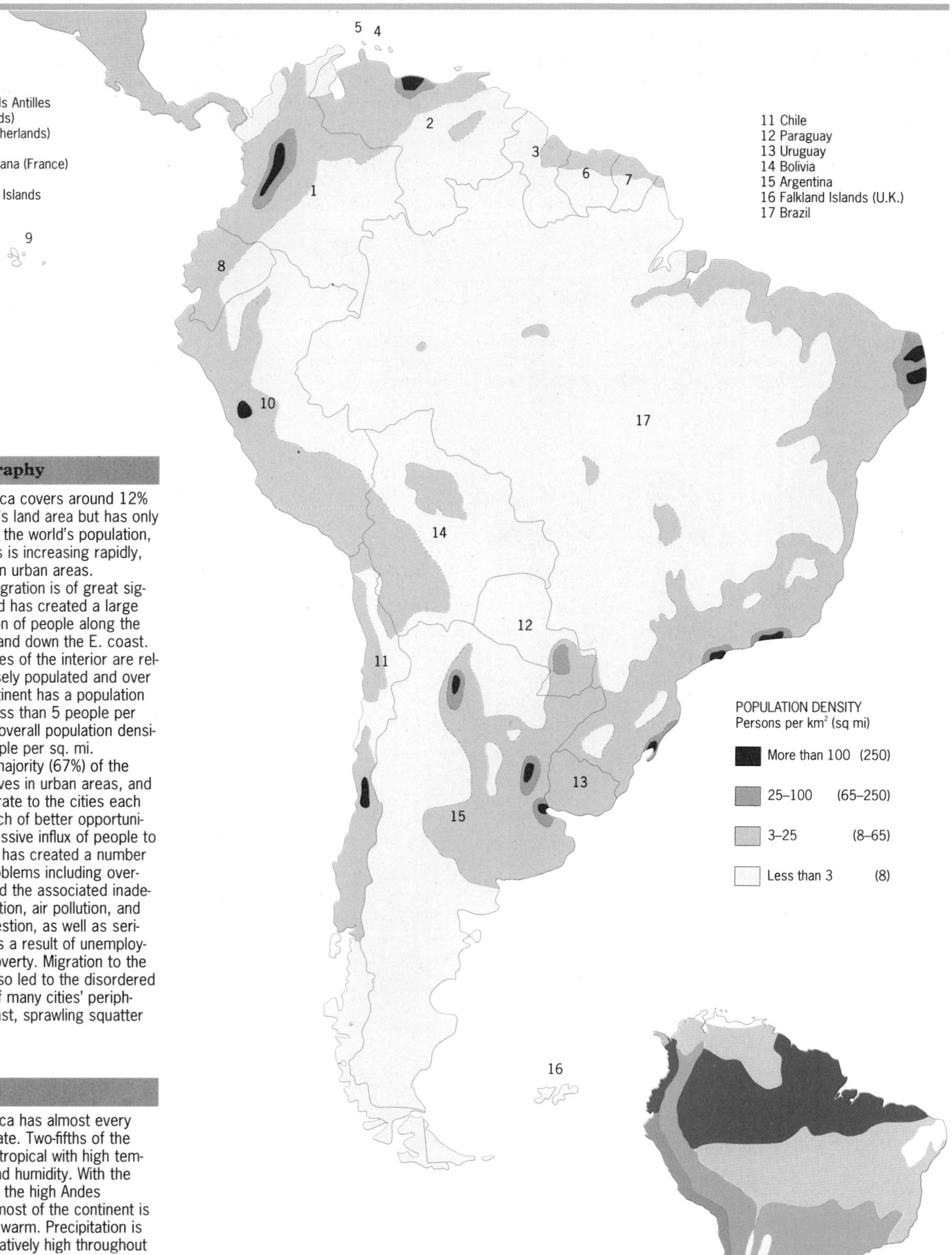

KEY
1 Colombia
2 Venezuela
3 Guyana
4 Netherlands Antilles
  (Netherlands)
5 Aruba (Netherlands)
6 Suriname
7 French Guiana (France)
8 Ecuador
9 Galápagos Islands
  (Ecuador)
10 Peru

11 Chile
12 Paraguay
13 Uruguay
14 Bolivia
15 Argentina
16 Falkland Islands (U.K.)
17 Brazil

Demography

South America covers around 12% of the world's land area but has only about 5% of the world's population, although this is increasing rapidly, particularly in urban areas.

Internal migration is of great significance and has created a large concentration of people along the N.W. coast and down the E. coast. Vast expanses of the interior are relatively sparsely populated and over half the continent has a population density of less than 5 people per sq. mi. The overall population density is 14 people per sq. mi.

The vast majority (67%) of the population lives in urban areas, and millions migrate to the cities each year in search of better opportunities. The massive influx of people to urban areas has created a number of social problems including overcrowding and the associated inadequate sanitation, air pollution, and traffic congestion, as well as serious crime as a result of unemployment and poverty. Migration to the cities has also led to the disordered expansion of many cities' peripheries with vast, sprawling squatter settlements.

Climate

South America has almost every type of climate. Two-fifths of the continent is tropical with high temperatures and humidity. With the exception of the high Andes Mountains, most of the continent is consistently warm. Precipitation is generally relatively high throughout South America, and Colombia, the wettest country, receives over 350 in./890 cm of rain a year. Coastal Peru and northern Chile, however, are among the driest places on Earth. The *El Niño* effect (*p. 72*), which occurs at irregular intervals, causes warm water to flow S. along the coast of Peru and N. Chile where there is usually a cold current. This increases rainfall in a normally dry climatic region.

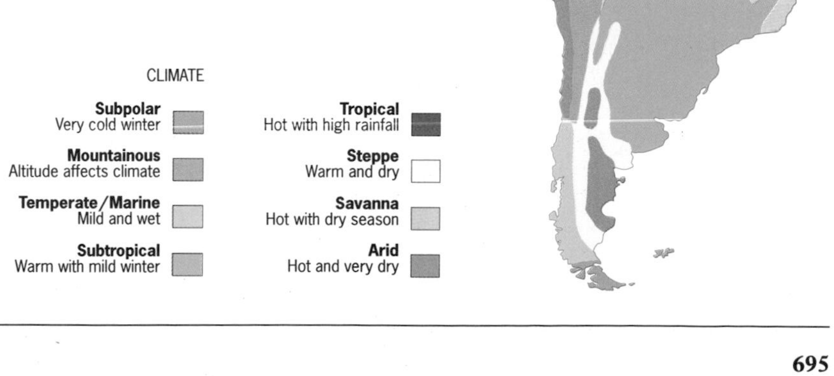

POPULATION DENSITY
Persons per km² (sq mi)

■ More than 100 (250)

▨ 25–100 (65–250)

▨ 3–25 (8–65)

□ Less than 3 (8)

CLIMATE

Subpolar
Very cold winter

Mountainous
Altitude affects climate

Temperate/Marine
Mild and wet

Subtropical
Warm with mild winter

Tropical
Hot with high rainfall

Steppe
Warm and dry

Savanna
Hot with dry season

Arid
Hot and very dry

COLOMBIA

Map labels:

Caribbean Sea · PANAMA · PACIFIC OCEAN · Punta Gallinas · Gulf of Venezuela · VENEZUELA · Santa Marta · Ríohacha · Barranquilla · Ciénaga · Cartagena · Pico Cristobal Colón 5,775 m 18,947 ft. · Sincelejo · Montería · Cauca · Perijá Mts. · Cúcuta · Barrancabermeja · Bucaramanga · Llanos · Medellín · Magdalena · Quibdó · Muzo · Tunja · Meta · Orinoco · Pereira · Ibagué · BOGOTA · Villavicencio · Buenaventura · Tuluá · Cordillera Occidental · Cordillera Central · Cordillera Oriental · Cali · Neiva · C O L O M B I A · Guaviare · Tumaco · San Augustín · Pasto · Selvas · Equator · ECUADOR · Putumayo · Caqueta · PERU · BRAZIL · Amazon · PACIFIC OCEAN · ATLANTIC OCEAN

mi. 0 — 200
km 0 — 200

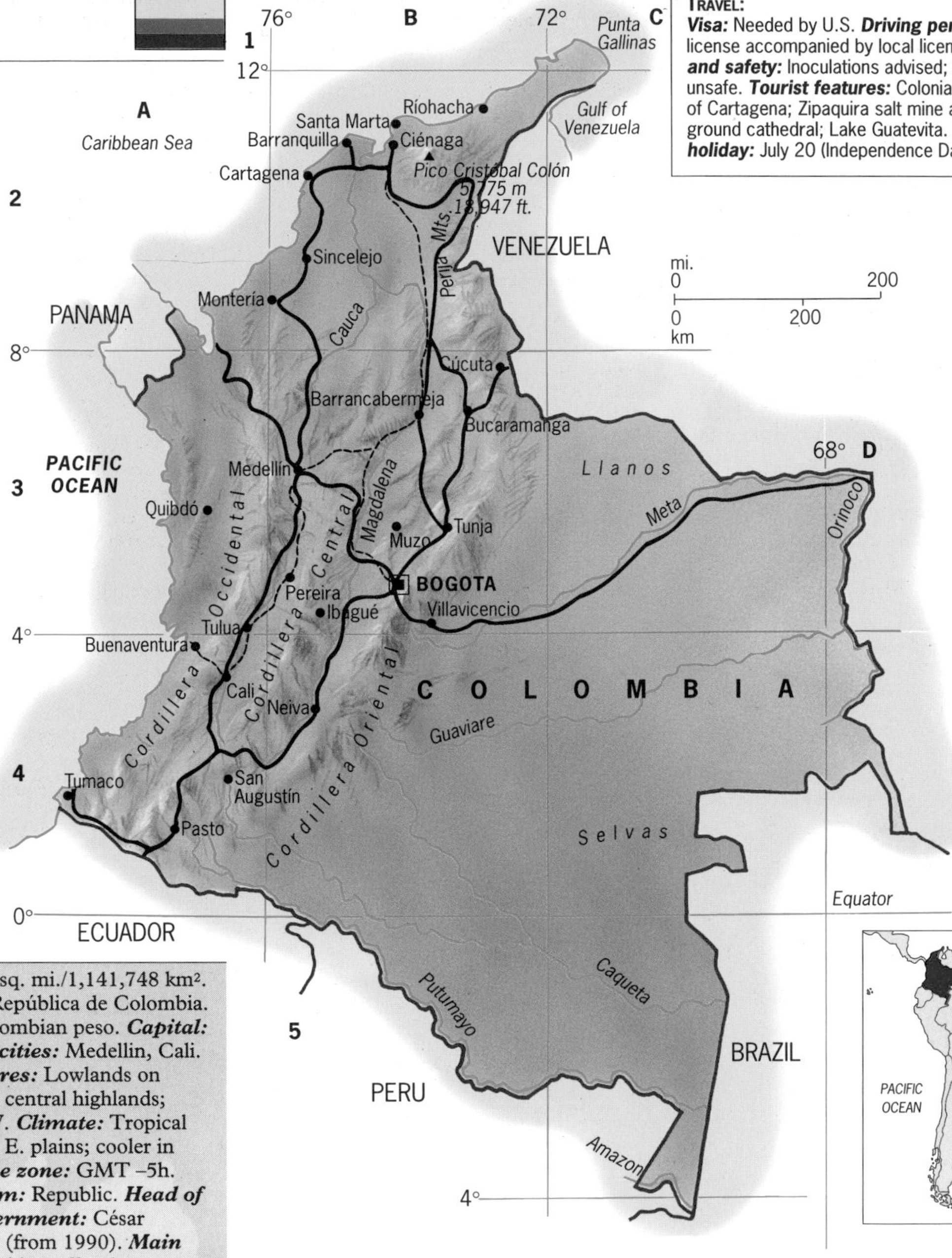

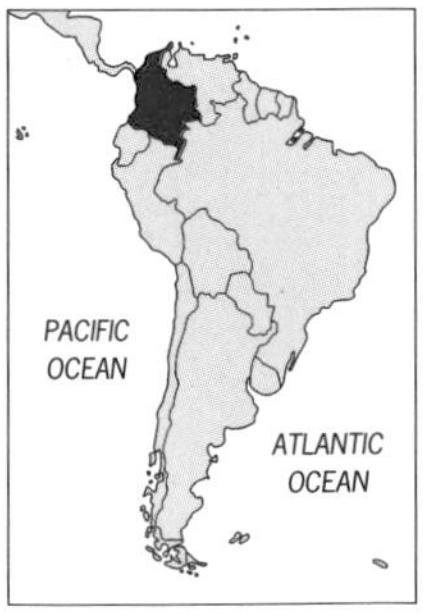

Area: 440,830 sq. mi./1,141,748 km². *Local name:* República de Colombia. *Currency:* Colombian peso. *Capital:* Bogotá. *Other cities:* Medellin, Cali. *Physical features:* Lowlands on coast and in E.; central highlands; mountains in W. *Climate:* Tropical along coast and E. plains; cooler in highlands. *Time zone:* GMT –5h. *Political system:* Republic. *Head of state and government:* César Gaviria Trujillo (from 1990). *Main exports:* Emeralds, coffee, bananas, petroleum, flowers. *Resources:* Oil, gas, coal, gold, copper, lead, emeralds.

PEOPLE

Population: 33,951,000. *Distribution urban/rural:* 65%/35%. *Life expectancy:* 69(m), 74(f). *Language:* Spanish. *Ethnic groups:* Mestizo 58%, European 20%, mulatto 14%, other 8%. *Religion:* Roman Catholic 95%. *Literacy rate:* 87%. *Per capita GDP:* $1,300.

KEY DATES

1525 Spanish arrive in Colombia.
1819 Independence achieved.
1948 Liberal Party leader Jorge Eliécer Gaitán, is assassinated, leading to riots and eventual civil war (*La Violencia*), that kills around 200,000.
1957 Liberal and Conservative Accord results in National Front coalition.
1970 National Popular Alliance (ANAPO) formed as a left-wing opposition to the National Front.
1974 National Front temporarily splits.
1975 Civil unrest.
1978 Liberals revive accord and begin intensive fight against drug dealers.
1982 Conservative president Belisario Betancur grants amnesty to left-wing guerrillas and frees political prisoners.
1984 Minister of Justice assassinated.
1986 Virgilio Barco Vargas (Liberal) elected president by record margin.
1989 Leading presidential candidate assassinated by drug cartel; Vargas declares war on drugs; police kill José Rodríguez Gacha, cartel leader.
1990 César Gaviria Trujillo president.
1991 New constitution prohibits extradition of Colombians.
1992 Pablo Escobar, drug cartel leader, escapes from prison.
1994 Escobar killed by police.
1995 Trade agreement signed with Mexico and Venezuela; many government officials arrested for accepting favors from Cali drug cartel.

VENEZUELA

Area: 352,143 sq. mi./912,050 km².
Local name: República de Venezuela.
Currency: Bolívar. **Capital:** Caracas.
Other cities: Maracaibo,
Barquisimeto, Valencia, Maracay.
Physical features: Mountains and
Maracaibo lowlands in N.W.; central
plains; Guyana highlands in S.E.
Climate: Tropical; more moderate in
highlands. **Time zone:** GMT –4h.
Political system: Federal republic.
Head of state and government:
Rafael Caldera (from 1993). **Main
exports:** Textiles, coffee, fruit, petro-
leum, bauxite, aluminum, iron ore.
Resources: Crude oil, natural gas,
iron, gold, bauxite.

PEOPLE
Population: 20,712,000. **Distribution
urban/rural:** 83%/17%. **Life expectancy:** 71(m), 78(f). **Language:** Spanish.
Ethnic groups: Mestizo 69%, European
20%, African 9%, Indian 2%. **Religion:**
Roman Catholic 96%. **Literacy rate:**
88%. **Per capita GDP:** $2,590.

KEY DATES
1498 Columbus lands in Venezuela.
1811 Independence declared.
1908–35 Petroleum industry begins to
develop, proceeds of which go to pay off
huge national debt and strengthen army.
1945 Acción Democrática (AD) seizes
power.
1948 Rómulo Gallegos (AD) becomes
president; later ousted in military coup.
1952 Beginning of Marcos Pérez
Jiménez's dictatorship.
1958 Revolt; Jiménez is forced into exile.
1969 Rafael Caldera president.
1984 Dr. Jaime Lusinchi president; social
pact established among government,
trade unions, and business; repayment
of national debt rescheduled.
1987 Civil unrest caused by inflation;
police fire on student demonstrators.
1988 Carlos Andrés Pérez president.
1989 Austerity program enforced;
Venezuela receives $4.3 billion loan
from the IMF; price increases trigger
riots, killing 300; Feb.: martial law
declared; May: general strike.
1992 Attempted antigovernment coups
fail; Pérez promises reform.
1993 Pérez resigns, accused of corruption;
Rafael Caldera reelected.
1995 Trade agreement signed with
Mexico and Colombia.

ECONOMY
Farming: Coffee is the leading cash
crop; other important crops include
cocoa beans, sugar, corn, rice, wheat,
tobacco, cotton, beans, fruit, and sisal;
millions of cattle and horses are raised.
Natural resources: Venezuela is a leading oil producer; there are also reserves
of bauxite, iron ore, nickel, diamonds,
gold, and phosphates.
Industry: Refineries process steel and
aluminum; factories produce petrochemicals, ammonia, fertilizers, machinery, cement, and vehicles.
Services: Service industries employ
about 60% of the population; tourism is
an important source of income.

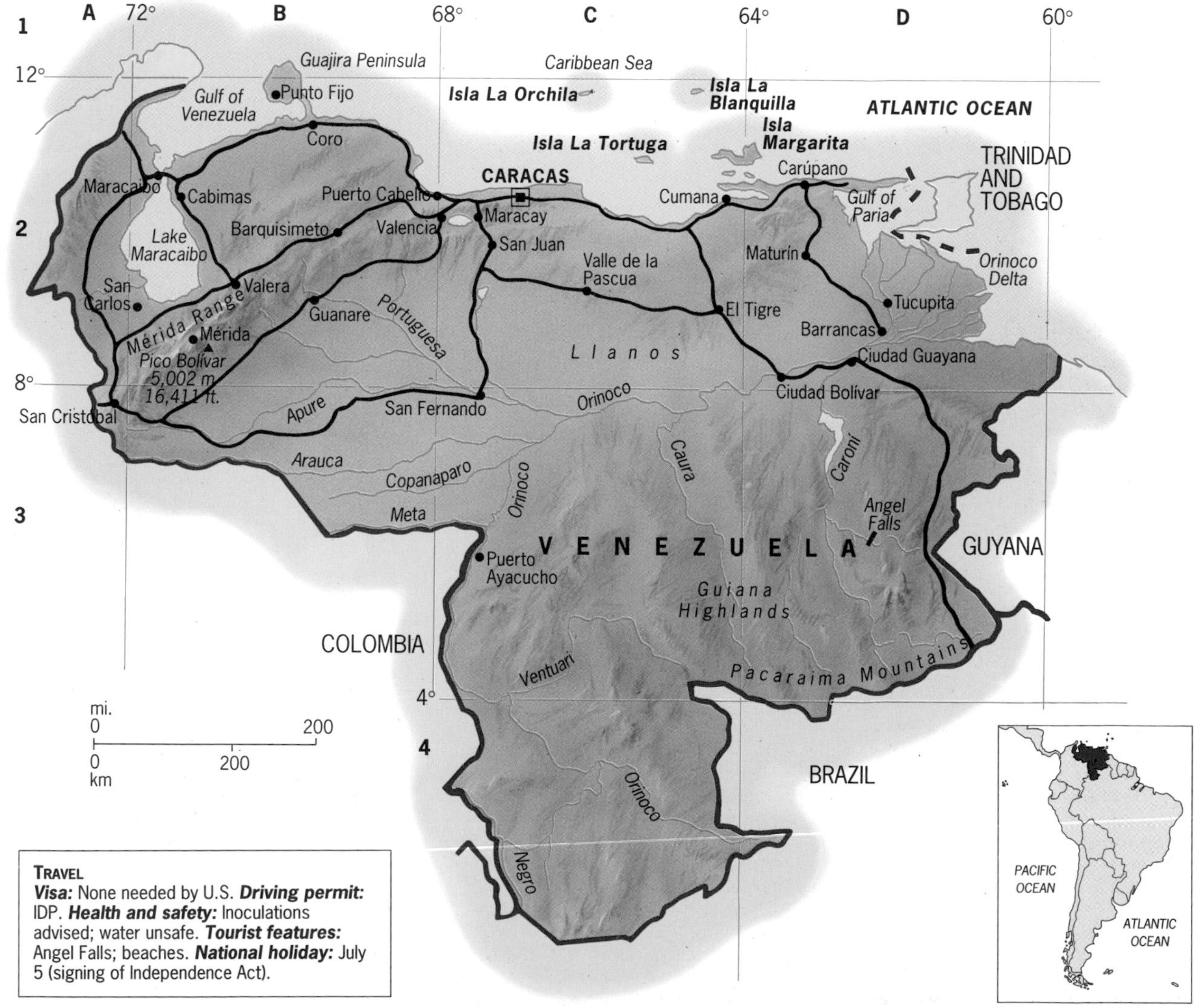

TRAVEL
Visa: None needed by U.S. **Driving permit:**
IDP. **Health and safety:** Inoculations
advised; water unsafe. **Tourist features:**
Angel Falls; beaches. **National holiday:** July
5 (signing of Independence Act).

GUYANA

Area: 83,000 sq. mi./214,969 km².
Local name: Cooperative Republic of
Guyana. *Currency:* Guyana dollar.
Capital: Georgetown. *Other cities:*
New Amsterdam, Linden. *Physical
features:* Highlands and fertile coastal
plains divided by savanna. *Climate:*
Tropical; two rainy seasons (May to
mid-Aug. and mid-Nov. to mid-Jan.).
Time zone: GMT –3h. *Political
system:* Cooperative republic. *Head
of state:* President Cheddi Jagan
(from 1992). *Head of government:*
Sam Hinds (from 1992). *Main
exports:* Bauxite, aluminum, sugar,
gold, rice, shrimp, molasses, wood,
rum. *Resources:* Bauxite, gold,
shrimp, diamonds, wood.

PEOPLE
Population: 816,000. *Distribution
urban/rural:* 35%/65%. *Life
expectancy:* 61(m), 68(f). *Languages:*
English, Indian dialects, Hindi, Urdu.
Ethnic groups: East Indian 51%,
African and mixed 43%, Indian 4%, other
2%. *Religions:* Christian 46%, Hindu
37%, Muslim 9%. *Literacy rate:* 95%.
Per capita GDP: $300.

KEY DATES
1814 British gain control from Dutch.
1953 New constitution; elections won by
left-wing People's Progressive Party
(PPP) under Cheddi Jagan; fearing a
Communist takeover, British suspend
constitution and remove Jagan from
power; an interim government is
installed.
1961 Internal self-government granted.
1962 Violence between East Indians and
blacks; Britain demands another election before full independence is granted.
1964 People's National Congress (PNC)

and United Force form coalition
government led by Forbes Burnham.
1966 Full independence achieved.
1970 Guyana becomes republic within
British Commonwealth.
1985 Forbes Burnham dies and is
succeeded by Desmond Hoyte.
1992 PPP wins assembly elections;
Cheddi Jagan becomes president.

TRAVEL
Visa: Needed by U.S. *Driving permit:* IDP.
Health and safety: Inoculations advised;
water unsafe. *Tourist features:* Kaieter
National Park, including Kaietur Falls on
Potaro River; tropical rain forests. *National
holidays:* February 23 (Day of Republic) and
August 4 (Day of Freedom).

NETHERLANDS ANTILLES

Area: 371 sq. mi./960 km². *Curren-
cy:* Netherlands Antillian guilder or
florin. *Capital:* Willemstad. *Physical
features:* Generally hilly. *Climate:*
Tropical. *Time zone:* GMT –4h.
Political system: Part of the Dutch
realm; self-government from 1954.
Head of state: Queen Beatrix
Wilhelmina Armgard represented by
Gov.-Gen. Jaime Saleh (from 1989).
Head of government: Maria Liberia-
Peters (from 1988). *Resources:*
Petroleum, phosphates, salt.

PEOPLE
Population: 184,325. *Distribution
urban/rural:* n.a. *Life expectancy:*
73(m), 77(f). *Languages:* Dutch (official), Papiamento (Dutch/Spanish/English/

Portuguese dialect). *Ethnic groups:*
Mixed African 85%; Caribbean Indian,
European, East Indian. *Religion:* Predominantly Roman Catholic. *Literacy
rate:* 94%. *Per capita GDP:* $7,600.

ARUBA

Area: 75 sq. mi./194 km². *Currency:*
Aruban florin. *Capital:* Oranjestad.
Physical features: Flat; scant vegeta-
tion. *Climate:* Tropical. *Time zone:*
GMT –3.5h. *Political system:* Part
of Dutch realm; full autonomy in
internal affairs granted in 1986. *Head
of state:* Queen Beatrix Wilhelmina
Armgard represented by Gov.-Gen.
Felipe B. Tromp (from 1986). *Head
of government:* Prime Minister
Nelson Oduber (from 1989).

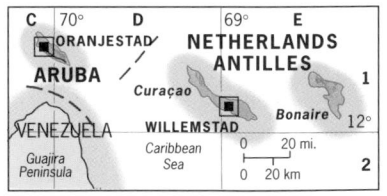

PEOPLE
Population: 64,692. *Distribution
urban/rural:* n.a. *Life expectancy:*
73(m), 80(f). *Languages:* Dutch (official), Papiamento (a Dutch/Spanish/
Portuguese/English) dialect), English and
Spanish widely understood. *Ethnic
groups:* Mixed European/Indian 80%,
Dutch, Spanish and other 20%; Spanish
and Indian influences greater than in the
Netherlands Antilles. *Religion:* Roman
Catholic 82%. *Literacy rate:* n.a. *Per
capita GDP:* $13,600.

SURINAM

Area: 63,256 sq. mi./163,820 km². **Local name:** Republiek Suriname. **Currency:** Suriname guilder. **Capital:** Paramaribo. **Physical features:** Mostly rolling forested hills with narrow coastal plains. **Climate:** Tropical with heavy rainfall. **Time zone:** GMT –3h. **Political system:** Republic. **Head of state and government:** Ronald Venetiaan (from 1991). **Main exports:** Bauxite, alumina, rice, wood, fish, bananas. **Resources:** Bauxite, aluminum, shrimp, wood, iron ore.

PEOPLE

Population: 446,000. **Distribution urban/rural:** n.a. **Life expectancy:** 66(m), 71(f). **Languages:** Dutch (official), English, Sranan tongo, Hindi Surinamese, Hindustani, and Javanese. **Ethnic groups:** Hindustani 37%, Creole 31%, Javanese 15%, African black 10%, American 3%, Chinese and other 4%. **Religions:** Hindu 27%, Protestant 25%, Roman Catholic 23%, Muslim 20%, indigenous beliefs around 5%. **Literacy rate:** 95%. **Per capita GNP:** $3,400.

KEY DATES

1667 Becomes Dutch colony.
1954 Internal autonomy granted.
1970s Creoles fight for independence.
1975 Full independence; nearly half the population emigrates to Netherlands.
1986 Antigovernment rebels bring economic chaos.
1991 Ronald Venetiaan president.
1992 Peace accord with guerrilla groups.

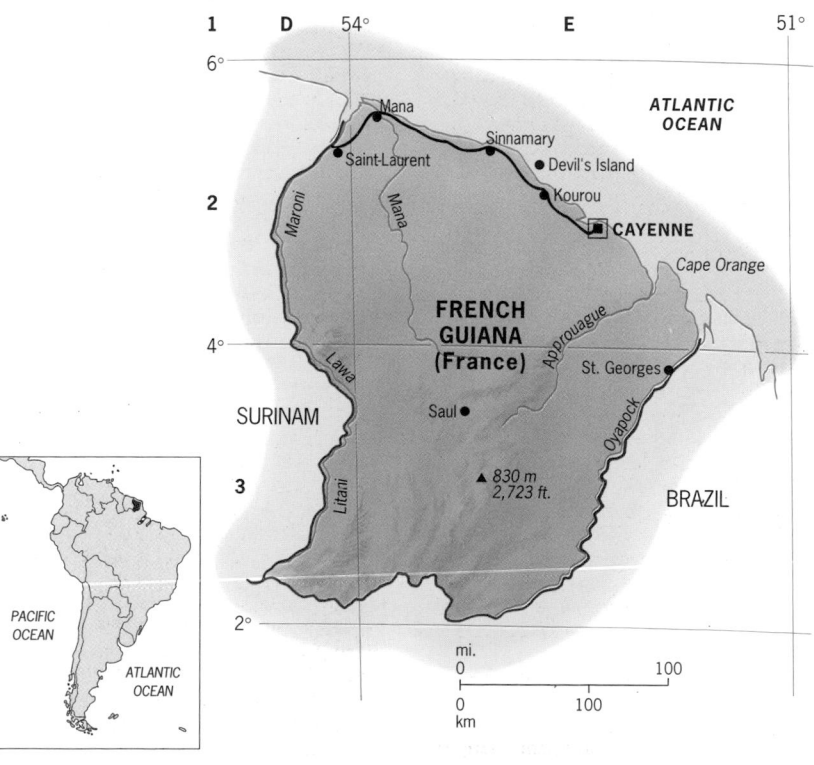

TRAVEL
Visa: Needed by U.S. **Driving permit:** IDP. **Health and safety:** Inoculations advised; water unsafe. **Tourist features:** Suriname River; rain forests. **National holiday:** November 25 (Independence Day).

FRENCH GUIANA

Area: 32,255 sq. mi./83,533 km². **Local name:** Guyane Française. **Currency:** French franc. **Capital:** Cayenne. **Physical features:** Low, marshy coastal plains; hills and small mountains, rain forest in interior. **Climate:** Tropical moderated by coastal breezes; temperatures average 80°F/27°C; two rainy seasons (peaks in Dec. and June). **Time zone:** GMT –3h. **Political system:** Overseas department of France. **Head of state:** President Jacques Chirac (from 1995). **Head of government:** Prefect of the Republic Jean-François Cordet (from 1992). **Main exports:** Shrimp, prawns, wood, metal and wood products, rum. **Resources:** Bauxite, wood, gold, cinnabar, kaolin, fish.

PEOPLE

Population: 108,000. **Distribution urban/rural:** n.a. **Life expectancy:** 71(m), 78(f). **Language:** French. **Ethnic groups:** African or mulatto 66%, European 12%, other 22%. **Religion:** Roman Catholic 78%, Protestant 4%. **Literacy rate:** 82%. **Per capita GDP:** $2,240.

ECUADOR

Area: 109,483 sq. mi./283,561 km². *Local name:* República del Ecuador. *Currency:* Sucre. *Capital:* Quito. *Other cities:* Guayaquil, Cuenca, Machala, Portoviejo. *Physical features:* Coastal plains rising to inter-Andean central highlands; flat to rolling jungle in E. *Climate:* Tropical along coast; cooler inland. *Time zone:* GMT –5h. *Political system:* Republic. *Head of state and government:* Sixto Duran Ballen (from 1992). *Main exports:* Petroleum, coffee, bananas, cocoa products, shrimp, fish products, rice. *Resources:* Natural oil, fish, wood.

PEOPLE

Population: 10,981,000. *Distribution urban/rural:* 54%/46%. *Life expectancy:* 67(m), 72(f). *Languages:* Spanish (official), Indian languages, especially Quechua. *Ethnic groups:* Mestizo 55%, Indian 25%, Iberian 10%, African 10%. *Religion:* Roman Catholic 95%. *Literacy rate:* 86%. *Per capita GDP:* $1,070.

KEY DATES

1809 Independence from Spain.
1830 Secedes from Gran Colombia.
1925–48 Ecuador has 22 presidents, none of whom serves a full term.
1941 War with Peru over Amazon Basin territory; most of the land lost to Peru.
1948–55 Liberals in power.
1956 First Conservative president in 60 years takes office.
1960 Liberals return to power with José Velasco as president.
1961 Velasco replaced by Vice-President Carlos Julio Arosemena Monroy.
1962 Military junta installed.

1966 Return to civilian government with new constitution.
1968 José Velasco returns as president.
1972 Coup and return to military rule.
1978 New democratic constitution.
1979 Liberals in power.
1982 Deteriorating economy prompts civil unrest; state of emergency declared.
1983 Austerity measures introduced.

1984 Narrow majority in elections brings Conservatives back into power.
1988 Rodrigo Borja Cevellos elected (moderate left-wing coalition).
1989 Left-wing guerrilla group Alfaro Vive, ¡Carajo! (AVC) lays down arms after nine years of fighting.
1992 Sixto Duran Ballen president.
1995 Border dispute with Peru.

GALÁPAGOS ISLANDS

The Galápagos Islands are a volcanic archipelago lying 600 miles (970 km) west of Ecuador. They are famed for their extraordinary wildlife, which includes a rare flightless cormorant, marine iguanas, and giant tortoises weighing more than 200 pounds (90 kg). It was here that the naturalist Charles Darwin began to formulate his theory of evolution. Human colonization has taken its toll, however, and animals introduced to the islands by farmers now pose an enormous threat. Whales, tortoises, and seals have proved easy pickings for commercial vessels, and the islands' wildlife has been further depleted by scientific missions taking specimens for research. But Ecuador has begun to confront the problem and is taking steps toward ensuring the survival of the Galápagos's wildlife.

KEY DATES

1832 Ecuador annexes islands.
1835 Charles Darwin visits Galápagos Islands.

1934 Ecuadorian government under Abelardo Motalvo takes first steps toward safeguarding the islands' wildlife by making a legal provision for the declaration of nature reserves and national parks and by limiting the number of specimens that scientific expeditions are allowed to collect.
1936 Fourteen islands made nature reserves.
1957 International mission to recommend site for research station; Ecuador makes all islands apart from those already assigned to Ecuadorian colonists a national park.
1959 Charles Darwin Foundation founded.
1960 Ecuador's first National Scientific Commission is set up.
1964 Authorization given for the extermination of feral animals damaging the environment and for the prevention of native animals being moved; first conservation officer appointed; regulations introduced for tour operators.
1972 Program initiated for the protection of

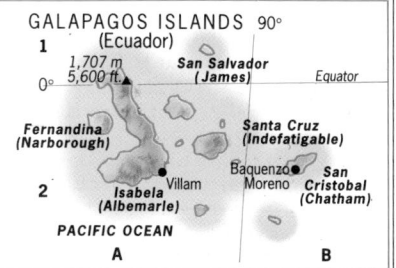

tortoises, including interim breeding in captivity; goats are eliminated on four islands and their numbers greatly reduced elsewhere.
1985 Fire on the islands threatens wildlife.
1994 Fire on island of Isabella destroys more than 15,000 acres (6,070 hectares) of forest; World Wide Fund for Nature organizes relocation of tortoises at risk.

PERU

Area: 480,418 sq. mi./1,244,284 km². **Local name:** República del Peru. **Currency:** Nuevo Sol. **Capital:** Lima. **Other cities:** Arequipa, Callao, Trujillo. **Physical features:** Western coastal plain (*costa*), high and rugged Andes in center (*sierra*), eastern lowland jungle of Amazon Basin (*selvas*). **Climate:** Varies from tropical in E. to dry desert in W. **Time zone:** GMT –5h. **Political system:** Republic. **Head of state:** Alberto Fujimori (from 1990). **Head of government:** Oscar de la Puente Raygada (from 1992). **Main exports:** Copper, fishmeal, zinc, crude petroleum and by-products, lead, refined silver, sugar, coffee, cotton. **Resources:** Copper, fish, zinc, oil, lead, silver, coffee, iron, cotton, molybdenum, wool.

PEOPLE

Population: 22,454,000. **Distribution urban/rural:** 70%/30%. **Life expectancy:** 63(m), 67(f). **Languages:** Spanish and Quechua (both official), Aymara. **Ethnic groups:** Indian 45%, Mestizo 37%, European 15%, African, Asian, and other 3%. **Religion:** Roman Catholic 90%. **Literacy rate:** 85%. **Per capita GDP:** $920.

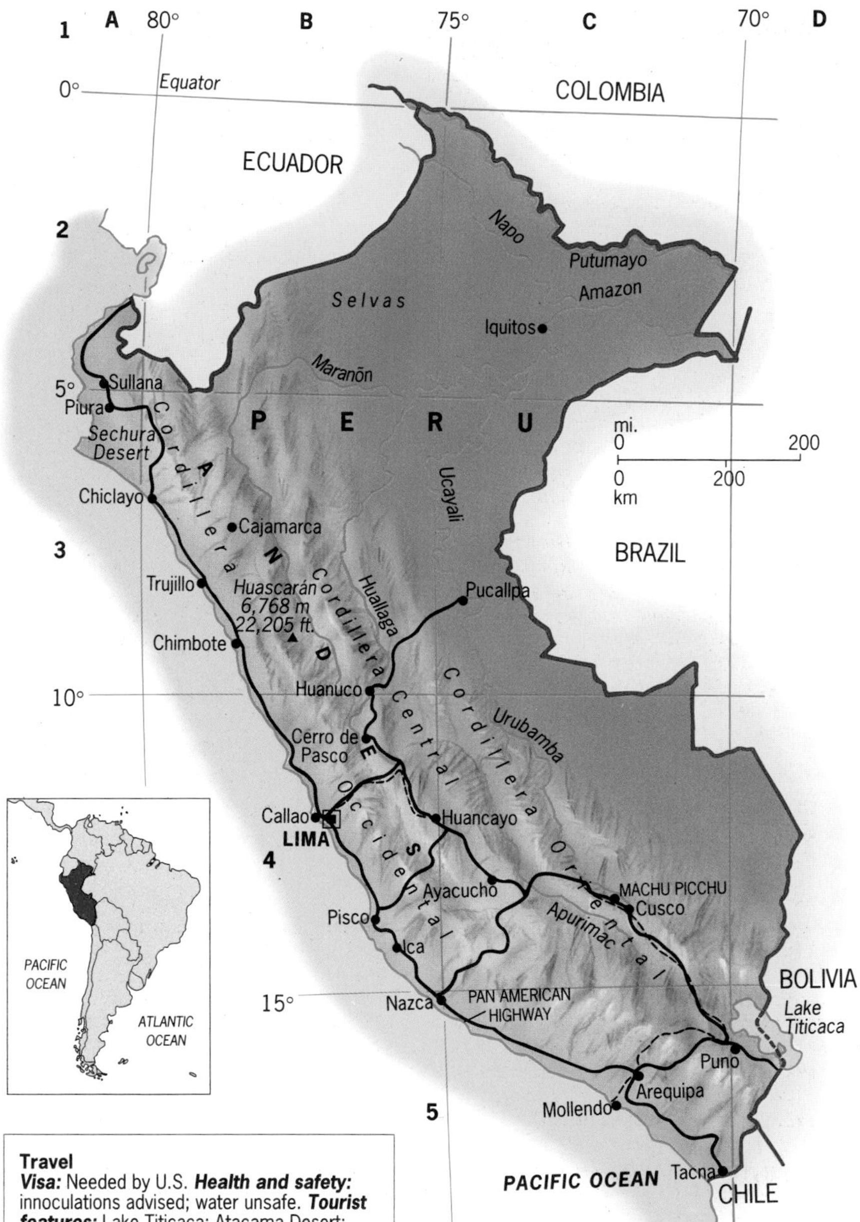

KEY DATES

1533 Spain conquers Peru.

1824 Independence from Spain.

1849–74 Around 80,000–100,000 Chinese laborers arrive in Peru to extract guano and work on plantations.

1879–84 Peru loses nitrate-rich southern provinces to Chile in the War of the Pacific.

1919 Augusto B. Leguia is elected president; he soon becomes a dictator and borrows large sums of money from U.S. banks to finance his projects.

1921 The International Petroleum Company, a branch of the Standard Oil Company, gains control of oil deposits in N.W. Peru.

1924 Victor Raúl Haya de la Torre founds Alianza Popular Revolucionaria Americana (APRA), Peru's first real socialist party.

1930 Alarmed by state of country's finances, army overthrows Augusto B. Leguia and installs Col. Luis Sánchez Cerro as president.

1931 Victor Raúl Haya de la Torre runs for president against Sánchez Cerro and loses; APRA suspects that the election is rigged and stages violent antigovernment demonstrations; hundreds of APRA supporters are jailed or killed, and APRA is banned from fielding political candidates.

1948 Further violence following general election leads to APRA being outlawed by President José Luis Bustamante; Bustamante overthrown by military and

replaced by Gen. Manuel Odría.

1956 Gen. Odría legalizes APRA.

1963 Return to civilian rule with Fernando Belaúnde Terry (Popular Action Party) as president; Belaúnde carries out social reforms.

1968 President Belaúnde makes agreement with International Petroleum Company over Peruvian oil fields; opponents accuse Belaúnde of favoring the U.S. company; Belaúnde is overthrown and military junta is imposed; Gen. Juan Velasco Alvarado named president.

1980 Civilian government elected with Fernando Belaúnde Terry as president again; Sendero Luminoso ("Shining

Path"), Maoist guerrilla group, formed.

1981 Boundary dispute with Ecuador.

1985 Alan García Pérez (Social Democrats) becomes president.

1988 García pressured to seek help from IMF; Sendero Luminoso steps up campaign of violence.

1990 Alberto Fujimori president; assassination attempt on him.

1992 Two coup attempts; U.S.A. suspends humanitarian aid; Sendero Luminoso leader Abimael Guzman Reynoso arrested and sentenced to life imprisonment; single-chamber legislature replaces two-chamber system.

1995 Border dispute with Ecuador.

Travel
Visa: Needed by U.S. **Health and safety:** innoculations advised; water unsafe. **Tourist features:** Lake Titicaca; Atacama Desert; Nazca lines; monuments of Machu Picchu, lost city of the Incas; Chan Chan. **National Holiday:** July 28 (Independence Day).

CHILE

Area: 284,520 sq. mi./736,905 km². *Local name:* República de Chile. *Currency:* Chilean peso. *Capital:* Santiago. *Other cities:* Valparaiso, Concepción. *Physical features:* Low coastal mountains, central valley, Andes in E. *Climate:* Desert in N., temperate in S. *Time zone:* GMT –4h. *Political system:* Democratic republic. *Head of state and government:* Eduardo Frei Rulz-Tagle (from 1994). *Main exports:* Copper, other metals, minerals, wood products, fish, fruit, wine. *Resources:* Copper, iron ore, nitrates, wood, precious metals.

PEOPLE

Population: 13,813,000. *Distribution urban/rural:* 84%/16%. *Life expectancy:* 71(m), 77(f). *Language:* Spanish. *Ethnic groups:* European and European-Indian 95%, Indian 3%, other 2%. *Religions:* Roman Catholic around 89%, Protestant and Jewish around 11%. *Literacy rate:* 93%. *Per capita GDP:* $2,300.

KEY DATES

1818 Independence from Spain.

1879–84 War of the Pacific; Chile wins new territory from Peru containing valuable copper and nitrate deposits.

1891 Civil war kills more than 10,000.

1920 Germany begins to produce synthetic nitrates, destroying Chile's export economy; widespread unemployment.

1939 Economic development body, the Corporación de Fomento de la Producción (CORFO), founded.

1960 Chile struck by series of earthquakes and tidal waves, killing thousands.

1970 Salvador Allende Gossens becomes first democratically elected Marxist leader in the world; massive nationalization and land reform program begun.

1971–73 Inflation soars to more than 350%; strikes and demonstrations.

1973 Allende overthrown in U.S.-sponsored coup and killed; Gen. Augusto Pinochet Ugarte becomes leader of military junta; thousands of Chileans are imprisoned without trial, tortured, and killed by the military; congress dissolved, freedom of press restricted, and political parties banned.

1980 New constitution provides for gradual return to democratic government.

1987 Partial lift of ban on political parties.

1988 Pinochet voted out in referendum.

1989 Patricio Aylwin of the Christian Democratic Party elected president.

1990 New government installed, although Pinochet remains commander-in-chief.

1992 Senior officials involved in arms sales to Croatia in violation of UN ban.

1994 Eduardo Frei Rulz-Tagle becomes president.

TRAVEL

Visa: Needed by U.S. *Driving permit:* IDP. *Health and safety:* Inoculations advised; water unsafe. *Tourist features:* Atacama Desert in N.; Andes; lakes in S.; Torres del Paine National Park; beaches. *National holiday:* September 19 (Independence Day).

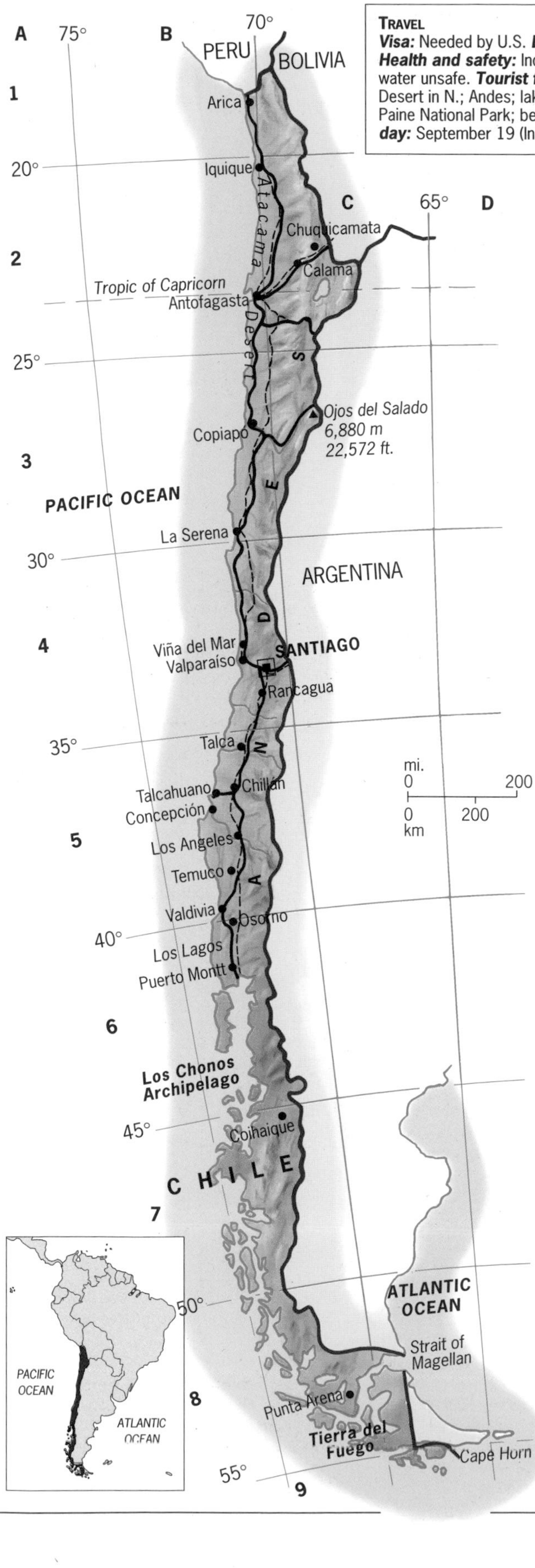

PERU
BOLIVIA
Arica
Iquique
Atacama
Chuquicamata
Calama
Tropic of Capricorn
Antofagasta
Ojos del Salado
6,880 m
22,572 ft.
Copiapo
PACIFIC OCEAN
La Serena
ARGENTINA
Viña del Mar
Valparaiso
SANTIAGO
Rancagua
Talca
Talcahuano
Chillan
Concepción
Los Angeles
Temuco
Valdivia
Osorno
Los Lagos
Puerto Montt
Los Chonos
Archipelago
Coihaique
CHILE
ATLANTIC OCEAN
Strait of Magellan
PACIFIC OCEAN
ATLANTIC OCEAN
Punta Arena
Tierra del Fuego
Cape Horn

mi.
0   200
0   200
km

PARAGUAY

Area: 157,047 sq. mi./406,752 km². *Local name:* República del Paraguay. *Currency:* Guaraní. *Capital:* Asunción. *Other cities:* San Lorenzo, Ciudad del Este. *Physical features:* Low marshy plains, some wooded hills. *Climate:* Varies from temperate in E. to semiarid in W. *Time zone:* GMT –4h. *Political system:* Republic. *Head of state and government:* Juan Carlos Wasmosy (from 1993). *Main exports:* Cotton, soy beans, wood, vegetable oils, hides, meat. *Resources:* Iron ore, manganese, limestone, hydropower, wood.

PEOPLE

Population: 4,643,000. *Distribution urban/rural:* 46%/54%. *Life expectancy:* 71(m), 74(f). *Languages:* Spanish, Guarani. *Ethnic groups:* Mestizo 95%, other 5%. *Religions:* Roman Catholic 90%, Mennonite and other Protestant denominations 10%. *Literacy rate:* 90%. *Per capita GDP:* $1,460.

KEY DATES

1537 Spanish arrive in Paraguay.
1811 Independence declared.

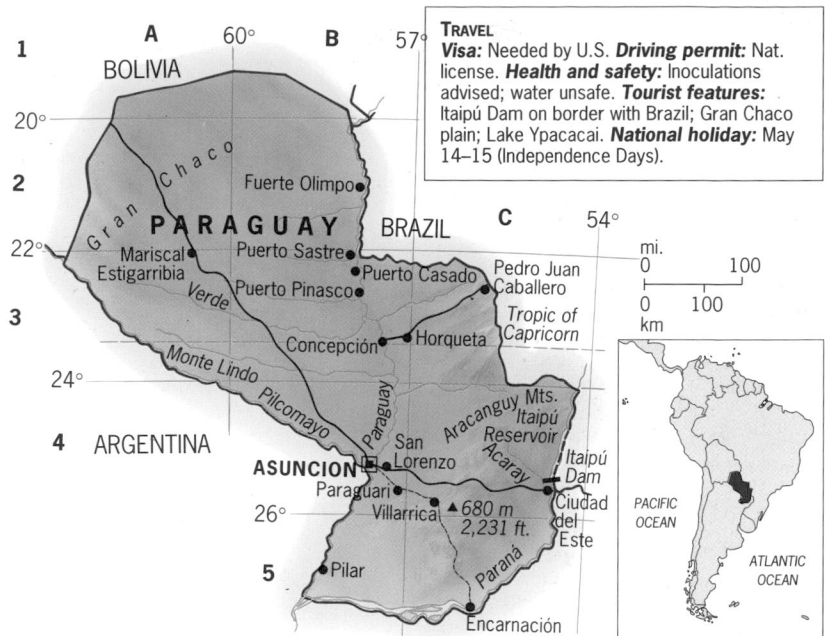

1865–70 War of the Triple Alliance.
1932 War with Bolivia over Chaco.
1938 Settlement with Bolivia gives Paraguay new territory in Chaco.
1948–54 Political instability.
1954 Alfredo Stroessner seizes power; he maintains political stability which enables him to develop the economy.
1989 Stroessner overthrown in coup led by Gen. Andrés Rodríguez; Rodríguez elected president.
1993 Juan Carlos Wasmosy president.

URUGUAY

Area: 68,041 sq. mi./176,215 km². *Local name:* República Oriental del Uruguay. *Currency:* Uruguayan peso. *Capital:* Montevideo. *Other cities:* Salto, Paysandú. *Physical features:* Plains and low hills, coastal plains in S. *Climate:* Temperate. *Time zone:* GMT –3h. *Political system:* Republic. *Head of state and government:* Luis Alberto Lacalle Herrera (from 1989). *Main exports:* Hides, beef, wool, fish. *Resources:* Minerals.

PEOPLE

Population: 3,149,000. *Distribution urban/rural:* 86%/14%. *Life expectancy:* 69(m), 76(f). *Language:* Spanish. *Ethnic groups:* European 88%, Mestizo 8%, African 4%. *Religions:* Roman Catholic 66%, Protestant, Jewish, and other 34%. *Literacy rate:* 96%. *Per capita GDP:* $2,935.

KEY DATES

1825 Independence from Spain.
1967 Emergence of leftist guerrilla organization, the Tupamaros.
1972 Juan Maria Bordaberry president; increase in terrorist activities; congress declares state of internal war.
1973 General strike; National Labor Confederation is banned.

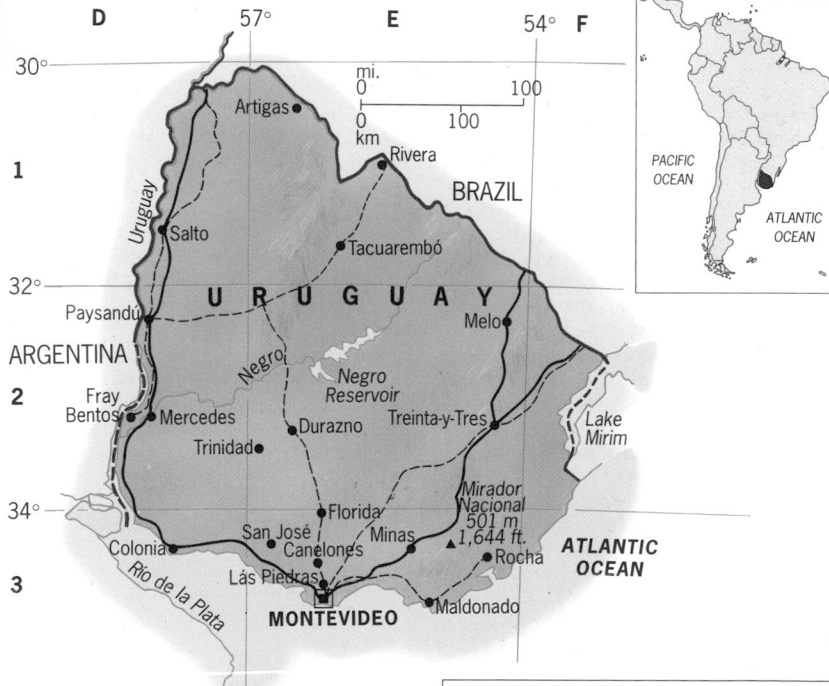

1976 Bordaberry deposed by army.
1981 Gen. Gregorio Alvarez Armellino president.
1984 Civil unrest precipitates return of democratically elected government.
1989 Luis Lacalle Herrera president.

BOLIVIA

Area: 424,162 sq. mi./1,098,581 km². **Local name:** República de Bolivia. **Currency:** Boliviano. **Capital**: La Paz/Sucre. **Other cities:** Santa Cruz, Cochabamba. **Physical features:** Rugged Andes Mountains; lowland plains of Amazon Basin. **Climate:** Tropical/semiarid. **Time zone:** GMT –4h. **Political system:** Republic. **Head of state and government:** Gonzalo Sanchez de Lozado (from 1993). **Main exports:** Metals, natural gas, coffee, soy beans, sugar, cotton. **Resources:** Tin, natural gas, oil, zinc, tungsten, antimony, silver, iron ore.

PEOPLE

Population: 7,065,000. **Distribution urban/rural:** 51%/49%. **Life expectancy:** 59(m), 64 (f). **Languages:** Spanish, Quechua, Aymara (all official). **Ethnic groups:** Quechua 30%, mixed 30%, Aymara 25%, European 15%. **Religions:** Roman Catholic 95%; active Protestant minority. **Literacy rate:** 78%. **Per capita GDP:** $630.

KEY DATES

1825 Independence from Spain.

1967 Uprising led by Ernesto "Che" Guevara put down by army.

1971 Col. Hugo Banzer Suárez president.

1974 Attempted coup; Banzer bans political and trade union activity.

1980 Gen. Luis García president after military coup; allegations of corruption lead to cancellation of U.S. and EC aid.

1981 García forced to resign; Gen. Celso Torrelio Villa becomes president.

1982 Siles Zuazo president.

1983 U.S./EC economic aid resumed.

1985 Dr. Paz Estenssoro president.

1989 Jaime Paz Zamora of the Movement of Revolutionary Left (MIR) president.

1993 Right-wing National Revolutionary Movement (MNR) wins elections.

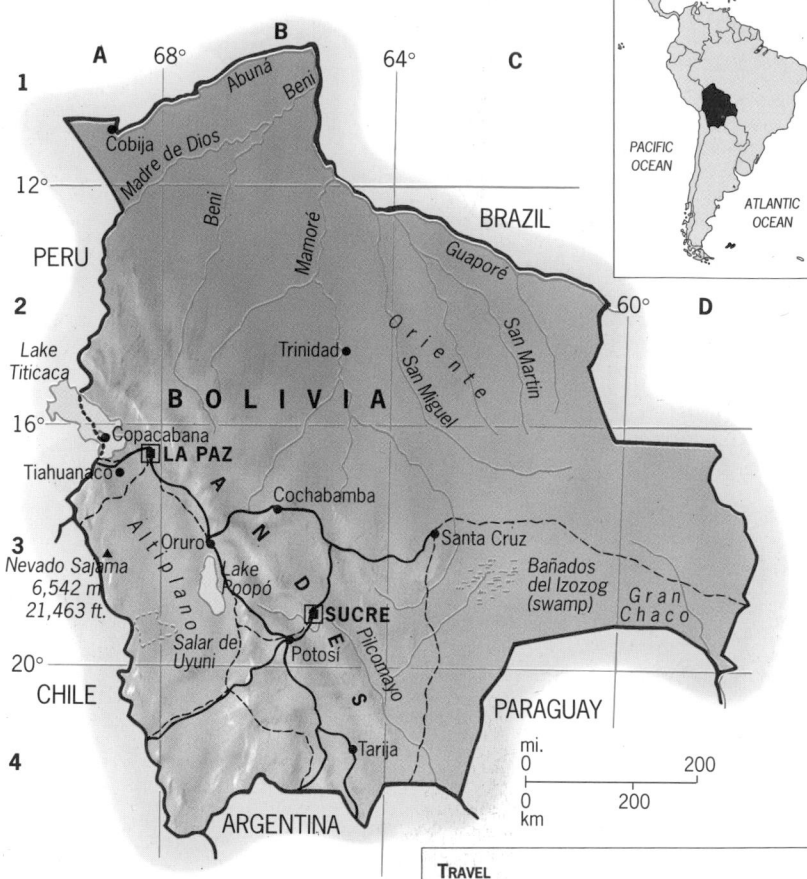

TRAVEL
Visa: Needed by U.S. **Driving permit:** IDP. **Health and safety:** Inoculations advised; water unsafe. **Tourist features:** Andes; Lakes Titicaca and Poopú; La Paz is world's highest capital city. **National holiday:** August 6 (Independence Day).

THE FALKLAND ISLANDS (ISLAS MALVINAS)

The Falkland Islands are a self-governing British dependency approximately 300 miles (500 km) east of the Strait of Magellan. They consist of two large islands, East Falkland and West Falkland, and about 200 small islands covering an area of 4,700 sq. mi. (12,175 km²). The capital, Stanley on the island of East Falkland, is home to about half of the islands' population.

Despite having negligible resources, infertile terrain, and a population of less than 2,000, the Falkland Islands have been the cause of a long-standing dispute between Argentina and Britain over sovereignty. In the early 1980s, this dispute resulted in a war between the two countries that, although short-lived, caused considerable loss of life, particularly on the Argentine side.

Argentina still claims that the Falklands are rightfully Argentinian territory (and, indeed, geologically they are a part of Patagonia in Argentina) but, despite ever-diminishing sympathy from the international community, the British government has consistently refused to engage in negotiations on the matter, and the situation looks unlikely to change.

KEY DATES

1592 Falkland Islands first sighted by British explorer John Davis.

1690 Captain John Strong makes the first landing on the Falkland Islands.

1764 Colonists from Saint-Malo in France establish a settlement on East Falkland.

1765 The first British settlement is established on West Falkland.

1770 Spain buys the territory on East Falkland from the French.

1774 British temporarily leave the islands.

1816 Argentina achieves independence.

1820 Argentina claims sovereignty of the Falkland Islands.

1833 Great Britain takes full control of the Falkland Islands.

1908 Great Britain formally annexes the Falkland dependencies.

1914 Naval battle of the Falkland Islands with decisive victory for Britain over Germany.

1960s UN negotiations begin.

1977 Present constitution comes into effect.

1982 April: Argentine troops occupy the Falklands and expel British governor; June: Argentines defeated by British and surrender; 725 Argentinians and 225 Britons are killed during the Falklands War.

1983 Falkland Islands Government Office opens in London.

1985 Islands of South Georgia and South Sandwich cease to be Falkland dependencies.

1990 Argentina's congress declares the Falkland Islands to be part of the new province of Tierra del Fuego; diplomatic relations between U.K. and Argentina are restored.

ARGENTINA

Area: 1,073,394 sq. mi./2,780,092 km². *Local name:* República Argentina. *Currency:* Peso. *Capital:* Buenos Aires. *Other cities:* Córdoba, Rosario. *Physical features:* Rich plains of the Pampas in N., flat to rolling plateau of Patagonia in S., Andes along western border. *Climate:* Mostly temperate; arid in S.E.; subpolar in S.W; subtropical in N.E. *Time zone:* GMT –3h. *Political system:* Republic. *Head of state and government:* Carlos Saúl Menem (from 1989). *Main exports:* Meat, wheat, corn, oilseed, tannin, hides, wool. *Resources:* Lead, zinc, tin, copper, iron ore, gold, silver, natural gas.

PEOPLE

Population: 33,778,000. *Distribution urban/rural:* 87%/13%. *Life expectancy:* 67(m), 74(f). *Languages:* Spanish (official), Italian. *Ethnic groups:* European 85%; Mestizo, Indian, and other groups 15%. *Religions:* Roman Catholic 90%; Protestant 2%; Jewish 2%; other 6%. *Literacy rate:* 95%. *Per capita GDP:* $3,100.

KEY DATES

1816 Argentina achieves independence.

1946 Col. Juan Perón elected president; freedom of speech suspended and constitution changed to increase his power.

1955 Perón is ousted and flees to Spain.

1962–72 Political instability; civil unrest.

1973 Perón returns to Argentina and is re-elected; his third wife, Isabel, is made vice-president.

1974 Col. Juan Perón dies; Isabel Perón becomes president; increased terrorist activity.

1976 Army arrests Isabel Perón and takes control of government; many people are imprisoned without trial, tortured, and killed by military.

1982 Falklands War with U.K.

1983 Raúl Alfonsin becomes president.

1985–86 Investigations into previous governments; many officials are brought to trial, including three former presidents.

1986 Assassination attempt on Alfonsin.

1989 Carlos Menem (Peronista) becomes president and pardons some of those convicted under Alfonsin.

1990 Full diplomatic relations with U.K. are restored.

1993 Agreement allows presidents to seek a second term of office.

1995 Menem re-elected by record margin.

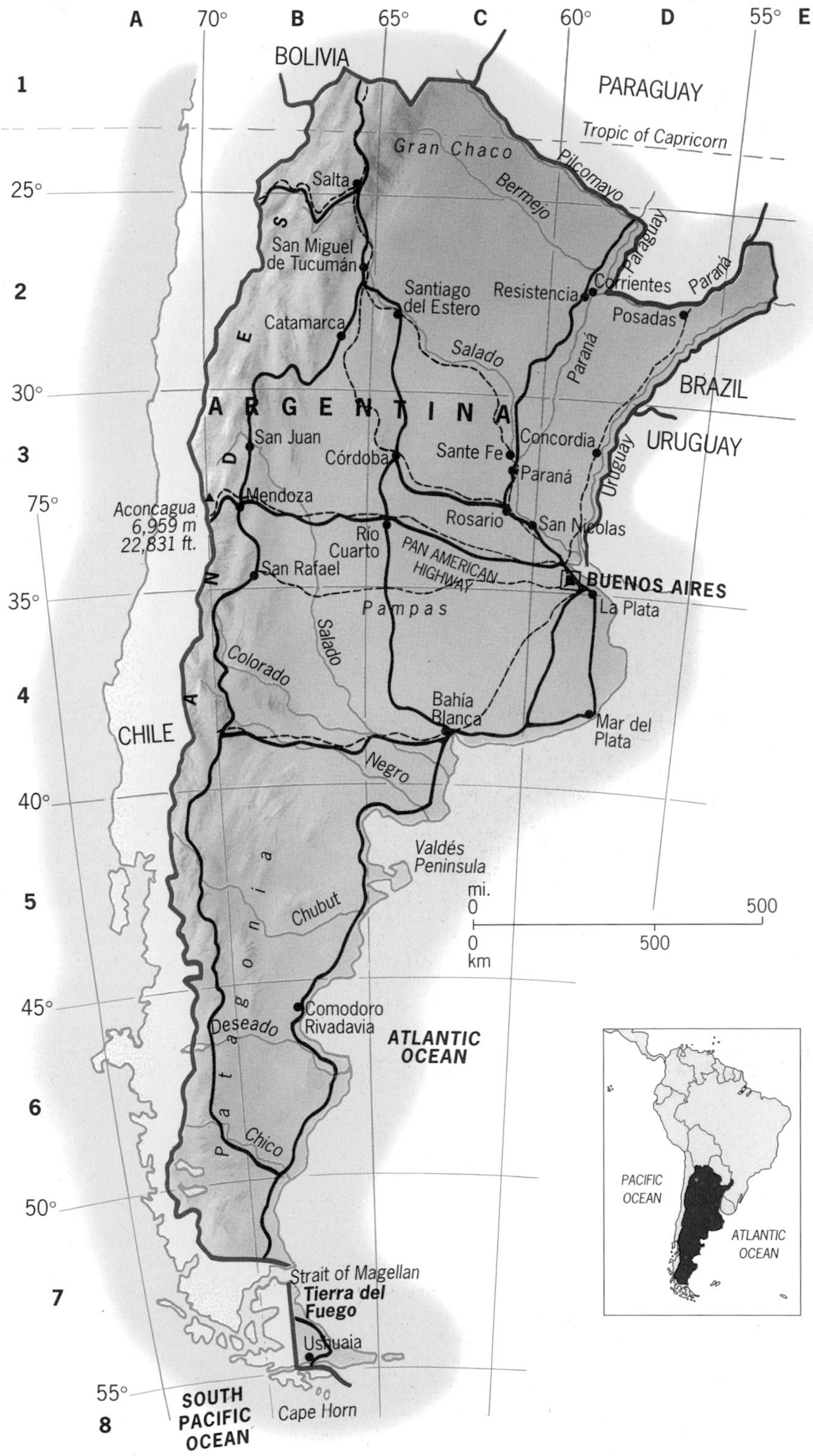

ECONOMY

Farming: Ranches support more than 50 million beef cattle and around 29 million sheep; crops include corn, wheat, fruit, cotton, flax, potatoes, sorghum, sugarcane, sunflower seeds, and soy beans.

Forestry: Trees in the Gran Chaco yield a very tough wood (Quebracho) from which tannin is extracted.

Natural resources: Gas and oil, coal, copper, iron ore, lead, zinc, gold, silver, and uranium.

Industry: Main industries are food processing, oil refining, and manufacture of chemicals, electrical goods, and vehicles.

TRAVEL
Visa: Needed by U.S. *Driving permit:* IDP.
Health and safety: Inoculations advised.
Tourist features: Andes Mountains; Iguaçu Falls. *National holiday:* May 25 (Revolution Day).

BRAZIL

Area: 3,286,485 sq. mi./8,511,996 km². *Local name:* República Federativa do Brasil. *Currency:* Real. *Capital:* Brasilia. *Other cities:* São Paulo, Rio de Janeiro, Belo Horizonte. *Physical features:* Mostly flat to rolling lowlands in N.; some plains, hills, mountains, and narrow coastal belt. *Climate:* Subtropical/savanna. *Time zone:* GMT –3h (E), –5h (W). *Political system:* Federal republic. *Head of state and government:* Fernando Henrique Cardoso (from 1995). *Main exports:* Iron ore, steel, soy beans, cocoa, orange juice, coffee, fruit. *Resources:* Quartz, iron ore, manganese, bauxite, nickel, uranium, phosphates, tin, hydropower, gold, platinum, crude oil.

PEOPLE

Population: 151,534,000. *Distribution urban/rural:* 76%/24%. *Life expectancy:* 62(m), 69(f). *Languages:* Portuguese (official), Indian languages, Spanish. *Ethnic groups:* European 55%, mixed 38%, African 6%, other 1%. *Religion:* Predominantly Roman Catholic; others Protestant, Jewish, Indian, and African religions. *Literacy rate:* 81%. *Per capita GDP:* $2,300.

KEY DATES

1500 Portuguese land in Brazil.

1808 Portugal's ruler, King João VI, flees occupied Portugal and makes Rio de Janeiro capital of Portuguese Empire.

1815 Brazil raised to status of kingdom.

1822 King João's son, Pedro, declares independence; Pedro crowned emperor.

1824 Pedro grants first constitution.

1865–70 War of the Triple Alliance.

1888 Slavery abolished.

1889 Brazil becomes a republic.

1891 First constitution adopted.

1917 Brazil joins Allies in World War I.

1926 Wáshington Luís made president without election.

1930 Wáshington Luís overthrown in coup led by Getúlio Vargas.

1932 Large-scale rebellion in São Paulo against Vargas regime lasts for three months before being quelled.

1934 New constitution increases wages, shortens working hours, gives trade unions greater powers, and introduces suffrage for women.

1937 New constitution installs Getúlio Vargas as dictator; most constitutional freedoms are lost; Vargas makes important social changes.

1942 Brazil declares war on Axis powers; 25,000 Brazilian troops go to Italy.

1945 Military leaders force Getúlio Vargas to resign; Eurico Gaspar Dutra is elected president.

1946 New constitution restores individual freedoms and democratic rule.

1951 Getúlio Vargas reelected.

1954 Civil unrest; military leaders demand Vargas's resignation; Vargas commits suicide.

1956 Juscelino Kubitschek is elected president.

1960 Government moves from Rio de Janeiro to new city of Brasilia; Jânio Quadros elected president and attempts to build economy; political pressures mount as a result of trade union action in the cities and peasant rebellions; Quadros resigns seven months after election and is succeeded by Vice-President João Goulart.

1964 Fearing that Goulart's economic policies will lead to a communist takeover, military leaders take power; Gen. Humberto Castelo Branco becomes dictator, outlaws political parties.

1974 General Ernesto Geisel becomes president.

1979 Gen. João Baptista Figueiredo becomes president and allows political and trade union activity to resume after 15 years of military rule; 300 trade unions stage strikes for higher wages.

1985 Military rule ends; Tancredo de Almeida Neves elected first civilian president for 21 years but is too ill to take office; replaced by José Sarney; economic austerity program imposed; constitutional amendment passed by congress provides for direct election of future presidents by the people rather than by representatives in the electoral college.

1986 Brazilians elect new congress and state legislatures.

1988 New constitution transfers power from president to congress; measures announced to halt large-scale burning of Amazonian rain forest for cattle grazing.

1989 Fernando Collor de Mello is elected president.

1992 Collor charged with corruption; replaced by vice-president.

1993 Collor is indicted for "passive corruption" and appears before the supreme court.

1994 Currency stabilization plan, new currency, and reduced inflation achieved.

1995 Fernando Henrique Cardoso becomes president.

ECONOMY

Farming: Brazil is the world's leading producer of coffee, bananas, cassava, oranges, papaya, and sugarcane. Cattle, poultry, pigs, horses, and sheep raised.

Forestry: Brazil is the third largest producer of forest products, including wood and especially paraná pine nuts, resins, rubber, oils, and medicines.

Fishing: Catches include lobsters, shrimp, and bony fish.

Mining: Minerals include quartz (the world's chief source), diamonds, gold, iron ore, lead, magnesium, copper, manganese, mica, uranium, and oil.

Industry: Products include vehicles, aircraft, cement, chemicals, machinery, textiles, foods, and pharmaceuticals.

A 70°

B

VENEZUELA

1

Neb
3,0
9,8

COLOMBIA

0°

Negro

Japurá

Yavari

Amazon

2

Purus

Pôrto Vel

10°

PERU

BOLIV

3

mi.
0   500

0   500
km

20°

C   60°   50°   **D**   40°   **E**

Highlands

GUYANA

SURINAM

FR. GUIANA

ATLANTIC OCEAN

Macapá

Equator

Marajó Island

Belém

São Luis

B a s i n

Amazon

Manaus

TRANS AMAZONIAN HIGHWAY

Madeira

Tucurui Reservoir

Fortaleza

Tapajós

Teresina

Natal

Juruena

Selvas

Teles Pires

Xingu

Araguaia

Tocantins

São Francisco

Campina Grande

João Pessoa

Recife

B   R   A   Z   I   L

Maceió

Aracaju

Feira de Santana

Salvador

Mato Grosso

Cuiabá

Brazilian Highlands

BRASILIA

Goiânia

Paranaiba

Uberlândia

Governador Valadares

Campo Grande

Uberaba

Belo Horizonte

Vitória

São José do Rio Prêto

Ribeirão Prêto

Juiz de Fora

Campos

Tropic of Capricorn

PARAGUAY

Londrina

Sorocaba

Campinas

Niterói

Rio de Janeiro

Ponta Grossa

São Paulo

Santos

4

Iguaçu Falls

Curitiba

Joinville

ARGENTINA

Uruguay

Florianópolis

Caxias do Sul

Santa Maria

Pôrto Alegre

30°

Patos Lagoon

Pelotas

5

Rio Grande

URUGUAY

Mirim Lake

PACIFIC OCEAN

ATLANTIC OCEAN

AFRICA

Area: 11,700,000 sq. mi./30,262,000 km². *Largest cities:* Cairo, Lagos, Kinshasa, Casablanca, Alexandria, Giza, Abidjan, Addis Ababa, Cape Town. *Organizations:* Organization of African Unity (OAU), Communauté Economique des Etats de l'Afrique Centrale (CEEAC), Economic Community of West African States (ECOWAS). *Main products (and percentage of world output):* Cocoa (52%), diamonds (48%), cobalt (41%), chromium (40%), gold (36%), coffee (23%).

PHYSICAL FEATURES
Africa is the world's second largest continent and covers one-fifth of the earth's land area. The continent consists of a vast central plateau broken by mountain ranges and bordered in places by narrow coastal plains. *Highest point:* Mount Kilimanjaro (19,340 ft./5,900 m). *Lowest point:* Lake Assal (–509 ft./–155 m). *Longest river:* Nile. *Largest lake:* Victoria. *Other features:* Sahara and Kalahari deserts, Great Rift Valley, Atlas Mountains. *Vegetation:* Mainly desert in N., savanna and tropical rain forest in center, savanna and semidesert in S.

PEOPLE
Population: 670,000,000 (12% of the total world population). *Growth rate:* 2.9%. *Density:* 58/sq. mi. *Distribution urban/rural:* 30%/70%. *Life expectancy:* 54(m), 58(f). *Languages:* More than 800 languages including 300 Bantu languages, of which Swahili is most common; Arabic and Hausa are also important. *Ethnic groups:* More than 800 black ethnic groups make up 75% of the total population and live mostly S. of the Sahara; Arabs and Berbers live in N. Africa; 2.5 million Asians live in Madagascar; some Europeans. *Religions:* Muslim, Christian, including Ethiopian Orthodox and Coptic Orthodox, indigenous beliefs; many Africans practice religions that combine the beliefs of Christianity with local faiths.

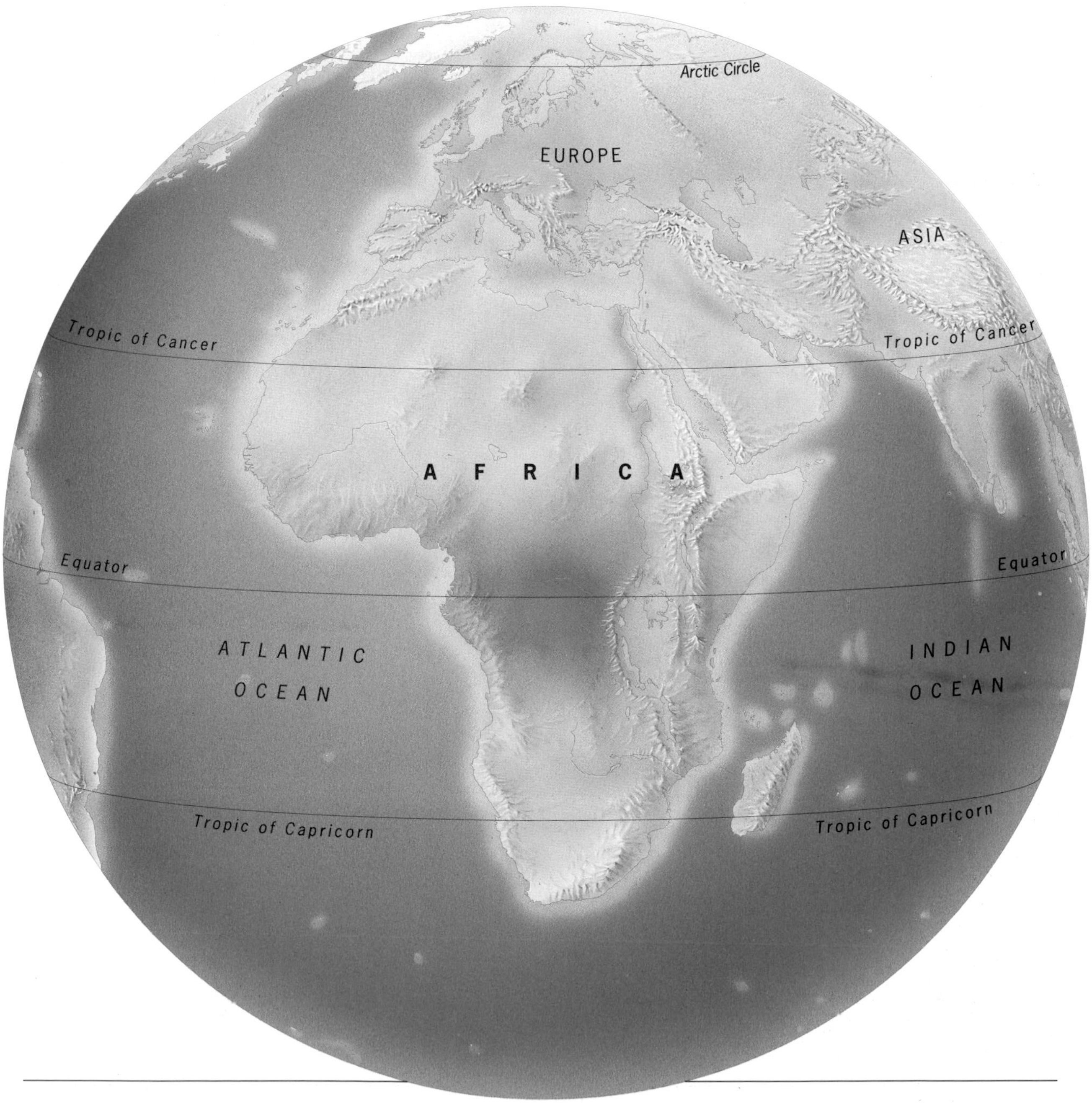

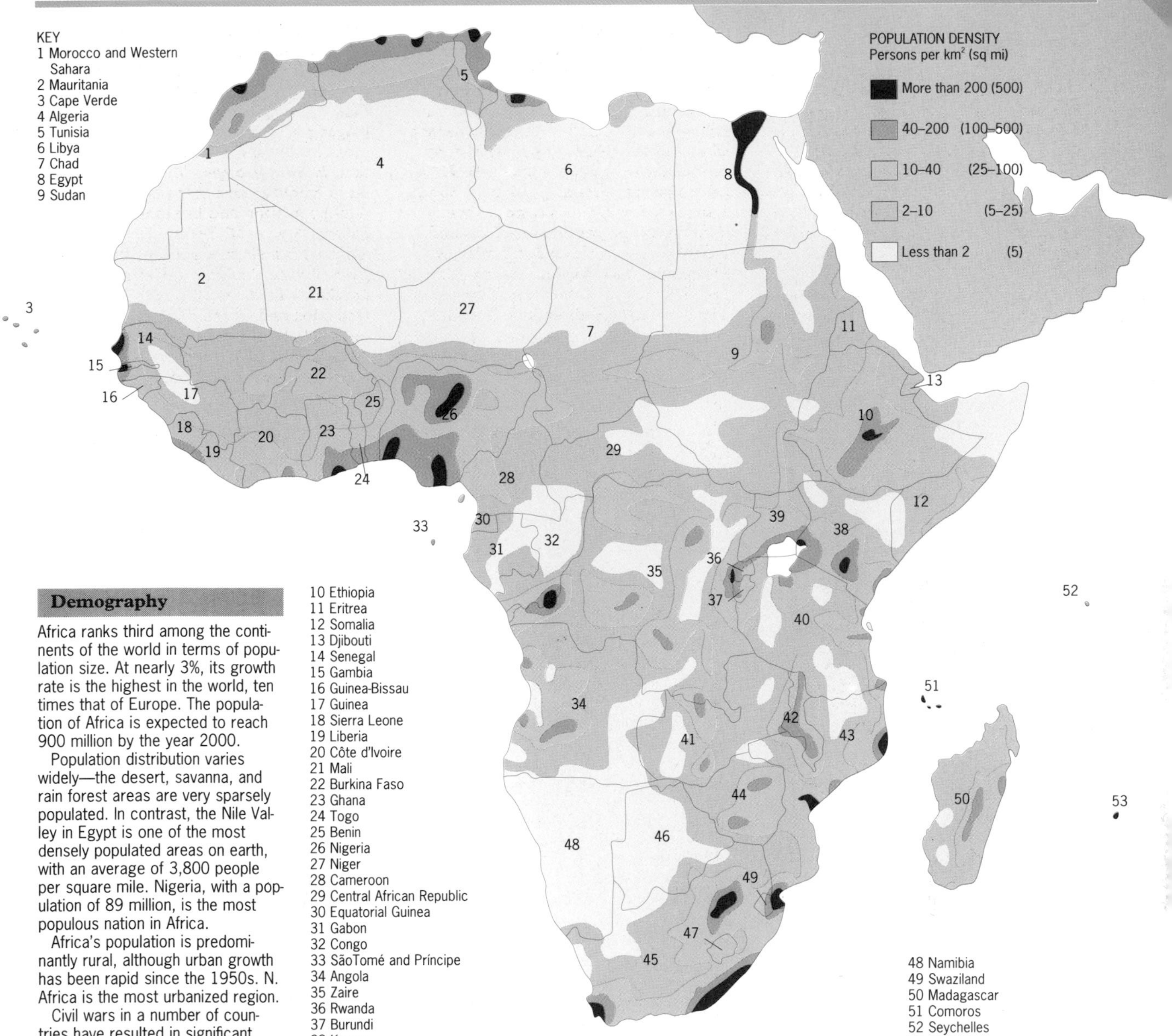

KEY
1 Morocco and Western
  Sahara
2 Mauritania
3 Cape Verde
4 Algeria
5 Tunisia
6 Libya
7 Chad
8 Egypt
9 Sudan

POPULATION DENSITY
Persons per km² (sq mi)

More than 200 (500)

40–200 (100–500)

10–40   (25–100)

2–10   (5–25)

Less than 2   (5)

10 Ethiopia
11 Eritrea
12 Somalia
13 Djibouti
14 Senegal
15 Gambia
16 Guinea-Bissau
17 Guinea
18 Sierra Leone
19 Liberia
20 Côte d'Ivoire
21 Mali
22 Burkina Faso
23 Ghana
24 Togo
25 Benin
26 Nigeria
27 Niger
28 Cameroon
29 Central African Republic
30 Equatorial Guinea
31 Gabon
32 Congo
33 SãoTomé and Príncipe
34 Angola
35 Zaire
36 Rwanda
37 Burundi
38 Kenya
39 Uganda
40 Tanzania
41 Zambia
42 Malawi
43 Mozambique
44 Zimbabwe
45 South Africa
46 Botswana
47 Lesotho

48 Namibia
49 Swaziland
50 Madagascar
51 Comoros
52 Seychelles
53 Mauritius

Demography

Africa ranks third among the continents of the world in terms of population size. At nearly 3%, its growth rate is the highest in the world, ten times that of Europe. The population of Africa is expected to reach 900 million by the year 2000.

Population distribution varies widely—the desert, savanna, and rain forest areas are very sparsely populated. In contrast, the Nile Valley in Egypt is one of the most densely populated areas on earth, with an average of 3,800 people per square mile. Nigeria, with a population of 89 million, is the most populous nation in Africa.

Africa's population is predominantly rural, although urban growth has been rapid since the 1950s. N. Africa is the most urbanized region.

Civil wars in a number of countries have resulted in significant refugee migration, as have the droughts and famines that have struck some African countries. Large-scale labor migration, particularly of central Africans to the mines and factories of Zambia, Zimbabwe, and South Africa, has also influenced population distribution.

Climate

Most of Africa has a warm or hot climate, but humidity and precipitation vary dramatically. Africa has the largest tropical area of any continent: about 90% lies within the tropics. The highest temperatures occur in the Sahara and in parts of Libya and Somalia. The Sahara also has the greatest seasonal range of temperatures in Africa. Rainfall is mostly seasonal, and more than half the continent receives less than 20 inches (50 cm) of rainfall annually.

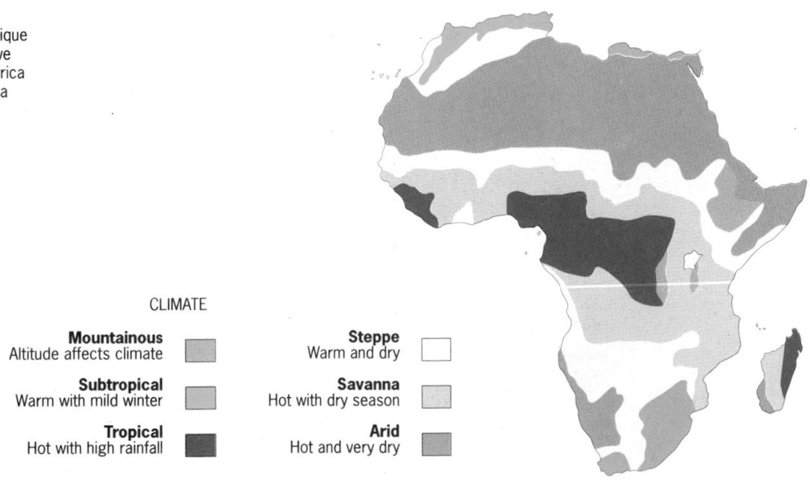

CLIMATE

Mountainous
Altitude affects climate

Subtropical
Warm with mild winter

Tropical
Hot with high rainfall

Steppe
Warm and dry

Savanna
Hot with dry season

Arid
Hot and very dry

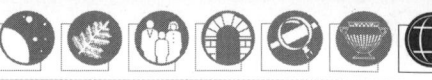

MOROCCO

Area: 177,116 sq. mi./458,730 km². *Local name:* Al-Mamlaka al-Maghrebia. *Currency:* Dirham. *Capital:* Rabat. *Other cities:* Fez, Casablanca, Marrakesh. *Physical features:* Mostly mountainous with fertile coastal plains. *Climate:* Subtropical, becoming semiarid in the interior. *Time zone:* GMT. *Political system:* Constitutional monarchy. *Head of state:* King Hassan II (from 1961). *Head of government:* Dr. Azzedine Laraki (from 1986). *Main exports:* Food and beverages, consumer goods, phosphates. *Resources:* Phosphates, iron ore, manganese, lead, zinc, fish, salt.

PEOPLE
Population: 26,069,000. *Distribution urban/rural:* 50%/50%. *Life expectancy:* 63(m), 67(f). *Languages:* Arabic (official), several Berber dialects, French. *Ethnic groups:* Arab-Berber 99%, non-Moroccan 1%. *Religions:* Muslim 98%, Christian and Jewish 2%. *Literacy rate:* 50%. *Per capita GDP:* $1,060.

KEY DATES
1912 Becomes a French territory.
1934 Plan of Reforms requesting guaranteed political rights for Moroccans is rejected by France.
1937 Widespread demonstrations; independence movement leaders arrested.
1943 Istiqlal Party founded.
1947 Riots after France rejects request for self-government.
1953 Sultan Muhammad V exiled and Istiqlal leaders imprisoned; civil unrest; National Liberation Army founded.
1955 French bring Muhammad V back to restore order and promise independence for Morocco.
1956 Independence achieved.

1957 Muhammad V changes title to King in move toward constitutional monarchy.
1961 Muhammad V dies and is succeeded by Hassan II.
1965–70 State of emergency declared when legislature rejects reform program.
1972 Attempted military coup.
1975 Spain cedes Western Sahara to Morocco and Mauritania; guerilla warfare ensues.
1977 New constitution.

1991 Cease-fire in Western Sahara.
1995 Referendum scheduled on independence of Western Sahara.

TRAVEL
Visa: Not needed by U.S. *Driving permit:* Nat. license for 90 days; IDP to rent car. *Health and safety:* Inoculations advised; water unsafe. *Tourist features:* Atlas Mountains; Great Hassan II Mosque. *National holiday:* June 25 (Independence Day).

WESTERN SAHARA

Western Sahara is a former province of Spain covering 97,344 sq. mi. (252,120 km²) on the Mediterranean coast of N.W. Africa. It is now a territory of Morocco, although the Western Saharan liberation movement, the Polisario Front, controls much of the territory and has declared independence as the Sahrawi Arab Democratic Republic (SADR). SADR is recognized as an independent state by 70 other countries worldwide.

KEY DATES
1509 Spanish occupy Western Sahara.
1524 Morocco takes control.
1884 Spain establishes protectorate.
1956 Attempted Moroccan invasion thwarted.
1965 Rich phosphate deposits are discovered at Bu Cra'a in north.
1973 Foundation of Polisario Front (Popular

Front for the Liberation of Saguia el Hamra and Rio de Oro); fighting begins.
1975 Morocco prepares invasion; Spain agrees to partition area between Mauritania and Morocco.
1976 Polisario Front forms government in exile and calls country Sahrawi Arab Democratic Republic (SADR); Spanish leave the territory.
1979 Mauritania gives up territories in Western Sahara; Morocco lays claim to Mauritanian territory and continues to fight Polisario Front.
1982 SADR admitted to the Organization of African Unity (OAU).
1987 Moroccans complete defensive earthwork separating the phosphate-rich north from the rest of the territory.
1988 Morocco and Polisario Front agree to UN-sponsored peace plan.
1989 Disagreement over terms of the refer

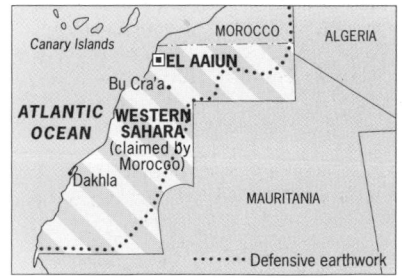

endum result in the cease-fire being broken.
1990 Seventy countries recognize SADR.
1991 UN agrees to fund a Mission for the Organization of a Referendum in Western Sahara (MINURSO); cease-fire declared.
1995 Referendum scheduled to take place.

MAURITANIA

Area: 397,954 sq. mi./1,030,700 km². *Local name:* République Islamique de Mauritanie. *Currency:* Ouguiya. *Capital:* Nouakchott. *Other city:* Kaédi. *Physical features:* Mostly barren, flat plains of the Sahara, some central hills. *Climate:* Arid. *Time zone:* GMT. *Political system:* Republic. *Head of state:* Col. Maaouya Ould Sid'Ahmed Taya (from 1984). *Head of government:* Sidi Mohammed Ould Boubacar (from 1992). *Main exports:* Iron ore, processed fish. *Resources:* Iron ore, gypsum, fish, copper, phosphate.

PEOPLE

Population: 2,206,000. *Distribution urban/rural:* 34%/66%. *Life expectancy:* 44(m), 50(f). *Languages:* French and Arabic (both official), Hasaniya Arabic. *Ethnic groups:* Mixed Maur/black 40%, Maur 30%, black 30%. *Religion:* Muslim. *Literacy rate:* 34%. *Per capita GDP:* $535.

KEY DATES

1920 Becomes a French colony.
1960 Full independence achieved but not recognized by Morocco.
1961 Moktar Ould Daddah becomes first president.
1965 Becomes one-party state.
1970 Morocco recognizes Mauritanian independence.
1978 Ould Daddah ousted in coup.
1979 Mauritania gives up claims to Western Sahara.
1984 Col. Maaouya Ould Sid'Ahmed Taya becomes president.
1991 Return to multiparty politics.
1992 Ahmed Taya reelected amid election fraud allegations.

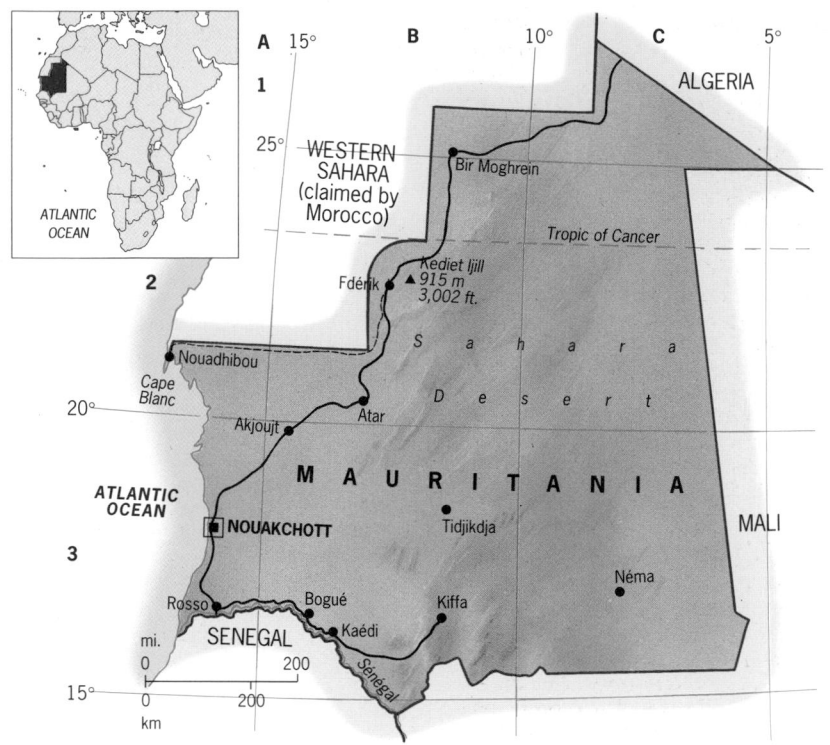

TRAVEL
Visa: Needed by U.S. *Driving permit:* IDP. *Health and safety:* Inoculations advised; water unsafe. *Tourist feature:* Part of the Sahara Desert. *National holiday:* November 28 (Independence Day).

CAPE VERDE

Area: 1,557 sq. mi./4,033 km². *Local name:* República de Cabo Verde. *Currency:* Cape Verde escudo. *Capital:* Praia. *Physical features:* Volcanic islands. *Climate:* Subtropical. *Time zone:* GMT –2h. *Political system:* Republic. *Head of state:* Antonio Monteiro Mascarenhas (from 1991). *Head of government:* Carlos Veiga (from 1991). *Main exports:* Salt, fish. *Resources:* Salt, fish.

PEOPLE

Population: 395,000. *Distribution urban/rural:* 29%/71%. *Life expectancy:* 60(m), 64(f). *Languages:* Portuguese (official), Crioulo. *Ethnic groups:* Mulatto 71%, African 28%, European 1%. *Religions:* Roman Catholic, indigenous beliefs. *Literacy rate:* 66%. *Per capita GDP:* $800.

KEY DATES

1975 Independence from Portugal.
1981 Becomes one-party state.
1991 First democratic elections.

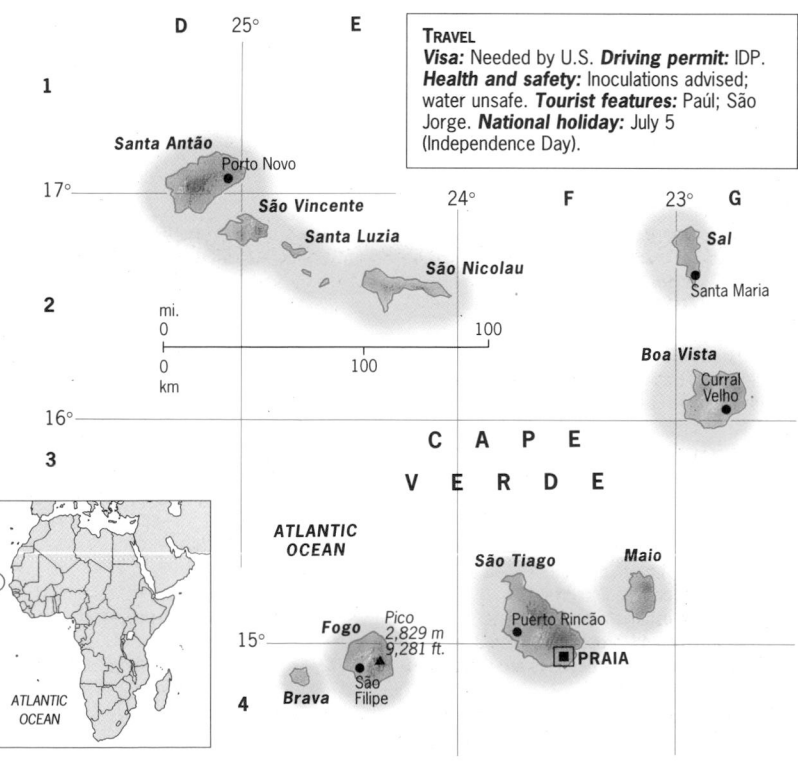

TRAVEL
Visa: Needed by U.S. *Driving permit:* IDP. *Health and safety:* Inoculations advised; water unsafe. *Tourist features:* Paúl; São Jorge. *National holiday:* July 5 (Independence Day).

ALGERIA

Area: 919,591 sq. mi./2,381,741 km². **Local name:** Al-Jumhuriya al-Jazāiriya ad-Dimuqratiya ash-Shabiya. **Currency:** Algerian dinar. **Capital:** Algiers. **Other cities:** Oran, Constantine, Annaba. **Physical features:** Mostly high plateau and desert with narrow coastal plain; some mountains. **Climate:** Arid/semiarid. **Time zone:** GMT +1h. **Political system:** Republic. **Head of state:** Gen. Lamine Zeroual (from 1994). **Head of government:** Mokdad Sifi (from 1994). **Main exports:** Petroleum, industrial products, natural gas, food. **Resources:** Crude oil, natural gas, iron ore, phosphates, uranium.

PEOPLE

Population: 27,070,000. **Distribution urban/rural:** 49%/51%. **Life expectancy:** 66(m), 68(f). **Languages:** Arabic (official), French, Berber dialects. **Ethnic groups:** Arab-Berber 99%, European 1%. **Religions:** Sunni Muslim 99%, Christian and Jewish 1%. **Literacy rate:** 50%. **Per capita GDP:** $2,130.

KEY DATES

1830 France invades N. Algeria.
1914 France gains control of all Algeria.
1954 Revolution launched by Front de Libération Nationale (FLN); in retaliation, French destroy Algerian orchards and cropland and send millions of Algerians to concentration camps.
1961 Peace talks begin.
1962 Independence achieved.
1963 Rebel leader Ahmed Ben Bella becomes first president; he proclaims Algeria a socialist state.
1965 Ben Bella overthrown by Houari Boumedienne.
1978 Houari Boumedienne dies.
1979 Chadli Benjedid elected president.
1989 Constitutional amendment introduces multiparty politics; foundation of Front Islamic du Salut (FIS).
1991 Economic crisis; first multiparty elections since independence; FIS wins national legislative elections, but government voids elections; FIS leader Abassi Madani calls general strike and threatens *jihad* (holy war); 50 die in demonstrations; state of emergency declared; 5,000 FIS members are arrested.
1992 Chadli Benjedid resigns; military council installed with Mohammed Boudiaf as leader; violence continues, more than 300 killed; FIS outlawed; 10,000 suspected Islamic activists detained; Boudiaf assassinated; 13 Islamic activists sentenced to death for killing three soldiers in 1991; postponement of elections leads to further violence.
1995 Violence worsens; thousands killed; foreigners, FIS supporters, intellectuals, journalists among those targeted; country on brink of civil war.

TRAVEL
Visa: None needed by U.S. **Driving permit:** IDP. **Health and safety:** Inoculations advised; extremely dangerous; seek advice. **Tourist features:** Atlas Mountains; Barbary Coast; Chou Melthir depression; Ahaggar Mountains. **National holiday:** November 1 (Anniversary of the Revolution).

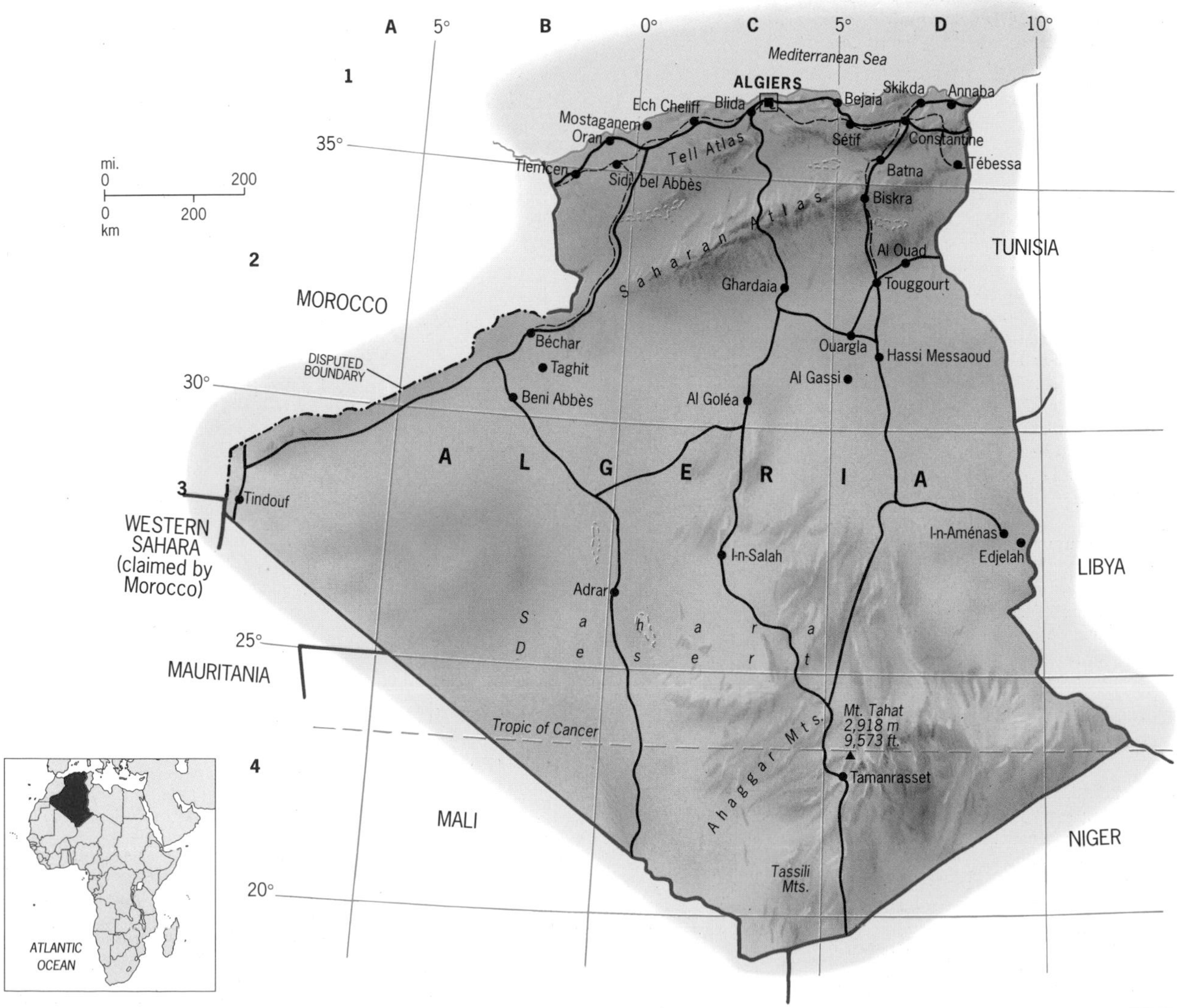

Map of Algeria showing cities including Algiers, Oran, Constantine, Annaba, Mostaganem, Ech Cheliff, Blida, Bejaia, Skikda, Tlemcen, Sidi bel Abbès, Sétif, Batna, Tébessa, Biskra, El Oued, Ghardaia, Touggourt, Béchar, Taghit, Beni Abbès, Ouargla, Hassi Messaoud, Al Gassi, Al Goléa, Tindouf, Adrar, I-n-Salah, I-n-Aménas, Edjelah, Tamanrasset. Physical features: Tell Atlas, Saharan Atlas, Sahara Desert, Ahaggar Mts, Mt. Tahat 2,918 m / 9,573 ft., Tassili Mts. Neighboring countries: MOROCCO, WESTERN SAHARA (claimed by Morocco), MAURITANIA, MALI, NIGER, LIBYA, TUNISIA. Mediterranean Sea to the north. Tropic of Cancer.

ATLANTIC OCEAN

TUNISIA

Area: 63,383 sq. mi./164,150 km². *Local name:* Al-Jumhuriya at-Tunisiya. *Currency:* Tunisian dinar. *Capital:* Tunis. *Other cities:* Sfax, Bizerte, Gabès. *Physical features:* Mountains in N., S. merges into the Sahara; hot, dry central plain. *Climate:* Subtropical in N. with mild, rainy winters and hot, dry summers; arid in S. *Time zone:* GMT +1h. *Political system:* Republic. *Head of state:* Gen. Zine al-Abidine Ben Ali (from 1987). *Head of government:* Hamed Karoui (from 1989). *Main exports:* Agricultural products, crude oil, textiles, electrical appliances, leather, phosphates, chemicals. *Resources:* Crude oil, phosphates, iron ore, lead, zinc, salt.

PEOPLE

Population: 8,579,000. *Distribution urban/rural:* 70%/30%. *Life expectancy:* 70(m), 74(f). *Languages:* Arabic (official), French. *Ethnic groups:* Arab-Berber 98%, European 1%, Jewish less than 1%. *Religions:* Sunni Muslim 98%, Christian 1%, Jewish less than 1%. *Literacy rate:* 65%. *Per capita GDP:* $1,320.

KEY DATES

1574 Becomes part of Ottoman Empire.

1881 Tunisia becomes a French protectorate.

1934 Neo-Destour (New Constitution) Party founded by Habib Bourguiba.

1952 Demonstrations against French rule; Bourguiba imprisoned.

1955 Internal self-government granted.

1956 Full independence achieved as monarchy with Habib Bourguiba as prime minister.

1957 Tunisia becomes a republic with Bourguiba as president.

1964 Appropriation of French lands; conflict with Algeria, which supports antigovernment group.

1967 Troops sent to assist Arab forces in the Six-Day War against Israel.

1969 Minister of Finance and Planning imprisoned after conviction on several charges.

1974 Merger with Libya proposed.

1974–76 Hundreds imprisoned for opposing the government.

1975 Having been reelected three times, Habib Bourguiba is named president for life.

1980 Raid on Gafsa probably organized by Tunisian dissidents with Libyan support; Tunisia requests assistance from France, leading to increased isolation from other countries in Maghreb.

1985 Tunisia suspends diplomatic relations with Libya.

1987 Prime Minister Zine al-Abidine Ben Ali removes Bourguiba from office.

1988 Relations with Libya restored.

1989 Ben Ali elected president.

1991 Tunisia expresses opposition to U.S. involvement in Persian Gulf War; government crackdown on religious fundamentalists begins.

1992 Amnesty International accuses government of illegally imprisoning thousands of Islamic activists and of routine torture of political prisoners.

TRAVEL
Visa: None needed by U.S. *Driving permit:* Nat. license for 90 days. *Health and safety:* Inoculations advised; water unsafe. *Tourist features:* Island of Jerba; Shott el Jerid salt lakes; holy city of Kairouan; ruins of Carthage; beaches. *National holiday:* March 20 (National Day).

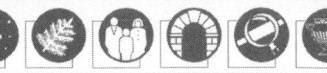

LIBYA

Area: 679,359 sq. mi./1,759,540 km². **Local name:** Al-Jamahiriya al-Arabiya al-Libya al-Shabiya al-Ishtirakiyaal-Uzma. **Currency:** Libyan dinar. **Capital:** Tripoli. **Other cities:** Benghazi, Misratah. **Physical features:** Mostly flat to rolling plains. **Climate:** Subtropical along coast; desert interior. **Time zone:** GMT +2h. **Political system:** Jamahiriya ("State of the masses"). **Head of state:** Col. Muammar Abu Minyar al-Qaddafi (from 1969). **Head of government:** Abu Zayd 'umar Durda (from 1990). **Main exports:** Petroleum, peanuts. **Resources:** Crude oil, natural gas, gypsum.

PEOPLE

Population: 4,700,000. **Distribution urban/rural:** 70%/30%. **Life expectancy:** 66(m), 71(f). **Languages:** Arabic; Italian and English widely understood. **Ethnic groups:** Arab-Berber 97%. **Religion:** Sunni Muslim 97%. **Literacy rate:** 64%. **Per capita GDP:** $6,800.

KEY DATES

1951 Independence achieved as kingdom.
1986 U.S.A. suspects Qaddafi's terrorist links; breaks off diplomatic relations.
1993 Tightening of UN sanctions imposed in 1992 after Libya failed to extradite suspected Lockerbie bombers.

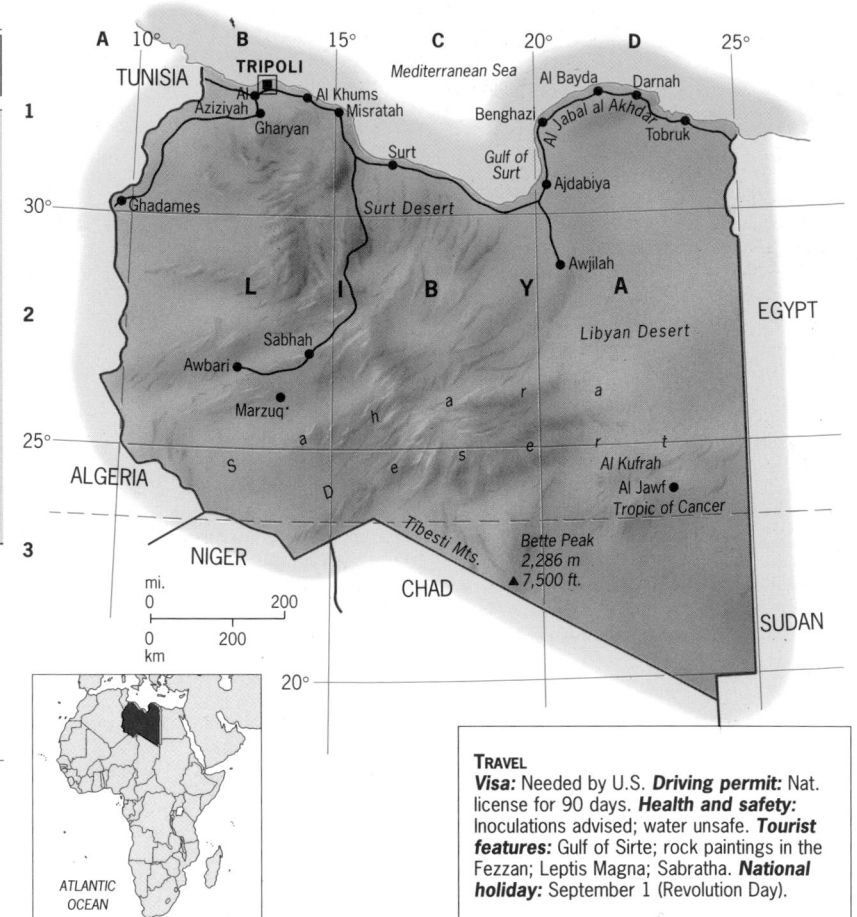

TRAVEL

Visa: Needed by U.S. **Driving permit:** Nat. license for 90 days. **Health and safety:** Inoculations advised; water unsafe. **Tourist features:** Gulf of Sirte; rock paintings in the Fezzan; Leptis Magna; Sabratha. **National holiday:** September 1 (Revolution Day).

CHAD

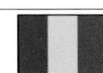

Area: 495,753 sq. mi./1,284,000 km². **Local name:** République du Tchad. **Currency:** C.F.A. franc. **Capital:** N'Djamena. **Other city:** Moundou. **Physical features:** Plains in center, desert in N., mountains in N.W., lowlands in S. **Climate:** Tropical in S., arid in N. **Time zone:** GMT +1h. **Political system:** Republic. **Head of state:** Col. Idriss Déby (from 1990). **Head of government:** Jean Alingue Bawoyeu (from 1991). **Main exports:** Cotton, cattle, textiles, fish. **Resources:** Crude oil (unexploited), uranium, natron, kaolin, fish.

PEOPLE

Population: 6,098,000. **Distribution urban/rural:** 32%/68%. **Life expectancy:** 39(m), 41(f). **Languages:** French and Arabic (both official); more than 100 different languages and dialects, including Sara and Sango in S. **Ethnic groups:** Approximately 200 ethnic groups, mostly Muslims in N. and non-Muslims in S. **Religions:** Muslim 44%, Christian 33%, indigenous beliefs 23%. **Literacy rate:** 30%. **Per capita GDP:** $205.

KEY DATES

1920 Becomes a French colony.
1960 Independence achieved.
1973 Libyan forces occupy Aouzou Strip.
1994 International Court of Justice confirms Chad's rights to Aouzou Strip.

TRAVEL

Visa: Needed by U.S. **Driving permit:** IDP. **Health and safety:** Inoculations advised; water unsafe. **Tourist feature:** Oldest prehistoric remains in Africa. **National holiday:** August 11 (Independence Day).

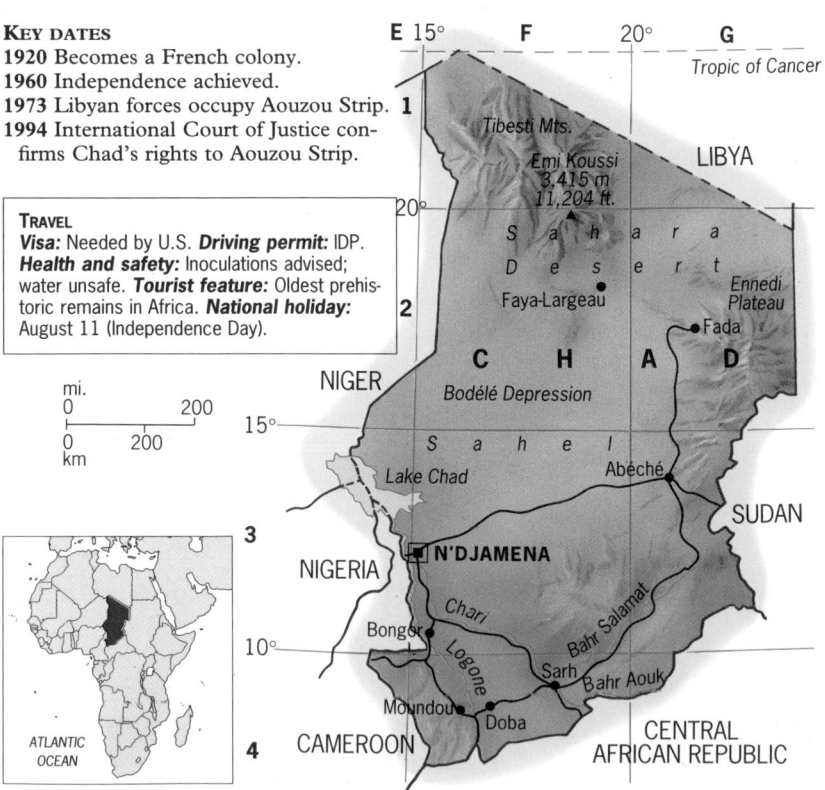

EGYPT

Area: 386,690 sq. mi./1,001,449 km². **Local name:** Jumhuriyat Misr al-Arabiya. **Currency:** Egyptian pound. **Capital:** Cairo. **Other cities:** Alexandria, Giza, Luxor Port Said. **Physical features:** Vast desert plateau dissected by Nile Valley. **Climate:** Arid. **Time zone:** GMT +2h. **Political system:** Republic. **Head of state:** Mohammed Hosni Mubarak (from 1981). **Head of government:** Atef Mohammed Najib Sedky (from 1986). **Main exports:** Crude oil and petroleum products, cotton, textiles, metals, chemicals. **Resources:** Crude oil, natural gas, iron ore, phosphates, manganese, limestone, gypsum, talc.

PEOPLE

Population: 56,488,000. **Distribution urban/rural:** 44%/56%. **Life expectancy:** 58(m), 62(f). **Languages:** Arabic (official), English and French. **Ethnic groups:** Eastern Hamitic 90%, Greek, Italian, Syro-Lebanese 10%. **Religions:** Sunni Muslim 94%, other 6%. **Literacy rate:** 48%. **Per capita GDP:** $720.

KEY DATES

1869 Suez Canal is opened.
1922 Independence achieved from U.K.
1953 Becomes a republic.
1956 Gamar Abdul Nasser seizes control of Suez Canal; Israel and U.K. invade.
1967 Six-Day War with Israel; Israel occupies Sinai and Gaza Strip.
1970 Nasser dies; Anwar Sadat president.
1973 Yom Kippur War with Israel.
1978 Camp David Accord returns Sinai peninsula to Egypt.
1979 Peace treaty with Israel signed; Egypt expelled from Arab League.
1981 Sadat assassinated by Islamic extremists; Hosni Mubarak president.
1989 Egypt rejoins Arab League.
1991 Enters Persian Gulf War.
1992 Violence between Muslims and Christians; Cairo hit by earthquake.
1995 Crackdown continues against Muslim fundamentalist violence and terrorist attacks, some against tourists.

ECONOMY

Farming: Cotton, sugarcane, tomatoes, corn, potatoes, and fruit are grown; livestock include cattle, goats, and camels. **Natural resources:** Oil is most valuable revenue source; also natural gas, phosphates, iron ore, and manganese. **Industry:** Large concerns are state run; products include fertilizers, vehicles, cement, sugar, steel, cotton, and jute. **Tourism:** Tourists make a significant contribution to the economy.

TRAVEL
Visa: Needed by U.S. **Driving permit:** IDP/nat. license. **Health and safety:** Inoculations advised; water unsafe. **Tourist features:** Remains of ancient Egypt; Aswan High Dam and Lake Nasser; Sinai. **National holiday:** July 23 (Anniversary of the Revolution).

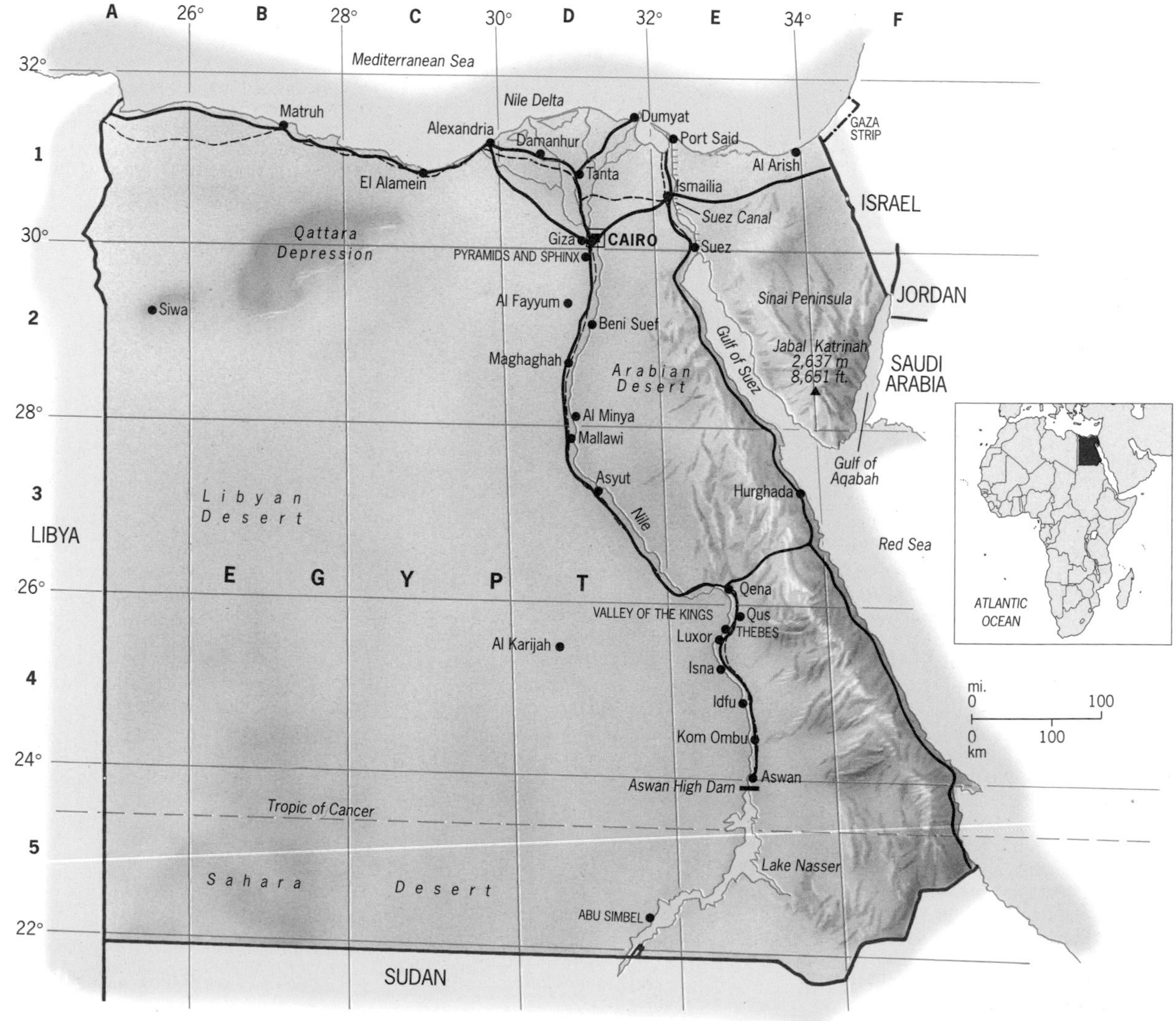

Map of Egypt showing major cities, deserts, the Nile, and neighboring countries.

SUDAN

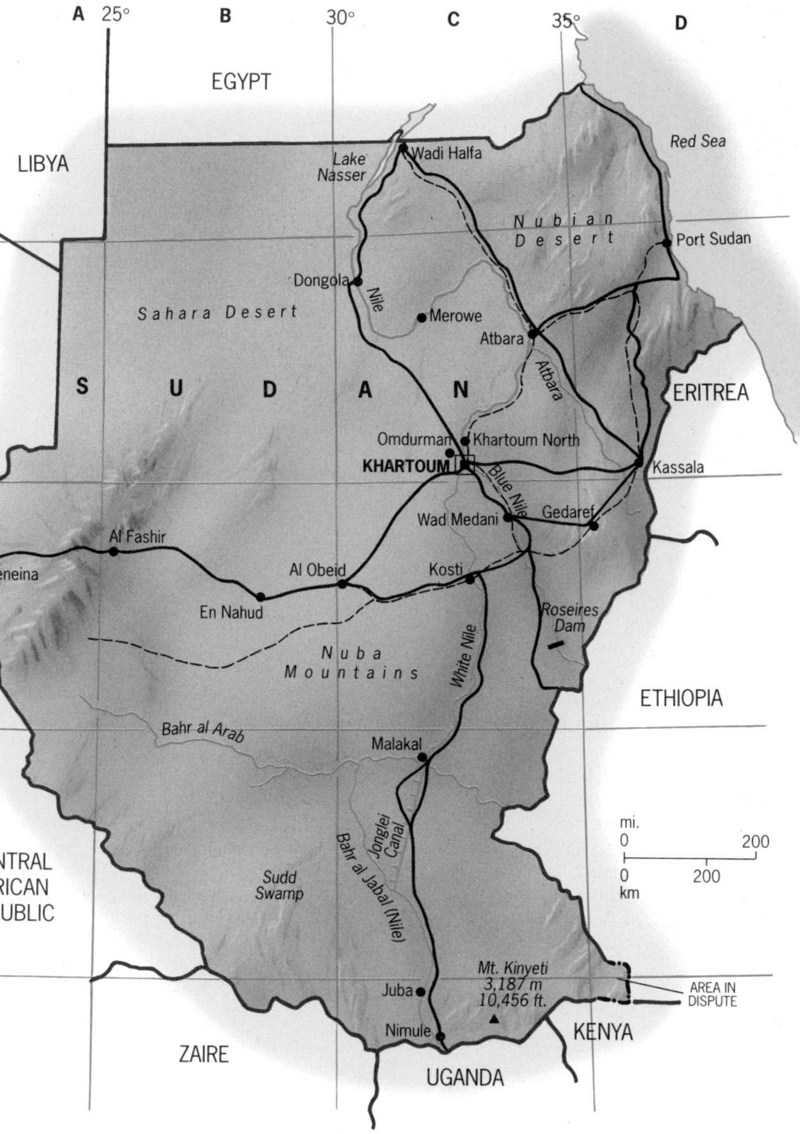

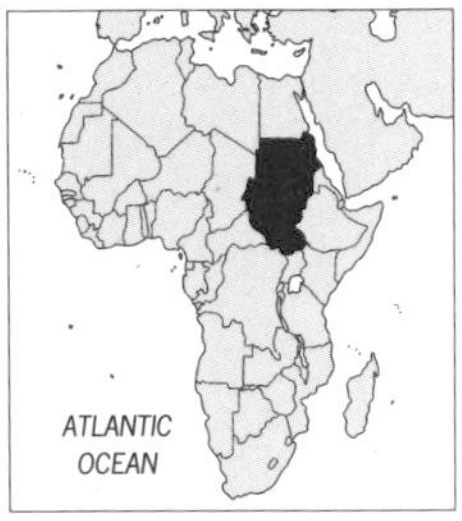

Map references

EGYPT
LIBYA
CHAD
S U D A N
CENTRAL
AFRICAN
REPUBLIC
ZAIRE
UGANDA
KENYA
ETHIOPIA
ERITREA
Red Sea

Lake Nasser
Wadi Halfa
Nubian Desert
Port Sudan
Dongola
Nile
Merowe
Atbara
Atbara
Sahara Desert
Kassala
Omdurman Khartoum North
KHARTOUM
Blue Nile
Gedaref
Wad Medani
Al Fashir
Al Obeid Kosti
Roseires Dam
Geneina
En Nahud
Nuba Mountains
White Nile
Bahr al Arab
Malakal
Bahr al Jabal (Nile)
Jonglei Canal
Sudd Swamp
Mt. Kinyeti
3,187 m
10,456 ft.
Juba
Nimule
AREA IN DISPUTE

ATLANTIC OCEAN

mi.
0   200
0   200
km

Area: 967,495 sq. mi./2,505,813 km². **Local name:** Jamhuryat es-Sudan. **Currency:** Sudanese pound. **Capital:** Khartoum. **Other cities:** Omdurman, Khartoum North, Port Sudan. **Physical features:** Generally flat, featureless plain; mountains in E. and W. **Climate:** Savanna in S., arid in N.; rainy season April–Oct. **Time zone:** GMT +2h. **Political system:** Military. **Head of state and government:** Revolutionary Command Council Chairman and Prime Minister Lt. Gen. Umar Hasan Ahmad al-Bashir (from 1989). **Main exports:** Sugar, nickel, medical products, shellfish, citrus, cotton, gum arabic, peanuts, sesame. **Resources:** Iron ore, copper, chromium ore, zinc, tungsten, mica, silver, nickel, shellfish, small reserves of crude oil.

PEOPLE
Population: 28,129,000. **Distribution urban/rural:** 22%/78%. **Life expectancy:** 53(m), 54(f). **Languages:** Arabic (official), Nubian, Ta Bedawie, various dialects, English. **Ethnic groups:** Black African 52%, Arab 39%, Beja 6%. **Religions:** Sunni Muslim 70%; indigenous beliefs, Christians 30%. **Literacy rate:** 27%. **Per capita GDP:** $450.

KEY DATES
1821 Egypt takes over Sudan.
1898 Battle of Omdurman: British and Egyptian forces join to crush Sudanese revolt and agree to joint rulership of Sudan.
1955 Civil war.
1956 Independence achieved.
1958 Gen. Ibrahim Abboud leads military coup; all political parties outlawed and many politicians imprisoned.
1964 Civil unrest; return to civilian rule.

1969 Col. Caafar Nimeiri seizes power.
1972 Single regional government for southern provinces set up.
1983 Islamic law established; regional government in S. abolished; government installations in S. attacked by non-Muslim guerrilla group, the Sudan People's Liberation Army (SPLA).
1985 Return to multiparty politics.
1989 Military coup; national legislature replaced by military council.
1990 New SPLA offensive.
1991 Major famine in S.; escalation of civil war.
1993 SPLA leaders announce cease-fire.

ETHIOPIA

Area: 446,951 sq. mi./1,157,603 km². **Local name:** Hebretesebawit Ityopia. **Currency:** Ethiopian birr. **Capital:** Addis Ababa. **Physical features:** High plateau with central mountain range. **Climate:** Arid/steppe. **Time zone:** GMT +3h. **Political system:** In transition. **Head of state:** Meles Zenawi (from 1991). **Head of government:** Timirat Layne (from 1991). **Main exports:** Coffee, hides, oilseed. **Resources:** Gold, platinum.

PEOPLE

Population: 56,900,000. **Distribution urban/rural:** 11%/89%. **Life expectancy:** 50(m), 53(f). **Languages:** Amharic (official), various Hamitic languages. **Ethnic groups:** Oromo 40%, Amhara and Tigrean 32%, Sidamo 9%, Shankella 6%, Somali and other 13%. **Religions:** Muslim 45%, Ethiopian Orthodox 35%, animist 15%, other 5%. **Literacy rate:** 62%. **Per capita GDP:** $130.

KEY DATES

1889 Ethiopian Empire united.
1930 Ras Tafari becomes emperor and takes title Haile Selassie I.
1936 Italy conquers Addis Ababa; Haile Selassie flees to Great Britain.
1941 Britain helps Ethiopia drive Italians out; Haile Selassie returns to throne.
1962 Ethiopia annexes Eritrea.
1974 Haile Selassie overthrown in military coup; Gen. Teferi Benti leader.
1977 Teferi Benti killed and replaced by

Col. Mengistu Haile Mariam.
1977–79 "Red Terror"—Mengistu's regime kills thousands.
1985 Millions die in worst famine in more than 10 years.
1991 Mengistu overthrown; transitional government installed.
1993 Eritrean independence recognized.

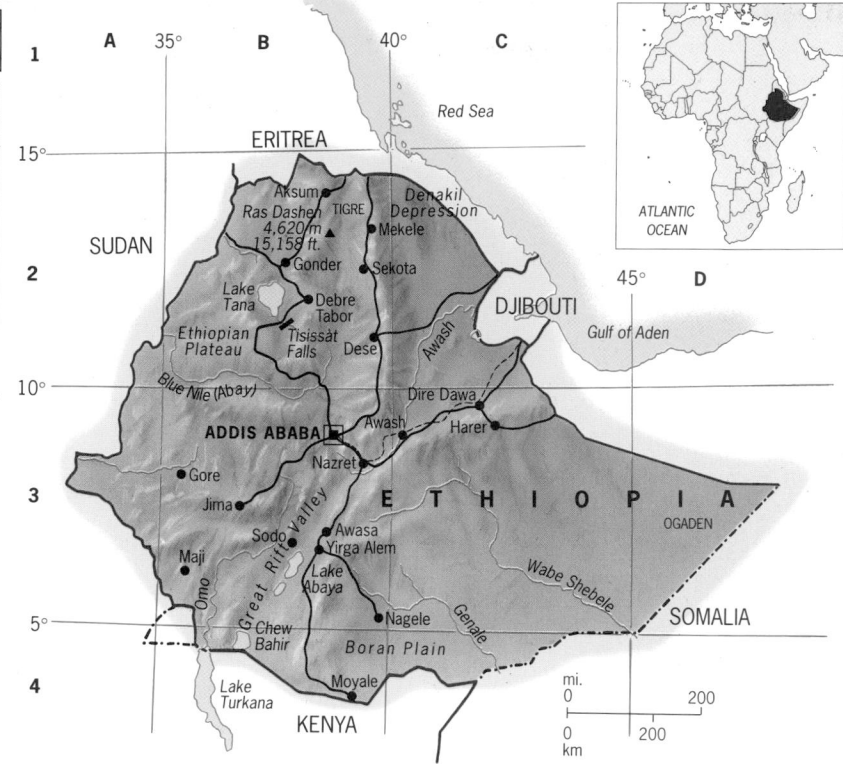

TRAVEL
Visa: Needed by U.S. **Driving permit:** Nat. license exchanged for local one at Licensing Office. **Health and safety:** Inoculations advised; water unsafe. **Tourist features:** Ancient remains. **National holiday:** September 11 (New Year's Day).

ERITREA

Area: 36,172 sq. mi./93,679 km². **Local name:** State of Eritrea. **Currency:** Birr. **Capital:** Asmera. **Physical features:** Low coastal plains in S., mountains in N. **Climate:** Arid. **Time zone:** GMT +3h. **Political system:** In transition. **Head of state and government:** Issaias Afewerki (from 1993). **Main exports:** Hides, salt, cement, gum arabic, coffee. **Resources:** Crude oil, salt, gum arabic.

PEOPLE

Population: 3,500,000. **Distribution urban/rural:** 14%/86%. **Life expectancy:** n.a. **Languages:** Amharic, Tigrinya. **Ethnic groups:** Tigrays 50%, Tigre and Kunama 40%, Afar 4%. **Religions:** Christian 50%, Muslim 50%. **Literacy rate:** n.a. **Per capita GDP:** n.a.

KEY DATES

1889 Italy conquers Eritrea.
1941 Comes under British control.
1945 Federated with Ethiopia.

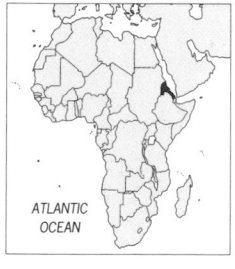

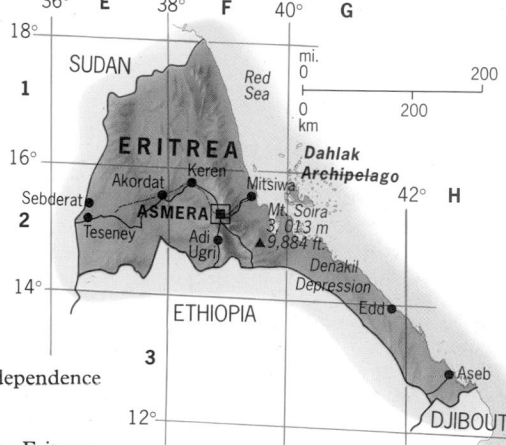

1962 Annexed by Ethiopia; independence movement begins.
1970s–80s Civil war.
1980s Ethiopian rule weakens as Eritrean rebels claim more military victories.
1991 Eritrean and Tigrean rebels overthrow Ethiopian government; Tigrean rebels establish new government for Ethiopia excluding Eritrea; Eritreans establish independent government.
1993 Referendum supports independence; new state formally recognized by Ethiopia.

TRAVEL
Visa: Needed by U.S. **Driving permit:** IDP. **Health and safety:** Inoculations advised; water unsafe. **Tourist feature:** Dramatic mountain scenery. **National holiday:** n.a.

SOMALIA

Area: 246,200 sq. mi./637,657 km². *Local name:* Jamhuriyadda Dimugradiga Somaliya. *Currency:* Somali shilling. *Capital:* Mogadishu. *Other cities:* Hargeysa, Borama, Kismaayo. *Physical features:* Mostly flat to undulating; plateau rising to hills in N. *Climate:* Arid; N.E. monsoon Dec.–Feb., cooler S.W. monsoon May–Oct. *Time zone:* GMT +3h. *Political system:* In transition. *Main exports:* Bananas, livestock, fish, hides, sugar, sorghum, corn, gum. *Resources:* Uranium, iron ore, tin, gypsum, bauxite, copper, salt.

PEOPLE

Population: 9,517,000. *Distribution urban/rural:* 36%/64%. *Life expectancy:* 56(m), 57(f). *Languages:* Somali (official), Arabic, Italian. *Ethnic groups:* Somali 85%, Bantu, Arab, European. *Religion:* Sunni Muslim 99%. *Literacy rate:* 24%. *Per capita GDP:* $210.

KEY DATES

1884–87 N. becomes British protectorate.
1889 Rest becomes Italian protectorate.
1960 Both Britain and Italy grant independence; Somalia unites.
1969 Bloodless coup led by Maj. Gen. Mohamed Siad Barre; constitution suspended; massive nationalization program begins.
1977–78 War with Ethiopia over Ogaden region; Somali troops defeated.
1979 Becomes one-party socialist state.
1981 Somali National Movement formed.
1988 Peace treaty with Ethiopia.
1989 Dissatisfaction with government leads to increased guerrilla activity in N.
1991 United Somali Congress (USC) overthrows military and takes control of Mogadishu area; USC divides into factions, intense fighting breaks out; Mohamed Siad Barre flees.
1992 Rival factions of USC agree to a cease-fire; fighting between other rebel groups; war and drought lead to widespread famine; UN sends in peacekeeping troops to protect relief operations.
1993 Leaders agree to federal system of government based on 18 autonomous regions; UN forces destroy headquarters of clan leader Gen. Mohammad Farah Aidid after UN Pakistani peacekeeping troops are killed.
1994 March: U.S.A. withdraws its peacekeeping troops; June: clan leaders sign peace accord; violence continues.

> TRAVEL
> **Visa:** Needed by U.S. **Driving permit:** IDP. **Health and safety:** Inoculations advised; water unsafe. **Tourist features:** Sinbusi and Gazira beaches; the Hammawein. **National holiday:** n.a.

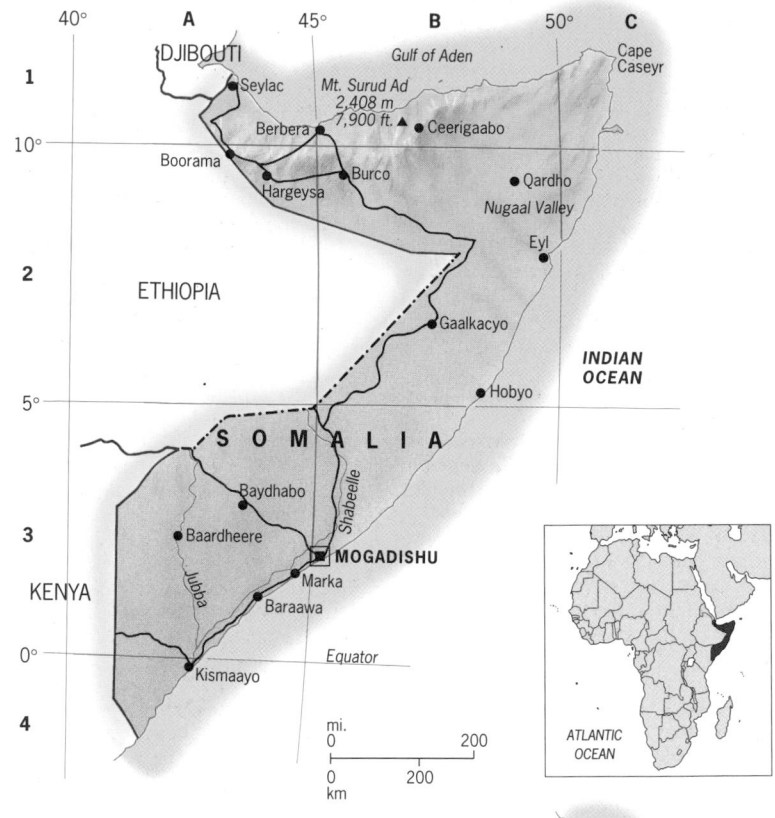

DJIBOUTI

Area: 8,958 sq. mi./23,200 km². *Local name:* Jumhouriya Djibouti. *Currency:* Djibouti franc. *Capital:* Djibouti. *Physical features:* Coastal plain separated by central mountains. *Climate:* Arid. *Time zone:* GMT +3h. *Political system:* Republic. *Head of state:* Hassan Gouled (from 1977). *Head of government:* Barkat Gourad Hamadou (from 1978). *Main exports:* Hides and skins, coffee. *Resources:* Geothermal energy.

PEOPLE

Population: 481,000. *Distribution urban/rural:* 81%/19%. *Life expectancy:* 47(m), 50(f). *Languages:* French and Arabic (both official), Somali, Afar. *Ethnic groups:* Somali 60%, Afar 35%, other 5%. *Religions:* Muslim 94%, Christian 6%. *Literacy rate:* 48%. *Per capita GDP:* $1,000.

KEY DATES

1884 Annexed by France.
1897 Menelik II of Ethiopia makes Djibouti the port for Ethiopian trade.
1967 People vote to continue association with France; becomes French Territory of the Afars and the Issas.

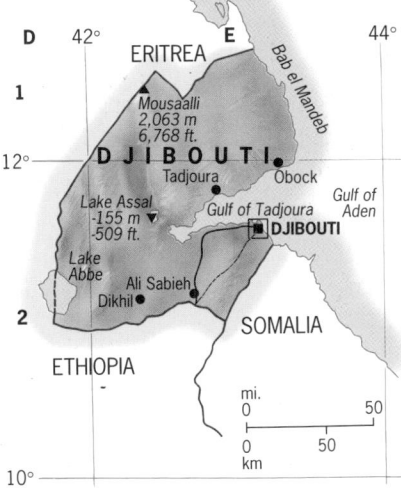

1977 Independence achieved.
1979 All political parties combine to form People's Progress Assembly (RPP).
1981 New constitution makes RPP the only legal party; treaties of friendship signed with neighbouring countries.
1992 Multiparty system in place.

> TRAVEL
> **Visa:** Needed by U.S. **Driving permit:** IDP. **Health and safety:** Inoculations advised; water unsafe. **Tourist feature:** Assal salt lake, second lowest point on earth. **National holiday:** June 27 (Independence Day).

SENEGAL

Area: 76,124 sq. mi./197,161 km². *Local name:* République du Sénégal. *Currency:* C.F.A. franc. *Capital:* Dakar. *Physical features:* Low, rolling plains. *Climate:* Tropical. *Time zone:* GMT. *Political system:* Democratic republic. *Head of state:* Abdou Diouf (from 1981). *Head of government:* Habib Thiam (from 1991). *Main exports:* Fish, peanuts, phosphates. *Resources:* Fish, phosphates.

PEOPLE

Population: 7,736,000. *Distribution urban/rural:* 30%/70%. *Life expectancy:* 54(m), 57(f). *Languages:* French (official), African languages. *Ethnic groups:* Wolof 36%, Fulani 17%, Serer 17%, Toucouleur 9%, Diola 9%, Mandingo 9%, other 3%. *Religions:* Muslim 92%, indigenous beliefs 6%, Christian 2%. *Literacy rate:* 38%. *Per capita GDP:* $615.

KEY DATES

1882 Senegal becomes a French colony.
1960 Independence achieved.
1982 Joins confederation of Senegambia.
1989 Senegambia federation abandoned.
1993 Abdou Siouf reelected president.

TRAVEL
Visa: None needed by U.S. *Driving permit:* Nat. license. *Health and safety:* Inoculations advised; water unsafe. *Tourist features:* Senegal River; Atlantic beaches. *National holiday:* April 4 (Independence Day).

GAMBIA

Area: 4,361 sq. mi./11,295 km². *Local name:* Republic of the Gambia. *Currency:* Dalasi. *Capital:* Banjul. *Physical features:* River flanked by low hills. *Climate:* Tropical. *Time zone:* GMT. *Political system:* Military. *Head of state and government:* Lt. Yahyah Jammeh (from 1994). *Main exports:* Peanuts, fish, cotton lint, hides, palm kernels. *Resources:* Fish.

PEOPLE

Population: 1,026,000. *Distribution urban/rural:* 21%/79%. *Life expectancy:* 47(m), 51(f). *Languages:* English (official), Mandinka, Wolof, other indigenous languages. *Ethnic groups:* African 99% (Mandinka 42%, Fula 18%, Wolof 16%, other 23%); non-African 1%. *Religions:* Muslim 90%, Christian 9%, indigenous beliefs 1%. *Literacy rate:* 27%. *Per capita GDP:* $235.

KEY DATES

1843 Becomes a British crown colony.
1965 Independence achieved.
1970 Becomes a republic.
1982 Joins Confederation of Senegambia.
1989 Senegambia federation abandoned.
1994 Military coup.

TRAVEL
Visa: None needed by U.S. *Driving permit:* Nat. license. *Health and safety:* Inoculations advised; water unsafe. *Tourist features:* Atlantic beaches; Karantaba obelisk. *National holiday:* February 18 (Independence Day).

GUINEA-BISSAU

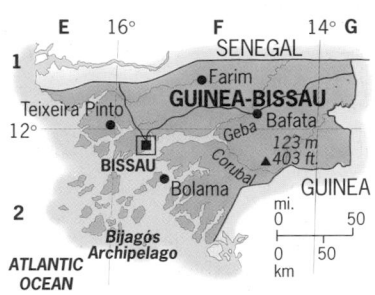

Area: 13,949 sq. mi./36,125 km². *Local name:* República da Guinée-Bissau. *Currency:* Guinea-Bissau peso. *Capital:* Bissau. *Physical features:* Mostly low coastal plain. *Climate:* Tropical. *Time zone:* GMT. *Political system:* Republic. *Head of state and government:* Brig. Gen. João Bernardo Vieira (from 1980). *Main exports:* Cashews, fish, peanuts, coconuts. *Resources:* Petroleum (unexploited), bauxite, fish.

PEOPLE

Population: 1,047,137. *Distribution urban/rural:* n.a. *Life expectancy:* 45(m), 48(f). *Languages:* Portuguese (official), Criolo, African languages. *Ethnic groups:* African *c.* 99% (Balanta 30%, Fula 23%, Manjaca 14%, other 32%); European and mulatto less than 1%. *Religions:* Indigenous beliefs 65%, Muslim 30%, Christian 5%. *Literacy rate:* 36%. *Per capita GDP:* $160.

KEY DATES

1879 Becomes a Portuguese colony.
1956 Foundation of African Party for the Independence of Guinea-Bissau and Cape Verde (PAIGC).
1974 Independence achieved.
1981 Becomes one-party state.
1991 Return to multiparty politics.

TRAVEL
Visa: Needed by U.S. *Driving permit:* IDP. *Health and safety:* Inoculations advised; water unsafe. *Tourist feature:* Bijagos archipelago. *National holiday:* September 10 (Independence Day).

GUINEA

Area: 94,925 sq. mi./245,857 km². **Local name:** République de Guinée. **Currency:** Guinean franc. **Capital:** Conakry. **Other city:** Kankan. **Physical features:** Flat coastal plain rising to hilly interior. **Climate:** Tropical. **Time zone:** GMT. **Political system:** Republic. **Head of state and government:** Gen. Lansana Conté (from 1984). **Main exports:** Alumina, bauxite, diamonds, coffee, pineapples, bananas, hides, palm kernels. **Resources:** Bauxite, iron ore, diamonds, gold, uranium, hydropower, fish.

PEOPLE

Population: 6,306,000. **Distribution urban/rural:** 26%/74%. **Life expectancy:** 41(m), 45(f). **Languages:** French (official), numerous African languages. **Ethnic groups:** Fulani 35%, Malinke 30%, Soussou 20%, other groups 15%. **Religions:** Muslim 85%, Christian 8%, indigenous beliefs 7%. **Literacy rate:** 24%. **Per capita GDP:** $410.

KEY DATES

1890 Becomes a French colony.
1958 Independence achieved.
1984 Bloodless coup establishes Military Committee for National Recovery.
1991 Antigovernment general strike.

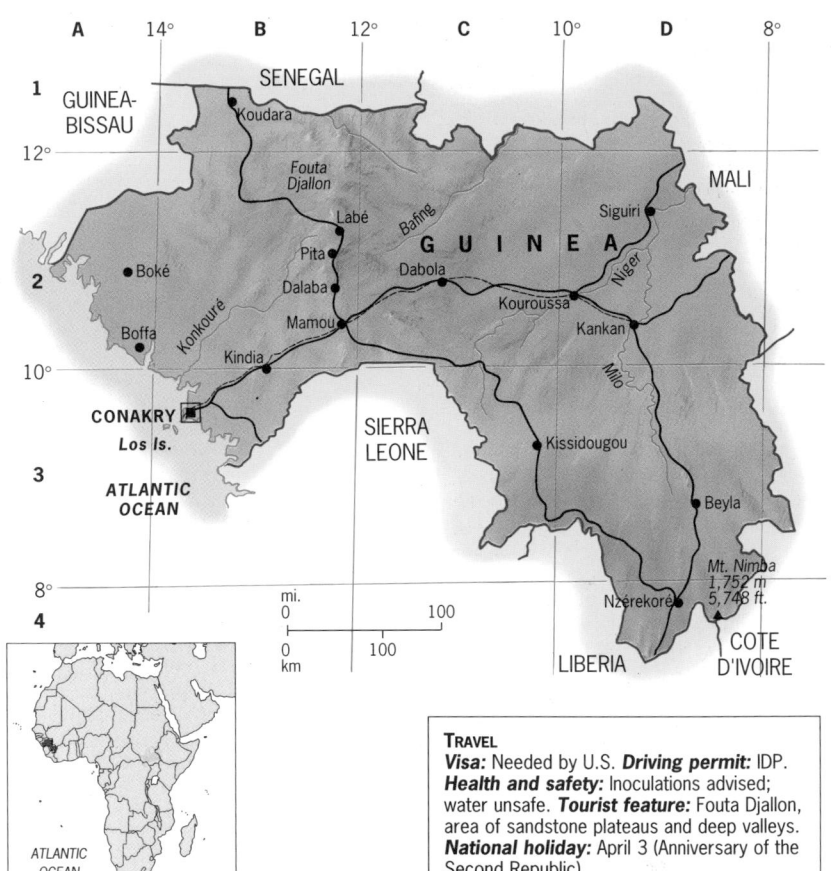

TRAVEL
Visa: Needed by U.S. **Driving permit:** IDP. **Health and safety:** Inoculations advised; water unsafe. **Tourist feature:** Fouta Djallon, area of sandstone plateaus and deep valleys. **National holiday:** April 3 (Anniversary of the Second Republic).

SIERRA LEONE

Area: 28,313 sq. mi./73,326 km². **Local name:** Republic of Sierra Leone. **Currency:** Leone. **Capital:** Freetown. **Physical features:** Varied; mountains in E. **Climate:** Tropical. **Time zone:** GMT. **Political system:** Military. **Head of state and government:** Capt. Valentine Strasser (from 1992). **Main exports:** Rutile, bauxite, cocoa, diamonds, gold, coffee. **Resources:** Diamonds, titanium ore, bauxite, iron ore, gold.

PEOPLE

Population: 4,494,000. **Distribution urban/rural:** 33%/67%. **Life expectancy:** 43(m), 48(f). **Languages:** English (official), Mende, Temne, Krio. **Ethnic groups:** Native African 99%, Creole and other 1%. **Religions:** Muslim 30%, indigenous beliefs 30%, Christian 10%, other 30%. **Literacy rate:** 21%. **Per capita GDP:** $330.

KEY DATES

1807 Becomes a British colony as a settlement for freed slaves.
1961 Independence granted.
1992 Military coup.

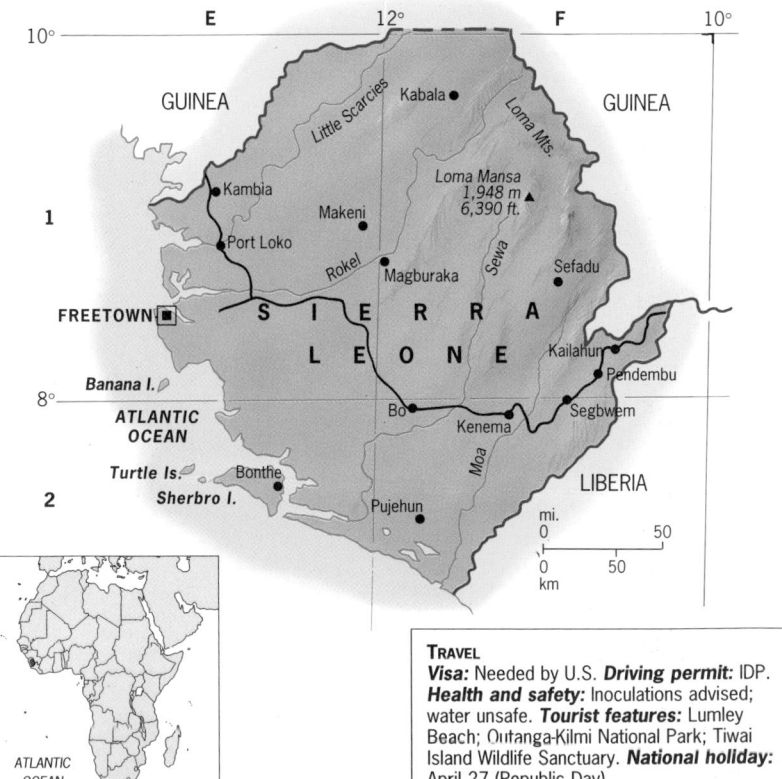

TRAVEL
Visa: Needed by U.S. **Driving permit:** IDP. **Health and safety:** Inoculations advised; water unsafe. **Tourist features:** Lumley Beach; Outanga-Kilmi National Park; Tiwai Island Wildlife Sanctuary. **National holiday:** April 27 (Republic Day).

LIBERIA

Area: 38,253 sq. mi./99,067 km². *Local name:* Republic of Liberia. *Currency:* Liberian dollar. *Capital:* Monrovia. *Physical features:* Flat to rolling coastal plains, low mountains in N.E. *Climate:* Tropical. *Time zone:* GMT. *Political system:* Republic. *Head of state and government:* David Kpormakor (from 1994). *Main exports:* Iron ore, rubber, wood, coffee. *Resources:* Iron ore, wood, gold.

PEOPLE

Population: 2,640,000. *Distribution urban/rural:* 46%/54%. *Life expectancy:* 54(m), 59(f). *Languages:* English (official), more than 20 indigenous languages. *Ethnic groups:* Indigenous African 95%, Americo-Liberians 5%. *Religions:* indigenous beliefs 70%, Muslim 20%, Christian 10%. *Literacy rate:* 40%. *Per capita GDP:* $400.

KEY DATES

1816 Founded by American Colonization Society (ACS) for repatriated slaves.
1822 First freed slaves arrive.
1847 Independence achieved.
1989 Civil war breaks out.
1993 Peace agreement signed in Benin.
1994 Renewed hostilities between rival ethnic groups.

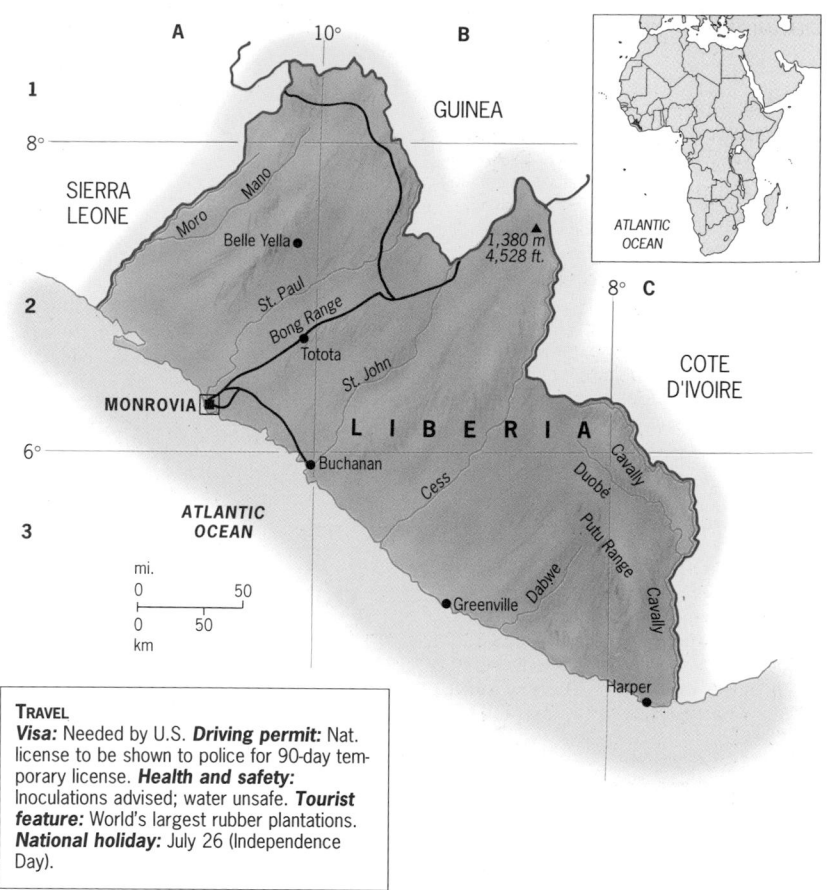

TRAVEL
Visa: Needed by U.S. *Driving permit:* Nat. license to be shown to police for 90-day temporary license. *Health and safety:* Inoculations advised; water unsafe. *Tourist feature:* World's largest rubber plantations. *National holiday:* July 26 (Independence Day).

COTE D'IVOIRE

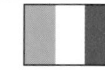

Area: 124,503 sq. mi./322,463 km². *Local name:* République de la Côte d'Ivoire. *Currency:* C.F.A. franc. *Capital:* Abidjan. *Physical features:* Mostly flat to rolling plains. *Climate:* Savanna. *Time zone:* GMT. *Political system:* Republic. *Head of state and government:* Henri Konan Bedie (from 1993). *Main exports:* Cocoa, coffee, tropical woods, cotton, bananas, pineapples, palm oil. *Resources:* Mercury, potash, marble, sulfur, natural gas, crude oil, fish.

PEOPLE

Population: 13,397,000. *Distribution urban/rural:* 40%/60%. *Life expectancy:* 74(m), 81(f). *Languages:* French; more than 60 dialects. *Ethnic groups:* About 60 ethnic groups; foreign Africans c. 2 million. *Religions:* Traditional 63%, Muslim 25%, Christian 12%. *Literacy rate:* 54%. *Per capita GDP:* $800.

KEY DATES

1893 Becomes a French colony.
1960 Independence achieved.
1990 First multiparty presidential elections held.

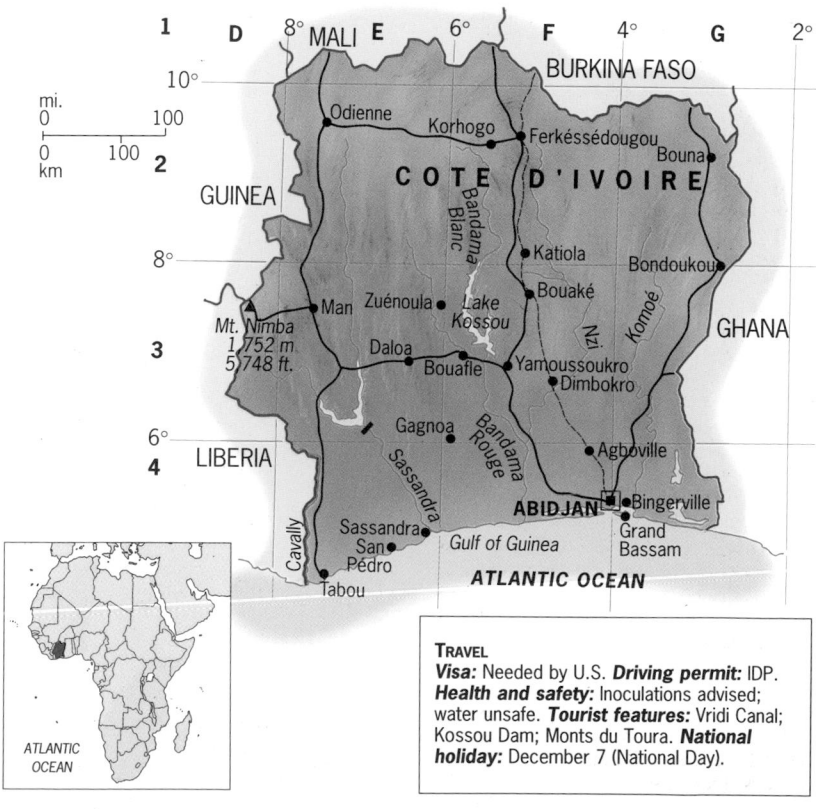

TRAVEL
Visa: Needed by U.S. *Driving permit:* IDP. *Health and safety:* Inoculations advised; water unsafe. *Tourist features:* Vridi Canal; Kossou Dam; Monts du Toura. *National holiday:* December 7 (National Day).

MALI

Area: 478,839 sq. mi./1,240,192 km².
Local name: République du Mali.
Currency: C.F.A. franc. **Capital:**
Bamako. **Other cities:** Mopti, Kayes,
Ségou, Timbuktu. **Physical features:**
Mostly flat to rolling plains in N.;
rugged hills in N.E. **Climate:**
Savanna/arid. **Time zone:** GMT.
Political system: Democratic repub-
lic. **Head of state:** Alpha Oumar
Konare (from 1992). **Head of gov-
ernment:** Abdoulaye Sekou Sow
(from 1993). **Main exports:**
Livestock, peanuts, fish, gold, cotton,
skins. **Resources:** Gold, phosphates,
kaolin, salt, limestone, uranium, bauxite, iron ore.

PEOPLE

Population: 10,137,000. **Distribution
urban/rural:** 25%/75%. **Life expectancy:** 43(m), 47(f). **Languages:** French
(official), Bambara, other African languages. **Ethnic groups:** Mande 50%,
Peul 17%, Voltaic 12%, Songhai 6%,
Tuareg and Moor 5%, other 10%.
Religions: Muslim 90%, indigenous
beliefs 9%, Christian 1%. **Literacy rate:**
32%. **Per capita GDP:** $265.

KEY DATES

1895 Becomes a French colony.
1959 Federation of Mali formed.
1960 Federation of Mali breaks up; Mali
becomes independent as republic.
1991 Antigovernment demonstrations;
president overthrown in military coup.
1992 Referendum endorses new constitution; Alpha Oumar Konare president.

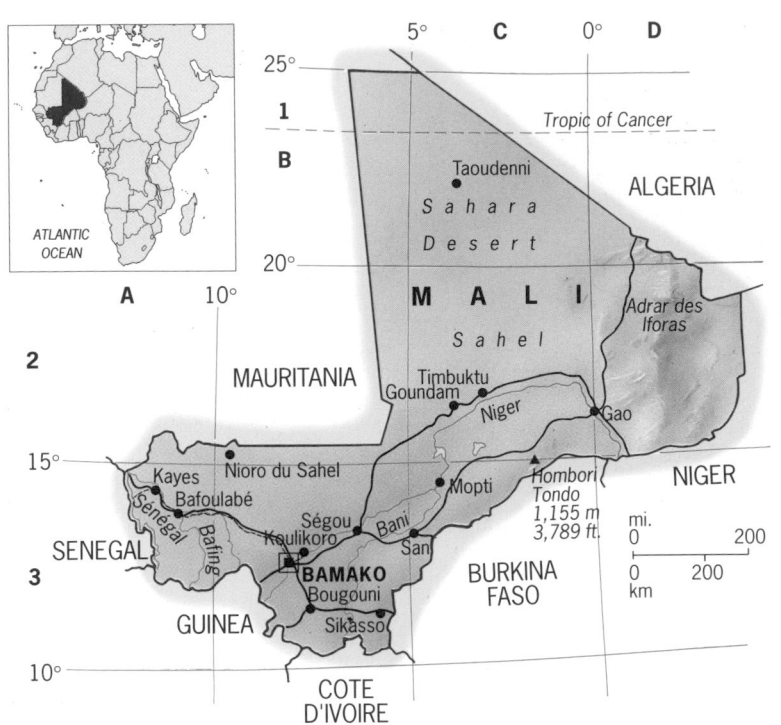

BURKINA FASO

Area: 105,946 sq. mi./274,400 km².
Local name: République de Burkina.
Currency: C.F.A. franc. **Capital:**
Ougadougou. **Physical features:**
Rolling plains; hills in W. and S.E.
Climate: Savanna. **Time zone:**
GMT. **Political system:** Military.
Head of state Capt. Blaise Compaoré
(from 1987). **Head of government:**
Roch Christian Kabore (from 1994).
Main exports: Oilseed, karite nuts,
gold. **Resources:** Manganese, lime-
stone, gold.

PEOPLE

Population: 9,682,000. **Distribution
urban/rural:** 8%/92%. **Life expectancy:** 52(m), 53(f). **Languages:** French,
indigenous languages. **Ethnic groups:**
More than 50 groups (Mossi most important). **Religions:** Indigenous beliefs 65%,
Muslim 25%, Christian 10%. **Literacy
rate:** 18%. **Per capita GDP:** $320.

KEY DATES

1897 Comes under French control.
1960 Independence achieved.
1991 New constitution.

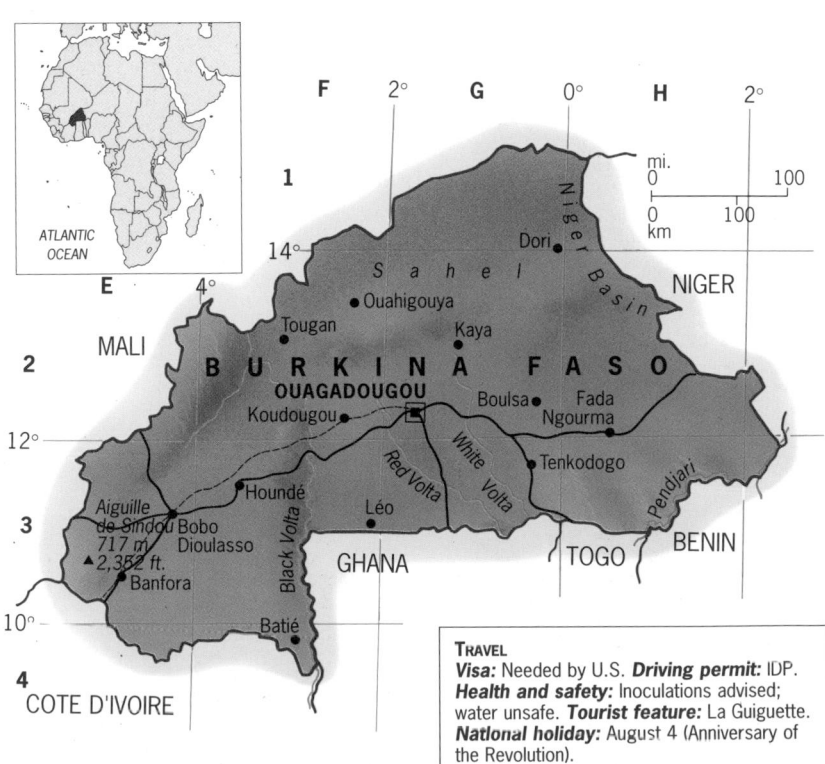

GHANA

Area: 92,100 sq. mi./238,537 km². *Local name:* Republic of Ghana. *Currency:* Cedi. *Capital:* Accra. *Other cities:* Kumasi, Sekondi-Takoradi. *Physical features:* Mostly low plains with dissected plateau in south-central area. *Climate:* Savanna. *Time zone:* GMT. *Political system:* Military. *Head of state and government:* Jerry Rawlings (from 1981). *Main exports:* Cocoa, gold, wood, tuna, manganese, bauxite, aluminum. *Resources:* Gold, wood, industrial diamonds, bauxite, manganese, fish, aluminum.

PEOPLE

Population: 16,446,000. *Distribution urban/rural:* 33%/67%. *Life expectancy:* 53(m), 57(f). *Languages:* English (official), indigenous languages including Akan, Moshi-Dagomba, Ewe, and Ga. *Ethnic groups:* Akan around 44%, Moshi-Dagomba 16%, Ewe 13%, Ga 8%, other 19%. *Religions:* Indigenous beliefs 38%, Muslim 30%, Christian 24%, other 8%. *Literacy rate:* 60%. *Per capita GDP:* $400.

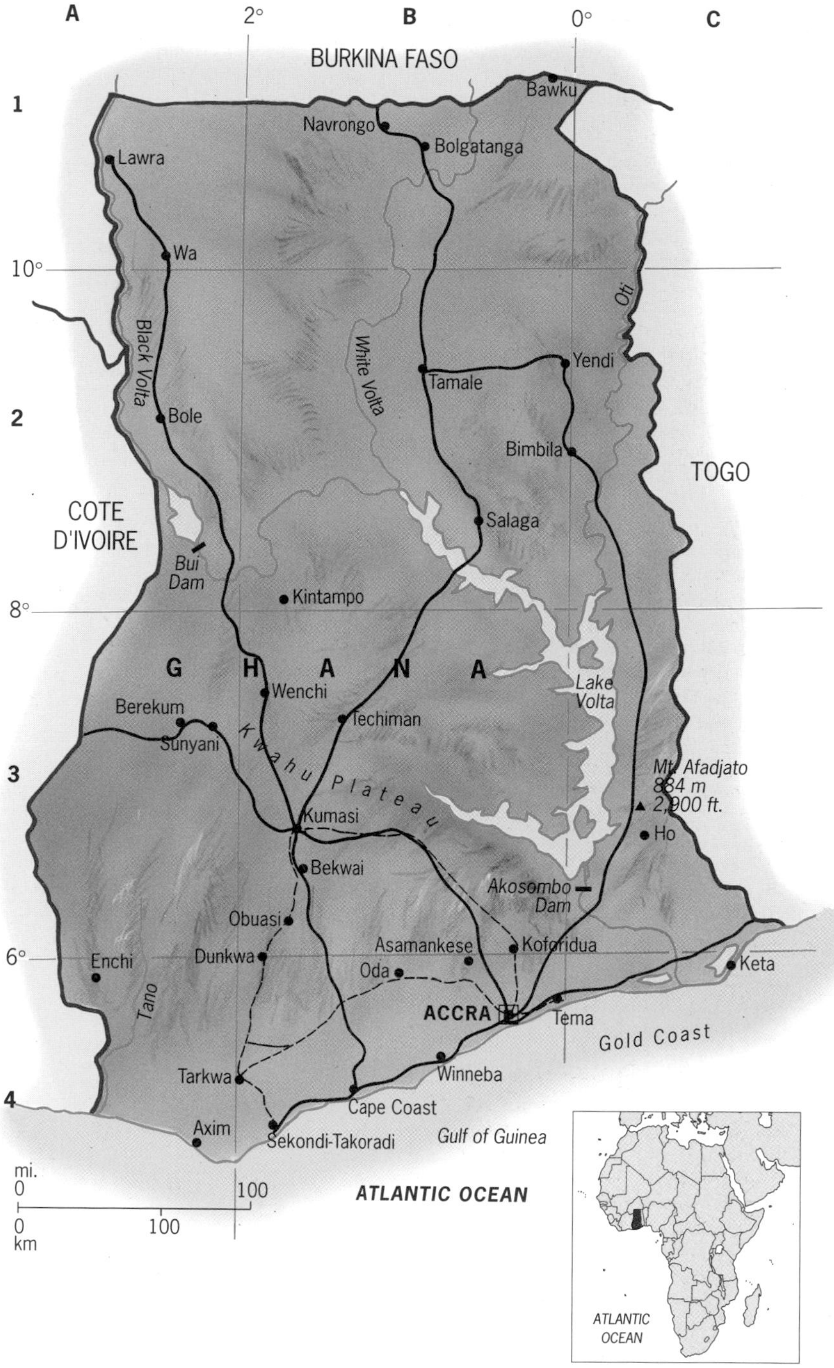

KEY DATES

1874 Great Britain makes territory between the coast and the Ashanti Empire a British colony.
1901 Most of Ghana becomes British.
1952 Kwame Nkrumah (Convention People's Party) becomes prime minister.
1954 Ghana is granted autonomy in internal affairs, although Britain retains responsibility for the police.
1957 Independence achieved with British Togoland becoming a part of the new nation.
1960 Ghana becomes a republic with Kwanae Nkrumah as president; badly managed state intervention in industry causes severe economic problems.
1961 State of emergency declared to end protest strikes.
1962 Assassination attempts against President Nkrumah.
1964 Nkrumah declares Ghana a one-party state.
1966 Military coup; Nkrumah charged with embezzling; constitution suspended and legislature dissolved; CPP abolished; Gen. Joseph Ankrah is named head of government.
1969 Ankrah resigns; Brig. Akwasi Amankwa Afrifa installed in his place; new constitution introduced; Ghana returns to civilian rule with Kofi Busia (Progressive Party) as prime minister.
1972 Military leaders seize government once again; Col. I. K. Acheampong becomes head of government.
1978 Acheampong forced to resign; Gen. Frederick William Kwasi Akuffo becomes head of government.

1979 Akuffo is overthrown by other military leaders led by Lieut. Jerry Rawlings; Afrifa, Acheampong, and Akuffo are executed; civilian government established, led by Hillia Limann.
1981 Rawlings leads another coup; all political parties are outlawed.
1981–83 Many people leave Ghana to work in Nigeria as a result of severe economic problems.
1983 Nigerian government forces about one million Ghanaians to return to Ghana, creating mass unemployment and shortages of food, housing, water.

1991 Trade pact with Cuba.
1992 New constitution; partial lifting of ban on political parties; Rawlings elected president in national elections.

TRAVEL
Visa: Needed by U.S. *Driving permit:* IDP. *Health and safety:* Inoculations advised; water unsafe. *Tourist features:* World's largest artificial lake, Lake Volta; relics of the ancient kingdom of Ashanti. *National holiday:* March 6 (Independence Day).

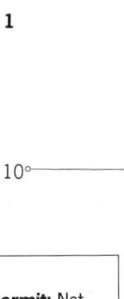

TOGO

Area: 21,926 sq. mi./56,785 km². *Local name:* République Togolaise. *Currency:* C.F.A. franc. *Capital:* Lomé. *Other city:* Sokodé. *Physical features:* Savanna in N.; central hills, plateau in S.; low coastal plains with extensive lagoons and marshes. *Climate:* Tropical in S., savanna in N. *Time zone:* GMT. *Political system:* Democratic republic. *Head of state:* Etienne Gnassingbé Eyadéma (from 1967). *Head of government:* Edem Kokjo (from 1994). *Main exports:* Phosphates, cocoa, coffee, cotton, palm kernels. *Resources:* Phosphates, limestone, marble.

PEOPLE

Population: 3,885,000. *Distribution urban/rural:* 25%/75%. *Life expectancy:* 54(m), 58(f). *Languages:* French (official), major African languages are Ewe, Mina, Dagomba, and Kabyè. *Ethnic groups:* 37 groups, of which the most important are Ewe, Mina, and Kabyè; others less than 1%. *Religions:* Indigenous beliefs about 70%, Christian 20%, Muslim 10%. *Literacy rate:* 43%. *Per capita GDP:* $400.

TRAVEL

Visa: Needed by U.S. *Driving permit:* Nat. license. *Health and safety:* Inoculations advised; water unsafe. *Tourist features:* Mono tableland; Oti River and plateau; Atlantic beaches. *National holiday:* April 27 (Independence Day).

KEY DATES

1884 Becomes a German protectorate.
1919 Britain and France divide Togo between them after World War I.
1960 Independence achieved.
1967 Military coup; Gnassingbé Eyadéma becomes president.
1973 Assembly of Togolese People (RPT) formed as sole legal party.
1991 Opposition parties legalized.
1992 Referendum calls for multiparty elections.
1994 First multiparty elections.

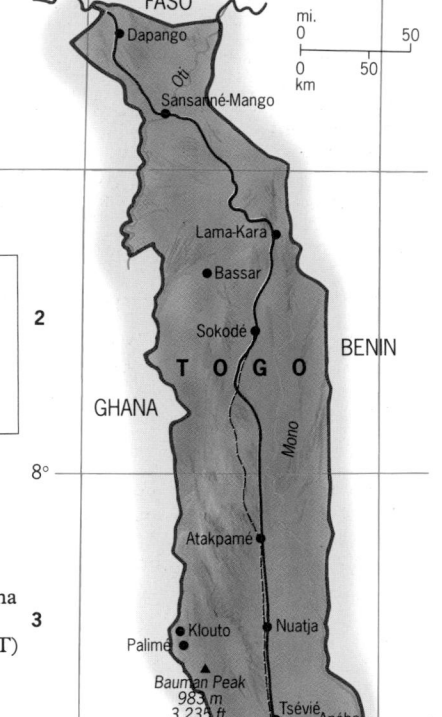

BENIN

Area: 43,486 sq. mi./112,622 km². *Local name:* République Populaire du Bénin. *Currency:* C.F.A. franc. *Capital:* Porto-Novo. *Physical features:* Mostly flat to rolling plains; some hills and low mountains. *Climate:* Tropical. *Time zone:* GMT +1h. *Political system:* Republic. *Head of state and government:* Nicéphore Soglo (from 1991). *Main exports:* Crude oil, cotton, palm products, cocoa, sugar. *Resources:* Small offshore oil deposits, limestone, marble, wood.

PEOPLE

Population: 5,215,000. *Distribution urban/rural:* 20%/80%. *Life expectancy:* 49(m), 53(f). *Languages:* French (official), Gur and Kwa languages. *Ethnic groups:* African 99% (42 ethnic groups); small European minority. *Religions:* Indigenous beliefs 70%, Muslim 15%, Christian 15%. *Literacy rate:* 23%. *Per capita GDP:* $410.

TRAVEL

Visa: Needed by U.S. *Driving permit:* IDP. *Health and safety:* Inoculations advised; water unsafe. *Tourist features:* Coastal lagoons with fishing villages on stilts; Niger River in N.E. *National holiday:* August 1 (National Day).

KEY DATES

1904 Becomes territory (known as Dahomey) of French West Africa.
1946 Becomes overseas territory of France.
1958 Self-government achieved.
1960 Independence achieved.
1960–72 Political instability leading to widespread civil unrest.
1972 Military regime established by Gen. Mathieu Kerekou.
1975 Name changes to Benin.
1978 Return to civilian rule under new constitution.
1980 Gen. Mathieu Kerekou formally elected president.
1989 Strikes and demonstrations against Kerekou; army deployed against protesters.
1991 Kerekou defeated in multiparty elections; Nicéphore Soglo president.

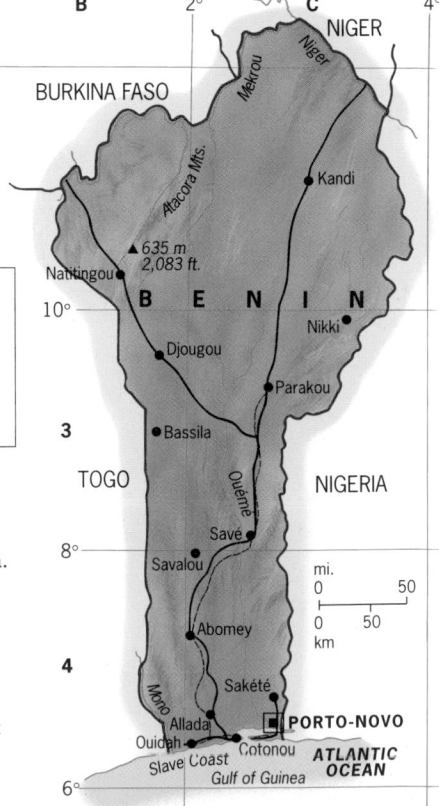

NIGERIA

Area: 356,670 sq. mi./923,773 km². **Local name:** Federal Republic of Nigeria. **Currency:** Naira. **Capital:** Abuja. **Other cities:** Lagos, Ibadan, Ogbomosho, Kano. **Physical features:** Lowlands in S. merge into central hills and plateaus; mountains in S.E., plains in N. **Climate:** Mainly tropical; savanna in N. **Time zone:** GMT +1h. **Political system:** Military. **Head of state and government:** Gen. Sani Abacha (from 1993). **Main exports:** Petroleum, cocoa, rubber. **Resources:** Crude oil, tin, columbite, iron ore, coal, limestone, lead, zinc.

PEOPLE

Population: 88,514,501. **Distribution urban/rural:** 35%/65%. **Life expectancy:** 48(m), 50(f). **Languages:** English (official), Hausa, Yoruba, Ibo, Fulani, several other African languages. **Ethnic groups:** More than 250 groups: Hausa and Fulani (N.), Yoruba (S.W.), and Ibo (S.E.) 65%. **Religions:** Muslim 50%, Christian 40%, other 10%. **Literacy rate:** 51%. **Per capita GDP:** $250.

KEY DATES

1960 Independence achieved.
1966 Military coup; Gen. Johnson Aguiyi-Ironsi (Ibo) is head of government; fear of Ibo domination prompts riots in which thousands are killed; Aguiyi-Ironsi killed in counter coup.
1967 Biafra secedes; civil war breaks out.
1970 Biafra surrenders; civil war ends.
1983 Economic problems due to declining oil prices; Maj.-Gen. Muhammadu Buhari seizes power.
1985 Buhari overthrown in coup led by Ibrahim Badamosi Babangida.
1992 Babangida wins elections.
1993 Results of elections suspended. Gen. Sani Abucha restores military rule and outlaws political parties.
1995 Ban on political activity lifted.

ECONOMY

Farming: About two-thirds of workers are employed in this sector, although it accounts for only about 20% of the GDP; cash crops include palm nuts, peanuts, and rubber; food crops include beans, cassava, corn, millet, sorghum, rice, and yams; cattle raising is important in N. **Forestry:** Wood, including sapele, mahogany, iroko, obechwe, and ebony; overexploitation is a problem. **Minerals:** A major oil-producing country; other minerals are coal, columbite, iron ore, tin, lead, and zinc. **Industry:** Factories produce foodstuffs, chemicals, textiles, rubber, plastics, and paper; large construction industry.

TRAVEL
Visa: Needed by U.S. **Driving permit:** IDP. **Health and safety:** Inoculations advised; water unsafe. **Tourist feature:** Rich artistic heritage, e.g. Benin bronzes. **National holiday:** October 1 (Independence Day).

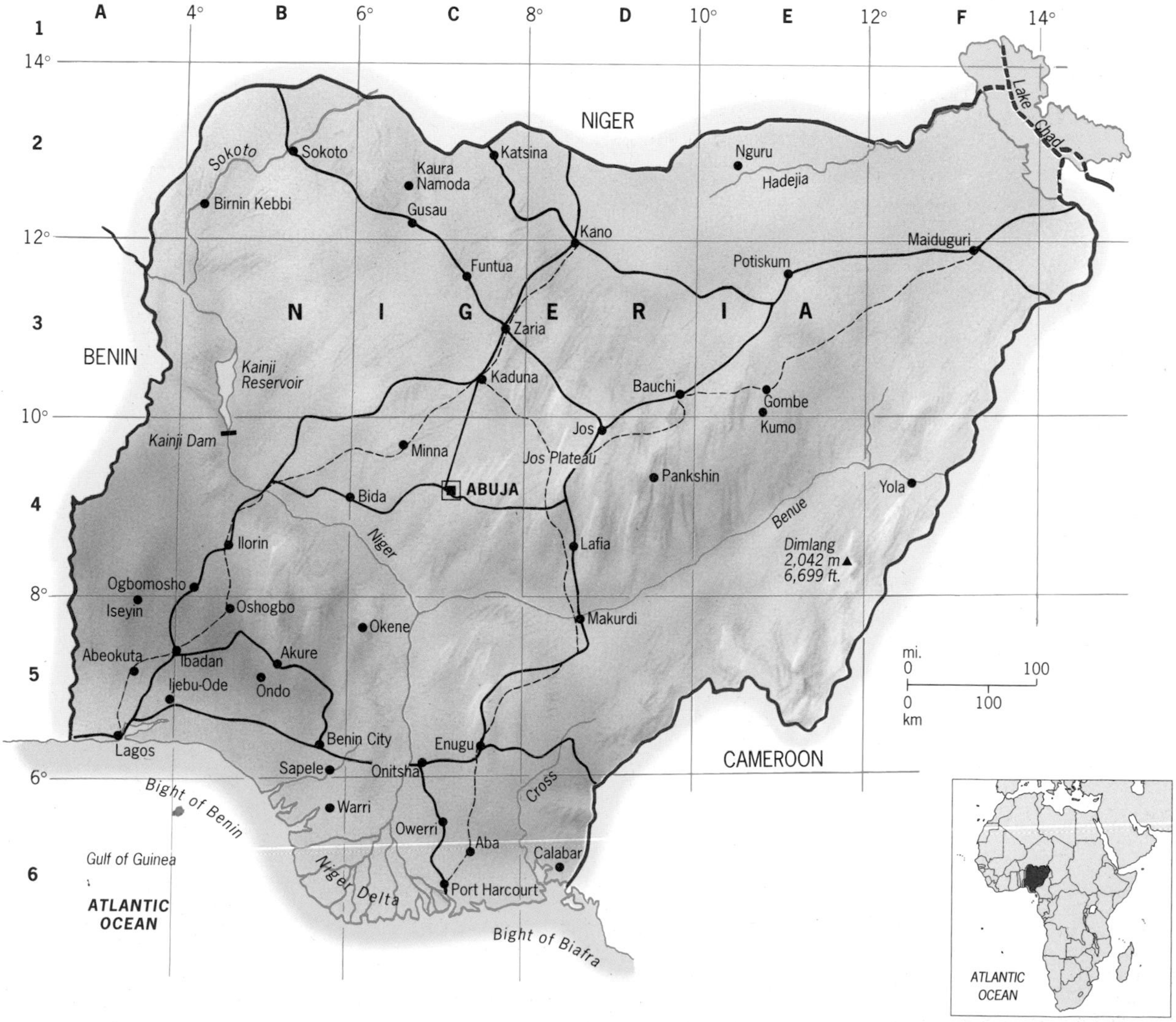

NIGER

Area: 489,190 sq. mi./1,267,000 km². **Local name:** République du Niger. **Currency:** C.F.A. franc. **Capital:** Niamey. **Other city:** Zinder. **Physical features:** Mainly desert; some hills and mountains. **Climate:** Mainly arid; savanna in S. **Time zone:** GMT +1h. **Political system:** Republic. **Head of state:** Mahamane Ousmane (from 1993). **Head of government:** Mahamadou Issoufou (from 1993). **Main exports:** Uranium, livestock, vegetables. **Resources:** Uranium, coal, iron ore.

PEOPLE

Population: 8,361,000. **Distribution urban/rural:** 21%/79%. **Life expectancy:** 42(m), 45(f). **Languages:** French (official), Hausa, Djerma. **Ethnic groups:** Hausa 56%, Djerma 22%, Fula 9%, Tuareg 8%, Beri Beri 4%; Arab, Toubou, and Gourmantche 1%. **Religions:** Muslim 80%, indigenous beliefs and Christian 20%. **Literacy rate:** 28%. **Per capita GDP:** $300.

KEY DATES

1922 Becomes part of French West Africa.
1960 Independence achieved with Hamani Diori of the Niger Progressive

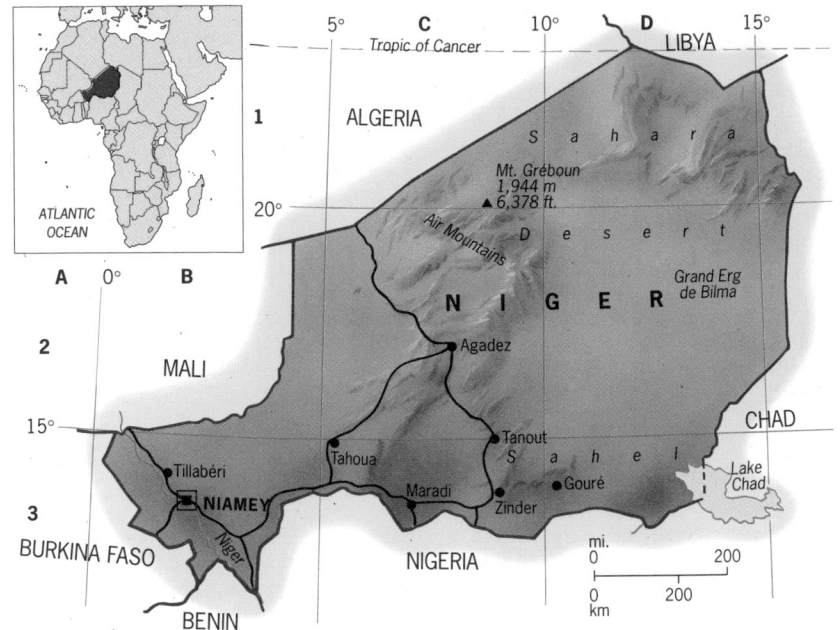

Party (PPN) as president.
1974 Hamani Diori overthrown; Seyni Kountché takes power; PPN outlawed, constitution suspended, and National Assembly dissolved.
1987 Seyni Kountché dies; Col. Ali Saibou becomes leader.
1989 New constitution.
1993 First free elections.

TRAVEL
Visa: Needed by U.S. **Driving permit:** IDP. **Health and safety:** Inoculations advised; water unsafe. **Tourist feature:** Part of the Sahara Desert. **National holiday:** December 18 (Republic Day).

CAMEROON

Area: 183,568 sq. mi./475,442 km². **Local name:** République du Cameroun. **Currency:** C.F.A. franc. **Capital:** Yaoundé. **Physical features:** Varies from plains in S.W. and N. to mountains in W. **Climate:** Tropical along coast, savanna in N. **Time zone:** GMT +1h. **Political system:** Republic. **Head of state:** Paul Biya (from 1982). **Head of government:** Simon Achidi Achu (from 1992). **Main exports:** Petroleum products, coffee, cocoa beans, wood. **Resources:** Crude oil, bauxite, iron ore, wood.

PEOPLE

Population: 12,547,000. **Distribution urban/rural:** 40%/60%. **Life expectancy:** 55(m), 60(f). **Languages:** English and French (both official), African languages. **Ethnic groups:** More than 200 groups, including Bamileke 30%, Fulani 7%. **Religions:** Indigenous beliefs 51%, Christian 33%, Muslim 16%. **Literacy rate:** 54%. **Per capita GDP:** $1,040.

KEY DATES

1884 Becomes a German protectorate.
1916 Captured by Allied forces.

1922 Divided between Britain and France.
1960 Independence achieved.
1970s Begins producing petroleum.
1990 Widespread civil unrest.
1992 Ruling Socialist RDPC party wins first multiparty elections in 28 years.

TRAVEL
Visa: Needed by U.S. **Driving permit:** IDP. **Health and safety:** Inoculations advised; water unsafe. **Tourist feature:** Active volcano Mount Cameroon. **National holiday:** May 20 (National Day).

CENTRAL AFRICAN REPUBLIC

Area: 240,323 sq. mi./622,436 km². *Local name:* República Centrafricaine. *Currency:* C.F.A. franc. *Capital:* Bangui. *Physical features:* Flat to rolling plateau. *Climate:* Tropical. *Time zone:* GMT +1h. *Political system:* Republic. *Head of state:* Ange Patasse (from 1993). *Head of government:* Jean-Luc Mandaba (from 1993). *Main exports:* Diamonds, cotton, coffee, wood, tobacco. *Resources:* Diamonds, uranium, wood, gold, oil.

PEOPLE

Population: 3,258,000. *Distribution urban/rural:* 47%/53%. *Life expectancy:* 46(m), 49(f). *Languages:* French (official), Sangho (lingua franca), Arabic, Hunsa, Swahili. *Ethnic groups:* Banda 27%, Baya 34%, Mandija 21%, Sara 10%. *Religions:* Christian 50%, indigenous beliefs 24%, Muslim 15%. *Literacy rate:* 27%. *Per capita GDP:* $440.

KEY DATES

1889 Comes under French control.
1960 Independence achieved.
1962 Becomes one-party state.
1993 First multiparty elections.

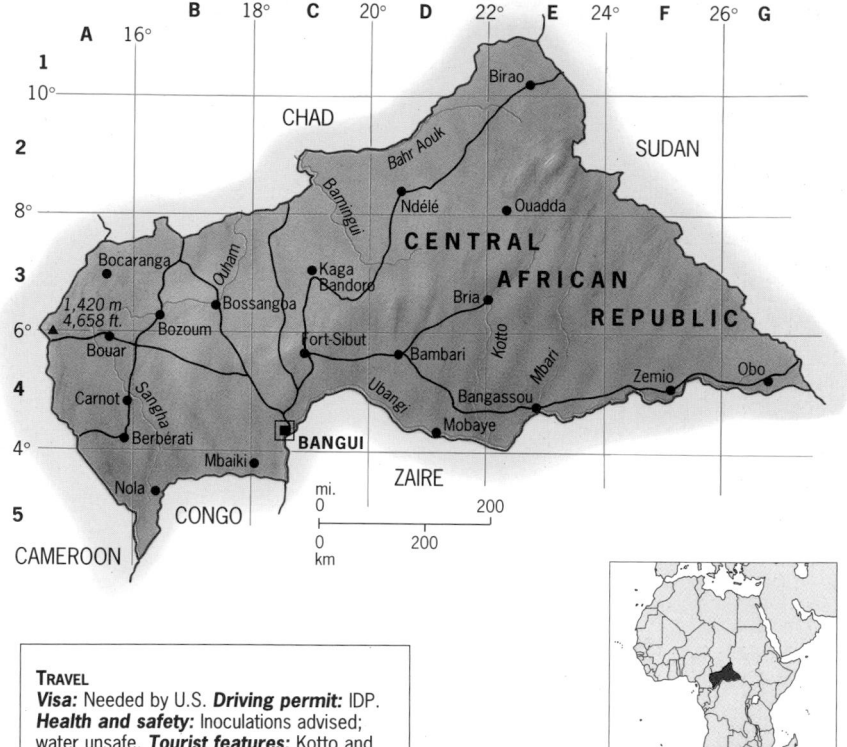

TRAVEL
Visa: Needed by U.S. *Driving permit:* IDP. *Health and safety:* Inoculations advised; water unsafe. *Tourist features:* Kotto and Mbali River falls; Oubangui River. *National holiday:* December 1 (National Day).

EQUATORIAL GUINEA

Area: 10,831 sq. mi./28,051 km². *Local name:* República de Guinea Ecuatorial. *Currency:* C.F.A. franc. *Capital:* Malabo. *Physical features:* Coastal plains rising to hills. *Climate:* Tropical. *Time zone:* GMT +1h. *Political system:* In transition. *Head of state:* Brig. Gen. Teodoro Obiang Nguema Mbasogo (from 1979). *Head of government:* Silvestre Siale Bileka (from 1993). *Main exports:* Coffee, wood, cocoa beans. *Resources:* Wood, crude oil, gold, manganese and uranium unexploited.

PEOPLE

Population: 379,000. *Distribution urban/rural:* n.a. *Life expectancy:* 49(m), 53(f). *Languages:* Spanish (official), Fang, Bubi, Ibo. *Ethnic groups:* Fang 80%, Bubi 15%. *Religion:* Roman Catholic. *Literacy rate:* 50%. *Per capita GDP:* $400.

KEY DATES

1885 Becomes Spanish colony.
1968 Independence achieved.
1968–79 Macias Nguema dictatorship.
1979 Military regime established.
1992 New constitution.

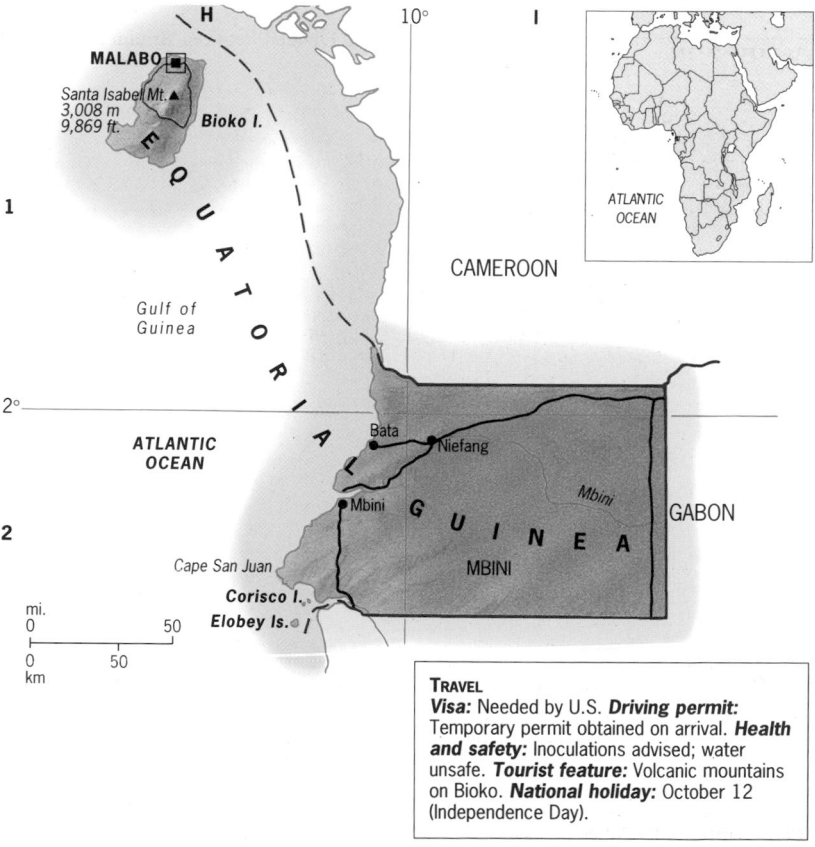

TRAVEL
Visa: Needed by U.S. *Driving permit:* Temporary permit obtained on arrival. *Health and safety:* Inoculations advised; water unsafe. *Tourist feature:* Volcanic mountains on Bioko. *National holiday:* October 12 (Independence Day).

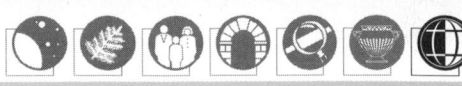

CONGO

Area: 132,046 sq. mi./342,000 km². *Local name:* République du Congo. *Currency:* C.F.A. franc. *Capital:* Brazzaville. *Physical features:* Coastal plain, central plateau. *Climate:* Tropical. *Time zone:* GMT +1h. *Political system:* Republic. *Head of state:* Pascal Lissouba (from 1992). *Head of government:* Jacques-Joachim Yhombi-Opango(from 1993). *Main exports:* Petroleum, lumber, plywood, coffee. *Resources:* Petroleum, wood, lead, zinc, uranium, copper, phosphates.

PEOPLE

Population: 2,441,000. *Distribution urban/rural:* 41%/59%. *Life expectancy:* 53(m), 56(f). *Languages:* French (official), African languages including Lingala and Kikongo. *Ethnic groups:* About 75 tribes including Bakongo 45%, Bateke 20%. *Religions:* Christian 50%, animist 48%, Muslim 2%. *Literacy rate:* 57%. *Per capita GDP:* $1,070.

KEY DATES

1880 Comes under French control.
1960 Full independence achieved.
1970 Marxist state announced.
1992 First free elections in 28 years.

TRAVEL
Visa: Needed by U.S. *Driving permit:* IDP. *Health and safety:* Inoculations advised; water unsafe. *Tourist features:* Brazzaville cathedral and mosque; Congo rapids. *National holiday:* August 15 (Congolese National Day).

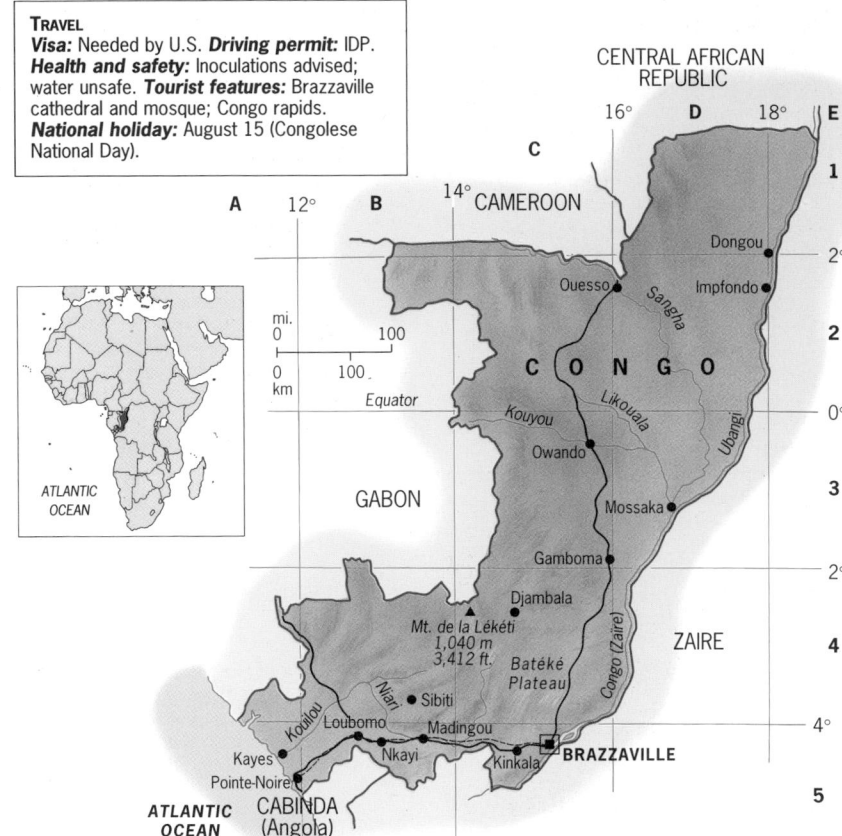

GABON

Area: 103,346 sq. mi./267,667 km². *Local name:* République Gabonaise. *Currency:* C.F.A. franc. *Capital:* Libreville. *Physical features:* Narrow coastal plain rising to hilly interior. *Climate:* Tropical. *Time zone:* GMT +1h. *Political system:* Republic. *Head of state:* El Hadj Omar Bongo (from 1967). *Head of government:* Casimir Oyé-Mba (from 1990). *Main exports:* Crude oil, manganese, wood, uranium. *Resources:* Crude oil, manganese, uranium, gold, wood, iron ore.

PEOPLE

Population: 1,012,000. *Distribution urban/rural:* 45%/55%. *Life expectancy:* 51(m), 56(f). *Languages:* French (official), African languages. *Ethnic groups:* About 40 Bantu groups, including Fang 25% and Bapounou 10%; about 100,000 foreign Africans and Europeans. *Religions:* Christian 55–75%, Muslim fewer than 1%, animist. *Literacy rate:* 61%. *Per capita GDP:* $3,090.

KEY DATES

1886 Becomes French colony.
1960 Independence achieved.
1990 First free elections since 1964.

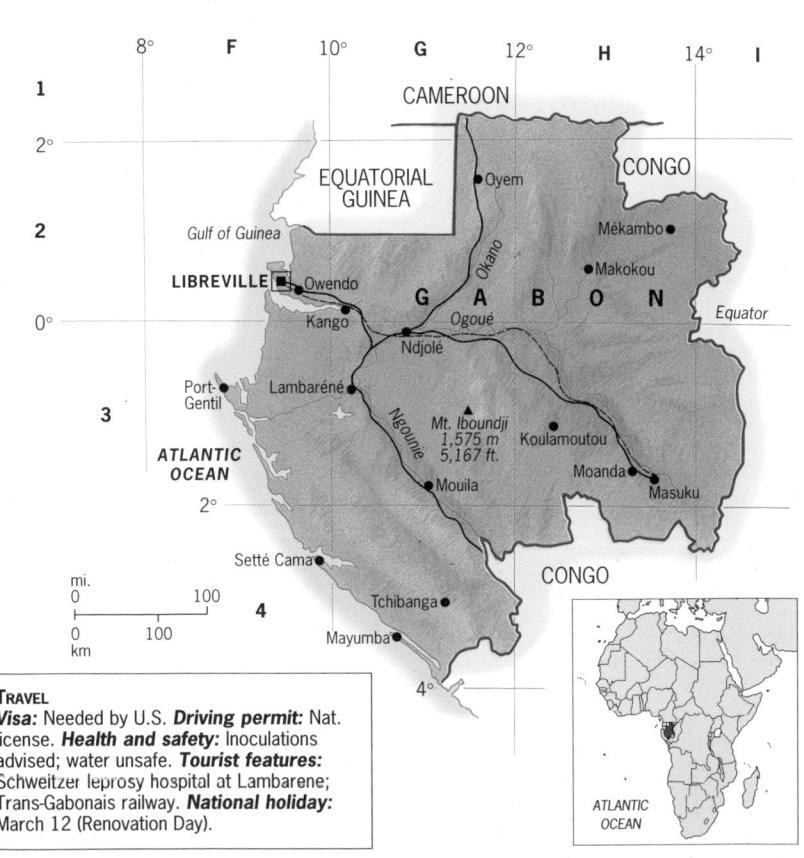

TRAVEL
Visa: Needed by U.S. *Driving permit:* Nat. license. *Health and safety:* Inoculations advised; water unsafe. *Tourist features:* Schweitzer leprosy hospital at Lambarene; Trans-Gabonais railway. *National holiday:* March 12 (Renovation Day).

SAO TOME AND PRINCIPE

Area: 387 sq. mi./1,001 km². *Local name:* República Democrática de São Tomé e Príncipe. *Currency:* Dobra. *Capital:* São Tomé. *Physical features:* Volcanic, mountainous. *Climate:* Tropical; rainy season Oct.–May. *Time zone:* GMT. *Political system:* Republic. *Head of state:* Miguel Trovoada (from 1991). *Head of government:* Noberto Costa Alegre Daio (from 1992). *Main exports:* Cocoa, copra, coffee, bananas, palm oil. *Resources:* Fish.

PEOPLE
Population: 122,000. *Distribution* *urban/rural:* n.a. *Life expectancy:* 64(m), 68(f). *Language:* Portuguese. *Ethnic groups:* Primarily mixed Portuguese-African; African minority. *Religions:* Christian sects including Roman Catholic, Evangelical Protestant, Seventh-Day Adventist. *Literacy rate:* 57%. *Per capita GDP:* $400.

KEY DATES
1485 Portugal begins to send convicts, exiles, and settlers to islands.
1522 Becomes Portuguese province.
1953 Batepa massacre: hundreds of black workers killed during protest against working conditions.
1975 Independence achieved with Manuel Pinto da Costa as president.
1988 Coup attempt against da Costa.
1991 First multiparty elections.

TRAVEL
Visa: Needed by U.S. *Driving permit:* IDP. *Health and safety:* Inoculations advised. *Tourist feature:* National museum of São Tomé; beaches on São Tomé. *National holiday:* July 12 (Independence Day).

ANGOLA

Area: 481,351 sq. mi./1,246,700 km². *Local name:* República de Angola. *Currency:* Kwanza. *Capital:* Luanda. *Other cities:* Lobito. *Physical features:* Narrow coastal plain rising to vast interior plateau. *Climate:* Savanna in S. and along coast; rainy season: Nov.–April in N. *Time zone:* GMT +1h. *Political system:* Republic. *Head of state:* José Eduardo dos Santos (from 1979). *Head of government:* Marcolino Moco (from 1992). *Main exports:* Oil, gas, diamonds, coffee, sisal, fish, wood, cotton. *Resources:* Petroleum, diamonds, wood, fish, iron ore, phosphates, copper, bauxite, uranium.

PEOPLE
Population: 10,276,000. *Distribution* *urban/rural:* 29%/71%. *Life expectancy:* 43(m), 47(f). *Languages:* Portuguese (official), numerous Bantu languages. *Ethnic groups:* Ovimbundu 38%; Kimbundu 25%, Bakongo 13%, Mestizo and other 24%. *Religions:* Indigenous beliefs 47%, Roman Catholic 38%, Protestant 15%. *Literacy rate:* 42%. *Per capita GDP:* $950.

KEY DATES
1500s Portuguese arrive in Angola.
1956 Foundation of Popular Movement for the Liberation of Angola (MPLA).
1961 MPLA guerrilla offensive begins.
1962 Front for the Liberation of Angola (FNLA) founded.
1966 Foundation of National Union for the Total Independence of Angola (UNITA).
1974 Portuguese government overthrown.
1975 Independence achieved; civil war between rival parties begins.
1976 MPLA gains control and establishes Marxist government with Soviet and Cuban support, but UNITA and FNLA continue guerrilla warfare with South African and U.S. assistance.
1988 Agreement signed with Cuba and South Africa to end military aid.
1991 Peace treaty between government and UNITA.
1992 First free elections followed by renewed fighting.
1994 Government–UNITA peace accord.

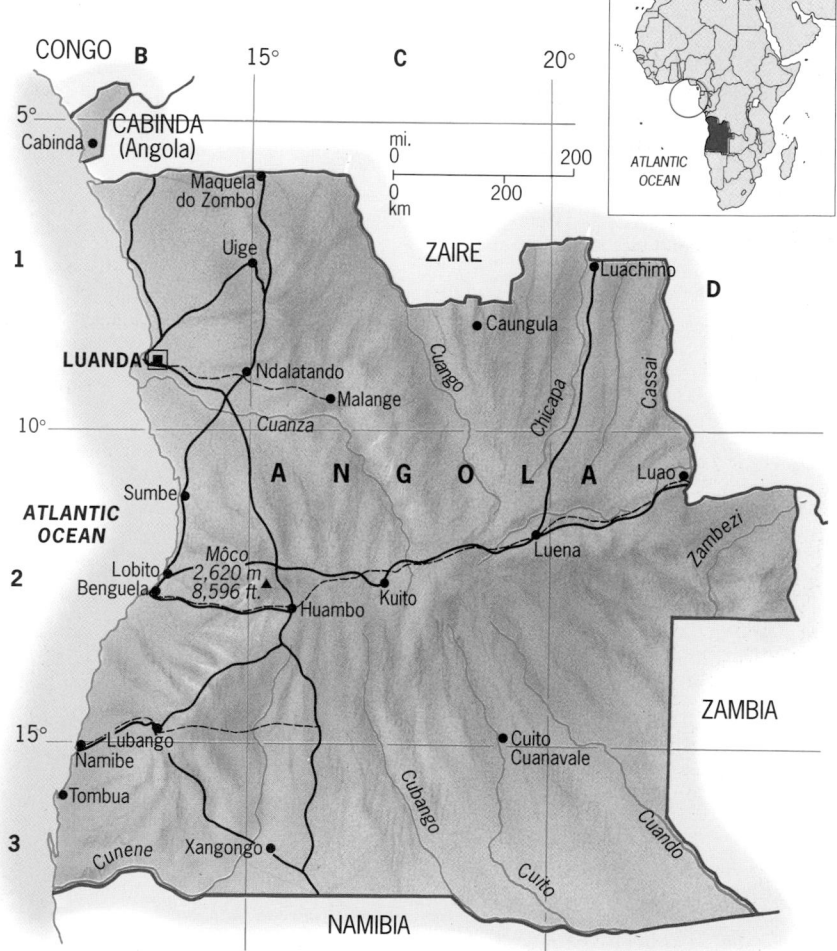

TRAVEL
Visa: Needed by U.S. *Driving permit:* Nat. license exchanged for local one on arrival. *Health and safety:* Inoculations advised; water unsafe. *Tourist features:* Cuanza, Cuito, Cubango, and Cunene rivers; Cabinda enclave. *National holiday:* November 11 (Independence Day).

ZAIRE

Area: 905,360 sq. mi./2,344,885 km². *Local name:* République du Zaíre. *Currency:* Zaire. *Capital:* Kinshasa. *Physical features:* Low-lying plateau; mountainous in E. *Climate:* Tropical. *Time zone:* GMT +1h (W), +2h (E). *Political system:* Republic. *Head of state:* Marshal Mobutu Sese Seko Kuku Ngbendu wa Za Banga (from 1965). *Head of government:* Kengo Wa Dondo (from 1994). *Main exports:* Cobalt, coffee, copper, diamonds, oil. *Resources:* Cobalt, copper, cadmium, crude oil, diamonds, zinc, manganese, uranium.

PEOPLE

Population: 41,166,000. *Distribution urban/rural:* 44%/56%. *Life expectancy:* 52(m), 56(f). *Languages:* French (official), Lingala, Swahili, Kingwana, Kikongo, Tshiluba. *Ethnic groups:* More than 200 African groups, the majority Bantu; also Mangbetu-Azande (Hamitic). *Religions:* Roman Catholic 50%, Protestant 20%, Kimbanguist 10%, Muslim 10%, other 10%. *Literacy rate:* 72%. *Per capita GDP:* $260.

KEY DATES

1885 Congo Free State becomes personal property of King Leopold II of Belgium.
1908 Belgian government takes control.
1960 Independence achieved; Katanga province declares independence; civil war; UN troops sent in to restore order.
1963 UN troops end Katanga secession; many Katangan rebels flee to Angola.
1965 Military takes over government with Gen. Joseph Désiré Mobutu as president; Africanization program begun.
1971 Congo renamed Zaire.
1977–78 Abortive Katangan invasions.
1980s Severe economic problems.
1991 Riots force Mobutu to share power with opposition; Etienne Tshisekedi becomes prime minister; Oct.: Mobutu dismisses Tshisekedi.
1992 Tshisekedi reinstated against Mobutu's wishes; Oct.: civil unrest.
1993 Army mutiny; c.1,000 killed in fighting; Tshisekedi dismissed again.
1994 Hundreds of thousands of Rwandan refugees arrive in Zaire.
1995 Over 100 die during outbreak of Ebola Virus.

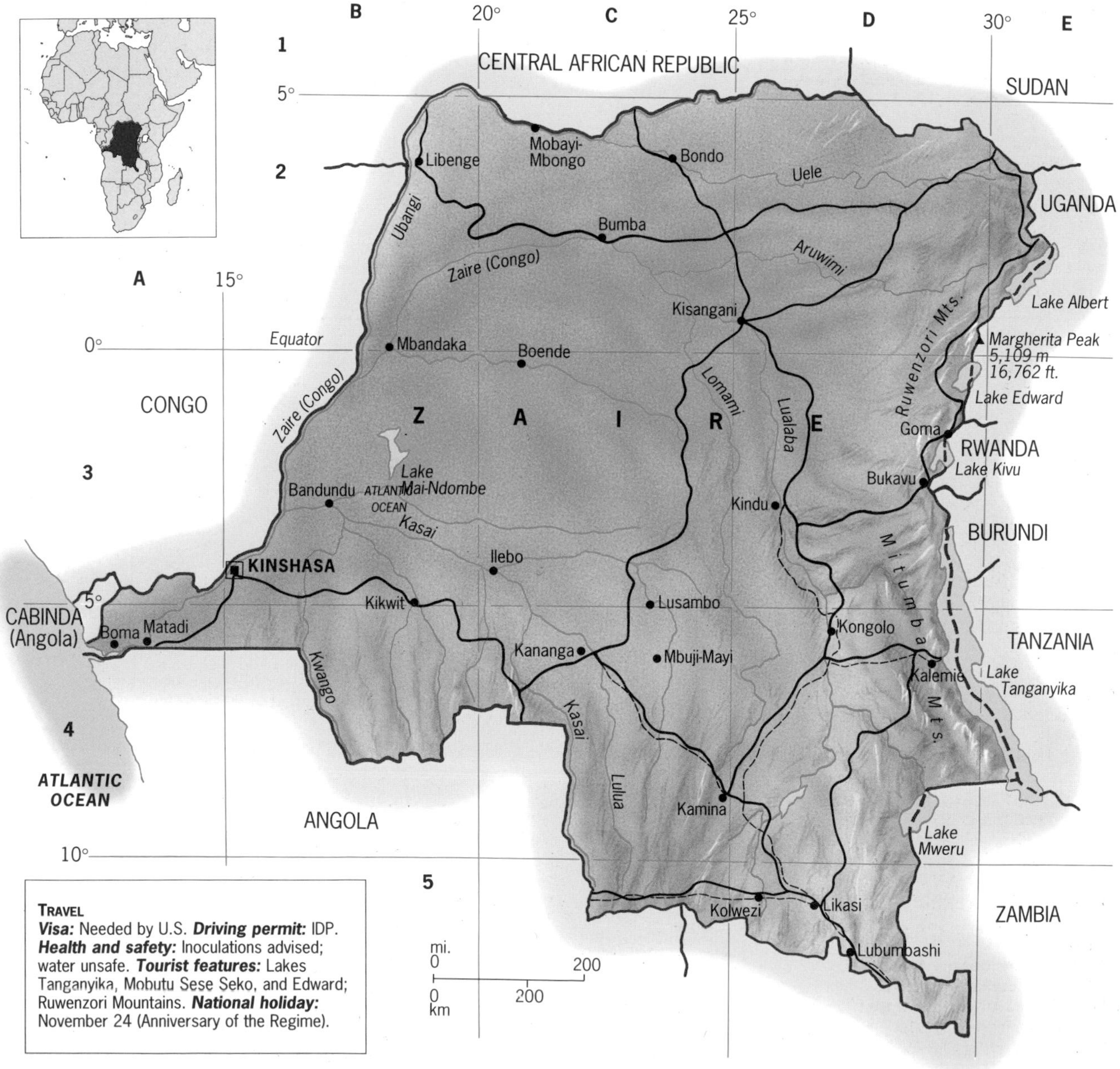

TRAVEL

Visa: Needed by U.S. *Driving permit:* IDP. *Health and safety:* Inoculations advised; water unsafe. *Tourist features:* Lakes Tanganyika, Mobutu Sese Seko, and Edward; Ruwenzori Mountains. *National holiday:* November 24 (Anniversary of the Regime).

RWANDA

Area: 10,170 sq. mi./26,338 km². **Local name:** Republika y'u Rwanda. **Currency:** Rwanda franc. **Capital:** Kigali. **Physical features:** Mostly grassy uplands and hills. **Climate:** Tropical. **Time zone:** GMT +2h. **Political system:** Military. **Head of state:** Pasteur Bizimungu (from 1994). **Head of government:** Faustin Twagiramungu (from 1994). **Main exports:** Coffee, tea, pyrethrum, tin. **Resources:** Gold, cassiterite, wolframite, natural gas.

PEOPLE

Population: 7,789,000. **Distribution urban/rural:** 5%/95%. **Life expectancy:** 51(m), 55(f). **Languages:** Kinyarwanda, French. **Ethnic groups:** Hutu 90%, Tutsi 9%, Twa 1%. **Religions:** Christian 74%, Muslim 1%, indigenous beliefs 25%. **Literacy rate:** 50%. **Per capita GDP:** $300.

KEY DATES

1897 Becomes a German colony.
1923 Comes under Belgian control.
1962 Independence achieved.
1990 Tutsi rebels launch offensive.
1992 Peace accord with Tutsi rebels.
1994 Civil war; thousands massacred; millions flee, mostly to Zaire.

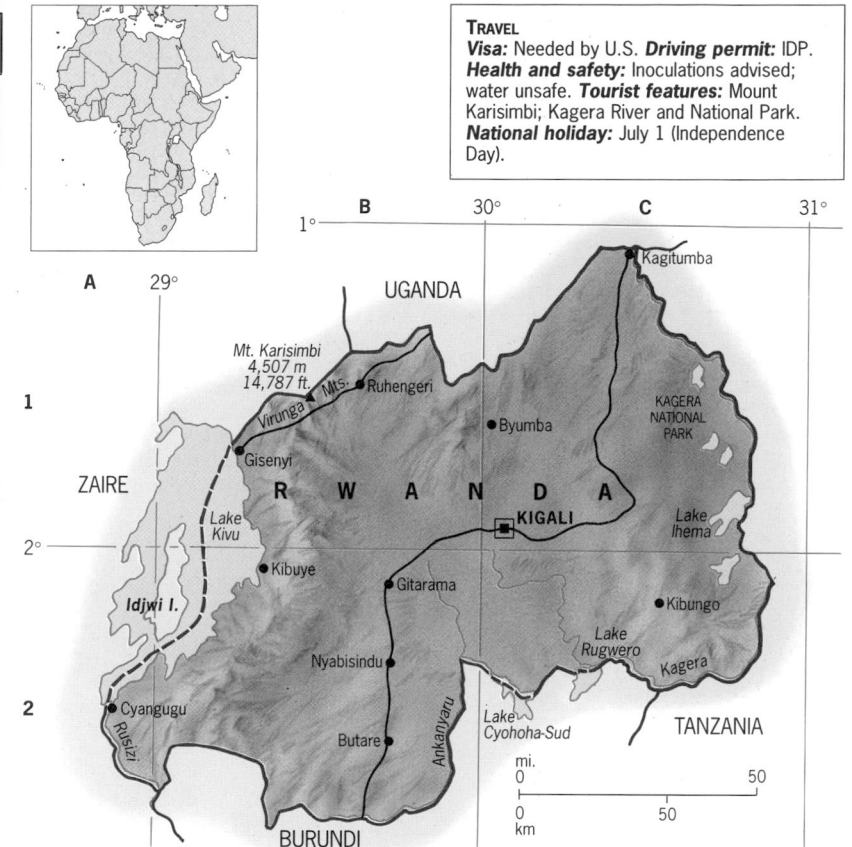

BURUNDI

Area: 10,748 sq. mi./27,834 km². **Local name:** Republika y'Uburundi. **Currency:** Burundi franc. **Capital:** Bujumbura. **Physical features:** Mostly rolling to hilly highlands. **Climate:** Tropical. **Time zone:** GMT +2h. **Political system:** Republic. **Head of state:** Sylvestre Ntibantunganya (from 1994). **Head of government:** Anatole Kanyenkiko (from 1994). **Main exports:** Coffee, tea, hides. **Resources:** Nickel, uranium, cobalt, copper, platinum.

PEOPLE

Population: 5,958,000. **Distribution urban/rural:** 8%/92%. **Life expectancy:** 51(m), 55(f). **Languages:** Kirundi and French (official), Swahili. **Ethnic groups:** Hutu 85%, Tutsi 14%, Twa 1%. **Religions:** Christian 67%, indigenous beliefs 32%, Muslim 1%. **Literacy rate:** 50%. **Per capita GDP:** $200.

KEY DATES

1916 Belgians occupy Burundi.
1962 Independence achieved.
1972 Hutu onslaught against Tutsi results in about 100,000 deaths.
1993 Ethnic violence kills 150,000.

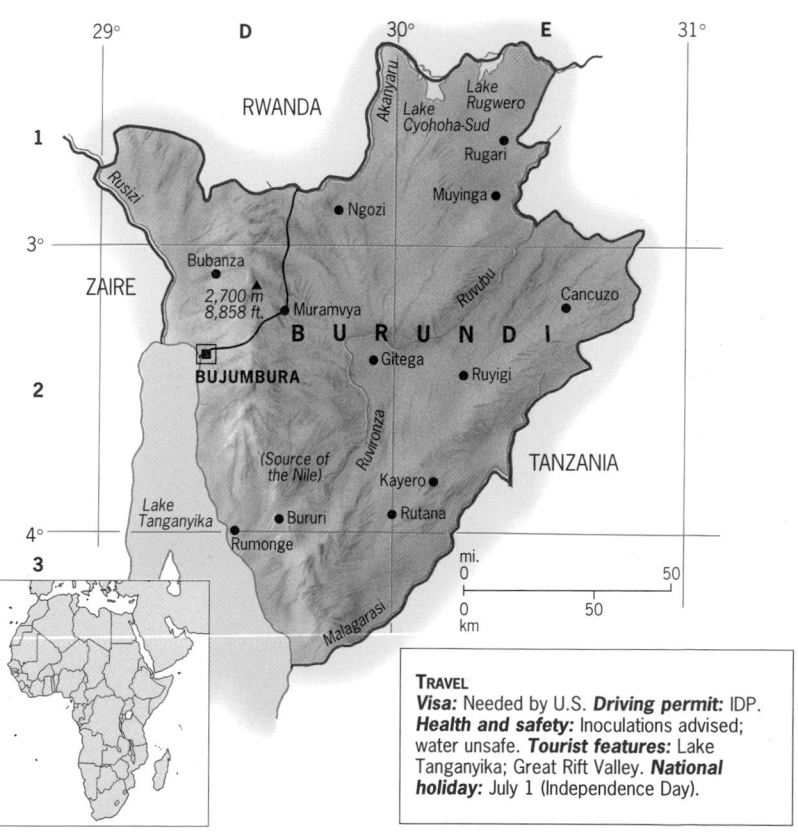

KENYA

Area: 224,960 sq. mi./582,646 km². **Local name:** Jamhuri ya Kenya. **Currency:** Kenya shilling. **Capital:** Nairobi. **Other cities:** Mombasa, Kisumu. **Physical features:** Low plains with central highlands. **Climate:** Savanna. **Time zone:** GMT +3h. **Political system:** Republic. **Head of state and government:** Daniel Teroitich arap Moi (from 1978). **Main exports:** Tea, coffee, petroleum products. **Resources:** Oil, gold, soda ash, salt.

PEOPLE

Population: 28,113,000. **Distribution urban/rural:** 26%/74%. **Life expectan-** cy: 60(m), 64(f). **Languages:** Swahili (official), English, numerous African languages. **Ethnic groups:** Kikuyu 21%, Luhya 14%, Luo 13%, Kalenjin 11%, Kisii 6%; Asian, European, and Arab. **Religions:** Protestant 38%, Roman Catholic 28%, indigenous beliefs 26%, Muslim 6%, other 2%. **Literacy rate:** 69%. **Per capita GDP:** $385.

KEY DATES

1895 Becomes a British colony.
1944 Foundation of Kenya African Union (KAU) by Kikuyu people.
1947 Jomo Kenyatta becomes leader of KAU.
1952 Mau Mau, splinter group of KAU, begins terrorist offensive; British take military action against movement; widespread fighting between government and nationalists kills *c.* 13,600.
1953 Jomo Kenyatta is convicted of leading Mau Mau and is imprisoned.
1961 Kenyatta released.
1963 Independence with Kenyatta as prime minister.
1964 Becomes republic.
1967 Joins East African Community with Tanzania and Uganda.
1977 East African Community dissolves.
1978 Jomo Kenyatta dies; Daniel Teroitich arap Moi becomes president.
1982 Unsuccessful coup attempt; government outlaws all opposition parties, although none have existed since 1960.
1984 More than 2,000 killed by government forces at Wajir.
1989 Daniel Teroiticharap Moi announces the release of political prisoners.
1990 Riots against one-party system.
1992 Moi reelected in multiparty elections, despite allegations of fraud.

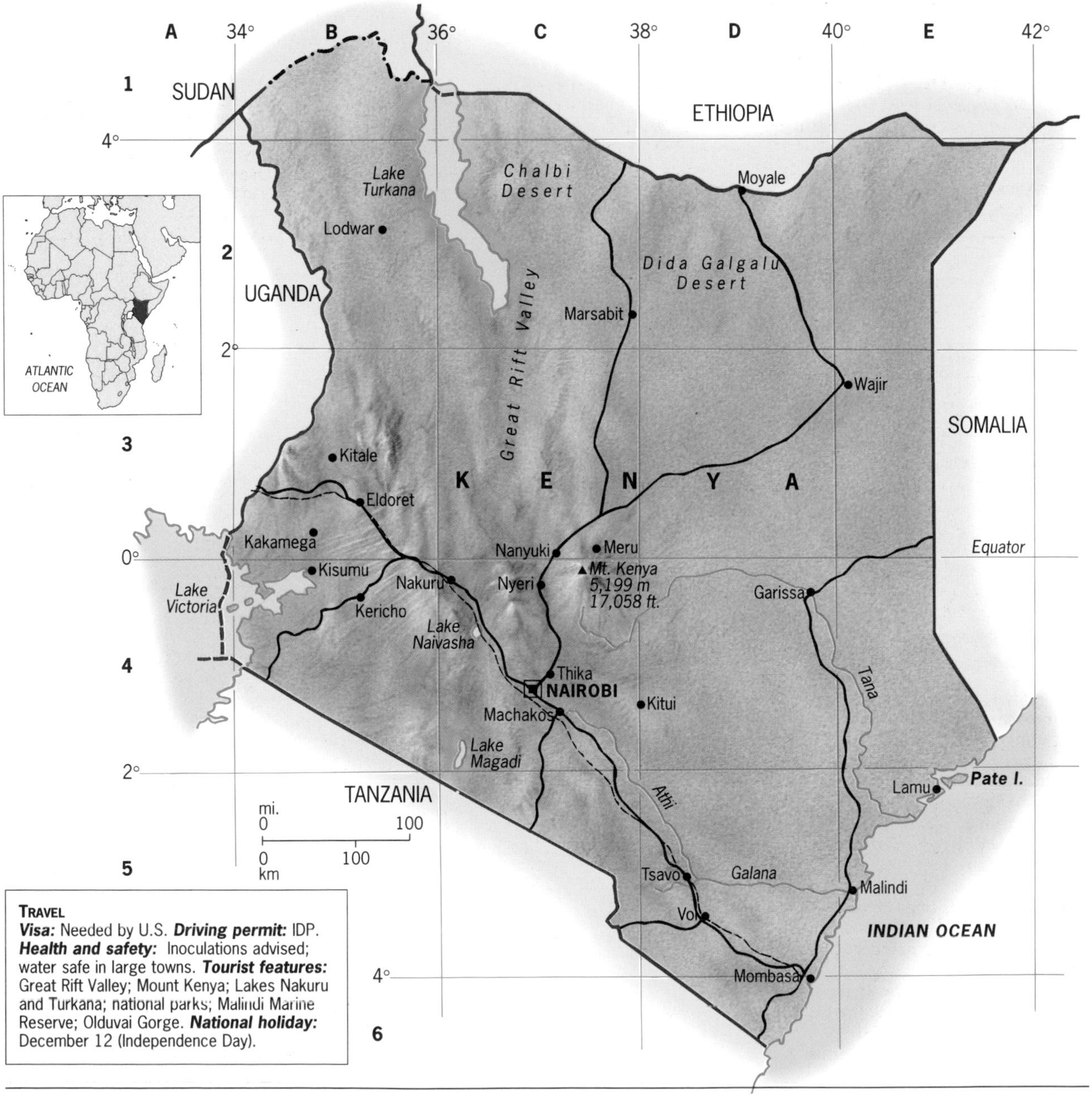

UGANDA

Area: 93,065 sq. mi./241,038 km². *Local name:* Republic of Uganda. *Currency:* Uganda shilling. *Capital:* Kampala. *Physical features:* Mostly plateau with rim of mountains. *Climate:* Tropical; semiarid in N.E. *Time zone:* GMT +3h. *Political system:* Republic. *Head of state:* Lt. Gen. Yoweri Kaguta Museveni (from 1986). *Head of government:* George Cosmas Adyebo (from 1991). *Main exports:* Coffee, cotton, tea, tobacco. *Resources:* Copper, cobalt.

PEOPLE

Population: 19,246,000. *Distribution urban/rural:* 11%/89%. *Life expectancy:* 50(m), 52(f). *Languages:* English (official), Luganda, Swahili, other Bantu and Nilotic languages. *Ethnic groups:* Bantu, Nilotic, Nilo-Hamitic, and Sudanic groups 99%. *Religions:* Roman Catholic 33%, Protestant 33%, Muslim 16%, indigenous beliefs 18%. *Literacy rate:* 48%. *Per capita GDP:* $300.

KEY DATES
1894 Becomes a British protectorate.

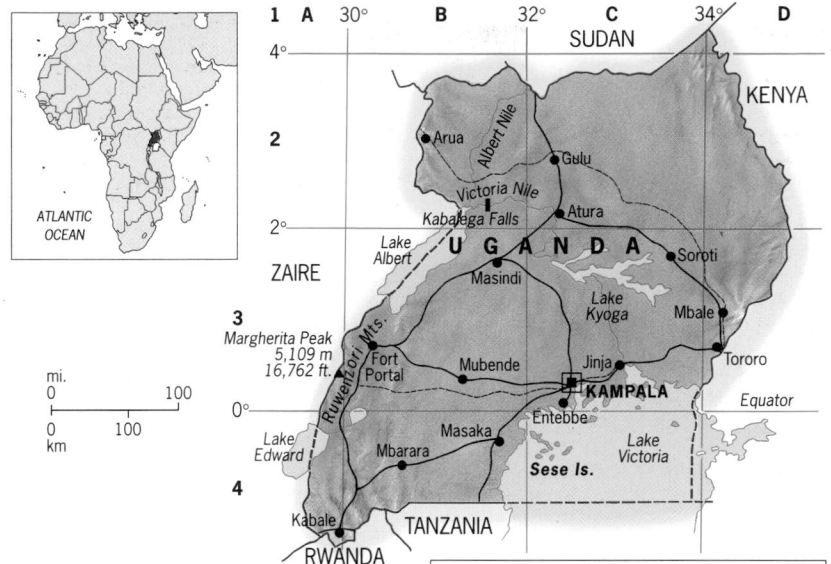

1962 Independence achieved.
1963 Proclaimed a republic.
1971–79 All Uganda's Asians are expelled, and more than 300,000 Ugandans are killed during dictatorship of Idi Amin.
1992 Draft constitution aims at creation of multiparty republic.

TRAVEL
Visa: Needed by U.S. *Driving permit:* Nat. license for 90 days. *Health and safety:* Inoculations advised; water unsafe. *Tourist features:* Ruwenzori Range; national parks; Owen Falls on White Nile where it leaves Lake Victoria; Lake Albert. *National holiday:* October 9 (Independence Day).

TANZANIA

Area: 364,880 sq. mi./945,037 km². *Local name:* Jamhuri ya Mwungano wa Tanzania. *Currency:* Tanzanian shilling. *Capital:* Dodoma. *Other city:* Dar es Salaam. *Physical features:* Coastal plains; central plateau; highlands in N. and S. *Climate:* Savanna. *Time zone:* GMT +3h. *Political system:* Republic. *Head of state:* Ali Hassan Mwinyi (from 1985). *Head of government:* John Malecela (from 1990). *Main exports:* Coffee, cotton, sisal, tea, nuts. *Resources:* Diamonds, gold.

PEOPLE

Population: 28,783,000. *Distribution urban/rural:* 32%/68%. *Life expectancy:* 50(m), 55(f). *Languages:* Swahili, English. *Ethnic groups:* Over 100 indigenous groups make up 99% of the population. *Religions:* Christian 33%, Muslim 33%, indigenous beliefs 33%. *Literacy rate:* 46%. *Per capita GDP:* $260.

KEY DATES
1890 Zanzibar becomes British protectorate.
1920 Tanganyika mandated to Britain.
1961 Tanganyika independent.
1964 Tanganyika and Zanzibar unite.
1977 One-party rule established.
1979 Help given to Uganda to oust Amin.

TRAVEL
Visa: Needed by U.S. *Driving permit:* IDP. *Health and safety:* Inoculations advised; water unsafe. *Tourist features:* Serengeti National Park; Mt. Kilimanjaro; Olduvai Gorge. *National holiday:* April 26 (Union Day).

ZAMBIA

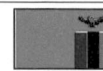

Area: 290,584 sq. mi./752,614 km². *Local name:* Republic of Zambia. *Currency:* Kwacha. *Capital:* Lusaka. *Other cities:* Kitwe, Ndola. *Physical features:* Mostly high plateau with some hills and mountains. *Climate:* Savanna; rainy season Oct.–April. *Time zone:* GMT +2h. *Political system:* Republic. *Head of state and government:* Frederick Chiluba (from 1991). *Main exports:* Copper, zinc, cobalt, lead, tobacco. *Resources:* Copper, cobalt, zinc, lead, coal, emeralds, gold, silver, uranium, hydropower potential.

PEOPLE

Population: 8,885,000. *Distribution urban/rural:* 49%/51%. *Life expectancy:* 55(m), 59(f). *Languages:* English (official), about 70 indigenous languages. *Ethnic groups:* African (chiefly Bantu) 99%, European and Asian 1%. *Religions:* Christian 66%, Muslim, Hindu, indigenous beliefs. *Literacy rate:* 73%. *Per capita GDP:* $600.

KEY DATES

1924 British government gains control.
1964 Independence achieved with Kenneth Kaunda as president.
1972 Becomes one-party state.
1970s–80s Severe economic problems.
1991 Frederick Chiluba becomes president in first free elections since 1972.
1992 Severe drought.

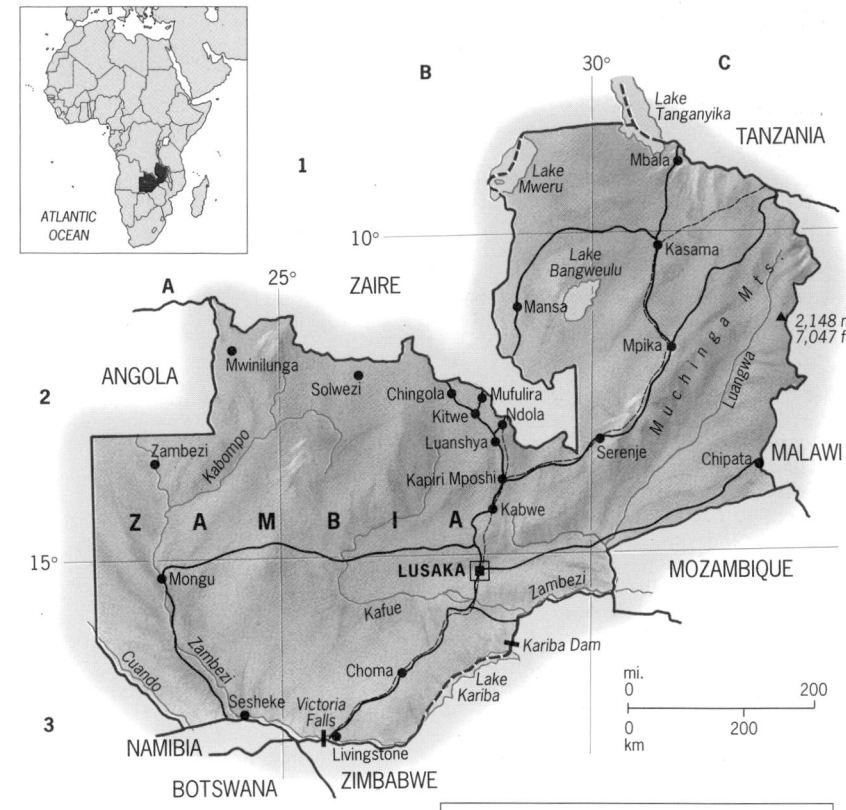

TRAVEL

Visa: Needed by U.S. *Driving permit:* IDP. *Health and safety:* Inoculations advised; water unsafe. *Tourist features:* Zambezi River; Victoria Falls; Kariba dam. *National holiday:* October 24 (Independence Day).

MALAWI

Area: 45,750 sq. mi./118,484 km². *Local name:* Republic of Malawi. *Currency:* Kwacha. *Capital:* Lilongwe. *Physical features:* Narrow plateau with rolling plains. *Climate:* Savanna. *Time zone:* GMT +2h. *Political system:* Multiparty republic. *Head of state and government:* Dr. Bakili Muluzi (from 1994). *Main exports:* Cotton, tobacco, tea, sugar, coffee, peanuts. *Resources:* Limestone, uranium, coal, bauxite.

PEOPLE

Population: 9,135,000. *Distribution urban/rural:* 15%/85%. *Life expectancy:* 48(m), 51(m). *Languages:* English and Chichewa (both official), indigenous languages. *Ethnic groups:* Chewa, Nyanja, Lomwe, and other Bantu groups 99%. *Religions:* Christian 75%, Muslim 20%, indigenous beliefs 5%. *Literacy rate:* 22%. *Per capita GDP:* $200.

KEY DATES

1891 Becomes a British protectorate.

1964 Independence achieved.
1966 Becomes one-party state.
1993 Return to multiparty politics.

TRAVEL

Visa: None needed by U.S. *Driving permit:* IDP. *Health and safety:* Inoculations advised; water unsafe. *Tourist features:* Great Rift Valley; Nyika, Kasungu, and Lengare national parks. *National holiday:* July 6 (Independence Day).

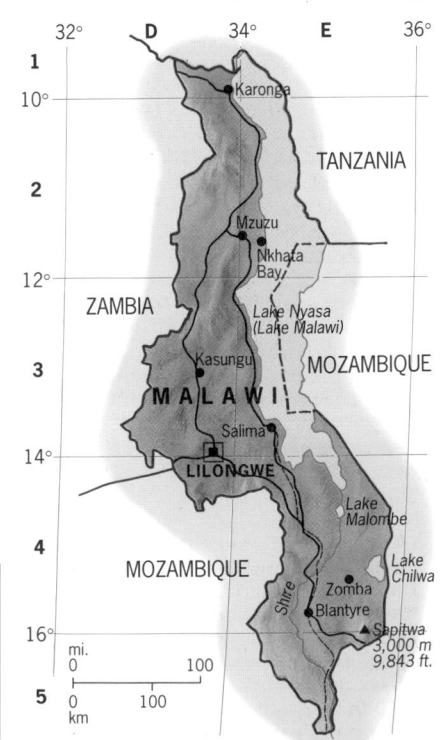

MOZAMBIQUE

Area: 308,640 sq. mi./799,380 km². **Local name:** República de Moçambique. **Currency:** Metical. **Capital:** Maputo. **Physical features:** Central highlands, mountains in W. **Climate:** Savanna/subtropical. **Time zone:** GMT +2h. **Political system:** Republic. **Head of state:** Joaqím Alberto Chissano (from 1986). **Head of government:** Mário da Graca Machungo (from 1986). **Main exports:** Shrimp, cashews, sugar, copra. **Resources:** Coal, titanium.

PEOPLE

Population: 15,322,000. **Distribution urban/rural:** n.a. **Life expectancy:** 46(m), 49(f). **Languages:** Portuguese (official), indigenous languages. **Ethnic groups:** Bantu groups 100%. **Religions:** Indigenous beliefs 60%, Christian 30%, Muslim 10%. **Literacy rate:** 33%. **Per capita GDP:** $120.

KEY DATES

1975 Independence from Portugal.
1980s Civil war and severe drought.
1989 Marxist economic policy ended.
1994 Free elections.

TRAVEL

Visa: Needed by U.S. **Driving permit:** IDP. **Health and safety:** Inoculations advised; water unsafe. **Tourist features:** Zambezi and Limpopo rivers. **National holiday:** June 25 (Independence Day).

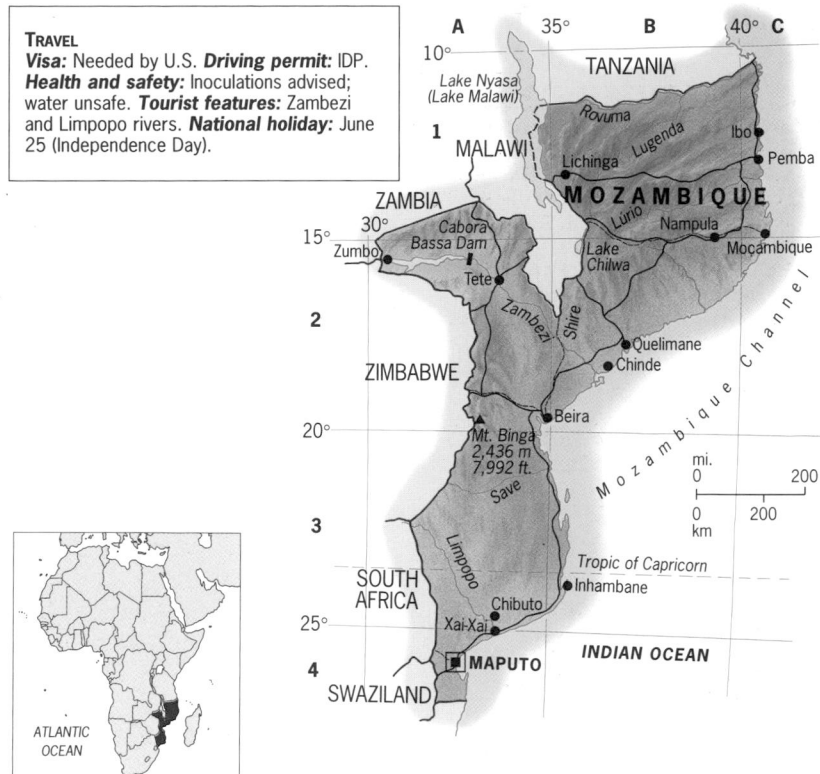

ZIMBABWE

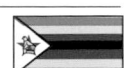

Area: 150,800 sq. mi./390,580 km². **Local name:** Republic of Zimbabwe. **Currency:** Zimbabwe dollar. **Capital:** Harare. **Physical features:** Mostly high plateau. **Climate:** Savanna/steppe. **Time zone:** GMT +2h. **Political system:** Republic. **Head of state and government:** Robert Gabriel Mugabe (from 1987). **Main exports:** Tobacco, manufactured goods, nickel, gold. **Resources:** Coal, chromium ore, gold, nickel.

PEOPLE

Population: 10,898,000. **Distribution urban/rural:** 25%/75%. **Life expectancy:** 60(m), 64(f). **Languages:** English (official), Shona, Sindebele. **Ethnic groups:** Shona and Ndebele 98%. **Religions:** Syncretic 50%, Christian 25%, indigenous beliefs 24%. **Literacy rate:** 67%. **Per capita GDP:** $660.

KEY DATES

1897 Becomes British territory of Southern Rhodesia.
1965 Unilateral Independence declared.
1966 UN imposes economic sanctions.
1979 First elections with universal suffrage bring predominantly black government to power.
1980 Independence finally recognized; name changes to Zimbabwe.

TRAVEL

Visa: None needed by U.S. **Driving permit:** IDP preferred. **Health and safety:** Inoculations advised; water unsafe. **Tourist features:** Hwange National Park, Victoria Falls; ruins of Great Zimbabwe. **National holiday:** April 18 (Independence Day).

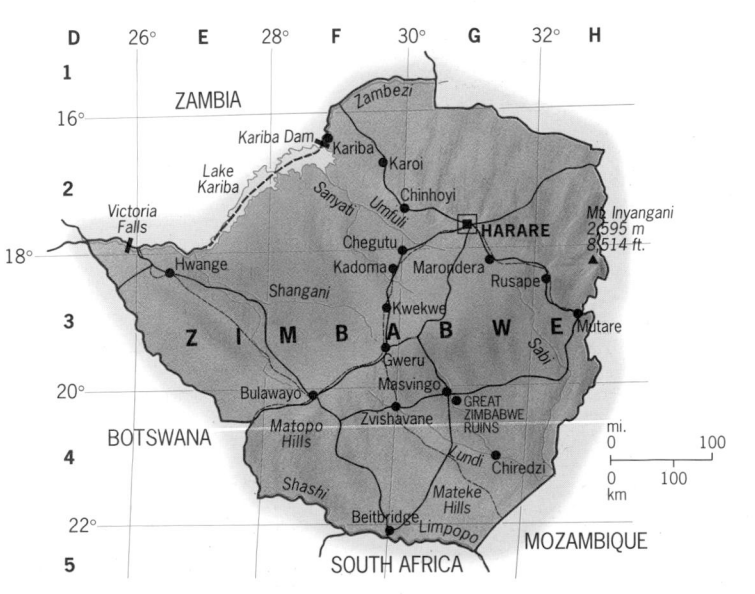

SOUTH AFRICA

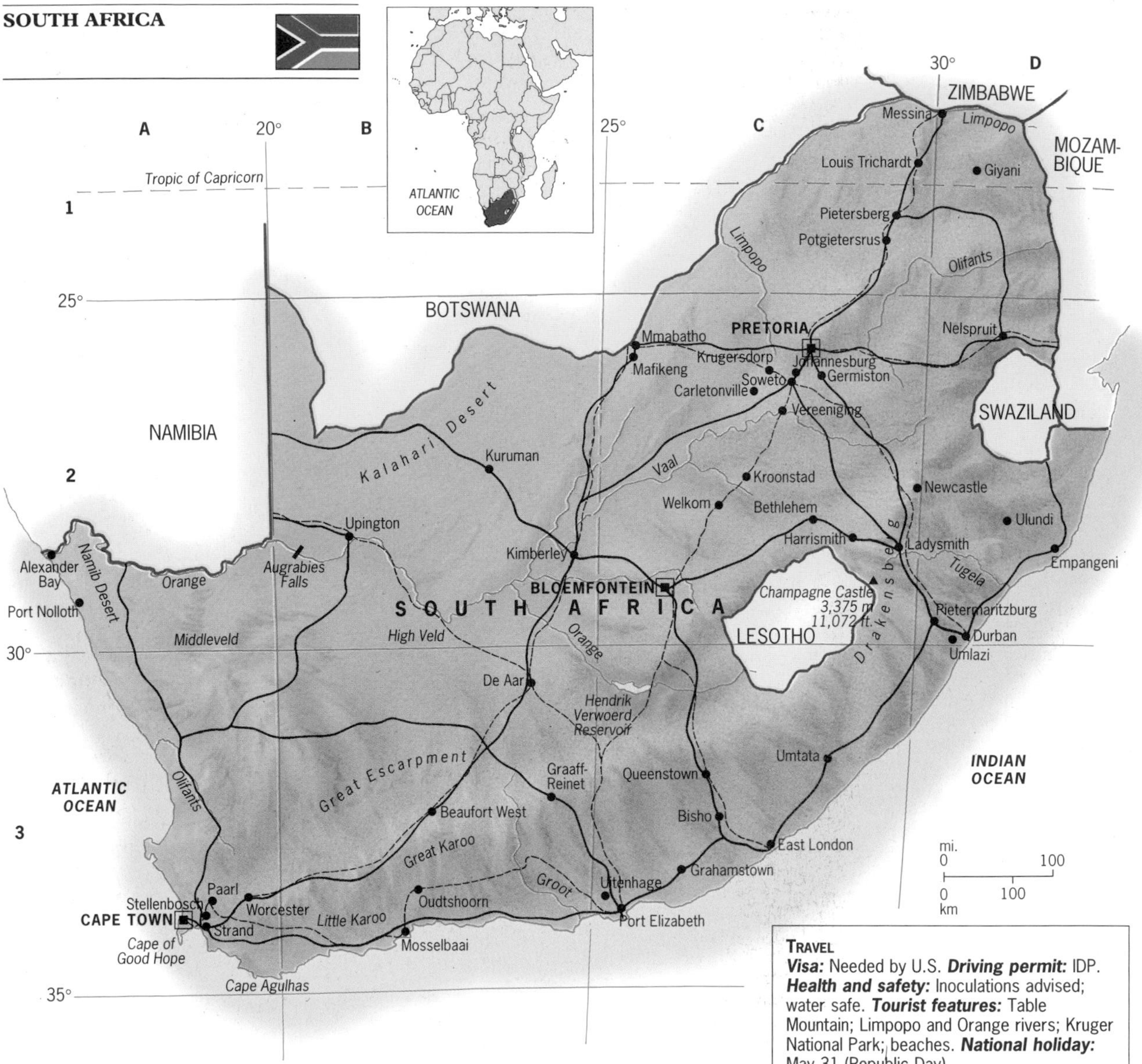

TRAVEL
Visa: Needed by U.S. **Driving permit:** IDP.
Health and safety: Inoculations advised;
water safe. **Tourist features:** Table
Mountain; Limpopo and Orange rivers; Kruger
National Park; beaches. **National holiday:**
May 31 (Republic Day).

Area: 435,047 sq. mi./1,126,771 km².
Local name: Republic of South
Africa/Republiek van Suid-Afrika.
Currency: Rand. **Capitals:** Pretoria
(administrative), Cape Town (legislative), Bloemfontein (judicial). **Other
cities:** Johannesburg, Durban.
Physical features: Vast interior
plateau surrounded by rugged hills
and narrow coastal plain. **Climate:**
Mostly savanna; subtropical along
coast. **Time zone:** GMT +2h.
Political system: Republic. **Head of
state and government:** Nelson
Mandela (from 1994). **Main exports:**
Gold, other minerals and metals, food,
machinery. **Resources:** Gold,
chromium, antimony, coal, iron ore,
manganese ore, nickel, diamonds.

PEOPLE
Population: 40,774,000. **Distribution
urban/rural:** 60%/40%. **Life expectancy:** 62(m), 67(f). **Languages:** 11 official
languages including Afrikaans, English,
Zulu, and Xhosa. **Ethnic groups:** Black
African (Zulu, Xhosa, Sotho, Tswana)
75%, white 14%, mixed and other 11%.
Religions: Dutch Reformed Church
40%, Anglican 11%, Roman Catholic
8%, other Christian 25%, Hindu,
Muslim. **Literacy rate:** 76%. **Per capita GDP:** $2,600.

KEY DATES
1652 First Dutch settlement established.
1795 British military occupation of Cape.
1814 Congress of Vienna recognizes
British occupation as permanent.
1836–38 More than 10,000 Boers leave
Cape colony (the Great Trek).

1837 Trekkers establish own government;
Zulu army attacks Boers, killing c. 500.
1838 Boers defeat Zulus at Battle of
Blood River; trekkers settle in Natal.
1868–71 Extensive alluvial diamond
deposits discovered.
1873–86 Gold discovered.
1879 Zululand comes under British control after Zulu War.
1909 Black political leaders meet to
protest exclusion of blacks from government in proposed constitution for new
South African union; convention sends
delegation to London, but it is unsuccessful.
1910 Two British colonies and two Boer
republics unite to form South Africa.
1912 South African Native National
Congress set up (later ANC).
1914 South Africa enters World War I on
Allied side.

1923 Residential segregation enforced.
1926 Blacks are banned from occupying certain skilled occupations.
1931 South Africa achieves independence within the Commonwealth of Nations.
1939 Joins World War II on Allied side.
1945 Becomes charter member of UN.
1948 National Party comes to power.
1950 System of racial segregation (apartheid) is made official under Daniel Malan; Population Registration Act classes all South Africans according to race; separate schools, universities, residential areas, and public facilities are established for each racial group.
1955 Legal obstacles to creation of further apartheid laws are removed.
1960 Major demonstrations against laws requiring blacks to carry identity papers at all times; 67 blacks are killed by police; state of emergency declared; ANC and breakaway Pan African Congress (PAC) are outlawed.
1961 South Africa leaves Commonwealth.
1962 ANC leader Nelson Mandela is imprisoned for sabotage and conspiracy.
1963 UN Security Council condemns apartheid and orders study of sanctions against South Africa.
1964 Eight ANC leaders sentenced to life imprisonment.
1965 UN General Assembly votes to terminate South African mandate over South West Africa, which is renamed Namibia; South Africa rejects all UN claims to authority and begins to integrate Namibia into its economy.
1976 Soweto uprising: 176 die when police open fire on demonstrators protesting against compulsory teaching of Afrikaans in all schools; violence breaks out within the black population.
1977 Continued violence in Soweto; death in custody of PAC activist Steve Biko; Transkei and Bophuthatswana homelands granted independence.
1978 P. W. Botha prime minister.
1981 South Africa begins military operations in Angola and covertly backs Renamo rebel forces in Mozambique.
1984 New constitution gives segregated representation to Coloureds and Asians and changes P. W. Botha's title to president; outbreaks of violence between rival black groups in townships; South Africa signs nonaggression pact with Mozambique.
1985 Violence increases in black townships; state of emergency imposed.
1986 Trade sanctions imposed by EC, Commonwealth, and U.S.A.
1988 South Africa agrees to withdraw from Angola and to grant Namibia independence in 1990.
1989 P. W. Botha suffers stroke and resigns; F. W. de Klerk president.
1990 Ban on ANC lifted; Nelson Mandela released from prison; fighting in townships continues.
1991 Remaining apartheid laws repealed; Mandela elected ANC president; revelations of government support for Zulu

Inkatha strains relationship with ANC; U.S.A. lifts sanctions; PAC and Zulu leader Mangosuthu Buthelezi boycott negotiations about constitutional reforms.
1992 New constitution leading to free elections is approved in all-white referendum; massacre of civilians at Boipatong by Inkatha, aided by police, threatens constitutional talks.
1993 ANC leader Chris Hani assassinated by white extremist; July: riots; Oct.: Mandela and de Klerk named as joint winners of Nobel Peace Prize.
1994 Nelson Mandela elected president.

ECONOMY

South Africa is one of the world's wealthiest countries in terms of mineral resources, which include vast deposits of diamonds and the largest deposits of gold in the world. Before World War I, the economy was based largely on mining. Since then, the industrial sector has developed rapidly to become the most advanced in Africa. In the 1950s–70s, government policies encouraging foreign investment led to phenomenal industrial growth, and under the old regime the exploitation of cheap labor among blacks benefited the economy.

In spite of sanctions during the 1980s, South Africa has managed to maintain profitable trade links with a number of countries including the U.S.A., U.K., Japan, Germany, Switzerland, France, and the Netherlands.

Industry by sector
Farming Despite harsh physical conditions in some areas that render only 15% of the land suitable for growing crops, South Africa is self-sufficient in food production. The chief food crops are corn, sorghum, wheat, oats, barley, and sugarcane. Livestock farming is important, and cattle, sheep, goats, and pigs are raised. Wool is a major export. Other products are fruit, tobacco, and wine.
Fishing Catches include anchovy, pilchard, herring, mackerel, and hake. The fleet has more than 4,000 vessels.
Mining South Africa has a vast mineral wealth and is by far the world's largest producer of gold. Other products include diamonds, coal, copper, iron ore, manganese, chromite, platinum, and uranium.
Industry Trade sanctions against South Africa spurred development of self-sufficient local industries, especially in the armaments, electronics, and chemicals fields. Machinery, iron and steel, vehicles, and processed foods are also produced.

PROVINCES OF SOUTH AFRICA

In November 1993, the South African transitional executive council, formed to prepare the country for its first free elections, created nine new provinces, each of which would send representatives to the National Assembly.

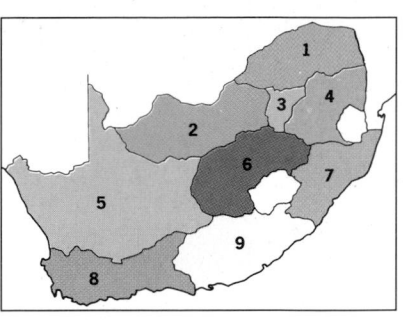

Northern Transvaal 1, Northwest 2, Gauteng 3, Eastern Transvaal 4, Northern Cape 5, Orange Free State 6, Kwazulu Natal 7, Western Cape 8, Eastern Cape 9.

(in alphabetical order)
EASTERN CAPE
Area: 65,880 sq. mi./170,616 km². *Population:* 6,665,400. *Racial composition:* Black 87.2%, Colored 6.7%, white 5.9%, Asian 0.2%. *Assembly seats:* 26.

EASTERN TRANSVAAL
Area: 31,592 sq. mi./81,816 km². *Population:* 2,838,500. *Racial composition:* Black 84.6%, white 14%, Colored 0.9%, Asian 0.5%. *Assembly seats:* 14.

GAUTENG
Area: 7,244 sq. mi./18,760 km². *Population:* 6,847,000. *Racial composition:* Black 70.6%, white 24.6%, Colored 3.2%, Asian 1.6%. *Assembly seats:* 43.

KWAZULU NATAL
Area: 35,324 sq. mi./91,481 km². *Population:* 8,549,000. *Racial composition:* Black 80%, Asian 11%, white 7.5%, Colored 1.5%. *Assembly seats:* 40.

NORTHERN CAPE
Area: 140,305 sq. mi./363,389 km². *Population:* 763,900. *Racial composition:* Colored 53.9%, black 31%, white 14.9%, Asian 0.2%. *Assembly seats:* 4.

NORTHERN TRANSVAAL
Area: 46,183 sq. mi./119,606 km². *Population:* 5,120,600. *Racial composition:* Black 97.1%, white 2.7%, Asian 0.1%, Colored 0.1%. *Assembly seats:* 20.

NORTHWEST
Area: 45,834 sq. mi./118,710 km². *Population:* 3,506,800. *Racial composition:* Black 86.5%, white 10.4%, Colored 2.8%, Asian 0.3%. *Assembly seats:* 17.

ORANGE FREE STATE
Area: 49,980 sq. mi./129,437 km². *Population:* 2,804,600. *Racial composition:* Black 85.2%, white 12.1%, Colored 2.7%. *Assembly seats:* 15.

WESTERN CAPE
Area: 49,960 sq. mi./129,386 km². *Population:* 3,620,200. *Racial composition:* Colored 59.7%, white 22.1%, black 17.8%, Asian 0.7%. *Assembly seats:* 21.

BOTSWANA

Area: 224,606 sq. mi./581,730 km². **Local name**: Republic of Botswana. **Currency**: Pula. **Capital**: Gaborone. **Other cities**: Mahalapye, Serowe. **Physical features**: Mostly flat to gently rolling plains. **Climate**: Steppe. **Time zone**: GMT +2h. **Political system**: Republic. **Head of state and government**: Quett K. J. Masire (from 1980). **Main exports**: Diamonds, beef, copper, nickel. **Resources**: Diamonds, copper, nickel, salt, potash, coal, iron ore, gas.

PEOPLE

Population: 1,143,000. **Distribution urban/rural**: 25%/75%. **Life expectancy**: 59(m), 65(f). **Languages**: English (official), Setswana (national). **Ethnic groups**: Tswana 95%; Kalanga, Basarwa, other 5%. **Religions**: Indigenous beliefs 50%, Christian 50%. **Literacy rate**: 23%. **Per capita GDP**: $2,800.

KEY DATES

1885 Becomes British Protectorate.
1960 Bechuanaland People's Party formed as independence movement.
1966 Full independence achieved.
1967 Diamonds discovered near Orapa.
1976 New unit of currency, the pula,

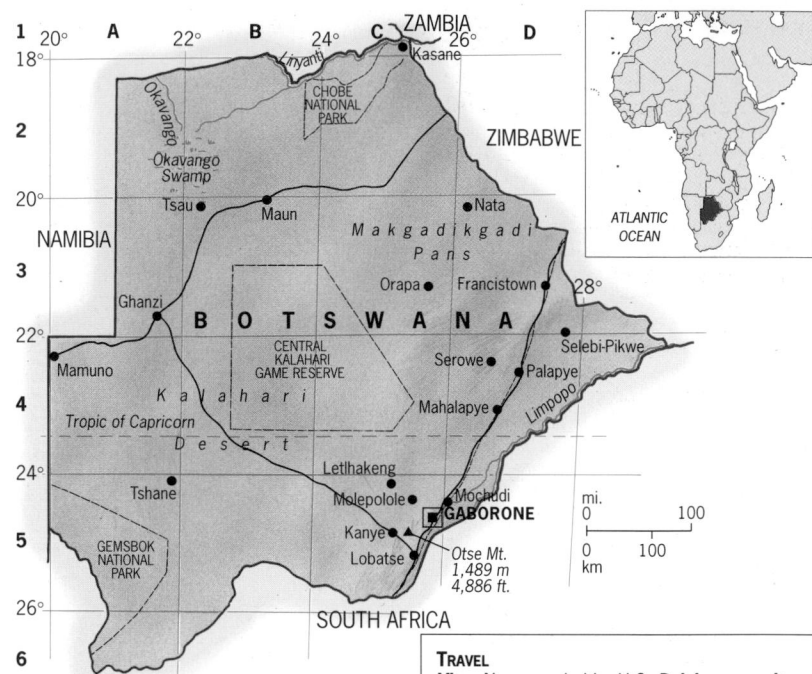

adopted instead of South African rand.
1986 Rapid economic growth; South Africa carries out raids on Gaborone in retaliation for suspected harboring of ANC members.

LESOTHO

Area: 11,721 sq. mi./30,355 km². **Local name**: Kingdom of Lesotho. **Currency**: Loti. **Capital**: Maseru. **Physical features**: Mostly highland. **Climate**: Subtropical. **Time zone**: GMT +2h. **Political system**: Constitutional monarchy. **Head of state**: King Moshoeshoe II (from 1995). **Head of government**: Ntsu Mokhehle (from 1993). **Main exports**: Wool, mohair, wheat, diamonds. **Resources**: Diamonds.

PEOPLE

Population: 1,882,000. **Distribution urban/rural**: n.a. **Life expectancy**: 60(m), 63(f). **Languages**: Sesotho and English (both official). **Ethnic groups**: Sotho nearly 100%. **Religions**: Christian 80%, indigenous beliefs 20%. **Literacy rate**: 59%. **Per capita GDP**: $240.

KEY DATES

1868 Becomes a British protectorate.
1966 Independence achieved as Kingdom of Lesotho.
1970 State of emergency declared and constitution suspended.
1985 Elections canceled because of lack of opposition candidates.
1986 South African border blockade

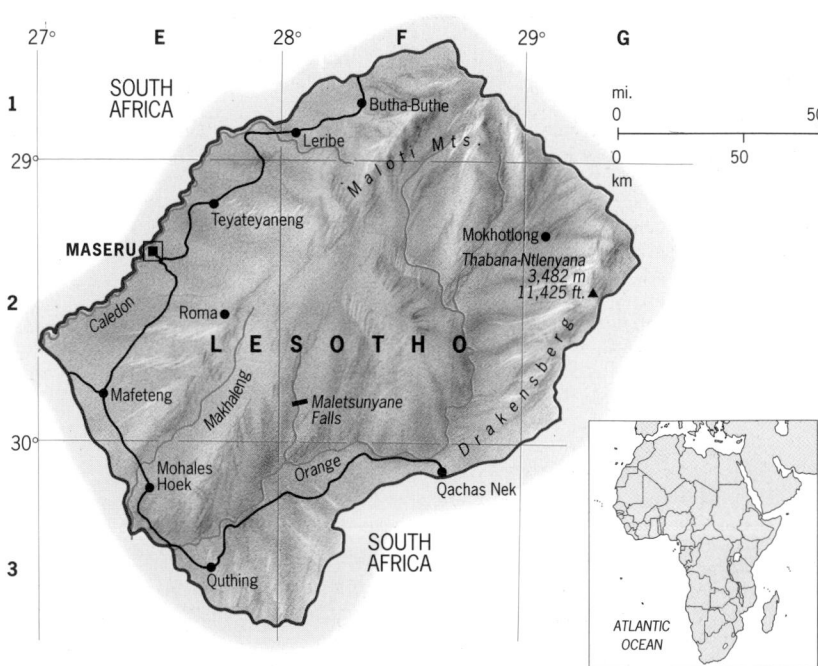

extradites 60 ANC members; military coup.
1990 King Moshoeshoe dethroned by military council; King Letsie III comes to the throne.
1991 Military coup.
1993 Free elections end military rule.
1995 Letsie III Steps down in favor of his father, Moshoeshoe II.

NAMIBIA

Area: 318,250 sq. mi./824,268 km². **Local name:** Republic of Namibia. **Currency:** Namibian dollar. **Capital:** Windhoek. **Physical features:** Mostly high plateau and desert. **Climate:** Arid. **Time zone:** GMT +2h. **Political system:** Republic. **Head of state and government:** Sam Nujoma (from 1990). **Main exports:** Diamonds, uranium, zinc, copper, cattle, fish. **Resources:** Diamonds, uranium, copper, gold, tin, lead, lithium, cadmium, zinc, salt.

PEOPLE

Population: 1,584,000. **Distribution urban/rural:** 33%/67%. **Life expectancy:** 58(m), 63(f). **Languages:** English (official), Afrikaans, German, about 15 indigenous languages. **Ethnic groups:** Ivambo 50%, Kavango 10%, Herero 7%, Damara 7%, white 7%, mixed and other 19%. **Religion:** Christianity. **Literacy rate:** 38%. **Per capita GDP:** $1,400.

KEY DATES

1884 Germany annexes South West Africa (Namibia).
1920 Mandated to South Africa.
1960 South West Africa People's Organization (SWAPO) formed.
1965 UN ends South African mandate.

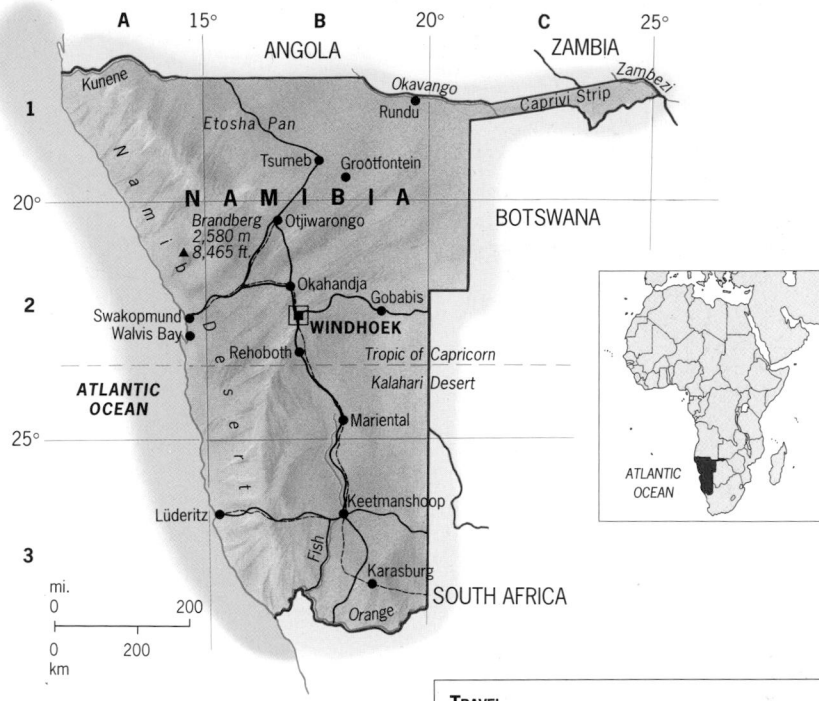

1966 Apartheid laws extend to Namibia; SWAPO launch guerilla war.
1968 South West Africa renamed Namibia.
1989 SWAPO assault from Angola.
1990 Independence achieved.

TRAVEL
Visa: None needed by U.S. **Driving permit:** IDP. **Health and safety:** Inoculations advised; water unsafe. **Tourist features:** Namib Desert; Etosha Game Park; Skeleton Coast; Orange River; Walvis Bay. **National holiday:** March 21 (Independence Day).

SWAZILAND

Area: 6,704 sq. mi./17,363 km². **Local name:** Kingdom of Swaziland. **Currency:** Lilangeni. **Capital:** Mbabane. **Physical features:** Mostly mountainous. **Climate:** Subtropical. **Time zone:** GMT +2h. **Political system:** Monarchy. **Head of state:** King Mswati III (from 1986). **Head of government:** Prince Jameson Moilini Dlamini (from 1994). **Main exports:** Soft drink concentrates, sugar, wood pulp, citrus. **Resources:** Asbestos, coal, clay, cassiterite, hydropower, wood, gold, diamonds, quarry stone.

PEOPLE

Population: 814,000. **Distribution urban/rural:** 30%/70%. **Life expectancy:** 52(m), 60(f). **Languages:** English and Swazi (both official). **Ethnic groups:** Black (chiefly Bantu) 97%, European 3%. **Religions:** Christian 60%, indigenous beliefs 40%. **Literacy rate:** 55%. **Per capita GDP:** $725.

KEY DATES

1894 South Africa gains control.
1902 Britain takes over.
1968 Independence achieved as constitu-

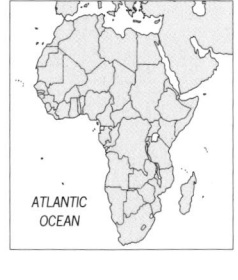

TRAVEL
Visa: None needed by U.S. **Driving permit:** IDP. **Health and safety:** Inoculations advised; water safe in towns. **Tourist features:** National parks, nature reserves. **National holiday:** September 6 (Independence Day).

tional monarchy under Sobhuza II; British draw up constitution.
1973 King Sobhuza II abolishes British constitution; commission appointed to draw up new Swazi constitution.
1982 Sobhuza dies after reign of 82 years.

1986 Sobhuza's son, Prince Makhosetive, installed as King Mswati III.
1987 Mswati dissolves parliament; new government elected.
1992 Mswati dissolves parliament again and assumes "executive powers."

MADAGASCAR

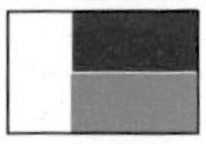

Area: 226,657 sq. mi./587,041 km². *Local name:* Repoblika Demokratikaȟi Malagasy. *Currency:* Malagasy franc. *Capital:* Antananarivo. *Other cities:* Fianarantsoa, Mahajanga. *Physical features:* Narrow coastal plain, mountains in center. *Climate:* Tropical. *Time zone:* GMT +3h. *Political system:* Republic. *Head of state:* Albert Zafy (from 1993). *Head of government:* Francisque Ravony (from 1993). *Main exports:* Coffee, sisal, vanilla, cloves, sugar, petroleum products. *Resources:* Graphite, chromite, coal, bauxite, salt, quartz, tar sands, semiprecious stones, mica, fish.

PEOPLE

Population: 13,259,000. *Distribution urban/rural:* 22%/78%. *Life expectancy:* 51(m), 55(f). *Languages:* French and Malagasy (both official). *Ethnic groups:* Chiefly groups of Malayo-Indonesian origin in highlands; groups of mixed African, Malayo-Indonesian, and Arab ancestry on coast. *Religions:* Indigenous beliefs 52%, Christian 41%, Muslim 7%. *Literacy rate:* 80%. *Per capita GDP:* $200.

KEY DATES

1810 Radama I becomes king; he plays on Franco-British rivalry to keep Madagascar independent and encourages modernization.

1896 Becomes a French colony.

1914–18 Malagasy leaders begin to demand independence.

1947–49 Independence activists lead armed revolt against French rule.

1958 Internal self-government achieved.

1960 Full independence achieved as Malagasy Republic with Philibert Tsiranana as president; he allows France to maintain much control.

1972 Demonstrations calling for Philibert Tsiranana's resignation; military takes over government and severs many ties with France.

1975 Martial law imposed under national military directorate; new Marxist constitution proclaims the Democratic Republic of Madagascar.

1977 National Front for the Defence of the Malagasy Socialist Revolution (FNDR) becomes sole legal political organization.

1980 Marxism abandoned.

1990 Opposition parties legalized.

1991 Antigovernment demonstrations and general strike almost result in government being overthrown.

1992 First multiparty elections won by Democrat coalition.

1993 Albert Zafy, leader of coalition, becomes president.

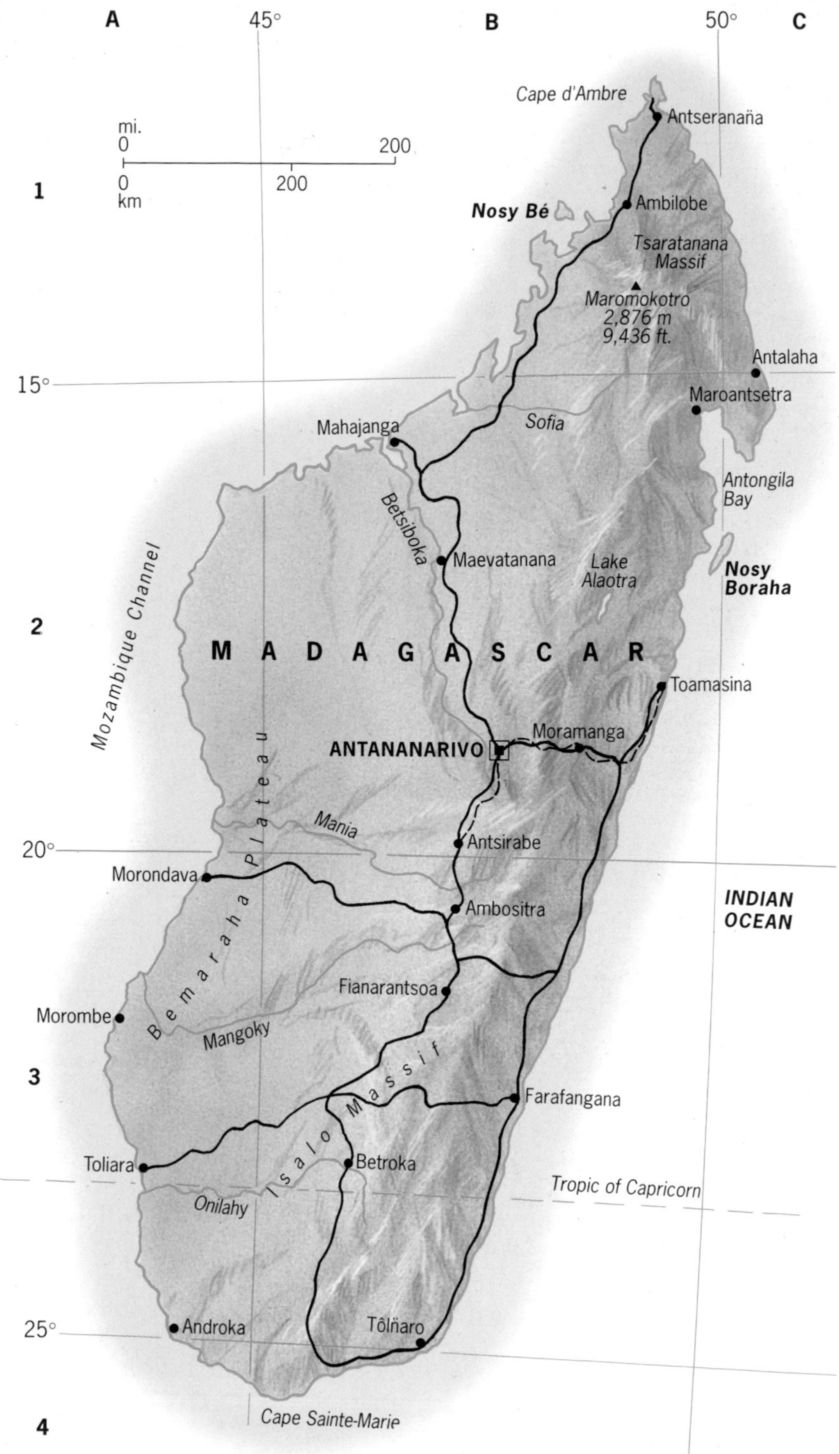

TRAVEL
Visa: Needed by U.S. *Driving permit:* Some licenses recognized. *Health and safety:* Inoculations advised; water unsafe. *Tourist feature:* Unique wildlife including endangered lemurs. *National holiday:* June 26 (Independence Day).

COMOROS

Area: 719 sq. mi./1,862 km². *Local name:* Jumhuriyat al-Qumur al-Itthadiyah al-Islamiyah. *Currency:* Comorian franc. *Capital:* Moroni. *Physical features:* Volcanic islands. *Climate:* Tropical. *Time zone:* GMT +3h. *Political system:* Republic. *Head of state:* Said Mohammad Djohar (from 1989). *Head of government:* Mohammed Abdou Mahd (from 1994). *Main exports:* Vanilla, cloves, essential oils, copra. *Resources:* Negligible.

PEOPLE
Population: 607,000. *Distribution urban/rural:* n.a. *Life expectancy:* 55(m), 59(f). *Languages:* Arabic and French (both official), Comoran. *Ethnic groups:* Antalote, Cafre, Makoa, Oimatsaha. *Religions:* Sunni Muslim 86%, Roman Catholic 14%. *Literacy rate:* 48%. *Per capita GDP:* $540.

KEY DATES
1841–86 France gains control.
1976 Islands of Njazidja, Mwali, and Nzwami gain independence.
1989 President Abdallah assassinated; Said Mohammad Djohar elected president.
1990–92 Unsuccessful coup attempts.

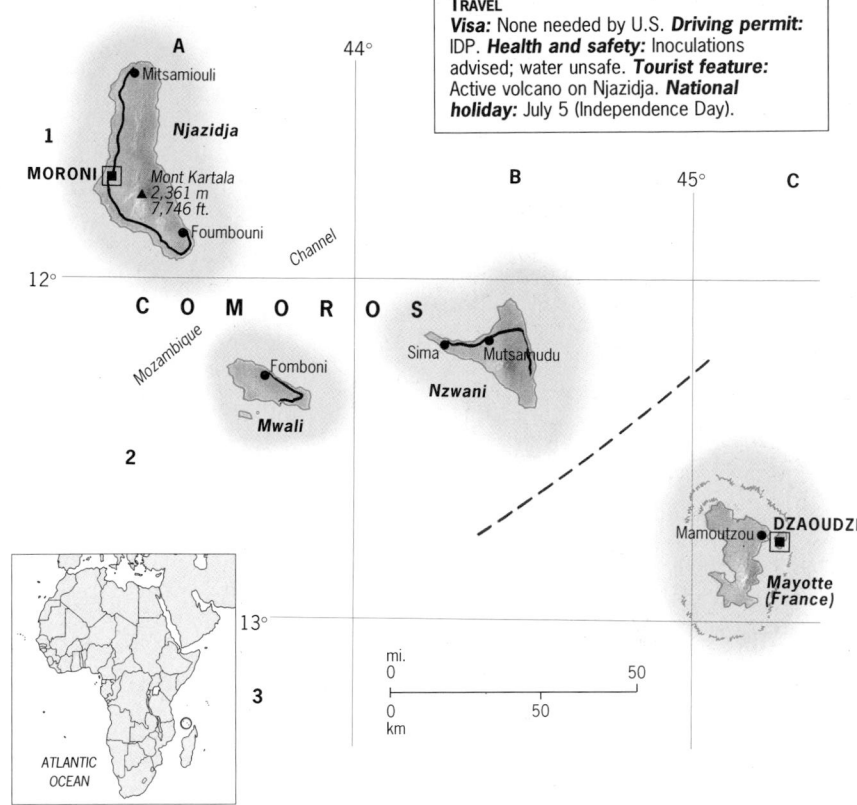

TRAVEL
Visa: None needed by U.S. *Driving permit:* IDP. *Health and safety:* Inoculations advised; water unsafe. *Tourist feature:* Active volcano on Njazidja. *National holiday:* July 5 (Independence Day).

SEYCHELLES

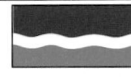

Area: 176 sq. mi./455 km². *Local name:* Republic of Seychelles. *Currency:* Seychelles rupee. *Capital:* Victoria. *Physical features:* More than 100 islands, half coral, half granite. *Climate:* Tropical marine. *Time zone:* GMT +4h. *Political system:* Republic. *Head of state and government:* France-Albert René (from 1977). *Main exports:* Fish, copra. *Resources:* Fish, copra, cinnamon.

PEOPLE
Population: 72,000. *Distribution urban/rural:* 60%/40%. *Life expectancy:* 65(m), 75(f). *Languages:* English and French (both official), Creole. *Ethnic groups:* Seychellois (mixed Asian/African/European) nearly 100%. *Religions:* Roman Catholic 90%, Anglican 8%, other 2%. *Literacy rate:* 85%. *Per capita GDP:* $5,200.

KEY DATES
1756 Becomes a French colony.
1814 Ceded to Britain.
1976 Independence achieved as a republic within British Commonwealth with James Mancham as president.
1977 France-Albert René president.
1979 Becomes one-party state.

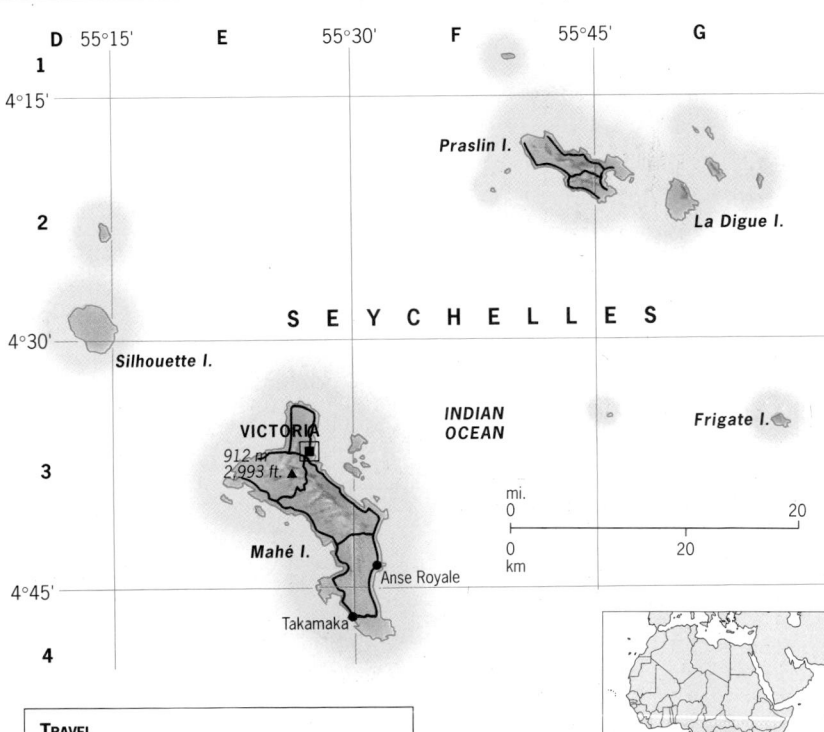

TRAVEL
Visa: None needed by U.S. *Driving permit:* Nat. license. *Health and safety:* Inoculations advised; water safe. *Tourist features:* Aklabra atoll; beaches. *National holiday:* June 5 (Liberation Day).

MAURITIUS

Area: 788 sq. mi./2,040 km². *Local name:* Mauritius. *Currency:* Mauritius rupee. *Capital:* Port Louis. *Physical features:* Mountainous volcanic island surrounded by coral reefs. *Climate:* Tropical moderated by trade winds. *Time zone:* GMT +4h. *Political system:* Parliamentary democracy. *Head of state:* Cassam Uteem (from 1992). *Head of government:* Sir Aneerood Jugnauth (from 1982). *Main exports:* Textiles, sugar, light manufacturing, toys, tea. *Resources:* Fish.

PEOPLE

Population: 1,098,000. *Distribution urban/rural:* 41%/59%. *Life expectancy:* 66(m), 73(f). *Languages:* English (official), Creole, French, Hindi, Urdu, Hakka, Bojpoori. *Ethnic groups:* Indo-Mauritian 68%, Creole 27%, Sino-Mauritian 3%, Franco-Mauritian 2%. *Religions:* Hindu 52%, Christian 28%, Muslim 17%, other 3%. *Literacy rate:* 83%. *Per capita GDP:* $2,300.

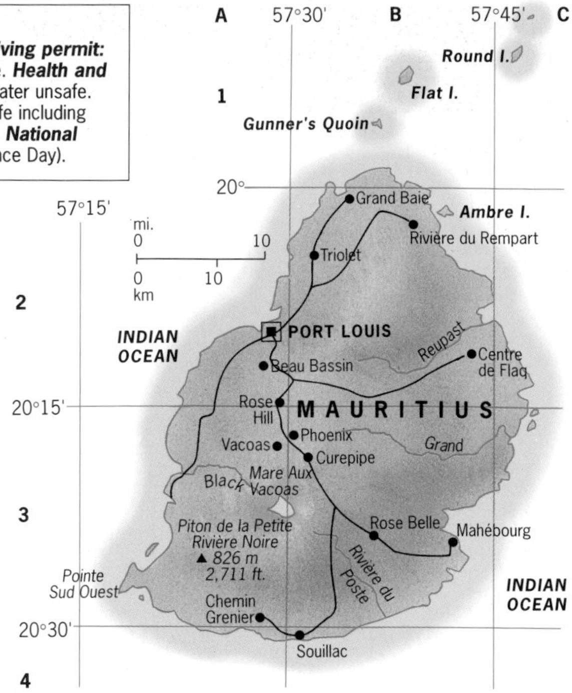

KEY DATES

1598 Dutch claim Mauritius.

TRAVEL
Visa: None needed by U.S. **Driving permit:** Nat. license endorsed by police. **Health and safety:** Inoculations advised; water unsafe. **Tourist feature:** Unusual wildlife including flying fox and ostrich; beaches. **National holiday:** March 12 (Independence Day).

1715 Becomes a French colony.
1814 Becomes a British colony.
1835–1907 Nearly 450,000 Indian laborers arrive to work on sugar plantations.

1968 Independence achieved.
1992 Becomes republic within the British Commonwealth; Cassam Uteem elected president.

INTERNATIONAL TIME ZONES

This map shows standard time zones around the world. Standard time zones begin at the prime meridian in Greenwich, U.K., and divide the world into 23 full time zones and two half-zones, going one hour forward from Greenwich Mean Time for every zone passed to the west, and one hour back for each zone passed to the east. The 12th zone east and the 12th zone west are each half a zone wide and are separated by the International Date Line.

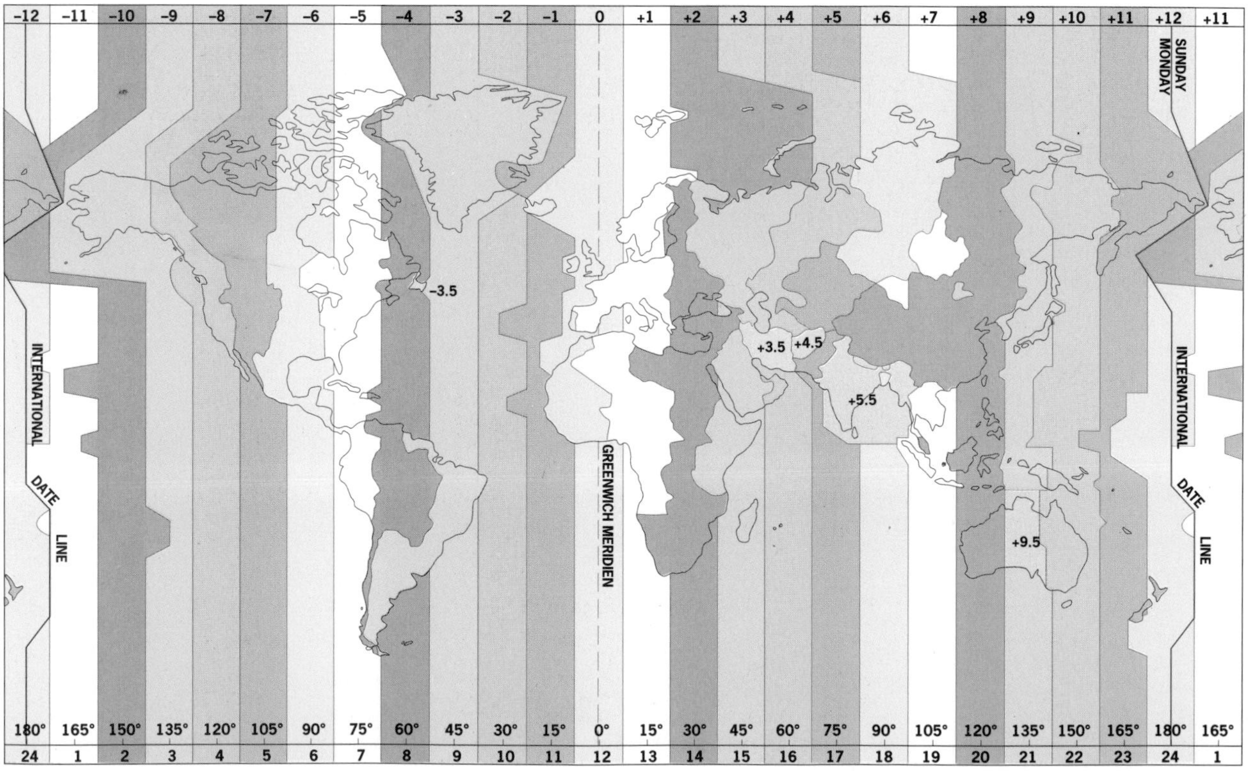

INDEPENDENT MEMBERS OF THE BRITISH COMMONWEALTH

Country	Year joined
Antigua and Barbuda	1981
Australia	1931
Bahamas	1973
Bangladesh	1972
Barbados	1966
Belize	1982
Botswana	1966
Brunei	1984
Canada	1931
Cyprus	1961
Dominica	1978
Gambia	1965
Ghana	1957
Grenada	1974
Guyana	1966
India	1947
Jamaica	1962
Kenya	1957
Kiribati	1968
Lesotho	1966
Malaysia	1957
Malawi	1964
Maldives	1982
Malta	1964
Mauritius	1968
Namibia	1990
Nauru	1931
New Zealand	1931
Nigeria	1960
Pakistan*	1947
Papua New Guinea	1975
St. Christopher Nevis	1983
St. Lucia	1979
St. Vincent and the Grenadines	1979
Seychelles	1976
Sierra Leone	1961
Singapore	1965
Solomon Islands	1978
South Africa**	1910
Sri Lanka	1948
Tanzania	1961
Tonga	1970
Trinidad and Tobago	1962
Tuvalu	1978
Uganda	1962
Vanuatu	1980
Western Samoa	1970
Zambia	1964
Zimbabwe	1980

* Withdrew in 1972; readmitted in 1989.

** Withdrew in 1961; readmitted in 1994.

LARGEST COUNTRIES

Country	Population (thousands)	Country	Area (thousands) sq m	km²
China	1,205,181	Russia	6,591	17,076
India	896,567	Canada	3,852	9,976
U.S.A.	254,521	China	3,696	9,573
Indonesia	189,136	U.S.A.	3,619	9,369
Brazil	151,534	Brazil	3,287	8,512
Russia	148,366	Australia	2,966	7,682
Japan	124,460	India	1,222	3,166
Pakistan	122,802	Argentina	1,073	2,780
Bangladesh	122,210	Kazakhstan	1,049	2,717
Mexico	92,381	Sudan	968	2,506
Nigeria	88,515	Algeria	920	2,382
Germany	81,187	Zaire	905	2,345
Vietnam	70,902	Saudi Arabia	849	2,200
Philippines	65,649	Mexico	760	1,967
Iran	63,180	Indonesia	741	1,919
Turkey	58,775	Libya	679	1,760
Thailand	58,584	Iran	636	1,648
U.K.	57,827	Mongolia	605	1,567
France	57,660	Chad	494	1,284
Italy	57,057	Niger	489	1,267
Ethiopia	56,900	Peru	480	1,244
Egypt	56,488	Angola	481	1,247
Ukraine	52,179	Mali	479	1,240
South Korea	44,149	Ethiopia	426	1,158
Zaire	41,166	Columbia	441	1,142
South Africa	40,774	South Africa	435	1,127
Spain	39,434	Bolivia	424	1,099
Poland	37,459	Mauritania	398	1,031
Myanmar (Burma)	35,308	Tanzania	364	945
Colombia	33,951	Nigeria	357	924
Argentina	33,778	Venezuela	352	912
Tanzania	28,783	Namibia	318	824
Sudan	28,129	Mozambique	309	799
Algeria	27,070	Pakistan	307	796
Morocco	26,069	Turkey	301	781

POPULATION

Fastest growing	Growth rate Annual (1960–92) (%)	Projected (1992–2000) (%)	Slowest growing	Growth rate Annual (1960–92) (%)	Projected (1992–2000) (%)
UAE	9.6	2.1	St. Christopher– Nevis	-0.6	-0.2
Qatar	7.5	2.3	Hungary	0.2	0.0
Djibouti	5.7	2.9	Austria	0.3	0.3
Saudi Arabia	4.4	3.3	Belgium	0.3	0.1
Libya	4.1	3.4	Germany	0.3	0.4
Bahrain	3.9	2.6	U.K.	0.3	0.2
Côte d'Ivoire	3.9	2.7	Barbados	0.4	0.4
Brunei	3.8	2.1	Bulgaria	0.4	-0.1
Oman	3.8	3.5	Czechoslovakia	0.4	0.4
Kenya	3.5	3.3	Denmark	0.4	0.2
Malawi	3.4	2.6	Finland	0.4	0.3
Syria	3.4	3.5	Italy	0.4	0.1
Solomon Islands	3.4	3.3	Malta	0.4	0.7
Honduras	3.3	2.8	Portugal	0.4	0.1
Iran	3.3	3.0	Sweden	0.5	0.5
Iraq	3.3	3.1	Antigua and Barbuda	0.6	0.7
Uganda	3.3	2.8	Dominica	0.6	-0.1
Botswana	3.2	2.9	Greece	0.6	0.2
Comoros	3.2	3.6	Luxembourg	0.6	0.7
Niger	3.2	3.2	Norway	0.6	0.6
Tanzania	3.2	3.2	Ukraine	0.6	0.4
Rwanda	3.2	3.3	Cyprus	0.7	0.8
Zambia	3.2	2.7	France	0.7	0.6
Zimbabwe	3.2	2.8	Ireland	0.7	-0.2
Liberia	3.1	3.2	Latvia	0.7	-0.1
Nicaragua	3.1	3.3	Romania	0.7	0.4
Venezuela	3.1	2.0	Russia	0.7	0.5
Costa Rica	3.0	2.2	Switzerland	0.7	0.6
Gabon	3.0	3.2	Uruguay	0.7	0.6
Gambia	3.0	2.5	Belarus	0.8	0.6
Jordan	3.0	3.4	Estonia	0.8	0.0
Paraguay	3.0	2.6	Poland	0.8	0.4
Zaire	3.0	3.1	Spain	0.8	0.2
Ecuador	2.9	2.1	Japan	0.9	0.4
Pakistan	2.9	2.7	Netherlands	0.9	0.7
Togo	2.9	3.1			

SMALLEST COUNTRIES

Country	Area km²	sq mi
Vatican City	0.16	0.4
Monaco	0.7	1.9
Nauru	8	21
Tuvalu	9	24
San Marino	24	61
Liechtenstein	62	160
Marshall Islands	70	181
St. Christopher- Nevis	101	261
Maldives	115	298
Malta	122	316
Grenada	133	344
St. Vincent and the Grenadines	150	388
Barbados	166	431
Antigua and Barbuda	170	442
Andorra	175	453
Seychelles	176	455
Palau	188	488
St. Lucia	238	616
Singapore	248	641
Bahrain	266	688
Micronesia, Fed States of	271	701
Kiribati	281	728
Tonga	289	748
Dominica	290	751
São Tomé and Príncipe	387	1,001
Comoros	719	1,862
Mauritius	788	2,040
Luxembourg	999	2,586
Western Samoa	1,093	2,831

LARGEST CITIES

City	Population (thousands)
Tokyo-Yokohama	27,245
Mexico City	20,899
São Paulo	18,701
Seoul	16,792
New York	14,625
Osaka-Kobe-Kyoto	13,872
Bombay	12,101
Calcutta	11,898
Rio de Janeiro	11,688
Buenos Aires	11,657
Moscow	10,446
Manila	10,156
Los Angeles	10,130
Cairo	10,099
Jakarta	9,882
Teheran	9,779
London	9,115
Delhi	8,778
Paris	8,720
Karachi	8,014
Lagos	7,998
Essen	7,452
Shanghai	6,936
Lima	6,815
Taipei	6,695
Istanbul	6,678
Chicago	6,529
Bangkok	5,955
Bogotá	5,913
Madras	5,896
Beijing	5,762
Santiago	5,378
Pusan	5,008
Tianjin	4,850
Bangalore	4,802
Nagoya	4,791
Milan	4,749
St Petersburg	4,672
Madrid	4,513
Dhaka	4,419

ECONOMIC GROWTH (1985–92)

Average annual increase in real GDP

Fastest

China	9.2	Laos	5.8
South Korea	8.9	Nigeria	5.7
Thailand	8.6	Pakistan	5.6
Botswana	7.5	Chad	5.5
Mauritius	6.9	Lesotho	5.5
Taiwan	6.5	Malta	5.5
Singapore	6.3	Oman	5.5
Chile	6.2	India	5.2
Malaysia	6.2	Nepal	5.0
Cyprus	6.1	Turkey	5.0
Hong Kong	6.1	Ireland	4.8
Bhutan	5.9	Vietnam	4.8
Cambodia	5.8	Burundi	4.7
Indonesia	5.8	Ghana	4.7

Slowest

Liberia	−0.6	Libya	−2.8
Bulgaria	−0.8	Cameroon	−3.2
Peru	−0.9	Afghanistan	−3.8
Belarus	−1.2	Albania	−4.5
Former		Latvia	−4.8
Czechoslovakia	−1.4	Slovenia	−5.1
Trinidad		Estonia	−5.1
and Tobago	−1.5	Azerbaijan	−5.4
Surinam	−1.5	Romania	−5.5
Kyrgyzstan	−1.7	Moldova	−5.5
Hungary	−1.7	Lithuania	−6.0
Haiti	−2.5	Armenia	−9.8
Nicaragua	−2.6	Iraq	−14.3
Ukraine	−2.8	Georgia	−14.5

POPULATION IN WORK (1991–92)

Highest

	%		%
Singapore	57.6	Switzerland	51.5
Denmark	56.7	Bahamas	51.0
Thailand	56.3	Ukraine	50.8
Latvia	55.1	Estonia	50.5
Burundi	52.9	U.S.A.	50.4
Japan	52.9	Germany	50.2
Russia	52.6	Finland	50.1
Belarus	52.5	Macao	50.1
Sweden	52.3	U.K.	49.9
Lithuania	51.7	Norway	49.8
Former		Canada	49.6
Czechoslovakia	51.6	Hong Kong	49.5

Lowest

	%		%
India	37.6	Senegal	34.0
South Africa	37.5	Guatemala	33.5
Mexico	37.5	Botswana	33.4
Chile	37.5	Morocco	32.5
Venezuela	37.3	Puerto Rico	32.4
Malta	37.2	Nigeria	31.1
Turkey	36.5	Egypt	30.7
Israel	36.5	Tunisia	29.8
Fiji	35.2	Pakistan	28.0
Honduras	34.8	Syria	27.8
Ecuador	34.8	Iran	26.0
Nicaragua	34.7	Surinam	21.2

Figures do not include part-time, temporary, or informal workers.

WOMEN IN THE WORKFORCE (1991–92)

	female workers %		female workers %
Highest			
Burundi	53	Finland	47
Malawi	51	Jamaica	47
Burkina Faso	49	Niger	47
Grenada	49	Thailand	47
Barbados	48	Trinidad and	
Mozambique	48	Tobago	47
Sweden	48	Vietnam	47
Tanzania	48	Bulgaria	46
Bahamas	47	Denmark	46
CAR	47	North Korea	46
Former		Romania	46
Czechoslovakia	47	Vanuatu	46

	%		%
Lowest			
Mauritania	22	Yemen	13
Guyana	21	Iran	10
Maldives	20	Jordan	10
Fiji	19	Libya	9
Bahrain	18	Afghanistan	8
Syria	18	Saudi Arabia	7
Chad	17	Qatar	7
Mali	16	Iraq	6
Dominica	15	UAE	6
Pakistan	14	Algeria	4

Figures do not include part-time, temporary, informal, or home workers.

HIGHEST HEALTH EXPENDITURE (1991)

	% of GDP spent
U.S.A.	13.3
Canada	9.9
France	9.1
Germany	9.1
Finland	8.9
Sweden	8.8
Netherlands	8.7
Australia	8.6
Nicaragua	8.6
Austria	8.5
Norway	8.4
Iceland	8.3
Italy	8.3
Belgium	8.1
Ireland	8.0
Switzerland	8.0
New Zealand	7.7
Algeria	7.0
Denmark	7.0
Japan	6.8
South Korea	6.6
Luxembourg	6.6
U.K.	6.6

ABSOLUTE POVERTY

People in absolute poverty

	(millions)
India	350.0
China	105.0
Bangladesh	93.2
Brazil	72.4
Indonesia	47.8
Nigeria	46.4
Vietnam	37.6
Philippines	35.2
Pakistan	35.0
Ethiopia	31.9
Zaire	28.0
Mexico	26.4
Thailand	16.8
Tanzania	16.2

CALORIE CONSUMPTION (1989–90)

	Calories per person per day	%* of daily needs
Highest		
Ireland	3,952	169
Belgium	3,925	167
Greece	3,775	161
Bulgaria	3,695	156
U.S.A.	3,642	155
Denmark	3,639	155
Hungary	3,608	154
France	3,593	153
Germany	3,591	153
Czechoslovakia	3,574	152
Yugoslavia	3,545	151
Switzerland	3,508	150
Italy	3,498	149
Austria	3,486	149
Iceland	3,473	148
Spain	3,472	148
New Zealand	3,461	148
Lowest		
Malawi	2,049	87
Sudan	2,043	87
Peru	2,037	87
Bangladesh	2,037	86
Zambia	2,016	86
Bolivia	2,013	85
Burundi	1,948	85
Rwanda	1,913	83
Sierra Leone	1,899	82
Namibia	1,889	80
Somalia	1,874	80
Chad	1,852	80
CAR	1,846	79
Mozambique	1,805	77
Comoros	1,760	75
Angola	1,725	73
Ethiopia	1,658	70

*based on the recommended daily intake of 2,345 (WHO).

EDUCATIONAL EXPENDITURE (1989)

	% of GDP spent
Highest	
Libya	10.1
Surinam	9.5
Algeria	9.4
Seychelles	9.1
Guyana	8.8
Zimbabwe	8.5
Botswana	8.2
Sweden	7.5
Denmark	7.3
Morocco	7.3
Canada	7.2
St. Lucia	7.2
Côte d'Ivoire	7.0
Grenada	6.9
Barbados	6.9
Egypt	6.8
Netherlands	6.8
U.S.A.	6.8
Norway	6.7
Cuba	6.6
Lowest	
Bolivia	2.3
Burkina Faso	2.3
Myanmar (Burma)	2.2
Bangladesh	2.2
UAE	2.1
Chad	2.0
El Salvador	2.0
Namibia	1.9
Turkey	1.8
Madagascar	1.8
Haiti	1.8
Guatemala	1.8
Afghanistan	1.8
Peru	1.5
Nigeria	1.5
Argentina	1.5
Laos	1.2
Zaire	0.9
Indonesia	0.9
Somalia	0.4

MILITARY EXPENDITURE (1990–91)

	% of GDP spent
Highest	
Angola	20.0
Syria	16.8
Oman	16.4
Iraq	16.0
Yemen	14.4
Saudi Arabia	14.0
Ethiopia	13.5
Mozambique	13.0
Cuba	12.5
Qatar	12.5
Jordan	10.6
Mongolia	10.0
U.S.S.R.	10.0
Zimbabwe	9.1
Brunei	9.0
Nicaragua	9.0
Israel	8.6
New Zealand	8.6
Libya	7.8
Honduras	6.9
Tanzania	6.9
Lowest	
Guatemala	1.1
Paraguay	1.0
Japan	1.0
Austria	1.0
Nigeria	0.9
Uganda	0.8
Niger	0.8
Malta	0.8
Dominican Republic	0.8
Sierra Leone	0.7
Jamaica	0.7
Trinidad and Tobago	0.6
Ghana	0.6
Gambia	0.6
Barbados	0.6
Costa Rica	0.5
Mexico	0.3
Mauritius	0.2

Map index

Bold indicates a country that receives individual treatment.

Italics denote a physical feature

CONVERSION FACTORS

CUSTOMARY TO METRIC

		Multiply by
Length		
inches	millimeters	25.4
inches	centimeters	2.54
feet	meters	0.3048
yards	meters	0.9144
statute miles	kilometers	1.6093
nautical miles	kilometers	1.852
Area		
square inches	square centimeters	6.4516
square feet	square meters	0.0929
square yards	square meters	0.8361
acres	hectares	0.4047
square miles	square kilometers	2.5899
Volume		
cubic inches	cubic centimeters	16.3871
cubic feet	cubic meters	0.0283
cubic yards	cubic meters	0.7646
Capacity		
U.K. fluid ounces	liters	0.0284
U.S. fluid ounces	liters	0.0296
U.K. pints	liters	0.5682
U.S. pints	liters	0.4732
U.K. gallons	liters	4.546
U.S. gallons	liters	3.7854
Weight		
ounces (avoirdupois)	grams	28.3495
ounces (troy)	grams	31.1035
pounds	kilograms	0.4536
tons (short)	tonnes	0.907
Energy		
calories	joules	4.186
Power		
horsepower	kilowatts	0.7457

METRIC TO IMPERIAL

		Multiply by
Length		
millimeters	inches	0.0394
centimeters	inches	0.3937
meters	feet	3.2808
meters	yards	1.0936
kilometers	statute miles	0.6214
kilometers	nautical miles	0.54
Area		
square centimeters	square inches	0.155
square meters	square feet	10.764
square meters	square yards	1.196
hectares	acres	2.471
square kilometers	square miles	0.386
Volume		
cubic centimeters	cubic inches	0.061
cubic meters	cubic feet	35.315
cubic meters	cubic yards	1.308
Capacity		
liters	U.K. fluid ounces	35.1961
liters	U.S. fluid ounces	33.8150
liters	U.K. pints	1.7598
liters	U.S. pints	2.1134
liters	U.K. gallons	0.2199
liters	U.S. gallons	0.2642
Weight		
grams	ounces (avoirdupois)	0.0353
grams	ounces (troy)	0.0322
kilograms	pounds	2.2046
tonnes	tons (short)	1.102
Energy		
joules	calories	0.238
Power		
kilowatts	horsepower	1.341

COMMON MEASURES

	METRIC UNITS	CUSTOMARY EQUIVALENTS
Length		
	1 millimeter	0.03937in
10mm	1 centimeter	0.39in
10cm	1 decimeter	3.94in
100cm	1 meter	39.37in
1,000m	1 kilometer	0.62mile
Area		
	1mm^2	0.0016 sq. in.
	1cm^2	0.155 sq. in.
100cm^2	1dm^2	15.5 sq. in.
10,000cm^2	1m^2	10.76 sq. ft.
10,000m^2	1 hectare	2.47 acres
Volume		
	1cm^3	0.016 cu in
1,000cm^3	1m^3	61.024 cu in
1,000dm^3	1dm^3	35.31 cu ft
		1.308 cu yd
Liquid volume		
	1 liter	1.76 pints
100 litres	1 hectoliter	26.4 gallons
Weight		
	1 gram	0.035oz
1,000 g	1 kilogram	2.2046lb
1,000kg	1 tonne	0.0842 tons

	CUSTOMARY UNITS	METRIC EQUIVALENT
Length		
	1 inch	2.54cm
12in	1 foot	30.48cm
3ft	1 yard	0.9144m
1,760yd	1 mile	1.6093km
Area		
	1 square inch	6.45cm^2
144 sq. in.	1 square foot	0.0929m^2
9 sq. ft.	1 square yard	0.836m^2
4,840 sq. yd.	1 acre	0.405ha
640 acres	1 square mile	259ha
Volume		
	1 cubic inch	16.3871cm^3
1,728 cu. in.	1 cubic foot	0.028m^3
27 cu. ft.	1 cubic yard	0.765m^3
Liquid volume		
	1 pint	0.57 liter
2 pints	1 quart	1.14 liters
4 quarts	1 gallon	3.79 liters
Weight		
	1 ounce	28.3495g
16oz.	1 pound	0.4536kg
20cwt.	1 ton	0.907 tonnes

TEMPERATURE CONVERSION EQUATIONS

To convert	To	Equation
°Fahrenheit	°Celsius	−32, x5, ÷9
°Fahrenheit	°Rankine	+459.67
°Fahrenheit	°Réaumur	−32, x4, ÷9
°Celsius	°Fahrenheit	x9, ÷5, +32
°Celsius	Kelvin	+273.15
°Celsius	°Réaumur	x4, ÷5
Kelvin	°Celsius	-273.15
°Rankine	°Fahrenheit	-459.67
°Réaumur	°Fahrenheit	x9, ÷4, +32
°Réaumur	°Celsius	x5, ÷4

Carry out operations in sequence.

TEMPERATURE: Degrees Farenheit/Celsius (centigrade)

°F	°C	°F	°C
33.8	1	123.8	51
35.6	2	125.6	52
37.4	3	127.4	53
39.2	4	129.2	54
41.0	5	131.0	55
42.8	6	132.8	56
44.6	7	134.6	57
46.4	8	136.4	58
48.2	9	138.2	59
50.0	10	140.0	60
51.8	11	141.8	61
53.6	12	143.6	62
55.4	13	145.4	63
57.2	14	147.2	64
59.0	15	149.0	65
60.8	16	150.8	66
62.6	17	152.6	67
64.4	18	154.4	68
66.2	19	156.2	69
68.0	20	158.0	70
69.8	21	159.8	71
71.6	22	161.6	72
73.4	23	163.4	73
75.2	24	165.2	74
77.0	25	167.0	75
78.8	26	168.8	76
80.6	27	170.6	77
82.4	28	172.4	78
84.2	29	174.2	79
86.0	30	176.0	80
87.8	31	177.8	81
89.6	32	179.6	82
91.4	33	181.4	83
93.2	34	183.2	84
95.0	35	185.0	85
96.8	36	186.8	86
98.6	37	188.6	87
100.4	38	190.4	88
102.2	39	192.2	89
104.0	40	194.0	90
105.8	41	195.8	91
107.6	42	197.6	92
109.4	43	199.4	93
111.2	44	201.2	94
113.0	45	203.0	95
114.8	46	204.8	96
116.6	47	206.6	97
118.4	48	208.4	98
120.2	49	210.2	99
122.0	50	212.0	100

TEMPERATURE

Degrees Fahrenheit (F)/Celsius (C)

°F	°C	°F	°C	°F	°C	°F	°C	°F	°C	°F	°C	°F	°C	°F	°C
1	−17.2	28	−2.2	55	12.8	82	27.8	109	42.8	136	57.8	163	72.8	190	87.8
2	−16.7	29	−1.7	56	13.3	83	28.3	110	43.3	137	58.3	164	73.3	191	88.0
3	−16.1	30	−1.1	57	13.9	84	28.9	111	43.9	138	58.9	165	73.9	192	88.8
4	−15.5	31	−0.5	58	14.4	85	29.4	112	44.4	139	59.4	166	74.4	193	89.4
5	−15.0	32	0.0	59	15.0	86	30.0	113	45.0	140	60.0	167	75.0	194	90.0
6	−14.4	33	0.5	60	15.5	87	30.5	114	45.5	141	60.5	168	75.5	195	90.5
7	−13.9	34	1.1	61	16.1	88	31.1	115	46.1	142	61.1	169	76.1	196	91.1
8	−13.3	35	1.7	62	16.7	89	31.7	116	46.7	143	61.7	170	76.7	197	91.7
9	−12.8	36	2.2	63	17.2	90	32.2	117	47.2	144	62.2	171	77.2	198	92.2
10	−12.2	37	2.8	64	17.8	91	32.8	118	47.8	145	62.8	172	77.8	199	92.8
11	−11.6	38	3.3	65	18.3	92	33.3	119	48.3	146	63.3	173	78.3	200	93.3
12	−11.1	39	3.9	66	18.9	93	33.9	120	48.9	147	63.9	174	78.9	201	93.9
13	−10.5	40	4.4	67	19.4	94	34.4	121	49.4	148	64.4	175	79.4	202	94.4
14	−10.0	41	5.0	68	20.0	95	35.0	122	50.0	149	65.0	176	80.0	203	95.0
15	−9.4	42	5.5	69	20.5	96	35.5	123	50.5	150	65.5	177	80.5	204	95.5
16	−8.9	43	6.1	70	21.1	97	36.1	124	51.1	151	66.1	178	81.1	205	96.1
17	−8.3	44	6.7	71	21.7	98	36.7	125	51.7	152	66.7	179	81.7	206	96.7
18	−7.8	45	7.2	72	22.2	99	37.2	126	52.2	153	67.2	180	82.2	207	97.2
19	−7.2	46	7.8	73	22.8	100	37.8	127	52.8	154	67.8	181	82.8	208	97.8
20	−6.7	47	8.3	74	23.3	101	38.3	128	53.3	155	68.3	182	83.3	209	98.3
21	−6.1	48	8.9	75	23.9	102	38.9	129	53.9	156	68.9	183	83.9	210	98.9
22	−5.5	49	9.4	76	24.4	103	39.4	130	54.4	157	69.4	184	84.4	211	99.4
23	−5.0	50	10.0	77	25.0	104	40.0	131	55.0	158	70.0	185	85.0	212	100.0
24	−4.4	51	10.5	78	25.5	105	40.5	132	55.5	159	70.5	186	85.5		
25	−3.9	52	11.1	79	26.1	106	41.1	133	56.1	160	71.1	187	86.1		
26	−3.3	53	11.7	80	26.7	107	41.7	134	56.7	161	71.7	188	86.7		
27	−2.8	54	12.2	81	27.2	108	42.2	135	57.2	162	72.2	189	87.2		

AREA

sq. in.	cm²	cm²	sq. in.	sq. ft.	m²	m²	sq. ft.	acres	ha	ha	acres
1	6.45	1	0.16	1	0.09	1	10.8	1	0.40	1	2.4
2	12.90	2	0.31	2	0.19	2	21.5	2	0.81	2	4.9
3	19.35	3	0.47	3	0.28	3	32.3	3	1.21	3	7.4
4	25.81	4	0.62	4	0.37	4	43.1	4	1.62	4	9.9
5	32.26	5	0.78	5	0.46	5	53.8	5	2.02	5	12.4
6	38.71	6	0.93	6	0.56	6	64.6	6	2.43	6	14.8
7	45.16	7	1.09	7	0.65	7	75.3	7	2.83	7	17.3
8	51.61	8	1.24	8	0.74	8	86.1	8	3.24	8	19.8
9	58.06	9	1.40	9	0.84	9	96.9	9	3.64	9	22.2
10	64.52	10	1.55	10	0.93	10	107.6	10	4.05	10	24.7
11	70.97	11	1.71	11	1.02	11	118.4	11	4.45	11	27.2
12	77.42	12	1.86	12	1.11	12	129.2	12	4.86	12	29.7
13	83.87	13	2.02	13	1.21	13	139.9	13	5.26	13	32.1
14	90.32	14	2.17	14	1.30	14	150.7	14	5.67	14	34.6
15	96.77	15	2.33	15	1.39	15	161.5	15	6.07	15	37.1
16	103.23	16	2.48	16	1.49	16	172.2	16	6.47	16	39.5
17	109.68	17	2.64	17	1.58	17	183.0	17	6.88	17	42.0
18	116.13	18	2.79	18	1.67	18	193.8	18	7.28	18	44.5
19	122.58	19	2.95	19	1.77	19	204.5	19	7.69	19	46.9
20	129.03	20	3.10	20	1.86	20	215.3	20	8.09	20	49.4
25	161.29	25	3.88	25	2.32	25	269.1	25	10.12	25	61.8
50	322.58	50	7.75	50	4.65	50	538.2	50	20.23	50	123.6
75	483.87	75	11.63	75	6.97	75	807.3	75	30.35	75	185.3
100	645.16	100	15.50	100	9.29	100	1,076.4	100	40.47	100	247.1
125	806.45	125	19.38	250	23.23	250	2,691.0	250	101.17	250	617.8
150	967.74	150	23.25	500	46.45	500	5,382.0	500	202.34	500	1,235.5
				750	69.68	750	8,072.9	750	303.51	750	1,853.3
				1,000	92.90	1,000	10,763.9	1,000	404.69	1,000	2,471.1

AREA

sq. mi.	km²	km²	sq. mi.	sq. mi.	km²	km²	sq. mi.
1	2.6	1	0.39	14	36.3	14	5.41
2	5.2	2	0.77	15	38.8	15	5.79
3	7.8	3	1.16	16	41.4	16	6.18
4	10.4	4	1.54	17	44.0	17	6.56
5	12.9	5	1.93	18	46.6	18	6.95
6	15.5	6	2.32	19	49.2	19	7.34
7	18.1	7	2.70	20	51.8	20	7.72
8	20.7	8	3.09	25	64.7	25	9.65
9	23.3	9	3.47	50	129.5	50	19.31
10	25.9	10	3.86	100	259.0	100	38.61
11	28.5	11	4.25	500	1,295.0	500	193.10
12	31.1	12	4.63	1,000	2,590.0	1,000	386.10
13	33.7	13	5.02	10,000	25,900.0	10,000	3,8861.00

LENGTH

in.	cm	cm	in.	in.	cm	cm	in.
1/8	0.3	1	0.39	7	17.8	14	5.51
1/4	0.6	2	0.79	8	20.3	15	5.91
3/8	1.0	3	1.18	9	22.9	16	6.30
1/2	1.3	4	1.57	10	25.4	17	6.69
5/8	1.6	5	1.97	20	50.8	18	7.09
3/4	1.9	6	2.36	30	76.2	19	7.48
7/8	2.2	7	2.76	40	101.6	20	7.87
1	2.5	8	3.15	50	127.0	50	19.69
2	5.1	9	3.54	60	152.4	60	23.62
3	7.6	10	3.94	70	177.8	70	27.56
4	10.2	11	4.33	80	203.2	80	31.50
5	12.7	12	4.72	90	228.6	90	35.43
6	15.2	13	5.12	100	254.0	100	39.37

LENGTH

ft.	m	m	ft.	yd.	m	m	yd.	mi.	km	km	mi
1	0.3	1	3.3	1	0.9	1	1.1	1	1.6	1	0.6
2	0.6	2	6.6	2	1.8	2	2.2	2	3.2	2	1.2
3	0.9	3	9.8	3	2.7	3	3.3	3	4.8	3	1.9
4	1.2	4	13.1	4	3.7	4	4.4	4	6.4	4	2.5
5	1.5	5	16.4	5	4.6	5	5.5	5	8.0	5	3.1
6	1.8	6	19.7	6	5.5	6	6.6	6	9.7	6	3.7
7	2.1	7	23.0	7	6.4	7	7.7	7	11.3	7	4.3
8	2.4	8	26.2	8	7.3	8	8.7	8	12.9	8	5.0
9	2.7	9	29.5	9	8.2	9	9.8	9	14.5	9	5.6
10	3.0	10	32.8	10	9.1	10	10.9	10	16.1	10	6.2
15	4.6	15	49.2	15	13.7	15	16.4	15	24.1	15	9.3
20	6.1	20	65.5	20	18.3	20	21.9	20	32.2	20	12.4
25	7.6	25	82.0	25	22.9	25	27.3	25	40.2	25	15.5
30	9.1	30	98.4	30	27.4	30	32.8	30	48.3	30	18.6
35	10.7	35	114.8	35	32.0	35	38.3	35	56.3	35	21.7
40	12.2	40	131.2	40	36.6	40	43.7	40	64.4	40	24.9
45	13.7	45	147.6	45	41.1	45	49.2	45	72.4	45	28.0
50	15.2	50	164.0	50	45.7	50	54.7	50	80.5	50	31.1
75	22.9	75	246.1	75	68.6	75	82.0	55	88.5	55	34.2
100	30.5	100	328.1	100	91.4	100	109.4	60	96.6	60	37.3
200	61.0	200	656.2	200	182.9	200	218.7	65	104.6	65	40.4
300	91.4	300	984.3	220	201.2	220	240.6	70	112.7	70	43.5
400	121.9	400	1,312.3	300	274.3	300	328.1	75	120.7	75	46.6
500	152.4	500	1,640.4	400	365.8	400	437.4	80	128.7	80	49.7
600	182.9	600	1,968.5	440	402.3	440	481.2	85	136.8	85	52.8
700	213.4	700	2,296.6	500	457.2	500	546.8	90	144.8	90	55.9
800	243.8	800	2,624.7	600	548.6	600	656.2	95	152.9	95	59.0
900	274.3	900	2,952.8	700	640.1	700	765.5	100	160.9	100	62.1
1,000	304.8	1,000	3,280.8	800	731.5	800	874.9	200	321.9	200	124.3
1,500	457.2	1,500	4,921.3	880	804.7	880	962.4	300	482.8	300	186.4
2,000	609.6	2,000	6,561.7	900	823.0	900	984.2	400	643.7	400	248.5
2,500	762.0	2,500	8,202.1	1,000	914.4	1,000	1,093.6	500	804.7	500	310.7
3,000	914.4	3,000	9,842.5	1,500	1,371.6	1,500	1,640.4	750	1,207.0	750	466.0
3,500	1,066.8	3,500	11,482.9	2,000	1,828.8	2,000	2,187.2	1,000	1,609.3	1,000	621.4
4,000	1,219.2	4,000	13,123.4	2,500	2,286.0	2,500	2,734.0	2,500	4,023.4	2,500	1,553.4
5,000	1,524.0	5,000	16,404.2	5,000	4,572.0	5,000	5,468.1	5,000	8,046.7	5,000	3,106.9

WEIGHT

oz.	g	g	oz.
1	28.3	1	0.04
2	56.7	2	0.07
3	85.0	3	0.11
4	113.4	4	0.14
5	141.7	5	0.18
6	170.1	6	0.21
7	198.4	7	0.25
8	226.8	8	0.28
9	255.1	9	0.32
10	283.5	10	0.35
11	311.7	20	0.71
12	340.2	30	1.06
13	368.5	40	1.41
14	396.9	50	1.76
15	425.2	100	3.53
16	453.6		

lb.	kg	lb.	kg
1	0.45	20	9.07
2	0.91	30	13.61
3	1.36	40	18.14
4	1.81	50	22.68
5	2.27	60	27.24
6	2.72	70	31.78
7	3.18	80	36.32
8	3.63	90	40.86
9	4.08	100	45.36
10	4.54	1,000	453.59

kg	lb.	kg	lb.
1	2.2	20	44.1
2	4.4	30	66.1
3	6.6	40	88.2
4	8.8	50	110.2
5	11.0	60	132.3
6	13.2	70	154.4
7	15.4	80	176.4
8	17.6	90	198.5
9	19.8	100	220.5
10	22.0	1,000	2,204.6

VOLUME

cu. in.	cm^3	cm^3	cu. in.	cu. ft.	m^3	m^3	cu. ft.
1	16.39	1	0.61	1	0.03	1	35.3
2	32.77	2	1.22	2	0.06	2	70.6
3	49.16	3	1.83	3	0.08	3	105.9
4	65.55	4	2.44	4	0.11	4	141.3
5	81.93	5	3.05	5	0.14	5	176.6
6	93.32	6	3.66	6	0.17	6	211.9
7	114.71	7	4.27	7	0.20	7	247.2
8	131.10	8	4.88	8	0.23	8	282.5
9	147.48	9	5.49	9	0.25	9	317.8
10	163.87	10	6.10	10	0.28	10	353.1
50	819.35	50	30.50	50	1.41	50	1,765.7
100	1,638.71	100	61.00	100	2.83	100	3,531.5

cu. yd.	m^3	m^3	cu. yd.
1	0.76	1	1.31
2	1.53	2	2.62
3	2.29	3	3.92
4	3.06	4	5.23
5	3.82	5	6.54
6	4.59	6	7.85
7	5.35	7	9.16
8	6.12	8	10.46
9	6.88	9	11.77
10	7.65	10	13.08
50	38.23	50	65.40
100	76.46	100	130.80

MOVABLE CHRISTIAN FEASTS

	1995	1996	1997	1998	1999	2000
Good Friday	14 Apr	5 Apr	28 Mar	10 Apr	2 Apr	21 Apr
Easter Sunday	16 Apr	7 Apr	30 Mar	12 Apr	4 Apr	23 Apr
Ascension Day	25 May	16 May	8 May	21 May	13 May	1 Jun
Pentecost (Whitsun)	4 Jun	26 May	18 May	31 May	23 May	11 Jun
Trinity Sunday	11 Jun	2 Jun	25 May	7 Jun	30 May	18 Jun
(Sundays after Trinity)	24	25	26	24	25	23
Advent Sunday	3 Dec	1 Dec	30 Nov	29 Nov	28 Nov	3 Dec

MAJOR IMMOVABLE CHRISTIAN FEASTS

1 Jan	Solemnity of Mary, Mother of God
6 Jan	Epiphany
7 Jan	Christmas Day (Eastern Orthodox)[1]*
11 Jan	Baptism of Jesus
25 Jan	Conversion of Apostle Paul
2 Feb	Presentation of Jesus (Candlemas Day)
22 Feb	The Chair of Peter. Apostle
25 Mar	Annunciation of the Virgin Mary
24 Jun	Birth of John the Baptist
6 Aug	Transfiguration
15 Aug	Assumption of the Virgin Mary
22 Aug	Queenship of Mary
8 Sep	Birthday of the Virgin Mary
14 Sep	Exaltation of the Holy Cross
2 Oct	Guardian Angels
1 Nov	All Saints
2 Nov	All Souls
9 Nov	Dedication of the Lateran Basilica
21 Nov	Presentation of the Virgin Mary
8 Dec	Immaculate Conception
25 Dec	Christmas Day
28 Dec	Holy Innocents

* Fixed feasts in the Julian Calendar fall 13 days later than the Gregorian Calendar date.

MAJOR JAPANESE FESTIVALS

1–3 Jan	Jan Oshogatsu (New Year)
3 Mar	Ohinamatsuri (Dolls' or Girls' Festival)
5 May	Tango no Sekku (Boys' Festival)
7 Jul	Hosh matsuri or Tanabata (Star Festival)
13–31 Jul	Obon (Buddhist All Souls)
15 Nov	Shichi-go-San (age celebrations for 7-year-old girls, 5-year-old boys and 3-year-old girls)

MAJOR CHINESE FESTIVALS

Jan–Feb	Chinese New Year
Feb–Mar	Lantern Festival
Mar–Apr	Festival of Pure Brightness
May–Jun	Dragon Boat Festival
Jun–Aug	Summer Retreat
Jul–Aug	Herd Boy and Weaving Maid
Aug	All Souls' Festival: Festival of Hungry Ghosts: Gautama Buddha's Birth: Kuan-yin
Sep	Mid-Autumn Festival
Sep–Oct	Double Ninth Festival
Nov–Dec	Winter Solstice

ISLAMIC CALENDAR AND FESTIVALS

Muhurram (May–Jun)	1 New Year's Day (Hegira: Muhammad's migration from Mecca to Medina, AD 622)
Safar (Jun–Jul)	
Rabi I (Jul–Aug)	12 Birthday of Muhammad (celebrated throughout month)
Rabi II (Aug–Sep)	
Jumad I (Sep–Oct)	
Jumad II (Oct–Nov)	
Rajab (Nov–Dec)	27 Laylat al-Miraj (Ascent of Muhammad to Heaven)
Sha'ban (Dec–Jan)	
Ramadan (Jan–Feb)	1 Beginning of month of fasting during day light hours; 27 Laylat al-Qadir (Transmission of Qur'an to Muhammad)
Shawwal (Feb–Mar)	1 Id al-Fitr (Celebration of end of fasting)
Dhu 'l-Qada (Mar–Apr)	
Dhu 'l-Hijjah (Apr–May)	8–13 Dhu 'l-Hijja (Annual pilgrimage to Mecca) 10 (Feast of the sacrifice)

JEWISH CALENDAR AND FESTIVALS

Tishri (Sept–Oct)	1–2 Rosh Hashana (New Year) 10 Yom Kippur (Day of Atonement) 5–21 Sukkot (Feast of Tabernacles)
Heshvan (Oct–Nov)	
Kislev (Nov–Dec)	25 Hannukah (Feast of Dedication)
Tevet (Dec–Jan)	
Shevat (Jan–Feb)	
Adar (Feb–Mar)	14–15 Purim (Feast of Lots)
Nisan (Mar–Apr)	15–22 Pesach (Passover)
Iyar (Apr–May)	5 Israel Independence Day
Sivan (May–Jun)	6–7 Shavuot (Feast of Weeks)
Tammuz (Jun–Jul)	
Av (Jul–Aug)	
Elul (Aug–Sep)	

BUDDHIST FESTIVALS

Myanmar
16–17 April	New Year
May–June	The Buddha's Birth, Enlightenment, and Death
July	The Buddha's First Sermon
October	Beginning of the Rains Retreat
November	Kathina Ceremony

Sri Lanka
13 April	New Year
May–June	The Buddha's Birth, Enlightenment, and Death
June–July	Establishment of Buddhism in Sri Lanka
July	The Buddha's First Sermon
July–August	Procession of the Month of Asala
September	The Buddha's First Visit to Sri Lanka
Dec–Jan	Arrival of Sanghamitta

Thailand
13–16 April	New Year
May	The Buddha's Enlightenment
May–Jun	The Buddha's Cremation
Jul–Oct	Rains Retreat
Oct	End of the Rains Retreat
Nov	Kathina Ceremony: Festival of Lights
Feb	All Saints Day

Tibet
Feb	New Year
May	The Buddha's Birth, Enlightenment, and Death
Jun	Dzamling Chisang
Jun–Jul	The Buddha's First Sermon
Oct	The Buddha's Descent from Tushita
Nov	Death of Tsongkhapa
Jan	The conjuction of Nine Evils and the conjuction of Ten Virtues

HINDU AND SIKH FESTIVALS

Hindu calendar with Hindu (H) and Sikh (S) festivals S: Sukla (fortnight of increasing Moon) K: Krishna (two weeks of decreasing Moon)

Chaitra (Mar–Apr)	S9 (H) Ramanavami (Rama's Birthday)
Vaisakha (Apr–May)	K15 (S) Baisakhi (Sikh New Year)
Jyaistha (May–Jun)	S4 (S) Martyrdom of Guru Arjan Dev
Asadha (Jun–Jul)	S2 (H) Rathayatra (Pilgrimage of the Chariot at Jagannath)
Sravana (Jul–Aug)	S11–15 (H) Jhulanayatra (Swinging of Krishna)
Bhadrapada (Aug–Sep)	K8 (H) Janamashtami (Krishna's Birthday)
Asvina (Sep–Oct)	S1–10 (H) Navaratri (Festival of Nine Nights) S7–10 (H) Durga-puja (Festival of Durga) S15 (H) Lakshmi-puja (Festival of Lakshmi) K15 (H and S) Diwali (Garland of Lights)
Kartikka (Oct–Nov)	S15 (S) Guru Nanak's Birthday
Margasirsa (Nov–Dec)	
Pausa (Dec–Jan)	S7 (S) Guru Gobind Singh's Birthday
Magha (Jan–Feb)	S5 (S) Martyrdom of Guru Teg Bahadur K5 (H) Sarasvati-puja (Festival of Sarasvati) K13 (H) Mahashivaratri (Great Night of Shiva)
Phalguna (Feb–Mar)	S14 (H) Holi (Spring festival)

How to use the index

There are several ways of using the index according to the level and type of information you want to find.

Look first under the most specific term for the subject you need. If you want to find an in-depth explanation of a subject, the main headings and the "mini-essays" in boxed sections are shown with **bold** page numbers. References to general topics have a **bold span** of page numbers, for example: transportation **468-77**. *Italic* page numbers indicate information in the *caption* to an illustration.

Some index entries have extra explanation given in brackets either to distinguish between the same term in different contexts, for example: scales (maps) 82; (music) 520, or to clarify a single term.

Occasionally entries have a common first element but are of different types. In this case the order of entry is as follows: personal names; company names; geographic names; subjects; titles. So, for example, Hudson, Rock (a personal name) is followed by Hudson River (a geographic name).

Acronyms are indexed under their fully expanded form, except where the subject is very well-known by the acronym.

ACKNOWLEDGMENTS
The publishers wish to thank the following for supplying photographs for this book:

t = top *l* = left *r* = right *b* = bottom *m* = middle
Page 11 SPL (*l*) NASA (*r*); 12 SPL; 14 SPL; 15 SPL; 16 SPL; 18 SPL; 19 SPL, Jet Propulsion Lab (*tr*); 20 SPL, Jet Propulsion Lab (*t*); 21 SPL, Jet Propulsion Lab (*b*); 22 Jet Propulsion Lab, SPL (*tl*); 23 SPL; 25 Armagh Planetarium (*t*) SPL (*b*); 26 SPL; 27 SPL; 28 Armagh Planetarium (*t*) SPL (*m*); 29 SPL; 31 NASA; 32 SPL; 34 SPL; 46 SPL; 47 US Geological Survey; 50 ZEFA; 51 SPL; 52 Natural History Museum; 53 Imitor, Natural History Museum, Geological Museum, Mike Grey; 54 ZEFA; 55 ZEFA; 65 ZEFA; 66 Life Science Images; 68 Robert Harding Picture Library; 69 Geoscience Features (*t*) Robert Harding Picture Library (*b*); 70 Robert Harding Picture Library; 76 J.Allan Cash; 77 SPL; 79 SPL; 80 SPL; 81 SPL; 82 ZEFA; 91 NHPA/Michael Tweedie; 103 Heather Angel; 114 ZEFA (*t*) NHPA/Stephen Dalton (*b*); 115 ZEFA (*t*) Bruce Coleman Pictures (*b*); 122 ARDEA; 128 NHPA/ANT; 145 Bruce Coleman Pictures, NHPA/ANT (*b*); 150 ZEFA (*l,b*) Robert Harding Picture Library (*t,m*) Bruce Coleman Pictures (*m*); 198 Natural History Museum; 199 French Government Tourist Office; 200 Werner Forman Archive; 202 Robert Harding Picture Library; 203 Hutchison Library (*t*) Werner Forman Archive (*b*); 205 South American Pictures; 208 James Hughes; 209 Michael Holford; 210 Werner Forman Archive (*t*) James Hughes (*b*); 211 Ancient Art & Architecture Collection (*t*) ZEFA (*b*); 212 Michael Holford (*t*) Images Colour Library (*b*); 213 Ancient Art & Architecture Collection (*t*) Images Colour Library (*b*); 214 Trip/Helene Rogers; 215 C.M.Dixon; 216 Ancient Art & Architecture Collection; 217 Michael Holford; 218 Trip; 219 Trip (*t,m*) Ancient Art & Architecture Collection (*b*); 220 Ancient Art & Architecture Collection; 221 Bridgeman Art Library/TheMaas Gallery (*t*) Catherine Rubinstein (*b*); 222 Michael Holford (*t*) Trip/Helene Rogers (*b*); 223 Ancient Art & Architecture Collection; 224 E.T.Archive (*t*) Images Colour Library; 225 Images Colour Library; 226 Images Colour Library (*t*) E.T.Archive (*b*); 227 Peter Newark Pictures; 228 Werner Forman Archive; 229 Mary Evans Picture Library (*t*) National Portrait Gallery (*b*); 230 Werner Forman Archive (*t*) Life File/Sean Finnigan (*b*);231 Life File/Ian Lochhead (*t*) Ancient Art & Architecture Collection (*b*);232 Images Colour Library; 233 Trip/Bob Turner; 234 Mary Evans Picture Library (*t*) Life File/Terence Waeland (*b*); 235 Mansell Collection; 236 Salvation Army (*t*) Trip/Joseph Okwesa (*b*); 237 Mary Evans Picture Library (*t*) James Hughes (*b*); 238 Camera Press (*t*) Trip/J.Novotny (*m*) Trip/T.Noorits (*b*); 240 Camera Press; 241 Mary Evans Picture Library; 246 Mary Evans Picture Library; 247 Range Pictures/Bettmann Archive (*l*) Rex Features (*r*); 254 ZEFA; 255 Panos Pictures; 258 ZEFA; 259 ZEFA; 262 Allsport; 263 Allsport; 264 Allsport; 269 Mary Evans Picture Library; 274 Allsport; 275 Allsport; 277 Allsport; 284 Allsport; 286 Allsport; 288 Allsport; 293 ZEFA; 296 ZEFA; 297 Popperfoto; 298 Robert Harding Picture Library (*t*) Popperfoto (*b*); 299 Popperfoto; 300 Popperfoto; 301 Popperfoto; 302 Popperfoto; 303 Popperfoto; 304 Peter Newark Pictures; 305 Sonia Halliday Photographs; 306 Range Pictures/Bettmann Archive; 307 Range Pictures/Bettmann Archive; 308 Range Pictures/Bettmann Archive; 313 ZEFA; 314 C.M.Dixon; 315 Michael Holford (*t*) ZEFA (*b*); 317 SCALA (*t*) Ancient Art & Architecture (*b*); 318 AKG,London; 319 SCALA (*tl*) Ancient Art &

Architecture (*tr,b*); 321 Michael Holford; 323 SCALA (*t*) ZEFA (*b*); 326 SCALA; 327 Mansell Collection (*t*) Bridgeman Art Library/Musee Conde, Chantilly (*m*); 328 Sonia Halliday Photographs (*l*) British Museum (*r*); 329 SCALA (*l*) Werner Forman Archive (*r*); 331 Bridgeman Art Library/British Library; 332 Mary Evans Picture Library; 333 Robert Harding Picture Library (*t*) Bridgeman Art Library/Christies, London (*b*); 336 South American Pictures; 335 Werner Forman Archive (*m*) ZEFA (*b*); 334 SCALA; 338 Mary Evans Picture Library; 339 E.T.Archive; 341 Bridgeman Art Library/Wallace Collection; 342 Guildhall Library,London; 343 Michael Holford; 344 AKG,London (*l*) Mary Evans Picture Library (*r*); 345 Bridgeman Art Library/Tate Gallery,London (*t*) India Office Library (*b*); 346 Bridgeman Art Library/Giraudon; 348 Bridgeman Art Library/Private Collection/Giraudon; 349 British Museum; 350 Bridgeman Art Library/Musee de la Ville de Paris,Musee Carnavalet; 351 Bridgeman Art Library/National Library of Australia; 353 Mansell Collection; 354 Mary Evans Picture Library; 355 Peter Newark's Pictures; 357 Peter Newark's Pictures; 358 The Granger Collection; 359 Peter Newark's Pictures (*l*) Illustrated London News (*r*) The Granger Collection (*b*); 360 Imperial War Museum; 361 AKG,London (*t*) Peter Newark's Pictures (*b*); 362 Mary Evans Picture Library; 363 Peter Newark's Pictures (*t*) Range Pictures/Bettmann Archive (*b*); 364 AKG,London; 365 Wiener Library (*t*) Peter Newark's Pictures (*b*); 367 Camera Press; 368 Rex Features; 369 Range Pictures/Bettmann Archive (*t*) SPL (*b*); 370 Panos Pictures; 371 Frank Spooner Pictures/Gamma (*t*) Popperfoto (*b*); 372 Mary Evans Picture Library; 373 Camera Press; 374 Peter Newark's Pictures; 375 Camera Press; 376 Range Pictures/Bettmann Archive; 377 Camera Press; 378 Camera Press; 380 Range Pictures/Bettmann Archive; 381 Mary Evans Picture Library (*t*) E.T.Archive (*b*); 382 Range Pictures/Bettmann Archive; 383 Mary Evans Picture Library; 384 Mary Evans Picture Library; 385 Peter Newark's Pictures (*t*) Camera Press (*b*); 386 Camera Press; 387 H.M. The Queen (*t*) Camera Press (*b*); 388 Peter Newark's Pictures; 406 ZEFA; 407 ZEFA; 408 Images Colour Library; 410 Michael Holford; 417 ZENECA Bio Products, 3M Health Care Ltd, Blatchford Products Division, ZEFA (*t*) Rex Features, Canon, Westland Group (*b*); 435 HP Bulmer Holdings plc; 436 Cephas; 437 Cephas; 438 Panos Pictures; 439 Panos Pictures; 440 ZEFA; 442 ZEFA; 445 Robert Harding Picture Library (*t*) British Coal (*b*); 446 ZEFA; 449 Robert Harding Picture Library; 452 Robert Harding Picture Library (*t*) Michael Holford (*b*); 453 Michael Holford; 454 SPL; 457 McLaren Cars Ltd; 458 ZEFA; 459 Rex Features; 460 ZEFA; 461 Q.A.Photo Library; 462 ZEFA; 463 Albert Haynen (*t*) Popperfoto (*bl*) ZEFA (*br*); 464 Hutchison Library; 465 Ford Archives (*t*) SPL (*b*); 466 SPL; 467 Popperfoto (*t*) SPL (*b*); 468 Robert Harding Picture Library (*t*) Michael Holford (*b*); 470 Quadrant Picture Library; 471 French Railways/Jean Marc Fabro; 473 ZEFA; 474 Robert Harding Picture Library (*t*) Reg Harman (*m*); 475 Mary Evans Picture Library (*t*) Panos Pictures (*b*); 476 Shell Photo Library; 477 ZEFA; 479 Grant Smith; 480 Science & Society Photo Library (*t*) SPL (*bl*) NHPA/M.Walker (*br*); 481 Colorific; 482 BT Pics; 483 SPL; 490 Michael Holford; 491 Bridgeman Art Library/Musee Conde,Chantilly/Lauros/Giraudon (*t*) Bridgeman Art Library/Victoria & Albert Museum,London (*b*); 492 British Museum; 493 Bridgeman Art Library/Giraudon; 494 Dover Publications, Inc (*t*) Bridgeman Art Library/Fitzwilliam Museum, University of Cambridge (*b*); 495 Aquarius Picture Library; 497 Riverside Press (*t*) The Writers' Museum,Edinburgh (*b*);

498 V.Poirson (*t*) Bridgeman Art Library/British Library (*b*); 499 Aquarius Picture Library; 500 Mansell Collection (*t*) Vintage Press (*b*); 501 National Portrait Gallery; 502 ZEFA; 503 Pica Pressfoto; 506 Victoria & Albert Museum,London; 507 Range Pictures/Bettmann Archive; 508 Mansell Collection (*t*) Prodeepta Das (*b*); 509 Mansell Collection (*t*) Bridgeman Art Library/Metropolitan Museum of Art, New York (*m*) Bridgeman Art Library/Private Collection (*b*); 510 Mary Evans Picture Library (*t*) Range Pictures/Bettmann Archive (*b*); 511 Aquarius Picture Library (*t*) Ronald Grant Archive (*b*); 512 Aquarius Picture Library (*r*) Ronald Grant Archive (*l*); 513 Aquarius Picture (*t*) Ronald Grant Archive (*b*); 514 National Film Archive (*t*) Aquarius Picture Library (*b*); 515 Ronald Grant Archive; 516 Kobal Collection (*t*) Ronald Grant Archive (*m,b*); 520 Michael Holford (*t*) E.T.Archive (*b*); 521 Bridgeman Art Library/Stadtische Museum,Erfurt (*t*) Mozart Museum,Salzburg (*b*); 522 Bridgeman Art Library/Staatsbibliothek Preussischer Kulterbesitz,Berlin; 523 Italian Tourist Board; 524 Mary Evans Picture Library; 525 Range Pictures/Bettmann Archive; 526 Range Pictures/Bettmann Archive (*t*) Redferns (*m*) Topham (*b*); 527 Topham (*t*) Camera Press (*m*) Redferns (*b*); 533 ZEFA (*m*) Catherine Rubinstein (*b*); 534 Bridgeman Art Library/Musee Cluny,Paris/Lauros/Giraudon (*t*) ZEFA (*b*); 535 Bridgeman Art Library/Galleria Degli Uffizi,Florence; 536 Bridgeman Art Library/Santa Maria della Vittoria,Rome (*t*) Rijksmuseum, Amsterdam (*b*); 538 Bridgeman Art Library/Kunsthalle,Hamburg (*t*) Bridgeman Art Library/Victoria & Albert Museum,London (*b*); 539 ZEFA; 540 British Museum (*t*) ZEFA/DACS 1995 (*b*); 541 Bridgeman Art Library/Demart Pro Arte BV/DACS 1995 (*t*) Bridgeman Art Library/Kunsthalle, Hamburg (*b*); 542 ARCAID (*t*) Bridgeman Art Library/Christies,London (*b*); 543 Grant Smith (*t*) Judy Chicago,1979/Donald Woodman (*b*); 544 AKG, London (*t*) ZEFA (*b*); 545 Catherine Rubinstein (*t*) ZEFA (*m*) Architectural Association/Andrew Higgott (*b*); 550 Robert Harding Picture Library (*t*) Michael Holford (*m*) Ancient Art & Architecture Collection (*b*); 551 Sonia Halliday Photographs; 552 British Museum (*t*) Sotheby's (*b*); 553 Sotheby's (*t*) Christie's (*b*); 554 Victoria & Albert Museum (*t*) Christie's (*b*); 555 Bridgeman Art Library/Christie's (*t*) E.T.Archive (*b*); 556 E.T.Archive (*t*) Christie's (*b*); 557 Art Resource,New York / National Museum of American Art, Washington DC (*t*) Christie's (*b*); 558 Angelo Hornak; 559 Victoria & Albert Museum (*t*) Bauhaus-Archiv, Museum fur Gestaltung (*b*); 562 Royal Photographic Society; 563 Range Pictures/Bettmann Archive (*t*) Camera Press (*m*) Magnum Photos/Robert Capa (*b*); 564 Range Pictures/Bettmann Archive (*t*) Magnum Photos/Henri Cartier-Bresson (*b*); 565 Range Pictures/Bettmann Archive; 566 Hulton-Deutsch Collection (*t,b*) Bridgeman Art Library/Private Collection (*m*); 567 Topham Picturepoint (*t*) Hulton-Deutsch Collection (*m*) Camera Press (*b*); 568 Camera Press (*t,m*) Topham Picturepoint (*b*).

All efforts have been made to contact the Artist's Estate and if notified we would be pleased to amend the acknowledgments in any future editions.

The publishers would like to thank the following for their assistance in checking facts and providing technical reference and advice:
Sara Anderson BA, Rob Bown MA, Imay Chan BA, Charles Cook Jr BA, Piers Gollop BA, Greville Healey BA, Sara Lazarus BA, Kevin Miller BA, Alex Monro BA (hons),.Simon O'Hana BSc CEng MICE, Mark Thomas PhD.